Ref.

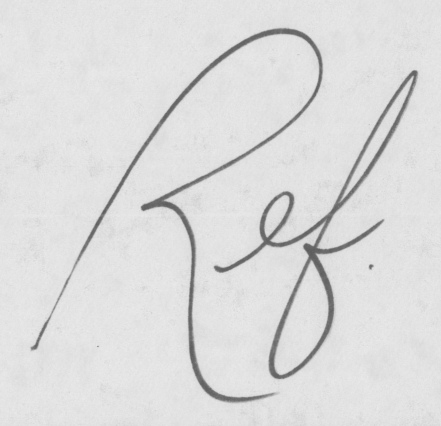

Contemporary Authors

NEW REVISION SERIES

Contemporary Authors

A Bio-Bibliographical Guide to
Current Writers in Fiction, General Nonfiction,
Poetry, Journalism, Drama, Motion Pictures,
Television, and Other Fields

ANN EVORY
Editor

NEW REVISION SERIES
volume 1

GALE RESEARCH COMPANY • THE BOOK TOWER • DETROIT, MICHIGAN 48226

Library of Congress Catalog Card Number 62-52046
ISBN 0-8103-1930-6

Preface

The new title on this volume, *Contemporary Authors New Revision Series,* reflects a major change in the preparation of *Contemporary Authors* revision volumes. No longer will all of the sketches in a given *Contemporary Authors* volume be updated and published together as a revision volume. Instead, sketches from a number of volumes will be assessed, and only those sketches requiring *significant change* will be revised and published in a *Contemporary Authors New Revision Series* volume. This change will enable us to provide *Contemporary Authors* users with updated information about active writers on a more timely basis, and will avoid printing sketches from previous volumes in which there has been little or no change. As always, the most recent *Contemporary Authors* cumulative index will continue to be the user's guide to the location of an individual author's listing.

Following are more detailed explanations about *Contemporary Authors New Revision Series.*

Questions and Answers About *Contemporary Authors • New Revision Series*

How do *New Revision Series* volumes differ from previous revision volumes?

In the past, all sketches in a given volume of *CA* were revised and published as a unit. For example, *CA* Volumes 41-44, First Revision, the last book published under the previous revision system, contained *all* of the 2,252 sketches listed in the original *CA* Volumes 41-44.

The *New Revision Series* differs from previous revisions of individual volumes in two basic ways: 1) The *New Revision Series* lists only those authors whose entries have undergone significant change since their last appearance in *CA*. For example, only 35% or 737 of the sketches in original *CA* Volumes 45-48 (published in 1974) have been revised for the *New Revision Series;* the remaining 65%, or 1,368 sketches, will be updated and placed in future *New Revision Series* volumes *when and if significant change* can be reflected in the entries. 2) *New Revision Series* volumes also contain sketches from *several CA volumes,* including previously revised editions. In addition to the numerous sketches drawn from *CA* Volumes 45-48, this volume also contains entries taken from *CA* Volumes 1-4, First Revision (published 1968), and *CA* Volumes 49-52 (published 1975). The new series name and single-volume numbering system reflect this mixture of sketches and serve to distinguish the *New Revision Series* from earlier revisions.

Why has the *CA* revision system been changed?

While the previous approach to revising *CA* sketches provided complete, accurate, and up-to-date information on all authors in a given volume, we feel the *New Revision Series* will even better meet the needs of *CA* users. By employing a selective approach to revisions, we can revise and publish sketches whenever they are out of date. The *New Revision Series* eliminates the need to publish entries with few or no changes.

How are sketches selected for the *New Revision Series*?

Clippings of all sketches in selected *CA* volumes published several years ago are sent to the authors at their last-known addresses. Authors mark material to be deleted or changed, and insert any new personal data, new affiliations, new books, new work in progress, new sidelights, and new biographical/critical sources. All author returns are assessed, additional research is done, if necessary, and those sketches with *significant change* are published in the *New Revision Series.*

If, however, authors fail to reply, or if authors are now deceased, biographical dictionaries are checked for new information (a task made easier through the use of Gale's *Biographical Dictionaries Master Index* and *Author Biographies Master Index),* as are bibliographical sources, such as *Cumulative Book Index, The National Union Catalog,* etc. Using data from such sources, revision editors select and revise nonrespondents' entries which need *substantial updating.* Sketches not personally reviewed by the authors are marked with a dagger (†) to indicate that these listings have been revised from secondary sources believed to be reliable, but they have not been personally reviewed for this edition by the authors sketched.

In addition, listings for active individual authors from *any* previous volume of *CA* may be included in a volume of the *New Revision Series.* Reviews and articles in major periodicals, lists of prestigious awards, and *requests from CA users* are monitored so that authors on whom new information is in demand can be identified and revised listings prepared promptly. For example, this volume includes a completely updated entry for Stephen King, who has written *The Shining, The Stand, Night Shift, The Dead Zone, Firestarter,* and *Stephen King's Danse Macabre* since his listing originally appeared in *CA* Volumes 61-64 (published 1976).

How much change is likely to occur in a *New Revision Series* entry?

The amount and type of change in any given sketch vary with the author, but all listings in this volume have been revised and/or augmented in various ways. Entries may include *new* degrees, mailing addresses, literary agents, career items, career-related and civic activities, memberships, work in progress, and biographical/critical sources. They may also include the following:

1) Major new awards—Isaac Singer's updated entry contains twelve awards not listed previously, including two National Book Awards and the Nobel Prize for Literature.

2) Extensive bibliographical additions—Eleven new books have been added to William F. Buckley's entry and nine to Milton Friedman's revised sketch; Robert Silverberg's listing includes thirty more nonfiction books and forty-five new science fiction titles, and he has edited over fifty additional books since his last appearance in *CA.*

3) Informative new sidelights—Original entries for both Stephen King and Gail Sheehy did not have sidelights. However, King's revised sketch includes amusing interview excerpts, and Sheehy's revised entry outlines some of the publicity associated with the publication of her book *Passages.*

Other notable people in this volume whose entries have undergone similarly extensive revision include Paul Bowles, Pearl Buck, Alex Comfort, Leon Edel, Robert Heinlein, Langston Hughes, Katherine Anne Porter, Philip Roth, John Steinbeck, and Kurt Vonnegut.

We invite *CA* users to compare original entries with revised listings and provide us with feedback on our revision procedures. To illustrate more specifically the amount and type of change that occurs in a *New Revision Series* entry, James Jackson Kilpatrick's original and revised sketches have been reprinted on the following page.

What happens to sketches not included in a *New Revision Series* volume?

Sketches not eligible for a *New Revision Series* volume because the author or a revision editor has verified that no significant change is required will, of course, be available to *CA* users in previously published *CA* volumes. When enough new information is accumulated, either through remailings to the authors or through such sources as reviews, articles, and interviews in periodicals, suggestions from *CA* users, publicity releases, book lists, award lists, etc., these sketches will be revised and placed in a *New Revision Series* volume. Some sketches, however, may never be revised if the existing entries

Original:

KILPATRICK, James Jackson 1920-

PERSONAL: Born 1920, in Oklahoma City, Okla.; married Marie Pietri, 1942; children: Michael Sean, Christopher Hawley, Kevin Pietri. *Education:* University of Missouri, B.J., 1941. *Home:* 1615 Hanover Ave., Richmond, Va.; and, 905 G St., S.E., Washington, D.C. *Office: Richmond News Leader,* 333 East Grace St., Richmond, Va.

CAREER: Richmond News Leader, Richmond, Va., reporter, 1941-49, associate editor, 1949, editor, 1949—. Syndicated columnist, 1964—. Member, Virginia Commission on Constitutional Government. Chairman, Magna Carta Commission of Virginia, 1965. *Member:* National Conference of Editorial Writers (chairman, 1956-57). *Awards, honors:* Medal of Honor for distinguished service to journalism, University of Missouri, 1953; Sigma Delta Chi Annual Award for editorial writing, 1954.

WRITINGS: The Sovereign States, Regnery, 1957; (co-editor) *The Lasting South,* Regnery, 1957; *The Smut Peddlers,* Doubleday, 1960; *The Case for Southern School Segregation,* Crowell-Collier, 1962.

Revised:

KILPATRICK, James Jackson 1920-

PERSONAL: Born November 1, 1920, in Oklahoma City, Okla.; son of James Jackson (a timberman) and Alma Mia (Hawley) Kilpatrick; married Marie Pietri (a sculptor), September 21, 1942; children: Michael Sean, Christopher Hawley, Kevin Pietri. *Education:* University of Missouri, B.J., 1941. *Home:* White Walnut Hill, Woodville, Va. 22749. *Office:* Rudasill's Mill Rd., Scrabble, Va. 22749.

CAREER: Richmond News Leader, Richmond, Va., reporter, 1941-49, associate editor, 1949, editor, 1949-66; nationally syndicated columnist, Washington Star Syndicate, 1964—; commentator, "60 Minutes," CBS-TV, 1971-79. *Member:* National Conference of Editorial Writers (chairman, 1956-57), Gridiron Club (Washington, D.C.). *Awards, honors:* Medal of Honor for distinguished service to journalism, University of Missouri, 1953; Sigma Delta Chi, annual award for editorial writing, 1954, fellowship, 1975; elected to Oklahoma Hall of Fame, 1978; William Allen White Medallion, University of Kansas, 1979.

WRITINGS: The Sovereign States, Regnery, 1957; (co-editor) *The Lasting South,* Regnery, 1957; (editor) *We the States,* Commonwealth of Virginia, 1958; *The Smut Peddlers,* Doubleday, 1960; *The Case for Southern School Segregation,* Crowell-Collier, 1962; *The Foxes' Union,* EPM Publications, 1977; (with Eugene J. McCarthy) *A Political Bestiary,* McGraw, 1978.

SIDELIGHTS: Known for his conservative political views, James Jackson Kilpatrick commented in an interview with Mary Hoffelt on the dour reputation of most avowed conservatives: "Taking the conservative stance is saying 'no' more often than not. If you think of the body politic as a machine, the liberals' habit is to accelerate. The conservatives' function is to apply the brakes. Certain aspects of the conservative point of view are by nature solemn. But I don't take myself too seriously." Kilpatrick is often called upon to take a conservative stance in an advocate role. But he's honest about the pitfalls of being a "front office conservative." He notes that he "was once asked to take the side of 'The Conservative's View of Watergate.' And I asked myself, 'Just what is a conservative's view of burglary?' "

But Kilpatrick believes it important for the press to present a balanced view of the issues, especially in newspaper columns. He told an interviewer from *Quill:* "I think ours is one area where we must try with diligence to present the other side. It's only in this way that we can hope through our readers to arrive at some sort of political wisdom, some sort of knowledge, some kind of truth. We get at it by fighting it out, this side against that side with reasoned arguments, responsible presentations, a responsible kind of advocacy—and then let the people make up their own minds."

[The remainder of Kilpatrick's sidelights, too lengthy to reprint here, can be found in his sketch on page 331.]

BIOGRAPHICAL/CRITICAL SOURCES: Time, November 30, 1970; *Seattle Post-Intelligencer,* November 12, 1974; *Quill,* October, 1975; *Authors in the News,* Gale, Volume I, 1976, Volume II, 1976.

remain accurate. *CA* users should always consult the *CA* cumulative index published in alternate new volumes of *CA* to determine the location of any author's entry.

Can any volumes of *Contemporary Authors* safely be discarded because they are obsolete?

As the chart on the following page indicates, *CA* users who have all First Revision volumes *and* both *Contemporary Authors Permanent Series* volumes can discard corresponding unrevised volumes 1 through 44.

Since the *New Revision Series* will not supersede any specific volumes of *CA,* all *revised* volumes, the two *Contemporary Authors Permanent Series* volumes, and *CA* Volumes 45-48 and subsequent *original* volumes must be retained in order to have information on all authors in the series.

How can information be located on a particular author?

The *CA* cumulative index published in alternate new volumes of *CA* will continue to be the user's guide to the location of an individual author's listing. Those authors appearing in the *New Revision Series* will be listed in the *CA* index with the designation CANR- in front of the specific volume number. For the convenience of those who do not have *New Revision Series* volumes, the index will also note the specific earlier volume of *CA* in which the sketch appeared. Below is a sample *New Revision Series* index citation:

Vonnegut, Kurt, Jr. 1922- CANR-1
Earlier sketch in CA 3R
See also CLC 1, 2, 3, 4, 5, 8, 12
See also AITN 1

For the most recent information on Vonnegut, users should refer to Volume 1 of the *New Revision Series,* as designated by "CANR-1"; if that volume is unavailable, refer to *CA* 1-4 First Revision, as indicated by "Earlier sketch in CA 3R," for his 1968 listing. (And if *CA* 1-4 First Revision is unavailable, refer to *CA* 3, published in 1963, for Vonnegut's original listing.)

For the convenience of *CA* users, the *CA* cumulative index also includes references to all entries in three related Gale series—*Contemporary Literary Criticism* (CLC), which is devoted entirely to current criticism on major novelists, poets, and playwrights, *Something About the Author* (SATA), a series of heavily illustrated sketches on juvenile authors and illustrators, and *Authors in the News* (AITN), a compilation of news stories and feature articles from American newspapers and magazines covering writers and other members of the communications media.

Summary

1) *CA* Volumes 41-44, First Revision, marks the end of the previous *CA* revision system.

2) Only authors whose entries have undergone *significant change* since their last appearance in *CA* will be listed in the *New Revision Series.*

3) Authors eligible for revised entries in the *New Revision Series* can be drawn from any *CA* volume.

4) Since only active authors will be selected for inclusion in the *New Revision Series,* in almost all cases their revised sketches will be significantly longer than their previous *CA* entries.

5) The most recent *CA* cumulative index will continue to be the user's guide to locating an author's original and revised *CA* entries.

As always, suggestions from users about any aspect of *CA* will be welcomed.

IF YOU HAVE:	YOU MAY DISCARD:
1-4 First Revision (1967)	1 (1962) 2 (1963) 3 (1963) 4 (1963)
5-8 First Revision (1969)	5-6 (1963) 7-8 (1963)
Both 9-12 First Revision (1974) AND *Contemporary Authors Permanent Series,* Volume 1 (1975)	9-10 (1964) 11-12 (1965)
Both 13-16 First Revision (1975) AND *Contemporary Authors Permanent Series,* Volumes 1 and 2 (1975, 1978)	13-14 (1965) 15-16 (1966)
Both 17-20 First Revision (1976) AND *Contemporary Authors Permanent Series,* Volumes 1 and 2 (1975, 1978)	17-18 (1967) 19-20 (1968)
Both 21-24 First Revision (1977) AND *Contemporary Authors Permanent Series,* Volumes 1 and 2 (1975, 1978)	21-22 (1969) 23-24 (1970)
Both 25-28 First Revision (1977) AND *Contemporary Authors Permanent Series,* Volume 2 (1978)	25-28 (1971)
Both 29-32 First Revision (1978) AND *Contemporary Authors Permanent Series,* Volume 2 (1978)	29-32 (1972)
Both 33-36 First Revision (1978) AND *Contemporary Authors Permanent Series,* Volume 2 (1978)	33-36 (1973)
37-40 First Revision (1979)	37-40 (1973)
41-44 First Revision (1979)	41-44 (1974)
45-48 (1974) 49-52 (1975) 53-56 (1975) 57-60 (1976) ↓ ↓ 93-96 (1980)	NONE: These volumes will not be superseded by corresponding revised volumes. Individual entries from these and all other volumes appearing in the left column of this chart will be revised and included in the *New Revision Series.*
Contemporary Authors New Revision Series, Volume 1 (1981)	NONE: The *New Revision Series* does not replace any single volume of *CA*. All volumes appearing in the left column of this chart must be retained to have information on all authors in the series.

CONTEMPORARY AUTHORS

NEW REVISION SERIES

† Indicates that a listing has been revised from secondary sources believed to be reliable, but has not been personally reviewed for this edition by the author sketched.

A

ACKERMAN, Gerald M(artin) 1928-

PERSONAL: Born August 21, 1928, in Alameda, Calif.; son of Alois M. (an accountant) and Eva (Sadler) Ackerman. *Education:* University of California, Berkeley, B.A., 1952; University of Munich, graduate study, 1956-58, Princeton University, M.F.A., 1960, Ph.D., 1964. *Politics:* Democrat. *Home:* 360 South Mills Ave., Claremont, Calif. 91711. *Office:* Department of Art, Pomona College, Claremont, Calif. 91711.

CAREER: Bryn Mawr College, Bryn Mawr, Pa., instructor in art history, 1960-64; Stanford University, Stanford, Calif., assistant professor of art history, 1964-70; Pomona College, Claremont, Calif., associate professor, 1970-76, professor of art history, 1976—, chairman of department, 1972—. *Member:* College Art Association, Deutsche Verein fuer Kunstwissenschaft.

WRITINGS: (With Richard Ettinghausen) *Gerome,* Dayton Art Institute, 1972; "Family and Friends" (play), first produced in Sacramento, Calif., 1979; "A Tradition" (play), first produced in Sacramento, Calif., 1980. Contributor to *Art News, Art News Annual, Burlington Magazine, Archive de Arte Espanol, Art Bulletin, Gazette des Beaux Arts, Listener,* and *Encyclopedia Universalis.*

WORK IN PROGRESS: A monograph on Gerome; several articles on realist painters.

* * *

ADAMS, Adrienne 1906-

PERSONAL: Born February 8, 1906, in Fort Smith, Ark.; daughter of Edwin Hunt (an accountant) and Sue (Broaddus) Adams; married John Lonzo Anderson (a writer, under name Lonzo Anderson), August 17, 1935. *Education:* Stephens College, B.A., 1925; attended University of Missouri, 1927, and American School of Design, New York, 1926. *Residence:* Glen Gardner, N.J.

CAREER: Artist, illustrator, author of children's books. Teacher in a rural school in Oklahoma, 1927; free-lance designer of displays, murals, textiles, greeting cards, and other materials, in New York City, 1929-45; Staples-Smith Displays, New York City, decorator of furniture and murals, and art director, 1945-52; full-time illustrator, 1952—. *Awards, honors:* Runner-up for Caldecott Medal, 1960, for illustration of *Houses from the Sea,* and 1962, for illustration of *The Day We Saw the Sun Come Up;* Rutgers Award from College of Library Services, Rutgers University, 1973, for contributions to children's literature.

WRITINGS—Self-illustrated; all published by Scribner: *A Woggle of Witches,* 1971; (compiler) *Poetry of Earth,* 1972; *The Easter Egg Artists,* 1976; *The Christmas Party,* 1978.

Illustrator: Lonzo Anderson, *Bag of Smoke,* Viking, 1942, revised edition, Knopf, 1968; Patricia Gordon, *The 13th Is Magic,* Lothrop, 1950; Gordon, *The Summer Is Magic,* Lothrop, 1952; Elizabeth Fraser Torjesen, *Captain Ramsay's Daughter,* Lothrop, 1953; Elizabeth Rogers, *Angela of Angel Court,* Crowell, 1954; Rumer Godden, *Impunity Jane,* Viking, 1954; Mary Kennedy, *Jenny,* Lothrop, 1954; Norma Simon, *The Baby House,* Lippincott, 1955; Beth Lipkin, *The Blue Mountain,* Knopf, 1956; Godden, *The Fairy Doll,* Viking, 1956; Priscilla Friedrich, *The Easter Bunny That Overslept,* Lothrop, 1957; Gordon, *The Light in the Tower,* Lothrop, 1957; Margaret Glover Otto, *Great Aunt Victoria's House,* Holt, 1957; Godden, *Mouse House,* Viking, 1957; Rachel Lyman Field, *The Rachel Field Story Book,* Doubleday, 1958; Godden, *Die Feenpuppe,* Boje Verlag, 1958; Godden, *The Story of Holly and Ivy,* Viking, 1958; Janice Udry, *Theodore's Parents,* Lothrop, 1958; Alice E. Goudey, *Houses from the Sea,* Scribner, 1959; Paula Hendrich, *Trudy's First Day at Camp,* Lothrop, 1959; Jeanne Massey, *The Little Witch,* Knopf, 1959.

Aileen Lucia Fisher, *Going Barefoot,* Crowell, 1960; Rumer Godden, *Candy Floss,* Viking, 1960; Jakob Ludwig Karl Grimm, *The Shoemaker and the Elves,* Scribner, 1960; Hans Christian Andersen, *Thumbelina,* Scribner, 1961; Fisher, *Where Does Everyone Go?,* Crowell, 1961; Alice E. Goudey, *The Day We Saw the Sun Come Up,* Scribner, 1961; Mary Francis Shura, *Mary's Marvelous Mouse,* Knopf, 1962; Clyde Robert Bulla, *What Makes a Shadow?,* Crowell, 1962; John Lonzo Anderson, compiler, *A Fifteenth Century Cookry Boke,* Scribner, 1962; W. Saboly, *Bring a Torch, Jeannette, Isabella,* Scribner, 1963; Virginia Haviland, *Favorite Fairy Tales Told in Scotland,* Little, Brown, 1963; Shura, *The Nearsighted Knight,* Knopf, 1964; Grimm, *Snow White and Rose Red,* Scribner, 1964; Goudey, *Butterfly Time,* Scribner, 1964; Frances Carpenter, *The Mouse Palace,* McGraw, 1964; Hans Christian Andersen, *The Ugly Duckling,* Scribner, 1965; Fisher, *In the Middle of the Night,* Crowell, 1965; Jan Wahl, *Cabbage Moon,* Holt, 1965; Anderson, *Ponies of Mykillengi,* Scribner, 1966; Andrew Lang, *The Twelve Dancing Princesses,* Holt, 1966; Barbara Schiller, *The White Rat's Tale*, Holt, 1967; Grimm, *Jorinda and Joringel*, Scribner, 1968; Anderson, *Two Hundred Rabbits*, Viking, 1968; Leclaire Alger, *The Laird of Cockpen*, Holt, 1969.

Natalia Belting, *Summer's Coming In*, Holt, 1970; Carl Withers, *Painting the Moon*, Holt, 1970; Lonzo Anderson, *Mr. Biddle and the Bird*, Scribner, 1971; Anderson, *Izzard*, Scribner, 1973; Irwin Shapiro, *Twice upon a Time*, Scribner, 1973; Anderson, *Halloween Party*, Scribner, 1974; Jakob and Wilhelm Grimm, *Hansel and Gretel*, Scribner, 1975; Kenneth Grahame, *The River Bank*, Scribner, 1977; Anderson, *Arion and the Dolphins*, Scribner, 1978; Peter Bankart, *The Wounded Duck*, 1979.

SIDELIGHTS: "I love children's books," Adrienne Adams once said, "and I feel very lucky to be involved in them. As I became involved, I discovered the satisfactions of a field which can be as sweetly innocent of the rank business-and-profit taint as any I can hope for, simply because a book cannot succeed unless little children love it and wear out its cover and pages so thoroughly that librarians must reorder it for the library shelves; you can not tell a child what to like."

BIOGRAPHICAL/CRITICAL SOURCES: Horn Book, April, 1965; *American Artist*, November, 1965; Diana Klemin, *The Art of Art for Children's Books*, C. N. Potter, 1966.

* * *

ADAMS, J(ames) Donald 1891-1968

PERSONAL: Born September 24, 1891, in New York, N.Y.; died August 23, 1968, in New York, N.Y.; son of James and Mary Louise (Barron) Adams; married Elvine G. Simeon, 1921 (divorced, 1949); married Jaqueline Ambler Winston, 1953; children: (first marriage) Mary Louise (Mrs. H. C. Orth-Pallavicini). *Education:* Harvard University, A.B., 1913. *Home:* 444 East 57th St., New York, N.Y. 10022. *Agent:* Mavis McIntosh, 30 East 60th St., New York, N.Y.

CAREER: University of Washington, Seattle, teaching fellow, 1913-15; *Evening Standard*, New Bedford, Mass., reporter, 1915; *Providence Journal*, Providence, R.I., reporter, 1916-17, assistant Sunday editor, 1919; *New York Sun and Herald*, New York City, reporter, 1920-21; *New York Herald*, New York City, editorial writer, 1922-24; *New York Times Book Review*, New York City, editor, 1925-43, contributing editor, 1943-64. *Military service:* U.S. Army, 1917-19; became sergeant. *Member:* P.E.N., Authors Guild, Authors League, Poetry Society of America (president, 1945-46), Academy of American Poets (chancellor, 1946-63), Harvard Club, Century Club, Dutch Treat Club. *Awards, honors:* Christopher Award, 1958.

WRITINGS: The Shape of Books to Come, Viking, 1944 (published in England as *The Writer's Responsibility*, Secker & Warburg, 1946), reprinted, Books for Libraries, 1971; (editor) *The Treasure Chest*, Dutton, 1946, reprinted, 1966; *Literary Frontiers*, Duell, 1951, reprinted, Kraus, 1969; *Triumph over Odds*, Duell, 1958; *Copey of Harvard*, Houghton, 1960; *The Magic and Mystery of Words*, Holt, 1963; *Speaking of Books and Life*, Holt, 1965; (compiler) Ralph Waldo Emerson, *Poems*, Crowell, 1965; *Naked We Came: A More or Less Lighthearted Look at the Past, Present, and Future of Clothes*, Holt, 1967. Contributor to many magazines.

WORK IN PROGRESS: An autobiography, tentatively entitled *The Rough and the Smooth*.

SIDELIGHTS: When J. Donald Adams took over as editor of the *New York Times Book Review* in 1925, "the *Times* thought that all you had to do was to tell people what was in the books," he once told an interviewer. "I wanted to make *The Book Review* something more than that." After his eighteen year stint as editor, Adams began writing the "Speaking of Books" column which was his regular contribution for the next 21 years. Conservative, even old-fashioned, Adams was nevertheless "a well-known and much respected figure in the literary world of New York," noted the *Times* obituary.

BIOGRAPHICAL/CRITICAL SOURCES: Choice, April, 1967; *New York Times Book Review*, November 12, 1967; *New Yorker*, January 6, 1968; *New York Times*, August 24, 1968.†

* * *

ADAMS, Joey 1911-

PERSONAL: Surname originally Abramowitz; legally changed in 1930; born January 6, 1911, in New York, N.Y.; son of Nathan (a tailor) and Ida (Chonin) Abramowitz; married second wife, Cindy Heller (a columnist and commentator), February 14, 1952. *Education:* Attended City College (now City College of the City University of New York), 1931. *Home:* 1050 Fifth Ave., New York, N.Y. 10028. *Office:* 160 West 46th St., Room 402A, New York, N.Y. 10036.

CAREER: Writer, actor, comedian, toastmaster. Nightclub and vaudeville entertainer throughout United States, 1930—; appeared in and produced films, including "Ringside," 1945, and "Singing in the Dark," 1956; appeared in stage productions, including "The Gazebo," 1959, and "Guys and Dolls," 1960; host of television and radio shows, including "Spend a Million," 1954-55, "The Joey Adams Show," 1957, "Rate Your Mate," 1958, "Back That Fact," 1958, and "Gags to Riches"; has appeared on numerous radio and television shows, including "The Ed Sullivan Show," "The Jackie Gleason Show," and "The Steve Allen Show"; host of daily radio show on WEVD, 1968—. U.S. State Department representative entertaining soldiers around the world, 1958; deputy commissioner and chairman of entertainment committee for youth of New York City Youth Board, 1959—; president of Actors Youth Fund, and Senior Citizens of America Fund; personal representative of U.S. President as entertainer to Asia and Africa, 1961; goodwill ambassador for Presidents Kennedy, Johnson, and Nixon. Member of board of directors, Central State Bank (New York), and Theatre Authority; chairman of special events committee, March of Dimes, 1955.

MEMBER: American Guild of Variety Artists (president, 1959—; president of retirement foundation; chairman of youth fund), Screen Actors Guild, American Federation of Television and Radio Artists, Actors Equity Association. *Awards, honors:* Doctor of Comedy, Columbia University, 1950, City College, 1952, and New York University, 1959; Man of the Year Award from March of Dimes, 1955, City of Hope, 1959, and New York City Police Department, 1960; honored by Israeli Government for work with United Jewish Appeal and Israel Bond drives, 1952; recipient of humanitarian awards from American Cancer Society, 1952, Crusade for Freedom, 1956, and Yiddish Theatrical Alliance, 1960; special honorary degree from Long Island University; Dr. of Letters, Chung-Au University, Korea; Ph.D., Fu-Jen University, Taiwan; recipient of Pope's Medal, 1971, and numerous other awards.

WRITINGS—Published by Fell, except as indicated: *From Gags to Riches*, 1946; *The Curtain Never Falls*, 1949; *Joey Adams' Joke Book: A Mad, Merry Mixture of Sly Stories,*

Tasty Tales, and Wise Witticisms, by the Master of Mirth, 1952; *Strictly for Laughs,* 1955, reprinted, Manor, 1979; *Cindy and I: The Real Life Adventures of Mr. and Mrs. Joey Adams,* Crown, 1957; *It Takes One to Know One: The Joey Adams Do-It-Yourself Laugh Kit,* Putnam, 1959; *The Joey Adams Joke Dictionary,* Citadel, 1961; *On the Road for Uncle Sam,* Geis, 1963; *LBJ's Texas Laughs,* 1964; *Joey Adams' Round-the-World Joke Book,* 1965.

Published by Bobbs-Merrill, except as indicated: (With Henry Tobias) *The Borscht Belt,* 1966; *You Could Die Laughing: Or, I Was a Comic for the F.B.I. and the Swingers,* 1968; *Encyclopedia of Humor,* 1968; *Son of Encyclopedia of Humor,* 1970; *Laugh Your Calories Away,* Crown, 1971; *Children's Joke Book,* Crown, 1971; *Speaker's Bible of Humor,* Doubleday, 1972; *The God Bit,* Mason and Lipscomb, 1974; *Joey Adams Ethnic Humor,* Manor, 1977; *Joey Adams Joke Diary,* Manor, 1978. Has written and recorded several comedy records, including "Cindy and I" and "Jewish Folk Songs," with Molly Picon and Sholum Secunda, for Roulette Records. Author of daily column "Strictly for Laughs," and feature writer on politics and humor for *New York Post;* syndicated humor columnist.

SIDELIGHTS: In 1960, the American Guild of Variety Artists created a "Joey Award" for talent in the variety field in honor of Joey Adams.

* * *

ADAMSON, Joseph III 1945-
(Joe Adamson, Warren Wintergreen)

PERSONAL: Born December 30, 1945, in Cleveland, Ohio; son of Joseph (a salesman) and Janet (Friday) Adamson. *Education:* Attended Gettysburg College, 1963-65; University of California, Los Angeles, B.A. (cum laude), 1967, M.A., 1970. *Politics:* "To the left of Hubert Humphrey." *Religion:* "Creative Evolution." *Home address:* P.O. Box 29561, Los Angeles, Calif. 90027. *Agent:* Russell & Volkening, Inc., 551 Fifth Ave., New York, N.Y. 10017.

CAREER: Pennsylvania State University, University Park, instructor, 1970-72, assistant professor of film, 1972-74; free-lance writer and film researcher, 1974—. Instructor at Los Angeles City College, 1975, California State Polytechnic University, Pomona, 1978, and University of California, Los Angeles, 1978-79. Producer, director, and cinematographer of films. Interviewer and historian for Oral History of the Motion Picture in America program, American Film Institute, 1968-69, Office of Special Projects, Directors Guild of America, 1977-79, and Oral History Program of the Astoria Motion Picture and Television Center, 1979. Script reader for United Artists Corp., 1978. *Awards, honors:* Second prize, Kodak Teen-Age Movie Contest and Eagle Award, Council on International Non-Theatrical Events, both 1964, both for film, "It's an Out of Its Mind World"; honorable mention, Kodak contest, 1965, for film, "The Man Who Owned America"; American Film Institute fellowship, 1969, and University Film Foundation fellowship, 1970, both for work on *Groucho, Harpo, Chico and Sometimes Zeppo;* Pennsylvania State University, two grants from Fund for Research and one from Institute for Arts and Humanistic Studies, 1972, all for production of "A Political Cartoon"; Judges' Prize, Santa Barbara Film Festival, Audience Prize, Midwest Film Festival, Francis Scott Key Award, Baltimore Film Festival, 1974, all for film, "A Political Cartoon."

WRITINGS—Under name Joe Adamson: *Groucho, Harpo, Chico and Sometimes Zeppo,* Simon & Schuster, 1973; *Tex Avery: King of Cartoons,* Popular Library, 1975; (contributor) *Dictionary of Literary Biography: American Screenwriters,* two volumes, Gale, 1980.

Screenplays: (Under pseudonym Warren Wintergreen, with James Bryan) "Escape to Passion," produced by Grads Corp., 1971; (with Jim Morrow) "A Political Cartoon," produced by Odradek Productions, 1973, published in *Scripts 1,* edited by Floren Harper, Houghton, 1973. Author or co-author of numerous additional screenplays, including "It's an Out of Its Mind World," "The Man Who Owned America," "In the Mist of Life," 1967, and "Bijou Dream," 1974. Also author of narration for 14 episodes of "Lowell Thomas Remembers," PBS-TV, 1975, and seven video presentations, "Introduction to Business" series, produced by Milan Herzog Associates, 1979.

Work represented in anthologies, including *Film Theory and Criticism: Introductory Readings,* edited by Gerald Mast and Marshall Cohen, Oxford University Press, 1974, 2nd edition, 1979. Contributor to many film journals, including *Film Comment, Take One, Filmakers Newsletter,* and *Cinema Journal.*

SIDELIGHTS: While still a student, Joseph Adamson made seventeen short films; one of these, "In the Mist of Life," was exhibited nationally with other films by the UCLA film program's students. "I enrolled in college as an English major," Adamson explained to *CA,* "and renounced my childhood fascination for movie making forever—only to find myself making 'one last film' and winning a nation-wide award with it. I dutifully trooped off to UCLA to study film and assume the anticipated post of Great American Director, but on the way I wrote a book [*Groucho, Harpo, Chico and Sometimes Zeppo*]."

This book, writes Robert Lasson in the *New York Times Book Review,* "is loaded with anecdotes and side trips that will endear it to every fan of Minnie's boys. Joe Adamson has evidently spoken to every writer, director, gagman and cinematographer who ever worked with—or against—them. Even the bibliography is interesting." In addition, *Variety* reviewer Don Carle Gillette finds that "reading this book . . . is almost like having a front seat at a complete retrospective of Marx Brothers films and stage attractions," because Adamson describes each production from the original idea to the final result. Moreover, "the marathon performance," Gillette continues, "is enlivened by the humorous narrative and commentaries by Adamson, an incisive wit himself, who really gets under the skin of the Marxes and fleshes them out so they come to life in all their zany hilarity." The volume is similarly praised by Richard T. Jameson in *Movietone News:* "Joe Adamson's response to the zanies' personalities, styles, and careers is exhilarating. . . . Besides being funny, [the book] is perceptive and instructive and dazzlingly personal. Rarity among film volumes, it is a *written* book that honors its subjects in the most integral way possible, not only evoking but coming near to embodying what the Marx Brothers and their movies are all about."

BIOGRAPHICAL/CRITICAL SOURCES: Variety, August 30, 1973; *Best Sellers,* September 15, 1973; *New York Times Book Review,* September 23, 1973; *Movietone News,* April, 1974.

* * *

AGETON, Arthur Ainsley 1900-1971

PERSONAL: Born October 25, 1900, in Fromberg (Gebo), Mont.; died April 23, 1971, in Bethesda, Md.; son of Peter Benjamin and Minnie Anna (Drummond) Ageton; married Jo Lucille Gallion, November 24, 1933; children: Mary Jo Ageton Binder, Arthur A., Jr. *Education:* Attended State College of Washington (now Washington State University), 1918-19; U.S. Naval Academy, B.S., 1923; U.S. Naval Post Graduate School, certificate, 1931; Johns Hopkins University, M.A., 1953. *Politics:* Republican. *Religion:* Episcopalian. *Home:* 3900 Connecticut Ave. N.W., Washington, D.C. 20008.

CAREER: U.S. Navy career officer, 1919-47, retired as rear admiral. Self-employed author and lecturer, Annapolis, Md., 1947-54; U.S. Department of State, Asuncion, Paraguay, ambassador extraordinary and minister plenipotentiary, 1954-57; Charles A. Koons & Co., Washington, D.C., and New York City, business executive and Washington representative, 1957-61; George Washington University, Washington, D.C., associate professor of creative writing and writing the short story, 1960-61; self-employed as consultant on international business to Dunlap & Associates, Inc., Stamford, Conn., Filmfax Productions, Inc., New York City, and Nuclear Utility Services, Inc., Washington, D.C., 1960-62. Active in fund drives and church organizations.

MEMBER: U.S. Naval Institute, Authors Guild, Army-Navy Club (Washington, D.C.), Army and Navy Country Club (Arlington). *Awards, honors:* Various military awards including Bronze Star and Legion of Merit for action during World War II; Orden Nacional del Merito en el Grado del Gran Cruz of the Republic of Paraguay.

WRITINGS: Dead Reckoning Altitude and Azimuth Table, Hydrographic Office, 1932; *Manual of Celestial Navigation,* Van Nostrand, 1942, 2nd edition, 1960; *Naval Officer's Guide,* McGraw, 1943, 8th edition (with W. P. Mack), U.S. Naval Institute, 1970; *Naval Leadership and the American Bluejacket,* McGraw, 1944; *Mary Jo and Little Liu* (juvenile), Whittlesey, 1945; *The Jungle Seas* (novel), Random House, 1954; (with Robert Heinl and G. C. Thomas) *The Marine Officer's Guide,* U.S. Naval Institute, 1955, 3rd edition, 1967; (with William H. Standley) *Admiral Ambassador to Russia,* Regnery, 1955; *Hit the Beach* (novel), New American Library, 1961. Contributor of stories and articles to national magazines.

WORK IN PROGRESS: Novel about Washington with World War II background, a study of the effect of the unification struggle on the life and career of one naval officer; *Memoirs,* about author's tour of duty with the U.S. Department of State.

SIDELIGHTS: Arthur Ainsley Ageton was noted for his contributions to navigation. His papers are part of the Ageton Collection at Boston University Library. His works have been translated into Italian, French, Danish, Swedish, and Finnish.†

* * *

AHERN, Thomas Francis 1947-
(Tom Ahern)

PERSONAL: Born August 3, 1947, in Holbrook, Mass.; son of Thomas Francis (a machinist) and Hazel (McKay) Ahern. *Education:* Brown University, B.A., 1970, M.A., 1973. *Home:* 71 Elmgrove Ave., Providence, R.I. 02906.

CAREER: Eyewitness, Cambridge, Mass., co-editor and art director, beginning 1973; Center for Career Education in the Arts, Providence, R.I., writing specialist, 1976-77; writer, Rhode Island Public Arts Program, 1977; writer-in-residence, Rhode Island State Council on the Arts, 1977-79; Electron Mover (videotape production studio), Providence, programming consultant, 1979—; *Real Paper,* Boston, Mass., columnist, 1979—.

WRITINGS—Under name Tom Ahern: *The Transcript,* Burning Deck Press, 1973; *Strangulation of Dreams,* Burning Deck Press, 1973; *A Movie Starring the Late Cary Grant and an As-Yet Unnamed Actress,* Treacle Press, 1976; *The Capture of Trieste,* Windfall Press, 1978. Work represented in anthologies, including: *Fresh Meats,* edited by Richard Goldstein, Bantam, 1973; *In Youth,* edited by Richard Kostelanetz, Ballantine, 1973; *Breakthrough Fictioneers,* edited by Kostelanetz, Something Else Press, 1973; *Alphabet Anthology,* edited by Joyce Holland, Collective Identities Press, 1973; *The Poets' Encyclopedia,* Unmuzzled Ox, 1979. Author of bi-weekly column, "Presidential Romance: The Continuing Story of Lust in High Places," *Point-in-Time.* Contributor to numerous literary journals, including *Ghost Dance, Center, Telephone, Tottel's, Curtains, Margins* and *Invisible City.* Editor, *Diana's Bimonthly,* 1972—.

WORK IN PROGRESS: The Tales of Petrus Borel, a retelling of the collected stories of the 19th century French author, Joseph Petrus Borel d'Hauterive; *Tales Friends Tell,* "collected gossip."

BIOGRAPHICAL/CRITICAL SOURCES: Booklist, May 1, 1977; *Philadelphia Inquirer,* May 8, 1977; *East Side,* November 3, 1977.

* * *

AIKEN, Henry David 1912-

PERSONAL: Born July 3, 1912, in Portland, Ore.; son of Frank Bethel and Miriam (Boskowitz) Aiken; married third wife, Helen Rowland Geer, November 17, 1958; children: (previous marriages) Katharine, Harriet, David; (present marriage) Paula, Henry. *Education:* Reed College, A.B., 1935; Stanford University, M.A., 1937; Harvard University, Ph.D., 1943. *Home:* 16 Fells Rd., Falmouth, Mass. 02540. *Agent:* Curtis Brown Ltd., 575 Madison Ave., New York, N.Y. *Office:* Department of Philosophy, Brandeis University, Waltham, Mass. 02154.

CAREER: Harvard University, Cambridge, Mass., instructor, 1943-44; Columbia University, New York, N.Y., associate, 1944-45; University of Washington, Seattle, assistant professor, 1945-46; Harvard University, associate professor of philosophy, 1946-54, professor, 1954-65; Brandeis University, Waltham, Mass., professor of philosophy and history of ideas, 1965-67, Charles Goldman Professor of Philosophy, 1967—. Visiting professor, University of Michigan, 1953, 1962, and 1965, University of California, Los Angeles, 1958. *Member:* American Philosophical Association, American Society for Aesthetics (trustee, 1947-50), American Psychological Association, American Society for Political and Legal Philosophy. *Awards, honors:* Guggenheim fellowship, 1960-61; Alfred North Whitehead fellow, Harvard University, 1968-69; National Foundation for Arts and Humanities grant, 1968-69.

WRITINGS: (Editor and author of introduction) David Hume, *Dialogues Concerning Natural Religion,* Hafner, 1944; (editor and author of introduction) *Moral and Political Philosophy,* Hafner, 1948; (editor) *The Age of Ideology,* Houghton, 1956; (contributor) Israel Scheffler, editor, *Philosophy and Education,* Allyn & Bacon, 1958; *Reason and Conduct,* Knopf, 1962, reprinted, Greenwood Press, 1978; (editor with William Barrett) *Philosophy of the Twentieth Century* (anthology), Random House, 1962; (contributor) Richard T. DeGeorge, editor, *Ethics and Society,* Anchor Books, 1966; (contributor) George Barnett, editor, *Philosophy and Educational Development,* Houghton, 1966; (with others) *The University and the New Intellectual Environ-*

ment, St. Martin's Press, 1968; (contributor) Arthur J. Bellinzoni, Jr., and Thomas V. Litzenburg, Jr., editors, *Intellectual Honesty and Religious Commitment,* Fortress Press, 1969; (editor and author of introduction) David Hume, *Hume's Moral and Political Philosophy,* Hafner, 1970; *Predicament of the University,* Indiana University Press, 1971; (contributor) Bruce Hilton and others, editors, *Ethical Issues in Human Genetics,* Plenum Press, 1973. Contributor to *New Republic, Commentary, Kenyon Review, New York Review,* and philosophy journals.

AVOCATIONAL INTERESTS: Music, literature, and fine arts.†

* * *

AKERS, Ronald L(ouis) 1939-

PERSONAL: Born January 7, 1939, in New Albany, Ind.; son of Charles Edward (a machinist) and Thelma (Johnson) Akers; married Caroline Rakes, June 20, 1958; children: Ronald Louis II, Tamara Noel, Levi Jeremiah. *Education:* Indiana State College (now University), B.S., 1960; Kent State University, M.A., 1961; University of Kentucky, Ph.D., 1966. *Politics:* Democrat. *Religion:* Baptist. *Address:* Rural Route 2, Box 101A, West Branch, Iowa 52358. *Office:* Department of Sociology, University of Iowa, Iowa City, Iowa 52242.

CAREER: University of Washington, Seattle, 1965-72, began as assistant professor, became associate professor of sociology; Florida State University, Tallahassee, professor of criminology, 1972-74; University of Iowa, Iowa City, professor of sociology, 1974—, chairman of department, 1978—. *Member:* American Society of Criminology (president, 1978-79); American Sociological Association (chairman of section on criminology), Society for the Study of Social Problems, Law and Society Association.

WRITINGS: Deviant Behavior: A Social Learning Approach, Wadsworth, 1973, 2nd edition, 1977; *Law and Control in Society,* Prentice-Hall, 1975; *Crime, Law, and Sanctions,* Sage Publications, Inc., 1978. Contributor of articles to journals in his field.

WORK IN PROGRESS: Research on adolescent drinking and drug use, and on adolescent smoking behavior.

* * *

ALBRECHT-CARRIE, Rene 1904-1978

PERSONAL: Born January 20, 1904, in Izmir, Turkey; naturalized U.S. citizen in 1923; died August 31, 1978, in New York; son of Ernest and Claire (Carrie) Albrecht-Carrie; married Eleanor Kingsley, 1932 (divorced, 1973); married Else B. Lorch, 1973; children: (first marriage) Claire, Pierre. *Education:* Columbia University, B.A. and M.A., 1923, Ph.D., 1938. *Home:* *9 Claremont Ave., New York, N.Y.* Office: *Barnard College, Columbia University, New York, N.Y.*

CAREER: City College (now City College of the City University of New York), New York City, instructor of mathematics, 1923-42; Queens College of the City of New York (now Queens College of the City University of New York), Flushing, N.Y., instructor in history, 1942-45; Barnard College, New York City, professor of history, 1946-69, professor emeritus, 1969-78. Special lecturer in history, Columbia University, 1969-70; distinguished visiting professor of history, Rockford College, 1970-72; visiting professor of history, St. Johns University, 1973-74. *Member:* American Historical Association, History of Science Society, Society for French Historical Studies, Society for Italian Historical Studies, America-Italy Society, Council on Foreign Relations. *Awards, honors:* George Louis Beer Prize, American Historical Association, 1938; grants from Rockefeller Foundation, 1952-53, Ford Foundation, 1967-68, and American Philosophical Society, 1967-68; medal of Middle States Association, 1965, for *The Meaning of the First World War;* Guggenheim fellowship, 1966-67.

WRITINGS: Italy at the Paris Peace Conference, Columbia University Press, 1938, reprinted, Shoe String, 1966; (contributor) *War as a Social Institution,* Columbia University Press, 1940; (contributor) *Contemporary Europe,* Van Nostrand, 1941; *Italy from Napoleon to Mussolini,* Columbia University Press, 1950; *A Diplomatic History of Europe since the Congress of Vienna,* Harper, 1958, revised edition, 1973; *France, Europe and the Two World Wars,* Droz, 1960, Harper, 1961; *Europe since 1815,* Harper, 1962, 5th edition, 1972; *One Europe,* Doubleday, 1965 (published in England as *The Unity of Europe,* Secker & Warburg, 1966); *The Meaning of the First World War,* Prentice-Hall, 1965; (contributor) *L'Europa fra le due guerre,* [Torino, Italy], 1966; *The Concert of Europe,* Harper, 1968; *Le rivoluzione nazionali,* Unione Tipografico-Editrice Torinese, 1969; *Britain and France: Adaptations to a Changing Context of Power,* Doubleday, 1970; *Twentieth Century Europe,* Littlefield, 1973; *Adolphe Thiers,* Twayne, 1977. Contributor of numerous articles to political science, history and scientific journals.

WORK IN PROGRESS: Ideology and Power.†

* * *

ALEXANDER, Lloyd Chudley 1924-

PERSONAL: Born January 30, 1924, in Philadelphia, Pa.; son of Alan Audley and Edna (Chudley) Alexander; married Janine Denni, January 8, 1946; children: Madeleine. *Education:* Attended West Chester State Teachers College, Lafayette College and Sorbonne University of Paris. *Home:* 1005 Drexel Ave., Drexel Hill, Pa. 19026. *Agent:* Brandt & Brandt, 1501 Broadway, New York, N.Y. 10036.

CAREER: Author of children's books; free-lance writer and translator, 1946—. Author-in-residence, Temple University, 1970. *Military service:* U.S. Army, Intelligence, 1942-46; became staff sergeant. *Member:* Authors Guild, P.E.N., Carpenter Lane Chamber Music Society (member of board of directors). *Awards, honors:* Isaac Siegel Memorial Juvenile Award, 1959, for *August Bondi: Border Hawk;* Newbery Medal, American Library Association, 1969, for *The High King;* National Book Award, 1971, for *The Marvelous Misadventures of Sebastian;* National Book Award nomination in children's literature, 1979, for *The First Two Lives of Lukas-Kasha.*

WRITINGS: And Let the Credit Go, Crowell, 1955; *My Five Tigers,* Crowell, 1956; *Janine Is French,* Crowell, 1958; *August Bondi: Border Hawk,* Farrar, Straus, 1959; *My Love Affair with Music,* Crowell, 1960; *Aaron Lopez and Flagship Hope,* Farrar, Straus, 1960; (with Louis Camuti) *Park Avenue Vet,* Holt, 1962; *Time Cat,* Holt, 1963; *Fifty Years in the Doghouse,* Putnam, 1963 (published in England as *Send for Ryan!,* W. H. Allen, 1965); *The Book of Three,* Holt, 1964; *The Black Cauldron,* Holt, 1965; *Coll and His White Pig,* Holt, 1965; *Castle of Llyr,* Holt, 1966; *Taran Wanderer,* Holt, 1967; *The Truthful Harp,* Holt, 1967; *The High King,* Holt, 1968; *The Marvelous Misadventures of Sebastian,* Dutton, 1970; *The King's Fountain,* Dutton, 1971; *The Four Donkeys,* Holt, 1972; *The Foundling and Other Tales of Prydain,* Holt, 1973; *The Cat Who Wished to Be a Man,* Dutton,

1973; *The Wizard in the Tree,* Dutton, 1975; *The Town Cats and Other Tales,* Dutton, 1977; *The First Two Lives of Lukas-Kasha,* Dutton, 1978.

Translator from the French; published by New Directions, except as indicated: Paul Eluard, *Uninterrupted Poetry,* 1950; Jean-Paul Sartre, *The Wall,* 1951; Paul Vialar, *The Sea Rose,* Spearman, 1951; Sartre, *Nausea,* 1953.

Work included in New Directions anthologies. Contributor to *Contemporary Poetry;* also contributor of articles to *School Library Journal, Harper's Bazaar, Horn Book Magazine,* and other periodicals.

SIDELIGHTS: "At fifteen, in my last year of high school, I announced to my family that I intended to be a poet," Lloyd Alexander told *CA.* "Poetry, my father warned, was no practical career, I would do well to forget it. My mother came to my rescue. At her urging, my father agreed I might have a try, on condition that I also find some sort of useful work.

"For my part, I had no idea how to find any sort of work; or, in fact, how to go about being a poet. During more than a year, I had been writing long into the nights, and studying verse form to the scandalous neglect of my homework. My parents could not afford sending me to college; my grades were too wretched for a scholarship.

"Adventure, I decided, was the best way to learn writing. The United States had already entered World War II and I joined the Army, convinced that here was a chance for real deeds of derring-do.

"They shipped me not into the thick of some bold fray, but to Texas, where I became in discouraging succession an artilleryman, a cymbal player in the band, a harmonium player in the post chapel, and a first aid man.

"I had been writing grimly . . . , in a stubborn kind of hopeless hopefulness, ready to admit I was no writer at all. . . . Looking back on those days, what seemed a catastrophe now struck me as deeply funny, I was able to laugh at it; and at myself. And enjoy it. I wrote a novel about it, as my fourth and last attempt. The novel was published.

"One thing I had learned was to write about things I knew and loved. . . . I was writing out of my own life and experience. But nearly ten more years passed before I learned a writer could know and love a fantasy world as much as his real one."

AVOCATIONAL INTERESTS: Music, particularly violin, piano, and guitar, and printmaking.

BIOGRAPHICAL/CRITICAL SOURCES: Philadelphia Sunday Bulletin, March 22, 1959; *Writer,* May, 1971; *Children's Literature Review,* Volume I, Gale, 1976; *New York Times,* March 19, 1979; *Los Angeles Times,* March 22, 1979.

* * *

ALEXANDROWICZ, Charles Henry 1902-1975

PERSONAL: Born October 13, 1902, in Lemberg, Austria; died October, 1975; son of Francis and Mary (Gregor) Alexandrowicz; married Marguerite G. Drabble, 1945. *Education:* Attended Scottish College, Vienna, Austria, 1912-18; Jagiellonian University, Krakow, Poland, LL.M., LL.D.; Council of Legal Education, Lincoln's Inn, London, England, Barrister-at-Law. *Office:* Faculty of Law, 167 Phillip St., Sydney, Australia.

CAREER: Polish Diplomatic Service, counsellor of the embassy in London, England, resigned after World War II; European Central Inland Transport Organisation, chairman, 1946-48; University of Madras, Madras, India, research professor of law, 1950-61; University of Sydney, Sydney, Australia, professor, 1961-68. Visiting professor at Hague Academy of International Law, 1960, 1968, Sorbonne, University of Paris, 1963, Institut des Hautes Etudes Internationales, 1969; professorial fellow, Sorbonne, University of Paris, 1969-70. *Military service:* Home Guard, London, England, 1943-45. *Member:* Royal Asiatic Society (fellow), Grotian Society (chairman), Old Scottish Club (Vienna, Austria). *Awards, honors:* Grotius Memorial Medal awarded by International Grotius Foundation, 1961.

WRITINGS: International Economic Organisations, Stevens, 1952; *Constitutional Developments in India,* Oxford University Press, 1957; *Treaty and Diplomatic Relations between European and Asian Powers in the XVII and XVIII Centuries,* Hague Academy of International Law, 1960; *World Economic Agencies,* Stevens, 1962; *History of the Law of Nations in the East Indies,* Oxford University Press, 1966; *Studies in the History of the Law of Nations,* Nijhoff, 1970; *Law of Global Communications,* Columbia University Press, 1971; *European-African Confrontation,* Sijthoff, 1973; *Law-Making Functions of the Specialised Agencies of the United Nations,* Fred B. Rothman, 1973. Editor, *Indian Year Book of International Affairs,* 1951-61.†

* * *

ALLABY, (John) Michael 1933-

PERSONAL: Born September 18, 1933, in Belper, Derbyshire, England; son of Albert (a chiropodist) and Jessie May (King) Allaby; married Ailsa Marthe McGregor, January 3, 1957; children: Vivien Gail, Robin Graham. *Home:* Penquite, Fernleigh Rd., Wadebridge, Cornwall, England. *Agent:* Curtis Brown Group Ltd., 1 Craven Hill, London W2 3EW, England.

CAREER: Variously employed as police cadet, 1949-51, and actor, 1954-64; Soil Association, Suffolk, England, member of editorial department, 1964-72, editor of *Span,* 1967-72; Ecosystems Ltd., Wadebridge, Cornwall, England, member of board of directors and editor of *Ecologist,* 1972-73; freelance writer, 1973—. *Military service:* Royal Air Force, 1951-54, served as pilot; became pilot officer. *Member:* National Union of Journalists.

WRITINGS: The Eco-Activists, Knight & Co., 1971; *Who Will Eat? The World Food Problem,* Stacey, 1972; (with others) *A Blueprint for Survival,* Houghton, 1972; (with Floyd Allen) *Robots behind the Plow,* Rodale Press, 1974; *Ecology,* Hamlyn, 1975; (with Marika Hanbury-Tenison, Hugh Sharman, and John Seymour) *The Survival Handbook: Self-Sufficiency for Everyone,* Macmillan (London), 1975; *Inventing Tomorrow: How to Live in a Changing World,* Hodder & Stoughton, 1976; (editor) *A Dictionary of the Environment,* Macmillan, 1977; (with Colin Tudge) *Home Farm: Complete Food Self-Sufficiency,* Macmillan, 1977; *World Food Resources: Actual and Potential,* Applied Science Publishers, 1977; *Animals That Hunt,* Hamlyn, 1979; *Wildlife of North America,* Hamlyn, 1979; *Making and Managing a Smallholding,* David & Charles, 1979; *The Earth's Resources,* Eurobook, 1980.

Contributor: John Barr, editor, *The Environmental Handbook,* Ballantine, 1971; Edward Goldsmith, editor, *Can Britain Survive?,* Stacey, 1971; Michael Schwab, editor, *Teach-in for Survival,* Robinson & Watkins Books, 1972; Jonathan Benthall, editor, *Ecology,* Longmans, Green, 1973. Contributor to *Encyclopaedia Britannica,* and to magazines, journals, and newspapers.

WORK IN PROGRESS: A Year in the Life of a Field, for David & Charles; *Tropical Rain Forests,* for Orbis Publishing; with Peter Bunyard, *The Politics of Self-Sufficiency,* for Oxford University Press; editing *Encyclopedia of the 21st Century,* for Macmillan.

SIDELIGHTS: Michael Allaby told *CA:* "As a small boy I longed to do two things: to be an actor and to write books. I have done both, and so I count myself among the most fortunate of people." Concerning the life of a free-lance writer Allaby comments: "I would have it no other way, but my economic survival is a mystery I do not altogether understand. Like most writers, I suspect, I write mainly about subjects chosen by others. This can be frustrating, but it brings its own rewards." Allaby explains that a great deal of his time is spent studying, understanding, and then interpreting the subject matter presented to him. He continues: "Because I cannot write until I become enthused by my subject, I have acquired a great love for new information, new ideas, new areas to explore. A famous actor is said to have offered a newcomer two words of advice to guide him through his career: 'Be delighted.' If I can communicate to others the delight I experience in examining the world about me, and if I can be paid for doing it, I rest content."

* * *

ALLARD, Dean C(onrad) 1933-

PERSONAL: Born October 19, 1933, in Kansas City, Mo.; son of Dean C. (a lawyer) and Elizabeth (Graves) Allard; married Constance Morgan, June 17, 1955; children: Scott, Hunt, Elizabeth. *Education:* Dartmouth College, B.A., 1955; Georgetown University, M.A., 1959; George Washington University, Ph.D., 1967. *Home:* 4823 North 15th St., Arlington, Va. 22205. *Office:* U.S. Naval Historical Center, Washington, D.C. 20374.

CAREER: U.S. Naval Historical Center, Washington, D.C., head of operational archives, 1958-72, senior archivist, 1972—. George Washington University, Washington, D.C., instructor, 1960-61, assistant professorial lecturer, 1965-66, 1970-72, professorial lecturer in history, 1979—; lecturer in history, University of Virginia, Northern Virginia Branch, 1969-71. Active in various Arlington County civic and political organizations. *Military service:* U.S. Naval Reserve, active duty, 1955-58; became commander. *Member:* North American Society for Oceanic History, American Historical Association, Organization of American Historians, American Military Institute (trustee, 1979—), Society of Historians of American Foreign Relations, American Committee on the History of the Second World War (director, 1975—), Naval Historical Foundation, U.S. Naval Institute, Arlington County Historical Commission (chairman), Arlington Historical Society (president, 1973-74), Phi Beta Kappa.

WRITINGS: (Co-editor) *U.S. Naval History Sources in the Washington Area and Suggested Research Subjects,* 3rd edition, U.S. Government Printing Office, 1970; (contributor) *Technology and Institutional Response: Emergence of Naval Ordnance,* Military Affairs Press, Kansas State University, 1972; (contributor) Rollin Higham, editor, *A Guide to the Sources for American Military History,* Archon Press, 1975, supplement, 1980; (co-author) *The United States Navy and the Vietnam Conflict,* Volume I, U.S. Government Printing Office, 1976; (author of foreword) Myron J. Smith, Jr., *Naval Bibliography of World War II,* Scarecrow, 1976; *Spencer Fullerton Baird and the U.S. Fish Commission: A Study in the History of American Science,* Arno, 1978; (contributor) Kenneth J. Hagan, editor, *In Peace and War: American Naval Policy,* Greenwood Press, 1978; (author of foreword) Paul Dull, *Battle History of the Japanese Navy in World War II,* Naval Institute Press, 1978; (contributor) *Versatile Guardian: Research in Naval History,* Howard University Press, 1979; (co-editor) *U.S. Naval History Sources in the United States,* U.S. Government Printing Office, 1979.

Contributor to *Encyclopedia of American History* and to *Dictionary of Scientific Biography, Dictionary of American Biography, Dictionary of American History,* and *Dictionary of American Military Biography;* contributor to *Newsletter of the Society for the Historians of American Foreign Relations, George Washington Magazine, American Neptune, Virginia Magazine of History and Biography, Arlington Historical Magazine, Military Affairs,* and *Oral History Review.* Member of editorial advisory board, *Military Affairs,* 1973—.

WORK IN PROGRESS: A study of U.S. naval policy during World War I.

* * *

ALLEN, Lee 1915-1969

PERSONAL: Born January 12, 1915, in Cincinnati, Ohio; died May 20, 1969, in Syracuse, N.Y.; son of Alfred Gaither and Clara (Forbes) Allen; married Adele Louise Felix, 1958; children: Randall and Roxann (twins). *Education:* Kenyon College, A.B., 1937; graduate study at Columbia University, 1937-38. *Home:* Westridge, Cooperstown, N.Y. *Office:* National Baseball Hall of Fame, Cooperstown, N.Y.

CAREER: Cincinnati Baseball Club, Cincinnati, Ohio, publicity writer, 1938-39, 1943-45; Gruen Watch Company, Cincinnati, publicity director, 1940-42; WSAI (radio station), Cincinnati, sports announcer, 1948-50; KYW (radio station), Philadelphia, Pa., sports announcer, 1951-53; *Cincinnati Times-Star* and *Cincinnati Enquirer,* Cincinnati, feature writer, 1955-58; Baseball Hall of Fame, Cooperstown, N.Y., historian, 1959-69. *Member:* Psi Upsilon.

WRITINGS: The Cincinnati Reds, Putnam, 1948; *One Hundred Years of Baseball,* Bartholomew, 1950; *The Hot Stove League,* A. S. Barnes, 1955; *The National League Story,* Hill & Wang, 1961, revised edition, 1965; *The American League Story,* Hill & Wang, 1962; *The Giants and the Dodgers,* Putnam, 1964; (with T. W. Meany) *Kings of the Diamond: The Immortals in Baseball's Hall of Fame,* Putnam, 1965; *Babe Ruth,* Putnam, 1966; *Dizzy Dean,* Putnam, 1967; *The World Series,* Putnam, 1969. Regular contributor to *Sporting News.*

AVOCATIONAL INTERESTS: Collected twentieth-century American fiction.

BIOGRAPHICAL/CRITICAL SOURCES: Sports Illustrated, April, 1959; *Sporting News,* April, 1959.†

* * *

ALMEDINGEN, Martha Edith von 1898-1971 (E. M. Almedingen)

PERSONAL: Born July 21, 1898, in St. Petersburg, Russia; died March 5, 1971; daughter of A. N. von Almedingen (a chemistry professor). *Education:* Educated privately; entered Xenia Nobility College, 1913, left with highest honors for history and literature; Petrograd University, doctoral study, 1916-20. *Home:* Brookleaze, Nettlebridge, Oakhill, Bath, England.

CAREER: University of Petrograd, Petrograd, Russia, lecturer on English mediaeval history and literature, 1921-22; Oxford University, Oxford, England, lecturer, Russian history and literature, 1951; novelist and biographer, 1951-71. *Member:* Royal Society of Literature (fellow).

WRITINGS: From Rome to Canterbury, Morehouse, 1933, 2nd edition, Faith Press, c.1937; *Pilgrimage of a Soul,* Morehouse, 1934; *Through Many Windows Opened by the Book of Common Prayer,* Morehouse, 1935; *Lion of the North: Charles XII, King of Sweden,* Constable, 1938; *She Married Pushkin,* Constable, 1939; *Young Catherine,* Constable, 1939; (translator) Hrabamus Maurus, *The Lord's Passion,* Mowbray, c.1940; *Tomorrow Will Come* (autobiography), Little, Brown, 1941, 2nd edition, Bodley Head, 1961, Dufour, 1964; *Poloniae Testamentum: A Poem,* John Lane, 1942; *Frossia* (novel), John Lane, 1943, Harcourt, 1944; *Out of Seir: A Poem,* John Lane, 1943; *Dasha* (novel), Harcourt, 1945; *Dom Bernard Clements: A Portrait,* John Lane, 1945; *The Almond Tree* (autobiography), John Lane, 1947; *The Golden Sequence* (novel), Westminster, 1949 (published in England as *The Inmost Heart,* John Lane, 1949).

Within the Harbour (autobiography), John Lane, 1950; *Flame on the Water,* Hutchinson, 1952; *Late Arrival* (autobiography), Westminster, 1952; *Storm at Westminster: A Play in Twelve Scenes,* Oxford University Press, 1952; *Stand Fast, Beloved City,* Hutchinson, 1954; *Ground Corn* (novel), Hutchinson, 1955; *Fair Haven* (novel), Hutchinson, 1956; *Stephen's Light* (novel), Hutchinson, 1956; *The Scarlet Goose* (novel), Hutchinson, 1957; (adaptor) *Russian Fairy Tales,* Muller, 1958; *Very Far Country,* Appleton, 1958 (published in England as *Life of Many Colours: The Story of Grandmother Ellen,* Hutchinson, 1958); *So Dark a Stream: A Study of the Emperor Paul I of Russia, 1754-1801,* Hutchinson, 1959.

Winter in the Heart (novel), Appleton, 1960 (published in England as *The Little Stairway,* Hutchinson, 1960); *The Young Pavlova* (juvenile), Parrish, 1960, Roy, 1961; *Catherine: Empress of Russia,* Dodd, 1961; *Dark Splendour* (novel), Hutchinson, 1961; *The Empress Alexandra, 1872-1918: A Study,* Hutchinson, 1961; (author of introduction) *Kittens in Color,* Studio Books, 1961; *The Emperor Alexander II: A Study,* Bodley Head, 1962, Dufour, 1964; *Catherine the Great: A Portrait,* Hutchinson, 1963; *One Little Tree: A Christmas Card of a Finnish Landscape,* Parrish, 1963; (adaptor) *Russian Folk and Fairy Tales,* Putnam, 1963; *The Knights of the Golden Table* (juvenile), Bodley Head, 1963, Lippincott, 1964; *The Young Leonardo da Vinci* (juvenile), Parrish, 1963, Roy, 1964; *The Emperor Alexander I,* Bodley Head, 1964, Vanguard, 1966; *A Picture History of Russia* (juvenile), C. A. Watts, 1964; *The Treasure of Siegfried* (juvenile), Bodley Head, 1964, Lippincott, 1965; *An Unbroken Unity: A Memoir of Grand Duchess Serge of Russia, 1864-1918,* Bodley Head, 1964; *The Ladies at St. Hedwig's* (novel), Hutchinson, 1965, Vanguard, 1967; *The Unnamed Stream and Other Poems,* Bodley Head, 1965; *The Young Catherine the Great* (juvenile), Roy, 1965; *Little Katia,* Oxford University Press, 1966, Farrar, Straus, 1967; *Retreat from Moscow,* Parrish, 1966; *Young Mark,* Oxford University Press, 1966; *The Romanovs,* Holt, 1966; *St. Francis of Assisi,* Knopf, 1967; *Charlemagne,* Bodley Head, 1968; *Candle at Dusk,* Farrar, Straus, 1969; *I Remember St. Petersburg,* Longmans, Green, 1969, Norton, 1970; *Ellen,* Farrar, Straus, 1970; *Fanny,* Farrar, Straus, 1970; *Too Early Lilac,* Hutchinson, 1970, Vanguard, 1974; *Land of Muscovy: The History of Early Russia,* Farrar, Straus, 1972; *Anna,* Farrar, Straus, 1972.

SIDELIGHTS: While Martha Edith von Almedingen wrote over sixty books during her lifetime, her biographical and autobiographical novels seemed to be the most popular and successful of her collection.

Writing in a review for the *School Library Journal,* Rosemary Neiswender felt the reason for Almedingen's success in this area was that she seemed "especially adept at translating history into terms dramatic enough to capture the imagination of younger readers without sacrificing accuracy."

Using *The Emperor Alexander I* was an example, *Saturday Review* critic, Hans Kohn explained that "Almedingen wrote her book not for the historian but for the general public, to which it can be warmly recommended. Not a 'romantic' or fictional biography but based on letters and memoirs of the period." Guy Davenport agrees with Kohn's explanation and goes on to describe Almedingen's style in more detail in his review in the *National Review.* Davenport wrote that "Almedingen offers no political opinions, makes no passionate statements about civilization, extracts no conclusions; she is not writing that kind of book. Brilliant historian that she is, she chose rather to write a book in which one can feel page by page the anguish of the revolution and the loss of the civilization it destroyed. But it is the kind of book every wise reader prefers to the cold diagrams of the history book. Facts hide the knowledge they pretend to convey; real history is knowing that there was a time in one of the most civilized of cities when a broken shoelace was the last shoelace in the world."

Almedingen once explained her philosophy of writing. As she told *CA:* "Work is as necessary as air and bread to me. I never feel satisfied, and am convinced that the day I write anything to please me I will lay down the pen. Have no regular hours for work. Broadly speaking, the mind is at it the whole time. Sometimes I re-write a page ten and more times. I have no secretary or dictaphone. Write everything before typing it. Environment never troubles me. Have done work in crowded trains, on top of London buses, in noisy tearooms. Can't write a novel unless I become the people I write about."

BIOGRAPHICAL/CRITICAL SOURCES: Saturday Review, September 17, 1966; *National Review,* October 22, 1968; *School Library Journal,* April. 1969; (under name E. M. Almedingen) *Contemporary Literary Criticism,* Volume XII, Gale, 1980.†

* * *

ALTENBERND, (August) Lynn 1918-

PERSONAL: Born February 3, 1918, in Cleveland, Ohio; son of Adolf Carl (a gardener) and Lucy (Cheyney) Altenbernd; married Mary Blazekovich, April 19, 1941; children: Toni (Mrs. Andrew J. Gold), Mark, Nicholas. *Education:* Ohio State University, B.Sc., 1939, M.A., 1949, Ph.D., 1954. *Home:* 710 West Washington Ave., Urbana, Ill. 61801. *Office:* Department of English, 100 English Bldg., University of Illinois, Urbana, Ill. 61801.

CAREER: High school English teacher in Yellow Springs, Ohio, 1942-44; Ohio State University, Columbus, instructor in English, 1949-54; University of Illinois at Urbana-Champaign, instructor, 1954-57, assistant professor, 1957-62, associate professor, 1962-65, professor of English, 1965—, chairman of department, 1966-71. *Military service:* U.S. Army, 1944-46; became second lieutenant. *Member:* American Association of University Professors, Modern Language Association of America, National Council of Teachers of English.

WRITINGS: (Editor with Leslie L. Lewis) *Introduction to Literature: Plays* (with handbook), Macmillan, 1963, 2nd edition, 1969, revised edition of handbook published separately as *A Handbook for the Study of Drama,* 1966; (editor with Lewis) *Introduction to Literature: Poems* (with handbook), Macmillan, 1963, 3rd edition, 1975, revised edition of handbook published separately as *A Handbook for the Study of Poetry,* 1966, 2nd revised edition, 1975; (editor with Lewis) *Introduction to Literature: Stories* (with handbook), Macmillan, 1963, 3rd edition, 1980, revised edition of handbook published separately as *A Handbook for the Study of Fiction,* 1966, 2nd revised edition, 1980; (editor) *Exploring Literature: Fiction, Poetry, Drama, Criticism,* Macmillan, 1970; (editor) *Anthology: An Introduction to Literature,* Macmillan, 1977. Contributor to *Journal of English and Germanic Philology, Criticism,* and *Modern Language Notes.*

WORK IN PROGRESS: A book on American writing on Europe in the nineteenth century, including the work of Henry James, Mark Twain, William Dean Howells, and Henry Adams.

* * *

ALTER, Robert B(ernard) 1935-

PERSONAL: Born April 2, 1935, in New York, N.Y.; son of Harry (a salesman) and Tillie (Zimmerman) Alter; married Judith Berkenbilt, June 4, 1961 (divorced February, 1973); married Carol Cosman (an editor and translator), June 17, 1973; children: (first marriage) Miriam, Dan; (second marriage) Gabriel. *Education:* Columbia University, B.A., 1957; Harvard University, M.A., 1958, Ph.D., 1962. *Religion:* Jewish. *Home:* 123 Tamalpais Rd., Berkeley, Calif. 94708. *Agent:* Georges Borchardt, 136 East 57th St., New York, N.Y. 10022. *Office:* Department of Comparative Literature, University of California, Berkeley, Calif. 94720.

CAREER: Columbia University, New York, N.Y., instructor, 1962-64, assistant professor of English, 1964-66; University of California, Berkeley, associate professor, 1967-69, professor of Hebrew and comparative literature, 1969—, chairman of comparative literature department, 1970-72. *Member:* American Comparative Literature Association, Association for Jewish Studies. *Awards, honors:* English Institute essay prize, 1965; Guggenheim fellow, 1966-67, 1979-80; National Endowment for the Humanities senior fellow, 1972-73.

WRITINGS: *Rogue's Progress: Studies in the Picaresque Novel,* Harvard University Press, 1965; *Fielding and the Nature of the Novel,* Harvard University Press, 1968; *After the Tradition: Essays on Modern Jewish Writing,* Dutton, 1969; *Partial Magic: The Novel as a Self-Conscious Genre,* University of California Press, 1975; *Defenses of the Imagination,* Jewish Publication Society, 1978; (with wife, Carol Cosman) *A Lion for Love: A Critical Biography of Stendhal,* Basic Books, 1979. *Commentary,* columnist, 1965—, contributing editor, 1973—.

WORK IN PROGRESS: A literary study of biblical narrative, for Basic Books.

SIDELIGHTS: In a *Commentary* review, John Gross writes that the essays in *After the Tradition* "are distinguished by their clarity, sober intelligence, and sureness of touch. It is a relief, for a start, to find a critic dealing so firmly with the fashion for sentimental misrepresentations of Jewish experience. . . . Without losing his temper or jeering at honest confusion, Mr. Alter makes short work of what he calls the 'tacit conspiracy afoot in recent years to foist on the American public as peculiarly Jewish various admired characteristics which in fact belong to the common humanity of us all.'" Gross also feels that Alter "is rewarding, too, on the subject of critics who talk gaily about the 'talmudic' qualities of Kafka's prose without giving any sign that they know the difference between an *aleph* and a *bet,* and on novelists whose acquaintance with classical Jewish tradition bears about as much relation to the real thing as 'When Irish Eyes Are Smiling' does to the collected poems of W. B. Yeats, but whose books are nevertheless somehow supposed to be replete with ancestral Jewish wisdom."

Meyer Levin of the *New York Times Book Review* finds that Alter's essays on Saul Bellow and Bernard Malamud "cover familiar ground," but that some, the one on Elie Wiesel for instance, are "rich in perceptions that escape the casual reader." Levin believes that the pieces on the Israeli literary scene have greater impact than those on American Jewish writers "because of the remoteness of Hebrew to that same casual reader." He calls Alter's treatment of Israeli literature "brilliant and erudite . . . from Agnon to Ziklag. Few critics are equipped for this."

Reviewing *A Lion for Love* for the *Washington Post Book World,* Julia Epstein calls the book "a splendid example of a rare and difficult critical genre; a biography which chronicles and interprets the development of a character of complex imaginative genius, and at the same time produces a lucid critical reading of his works which is accessible to general readers." Epstein concludes that "*A Lion for Love* is a gentle book, a rigorous scholarly biography that remains honestly affectionate toward its subject." And John Sturrock writes: "In this excellent short biography, Robert Alter (in collaboration with Carol Cosman) brings out both the charms and the complexities of Stendhal. The tone of the book is discreetly admiring, but ironic enough when need be to remind one of the saving and consummate irony of its subject. There is a wide choice of biographies of Stendhal by now, but I know of none more coherent or civilized than this one."

BIOGRAPHICAL/CRITICAL SOURCES: *New York Times Book Review,* January 26, 1969, October 7, 1979; *Commentary,* April, 1969; *Georgia Review,* spring, 1969; *Washington Post Book World,* September 16, 1979; *Los Angeles Times,* October 19, 1979.

* * *

ALTER, Robert Edmond 1925-1965 (Robert Raymond, Robert Retla)

PERSONAL: Born December 10, 1925, in San Francisco, Calif.; died, 1965; son of Retla and Irene (Kerr) Alter; married Maxine Louise Outwater, 1947; children: Sande. *Education:* Attended University of Southern California, 1944, Pasadena City College, 1946, Pasadena Playhouse, 1948. *Home:* 2811 Alexander Dr., Laguna Beach, Calif. *Agent:* Larry Sternig Literary Agency, 742 Robertson St., Milwaukee, Wis. 53213.

CAREER: In his youth was a migratory worker in Santa Paula, Calif., 1942, a stock boy for Vroman's Books, Pasadena, Calif., 1943-44, and a farm hand in Hamilton, N.D., 1945; U.S. Post Office, Altadena, Calif., carrier, 1949-62. *Military service:* U.S. Army, one year; National Guard, two years; became sergeant.

WRITINGS—All published by Putnam, except as indicated: *Swamp Sister,* Gold Medal, 1961; *Dark Keep,* 1962; *Listen, the Drum,* 1963; *Time of the Tomahawk,* 1963; *Shovel Nose and the Gator Grabbers,* 1963; *Treasure of Tenakertom,*

1964; *Rabble on a Hill,* 1964; *The Day of the Arkansas,* 1965; *Heroes in Blue and Gray,* Whitman Publishing, 1965; *Two Sieges of the Alamo,* 1965; *Who Goes Next,* 1966; *High Spy,* 1967; *Henry M. Stanley: The Man from Africa,* 1967; *Red Water,* 1968; *First Comes Courage,* 1969; *Path to Savagery,* Avon, 1969; *The Trail of Billy the Kid,* Belmont-Tower, 1975. Also author of *Carney Hill* and of a television script for "World of Disney."

AVOCATIONAL INTERESTS: Skin diving, history, and book collecting.

BIOGRAPHICAL/CRITICAL SOURCES: Publishers' Weekly, June 20, 1966.†

* * *

AMAN, Mohammed M(ohammed) 1940-

PERSONAL: Born January 3, 1940, in Alexandria, Egypt; son of Mohammed Aman (an army officer) and Fathia Ali (al-Maghrabi) Mohammed; married Mary Jo Parker (a librarian), September 15, 1972. *Education:* Cairo University, B.A., 1961; Columbia University, M.S., 1964; University of Pittsburgh, Ph.D., 1968. *Religion:* Islam. *Home:* 4020 West Mequon Rd., Mequon, Wis. 53092. *Office:* School of Library Science, University of Wisconsin, Milwaukee, Wis. 53201.

CAREER: Egyptian National Library, Cairo, bibliographer and reference librarian, 1961-63; Arab Information Center, New York City, head librarian, 1963-64; Duquesne University Library, Pittsburgh, Pa., reference librarian, 1966-68; Pratt Institute, New York City, assistant professor of library science and head of Library Science Library, 1968-69; St. John's University, Jamaica, N.Y., assistant professor, 1969-71, associate professor, 1971-74, professor of library science, 1974-76, chairman of department, 1973-76; Long Island University, C. W. Post Center, Greenvale, N.Y., professor and dean of Palmer Graduate Library School, 1976-79; University of Wisconsin—Milwaukee, professor and dean of School of Library Science, 1979—. *Member:* American Library Association, American Society for Information Science, American Association of University Professors, Egyptian American Scholars Association, Middle East Studies Association, Wisconsin Library Association.

WRITINGS: Analysis of Terminology, Form, and Structure of Subject Headings in Arabic Literature and Formulation of Rules for Arabic Subject Headings, University of Pittsburgh Press, 1968; *Arab States Author Headings,* St. John's University Press, 1973; (with A. Huq) *Librarianship and the Third World,* Garland Publishing, 1976; *Plan for a National Education Documentation Center in Bahrain,* UNESCO (Paris), 1977; (with M. Zehery) *Kuwait University Libraries: A Management Study,* Kuwait University, 1978; *Arab Serials and Periodicals: A Subject Bibliography,* Garland Publishing, 1979; *Cataloging and Classification of Non-Western Library Material: Issues, Trends and Practices,* Oryx, 1980.

Contributor; published by Scarecrow, except as indicated: E. J. Josey, editor, *What Black Librarians Are Saying,* 1972; Jean Lowrie, editor, *School Libraries: International Developments,* 1972; Josey, editor, *New Dimensions in Academic Librarianship,* 1974; John Harvey, editor, *Significant Recent Trends in Comparative and International Library Science,* 1977; Josey and Ann Schockley, editors, *Handbook on Black Librarianship,* Libraries Unlimited, 1977; Josey and Kenneth E. Peeples, editors, *Opportunities for Minorities in Librarianship,* 1977.

Contributor to *Encyclopedia of Library and Information Science;* book reviewer for *American Reference Books Annual* and *Annual Review of Library and Information Science,* 1974—. Honorary contributing editor, *International Library Review,* 1969—.

WORK IN PROGRESS: Education and Librarianship in the Arab World.

SIDELIGHTS: Mohammed M. Aman told *CA:* "My writings on library and information science in general and international librarianship in particular aim at increasing international understanding through unrestricted and free access to books and other media and the availability of quality library services, especially to those who have been deprived from such essential services. Libraries and books are essential ingredients for an educated society and for its aspiring young writers. I hope that my writings on the subject will help those who plan for the betterment of their societies."

AVOCATIONAL INTERESTS: Tennis, swimming, gardening, travel.

* * *

AMANUDDIN, Syed 1934-

PERSONAL: Born February 4, 1934, in Mysore, India; son of Syed (a businessman) and Shahzadi (Begum) Jamaluddin; married Ashraf Basith (a social worker), February 18, 1960; children: Irfan, Rizwan. *Education:* University of Mysore, B.A. (with honors), 1956, M.A., 1957; Bowling Green State University, Ph.D., 1970; postdoctoral study at University of London, summer, 1973, New York University, summer, 1974, and Duke University, 1976-77. *Home address:* P.O. Box 391, Sumter, S.C. 29150. *Office:* Department of English, Morris College, Sumter S.C. 29150.

CAREER: College of Arts, Karimnagar, India, lecturer in English, 1958-61; Osmania University, Hyderabad, India, lecturer in English, 1961-67; Morris College, Sumter, S.C., associate professor, 1970-73, professor of English, 1976—, chairman of Division of Humanities, 1973—. *Member:* Modern Language Association of America, South Asian Literary Association (co-founder; secretary, 1976-79), Sumter Poetry Club (founder; chairman, 1974-77).

WRITINGS—Published by Poetry Eastward, except as indicated: *Hart Crane's Mystical Quest and Other Essays,* Kavyalaya (Mysore, India), 1967; *The Forbidden Fruit* (poems), Kavyalaya, 1967; *Tiffin State Hospital* (poems), 1970; *Shoes of Tradition,* 1970; *The Children of Hiroshima* (poems), 1970; *Poems of Protest,* 1972; *System Shaker* (plays), 1972; (editor with Margaret Diesendorf) *New Poetry from Australia,* 1973; *Lightning and Love* (poems), 1973; *The Age of the Female Eunichs* (poems), 1974; *Adventures of Atman: An Epic of the Soul,* 1977; *The King Who Sold His Wife* (play), Prayer Books (Calcutta), 1978; *Gems and Germs,* 1978; (contributor) C. D. Narasimhaiah, editor, *Awakened Conscience: Studies in Commonwealth Literature,* Sterling Publishers (New Delhi), 1978; *Passage to the Himalayas* (novel), Prayer Books, 1979.

Contributor of reviews, articles, and poems to periodicals, including *Indian Verse, Poetry Australia, Descant, World Literature Today, Journal of South Asian Literature,* and *Journal of Indian Writing in English.* Editor of *Poetry Eastward,* 1967-75, and of *Creative Moment: World Poetry and Criticism,* 1972-81.

WORK IN PROGRESS: Studies in World Poetry in English; Goodbye, America and *Domestic from Bombay,* both novels; *Anarkali,* a play.

SIDELIGHTS: Syed Amanuddin writes: "Creativity is, I think, a characteristic of our being human. Without creativity the caveman could not have come out of his cave and the astronaut could not have reached the moon. Cultures that block creativity are doomed, for creativity means freedom to think, imagine, and create what one wants to and the way one wants to.

"I feel alive only when I am engaged in a creative act. Experiences rush to me as visual and audial experiences. Sometimes I try to express these experiences with the help of the canvas or camera, but I am primarily a poet or artist in words. I care for the freshness of image and phrase. At the same time, I lry to establish a dialogue with my readers. I am fascinated by Sir Philip Sidney's definition of poetry as a speaking picture. Some of my poems are dramatic monologues where I imagine the reader himself playing the role of the mute but involved listener.

"While in my poetry I try to explore three contexts of human experiences—personal, social, and cosmic—my plays and novels are mostly about men and women whose lives are involved in the clashes of values and actions.

"I am also involved in using television for creative expression and social criticism. My arrangement of my poetry, photography, and paintings was produced by South Carolina Educational Television in Sumter in the spring of 1976. The same station produced a seven-part series of discussions developed and moderated by me in the spring of 1979 on aspects of the relationship between the humanities and mental health. The series which was aired in the fall of 1979 emphasized the fact that creativity is essential for human happiness and sanity."

* * *

AMBROSE, Alice 1906-

PERSONAL: Born November 25, 1906, in Lexington, Ill.; daughter of Albert Lee (a florist) and Bonnie Belle (Douglass) Ambrose; married Morris Lazerowitz (a writer and professor emeritus of philosophy), June 15, 1938. *Education:* Millikin University, A.B., 1928; University of Wisconsin, M.A., 1929, Ph.D., 1932; Cambridge University, Ph.D., 1938. *Home:* 126 Vernon St., Northhampton, Mass. 01060. *Office:* Department of Philosophy, Smith College, Northampton, Mass. 01060.

CAREER: University of Michigan, Ann Arbor, instructor in philosophy, 1935-37; Smith College, Northampton, Mass., assistant professor, 1943-51, professor, 1951-64, Sophia and Austin Smith Professor of Philosophy, 1964-72, professor emeritus, 1972—. *Member:* American Philosophical Association (vice-president of Eastern Division, 1966), American Association of University Professors, Association for Symbolic Logic, Phi Kappa Phi. *Awards, honors:* LL.D., Millikin University, 1958.

WRITINGS—With husband, Morris Lazerowitz, except as indicated: *Fundamentals of Symbolic Logic,* Holt, 1948, revised edition, 1962; *Logic: The Theory of Formal Inference,* Holt, 1961, revised edition, Scientia, 1972; (sole author) *Essays in Analysis,* Allen & Unwin, 1966; (editors) *G. E. Moore: Essays in Retrospect,* Allen & Unwin, 1970; (editors) *Ludwig Wittgenstein: Philosophy and Language,* Allen & Unwin, 1972; *Philosophical Theories,* de Gruyter, 1976; (sole editor) *Wittgenstein's Lectures: Cambridge, 1932-1935,* Rowman & Littlefield, 1979; *Necessity and Philosophy* (in Spanish), University of New Mexico Press, in press. Contributor to proceedings and to professional journals. Editor of *Journal of Symbolic Logic,* 1953-68.

WORK IN PROGRESS: Research on philosophy of mathematics.

ANASTAS, Peter 1937-

PERSONAL: Born November 15, 1937, in Gloucester, Mass.; son of Panos Nicholas (a restaurateur) and Catherine (Polisson) Anastas; married Jeane Wiener, November 14, 1964 (divorced November, 1972); children: Jonathan Peter, Benjamin Thomas, Rhea. *Education:* Bowdoin College, B.A., 1959; University of Florence, graduate study, 1959-61; Tufts University, M.A., 1967. *Home:* 15 Vine St., Gloucester, Mass. 01930.

CAREER: International Academy, Florence, Italy, instructor in English, 1960-62; high school English teacher in Winchester, Mass., 1962-64; Tufts University, Medford, Mass., teaching assistant in English, 1964-67; full-time writer, 1967-72; North Shore Community College, Beverly, Mass., instructor in English, 1972—. Instructor in humanities at Montserrat School of Visual Art, 1972-74. Action, Inc., family services administrator of Home Start Program, 1972-75, director of advocacy, 1976—; rector, Dogtown College (alternative adult education center), 1979—. *Member:* American Civil Liberties Union, Concerned Clergy and Laymen, Citizens for Participatory Politics, Massachusetts Civil Liberties Union, Cape Ann Concerned Citizens, Gloucester Historical Commission.

WRITINGS: (Translator) Giorgio Piccardi, *The Chemical Basis of Medical Climatology,* C. C Thomas, 1962; (with Peter Parsons) *When Gloucester Was Gloucester: Toward an Oral History of the City,* Gloucester Three Hundred Fiftieth Anniversary Celebration, Inc., 1973; *Glooskap's Children: Encounters with the Penobscot Indians of Maine,* Beacon Press, 1973; *Landscape with Boy* (novella), Kite Books, 1974; *Siva Dancing: A Memoir,* Pressroom, 1979. Contributor of stories and reviews to magazines in the United States and abroad, including *Numero, Le Arti, Tension, Falmouth Review of Literature,* and *Stations One.*

WORK IN PROGRESS: Decline of Fishes, a novel based on the history of Gloucester, Mass.; research for a documentary book on the Greek experience in America; continued research on the oral history of Gloucester; short stories, essays, and journals.

SIDELIGHTS: Peter Anastas told *CA:* "The entire thrust of my life in writing, teaching and social work (three activities which I have pursued simultaneously for many years) has been to the end of being of use to other people. The ultimate statement is not, I believe, the one you make on paper, but the one you make with your life—how you live it, what you do with it. The true 'responsibility of intellectuals' (especially in times of crisis) lies in this. Hence, political and social action is an imperative; and writing can be such an action. Witness: Sartre, Camus and de Beauvoir.

"In terms of the daily work of writing whatever it is you need to write (categories are no longer of any use—'fiction, nonfiction'—no one needs to 'make up' anything anymore) the work and teaching of the late poet Charles Olson has been of most help to me, especially his statement to the effect that 'there is simply ourselves and where we are has a particularity which we'd better use because that's about all we got . . . the literal essence and exactitude of your own. I mean the streets you live on, or the clothes you wear, or the color of your own hair. Truth lies solely in what you do with it.'"

Anastas has a special interest in American Indian culture. He feels that Indians can teach white America a great deal about the quality of life and how to find inner peace. Convinced that white culture contains the seeds of its own destruction, he also sees a correlation between "the destruction of the environment in America and the annihilation of the Indian."

* * *

ANAYA, Rudolfo A(lfonso) 1937-

PERSONAL: Born October 30, 1937, in Pastura, N.M.; son of Martin (a laborer) and Rafaelita (Mares) Anaya; married Patricia Lawless (a counselor), July 21, 1966. *Education:* University of New Mexico, B.A., 1963, M.A. (English), 1968, M.A. (guidance and counseling), 1972. *Home:* 5324 Canada Vista N.W., Albuquerque, N.M. 87120. *Office:* Department of English, University of New Mexico, Albuquerque, N.M. 87131.

CAREER: Teacher in public schools of Albuquerque, N.M., 1963-70; University of Albuquerque, Albuquerque, N.M., director of counseling, 1971-73; University of New Mexico, Albuquerque, assistant professor of English, 1974—. Summer lecturer, Universidad Anahuac, Mexico City, Mexico, 1974. Lecturer and consultant. Associate editor, La Academia Publications. *Member:* Modern Language Association of America, American Association of University Professors, Coordinating Council of Literary Magazines, Writers West, Rio Grande Writers Association, La Academia Society, La Compania de Teatro de Albuquerque. *Awards, honors:* Premio Quinto Sol literary award, 1971, for *Bless Me, Ultima;* University of New Mexico Mesa Chicana literary award, 1977; New Mexico Governor's Public Service Award, 1978; National Chicano Council on Higher Education fellow, 1978-79.

WRITINGS: Bless Me, Ultima (novel), Tonatiuh International, 1972; *Heart of Aztlan* (novel), Editorial Justa, 1976; *Bilingualism: Promise for Tomorrow* (screenplay), Bilingual Educational Services, 1976; (author of introduction) Sabine Ulibarri, *Mi Abuela Fumaba Puros,* Tonatiuh International, 1978; *Tortuga* (novel), Editorial Justa, 1979; "The Season of la Llorona" (one-act play), first produced at El Teatro de la Compania de Albuquerque, October 14, 1979; *Cuentos: Tales from the Hispanic Southwest,* Museum of New Mexico Press, 1980.

Contributor: (And co-editor) *Voices from the Rio Grande,* Rio Grande Writers Association Press, 1976; Lee and Galati, editors, *Oral Interpretations,* 5th edition, Houghton, 1977; *New Voices 4 in Literature, Language and Composition,* Ginn, 1978; *Anuario de Letras Chicanas,* Editorial Justa, 1979; *Grito del Sol,* Quinto Sol Publications, 1979.

Also author of dramas for the Visions Project, KCET-TV (Los Angeles), as yet neither published nor produced. Contributor of short stories, articles, and reviews to *La Luz, Bilingual Review-Revista Bilingue, New Mexico Magazine, La Confluencia, Contact II,* and the *Albuquerque News.* Associate editor, *American Book Review.*

WORK IN PROGRESS: Novels, plays, short stories.

SIDELIGHTS: Rudolfo A. Anaya told *CA:* "I write because I am filled with the urge to create. Writing novels seems to be the medium which allows me to bring together all the questions I ask about life, the characters I have met, the haunting beauty of the people and the land.

"I began to write 'in my mind' from the time I first heard words. I was raised in a very rich oral literary ambience. In New Mexico everyone tells stories, it is a creative pastime. I was hooked early on the power of the word, in the relationships between the characters of the stories. The old Spanish and indigenous *cuentos* (stories) of the Mexican American peoples of the Southwest are a rich, fantastic storehouse. I learned from the old storytellers how to recreate the narrative and pass it on.

"I've [also] been influenced by every writer I ever read. I read and absorb, not details, but the mood and style and the force of the voice in the writer. I tell my students that writing is not learned by formula, it is learned by writing a lot. There is no short cut for work in writing.

"Perhaps the greatest problem I had to solve was the shift from Spanish to English. I was raised in a Spanish-speaking family and community. I read a lot when I was growing up. I learned to translate Spanish thoughts into English phrases.

"When I am working on a novel I try to write every day. I used to write at night, but the psychological progression of my life has made me a morning writer now. Finding the time to write every morning is difficult, but it's a must. I feel somewhat satisfied that I have completed the trilogy I set out to write years ago, [for] *Bless Me, Ultima, Heart of Aztlan* and *Tortuga* are a definite trilogy in my mind. They are not only about growing up in New Mexico, they are about life. Since I completed the novels I've been writing plays and a few short stories. But I feel those are breathing spaces.

"The contemporary [literary] scene is very active and exciting. The literary magazines are providing a forum for many young writers. Of particular importance to readers in this country are not only the experimentations going on in fiction, but the role of ethnic writers. Chicano, Native American, Asian American and Black writers, and the role of women as a community of writers, is one of the most exciting things happening to writing in this country."

Bless Me, Ultima has been optioned as a possible television series.

BIOGRAPHICAL/CRITICAL SOURCES: University of Albuquerque Alumni Magazine, January, 1973; *University of New Mexico Alumni Magazine,* January, 1973; *La Luz,* May, 1973.

* * *

ANDERSON, Mary 1939-

PERSONAL: Born January 20, 1939, in New York, N.Y.; daughter of Andrew Joseph and Nellie (DeHaan) Quirk; married Carl Anderson (a commercial artist), March 1, 1958; children: Lisa, Maja, Chersteen. *Education:* Attended Hunter College of the City University of New York and New School for Social Research. *Home:* 270 Riverside Dr., New York, N.Y. 10025.

CAREER: Writer. Actress in Off-Broadway productions, New York City, 1956-58; secretary in advertising and television fields, New York City, 1958-59; teacher of creative writing in New York City schools in conjunction with Teachers and Writers Collaborative. Lecturer. *Awards, honors:* Sequoyah Children's Book Award nomination, 1976, for *F.T.C. Superstar!*; Dorothy Canfield Fisher Award nomination, 1979-80, for *Step On a Crack.*

WRITINGS—For young people; published by Atheneum, except as indicated: (With Hope Campbell) *There's a Pizza Back in Cleveland,* Four Winds, 1972; *Matilda Investigates,* 1973; *Emma's Search for Something,* 1973; *I'm Nobody! Who Are You?* (Junior Literary Guild selection), 1974; *Just the Two of Them,* 1974; *F.T.C. Superstar!,* 1976; *Matilda's Masterpiece,* 1977; *The Mystery of the Missing Painting,* Scholastic Book Services, 1977; *Step On a Crack,* 1978; *F.T.C. and Company,* 1979; (contributor) *The New York Kid's Book,* Doubleday, 1979; *The Rise and Fall of a Teenage Wacko,* 1980. Also author of libretto, "Sara Crewe: The

Orphan Princess" (musical adaptation of Frances Hodgson Burnett's classic, *A Little Princess*), produced by Performing Arts Repertory Theatre.

SIDELIGHTS: Mary Anderson told *CA:* "I think I've always wanted to write, though I didn't always know it. When I was younger, I had visions of being a famous actress. But a year or two of acting school and a brief flirtation with Off-Broadway cured me! No matter what play I was in, I kept wanting to rewrite the dialogue—including Shakespeare! That was my first clue I'd chosen the wrong profession.

"But at the time, it seemed a natural choice, since I'd always been fascinated by plays. As a child, I practically by-passed the entire world of children's literature. I was too busy reading ten-pound play anthologies. I didn't know it then, but it was *dialogue*, not the theatre, which truly intrigued me.

"When I was twelve, my best friend, Ann, took pity on me and lent me her copy of *Mary Poppins*. I was insulted. A *children's* book? My reading was far more advanced than that! As a favor, I read it. Almost overnight a new world opened up for me, the very special world of children's literature. I'd cheated myself out of a tremendous chunk of good reading and proceeded to make up for lost time. I haven't stopped since.

"With so much competition from television, writing a book which young people will take time to read is not only exciting, but very challenging. Of course, it isn't always easy trying to raise a family and write as well. But my husband, a commercial artist, also works at home. Between the two of us we've managed, despite the telltale remnants of peanut butter and tuna fish often found on our typewriter paper and art pads. Rooting out a pencil without a chewed-off eraser is always a pleasant surprise!

"Our three daughters, Lisa, Maja, and Chersteen, have always been built-in resident critics for everything I've written. My daily allotment of pages would pop hot from the typewriter, into the hands of a waiting audience.

"My oldest, Lisa, was the first to sample my material. Her criticism was diplomatic, but pointed: 'It's good, Mommy, except for the bore parts. But don't worry. Even the best books have some bore parts.' Since then, it's been a constant goal to keep the 'bore parts' to a minimum.

"Maja has a drawing board, just like her dad. And Chersteen has an 'office' just like her mom: a typewriter in the center of her table, with file folders tucked at the side. We share the typewriter paper, so things work out just fine.

"While Chersteen's stories are varied, mine have a running theme through all of them. I like to think of my books as a patchwork sampler of city life. I was born in Manhattan and have never lived anywhere else. Whether I'm writing comedy or mystery, New York is always the background, and often a main character. This also gives me the opportunity to indulge in the aspect of writing I enjoy most—research. The hours I spend browsing through library shelves and ferreting through second-hand book stalls are always a pleasure.

"Which brings me to one of my more passionate hobbies: collecting children's books. Which brings up the question that rivals 'how many angels can fit on the head of a pin?' Name 'how many children's books can fit in a Manhattan apartment?' My husband keeps insisting we don't have room for one more, while I busily build another book shelf! I no longer hear from my childhood friend, Ann, who lent me *Mary Poppins* so many years ago. But I keep reminding him it's all her fault!

"When not collecting books, several other hobbies keep me busy. My husband and I collect and make miniature rooms. I also love to quilt, bike ride, and tend my jungle of plants which kindly share our apartment with us."

* * *

ANDREW, Prudence (Hastings) 1924-

PERSONAL: Born May 23, 1924, in London, England; daughter of Percy and Margaret (Bridge) Petch; married G.H.L. Andrew, 1946; children: Jane, Sarah. *Education:* St. Anne's College, Oxford, honors degree in history, 1946. *Home:* Elmhurst, Linden Ave., Abergavenny, Monmouthshire, England.

CAREER: Joseph Lucas Ltd., Birmingham, England, on staff of personnel department, 1944-45; Nuffield Institute of Colonial Affairs, Oxford, England, member of staff, 1945-47; St. Michael's Convent School, Monmouthshire, England, history teacher, 1956-60; author.

WRITINGS: The Hooded Falcon, New Authors (London), 1960, New Authors Guild (New York), 1961; *Ordeal by Silence: A Story of Medieval Times,* Putnam, 1961; *A Question of Choice,* Putnam, 1962; *The Earthworms,* Hutchinson, 1963; *The Constant Star,* Putnam, 1964; *A Sparkle from the Coal,* Hutchinson, 1964; *The Christmas Card,* Hamish Hamilton, 1966; *Mr. Morgan's Marrow,* Hamish Hamilton, 1967; *Dog!,* Hamish Hamilton, 1968, Thomas Nelson, 1973; *A New Creature,* Putnam, 1968; *A Man with Your Advantages,* Hutchinson, 1970.

Published by Heinemann, except as indicated: *Mister O'-Brien,* 1972, Thomas Nelson, 1973; *Una and Grubstreet,* 1972, published as *Una and the Heaven Baby,* Thomas Nelson, 1975; *Roger, Sylvie and Munch,* 1973; *Goodbye to the Rat,* 1974; *The Heroic Deeds of Jason Jones,* 1975; *Where Are You Going to, My Pretty Maid?,* 1977; *Robinson Daniel Crusoe,* 1978; *Close within My Own Circle,* Elsevier/Nelson Books, 1979.

"Ginger" series, published by Lutterworth: *Ginger over the Wall,* 1962; *. . . and Batty Billy,* 1963; *. . . and No. 10,* 1964; *. . . among the Pigeons,* 1966.

WORK IN PROGRESS: A novel about England in the eighteenth century.

AVOCATIONAL INTERESTS: Music (jazz and classical), ballet, history, cats and dogs.†

* * *

ANDREWS, Allen 1913-

PERSONAL: Born April 25, 1913, in London, England; son of Ernest Samuel and Jessie (Hammond) Andrews; married Joyce Antonietta Garbutt, January 16, 1957; children: Robert Allen. *Education:* Oxford University, M.A., 1935. *Home:* 72 Princes Ct., Brompton Rd., London SW3 1ET, England.

CAREER: Sunday Pictorial, London, England, feature writer and film critic, 1946; feature writer for *Public Opinion,* 1949, *Sunday Pictorial,* 1950, and *Illustrated,* 1952 (all in London); *Daily Herald,* London, feature writer and features editor, 1954-56; writer and free-lance journalist, 1957—. *Military service:* Royal Air Force, 1940-46; became sergeant. *Member:* Society of Authors, National Union of Journalists.

WRITINGS: Proud Fortress: The Fighting History of Gibraltar, Evans Brothers, 1958, Dutton, 1959; *Earthquake,* Angus & Robertson, 1963; *The Mad Motorists: The Great Peking-Paris Race of 1907,* Harrap, 1964, Lippincott, 1965; *Those Magnificent Men in Their Flying Machines,* illustrations by Ronald Searle, Norton, 1965; *She Doubles Her Money*, Ebury Press, 1966; *The Splendid Pauper: Moreton Frewen*, Harrap, 1968, Lippincott, 1969; *The Prosecutor: Mervyn Pugh*, Harrap, 1968; *Monte Carlo or Bust: Those Daring Young Men in Their Flying Jalopies*, illustrations by Searle, Dobson, 1969; *Quotations for Speakers and Writers*, George Newnes, 1969.

The Air Marshals: The Air War in Western Europe, Morrow, 1970; *The Royal Whore: Barbara Villiers, Countess of Castlemaine*, Chilton, 1970; *Lafayette in London*, Genevieve, 1972; *Intensive Inquiries: Britain's Best Detection Chosen by Britain's Best Detectives*, St. Martin's, 1973; *Executioner Pierrepoint*, Harrap, 1974; *The Follies of King Edward VII*, Lexington Books, 1975; *The King Who Lost America*, Jupiter, 1976; *Kings and Queens of England and Scotland*, Cavendish, 1976; *Exemplary Justice: The Stalag Luft III Murders Investigation*, Harrap, 1976; *The Whisky Barons*, Jupiter, 1977; *The Life of L. S. Lowry*, Jupiter, 1977; *The Flying Machine*, Putnam, 1977 (published in England as *Back to the Drawing Board*, David & Charles, 1977); *Victorian Engineering*, Jupiter, 1978; *The Technology of Man*, United Technologies, 1979; *The Pig Plantagenet*, Viking, 1980. Ghost writer of company histories and of several autobiographies. Contributor to periodicals.

WORK IN PROGRESS: Love and Death in Man and Beast, a novel, for Hutchinson.

SIDELIGHTS: Allen Andrews told *CA:* "My deep pleasure is to get tangled, but not drowned, in a morass of facts and to discipline them into understandable order. . . . After concentrating on creative history and biography, with relaxation in documentary crime, in show business, and in the lovely land of Italy, I have eased into the historical novel, and histories of technology."

Andrews's books have been published in Australia, Germany, the Netherlands, Sweden, Italy, Japan, France, Spain, and Czechoslovakia. Feature length films have been produced of *The Mad Motorists, Those Magnificent Men in Their Flying Machines*, and *Monte Carlo or Bust*.

* * *

ANDREWS, F(rank) Emerson 1902-1978

PERSONAL: Born January 26, 1902, in Lancaster, Pa.; died August 7, 1978, in Burlington, Vt.; son of Harry and Ellen (Wiggins) Andrews; married Edith Lilian Severance, July 5, 1932; children: Frank M., Peter Bruce, Bryant. *Education:* Franklin and Marshall College, B.A., 1923. *Religion:* Protestant. *Home:* 34 Oak St., Tenafly, N.J. 07670.

CAREER: Macmillan Publishing Co., Inc., New York City, manager of advertising printing, 1923-26, director of mail service department, 1926-28; Russell Sage Foundation, New York City, director of publications, 1928-56, director of philanthropic research, 1944-56; Foundation Library Center, New York City, director, 1956-64, president, 1964-67; consultant, 1967-78. Consultant on publications to Twentieth Century Fund, 1940-55, and to National Science Foundation, 1958-68. Member and sometime chairman of Tenafly Planning Board, 1936-62. Trustee, Franklin and Marshall College and Tenafly Library Board. *Member:* Duodecimal Society of America (president, 1944-50; chairman of board, 1950-64), American Institute of Graphic Arts (director), Authors League of America, National Conference on Social Welfare, Phi Beta Kappa. *Awards, honors:* First annual award, Duodecimal Society; L.H.D. from Franklin and Marshall College, 1952.

WRITINGS: New Numbers, Harcourt, 1935; *The Gingerbread House*, Oxford University Press, 1943; *I Find Out*, Essential Books, 1946; (with Shelby M. Harrison) *American Foundations for Social Welfare*, Russell Sage, 1946; (with Lilian Brandt and J. M. Glenn) *Russell Sage Foundation: 1907-1946*, Russell Sage, 1947; *For Charlemagne!*, Harper, 1949; *Philanthropic Giving*, Russell Sage, 1950; *Corporation Giving*, Russell Sage, 1952; *Attitudes toward Giving*, Russell Sage, 1953; *Grugan's God*, Muhlenberg, 1955; *Philanthropic Foundations*, Russell Sage, 1956; *Upside-Down Town*, Little, Brown, 1958; (editor) *Legal Instruments of Foundations*, Russell Sage, 1958; (editor with Ann Walton) *The Foundation Directory*, Russell Sage, 1960; *Numbers, Please*, Little, Brown, 1961, 2nd enlarged edition, Teachers College Press, 1977; (editor) *Foundations: Twenty Viewpoints*, Russell Sage, 1965; *Knights and Daze*, Putnam, 1966; *The Tenafly Public Library: A History, 1891-1970*, Tenafly Public Library, 1970; *Foundation Watcher*, Franklin & Marshall College, 1973; *Nobody Comes to Dinner*, Little, Brown, 1977. Contributor of nearly 300 articles to national magazines, including *Atlantic Monthly, Harper's, New Yorker*, and *Ladies Home Journal*.

WORK IN PROGRESS: Research on American philanthropic foundations for encyclopedias, magazines, and the *Foundation Directory; Upside-Down Circus*, for Little, Brown.

AVOCATIONAL INTERESTS: Mountain climbing, tennis, mathematics.

BIOGRAPHICAL/CRITICAL SOURCES: New York Times, July 11, 1960.†

* * *

ANTICAGLIA, Elizabeth 1939-

PERSONAL: Surname pronounced without "g" sound; born September 14, 1939, in New York, N.Y.; daughter of Harold William (a construction rigger) and Hilma Elizabeth (Nevalainen) Ahlfors; married Joseph R. Anticaglia (a facial plastic surgeon and otolaryngologist), September 21, 1962; children: Jeannine, Jason. *Education:* New York University, B.A., 1961. *Politics:* Democrat. *Religion:* Unitarian Universalist. *Home address:* R.D. 2, Box 149A, Hockessin, Del. 19707.

CAREER: Living for Young Homemakers, New York City, assistant production editor, 1961; *Vogue*, New York City, assistant production editor, 1961-62; Speaker's Showcase (lecture bureau), Philadelphia, Pa., lecturer, 1973—. *Member:* Authors Guild, National Organization for Women.

WRITINGS: A Housewife's Guide to Women's Liberation, Nelson-Hall, 1972; *Twelve American Women*, Nelson-Hall, 1975; *Heroines of '76* (juvenile), Walker & Co., 1975. Contributor to *Yankee, Coronet*, and other magazines. Author of two columns, "The Doctor's Bag," for *Companion*, 1971, and "Woman Today," for *Today's Post*, 1971-73.

WORK IN PROGRESS: Literature to interest older children who read at a low level, for inclusion in textbooks and educational packets.

* * *

APPS, Jerold W(illard) 1934- (Jerry Apps)

PERSONAL: Born July 25, 1934, in Wild Rose, Wis.; son of Herman E. (a farmer) and Eleanor (Witt) Apps; married Ruth E. Olson (a home economist), May 20, 1961; children: Susan, Steven, Jeffrey. *Education:* University of Wisconsin,

B.S., 1955, M.S., 1957, Ph.D., 1967. *Politics:* Independent. *Religion:* Lutheran. *Home:* 522 Togstad Glen, Madison, Wis. 53711. *Agent:* Larry Sternig Literary Agency, 742 Robertson, Milwaukee, Wis. 53212. *Office:* Department of Continuing and Vocational Education, University of Wisconsin, 208 Agriculture Hall, Madison, Wis. 53706.

CAREER: County extension agent in Wisconsin, 1957-62; University of Wisconsin—Madison, assistant professor, 1962-67, associate professor, 1967-70, professor of adult education, 1970—, chairman of department of continuing and vocational education, 1977-79. Assistant state 4-H leader in Wisconsin, 1962-64. Teacher of creative writing at Rhinelander School of Arts, summers, 1971—. Consulting editor, McGraw-Hill Book Co. *Military service:* U.S. Army Reserve, 1956-66; active duty in Transportation Corps, 1956; became captain. *Member:* Adult Education Association, Commission of Professors of Adult Education (president), Adult Education Association of Wisconsin (past president), Gamma Sigma Delta. *Awards, honors:* Award for best nonfiction book by a Wisconsin author from Wisconsin Council for Writers, 1977, and Nonfiction Book Award of Merit from Wisconsin Historical Society, 1978, both for *Barns of Wisconsin*.

WRITINGS: (Under name Jerry Apps) *The Land Still Lives,* Wisconsin House, 1970; (under name Jerry Apps) *Cabin in the Country,* Argus, 1972; *How to Improve Adult Education in Your Church,* Augsburg, 1972; *Toward a Working Philosophy of Adult Education,* Syracuse University, 1973; *Tips for Article Writers,* Wisconsin Regional Writers, 1973; (under name Jerry Apps) *Village of Roses,* Wild Rose Historical Society, 1973; *Ideas for Better Church Meetings,* Augsburg, 1975; *Barns of Wisconsin,* Tamarack Press, 1977; *Study Skills: For Those Adults Returning to School,* McGraw, 1978; *Problems in Continuing Education,* McGraw, 1979; *Mills of the Midwest,* Tamarack Press, 1980; (editor with Robert Boyd) *Redefining the Discipline of Adult Education,* Jossey-Bass, 1980. Author of weekly column "Outdoor Notebook" appearing in three Wisconsin newspapers. Contributor of numerous articles to periodicals, including *Life Long Learning, Hospital Progress, Resource, Wisconsin Trails, Outdoor World,* and *Wisconsin Academy Review.* Book editor, *Journal of Adult Education,* 1967-69; editor, *Journal of Extension,* 1969-70.

WORK IN PROGRESS: A second edition of *Study Skills: For Those Adults Returning to School; The Returning Student on Campus,* for Follett.

SIDELIGHTS: Jerold W. Apps writes: "I am committed to helping the university relate to the real needs of people. In doing that I'm constantly trying to combine theory and practice, and stress the importance of doing this in the classroom and the community.

"I believe that action without careful thought can be dangerous, that thought without action can be irrelevant. Thus the necessity for combining the two.

"As the population of the country grows older, I am committed to the concept of continuing education for all ages. Through education people will be able to discover latent talents, will learn to know more about themselves, and how to relate to others. Through education I believe that people can reach their highest potentials, and can learn how to work together to solve the problems they face collectively in their communities.

"I believe that religion is an important force in the lives of people, but must be viewed in ways that transcend the traditional institutional church."

AVOCATIONAL INTERESTS: Wild flower study, bird study, nature photography, hiking, camping, canoeing, fishing, farming.

* * *

ARIAN, Alan (Asher) 1938-

PERSONAL: Born 1938, in Cleveland, Ohio. *Education:* Western Reserve University (now Case Western Reserve University), B.A. (cum laude), 1961; Michigan State University, M.A., 1963, Ph.D., 1965. *Office:* Faculty of Social Sciences, Tel-Aviv University, Ramat-Aviv, Israel.

CAREER: Western Reserve University (now Case Western Reserve University), Cleveland, Ohio, assistant professor, 1965-66; Tel-Aviv University, Ramat-Aviv, Israel, lecturer, 1966-68, senior lecturer, 1968-71, associate professor of political science, 1976—, chairman of department, 1966-70, 1971-73, dean of faculty of social sciences, 1977—. Guest research associate at Israel Institute of Applied Social Research, 1967; guest lecturer at Communications Institute of Hebrew University, 1967-70; visiting associate professor at University of Minnesota, autumn, 1968; guest research associate at Center for Political Studies, University of Michigan, spring, 1971; visiting professor of politics and Near East and Jewish studies, Brandeis University, spring, 1976. *Member:* International Political Science Association (member of executive committee, 1979—), Israel Association of Political Science (president, 1979—). *Awards, honors:* Naftali Award for social and economic research, 1973.

WRITINGS: (Editor with Charles Press, and contributor) *Empathy and Ideology: Aspects of Administrative Innovation,* Rand McNally, 1966; *Ideological Change in Israel,* Case Western Reserve University Press, 1968; *Consensus in Israel* (monograph), General Learning Corp., 1971; (editor and contributor) *The Elections in Israel: 1969,* Jerusalem Academic Press, 1972; (with Aaron Antonovsky) *Hopes and Fears of Israelis: Consensus in a New Society,* Jerusalem Academic Press, 1972; (with Roger W. Benjamin, Richard N. Blue, and Stephen Coleman) *Patterns of Political Development: Japan, India, Israel,* McKay, 1972; *The Choosing People: Voting Behavior in Israel,* Case Western Reserve University Press, 1973; (editor and contributor) *The Elections in Israel: 1973,* Jerusalem Academic Press, 1975; (editor and contributor) *The Elections in Israel: 1977,* Jerusalem Academic Press, 1979; (editor) *Israel: A Developing Society,* Van Gorcum, 1979; (contributor with Michael Keren) Candido Mendes, editor, *The Controls of Technocracy,* Educam, 1979.

Contributor to political science and social science journals, including *Journal of Politics, Public Opinion Quarterly, Jewish Journal of Sociology, Western Political Quarterly, Sociological Review,* and *Journal of Human Relations.*

* * *

ARMSTRONG, J(on) Scott 1937-

PERSONAL: Born March 26, 1937, in Philadelphia, Pa.; son of William W. and Helen (Lloyd) Armstrong; married Kay Anderson, August 1, 1964; children: Kathy Jean, Jennifer Lynn. *Education:* Lehigh University, B.A., 1959, B.S., 1960; University of Rochester, graduate study, 1960-63; Carnegie-Mellon University, M.S., 1965; Massachusetts Institute of Technology, Ph.D., 1968. *Home:* 645 Harper Ave., Drexel Hill, Pa. 19026. *Office:* Department of Marketing, Wharton School, University of Pennsylvania, Philadelphia, Pa. 19104.

CAREER: Eastman Kodak, Rochester, N.Y., industrial engineer, 1960-63; Xerox Corp., Rochester, systems analyst, 1964; Polaroid Corp., Cambridge, Mass., marketing researcher, 1966; Massachusetts Institute of Technology, Sloan School, Cambridge, instructor in applied statistics for the behavioral sciences, 1967; University of Pennsylvania, Wharton School, Philadelphia, assistant professor, 1968-72, associate professor of marketing management and marketing research, 1972—. Visiting professor at Stockholm School of Economics, 1974-75, and University of Hawaii, 1976. Senior staff member of Management and Behavioral Science Center, 1968-69, 1971-72; research associate of University City Science Institute, 1970-71. Consultant to Royal Packaging Industries of the Netherlands, General Foods, General Mills, Ford Motor Co., U.S. Department of Transportation, and other industries. *Military service:* U.S. Army, 1961.

WRITINGS: (Contributor) Johan Arndt, editor, *Insights into Consumer Behavior,* Allyn & Bacon, 1968; (contributor) Robert L. King, editor, *Marketing and the New Science of Planning,* American Marketing Association, 1968; *Long-Range Forecasting: Crystal Ball to Computer,* Wiley, 1978. Contributor of about two dozen articles to professional journals.

WORK IN PROGRESS: Further work to assess the relative value of different forecasting methods in the social sciences.

SIDELIGHTS: Reviewing J. Scott Armstrong's book *Long-Range Forecasting* Jay S. Mendell writes in *Business Tomorrow:* "If a book ever deserved to be a best-seller, this is it. The author organized the material systematically so that in a given situation, you can decide whether to use high-power methods and whether you can expect accurate results." Robert N. White comments in *Decision Line:* "This book will stun you with its scholarship, entertain you with its comedic style, enlighten you with its perceptive analysis." Armstrong says of his book: "I believe that technical books can be interesting, easy to read, practical, and worthwhile. That's what I tried to do with *Long-Range Forecasting.* And it only took me 10 years! After that type of investment, it was nice to see that the reviewers agreed with me."

BIOGRAPHICAL/CRITICAL SOURCES: Business Tomorrow, summer, 1978; *Simulation,* August, 1978; *Journal of Accountancy,* November, 1978; *Decision Line,* January, 1979; *Accountant,* January, 1979; *Journal of Marketing Research,* April, 1979; *Thresholds and Turning Points,* April, 1979; *Journal of the Operational Research Society,* July, 1979; *Contemporary Sociology,* July, 1979.

* * *

ARNOLD, Peter 1943-

PERSONAL: Born January 25, 1943, in Newton, Mass.; son of Israel Isaac (a businessman) and Edith (Gordon) Arnold; married Kirsten Ellen Hannibal, July 25, 1966 (divorced July 10, 1979); children: Jeremy Gordon. *Education:* University of Michigan, B.A., 1966; University of Southern California, M.A., 1969. *Residence:* Boston, Mass. *Agent:* Max Gartenberg, 331 Madison Ave., New York, N.Y. 10017. *Office:* 10 Emerson Pl., Boston, Mass. 02114.

CAREER: Universal Studios, Universal City, Calif., writer and producer, 1967-68; free-lance film writer, Los Angeles, Calif., 1968-73; free-lance nonfiction book writer, Los Angeles, 1969-77; California Institute of Technology, Development Office, Pasadena, head of writing staff, 1973-74; Occidental College, Los Angeles, director of special projects, 1974-76; Hugh O'Brian Youth Foundation, Los Angeles, director, 1976-77; Peter Arnold Associates (writing and editing), Boston, Mass., president, 1977—. *Member:* Writer's Guild of America, Author's Guild, Authors League of America, Word Guild.

WRITINGS: Burglar-Proof Your Home and Car, Nash Publishing, 1971; *Off the Beaten Track in Copenhagen,* Nash Publishing, 1972; *Lady Beware,* Doubleday, 1974; *Check List for Emergencies,* Doubleday, 1974; *Crime and Youth,* Messner, 1976; *How to Protect Your Child against Crime,* Follett, 1977; *Job and Career Building,* Harper, 1980; *The Everyday Handbook,* Doubleday, 1980. Contributor to *National Observer, Woman's Day, Coronet, Seventeen,* and *New Idea.*

WORK IN PROGRESS: CPR for the Layman, for Van Nostrand; *Career Advancement for Women.*

* * *

ARRIGHI, Mel 1933-

PERSONAL: Born October 5, 1933, in San Francisco, Calif.; son of Enrico (a wholesale produce merchant) and Gemma (Casentini) Arrighi; married Patricia Bosworth (a writer and magazine editor), February 15, 1966. *Education:* Attended Reed College, 1951-53; University of California, Berkeley, B.A., 1955. *Politics:* Liberal Democrat. *Home:* 344 East 79th St., New York, N.Y. 10021. *Agent:* (Literary) McIntosh & Otis, Inc., 475 Fifth Ave., New York, N.Y. 10017; (dramatic) Robert Freedman, Brandt & Brandt, 1501 Broadway, New York, N.Y. 10036.

CAREER: Professional actor in New York, N.Y., 1956-62; writer, 1962—. As an actor, worked in Off-Broadway productions, on national tours, in summer theatre, and on television. *Member:* Authors Guild, Dramatists Guild, Authors League of America, Writers Guild of America East.

WRITINGS—Novels: *Freak-Out,* Putnam, 1968; *An Ordinary Man,* Peter H. Wyden, 1970; *Daddy Pig,* Bobbs-Merrill, 1974; *The Death Collection,* Popular Library, 1975; *The Hatchet Man,* Harcourt, 1975; *Navona 1000,* Bobbs-Merrill, 1976; *Turkish White,* Harcourt, 1977; *Delphine,* Atheneum, 1978; *On Tour,* Atheneum, 1979.

Plays: *An Ordinary Man* (first produced Off-Broadway at Cherry Lane Theatre, September 9, 1968), Dramatists Play Service, 1969; *The Castro Complex* (first produced in New York, N.Y., at Stairway Theatre, November 18, 1970), Dramatists Play Service, 1971; "The Unicorn in Captivity," first produced in New York, N.Y. at Impossible Ragtime Theatre, November 3, 1978.

Author of scripts for television series, including "NYPD" and "McCloud."

SIDELIGHTS: Mel Arrighi told *CA:* "My impulse is to tell stories that investigate the relation of the individual to his society. I have no answers or solutions to propose. Instead, I am interested in questioning too-readily-accepted assumptions, and where possible, inspiring in the reader new lines of inquiry. In short, I am one of those who regard the creative artist as the responsive conscience of his society."

* * *

ASBELL, Bernard 1923-
(Nicholas Max)

PERSONAL: Born May 8, 1923, in Brooklyn, N.Y.; son of Samuel and Minnie (Zevin) Asbell; married Mildred Sacarny, January 2, 1944 (divorced April 2, 1971); married Marjorie Baldwin, June 11, 1971 (divorced August, 1977); children: (first marriage) Paul, Lawrence, Jonathan, Jody.

Education: Attended University of Connecticut, 1943-44. *Home and office:* 49 Mohawk Trail, Guilford, Conn. 06437.

CAREER: Richmond Times-Dispatch, Richmond, Va., reporter, 1945-47; public relations agent in Chicago, Ill., 1947-55; *Chicago* (magazine), Chicago, managing editor, 1955-56; University of Chicago, Chicago, lecturer in nonfiction writing, 1956-60; Middlebury College, Middlebury, Vt., lecturer in nonfiction writing at Breadloaf Writers' Conference, 1960-61; University of Bridgeport, Bridgeport, Conn., lecturer in journalism, 1961-63; currently full-time writer. Lecturer, Yale University, 1979. Founder and director, New England Writers Center, 1979—. Consultant to Educational Facilities Laboratories, 1963, 1970, Ford Foundation, 1963, 1968-69, Secretary of Health, Education, and Welfare, 1965-68, Carnegie Corp., and International Business Machines Corp. Justice of the Peace in Wilton, Conn., 1966-67. *Military service:* U.S. Army, 1943-45. *Member:* American Society of Journalists and Authors (president, 1963), P.E.N. American Center, Authors Guild, National Press Club, Coffee House (New York). *Awards, honors:* Educational Writers Association, first prize for magazine coverage of education, 1956, citation, 1966; National Education Association School Bell Award, 1965; National Council for the Advancement of Educational Writing, second place award for best educational writing in magazines, 1968; L.H.D., University of New Haven, 1978.

WRITINGS: When F.D.R. Died, Holt, 1961; *The New Improved American,* McGraw, 1965; *Careers in Urban Affairs,* Peter H. Wyden, 1970; *What Lawyers Really Do,* Peter H. Wyden, 1970; (under pseudonym Nicholas Max) *President McGovern's First Team,* Doubleday, 1973; *The F.D.R. Memoirs,* Doubleday, 1973; (with Clair F. Vough) *Tapping the Human Resource,* American Management Association, 1975; *The Senate Nobody Knows,* Doubleday, 1978. Contributor to periodicals.

* * *

ASHLEY, Franklin 1942-

PERSONAL: Born in 1942, in Charlotte, N.C.; son of Frank W. (a professor) and Alice (Wilson) Ashley; married Dottie Sitton. *Education:* Newberry College, B.A., 1964; University of South Carolina, M.A., 1966, Ph.D., 1970. *Politics:* Democrat. *Religion:* Presbyterian. *Home:* 125 Shannondale Ct., Columbia, S.C. 29209. *Agent:* Pat Berens, The Sterling Lord Agency, 660 Madison Ave., New York, N.Y. 10021. *Office:* College of General Studies, University of South Carolina, Columbia, S.C. 29208.

CAREER: Citadel, Charleston, S.C., assistant professor of English and coach of debating team, 1966-68; University of South Carolina, Aiken, assistant professor, 1970-72, associate professor of English, 1972-75, associate professor, College of General Studies, 1975-80, professor, 1980—. Poet-in-residence for South Carolina Arts Commission and Indiana Arts Commission; organizer and director of Aiken Literary Festival, 1971, coordinator, 1972—. Speechwriter for Lieutenant Governor Earle Morris, Jr., and for Congressman Mendel Davis; director and producer of radio and television spots for gubernatorial campaign of Richard Riley. Organizer and leader of Franklin Ashley Trio. *Member:* American Association of University Professors. *Awards, honors:* Fiction award from *Miscellany,* 1972.

WRITINGS: James Dickey: A Checklist, Gale, 1973; *Hard Shadows,* Peaceweed, 1975. Work is represented in several anthologies, including *Best Sports Stories,* Dutton, 1980.

Author of "Amber Keyhold" and "Midnight Ride," plays first performed in Columbia, S.C., at Workshop Theatre, May, 1972; also author, with William Fox and Shel Silverstein, of "Southern Fried," first performed in Columbia, S.C., at Town Theatre, 1977. Composer of music to accompany his own plays; South Carolina correspondent for *New Democrat.* Contributor of stories, poems, and articles to literary journals, national magazines, and little poetry magazines, including *Harper's, Sandlapper, People, New Republic, New Times,* and *College English.* Editor and director of *Faces of South Carolina,* 1973; founder of *Broken Ink;* senior editor, *Sandlapper.*

WORK IN PROGRESS: Essays on the South.

* * *

ASQUITH, Glenn Hackney 1904-

PERSONAL: Born October 21, 1904, in Knoxville, Tenn.; son of George Hurst and Mary (McCrary) Asquith; married Helen Underdown, 1935; children: Nancy, Helen, Glenn, Jr. *Education:* Eastern Baptist Theological Seminary, Th.B., 1935; Eastern Baptist College (now Eastern College), A.B., 1943. *Home:* 37 Edison Ave., Cherry Hill, N.J.

CAREER: Pastor of Baptist churches in Pennsylvania, New Jersey, Rhode Island, and Connecticut, 1935-50; New York State Baptist Convention, Syracuse, N. Y., executive secretary, 1950-56; First-United Baptist Church, Lowell, Mass., pastor, 1956-60; Philadelphia Baptist Association, Philadelphia, Pa., executive secretary, 1960-61; American Baptist Board of Education and Publication, Valley Forge, Pa., editor-in-chief, 1961-67; First Baptist Church, Montclair, N.J., pastor, 1967-70; free-lance writer, 1970—. Director, Christian Writers and Editors Conference, Green Lake, Wis., 1962-68. Delegate to Baptist World Alliance, London, England, 1955; member of Governor Harriman's Citizens' Advisory Committee on the Problems of Aging, 1955; delegate to the White House Conference on the Problems of the Aging, 1961. Member of the Associated Church Press. *Awards, honors:* D.D., Eastern Baptist Theological Seminary, 1952; Freedoms Foundation Award, 1954; Eastern Baptist Theological Seminary alumni award.

WRITINGS: A Two-Century Church, Baptist Church, Scotch Plains, N.J., 1948; *Church Officers at Work,* Judson, 1950, revised edition, 1977; *Lively May I Walk,* Abingdon, 1960; *The Selected Works of Ryters Krampe,* Judson, 1962; *Cousin Tom,* Bethany, 1964; *God in My Day,* Abingdon, 1967; *Preaching According to Plan,* Judson, 1968; *The Person I Am,* Abingdon, 1969; *Death Is All Right,* Abingdon, 1970; *Living in the Presence of God,* Judson, 1972; *Footprints in the Sand,* Judson, 1975; *Living Creatively as an Older Adult,* Herald Press, 1975. Contributor of seventeen hundred articles to religion journals. Editor, *Baptist New Yorker,* 1950-56, and *Baptist Leader,* 1962-67.

AVOCATIONAL INTERESTS: Photography, art, reading.

* * *

ATCHITY, Kenneth John 1944-

PERSONAL: Born January 16, 1944, in Eunice, La.; son of Fred J. (an accountant) and Myrza (a registered nurse; maiden name, Aguillard) Atchity; married Kathleen Dillon, June 12, 1964 (divorced, 1973); married Bonnie Fraser, February 1, 1974; children: (first marriage) Vincent, Rosemary. *Education:* Georgetown University, A.B., 1965; Yale University, M.Phil., 1969, Ph.D., 1970. *Politics:* "Depends on the issue." *Religion:* "Jesuit." *Office:* Department of English and Comparative Literature, Occidental College, Los

Angeles, Calif. 90041; and L/A House, P.O. Box 41110, Los Angeles, Calif. 90041.

CAREER: American Telephone & Telegraph (AT&T), Government Communications, Washington, D.C., communications engineer and National Aeronautics and Space Administration headquarters account manager, 1965-66; Occidental College, Los Angeles, Calif., 1970—, began as assistant professor, currently professor of English and comparative literature; L/A House (publishing, editing, and research company), Los Angeles, founder and president, 1976—. Visiting instructor at California State College (now University), Los Angeles, 1970-71; instructor at U.S. Postal Service Management Institute, 1973; Fulbright professor at University of Bologna, 1974-75. Newscaster for WGTB-FM Radio, 1962-65. Editorial consultant, Southern California Research Council, Pasadena Research Institute, Mark Taper Forum, and Afro-American Urban Center.

MEMBER: Modern Language Association of America, P.E.N. American Center, American Association of Teachers of Italian, American Comparative Literature Association (national membership chairman, 1978-79), Renaissance Society of America, Dante Society of America, Vergilian Society, California Educational Research Association, California State Poetry Society, Eta Sigma Phi. *Awards, honors:* Woodrow Wilson fellowship, 1966; third place in international essay contest of Dante Society of America, 1968, for "Inferno VII: The Idea of Order"; Readers' Choice award from *Bardic Echoes,* 1970, for poem "Noasis"; National Federation of State Poetry Societies Lubbe award, 1971, for poem "e e cummings i hate you," Modern Award, 1971, for poem "What Horace Meant to Say"; National Endowment for the Humanities grant, 1972; American Council of Learned Societies, grant, 1973, for work in Florence, Italy; annual Mentor Poetry Award, 1974; Mellon Foundation grant and Graves Award, both for research in Greece, 1978; American Council of Learned Societies grant for address to International Comparative Literature Association, Innsbruck, Austria, 1979; California Council for the Humanities in Public Policy grant for "Communication in the Public Interest" series appearing in *Follies-Avanti,* 1979-80; four grants from Coordinating Council of Literary Magazines for work with *Contemporary Quarterly.*

WRITINGS: (Editor) *Eterne in Mutabilitie: The Unity of "The Faerie Queene,"* Archon, 1972; (co-editor and contributor) *Italian Literature: Roots and Branches,* Yale University Press, 1976; *Sleeping with an Elephant: Selected Poems, 1965-1976,* Valkyrie, 1978; *Homer's "Iliad": The Shield of Memory,* foreword by John Gardner, Southern Illinois University Press, 1978.

Contributor: Henry Grosshans, editor, *To Find Something New,* Washington State University Press, 1969; Donald K. Adams, editor, *The Mystery and Detection Annual,* Donald K. Adams Publishing, 1972; Frank N. Magill, editor, *Magill's Literary Annual: 1976,* Salem Press, 1977; Magill, editor, *Magill's Literary Annual: 1977,* Salem Press, 1977; Alida Becker, editor, *The Tolkien Scrapbook,* Grosset, 1978; *Contemporary Literary Scene,* Salem Press, 1979; Magill, editor, *Magill's Literary Annual: 1979,* Salem Press, 1979.

Author of libretto for *In Praise of Love* (performed at New York Philharmonic, 1974), Erik K. Marcus, 1974; also author of "Homer," a three-part television program for KNXT-TV, 1976. Guest columnist and reviewer, *Los Angeles Times Book Review,* 1970—. Contributor of numerous articles, poems, and reviews to literary journals, popular magazines, and newspapers, including *American Quarterly, Classical Philology, Italian Quarterly, Kenyon Review, Western Humanities Review,* and *Washington Post.* Editor-in-chief, *Hoya,* 1962-65; features editor, *Moneysworth,* 1971; contributing editor, *California State Poetry Quarterly,* 1972-75, *San Francisco Review of Books,* 1977—, *Italia-America,* 1977—, and *Literary Review* (Edinburgh, Scotland), 1980—; editor, *Contemporary Quarterly,* 1976-79, and *Follies,* 1978-79; co-founder and co-editor, *Dreamworks,* 1980—.

SIDELIGHTS: Kenneth John Atchity told *CA:* "I am presently interested in the relationship between dream and memory, two highly artistic aspects of imagination. The dreams of memory are what we call, in waking life, fiction and poetry; they provide our identities for us, our only relatively stable reference points in the flux of experience and perception. *Dreamworks* is dedicated to studying the relationship between dream and art, on the premise that the roots of art lead through our personal dreams back into the great myths which we share with all those in our culture. The dream expresses at one and the same time the unconscious imagination of a culture and the individual's own artistic contribution to his culture. The dream of the poet is to make his return to the unlimited freedom of dream. Some artists want to take us with them, others don't care whether we go or not. But we can always go as far as we ourselves can imagine. The successful poem read successfully is a shared dream, an ideal experience of communication between poet and reader that takes place in the time-defying air between them, like the experience of a holograph, like the words of the ancient Greek drama, projected from megaphonic masks, that made the myth alive in the theatrical air so that the individuals in the audience became, as they experienced together the resonant words, no longer only individuals, but now, for the time of the drama, a true community. Poetry is the waking expression of that communal consciousness expressed by dream, in which we all see the same things but from our own individual viewpoints."

Atchity offers this advice for aspiring writers: "Exceed your limits so you can discover what they are. Write from the heart about things that matter to us all. Remember what John Cage said, that 'there are no aesthetic emergencies,' that you have as much time as your art needs. Work daily; make lists or road-maps instead of rigid outlines; use file folders instead of notebooks for ideas a-building, reviewing the notes randomly added from time to time until their proper order and connection gells—the folders more accurately represent the way your mind works; when in a slump, don't fight it—do things you don't do otherwise, extra research, reading—then don't sit down to write until the pressure in your head is unbearable and the sentences have become clear paragraphs; remember that life itself is a cycle and that you don't scale the next mountain until you've crossed the valley; also remember, mountains are your goal—as my brother Fred says, you can walk over a hundred pebbles and not make progress but all it takes is one mountain and you're in another world. When working on a long project that demands interruptions, stop in the middle of a page, paragraph, and sentence when you know how the sentence will end. When you return, whether the next day or weeks later, retype the half-page and by the time you've reached the half-sentence you'll be back on track; I guarantee it. If you feel you can't write an opening paragraph, give youself a half hour to think of the opening sentence; if that doesn't work, take a half hour to write the opening word—you'll be on your way in less than an hour. I agree with Norman Mailer's observation: 'Writer's block is only a failure of the ego.'"

ATCHLEY, Robert C. 1939-
(Bob Atchley)

PERSONAL: Born September 18, 1939, in San Antonio, Tex.; son of Ray C. (an optometrist) and Roberta (a retail supervisor; maiden name, Maddox) Atchley; married Sue Hyser, June 10, 1961 (divorced May, 1976); children: Christopher, Melissa. *Education:* Miami University, Oxford, Ohio, A.B., 1961; American University, M.A., 1965, Ph.D., 1968. *Religion:* Humanist. *Home:* 5991 Contreras Rd., Oxford, Ohio 45056. *Office:* 351 Hoyt Library, Miami University, Oxford, Ohio 45056.

CAREER: George Washington University, Washington, D.C., researcher and assistant professor of sociology, 1965-66; Miami University, Oxford, Ohio, 1966—, began as researcher and associate professor, now professor of sociology. *Military service:* U.S. Marine Corps, computer systems analyst, 1962-65; became captain. *Member:* International Congress of Gerontology, Gerontological Society, American Sociological Association, American Psychological Association, North Central Sociological Association, Sigma Xi.

WRITINGS: The Population of the Ohio-Kentucky-Indiana Metropolitan Region, Hamilton County Regional Planning Commission, 1969; *American Social Institutions,* Wadsworth, 1969; *Using Population Data in Community Planning,* Scripps Foundation, 1969; *Retired Women: A Preliminary Report,* Scripps Foundation, 1969; *Population Estimates and Projections for Local Areas,* Scripps Foundation, 1970; *The Use of Community Information in Educational Planning,* U.S. Office of Education, 1971; *Understanding American Society,* Wadsworth, 1971; *Ohio's Older People,* Scripps Foundation, 1972; *The Social Forces in Later Life,* Wadsworth, 1972, 3rd edition, 1980; *The Sociology of Retirement,* Schenkman, 1976; *Rural Environments and Aging,* Gerontological Society, 1977; *The Sociology of Aging,* Wadsworth, 1977; *Social Problems of the Aged,* Wadsworth, 1978; *Families in Later Life,* Wadsworth, 1979. Contributor of articles to professional journals, under name Bob Atchley.

WORK IN PROGRESS: The Retirement Revolution, for Wadsworth.

AVOCATIONAL INTERESTS: Playing bluegrass and blues on the guitar, making transfer prints, collecting original paintings, sports.

* * *

ATKINS, Russell 1926-

PERSONAL: Born February 25, 1926, in Cleveland, Ohio; son of Perry Kelly and Mamie (Harris) Atkins. *Education:* Attended Cleveland School of Art (now Cleveland Institute of Art), 1943-44, and Cleveland Institute of Music, 1944-45; private music study, 1950-54. *Politics:* "Nothing particular." *Religion:* None. *Home:* 6005 Grand Ave., Cleveland, Ohio 44104.

CAREER: Editor, writer, and composer; founder and editor of *Free Lance* magazine, 1950—. Publicity manager and assistant to director, Sutphen School of Music (of National Guild of Community Music Schools), Cleveland, Ohio, 1957-60; lecturer, Poets and Lecturers Alliance, 1963-65, and elsewhere; writing instructor at Karamu House, 1972; writer-in-residence, Cuyahoga Community College, summer, 1973; member of Artists-in-Schools Program of Ohio Arts Council and National Endowment for the Arts, 1973—. Participant, Bread Loaf Writers' Conference, 1956; member of Cleveland State University Poetry Forum; member of Coordinating Council of Literary Magazines of National Endowment for the Arts. Consultant to writers conferences and workshops; consultant to WVIZ—NET-TV, 1969-71, and to Cleveland Board of Education, 1972-73; member of literary advisory panel, Ohio Arts Council, 1973-76.

MEMBER: International Platform Association, Committee of Small Magazine Editors and Publishers, Ramakah, Inc. (president, 1972), Ohio Poets Association, Ohio Poetry Society, Poets League of Greater Cleveland (member of board of trustees), East Side Music Guild. *Awards, honors:* Honorary doctorate, Cleveland State University, 1976; Individual Artist grant, Ohio Arts Council, 1978.

WRITINGS—All poetry: *Phenomena,* Wilberforce University Press, 1961; *Objects,* Hearse Press, 1963; *Objects 2,* Renegade Press, 1963; *Heretofore,* Paul Breman, 1968; *Presentations,* Podium Press, 1969; *The Nail and Maleficium,* Free Lance Press, 1971; *Here in The,* Poetry Center, Cleveland State University, 1976; *Whichever,* Free Lance Press, 1978.

Musical compositions: (With Langston Hughes and Hale Smith) *Elegy* (poetry set to music), Highgate Press, 1968; *Objects* (for piano), Free Lance Press, 1969. Also composer of unpublished musical works.

Work represented in anthologies, including: *Sixes and Sevens,* edited by Paul Breman, Paul Breman (London), 1962; *Silver Cesspool,* edited by Adelaide Simon, Renegade Press, 1964; *Four, Six, Five,* edited by D. A. Levy, Seven Flowers Press, 1966; *Sounds and Silences: Poetry for Now,* edited by Richard E. Peck, Delacorte, 1969; *Soulscript: Afro-American Poetry,* edited by June Jordan, Doubleday, 1970; *Yearbook of Modern Poetry,* edited by Jeanne Hollyfield, Young Publications, 1972; *Anthologies in Braille,* Bell Telephone Laboratories, 1970; *Poetry: An Introduction through Writing,* edited by Lewis Turco, Prentice-Hall, 1972; *The Strong Voice Two,* edited by Robert McGovern and Richard Snyder, Ashland Poetry, 1972; *Penguin Book of Verse,* edited by Willemien Vroom, Penguin (England), 1973; *The Forerunners,* edited by Woodie King, Jr., Howard University Press, 1975; *Celebrations,* edited by Arnold Adoff, Follett, 1977; *Forum,* edited by Peter Hargitai and Lolette Kuby, Mentor Press, 1978; *Seventy-three Ohio Poets,* edited by Citino, Turner, and Bennett, Ohio State University, 1978.

Also author of "The Theory of Psychovisualism," originally published in *Free Lance* and reprinted several times. Contributor of poems and articles to *New York Times Book Review, Beloit Poetry Journal, Western Review, Minnesota Quarterly, Poetry Now,* and numerous other journals.

WORK IN PROGRESS: Revision of theoretical articles and monographs; *Children's Bones,* a poem-play; "Twenty Spirituals," a musical composition for piano.

SIDELIGHTS: Russell Atkins's poems were read over radio by poets Langston Hughes, in 1950, and Marianne Moore, in 1951. *Elegy* was recorded as "In Memoriam," in 1964, by the Kulas Chorus conducted by Robert Shaw with the Cleveland Orchestra. Karamu House presented an evening called "A Tribute to Russell Atkins" in 1971.

Atkins told *CA:* "My work seeks to go beyond the mere distributing of a few good images throughout an argumentative poetic context of 'insights' and 'observations.' To me, a poet's task is to use the imagination to exploit range, to create a body of effect, event, colors, characteristics, moods, verbal stresses pushed to a maximum."

BIOGRAPHICAL/CRITICAL SOURCES: H. H. Stuckenschmidt, *20th Century Music,* McGraw, 1969; *You Better*

Believe It, Penguin, 1973; Eugene B. Redmond, *Drumvoices,* Doubleday, 1976.

* * *

ATTNEAVE, Carolyn L(ewis) 1920-

PERSONAL: Surname rhymes with "sleeve"; born July 2, 1920, in El Paso, Tex.; daughter of James Irwin (a marketing representative) and Carrie F. (a florist; maiden name, Adams) Lewis; married Fred Attneave II, October 7, 1949 (divorced, 1956); children: Dorothy Maud Jackson, Philip Henry. *Education:* Attended Occidental College and California College of Arts and Crafts; Yuba College, A.A., 1939; Chico State College (now California State University, Chico), B.A., 1940; Stanford University, M.A., 1947, Ph.D., 1952; postdoctoral study at University of Chicago and University of Oklahoma Medical School. *Home:* 5206 Ivanhoe N.E., Seattle, Wash. 98105. *Office:* Department of Psychology, University of Washington, Seattle, Wash. 98195.

CAREER: Texas Woman's University, Denton, director of student personnel, 1956-57; Texas Technological College (now Texas Tech University), Lubbock, assistant professor of psychology and human development, 1957-61; Oklahoma State Department of Health, Community Guidance Center, Shawnee, coordinator, 1962-69; Philadelphia Child Guidance Clinic, Philadelphia, senior psychologist, 1969-71; Tufts University, School of Medicine, Medford, Mass., assistant professor of clinical psychology, 1971; Massachusetts Department of Mental Health, Boston, coordinator of public service careers programs, 1971-72; Boston University, Boston, supervisor of family therapy, 1972-75; Harvard University, School of Public Health, Boston, research associate and lecturer, 1973-75; University of Washington, Seattle, professor of psychology and adjunct professor of behavorial sciences, 1975—, director of American Indian studies, 1975-77. Consulting psychologist and family therapist in private practice; president of Psychiatric Outpatient Centers of America, 1973-74. *Military service:* U.S. Coast Guard Women's Auxiliary (SPARS), 1942-46; became lieutenant senior grade.

MEMBER: American Psychological Association, American Orthopsychiatric Association (fellow), American Family Therapy Association (member of board of directors, 1978—), Society for Family Therapy and Research (vice-president, 1973), Massachusetts Psychological Association, Delaware-Cherokee Tribe of Oklahoma. *Awards, honors:* Research grant from Oklahoma Public Health Association, 1965.

WRITINGS: (With Ross Speck) *Family Networks,* Pantheon, 1973; (editor with Alan Tulipan) *Beyond Clinic Walls,* University of Alabama Press, 1975; (with Diane Kelso) *Annotated Bibliography of American Indian Mental Health,* University of Washington and Whitecloud Center, 1978. Also author of *Service Networks and Patterns of Utilization: Mental Health Services Involving American Indians,* 1976. Contributor of chapters to books. Contributor of articles on American Indian mental health and the problems of family therapy to professional journals.

AVOCATIONAL INTERESTS: American Indian art and artists, family histories, natural history.

* * *

AXELROD, D(avid) B(ruce) 1943-

PERSONAL: Born July 29, 1943, in Beverly, Mass.; son of Samuel Robert (a factory supervisor) and Irene (Kransberg) Axelrod; married Joan Carole Hand (a writer and teacher), May 29, 1966; children: Jessica Ellen, Emily Elizabeth. *Education:* University of Massachusetts, B.A., 1965; Johns Hopkins University, M.A., 1966; University of Iowa, M.F.A., 1968; Union Graduate School, Ph.D., 1977. *Home:* 194 Soundview Dr., Rocky Point, N.Y. 11778. *Agent:* (Literary) Alliance of New York Writers and Publishers, Inc., Rocky Point, N.Y. 11778; (lectures) Stanley H. Barkan, Cross-Cultural Communications, 239 Wynsum Ave., Merrick, N.Y. 11566.

CAREER: Suffolk County Community College, Selden, N.Y., associate professor of English, 1969—, advisor to visiting writers program, 1971—. Teacher of creative writing to high school students at summer seminars, 1966-68; toured the United States and Italy as a teacher and organizer of creative writing and poetry workshops, 1966, 1979-80. Founder and co-director of nonprofit literary agency, Writers Unlimited Agency, Inc., 1972—; active in arts administration and real estate management on Long Island; founder of North Shore Beach Community Center, 1970.

MEMBER: East End Arts and Humanities Association (member of executive council), North Shore Committee against Nuclear and Thermal Pollution (member of executive council), North Shore Beach Association (former president), North Shore Beach Property Owners Association (member of board of directors), Lloyd Harbor Study Group (member of executive council). *Awards, honors:* Doctor of Disseminating Arts, Free University of Northampton, 1971; Poets and Writers, Inc., grant, 1972—; America the Beautiful grant, 1976; first prize in journalism, National Teachers Press Association, 1976; National Education Association community service grant, 1976-77; New York State Council on the Arts grants, 1976, 1978, 1979, 1980; Suffolk County cultural affairs grant, 1977—; C. W. Post Poetry Award, 1977; Westbury Arts Council award, 1979.

WRITINGS: *Stills from a Cinema: Poems, 1964-68,* Despa Press, 1968, revised edition, 1972; (with others) *Starting from Paumanok: Five Long Island Poets,* Despa Press, 1971; *Myths, Dreams and Dances: Poems, 1968-73,* Despa Press, 1973; *A Dream of Feet,* Cross-Cultural Communications, 1976; *A Meeting with David B. Axelrod and Ignazino Russo* (bilingual edition in English and Italian), Cross-Cultural Communications, 1979; *The Man Who Fell in Love with a Chicken* (chapbook), Cross-Cultural Communications, 1979. Also author of play, "The Performance," produced at University of Massachusetts, 1965; contributor to numerous anthologies, including *Introduction to Poetry* and *Introduction to Literature,* both edited by X. J. Kennedy. Contributor to over 150 periodicals, including *Western Humanities Review, Kansas Quarterly, Descant,* and *Carolina Quarterly.*

WORK IN PROGRESS: The Salaried Person's Guide to Paying No Income Tax, with Alan J. Pomerantz; *The Spot and Other Poems: 100 New Poems and Experiences; Eight Interviews with American Writers.*

SIDELIGHTS: Axelrod, an experienced actor, gives frequent readings and performances, often with composer-musician Lou Stevens, endeavoring to make poetry a vital performing art. He has appeared at nearly two hundred colleges and festivals, touring two or three months each year. He calls himself "a business person among the poets" and says that he melds his "administrative and writing abilities to further the arts."

AZRIN, Nathan H(arold) 1930-

PERSONAL: Born November 26, 1930, in Boston, Mass.; son of Harry (a grocer) and Esther (Alper) Azrin; married Victoria Besalel (a rehabilitation worker), January 25, 1953; children: Rachel, Michael, David, Richard. *Education:* Boston University, B.A. (cum laude), 1951, M.A., 1952; Harvard University, Ph.D., 1956. *Home:* 1200 West Schwartz St., Carbondale, Ill. 62901. *Agent:* Georges Borchardt, Inc., 136 East 57th St., New York, N.Y. 10022. *Office:* Anna State Hospital, 1000 North Main St., Anna, Ill. 62901.

CAREER: Anna State Hospital, Anna, Ill., research supervisor, 1957—; Southern Illinois University at Carbondale, professor of rehabilitation, 1958—. *Military service:* U.S. Army, Ordnance, 1956-58. *Member:* American Psychological Association (division president, 1967-70), Phi Beta Kappa, Sigma Xi.

WRITINGS: (With Teodoro Ayllon) *Token Economy,* Appleton, 1968; (with Richard M. Foxx) *Rapid Toilet Training of the Retarded: Day and Nighttime Independent Toileting,* Research Press, 1973; (with Foxx) *Toilet Training in Less than a Day,* Simon & Schuster, 1974; (with Nunn) *Habit Control,* Simon & Schuster, 1977; (with wife, Victoria Besalel) *Parent's Guide to Bedwetting Control,* Simon & Schuster, 1979; (with V. Besalel) *Job Club Counselor's Manual,* University Park Press, 1979. Contributor to proceedings and to professional journals, including *Journal of Research and Training, Behavior Research and Therapy, American Journal of Mental Deficiency,* and *Journal of Applied Behavioral Analysis.* Editor of *Journal of Experimental Analysis of Behavior,* 1958—.

B

BADAWI, M(ohamed) M(ustafa) 1925-
(Muhammad Mustafa Badawi)

PERSONAL: Given name is sometimes listed as Muhammad; born June 10, 1925, in Alexandria, Egypt; son of Mustafa (a contractor) and Aziza (Ibrahim) Badawi; married Wilemina Herderschee (a medical social worker), July 27, 1954; children: Salma, Randa, Kareema, Ramsey. *Education:* Alexandria University, B.A. (honors), 1946; University of London, B.A. (honors), 1950, Ph.D., 1954. *Office:* St. Antony's College, Oxford University, Oxford, England.

CAREER: Alexandria University, Alexandria, Egypt, research fellow, 1947-54, lecturer, 1954-60, professor of English, 1960-64; Oxford University, Oxford, England, university lecturer in Arabic and lecturer at Brasenose College, 1964—, fellow of St. Antony's College, 1967—. *Member:* Association of University Teachers. *Awards, honors:* M.A., Oxford University, 1964.

WRITINGS: Rasa'il min London (title means "Letters from London: A Volume of Arabic Verse"), Dar al-Talib (Alexandria), 1956; *Coleridge,* Dar al-Ma'arif (Cairo), 1958; *Dirasat fi'l shi'r wa'l masrah* (title means "Studies in Poetry and Drama: A Comparative Study of the Form and Language of Classical and Modern Arabic Poetry"), Dar al-Marif, 1960; (editor) *Mukhtarat min alshi'r al-'arabi al-hadith,* Dar al-Nahar (Beirut), 1969, translation published as *An Anthology of Modern Arabic Verse,* Oxford University Press, 1970; *Coleridge: Critic of Shakespeare,* Cambridge University Press, 1973; (translator from the Arabic) Yahya Haqqi, *The Saint's Lamp and Other Stories,* E. J. Brill, 1973; *A Critical Introduction to Modern Arabic Poetry,* Cambridge University Press, 1975; (contributor of translation from the Arabic) Tewfik El Hakim, *Arabic Writing Today,* edited by M. Manzaloui, American Research Center in Egypt (Cairo), 1977; (translator from the Arabic) Abbas El Akkad, *Sara* (novel), General Egyptian Book Organization (Cairo), 1978; *At lal* (title means "Ruins: A Volume of Arabic Verse"), Al-Hay'a al-Misriyya al-'Amma li'l Kitab, 1979; *Studies Mainly in Arabic Literature,* Macmillan (London), 1980.

Translator into Arabic: George Santayana, *Al-Ihsas bi'l jamal* ("The Sense of Beauty"), Mu'assasat Franklin (Cairo), 1960; I. A. Richards, *Al-'Ilm wa'l shi'r* ("Science and Poetry"), Matba'at al-Anglo (Cairo), 1960; Stephen Spender, *Al-Hayat wa'l sha'ir* ("Life and the Poet"), Matba'at al-Anglo, 1960; G. Rostrevor Hamilton, *Al-Shi'r wa'l ta'ammul* ("Poetry and Contemplation"), al-Mu'assasa al-Misriyya (Cairo), 1963; Richards, *Mabadi' al-naqd aladabi* ("Principles of Literary Criticism"), al-Mu'assasa al-Misriyya, 1963; William Shakespeare, *Al-Malik Lir* ("King Lear"), Wazarat al-I'lam (Kuwait), 1976.

Contributor of essays to journals in his field. Member of committee of correspondents for the Annual Bibliography of *Shakespeare Quarterly,* 1961-80. Co-editor, *Journal of Arabic Literature,* 1970—; member of editorial advisory board, *Cambridge History of Arabic Literature,* 1971—.

WORK IN PROGRESS: Attitudes and Assumptions in Eighteenth-Century Shakespearean Criticism.

BIOGRAPHICAL/CRITICAL SOURCES: Bulletin of the School of Oriental and African Studies, Volume XXXI, Part I, 1968; *Journal of Arabic Literature,* Volume III, 1972; R. C. Ostle, editor, *Studies in Modern Arabic Literature,* Aris & Phillips, 1975; S. Moreh, *Modern Arabic Poetry, 1800-1970,* E. J. Brill, 1976; S. K. Jayyusi, *Trends and Movements in Modern Arabic Poetry,* E. J. Brill, 1977.

* * *

BAILEY, Charles W(aldo) II 1929-

PERSONAL: Born April 28, 1929, in Boston, Mass.; son of David Washburn and Catherine (Smith) Bailey; married Ann Card Bushnell, September 9, 1950; children: Victoria Britton, Sarah Tilden. *Education:* Harvard University, A.B. (magna cum laude), 1950. *Home:* 2500 Lake Pl., Minneapolis, Minn. 55405. *Office:* 425 Portland Ave., Minneapolis, Minn. 55488.

CAREER: Minneapolis Tribune, Minneapolis, Minn., reporter, 1950-54, correspondent in Washington, D.C., 1954-67, Washington bureau chief, 1968-72, editor in Minneapolis, 1972—. Washington correspondent for *Des Moines Register* and *Look,* 1954-67. Standing committee of correspondents, U.S. Congress, member, 1962-63, secretary, 1963. Trustee, Carnegie Endowment for International Peace. *Member:* American Society of Newspaper Editors (director, 1977—), Asia Society (co-chairman of China Council), National Press Club, White House Correspondents Association (president, 1969), Federal City Club, Minneapolis Club. *Awards, honors:* Honorable mention, Raymond Clapper Award, 1961 and 1964.

WRITINGS: (Contributor) *Candidates 1960,* Basic Books, 1959; (with Fletcher Knebel) *No High Ground,* Harper,

1960; (with Knebel) *Seven Days in May,* Harper, 1962; (with Knebel) *Convention,* Harper, 1964; (contributor) *Exeter Remembered,* Phillips Exeter Academy, 1965; (contributor) *The President's Trip to China,* Bantam, 1972.

SIDELIGHTS: A reviewer in *Booklist* calls *Seven Days in May,* a novel about an attempted military takeover of the U.S. government, "an intriguing story which, despite its prosaic style and superficial characterization, will hold reader attention." A critic in *Christian Century* also notes the book's "crude characterizations and . . . improbable situations," but agrees that it has a "disturbing ring of truth" and that "chances are, once you start reading it you won't [be able to] put it down." S.L.A. Marshall of the *New Republic* also found the book disturbing, but not exactly in the way the authors intended: "One might dismiss [this novel] by saying that writing a stunt book for fun and a fast buck is done every day. But it's too late for that. Knebel and Bailey so love their thesis that they are essayists in *Look* magazine warning that their novel outlines a palpable danger. When they go that far, knowing so little, they match in recklessness the insidious characters which they themselves imagine." *Seven Days in May* was filmed by Paramount in 1963. It starred Burt Lancaster and Kirk Douglas.

BIOGRAPHICAL/CRITICAL SOURCES: Christian Century, September 26, 1962; *New Republic,* October 1, 1962; *Booklist,* November 15, 1962.

* * *

BAKER, Dorothy 1907-1968

PERSONAL: Born April 21, 1907, in Missoula, Mont.; died June 17, 1968, in Springville, Calif.; buried in Porterfield, Calif.; daughter of Raymond Branson and Alice (Grady) Dodds; married Howard Baker, September 2, 1930; children: Ellen, Joan. *Education:* University of California, Los Angeles, A.B., 1929, M.A., 1934; Occidental College, B.E., 1930. *Politics:* Democrat. *Home address:* Route 1, Box 11, Terra Bella, Calif. *Agent:* Annie Laurie Williams, Inc., 18 East 41st St., New York, N.Y.

CAREER: Writer. *Awards, honors:* Houghton Mifflin literary fellowship, 1938, for *Young Man with a Horn;* Guggenheim fellowship, 1942; General Literature Gold Medal, Commonwealth Club of California, 1943, for *Trio;* National Institute of Arts and Letters fellowship, 1964.

WRITINGS: Young Man with a Horn, Houghton, 1938, reprinted, Queens House, 1977; *Trio,* Houghton, 1943, reprinted, Greenwood Press, 1977; *Our Gifted Son,* Houghton, 1948; *Cassandra at the Wedding,* Houghton, 1962. Also author of television play with husband, Howard Baker, "The Ninth Day." Contributor of short stories to *McCall's, Harper's,* and other national magazines.

SIDELIGHTS: Dorothy Baker once told an interviewer: "When I first began to write, I was seriously hampered by an abject admiration for Ernest Hemingway, and I found that the only way I could grow up and get over it was simply to quit writing any direct discourse.

"I didn't allow myself any quotation marks until I felt confident that I could write, for good or ill, my own stuff. . . . On the other hand, I have very deliberately studied and have been influenced by the nonfiction method of Otis Ferguson. In fiction I admire above all else simplicity and clarity in both phrase and story."

Young Man with a Horn was filmed by Warner Brothers in 1950.

AVOCATIONAL INTERESTS: Cooking, sports, and music.

BIOGRAPHICAL/CRITICAL SOURCES: New York Times, June 19, 1968; *Newsweek,* July 1, 1968; *Publishers Weekly,* July 8, 1968; *Antiquarian Bookman,* July 29, 1968.†

* * *

BAKER, Jeffrey J(ohn) W(heeler) 1931-

PERSONAL: Born February 2, 1931, in Montclair, N.J.; son of Jefferson Wheeler (a stockbroker) and Monica L. (Deakin) Baker; married Barbara Bernache, August 20, 1955; children: Rebekah Monica, Deborah Ann, Jennifer Deakin, Jefferson Jonathan Farrar. *Education:* Attended University of Vermont, 1950-51; University of Virginia, B.A., 1953, M.S., 1959. *Politics:* Independent. *Religion:* None. *Home:* 13 Sunset Ter., Portland, Conn. 06480. *Office:* Science Program, Wesleyan University, Middletown, Conn. 06457.

CAREER: Mt. Hermon School, Mt. Hermon, Mass., instructor in biology, 1954-58, 1959-62; Wesleyan University, Middletown, Conn., lecturer in science, 1962-66; George Washington University, Washington, D.C., associate professor, 1966-68; University of Puerto Rico, Rio Piedras, professor of biology, 1968-69; Wesleyan University, lecturer in science and chairman of science program, 1969—, senior fellow, College of Science in Society, 1975—. Editorial director and staff biologist, Commission on Undergraduate Education in the Biological Sciences (CUEBS), 1966-68. *Member:* American Institution of Biological Sciences, American Association for the Advancement of Science, National Association of Biology Teachers, Society for the Scientific Study of Sex, American Association of Sex Educators, Counselors and Therapists, National Association of Science Writers, Authors Guild. *Awards, honors: Patterns of Nature* was selected by the *New York Times* as one of the fifty best books for children, 1967.

WRITINGS: (With Rudolph E. Hafner) *The Vital Wheel: Metabolism,* American Education Publications, 1963; *In the Beginning: A Survey of Modern Embryology,* American Education Publications, 1964; *Cell,* American Education Publications, 1965; *Patterns of Nature* (juvenile), Doubleday, 1967; *The Vital Process: Photosynthesis* (young adult), Doubleday, 1969; *Strike the Tent,* Doubleday, 1970; *Learn About Genetics,* American Education Publications, 1977.

With Garland E. Allen: *Matter, Energy and Life: An Introduction for Biology Students,* Addison-Wesley, 1965, 3rd edition, 1976; *The Study of Biology,* Addison-Wesley, 1967, 3rd edition, 1977, abridged edition published as *A Course in Biology,* 1968, 3rd edition, 1979; *Hypothesis: Prediction and Implication in Biology,* Addison-Wesley, 1968; (compilers) *The Process of Biology: Primary Sources,* Addison-Wesley, 1970, 2nd edition, 1971; (and Preston Adams) *The Study of Botany,* Addison-Wesley, 1970.

Editor and contributor of *Biology in Liberal Education,* 1966, and numerous other publications published by the Commission on Undergraduate Education in the Biological Sciences, 1967-69, and *Conference on Explanation in Biology: Historical, Philosophical and Scientific Aspects,* Harvard University Press, 1969. Contributor of over 200 articles to periodicals. Biology editor, *Science and Math Weekly* and *Current Science,* 1962-66.

WORK IN PROGRESS: Books in fields of science, religion, and music.

AVOCATIONAL INTERESTS: The American Civil War; playing flamenco guitar and the accordion.

BALLANTINE, Richard 1940-

PERSONAL: Born July 25, 1940, in Kingston, N.Y.; son of Ian (a publisher) and Elizabeth (Jones) Ballantine. *Address:* 30 Oppidan's Rd., London N.W.3, England.

CAREER: Has worked as a shooting gallery attendant, pinticket machine operator, electronics technician, shipping clerk, salesman, book editor, publicity director, indexer, inventor, and toy designer; free-lance writer.

WRITINGS: (With John Cohen) *Africa Addio,* Ballantine, 1966; (with Joel Griffiths) *Silent Slaughter,* Regnery, 1972; *Richard's Bicycle Book,* Ballantine, 1972 (published in England as *How to Choose and Use a Bicycle,* Foulis, 1975), revised edition, Pan Books, 1976; *The Piccolo Bicycle Book,* Pan Books, 1977; (editor) *Yachting: The Photography of Beken of Cowes,* Bantam, 1977.

WORK IN PROGRESS: The First Book; Richard's Boat Book.

* * *

BALLINGER, William Sanborn 1912-1980 (Bill S. Ballinger; pseudonyms: Frederic Freyer, B. X. Sanborn)

PERSONAL: Born March 13, 1912, in Oskaloosa, Iowa; son of William M. and Ella (Satia) Ballinger; married Geraldine Taylor (divorced February, 1948); married Laura Dunham, 1949 (divorced December, 1964); married Lucille Rambeau, December 11, 1964; children: (first marriage) William B., Bruce R.; (second marriage) Constance V., Julia P. *Education:* University of Wisconsin, B.A., 1934; Northern College, Philippines, LL.D., 1940. *Agent:* Russell & Volkening, Inc., 551 Fifth Ave., New York, N.Y. 10017.

CAREER: Magazine, newspaper, and radio work, 1935-50; self-employed novelist, screen writer, and dramatist, 1950-77; California State University, Northridge, associate professor, beginning 1977. Frequent university lecturer on creative writing. *Member:* Authors Guild, Screen Writers Guild (West), Mystery Writers of America (executive vice-president, 1957), Delta Kappa Epsilon, Lambs Club (New York, N.Y.), The Coral Casino (Santa Barbara, Calif.). *Awards, honors:* Prix roman policier, Presses de la Cite, 1953; Edgar Allan Poe Award for best half-hour suspense show in television, 1961.

WRITINGS: The Body in the Bed, Harper, 1948; *The Body Beautiful,* Harper, 1949; *Portrait in Smoke,* Harper, 1950; *The Darkening Door,* Harper, 1952; *Rafferty,* Harper, 1953; *The Tooth and the Nail,* Harper, 1955; (under pseudonym Frederic Freyer) *The Black Black Hearse,* St. Martin's, 1955; *The Wife of the Red-Haired Man,* Harper, 1956; *The Longest Second,* Harper, 1957; *Formula for Murder,* New American Library, 1958; *Beacon in the Night,* Harper, 1958; (under pseudonym B. X. Sanborn) *The Doom-Maker,* Dutton, 1959.

The Fourth of Forever, Harper, 1963; *Not I, Said the Vixen,* Gold Medal, 1964; *The Spy in the Jungle,* New American Library, 1965; *The Chinese Mask,* New American Library, 1965; *The Spy in Bangkok,* New American Library, 1965; *The Heir-Hunters,* Harper, 1966; *The Spy at Angkor Wat,* New American Library, 1966; *The Spy in the Java Sea,* New American Library, 1966; *49 Days of Death,* Sherbourne, 1969; *The Corsican,* Dodd, 1974; *The Lost City of Stone,* Simon & Schuster, 1978. Author of seven motion pictures, approximately 200 films for television suspense, western, adventure, situation comedy, juvenile, and drama shows, and twenty-five short stories. Contributing editor, *True* (magazine), 1975.

WORK IN PROGRESS: Untitled novels.

SIDELIGHTS: William Ballinger spent a great deal of time in Europe and the Near East. He spoke some French and Spanish. Ballinger's books have been translated into eleven languages and sold in twenty-eight foreign countries. Ballinger told *CA:* "I'm now retired from script writing and working harder than ever on my books."

(Died March 23, 1980, in Tarzana, Calif.)

* * *

BANGERT, Ethel E(lizabeth) 1912-

PERSONAL: Surname is pronounced *Ban*-gert; born September 28, 1912, in Oakland, Calif.; daughter of William Duncon (a salesman) and Georgina (Mann) Patterson; married Nelson Bangert (a civil engineer), December 5, 1930; children: Beverly D., Dolores (Mrs. E. Rhode), Virginia D. (died, 1970). *Education:* Correspondence courses, University of California Extension, 1936, 1937; attended University of California, Berkeley, summer, 1971. *Agent:* Larry Sternig Literary Agency, 742 Robertson St., Milwaukee, Wis. 53213.

CAREER: Sacramento City Schools, Sacramento, Calif., adult education teacher of creative writing, 1955-77. *Member:* Authors League, Outdoor Writers of America, California Writer's Club (vice-president, 1940), Sacramento Writer's Club (vice-president, 1951).

WRITINGS—All novels: *Her Best Man,* Gramercy, 1943; *Desert Flower,* Gramercy, 1944; *Rosemary and Rue,* Gramercy, 1945; *A Time to Dance,* Gramercy, 1946; *Wait for Tomorrow,* Arcadia House, 1948; *Delta Girl,* Arcadia House, 1949; *Once and Forever,* Arcadia House, 1950; *Dawn of Romance,* Arcadia House, 1950; *Behold This Hour,* Arcadia House, 1952, revised edition published as *Thoughts of Love,* Prestige Books, 1979; *Bird in the Forest,* Arcadia House, 1954; *Child of the Wind,* Arcadia House, 1957; *Polly Perry: TV Cook,* Putnam, 1959; *Clover Hill,* Arcadia House, 1962; *Nurse on Vacation,* Avalon, 1970; *Nurse of the Sacramento,* Avalon, 1971; *Nurse of the Gold Country,* Avalon, 1972; *Down under Nurse,* Avalon, 1972; *Nurse under Suspicion,* Avalon, 1973; *Nurse in Spain,* Avalon, 1973; *Nurse Suzanne's Bold Journey,* Avalon, 1975; *The Secret of the Peony Vase,* Avalon, 1975; *An Opal for Nurse Kate,* Bouregy, 1979. Author of column, "Collectibles Corner," for the *Valley Pioneer* (newspaper). Contributor of articles and short stories to periodicals.

WORK IN PROGRESS: A nonfiction book, *Fun Things to Collect,* for Messner.

* * *

BANNER, Lois W(endland) 1939-

PERSONAL: Born July 26, 1939, in Los Angeles, Calif.; daughter of Harry J. (a medical writer) and Melba (a teacher; maiden name, Parkes) Wendland; married James M. Banner, Jr. (a university professor), May 23, 1962; children: Olivia Parkes. *Education:* University of California, Los Angeles, B.A., 1960; Columbia University, M.A., 1962, Ph.D., 1970. *Politics:* Democrat. *Religion:* None. *Office:* Department of History, University of Scranton, Scranton, Pa. 18510.

CAREER: Rosemary Hall, Greenwich, Conn., teacher of history, 1962-66; Rutgers University, Douglass College, New Brunswick, N.J., instructor, 1966-71, assistant professor of history, 1971-77; Princeton University, Princeton, N.J., instructor, 1977-78; University of Scranton, Scranton, Pa., National Endowment for the Humanities Lecturer, 1979—. *Member:* Organization of American Historians,

American Historical Association, Coordinating Committee on Women in the Historical Profession, Berkshire Conference of Women Historians.

WRITINGS: Women in Modern America: A Brief History, Harcourt, 1974; *Clio's Consciousness Raised: New Perspectives on the History of Women,* Harper, 1974; *Elizabeth Cady Stanton: A Radical for Woman's Rights,* Little, Brown, 1980. Contributor of articles on women and on religion in early America to professional journals.

WORK IN PROGRESS: On Being Beautiful in America: Fashion, Feminism, and Physical Appearance.

* * *

BARBA, Harry 1922-
(Baron Mikan, Ohon)

PERSONAL: Born June 17, 1922, in Bristol, Conn.; son of Michael and Sulton (Manatsikanian) Barba; married Roberta Ashburn,1956 (divorced, 1963); married Marian Homelson, 1965; children:(first marriage) Gregory Robert. *Education:* Bates College, A.B., 1944; Harvard University, M.A., 1951; graduate study at City College of the City University of New York, 1955-56, New York University, 1956-57, and Columbia University, 1957-58; University of Iowa, M.F.A., 1960, Ph.D., 1963. *Home and office:* 47 Hyde Blvd., Ballston Spa, N.Y. 12020.

CAREER: Wilkes College, Wilkes-Barre, Pa., instructor, 1947; University of Connecticut, Hartford Branch, instructor, 1947-49; Seward Park High School, New York, N.Y., teacher, 1955-59; University of Iowa, Iowa City, instructor, 1959-63; University of Damascus, Damascus, Syria, Fulbright professor, 1963-64; Skidmore College, Saratoga Springs, N.Y., 1964-68, began as assistant professor, became associate professor of English and creative writing; Marshall University, Huntington, W.Va., professor of English and director of writing, 1968-70; free-lance writer and lecturer, consultant, and workshop coordinator in the field of creative writing, 1970—. Director and writer-in-residence, Adirondack-Metroland Writers and Educators Conference, 1970—; distinguished visiting lecturer, State University of New York at Albany, 1977-78; established writing programs at Skidmore College and Marshall University. Publisher, Harian Creative Press, Ballston Spa, N.Y. Consultant to numerous national organizations, including National Education Association, National Endowment for the Arts, and National Endowment for the Humanities; editorial consultant, Bantam Books, Inc., 1967, Random House, Inc., 1969-71, and Macmillan Publishing Co., Inc., 1972.

MEMBER: P.E.N., Authors Guild, Authors League of America, Poets and Writers, Inc., Modern Language Association of America, College English Association, Harvard Graduate Research Foundation, Harvard Club of Eastern New York (member of board of directors, 1975—). *Awards, honors:* Yaddo fellowship, 1950; University of Iowa graduate fellowship, 1961-62; Skidmore College research grant, 1964-68; Benedeum research grant,1969; Higher Education Act grant, 1969-70; Macdowell Colony fellow, 1970.

WRITINGS—Published by Harian Creative Press, except as indicated: *For the Grape Season* (novel), Macmillan, 1960; *The Bulbul Bird* (novel), University Microfilm, 1963; *3 by Harry Barba* (short stories), 1967; *3x3* (short stories), 1969; *How to Teach Writing,* 1969; *Teaching in Your Own Write,* 1970; *The Case for Socially Functional Education,* 1973; *The Three Crashes at Marshall University,* 1974; *One of a Kind: The Many Faces and Voices of America* (short stories), 1976; *The Day the World Went Sane* (science fiction novelette), 1979; (editor with wife, Marian Barba) *What's Cooking in Congress?* (cookbook), 1979. Also author of a play, "All Hallowmas," first produced at the University of Iowa, spring, 1961; contributor of stories to several anthologies. Contributor of articles, novellas, and stories to periodicals.

WORK IN PROGRESS: An autobiography; a novel.

SIDELIGHTS: According to Harry Barba, of the few contemporary authors who may last, he is sure of only three: William Faulkner, John Barth, and Harry Barba. "I suppose that sounds egotistical," he told Gioia Diliberto in an interview, "but I'm really very insecure." Diliberto says that the author "feels slighted by the literary world. That's why he's both insecure and arrogant. If Harry Barba doesn't sing Harry Barba's praises, no one will."

Nona Balakian praises Barba's work—especially his short stories—and calls him a "highly accomplished but insufficiently recognized" writer who, although born in New England, "has the Southern writer's sense of the eccentric, the larger-than-life character who thrives on his individualism. His social criticism is subtly masked behind a gusty humor which he sometimes indulges to excess. But, whether he is writing about the New England scene or the Middle East (which he also knows first-hand), he keeps his stories moving from episode to episode with unfailing exuberance and aplomb." The comparison to southern writers is not a new one. Barba told Bill Belanger: "Thomas Wolfe, Saroyan, Faulkner ... the southern writers influenced me most. Faulkner probably most of all. I'd like to have been audacious like him. In fact, I'd rather be significant than great; significance comes to a man for what he does; greatness is for the man himself."

Barba's main interest, however, is not his own writing; he says that the most important thing in his life is the establishment of workshops for writers. As he told Belanger: "I like to bring author and editor together to help the author get ahead, and there are many ways, direct and indirect, to do this. But most of all, best of all, I like to get them interested in writing. . . . A writer's life is lonely, and he needs classes or workshops for a strong socializing force. Students learn more from each other than they do from parents. . . ." Barba's desire to help new authors led him to found the Harian Press which is devoted to publishing the work of essentially unknown writers. When asked about hobbies, he replied, "My hobby . . . is Harian Press. That's how I like to relax."

BIOGRAPHICAL/CRITICAL SOURCES: Herald-Advertiser (Huntington, W.Va.), November 16, 1969; *Times-Union* (Albany, N.Y.), October 3, 1975; *Times-Record* (Troy, N.Y.), December 1, 1975; *Ararat,* winter, 1977; *Choice,* February, 1977; *Knoxville News-Sentinel,* November 26, 1979; *Evening News* (Harrisburg, Pa.), January 18, 1980.

* * *

BARKER, Dudley 1910-
(Lionel Black, Anthony Matthews)

PERSONAL: Born March 25, 1910, in London, England; son of Theodore Edwin and Katie (Bradgate) Barker; married Muriel Irene Griffiths, 1935; children: Raymond, Jane. *Education:* Oriel College, Oxford, B.A. (with honors), 1933. *Home:* French Court, Barn, Pett, Sussex TN35 4JA, England. *Office:* 12 Wharfedale St., London SW10 9AL, England.

CAREER: Has been employed as a reporter, features editor, news editor, feature writer, and magazine editor in London,

England, 1933-60; Curtis Brown Ltd., London, literary agent, 1960-63; author and free-lance journalist, 1964—. *Military service:* Royal Air Force, 1940-46; became wing commander; mentioned in dispatches. *Member:* Crime Writers Association, National Union of Journalists, Savage Club, Whitefriars Club.

WRITINGS—Novels: *A Few of the People,* Jarrolds, 1946; *Grandfather's House,* Heinemann, 1951; *The Voice,* Heinemann, 1953; *Green and Pleasant Land,* Heinemann, 1955, Holt, 1956; *Toby Pinn,* Heinemann, 1956; *Private Company,* Longmans, Green, 1959; *The Ladder,* Cassell, 1968; *A Pillar of Rest,* Cassell, 1970.

Nonfiction: *Laughter in Court,* Methuen, 1935; *Palmer,* Duckworth, 1935; *Lord Darling's Famous Capes,* Hutchinson, 1936; *People for the Commonwealth,* Werner Laurie, 1958; *Grivas,* Harcourt, 1960; *The Commonwealth We Live In,* H.M.S.O., 1960; *The Man of Principle: A View of John Galsworthy,* Heinemann, 1963, published as *The Man of Principle: A Biography of John Galsworthy,* Stein & Day, 1969; *The Young Man's Guide to Journalism,* Hamish Hamilton, 1963; *Swaziland,* H.M.S.O., 1965; *Writer By Trade: A View of Arnold Bennett,* Atheneum, 1966; *Prominent Edwardians,* Atheneum, 1969; *G. K. Chesterton,* Stein & Day, 1973.

Under pseudonym Lionel Black, except as indicated: *A Provincial Crime,* Cassell, 1960; *Chance to Die,* Cassell, 1965; *The Bait,* Cassell, 1966, Paperback Library, 1967; *Two Ladies in Verona,* Cassell, 1967, Paperback Library, 1968; *Outbreak,* Stein & Day, 1968; *Swinging Murder,* Cassell, 1969, published under pseudonym Anthony Matthews, Walker, 1969; *Breakaway,* Collins, 1970, Stein & Day, 1971; *Death Has Green Fingers,* Collins, 1971, published under pseudonym Anthony Matthews, Walker, 1971; *Ransom for a Nude,* Stein & Day, 1972; *The Life and Death of Peter Wade,* Collins, 1973, Stein & Day, 1974; *Death By Hoax,* Collins, 1974, Avon, 1978; *Arafat Is Next,* Stein & Day, 1975; *A Healthy Way To Die,* Collins, 1976, Avon, 1978; *The Foursome,* Collins, 1978; *The Penny Murders,* Collins, 1979.

Also author of radio plays. Contributor of numerous articles and short stories to various periodicals.

WORK IN PROGRESS: A novel.

SIDELIGHTS: The movie rights for *Outbreak* were purchased by Universal.

* * *

BARKER, Ralph 1917-

PERSONAL: Born October 21, 1917, in Feltham, Middlesex, England; son of Frederick Charles and Alma (Golding) Barker; married Joan Muriel Harris, 1948; children: Sarah Geraldine. *Education:* Studied at Hounslow College, 1926-34. *Religion:* Church of England. *Home and office:* Old Timbers, 16 Aldercombe Lane, Caterham, Surrey, England.

CAREER: Sporting Life (newspaper), London, England, sub-editor, 1935; Barclays Bank, Ltd., London, clerk and cashier, 1936-48; Royal Air Force, aircrew, 1940-46, intelligence, 1948-61, retired as flight lieutenant. *Member:* Royal Aeronautical Society (associate member), Society of Authors.

WRITINGS—Published by Chatto & Windus, except as indicated: *Down in the Drink,* 1955; *The Ship-Busters,* 1957; *The Last Blue Mountain,* 1959, Doubleday, 1960, reprinted, Mountaineers, 1979; *Strike Hard, Strike Sure,* 1963; *Ten Great Innings,* 1964; *The Thousand Plan,* 1965; *Ten Great Bowlers,* 1966; *Great Mysteries of the Air,* 1966, Macmillan (New York), 1967; *Aviator Extraordinary,* 1969; *Test Cricket: England vs. Australia,* Batsford, 1969; *Verdict on a Lost Flyer,* Harrap, 1969; *The Schneider Trophy Races,* 1971; *Against the Sea,* 1972; *One Man's Jungle,* 1975; *The Blockade Busters,* 1976, Norton, 1977; *Survival in the Sky,* Kimber, 1976; *The Cricketing Family Edrich,* Pelham Books, 1976; *The Hurricats,* Pelham Books, 1978. Contributor to *Sunday Express* (London).

WORK IN PROGRESS: The story of the South Moluccan sieges in Holland in 1975 and 1977, for St. Martin's, as yet untitled.

SIDELIGHTS: The Thousand Plan was made into a movie called "The Thousand Plane Raid" by United Artists in 1969. Many of Ralph Barker's books have been published in translation. *Avocational interests:* Flying, cricket, and contract bridge.

* * *

BARKER, W(illiam) Alan 1923-

PERSONAL: Born October 1, 1923, in Edinburgh, Scotland; son of Thomas Ludwig and Isobel (MacEwan) Barker; married Jean Alys Campbell-Harris, 1954; children: Adam Campbell. *Education:* Jesus College, Cambridge, M.A., 1948; Yale University, M.A., 1952. *Religion:* Anglican. *Home:* Luckboat House, King St., Sandwich, Kent, England. *Office:* University College School, Hampstead, London NW3 6X4, England.

CAREER: Eton College, Windsor, England, assistant master, 1947-53, 1955-58; Cambridge University, Queen's College, Cambridge, England, fellow, 1953-55; The Leys School, Cambridge, headmaster, 1958-75; University College School, London, England, headmaster, 1975—. Member, Cambridgeshire County Council; governor of 3 schools. British Information Services lecturer in United States, 1962; Paul M. Angle Memorial Lecturer, Chicago, 1978. *Military service:* Royal Artillery, 1941-45; became lieutenant. *Member:* British Association of American Studies, Headmasters' Conference, Historical Association, Brooks's Club (London), Pitt Club (Cambridge), Royal St. Georges Club (Sandwich), Public Schools Club (London), Elizabethan Club (Yale).

WRITINGS: (With others) *General History of England, Volume I, 1688-1832,* A. & C. Black, 1951, 3rd edition, 1963; (with others) *General History of England, Volume II, 1832-1950,* A. & C. Black, 1952-53, 2nd edition published as *General History of England, Volume II, 1832-1960,* 1960; (editor with others) *Documents of English History, 1688-1832,* A. & C. Black, 1952; (editor with others) *Documents of English History, 1832-1950,* A. & C. Black, 1954; *Religion and Politics, 1558-1603,* Historical Association, 1957; *The Civil War in America,* Doubleday, 1961, revised edition, 1977; (contributor) *Rebirth of Britain,* Pan Books, 1964; *Local Government Statistics,* Institute of Municipal Treasures and Accountants, 1965. Contributor of historical reviews to professional journals.

WORK IN PROGRESS: An anthology of the writings of C. A. Alington.

* * *

BARMASH, Isadore 1921-

PERSONAL: Born November 16, 1921, in Philadelphia, Pa.; son of Samuel (a tailor) and Sarah (Griff) Barmash; married Sarah Jasnoff; children: Elaine (Mrs. Morris Charnow), Stanley, Marilyn (Mrs. Michael Weinberger), Pamela. *Edu-*

cation: Charles Morris Price School, diploma in journalism, 1941. *Home:* 85-33 215th St., Hollis Hills, New York, N.Y. 11427. *Agent:* International Creative Management, 40 West 57th St., New York, N.Y. 10019. *Office: New York Times,* 229 West 43rd St., New York, N.Y. 10036.

CAREER: Fairchild Publications, New York City, bureau chief, copy chief, managing editor, and editor-in-chief, 1946-62; *New York Herald Tribune,* New York City, feature writer, 1962-65; *New York Times,* New York City, assistant to financial editor, 1965—. Lecturer at School of Journalism, University of Missouri, 1979. *Military service:* U.S. Army, 1942-45; became staff sergeant. *Member:* Authors Guild, Authors League of America, American Newspaper Guild, Actor's Studio (member of playwriting unit). *Awards, honors:* Certificate of distinction, Charles Morris Price School, 1975.

WRITINGS: The Self-Made Man, Macmillan, 1969; *Welcome to Our Conglomerate: You're Fired* (Book-of-the-Month Club selection), Delacorte, 1971; *Net Net* (novel), Macmillan, 1972; (editor) *Great Business Disasters,* Playboy Press, 1973; *The World Is Full of It,* Delacorte, 1974; *For the Good of the Company,* Grossett, 1976; *The Chief Executives,* Lippincott, 1978. Also author of two plays. Columnist for *Harper's Bazaar,* 1971-72. Contributor to *New York Times Sunday Magazine.*

BIOGRAPHICAL/CRITICAL SOURCES: Saturday Review, September 10, 1971; *New York Times Book Review,* December 26, 1976.

* * *

BARNARD, Charles N(elson III) 1924-

PERSONAL: Born October 5, 1924, in Arlington, Mass.; son of Charles Nelson, Jr. (a horse dealer) and Mae Esther (Johnson) Barnard; married Diana Lee Pattison, August 6, 1949 (divorced August, 1970); married Karen Louise Zakrison (an editor), April 18, 1971; children: (first marriage) Jennifer Lee, Rebecca, Charles Nelson IV, Patrick. *Education:* University of Missouri, B.J., 1949. *Politics:* Independent. *Religion:* Christian. *Home:* 225 Valley Rd., Cos Cob, Conn. 06807. *Agent:* John A. Ware Literary Agency, 392 Central Park W., New York, N.Y. 10025.

CAREER: Dell Publishing Co., New York City, editor, 1949; Fawcett Publications, New York City, associate editor of *True* magazine, 1949-54, managing editor, 1954-63; *Saturday Evening Post,* New York City, senior editor, 1964-65; Fawcett Publications, executive editor of *True,* 1965-67, editor, 1968-70; free-lance writer and editorial consultant, 1971—. War correspondent, 1943-46. *Military service:* U.S. Army, 1943-45; became sergeant. *Member:* Alpha Tau Omega, Sigma Delta Chi, Kappa Tau Alpha.

WRITINGS: (Editor) *A Treasury of "True,"* A. S. Barnes, 1957; (editor) *Official Automobile Handbook,* A. S. Barnes, 1959; (editor) *Anthology of "True,"* A. S. Barnes, 1962; *The Winter People,* Dodd, 1973; *20,000 Alarms,* Dodd, 1974; *I Drank the Water Everywhere,* Dodd, 1975; *The Money Pit,* Dodd, 1976; *It Was a Wonderful Summer for Running Away,* Dodd, 1977. Contributor to *Encyclopaedia Britannica.*

AVOCATIONAL INTERESTS: World travel.

* * *

BARNES, Thomas Garden 1930-

PERSONAL: Born April 29, 1930, in Pittsburgh, Pa.; son of Demas Ellsworth and Helen (Garden) Barnes; married Jeanne-Marie Dubus, 1955; children: Claudine, Demas Andre (died, 1961), Francoise, Marc. *Education:* Harvard University, A.B., 1952; Oxford University, D. Phil., 1955. *Religion:* Anglican. *Home:* 456 Vermont Ave., Berkeley, Calif. 94707; and Gardenia Lodge, Savary House, Plympton, Nova Scotia, Canada (summer). *Office:* Department of Law, University of California, Berkeley, Calif. 94720.

CAREER: Lycoming College, Williamsport, Pa., assistant professor, 1956-59, associate professor of history, 1959-60; University of California, Berkeley, lecturer, 1960-61, assistant professor, 1961-63, associate professor, 1963-67, professor of history, 1967—, professor of law, 1974—. Vice-provost and praelector in ecclesiastical history, St. Joseph of Arimathea Anglican Theological College, 1978—. Project director, American Bar Foundation Anglo-American Legal History Project, 1965—; editor, Public Record Office, London, England. Member of board of directors, St. Joseph of Arimathea Foundation, 1961—. *Member:* Royal Historical Society (fellow), American Historical Association, American Society for Legal History, Conference on British Studies, Selden Society (England; member of council, 1971—), Somerset Record Society (England; member of council, 1959—), Lincoln's Inn (London). *Awards, honors:* Alexander Prize from Royal Historical Society, 1958; American Council of Learned Societies fellow, 1962-63; Guggenheim fellow, 1970-71.

WRITINGS: Somerset Assize Orders, Somerset Record Society (England), 1959; *Somerset, 1625-1640: A County's Government during the "Personal Rule,"* Harvard University Press, 1961; *The Clerk of the Peace in Caroline Somerset,* University of Leicester Press (England), 1961; (with Jerome Blum and Rondo Cameron) *The European World: A History,* four parts, Little, Brown, 1966, 2nd edition, 1970, Parts I and II published as *The Emergence of the European World,* 1966, 2nd edition, 1970, Parts III and IV published as *The European World since 1815: Triumph and Transition,* 1966; (editor with Gerald Feldman) *A Documentary History of Modern Europe,* Little, Brown, Volume I: *Renaissance, Reformation, and Absolutism: 1400-1660,* 1972, Volume II: *Rationalism and Revolution: 1660-1815,* 1972, Volume III: *Nationalism, Industrialization, and Democracy: 1815-1914,* 1972, Volume IV: *Breakdown and Rebirth: 1914 to the Present,* 1972; (editor) *List and Index to the Proceedings in Star Chamber for the Reign of James I (1603-1625) in the Public Record Office, London,* three volumes, American Bar Foundation, 1975; (editor and author of introduction) *The Book of the General Lawes and Libertyes Concerning the Inhabitants of the Massachusets,* Henry E. Huntington, 1975; (with Joseph Henry Smith) *The English Legal System: Carryover to the Colonies,* William Andrews Clark Memorial Library, University of California, 1975; *Hastings College of the Law: The First Century,* Hastings College of the Law Press, 1978. Contributor to *Bulletin* of Institute of Historical Research, *Transactions of the Royal Historical Society,* and *Huntington Library Quarterly.*

AVOCATIONAL INTERESTS: Fishing, boating.

* * *

BAROLINI, Antonio 1910-1971

PERSONAL: Born May 29, 1910, in Vicenza, Italy; died January 21, 1971, in Rome, Italy; son of Giuseppe and Maria Lucia (Albarello) Barolini; married Helen Frances, 1950; children: Teodolinda Lucia, Susanna Giulia, Nicoletta Ellen. *Agent:* Anne Curtis Brown, 821 Second Ave., New York, N.Y.

CAREER: Self-employed writer; U.S. correspondent for *La*

Stampa, daily newspaper in Turin, Italy; at time of death, was producer of a cultural program for Italian television. *Member:* Authors League, United Nations Correspondents Association, Societa degli Scrittori Italiani, Albo dei Giornalisti Professionisti Italiani, P.E.N., Overseas Press Club. *Awards, honors:* Saint Vincent Prize, Val d'Aosta, Italy, 1953; Bagutta Prize, Milano, Italy, 1960.

WRITINGS: *La Gaia gioventu,* Neri Pozza, 1938; *Il Meraviglioso giardino,* Il Pellicano, 1941; *Giornate di Stefano,* Tolomei, 1943; *Poesie di dolore,* Il Pellicano, 1943; *Viaggio col veliero San Spiridione,* Il Pellicano, 1946; *Il Veliero sommerso,* Il Pellicano, 1949; *Elegie di croton,* Feltrinelli, 1959; *Our Last Family Countess and Related Stories,* Harper, 1960; *Poesie alla madre,* Neri Pozza, 1960; *Una Lunga Pazzia,* Feltrinelli, 1962, translation by wife, Helen Barolini, published as *A Long Madness,* Pantheon, 1964; *Un Fils pour le ciel,* Stock (Paris), 1964; *Il Meraviglioso giardino* (anthology of his complete poetic works), Feltrinelli, 1964; *Le notti della paura* (novel), Feltrinelli, 1967; (contributor) *Antologia del Campiello millenovecentossantasette,* Scuola grafica del Centro arti e mestieri della Fondazione Giorgio Cini, 1968; *La memoria di Stefano* (novel), Feltrinelli, 1969; (author of preface) *L'omino del pepe e altri racconti,* La nuova Italia, 1970; *Il paradiso che verra: Momenti di un'esperienza religiosa,* Vallecchi, 1972. Contributor to Italian and American magazines.

SIDELIGHTS: In 1968, Antonio Barolini became embroiled in a controversy over the awarding of Italy's most important literary prize, the Premio Strega. To protest the tendency of the jury to vote for friends or in return for favors, four of the five candidates, including Barolini, attempted to withdraw their books from competition. As a result of their protest, the patronage system for judging entries was abandoned.

BIOGRAPHICAL/CRITICAL SOURCES: *New York Times Book Review,* May 3, 1964; *Christian Science Monitor,* May 6, 1964; *Reporter,* May 7, 1964; *Commonweal,* May 8, 1964; *Saturday Review,* May 9, 1964; *Times Literary Supplement,* October 8, 1964; *Books Abroad,* winter, 1971; *New York Times,* January 23, 1971.†

* * *

BARONDESS, Sue K(aufman) 1926-1977 (Sue Kaufman)

PERSONAL: Born August 7, 1926, on Long Island, N.Y.; died June 25, 1977, in New York, N.Y.; daughter of Marcus and Anna (Low) Kaufman; married Jeremiah A. Barondess, 1953; children: James. *Education:* Vassar College, A.B., 1947. *Home and office:* 544 East 86th St., New York, N.Y. 10028. *Agent:* Russell & Volkening, Inc., 551 Fifth Ave., New York, N.Y. 10017.

CAREER: *Mademoiselle,* New York, N.Y., assistant to fiction editor, 1947-49, part-time assistant fiction editor. Freelance fiction writer, 1949-77. *Member:* Authors League. *Awards, honors:* Twice received honorable mention in Martha Foley collections of short stories.

WRITINGS—All published under the name Sue Kaufman: *The Happy Summer Days,* Scribner, 1959; *Green Holly,* Scribner, 1962; *Diary of a Mad Housewife,* Random House, 1967; *The Headshrinker's Test,* Random House, 1969; *Life with Prudence: A Chilling Tale,* M. Joseph, 1970; *Falling Bodies,* Doubleday, 1974; *The Master, and Other Stories,* Doubleday, 1976. Contributor of numerous short stories in national magazines.

SIDELIGHTS: "Sue Kaufman is the minor poet of the big city's minor neuroses," a reviewer for *Harper's* wrote. "*Diary of a Mad Housewife* caught, better than any novel I know, the manner in which the pressure of urban inconvenience . . . combined with the driving need to make it and to convincingly prove to others that you are making it, can together bring a no more than normally sensitive woman close to the edge of insanity. In *Life with Prudence: A Chilling Tale,* which is a trifle thinner, a trifle less believable, but good nonethless, we see one of her characters going over that edge. . . . [Kaufman] is obviously a battle-scarred veteran of the fight for urban survival who has learned from her experiences. She is also a slyly funny, wonderfully precise observer and it seems to me she has no peer as a recorder of our nickel miseries, anxieties, and hysterics."

In agreement Barbara Nelson felt that in *Diary of a Mad Housewife,* Kaufman exposes the frustration, dangers, and foibles of life in 'fun city' with a shrewd and knowing eye."

In a review of *Falling Bodies,* V. A. Salamone stated: "Sue Kaufman does a commendable job in explication the decadent ethos of contemporary middle-class America. The waste, the delusion that money answers all wants, the quick solutions, the running away from the truth, all negative features prevalent in American society are interwoven into the fabric of the story. . . . [The book] is a brilliant production."

Diary of a Mad Housewife was filmed by Universal in 1970.

BIOGRAPHICAL/CRITICAL SOURCES: *Library Journal,* April 15, 1967; *New Yorker,* June 24, 1967; *Books and Bookmen,* March, 1968; *Harper's,* February, 1970; *Best Sellers,* February, 1974; (under name Sue Kaufman) *Contemporary Literary Criticism,* Gale, Volume III, 1975, Volume VIII, 1978; *New York Times,* June 26, 1977; *Washington Post,* June 28, 1977; *Newsweek,* July 11, 1977; *Time,* July 11, 1977.†

* * *

BARR, George 1907-

PERSONAL: Born November 11, 1907, in Brooklyn, N.Y.; son of Samuel and Sarah (Horowitz) Barr; married Hylda Newfield, 1936; children: Michael, Elsa. *Education:* City College (now City College of the City University of New York), B.S., 1930; Brooklyn College (now Brooklyn College of the City University of New York), M.S., 1940. *Office:* New York City Board of Education, 133 East 53rd St., Brooklyn, N.Y.

CAREER: Color Photography Supply Co., New York City, research chemist, 1930-33; Board of Education, New York City, teacher and science consultant, 1934—. *Member:* National Science Teachers Association, General Science Teachers Association, Elementary School Science Association, Queens County Bird Club (president), Emile Society, Knights of Magic, Nature Conservancy.

WRITINGS—Published by McGraw, except as indicated: *Research Ideas for Young Scientists,* 1958; *Young Scientist Takes a Walk,* 1959; *Young Scientist Takes a Ride,* 1960; *More Research Ideas for Young Scientists,* 1961; *Young Scientist and Sports,* 1962; *Young Scientist Looks at Skyscrapers,* 1963; *Experiments with Everyday Things,* Harrap, 1963; *Research Adventures for Young Scientists,* 1964; *Here's Why: Science in Sports,* Scholastic Book Services, 1964; *Show Time for Young Scientists,* 1965; *Young Scientist in the Fire Department,* 1966; *Young Scientist and the Police Department,* 1967; *Fun and Tricks for Young Scientists,* 1968; *Young Scientists and the Doctor,* 1969; *Young Scientist and the Dentist,* 1970; *Entertaining with Number Tricks,*

1971. Also author of the teachers' guide for Book 1 of *Science for Work and Play*, by Herman and Nina Schneider, Heath. Author of monthly page, "Magic You Can Make" in *Popular Science*. Co-author of teachers' manuals in elementary science. Contributor to publications for teachers.

SIDELIGHTS: A man of many talents with a zest for his work, George Barr lists his interests as nature, photography, magic, whittling, bird watching, geology, hiking, and home workshop. "I'm the luckiest fellow in the world," Barr told *CA*. "My job as science consultant was made to order for me. I am doing what I like to do. I teach teachers and have assembly shows for children to awaken their interest in science around them."

At one time, Barr ran magic clubs in libraries for teenagers, and sponsored whittling clubs. Feature stories were written about his work in running clubs to help combat juvenile delinquency in poor neighborhoods; *Look* and the *New York Times* published articles about his whittling of humorous eating utensils.†

* * *

BARR, Stringfellow 1897-

PERSONAL: Born January 15, 1897, in Suffolk, Va.; son of William Alexander and Ida (Stringfellow) Barr; married Gladys Baldwin, August 13, 1921. *Education:* University of Virginia, B.A., 1916, M.A., 1917; Oxford University (Rhodes Scholar), B.A., 1921, M.A., 1927; University of Paris, diploma, 1922; University of Ghent, postgraduate study, 1922-23. *Politics:* Democrat. *Religion:* Episcopalian. *Home:* Goodwin House, 4800 Fillmore Ave., Alexandria, Va. 22311.

CAREER: University of Virginia, Charlottesville, assistant professor, 1924-27, associate professor, 1927-30, professor of modern European history, 1930-37; St. John's College, Annapolis, Md., president, governor, and member of board of visitors, 1937-46; president, Foundation for World Government, 1948-58; Rutgers University, Newark, N.J., professor of humanities, 1955-64; fellow, Center for the Study of Democratic Institutions, 1966-69. Visiting professor of liberal arts, University of Chicago, 1936-37; visiting professor of political science, University of Virginia, 1951-53; visiting fellow, New College, Hofstra University, 1966-67. Public lecturer on liberal education and American foreign policy. *Military service:* U.S. Army, 1917-19; on ambulance service, 1917-18; served with Surgeon General's Office, 1918-19; became sergeant. *Member:* Authors League, Alpha Tau Omega, Phi Beta Kappa. *Awards, honors:* Lindback Award for distinguished teaching, 1961; Marjorie Peabody Waite Award, National Institute of Arts and Letters, 1967.

WRITINGS: Mazzini: Portrait of an Exile, Holt, 1935, reprinted, Octagon, 1975; *Pilgrimage of Western Man*, Harcourt, 1949, revised edition, Lippincott, 1962; *Let's Join the Human Race*, University of Chicago Press, 1950; *Citizens of the World*, Doubleday, 1952; *Copydog in India* (children's book), Viking, 1955; (with Stella Standard) *The Kitchen Garden Book: Vegetables from Seed to Table*, Viking, 1956, reprinted, Penguin, 1977; *Purely Academic* (novel), Simon & Schuster, 1958, reprinted, Queens House, 1976; (with others) *American Catholics: A Protestant-Jewish View*, edited by Philip Scharper, Sheed, 1959; *The Will of Zeus: A History of Greece from the Origins of Hellenic Culture to the Death of Alexander* (also see below), Lippincott, 1961; *The Three Worlds of Man* (essays and lectures), University of Missouri Press, 1963; *The Mask of Jove: A History of Graeco-Roman Civilization from the Death of Alexander to the Death of Constantine* (sequel to *The Will of Zeus*), Lippincott, 1966; *Voices That Endured: The Great Books and the Active Life*, Prentice-Hall, 1971. Advisory editor, "Great Books" series, Encyclopaedia Britannica, 1944-46. Contributor to numerous publications, including *Atlantic Monthly, Nation, New York Times Book Review*, and *New York Herald Tribune Book Week*. *Virginia Quarterly Review*, advisory editor, 1926-30, 1934-37, editor, 1930-34.

SIDELIGHTS: While president of St. John's College, Stringfellow Barr abolished the elective system and inaugurated the Great Books curriculum, a four-year, required course of study with heavy emphasis on mathematics and science. Barr has made frequent radio and television appearances and, in 1940, he initiated the CBS program, "Invitation to Learning." Barr has also travelled extensively; between 1950 and 1954 he visited every continent except Australia.

AVOCATIONAL INTERESTS: Gardening.

* * *

BARSTOW, Stan(ley) 1928-

PERSONAL: Born June 28, 1928, in Horbury, Yorkshire, England; son of Wilfred and Elsie (Gosnay) Barstow; married Constance Mary Kershaw, 1951; children: Richard Neil, Gillian Rosemary. *Education:* Attended local schools. *Home:* Goring House, Goring Park Ave., Ossett, West Yorkshire WF5 0HX, England. *Agent:* Harvey Unna and Stephen Durbridge, Ltd., 14 Beaumont Mews, Marylebone High St., London W1N 4HE, England.

CAREER: Full-time writer, 1962—. *Member:* Society of Authors, P.E.N. English Centre, Writers' Guild of Great Britain. *Awards, honors:* Best dramatization award, Writers' Guild of Great Britain, and best drama series award, British Broadcasting Press Guild, both 1974, for "South Riding"; Royal Television Society's Writer's award, for dramatizations of "South Riding," *A Raging Calm*, and *Joby*.

WRITINGS—Novels, except as indicated; all published by M. Joseph, except as indicated: *A Kind of Loving*, 1960, Doubleday, 1961; *The Desperadoes*, 1961; *Ask Me Tomorrow*, 1962; *Joby*, 1964; *The Watchers on the Shore*, 1965, Doubleday, 1967; *A Raging Calm*, 1968, published as *The Hidden Part*, Coward, 1969; *A Season with Eros*, 1971; *Casual Acquaintance and Other Stories*, (short stories), Longman, 1976; *The Right True End*, 1976; *A Brother's Tale*, 1980.

Plays: (With Alfred Bradley) *Ask Me Tomorrow* (based on Barstow's novel of same title; also see above), Samuel French, 1966; (with Alfred Bradley) *A Kind of Loving* (based on Barstow's novel of same title; also see above), Blackie & Son, 1970; (with Bradley) *Stringer's Last Stand*, Samuel French, 1972; (adapter) Henrik Ibsen, *An Enemy of the People*, J. Calder, 1978.

Television plays: "South Riding" (based on novel by Winifred Holtby), produced by Yorkshire Television, 1974; "A Raging Calm" (based on Barstow's novel of same title; also see above), produced by Independent Television on Canadian television, 1974; "Joby" (based on Barstow's novel of same title; also see above), 1975; "The Cost of Loving," 1977; "Travellers," 1978.

Radio plays: "A Kind of Loving" (based on Barstow's novel of same title; also see above), "The Watchers on the Shore" (based on Barstow's novel of same title; also see above), "The Right True End" (based on Barstow's novel of same title; also see above), and "Bright Day" (based on J. B. Priestley's novel of same title).

SIDELIGHTS: Stan Barstow told *CA:* "[I] came to prominence about the same time as several other novelists from north of England working-class backgrounds, . . . and saw with satisfaction and occasional irritation the gains made in the opening up of the regions and the 'elevation' of the people into fit subjects for fictional portrayal absorbed into the popular cultures of cinema and TV drama series and comedy shows. Still, living in the provinces and using mainly regional settings, [I] consider myself non-metropolitan oriented. The publication of some of my work in the U.S. and its translation into several European languages reassures me that I have not resisted the neurotic trendiness of much metropolitan culture for the sake of mere provincial narrowness; and the knowledge that some of the finest novels in the language are 'regional' leads me to the belief that to hoe one's own row diligently, thus seeking the universal in the particular, brings more worthwhile satisfactions than the frantic pursuit of an often phoney jet-age internationalism.

"I enjoy writing for television, radio, and the theatre as a means of exercising other muscles, for the pleasure of casting existing material in dramatic forms and as an antidote to the loneliness of the novelist's and short-story writer's life."

* * *

BARTH, Roland S(awyer) 1937-

PERSONAL: Born May 18, 1937, in Boston, Mass.; son of Joseph and Ramona (Sawyer) Barth; married Beth Rosenthal (a teacher), June 23, 1962; children: Joanna, Carolyn. *Education:* Princeton University, A.B. (magna cum laude), 1959; Harvard University, Ed.M., 1962, Ed.D., 1970. *Home:* 124 Hunnewell Ave., Newton, Mass. 02158. *Office:* Graduate School of Education, Harvard University, Cambridge, Mass. 02138.

CAREER: Princeton University, Princeton, N.J., assistant to director of admissions, 1959-60; elementary school teacher in Princeton, 1960-61, Corte Madera, Calif., 1962-63, and Palo Alto, Calif., 1963-65; Harvard University, Graduate School of Education, Cambridge, Mass., assistant to dean, 1965-68; Baldwin-King School Program, New Haven, Conn., instructional principal, 1968-69; Yale University, Child Study Center, New Haven, research associate, 1968-69; Edward Devotion School, Brookline, Mass., assistant principal, 1970-71; Angier School, Newton, Mass., principal, 1971-77; Harvard University, Graduate School of Education, lecturer, 1979—. Master teacher, Harvard-Newton Summer School, 1966; faculty member, Center for Adult Education, Cambridge, 1968, and Transitional Year Program, Yale University, 1970; Greater Boston Teachers' Center, faculty member, 1973-76, member of executive committee, 1974-76; lecturer at colleges and universities and to numerous professional conferences. Director of study of public school reorganization in Maine, New England Educational Data System and National Council for Improvement of Public Schools, 1967. Consultant to New York State Follow Through Leadership Conference, 1969; member of advisory council, department of psychology, Princeton University, 1971; member of board of counselors, Smith College, 1976—; consultant to various state and local boards of education and to numerous colleges and universities.

MEMBER: National Education Association (life member), National Froebel Foundation (life member), Association for Childhood Education, National Association of Elementary School Principals (member of publications advisory committee, 1974-75), Newton Elementary Principals' Group (chairman, 1976-77), Phi Delta Kappa (member of executive board of Harvard chapter, 1966; president, 1967-68), Harvard Graduate School of Education Alumni Association (chairman, 1976-78). *Awards, honors:* First prize in First Annual Karl Spangenberg Memorial Lecture Series, 1965, for paper "Science: Learning through Failure"; Milton Fund field research grant, 1968, for studying primary schools in Great Britain; Guggenheim fellow, 1977-78.

WRITINGS: Open Education and the American School, Agathon Press, 1972; (author of foreword) Donald A. Myers and Lilian Myers, *Open Education Re-Examined,* Lexington Books, 1973; (with Kathryn A. Moe) *Selecting Educational Equipment and Materials for School and Home,* Association for Childhood Education International, 1976; *Run School Run: Inside Looking In at American Elementary Education,* Harvard University Press, 1980.

Contributor: *Follow Through Workshop,* New York State Department of Education, 1970; Wassman, editor, *Selected Readings in Elementary Education,* Simon & Schuster, 1970; F. Leibe, editor, *The Integrated Day in Theory and Practice,* Ward, Lock, 1971; C. H. Rathbone, editor, *Readings in Open Education,* Citation Press, 1971; S. P. Stoff and H. Schwartzberg, editors, *The Human Encounter: Readings in Education,* Harper, 1971, 2nd edition, 1973; H. W. Sobel and A. B. Salz, editors, *The Radical Papers: Readings in Education,* Harper, 1972; Bernard Sherman, editor, *The Open Classroom: Readings,* Educational Methods, 1972; David Purpel and Maurice Belanger, editors, *Curriculum and the Cultural Revolution,* McCutchan, 1972; Donald E. Hawkins and Dennis A. Vinton, editors, *The Environmental Classroom,* Prentice-Hall, 1973; Henry Ehlers, *Crucial Issues in Education,* Holt, 1973; Frank Krahewski and Gary Peltier, editors, *Education: Where It's Been, Where It's At, Where It's Going,* C. E. Merill, 1973; Thomas Sergiovanni, editor, *Living with Children: The Modern Elementary School Principalship,* Prentice-Hall, 1973.

Evelyn M. Carswell and Darrell L. Roubinek, *Open Sesame: A Primer in Open Education,* Goodyear Publishing, 1974; Sidney M. Tiedt, *The Social Cultural Foundations of Education,* San Jose State University, 1974; Keith Tronc, *The Open Area Primary School in Australia,* [Queensland], 1974; Thomas B. Glass, editor, *Readings in Education,* Mss Information, 1974; J. Michael Palardy, *Teaching Today,* Macmillan, 1975; H. D. Lindgren, *Educational Psychology in the Classroom,* Wiley, 1976; Robert Nye and Vernice Nye, *Music in the Elementary School,* Prentice-Hall, 1976; Peter Martorella, *Social Studies Strategies: Theory into Practice,* Harper, 1976; M. Dembo, *Analyzing the Teaching Learning Process,* Goodyear Publishing, 1977.

Contributor of numerous articles to professional journals, including *Elementary School Journal, Journal of Educational Philosophy and Theory, Grade Teacher, Childhood Education, Norwegian Journal of Education, Froebel Journal,* and *National Elementary Principal.* Member of editorial advisory board, *Harvard Educational Review,* 1968, and *Open Education in America,* 1974—.

* * *

BARTON, Thomas Frank 1905-

PERSONAL: Born December 3, 1905, in Cornell, Ill.; son of Frank Douglas (a professional agriculturalist) and Martha (Gamblin) Barton; married Erselia Marie A. Monticello, September 26, 1931; children: Thomas Frank Monticello, Jr. *Education:* Illinois State University, B.Ed., 1930; University of Wisconsin, Ph.M., 1931; University of Nebraska, Ph.D., 1935. *Politics:* "Progressive (for progressive men in either party).'' *Religion:* Presbyterian. *Home:* 940 South Jourdan Ave., Bloomington, Ind. 47401. *Office:* Department of Geography, Indiana University, Bloomington, Ind. 47401.

CAREER: Rural school teacher, 1925-27; West Tennessee State Teachers College (now Memphis State University), Memphis, assistant professor of geography, summers, 1933-34; Nebraska State Teachers College (now Kearney State College), Kearney, assistant professor of social studies, 1934-35; Southern Illinois University at Carbondale, professor of geography and geology, 1935-47, chairman of department, 1935-47; Indiana University at Bloomington, professor of geography, 1947—. Visiting professor at University of Nebraska, 1947, University of San Francisco, 1954, College of Education (Bangkok), 1955-57, and University of Colorado, 1965. Collaborator and adviser on educational films. Supervisor of U.S. Airway Weather Station, 1941-47.

MEMBER: National Council for Geographical Education (president, 1948), American Geographical Society, Association of American Geographers, Royal Geographical Society, American Association for the Advancement of Science (fellow), American Association of University Professors, Association for Asian Studies, Southeast Asia Development Advisory Group, Nebraska Academy of Sciences (president, 1935), Illinois Academy of Sciences (president, 1939-40), Indiana Academy of Sciences (president, 1972-73), Illinois Education Association, Indiana State Teachers Association, Indiana Academy of Social Science, Indiana Planning Association, Sigma Xi, Phi Delta Kappa, Kappa Phi Kappa, Pi Kappa Delta, Kappa Delta Pi, Phi Gamma Mu, Gamma Theta Upsilon. *Awards, honors:* Distinguished service award from National Council for Geographical Education, 1965; distinguished alumni award, Alumni Association of Illinois State University, 1975; Rocking Chair Award, Sigma Delta Chi, 1976; LL.D., Illinois State University, 1977; distinguished service award, Geographical Society of Chicago, 1978.

WRITINGS: *Living in Illinois* (juvenile), Rand McNally, 1941; *The National Council of Geography Teachers as a Working Organization,* National Council of Geography Teachers, 1941; *The Sequential Landscapes and Land Utilization of Hastings, Nebraska: An Urban Center Dominated by a Great Plains Physical Environment,* University of Nebraska Press, 1942; (with Sedman P. Poole and Clara Belle Baker) *Through the Day* (juvenile), Bobbs-Merrill, 1947; (with Poole and Baker) *From Season to Season* (juvenile), Bobbs-Merrill, 1947; (with Poole and Baker) *In Country and City* (juvenile), Bobbs-Merrill, 1947; *A Plan for Forestry in Illinois,* Technical Forestry Association, 1947; (with Poole and Irving Robert Melbo) *The World about Us* (juvenile), Bobbs-Merrill, 1948; (contributor) *Southern Illinois,* University of Illinois Press, 1949; (contributor) *Geography in the High Schools,* McKnight, 1949.

(Contributor) *A Handbook of Suggestions on the Teaching of Geography,* UNESCO, 1951; *Economic Survey of the Terre Haute Area,* Indiana Economic Council, 1951; (contributor) *Geography Teaching for International Understanding,* UNESCO, 1952; (contributor) John Henry Garland, editor, *The North American Midwest,* Wiley, 1955; (contributor) E. W. Miller and George T. Renner, editors, *Global Geography,* Crowell, 1957; *An Economic Geography of Thailand: An Outline Study,* originally written in English, translation into Thai language by Sawat Senanarong published by Ministry of Education (Bangkok), 1958.

Patrick Henry: Boy Spokesman (juvenile), Bobbs-Merrill, 1960; (contributor) Nila Banton Smith, Hazel C. Hart, and Baker, editors, *Time for Adventure* (juvenile), Bobbs-Merrill, 1960; (contributor) Theo L. Hills, editor, *A Selected Annotated Bibliography of the Humid Tropics,* International Geographical Union, 1960; (contributor) Wilhelmina Hills, editor, *Curriculum Guide for Geographic Education,* Publications Center, National Council for Geographical Education, 1963; (contributor) John Jarolimek and Huber M. Walsh, editors, *Readings for Social Studies in Elementary Education,* Macmillan, 1965; *John Smith: Jamestown Boy* (juvenile), Bobbs-Merrill, 1966; (contributor) Howard Roepke, editor, *Readings in Economic Geography,* Wiley, 1967; (contributor) John W. Morris, editor, *Methods of Geographic Instruction,* Blaisdell, 1968.

(With Robert C. Kingsbury and Gerald R. Showalter) *Southeast Asia in Maps,* Denoyer-Geppert, 1970; (contributor) *An Overall Economic Development Study of Southeastern Indiana,* U.S. Office of Economic Opportunity, 1970; (contributor) John W. Morris, editor, *World Geography,* McGraw, 1972; *Lyndon B. Johnson: Young Texan* (juvenile), Bobbs-Merrill, 1973; (contributor) Ashok K. Dott, editor, *Asia: Realm of Contrasts,* Kendall/Hunt, 1974.

Also author of several map series and of numerous educational films. Contributor to proceedings, transactions, to *Yearbook of the National Council for the Social Studies,* to *Encyclopaedia Britannica, Collier's Encyclopedia, Book of Knowledge,* and to *U.S. Congressional Record.* Contributor of more than a hundred articles to professional journals, including *Journal of Geography, Science Education, Economic Geography, Social Education, Interplay: The Magazine of International Affairs, Journal of the Bangladesh National Geographical Association,* and *Time for Adventure.* Editor of *Journal of Geography,* 1950-65.

WORK IN PROGRESS: Research on various facets of the Web Theory of internal city structure, growth, and planning, on rural non-farm dwellers in the United States, and on Southeast Asia geography.

BIOGRAPHICAL/CRITICAL SOURCES: *Journal of Geography,* January, 1972.

* * *

BARTON, William (Renald III) 1950-

PERSONAL: Born September 28, 1950, in Boston, Mass.; son of William Renald, Jr. (a geologist) and Hazel (Jones) Barton; married Lois A. Sandy, May 20, 1977; children: Matthew Benjamin. *Education:* Attended Northern Virginia Community College, 1969-72, and New Hampshire Vocational-Technical College, 1979-80. *Politics:* ''Nihilist-Superrevolutionary.'' *Religion:* Mani Koi. *Home:* 16 George St., Dover, N.H. 03820.

CAREER: Writer. Has been employed in a variety of jobs, many under the Comprehensive Employment and Training Act (CETA), including cook, assistant manager of a 7-11 store, technician, machinist, map encoder, operator trainee at a sewage treatment plant, lawnmower operator, and auto mechanic. In the near future, he envisions ''a brief period of unemployment, followed by forty weeks on CETA-OJT [On the Job Training] doing whatever those stolid bureaucratic types imagine (in their power-crazed state) that I am capable of doing.''

WRITINGS: *Hunting on Kunderer* (science fiction novel), Ace Books, 1973; *A Plague of All Cowards* (science fiction novel), Ace Books, 1976. Also author of *This Dog/Rat World* and, with Michael Capobianco, *Under Twilight;* author of short stories.

WORK IN PROGRESS: The Lord of Skyhaven; Crimson Darkness, with Michael Capobianco.

SIDELIGHTS: William Barton says that the manuscript of *This Dog/Rat World,* a history book, was "kept prisoner by Ace Books for eighteen months, then kept prisoner by Doubleday for twelve months—in both instances finally returned after many plaintive demands. Since then, a steady stream of inquiries to many publishers either ignored or declined. No one wants to look at it, apparently." He feels that the manuscript of *Under Twilight* was similarly "kept prisoner" by Ace Books for twenty one months and that now no other publisher will look at it.

Barton writes: "'We are sorry to tell you that your manuscript/proposal is not suited to the present requirements of %$#!!! Books. Unfortunately, the great number of proposals received makes it impossible for us to provide individual comment. However, we do wish to thank you for giving us the opportunity to see your work, and we wish you much success in finding a more suitable publisher. Sincerely yours, Editorial Department.' Well, golly there, Mr/Ms Department (may I call you Deppie, for short?), and while I'm at it, I shore dew appreciate the invisible autograph you put on that rejection notice.

"When I began to write (and I had every intention of being a novelist, from day one—so rejected short stories never upset me), I fully expected I would receive little gems like the above. Imagine my astonishment when I finished *Hunting on Kunderer,* sent it in, and six weeks later received a letter of acceptance from Fred Pohl, whose books I even admired. The world is real! thought I. I was so pleased I wrote and sold *A Plague of All Cowards* to his successor, whose name no longer passes my lips without the accompaniment of some rather bad words. End of illustrious career. I wrote two more books and spent nearly three years trying to get them back from a man who wasn't interested in them! I still don't know why all this happened.

"Since then I have received a host of formletter rejections; not of my books, the publishers won't take manuscripts anymore, just answers to letters-of-inquiry (when they bother to reply at all). Only a few publishers still send out personal sorry-charlies—one fine fellow wrote me to boast about his recent trip to England, but he still didn't want to read my book—I thought you were supposed to 'pay your dues' at the beginning of a career, not in the middle."

He adds, "by the way, my personal religion, Mani Koi, has been defined as 'the worship of bad weather.'"

AVOCATIONAL INTERESTS: Music, art, cartography, guitar-playing, strenuous dieting, collecting old "78s," carpentry, cabinetmaking, bar-hopping, bicycling, speculative engineering designs, gourmand cooking.

* * *

BASART, Ann Phillips 1931-

PERSONAL: Born August 26, 1931, in Denver, Colo.; daughter of Burrill and Alberta (Mayfield) Phillips; married Robert David Basart, 1955; children: Kathryn Miriam, Nathaniel. *Education:* University of California, Los Angeles, B.A., 1954; University of California, Berkeley, M.L.S., 1958, M.A., 1961. *Home:* 2419 Oregon St., Berkeley, Calif. 94705. *Office:* Musical Library, University of California, Berkeley, Calif. 94720.

CAREER: University of California, Berkeley, librarian, 1958-61; San Francisco College for Women (now Lone Mountain College), San Francisco, Calif., instructor in music, 1964-67; University of California, Berkeley, librarian, 1970—. *Member:* International Association of Music Libraries, Music Library Association (member of board of directors, 1978-80, Phi Beta Kappa, Sigma Alpha Iota. *Awards, honors:* Fulbright grant to Italy, 1956-57.

WRITINGS: Serial Music: A Classified Bibliography, University of California Press, 1961; (with Richard Crocker) *Listening to Music,* McGraw, 1971. Contributor of articles to *Notes* and *Cum notis variorum.* Music review editor, *Notes,* 1972-73; editor, *Cum notis variorum,* 1976—.

* * *

BASS, Herbert Jacob 1929-

PERSONAL: Born January 25, 1929, in Bridgeport, Conn.; son of William Benjamin and Lillian (Nemzoff) Bass; married Barbara Spivack, 1952; children: Laurie Ellen, Kenneth Edward, Carolyn Ann. *Education:* Boston University, A.B., 1950; University of Rochester, Ph.D., 1956. *Home:* 411 Waring Rd., Elkins Park, Pa. *Office:* Department of History, Temple University, Philadelphia, Pa. 19122.

CAREER: Clark University, Worcester, Mass., instructor, 1956-57; University of Maine at Orono, instructor, 1957-59, assistant professor, 1959-63, associate professor of history, 1963-65; Temple University, Philadelphia, Pa., associate professor, 1965-68, professor of history, 1968—, chairman of department, 1974-80. *Military service:* U.S. Army, 1954-56. *Member:* American Historical Association, American Association of University Professors, Organization of American Historians.

WRITINGS: "I Am A Democrat": The Political Career of David Bennett Hill, Syracuse University Press, 1961; (editor with Glyndon G. Van Deusen) *Readings in American History,* Macmillan, two volumes, 1963, revised edition, 1968; *America's Entry into World War I,* Holt, 1964; (editor) *The State of American History,* Quadrangle, 1970; *Our American Heritage,* Silver Burdett, 1979. Contributor of articles to *New York History.*

* * *

BATTAGLIA, Elio Lee 1928-

PERSONAL: Born October 11, 1928, in Messina, Italy; son of Rocco and Laura (DeLuca) Battaglia; married Kathleen Haden, 1957; children: David, Rebecca, Jessica, Brian. *Education:* Attended University of Naples, two years; University of Missouri, B.J., M.A. *Home:* 1301 Cottage St. S.W., Vienna, Va. 22180. *Office:* International Communications Agency, 1776 Pennsylvania Ave., Washington, D.C.

CAREER: Time and *Life* Inc., New York City, assistant photographer, one year; American Export Lines, New York City, photographer, eighteen months; University of Missouri Press, Columbia, editorial assistant, two years; National Geographic Society, Washington, D.C., picture editor, 1960-66; photo editor, *America Illustrated,* 1966-72, and *Horizons/USA,* 1972-76; U.S. Information Agency, Washington, D.C., special assistant to director of press and publications, 1976-77; International Communications Agency, Washington, D.C., director of photography, 1977—. Assistant professorial lecturer in art, George Washington University. *Military service:* U.S. Army, 1949-52; became staff sergeant, received Bronze Star.

WRITINGS: The Face of Missouri, University of Missouri Press, 1960. Contributor of articles and photographs to *Life, Sports Illustrated, Smithsonian, National Geographic, Paris Match,* and other magazines.

WORK IN PROGRESS: A study of the impact of technology on the twentieth century.

* * *

BAUMER, William H(enry) 1909-

PERSONAL: Born November 27, 1909, in Omaha, Neb.; son of William Henry and Winifred (Mitchell) Baumer; married Alice Hull Brough, August 29, 1936 (died, 1970); married Peggy O'Neill Bruen, September 3, 1970 (divorced, 1978); children: (first marriage) Winifred Joan, Natalie Brough, Marjorie Anne, William H., Jr., Carolyn Jean. *Education:* Attended Creighton University, 1927-29; U. S. Military Academy, B.S., 1933; Columbia University, M.A., 1941. *Religion:* Roman Catholic. *Address:* Box 1045, La Jolla, Calif. 92038.

CAREER: U.S. Army, 1933-50, commissioned second lieutenant, 1933, became colonel; U.S. Army Reserve, 1950-69, retired as major general; Johnson & Johnson, New Brunswick, N.J., assistant to president and chairman, 1950-62; Atlas General Industries, New York, N.Y., executive vice-president, 1962-63; International General Industries, Inc. and IB Industries, Inc., both Washington, D.C., president and member of board, 1963-72. Served on General Eisenhower's staff in Europe during World War II; member of U.S. mission to Moscow; sole American member of British Planning Board; military advisor at Paris Peace Conference, 1946. Former vice-president, International Bank; former member of board, Kliklok Corp., Foster Wheeler Corp., Pierce Governor Co., Woodman Co., Globe Industries, and Avis International Corp. Secretary, Middlesex County (N.J.) Sewerage Authority, 1950-55; city councilman, Westfield, N.J., 1959-60; chairman, National Institute for Disaster Mobilization, 1961-62; former member of Water Resources Association of Delaware River Basin; chairman of associate board of trustees, St. Peter's Hospital, New Brunswick, 1961-62; former member of national capital area advisory committee, Boy Scouts of America; former member of advisory board, Blinded Veterans Association; member of board, Philadelphia Fund. *Member:* Council on Foreign Relations, West Point Society, Army-Navy Club. *Awards, honors*—Military: Legion of Merit with two oak-leaf clusters; Order of Leopold; Croix de Guerre avec Palme, 1945 (Belgium).

WRITINGS: Sports as Taught and Played at West Point, Stackpole, 1939; *How to Be an Army Officer,* McBride, 1940; (with S. F. Griffin) *18-35: The Draft and You,* Prentice-Hall, 1940; *He's in the Army Now,* McBride, 1941; *Not All Warriors,* Smith & Durrell, 1941, reprinted, Books for Libraries, 1971; *West Point: Moulder of Men,* Appleton, 1942; (with Donald G. Herzberg) *Politics Is Your Business,* Dial, 1960; (with R. Ernest Dupuy) *The Little Wars of the United States,* Hawthorn, 1968; (with Leo J. Northart) *Buy, Sell, Merge: How to Do It,* Prentice-Hall, 1971; *We Led the Way: Darby's Rangers,* Presidio Press, 1980. Contributor to *Encyclopaedia Britannica;* contributor to magazines.

AVOCATIONAL INTERESTS: Politics.

* * *

BAXTER, Gordon F(rancis), Jr. 1923-
(Bax)

PERSONAL: Born December 25, 1923, in Port Arthur, Tex.; son of Gordon F. and Mary Baxter; married Mary O'Dailey, May 14, 1943 (divorced December 21, 1973); married Diane Tittle (an airline hostess), December 30, 1973; children: (first marriage) five daughters, three sons; (second marriage) Jenny. *Education:* Attended U.S. Merchant Marine Academy. *Politics:* "Right of center most of the time." *Religion:* "God." *Home address:* Village Creek, Silsbee, Tex. 77656. *Office: Flying* Magazine, One Park Ave., New York, N.Y. 10016.

CAREER: Deck hand on a river boat, 1941-42; broadcaster, 1945-55; author of syndicated column, "Gordon Baxter," appearing in weekly newspapers in eastern Texas, 1955—; television producer, 1960-69; KLVI-Radio, Beaumont, Tex., commentator and producer of morning show, 1968-70; *Flying* Magazine, New York, N.Y., associate editor, 1970—. *Military service:* U.S. Merchant Marine, Navy Reserve, 1942-43, U.S. Army Air Forces, 1943-45. *Awards, honors:* Named best columnist by Gulf Coast Press Association, 1970.

WRITINGS: Best of Bax, Becker, Volume I, 1965, Volume II, 1967, Volume III, 1969, Volume IV, 1972, Volume V, 1974, Volume VI, 1976; *13/13 Vietnam: Search and Destroy,* World Publishing, 1967; *Bax Seat: Log of a Pasture Pilot,* McGraw, 1978; *Village Creek,* Summit Books, 1980; *How to Fly: For Real Beginners,* Summit Books, 1980; *Growing Up with Jenny,* Summit Books, 1981.

* * *

BAYLES, Michael D(ale) 1941-

PERSONAL: Born January 21, 1941, in Charleston, Ill.; son of Dale M. (a clothier) and Elizabeth (a librarian; maiden name, Widger) Bayles; married Janice E. Morgan, January 14, 1961 (divorced November 3, 1976); married Marjorie L. Watts, November 23, 1979; children: (first marriage) Melanie, Michele. *Education:* University of Illinois, B.A., 1962; University of Missouri, M.A., 1963; Indiana University, Ph.D., 1967. *Home:* 1491 Richmond St., London, Ontario, Canada N6G 2M1. *Office:* Westminster Institute for Ethics and Human Values, Westminster College, London, Ontario, Canada N6G 2M2.

CAREER: University of Idaho, Moscow, instructor in philosophy, 1965-67; Brooklyn College of the City University of New York, Brooklyn, N.Y., assistant professor of philosophy, 1967-70; University of Kentucky, Lexington, associate professor, 1970-74, professor of philosophy, 1974-79; University of Western Ontario, London, Ontario, professor of philosophy, 1979—; Westminster College, Westminster Institute for Ethics and Human Values, London, Ontario, director, 1979—. *Member:* International Association for Philosophy of Law and Social Philosophy (executive director, American section, 1975—), American Philosophical Association, American Society for Political and Legal Philosophy, Society for Philosophy and Public Affairs (member of executive board, 1973), Canadian Philosophical Association. *Awards, honors:* American Council of Learned Societies study fellowship, 1974-75; Harvard Law School liberal arts fellowship, 1974-75; Institute of Society, Ethics, and the Life Sciences fellowship, 1976-77.

WRITINGS: (Editor) *Contemporary Utilitarianism,* Doubleday, 1968; (editor) *Ethics and Populations,* Schenkman, 1976; (co-editor) *Medical Treatment of the Dying: Moral Issues,* G. K. Hall, 1978; *Principles of Legislation,* Wayne State University Press, 1978; *Morality and Population Policy,* University of Alabama Press, 1980.

Contributor: Ervin H. Pollack, editor, *Human Rights: Amintaphil I,* Jay Stewart, 1971; J. Roland Pennock and John W. Chapman, editors, *Coercion: Nomos XIV,* Aldine-Atherton, 1972; Norman S. Care and Thomas K. Trelogan, editors, *Issues in Law and Morality,* Press of Case Western Reserve

University, 1973; Pennock and Chapman, editors, *The Limits of Law: Nomos XV*, Lieber-Atherton, 1974; Milton Goldinger, editor, *Punishment and Human Rights*, Schenkman, 1974; Ransom Baine Harris, editor, *Authority: A Philosophical Analysis*, University of Alabama Press, 1976; Gray Dorsey, editor, *Equality and Freedom*, Oceana, 1977; Eugene Dais, editor, *Law and the Ecological Challenge: Amintaphil II*, William S. Hein, 1978; Richard T. DeGeorge and Joseph Pichler, editors, *Ethics, Free Enterprise, and Public Policy*, Oxford University Press, 1978; John W. Davis, C. B. Hoffmaster, and S. J. Shorten, editors, *Contemporary Issues in Biomedical Ethics*, Humana, 1978; Wade L. Robison and Michael S. Pritchard, editors, *Medical Responsibility*, Humana, 1979.

Contributor to *Personalist, Review of Metaphysics, Analysis, Social Theory and Practice, Wayne Law Review, Journal of Value Inquiry, Metaphilosophy, Modern Schoolman*, and *Idealistic Studies*, and many other periodicals. Member of editorial board, *National Forum, Southern Journal of Philosophy*, and *Social Theory and Practice*.

WORK IN PROGRESS: The Uses of Political Authority.

SIDELIGHTS: Michael D. Bayles wrote *CA:* "While my new position as director of Westminster Institute for Ethics and Human Values provides less time for writing, it affords an opportunity to be involved in multi-disciplinary studies addressing the important moral issues of our time."

* * *

BEAKLEY, George Carroll, Jr. 1922-

PERSONAL: Born February 3, 1922, in Marble Falls, Tex.; son of George Carroll (a rancher) and Tessielea (Poage) Beakley; married Oletta B. Zeh, August 4, 1944; children: George Carroll III, William Don, Martha Ann, David Lee. *Education:* Texas Technological College (now Texas Tech University), B.S.M.E., 1947; University of Texas, M.S.M.E., 1952; Oklahoma State University, Ph.D., 1956. *Politics:* Democrat. *Religion:* Southern Baptist. *Office:* School of Engineering, Arizona State University, Tempe, Ariz. 85281.

CAREER: Tarleton State College, Stephenville, Tex., associate professor of engineering, 1947-53; Bell Helicopter Corp., Hurst, Tex., design engineer, 1953-54; Airesearch Mfg. Co., Phoenix, Ariz., development engineer, 1956; Arizona State University, Tempe, professor of engineering, 1956—, chairman of mechanical engineering, 1956-67, associate dean and director of engineering science, 1957—. *Military service:* U.S. Army, Infantry, 1943-46; became first lieutenant. *Member:* National Society of Professional Engineers, American Society of Mechanical Engineers, American Institute of Industrial Engineers, American Society for Engineering Education, Tau Beta Pi, Kappa Mu Epsilon, Phi Kappa Phi, Pi Tau Sigma, Sigma Xi, Alpha Pi Mu.

WRITINGS—Published by Macmillan, except as indicated; with H. W. Leach, except as indicated: *Elementary Problems in Engineering*, 1951, 2nd edition published as *Engineering: The Profession and Elementary Problem Analysis*, 1960, 3rd edition published as *Engineering: An Introduction to a Creative Profession*, 1967, 4th edition published as *Careers in Engineering and Technology*, 1969, 6th edition published as *Engineering: An Introduction to a Creative Profession*, 1977, 7th edition published as *Careers in Engineering and Technology*, 1979; *The Slide Rule*, 1953; *The Slide Rule and Technical Problem Solving*, 1963, 2nd edition published as *The Slide Rule and Its Use in Problem Solving*, 1969, 3rd edition published as *The Slide Rule, Electronic Hand Calculator, and Metrification in Problem Solving*, 1975; (with John Hawley and Donald D. Autore) *Graphics for Design and Visualization: Problems*, 1973; (with E. G. Chilton) *Introduction to Engineering Design and Graphics*, 1973; (with Chilton) *Design: Serving the Needs of Man*, 1974; *Introduction to Engineering Graphics*, 1975; (with Autore) *Electronics Drafting*, Harper, in press. Contributor to professional journals.

AVOCATIONAL INTERESTS: Music, fishing, camping, sports.

* * *

BECK, Carl 1930-

PERSONAL: Born January 14, 1930, in Pittsburgh, Pa.; son of Edward F. W. and Leigh (Lester) Beck; married Isabel Lubovsky, 1954; children: Elizabeth Leigh, Mark Edward. *Education:* Attended Wesleyan University, 1948-51; University of Pittsburgh, B.A., 1952, M.A., 1954; Duke University, Ph.D., 1958; additional study at University of Munich, 1958-59. *Politics:* Democrat. *Religion:* Unitarian Universalist. *Home:* 1425 Wightman St., Pittsburgh, Pa. 15217. *Office:* Department of Political Science, University of Pittsburgh, Pittsburgh, Pa. 15213.

CAREER: Kingsley Association, Pittsburgh, Pa., group worker, 1951-53; University of Pittsburgh, Pittsburgh, lecturer, 1952-54, assistant professor, 1959-62, associate professor, 1962-66, professor of political science, 1966—. Member of council of representatives, Inter-University Consortium for Political Research. Fulbright fellow and Social Science Research Council fellow in Munich, 1958-59. *Military service:* U.S. Army, 1954-56. *Member:* American Political Science Association, International Political Science Association, International Studies Association (executive director, 1974—), American Association for the Advancement of Science, American Association for the Advancement of Slavic Studies. *Awards, honors:* Social Science Research Council travel grant, 1964.

WRITINGS: Contempt of Congress, Hauser, 1959, reprinted, Oceania, 1977; (contributor) J. LaPalombara, editor, *Bureaucracy and Political Development*, Princeton University Press, 1963; (with Thomas McKechnie) *Political Elites*, M.I.T. Press, 1968; (contributor) R. Barry Farrell, editor, *Soviet and East European Leadership*, Aldine, 1970; (contributor) Roger Kanet, editor, *The Behavioral Revolution and Communist Studies*, Free Press, 1971; (with others) *Comparative Communist Leadership*, McKay, 1972; (editor with Carmelo Mesa-Lago) *Comparative Socialist Systems: Essays on Politics and Economics*, University Center for International Studies, 1975; *Political Succession in Eastern Europe*, University Center for International Studies, 1976; (contributor) Donald Freeman, editor, *Foundation of Political Science: Scope, Research, Method*, Free Press, 1977. Editor, *Law and Justice: Essays in Honor of Professor Robert S. Rankin*, Duke University Press, 1969, *Political Science Thesaurus*, American Political Science Association, 1975, and *Detente: An International Overview*, 1978. Contributor to *Encyclopedia on Higher Education*, 1977; also contributor of articles to *Comparative Communism, Journal of Politics, American Behavioral Scientist*, and other journals.

WORK IN PROGRESS: An analysis of political perceptions and motivations; research on cybernetics and political analysis.

BEEBE, Maurice (Laverne) 1926-

PERSONAL: Born January 26, 1926, in Anacortes, Wash.; son of Cecil Henry and Eleanor (Dobers) Beebe; married second wife, Anna Lurline Olson Smith, 1961 (divorced, 1976); children: (first marriage) Brent Alan, Paul Playford, Mark David. *Education:* University of Washington, B.A. and M.A., 1947; Cornell University, Ph.D., 1952. *Home:* 1011 Serpentine Lane, Wyncote, Pa. 19095. *Office:* 1241 Humanities Building, Temple University, Philadelphia, Pa. 19122.

CAREER: University of Kansas, Lawrence, instructor, 1951-52; Purdue University, Lafayette, Ind., 1952-68, began as instructor, became professor; Temple University, Philadelphia, Pa., professor of English 1968—. Consultant, National Endowment for the Humanities, 1976-78. *Member:* Modern Language Association of America (member of advisory council, American literature section, 1976-78), Phi Beta Kappa.

WRITINGS: (Editor) *Ernest Hemingway: Configuration Critique,* Lettres Modernes, 1957; (with others) *William Faulkner: Configuration Critique,* Folcroft Library Editions, 1957; (editor) *Literary Symbolism,* Wadsworth 1960; *Ivory Towers and Sacred Founts: The Artist as Hero in Fiction from Goethe to Joyce,* New York University Press, 1964; (with Leslie A. Field) *Robert Penn Warren's "All the King's Men": A Critical Handbook,* Wadsworth, 1966; (contributor) *The Reader's Advisor,* Bowker, 1974. Editor, "Modern Fiction Studies," 1955-68. Contributor to professional journals. Editor, *Journal of Modern Literature,* 1968—.

WORK IN PROGRESS: An Anatomy of Modernism.

* * *

BEERS, V(ictor) Gilbert 1928-

PERSONAL: Born May 6, 1928, in Sidell, Ill.; son of Ernest S. (a farmer) and Jean (Bloomer) Beers; married Arlisle Felten, August 26, 1950; children: Kathleen, Douglas, Ronald, Janice, Cynthia. *Education:* Wheaton College, Wheaton, Ill., A.B., 1950; Northern Baptist Seminary, Chicago, M.R.E., 1953, M.Div., 1954, Th.M., 1955, Th.D., 1960; Northwestern University, Ph.D., 1963. *Politics:* Republican. *Home and office address:* Route 1, Box 321, Elgin, Ill. 60120.

CAREER: Northern Baptist Seminary, Chicago, Ill., professor of religion, 1954-57; David C. Cook Publishing Co., Elgin, Ill., editor of senior high publications, 1957-59, executive editor, 1959-61, editorial director, 1961-67; Creative Designs, Elgin, president, 1967—. Presently member of board of directors, Wheaton College, Wheaton, Ill., Scripture Press, and Deerfoot Lodge (boys camp), Speculator, N.Y.; member of board of directors, Wheaton Youth Symphony, 1962-64, president, 1963-64; trustee of David C. Cook Foundation, 1965-67. *Member:* Children's Reading Round Table (Chicago), Wheaton College Alumni Association (president, 1972-73). *Awards, honors:* Distinguished Service Award of Midland Authors, 1973, for *Cats and Bats and Things Like That* and *The ABQ Book.*

WRITINGS—Adult: *Family Bible Library,* ten volumes, Southwestern Co., 1971; *Patterns for Prayer from the Gospels,* Revell, 1972; *Joy Is . . . ,* Revell, 1974; *The Discovery Bible Handbook,* Victor Books 1974. Also author of *The Book of Life,* twenty-three volumes, Zondervan.

Juvenile books; all published by Moody, except as indicated: *A Child's Treasury of Bible Stories,* four volumes, Parent and Child Institute, 1970; *Cats and Bats and Things Like That,* 1972; *The ABQ Book,* 1972; *The House in the Hole in the Side of the Tree,* 1973; *Coco's Candy Shop,* 1973; *Helping Hands,* Southwestern Co., 1973; *Around the World with My Red Balloon,* 1973; *The Magic Merry-Go-Round,* 1973; *A Gaggle of Green Geese,* 1974; *Honeyphants and Elebees,* 1974; *Through Golden Windows,* 1975; *Under the Tagalong Tree,* 1976; *With Sails to the Wind,* 1977; *Over Buttonwood Bridge,* 1978.

Juvenile series: "Learning to Read from the Bible" series, published by Zondervan, 1973: *God Is My Helper, Jesus Is My Teacher, God Is My Friend, Jesus Is My Guide;* "Learning to Read from the Bible Primer" series, published by Zondervan, 1979: *May I Help You, Do You Know My Friend, Do You Love Me, Will You Come With Me.*

SIDELIGHTS: V. Gilbert Beers wrote *CA:* "As father of five inquisitive children, I have spent many hours interacting with them where fun and learning touch. It has been my concern that we make learning fun and we make fun a means of learning. Add to this the dimension of Bible and Christian education, and we have the reason for my writing.

"Too often, the Bible and Christian education are presented in somber tones. This is inconsistent with the 'Good News' of One who came to bring life, and joy, and hope, and a new way. Thus *Honeyphants and Elebees* and *A Gaggle of Green Geese* help happy children learn about those happy truths."

* * *

BEILER, Edna 1923-

PERSONAL: Born October 24, 1923, in New Paris, Ind.; daughter of John A. and Magdalena (Byler) Beiler. *Education:* Attended Arizona State University, 1944-45; Goshen College, graduate, 1968. *Home:* 125 North Munsie, Cumberland, Ind. 46229. *Office:* State Department of Public Welfare, 100 North Senate, Room 701, Indianapolis, Ind. 46204.

CAREER: Mennonite Publishing House, Scottdale, Pa., free-lance writer, 1950-55; Mennonite Relief and Service Committee, Elkhart, Ind., roving reporter, 1955-58; Mennonite Board of Missions and Charities, Elkhart, editorial assistant, 1959-66; Department of Public Welfare, Hancock County, Ind., social worker, 1968-76; Indiana State Department of Public Welfare, Indianapolis, institutional specialist, 1976—.

WRITINGS—All published by Herald Press, except as indicated: *Ten of a Kind,* 1953; *Adventures with the Buttonwoods,* 1960; *Bringing Jesus to Our Neighbors,* 1962; *Yuishu Sahai,* 1963; *Mitsy Buttonwood,* 1963; *Tres Casas, Tres Famillias,* Friendship, 1964; *Fly High!* (study course), 1965; *White Elephant for Sale,* Friendship, 1966; *Mattie Mae,* 1967.

WORK IN PROGRESS: A devotional book for adults, tentatively entitled *Overflowings.*

AVOCATIONAL INTERESTS: Oil painting, piecing quilt tops, gardening, ecology.

* * *

BEITZ, Charles R(ichard) 1949-

PERSONAL: Born July 20, 1949, in Buffalo, N.Y.; son of Richard C. and Jean (Harris) Beitz. *Education:* Colgate University, B.A., 1970; University of Michigan, M.A., 1974; Princeton University, M.A., 1976, Ph.D., 1978. *Office:* Department of Political Science, Swarthmore College, Swarthmore, Pa. 19081.

CAREER: Colgate University, Hamilton, N.Y., coordinator

of Peace Studies Program, 1970-71; Institute for World Order, New York, N.Y., assistant director of University Program, 1971-72; Trenton State College, Trenton, N.J., instructor in philosophy, spring, 1974; Princeton University, Princeton, N.J., preceptor in philosophy and politics, 1974-76; Swarthmore College, Swarthmore, Pa., assistant professor of political science, 1976—. *Awards, honors:* Rockefeller Foundation Humanities fellowship, 1979-80.

WRITINGS: (Editor with Theodore Herman) *Peace and War,* W. H. Freeman, 1973; (with Michael Washburn) *Creating the Future: A Guide to Living and Working for Social Change,* Bantam, 1974; *Political Theory and International Relations,* Princeton University Press, 1979. Contributor of articles to *Philosophy and Public Affairs, Political Theory, International Organization, Dissent, Nation,* and *Ethnics.*

WORK IN PROGRESS: Research on human rights, rationality, and risk.

* * *

BELL, David Victor John 1944-

PERSONAL: Born, 1944, in Toronto, Ontario, Canada; son of Herbert McLean and Violet (Bryan) Bell; married Kaaren Cambelle Macdonald, 1966; children: Kristin Cassandra, Jason David. *Education:* Attended York University, 1962-65; University of Toronto, B.A. (first class honors), 1965; Harvard University, A.M., 1967, Ph.D., 1969. *Residence:* Thornhill, Ontario, Canada. *Office:* Department of Political Science, York University, 4700 Keele St., Downsview, Ontario, Canada M3J 1P3.

CAREER: Michigan State University, East Lansing, assistant professor of political science, 1969-71; York University, Downsview, Ontario, assistant professor, 1971-73, associate professor of political science, 1973—. Co-founder and president, Grindstone Cooperative Ltd., 1976—; chairman, Leave Fellowship Selection Committee, Social Science and Humanities Research Council, 1978. Lecturer; has appeared on television and radio programs.

MEMBER: Canadian Political Science Association, Canadian Association for American Studies (vice-president, 1972-74; president, 1974-76), Canadian Peace Research and Education Association, International Studies Association. *Awards, honors:* Woodrow Wilson fellowships, 1965, 1967; Canada Council leave fellowship, 1976-77.

WRITINGS: (With Karl W. Deutsch) *Instructor's Manual to Accompany "Politics and Government",* Houghton, 1970, 2nd edition (with wife, Kaaren C. M. Bell), 1974; (editor with Deutsch and Seymour Martin Lipset) *Issues in Politics and Government,* Houghton, 1970; *Resistance and Revolution,* Houghton, 1973; *Power, Influence, and Authority,* Oxford University Press, 1975; (with Lorne J. Tepperman) *The Roots of Disunity: A Study of Canadian Political Culture,* McClelland & Stewart, 1979.

Co-editor of "Canada in Transition: Crises in Development," a series of monographs, McClelland & Stewart. Contributor of articles and reviews to periodicals, including *Issues in Politics and Government, Journal of Canadian Studies, Yale Review, Newsletter* of Association for Canadian Studies in American Universities, *Windsor Review, Harvard Alumni Bulletin,* and *Canadian Journal of Political Science.* Member of editorial board, *Teaching Political Science* and *International Interactions,* both 1972—; guest editor of a special issue of *International Interactions,* 1979.

AVOCATIONAL INTERESTS: Tennis, squash, touch football, music (has been a professional chorister and jazz bassist).

BELL, Margaret E(lizabeth) 1898-

PERSONAL: Born December 29, 1898, in Thorn Bay, Alaska; daughter of Robert Biggar and Florence (Millar) Bell; married Sam R. Wiks, 1963. *Education:* Annie Wright Seminary, graduate, 1918; attended University of Washington, Seattle, two years. *Home:* Route 1, Pond Reef Rd., Ketchikan, Alaska 99901. *Agent:* McIntosh & Otis, Inc., 475 Fifth Ave., New York, N.Y. 10017.

CAREER: American Trust Co., San Francisco, Calif., auditor, 1929-37. Writer, 1938—. Red Cross war work in Canada, Alaska, and the Aleutian Islands, 1942-46. *Awards, honors:* National Mass Media Award, Thomas Alva Edison Foundation, 1960; D.Litt., University of Alaska, 1970.

WRITINGS—All published by Morrow, except as indicated: *The Pirates of Icy Strait,* 1943; *Danger on Old Baldy,* 1944; *Enemies in Icy Strait,* 1945; *Watch for a Tall White Sail,* 1948, reprinted, Grosset, 1972; *The Totem Casts a Shadow,* 1949; *Ride out the Storm,* 1951; *Kit Carson: Mountain Man* (biography), 1952; *Love Is Forever,* 1954; *Daughter of Wolf House,* 1957; *Touched with Fire* (biography), 1960; *Flight from Love,* 1968; *To Peril Straight,* Viking, 1971.

WORK IN PROGRESS: Articles on Alaska's wildlife; a book for young people, *The Raft;* a book, *The Ravens;* a story of modern Alaska for the young; *Memoirs of Loring.*

SIDELIGHTS: For twenty-three years, Margaret E. Bell lived at Loring, an abandoned town site north of Ketchikan, where the population varies from two to eight. Her principal contact with the outside world was a weekly mail and supply boat. Bell's book, *Ride out the Storm,* is based on her childhood in the Icy Straits country; her other books with a northern locale have been based on research and explorations in the region, including a trip to the Alaskan Arctic in 1954. During her trips to New York and other cities, she is a frequent lecturer and television guest. Her books have been published in Spain, Germany, Czechoslovakia, Austria, and Japan.

AVOCATIONAL INTERESTS: Nature study and wood sculpture.

* * *

BELL, Norman W. 1928-

PERSONAL: Born February 18, 1928, in Canada; son of David Harvie and Mabel (Shepherd) Bell; married Lucille Hammond, 1953; children: Jane, Peter. *Education:* University of Toronto, B.A., 1950, M.A., 1953; Harvard University, Ph.D., 1959. *Office:* Department of Sociology, Faculty of Fine Arts and Sciences, University of Toronto, Toronto, Ontario, Canada.

CAREER: Harvard University, Cambridge, Mass., Laboratory of Social Relations, assistant, 1954-59, research associate, 1959-66, Family Guidance Center, research assistant, 1957-58, School of Medicine, assistant, 1960-61, research associate, 1961-66, assistant professor, 1966-67; University of Toronto, Faculty of Fine Arts and Sciences, Toronto, Ontario, professor of sociology, beginning 1967. McLean Hospital, Belmont, Mass., assistant sociologist, 1958-67, department of social science, acting chief, 1961-62, chief, 1962-67. Consultant in organization, Worchester State Hospital, Worchester, Mass., 1959-64. *Member:* American Sociological Association, Canadian Political Science Association.

WRITINGS: (With John R. Seeley and others) *Crestwood Heights,* University of Toronto Press, 1956; (contributor with J. P. Spiegel) S. Arieti, editor, *American Handbook of*

Psychiatry, Basic Books, 1959; (editor with Ezra F. Vogel) *A Modern Introduction to the Family,* Free Press of Glencoe, 1960, revised edition, Free Press, 1968; (with Colette Carisse) *Family Research in Canada: Notes from the Stanley House Conference,* Vanier Institute of the Family (Ottawa), 1971. Also author of *The Family and the Doctor,* 1964, and, with others, *Social Psychiatry: Vagaries of a Term,* 1966. Editor, *Bulletin* of the Laboratory of Social Relations, Harvard University, 1954-55; advisory editor, *Family Process.*

WORK IN PROGRESS: Origins of Social Psychiatry.†

* * *

BELL, Robert Roy 1924-

PERSONAL: Born September 9, 1924; son of Ollie Roy and Lillian (Pepperell) Bell; married Phyllis Lowry, 1950; children: Marta Lee, Robin Ann. *Education:* Michigan State College of Agriculture and Applied Science (now Michigan State University), B.A., 1951; Indiana University, M.A., 1953. *Home:* 1347 Harris Rd., Dresher, Pa. *Office:* Department of Sociology, Temple University, Philadelphia, Pa. 19122.

CAREER: Temple University, Philadelphia, Pa., instructor, 1953-61, assistant professor, 1961-65, associate professor, 1965-70, professor of sociology, 1970—. *Military service:* U.S. Army, 1943-45. *Member:* American Association of University Professors, National Council on Family Relations, American Sociological Association, Society for Study of Social Problems, Eastern Sociological society.

WRITINGS: (Editor) *The Sociology of Education,* Dorsey, 1962, 3rd edition, 1975; *Marriage and Family Interaction,* Dorsey, 1963, 5th edition, 1979; *Premarital Sex in a Changing Society,* Prentice-Hall, 1966; (compiler) *Studies in Marriage and Family,* Crowell, 1968, 2nd edition, 1973; *Social Deviance: A Substantive Analysis,* Dorsey, 1971, revised edition, 1976. Contributor of articles and papers to professional journals.

WORK IN PROGRESS: The One-Parent Family in the United States.†

* * *

BELL, Sallie Lee

PERSONAL: Born in New Orleans, La.; daughter of Robert Lee (a physician) and Sallie (O'Pry) Riley; married Thaddeus Park Bell (a physician), 1909 (deceased). *Education:* Attended Newcomb College.

CAREER: Writer.

WRITINGS—All published by Zondervan: *Until the Day Break,* 1950; *The Street Singer,* 1951; *Through Golden Meadows,* 1951, reprinted, 1971; *The Queen's Jest,* 1952, reprinted, 1979; *By Strange Paths,* 1952, reprinted, 1974; *Riven Fetters,* 1953; *Unto the Uttermost,* 1954; *The Substitute,* 1955, reprinted, 1976; *The Thunderbolt,* 1956; *The Torchbearer,* 1956; *The Wayward Heart,* 1957; *The Bond Slave,* 1957; *The Barrier,* 1957, reprinted, 1972; *The Silver Cord,* 1958; *Ginger,* 1958; *The Long Search,* 1959, new edition, 1974; *The Snare,* 1959; *The Last Surrender,* 1959, new edition, 1974.

The Hidden Treasure, 1960; *Beyond the Shadows,* 1960; *The Shattered Wall,* 1961; *Her Bridge to Happiness,* 1961; *The Singing Angel,* 1961; *The Love That Lingered,* 1962; *The Secret Conflict,* 1963; *Love at the Crossroads,* 1963; *The Interrupted Melody,* 1963; *Romance along the Bayou,* 1964, new edition, 1974; *The Scar,* 1965, new edition, 1974; *Light from the Hill,* 1965; *The Trail,* 1966; *The Promise,* 1966; *Last Cry,* 1967; *The Hidden Dream,* 1967; *Down a Dark Road,* 1968; *Tangled Threads,* 1968; *Overshadowed,* 1969. Also author of plays for amateur theatre groups and of short stories for children.

SIDELIGHTS: Sallie Lee Bell wrote *CA* that her novels are "Christian novels, and my one desire is that in my writings I may have the privilege of helping someone to live a better life." Several of Bell's books have been published in Europe. She has travelled throughout the United States, Canada, South and Central America, Europe, the Middle East, New Zealand, and Australia.†

* * *

BENNETT, Jonathan (Francis) 1930-

PERSONAL: Born February 17, 1930, in Greymouth, New Zealand; son of Francis Oswald (a physician) and Pearl (Brash) Bennett; married Gillian Quentin-Baxter, April 13, 1957; children: Sara, Guy Francis. *Education:* University of New Zealand, B.A., 1950, M.A., 1952; Oxford University, B.Phil., 1955. *Politics:* Socialist. *Religion:* Atheist. *Home:* 128 Dorset Rd., Syracuse, N.Y. 13210. *Office:* Department of Philosophy, Syracuse University, Syracuse, N.Y. 13210.

CAREER: Cambridge University, Cambridge, England, lecturer in moral science, 1956-68; Simon Fraser University, Burnaby, British Columbia, professor of philosophy, 1968-70; University of British Columbia, Vancouver, professor of philosophy, 1970-79; Syracuse University, Syracuse, N.Y., professor of philosophy, 1979—.

WRITINGS: (Compiler with Robert McDonald Chapman) *An Anthology of New Zealand Verse,* Oxford University Press, 1956; *Rationality: An Essay towards an Analysis,* Humanities, 1964; *Kant's Analytic,* Cambridge University Press, 1966; *Locke, Berkeley, Hume: Central Themes,* Oxford University Press, 1971; *Kant's Dialectic,* Cambridge University Press, 1974; *Linguistic Behaviour,* Cambridge University Press, 1976.

WORK IN PROGRESS: Research in ethics and on Spinoza's philosophy.

* * *

BENSE, Walter F(rederick) 1932-

PERSONAL: Surname rhymes with "sense"; born February 17, 1932, in Jena, Germany; son of Frederick H. (an American citizen) and Marie (Mueller) Bense; divorced. *Education:* University of Washington, B.A. (cum laude), 1954; University of Oregon, graduate study, summers, 1955, 1959; Western Baptist Seminary, B.D. (with highest honors), 1957; Portland State University, emergency teaching certificate, 1957; Harvard University, Ph.D., 1967. *Politics:* Independent. *Home:* 305 Twelfth St., Neenah, Wis. 54956. *Office:* Department of Religion, University of Wisconsin, Oshkosh, Wis. 54901.

CAREER: Ordained Baptist minister in 1957. Teacher of English and social studies in junior high school in The Dalles, Ore., 1957-59; Harvard University, Divinity School, Cambridge, Mass., member of faculty, 1961-68; Emerson College, Boston, Mass., member of faculty in philosophy and history, 1964-65; University of Massachusetts—Boston, instructor in history, 1965-67; University of Wisconsin—Oshkosh, assistant professor of history, 1967-68, assistant professor of religion, 1968-69, associate professor of religion, 1969—, chairperson of department of religion, 1968—. Part-time minister, 1957-59; chairperson of subcommittee on religion, Wisconsin Committee on Social Studies, 1972-74. *Member:* American Society of Church History, American Society for Reformation Research, Renaissance Society of America, American Catholic Historical Association, Conference on Peace Research in History, Societe Europeene de Culture, American Civil Liberties Union, Americans United for Separation of Church and State, Luther Gesellschaft. *Awards, honors:* Fulbright fellowship to Paris, 1963-64.

WRITINGS: (Contributor) F. N. Magill and I. P. McGreal, editors, *Masterpieces of Christian Literature in Summary Form,* Volume I, Salem Press, 1963; *An Introduction to Theological German,* Divinity School, Harvard University, 1964; (translator) Georg Kretschmar and others, *Councils of the Church: History and Analysis,* Fortress, 1966; (editor with J. L. Adams, and author of introduction) Karl Holl, *What Did Luther Understand by Religion?,* Fortress, 1977; (editor with Adams and author of introduction) Holl, *The Reconstruction of Morality,* Augsburg, 1979.

Also author of introductions to four volumes in the "Garland Library of War and Peace" reprint series, 1972-73: G. J. Heering, *The Fall of Christianity;* Harald Fuchs, *Augustin und der antike Friedensgedanke;* Dante Alighieri, *Monarchy;* S. J. Hemleben, *Plans for World Peace through Six Centuries.*

WORK IN PROGRESS: Editing three volumes of essays by Ernst Troeltsch in English translation, *Theology, Philosophy, and History in the Study of Religion according to Ernst Troeltsch, Christian Faith and Ethics according to Ernst Troeltsch,* and *The Modernism of Ernst Troeltsch,* all for T. & T. Clark; editing additional works by Holl; *Champion of Discipline: Noel Beda at the University of Paris, 1504-1534.*

* * *

BENSON, Mary 1919-

PERSONAL: Born December 9, 1919, in Pretoria, South Africa; daughter of Cyril (an administrator) and Lucy (Stubbs) Benson. *Education:* Attended schools in Australia. *Home:* 34 Langford Ct., Abbey Rd., London N.W.8, England.

CAREER: Secretary with British High Commission, Pretoria, South Africa, 1940-41, and David Lean (film director), London, England, 1947-49; Africa Bureau, London, cofounder and secretary, 1950-57 (lobbied in England and at United Nations on South African issues during that period and later); writer. Active in African Development Trust and National Campaign for the Abolition of Capital Punishment. *Military service:* South African Women's Army, 1941-45; served in Cairo, Algiers, Italy, Greece, and Austria; became captain.

WRITINGS: Tshekedi Khama, Verry, 1960; *Chief Albert Lutuli of South Africa,* Oxford University Press, 1963; *The African Patriots: The Story of the African National Congress of South Africa,* Faber, 1963, Encyclopaedia Britannica (Chicago), 1964, revised and enlarged edition published as *South Africa: The Struggle for a Birthright,* Penguin (London), 1966, Funk, 1969; (contributor) Nadine Gordimer, editor, *South African Writing Today,* Penguin, 1967; *At the Still Point* (novel; also see below) Gambit, 1970; (contributor) R. L. Markovitz, editor, *African Politics and Society,* Free Press, 1970; (editor) *The Sun Will Rise: Statements from the Dock by Southern African Political Prisoners,* International Defence and Aid Fund, 1974; *Nelson Mandela,* Panaf Books, 1980.

Radio plays; produced by British Broadcasting Corp.: "At the Still Point" (based on novel of same title), 1972; "Nelson Mandela and the Rivona Trial," 1972; "The Hour Is Getting Late," 1973; (adaptor) Sheila Fugard, "The Castaways," 1974; "Robben Island," 1976; "Rainer Maria Rilke: Four Documentaries," 1979-80; (adaptor) Ngugiwa Thiong'o, "Petals of Blood," 1980.

Contributor to *London Magazine, Times, Guardian, Observer, New Statesman, Spectator, New York Times,* and other publications.

WORK IN PROGRESS: Her autobiography.

SIDELIGHTS: An outspoken activist and critic on South Africa's policy of apartheid, Mary Benson remarks that she had the "normal prejudiced attitude of white South Africans" until she read Paton's *Cry the Beloved Country* in 1948. She has since studied, lobbied, written, and lectured about her country, testifying before United Nations committees on apartheid and human rights between 1963 and 1970, and before the United States Congressional Committee on South Africa in 1966. While reporting on political trials in South Africa she was put under house arrest and banned from all writing. Finally, in March of 1966, Benson left South Africa, a political exile.

BIOGRAPHICAL/CRITICAL SOURCES: Times Literary Supplement, January 12, 1967; *New York Times,* December 23, 1969; *New York Time's Book Review,* January 4, 1970; *New Republic,* February 7, 1970; *Observer,* May 30, 1971.

* * *

BENTON, Kenneth (Carter) 1909-

PERSONAL: Born March 4, 1909, in Sutton Coldfield, England; son of William Alfred (an engineer) and Amy Adeline (Kirton) Benton; married Peggie Pollock Lambert (an author), March 2, 1938; children: Timothy John; stepchildren: Alexander Pollock Lambert, Charles Mark Lambert. *Education:* University of London, B.A., 1936; additional study at University of Florence and University of Vienna. *Religion:* Church of England. *Home:* Vine House, Appledore, Ashford, Kent, England.

CAREER: British Foreign Service, London, England, 1937-68, assistant passport control officer at British Legation in Vienna, Austria, 1937-38, vice-consul in Riga, Latvia, 1938-40, British Embassy in Madrid, Spain, third secretary, 1941-42, second secretary, 1942-43, first secretary, 1953-56, member of foreign office staff, 1956-52, British Embassy in Rome, Italy, second secretary, 1944-46, first secretary, 1946-48, member of foreign office staff, 1948-50, British Embassy in Lima, Peru, first secretary and member of consul, 1962-63, member of foreign office staff, 1964-66, counsellor of British Embassy in Rio de Janeiro, Brazil, 1966-68; writer.

MEMBER: Author's Society, Crime Writers Association (vice-chairman, 1973-74; chairman, 1974-75), Detection Club. *Awards, honors:* Named Companion of the Order of St. Michael and St. George (CMG), 1966.

WRITINGS: Twenty-Fourth Level, Dodd, 1969; (contributor) *Peru's Revolution from Above,* Institute for the Study of Conflict, 1970; *Sole Agent,* Collins, 1970, Walker & Co., 1974; *Spy in Chancery,* Collins, 1972, Walker & Co., 1973; *Craig and the Jaguar,* Macmillan (London), 1973, Walker & Co., 1974; *Craig and the Tunisian Tangle,* Macmillan, 1974, Walker & Co., 1975; *Death on the Appian Way* (historical novel), Chatto & Windus, 1974; *Craig and the Midas Touch,* Macmillan, 1975, Walker & Co., 1976; *A Single Monstrous Act,* Macmillan, 1976; *The Red Hen Conspiracy,* Macmillan,

1977; *Craig and the Living Dead,* Mondadori (Italy), 1979. Also contributor to *The Security of the Cape Oil Route,* 1973, *A Manual of Counter-Subversion,* and *Conflict Studies,* for the Institute for the Study of Conflict. Author of reports. Contributor of reviews to professional publications.

WORK IN PROGRESS: An espionage novel based in Morocco; an historical novel dealing with the events at the end of the Roman Republic.

SIDELIGHTS: Kenneth Benton told *CA:* "I started writing fiction late in life, and my first adventure-suspense story was published when I was sixty. Having spent my whole career dealing with political problems, with some practical experience of both espionage and counter-espionage, it was perhaps natural that my stories have dealt mainly with such matters. I've also drawn on my knowledge of foreign countries and customs. On the nonfiction side I write reports and reviews, mainly on political movements, subversion, and intelligence."

* * *

BERCKMAN, Evelyn Domenica 1900-
(Joanna Wade)

PERSONAL: Born October 18, 1900, in Philadelphia, Pa.; daughter of Aaron and Ann (Altman) Berckman. *Education:* Attended Columbia University.

CAREER: Writer and musician. *Member:* Curzon Club and Hamilton Club (both London, England), West Kent Club (Tunbridge Wells, England). *Awards, honors:* Red Badge Award, Dodd, Mead & Co., 1954.

WRITINGS: The Evil of Time, Dodd, 1954, reprinted, Queens House, 1977; *The Beckoning Dream,* Dodd, 1955, reprinted, Queens House, 1977; *The Strange Bedfellows,* Dodd, 1956, reprinted, Queens House, 1977; *The Blind Villain,* Dodd, 1957; *The Hovering Darkness,* Dodd, 1958, reprinted, Queens House, 1977; *Lament for Four Brides,* Dodd, 1959, reprinted, Queens House, 1977; *No Known Grave,* Eyre & Spottiswoode, 1959, reprinted, Hamish Hamilton, 1975.

Do You Know This Voice?, Dodd, 1960; *Nelson's Dear Lord* (biography), Macmillan, 1962, *Blind Girl's Buff,* Dodd, 1962; *A Thing That Happens to You,* Dodd, 1964; *A Simple Case of Ill-Will,* Eyre & Spottiswoode, 1964, Dodd, 1965; *Keys from a Window,* Eyre & Spottiswoode, 1965; *Stalemate,* Doubleday, 1966; *The Heir of Starvelings,* Doubleday, 1967; *A Case of Nullity,* Eyre & Spottiswoode, 1967, Doubleday, 1968; *The Long Arm of the Prince,* R. Hale, 1968; *She Asked for It,* Doubleday, 1969.

The Voice of Air, Doubleday, 1970; *A Finger to Her Lips,* Doubleday, 1971; *The Stake in the Game,* Hamish Hamilton, 1971, Doubleday, 1973; *The Fourth Man on the Rope,* Doubleday, 1972; *The Victorian Album,* Dell, 1973; *The Hidden Navy,* Hamish Hamilton, 1973; *Wait,* Hamish Hamilton, 1973, published as *Wait, Just You Wait,* Doubleday, 1974; *Creators and Destroyers of the English Navy,* Hamish Hamilton, 1974; *The Nightmare Chase,* Doubleday, 1975; *Indecent Exposure,* Hamish Hamilton, 1975; *A Hidden Malice,* Belmont Books, 1976; *The Crown Estate,* Doubleday, 1976; *The Blessed Plot,* Hamish Hamilton, 1976; *Be All and End All,* Hamish Hamilton, 1976; *Journey's End,* Doubleday, 1977; *Victims of Piracy,* Hamish Hamilton, 1978.

SIDELIGHTS: Evelyn Berckman is a composer and musician whose works have been performed by the Philadelphia Orchestra and the Rochester Symphony. *Avocational interests:* Bridge, two-piano playing, the protection of animals.

BIOGRAPHICAL/CRITICAL SOURCES: New York Times Book Review, August 27, 1967, April 14, 1968, April 30, 1972; *New Yorker,* September 2, 1967, August 19, 1974; *Books & Bookmen,* September, 1970; *Book World,* February 20, 1972; *Times Literary Supplement,* April 28, 1972; *Spectator,* March 17, 1973; *Listener,* March 22, 1973; *Economist,* June 8, 1974; *Observer,* February 1, 1976.†

* * *

BERGER, Peter Ludwig 1929-

PERSONAL: Born March 17, 1929, in Vienna, Austria; came to United States, 1946; naturalized citizen, 1952; son of George William and Jelka (Loew) Berger; married Brigitte Kellner, 1959; children: Thomas Ulrich, Michael George. *Education:* Attended University of London, 1946; Wagner College, B.A., 1949; New School for Social Research, M.A., 1950, Ph.D., 1954; additional study at Lutheran Theological Seminary at Philadelphia, University of Michigan, and Yale University. *Office:* Department of Sociology, Rutgers University, New Brunswick, N.J. 08903.

CAREER: University of Georgia, Columbus, extension, lecturer, 1954-55; Evangelical Academy, Bad Boll, Germany, research director, 1955-56; Women's College of the University of North Carolina (now University of North Carolina at Greensboro), assistant professor, 1956-58; Hartford Seminary Foundation, Hartford, Conn., associate professor and director of Institute of Church and Community, 1958-63; New School for Social Research, New York, N.Y., associate professor, 1963-66; Brooklyn College of the City University of New York, Brooklyn, N.Y., professor, 1966-70; Rutgers University, New Brunswick, N.Y., professor of sociology, 1970—. Lecturer and visiting professor at European and American universities. *Military service:* U.S. Army, two years. *Member:* American Sociological Association, Society for the Scientific Study of Religion (president, 1966-68), Eastern Sociological Association. *Awards, honors:* LL. D., Loyola University, 1970; American Book Award nomination, 1980, for *The Heretical Imperative.*

WRITINGS: The Noise of Solemn Assemblies, Doubleday, 1961; *The Precarious Vision,* Doubleday, 1961; *Invitation to Sociology: A Humanistic Perspective,* Doubleday, 1963; (editor) *The Human Shape of Work,* Macmillan, 1964; (with Thomas Luckmann) *The Social Construction of Reality,* Doubleday, 1966; *The Sacred Canopy: Elements of a Sociological Theory of Religion,* Doubleday, 1967 (published in England as *The Social Reality of Religion,* Faber, 1969); (editor) *Marxism and Sociology: Views from Eastern Europe,* Appleton, 1969; *A Rumor of Angels: Modern Society and the Rediscovery of the Supernatural,* Doubleday, 1969.

(With Richard J. Neuhaus) *Movement and Revolution,* Doubleday, 1970; (with wife, Brigitte Berger) *Sociology: A Biographical Approach,* Basic Books, 1972, 2nd edition, 1975; *The Homeless Mind: Modernization and Consciousness,* Random House, 1973; *Pyramids of Sacrifice: Political Ethics and Social Change,* Basic Books, 1974; (with Neuhaus) *Against the World for the World,* Seabury, 1976; *Facing Up to Modernity,* Basic Books, 1977; (with Neuhaus) *To Empower People: The Role of Mediating Structures in Public Policy,* American Enterprise Institute for Public Policy Research, 1977; *The Heretical Imperative: Contemporary Possibilities of Religious Affirmation,* Doubleday, 1979. Contributor of articles and reviews to professional and religious journals.†

BERKMAN, Richard Lyle 1946-

PERSONAL: Born September 4, 1946, in Pittsburgh, Pa.; son of Allen H. (a lawyer) and Selma (Wiener) Berkman; married Judy Fromson (a lawyer), June 23, 1968. *Education:* Harvard University, A.B. (magna cum laude), 1968, J.D. (cum laude), 1973. *Home:* 1704 Panama St., Philadelphia, Pa. 19103. *Office:* Dechert, Price & Rhoads, 3400 Centre Square West, 1500 Market St., Philadelphia, Pa. 19102.

CAREER: Admitted to Bar of the State of Pennsylvania, 1973. Executive Office of the President, Office of Emergency Preparedness, Washington, D.C., special assistant to director on wage-price freeze policy, summer, 1971; Center for the Study of Responsive Law, Washington, D.C., project director, summer, 1971; Cleary, Gottlieb, Steen & Hamilton, Washington, D.C., law clerk, summer, 1972; law clerk to U.S. District Court Judge Edward Becker, Philadelphia, Pa., 1973-74; Dechert, Price & Rhoads, Philadelphia, associate, 1974—. *Military service:* U.S. Naval Reserve, 1968-70; became lieutenant junior grade. *Member:* Phi Beta Kappa.

WRITINGS: Damming the West, Grossman, 1971; (with F. Hastings Griffin, Jr.) *Pennsylvania Evidence—1974,* Pennsylvania Bar Institute, 1974. President, *Harvard Journal on Legislation,* 1972-73. Contributor to professional journals.

AVOCATIONAL INTERESTS: Playing squash and tennis.

* * *

BERKOWITZ, Sol 1922-

PERSONAL: Born April 27, 1922, in Warren, Ohio; son of Jacob (a decorator) and Lillie (Bresovitz) Berkowitz; married Pearl Schwartz (a psychologist), June 27, 1945. *Education:* Queens College (now Queens College of the City University of New York), B.A., 1942; Columbia University, M.A., 1947. *Home:* 46-36 Hanford St., Douglaston, N.Y. 11362. *Agent:* Helen Harvey, Harvey & Hutto, Inc., 110 West 57th St., New York, N.Y. 10019. *Office:* School of Music, Queens College of the City University of New York, Flushing, N.Y. 11367.

CAREER: Composer of music for stage, television, motion pictures, and radio, 1955—. Queens College of the City University of New York, Flushing, N.Y., instructor, 1946-52, assistant professor, 1952-55, associate professor, 1955-71, professor of music, 1971—. *Military service:* U.S. Army, Signal Corps and Special Services, 1942-46; became staff sergeant. *Member:* Dramatists Guild, American Society of Composers, Authors and Publishers. *Awards, honors:* Ford Foundation grant, 1955-56, for composition.

WRITINGS: New Approach to Sight Singing, Norton, 1960; *Improvisation through Keyboard Harmony,* Prentice-Hall, 1973.

Music; all published by Frank Music Corp.: *Paradigm* (for concert band), 1969; *Ye Gods, You Gave to Me a Wife* (for chorus), 1970; *Five Sad and Humorous Songs* (for chorus), 1970; *Game of Dance* (for concert band), 1970; *Three Tongue Twisters* (for chorus), 1971; *Twenty-Seven Jazzettes* (for piano), 1971; *Diversion* (for orchestra), 1972; *Folk Song Preludes* (for piano), 1972.

Ten Duets (for treble instruments), Boston Music Co., 1971; *Letter to a Mother* (for chorus), Elkan-Vogel, 1973; *Letter to a Brother* (for chorus), Elkan-Vogel, 1973; *To Have and to Be* (for chorus), Lawson-Gould, 1977; *We Would Rather Whistle* (for chorus), Elkan-Vogel, 1978; *Some Guides to Dining* (for chorus), Elkan-Vogel, 1978; *Father William* (for chorus), Lawson-Gould, 1979; *Don't Ask Me* (for chorus), Lawson-Gould, 1979; *I Had a Little Pup* (for chorus), Lawson-Gould, 1979. Also author of about forty other musical compositions published by Chappell, Presser, and Lawson-Gould.

Music for stage productions: "Jazz Ballet," first performed in New York at 92nd St. Young Men's-Young Women's Hebrew Association, December, 1952; "Fat Tuesday" (opera), first produced in Tamiment, Pa. at Tamiment Playhouse, August, 1956; "The Littlest Revue," first produced Off-Broadway at Phoenix Theatre, May 22, 1956; (composer of score) "Miss Emily Adam," first produced in New York at Theatre Marquee, March 29, 1960; (composer of incidental music) "The Unsinkable Molly Brown," first produced on Broadway at Winter Garden Theatre, November 3, 1960; (composer of score) *Nowhere to Go but Up* (first produced on Broadway at Winter Garden Theatre, November 10, 1962), Chappell, 1962; (composer of ballet and incidental music) "Mornin' Sun," first produced Off-Broadway at Phoenix Theatre, October 6, 1963; (composer and orchestrator) "Diamond Fair" (nightclub production), first performed in New York at Latin Quarter, November, 1963.

Composer of music for concert stage, including: "Duo Concertante for Two Pianos," first performed in New York at Carnegie Hall, January, 1947; "Scherzo for Piano," first performed at Carnegie Hall, November, 1948; "Sonata for Piano," first performed in New York at Brooklyn Museum, February, 1948; "Suite for Piano," first performed at New York City Center, March, 1949; "Concerto for Oboe," first performed at American Festival of Music, February, 1950; "Quintet for Winds," first performed in New York at Town Hall, November, 1951. Has also composed music for ninety television programs, including "Jazz of This Hotel," broadcast by ABC, February, 1952; staff composer for "The Garry Moore Show," 1963-64, and for "The Entertainers," 1964, both produced by Columbia Broadcasting System. composer of music scores for films, "IS-ES," 1967, and "American Can" (documentary), 1967.

* * *

BERMAN, Daniel M(arvin) 1928-1967

PERSONAL: Born June 15, 1928, in Paterson, N.J.; died November 19, 1967, in New Delhi, India; son of Isidor and Roselyn (Pollock) Berman; married Aline Fugh, 1957; children: Stuart, Adriane. *Education:* Rutgers University, A.B., 1947, Ph.D., 1957; University of Wisconsin, A.M., 1948. *Office:* American University, 1901 F St. N.W., Washington, D.C.

CAREER: State Teachers College (now State University of New York College at Fredonia), instructor, 1957-58; Washington College, Chestertown, Md., assistant professor, 1958-61; staff consultant to U.S. Senate sub-committee on constitutional rights, 1960-61; American University, Washington, D.C., associate professor, 1961-64, professor of government and public administration, 1964-67. Executive director, Institute on American Freedoms, beginning 1965; national vice-chairman, National Committee to Abolish the House Un-American Activities Committee. Member, Washington Professors for World Peace. *Member:* American Political Science Association, American Association of University Professors. *Awards, honors:* American Political Science Association congressional fellowship, 1959-60; Eagleton Institute of Politics and Citizenship Clearing House national convention fellowship, 1960; American Bar Association Scribe's Award, 1963; University of Pennsylvania special study grant for research in India.

WRITINGS: A Bill Becomes Law: The Civil Rights Act of

1960, Macmillan, 1962, 2nd edition published as *A Bill Becomes Law: Congress Enacts Civil Rights Legislation,* 1966; *In Congress Assembled: The Legislative Process in the National Government,* Macmillan, 1964; *It Is So Ordered: The Supreme Court Rules on School Segregation,* W. W. Norton, 1967; *Urban Renewal: Bonanza of the Real Estate Business,* Prentice-Hall, 1969; (with L. S. Loeb) *Laws and Men: The Challenge of American Politics,* Macmillan, 1970, published as *American Politics: Crisis and Challenge,* 1975. Also author of *Death on the Job.* Contributor to professional journals.

WORK IN PROGRESS: Towards a Color-Blind Constitution, for Appleton; *The American Way: The National Government in the United States,* for Macmillan.†

* * *

BERNE, Stanley 1923-

PERSONAL: Born June 8, 1923, in Staten Island, N.Y.; son of William (a businessman) and Irene (Daniels) Berne; married Arlene Zekowski (a writer and university professor), May 17, 1953. *Education:* Rutgers University, B.S., 1951; New York University, M.A., 1952; Louisiana State University, additional study, 1958-62. *Office:* Department of English, Eastern New Mexico University, Portales, N.M. 88130.

CAREER: Eastern New Mexico University, Portales, assistant professor, 1963-67, associate professor of English, 1968—. Guest lecturer at University of the Americas, 1965, University of South Dakota, 1968, and Styrian Hauptschulen Paedagogische Akademie (Graz, Austria), 1969. Producer and host with wife, Arlene Zekowski, of television series, "Future Writing Today," for Public Broadcasting System. Has participated in lecture tour through Mexico, sponsored by U.S. Department of State and U.S. Embassy, 1965; has appeared on over 150 radio and television interview programs in the United States and Canada, speaking about art and literature, and on television programs including "Avant-Garde Goes West" and "Noonday." *Military service:* U.S. Army Air Forces, 1942-45; served in South Pacific theater; received Philippine Liberation Medal. *Member:* P.E.N., Committee of Small Magazine Editors and Publishers, Western Independent Publishers.

WRITINGS—All published by Wittenborn, except as noted: (With wife, Arlene Zekowski) *A First Book of the Neo-Narrative,* 1954; (with A. Zekowski) *Cardinals and Saints,* 1958; *The Dialogues,* 1962; *The Multiple Modern Gods and Other Stories,* 1964; *The Unconscious Victorious and Other Stories,* 1968; *The New Rubaiyat of Stanley Berne* (poetry), American-Canadian Publishers, 1973; *Future Language,* Horizon Press, 1977; *The Great American Empire,* Horizon Press, 1979. Work represented in anthologies: *Breakthrough Fictioneers,* edited by Richard Kostelanetz, Something Else Press, 1973; *First Person Intense* edited by Sasha Newborn, Mudborn Press, 1978.

SIDELIGHTS: Stanley Berne told *CA:* "We [Berne and his wife, Alene Zekowski] proposed in our books that grammar be reformed for purposes of artistic communication in prose. We proposed . . . that grammar be made sensibly simpler. Everybody got angry. They thought we were advocating anarchy. Does reducing the 300 rules and elements of grammar to two sound anarchic? Well, that's what we proposed. We simply called attention to the four great writers of the 20th century who, working by artistic instinct, had already indicated the direction of English (and all modern language communication) for the future. They are Virginia Woolf, Gertrude Stein, William Faulkner, and James Joyce. Some think these writers were eccentrics, or merely interesting but impractical dreamers. We discovered, in the course of writing *Future Language* [by Berne] and *Image Breaking Images* [by Zekowski], that they were harbingers of the future.

"It is clear that people will resist change in language as passionately as in religion. But it appeared to us unthinkable, that in the age of space travel, jet aircraft, new electronic storage and retrieval systems, that language would remain frozen in the linear form of the sentence. It cannot be, because of the assault on our sensibilities by electronic communication devices, and the overwhelming flood of information coming at us as we approach the year 2000. Above all, we, as authors, are interested in the beauty of language, in its elasticity as a human organ, and in authors and poets providing solutions to the stunning and compounding loss of interest in reading and in books rather than in linguistitioners and grammarians making rules, from which masses of people are daily fleeing. I believe with Shelley that writers and poets are the true legislators of the spirit. If we are, then we must turn our minds to the problem of the fading away of reading interest (which is nothing more than the failure of language forms to communicate contemporary thought and feeling) and to the solution of providing new and reliable forms for the future of communication."

BIOGRAPHICAL/CRITICAL SOURCES: New World Writing, number 11, 1958; *Times Literary Supplement,* August 6, 1964; *Denver Quarterly,* autumn, 1969; *Saturday Review,* September 29, 1979; *X: A Journal of the Arts,* winter, 1979.

* * *

BERNSTEIN, Harry 1909-

PERSONAL: Born October 13, 1909; son of Louis and Rose (Katz) Bernstein; married Florence I. Borenstein, June 21, 1936; children: Stefanie Ruth, Walter Ted. *Education:* City College (now City College of the City University of New York), B.A., 1933; Columbia University, M.A., 1934, Ph.D., 1945. *Home:* 191 Lexington Ave., Freeport, N.Y. 11520.

CAREER: City College (now City College of the City University of New York), New York, N.Y., instructor, 1939-43; Brooklyn College of the City University of New York, Brooklyn, N.Y., instructor, 1945-47, assistant professor, 1948-54, associate professor, 1954-58, professor of history, beginning 1958; became professor of Ibero-American history, Graduate Center, City University of New York. Visiting professor of Brazilian history, Graduate School, New York University, 1959-69, and University of Rochester, summer, 1961; lecturer in Spanish, Columbia University, 1959-60, and in Brazilian history, University of California, Berkeley, 1962. *Member:* Hispanic Society of America, Societe des Americanistes, Sociedade Geografica de Lisboa, Conference of Latin-American Historians, Latin American Studies Association, American Historical Association. *Awards, honors:* Beveridge award, 1945; fellowships from Social Science Research Council, 1943-44, Ford Foundation, beginning 1953, Fund for the Advancement of Education, 1953-54, and Fulbright-Hays Foundation, 1964.

WRITINGS: Origins of Inter-American Interest, 1700-1812, University of Pennsylvania Press, 1945, reprinted, Russell, 1965; (contributor) B.W. Diffie, *Latin American Civilization: Colonial Period,* Stackpole, 1945, reprinted, Octagon, 1967; *Modern and Contemporary Latin America,* Lippincott, 1952; *Making an Inter-American Mind,* University of Florida Press, 1961; *Venezuela and Colombia,* Prentice-Hall, 1964; (contributor) *Boletim Internacional de Bibliografia*

Luso-Brasileira, Gulbenkian, 1972; *Dom Pedro II,* Twayne, 1973; *Matias Romero,* Fondo de Cultura Economica, 1973; (contributor) *Arquivos Centro Cultural Portuguens,* Gulbenkian, 1978; *Alexandre Herculano, Portuguese Historian,* Gulbenkian, in press; *The Craesbeecks of Lisbon: 17th-Century Publishers to Brazil and Portugal,* Cambridge University Press, in press. Also author: *The Lisbon Juiz do Povo and His 24 Guildsmen; Brazilian Diamonds, Portuguese Loans, and Anglo-Dutch Bankers; The White Working Man and Artisan of Brazil, 1640-1934.*

* * *

BERRIEN, F. Kenneth 1909-1971

PERSONAL: Born December 22, 1909, in Philadelphia, Pa.; died February 9, 1971, in New Brunswick, N.J.; son of Fred C. and May (Croshaw) Berrien; married Alice Elizabeth Brown, December 29, 1932 (divorced, 1952); married Betty Anne Rutherford, July 12, 1952; children: (first marriage) Barbara (Mrs. Robert Ewen), Frederick B. *Education:* Colgate University, A.B., 1931; Ohio State University, M.A., 1932, Ph.D., 1938. *Residence:* Somerville, N.J. *Office:* Department of Psychology, Rutgers University, 77 Hamilton St., New Brunswick, N.J.

CAREER: Hightstown High School, Hightstown, N.J., teacher, 1933-35; Ohio State University, Columbus, graduate assistant and assistant, 1935-37; University of Pennsylvania, Philadelphia, instructor in psychology, 1937-38; Colgate University, Hamilton, N.Y., instructor, 1938-42, assistant professor, 1942-45, associate professor, 1945-49, professor of psychology, 1949-51; Institute for Research in Human Relations, Philadelphia, research director, 1951-55; Central Intelligence Agency, Washington, D.C., psychologist, 1955-56; Rutgers University, New Brunswick, N.J., professor of psychology, 1956-71, chairman of graduate psychology, 1956-61. Diplomate (counseling) of American Board of Examiners in Professional Psychology. Research fellow in human relations, Harvard University, 1945; summer instructor in psychology, San Diego State College (now University), 1949; visiting lecturer, Columbia University, 1954; professor of psychology, George Washington University, 1955-56; visiting exchange professor, University of Hawaii, 1958-59, 1963-64. Delegate to International Congress of Scientific Psychology, 1958 and 1960, and to Japanese Association of Educational Psychology, 1963. Senior specialist, East-West Center for Cultural Exchange, University of Hawaii, 1965-66, 1966-67. Lecturer. Consultant at various times to government agencies and business firms, including Curtiss-Wright Corp., Hughes Aircraft Co., Douglass Aircraft Co., Sperry Gyroscope Co., General Electric Co., Office of Naval Research, National Research Council, and Office of Scientific Research and Development. Administrator, Utica-Colgate Counseling Service, 1946-47. Former member, national YMCA Committee on Youth Program and Camping. *Member:* International Studies Association, American Psychological Association (fellow; member of council of representatives, 1960-66), American Association for the Advancement of Science (fellow), American Management Association, American Association of University Professors, Eastern Psychological Association (chairman of membership committee, 1962-63), New Jersey Psychological Association, New York State Psychological Association, Huguenot Society of New Jersey.

WRITINGS: Practical Psychology, Macmillan, 1944, revised edition (with J. M. Brown, D. L. Russell, and W. D. Wells) published as *Applied Psychology,* 1966; *Comments and Cases on Human Relations,* Harper, 1951, revised edition (with Wendell H. Bash), 1957; (editor with Bernard P. Indik) *People, Groups, and Organizations,* Teachers College Press, 1968; *General and Social Systems,* Rutgers University Press, 1968. Also author of technical reports. Contributor to *Encyclopedia Americana Yearbook,* 1948; also contributor of over 100 articles to popular magazines and journals in his field. Consulting editor, *International Journal of Psychology,* 1968-71.

AVOCATIONAL INTERESTS: Photography, boating, and hunting.†

* * *

BERTOLINO, James 1942-

PERSONAL: Born October 4, 1942, in Pence, Wis.; son of James A. (a sales manager) and Doris (a teacher; maiden name, Robbins) Bertolino; married Lois Behling (director of craft studios at Cornell University), November 29, 1966. *Education:* University of Wisconsin—Oshkosh, B.S., 1970; Washington State University, graduate study, 1970-71; Cornell University, M.F.A., 1973. *Office:* Department of English, University of Cincinnati, Cincinnati, Ohio 45211.

CAREER: Cornell University, Ithaca, N.Y., lecturer in English, 1973-74; University of Cincinnati, Cincinnati, Ohio, associate professor of English, 1974—. Has taught high school poetry. Member of board of directors, Print Center, Inc., 1972-74; Cincinnati Comprehensive Employment and Training Act artists' program, member of performance panel, 1977, chairman of literature panel, 1978; member of literature panel, Ohio Arts Council, 1979-80. Founder, Elliston Book Award for small press poetry books, 1975, *Cincinnati Poetry Review,* 1975, and Cincinnati Area Poetry Project, 1977. *Member:* Committee of Small Magazine Editors and Publishers, Coordinating Council of Literary Magazines (member of board of consultants, 1975—). *Awards, honors:* Hart Crane Memorial Foundation award, 1969, for poems appearing in *Foxfire;* Book-of-the-Month Club award for poetry, 1970; winner of Discovery-72 poetry competition sponsored by the New York City YM-YWHA Poetry Center, 1972; National Endowment for the Arts creative writing grant, 1974-75; William Howard Taft summer research fellowship, 1976; Charles Phelps Taft Memorial Fund grant, 1977; Ohio Arts Council individual artist grant, 1979.

WRITINGS—Poetry: (Editor) *Northwest Poets Anthology,* Quixote Press, 1968; *Day of Change,* Gunrunner Press, 1968; *Drool,* Quixote Press, 1968; *Ceremony,* Morgan Press, 1969; *Mr. Nobody,* Ox Head Press, 1969; *Stone-Marrow,* Abraxas Press, 1969; *Becoming Human,* Road Runner Press, 1970; *Employed,* Ithaca House, 1972; *Edging Through,* Stone-Marrow Press, 1972; (editor) *Young Poets Anthology,* Stone Drum and Stone-Marrow Press, 1973; *Soft Rock,* Charas Press, 1973; *Making Space for Our Living,* Copper Canyon Press, 1975; *Terminal Placebos,* New Rivers Press, 1975; *The Gestures,* Bonewhistle Press, 1975; *The Alleged Conception,* Granite Publications, 1976; *New and Selected Poems,* Carnegie-Mellon University Press, 1978; *Are You Tough Enough for the Eighties?,* New Rivers Press, 1979.

Poems are represented in anthologies: *New Poetry Out of Wisconsin,* edited by August Derleth, Stanton & Lee, 1969; *Stoney Lonesome,* edited by Roger Pfingston, Stoney Lonesome Press, 1970; *I Love You All Day/It Is That Simple,* edited by Phillip Dacey, Abbey Press, 1970; *Poems One Line and Longer,* edited by William Cole, Grossman, 1973; *Heartland II: Poets of the Midwest,* edited by Lucien Stryk, Northern Illinois University Press, 1975.

Editor of pamphlets for Abraxas Press, 1969-71, and Stone-Marrow Press, 1970—. Contributor of poems and articles to magazines and newspapers, including *Poetry, Partisan Review, Foxfire, Minnesota Review, Greenfield Review, Sou'wester,* and *Choice*. Editor, *Abraxas,* 1968-71; *Epoch,* assistant editor, 1971-73, poetry editor, spring, 1973; co-editor, *Cincinnati Poetry Review,* 1975—; poetry editor, *Eureka Review,* 1976—.

SIDELIGHTS: James Bertolino told *CA:* "The phenomenon of little magazines and small presses in America over the last [twenty] years, explosive in nature, has brought on a kind of renaissance in American poetry, and to a lesser extent, fiction. The energy and health of the wildly proliferate accomplishments in this field have sustained my hopes for the future of American literature."

* * *

BETHELL, Nicholas William 1938-

PERSONAL: Born July 19, 1938, in London, England; son of William Gladstone (a stockbroker) and Ann Margaret (Barlow) Bethell; married Cecilia Mary Honeyman, April 7, 1964 (divorced July, 1971); children: James Nicholas, William Alexander. *Education:* Pembroke College, Cambridge, M.A., 1961. *Politics:* Conservative. *Religion:* Church of England. *Home:* 73 Sussex Square, London W.2., England.

CAREER: Times Literary Supplement, London, England, sub-editor, 1962-64; British Broadcasting Corp., London, script editor of radio dramas, 1964-67. Member of the House of Lords (government Whip, 1970-71). Nominated member of European Parliament, 1975-79; elected member of European Parliament for London North-West, 1979—. Writer. *Military service:* British Army, 1956-58. *Member:* Garrick Club (London). *Awards, honors:* Pilsudski Institute annual prize, 1973, for *The War Hitler Won.*

WRITINGS: (Editor and translator) Joseph Brodsky, *Elegy to John Donne and Other Poems,* Longmans, 1967; (translator) Slawomir Mrozek, *Six Plays,* Grove, 1967; *Gomulka: His Poland and His Communism,* Holt, 1969; (translator with David Burg) Alexander Solzhenitsyn, *Cancer Ward,* Farrar, Straus, 1969; (translator with Burg) Solzhenitsyn, *The Love-Girl and the Innocent* (play), Bodley Head, 1969, Farrar, Strauss, 1970; *The War Hitler Won,* Holt, 1973; *The Last Secret,* Basic Books, 1974; *The Palestine Triangle,* Putnam, 1979. Also author of radio and television scripts for BBC.

WORK IN PROGRESS: Research on the alliance between Hitler and Stalin, 1939-41.

BIOGRAPHICAL/CRITICAL SOURCES: Times Literary Supplement, July 17, 1969, December 8, 1972; *New York Times Book Review,* June 3, 1973, September 16, 1979; *National Review,* February 28, 1975.

* * *

BEVIS, Em Olivia 1932-

PERSONAL: Born March 20, 1932, in Graceville, Fla.; daughter of James Edison and Willie (an educator; maiden name, Bullock) Bevis. *Education:* Attended University of Florida, 1950-52; Emory University, B.A., 1955; University of Chicago, M.A., 1958. *Religion:* Jewish. *Office:* Department of Nursing, Georgia Southern College, Statesboro, Ga.

CAREER: Emory University Hospital, Atlanta, Ga., staff nurse, 1955-56; University of North Carolina at Chapel Hill, instructor in medical-surgical nursing, 1958-62; San Jose State University, San Jose, Calif., 1962-74, became professor of nursing; Georgia Southern College, Statesboro, professor of nursing and chairman of department, 1974—. *Member:* American Nurses Association, National League for Nursing, American Academy of Nursing (fellow), Pi Lambda Theta, Sigma Theta Tau.

WRITINGS: (With Laura Mae Douglass) *Team Leadership in Action: Principles and Application to Staff Nursing Situations,* Mosby, 1970, revised edition published as *Nursing Leadership in Action: Principles and Application to Staff Situation,* 1974, 2nd revised edition published as *Nursing Leadership and Management in Action,* 1978; (contributor) Harriet Moidel and others, editors, *Nursing Care of the Patient with Medical-Surgical Disorders,* McGraw, 1971; *Curriculum Building in Nursing: A Process,* Mosby, 1973, 2nd edition, 1978; (with Gwen D. Marram and Shirley Schelagle) *Primary Nursing: A Model for Individualized Care,* Mosby, 1974, 2nd edition, 1978; (with Fay L. Bower) *Fundamentals of Nursing Practice: Concepts, Roles and Functions,* Mosby, 1979.

* * *

BICKEL, Alexander M(ordecai) 1924-1974

PERSONAL: Born December 17, 1924, in Bucharest, Rumania; came to United States in 1939, naturalized citizen in 1943; died November 7, 1974, of cancer, in New Haven, Conn.; son of Solomon (a writer) and Yetta (Schafer) Bickel; married Josephine Ann Napolino, October 17, 1959; children: Francesca Ann, Claudia Rose. *Education:* City College of New York (now City College of the City University of New York), B.S., 1947; Harvard University, LL.B., 1949. *Office:* Yale Law School, New Haven, Conn.

CAREER: U.S. Court of Appeals, Boston, Mass., law clerk to Chief Judge Calvert Magruder, 1949-50; law officer, U.S. State Department, 1950-52; Supreme Court of the United States, Washington, D.C., law clerk to Mr. Justice Frankfurter, 1952-53; special assistant to director, policy planning staff, U.S. State Department, 1953-54; Harvard University, Cambridge, Mass., research associate, 1954-56; Yale University, New Haven, Conn., 1956-74, professor of law, 1960-74, Chancellor Kent Professor of Law and Legal History, beginning 1966, William C. DeVane Professor, 1971-74, Sterling Professor of Law. Oliver Wendell Holmes Lecturer, Harvard Law School, 1969. Consultant to subcommittee on separation powers, Senate Committee on the Judiciary, 90th-93rd Congresses. *Military service:* U.S. Army, 1943-45. *Member:* American Academy of Arts and Sciences. *Awards, honors:* Guggenheim fellow; M.A., Yale University, 1960; Center for Advanced Study in Behavioral Sciences fellow, 1970-71.

WRITINGS: (Editor) *The Unpublished Opinions of Mr. Justice Brandeis,* Belknap Press, 1957; *The Least Dangerous Branch,* Bobbs-Merrill, 1962; *Politics and the Warren Court,* Harper, 1965; *The New Age of Political Reform: The Electoral College, the Convention, and the Party System* Harper, 1968, revised and expanded edition published as *Reform and Continuity: The Electoral College, the Convention, and the Party System,* 1971; *The Supreme Court and the Idea of Progress,* Harper, 1970; *The Caseload of the Supreme Court: And What, if Anything, to Do about It,* American Enterprise Institute for Public Policy Research, 1973; (with others) *Watergate, Politics, and the Legal Process,* American Enterprise Institute for Public Policy Research, 1974; *The Morality of Consent,* Yale University Press, 1975. Contributor to professional journals. Contributing editor, *New Republic,* 1957-74.

WORK IN PROGRESS: A volume covering the period from 1910-30, for a multi-volume history of U.S. Supreme Court.

SIDELIGHTS: Martin Weil describes Alexander Bickel as "a pungent and powerful speaker and writer of great intellectual force.... [He] was heard, seen, read, and consulted often on the great constitutional issues of the past decade.

"In national debates over such questions as impeachment, Watergate, war powers of the president, the powers of Congress versus those of the courts, school integration and busing, Mr. Bickel shaped the thinking of law students and government policymakers alike, by appearances in court and before congressional committees, through articles in publications . . . and as law school lecturer and legal adviser."

Lawrence Van Gelder has said that Bickel's "thoughts, speeches, and writings . . . resounded with profound impact at the highest levels of government . . . [and] figured formidably in the nation and the legal community at large." Another reviewer comments that "Bickel shared Leonard Hand's conviction that when liberty dies in the hearts of the people, 'no constitution, no law, no court can save it [or] even do much to help it.'"

Bickel's last book, *The Morality of Consent,* bears this out. A reviewer for *Publishers' Weekly* writes: "The impassioned urgency and depth of thought in this . . . volume . . . can only make acute the serious reader's sense of loss in his recent death.... Bickel has . . . moved beyond transient emotions to address himself to the fundamental issues involving his own belief in our democratic system as an imperfect but continually evolving reflection of morality and law in mutual accommodation.... He makes a persuasive and fervent plea for a fresh understanding."

While Bickel's influence on legal thought will be felt for years to come, he will probably be best remembered for his successful defence of the *New York Times* in the controversial Pentagon Papers case of 1971. To many people's surprise he did not base his argument on First Amendment freedoms in general, but on the principle that publication did not create a clear and present danger to the nation's security, thus freeing the courts to suppress other publications if the situation warranted it.

BIOGRAPHICAL/CRITICAL SOURCES: New York Times Book Review, April 21, 1963, January 16, 1966, March 1, 1970, June 7, 1970, December 6, 1970, September 21, 1975; *Book Week,* December 19, 1965; *Harper's,* April, 1970; *National Review,* April 21, 1970; *Commonwealth,* May 15, 1970; *Nation,* September 21, 1970; *New York Times,* November 8, 1974; *Washington Post,* November 9, 1974; *Publisher's Weekly,* August 11, 1975; *New Republic,* October 18, 1975; *Commentary,* January, 1976.†

* * *

BICKERS, Richard Leslie Townshend 1917- (Mark Charles, Ricardo Cittafino, Philip Dukes, Paul Kapusta, Burt Keene, Fritz Kirschner, Gui Lefevre, Gerhardt Mueller, David Richards, Richard Townshend)

PERSONAL: Born July 5, 1917, in Shillong, Assam, India; son of Maurice Henry Townshend (an official of the British Government in India) and Gladwys Mary (Williams) Bickers; married Winifred Warne Richardson, November 21, 1938; children: Richard Paul Townshend, David Charles Townshend. *Education:* Attended Monkton Combe School and St. Paul's School, England. *Politics:* Conservative. *Religion:* Roman Catholic. *Home:* 15 Fox Rd., Holmer Green, High Wycomb, Buckinghamshire HP15 6SF, England. *Agent:* A. M. Heath & Co. Ltd., 40-42 William IV St., London WC2N 4DD, England.

CAREER: Royal Air Force, 1939-57, serving as regular officer in Fighter Command, Mediterranean Allied Air Forces, Far East Command, and Desert Air Force; Richard Bickers and Associates Ltd. (international marketing consultants), managing director. *Member:* Institute of Marketing, Institute of Export, Society of Authors.

WRITINGS—Nonfiction: *Ginger Lacey: Fighter Pilot* (biography), R. Hale, 1962; *Marketing in Europe,* Gower Press, 1971.

Fiction; under name Richard Townshend Bickers; all published by Brown, Watson; all 1958: *Air Patrol: Biscay; Full Ahead—Both!; Italian Episode; Jungle Pilot; The Liberators; Night Intruder; Ten Hundred Hours; "Scramble!"; Volunteers for Danger.*

All published by R. Hale, except as indicated: *The Guns Boom Far,* Hutchinson, 1960; *The Savage Sky,* 1961; *Jagger's Secret Challenge,* Macdonald, 1964; *The Hellions,* 1965; *Scent of Mayhem,* 1965; *Maraskar Bound,* 1968; *Hunt and Kill,* 1969; *Summer of No Surrender,* 1976; *My Enemy Came Nigh,* 1978; *The Desert Falcons,* 1978; *Their Flarepath the Moon,* 1979. Also author of *The Beaufighters* and *Dusk Patrol.*

Under pseudonyms as shown; all published by Brown, Watson; all 1958: (Mark Charles) *Here Come the Marines!;* (Ricardo Cittafino) *Conscript;* (Philip Dukes) *Kidnap;* (Paul Kapusta) *Avenging Eagle;* (Burt Keene) *Death but No Glory;* (Fritz Kirschner) *S.S.;* (Gui Lefevre) *We Were Three;* (Gerhardt Mueller) *Luftwaffe;* (David Richards) *Double Game;* (David Richards) *Hurricane Squadron;* (David Richards) *Four Men.*

Under pseudonym Richard Townshend; all published by Edwin Self: *Angels Twenty-five,* 1955; *Malayan Episode,* 1956; *Japanese Encounter,* 1956; *Terror in Cyprus,* 1957.

Author with Berkely Mather of "The Pagoda Well," a six-part serial for BBC radio; author of "Hunt for Zalek" and "Zero Fuel," for BBC radio. Author of numerous plays and scripts for television and radio, and of about one hundred short stories broadcast and published in various languages. Contributor to magazines and newspapers.

WORK IN PROGRESS: A novel, tentatively entitled *Satan's Whirlpool;* a biography of race-car driver Alan Jones.

AVOCATIONAL INTERESTS: Small boat sailing, skiing, tennis, squash, and riding.

* * *

BIESTERVELD, Betty Parsons 1923-

PERSONAL: Born February 2, 1923, in Paducah, Ky.; daughter of George Arthum (a Methodist minister) and Elizabeth (Dimmick) Parsons; married Lavern Perry Biesterveld, August 11, 1951; children: Julia Elizabeth, Rebekah Jo. *Education:* Attended Muskingum College, 1941-42; Mount Union College, B.A., 1945; also attended University of Akron, 1946-47. *Religion:* Presbyterian. *Home:* 2607 Shangri La Rd., Phoenix, Ariz. 85028.

CAREER: Elementary school teacher in New Philadelphia, Ohio, 1945-46, Williamsfield, Ohio, 1947-54, Akron, Ohio, 1954-57, Oraibi, Ariz., 1968-69, and Akron, beginning 1969; currently part-time secretary for First Baptist Church of Sunnyslope, Phoenix, Ariz. Sunday school teacher. *Member:* Alpha Chi Omega. *Awards, honors:* Friends of American Writers Award for *Six Days from Sunday.*

WRITINGS—All published by Western Publishing, except as indicated: *Run, Reddy, Run,* Thomas Nelson, 1962; *Peter's Junk,* 1965; *Wags,* 1965; *Two Stories about Wags,* 1966; (adapter) *Cinderella,* 1967; *Gumby,* 1968; *Peter's Wagon,* 1969; *Michael's Treasure,* 1969; *Six Days from Sunday,* Rand McNally, 1973. Contributor of poems and articles to Christian magazines.

WORK IN PROGRESS: A children's book.

SIDELIGHTS: As the daughter of a Methodist minister, Betty Parsons Biesterveld says she grew up "constantly on the move." From her parents she derived a love and appreciation for the many types of people that a minister's family comes in contact with. Also, she remarks, "I was taught tenderness for animals, their not being much different from people when it came to being wanted and loved. So, I was constantly dragging stray cats and dogs home." She turned to teaching to fulfill a desire to guide children toward happy and full lives. "It was from these experiences as a P.K. (preacher's kid), my love of animals, children, and the personal contact later in life with the loggers and my pet fox that the story of *Run, Reddy, Run* was written," Biesterveld says. Her father, sister, and brother are also authors of juvenile books.

AVOCATIONAL INTERESTS: Painting, ceramics, raising birds.

* * *

BIKEL, Theodore 1924-

PERSONAL: Born May 2, 1924, in Vienna, Austria; came to United States in 1954, naturalized in 1961; son of Joseph and Miriam (Riegler) Bikel; married Rita Weinberg, 1967; children: two sons. *Education:* University of London, B.A., 1944; Royal Academy of Dramatic Art, diploma, 1948. *Politics:* "Reform Democrat." *Agent:* William Morris Agency, 1350 Avenue of the Americas, New York, N.Y. 10019.

CAREER: Actor, singer, linguist, and photographer. Apprentice with Habimah Theatre, Tel Aviv, 1942-44; founder, Tel Aviv Chamber Theatre, 1944-46. Has performed in numerous theatrical productions, including "A Streetcar Named Desire," 1950, "The Love of Four Colonels," 1951, "Tonight in Samarkand," 1955, "The Rope Dancers," 1957, "The Sound of Music," 1959, "Brecht on Brecht," 1962, "Cafe Crown," 1964, "Fiddler on the Roof," 1967, "The Rothschilds," 1972, "Jacques Brel Is Alive and Well and Living in Paris," 1972, "The Marriage Go Round," 1973, "The Sunshine Boys," 1973, "I Do, I Do," 1974, "The Good Doctor," 1975, and "Zorba," 1976. Has also appeared in numerous motion pictures, including "The African Queen," "Moulin Rouge," "The Little Kidnappers," "I Want to Live!," "The Defiant Ones," "The Blue Angel," "My Fair Lady," "Sands of the Kalahari," "The Russians Are Coming! The Russians Are Coming!," "Sweet November," "Darker Than Amber," and "The Little Ark." Host of radio show, "At Home with Theodore Bikel," 1957-62. Has made regular television appearances on most major shows and in several plays produced especially for television, 1954—. Writer and performer, "The Eternal Light," NBC-TV, 1958-60, "Look Up and Live," CBS-TV, 1958-60; host-editor, "Directions '61," ABC-TV, 1961. Photographs have been exhibited at Bank Street Gallery. Delegate to Democratic National Convention, 1968. Member of National Council on the Arts, 1977.

MEMBER: Actors Equity Association (member of council, 1961-64; first vice-president, 1964-73; president, 1973—), American Academy of Television Arts and Sciences (member of board of governors, 1962-65), American Federation of Television and Radio Artists, Screen Actors' Guild, American Federation of Musicians, American Jewish Congress (founder of arts chapter; national vice-president, 1963-70; chairman of governing council, 1970—). *Awards, honors:* Tony Award nomination, 1958, for role in "The Rope Dancers," and 1960, for role in "The Sound of Music"; Academy Award nomination, 1959, for role in "The Defiant Ones"; Brandeis University Women's Committee citation as "Citizen of the World and Friend of Humanity," 1960; National Jewish Hospital citation for distinguished philanthropic service, 1960; Mt. Sinai Hospital Man of the Year award, 1960; Joint Defense Appeal of the American Jewish Committee and the Anti-Defamation League citation for distinguished service in the cause of human rights, 1961; American Jewish Congress Arts Chapter citation, 1964; Israel Bonds annual award, 1966; Goodwill Industries of Philadelphia distinguished achievement award, 1966; B'nai B'rith Man of the Year award, 1967; Hebrew University of Jerusalem certificate of honor, 1969; National Press Club certificate of appreciation, 1972; Jewish Heritage Award of Farband Labor Zionist Organization, 1973.

WRITINGS: *Folksongs and Footnotes,* Meridian, 1960. Contributor to *Book of Knowledge.* Also contributor to *Hootenanny, Popular Photography,* and other magazines.

WORK IN PROGRESS: A book of folksongs of Israel, with annotations.

BIOGRAPHICAL/CRITICAL SOURCES: *Washington Post,* May 5, 1971; *New Yorker,* April 29, 1974; *Biography News,* September, 1974.

* * *

BIRNBAUM, Philip 1904-

PERSONAL: Born April 15, 1904, in Zarnowiec, Poland; son of Abraham Joel (a mechanic) and Roza (Rozen) Birnbaum. *Education:* Howard College, B.A., 1933; Dropsie College (now University), Ph.D., 1939. *Home:* 41 West 86th St., New York, N.Y. 10024. *Office:* Hebrew Publishing Co., 80 Fifth Ave., New York, N.Y. 10011.

CAREER: Teacher; director of Hebrew school in Wilmington, Del. 1943-63, and of Hebrew schools in Birmingham, Ala. and Camden, N.J.; translator and editor of Jewish classical and liturgical literature; currently editor and consultant, Hebrew Publishing Co., New York, N.Y. Director of Associated Hebrew Schools and School for Advanced Jewish Studies. *Member:* National Council of Jewish Education, National Association of Professors of Hebrew, American Academy for Jewish Research, Zionist Organization of America, Histadruth Ivrith, Jewish Center.

WRITINGS—All published by Hebrew Publishing, except as indicated: *The Arabic Commentary of Yefet ben Ali, the Karaite, on the Book of Hosea,* Dropsie College, 1942; (editor, translator and annotator) Moses ben Maimon, *Mishnen Torah,* 1944, reprinted 1967; (translator and annotator) *The Daily Hebrew Prayer Book,* 1949; *Ethics of the Fathers,* 1949; (translator and annotator) *The High Holyday Prayer Book,* 1951; (translator and annotator) *Selihoth* (title means "Penitential Prayers"), 1952; (translator and annotator) *The Passover Haggadah,* 1953; (editor and translator) *A Treasury of Judaism,* 1957.

A Book of Jewish Concepts (dictionary), 1964; *Fluent Hebrew,* 1966; *Mahzor Ha-Shalem* (title means "Complete High Holyday Prayer Book"), Sephardic, 1967; *Hebrew-English Edition of Maimonides Code of Law and Ethics,*

1967, (compiler) *Prayer Book for Three Festivals*, 1971; *Tefilloth Yisrael u-Musar Ha-Yahaduth* (anthology; title means "Prayers and Ethics of Judaism"), Shulsinger, 1971; (editor and author of introduction) *Karaite Studies*, Herman Press, 1971; *Pletat Soferim* (collected essays; title means "Remnant of Sages"), Mossad Harav Kook, 1971; *Five Megilloth*, 1973; (editor) *The Concise Jewish Prayer Book*, 1976; *The Birnbaum Haggadah*, 1976; *The New Treasury of Judaism*, Sanhedrin Press, 1977; *Death and Mourning in Jewish Tradition*, 1980; *Jewish Holidays*, 1980.

Also editor and translator of *Ha-Sidur ha-shalem* (title means "Complete Daily Prayer Book"), 1949, *Sidur le-Shabat ve-yom tov*, 1950, *Sidur le-Shabat ve-yon tov*, 1964, *Mahazor le-shalosh regalim*, 1971; also translator and annotator of *Megillah Reading Service for Purim Evening*, 1973, and *Kinnoth Reading Service for Jishalt b' Av*, 1973. Contributor to *Hadoar, Bitzaron*, and *Hatzofeh*.

* * *

BISHOP, Thomas W(alter) 1929-

PERSONAL: Born February 21, 1929, in Vienna, Austria; son of Martin M. and Katherine (Abeles) Bishop; married Muriel Hausman, 1950 (divorced, 1967); married Helen Gary, 1967; children: (first marriage) Jeffrey Lawrence, Katherine Michelle. *Education:* New York University, A.B., 1950; attended University of Paris, 1950-51; University of Maryland (Paris center), A.M., 1951; University of California, Berkeley, Ph.D., 1957. *Home:* 56 Washington Mews, New York, N.Y. 10003. *Office:* Department of French and Italian, New York University, 19 University Pl., New York, N.Y. 10003.

CAREER: New York University, New York, N.Y., instructor, 1956-59, assistant professor, 1959-61, associate professor of French, 1961-64, director of La Maison Francaise, 1959-64, professor of French and comparative literature, 1964—, Florence Gould Professor of French Literature, 1974—, director of French graduate studies, 1964-66, chairman of French department, 1964-70, chairman of department of French and Italian, 1970—. Professor, Ecole Libre des Hautes Etudes, New York, N.Y., beginning 1960; teacher of television course on modern French novel and theater, CBS-TV, 1969 and 1976. Member of board of directors, French-American Foundation, 1976. Consultant, National Endowment for the Humanities, 1975—. Assistant chief of protocol, Tenth Commemorative Session of the United Nations, 1955.

MEMBER: Association Internationale des Etudes Francaises, Modern Language Association of America, American Association of Professors of French, Alliance Francaise de New York (member of advisory board, 1961-71; president, 1964-68), Phi Beta Kappa, Pi Delta Phi. *Awards, honors:* Arts and Science Research Fund grants, 1959, 1960, 1962, 1963, and 1968; French-American Cultural Service and Educational Aid grant, 1962; Palmes Academiques, Chevalier, 1965, Officier, 1971; Fulbright senior research scholar, 1965-66; Officier, Ordre National du Merite, Republic of France, 1977; National Endowment for the Humanities grants, 1977 and 1979; Obie Award, 1979.

WRITINGS: *Pirandello and the French Theater*, New York University Press, 1960; (editor) Jean Giraudoux, *La Folle de Chaillot* [and] *L'Apollon de Bellac*, Dell, 1963; (editor) *Deux paces modernes*, Harcourt, 1965; (editor) Marguerite Duras, *Moderato Cantabile*, Prentice-Hall, 1968; (editor) *L'Avant-Garde Theatrale: The French Theatre since 1950*, Heath, 1970; (contributor) *Nouveau roman: hier et aujourd'hui*, Union Generale d'Edition, 1972; (translator with wife, Helen Gary) Fernando Arrabal, *Garden of Delights*, Grove, 1974; (editor) Jean-Paul Sartre, *Huit Clos*, Hachette, 1975; (contributor) *Robbe-Grillet: Colloque de Cerisy*, Union Generale d'Edition, 1976; (editor) *Samuel Beckett*, Editions de l'Herne, 1976. Also contributor to *Albert Camus: A Symposium*, 1976. Contributor to *Encyclopedia Americana;* contributor to professional journals and to *Saturday Review*, *Nation*, and *New York Times Book Review*.

WORK IN PROGRESS: An analysis of French views of the United States and American views of France as exemplified by television.

* * *

BLANKSTEN, George I(rving) 1917-

PERSONAL: Born September 19, 1917, in Chicago, Ill.; son of Hymen Irving and Dinah (Sachs) Blanksten; married Deborah Schussler, 1950. *Education:* Attended University of Illinois, 1935-37; University of Chicago, A.B., 1939, A.M., 1940; University of California, Los Angeles, Ph.D., 1949. *Home address:* Route 4, Box 536 D, Antioch, Ill. 60002. *Office:* Department of Political Science, Northwestern University, Evanston, Ill. 60201.

CAREER: Instructor in public junior colleges, Chicago, Ill., 1940-42; Office of U.S. Co-ordinator of Inter-American Affairs, Washington, D.C., analyst, 1943-45; analyst for U.S. Department of State, 1945-46; Northwestern University, Evanston, Ill., instructor, 1947-50, assistant professor, 1950-52, associate professor, 1952-57, professor of political science, 1957—. Member, All-Chicago Citizen's Committee, 1956—. *Member:* American Political Science Association, American Society of International Law, Midwest Conference of Political Scientists. *Awards, honors:* Various foundation awards and fellowships, 1948-60.

WRITINGS: *Ecuador: Constitutions and Caudillos*, University of California Press, 1951; *Peron's Argentina*, University of Chicago Press, 1953, reprinted, 1974; *The United States' Role in Latin America*, edited by Martha J. Porter, Laidlaw Brothers, 1962; (with Leften Stavros Stavrianos) *Latin America: A Culture Area in Perspective*, Allyn & Bacon, 1964; (editor with Herbert R. Barringer) *Social Change in Developing Areas: A Reinterpretation of Evolutionary Theory*, Schenkman, 1965; *Argentina and Chile*, Ginn, 1969.

Contributor: H. E. Davis, editor, *Government and Politics in Latin America*, Ronald, 1958; R. C. Macridis, editor, *Foreign Policy in World Politics*, Prentice-Hall, 1958; G. A. Almond and J. S. Coleman, editors, *Politics of the Developing Areas*, Princeton University Press, 1960; *World History*, Laidlaw Brothers, 1962; Morton A. Kaplan, editor, *The Revolution in World Politics*, Wiley, 1962. Contributor to professional journals.

SIDELIGHTS: George I. Blanksten has traveled and worked in Argentina, Brazil, Chile, Costa Rica, Cuba, Ecuador, Guatemala, Mexico, Paraguay, Peru, Uruguay, and Venezuela.

* * *

BLAU, Peter M(ichael) 1918-

PERSONAL: Born February 7, 1918, in Vienna, Austria; came to United States in 1939, naturalized in 1943; son of Theodore I. and Bertha (Selka) Blau; married Zena Smith, August 7, 1948; married second wife, Judith Rae Fritz, July 31, 1968; children: (first marriage) Pamela Lisa; (second marriage) Reva Theresa. *Education:* Elmhurst College, B.A., 1942; Columbia University, Ph.D., 1952; Cambridge

University, M.A., 1966. *Home:* 726 Western Ave., Albany, N.Y. *Office:* Department of Sociology, Columbia University, New York, N.Y. 10027.

CAREER: Wayne University (now Wayne State University), Detroit, Mich., instructor, 1949-51; Cornell University, Ithaca, N.Y., instructor, 1951-53; University of Chicago, Chicago, Ill., assistant professor, 1953-58, associate professor, 1958-63, professor of sociology, 1963-70; Columbia University, New York, N.Y., professor, 1970—, Quetelet Professor of Sociology, 1977—; State University of New York at Albany, professor, 1978—. Pitt Professor of American History and Institutions, Cambridge University, 1966-67. Member of board, Social Science Research Council, 1967-69; member of advisory committee for research, National Science Foundation, 1973-74. *Military service:* U.S. Army, Intelligence, 1943-45; received Bronze Star. *Member:* American Sociological Association (councillor, 1968-71, 1972-75; president, 1973-74), American Academy of Arts and Sciences (fellow), American Association of University Professors, American Civil Liberties Union. *Awards, honors:* Social Science Research Council fellow, 1948-49; Ford Foundation Master's fellow, 1959-64; Center for Advanced Study in the Behavioral Sciences fellow, 1962-63; National Science Foundation senior postdoctoral fellow, 1962-63; Fulbright Distinguished Visitor Award, 1965; Sorokin Award, 1968, for *The American Occupational Structure;* LL.D., Elmhurst College, 1973; Netherlands Institute for Advanced Study fellow, 1975-76.

WRITINGS: The Dynamics of Bureaucracy, University of Chicago Press, 1955, 2nd revised edition, 1963; *Bureaucracy in Modern Society,* Random House, 1956, revised edition (with M. W. Meyer), 1971; (with W. Richard Scott) *Formal Organizations: A Comparative Approach,* Chandler Publishing, 1962; *Exchange and Power in Social Life,* Wiley, 1964; (with Otis Dudley Duncan) *The American Occupational Structure,* Wiley, 1967; (with Richard A. Schoenherr) *The Structure of Organizations,* Basic Books, 1971; *The Organization of Academic Work,* Wiley, 1973; *On the Nature of Organizations,* Wiley, 1974; (editor and contributor) *Approaches to the Study of Social Structure,* Free Press, 1975; *Inequality and Heterogeneity: A Primitive Theory of Social Structure,* Free Press, 1977. Contributor to professional journals. Editor, *American Journal of Sociology,* 1961-67.

* * *

BLAU, Zena Smith 1922-

PERSONAL: Born August 4, 1922, in New York, N.Y.; daughter of Joseph (a painting contractor) and Lena (Kretzmer) Smith; married Peter M. Blau, August 7, 1948 (divorced, 1968); children: Pamela. *Education:* Wayne University (now Wayne State University), A.B., 1943, M.S.W., 1946; Columbia University, Ph.D., 1957. *Religion:* Jewish. *Office:* Department of Sociology, University of Houston, Houston, Tex. 77004.

CAREER: Adelphi University, Garden City, N.Y., instructor in sociology, 1948-49; Wayne University (now Wayne State University), Detroit, Mich., special instructor, 1950-52; Cornell University, Ithaca, N.Y., research associate, department of child development and family relations, 1952-53; Smith College, Northampton, Mass., lecturer in School of Social Work, 1957-58; University of Illinois at the Medical Center, College of Nursing, Chicago, instructor, 1958-60, assistant professor of sociology, 1961-65; Institute for Juvenile Research, Chicago, Ill., senior research scientist, 1965-74; Northwestern University, Evanston, Ill., associate professor of sociology, 1969-74; City University of New York, New York, N.Y., professor of sociology at Richmond College and Graduate School and University Center, 1975-76; University of Houston, Houston, Tex., professor of sociology, 1976—. *Member:* American Sociological Association, Society for the Study of Social Problems, Association for the Sociological Study of Jewry (member of executive committee, 1972-73). *Awards, honors:* Research grants from Welfare Administration and Institute of Mental Health.

WRITINGS: Old Age in a Changing Society, F. Watts, 1973, 2nd edition, 1980; *Lebens Muster fuer das Alter,* Walter Verlag, 1979; *Black and White Children: Competence, Socialization and Social Structure,* Free Press, 1980.

Contributor: Rose L. Coser, editor, *Life Cycle and Achievement in America,* Harper, 1969; Marcel Goldschmidt, editor, *Black Americans,* Holt, 1970; Charles Willie, editor, *The Family Life of Black People,* C. E. Merrill, 1970. Contributor to *Midstream, American Sociological Review,* and other journals.

WORK IN PROGRESS: A book on successful aging from a life cycle perspective; an article on patterns of adaptation in retirement and interest in working again.

* * *

BLAUG, Mark 1927-

PERSONAL: Born 1927, in The Hague, Netherlands; children: David Ricardo, Tristan Bernard. *Education:* Columbia University, M.A., 1952, Ph.D., 1955. *Home:* 169 Walm Lane, London N.W. 2, England. *Office:* Institute of Education, University of London, Bedford Way, London W.C. 1, England.

CAREER: Queens College of the City of New York (now Queens College of the City University of New York), Flushing, N.Y., lecturer, 1951-52; Yale University, New Haven, Conn., assistant professor, 1954-62; University of London, Institute of Education, London, England, professor of the economics of education, 1967—, director of research unit in the economics of education. *Member:* American Economic Association, Royal Economic Society. *Awards, honors:* Guggenheim fellow, 1958-59; Social Science Research Council fellow, 1962-63.

WRITINGS: Ricardian Economics: A Historical Study, Yale University Press, 1958; *Economic Theory in Retrospect,* Irwin, 1962, 3rd edition, Cambridge University Press, 1978; *The Role of Education in Enlarging the Exchange Economy in Middle Africa: The English-Speaking Countries,* United Nations Educational, Scientific and Cultural Organization, 1964; *Economics of Education: A Selected Annotated Bibliography,* Pergamon, 1966, 3rd edition, 1978; (with Maurice Preston and Adrian Ziderman) *The Utilization of Educated Manpower in Industry,* Oliver & Boyd, 1967; (editor) *Economics of Education: Selected Readings,* Penguin, Volume I, 1968, Volume II, 1969, 2nd edition, Pergamon, 1970; (with Richard Layard and Maureen Woodhall) *The Causes of Graduate Unemployment in India,* Lane, 1969; *An Introduction to the Economics of Education,* Lane, 1970; (editor with B. Ahamad) *The Practice of Manpower Forecasting,* Elsevier, 1973; *The Cambridge Revolution: Success or Failure?,* Institute of Economic Affairs, 1974; (editor) *The Economics of the Arts,* Westview, 1976. Contributor of articles to various economic journals.

WORK IN PROGRESS: Methodology of Economics, for Cambridge University Press.

AVOCATIONAL INTERESTS: Music, archaeology.

BLAUSTEIN, Albert Paul 1921-
(Allen De Graeff)

PERSONAL: Born October 12, 1921, in New York, N.Y.; son of Karl Allen (a lawyer) and Rose (Brickman) Blaustein; married Phyllis Migden, December 21, 1948; children: Mark Allen, Eric Barry, Dana Beth. *Education:* University of Michigan, A.B., 1941; Columbia University, J.D., 1948. *Religion:* Jewish. *Home:* 415 Barby Lane, Cherry Hill, N.J. 08003. *Office:* School of Law, Rutgers University, Camden, N.J. 08102.

CAREER: Admitted to New York State Bar, 1948, and New Jersey State Bar, 1962; City News Bureau, Chicago, Ill., reporter and rewrite man, 1941-42; private law practice, New York City, 1948-50, 1952-55; New York Law School, New York City, assistant professor of law and law librarian, 1953-55; Rutgers University, School of Law, Camden, N.J., associate professor, 1955-59, professor of law, 1959—, law librarian, 1959-68. President, Human Rights Advocates International, Inc. (public service legal corporation). Counsel, Nierenberg, Zeif, & Weinstein (New York). Special studies consultant for survey of the legal profession, 1948-55; professional relations consultant, National Association of Claimants Compensation Attorneys (now National Trail Lawyers Association), 1955-57; consultant on desegregation to U.S. Commission on Civil Rights, 1962-63, School District of Philadelphia, 1963-64, and New Jersey Division on Civil Rights, 1971-72; law school and law library development consultant to various African and Asian universities, 1963—; constitutional consultant and legal advisor to governments and liberation movements in Africa, Asia, and South America, 1966—; chairman, Constitutions Associates; consultant to Commission on Age of Majority (Great Britain), 1967. Expert witness on legal aspects of population control for U.S. Senate commission, 1966. Chairman, American Committee for Asians in Africa; president, Human Rights International, Bangladesh-American Foundation, and Population Information Center, Inc., 1972-74; senior vice-president, English Simplified, Inc.; member of board of directors, National Committee on American Foreign Policy and Americans for a Safe Israel. Founder, Law Day, U.S.A. Member of board of managers, Jewish Community Center (Camden), 1966-71. *Military service:* U.S. Army, Judge Advocate General's Corps, 1942-46, 1950-52; fourteen years in reserves; became major; now retired.

MEMBER: International Bar Association, International Law Association, International Society for Military Law and Law of War, Commission for International Due Process of Law, International Association of Jewish Lawyers and Jurists (representative to United Nations, 1975—), International League for Human Rights, Anti-Slavery Society (Great Britain), Institute for Twenty-First Century Studies, World Peace through Law Center, Zero Population Growth (member of board of directors, 1968-75; representative to United Nations, 1974-75), Scribes (co-founder; member of board of directors, 1977—), Copyright Society of the United States of America, Association of American Law Schools, American Society of International Law, Association of the Bar of the City of New York, Camden County Bar Association. *Awards, honors:* Ford fellow, summer, 1962.

WRITINGS: (With Richard P. Tinkham and Charles O. Porter) *Public Relations for Bar Associations,* American Bar Association, 1952, 2nd revised edition, 1953; (with Charles T. Duncan and Porter) *The American Lawyer: A Summary of the Survey of the Legal Profession,* University of Chicago Press, 1954; (with C. C. Ferguson) *Desegration and the Law: The Meaning and Effect of the School Segregation Cases,* Rutgers University Press, 1957, 2nd revised edition, Vintage Books, 1962; *Manual on Foreign Legal Periodicals and Their Index,* Oceana, 1962; *Civil Rights U.S.A.: Public Schools in Cities in the North and West,* U.S. Commission on Civil Rights, 1962; *Civil Rights U.S.A. 1963: Public Schools in Camden and Environs,* U.S. Commission on Civil Rights, 1964; (with Robert L. Zangrando) *Civil Rights and the American Negro,* Trident, 1968, published as *Civil Rights and the Black American: A Documentary History,* Washington Square Press, 1970; (with Allan R. Koritzinsky) *Law and the Military Establishment,* Schools of Law, Rutgers University—Camden and University of Wisconsin—Madison, 1970; (with Robert A. Gorman) *Intellectual Property: Cases and Materials 1960-1970,* Schools of Law, Rutgers University—Camden and University of Pennsylvania, 1971, expanded edition published as *Intellectual Property: Cases and Materials, 1960-1971,* Foundation Press, 1971, supplement published as *Intellectual Property: Cases and Materials, 1972-1973,* Schools of Law, Rutgers University—Camden and University of Pennsylvania, 1973; *Housing Discrimination in New Jersey,* New Jersey Division on Civil Rights, 1972; (with Jordon J. Paust) *Human Rights and the Bangladesh Trials,* Editorial Correspondents, 1973; (with Paust) *The Arab Oil Weapon,* Oceana, 1977; (with Roy M. Mersky) *The First One Hundred Justices: Statistical Studies on the Supreme Court of the United States,* Archon Books, 1978.

Editor: *Fiction Goes to Court: Favorite Stories of Lawyers and the Law Selected by Famous Lawyers,* Holt, 1954, reprinted, Greenwood Press, 1977; (with Edith Fisch and Matthew Foner) *Lawyers in Industry,* Oceana, 1956; (with wife, Phyllis M. Blaustein) *Doctor's Choice: Sixteen Stories about Doctors and Medicine Selected by Famous Physicians,* Funk, 1957; (with Basil Davenport) *Deals with the Devil,* Dodd, 1958, published as *Twelve Stories from Deals with the Devil,* Ballantine, 1959; (with Davenport) *Invisible Men,* Ballantine, 1960; (with Harold Cunningham and James Kelly) *Civil Affairs Legislation: Cases and Materials,* Judge Advocate General's School, U.S. Army, 1960; *Fundamental Legal Documents of Communist China,* Fred B. Rothman, 1962; (under pseudonym Allen De Graeff) *Human and Other Beings,* P. Collier, 1963; (with Davenport) *Famous Monster Tales,* D. Van Nostrand, 1967; (with Iris J. Wildman) *Cataloging Manual for Use in Vietnamese Law Libraries,* Yale University Law School, 1971; (with Gisbert H. Flanz) *Constitutions of the Countries of the World,* fifteen volumes, Oceana, 1971—; (with Jessie L. Matthews and Adrienne de Vergie) *A Bibliography on the Common Law in French,* Oceana, 1974; (with son, Eric B. Blaustein) *Constitutions of Dependencies and Special Sovereignties,* six volumes, Oceana, 1975—; (with Jay A. Sigler and Benjamin R. Beebe) *Independence Documents of the World,* two volumes, Oceana, 1977; (with Donald N. Zillman and Edward F. Sherman) *The Military and American Society: Cases and Materials,* Matthew Bender, 1979. Also editor of *The Influence of the United States Constitution Abroad.*

Contributor: Kenneth Redden, editor, *So You Want to Be a Lawyer,* Bobbs-Merrill, 1951; Redden, editor, *Career Planning in the Law,* Bobbs-Merrill, 1951; Elliot E. Cheatam and others, editors, *Cases and Materials on the Legal Profession,* 2nd revised edition (Blaustein was not associated with earlier edition), Foundation Press, 1955; William M. Trumbull, editor, *Materials on the Lawyer's Professional Responsibility,* Prentice-Hall, 1957; Robert Scigliano, *The Courts: A Reader in the Judicial Process,* Little, Brown, 1962; William

R. Roalfe, general editor, *How to Find the Law and Legal Writing,* 6th edition (Blaustein was not associated with earlier editions), West Publishing, 1965, 7th edition, Morris L. Cohen, general editor, 1976; Vern Countryman and Ted Finman, editors, *The Lawyer in Modern Society,* Little, Brown, 1966; Theodore L. Becker, editor, *The Impact of Supreme Court Decisions,* Oxford University Press, 1969, 2nd edition, 1973; Leon Friedman and Fred I. Israel, editors, *The Justices of the United States Supreme Court, 1789-1969,* four volumes, Chelsea House, 1969; Charles A. Tesconi, Jr. and Emanuel Hurwitz, Jr., editors, *Education for Whom?: The Question of Equal Educational Opportunity,* Dodd, 1974; Richard B. Lillich, editor, *Economic Coercion and the New International Economic Order,* Michie Co., 1976; John Norton Moore, editor, *The Arab-Israeli Conflict,* Princeton University Press, 1977. Contributor of articles and book reviews to professional journals. Co-founder and first editor-in-chief, *Columbia Law School News,* 1947; editor, *American Bar Association Public Relations Bulletin,* 1953-54; co-editor, *Legal Malpractice Reporter,* 1976-77.

WORK IN PROGRESS: Overruling Opinions of the Supreme Court; Human Rights Reader; Human Rights Classified; Legal Research Annotated.

* * *

BLEVINS, Winfred (Ernest, Jr.) 1938-

PERSONAL: Born October 21, 1938, in Little Rock, Ark.; son of Winfred Ernest (an electrical engineer) and Hazel (Dickson) Blevins; married Patricia Ann Adams, August 20, 1959 (divorced, 1964); married Martha Gene Stearn, May 26, 1978; children: (first marriage) Pamela Jo, Adam. *Education:* Hannibal-LaGrange Junior College, A.A., 1958; University of Missouri, A.B. (with honors), 1960; Columbia University, A.M. (with honors), 1962; further graduate study at University of Wisconsin, 1961-62, and Purdue University, 1964-66; University of Southern California, certificate in music criticism, 1967. *Politics:* None. *Religion:* None. *Residence:* Malibu, Calif. *Agent:* Candace Lake, 1107 Glendon Ave., Los Angeles, Calif. 90024.

CAREER: Franklin College, Franklin, Ind., instructor in American literature, 1962-64; Purdue University, West Lafayette, Ind., instructor in English, 1964-66; *Los Angeles Times,* Los Angeles, Calif., music and stage reviewer, 1967-68; *Los Angeles Herald-Examiner,* Los Angeles, music and stage critic, 1968, entertainment editor, stage critic, and film critic, 1969-72; writer, 1972—. Los Angeles Drama Critics Circle, charter member, 1968-72, president, 1972. *Awards, honors:* Woodrow Wilson fellowship, 1960-61; Rockefeller Foundation Program for the Training of Music Critics fellow, 1966-68.

WRITINGS: Give Your Heart to the Hawks: A Tribute to the Mountain Men, Nash Publishing, 1973; *Charbonneau: Man of Two Dreams* (novel), Nash Publishing, 1975. Also author of several screenplays. Contributor of poems, stories, articles, and reviews to newspapers and magazines.

WORK IN PROGRESS: Half of the Sky, a novel on the life of Jedediah Smith; an untitled novel on a family in the time of the Indian Wars, for Houghton; an original mountaineering adventure screenplay.

SIDELIGHTS: Winfred Blevins told *CA:* "I want to take more and more time to fashion simpler, more eloquent, more mythic novels about the American Western experience, and to live long enough to see the best Western writers—Abbey, Bradford, Manfred, Guthrie, Stegner—get the credit they're due." *Avocational interests:* Mountaineering, river-running, trekking, travelling in the West.

BIOGRAPHICAL/CRITICAL SOURCES: Los Angeles Times, October 14, 1973.

* * *

BLODGETT, Richard 1940-

PERSONAL: Born August 24, 1940, in Bristol, Conn.; son of Harley E. and Doris (Dutton) Blodgett; married Carolyn S. Virgil, June 24, 1979. *Education:* Middlebury College, B.A., 1962. *Home:* 29 Charlton St., New York, N.Y. 10014. *Agent:* A. L. Hart, Fox Chase Agency, 419 East 57th St., New York, N.Y. 10022.

CAREER: Wall Street Journal, New York City, writer, 1962-66; *Business Week* (magazine), New York City, writer, 1966-68; Corporate Annual Reports, Inc., New York City, writer, 1968-70; free-lance writer, 1970—.

WRITINGS: (Contributor) *The Anatomy of Wall Street,* Lippincott, 1967; *The New York Times Book of Money,* Quadrangle, 1974; *Investing in Art,* Peter H. Wyden, 1975; *Conflicts of Interest: Union Pension Fund Asset Management,* Twentieth Century Fund, 1977; *Photographs: A Collector's Guide,* Ballantine, 1979.

WORK IN PROGRESS: The Merrill Lynch Family Guide to Financial Planning.

* * *

BLUE, Betty (Anne) 1922-

PERSONAL: Born September 16, 1922, in Danville, Ill.; daughter of Frank P. and Mary (Hayes) Unger; married Thomas Robert Blue, January 20, 1946; children: Robert Dean, John Richard. *Education:* Blackburn College, A.A., 1942; University of Illinois, B.A., 1944, M.A., 1946; Interamerican University, Ph.D., 1962. *Politics:* Republican. *Religion:* Methodist. *Home:* 1001 Lawton Circle, Magnolia, Ark. 71753. *Office:* Division of Language Arts, Southern Arkansas University, Magnolia, Ark. 71753.

CAREER: Southern Arkansas University, Magnolia, instructor, 1956-61, assistant professor, 1961-64, associate professor, 1964-68, professor of foreign languages, 1968—, chairman of department, 1964—, chairman of Division of Language Arts, 1976—. Teacher of Spanish course for children, "Pedro Dice," KTVE-TV, El Dorado, Ark. Member, Arkansas Governor's Commission on Crime and Law Enforcement, 1967—; secretary-treasurer, Southern Criminal Justice Planning Council, 1970—; member of national Fulbright scholarship to Spain and Portugal selection committee, 1975-76. *Member:* American Association of Teachers of Spanish and Portuguese, National Education Association, American Association of University Women, National Federation of Republican Women, South Central Modern Language Association, Arkansas Association of Foreign Language Teachers (former vice-president), Arkansas Education Association, Sigma Delta Pi. *Awards, honors:* Fulbright grant to University of Valladolid, 1966; Durango State University scholar, 1976; selected for Prentice-Hall Hall of Fame, 1979, for *Authentic Mexican Cooking.*

WRITINGS: Fundamentals of Teaching a Foreign Language, Whitehall, 1970; *Authentic Mexican Cooking,* Prentice-Hall, 1977; *Authentic Spanish Cooking,* Prentice-Hall, in press.

WORK IN PROGRESS: Hispanic Civilization: Spain; Hispanic Civilization: Latin America; Cooking with Friends.

SIDELIGHTS: Betty Blue writes: "I have often been asked why as a college professor and professional person, I have switched my writing to cookbooks. However, my current writing is not that alien to my chosen field. Having lived with Mexican families off and on over a period of sixteen years and collecting wonderful recipes, I decided to attempt to correct the popular misconception that Mexicans live on tacos, chalupas, tortillas and beans. Although there is a long chapter in *Authentic Mexican Cooking* for preparing this type of food, most of the book is devoted to recipes for soups, casseroles, sea food, meat, poultry, egg dishes, vegetables, salads and desserts.

"The original recipes were written in Spanish and in the metric system, and a word for word translation was impossible. I practically gave up sleeping for writing and rewriting. Perhaps, in my small way, I have been able to draw a different picture of our wonderful neighbors south of the border through an understanding of the cuisine of their country. This has also been my purpose for writing *Authentic Spanish Cooking*."

AVOCATIONAL INTERESTS: Golf, coin collecting, and cooking.

* * *

BLUESTONE, George 1928-

PERSONAL: Born August 25, 1928, in Brooklyn, N.Y.; son of Samuel and Becky Bluestone; married Natalie Suzanne Harris, August 1, 1954. *Education:* Harvard University, B.A. (magna cum laude), 1949; University of Iowa, M.F.A., 1951; Johns Hopkins University, Ph.D., 1956. *Home:* 90 Babcock St., Brookline, Mass. 02146. *Office:* School of Public Communication, Boston University, 640 Commonwealth Ave., Boston, Mass. 02215.

CAREER: University of Washington, Seattle, assistant professor, 1957-61, associate professor of American literature and creative writing, 1962-66; film writer and producer in London, England, 1967-72; Boston University, Boston, Mass., professor of film, 1972—. *Member:* Modern Language Association of America, American Association of University Professors, Writers Guild of America, Phi Beta Kappa. *Awards, honors: Atlantic Monthly* first prize, 1952; Emily Clark Balch Prize from *Virginia Quarterly Review,* 1961.

WRITINGS: Novels into Film, Johns Hopkins Press, 1957; *The Private World of Cully Powers,* Doubleday, 1960; *The Send-Off,* Secker & Warburg, 1969. Also author and producer of a half hour film version of Herman Melville's *Bartleby,* 1961; other films include "The American Dream," 1963, "The Monkey and the Fox," 1965, "The Walking Stick," 1970, and "The Agency," 1975. Contributor of articles, reviews, stories, and poems to literary journals and to *Atlantic, Film Culture, Film Quarterly,* and *Coastlines.*

WORK IN PROGRESS: A novel, tentatively entitled *The Hyphenated House;* two screenplays, "Steam-Pipe" and "Elijah and the Rebels."

SIDELIGHTS: George Bluestone told *CA:* "I think the main task for America's cunning apostates is to discover a meaningful sense of the future. Futopias and Utopias are both out of style." *Avocational interests:* Collecting owl artifacts—photographs, drawings, and ceramics.

* * *

BLYTH, Alan 1929-

PERSONAL: Born July 27, 1929, in London, England; married Ursula Zumloh. *Education:* Pembroke College, Oxford, M.A., 1951. *Home:* 11 Boundary Rd., London NW8 0HE, England. *Agent:* A. M. Heath & Co. Ltd., 40-42 William IV St., London WC2N 4DD, England. *Office: Daily Telegraph,* 135 Fleet St., London, England.

CAREER: Encyclopedia Britannica, London, England, subeditor, 1951-53; Fabian Society, London, bookshop manager, 1953-56; feature editor and writer in London, 1956-63; *Times,* London, music critic, 1963-76; *Daily Telegraph,* London, music critic, 1976—. Music editor for *Encyclopedia Britannica,* 1971-73. *Member:* Critics' Circle (chairman of music section, 1971-74).

WRITINGS: The Enjoyment of Opera, Oxford University Press, 1969; *Colin Davis: A Short Biography,* Ian Allan, 1972; *Janet Baker,* Ian Allan, 1973; (contributor of section on vocal music) *New Companion to Music,* Gollancz, 1978; (editor) *Opera on Record,* Hutchinson, 1979; *Wagner's "Ring": An Introduction,* Hutchinson, 1980; *Remembering Britten,* Hutchinson, 1980. Also contributor to *Grove's Dictionary,* 1980. Contributor and interviewer, *Gramophone,* 1966—. Associate editor, *Opera,* 1969—.

WORK IN PROGRESS: Editing *More Opera on Record,* for Hutchinson.

AVOCATIONAL INTERESTS: History of the recorded voice, music of Verdi and Wagner, gardening, wine.

* * *

BLYTHE, (William) LeGette 1900-

PERSONAL: Born April 24, 1900, in Huntersville, N.C.; son of William Brevard and Hattye (Jackson) Blythe; married Esther Farmer, May 31, 1926; children: William Brevard, Samuel LeGette, Esther Lovelace Blythe Pugh. *Education:* University of North Carolina, B.A., 1921. *Politics:* Democrat. *Religion:* Presbyterian. *Home:* College St., Huntersville, N.C. 28078.

CAREER: Public school teacher in Greensboro, N.C., 1921-22; *Charlotte News,* Charlotte, N.C., reporter, 1922-25; *New York Evening Post* and other newspapers, New York, N.Y., reporter, 1925; *Mecklenburg Times,* Charlotte, editor, 1926-27; *Charlotte Observer,* Charlotte, reporter, columnist, editorial writer, feature writer, and literary editor, 1927-50; full-time writer, 1950—; University of North Carolina at Charlotte, writer-in-residence, 1967—. Member of Mayflower Award Jury, 1938, 1947, and 1952; member of governor's commission on library resources, 1964; chairman of North Carolina Writers Conference, 1965. Chairman of President Andrew Johnson Sesquicentennial Commission, 1958; member of Mecklenburg County Economic Development Commission, 1966—, and Huntersville Planning and Zoning Commission, 1967—; member of Charlotte Bicentennial Committee, 1968, and Charlotte-Mecklenburg Bicentennial Committee, 1975-76. Commissioner of general assembly, Presbyterian Church of the United States, 1952; Mecklenburg Presbytery, moderator, 1955-56, member of centennial commission, 1968; Presbyterian Synod of North Carolina, member of sesquicentennial observance committee, 1963, member of permanent commission on historical matters, 1967—. Member of board of directors, North Carolina Boys Home, 1971—.

MEMBER: North Carolina State Literary and Historical Association, North Carolina Society for the Preservation of Antiquities, North Carolina Folklore Society, Mecklenburg Historical Association (director), Phi Beta Kappa, Omega Delta, Sigma Upsilon, Delta Tau Delta, Huntersville Lions Club. *Awards, honors:* Litt.D., Davidson College, 1950; Mayflower Society Awards, 1953 and 1961, for the best books by a North Carolinian; Huntersville Man of the Year Award, 1955; Cannon Cup for historical research, 1961; LL.D., University of North Carolina, 1969.

WRITINGS: Marshall Ney: A Dual Life, Stackpole, 1937; *Alexandriana,* Stackpole, 1940; *Bold Galilean,* University of North Carolina Press, 1948; *William Henry Belk: Merchant of the South,* University of North Carolina Press, 1950; *A Tear for Judas,* Bobbs-Merrill, 1951; (with Mary Martin Sloop) *Miracle in the Hills,* McGraw, 1953; *James W. Davis: North Carolina Surgeon,* Heritage House, 1956; *The Crown Tree,* John Knox, 1957; (with Mary Wilson Gee) *Yes, Ma'am, Miss Gee,* Heritage House, 1957; (with Lucy Morgan) *Gift from the Hills,* Bobbs-Merrill, 1958; *Call Down the Storm,* Holt, 1958.

(With Mabel Wolfe Wheaton) *Thomas Wolfe and His Family,* Doubleday, 1961; *Hear Me, Pilate!,* Holt, 1961; (with Charles Brockmann) *Hornets' Nest: The Story of Charlotte and Mecklenburg County,* McNally & Loftin, 1961; (with Septima Poinsette Clark) *Echo in My Soul,* Dutton, 1962; *Mountain Doctor,* Morrow, 1964; *Man on Fire,* Funk, 1964; *Robert Lee Stowe: Pioneer in Textiles,* McNally & Loftin, 1965; *38th Evac,* McNally & Loftin, 1966; *Brothers of Vengeance,* Morrow, 1969; *Meet Julius Abernethy: Trader and Philanthropist,* Loftin, 1970; *When Was Jesus Born?,* Loftin, 1974; *The Stableboy Who Stayed at Bethlehem,* Loftin, 1974; *Looking to the One Beckoning Star,* Thomas Williams, 1979. Also author of a play, "The Chatham Rabbit," first produced in Chapel Hill, N.C., April 29, 1921.

Symphonic dramas: "Shout Freedom!," first produced in Charlotte, N.C., May, 1948; *Voice in the Wilderness* (first produced in Charlotte, 1955), Loftin, 1955; *The Hornet's Nest* (first produced in Charlotte, June, 1968), McNally & Loftin, 1968; "First in Freedom," first produced in Charlotte, 1975; "Thunder over Carolina," first produced in Charlotte, 1976. Contributor of articles, reviews, and short stories to magazines and newspapers.

WORK IN PROGRESS: Biblical novels; a series of children's books on biblical characters.

SIDELIGHTS: A reviewer in *Best Sellers* calls LeGette Blythe's *Brothers of Vengeance* "a story of early Christianity which is authentic, gripping and vibrant with life. . . . One can feel the intensity of modern life in modern Israel and if it is any reflection of past history, this novel has caught it. . . . Mr. Blythe . . . is long overdue for national fame as a storyteller who can spin a fascinating tale."

Some of Blythe's books have been translated into Spanish, French, German, Japanese, Arabic, Bengali, Portuguese, and Marathi.

AVOCATIONAL INTERESTS: Sports, gardening.

BIOGRAPHICAL/CRITICAL SOURCES: Archibald Henderson, *North Carolina: The Old North State and the New,* Lewis, 1941; Frederick H. Kock, *Carolina Folk Plays,* Henry Holt, 1941; Bernadette Hoyle, *Tar Heel Writers I Know,* Blair, 1956; *Best Sellers,* August 1, 1969.

* * *

BOLLES, Richard Nelson 1927-

PERSONAL: Surname is pronounced like "bowls"; born March 19, 1927, in Milwaukee, Wis.; son of Donald Clinton and Frances (Fifield) Bolles; married Janet Price, December 30, 1949 (divorced, 1971); married Geralyn Nase, February 17, 1971 (divorced, 1978); children: (first marriage) Stephen, Mark, Gary, Sharon. *Education:* Attended Massachusetts Institute of Technology, 1946-48; Harvard University, B.A. (cum laude), 1950; General Theological Seminary, New York, N.Y., S.T.M., 1957. *Residence:* San Francisco, Calif. *Office address:* National Career Development Project, United Ministries in Education, P.O. Box 379, Walnut Creek, Calif. 94596.

CAREER: Rector of Episcopalian church in Passaic, N.J., 1958-66; Grace Cathedral, San Francisco, Calif., canon pastor, 1966-68; United Ministries in Education, San Francisco, Western regional secretary, 1968—, director of National Career Development Project, 1974—. *Military service:* U.S. Navy, 1945-46. *Member:* American Personnel and Guidance Association, American Society of Training Directors, Mensa.

WRITINGS—All published by Ten Speed Press: *What Color Is Your Parachute?: A Practical Manual for Job-Hunters and Career-Changers,* 1972, 5th revised edition, 1979; (with John Crystal) *Where Do I Go from Here with My Life?,* 1974; *Quick Job-Hunting Map,* 1975; *Tea Leaves: A New Look at Resumes,* 1977; *The Three Boxes of Life and How to Get Out of Them,* 1978. Editor, *Newsletter about Higher Education.*

SIDELIGHTS: Richard Bolles, author of the highly-acclaimed job-hunting manual, *What Color Is Your Parachute?,* told *CA* that he is "glad to be a best-selling author. It's nice to have people recognize that you know something about a helpful subject. But I get my real kicks from other areas. I love the act of writing, in and of itself, because of my philosophy about writing: namely, if I think a thought, I must write it—unless it is mean, or is more self-revelatory than I can bear. Not for me to sit at the typewriter and wait for the right sentence to come. If I think it, I write it. That makes writing fun.

"Also fun for me is the unique freedom that Phil Wood, owner of Ten Speed Press, gives to me: that my first draft can be (and usually is) my last, that no editor lays a hand upon my manuscripts except for proof-reading and spelling, that I have the oversight of the layout of the whole book (in tandem with Bev Anderson, my incredibly talented friend and layout artist), *and* can work with her on each page of the book so that it looks the way I want it to look, *and* that economics are not the key consideration in the layout, but only whether or not we have produced a book as good to look at as it is to read (appealing to both the right and the left sides of the brain). I am sure he gives me this kind of freedom as his compliment to my judgment and my brain; but since there are many other such authors, who yet are not granted such freedom, it is also a tribute to the kind of man he is. As the trade journals are full of adversary relationships between author and publisher, I am glad to be able to contribute a more positive model to the literature. Apparently readers enjoy the fruits thereof: *What Color Is Your Parachute?* sells as many as 64,000 copies a month, and does this sort of thing year in and year out.

"I am certainly awed, that when you try to do a thing (like writing) in the manner you enjoy the most, rather than approaching it as a drudgery, it works. But then, that's what I preach in all my books; so it's nice that my life is consistent with the advice I give others."

BIOGRAPHICAL/CRITICAL SOURCES: Money, May, 1978.

* * *

BOLTON, Carole 1926-

PERSONAL: Born January 10, 1926, in Uniontown, Pa.; daughter of Harry M. and Leone (Shomo) Roberts; married

John J. Bolton, February 1, 1947; children: Timothy Duke, John Christopher. *Education:* Attended Ramsey Streett School of Acting, Baltimore, Md., for three years. *Politics:* Democrat. *Religion:* "Former Catholic—now I do not go to church." *Residence:* Montville, Me. *Address:* Box 137, Route 1, Freedom, Me. 04941.

CAREER: William Morrow & Co., Inc., New York City, N.Y., 1958-64, began as a secretary, became assistant editor of children's books; Meredith Press, New York City, N.Y., assistant editor of children's books, 1964-67; Lothrop, Lee & Shepard Co., New York City, associate editor of children's books, 1967-70; Thomas Nelson, Inc., New York City, associate editor of children's books, 1972-79; full-time writer, 1979—. Has acted with little theatre groups. *Member:* Authors Guild, Authors League of America.

WRITINGS—Juvenile; published by Morrow, except as indicated: *Christy,* 1960; *The Callahan Girls,* 1961; *Reunion in December,* 1962; *The Stage Is Set,* 1963; *The Dark Rosaleen,* 1964; *Never Jam Today* (Junior Literary Guild selection), Atheneum, 1971; *The Search of Mary Katherine Mulloy* (Junior Literary Guild selection), Elsevier-Nelson, 1974; *Little Girl Lost,* Elsevier-Nelson, 1980.

SIDELIGHTS: On the subject of what advice she would give to aspiring young writers, Carole Bolton comments: "If a young person were to ask me whether or not he or she should become a writer, I think my answer would be, 'not unless you can't help yourself.' Many times I have said I was going to give the whole thing up, but I soon find myself back at my desk again. Right now, I feel I am at a turning point. This year, for the first time, I am giving myself a chance to write full-time, and I hope something better than I have done before will be the result."

* * *

BOND, Horace Mann 1904-1972

PERSONAL: Born November 8, 1904, in Nashville, Tenn.; died December 21, 1972, in Atlanta, Ga.; son of James and Jane (Browne) Bond; married Julia Agnes Washington, 1929; children: Jane, Horace Julian, James. *Education:* Lincoln University (Pa.), A.B., 1923; University of Chicago, M.A., 1926, Ph.D., 1936. *Office:* Atlanta University, 223 Chestnut St. S.W., Atlanta, Ga.

CAREER: Colored Agricultural and Normal School (now Langston University), Langston, Okla., professor and head of department of education, 1924-27; State Normal School for Colored Students (now Alabama State University), Montgomery, Ala., director of department of extension, 1927-28; Fisk University, Nashville, Tenn., instructor, 1928-29, assistant professor of social science, 1932-34; Dillard University, New Orleans, La., dean, 1934-37; Fisk University, professor of education and head of department, 1937-39; Fort Valley State College, Fort Valley, Ga., president, 1939-45; Lincoln University, Lincoln University, Pa., president, 1945-57; Atlanta University, Atlanta, Ga., dean of school of education, 1957-66, director of Bureau of Educational and Social Research, 1966-71. Research assistant, Julius Rosenwald Fund, 1934-37. Lecturer, Tuskegee Normal and Industrial Institute (now Tuskegee Institute), 1929, and Garrett Biblical Institute (now Garrett-Evangelical Theological Seminary), 1943. Member, President's Committee on Higher Education, University of Ghana Committee, and International Congress of Africanists permanent council, beginning 1962. *Military service:* Joint Army and Navy Command. *Member:* American Teachers Association (life member), American Association of School Administrators, National Society for the Study of Education, African Studies Association, American Educational Research Association, American Society of African Culture (president, 1958-63; chairman of board, 1963-72), Southern Sociological Society, Kappa Alpha Psi. *Awards, honors:* American Educational Research Award, 1939, for *Negro Education in Alabama: A Study in Cotton and Steel;* Association for the Study of Negro History Award, 1943; LL.D. from Lincoln University (Pa.), 1941, and Temple University, 1955.

WRITINGS: Education of the Negro in American Social Order, Prentice-Hall, 1934, revised edition, Octagon, 1966; *Negro Education in Alabama: A Study in Cotton and Steel,* Associated Publishers, 1939, reprinted, Octagon, 1969; *Education for Production,* University of Georgia Press, 1944; *The Search for Talent,* Harvard University Press, 1959; *Black American Scholars: A Study of Their Beginnings,* Balamp, 1972; *Education for Freedom: A History of Lincoln University, Pennsylvania,* Lincoln University, 1976. Contributor to professional magazines and encyclopedic works.

SIDELIGHTS: The Horace Mann Bond Center for Equal Education of the University of Massachusetts—Amherst was established in 1979 to serve as a clearinghouse for information on racial and other social factors related to educational quality. The Center houses Bond's papers, correspondence, and unpublished manuscripts.

BIOGRAPHICAL/CRITICAL SOURCES: Roger M. Williams, *The Bonds: An American Family,* Atheneum, 1971; *New York Times,* October 24, 1979.†

* * *

BONINGTON, Christian (John Storey) 1934-

PERSONAL: Born August 6, 1934, in London, England; son of Charles (a journalist) and Helen (Storey) Bonington; married Muriel Wendy Marchant (an illustrator), May 26, 1962; children: Daniel, Rupert. *Education:* Attended Royal Military Academy, Sandhurst, 1954-56. *Religion:* Agnostic. *Home and office:* Badger Hill, Hesket Newmarket, Wigton, Cumbria, England. *Agent:* John Farquharson Ltd., 15 Red Lion Sq., London WC1R 4QW, England.

CAREER: British Army, troop commander of Royal Tank Regiment, 1956-58, instructor in Army Outward Bound School, 1958-61; Unilever, London, England, management trainee, 1962; free-lance writer, photographer, and mountaineer, 1962—. Member of team making first descent of Blue Nile, 1968; leader of Annapurna South Face Expedition, 1970,British Everest Expedition, 1972, and Everest South West Face Expedition, 1975. *Member:* Alpine Climbing Group (president, 1964-66), Climbers Club, Alpine Club, Army and Navy Club. *Awards, honors:* Royal Geographic Society Founders Medal, 1974; Commander, Order of the British Empire, 1976.

WRITINGS: I Chose to Climb, Doubleday, 1966; *Annapurna South Face,* McGraw, 1970; *The Next Horizon,* Gollancz, 1972; *The Ultimate Challenge: The Hardest Way up the Highest Mountain in the World,* Stein & Day, 1973 (published in England as *Everest South West Face,* Hodder & Stoughton, 1973); *Everest the Hard Way,* Random House, 1977.

SIDELIGHTS: In his review of Christian Bonington's *The Next Horizon,* Robin James of *Books and Bookmen* notes that "the author is as energetic in his writing as he is in his life. . . . Gripped by the danger of some climb or expedition, I found that we were either at the top of the mountain or at the end of the journey while my mind was still catching mental breath. Perhaps this is a good thing . . . [for, while] I am not inclined to rush the south col of Box Hill next weekend, . . . I have now a stronger (and more down to earth) respect for those who will, and certainly for those, like Bonington, aiming for higher things. . . . This is not a totally absorbing book, but one which says far more for the men than it does for the mountains."

Robin Campbell of the *Spectator* is suspicious of the true motivation behind the writing of *The Ultimate Challenge*. In short, he criticizes Bonington for negotiating the book, film, and television rights to the story of the Everest expedition *prior to* the actual event. Nevertheless, Campbell admits, Bonington "does not completely gloss over the Janus-faced nature of modern Greater Mountaineering. It is made clear to the reader . . . that not only mountaineering values are involved. However, much is still left unsaid. For example, nowhere is the *quality* of the route discussed—a factor considered important in mountaineering circles—and the quality of the south-west face is exceedingly low. . . . Why then was it chosen? . . . In short, because of its news value. The standards which must be applied to [this book] are therefore those which apply to any contemporary adventure thriller. How has Bonington coped with plot, characterization, tempo, etc., bearing in mind that the expedition was a total failure due to impossible weather conditions? Pretty well, under the circumstances. The story has a good deal of human interest. . . . Narrative responsibility shifts occasionally to other members. . . . The Sherpas provide useful light relief. . . . Those essential ingredients of the modern thriller, sex and violence, are more difficult. However, Bonington does his best. . . . All in all, [the result] is not unworthy of, say, Alister MacLean."

Finally, commenting on *Everest the Hard Way*, John Naughton of the *Times Literary Supplement* contends that "this book will confirm the worst suspicions of those who believe that all mountaineers are crazy. Everest is not exactly an easy climb at the best of times; but to attempt an ascent by what is generally acknowledged to be the most difficult route . . . is to give to fortune rather more hostages than she has a right to expect. . . . Chris Bonington is acutely aware of this, and the cautious, self-effacing, almost apologetic, tone of [*Everest the Hard Way*] is the result. . . . [It] is an admirable book."

BIOGRAPHICAL/CRITICAL SOURCES: Books and Bookmen, August, 1973; *Spectator*, September 29, 1973; *New York Times Book Review*, April 17, 1977; *Times Literary Supplement*, October 21, 1977.

* * *

BONNEY, Lorraine G(agnon) 1922-

PERSONAL: Born November 28, 1922, in Edmonton, Alberta, Canada; daughter of Napoleon and Marie (Schlereth) Gagnon; married Orrin H. Bonney (a lawyer), June 5, 1955 (died June 18, 1979). *Education:* University of Alberta, B.A., 1948; University of Houston, graduate study, 1972. *Politics:* Democrat. *Home:* 625 East 14th St., Houston, Tex. 77008; and P.O. Box 15, Kelly, Wyo. 83011 (summer).

CAREER: Free-lance writer. *Member:* American Society of Journalists and Authors, Outdoor Writers Association of America, American Alpine Club, Sierra Club, Scribblers Club (president, 1965). *Awards, honors:* Wyoming Historical Society Book Awards, 1965, for *Guide to the Wyoming Mountains and Wilderness Areas*, 1970, for *Battle Drums and Geysers*, and 1979, for *Field Book: Big Horn Range;* Outdoor Writers Association of America category award, 1968-69, for *Field Book: The Wind River Range*.

WRITINGS—All with husband, Orrin H. Bonney: *Guide to the Wyoming Mountains and Wilderness Areas* (also see below), Sage Books, 1960, 3rd revised edition, Swallow Press, 1977; *Bonney's Guide: Jackson's Hole and Grand Teton National Park*, Orrin H. Bonney, 1961, published as *Bonney's Guide: Grand Teton National Park and Jackson's Hole*, 1966, revised edition, 1972; *Field Book: The Wind River Range* (includes material from *Guide to the Wyoming Mountains and Wilderness Areas*), Sage Books, 1962, 3rd revised edition, Swallow Press, 1977; *Field Book: The Absaroka Range, Yellowstone Park* (includes material from *Guide to the Wyoming Mountains and Wilderness Areas*), Sage Books, 1963, 2nd revised edition, Swallow Press, 1977; *The Teton Range and Gros Ventre Range: The Complete Guide to All Climbing Routes and Back Country* (includes material from *Guide to the Wyoming Mountains and Wilderness Areas*), Sage Books, 1963, 2nd revised edition, Swallow Press, 1977; (editor) *Battle Drums and Geysers: The Life and Journals of Lt. Gustavus Cheyney Doane, Soldier and Explorer of the Yellowstone and Snake River Regions*, Sage Books, 1970, published in three volumes, Orrin H. Bonney, 1978, Volume I: *Lt. Gustavus C. Doane: His Life and Remarkable Military Career*, Volume II: *Exploration of Yellowstone Park: Lt. Doane's Yellowstone Journal*, Volume III: *Lt. G. C. Doane's Snake River Journal of 1876; Field Book: Big Horn Range*, Swallow Press, 1977. Contributor to magazines and newspapers, including *Popular Science*, *American Weekly*, *True West*, *American West*, *Sierra Club Bulletin*, and *Houston Chronicle*.

WORK IN PROGRESS: Beginnings of Teton Climbing; Guide to Big Thicket.

AVOCATIONAL INTERESTS: Photography, travel.

* * *

BOOKCHIN, Murray 1921-
(Lewis Herber)

PERSONAL: Born January 14, 1921, in New York, N.Y.; son of Nathan and Rose Bookchin; children: one daughter, one son. *Home:* 118 Hayward St., Burlington, Vt. 05401.

CAREER: Free-lance writer; lecturer. Professor, Ramapo College of New Jersey. Director, Institute for Social Ecology, Goddard College, Plainfield, Vt.

WRITINGS: (Under pseudonym Lewis Herber) *Our Synthetic Environment*, Knopf, 1962, revised edition (under real name), Harper, 1974; (under pseudonym Lewis Herber) *Crises in Our Cities*, Prentice-Hall, 1965; (with others) *Hip Culture: Six Essays on Its Revolutionary Potential*, Times Change Press, 1971; *Post-Scarcity Anarchism*, Ramparts, 1971; *Spanish Anarchists*, Harper, 1978. Former associate editor, *Contemporary Issues;* editor, *Radiation Information*.

WORK IN PROGRESS: Ecology of Freedom; Toward an Ecological Society, for Black Rose Books; *Urbanization without Cities*, for Sierra Club Books.

SIDELIGHTS: An enthusiastic student of the biological and social sciences as well as natural history, Murray Bookchin spends much of his free time in wilderness areas.

BIOGRAPHICAL/CRITICAL SOURCES: Nation, March 6, 1972; *Dissent*, summer, 1972; *Village Voice*, September 6, 1973; *Books & Bookmen*, June, 1974; *Times Literary Supplement*, June 21, 1974; *Science & Society*, summer, 1975.

* * *

BOORSTIN, Daniel J(oseph) 1914-

PERSONAL: Born October 1, 1914, in Atlanta, Ga.; son of

Samuel A. (an attorney) and Dora (Olsan) Boorstin; married Ruth Carolyn Frankel, April 9, 1941; children: Paul, Jonathan, David. *Education:* Harvard University, B.A. (summa cum laude), 1934; Oxford University, Balliol College (Rhodes Scholar), B.A. (first class honors), 1936, B.C.L. (first class honors), 1937; Yale University (Sterling fellow), J.S.D., 1940. *Politics:* Independent. *Religion:* Jewish. *Home:* 3541 Ordway St. N.W., Washington, D.C. 20016. *Office:* Library of Congress, Washington, D.C. 20540.

CAREER: Admitted as barrister-at-law, Inner Temple, London, England, 1937; admitted to the Massachusetts Bar, 1942; Harvard University, Cambridge, Mass., history instructor, 1939-42; Office of Lend-Lease Administration, Washington, D.C., senior attorney, 1942; Swarthmore College, Swarthmore, Pa., assistant professor of history, 1942-44; University of Chicago, Chicago, Ill., 1944-69, began as assistant professor, Preston and Sterling Morton Distinguished Professor of History, 1956-69; Smithsonian Institution, Washington, D.C., director of National Museum of History and Technology, 1969-73, senior historian, 1973-75; appointed Librarian of Congress, 1975—. Fulbright visiting lecturer at University of Rome, 1950-51, and Kyoto University, 1957; lecturer for U.S. Department of State in Turkey, Iran, Nepal, India, and Ceylon, 1959-60. First occupant of newly established chair of American history at the Sorbonne, Paris, 1961-62; fellow of Trinity College, and Pitt Professor of American History and Institutions at Cambridge University, 1964-65; Shelby and Kathryn Cullom Davis Lecturer, Graduate Institute of International Studies, Geneva, Switzerland, 1973-74.

MEMBER: American Studies Association (president, 1969-70), American Historical Association, American Antiquarian Society, Authors Guild, National Press Club, Association of Southern History, International House of Japan, Phi Beta Kappa, Quadrangle Club (Chicago), Elizabethan Club (Yale University), Reform Club (London), Cosmos Club (Washington, D.C.). *Awards, honors:* Bancroft Prize, 1959, for *The Americans: The Colonial Experience;* Friends of American Literature Prize, 1959; Francis Parkman Medal of American Society of Historians, 1966, and Patron Saints award of Society of Midland Authors, 1966, both for *The Americans: The National Experience;* Dexter Prize and Pulitzer Prize for history, 1974, both for *The Americans: The Democratic Experience;* D.Litt. from Cambridge University, 1968.

WRITINGS: The Mysterious Science of the Law, Harvard University Press, 1941, reprinted, Peter Smith, 1973; *Delaware Cases, 1792-1830,* three volumes, West, 1943; *The Lost World of Thomas Jefferson,* Holt, 1948; *The Genius of American Politics,* University of Chicago Press, 1952; *The Americans: The Colonial Experience,* Random House, 1958; *America and the Image of Europe,* Meridian, 1959; (editor) *A Lady's Life in the Rocky Mountains,* University of Oklahoma Press, 1960; *The Image: What Happened to the American Dream,* Atheneum, 1961, paperback edition published as *The Image: A Guide to Pseudo-Events in America,* Harper, 1964; *The Americans: The National Experience,* Random House, 1965; (editor) *American Primer,* two volumes, University of Chicago Press, 1966; *Landmark History of the American People,* Random House, Volume I: *From Plymouth to Appomattox,* 1968, Volume II: *From Appomattox to the Moon,* 1970; *The Decline of Radicalism: Reflections of America Today,* Random House, 1969; *The Sociology of the Absurd,* Simon & Schuster, 1970; (editor) *American Civilization,* McGraw, 1972; *The Americans: The Democratic Experience,* Random House, 1973; *Democracy and Its Discontents: Reflections on Everyday America,* Random House, 1974; *The Exploring Spirit: America and the World, Then and Now,* Random House, 1976; (editor) *America in Two Centuries: An Inventory,* Arno, 1976; *Visiting Our Past: America's Historylands,* National Geographic Society, 1977; *The Republic of Technology,* Harper, 1978. Editor of the 25-volume *History of American Civilization,* University of Chicago Press. Former editor of American history for *Encyclopaedia Britannica.* Contributor to *Harper's, Newsweek, U.S. News & World Report, New York Times Book Review, Fortune, Esquire,* and *Look.*

SIDELIGHTS: Mary Anne Dolan describes Daniel Boorstin as "an anti-historian historian, a lawyer-in-academe.... A proud conservative in the primarily liberal world of American scholars, one who is unafraid of materialism and in fact builds his view of democracy around entrepreneurs and inventions.... [He] unabashedly calls television watching a prerequisite for modern-day literacy.... [Boorstin] is one of those rare intellectuals, whose opinions—sometimes outrageous, nearly always against the grain—are carried to classrooms and cocktail parties alike. And whether from friend or enemy, an opinion of Daniel Boorstin is bound to be emphatic."

As if to illustrate this, in his review of *The Decline of Radicalism: Reflections of America Today,* Norman Birnbaum calls the book "garrulous and empty, pompous and trivial, self-congratulatory and unashamed.... [It] is a painful record of the decomposition of critical intelligence.... Not without a patronizing tone toward the social sciences, Boorstin denies that there is inauthenticity at all [in the current 'consumption community']; and with sovereign contempt for three generations of social criticism in this country, praises American capitalism not for producing goods but for shaping citizens." Boorstin "does call for new political measures to record the votes of the disintegrated majority," apparently out of his own "revulsion from some of the newer forms of politics: minority group movements, direct attacks on the functioning of bureaucracies, [and] demonstrations."

Birnbaum continues: "The book appears to have been put together to justify the publication of the final chapter.... In it, we are given a conceptual analysis of the difference between 'disagreement' and 'dissent.' ... An intelligent conservative could tell us much.... What we have here, however, is ... liberalism reduced not to its assumptions but to a set of attitudes—defensive and rigidified."

Continuing in that vein, William McPherson writes: "What Dr. Boorstin seems to be saying is that disagreement is acceptable as long as those who disagree are few, generally polite, and relatively powerless in relation to ... [the] 'silent majority'; unacceptable when they are many, highly visible, occasionally rude, and powerful." With regard to the author himself, McPherson writes: "Every little victory for the sort of intellectual violence Boorstin inflicts on rational discourse is a very sad sort of victory indeed. It is one of the grotesque ironies in the world around us that Dr. Boorstin's occasionally reasonable voice is drowned out by his own invective, just as the cries of the Crazies, the Mad Dogs, and the Yippies drown out the more sober sounds of legitimate protest."

Jack Newfield comments: "There is a growing library of literature by respected academic liberals who seem to celebrate their intellectual menopause by joining the war on puberty and attacking the New Left.... That [Daniel] Boorstin should contribute to this trend ... is a depressing development, because he has always struck me as an original and trenchant interpreter of the image-making role of the mass media, and of the American colonial experience."

Kenneth S. Lynn is more ambivalent about Boorstin. While he admits "*The Americans* . . . displays an immense zest for historical research, an analytical skill which is often brilliant, and a supple literary style," he also writes: "What robs these volumes of their potential greatness, incredibly vulgarizes their argument at every turn, is the author's obsessive desire to turn the education of Daniel Boorstin into an American history textbook. . . . The philosophical bias . . . is nothing less than appalling. What makes it so is not the fact that Boorstin rejects Marxist ideas but that he rejects *all* logical systems of thought."

Lynn continues: "Boorstin's boosterism is as nauseating as it is incredible. Yet for all the vulgarity, the blatant myth-making, and the philistine enthusiasms, it is also true that he has produced a path-breaking and important book. Boorstin has a wonderful instinct for institutions in American life that have been left unexplored by other historians, and he approaches those institutions not in a traditional, formalistic way but in terms of the problems that people have to solve in order to subdue and settle a new country. . . . In such analyses as these [he] gives us glimpses of the truly eminent historian he still has time to become."

BIOGRAPHICAL/CRITICAL SOURCES: Kenyon Review, January, 1966; *Book Week,* March 5, 1967; *Best Sellers,* November 1, 1968; *Children's Book World,* November 3, 1968; *New York Times Book Review,* November 24, 1968; M. Cunliffe and R. Winks, editors, *Pastmasters,* Harper, 1969; *Village Voice,* October 2, 1969; *Washington Star,* November 9, 1969, July 27, 1975; *Washington Post,* November 18, 1969; *New York Review,* February 12, 1970; *National Review,* April 7, 1970; *American Historical Review,* February, 1971; *Nation,* March 6, 1971; *Authors in the News,* Volume II, Gale, 1976.

* * *

BOROWITZ, Eugene B(ernard) 1924-

PERSONAL: Born February 20, 1924, in New York, N.Y.; son of Benjamin and Molly (Shafranik) Borowitz; married Estelle Covel, September 7, 1947; children: Lisa, Drucy, Nan. *Education:* Ohio State University, B.A., 1943; Hebrew Union College, M.H.L. and Rabbi, 1948, D.H.L., 1952; Columbia University, Ed.D., 1958. *Office:* Hebrew Union College—Jewish Institute of Religion, New York Campus, 1 West Fourth St., New York, N.Y., 10012.

CAREER: Rabbi in Port Washington, N.Y., 1953-57; Union of American Hebrew Congregations, New York City, director of education, 1957-62; Hebrew Union College—Jewish Institute of Religion, New York Campus, New York City, professor of education and Jewish religious thought, 1962—. Visiting professor at City College of the City University of New York, Princeton University, Jewish Theological Seminary, Woodstock College, Temple University, and Columbia University. *Military service:* U.S. Naval Reserve, 1951-53; served as chaplain in active duty; became lieutenant junior grade. *Awards, honors:* National Jewish Book Award, 1973, for *The Mask Jews Wear.*

WRITINGS: A Layman's Introduction to Religious Existentialism, Westminster, 1965; *Toward a New Jewish Theology,* Westminster, 1967; *How Can a Jew Speak of Faith Today?,* Westminster, 1968; *Choosing a Sex Ethic,* Schocken, 1968; *A New Jewish Theology in the Making,* Westminster, 1969; *The Mask Jews Wear,* Simon & Schuster, 1973; *Reform Judaism Today,* Behrman, 1977; *Understanding Judaism,* Union of American Hebrew Congregations, 1979; *Contemporary Christologies: A Jewish Response,* Paulist/Newman, 1980. Contributor to journals. Founder and editor of *Sh'ma* (a journal of Jewish responsibility), 1970—.

SIDELIGHTS: Eugene B. Borowitz is a noted Jewish theologian and scholar whose belief that it is essential to develop a clearcut Jewish theology has prompted much critical response. The *Christian Century*'s Donald L. Rogan notes that in *A New Jewish Theology in the Making,* Borowitz's concern is "to liberate Jewish theology from its long bondage to 'Jewish philosophy.'" Louis Jacobs of *Commentary* explains that although "some Jews have tended to look askance" at the idea of an actual Jewish theology, in "a comparatively secure Jewish community like the American it is precisely theological thinking to which many sensitive Jews have now become attracted." He continues: "No longer content with pious exhortations to follow the Jewish way of life, these younger thinkers wish to explore the meaning of that which has provided Jewish life with its inspiration. They want to know what it is that Judaism would have them believe. Eugene Borowitz is prominent among these new Jewish theologians on the American scene."

BIOGRAPHICAL/CRITICAL SOURCES: New Republic, March 15, 1969; *Christian Century,* March 19, 1969; *Commentary,* November, 1969; *Commonweal,* January 16, 1970; *Kirkus Reviews,* July 1, 1973; *Choice,* October, 1978.

* * *

BOTTING, Douglas (Scott) 1934-

PERSONAL: Born February 22, 1934, in London, England; son of Leslie William (a civil servant) and Bessie (Cruse) Botting; married Louise Young (a financial consultant and broadcaster), August 29, 1964; children: Catherine, Anna. *Education:* St. Edmund Hall, Oxford, M.A. (honors), 1958. *Home and office:* 44 Worcester Rd., London S.W.19, England. *Agent:* Deborah Rogers Ltd., 5-11 Mortimer St., London W1H 7RH, England.

CAREER: British Broadcasting Corp. (BBC), London, England, writer and independent producer for television, 1958—; explorer, writer, and photographer. *Military service:* British Army, King's African Rifles, 1952-54; served in East Africa; became lieutenant. *Member:* Society of Authors, Royal Geographical Society (fellow), Royal Institute of International Affairs.

WRITINGS: Island of the Dragon's Blood (travels in Arabia), Funk, 1958; *The Knights of Bornu* (travels in Tchad), Hodder & Stoughton, 1961; *One Chilly Siberian Morning* (travels in Siberia), Macmillan, 1965; *Humboldt and the Cosmos* (biography), Harper, 1973; *Pirates of the Spanish Main* (juvenile), Puffin, 1973; *Shadow in the Clouds* (juvenile), Puffin, 1974; *Wilderness Europe,* Time-Life, 1976; *Rio de Janeiro,* Time-Life, 1977; *The Pirates,* Time-Life, 1978; *The Second Front,* Time-Life, 1979; *The U-Boats,* Time-Life, 1980; *The Great Airships,* Time-Life, 1980.

WORK IN PROGRESS: The Second World Peace: The Struggle for Europe, 1945-49.

SIDELIGHTS: Douglas Botting has traveled in Siberia, the Soviet Arctic, the Amazon, Orinoco, Mato Grosso, the Sahara, Southern Arabia, and many parts of Africa. He has participated in scientific and archaeological expeditions, including a balloon flight over East Africa for a study of game migration. Botting speaks French, Portuguese, German, and Swahili. *Avocational interests:* Playing classical guitar.

* * *

BOULWARE, Marcus H(anna) 1907-

PERSONAL: Surname is pronounced Bool-wah; born May

17, 1907, in Chester, S.C.; son of Musco James (a plastering contractor) and Lizzie (Wilson) Boulware; married N. Ruth Boyce, July, 1937 (divorced, 1963); married Bernice Allen Reeves, 1963 (divorced, 1969); children: (first marriage) Marguerite Boulware Popov, Marcus Hanna, Jr., Philomena Boulware Martin, James Monroe (died March, 1970), James Musco. *Education:* Johnson C. Smith University, A.B. (cum laude), 1931; University of Michigan, M.A., 1936; University of Wisconsin, Ph.D., 1952; postdoctoral studies at George Peabody College for Teachers, Wayne State University, Florida State University, and Indiana University. *Politics:* Democrat. *Religion:* African Methodist Episcopal Zion and Presbyterian. *Address:* 430 Mercury Dr., Tallahassee, Fla. 32304.

CAREER: Instructor in English composition at Prairie View State Normal and Industrial College (now Prairie View Agricultural and Mechanical College), Prairie View, Tex., 1936-37, at Arkansas Agricultural, Mechanical, and Normal College (now University of Arkansas at Pine Bluff), 1937-39, and at State Teachers College (now Alabama State University), Montgomery, 1939-44; *Afro-American* (newspaper), Baltimore, Md., copy editor, 1944; speech therapist in public schools of Charlotte, N.C., 1949-52; Albany State College, Albany, Ga., instructor in English and speech, 1952-53; St. Augustine's College, Raleigh, N.C., professor of English, 1953-60; Florida Agricultural and Mechanical University, Tallahassee, professor of speech, 1960-77. Coordinator of training program in speech, pathology, and audiology, Tennessee State University, 1967-68. *Member:* American Speech and Hearing Association, Speech Association of America, American Communications Association, Association for the Study of Negro Life and History, National Association for the Advancement of Colored People, Florida Speech and Hearing Association, Kappa Alpha Psi.

WRITINGS: Bibliography on Snoring, privately printed, 1969; *The Riddle of Snoring,* Health Research, 1969; *The Oratory of Negro Leaders: 1900-1968,* Negro Universities Press, 1969; *Snoring: New Answers to an Old Problem,* American Faculty Press, 1974; *Metropolitan A.M.E. Zion Church, Chester, S.C.: 1866-1979,* Bryan, 1979. Contributor to *Encyclopedia of World Biography*. Contributor of more than fifty articles on speech, exceptional child education, and snoring to professional and lay journals.

WORK IN PROGRESS: Sleep Gets in Your Eyes, a layman's book on sleep; *Black Women Speakers in the Anti-Slavery and Anti-Lynching Movements; The Black Woman Agent-Lecturer in the American Temperance Crusade, 1848-1920: Anthology of Participation.*

* * *

BOWLE, John (Edward) 1905-

PERSONAL: Born December 19, 1905, in Salisbury, England; son of Edward Francis and Edith (Taunton) Bowle. *Education:* Balliol College, Oxford, B.A., 1927, M.A., 1932. *Home:* 24 Woodstock Close, Oxford, England. *Agent:* Curtis Brown Group Ltd., 1 Craven Hill, London W2 3EW, England; and Harold Ober Associates, Inc., 40 East 49th St., New York, N.Y. 10017.

CAREER: Westminster School, London, England, assistant master and history master, 1930-40; Eton College, Eton, England, history master, 1940-41; served in Air Ministry and in Foreign Office, London, 1941-45; Oxford University, Wadham College, Oxford, England, lecturer in modern history, 1947-49, Leverhulme research fellow, 1949-50; College of Europe, Bruges, Belgium, professor of political theory, 1950. Visiting professor in United States at Columbia University, 1949, Grinnell College, 1961, Occidental College, 1965, Indiana University, 1966, and Smith College, 1968. *Member:* Travellers Club, Pall Mall (London).

WRITINGS: Western Political Thought, Oxford University Press, 1947; *The Unity of European History,* Oxford University Press, 1948, revised edition, 1970; *Hobbes and His Critics,* Oxford University Press, 1951, reprinted, Biblio Distribution Centre, 1969; *Politics and Opinion in the 19th Century,* Oxford University Press, 1954, reprinted, CORE Collection, 1980; (editor with John Bradford) *Concise Encyclopedia of World History,* Hutchinson, 1958, reprinted, Greenwood Press, 1975; *Viscount Samuel,* Gollancz, 1958; *Man through the Ages,* Little, Brown, 1963; *Henry VIII,* Little, Brown, 1965; *England: A Portrait,* Praeger, 1966; *The English Experience,* Weidenfeld & Nicolson, 1971; *Napoleon,* Weidenfeld & Nicolson, 1973, Follett, 1975; *Imperial Achievement: The Rise and Transformation of the British Empire,* Secker & Warburg, 1974, Little, Brown, 1975; *Charles I,* Weidenfeld & Nicolson, 1975, Little, Brown, 1976; *A History of Europe,* Secker & Warburg, 1979. Editor, *World Today,* Royal Institute of International Affairs, London, 1949-51. Contributor to *Punch* and other periodicals.

* * *

BOWLES, Paul (Frederick) 1910-

PERSONAL: Born December 30, 1910, in New York, N.Y.; son of Claude Dietz (a dentist) and Rena (Winnewisser) Bowles; married Jane Auer (a playwright), February 21, 1938 (died, 1973). *Education:* Studied music with Aaron Copland in New York and Berlin, 1930-32, and Virgil Thomson in Paris, 1933-34. *Home:* Inmueble Itesa, Calle Campoamor, Tangier, Morocco. *Agent:* William Morris Agency, 1350 Ave. of the Americas, New York, N.Y. 10019.

CAREER: Writer. Composer for stage, and of operas, film scores, ballets, songs, and chamber music. Musical works include scores for "Glass Menagerie," "Sweet Bird of Youth," and for the ballets, "Pastorelas," "Yankee Clipper," and "Sentimental Colloquy." *Awards, honors:* Guggenheim fellowship, 1941; Rockefeller grant, 1959; American Book Award nomination, 1980, for *Collected Stories of Paul Bowles.*

WRITINGS—Novels: *The Sheltering Sky,* New Directions, 1949, reprinted, Ecco Press, 1978; *Let It Come Down,* Random House, 1952; *The Spider's House,* Random House, 1955; *Up above the World,* Simon & Schuster, 1966.

Short stories: *The Delicate Prey and Other Stories,* Random House, 1950, reprinted, Ecco Press, 1972; *A Little Stone,* J. Lehmann, 1950; *The Hours after Noon,* Heinemann, 1959; *A Hundred Camels in the Courtyard,* City Lights, 1962; *The Time of Friendship,* Holt, 1967; *Pages from Cold Point and Other Stories,* P. Owen, 1968; *Three Tales,* F. Hallman, 1975; *Things Gone and Things Still Here,* Black Sparrow Press, 1977; *Collected Stories of Paul Bowles,* Black Sparrow Press, 1979.

Poetry: *Scenes,* Black Sparrow Press, 1968; *The Thicket of Spring: Poems, 1926-1969,* Black Sparrow Press, 1972.

Other: *Yallah* (travel essays), McDowell, Obolensky, 1957; *Their Heads Are Green and Their Hands Are Blue* (travel essays), Random House, 1963 (published in England as *Their Heads Are Green,* P. Owen, 1963); *Without Stopping* (autobiography), Putnam, 1972.

Translator from the Moghrebi; books by Mohammed Mrabet, except as indicated: Driss ben Hamed Charhadi, *A Life*

Full of Holes, Grove, 1963; *Love with a Few Hairs,* P. Owen, 1967; *The Lemon,* P. Owen, 1969; *M'Hashish,* City Lights, 1969; *The Boy Who Set the Fire and Other Stories,* Black Sparrow Press, 1974; *Hadidan Aharam,* Black Sparrow Press, 1975; *Harmless Poisons, Blameless Sins,* Black Sparrow Press, 1976; *Look and Move On,* Black Sparrow Press, 1976; *The Big Mirrow,* Black Sparrow Press, 1977.

Translator from other languages: (From the French) Jean-Paul Sartre, *No Exit,* Samuel French, 1946; (from the Arabic) Mohamed Choukri, *For Bread Alone,* P. Owen, 1973; (from the Arabic) Choukri, *Jean Genet in Tangier,* Ecco Press, 1974; (from the French) Isabelle Eberhardt, *The Oblivion Seekers,* City Lights, 1975. Also translator of other works from French, Spanish, and Italian.

SIDELIGHTS: Paul Bowles's short stories and novels present an attempt to escape the sterile conformity of modern life in the West. Bowles himself first left the United States when he was eighteen and, with the encouragement of Gertrude Stein, finally settled in North Africa where he has lived for many years. He once told an interviewer: "I first came to North Africa when I was a college student back in the States, and then one summer, a year or two later, I met Gertrude Stein in Paris. I was thinking of going on to Villefranche where Cocteau and a lot of other writers were living at the time. But Gertrude Stein insisted, instead, that I should come to Tangier, which wasn't well known then to Europeans as it is now. 'You must break new ground,' she told me. 'Besides, what is the use of going to Villefranche where you'll just sit about discussing literature with other writers instead of trying to create it yourself?'. . . . But for her, I should probably never have become a writer at all."

Bowles's characters are inveterate travellers, escapees from Europe or North America, who wander to exotic ports and desert lands. A reviewer for *Time* comments: "His characters, robbed of purpose, their spirits rubbed flat, move zombielike through exquisitely desolate landscapes—Moroccan ghettos, Algerian deserts, New York subway tunnels. Displaced in the present, they have vague pasts and menacing futures; sighing despair, they search for something unnameable. Perhaps their quest is for what they find: hostility, hallucination, more intense dislocation, the last retreat of death—Bowles doesn't say. . . . His warped people are beyond help because they will not help themselves. They have surrendered, and Bowles, the devil's advocate, grinds them further into defeat."

The scenario Bowles creates reflects the arid desert in which his characters wander and in which he himself lives. Melvin Maddocks notes that "his hell is a brilliant composite landscape, half North African, half the terrain of puritan conscience. Color Bowles's inferno flame-orange, hot and sand-arid, with a sky of violent blue, suffocating and quite opaque. Enter stage right, Bowles's repertory company of about-to-be damned Americans and Europeans—fascinated tourists solemnly inspecting animal totems and side-stepping with delicious shudders a one-legged boy here, an old Arab peddler with six fingers there." Reflecting on this scenario, Daniel Stern comments: "Paul Bowles's universe (and it is a mark of distinction that there *is* a Bowlesian universe) is made up of primitive but wise natives and effete children of the West searching for escape from the self—that self that supposedly hangs like an albatross around the neck of modern literature, from Hemingway to Herzog, feeding thought and stifling feeling."

Other than travel, the only escape route that Bowles provides his characters is the use of drugs. Disdaining alcohol as a Western ploy to obliterate individuality, he prefers hashish or marijuana (known collectively to Bowles as kif), which he believes help the individual find himself in a world devoted to conformity. As Frances Fytton notes: "Devotion to hashish is as important to the writing of Paul Bowles as it is to the literature of his favoured civilization: Islam. He praises the drug not merely for its powers of intoxication but for the escape it can provide from the spreading monotone of the modern world: for the typical Bowles character is condemned to perpetual wandering in search of a place of refuge from his own culture; when the wandering fails he falls back upon kif to provide the required hallucination. Travel becomes an end in itself: kif is the extension of the journey."

Although some critics find Bowles's writing horrific and sensationalistic, Maddocks believes that "Bowles survives his own sensationalism as well as the pat explicitness with which he allows his model of hell to stand as a metaphor for the contemporary world. . . . He survives, a unique trader in African Gothic, because he is a superb storyteller and because he avoids the one unforgiveable sin of his genre: voyeurism. He extends to his characters a frail but consistent humanity they do not extend to one another or to themselves." Other reviewers point to the contradiction in Bowles's scenario. The travellers seek comfort in static and unchanging societies because of the contrast they provide to their native West. Yet what the travellers are trying to escape is the conformity and conservatism of their own countries. Bowles has what Fytton calls "an ambivalent attitude towards his Mecca: explicit in his essays, implicit in his fiction. He is ultraconservative, rejecting social reform on the grounds that it is the prelude to international conformity; yet demanding luxury hotels which provide American standards of comfort."

Walter Allen compares Bowles to Edgar Allen Poe, noting that "like Poe's, his theme is the disintegration of the psyche." Bowles has admitted the debt to Poe, dedicating his first collection of short stories to "my mother, who first read me the stories of Poe." Charles T. Samuels thinks that "Bowles has improved on his master. With muted prose, he refined Poe's menacing but frequently hysterical atmosphere, while his tropical and African settings provide a more plausible backdrop for terror than Poe could dream up in his New York Grub Street. More important, Bowles writes out of an ironist's vision of human beastiality, whereas Poe writes mostly for emotional effect."

Despite the comparison to Poe, Oliver Evans notes that "Bowles does not usually indulge in horror for its own sake; it is nearly always related to his central obsession . . . that psychological well-being is in inverse ratio to what is commonly known as progress, and that a highly evolved culture enjoys less peace of mind that one which is less highly evolved." The tension in Bowles's work, Evans observes, "arises from a contrast between alien cultures: in a typical Bowles story, a civilized individual comes in contact with an alien environment and is defeated by it. . . . There is still another reason for Bowles's choice of remote locales. Deserts and jungles are places in which people can easily get lost, and Bowles believes that modern man, if not already lost in a spiritual and moral sense, is in serious danger of becoming so."

BIOGRAPHICAL/CRITICAL SOURCES: John W. Adridge, *After the Lost Generation,* Noonday, 1951; *Critique,* Volume III, number 1, 1959; *Harper's,* October, 1959; *London Magazine,* November, 1960, February, 1967, June, 1968; Walter Allen, *The Modern Novel,* Dutton, 1965; *New Statesman,* January 27, 1967; *Illustrated London News,*

January 28, 1967; *Times Literary Supplement,* February 2, 1967, May 9, 1968; *Listener,* February 2, 1967; *Life,* July 21, 1967; *National Observer,* July 24, 1967; *Time,* August 4, 1967; *New York Times Book Review,* August 6, 1967, September 30, 1979; *Nation,* September 4, 1967; *New York Review of Books,* November 9, 1967; *Books and Bookmen,* June, 1968; *Partisan Review,* winter, 1968; Theodore Solotaroff, *The Red Hot Vacuum and Other Pieces on the Writing of the Sixties,* Atheneum, 1970; Paul Bowles, *Without Stopping,* Putnam, 1972; *New York Times,* March 21, 1972; *New Republic,* April 22, 1972; *Contemporary Literary Criticism,* Gale, Volume I, 1973, Volume II, 1974; Lawrence D. Stewart, *The Illumination of North Africa,* Southern Illinois University Press, 1974; *Washington Post Book World,* September 9, 1979.

—*Sketch by Linda Metzger*

* * *

BOYER, Paul Samuel 1935-

PERSONAL: Born August 2, 1935, in Dayton, Ohio. *Education:* Harvard University, A.B. (magna cum laude), 1960, M.A., 1961, Ph.D., 1966. *Office:* Department of History, University of Massachusetts, Amherst, Mass. 01002.

CAREER: Harvard University Press, Cambridge, Mass., assistant editor, 1964-67; University of Massachusetts—Amherst, assistant professor, 1967-70, associate professor, 1970-75, professor of history, 1975—, chairman of department, 1978. Visiting lecturer, Smith College, spring, 1969, fall, 1975, and Mount Holyoke College, spring, 1977. *Member:* Phi Beta Kappa. *Awards, honors:* American Philosophical Society grant, 1969; Guggenheim fellowship, 1973-74; John H. Dunning Prize from American Historical Association, 1974, and National Book Award nomination, 1975, both for *Salem Possessed.*

WRITINGS: Purity in Print: Book Censorship in America, Scribner, 1968; (editor with E. T. James and J. W. James) *Notable American Women: 1607-1950,* three volumes, Harvard University Press, 1971; (editor with Stephen Nissenbaum) *Salem Village Witchcraft: A Documentary Record of Local Conflict in Colonial New England,* Wadsworth, 1972; (with Nissenbaum) *Salem Possessed: The Social Origins of Witchcraft,* Harvard University Press, 1974; (editor with Nissenbaum) *The Salem Witchcraft Papers,* three volumes, Da Capo Press, 1977; *Urban Masses and Moral Order in America, 1820-1920,* Harvard University Press, 1978.

Contributor to *Dictionary of American History, Dictionary of American Biography, Encyclopedia Americana,* and *Encyclopedia of American History;* contributor of articles and reviews to *William and Mary Quarterly, American Quarterly, Massachusetts Alumnus, American Historical Review, Journal of American History,* and *Historian.*

WORK IN PROGRESS: A social and intellectual history of the United States, 1860-1920.

SIDELIGHTS: In response to *CA*'s question about his advice to aspiring writers, Paul Samuel Boyer wrote: "Jonathan Swift said it all: 'Blot out, correct, insert, refine, enlarge, diminish, interline; be mindful; when invention fails, to scratch your head, and bite your nails.'"

* * *

BOYLAN, James (Richard) 1927-

PERSONAL: Born December 13, 1927, in Charles City, Iowa; son of Charles Clifford (a teacher) and Irene (Imus) Boylan; married Betsy Wade (a newspaper copy editor), December 27, 1952; children: Richard Wade, Benjamin Mark. *Education:* Cornell College, A.B., 1950; Columbia University, M.S., 1951, M.A., 1960, Ph.D., 1971. *Office:* Journalistic Studies, University of Massachusetts, Amherst, Mass. 01002.

CAREER: This Week, New York City, copy editor, 1951-56; Columbia University, Graduate School of Journalism, New York City, assistant to dean, 1957-60, assistant professor, 1960-64, adjunct associate professor of journalism, 1970-76; University of Massachusetts—Amherst, lecturer, 1977-79, associate professor of journalism, 1979—.

WRITINGS: School Teaching as a Career, Walck, 1962; (co-editor) *Our Troubled Press,* Little, Brown, 1970; (editor) *The World and the 20's,* Dial, 1973; (co-author) *Mass Media: Systems and Effects,* Praeger, 1976. *Columbia Journalism Review,* managing editor, 1961-64, editor, 1964-69, and 1976-79, contributing editor, 1970-75.

BIOGRAPHICAL/CRITICAL SOURCES: Newsweek, October 9, 1961.

* * *

BRACHER, Karl Dietrich 1922-

PERSONAL: Born March 13, 1922, in Stuttgart, Germany; son of Theodor (an educator) and Gertrud (Zimmermann) Bracher; married Dorothee Schleicher, May 13, 1951; children: Christian, Susanne. *Education:* University of Tuebingen, Ph.D., 1948; Harvard University, postdoctoral study, 1949-50. *Religion:* Protestant. *Home:* Stationsweg 17, Bonn, Germany. *Office:* University of Bonn, Am Hofgarten 15, Bonn, Germany.

CAREER: Free University, Berlin, Germany, assistant, 1950-53, lecturer, 1954-55, professor of modern history and political science, 1955-58; University of Bonn, Bonn, Germany, professor of political science and contemporary history, 1959—. Guest professor in Sweden, 1962, Athens, 1966 and 1978, London, 1967, at Oxford University, 1971, at Tel Aviv University, 1974, in Jerusalem, 1974, Japan, 1975, Florence, 1976, Madrid, 1976, and Rome, 1979. Member of Institute for Advanced Study, 1967-68 and 1974-75. Consultant to and member of government committees of the Federal Republic of Germany. *Member:* German Association of Political Science (chairman, 1965-67), Association of German Scientists, German Association of Foreign Policy, Historical Association, Commission on History of Parliamentarism and Political Parties (chairman, 1962-68), Institute for Contemporary History (member of board), German P.E.N. Center, British Academy (corresponding fellow), American Philosophical Society, American Academy of Arts and Sciences (honorary member). *Awards, honors:* Doctor of humane letters from Florida State University; Center for Advanced Studies in the Behavioral Sciences fellow, 1963-64.

WRITINGS: (Compiler with Annedore Leber and Willy Brandt) *Das Gewissen steht auf: 64 Lebensbilder aus dem deutschen Widerstand 1933-1945,* Mosaik Verlag, 1954, translation by Rosemary O'Neill published as *Conscience in Revolt: Sixty-four Stories of Resistance in Germany, 1933-45,* Associated Booksellers, 1957; *Die Aufloesung der Weimarer Republik: eine Studie zum Problem des Machtverfalls in der Demokratie* (title means "The Dissolution of the Weimar Republic"), Ring-Verlag, 1955, 16th edition, 1978; *Nationalsozialistische Machtergreifung und Reichskonkordat* (title means "Nazi Seizure of Power and the Concordat"), C. Ritter, 1956; (editor with Ernst Fraenkel) *Staat und Politik* (title means "State and Politics"), Fischer Buecherei, 1957; (compiler with Leber and Brandt) *Das Gewissen entscheidet: Bereiche des deutschen Widerstandes von 1933-45 in Lebensbildern* (sequel to *Das Gewissen steht auf;* title means "Conscience Decides"), Mosaik Verlag, 1957.

Die Nationalsozialistische Machtergreifung (title means "The National Socialist Seizure of Power"), Westdeutscher Verlag, 1960, 3rd edition, 1974; *Ueber das Verhaeltnis von Politik und Geschichte* (title means "On the Relation of Politics and History"), Peter Hanstein, 1961; *Die Entstehung der Weimarer Verfassung* (title means "The Genesis of the Weimar Constitution"), [Hannover], 1963; *Adolf Hitler,* Scherz Verlag, 1964; *Deutschland Zwischen Demokratie und Diktatur* (title means "Germany between Democracy and Dictatorship"), Scherz, 1964; *Theodor Heuss und die Wiederbefruendung der Demokratie in Deutschland* (title means "Theodor Heuss and the Refounding of Democracy in Germany"), R. Wunderlich Verlag, 1965; (editor with others) *Modern Constitutionalism and Democracy,* two volumes, J.C.B. Mohr, (Tuebingen), 1966; (editor with Fraenkel) *Internationale Beziehungen,* Fischer-Buecherei, 1969; *Die deutsche Diktatur: Entstehung, Struktur, Folgen des Nationalsozialismus,* Koeln, Kiepenheuer & Witsch, 1969, 6th edition, 1979, translation by Jean Steinberg published as *The German Dictatorship: The Origins, Structure, and Effects of National Socialism,* Praeger, 1970.

(Editor) *Nach 25 [fuenfundzwanzig] Jahren* (title means "After Twenty-five Years"), Kindler, 1970; (editor with others) *Bibliographie zur Politik,* Droste, 1970; *Das deutsche Dilemma: Leidenswege der politischen Emanzipation* (title means "The German Dilemma . . ."), R. Piper, 1971, English translation, Weidenfeld & Nicolson, 1974; *Zeitgeschichtliche Kontroversen* (title means "Controversies in Contemporary History"), Piper, 1976, 3rd edition, 1979; *Die Krise Europas 1917-1975* (title means "The Crisis of Europe 1917-1975"), Propylaen, 1976, new edition, 1979; *Schluesselwoerter in der Geschichte* (title means "Key Words in History"), Droste, 1978.

Contributor: Max Beloff, editor, *On the Track of Tyranny,* Valentine, Mitchell, 1960; J. E. Black and K. W. Thompson, editors, *Foreign Policies in a World of Change,* Harper, 1963; H. W. Ehrmann, editor, *Democracy in a Changing Society,* Praeger, 1964; Stephen R. Graubard, editor, *A New Europe?,* Houghton, 1964; *The Times History of Our Times,* [London], 1971; R. Mayne, editor, *Europe Tomorrow,* Fontana, 1972; Hajo Holborn, editor, *Republic to Reich,* Pantheon, 1972; Walter Laqueur, editor, *Fascism: A Reader's Guide,* University of California Press, 1976.

Contributor to *International Encyclopedia of the Social Sciences* and *Dictionary of the History of Ideas.* Editor, *Neue Politische Literatur;* member of editorial boards of *Politische Vierteljahresschrift, Vierteljahrshefte fuer Zeitgeschichte, Bonner Historische Forschungen, Journal of Contemporary History, Government and Opposition, Societas, History of the Twentieth Century,* and *Bonner Schriften zur Politik und Zeitgeschichte.*

WORK IN PROGRESS: Analysis of the Federal Republic of Germany; History of the Twentieth Century; History of Political Ideas.

AVOCATIONAL INTERESTS: Playing the piano, mountain hiking.

* * *

BRACKETT, Leigh (Douglass) 1915-1978

PERSONAL: Born December 7, 1915, in Los Angeles, Calif.; died March 18, 1978, in Lancaster, Calif.; daughter of William Franklin and Margaret (Douglass) Brackett; married Edmond Hamilton, 1946 (died February 1, 1977). *Education:* Attended private schools. *Home and office address:* R.D. 2, Kinsman, Ohio.

CAREER: Free-lance writer, 1939-78. *Member:* Authors Guild, Writers Guild of America West, Western Writers of America. *Awards, honors:* Jules Verne Award for Fantasy; Silver Spur Award, Western Writers of America, 1963, for *Follow the Free Wind.*

WRITINGS: No Good from a Corpse, Coward, 1944, reprinted, Collier, 1964; *The Starmen,* Gnome, 1952, published as *The Starmen of Llyrdis,* Ballantine, 1976; *The Big Jump,* published with P. K. Dick's *Solar Lottery,* Ace Books, 1955, published separately, 1976; *The Long Tomorrow,* Doubleday, 1955, reprinted, Ballantine, 1975; *Eye for an Eye,* Doubleday, 1957; *The Tiger among Us,* Doubleday, 1957; *Follow the Free Wind,* Doubleday, 1963; *Alpha Centauri or Die!,* published with G. M. Wallis's *Legend of the Lost Earth,* Ace Books, 1963, published separately, 1976; *The People of the Talisman* [and] *Secret of Sinharat,* Ace Books, 1964; *Silent Partner,* Putnam, 1969; *The Halfling, and Other Stories,* Ace Books, 1973; *The Ginger Star,* Ballantine, 1974; *The Sword of Rhiannon,* Ace Books, 1975; *The Coming of the Terrans,* Ace Books, 1976; *The Hounds of Skaith,* Ballantine, 1976; *The Nemesis from Terra,* Ace Books, 1976; *The Reavers of Skaith,* Ballantine, 1976; (editor and author of introduction) Edmond Hamilton, *The Best of Edmond Hamilton,* Doubleday, 1977. Work has been anthologized in *Three Times Infinity,* edited by Leo Margulies, Fawcett, 1958.

Screenplays: (With Jules Furthman) "Rio Bravo," (with Furthman and W. Faulkner) "The Big Sleep," "Hatari," "Eldorado," "The Long Goodbye," and "The Empire Fights Back." Writer and contributor of material for "Checkmate" and "Suspense" (television series).

WORK IN PROGRESS: Two novels, *Night of the Darkbirds* and *The Psirens.*

AVOCATIONAL INTERESTS: Photography, music, history, gardening, and travel.†

* * *

BRADBURY, Malcolm (Stanley) 1932-

PERSONAL: Born September 7, 1932, in Sheffield, England; son of Arthur and Doris (Marshall) Bradbury; married Elizabeth Salt, 1959; children: two sons. *Education:* University College, University of Leicester, B.A. (with honors), 1953; University of London, M.A., 1955; additional graduate study at Indiana University, 1955-56; University of Manchester, graduate study, 1956-58, Ph.D., 1964. *Home:* 14 Heigham Grove, Norwich NOR 14G, England; and Lockington House Cottage, Lockington near Driffield, East Yorkshire, England. *Agent:* John Cushman Associates, Inc., 25 West 43rd St., New York, N.Y. 10036. *Office:* School of English and American Studies, University of East Anglia, Norwich, Norfolk NR4 7TJ, England.

CAREER: University of Hull, Hull, England, staff tutor in literature in department of adult education, 1959-61; University of Birmingham, Birmingham, England, lecturer, 1961-65; University of East Anglia, Norwich, England, lecturer, 1965-67, senior lecturer, 1967-69, reader in English, 1969-70, professor of American studies, 1970—. Visiting fellow, All Souls College, Oxford University, 1969. *Member:* British Association of American Studies, Society of Authors, P.E.N., Royal Society of Literature (fellow). *Awards, honors:* British Association of American Studies junior fellow in

United States, 1958-59; American Council of Learned Societies fellow, 1965-66.

WRITINGS: Eating People Is Wrong (novel), Secker & Warburg, 1959, Knopf, 1960; *Phogey!, or How to Have Class in a Classless Society,* Parrish, 1960; *All Dressed Up and Nowhere to Go: The Poor Man's Guide to the Affluent Society,* Parrish, 1962; *Evelyn Waugh,* Oliver & Boyd, 1964; *Stepping Westward* (novel), Secker & Warburg, 1965, Houghton, 1966; (with Allan Rodway) *Two Poets* (verse), Byron Press, 1966; *What Is a Novel?,* Edward Arnold, 1969; *The Social Context of Modern English Literature,* Schocken, 1971; *Possibilities: Essays on the State of the Novel,* Oxford University Press, 1973; *The History Man* (novel), Secker & Warburg, 1975, Houghton, 1976; *Who Do You Think You Are?: Stories and Parodies,* Secker & Warburg, 1976.

Editor: *Forster: A Collection of Critical Essays,* Prentice-Hall, 1966; Mark Twain, *"Pudd'nhead Wilson" and "Those Extraordinary Twins,"* Penguin, 1969; E. M. Forster, *"A Passage to India": A Casebook,* Macmillan, 1970; (with David Palmer) *Contemporary Criticism,* Edward Arnold, 1970, St. Martin's, 1971; (with Eric Mottram and Jean France) *The Penguin Companion to American Literature,* McGraw, 1971 (published in England as *The Penguin Companion to Literature,* Volume III: *U.S.A.,* Allen Lane, 1971); (with Palmer) *Metaphysical Poetry,* Indiana University Press, 1971; (with Palmer) *The American Novel and the Nineteen Twenties,* Edward Arnold, 1971; (with Palmer) *Shakespearian Comedy,* Edward Arnold, 1972; (with James McFarlane) *Modernism: 1890-1930,* Penguin, 1976; *The Novel Today: Contemporary Writers on Modern Fiction,* Rowman & Littlefield, 1977; (with Palmer) *Decadence and the 1890s,* Edward Arnold, 1979; (with Palmer) *The Contemporary English Novel,* Edward Arnold, 1979; (with Howard Temperley) *An Introduction to American Studies,* Longman, 1980.

Plays: (With David Lodge and James Duckett) "Between These Four Walls," first produced in Birmingham, England, 1963; (with Lodge, Duckett, and David Turner) "Slap in the Middle," first produced in Birmingham, England, 1965. Author, with wife, Elizabeth Bradbury, of radio play, "This Sporting Life," 1974-75; author, with Christopher Bigsby, of television plays, "The After Dinner Game," 1975, and "Stones," 1976; also author of television plays, "Love on a Gunboat," 1977, and "The Enigma," 1980.

Contributor: A. Kazin, editor, *The Open Form: Essays for Our Time,* Harcourt, 1961; G. Levin, editor, *Prose Models,* Harcourt, 1964; J. R. Brown and B. Harris, editors, *Modern American Poetry,* Edward Arnold, 1965; Edgell Rickword and Douglas Garman, editors, *The Calendar of Modern Letters: March, 1925-July, 1927,* Barnes & Noble, 1966. Contributor to periodicals.

WORK IN PROGRESS: A History of American Literature; a novel, *Rates of Exchange;* a study of American images of Europe and European images of America.

SIDELIGHTS: Herbert Burke calls Malcolm Bradbury's first novel, *Eating People Is Wrong,* "a novel . . . about how weary academic life is in the English Midlands of the '50s—but this is not a weary novel. Often truly comic, its satire has many barbs and they often draw blood. . . . If seriousness of intent—a sociology of the British establishment of the times as seen through the microcosm of the academy—gets in the way of hearty satire, bawdiness is not lacking." According to Martin Tucker, the author "has written a first novel that is sloppy, structurally flabby, occasionally inane, frequently magnificent and ultimately successful. It is as if Dickens and Evelyn Waugh sat down together and said, 'Let's write a comic novel in the manner of Kingsley Amis about a man in search of his lost innocence who finds it.' The result is one of the most substantial and dazzling literary feasts this year." Not all reviewers have been so generous in their appraisal of the book, however. Patrick Dennis writes: "While Malcolm Bradbury's first novel is brilliant, witty, sensitive, adult, funny and a lot of other pleasant and desirable things, it is not a good novel. And I know why: Mr. Bradbury has been so busy entertaining himself with his brilliance, wit, etc., that he has quite forgotten about those less gifted people who are expected to buy, read and enjoy his book. . . . While his knaves and fools are elegantly written, his 'sympathetic' characters are so feckless or so grotesque that one has almost no feeling for them." And a *New Yorker* critic finds that "there are no funny situations, and the few comic episodes that occur are much too light, and perhaps also too tired, to stand up against the predominant, tragic predicament that is [the main character's] life . . . and even if this spectacle were more richly decorated that it is with jokes and puns and so on, it would not be good enough. Mr. Bradbury has created a serious and very human character, and has obscured him with jugglers."

Stepping Westward, Bradbury's second novel, also about university life, has been hailed by a *Times Literary Supplement* reviewer as "a *vade mecum* for every youthful or aspiring first visitor to the United States. Every situational joke, every classic encounter is exactly and wittily exploited. The dialogue is often marvellously acute, the tricks of American speech expertly 'bugged.'" On the other hand, however, Rita Estok says that "the school, faculty and students do not ring true; in fact, it is almost a travesty on university life. James Walker, the principal character, never becomes believable and remains unsympathetic throughout the story. *Stepping Westward,* be it a travesty or satire on university life, fails to hit the mark as either." And Bernard McCabe writes: "Within this very funny book Mr. Bradbury proposes a serious novel about freedom and community and friendship's inevitable failures. The result is interesting, but too schematic and analytical to be really successful. The comedy works, though, thanks to Bradbury's artful writing. I leave to some future scholar the precise significance of the recurrent buttocks-motif and ear-motif. . . . [The author's] exaggerated versions of [university life] work by lending a British ear and eye to the oddities of the American scene."

Robert Nye says that Bradbury, in his third novel, *The History Man,* "achieves some charming comic efforts—and not a few cruel ones. Bradbury has a baleful eye for human weakness. He describes with skill and obvious relish. The result is a clever, queer, witty, uncomfortable sort of book—a book whose prose possesses considerable surface brilliance but with a cutting edge concealed beneath." Margaret Drabble calls the book "a small narrative masterpiece," and she feels that "one of the reasons why this novel is so immensely readable is its evocation of physical reality; it may be a book about ideas, but the ideas are embodied in closely observed details. . . . A thoroughly civilized writer, [Bradbury] has written a novel that raises some very serious questions about the nature of civilization without for a moment appearing pretentious or didactic—a fine achievement." But again, some critics seem to be less convinced of the merits of the book. For instance, Hilary Spurling finds that the bulk of *The History Man* "seems at times in danger of being swamped by elaborately detailed, oddly flat descriptions of supermarkets, shopping precincts, clothes, cutlery, furniture and floor coverings.... One set of stripped pine kitchen shelves is described three times, and its contents listed twice, in tones not so much ironic as admiring. One cannot help feeling that inside this fat catalogue of very superior goods a thinner, sharper and altogether more disconcerting novel is struggling to get out."

Malcolm Bradbury told *CA:* "For most of my adult life I have been two things, not always compatible: a university teacher—now a professor of American studies—and a writer of fiction. In some ways these activities feed on each other; in others, particularly in the conflict of time, they clash. The competences that make me a critic and scholar are not quite of the same kind that make me a novelist, yet there are connections. The persistent study of literature, the debates surrounding it, a preoccupation with style, language and form—these all seem to me a proper environment in which to pursue artistic expression. Serious writing is not an innocent act; it is an act of connection with the major acts of writing achieved by others. It is also, though, a new set of grammars, forms, and styles for the age we live in."

BIOGRAPHICAL/CRITICAL SOURCES: New Statesman, October 31, 1959; *Times Literary Supplement,* November 13, 1959, August 5, 1965, November 7, 1975; *Library Journal,* March 1, 1960, June 1, 1966; *Saturday Review,* April 9, 1960, May 21, 1966; *New York Times,* April 10, 1960; *Booklist,* April 15, 1960; *Commonweal,* April 22, 1960; *San Francisco Chronicle,* April 26, 1960; *National Review,* May 2, 1960; *New Yorker,* July 16, 1960, May 3, 1976; *Time,* June 3, 1966; *New York Times Book Review,* February 8, 1976; *Christian Science Monitor,* February 18, 1976.

* * *

BRAINE, John (Gerard) 1922-

PERSONAL: Born April 13, 1922, in Bradford, Yorkshire, England; son of Fred and Katherine (Henry) Braine; married Helen Patricia Wood, 1955; children: Anthony, Frances, Felicity. *Education:* Leeds School of Librarianship, A.L.A., 1949. *Politics:* Conservative. *Religion:* Roman Catholic. *Home:* Pentons, Onslow Crescent, Woking, Surrey, England. *Agent:* David Higham Associates Ltd., 5-8 Lower John St., Golden Sq., London W1R 4HA, England.

CAREER: Bingley Public Library, Bingley, England, assistant, 1940-48, chief assistant librarian, 1948-51; librarian at Northumberland County Library, England, 1954-56, and West Riding County Library, England, 1956-57; full-time writer, 1957—. Member of North Regional Advisory Council, British Broadcasting Corp., 1960-64. *Military service:* Royal Navy, 1942-43. *Member:* Arts Theatre Club, Library Association, Authors' Club, Bingley Little Theatre, Bradford Civic Theatre.

WRITINGS: Room at the Top, Houghton, 1957, reprinted, Methuen, 1980; *The Vodi,* Eyre & Spottiswoode, 1959, published as *From the Hand of the Hunter,* Houghton, 1960; *Life at the Top,* Houghton, 1962; *The Jealous God,* Eyre & Spottiswoode, 1964, Houghton, 1965; *The Crying Game,* Houghton, 1968; *Stay with Me till Morning,* Eyre & Spottiswoode, 1970, published as *The View from Tower Hill,* Coward, 1971; *The Queen of a Distant Country,* Methuen, 1972, Coward, 1973; *Writing a Novel,* Coward, 1974; *The Pious Agent,* Eyre Methuen, 1975, Atheneum, 1976; *Waiting for Sheila,* Eyre Methuen, 1976; *Finger of Fire,* Eyre Methuen, 1977; *J. B. Priestley,* Barnes & Noble, 1979. Also author of play, "The Desert in the Mirror," produced in Bingley, England, 1951, and television series "Man at the Top," for Thames Television (England), 1970 and 1972. Contributor to numerous newspapers and periodicals in England and the United States.

WORK IN PROGRESS: A novel, *Praise to the Evening.*

SIDELIGHTS: With the publication of his first novel, *Room at the Top,* John Braine achieved almost instant literary recognition. The story of a young and ambitious working-class Englishman who eventually joins the urban upper-class that he pretends to disdain drew an overwhelmingly favorable response from both readers and critics. Of the book's theme, Anthony Burgess writes: "*Room at the Top* was taken by many to be a straight account of achieved ambition. Young man puts boss's daughter in family way and then has it made. But there was much more to the book than that—there was guilt, betrayal of love, . . . the sense that the price of success can be too high and that this, alas, is usually only discovered when success is attained." James W. Lee believes that *Room at the Top* "is a novel which epitomizes its age. Like Ernest Hemingway's *The Sun Also Rises* and F. Scott Fitzgerald's *The Great Gatsby, Room at the Top* probes deeply and tellingly into a central problem of the times. Braine's Joe Lampton is a creation of the postwar British welfare state."

Yet Braine's succeeding novels apparently failed to evoke the same high praise. "Nearly a decade later," writes John Lahr in his review of *The Crying Game,* "Braine is still scrutinizing English mores with a vicar's scowl, obsessed by evil but unable to fathom it, shocked by the inhumanity of permissiveness without the ability to create characters of human sinew." Felicia Lamport describes *The View from Tower Hill* as a "curiously tepid work" and adds: "Over another signature, *The View from Tower Hill* might have seemed less pallid, but Braine's name triggers expectations of the kind of vitality, power, and urgency that filled his *Room at the Top*.... John Braine's bodies are no longer smoldering with life but serenely and prosperously middle-aged." Pamela Marsh, in perhaps the harshest assessment of Braine's later work, states, "John Braine is one of those who have become tagged as a 'one-novel man.'"

According to R.G.G. Price, however, this kind of criticism is unjust: "Early reviews of Mr. Braine took him as more of a highbrow novelist than he ever set out to be and later ones became disgruntled and even hinted at metropolitan corruption of standards. This was unfair. He's no Proust but on the level he aims at he is very good." Moreover, reviews of Braine's later novel, *The Queen of a Distant Country,* indicate a renewed understanding between the author and his critics. "After some dreadful potboiling," writes a critic for the *Times Literary Supplement,* "John Braine has produced a novel of real unforced style and feeling." Jan B. Gordon believes that "Braine continues to speak to us with a certain urgency," and that *The Queen of a Distant Country* "talks directly to a civilization which must now cope with the apathy of a youth which has plugged itself into the system and finds its ideals either co-opted or commercialized."

In an interview with Kenneth Allsop, Braine says that the novelist's responsibility is "to show his age as it really is.... But a writer must be a civilized and tolerant human being, possessing, above all, intellectual integrity.... The writer doesn't have to inhabit a rarified moral or intellectual plane, but he must always be, no matter how imperfectly, the conscience of society."

Braine has made several radio and television appearances in England and the United States. *Room at the Top* was filmed by British Lion Films Ltd. in 1959; *Life at the Top* was produced by Royal Films in 1966.

BIOGRAPHICAL/CRITICAL SOURCES: Kenneth Allsop, *The Angry Decade,* P. Owen, 1958; *New York Times Book Review,* April 19, 1959, October 27, 1968, May 27, 1973, May 2, 1976; Frederick R. Karl, *The Contemporary English Novel,* Farrar, Straus, 1962; *Saturday Review,* October 6, 1962, February 27, 1971; *Harper's,* April, 1965; *Commonweal,* April 23, 1965, December 14, 1973; James W. Lee, *John Braine,* Twayne, 1968; *Books and Bookmen,* April, 1968; *Punch,* September 4, 1968; *National Observer,* November 25, 1968; *Christian Science Monitor,* December 12, 1968; *Writer,* May, 1972; *Times Literary Supplement,* October 27, 1972, June 20, 1975; *Contemporary Literary Criticism,* Gale, Volume I, 1973, Volume III, 1975; *Newsweek,* April 30, 1973; *Observer,* February 18, 1979.

* * *

BRANDNER, Gary 1933-
(Garrison Brand, Clayton Moore, Barnaby Quill)

PERSONAL: Born May 31, 1933, in Sault Sainte Marie, Mich.; son of Henry Phil and Beada (Gehrman) Brandner; married Paula Moon, 1958 (divorced, 1963); married Barbara Grant Nutting, 1979. *Education:* University of Washington, B.A., 1955. *Home:* 2134 Santa Ynez St., Apt. 3, Los Angeles, Calif. 90026. *Agent:* Jay Garon, 415 Central Park W., 17-D, New York, N.Y. 10025.

CAREER: Dan B. Miner (advertising agency), Los Angeles, Calif., copy writer, 1955-57; Douglas Aircraft, Santa Monica, Calif., technical writer, 1957-59; North American Rockwell, Downey, Calif., technical writer, 1959-67; full-time free-lance writer, 1969—. *Member:* Mystery Writers of America, Writers Guild of America West.

WRITINGS: Vitamin E: Key to Sexual Satisfaction, Nash Publishing, 1971, revised edition, Paperback Library, 1972; (contributor) Richard Davis, editor, *Year's Best Horror Stories,* Sphere Books, 1971; *Living Off the Land,* Nash Publishing, 1971; *Off the Beaten Track in London,* Nash Publishing, 1972; (with Clayton Matthews) *Saturday Night in Milwaukee,* Curtis Books, 1973; (under pseudonym Clayton Moore) *Wesley Sheridan,* Berkley Publishing, 1974; *The Aardvark Affair,* Zebra Publications, 1975; *The Beelzebub Business,* Zebra Publications, 1975; *The Players,* Pyramid Publications, 1975; *London,* Pocket Books, 1976; *Billy Lives!,* Manor, 1976; *The Howling,* Fawcett, 1977; *The Howling II,* Fawcett, 1978; *Offshore,* Pinnacle Books, 1978; *Walkers,* Fawcett, 1980. Contributor of over fifty short stories, sometimes under pseudonyms, to *Ellery Queen's Mystery Magazine, Alfred Hitchcock's Mystery Magazine, Mike Shayne Mystery Magazine, Zane Grey, Cavalier, Gem,* and *Witchcraft and Sorcery.*

WORK IN PROGRESS: Three novels, one for Fawcett, *Tsunami,* for Playboy Press, and *The Sterling Standard;* a screenplay for Universal Pictures.

SIDELIGHTS: Gary Brandner told *CA:* "It is, in a way, lucky for those of us who write for a living that it is so difficult. Otherwise, everyone would be doing it, because it is a fine way to live, and there would be no one left to read.

"The best things about writing are that you can wear whatever you want to work, and you can set your own schedule, and you get to hang around with other writers. The worst thing is that your family never believes you have a real job.

"My advice to aspiring writers is (a) never identify yourself as an aspiring writer, and (b) don't read your stuff to friends."

BRANSON, Margaret Stimmann 1922-

PERSONAL: Born August 7, 1922, in Modesto, Calif.; daughter of Georg August and Dora (Schramm) Stimmann; married Rodney B. Branson (manager of Melrose Lumber Co.), June 15, 1946; children: Rodney Thomas, Martha Elizabeth (deceased), David George. *Education:* University of the Pacific, A.B. (with high honors), 1944; University of California, Berkeley, M.A. in Ed., 1952; Holy Names College, M.A. (history), 1962; post-graduate study, University of San Francisco. *Religion:* Lutheran. *Home:* 523 Hampton Rd., Piedmont, Calif. 94611. *Office:* Holy Names College, 3500 Mountain Blvd., Oakland, Calif. 94619.

CAREER: Oakland public schools, Oakland, Calif., teacher, counselor, and curriculum assistant, 1945-59, vice-principal, 1959-64, supervisor of secondary social sciences, 1964-69; associate professor of education at Holy Names College and instructor in teacher education at Mills College, both Oakland, Calif., 1969—. Lecturer at other colleges and universities. Consultant to Law in Free Society Project, 1969-78, and to History Education Project of American Historical Association. *Member:* American Historical Association, American Academy of Political and Social Science, Organization of American Historians, National Council for the Social Studies, Association for Supervision and Curriculum Development, League of Women Voters, Oakland Museum Association (member of board of directors), Pi Lambda Theta, Alpha Delta Kappa, Delta Kappa Gamma, Delta Delta Delta, Phi Delta Kappa. *Awards, honors:* Hilda-Taba award for contributions to the social studies.

WRITINGS: American History for Today, Ginn, 1970, 3rd edition, 1977; *Inquiry Experiences in American History,* Ginn, 1970, 2nd edition, 1975; (with Evarts Erickson) *Urban America,* Scott, Foresman, 1970; (with Edward E. France) *The Human Side of Afro-American History,* Ginn, 1972; (with Raymond Calkins and Charles Quigley) *The Environments We Live In,* Follett, 1973; (with June Chapin) *Women: The Majority Minority,* Houghton, 1973; *Land of Promise,* Ginn, 1974; *The Way People Live,* Houghton, 1976; (with others) *Urban Communities,* C. E. Merrill, 1978; *Civics for Today,* Houghton, 1980; *Around Our World,* Houghton, 1980. Writer of guides. Contributor to professional journals.

WORK IN PROGRESS: Revising *American History for Today;* contributing to a book on law and education; a human rights *Primer for Educators;* editing *International Human Rights and the Social Studies;* a collection of multiethnic folk tales adapted for young children.

* * *

BREIHAN, Carl W(illiam) 1916-

PERSONAL: Born February 3, 1916, in St. Louis County, Mo.; son of William A. and Cecelia (Schnieders) Breihan; married May 17, 1944; wife's name, Venarde; children: Carol Ann, Carl, Jr., Janis Sue. *Education:* Attended parochial high schools. *Politics:* Republican. *Religion:* Roman Catholic. *Home:* 4939 Mattis Rd., St. Louis, Mo.

CAREER: Former office manager, McLean-Hayes-Chicago Express Trucking Co., St. Louis, Mo. Member of Board of Traffic Commissioners, St. Louis County, Mo., 1956-62; chairman of roads and traffic, St. Louis County South Central Council, beginning 1963. Deputy sheriff, St. Louis County, 1944-56; deputy marshall, Marlborough, St. Louis County, beginning 1962; president, Longstreet Memorial Association. *Member:* Big Brothers Organization (associate member), Western Writers of America, Missouri Writers Guild, Denver Posse of Westerners, Los Angeles Westerners, Concord Township Republican Club (president, 1958-60, and beginning 1961).

WRITINGS: The Complete and Authentic Life of Jesse James, Fell, 1953, revised edition, 1969; *Badmen of the Frontier Days,* McBride, 1957 (published in England as *Outlaws of the Old West,* John Long, 1959); *Quantrill and His Civil War Guerrillas,* Sage Publications, 1959; *Younger Brothers,* Naylor, 1961; *The Day Jesse James Was Killed,* Fell, 1961; *Great Gunfighters of the West,* Naylor, 1962; *Great Lawmen of the West,* Bonanza, 1963; (with Charles A. Rosamond) *The Bandit Belle,* Hangman Press, 1970; (with Marion Ballert) *Billy the Kid: A Date with Destiny,* Hangman Press, 1970; *The Killer Legions of Quantrill,* Hangman Press, 1971; *The Escapades of Frank and Jesse James,* Fell, 1974; *The Man Who Shot Jesse James,* A. S. Barnes, 1978; (with Wayne Montgomery) *Forty Years on the Wild Frontier,* Devin-Adair, 1979.

AVOCATIONAL INTERESTS: Bowling.†

* * *

BRICKMAN, William Wolfgang 1913-

PERSONAL: Born June 30, 1913, in New York, N.Y.; son of David Shalom and Sarah (Shaber) Brickman; married Sylvia Schnitzer, February 26, 1958; children: Joy, Chaim, Sara. *Education:* City College (now City College of the City University of New York), B.A., 1934, M.S. in Education, 1935; New York University, Ph.D., 1938. *Home:* 15 Jade Lane, Cherry Hill, N.J. 08002. *Office:* Graduate School of Education, University of Pennsylvania, Philadelphia, Pa. 19104.

CAREER: City College (now City College of the City University of New York), New York City, tutor in German, 1937; New York University, New York City, instructor, 1940-42, 1946-48, lecturer, 1948-50, assistant professor, 1950-51, associate professor, 1951-57, professor of education, 1957-62; University of Pennsylvania, Philadelphia, professor of educational history and comparative education, 1962—; Touro College, New York City, dean, 1977-79. President's research fellow, Brown University, 1950-51. Visiting professor, University of California, Los Angeles, 1953 and 1954, Yeshiva University, 1953-57, 1959, and 1964, University of Hamburg, 1957, University of Illinois, 1958, Teachers College, Columbia University, 1964, University of Pittsburgh, 1965, and University of Wyoming, 1968. Member of committee on international education, College Entrance Examination Board, 1969-70; member of National Fulbright Selection Committee; member of committee of religion and education, University of Notre Dame; member of academic advisory board, Yeshiva University. *Military service:* U.S. Army, 1943-46; became staff sergeant. *Member:* International Association for the Advancement of Educational Research (member of council), Comparative Education Society (president, 1956-59), American Historical Association, National Society for the Study of Education, History of Education Society. *Awards, honors:* M.A., University of Pennsylvania, 1972.

WRITINGS: Guide to Research in Educational History, New York University Bookstore, 1949, published as *Research in Educational History,* Folcroft Library Editions, 1976; (co-author) *The Changing Soviet School,* Houghton, 1960; *Educational Systems in the United States,* Center for Applied Research in Education, 1964; *Foreign Students in American Elementary and Secondary Schools,* International House, 1967; *Bibliographical Essays on Curriculum and Instruction,* Norwood, 1974; *Bibliographical Essays on Comparative and International Education,* Norwood, 1975; *Bibliographical Essays on Educational Psychology and Sociology of Education,* Norwood, 1975; *Bibliographical Essays on the History and Philosophy of Education,* Norwood, 1975; *Bibliographical Essays on the System of Education,* Norwood, 1975; *Two Millenia of International Relations in Higher Education,* Norwood, 1976; *The Jewish Community in America: An Annotated and Classified Bibliographical Guide,* Burt Franklin, 1977; (co-author) *Ideas and Issues in Educational Thought: Past and Recent,* Norwood, 1978.

Editor: (With Stanley Lehrer) *John Dewey: Master Educator,* Society for the Advancement of Education, 1959, 2nd edition, 1961; (with Lehrer) *The Countdown on Segregated Education,* Society for the Advancement of Education, 1960; (with Lehrer) *Religion, Government, and Education,* Society for the Advancement of Education, 1961; (with Lehrer) *A Century of Higher Education,* Society for the Advancement of Education, 1962; John Dewey, *Impressions of Soviet Russia and the Revolutionary World,* Columbia University, 1964; (with Lehrer) *Automation, Education, and Human Values,* School & Society Books, 1966; *Educational Imperatives in Changing Culture,* University of Pennsylvania Press, 1967; (with Stewart E. Fraser) *A History of International and Comparative Education,* Scott, Foresman, 1968.

(With Lehrer) *Conflict and Change on the Campus: The Response to Student Hyperactivism,* School & Society Books, 1970; (with Lehrer) *Education and the Many Faces of the Disadvantaged: Cultural and Historical Perspectives,* Wiley, 1972; *Comparative Education: Concept, Research, and Application,* Norwood, 1973; (with Francesco Cordasco) *A Bibliography of American Educational History: An Annotated and Classified Guide,* AMS Press, 1975. Also editor of over forty books in the Norwood educational reprints series, including *The Use and Abuse of Examinations,* by David Murray, *Higher Schools and Universities in Germany,* by Matthew Arnold, *Reformatory Education,* by Henry Barnard, *The Soviet Challenge to America,* by George S. Counts, *Child Life in Colonial Days,* by Alice M. Earle, *Methods of Teaching History,* by G. Stanley Hall, *Outlines of Educational Doctrine,* by J. F. Herbart, *History of Education,* by Henry I. Smith, and *New Minds, New Men?,* by Thomas Woody.

Contributor to *Encyclopaedia Britannica, Encyclopedia of Educational Research, Encyclopedia of Education,* and *Encyclopedia Americana.* Contributor of numerous articles and reviews to professional journals, literary periodicals, and newspapers. Editor, *School and Society,* 1953-76; assistant managing editor, *Modern Language Journal;* member of editorial board, *Paedagogica Historica.*

WORK IN PROGRESS: Anna Maria van Schurman: Learned Lady; Bengt Skytte's Plan for an International University; History of Educational Historiography; Multilingual Education in Historical and International Perspectives.

SIDELIGHTS: William Wolfgang Brickman has a reading knowledge of most European languages. *Avocational interests:* Music history and appreciation.

* * *

BRIGGS, Charlie 1927-

PERSONAL: Born July 10, 1927, in Paducah, Ky.; daughter of Frank (Kentucky agricultural commissioner) and Ora Lee (Lipford) Irwin; married Andrew Jackson Briggs (owner of Topix, Inc.), June 7, 1948; children: Clark H., Charles A. *Education:* Attended University of Kentucky, 1946-48. *Poli-*

tics: Republican. *Religion:* Christian. *Home:* 420 South Harbor Dr., Venice, Fla. 33595. *Office:* 530 U.S. 41 Bypass, South Venice, Fla. 33595.

CAREER: Transylvania Times, Brevard, N.C., author of "Backtalk" column, 1956-60; *Tampa Tribune,* Tampa, Fla., reporter, 1963-73; currently editor and publisher of *Business & Pleasure* magazine. Teacher of creative writing, Manatee Junior College. Has worked as circus press agent.

WRITINGS: (With Rosemary K. Collett) *My Orphans of the Wild,* Lippincott, 1974. Work is represented in anthologies. Contributor of short stories and articles to magazines, including *American Girl, Ladies Circle, Southern Living,* and *Floridan,* and to newspapers. Former editor of *North Port News* (Northport, Fla.), and *Port Charlotte Chronicle* (Port Charlotte, Fla.).

SIDELIGHTS: Charlie Briggs told *CA:* "After thirty years as a free lancer, I have developed a bottom-line creed of trying to be honest and upbeat, trying to write the best I can, and not be tempted to 'play writer.' The disciplines of any writing craft are very important to me, and the freedom within those disciplines are there and possible only because the disciplines exist in the first place."

* * *

BRINNIN, John Malcolm 1916-

PERSONAL: Born September 13, 1916, in Halifax, Nova Scotia, Canada; brought to United States in 1920; son of John Thomas and Frances (Malcolm) Brinnin (American citizens). *Education:* University of Michigan, B.A., 1941; Harvard University, additional study, 1941-42. *Home:* 100 Memorial Dr., Cambridge, Mass. *Agent:* Harold Ober Associates, 40 East 49th St., New York, N.Y. 10017. *Office:* Department of English, Boston University, Boston, Mass. 02215.

CAREER: Vassar College, Poughkeepsie, N.Y., instructor, 1942-47; Dodd, Mead & Co., New York, N.Y., associate editor, 1948-50; University of Connecticut, Storrs, associate professor of English, 1951-62; Boston University, Boston, Mass., professor of English, 1962—. Poet-in-residence, Stephens College, 1947. Director, Young Men's and Young Women's Hebrew Association's Poetry Center (New York, N.Y.), 1949-56; U.S. State Department lecturer and delegate in Europe, 1954, 1956, and 1961. *Member:* Connecticut Academy of Arts and Sciences, Signet Society. *Awards, honors:* Levinson Prize, 1943; received gold medal, Poetry Society of America, 1955, for distinguished service; National Institute of Arts and Letters grant, 1968.

WRITINGS—Poetry: *The Garden Is Political,* Macmillan, 1942; *The Lincoln Lyrics,* New Directions, 1942; *No Arch, No Triumph,* Knopf, 1945; *The Sorrows of Cold Stone: Poems 1940-1950,* Dodd, 1951, reprinted, Greenwood Press, 1971; *The Selected Poems of John Malcolm Brinnin,* Little, Brown, 1963; *Skin Diving in the Virgins and Other Poems,* Delacorte, 1970.

Other: *Dylan Thomas in America: An Intimate Journal,* Little, Brown, 1955, reprinted, 1971; *The Third Rose: Gertrude Stein and Her World,* Little, Brown, 1959; *Arthur: The Dolphin Who Didn't See Venice* (juvenile), Little, Brown, 1961; *William Carlos Williams* (pamphlet), University of Minnesota Press, 1963; *Dylan,* Random House, 1964; *The Sway of the Grand Saloon: A Social History of the North Atlantic,* Delacorte, 1971.

Editor: (With Kimon Friar) *Modern Poetry: American and British,* Appleton, 1951; *Casebook on Dylan Thomas,* Crowell, 1960; *Emily Dickinson: Poems,* Dell, 1960; (with Bill Read) *The Modern Poets: An American-British Anthology,* McGraw, 1963, 2nd edition, 1970; *Selected Operas and Plays of Gertrude Stein,* University of Pittsburgh Press, 1970; (with Read) *Twentieth Century Poetry, American and British (1900-1970): An American-British Anthology,* McGraw, 1970. Contributor of numerous articles and stories to periodicals.

SIDELIGHTS: Discussing his philosophy of poetry, John Malcolm Brinnin once wrote in *Poets on Poetry* that he has always been "less interested in understanding a poem than in feeling it. What moved me then, as now, was the language and the music of language, the perception of the sheer poetic thing, without reference to the ideas which it is meant to serve or to promote. . . . In other words, poetry for me was, from the very beginning, not a vehicle, nor an agent, nor a means to salvation, but the liveliest art, the most gloriously useless and the most necessary."

BIOGRAPHICAL/CRITICAL SOURCES: Poetry, April, 1945; *New Republic,* April 2, 1945; *New Statesman,* September 27, 1963; *Book Week,* October 27, 1963; *New York Times Book Review,* December 22, 1963; Howard Nemerov, editor, *Poetry and Fiction,* Rutgers University Press, 1963; *Saturday Review,* February 1, 1964; Nemerov, editor, *Poets on Poetry,* Basic Books, 1966; *Library Journal,* July, 1970.†

* * *

BRITTON, Dorothea S(prague) 1922-

PERSONAL: Born October 30, 1922, in Cleveland, Ohio; daughter of Paul Epworth (executive vice-president of Glidden Co.) and Ruth (Horrocks) Sprague; married Alan Beckwith Britton (president of Steinkemp & Britton, Inc., realtors), September 27, 1952; children: Dana Sprague, Deborah Beckwith, Tracy Tuttle. *Education:* University of Michigan, A.B., 1948. *Politics:* Republican. *Religion:* Protestant. *Home:* 4 Rock Hill Lane, Scarsdale, N.Y. 10583. *Agent:* Julia Fallowfield, McIntosh & Otis, 475 Fifth Ave., New York, N.Y. 10017. *Office:* Norwalk Hospital, Norwalk, Conn.

CAREER: George Worthington Co., Cleveland, Ohio, director of personnel, 1950-52; Tracydot Products, Scarsdale, N.Y., founder, 1958-70; Nellie J. Crocker Health Center, Ossining, N.Y., director of program development, 1970-72; Roosevelt Hospital, New York, N.Y., director of voluntary personnel, 1973-77; People's Bank for Savings, New Rochelle, N.Y., manager of community relations and marketing, 1977-79; Norwalk Hospital, Norwalk, Conn., administrative director of volunteer services, 1979—. Free-lance writer. *Member:* Pi Beta Phi, Scarsdale (N.Y.) Women's Club, Scarsdale Golf Club.

WRITINGS: Dot Britton's Plans for an Op-Art Spring and Easter Bazaar, privately printed, 1969; *Dot Britton's 1970 Christmas Bazaar Book,* privately printed, 1970; *Dot Britton's Christmas and Easter Bazaar Book,* privately printed, 1970; *The Complete Book of Bazaars,* Coward, 1973; *The Legends of Christmas,* Coward, 1980. Contributor to *Better Homes and Gardens* and *Westchester Illustrated Magazine.*

WORK IN PROGRESS: A book on crafts for the elderly and handicapped; a sequel to *The Complete Book of Bazaars;* a book, *Development of Women's Job Opportunities.*

BIOGRAPHICAL/CRITICAL SOURCES: Family Circle, April, 1969; Mary Bass Gibson, *The Family Circle Book of Careers at Home,* Cowles, 1972.

BRODERICK, Richard L(awrence) 1927-
(Kenny Richards)

PERSONAL: Born November 12, 1927, in New York, N.Y.; son of Robert (a sales executive) and Winifred (Cantwell) Broderick; married Mary Ann Hammel (a travel consultant), September 30, 1950; children: Barbara, Virginia, Richard, Jr., Marianne, Maureen, Colleen. *Education:* Fordham University, B.A., 1947. *Politics:* Independent. *Religion:* Roman Catholic. *Home:* 106 Norma Rd., Harrington Park, N.J. 07640. *Office:* Topaz Marketing Corp., 150 East 52nd St., New York, N.Y.

CAREER: M.C.A. Records International, New York City, vice-president, 1968-71; Tara International, New York City, president, 1971-73; Audio Quest International, New York City, president, 1973-76; Topaz Marketing Corp., New York City, managing director, 1978—. Assistant professor, New York University, 1979—. Director of Hawaiian Music Association, 1971—. *Military service:* U.S. Army, 1947-52; became second lieutenant. *Member:* Country Music Association (chairman of the board, 1971-72), National Academy of Recording Arts and Sciences.

WRITINGS: (With Ellis Nassour) *Rock Opera,* Hawthorn, 1973; (editor) *New York Times One Hundred Latin Songs,* Quadrangle, 1973; (editor) *New York Times One Hundred Country Songs,* Quadrangle, 1974; *Our Musical Heritage,* Meredith, 1976. Editor of *Roller Derby News,* 1949-53, and *Hosiery Industry News,* 1953-54.

WORK IN PROGRESS: Up, Up and Away the Organization: A Travesty of the Airline Travel Business; A Funny Thing Happened on the Way to the World Series.

* * *

BROOKE, Bryan (Nicholas) 1915-

PERSONAL: Born February 21, 1915, in Croydon, Surrey, England; son of George Cyril (a numismatist) and Margaret Florence (Parsons) Brooke; married Naomi Winefride Mills, December 21, 1940; children: Marian (Mrs. Michael Shaw), Nicola (Mrs. Christopher Brooker), Penelope. *Education:* Attended Bradfield College, Berkshire, England, 1928-33; Corpus Christi College, Cambridge, B.A., 1936, M.B., B.Chir., 1940; St. Bartholomew's Hospital, London, M.Chir., 1944; University of Birmingham, M.D. (honors), 1954. *Home:* 112 Balham Park Rd., Balham SW12 8EA, England. *Agent:* Curtis Brown Ltd., 1 Craven Hill, London W2 3EW, England. *Office:* St. James' Hospital, Sarsfeld Rd., Balham SW12 8HW, England.

CAREER: University of Aberdeen, Aberdeen, Scotland, lecturer in surgery, 1946-47; University of Birmingham, Birmingham, England, reader in surgery, 1947-63; University of London, St. George's Hospital, London, England, professor of surgery, 1963-76, professor emeritus, 1976—, consultant surgeon, 1976—; St. James' Hospital, Balham, England, consultant surgeon, 1976—. Royal College of Surgeons, Hunterian Professor, 1951, chairman of court of examiners, 1978; examiner in surgery at University of Birmingham, 1951-63, Cambridge University, 1958-68, University of Bristol, 1961-70, University of London, 1962—, University of Glasgow, 1969-72, and Oxford University, 1970. Member of Medical Appeals Tribunal, 1948—. *Military service:* British Army, Royal Medical Corps, 1944-46; became lieutenant colonel.

MEMBER: Royal College of Surgeons (fellow), British Society of Gastroenterology (honorary member), Surgical Research Society (England), Royal Australasian College of Surgeons (honorary fellow), American Gastroenterology Society, American Society for Colon and Rectal Surgeons (honorary fellow). *Awards, honors:* Copeman Medal for Scientific Research, 1960; Graham Award (of American Proctologic Society), 1961; New York Society of Colon and Rectal Surgeons Award, 1967.

WRITINGS: United Birmingham Cancer Reports, United Birmingham Hospital, 1953, 3rd edition, 1957; *Ulcerative Colitis and Its Surgical Treatment,* E. S. Livingstone, 1954; *You and Your Operation,* Faber, 1956; (editor with John Badenock) *Recent Advances in Gastroenterology,* Little, Brown, 1965, 2nd edition, Williams & Wilkins, 1972; (with Geoffrey Slaney) *Metabolic Derangements in Gastrointestinal Surgery,* C. C Thomas, 1967; *Understanding Cancer,* Heinemann, 1971, Holt, 1973; (editor) *Clinics in Gastroenterology,* Saunders, 1972; (editor) *Crohn's Disease,* Saunders, 1972; *Inflammatory Diseases of the Bowel,* Pitman, 1980. Contributor of articles on medicine and medical education to professional journals.

WORK IN PROGRESS: Research on inflammatory diseases of the intestine.

AVOCATIONAL INTERESTS: Painting, pottery.

* * *

BROOKS, Anne Tedlock 1905-
(Ann Carter, Anne Carter, Cynthia Millburn)

PERSONAL: Born April 8, 1905, in Columbus, Kan.; daughter of James Matthew and Alice (Hall) Tedlock; married Mark L. Brooks, 1924; children: Marcus William. *Education:* Attended Kansas State Teachers College (now Pittsburg State University), 1925-27; University of Oregon, B.S. in Education (magna cum laude), 1955; University of San Francisco, graduate study, 1957. *Residence:* Gladstone, Ore. *Agent:* Gerald Pollinger, Laurence Pollinger Ltd., 18 Maddox St., London W1R 0EU, England.

CAREER: Free-lance writer, 1936—. *Member:* National League of American Penwomen (Missouri state president, 1944-45), American Association of University Women, Oregon Freelance Club. *Awards, honors:* Missouri Writers Guild award, 1938; National League of American Pen Women novel award, 1946; Daughters of the American Revolution citation as Missouri Woman of Achievement, 1950.

WRITINGS—Published by Arcadia House, except as indicated: *Romance in the Sky,* Gramercy, 1940; *Paddlewheels Churning: A Tale of Old Missouri,* Burton Publishing, 1942; *This Side of Heaven,* 1943; *Undertow,* 1943; *The Girl Next Door,* 1944; *Only the Gulls Cry,* 1947; *Love Came Laughing,* Samuel Curl, 1947 (published in England as *Jane Finally Decides,* Foulsham, 1957); *Fair Sailing,* 1948; *The Romantic Journey,* 1948; *Smoke on the River,* 1949; *Fire in the Wind,* 1950; *The Singing Fiddles: A Story of the Jason Lee Missions in Early Oregon,* 1950; *White Gulls Flying,* 1953; *Castle on the Coast,* 1954; *Tawn Delaney,* 1955; *The Peacock Feather,* 1956, published as *With a Heart Full of Love,* Paperback Library, 1966; *Island Neighbor,* 1956; *Evergreen Girl,* 1957; *One Enchanted Summer,* 1958; *Centennial Summer,* 1960; *White Camellias,* 1960; *Once upon a Cruise,* 1961; *Holiday Cove,* 1962; *One More Camellia,* Lenox Hill, 1971; *Point Virtue,* Belmont Tower, 1979.

Under pseudonym Ann Carter; originally published by Arcadia House: *Prudent Angel,* 1948; *You'll Remember,* 1949; *Lucky the Bride,* 1950; *Huckleberry Hill,* 1950 (published in England as *Valerie's Two Loves,* Foulsham, 1952); *Prelude to Summer,* 1951; *Villa by the Sea,* 1952 (published in England as *The Cottage l'Amour,* Foulsham, 1955).

Under pseudonym Anne Carter: *The Enchanted Year,* Arcadia House, 1949, published in England under pseudonym Ann Carter, T. V. Boardman, 1950.

Under pseudonym Cynthia Millburn: *Pilot Judy,* Gramercy, 1943; *Yours Truly,* Gramercy, 1943; *Thanks, Angel,* Gramercy, 1945; *I Take This Man,* Gramercy, 1946; *A Lady's Fancy,* Gramercy, 1948; *Golden Acres,* Arcadia House, 1950; *Pirate's Cove,* Arcadia House, 1951; *Bow without Arrow,* Arcadia House, 1951; *Bright Lamp,* Arcadia House, 1953; *Spin a Dream,* Arcadia House, 1962.

Stories represented in anthologies: *Something Singing: An Anthology of Verse by Members of the Jefferson City Chapter of the Missouri Writers Guild,* Bard Press, 1936; *We Are Neighbors,* edited by Odille Ousley and David H. Russell, revised edition, Ginn, 1957; *Trails to Treasure,* edited by Russell, Constance M. McCullough, and Doris Gates, revised edition, Ginn, 1961.

Also author of three serials syndicated by *Philadelphia Ledger,* 1939-43, and six short novels syndicated by *Chicago Daily News.* Contributor of short stories and serials to *Parents' Magazine, Mother's Activities, Children's Activities, Writer's Monthly, Christian Herald,* and other periodicals. Editor, *Universal Tips,* 1944-45.

WORK IN PROGRESS: Two historical novels, *Peacock Spit* and *These Boys Became Presidents.*

* * *

BROOKS, Gwendolyn 1917-

PERSONAL: Born June 7, 1917, in Topeka, Kan.; daughter of David Anderson and Keziah Corinne (Wims) Brooks; married Henry L. Blakely, September 17, 1939; children: Henry L., Nora. *Education:* Graduate of Wilson Junior College, 1936. *Home:* 2528-A Jerome, Chicago, Ill. 60645.

CAREER: Author. Taught poetry at numerous colleges and universities, including Columbia College, Elmhurst College, Northeastern Illinois State College (now Northeastern Illinois University), and University of Wisconsin—Madison, 1969; Distinguished Professor of the Arts, City College of the City University of New York, 1971. Member, Illinois Arts Council. *Member:* American Academy of Arts and Letters, National Institute of Arts and Letters, Society of Midland Authors (Chicago). *Awards, honors:* Named one of ten women of the year, *Mademoiselle* magazine, 1945; National Institute of Arts and Letters grant in literature, 1946; American Academy of Arts and Letters award for creative writing, 1946; Guggenheim fellowships, 1946, 1947; Eunice Tietjens Memorial Prize, *Poetry* magazine, 1949; Pulitzer Prize in poetry, 1950, for *Annie Allen;* Friends of Literature Poetry Award, 1963; Thormod Monsen Literature Award, 1964; Anisfield-Wolf Award, 1968; named Poet Laureate of Illinois, 1969; Black Academy of Arts and Letters Award, 1971, for outstanding achievement in letters; Shelley Memorial Award; thirty-eight honorary degrees from universities and colleges, including Columbia College, 1964, Lake Forest College, 1965, and Brown University, 1974.

WRITINGS: Maud Martha (novel), Harper, 1953; (with others) *A Portion of That Field,* University of Illinois Press, 1967; *The World of Gwendolyn Brooks* (collection of verse and prose), Harper, 1971; (editor) *A Broadside Treasury* (poems), Broadside Press, 1971; (editor) *Jump Bad: A New Chicago Anthology,* Broadside Press, 1971; *Report from Part One* (autobiography), Broadside Press, 1972; (with Keorapetse Kgositsile, Haki R. Madhubuti, and Dudley Randall) *A Capsule Course in Black Poetry Writing,* Broadside Press, 1975.

Poems; published by Harper, except as indicated: *A Street in Bronzeville,* 1945; *Annie Allen,* 1949, reprinted, Greenwood Press, 1972; *Bronzeville Boys and Girls,* 1956; *The Bean Eaters* (juvenile), 1960; *Selected Poems,* 1963; *In the Mecca,* 1968; *For Illinois 1968: A Sesquicentennial Poem,* [Chicago], 1968.

Published by Broadside Press, except as indicated: *Riot,* 1969; *Family Pictures,* 1970; *Aloneness,* 1971; *Aurora,* 1972; *The Tiger Who Wore White Gloves: Or, What You Are You Are,* Third World Press, 1974; *Beckonings,* 1975. Also author of *The Wall* and *We Real Cool,* for Broadside Press, and *I See Chicago,* 1964. Contributor of reviews to *Chicago Sun-Times* and *Chicago Daily News.* Editor, *Black Position.*

WORK IN PROGRESS: The second volume of her autobiography.

SIDELIGHTS: In 1950, Gwendolyn Brooks, a highly regarded poet, became the first black author to win the Pulitzer Prize. Her poems from this period, specifically *A Street in Bronzeville* and *Annie Allen,* were "devoted to small, carefully cerebrated, terse portraits of the Black urban poor," Richard K. Barksdale comments. Jeanne-Marie A. Miller calls this "city-folk poetry" and describes Brooks' characters as "unheroic black people who fled the land for the city—only to discover that there is little difference between the world of the North and the world of the South. One learns from them," she continues, "their dismal joys and their human grief and pain." Although, as Martha Liebrum notes, Brooks "wrote about being black before being black was beautiful," in retrospect her first poems have been "characterized as 'establishment,' 'safe' 'conservative,'" writes Hollie I. West. Barksdale states that by avoiding any "rhetorical involvement with causes, racial or otherwise," Brooks was merely reflecting the "the literary mood of the late 1940's." He suggests that there was little reason for Brooks to confront the problems of racism on a large scale since, in her work, "each character, so neatly and precisely presented, is a racial protest in itself and a symbol of some sharply etched human dilemma."

However, Brooks' later poems show a marked change in tone and content. Just as her first poems reflected the mood of their era, her later works mirror their age by displaying what Bruce Cook calls "an intense awareness of the problems of color and justice." Toni Cade Bambara comments that, at the age of fifty "something happened [to Brooks], a something most certainly in evidence in 'In the Mecca' (1968) and subsequent works—a new movement and energy, intensity, richness, power of statement and a new stripped, lean, compressed style. A change of style prompted by a change of mind." *In the Mecca* "sets the brutal slaying of a child against the vast, indifferent misery of others trapped in Mayor Daley's slums," writes James N. Johnson. The poem exemplifies what he and others term Brooks' new "toughness."

Although these later works are characterized as tougher and possess what a reviewer for the *Virginia Quarterly Review* describes as "raw power and roughness," critics are quick to indicate that these poems are neither bitter nor vengeful. Instead, according to Cook, they are more "about bitterness" than bitter in themselves. Johnson believes that while Brooks writes of "the solemn hungers and hellish silences of the ghetto," she does not preach, "she simply observes, with quiet and merciless accuracy."

Brooks' objectivity is perhaps the most widely acclaimed feature of her poetry. Janet Overmeyer notes that Brooks' "particular, outstanding, genius is her unsentimental regard and respect for all human beings. . . . She neither foolishly pities nor condemns—she creates." Overmeyer continues, "From her poet's craft bursts a whole gallery of wholly alive persons, preening, squabbling, loving, weeping; many a novelist cannot do so well in ten times the space." Brooks achieves this effect through a high "degree of artistic control," claims David Littlejohn. "The words, lines, and arrangements," he states, "have been worked and worked and worked again into poised exactness: the unexpected apt metaphor, the mock-colloquial asides amid jewelled phrases, the half-ironic repetitions—she knows it all." More importantly, Brooks' objective treatment of issues such as poverty and racism "produces genuine emotional tension," writes Littlejohn. Johnson agrees and adds that it is "her restraint which enables Miss Brooks to put a living character before you."

Johnson refers to Brooks' objectivity as "detached compassion." This quality not only gives her work excitement, tension, and depth, it also provides her poems with universal appeal. Blyden Jackson believes that Brooks "is one of those artists of whom it can truthfully be said that things like sex and race, important as they are, . . . appear in her work to be sublimated into insights and revelations of universal application." Although Brooks' characters are primarily black and poor, and live in Northern urban cities, she provides, according to Jackson, through "the close inspection of a limited domain, . . . a view of life in which one may see a microscopic portion of the universe intensely and yet, through that microscopic portion see all truth for the human condition wherever it is." In Roy Newquist's *Conversations,* Brooks comments: "I think that my poetry is related to life in the broad sense of the word, even though the subject matter relates closest to the Negro. Although I called my first book *A Street in Bronzeville,* I hoped that people would recognize instantly that Negroes are just like other people; they have the same hates and loves and fears, the same tragedies and triumphs and deaths, as people of any race or religion or nationality."

BIOGRAPHICAL/CRITICAL SOURCES: David Littlejohn, *Black on White: A Critical Survey of Writing by American Negroes,* Viking, 1966; Roy Newquist, *Conversations,* Rand McNally, 1967; *Negro Digest,* January, 1968; *Christian Science Monitor,* September 19, 1968; *National Observer,* November 9, 1968; *Ramparts,* December, 1968; *Virginia Quarterly Review,* winter, 1969; *New York Times Book Review,* March 2, 1969, January 7, 1973; *Journal of Negro Education,* winter, 1970; *Black World,* August, 1970; *Washington Post,* May 19, 1971, April 19, 1973; Donald B. Gibson, editor, *Modern Black Poets: A Collection of Critical Essays,* Prentice-Hall, 1973; *Contemporary Literary Criticism,* Gale, Volume I, 1973, Volume II, 1974, Volume IV, 1975, Volume V, 1976; Blyden Jackson and Louis D. Rubin, Jr., *Black Poetry in America: Two Essays in Historical Interpretation,* Louisiana State University Press, 1974; *Houston Post,* February 11, 1974; *Authors in the News,* Volume I, Gale, 1976.

—Sketch by Denise Gottis

* * *

BROOKS, Peter 1938-

PERSONAL: Born April 19, 1938, in New York, N.Y.; son of Ernest, Jr. and Mary (Schoyer) Brooks; married Margaret Waters (a teacher), July 18, 1959; children: three. *Education:* Harvard University, A.B., 1959, Ph.D., 1965. *Residence:* New Haven, Conn. *Office:* Department of French, Yale University, New Haven, Conn. 06520.

CAREER: Yale University, New Haven, Conn., instructor, 1965-67, assistant professor, 1967-71, associate professor, 1971-75, professor of French and comparative literature, 1975—. Director, The Literature Major, 1974—. *Member:* Modern Language Association of America. *Awards, honors:* Guggenheim fellow, 1973-74.

WRITINGS: The Novel of Worldliness, Princeton University Press, 1969; (editor) *The Child's Part,* Beacon Press, 1972; (editor with Alvin B. Kernan and J. Michael Holquist) *Man and His Fictions,* Harcourt, 1973; *The Melodramatic Imagination,* Yale University Press, 1976; (editor with Joseph Halpern) *Genet: A Collection of Critical Essays,* Prentice-Hall, 1979. Contributor of articles and reviews to literature journals, including *New Republic* and *New York Times Book Review.* Associate editor, *Yale French Studies,* 1966—; contributing editor, *Partisan Review,* 1972—.

WORK IN PROGRESS: Research on the sense of plot in the nineteenth and twentieth century novel; psychoanalysis and the study of narrative.

* * *

BROWN, Benjamin F. 1930-

PERSONAL: Born June 24, 1930; son of Ben F. and Mary (Hunt) Brown. *Education:* Baylor University, B.A., 1950; University of Colorado, M.A., 1953; University of California, Berkeley, graduate study, 1955-56; Harvard University, Ph.D., 1966. *Politics:* Democrat. *Religion:* Episcopalian. *Home:* 806 Carroll St., Brooklyn, N.Y. 11215.

CAREER: University of Florence, Florence, Italy, lecturer in modern and contemporary history, 1959-61, 1970-71; Sonoma State College (now California State College, Sonoma), Sonoma, Calif., assistant professor of history, 1962-66; University of Kansas, Lawrence, assistant professor, 1967-69, associate professor, 1969-77, professor of modern European history, 1977-79. *Member:* American Historical Association, American Association of University Professors, Society for Italian Historical Studies. *Awards, honors:* Fulbright scholar at University of Rome, 1954-55; Harvard Travelling fellow, 1959-61; American Philosophical Society fellow, 1967, and 1973; Marraro Prize, American Historical Association, 1974; Guggenheim Foundation fellow, 1977.

WRITINGS—General editor with P. Pastorelli; all published by Giuseppi Laterza (Rome): *Opera omnia di Sidney Sonnino, Diario, 1866-1922,* three volumes, 1972; *Scritti e discorsi extra-parlamentari,* two volumes, 1972; *Carteggio, 1891-1922,* three volumes, 1974-79.

AVOCATIONAL INTERESTS: Photography, skiing, swimming.

* * *

BROWN, Vinson 1912-

PERSONAL: Born December 7, 1912, in Reno, Nev.; son of Henry Alexander and Bertha (Bender) Brown; married Barbara Black, June 18, 1950; children: Kirby W., Jerrold V., Tamara L., Roxana L., Keven A. *Education:* University of California, Berkeley, B.A., 1939; Stanford University, M.A., 1947. *Religion:* Baha'i Faith. *Address:* P.O. Box 1045, Happy Camp, Calif. 96039. *Office:* Naturegraph Co., P.O. Box 1075, Happy Camp, Calif. 96039.

CAREER: Boy Naturalists' Club, Berkeley, Calif., director, 1936-41; Westinghouse Electric Co., Emeryville, Calif., electrician, 1942-43; Office of War Information, San Francisco, Calif., writer, 1943-44; Naturegraph Co. (publishers), Happy Camp, Calif., owner, 1946—. Affiliated with National

School Assemblies, Los Angeles, Calif., 1949-50; produced records on nature for San Mateo County Schools, Calif., 1951; member of editorial staff, Stanford University Press, 1952. *Military service:* U.S. Army, 1945-46; became technical sergeant.

WRITINGS: The Amateur Naturalist's Handbook, Little, Brown, 1946, revised edition, Prentice-Hall, 1980; *John Paul Jones,* Wheeler, 1949; *Black Treasure,* Little, Brown, 1951; (editor and rewriter) *Education in California,* Stanford University Press, 1952; *California Wildlife Region,* Naturegraph, 1953; *How to Make a Home Nature Museum,* Little, Brown, 1954; *It All Happened Right Here,* Stanford University Press, 1954; *The Sierra Nevada Wildlife Region,* Naturegraph, 1954, revised edition (with Robert Livezey), Naturegraph, 1961; (with David Allan III) *Rocks and Minerals of California,* Naturegraph, 1955; *How to Make a Miniature Zoo,* Little, Brown, 1956; (editor) Charles Yocom and Raymond Dasmann, *The Pacific Coastal Wildlife Region,* Naturegraph, 1957, revised edition, 1965; *How to Understand Animal Talk,* Little, Brown, 1958; (with Yocom and Aldine Starbuck) *Wildlife of the Intermountain West,* Naturegraph, 1958; (editor) *An Illustrated Guide to Fossil Collecting,* Naturegraph, 1959; (with Henry G. Weston, Jr.) *Handbook of California Birds,* Naturegraph, 1961; *How to Explore the Secret Worlds of Nature,* Little, Brown, 1962; *Explorations in Ancient Life,* Science Materials Center, 1962; (with William Willoya) *Warriors of the Rainbow,* Naturegraph, 1962; *Backyard Wild Birds of California and the Pacific Northwest,* T.F.H. Publications, 1965; *How to Follow the Adventures of the Insects,* Little, Brown, 1968; (with Yocom) *Wildlife and Plants of the Cascades,* Naturegraph, 1971; *Backyard Wild Birds of the East and Midwest,* T.F.H. Publications, 1971; *Reading the Woods,* Stackpole, 1972; *How to Know the Outdoors in the Dark,* Stackpole, 1972; *Great Upon the Mountain: Crazy Horse, Legendary Mystic and Warrior,* Macmillan, 1973; *Reptiles and Amphibians of the West,* Naturegraph, 1974; *Sea Mammals and Reptiles of the Pacific Coast,* Macmillan, 1976; *Peoples of the Sea Wind: Native Americans of the Pacific Coast,* Macmillan, 1977; *The Explorer Naturalist,* Macmillan, 1977. Contributor to *Encyclopedia of the Indians of America.* Columnist, *Gilroy Dispatch,* 1954-59; author of column, "Exploring Sonoma County," for four local newspapers, 1960—.

SIDELIGHTS: Vinson Brown has been on several natural history expeditions to Panama and Costa Rica jungles and in the western United States.

BIOGRAPHICAL/CRITICAL SOURCES: San Francisco Chronicle, August, 1961.

* * *

BRUBACHER, John Seiler 1898-

PERSONAL: Born October 18, 1898, in Easthampton, Mass.; son of A. R. and Rosa M. (Haas) Brubacher; married Winifred Wemple, 1924; children: John W., Paul W. *Education:* Yale University, A.B., 1920; Harvard University, J.D., 1923; Columbia University, Ph.D., 1927. *Religion:* Congregational Church. *Home:* 3030 Park Ave., Bridgeport, Conn.

CAREER: Dartmouth College, Hanover, N.H., instructor, 1924; Columbia University, New York, N.Y., assistant professor, 1928; Yale University, New Haven, Conn., 1928-58, began as assistant professor, became professor of history and philosophy of education, Reuben Post Halleck Professor of History and Philosophy of Education, 1948; University of Michigan, Ann Arbor, professor of higher education, 1958-69. Taught at American University, Beirut, Lebanon, 1951-52, and 1956-57. *Military service:* U.S. Army, Field Artillery; became second lieutenant. *Member:* National Education Association, Philosophy of Education Society (president, 1942-46), National Society of College Teachers of Education (vice-president, 1962-63; presdent-elect, 1963-64), Phi Beta Kappa. *Awards, honors:* Fulbright fellow at Kyushu University, Japan, 1957; John Dewey Society Award for distinguished service to education, 1973.

WRITINGS: Modern Philosophies of Education, McGraw, 1939, 4th edition, 1969; *A History of the Problems of Education,* McGraw, 1947, 2nd edition, 1966; (with Willis Rudy) *Higher Education in Transition,* Harper, 1958, 3rd edition, 1976; *Bases for Policy in Higher Education,* McGraw, 1965; *Case Book in the Law of Higher Education,* two volumes, University of Michigan, 1969, published as *The Law and Higher Education: A Casebook,* Fairleigh Dickinson University Press, 1971; *The Courts and Higher Education,* Jossey-Bass, 1971; *On the Philosophy of Higher Education,* Jossey-Bass, 1977. Also author of *The Importance of Theory in Education.*

Editor: *The Public School and Spiritual Values,* Harper, 1944; *Eclectic Philosophy of Education,* Prentice-Hall, 1951, 2nd edition, 1962; *Henry Barnard on Education,* Russell, 1965. Contributor to professional journals.

AVOCATIONAL INTERESTS: Travel, gardening, chess.

* * *

BRUNER, Jerome S(eymour) 1915-

PERSONAL: Born October 1, 1915, in New York, N.Y.; son of Herman and Rose (Glucksmann) Bruner; married Katherine Frost, November 10, 1940 (divorced, 1956); married Blanche Marshall McLane, January 16, 1960; children: (first marriage) Whitley, Jane. *Education:* Duke University, A.B., 1937; Harvard University, A.M., 1939, Ph.D., 1941. *Home:* 18 Hawkswell Gardens, Summertown, Oxford, England. *Office:* Department of Experimental Psychology, Oxford University, South Parks Rd., Oxford OX1 3PS, England.

CAREER: Harvard University, Cambridge, Mass., lecturer, 1945-48, associate professor, 1948-52, professor of psychology, 1952-72, director of Center for Cognitive Studies, 1961-72, master of Currier House of Harvard-Radcliffe College, 1970-71; Oxford University, Oxford, England, Watts Professor of Psychology, 1972—. Visiting member of Princeton Institute for Advanced Study, 1951-52; lecturer at Salzburg Seminar, 1952; Bacon Professor (Harvard) at University of Aix-en-Provence, 1965. Member of board of syndics, Harvard University Press, 1962-63; member of numerous other boards of directors and advisory boards for government and private agencies, including John F. Kennedy Center for Research on Human Development, National Science Foundation, United Nations, Educational Testing Service, National Institutes of Health, Educational Development Center, U.S. Department of State, Hampshire College, and Wheaton College. *Military service:* U.S. Army, Intelligence Corps, 1941-44; worked on analysis of public opinion and propaganda.

MEMBER: International Union of Scientific Psychology (member of executive committee), American Psychological Association (president, 1964-65), American Academy of Arts and Sciences (fellow), American Association for the Advancement of Science (fellow), National Academy of Education (founding fellow), Society for the Psychological Study of Social Issues (former president), American Association of University Professors, Federation Suisse de Psychologie (honorary foreign fellow), Officier de l'Instruction

Publique (honorary), Puerto Rican Academy of Arts and Sciences (honorary), Cruising Club of America, Royal Cruising Club, Harvard Club (New York), Cosmos Club.

AWARDS, HONORS: Guggenheim fellowship, Cambridge University, 1955-56; Distinguished Science Contribution Award, American Psychological Association, 1962; D.Litt. from Lesley College, 1964, Duke University, 1969, and Northern Michigan University, 1969; D.Sc. from Northwestern University, 1965, and University of Sheffield, 1970; LL.D. from Temple University, 1965, University of Cincinnati, 1966, and University of New Brunswick, 1969; first joint award of American Educational Research Association and American Educational Publishers Institute, 1969; citation from Merrill-Palmer Institute, 1970.

WRITINGS: Public Thinking on Post-War Problems, National Planning Association, 1943; *Mandate from the People,* Duell, Sloan, & Pearce, 1944; (editor) *Perception and Personality: A Symposium,* Duke University Press, 1950, reprinted, Greenwood Press, 1968; (with Jacqueline J. Goodnow and George A. Austin) *A Study of Thinking,* Wiley, 1956, reprinted, Robert E. Krieger, 1977; (with Mortimer B. Smith and R. W. White) *Opinions and Personality,* Wiley, 1956; (contributor with others) *Contemporary Approaches to Cognition,* Harvard University Press, 1957; (contributor with others) *Logique et perception,* Presses Universitaires de France, 1958; (contributor with others) Henry Alexander Murray, editor, *Myth and Mythmaking,* [Cambridge, Mass.], 1959.

The Process of Education, Harvard University Press, 1960, reprinted, 1977; *On Knowing: Essays for the Left Hand,* Harvard University Press, 1962, reprinted, 1979; *Man: A Course of Study,* Educational Services, 1965; (editor) *Learning about Learning: A Conference Report,* U.S. Department of Health, Education and Welfare, 1966; (with others) *Studies in Cognitive Growth,* Wiley, 1966; *Toward a Theory of Instruction,* Belknap Press, 1966; *Process of Cognitive Growth: Infancy* (Heinz Werner Lectures), Clark University Press, 1968; (contributor with others) *La sfida pedagogica americana,* A. Armando, 1969.

(Contributor) Victor H. Denenberg, editor, *Education of the Infant and Young Child,* Academic Press, 1970; (contributor with others) Robert Leeper, editor, *Dare to Care/Dare to Act: Racism and Education,* [Washington, D.C.], 1971; (contributor) Merle E. Meyer and F. Herbert Hite, editors, *The Application of Learning Principles to Classroom Instruction* (symposium), Western Washington State College, 1971; *The Relevance of Education,* edited by Anita Gil, Norton, 1971, new edition, 1973; *Beyond the Information Given: Studies in the Psychology of Knowing,* edited by Jeremy M. Anglin, Norton, 1973; (editor with Kevin Connolly) *The Growth of Competence* (conference proceedings), Academic Press, 1974; (editor with Alison Jolly and Kathy Sylva) *Play: Its Role in Development and Evolution,* Basic Books, 1976; (editor with Alison Garton) *Human Growth and Development: The Wolfson College Lectures, 1976,* Oxford University Press, 1978.

General editor with others, "Developing Child" series, Harvard University Press. Contributor to numerous professional journals. Editor, *Public Opinion Quarterly,* 1943-44.

WORK IN PROGRESS: The Growth of Language.

AVOCATIONAL INTERESTS: Sailing, politics.

BRYANT, Edward (Winslow, Jr.) 1945-
(Lawrence Talbot)

PERSONAL: Born August 27, 1945, in White Plains, N.Y.; son of Edward Winslow (a postal employee) and Anne (Van Kleeck) Bryant. *Education:* University of Wyoming, B.A., 1967, M.A., 1968. *Politics:* Independent. *Religion:* Protestant. *Home:* 300 Park Ave., Wheatland, Wyo. 82201. *Agent:* Robert Mills Ltd., 156 East 52nd St., New York, N.Y. 10022. *Office address:* P.O. Box 18162, Denver, Colo. 80218.

CAREER: Writer of science fiction and fantasy. Worked as disc jockey for KYCN-Radio, 1961-63, and as broadcaster, disc jockey, and news director for KOWB-Radio, 1965-66; shipping clerk, Blevins Manufacturing Co., 1968-69; taught high school and college courses in science fiction and in writing; lecturer for Science Fiction Writers Speakers Bureau and Western States Art Foundation; attended Clarion Science Fiction and Fantasy Writers Workshop, 1968, 1969. *Member:* Science Fiction Writers of America. *Awards, honors:* General Motors scholar; First Place, New American Library Fiction Competition, 1971; Science Fiction Writers of America, nominated for Nebula awards for best novelette and for best short story, both 1978, received Nebula award for best short story, 1979; nominated for Hugo award for best short story, World Science Fiction Convention, 1979.

WRITINGS: Among the Dead: And Other Events Leading up to the Apocalypse, Macmillan, 1973; (with Harlan Ellison) *Phoenix without Ashes,* Fawcett, 1975; *Cinnabar,* Macmillan, 1976; (editor) *2076: The American Tricentennial,* Pyramid Publications, 1977; *Particle Theory,* Pocket Books, in press; *Prairie Sun,* Jelm Mountain Press, in press. Work represented in many anthologies, including *Universe,* edited by Terry Carr, Random House, 1971, *Prejudice,* edited by Roger Elwood, Prentice-Hall, 1974, *High Terror,* edited by Kirby McCauley, Viking, 1980, and *Interfaces,* edited by Ursula K. LeGuin, Ace Books, 1980. Author of quarterly column, "Film," *Eternity* Magazine.

Also author of "The Synar Calculation," a film script for CVD Studios, 1973. Contributor of more than one hundred short stories and articles to science fiction magazines, popular national journals, and literary publications, including *National Lampoon, Rolling Stone, Omni, Penthouse,* and *Magazine of Fantasy and Science Fiction.*

WORK IN PROGRESS: Formal Wreckage, a mosaic novel composed of stories about a future American West; *Tiburon,* a novel; *Caged Eagles,* a book about America's future.

SIDELIGHTS: Edward Bryant told *CA:* "I keep finding myself arguing both with science fiction readers who feel my stories are not science-fictional enough and general readers who shy off because of the science fiction or fantasy label. My contention is that good science fiction possesses the same virtues and acquiesces to the same demands of art and craft as any other sort of fiction. I attempt to adhere to that: I write about people and their problems and relationships. But in addition, I'm intensely curious about what the future's influence through science and technology will be when applied to the basic human relationships of person-to-person and person-to-society. My wish for the moment is that more good writers in all fields would toss aside the knee-jerk anti-technology reaction and exercise a healthy, non-judgmental curiosity about this increasingly complex and fascinating universe."

BRYDEN, John Marshall 1941-

PERSONAL: Born December 18, 1941, in Perth, Scotland; son of William James and Christina (Marsh[illegible]ryden; married Elspeth Mowat, September 2, 1967; children: Tanera Mowat, Douglas Tyrie, Rory Marshall Anderson, Christina Naomi Elliot. *Education:* University of Glasgow, B.Sc. (honors), 1965; University of the West Indies, graduate study, 1965-66; University of East Anglia, Ph.D., 1972. *Office:* Coulnakyle, Nethybridge, Inverness-shire PH25 3EA, Scotland.

CAREER: Ministry of Overseas Development, London, England, economic assistant, 1966-67, Caribbean regional development advisor, 1968-70; University of East Anglia, Norwich, England, lecturer in economics, 1967-72; Highlands-Islands Development Board, Inverness, Scotland, head of land development division, 1972-79; farmer and development policy specialist, 1979—. *Member:* Agricultural Economics Society, Scottish Economic Society, Royal Highlands Agricultural Society, Royal Scottish Forestry Society. *Awards, honors:* Arkleton fellow, 1980-81.

WRITINGS: Tourism and Development: A Case Study of the Commonwealth Caribbean, Cambridge University Press, 1973; (with George Houston) *Agrarian Change in the Scottish Highlands,* Martin Robinson, 1976; (contributor) Seers, editor, *Underdeveloped Europe,* Harvester Press, 1979. Contributor to *Social and Economic Studies* and *Journal of Agricultural Economics.* Resource editor, *Annals of Tourism Research,* 1980—.

WORK IN PROGRESS: Research on institutional approaches to rural development in less favored areas of Europe; some theoretical aspects of tourism developments.

* * *

BUCHANAN, Cynthia 1942-

PERSONAL: Born October 23, 1942, in Des Moines, Iowa; daughter of Henry Rogers Buchanan and Marguerite (a teacher; maiden name, Parker) Noble. *Education:* Arizona State University, B.A. (cum laude), 1964; University of the Americas, Mexico City, M.A., 1966. *Home and office address:* P.O. Box 520, Cottonwood, Ariz. 86326. *Agent:* Lynn Nesbit, International Creative Management, 40 West 57th St., New York, N.Y. 10019.

CAREER: Worked with South Phoenix Area Cultural Enrichment (SPACE) program, Phoenix, Ariz., 1966-68; Batten, Barton, Durstine & Osborne, San Francisco, Calif., copywriter, 1968; full-time writer, 1970—. *Awards, honors:* Fulbright scholar in creative writing, Madrid, Spain, 1968-70; MacDowell Colony fellowship, 1970; *Maiden* included in the American Library Association's list of notable books, 1972, in the *New York Times* noteworthy titles, 1972, and in the *Encyclopaedia Britannica Yearbook* list of distinguished fiction, 1973; "Mlle" award, *Mademoiselle,* 1972, for *Maiden;* New York State Council on the Arts playwright grant, 1975-76.

WRITINGS: Maiden (novel), Morrow, 1972; "Cabrona" (play), first produced in Washington, D.C., 1976, produced Off-Off-Broadway by Circle Repertory Co., 1980. Work represented in anthologies, including *The Best Little Magazine Fiction,* edited by Curt Johnson, New York University Press, 1970, and *The Realm of Fiction,* edited by James B. Hall and Elizabeth C. Hall, McGraw, 1977. Also author of a screenplay adaptation of *Maiden* and material for Lily Tomlin, including television monologues and two screenplays, "Backstretch" and "The Psychoanalyst." Contributor to numerous periodicals, including *Newsweek, New York Times, Oui, Transatlantic Review, North American Review, Harvard Advocate, American Women Poets, American Poet,* and *Mexico Quarterly Review.* Guest editor, *Mademoiselle,* 1964.

WORK IN PROGRESS: A novel, *Cock Walk in Exile.*

SIDELIGHTS: Maiden has been described as the story of a woman who is much like Arthur Miller's Willy Loman, a victim of the now dying American dream, out of sync with the times. "Buchanan is a master puppeteer," writes Lael Pritchard in *Best Sellers,* "using her characters to show us how macabre, how vacant, how desperate life can be, without our even guessing at this truth. . . . This novel is a work of distinction whose narrative form supports at every juncture the author's point." *Nation* reviewer Catherine Stimpson calls Fortune Dundy, the novel's main character, "an exemplary creation," and Buchanan's writing "brilliant" as she verbally attacks "the culture that advocates sex as a woman's only redemptive interlude." Similarly, Annie Gottlieb, writing in the *New York Times Book Review,* sees *Maiden* as a satire on "the world that hard-sells life, death, sex and the five senses back to their bewildered possessors" and describes its author as the finest satirist of this theme since Evelyn Waugh wrote *The Loved One.*

"The reason I am a writer," Buchanan told *CA,* "probably has something to do with my father, a poetic dreamer from Philadelphia who went West in the 1930's to seek his fortune (and in middle age, the 1960's, tried to publish his only novel, unsuccessfully). So, from my father, vision. And from my mother, grit maybe. Another reason I am a writer also may have something to do with the fact my parents were divorced, and I learned a lot about conflict at an early age and how insipid life (and literature) can be without it."

AVOCATIONAL INTERESTS: Horseback riding, tennis.

BIOGRAPHICAL/CRITICAL SOURCES: Arizona Living, October 22, 1971; *New York Times Book Review,* January 9, 1972; *Best Sellers,* January 15, 1972; *Nation,* January 24, 1972; *Life,* April 7, 1972.

* * *

BUCHMAN, Randall L(oren) 1929-

PERSONAL: Born May 12, 1929, in Oak Harbor, Ohio; son of Charles C. (a miner) and Cora (Scholt) Buchman; married Marilyn Patterson (a teacher), August 16, 1952; children: Deborah, Randall II, Kevin. *Education:* Heidelberg College, A.B., 1952; Ohio State University, M.A., 1958; Ball State University, D.Ed., 1973. *Religion:* United Church of Christ. *Home:* 730 E. High St., Defiance, Ohio 43512. *Office:* Department of History, Defiance College, Defiance, Ohio 43512.

CAREER: Ohio Historical Society, Columbus, research historian and librarian, 1953-55; Jefferson Local Schools, West Jefferson, Ohio, teacher and coach, 1955-58; Ravenna City Schools, Ravenna, Ohio, teacher and coach, 1958-64; Defiance College, Defiance, Ohio, assistant professor, 1964-67, associate professor of history, 1967—, director of Social Studies Center, 1968—, vice president, 1977—. Visiting professor, Heidelberg College, 1975, Ohio State University, 1976, and Bowling Green State University, 1978-79. Chairperson, historical council of United Church of Christ; member of Ohio American Revolution Bicentennial Commission. Consultant to Ohio State Department of Education; research assistant, U.S. Department of Justice, Indian Land Claim Division, 1954. *Member:* Society of Historical Archaeology,

Society of American Archaeology, National Council for the Social Studies, Ohio Academy of History, Pi Gamma Mu, Phi Alpha Theta, Lambda Alpha.

WRITINGS: A Bibliography for Social Studies Teachers, Hubbard Press, 1970; (contributor) B. K. Swartz, Jr., editor, *Adena: The Seeking of an Identity,* Ball State University, 1971; (editor) *Journal of the Northwestern Campaign of 1812-1813,* Defiance College Press, 1975; (editor) *The Historic Indians of Ohio,* Ohio American Revolution Bicentennial Commission, 1976; (contributor) *Ohio in the American Revolution,* Ohio Historical Society, 1976. Contributor to *Ohio History, Ohio Archaeologist.* Editor of archaeological field reports. Member of editorial board, *Ohio History.*

WORK IN PROGRESS: The White House and Archaeology: Presidential Interest in New World Archaeology.

SIDELIGHTS: Randall L. Buchman has been director of archaeological excavations at Fort Winchester, Fort Gower, and Fort Meigs, Ohio, Fort Mason, Ariz., and Webster Station, W.Va.

* * *

BUCK, Pearl S(ydenstricker) 1892-1973
(John Sedges)

PERSONAL: Born June 26, 1892, in Hillsboro, W.Va.; died March 6, 1973, in Danby, Vt.; buried on Green Hills Farm, Perkasie, Pa.; daughter of Absalom and Caroline (Stulting) Sydenstricker (both Presbyterian missionaries); married John Lossing Buck (an agriculture instructor), May 13, 1915 (divorced, June 11, 1935); married Richard John Walsh (president of John Day Co., publishers), June 11, 1935 (died May, 1960); children: (first marriage) Carol, Janice (adopted); (second marriage) Richard, John, Edgar, Jean C., Henriette, Theresa, Chieko, Johanna (all adopted). *Education:* Randolph-Macon Woman's College, B.A., 1914; Cornell University, M.A., 1926. *Home and office:* Pearl S. Buck Foundation, Green Hills Farm, Perkasie, Pa. 18944.

CAREER: Teacher, Randolph-Macon Woman's College, Lynchburg, Va., 1914, University of Nanking, Nanking, China, 1921-31, Southeastern University, Nanking, 1925-27, and Chung Yang University, Nanking, 1928-30; writer. Founder-director, East and West Association, 1941-51; founder, Welcome House, Inc. (adoption agency for Asian-American children), 1949, and Pearl S. Buck Foundation, Inc., 1964. Also active in numerous other child welfare and retarded children's organizations. Member of board of directors, Weather Engineering Corp., 1966. *Member:* National Institute of Arts and Letters, American Academy of Arts and Letters, Phi Beta Kappa, Kappa Delta, Cosmopolitan Club (New York).

AWARDS, HONORS: Pulitzer Prize for Fiction, 1932, and William Dean Howells Medal for the most distinguished work of American fiction published in the period 1930-35, 1935, both for *The Good Earth;* Nobel Prize for Literature, 1938; Women's National Book Association Skinner Award, 1960; Pennsylvania Governor's Award for Excellence, 1968; Philadelphia Club of Advertising Women Award, 1969. Recipient of numerous honorary degrees, including M.A., Yale University, 1933, D.Litt., University of West Virginia, 1940, St. Lawrence University, 1942, and Delaware Valley College, 1965, LL.D., Howard University, 1942, and Muhlenberg College, 1966, L.H.D., Lincoln University, 1953, Woman's Medical College of Philadelphia, 1954, and Rutgers University, 1969, D.H.L., University of Pittsburgh, 1960, Bethany College, 1963, and Hahnemann Hospital, 1966, D.Mus., Combs College of Music, 1962, and H.H.D., West Virginia State College, 1963. Recipient of over 300 humanitarian awards, including President's Committee on Employment of Physically Handicapped Citation, 1958, and Big Brothers of America Citation, 1962.

WRITINGS—Fiction; all published by John Day, except as indicated: *East Wind: West Wind,* 1930, reprinted, 1967; *The Good Earth* (also see below), 1931, reprinted, Pocket Books, 1975; *Sons* (also see below), 1932, reprinted, Pocket Books, 1975; *The Young Revolutionist* (juvenile), Friendship Press, 1932; (translator) Shui-hu Chuan, *All Men Are Brothers,* 1933, reprinted, 1968; *The First Wife and Other Stories* (also see below), 1933, reprinted, Methuen, 1963; *The Mother,* 1934, reprinted, 1973; *A House Divided,* Reynal & Hitchcock, 1935, reprinted, Pocket Books, 1975; *House of Earth* (contains *The Good Earth* and *Sons*), Reynal & Hitchcock, 1935; *This Proud Heart,* Reynal & Hitchcock, 1938, reprinted, John Day, 1965; *The Patriot,* 1939.

Stories for Little Children, (juvenile), 1940; *Other Gods: An American Legend,* 1940, reprinted, Severn House, 1976; *Today and Forever: Stories of China* (also see below), 1941; *Dragon Seed,* 1942, reprinted, Pocket Books, 1972; *China Sky,* Triangle Books, 1942; *The Chinese Children Next Door* (juvenile), 1942; *The Water-Buffalo Children* (juvenile; also see below), 1943; *Twenty-Seven Stories,* Sun Dial Press, 1943; *The Promise,* 1943; *The Story of Dragon Seed,* 1944; *The Dragon Fish* (juvenile; also see below), 1944; (under pseudonym John Sedges) *The Townsman,* 1945, reprinted, Pocket Books, 1975, published under real name as *The Townsman: A "John Sedges" Novel,* John Day, 1967; *Portrait of a Marriage,* 1945, reprinted, Pocket Books, 1975; *China Flight,* Triangle Books, 1945; *Yu Lan: Flying Boy of China* (juvenile), 1945; *Pavilion of Women,* 1946, reprinted, Pocket Books, 1978; *Far and Near: Stories of Japan, China, and America,* 1947 (published in England as *Far and Near: Stories of East and West,* Methuen, 1949); (under pseudonym John Sedges) *The Angry Wife,* 1947, reprinted under real name, Pocket Books, 1975; *Peony,* 1948, reprinted, Pocket Books, 1978 (published in England as *The Bondmaid,* Methuen, 1949); *The Big Wave* (juvenile), 1948, reprinted, 1973; (under pseudonym John Sedges) *The Long Love,* 1949, reprinted under real name, Pocket Books, 1975; *Kinfolk,* 1949, reprinted, Pocket Books, 1978.

One Bright Day (juvenile), 1950 (published in England as *One Bright Day and Other Stories for Children,* Methuen, 1952); *God's Men,* 1951, reprinted, Pocket Books, 1978; *The Hidden Flower,* 1952; (under pseudonym John Sedges) *Bright Procession,* 1952; *Come, My Beloved,* 1953, reprinted, Pocket Books, 1975; (under pseudonym John Sedges) *Voices in the House,* 1953, reprinted, White Lion Publishers, 1977; *Johnny Jack and His Beginnings* (juvenile; also see below), 1954; *The Beech Tree* (juvenile; also see below), 1954; *Imperial Woman,* 1956, reprinted, White Lion Publishers, 1977; *Letter from Peking,* 1957, reprinted, Pocket Books, 1975; *Christmas Miniature* (juvenile), 1957 (published in England as *The Christmas Mouse,* Methune, 1958); *American Triptych: Three "John Sedges" Novels,* 1958; *Command the Morning,* 1959, reprinted, Pocket Books, 1975.

The Christmas Ghost (juvenile), 1960; *Fourteen Stories,* 1961, reprinted, Pocket Books, 1976 (published in England as *With a Delicate Air and Other Stories,* Methuen, 1962); *Satan Never Sleeps,* Pocket Books, 1962; *Hearts Come Home and Other Stories,* Pocket Books, 1962; *The Living Reed,* 1963, reprinted, Pocket Books, 1979; *Stories of China* (contains contents of *The First Wife and Other Stories* and *Today and Forever*), 1964; *Escape at Midnight and Other*

Stories, Dragonfly Books, 1964; (editor) *Fairy Tales of the Orient,* Simon & Schuster, 1965; *Death in the Castle,* 1965; *The Big Fight* (juvenile) 1965; *The Little Fox in the Middle* (juvenile), Collier Books, 1966; *The Water-Buffalo Children* [and] *The Dragon Fish,* Dell, 1966; *The Time Is Noon,* 1967; *Matthew, Mark, Luke, and John* (juvenile), 1967; *The Beech Tree* [and] *Johnny Jack and His Beginnings,* Dell, 1967; *The New Year,* 1968; *The Three Daughters of Madame Liang,* 1969; *The Good Deed and Other Stories of Asia, Past and Present,* 1969.

Mandala, 1970; *The Chinese Story Teller,* 1971; *Once Upon a Christmas,* 1972; *The Goddess Abides,* 1972; *A Gift for the Children,* 1973; *Mrs. Starling's Problem,* 1973; *All under Heaven,* 1973; *Words of Love* (poetry), 1974; *The Rainbow,* 1974; *East and West: Stories,* 1975; *Secrets of the Heart: Stories,* 1976; *The Lovers and Other Stories,* 1977; *Mrs. Stoner and the Sea and Other Works,* Ace Books, 1978; *The Woman Who Was Changed and Other Stories,* Crowell, 1979.

Nonfiction; all published by John Day, except as indicated: *East and West and the Novel: Sources of the Early Chinese Novel,* College of Chinese Studies (Peking), 1932; *Is There a Case for Foreign Missions?* (pamphlet), North China Language School, 1932; *The Exile* (biography of author's mother; also see below), Reynal & Hitchcock, 1936, reprinted, Pocket Books, 1976; *Fighting Angel: Portrait of a Soul* (biography of author's father; also see below), Reynal & Hitchcock, 1936, reprinted, Pocket Books, 1976; *The Chinese Novel* (lecture), 1939.

Of Men and Women, 1941, reprinted, 1971; *When Fun Begins* (juvenile), Methuen, 1941; *American Unity and Asia,* 1942, reprinted, Books for Libraries, 1970 (published in England as *Asia and Democracy,* Macmillan, 1943); *Pearl Buck Speaks for Democracy,* New York City Common Council for Unity, 1942; *What America Means to Me,* 1943, reprinted, Books for Libraries, 1971; *The Spirit and the Flesh* (contains *Fighting Angel* and *The Exile*), 1944; (compiler) *China in Black and White: An Album of Woodcuts,* 1945; *Tell the People: Mass Education in China,* Institute of Pacific Relations, 1945, published as *Tell the People: Talks with James Yen about the Mass Education Movement,* John Day, 1945; *Talk about Russia with Masha Scott,* 1945; (with Erna von Pustau) *How It Happens: Talk about the German People, 1914-1933,* 1947; (with Eslanda Goode Robeson) *American Argument,* 1949.

The Child Who Never Grew, 1950; *The Man Who Changed China: The Story of Sun Yat-sen* (juvenile), Random House, 1953; *My Several Worlds: A Personal Record,* 1954, reprinted, Pocket Books, 1975; *Friend to Friend: A Candid Exchange between Pearl S. Buck and Carlos P. Romulo,* 1958; *The Delights of Learning,* University of Pittsburgh Press, 1960; *A Bridge for Passing* (autobiography), 1962; *Welcome Child* (juvenile), 1964; *The Joy of Children,* 1964; (with Gweneth T. Zarfoss) *The Gifts They Bring: Our Debts to the Mentally Retarded,* 1965; *Children for Adoption,* Random House, 1965; (with others) *My Mother's House,* Appalachia Press, 1966; *The People of Japan,* Simon & Schuster, 1966; (with Theodore F. Harris) *For Spacious Skies: Journey in Dialogue,* 1966; *To My Daughters, with Love,* 1967.

The Kennedy Women: A Personal Appraisal, Cowles Book Co., 1970; *China as I See It,* 1970; *The Story Bible,* Bartholomew House, 1971; *Pearl Buck's America,* Bartholomew House, 1971; *Pearl S. Buck's Oriental Cookbook,* Simon & Schuster, 1972; *China Past and Present,* 1972; *A Community Success Story: The Founding of the Pearl Buck Center,* 1972; (editor) *Pearl Buck's Book of Christmas,* Simon & Schuster, 1974.

Plays: "Flight into China," produced in New York, 1939; *Sun Yat Sen: A Play, Preceded by a Lecture by Dr. Hu-Shih,* Universal Distributors, 1944; "The First Wife," produced in New York, 1945; "A Desert Incident," produced in New York, 1959; "Christine," produced in New York, 1960; "The Guide" (adaptation of novel by N. K. Narayan), produced on Broadway at Lincoln Art Theatre, 1965. Also author of a television drama, "The Big Wave," produced by the National Broadcasting Co., 1956. Contributor of articles and stories to numerous magazines. Co-editor, *Asia,* 1941-46.

SIDELIGHTS: "One pays the price for being prolific," best-selling author Pearl Buck once told an interviewer. "Heaven knows the literary Establishment can't forgive me for it, nor for the fact that my books sell." In retrospect, Buck's assessment of her own career seems to ring true. Despite the fact that she enjoyed world-wide popularity throughout most of her life (at the time of her death, her books had been translated into more languages than any other American writer), critical success eluded her after the prize-winning decade that produced *The Good Earth* and the biographical work *The Spirit and the Flesh.* Suspicious of her tremendously high output and annoyed by her all-too-frequent lapses into didacticism and sentimentality, post-1938 critics regarded her for the most part as a prime example of a "too much, too often" writer.

The only child of Absalom and Caroline Sydenstricker to be born in the United States, Pearl Buck lived in America for only a few months before accompanying her missionary parents on their return to Chinkiang, China. She remained there until reaching the age of seventeen, learning to speak Chinese before English (her parents declined to live in the foreigners' compound in Chinkiang, choosing instead to live among the Chinese) but beginning to read and write in the less difficult English alphabet system. Although her mother encouraged her as a very young child to write something every week, her first direct literary influence was her Chinese nurse, who fascinated her with numerous folk tales of magic and adventure.

Buck's first published works appeared in the *Shanghai Mercury,* an English-language newspaper which had a weekly edition for children; she also wrote for the Randolph-Macon Woman's College paper after returning to the United States for further schooling. In 1927, Buck found herself back in China, this time in Nanking at the time Communists were invading the city with the intention of killing all foreigners. Thanks to the aid of a few loyal friends and servants, Buck and her family managed to escape death by the narrow margin of ten minutes. Her home, however, as well as the manuscript of her first novel, was destroyed in the fire following the raid.

Her second novel, *East Wind: West Wind,* was written in 1925 aboard a ship bound for America. In 1930, after contacting a literary agent she had chosen at random from a handbook, the author received her first taste of success when John Day Co. agreed to publish her work. Ten months after *East Wind: West Wind*'s third printing, *The Good Earth* (which had taken Buck only three months to write) appeared and began an almost two-year stay on the best-seller lists, winning its author a Pulitzer Prize in 1931. This book, along with her 1936 biographies of her parents, *The Exile* and *Fighting Angel,* established Buck's early literary reputation and served as the basis of comparison for all of her later works.

The major goal of Buck's writings throughout her long career was to teach the Western world about Asia, especially China, which she naturally knew and loved best. She often described her unique Chinese-American background as one which afforded her the ability to be "mentally bifocal"—that is, she was able to look at two distinctly different cultures and understand and love both of them, each on its own terms. As critic Malcolm Cowley once observed in 1935: "Mrs. Buck has spent so many years in [China], has studied the language so well, has lived on such terms of friendship with the people, that she makes [other writers like] Tretiakov and Malraux seem like tourists dropping ashore from a round-the-world cruise. She has a truly extraordinary gift for presenting the Chinese, not as quaint and illogical, yellow-skinned, exotic devil-dolls, but as human beings merely, animated by motives we can always understand even when the background is strange and topsy-turvy. . . . She seems to know China so well that she no longer judges it even from the standpoint of 'the native Chinese'—whoever he may be—but rather from the standpoint of a particular class, the one that includes the liberal, three-quarters Westernized scholars who deplore the graft and cruelty of the present government but nevertheless keep their heads on their shoulders and hold their noses, and support General Chiang Kaishek because they are afraid of what would happen if he were overthrown."

Phyllis Bentley, commenting during the same period as Cowley, also praised Buck's ability to write knowledgeably of Chinese culture: "Mrs. Buck's chosen scene . . . is modern China. There are parts of that vast country where modern China means the same as ancient China; there are parts where the change of date implies a profound social change. These two Chinas, the old and the new, form the material for Mrs. Buck's art. . . . [An] attempt is made to present China from within, as the Chinese see it. . . . [The] landscape in Mrs. Buck's novels is always presented as seen by familiar eyes. . . . [She] has lived in China so long that she really knows the landscape, and she never once, in all the volumes of her work, forgets it and goes into raptures as over an alien scene. . . . In the same way Mrs. Buck aims to present the Chinese customs as familiar, natural and correct, because so would her characters regard them. [These customs] . . . are all copiously illustrated, but always presented, as it were, unself-consciously, as part of the natural process of living; never by the slightest word or turn of phrase does Mrs. Buck call our attention to the difference of these customs from our own."

Buck was "mentally bifocal" in another sense as well, for her writing style also reflected her dual background. Time and time again critics refer to her "biblical" prose—mellifluous, stately, serious, and lyrical. This was often combined with a narrative style reminiscent of the ancient Chinese saga—straightforward, simple, precise, and concrete—and an emphasis on the role of the novel as a form of entertainment for the common people. Some reviewers have also identified a few key elements that are characteristic of nineteenth-century French Naturalism, such as the author's documentary approach to her subject matter, her detached and objective narration, her preoccupation with the effects of environment and heredity, and her interest in depicting the lifestyle of members of lower social classes. She also exhibited a typically Chinese respect for tradition and a deep commitment to the family and to what Phyllis Bentley referred to as "the continuity of life"; that is, "the passing of life on from generation to generation." And even though her characters were almost exclusively Chinese, her stories were designed to have a universal appeal, for she believed very strongly that people the world over, regardless of race, share essentially the same hopes and fears.

The Good Earth is perhaps the best known example of the Pearl Buck style. Malcolm Cowley described it as "a parable of the life of man, in his relation to the soil that sustains him. The plot, deliberately commonplace, is given a sort of legendary weight and dignity by being placed in an unfamiliar setting. The biblical style is appropriate to the subject and the characters. If we define a masterpiece as a novel that is living, complete, sustained, but still somewhat limited in its scope as compared with the greatest works of fiction—if we define it as *Wuthering Heights* rather than *War and Peace*—then [*The Good Earth* is a masterpiece]."

Other reviewers were equally impressed. The *New York Times* critic, for example, noted that "In *East Wind: West Wind,* Pearl S. Buck wrote a novel of China which was generally hailed as a very promising first novel. In her second book, *The Good Earth,* she has fulfilled that promise with a brilliance which passes one's most optimistic expectations. Laying aside the question of the locale, *The Good Earth* is an excellent novel. It has style, power, coherence and a pervasive sense of dramatic reality."

A *Books* reviewer claimed that *The Good Earth* depicts "China as it has never before been portrayed in fiction, the China that Chinese live in and as Chinese live. . . . [The story] is, however, much more than China. One need never have lived in China or know anything about the Chinese to understand it or respond to its appeal."

The *Spectator* critic also praised its universality: "It is a familiar story; there is not startling psychological observation, though it is complete and whole. We are satisfied of its essential truth; confident, interested, never ruffled: it is a universal story, very well told, honestly, sympathetically, without any self-consciousness whatever. . . . [*The Good Earth*] is a tender and charming book, written in a very personal, but in no way irritating idiom."

Finally, a *Bookman* reviewer observed: "To read this story of Wang Lung is to be slowly and deeply purified; and when the last page is finished it is as if some significant part of one's own days were over. Though I may never see a rice-field, I shall always feel that I have lived for a long time in China. The strange power of a western woman to make an alien civilization seem as casual, as close, as the happenings of the morning is surprising; but it is less amazing than her power to illuminate the destiny of man as it is in all countries and at all times by quietly telling the story of one poor Wang Lung."

Younghill Kang of the *New Republic,* however, did not feel that *The Good Earth* was truly representative of Chinese life. He wrote: "Since Mrs. Buck does not understand the meaning of the Confucian separation of man's kingdom from that of woman, she is like someone trying to write a story of the European Middle Ages without understanding the rudiments of chivalric standards and the institution of Christianity. None of her major descriptions is correct except in minor details. . . . *The Good Earth,* though it has no humor or profound lyric passion, shows good technique and much artistic sincerity. Thus, it is discouraging to find that the novel works toward confusion, not clarification. Its implied comparison between Western and Eastern ways is unjust to the latter."

Sons and *A House Divided* continued the saga of the house of Wang, but neither achieved quite the critical and popular acclaim of *The Good Earth.* Reviewers found *Sons,* for example, to be an adequate enough novel in and of itself, but not as a sequel to a work such as *The Good Earth*. In general, they found it suffered from colorless and unsympathetic characterization and a lack of universality due to its thematic emphasis on warlords and brigands. *A House Divided* was judged to be an even weaker novel; it, too, was criticized for its lack of credible characterization, as well as for its wandering, overburdened plot and an increasingly exaggerated and inappropriate biblical style. For the most part, reviewers felt that neither novel possessed that indefinable "something" that made *The Good Earth* so memorable.

When Pearl Buck won the Nobel Prize for Literature in 1938, the judges, though making it clear that the award was for the body of her work, specifically mentioned the biographies of her mother (*The Exile*) and her father (*Fighting Angel*) as particularly outstanding examples of her talent. Commenting on *The Exile*, a *Books* critic wrote: "The events of the story are stirring, but they pale beside the story of the woman and her mastery of circumstance. . . . Restrained, temperate, the book of a novelist who not only loves life but looks at it clear-eyed, *The Exile* is a story of fact as exciting and as moving as any of the fiction in which Pearl Buck has showed life as Carie [her mother] helped her to see it."

A *Christian Century* reviewer agreed: "The subject of this story—which is at once a story, a study, a memoir, and a tribute of discerning affection—was evidently a very unusual missionary as well as a very remarkable woman. The book is quite different in style from Mrs. Buck's novels, but is of the same piece of quality and insight."

Several reviewers, however, felt the book lacked the customary universal appeal of a Pearl Buck story due to its focus on one individual. For example, a *Times Literary Supplement* critic wrote: "This is not a story—however vivid and moving in its detail and its portrait of the martyred Carie—which exhibits Mrs. Buck's peculiar gifts in their finest expression. She so manifestly suffers from her inability to give free play to her imagination. In her studies of Chinese life she can create for us a type that may or may not be true of any single individual. In *The Exile* she labours to present the whole truth about one particular woman and succeeds only at the cost of artistic verisimilitude."

A *Christian Science Monitor* reviewer expressed a similar sentiment: "In this latest work Mrs. Buck has, to our discomfiture, lost touch with that quality so conspicuous in *The Good Earth*, a flowing style which is thrillingly beautiful in rhythm and cadence. One hears its whisper now too seldom. For *The Exile* is not, like its predecessor, by implication a record of the labor and struggle of all humankind; its scope is narrowed until, in essence at least, it includes only one woman."

Fighting Angel was generally regarded as the better biography of the two, primarily because it contained the quality of universality that *The Exile* lacked. According to Paul A. Doyle, this universal appeal is a result of Buck's "compelling delineation of the nineteenth-century type of crusader—the very essence of rock-ribbed individualism, a fiery zeal. . . . [In short,] Pearl Buck sees her father as a manifestation of a spirit which especially permeated America at a particular time." As a *New York Times* reviewer noted: "In the limpid flowing beauty of Pearl Buck's writing, in the unerring clarity and directness of every word and image and expression, she has done in *Fighting Angel* what she did in *The Exile*—has drawn a portrait with far more than personal vividness, touched problems as deep as all humanity. And her incandescent realism lights the very heart of our thought."

A *Books* critic felt that "its very difficulty makes this an even finer book than its companion piece. . . . This is the work of maturity—hard-won maturity of heart. A good many layers of soil had to be lived away and written away before this rock could be laid bare. And nobody who has not read the earlier book can know quite what an achievement this one is."

A *Christian Science Monitor* reviewer declared that "with true artistry Mrs. Buck has offered us this portrait of her father. . . . It is an experience to read and ponder this book, for it has the ring of universal truth. One has known just such reformers as was Andy." A *Christian Century* critic admitted that "his daughter's portrayal does not paint out his warts, but it makes him a giant in character and personality, and a giant can carry some warts. No missionary has had a nobler monument."

A *Commonweal* reviewer who enjoyed *The Exile* more than *Fighting Angel* concluded: "If the appeal of *Fighting Angel* is less that of its companion book, *The Exile*, doubtless it is because most of us feel keener response to the flesh than to the spirit. If the book is less vivid, it is less direct, as its author relies for the most of its material upon relation rather than observation. . . . Although there can be no doubt as to where the major part of [the author's] loyalty lay, she gives a thoroughly admirable and sympathetic account of her father's stalwart faith and indefatigable labors, both in scholarship and evangelism."

In a critical study of Pearl Buck's work, Paul A. Doyle offers this summation of the author's contributions to literature: "Although she has been virtually ignored by critics for over twenty years, it may be maintained with much justification that [Buck] has written at least three books of undoubted significance: *The Good Earth* and the biographies of her father and mother." Due to these successes, Doyle continues, "at about the time of the Nobel Award . . . Pearl Buck's writing career certainly seemed to be in the ascent, and to promise further important achievement. After this period, however, Pearl Buck's humanitarian preoccupations seemed to increase. These interests, carried into her fiction, immediately weakened the objectivity of her creation. She began to assert didactic considerations to such an excessive degree that [certain later novels] become propaganda efforts on behalf of China's struggle against Japan. . . . After 1939 she became more facile at constructing her plots, handling dialogue, and in the technical aspects of her craft; but no subsequent significant growth in the artistic features of novel writing occurred in Pearl Buck's work. No experimentation in technique took place, and she made no attempt to penetrate more deeply into character analysis, showed no willingness to seek subtleties of tone or mood, and indicated no interest in using myth or symbolism or other elements characteristic of the modern novel. On this account alone Miss Buck must be neglected by some of the more recent literary critics, . . . [for] her novels do not furnish the layers of meaning and the complexity which modern literary criticism demands. . . . [In addition,] her work has suffered from the inevitable reaction against her best-seller status."

Furthermore, notes Doyle, "another factor in Pearl Buck's loss of prestige in serious literary circles stems from her optimistic, affirmative point of view. She has not lost her faith in progress, and she exalts a Rousseau-Thomas Paine Transcendental type of belief in the innate goodness of most men. . . . [But] judged by her standards—'to please and to amuse,' to relate a captivating story, and to deal with significant problems—Miss Buck must be granted considerable success."

Several of Pearl Buck's novels have been made into motion pictures. *A House Divided* was filmed by Universal Pictures in 1932; *The Good Earth* and *Dragon Seed* were both filmed by Metro-Goldwyn-Mayer, Inc., the former in 1937 and the latter in 1944; *China Sky* was filmed by RKO General, Inc., in 1945; and *Satan Never Sleeps* was filmed by Twentieth Century-Fox Film Corp. in 1962.

BIOGRAPHICAL/CRITICAL SOURCES: Books, March 1, 1931, September 25, 1932, January 20, 1935, February 9, 1936, November 29, 1936; *New York Times,* March 15, 1931, September 25, 1932, January 20, 1935, February 9, 1936, November 29, 1936, September 10, 1969, March 7, 1973, March 10, 1973; *Outlook,* March 18, 1931; *Saturday Review of Literature,* March 21, 1931, September 24, 1932, February 8, 1936, December 5, 1936; *Bookman,* May, 1931, October, 1932; *Spectator,* May 2, 1931; *Nation,* May 13, 1931, November 16, 1932, February 6, 1935; *New Statesman and Nation,* May 16, 1931, December 3, 1932; *Saturday Review,* May 16, 1931, November 5, 1932, March 31, 1956, November 22, 1958, July 12, 1969; *Christian Century,* May 20, 1931, October 5, 1932, March 13, 1935, February 5, 1936, April 7, 1937, December 9, 1970; *New Republic,* July 1, 1931, October 26, 1932, January 23, 1935, December 9, 1936; *Chicago Daily Tribune,* September 24, 1932; *Times Literary Supplement,* October 6, 1932, January 24, 1935, February 15, 1936, October 19, 1967, March 21, 1980; *New York Herald Tribune,* January 21, 1935; *Forum,* March, 1935; *Christian Science Monitor,* February 7, 1936, December 1, 1936, December 24, 1958, July 10, 1969; *Commonweal,* December 11, 1936; *Atlantic,* March, 1937, July, 1969; *Best Sellers,* February 1, 1965, April 1, 1968, April 1, 1969, June 1, 1970, November 1, 1970; *National Observer,* April 29, 1968; *New York Times Book Review,* February 23, 1969, March 11, 1979; *Time,* July 25, 1969, March 19, 1973; *Detroit News,* January 16, 1972, November 20, 1979; *Washington Post,* March 7, 1973; *Publishers Weekly,* March 12, 1973; *Antiquarian Bookman,* March 19, 1973; *Newsweek,* March 19, 1973; *Authors in the News,* Volume I, Gale, 1976; *Contemporary Literary Criticism,* Gale, Volume VII, 1977, Volume XI, 1979.†

—*Sketch by Deborah A. Straub*

* * *

BUCKLEY, William F(rank), Jr. 1925-

PERSONAL: Born November 24, 1925, in New York, N.Y.; son of William Frank (a lawyer and oilman) and Aloise (Steiner) Buckley; married Patricia Austin Taylor, July 6, 1950; children: Christopher. *Education:* Attended University of Mexico, 1943-44; Yale University, B.A. (with honors), 1950. *Politics:* Republican. *Religion:* Roman Catholic. *Office: National Review,* 150 East 35th St., New York, N.Y. 10016.

CAREER: Affiliated with Central Intelligence Agency (C.I.A.) in Mexico; Yale University, New Haven, Conn., instructor in Spanish, 1947-51; *American Mercury* (magazine), New York City, associate editor, 1952; free-lance writer and lecturer, 1952-55; *National Review* (magazine), New York City, founder, president, and editor-in-chief, 1955—; syndicated columnist, 1962—; host of "Firing Line" weekly television program, 1966—. Conservative Party candidate for mayor of New York City, 1965; member of advisory commission, U.S. Information Agency, 1969-72; public member of the U.S. delegation to the United Nations, 1973. Lecturer, New School for Social Research, 1967-68; Froman Distinguished Professor, Russell Sage College, 1973. Former chairman of the board, Starr Broadcasting Group, Inc. *Military service:* U.S. Army, 1944-46; became second lieutenant.

MEMBER: Century Association, Bohemian Club. *Awards, honors:* Freedom Award, Order of Lafayette, 1966; George Sokolsky Award, American Jewish League Against Communism, 1966; University of Southern California Distinguished Achievement Award in Journalism, 1968; Liberty Bell Award, New Haven County Bar Association, 1969; Emmy Award, National Academy of Television Arts and Sciences, 1969, for "Firing Line"; Man of the Decade Award, Young Americans for Freedom, 1970; fellow, Sigma Delta Chi, 1976; Bellarmine Medal, 1977; Americanism Award, Young Republican National Federation, 1979, for contributions to the American principles of freedom, individual liberty, and free enterprise; American Book Award, 1980, for *Stained Glass.* Honorary degrees: L.H.D. from Seton Hall University, 1966, Niagara University, 1967, and Mount Saint Mary's College, 1969; LL.D. from St. Peter's College, 1969, Syracuse University, 1969, Ursinus College, 1969, LeHigh University, 1970, Lafayette College, 1972, St. Anselm's College, 1973, St. Bonaventure University, 1974, and University of Notre Dame, 1978; D.Sc.O. from Curry College, 1970; Litt.D. from St. Vincent College, 1971, Fairleigh Dickinson University, 1973, and Alfred University, 1974.

WRITINGS: God and Man at Yale: The Superstitions of "Academic Freedom," Regnery, 1951, reprinted, Gateway Editions, 1977; (with L. Brent Bozell) *McCarthy and His Enemies,* Regnery, 1954; *Up from Liberalism,* Obolensky, 1959; *Rumbles Left and Right,* Putnam, 1963; (editor) *The Committee and Its Critics,* Constructive Action, 1963; *The Unmaking of a Mayor,* Viking, 1966; (author of introduction) Edgar Smith, *Brief against Death,* Knopf, 1968; *The Jeweler's Eye: A Book of Irresistible Political Reflections,* Putnam, 1968; (author of introduction) *Will Mrs. Major Go to Hell?: The Collected Work of Aloise Buckley Heath,* Arlington House, 1969; *Quotations from Chairman Bill: The Best of William F. Buckley, Jr.,* compiled by David Franke, Arlington House, 1970; *The Governor Listeth: A Book of Inspired Political Revelations,* Putnam, 1970; (editor) *Odyssey of a Friend: Whittaker Chambers' Letters to William F. Buckley, Jr., 1954-1961,* Putnam, 1970; (editor) *Did You Ever See a Dream Walking?: American Conservative Thought in the Twentieth Century,* Bobbs-Merrill, 1970; *Cruising Speed: A Documentary,* Putnam, 1971; *Inveighing We Will Go,* Putnam, 1972; *Four Reforms: A Guide for the Seventies,* Putnam, 1973; *United Nations Journal: A Delegate's Odyssey,* Putnam, 1974; *Execution Eve and Other Contemporary Ballads,* Putnam, 1975; *Airborne: A Sentimental Journey,* Macmillan, 1976; *Saving the Queen* (novel), Doubleday, 1976; *A Hymnal: The Controversial Arts,* Putnam, 1978; *Stained Glass* (novel), Doubleday, 1978; *Who's on First* (novel), Doubleday, 1980.

Contributor: *Ocean Racing,* Van Nostrand, 1959; *The Intellectuals,* Free Press, 1960; F. S. Meyer, editor, *What Is Conservatism?,* Holt, 1964; *Dialogues in Americanism,* Regnery, 1964; Edward E. Davis, editor, *The Beatles Book,* Cowles, 1968; S. Endleman, editor, *Violence in the Streets,* Quadrangle, 1968; R. Campbell, editor, *Spectrum of Catholic Attitudes,* Bruce Publishing, 1969; *Great Ideas Today Annual, 1970,* Encyclopaedia Britannica, 1970; Fritz Machlup, editor, *Essays on Hayek,* New York University Press, 1976.

Author of syndicated column "On the Right," 1962—. Contributor to *Esquire, Saturday Review, Harper's, Atlantic,* and other publications.

WORK IN PROGRESS: Several books.

SIDELIGHTS: William F. Buckley, Jr. is a conservative

spokesman in several media whose personal style appeals to both conservatives and liberals alike. Noting Buckley's popularity among even some of his political adversaries, a writer for *Time* points out that "the Buckley substance is forgiven for the Buckley style." Frederick C. Klein agrees, "Buckley has a growing following among liberals who detest his views but frankly admire his panache."

Opinions vary about Buckley's personal style and the degree of its appeal. According to Mario Puzo, "Buckley is . . . one of the few men in politics whose style can be called literary [and who] has an intelligence to match." "What Buckley has," Malcolm Muggeridge believes, "is a sort of sparkle and grace, equally in his speaking, writing, and television appearances, so dismally lacking in most other practitioners." Larry L. King is of the mixed opinion that "Mr. Buckley can, indeed, charm the socks off a rooster; that his wit is no mere illusion; that he is an instinctive aristocrat . . . and that he is a refined, polished gentleman who, sitting among artifacts of culture in his own home, can call a guest a son-of-a-bitch in an Oxford accent and with the cold eyes of a lynch-mob leader." Buckley's more severe critics find little to praise. Congressman Michael Harrington describes Buckley as "an urbane front man for the most primitive and vicious emotions in the land." Gore Vidal's opinions of Buckley, broadcast on national television in 1968, were met by a Buckley lawsuit for libel.

Buckley is something unique to the political right. "Before Buckley . . . ," Donald Phelps writes, "many intellectually virile conservatives . . . tended toward the dry [and] the livelier conservatives tended to be goofballs and semi-illiterates." Phelps believes that Buckley has "soldered a long-time break" among the nation's conservatives, bringing "a humming action, both authentic and mock-up, which, in its own way, re-created the pyro-technics of old-fashioned preachers, or the more prominent literary figures of the 1920's." Irving Howe believes that when one thinks of "the archetypal American reactionary" one sees "an image of a stumbling primitive." Buckley is an anomaly, Howe argues, being a right-winger who can "write a paragraph of lucid prose and make a clever wisecrack."

Buckley first came to public attention in 1951 when he published *God and Man at Yale,* an attack against his alma mater, Yale University. The book charged Yale with suppressing its students' political freedom while encouraging agnosticism and collectivism. These charges stemmed from Buckley's own experiences while attending Yale, where his staunchly conservative views found little support in the academic community. Buckley proposed that the Yale alumni withhold their donations to the school until changes had been made in the school's staff and curriculum. The book alarmed and enraged a number of Yale faculty and alumni and the resulting controversy made Buckley well-known among conservatives.

This position as conservative spokesman was vastly strengthened in 1955 when Buckley founded *National Review,* now the nation's largest conservative magazine, with a circulation of some one hundred thousand. Although the magazine habitually loses money, made up in part by reader contributions and Buckley's own subsidy, he sees the publication as his best means of reaching the nation's conservatives, particularly those in the Republican Party's leadership. Klein describes *National Review* as Buckley's "primary tool in 'reforming' the Republican Party." Buckley states that "what we are trying for is the maximum leverage that conservative opinion can exert."

A broad range of conservative thought is presented in *National Review,* Buckley believing that such a policy is healthy for both the magazine and its readers. However, several conservative spokesmen, including Robert Welch and Ayn Rand, are omitted from the magazine's serious attention. Buckley believes that Welch, founder and head of the John Birch Society, speaks "drivel." About Welch's fondness for Communist conspiracy theories, Buckley has said: "For all I know, Robert Welch thinks *I'm* a Communist plot." As for Ayn Rand, founder of the Objectivist school of conservative thought, Buckley has criticized her individualist ideas to the point where Rand, as a writer for *Time* reports, "refuses even to appear in the same room with Buckley."

Buckley's own political opinions, expressed most often in his syndicated column "On the Right," include calls for abolishing federal unemployment compensation, federal welfare, and certain other federal social programs, support for the use of nuclear weapons if necessary for national sovereignty, and an unswerving trust in the laissez-faire economic system. These opinions have drawn fire from many of his critics. Walter Karp, for example, states that Buckley "is far more willing than most men to contemplate nuclear war against Communism." "If it is right that a single man is prepared to die for a just cause," Buckley writes in *The Jeweler's Eye,* "it is arguably right that an entire civilization be prepared to die for a just cause." "So much," Karp notes, "for conserving."

Perhaps Buckley's most influential popular means of spreading conservative thought is through his weekly television program "Firing Line," which reaches several million people over the Public Broadcasting System. "Firing Line" has featured debates between Buckley and such prominent figures as Richard Nixon, Arthur Schlesinger, Allen Ginsberg, Norman Mailer, and Dean Rusk. As Russ Drake writes, paraphrasing "Firing Line" producer Warren Steibel, "Buckley isn't intimidated by anyone, and very few guests are off limits." "The chief reason for [the program's] success," claims Phil Garner, "is the image of . . . Buckley as a mean and unrelenting interrogator of his guests—always on the most impeccably intellectual level." Drake notes that "Buckley can be lethal in rejoinder, flashing a hypnotically facile vocabulary, and spinning logic in crisp arabesques." Klein compares "the spectacle of William F. Buckley, Jr. spearing a foe" to "the sight of a cat stalking a bird. If you sympathize with the bird, you can still find it possible to admire the grace and ferocity of its pursuer."

Despite his involvement and concern with the nation's political life, Buckley has only once sought public office. In 1965, he ran for mayor of New York City in a highly-visible, perhaps not-quite-serious campaign. Or, as Buckley explained, it was just that he couldn't work up the "synthetic optimism" his followers expected. When asked, for example, what he would do if elected, Buckley replied, "Demand a recount." When questioned as to the number of votes he expected to receive, "conservatively speaking," Buckley answered: "Conservatively speaking, one." Although he lost the election, receiving 13.4% of the vote, Buckley managed to draw public attention to several issues he felt to be of importance, including welfare reform, the New York City traffic problem, and the treatment of criminals. Buckley now considers his political career over. "The only thing that would convince me to run again," he states, "would be a direct order from my Maker, signed in triplicate by each member of the Trinity."

In 1973, Buckley found himself again being considered for

governmental office, this time as a public member of the U.S. delegation to the 28th General Assembly of the United Nations. He was appointed to the post by President Richard Nixon. Although a critic of the U.N. and skeptical of its effectiveness, Buckley took the job. "I saw myself there," Buckley writes of his reasons for accepting the post, "in the center of the great assembly at the U.N. . . . holding the delegates spellbound . . . I would cajole, wheedle, parry, thrust, mesmerize, dismay, seduce, intimidate. The press of the world would rivet its attention on the case the American delegate was making for human rights." Buckley's dream was not to be. "[If] the Gettysburg Address were to be delivered from the floor of the United Nations," Buckley later told an interviewer, "it would go unnoticed. . . . I soon became aware that the role of oratory was purely ceremonial. No one takes any notice of what is actually said. One listens for the overtones." Why did he stay as long as he did? "If you quit too soon," he says, "you look like a horse's ass for having taken it on."

Leaving his governmental work behind him, Buckley has explored yet another field, that of fiction writing. His novels, *Saving the Queen, Stained Glass,* and *Who's on First,* feature the character Blackford Oakes, a C.I.A. operative in post-war Europe. Buckley told an interviewer that some of the events in these novels stem from his own experiences in the C.I.A. "In my first book *Queen,*" he says, "the training received by Blackford Oakes is, in exact detail, the training I received. In that sense, it's autobiographical."

Through these novels, Buckley dramatizes some of his ideas concerning East-West relations in a manner that several critics have praised. Robin W. Winks, writing of *Saving the Queen,* finds that it is "replete with ambiguity, irony, suspense—all those qualities we associate with [Eric] Ambler, [Graham] Greene, [and John] le Carre," and that *Stained Glass* is a "chilling, compelling book" which is "closer to the bone than le Carre has ever cut." *Stained Glass,* Jane Larkin Crain writes, is "an elegant and engaging tale" that contains "the ample wit and intelligence that one by now takes for granted in Buckley." Robert W. Smith, writing of *Who's on First,* notes that "Buckley crafts well. His yarn is no yawner. The plot keeps moving and what the story lacks in verisimilitude it compensates for in vivacity." Christopher Lehmann-Haupt believes that "not only can Buckley execute the international thriller as well as nearly anyone working in the genre . . . he threatens to turn this form of fiction into effective propaganda for his ideas."

As author, columnist, television host, lecturer, and magazine editor, Buckley has managed to make the conservative position known to a large number of Americans. In the process he has become, as Klein notes, "conservatism's one-man band" and "the most conspicuous and articulate spokesman for the Right in America."

AVOCATIONAL INTERESTS: Ocean racing, swimming, skiing; plays the piano and harpsichord.

BIOGRAPHICAL/CRITICAL SOURCES—Periodicals: *New Republic,* October 19, 1959, June 10, 1978; *Catholic World,* November, 1959; *Yale Review,* November, 1959; *Time,* October 31, 1960, November 4, 1966, November 3, 1967, August 2, 1971, November 18, 1974, January 5, 1976, June 19, 1978, February 19, 1979; *Esquire,* January, 1961, November, 1966, January, 1968, August, 1969, September, 1969, February, 1972, July, 1976; *Mademoiselle,* June, 1961; *New York Times Book Review,* March 25, 1962, April 28, 1963, August 2, 1970, December 26, 1976, January 11, 1978, May 14, 1978, February 17, 1980, March 30, 1980; *Saturday Review,* April 27, 1963, August 8, 1970, May 13, 1978; *Commonweal,* May 3, 1963, December 23, 1966, March 1, 1974; *National Review,* May 7, 1963, November 15, 1966, September 13, 1974, February 20, 1976, May 13, 1977, June 9, 1978, November 24, 1978; *New York Times Magazine,* September 5, 1965; *Life,* September 17, 1965; *Newsweek,* October 17, 1966, March 25, 1968, August 2, 1971, September 30, 1974, January 5, 1976, February 19, 1979; *Wall Street Journal,* November 15, 1966, January 31, 1967; *Harper's,* March, 1967, November, 1971; *Modern Age,* summer, 1967, summer, 1974; *Bookworld,* June 30, 1968, January 23, 1972, February 12, 1980; *Atlantic,* July, 1968; *Christian Century,* July 3, 1968; *Christian Science Monitor,* August 29, 1968; *Progressive,* January, 1969; *Negro Digest,* April, 1969.

New Yorker, August 8, 1970, August 21, 1971, August 28, 1971; *Reader's Digest,* September, 1971; *New York Times,* October 6, 1971, April 5, 1978, February 6, 1980; *Nation,* October 2, 1972; *Village Voice,* February 21, 1974, December 8, 1975; *New York Review of Books,* July 18, 1974; *Publishers Weekly,* August 26, 1974; *Observer,* June 8, 1975; *Spectator,* June 21, 1975; *Listener,* July 3, 1975; *New Statesman,* March 12, 1976; *Times Literary Supplement,* March 12, 1976; *Yachting,* January, 1977; *Saturday Evening Post,* April, 1977; *Punch,* July 12, 1978; *Washington Post,* February 12, 1980.

Books: Edward R. Cain, *They'd Rather Be Right: Youth and the Conservative Movement,* Macmillan, 1963; Arnold Forster and B. R. Epstein, *Danger on the Right,* Random House, 1964; William F. Buckley, Jr., *The Unmaking of a Mayor,* Viking, 1966; Donald Phelps, *Covering Ground: Essays for Now,* Croton Press, 1969; Buckley, *Cruising Speed: A Documentary,* Putnam, 1971; J. Tuccille, *It Usually Begins with Ayn Rand: A Libertarian Odyssey,* Stein & Day, 1972; Charles L. Markmann, *The Buckleys: A Family Examined,* Morrow, 1973; Buckley, *United Nations Journal: A Delegate's Odyssey,* Putnam, 1974; *Contemporary Literary Criticism,* Volume VII, Gale, 1977.

—Sketch by Thomas Wiloch

* * *

BUENKER, John D(avid) 1937-

PERSONAL: Born August 11, 1937, in Dubuque, Iowa; son of Joseph F. (a brewer) and Melita (Ferring) Buenker; married Claralee O'Leary (a teacher), September 1, 1962; children: Jeanne Marie, Catherine, Eileen, Thomas, Joseph. *Education:* Loras College, B.A. (maxima cum laude), 1959; Georgetown University, M.A., 1962, Ph.D. (with distinction), 1964. *Politics:* Democrat. *Religion:* Roman Catholic. *Home:* 3901 Western Way, Racine, Wis. 53404. *Office:* University of Wisconsin—Parkside, Kenosha, Wis. 53140.

CAREER: Prince Georges Community College, Largo, Md., instructor in history, 1962-65; Eastern Illinois University, Charleston, assistant professor, 1965-68, associate professor of history, 1968-70; University of Wisconsin—Parkside, Kenosha, professor of history, 1970—, director, Center for Multicultural Studies, 1977—. Lecturer to Peace Corps trainees, 1962-63; summer lecturer, Georgetown University, 1964-65; visiting professor, District of Columbia Teachers College, summer, 1964, Indiana State College (now Indiana University of Pennsylvania), summer, 1965, and Holy Redeemer College, 1971—. *Member:* American Historical Association, Organization of American Historians, Academy of Political and Social Science, Immigration History Group, American Association of University Professors, Illinois State Historical Society, Teachers Association of Wisconsin

University Faculties, Phi Alpha Theta, Delta Epsilon Sigma, Alpha Sigma Nu. *Awards, honors:* Indiana Historical Society Book Review Award, 1969; William Adee Whitehead Award from New Jersey Historical Society, 1970; Harry E. Pratt Award from Illinois State Historical Society, 1971; Wisconsin Alumni Research Foundation fellow, 1971; American Philosophical Society grant, 1972; University of Wisconsin—Parkside summer grant, 1975; Wisconsin Humanities Committee grant, 1975; Guggenheim Memorial Fellowship, 1975-76.

WRITINGS: (With Donald F. Tingley) *Essays in Illinois History,* Southern Illinois University Press, 1967; (contributor) Blaine A. Brownell and Warren E. Stickle, editors, *Bosses and Reformers: Urban Politics in America,* Houghton, 1972; *Urban Liberalism and Progressive Reform,* Scribner, 1973; (with others) *American History: 1973,* Dushkin, 1973; (contributor) Arthur Mann, editor, *The Progressive Era,* Wiley, 1974; (contributor) John A. Neuenschwander, editor, *Kenosha County in the Twentieth Century,* Kenosha County Bicentennial Commission, 1976; (contributor) John B. Duff, *Irish Americans,* Arno, 1976; (with Robert Crunden and John Burnham) *Progressivism,* Schenkman, 1977; (editor with Nicholas C. Burckel) *Immigration and Ethnicity: A Guide to Information Sources,* Gale, 1977; (contributor) Burckel, editor, *Racine: Growth and Change in a Wisconsin County,* Racine County Bicentennial Commission, 1977; (with Burckel) *Progressive Reform: A Guide to Information Sources,* Gale, 1980; (with Gerald Greenfield and William Murin) *Urban History and Urbanization: A Guide to Information Sources,* Gale, 1980; (with Greenfield and Murin) *Public Policy and Administration: A Guide to the Information Sources,* Gale, in press; (contributor) Sally M. Miller, editor, *Flawed Liberation: Socialism and Feminism,* Greenwood Press, in press; (contributor) Stanley Coben and Lorman Ratner, editors, *The Development of an American Culture,* St. Martin's, in press.

Contributor to *Encyclopedia Americana, Sourcebook in American History, Biographical Director of American Mayors,* and *Dictionary of American Biography.* Contributor of about forty articles to history and political science journals, including *Historians, Journal of American History, Mid-America, American Historical Review, Catholic Historical Review,* and *New England Quarterly.*

WORK IN PROGRESS: A comparative study of the sixteenth and nineteenth amendments; an examination of coalition politics as a synthesis for explaining Progressive Era reform; and examination of the growth patterns of medium-sized industrial cities.

* * *

BUGBEE, Ruth Carson 1903-
(Ruth Carson)

PERSONAL: Born July 10, 1903, in Indianapolis, Ind.; son of Oliver Howard and Mary (Dowdigan) Carson; married Burton Ashford Bugbee, 1936; children: Mary Carson. *Education:* University of Michigan, B.A., 1926. *Home:* 4 Signal Hill Rd., Brookfield, Conn. 06804. *Agent:* McIntosh & Otis, Inc., 475 Fifth Ave., New York, N.Y. 10017.

CAREER: Crowell-Collier Publishing Company, New York City, contributing editor, 1933-48; free-lance writer, 1948—. Has done public relations work for Lobenz Public Relations Co., New York City. *Member:* Fashion Group (former member of executive council), Phi Beta Kappa, Delta Delta Delta.

WRITINGS: *You and Tuberculosis,* Knopf, 1952; (under name Ruth Carson; with others) *Your New Baby and You,* edited by Jules Saltman, Grosset, 1966; (with Patricia Poore) *Teeth for Life,* Charles B. Slack, 1974. Also author, under name Ruth Carson, of pamphlets on health, babies, and children, published by Public Affairs Committee, and of numerous pamphlets for Salvation Army, Children's Psychiatric Center of Monmouth, N.J., and for Holland Estill Co. (fundraisers). Contributor to *Parents' Magazine, Coronet, Lifetime Living, Look, McCall's, Redbook,* and *Woman's Day.*

* * *

BULLIS, Jerald 1944-

PERSONAL: Born May 5, 1944, in Sioux City, Iowa; son of L. H. (an electrician) and Hattie (Miller) Bullis; married Frances Meyers, June 1, 1968. *Education:* Attended Central Methodist College, 1962-64; Washington University, St. Louis, Mo., A.B., 1966; Cornell University, M.A., 1969, Ph.D., 1970. *Home:* RD 2, Seneca Rd., Trumansburg, N.Y. 14886.

CAREER: Lawrence University, Appleton, Wis., assistant professor of English, 1970-78; lecturer in English, Cornell University, 1978-80, and Ithaca College, 1979-80. Visiting assistant professor and poet in residence, Wake Forest University, 1975-76. *Member:* Modern Language Association of America, Phi Beta Kappa. *Awards, honors:* Woodrow Wilson fellowship, 1966-67; National Endowment for the Arts research grant, 1972-73; received Wisconsin Arts Board grant to writers, 1977.

WRITINGS: *Taking Up the Serpent: A Book of Poems,* Ithaca House, 1973; *Adorning the Buckhorn Helmet,* Ithaca House, 1976; *Orion: A Poem,* Jackpine Press, 1976; *Inland,* Editions Generation, 1978. Work is represented in many anthologies. Contributor of reviews, literary criticism, and essays to numerous journals including *Massachusetts Review, Epoch, New England Review,* and *Articules.* Contributor to journals.

WORK IN PROGRESS: Poetry, nonfiction, and literary criticism.

AVOCATIONAL INTERESTS: Hunting.

* * *

BURKE, Gerald 1914-

PERSONAL: Born August 3, 1914; married; children: two. *Education:* University of London, B.Sc., M.Sc., Ph.D. *Home:* Longwood Hartley Wespall Near Basingstoke, Hampshire, England. *Office:* Oxford Polytechnic, Gypsy Lane, Headington, Oxford OX3 0BP, England.

CAREER: Former member of faculty, University of Reading, Berkshire, England, and University of London, London, England; Oxford Polytechnic, Oxford, England, currently department head. Chartered surveyor; chartered town planner.

WRITINGS: *The Making of Dutch Towns,* Cleaver-Hume Press, 1956; *Greenheart Metropolis,* Macmillan, 1966; *Towns in the Making,* Edward Arnold, 1971; *Townscapes,* Penguin, 1976. Also author of *Town Planning and the Surveyor.*

* * *

BURKE, James Wakefield 1916-

PERSONAL: Born February 7, 1916; son of Richard E. and Bessie Mae (Clay) Burke; married July 16, 1952; wife's name, Angela. *Education:* Attended University of Tennessee; University of Southern California, B.S. and M.A.; University of Chicago, Ph.D. *Politics:* Independent. *Agent:* Bertha Klausner International Literary Agency, Inc., 71 Park Ave., New York, N.Y. 10016.

CAREER: Salesman and executive sales manager in Chicago, Ill., until 1941; war correspondent at Nuremberg trials for *Esquire* magazine, 1945-46; public relations adviser to General Lucius D. Clay, military governor for occupied Germany, 1947-48; *Indianapolis News,* Indianapolis, Ind., staff correspondent in Berlin, Germany; free-lance writer. Has lectured nationally on missions of old Texas and on the Nuremberg trials. *Military service:* U.S. Army Air Forces, test pilot; became lieutenant colonel. *Member:* Military Order of the World Wars, Retired Officers Club, Quiet Birdman, Delta Sigma Phi, Elks, University of Chicago Emeritus Club.

WRITINGS: The Big Rape, F. Rudl Verleger-Union (Frankfurt-am-Main), 1951, Farrar, Strauss, 1952; *Thirsty People in the Rain,* World Wide Productions (Berlin), 1952, published as *Of a Strange Woman,* 1954; *Fraulein Lili Marlene, and Other Stories,* World Wide Productions, 1953; *Three Day Pass—To Kill,* World Wide Productions (Berlin), 1954; *Taboo,* World Distributors (London), 1959; *Ami Go Home,* Amsel Verlag (Berlin), 1960; *The Sweet Dream,* Fountainhead, 1964; *Frau Geh,* Amsel Verlag, 1966; *Missions of Old Texas,* A. S. Barnes, 1971; *The Blazing Dawn,* Harcourt, 1976; *Sunbelt,* Fawcett-Gold Medal, 1977; *Arli,* Caroline House, 1978. Also author of *Sisters of the Sun,* published by World Wide Productions. Contributor of hundreds of articles and short stories to national magazines.

WORK IN PROGRESS: Further work on Texas missions, tentatively entitled *A Forgotten Glory;* the diary of George and Jeanne Mohrenschildt's walk from Texas to Panama, tentatively entitled *A Walk from It All; Requiem for Elvis;* a television mini-series based on *Sunbelt;* a book from a story John Wayne wanted to film before he died, tentatively entitled *The Judge; A Woman of Hitler's Berlin,* completion expected 1981.

* * *

BURN, Andrew Robert 1902-

PERSONAL: Born September 25, 1902, in Kynnersley, Shropshire, England; son of Andrew Ewbank (a clergyman) and Celia Mary (Richardson) Burn; married Mary Wynn Thomas, December 31, 1938. *Education:* Christ Church, Oxford, B.A., 1925, M.A., 1928. *Politics:* "Academic socialist. Not a party member." *Religion:* Anglican ("skeptical"). *Home:* Flat 23, 380 Banbury Rd., Oxford OX2 7PW, England.

CAREER: Uppingham School, Uppingham, England, senior classical master, 1927-40; British Embassy, Athens, Greece, second secretary, 1944-46; University of Glasgow, Glasgow, Scotland, senior lecturer, 1946-65, reader in ancient history, 1965-69. Gillespie Professor, College of Wooster, Ohio, 1958-59; member of Institute for Advanced Study, Princeton, N.J., 1961-62; professor, A College Year in Athens, Inc., 1969-72. *Military service:* Intelligence Corps, 1941-43; became captain. *Member:* Society for the Promotion of Hellenic Studies (member of council, 1959-62), Society for the Promotion of Roman Studies, Glasgow Archaeological Society (president, 1969-72). *Awards, honors:* Silver Cross, Order of the Phoenix (Greece), 1975.

WRITINGS: Minoans, Philistines, and Greeks, Knopf, 1930, reprinted, Greenwood Press, 1975; *The Romans in Britain: An Anthology of Transcriptions,* Basil Blackwell, 1932, 2nd edition, 1968, University of South Carolina, 1968; *The World of Hesiod,* Knopf, 1936, reprinted, Blom, 1968; *This Sceptered Isle: An Anthology of English Poetry,* Pyrsos (Athens), 1940; *Philoi toi Vivliou,* [Alexandria], 1942, translation published as *The Modern Greeks,* Thomas Nelson, 1944; *Alexander the Great and the Mid-East,* English Universities Press, 1947, enlarged edition, Collier, 1962; *Pericles and Athens,* English Universities Press, 1948, Collier, 1962; *Agricola and Roman Britain,* English Universities Press, 1953, revised edition, Collier, 1962; (contributor) John Bowle, editor, *An Encyclopaedia of World History,* Hutchinson, 1958; *The Lyric Age of Greece,* Edward Arnold, 1960; *Persia and the Greeks,* St. Martin's, 1962; (contributor) Michael Grant, editor, *The Birth of Western Civilization,* Thames & Hudson, 1964; *A Traveller's History of Greece,* Hodder & Stoughton, 1965, published as *The Pelican History of Greece,* Pelican, 1966; *Greece and Rome,* Scott, Foresman, 1971. Contributor to encyclopedias and professional journals.

WORK IN PROGRESS: A one-volume history of civilization, tentatively entitled *Man: A Brief History,* for Hodder & Stoughton; *Greece Has Four Dimensions,* an autobiography.

SIDELIGHTS: A reviewer for *Times Literary Supplement* describes Andrew Burn as "a scholar whose detailed grasp of the minutiae of ancient history is reinforced by wide personal and topographical knowledge, great imaginative insight, and a pleasantly warm style. . . . [He] could not be dull if he tried." *Avocational interests:* Formerly mountaineering and gliding; now travel.

BIOGRAPHICAL/CRITICAL SOURCES: Times Literary Supplement, April 21, 1961.

* * *

BURNFORD, Sheila (Philip Cochrane Every) 1918-

PERSONAL: Born May 11, 1918, in Scotland; daughter of Wilfred George Cochrane and Ida Philip (Macmillan) Every; married David Burnford, 1941; children: Peronelle Philip, Elizabeth Jonquil, Juliet Sheila. *Education:* Privately educated in England, France, and Germany. *Religion:* Anglican. *Home:* R.R.I, Pass Lake, Ontario, Canada POT 2MO. *Agent:* Harold Ober Associates, Inc., 40 East 49th St., New York, N.Y. 10017; David Higham Associates, Ltd., 5-8 Lower John St., London W1R 4HA, England.

CAREER: Writer. *Member:* Society of Authors (England), Canadian Authors Association, Authors Guild (United States). *Awards, honors:* Canadian Book of the Year for Children medal, 1963, and Lewis Carroll Shelf Award, 1971, both for *The Incredible Journey.*

WRITINGS: The Incredible Journey, Little, Brown, 1961; *The Fields of Noon* (autobiographical essays), Little, Brown, 1964; *Without Reserve,* Atlantic, 1969; *One Woman's Arctic,* Little, Brown, 1973; *Mr. Noah and the Second Flood,* Praeger, 1973; *Bel Ria,* Little, Brown, 1978. Contributor to magazines and newspapers.

SIDELIGHTS: Sheila Burnford's first book, *The Incredible Journey,* has often been described as "remarkable," "convincing," and "compelling." It has been praised for its "restraint and integrity," in that the animals are "never humanized or sentimentalized." It has been translated into sixteen languages and made into a movie by Walt Disney Studios.

Perhaps understandably, then, Sheila Egoff finds that *The Incredible Journey* "represents almost all the virtues and failings characteristic of popular films" which, among other things, contain simple plots, "a strong emphasis on characterization, a large measure of sentimentality, and a compelling vividness, pace, and charm." The animals are given "all the human attributes that pet lovers are apt to ascribe to their charges." The events of the story are related "so graphically and even poetically that it very nearly convinces. But not quite. The journey remains incredible and, despite its undoubted emotional impact, the book is not entirely honest."

Of Burnford's book of essays, *The Fields of Noon,* G. F. Dole writes, "The quality of the writing . . . seems uneven." Dole finds that "some of the passages sparkle with beauty while others are in lengthy, rather complicated sentences with philosophic overtones." Still, Edward Weeks comments, "[The essays] establish at once . . . a degree of trust, of intimacy between the writer and the reader, and an expectation for the self-reliance, the quiet humor, and the lively sense of observation so characteristic" of Sheila Burnford's writing. C. M. Siggins goes so far as to say that "these essays are the greatest of their kind and this is not merely a subjective comment. . . . [Burnford] is quite a yarner; her style and her subject matter cause the reader to talk back to her. . . . By means of diction and cadence she gives [the animals] something like life and vigor, and warmth. Yet the sensuousness in her language is only one aspect of her style. Brevity and clarity are other aspects; and those turns of phrase, speedy and forceful and neat . . . always with a sense of fun, make this a most re-readable book."

Without Reserve, Burnford's third book, presents a "vivid and sympathetic account" of her stay on Cree and Ojibwa reservations in Canada. Dennis Linehan points out that "the author makes no claim to objectivity, so she must not be faulted for her failure to achieve it. Rather, she is to be congratulated for producing a highly readable and pleasant memoir" which, in Edith Fowke's opinion, "should be required reading for every official connected with the Department of Indian Affairs." In the same way, *One Woman's Arctic* has been dubbed an "interesting and sensitive account" of her visits with the Eskimos. The reviewer calls it "a delightful, informative book that reflects Burnford's good humor and natural curiosity."

Mr. Noah and the Second Flood, though in some ways considered too subtle for young children, explores the plight of the modern-day ark builder with the same sort of wry humor. Some of the original animals are now extinct, while others are hard to keep fed. Judy Noyes comments that "the story has bite and meaning," as it takes a new approach to the subject of destruction of the environment through pollution.

Finally, *Bel Ria,* is said to rank with *The Incredible Journey* in its emotional warmth and charm. Once again, the animals and people are vivid and alive. As one reviewer describes it, "This is a real tear-jerker, but in the very best way." To illustrate its widespread appeal, less than a year after its publication, *Bel Ria* had already been translated into twelve languages.

AVOCATIONAL INTERESTS: Hunting, mycology, and astronomy.

BIOGRAPHICAL/CRITICAL SOURCES: *Christian Science Monitor,* December, 1961; *Library Journal,* August, 1964, June 1, 1973; *Best Sellers,* August 15, 1964, November 1, 1969; *Atlantic,* September, 1964; *Canadian Forum,* January, 1970; M. H. Arbuthnot and Z. Sutherland, *Children and Books,* 4th edition, Scott, Foresman, 1972; *New York Times Book Review,* December 16, 1973; S. Egroff, *The Republic of Childhood: A Critical Guide to Canadian Children's Literature in English,* 2nd edition, Oxford University Press, 1975; *Children's Literature Review,* Volume II, Gale, 1976; *Publisher's Weekly,* November 28, 1977.

* * *

BURNS, Wayne 1918-

PERSONAL: Born August 26, 1918, in Fincastle, Ohio; son of William and Lillian (Juillerat) Burns; married, 1939 (divorced); married, 1946 (divorced). *Education:* Miami University, Oxford, Ohio, A.B., 1938; Duke University, additional study, 1939-40; Harvard University, A.M., 1940; Cornell University, Ph.D., 1946. *Home:* 212 East Howe St., Seattle, Wash. 98102. *Office:* Department of English, University of Washington, Seattle, Wash. 98195.

CAREER: Harvard University, Cambridge, Mass., instructor, 1945-46; University of California, Berkeley, instructor, 1946-48; University of Washington, Seattle, associate professor, 1948-63, professor of English, 1963—. *Member:* Modern Language Association of America, American Society for Aesthetics.

WRITINGS: *Charles Reade: A Study in Victorian Authorship,* Twayne, 1961, reprinted, Irvington Books, 1980; *Towards a Contextualist Aesthetic of the Novel,* Genitron, 1968; *The Panzaic Principle,* Pendejo Press, 1972. Contributor of essays, articles, and studies to journals.

WORK IN PROGRESS: *A Study of Thomas Hardy's Later Novels.*

AVOCATIONAL INTERESTS: Tennis, golf, sports car racing, boating.

* * *

BURTON, Robert (Wellesley) 1941-

PERSONAL: Born June 18, 1941, in Sherbourne, Dorsetshire, England; son of Maurice (a zoologist) and Margaret (Maclean) Burton. *Education:* Attended Downing College, Cambridge, 1960-63. *Home and office:* Manor Cottage, 46 West St., Great Gransden, Sandy, Bedfordshire SG19 3AU, England. *Agent:* Murray Pollinger, 4 Garrick St., London WC2E 9BH, England.

CAREER: Author, 1967—. Meteorologist and biologist for British Antarctic Survey, 1963-66; biologist, 1971-72. *Member:* Society of Authors, Institute of Biology, Zoological Society of London.

WRITINGS: *Animals of the Antarctic,* Abelard Schuman, 1970; *Animal Senses,* David & Charles, 1970; *The Life and Death of Whales,* Deutsch, 1973; *How Birds Live,* Elsevier Phaidon, 1975; *The Mating Game,* Elsevier Phaidon, 1976; *Ponds,* David & Charles, 1976; *The Cat Family,* Macmillan, 1976; *The Language of Smell,* Routledge & Kegan Paul, 1976; *Love of Baby Animals,* Octopus Press, 1976; *Exploring Hills and Moors,* Elsevier Phaidon, 1976; *Nature by the Roadside,* Elsevier Phaidon, 1977; *The Seashore,* Orbis, 1977; (co-author) *Inside the Animal World,* Macmillan, 1977; *Seals,* Bodley Head, 1978; *Carnivores of Europe,* Batsford, 1979; *Horses and Ponies,* Macmillan, 1979. Contributor to *Animals* and *Sea Frontiers.* Co-editor of *Purnell's Encyclopedia of Animal Life* (published in the United States as *International Wildlife Encyclopedia*).

AVOCATIONAL INTERESTS: Whaling, the history of polar expeditions.

* * *

BURTON, William H(enry) 1890-1964

PERSONAL: Born October 9, 1890, in Fort Worth, Tex.;

died April 3, 1964; son of George Charles and Agnes Ann (Selbie) Burton; married Virginia Lee Nottingham, August 4, 1920. *Education:* University of Oregon, B.A., 1915; Columbia University, Ed.M., 1917; University of Chicago, Ph.D., 1924. *Politics:* Democrat. *Religion:* Episcopalian. *Home and office:* 3434 Willamette Ave., Corvallis, Ore.

CAREER: Taught in rural, elementary, and secondary schools in Oregon, intermittently, 1914-18, and at Oregon Normal School (now Oregon College of Education), Monmouth, 1918; State College of Washington (now Washington State University), Pullman, assistant professor, 1919-21; Winona State Teachers College (now Winona State College), Winona, Minn., director of student teaching and principal training, 1921-23; University of Cincinnati, Cincinnati, Ohio, director of student teaching, 1924-26; University of Chicago, Chicago, Ill., professor of education, 1926-31; University of Southern California, Los Angeles, professor of education, 1932-38; Harvard University, Cambridge, Mass., director of student teaching, 1938-54. Visiting summer instructor, University of California, 1932, University of Puerto Rico, 1933, University of Nebraska, 1934, Harvard University, 1938, and University of Maine, 1944. Consultant, Oregon State Department of Education.

MEMBER: National Education Association (member of executive committee, 1927-32; member of editorial board, 1927-38), Association for Curriculum Development, (president, 1927), National Society for Study of Education (yearbook commission, 1950), International Reading Association, John Dewey Society, Association for Student Teaching, National Society of Teachers of Education, Phi Delta Kappa. *Awards, honors:* S.C. Rosenberger Prize from University of Chicago, 1925; Litt.D. from Pacific University, 1955.

WRITINGS—Published by Appleton, except as indicated: *Supervision and the Improvement of Teaching,* 1922; (with A. S. Barr) *The Supervision of Instruction,* 1926; *The Nature and Direction of Learning,* 1929; *An Introduction to Education,* 1934; (with Barr and L. J. Brueckner) *Supervision: A Social Process,* 1938, 3rd edition (with Brueckner), 1955; *Guidance of Learning Activities,* 1944, 3rd edition, 1962; (with A. W. Blair) *Growth and Development of the Preadolescent,* 1951; (with Grace K. Kemp and Clara Belle Baker) *Reading in Child Development,* Bobbs-Merrill, 1956; (with R. B. Kimball and R. L. Wing) *Education for Effective Thinking,* 1960; *The Profession of Education,* 1967. Also contributor to *The Supervision of Elementary Subjects,* 1929.

(With others) "Reading for Living" series, published with teacher's manuals and workbooks by Bobbs-Merrill, 1950: *Get Ready to Read, Don and Peggy, Come and See, Here We Play, Days of Fun, Our Happy Ways, Meet Our Friends, Our Good Neighbors.*

(With others) "Developmental Reading Text-Workbooks" series, published with teacher's manuals and workbooks by Bobbs-Merrill, 1961: *Up and Away, Animal Parade, Picnic Basket, Blazing New Trails, Flying High, Shooting Stars.*

Monographs: (With others) *Children's Civic Information, 1924-35,* University of Southern California Press, 1936; (with Mary O'Rourke) *Workshops for Teachers,* Appleton, 1957; *Teaching as a Career,* Bellman Publishing, 1963; (with Helen Hefferman) *The Step Beyond: Creativity,* National Education Association, 1964. Contributor of more than fifty articles to periodicals.

AVOCATIONAL INTERESTS: Local history, golf, and gardening.†

BUSKIRK, Richard H(obart) 1927- (Qass Aquarius)

PERSONAL: Born January 24, 1927, in Bloomington, Ind; son of Cyrus Hobart and Ruth (Borland) Buskirk; married Barbara J. Lusk, June 14, 1947; children: Bruce David, Carol Ann. *Education:* Indiana University, B.S., 1948, M.B.A., 1949; University of Washington, D.B.A., 1955. *Home:* 13228 Hughes Lane, Dallas, Tex. 75240. *Office:* School of Business, Southern Methodist University, Dallas, Tex. 75275.

CAREER: Assistant to sales manager, Stewart-Warner, 1948; University of Kansas, Lawrence, instructor in marketing, 1949-53; University of Washington, Seattle, instructor in marketing, 1953-55; University of Oklahoma, Norman, assistant professor of marketing, 1955-57; University of Colorado, Boulder, associate professor, 1957-61, professor of marketing, 1961-70; California State University, Fullerton, professor of marketing and chairman of department, 1970-73; University of Southern California, Los Angeles, professor of business administration, 1973-74; Southern Methodist University, Dallas, Tex., Herman W. Lay Professor of Marketing, 1974—. Director, ARF Products, Inc., 1960-70, Ampco, 1960-63, The Regiment, Ltd., 1965-70, Thomas Horton & Co., 1972—, Health Wheels, 1972-74, and Oak Tree Press, 1973-79; consultant, Weyerhauser Co., 1963-64, and Delta Drilling Co., 1978—. *Military service:* U.S. Navy, 1944-46. *Member:* American Marketing Association, American Academy of Management, Beta Gamma Sigma, Delta Sigma Pi, Alpha Delta Sigma, Theta Chi.

WRITINGS: (With William Stanton) *Management of the Sales Force,* Irwin, 1959, 5th edition, 1978; *Principles of Marketing: The Management View,* Holt, 1961, 4th edition, 1975; *Cases and Readings in Marketing,* Holt, 1961, 2nd edition, 1970; (with Frederic Arthur Russell and Frank H. Beach) *Textbook of Salesmanship,* 7th edition (Buskirk was not associated with earlier editions), McGraw, 1963, 10th edition, 1979; (with Benjamin R. Howe) *Preplanning a Profitable Call Writing Program,* Investors Intelligence, 1970; *Business and Administrative Policy: Text, Cases, Incidents and Readings,* Wiley, 1971; (under pseudonym Qass Aquarius) *The Corporate Prince,* Van Nostrand, 1971; (With Donald J. Green and William C. Rodgers) *Concepts of Business: An Introduction to the Business System,* Rinehart Press, 1972; *Modern Management and Machiavelli,* Cahners, 1974; *Retail Selling: A Vital Approach,* Harper, 1975; *Handbook of Managerial Tactics,* Cahners, 1976; (with Percy J. Vaughn, Jr.) *Managing New Enterprises,* West Publishing, 1976; *Your Career: How to Plan It, Manage It, Change It,* Cahners, 1976; (with son, Bruce D. Buskirk) *Retailing,* McGraw, 1979.

* * *

BUTWELL, Richard 1929-

PERSONAL: Born April 19, 1929, in Portland, Me.; son of Walter (a salesman) and Jenny Butwell; married Charlene Bell, December 18, 1965; children: Michael Lee, Scot Andrew. *Education:* Tufts University, B.A., 1951; Indiana University, M.S., 1952; St. Antony's College, Oxford, D.Phil., 1954. *Home:* 1523 London Dr., Murray, Ky. 42071. *Office:* Vice-President for Academic Programs, Murray State University, Murray, Ky. 42071.

CAREER: University of Illinois at Urbana-Champaign, 1958-65, began as assistant professor, became professor of political science; University of Kentucky, Lexington, professor of political science and director of William Andrew

Patterson School of Diplomacy and International Commerce, 1965-68; American University, Washington, D.C., professor of Southeast Asian politics and director of program for international business executives, 1968-71; State University of New York College at Brockport, professor of political science and chairman of department, 1971-74; State University of New York College at Fredonia, professor of political science and dean of arts and sciences, 1974-78; Murray State University, Murray, Ky., professor of political science and vice-president for academic programs, 1978—. Fulbright professor, University of Rangoon, 1959-60; visiting professor and director of Asian studies, National War College, 1970-71. *Member:* American Political Science Association, Association for Asian Studies. *Awards, honors:* Fulbright scholar at Oxford University, 1952-54; SEATO research fellow in Thailand, 1962.

WRITINGS: (With Amry Vandenbosch) *Southeast Asia among the World Powers,* University Press of Kentucky, 1958; *Southeast Asia Today and Tomorrow,* Praeger, 1961, revised edition, 1969; *U Nu of Burma,* Stanford University Press, 1963, revised edition, 1969; (with Vandenbosch) *Southeast Asia in the Changing World,* University Press of Kentucky, 1966; *Indonesia,* Ginn, 1967; *Southeast Asia: A Survey,* Foreign Policy Association, 1968; (editor) *Foreign Policy and the Developing Nation,* University Press of Kentucky, 1969; (contributor) Abdul A. Said, editor, *America's World Role in the 70's,* Prentice-Hall, 1970; (contributor) Said, editor, *Protagonists of Change: Subcultures in Development and Revolution,* Prentice-Hall, 1971; *Southeast Asia: A Political Introduction,* Praeger, 1975; (contributor) Arthur W. Banks, editor, *Political Handbook of the World,* McGraw, for Council on Foreign Relations, 1978. Also contributor to *Nationalism, Revolution, and Evolution in Southeast Asia* (University of Hull monograph series), edited by Michael Leifer, 1970. Contributor to journals. Member of editorial boards of *Journal of Politics, Asian Survey,* and *Current History.*

C

CADWALLADER, Sharon 1936-

PERSONAL: Born January 12, 1936, in Jamestown, N.D.; daughter of Herman Julius and Mildred (Hull) Wulfsberg; married Mervyn Leland Cadwallader, July 4, 1959 (divorced, 1966); children: Leland Hull. *Education:* San Jose State College (now University), A.B., 1958. *Politics:* Democrat. *Religion:* None. *Home and office:* 174 12th Ave., Santa Cruz, Calif. 95062.

CAREER: Has taught mentally retarded children; taught English to speakers of foreign languages; medical social worker in public clinic in Santa Cruz County, Calif.; organized and operated Whole Earth Restaurant at University of California, Santa Cruz; writer, 1972—.

WRITINGS: (With Judi Ohr) *Whole Earth Cookbook,* Houghton, 1972; *In Celebration of Small Things,* Houghton, 1975; *Cooking Adventures for Kids,* Houghton, 1975; *Whole Earth Cookbook 2,* Houghton, 1975; *Sharon Cadwallader's Complete Cookbook,* San Francisco Book Co., 1977; *Sharing in the Kitchen: A Cookbook for Single Parents and Children,* McGraw, 1979. Food columnist, *Bon Appetit, Christian Science Monitor,* and *San Francisco Chronicle;* restaurant reviewer, *San Jose Mercury.*

WORK IN PROGRESS: Through the Kitchens of Mexico: A Travel Cookbook, for McGraw.

SIDELIGHTS: Sharon Cadwallader told *CA:* "People ask me quite frequently how I created a career such as mine—a food writer with a healthy emphasis. I always respond that I like to write, I like to cook, I like to eat, and I like to eat well. What else can I do but what I am doing? I am, however, doing some writing for children now. It's also writing of a nurturing nature, I think."

* * *

CAEN, Herb (Eugene) 1916-

PERSONAL: Born April 3, 1916, in Sacramento, Calif.; son of Lucien and Augusta (Gross) Caen; married second wife, Sally Gilbert, February 15, 1952 (divorced, 1959); married Maria Theresa Shaw, March 9, 1963; children: (second marriage) Deborah (stepdaughter); (third marriage) Christopher. *Education:* Attended Sacramento Junior College, 1934. *Residence:* Pacific Heights, Calif. *Office: San Francisco Chronicle,* 925 Mission St., San Francisco, Calif. 94103.

CAREER: Sacramento Union, Sacramento, Calif., reporter, 1932-36; columnist, *San Francisco Chronicle,* San Francisco, Calif., 1936-50, *San Francisco Examiner,* San Francisco, 1950-58, and *San Francisco Chronicle,* 1958—. *Military service:* U.S. Army Air Forces, 1942-45; became captain; received battle star for Normandy campaign. *Member:* California Tennis Club, San Francisco Press Club.

WRITINGS—All published by Doubleday, except as indicated: *The San Francisco Book,* Houghton, 1948; *Baghdad-by-the-Bay,* 1949; *Baghdad, 1951,* 1950; *Don't Call It Frisco,* 1953; *Guide to San Francisco,* 1957, revised edition published as *New Guide to San Francisco and the Bay Area,* 1958, 2nd revised edition published as *Herb Caen's San Francisco: The Guide to the City and the Bay Area Today,* 1965; *Only in San Francisco,* 1960; (with Dong Kingman) *San Francisco: City on Golden Hills,* 1967; *The Cable Car and the Dragon* (juvenile), 1972; *One Man's San Francisco,* 1976.

SIDELIGHTS: "It's News to Me," Herb Caen's popular column of anecdotes and news briefs on the city of San Francisco and its residents, is syndicated to various newspapers throughout the United States.

BIOGRAPHICAL/CRITICAL SOURCES: Authors in the News, Volume I, Gale, 1976.†

* * *

CAESAR, (Eu)Gene (Lee) 1927- (Johnny Laredo, Anthony Sterling)

PERSONAL: Born December 10, 1927, in Saginaw, Mich.; son of Ernest Thor and Eunice (Lee) Caesar; married Judith May Hall, 1953; children: Cheryl Lee, Craig Arthur. *Education:* Attended Central Michigan College (now University), 1945, Case Institute of Technology (now Case Western Reserve University), 1945-46, and University of Miami, Coral Gables, Fla., 1947-49. *Agent:* Curtis Brown Ltd., 575 Madison Ave., New York, N.Y. 10022.

CAREER: Saginaw Steering Gear, Saginaw, Mich., machine operator, 1950-53; Republic Aviation, Farmingdale, Long Island, N.Y., mechanic, 1954-55; professional writer, 1955—. *Military service:* U.S. Naval Air Corps, 1945-46. *Awards, honors:* Western Heritage Award, 1961, for *King of the Mountain Men.*

WRITINGS: Mark of the Hunter, William Sloane Associates, 1953; (under pseudonym Johnny Laredo) *Come and Get Me,* Popular Library, 1956; *The Wild Hunters: The*

Wolves, the Bears, and the Big Cats, Putnam, 1957; *King of the Mountain Men: The Life of Jim Bridger,* Dutton, 1961; *Rifle for Rent,* Monarch, 1963; *Incredible Detective: The Biography of William J. Burns,* Prentice-Hall, 1968; (with Robert N. McKerr and James Phelps) *New Equity in Michigan School Finance,* Michigan Senate Committee on Education, 1973. Contributor of articles to *True, Holiday, Saturday Evening Post, Argosy, Virginia Quarterly Review, Field and Stream, Stag,* and *Bluebook.*

SIDELIGHTS: Gene Caesar became interested in writing while studying engineering as a Navy student. "Somehow found myself" he told *CA,* "in a creative writing course taught by Pulitzer Prize-winning Dr. S. I. Hayakawa." After attempting novels, Caesar found what he calls his "stock in trade," a full-fledged short story with an outdoor background. His writing interest in wild animals has been supplanted more recently by an interest in Western Americana. "America's past is more colorful and exciting than anything the human imagination could conjur up." Caesar states, "This is especially true of the lusty, fast-paced chronicle of the West." *Avocational interests:* Wildlife, American history, travel.†

* * *

CAFFREY, Kate (Kate Caffrey Toller)

PERSONAL: Born in Preston, Lancashire, England; daughter of Louis John and Mary (Bracher) Caffrey; married Roland Toller, January 21, 1954 (divorced, 1958); children: Owen Louis Caffrey. *Education:* University of Exeter, B.A. (honors); College of William and Mary, M.A. *Home:* 82 Castleton Ave., Wembley, Middlesex HA9 7QF, England. *Agent:* Elaine Greene Ltd., 31 Newington Green, London N16 9PJ, England.

CAREER: Teacher in London schools, 1955-67; Middlesex Polytechnic, Trent Park College of Education, Barnet, Hertfordshire, England, senior lecturer in English, 1967—. *Member:* Royal Society of Arts (fellow).

WRITINGS: *The British to Southern Africa,* Gentry Books, 1973; *Out in the Midday Sun: Singapore, 1941-1945,* Stein & Day, 1973; *The Mayflower* (Book-of-the-Month Club alternate selection), Stein & Day, 1974; *The 1900s Lady,* Gordon & Cremonesi, 1976; *The Twilight's Last Gleaming: Britain vs. America, 1812-1815,* Stein & Day, 1977 (published in England as *The Lion and the Union: Anglo-American War, 1812-1815,* Deutsch, 1978); *1937-1939: Last Look Round,* Gordon & Cremonesi, 1978; *Farewell, Leicester Square: The Old Contemptibles, 1914,* Deutsch, 1980.

SIDELIGHTS: Kate Caffrey told *CA:* "I cannot remember the time when I did not try to write. I took years to realize that I should never be a novelist because I can't invent plots. It never occurred to me to write histories until I became interested in the Singapore campaign. . . . My favorite period is, roughly, 1860-1945, in both history and literature.

"The thing that has given me the greatest pleasure [about my writing] is that every critic has commented favourably upon my style. This matters a lot to me; I love good English and detest seeing it debased. . . . All I could ever say to aspiring writers is, I suppose, what I have found most important—practise, practise all the time; strive for improvement; never give up."

* * *

CALAFERTE, Louis 1928-

PERSONAL: Born July 14, 1928, in Turin, Italy; son of Ugo (a mason) and Marguerite (Crepet) Calaferte; married Guillemette Maurice, January 10, 1956. *Education:* Attended primary school in Lyon, France. *Religion:* Christian. *Home:* 9 bis, rue Roux-Soignat, Lyon 3, France.

CAREER: Held various jobs from age of fourteen, in factories, as movie extra, and as newspaper vendor; Office de Radio Television Francais, Lyon and Paris, France, radio and television producer, 1956—. *Awards, honors:* Laureat de la Bourse Del Duca, 1953; Bourse Nationale des Lettres, 1956; Prix Ponceton de la Societe des Gens de Lettres, 1976; Prix Ibsen, 1979; Prix Lugne-Poe, 1979.

WRITINGS: *Requiem des innocents,* Julliard, 1952; *Partage des vivants* (novel), Julliard, 1953; "Clotilde du Nord" (one-act play), first produced in Paris, France, at Comedie de Paris, March, 1955; *Septentrion* (novel), Cercle du Livre Precieux, 1963; *No Man's Land,* Julliard, 1963; *Satori,* Denoel, 1968; *Rosa mystica* (novel), Denoel, 1968; *Portrait de l'Enfant,* Denoel, 1969.

Hinterland, Denoel, 1971; *Limitrophe: Recit,* Denoel, 1972; *Megaphonie* (full-length play), Stock, 1972; *Rag-Time* (poems), Denoel, 1972; "Chez les Titch" (one-act play; also see below), first produced in Paris at Theatre National du Petit Odeon, 1973; *Paraphe,* Denoel, 1974; *La Vie parallele,* Denoel, 1974; *Episodes de la vie des mantes religieuses,* Denoel, 1976; *Mo* (one-act play; first produced in Paris at Theatre National du Petit Odeon, 1976), Stock, 1976; *Les Mandibules* (full-length play; first produced in Paris at Centre National Beaubourg, 1977), Stock, 1976; *Campagnes,* Denoel, 1979; *L'Amour des mots* (one-act play), Revue de Centre Dramatique National de Reims, 1979.

Trafic (also see below; one-act play; first produced in Paris at Theatre National du Petit Odeon, 1976), Stock, 1980; *Les Miettes* (also see below; one-act play; first produced in Paris at Theatre Essaion, 1978), Stock, 1980; *Theatre intimiste* (contains "Chez les Titch," "Trafic," "Les Miettes," and "Tu as bien fait de venir, Paul"), Stock, 1980; *Le Chemin de Sion,* Denoel, 1980; "Les Beaux Dimanches" (screenplay), produced by French television, 1980. Contributor to newspapers.

WORK IN PROGRESS: *Langages,* poems and paintings; "Opera Bleu," a full-length play.

SIDELIGHTS: Louis Calaferte told *CA* that drawing and painting have become as important to him as writing. His gouaches and tint-drawings were exhibited in France, at Lyon-Miribel, Gallery Corine Martin, in 1973.

* * *

CALDER, Jenni 1941-

PERSONAL: Born December 3, 1941, in Chicago, Ill.; daughter of David and Isabel (Mackay) Daiches; married Angus Calder (an author), October 1, 1963; children: Rachel Elizabeth, Gowan Lindsay, Gideon James. *Education:* Cambridge University, B.A. (first class honors), 1963; University of London, M.Phil., 1965. *Politics:* Socialist. *Religion:* Atheist. *Home:* Philipstoun House, Linlithgow, West Lothian, Scotland. *Agent:* A. D. Peters & Co., 10 Buckingham St., London WC2N 6BU, England.

CAREER: University of Nairobi, Nairobi, Kenya, lecturer in literature, 1968-69; Royal Scottish Museum, Edinburgh, lecturer in education department, 1978—. Part-time adult education teacher.

WRITINGS: *Chronicles of Conscience: A Study of George Orwell and Arthur Koestler,* University of Pittsburgh Press, 1968; (with husband, Angus Calder) *Sir Walter Scott,* Arco,

1969; *There Must Be a Lone Ranger,* Hamish Hamilton, 1974, Taplinger, 1975; *Women and Marriage in Nineteenth-Century Fiction,* Thames & Hudson, 1976; *Heroes: From Byron to Guevara,* Hamish Hamilton, 1977; *The Victorian and Edwardian Home from Old Photographs,* Thames & Hudson, 1977, Hippocrene, 1979; *RLS: A Like Study,* Hamish Hamilton, 1980.

WORK IN PROGRESS: Research on museum history.

SIDELIGHTS: Jenni Calder told *CA:* "My motivations in writing are compounded of curiosity, a love of writing and reading, and an urge to communicate. I am a socialist, an internationalist and a feminist in instinct and intellect, and most of my interests and activities, professional or recreational, stem from this. I have a deep concern for the fates of Israel and Scotland, disbelieve in patriotism."

AVOCATIONAL INTERESTS: Walking, cooking, music.

BIOGRAPHICAL/CRITICAL SOURCES: Times Literary Supplement, June 6, 1980.

* * *

CALISHER, Hortense 1911-

PERSONAL: Born December 20, 1911, in New York, N.Y.; daughter of Joseph Henry (a manufacturer) and Hedwig (Lichtstern) Calisher; married Heaton Bennet Heffelfinger, September 27, 1935; married Curtis Arthur Harnack (a novelist), March 27, 1959; children: (first marriage) Bennet Hughes (daughter), Peter Hughes. *Education:* Barnard College, A.B., 1932. *Agent:* Candida Donadio & Associates, Inc., 111 West 57th St., New York, N.Y. 10019.

CAREER: Adjunct professor at Barnard College, 1957, Columbia University, 1968-70, and Columbia School of the Arts, 1972-73. Visiting professor at Brandeis University, 1963-64, City College of the City University of New York, 1970-71, and State University of New York at Purchase, 1971-72. Regents Professor, University of California at Irvine, 1975. Visiting lecturer at University of Iowa, 1957, 1959-60, Stanford University, 1958, Sarah Lawrence College, 1962, and at University of Pennsylvania, 1969. Clark Lecturer, Scripps College, 1968. Visiting writer at Bennington College, 1978. *Member:* P.E.N., American Academy and Institute. *Awards, honors:* Guggenheim fellow, 1951-52, 1953-54; American Specialist's Grant, U.S. Department of State, 1958, for visiting Southeast Asia; National Council of the Arts award, 1967; Academy of Arts and Letters award, 1967; four O. Henry prize story awards; Hurst Fellow, Washington University.

WRITINGS—Novels: *False Entry,* Little, Brown, 1961; *Textures of Life,* Little, Brown, 1963; *Journal from Ellipsia,* Little, Brown, 1965; *The New Yorkers,* Little, Brown, 1969; *Queenie,* Arbor House, 1971; *Standard Dreaming,* Arbor House, 1972; *Eagle Eye,* Arbor House, 1973; *On Keeping Women,* Arbor House, 1977.

Collections: *In the Absence of Angels* (stories), Little, Brown, 1951; *Tale for the Mirror* (novella and stories), Little, Brown, 1962; *Extreme Magic* (novella and stories), Little, Brown, 1964; *The Railway Police* [and] *The Last Trolley Ride* (two novellas), Little, Brown, 1966; *The Collected Stories of Hortense Calisher,* Arbor House, 1975.

Other: *Herself* (autobiographical memoir), Arbor House, 1972.

Work appears in numerous anthologies, including: *50 Best American Short Stories, 1915-1965, Great American Short Stories, Mid-Century: An Anthology of Distinguished American Short Stories,* and *O. Henry Memorial Award Prize Stories.* Contributor of short stories, articles, and reviews to *New York Times, Evergreen Review, Texas Quarterly, American Scholar, New Yorker,* and *Harper's.*

WORK IN PROGRESS: Further prose works.

SIDELIGHTS: In her short stories and novels, Hortense Calisher explores through a psychological writing style what Doris Grumbach calls "the private depths of lives." Her short stories in particular have received considerable praise. "Hortense Calisher," Robert Phillips writes, "not only is best at writing short stories, she is one of *the* best." He goes on to note that "it is impossible to overpraise the psychological acumen which the author brings to each story." Eugenie Bolger concludes that "her stories, symmetrical, conclusive, polished to the glint, are classics of their kind."

Calisher's novels have also been well-received, although her style has not always been appreciated. A reviewer for *Virginia Quarterly Review,* for instance, writes that *The New Yorkers* contains Calisher's "predilection for ambiguity, opacity, ellipses, and prolixity" while praising her "charm, deftness, fluency, and sureness of touch."

Other critics, however, have found Calisher's novels praiseworthy in all respects. Lucy Rosenthal describes *Queenie* as "dense with insight and written intensely, with wit and love of life and of ideas." Bonnie Stowers, reviewing *Eagle Eye* in *Nation,* considers it "a durable masterpiece" and "a work of art."

BIOGRAPHICAL/CRITICAL SOURCES: Wisconsin Studies in Contemporary Literature, summer, 1965; Brigid Brophy, *Don't Never Forget: Collected Views and Reviews,* Holt, 1966; *New York Review of Books,* December 15, 1966; Roy Newquist, *Conversations,* Rand McNally, 1967; *Kenyon Review,* Volume XXX, number 1, 1968; *New York Times Book Review,* June 2, 1968, October 23, 1977; *Writer's Digest,* March, 1969; *New York Times,* April 18, 1969, November 9, 1972; *Publishers' Weekly,* April 21, 1969; *Book World,* April 27, 1969, September 18, 1977; *Best Sellers,* May 1, 1969; *Time,* May 16, 1969; *Times Literary Supplement,* January 15, 1970; *New Statesman,* January 16, 1970; *Guardian Weekly,* January 24, 1970; *Harper's,* March, 1971; *National Review,* May 18, 1971; Hortense Calisher, *Herself,* Arbor House, 1972; *Hudson Review,* spring, 1972; *Newsweek,* October 16, 1972; *Minnesota Review,* spring, 1973; *Atlantic,* November, 1973; *New Republic,* November 3, 1973, October 25, 1975; *New Yorker,* November 12, 1973; *Contemporary Literary Criticism,* Gale, Volume II, 1974, Volume IV, 1975, Volume VIII, 1977; *Ms,* January, 1974; *Nation,* June 29, 1974; *Saturday Review,* October 18, 1975; *National Observer,* November 22, 1975; *New Leader,* January 19, 1976; *Commonweal,* May 7, 1976; *Christian Century,* December 7, 1977; *Antioch Review,* winter, 1978.

* * *

CAMERON, Elizabeth Jane 1910-1976 (Jane Duncan, Janet Sandison)

PERSONAL: Born March 10, 1910, in Dunbartonshire, Scotland; died October 20, 1976; daughter of Duncan and Janet (Sandison) Cameron; widow. *Education:* University of Glasgow, M.A., 1930. *Religion:* Presbyterian. *Agent:* A. M. Heath & Co. Ltd., 40-42 William IV St., London WCZN 4DD, England; and Brandt & Brandt, 101 Park Ave., New York, N.Y. 10017.

CAREER: Worked as private secretary in Great Britain, 1931-39. *Military service:* Royal Air Force, Women's Auxiliary, 1939-45; became flight officer. *Member:* P.E.N. International.

WRITINGS—All published by Grosset: *The Big Book of Real Trains,* 1963; *The Big Book of Real Fire Engines,* 1964; *The Big Book of Real Trucks,* 1970.

Under pseudonym Jane Duncan; "My Friend" series, all originally published by St. Martin's, except as indicated: *My Friends the Miss Boyds,* 1959; *My Friend Muriel,* 1959; ... *Monica,* 1960; ... *Annie,* 1961; ... *Sandy,* Macmillan (London), 1961, St. Martin's, 1962; ... *Flora,* Macmillan (London), 1962, St. Martin's 1963; ... *Martha's Aunt,* 1962; ... *Madame Zora,* 1963; ... *Rose,* 1964; ... *Cousin Emmie,* 1965; *My Friends the Mrs. Millers,* 1965; ... *My Father,* Macmillan (London), 1966, St. Martin's, 1967; *My Friends from Cairnton,* 1966; *My Friends the Macleans,* 1967; *My Friends the Hungry Generation,* 1968; ... *the Swallow,* 1970; ... *Sashie,* 1972; *My Friends the Misses Kindness,* 1974; *My Friends George and Tom,* 1976.

"Camerons" series, all originally published by Macmillan, except as indicated: *Camerons on the Hills,* 1963; ... *on the Train,* 1963; ... *at the Castle,* 1965; ... *Calling,* 1965, St. Martin's, 1966; ... *Ahoy!,* St. Martin's, 1968.

"Janet Reachfar" series: *Brave Janet Reachfar,* Seabury, 1975; *Herself and Janet Reachfar,* Macmillan (London), 1975; *Janet Reachfar and the Kelpie,* Seabury, 1976; *Janet Reachfar and Chickabird,* Seabury, 1978.

Letter from Reachfar (a memoir), Macmillan (London), 1975, St. Martin's 1976.

Under pseudonym Janet Sandison; all originally published by St. Martin's, except as indicated: "An Apology for the Life of Jean Robertson," Volume I: *Jean in the Morning,* 1964, Volume II: *Jean at Noon; or, Summer's Treasure,* Macmillan (London), 1971, St. Martin's, 1972, Volume III: *Jean in the Twilight; or, the Mists of Autumn,* 1973, Volume IV: *Jean towards Another Day; or, Can Spring Be Far Away?,* 1975.

WORK IN PROGRESS: More novels of "My Friend" series.

SIDELIGHTS: Elizabeth Jane Cameron once told *CA* that the "only item of interest" about her as a writer was that "in late 1958 and early 1959 I submitted the manuscripts of [my] first seven novels . . . to Macmillan of London and they were accepted *en bloc.* I am led to believe that this was new in British publishing."

Reviews of Cameron's books emphasize many of the same strengths. One critic writes about the simplicity of her stories: "If you think [the events in *My Friends George and Tom*] are too insignificant to sustain a novel, then you haven't been reading the 'My Friends' novels. . . . Jane Duncan has a gift for converting activity into action. . . . [The plots' details] carry as much excitement as the solution of a difficult crime in a mystery novel. . . . This [book] is full of meaningful bustle."

Elizabeth O'Rourke comments: "Duncan's forte is 'her ability to portray the complexity and richness of human relationships.' There is much interplay among the characters of the book, ... [much] insight into human nature." Other critics agree, often using such adjectives as "refreshing," "wholesome," and "delightful" to describe her work, even though they may consider such wholesome simplicity unrealistic.

BIOGRAPHICAL/CRITICAL SOURCES: Best Sellers, November 15, 1967, September 15, 1968; *Books and Bookmen,* August, 1968; *Letter from Reachfar,* Macmillan (London), 1975, St. Martin's, 1976; *Book World,* September 8, 1968; *Publishers Weekly,* March 8, 1976; *New York Times Book Review,* October 31, 1976.†

* * *

CANDLIN, Enid Saunders 1909-

PERSONAL: Born October 7, 1909, in Shanghai, China; daughter of Norman Thorpe (a businessman) and Vesta (Baldwin) Saunders; married A. H. Stanton Candlin (a writer), October 10, 1939 (died August, 1977); children: Rosalind (Mrs. W. R. Benedict), Celia. *Education:* Attended Smith College, 1928-29, 1930-31. *Home:* Apt. 5H, 49 East 73rd St., New York, N.Y. 10021.

CAREER: Worked in offices in Nanking and Shanghai, China, 1932-38, holding position as secretary to John Lossing Buck (first husband of Pearl S. Buck), 1936-38. *Member:* Royal Society for Asian Affairs, Asia Society, English-Speaking Union. *Awards, honors:* Ella Lyman Cabot Trust grant, 1975.

WRITINGS: A Breach in the Wall: A Memoir of the Old China, Macmillan, 1971; *A Traveler's Tale,* Macmillan, 1974. Also author of a nonfiction book on Oriental philosophies, *A Sage in the Wind,* a history of Chinese painting, *A Comprehensive Mirror of Chinese Painting,* a memoir on Germany, *Polyhedron,* and two novels, *Balticum* and *Lovely Is My Quiet Girl.* Contributor of articles and reviews to *Journal of the Royal Central Asian Society, Asian Affairs, Christian Science Monitor,* and other publications.

SIDELIGHTS: Enid Saunders Candlin told *CA:* "I love a pure, incisive, beautifully phrased style in writing, a clear, concise, cogent use of words, the cadence and balance of a well-conceived sentence, something able to evoke a fleeting moment. Conversely I detest sloppy ugly writing, hence I feel it extremely important that those sensitive to these matters should write as elegantly, as lyrically, as they can. We have a marvellous language within our reach, and we must honor it to the best of our capacity.

"Certainly I have been greatly influenced by the masters of prose and poetry, especially by the writers of the eighteenth and nineteenth centuries both French and English, and to some extent German, as well as by the Chinese. I read extensively in the fields of history, biography, and the arts, and I love belles lettres. Of recent writers I like to read some of the novels of Rose Macaulay, all of Maurice Collis, or almost all, the Sitwells, the Pope-Hennessys. I find little of pleasure or value in most contemporary writers, who write of ugly and wicked scenes in an ugly and brutal way.

"One writes because one has something to say, to crystallize one's views and impressions, and in the hope of giving others pleasure and inspiration, instruction, interest. One hopes to open closed doors, to lift thought. I love a book that enlarges my vision and I would be glad if anything I write does this for others. Also, I write because I love doing it—it gives me pleasure in itself. I often feel I am only an amenuensis and am surprised at what appears."

* * *

CANO-BALLESTA, Juan 1932-

PERSONAL: Born March 12, 1932, in Murcia, Spain; son of Jose and Marcelina (Ballesta) Cano; married Mercedes Alonso, September 12, 1969. *Education:* University of Munich, Ph.D., 1961. *Office:* Department of Hispanic Literatures, University of Pittsburgh, 1309 Cathedral of Learning, Pittsburgh, Pa. 15260.

CAREER: University of Goettingen, Goettingen, Germany, lecturer, 1962-65; Yale University, assistant professor, 1966-68, research associate, 1968-70, associate professor of Spanish, 1970-71; Boston University, Boston, Mass., associate professor of Spanish, 1971-76; University of Pittsburgh, Pittsburgh, Pa., professor of Spanish, 1976—. *Member:* Asociacion Internacional de Hispanistas, Modern Language Association of America, American Association of Teachers of Spanish and Portuguese, Northeast Modern Language Association. *Awards, honors:* Morse research fellowship from Yale University, 1968-70; senior research fellowship from American Council of Learned Societies, 1975-76.

WRITINGS: Die Dichtung des Miguel Hernandez: Eine stilistische Untersuchung (title means "The Poetry of Miguel Hernandez: A Stylistic Study"), Fernando Walter, 1962; *La poesia de Miguel Hernandez* (title means "The Poetry of Miguel Hernandez"), Editorial Gredos, 1962, revised edition, 1971; *La poesia espanola entre pureza y revolucion, 1930-1936* (title means "Spanish Lyric between Pure Poetry and Revolution"), Editorial Gredos, 1972; (editor) *Miguel Hernandez: El hombre y su poesia* (title means "Miguel Hernandez: The Man and His Poetry"), Ediciones Catedra, 1974, 4th edition, 1979; (editor) *Maestros del cuento espanol moderno* (title means "Masters of the Modern Spanish Short Story"), Scribner, 1974; (editor with Robert Marrast) *Poesia y prosa de guerra y otros textos olvidados de Miguel Hernandez* (title means "War Poetry and Prose and Other Forgotten Texts by Miguel Hernandez"), Peralta Ediciones, 1977; (editor) *En torno a Miguel Hernandez* (title means "Studies on Miguel Hernandez"), Editorial Castalia, 1978; *Literatura y tecnologica: Las letras ante el proceso industrializador* (title means "Literature and Technology: Letters Confronting the Industrial Revolution"), Editorial Gredos, 1980.

Contributor to *Romanische Forschungen, Tribuna, Insula, La Torre, Papeles de Son Armadans, Hispania, Litoral, Puerto,* and *Revista Hispanica Moderna.*

WORK IN PROGRESS: An edition of Mariano Jose de Larra's social, political, and critical writings; articles on Lope de Vega's *graciosos* and the comic popular culture of medieval tradition.

BIOGRAPHICAL/CRITICAL SOURCES: Alfredo Gomez Gil, *Cerebros espanoles en USA,* Plaza y Janes, 1971.

* * *

CARDEN, Karen W(ilson) 1946-

PERSONAL: Born February 7, 1946, in Knoxville, Tenn.; daughter of Ralph S. and Katherine (Pardue) Wilson. *Education:* Attended University of Tennessee. *Home address:* Route 11, Loyston Rd., Knoxville, Tenn. 37918.

CAREER: Free-lance writer and photographer. Instructor, University of Tennessee. *Member:* Authors Guild, Authors League of America, American Quarter Horse Association.

WRITINGS: (With Robert W. Pelton) *Snake Handlers: God-Fearers? or Fanatics?,* Thomas Nelson, 1974; (with Pelton) *The Persecuted Prophets,* A. S. Barnes, 1976; *Western Rider's Handbook,* A. S. Barnes, 1976; (with Pelton) *In My Name Shall They Cast Out Devils,* A. S. Barnes, 1976; (with David Litz) *A Photographic Guide to Tennis Fundamentals,* Arco, 1978. Contributor of articles and poems to magazines, including *Grit, Babytalk, Home Life, Western Horseman, American Square Dance, Today's Art, Mother Earth News,* and numerous other periodicals.

WORK IN PROGRESS: Rodeo Today, a photo documentary; *The Modern Work Horse Handbook,* a practical guide to using stock; *Going Back,* a photo documentary of one family's journey from dependency on space-age gadgetry to greater self-sufficiency.

SIDELIGHTS: Karen Carden wrote *CA:* "As for why I am a writer, I simply can't help it. In my role of helping others become writers, I try to persuade them that it is not a mysterious, romance-cloaked pursuit. I hold fast to the theory that special talent is more a luxury than a necessity. The key to successful writing always has been and always will be hard work. I encourage my students to spend as much time on researching the markets as they do on birthing their literary creations.

"I have met artists who lack direction. I have met people to whom becoming a writer will be a burdensome life-long self-deception. And I have met semi-talented word crafters who learn quickly to meet writing head-on as a difficult and demanding job, and they are the ones who sell. Free-lancers today must view writing as a business, nonetheless.

"My advice to beginning writers is descend from your lofty aspirations and sit humbly through hours of perspiration. Don't wait on inspiration, employ dedication. Cast off the robe of artistic temperament and slip into the jeans and sweatshirt of the common phrase laborer."

AVOCATIONAL INTERESTS: Horses, mountain dancing and music, regional folk and crafts, antiques.

* * *

CARDINAL, Roger (Thomas) 1940- (Peter Bridgecross)

PERSONAL: Born February 27, 1940, in Bromley, England; son of Thomas (an engineer) and Ada (Melbourne) Cardinal; married Agnes Meyer, August, 1965; children: Daniel, Felix. *Education:* Attended St. Dunstan's College, 1951-58; Cambridge University, B.A., 1962, Ph.D., 1965. *Politics:* "Anarchist-surrealist." *Religion:* None. *Home:* Heath Field, Chartham Hatch CT4 7NS, Kent, England. *Office:* Department of French, Keynes College, University of Kent, Canterbury, England.

CAREER: University of Manitoba, Winnipeg, assistant professor of French, 1965-67; University of Warwick, Coventry, Warwick, England, lecturer in French, 1967-68; University of Kent, Keynes College, Canterbury, Kent, England, lecturer, 1968-76, senior lecturer in French, 1976—. Visiting associate professor, University of Toronto, 1976-77.

WRITINGS: (With Robert S. Short) *Surrealism Permanent Revelation,* Dutton, 1970; *Outsider Art,* Praeger, 1972; *German Romantics,* Studio Vista, 1975; (editor) *Sensibility and Creation: Studies in Twentieth-Century French Poetry,* Barnes & Noble, 1977; *Primitive Painters,* St. Martin's, 1978; *Outsiders,* Arts Council of Great Britain, 1979. Contributor to *Times Literary Supplement, Queen's Quarterly, Moment, Melmoth,* and *L'Art Brut.* Contributor under pseudonym Peter Bridgecross to *Wheels* and *Red River Poems.*

WORK IN PROGRESS: Figures of Reality: A Perspective on the Poetic Imagination, for Croom Helm; *Andre Breton's Nadja: A Critical Study,* for Grant & Cutler; research into imaginative process in fields of French poetry, surrealism, symbolism, Art Brut, and psychopathological creation.

SIDELIGHTS: Roger Cardinal told *CA:* "My intellectual awareness of so many things has been stimulated by Surrealism, and it is by the light of the work of Andre Breton and of the surrealist poets and painters that I have travelled into the territories of modern European poetry, German Romanticism, French Symbolism, psychotic and mediumistic drawing and writing, native and folk art, the cinema. My interests extend into such areas as response to landscape and the sense of place, the analysis of metaphoric forms of expression, tribal cultures and their art, and the role of imagination in scientific research.

"My work obliges me to seek to eradicate the orthodox division between 'creative' and 'critical' writing. My aim is to illuminate the processes of the creative imagination in its handling of the inner and outer worlds, and to contribute to a widening of critical perspectives on the arts in highlighting the sensibility of the individual creator and his personal imagery, whether verbal or visual. My hope as a writer is to be able to speak of poetry, painting or any other experience in my life without the change in subject entailing any shift in style or seriousness.

"Since 1966 I have kept a journal in many volumes, containing poems, drawings, reflections, reading notes and cuttings. This provides me with a pool of stimuli from which I constantly benefit. In my teaching I have been lucky enough to establish courses in areas corresponding to my enthusiasms: rather than being typecast as exclusively a teacher of French literature, I currently work in comparative literary studies, and deal in modern poetry, the literature of the Fantastic, the visual arts, psychopathology and even political theory.

"I hope to contribute towards a view of creativity as an impulse springing from identifiable and essential needs, both private and collective, and hence capable of elucidation in a language which will transcend traditional disciplines and herald an integral definition of the ways followed by the imaginative faculty."

* * *

CARNEY, T(homas) F(rancis) 1931-

PERSONAL: Born February 7, 1931, in Brooklyn, N.Y.; son of Felix Francis (a civil servant) and Cecelia (Burke) Carney; married Barbara Parr (a teacher), August 17, 1954; children: Michael, Judith. *Education:* University of London, B.A. (honors), 1952, Ph.D., 1957; University of South Africa, D.Litt. et Phil., 1959. *Residence:* Windsor, Ontario, Canada. *Office:* Department of Communication Studies, University of Windsor, Windsor, Ontario, Canada N9B 3P4.

CAREER: Victoria University, Wellington, New Zealand, lecturer in classics, 1953-57; University College of Rhodesia and Nyasaland, Salisbury, South Rhodesia, professor of classics and head of department, 1957-62; University of Sydney, Sydney, Australia, associate professor of history, 1962-66; University of Manitoba, Winnipeg, associate professor, 1966-67, professor of history, 1967-77, professor of resource management in Natural Resource Institute, 1974-77, head of department of history, 1968-69; University of Windsor, Windsor, Ontario, professor of communication studies, 1977—. Visiting research scholar at University of Vienna, 1957-58, University of Pisa, 1959-60, University of Athens and University of Thessaloniki, 1961-62, Birkbeck College, University of London, 1969-70, and Princeton University, 1972-73. *Member:* Belongs to various professional organizations. *Awards, honors:* Senior Fulbright scholar, Center for International Studies, Massachusetts Institute of Technology, 1965-66; Killam Award, 1969; Canada Council fellowship, 1972-73; RK Institute Award, 1974, and Zubek Award, 1975, both from University of Manitoba; Ontario Confederation of University Faculty Associations Award for excellence in teaching, 1979.

WRITINGS: A Biography of Caius Marius (monograph), Classical Association of Rhodesia and Nyasaland, 1961; (translator) A. P. Vacalopoulos, *History of Thessaloniki,* Institute of Balkan Studies, 1963; (editor) Terence, *Hecyra,* Classical Association of Rhodesia and Nyasaland, 1964; (translator) John the Lydian, *On the Magistracies of the Roman Constitution,* Wentworth Press, 1965; (editor and translator) John the Lydian, *De Magistratibus,* Coronado Press, 1971; *Bureaucracy in Traditional Society,* Coronado Press, 1971; *Content Analysis: A Technique for Systematic Inference from Communications,* University of Manitoba Press, 1972; *The Economies of Antiquity,* Coronado Press, 1973; *Time-Budgeting a Thesis: The Critical Path Method,* Faculty of Graduate Studies, University of Manitoba, 1973; *Constructing Instructional Simulations Games,* Natural Resource Institute, University of Manitoba, 1974, revised edition, 1975; *The Shape of the Past: Models and Antiquity,* Coronado Press, 1975; *Communications and Society: A Social History of Communications,* Natural Resource Institute, University of Manitoba, 1975; *Historical Methods: A Reader,* University of Manitoba Bookstore, 1976; *No Limits to Growth: Mind-Expanding Techniques,* Harbeck & Associates (Winnipeg), 1976; *The Revolution in Interpersonal Communication Skills,* Natural Resource Institute, University of Manitoba, 1978. Contributor of over 100 articles and reviews, mostly to academic journals in North America and Europe.

WORK IN PROGRESS: Organizational Communications as if People Matter, for Sage Publications, Inc.

SIDELIGHTS: T. F. Carney told *CA:* "Probably my most creative work takes the form of workshops: short (one- or two-day) intensive experimental learning sessions. I design the 'instruments' as well as the game plan for these—for instance, for a workshop on stress, there's a 'stress board' (a self-inventory, keyed to a display diagram, showing overall pattern of stress, high stress areas and levels of stress) keyed to a 'sensurround' approach (visuals and music, as well as lecture/commentary). When they're well designed, workshops like this have a most impressive impact on participants."

* * *

CARPENTER, Don(ald Richard) 1931-

PERSONAL: Born March 16, 1931, in Berkeley, Calif.; son of Eugene P. and Genevieve (Cody) Carpenter; married Martha Ryherd, June 16, 1956; children: Marie Ryherd, Julie Ryherd. *Education:* Portland State College (now University), B.S., 1959; San Francisco State College (now University), M.A., 1960. *Politics:* None. *Religion:* None. *Residence:* Mill Valley, Calif. *Agent:* Brann-Hartnett Agency, 14 Sutton Pl. S., New York, N.Y. 10022.

CAREER: Free-lance writer. *Military service:* U.S. Air Force, 1952-56. *Member:* Writers Guild of America, West.

WRITINGS—Fiction: *Hard Rain Falling,* Harcourt, 1965; *Blade of Light,* Harcourt, 1966; *The Murder of the Frogs and Other Stories,* Harcourt, 1968; *Getting Off,* Dutton, 1971; *The True Life Story of Jody McKeegan,* Dutton, 1974; *A Couple of Comedians,* Simon & Schuster, 1979. Also author of filmscript, "Payday," 1973.

WORK IN PROGRESS: Peaches and Whiskey, a novel.

SIDELIGHTS: A Couple of Comedians was inspired by Don Carpenter's experiences in Hollywood as a writer for television and movies. "Hollywood to me," he writes, "is a civilization easily as complex, fascinating and mysterious as ancient Egypt." The novel details the lives and times of a comedy team, a duo reminiscent of Dean Martin and Jerry Lewis. Robert Kiely, writing in the *New York Times Book Review,* objects that Carpenter blunts his satire of Hollywood by sentimentalizing his central characters. *New York Times* critic John Leonard also finds some weaknesses in the book. In particular, he contends that *Comedians* displays too many of the cliches of Hollywood novels, including "the parties, the pills, the starlets and the power brokers." Yet Leonard goes on to say that the real subject of the book is not Hollywood but "the way we try to complete ourselves, to fill in the gaps with other people whose behavior and commitment will authenticate or betray the self we think we are. A comedy team is a marvelous paradigm to explain the anxious set." "*A Couple of Comedians,*" Leonard continues, "for all its breeziness and scoring and flimflam, . . . seizes the heart precisely because it makes us see ourselves as fragmentary and dependent."

BIOGRAPHICAL/CRITICAL SOURCES: New Statesman, January 15, 1966; *New York Times Book Review,* January 30, 1966, May 16, 1971, February 9, 1975, January 6, 1980; *Best Sellers,* July 15, 1971; *New York Times,* December 24, 1979; *Washington Post Book World,* February 10, 1980.

* * *

CARR, Albert H. Z(olotkoff) 1902-1971 (A.H.Z. Carr; A. B. Carbury, a pseudonym)

PERSONAL: Born January 15, 1902, in Chicago, Ill.; died October 28, 1971, of a heart attack, in New York, N.Y.; son of Leon Zolotkoff and Fannie (Ogus) Carr; married Anne Kingsbury, December 13, 1943. *Education:* University of Chicago, B.S., 1921; graduate study, Columbia University, 1926-27 and London School of Economics, 1936. *Home:* Castle Rd., Truro, Mass. *Office:* 290 Ninth Ave., New York, N.Y.

CAREER: Editor, Business Training Corp., 1927-30; Tradeways, Inc. (business consultants), New York City, assistant to president, 1927-34; free-lance writer, 1931-41; War Production Board, Washington, D.C., assistant to chairman, 1942-44; White House Staff, Washington, D.C., economic adviser, 1944-46; consultant to President Truman, 1948-52; Caravel, Inc. (film producers), New York City, vice-president, 1953-56; Cape Lands, Inc., vice-president, director, beginning 1957; special consultant to American Paper Institute. Member of government missions to England, 1943, to China, 1944, 1945, and of Inter-Allied Reparations mission to Germany, 1947. *Member:* Authors Guild. *Awards, honors:* Order of Victory, Republic of China, 1945; *Ellery Queen's Mystery Magazine* award, first prize, 1955, for "The Black Kitten," a short story.

WRITINGS: Juggernaut: The Path of Dictatorship, Viking, 1939, reprinted, Books for Libraries, 1969; *America's Last Chance,* Crowell, 1940; *Men of Power,* Viking, 1941, revised edition, 1956; *Napoleon Speaks,* Viking, 1942; *Truman, Stalin and Peace,* Doubleday, 1950; *How to Attract Good Luck and Make the Most of It in Your Daily Life,* Simon & Schuster, 1952, revised edition, Cornerstone, 1965; *The Coming of War,* Doubleday, 1960; *John D. Rockerfeller's Secret Weapon,* McGraw, 1962; *The World and William Walker,* Harper, 1963; *A Matter of Life and Death: How Wars Get Started or Are Prevented,* Viking, 1966 (published in England as *A Matter of Life and Death: How the Conflicts of Our Century Arose,* Gollancz, 1967); (under pseudonym A. B. Carbury) *The Girl with the Glorious Genes,* Bantam, 1968; *Business as a Game,* New American Library, 1968; *Finding Maubee,* Putnam, 1971. Contributor of short stories and articles to *Saturday Evening Post, Cosmopolitan, Harper's Bazaar, This Week, Life, Harper's,* and other magazines. Also author of several film and television plays.

WORK IN PROGRESS: A novel.†

* * *

CARRICK, Carol 1935-

PERSONAL: Born May 20, 1935, in Edgartown, Mass.; daughter of Chauncey L. (a salesman) and Elsa (Schweizer) Hatfield; married Donald Carrick (an artist), March 26, 1965; children: Christopher, Paul. *Education:* Hofstra University, B.A., 1957. *Home:* High St., Edgartown, Mass. 01539.

CAREER: Writer for children.

WRITINGS—Books for children; all illustrated by husband, Donald Carrick: *The Old Barn,* Bobbs-Merrill, 1966; *The Brook,* Macmillan, 1967; *Swamp Spring,* Macmillan, 1969; *The Pond,* Macmillan, 1970; *The Dirt Road,* Macmillan, 1970; *The Clearing in the Forest,* Dial, 1970.

The Dragon of Santa Lalia, Bobbs-Merrill, 1971; *The Sleep Out,* Seabury, 1973; *Beach Bird,* Dial, 1973; *Lost in the Storm,* Seabury, 1974; *Old Mother Witch,* Seabury, 1975; *The Blue Lobster,* Dial, 1975; *The Accident,* Seabury, 1976; *The Sand Tiger,* Seabury, 1977; *The Highest Balloon on the Common,* Greenwillow, 1977; *The Foundling,* Seabury, 1977; *The Octopus,* Seabury, 1978; *The Washout,* Seabury, 1978; *Paul's Christmas Birthday,* Greenwillow, 1978; *A Rabbit for Easter,* Greenwillow, 1979; *Some Friend!,* Houghton, 1979; *The Crocodiles Still Wait,* Houghton, 1980.

SIDELIGHTS: There have been Swedish, Danish, and German editions of *The Sleep Out, Lost in the Storm,* and *The Washout.*

* * *

CARRIGAN, Andrew G(ardner) 1935-

PERSONAL: Born March 7, 1935, in Battle Creek, Mich.; son of Robert Gardener (a carpenter) and Katherine (Dinkel) Carrigan; married Susan J. Clegg (an art teacher), June, 1972; children: Robert Jason. *Education:* Attended Western Michigan University, 1953, and Olivet College, 1954-55; University of Michigan, B.A., 1961, M.A., 1966. *Home:* 212 West Henry St., Saline, Mich. 48176. *Office:* Ann Arbor Huron High School, Ann Arbor, Mich. 48104.

CAREER: Ann Arbor (Mich.) Public Schools, teacher of English, 1961—. Teacher of creative writing at University of Michigan, 1973-77. *Military service:* U.S. Naval Reserve, 1956-58. *Awards, honors:* Periodical Lunch Poetry Award from *Periodical Lunch,* 1973.

WRITINGS: (With Greg Kohl and Daniel Rosochaki) *Book 3* (poems), Sumac Press, 1972; (with Warren Hecht) *Babyburgers,* Street Fiction Press, 1975; *The Threshold of Heaven,* Crowfoot Press, 1978; *You Poems,* Crowfoot Press, 1979; *Poems Selected and New,* Crowfoot Press, 1980. Also author with Ruth Clay and Stephen Dunning of a textbook, *Poetry: Voices, Language, Forms.*

SIDELIGHTS: Andrew G. Carrigan told *CA:* "I get up at 4:00 a.m. every morning to write before leaving for work. I work on individual poems until they 'feel' complete. Usually this means about 10 drafts, informal readings to friends and colleagues, and then a draft or two for fine tuning. There are poems that have taken extended periods (more than a year), but usually the process takes about a week. Working longer on poems seems to rob them of life and rivet them to the page.

"The works of many poets have influenced my work. Among the most important are William Stafford, Robert Hayden, Tom Raworth, Anselm Hollo, Ted Berrigan, Donald Hall, and Frank O'Hara. With the exception of O'Hara, all of these poets have been generous with their comments. Still, the works of these writers have been most influential.

"It seems to me that the contemporary scene does not broaden the audience for poetry as it should. We seem to add to the audience of poetry by adding poets. The availability of free money through the National Endowment for the Arts encourages the publishing of too much work that would be better left on the shelf. I take exception to the idea that publishers and writers need to be placed on this kind of 'relief.' Poets need to write more poems to people and fewer to fellow poets."

BIOGRAPHICAL/CRITICAL SOURCES: Booklist, February 15, 1980.

* * *

CARROLL, Ruth (Robinson) 1899-

PERSONAL: Born September 24, 1899, in Lancaster, N.Y.; daughter of Frank Howard and Sallie (Underhill) Robinson; married Latrobe Carroll, January 24, 1928. *Education:* Vassar College, A.B., 1922; attended Art Students League, 1922-24 and Cecelia Beaux's School of Portrait Painting, 1925 (both New York). *Home and office:* 2 Fifth Ave., Apt. 16-0, New York, N.Y. 10011.

CAREER: Author; artist and illustrator of books. *Member:* Delta Kappa Gamma. *Awards, honors:* Juvenile award of American Association of University Women (North Carolina division), 1953, for *Peanut,* and 1955, for *Digby: The Only Dog.*

WRITINGS: (Self-illustrated) *What Whiskers Did,* Macmillan, 1932, reprinted, Walck, 1965; *Chimp and Chump,* Reynal, 1933; *Bounce and the Bunnies,* Reynal, 1934, revised edition, Walck, 1959; *Chessie,* Messner, 1936; *Chessie and Her Kittens,* Messner, 1937; *Where's the Bunny?* Walck, 1950; *Old Mrs. Billups and the Black Cats,* Walck, 1961; *Where's the Kitty?* Walck, 1962; *From the Appalachians* (portfolio of paintings and drawings) introduction by husband, Latrobe Carroll, Walck, 1964; *The Chimp and the Clown,* Walck, 1968; *Rolling Down Hill,* Walck, 1973; *The Witch Kitten,* Walck, 1973; *The Dolphin and the Mermaid,* Walck, 1974.

With L. Carroll: *Luck of the Roll and Go,* Macmillan, 1935; *Flight of the Silver Bird,* Messner, 1939; *Scuffles,* Walck, 1943; *School in the Sky,* Macmillan, 1945; *The Flying House,* Macmillan, 1946; *Pet Tale,* Walck, 1949; *Peanut,* Walck, 1951; *Salt and Pepper,* Walck, 1952; *Beanie,* Walck, 1953; *Tough Enough,* Walck, 1954; *Digby: The Only Dog,* Walck, 1955; *Tough Enough's Trip,* Walck, 1956; *Tough Enough's Pony,* Walck, 1957; *Tough Enough and Sass,* Walck, 1958; *Tough Enough's Indians,* Walck, 1960; *Runaway Pony: Runaway Dog,* Walck, 1963; *Danny and the Poi Pup,* Walck, 1965; *The Picnic Bear,* Walck, 1966; *The Christmas Kitten,* Walck, 1970; *The Managing Hen and the Floppy Hound,* Walck, 1972; *Hullaballoo: The Elephant Dog,* Walck, 1975.

AVOCATIONAL INTERESTS: Photography, travel, the theatre, natural history, botany, and hiking.

* * *

CARSE, Robert 1902-1971

PERSONAL: Born July 9, 1902, in New York, N.Y.; died January 14, 1971, in East Hampton, Long Island, N.Y.; son of Bradley David and Birdelle (Switzer) Carse; married Janet Wood, 1925; children: Mrs. Sanford H. Wachtel. *Education:* Attended Horace Mann School and Hill School. *Agent:* Malcolm Reiss, Paul R. Reynolds, Inc., 12 East 41st St., New York, N.Y. 10017.

CAREER: Formerly professional seaman in U.S. Merchant Marine for seven years; became chief mate; received combat bar with star, citation for convoy duty to Russia, and other decorations for wartime service; also held a variety of other jobs, including a foundry, shipyard, and railroad worker as well as a writer on the *New York Times* news staff. Freelance writer. *Member:* P.E.N., Marine Historical Association (Mystic, Conn.).

WRITINGS—Fiction: *Horizon,* Dodd, 1927; *Siren Song,* Farrar & Rinehart, 1930; *Pacific,* Farrar & Rinehart, 1932; *Heart's Desire,* Arthur Barker, 1934; *Deep Six,* Morrow, 1946; (contributor) *Teen-Age Sea Stories,* Lantern, 1948; *From the Sea and the Jungle,* Scribner, 1951; *The Beckoning Waters,* Scribner, 1953; *Great Circle,* Scribner, 1956; *The Wicked Blade,* Popular Library, 1959; *Drums of Empire,* Popular Library, 1959; *The Wide Sea* (short stories), Avon, 1962.

Nonfiction: *The Unconquered,* McBride, 1942; *There Go the Ships,* Morrow, 1942; *Lifeline,* Morrow, 1943; (contributor) *Amateurs at War,* Houghton, 1943; *History of the Second World War,* Pocket Books, 1945; *The Age of Piracy,* Rinehart, 1957; *Blockade,* Rinehart, 1958; *Rum Row,* Rinehart, 1959; *Department of the South,* South Carolina Publishing Society, 1961; *The Moonrakers,* Harper, 1961; (contributor) *Counterattack,* Bantam, 1962; *The Seafarers: A History of Maritime America, 1620-1820,* Harper, 1964; (contributor) *Battle: True Stories of Combat in World War II* (anthology), Curtis Books, 1965; *The Twilight of Sailing Ships,* Grosset, 1965; *The Castaways: A Narrative History of Some Survivors from the Dangers of the Sea,* Rand McNally, 1966; *A Cold Corner of Hell: The Story of the Murmansk Convoys, 1941-1945,* Doubleday, 1969; *Dunkirk, 1940: A History,* Prentice-Hall, 1970.

Juvenile fiction; all novels: *Great Venture,* Scribner, 1952; *The Winner,* Scribner, 1955; *Winter of the Whale,* Putnam, 1961; *Friends of the Wolf,* Putnam, 1961; *Glory Haul,* Putnam, 1962; *Turnabout,* Putnam, 1962; *Hudson River Hayride,* New York Graphic Society, 1962; *Go Away Home,* W. W. Norton, 1964; *Fire in the Night,* W. W. Norton, 1965; *Ocean Challenge,* W. W. Norton, 1967.

Juvenile nonfiction: *The Young Colonials,* W. W. Norton, 1963; *Great American Habors,* W. W. Norton, 1963; *Your Place in the Merchant Marine,* Macmillan, 1964; *The Long Haul: The United States Merchant Service in World War II,* W. W. Norton, 1965; *The Young Mariners: A History of Maritime Salem,* W. W. Norton, 1966; *The High Country: A History of the Explorations of Northwest America,* W. W. Norton, 1966; *Ports of Call,* Scribner, 1967; *Early American Boats,* World Publishing, 1968; *The Great Lakes Story,* W. W. Norton, 1968; *Keepers of the Lights: A History of American Lighthouses,* Scribner, 1969; *The River Men,* Scribner, 1969; *A Book of Smugglers,* Scribner, 1970; *Towline: The Story of American Tugboats,* W. W. Norton, 1970.

Contributor of short stories, serials, and articles to numerous popular magazines, including *Saturday Evening Post, Argosy, Collier's, American, Redbook,* and *Blue Book.*

SIDELIGHTS: As a basis for his book, *A Cold Corner of Hell,* Robert Carse drew upon his experiences as a merchant seaman who, in the words of a reviewer for *Best Sellers,* "underwent the terror of the Arctic blasts, the frigid waters, the lurking German U-boats, and the omni-present Luftwaffe, to carry supplies to Russia by way of Murmansk and Archangel." He continues: "Carse has not painted a pretty picture, but rather has gathered eye-witness accounts into one small history. . . . This story is not a literary work, but it is a vivid picture of what was."

Richard L. Tobin of *Saturday Review*, another man personally familiar with the dangerous Murmansk run, also praises Carse's "no frills" approach to writing: "Robert Carse does not write in the limpid style of Bruce Catton or the lovely rhythms of Barbara Tuchman for he is a seafaring historian with a love for stark sentence structure and simple, factual phrasing. This new book of his is a very masculine work, written in lean male terms."

AVOCATIONAL INTERESTS: Small-craft sailing, tennis.

BIOGRAPHICAL/CRITICAL SOURCES: Best Sellers, January 1, 1968, June 1, 1969, August 1, 1969, December 15, 1969, March 15, 1970; *New York Times Book Review*, January 7, 1968, November 3, 1969; *Saturday Review*, August 30, 1969.†

* * *

CARSON, Gerald (Hewes) 1899-

PERSONAL: Born July 6, 1899, in Carrollton, Ill.; son of James Anderson and Minnie (Hewes) Carson; married Lettie Gay, 1923; children: Nancy Payne, Sara Ann (Mrs. David W. Forden). *Education:* University of Illinois, A.B., 1921, M.A., 1922. *Home:* Pennswood, Apt. H 110, Newtown, Pa. 18940. *Agent:* Willis Kingsley Wing, Apt. 90, Crosslands, Kennett Sq., Pa. 19348.

CAREER: Has worked as reporter and editor, but mainly in advertising field in New York, N.Y. 1922-51, last associated with Kenyon & Eckhardt, Inc., as vice-president and member of board of directors, 1947-51; writer, 1951—. Chairman, Francis Parkman Award, 1972 and 1974. *Member:* Society of American Historians (fellow; member of executive board, 1974—), Authors Guild, Authors League, Manuscript Society (director, 1955), Society of Colonial Wars, New York Historical Society, Sigma Delta Chi, University Club (New York), Williams Club. *Awards, honors:* Received John H. Dunning Prize, and listed as one of thirty-five notable books of 1954 by American Library Association, both 1954, for *The Old Country Store;* award of merit, American Association for State and Local History, 1954.

WRITINGS: The Old Country Store, Oxford University Press, 1954; *Cornflake Crusade,* Rinehart, 1957, reprinted, Arno, 1976; *The Roguish World of Doctor Brinkley,* Rinehart, 1960; *One for a Man, Two for a Horse,* Doubleday, 1961; *The Social History of Bourbon,* Dodd, 1963; *The Polite Americans: A Wide-Angle View of Our More or Less Good Manners Over 300 Years,* Morrow, 1966; *Men, Beasts, and Gods: A History of Cruelty and Kindness to Animals,* Scribner, 1972; *The Golden Egg: The Personal Income Tax, Where It Came From, How It Grew,* Houghton, 1977; *A Good Day at Saratoga,* American Bar Association, 1978. Also author of *Country Store in Early New England* and *Rum and Reform in Old New England.*

Contributor: Edward C. Bursk, Donald T. Clark, and Ralph W. Hidy, editors, *The World of Business,* Simon & Schuster, 1962; *The American Heritage Cook Book and Illustrated History of American Eating and Drinking,* American Heritage Publishing, 1964; *Best-in-Books,* Doubleday, 1966; Stanley J. Shapiro and Alton F. Doody, compilers, *Readings in the History of American Marketing: Settlement to Civil War,* Irwin, 1968; Norman F. Cantor and Michael S. Werthman, editors, *The History of Popular Culture Since 1815,* Macmillan, 1968; John A. Garraty, editor, *Historical Viewpoints: Since 1865,* Harper, 1970, 3rd edition, 1979; Raymond Friday Locke, editor, *The Human Side of History: Man's Manners, Morals and Games,* Mankind Publishing Co., 1970; Leonard Dinnerstein and Kenneth T. Jackson, editors, *American Vistas, 1607-1877,* Oxford University Press, 1971, 3rd edition, 1979; Don Dooley, editor, *Better Homes and Gardens Golden Treasury of Cooking,* Meredith Corp., 1973; Robert M. Warner and C. Warren Vander Hill, editors, *A Michigan Reader, 1865 to the Present,* Eerdmans, 1974; Timothy T. Clarke, editor, *The Dog Lover's Reader,* Hart Publishing, 1974; Roger Lane and John J. Turner, editors, *Riot, Rout, and Tumult: Readings in American Social and Political Violence,* Greenwood Press, 1978; William E. Maloney and Jean-Claude Suares, editors, *The Literary Dog,* Berkeley Publishing, 1978.

Contributor of articles and reviews on popular culture, sociology, economics, and intellectual history to magazines and journals. Member of advisory board, *American Heritage,* 1964-76; member of usage panel, *American Heritage Dictionary of English Language,* 1969—.

WORK IN PROGRESS: Dr. Evans: An American in Paris during the Second Empire, for Houghton.

AVOCATIONAL INTERESTS: Reading, and research into the fields of American manners and folkways, economics, and popular culture.

BIOGRAPHICAL/CRITICAL SOURCES: Saturday Review, May 1, 1954; *Time,* September 1, 1961.

* * *

CATER, (Silas) Douglass 1923-

PERSONAL: Born August 24, 1923, in Montgomery, Ala.; son of Silas D. and Nancy (Chesnutt) Cater; married Libby Anderson, 1950; children: Silas Douglass III, Rebecca Sage, Libby Morrow, Benjamin Winston. *Education:* Harvard University, B.A., 1947, M.A., 1948. *Office:* 2010 Massachusetts Ave. N.W., Washington, D.C. 20036; and *The Observer,* 8 St. Andrew's Hill, London, England.

CAREER: The Reporter magazine, Washington, D.C., Washington editor, 1950-63, national affairs editor, 1963-64; special assistant to President Lyndon B. Johnson, 1964-68; writer and consultant, 1968—; vice-chairman, *The Observer,* London, England, 1976—. Temporary appointment as assistant to Secretary of Army (on leave from *The Reporter*), 1951. Ferris Lecturer, Princeton University, 1959; Wesleyan University, visiting fellow, 1961-62, visiting professor and associate director, 1963-64; Regent's professor, University of California, San Francisco, 1971-72. Founding fellow and trustee, Aspen Institute. *Member* Overseas Writers, Sigma Delta Chi, Metropolitan Club and National Press Club (both Washington, D.C.), University Club (New York), Garrick Club and Rac Club (both London). *Awards, honors:* Guggenheim fellowship, 1954, to study the interaction of press and government in Washington; Eisenhower exchange fellow, for extended around-the-world trips, 1957; Special George Polk Memorial Citation, 1961; Newspaper Guild Page One Award, 1961.

WRITINGS: (With Marquis Childs) *Ethics in a Business Society,* Harper, 1953, reprinted, Greenwood Press, 1973; *The Fourth Branch of Government,* Houghton, 1959; *Power in Washington,* Random House, 1964; *Dana: The Irrelevant Man,* McGraw, 1970; (editor with Philip R. Lee) *Politics of Health,* Medcom, 1972; (with Stephen Strickland) *Television*

Violence and the Child, Russell Sage, 1975; (editor with Richard Adler) *Television As a Social Force: New Approaches to TV Criticism,* Praeger, 1975; (editor with Michael J. Nyhan) *The Future of Public Broadcasting,* 1976. Contributor to *New York Times Magazine, Horizon,* and *Annals* of the American Academy of Political and Social Science.

* * *

CATTON, William Bruce 1926-

PERSONAL: Born March 21, 1926, in Cleveland, Ohio; son of Bruce (an author) and Hazel (Cherry) Catton; married Mina Kathryn Sweeney, 1957 (divorced, 1978); married Frances Lyn Casman, 1978; children: (first marriage) David Bruce. *Education:* University of Maryland, A.B., 1951, M.A., 1952; Northwestern University, Ph.D., 1959. *Politics:* Democrat. *Office:* Department of History, Middlebury College, Middlebury, Vt. 05753.

CAREER: University of Maryland, College Park, instructor in history, 1955-58; Princeton University, Princeton, N.J., instructor, 1958-61, assistant professor of history, 1961-64; Middlebury College, Middlebury, Vt., associate professor, 1964-68, professor, 1968-80, Charles A. Dana Professor of History, 1969-80, professor emeritus and historian in residence, 1980—. *Military service:* U.S. Army, 1945-46; became technician third grade.

WRITINGS: (With father, Bruce Catton) *Two Roads to Sumter,* McGraw, 1963; (with Arthur Link) *American Epoch,* 2nd revised edition (Catton was not associated with earlier edition), Knopf, 1963, 5th edition, 1980; (with B. Catton) *The Bold and Magnificent Dream: America's Founding Years, 1492-1815,* Doubleday, 1978.

WORK IN PROGRESS: A history of the United States since 1815, for Doubleday.

SIDELIGHTS: As the son of Civil War historian Bruce Catton, it is not surprising that William Bruce Catton found himself drawn to the same field. Yet he apparently never set out to follow in his father's footsteps, at least not consciously. Prior to his success as a historian, the elder Catton was a newspaperman and government speechwriter and information specialist; his son was already pursuing his Ph.D. studies in history when Catton first began to gain recognition for his Civil War books. As the younger Catton explains: "I went into history simply because I found it interesting. I've often wondered if I would have done the same thing if I'd known what a famous name [my father] was going to become in the same field. It isn't the easiest thing in the world to be a famous man's son."

Nevertheless, a strong bond of mutual love and respect, as well as a common interest in the subject matter, enabled the father-and-son combination to collaborate successfully on two books, *Two Roads to Sumter* and *The Bold and Magnificent Dream.* Though completed just over a year before Bruce Catton's death in 1978, the idea for the latter book was conceived by Doubleday in the late 1950's as a means of replacing an out-of-date U.S. history text it was then publishing. Neither man, however, could find the time to get together and begin what would surely be an extensive project. Contracts were revised and re-revised, but the book never even reached the planning stages. During this same period, though, the two men collaborated on *Two Roads to Sumter,* convincing both father and son that "we could do [the U.S. history] someday, once we found the time."

Yet it was not until 1973 that the Cattons finally managed to find the time. William took a leave of absence and journeyed to his father's home in Michigan, at which time the men began working on an outline. They also decided that theirs would not be a conventional history; rather than writing a college textbook or a historical monograph, they chose to combine narrative and interpretive essays in order to appeal to the general reader.

The working plan called for William to draft the chapters and then for Bruce to edit them; for the most part, this plan was followed throughout the book, except for chapters on the Revolutionary War and the War of 1812 (the senior Catton was more knowledgeable about military history than his son). "Dad was a magnificent editor as well as a good writer," William explains, "and we never had any trouble about my resenting what he might do to my prose. . . . On historical matters, we would sometimes not see eye to eye—usually on matters of emphasis. I was the one who felt the book should contain a lot about America's European background. . . . My father was dubious at first, but when he saw what I had done, he agreed. By the same token, he showed me that certain touches about George Washington's generalship also added something."

Based on the two men's previous research and conversations, William feels that he can complete volume two of the series in the same style as volume one, though he finds the prospect "exciting and a little scary." In any case, it will be the first book he has written on his own. "I like to write," he says, "but teaching has taken up so much of my energy that I don't have the time to do what Dad did, even if I could."

Publishers Weekly calls *The Bold and Magnificent Dream* an "eminently readable account [in which] the Cattons evaluate the most recent historical theories, sometimes agreeing with and sometimes debunking the revisionists. They don't glamorize our past, but face squarely the flaw in the American way—espcially the treatment of Indians and blacks." Eugene McCarthy, writing in the *Chicago Tribune,* comments: "Bruce Catton and his son William have written what can properly be called a 'history' of America from 1492 to 1815, in contrast with other writings about men and events of those 300-plus years—writings that have, for the most part, been little more than anecdotes or scattered reports, isolated from any contest of ideas or of historical movement. . . . The book emerges much as a tapestry; complex but with form."

BIOGRAPHICAL/CRITICAL SOURCES: Publishers Weekly, October 16, 1978, December 4, 1978; *Chicago Tribune,* December 17, 1978.

* * *

CAULEY, Troy Jesse 1902-
(Terry Cauley)

PERSONAL: Born July 23, 1902, in Comanche, Tex.; son of William Carter and Daisy (Ewing) Cauley; married Clara Millicent Harris, 1926; children: Carolyn Irene (Mrs. Joseph E. Barry, Jr.), Peyton Dabney. *Education:* University of Texas, B.A., M.A., 1926; University of Wisconsin, Ph.D., 1931. *Politics:* Democrat. *Religion:* Episcopalian. *Home:* 5005 Timberline Dr., Austin, Tex. 78746. *Office:* Department of Economics, Indiana University, Bloomington, Ind.

CAREER: Taught economics at University of Texas at Austin, University of Wisconsin—Madison, University of Vermont, Burlington, Emory University, Atlanta, Ga., and Georgia School of Technology (now Georgia Institute of Technology), Atlanta, 1929-35; with U.S. government as economist and soil conservationist, 1935-47, in last period as director of Wage Stabilization Division of National Wage

Stabilization Board; Indiana University at Bloomington, associate professor, 1947-64, professor of economics, 1964—. *Military service:* U.S. Army, Military Government, 1943-44, assistant military attache at U.S. Embassy in London, 1944-46; became major. U.S. Army Reserve, 1946—. *Member:* American Economic Association, American Farm Economic Association, Midwest Economic Association, Southwestern Social Science Association, Indiana Academy of the Social Sciences, Phi Beta Kappa, Indiana University Club.

WRITINGS: Agrarianism: A Program for Farmers, University of North Carolina Press, 1935; (contributor) *Democratic Collectivism,* H. W. Wilson, 1935; (contributor) *Who Owns America?,* Houghton, 1936; *Agriculture in an Industrial Economy,* Bookman Associates, 1956; *Public Finance and the General Welfare,* C. E. Merrill, 1960; *Texas Town,* Tippecanoe Press, 1962; *Our Economy,* International Textbook, 1963; *Economics: Principles and Institutions,* Intext Press, 1968; *Winnpwac State University,* FAS Publishers, 1977. Contributor of more than twenty-five articles to *Texas Monthly, Cattleman,* economics journals and regional reviews.

WORK IN PROGRESS: The Theory and Practice of Public Expenditures.

AVOCATIONAL INTERESTS: Gardening, bird-watching, fishing, hunting.

* * *

CAUTE, David 1936-

PERSONAL: Born December 16, 1936. *Education:* Wadham College, Oxford, M.A., and D.Phil.

CAREER: Author and playwright. Fellow, All Souls College, Oxford University, 1959-65. Visiting professor, New York University, 1966-67. *Military service:* British Army, 1955-56. *Member:* International P.E.N. *Awards, honors:* London Authors' Club award, 1960; John Llewelyn Rhys Prize, 1960.

WRITINGS: At Fever Pitch, Deutsch, 1959, Pantheon, 1961; *Comrade Jacob,* Deutsch, 1961, Pantheon, 1962; *Communism and the French Intellectuals, 1914-1960,* Macmillan, 1964; *The Left in Europe since 1789,* McGraw, 1966; *The Decline of the West* (novel), Macmillan, 1966; *The Demonstration* (play; also see below), Deutsch, 1970; *Frantz Fanon,* Viking, 1970; *The Occupation* (novel), Deutsch, 1971, McGraw, 1971; *The Illusion,* Deutsch, 1971, Harper, 1972; *The Fellow Travellers,* Macmillan, 1973; *Cuba, Yes?,* McGraw, 1974; *Collisions: Essays and Reviews,* Quartet, 1974; *The Great Fear: The Anti-Communist Purge under Truman and Eisenhower,* Simon & Schuster, 1978.

Produced plays: "Songs for an Autumn Rifle," first produced at the Edinburgh Festival by the Oxford Theatre Group, 1961; "The Demonstration," first produced in London at Nottingham Playhouse, 1969; "Fallout," first produced on British Broadcasting Corp.-Radio, 1973. Contributor to *New Statesman, Times Literary Supplement, Spectator,* and other magazines.

* * *

CHACE, James (Clarke) 1931-

PERSONAL: Born October 16, 1931, in Fall River, Mass.; son of Hollister Remington and H. Mildred (Clarke) Chace; married Jean Valentine, 1957 (divorced, 1968); married Susan Denvir, 1975; children: (first marriage) Sarah, Rebecca. *Education:* Harvard University, A.B., 1953; University of Paris, graduate study at Institut d'Etudes Politiques, 1954. *Home:* 333 Central Park W., New York, N.Y. 10025. *Office: Foreign Affairs,* 58 East 68th St., New York, N.Y. 10021.

CAREER: Esquire, Inc., New York City, assistant editor, 1957-58; *East Europe,* New York City, managing editor, 1958-64; *Interplay,* New York City, managing editor, 1964-69; *Foreign Affairs,* New York City, managing editor, 1970—. *Military service:* U.S. Army, 1954-56. *Member:* Phi Beta Kappa.

WRITINGS: The Rules of the Game, Doubleday, 1960; (editor) *Conflict in the Middle East,* H. W. Wilson, 1969; *A World Elsewhere: The New American Foreign Policy,* Scribner, 1973; (editor with Earl C. Ravenal) *U.S.-European Relations after the Cold War,* New York University Press, 1976. Contributor to *New Republic, Esquire, Harper's,* and *New York Times Magazine.*

WORK IN PROGRESS: A novel; a book on foreign policy.

SIDELIGHTS: After his graduation from Harvard, where he edited the *Advocate,* a campus literary magazine, James Chace spent two years in France, following up a year of study by working on a novel and the libretto of a comic opera. *Avocational interests:* Sailing.

* * *

CHACHOLIADES, Miltiades 1937-

PERSONAL: Born June 22, 1937, on Cyprus; naturalized U.S. citizen; son of Panayiotis and Chericlea (Miltiadou) Chacholiades; married Mary Modenos, December 30, 1962; children: Lea, Marina. *Education:* Athens School of Economics and Business Science, diploma, 1962; Massachusetts Institute of Technology, Ph.D., 1965. *Home:* 5219 Forest Springs Dr., Dunwoody, Ga. 30338. *Office:* Department of Economics, Georgia State University, Atlanta, Ga. 30303.

CAREER: New York University, New York, N.Y., assistant professor, 1965-68, associate professor of economics, 1968; Georgia State University, Atlanta, associate professor, 1968-71, professor, 1971-73, research professor of economics, 1973—. Visiting associate professor at University of California, Los Angeles, spring, 1970.

WRITINGS: (Contributor) C. P. Kindleberger, *International Economics,* Irwin, 4th edition (Chacholiades was not associated with earlier editions), 1968, 5th edition, 1973; *The Income-Specie-Flow Mechanism,* Bureau of Business and Economic Research, School of Business Administration, Georgia State University, 1970; *The Pure Theory of International Trade,* Aldine-Atherton, 1973; *International Monetary Theory and Policy,* McGraw-Hill, 1978; *International Trade Theory and Policy,* McGraw-Hill, 1978; *Principles of International Economics,* McGraw-Hill, in press. Contributor to economics journals.

* * *

CHADWICK, W(illiam) Owen 1916-

PERSONAL: Born May 20, 1916, in Bromley, Kent, England; son of John (a lawyer) and Edith Mary (Horrocks) Chadwick; married Ruth Hallward, December 28, 1949; children: Charles, Stephen, Helen, Andre. *Education:* St. John's College, Cambridge, B.A., 1939, D.D., 1955. *Religion:* Church of England. *Home:* Selwyn Lodge, Cambridge, England.

CAREER: Cambridge University, Cambridge, England, dean of Trinity Hall, 1949-56, master of Selwyn College, 1956—, Dixie Professor of Ecclesiastical History, 1958-68,

Regius Professor of Modern History, 1968—. *Member:* British Academy (fellow), Royal Historical Society (fellow). *Awards, honors:* D.D., University of St. Andrews and Oxford University; D.L., University of Kent, Columbia University, University of East Anglia, and University of Bristol.

WRITINGS: John Cassian, Cambridge University Press, 1950, revised edition, 1968; *The Founding of Cuddesdon,* Oxford University Press, for Cuddesdon College, 1954; *From Bossuet to Newman,* Cambridge University Press, 1957; *Western Asceticism,* S.C.M. Press, 1958, Westminster, 1979; *Creighton on Luther,* Cambridge University Press, 1959; *Mackenzie's Grave,* Hodder & Stoughton, 1959; *Victorian Miniature,* Hodder & Stoughton, 1960; (editor) *The Mind of the Oxford Movement,* A. & C. Black, 1960, Stanford University Press, 1961; (editor with G. Nuttall) *From Uniformity to Unity, 1662-1962,* S.P.C.K., 1962; *Westcott and the University,* Cambridge University Press, 1962; *The Reformation,* Pelican, 1964; *The Victorian Church,* A. & C. Black, Volume I, 1966, 3rd edition, Barnes & Noble, 1979, Volume II, 1970, 2nd edition, Barnes & Noble, 1979; *Acton and Gladstone,* Athlone Press, 1976; *The Secularization of the European Mind,* Cambridge University Press, 1977; *Catholicism and History,* Cambridge University Press, 1978. Contributor to *London Times, New Statesman, Spectator, Manchester Guardian, Sunday Times, Observer,* and to history and ecclesiastical history journals.

WORK IN PROGRESS: Studies in the modern papacy.

SIDELIGHTS: Mackenzie's Grave was adapted for a radio drama.

BIOGRAPHICAL/CRITICAL SOURCES: Christian Century, March 24, 1971.

* * *

CHAKRAVARTY, Amiya (Chandra) 1901-

PERSONAL: Born April 10, 1901, in Serampore, West Bengal, India; son of Dijesh Chandra and Anindita (Maitra) Chakravarty; married Hjordis, 1927; children: Semanti Bhattacharya. *Education:* University of Patna, B.A. (first class honors), 1921, M.A., 1926; Oxford University, Ph.D., 1936. *Office:* Department of Philosophy, State University of New York College, New Paltz, N.Y. 12561.

CAREER: Literary secretary to Dr. Rabindranath Tagore, 1926-33; Oxford University, Brasenose College, Oxford, England, senior research fellow, 1934-37; professor of literature and humanities, Forman Christian College, 1936-39; University of Calcutta, Calcutta, India, professor of English and comparative modern literature, 1940-48; visiting professor at various universities, including Harvard University, Yale University, and University of Kansas, 1948-52; Boston University, Boston, Mass., professor of comparative Oriental religions and literature, 1952-67, University Lecturer, 1965; State University of New York College at New Paltz, professor of philosophy, beginning 1967, currently professor emeritus. First occupant of Tagore Chair of Humanities, University of Madras, 1963; lecturer throughout United States and abroad. Adviser to Indian delegation to United Nations, 1952; delegate to UNESCO conferences, 1955, 1957; delegate and commissioner, Conference on Tradition and Technology, Bangkok, Thailand, 1958; member of board of India Committee, Danforth Foundation, beginning 1960. *Member:* P.E.N., International Writers Organization, American Association of University professors, Association for Asian Studies, Asia Society (board member, India Committee, beginning 1960), American Friends Service Committee, Phi Beta Kappa. *Awards, honors:* Rockefeller Foundation research scholar, 1951; fellow, Institute for Advanced Study, Princeton, N.J., 1951; Canada Council award, 1961-62; D.Litt. from Santiniketam University, 1963, and Visva-Bharati University, 1965; Padma Bhushan Award, India, 1966.

WRITINGS: The Dynasts and the Post-War Age in Poetry, Oxford University Press, 1938, reprinted, Arden Library, 1978; *The Indian Testimony,* Pendle Hill, 1954; *The Saint at Work,* American Friends Service Committee, 1956; (editor) *A Tagore Reader,* Macmillan, 1961; (contributor) Marion Edman, editor, *The Horizon of Man,* Wayne State University Press, 1963; (with A. Ghosh) *Union Budgets and Prices,* Asia Publishing House, 1964; (editor and author of introduction; translator with Mary Lago and Tarun Gupta) Rabindranath Tagore, *The Housewarming and Other Selected Writings,* New American Library, 1965; *Modern Humanism: An Indian Perspective,* University of Madras, 1968.

Also author of books in Bengali language, except as indicated, published in Calcutta, 1938—, including *Parapara,* 1953, *Duhswapna* (in Assamese), 1961, *Caio Yai,* 1962, *Sampratika,* 1963, *Ghare-pherara Dina,* 1964, *Harano Arkida,* 1966, *Pushpita Imeja,* 1967, *Amarabati,* 1972, and *Amiya Cakrabartira Sreshtha Kabita,* 1973. Contributor to *Saturday Review, Atlantic Monthly,* and periodicals in India.

WORK IN PROGRESS: Research studies on comparative religions.

SIDELIGHTS: Amiya Chakravarty works for international peace. He joined Mahatma Gandhi in his "peace-marches" in Indian villages during the disturbances in 1946-48, and he was associated with Dr. Albert Schweitzer in England and France. He traveled in Africa to study the impact of modern society on the cultural life of Africa and in the West Indies and Caribbean area to survey multi-cultural and linguistic patterns and the problem of religious minority groups. Chakravarty has also traveled widely in Asia, the Middle East, and Europe.†

* * *

CHALK, Ocania 1927-

PERSONAL: Born March 27, 1927, in Mallory, Tenn.; son of Shadrick (a businessman) and Odessa (Graham) Chalk; married Barbara Ann Maxfield (a clerk), October, 1964 (separated, 1976); children: Darryl, Lotus. *Education:* Attended Johnson C. Smith University. *Politics:* Independent. *Religion:* Protestant. *Home address:* RD1, McConnells, S.C.

CAREER: Public assistance caseworker in York, Pa., 1960-69; owner of a bookstore in York, Pa., 1969-70; *Washington Star,* Washington, D.C., reporter, 1970-71; U.S. Department of Labor, Washington, D.C., writer and editor, beginning 1972; currently affiliated with Cannon Mills, York, S.C. *Military service:* U.S. Army, 1950-53.

WRITINGS: Pioneers of Black Sport, Dodd, 1974; *Black College Sport,* Dodd, 1976. Contributor to *Black Sport* and *Liberator.*

WORK IN PROGRESS: A biographical novel, *The Last Warrior: The Story of Battling Siki.*

* * *

CHAMPLIN, Joseph M(asson) 1930-

PERSONAL: Born May 11, 1930, in Hammondsport, N.Y.; son of Francis Mulburn and Katherine (Masson) Champlin. *Education:* Attended Yale University, 1947-48, University of Notre Dame, 1948-49, St. Andrew's Seminary, 1949-50, and St. Bernard's Seminary, 1950-56. *Home:* St. Joseph's Rectory, 5600 West Genesee St., Camillus, N.Y. 13031. *Office:* The Chancery, 240 East Onondaga, St., Syracuse, N.Y. 13202.

CAREER: Ordained Roman Catholic priest, 1956; Immaculate Conception Cathedral, Syracuse, N.Y., assistant pastor, 1956-68; Bishops' Committee on the Liturgy, Washington, D.C., associate director of secretariat, 1968-71; Holy Family Church, Fulton, N.Y., pastor, beginning 1971; Diocese of Syracuse, Syracuse, vicar for parish life and worship, 1979—. Diocese of Syracuse, director of vocations, 1957-60, secretary of liturgical commission, 1961-65, chairman of commission, 1973-76. Visiting lecturer in liturgy, Princeton Theological Seminary, winter, 1973; pastor-in-residence, North American College, Rome, Italy, 1976-77. Has made network radio and television appearances; host of daily radio program, "The Lord in Your Life"; lecturer. Chairman of board of directors, Lee Memorial Hospital, Fulton, N.Y., 1973-77. *Awards, honors:* Named honorary prelate by Pope Paul VI, 1974.

WRITINGS—All published by Ave Maria Press, except as indicated: *Don't You Really Love Me?,* 1968; (editor and contributor) *The Priest Today and Tomorrow,* Collegeville Press, 1969; *Together for Life,* 1970; *Christ Present and Yet to Come,* Orbis Books, 1971; *The Mass in a World of Change,* 1973; *The Sacraments in a World of Change,* 1973; *Together in Peace,* 1975, children's edition (with Brian A. Haggerty), 1976; *Preparing for the New Rite of Penance,* 1975; *The Living Parish,* 1977; *The New, Yet Old Mass,* 1977; *Alone No Longer,* 1977; *Preaching and Teaching about the Eucharist,* 1977; *Through Death to Life,* 1979; *Together by Your Side: A Book for Comforting the Sick and Dying,* 1979; *An Important Office of Immense Love,* 1980. Also author of a cassette tape to accompany *Together by Your Side.* Author of weekly column, "The Altar of God," for Diocese of Syracuse paper, 1958-62; author of syndicated column, "Worship and the World," 1969—.

SIDELIGHTS: Joseph M. Champlin told *CA:* "With an older brother who is entertainment editor of the *Los Angeles Times* and a nationally recognized film critic, it would seem that my own writing career grew out of my brother Chuck's model and inspiration. However, we seemed to have gone in different paths and I am not sure that really is accurate.

"After entering the seminary and just prior to ordination to priesthood, I began writing a few things and soon after the priesthood started a weekly column in our local Catholic paper. That was really the beginning, and in my twenty-five years as a priest, I have written either a local column for the diocesan paper or a syndicated one for half of those years. I have always enjoyed the column as a vehicle for my writing. A column can be done in an hour and a half. One does not have to carry the thoughts along or labor through an extended process as one does writing a book. All my writing has been done as a sideline while still being a full-time parish priest or a priest in an administrative position. The column fits very well into that kind of behavior.

"After a few years in the priesthood I tried my hand at a little pamphlet. It was quite specific and grew out of my own experience in the pastoral ministry of preparing young women to enter the religious life. It was turned down by a half dozen publishers and finally accepted by Our Sunday Visitor. The first royalty check was for $4.68 and covered the sale of about 500 copies. At that point I decided my real vocation was to concentrate more on my priestly ministry and less on writing. However, a year later the next royalty check was for a more substantial amount and included the sale of some 5,000 copies. That was an exciting, unexpected day and really launched my career.

"After several articles in clerical journals and a few pamphlets, I had a bit of extra time because of some complications on the local scene. I began doing a book growing out of my experience teaching about sex and love to high school students in the public school. It was based on the modern novel and contemporary psychology and was written on my day off and on Tuesday nights. I kept testing each chapter with some high school students and an interesting janitor at the Cathedral where I was stationed who did a lot of reading. The feedback was quite positive. I sent it around to several publishers, sure I had a best seller, only to have it turned down. Finally, Ave Maria Press accepted the manuscript. That too was, as they would say today, a very 'affirming' moment.

"I remember a priest in our diocese who had written several books of poetry, a brilliant, but erratic and sort of eccentric person telling me one day that 'the way you learn to write is by writing.' He also said that because a particular manuscript is turned down does not mean the manuscript lacks merit. The choice often is simply a matter of what a particular magazine or publisher needs at this moment. Both of those I found very good advice.

"Writing is not something I enjoy, but a compulsion which I must follow. It is neither relaxation nor fun, although highly satisfying. One thing is always very clear to me: if I have a deep experience of anything—death, love, life, etc.—it will work its way into print, normally in some kind of column.

"I recall some words of Jacqueline Susann, who said that the sale of books is applause. I feel the same way. The money for me is rather irrelevant since in my situation I try to give almost all of it away. But the sales indicate acceptance and applause and I welcome those. Since I am older now and my books have sold about 3,000,000 copies, I am beginning to feel in the last year or so some very satisfying moments from people around the country who recognize me or comment on one of my books which they have used. That started in intensity only about a year or so ago, but needless to say it makes all the efforts of the years very worthwhile.

"I still dread the thought of doing a book because it means going through another pregnancy. All the pain and labor and exhaustion afterwards still is part of the process. But when the child is born and the book hits the market, the pain was all worthwhile, especially when the sales are satisfying and the comments are positive."

* * *

CHANDLER, David Leon

EDUCATION: Self-educated. *Home and office address:* P.O. Box 126, Norfolk, Va. 23501. *Agent:* Roberta Pryor, International Creative Management, 40 West 57th St., New York, N.Y. 10019.

CAREER: Has worked as merchant seaman and farm laborer; *Panama City News-Herald,* Panama City, Fla., reporter, 1959-61; *New Orleans States-Item,* New Orleans, La., reporter, 1961-64; *Life* (magazine), New York, N.Y., contract reporter and correspondent, 1965-71; free-lance writer, 1972-78; *Ledger-Star,* Norfolk, Va., investigative reporter, 1979—. *Member:* Dramatists Guild. *Awards, honors:* Shared Pulitzer Prize for investigative reporting, 1962; Sigma Delta Chi prize for national magazine reporting, 1970; named outstanding journalist by Virginia chapter of Sigma

Delta Chi, 1979; Virginia Press Association Investigative Reporting Award, 1980.

WRITINGS—Nonfiction: *Dragon Variation,* Dutton, 1974; *Brothers in Blood: The Rise of the Criminal Brotherhoods,* Dutton, 1975; *The Natural Superiority of Southern Politicians: A Revisionist History,* Doubleday, 1977; *One Hundred Tons of Gold,* Doubleday, 1978.

WORK IN PROGRESS: A novel, for Doubleday.

SIDELIGHTS: In his 1977 contribution to regional social and historical analysis, *The Natural Superiority of Southern Politicians,* "David Leon Chandler has let his chauvinism run rampant," according to the *New York Times Review* critic. "His thesis is that 'the South has produced the preeminent geniuses of all American political history,' a contribution unrecognized by the nation because 'conquerors, not losers, write history.'" In essence, the critic continues, "the author seeks to set the record straight. . . . [The result is] a presentation of Southerners without warts, a song to the South *in excelsis Deo,* the leadership always cloaked in first principles, protectors of tradition and stability, the embodiment of the Constitution as they interpret it. It's a puzzling argument to deal with since no one who has suffered through the bicentennial could have detected any lack of tribute to the founding Virginians who gave the nation life. . . . What seems to be bothering the author is the reluctance of the nation to acknowledge the wisdom and contribution of the Congressional leaders of the last forty years and to link them to the legends of the Colonial era as products of the same ground and tradition. Lord knows, every Southern Senator believes it. But another book could have been written calling the Southern-dominated Senate obstructionist, filibustered to ineptitude, shot through with Southern arrogance of power, cynically protecting white supremacy until the sit-ins and the civil rights movement forced the Congress to act."

Victor Gold of the *National Review* agrees that the author's chauvinism is rather obvious. He writes: "Chandler, understand, has written a Theses history, capital T; which is to say, he proceeds from Sonnenberg's Principle of perceived truth and interpretation—after Ben Sonnenberg, the public relations entrepreneur, who compared the skill involved in successfully handling a PR account to a dart game in which, 'First you throw your dart, then you draw a circle around wherever it hit: *that* was the target.' Here the author's title is his dart; the 373 pages of Southern political lore, his circle. . . . Chandler is only marketing to a national audience the revanchist pap that Southerners have been spoonfeeding their young for generations: the idea that though the Yankees won the 'War between the States,' it was not because of any intellectual (and certainly not any *moral*) superiority. . . . Be that as it may, let me suggest that whether the reader be revanchist Southerner or crass, crude Yankee, there is only one way to absorb this book: in a hammock, sipping a mint julep, background music by the University of Georgia band playing 'The Bonnie Blue Flag,' up tempo."

BIOGRAPHICAL/CRITICAL SOURCES: New York Times Book Review, January 16, 1977; *New Republic,* January 22, 1977; *Best Sellers,* April, 1977; *National Review,* July 8, 1977.

* * *

CHAPLIN, James P(atrick) 1919-

PERSONAL: Born January 6, 1919, in Santa Monica, Calif.; son of William and Mary (Mahoney) Chaplin; married Madeline Wright, 1940; children: Paul W. *Education:* University of New Mexico, B.A., 1940, M.S., 1940; University of Illinois, Ph.D., 1947. *Home:* 1741 Spear St., South Burlington, Vt. *Office:* Department of Psychology, St. Michael's College, Winooski, Vt. 05404.

CAREER: University of Vermont, Burlington, 1947-70, began as assistant professor, professor of psychology and chairman of department, 1956-70; St. Michael's College, Winooski, Vt., professor of psychology and chairman of department, 1970—. *Military service:* U.S. Army Air Forces, 1942-45; became staff sergeant.

WRITINGS: Rumor, Fear, and the Madness of Crowds, Ballantine, 1959; *The Unconscious,* Ballantine, 1960; *Systems and Theories of Psychology,* Holt, 1960, 4th edition, 1979; *Dictionary of Psychology,* Dell, 1975; *Dictionary of the Occult and Paranormal,* Dell, 1977; *Primer of Neurology and Neurophysiology,* Wiley, 1978.

WORK IN PROGRESS: The Search for Human Nature.

SIDELIGHTS: James P. Chaplin told *CA:* "I have always been fascinated by the concepts that we formulate into the words of our language. I have been especially concerned with trying to make the technical language of psychology clear to the layman in my dictionaries and other writings. My hero in this respect is William James, and I am sure if I wrote novels it would be his brother, Henry." *Avocational interests:* Gardening, hiking.

* * *

CHARLES, C(arol) M(organ) 1931-

PERSONAL: Born January 11, 1931, in Lorraine, Tex.; son of Joe M. and Lois (Jackson) Charles; married Ruth Kimbell (a teacher), June 3, 1951; children: Gail, Timothy. *Education:* Eastern New Mexico University, B.A., 1953, M.A., 1975; University of New Mexico, Ph.D., 1961. *Office:* School of Education, San Diego State University, San Diego, Calif. 92182.

CAREER: Teacher of English and general science in public schools in Estancia, N.M., 1953-59; University of New Mexico, Albuquerque, research assistant and visiting professor of education, 1959-61; San Diego State University, San Diego, Calif., assistant professor, 1961-63, associate professor, 1964-68, professor of education, 1969—. Associate professor at Columbia University, 1966-68. Consultant to ministries of education in Peru and Brazil.

WRITINGS: Creative Writing Skills, Books I and II, Denison, 1968; *Educational Psychology,* Mosby, 1972, revised edition, 1976; *Teacher's Petit Piaget,* Fearon, 1974; *Individualizing Instruction,* Mosby, 1976, revised edition, 1980; *Schooling, Teaching, and Learning: American Education,* Mosby, 1978; *The Special Student in the Regular Classroom,* Mosby, 1980; *Total Discipline for Classroom Teachers,* Longman, 1980. Contributor of articles to education journals in English, Spanish, and Portuguese.

WORK IN PROGRESS: Adult fiction.

* * *

CHARLES, Gerda

PERSONAL: Born in Liverpool, England; daughter of Gertrude Lipson. *Education:* Attended Liverpool, England, public schools. *Religion:* Jewish. *Home:* 22 Cunningham Ct., Maida Vale, London W9 1AE, England.

CAREER: Novelist, critic, and lecturer. *Awards, honors:* James Tait Black Award, for *A Slanting Light;* Whitbread Literary Award, 1971, for *The Destiny Waltz;* Arts Council Award, 1972.

WRITINGS: *The True Voice,* Eyre & Spottiswoode, 1959; *The Crossing Point,* Knopf, 1960; *A Slanting Light,* Knopf, 1963; (editor) *Modern Jewish Stories,* Faber, 1963, Prentice-Hall, 1965; *A Logical Girl,* Eyre & Spottiswoode, 1966, Knopf, 1967; *The Destiny Waltz,* Eyre & Spottiswoode, 1971, Scribner, 1972. Also editor of *Great Short Stories of the World,* Hamlyn Publishing. Contributor to numerous magazines and newspapers, including *New Statesman, Daily Telegraph, New York Times,* and *Jewish Chronicle.* Television columnist, *Jewish Observer and Middle East Review,* 1978.

WORK IN PROGRESS: A sixth novel.

SIDELIGHTS: Gerda Charles' *A Logical Girl* tells the story of the 1943 Allied "invasion" of an English seaside town as seen through the eyes of Rose Morgan, an immature young woman who, along with her father and sister-in-law, runs a boarding house which serves American GIs. "Whatever else may be said for the underdog . . . ," writes Marilyn Gardner of the *Christian Science Monitor,* "one fact remains too often sure: his still infrequent ability to come out on top. The 26-year-old underdog-narrator of Gerda Charles' third novel is no exception to this, but her story makes exceptional reading just the same. . . . What gives the story vitality and sensitivity . . . is Miss Charles' deft appraisal of the internal changes Rosie undergoes. . . . Against the backdrop of a global conflict, her private war against falseness, dishonesty, and hypocrisy becomes a less futile cause."

R.G.G. Price of *Punch* writes: "*A Logical Girl* is so good that it's difficult to praise it without tearing bits off and holding them up for approval. It is a very ambitious novel and a very bold one. . . . Its many virtues include a swinging narrative vigour. . . . After I had finished, I kept seeing new points in what at the time of reading seemed to be just casual snatches of setting or amusing minor characters or even faults of tone. I admired, learned and enjoyed."

Not all the critics, however, were as equally impressed with the novel. Louise Armstrong of the *New York Times Book Review* calls Rose Morgan a "non-heroine" who is "one of the most tiresome women fiction has produced in a long time. . . . Rose's pattern of dream fancy and rude awakening treads monotonously on. Here is the most tenacious adolescence I have ever seen outside of real life." There is, however, a hint of faint praise for Charles' ability to create a vivid character. "Say this for Rosie—and for her author—she is so real, so specific, she details her relationships so minutely and makes her own limitations so clear, that in the end one is just annoyed and anxious to be rid of her, as though she had actually been around for months."

A reviewer in the *Nation* comments: "Miss Charles is an extremely gifted writer, a writer of unfashionable moral seriousness and exceptional narrative power, but *A Logical Girl* is the least impressive of her three novels so far. One can take her female protagonist seriously, or regard her as an object for subtle satire: Miss Charles has not quite brought her themes and characters under the control of her hard, unsentimental intelligence, and there is an ambiguity at the core of *A Logical Girl* that is not willed."

A critic in *Newsweek* offers what is perhaps the best summation of the pros and cons of *A Logical Girl:* "Miss Charles charts Rose's futile puritanical reactions to the human frailties in her wartime world with an almost cruel satisfaction, which makes it rather difficult to sympathize with the poor girl. . . . Still, indelibly etched on our memory, we can never forget poor Rose—at least as a brilliant portrait of the arrested adolescent as compulsive old maid."

BIOGRAPHICAL/CRITICAL SOURCES: *Critique,* winter, 1964-1965; *Jewish Quarterly,* spring, 1967; *Observer,* April 30, 1967; *Illustrated London News,* May 20, 1967; *Punch,* May 24, 1967; *Times Literary Supplement,* May 25, 1967, April 23, 1971; *New York Times Book Review,* June 6, 1967; *Newsweek,* July 14, 1967; *Christian Science Monitor,* July 27, 1967; *Nation,* October 2, 1967.

* * *

CHARLTON, Donald Geoffrey 1925-

PERSONAL: Born April 8, 1925, in Bolton, Lancashire, England; son of Harry and Hilda (Whittle) Charlton; married Thelma D. E. Masters, 1952; children: Katharine Penelope, Nicholas John, Jane Victoria. *Education:* Attended St. Edmund Hall, Oxford, 1943-44; Emmanuel College, Cambridge, B.A., 1948, M.A., 1953, Ph.D. (London), 1955. *Home:* 3 Clarendon Cres., Leamington Spa, Warwickshire, England. *Office:* Department of French Studies, University of Warwick, Coventry, England.

CAREER: University of Hull, Hull, England, lecturer, 1949-60, senior lecturer in French, 1960-64; University of Warwick, Coventry, England, professor of French, 1964—. Visiting professor of French, Trinity College, University of Toronto, Toronto, Ontario, 1961-62, and University of California, Berkeley, 1966. *Military service:* Royal Navy, 1944-46; became petty officer. *Member:* Society for French Studies (secretary, 1961-62).

WRITINGS: *Positivist Thought in France during the Second Empire, 1852-1870,* Clarendon Press, 1959, reprinted, Greenwood Press, 1976; *Secular Religions in France, 1815-1870,* Oxford University Press, 1963; *France: A Companion to French Studies,* Methuen, 1972, 2nd edition, 1979; (editor with others) *Balzac and the Nineteenth Century: Studies in French Literature Presented to Herbert J. Hunt by Pupils, Colleagues and Friends,* Humanities Press, 1972; (with D. C. Potts) *French Thought since 1600,* Methuen, 1974. Contributor to professional journals in England and the United States.

WORK IN PROGRESS: Writing on Romanticism and on French intellectual and cultural history, 1750-1800.

* * *

CHEESMAN, Paul R. 1921-

PERSONAL: Born May 31, 1921, in Brigham City, Utah; married Millie Rubey Foster, June 29, 1944; children: Brian, Ross, Douglas, Larry, LuAnn, Jay. *Education:* San Diego State College (now University), B.A., 1944; graduate study at University of California, Los Angeles, 1945, and University of Miami, Coral Gables, Fla., 1955; Brigham Young University, M.R.S., 1964, D.R.E., 1967. *Home:* 1146 Old Willow Dr., Provo, Utah 84601. *Office:* Brigham Young University, Provo, Utah 84602.

CAREER: Ordained Mormon clergyman, 1941; bishop in Linda Vista, Calif., and Provo, Utah; teacher in public schools of San Diego, Calif., 1944-49; self-employed photographer, 1949-53; corporation president in Miami, Fla., 1955-63; Brigham Young University, Provo, instructor, 1963-67, assistant professor, 1967-70, associate professor, 1970-74, professor, 1975—. Associate producer of motion pictures. *Military service:* U.S. Naval Reserve, chaplain, 1953-55; became lieutenant. *Member:* Lions Club.

WRITINGS: *Great Leaders of the Book of Mormon,* Community Press, 1970; *Early America and the Book of Mormon,* Deseret, 1972; *Keystone of Mormanism,* Deseret,

1973; *These Early Americans,* Deseret, 1974; *The Polynesians and the Book of Mormon,* Community Press, 1975; *The World of the Book of Mormon,* Deseret, 1978; *The Land of the Book of Mormon,* Hudson Press, 1979.

WORK IN PROGRESS: A book about the American Indian, *Children of the Son.*

* * *

CHEN, Theodore Hsi-En 1902-

PERSONAL: Born July 14, 1902, in China; married Wen-Hui Chung, June 6, 1932; children: Helen Cheng. *Education:* Fukien Christian University, A.B., 1922; Columbia University, A.M., 1929; University of Southern California, Ph.D., 1939. *Home:* 5564 Village Green, Los Angeles, Calif. 90016. *Office:* 804 WPH, University of Southern California, Los Angeles, Calif. 90007.

CAREER: Fukien Christian University, Foochow, China, dean of faculty, 1929-37, president, 1946-47; University of Southern California, Los Angeles, professor of education and Asian studies, 1938-74, professor emeritus, 1974—. *Member:* Phi Beta Kappa, Phi Kappa Phi, Phi Delta Kappa. *Awards, honors:* LL.D., University of Southern California, 1967.

WRITINGS: Developing Patterns of the College Curriculum in the United States, University of Southern California Press, 1940; *Elementary Chinese Reader and Grammar,* Perkins Oriental Books, 1945; *Chinese Communism and the Proletarian-Socialist Revolution,* University of Southern California Press, 1955; *Thought Reform of the Chinese Intellectuals,* Oxford University Press, 1960; *Teacher Training in Communist China,* U.S. Office of Education, 1960; *The Chinese Communist Regime: Documents and Commentary,* Praeger, 1967; *Maoist Educational Revolution,* Praeger, 1974.

Contributor: J. S. Roucek and Moehlman, editors, *Comparative Education,* Dryden, 1952; Roucek, editor, *Contemporary Political Ideologies,* Philosophical Library, 1961; S. H. Gould, editor, *Sciences in Communist China,* American Association for the Advancement of Science, 1961; Roucek and K. V. Lottich, editors, *Behind the Iron Curtain,* Caxton, 1964; Stewart Fraser, editor, *Governmental Encouragement and the Control of International Education in Communist China,* Wiley, 1965; Ruth Adams, editor, *Contemporary China,* Pantheon, 1966; George P. Jan, editor, *Government of Communist China,* Chandler Publishing, 1966; *The China Giant: Perspective on Communist China,* Scott, Foresman, 1967; Paul K. T. Sih, editor, *The Strenuous Decade: China's Nation-Building Efforts, 1927-1937,* St. John's University Press, 1970; Frank Traeger and William Henderson, editors, *Communist China: 1949-1969,* New York University, 1970.

Contributor to *Encyclopaedia Britannica, Encyclopedia Americana, World Book Encyclopedia, Encyclopedia of Modern Education,* and *Encyclopedia of Vocational Guidance.* Contributor of numerous articles to newspapers and professional journals, including the *Los Angeles Times, Christian Science Monitor, School and Society, Current History, Far Eastern Survey,* and *Sociology and Social Research.*

BIOGRAPHICAL/CRITICAL SOURCES: Book World (Chicago Tribune), March 17, 1968.

* * *

CHESTER, Michael (Arthur) 1928-

PERSONAL: Born November 23, 1928, in New York, N.Y.; son of Arthur Vincent and Irene (Greenberg) Chester; married Jacqueline Sapsis, 1950; children: Thomas, Teresa, Barbara. *Education:* University of California, B.A., 1952.

CAREER: Tracerlab, Inc., Berkeley, Calif., physicist, 1952-53; Northrop Aircraft, Inc., Hawthorne, Calif., research analyst, 1953-55; Coleman Engineering Co., Los Angeles, Calif., engineer, 1955-56; Northrop Aircraft, Inc., engineer, 1956-57; Lockheed Missiles & Space Co., Sunnyvale, Calif., scientist, beginning 1957.

WRITINGS—Juvenile; published by Putnam: (With William Nephew) *Moon Trip: True Adventure in Space,* 1958; (with Nephew) *Moon Base,* 1959; (with Nephew) *Planet Trip,* 1960; (with Nephew) *Beyond Mars,* 1960; (with Saunders B. Kramer) *Discoverer: The Story of a Satellite,* 1960; *The Mystery of the Lost Moon,* 1961; *The Wonders of Robots,* 1962; (with David McClinton) *The Moon: Target for Apollo,* 1963; *Robots in Space,* 1965; *First Wagons to California,* 1965; *Joseph Strauss, Builder of the Golden Gate Bridge,* 1965; *Forts of Old California,* 1967.

Rockets and Spacecraft of the World, Norton, 1964; *Relativity: An Introduction for Young Readers,* Norton, 1967; (with Thomas Chester) *Submersibles and Undersea Labs of the World,* Grosset, 1970; *Water Monsters,* Grosset, 1973; *Deeper than Speech: Frontiers of Language and Communication,* Macmillan, 1975; *Particles: An Introduction to Particle Physics,* Macmillan, 1978.

"Let's Go" series, published by Putnam: *Let's Go to a Rocket Base,* 1961; *. . . on a Space Trip,* 1963; *. . . to the Moon,* 1965, revised edition, 1974; *. . . to Build a Suspension Bridge,* 1966; *. . . to Stop Air Pollution,* 1968; *. . . to Stop Water Pollution,* 1969; *. . . on a Space Shuttle,* 1975; *. . . to a Recycling Center,* 1977; *. . . to Fight a Forest Fire,* 1978.

SIDELIGHTS: Michael Chester grew up in LaCanada, Calif. and has been interested since boyhood in science and creative writing, "the latter probably due to some degree to my father, Arthur Chester, a published writer of mystery stories," he told *CA.* Chester's reading interests include James Joyce, Herman Melville, William Faulkner, and Mark Twain.

AVOCATIONAL INTERESTS: Chess and sailing.†

* * *

CHINOY, Ely 1921-1975

PERSONAL: Born September 5, 1921, in Newark, N.J.; died April 21, 1975, in an automobile accident; son of Solomon and Bella (Traskanoff) Chinoy; married Helen Krich, June 6, 1948; children: Michael Avrum, Claire Nicole. *Education:* Rutgers University, B.A., 1942; Columbia University, Ph.D., 1953. *Home:* 230 Crescent St., Northampton, Mass. *Office:* Department of Sociology and Anthropology, Smith College, Northampton, Mass. 01060.

CAREER: Newark College of Engineering (now New Jersey Institute of Technology), Newark, N.J., instructor, 1942-44; New York University, New York, N.Y., instructor in sociology, 1945-46; University of Toronto, Toronto, Ontario, lecturer in sociology, 1947-51; Smith College, Northampton, Mass. instructor, 1951-53, assistant professor, 1953-57, associate professor, 1957-61, professor of sociology, 1961-75, Mary Huggins Gamble Professor of Sociology, 1969-75, chairman of department of sociology and anthropology. Fulbright visiting professor, University of Leicester, 1963-64; Fulbright lecturer in the Philippines, summer, 1971. *Member:* American Sociological Association, American Association of University Professors, American Civil Liberties

Union, Eastern Sociological Society, Phi Beta Kappa. *Awards, honors:* Social Science Research Council fellow, 1946-47.

WRITINGS—All published by Random House, except as indicated: *Sociological Perspectives,* 1954, 3rd edition, edited by S. G. McNall, Little, Brown, 1975; *Automobile Workers and the American Dream,* 1955; *Society: An Introduction to Sociology,* 1961, 2nd edition, 1967; (editor) *The Urban Future,* Lieber-Atherton, 1973.

Contributor: C. H. Page, editor, *Sociology and Contemporary Education,* Random House, 1964; P. L. Berger, editor, *The Human Shape of Work,* Macmillan, 1964; J. Gould and W. L. Kolb, editors, *A Dictionary of the Social Sciences,* Free Press, 1964. Contributor of articles and reviews to sociology journals in United States, Canada, Yugoslavia, and Great Britain. *American Sociological Review,* assistant editor, 1957-60, associate editor, 1961-64; consulting editor in sociology, Lieber-Atherton Press, 1964-75; member of editorial board, Cambridge Studies in Sociology, 1972-75.†

* * *

CHORAO, (Ann Mc)Kay (Sproat) 1936-

PERSONAL: Surname is pronounced Shoe-*row;* born January 7, 1936, in Elkhart, Ind.; daughter of James McKay (a lawyer) and Elizabeth (Fleming) Sproat; married Ernesto A. K. Chorao (an artist), June 10, 1960; children: Jamie, Peter, Ian. *Education:* Wheaton College, Norton, Mass., B.A., 1958; graduate study at Chelsea School of Art, 1958-59. *Home:* 290 Riverside Dr., Apt. 12A, New York, N.Y. 10025.

CAREER: Artist; illustrator and writer of children's books. *Awards, honors:* American Institute of Graphic Arts Certificate of Excellence, 1974, for *Ralph and the Queen's Bathtub;* Christopher Award, 1979, for *Chester Chipmunk's Thanksgiving.*

WRITINGS—Self-illustrated books for children: *The Repair of Uncle Toe,* Farrar, Straus, 1972; *A Magic Eye for Ida,* Seabury, 1973; *Ralph and the Queen's Bathtub,* Farrar, Straus, 1974; *Ida Makes a Movie,* Seabury, 1974; *Maudie's Umbrella,* Dutton, 1975; *Molly's Moe,* Seabury, 1976; *Lester's Overnight,* Dutton, 1977; *The Baby's Lap Book,* Dutton, 1977; *Molly's Lies,* Seabury, 1979.

Illustrator: Judith Viorst, *My Mama Says,* Atheneum, 1973; Madeline Edmonson, *The Witch's Egg,* Seabury, 1974; Barbara Williams, *Albert's Toothache,* Dutton, 1974; Williams, *Kevin's Grandma,* Dutton, 1975; Winifred Rosen, *Henrietta, the Wild Woman of Borneo,* Four Winds Press, 1975; Ann Schweninger, *The Hunt for Rabbit's Galosh,* Doubleday, 1976; Williams, *Someday Said Mitchell,* Dutton, 1976; *Monster Poems,* edited by Daisy Wallace, Holiday House, 1976; Robert Crowe, *Clyde Monster,* Dutton, 1976; Marjorie Sharmat, *I'm Terrific,* Holiday House, 1977; Jan Whal, *Frankenstein's Dog,* Prentice-Hall, 1977; Susan Pearson, *That's Enough for One Day, J. P.,* Dial, 1977; Whal, *Dracula's Cat,* Prentice-Hall, 1978; Williams, *Chester Chipmunk's Thanksgiving,* Dutton, 1978; Rosen, *Henrietta and the Day of the Iguana,* Four Winds Press, 1978; Sharmat, *Thornton the Worrier,* Holiday House, 1978; Norma Klein, *Visiting Pamela,* Dial, 1979; A. E. Hoffman, *Nutcracker,* edited by Janet Shulman, Dutton, 1979; Williams, *A Valentine for Cousin Archie,* Dutton, 1980; Sharmat, *Sometimes Mama and Papa Fight,* Harper, 1980; Crowe, *Tyler Toad and the Thunder,* Dutton, 1980; Sharmat, *Grumley the Grouch,* Holiday House, 1980.

SIDELIGHTS: Kay Chorao writes: "Basically I am an illustrator; my training is in fine arts. The books I have written . . . have grown out of observations of my own children—but often filtered through memories of my own childhood."

* * *

CHRISTIAN, Mary Blount 1933-

PERSONAL: Born February 20, 1933, in Houston, Tex.; daughter of George D. and Anna (Dill) Blount; married George L. Christian, Jr. (a book review editor), September 22, 1956; children: Scott, Karen, Devin. *Education:* University of Houston, B.S., 1954. *Home:* 1108 Danbury Rd., Houston, Tex. 77055.

CAREER: Houston Post, Houston, Tex., reporter and columnist, 1953-57; free-lance writer in Houston, Tex., 1959—. Has taught writing for children at university workshops and adult education programs. Instructor in creative writing, Houston Community College, 1973-78; instructor, Institute of Children's Literature, 1979—. Creator and moderator for "Children's Bookshelf," PBS-TV, syndicated through Eastern Educational Television. *Member:* Society of Children's Book Writers (charter member; member of board of advisors, 1975-76), Mystery Writers of America, Authors Guild.

WRITINGS—For children: *Scarabee: The Witch's Cat,* Steck, 1973; *The First Sign of Winter,* Parents' Magazine Press, 1973; *Nothing Much Happened Today* (also see below), Addison-Wesley, 1973; *Sebastian: Super Sleuth,* J. Philip O'Hara, 1974; *Devin and Goliath,* Addison-Wesley, 1974; *No Dogs Allowed, Jonathan!* (also see below), Addison-Wesley, 1975.

Hats Are for Watering Horses, Rand McNally, 1976; *When Time Began,* Concordia, 1976; *Jonah, Go to Nineveh!,* Concordia, 1976; *Daniel Who Dared,* Concordia, 1977; *The Goosehill Gang Cookbook,* Concordia, 1978; *The Goosehill Gang Craft Book,* Concordia, 1978; *The Sand Lot,* Harvey House, 1978; *Felina,* Scholastic Action, 1978; *His Brother's Keeper,* Concordia, 1978; *J. J. Leggett, Secret Agent,* Lothrop, 1978; *The Lucky Man,* Macmillan, 1979; *The Devil Take You, Barnabas Beane!,* Crowell, 1979; *Anah and the Strangers,* Abingdon, 1980; *Christmas Reflections,* Concordia, 1980; *The Doggone Mystery,* A. Whitman, 1980.

"The Goosehill Gang," Series I, published by Concordia, 1976: *The Vanishing Sandwich; The Test Paper Thief; The Disappearing Dues; The Chocolate Cake Caper.*

"The Goosehill Gang," Series II, published by Concordia, 1977: *The C.B. Convoy Caper; The Pocket Park Problem; The Runaway House Mystery; The May Basket Mystery.*

"The Goosehill Gang," Series III, published by Concordia, 1978: *The Stitch in Time Solution; The Ghost in the Garage; The Shadow on the Shade; The Christmas Shoe Thief.*

Film strips: "No Dogs Allowed, Jonathan!," Taylor Associates, 1976; "Nothing Much Happened Today," Taylor Associates, 1976.

Work represented in anthologies, including *Hootnanny,* Scott, Foresman, and *Twentieth Century Children's Authors,* St. Martin's. Juvenile book critic, *Houston Chronicle.*

WORK IN PROGRESS: Two bible retellings, for Concordia; a mystery series for the early reader; "high-interest/low vocabulary" novellas; an adaptation to play form of *The C.B. Convoy Caper,* for Lippincott language series.

SIDELIGHTS: Mary Blount Christian writes: "Everything I write comes both from a deep inner feeling and an experience (my own or someone else's), but they are so evolved by the time they are written that the original stimuli is invisible.

I feel a deep responsibility for the reader. While I start out to entertain I never send anything out without being very sure that it contains nothing that will mislead or misinform a child about the world as I know it. I try to tell myself in one sentence just what theme, what universal message, each story conveys. After all, we can't follow the book around and add footnotes to the reader. It leads its own life apart from us and nothing we could say later can erase a misconception we may have caused. Children look much deeper into stories than adults—perhaps not consciously, but they decode everything into validity to life.''

BIOGRAPHICAL/CRITICAL SOURCES: Houston Chronicle, December 24, 1972; *Westside Reporter* (Houston), June 1, 1979.

* * *

CLAERBAUT, David 1946-

PERSONAL: Born February 27, 1946, in Tomahawk, Wis.; son of Erwin Peter (a postal distribution clerk) and Wilma (Gabrielse) Claerbaut; married present wife, Carole Patricia, March 15, 1979; children: (first marriage) Wilma Rochelle. *Education:* Calvin College, A.B., 1969; University of Michigan, M.A., 1970; Loyola University, Chicago, Ill., Ph.D., 1976. *Home:* 5061 North St. Louis, Chicago, Ill. 60625. *Office:* Department of Sociology, North Park College, 5125 North Spaulding, Chicago, Ill. 60625.

CAREER: Teacher of English and social studies in public schools of Grand Rapids, Mich., 1969-70; North Park College, Chicago, Ill., 1970—, began as assistant professor, currently associate professor of sociology and psychology, chairman of department of sociology, 1978—. President of board of directors, Oak Therapeutic School, 1979—, and Cabrini-Green Legal Aid Clinic. Lecturer at Loyola University and De Paul University.

WRITINGS: Black Jargon in White America, Eerdmans, 1972; *Social Problems,* Christian Academic Publications, 1977; *Black Student Alienation: A Study,* R & E Research Associates, 1978; *The Reluctant Defender,* Tyndale, 1978.

WORK IN PROGRESS: Urban Ministry.

AVOCATIONAL INTERESTS: Public speaking, sports.

* * *

CLARK, Dennis J. 1927-

PERSONAL: Born June 30, 1927, in Philadelphia, Pa.; son of John A. and Geraldine Clark; married Josepha T. O'Callaghan (a librarian), March 28, 1952; children: Conna, Brendan, Patrick, Ciaran, Brian, Drigid. *Education:* St. Joseph's College, B.S., 1951; Temple University, M.A., 1966, Ph.D., 1971. *Home:* 644 Bridle Rd., Glenside, Pa. 19038. *Office:* Samuel S. Fels Fund, 2 Penn Center, Philadelphia, Pa. 19102.

CAREER: Philadelphia Housing Authority, Philadelphia, Pa., information specialist, 1951-54; Philadelphia Fellowship Commission, Philadelphia, housing specialist, 1954-57; Philadelphia Commission on Human Relations, Philadelphia, supervisor in housing division, 1957-61; New York Catholic Interracial Council, New York, N.Y., director, 1962-63; Temple University, Center for Community Studies, Philadelphia, staff member, 1964-71; Samuel S. Fels Fund, Philadelphia, secretary and executive director, 1971—. Teacher in evening division, St. Joseph's College, 1956-57, 1964, and 1973; teacher, Pennsylvania State University, 1963. Consultant to National Association of Housing and Redevelopment Officials, 1966, U.S. Department of Health, Education, and Welfare, 1967, and Urban Poverty Neighborhood Data Resources Project, 1968. Lecturer. *Military service:* U.S. Army, 1945-47. *Member:* Organization of American Historians, National Catholic Conference for Interracial Justice (member of board), American Irish Historical Society, American Committee for Irish Studies, Historical Society of Pennsylvania.

WRITINGS: Cities in Crisis, Sheed, 1960; *The Ghetto Game,* Sheed, 1962; (contributor) Roger L. Shinn, editor, *The Search for Identity,* Harper, 1964; (contributor) C. E. Elias and others, editors, *Metropolis: Values in Conflict,* Wadsworth, 1965; *Work and the Human Spirit,* Sheed, 1967; (contributor) John O'Connor, editor, *The American Catholic Exodus,* Corpus Books, 1968; (contributor) Miriam Ershkowitz and Joseph Zikmund, editors, *Black Politics in Philadelphia,* Basic Books, 1972; (contributor) Allen Davis and Mark Haller, editors, *Peoples of Philadelphia,* Temple University Press, 1973; *The Irish in Philadelphia: Ten Generations of Urban Experience,* Temple University Press, 1973; (editor) *Philadelphia 1776-2076: A Three Hundred Year View,* National University Publications, 1976; *Irish Blood: Northern Ireland and the American Conscience,* Kennikat, 1977. Also author of monographs. Contributor of articles to professional journals. Editor, *Interracial Review,* 1961-63.

WORK IN PROGRESS: A novel and a collection of historical essays.

AVOCATIONAL INTERESTS: Writing, folk song collections, camping.

* * *

CLARK, Gordon H(addon) 1902-

PERSONAL: Born August 31, 1902, in Philadelphia, Pa.; son of David Scott and Elizabeth (Haddon) Clark; married Ruth Schmidt, March 27, 1929; children: Lois A. Zeller, Nancy Elizabeth George. *Education:* University of Pennsylvania, A.B., 1924, Ph.D., 1929; attended Sorbonne, University of Paris, 1931; Reformed Episcopal Seminary, D.D., 1966. *Religion:* Presbyterian. *Home address:* Route 2, Box 219, Rising Fawn, Ga. 30738. *Office:* Department of Philosophy, Covenant College, Lookout Mountain, Tenn. 37350.

CAREER: University of Pennsylvania, Philadelphia, instructor, 1924-36; Reformed Episcopal Seminary, Philadelphia, lecturer, 1932-36; Wheaton College, Wheaton, Ill., associate professor of philosophy, 1936-43; ordained minister of Presbyterian Church, 1944; Butler University, Indianapolis, Ind., professor of philosophy and chairman of department, 1945-73; Covenant College, Lookout Mountain, Tenn., professor of philosophy, 1974—. Moderator of General Synod, Reformed Presbyterian Church, 1961. *Member:* American Philosophical Association, Evangelical Theological Society, Indiana Philosophical Society, Phi Beta Kappa.

WRITINGS: (Editor with Thomas V. Smith) *Readings in Ethics,* Appleton, 1931, 2nd edition, 1935; (editor) *Selections from Hellenistic Philosophy,* Appleton, 1940, reprinted, 1964; (with others) *A History of Philosophy,* F. S. Crofts, 1941; *A Christian Philosophy of Education,* Eerdmans, 1946; (contributor) Vergilius Ferm, editor, *History of Philosophical Systems,* Philosophic Library, 1950; *A Christian View of Men and Things,* Eerdmans, 1952; *What Presbyterians Believe,* Presbyterian & Reformed, 1956, 2nd edition published as *What Do Presbyterians Believe?*, 1965; *Thales to Dewey,* Houghton, 1956; (contributor) Carl F.H. Henry, editor, *Contemporary Evangelical Thought,* Channel, 1957; (contributor) Henry, editor, *Revelation and the Bible,* Baker Book, 1958.

Dewey, Presbyterian & Reformed, 1960; *Religion, Reason, and Revelation*, Presbyterian & Reformed, 1961; *Karl Barth's Theological Method*, Presbyterian & Reformed, 1963; (contributor) *Can I Trust My Bible?*, Moody, 1963; (contributor) Henry, editor, *Christian Faith and Modern Theology*, Channel, 1964; *The Philosophy of Science and Belief in God*, Craig, 1964; (contributor) Henry, editor, *Jesus of Nazareth: Savior and Lord*, Eerdmans, 1966; *Peter Speaks Today*, Presbyterian & Reformed, 1967; (contributor) Henry, editor, *Fundamentals of the Faith*, Zondervan, 1969; *Biblical Predestination*, Presbyterian & Reformed, 1969; *Historiography: Secular and Religious*, Craig, 1971; *Three Types of Religious Philosophy*, Presbyterian & Reformed, 1974; *First Corinthian Commentary*, Presbyterian & Reformed, 1975; *Language and Theology*, Presbyterian & Reformed, 1980. Contributor to *Dictionary of Theology*, *Dictionary of Christian Ethics*, *American People's Encyclopedia*, *Collier's Encyclopedia*, and *Encyclopedia of Christianity*. Contributor to professional journals.

WORK IN PROGRESS: The Pastoral Epistles; Behaviorism and Christianity.

AVOCATIONAL INTERESTS: Chess, oil painting.

BIOGRAPHICAL/CRITICAL SOURCES: The Philosophy of Gordon H. Clark: A Festschrift, Presbyterian & Reformed, 1968.

* * *

CLARK, L. D. 1922-

PERSONAL: Born October 22, 1922, in Gainesville, Tex.; son of Thomas H. and Ruby (Loyd) Clark; married LaVerne Harrell, September 15, 1951. *Education:* Attended Gainesville College (now Cooke County Junior College); Columbia University, B.A., 1953, M.A., 1954, Ph.D., 1963. *Home:* 4690 North Campbell Ave., Tucson, Ariz. 85718. *Office:* Department of English, University of Arizona, Tucson, Aiz. 85721.

CAREER: Agricultural and Mechanical College of Texas (now Texas A&M University), College Station, instructor, 1954-55; University of Arizona, Tucson, instructor, 1955-58; Columbia University, New York, N.Y., lecturer, 1958-59; University of Arizona, lecturer, 1959-63, assistant professor, 1963-65, associate professor, 1965-70, professor of English, 1970—. Lecturer on writing, Texas Woman's University, summer, 1962. *Military service:* U.S. Army Air Forces, 1941-46; served in Pacific; became master sergeant; received Air Medal. *Member:* Modern Language Association of America, D. H. Lawrence Society, Cooke County Heritage Society, Phi Beta Kappa (president of University of Arizona chapter). *Awards, honors:* William Bayard Cutting fellowship from Columbia University, 1960-61, for research in Mexico; Ford Foundation publication grant, 1964; faculty research grants from University of Arizona, 1967-68, 1969; Fulbright travel grant to University of Nice, 1973-74; research grant from National Endowment for the Humanities, 1978.

WRITINGS: The Dove Tree (novel), Doubleday, 1961; *Dark Night of the Body: D. H. Lawrence's "The Plumed Serpent,"* University of Texas Press, 1964; (contributor) John Unterecker, editor, *Approaches to the Twentieth Century Novel*, Crowell, 1965; (contributor) *Voices from the Southwest*, Northland Press, 1976; *Is This Naomi and Other Stories*, Blue Moon Press, 1980; *The Minoan Distance: The Symbolism of Travel in D. H. Lawrence*, University of Arizona Press, 1980.

Contributor of short stories to anthologies, including *Stories Southwest*, edited by A. Wilbur Stevens, Prescott College Press, 1972, and *Southwest: A Contemporary Anthology*, edited by Karl Kopp and Jane Kopp, Red Earth Press, 1977. Also contributor of short stories and articles to professional journals, including *Real*, *Forum*, *Blue Cloud Quarterly*, *Rocky Mountain Review*, *Parabola*, *Texas Quarterly*, *D.H. Lawrence Review*, and *Southwest Heritage*. Advisory editor, *D. H. Lawrence Review*.

WORK IN PROGRESS: A novel, *The Fifth Wind*, for Blue Moon Press; a definitive edition of D. H. Lawrence's *The Plumed Serpent*.

* * *

CLARKE, George Timothy

PERSONAL: Son of George Samuel and Mary (Carrigan) Clarke; married Mildred Shanley, 1937; children: Jane Lee (Mrs. G. Robert Boller), Judith (Mrs. William H. Turner). *Education:* Fordham University, B.A., 1931; New York University, M.B.A., 1950. *Residence:* Greenwich, Conn.

CAREER: Bendix Aviation Corp., Pioneer Instrument Division, Teterboro, N.J., publications manager, 1940-43; *Look* Magazine, New York City, promotion executive, 1943-47; Scholastic Magazines, New York City, promotion director, 1947-49; New York University, New York City, assistant professor, 1949-52, associate professor of marketing, 1952-74, associate professor emeritus, 1974—. Advertising Federation of America, director of Bureau of Education and Research, 1959-74, director of Club Services department, 1962-64, director of seminars in marketing management and advertising presented by Harvard Business School faculty, 1962-74. *Member:* American Marketing Association, American Academy of Advertising (national bursar, 1959-62), Financial Executives Institute, Alpha Delta Sigma.

WRITINGS: Copywriting: Theory and Technique, Harper, 1959; (co-author) *Effective Marketing Action*, Harper, 1959; *Advertising and Marketing Theses for the Doctorate in United States Colleges and Universities: A Bibliography*, Advertising Educational Foundation, 1961; *Opportunities in Advertising*, Universal Publishing, 1967; *Transit Advertising*, Transit Advertising Association, 1970. Contributor to professional journals.

* * *

CLEEVE, Brian (Talbot) 1921-

PERSONAL: Born November 22, 1921, in Essex, England; son of Charles Edward (a businessman) and Josephine (Talbot) Cleeve; married Veronica McAdie (a business director), September 24, 1945; children: Berenice Cleeve Dezalay, Tanga. *Education:* Attended St. Edward's College, Oxford, 1935-38; University of South Africa, B.A. (honors), 1954; National University of Ireland, Ph.D., 1956. *Politics:* None. *Religion:* Catholic. *Home:* 60 Heytesbury Lane, Ballsbridge, Dublin 4, Ireland.

CAREER: Free-lance journalist in South Africa, 1948-54, and in Ireland, 1954—. Broadcaster for Radio Telefis Eireann, 1962-72. *Wartime service:* British Merchant Navy, 1938-45. *Member:* National Union of Journalists (Ireland), Society of Authors.

WRITINGS: Dictionary of Irish Writers, Mercier Press, Volume I: *Fiction in English*, 1967, Volume II: *Nonfiction in English and Latin*, 1969, Volume III: *All Writing in Gaelic and Latin*, 1972; (editor) *W. B. Yeats and the Designing of Ireland's Coinage*, Dolman Press, 1972.

Novels, except as indicated: *The Far Hills,* Jarrolds, 1952; *Portrait of My City,* Jarrolds, 1953; *Birth of a Dark Soul,* Jarrolds, 1953, published as *The Night Winds,* Houghton, 1954; *Assignment to Vengeance,* Hammond, 1961; *Death of a Painted Lady,* Hammond, 1962, Random House, 1963; *Death of a Wicked Servant,* Hammond, 1963, Random House, 1964; *Vote X for Treason,* Collins, 1964, Random House, 1965; *Dark Blood Dark Terror,* Random House, 1965; *Vice Isn't Private,* Random House, 1966 (published in England as *The Judas Goat,* Hammond, 1966); *The Horse Thieves of Ballysaggert* (short stories), Mercier Press, 1966; *Violent Death of a Bitter Englishman,* Random House, 1967; *You Must Never Go Back,* Random House, 1968; *Exit from Prague,* Corgi Books, 1970, published as *Escape from Prague,* Pinnacle Books, 1973; *Cry of Morning,* M. Joseph, 1971, published as *The Triumph of O'Rourke,* Doubleday, 1972; *Tread Softly in This Place,* Cassell, 1972, John Day, 1973; *The Dark Side of the Sun,* Cassell, 1973; *A Question of Inheritance,* Cassell, 1974; *For Love of Crannagh Castle,* Dutton, 1975; *Sara* (Book Club Associates selection), Coward, 1976; *Kate,* Coward, 1977; *Judith* (Book Club Associates selection), Coward, 1978; *Hester* (Book Club Associates selection), Cassell, 1979, Coward, 1980; *The House on the Rock,* Watkins, 1980; *The Seven Mansions,* Watkins, 1980. Contributor of short stories to magazines, including the *Saturday Evening Post.*

WORK IN PROGRESS: The Fourth Mary, for Watkins; *The Holy Grail,* a novel in four parts.

SIDELIGHTS: Prior to *The House on the Rock* and *The Seven Mansions,* most of Brian Cleeve's books were of the "light entertainment" variety, full of secret agents, murderers, Gothic heroines, and so on. But in 1980, Cleeve turned to a different type of writing. As he explained to *CA:* "I think that all writers feel about the books that mean most to them that their substance came to them from somewhere outside themselves. This is certainly my case with *The House on the Rock* and *The Seven Mansions.* I not only feel it, I claim it, in the books, and on their covers. They are books of mysticism, or metaphysics if that sounds more respectable. In a way I have been working towards them all my writing life, but I could not so much as have begun them out of my own mental resources. I have no idea whether they will achieve a wide readership, but I feel that in time they must. They are about the questions that every intelligent individual asks at some time in his or her life: the reasons for evil and suffering; the purpose of our lives; the inexplicable cruelty, in human terms, of religion towards women; the possibility of finding God; and a hundred or more similar questions. If the answers were mine they would have no value at all. But what I believe, and say in the books, is that they are God's.

"Having said that, I obviously qualify in your eyes for whatever corner of *CA* you reserve for harmless lunatics, or shameless liars. I'm sorry about that, and there is no possible defence against such easy and immediate accusations—except to say, 'please read the books. If they seem to you the work of a lunatic or a liar, then you are satisfied and there is no harm done. While if the books convince you, if the answers seem plausible, however surprising, then you will cease to have any interest in me and will be concerned only with the books.'"

* * *

CLEPPER, Henry (Edward) 1901-

PERSONAL: Born March 21, 1901, in Columbia, Pa.; son of Martin Neil (a businessman) and Charlotte (Keech) Clepper; married Clorinda McFerren, August 14, 1921 (deceased); children: Charlotte Mae (Mrs. I. I. Davidson), Albert Lynn. *Education:* Pennsylvania State Forest Academy (affiliated with Pennsylvania State University), B. Forestry, 1921. *Home:* Brandywine, Apt. 514, 4545 Connecticut Ave. N.W., Washington, D.C. 20008. *Office:* American Forestry Association, 1319 18th St. N.W., Washington, D.C. 20036.

CAREER: Pennsylvania Department of Forests and Waters, Harrisburg, forester, 1921-36; U.S. Department of Agriculture, Forest Service, Washington, D.C., forester, 1936-37; Society of American Foresters, Washington, D.C., executive secretary and managing editor of *Journal of Forestry,* 1937-66; Forest History Society, New Haven, Conn., director of history project, 1966-69. Adviser on forestry to United Nations Food and Agricultural Organization, Rome, Italy, 1957-66.

MEMBER: Forest History Society (fellow), Society of American Foresters (fellow), American Fisheries Society, American Forestry Association (honorary life member), Canadian Institute of Forestry, Soil Conservation Society of America, Natural Resources Council of America, Cosmos Club (Washington, D.C.). *Awards, honors:* Gifford Pinchot Medal of Society of American Foresters, 1957; American Forestry Association Distinguished Service Award, 1970; John Aston Warder Medal, 1977.

WRITINGS: (With Arthur B. Meyer) *The World of the Forest,* Heath, 1965; *Professional Forestry in the United States,* Johns Hopkins Press, 1971; *Crusade for Conservation,* American Forestry Association, 1975.

Editor: *Forestry Education in Pennsylvania,* Pennsylvania State Forestry Alumni Association, 1957; *American Forestry: Six Decades of Growth,* Society of American Foresters, 1960; *Careers in Conservation,* Ronald, 1963; *Origins of American Conservation,* Ronald, 1966; *Leaders of American Conservation,* Ronald, 1971; *Predator–Prey Systems in Fisheries Management,* Sport Fishing Institute, 1979. Also editor of *Black Bass Biology and Management,* 1976, and *Marine Recreational Fisheries,* Volume I, 1976, Volume II, 1977, Volume III, 1978, Volume IV, 1979.

Contributor of more than two hundred articles on conservation and management of natural resources to magazines and professional journals. Associate editor, *Forest Science,* 1947-66; consulting editor, American Fisheries Society, 1970-72, Natural Resources Council of America, and Sport Fishing Institute.

SIDELIGHTS: Henry Clepper told *CA* that he has long worked for "the conservation of renewable natural resources and the soil and water that support them. Their scientific management for the benefit of society is one of the critical challenges facing the world."

* * *

COATS, Peter 1910-

PERSONAL: Born June 26, 1910, in Sundrum, Ayr, Scotland; son of Ernest Symington (a company director) and Nora (Pountney) Coats. *Education:* Attended Eton College, 1923-27. *Religion:* Church of England. *Home:* A I Albany, Piccadilly, London W. 1., England. *Office:* Conde Nast Publications, Vogue House, Hanover Sq., London W. 1., England.

CAREER: Advertising agent in London, England, 1931-39; Conde Nast Publications, London, *House and Garden* (magazine), garden editor, 1948—, garden designer, 1958—. *Military service:* British Army, 1939-46; served in Egypt, Middle

East, and India as aide to F. M. Lord Wavell (commander-in-chief in Middle East, then viceroy of India); became major; mentioned in dispatches. *Member:* Royal Horticulture Society (fellow), Travellers Club (London).

WRITINGS: Roses, Weidenfeld & Nicolson, 1962; *Great Gardens of the Western World,* Weidenfeld & Nicolson, 1963; *Great Gardens of Britain,* Weidenfeld & Nicolson, 1968; *Flowers in History,* Weidenfeld & Nicolson, 1970; *Garden Decoration,* Conde Nast, 1971; *Plants for Connoisseurs,* Conde Nast, 1973; *Of Generals and Gardens* (autobiography), Weidenfeld & Nicolson, 1976; *Gardens of Buckingham Palace,* M. Joseph, 1978.

* * *

COE, Ralph T(racy) 1929-

PERSONAL: Born August 27, 1929, in Cleveland, Ohio; son of Ralph M. Coe; married Sarah Foresman, August, 1961 (divorced). *Education:* Oberlin College, B.A., 1953; Yale University, M.A., 1957. *Home:* San Francisco Towers, No. 704, 2510 Grand, Kansas City, Mo. 64108. *Office:* W. R. Nelson Gallery of Art, 4525 Oak, Kansas City, Mo. 64111.

CAREER: Victoria and Albert Museum, London, England, visiting research assistant, 1957-58; National Gallery of Art, Washington, D.C., assistant curator, 1958-59; W. R. Nelson Gallery of Art, Kansas City, Mo., curator of paintings and sculpture, 1959-65, assistant director, 1965-77, director, 1977—.

WRITINGS: (Co-editor) *American Architecture and Other Writings by Montgomery Schuyler,* Harvard University Press, 1961; *The Imagination of Primitive Man* (book-length exhibition catalogue), Nelson Gallery of Art, 1962; *Popular Art: Artistic Projections of Common Symbols* (catalog essay), Nelson Gallery of Art, 1963; *The Magic Theater: Art Technology Spectacular,* Circle Press, 1970; *Sacred Circles: Two Thousand Years of North American Indian Art* (book-length exhibition catalogue), Arts Council of Great Britain, 1976; *Dale Eldred: Sculpture into Environment,* Regents Press of Kansas, 1978. Also author of several brief exhibition catalogues. Contributor of articles to art periodicals.

WORK IN PROGRESS: A textbook on primitive art.

BIOGRAPHICAL/CRITICAL SOURCES: Kansas City Star, March 21, 1962.†

* * *

COELHO, George Victor 1918-

PERSONAL: Surname is pronounced *Quail*-leo; born November 9, 1918, in Bombay, India; son of Joachim Joseph and Maria Francisca (Souza) Coelho; married Rani Chari, December 23, 1950; children: George, Jr., Anand, Sumangali. *Education:* Bombay University, B.A., 1939, M.A., 1941; University of London, M.A., 1952; Harvard University, Ph.D., 1956. *Home:* 18 Lochs Pond Ct., Rockville, Md. *Office:* National Institute of Mental Health, Rockville, Md. 20057.

CAREER: Haverford College, Haverford, Pa., acting chairman of department of psychology, 1956-58; National Institute of Mental Health, Rockville, Md., visiting scientist at Adult Psychiatry Branch of Intramural Research Division, 1958-64; United Nations Educational, Scientific and Cultural Organization (UNESCO), Paris, France, program specialist, 1964-66; National Institute of Mental Health, chief of Field Studies Section of Division of Extramural Research Programs, 1966-69, deputy to assistant director for behavioral sciences, 1969-72, behavioral science coordinator of Office of Program Planning and Evaluation, 1972—, senior social scientist, Office of Assistant Director for Children and Youth, 1977-79, member of staff, Health Science Administration, 1979—. *Military service:* Indian Army, 1943-50; became major. *Member:* American Psychological Association (fellow), American Association for the Advancement of Science (fellow), American Anthropological Association (fellow).

WRITINGS: Changing Images of America, Free Press of Glencoe, 1958; (editor) *Impacts of Studying Abroad,* American Psychological Association, 1962; (editor with Eli A. Rubinstein) *Behavioral Sciences and Mental Health,* National Institute of Mental Health, 1970; (editor) *Social Change and Mental Health,* National Institute of Mental Health, 1970; (editor) *Coping and Adaptation,* Basic Books, 1974; (editor with P. I. Ahmed) *Toward a New Definition of Health,* Plenum, 1979; (editor with Ahmed) *Uprooting and Development,* Plenum, 1980. Contributor to professional journals.

* * *

COHEN, Arthur A(llen) 1928-

PERSONAL: Born June 25, 1928, in New York, N.Y.; son of Isidore M(eyer) and Bess (Junger) Cohen; married Elaine Firstenberg Lustig (a painter), October 14, 1956; children: Tamar Judith. *Education:* Attended Friends Seminary, New York, N.Y., 1941-44; University of Chicago, B.A., 1946, M.A., 1949, graduate study, 1949-51; additional studies at Union Theological Seminary, 1950, New School for Social Research, 1950, and Columbia University, 1950. *Politics:* "Liberal, if not left, Democrat." *Religion:* Jewish. *Home:* 160 East 70th St., New York, N.Y. 10021. *Agent:* Russell & Volkening, Inc., 551 Fifth Ave., New York, N.Y. 10017. *Office:* 160A East 70th St., New York, N.Y. 10021.

CAREER: Noonday Press, New York City, co-founder and managing director, 1951-55; Meridian Books, Inc., New York City, founder and president, 1955-60; World Publishing Co., New York City, vice-president, 1960-61; Holt, Rinehart & Winston, Inc., New York City, director of religion department, 1961-64, editor-in-chief and vice-president of General Books Division, 1964-68; Viking Press, Inc., New York City, managing editor, 1968-75; Ex Libris (rare book dealer), New York City, founder and president, 1974—. Visiting lecturer, Brown University, 1972, and Jewish Institute of Religion, 1977; Tisch Lecturer in Judaic Theology, Brown University, 1979. Consultant, Fund for the Republic "Religion and the Free Society" project, 1956-59; member of advisory board, Institute for Advanced Judaic Studies, Brandeis University. *Awards, honors:* Edward Lewis Wallant Prize, 1973, for *In the Days of Simon Stern.*

WRITINGS: Martin Buber, Hillary House, 1958; (contributor) *Religion and the Free Society,* Fund for the Republic, 1958; (contributor) *American Catholics: A Protestant-Jewish View,* Sheed, 1959; (editor) *The Anatomy of Faith: Theological Essays of Milton Steinberg,* Harcourt, 1960; *The Natural and the Supernatural Jew: An Historical and Theological Introduction,* Pantheon, 1963; (contributor) *Religion and Contemporary Society,* Macmillan, 1963; (editor) *Humanistic Education and Western Civilization: Essays in Honor of Robert Maynard Hutchins,* Holt, 1964; (contributor) *Christianity: Some Non-Christian Appraisals,* McGraw, 1964; (contributor) *What's Ahead for the Churches?,* Sheed, 1964; (contributor) *Varieties of Jewish Belief,* Reconstructionist Press, 1966; (contributor) *Confrontations with Judaism,* Anthony Blond, 1966; *The Carpenter Years,* New

American Library, 1967; (contributor) *Negro and Jew*, Macmillan, 1967; (contributor) *McLuhan: Pro and Con*, Funk, 1968.

(Editor) *Arguments and Doctrines: A Reader of Jewish Thinking in the Aftermath of the Holocaust*, Harper, 1970; *The Myth of the Judeo-Christian Tradition*, Harper, 1970; *A People Apart: Hasidic Life in America*, Dutton, 1970; *If Not Now, When? Conversations between Mordecai M. Kaplan and Arthur A. Cohen*, Schocken, 1970; *In the Days of Simon Stern*, Random House, 1973; *Osip Emilevich Mandelstam: An Essay in Antiphon*, Ardis, 1974; *Sonia Delaunay*, Abrams, 1975; *A Hero in His Time*, Random House, 1976; (editor) *The New Art of Color: The Writings of Robert and Sonia Delaunay*, Viking, 1978; (contributor) *Dada Spectrum*, Coda Press, 1979; (editor) *The Jew: Essays from Martin Buber's Journal "Der Jude,"* University of Alabama Press, 1980; *Acts of Theft*, Harcourt, 1980.

Managing editor, "Documents of 20th Century Art" series, Viking, 1968-75. Contributor of articles and short stories to numerous publications, including *TriQuarterly*, *Commonweal*, *Partisan Review*, *Cross Currents*, *Midstream*, *Commentary*, *Harper's*, *Saturday Review*, and the *New York Times Book Review*. Member of editorial board, *Judaism*.

WORK IN PROGRESS: A novel, *An Admirable Woman*.

SIDELIGHTS: After spending over twenty (successful) years working and writing in the field of nonfiction, Arthur A. Cohen left the publishing world in 1975 in order to try his luck as a fiction writer. "I was terrified of writing fiction," he recalls, "[and] for years put it off and, as a result, have no drawerful of partial manuscripts or shards from broken ideas. My training was in philosophy and theology, and my passion remains philosophy and theology. People, unfortunately, don't read philosophy and theology, certainly not Jewish theology." Yet despite this awareness of the reading preferences of the general public, Cohen has chosen to draw heavily from philosophy and Jewish theology as a basis for his novels.

The Carpenter Years, for example, tells the story of a Jewish man who, perceiving himself as a failure, abandons his faith, his job, and his family and creates a new identity for himself as a successful and respected "WASP." A *Book World* critic observes: "Can a man who is not a novelist write a good novel? Mr. Cohen is not a novelist. He has mastered the ordinary techniques of modern fiction . . . but he is content to use these techniques passively, never suggesting that he has something *novel* to contribute to the history of the form. Yet *The Carpenter Years* is a good novel. It is good because the man who made it, though not imaginatively gifted, has known how to take advantage of the possibilities of conventional fiction as a medium of discourse and as a tool of investigation. As philosophers use myth, as novelists have sometimes used theology, so Mr. Cohen, a theologian, uses fiction—for purposes foreign to its ends, but proper to his."

"Although I do not think that Mr. Cohen has been particularly successful," notes a *Nation* reviewer, "he has been daring in his choice of a theme. . . . *The Carpenter Years* is apparently an effort at creating a contemporary parable about religion in the United States. Unfortunately, Cohen's protagonist exists only on the edges of the reader's perceptions. . . . [The story] leaves one in a kind of spiritual torpor. . . . The failure in this novel is [the author's] inability to make his religious consciousness decisive for the reader."

A *Christian Century* reviewer, on the other hand, finds that the novel's characters are "vividly drawn and all are observed at close range, as through a zoom lens. Hence the air of claustrophobic tension throughout. The story holds the reader's attention as it speeds to its climax." An *Illustrated London News* critic pronounces it to be a "strong, simple narrative" which is "beautifully written, . . . well observed, and full of implicit wisdom." A *New York Review of Books* critic, however, feels almost exactly the opposite: "Mr. Cohen pushes along a wooden melodramatic plot in the flat, gray no-style of standard commercial fiction. His seriousness exists only on the level of intention, not of imaginative enactment."

Finally, a *Commonweal* reviewer notes: "The barest outline of Arthur Cohen's first novel is intriguing, exciting, filled with promise. . . . It would have to be sure-fire, it would seem, especially if it were by a writer of Arthur Cohen's demonstrated intelligence, cultivation and sensitivity. Unfortunately, it isn't sure-fire at all. *The Carpenter Years* is not a successful novel, which makes for particularly keen disappointment because it is—or has—a number of other very good things. . . . But because Mr. Cohen is not a novelist—at least not yet a novelist—his interests, reflections and ideas are only hung on his characters and events, not embodied in them. . . . It is hard to believe in any of the characters, in fact, and therefore hard to take very seriously the objectively very serious things that happen in the novel. . . . I am afraid that what [the author] was trying to convey in *The Carpenter Years* would have been clearer—and better realized—in one of his philosophic essays."

In the Days of Simon Stern, the story of a post-World War II messiah who uses his vast financial resources to set up a haven for victims of the Holocaust, came under fire for its often obscure and confusing references to personages and concepts of Jewish theology. A *Book World* critic writes: "*In the Days of Simon Stern* is hollow. It blunders about in sociology, psychology, philosophy, all gracelessly, but never tells a convincing story. Instead, Arthur Cohen . . . over-explains every moment to prepare us for any surprise the plot holds in store. . . . And the dialogue—wooden? Solid oak. . . . The writer's fiction is not adequate to his sense of history."

A *Books and Bookmen* critic is even more harsh in his appraisal of *In the Days of Simon Stern*. "Although no human being can be other than harrowed and driven to compassion by the sufferings the Jews have undergone this century, few Gentiles will be able (or willing) to follow Mr. Cohen through this fictional labyrinth, with its theological meanderings, symbolical cobwebberies, stylistic obfuscations and anecdotal cul-de-sacs. . . . No doubt some discerning critics will discover monumental significance in it. Certainly some Jews will be moved by it. I regret to say that I found the book not so much 'deeply moving' as profoundly boring."

A *New York Times Book Review* critic, however, declares that "for a small mountain of reasons, this book ensnares one of the most extra-ordinarily daring ideas to inhabit an American novel in a number of years. . . . In its teeming particularity every vein of this book runs with a brilliance of Jewish insight and erudition to be found in no other novelist. . . . Arthur Cohen is the first writer of any American generation to compose a profoundly Jewish fiction on a profoundly Western theme." A *Commonweal* reviewer refers to *In the Days of Simon Stern* as "a jewel to be treasured; a majestic work of fiction that should stand world literature's test of time, to be read and reread in a search for new meanings and interpretations."

A Hero in His Time was greeted with less polarized reactions. It tells the story of an obscure Soviet Jewish poet who is chosen to attend a writers' conference in New York to read a special poem which, unknown to him, is really a coded message intended for a KGB agent. It is, according to a *Commentary* reviewer, "politically and artistically a more complex work" than the plot suggests, and its focus is quite different from the strong religious and philosophical orientation of Cohen's previous novels. "Well-written and engaging in its ideas, this novel steers an uneven course between comedy and high seriousness. . . . Some of the characters are mere occasions for aspects of social history, and even the hero, though witty and interesting, seems emotionally underdone, too flat for the fictional load he must carry."

A *Time* critic writes that *A Hero in His Time* is "a delightful minor-key farce. . . . [The author] uncannily manages to sound like a U.S.S.R. satirist writing riskily for *Samizdat* circulation. The New York section of the book is weaker; perhaps it should have been written by a Soviet. For the satire of the left-wing academic community lacks teeth, and too many plot turns seem to occur in the last third of the novel, simply because something has to happen." A *National Observer* reviewer thinks that *A Hero in His Time* "may well be the most deceptive book of the season. In tone, in 'feel,' Arthur A. Cohen's novel seems at the outset a kind of fable. . . . [It] is indeed an acidly funny fable, but it is a deeply human, moving fable as well. It is the sort of book that a rummager always hopes to find."

Finally, a critic in *New Statesman* writes: "It takes, perhaps, a scholarly Jewish writer such as Arthur Cohen . . . to be able to get inside the imaginative life of Russian Jews. . . . But important though the author's Jewish sympathies and inside knowledge are, they're not by themselves enough to guarantee the amazing *tour de force* that *A Hero in His Time* represents. . . . [It] is solid, believable, and quite astonishing from an American, even a Jewish-American, writer."

Acts of Theft represents somewhat of a departure from Cohen's previous novels in that it does not deal specifically with American Judaism; instead, it tells the story of a European sculptor residing in Mexico who supplements his income by stealing various pieces of pre-Colombian art from archaeological sites in order to sell them to collectors. The tone of the novel is decidedly philosophical, however, for in the confrontation between the thief and the clever Mexican detective who tracks him down, the author's real concerns come to the forefront. As the *New York Times'* John Leonard explains, *Acts of Theft* is an exploration of "the artist as God, art as theft, the ransom of the past, the ancient made modern, pride and sacrifice"; Mark Shechner of the *New York Times Book Review* describes it as a study of "the corruptions that attend the worship of graven images."

As a result of this preoccupation, continues Shechner, "those who buy this book expecting a straightforward drama of crime and detection will find Mauger [the main character] sadly easy to catch. He drops clues everywhere. This is because, I guess, Mr. Cohen doesn't want the dramatics of pursuit and evasion to distract us from his ruminations on the morality of art. Hence he short-circuits his plot with flashbacks, asides, interior monologues, lectures, the works, for the sake of depth, weight and moral tone. But rather than challenging the reader, this strategy only exasperates him. . . . Mr. Cohen plies us with vivid and passionate yearnings that overpower his plot and overwhelm his sentences. . . . The trouble with *Acts of Theft* is that Mr. Cohen wants the sublime but can achieve only the breathless, which works in fiction about as well as it does in religion."

The *Washington Post*'s Joseph McLellan, on the other hand, feels that Cohen *has* achieved a successful blend of philosophy and drama in *Acts of Theft*. He notes: "On one level, *Acts of Theft* is a very elaborate story of cops and robbers—but it aspires to much more and its aspirations are largely fulfilled. The parallels that spring to mind are *Crime and Punishment* or *Les Miserables,* and if it does not have quite the depth of the one or the sweeping scope of the other, it is certainly more than a routine novel. Its texture is rich. . . . Its central characters are deeply pondered, and the metaphysical concerns that drive them are rendered not only in occasional dialogues a la Plato but in gestures both concrete and symbolic that add up to a well-engineered plot. . . . Underlying all these is the subject of sculpture—though the intricate weaving of thematic strands makes Arthur Cohen's technique seem more like that of a tapestry."

In conclusion, the *New York Times'* Leonard writes: "In his new novel, Arthur A. Cohen assigns himself the formidable task of making us believe in art—sculpture—that we can't see, of evoking space shaped in silence, 'essential things,' by a piling on of words. That he succeeds should come as no surprise. . . . We believe in [the main character]. . . . We believe because Mr. Cohen has somehow found words that amount to a revelation instead of an excuse."

As Cohen himself explained to *CA:* "Writing fiction is a moral act, even if the substantive vision is indifferent to morality. This is only to say that I try to tell the truth even if it persuades no one."

AVOCATIONAL INTERESTS: Horseback riding, traveling, learning languages.

BIOGRAPHICAL/CRITICAL SOURCES: Library Journal, October 1, 1966; *Christian Science Monitor,* February 23, 1967; *Christian Century,* March 1, 1967, March 10, 1971; *Book World,* March 12, 1967, July 29, 1973; *Commentary,* April, 1967, November, 1969, November, 1970, October, 1976; *Observer,* April 2, 1967; *Illustrated London News,* April 22, 1967; *Times Literary Supplement,* April 27, 1967, November 9, 1967; *New York Review of Books,* June 1, 1967; *Books and Bookmen,* July, 1967, March, 1976; *Nation,* July 3, 1967; *Commonweal,* September 8, 1967, September 28, 1973; *New York Times,* January 27, 1968, February 12, 1980, February 22, 1980; *New York Times Book Review,* June 3, 1973, March 9, 1980; *Time,* January 5, 1976; *Newsweek,* January 12, 1976; *Publishers Weekly,* January 19, 1976; *New Statesman,* February 27, 1976; *National Observer,* April 3, 1976; *Contemporary Literary Criticism,* Volume VII, Gale, 1977; *Washington Post,* March 21, 1980.

—*Sketch by Deborah A. Straub*

* * *

COHEN, Daniel 1936-

PERSONAL: Born March 12, 1936, in Chicago, Ill.; son of M. Milton and Sue (Greenberg) Cohen; married Susan Handler (a writer), February 2, 1959; children: Theodora. *Education:* University of Illinois, journalism degree, 1959. *Home and office:* 24 Elizabeth St., Port Jervis, N.Y. 12771. *Agent:* Henry Morrison, Inc., 58 West 10th St., New York, N.Y. 10011.

CAREER: Science Digest (magazine), New York, N.Y., managing editor, 1960-69; writer for adults and young people, 1969—. *Member:* Author's Guild, National Association of Science Writers, Audubon Society, Committee for the Scientific Investigation of Claims of the Paranormal, Appalachian Mountain Club.

WRITINGS—Published by Dodd, except as indicated:

Myths of the Space Age, 1967; *Mysterious Places,* 1969; *A Modern Look at Monsters,* 1970; *Masters of the Occult,* 1971; *Voodoo, Devils, and the New Invisible World,* 1972; *The Far Side of Consciousness,* 1974; *Biorhythms in Your Life,* Fawcett, 1976; *Close Encounters with God,* Pocket Books, 1979.

Young adult nonfiction: *Secrets from Ancient Graves,* Dodd, 1968; *Vaccination and You,* Messner, 1968; *The Age of Giant Mammals,* Dodd, 1969; *Animals of the City,* McGraw, 1969.

Night Animals, Messner, 1970; *Conquerors on Horseback,* Doubleday, 1970; *Talking with Animals,* Dodd, 1971; *Superstition,* Creative Education Press, 1971; *A Natural History of Unnatural Things,* Dutton, 1971; *Ancient Monuments and How They Were Built,* McGraw, 1971; *Watchers in the Wild,* Little, Brown, 1972; *In Search of Ghosts,* Dodd, 1972; *The Magic Art of Foreseeing the Future,* Dodd, 1973; *How Did Life Get There?,* Messner, 1973; *Magicians, Wizards, and Sorcerers,* Lippincott, 1973; *How the World Will End,* McGraw, 1973; *Shaka: King of the Zulus,* Doubleday, 1973; *ESP: The Search beyond the Senses,* Harcourt, 1973; *The Black Death,* F. Watts, 1974; *The Magic of the Little People,* Messner, 1974; *Curses, Hexes, and Spells,* Lippincott, 1974; *Intelligence: What Is It?,* M. Evans, 1974; *Not of the World,* Follett, 1974; *Human Nature, Animal Nature,* McGraw, 1974.

The Mysteries of Reincarnation, Dodd, 1975; *The Greatest Monsters in the World,* Dodd, 1975; *The Body Snatchers,* Lippincott, 1975; *The Human Side of Computers,* McGraw, 1975; *Monsters, Giants, and Little Men from Mars,* Doubleday, 1975; *The New Believers,* M. Evans, 1975; *The Spirit of the Lord,* Four Winds, 1975; *Animal Territories,* Hastings House, 1975; *Mysterious Disappearances,* Dodd, 1976; *The Ancient Visitors,* Doubleday, 1976; *Dreams, Visions, and Drugs,* F. Watts, 1976; *Gold,* M. Evans, 1976; *Supermonsters,* Dodd, 1977; *Ghostly Animals,* Doubleday, 1977; *The Science of Spying,* McGraw, 1977; *Real Ghosts,* Dodd, 1977; *Meditation,* Dodd, 1977; *What Really Happened to the Dinosaurs?,* Dutton, 1977; *Creativity: What Is It?,* M. Evans, 1977; *Ceremonial Magic,* Four Winds, 1978; *The World of UFOs,* Lippincott, 1978; *The World's Most Famous Ghosts,* Dodd, 1978; *Young Ghosts,* Dutton, 1978; *Frauds, Hoaxes, and Swindles,* F. Watts, 1979; *Missing,* Dodd, 1979; *Mysteries of the World,* Doubleday, 1979; *What's Happening to Our Weather,* M. Evans, 1979; *Dealing with the Devil,* Dodd, 1979; *Famous Curses,* Dodd, 1979; *Great Mistakes,* M. Evans, 1979.

The Monsters of "Star Trek," Pocket Books, 1980; *Monsters You Never Heard Of,* Dodd, 1980; *The Tomb Robbers,* McGraw, 1980; *Bigfoot: America's Number One Monster,* Pocket Books, 1980. Contributor to *People's Almanac, New York Kids' Book, Doubleday Encyclopedia of UFOs,* and *Science and the Paranormal.* Contributing editor to *Science Digest.*

WORK IN PROGRESS: Several books about monsters, a book on conspiracies, and a book on legends of contemporary teenagers.

SIDELIGHTS: Daniel Cohen told *CA:* "I am a professional writer and a fairly prolific one, though I have set no speed records and am not trying for any. With Asimov around there is no chance for a record anyway. I simply try to do the best work that I possibly can and still make a living."

BIOGRAPHICAL/CRITICAL SOURCES: Christian Science Monitor, April 1, 1971; *New York Times Book Review,* April 16, 1972, July 6, 1975; *Teacher,* December, 1974; *Scientific American,* December, 1976; *Childhood Education,* April, 1977; *Books & Bookmen,* December, 1977; *Children's Literature Review,* Volume III, Gale, 1978; *Times Educational Supplement,* February 3, 1978; *Commonweal,* November 10, 1978.

* * *

COLBERG, Marshall R(udolph) 1913-

PERSONAL: Born June 11, 1913, in Chicago, Ill.; son of Rudolph Emanuel and Elvira (Wester) Colberg; married Peggy Lou Dean, 1942 (died, 1964); marreid Grace G. Metz, 1976; children: (first marriage) Marsha, Daniel. *Education:* University of Chicago, A.B., 1934, A.M., 1938; University of Michigan, Ph.D., 1950. *Home:* 4509 Andrew Jackson Way, Tallahassee, Fla. 32303. *Office:* Department of Economics, Florida State University, Tallahassee, Fla. 32306.

CAREER: War Production Board, Washington, D.C., statistician, 1940-43; Civilian Production Administration, Washington, D.C., economist, 1946-47; U.S. Air Force, Washington, D.C., program analyst, 1947-50; Florida State University, Tallahassee, associate professor, 1950-53, professor of economics, 1953—, head of department, 1955-67. *Military service:* U.S. Army Air Forces, 1943-46. *Member:* Southern Economic Association (vice-president, 1960; president-elect, 1961; president, 1962), American Economic Association (member of committee on economic education, 1964-71), Mount Pelerin Society. *Awards, honors:* Grant from Inter-University Committee for research on the South; grant from Social Security Administration.

WRITINGS: (Co-author) *Prices, Income, and Public Policy,* McGraw, 1954, 2nd edition, 1959; (co-author) *Business Economics,* Irwin, 1957, 5th edition, 1975; (co-author) *Factors in the Location of Florida Industry,* Florida State University Press, 1962; *Human Capital in Southern Development: 1939-63,* University of North Carolina Press, 1965; *Consumer Impact of Repeal of 14-B,* Heritage Foundation, 1978; *The Social Security Retirement Test: Right or Wrong?,* American Enterprise Institute for Public Policy Research, 1978. Contributor to economics journals.

WORK IN PROGRESS: Universal Coverage under Social Security, for American Enterprise Institute for Public Policy Research; 6th edition, *Business Economics.*

* * *

COLEMAN, James C(ovington) 1914-

PERSONAL: Born October 19, 1914, in Salem, N.H.; son of J. C. and Mary (Lillie) Coleman; divorced. *Education:* University of California, Los Angeles, B.A. (with highest honors), 1938, Ph.D., 1942. *Home:* 20178 Rockport Way, Malibu, Calif. 90265. *Office:* Department of Psychology, University of California, Los Angeles, 405 Hilgard, Los Angeles, Calif. 90024.

CAREER: University of California, Los Angeles, instructor, 1942-45; University of Kansas, Lawrence, assistant professor, 1945-47; University of New Mexico, Albuquerque, assistant professor of psychology and head of psychology clinic, 1947-48; University of Southern California, Los Angeles, assistant professor of psychology, 1948-50; University of California, Los Angeles, 1950—, began as assistant professor, professor of education, 1963—, director, Psychology Clinic School, 1950-64. Member of board of directors, Los Angeles Psychiatric Service, 1956-58; consultant, Adams Schools, 1956-57. *Member:* American Psychological Association, Western Psychological Association, Los Angeles

County Psychological Association, International Reading Association.

WRITINGS—Published by Scott, Foresman, except as indicated: (With others) *Abnormal Psychology and Modern Life,* 1950, 6th edition, 1979; *Personality Dynamics and Effective Behavior,* 1960, 2nd edition published as *Psychology and Effective Behavior,* 1969, 3rd edition (with Constance L. Hammen), published as *Contemporary Psychology and Effective Behavior,* 4th edition, 1979; (with Frieda Bernston Libaw and William D. Martinson) *Success in College,* 1960; (with F. B. Libaw) *Successful Study,* 1960; *Abnormal Behavior,* William C. Brown, 1966, 2nd edition (with Richard L. Hagen), 1973.

"Deep-Sea Adventure" series for slow readers; with Frank Hewett, Frances Berres, and William Briscoe; all published by H. Wagner: *Danger Below,* 1962, 2nd edition, 1967; *Rocket Divers,* 1962, 2nd edition, 1967; *Whale Hunt,* 1962, 2nd edition, 1967; *Frogmen in Action,* 1962, 2nd edition, 1967; *The Sea Hunt,* 1962, 2nd edition, 1967; *The Pearl Divers,* 1962, 2nd edition, 1967.

Also author of screenplay for film on abnormal behavior, American Broadcasting Corp., 1970. Contributor of articles to journals.

WORK IN PROGRESS: Integration of research literature on relation of stress to bodily and psychological disorders.

SIDELIGHTS: James C. Coleman told *CA* that his "primary motivation in writing is twofold—to contribute materials helpful to children experiencing serious learning difficulties (and to their parents) [and] to contribute instructional materials that bring [the] latest scientific findings and trends in an integrated way to college and university students—and hopefully to be of assistance to instructors in providing up-to-date instructional materials and programs."†

* * *

COLEMAN, John R(oyston) 1921-

PERSONAL: Born June 24, 1921, in Copper Cliff, Ontario, Canada; came to United States in 1946, became citizen in 1954; son of Richard M. (an engineer) and Mary Irene (Lawson) Coleman; married Mary N. Irwin, October 1, 1943 (divorced, 1966); children: John M., Nancy J., Patty A., Paul R., Stephen W. *Education:* University of Toronto, B.A., 1943; University of Chicago, M.A., 1949, Ph.D., 1950. *Home:* 300 Central Park W., New York, N.Y. 10024. *Office:* Edna McConnell Clark Foundation, 250 Park Ave., New York, N.Y. 10017.

CAREER: Massachusetts Institute of Technology, Cambridge, instructor, 1949-51, assistant professor of economics, 1951-55; Carnegie Institute of Technology (now Carnegie-Mellon University), Pittsburgh, Pa., associate professor, 1957-60, professor of economics and head of department, 1960-62, dean of humanities and social sciences, 1963-65; Ford Foundation, New York City, associate director of economic development and administration, 1965-66, program officer in charge of social development, 1966-67; Haverford College, Haverford, Pa., president, 1967-77; Edna McConnell Clark Foundation, New York City, president, 1977—. Teacher on CBS College of the Air, "American Economy" program, 1962-63. Consultant in India, Ford Foundation, 1960-61; chairman of board of directors, Federal Reserve Bank of Philadelphia, 1973-76; director, Provident Mutual Life Insurance Co.; trustee, Philadelphia Savings Fund Society. *Military service:* Royal Canadian Navy, 1943-45; became lieutenant. *Member:* American Economic Association, Industrial Relations Research Association, National Academy of Arbitrators, United Nations Association of Pittsburgh (president, 1962-65), Western Pennsylvania Council on Economic Education (chairman, 1964-65). *Awards, honors:* LL.D. from Beaver College, 1963, University of Pennsylvania, 1968, and Gannon College, 1975; Atheneum Medal for best book by a Philadelphian, 1974; L.H.D. from Manhattanville College, 1975, and Emory and Henry College, 1977; D.Litt. from Haverford College, 1980; Christopher Award for *Blue Collar Journal;* two Myrtle Awards from Hadassah.

WRITINGS: Goals and Strategy in Collective Bargaining, Harper, 1951; *Readings in Economics,* McGraw, 1952, 5th edition, 1967; *Labor Problems,* McGraw, 1953, 2nd edition, 1959; *Television Study Guide for the American Economy,* McGraw, 1962; *Comparative Economic Systems,* Holt, 1966, 2nd edition, 1968; *The Changing American Economy,* Basic Books, 1967; *Blue Collar Journal,* Lippincott, 1974. Author of column in *Philadelphia Sunday Bulletin.* Contributor of articles to *American Economic Review, American Journal of Sociology, Labor Law, New York Times Magazine, TV Guide, Industrial and Labor Relations Review,* and other periodicals.

WORK IN PROGRESS: We Are What We Do; . . . And Throw Away the Key.

SIDELIGHTS: At his inauguration as president of Haverford College, John R. Coleman expressed the opinion that college students should integrate travel and work experience into their formal education; students who break their educational "lockstep," according to Coleman, often reflect more maturity and increased awareness of what they want from their college experience. Distressed by the attack of construction workers on student peace demonstrators in the Wall Street area of New York City and by the building trades council parade against the peace movement, Coleman decided to break his own academic "lockstep" and reenter the blue-collar world. During the spring semester of 1973, he worked as a sewer worker and ditch digger in Atlanta, as a sandwich and salad maker in a Boston restaurant, and as a garbage collector in a Maryland suburb of Washington D.C. He continued to meet monthly with the board of directors of the Federal Reserve Bank of Philadelphia as his only contact with the white collar world.

In *Blue Collar Journal,* Coleman wrote about the new perspective his work as a manual laborer had given him on his own academic and white collar life. "I'm learning more about what we have in common than about what drives us apart. The truth is that we are all somewhat mixed-up and some of us in both worlds are happy about even that fact." The book, which was well-received, lent credence to Coleman's educational philosophy. C. C. Walton wrote: "Other college presidents (and I am one of that beleaguered breed) will read this journal with envy or cynicism. . . . His journal teaches us lessons once learned and then, often, soon forgot. . . . [Coleman learned] many things. He recognized the stupidity of facile generalizations regarding workers and their views. . . . Economic theory took on bruising meaning for Coleman, the professional economist, when he compared income and expenses and experienced the chagrin of being marginally solvent." Benjamin DeMott commented that the journal "summons memories of the best American dream, namely that our purpose, the national destiny, was nothing other than to achieve a full democratization of mind." According to Janet Chusmir, Coleman "learned how many other people want to do what he did. They, too, have their

Walter Mitty dreams.... 'Humble dreams like mine,' he says."

BIOGRAPHICAL/CRITICAL SOURCES: Miami Herald, January 17, 1974; *New Republic,* March 16, 1974; *Atlantic,* August, 1974; *Authors in the News,* Volume I, Gale, 1976.

* * *

COLLINS, George R(oseborough) 1917-

PERSONAL: Born September 2, 1917, in Springfield, Mass.; son of Harold Fisher and Lucy Roseborough (Mackay) Collins; married Rosanne G. Walker, 1947 (died, 1948); married Christiane Crasemann, 1950; children: David Walker, Nicolas Bernd, Luke Malte. *Education:* Princeton University, B.A., 1939, M.F.A., 1942. *Home:* 448 Riverside Dr., New York, N.Y. 10027. *Office:* Department of Art History, Columbia University, New York, N.Y. 10027.

CAREER: United Nations Relief and Rehabilitation Administration Displaced Persons Operations, director of refugee center in Germany, 1945-46; Columbia University, New York, N.Y., instructor, 1946-49, assistant professor, 1949-54, associate professor, 1954-62, professor of art history, 1962—, member of departmental executive committee, 1957—, departmental representative to School of General Studies, 1951-57, member of committee on instruction, 1954-57, executive secretary of university art program, 1958—, director of Amigos de Gaudi—U.S.A., 1958—, member of advisory committee of Center for Mass Communications, 1959. Visiting scholar, Vassar College, 1967; Hans Vetter Memorial Lecturer, Carnegie-Mellon University, 1973. Member of board of directors, American Field Service Scholarship Program, 1946-48, Gardens Nursery School, 1957-61, Spanish Institute, Inc., 1961—, Drawing Center, 1977—. *Wartime service:* American Field Service, 1942-45, director of training for Italian Theatre of Operations; received three battle stars. *Member:* Society of Architectural Historians, College Art Association, William Morris Society, Medieval Club (New York). *Awards, honors:* Columbia University Council on Research in Humanities grant, 1958, for research in Spain; American Council of Learned Societies grants, 1959, to secure materials for establishment of an archive of Catalan art and architecture at Columbia University, and 1964, to study Catalan vaulting in the United States; Guggenheim fellow, 1962-63; Rockefeller humanities fellowship, 1976-77; honorary doctorate from Universidad Politecnica de Barcelona, 1977.

WRITINGS: (Editor and contributor) *Introduction to the Arts,* Columbia University Press, 1955; *Antonio Gaudi,* Braziller, 1960; (translator and editor with wife, Christiane C. Collins) *Architecture of Fantasy,* Praeger, 1963 (translator with C. C. Collins) Camillo Sitte, *City Planning According to Artistic Principles,* Phaidon, 1965; (with C. C. Collins) *Camillo Sitte and the Birth of Modern City Planning,* Random House, 1965; (compiler with Maurice E. Farinas) *A Bibliography of Antonio Gaudi and the Catalan Movement, 1870-1930,* University Press of Virginia, 1973; (editor with William Alex) Nikolai A. Miliutin, *Sotsgorod: The Problem of Building Socialist Cities,* MIT Press, 1974; *Visionary Drawings of Architecture and Planning: The 20th Century through the 1960's,* MIT Press, 1979. Also author of several booklets. General editor, "Cities and Planning" series, Braziller, 1966—. Contributor to encyclopedias and journals. Editor and contributor, *Proceedings of the Modern Architecture Symposium,* Columbia University, 1962, 1964.

COMFORT, Alex(ander) 1920-

PERSONAL: Born February 10, 1920, in London, England; son of Alexander Charles and Daisy Elizabeth (Fenner) Comfort; married Ruth Muriel Harris, 1943 (divorced, 1973); married Jane Tristram Henderson, 1973; children: (first marriage) Nicholas Alfred Fenner. *Education:* Trinity College, Cambridge, B.A., 1943, M.B., B.Ch., 1944, M.A., 1945; London Hospital, M.R.C.S., L.R.C.P., 1944; University of London, D.C.H., 1946, Ph.D. (biochemistry), 1949, D.Sc. (gerontology), 1963. *Politics:* "Anarchist." *Home:* 683 Oak Grove Dr., Santa Barbara, Calif. 93108.

CAREER: London Hospital, London, England, house physician, 1944; Royal Waterloo Hospital, London, resident medical officer, 1944-45; London Hospital Medical College, London, lecturer in physiology, 1945-51; University of London, University College, London, Nuffield research fellow in gerontology in department of zoology, 1952-64, director of Medical Research Council Group on Aging, 1965-73; Stanford University, Stanford, Calif., clinical lecturer in department of psychiatry, 1974—; Institute for Higher Studies, Santa Barbara, Calif., fellow, 1975—; University of California, School of Medicine, Irvine, professor in department of pathology, 1976-79; University of California, Los Angeles, Neuropsychiatric Institute, adjunct professor, 1979—. Consultant psychiatrist, Brentwood VA Hospital, 1977—. *Wartime service:* Conscientious objector during World War II. *Member:* British Society for Research on Aging, Royal Society of Medicine, American Medical Association, American Psychiatric Association, Gerontological Society, American Association of Sex Educators, Counselors, and Therapists, Conchological Society, Malacological Society, Peace Pledge Union (sponsor). *Awards, honors:* Ciba Foundation Prize for research in gerontology, 1958; Borestone Poetry Award, second prize, 1962; Karger Memorial Prize, 1969.

WRITINGS: First Year Physiological Technique, Staples, 1948; *Sexual Behavior in Society,* Viking, 1950, published as *Sex in Society,* Duckworth, 1963, Citadel, 1966; *Authority and Delinquency in the Modern State: A Criminological Approach to the Problem of Power,* Routledge & Kegan Paul, 1950, published as *Authority and Delinquency,* Sphere, 1970; *The Biology of Senescence,* Rinehart, 1956, published as *Ageing: The Biology of Senescence,* Holt, 1964; *The Process of Ageing,* New American Library, 1964; *The Anxiety Makers: Some Curious Preoccupations of the Medical Profession,* Thomas Nelson (London), 1967, Dell, 1969; (editor) *The Joy of Sex: A Cordon Bleu Guide to Lovemaking,* Simon & Schuster, 1972, revised edition published as *The Joy of Sex: A Gourmet Guide to Lovemaking,* Crown, 1972; (editor) *More Joy,* Mitchell Beazley, 1973, published as *More Joy: A Lovemaking Companion to "The Joy of Sex,"* Crown, 1974; *A Good Age,* Crown, 1975; *Sexual Consequences of Disability,* Stickley, 1978; *I and That: Notes on the Biology of Religion,* Crown, 1979; (with wife, Jane T. Comfort) *The Facts of Love,* Crown, 1979; *A Practice of Geriatric Psychiatry,* American Elsevier, 1980.

Essay and lecture collections: *Art and Social Responsibility: Lectures on the Ideology of Romanticism,* Falcon Press, 1946, reprinted, Pendejo Press, 1971; *The Novel and Our Time,* Phoenix House, 1948, reprinted, Pendejo Press, 1969; *Barbarism and Sexual Freedom: Lectures on the Sociology of Sex from the Standpoint of Anarchism,* Freedom Press, 1948, reprinted, Haskell House, 1977; *Darwin and the Naked Lady: Discursive Essays on Biology and Art,* Routledge & Kegan Paul, 1961, Braziller, 1962; *The Nature of Human Nature,* Harper, 1966 (published in England as *Nature and*

Human Nature, Weidenfeld & Nicolson, 1966); *What Is a Doctor?,* Stickley, 1980.

Novels: *The Silver River,* Chapman & Hall, 1937; *No Such Liberty,* Chapman & Hall, 1941; *The Almond Tree,* Chapman & Hall, 1943; *The Powerhouse,* Viking, 1945; *On This Side Nothing,* Routledge & Kegan Paul, 1948, Viking, 1949; *A Giant's Strength,* Routledge & Kegan Paul, 1952; *Come out to Play,* Eyre & Spottiswoode, 1961; *Tetrarch,* Shambhala, 1980.

Poetry: *France and Other Poems,* Favil Press, 1942; *A Wreath for the Living,* Routledge & Kegan Paul, 1942; (contributor) *Three New Poets: Roy McFadden, Alex Comfort, Ian Serraillier,* Grey Walls Press, 1942; *Elegies,* Routledge & Kegan Paul, 1944; *The Song of Lazarus,* Viking, 1945; *The Signal to Engage,* Routledge & Kegan Paul, 1946; *And All But He Departed,* Routledge & Kegan Paul, 1951; *Haste to the Wedding,* Eyre & Spottiswoode, 1962; *All But a Rib: Poems Chiefly of Women,* Mitchell Beazley, 1973; *Poems for Jane,* Crown, 1979.

Plays: *Into Egypt,* Grey Walls Press, 1942; *Cities of the Plain: A Democratic Melodrama,* Grey Walls Press, 1943.

Other: *Letters from an Outpost* (stories), Routledge & Kegan Paul, 1947; *The Pattern of the Future* (radio programs), Routledge & Kegan Paul, 1949; *Are You Sitting Comfortably?* (political songs), Sing Magazine, 1962; (editor and translator) Kokkoka, *The Koka Shastra and Other Mediaeval Writings on Love,* Allen & Unwin, 1964, Stein & Day, 1965; (editor) Inge and Sten Hegeler, *An Abz of Love,* Nevill Spearman, 1969.

Contributor of more than 500 articles to literary and professional journals. Editor, with Peter Wells, of *Poetry Folios,* 1942-44; editor, *New Road,* 1943-44.

WORK IN PROGRESS: Tiger, Tiger, a novel set in modern India; the fictional diary of Nero's physician; studies relating neurology to physics and philosophy.

SIDELIGHTS: "Alex Comfort," writes Theodore Solotaroff, "is a remarkable English writer in whom the 'two cultures' have come together in a sturdy, companionable, and fertile marriage. A biologist who publishes good fiction and poetry, a specialist in the problems of aging as well as of the erotic literature of India, a planner of a new 'technology of the emotions,' and an anarchist who writes lyrics for Pete Seeger, Comfort is a genuine man of parts: a C. P. Snow raised to the next power." Wayne Burns calls Comfort a "scientific humanist"; that is, a scientist who has a clear understanding of how his knowledge can be applied to human problems. "In his own work," Burns writes, "he makes the fullest use of scientific knowledge, drawing most heavily upon the discoveries of advanced psychiatrists and anthropologists. Finally, and perhaps most important in this connection, he realizes that science is not opposed to art, that, rather, the two modes of knowledge complement one another."

Though well-known and highly respected in professional circles for his pioneering work in gerontological research, Comfort is perhaps best known to the general reading public as the author of *The Joy of Sex* and its sequel, *More Joy.* A *Saturday Review* critic contends that "the only self-help book ever worth a dang was Alex Comfort's *The Joy of Sex,* which was also one of the few *huge* best-sellers that deserved to be so. Indeed, Dr. Comfort is to sex what Dr. Spock is to child-rearing." On the other hand, a *New Statesman* reviewer, noting that the book is "full of gastronomic imagery" (for example, sections have headings such as "Starters" and "Main Courses"), finds *The Joy of Sex* quite "ludicrous" and wonders how any intelligent person can take it seriously. The book, he says, is "a rather depressing sex manual . . . written in the illiterate, folksy style one associates with holiday camps and *Blue Peter.*"

More Joy was also criticized for its somewhat "folksy" approach. This book, according to an *Atlantic* reviewer, "commits itself unreservedly to the cool-sex cause. . . . The latter tone wasn't noticeable in Dr. Comfort's *The Joy of Sex,* but here it's pervasive. . . . The author's easygoing diction . . . is unchanged, as is his assurance that 'we manufacture our own nonsenses,' and his adeptness at *Village Voice* patter. . . . It's Easyrider cool that the mass audience is offered as a model. . . . Some will contend that this second volume . . . is less an attempt at consolidation and understanding of The Revolution than a fresh exploitation of the middle-class porn markets. . . . But at the risk of solemnity, it needs to be repeated that the point of real moment lies elsewhere, in the fact that, like its predecessor, this volume of instruction in how to think, feel and do has won a mass audience. Its endorsement of cool-sex larking, its tutoring in disengagement, is being heard."

A Good Age represents Comfort's attempt to portray the joys of aging in the same basic encyclopedic style as *The Joy of Sex.* "Dr. Comfort has progressed quite naturally to the joy of age," notes a *New York Times* critic. "But while most of his remarks are both useful and reasonable, he sometimes seems unduly optimistic in both of these areas. . . . A man who writes two books about joy in the 1970s shows what might be called a prejudice in favor of the positive. . . . He seems not to realize that what he is suggesting [viewing the middle age identity crisis as a second chance to 'seize life in a passionate embrace'] requires an effort not very far short of moral and physical heroism."

A *New York Times Book Review* critic agrees that "much of the spirit of [*The Joy of Sex* and *More Joy*] illuminates [*A Good Age.* It] is at once poetic, passionate, gently ironic, humane—and lucid, practical, tough-minded and detailed. . . . It is not a handbook, a manual, a list of agencies, drugs or diets. Sometimes there is advice . . . but most often it offers a different point of view, another way of looking at oldness, and therefore a rationale for a different kind of problem-solving. . . . There is a weakness in *A Good Age,* but it is a minor one. Dr. Comfort understands that 'the real curse of being old is the ejection from a citizenship traditionally based on work.' . . . [But] nowhere does *A Good Age* really address change on this political and economic level—but it is a magnificent preamble to that effort."

A *Book World* reviewer writes that *A Good Age* "has the same kind of refreshingly unclouded perceptions as *The Joy of Sex*. . . . This compendium consolidates some recent gains in what amounts to a revolution in popular opinion, and it would be well for the young as the old to become familiar with its ideas."

When asked to describe himself, Comfort replies that he is a "medical biologist, writer, and pamphleteer, dividing time equally between science, literature, and politico-social agitation of various kinds, chiefly connected with anarchism, pacifism, sex law reforms, and application of sociological ideas to society generally." In 1962, he was jailed along with Bertrand Russell and others for organizing an anti-nuclear sit-down in London's Trafalgar Square.

BIOGRAPHICAL/CRITICAL SOURCES: Derek Stanford, *The Freedom of Poetry,* Falcon Press, 1947; *Humanist,* November/December, 1951; *Times Literary Supplement,*

January 12, 1967, July 20, 1967; *Observer,* June 11, 1967, July 30, 1967; *Listener,* July 13, 1967; *New Leader,* August 14, 1967; *New Republic,* October 14, 1967; *New Statesman,* April 12, 1974; *Saturday Review,* September 7, 1974; *Time,* October 7, 1974; *Atlantic,* April, 1975; *New York Times,* November 10, 1976; *New York Times Book Review,* November 28, 1976; *Book World,* December 5, 1976, November 11, 1979; *Best Sellers,* January, 1977; *Contemporary Literary Criticism,* Volume VII, Gale, 1977.

—*Sketch by Deborah A. Straub*

* * *

CONDON, George Edward 1916-

PERSONAL: Born November 6, 1916, in Fall River, Mass.; son of John J. (an expert on cotton weaving) and Mary (O'Malley) Condon; married Marjorie P. Smith (a school teacher), May 9, 1942; children: Theresa A., John R., George E., Jr., Katherine E., Mary P., Susan E. *Education:* Ohio State University, B.S., 1940. *Politics:* Independent. *Religion:* Roman Catholic. *Home:* 1096 Erie Cliff Dr., Lakewood, Ohio 44107. *Office: Cleveland Plain Dealer,* 1801 Superior Ave., Cleveland, Ohio 44114.

CAREER: Mount Union College, Alliance, Ohio, publicity director, 1941; U.S. Department of Agriculture, Agricultural Adjustment Administration, Columbus, Ohio, information director, 1942-43; *Cleveland Plain Dealer,* Cleveland, Ohio, reporter, copy editor, radio and television editor, 1943-62, columnist, 1962—. *Member:* Cleveland Press Club, Sigma Delta Chi, Pi Sigma Alpha.

WRITINGS: Cleveland: The Best Kept Secret, Doubleday, 1967; *Laughter from the Rafters,* Doubleday, 1968; *Stars in the Water,* Doubleday, 1974; *Yesterday's Cleveland,* E. A. Seemann, 1976; *Yesterday's Columbus,* E. A. Seemann, 1977; *Cleveland: Prodigy of the Western Reserve,* Continental Heritage, 1979.

* * *

CONE, Molly Lamken 1918-
(Caroline More)

PERSONAL: Born October 3, 1918, in Tacoma, Wash.; daughter of Arthur and Frances (Sussman) Lamken; married Gerald J. Cone, September 9, 1939; children: Susan, Gary, Ellen. *Education:* Attended University of Washington, 1936-39. *Politics:* Democrat. *Religion:* Jewish. *Home address:* Box 1005, Suquamish, Wash. 98392. *Agent:* McIntosh and Otis, Inc., 475 Fifth Ave., New York, N.Y. 10017.

CAREER: Advertising copywriter. Writer of books for children. *Awards, honors:* Theta Sigma Phi, woman of achievement award, 1960, Matrix Table Award, 1968; citation by the *New York Times* as one of the 100 outstanding books for young readers, 1962, for *Mishmash;* Governor's Festival of Arts Certificate of Recognition, State of Washington, 1966, 1970; Myrtle Wreath Achievement Award, Hadassah (Seattle chapter), 1967; literary creativity citation, Music and Art Foundation of Seattle, 1968; Washington Press Women first place award for juvenile books, 1969, for *Annie, Annie,* 1970, for *Simon,* 1974, for *Dance around the Fire,* second place award for juvenile books, 1971, for *You Can't Make Me If I Don't Want To,* Sugar Plum Award, 1972; Neveh Shalom Centennial Award, 1970; Shirley Kravitz Children's Book Award, Association of Jewish Libraries, 1973.

WRITINGS—All juveniles: *Only Jane* (Junior Literary Guild selection), Thomas Nelson, 1960; *Too Many Girls,* Thomas Nelson, 1960; *The Trouble with Toby,* Houghton, 1961; *Reeney,* Houghton, 1963; (under pseudonym Caroline More, with Margaret Pitcairn Strachan) *Batch of Trouble,* Dial, 1963; *Stories of Jewish Symbols,* Bloch Publishing, 1963; *The Real Dream,* Houghton, 1964; *A Promise Is a Promise,* Houghton, 1964; *Who Knows Ten: Children's Tales of the Ten Commandments,* Union of American Hebrew Congregations, 1965, teacher's guide, 1967; *The Sabbath,* Crowell, 1966; *Crazy Mary,* Houghton, 1966; *Hurry Henrietta,* Houghton, 1966; *Jewish New Year,* Crowell, 1966; *Purim,* Crowell, 1967; *The Other Side of the Fence,* Houghton, 1967; *The House in the Tree,* Crowell, 1968; *The Green Green Sea,* Crowell, 1968; *Annie, Annie,* Houghton, 1969; *Leonard Bernstein,* Crowell, 1970; *Simon,* Houghton, 1970; *The Ringling Brothers,* Crowell, 1971; *You Can't Make Me If I Don't Want To,* Houghton, 1971; *Number Four,* Houghton, 1972; *Dance around the Fire,* Houghton, 1974; *Call Me Moose,* Houghton, 1978; *The Amazing Memory of Harvey Bean,* Houghton, 1980.

"Mishmash" series; all published by Houghton: *Mishmash,* 1962; *. . . and the Substitute Teacher,* 1963; *. . . and the Sauerkraut Mystery,* 1965; *. . . and Uncle Looey,* 1968; *. . . and the Venus Flytrap,* 1976.

"Shema" (title means "Hear O Israel") series; all published by Union of American Hebrew Congregations: *First I Say the Shema,* 1971; *About Belonging,* 1972; *About Learning,* 1972; *About God,* 1973.

Work included in anthologies, including *Bold Journeys,* Macmillan, 1966, *The Young America Basic Reading Program,* Rand McNally, 1972, and *Stories My Grandfather Should Have Told Me,* Bonim Books, 1977. Also author of "A Storyteller's Journey," POM Records, 1975. Contributor to juvenile magazines.

WORK IN PROGRESS: Mishmash and the Robot, for Houghton.

SIDELIGHTS: Molly Cone's humorous "Mishmash" series concerns a mischievous little dog. Cone's inspiration for the series came from her own dog, Tiny, who was so eagerly affectionate that she upset the entire Cone household. *Only Jane* was recorded by the Library of Congress for the blind.

BIOGRAPHICAL/CRITICAL SOURCES: Commonweal, May 26, 1967; *Christian Science Monitor,* February 1, 1968; *Young Readers' Review,* March, 1968; *New York Times Book Review,* November 5, 1972.

* * *

CONNOLLY, Vivian 1925-
(Andrea Harris, Susanna Rosse)

PERSONAL: Born August 22, 1925, in Pittsburgh, Pa.; daughter of James N. (a management consultant) and Esther (Reedy) Hauser; married Harry H. Eckstein, September, 1946 (divorced March, 1953); married John R. Connolly (a clockmaker), October, 1969. *Education:* Ohio State University, B.A., 1946, B.Sc., 1946; Manhattan State Hospital School of Nursing, diploma in nursing, 1960; University of California, San Francisco, M.S., 1967. *Residence:* New Orleans, La. *Agent:* Ray Peekner Literary Agency, 2625 North 36th St., Milwaukee, Wis. 53210.

CAREER: International Theatre Co., England and Malta, actress, 1952-53; nursing positions in New York and California, 1960-69; Visalia Day Treatment Center, Visalia, Calif., psychiatric nurse specialist, 1969-70; free-lance writer. Instructor, School of Nursing, Louisiana State University, 1975-77. *Member:* Phi Beta Kappa.

WRITINGS—Novels: *South Coast of Danger,* Tower, 1973;

The Fires of Ballymorris, Dell, 1975; *The Velvet Prison,* Dell, 1977; (under pseudonym Andrea Harris) *An Irish Affair,* Playboy Press, 1978; (under pseudonym Andrea Harris) *Byzantine Encounter,* Playboy Press, 1979; (under pseudonym Susanna Rosse) *To Love as Eagles,* Playboy Press, 1979; (under pseudonym Susanna Rosse) *Dance on the Tightrope,* Playboy Press, in press; *The Counterfeit Bride,* Fawcett, in press. Contributor to *American Mercury, American Journal of Nursing, Irish Times,* and *Irish Independent.*

WORK IN PROGRESS: The Reluctant Landlord, for Fawcett.

AVOCATIONAL INTERESTS: Traveling, making beaded Indian headbands.

* * *

COOK, Albert Spaulding 1925-

PERSONAL: Born October 28, 1925, in Exeter, N.H.; son of Albert Spaulding and Adele (Farrington) Cook; married Carol S. Rubin (a librarian), June 19, 1948; children: David, Daniel, Jonathan. *Education:* Harvard University, A.B., 1946, A.M., 1947. *Religion:* Episcopalian. *Home:* 92 Elmgrove, Providence, R.I. 02906. *Office:* Department of Comparative Literature, Box E, Brown University, Providence, R.I. 02912.

CAREER: Harvard University, Cambridge, Mass., junior fellow, 1948-51; University of California, Berkeley, assistant professor, 1953-56; Western Reserve University (now Case Western Reserve University), Cleveland, Ohio, associate professor, 1957-62, professor of English and comparative literature, 1962-63; State University of New York at Buffalo, professor of English and chairman of department, 1963-66; currently affiliated with department of comparative literature and department of classics, Brown University, Providence, R.I. Fulbright research professor, University of Munich, 1956-57; professor of American literature, University of Vienna, 1960-61. *Military service:* U.S. Army, 1943-44. *Member:* American Philological Association, Modern Language Association of America, American Comparative Literature Association, Modern Poetry Association. *Awards, honors:* Fulbright fellow at University of Paris, 1952-53; Center for Advanced Study in the Behavioral Sciences senior fellow, 1966-67; American Council of Learned Societies summer fellow in Athens, Geneva, and Paris, 1968; Fondation Hardt fellow in classical studies, Geneva, 1968, 1975; Guggenheim fellow in Paris, 1969-70; Soviet Ministry of Education, International Research and Exchange Board senior fellow, 1972; Camargo Foundation fellow, 1977.

WRITINGS: The Dark Voyage and the Golden Mean, Harvard University Press, 1949; (translator) Sophocles, *Oedipus Rex,* Houghton, 1957; *The Meaning of Fiction,* Wayne State University Press, 1960; *Progressions and Other Poems,* University of Arizona Press, 1963; *Oedipus Rex: A Mirror for Greek Drama,* Wadsworth, 1963; *The Classic Line: A Study of Epic,* Indiana University Press, 1966; (translator) Homer, *The Odyssey,* Norton, 1967; *Prisms,* Indiana University Press, 1967; *The Root of the Thing: A Study of Job and the Song of Songs,* Indiana University Press, 1968; *The Charges,* Swallow Press, 1970; *Enactment: Greek Tragedy,* Swallow Press, 1971; (with E. Dolin) *Plays for the Greek Theatre,* Bobbs-Merrill, 1972; *The Odyssey: A Critical Edition,* Norton, 1972; *Shakespeare's Enactment,* Swallow Press, 1976; *Adapt the Living,* Swallow Press, 1980; *French Tragedy: The Power of Enactment,* Swallow Press, 1980; *Myth and Language,* Indiana University Press, 1980. Author of verse plays, some of which have been produced on radio. Editor, *Halcyon,* 1947-48.

WORK IN PROGRESS: Thresholds, a study of some aspects of Romanticism; plays, poem, and prose; related studies in art and literature.

BIOGRAPHICAL/CRITICAL SOURCES: Criticism, summer, 1967; *Motive,* March, 1968.

* * *

COOK, Stuart W(ellford) 1913-

PERSONAL: Born April 17, 1913, in Richmond, Va.; son of Arthur B. and Lois (Leonard) Cook; married Annabelle Hurley, July 14, 1938; children: Jonathan B., Timothy Q., Stephen H., Joanna H. *Education:* University of Richmond, B.A., 1934, M.A., 1935; University of Minnesota, Ph.D., 1938. *Home:* 1540 Columbine, Boulder, Colo. 80302. *Office:* Department of Psychology, University of Colorado, Boulder, Colo. 80302.

CAREER: University of Minnesota, Minneapolis, instructor in psychology and clinical psychologist in psychiatric clinic for children, 1938-41; head of bureau for psychological services, State of Minnesota, 1941-42; director of research for Commission on Community Inter-relations, American Jewish Congress, 1946-50; New York University, New York, N.Y., director of research for Research Center for Human Relations, 1949-56, chairman of department of psychology, 1950-63; University of Colorado, Boulder, chairman of department of psychology, 1963-68, professor of psychology, 1968—. *Military service:* U.S. Army Air Forces, 1942-46; became captain. *Member:* World Federalists Association, American Academy of Arts and Sciences, American Association of University Professors, Society for the Psychological Study of Social Issues (president, 1952), American Association for the United Nations, American Psychological Association, Eastern Psychological Association (president, 1957-58), New York State Psychologists, New York Psychological Association (president, 1955-56), Colorado Psychological Association, Phi Beta Kappa, Sigma Xi, Psi Chi, Omicron Delta Kappa.

WRITINGS: (Editor) *Psychological Research in Radar Observer Training,* U.S. Government Printing Office, 1947; (with M. Jahoda and M. Deutsch) *Research Methods in Social Relations,* Dryden Press, 1951, 3rd edition, Holt, 1976; (with Daniel M. Wilner and Rosabelle Price Walkley) *Human Relations in Interracial Housing,* University of Minnesota Press, 1955; (with C. Selltiz, J. Christ, and J. Havel) *Attitudes and Social Relations of Foreign Students,* University of Minnesota Press, 1963; *Studies of Attitude and Attitude Measurement,* Institute of Behavioral Science, University of Colorado, 1968; (editor with Frances F. Korten and John I. Lacey) *Psychology and the Problems of Society,* [Washington], 1970. Also author, with John Carl Brigham, of *The Influence of Attitude on the Recall of Controversial Material,* Institute of Behavioral Science, University of Colorado. Contributor to professional journals.

* * *

COOKE, Hereward Lester 1916-1973

PERSONAL: Born February 16, 1916, in Princeton, N.J.; died October 5, 1973, in McLean, Va.; son of Hereward Lester and Olive (McCallum) Cooke; married Elizabeth Miles, November 11, 1942. *Education:* Oxford University, B.A., 1937; Princeton University, M.F.A., 1946, Ph.D., 1956; also attended Yale University and Art Students League. *Home:* Swink's Mill, McLean, Va. *Office:* National Gallery of Art, Washington, D.C.

CAREER: Free-lance artist and cartographer in New York and New Jersey, 1937-41; Princeton University, Princeton, N.J., instructor and artist-in-residence, 1946-51; National Gallery of Art, Washington, D.C., museum curator, 1955-62, curator of painting, 1962-73. Lecturer. Instructor in drawing, Corcoran Gallery of Art, 1957-58. Art advisor, National Aeronautics and Space Administration. U.S. Army combat artist in South Vietnam, 1967. Has had one-man shows in New York and Philadelphia, and at Princeton University Museum, Bowdoin College Museum, and other locations. *Military service:* U.S. Army Air Forces, 1942-46; became captain; awarded Bronze Star and Air Medal. *Member:* College Art Association, Cosmos Club (Washington, D.C.), Vincents Club (Oxford). *Awards, honors:* Fulbright fellow, Sorbonne, University of Paris, 1952-53; senior fellow, American Academy of Rome; Prix-de-Rome, 1953-55; Knight of the Order of Merit from Republic of Italy, 1963.

WRITINGS: (Illustrator) *Atlas of Islamic History,* Princeton University Press, 1951, 3rd revised edition, 1954; (with Sir A. Blunt) *Roman Drawings at Windsor,* Phaidon, 1960; (author of introduction) Pinckney Alston Trapier, *The Cities of America: An Artist's Panorama,* Saint Albans School, 1962; *La Galeria Nacional de Washington,* translated by Maria Teresa de la Cruz, Aquilar Press (Madrid), 1965; *Painting Lessons from the Great Masters,* Watson-Guptill, 1967, revised edition published as *Painting Techniques of the Masters,* 1972; *The National Gallery of Art in Washington,* Knorr & Hirth Verlag, 1971; (with James D. Dean) *Eyewitness to Space,* Abrams, 1971; *Fletcher Martin,* Abrams, 1977. Also author of museum catalogs. Contributor of numerous articles on art to popular magazines.

BIOGRAPHICAL/CRITICAL SOURCES: American Artist, February, 1967.†

* * *

COOMBS, Patricia 1926-

PERSONAL: Born July 23, 1926, in Los Angeles, Calif.; daughter of Donald Gladstone and Katherine (Goodro) Coombs; married C. James Fox (a technical writer and editor), July 13, 1951; children: Ann Fox Austin, Patrica Taylor. *Education:* Attended DePauw University, 1944, and Michigan State University of Agriculture and Applied Science (now Michigan State University), 1945-46; University of Washington, B.A., 1947, M.A., 1950. *Politics:* Independent. *Religion:* Episcopalian. *Home:* 178 Oswegatchie Rd., Waterford, Conn. 06385. *Agent:* Dorothy Markinko, McIntosh & Otis, Inc., 475 Fifth Ave., New York, N.Y. 10017.

CAREER: Writer. *Awards, honors: Dorrie's Magic* was named one of the ten best books of the year by the *New York Times,* 1962; *Mouse Cafe* was named one of the ten best illustrated books of the year by the *New York Times,* 1972; Child Study Association citation for one of the Children's Books of the Year, 1970, for *Dorrie and the Haunted House.*

WRITINGS: "Dorrie" series; all self-illustrated; all published by Lothrop: *Dorrie's Magic,* 1962; *Dorrie and the Blue Witch* (Junior Literary Guild selection), 1964; *Dorrie's Play,* 1965; *Dorrie and the Weather Box* (Junior Literary Guild selection), 1966; *. . . and the Witch Doctor* (Weekly Reader Book Club selection), 1967; *. . . and the Wizard's Spell,* 1968; *. . . and the Haunted House,* 1970; *. . . and the Birthday Eggs,* 1971; *. . . and the Goblin,* 1972; *. . . and the Fortune Teller,* 1973; *. . . and the Amazing Magic Elixir,* 1974; *. . . and the Witch's Imp,* 1975; *. . . and the Halloween Plot,* 1976; *. . . and the Dreamyard Monsters,* 1978; *. . . and the Screebit Ghost,* 1979; *. . . and the Witchville Fair,* 1980.

Other juveniles; all self-illustrated; all published by Lothrop: *The Lost Playground,* 1963; *Waddy and His Brothers,* 1963; *Lisa and the Grompet,* 1970; *Mouse Cafe,* 1972; *Molly Mullett,* 1975; *The Magic Pot* (Weekly Reader Book Club selection), 1977; *Tilabel,* 1978.

Illustrator: Shelagh Williamson, *Pepi's Bell,* Singer, 1961; Noel B. Gerson, *P.J., My Friend,* Doubleday, 1969; Gladys Yessayan Cretan, *Lobo,* Lothrop, 1969; Cretan, *Lobo and Brewster,* Lothrop, 1971.

Contributor of poetry to *Partisan Review, Poetry, Western Review,* and other magazines.

SIDELIGHTS: Patricia Coombs' "Dorrie" series concerns the humorous adventures of a little girl witch "whose hat is always on crooked and whose socks never match," as a reviewer for *Book World* once put it. The series is popular with many young readers and has received critical acclaim. A reviewer for *Horn Book* called *Dorrie's Magic* "an original and imaginative story," while M. F. O'Connell, writing in the *New York Times Book Review,* spoke of its "spellbinding naturalness." *Avocational interests:* Organic gardening, beach combing, bicycling.

BIOGRAPHICAL/CRITICAL SOURCES: New York Times Book Review, September 16, 1962, October 25, 1964, June 19, 1977; *Horn Book,* October, 1962; *Saturday Review,* October 17, 1964; *Christian Science Monitor,* October 22, 1964; *Book World,* October 20, 1968; *Kirkus Reviews,* March 15, 1978.

* * *

COOPER, Darien B(irla) 1937-

PERSONAL: Born September 27, 1937, in Mohawk, Tenn.; daughter of George P. (a farmer) and Mildred (Johnson) Brown; married DeWitt T. Cooper (a builder-contractor), September 27, 1957; children: Craig, Brian, Ken. *Education:* Carson-Newman College, B.A., 1958. *Politics:* Republican. *Religion:* Baptist. *Home:* 3975 Kimball Bridge Rd., Alpharetta, Ga. 30201.

CAREER: High school teacher of mathematics in Clarkston, Ga., 1958-61; staff member of Campus Crusade for Christ, Inc., 1970-72; teacher of course on the home in metropolitan area of Atlanta, Ga., fall and spring, 1972—.

WRITINGS: You Can Be the Wife of a Happy Husband, Victor, 1974; *We Became Wives of Happy Husbands,* Victor, 1976; *How to be Happy though Young,* Revell, 1979.

SIDELIGHTS: Darien B. Cooper wrote *CA:* "Each of my books came about as a result of God changing my life and my wanting to share these truths with others, and realizing the tremendous needs in these areas." *Avocational interests:* Painting, interior decorating, sewing, decoupage, flower arranging, tennis, swimming.

BIOGRAPHICAL/CRITICAL SOURCES: Atlanta Journal, February 10, 1974; *Christian Life,* July, 1974.

* * *

COOPER, Elizabeth Keyser

PERSONAL: Born in Erie, Pa.; daughter of George Almer (a chemist) and Susan (Koch) Keyser; married Clancy Cooper (an actor, director, and producer; died, 1976); children: Padraic. *Education:* Western Reserve University (now Case Western Reserve University), A.B.; University of California, Los Angeles, M.A., Ph.D. *Home:* Wheat Ridge, Colo. *Agent:* McIntosh & Otis, Inc., 475 Fifth Ave., New York, N.Y. 10017.

CAREER: Public school teacher, Cleveland Heights, Ohio; Ethical Culture Schools, New York, N.Y., teacher; University of California, Los Angeles, lecturer and assistant professor; Lennox and Wiseburn School District, Los Angeles County, Calif., director of guidance and curriculum; Santa Monica (Calif.) public schools and University of California, Los Angeles, director of elementary education, coordinator of teacher training, and instructor in psychology; full-time writer, 1960—. *Member:* Phi Beta Kappa. *Awards, honors:* Thomas A. Edison Award for best children's science book, 1958, for *Science in Your Own Back Yard.*

WRITINGS—All published by Harcourt, except as indicated: (With Herbert S. Zim) *Minerals,* 1943; *Science in Your Own Back Yard,* 1958; *Discovering Chemistry,* 1959; *Science on the Shores and Banks,* 1960; *Silkworms and Science,* 1961; *Insects and Plants: The Amazing Partnership,* 1963; *And Everything Nice: The Story of Sugar, Spice, and Flavoring,* 1966; (with Paul F. Brandwein and others) *Concepts in Science,* 1967, 6th edition, 1980; (with Harriet Pincus) *Who Is Paddy?,* 1968; *The Fish from Japan,* 1969; (with son, Padraic Cooper) *A Tree Is Something Wonderful,* Golden Gate Junior Books, 1972; *The Wild Cats of Rome,* Golden Gate Junior Books, 1972; (with P. Cooper) *Sweet and Delicious: Fruits of Tree, Bush, and Vine,* Golden Gate Junior Books, 1973. Also author, with Margaret Early, of "Bookmark Reading Program" series, Harcourt, beginning 1970. Has done assorted theatrical writing in collaboration with husband, Clancy Cooper. Contributor of articles to education journals.

WORK IN PROGRESS: A new and different series, for Harcourt.

SIDELIGHTS: Elizabeth Keyser Cooper writes *CA* that she is very active in "community, religious, and political groups that are trying to improve conditions for children and for our growing population of aging persons." *Avocational interests:* Hiking, mountain climbing, and wildlife exploration.

BIOGRAPHICAL/CRITICAL SOURCES: Christian Science Monitor, November 2, 1967; *National Observer,* November 27, 1967; *Book World,* December 17, 1967; *Saturday Review,* April 19, 1969.

* * *

COOPER, Kay 1941-

PERSONAL: Born July 26, 1941, in Cleveland, Ohio; daughter of Jack Edwin (an engineer) and Margaret (Stevens) Cooper; married John James Watt III (a pharmacist), June 20, 1964; children: Ann Michelle, Susan Kathleen. *Education:* University of Michigan, B.A., 1963. *Politics:* Independent. *Religion:* Protestant. *Home:* 222 East Hazel Dell Lane, Springfield, Ill. 62707.

CAREER: Reporter, *Indianapolis News,* Indianapolis, Ind., 1960, *Freeport Journal-Standard,* Freeport, Ill., 1963-64, and *Springfield Sun,* Springfield, Ill., 1966-67. Trail guide, Lincoln Memorial Garden and Nature Center, 1966-69, 1972—. *Member:* P.E.O., Springfield Children's Reading Round Table (president, 1976), Springfield Audubon Society, Kappa Delta (president of Springfield alumnae chapter, 1968-69; vice-president, 1969-70).

WRITINGS—All published by Messner: *A Chipmunk's Inside-Outside World,* 1973; *All about Rabbits as Pets,* 1974; *All about Goldfish as Pets,* 1976; *C'mon Ducks!,* 1978; *Journeys on the Mississippi,* 1981.

WORK IN PROGRESS: The Truth beyond Science Fiction; Voyage through the Solar System.

CORBETT, Scott 1913-

PERSONAL: Born July 27, 1913, in Kansas City, Mo.; son of Edward Roy and Hazel Marie (Emanuelson) Corbett; married Elizabeth Grosvenor Pierce, 1940; children: Florence Lee. *Education:* University of Missouri, B.J., 1934. *Religion:* Episcopalian. *Home:* 149 Benefit St., Providence, R.I. *Agent:* Curtis Brown Ltd., 575 Madison Ave., New York, N.Y. 10022.

CAREER: Writer. *Military service:* U.S. Army, 1943-46; became sergeant; army correspondent and final editor, continental edition, *Yank. Member:* Authors Guild, Authors League of America. *Awards, honors:* Edgar Allan Poe Award, Mystery Writers of America, 1962, for *Cutlass Island;* Mark Twain Award, Missouri Library Association, 1975, for *The Home Run Trick;* Golden Archer Awards, University of Wisconsin, 1978, for *The Home Run Trick.*

WRITINGS—All juveniles; all published by Atlantic-Little, Brown, except as indicated: *The Reluctant Landlord,* Crowell, 1950; *Sauce for the Gander,* Crowell, 1951; *We Chose Cape Cod,* Crowell, 1953; *Cape Cod's Way,* Crowell, 1955; *The Sea Fox,* Crowell, 1956; *Susie Sneakers,* Crowell, 1956; *Midshipman Cruise,* 1957; *Tree House Island,* 1959; *Dead Man's Light,* 1960; *The Mailbox Trick,* 1961; *Danger Point,* 1962; *Cutlass Island,* 1962; *What Makes a Car Go?,* 1963; *One By Sea,* 1965; *What Makes TV Work?,* 1965; *The Cave above Delphi,* Holt, 1965; *What Makes a Light Go On?,* 1966; *Pippa Passes,* Holt, 1966; *The Case of the Gone Goose,* 1966; *Diamonds Are Trouble,* Holt, 1967; *Cop's Kid,* 1968; *The Case of the Fugitive Firebug,* 1969; *Ever Ride a Dinosaur?,* Holt, 1969; *Diamonds Are More Trouble,* Holt, 1969.

The Baseball Bargain, 1970; *The Mystery Man,* 1970; *Steady, Freddie!,* Dutton, 1970; *The Case of the Ticklish Tooth,* 1971; *The Red Room Riddle,* 1972; *Dead before Docking,* 1972; *The Big Joke Game,* Dutton, 1972; *Run for the Money,* 1973; *Dr. Merlin's Magic Shop,* 1973; *What about the Wankel Engine?,* Four Winds Press, 1973; *Here Lies the Body,* 1974; *The Case of the Silver Skull,* 1974; *The Great Custard Pie Panic,* 1974; *Take a Number,* Dutton, 1974; *The Case of the Burgled Blessing Box,* 1975; *The Boy Who Walked on Air,* 1975; *Captain Butcher's Body,* 1976; *The Hockey Girls,* Dutton, 1976; *The Foolish Dinosaur Fiasco,* 1978; *Bridges,* Four Winds Press, 1978; *The Discontented Ghost,* Dutton, 1978; *The Mysterious Zetabet,* 1979; *The Donkey Planet,* Dutton, 1979; *Jokes to Read in the Dark,* Dutton, 1980; *Home Computers: The Simple Facts,* Little-Brown, 1980.

"Trick" series; all published by Atlantic-Little, Brown: *The Lemonade Trick,* 1960; *The Mailbox Trick,* 1961; *The Limerick Trick,* 1964; *The Baseball Trick,* 1965; *The Turnabout Trick,* 1967; *The Hairy Horror Trick,* 1969; *The Hateful Plateful Trick,* 1971; *The Home Run Trick,* 1973; *The Hockey Trick,* 1974; *The Black Mask Trick,* 1976; *The Hangman's Ghost Trick,* 1977.

"The Great McGoniggle" series; all published by Atlantic-Little, Brown: *The Great McGoniggle's Gray Ghost,* 1975; *The Great McGoniggle's Key Play,* 1976; *The Great McGoniggle Rides Shotgun,* 1977.

SIDELIGHTS: Scott Corbett, a prolific author of children's books, told *CA:* "I was surprised to see that in the four years from 1973 to 1976 I published sixteen books. In my own defense I can only point out that I give my full time to the effort. I don't teach, lecture, work on a magazine, or write book reviews—I write books. Estimates of how many writers in this country make their living solely from their books usually range between 100 and 200."

Corbett has done much of his writing while at sea. "In the past fourteen years," he said, "my wife and I have traveled extensively, mostly on freighters. During this time we have been at sea a total of over three years. This has been possible because I find I can get as much productive work done at sea as I do at home, and *productive* work (this fact is sometimes overlooked by busy-work experts) is the work that really matters."

BIOGRAPHICAL/CRITICAL SOURCES: Times Literary Supplement, May 29, 1959; *Saturday Review,* November 12, 1960, May 27, 1978; *Children's Literature in the Elementary School,* Holt, 1961; *Atlantic Monthly,* December, 1962; *Christian Science Monitor,* August 8, 1963; *New York Times Book Review,* November 7, 1965, July 16, 1972, April 30, 1978, April 27, 1980; *Books for Children: 1960-1965,* American Library Association, 1966; *Horn Book,* February, 1967; Nancy Larrick, *A Parent's Guide to Children's Reading,* 3rd edition, Doubleday, 1969; *Book World,* May 4, 1969; *Science Books,* September, 1970; *Commonweal,* November 19, 1971; *America,* December 2, 1972; *Booklist,* May 1, 1974; *Parents' Magazine,* October, 1975; *Children's Literature Review,* Volume I, Gale, 1976; *Language Arts,* September, 1976; *West Coast Review of Books,* September, 1977.

* * *

CORLISS, William R(oger) 1926-

PERSONAL: Born August 28, 1926, in Stamford, Conn.; son of George Martin (a farmer) and Hazel (Brown) Corliss; married Virginia Odabashian, July 22, 1950; children: Cathleen, Steven, James, Laura. *Education:* Rensselaer Polytechnic Institute, B.S., 1950; University of Colorado, M.S., 1953; University of Wisconsin, additional graduate study, 1953-54. *Home and office address:* P.O. Box 107, Glen Arm, Md. 21057.

CAREER: University of California, Radiation Laboratory, Berkeley, senior accelerator technician, 1951; Pratt & Whitney Aircraft, East Hartford, Conn., supervisor of heat transfer and hydrodynamics, 1954-56; General Electric Co., Flight Propulsion Laboratory, Cincinnati, Ohio, space propulsion systems specialist, 1956-59; Martin Co., Nuclear Division, Baltimore, Md., director of advanced programs, 1959-63; free-lance science writer, 1963—. *Military service:* U.S. Navy, 1944-46. *Member:* American Association for the Advancement of Science.

WRITINGS: Propulsion Systems for Space Flight, McGraw, 1960; (with D. G. Harvey) *Radioisotopic Power Generation,* Prentice-Hall, 1964; *Space Probes and Planetary Exploration,* Van Nostrand, 1965; *Scientific Satellites,* U.S. Government Printing Office, 1967; *Mysteries of the Universe,* Crowell, 1967, revised edition edited by Patrick Moore, published as *Some Mysteries of the Universe,* A. & C. Black, 1969; (with E. G. Johnsen) *Teleoperator Controls,* U.S. Government Printing Office, 1968.

(Editor) *Encyclopedia of Satellites and Sounding Rockets,* Goddard Space Flight Center, 1970; *Mysteries beneath the Sea,* Crowell, 1970; (with Johnsen) *Human Factors Applications in Teleoperator Design and Operation,* Wiley, 1971; *History of NASA Sounding Rockets,* U.S. Government Printing Office, 1971; (with Glenn T. Seaborg) *Man and Atom,* Dutton, 1971; *History of the Goddard Networks,* Goddard Space Flight Center, 1972; *The Interplanetary Pioneers,* three volumes, U.S. Government Printing Office, 1972; *Strange Phenomena: A Sourcebook of Unusual Natural Phenomena,* privately printed, 1974; *Strange Artifacts: A Sourcebook on Ancient Man,* privately printed, 1974; *The Unexplained,* Bantam, 1976; *Handbook of Unusual Natural Phenomena,* Sourcebook Project, 1977; *Ancient Man: A Handbook of Puzzling Artifacts,* Sourcebook Project, 1978; *Mysterious Universe: A Handbook of Astronomical Anomalies,* Sourcebook Project, 1979.

Author of several dozen booklets for the U.S. Government. Consulting editor, *McGraw-Hill Encyclopedia of Science and Technology.* Contributor to *International Science and Technology* and *Mosaic.*

* * *

CORNELL, Jean Gay 1920-

PERSONAL: Born August 17, 1920, in Streator, Ill.; daughter of John Charles (a certified public accountant) and Florence (Dixon) Werckman; married Francis G. Cornell, June 14, 1968 (divorced March 26, 1973); children: (previous marriage) Steven C. Howard, David G. Howard. *Education:* Attended Beloit College, 1938-40; University of Illinois, B.A., 1942. *Politics:* Republican. *Religion:* Episcopalian. *Home:* 182 Garth Rd., Scarsdale, N.Y. 10583.

CAREER: Spencer Press, Champaign, Ill., executive assistant to managing editor, 1953-62; University of Illinois, College of Electrical Engineering, Champaign, head of publications department, 1964-66; Garrard Publishing, Scarsdale, N.Y., head of production department, 1966-68; Educational Research Services, White Plains, N.Y., vice-president, 1968-72; free-lance writer, 1972-74; *Reader's Digest,* Pleasantville, N.Y., copy editor, 1975—.

WRITINGS—Published by Garrard, except as indicated: (Editor with A. Atwood) *Sports Alive,* Spencer Press, 1960; *Louis Armstrong: Ambassador Satchmo,* 1972; *Mahalia Jackson: Queen of Gospel,* 1974; *Ralph Bunche: Champion of Peace,* 1976.

* * *

CORWIN, Norman 1910-

PERSONAL: Born May 3, 1910, in Boston, Mass.; son of Samuel Haskell and Rose (Ober) Corwin; married Katherine Locke, March 17, 1947; children: Anthony, Diane. *Education:* Attended public schools in Boston and Winthrop, Mass. *Home:* 1840 Fairburn Ave., Los Angeles, Calif. 90025. *Agent:* William Morris Agency, 151 El Camino, Beverly Hills, Calif. 90212.

CAREER: Greenfield Daily Recorder, Greenfield, Mass., sports editor, 1927-29; *Springfield Daily Republican* and *Springfield Sunday Republican,* Springfield, Mass., radio editor, 1929-36; Columbia Broadcasting System, Inc., New York City, writer, director, and producer, 1938-47; screen writer for various production companies, including Metro-Goldwyn-Mayer, RKO General, Twentieth Century-Fox, and CBS, 1945—; United Nations Radio, New York City, chief of special projects, 1949-52; writer, director, and producer of radio and television programs. University of California, Los Angeles, director of theater group, 1960—, teacher, 1967-69; University of Southern California, teacher of telecommunications, 1970, and creative radio, 1979-80; director of creative writing, University of Southern California, Idyllwild, 1971—; lecturer, University of North Carolina, 1972; distinguished visiting lecturer, San Diego State University, 1977-78. *Member:* Academy of Motion Picture Arts and Sciences (chairman of documentary awards committee, 1963-74; co-chairman of scholarship committee,

1970-76), Authors League of America, Directors Guild of America, Screen Writers Guild (West), Dramatists League, American Society of Composers, Authors and Publishers.

AWARDS, HONORS: Has received numerous awards for individual radio programs and for general contributions to broadcasting, including Institute for Education by Radio Award, 1939, for "Words without Music" and "They Fly through the Air," and 1940, for "Pursuit of Happiness"; Bok Medal, 1942; American Academy of Arts and Letters Award, 1942; Peabody Medal, 1942, for "We Hold These Truths"; American Newspaper Guild Page One Award, 1944; National Council of Teachers of English Citation, 1945, Page One Award, 1945, and Institute for Education by Radio Award, 1946, all for "On a Note of Triumph!"; Wendell Willkie One World Award, 1946; Freedom Foundation Honor Medal, 1950, for "Between Americans"; National Conference of Christians and Jews Award, 1951, for "Document A/777"; admitted to Radio Hall of Fame, 1962; Pacific Pioneer Broadcasters Carbon Mike Award, 1974; American College of Radio Arts, Crafts and Sciences fellow. Foreign Language Press Film Critics Circle Award and Academy Award nomination, both 1957, both for "Lust for Life"; Women's ORT Award, 1960, for "The Story of Ruth"; Litt.D., Columbia College, 1967; Emmy Award, 1970, for "The Plot to Overthrow Christmas"; Writers Guild of America Valentine Davis Award, 1972.

WRITINGS: They Fly through the Air (radio script), Vrest Orton, 1939; *Thirteen by Corwin* (radio dramas), Holt, 1942; *More by Corwin* (radio dramas), Holt, 1944; *On a Note of Triumph!,* Simon & Schuster, 1945; *The Warrior* (opera; first produced in New York at Metropolitan Opera House, November, 1947), Rullman, 1946; *"Untitled" and Other Radio Dramas,* Holt, 1947; *Dog in the Sky: The Authentic and Unexpurgated Odyssey of Runyon Jones* (first produced as "The Odyssey of Runyon Jones" in Los Angeles at Valley Music Theater, December 16, 1972), Simon & Schuster, 1952; *The Plot to Overthrow Christmas,* Holt, 1952; "The Golden Door" (cantata), first produced in Cleveland, Ohio at Music Hall, March 23, 1955.

The Rivalry (first produced in Vancouver at Georgia Auditorium, September 23, 1957; produced on Broadway at Bijou Theater, February 7, 1959), Dramatists' Play Service, 1960; *The World of Carl Sandburg* (first produced in Portland, Me. at State Theater, October 12, 1959; produced on Broadway at Henry Miller's Theater, September 14, 1960), Harcourt, 1961, acting edition, Samuel French, 1961; *Overkill and Megalove* (first produced in Hollywood at Desilu Theater, July 24, 1964), World Publishing, 1963; *Prayer for the Seventies,* Doubleday, 1969; "Jerusalem Printout," first produced in Los Angeles at Convention Center Auditorium, November 22, 1972; "Cervantes," first produced in Washington, D.C. at American Theater, September 6, 1973; "Together Tonight: Jefferson, Hamilton, Burr," first produced in Bloomington, Ind., 1976; *Holes in a Stained Glass Window,* Lyle Stuart, 1978; *Network at Fifty,* Ritchie, 1979.

Also author of scripts for numerous other radio series and special broadcasts. Author of screenplays, "The Blue Veil," 1951, "Scandal at Scourie," 1953, "Lust for Life," 1956, "The Story of Ruth," 1959, and "Winds of Change," and of television scripts for "F.D.R.," "Inside the Movie Kingdom," "The Court Martial of the Tiger of Malaya," "Norman Corwin Presents," "The Last GIs," "The Trial of Yamashita," and "Academy Leaders" (PBS series).

Work represented in numerous anthologies, including: *This Is War,* Dodd, 1942; *Radio in Wartime,* Greenberg, 1942; *Off Mike,* Duell, Sloan & Pearce, 1944; *While You Were Gone,* Simon & Schuster, 1946; *The American System of Government,* McGraw, 1959; *War Poems of the United Nations,* Dial, 1961; *Lincoln: A Contemporary Portrait,* Doubleday, 1962.

Author of column, "Corwin on Media," *Westways.*

SIDELIGHTS: Norman Corwin is regarded as one of the great radio dramatists of the 1930s and 1940s.

His radio play, "My Client Curley," was made into a movie entitled "Once upon a Time." It starred Cary Grant.

BIOGRAPHICAL/CRITICAL SOURCES: New York Times Magazine, August 2, 1942; *Theater Arts Monthly,* September, 1942; *Liberty,* February 10, 1945; *Coronet,* December, 1945; Erik Barnouw, *The Golden Web,* Oxford University Press, 1968; Joseph Julian, *This Was Radio,* Viking, 1975; *Authors in the News,* Volume II, Gale, 1976; *Readers Theatre News,* fall/winter, 1978; *San Diego Union,* February 4, 1979; *Washington Star,* February 5, 1979; *About Norman Corwin,* Santa Susana Press, 1980.

* * *

COSGRAVE, John O'Hara II 1908-1968

PERSONAL: Born October 10, 1908, in San Francisco, Calif.; died May 9, 1968, in Pocasset, Mass. after a brief illness; son of Charles O'Malley and Margaret (Mahoney) Cosgrave; married Mary Silva (a children's book editor), November 21, 1952. *Education:* Attended Marin Junior College, 1926-29, University of California, Berkeley, 1929-30, California School of Fine Arts, 1930, and Academie d'Andre L'Hote, 1931-32. *Home address:* Box 645, Pocasset, Mass.

CAREER: Free-lance commercial artist, Brooklyn, N.Y., 1933-62. *Military service:* U.S. Army, Office of Strategic Services, 1942-45; became staff sergeant. *Member:* Dutch Treat Club, Buzzards Yacht Club. *Awards, honors:* Watercolor prize, Brooklyn Society of Artists, 1941.

WRITINGS—Author and illustrator: *America Sails the Seas,* Houghton, 1962; *Clipper Ship,* Macmillan, 1963.

Illustrator: Antoine de Saint Exupery, *Wind, Sand and Stars,* Reynal & Hitchcock, 1939, reprinted, Harcourt, 1967; Julian Meade, *Bouquets and Bitters: A Gardener's Medley,* Longmans, Green, 1940; William G. Morse, *Pardon My Harvard Accent,* Farrar & Rinehart, 1941; Walter Havighurst, *The Long Ships Passing,* Macmillan, 1942, reprinted, 1961; Frederick Way, Jr., *Pilotin' Comes Natural,* Farrar & Rinehart, 1943; Robert Frost, *Come In, and Other Poems,* Holt & Co., 1943; Clara Ingram Judson, *Donald McKay: Designer of Clipper Ships,* Scribner, 1943; George Washington Cable, *Old Creole Days,* Limited Editions Club, 1943; Edward Downes, *Adventures in Symphonic Music,* Farrar & Rinehart, 1944, reprinted, Kennikat, 1972; James Branch Cabell, *There Were Two Pirates,* Farrar, Straus, 1946; Carl Lamson Carmer, *Listen for a Lonesome Drum,* Sloane, 1950; Anne Stearns Molloy, *Lucy's Christmas* (juvenile), Houghton, 1950; Jean Lee Latham, *Carry On, Mr. Bowditch* (juvenile), Houghton, 1955; Frost, *A Pocket Book of Robert Frost's Poems,* Washington Square Press, 1962; Samuel Epstein, *The Sacramento,* Garrard, 1968.

WORK IN PROGRESS: A book about early American railroads; books on oil, coal, iron and early American ships.

AVOCATIONAL INTERESTS: Racing and sailing boats, fishing.†

COTTER, Cornelius Philip 1924-

PERSONAL: Born March 18, 1924, in New York, N.Y.; son of Cornelius Joseph and Charlotte (Keller) Cotter; married; children: (previous marriage) Cornelia Marie, Lawrence P., Charles Rudolph, Steven Ackerl. *Education:* Stanford University, A.B., 1949; Harvard University, M.P.A., 1951, Ph.D., 1953. *Home:* 3965 North Harcourt Pl., Milwaukee, Wis. 53211. *Office:* Department of Political Science, University of Wisconsin, Milwaukee, Wis. 53201.

CAREER: Columbia University, New York, N.Y., instructor in government, 1952-53, assistant professor of political science, 1953-56; Stanford University, Stanford Calif., associate professor of political science, 1956-61; Republican National Committee, Washington, D.C., assistant to chairman, 1958-61; U.S. Commission on Civil Rights, Washington, D.C., assistant staff director, 1961-63; University of Wichita (now Wichita State University), Wichita, Kan., professor of political science and head of department, 1963-67; University of Wisconsin—Milwaukee, professor of political science, 1967—. Executive director, Republican Committee on Program and Progress. *Military service:* U.S. Navy, Construction Battalion, 1943-46; became yeoman first class. *Member:* American Political Science Association.

WRITINGS: Government and Private Enterprise, Holt, 1960; (with J. Malcolm Smith) *Powers of the President During Crises,* Public Affairs Press, 1960; (editor) *Decisions for a Better America,* Doubleday, 1960; (with Leonard Freedman) *Issues of the Sixties,* Wadsworth, 1961; (with Bernard C. Hennessy) *Politics without Power,* Atherton, 1964; *Jet Tanker Crash: Urban Response to Military Disaster,* University Press of Kansas, 1968; (editor and co-author) *Practical Politics in the United States,* Allyn & Bacon, 1969; *The Black Student in the Wisconsin State Universities System,* U.S. Government Printing Office, 1971; (editor) *Political Science Annual,* Bobbs-Merrill, Volume IV, 1973, Volume V, 1974, Volume VI, 1975. Contributor to professional journals and reference works. Member of editoral board, *Political Science Annual,* 1970-72.

WORK IN PROGRESS: Study of party organizational strength at the national and state levels.

AVOCATIONAL INTERESTS: Reading, writing, camping.

* * *

COTTERELL, (Francis) Peter 1930-

PERSONAL: Born May 4, 1930, in Malta; son of Leonard Charles and Edith (Stead) Cotterell; married Geraldine Brodie, June 1, 1957; children: Anne, Janet. *Education:* Brunel College (now University), B.Sc., 1955; Spurgeon's Theological College, B.D., 1960; University of London, Ph.D., 1970. *Home:* London Bible College, Green Lane, Northwood, Middlesex HA6 2UW, England.

CAREER: Brunel College (now University), London, England, lecturer in physics, 1955-57; Christian missionary in Ethiopia, 1957-76; London Bible College, Middlesex, England, director of overseas studies, 1976—. Visiting professor at Fuller Theological Seminary, 1973. Member of theological and religious studies board, Council for National Academic Awards, 1978—. *Member:* International African Institute.

WRITINGS: Born at Midnight, Moody, 1973; *Language and the Christian,* Bagster, 1978; *What Next?,* Marshall, Morgan & Scott, 1979; *What the Bible Teaches about Death,* Kingsbury, 1979; *What the Bible Teaches about Salvation,* Kingsbury, 1980. Also author of more than twenty books in the Amharic language, including primers with distribution of more than one million copies. Contributor to *Journal of Ethiopian Studies.*

WORK IN PROGRESS: Biblical Missiology and *Church Growth and Communications.*

SIDELIGHTS: Cotterell is involved with making Christianity relevant to the younger generation, particularly through drama, radio, and in the church itself. He told *CA* that he writes the books "no one else will write."

* * *

COUFFER, Jack 1924-

PERSONAL: Born December 7, 1924, in Upland, Calif.; son of L. P. and Ruth Couffer; married Joan Burger, 1948 (divorced); children: Michael. *Education:* University of Southern California, B.A., 1949. *Home:* 500½ Poinsettia Ave., Corona Del Mar, Calif. *Agent:* Elizabeth McKee, Harold Mattson Co., Inc., 22 East 40th St., New York, N.Y. 10016; and Ben Benjamin, International Creative Management, 8899 Beverly Blvd., Los Angeles, Calif. 90048.

CAREER: Writer and motion picture director, producer, and cameraman. *Military service:* U.S. Army Air Forces, 1943-46; became sergeant. *Member:* International Alliance of Theatrical Stage Employees, American Society of Cinematographers, Academy of Motion Picture Arts and Sciences, Director's Guild of America, Writer's Guild of America.

WRITINGS: Swim, Rat, Swim, Lippincott, 1960; *Song of Wild Laughter,* Simon & Schuster, 1963; *The Concrete Wilderness,* Meredith Press, 1967; *The Lions of "Living Free,"* Dutton, 1972; *Nights with Sasquatch,* Berkley Publishing, 1977.

With son, Mike Couffer; all published by Putnam: *Galapagos Summer,* 1975; *African Summer,* 1976; *Canyon Summer,* 1977; *Salt Marsh Summer,* 1978.

BIOGRAPHICAL/CRITICAL SOURCES: New York Times Book Review, October 1, 1967; *Best Sellers,* November 1, 1967; *National Review,* November 28, 1967.

* * *

COUSINS, Margaret 1905-
(Avery Johns, William Masters, Mary Parrish)

PERSONAL: Born January 26, 1905, in Munday, Tex.; daughter of Walter Henry (a pharmacist and editor) and Sue (Reeves) Cousins. *Education:* University of Texas, A.B., 1926. *Politics:* Democrat. *Religion:* Episcopalian. *Home:* 429 East Commerce St., San Antonio, Tex. 78205. *Agent:* Harold Matson Co., 22 East 40th St., New York, N.Y. 10016.

CAREER: Southern Pharmaceutical Journal, Dallas, Tex., associate editor, 1927-32, editor-in-chief, 1932-37; *Pictorial Review,* New York City, associate editor, 1937-38; Hearst Promotion Service, New York City, copywriter, 1938-42; *Good Housekeeping,* New York City, associate editor, 1942-45, managing editor, 1945-58; *McCall's,* New York City, managing editor, 1958-61; Doubleday & Co., New York City, senior editor, 1961-70; Holt, Rinehart & Winston, New York City, special editor, 1970; *Ladies Home Journal,* New York City, fiction and book editor, 1971-73. Member of San Antonio River Authority Advisory Commission. *Member:* Authors Guild (member of board of governors, 1959-74), Authors League of America (secretary, 1965-66), American Institute of Interior Designers, Fashion Group (member of board of governors, 1960-62), Texas Institute of Letters,

Philosophical Society of Texas, San Antonio Conservation Society, San Antonio Fine Arts Commission, Arts Council of San Antonio (member of board of directors), Theta Sigma Phi, Alpha Chi Omega, Cosmopolitan Club. *Awards, honors:* Award of achievement, Alpha Chi Omega, 1955; J.C. Penney-Missouri School of Journalism award for magazine writing. 1968; George Washington Medal, Freedoms Foundation of Valley Forge, 1969; Distinguished Alumna Award, University of Texas, 1973.

WRITINGS: Uncle Edgar and the Reluctant Saint, Farrar, Straus, 1948; *Ben Franklin of Old Philadelphia* (juvenile), Random House, 1952; *Christmas Gift* (collection of short stories), Doubleday, 1952; (with Margaret Truman) *Souvenir* (biography), McGraw, 1955; *We Were There at the Battle of the Alamo* (juvenile), Grossett, 1958; (editor) *Love and Marriage* (anthology), Doubleday, 1961; (under pseudonym Avery Johns) *Traffic with Evil,* Doubleday, 1962; *Thomas Alva Edison* (juvenile), Random House, 1965. Contributor, sometimes under pseudonyms, of fiction to magazines. Member of advisory board, *San Antonio.*

WORK IN PROGRESS: A Happy Childhood, an autobiography, for Doubleday.

SIDELIGHTS: Margaret Cousins told *CA:* "I was born on the Knox Prairie and I did not know another child until my brother was born when I was five, so that I was strongly influenced by my father and mother. My father, a self-educated man, was a prodigious reader and a frustrated writer. He had natural taste and exposed me early to the classics. I learned to read when I was four years old, and I never had any other intention but to read and write. I wrote verse originally, due possibly to a strong dose of English poets. I had a poem published in a Dallas, Texas newspaper when I was twelve, and I sold a good deal of light verse when I was in college.

"My father always read aloud to my brother and me, everything from the complete works of Edgar Allen Poe to the *Saturday Evening Post.* He read nine volumes of the short stories of O. Henry to us. I believe this is why I became a short story writer. I actually wanted to be a novelist and to write novels of social history. I was embarked on such a novel, after I was a grown woman, but I came to the conclusion one day that I was not profound enough to be a really important novelist. This was a personal crisis of enormous dimensions. Although I managed to survive, I have never written a novel. I decided that I would write simply to entertain, so I have turned to the short story for the popular mass-circulation market of magazines. Over a twenty-five year period, I published upward of two hundred short stories in this market in the United States and in seventeen foreign countries."

* * *

COWEN, Zelman 1919-

PERSONAL: Born October 7, 1919, in Melbourne, Australia; son of Bernard and Sara (Granat) Cowen; married Anna Wittner, 1945; children: Simon David, Nicholas Robert, Katherine Jane, Benjamin John. *Education:* University of Melbourne, B.A., 1939, LL.B., 1940, LL.M., 1941; Oxford University, M.A., D.C.L., 1947. *Home and office:* Government House, Canberra, Australian Capital Territory, 2600 Australia.

CAREER: Barrister-at-law, Gray's Inn, London, England, and Victoria, Australia; Oxford University, Oxford, England, fellow of Oriel College, 1947-50; University of Melbourne, Melbourne, Australia, professor of public law and dean of the faculty of law, 1951-66, professor emeritus, 1967—; vice-chancellor, University of New England, 1967-70; vice-chancellor, University of Queensland, 1970-77; governor-general of Australia, 1977—. Academic governor of the board of governors, Hebrew University of Jerusalem, 1969-77; member of board of directors, Australian Opera, 1969-77; president of Australian Institute of Urban Studies, 1973-77, and Club of Rome, 1974-77; chairman of board of governors, Utah Foundation, 1975-77; law reform commissioner, Commonwealth of Australia, 1976-77; member of council, University of Lesotho, 1976-77; chairman, Australian Vice-Chancellor's Committee, 1977. *Military service:* Royal Australian Navy, 1941-45; became lieutenant. *Member:* Academy of Social Sciences in Australia (honorary fellow), Australian College of Education (honorary fellow), American Academy of Arts and Sciences (foreign honorary member), Royal Society of the Arts (fellow). *Awards, honors:* Oxford University, honorary fellow of Oriel College, 1977, and New College, 1978; honorary master of bench, Gray's Inn, 1978.

WRITINGS: (Co-editor) *Dicey: Conflict of Laws,* 6th edition, Stevens & Sons, 1949; *Australia and the United States: Some Legal Comparisons,* University of Buffalo Press, 1954; (with P. B. Carter) *Essays on the Law of Evidence,* Clarendon Press, 1956; *American-Australian Private International Law,* Oceana, 1957; *Federal Jurisdiction in Australia,* Oxford University Press, 1959, 2nd edition (with Leslie Zines), 1978; (with D. Mendes da Costa) *Matrimonial Causes Jurisdiction,* Law Book Company of Australia, 1961; *Great Australians: Sir Isaac Isaacs,* Oxford University Press, 1962; (with Cheshire) *The British Commonwealth of Nations in a Changing World,* Northwestern University Press, 1965; *Sir John Latham and Other Papers,* Oxford University Press, 1965; (author of introduction) *Evatt: The King and His Dominion Governors,* 2nd edition, F. W. Cheshire, 1967; *The Private Man* (Boyer Lectures), Australian Broadcasting Commission, 1969; *Individual Liberty and the Law* (Tagore Law Lectures), Eastern Law House (Calcutta), 1977. Contributor of chapters to books and articles and essays on legal, political, social, and university matters. to journals in Australia, United Kingdom, United States, Canada, and Europe.

AVOCATIONAL INTERESTS: Music, the theatre, films, tennis.

* * *

COWIE, Peter 1939-

PERSONAL: Born December 24, 1939, in Boscombe, England; son of Donald John (a writer) and Ruth Mary (Woods) Cowie; married Elisabeth von Waldow, September 22, 1962; children: Monica Anne, Felicity May. *Education:* Magdalene College, Cambridge, B.A., 1962, M.A., 1967. *Home:* 69 York Ave., London S.W. 14, England. *Office:* Tantivy Press, 136-148 Tooley St., London S.E.I., England.

CAREER: Tantivy Press, London, England, publisher, 1963—. Sometime Regent's Lecturer, University of California, Santa Barbara. Consultant to various international film festivals.

WRITINGS—All published by A. S. Barnes: *Antonioni-Bergman-Resnais,* 1963; *The Cinema of Orson Welles,* 1965, revised edition, 1973; *Swedish Cinema,* 1966, revised edition, 1970; *Seventy Years of Cinema,* 1969, revised edition published as *Eighty Years of Cinema,* 1978; (editor) *A Concise History of the Cinema,* 1971; *Fifty Major Film Makers,* 1976; *Finnish Cinema,* 1976; *Film in Sweden: Stars and*

Players, 1977; *Dutch Cinema,* 1979. Also author of annual, *International Film Guide,* A. S. Barnes, 1964—. Contributor to periodicals in England.

WORK IN PROGRESS: A critical biography of Ingmar Bergman, for Scribner.

* * *

COX, Fred(erick) M(oreland) 1928-

PERSONAL: Born December 8, 1928, in Los Angeles, Calif.; son of Frederick Alfred Edward (a businessman) and Ethel (Moreland) Cox; married Margaret Gay Campbell (a social worker), June 29, 1951; children: Larry, Elizabeth, Sherman. *Education:* University of California, Los Angeles, B.A. (with honors), 1950, M.S.W., 1954; University of California, Berkeley, D.S.W., 1968. *Office:* School of Social Work, Michigan State University, 254 Baker Hall, East Lansing, Mich. 48824.

CAREER: Bureau of Public Assistance, Los Angeles, Calif., child welfare caseworker, 1952-53; Superior Court, Los Angeles, deputy counselor in mental health, 1953; Family Service Bureau, Oakland, Calif., caseworker, 1954-57; Easter Seal Society, Oakland, program director, 1957-60; University of Michigan, Ann Arbor, assistant professor, 1964-69, associate professor of social work, 1969-76; Michigan State University, East Lansing, professor of social work and director of School of Social Work, 1976—. Part-time teacher at Contra Costa College, 1957-60. Member of Ann Arbor Community Development, Inc.; president of Port St. James Association and of University Credit Unions Non-Profit Housing Development Corp.; member of Ann Arbor Housing Commission, 1970-72, chairman, 1970-71.

MEMBER: American Sociological Association, National Association of Social Workers, Academy of Certified Social Workers, Council on Social Work Education, Phi Beta Kappa.

WRITINGS: (Editor with John L. Erlich, Jack Rothman, and John E. Tropman, and contributor) *Strategies of Community Organization: A Book of Readings,* F. E. Peacock, 1970, 3rd edition, 1979; (with Erlich, Rothman, and Tropman) *Community—Action, Planning, Development: A Casebook,* F. E. Peacock, 1974; (with Erlich, Rothman, and Tropman) *Tactics and Techniques of Community Practice,* F. E. Peacock, 1977.

WORK IN PROGRESS: Issues in Social Welfare Policy; Housing Policy for the Aged.

* * *

CRAIK, Kenneth H(enry) 1936-

PERSONAL: Born April 10, 1936, in Pawtucket, R.I.; son of Robert Johnstone (a heating engineer) and Maggie (Conlon) Craik; married Janice Ruth Hebner, September 7, 1957; children: Jennifer, Kenneth J. P., Amy. *Education:* Brown University, B.A. (magna cum laude), 1958; University of California, Berkeley, Ph.D., 1964. *Politics:* Liberal Democrat. *Religion:* Unitarian. *Home:* 2737 Prince St., Berkeley, Calif. 94705. *Office:* Department of Psychology, 3210 Tolman Hall, University of California, Berkeley, Calif. 94720.

CAREER: University of California, Berkeley, assistant professor and assistant research psychologist, 1964-70, associate professor and associate research psychologist, 1970-78, professor of psychology and research psychologist, 1978—. Member of directorate, U.S. committee of Man and the Biosphere Project, United Nations. *Member:* American Psychological Association, Association for the Study of Man-Environment Relations (member of board of directors, 1960-72), Environmental Design Research Association, Western Psychological Association.

WRITINGS: (With others) *New Directions in Psychology 4,* Holt, 1970; (editor with E. H. Zube) *Perceiving Environmental Quality: Research and Application,* Plenum, 1976; (editor with G. E. McKechnie) *Personality and the Environment,* Sage Publications, Inc., 1978.

Contributor: P. McReynolds, editor, *Advances in Psychological Assessment,* Volume II, Science and Behavior Books, 1971; W. M. Smith, editor, *Behavior, Design and Policy: Aspects of Human Habitats,* University of Wisconsin, 1972; J. V. Krutilla, editor, *Natural Environments: Studies in Theoretical and Applied Analysis,* Johns Hopkins Press, 1972; P. H. Mussen and M. R. Rosenzweig, editors, *Annual Review of Psychology,* Volume XXIV, Annual Reviews, 1973; E. H. Zube, R. O. Brush, and J. Fabos, editors, *Landscape Assessment: Values, Perceptions, and Resources,* Dowden, 1975; S. Wapner, S. Cohen, and B. Kaplan, editors, *Experiencing Environments,* Plenum, 1976. Contributor to professional journals.

WORK IN PROGRESS: Contributing to *The Psychology of Situations: An Interactionist Perspective,* edited by D. Magnusson; articles on environmental psychology, styles of humorous behavior, and application of personality research techniques to assessment of historical figures.

* * *

CREGAN, David (Appleton Quartus) 1931-

PERSONAL: Born September 30, 1931, in Buxton, England; son of James Grattan and Gertrude (Fraser) Cregan; married Ailsa Mary Wynne Willson (a teacher of mentally handicapped children), August 6, 1960; children: Timothy James Beaumont, Alexis David, Benjamin Luke, Rebecca Sally Mary. *Education:* Clare College, Cambridge, B.A., 1955. *Politics:* Socialist. *Religion:* None. *Home:* 76 Wood Close, Hatfield, Hertfordshire, England. *Agent:* Margaret Ramsay Ltd., 14A Goodwin's Ct., London WC2N 4LL, England.

CAREER: Palm Beach Private School, Palm Beach, Fla., head of English department, 1955-57; Burnage Grammar School, Manchester, England, assistant in English, 1957; salesman of mouse poison and clerk for Automobile Association, 1958; Hatfield School, Hatfield, England, assistant in English and head of drama, 1958-62, part-time teacher of drama, 1962-67; playwright and novelist. Member of steering committee, Guggenheim New Theatre Writing Project, 1979. Chairman of drama advisory council, West Midlands Arts Association, 1973-74. *Military service:* Royal Air Force, 1950-51. *Member:* Theatre Writers Union. *Awards, honors:* Charles Henry Foyle Award for new plays, 1966, for *Transcending* [and] *The Dancers;* Arts Council award, 1967, for *Three Men for Colverton;* Arts Council bursary for *How We Held the Square,* 1971; British Council visit to Hungary, 1971, and Romania, 1979.

WRITINGS—Plays, published by Methuen, except as indicated: *Ronald Rossiter* (novel), Hutchinson, 1959; *Miniatures* (first produced in London at Royal Court Theatre, April 25, 1965), 1970; *Transcending* [and] *The Dancers* (first produced in London at Royal Court Theatre, January 23, 1966), 1967; *Three Men for Colverton* (first produced in London at Royal Court Theatre, September 21, 1966), 1967; *The Houses by the Green* (first produced in London at Royal Court Theatre, November 2, 1968), 1969; *How We Held the Square* (juvenile; first produced in Birmingham, England at Midlands Arts Centre, October, 1971), 1973; *George Reborn* (two-act; first produced in Richmond at Orange Tree Theatre, February 2, 1973), 1973; *The Land of Palms* (two-act; first produced in Devonshire, England at Barn Theatre, November, 1972), 1974; *Poor Tom* [and] *Tina* (contains "Tina" [first produced in Richmond at Orange Tree Theatre, October 24, 1975] and "Poor Tom" [first produced at University Theatre, University of Manchester, April 7, 1976]), 1976. Author of *Liebestraum,* a one-act play first produced in Birmingham, England at Midlands Arts Centre, December 11, 1972, and published by Methuen; also author of *Arthur,* a one-act juvenile play published in Hutchinson's *Playbill,* 1969.

Unpublished plays: "A Comedy of the Changing Years," first produced in London at Theatre Upstairs of the Royal Court Theatre, February 23, 1969; "Tipper," first produced at the Oxford Union, November, 1969; "Cast Off," first produced in Sheffield, England at Crucible Studio, April, 1973; "The King," first produced on the West End at Shaw Theatre, May 23, 1974; "Tigers," first produced in Richmond at Orange Tree Theatre, September 22, 1978; "Young Sir" (one-act), first produced in Richmond at Orange Tree Theatre, June 22, 1979.

Author of radio plays, including "The Latter Days of Lucy Trenchard," "The Monument," "Hope," and "Inventor's Corner," all broadcast on British Broadcasting Corp. Radio Three; also author of several very short plays and some television scripts.

SIDELIGHTS: David Cregan writes: "The agnostic, scientific world, in which lies most of our hope, is unhappily as much bedevilled by orthodoxy as the Catholic Middle Ages. Orthodoxy, once in power, automatically sets about bereaving those who must live by it, for it separates people from their relationships, whether those relationships are with other people, or with ideas, or with the very objects of their daily lives. The contradiction of modern life is that often this separation is the only hope of renewal. Also it is the foundation of monolithic conservatism, and the legalising of violence. It is therefore the cause of a central human pain, polarising the public (external) and the personal (internal) in a classic and uncompassionate manner, as well as giving hope of future human success through a renewed, or revolutionised society.

"My own work, driven by observation of this painful and uncertain process, is anti-rhetorical. This is because uncertainty doesn't inspire rhetoric, which is the language of monolithism. As it is anti-rhetorical, and also, since I am made that way, comic, it derives from traditions of character presentation and play structure that are close to the *commedia dell'Arte.* This tradition gave emphasis to words as actions, somewhat sheer, confronting things, rather than to words as paint. The terseness of such techniques—necessarily funny, otherwise they would be merely melodramatic—produces forms which are only realisable as three dimensional stage plays, and often plays that are gratifyingly complicated in their unfolding, though wonderfully easy to assimilate. For reasons I am not very clear about, working for radio seems to be much closer to this sort of theatre writing than working in television, perhaps because the current strength of television lies in its deceptively documentary appearance.

"Although I have strongly-held views deriving from the above, I am very aware of the straitjacket of theorising about one's self, sealing one's self off from cataclysm or chance. Suffice it to say that space is the physical material from which plays are made, and absolute accuracy the prime skill with which to make them. Given that, it is also my view that a play should explode and not creep about. Among other unpleasantnesses, creeping leads to cliches.

"For the rest, I travel whenever possible and wherever possible. I like holidays more than anything else in the world, provided I am with my wife and family and no one else. I have always been influenced by Keith Johnstone, Bill Gaskill, and Philip Hedley. I greatly admire Grotowski, Kantor, and the expatriate Hungarian Squat Theatre Company."

BIOGRAPHICAL/CRITICAL SOURCES: Plays and Players, December, 1970.

* * *

CREWS, Frederick C(ampbell) 1933-

PERSONAL: Born February 20, 1933, in Philadelphia, Pa.; son of Maurice Augustus and Ruby (Gaudet) Crews; married Elizabeth Peterson, September 9, 1959; children: Gretchen Elizabeth, Ingrid Anna. *Education:* Yale University, A.B., 1955; Princeton University, Ph.D., 1958. *Home:* 636 Vincente Ave., Berkeley, Calif. 94707. *Office:* Department of English, University of California, Berkeley, Calif. 94720.

CAREER: University of California, Berkeley, 1958—, began as instructor, currently professor of English. Fulbright lectureship in American literature, University of Turin, Italy, 1961-62. *Member:* Modern Language Association of America, National Council of Teachers of English. *Awards, honors:* American Council of Learned Societies study fellowship, and fellow, Center for Advanced Study in the Behavioral Sciences, 1965-66; National Endowment for the Arts essay prize, 1967; Guggenheim fellowship, 1970-71.

WRITINGS: The Tragedy of Manners: Moral Drama in the Later Novels of Henry James, Yale University Press, 1957; *E. M. Forster: The Perils of Humanism,* Princeton University Press, 1962; *The Pooh Perplex: A Freshman Casebook,* Dutton, 1963; (editor) Stephen Crane, *The Red Badge of Courage,* Bobbs-Merrill, 1964; *The Sins of the Fathers: Hawthorne's Psychological Themes,* Oxford University Press, 1966; (editor) *Great Short Works of Nathaniel Hawthorne,* Harper, 1967; *The Patch Commission,* Dutton, 1968; (editor with Orville Schell) *Starting Over: A College Reader,* Random House, 1970; (editor) *Psychoanalysis and Literary Process,* Winthrop Publishing, 1970; *The Random House Handbook,* Random House, 1974, 3rd edition, 1980; *Out of My System: Psychoanalysis, Ideology, and Critical Method,* Oxford University Press, 1975. Advisory editor, *Anthology of American Literature,* Macmillan, 1974, 2nd edition, 1980. Contributor to literary journals.

WORK IN PROGRESS: Editing *The Random House Reader,* completion expected in 1981.

SIDELIGHTS: Although Frederick C. Crews has long been established as a practitioner of psychoanalytical literary criticism, he is probably best known for his mock-serious book, *The Pooh Perplex.* According to Eliot Fremont-Smith, "The book was a satirical triumph; it was also one of the best guides to literary absolutism since Stanley Edgar Hyman's *The Armed Vision.*" "Those of us who relish the more scholarly periodicals of literary criticism will be taken aback by the author's merciless parodies," notes Gerald Gardner, "for here are all the hilarious abuses of the somber breed whose pomposities parade across the pages of the learned quarterlies. . . . Crews has mounted a withering attack on the pretensions and excesses of academic criticism that both students and scholars should study for more than mere entertainment."

"Literary critics are traditionally and properly objects of derision," R. M. Adams concedes. "But if they are to be executed, it should be with a sharp knife and a devout spirit, on the altar of that intelligence which they themselves profess to serve. Clubbing them to death indiscriminately as too trivial and too ambitious, too learned and too ignorant, too subtle and too stupid, doesn't make for literate entertainment."

In *The Patch Commission,* Crews attempts another parody, this time of politics and *Baby and Child Care.* Fremont-Smith finds that the result "is funny in spots but with a fang-toothed bite; in fact, [it is] generally more bitter than funny, which in turn gives rise more often to impatience than to laughter. . . . Perhaps we have been surfeited with political satire; or perhaps, at the moment, our mood is too grim for this sort of wit; real events may have provided us with all the laceration we can take." Nevertheless, Carolyn F. Ruffin finds that "Crews's book is well-timed to fall into the generation gap and the credibility gap, like a wedge. It is as humor a little too perceptive for comfort, but still a little too brittle to work as solder from either side of the rift." To add his own wry twist, Leonard C. Lewin comments that "it is hard to understand . . . why [the] publishers timidly insist that the book and its characters are fictitious," and thinks the book "should be required reading for all serious students of government-where-it's-at."

In examining Crews's more serious works, one still finds him at his best where he injects some humor. Benjamin DeMott laments that "most readers of [*The Pooh Perplex*] knew from the first—with delight—that its author possessed a fine measuring eye for the gap between the words literary professionals utter about imaginative literature and the full life of that literature as experienced by ideal 'ordinary' readers. . . . It is this awareness that is absent [in *The Sins of the Fathers*]." On that point, critics often agree. On the subject of the book's projected impact, the consensus is less clear. "[This book] does little to shake the immense reputation of a classic American novelist whose complexities must continue to elude the most painstaking academic dissection," declares Allan Angroff. Such a view does not deter Lawrence Thompson from seeing *The Sins of the Fathers* as a book of "so much merit that it should create an important turning point in the study of Hawthorne's ambiguous art." Thompson feels that "some of Crews's best pages are those which clarify Hawthorne's art and thought by recourse to concepts that stem from psychoanalytic theories."

David Galoway tempers this opinion somewhat, calling it "a limited study . . . [in which] one could easily quarrel with some of the critic's interpretations of individual works. But this is, essentially, an admirable book—first, as an example of a highly disciplined and informed psychoanalytic study, and secondly as an important contribution to an understanding of a writer who, 'good Romantic that he was, located reality squarely in the buried life of the mind.'"

In *Out of My System,* Crews's sense of humor is more in evidence. "With wit and lucidity [he] examines and largely refutes the standard objections" to psychoanalytic criticism, writes Robert Towers. At the same time, "he argues against its reductionist excesses," another reviewer notes. "He plays the role of skeptical believer, so much so that often, in the prefatory remarks to each essay, he indicates his present reservations to his earlier positions. [He] gives the impression of challenging current positions while at the same time wittily enjoying his participation in them."

BIOGRAPHICAL/CRITICAL SOURCES: New York Times Book Review, September 29, 1963, May 22, 1966, October 6, 1968, December 21, 1975; *Virginia Quarterly Review,* winter, 1964, spring, 1976; *Book Week,* May 8, 1966; *Library Journal,* May 15, 1966; *Listener,* February 23, 1967; *New York Times,* July 26, 1968; *Christian Science Monitor,* October 24, 1968; *Book World,* August 25, 1968; *Western Humanities Review,* autumn, 1970.

* * *

CROMIE, Robert (Allen) 1909-

PERSONAL: Born February 28, 1909, in Detroit, Mich.; son of Robert and Annie Gertrude (Crosby) Cromie; married Alice Louise Hamilton, May 22, 1937; children: Michael, Richard, Barbara, James. *Education:* Oberlin College, A.B., 1930. *Home address:* Route 1, Box 42, Grayslake, Ill. 60030. *Agent:* Blassingame, McCauley & Wood, 60 East 42nd St., New York, N.Y. 10017.

CAREER: Pontiac Daily Press, Pontiac, Mich., reporter, 1935; *Pontiac News,* Pontiac, reporter, 1936-37; *Chicago Tribune,* Chicago, Ill., reporter, 1937-42, war correspondent, 1942-46, news reporter, 1946-48, sportswriter, 1948-60, book editor, 1960-69, daily columnist, 1969-74. Host of "Book Beat," WTTW-TV, Chicago, 1963-79, and of "The Cromie Circle," WGN-TV, Chicago, 1969—. Member of museum committee, U.S. Golf Association. *Member:* Authors Guild, Authors League of America, American Federation of Television and Radio Artists, Society of Midland Authors, Chicago Historical Society, Chicago Arts Club, Chicago Press Club. *Awards, honors:* Emmy award, National Academy of Television Arts and Sciences (Chicago branch), 1966; Irita Van Doren Award, American Booksellers Association, 1968; Peabody Award for "Book Beat" television program, 1969.

WRITINGS: The Great Chicago Fire, McGraw, 1959; (reviser) Mark Harris, *New Angles on Putting and Chip Shots,* Reilly & Lee, 1960; (with Joseph Pinkston) *Dillinger: A Short and Violent Life,* McGraw, 1962; (editor) *Par For the Course: A Golfer's Anthology,* Macmillan, 1964; *Golf for Boys and Girls,* Follett, 1965; (editor) *Where Steel Winds Blow: Poets on War,* McKay, 1968; (with Archie Lieberman) *Chicago in Color,* Hastings House, 1969; (with Herman Kogan) *The Great Fire: Chicago, 1871,* Putnam, 1971. Also author with Art Haug, of *Chicago.* Contributor of articles to golf magazines; contributor to popular periodicals; contributor of light verse to *Saturday Evening Post.*

SIDELIGHTS: A *Variety* critic notes that the Chicago public television station that produces the "Book Beat" series had some difficulty selling the N.E.T. network on the show because of the large number of book review-interview shows already on the air in many cities. However, "NET became interested in the Cromie show when authors began reporting and complaining that Cromie was the only one of the interviewers who had obviously read all of the book under discussion. . . . More than just a literary man, Cromie brings a widely-diversified journalistic background to his interviews that allows him to put the book and author in a wider perspective." And Cleveland Amory writes that "the average author is a difficult interview subject. All too often he exhibits that one unpardonable combination—nervousness and ego together. A man becomes an author, Somerset Maugham once said, because he is the kind of man who thinks of what he should have said on the way home from the party. We have often thought of that line as we watched some interview program and saw some author mumbling along. During one program, however, we never think of it. It is Robert Cromie's 'Book Beat,' telecast out of Chicago on some 150 educational stations. Mr. Cromie is strictly upbeat—a cheerful, gentle man. A refugee from the sports desk, he is, compared to the average literary critic, no intellectual giant. Compared to the average TV host, however, he is a think tank."

AVOCATIONAL INTERESTS: Photographic memorabilia; golf.

BIOGRAPHICAL/CRITICAL SOURCES: TV Guide, February 15, 1969; *Variety,* October 14, 1970.

* * *

CRONON, E(dmund) David 1924-

PERSONAL: Born March 11, 1924, in Minneapolis, Minn.; son of Edmund David and Florence Ann (Meyer) Cronon; married Mary Jean Hotmar, May 13, 1950; children: William John, Robert David. *Education:* Oberlin College, B.A., 1948; University of Wisconsin, M.A., 1949, Ph.D., 1953; attended University of Manchester, 1950-51. *Office:* Department of History, University of Wisconsin, Madison, Wis. 53706.

CAREER: Yale University, New Haven, Conn., instructor, 1953-57, assistant professor of history, 1957-59; University of Nebraska, Lincoln, associate professor, 1959-61, professor of history, 1961-62; University of Wisconsin—Madison, professor of history, 1962—, chairman of department, 1966-69, director of Institute for Research in the Humanities, 1969-74, dean of College of Letters and Science, 1974—. Lecturer, American Specialists Program, Department of State, 1966. Consultant on programs and research projects, National Endowment for the Humanities, 1969—. Member of executive committee, Wisconsin American Revolution Bicentennial Commission, 1972-77; chairman of advisory screening committee in American history, Council for International Exchange of Scholars, 1974-76; member of board of trustees, Ripon College, 1976—; member of board of directors, Council of Colleges of Arts and Sciences, 1977-80. *Military service:* U.S. Army, Infantry, 1943-46; became first lieutenant. *Member:* Society of American Historians (fellow), American Historical Association (chairman of committee on Ph.D. programs, 1968-70; chairman of Tocqueville Prize committee, 1978—), Organization of American Historians (member of executive board, 1970-73; chairman of Binkley-Stephenson Award committee, 1970), Southern Historical Association (member of executive council, 1975-76), State Historical Society of Wisconsin (member of board of curators, 1964—; president, 1970-73), Phi Beta Kappa. *Awards, honors:* Fulbright fellowship, 1950-51; University fellow, University of Wisconsin—Madison, 1952-53; Henry L. Stimson fellowship, Yale University, 1958-59.

WRITINGS: (Contributor) Howard K. Beale, editor, *Charles A. Beard: An Appraisal,* University of Kentucky Press, 1954; *Black Moses,* University of Wisconsin Press, 1955; *Josephus Daniels in Mexico,* University of Wisconsin Press, 1960; (editor) *Government and the Economy: Some Nineteenth Century Views,* Holt, 1960; *Contemporary Labor-Management Relations,* Holt, 1960; (with David M. Potter and Howard R. Lamar) *The Railroads,* Holt, 1960; (with Thomas G. Manning and Lamar) *The Standard Oil Company,* Holt, 1960; (contributor) Martin Borden, editor, *America's Ten Greatest Presidents,* Rand McNally, 1961; *Labor and the New Deal,* Rand McNally, 1963; (editor) *The Cabinet Diaries of Josephus Daniels, 1913-1921,* University of Nebraska Press, 1963; (contributor) Howard Quint, Dean Albertson, and Milton Cantor, editors, *Main Problems in American History,* Dorsey, 1964; (editor) *The Political Thought of Woodrow Wilson,* Bobbs-Merrill, 1965; (editor) *Twentieth Century America,* Dorsey, Volume I: *1900-1933,* 1965, Volume II: *1929-Present,* 1966; (editor) *Marcus Garvey,* Prentice-Hall, 1973; (editor with Theodore Rosenhof) *The Second World War and the Atomic Age, 1940-1973,* AHM Publishing, 1975.

* * *

CROSLAND, Margaret 1920-

PERSONAL: Born June 17, 1920, in Bridgnorth, Shropshire, England; daughter of Leonard and Beatrice Masterman (Wainwright) Crosland; married Max Denis, 1950 (divorced, 1959); children: Patrick Leonard Dagobert. *Education:* University of London, B.A. (honors), 1941. *Politics:* Labour Party. *Religion:* Church of England. *Home:* The Long Croft, Upper Hartfield, Sussex, England.

CAREER: Writer and translator. Literary adviser, British Broadcasting Corp. television film, "A Window on the War" (Colette), 1973. *Member:* Society of Authors.

WRITINGS: Strange Tempe (poems), Fortune Press, 1946; (compiler with Patricia Ledward) *The Happy Yes: An Anthology of Marriage Proposals, Grave and Gay,* Benn, 1949; *Madame Colette: A Provincial in Paris,* P. Owen, 1953, published as *Colette: A Provincial in Paris,* British Book Centre, 1954; *Jean Cocteau,* P. Neville, 1955, published as *Jean Cocteau: A Biography,* Knopf, 1956; *Ballet Carnival: A Companion to Ballet,* Arco, 1955, new edition, 1957; *Home Book of Opera,* Arco, 1957.

Ballet Lovers' Dictionary, Arco, 1962; *Louise of Stolberg, Countess of Albany,* Oliver & Boyd, 1962; *The Young Ballet Lover's Companion,* Souvenir Press, 1962; (adapter) Ornella Volta and Valeria Riva, compilers, *The Vampire: An Anthology,* Neville Spearman, 1963; *Philosophy Pocket Crammer,* Ken Publishing Company, 1964; (editor) Marquis de Sade, *Selected Letters,* P. Owen, 1965, October House, 1966; (editor) *A Traveller's Guide to Literary Europe,* H. Evelyn, 1965, published as *A Guide to Literary Europe,* Chilton, 1966; (editor) Jean Cocteau, *My Contemporaries,* P. Owen, 1967, Chilton, 1968; (author of introduction) Madame de Stael, *Ten Years' Exile,* Centaur Press, 1968; (editor) *Foliejon Park: A Short History,* Mining and Chemical Products Ltd., 1970; (editor) Cocteau, *Cocteau's World: An Anthology of Major Writings by Jean Cocteau,* P. Owen, 1972, Dodd, 1973; *Colette—The Difficulty of Loving: A Biography,* Bobbs-Merrill, 1973; *Raymond Radiguet: A Biographical Study with Selections from His Work,* P. Owen, 1976; *Women of Iron and Velvet: French Women Writers after George Sand,* Taplinger, 1976 (published in England as *Women of Iron and Velvet and the Books They Wrote in France,* Constable, 1976); (compiler and author of introduction) *The Leather Jacket: Stones by Cesare Pavese,* Quartet Books, 1980.

Translator: Felicien Marceau, *The Flesh in the Mirror,* Vision Press, 1953; Jean Cocteau, *Paris Album, 1900-1914,* W. H. Allen, 1956; Minou Drouet, *First Poems,* Hamish Hamilton, 1956; Drouet, *Then There Was Fire,* Hamish Hamilton, 1957; (with Sinclair Road) Cocteau, *Opium,* P. Owen, 1957, Grove, 1958, new translation with introduction by translators, Icon Books, 1961; Edmund de Goncourt, *Elisa,* Neville Spearman, 1959; *The Story of Reynard,* Hamish Hamilton, 1959; Vladimir Jankelevitch, *Ravel,* Grove, 1959; Pierre Lacroix, *The Conquest of Fire,* Burke Publishing, 1959; Joseph Rovan, *Germany,* Viking, 1959; Rene Poirier, *The Fifteen Wonders of the World,* Gollancz, 1960; Emile Zola, *Earth,* New English Library, 1962; Marcel

Mouloudji, *French Leave,* Neville Spearman, 1962; (and editor) Marquis de Sade, *De Sade Quartet,* P. Owen, 1963; (with Alan Daventry) Maurice Bessy, *A Pictorial History of Magic and the Supernatural,* Spring Books, 1963; (with Road) Octave Aubry, *Napoleon,* Paul Hamlyn, 1964; (and editor) *Selected Writings of de Sade,* P. Owen, 1964; Cecile Arnaud, *The Gift of Indifference,* Heinemann, 1965; Ghislain de Diesbach, *Secrets of the Gotha,* Chapman & Hall, 1967, Meredith, 1968; (with Daventry) Raymond de Becker, *The Other Face of Love,* Neville Spearman, 1967, Grove, 1969; Giorgio de Chirico, *Hebdomeros,* P. Owen, 1968; (and editor) Cesare Pavese, *A Mania for Solitude: Selected Poems, 1930-1950,* P. Owen, 1969; Drouet, *Donatella,* Neville Spearman, 1969; de Chirico, *Memoirs of Giorgio de Chirico,* University of Miami Press, 1971; Colette, *The Other Woman,* P. Owen, 1971, Bobbs-Merrill, 1972; (with David Le Vay) Colette, *The Thousand and One Mornings,* Bobbs-Merrill, 1973; (and author of introduction) Colette, *Retreat from Love,* Bobbs-Merrill, 1974; (and author of introduction) Colette, *Duo* (two novels), Bobbs-Merrill, 1974.

Contributor to *Spectator* and *Observer* (London).

WORK IN PROGRESS: Books on the painter and writer, Giorgio de Chirico; *Beyond the Lighthouse: English Women Novelists in the Twentieth Century.*

SIDELIGHTS: One of the first words Olivia Manning of the *Spectator* uses to describe Margaret Crosland's *Women of Iron and Velvet: French Women Writers after George Sand* is "dashing." Continues the critic: "[Crosland] sweeps the reader along with her vivacious prose, her enthusiasm and her intense interest in the personal lives of her subjects. [*Women of Iron and Velvet*] is a feminine book, deliciously feminine, . . . and is written from a frankly feminist viewpoint. The sweep of [Crosland's] study is enormous. . . . [Her subjects] are a delightful lot. . . . The reader enjoys them. In fact, this one of the most enjoyable nonfiction books I have read in a long time. . . . [*Women of Iron and Velvet*] is a brilliantly written, informative and often amusing book. Let us be grateful for it." Jean Stubbs of *Books and Bookmen* agrees. "Amused and awed by the iron energy and velvet fascination" of the writers Crosland profiles, she writes that "the vignettes in this study are riveting. . . . Anecdotes remain with me. . . . What a magnificent set [these women] are!"

The critics' *Yale Review* colleague, however, does not share their enthusiasm for Crosland's book. He calls the introductory chapters, which include "a panoramic presentation" of the French women writers who preceded George Sand, "superficial and cliche-ridden. . . . They are marred by breezy inaccuracies and flip oversimplifications. . . . The body of the book does not provide much more detailed discussion than the introductory chapters. . . . A more serious failing is the lack of a point of view that would tie these extremely varied writers together and raise the question of their sex vis-a-vis their art. The helter-skelter enumeration rarely rises above the encyclopedic." Futhermore he states "Crosland's likes and dislikes are allowed free rein, but one would wish them more responsibly argued. . . . Throughout the book the criteria are unclear, the historical assumptions unexamined. There is a disorderly quality to the writing itself which does not do justice to its tantalizing glimpses of real questions. . . . The implicit question raised by this book remains the unformulated one of what distinguishes a woman writer."

BIOGRAPHICAL/CRITICAL SOURCES: Spectator, November 27, 1976; *Books and Bookmen,* February, 1977; *Yale Review,* summer, 1977.

CROWDER, Michael 1934-

PERSONAL: Born June 9, 1934, in London, England; son of Henry Cussons (a businessman) and Molly (Burchell) Crowder. *Education:* Hertford College, Oxford, B.A. (first class honours in politics, philosophy and economics), 1957, M.A., 1962. *Politics:* "Radical/anti-colonial." *Home:* Flat 5, 5 Colville Houses, London W. 11, England. *Agent:* Curtis Brown Ltd., 1 Craven Hill, London W2 3EW, England. *Office:* c/o Longman Group Ltd., Longman House, Burnt Mill, Harlow, Essex, England.

CAREER: Writer specializing in African affairs, 1957-59; *Nigeria* Magazine, Lagos, Nigeria, editor, 1959-62; University of Ibadan, Institute of African Affairs, Ibadan, Nigeria, secretary, 1962-64; Fourah Box College, Freetown, Sierra Leone, director of Institute of African Studies, 1965-57; University of Ife, Ile-Ife, Nigeria, research professor and director of Institute of African Studies, 1968-71; Ahmadu Bello University, Zaria and Kano, Nigeria, professor of history and director of Center for Nigerian Cultural Studies, 1971-75; University of Lagos, Lagos, Nigeria, research professor at Centre for Cultural Studies, 1975-78. Visiting professor of African history, Columbia University, summers, 1963 and 1964; lecturer in African history, University of California, Berkeley, 1964-65. Executive secretary, Bureau of the International Congress of Africanists, 1962-68. *Military service:* British Army, Middlesex Regiment, temporary duty with Nigerian Regiment, 1952-54; became second lieutenant. Territorial Army, 1954-56; became lieutenant. *Member:* African Studies Association (United States; fellow), African Studies Association (England). *Awards, honors:* Officer of the National Order of Senegal, 1964.

WRITINGS: Pagans and Politicians, Hutchinson, 1959; *A Short History of Nigeria,* Praeger, 1962 (published in England as *The Story of Nigeria,* Faber, 1962, 4th edition, 1978), 4th edition, 1977; *Senegal: A Study in French Assimilation Policy,* Oxford University Press, 1962, revised edition, 1968; (with Onoura Nzekwu) *Eze Goes to School,* African Universities Press, 1963; (editor with Lalage Brown) *Proceedings of the International Congress of Africanists,* Northwestern University Press, 1964; (with Rex Akpofure) *Nigeria: A Modern History for Schools,* Faber, 1966; (editor with David Brokensha) *Africa in the Wider World: The Interrelationship of Area and Comparative Studies,* Pergamon, 1967; *West Africa under Colonial Rule,* Northwestern University Press, 1968; (editor with J. F. Ade Ajayi) *History of West Africa,* Longman, Volume I, 1971, Volume II, 1974; (editor) *West African Resistance: The Military Response to Colonial Occupation,* Africana Publishing, 1971; (editor with Obaro Ikime) *West African Chiefs,* Africana Publishing and Ife University Press, 1972; *Revolt in Bussa: A Study in British Native Administration in Nigerian Borgu, 1902-1935,* Northwestern University Press, 1973; *West Africa: An Introduction to Its History,* Longman, 1977; *Colonial West Africa: Collected Essays,* Cass & Co., 1978; (with Guda Abadullabu) *Nigeria: An Introduction to Its History,* Longman, in press. Contributor of articles on, African affairs to newspapers and periodicals. Editor of *African Notes,* 1963-64, *Sierra Leone Studies,* 1965-68, and *Odu,* 1968.

WORK IN PROGRESS: Editing volume eight of *Cambridge History of Africa;* editing with J. F. Ade Ajayi, *Historical Atlas of Africa,* for Longman.

AVOCATIONAL INTERESTS: Travel, gardening, photography, and French.

BIOGRAPHICAL/CRITICAL SOURCES: Observer Review, August 11, 1968; *Spectator,* August 23, 1968; *Punch,* September 25, 1968.

CULLINGWORTH, J(ohn) Barry 1929-

PERSONAL: Born September 11, 1929, in Nottingham, England; son of Sidney and Winifred (Tomlin) Cullingworth; married, 1950; children: Wendy, Peter, Jane. *Education:* Trinity College of Music, London, graduate, 1950; London School of Economics and Political Science, B.Sc., 1955. *Office:* Department of Urban and Regional Planning, University of Toronto, Toronto, Ontario, Canada M5S 1A1.

CAREER: University of Manchester, Manchester, England, research assistant, 1955-57, assistant lecturer, 1957-59, lecturer in social administration, 1959-60; University of Durham, Durham, England, lecturer in social studies, 1960-63; University of Glasgow, Glasgow, Scotland, senior lecturer in urban studies, 1963-66; University of Birmingham, Birmingham, England, director of Centre for Urban and Regional Studies, 1966-72, professor of urban and regional studies, 1968-72; Scottish Planning Exchange, Glasgow, director, 1972-75; Cabinet Office, Whitehall, London, England, official historian, 1975-77; University of Toronto, Toronto, Ontario, professor of urban and regional planning and chairman of department, 1977—. Visiting professor of regional and urban planning, University of Strathclyde. Vice-president, Housing Centre Trust; member of West Midlands Economic Planning Council, 1966-70, and Greater Glasgow Passenger Transport Authority, 1973-75. Consultant to Economic Commission for Europe, 1964-66, Organization for Economic Co-operation and Development, 1967, World Health Organization, 1971, United Nations Development Program on Regional Planning for the Suez Canal Zone, 1975-76, National Economic Development Council on Housing Policy, 1977, and Expenditure Committee of the House of Commons, 1977; member of advisory council, National Corporation for the Care of Old People, 1959-65; member of Secretary of State's Advisory Group on Housing Finance Review, 1975-77; member of Central Housing Advisory Committee, British Ministry of Housing. *Military service:* British Army, Education Corps; became sergeant. *Member:* British Sociological Association, Royal Institute of Public Administration, Social Administration Association, Architectural Association, Canadian Institute of Public Administration, Town and Country Planning Association, Ontario Council of Health.

WRITINGS: Restraining Urban Growth, Fabian Society, 1960; *Housing Needs and Planning Policy,* Routledge & Kegan Paul, 1960; *New Towns for Old,* Fabian Society, 1962; *Housing in Greater London,* London School of Economics and Political Science, 1962; *Housing in Transition,* Heinemann, 1963; *Town and Country Planning in England and Wales: An Introduction,* Allen & Unwin, 1964, 4th edition published as *Town and Country Planning in Britain,* 1972, 7th edition, 1979; *English Housing Trends,* G. Bell, 1965; *Housing and Local Government in England and Wales,* Allen & Unwin, 1966; *Scottish Housing in 1965,* H.M.S.O., 1968; *A Profile of Glasgow Housing,* Oliver & Boyd, 1968; (with Valerie A. Karn) *The Ownership and Management of Housing in the New Towns,* H.M.S.O., 1968; *Housing and Labour Mobility,* Organization for Economic Co-operation and Development, 1969; (editor with Sarah C. Orr) *Regional and Urban Studies,* Allen & Unwin, 1969.

The Politics of Research, Centre for Urban and Regional Studies, University of Birmingham, 1970; (with C. J. Watson) *Housing in Clydeside,* H.M.S.O., 1971; *Problems of an Urban Society,* three volumes, Allen & Unwin, 1973; *Reconstruction and Land Use Planning,* H.M.S.O., 1975; *Communication and Understanding in Planning Research: The Case of the Scottish Planning Exchange,* Department of Urban and Regional Planning, University of Toronto, 1978; *Ontario Planning: Notes on the Comay Report on the Ontario Planning Act,* Department of Urban Planning, University of Toronto, 1978; *Essays on Housing Policy,* Allen & Unwin, 1979; *New Towns Policy,* H.M.S.O., 1979; *Land Values Compensation and Betterment,* H.M.S.O., 1979. Also author of *Occasional Papers* for Centre for Urban and Regional Studies, University of Birmingham, 1966-72. Contributor to professional journals. *Urban Studies,* editor, 1964-66, member of editorial board, 1966—; member of editorial board, *Urban Abstracts,* 1968—; associate editor, *Urban Law and Policy,* 1978—.

* * *

CULLY, Iris V(irginia Arnold) 1914-

PERSONAL: Born September 12, 1914, in Brooklyn, N.Y.; daughter of James Aikman and Myrtle Marie (Michael) Arnold; married Kendig Brubaker Cully (a professor and clergyman), September 9, 1939; children: Melissa Iris Mueller, Patience Allegra Ecklund. *Education:* Adelphi College, B.A., 1936; Hartford Seminary Foundation, M.A., 1937; Garrett Theological Seminary, B.D., 1954; Northwestern University, Ph.D., 1955. *Politics:* Democrat. *Religion:* Episcopalian. *Home:* 1027 Gainesway Dr., Lexington, Ky. *Office:* Lexington Theological Seminary, 631 South Limestone St., Lexington, Ky. 40508.

CAREER: Garrett Theological Seminary, Evanston, Ill., part-time teacher of religious education, 1958-61; Northwestern University, Evening Division, Chicago and Evanston campuses, part-time teacher of religion, 1960, 1963; Chicago Lutheran Seminary, Chicago, part-time teacher, 1963; Yale University Divinity School, New Haven, Conn., associate professor of Christian education, 1965-72; *Review of Books and Religion,* White River Junction, Vt., editor, 1972-76; Lexington Theological Seminary, Lexington, Ky., Alexander Campbell Hopkins Professor of Religious Education, 1976—. Visiting professor, Drew University School of Theology, 1964, New York University, 1964-65, Union Theological Seminary, 1964-66, and Fordham University. *Member:* Religious Education Association (member of board of trustees, 1975-79), Association of Professors and Researchers in Religious Education (vice-president, 1972-73; president, 1973-74).

WRITINGS: (With husband, Kendig Brubaker Cully) *Two Seasons: Advent and Lent,* Bobbs-Merrill, 1954; *The Dynamics of Christian Education,* Westminster, 1958; *Children in the Church* (Pastoral Psychology Book Club selection and Religious Book Club alternate selection), Westminster, 1960; *Imparting the Word: The Bible in Christian Education,* Westminster, 1962; (with K. B. Cully) *An Introductory Theological Wordbook,* Westminster, 1964; *Ways to Teach Children,* Lutheran Church Press, 1966; *Christian Worship and Church Education,* Westminster, 1967; (contributor) Alois Mueller, editor, *Catechetics for the Future,* Herder & Herder, 1970; *Change, Conflict and Self-Determination,* Westminster, 1972; *New Life for Your Sunday School,* Hawthorn, 1976; (with K. B. Cully) *From Aaron to Zerubbabel,* Hawthorn, 1976; (editor with K. B. Cully) *Process and Relationship,* Religious Education Press, 1978; *Christian Child Development,* Harper, 1979. Also author of curriculum materials. Contributor of articles and book reviews to magazines. *Religious Education,* associate editor, 1974-78, consulting editor, 1978—; editor-in-chief, *New Review of Books and Religion,* 1976-78.

SIDELIGHTS: Iris Cully observed and studied religious education in western Europe in 1956. She conducted similar studies in the Caribbean area, South America, Mexico, 1962, Asia, 1970, and the Middle East, 1979.

* * *

CULLY, Kendig Brubaker 1913-

PERSONAL: Born November 30, 1913, in Millersville, Pa.; son of William Bigler and Emma Lavina (Kendig) Cully; married Iris Virginia Arnold, 1939; children: Melissa Iris (Mrs. William K. Mueller), Patience Allegra (Mrs. Laverne N. Ecklund). *Education:* American International College, A.B. (cum laude), 1934; Hartford Theological Seminary, B.D., 1937; Hartford School of Religious Education, M.R.E., 1938; Hartford Seminary Foundation, Ph.D., 1939; Seabury-Western Theological Seminary, S.T.M., 1953. *Home:* 1027 Gainesway Dr., Lexington, Ky.

CAREER: Minister of Congregational churches in Southwick, Belchertown, Melrose, and Haverhill (all Mass.), 1939-51; First Methodist Church, Evanston, Ill., minister of education, 1951-54; ordained Episcopal priest, 1955; Seabury-Western Theological Seminary, Evanston, professor of religious education, 1955-64; New York Theological Seminary, New York, N.Y., professor of Christian education, 1964-72, dean, 1965-72. Guest professor at Pacific School of Religion, Union Theological Seminary, Yale University, University of Pittsburgh, Lutheran School of Theology, Christian Theological Seminary, and Bethany Theological Seminary; visiting professor of Anglican Studies, Louisville Presbyterian Theological Seminary, 1977—; dean, Episcopal Theological Seminary in Kentucky, 1980—. Has studied religious education in Europe, 1956, Latin America, 1962, Asia, 1970, and the Middle East, 1979. *Member:* Religious Education Association, American Theological Society (midwest division), Professors and Researchers in Religious Education, American Academy of Religion, Tau Kappa Epsilon, Masons.

WRITINGS: (With wife, Iris V. Cully) *Two Seasons: Advent and Lent,* Bobbs-Merrill, 1954; (editor) *Basic Writings in Christian Education,* Westminster, 1960; *Exploring the Bible,* Morehouse, 1960; (contributor) *Religious Education,* Abingdon, 1960; *Sacraments: A Language of Faith,* Christian Education Press, 1961; (editor) *Prayers for Church Workers,* Westminster, 1961; (editor) *Confirmation: History, Doctrine, Practice,* Seabury, 1962; *The Teaching Church,* United Church Press, 1963; (contributor) *Preaching the Passion,* Fortress, 1963; (editor) *The Westminster Dictionary of Christian Education,* Westminster, 1963; *The Lord of Life,* Morehouse, 1964; (with I. V. Cully) *An Introductory Theological Wordbook,* Westminster, 1964; *The Search for a Christian Education: Since 1940,* Westminster, 1965; *The Episcopal Church and Education,* Morehouse, 1966; (editor) *Does the Church Know How to Teach?,* Macmillan, 1970; (editor with F. Nile Harper) *Will the Church Lose the City?,* World Publications, 1970; *Decisions and Your Future,* [Geneva], 1970; (with I. V. Cully) *From Aaron to Zerubbabel: Profiles of Bible People,* Seabury, 1976; (editor with I. V. Cully) *Process and Relationship: Issues in Theology, Philosophy, and Religious Education,* Religious Education Press, 1978. General editor of eleven volumes in "The Westminster Studies in Christian Communication" series. Contributor of articles, poems and reviews to periodicals. Founding editor, with I. V. Cully, of *Review of Books and Religion,* 1971-76, and *New Review of Books and Religion,* 1976-78.

CUNNINGHAM, J(ames) V(incent) 1911-

PERSONAL: Born August 23, 1911, in Cumberland, Md.; son of James Joseph and Anna (Finan) Cunningham; married Barbara Gibbs (a poet), 1937 (divorced, 1942); married Dolora Gallagher, 1945 (divorced, 1949); married Jessie Campbell, 1950; children: Marjorie Lupien. *Education:* Stanford University, A.B., 1934, Ph.D., 1945. *Home:* 17 Singletary Lane, Sudbury, Mass. 01776. *Office:* Brandeis University, Waltham, Mass. 02254.

CAREER: Stanford University, Stanford, Calif., instructor, 1937-45; University of Hawaii, Honolulu, assistant professor, 1945-46; University of Chicago, Chicago, Ill., assistant professor, 1946-52; University of Virginia, Charlottesville, assistant professor, 1952-53; Brandeis University, Waltham, Mass., professor of English, 1953—, University Professor, 1976—. Visiting professor at Harvard University, 1952, University of Washington, 1956, Indiana University at Bloomington, 1961, University of California, Santa Barbara, 1963, and Washington University, 1976. *Wartime service:* Mathematics teacher at an Air Force base in southern California. *Awards, honors:* Guggenheim fellowship in poetry, 1959-60, 1966-67; National Institute of Arts and Letters grant, 1965; National Endowment for the Arts grant, 1966; Academy of American Poets fellowship, 1976.

WRITINGS: (Translator) P. Nicole, *Essay on True and Apparent Beauty . . . ,* Augustan Reprint, 1950; *Woe or Wonder,* University of Denver Press, 1951; *Tradition and Poetic Structure,* A. Swallow, 1960; *The Journal of John Cardan,* [together with] *The Quest of the Opal* [and] *The Problem of Form,* A. Swallow, 1964; (contributor) Howard Nemerov, editor, *Poets on Poetry,* Basic Books, 1966; (editor) *The Renaissance in England,* Harcourt, 1966; (editor) *Problem of Style,* Fawcett, 1966; (editor) *In Shakespeare's Day,* Fawcett, 1970; *The Collected Essays of J. V. Cunningham,* Swallow Press, 1977.

Poetry: *The Helmsman,* Colt, 1942; *The Judge Is Fury,* Morrow, 1947; *Doctor Drink,* Cummington, 1950; *Trivial, Vulgar and Exalted: Epigrams,* Poems in Folio, 1957; *The Exclusions of a Rhyme,* A. Swallow, 1960; *To What Strangers, What Welcome,* A. Swallow, 1964; *Some Salt: Poems and Epigrams,* Perishable Press, 1967; *The Collected Poems and Epigrams of J. V. Cunningham,* Swallow Press, 1971.

SIDELIGHTS: "J. V. Cunningham seems to me the most consistently distinguished poet writing in English today, and one of the finest in the language, . . ." writes Yvor Winters. He is "the most finished master of the [epigram] form in English." His epigrams are precise and witty, and as Joseph Slater writes, Cunningham "distills not merely wisdom . . . but fun." Of this light touch in Cunningham's poetry, W. T. Scott writes: "The tone is doggedly minor, . . . [and] some of the epigrams are so slyly naughty that innocence could read them unbetrayed." His poems are not widely known, however, even among readers of poetry. As Hayden Carruth describes them, "the volume of Cunningham's output is small, but compact and without waste, tough, distinctive, filled with strange, flint-like intensity." Robert A. Stein finds "it sustains poetry's traditional resources at their very highest level."

BIOGRAPHICAL/CRITICAL SOURCES: *Yale Review,* September, 1960; *Times Literary Supplement,* September 23, 1960; *Saturday Review,* October 29, 1960; *New York Times Book Review,* November 13, 1960, August 7, 1977; *Poetry,* December, 1960; Yvor Winters, *J. V. Cunningham,* A. Swallow, 1961; Edward Hungerford, editor, *Poets in Progress,* Northwestern University Press, 1962; D. Donoghue, *Connoisseurs of Chaos,* Macmillan, 1965; *Spectator,* October 23, 1971; *Michigan Quarterly Review,* spring, 1972; *Western Humanities Review,* winter, 1973; *Contemporary Literary Criticism,* Volume III, Gale, 1975; *New Republic,* January 28, 1978.

* * *

CUNNINGHAM, Robert M(aris), Jr. 1909-

PERSONAL: Born May 28, 1909, in Chicago, Ill.; son of Robert Maris (a businessman) and Beda (Dickson) Cunningham; married Deborah Libby, November 24, 1934; children: Dennis, Damon, Margaret (deceased), Robert Maris III. *Education:* University of Chicago, Ph.B., 1931. *Home:* 2126 North Dayton St., Chicago, Ill. 60614. *Office:* Blue Cross and Blue Shield Associations, 840 North Lake Shore Dr., Chicago, Ill. 60611.

CAREER: Armour Institute of Technology (now Illinois Institute of Technology), Chicago, Ill., assistant to president, 1932-34; Shell Petroleum Co., Chicago, employed in sales and promotion, 1934-37; Chicago Blue Cross, Chicago, director of public relations, 1938-41; American Medical Association, Chicago, associate editor, *Hygeia,* 1941-45; McGraw-Hill Publications Co., Chicago, managing editor of *Modern Hospital,* 1945-51, editor, 1951-74; publisher, 1963-67, editorial director and publisher of *Nation's Schools and Colleges,* 1963-67, publisher of *College and University Business,* 1963-67, editorial director, 1967-74, editor of *Modern Nursing Home,* 1964-74, publisher, 1964-67, chairman of editorial board, *Modern Healthcare,* 1974-75, contributing editor, 1976—; Blue Cross and Blue Shield Associations, Chicago, publications consultant, 1974—. Vice-president and member of board of directors, F. W. Dodge Corp., 1959-63. Lecturer on hospital administration at Northwestern University and University of Chicago, 1946-51; consultant to American College of Surgeons, 1955-59, and U.S. Department of Health, Education, and Welfare.

MEMBER: National Association of Science Writers, Health Industries Association (member of board of directors, 1966-69; president, 1968-69), American College of Hospital Administrators (honorary fellow), American Hospital Association (honorary member), Psi Upsilon.

WRITINGS: Hospitals, Doctors and Dollars, F. W. Dodge, 1961; *The Third World of Medicine,* McGraw, 1968; *Governing Hospitals,* American Hospital Association, 1976; *Asking and Giving,* American Hospital Association, 1980. Contributor of articles on medical and hospital topics to journals.

* * *

CUSSLER, Clive (Eric) 1931-

PERSONAL: Born July 15, 1931, in Aurora, Ill.; son of Eric E. and Amy (Hunnewell) Cussler; married Barbara Knight, August 28, 1955; children: Teri, Dirk, Dana. *Education:* Attended Pasadena City College, Orange Coast College, and California State University, Los Angeles; San Jose State College (now University), B.S., 1957. *Politics:* Non-partisan. *Religion:* None. *Home:* 7731 West 72nd Pl., Arvada, Colo. 80002. *Agent:* Peter Lampack, The Lampack Agency, 551 Fifth Ave., New York, N.Y. 10017.

CAREER: Bestgen & Cussler Advertising, Newport Beach, Calif., owner, 1961-65; Darcy Advertising, Hollywood, Calif., copy director, 1965-67; Aquatic Marine Corp., Newport Beach, Calif., advertising director, 1967-69; Mefford Advertising, Denver, Colo., vice-president and creative director, 1970-75. Chairman, National Underwater and Marine Agency, Washington, D.C. *Military service:* U.S. Air Force, 1950-54; became sergeant. *Member:* Royal Geographic Society (London; fellow), Writers Guild, Colorado Author's League (president), Explorers Club (New York; fellow). *Awards, honors:* Ford Foundation Consumer Award, 1965-66, for best promotional presentation; Los Angeles Advertising Club awards, 1965, 1967, both for best sixty-second live commercial; Los Angeles Art Directors' Club certificates of merit, 1965, 1966, distinguished merit award, 1968; First Prize, Chicago Film Festival, 1966, for best thirty-second live action commercial; International Broadcasting Awards, 1967, for one of the year's ten best commercials, and 1968, for best sixty-second commercial; New York Art Directors' Club certificate of merit, 1968; Venice Film Festival second place award, 1972, for sixty-second live commercial; and numerous other advertising awards.

WRITINGS: The Mediterranean Caper (novel), Pyramid Publications, 1973; *Iceberg,* Dodd, 1975; *Raise the Titanic,* Viking, 1976; *Vixen O-3,* Viking, 1978. Writer of television scripts for segments of "The Courtship of Eddie's Father," "Here Come the Brides," "I Spy," "The Good Guys," "The Mothers-In-Law," and "Twelve O'Clock High." Also author of two pilot scripts, "Aces of the 86th" and "Once over Lightly," as yet unproduced.

WORK IN PROGRESS: A suspense-adventure novel with the continuing hero of Dirk Pitt.

SIDELIGHTS: Cussler told *CA* that "love of adventure based in and around the field of oceanography is [his] primary motivation for the Dirk Pitt series of books." He is an expert diver and an amateur marine archaeologist who financially backs expeditions to find lost historical ships, such as John Paul Jones's famous frigate, the "Bonhomme Richard." Cussler also closely follows and researches unexplained marine phenomena.

BIOGRAPHICAL/CRITICAL SOURCES: Washington Post, October 24, 1978; *Los Angeles Times,* June 21, 1979; *Chicago Tribune,* February 10, 1980.

* * *

CUTHBERTSON, Tom 1945-

PERSONAL: Born May 7, 1945, in San Mateo, Calif.; son of Kenneth McLean (vice-president for finance of Stanford University) and Coline (Upshaw) Cuthbertson; married Patricia Zylius, July 12, 1969; children: Ian, Cory. *Education:* University of California, Santa Cruz, B.A. (with honors), 1967; San Francisco State College (now University), M.A., 1971. *Residence:* Santa Cruz, Calif.

CAREER: Writer. Has worked as gardener, ranch hand, construction laborer, truck driver, hospital orderly, missionary, bicycle mechanic, library employee, field hand in a vineyard, boatman, lecturer, and actor in educational movies. *Member:* Amateur Bicycle League of America.

WRITINGS—Published by Ten Speed Press, except as indicated: *Anybody's Bike Book,* 1971; *Bike Tripping,* 1972; *My Lawnmower Hates Me,* 1974; *Anybody's Skateboard Book,* 1975; *Alan Chadwick's Enchanted Garden,* Dutton, 1978; *Anybody's Roller Skating Book,* 1979; *I Can Swim, You Can Swim,* 1979.

WORK IN PROGRESS: Bikes That Do a Car's Work, for Ten Speed Press.

AVOCATIONAL INTERESTS: Tinkering, Chinese puzzles, riding bicycles, listening to his wife sing madrigals.

D

DABNEY, Virginius 1901-

PERSONAL: Born February 8, 1901, in University (now Charlottesville), Va.; son of Richard Heath (a professor) and Lily Heth (Davis) Dabney; married Douglas Harrison Chelf, October 10, 1923; children: Douglas G. (Mrs. James S. Watkinson), Lucy D. (Mrs. Alexander P. Leverty II), Richard Heath II. *Education:* University of Virginia, B.A., 1920, M.A., 1921. *Politics:* Independent. *Religion:* Episcopalian. *Home:* 14 Tapoan Rd., Richmond, Va. 23226.

CAREER: Episcopal High School, Alexandria, Va., teacher of French and algebra, 1921-22; *Richmond News Leader,* Richmond, Va., reporter, 1922-28; *Richmond Times-Dispatch,* Richmond, member of editorial staff, 1928-34, chief editorial writer, 1934-36, editor, 1936-69. Member of board of trustees, Episcopal High School, 1935-38, 1940-43, 1944-54, and Institute of Early American History and Culture during the early 1940s; member of board of directors, Richmond Public Library, 1943-61, and University Press of Virginia, 1966-70; chairman of board of directors, Southern Education Reporting Service, 1954-57; chairman of Virginia Governor's Statewide Conference on Education, 1966. Visiting lecturer, Princeton University, 1939-40, Cambridge University, 1954.

MEMBER: American Society of Newspaper Editors (member of board of directors, 1946-59; president, 1957-58), Virginia Historical Society (president, 1969-72), Raven Society, Phi Beta Kappa, Omicron Delta Kappa, Delta Kappa Epsilon, Sigma Delta Chi (fellow), Society of the Cincinnati, Jamestowne Society, Country Club of Virginia (member of board of directors, for three terms). *Awards, honors:* Oberlaender Trust grant, 1934, for travel and study in Central Europe; Lee Award of Virginia Press Association and Washington and Lee School of Journalism, 1937, for distinguished editorial writing; D.Litt., University of Richmond, 1940; LL.D., College of Lynchburg and College of William and Mary, both 1944; Pulitzer Prize, 1947, for editorial writing; Sigma Delta Chi National Editorial Award, 1948, 1952; Virginians of Maryland Society Medallion of Honor, 1961; B'nai B'rith (Richmond) Man of the Year Award, 1963; Guggenheim fellowship, 1968; Sigma Delta Chi George Mason Award, 1969, for outstanding contribution to journalism; National Endowment for the Humanities grant, 1970; National Conference of Christians and Jews Brotherhood Award, 1971; Raven Society award, 1972, for service to the University of Virginia; Thomas Jefferson Award for public service, 1972; Virginia Social Science Association District Service Award, 1975; Jackson Davis Medal, 1975, for service to higher education, 1975; received special award from Virginia State Chamber of Commerce, 1975; Richmond Bar Association Liberty Bell Award, 1976; L.H.D., Virginia Commonwealth University, 1976.

WRITINGS: Liberalism in the South, University of North Carolina Press, 1932, reprinted, AMS Press, 1970; *Below the Potomac: A Book about the New South,* Appleton, 1942, reprinted, Kennikat, 1969; *Dry Messiah: The Life of Bishop Cannon,* Knopf, 1949, reprinted, Greenwood Press, 1970; *Virginia: The New Dominion,* Doubleday, 1971; (editor) *The Patriots: The American Revolution Generation of Genius,* Atheneum, 1975; *Richmond: The Story of a City,* Doubleday, 1976; *Across the Years: Memories of a Virginian,* Doubleday, 1978. Contributor to *Dictionary of American Biography* and *Encyclopaedia Britannica,* and to numerous periodicals, including *Economist, Atlantic, Saturday Review, New Republic, Nation, Life, Reader's Digest, Saturday Evening Post, New York Times Magazine, Virginia Quarterly Review.*

WORK IN PROGRESS: Mr. Jefferson's University, University Press of Virginia, publication expected in 1981.

SIDELIGHTS: In *Virginia: The New Dominion,* Virginius Dabney, the long-time editor of what Cabell Phillips calls Virginia's "most influential newspaper," chronicles his native state's growth from its beginnings as a colony to the early 1970's. According to Phillips, "Virginia's history is the oldest, and at some points the most glamourous, of any of the states of the Union." Its contributions to the American Revolution and to the founding of the United States are highlighted in Dabney's book. *Virginia Quarterly Review* critic Allen W. Moger writes: "The account of Virginia's majestic accomplishments and contributions during the period of the Revolution and the few years that followed is one of the best in the book. Virginians can wonder with justifiable pride how independence could have been secured and the new nation established without the enlightened and determined leadership of the commonwealth's great men: Patrick Henry, Thomas Jefferson, George Washington, George Mason, Peyton Randolf, Richard Henry Lee, and James Madison." Phillips comments that this history is the "obsessive pride" of Virginians and claims that "Virginia is both a state and a state of mind."

Although many books detailing Virginia's history and heritage have been published over the years, Dabney's has the distinction of retracing "this well-worn literary trail with absorbing detail and insight," Phillips remarks. Moger agrees with this assessment and finds that "the narrative is woven around men and events, ideas and accomplishments, and Virginia is made a vital part of the nation's history." Moreover, he believes that in *Virginia: The New Dominion* Dabney "demonstrates that his personal skill and long experience as a journalist have made him the master of writing, and he has a distinctive appreciation for the facts and trends of history."

BIOGRAPHICAL/CRITICAL SOURCES: New York Times Book Review, February 2, 1972; *Virginia Quarterly Review,* spring, 1972, spring, 1976; *Atlantic,* December, 1975; *Kirkus Review,* July 1, 1978; *New Yorker,* September 4, 1978; *Washington Post,* September 26, 1978.

* * *

DAEMMRICH, Horst S. 1930-

PERSONAL: Born January 5, 1930, in Pausa, Germany; naturalized U.S. citizen in 1959; son of Arthur M. (a factory owner) and Gertrud (Orlamuende) Daemmrich; married Ingrid Guenther (a press editor), June 10, 1962; children: JoAnn, Arthur. *Education:* Wayne State University, B.A. and M.A., 1958; University of Chicago, Ph.D., 1964. *Home:* 14531 Stahelin, Detroit, Mich. 48223. *Office:* Department of German, Wayne State University, Detroit, Mich. 48202.

CAREER: Wayne State University, Detroit, Mich., assistant professor, 1963-67, associate professor, 1967-71, professor of German, 1971—. *Member:* American Association for Aesthetics, Modern Language Association of America, American Association of Teachers of German, American Lessing Society, Phi Beta Kappa. *Awards, honors:* Board of Governors recognition award, Wayne State University, 1975; distinguished graduate faculty award, 1978.

WRITINGS: (Editor with Diether Haenieke) *The Challenge of German Literature,* Wayne State University Press, 1972; *The Shattered Self: E.T.A. Hoffmann's Tragic Vision,* Wayne State University Press, 1973; *Literaturkritik in Theorie und Praxis,* Francke Verlag, 1974; (with wife, Ingrid Daemmrich) *Wiederholte Spiegelungen: Themen und Motive in der Literatur,* Francke Verlag, 1978; *Wilhelm Raabe,* Twayne, 1980; *Karl Krolow,* C. H. Beck, 1980. Contributor to *Journal of Aesthetics and Art Criticism, Germanic Review, Weimarer Beitrage, Mosaic, Modern Language Quarterly, Papers on English Language and Literature, Bucknell Review,* and *Publications of English Geothe Society.*

WORK IN PROGRESS: Books and articles on German literature.

* * *

DAHLSTEDT, Marden 1921-

PERSONAL: Born August 14, 1921, in Pittsburgh, Pa.; daughter of Glenn Stewart (a hardware store owner) and Lillian (Seigler) Armstrong; married Richard Robert Dahlstedt (a newspaperman), May 26, 1945; children: Ellen Christina (Mrs. Richard Douglas Irwin, II). *Education:* Chatham College, A.B., 1942; Slippery Rock State College, certification in high school library science, 1965. *Politics:* Democrat. *Religion:* Protestant. *Home:* 2613 Bay Ave., Beach Haven Gardens, N.J. 08008. *Office:* Beach Haven Public Library, Beach Haven, N.J. 08008. *Agent:* McIntosh & Otis, Inc., 475 Fifth Ave., New York, N.Y. 10017.

CAREER: West Deer Junior High School, Cheswick, Pa., librarian, 1964-68; Beach Haven Elementary School, Beach Haven, N.J., librarian, beginning 1971; Beach Haven Public Library, Beach Haven, director, 1978—. Co-owner, with husband, of The Attic (an antique shop) in Beach Haven Gardens. *Member:* American Association of University Women, Authors Guild, New England Poetry Society, Pittsburgh Poetry Society. *Awards, honors:* Borestone Mountain Poetry Award, 1960.

WRITINGS: The Terrible Wave, Coward, 1972; *Shadow of the Lighthouse,* Coward, 1974; *The Stopping Place,* Putnam, 1976. Author of a column on antiques, "The Corner Cupboard," in *Beach Haven Times.*

WORK IN PROGRESS: A contemporary juvenile novel.

* * *

DALE, Peter (John) 1938-

PERSONAL: Born August 21, 1938, in Addlestone, Surrey, England; son of Ernest John (a salesman) and Elizabeth Dale; married Pauline Strouvelle; children: Piers Graham, Kim Paula. *Education:* St. Peter's College, Oxford, B.A. (second class honors), 1963. *Politics:* Socialist. *Home and office:* 10 Selwood Rd., Sutton, Surrey, England.

CAREER: Knaphill County Secondary School, Woking, Surrey, England, assistant teacher of English, 1963; Howden C.S. School, Howden, East Yorkshire, England, assistant teacher of English, 1964-65; Glastonbury C.S. School, Morden, Surrey, assistant teacher of English, 1965-72; Hinchley Wood C.S. School, Hinchley Wood, Surrey, head of English department, 1972—. *Member:* Assistant Masters Association.

WRITINGS: Nerve, privately printed, 1959; *Walk from the House,* Fantasy Press (Oxford), 1962; *The Storms* (poems), Dufour, 1968; *Mortal Fire* (poems), Dufour, 1970; (translator) Francois Villon, *"The Legacy" and Other Poems,* Agenda, 1971; (translator) Villon, *"The Legacy," "The Testament" and Other Poems,* St. Martin's, 1973; (translator with Kokilam Subbiah) Tamil, *The Seasons of Cankam,* Agenda, 1975; *Mortal Fire* (collected poems), Ohio University Press, 1976; (translator) Villon, *Selected Poems of Francois Villon,* Penguin (London), 1978; *One Another* (sonnet sequence), Agenda, 1978. Contributor to *Agenda, Times Literary Supplement, Review, Listener, Canto, Green River Review, Paideuma, Poetry Review, Stand, Shenandoah, Southern Review,* and other publications. Associate editor, *Agenda,* 1972—.

WORK IN PROGRESS: A verse play, *Sephe;* a verse translation of the collected poems of Jules Laforgue; a book of poems.

* * *

DALLIN, Leon 1918-

PERSONAL: Born 1918, in Silver City, Utah; son of Glenn L. and Elizabeth (Jolley) Dallin; married Lynn Nicholes. *Education:* University of Rochester, Eastman School of Music, B.M., 1940, M.M., 1941; University of Southern California, Ph.D., 1949. *Address:* P.O. Box 2400, Seal Beach, Calif. 90740. *Office:* Department of Music, California State University, Long Beach, Calif. 90840.

CAREER: Colorado State College of Agriculture and Mechanic Arts (now Colorado State University), Fort Collins, assistant professor, 1946; University of Southern California, Los Angeles, instructor, 1946-48; Brigham Young University, Provo, Utah, professor, 1948-55; California State University, Long Beach, professor of music, 1955—. Program annotator, Long Beach Symphony Orchestra, 1959-61;

preview lecturer, Los Angeles Philharmonic and Long Beach Symphony; member of board and talent chairman, Long Beach Community Concert Association, 1962. Guest conductor and composer. *Military service:* U.S. Army Air Forces, 1942-45; became technical sergeant.

MEMBER: American Musicological Society (president of Rocky Mountain chapter, 1954-55), National Association of Composers, U.S.A., Music Educators National Conference (life member), American Association of University Professors, American Society of Composers, Authors and Publishers, Phi Mu Alpha Sinfonia.

WRITINGS—All published by W. C. Brown, except as indicated: *Techniques of Twentieth Century Composition,* 1957, 3rd edition, 1974; (with R. W. Winslow) *Music Skills for Classroom Teachers,* 1958, 5th edition, 1979; *Listener's Guide to Musical Understanding,* with workbook, 1959, 4th edition, 1977; *Foundations in Music Theory,* Wadsworth, 1962, 2nd edition, 1967; *Introduction to Music Reading,* Scott, Foresman, 1966; (with wife, L. Dallin) *Heritage Songster,* 1966, 2nd edition, 1980; (with L. Dallin) *Folk Songster,* 1967; *Basic Music Skills: A Supplementary Program for Self-Instruction,* 1971. Composer of a number of published musical compositions for orchestra, band, chorus, solo instruments, and chamber groups.

* * *

DALLMAYR, Fred R(einhard) 1928-

PERSONAL: Born October 18, 1928, in Ulm, Germany; son of Albert (a realtor) and Olga (Schnell) Dallmayr; married Ilse Balzer, August 24, 1957; children: Dominique Brigit, Philip Gregory. *Education:* Attended University of Munich, 1949-53, and University of Brussels, 1953-54; University of Munich, LL.D., 1955; Southern Illinois University, M.A., 1956; Duke University, Ph.D., 1960. *Home:* 51888 Old Mill Rd., South Bend, Ind. 46637. *Office:* Department of Government, University of Notre Dame, Notre Dame, Ind. 46556.

CAREER: Milwaukee-Downer College, Milwaukee, Wis., instructor, 1961-62, assistant professor of political science, 1962-63; Purdue University, Lafayette, Ind., assistant professor, 1963-65, associate professor, 1965-68, professor of political science, 1968-71; University of Georgia, Athens, professor of political science, 1971-73; Purdue University, professor of political science and chairman of department, 1973-78; University of Notre Dame, Notre Dame, Ind., Dee Professor of Government, 1978—. Visiting professor, University of Hamburg, 1969, 1971, and 1976. *Member:* American Political Science Association, Conference for the Study of Political Thought, Society for Phenomenology and Existential Philosophy, Phi Beta Kappa. *Awards, honors:* National Endowment for the Humanities fellowship, 1978-80.

WRITINGS: (With Robert S. Rankin) *Freedom and Emergency Powers,* Appleton, 1964; (contributor) R. Koselleck and R. Schnur, editors, *Hobbes-Forschungen* (title means "Essays on Hobbes"), Duncker & Humblot, 1969; (contributor) Carl Beck, editor, *Law and Justice,* Duke University Press, 1970; (contributor) Glen Gordon and William E. Connolly, editors, *Social Structure and Political Life,* Heath, 1973; (contributor) George Psathas, editor, *Phenomenological Sociology,* Wiley, 1973; (contributor) E. S. Casey and D. Carr, editors, *Explorations in Phenomenology,* Nijhoff, 1974; (editor and author of introduction and epilogue) *Materialienband zu Habermas' Erkenntnis und Interesse* (title means "Essays on Habermas' 'Knowledge and Human Interests'"), Suhrkamp, 1974; (with Thomas A. McCarthy) *Understanding and Social Inquiry,* University of Notre Dame Press, 1977; (editor and author of introduction) *From Contract to Community: Political Theory at the Crossroads,* Dekker, 1978; (contributor) Joseph Bien, editor, *Phenomenology and Social Science,* Nijhoff, 1978; (contributor) Maria J. Falco, editor, *Through the Looking Glass,* University Press of America, 1979; *Phenomenology of Politics,* University of Notre Dame Press, 1980. Contributor to *Law and Contemporary Problems, Ethics, Journal of General Education, American Political Science Review, Review of Politics, Social Research, Journal of Politics, Polity, Politics and Society, Man and World, Philosophy of the Social Sciences, Philosophische Rundschau,* and *Inquiry.*

WORK IN PROGRESS: Man and Polis: Contributions to a Post-Individualist Theory of Politics, for University of Massachusetts Press.

* * *

D'AMATO, Janet Potter 1925-

PERSONAL: Born June 5, 1925, in Rochester, N.Y.; daughter of Earle H. and Florence (an artist; maiden name, Cowles) Potter; married Alex D'Amato (a book designer), February 28, 1949; children: Sandra (Mrs. Harry Tompkins, Jr.), Donna (Mrs. James Lee). *Education:* Pratt Institute, diploma, 1946. *Residence:* Bronxville, N.Y.

CAREER: Display designer; Art Studio, Mt. Vernon, N.Y., illustrator for filmstrips, 1946-47; free-lance artist, 1952—.

WRITINGS—With husband, Alex D'Amato: *Wendy and the Wind,* Grosset, 1957; *U.S.A. Fun and Play,* Doubleday, 1960; *Blow, Wind, Blow,* Grosset, 1960; *The Costume Party,* Grosset, 1962; *My First Book of Jokes,* Grosset, 1962; *Animal Fun Time,* Doubleday, 1964; *Fun till Christmas,* Whitman Publishing, 1965; *Cardboard Carpentry,* Lion Press, 1966; *Handicrafts for Holidays,* Lion Press, 1967; *Indian Crafts,* Lion Press, 1968; *African Crafts for You to Make,* Messner, 1968; *African Animals through African Eyes,* Messner, 1971; *What's in the Sky?,* Nutmeg Press, 1971; *Houses,* Nutmeg Press, 1971; *Animals,* Nutmeg Press, 1971; *American Indian Craft Inspirations,* M. Evans, 1972; *Gifts to Make for Love or Money,* Golden Press, 1973; *Colonial Crafts for You to Make,* Messner, 1975; *Quillwork: The Craft of Paper Filigree,* M. Evans, 1975; *More Colonial Crafts for You to Make,* Messner, 1977; *Italian Crafts: Inspirations from Folk Art,* M. Evans, 1977; *Algonquin and Iroquois Crafts for You to Make,* Messner, 1979.

Illustrator: Sophie Ruskay, *Discovery at Aspen,* A. S. Barnes, 1960; Shari Lewis and Jacquelyn Reinach, *Headstart Book of Looking and Listening,* McGraw, 1960; Constantine Georgiou, *Wait and See,* Harvey House, 1962; Azriel Eisenberg, editor, *Tzedakah,* Behrman, 1963; Hyman Ruchlis, *Your Changing Earth,* Harvey House, 1963; Mary Elting, *Water Come, Water Go,* Harvey House, 1964; Elting, *Aircraft at Work,* Harvey House, 1964; Norah Smaridge, *The Light Within,* Hawthorn, 1965; Evelyn Fiore, *Wonder Wheel Book of Birds,* Rutledge Books, 1965; A. Sundgaard, *How Lovely Is Christmas,* Western Publishing, 1966; Joan W. Jenkins, *A Girl's World,* Hawthorn, 1967; Samm S. Baker, *Miracle Gardening Encyclopedia,* Grosset, 1967; Arthur Liebers, *Fifty Favorite Hobbies,* Hawthorn, 1968. M. Bevans, *Weather and Weather Forecasting,* Nutmeg Press, 1975; Arnold Madison, *Don't Be a Victim!,* Messner, 1978; Barbara Ford, *Animals That Use Tools,* Messner, 1978; Lorraine Henriod, *Ancestor Hunting,* Messner, 1979. Also creator, with husband, of kits and book and record cover designs. Contributor to *Creative Crafts* and *Humpty Dumpty.*

WORK IN PROGRESS: Galaxy Games, for Doubleday.

SIDELIGHTS: Janet D'Amato told *CA:* "Basically I'm an artist; writing just slipped in along the way. I started writing stories to have something to illustrate for children's books. My husband, a book designer, worked with me and we sold our first book when our daughter was three.

"Later, my interests in crafts and their origins was turned into how-to books. I write, create craft adaptations, and illustrate various types of books with games, activities or crafts, mostly for children. A product of our technological age, today's youngsters seldom realize early crafts were produced as household necessities. They think of crafts as only pastimes. With historical background on each project, we try to help them realize the origins of crafts and encourage them to feel the satisfaction of working with their own hands. Hopefully, along with the sense of personal achievement, they may also feel a relationship to an era when an individual was more part of all that was made and used in daily living."

* * *

DANCE, F(rancis) E(sburn) X(avier) 1929-
(Frank E. X. Dance)

PERSONAL: Born November 9, 1929, in Brooklyn, N.Y.; son of Clifton L. (a physician) and Catherine (Tester) Dance; married Nora Alice Rush, 1954 (divorced, 1973); married Carol C. Zak, July 4, 1974; children: (first marriage) Clifton L. III, Charles Daniel, Alison Catherine, Andrea, Frances, Brendan; (second marriage) Zachary Esburn. *Education:* Fordham University, B.S., 1951; Northwestern University, M.A., 1953, Ph.D., 1959. *Religion:* Roman Catholic. *Home:* 99 South Emerson St., Denver, Colo. 80209. *Office:* Department of Speech Communication, University of Denver, Denver, Colo. 80208.

CAREER: University of Illinois at Chicago Circle, instructor in humanities and coordinator of radio and television, 1953-54; Chicago City Junior College, Wilson Branch, Chicago, instructor in speech, 1957-58; St. Joseph's College, Rensselaer, Ind., assistant professor, 1958-60; University of Kansas, Lawrence, assistant professor of speech, 1960-62; University of Wisconsin—Milwaukee, 1962-71, began as associate professor, became professor of speech and director of Speech Communication Center; University of Denver, Denver, Colo., professor of speech, 1971—. Visiting distinguished professor, University of Montana, 1971; visiting scholar, Western Michigan University, 1977. *Military service:* U.S. Army, 1954-56; became first lieutenant. *Member:* International Communication Association (president, 1967; fellow, 1978), American Association for the Advancement of Science, American Association of University Professors (president of St. Joseph's chapter, 1959-60), Speech Communication Association, Eastern Communication Association, Western Speech Communication Association, Central States Speech Communication Association.

WRITINGS—Under name Frank E. X. Dance: *The Citizen Speaks,* Wadsworth, 1962; (with Harold P. Zelko) *Business and Professional Speech Communication,* Holt, 1965; (editor) *Human Communication Theory: Original Essays,* Holt, 1967; (editor with Carl E. Larson) *Perspectives on Communication,* Helix Press, 1970; (with Larson) *Speech Communication: Concepts and Behavior,* Holt, 1972; (with Larson) *The Functions of Human Communication: A Theoretical Approach,* Holt, 1976. Contributor of over fifty articles and book reviews to professional journals. Editor, *Journal of Communication,* 1962-64, and *Communication Education,* 1970-72; contributing editor or member of editorial board of *Journal of Psycholinguistic Research, Journal of Black Studies, Western Journal of Speech Communication, Communication, Communication Education, Health Communications and Informatics,* and *Preaching: A Journal of Homiletics.*

WORK IN PROGRESS: A study concerning the oral intellect; a text book in comparative human communication theory; and an extended essay dealing with the creative aspects of tension in the individual life.

SIDELIGHTS: Frank E. X. Dance told *CA:* "The fact that humans speak is central to an understanding of the human condition. My efforts are aimed toward a fuller explication of the difference it makes to the human individual and to human society . . . that our natural communicative mode is through the spoken word."

* * *

DANNAY, Frederic 1905-
(Ellery Queen, Ellery Queen, Jr., and Barnaby Ross, joint pseudonyms; Daniel Nathan)

PERSONAL: Original name, Daniel Nathan; name legally changed; born October 20, 1905, in Brooklyn, N.Y.; son of Meyer H. and Dora (Walerstein) Nathan; married Mary Beck (deceased); married Hilda Wiesenthal (died, 1972); married Rose Koppel; children: (first marriage) Douglas, Richard; (second marriage) Stephen (deceased). *Home:* 29 Byron Lane, Larchmont, N.Y. 10538.

CAREER: After what he calls a "patchwork" of jobs, Dannay worked in advertising, becoming a copywriter, art director, and account executive for various advertising agencies; he was also a typographic consultant. He left advertising just after publication of the first Ellery Queen novel in 1929. Since then, he has been a full-time writer and editor. In 1933-34, he made lecture tours with Manfred B. Lee; in 1958-59, he was visiting professor at the University of Texas at Austin.

MEMBER: Mystery Writers of America (co-founder and co-president, with Manfred B. Lee), Crime Writers' Association (London), Baker Street Irregulars. *Awards, honors:* Mystery Writers of America, Edgar Allan Poe Annual Award, 1945, for best radio program, 1947, for outstanding contribution in the field of the mystery short story, 1949, to *Ellery Queen's Mystery Magazine,* for outstanding contribution in the field of the mystery short story, Special Book Award, 1951, Grand Master Award, 1960; Pocket Books, Silver Gertrude (signifying membership in Million Copy Club), Gold Gertrude (signifying membership in Five Million Copy Club); American Red Cross citation for outstanding national service, 1945; National War Fund citation for meritorious service, 1945; Youth Oscar Award, Youth United, 1949, as distinguished ex-Brooklynite; *TV Guide* Gold Medal Award, 1950, to the Ellery Queen TV series as "Mystery Show of the Year"; Ellery Queen ranked third in Gallup Poll of Best Mystery Writers of All Time, 1950; Ellery Queen was ranked, in an international poll of experts, among the ten best active mystery writers, 1951; *True* magazine citation to Ellery Queen TV series, 1952; Edgar Allan Poe Ring, Mystery Writers of Japan, 1956; Grand Prix de Litterature Policiere, 1978, for *And On the Eighth Day;* honorary doctorate, Carroll College, 1979; many awards during 1979 for the fiftieth anniversary of *The Roman Hat Mystery,* the first Ellery Queen book.

WRITINGS—All with Manfred B. Lee under joint pseudonym Ellery Queen; novels: *The Roman Hat Mystery,*

Stokes, 1929, reprinted, Mysterious Press, 1979; *The French Powder Mystery,* Stokes, 1930; *The Dutch Shoe Mystery,* Stokes, 1931; *The Greek Coffin Mystery,* Stokes, 1932; *The Egyptian Cross Mystery,* Stokes, 1932; *The American Gun Mystery,* Stokes, 1933; *The Siamese Twin Mystery,* Stokes, 1933; *The Chinese Orange Mystery,* Stokes, 1934; *The Spanish Cape Mystery,* Stokes, 1935; *Halfway House,* Stokes, 1936; *The Door Between,* Stokes, 1937; *The Devil to Pay,* Stokes, 1938; *The Four of Hearts,* Stokes, 1938; *The Dragon's Teeth,* Stokes, 1939; *Calamity Town,* Little, Brown, 1942; *There Was an Old Woman,* Little, Brown, 1943; *The Murderer Is a Fox,* Little, Brown, 1945; *Ten Days' Wonder,* Little, Brown, 1948; *Cat of Many Tails,* Little, Brown, 1949; *Double, Double,* Little, Brown, 1950; *The Origin of Evil,* Little, Brown, 1951; *The King Is Dead,* Little, Brown, 1952; *The Scarlet Letters,* Little, Brown, 1953; *The Glass Village,* Little, Brown, 1954; *Inspector Queen's Own Case,* Simon & Schuster, 1956; *The Finishing Stroke,* Simon & Schuster, 1958; *The Player on the Other Side,* Random House, 1963; *And On the Eighth Day,* Random House, 1964; *The Fourth Side of the Triangle,* Random House, 1965; *A Study in Terror,* Lancer Books, 1966; *Face to Face,* New American Library, 1967; *The House of Brass,* New American Library, 1968; *Cop Out,* World Publishing, 1969; *The Last Woman in His Life,* World Publishing, 1970; *A Fine and Private Place,* World Publishing, 1971.

Omnibus volumes: *The Ellery Queen Omnibus* (contains *The French Powder Mystery, The Dutch Shoe Mystery,* and *The Greek Coffin Mystery*), Gollancz, 1934; *The Ellery Queen Omnibus* (contains *The Roman Hat Mystery, The French Powder Mystery,* and *The Egyptian Cross Mystery*), Grosset, 1936; *Ellery Queen's Big Book* (contains *The Siamese Twin Mystery* and *The Greek Coffin Mystery*), Grosset, 1938; *Ellery Queen's Adventure Omnibus* (contains *The Adventures of Ellery Queen* and *The New Adventures of Ellery Queen*), Grosset, 1941; *Ellery Queen's Parade* (contains *The Greek Coffin Mystery* and *The Siamese Twin Mystery*), World Publishing, 1944; *The Case Book of Ellery Queen* (contains *The Adventures of Ellery Queen* and *The New Adventures of Ellery Queen*), Gollancz, 1949; *The Wrightsville Murders* (contains *Calamity Town, The Murderer Is a Fox,* and *Ten Days' Wonder*), Little, Brown, 1956; *The Hollywood Murders* (contains *The Devil to Pay, The Four of Hearts,* and *The Origin of Evil*), Lippincott, 1957; *The New York Murders* (contains *Cat of Many Tails, The Scarlet Letters, The American Gun Mystery*), Little, Brown, 1958; *The XYZ Murders* (contains *The Tragedy of X, The Tragedy of Y,* and *The Tragedy of Z;* also see below), Lippincott, 1961; *The Bizarre Murders* (contains *The Siamese Twin Mystery, The Chinese Orange Mystery,* and *The Spanish Cape Mystery*), Lippincott, 1962.

Short story collections: *The Adventures of Ellery Queen,* Stokes, 1934; *The New Adventures of Ellery Queen,* Stokes, 1940; *The Case Book of Ellery Queen,* Bestseller, 1945; *Calendar of Crime,* Little, Brown, 1952; *Q.B.I.: Queen's Bureau of Investigation,* Little, Brown, 1955; *Queens Full,* Random House, 1965; *Q.E.D.: Queen's Experiments in Detection,* New American Library, 1968.

Nonfiction books about the mystery genre: *The Detective Short Story: A Bibliography,* Little, Brown, 1942, reprinted, Biblo & Tannen, 1969; *Queen's Quorum: A History of the Detective-Crime Short Story,* Little, Brown, 1951, new edition, Biblo & Tannen, 1969; *In the Queen's Parlor, and Other Leaves from the Editor's Notebook* (criticism), Simon & Schuster, 1957, reprinted, Biblo & Tannen, 1969.

Nonfiction books of true crime: *Ellery Queen's International Case Book,* Dell, 1964; *The Woman in the Case,* 1966 (published in England as *Deadlier than the Male,* Transworld Publishers, 1966).

Editor of anthologies; with Manfred B. Lee until 1971, sole editor after 1971; all under pseudonym Ellery Queen: *Challenge to the Reader,* Stokes, 1938; *101 Years' Entertainment: The Great Detective Stories, 1841-1941,* Little, Brown, 1941; *Sporting Blood: The Great Sports Detective Stories,* Little, Brown, 1942 (published in England as *Sporting Detective Stories,* Faber, 1946); *The Female of the Species: The Great Women Detectives and Criminals,* Little, Brown, 1943 (published in England as *Ladies in Crime: A Collection of Detective Stories by English and American Writers,* Faber, 1947); *The Misadventures of Sherlock Holmes,* Little, Brown, 1944; *Best Stories from Ellery Queen's Mystery Magazine,* Detective Book Club, 1944; *Rogues' Gallery: The Great Criminals of Modern Fiction,* Little, Brown, 1945; *To the Queen's Taste: The First Supplement to 101 Years' Entertainment,* Little, Brown, 1946; *Murder by Experts,* Ziff-Davis Publications, 1947; *20th Century Detective Stories,* World Publishing, 1948, 2nd edition, Pocket Books, 1964; *The Literature of Crime: Stories by World-Famous Authors,* Little, Brown, 1950, published as *Ellery Queen's Book of Mystery Stories,* Pan, 1957; *Ellery Queen's 12,* Dell, 1964; *Ellery Queen's Lethal Black Book,* Dell, 1965; *Poetic Justice: 23 Stories of Crime, Mystery, and Detection by World-Famous Poets from Geoffrey Chaucer to Dylan Thomas,* New American Library, 1967; *Minimysteries: 70 Short-Short Stories of Crime, Mystery, and Detection,* World Publishing, 1969; *Ellery Queen's Murder—in Spades,* Pyramid, 1969; *Ellery Queen's Shoot the Works,* Pyramid, 1969; *Ellery Queen's Mystery Jackpot,* Pyramid, 1970; *The Golden 13: 13 First Prize Winners from Ellery Queen's Mystery Magazine,* World Publishing, 1971; *Ellery Queen's Best Bets,* Pyramid, 1972; *Ellery Queen's Japanese Golden Dozen: The Detective Story World in Japan,* Tuttle, 1978.

Editor of "Mystery Annual Anthology" series; with Manfred B. Lee until 1971, sole editor after 1971; all under pseudonym Ellery Queen; published by Little, Brown except as indicated: *The Queen's Awards, 1946,* 1946; . . . , *1947,* 1947; . . . , *1948,* 1948; . . . , *1949,* 1949; . . . , *Fifth Series,* 1950; . . . , *Sixth Series,* 1951; . . . , *Seventh Series,* 1952; . . . , *Eighth Series,* 1953.

Ellery Queen's Awards, Ninth Series, 1954; . . . , *Tenth Series,* 1955; . . . , *Eleventh Series,* Simon & Schuster, 1956; . . . , *Twelfth Series,* Simon & Schuster, 1957; . . . , *Thirteenth Annual,* Random House, 1958 (published in England as *Ellery Queen's Choice: Thirteenth Series,* Collins, 1960); . . . , *14th Mystery Annual,* Random House, 1960 (published in England as *Ellery Queen's Choice: Fourteenth Series,* Collins, 1961); . . . , *15th Mystery Annual,* Random House, 1960; . . . , *16th Mystery Annual,* Random House, 1961; *To Be Read before Midnight,* Random House, 1962.

Ellery Queen's Mystery Mix #18, Random House, 1963; . . . *Double Dozen,* Random House, 1964 (published in England as *Ellery Queen's 19th Mystery Annual,* Gollancz, 1965); . . . *20th Anniversary Annual,* Random House, 1965; . . . *Crime Carousel,* New American Library, 1966; . . . *All-Star Lineup,* New American Library, 1967; . . . *Mystery Parade,* New American Library, 1968; . . . *Murder Menu,* World Publishing, 1969; . . . *Grand Slam,* World Publishing, 1970; . . . *Headliners,* World Publishing, 1971; . . . *Mystery Bag,* World Publishing, 1972; . . . *Crookbook,* Random House, 1974; . . . *Murdercade,* Random House, 1975; . . . *Crime Wave,* Putnam, 1976; . . . *Searches and Seizures,* Dial, 1977;

. . . *A Multitude of Sins,* Davis Publications (New York), 1978; *The Scenes of the Crime,* Davis Publications (New York), 1979; *Circumstantial Evidence,* Davis Publications (New York), 1980.

Editor of "Ellery Queen's Anthology" series; with Manfred B. Lee until 1971, sole editor after 1971; all under pseudonym Ellery Queen; published in magazine format by Davis Publications (New York), 1959—.

Editor of "Masterpieces of Mystery" series; all under pseudonym Ellery Queen; published by Meredith Corp., 1976-79.

Editor of short story collections; all under pseudonym Ellery Queen: Dashiell Hammett, *The Adventures of Sam Spade and Other Stories,* Bestseller, 1944, published as *They Can Only Hang You Once and Other Stories,* Mercury, 1949; Hammett, *The Continental Op,* Bestseller, 1945; Hammett, *The Return of the Continental Op,* Jonathan, 1945; Hammett, *Hammett Homicides,* Bestseller, 1946; Hammett, *Dead Yellow Women,* Jonathan, 1947; Stuart Palmer, *The Riddles of Hildegarde Withers,* Jonathan, 1947; John Dickson Carr, *Dr. Fell, Detective, and Other Stories,* Mercury, 1947; Roy Vickers, *The Department of Dead Ends,* Bestseller, 1947; Margery Allingham, *The Case Book of Mr. Campion,* Mercury, 1947; O. Henry, *Cops and Robbers,* Bestseller, 1948; Hammett, *Nightmare Town,* Mercury, 1948; Stuart Palmer, *The Monkey Murder and Other Stories,* Bestseller, 1950; Hammett, *The Creeping Siamese,* Jonathan, 1950; Hammett, *Woman in the Dark,* Jonathan, 1952; Hammett, *A Man Named Thin and Other Stories,* Mercury, 1962; Erle Stanley Gardner, *The Case of the Murderer's Bride and Other Stories,* Davis Publications (New York), 1969; Lawrence Treat, *P As in Police,* Davis Publications (New York), 1970; Edward D. Hoch, *The Spy and the Thief,* Davis Publications (New York), 1971; Michael Gilbert, *Amateur in Violence,* Davis Publications (New York), 1973; Stanley Ellin, *Kindly Dig Your Grave and Other Wicked Stories,* Davis Publications (New York), 1975; Julian Symons, *How to Trap a Crook and Twelve Other Mysteries,* Davis Publications (New York), 1977; Gardner, *The Amazing Adventures of Lester Leith,* Davis Publications (New York), 1980.

With Manfred B. Lee under joint pseudonym Barnaby Ross; novels: *The Tragedy of X,* Viking, 1932, reissued under pseudonym Ellery Queen, Stokes, 1940; *The Tragedy of Y,* Viking, 1932, reissued under pseudonym Ellery Queen, Stokes, 1941; *The Tragedy of Z,* Viking, 1933, reissued under pseudonym Ellery Queen, Little, Brown, 1942; *Drury Lane's Last Case,* Viking, 1933, reissued under pseudonym Ellery Queen, Little, Brown, 1946.

Under name Daniel Nathan: *The Golden Summer* (autobiographical novel), Little, Brown, 1953.

Co-author with Manfred B. Lee under joint pseudonym Ellery Queen of radio scripts for "The Adventures of Ellery Queen" radio show, 1938-49 and of short stories and articles for numerous magazines including *Cosmopolitan, Playboy, Argosy, Saturday Evening Post, Today's Family,* and *Redbook.* Co-editor with Manfred B. Lee under joint pseudonym Ellery Queen, *Mystery League,* 1933-34, and *Ellery Queen's Mystery Magazine,* 1941-71, sole editor, 1971—.

SIDELIGHTS: Ellery Queen, the joint pseudonym of Frederic Dannay and his cousin, the late Manfred B. Lee, is a prominent figure in the detective/mystery genre as author, anthologist, and founder of *Ellery Queen's Mystery Magazine.* "Few writers," Allen J. Hubin notes, "have made as great an impact on 20th century American detective fiction as Ellery Queen."

Ellery Queen was created in 1929 when Dannay and Lee wrote a mystery novel for a writing contest. They used the name Ellery Queen for the novel's protagonist, a clever young detective, as well as for their own pseudonym, reasoning that the public would more easily remember the name if it were used twice. Although their novel, *The Roman Hat Mystery,* did not win the contest, the firm of Frederick A. Stokes accepted it for publication. It sold well, and what Francis M. Nevins, Jr. calls "the most successful collaboration in the history of prose fiction" was on its way.

The Queen novels of the 1930s are complex, logically-solved puzzles containing, as Julian Symons notes, "a relentlessly analytical treatment of every possible clue and argument. Judged as exercises in rational deduction," he continues, "these are certainly among the best detective stories ever written." Although praising the deductive complexity of the stories, some critics found these early mysteries too cold, favoring intellectual passions over emotional ones.

Queen's novels since this time have had a variety of goals, concerning themselves less strictly with the mystery than did the earlier books. *The Glass Village,* for instance, is a political statement against the McCarthy witch hunts of the fifties. *Calamity Town* carefully delineates the varied customs and inhabitants of a small town. Other novels, like *Ten Days' Wonder,* create what Francis M. Nevins, Jr. calls "a private, topsy-turvy, Alice-in-Wonderland otherworld" in which the mystery is unraveled.

In addition to being successful novelists, Dannay and Lee are also known for their mystery anthologies. In over 100 anthologies, they have gathered together not only the best of contemporary mystery fiction (most of which is taken from *Ellery Queen's Mystery Magazine*) but hard-to-find classics of the genre as well. These anthologies have popularized the mystery field while preserving in print historically important examples of the form. Anthony Boucher writes that "much though we may admire . . . Queen the writer, it is Queen the editor who is unquestionably immortal."

Another aspect of the Ellery Queen popularity lies in *Ellery Queen's Mystery Magazine,* the largest-selling mystery magazine in the world, which Dannay and Lee founded in 1941. During a time when many popular fiction magazines have gone out of business, forcing mystery writers to abandon the short story in favor of the novel, *Ellery Queen's* has published and encouraged short mystery fiction. It has done much to keep the mystery and crime short story alive. "It is not too much to say," Julian Symons writes, "that the continuation of the crime short story as we know it, like its development during the past twenty years, seems largely dependent upon *Ellery Queen's Mystery Magazine.*"

About his writing, Dannay told *CA:* "I've written three critical works on the [mystery] field (one a bibliography, one a history and critical estimate, and one a book of essays and opinions), and have come to this decision: no more 'invasions' of the critics' and historians' provinces until I hang up my gloves as a writer and editor in the field."

Dannay revealed in the 1960s that his original name was Daniel Nathan. About his present name he told *CA:* "Frederic was chosen because of my deep affection for Chopin—Chopin's first name was Frederic, so spelled. Dannay [consists of] the first half of real first name, Daniel, plus nay, the phonetic spelling of first half of real last name, Nathan."

Queen books have sold some 150,000,000 copies in numerous hardcover and paperback editions in America and abroad. A radio series and three television series have been based on the character and thirteen Queen novels have been made into movies.

AVOCATIONAL INTERESTS: Book and stamp collecting.

BIOGRAPHICAL/CRITICAL SOURCES: Henry Douglas Thomson, *Masters of Mystery: A Study of the Detective Story,* Collins, 1931; *Publishers' Weekly,* October 10, 1936, November 20, 1943, March 10, 1969; *Newsweek,* June 26, 1939; *Time,* October 23, 1939; *New Yorker,* March 16, 1940; *New York Times,* November 15, 1940, February 22, 1969, April 5, 1971; Howard Haycraft, *Murder for Pleasure: The Life and Times of the Detective Story,* Appleton-Century, 1941; *Wilson Library Bulletin,* April, 1942; *Coronet,* December, 1942; *Life,* November 22, 1943; John Richmond and Abril Lamarque, *Brooklyn, U.S.A.,* Creative Age Press, 1946; Frank Luther Mott, *Golden Multitudes,* Macmillan, 1947; Anthony Boucher, *Ellery Queen: A Double Profile* (pamphlet), Little, Brown, 1951; *A Silver Anniversary Tribute to Ellery Queen from Authors, Critics, Editors, and Famous Fans* (pamphlet), Little, Brown, 1954.

New York Times Book Review, February 26, 1961, October 8, 1967, December 1, 1968; *MD,* December, 1967; *The Ellery Queen Review* (magazine for collectors of Ellery Queen books), 1968-71; *The Armchair Detective,* January, 1970, October, 1972; *Look,* April 21, 1970; *London Sunday Express,* December 13, 1970; Jacques Barzun and Wendell Hertig Taylor, *A Catalogue of Crime,* Harper, 1971; Julian Symons, *Mortal Consequences: A History from the Detective Story to the Crime Novel,* Harper, 1972; Francis M. Nevins, Jr., *Royal Bloodline: Ellery Queen, Author and Detective,* Bowling Green University Press, 1973; *Book World,* August 18, 1974; *Contemporary Literary Criticism,* Gale, Volume III, 1975, Volume XI, 1979; *Observer,* October 5, 1975; *Times Literary Supplement,* November 12, 1976; *Spectator,* January 1, 1977; *New Republic,* November 26, 1977; *People,* March 5, 1979; *Detroit News,* April 26, 1979.

* * *

DAUBE, David 1909-

PERSONAL: Born February 8, 1909, in Freiburg im Breisgau, Germany; son of Jakob and Selma (Ascher) Daube; married Herta Babette Aufseesser, 1936 (divorced, 1964); children: Jonathan Mahram, Benjamin Jeremy, Michael Matthew. *Education:* University of Freiburg im Breisgau, Referendar, 1930; University of Goettingen, Dr.Jur. (with distinction), 1932; Cambridge University, Ph.D., 1936; Oxford University, M.A., D.C.L., both 1955. *Office:* School of Law, University of California, Berkeley, Calif. 94720.

CAREER: Cambridge University, Cambridge, England, fellow of Caius College, 1938-46, university lecturer in law, 1946-51; Aberdeen University, Aberdeen, Scotland, professor of jurisprudence, 1951-55; Oxford University, Oxford, England, Regius Professor of Civil Law, 1955-70, Regius Professor Emeritus, 1970—, fellow of All Souls College, 1955-70, fellow emeritus, 1980—; University of California, Berkeley, professor of law and director of Robbins Collection, 1970—. Member of academic board, Institute of Jewish Study, London, 1953—; senior fellow, Yale University, 1962; Delitzsch Lecturer, University of Muenster, 1962; Gifford Lecturer, Edinburgh University, 1962-63; Olaus Petri Lecturer, Uppsala University, 1963; Ford Professor of Political Science, University of California, Berkeley, 1964; Riddell Lecturer, University of Newcastle, 1965; Gray Lecturer, Cambridge University, 1966; Lionel Cohen Lecturer, University of Jerusalem, 1970; Messenger Lecturer, Cornell University, 1971. Honorary professor of history, University of Konstanz, 1966—; honorary fellow, Caius College, Cambridge University, 1974—. *Member:* Classical Association of Great Britain (president, 1976-77), British Academy (fellow), American Academy of Arts and Sciences (fellow), World Academy of Art and Sciences (fellow), Royal Irish Academy (corresponding fellow), Akademie der Wissenschaften (Goettingen; corresponding fellow), Akademie der Wissenschaften (Munich; corresponding fellow). *Awards, honors:* LL.D., Edinburgh University, 1958, and University of Leicester, 1964; Doctorat, University of Paris, 1963; D.H.L., Hebrew Union College, 1971; Dr.Jur., University of Munich, 1972; Oxford Centre for Postgraduate Hebrew Studies fellow, 1973.

WRITINGS: Studies in Biblical Law, Cambridge University Press, 1947, reprinted, Ktav, 1969; *The New Testament and Rabbinic Judaism,* Athlone Press, 1956, reprinted, Arno, 1973; *Forms of Roman Legislation,* Clarendon Press, 1956, reprinted, Greenwood Press, 1979; (editor with William D. Davies) *The Background of the New Testament and Its Eschatology,* Cambridge University Press, 1956; (editor) *Studies in the Roman Law of Sale,* Clarendon Press, 1959; *The Exodus Pattern in the Bible,* Faber, 1963, reprinted, Greenwood Press, 1979; *The Sudden in the Scriptures,* E. J. Brill, 1964; *Collaboration with Tryanny in Rabbinic Law: The Riddell Memorial Lectures,* Oxford University Press, 1965; *Roman Law: Linguistic, Social, and Philosophical Aspects,* Aldine, 1969; *Civil Disobedience in Antiquity,* Edinburgh University Press, 1972.

SIDELIGHTS: David Daube is a highly respected biblical and legal scholar. Of *Roman Law,* the *Times Literary Supplement* reviewer writes: "Professor Daube fully displays his many talents and his great learning in a style both lively and humorous. . . . [He] enjoys himself and delights the reader with a miscellany of ideas . . . brought together to give a fresh slant on institutions normally dealt with separately and from a very staid standpoint." Three festschriften have been published in Daube's honor.

BIOGRAPHICAL/CRITICAL SOURCES: Times Literary Supplement, June 26, 1969, March 30, 1973; Bernard S. Jackson, editor, *Studies in Jewish Legal History: Essays in Honour of David Daube,* Jewish Chronicle Publications, 1974; Alan Watson, editor, *Daube Noster: Essays in Legal History for David Daube,* Scottish Academic Press, 1974; E. Bammel, editor, *Donum Gentilicium: New Testament Studies in Honor of David Daube,* Clarendon Press, 1978.

* * *

DAVIDSON, Basil 1914-

PERSONAL: Born November 9, 1914, in Bristol, England; son of Thomas and Jessie (Craig) Davidson; married Marion Ruth Young, 1943; children: Nicholas, Keir, James. *Home:* 2 Palace Yd., Hereford, England. *Agent:* Curtis Brown Ltd., 575 Madison Ave., New York, N.Y. 10022.

CAREER: The Economist, London, England, member of editorial staff, 1938-39; *The Times,* London, Paris correspondent, 1945-47, European leader writer, 1947-49; writer for other journals, England; author. *Military service:* British Army, 1940-45, became lieutenant colonel: awarded Military Cross, Bronze Star (U.S. Army), twice mentioned in dispatches. *Member:* Savile Club (London). *Awards, honors:* Anisfield-Wolf Award for best book concerned with racial problems in field of creative literature, 1960, for *The Lost Cities of Africa;* gold medal from Haile Selassie for his work on African history, 1970; Litt.D., University of Ibadan, 1975; Medalha Amilcar Cabral, 1976.

WRITINGS: Partisan Picture: Jugoslavia 1933-44, Bedford, 1946; *Highway Forty* (novel), Frederick Muller, 1949; *Ger-*

many: What Now: From Potsdam to Partition, Frederick Muller, 1950; *Report on Southern Africa,* Cape, 1952; *Golden Horn* (novel), J. Cape, 1952; *Daybreak in China,* J. Cape, 1953; *The African Awakening,* Macmillan, 1955; *The Rapids* (novel), Houghton, 1956; *Turkestan Alive,* J. Cape, 1957; *Lindy* (novel), J. Cape, 1958, published as *Ode to a Young Love,* Houghton, 1959; *The Lost Cities of Africa,* Little, Brown, 1959 revised edition, 1970.

Black Mother, Little, Brown, 1961, published as *The African Slave Trade,* 1965; *Guide to African History,* Allen & Unwin, 1963, Doubleday, 1965, revised edition, edited by Haskel Frankel, Zenith Books, 1971; *Which Way Africa?: The Search for a New Society,* Penguin, 1964, 3rd edition, 1971; (editor) *The African Past: Chronicles from Antiquity to Modern Times,* Little, Brown, 1964; (with F. K. Buah) *The Growth of African Civilization: West Africa 1000-1800,* Longmans, Green, 1965, revised edition published as *A History of West Africa to the Nineteenth Century,* Doubleday Anchor, 1966, new edition published under original title, Longmans, Green, 1967; (with the editors of Time-Life) *African Kingdoms,* Time-Life, 1966; *Africa: History of a Continent,* Macmillan, 1966, revised edition, Spring Books, 1972, published as *Africa in History: Themes and Outlines,* Macmillan, 1968, revised edition, 1974; *The Andrassy Affair* (novel), Whiting & Wheaton, 1966; *History of West Africa,* Doubleday, 1966, revised edition, Longmans, 1978; *East and Central Africa to the Late Nineteenth Century,* Longmans, Green, 1967, revised edition, Doubleday, 1969; (with Paul Strand) *Tir a'mhurain: Outer Hebrides,* Grossman, 1968; *The Liberation of Guine: Aspects of an African Revolution,* Penguin, 1969; *The Africans: An Entry to Cultural History,* Longmans, Green, 1969; *The African Genius: An Introduction to African Cultural and Social History,* Little, Brown, 1969.

Old Africa Rediscovered, Longmans, Green, 1970; *Walking 300 Miles with Guerrillas through the Bush of Eastern Angola,* Munger Africana Library, 1971; *In the Eye of the Storm: Angola's People,* Doubleday, 1972, revised edition, Penguin, 1975; *Black Star: A View of the Life and Times of Kwame Nkrumah,* Allen Lane, 1973; *Growing from Grass Roots: The State of Guinea-Bissau,* Committee for Freedom in Mozambique, Angola, and Guinea, 1974; *Can Africa Survive?: Arguments against Growth without Development,* Little, Brown, 1974; (with Joe Slovo and Anthony R. Wilkinson) *Southern Africa: The New Politics of Revolution,* Penguin, 1976; *Ghana: An African Portrait,* Aperture, 1976; *Let Freedom Come: Africa in Modern History,* Little, Brown, 1978.

WORK IN PROGRESS: Scenes from the Anti-Nazi War.

SIDELIGHTS: Basil Davidson is a prominent figure in the field of African history who has, in the words of Benedict Wengler, "almost singlehandedly reversed the ethnocentric trend of considering anything African inferior" and "developed a whole new school of modern African history based on archaeology rather than on presumptions." In such books as *Lost Cities of Africa,* Davidson has compiled the archaeological evidence for ancient African civilizations and recounted their technological, cultural, and religious developments. His books have been translated into numerous languages.

AVOCATIONAL INTERESTS: Country life.

BIOGRAPHICAL/CRITICAL SOURCES: Social Education, February, 1965; *Geographical Journal,* June, 1965; *Journal of Negro Education,* summer, 1966; *Punch,* November 23, 1966; *New York Times Book Review,* December 4, 1966; *History Today,* March, 1967; *Nation,* July 31, 1967; *New York Times,* December 3, 1968; *Saturday Review,* March 22, 1969, April 25, 1970; *Christian Science Monitor,* May 17, 1969, December 16, 1974; *Spectator,* June 21, 1969; *Journal of Negro History,* July, 1969; *Christian Century,* February 18, 1970; *New Yorker,* June 20, 1970; *Best Sellers,* December 15, 1970; *New York Review of Books,* December 17, 1970; *Times Literary Supplement,* June 4, 1971, January 4, 1974; *New Statesman,* October 27, 1972; *Observer,* February 4, 1973; *Current History,* March, 1973; *American Anthropologist,* April, 1973; *Black World,* August, 1974; *Book World,* September 1, 1974; *Economist,* May 3, 1975; *Book Forum,* winter, 1977; *Business Week,* July 31, 1978; *Progressive,* October, 1978; *Times Educational Supplement,* October 13, 1978.

* * *

DAVIDSON, Lionel 1922-

PERSONAL: Born March 31, 1922, in Hull, Yorkshire, England; married Fay Jacobs, 1949. *Agent:* Curtis Brown Ltd., 1 Craven Hill, London W2 3EP, England.

CAREER: Writer and editor for several British magazines, 1946-59; novelist and screenwriter, 1959—. *Military service:* Royal Navy, Submarine Service, five years. *Member:* Society of Feature Writers, Authors' Society, London Press Club. *Awards, honors:* Authors' Club Award for most promising first novel, 1960, for *The Night of Wenceslas;* Crime Writers' Association award for best crime novel of year, 1960, for *The Night of Wenceslas,* 1967, for *The Menorah Men,* and 1978, for *The Chelsea Murders.*

WRITINGS: The Night of Wenceslas, Harper, 1960, reprinted, Penguin, 1977; *The Rose of Tibet,* Harper, 1962, reprinted, Penguin, 1977; *The Menorah Men,* Harper, 1966 (published in England as *A Long Way to Shiloh,* Gollancz, 1966, reprinted, Penguin, 1977); *Making Good Again,* Harper, 1968; *Smith's Gazelle,* Knopf, 1971; *The Sun Chemist,* Knopf, 1976; *Murder Games,* Coward, 1978 (pubished in England as *The Chelsea Murders,* J. Cape, 1978).

SIDELIGHTS: Though best known for his suspense novels—"rattling good yarn[s]," in the words of a *New Statesman* critic—Lionel Davidson's *Making Good Again* represents somewhat of a departure from his normal genre. In this particular novel, the plot centers around the post-World War II efforts of three lawyers—an Englishman, a German, and an Israeli—to discover the fate of a missing German Jewish banker in order to determine what should be done with his fortune (the title of the book refers to the German Federal Indemnification Law, a complex network of legal provisions by which the government makes amends for war crimes against Germany Jewry). Most reviewers, accustomed to Davidson's earlier work, do not quite seem to know how to approach *Making Good Again.* For example, a *Punch* reviewer writes: "Before reading *Making Good Again* I'd have made Lionel Davidson my choice for the title of best thriller writer in the business. This present book alters that position. For better? For worse?—it's hard to be sure. . . . [He] has great talent. His dialogue is supple, subtle and tempts you on. He can rise to high comedy and even to high seriousness. But to the very end of this one I remained in doubt whether he had wholly made up his mind about the kind of novel he meant to write."

A *Jewish Quarterly* critic notes: "This book has all the qualities which have distinguished Lionel Davidson's earlier books—a crackling tale told at a crackling pace; vivid characterisation; humour—but on this occasion he has attempted to do more, and one wishes he hadn't. On one level, *Making*

Good Again is a thriller. . . . On another it is a parable on guilt and reparation. . . . Mr. Davidson raises the questions [about German guilt], but does not come near to providing an answer. And there, I think, one touches upon the most serious failure of this book. . . . It may be ungracious to complain of this in a book which offers so much, but one has a right to expect more of Mr. Davidson."

Though a *Times Literary Supplement* reviewer finds *Making Good Again* to be "an uncomfortable blend of heavy documentary and mystifying symbolism," a *Time* reviewer, on the other hand, seems to be attracted to this sort of blend. He writes: "[*Making Good Again* is] an odd, quiet novel that contemplates the limits of private responsibility and public guilt. This moral terrain, though fascinating, is often overwrought in literature. And Davidson's low-key philosophic inquiry, conducted in a wonderfully conversational tone and decked out with the trapping of an international suspense tale, runs the risk of seeming schematic or frivolous. . . . [But] cleverly, wisely, Davidson offers no final solution [to the story]. Instead he slowly turns the book into a rueful seminar on the possibilities that men have of ever 'making good again' after various sorts of failure."

Both the *New York Times Book Review* critic and the *New Yorker* reviewer see Davidson's exploration of the human element in his story as one of the most successful parts of the book. "With the legal machinery as a *modus operandi*," writes Martin Levin of the *New York Times Book Review*, "Mr. Davidson proceeds to explore a variety of elusive human situations. . . . The denouement of [the lawyers'] search for restitution is a bit anti-climactic, but their journey is nonetheless rewarding for the reader." The *New Yorker* reviewer concludes: "[*Making Good Again*] is essentially a story of suspence, but Mr. Davidson is in manner, tempo, and tone an apt and interesting pupil of Graham Greene, and he has given his entertainment a bottom of human doubt and human certitude."

BIOGRAPHICAL/CRITICAL SOURCES: Punch, October 9, 1968; *Time,* October 11, 1968; *Times Literary Supplement,* October 17, 1968; *New York Times Book Review,* October 20, 1968, June 25, 1978; *New Statesman,* November 8, 1968, May 21, 1971; *Best Sellers,* December 1, 1968; *New Yorker,* December 7, 1968; *Jewish Quarterly,* winter, 1968-69; *Observer Review,* May 23, 1971; *New York Times,* October 16, 1976.

* * *

DAVIE, Donald (Alfred) 1922-

PERSONAL: Born July 17, 1922, in Barnsley, Yorkshire, England; son of George Clarke and Alice (Sugden) Davie; married Doreen John, January 13, 1945; children: Richard Mark, Diana Margaret, Patrick George. *Education:* St. Catharine's College, Cambridge, B.A., 1947, M.A., 1949, Ph.D., 1951. *Religion:* Episcopalian. *Home:* 31 Fore St., Silverton, Exeter, England. *Office:* Department of English, Vanderbilt University, Nashville, Tenn. 37235.

CAREER: Trinity College, Dublin, Ireland, lecturer, 1950-54, fellow, 1954-57; Cambridge University, Gonville and Caius College, Cambridge, England, lecturer in English and fellow, 1959-64; University of Essex, Colchester, England, professor of literature and dean of comparative studies, 1964-68; Stanford University, Stanford, Calif., professor of English, 1968-78; Vanderbilt University, Nashville, Tenn., Andrew Mellon Professor of Humanities, 1978—. Visiting professor, University of California, Santa Barbara, 1957-58; Bing Professor of English and American Literature, University of Southern California, 1968-69. British Council lecturer, Budapest, 1961; Elliston Lecturer, University of Cincinnati, 1963; lecturer in English, Cambridge University. *Military service:* Royal Navy, 1941-46; became sub-lieutenant. *Member:* London Library, Savile Club (London). *Awards, honors:* Honorary fellow, St. Catharine's College, 1973; Guggenheim fellow, 1973; fellow, American Academy of Arts and Sciences, 1973; D. Litt., University of Southern California, 1978; honorary fellow, Trinity College, Dublin, 1978.

WRITINGS—Verse: *Brides of Reason,* Fantasy Press, 1955; *A Winter Talent,* Routledge & Kegan Paul, 1957; *The Forests of Lithuania* (adapted from a poem by Adam Mickiewicz; Poetry Book Society selection), Marvell Press, 1960; *New and Selected Poems,* Wesleyan University Press, 1961; *A Sequence for Francis Parkman,* Marvell Press, 1962; *Events and Wisdoms: Poems 1957-1963,* Routledge & Kegan Paul, 1964, Wesleyan University Press, 1965; *Poems,* Turret Books, 1969; *Essex Poems: 1963-1967,* Routledge & Kegan Paul, 1969; *Six Epistles to Eva Hesse,* London Magazine Editions, 1970; *Collected Poems: 1950-1970,* Oxford University Press, 1972; *Orpheus,* Poem-of-the-Month-Club, 1974; *The Shires: Poems,* Routledge & Kegan Paul, 1974, Oxford University Press, 1975; *In the Stopping Train,* Carcanet, 1977.

Criticism: *Purity of Diction in English Verse,* Chatto & Windus, 1952, Oxford University Press, 1953, reprinted, Schocken, 1967; *Articulate Energy,* Routledge & Kegan Paul, 1955, Harcourt, 1958, reprinted, Folcroft, 1974; *The Heyday of Sir Walter Scott,* Barnes & Noble, 1961; *The Language of Science and the Language of Literature, 1700-1740,* Sheed, 1963; *Ezra Pound: Poet as Sculptor,* Oxford University Press , 1964, new edition, Viking, 1976; *Thomas Hardy and British Poetry,* Oxford University Press, 1972; *The Augustan Lyric,* Barnes & Noble, 1974; *A Gathered Church: The Literature of the English Dissenting Interest, 1700-1930,* Oxford University Press, 1978; *The Poet in the Imaginary Museum,* edited by Barry Alpert, Persea Books, 1978.

Editor: *The Late Augustans: Longer Poems of the Later Eighteenth Century,* Macmillan, 1958; *Poems: Poetry Supplement,* Poetry Book Society, 1960; *Poetics Poetyka,* Panstwowe Wydawn (Warsaw), 1961; William Wordsworth, *Selected Poems of Woodsworth,* Harrap, 1962; *Russian Literature and Modern English Fiction: A Collection of Critical Essays,* University of Chicago Press, 1965; (with Angela Livingstone) *Pasternak,* Macmillan, 1969.

Translator: Boris Pasternak, *The Poems of Doctor Zhivago,* Barnes & Noble, 1965, reprinted, Greenwood Press, 1977.

Work has appeared in numerous anthologies. Contributor of poetry to *New Republic, Yale Review, PN Review, Times Literary Supplement,* and other publications. Member of editorial board, *Poetics,* Mouton, 1963.

SIDELIGHTS: Donald Davie is a literary traditionalist interested in the "purity of language" in both his poetry and his literary criticism. "[The poet] is responsible to the community in which he writes," Davie explains in his *Purity of Diction,* "for purifying and correcting the spoken language."

This purification of language is expressed in Davie's poetry by a careful concern for, and an attempt to enlighten the reader in, the proper use of language. Subtle differences between the meanings of similar words, for instance, are carefully made clear by their contrasting use in a Davie poem. This practice, Davie states, "purifies the spoken tongue, for it makes the reader alive to nice meanings."

Davie's purification of language is also accomplished through his use of metaphor. "If the poet who coins new metaphors *enlarges* the language," he writes, "the poet who enlivens dead metaphors can be said to *purify* the language." By using a familiar metaphor in a new way, Davie believes the poet can give it renewed life. "Davie's object," George Dekker points out, "[is] to draw attention to the cultural power these 'dead' metaphors of dead cultures still have to control our living processes of thought and feeling."

Davie's literary criticism is alert to the purity of language in the works of others. He especially notes with concern the tendency of modern poetry to abandon or disregard syntax. Noting the relationship between "law in language and law in conduct," Davie writes that "one could almost say . . . that to dislocate syntax in poetry is to threaten the rule of law in the civilized community." He asserts that "systems of syntax are part of the heritable property of past civilization, and to hold firm to them is to be traditional in the best and most important sense."

BIOGRAPHICAL/CRITICAL SOURCES: *Poetry*, May, 1962, August, 1973, January, 1976; William Van O'Connor, *The New University Wits and the End of Modernism*, Southern Illinois University Press, 1963; *The Review*, December, 1964; *Western Humanities Review*, winter, 1965, summer, 1974; *New York Times Book Review*, February 6, 1966, January 7, 1973, March 26, 1978; *Hudson Review*, spring, 1967, summer, 1973, winter, 1973-74; *London Magazine*, December, 1969, November, 1970; *Agenda*, autumn-winter, 1970, summer, 1976; *Times Literary Supplement*, November 27, 1970, December 22, 1972, July 13, 1973, October 4, 1974; *New Statesman*, September 25, 1970, December 1, 1972, March 23, 1973, October 18, 1974; *Virginia Quarterly Review*, spring, 1973; *South Atlantic Quarterly*, summer, 1974; *Poetry Nation*, Number 3, 1974; *Parnassus: Poetry in Review*, fall-winter, 1974; *Southwest Review*, autumn, 1975; *Contemporary Literary Criticism*, Gale, Volume V, 1976, Volume VIII, 1978, Volume X, 1979; *Book World*, March 7, 1976; *Booklist*, March 15, 1976; *New York Review of Books*, May 27, 1976; *Harper's*, July, 1976; *New Yorker*, August 16, 1976; *Best Sellers*, September, 1976; *New Republic*, October 2, 1976, November 27, 1976, October 22, 1977; *Yale Review*, June, 1977; *Sewanee Review*, October, 1977, October, 1978.

* * *

DAVIES, William David 1911-

PERSONAL: Born December 9, 1911, in Wales; son of David and Rachel (Powell) Davies; married Eurwen Llewelyn, 1942; children: Rachel Mary. *Education:* University of Wales, B.A., 1934, B.D., 1938, D.D., 1948; Cambridge University, M.A., 1942. *Office:* Department of Christian Origins, Duke University, Durham, N.C. 27706.

CAREER: Congregational minister in Cambridgeshire, England, 1942-46; Yorkshire United College, Bradford, Yorkshire, England, professor of New Testament studies, 1946-50; Duke University, Durham, N.C., professor of Biblical theology, 1950-55; Princeton University, Princeton, N.J., professor of religion, 1955-59; Union Theological Seminary, New York, N.Y., Edward Robinson Professor of Biblical Theology, 1959-66; Duke University, George Washington Ivey Professor of Advanced Studies and Research in Christian Origins, 1966—. *Member:* British Academy (fellow), American Society of Biblical Literature (honorary president), Society of New Testament Studies (president, 1976-77), American Society for Oriental Research. *Awards, honors:* New Testament Seminar fellow, Uppsala, Sweden; Guggenheim fellow, 1960 and 1966-67; Burkitt Medal, 1964.

WRITINGS: *Paul and Rabbinic Judaism*, S.P.C.K., 1948, 2nd edition, 1955; *Torah in the Messianic Age*, American Society of Biblical Literature, 1952; (editor, with D. Daube) *The Background of the New Testament and Its Eschatology*, Cambridge University Press, 1956; *Christian Origins and Judaism*, Darton, Longman & Todd, 1962; *The Setting of the Sermon on the Mount*, Cambridge University Press, 1964; *The Sermon on the Mount*, Cambridge University Press, 1966; *Invitation to the New Testament*, Doubleday, 1966; *Introduction to Pharisaism*, Fortress, 1967; *The Gospel and the Land: Early Christianity and Jewish Territorial Doctrine*, University of California Press, 1974. Assistant editor, *Journal of Biblical Literature*, 1954-59.

WORK IN PROGRESS: Translating Epistle to the Hebrews; editing with Louis Finkelstein, volumes I-IV of *Cambridge History of Judaism*, for Cambridge University Press.

* * *

DAVIS, Bertram H(ylton) 1918-

PERSONAL: Born November 30, 1918, in Ozone Park, Long Island, N.Y.; son of Hubert Edwin (a businessman) and Gladys (Greenidge) Davis; married Ruth Benedict, January 11, 1946; children: Ralph, Kathryn, Richard. *Education:* Attended Hamilton College, 1937-39; Columbia University, B.A., 1941, M.A., 1948, Ph.D., 1956. *Home:* 2309 Domingo Dr., Tallahassee, Fla. 32304. *Office:* Department of English, Florida State University, Tallahassee, Fla. 32304.

CAREER: Hunter College (now Hunter College of the City University of New York), New York, N.Y., lecturer in English, 1947-48; Dickinson College, Carlisle, Pa., instructor, 1948-51, assistant professor of English, 1951-57; American Association of University Professors, Washington, D.C., staff associate, 1957-62, deputy general secretary, 1963-67, general secretary, 1967-74; Florida State University, Tallahassee, professor of English, 1974—. *Military service:* U.S. Army, 1941-46; served forty-six months in Australia and New Guinea; became captain. *Member:* American Association of University Professors, Modern Language Association of America, American Society for Eighteenth-Century Studies, Johnsonians. *Awards, honors:* American Philosophical Society research grants, 1962 and 1966; Guggenheim fellow, 1974; LL.D., Dickinson College, 1974.

WRITINGS: *Johnson before Boswell*, Yale University Press, 1960; (editor) Sir John Hawkins, *The Life of Samuel Johnson, LL.D.*, Macmillan, 1961; *A Proof of Eminence*, Indiana University Press, 1973. Field editor, Twayne's English authors series, 1977—.

WORK IN PROGRESS: *Thomas Percy*.

* * *

DAVIS, Harold Eugene 1902-

PERSONAL: Born 1902, in Girard, Ohio; son of Henry E. and Catherine (Zeller) Davis; married Audrey Hennen, 1929; children: Barbara Lee Davis Owen. *Education:* Western Reserve University (now Case Western Reserve University), student, 1923-24, Ph.D., 1933; Hiram College, B.A., 1924; University of Chicago, M.A., 1927. *Religion:* Disciples of Christ. *Home:* 4842 Langdrum Lane, Chevy Chase, Md. 20015. *Office:* School of International Service, American University, Washington, D.C. 20016.

CAREER: Hiram College, Hiram, Ohio, professor, 1927-47, dean, 1944-47; Office of Inter-American Affairs, Washington, D.C., director, division of education and teacher aids, 1943-45; U.S. Army University, Biarritz, France, instructor in Latin American history, 1945-46; American University, Washington, D.C., professor of Latin American history and government, 1947-63, dean, College of Arts and Sciences, 1953-58, University Professor, 1963-73, University Professor emeritus, 1973—. Fulbright lecturer in American history, University of Chile, 1959; visiting professor at India School of International Studies, 1965-66, and at University of West Virginia, Oberlin College, Western Reserve University (now Case Western Reserve University), and Johns Hopkins University. Has lectured on Latin American subjects at various universities and organizations including Inter-American Defense College, United States Foreign Service Institute, Washington International Center, National University of Mexico. Member of Governor's Commission on the History of Ohio. Representative of Hiram College in Cooperative Study in General Education, 1938-40. Consultant to colleges.

MEMBER: American Historical Association, Inter-American Council, American Political Science Association, American Society of International Law, Institute on History of Law (Buenos Aires; corresponding member), American Peace Society (director), Inter-American Indianist Institute, Societe des Americanistes, Ohio Academy of History (president, 1937), Garfield Society, Cosmos Club (Washington). *Awards, honors: Washington Evening Star* grant for research in Latin American social thought, 1958; faculty author award, American University, 1950; distinguished service award from Inter-American Council, 1978, and Ohio Academy of History, 1978; certificate for distinguished service from Office of Inter-American Affairs; Order of Colon, Dominican Republic.

WRITINGS: Garfield of Hiram, Historical Society (Hiram, Ohio), 1931; *Makers of Democracy in Latin America,* H. W. Wilson, 1945, reprinted, Cooper Square, 1968; (contributor) *Twentieth Century Political Thought,* Philosophical Publishing, 1946; (contributor) *Origins and Consequences of World War II,* Dryden, 1948; *A History of America: Civilization in the Western Hemisphere,* American University Press, 1948; *Latin American Leaders,* H. W. Wilson, 1949, reprinted, Cooper Square, 1968; *Social Science Trends in Latin America,* American University Press, 1950; *The Americas in History,* Ronald, 1953; (contributor) *Contemporary Social Science,* Volume I, Stackpole, 1953; (contributor) *The Caribbean: Contemporary Trends,* University of Florida Press, 1953; (contributor) *The Development of Historiography,* Stackpole, 1954; (with others) *Government and Politics in Latin America,* Ronald, 1958; *Material and Spiritual Factors in American History,* American University Language Center, 1958; *Latin American Social Thought,* University Press of Washington, 1961, 2nd edition, 1967; (with Harold A. Durfee) *The Teaching of Philosophy in Universities of the United States,* Pan American Union, 1965; (editor) Samuel Guy Inman, *Inter-American Conferences, 1826-1954,* University Press of Washington, 1965; *History of Latin America,* Ronald, 1968; *Hinsdale of Hiram: The Life of Burke Aaron Hinsdale, Pioneer Educator,* University Press of Washington, 1971; *Latin American Thought: A Historical Introduction,* Louisiana State University Press, 1972; *Revolutionaries, Traditionalists, and Dictators in Latin America,* Cooper Square, 1973; (with others) *Latin American Foreign Policies: An Analysis,* Johns Hopkins University Press, 1975; (with others) *Latin American Diplomatic History: An Introduction,* Louisiana State University Press, 1977. Contributor to *Encyclopedia Americana, Encyclopaedia Britannica, Collier's Encyclopedia, World Book Encyclopedia, Dictionary of American History.* Also author of notes for a dictionary of Ohio Indian place names, 1979. Contributor of over one hundred articles to journals including *Inter-American Law Review, Latin American Research Review, The Americas, Journal of Inter-American Studies, World Affairs,* and *Hispanic American Historical Review.* Editorial consultant to *Jefferson Encyclopedia.* Member of board of editors, *World Affairs.*

WORK IN PROGRESS: Two books.

SIDELIGHTS: Harold Davis told *CA:* "All of my professional life and all of my writing, in one way or another, have been devoted to enriching my teaching. . . . I am pleased to have a considerable number of . . . students who have followed in my footsteps. . . . My epitaph, which I have written out and circulated to a few friends, with a collection of my poems, is: 'He lived to teach, and hoped to leave behind the loving flame of knowledge in some mind.'"

AVOCATIONAL INTERESTS: Music (violin), poetry, and woodworking.

* * *

DAVIS, Herbert (John) 1893-1967

PERSONAL: Born May 24, 1893, in Long Buckby, Northamptonshire, England; came to United States in 1938; died March 28, 1967, in Oxford, England; son of Carter and Martha Ann (Sheldon) Davis; married Gertrud Lucas, 1922 (died, 1928); married Gladys Emily Wookey, April 17, 1930; children: (second marriage) Elisabeth Ann Davis Falconer, Jane Sheldon Davis Knowles. *Education:* St. John's College, Oxford, M.A., 1919. *Home:* Townsend Close, Iffley, Oxford, England.

CAREER: University of Leeds, Leeds, England, lecturer in English, 1920-22; University of Toronto, Toronto, Ontario, associate professor, 1922-35, professor of English, 1935-38; Cornell University, Ithaca, N.Y., professor of English, 1938-40; Smith College, Northampton, Mass., president, 1940-49; Oxford University, Oxford, England, reader and professor of English, 1949-60, professor emeritus, 1960-67. Frederick Ives Carpenter Visiting Professor, University of Chicago, 1937; visiting professor at University of Toronto and Columbia University, 1957, University of Minnesota, 1960-61, Stanford University, 1964, and Brown University, 1964. *Military service:* British Army, 1916-19; became lieutenant. *Member:* American Academy of Arts and Sciences, British Academy (fellow), Phi Beta Kappa (honorary); Century Association and Grolier Club (both New York); Malone Society (president, 1965). *Awards, honors:* LL.D. from Amherst College, 1940, and Queens' University, Kingston, Ontario, 1945; Huntington Library fellow, 1963-64; Clark Library senior fellow, 1966.

WRITINGS: Stella, a Gentlewoman of the Eighteenth Century, Macmillan, 1942; *The Satire of Swift,* Macmillan, 1947; *Jonathan Swift: Essays on His Satire, and Other Studies,* Oxford University Press, 1964; (with Maximillian E. Novak) *The Uses of Irony,* William Andrews Clark Memorial Library, University of California, 1966. Also author of *Swift's View of Poetry,* 1931, and *The Challenge to the Intellect,* 1941.

Editor: Jonathan Swift, *Drapier's Letters,* Clarendon Press, 1935, 2nd revised edition, 1965; *The Prose Works of Jonathan Swift,* fourteen volumes, Basil Blackwell, 1939-68, reprinted, Barnes & Noble, 1964-68; (with William C. DeVane and R. C. Bald) *Nineteenth-Century Studies,* Cornell University Press, 1940, reprinted, Greenwood Press, 1968; (with H. L. Gardner) *Elizabethan and Jacobean Studies,* Oxford University Press, 1959; (with Harry Carter) Joseph Moxon,

Mechanick Exercises on the Whole Art of Printing, Oxford University Press, 1958, 2nd revised edition, 1962, reprinted, Dover, 1978; Alexander Pope, *Poetical Works,* Oxford University Press, 1966; *The Complete Plays of William Congreve,* University of Chicago Press, 1967; Jonathan Swift, *Poetical Works,* Oxford University Press, 1967. General editor, "Oxford English Novels," Oxford University Press, 1964-67. Contributor to professional journals.

BIOGRAPHICAL/CRITICAL SOURCES: New York Times, March 30, 1967; *Times Literary Supplement,* June 8, 1967, December 21, 1967; *South Atlantic Quarterly,* Volume LXVII, number 1, 1968.†

* * *

DAVIS, James Allan 1929-

PERSONAL: Born November 2, 1929, in Chicago, Ill.; son of Robert G. and Mary (McMurray) Davis; married Martha Hocking, January 28, 1950; children: Mary, James, Andrew, Martha. *Education:* Northwestern University, B.S., 1950; University of Wisconsin, M.S., 1952; Harvard University, Ph.D., 1955. *Home:* Winthrop House, Harvard University, Cambridge, Mass. 02138. *Office:* Department of Sociology, William James Hall, Harvard University, Cambridge, Mass. 02138.

CAREER: Harvard School of Public Health, Boston, Mass., research associate, 1954-56; Yale University, New Haven, Conn., assistant professor, 1956-57; University of Chicago, Chicago, Ill., 1957-67, began as assistant professor, became associate professor of sociology and senior study director of National Opinion Research Center; Dartmouth College, Hanover, N.H. , professor of sociology, 1967-71; University of Chicago, professor of sociology and director of National Opinion Research Center, 1971-75, senior study director of National Opinion Research Center, 1975—; Dartmouth College, professor of sociology, 1975-77; Harvard University, Cambridge, Mass., professor of sociology, 1977—. Visiting associate professor of sociology, University of Washington, summer, 1963; visiting professor of social relations, Johns Hopkins University, 1963-64; visiting professor of sociology, Harvard University, summer, 1968. Member of sociology panel, National Science Foundation, 1964-65; co-chairman of sociology panel, behavior and social science survey committee of National Academy of Science and Social Science Research Council, 1967-68; member of behavorial science advisory panel, National Institute of Mental Health, 1969. *Member:* American Sociological Association, American Association for Public Opinion Research, American Statistical Association, American Council on Education (member of research advisory committee, 1972—).

WRITINGS: A Study of Participants in the Great Books Program, 1957, Fund for Adult Education, 1960; *Great Books and Small Groups,* Free Press of Glencoe, 1961, reprinted, Greenwood Press, 1977; *Stipends and Spouses: The Finances of American Arts and Science Graduate Students,* University of Chicago Press, 1962; *Great Aspirations: The Graduate School Plans of America's College Seniors,* Aldine, 1964; *Undergraduate Career Decisions,* Aldine, 1965; *Education for Positive Mental Health,* Aldine, 1965; (editor with Neil J. Smelser) *Sociology,* Prentice-Hall, 1969; *Elementary Survey Analysis,* Prentice-Hall , 1971. Also author of numerous social research monographs and surveys for National Opinion Research Center. Contributor to professional journals.

WORK IN PROGRESS: Principal investigator of a national survey of young men's attitudes and experiences regarding military service and the draft.

DAVIS, Julia 1900-
(F. Draco)

PERSONAL: Born July 23, 1900, in Clarksburg, W.Va.; daughter of John W. and Julia (McDonald) Davis; married William Adams, October 13, 1923 (divorced); married Charles P. Healy, June 18, 1951 (died, 1955); married William M. Adams, March 30, 1974. *Education:* Attended Wellesley College, 1918-20; Barnard College, B.A., 1922. *Home:* 115 Brookstone Dr., Princeton, N.J. 08540. *Agent:* Curtis Brown Ltd., 575 Madison Ave., New York, N.Y. 10022.

CAREER: Associated Press, New York City, reporter, 1925; children's agent, State Charities Aid Association, 1933-38; writer. Chairman of child adoption service, Children's Aid Society, 1962-65. *Member:* Authors League, Authors Guild, Mystery Writers of America, Cosmopolitan Club.

WRITINGS: Sword of the Vikings, Dutton, 1927; *Vaino,* Dutton, 1928; *Mountains Are Free,* Dutton, 1929; *Stonewall,* Dutton, 1930; *Remember and Forget,* Dutton, 1931; *Peter Hale,* Dutton, 1932; *No Other White Men,* Dutton, 1937; *The Sun Climbs Slow,* Dutton, 1940; *The Shenandoah,* Rinehart, 1944; Cloud on the Land, Rinehart, 1950; *Bridle the Wind,* Rinehart, 1951; *Eagle on the Sun,* Rinehart, 1956; *Legacy of Love,* Harcourt, 1962; *Ride with the Eagle,* Harcourt, 1962; *The Anvil* (play; produced, 1962), Harper, 1963; *A Valley and a Song,* Holt, 1963; *Mount Up,* Harcourt, 1967; *Never Say Die,* Norwood, 1980. Contributor to magazines.

Under pseudonym F. Draco: *The Devil's Church,* Rinehart, 1951; *Cruise with Death,* Rinehart, 1952.

WORK IN PROGRESS: An historical novel.

* * *

DAWSON, Carl 1938-

PERSONAL: Born May 2, 1938, in Leeds, England; son of Cecil and Lorna (Woodhouse) Dawson; married Hannelore Klages, October 25, 1963; children: Geoffrey, Sarah. *Education:* Occidental College, A.B. (magna cum laude), 1959; Columbia University, M.A., 1960, Ph.D., 1966; University of Munich, additional study, 1961-62. *Home:* 5 Emerson Rd., Durham, N.H. 03824. *Office:* Department of English, University of New Hampshire, Durham, N.H. 03824.

CAREER: Dartmouth College, Hanover, N.H., instructor in English, 1964-66; University of California, Berkeley, assistant professor of English, 1966-70; University of New Hampshire, Durham, associate professor, beginning 1970, professor of English, 1976—. Fulbright lecturer, Free University of Berlin, 1967-68. *Member:* Phi Beta Kappa. *Awards, honors:* American Council of Learned Societies fellow, 1973-74; Guggenheim fellow, 1974-75; Woodrow Wilson fellow.

WRITINGS: (Translator from the French, with Elliot Coleman, in collaboration with the author) Georges Poulet, *The Metamorphoses of the Circle,* Johns Hopkins Press, 1966; *Thomas Love Peacock,* Routledge & Kegan Paul, 1968; *His Fine Wit: A Study of Thomas Love Peacock,* University of California Press, 1970; (editor) *Matthew Arnold, the Poetry: The Critical Heritage,* Routledge & Kegan Paul, 1973; *Victorian Noon: English Literature in 1850,* Johns Hopkins Press, 1979. Also author of essays on nineteenth and twentieth century literature.

BIOGRAPHICAL/CRITICAL SOURCES: Times Literary Supplement, April 23, 1970; *Yale Review,* winter, 1971; *New York Times Book Review,* July 8, 1979.

DEAL, Babs H(odges) 1929-

PERSONAL: Born June 23, 1929, in Scottsboro, Ala.; daughter of Hilburn Tyson and Evelyn (Coffey) Hodges; married Borden Deal (a novelist), 1952, (divorced, 1975); children: Ashley, Brett, Shane. *Education:* University of Alabama, B.A., 1952. *Politics:* Democrat.

CAREER: Jackson County School System, Scottsboro, Ala., substitute teacher, 1950; U.S. Army, Judge Advocate General, Washington, D.C., clerk-typist, 1951; Anderson Brass Co., Birmingham, Ala., typist, 1952; writer. *Member:* Authors Guild, P.E.N.

WRITINGS—Published by Doubleday, except as indicated: *Acres of Afternoon,* McKay, 1959; *It's Always Three O'Clock,* McKay, 1961; *Night Story,* McKay, 1962; *The Grail,* McKay, 1964; *Fancy's Knell,* 1966, *The Walls Came Tumbling Down,* 1968; *High Lonesome World: The Death and Life of a Country Music Singer,* 1969; *Summer Games,* 1972; *The Crystal Mouse,* 1973; *The Reason for Roses,* 1974; *Waiting to Hear from William,* 1975; *Goodnight Ladies,* 1978; *Friendships, Secrets and Lies,* Fawcett, 1979. Stories anthologized in *Love and Marriage, Best Detective Stories of 1961,* and *Love, Love, Love.* Contributor of stories to magazines and journals in the United States and Europe, including *McCall's, Southwest Review, Redbook,* and *Cosmopolitan.*

WORK IN PROGRESS: A novel.

AVOCATIONAL INTERESTS: Cooking, reading, football, hillbilly music.†

* * *

DEAN, Burton V(ictor) 1924-

PERSONAL: Born June 3, 1924, in Chicago, Ill.; son of Samuel and Dorothy (Eisner) Dean; married Barbara Arnoff, November 26, 1958; children: David, Paul, Heather, Theodore. *Education:* Northwestern University, B.S., 1947; Columbia University, M.S., 1948; University of Illinois, Ph.D., 1952. *Home:* 2920 Broxton, Shaker Heights, Ohio. *Office:* Department of Operations Research, Case Western Reserve University, 10900 Euclid, Cleveland, Ohio 44106.

CAREER: National Security Agency, Washington, D.C., mathematician, 1952-55; Operations Research, Inc., Washington, D.C., research mathematician, 1955-57; Case Western Reserve University, Cleveland, Ohio, associate professor, 1957-65, professor of operations research, 1965—, chairman of department, 1965—. Visiting professor at Israel Institute of Technology, 1962-63, University of Louvain, Tel-Aviv University, and Ben-Gurion University. Lecturer at Japan-America Institute of Management Sciences Tenth International Business Forum, 1979. Consultant to government agencies and business firms, and to Battelle Memorial Institute and RAND Corp.

MEMBER: Institute of Management Sciences (member of council, 1966-67), Operations Research Society (member of council, 1973-76), Association for Computing Machinery, American Mathematical Society, American Association for the Advancement of Science (fellow; member of council, 1964-70). *Awards, honors:* Fulbright scholar in Israel, 1962-63.

WRITINGS: (Contributor) C. West Churchman and Michael Verhulst, editors, *Management Science Models and Techniques,* Pergamon, 1960; (contributor) R. L. Ackoff, editor, *Progress in Operations Research,* Volume I, Wiley, 1961; *Applications of Operations Research in Research and Development,* Wiley, 1963; (editor) *Operations Research in Research and Development,* Wiley, 1963; (with Maurice W. Sasieni and Shiv K. Gupta) *Mathematics of Modern Management,* with instruction manual, Wiley, 1963; (contributor) M. C. Yovits and other editors, *Research Program Effectiveness,* Gordon & Breach, 1966; (contributor) *Transportation and Community Values,* Highway Research Board, National Academy of Science, 1969; *Evaluating, Selecting, and Controlling Research and Development Projects,* American Management Association, 1968.

(Editor) *Studies in Operations Research,* Gordon & Breach, 1970; (contributor) H. B. Maynard, editor, *Industrial Engineering Handbook,* McGraw, 1971; (with Arnold Reisman, Muhatim Oral, and Michael Salvador) *Industrial Inventory Control,* Gordon & Breach, 1972; (contributor) Arnold Reisman and Marylou Kiley, editors, *Health Care Delivery Planning,* Gordon & Breach, 1973; *Studies in Management Science and Systems,* North-Holland, 1974; (contributor) Shaul P. Ladany, editor, *Management Science Applications to Leisure Time Operations,* North-Holland, 1975; (contributor) *Studies in Linear Programming,* North-Holland, 1975. Contributor to *Encyclopedia of Professional Management.* Contributor to proceedings, symposia, and transactions. Contributor to professional journals. Member of editorial board, *Institute of Electrical and Electronics Engineers Transactions on Engineering Management,* 1968—; associate editor, *Opsearch: Journal of the Operations Research Society of India,* 1968—; editor, *Management Science,* 1970—.

WORK IN PROGRESS: A book on research and development management.

SIDELIGHTS: Dean's books have been translated into Japanese and Yugoslavian.

* * *

de CAMP, L(yon) Sprague 1907-
(Lyman R. Lyon, J. Wellington Wells)

PERSONAL: Born November 27, 1907, in New York, N.Y.; son of Lyon and E. Beatrice (Sprague) de Camp; married Catherine A. Crook, August 12, 1939; children: Lyman Sprague, Gerard Beekman. *Education:* California Institute of Technology, B.S., 1930; attended Massachusetts Institute of Technology, 1932; Stevens Institute of Technology, M.S., 1933. *Politics:* Democrat. *Home:* 278 Hothorpe Lane, Villanova, Pa.

CAREER: Inventors Foundation, Inc., Hoboken, N.J., editor and instructor, 1933-36; International Correspondence Schools, Scranton, Pa., principal, 1936-37; Fowler-Becker Publishing Co., New York City, editor, 1937-38; American Society of Mechanical Engineers, New York City, editor, 1938; free-lance writer. Member of board of elections, Nether Providence Township, Pa., 1955-60. *Military service:* U.S. Navy, World War II; became lieutenant commander. *Member:* History of Science Society, Society for the History of Technology (member of advisory board), Association Phonétique Internationale, Bread Loaf Writers Conference (fellow), University of Pennsylvania Museum, Trap Door Spiders Club, Hyborian Legion, Philadelphia Academy of Natural Science. *Awards, honors:* International Fantasy Award, 1953, for *Lands Beyond;* Cleveland Science Fiction Association award, 1953, for *Tales from Gavagan's Bar;* fiction award, Athenaeum of Philadelphia, 1958, for *An Elephant for Aristotle;* Grand Master (Gandalf Award), World Science Fiction Convention, 1976; Nebula Grand Master, Science Fiction Writers of America, 1979.

WRITINGS—Science fiction and fantasy: *Lest Darkness*

Fall, Holt, 1941, reprinted, Remploy, 1973; (with Fletcher Pratt) *The Incomplete Enchanter,* Holt, 1941; (with Pratt) *The Land of Unreason,* Holt, 1942, reprinted, Ballantine, 1970; (with Pratt) *The Carnelian Cube,* Gnome, 1948, reprinted, Lancer Books, 1967; *Divide and Rule,* Fantasy Press, 1948; *The Wheels of If,* Shasta, 1948, reprinted, Berkeley Publishing, 1970; (with Pratt) *The Castle of Iron,* Gnome, 1950, reprinted, Pyramid Publications, 1962; (with P. Schuyler Miller) *Genus Homo,* Fantasy Press, 1950; *The Undesired Princess,* Fantasy Press, 1951; *Rogue Queen,* Doubleday, 1951; *The Continent Makers,* Twayne, 1953; (with Pratt) *Tales from Gavagan's Bar,* Twayne, 1953; *The Tritonian Ring* (short stories), Twayne, 1953, reprinted, Ballantine, 1977; *Cosmic Manhunt,* Ace, 1954; *Solomon's Stone,* Avalon, 1957; *The Tower of Zanid,* Avalon, 1958; *The Glory That Was,* Avalon, 1960; (with Pratt) *Wall of Serpents,* Avalon, 1960; *The Search for Zei,* Avalon, 1962; *A Gun for Dinosaur* (short stories), Doubleday, 1963; *The Hand of Zei,* Avalon, 1963; (editor) *Swords and Sorcery,* Pyramid Publications, 1963; (editor) *The Spell of Seven,* Pyramid Publications, 1965; (editor) *The Fantastic Swordsmen,* Pyramid Publications, 1967; *The Goblin Tower,* Pyramid Publications, 1968; *The Reluctant Shaman and Other Fantastic Tales,* Pyramid Publications, 1970; (editor) *Warlocks and Warriors,* Putnam, 1970; *The Clocks of Iraz,* Pyramid Publications, 1971; (author of introduction) Abdul Alhazred, *Al Azif (The Necronomicon),* Owlswick Press, 1973; *The Fallible Fiend,* Pyramid Publications, 1973; (with Pratt) *The Compleat Enchanter,* Doubleday, 1975; *The Hostage of Zir,* Putnam, 1977; *The Best of L. Sprague de Camp,* Doubleday, 1978; *The Great Fetish,* Doubleday, 1978; *The Purple Pterodactyls,* Ace Books, 1979.

"Conan" series; all published by Lancer Books, except as indicated: (With Robert E. Howard) *Tales of Conan,* Gnome, 1955; (with Bjoern Nyberg) *The Return of Conan,* Gnome, 1957; (with Howard) *Conan the Adventurer,* 1966; (with Lin Carter and Howard) *Conan,* 1967; (with Howard) *Conan the Warrior,* 1967; (with Howard) *Conan the Usurper,* 1967; *The Conan Reader,* Mirage Press, 1968; (with Howard and Nyberg) *Conan the Avenger,* 1968; (editor) Howard, *Conan the Conquerer,* 1968; (with Howard and Carter) *Conan the Wanderer,* 1968; (with Carter) *Conan of the Isles,* 1968; (editor with George H. Scithers) *The Conan Swordbook,* Mirage Press, 1969; (with Howard and Carter) *Conan of Cimmeria,* 1969; (with Carter) *Conan the Buccaneer,* 1971; (editor with Scithers) *The Conan Grimoire,* Mirage Press, 1972; (with Carter) *Conan of Aquilonia,* 1977; (with Carter) *Conan the Swordsman,* Bantam, 1978; (with Carter) *Conan the Liberator,* Bantam, 1979.

Nonfiction: (With Alf K. Berle) *Inventions and Their Management,* International Textbook Company, 1937, reprinted, Van Nostrand, 1959; *The Evolution of Naval Weapons,* U.S. Government Printing Office, 1947; (with Willy Ley) *Lands Beyond,* Rinehart, 1952; *Lost Continents: The Atlantis Theme in History, Science, and Literature,* Gnome, 1954, reprinted, Dover, 1970; *The Heroic Age of American Invention,* Doubleday, 1961; *The Ancient Engineers,* Doubleday, 1963; *Elephant,* Pyramid Publications, 1964; *The Great Monkey Trial,* Doubleday, 1968; *Scribblings,* NESFA Press, 1972; *Great Cities of the Ancient World,* Doubleday, 1972; *Lovecraft: A Biography,* Doubleday, 1975; *The Miscast Barbarian: A Biography of Robert E. Howard, 1906-1936,* Gerry de la Ree, 1975; *Literary Swordsmen and Sorcerers,* Arkham, 1976.

With wife, Catherine C. de Camp: *Science Fiction Handbook,* Hermitage, 1953, revised edition, Owlswick Press, 1975; *Ancient Ruins and Archaeology,* Doubleday, 1964, published as *Citadels of Mystery,* Ballantine, 1973; *Spirits, Stars, and Spells,* Canaveral, 1967; *The Story of Science in America* (juvenile), Scribner, 1967; *The Day of the Dinosaur,* Doubleday, 1968; *Darwin and His Great Discovery* (juvenile), Macmillan, 1972; (co-editors) *Three Thousand Years of Fantasy and Science Fiction,* Lothrop, 1972; (co-editors) *Tales Beyond Time,* Lothrop, 1973.

Juveniles: *Engines,* Golden Press, 1959, revised edition, 1961; *Man and Power,* Golden Press, 1962; *Energy and Power,* Golden Press, 1962.

Historical fiction: *An Elephant for Aristotle,* Doubleday, 1958; *The Bronze God of Rhodes,* Doubleday, 1960; *The Dragon of the Ishtar Gate,* Doubleday, 1961; *The Arrows of Hercules,* Doubleday, 1965; *The Golden Wind,* Doubleday, 1969.

Verse: *Demons and Dinosaurs,* Arkham, 1970; *Phantoms and Fancies,* Mirage Press, 1972.

Contributor to *Visual Encyclopedia of Science Fiction.* Contributor of over 350 short stories and articles to periodicals. Author of 76 radio scripts for "Voice of America" on scientific topics.

WORK IN PROGRESS: Conan and the Spider God; Dark Valley Destiny: The Life and Death of Robert E. Howard, with Jane W. Griffin; *The Ragged Edge of Science; Heroes and Hobgoblins,* verse.

SIDELIGHTS: L. Sprague de Camp has written many of the popular Conan books, based upon the character created by the late fantasy writer, Robert E. Howard. Conan is a muscular barbarian who lives in an ancient, untamed land and overcomes all obstacles with a well-placed sword. Howard created Conan for the pulp magazines of the thirties, but it wasn't until the sixties when de Camp reworked much of Howard's writings into novels and completed Howard's unfinished manuscripts that the character's popularity soared. Conan now appears successfully in several media.

BIOGRAPHICAL/CRITICAL SOURCES: Horn Book, April, 1965; *Classical World,* November, 1965; Sam Moskowitz, *Seekers of Tomorrow,* World, 1966; *New York Times Book Review,* November, 1967, February 24, 1974; *Natural History,* February, 1969; *Quarterly Journal of Speech,* April, 1969; *Scientific American,* December, 1969; *Science Fiction Review,* August, 1970; *American Historical Review,* June, 1971; *New York Review of Books,* June 3, 1971; *New York Times,* January 29, 1975; *Atlantic,* March, 1975; *Times Literary Supplement,* March 26, 1976; *Magazine of Fantasy and Science Fiction,* July, 1976, September, 1978; *Analog,* November, 1977; *Book World,* March 5, 1978.

* * *

de CHAIR, Somerset (Struben) 1911-
(Honourable Member for X)

PERSONAL: Born August 22, 1911, in Sunningdale, Berkshire, England; son of Dudley (an admiral, and governor of New South Wales, Australia) and Enid (Struben) de Chair; married Thelma Arbuthnot, 1932 (divorced, 1950); married Carmen Bowen Appleton, 1950 (divorced, 1958); married Margaret Patricia Field-Hart Manlove, 1958; children: (first marriage) two sons (one deceased); (second marriage) two sons; (third marriage) one daughter. *Education:* Balliol College, Oxford, honors degree in politics, philosophy, and economics, 1932. *Politics:* Conservative. *Home:* St. Osyth Priory, St. Osyth, Essex, England; and Farm of the Running Waters, Kortright, N.Y.

CAREER: Member of Parliament for South West Norfolk, England, 1935-45, and South Paddington, England, 1950-51; parliamentary private secretary to minister of production, 1942-44; writer. National appeal committee, United Nations Association, member of national executive board, 1947-50, chairman, 1948-50. *Military service:* British Army, Royal Horse Guards, 1938-42; served in Middle East campaigns; became captain. *Member:* Carlton Club.

WRITINGS: The Impending Storm, R. R. Smith, 1930; *Divided Europe,* J. Cape, 1931; (under pseudonym Honourable Member for X) *Peter Public: A Play in Three Acts,* J. Cape, 1932; *Enter Napoleon* (novel), Hutchinson, 1935, reprinted, World Distributors, 1965; *Red Tie in the Morning* (novel), Hutchinson, 1937; *The Silver Crescent* (also see below), Golden Cockerel, 1943; *The Golden Carpet* (also see below), Golden Cockerel, 1943; *The Golden Carpet* (contains "The Golden Carpet" and "The Silver Crescent"), Faber, 1944, Harcourt, 1945; *A Mind on the March,* Faber, 1945; (translator from the "Gesta Francorum et aliorum Hierosolimitanorum") *The First Crusade,* Golden Cockerel, 1945; (editor and translator) Napoleon I, *Supper at Beaucaire,* Golden Cockerel, 1945; (editor and translator) Napoleon I, *Napoleon's Memoirs,* Volume I: *Corsica to Marengo,* Volume II: *The Waterloo Campaign* (also see below), Golden Cockerel, 1945, Harper, 1948; *The Teetotalitarian State* (novel), Falcon Press, 1947; *The Dome of the Rock,* Falcon Press, 1948; *The Millennium, and Other Poems,* Falcon Press, 1949.

(Editor and translator) Caius Julius Caesar, *Commentaries: A Modern Rendering by Somerset de Chair,* Golden Cockerel, 1951; *The Story of a Lifetime,* Golden Cockerel, 1954; (editor and translator) Napoleon I, *The Waterloo Campaign,* Folio, 1957; (editor) Dudley de Chair, *The Sea Is Strong,* Harrap, 1961; *Bring Back the Gods: The Epic Career of the Emperor Julian, the Great,* Harrap, 1962; *Collected Verse,* Regency Press, 1970; *The Somerset de Chair Collection at Osyth's Priory, Essex,* English Life, 1971; *Friends, Romans, Concubines* (novel), Constable, 1973; *The Star of the Wind,* Constable, 1974; *Legend of the Yellow River,* Constable, 1979.

* * *

de GRUMMOND, Lena Young

PERSONAL: Born in Centerville, La.; daughter of William J. (a merchant) and Amy (Etienne) Young; married Will White de Grummond (deceased); children: Jewel Lynn (Mrs. Richard K. Delaune), Will White. *Education:* Southwestern Louisiana Institute of Liberal and Technical Learning (now University of Southwestern Louisiana), B.A., 1929; Louisiana State University, M.S., Ph.D., 1956. *Religion:* Protestant. *Home:* Heritage Apt. 216, 209 South 29th Ave., Hattiesburg, Miss. 39401.

CAREER: Teacher and librarian in Louisiana; Louisiana Department of Education, Baton Rouge, state supervisor of school libraries, 1950-65; University of Southern Mississippi, Hattiesburg, professor of library science, beginning 1965. Deep South Writers Conference, director, 1962-64, president, 1970-72; book reviewer. Member of East Baton Rouge Community Service Commission. *Member:* National League of American Pen Women, American Library Association (former council member), Delta Kappa Gamma, Theta Sigma Phi, Phi Kappa Phi. *Awards, honors:* Modisette Award for best school library, 1959; University of Southern Mississippi collection of original manuscripts and illustrations for children's books named Lena Young de Grummond Collection, 1970; Phi Lambda Pi National Award, 1972.

WRITINGS: (With M. S. Robertson) *How to Have What You Want in Your Future,* privately printed, 1959; (with daughter, Lynn de Grummond Delaune) *Jeff Davis: Confederate Boy,* Bobbs-Merrill, 1960; *Books Suitable for Use in Schools, Grades 1-12,* Louisiana Department of Education, 1961; (with Delaune) *Jeb Stuart,* Lippincott, 1962, reprinted, Pelican Press, 1979; (with Delaune) *Babe Didrikson: Girl Athlete,* Bobbs-Merrill, 1963; (with Delaune) *Jean Felix Piccard: Boy Baloonist,* Bobbs-Merrill, 1968. Contributor of articles to professional journals.

WORK IN PROGRESS: Further biographies, to be written with daughter, Lynn de Grummond Delaune.

* * *

de HARTOG, Jan 1914-
(F. R. Eckmar)

PERSONAL: Born April 22, 1914, in Haarlem, Netherlands; son of Arnold Hendrik (a minister and professor of theology) and Lucretia (a lecturer in medieval mysticism; maiden name, Meijjes) de Hartog; married Angela Priestly (daughter of English writer, J. B. Priestly), 1946; married Marjorie Eleanor Mein, 1961; children: (first marriage) Arnold, Sylvia, Nicholas, Catherine; (second marriage) Eva Kim, Julia Kim (both adopted). *Education:* Attended Amsterdam Naval College, 1930-31. *Religion:* Society of Friends (Quaker). *Residence:* Florida.

CAREER: Writer. Worked as a sailor on fishing boats, steamers, tugboats, and as adjunct inspector with the Amsterdam Harbor Police until 1932; member of staff, Amsterdam Municipal Theatre, 1932-37. Writer-in-residence and lecturer in creative play-writing, University of Houston, 1962. *Military service:* Netherlands Merchant Marine, correspondent, 1943-45; became captain; received Netherlands Cross of Merit. *Member:* Dramatists Guild, Societe des Auteurs (France). *Awards, honors:* Great National Drama Prize, 1939, for "De Ondergang van de Vrijheid"; Antoinette Perry (Tony) Award, 1952, for *The Fourposter;* Officier de l'Academie, France.

WRITINGS: Het Huis met den Handen, Dishoeck, 1934; *Ave Caesar,* Dishoeck, 1936; *Oompje Owadi,* Elsevier, 1938; *Hollands Glorie,* Elsevier, 1940, reprinted, 1970, translation published as *Captain Jan,* White Lion, 1976; *Gods Geuzen,* Elsevier, 1948, translation published as *The Spiral Road,* Harper, 1957, reprinted, Queens House, 1976; *Stella,* Elsevier, 1950, reprinted, 1970, translation published as *The Distant Shore: A Story of the Sea,* Harper, 1952 (also see below); (editor) *Feestelijke Ondergang: Leven en Werk van Johan C. P. Alberts,* Elsevier, 1950; *Mary,* Elsevier, 1951; *The Lost Sea,* Harper, 1951 (also see below); *Thalassa,* Elsevier, 1951; *The Little Ark,* Harper, 1953, reprinted, Grosset, 1971; *A Sailor's Life,* Harper, 1955, reprinted, White Lion, 1976 (also see below).

De Inspecteur, Elsevier, 1958, translation published as *The Inspector,* Atheneum, 1960; *De Kunstenaar,* Elsevier, 1959, translation published as *The Artist,* Atheneum, 1963; *Omnibus,* Elsevier, 1962; *The Hospital,* Atheneum, 1964; *Waters of the New World: Houston to Nantucket,* Atheneum, 1964; *The Call of the Sea* (contains *The Lost Sea, The Distant Shore,* and *A Sailor's Life*), Atheneum, 1966; *The Captain,* Atheneum, 1966; *Die Kinderen,* Elsevier, 1968, translation published as *The Children: A Personal Record for the Use of Adoptive Parents,* Atheneum, 1969; *The Peaceable Kingdom: An American Saga,* Atheneum, 1972 (published in two volumes in England as *The Peaceable Kingdom,* Cornet, 1973, Volume I: *The Children of Light,* Volume II: *The Holy*

Experiment); De Oorlong van het Lam, Elsevier, 1975, translation published as *Lamb's War,* Harper, 1980.

Plays: "De Ondergang van de Vrijheid," first produced in Amsterdam at Amsterdam Municipal Theatre, 1939; *Skipper next to God* (first produced on the West End at Embassy Theatre, November 27, 1945), Dramatists Play Service, 1949; "This Time Tomorrow," first produced on Broadway at Guild Theatre, November 3, 1947; *The Fourposter* (first produced on Broadway at Ethel Barrymore Theatre, October 24, 1951), Random House, 1951, acting edition, Samuel French, 1954; *De dood van een rat,* Elsevier, 1956; "William and Mary," first produced in Houston at University of Houston Theatre, 1963. Also author of play, "Mist," 1938, and screenplays, "Ergens in Nederland," Filmex, 1939, and "Maitre apres Dieu," Cooperative du Cinema Francais, 1949.

Detective novels; under pseudonym F. R. Eckmar: *Een Linkerbeen gezocht,* Dishoeck,1934; *Spoken te Koop,* Dishoeck, 1935; *Ratten op de Trap,* Dishoeck, 1937; *Drie Dode Dwergen,* Querido, 1938; *De Maagd ende Moordenaar,* Querido, 1939.

SIDELIGHTS: When he was ten years old, Jan de Hartog ran away to sea. Since then he has spent most of his life on the water, including many years living with his family aboard *Rival,* an oceangoing fishing barge which he converted into a houseboat. One of his earliest novels, *Hollands Glorie,* published in 1940, dealt with the oceangoing tugboats on which the author had worked for a number of years. Although it was not intended to be a book about war, this work became a symbol of the Dutch Resistance movement and sold 500,000 copies in the Netherlands. As a result, de Hartog was charged with exciting the "national passions" and the book was banned in 1942. He was forced to flee from the subsequent Nazi manhunt and hid in a senior citizens' home in Amsterdam disguised as an old lady. During his stay there, he made use of the idle hours by writing *The Fourposter,* the play which was to become one of his best-known works. Eventually, through the efforts of the Dutch Resistance, Basque shepherds, and the Spanish underground, he was able to make his way to England where, in 1943, he joined the Netherlands Merchant Marine as a correspondent. He later found that during his escape from Holland he had been sentenced to death *in absentia* by the Nazis. The book, however, remained a symbol of a country's resistance to occupation and de Hartog told interviewer William R. MacKaye that, to this day, when he is approached by Dutch readers, they invariably comment about his latest work, "It's very nice, mijnheer, but it's not *Holland's Glory.*"

Although de Hartog's novels about the sea have prompted critics to compare his work with the best of Joseph Conrad and C. S. Forester, and despite the acclaim he won with *The Fourposter* which enjoyed a 632-performance run on Broadway, it was a nonfiction work, *The Hospital,* that catapulted his name into headlines in this country. In 1962 Jan de Hartog arrived in Houston where he was to lecture on play writing. Since he and his wife, Marjorie, are Quakers they sought some means of doing volunteer community service during their stay in the city, and began working at Jefferson Davis County Hospital (now the Ben Taub Memorial Hospital), which was mainly a charity institution. His effort to call attention to the intolerable conditions at the hospital, particularly those resulting from overcrowding and understaffing, elicited wide local and national response. Within a week of the book's release, nearly four hundred citizens asked to become volunteer workers. The de Hartogs worked there only until the situation became public knowledge and their help was no longer needed; he told Bruce Paisner: "By nature and sanguinity I am a resistance fighter.... The moment we shift from wartime to reconstruction, it's time for me to get out." But the book had served its social purpose and had gained critical acclaim as well. Frank G. Slaughter writes: "In less inspired hands, this book might seem a muckracking exercise in sensationalism. Instead, it is a deeply moving account of the efforts of a group of dedicated people.... There is suspense in these pages that will make the average mystery novel seem tame; characters who could only be drawn from life because they could not be imagined: pain, horror, brutality, tenderness, courage."

Jan de Hartog was taught the value of service to mankind by his Quaker mother and, as a result of his dedication and his training as a nurse's aide, he has been able to offer assistance in several crises in various parts of the world. During the severe floods in Holland in 1953, he and his family turned their houseboat into a floating hospital. He later detailed many of their experiences in *The Little Ark.* In 1966, de Hartog and his wife worked at a reception center for war orphans about to be adopted by U.S. families. They later were instrumental in repealing a Dutch law forbidding the admission of Vietnamese and Korean orphans into the Netherlands. The de Hartogs themselves adopted two Korean orphans, Eva Kim and Julia Kim. De Hartog wrote *The Children: A Personal Record for the Use of Adoptive Parents,* a chronicle of their first few months with their new daughters, to offer advice and comfort to others who have taken similar children into their families. Having worked on many projects with people of all denominations, de Hartog has found that differing theologies tend to divide people, but service can bring them back together.

Several of Jan de Hartog's books have been produced as films: "The Fourposter," Columbia, 1952 (the play was also adapted into a musical, "I Do! I Do!," which opened on Broadway in 1966); "The Key," based on the novel, *Stella,* Columbia, 1958; "The Spiral Road," Universal, 1962; "Lisa," based on the novel, *The Inspector,* Twentieth Century-Fox Film Corp., 1962; and "The Little Ark," Cinema Century Films, 1972. His books have been translated into seventeen languages and his plays have been performed in twenty-three.

BIOGRAPHICAL/CRITICAL SOURCES: Atlantic, November, 1961; *New York Times,* November 18, 1961, January 7, 1972; *New Statesman,* March 16, 1962; *National Observer,* May 20, 1963; *New York Times Book Review,* July 7, 1963, November 15, 1964; *Times Literary Supplement,* December 5, 1963, July 24, 1969; *Book Week,* January 10, 1965; *Life,* March 26, 1965; *Detroit News,* January 30, 1972; *Washington Post,* February 25, 1972, February 9, 1980; *Los Angeles Times,* January 10, 1980.†

* * *

DeLEEUW, Adele Louise 1899-

PERSONAL: Born August 12, 1899, in Hamilton, Ohio; daughter of Adolph Lodewyk (a consulting engineer) and Katherine (Bender) DeLeeuw. *Education:* High school graduate, 1918. *Home:* 1763 Sleepy Hollow Lane, Plainfield, N.J. 07060.

CAREER: Public library, Plainfield, N.J., assistant librarian, 1919; secretary to father, New York, N.Y., 1919-26; author and lecturer. Founder and president, Words and Music, 1969—. Member, Rutgers University advisory council on children's literature; member of literature panel, New Jersey Council on the Arts; member of executive committee, New

Jersey Theatre Forum. *Member:* Authors League of America, Pen and Brush Club (member of board of governors; chairman of literature department), Plainfield Art Association (past president), Listen-to-Me Club (Orange, N.J.; president, 1963, 1964—). *Awards, honors:* Rachel Mark Wilson prize for poetry; Southland Club prize for poetry; joint citation with Cateau DeLeeuw from Martha Kinney Cooper Ohioana Library Association, 1958, for "outstanding work over the years for children."

WRITINGS—Poetry: *Berries of the Bittersweet,* Brimmer, 1924; *Life Invited Me,* Harrison, 1936.

Fiction: *Rika,* Macmillan, 1932; *Island Adventure,* Macmillan, 1934; *Year of Promise,* Macmillan, 1935; *A Place for Herself,* Macmillan, 1937; *Doll Cottage,* Macmillan, 1938; (with sister, Cateau DeLeeuw) *Anim Runs Away,* Macmillan, 1938; *Dina and Betsy,* Macmillan, 1940; *Career for Jennifer,* Macmillan, 1941; *Gay Design,* Macmillan, 1942; *The Patchwork Quilt,* Little, Brown, 1943; *Linda Marsh,* Macmillan, 1943; *Doctor Ellen,* Macmillan, 1944; *With a High Heart,* Macmillan, 1945, reprinted, 1964; *Nobody's Doll,* Little, Brown, 1946; *Future for Sale,* Macmillan, 1946; *Title to Happiness,* Macmillan, 1947; *Clay Fingers,* Macmillan, 1948; *Curtain Call,* Macmillan, 1949.

Blue Ribbons for Meg, Little, Brown, 1950; *Hawthorne House,* Macmillan, 1950; *The Rugged Dozen,* Macmillan, 1950; (with Marjorie Paradis) *The Golden Shadow,* Macmillan, 1951; (with C. DeLeeuw) *Mickey the Monkey,* Little, Brown, 1952; (with C. DeLeeuw) *Hideaway House,* Little, Brown, 1953; *The Barred Road,* Macmillan, 1954; (with Margaret Dudley) *The Rugged Dozen Abroad,* Macmillan, 1955; (with C. DeLeeuw) *The Expandable Browns,* Little, Brown, 1955; (with C. DeLeeuw) *Showboat's Coming!,* World Publishing, 1956; (with Paradis) *Dear Stepmother,* Macmillan, 1956; *Donny,* Little, Brown, 1957; (with C. DeLeeuw) *The Caboose Club,* Little, Brown, 1957; (with C. DeLeeuw) *Breakneck Betty,* World Publishing, 1957; (with C. DeLeeuw) *The Strange Garden,* Little, Brown, 1958; *The Goat Who Ate Flowers,* Steck, 1958; *A Heart for Business,* Macmillan, 1958; (with C. DeLeeuw) *Where Valor Lies* (Catholic Youth Book Club selection), Doubleday, 1959; (with C. DeLeeuw) *Apron Strings,* World Publishing, 1959.

(With C. DeLeeuw) *Love Is the Beginning,* World Publishing, 1960; (with C. DeLeeuw) *The Salty Skinners,* Little, Brown, 1964; *Miss Fix-It,* Macmillan, 1966; *Who Can Kill the Lion?,* Garrard, 1966; *Paul Bunyan and His Blue Ox,* Garrard, 1968; *Behold This Dream,* McGraw, 1968; *Paul Bunyon Finds a Wife,* Garrard, 1969; *Uncle Davy Lane: Mighty Hunter,* Garrard, 1970; *Casey Jones Drives an Ice Cream Train,* Garrard, 1971; *Boy with Wings,* Nautilus Books, 1971; *Horseshoe Harry and the Whale,* Parents' Magazine Press, 1976.

Biography: *The Story of Amelia Earhart,* Grosset, 1955; (with C. DeLeeuw) *Nurses Who Led the Way,* Whitman Publishing, 1961; *Richard E. Byrd: Adventurer to the Poles,* Garrard, 1963; *James Cook,* Garrard, 1963; *Sir Walter Raleigh,* Garrard, 1964; *John Henry: Steel Drivin' Man,* Garrard, 1966; *George Rogers Clark,* Garrard, 1967; *Old Stormalong: Hero of the Seven Seas,* Garrard, 1967; *Edith Cavell: Nurse, Spy, Heroine,* Putnam, 1968; *Lindbergh: Lone Eagle,* Westminster, 1968; *Marie Curie: Woman of Genius,* Garrard, 1969; *Peter Stuyvesant: A Colony Leader,* Garrard, 1970; *Maria Tallchief: American Ballerina,* Garrard, 1971; *Civil War Nurse: Mary Ann Bickerdyke,* Messner, 1973; (with C. DeLeeuw) *Anthony Wayne: Washington's General,* Westminister, 1974; *Carlos P. Romulo: The Barefoot Boy of Diplomacy,* Westminster, 1976.

Other: *The Flavor of Holland,* Century, 1928; *It's Fun to Cook,* Macmillan, 1952; (with C. DeLeeuw) *Make Your Habits Work for You* (Executive Book Club selection), Farrar, Straus, 1952; *Indonesian Legends and Folk Tales,* Thomas Nelson, 1961; *Legends and Folk Tales from Holland,* Thomas Nelson, 1963; *The Girl Scout Story,* Garrard, 1965.

Author of weekly column for *Courier-News,* Somerville, N.J. Contributor of hundreds of poems, stories, and articles to magazines in the United States and abroad.

SIDELIGHTS: "I've written all kinds of things and on all kinds of subjects and for all different age groups because I like the variety—it keeps me fresh—and the challenge," writes Adele Louise DeLeeuw. "If it's a story I try to make it a good one, with overtones and undertones, so that the reader can get as much from it as he is capable of getting, regardless of the 'age group' rating; I think a story should have not only a good story line, but more subtle values—courage, independence, a new way of looking at life, the satisfaction of work well done, the joy of reaching toward a goal—whatever it is that can open a window on the world. If it's a biography, I hope to make the life of the person I'm writing about so interesting that, unconsciously perhaps, the child knows an inner reaching upward. Here is a person who did things, who overcame obstacles, who contributed to the world—an example of the often-forgotten fact that man can do anything he really wants to do. If it's a fantasy—well, that's fun for me and, I hope, for the reader!"

AVOCATIONAL INTERESTS: Ceramics, color photography, and the piano.

* * *

de LERMA, Dominique-Rene 1928-

PERSONAL: Born December 8, 1928, in Miami, Fla. *Education:* University of Miami, Coral Gables, Fla., B.M., 1952; Indiana University, Ph.D., 1958; also attended Berkshire Music Center, 1949, Curtis Institute of Music, 1949, and University of Oklahoma, 1962-63. *Politics:* Liberal. *Home:* 711 Stoney Springs Dr., Baltimore, Md. 21210. *Office:* Graduate Music Department, Morgan State University, Baltimore, Md. 21239.

CAREER: University of Miami, Coral Gables, Fla., associate professor of musicology, 1951-61; University of Oklahoma, Norman, associate professor of musicology, 1962-63; Indiana University at Bloomington, associate professor of musicology and music librarian, 1963-76; Morgan State University, Baltimore, Md., professor of music and graduate music coordinator, 1976—. Associate director for special projects of Afro-American Music Opportunities Association, 1972-75. Chairman of the board, Institute for Research in Black American Music, Fisk University; member of council, Brooklyn Philharmonia and Dance Theatre of Harlem; member of advisory board of Foundation for Research in the Afro-American Creative Arts. President, Sonorities in Black Music, Inc. Chief consultant to Columbia Records, Inc., on Black composers series.

MEMBER: International Association of Music Libraries, Internationale Bach Gesellschaft, Music Library Association (member of board of directors), American Musicological Society, Society of Black Composers, College Music Society (member of council), Society for Ethnomusicology, Deutsche Mozart Gesellschaft. *Awards, honors:* Awards from Svenska Institutet foer Kulturelit Utbyte, 1969-70, Fundacao Calouste Gulbenkian, 1969-70, Fondation Pro Helvetia, 1969-70, National Endowment for the Arts, 1969-

73, National Endowment for the Humanities, 1969-73, and Irwin-Sweeney-Miller Foundation, 1969-74; Alice and Corin Strong Award from Scandinavian-American Foundation, 1969-70.

WRITINGS: The Black-American Musical Heritage, Music Library Association, 1969; *Black Music in Our Culture,* Kent State University Press, 1970; *Charles Edward Ives,* Kent State University Press, 1970; *The Fritz Busch Collection,* Indiana University Library, 1972; *Reflections on Afro-American Music,* Kent State University Press, 1973; *Igor Fedorovitch Stravinsky,* Kent State University Press, 1974; *Resources for Music Research,* Harper, 1976. Editor of various works by the Chevalier de Saint-Georges, for Peer International and Merion Music, and of works by Jose Nunes-Garcia, for Associated Music Publishers. Contributor to *Library Journal, Black Perspective in Music, Choice,* and other professional publications.

WORK IN PROGRESS: The Legacy of Black Music, a multi-volume international bibliography, for Greenwood Press; a comprehensive bibliography of international music periodicals and related serials.

SIDELIGHTS: Dominique-Rene de Lerma told *CA:* "I began writing about performance matters for music journals when I was twenty-two and soon absorbed this activity as part of the obligations of a university professor. Until the death of Martin Luther King, my work was mainly in the area of eighteenth-century music. From the moment of his death, however, I pledged to dedicate my skills and time toward the fuller recognition of Black music and musicians. Because I seem to have been the only one trying to accomplish any research in this area, my assistance was requested by scholars, performers and educators to a growing extent. In the course of my work, I have been able to reconstruct the history of five centuries in which Black composers have been active, often to arrange for the performance, publication and even recording of this music. My primary concern is to make the public aware of the rich and distinguished history of all Black music and to help in opening the doors for younger Black talents to achieve what they want, regardless of idiom, without consideration for stereotypic images of the culture."

AVOCATIONAL INTERESTS: Travel, cooking, hiking.

* * *

DELIBES SETIEN, Miguel 1920-
(Miguel Delibes)

PERSONAL: Born October 17, 1920, in Valladolid, Spain; son of Adolfo (a professor) and Maria (Setien) Delibes; married Angeles de Castro Ruiz, April 23, 1946 (died November, 1974); children: Miguel, Angeles, German, Elisa, Juan, Adolfo, Camino. *Education:* Hermanos Doctrina Cristiana, Bachillerato; Universidad de Valladolid, Doctor en Derecho; attended Escuela Altos Estudios Mercantiles, and Escuela Periodismo. *Religion:* Roman Catholic. *Home:* Paseo Zorrilla 5, Valladolid, Spain.

CAREER: Novelist and writer. Visiting professor, University of Maryland, 1964. *Military service:* Spanish Navy, 1938-39. *Member:* Academico de Numero, Real Academia Espanola, Hispanic Society. *Awards, honors:* Nadal Prize, 1947, for *La sombra del cipres es alargada;* Spanish national prize for literature, 1955, for *Diario de un cazador.*

WRITINGS—All under name Miguel Delibes; novels, except as indicated; published by Ediciones Destino, except as indicated: *La sombra del cipres es alargada* (also see below), 1948, 8th edition, 1969; *Aun es de dia,* 1949, 2nd edition, 1962; *El camino* (also see below), 1950, 11th edition, 1974, self-illustrated edition, Holt, 1960, translation by Brita Haycraft and John Haycraft published as *The Path,* John Day, 1961; *Mi Idolatrado hijo Sisi* (also see below), 1953, 3rd edition, 1969; *El loco* (novella; also see below), Editorial Tecnos, 1953; *La partida* (fiction; contains "La Partida," "El refugio," "Una peseta para el tranvia," "El manguero," "El campeonato," "El traslado," "El primer pitillo," "La contradiccion," "En una noche asi," "La conferencia"), L. de Caralt, 1954, 2nd edition, Alianza Editorial, 1969; *Diario de un cazador,* 1955, 6th edition, 1971; *Siestas con viento sur* (novellas; contains "La mortaja," "El loco," "Los nogales," "Los railes"), 1957, 2nd edition, 1967; *Diario de un emigrante,* 1958, 2nd edition, 1965; *La hoja roja,* 1959, 3rd edition, 1975.

Las ratas, 1962, 7th edition, 1971, Harrap, 1969; *Obra completa* (contains "Prologo," "La sombre del cipres es alargada," "El camino," and "Mi idolatrado hiji Sisi"), Part I, 1964; *Cinco horas con Mario,* 1966, 9th edition, 1975; *La Mortaja* (novellas; also see above; contains "La mortaga," "El amor propio de Juanito Osuna," "El patio de vecindad," "El sol," "La fe," "El conejo," "La perra," and "Navidad sin ambiente"), Alianza Editorial, 1969, 2nd edition, 1974; *Parabola del naufrago,* 1969, 3rd edition, 1971; (with others) *La sombra del cipres es alargada [por] Miguel Delibes. Sobre las piedras grises [por] Sebastian Juan Arbo. Las ultimas horas [por] Jose Suarex Carreno,* 1970; *Mi mundo y el mundo: seleccion antologica de obras del autor, para ninos de 11 a 14 anos,* Minon, 1970; *Smoke on the Ground,* translation by Alfred Johnson, Doubleday, 1972; *El principe destronado,* 1973, 6th edition, 1975; *Las guerras de neustros antepasados,* 1974, 2nd edition, 1975; *El disputado voto del senior Cape,* 1978.

Nonfiction: *Un novelista descrube America,* Editora Nacional, 1956; *La barberia: portada de Coll,* G. P. Ediciones, 1957; *Castilla,* Editorial Lumen, 1960, published as *Viejas historias de Castilla la Vieja,* 1964, 3rd edition, 1974; *Por esos mundos: Sudamerica con escala en las Canarias,* Ediciones Destino, 1971; *La Caza de la perdiz roja,* Editorial Lumen, 1963; *Europa: Parada y fonda,* Ediciones Cid, 1963; *El libro de la caza menor,* Ediciones Destino, 1964, 3rd edition, 1973; *USA y yo,* Ediciones Destino, 1966, Odyssey, 1970; *Vivir al dia* (also see below), Ediciones Destino, 1968; (contributor) Susanne Filkau, editor, *Historias de la guerra civil,* Edition Langewiesche-Brandt, 1968; *La primavera de Prage,* Alianza Editorial, 1968; *Con la escopeta al hombro* (also see below), Ediciones Destino, 1970, 2nd edition, 1971; *Un ano de mi vida* (also see below), Ediciones Destino, 1972; *La caza en Espana,* Alianza Editorial, 1972; *Castilla en mi obra,* Editorial Magistero Espanal, 1972; *S.O.S.,* Ediciones Destino, 1975; *Aventuras, venturas, y desventuras de un cazador a rabo,* Ediciones Destino, 1976; *Mis amigas las truchas,* Ediciones Destino, 1977; *Castilla, lo castellano y los castellanos,* Editorial Planeta, 1979. Also author of another volume of *Obra completa* containing "Vivir al dia," "Con la escopeta al hombro," and "Un ano de mi vida," for Ediciones Destino.

SIDELIGHTS: Miguel Delibes Setien is considered one of Spain's most important novelists; his work is distinguished by its stark realism, rural subject matter, and well-developed characters. Ronald Schwartz explains: "Delibes has been always considered a major novelist whose career is constantly developing, growing in quantity and quality, and becoming more prestigious because of his consistent use of Realism and his attachment to rural themes, which display a variety of character types. . . . Critics acknowledge his skepticism, pessimism, reactionary vision of nature, his love for the man of instinct, of nature in contrast to a 'civilized' product, in short, his negative view of progress and 'civilization,' his black humor and cold intellectualism."

The realism and themes of nature in Delibes Setien's work have been widely praised. Schwartz believes that the author demonstrates "an enormous capacity to capture within his writings the essence of nature by means of his starkly Realist style." In the *New York Times Book Review,* Martin Levin contrasts the "charming and nostalgic" view of nature rendered by "Anglo-Saxon novels" to the harsh atmosphere of *Smoke on the Ground.* "The land is wretchedly poor," he writes, "the climate is harsh, and the atmosphere has a haunting, 19th-century bleakness, although it is set in the age of moon missions." Schwartz believes that with the "harmonious" combination of "humor, tenderness, nature and tragedy" evident in Delibes Setien's later work, he is "reviving the theme of nature as a literary element indispensable to the human condition and portraying this harmony through his extremely personal style."

Some of Delibes Setien's works have been adapted for Spanish television. Feature-length film adaptions of his work include "Retrato de familia," based on his novel *Mi idolatrado hijo Sisi,* filmed in 1975, and "La guerra de papa," produced in 1978, and based on the novel *El principe destronado. Cinco horas con Mario* has also been filmed.

BIOGRAPHICAL/CRITICAL SOURCES: Times Literary Supplement, April 20, 1967, June 11, 1970; *Booklist,* February 15, 1971; *Hispania,* December, 1971, December, 1972, March, 1974, May, 1974, May, 1976; *New York Times Book Review,* August 20, 1972; *Antioch Review,* June, 1973; Ronald Schwartz, *Spain's New Wave Novelists: 1950-1974,* Scarecrow Press, 1976; *World Literature Today,* summer, 1977; (under name Miguel Delibes) *Contemporary Literary Criticism,* Volume VIII, Gale, 1978.

* * *

DEMARAY, Donald E(ugene) 1926-

PERSONAL: Born December 6, 1926, in Adrian, Mich.; son of C. Dorr and Grace (Vore) Demaray; married Kathleen Bear, 1948; children: Cherith, Elyse, James. *Education:* Azusa Pacific College, B.A., 1946; Asbury Theological Seminary, B.D., 1949; graduate study at University of Southern California, 1949-50, and University of Zurich, 1951; University of Edinburgh, Ph.D., 1952; University of Manchester, postdoctoral research, 1962. *Home:* 409 Talbot, Wilmore, Ky. 40390. *Office:* Dean of Students, Asbury Theological Seminary, Wilmore, Ky. 40390.

CAREER: Ordained minister of Free Methodist Church. Seattle Pacific College (now University), Seattle, Wash., 1952-66, began as lecturer, became professor of religion, dean of School of Religion, 1959-66; Asbury Theological Seminary, Wilmore, Ky., associate professor, 1966-67, professor of preaching and dean of students, 1967-75, Fisher Professor of Preaching, 1975—. Minister of youth, Seattle Pacific College Church, 1952-53.

WRITINGS: "Amazing Grace!," Light & Life Press, 1957; (editor) *Devotions and Prayers of John Wesley,* Baker Book, 1957, reprinted, 1977; *Basic Beliefs: An Introductory Guide to Christian Theology,* Baker Book, 1958; *Loyalty to Christ,* Baker Book, 1958; *The Book of Acts: A Study Manual,* Baker Book, 1959; *A Pulpit Manual,* Baker Book, 1959; (editor) *Devotions and Prayers of Charles Spurgeon,* Baker Book, 1960, reprinted, 1976; *Acts A and B,* Light & Life Press, 1961; *Questions Youth Ask,* Baker Book, 1961; *Cowman Handbook of the Bible,* Cowman, 1964, published as *Bible Study Sourcebook,* Zondervan, 1973; *Alive to God through Prayer,* Baker Book, 1965; *Preacher Aflame!,* Baker Book, 1972; *Pulpil Giants: What Made Them Great,* Moody, 1973; *An Introduction to Homiletics,* Baker Book, 1974; *The Minister's Ministries,* Light & Life Press, 1974; *A Guide to Happiness,* Baker Book, 1974; (editor) *Blow, Wind of God: Spirit Powered Passages from the Writing and Preaching of Billy Graham,* Baker Book, 1975; (editor) *Alive to God through Praise,* Baker Book, 1976; *Near Hurting People: The Pastoral Ministry of Robert Moffat Fine,* Light & Life Press, 1978; *Proclaiming the Truth: Guides to Scriptural Preaching,* Baker Book, 1979. Contributor to religion journals.

AVOCATIONAL INTERESTS: Collecting books and stamps, reading, gardening, tennis.

* * *

DEMPEWOLFF, Richard F(rederic) 1914- (Michael Day, Dick Frederick, Frederick Wolf)

PERSONAL: Born October 30, 1914, in New York, N.Y.; son of Augustus Frederic (a physician) and Katherine (Rubsamen) Dempewolff; married Rita M. Fitzpatrick (an editorial assistant), October 16, 1939; children: Judith Ann. *Education:* Middlebury College, B.S., 1936. *Politics:* Independent. *Religion:* Congregationalist. *Home address:* Box 61, Hunter Farm, R.D., Henryville, Pa. 18332.

CAREER: Literary Digest, New York City, associate editor, 1936-37; Fawcett Publications, New York City, managing editor of *True,* 1937-40; *Newsweek,* New York City, press editor, education editor, 1940-42, 1946; Street & Smith, New York City, article editor, *PIC,* 1946-49; *Popular Mechanics,* eastern editor, Chicago, Ill., 1949-62, executive editor, New York City, 1962-67; *Science Digest,* New York City, editor, 1967-74; free-lance writer, 1974—. *Military service:* U.S. Navy, 1942-46; became lieutenant junior grade. *Member:* National Press Club, Overseas Press Club of America (member of board of governors, 1974-78), National Association of Science Writers, Sigma Delta Chi, Kappa Delta Rho, Lake Swiftwater Club (director; secretary, 1952-57, 1959-62).

WRITINGS: Famous Old New England Murders, Daye, 1942; *Animal Reveille,* Doubleday, 1943; *Precut House,* Popular Mechanics Press, 1955; *Adventure with Nature Craft,* Capitol, 1960; *Tabletop Car Racing,* Hawthorn, 1963; *Lost Cities and Forgotten Tribes,* Hearst Books, 1974; (with Mortimer Feinberg) *Corporate Bigamy,* Morrow, 1980. Contributor to national magazines.

SIDELIGHTS: Richard F. Dempewolff was a correspondent member of Byrd Antarctic Expedition, 1955, and Deepfreeze Six, 1960-61. He told *CA:* "Like any creative endeavor, writing for most authors is something akin to a compulsion; for some, like my friend Isaac Asimov, it is a very real compulsion. While I tend to labor over many of the writings I produce, I have learned that it is far more important—as Michelangelo's aged teacher Bertoldo impressed upon that great artist—'to produce a body of work . . .' than to strive endlessly for perfection. Learning to write copy that is good, bad or indifferent—but WRITTEN—is one of the toughest lessons for a writer to learn; at least it was for me. And I have often discovered to my great surprise that some of the things that I thought I was writing for the wastebasket, were among my best."

DENTLER, Robert A(rnold) 1928-

PERSONAL: Born November 26, 1928, in Chicago, Ill.; son of Arnold E. and Jennie (Munsen) Dentler; married Helen Hosmer, 1950; children: Deborah, Eric A., Robin H. *Education:* Northwestern University, B.S., 1949, M.A., 1950; American University, M.A., 1954; University of Chicago, Ph.D., 1960. *Religion:* Unitarian Universalist. *Home:* 11 Childs Rd., Lexington, Mass. 02173. *Office:* Dean of Education, Boston University, 765 Commonwealth Ave., Boston, Mass. 02215.

CAREER: Dickinson College, Carlisle, Pa., member of faculty, 1954-57; University of Chicago, Chicago, Ill., university fellow, 1957-59; University of Kansas, Lawrence, researcher, 1959-61; Dartmouth College, Hanover, N.H., assistant professor, 1961-62; Columbia University, Teachers College, New York, N.Y., associate professor, 1962-65, professor, 1966-72; Boston University, Boston, Mass., dean of education and university professor, 1972—. Director of Center for Urban Education, 1966-72.

WRITINGS: The Young Volunteers, National Opinion Research Center, 1959; (co-author) *The Politics of Urban Renewal,* Free Press of Glencoe, 1962; (co-author) *Hostage America,* Beacon Press, 1963; (co-author) *Politics and Social Life,* Houghton, 1963; *Major American Social Problems,* Rand McNally, 1967, 2nd edition published as *Major Social Problems,* 1972; (with Mary Ellen Warshauer) *Big City Dropouts and Illiterates,* Praeger, 1967; (co-author) *The Urban R's,* Praeger, 1967; (co-editor) *Readings in Educational Psychology,* Harper, 1976; *Urban Problems,* Rand McNally, 1977. Contributor of sixty articles to social and behavioral science journals.

WORK IN PROGRESS: Co-authoring *Boston School Desegregation.*

* * *

DEVEREUX, Frederick L(eonard), Jr. 1914-

PERSONAL: Born April 20, 1914, in New York, N.Y.; son of Frederick Leonard (an executive) and Frances (Clark) Devereux; married Ruth Wentworth Foster, June 26, 1936 (died, 1974); married Elizabeth H. Robinson, December 30, 1978; children: (first marriage) Foster, Frances Clark, Frederick Leonard III. *Education:* University of Chicago, A.B., 1937; U.S. Army Command and General Staff College, Diploma, 1943. *Politics:* Republican. *Religion:* Episcopalian. *Home:* Fiddler's Green, Woodstock, Vt. 05091.

CAREER: R. H. Macy & Co., New York City, buyer, 1936-38; Young & Rubicam, Inc., New York City, merchandizing executive, 1939-40, 1946-52; Oneita Knitting Mills, Utica, N.Y., general sales manager, 1953-59; Allied Stores Corp., New York City, marketing manager, 1960-64; Merit Stores, Inc., Middletown, N.Y., president, 1964-66. Lecturer at Graduate School of Business Administration, New York University, 1959-60; instructor for U.S. Power Squadrons classes, 1969-72. Judge at National Horse Show and other horse shows and hunter trials. *Military service:* U.S. Army, Cavalry, 1941-45; instructor in horsemanship at U.S. Military Academy, 1942-43; later assistant chief of staff, Intelligence, 86th Infantry Division; became lieutenant colonel. *Member:* Institute of Navigation, American Horse Shows Association, U.S. Power Squadrons, Lucy Mackenzie Humane Society, American Yacht Club, Quechee Polo Club (vice-president).

WRITINGS: Practical Navigation for the Yachtsman, Norton, 1972; *Famous Horses: Past and Present* (juvenile), Devin-Adair, 1972; *Ride Your Pony Right* (juvenile), Dodd, 1974; *Horses: A First Book,* F. Watts, 1974; *The Backyard Pony,* F. Watts, 1975; (editor) *The Cavalry Manual of Horse Management,* revised edition, A. S. Barnes, 1979; *Horse Problems and Problem Horses,* Houghton, 1980. Former editor, *Vermont Horse.*

* * *

DEVINE, D(avid) M(cDonald) 1920-
(Dominic Devine, David Munro)

PERSONAL: Born August 16, 1920, in Greenock, Scotland; son of David and Elizabeth (Gray) Devine; married Betsy Findlay Munro, 1946; children: Sheena. *Education:* University of Glasgow, M.A., 1945; University of London. LL.B., 1953. *Home:* Melvaig, Lade Braes, St. Andrews, Scotland. *Office:* University of St. Andrews, North St., St. Andrews, Scotland.

CAREER: North-West Engineering Employers' Association, Glasgow, Scotland, assistant secretary, 1944-46; University of St. Andrews, St. Andrews, Scotland, assistant secretary, 1946-61, deputy secretary, 1961-72, secretary and registrar, 1972—. *Member:* Royal and Ancient Golf Club and Bridge Club (both St. Andrews).

WRITINGS: My Brother's Killer, Dodd, 1962; *Doctors Also Die,* Dodd, 1963; *The Royston Affair,* Dodd, 1965; *His Own Appointed Day,* Walker, 1965; *Devil at Your Elbow,* Walker, 1967; *The Fifth Cord,* Walker, 1967.

Under pseudonym Dominic Devine: *The Sleeping Tiger,* Walker, 1968; *Death Is My Bridegroom,* Walker, 1969; *Illegal Tender,* Walker, 1970; *Dead Trouble,* Doubleday, 1971; *Three Green Bottles,* Doubleday, 1972; *Sunk without Trace,* St. Martin's, in press.

SIDELIGHTS: D. M. Devine's work has been favorably compared to "whodunits" of the classic school. A critic in the *New York Times Book Review* notes that his books contain "more fully developed characters and locale . . . than that school could usually boast." *Avocational interests:* Reading, music, bridge, cricket, golf.

BIOGRAPHICAL/CRITICAL SOURCES: New York Times Book Review, March 26, 1967, October 29, 1967, September 7, 1969; *Punch,* April 16, 1969; *Best Sellers,* January 15, 1971.

* * *

DEVINE, George 1941-

PERSONAL: Born February 4, 1941, in San Francisco, Calif.; son of George Edward, Jr. (an attorney) and Dorothy Vasserot (Merle) Devine; married Joanne Catherine Donohue (a college instructor), December 27, 1968; children: George Edward IV, Annemarie Victoria. *Education:* University of San Francisco, A.B., 1962; Marquette University, M.A., 1964. *Politics:* Democratic Party. *Religion:* Roman Catholic. *Home and office:* 1960 Tenth Ave., San Francisco, Calif. 94116.

CAREER: Marquette University, Milwaukee, Wis., lecturer in religion in Division of Continuing Education, 1963-64; Seton Hall University, South Orange, N.J., instructor, 1964-67, assistant professor of theology, 1967-71, assistant professor, 1971-72, associate professor of religious studies, 1972-76, chairman of department, 1971-74; University of San Francisco, San Francisco, Calif., scholar-in-residence, 1975-76; Anthony Schools of San Francisco, San Francisco, instructor in real estate, 1976—. Teacher, St. John's University, New York City, 1969-70, and Manhattan College, New

York City, 1969-70. Realtor-associate, Klein & Co., San Francisco, 1976—. Staff assistant in public information/development, University of San Francisco, 1962-63; director of public relations, F.E.L. Church Publications, Chicago, Ill., 1963-64. Member, San Francisco Board of Realtors, 1976—. *Member:* American Society of Journalists and Authors, National Press Club.

WRITINGS: *Our Living Liturgy,* Claretian Publications, 1966; *Why Read the Old Testament?,* Claretian Publications, 1966; *Transformation in Christ,* Alba, 1972; *Liturgical Renewal: An Agonizing Reappraisal,* Alba, 1973; *If I Were to Preach,* Alba, Volume I, 1974, Volume II, 1975, Volume III, 1976; *American Catholicism: Where Do We Go from Here?,* Prentice-Hall, 1975; *A Case for Roman Catholicism,* Silver Burdett, 1975.

Editor of annual publications, College Theology Society, 1968-73, including: *To Be a Man,* Prentice-Hall, 1969; *Theology in Revolution,* Alba, 1970; *New Dimensions in Religious Experience,* Alba, 1971; *That They May Live: Theological Reflections on the Quality of Life,* Alba, 1972; *A World More Human, a Church More Christian,* Alba, 1973. Contributor to *Commonweal, America, New York Times Book Review, National Observer, San Francisco Examiner, Lutheran, Cross Currents, National Catholic Reporter, Catholic Digest, Worship, U.S. Catholic,* and *Jubilee.* Associate editor, *Pius XII Newsletter,* 1963-64, and *Christian Art,* 1963-66; member of editorial board, *Advocate* (offical newspaper of Archdiocese of Newark), 1973-77.

WORK IN PROGRESS: *Jesus, Lord and Savior,* for Silver Burdett.

SIDELIGHTS: George Devine told *CA:* "For me, good writing is not so much a matter of technique as a matter of having something to say. There are all too many people who know how to say things but have nothing to say—no expertise in any subject, no convictions, no distinctive point of view. People like these seldom become known as good writers. On the other hand, there are many intelligent people who know their subjects well and who feel strongly about what they want to communicate—and whose knowledge and enthusiasm compel them to put their message onto paper in a lively and effective way. People in this latter group frequently become known as very good writers. Sometimes they even break the 'rules' of 'technique' and their vital style is aided and not hindered by this fact (although it is hard to achieve any effect in breaking a rule unless one first knows the rule and knows why there is reason to break it).

"Most good writers in our society are professional in the sense that good editors (in publishing houses or magazines or newspapers or the broadcast media) will pay these writers for their copy and then publish it for a discriminating readership. But many good writers are not professional in the sense of earning a full living by doing nothing professionally except writing. Many good writers must perform some other kind of paying work which supports a lifestyle that includes some professional writing. As the number of outlets for writers decreases in proportion to the number of well-written works seeking to be published, more and more of our professional writers will also have paying jobs doing something quite apart from their writing careers."

AVOCATIONAL INTERESTS: Drama and fiction.

BIOGRAPHICAL/CRITICAL SOURCES: *Catholic Layman,* April, 1964; *Advocate,* November 9, 1972.

De WELT, Don Finch 1919-

PERSONAL: Born February 19, 1919, in Astoria, Ore.; son of Charles Wallace and Marie (Stewart) De Welt; married, 1942; wife's name, Elsie; children: Daniel, Anne Louise, Christopher. *Education:* Attended Pacific Bible Seminary, 1938-40; San Jose Bible College, B.Th. and B.D.; additional study at San Jose State College (now University), 1951-52, and Abilene Christian College (now University), 1956. *Home:* 124 Sergeant, Joplin, Mo. *Office:* College Press, 205 North Main St., Joplin, Mo. 64801.

CAREER: Ordained minister in Christian Church, 1941, served in California and Missouri; San Jose Bible College, San Jose, Calif., professor, 1943-57; Ozark Bible College, Joplin, Mo., professor, 1957—, currently affiliated with College Press.

WRITINGS—All published by College Press, except as indicated: *Acts Made Actual,* 1953, revised edition, 1975; *Sacred History and Geography,* Baker Book, 1955; *If You Want to Preach,* Baker Book, 1957, 2nd edition, 1964; *The Church in the Bible,* 1958; *Romans Realized,* 1959; *Paul's Letters to Timothy and Titus,* 1961; *The Power of the Holy Spirit,* four volumes, 1962-76; (with B. W. Johnson) *The Gospel of Mark,* 1965; *Leviticus,* 1975; *Song of Solomon,* 1977; *The Acts of the Apostles,* 1979; *What the Bible Says About Fasting and Prayer,* 1980. Contributor to *Christian Standard.* Editor of Bible Study Text Book Club, Joplin, Mo., which has published study texts on the 66 books of the Bible.

AVOCATIONAL INTERESTS: Oil painting.†

* * *

DEWEY, Thomas B(lanchard) 1915- (Tom Brandt, Cord Wainer)

PERSONAL: Born March 6, 1915, in Elkhart, Ind.; son of Henry Evert and Elizabeth (Blanchard) Dewey; married Maxine Morley Sorensen, 1951; married Doris L. Smith, 1972; children: (previous marriage) Thomas B., Deborah. *Education:* Kansas State Teachers College (now Emporia State University), B.S. in Ed., 1936; State University of Iowa, graduate study, 1937-38; University of California, Los Angeles, Ph.D., 1973.

CAREER: Harding Market Co., Chicago, Ill., clerical worker, 1936-37; Storycraft, Inc. (correspondence school), Hollywood, Calif., editor, 1938-42; U.S. Department of State, Washington, D.C., administrative and editorial assistant, 1942-45; worked for advertising agency, Los Angeles, Calif., 1945-52; Arizona State University, Tempe, assistant professor of English, 1971-77; currently free-lance writer. *Member:* Mystery Writers of America (director-at-large, 1960-62).

WRITINGS: *Hue and Cry,* Morrow, 1944; *As Good as Dead,* Morrow, 1946; *Draw the Curtain Close,* Morrow, 1947; *Mourning After,* Morrow, 1950; *Handle with Fear,* Morrow, 1951; *Murder of Marion Mason,* Dakers, 1952; *Every Bet's a Sure Thing,* Simon & Schuster, 1953; *Prey for Me,* Simon & Schuster, 1954; *The Mean Streets,* Simon & Schuster, 1955; *My Love is Violent,* Popular Library, 1956; *The Brave, Bad Girls,* Simon & Schuster, 1956; *And Where She Stops,* Popular Library, 1957; *You've Got Him Cold,* Simon & Schuster, 1958; (with Harold M. Imerman) *What Women Want to Know,* Crown, 1958; *I.O.U. Murder,* T. V. Boardman, 1958; *The Case of the Chased and the Unchaste,* Random House, 1959.

The Girl Who Wasn't There, Simon & Schuster, 1960; *Go to Sleep, Jeannie,* T. V. Boardman, 1960; *Too Hot for Hawaii,*

Popular Library, 1960; *Hunter at Large*, Simon & Schuster, 1961; *The Golden Hooligan*, Dell, 1961; *Mexican Slay Ride*, T. V. Boardman, 1961; *How Hard to Kill*, Simon & Schuster, 1962; *Go, Honeylou*, Dell, 1962; *The Girl with the Sweet Plump Knees*, Dell, 1963; *A Sad Song Singing*, Simon & Schuster, 1963; *Only on Tuesdays*, T. V. Boardman, 1964; *Don't Cry for Long*, Simon & Schuster, 1964; *Can a Mermaid Kill?*, Tower, 1965; *Portrait of a Dead Heiress*, Simon & Schuster, 1965; *The Girl in the Punchbowl*, T. V. Boardman, 1965; *Nude in Nevada*, T. V. Boardman, 1966; *Deadline*, Simon & Schuster, 1966; *Sleuths and Consequences*, Simon & Schuster, 1966; *A Season for Violence*, Gold Medal, 1966; *Death and Taxes* (Detective Book Club selection), Putnam, 1967; *The King Killers*, Putnam, 1968; *The Love-Death Thing*, Simon & Schuster, 1969; *The Taurus Trip*, Simon & Schuster, 1970.

Under pseudonym Cord Wainer: *Mountain Girl*, Gold Medal, 1953.

Under pseudonym Tom Brandt: *Kiss Me Hard*, Popular Library, 1954; *Run, Brother, Run*, Popular Library, 1954.

WORK IN PROGRESS: Detective novels in collaboration with Jerry Burnette.

SIDELIGHTS: Two of Thomas B. Dewey's books, *Every Bet's a Sure Thing* and *A Sad Song Singing*, have been adapted for television.

BIOGRAPHICAL/CRITICAL SOURCES: Book World, July 21, 1968; *New York Times Book Review*, July 28, 1968; *Best Sellers*, November 1, 1970.

* * *

DIBB, Paul 1939-

PERSONAL: Born October 3, 1939, in Yorkshire, England; son of Cyril William and Ethel (Greenwood) Dibb; married Joyce Valerie Redfern (a research assistant in adult education), 1960; children: Martin Richard. *Education:* University of Nottingham, B.A. (honors), 1960. *Home:* 1 Dugdale St., Cook, Canberra 2614, Australia. *Office:* Defense Department, Russell Offices, Canberra 2600, Australia.

CAREER: Australian Trade Department, Canberra, research economist, 1961-64; Australian Bureau of Agricultural Economics, Canberra, research economist, 1964-67; Australian National University, Canberra, research fellow, 1967-70; Defense Department, Canberra, Australia, member of national assessments staff, 1970-73, staff head, 1974-78, deputy director of Joint Intelligence Organization, 1978—.

WRITINGS: (Contributor) M. I. Goldman, editor, *Comparative Economic Systems*, Random House, 1971; *Siberia and the Pacific*, Praeger, 1972; (contributor) *Advance Australia: Where?*, Oxford University Press (Australia), 1975; *The Balance of Power in North-East Asia*, University of Sydney Press, 1976. Contributor to *Australian Outlook*.

SIDELIGHTS: Dibb has traveled in the Soviet Union (including Siberia), China, Japan, Indonesia, New Zealand, the United States, and England.

* * *

Di FRANCO, Fiorenza 1932-

PERSONAL: Born June 19, 1932, in Budapest, Hungary; daughter of Oscarre and Olga (Czako) Di Franco. *Education:* Attended Universita di Roma, 1951-53; Western Reserve University (now Case Western Reserve University), M.A., 1965, Ph.D., 1969. *Home:* Angelo Olivieri 91, Ostia (Roma), Italy. *Office:* Department of Humanities, John Cabot International College, Via Massaua, 6, Rome, Italy.

CAREER: Notre Dame College, Cleveland, Ohio, instructor in French and Latin, 1965-66; Kent State University, Kent, Ohio, instructor in French, 1966-67; Case Western Reserve University, Cleveland, assistant professor of French and Italian, 1968-72; University of Missouri—St. Louis, assistant professor of French and Italian, 1972-74; John Cabot International College, Rome, Italy, professor of French and Italian, 1976—. Visiting professor at Oberlin College, 1969-72. *Member:* Modern Language Association of America. *Awards, honors:* Wright-Plaisance fellowship to France, 1967-68; grant from Italian Government, for study, 1974-77.

WRITINGS: Le theatre de Salacrou, Gallimard, 1970; (contributor) Roger Johnson, editor, *Moliere and the Commonwealth of Letters*, University of Southern Mississippi Press, 1973; *Il teatro di Eduardo*, Laterza, 1975; *Eduardo De Filippo*, Gremese, 1978.

WORK IN PROGRESS: Peppino De Filippo, for Gremese; *Pier Paolo Pasolini*.

* * *

DOAN, Eleanor Lloyd

PERSONAL: Born in Boise, Idaho; daughter of Fred (a railroad official) and Gladys (Werth) Doan. *Education:* University of Nevada, B.A., 1936; graduate study at Wheaton College, Wheaton, Ill., 1936-37, and University of California. *Home:* 1240 Moncado Dr., Glendale, Calif. 91207. *Office:* Gospel Light Publications, 110 West Broadway, Glendale, Calif.

CAREER: Nevada State Journal, Reno, Nev., reporter, 1933-36; high school teacher, Austin, Nev., 1937-38; merchandising manager and writer with various religious periodicals in New York, N.Y., 1938-45; Gospel Light Publications, Glendale, Calif., 1945—, currently promotional publicist and writer. Partner, Tot 'n Teen Dress Shop, Elko, Nev., 1948-58. Trustee, Mustard Seed Missionary Organization, 1956—; member of executive committee, Glint (Gospel Light International), 1961—. *Member:* Doane Family Association of America (regional vice-president and president of California chapter), Chi Delta Chi, Kappa Tau Alpha, Gamma Phi Beta Alumnae.

WRITINGS—All published by Gospel Light Publications: *Teaching Two and Threes*, 1951; *Two and Three Time*, 1951, 2nd edition, 1956; *Worship Services*, four books, 1951; *Handcraft Adventures*, 1958; *Handcraft for Everyone*, 1959; *Teach Worship in Your Sunday School*, 1959; *Handcraft for All Ages*, 1960; *Handcraft Encyclopedia*, 1961; *Equipment Encyclopedia*, 1962; *Pattern Encyclopedia*, 1962; *Teaching Junior Highs Successfully*, 1962; *Kid Stuff*, 1970; *The Bible Story Picture Book*, 1972.

All published by Zondervan: *Finger Fun*, 1952; *251 Handcrafts and Fun for Little Ones*, 1953; *How to Plan and Conduct a Junior Church*, 1954; *Handcrafts and Fun*, 1956; *Hobby Fun*, 1956; *The Speaker's Sourcebook*, 1960; (with Frances Blankenbaker) *How to Plan and Conduct a Primary Church*, 1961; (with Gladys McElroy) *Food and Fun Craft*, 1963; *More Handcrafts and Fun for Little Ones*, 1966; *Sourcebook for Speakers*, 1967; *Mother's Day Sourcebook*, 1967; *Mother's Day Treasury of Inspiration*, 1969; *Treasury of Inspiration*, 1970; *157 Handcrafts for Juniors and Junior Highs*, 1972; *145 Fun to do Handcrafts for Juniors and Junior Highs*, 1972; *A Child's Treasury of Verse*, 1977; *Find the Words Puzzle Book*, 1980.

Also author of "Summer Bible School Course" series, seventeen books, Christian Publications, 1941, "Missionary

Stories'' series, four books, Gospel Light Publications, 1963, and ''Creative Handcraft'' series, four books, Gospel Light Publications, 1973.

Editor; all published by Gospel Light Publications: *Teaching Adults Successfully,* 1962; *Teaching Primaries Successfully,* 1962; *Teaching Juniors Successfully,* 1962; *How to Get Along with Teenagers,* 1962; *431 Quotes from the Notes of Henrietta C. Mears,* 1970. Creative research editor, *Teach* (magazine), 1959—; compiler of five ''Teach Tips'' booklets, 1966. Contributor to encyclopedias and periodicals.

WORK IN PROGRESS: A new series of handcraft books for Zondervan; inspirational books for Gospel Light Publications.

SIDELIGHTS: Eleanor Lloyd Doan told *CA:* ''From the time I learned to read, I wanted to be a writer. I wanted to help children and adults know about the world in which they lived, how to use their time profitably and creatively, to have bits of inspiration along the way, and to be encouraged to love God and live a Christian life. Journalism was my chosen profession by the time I was in Junior High School and the aroma of printer's ink was magnetic in keeping me tracking in that direction.

''Although I was a full-fledged, employed journalist while still in college, I tried my wings at poetry, inspirational, and 'how-to' articles. The English poets, particularly Kipling, [along with] H. L. Mencken, Richard Haliburton, Horace Greeley, and Mark Twain were writers I particularly enjoyed plus a smorgasbord of contemporary and classic writers whose works were devoured and probably contributed to broadening my interests and sharpening my skills. The Bible was my inspiration and Guidebook!

''My writing career has followed a dual pathway: journalism and creative/inspirational writing. They complement and motivate each other. For the most part, my writing is not for the literati, it is for the common people, to meet their need. My goal has not been motivated by dollars but by a desire to help people, to serve them practically in various areas of need.

''I receive great satisfaction from my writing because it has met needs, changed lives, and encouraged and inspired people in the English speaking world—and to some extent in countries where [my] books have been translated. . . . Some of my books I have initiated; some were initiated by my publishers. None have been easy, but all have been a challenge. To achieve, particularly in the area of freelance, self-discipline, is paramount. It is a combination of inspiration and a coat of glue to the seat of the chair—a thick coat!

''My challenge to aspiring writers: Don't write just because you want to write. Have a specific purpose that meets needs other than your need for self-expression. Be sensitive to the world around you. Be aware of its needs. And, get a BIG bottle of glue!''

AVOCATIONAL INTERESTS: Coin collecting, doll collecting, entertaining, reading, desert life and lore, travel, genealogy.

* * *

DOLINER, Roy 1932-

PERSONAL: Born April 9, 1932, in New York, N.Y.; son of George and Sylvia (Seigel) Doliner. *Education:* New York University, B.A., 1954. *Home and office:* 316 East 18th St., New York, N.Y. 10003.

CAREER: Novelist. *Military service:* U.S. Army, two years. *Member:* Authors Guild.

WRITINGS: Young Man Willing, Scribner, 1960; *The Orange Air,* Scribner, 1961; *Sandra Rifkin's Jewels,* New American Library, 1966; *The Antagonists,* Doubleday, 1967; *Rules of the Game,* Doubleday, 1970; *For Love or Money,* Simon & Schuster, 1974; *On the Edge,* Viking, 1978.

WORK IN PROGRESS: Apple Dome.

AVOCATIONAL INTERESTS: Oceanography.†

* * *

DOMARADZKI, Theodore F(elix) 1910-

PERSONAL: Born October 27, 1910, in Warsaw, Poland; son of Joseph (an engineer) and Maria (Tomaszewska) Domaradzki; married Maria T. Dobija (a professor and physician), April 24, 1954. *Education:* Academy of Political Sciences, Warsaw, diploma, 1936; University of Warsaw, M.A., 1939; University of Rome, Litt.D., 1941. *Religion:* Roman Catholic. *Home:* 5601 Ave. des Cedres, Montreal, Quebec, Canada H1T 2V4. *Office:* Institute of Comparative Civilizations of Montreal, 5214 Ave. du Parc, Montreal, Quebec, Canada H2V 4G7.

CAREER: University of Rome, Rome, Italy, lecturer in Polish philology, 1941-47; Pontifical Institute of Oriental Studies, Rome, associate professor of Slavic institutions and literatures, 1943-47; University of Montreal, Montreal, Quebec, associate professor, 1948-52, professor of Polish literature and Slavic civilization and director of department of Slavic studies, 1952-76; Institute of Comparative Civilizations, Montreal, professor and president, 1976—. Visiting professor at Fordham University, 1948-50. Vice-president, Canadian Inter-American Research Institute, 1964—; president, Canadian World University Committee, 1964—, and Committee for Canadian-Polish University and Scientific Cooperation P.Q. Section, 1969—; vice-president, Canadian International Academy of Humanities and Social Sciences, 1975—, and Quebec Ethnic Press Association, 1979—. Representative of the Polish Ministry of Education in exile, Rome, 1942-45; Canadian negotiator of university and cultural agreements with Poland, 1970—. *Military service:* Polish Corps, British Command, 1944-45; served in Italy; became major.

MEMBER: International Association for Modern Languages and Literature, Societe Polonaise Historique et Litteraire, Societe des Ecrivains Canadiens, Association Canadienne-Francaise pour l'Avancement des Sciences, Association of Polish University Professors and Lecturers Abroad, Polish Union of Journalists, Polish Veterans Association, Canadian Institute for International Affairs, Canadian Comparative Literature Association, Canadian Association of Slavists (honorary life member; vice-president, 1954-68), Canadian Association of University Teachers, Royal Canadian Legion, Canadian Society for the Comparative Study of Civilizations (honorary life member; president, beginning 1972), Paderewski Foundation-Canada (president, 1952—), Polish Institute of Arts and Sciences in America (member of council, 1964-72), Polish American Historical Association, Association of Professors of University of Montreal, Association des Combattants Allies de la Deuxieme Guerre Mondiale de la Resistance, United Services Club. *Awards, honors:* Defender of the Fatherland (Poland), 1945; Karpatian Brigade (Poland), 1945; 2nd Polish Corps Medal, 1945; Polish Golden Cross of Merits, 1962; Knight Commander, Papal Order of St. Gregory the Great, 1963; Great Officer, Sovereign Order of Cyprus, 1964; Great Officer, Holy Cross of Jerusalem, 1968; Commander, Royal Order of St. Sava, 1969; Alliance Combatants and Underground Army Cross, 1969; Polish

Medal for Scientific Merit, 1970; British Certificate for Distinguished Service in Literary and Cultural Studies, 1972; French Knight Military Merits Cross, S.R., 1973; Knight of Justice, Constantinian Order, 1975, St. Agatha Order, 1978, and O.S.J., 1979.

WRITINGS: Idea Pokoju na przestrzeni wiekow (title means "Peace Told through the Centuries"), Kolo Studiow Politycznych, 1938; *Le Concezioni antiche della guerra e della pace,* [Warsaw], 1939; *Il problema sociale nell'opera di B. Prus* (title means "The Social Problem in the Works of B. Prus"), [Rome], 1941; *Les Considerations de C. K. Norwid sur la liberte de la parole,* Les Presses de l'Universite Laval, 1971; *Le Symbolisme et l'universalisme de C. K. Norwid,* Volume I, Les Presses de l'Universite Laval, 1974. Contributor to *New Catholic Encyclopedia* and to *Zycie, Polish American Studies,* and *Revue Dominicaine.* Editor, *Slavic and East European Studies,* 1954-76; associate editor, *Canadian Slavonic Papers,* 1968—.

WORK IN PROGRESS: The second volume of the studies on C. K. Norwid.

BIOGRAPHICAL/CRITICAL SOURCES: L. Kos-Rabcewicz-Zubkowski, *The Poles in Canada,* Polish-Canadian Congress, 1968; Andrzej Wolodkowicz, *Polish Contributions to Arts and Sciences in Canada,* White Eagle Press, 1969.

* * *

DOMINOWSKI, Roger L. 1939-

PERSONAL: Born February 21, 1939, in Chicago, Ill.; son of Annette (Bochniak) Dominowski; married Nancy Ricketts, May 27, 1961 (divorced March 3, 1976); children: Barbara, Andrew, Tracy, Matthew. *Education:* DePaul University, A.B., 1960, M.A., 1963; Northwestern University, Ph.D., 1965. *Home:* 125 South Kenilworth, Oak Park, Ill. 60302. *Office:* Department of Psychology, University of Illinois at Chicago Circle, Chicago, Ill. 60680.

CAREER: DePaul University, Chicago, Ill., 1961-66, began as administrative assistant to the dean, 1961-62, became assistant professor of psychology; University of Illinois, Chicago, 1966—, began as assistant professor, professor of psychology, 1973—. Research fellow at University of Aberdeen, Scotland, 1972-73. *Member:* Society for Research in Child Development, Psychonomic Society, Midwestern Psychological Association, Sigma Xi.

WRITINGS: (With L. E. Bourne, Jr. and B. R. Ekstrand) *The Psychology of Thinking,* Prentice-Hall, 1971; (with Bourne and E. F. Loftus) *Cognitive Processes,* Prentice-Hall, 1979; *Research Methods,* Prentice-Hall, 1980. Contributor to *Journal of Experimental Psychology, Psychological Bulletin, Canadian Journal of Psychology, Psychonomic Science, Annual Review of Psychology,* and other journals.

WORK IN PROGRESS: Research project on how people resolve conflicts involved in making choices.

AVOCATIONAL INTERESTS: Tennis, golf.

* * *

DONCEEL, Joseph F. 1906-

PERSONAL: Born September 16, 1906, in Antwerp, Belgium. *Education:* University of Louvain, Ph.D., 1935. *Home and office:* Fordham University, New York, N.Y.

CAREER: Roman Catholic priest, member of Society of Jesus. Berchmans' Philosophicum, Eegenhoven, Louvain, Belgium, assistant professor of psychology, 1934-39; Loyola College, Baltimore, Md., assistant professor of philosophy, 1940-44; Fordham University, New York, N.Y., associate professor, 1944-66, professor of philosophy, 1966-72, professor emeritus, 1972—.

WRITINGS: Philosophical Psychology, Sheed, 1955, 2nd revised edition, 1961; *Elements of Natural Theology,* Sheed, 1962; *Philosophical Anthropology,* Sheed, 1967; (translator) Emerick Coreth, *Metaphysics,* Herder, 1968; *A Marechal Reader,* Herder, 1970; *The Searching Mind,* University of Notre Dame Press, 1979. Co-founder, coordinating editor, *International Philosophical Quarterly.*

* * *

DORESKI, William 1946-

PERSONAL: Born January 10, 1946, in Stafford, Conn.; son of Lawrence Howard (a store clerk) and Mildred (McGuire) Doreski; married Jean Eddy (a stockbroker), June 24, 1967 (divorced, 1978). *Education:* Attended University of Hartford, 1963-67; Goddard College, M.A., 1976; Boston University, Ph.D., 1980. *Politics:* "Utter and irresponsible anarchy." *Home:* 12 Margaret St., Arlington, Mass. 02174. *Office:* Goddard College, Plainfield, Vt. 05667.

CAREER: Pratt and Whitney Aircraft Co., East Hartford, Conn., inspector, 1965; Connecticut Department of Highways, Warehouse Point, mechanic, 1966-67; John Hancock Life Insurance Co., Boston, Mass., supervisor, 1967-68; Ahab Rare Books, Boston, owner, 1970-77; Goddard College, Plainfield, Vt., teacher, 1976—. Teacher at Emerson College, 1973 and 1976. Trustee, Pym-Randall Press, 1972—. Has worked as volunteer fireman, 1963-67. *Awards, honors:* Poet Lore subjective poem award, 1972, translation award, 1973; Black Warrior Poetry Prize, 1978.

WRITINGS—Poetry: *To Face the Sea,* Windy Row Press, 1969; *Running the Bitch Down,* Barn Dream Press, 1970; *Roxbury 1968,* Beanbag Press, 1972; *The Testament of Israel Potter,* Seven Woods Press, 1976; *Half of the Map,* Burning Deck, 1980. Also author of a two-act play, "The Fourth Man's Work," first produced in Boston at Boston Dramatic Arts Workshop Theatre, March, 1970. Contributor to *Hartford Times, Antioch Review, Yale Review,* and *Massachusetts Review.*

WORK IN PROGRESS: A book of poems.

SIDELIGHTS: William Doreski told *CA:* "I write out of necessity, which is, of course, the grandaddy of motives. Every poem has its own sub-motive, determined partly by its content, partly by the form the poem takes for itself. I subscribe to no theories, am interested in no programs, politics, etc. These things can come between the poem and its self-imposed shape, and therefore, I believe, must be avoided. That is not a comment on 'social' responsibilities; but those are outside the work—in the conscious, rather than the unconscious place where poems appear."

* * *

DORNBERG, John Robert 1931-

PERSONAL: Born August 22, 1931, in Erfurt, Germany; naturalized U.S. citizen; son of Robert Egon and Lily (Farkash) Dornberg; married Jane Haynes, 1951; married second wife, Ursula Stalph, 1956; remarried Jane Haynes, 1977; children: Stephen. *Education:* Attended University of Denver, three years. *Home and office:* Kafka Str. 8, 8 Munich 83, Germany. *Agent:* Sterling Lord Agency, 660 Madison Ave., New York, N.Y. 10021.

CAREER: Harry E. Shubart Co., Denver, Colo., editor,

1951-54; *Overseas Weekly,* Frankfurt, Germany, reporter, 1956-58, news editor, 1958-63; foreign correspondent for *Newsweek, New York Herald Tribune, Toronto Daily Star,* and World Wide Press Service, New York, 1963-65; *Newsweek,* foreign correspondent in Bonn, Germany, and bureau chief in Vienna, Austria, Moscow, U.S.S.R., and Munich, Germany, 1965-73; free-lance correspondent in Munich, covering Germany and Eastern Europe, 1973—. *Military service:* U.S. Army, 1954-56; assigned overseas as publicity and advertising director for touring 7th U.S. Army Symphony Orchestra.

WRITINGS: Schizophrenic Germany, Macmillan, 1961; *The Other Germany,* Doubleday, 1968; *The New Tsars: Russia under Stalin's Heirs,* Doubleday, 1972; *Brezhnev: The Masks of Power,* Basic Books, 1973; *The Two Germanys,* Dial, 1974; *The New Germans,* Macmillan, 1975; *The Soviet Union Today,* Dial, 1976; *Eastern Europe: The Communist Kaleidoscope,* Dial, 1979. Translator, from the German, of *Guide to Germany's Historic Inns* and *Germany: A Panorama,* both published by Umschau Verlag, 1962; author of a column syndicated in forty U.S. newspapers. Contributor to numerous periodicals, including *Nation, Saturday Review, Reader's Digest, Ms., Quest,* and *Popular Science.*

SIDELIGHTS: In a review of *The Other Germany,* Paul Wohl says that it is "not merely a book of ideas, but first of all a book of facts. The story of the emergence of a new country under communism is not always a pleasant one. For anyone who wants to understand the new Germany of the East it is an indispensable and objective guide." Another reviewer, Vincent Sheean, calls the book an authoritative account of what East Germany is like today and writes that John Dornberg is an author "who has devoted serious study to his subject for years past. He employs a Guntheresque technique without Gunther's personal style, which means that he has not Gunther's fluency or wit, and indeed his writing is at times awkward. Never mind. The content of the book is what matters, not its manner. It gives the best account you could find in English of that land, to us so strange—stranger than China!—which lies between the Berlin Wall and the West Polish frontier."

AVOCATIONAL INTERESTS: Music, photography.

BIOGRAPHICAL/CRITICAL SOURCES: Book World, July 28, 1968; *Christian Science Monitor,* September 27, 1968; *New York Times Book Review,* October 27, 1968.

* * *

DOTY, William Lodewick 1919-1979

PERSONAL: Born March 7, 1919, in New York, N.Y.; died December 23, 1979, in Mt. Kisco, N.Y.; son of George Espy and Lillian (Bergen) Doty. *Education:* Fordham University, A.B., 1939, graduate study, 1939-40; attended St. Joseph's Seminary (Yonkers, N.Y.), 1940-45. *Home and office:* St. John's Church, Pawling, N.Y. 12564.

CAREER: Ordained Roman Catholic priest, 1945; named papal chamberlain with title of very reverend monsignor, 1964. Parish priest, 1945-46; Cardinal Hayes High School, Bronx, N.Y., instructor, 1946-55; St. Patrick's Cathedral, New York City, curate, 1955-58; Society for the Propagation of the Faith, New York City, assistant director, 1958-59; College of New Rochelle, New Rochelle, N.Y., chaplain and instructor in senior theology, 1959-64; director of Westchester Catholic Hour and chaplain of Rosary Hill Home, Hawthorne, N.Y., 1964-66; Instructional Television Center, Archdiocese of New York, Yonkers, N.Y., staff member, 1966-68, director of suburban radio and TV, 1968-72; St. John's Church, Pawling, N.Y., pastor, 1972—.

WRITINGS: Catechetical Stories for Children, Joseph F. Wagner, 1948; *Stories for Discussion,* Joseph F. Wagner, 1951; *Fire in the Rain,* Bruce Publishing, 1951; *The Mark,* Bruce Publishing, 1953; *Crusaders of the Great River,* Benziger, 1958; *The Rise of Father Roland,* Bruce Publishing, 1961; *Trends and Counter-Trends Among American Catholics,* Herder, 1962; *Virtues for Our Time,* Herder, 1964; *Pathways to Personal Peace,* Herder, 1965; *One Season Following Another,* Franciscan Herald, 1968; *Holiness for All,* Herder, 1969; *Where Is Your Victory?,* St. Antony's Guild, 1970; *The On-Going Pilgrimage,* Alba, 1970; *A View from the Middle,* Liguori Publications, 1972; *Encountering Christian Crises,* Liguori Publications, 1973; *Prayer in the Spirit,* Alba, 1973; *Waiting for the Lord,* Alba, 1977; *Meet Your Pastor,* Alba, 1978; *Button, Button: A Mystery Story,* Our Sunday Visitor, 1979.

* * *

DOUBTFIRE, Dianne (Abrams) 1918-

PERSONAL: Born October 18, 1918, in Leeds, Yorkshire, England; daughter of Frederick Samuel and Etty (Heslewood) Abrams; married Stanley Doubtfire, 1946; children: Ashley Graham. *Education:* Studied at Harrogate School of Art, Yorkshire; Slade School of Fine Art, University of London, diploma, 1941; Institute of Education, University of London, A.T.D., 1947. *Home:* Folly Cottage, Ventnor, Isle of Wight, England. *Agent:* Curtis Brown Ltd., 1 Craven Hill, London W2 3EW, England.

CAREER: Free-lance writer, 1952—. Adult education lecturer in creative writing for Surrey County Council and Isle of Wight County Council. *Military service:* Women's Auxiliary Air Force, 1941-46; became flight sergeant; served in the Middle East in administrative capacity, 1944-46. *Member:* International P.E.N., Society of Authors, National Book League.

WRITINGS: Fun with Stamps, Hutchinson, 1957; *More Fun with Stamps,* Hutchinson, 1958; *Lust for Innocence,* Morrow, 1960; *Reason for Violence,* P. Davies, 1961; *Kick a Tin Can,* P. Davies, 1964; *The Flesh Is Strong,* P. Davies, 1966; *Behind the Screen,* P. Davies, 1969; *Escape on Monday,* Macmillan, 1970; *This Jim,* Heinemann, 1974; *Girl in Cotton Wool,* Scholastic Book Services, 1975; *A Girl Called Rosemary,* Scholastic Book Services, 1977; *Sky Girl,* Macmillan, 1978; *The Craft of Novel Writing,* Allison & Busby, 1978.

WORK IN PROGRESS: A novel.

SIDELIGHTS: "There should be no aspect of human affairs," Dianne Doubtfire told *CA,* "which the serious novelist cannot introduce, with taste and compassion, into his books. . . . I try to work six hours a day, during which I am lucky if I complete one thousand words. When I reach a temporary deadlock (a frequent occurrence) I go for a walk, talking aloud to myself, battling the thing out. I never prepare a rigid plot in advance; the story grows as the characters develop. . . . My greatest ambition is to write a novel that really satisfies *me!*"

AVOCATIONAL INTERESTS: Motoring, cinematography, cooking, travel.

BIOGRAPHICAL/CRITICAL SOURCES: Books and Bookmen, March, 1960, September, 1961; *Everywoman,* August, 1961; *Times Literary Supplement,* December 11, 1970; *Observer,* December 8, 1974.

* * *

DOWNEY, Fairfax D(avis) 1893-

PERSONAL: Born November 28, 1893, in Salt Lake City,

Utah; son of George Faber (an Army officer) and Mattie Louise (Davis) Downey; married Mildred Adams, October 19, 1918; children: F. Davis, Jr. (deceased), Marjorie Adams (Mrs. William A. Knowlton). *Education:* Yale University, A.B., 1916. *Politics:* Republican. *Religion:* Episcopalian. *Residence:* West Springfield, N.H. 03284. *Agent:* Paul R. Reynolds, Inc., 12 East 41st St., New York, N.Y. 10017.

CAREER: Kansas City Star, staff member, 1918-21; *New York Tribune* and *Herald Tribune,* New York City, staff member, 1921-27; free-lance writer, 1929—. *Military service:* U.S. Army, 1917-18, 1942-44; received Silver Star, World War I. U.S. Army Reserve, retired as lieutenant colonel. *Member:* Authors League, American Society of Composers, Authors and Publishers, Society of American Historians, Company of Military Historians (fellow), Order of St. Barbara, Aztec Club of 1847 (honorary member). *Awards, honors:* Class Secretaries Award for *Reunion in Print,* 25-year book of Class of 1916, Yale University; Honorary Doctorate of Humane Letters, Keene State College.

WRITINGS: Disaster Fighters, Putnam, 1938; *Indian-Fighting Army,* Scribner, 1941; *Our Lusty Forefathers,* Scribner, 1947; *Horses of Destiny,* Scribner, 1949; *Dogs of Destiny,* Scribner, 1949; *Clash of Calvary: The Battle of Brandy Station,* McKay, 1949; *Cats of Destiny,* Scribner, 1950; *Mascots,* Coward, 1954; *Dogs for Defense,* 1955; *Sound of the Guns,* McKay, 1955; *General Crook: Indian Fighter,* Westminster, 1957; *The Guns at Gettysburg,* McKay, 1958; *Famous Horses of the Civil War,* Thomas Nelson, 1959; *Storming of the Gateway: Chattanooga,* McKay, 1960; *Texas and the War with Mexico,* American Heritage Publishing, 1961; *Indian Wars of the U.S. Army, 1776-1865,* Doubleday, 1964; *Louisbourg, Key to a Continent,* Prentice-Hall, 1965; *Cannonade,* Doubleday, 1966; *Fife, Drum, and Bugle,* Old Army Press, 1971; (with Jacques Jacobsen, Jr.) *The Red Bluecoats,* Old Army Press, 1973.

Historical novels; juveniles: *War Horse,* Dodd, 1942; *Dog of War,* Dodd, 1943; *Jezebel the Jeep,* Dodd, 1944; *Army Mule,* Dodd, 1945; *Cavalry Mount,* Dodd, 1946; *The Seventh's Staghound,* Dodd, 1948; *Free and Easy,* Scribner, 1951; *Trail of the Iron Horse,* Scribner, 1952; *A Horse for General Lee,* Scribner, 1953; *The Shining Filly,* Scribner, 1954; *Guns for General Washington,* Thomas Nelson, 1961; *The Buffalo Soldiers in the Indian Wars,* McGraw, 1969.

Biography: *The Grande Turke: Suleyman the Magnificent,* Minton, Balch, 1929; *Burton, Arabian Nights Adventurer,* Scribner, 1931; *Richard Harding Davis: His Day,* Scribner, 1933; *Portrait of an Era,* Scribner, 1936.

Editor: *Laughing Verse,* Crowell, 1946; *My Kingdom for a Horse,* Doubleday, 1960; *Great Dog Stories of All Time,* Doubleday, 1962; *Races to the Swift,* Doubleday, 1967.

Humor, light verse: *A Comic History of Yale,* 1923; *Father's First Two Years,* Minton, Balch, 1925; *When We Were Rather Older,* Minton, Balch, 1926; *Young Enough to Know Better,* Minton, Balch, 1927.

Other: (With W. A. James) *Reunion in Print,* 25-year book of Class of 1916, Yale University Press, 1942; (editor) E. H. Southern, *Julia Marlowe's Story,* Rinehart, 1954. Also author of radio scripts and song lyrics. Contributor to magazines.

WORK IN PROGRESS: The Color-Bearers.

SIDELIGHTS: Several of Fairfax D. Downey's books have been published in French, Spanish, Italian, and Turkish. He has traveled throughout the United States, Europe, Asia, and North Africa. *Avocational interests:* Forestry, carpentry, and guitar.

DOWNEY, Glanville 1908-

PERSONAL: Born June 14, 1908, in Baltimore, Md.; son of Emory Kelly and Katherine Joyce (Glanville) Downey; married Sarah Sawyer Atherton, 1942; children: Katherine Glanville, Sarah Sawyer. *Education:* Princeton University, A.B., 1931, Ph.D., 1934. *Home:* 3033 Golden Rain Rd., Apt. 3, Walnut Creek, Calif. 94595.

CAREER: Yale University, New Haven, Conn., School of Fine Arts, librarian, 1939-42; Dumbarton Oaks Research Library and Collection of Harvard University, Washington, D.C., 1945—, professor of Byzantine literature, 1960-64; Indiana University at Bloomington, professor of history and classics, 1964-73, distinguished professor, 1973-78, professor emeritus, 1978—. American School of Classical Studies in Athens, Greece, member of managing committee, 1956—, member of executive committee, 1957—. Associate, Clare Hall, Cambridge University. *Military service:* U.S. Army, Signal Corps, 1942-45, became first lieutenant. *Member:* Archaeological Institute of America (former member of executive committee), American Philological Association, German Archaeological Institute (corresponding member), Royal Belgian Academy (associate of history and literature section), Phi Beta Kappa. *Awards, honors:* Guggenheim fellow; member, Institute for Advanced Study, Princeton, N.J., 1956-57.

WRITINGS: Constantinople in the Age of Justinian, University of Oklahoma Press, 1960; *Belisarius: Young General of Byzantium* (juvenile), Dutton, 1960; *A History of Antioch in Syria,* Princeton University Press, 1961; *Antioch in the Age of Theodosius the Great,* University of Oklahoma Press, 1962; *Aristotle, Dean of Early Science* (juvenile), F. Watts, 1962; *Gaza in the Early Sixth Century,* University of Oklahoma Press, 1963; *Ancient Antioch,* Princeton University Press, 1963; *Stories from Herodotus* (juvenile), Dutton, 1965; (editor with A. F. Norman) *Themistii Orations* (Greek text), Teubner, Volume I, 1965, Volume II, 1970, Volume III, 1974; *The Later Roman Empire,* Holt, 1969. Editor-in-chief, *American Journal of Archaeology,* 1949-52; associate editor, *Archaeology,* 1948-51. Contributor to philological, historical, and archaeological journals in the United States, England, Germany, Holland, Belgium, and Syria.

* * *

DOWNEY, Murray William 1910-

PERSONAL: Born July 13, 1910, in Toronto, Ontario, Canada; son of James Henry and Hattie (Williamson) Downey; married Edna Lillian Hawken, 1939; children: Deane, Raymur, Neil, Lois, Stanford, Lucille, Glendyne. *Education:* Attended Moody Bible Institute, 1930-33; Wheaton College, Wheaton, Ill., A.B., 1935, A.M., 1955; Chicago Graduate School of Theology, M.Div., 1970. *Home:* 235-2821 Tims St., Clearbrook, British Columbia, Canada V2T 4B1.

CAREER: Independent pastor-evangelist in Ontario, 1935-37; Peace River Bible Institute, Peace River, Alberta, Bible educator, 1937-41; Canadian Bible College, Regina, Saskatchewan, teacher, 1941-72, dean of education, 1954-61; professor of theology, Alliance College of Theology, 1972-76; Melbourne Bible Institute, Melbourne, Australia, teacher of evangelism, 1973-74; affiliated with Theological Education by Extension, 1977—.

WRITINGS: Manual on Soul-Winning, Baker Book, 1958; *The Art of Soul-Winning,* Baker Book, 1958; *Sermons on Christian Commitment,* Baker Book, 1964. Also author of "Book of Books" series, ten volumes, Christian Publications, 1976—. Contributor to Christian magazines.

DOWNIE, Leonard, Jr. 1942-

PERSONAL: Born May 1, 1942, in Cleveland, Ohio; son of Leonard (a sales executive) and Pearl (Evenheimer) Downie; married second wife, Geraldine Rebach (a nurse), August 15, 1971; children: (first marriage) David, Scott; (second marriage) Joshua. *Education:* Ohio State University, B.A., 1964, M.A., 1965. *Residence:* London, England. *Office: Washington Post,* 25 Upper Brook St., London W.1, England.

CAREER: Washington Post, Washington, D.C., reporter, 1965-70, day city editor, 1970-71, deputy metropolitan editor, 1972-79, London correspondent, 1979—. Instructor in communications at American University, 1972-73. *Awards, honors:* Washington-Baltimore Newspaper Guild Front Page Award for newswriting, 1967 and 1968; American Bar Association gavel award, 1967; Alicia Patterson Foundation fellow, 1971-72.

WRITINGS: (Contributor) Ben W. Gilbert, editor, *Ten Blocks from the White House,* Praeger, 1968; *Justice Denied: The Case for Reform of the Courts,* Praeger, 1971; *Mortgage on America,* Praeger, 1974; *The New Muckrakers,* New Republic Books, 1976. Contributor to *Nation, Potomac,* and *Washington Monthly.*

SIDELIGHTS: Leonard Downie, Jr.'s *The New Muckrakers,* a series of profiles of contemporary investigative reporters, is hailed by Richard Reeves of the *New York Times Book Review* as "the best book I have ever read on the subject. It is not an exciting book. It is not particularly well-written or well-organized. But Downie . . . knows what he's talking about and he gets his points across, including some non-mythical analysis of the work of the *Post*'s Bob Woodward and Carl Bernstein. . . . Investigative reporters are different, a point Downie makes in the first 40 pages, his best pages. . . . *The New Muckrakers* also goes out of its way to give credit to some older muckrakers, the people who kept the sport alive between the glamorous peaks." Admitting that "muckraking does seem to run in cycles," Reeves concludes his review by noting that "it is possible that it is not quite as influential as Downie sometimes tends to make it. My own experience indicated that no matter where you went, someone else had been there 10 years before and a couple of people had lost their jobs or gone to jail. But the real villain, institutional oppression routinely ignored by the press, reverts to type when the spotlights turn away."

BIOGRAPHICAL/CRITICAL SOURCES: New York Times Book Review, August 29, 1976.

* * *

DOWNS, Robert C. S. 1937-

PERSONAL: Born November 23, 1937, in Chicago, Ill.; son of Norbert Henry (an executive) and Laura C. (Smith) Downs; married Barbara Lewry, September 6, 1968; children: Christina Elizabeth, Susan Laura. *Education:* Harvard University, A.B., 1960; University of Iowa, M.F.A., 1965. *Agent:* Don Congdon, Harold Matson Co., Inc., 22 East 40th St., New York, N.Y. 10016. *Office:* Department of English, Burrowes Hall, Pennsylvania State University, University Park, Pa. 18602.

CAREER: Phillips Exeter Academy, Exeter, N.H., instructor in English, 1962-63; Hunter College of the City University of New York, New York City, lecturer in English, 1965-66; *Life,* New York City, sales promotion writer, 1966-68; Colby Junior College, New London, N.H., assistant professor of English, 1968-73; University of Arizona, Tucson, associate professor of English and director of creative writing program, 1973-80; Pennsylvania State University, University Park, professor of English and director of writing program, 1980—. *Awards, honors:* Guggenheim fellowship, 1979-80.

WRITINGS: Going Gently, Bobbs-Merrill, 1973; *Peoples,* Bobbs-Merrill, 1974; *Country Dying,* Bobbs-Merrill, 1976; *White Mama* (also see below), Ballantine, 1980. Also author of screenplay, "White Mama" (based on novel of same title), CBS-TV, 1980.

SIDELIGHTS: In addition to "White Mama," Robert C. S. Downs' adaptation of his own novel for television (which starred Bette Davis), two other novels by Downs have been filmed. "Billy: Portrait of a Street Kid," a 1977 NBC-TV World Premier Movie, was adapted by Stephen Gethers from Downs' novel *Peoples; Going Gently,* adapted by Thomas Ellice, is being produced by BBC-TV.

* * *

DOZER, Donald Marquand 1905-

PERSONAL: Born June 7, 1905, in Zanesville, Ohio; son of Perley W. and Minnie Bell (Marquand) Dozer; married Alice Louise Scott, August 2, 1941 (died October 26, 1972); children: Charles Scott, Jane Blythe, Hilary Marquand. *Education:* College of Wooster, A.B., 1927; attended Ohio State University, summers, 1927 and 1928; Harvard University, M.A., 1930, Ph.D., 1936. *Home:* 421 Miramonte Dr., Santa Barbara, Calif. 93109. *Office:* Department of History, University of California, Santa Barbara, Calif.

CAREER: High school and college instructor, 1927-29, 1934-35; National Archives, Washington, D.C., junior archivist, 1936-37; University of Maryland, College Park, instructor in history, 1937-41; Office of Strategic Services, Washington, D.C., research analyst, 1941-43; Office of Lend-Lease Administration, Washington, D.C., liaison officer, 1943-44; U.S. Department of State, Washington, D.C., held various intelligence and policy research positions, 1944-56, assistant to chief of historical policy research, 1951-56; American University, Washington, D.C., lecturer in history, 1950-59; University of California, Santa Barbara, associate professor, 1959-64, professor of Latin American history and inter-American relations, 1964-72, professor emeritus, 1972—. Lecturer in history, Montgomery Junior College, 1956-59, and University of Maryland, 1956-59; Lilly Endowment Lecturer, Eastern Baptist College, 1966; Fulbright lecturer in history, Argentina, 1971. State Department representative to intelligence conference, Panama Canal Zone, 1948; assistant technical secretary of U.S. delegation, 9th International Conference of American States, Bogota, Colombia, 1948; consultant on Latin America, Brookings Institution, 1950-51; Georgetown University Center for Strategic Studies, coordinator of colloquium on "The Strategic Importance of Latin America," 1964, consultant, 1966-67. American Revolution Bicentennial Commission of California, vice-chairman, 1968—, acting chairman, 1975—.

MEMBER: American Historical Association (Latin American Conference), Geographic Society (corresponding member), Pacific Coast Council on Latin American Studies (member of governing board; chairman, 1969-70), Phi Beta Kappa, Omicron Delta Kappa, Delta Sigma Rho, Mont Pelerin Society. *Awards, honors:* Research grants from University of California, 1959—; Relm Foundation fellow and grants for travel in South America, 1963 and 1965; Alberdi-Sarmiento Award from *La Prensa,* 1972, for distinguished contributions to inter-American friendship.

WRITINGS: (Contributor) Asher N. Christensen, editor,

The Evolution of Latin American Government: A Book of Readings, Henry Holt, 1951; (contributor) Olen E. Leonard and Charles P. Loomis, editors, *Readings in Latin American Social Organization and Institutions,* Michigan State College Press, 1953; (contributor) William A. Williams, editor, *The Shaping of American Diplomacy,* Rand McNally, 1956; (contributor) A. Curtis Wilgus, editor, *The Caribbean: Contemporary International Relations,* University of Florida Press, 1957; *Are We Good Neighbors?: Three Decades of Inter-American Relations, 1930-1960,* University of Florida Press, 1959; (editor) *Foreign Relations of the United States: The Conferences of Cairo and Tehran, 1943,* U.S. Government Printing Office, 1961; *Latin America: An Interpretative History,* McGraw, 1962, revised edition, Center for Latin American Studies, Arizona State University, 1980; (with others) *Trouble Abroad,* Crestwood, 1965; (contributor) Norman A Bailey, editor, *Latin America: Politics, Economics, and Hemispheric Security,* Center for Strategic Studies, Georgetown University, 1965; *The Monroe Doctrine: Its Modern Significance,* Knopf, 1965, revised edition, Center for Latin American Studies, Arizona State University, 1976; (contributor) Armin Rappaport, editor, *Issues in American Diplomacy,* Macmillan, 1965; (with others) *Panama Canal Issues and Treaty Talks,* Center for Strategic Studies, Georgetown University, 1967; *Portrait of the Free State: A History of Maryland,* Tidewater, 1976; *The Panama Canal in Perspective,* Council on American Affairs, 1978; *A New Interpretive History of Latin America,* Center for Latin American Studies, Arizona State University, 1979. Contributor of numerous articles to professional journals.

WORK IN PROGRESS: Inter-American Relations in Historical Perspective; Problems and Prospects in Latin American Policy; Politics of Appeasement: A Case Study of the Panama Canal Treaties.

SIDELIGHTS: Donald M. Dozer told *CA:* "I write history because writing it is the best way of learning it and, in these agitated times, [it] is much safer than making history. The historian is the ultimate arbiter of events; he makes the final judgements on the past, and he can hope to exert through his writings some influence on the future shape of things."

BIOGRAPHICAL/CRITICAL SOURCES: La Prensa, Buenos Aires, Argentina, May 12, 1972, May 20, 1972.

* * *

DRABEK, Thomas E(dward) 1940-

PERSONAL: Born February 29, 1940, in Chicago, Ill.; son of Thomas F. (a salesman) and Glenna (a fashion buyer; maiden name, Martin) Drabek; married Ruth Ann Obduskey, June 10, 1960; children: Deborah Kaye, Russell Ray. *Education:* University of Denver, B.A. (magna cum laude), 1961; Ohio State University, M.A., 1962, Ph.D., 1965. *Home:* 7643 Navarro Pl., Denver, Colo. 80237. *Office:* Department of Sociology, University of Denver, Denver, Colo. 80210.

CAREER: Ohio State University, Disaster Research Center, Columbus, research associate, 1963-65; University of Denver, Denver, Colo., assistant professor, 1965-69, associate professor, 1969-74, professor of sociology, 1974—, chairperson, 1974-79. Vice-chairman for disaster planning and inter-organizational coordinator, Denver Region of American Red Cross, 1970-72; chairman, committee on U.S. emergency preparedness, National Academy of Sciences, 1978-80. Consultant to chairman for disaster planning, Rocky Mountain Division, American Red Cross, 1975—. *Member:* American Sociological Association, Society for the Study of Social Problems, Western Social Science Association (member of executive council, 1967-70; president, 1971-72), Midwest Sociological Society, Phi Beta Kappa. *Awards, honors:* National Institute of Mental Health grants, 1965-67, 1969-72; National Science Foundation grants, 1966-68, 1977-80; Air Force Office of Scientific Research grant, 1967-68; Exxon Education Foundation grant, 1975-77.

WRITINGS: Disaster in Aisle Thirteen, College of Administrative Sciences, Ohio State University, 1968; (with Gresham M. Sykes) *Law and the Lawless,* Random House, 1969; *Laboratory Simulation of a Police Communication System under Stress,* College of Administrative Sciences, Ohio State University, 1969; (contributor) Dwight G. Dean, editor, *Dynamic Issues in Social Psychology,* Random House, 1969; (contributor) Joseph McGrath, editor, *Social and Psychological Factors in Stress,* Holt, 1970; (with J. Eugene Haas) *Complex Organizations: A Sociological Perspective,* Macmillan, 1973; (with Haas) *Understanding Complex Organizations,* W. C. Brown, 1974; (with Haas and D. Mileti) *Human Systems in Extreme Environments,* Institute of Behavioral Sciences, University of Colorado, 1975; (with D. Brodie, J. Edgerton, and P. Munson) *The Floor Breakers,* Institute of Behavioral Sciences, University of Colorado, 1979. Contributor to social science journals.

WORK IN PROGRESS: Research on the longitudinal impact of diasaster on family functioning, and on search and rescue missions in natural disaster and remote area settings.

* * *

DREIFUS, Claudia 1944-

PERSONAL: Born November 24, 1944. *Education:* New York University, B.S., 1966. *Politics:* "Radical feminist." *Home and office:* 158 Ninth Ave., New York, N.Y. 10011. *Agent:* Elaine Markson, 44 Greenwich Ave., New York, N.Y. 10011.

CAREER: Organizer of drug and hospital workers union in New York, N.Y., 1967-68; free-lance writer, 1968—. Associate adjunct professor of journalism, New York University, 1974; instructor, New School for Social Research, 1975. *Member:* Society of Magazine Writers.

WRITINGS: Radical Lifestyles, Lancer, 1971; *Woman's Fate: Raps from a Feminist Consciousness-Raising Group,* Bantam, 1973; (editor) *Seizing Our Bodies: The Politics of Women's Health Care,* Vintage Books, 1978. Work is represented in anthologies, including *Radical Feminism, Women's Liberation Blueprint for the Future,* and *Seeing through the Shuck.* Contributor to *McCall's, Evergreen Review, Nation, New York Times Book Review, Rolling Stone, Realist, Family Circle, Ms., Newsday, Penthouse, New York Daily News Sunday Magazine, Signature, Social Policy, Viva, Glamour,* and *Progressive.* News editor, *East Village Other,* 1969-71.

* * *

DREIFUSS, Kurt 1897-

PERSONAL: Born September 18, 1897, in Offenburg, Baden, Germany; son of Adolph Simon and Augusta (Spitzer) Dreifuss; married Bessie Barth; children: Pauline, Frank. *Education:* University of Chicago, Ph.B., 1924. *Home:* 2058 Alpine Rd., Apt. 20, Clearwater, Fla. 33515. *Office:* Society for a World Service Federation, 1600 Jarvis Ave., Chicago, Ill. 60626.

CAREER: Jewish Vocational Service, Chicago, Ill., vocational supervisor, 1940-45; Chicago Consumers Cooperative,

Chicago, organization director, 1945-47; Chicago Department of Welfare, Chicago, director of rehabilitation, 1947-52; U.S. Department of Interior, Bureau of Indian Affairs, Chicago, industrial development specialist, 1952-64; Society for a World Service Federation; Chicago, founder and president, 1964—. Founder and first president of Northside Symphony Orchestra and Community Symphony Orchestra, Chicago; membership chairman, United World Federalists, 1962.

WRITINGS: The Other Side of the Universe, Twayne, 1961; *Creative World Government,* Society for a World Service Federation, 1964; *A Voluntary World Service Federation,* Society for a World Service Federation, 1974. Also author of three plays: "Ode to a River Rat," "All Ends Disgracefully," and "A Man to Remember".

WORK IN PROGRESS: The Endangered Human Animal.

SIDELIGHTS: Kurt Dreifuss told *CA:* "I attribute my writing compulsion to an irrepressible and to me incomprehensible drive to put into the written word my rebellion against the still barbaric life-style of contemporary primitive society. Alas, it puts me badly out of step with most people around me except, fortunately, with my understanding wife.

"My addiction to this kind of writing does, however, provide its own medium of silent communication without having to talk to myself out loud [which would] cause people to think I've gone completely off my rocker; and in all honesty, there are times when I want to do just that. But I take comfort in the fact that Ibsen and Shaw had to live with the same problem and they did it quite well."

* * *

DRESCHER, John M(ummau) 1928-

PERSONAL: Born September 15, 1928, in Manheim, Pa.; son of John Lenhart (a builder) and Anna (Mummau) Drescher; married Betty Keener (a teacher), August 30, 1952; children: John Ronald, Sandra Kay, Rose Marie, Joseph Dean, David Carl. *Education:* Attended Elizabethtown College, 1947-49; Eastern Mennonite College, A.B., 1951, Th.B., 1953; Goshen Biblical Seminary, B.D., 1954. *Home:* 1126 Waterman Dr., Harrisonburg, Va. 22801. *Office:* Eastern Mennonite Seminary, Harrisonburg, Va. 22801.

CAREER: Ordained minister of the Mennonite Church, 1954; pastor in Rittman, Ohio, 1954-62; bishop overseer of Ohio and Eastern Mennonite Conference, 1958-63; Mennonite Church, assistant moderator, 1967-69, moderator, 1969-71; Scottdale Mennonite Church, Scottdale, Pa., pastor, 1973-78; Eastern Mennonite Seminary, Harrisonburg, Va., professor, 1979—. President of Ohio Mennonite Mission Board, 1956-62. Member of board of directors of Associated Church Press, 1970-73; member of Mennonite General Board, 1971-76.

WRITINGS: (Contributor) John C. Wenger, editor, *They Met God,* Herald Press, 1964; *Meditations for the Newly Married,* Herald Press, 1969; *Now Is the Time to Love,* Herald Press, 1970; *Heartbeats,* Zondervan, 1970; *Follow Me,* Herald Press, 1971; (contributor) J. Allan Petersen, editor, *The Marriage Affair,* Tyndale, 1971; *Spirit Fruit,* Herald Press, 1974; *Talking It Over,* Herald Press, 1975; *Seven Things Children Need,* Herald Press, 1976; *The Way of the Cross and Resurrection,* Herald Press, 1978; *For Better, for Worse,* Beacon Hill, 1979; *When Opposites Attract,* Abbey Press, 1979; *If I Were Starting My Family Again,* Abingdon, 1979; *What Should Parents Expect?,* Abingdon, 1980; *Testimony of Triumph,* Zondervan, 1980. Also author of a series of ten visitation booklets for doctors, pastors, and hospital chaplains, published by Herald Press, 1969. Contributor to more than ninety magazines and journals. Editor of *Gospel Herald,* 1962-73.

* * *

DRINKWATER, Francis Harold 1886-

PERSONAL: Born August 3, 1886, in Wednesbury, Staffordshire, England; son of Francis James and Frances Angela (Moore) Drinkwater. *Education:* Attended Cotton College, 1898-1903, and Oscott College, 1903-10. *Home and office:* 55 Lichfield Rd., Sutton, Coldfield, Warwickshire, England.

CAREER: Ordained Roman Catholic priest, 1910; served parishes in Leamington Spa, Warwickshire, England, 1910-15, Small Heath, Birmingham, England, 1919-45, and Lower Gornal, Staffordshire, England, 1945-64. Diocesan inspector of schools, Birmingham, 1922-58. *Military service:* British Army, chaplain, 1915-19; became major; mentioned in dispatches.

WRITINGS: Twelve and After, Burns, 1924, Newman, 1948; *Givers,* Benziger, 1926; *Short Instruction on the Mass for Children,* Benziger, 1927, Burns, 1960; *Homily Notes on the Sunday Gospels,* Herder, 1927, revised edition, Sands, 1938; *Two Hundred Sermon Notes,* Herder, 1928; *Prayers Worth Learning by Heart,* Sheed, 1929; (editor) Joseph Tahon, *First Instruction of Children and Beginners,* Herder, 1930; *Sermon Notes on the Sunday Propers,* Herder, 1931, Newman, 1950; *Doctrine for the Juniors,* Burns, 1933, reprinted, 1956; *Readings and Addresses for the Holy Hour and Other Occasions,* Burns, 1934, Newman, 1948; *Money and Social Justice,* Burns, 1934; *Why Not End Poverty?,* Burns, 1935; *Religion in School Again,* Burns, 1935; *Teaching the Catechism,* Burns, 1936, reprinted, 1958; *Gabriel's Ave.: Fourteen Religious Plays,* Burns, 1936; *Seven Addresses on Social Justice,* Burns, 1937; *Catechism Stories,* Burns, 1939, reprinted, 1958; *My Church Book for Children of First Communion Age and After,* Burns, 1942; *Catechism at Early Mass,* Burns, 1943; *Another Two Hundred Sermon Notes,* Burns, 1948; *Stories in School* (reprint), Burns, 1949, 2nd edition, 1962; *More Catechism Stories,* Newman, 1949.

Educational Essays, Burns, 1951; *Catholic Schools Assembly Book,* University of London Press, 1953; *Talks to Teenagers,* Newman, 1954, published as *Talking to Teen-Agers,* Burns, 1964; *Third Book of Catechism Stories,* Newman, 1956; *The Abbreviated Catechism with Explanations,* Burns, 1956, revised edition, Croydon, 1977; (contributor) Charles Thompson, editor, *Morals and Missiles,* J. Clarke, 1959; *Two Hundred Evening Sermon Notes,* More, 1960; *Telling the Good News,* Macmillan, 1960; *God and the Under-elevens,* Macmillan, 1962; *Religious Schools Inspector,* Darton, Longman & Todd, 1962; *New Sermons and Readings,* Burns, 1962, enlarged edition, 1964; *Fourth Book of Catechism Stories,* Macmillan, 1962; *Birth Control and the Natural Law,* Burns, 1965; *The Question of God,* Chapman, 1967; *Our Lord's Church and Her Message,* Society of St. Paul, 1972; *Sermon Notes for the New Missal,* Mayhew-McCrimmon, Volume I, 1976, Volume II, 1977, Volume III, 1978; *The Fact of the Resurrection,* Clowes, 1979.

Also author teacher's aid books and of religious plays for schools. Contributor of articles on social justice, money reform, nuclear warfare, and religion to periodicals. *Sower,* founder and editor, 1919-28, 1939-60.

SIDELIGHTS: Francis H. Drinkwater told *CA* that his "lifelong interest in better religious teaching was a result of four year's service as a priest with British front-line soldiers in the first World War." He "gained the impression that the Protestant soldiers seldom had a workable religion, whereas the Catholic soldiers did have one to come back to because they had attended a Catholic school, though they had usually neglected it after school days. The conclusion was that Catholic schools were a good thing (especially after Pious X's then recent introduction of earlier first communion) but that they needed further improvement in their methods and even in some points of content (E.G. less compulsion about Mass-attendance and catechism-learning, especially with children from careless homes; and more carefulness in using the phrase 'mortal sin,' notably about sexual matters)." He cites this as an explanation for his "ever-developing output of aid books for teachers and sermon notes for clergy. After Vatican II, when there seemed something like a split between past and future in the Roman Catholic Church, [he] stayed with the traditionalists but also held to catechetical reforms."

Drinkwater has taken a stand against nuclear war, he says, not as a pacifist, but because nuclear weapons are "indiscriminate and therefore immoral." Many of his books of "Catechism Stories" have been translated into Spanish and into some of the languages of India.

* * *

DRIVER, Tom F(aw) 1925-

PERSONAL: Born May 31, 1925, in Johnson City, Tenn.; son of Leslie R. and Sarah (Broyles) Driver; married Anne Barstow, June 7, 1952; children: Katharine Anne, Paul Barstow, Susannah Ambrose. *Education:* Duke University, B.A., 1950; Union Theological Seminary, New York, N.Y., B.D., 1953; Columbia University, Ph.D., 1957. *Home:* 606 West 122nd St., New York, N.Y. 10027. *Agent:* James O. Brown, 25 West 43rd St., New York, N.Y. 10036. *Office:* Union Theological Seminary, 3041 Broadway, New York, N.Y. 10027.

CAREER: Ordained Methodist minister, 1953; Riverside Church, New York City, supervisor of youth work, 1955-56; Union Theological Seminary, New York City, instructor, 1956-58, assistant professor, 1958-62, associate professor of Christian theology, 1962-67, professor of theology and literature, 1967-73, Paul J. Tillich Professor of Theology and Culture, 1973—. Visiting associate professor of English, Columbia University, 1965; visiting associate professor of religion, Barnard College, 1966; visiting associate professor of theology, Fordham University, 1967; visiting professor of religion at University of Otago, 1976, and Vassar College, 1978. Consultant in humanities and the arts, State University of New York College at Old Westbury, 1970-71. Drama critic, WBAI-FM, New York, 1959-61. Lecturer. *Military service:* U.S. Army, 1943-46. *Member:* American Academy of Religion, Modern Language Association of America, Society for Values in Higher Education, P.E.N., Phi Beta Kappa, Omicron Delta Kappa. *Awards, honors:* Kent fellow, 1953; Guggenheim fellow, 1962; D.Litt., Dennison University, 1970.

WRITINGS: (Librettist) *The Invisible Fire* (oratorio with music by Cecil Effinger), H. W. Gray, 1958; *The Sense of History in Greek and Shakespearean Drama,* Columbia University Press, 1960; (contributor) Henry P. Van Dusen, editor, *Christianity on the March,* Harper, 1963; (editor with Robert Pack) *Poems of Doubt and Belief: An Anthology of Modern Religious Poetry,* Macmillan, 1964; (contributor) Samuel A. Weiss, editor, *Drama in the Modern World,* Heath, 1964; (contributor) John Gassner, editor, *O'Neill,* Prentice-Hall, 1964; (contributor) Eric Bentley, editor, *The Storm Over "The Deputy,"* Grove, 1964; (contributor) Nathan A. Scott, Jr., editor, *Men in Modern Literature,* John Knox, 1965; (contributor) M. E. Marty and D. G. Peerman, editors, *New Theology, 3,* Macmillan, 1966; *Jean Genet,* Columbia University Press, 1966; *Romantic Quest and Modern Query: A History of the Modern Theater,* Delacorte, 1970; (contributor) Donald L. Grummon and others, editors, *Sexuality: A Search for Perspective,* Van Nostrand, 1971; *Patterns of Grace: Human Experience as Word of God,* Harper, 1977.

Contributor of articles on religion, culture, and drama to professional and literary journals. Drama critic, *motive,* 1953-55, *Christian Century,* 1956-63, *New Republic,* 1958-59, and *Reporter,* 1963-64.

SIDELIGHTS: Commenting on Tom F. Driver's *Romantic Quest and Modern Query: A History of the Modern Theater,* a reviewer in *Christian Century* writes: "In [this book, the author] attempts and largely succeeds in accomplishing what, to my knowledge, no other author of a study of modern drama has done: he combines historical exposition, critical analysis and cultural interpretation to provide a lengthy survey of the origins, development and consummation of the modernist movement in the theater. In so doing, Driver has written a book that is worthy of the historian, useful to the specialist and extraordinarily illuminating to the average theater-goer.... [He] manages to keep his attention focused on important currents within the modern theater and on significant dramatists who have brought those currents to their fullest expression.... He has given his book richness and complexity.... Yet the book acquires its real substantiality and power from the sheer bulk of the material it gathers, orders and evaluates. It is at once a Baedeker to the modern theater and a major repossession of its history. And while the book no doubt will ultimately be assessed in terms of its largest ambitions and claims, it is nonetheless from its multitude of acute minor observations and judgments that it derives its greatest authority."

Norris Houghton of *Saturday Review* comments: "Offhand, one would be led to conclude that the author . . . has set himself an impossible task [by attempting to prove that a current of romanticism exists in all realism]. He manages to pull it off [though].... He offers new insights that are challenging and exceptionally well thought out." Unlike the *Christian Century* reviewer, however, Houghton finds the scope of the book a bit too overwhelming. "If one were to fault *Romantic Quest and Modern Query,* it would be to say that the work spreads itself too widely, introduces too many plays and playwrights only to dismiss them in a sentence or a paragraph. As a result, the book swings between the brilliant and the pedestrian. The dramatists Driver deals with in depth . . . are masterfully served. The dozens of others only clutter the scene, and we learn little about them we had not known before. Nevertheless, Tom Driver's book is a valuable and most thoughtful addition to the critical assessment of the theater from 1860 to 1960."

In addition to his studies of drama, Driver has written *Patterns of Grace,* which Harold H. Ditmanson in *Christian Century* terms "an unconventional treatment of a classic Christian theme." According to Ditmanson, the book explores "standard items of doctrine" such as God, transcendence, grace, sin, faith, and revelation through autobiographical examination and philosophical interpretation and exposition. Overall, Ditmanson finds it a "rich, eloquent, provocative book." Similarly, John Shea of *Commonweal* calls the work a "fascinating, reflective, autobiographical excursion into human experience and religious reflection," and he singles out one chapter as a "small masterpiece . . . that expands consciousness and brings the reader to an appreciation of the sacrality of human life."

AVOCATIONAL INTERESTS: Photography, anthropology (made a field trip to Papua, New Guinea in 1976).

BIOGRAPHICAL/CRITICAL SOURCES: *Saturday Review,* May 16, 1970; *Christian Century,* June 7, 1970, April 12, 1978; *Commonweal,* May 12, 1978; *Choice,* September, 1978.

* * *

DRUXMAN, Michael Barnett 1941-

PERSONAL: Born February 23, 1941, in Seattle, Wash.; son of Harry (a jeweler) and Florence (Barnett) Druxman; married Theresa M. Lundy (a park director), March 18, 1966 (divorced, 1979); children: David Michael. *Education:* University of Washington, Seattle, B.A., 1963. *Residence:* Calabasas, Calif. *Office:* Michael B. Druxman, Public Relations, 8831 Sunset Blvd., Los Angeles, Calif. 90069.

CAREER: Pope & Talbot, Inc., Seattle, Wash., real estate salesman, 1963; Retail Credit Co., Los Angeles, Calif., credit investigator, 1964-65; Micheal B. Druxman (public relations firm), Los Angeles, Calif., owner, 1965—.

WRITINGS—All published by A. S. Barnes, except as indicated: *Paul Muni: His Life and His Films,* 1974; *Basil Rathbone: His Life and His Films,* 1975; *Make It Again, Sam: A Survey of Movie Remakes,* 1975; *Merv,* Award Books, 1976; *Charlton Heston,* Pyramid Books, 1976; *One Good Film Deserves Another: A Survey of Movie Sequels,* 1977; *The Musical: From Broadway to Hollywood,* 1980. Author of column in *Coronet,* "Yesterday at the Movies," 1973-74.

WORK IN PROGRESS: Several novels and screenplays.

SIDELIGHTS: Michael Druxman writes: "My interest in motion pictures stems from childhood, I appeared in and directed many plays in the Seattle area and even had two theatrical groups which I managed."

* * *

DUBERSTEIN, Helen 1926-

PERSONAL: Born June 3, 1926, in New York, N.Y.; daughter of Jacob M. and Bessie (Lieberman) Duberstein; married Victor Lipton (a writer), April 10, 1949; children: Jacqueline Frances, Irene Judith. *Education:* City College (now City College of the City University of New York), B.S., 1947. *Home:* Westbeth, 463 West St., 904D, New York, N.Y. 10014.

CAREER: Writer. Playwright-in-residence at Circle Theatre Co., New York City, 1968-72, University of Hartford, Hartford, Conn., 1978, Yaddo and Cummington Community of the Arts, 1978-79, and Interlochen Academy of the Arts, 1979. Coordinator of poetry readings in New York City for Westbeth Poets' Workshop, 1971-72, Theatre for the New City, 1972-73, and First New York Festival Playwrights Cooperative, 1973. Artistic director, Theatre for the New City, 1974-75; president, Playwrights Group, Inc., 1974-76. *Member:* Dramatists Guild, Poetry Society of America. *Awards, honors:* Honorable mention, Poetry Society of Virginia, 1965; first prize, North American Mentor Contest, 1967; Coordinating Council of Literary Magazines award and Herman Hirschfield Foundation award, both 1970, for *The Human Dimension;* finalist, Iowa School of Short Fiction award, 1971 and 1975; finalist, A.W.P. Poetry award, 1975, 1977, 1978, and 1979; grants from National Council for the Arts and New York State Council on the Arts.

WRITINGS—Poems: *Succubus, Incubus,* Ghost Dance Publishers, 1970; *The Human Dimension,* Gnosis, 1970; *The Voyage Out,* Fallen Angels Press, 1978; *Arrived Safely,* Four Corners Press, 1979. Also author of *Changes,* 1978, *Shadow Self,* 1979, and *Hotel Europe,* 1979.

Plays: "The Kingdom by the Sea" (also see below; contains five one-act plays, including "Kingdom by the Sea" and "The Affair"), first produced off-Broadway at Circle in the Square, May 14, 1967; *Five Thousand Feet High* (one-act; first produced in New York City at Westbeth Cabaret, May 25, 1970), privately printed, 1970; *The Affair* (one-act; first produced off-off Broadway at The Old Reliable, October 26, 1970), privately printed, 1966; *Your Unhappiness with Me Is of No Concern to Readers* (one-act; first produced off-off Broadway at Omni Theatre Club, May 7, 1971), privately printed, 1970; "The Visit," first produced off-off Broadway at The Assembly, May, 1971; *Time Shadows* (first produced off-off Broadway at The Circle Theatre Co., June 21, 1971), privately printed, 1970; *The Kingdom by the Sea* (one-act; produced off-off Broadway at The Cubicle, October 20, 1971), privately printed, 1966; "Street Scene" (first produced off-off Broadway at New York Theatre Ensemble, May, 1973); "The Play Within," first produced off-off Broadway at New York Theatre Ensemble, May, 1973; "The Monkey of the Inkpot," first produced off-off Broadway at Actors Experimental Unit, May, 1973; "Under the Bridge There Is a Lonely Spot with Gregory Peck" (two-act), produced in New York City at Theatre for the New City, May, 1974; "We Never Thought a Wedding," produced in New York City at Theatre for the New City, 1979.

Also author of numerous other plays, including "A Visit from Grandma," produced off-off Broadway at Dove Company, "Love/Hate," produced off-off Broadway at Omni Theatre Club, "When I Died My Hair in Venice," produced off-off Broadway at The Circle Theatre Co., and "The Brain," produced at The Open Space. Contributor of stories and poems to journals.

WORK IN PROGRESS: Two books of poetry, *Saturday Night Prizes at Loew's Spoon* and *The Vernal Equinox;* a novel, *From Here to Halifax;* a full-length play based on the biblical Judith.

SIDELIGHTS: Helen Duberstein told *CA:* "I am involved with the use of the stage to break down time. The interplay of time, dream and myth form the fabric of my work. The mythic as it manifests itself in the everyday life structure . . . the interplay of the day to day existence and the dream superstructure that manifests itself in spite of the rationalistic involvement WORK demands."

* * *

DUBIN, Robert 1916-

PERSONAL: Born March 19, 1916, in Chicago, Ill.; son of Aaron Joseph (a dentist) and Gertrude (Rozzett) Dubin; married Elisabeth Ruch (a counseling psychologist), January 16, 1937; children: Thomas Joseph (deceased), John Robert, Lucy Sarah, Amy Christina, George Ruch. *Education:* University of Chicago, A.B., 1936, A.M., 1940, Ph.D., 1947. *Home:* 2639 Bunya St., Newport Beach, Calif. 92660. *Office:* Department of Sociology, University of California, Irvine, Calif. 92664.

CAREER: U.S. Army, Chicago Ordnance District, Chicago, Ill., civilian head of labor relations and training section,

1940-43; University of Chicago, Chicago, assistant professor of sociology, 1947-48; University of Illinois at Urbana-Champaign, associate professor, 1948-52, professor of sociology, 1952-54; University of Oregon, Eugene, research professor of sociology, 1954-69; University of California, Irvine, research professor of sociology and professor of sociology and administration, 1969—. *Military service:* U.S. Army, 1943-46; became captain.

MEMBER: American Sociological Association (member of council, 1964-66; member of executive committee, 1965-66), Sociological Research Association, Industrial Relations Research Association (member of board of directors, 1953-55), Society for General Systems Research, Pacific Sociological Association (president, 1978-79). *Awards, honors:* Center for Advanced Studies in the Behavioral Sciences fellow, 1956-57; Guggenheim fellowship, 1963-64; Fulbright research fellowships in Germany and England, 1963-64, 1968-69; American Association for the Advancement of Science fellow, 1978.

WRITINGS: (With F. H. Harbison) *Patterns of Union-Management Relations,* Science Research Associates, 1947; (editor) *Human Relations in Administration,* Prentice-Hall, 1951, 4th edition, 1974; (editor with Arthur W. Kornhauser and A. Ross) *Industrial Conflict,* McGraw, 1954; *The World of Work,* Prentice-Hall, 1958; *Working Union-Management Relations,* Prentice-Hall, 1958; (with G. C. Homans and others) *Leadership and Productivity,* Chandler Publishing, 1965; (editor with T. C. Traveggia) *The Teaching-Learning Paradox: A Comparative Analysis of College Teaching Methods,* Center for the Advanced Study of Education Administration, University of Oregon, 1968; *Theory Building,* Free Press, 1969, revised edition, 1978; (with others) *The Medium May Be Related to the Message: College Instruction by T.V.,* Center for the Advanced Study of Education Administration, University of Oregon, 1969; (editor and contributor) *Handbook of Work, Organization, and Society,* Rand McNally, 1976. Contributor to professional journals.

* * *

DUBOFSKY, Melvyn 1934-

PERSONAL: Born October 25, 1934, in Brooklyn, N.Y.; son of Harry (a projectionist) and Lillian (Schneider) Dubofsky; married Joan S. Klores (a speech pathologist), January 16, 1959; children: David Mark, Lisa Sue. *Education:* Brooklyn College (now Brooklyn College of the City University of New York), B.A., 1955; University of Rochester, Ph.D., 1960. *Home:* 23 Devon Blvd., Binghamton, N.Y. 13903. *Office:* Department of History, State University of New York, Binghamton, N.Y. 13903.

CAREER: Northern Illinois University, DeKalb, assistant professor of history, 1959-67; University of Massachusetts—Amherst, associate professor of history, 1967-69; University of Wisconsin—Milwaukee, professor of history, 1970-71; State University of New York at Binghamton, professor of history, 1971—. *Member:* American Historical Association, Organization of American Historians, Labor Historians Society. *Awards, honors:* Grants from American Philosophical Society and from American Council of Learned Societies, 1965; National Endowment for the Humanities senior fellow, 1973-74.

WRITINGS: When Workers Organize, University of Massachusetts Press, 1968; *We Shall Be All: A History of the IWW,* Quadrangle, 1969; (editor) *American Labor Since the New Deal,* Quadrangle, 1971; *Industrialism and American Workers, 1865-1920,* Crowell, 1975; (with Warren W. Van Tine) *John L. Lewis: A Biography,* Quadrangle, 1977; (with Daniel Smith and Athan Theoharis) *The U.S. in the Twentieth Century,* Prentice-Hall, 1978.

SIDELIGHTS: Ward Sinclair of the *Progressive* writes of Melvyn Dubofsky's and Warren W. Van Tine's *John L. Lewis: A Biography:* "It is fortuitously coincidental that as a nation puzzles over the anarchic state of the coal industry, along comes a massive historical research work that helps put the situation into a badly needed perspective. . . . As this splendid (the term is used advisedly) new biography of John L. Lewis points out, we have been in this same spot—and worse—before and have survived. . . . [The authors] have written what is for now, and perhaps for all time, the definitive biography of John L. Lewis. Their research is impressive; their sources in many instances new and previously untapped; their organization skillful."

"For all that," Sinclair continues, "the biography is not as good as it could have been or should have been. My principal complaint is that while Dubofsky and Van Tine acknowledge that the miners themselves usually were ahead of Lewis ideologically, they do next to nothing to illustrate the case. The point is vital to understanding Lewis. The authors recognized that Lewis succeeded because he knew how to respond to the miners' emotional needs, but they do little to show just what those needs were. A deeper exploration of the statistical and sociological data—even interviews with surviving rank-and-filers from the darkest days—would have enhanced this biography, and perhaps would have added wider perspective to the Lewis persona."

Furthermore, notes Sinclair, though Dubofsky and Van Tine offer convincing evidence which contradicts some of the "time-honored folklore" regarding Lewis, their "academic arrogance shows through in a demeaning way. The first line of their book advertises it as a work of scholarship, but it is quickly marred by egregious sloppiness. . . . Throughout, they seem almost polemical in refuting the works of others who have added to the Lewis hagiography, and they reach a gleeful and unseemly level when they cut up the Lewis biography written by the late Saul Alinsky. . . . Beyond that, there are some rather glaring errors of academic omission, plus a dependence on some questionable recent sources." Yet despite these criticisms, the reviewer concludes, "Dubofsky and Van Tine have written a book that contributes vastly to our understanding of a man who was one of the titanic figures of the American century."

Raymond Sokolov of *Newsweek* asserts that the story of John L. Lewis "has never been told in such detail or with such objectivity before [as it has been in *John L. Lewis: A Biography*]. Dubofsky and Van Tine are labor historians who have drawn on hitherto unpublished UMW archives and various oral accounts to produce a vivid history of Lewis's rise from obscurity in a humble Iowa mining town to power and wealth. In their zeal to make this a definitive biography, they have perhaps set down more than most people will want to read about Lewis's unending conflicts with big business, big labor and FDR. Their prose is plodding, but the Lewis saga has its own warty, knotted fascination and carries the book along. . . . Lewis was not a likable man, and Dubofsky and Van Tine have not tried to whitewash him. Indeed, they suggest that his legacy to miners was, in part, a tradition of undemocratic, strong-arm leadership tinged with violence."

Finally, a *Best Sellers* critic calls the book "an excellent biography. . . . The authors are to be commended. This was clearly intended to be a scholarly effort, seeking to distinguish fact from the alleged hearsay and gossip of earlier books, particularly Saul Alinsky's *John L. Lewis: An Unauthorized Biography*. Though they pick a bit too much at Mr. Alinsky and engage in some questionable conjecture of their own, their work reveals more than ever before about an intensely private man. There is tedium in the text and documentation. . . . But let the graduate student wrestle with the infinite detail while the general reader sifts for the romance of the greatest force American labor has ever known. . . . Biographical 'textbooks' of this type should leave little to doubt. Dubofsky and Van Tine have done their job well.''

BIOGRAPHICAL/CRITICAL SOURCES: Book World, November 9, 1969; *New York Times Book Review,* November 23, 1969; *Washington Post,* November 28, 1969; *Newsweek,* August 8, 1977; *Best Sellers,* November, 1977; *Progressive,* February, 1978.

* * *

DUCHACEK, Ivo D(uka) 1913-

PERSONAL: Born February 27, 1913, in Prostejov, Czechoslovakia; son of Francis and Irena (Cermak) Duchacek; married second wife, Helena Kolda, 1956; children: (first marriage) Ivo-Jan, Sylvia. *Education:* Masaryk University, JuDr., 1935. *Home:* Maple Ave. Ext., Kent, Conn. 06757. *Office:* Graduate School, City University of New York, 33 West 42nd St., New York, N.Y. 10036.

CAREER: Czechoslovakian Government, diplomatic service in Paris and London, 1939-45, member of parliament, Prague, 1945-48; Yale University, New Haven, Conn., visiting lecturer, 1949-51; City College and Graduate School of the City University of New York, New York, N.Y., lecturer, 1949-54, assistant professor, 1954-58, associate professor, 1958-63, professor of political science, 1963—. Visiting lecturer, Air War College, 1958-63, Army War College, 1961-68, and Army Command and General Staff College, 1964-67; visiting professor, Columbia University, 1963-67; visiting lecturer, Executive Seminar Center, U.S. Civil Service Commission, 1972—. Editor-in-chief, U.S. Department of State and U.S. Information Agency, 1949-54. *Military service:* U.S. Army, liason officer, 1945; became major; received Bronze Star Medal, British King's Medal, Belgian War Cross, made officer of French Legion of Honor. *Member:* American Political Science Association. *Awards, honors:* Junior Book Award, Boys' Clubs of America, 1955; Best Teacher Award and Sigma Alpha Student Award, 1960; City College of the City University of New York 125th Anniversary Medal, 1973; City University of New York Excellence in Teaching Award, 1974.

WRITINGS: The Secret of the Two Feathers (fiction), Harper, 1954; *Martin and His Friend from Outer Space* (fiction), 1955; (with K. W. Thompson) *Conflict and Cooperation among Nations,* Holt, 1960; (contributor) *The Fate of East Central Europe: Hopes and Failures of American Foreign Policy,* University of Notre Dame Press, 1960; *Nations and Men,* Holt, 1966, 3rd edition, 1975; *Comparative Federalism: The Territorial Dimension of Politics,* Holt, 1970; *Discord and Harmony,* Holt, 1972; *Rights and Liberties in the World Today,* American Bibliographic Center-Clio Press, 1973; *Power-Maps: Comparative Politics of Constitutions,* American Bibliographic Center-Clio Press, 1973. Contributor of chapters to books, including *East Central Europe and the World, Europe and the World, The Strategy of Deception,* and *Comparative Politics: Notes and Readings.* Contributor of articles to political science journals, including *World Politics, Comparative Politics, Current History, Publius,* and *Journal of Constitutional and Parliamentary Studies* (New Delhi).

SIDELIGHTS: Rights and Liberties in the World Today and *Power-Maps: Comparative Politics of Constitutions* have been translated into Spanish.

* * *

DUCKWORTH, George E(ckel) 1903-1972

PERSONAL: Born February 13, 1903, in Little York, N.J.; died April 5, 1972, in Princeton, N.J.; son of Edwin J. and Eva (Eckel) Duckworth; married Dorothy Elwood Atkin, July 8, 1929; children: Dorothy Ann (Mrs. Donald L. Brown), Thomas Atkin. *Education:* Princeton University, A.B., 1924, M.A., 1926, Ph.D., 1931. *Home:* 25 Haslet Ave., Princeton, N.J.

CAREER: Princeton University, Princeton, N.J., instructor in classics, 1924-25; University of Nebraska, Lincoln, instructor in classics, 1926-28; Princeton University, 1929-71, began as instructor, Giger Professor of Classics, 1946-71, professor emeritus, 1971-72, acting chairman of department, 1943-46. Professor-in-charge, School of Classical Studies, American Academy in Rome, summers, 1952-55; visiting professor, Harvard University, 1955-56; visiting scholar, University Center in Virginia, 1958-59. Trustee, Rider College, 1937-56, and American Academy in Rome, 1947-59. *Member:* American Philogical Association (president, 1956), Archaeological Institute of America, Classical Association of the Atlantic States, Phi Beta Kappa. *Awards, honors:* Guggenheim fellowship, 1957-58.

WRITINGS: Foreshadowing and Suspense in the Epics of Homer, Appolonius, and Vergil, Princeton University Press, 1933, reprinted, 1966; (editor) *T. Macci Plauti Epidicus,* Princeton University Press, 1940; (editor and author of introduction) *The Complete Roman Drama,* two volumes, Random House, 1942, one volume published as *Roman Comedies,* Modern Library, 1963, both volumes reprinted, Random House, 1966; *The Nature of Roman Comedy,* Princeton University Press, 1952, reprinted, 1967; *Recent Work on Vergil,* Vergilian Society, 1958; *Structural Patterns and Proportions in Vergil's Aeneid,* University of Michigan Press, 1962; *Vergil and Classical Hexameter Poetry: A Study in Metrical Variety,* University of Michigan Press, 1969. Contributor to encyclopedias; contributor of articles to classical journals.†

* * *

DUDEK, Louis 1918-

PERSONAL: Born February 6, 1918, in Montreal, Quebec, Canada; son of Vincent and Stasia (Rozynski) Dudek; married Stephanie Zuperko, 1943 (divorced, 1965); married Aileen Collins, 1970; children: Gregory. *Education:* McGill University, B.A., 1939; Columbia University, M.A., 1946, Ph.D., 1951. *Home:* 5 Ingleside Ave., Montreal, Quebec, Canada H3Z 1N4. *Office address:* Department of English, McGill University, Box 6070, Station A, Montreal, Quebec, Canada H3C 3G1.

CAREER: City College (now City College of the City University of New York), New York, N.Y., instructor in English, 1946-51; McGill University, Montreal, Quebec, lecturer, 1951-53, assistant professor, 1953-62, associate professor, beginning 1962, professor of English, beginning 1969, Greenshields Professor of English, 1972—. Editor, Delta Canada (book publishers), 1966-71; co-founder, Contact Press; publisher, DC Books. Member, Humanities Research Council of Canada, beginning 1971. *Member:* Canadian Council of Teachers of English (director-at-large). *Awards, honors:* Quebec Literary Award, 1968.

WRITINGS: Literature and the Press: A History of Printing, Printed Media, and Their Relation to Literature, Ryerson, 1966; (translator) Michel Regnier, *Montreal, Paris d'Amerique,* [Montreal], 1961; *The First Person in Literature,* Canadian Broadcasting Corp., 1967; *Eprigrams,* DC Books, 1975; *Selected Essays and Criticism,* Tecumseh Press, 1978; *Technology and Culture,* Golden Dog Press, 1979.

Poems: (With others) *Unit of Five,* Ryerson, 1944; *East of the City,* Ryerson, 1946; *The Searching Image,* Ryerson, 1952; (with Irving Layton and Raymond Souster) *Cerberus,* Contact Press, 1952; *Twenty-Four Poems,* Contact Press, 1952; *Europe,* Contact Press, 1954; *The Transparent Sea,* Contact Press, 1956; *En Mexico,* Contact Press, 1958; *Laughing Stalks,* Contact Press, 1958; *Atlantis,* Delta Canada, 1967; *Collected Poetry,* Delta Canada, 1971; *Selected Poems,* Golden Dog Press, 1975.

Editor: (With Layton) *Canadian Poems, 1850-1952,* Contact Press, 1952; Souster, *Selected Poems,* Contact Press, 1956; *Poetry of Our Time: An Introduction to Twentieth Century Poetry, Including Modern Canadian Poetry,* Macmillan (Toronto), 1966; (with Michael Gnarowski) *The Making of Modern Poetry in Canada: Essential Articles on Contemporary Canadian Poetry in English,* Ryerson, 1967; *All Kinds of Everything,* Clarke, Irwin, 1973; Ezra Loomis Pound, *Some Letters of Ezra Pound,* DC Books, 1974.

Recordings: *The Green Beyond,* Canadian Broadcasting Corp., 1973. Contributor to numerous publications, including *Dalhousie Review, Queen's Quarterly, Culture, Canadian Forum,* and *Delta.* Editor, *Delta,* 1956-67.

WORK IN PROGRESS: An essay, *Theory of the Image in Modern Poetry;* poems, *Continuation I.*

SIDELIGHTS: Louis Dudek is a noted Canadian poet whose work, especially during the 1940s, greatly influenced the modern poetry movement of his country. *Saturday Night*'s Robert Weaver states that "Dudek was one of the Montreal poets of the 1940s, when so much of the energy of Canadian poetry in English seemed to come from that city." Weaver remarks that while Dudek's earlier poems reflect the "lyrical and socially involved" mood of Montreal during that period, his later work is "sombre in tone, disaffected, and out of sympathy with the emotional self-involvement of much recent Canadian poetry." Critics, such as Douglas Barbour, suggest that Dudek is essentially a philosophical poet whose "qualities of meditative vision and intense ratiocination" are rarely found in other Canadian poets.

Barbour views Dudek as consistently "striving for an intellectually tough poetry." He comments: "One of Dudek's continuing interests has been the process of thought. His poems often provide paradigms of that process, or icons of the results of that process." Barbour explains that as a "student of modern poetry and a follower of Ezra Pound," Dudek is opposed to "the popular poetry of primitivism," favoring instead "poetic tradition, especially . . . twentieth-century modernism."

Pound's influence is apparent in the simple, prose-like language of Dudek's poems. Dorothy Livesay of *Canadian Literature* notes that Dudek uses adjectives sparingly, and shows a "strong reliance on nouns, verbs, clauses." Barbour believes that "Dudek has carried Pound's dictum, 'that poetry should be written at least as well as prose' to its limit." He describes Dudek's style as "witty, and provocative of thought," but adds: "Despite its appearance, and the rhythmic control of certain parts, it would strike many readers as very different, at bottom, from what they know as poetry. . . . The periodic sentences and the syntax of those grand periods are surely qualities normally associated with scintillating prose."

Livesay agrees, to a point. She believes that Dudek is "the contemporary Canadian poet most consciously concerned with shape, form and sound: the origins of rhythm." Although Dudek employs a "simple, straight-forward use of language," Livesay argues, it would be a "mistake" to call it the "language of prose." Dudek is "opposed to 'musicality' a la Keats," she writes. "He [wants] poetry to reveal itself naked, without the props and embellishments of sound. His best poetry is unified, of a piece, and not discursive as is prose."

Finally, some critics compare the effect of Dudek's poetry to that produced by the visual arts, such as drawings and sculpture. In the *University of Toronto Quarterly,* Northrop Frye notes: "Some of his best poems have the quality of the wet water-colour that is done quickly and makes its point all at once. . . . One often feels that a poem is inconclusive, but then one often feels too that the inconclusiveness is part of the effect, as it is in a sketch." And Livesay comments that "order and control are the keynotes to this poet's work: as in sculpture, the whole must be visible at a glance, but the detail must be exact, and highlighted where essential."

BIOGRAPHICAL/CRITICAL SOURCES: University of Toronto Quarterly, April, 1957; *Canadian Literature,* autumn, 1964, autumn, 1966, summer, 1972; *Yes,* September, 1965; *Canadian Forum,* January, 1969, January, 1972; *Saturday Night,* November, 1971; George Woodcock, editor, *Poets and Critics: Essays from "Canadian Literature," 1966-1974,* Oxford University Press, 1974; *Books in Canada,* February, 1979; *Contemporary Literary Criticism,* Volume XI, Gale, 1979.

* * *

DUFF, John B. 1931-

PERSONAL: Born July 1, 1931, in Orange, N.J.; son of John B. (a Teamster) and Mary (Cunningham) Duff; married Helen Mezzanotti, October 8, 1955; children: Michael, Maureen, Patricia, John, Robert, Emily. *Education:* Fordham University, B.S., 1953; Seton Hall University, M.A., 1958; Columbia University, Ph.D., 1964. *Politics:* Democrat. *Religion:* Roman Catholic. *Home:* 124 Mansur St., Lowell, Mass. 01852. *Office:* University of Lowell, Lowell, Mass. 01854.

CAREER: Remington Rand Corp., Newark, N.J., sales representative, 1955-57, district manager, 1957-60; Seton Hall University, South Orange, N.J., instructor, 1960-63, assistant professor, 1963-66, associate professor, 1966-69, professor of history, beginning 1969, vice-president of instruction, 1970-73, executive vice-president, 1971-73, provost, 1973-76; University of Lowell, Lowell, Mass., president, 1976—. Visiting professor, Rutgers University, summer, 1967, Columbia University, summer, 1970, and Loyola University, Los Angeles, summer, 1971. Member of New Jersey Governor's Commission to study capital punishment, 1971—, and Massachusetts Post Secondary Commission, 1979—. Chairman, Lowell Historic Preservation Commission, 1979—. Member of advisory board, Wang Institute, 1979—; chairman of advisory council, Massachusetts Board of Higher Education, 1979—. *Military service:* U.S. Army, 1953-55. *Member:* American Historical Association, Organization of American Historians, American Catholic Historical Association, Academy of Political Science, American Association of University Professors, Immigration History Research Group, American Italian Historical Association.

WRITINGS: (Editor with Davis R. Ross and Alden Vaughan) *The Structure of American History,* Crowell, 1970; *The Irish in the United States,* Wadsworth, 1971; (editor with Peter M. Mitchell) *The Nat Turner Rebellion: The Historical Event and the Modern Controversy,* Harper, 1971; (editor with Larry A. Greene) *Slavery: Its Origins and Legacy,* Crowell, 1975.

AVOCATIONAL INTERESTS: Travel.

* * *

DULLES, John W(atson) F(oster) 1913-

PERSONAL: Born May 20, 1913, in Auburn, N.Y.; son of John Foster (the U.S. Secretary of State during the Eisenhower administration) and Janet (Avery) Dulles; married Eleanor Ritter, June 15, 1940; children: Edith, John, Ellen, Avery. *Education:* Princeton University, A.B., 1935; Harvard University, M.B.A., 1937; University of Arizona, B.S. Met.E. (with highest distinction), 1943, Met.E., 1951. *Home:* 1904 Hill Oak Court, Austin, Tex. *Office:* University of Texas, Box 7934, University Station, Austin, Tex. 78712.

CAREER: Cia. Metalurgica Penoles, S.A., Monterrey, Nuevo Leon, Mexico, assistant manager, 1946-48, manager of ore department, 1948-52; Cia. Minera de Penoles, S.A., Monterrey, Nuevo Leon, director of commercial division, 1952-54, assistant general manager, 1954-59, executive vice-president, 1959; Cia. de Mineracao Novalimense, Rio de Janeiro, Brazil, executive vice-president, 1959, vice-president, 1960-62; University of Texas at Austin, professor of Latin American studies, 1962—. Professor of history, University of Arizona, spring semesters, 1966—. Member of U.S. delegation to Inter-American Economic and Social Council of Organization of American States, Chile, 1967; participant in U.S. State Department Consultation on Communism in Latin America, 1968; consultant, Bureau of Intelligence and Research, U.S. Department of State, 1968—. Member, Texas Institute of Letters and Venerable Order of St. John of Jerusalem. *Member:* American Historical Association, Phi Alpha Theta, Phi Kappa Phi, Tau Beta Pi, Theta Tau, Phi Lambda Upsilon, Pi Mu Epsilon, Headliners Club (Austin), Westwood Country Club (Austin). *Awards, honors:* University of Arizona 75th Anniversary Award of Merit, 1960; Brown-Lupton Foundation lecture grant, 1964-66; Partners of Alliance for Progress Medal, 1966; University of Denver Social Science Foundation and Graduate School of International Studies grant, 1968; Tinker Foundation grant, 1968.

WRITINGS: Yesterday in Mexico: A Chronicle of the Revolution, 1919-1936, University of Texas Press, 1961; (contributor) Eric Baklanoff, editor, *New Perspectives of Brazil,* Vanderbilt University Press, 1965; *Vargas of Brazil: A Political Biography,* University of Texas Press, 1967; (contributor) Baklanoff, editor, *The Shaping of Modern Brazil,* Louisiana State University Press, 1969; *Unrest in Brazil: Political-Military Crises, 1955-1964,* University of Texas Press, 1970; (contributor) Sheldon B. Liss and Peggy K. Liss, editors, *Man, State and Society in Latin American History,* Praeger, 1972; (contributor) Donald L. Herman, editor, *The Communist Tide in Latin America,* University of Texas Press, 1973; *Anarchists and Communists in Brazil, 1900-1935,* University of Texas Press, 1973; (contributor) Jean-Claude Garcia-Zamor, editor, *Politics and Administration in Brazil,* University Press of America, 1978; *Castello Branco: The Making of a Brazilian President,* Texas A & M University Press, 1978.

SIDELIGHTS: Several of John W. F. Dulles' books have been translated into Spanish and Portuguese. *Avocational interests:* Tennis.

* * *

DUNCAN, Thomas (William) 1905-

PERSONAL: Born August 15, 1905, in Casey, Iowa; son of William Thomas and Irene (Valentine) Duncan; married Actea Carolyn Young (a writer, under pseudonym Carolyn Thomas) 1942. *Education:* Drake University, student, 1922-26, M.A., 1931; Harvard University, A.B. (cum laude), 1928. *Home address:* Box 308, Mesilla, N.M. 88046.

CAREER: Des Moines Register and *Des Moines Tribune,* Des Moines, Iowa, reporter, feature writer, and book reviewer, 1926-35; Des Moines College of Pharmacy, Des Moines, professor of English, 1934-38; Grinnell College, Grinnell, Iowa, director of public relations, 1942-44; full-time writer, 1944—. *Member:* Hollywood Authors Club, Sigma Delta Chi, Delta Theta Phi, Sigma Tau Delta, Masons. *Awards, honors:* Lloyd McKim Garrison Award, Harvard University, for *From a Harvard Notebook;* Johnson Brigham Medal, Iowa Library Association, 1947, for most distinguished contribution to literature by an Iowa-born author.

WRITINGS—Novels: *O, Chautauqua,* Coward, 1935; *We Pluck This Flower,* Coward, 1937; *Ring Horse,* Doubleday, 1940; *Gus the Great* (Book-of-the-Month Club selection), Lippincott, 1947; *Big River, Big Man,* Lippincott, 1959; *Virgo Descending,* Doubleday, 1961; *The Labyrinth,* Doubleday, 1967; *The Sky and Tomorrow,* Doubleday, 1974.

Verse: *House from a Life,* Victor Schultz, 1927; *From a Harvard Notebook,* Maizeland Press, 1929; *Elephants at War,* Prairie Press, 1935.

Contributor of short stories, articles, and verse to a wide range of publications.

WORK IN PROGRESS: A novel.

SIDELIGHTS: Thomas Duncan told *CA:* "During my long-lost and much-mourned youth when I was torn between desires to become a lawyer *or* an actor *or* a writer, I decided that being a writer was the only career for which I would be willing to starve if necessary. (Happily, this necessity has not actually arisen, although there have been those periods of touch-and-go which most freelances experience.)" He says that his writing career began when he was sixteen, "in the small Iowa town of Casey. A farmer in the adjacent countryside had a herd of elk. This excited me so much that I felt compelled to share my excitement and wrote an article on the subject for which a magazine published in Kansas City, *Rural Mechanics,* paid me one dollar."

Several of Duncan's novels have been published in Denmark, Norway, Sweden, Italy, Germany, Czechoslovakia, Poland, and England. *Ring Horse, Gus the Great,* and *Big River, Big Man* have been sold to major motion picture studios.

AVOCATIONAL INTERESTS: Photography, magic.

* * *

DUNNE, Gerald T. 1919-

PERSONAL: Born September 24, 1919, in St. Louis, Mo.; son of Patrick J. (a municipal employee) and Anne (Smyth) Dunne; married Nancy O'Neill, April 22, 1950; children: Mimi, Gerald, Katie, Peter, Nancy, Brian. *Education:* Georgetown University, B.S.B.A., 1943; St. Louis University, LL.B., 1948. *Religion:* Catholic. *Home:* 7301 Princeton,

University City, Mo. 63130. *Office:* St. Louis University, 3642 Lindell Blvd., St. Louis, Mo. 63108.

CAREER: Federal Reserve Bank of St. Louis, St. Louis, Mo., member of staff, 1949-73, vice-president, 1967-73; St. Louis University, St. Louis, professor of law, 1973—. Visiting professor of law, University of Missouri, 1970-71. Vice-president, St. Louis Mercantile Library, beginning 1975. Trustee, Missouri Historical Society, 1973-76. *Military service:* U.S. Navy, 1943-46; became lieutenant; received Silver Star and Purple Heart. *Member:* American Law Institute, American Bar Association, Selden Society, American Judicature Society. *Awards, honors:* American Bar Association Certificate of Merit and Scribes Meritorious Book Award, both in 1978, for *Hugo Black and the Judicial Revolution.*

WRITINGS: Monetary Decisions of the Supreme Court, Rutgers University Press, 1960; *Justice Joseph Story and the Rise of the Supreme Court,* Simon & Schuster, 1971; *Hugo Black and the Judicial Revolution,* Simon & Schuster, 1977. Contributor to *Harvard Law Review, Yale Law Journal,* and *Harvard Business Review.* Editor-in-chief, *Banking Law Journal.*

WORK IN PROGRESS: Grenville Clark: The Public Life of a Private Man.

SIDELIGHTS: In *Hugo Black and the Judicial Revolution,* Gerald T. Dunne recounts the career of this controversial and influential Supreme Court Justice. Alan M. Dershowitz of the *New York Times Book Review* calls Black "an enigma," and explains the purpose of Dunne's biography: "Dunne asks how a man, once an honored citizen of the "Invisible Empire" (the Ku Klux Klan), then the unscrupulous chairman of a witch-hunting Senate committee, could emerge as the judicial apostle of racial equality and civil liberties. And why, in the waning years of his illustrous career, he seemed to revert to some of the less compassionate residues of his past."

In addition to detailing the Court's major decisions and Black's influence upon them, Dunne affords a behind the scenes look at the machinations and people of government. According to Dershowitz, Dunne penetrates the "generally unbreachable barriers" of "Senate caucus rooms" and "the closed conferences and private correspondence of the least public of all Government institutions, the Supreme Court." Moreover, Dunne's book offers insight into the conflicts, rivalries, and affinities among the Judges, as well as a glimpse of their thought processes and motives. "Dunne's achievement," Martin Mayer of *Saturday Review* comments, "is that he has shown all these pieces of paper we call court decisions in terms of the people who wrote them and what they thought they were doing."

Lincoln Caplan finds that "the chief strength of Dunne's volume is its thoroughness." He continues: "This, plus his knowledge of specific cases and general history, has resulted in a host of provocative details on the Justice's intellectual work, on key actors in the drama of politics and law making, and on Black's effect on the public affairs of this country." Critics such as Mayer and *Commonweal*'s Isodore Silver contend that Dunne has provided a sensitive, fair, and readable account of Black's public life. "Dunne's depiction . . . is . . . rich, complex, and sensitive to nuance, ambiguity, and paradox," Silver writes. Mayer finds *Hugo Black and the Judicial Revolution* "an affectionate and graceful, yet scholarly biography," and concludes, "by dealing scrupulously with both Justice Black and his antagonists, . . . Dunne has placed this traditional yet unconventional American in a historical mainstream from which no subsequent revisionism is ever likely to dislodge him."

BIOGRAPHICAL/CRITICAL SOURCES: New York Times Book Review, May 30, 1971, April 10, 1977; *St. Louis Globe Democrat,* July 14, 1971; *Best Sellers,* November 1, 1971; *Saturday Review,* March 5, 1977; *New Leader,* August 1, 1977; *Commonweal,* August 19, 1977.

* * *

DURZAK, Manfred 1938-

PERSONAL: Born December 10, 1938, in Merkstein, Germany; son of Ludwig (a lawyer) and Helene (Grondzewski) Durzak; married Margund Klinke, November 29, 1963; children: Malte, Nike. *Education:* Attended University of Bonn, 1958-59; Free University of Berlin, D.Phil., 1961, Ph.D., 1963. *Home:* Unterer Muehlenberg, 2321 Grebin, Germany. *Office:* Department of German, Indiana University, Bloomington, Ind. 41401.

CAREER: Free University of Berlin, Berlin, Germany, university assistant in Germanistics, 1963-64; Yale University, New Haven, Conn., research scholar, 1964-65; Indiana University at Bloomington, assistant professor, 1965-68, associate professor, 1968-71, professor of German literature, 1971—; University of Kiel, Kiel, Germany, professor of German, 1969—. *Member:* Modern Language Association of America, American Association of Teachers of German, Deutsche Hochschulgermanisten, Lessing Society, Kleist-Gesellschaft, Hebbel-Gesellschaft. *Awards, honors:* Volkswagenstiftung grant, 1963; Ford Foundation grant, 1967

WRITINGS: Der junge Stefan George: Kunsttheorie und Dichtung (title means "The Young Poet Stefan George: His Poetry and Theory of Poetry"), W. Fink, 1968; *Hermann Broch: Der Dichter und seine Zeit* (title means "Broch: The Novelist and His Contemporaries"), W. Kohlhammer, 1968.

Poesie und Ratio: Vier Lessing-Studien (title means "Literature and Reason: Four Studies on G. E. Lessing"), Athenaeum, 1970; *Der deutsche Roman der Geganwart* (title means "The Contemporary German Novel"), W. Kohlhammer, 1971; (editor) *Die deutsche Literatur der Gegenwart* (title means "Contemporary German Literature"), Reclam, 1971; *Hermann Broch: Perspektiven der Forschung* (title means "Hermann Broch: Aspects of Broch-Scholarship Research"), W. Fink, 1972; *Duerrenmatt, Frisch, Weiss: Deutsches Drama der Gegenwart zwischen Kritik und Utopie* (title means "Duerrenmatt, Frisch, Weiss: Contemporary German Drama between Critique and Utopian Thought"), Reclam, 1972; *Die deutsche Exilliteratur, 1933-1945* (title means "German Literature of Exile, 1933-1945"), Reclam, 1973; *Texte und Kontexte: Studien zur deutschen und vergleichenden Literaturwissenschaft* (title means "Texts and Contexts: Studies on German and Comparative Literature"), Francke, 1973; *Zwischen Symbolismus und Expressionismus: Stefan George* (title means "Between Symbolism and Expressionism: Stefan George"), W. Kohlhammer, 1974.

Gespraeche ueber den Roman (mit Joseph Breitbach, Elias Canetti, Heinrich Boell, Siegfried Lenz, Hermann Lenz, Wolfgang Hildesheimer, Peter Handke, Hans Erich Nossack, Uwe Johnson, Walter Hoellerer): Formbestimmungen und Analysen (title means "Discussions on the Form of the Novel with . . . : Definitions and Interpretations of the Novel"), Suhrkamp, 1976; *Das expressionistische Drama I: Carl Sternheim, Georg Kaiser* (title means "Expressionist Drama I: Carl Sternheim, Georg Kaiser"), Nymphenburg, 1978; *Das expressionistische Drama II: Ernst Barlach, Ernst Tol-*

ler, Fritz von Unruh (title means "Expressionist Drama II: Ernst Barlach, Ernst Toller, Fritz von Unruh"), Nymphenburg, 1979; *Das Amerika-Bild in der deutschen Gegenwartsliteratur* (title means "The Image of America in Contemporary German Literature"), W. Kohlhammer, 1979; *Hermann Broch: Dichtung und Erkenntnis—Studien zum dichterischen Werk* (title means "Hermann Broch: Poetry and Reason—Studies on Broch's Literary Works"), W. Kohlhammer, 1979; *Die deutsche Kurzgeschichte seit 1945: Autorenportraets, Werkstattgespraeche und Interpretationen* (title means "The German Short Story since 1945: Essays, Interviews and Interpretations"), Reclam, 1980.

* * *

DUTTON, Geoffrey (Piers Henry) 1922-

PERSONAL: Born August 2, 1922, in Anlaby, Kapunda, South Australia; son of Henry Hampden and Emily (Martin) Dutton; married Ninette Trott (an enameler), July 31, 1944; children: Francis, Teresa, Sam. *Education:* Attended University of Adelaide, 1940-41; Magdalen College, Oxford, B.A., 1949. *Home:* Piers Hill, Williamstown, South Australia. *Agent:* Howard Moorepark, 444 East 82nd St., New York, N.Y. 10028.

CAREER: Writer in Europe and Australia, 1949-54; University of Adelaide, Adelaide, South Australia, lecturer, 1954-58, senior lecturer in English, 1958-62; writer and farmer, 1962—. Commonwealth Lecturer in Australian Literature at University of Leeds, 1960; visiting professor at Kansas State University, 1962. Editor, Penguin Books Ltd., Melbourne, Australia, 1961-65; Sun Books Ltd., Melbourne, co-founder, 1966, currently editorial director. Member, Australian Council for the Arts, 1968-70, Commonwealth Literary Fund Advisory Board, 1972-73, Australian Literature Board, beginning 1973, and Australian National University. Has appeared on television. *Military service:* Royal Australian Air Force, pilot, 1941-45; became flight lieutenant.

WRITINGS—Poems: *Nightflight and Sunrise,* Reed & Harris, 1944; *Antipodes in Shoes,* Edwards & Shaw, 1955; *Flowers and Fury,* F. W. Cheshire, 1962; *On My Island: Poems for Children,* F. W. Cheshire, 1967; *Poems Soft and Loud,* F. W. Cheshire, 1967; *Findings and Keepings: Selected Poems, 1940-70,* Australian Letters, 1970; *New Poems to 1972,* Australian Letters, 1972; *A Body of Words,* Edwards & Shaw, 1977. Also author of *Night Fishing,* Australian Letters.

Novels: *The Mortal and the Marble,* Chapman & Hall, 1950; *Andy,* Collins, 1968; *Tamara,* Collins, 1970; *Queen Emma of the South Seas,* St. Martin's, 1976.

Biographies: *Founder of a City: The Life of William Light,* F. W. Cheshire, 1960; *The Hero as Murderer: The Life of Edward John Eyre,* F. W. Cheshire, 1967, published as *Edward John Eyre: The Hero as Murderer,* Penguin (London), 1977; *Australia's Last Explorer: Ernest Giles,* Barnes & Noble, 1970.

Travel and history: *A Long Way South,* Chapman & Hall, 1953; *Africa in Black and White,* Chapman & Hall, 1956; *States of the Union,* Chapman & Hall, 1958; *Australia since the Camera: 1901-1914,* F. W. Cheshire, 1971, published as *From Federation to War,* Longman Cheshire, 1972; *Swimming Free: On and below the Surfaces of Lake, River, and Sea,* St. Martin's, 1972; *A Taste of History: Geoffrey Dutton's Australia,* Rigby, 1978.

Books for children: *Tisi and the Yabby,* Collins, 1965; *Seal Bay,* Collins, 1966; *Tisi and the Pageant,* Rigby, 1968.

Criticism: *Patrick White,* Landsdowne Press, 1961, 4th edition, Oxford University Press, 1971; *Whitman,* Grove, 1971 (published in England as *Walt Whitman,* Oliver & Boyd, 1971); Samuel Thomas Gill, *Paintings,* Rigby, 1962; *Russell Drysdale,* Thames & Hudson, 1964, revised edition, 1969; (with Elisabeth Weis) *A Checklist of Books for the Study of Science in Human Affairs,* Columbia University, 1969; *White on Black: The Australian Aborigine Portrayed in Art,* Macmillan (London), 1974.

Editor; published by Sun Books, except as indicated: *The Literature of Australia,* Penguin, 1964, revised edition, 1976; *Modern Australian Writing,* Fontana, 1966; *Australia and the Monarchy,* 1966; (with Max Harris) *The Vital Decade: Ten Years of Australian Art and Letters,* 1968; (with Harris) *Australia's Censorship Crisis,* 1970; (with Harris) *Sir Henry Bjelke: Don Baby and Friends,* 1971; *The Australian Uppercrust Book,* 1971; *Australian Verse from 1805,* Rigby, 1976; *Republican Australia?,* 1977.

Translator: (With Igor Mezhakoff-Koriakin) Evgenii Aleksandrovich Evtushenko, *The Bratsk Station and Other Poems,* Sun Books, 1966, Doubleday, 1967; (with Mezhakoff-Koriakin) Bella Akhmadulina, *Fever and Other Poems,* Sun Books, 1968, Morrow, 1969; Robert Ivanovich Rozhdestvenskii, *A Poem on Various Points of View and Other Poems,* Sun Books, 1968; Evtushenko, *Bratsk Station, The City of Yes and the City of No and Other Poems,* Sun Books, 1970; Andre Andreevich Voznesenskii, *Little Woods,* Sun Books, 1972; (with Eleanor Jacka) Evtuschenko, *Kazan University and Other New Poems,* Sun Books, 1973.

Co-founder of *Literary Quarterly, Australian Letters,* 1957, and *Fortnightly Australian Book Review,* 1962.

BIOGRAPHICAL/CRITICAL SOURCES: Books and Bookmen, June, 1966, March, 1970; *Spectator,* June 3, 1966, January 17, 1970; *Times Literary Supplement,* January 4, 1968, October 2, 1970, August 16, 1974, November 12, 1976; *New Statesman,* January 12, 1968; *Observer,* February 1, 1970, December 19, 1976; *Best Sellers,* September, 1978.

* * *

DUVALL, Evelyn Millis 1906-

PERSONAL: Born July 28, 1906, in Oswego, N.Y.; daughter of Charles Lieb and Bertha (Palmer) Millis; married Sylvanus Milne Duvall, December 19, 1927; children: Jean (Mrs. Paul Walther), Joy (Mrs. Ray M. Johnson, Jr.). *Education:* Syracuse University, B.S. (summa cum laude), 1927; Vanderbilt University, M.S., 1929; Northwestern University, graduate study, 1935-40; University of Chicago, Ph.D., 1946. *Home and office:* 700 John Ringling Blvd., Plymouth Harbor No. 804-805, Sarasota, Fla. 33577.

CAREER: Chicago Association for Child Study and Parent Education, Chicago, Ill., professional staff leader, 1934-40; Association for Family Living, Chicago, founding director, 1940-45; National Council on Family Relations, Chicago, executive director of family life, 1945-51, member of executive committee, 1951—. Lecturer at various universities in the United States and abroad, 1954-69; Distinguished Visiting Professor of Family Life, Southern Illinois University at Carbondale, 1962. Founder, Town Hall Marriage Course, New York, N.Y., 1947-48; University of Chicago, director of workshop on marriage and family research, 1950, consultant on family life education, 1952; director of adolescent study course, National Congress of Parents and Teachers, beginning 1954; co-leader with husband, Sylvanus M. Duvall, of family life conferences in Asia and the Middle East,

1954-55; leader of seminars through Scandinavia, 1958, and British West Indies, 1963-64; worked with New Zealand departments of health, justice, and social welfare, 1966; general chairman, Creative Retirement Conference, Sarasota, Fla., 1972; member of advisory council, Florida Division of Aging, 1972-75; founder and program coordinator, Sarasota Institute of Lifetime Learning, 1972—.

MEMBER: International Union of Family Organizations (member of general council, 1960—; member of U.S. committee, 1964-75), National Council on Family Relations (honorary life member; chairman of committee on international liaison, 1960-74), American Association of Marriage and Family Counselors (fellow; member of executive committee, 1949-50), American Institute of Family Relations (regional consultant), American Sociological Association (fellow), Child Study Association of America (member of advisory board), Sex Information and Education Council of the United States (charter member of board of directors, 1964—), Society for Research in Child Development, National Conference on Family Life, National Committee on Parent Education, Phi Kappa Phi, Pi Delta Nu, Pi Lambda Theta, Sigma Xi. *Awards, honors:* George Arents Medal from Syracuse University, 1952; L.H.D., Hood College, 1970.

WRITINGS: (With Reuben Hill) *When You Marry,* Heath, 1945, revised edition (with husband, Sylvanus M. Duvall), 1953, high school edition (with S. M. Duvall), 1962, revised high school edition, 1967; (with S. M. Duvall) *Leading Parents' Groups,* Abingdon, 1946; *Family Living* (high school textbook), Macmillan, 1950, revised edition, 1955; *Facts of Life and Love for Teen-Agers,* Association Press, 1950, 3rd edition published as *Love and the Facts of Life,* 1963; *In-Laws: Pro and Con,* Association Press, 1954, 2nd edition, 1961; *Family Development,* Lippincott, 1957, 5th edition published as *Marriage and Family Development,* Harper, 1977; (with daughter, Joy Duvall Johnson) *The Art of Dating,* Association Press, 1958, revised edition, 1968; (with Hill) *Being Married* (textbook), Heath, 1961; (editor with S. M. Duvall) *Sex Ways—in Fact and Faith,* Association Press, 1961; (with S. M. Duvall) *Sense and Nonsense about Sex,* Association Press, 1962; (with David Mace and Paul Popenoe) *The Church Looks at Family Life,* Broadman, 1964; *Why Wait Till Marriage?,* Association Press, 1965; *Today's Teen-Agers,* Association Press, 1966; (contributor) *The Responsible Christian Family,* Abingdon, 1966; *About Sex and Growing Up,* Association Press, 1968; *Faith in Families,* Rand McNally, 1970; *Evelyn Duvall's Handbook for Parents,* Broadman, 1974; *Parent and Teenager: Living and Loving,* Broadman, 1976. Also author, with S. M. Duvall, of daily syndicated column, "Let's Explore Your Mind," 1957-67. Contributor to journals, including *Coordinator* and *Journal of Marriage and the Family.* Member of editorial board, *Marriage and Family Living,* 1945-51.

AVOCATIONAL INTERESTS: Philately, photography.

* * *

DYKEMAN, Wilma

PERSONAL: Born in Asheville, N.C.; daughter of Willard J. and Bonnie (Cole) Dykeman; married James R. Stokely, Jr. (died, 1977); children: Dykeman Cole, James R. III. *Education:* Northwestern University, B.A. *Home and office:* 405 Clifton Heights, Newport, Tenn.

CAREER: Writer. Lecturer at universities and colleges, to civic, religious and social organizations. Member of board of trustees, Berea College. *Member:* P.E.N. International, Authors Guild, Authors League of America, Southern Historical Association, North Carolina Literary and Historical Association, Western North Carolina Historical Association, East Tennessee Historical Society, Tennessee Historical Society, Phi Beta Kappa. *Awards, honors:* Guggenheim fellowship, 1955; Thomas Wolfe Memorial Trophy, 1955, for *The French Broad;* Hillman Award, shared with her husband, for best book of year on world peace, race relations, or civil liberties, 1958, for *Neither Black Nor White;* Chicago Friends of American Writers, special Waukegan Club award, 1963, for *The Tall Woman;* National Endowment for the Humanities senior fellowship; named Tennessee Conservation Writer of the Year; honorary doctor of literature, Maryville College; named Tennessee Outstanding Speaker of the Year by State Association of Speech Arts Teachers and Professors; Distinguished Service Award, University of North Carolina at Asheville.

WRITINGS: The French Broad, Rinehart, 1955; (with husband, James R. Stokely, Jr.) *Neither Black Nor White,* Rinehart, 1957; (with J. R. Stokely) *Seeds of Southern Change,* University of Chicago Press, 1962; *The Tall Woman* (novel), Holt, 1962; (contributor) *The Southern Appalachian Region: A Survey,* University of Kentucky Press, 1962; *The Far Family* (novel), Holt, 1966; *Prophet of Plenty: The First Ninety Years of W. D. Weatherford,* University of Tennessee Press, 1966; *Look to This Day* (essays), Holt, 1968; (with J. R. Stokely) *The Border States,* Time-Life, 1970; *Return the Innocent Earth* (novel), Holt, 1973; *Too Many People, Too Little Love* (biography of Edna Rankin McKinnon), Holt, 1974; *Tennessee: A History,* Norton, 1976; (with son, James R. Stokely III) *Highland Homeland: The People of the Great Smokies,* National Park Service, 1978. Contributor to *Encyclopaedia Britannica;* columnist, *Knoxville News-Sentinel.* Contributor of articles to numerous publications, including *New York Times Magazine, Harper's, Reader's Digest,* and *New Republic;* contributor of book reviews to periodicals, including *New York Times, Chicago Tribune, Journal of Southern History,* and *South Atlantic Bulletin.*

SIDELIGHTS: Wilma Dykeman writes: "In an article, 'The Philosophy of Travel,' George Santayana spoke of 'the rooted heart and the ranging intellect.' From where I frequently write I can see in the distance the whole range of the Great Smoky Mountains through the changing seasons of the year. Through the 10,000 books in my personal library and through many trips across the U.S.A. and travels to familiar and remote parts of Mexico, Canada, most of the countries of Europe, and China, I reach out to know and understand other people, other landscapes. The rooted heart suggests an intense sense of place; the ranging intellect reveals concern for the human values and issues of our time. I believe that both of these are central to all that I have written.

"My writing has been divided between fiction and nonfiction. I have received awards for books in both categories and most of my books have stayed in print for five to ten years; my first novel, *The Tall Woman,* has never gone out of print in hardcover (now in its twentieth printing) despite paperback editions. Race, sex, nationality, class—any condition that limits an individual's fulfillment of total potential is of concern to me, as a person, as a writer.

"Being considered a Southern, an Appalachian, a regional writer has diminished serious evaluation of my work in some circles. I believe that much of the world's best literature is regional, in the largest sense of that word. Discovering all that is unique to a place, or a person, and relating that to the universals of human experience may be old-fashioned, but I feel it is one of the challenges of writing. This sounds very earnest (the work to which we devote our lives is a serious matter) but it is also delightful—toilsome and imaginative, heavy with frustration and rewarding with occasional joy.

"I have taught at several colleges and universities and writer's workshops for brief intervals, and my advice usually begins and ends with one word: Practice. Because words are tools and jewels that we use every day we tend to forget that they need sharpening and polishing. They cannot accomplish the task we wish them to, they cannot sparkle with maximum brilliance unless we care for them. Lack of respect for language is one of the tragedies of our time."

E

EAKIN, Mary K(atherine) 1917-

PERSONAL: Born August 20, 1917, in Nashville, Tenn.; daughter of Joseph Walter (a horticulturist) and Hela (Blakely) Eakin. *Education:* Drake University, B.A., 1943; University of Chicago, B.L.S., 1946, M.A., 1954. *Politics:* Democrat. *Home:* 3104 McClain Dr., Cedar Falls, Iowa 50613.

CAREER: University of Chicago, Center for Children's Books, Chicago, Ill., assistant librarian, 1946-49, librarian and editor, 1949-57; University of Northern Iowa, Cedar Falls, librarian of youth collection, 1958-68, associate professor in College of Education, beginning 1968. *Member:* American Library Association (council member, 1962-65), National Education Association, American Association of University Women, American Association of University Professors (chapter president, 1963-64), United World Federalists, American Civil Liberties Union, Iowa Library Association, Iowa Association of School Libraries.

WRITINGS—Editor: *Good Books for Children,* University of Chicago Press, 1959, 3rd edition, 1967; *Library Materials for Gifted Children,* State College of Iowa Press, 1959; *Library Materials for Holidays,* State College of Iowa Press, 1959; *Library Materials for Remedial Reading,* State College of Iowa Press, 1959; *Library Materials on Asia,* State College of Iowa Press, 1961; (with Eleanor Merritt) *Subject Index of Books for Primary Grades,* American Library Association, 1961, revised edition, 1967; *Subject Index to Books for Intermediate Grades,* American Library Association, 1963; (with Albert C. Haman) *Library Materials for Elementary Science,* State College of Iowa Press, 1964; *Library Materials for Beginning Independent Reading,* University of Northern Iowa Press, 1967. Contributor to *Britannica Book of the Year, American Educator Encyclopedia,* and *Britannica Junior,* and to professional journals and popular periodicals.

* * *

ECKSTEIN, Harry 1924-

PERSONAL: Born January 26, 1924, in Schotten, Germany; son of Moritz and Bella (Bachenheimer) Eckstein; married Joan J. Campbell, April 1, 1953; children: Jonathan. *Education:* Harvard University, B.A., 1948, M.A., 1950, Ph.D., 1954. *Office:* Woodrow Wilson Hall, Princeton University, Princeton, N.J.

CAREER: Harvard University, Cambridge, Mass., instructor, 1954-56, assistant professor of political science, 1956-58; Princeton University, Princeton, N.J., associate professor, 1959-61, professor of political science, 1961—, I.B.M. Professor of International Studies, 1968—, faculty associate of center for International Studies, 1959—, director of workshop in comparative politics, 1966—. *Military service:* U.S. Army, 1943-45; became staff sergeant; awarded Bronze Star. *Member:* American Political Science Association, American Academy of Arts and Sciences (fellow). *Awards, honors:* Fellowships from Social Science Research Council and Center for Advanced Study in Behavioral Sciences.

WRITINGS: The English Health Service, Harvard University Press, 1958; *Patterns of Government,* Random House, 1958; *Pressure Group Politics,* Stanford University Press, 1960; (editor with David E. Apter) *Comparative Politics,* Free Press, 1963; *Internal War: Problems and Approaches,* Free Press, 1964; *Division and Cohesion in Democracy,* Princeton University Press, 1966; *The Evaluation of Political Performance,* Sage Publications, 1971; (contributor) Lucian W. Pye, editor, *Political Science and Area Studies: Rivals or Partners?,* Indiana University Press, 1975; (with Ted R. Gurr) *Patterns of Authority: A Structual Basis for Political Inquiry,* Wiley, 1975. Contributor to professional journals. Editor, *World Politics,* 1960-71.

AVOCATIONAL INTERESTS: Theater, literature. †

* * *

EDEL, (Joseph) Leon 1907-

PERSONAL: Born September 9, 1907, in Pittsburgh, Pa.; son of Simon and Fannie (Malamud) Edel; married Roberta Roberts, December 2, 1950 (separated, 1974). *Education:* McGill University, B.A. , 1927, M.A. (honors in English), 1928; University of Paris, Docteur es Lettres, 1932. *Agent:* William Morris Agency, Inc., 1350 Avenue of the Americas, New York, N.Y. 10019. *Home:* 2943 Kalakava Ave., Honolulu, Hawaii 96815.

CAREER: Sir George Williams University, Montreal, Canada, assistant professor of English, 1932-34; work in journalism, broadcasting, and writing, 1934-43; New York University, New York, N.Y., associate professor, 1953-55, professor of English, 1955-66, Henry James Professor of English and American Letters, 1966-72, professor emeritus, 1972—; University of Hawaii, Honolulu, Citizens Professor of English, 1972-78. Visiting professor at New York University, 1950-52, Indiana University, 1954-55, University of Hawaii, 1955, 1969-70, Harvard University, 1959-60, Center for Advanced Study, Wesleyan University, 1965, and University of Toronto, 1967; Christian Gauss Lecturer in Criticism, Princeton University, 1952-53; Alexander Lecturer, University of Toronto, 1955-56. President, Hawaii Literary Arts Council, 1979. *Military Service:* U.S. Army, 1943-47; became first lieutenant; received Bronze Star Medal.

MEMBER: P.E.N. (president, U.S. Center, 1957-59), American Academy of Arts and Sciences (fellow), National Institute of Arts and Letters (secretary, 1964-65), Royal Society of Literature (fellow), Modern Humanities Research Association, American Association of University Professors, International Association of University Professors of English, Authors' Guild (member of council; president, 1969-70), Century Club, Athenaeum Club (London), Outrigger Canoe Club (Honolulu). *Awards, honors:* Guggenheim fellow, 1936-38, 1966; Bollingen Foundation fellow, 1958-60; National Institute of Arts and Letters grant, 1959; National Book Award in nonfiction and Pulitzer Prize for biography, both 1963, for *Henry James,* Volumes II and III; Litt. D. from Union College, Schenectady, N.Y., 1963, and McGill University, 1963; American Academy of Arts and Letters grant, 1972; Gold Medal for biography, National Institute of Arts and Letters-American Academy of Arts and Letters, 1976; Hawaii Writers Award, 1977.

WRITINGS: Henry James: Les Annees Dramatiques, Jouve (Paris), 1931, reprinted, Norwood, 1978; *The Prefaces of Henry James,* Jouve, 1931, reprinted, Folcroft, 1970; *James Joyce: The Last Journey,* Gotham Bookmart, 1947, reprinted, Haskell House, 1977; *Henry James,* Lippincott, Volume I: *The Untried Years, 1843-1870,* 1953, Volume II: *The Conquest of London, 1870-1881,* 1962, Volume III: *The Middle Years, 1882-1895,* 1962, Volume IV: *The Treacherous Years, 1895-1901,* 1969, Volume V: *The Master, 1901-1916,* 1972, published as *The Henry James Biography,* five volumes, Avon, 1978, revised edition published as *The Life of Henry James,* two volumes, Penguin, 1977; (with Edward K. Brown) *Willa Cather,* Knopf, 1953; *The Psychological Novel: 1900-1950,* Lippincott, 1955, revised edition published as *The Modern Psychological Novel,* Grosset, 1964; *Literary Biography,* University of Toronto Press, 1957, Doubleday, 1959, reprinted, Indiana University Press, 1973; (with Dan H. Laurence) *Bibliography of Henry James,* Hart-Davis, 1957, revised edition, 1961; *Willa Cather: The Paradox of Success* (pamphlet), Library of Congress, 1959; *Henry James* (pamphlet), University of Minnesota Press, 1960, revised edition, 1963; *The Age of the Archive,* Center for Advanced Study, Wesleyan University, 1966; *Henry David Thoreau* (pamphlet), University of Minnesota Press, 1970; *Henry James in Westminster Abbey,* Petronium Press, 1976; *Bloomsbury: A House of Lions,* Lippincott, 1979.

Editor: (And author of introduction with Gordon Ray) *Henry James and H. G. Wells,* University of Illinois Press, 1958; *Howells and James: A Double Billing,* New York Public Library, 1958; (with others) *Masters of American Literature,* two volumes, Houghton, 1959; (with others) *5 World Biographies,* Harcourt, 1961; *Henry James: A Collection of Critical Essays,* Prentice-Hall, 1963; *The Diary of Alice James,* Dodd, 1965; (with others) *Literary History and Literary Criticism,* New York University Press, 1965; (and author of introduction) Edmund Wilson, *The Devils and Canon Barham,* Farrar, Straus, 1973; (and author of introduction) Harold Clarke Goddard, *Alphabet of the Imagination,* Humanities, 1974; (and author of introduction) Wilson, *The Twenties: From Notebooks and Diaries of the Period,* Farrar, Straus, 1975; Wilson, *Israel and the Dead Sea Scrolls,* Farrar, Straus, 1978; Wilson, *The Thirties,* Farrar, Straus, 1980.

Editor and author of introduction; all written by Henry James: *The Ghostly Tales of Henry James,* Rutgers University Press, 1949, revised edition published as *Stories of the Supernatural,* Taplinger, 1970; *The Complete Plays of Henry James,* Lippincott, 1949; *Selected Fiction,* Dutton, 1953; *The Sacred Fount,* Grove, 1953; *Selected Letters of Henry James,* Farrar, Straus, 1955; *The Portrait of a Lady,* Houghton, 1956; *The Future of the Novel,* Vintage, 1956; *American Essays,* Vintage, 1956; (with Ilse D. Lind) *Parisian Sketches,* New York University Press, 1957, reprinted, Greenwood Press, 1978; *House of Fiction,* Hart-Davis, 1957, reprinted, Greenwood Press, 1973; *The Sacred Fount,* Hart-Davis, 1959; *Roderick Hudson,* Harper, 1960; *Guy Domville,* Lippincott, 1960; *The Tragic Muse,* Harper, 1960; *Watch and Ward,* Grove, 1960; *The Ambassadors,* Houghton, 1960; *The Complete Tales of Henry James,* twelve volumes, Lippincott, 1962-65; *The American,* New American Library, 1963; *French Poets and Novelists,* Grosset, 1964; *The Henry James Reader,* Scribner, 1965; *The Spoils of Poynton,* Hart-Davis, 1967; *The American Scene,* Indiana University Press, 1968; *Henry James: Letters,* Harvard University Press, Volume I: *1843-1875,* 1974, Volume II: *1875-1883,* 1975, Volume III: *1883-1895,* 1980.

Contributor: *Canadian Accent,* Penguin, 1944; *Reader's Companion to World Literature,* Dryden, 1956; *Comparative Literature,* Southern Illinois University Press, 1961; *New World Writing 18,* Lippincott, 1961; *Hemingway: A Collection of Critical Essays,* Prentice-Hall, 1962; *Biography as an Art,* Oxford University Press, 1962; *Varieties of Literary Experience,* New York University Press, 1962; Hilda Schiff, editor, *Contemporary Approaches to English Studies,* Heinemann, 1977; Van Tassel, editor, *Agony, Death and the Completion of Being,* University of Pennsylvania Press, 1979; Marc Pachter, editor, *Telling Lives: The Biographer's Art,* New Republic, 1979.

Author of introduction or preface: Edouard Dujardin, *We'll to the Woods No More,* New Directions, 1958; Henry James, *The Bodley Head Henry James,* eleven volumes, Bodley Head, 1967-74; John Glassco, *Memoirs of Montparnasse,* Viking, 1970; Leo Kennedy, *The Shrouding,* Golden Dog Press (Ottowa), 1975; Glenda Leeming, *Who's Who in Henry James,* Hamish Hamilton, 1976; Henry James, *Roderick Hudson,* Houghton, 1977; Graeme Gibson, *Five Legs,* Anansi Press (Toronto), 1979; Gibson, *Communion,* Anansi Press, 1979. Also author of introductions to Henry James, *The Other House,* New Directions, Gillet, *Claybook for James Joyce,* Abelard, and *The Pulitzer Prize Reader,* Popular Library.

Contributor to literary journals. Editor of Edmund Wilson papers, beginning 1972.

SIDELIGHTS: Leon Edel's major work is the five volume biography of Henry James, which Joseph Epstein terms "the single greatest work of biography produced in our century." *Henry James* is praised for its debunking of the myths surrounding James' life. As Hilton Kramer comments: "Mr. Edel has buried forever the notion that James was a writer to whom 'nothing happened,' that he was a sort of inspired dilettante, living out his sheltered life on inherited wealth, spinning his verbal intricacies in an existential void. If we can smile now at such an absurd characterization . . . it is largely because Mr. Edel has established the incontrovertible evidence to the contrary. Out of his painstaking researches and his large imaginative grasp of the literary mind, he has given us a biographical James in whom we can at last believe." Adds Epstein, "Edel has delivered James from the stultifying hand of legend and in the process allowed us a clearer focus upon his work than had seemed possible. . . ."

Edel has also been applauded for the interpretative skills he brings to biography. "He has imposed order on the facts," remarks C. W. McCue, "and dared discreet interpretation to the end that [Volumes II and III] . . . provide us with a coherent and sensitive study. . . ." In accepting the 1963 National Book Award, Edel elaborated on the importance of ordering the facts: "To illustrate rather than explain, to select, discriminate and above all to have some narrative design—for the biographer who feels obliged to include everything, this may seem like an impatience with facts and dates. It is the reverse. It is a recognition that all history can never be told; that without selection, all we have is clutter. We must disengage history and the lives of men from the clutter of events."

Some reviewers have expressed reservations about Edel's psychological analysis of James. Christopher Lehmann-Haupt, who calls *Henry James* "magnificent," comments: "There does remain one troublesome question about Edel's work: how long into the future will this particularly Freudian reading of James's life have resonance? For it is entirely possible that Edel is simply speaking in the idiom of our age, an idiom whose strictures are already beginning to create a sense of discomfort, if recent attacks on Freud are any evidence." Piers Brendon, writing in *Books,* wonders "how far the psychological connections, which Mr. Edel adduces between James's life and his art, are based on specific evidence and how much on ingenious Freudian speculation."

In a critique of Volume V, John W. Aldridge, on the other hand, commends Edel's reading: "Edel offers an account of James's development through these years that is both a triumph of biographical reportage and the subtlest kind of psychological portraiture. The suffering man and the creative mind are beautifully integrated; large masses of information are given their appropriate meaning through being placed within the context of James's emotional torments; and the result is not only a new creation of James, the most complete and satisfying we are likely to have, but a fresh interpretation of mysteries that have often led to serious misunderstandings about his life and work."

After completing *Henry James,* Edel focused his myth challenging and analytical abilities on the Bloomsbury group, a coalition of modernist writers, artists, and critics, in *Bloomsbury: A House of Lions.* Lehmann-Haupt praises Edel's "sensitive psycho-biographical approach to the complex characters of the Bloomsbury group" and adds that "Mr. Edel not only explains the individual contributions to modern thought and art of the members of Bloomsbury, he also makes clear in his narrative how their association with one another made possible those contributions."

Edel delivered an address at the placing of a plaque to Henry James in Poet's Corner of Westminster Abbey.

BIOGRAPHICAL/CRITICAL SOURCES: New Yorker, June 11, 1955, March 31, 1971; *Christian Science Monitor,* November 8, 1962, July 3, 1969; *Nation,* November 10, 1962; *America,* February 9, 1963; *National Review,* February 26, 1963; *Publisher's Weekly,* March 25, 1963; *New Statesman,* April 26, 1963; *New York Times,* June 5, 1969, February 14, 1972, June 20, 1979; *Saturday Review,* June 7, 1969, February 12, 1972; *New Republic,* June 14, 1969; *Newsweek,* June 23, 1969; *Virginia Quarterly Review,* summer, 1969; *Observer,* October 26, 1969; *Times Literary Supplement,* October 30, 1969, August 18, 1972, November 23, 1979; *Commentary,* November, 1969; *Books,* January, 1970; *Book World,* February 6, 1972; *New York Times Book Review,* February 6, 1972, July 1, 1979; *Time,* February 14, 1972; *Chicago Tribune Book World,* June 10, 1979; *Washington Post Book World,* June 24, 1979; *Detroit News,* July 8, 1979.

* * *

EDWARDS, Frank Allyn 1908-1967

PERSONAL: Born August 4, 1908, in Mattoon, Ill.; died June 23, 1967, in Indianapolis, Ind.; son of Isaac Wright and Nellie (Meneou) Edwards; married Mary Louise Conlin, December 15, 1949. *Education:* Attended University of California, Los Angeles, two years. *Office:* WLWI-TV, 1401 North Meridian, Indianapolis, Ind.

CAREER: Radio and television broadcaster; began radio career with KDKA, Pittsburgh, Pa., 1924; affiliated with WHAS and WLAP, Louisville, Ky., 1925-34; Mutual Broadcasting System, news analyst, 1942-54, 1959-61, White House correspondent, 1949-54; commentator for WTTV, 1955-59, 1961-62, WXLW, 1964-67, and WLWI-TV, Indianapolis, Ind., beginning 1965. Lecturer on broadcast journalism, Butler University, 1963-64. Consultant, Polycultural Institute, 1954-57. Director, Radiozark, beginning 1962, and Central Power, Inc., beginning 1963. Member of board of governors, National Investigating Commission on Aerial Phenomena, beginning 1957. *Member:* Radio-TV Correspondents Association, Indianapolis Press Club, Elks, Columbia Club (Indianapolis). *Awards, honors:* Cited, with Edward R. Murrow and Lowell Thomas, as one of nation's top three broadcasters in *Radio Daily* poll, 1953.

WRITINGS: My First Ten Million Sponsors, Ballantine, 1956; *Strangest of All,* Citadel, 1956; *Stranger Than Science,* Lyle Stuart, 1959; *Strange People,* Lyle Stuart, 1962; *Strange World,* Lyle Stuart, 1964; *Flying Saucers–Serious Business,* Lyle Stuart, 1966; *Flying Saucers–Here and Now!,* Lyle Stuart, 1967; *The Strange World of Frank Edwards,* edited by Rory Stuart, Lyle Stuart, 1977. Author of column syndicated in more than four hundred newspapers, 1950-54; column, "Strange to Relate," syndicated internationally to some three hundred newspapers by Central Newsfeatures, London, 1966. Contributing editor, *Fate,* beginning 1957.

WORK IN PROGRESS: A book, *Strange to Relate.*

AVOCATIONAL INTERESTS: Color photography, golf, deep-sea fishing.†

* * *

EDWARDS, Page L., Jr. 1941-

PERSONAL: Born January 15, 1941, in Gooding, Idaho; son of Page Lawrence (a mining engineer) and Mary Elizabeth (Smith) Edwards; married Frances de Forest Smith, June 10, 1967 (divorced, June 23, 1980); children: Amy de Forest, Benjamin Carter. *Education:* Stanford University, B.A., 1963; University of Iowa, M.F.A., 1973. *Home:* 2580 Parfet St., Lakewood, Colo. 80215. *Office:* Haverhill Public Library, Haverhill, Mass. 01830.

CAREER: Viking Press, New York City, editor, 1968; Grossman Publishers, New York City, editor, 1969-71; University Press of New England, Hanover, N.H., assistant director, 1972-73; David R. Godine, Publishers, Boston, Mass., editor, 1974-75; Haverhill Public Library, Haverhill, Mass., reference librarian, 1975—. *Military service:* U.S. Navy, 1963-67; became lieutenant junior grade.

WRITINGS: The Mules that Angels Ride, J. P. O'Hara, 1972; *Touring,* Marion Boyars, 1976; *Staking Claims: Stories,* Marion Boyars, 1980.

WORK IN PROGRESS: A novella, tentatively entitled *Crabbes' Retreat;* a novel, tentatively entitled *Three Old Men.*

AVOCATIONAL INTERESTS: Paintings of Edward Hopper and C. F. Childs, landscapes, long-distance running and cross-country skiing.

* * *

EHRLICH, Max 1909-

PERSONAL: Born October 10, 1909, in Springfield, Mass.; son of Simon (an accountant) and Sarah (Siegel) Ehrlich; married Doris Rubinstein, 1940 (divorced); children: Amy, Jane (Mrs. Carl Baver). *Education:* University of Michigan, B.A., 1933. *Home:* 818 North Doheny Dr., Los Angeles, Calif. 90069. *Agent:* Scott Meredith Literary Agency, Inc., 845 Third Ave., New York, N.Y. 10022.

CAREER: Has worked in machine shops and tobacco fields, sold magazines, and caddied at golf courses; reporter for *Knickerbocker Press* and *Evening News,* Albany, N.Y., and for *Republican* and *Daily News,* Springfield, Mass; full-time writer, 1949—. Guest lecturer in creative writing at various universities, including New York University and Columbia University. *Member:* Authors Guild, Authors League of America, Writers Guild of America West, Radio Writers Guild. *Awards, honors:* Huntington Hartford Foundation fellow.

WRITINGS—All novels: *The Big Eye* (Dollar Book Club selection), Doubleday, 1947; *Spin the Glass Web,* Harper, 1951; *First Train to Babylon* (*Readers' Digest* Book Club selection), Harper, 1955; *The Takers,* Harper, 1961; *Deep Is the Blue,* Doubleday, 1964; *The High Side,* Fawcett, 1970; *The Edict* (based on his screenplay of the same title; also see below), Bantam, 1974; *The Reincarnation of Peter Proud,* Bobbs-Merrill, 1974; *The Cult,* Simon & Schuster, 1978; *Reincarnation in Venice,* Simon & Schuster, 1979; *Naked Beach,* Playboy Press, 1979.

Screenplays: (With Frank De Felitta) "Z.P.G.," Sagittarius Productions, 1972; (with De Felitta) "The Savage Is Loose," United Artists, 1972; (with Gerald Schnitzer) "Waldo," American International, 1972; "The Reincarnation of Peter Proud" (based on his novel of the same title), American International, 1975. Also author of "The Liar" for Princess Pictures, and "Sail to Glory," a feature-length documentary, for Schnitzer Productions; author of documentary film scripts for various organizations, including American Red Cross, Boys Club of America, and U.S. Department of Defense.

Author of scripts for numerous television programs, including "Studio One," "The Defenders," "G.E. Theater," "Arrest and Trail," "Wild Wild West," and "Star Trek." Contributor of articles to periodicals.

SIDELIGHTS: Max Ehrlich told *CA:* "I love to write. Have been a professional author for thirty-five years, and still find it tremendously exciting. If you can make your way in it, earn your bread, then it is the aristocrat of all professions. Where else can you make your fantasies, or dreams, come true?

"I tend to shy away from rigid classification. Yet, in a loose sort of way, I suppose I could be called an author of suspense. The essence of my craft is to make the reader turn the page, by goading him into the question: 'What happens next?' Note that I use the word 'author' and not writer. There is a difference. An author is a creator, an orginator, an innovator. In a broad sense, he writes the novel or the play. But a 'writer' can write anything. Classified ads, articles, publicity, newspaper stories, pornography.

"To any author or dramatist, reality is an enemy. It is useful in the sense that you need reference points on which to hang your story. But the art is an exaggeration, making it all larger than life. Making it *seem* like reality, and making the reader believe in it, because he becomes absorbed in it. I am a story teller. Whatever I write has a beginning, middle and end, and I only hope that it entertains. But I always make some kind of important statement somewhere in the work, something in which I sincerely believe. Not necessarily to uplift the reader; but to uplift myself."

Spin the Glass Web was produced as a film starring Edward G. Robinson and John Forsythe; *First Train to Babylon* was made into a film, "The Naked Eye," starring Gary Cooper and Deborah Kerr. *The Big Eye, The Takers,* and *Deep Is the Blue* have been purchased by major motion picture studios. All of Max Ehrlich's novels have been translated into several foreign languages.

AVOCATIONAL INTERESTS: Golf, swimming, bridge, travel (has travelled extensively in Europe, the Near East, and the Caribbean.

* * *

ELEGANT, Robert S(ampson) 1928-

PERSONAL: Born March 7, 1928, in New York, N.Y.; son of Louis and Lillie (Sampson) Elegant; married Moira Clarissa Brady, April 16, 1956; children: Victoria Ann, Simon David Brady. *Education:* University of Pennsylvania, A.B., 1946; Yale University, Certificate in Chinese, 1948; Columbia University, M.A., 1950, M.S., 1951. *Address:* Loongshan House, Greystones, County Wicklow, Ireland. *Agent:* Julian Bach Literary Agency, Inc., 3 East 48th St., New York, N.Y. 10017.

CAREER: Overseas News Agency, correspondent in Far East, 1951-52; International News Service, correspondent in Japan and Korea, 1953; Ford Foundation fellow in Southeast Asia, 1954-56, and part-time correspondent for Columbia Broadcasting System, North American Newspaper Alliance, and McGraw-Hill News Service; *Newsweek,* South Asian correspondent stationed in India, 1956-57, and in Hong Kong, 1958-61, chief of bureau, Central Europe, with headquarters in Bonn, Germany, 1962-65; *Los Angeles Times,* chief of Hong Kong Bureau, 1965-69; foreign affairs columnist operating from Munich, Germany, 1970-72, and Hong Kong, 1973-75; visiting professor, University of South Carolina, autumn, 1976; free-lance writer, 1977—. *Military service:* U.S. Army, Infantry, 1946-48; became sergeant; studied and taught Japanese at Army Language School. *Member:* Authors League, Asia Society, Hong Kong Foreign Correspondent Club (president, 1960), Lausdowne Club (London), Royal Hong Kong Yacht Club, Phi Beta Kappa. *Awards, honors:* Pulitzer traveling fellow, 1951; Overseas Press Club, citation for best magazine reporting from abroad, 1961, annual awards for best interpretation of news from abroad, 1967, 1969, 1972; Edgar Allan Poe Award runner-up for best first mystery, 1967, for *A Kind of Treason;* Sigma Delta Chi award for correspondence, 1967; Columbia University Alumni Award, 1971.

WRITINGS: China's Red Masters, Twayne, 1951, reprinted, Greenwood Press, 1971; *The Dragon's Seed,* St. Martin's, 1959; *The Center of the World,* Doubleday, 1964, revised edition, Funk & Wagnalls, 1968; (contributor) *Journalists in Action,* Cresset, 1964; *A Kind of Treason* (novel), Holt, 1966; *The Seeking,* Funk & Wagnalls, 1969; *Mao's Great Revolution,* World Publishing, 1971; *Mao vs. Chiang,* Grosset, 1972; *Dynasty* (novel), McGraw, 1976; *Manchu* (novel), McGraw, 1979. Contributor to *Reporter* and *New Leader.*

SIDELIGHTS: As a former journalist who now writes novels, Robert S. Elegant comments in an interview with Robert Dahlin on the advantages of having spent many years reporting news and writing nonfiction: "[Journalists] have been trained to observe not only unconsciously, but also consciously. If you're a journalist, you make judgments in your mind, assessing people and events. And, it is a trained faculty, this communication. Reporters aren't rewarded for obscurity." Elegant believes that writing fiction does allow the writer certain freedoms not available to writers of nonfiction. "We all know things about people, things that would be unfair to use in nonfiction because we can't prove them," he comments. "And there are other issues. I know that at one time we led the Chinese to believe we were willing to commit ourselves to their defense against Russia, if anything should happen. But there's nothing I would be able to use in nonfiction to prove it."

Commenting on his novel, *Dynasty,* which is set in China, Elegant said: "What I hope I've been able to convey . . . is an atmosphere. And to show that the people themselves are not simply the inscrutable East. They have real and personal problems just like everyone else. Making that observation journalistically can be bloodless. In a novel, you can develop character. You can find your own length." Although Robert Lask, reviewing *Dynasty* for the *New York Times,* calls it an "uneven, sprawling novel [which] recapitulates the violent history of the Orient since 1900," he also writes that the book is filled with "highly colored incidents and characters." Particularly impressed with the novel's setting, Lask adds that Elegant's career as a newspaper correspondent in Hong Kong enabled him to include "those small details, customs, ceremonies and touches of folklore that make the time and place more vivid than the characters he has created. And history fascinates him. . . . You can read *Dynasty* as a short course in Chinese history since 1900. Anything additional is a pure dividend."

BIOGRAPHICAL/CRITICAL SOURCES: New York Times, April 1, 1971, September 22, 1977; *National Review,* May 18, 1971; *Publishers Weekly,* October 10, 1977.

* * *

ELIOT, Alexander 1919-

PERSONAL: Born April 28, 1919, in Cambridge, Mass.; son of Samuel Atkins, Jr. (a professor) and Ethel (an author; maiden name, Cook) Eliot; married Jane Winslow Knapp (a weaver, writer, and photographer), May 3, 1952; children: May Rose, Jefferson, Winslow. *Education:* Attended Black Mountain College, 1936-38, Boston Museum School, 1938-39, and Loomis Institute. *Agent:* James Brown Associates, 25 West 43rd St., New York, N.Y. 10036.

CAREER: Film writer for "March of Time" and government wartime agencies, 1940-45; *Time* (magazine), New York, N.Y., art editor, 1945-60. *Member:* P.E.N., Authors Guild, Free Lance Council, Society of American Travel Writers, Century Association, Dutch Treat Club. *Awards, honors:* Guggenheim fellowship. 1960; Japan Foundation senior fellowship, 1975.

WRITINGS: Proud Youth, Farrar, Straus, 1953; *Three Hundred Years of American Painting,* Time, 1957; *Sight and Insight,* McDowell-Obolensky, 1959; *Earth, Air, Fire, and Water,* Simon & Schuster, 1962; *Greece,* Life World Library, 1963; *Love Play,* New World Library, 1966; *Creatures of Arcadia,* Bobbs-Merrill, 1967; *Socrates,* Crown, 1967; *Concise History of Greece,* American Heritage, 1972; *Myths,* McGraw, 1976; *Zen Edge,* Seabury, 1979.

Author of "The Secret of Michelangelo: Every Man's Dream," for ABC-TV, 1968. Contributor of over 200 articles to periodicals, including *Texas Quarterly, Holiday, Greek Heritage, Horizon, Sports Illustrated, Atlantic, Vogue, Saturday Evening Post, Time, Life, Panorama* (Italy), *Embros* (Greece), and *Smithsonian.* Contributing editor, *Art in America,* 1960-65.

SIDELIGHTS: Alexander Eliot told *CA:* "I try to make each new book, and every article as well, a new departure from a position of stillness. Not to repeat old convictions, but to build new understanding on thin air, and take it from there. When I write, I'm in rapid motion of the mind; motion between what I was a moment ago and what I'll be a moment from now. Not ripeness, in my view, but readiness, is all."

* * *

ELKIND, David 1931-

PERSONAL: Born March 11, 1931, in Detroit, Mich.; married Sally Faye Malinsky, December 21, 1960; children: Paul Steven, Robert Edward, Eric Allen. *Education:* University of California, Los Angeles, B.A. (with highest honors), 1952, Ph.D., 1955. *Home:* 8 Linmoor Ter., Lexington, Mass. 02173. *Office:* Department of Child Study, Tufts University, Medford, Mass. 02155.

CAREER: Austen Riggs, Inc., Stockbridge, Mass., research assistant to David Rapaport, 1956-57; Beth Israel Hospital, Boston, Mass., staff psychologist, 1957-59; Wheaton College, Norton, Mass., assistant professor of psychology, 1959-61; University of California, Los Angeles, School of Medicine, assistant professor of medical psychology, 1961-62; University of Denver, Denver, Colo., associate professor of psychology and director of Child Study Center, 1962-66; University of Rochester, Rochester, N.Y., professor of psychology, 1966-78; Tufts University, Medford, Mass., professor of child study and chairman of department, 1978—. Member of visiting faculty, Cambridge Junior College, 1958-59, and Rhode Island College of Education, 1960-61. Psychological consultant to DePaul Child Guidance Clinic, Rochester Mental Health Center, and Family Court. Diplomate in child clinical psychology, American Board of Professional Examiners in Psychology.

MEMBER: American Psychological Association (fellow), British Psychological Society (foreign affiliate), Society for Research in Child Development, Interamerican Society of Psychology, Society for the Scientific Study of Religion, American Association for the Advancement of Science (fellow), American Educational Research Association, Sigma Xi, Phi Beta Kappa. *Awards, honors:* National Science Foundation postdoctoral fellow in Geneva, Switzerland, 1964-65.

WRITINGS: (Editor, author of introduction and notes, and translator with Anita Tenzer) Jean Piaget, *Six Psychological Studies,* Random House, 1968; (editor with John H. Flavell) *Studies in Cognitive Development: Essays in Honor of Jean Piaget,* Oxford University Press, 1969; *Children and Adolescents: Interpretive Essays on Jean Piaget,* Oxford University Press, 1970, 2nd edition, 1974; *Exploitation in Middle Class Delinquency: Issues in Human Development,* U.S.

Government Printing Office, 1971; *A Sympathetic Understanding of the Child: Six to Sixteen,* Allyn & Bacon, 1971, 2nd edition, 1978; (editor) Kenneth Lovell, *An Introduction to Human Development,* Scott, Foresman, 1971; (editor with Irving B. Weiner) *Readings in Child Development,* Wiley, 1972; (with Weiner) *Child Development: A Core Approach,* Wiley, 1972; (with others) *Introduction to Psychology,* Heath, 1974; *Child Development and Education,* Oxford University Press, 1976; (with D. Hetzel) *Readings in Human Development,* Harper, 1977; (with Weiner) *Development of the Child,* Wiley, 1978; *The Child's Reality: Three Developmental Themes,* Lawrence Erlbaum Associates, 1978; *The Child and Society,* Oxford University Press, 1979. Also author of film script, "What Do You Think?" Contributor to symposia and to journals.

WORK IN PROGRESS: A Sympathetic Understanding of the Person: Birth to Senescence.

* * *

ELLIS, Alec (Charles Owen) 1932-

PERSONAL: Born September 1, 1932, in Liverpool, England; son of Eric Vernon and Eva (Strafford) Ellis; married Anne Weir Struthers (a librarian), August 3, 1959; children: Malcolm Lamberton, Alison Strafford. *Education:* Attended Liverpool College of Commerce, 1949-58; University of Liverpool, M.A., 1970. *Politics:* Radical. *Home:* 53 Beechfield Rd., Liverpool L18 3EQ, England. *Office:* Liverpool Polytechnic, Tithebarn St., Liverpool L2 2ER, England.

CAREER: City Libraries, Liverpool, England, assistant librarian, 1949-61; St. Katharine's College, Liverpool, England, librarian, 1961-64; Liverpool Polytechnic, Liverpool, England, lecturer, 1965-68, senior lecturer, 1968-72, principal lecturer, 1972-78, head of department of library and information studies, 1978—. External examiner for University of Liverpool, 1968-71, and University of Wales, 1980—. *Member:* Library Association, Association of Teachers in Technical Institutions.

WRITINGS: How to Find Out about Children's Literature, Pergamon, 1966, 3rd edition, 1973; *A History of Children's Reading and Literature,* Pergamon, 1968; *Library Services for Young People in England and Wales: 1830-1970,* Pergamon, 1971; *Books in Victorian Elementary Schools,* Library Association, 1971; *Public Libraries and the First World War,* Ffynnon, 1974; *The Parish of All Hallows, Allerton, 1876-1976,* All Hallows, 1976; *Chosen for Children,* Library Association, 1977; *Public Libraries at the Time of the Adams Report,* Clover, 1979. Contributor to *British Journal of Educational Studies, Journal of Librarianship, Library Association Record, Junior Bookshelf,* and *School Librarian.*

AVOCATIONAL INTERESTS: Collecting British postage stamps.

* * *

ELLISON, James Whitfield 1929-

PERSONAL: Born May 15, 1929, in Lansing, Mich.; son of Chester Whitfield and Clara (Weber) Ellison; married Virginia Howell, April 11, 1955; children: David, Nicholas. *Education:* University of Michigan, B.A., 1950. *Religion:* Congregationalist. *Home:* Mather Rd., Stamford, Conn. *Agent:* Harold Ober Associates, 40 East 49th St., New York, N.Y. 10017. *Office:* E. P. Dutton and Elsevier Book Operations, 2 Park Ave., New York, N.Y. 10016.

CAREER: Columbia Pictures Industries, Inc., Hollywood, Calif., screen writer, 1955-58; Fawcett Publications, New York City, editor, 1958-59; Holt, Rinehart & Winston, New York City, editor, 1960-62; Coward-McCann, Inc., New York City, senior editor, 1962; E. P. Dutton, Inc., New York City, editor, 1962—. *Military service:* U.S. Army, 1951-53. *Member:* Author's Guild, Authors League of America. *Awards, honors:* Bread Loaf Writers' Conference life fellowship.

WRITINGS: I'm Owen Harrison Harding (novel), Doubleday, 1955, reprinted, Pocket Books, 1975; *The Freest Man on Earth,* Doubleday, 1958; *Master Prim* (novel), Little, Brown, 1968; *Descent* (novel), McCall, 1970; *The Summer after the War,* Dodd, 1972; *Proud Rachel* (novel), Stein & Day, 1975.

SIDELIGHTS: John Coleman calls *Master Prim* "beautifully neat, as deliberate as its title conveys. A good notion for a book (a 19-year-old American chess-master is pursued by a decent journalist with some sort of *Life* coverage of him in mind) is converted into a good book. The operation is conducted with the maximum of literate tidiness and, so far as I can judge, some wiliness around a chess-board." And A. H. Weiler writes: "Mr. Ellison has succinctly caught the feel of the game, the special atmosphere in which it is played and the kind of dedication it takes to get to the top. Master Prim in his early stages is as unlovable a chap as you will come across, but a man with the goods. The combination of great gifts and great coarseness of spirit is not new in life or in fiction. In Mr. Ellison's book it makes for a highly individual portrait."

John Leonard feels that, in *Descent,* Ellison "has produced a book full of so many good things, so much anger and precision and perception, that when it goes out of control—when the novel itself seems to suffer a nervous breakdown—you want to take the bolts off the back of it and inspect the circuitry." The reviewer says that "for the first half of the book, the juxtapositions and revelations work compellingly. The quartet of [characters] seems to move in broken boxes across the floor of some dark aquarium in a death-dance, wounding one another even as they embrace. The aquarium is language, of which Mr. Ellison is a master; and the members of the quartet are dangerous toys, essences whose springs we know are soon to snap. But the snapping does not occur in the characters; it occurs in the conception. We are asked to accept an orgy so explicit and so unlikely, so extravagant and so debasing, that one simply stops believing. Suggestion would have deepened the spell; detail makes a dreary tabloid of it."

BIOGRAPHICAL/CRITICAL SOURCES: New York Times Book Review, February 18, 1968, July 26, 1970; *New York Times,* June 15, 1968, May 28, 1970; *Observer Review,* August 4, 1968; *Punch,* August 14, 1968; *Library Journal,* June 15, 1970.†

* * *

ELSTOB, Peter 1915-

PERSONAL: Born December 22, 1915, in London, England; son of Frederick Charles and Lillian (Page) Elstob; married Medora Leigh-Smith, 1936; married second wife, Barbara Jean Zacheisz, 1952; children: (first marriage) Ann Elstob Hithersay, Penelope Elstob West, Blair, Michael, Harry; (second marriage) Mayo, Sukey. *Education:* Attended University of Michigan, 1934-35. *Home:* 22 Belsize Park Gardens, London N.W.3, England; and Coocderry, Hatchett's Pond, Beaulieu, Hampshire, England.

CAREER: Yeast-pac Co. Ltd., London, England, managing director, 1938—; Arts Theatre Club, London, England, director, 1941-54; Peter Arnold Properties, London, England, director, 1947—; Peter Arnold Studios, Ajijic, Mexico, manager, 1950-52; ABC Expeditions, London, England, director of publicity, 1958-62; Trade Wind Films, London, England, director, 1958-62; Archive Press, London, England, chairman, 1963—. *Military service:* Royal Air Force, 1935-36; International Brigade, 1936-37; Royal Tank Regiment, 1940-46; prisoner of war in Spain; mentioned in dispatches. *Member:* International P.E.N. (secretary-general, 1974—), Authors Guild, Society of Authors, Garrick Club, Savage Club.

WRITINGS: Spanish Prisoner, Carrick & Evans, 1939; *The Flight of the Small World,* Norton, 1959; *Warriors for the Working Day,* Coward, 1960; *The Armed Rehearsal,* Secker & Warburg, 1964; *Bastogne: The Road Block,* Ballantine, 1968; *The Battle of the Reichswald,* Ballantine, 1970; *Hitler's Last Offensive,* Macmillan, 1973; *Condor Legion,* Ballantine, 1973. Editor of books for International P.E.N. Contributor to magazines.

WORK IN PROGRESS: Scoundrel, a novel.

SIDELIGHTS: Peter Elstob has traveled in sixty countries and lived and worked in thirty-four countries, holding a variety of jobs. Many of his books have been translated into German, French, Italian, Spanish, Dutch, Portuguese, Norwegian, and Japanese. *Avocational interests:* Painting, theatre, films, collecting modern first editions.

* * *

ELZINGA, Kenneth G(erald) 1941-
(Marshall Jevons, a joint pseudonym)

PERSONAL: Born August 11, 1941, in Coopersville, Mich.; son of Clarence Albert (an engineer) and Lettie Elizabeth (Albrecht) Elzinga; married Barbara Brunson, June 17, 1967 (died December 6, 1978). *Education:* Kalamazoo College, B.A., 1963; Michigan State University, M.A., 1966, Ph.D., 1967. *Religion:* Christian. *Home:* Longbrook Farm, Keswick, Va. 22947. *Office:* Department of Economics, University of Virginia, Charlottesville, Va. 22903.

CAREER: University of Virginia, Charlottesville, assistant professor, 1967-71, associate professor, 1971-74, professor of economics, 1974—, assistant dean of College of Arts and Sciences, 1971-73. Fellow in law and economics at University of Chicago, 1974. Member of Nuclear Regulatory Commission Licensing and Safety Board Panel, 1971-79. *Member:* Industrial Organization Society (president, 1979). *Awards, honors:* Woodrow Wilson fellow, 1964; Phi Beta Kappa visiting scholar, 1973-74; Sesquicentennial Associateship in Center for Advanced Studies at University of Virginia, 1973-74; Distinguished Professor Award, University of Virginia, 1979.

WRITINGS: (Contributor) Walter Adams, editor, *The Structure of American Industry,* 4th edition (Elzinga was not associated with earlier editions), Macmillan, 1971, 5th edition, 1977; (editor) *Economics: A Reader,* Harper, 1972, 3rd edition, 1978; (with William Breit) *The Antitrust Penalties: A Study in Law,* Yale University Press, 1978; (with Breit; under joint pseudonym Marshall Jevons) *Murder at the Margin,* Thomas Horton, 1978. Contributor to *Social Science Quarterly, Journal of Law and Economics, Harvard Law Review, Antitrust Bulletin, Industrial Organization Review, Southern Economic Journal,* and other periodicals. Member of editorial board of *Industrial Organization Review,* 1972, and *Antitrust Bulletin,* 1977—.

WORK IN PROGRESS: Research on delivered pricing systems and the conditions of entry in American industry.

ENGLISH, Fenwick Walter 1939-

PERSONAL: Born February 9, 1939, in Los Angeles, Calif.; son of Melvin Mitchell (a teacher) and Phyllis (Steeves) English; married Lolita Rae Kennedy; children: Erin, Eric, Daphne. *Education:* University of Southern California, B.S., 1961, M.S., 1963; Arizona State University, Ph.D., 1972. *Politics:* Republican. *Home:* 4112 Whitacre Rd., Fairfax, Va. 22032. *Office:* Peat, Marwick, Mitchell & Co., 1990 K St., Washington, D.C. 20006.

CAREER: Temple City public schools, Temple City, Calif., principal, 1965-68, project director, 1968-70; assistant superintendent for personnel and program development, Sarasota County, Fla., 1972-74; superintendent of schools, Hastings-on-Hudson, N.Y., 1974-77; American Association of School Administrators, Arlington, Va., associate director, 1977-78; Peat, Marwick, Mitchell & Co., Washington, D.C., practice director of elementary-secondary education, 1979—. *Member:* American Association of School Administrators, Association for Supervision and Curriculum Development, Association of School Business Officials, Council for Basic Education, Phi Delta Kappa.

WRITINGS: (With Donald K. Sharpes) *Strategies for Differentiated Staffing,* McCutchan, 1972; *School Organization and Management,* Charles A. Jones Publishing, 1975; (with Frank L. Steeves) *Secondary Curriculum for a Changing World,* C. E. Merrill, 1978; (with Roger A. Kaufman) *Needs Assessment: Concept and Practice,* Educational Technology Publications, 1979.

WORK IN PROGRESS: Development of educational performance audit improved curriculum management in school systems.

* * *

ENRIGHT, D(ennis) J(oseph) 1920-

PERSONAL: Born on March 11, 1920, in Leamington, Warwickshire, England; son of George (a postman) and Grace (Cleaver) Enright; married Madeleine Harders, November 3, 1949; children: Dominique (daughter). *Education:* Downing College, Cambridge, B.A. (with honors), 1944, M.A., 1946; University of Alexandria, D. Litt., 1949. *Agent:* Bolt & Watson Ltd., 8-12 Old Queen's St., London SW1, England. *Office:* c/o Chatto & Windus Ltd., 40 William IV St., London WC2N 4DF, England.

CAREER: University of Alexandria, Alexandria, Egypt, assistant lecturer in English, 1947-50; University of Birmingham, Birmingham, England, lecturer, 1950-53; Konan University, Kobe, Japan, visiting professor, 1953-56; Free University of Berlin, Berlin, Germany, visiting professor, 1956-57; Chulalongkorn University, Bangkok, Thailand, British Council Professor, 1957-59; University of Singapore, Singapore, professor of English, 1960-70; co-editor, *Encounter* (magazine), 1970-72; Chatto & Windus Ltd. (publishers), London, England, director, 1974—. *Member:* Royal Society of Literature (fellow). *Awards, honors:* Cholmandeley Award, 1974.

WRITINGS: A Commentary on Goethe's "Faust," New Directions, 1949; *The World of Dew: Aspects of Living Japan,* Secker & Warburg, 1955, Dufour, 1959; *Robert Graves and the Decline of Modernism* (text of lecture), Craftsman Press (Singapore), 1960; *Memoirs of a Mendicant Professor* (autobiography), Chatto & Windus, 1969; *Shakespeare and the Students,* Chatto & Windus, 1970, Schocken, 1971; *A Faust Book,* Oxford University Press, 1980.

Poetry; published by Chatto & Windus, except as indicated:

The Laughing Hyena and Other Poems, Routledge & Kegan Paul, 1953; *Bread Rather than Blossoms,* Secker & Warburg, 1956; *The Year of the Monkey,* privately printed, 1956; *Some Men Are Brothers,* 1960; *Addictions,* 1962; *The Old Adam,* 1965; *Unlawful Assembly,* Wesleyan University Press, 1968; *Selected Poems,* 1969; *The Typewriter Revolution and Other Poems,* Library Press, 1971; *In the Basilica of the Annunciation,* Poem-of-the-Month Club, 1971; *Daughters of Earth,* 1972; *Foreign Devils,* Covent Garden Press, 1972; *The Terrible Shears: Scenes from a Twenties Childhood,* 1973, Wesleyan University Press, 1974; *Rhyme Times Rhyme* (juvenile), 1974; *Sad Ires,* 1975; (contributor) *Penguin Modern Poets 26: Dannie Abse, D. J. Enright, Michael Longley,* Penguin, 1975; *Paradise Illustrated,* 1978.

Novels: *Academic Year,* Secker & Warburg, 1955; *Heaven Knows Where,* Secker & Warburg, 1957; *Insufficient Poppy,* Chatto & Windus, 1960; *Figures of Speech,* Heinemann, 1965; *The Joke Shop* (juvenile), McKay, 1976; *Wild Ghost Chase* (juvenile), Chatto & Windus, 1978; *Beyond Land's End* (juvenile), Chatto & Windus, 1979.

Essays: *Literature for Men's Sake,* Kenkyusha Ltd. (Tokyo), 1955, reprinted, Richard West, 1976; *The Apothecary's Shop: Essays on Literature,* Secker & Warburg, 1957, Dufour, 1959, reprinted, Greenwood Press, 1975; *Conspirators and Poets,* Dufour, 1966; *Man Is an Onion: Reviews and Essays,* Chatto & Windus, 1972, Library Press, 1973.

Editor: (And author of introduction) *Poetry of the 1950's: An Anthology of New English Verse,* Kenkyusha Ltd. (Tokyo), 1955; (with Takamichi Nimomiya) *The Poetry of Living Japan,* Grove, 1957; (with Ernst de Chickera) *English Critical Texts: 16th Century to 20th Century,* Oxford University Press, 1962; (and author of introduction) John Milton, *A Choice of Milton's Verse,* Faber, 1975; (and author of introduction) Samuel Johnson, *The History of Rasselas, Prince of Abissinia,* Penguin, 1976.

Contributor to *Encounter, Scrutiny, Listener,* and *Times Literary Supplement.*

WORK IN PROGRESS: A sequence of poems on Faust; an anthology of modern poetry in English.

SIDELIGHTS: D. J. Enright is noted for his quiet, almost-casual poetry. "Enright's form," M. L. Rosenthal observes, "is usually very flat and conversational, approaching in a way the 'minimal' style of Robert Creeley, and though actually the poetry is intellectually oriented the statement is kept as simple as possible." Speaking of the collection *The Terrible Shears,* Dan Jacobson notes that "many of the poems have the appearance of being as casual as they can be without lapsing into prose; they are given to unrhymed, conjunctional line-endings, broken rhythms, and a deliberate avoidance of sonority. Yet one does not feel for a moment that they have been easy to write. Candour is never easily come by." David Bromwich writes that "the plainness of forms leads into a peculiarly stringent mode of vision, so that the most important notes are those struck most quietly."

Many of Enright's poems are about the Far East, where he taught for a number of years, and often contain social commentary. "Many of [Enright's] Eastern poems," Douglas Dunn writes, "conjure situations of the underdog beset by politicians." Enright's many poems about Japan, Philip Gardner remarks, are not "testimonials to the Japan of the tourist brochures, the Japan of cherry-blossom, Mount Fuji, Kyoto temple, Noh, Tea Ceremony, Flower Arrangement, and Zen. All these aspects appear, but as a background." Gardner emphasizes Enright's "concern for individuals rather than governments" and his depictions of "a Japan of overpopulation, poverty, landslides, suicides, [and] streetwalkers."

The collection *The Terrible Shears* concerns Enright's childhood in England. "Enright shows us vividly," a reviewer for *Times Literary Supplement* states, "what it was like to grow up in a particular town in circumstances of poverty and an atmosphere of disease and death." "In the face of the large facts of death and poverty," Jacobson writes, "the poems in this collection have the courage to speak repeatedly of the enduring littleness of a child's bewilderment and shame. Hence it is a measure of their painful exactness and truth that they should often be extremely funny. . . . but the funnier they are, the more poignant they are too."

Enright has travelled in India, Greece, Hong Kong, People's Republic of China, Cambodia, Australia, Burma, Ireland, and North America.

BIOGRAPHICAL/CRITICAL SOURCES: William Van O'Connor, *The New University Wits and the End of Modernism,* Southern Illinois University Press, 1963; *Times* (London), February 27, 1964; *Times Literary Supplement,* March 18, 1965, July 29, 1965, June 9, 1972, June 8, 1973, December 10, 1976; *Punch,* April 7, 1965, January 15, 1969; *New Statesman,* June 18, 1965, September 28, 1973, June 28, 1974, May 19, 1978; *New York Review of Books,* March 31, 1966; *Observer,* November 20, 1966; M. L. Rosenthal , *The New Poets: American and British Poetry since World War II,* Oxford University Press, 1967; *Commonweal,* December 1, 1967; *Contemporary Literature,* winter, 1968, autumn, 1976; *Listener,* September 5, 1968, August 20, 1970, November 20, 1975; *London Magazine,* December, 1968, September, 1973; D. J. Enright, *Memoirs of a Mendicant Professor,* Chatto & Windus, 1969; *Economist,* January 18, 1969; *Saturday Review,* March 15, 1969; *Hudson Review,* summer, 1969; *Nation,* December 6, 1971; *New York Times Book Review,* February 13, 1972, April 6, 1975; *Poetry,* April, 1973, February, 1976; *Spectator,* August 25, 1973; *Book World,* September 23, 1973; *New Republic,* October 13, 1973; *Books & Bookmen,* November, 1973, October, 1978; William Walsh, *D. J. Enright: Poet of Humanism,* Cambridge University Press, 1974; *Contemporary Literary Criticism,* Gale, Volume IV, 1975, Volume VIII, 1978; *Encounter,* February, 1976, November, 1978; *Times Educational Supplement,* June 16, 1978.

* * *

ENSMINGER, Marion Eugene 1908-

PERSONAL: Born May 28, 1908, in Stover, Mo.; son of Jacob and Ella (Belt) Ensminger; married Audrey Helen Watts (a nutritionist), June 11, 1941; children: John Jacob, Janet Aileen (deceased). *Education:* University of Missouri, B.S., 1931, M.S., 1932; University of Massachusetts, graduate study, 1938-40; University of Minnesota, Ph.D., 1941. *Politics:* Democrat. *Religion:* Presbyterian. *Home and office:* 648 West Sierra Ave., Clovis, Calif. 93612.

CAREER: Northwest Missouri State Teachers College (now Northwest Missouri State University), Maryville, instructor in agriculture, summers 1931-32; U.S. Department of Agriculture, assistant to superintendent of Soil Erosion Station, Bethany, Mo., 1933-34, soil erosion specialist in Urbana, Ill., 1934, manager of Dixon Springs Experiment Station in Robb, Ill., 1934-37; University of Massachusetts—Amherst, assistant professor of animal husbandry, 1937-40; Washington State University, Pullman, professor of animal science and chairman of department, 1941-62; Agriservices Foundation, Clovis, Calif., president, 1962—. Distinguished visiting professor at Wisconsin State University—River Falls (now University of Wisconsin—River Falls) 1963; adjunct professor at California State University, Fresno, 1973—, and University of Arizona, Tucson, 1977—. President of Consultants-Agriservices and Pegus Co., both 1962—. Director of Horse Science School and Beef Cattle Stud Managers School, both 1963—, and American National Bank, 1974-79. Member of technical committee of Western Cattle Breeding Laboratory and collaborator on Western Sheep Breeders Laboratory, both for U.S. Department of Agriculture, Member of national board of field advisers of U.S. Small Business Administration. Consultant to General Electric Co. and U.S. Atomic Energy Commission.

MEMBER: American Society of Agricultural Consultants (first president, 1963-64), American Society of Animal Sciences (member of executive committee; vice-president of western section, 1957-58; president, 1958-59; fellow), American Society of Range Management, American Dairy Science Association, American Genetic Association, Soil Conservation Society of America, American Association for the Advancement of Science (fellow), American Medical Writers Association, Future Farmers of America (honorary member), New York Academy of Sciences, Sigma Xi, Alpha Zeta, Lambda Gamma Delta. *Awards, honors:* Elected to Washington State University Animal Science Hall of Fame, 1958; distinguished teacher award from American Society of Animal Science, 1960.

WRITINGS: Animal Science, Interstate, 1950, 7th edition, 1977; *Beef Cattle Science,* Interstate, 1951, 5th edition, 1976; *Sheep and Wool Science,* Interstate, 1951, 4th edition, 1970; *Horses and Horsemanship,* Interstate, 1951, 5th edition, 1977; *Swine Science,* Interstate, 1952, 4th edition, 1970; *The Stockman's Handbook,* Interstate, 1955, 5th edition, 1978; (Contributor) John Hammond, Ivar Johannson, and Fritz Haring, *Handbuch Der Tier-Zuechtung* (title means "Handbook of Animal Breeding"), three volumes, Verlag Paul Parey, 1961; *Horses! Horses! Horses!,* Pegus Co., 1964; *Tack! Tack! Tack!,* Pegus Co., 1965; *Dairy Cattle Science,* Interstate, 1971, 2nd edition, 1980; *Poultry Science,* Interstate, 1971, 2nd edition, 1980; (with wife, Audrey Ensminger) *China: The Impossible Dream* (illustrated with photographs), Agriservices Foundation, 1973; *The Complete Book of Dogs,* A. S. Barnes, 1977; *The Complete Encyclopedia of Horses,* A. S. Barnes, 1977; *Horses and Tack,* Houghton, 1977; *Feeds and Nutrition,* privately published, 1978. Also author of *Food and Animals: A Global Perspective,* 1977.

Author of bulletins. Author of "The Stockman's Guide," a monthly syndicated column in magazines in the United States and Canada, 1956—, and "Horses, Horses, Horses!," 1962—. Contributor of more than five-hundred articles to scientific and popular magazines. Editor of *Horse Science Handbook, Beef Cattle Science Handbook, Dairy Science Handbook, Sheep and Goat Handbook,* and *Stud Managers Handbook,* annual publications of Agriservices Foundation, 1964—.

* * *

ERDMAN, David V(orse) 1911-

PERSONAL: Born November 4, 1911, in Omaha, Neb.; son of Carl Morris and Myrtle (Vorse) Erdman; married Virginia Bohan, 1937; children: Heidi, Wendy. *Education:* Carleton College, B.A., 1933; Princeton University, Ph.D., 1936. *Home:* 58 Crane Neck Rd., Setauket, N.Y. 11733. *Office:* Department of English, State University of New York, Stony Brook, N.Y. 11794.

CAREER: Agriculture, Mechanical and Normal College (now University of Arkansas at Monticello), English professor, 1936-37; University of Wisconsin—Madison, English instructor, 1937-41; Olivet College, Olivet, Mich., English instructor, 1941-42; The Citadel, Charleston, S.C., assistant professor, 1942-43; United Auto Workers-Congress of Industrial Organizations (UAW-CIO), Detroit, Mich., editor in education department, 1943-46; University of Minnesota, St. Paul, assistant professor, 1948-54; New York Public Library, New York, N.Y., editor of publications, 1956-68, part-time editor, 1968—; State University of New York at Stony Brook, professor, 1968—. Visiting professor, Duke University, 1952-53; adjunct professor, Temple University, 1964; instructor, University of Massachusetts summer school in Bologna, 1966; John Cranford Adams Chair, Hofstra University, 1966-67. *Member:* Modern Language Association of America, Keats-Shelley Association, Shaw Society, English Institute (chairman, 1960). *Awards, honors:* Guggenheim fellow, 1947, 1954; Emily S. Hamblen Memorial Award for best work on William Blake, 1955, for *Blake: Prophet against Empire;* awarded Committee on Scholarly Editions emblem, 1980, for *The Complete Poetry and Prose of William Blake.*

WRITINGS: Blake: Prophet against Empire, Princeton University Press, 1954, 3rd edition, 1977; (editor) *The Poetry and Prose of William Blake,* Doubleday, 1965, revised edition published as *The Complete Poetry and Prose of William Blake,* 1980; (editor with Ephim Fogel, and contributor) *Evidence for Authorship: Essays in Attribution,* Cornell University Press, 1966; (principal editor) *A Concordance to the Poetry and Prose of William Blake,* Cornell University Press, 1968; (editor with Donald K. Moore) *The Notebook of William Blake,* Oxford University Press, 1973, revised edition, Readex Books, 1977; (editor) S. T. Coleridge, *Essays on His Times,* three volumes, Princeton University Press, 1978. Editor of Byron papers, *Shelley and His Circle,* Harvard University Press, Volumes III-IV, 1970, Volumes V-VI, 1973. Also contributor of over sixty articles to professional journals. Critic-reviewer of Byron and Blake studies, 1947—, and Coleridge studies, 1958—, for *Annual Bibliography of the Romantic Movement.* Editor, *Bulletin* of the New York Public Library, 1956-77, and *Bulletin* of Research in the Humanities, 1978—; guest editor, *Keats-Shelley Journal,* 1966.

WORK IN PROGRESS: The Passionate Wordsworth; co-editing, *The Political Coleridge;* coordinating editor, *Blake's Designs for Young's Night Thoughts,* for Oxford University Press.

* * *

ETULAIN, Richard W(ayne) 1938-

PERSONAL: Surname is pronounced *Ed*-a-lane; born August 26, 1938, in Wapato, Wash.; son of Sebastian (a rancher and businessman) and Mary (Gillard) Etulain; married Joyce Oldenkamp (a librarian), August 18, 1961; children: Jacqueline Joyce. *Education:* Northwest Nazarene College, B.A. (history) and B.A. (English), 1960; University of Oregon, M.A., 1962, Ph.D., 1966; post-doctoral study at Dartmouth College, 1969-70, and University of Nevada, 1973-74. *Politics:* Independent. *Religion:* Church of the Nazarene. *Home:* 322 Wellesley Pl. N.E., Albuquerque, N.M. 87106. *Office:* Department of History, University of New Mexico, Albuquerque, N.M. 87131.

CAREER: High school teacher in Lowell, Ore., 1961-62, and Eugene, Ore., 1962-64; Lane Community College, Eugene, part-time instructor in history, 1965-66; Northwest Nazarene

College, Nampa, Idaho, assistant professor of American studies, 1966-68; Idaho State University, Pocatello, associate professor, 1970-76, professor of history, 1976-79, chairman of department, 1972-74; University of New Mexico, Albuquerque, professor of history, 1979—. Member of European seminar at Gordon College, summer, 1969; visiting associate professor, Eastern Nazarene College, 1968-69, and University of Oregon, summer, 1973; visiting professor, University of California, Los Angeles, winter, 1978, and University of Oregon, spring, 1978. American Specialist Lecturer, U.S. Information Agency, 1977; lecturer in American western literature and culture, Falkenstein seminar, 1978.

MEMBER: Organization of American Historians, Faith and History, Popular Culture Association, Western Literature Association (member of executive council, 1965-68, 1975-78; president, 1978-79), Western History Association, Association for the Humanities in Idaho. *Awards, honors:* National Historical Publications Commission fellowship, 1969-70; National Endowment for the Humanities fellowship, 1973-74; Huntington Library fellow, summer, 1974; American Philosophical Society research grant, 1976-77; Louis Knott Koontz Award, 1976, for best article appearing in *Pacific Historical Review;* award for best journal article on western history, Western History Association, 1976.

WRITINGS: Western American Literature: A Bibliography of Interpretive Books and Articles, University of South Dakota Press, 1972, 2nd edition, University of Nebraska Press, in press; (editor with others) *Interpretive Approaches to Western American Literature,* Idaho State University Press, 1972; *Owen Wister,* Boise State College, 1973; (editor with Bert W. Marley) *The Idaho Heritage: A Collection of Historical Essays,* Idaho State University Press, 1974; (editor with Michael Marsden) *The Popular Western: Essays Toward a Definition,* Popular Culture Press, 1974; (editor with Merwin R. Swanson) *Idaho History: A Bibliography,* Idaho State University Press, 1974, 2nd edition, 1979; (editor) *The American West: The Frontier Era,* Everett/Edwards, 1976; (editor with Rodman W. Paul) *The Frontier and the American West,* AHM Publishing, 1977; (editor with W. A. Douglass and W. Jacobson) *Anglo-American Contributions to Basque Studies,* Desert Research Institute, 1977; (editor) *The New Frontier: The Twentieth Century West,* Everett/Edwards, 1979; (editor) *Jack London on the Road: The Tramp Diary and Other Hobo Writings,* Utah State University Press, 1979; (editor) *The Basques* (bibliography), Gale, in press.

Contributor of nearly two hundred articles and reviews to scholarly journals. Editor, with Marsden, of "Popular Western Writers" series (monographs), Bowling Green University Popular Press, 1977—; editor, *The American Literary West,* special issue of *Journal of the West,* Sunflower University Press, 1980, and *Cultural History of the American West,* special issue of *Journal of American Culture,* Bowling Green University Popular Press, 1980. Editor, *New Mexico Historical Review,* 1979—; member of editorial board, *Rendezvous,* 1976-79, *Pacific Historical Review,* 1976-79, *Idaho Yesterdays,* 1976—, *Journal of the West,* 1978—, *Western Historical Quarterly,* 1978—, and *Great Plains Quarterly,* 1979—.

WORK IN PROGRESS: Two monographs, *Ernest Haycox and the Western* and *The Closing Frontier: The West in American Thought, 1890-1930; A Guide to Western American Literature; The Western: A Reference Guide;* editing *The Rise of the Western* with Marsden, *Fifty Western Writers,* with Fred Erisman, and *The Basques of the Pacific Northwest: A Collection of Essays.*

* * *

EVANS, Max 1925-

PERSONAL: Born August 29, 1925, on Texas-New Mexico border; son of W. B. and Hazel (Swafford) Evans; married Pat James, August 4, 1949; children: Charlotte and Sheryl (twins). *Education:* Studied art privately. *Residence:* Taos, N.M. *Agent:* Russell & Volkening, Inc., 551 Fifth Ave., New York, N.Y. 10017.

CAREER: Began work on a cattle ranch at the age of twelve; has worked as cowboy, ranch owner, trapper, prospector, and mining promoter; currently writer and artist. *Awards, honors:* Commendation from City of Los Angeles; named honorary member of board of chancellors of University of Texas.

WRITINGS: Southwest Wind (short stories), Naylor, 1958; *Long John Dunn of Taos* (biography), Westernlore, 1959; *The Rounders,* Macmillan, 1960; *The Hi Lo Country,* Macmillan, 1961; *Three Short Novels: The Great Wedding, The One-eyed Sky, My Pardner,* Houghton, 1963; *Mountain of Gold,* Berg, 1965; *Shadow of Thunder,* Swallow Press, 1967; *Sam Peckinpah: Master of Violence,* Dakota Press, 1972; *Bobby Jack Smith: You Dirty Coward,* Nash Publishing, 1974; *The White Shadow,* Joyce Press, 1977. Contributor of over sixty articles to periodicals, including *Field and Stream, Empire,* and *Contact.*

WORK IN PROGRESS: Silver City Millie, a biography of the famous madame.

SIDELIGHTS: The Rounders was filmed by M.G.M. and starred Henry Fonda and Glen Ford; the book was also adapted for a television series by A.B.C. in 1966. *The Hi Lo Country* and *Mountain of Gold* were also sold to motion picture companies.

* * *

EVERSLEY, D(avid) E(dward) C(harles) 1921- (William Small)

PERSONAL: Name legally changed; born November 22, 1921, in Frankfurt, Germany; son of Otto Robert and Adele (Morel) Eberstadt; married Edith E. Wembridge, 1945 (died, 1978); children: Patricia, Judith, Ruth, John. *Education:* London School of Economics and Political Science, B.Sc., 1949; University of Birmingham, Ph.D., 1960. *Politics:* Socialist. *Religion:* Quaker. *Home:* Hummerstons, Cottered, Buntingford, Hertfordshire SG9 9QP, England. *Office:* Policy Studies Institute, 1-2 Castle Lane, London SW1E 6DR, England.

CAREER: University of Birmingham, Birmingham, England, 1949-65, began as assistant lecturer, became reader in social history, director of West Midlands Social and Political Research Unit, 1963-65; University of Sussex, Sussex, England, 1966-71, began as reader, became professor of population and regional studies and director of Social Research Unit; Greater London Council, London, England, chief planner, 1969-72; senior research worker, Centre for Environmental Studies, 1972-76; senior research fellow, Centre for Studies in Social Policy, 1976-78; Policy Studies Institute, London, senior research fellow, 1978—. Visiting professor of demography, University of California, Berkeley, 1965; visiting professor, Bartlett School of Architecture and Planning, 1976—. Member of West Midlands Regional Economic Planning Council, 1965-66. *Military service:* British Army, 1940-45. *Member:* Royal Town Planning Institute (honorary member).

WRITINGS: *Rents and Social Policy,* Fabian Society, 1955; *Social Theories of Fertility and the Malthusian Debate,* Oxford University Press, 1959, reprinted, Greenwood Press, 1976; (editor with D. V. Glass) *Population in History,* Edward Arnold, 1965; (editor) Creighton, *History of Epidemics,* new edition, with introductory essays, Cass & Co., 1965; (with V. J. Jackson and G. M. Lomas) *Population Growth and Planning Policy,* Cass & Co., 1965; (with others) *English Historical Demography,* Weidenfeld & Nicolson, 1966; (with F. Sukdeo) *The Dependents of the Coloured Commonwealth Population of England and Wales,* Institute of Race Relations (London), 1969; (editor) *Demography and Economy,* [Paris], 1972; *The Planner in Society,* Faber, 1973; (editor with D. V. Donnison) *London: Urban Patterns, Problems, and Policies,* Heinemann, 1973; *Question of Numbers,* Runnymede Trust, 1973; *Planning without Growth,* Fabian Society, 1975; (editor with J. Platts) *Public Spending and Private Lives,* [London], 1976; (editor with Alan Evans) *The Inner City: Employment and Industry,* Heinemann, 1979. Contributor of articles and reviews to professional journals.

AVOCATIONAL INTERESTS: Hill-walking.

F

FABRE, Michel J(acques) 1933-

PERSONAL: Born October 31, 1933, in Le Puy, France; son of Jean and Marcelle (Mazoyer) Fabre; married Genevieve Moreau (a university professor), July 13, 1960; children: Pierre, Jean-Marc. *Education:* University of London, diploma of international phonetics, 1958; Universite de Paris and Ecole Normale Superieure, licence d'anglais, 1955, D.E.S. d'anglais, 1956, agregation d'anglais, 1959, doctorat d'etudes americaines, 1970, diplome d'etudes approfondies d'anthropologie, 1976. *Home:* 12 Square Montsouris, 75014 Paris, France. *Agent:* Ellen Wright, 20 rue Jacob, 75006 Paris, France. *Office:* UER d'Anglais, 5 rue Ecole de Medecine, 75006 Paris, France.

CAREER: Wellesley College, Wellesley, Mass., instructor in French, 1962-63; Harvard University, Cambridge, Mass., instructor in French, 1963-64; University of Paris (X), Nanterre, France, assistant professor of English, 1964-69; University of Paris (VIII), Vincennes, France, associate professor of American studies, 1969-70; Universite de la Sorbonne Nouvelle of University of Paris (III), Paris, France, professor of American and Afro-American studies, 1970—, director of Afro-American studies and Third World literatures program, 1973—. Adviser to Center for Southern Culture, University of Mississippi, 1979—. *Military service:* French Navy, 1959-62; interpreter and cipher officer; became lieutenant. *Member:* French Association of American Studies (A.F.E.A.; secretary, 1969-75), French Association of English Studies, Association des Ecrivains de Langue Francaise, Association des Gens de Lettres, Societe d'Etude des Pays du Commonwealth. *Awards, honors:* Anisfield-Wolf Award in Race Relations, 1973.

WRITINGS: *Les Noirs Americains,* A. Colin, 1967; *The British Isles* (geography text), Europe Editions, 1968; (with wife, Genevieve Fabre, and Andre Le Vot) Bernard Poli, editor, *Francis Scott Fitzgerald,* A. Colin, 1969; *Esclaves et planteurs dans le Sud Americain au XIX siecle,* Julliard, 1970; (with Paul Orean) *Harlem, ville noire,* A. Colin, 1971; (with others) *Guide de l'etudiant d'anglais,* Presses Universitaires de France, 1971; (author of introduction and notes) Richard Wright, *L'Homme qui vivait sous terre* (bilingual edition), Aubier, 1971; *The Unfinished Quest of Richard Wright,* Morrow, 1973; (editor with Ellen Wright) *Richard Wright Reader,* Harper, 1978; (with G. Fabre, William French, and Ameritjit Singh) *Afro-American Poetry and Drama,* Gale, 1979. Contributor of reviews to *Le Monde, La Nouvelle Critique, Etudes Anglaises, Presence Africaine,* and professional journals. Contributing editor of *New Letters,* 1972-75, *World Literature Written in English,* 1978—, *Melus,* 1978—, and *French-American Review,* 1979—.

WORK IN PROGRESS: Co-editing Wright correspondence, with Edward Margolies, for Harper; an international Richard Wright bibliography; a bibliography of Wright primary sources, for G. K. Hall; research on the relationship between Afro-American writers and France and French-speaking Black writers in the twentieth century; a collection of essays on Richard Wright, a collection on Ernest Gaines, and a collection on Erskine Caldwell for University of Mississippi Press.

SIDELIGHTS: In addition to English and French, Michel J. Fabre speaks Spanish, German, and Portuguese. He has travelled throughout Europe, North Africa, and the Caribbean. Fabre told *CA* that his interest in Wright and Afro-American writers made him "discover cultural relativity and new possibilities in cultural pluralism and world civilization."

* * *

FARR, Finis (King) 1904-

PERSONAL: Born December 31, 1904, in Lebanon, Tenn.; son of Finis King and Ethel (Riley) Farr. *Education:* Princeton University, A.B. (cum laude), 1926. *Home address:* Box 4352, Station A, Portland, Maine 04101. *Agent:* International Creative Management, 40 West 57th St., New York, N.Y. 10019.

CAREER: Free-lance writer. *Military service:* U.S. Army, Infantry, 1942-46; served in China-Burma-India Theater; became major; received Bronze Star.

WRITINGS: *Frank Lloyd Wright: A Biography* (British Book Society selection), Scribner, 1961; *Black Champion: The Life and Times of Jack Johnson* (American Heritage Book Club selection), Scribner, 1964; *Margaret Mitchell of Atlanta: The Author of "Gone with the Wind,"* Morrow, 1965; *The Elephant Valley* (novel), Arlington House, 1966; *FDR: A Political Biography,* Arlington House, 1969; *Chicago: A Personal History,* Arlington House, 1970; *O'Hara* (biography), Little, Brown, 1973; *Fair Enough: The Life of Westbrook Pegler,* Arlington House, 1975; *Rickenbacker's Luck: An American Life* (biography), Houghton, 1979.

WORK IN PROGRESS: A social history of the 1930s.

SIDELIGHTS: Frank Lloyd Wright: A Biography was selected by the English-Speaking Union for distribution abroad and was placed in the White House Library by Booksellers of America. Farr's books have been translated throughout the world.

BIOGRAPHICAL/CRITICAL SOURCES: New York Times Book Review, June 3, 1979; *Chicago Tribune Book World*, June 10, 1979; *New York Times*, August 21, 1979.

* * *

FAST, Howard (Melvin) 1914-
(E. V. Cunningham, Walter Ericson)

PERSONAL: Born November 11, 1914, in New York, N.Y.; son of Barney (a designer) and Ida (Miller) Fast; married Bette Cohen (an artist), June 6, 1937; children: Rachel, Jonathan. *Education:* Attended National Academy of Design. *Religion:* Jewish. *Agent:* Sterling Lord Agency, 660 Madison Ave., New York, N.Y. 10021.

CAREER: Worked at several odd jobs and as a page in the New York Public Library prior to 1932; full-time writer, 1932—. Member of overseas staff, U.S. Office of War Information, 1942-44; correspondent with special Signal Corps unit and war correspondent in China-India-Burma Theater, 1944-45; foreign correspondent, *Esquire* and *Coronet*, 1945. Member of World Peace Council, 1950-55; American Labor Party candidate for U.S. Congress, 23rd New York District, 1952. Lecturer; has appeared on radio and television programs. *Awards, honors:* Breadloaf Literary Award, 1937; Schomburg Award for Race Relations, 1944; Newspaper Guild award, 1947; Jewish Book Council of America annual award, 1947; Stalin International Peace Prize of the U.S.S.R., 1954; Screen-writers annual award, 1960; Secondary Education Board annual book award, 1962; American Library Association Notable Book Award, 1972, for *The Hessian*.

WRITINGS: Two Valleys, Dial, 1933; *Strange Yesterday*, Dodd, 1934; *Place in the City*, Harcourt, 1937; *Conceived in Liberty: A Novel of Valley Forge*, Simon & Schuster, 1939; *Last Frontier*, Duell, Sloan & Pearce, 1941; *The Romance of a People*, Hebrew Publishing, 1941; *Lord Baden-Powell of the Boy Scouts*, Messner, 1941; *Haym Salomon, Son of Liberty*, Messner, 1941; *The Unvanquished*, Duell, Sloan & Pearce, 1942; *The Tall Hunter*, Harper, 1942; (with wife, Bette Fast) *The Picture-Book History of the Jews*, Hebrew Publishing, 1942; *Goethals and the Panama Canal*, Messner, 1942; *Citizen Tom Paine*, Duell, Sloan & Pearce, 1943; *The Incredible Tito*, Magazine House, 1944; *Freedom Road*, Duell, Sloan & Pearce, 1944; *Patrick Henry and the Frigate's Keel and Other Stories of a Young Nation*, Duell, Sloan, & Pearce, 1945; *The American: A Middle Western Legend* (Literary Guild selection), Duell, Sloan & Pearce, 1946; (with William Gropper), *Never Forget: The Story of the Warsaw Ghetto*, Book League of the Jewish Fraternal Order, 1946; (editor) *The Selected Works of Tom Paine*, Modern Library, 1946; *The Children*, Duell, Sloan & Pearce, 1947; (editor) *Best Short Stories of Theodore Dreiser*, World Publishing, 1947; *Clarkton*, Duell, Sloan & Pearce, 1947; *Tito and His People*, Contemporary Publishers, 1948; *My Glorious Brothers*, Little, Brown, 1948; *Departure and Other Stories*, Little, Brown, 1949.

The Proud and the Free, Little, Brown, 1950; *Literature and Reality*, International Publishers, 1950; *Spartacus*, privately printed, 1951, Citadel, 1952; *Peekskill, U.S.A.: A Personal Experience*, Civil Rights Congress, 1951; *Tony and the Wonderful Door*, Blue Heron, 1952; *The Passion of Sacco and Vanzetti: A New England Legend*, Blue Heron, 1953; *Silas Timberman*, Blue Heron, 1954; *The Last Supper, and Other Stories*, Blue Heron, 1955; *The Story of Lola Gregg*, Blue Heron, 1956; *The Naked God: The Writer and the Communist Party*, Praeger, 1957; *Moses, Prince of Egypt*, Crown, 1958; *The Winston Affair*, Crown, 1959.

The Howard Fast Reader, Crown, 1960; *April Morning*, Crown, 1961; *The Edge of Tomorrow* (stories), Bantam, 1961; *Power*, Doubleday, 1962; *Agrippa's Daughter*, Doubleday, 1964; *Torquemada*, Doubleday, 1966; *The Hunter and the Trap*, Dial, 1967; *The Jews: Story of a People*, Dial, 1968; *The General Zapped an Angel*, Morrow, 1970; *The Crossing* (based on his play of the same title; also see below), Morrow, 1971; *The Hessian* (based on his screenplay of the same title; also see below), Morrow, 1972; *A Touch of Infinity: Thirteen Stories of Fantasy and Science Fiction*, Morrow, 1973; *The Immigrants*, Houghton, 1977; *The Second Generation*, Houghton, 1978; *The Establishment*, Houghton, 1979.

Plays: "The Hammer," first produced in New York, 1950; *Thirty Pieces of Silver* (first produced in Melbourne, 1951), Blue Heron, 1954; *George Washington and the Water Witch*, Bodley Head, 1956; "The Crossing," first produced in Dallas, Tex., 1962; *The Hill* (screenplay), Doubleday, 1964. Author of screenplays, "Spartacus" (based on his novel of the same title), with Dalton Trumbo, 1960, "The Hill" (based on his play of the same title), 1965, and "The Hessian," 1971; also author of television script, "What's a Nice Girl Like You . . . !," based on his novel *Shirley*.

Novels; under pseudonym E. V. Cunningham; published by Doubleday, except as indicated: *Sylvia*, 1960; *Phyllis*, 1962; *Alice*, 1963; *Shirley*, 1963; *Lydia*, 1964; *Penelope*, 1965; *Helen*, 1966; *Margie*, Morrow, 1966; *Sally*, Morrow, 1967; *Samantha*, Morrow, 1967; *Cynthia*, Morrow, 1968; *The Assassin Who Gave Up His Gun*, Morrow, 1969; *Millie*, Morrow, 1973; *The Case of the One-Penny Orange*, Holt, 1977; *The Case of the Russian Diplomat*, Holt, 1978.

Under pseudonym Walter Ericson: *Fallen Angel*, Little, Brown, 1951.

SIDELIGHTS: Although Howard Fast has enjoyed success as a playwright, historian, mystery novelist, and screenwriter, he is best known, and most highly praised, for his historical novels. His first book, *Two Valleys*, published when he was eighteen years old, dealt with life on the American frontier during the days of the Revolutionary War. In 1933, a reviewer for the *Springfield Republican* wrote: "There is plenty of bloodshed and thrilling escapes before the story comes to a satisfactory ending. These scenes are handled with a maturity surprising in one so young." And a *New York Times* critic said that "Mr. Fast is unusually successful in conveying the mood and impression he depicts. He possesses also the knack of creating life-like characters; his leading figures, in their outlines, have reality and act on their own volition, and the minor figures emerge as distinct individualities."

Conceived in Liberty: A Novel of Valley Forge is notable for its stark, realistic portrayal of the downtrodden American army's grim winter at Valley Forge, Pa., as seen through the eyes of a young private. David Tilden called the book, "a picture of one of the Revolutionary episodes less well known to fiction, told with rude vigor and blending with historical veracity. . . ." A *Christian Science Monitor* reviewer noted that "human nature rather than history is Howard Fast's field. In presenting these harassed human beings without any heroics he makes us all the more respectful of the price paid for American liberty." Stephen Vincent Benet criticized Fast's flamboyant style, but he felt that "in spite of its hectic overwriting, *Conceived in Liberty* has points. It is an honest attempt to tell a great story from the reverse of the conventional point of view. . . . And Mr. Fast will bear watching, as soon as he gets the lightning bugs out of his style."

With *Citizen Tom Paine* Fast ventured into the sometimes controversial area of fictional biography. Marion Neville echoed the sentiments of many critics and historians when he wrote that "Paine's *real* biography still remains to be written." But as Neville explained, "The virtues of this fictional life story are its timeliness, its inspirational force, its sincerity and its very great dignity." And, as Rose Feld put it, "Whether this portrait is the whole of Paine is questionable; but, granting Mr. Fast's clearly avowed sympathy with this strange and twisted character, it is both a provocative and impressive one." Elmer Rice was even more impressed with the book; he wrote: "To the ever-increasing number of books that deal with the events and the personages of our own brief American past, Howard Fast has made an interesting and valuable addition. . . . He has succeeded, to a laudable degree, not only in sketching a vivid portrait of one of the most extraordinary figures of the eighteenth century, but in projecting it against the stormy background of the times in which he lived and played a part, whose importance has been far too little recognized."

The most popular of Fast's recent work is probably the trilogy composed of *The Immigrants, The Second Generation,* and *The Establishment.* The first of these novels, *The Immigrants,* has been hailed as the author's finest work and, at the same time, condemned (by *Time* critic, R. Z. Sheppard) as "soap history." Joanne Leedom-Ackerman says that Fast is "a facile writer. He writes in short scenes which rarely run more than half a dozen pages, and out of these hundreds of quick scenes, he compiles his book. His novel is entertainment fiction—not profound or artistically remarkable, but a good easy read." But Donald Newlove calls the book "the opener of a trilogy that is likely to be Fast's big bid for recognition as an artist. He does a lot of things right in this novel." Sheppard, however, maintains that "the author is still a pro at milking emotions out of his characters' complicated personal relationships, and still a hacker when it comes to pumping life into his historical props. An overripe description of the Statue of Liberty, for example, ends with the line, 'Across the water, there was the mass of buildings on the battery, but the lady of liberty was something else.' It is a long way from Emma Lazarus' New York to Fast's Beverly Hills, where descendants of immigrants cater to huddled masses yearning for TV." *The Second Generation* has been received somewhat unenthusiastically by critics. Robert H. Donahugh says that "although there are a few vivid scenes, this book reads like a treatment for a TV miniseries. . . . Strikes, Nazis, wine growing, and banking keep the large and predictable cast of characters occupied." Anthony Salamone found the book a bit more enjoyable, citing its "lucid characterizations" and "enthralling, if somewhat imitative plot." Joseph McLellan finds that *The Establishment* is "the least satisfying" book in the trilogy. He feels that Fast was better in *The Second Generation,* particularly in his description of the San Francisco dock strikes of 1934. McLellan writes: "Here the author is in his element, writing about people and scenes he knows at first hand, and the effect is striking. In contrast, the scene in *The Establishment* where a group of establishmentarians begin grooming a sleazy Republican congressman from California for the 1952 vice-presidential nomination seem lifeless and warmed-over."

Of the more than fifty books written by Howard Fast, the title that is probably most recognizable is *Spartacus,* his fictional account of a slave revolt in ancient Rome. The book's familiarity is unquestionably due to the popular 1960 film, which starred Kirk Douglas and Laurence Olivier; the script was co-authored by Fast and Dalton Trumbo. When the novel was first written, Fast was unable to find a company willing to publish it. Having unsuccessfully approached several commercial houses, he resorted to having the book privately printed in 1951 (the next year it was picked up by the Citadel Press for subsequent printings). *Spartacus* met with lackluster reviews. Although several critics admired Fast's historical sense and his ability as a storyteller, many felt that the book was inferior to some of his earlier work. A *Saturday Review* writer offered a possible explanation for the cool reception, calling *Spartacus* "a good novel which may suffer from the fact that attention to Mr. Fast has shifted from the book page to the front page." In 1950 the author had served a federal prison sentence for withholding information from the House Committee on Un-American Activities concerning the Joint Anti-Fascist Refugee Committee, which was listed as a subversive organization by the attorney general. Fast, who had a long history of association with left-wing political groups, invoked the Fifth Amendment when asked whether he was a member of the Communist Party. There can be little doubt that his political activities adversely affected the critical reception of his work at the time, and even today some reviewers point out socialist leanings in some of his books.

More than ten of Howard Fast's novels and stories have been adapted for production as motion pictures, including "Man in the Middle," based on his novel, *The Winston Affair,* 1964, "Mirage," based on a story he wrote under the pseudonym Walter Ericson, 1965, "Penelope," based on his novel of the same title, 1966, and "Jigsaw," based on his novel, *Fallen Angel,* 1968. "The Immigrants" was broadcast as a television miniseries in 1979.

AVOCATIONAL INTERESTS: "My home, my family, the theater, the film, and the proper study of ancient history. And the follies of mankind."

BIOGRAPHICAL/CRITICAL SOURCES: New York Times, October 15, 1933, June 25, 1939, April 25, 1943, February 3, 1952; *Springfield Republican,* November 5, 1933; *Books,* September 23, 1934, June 25, 1939; *New Yorker,* July 1, 1939, May 1, 1943; *Saturday Review of Literature,* July 1, 1939, May 1, 1943; *Christian Science Monitor,* July 8, 1939, August 23, 1972, November 7, 1977; *Times Literary Supplement,* November 11, 1939; *Weekly Book Review,* April 25, 1943; *Book Week,* May 9, 1943; *Masses and Mainstream,* December, 1950; *Saturday Review,* March 8, 1952; *Catholic World,* September, 1953; Hershel D. Meyer, *History and Conscience: The Case of Howard Fast,* Anvil-Atlas, 1958; *Spectator,* April 3, 1959; *Nation,* May 30, 1959; *New Statesman,* August 8, 1959; *New York Times Book Review,* July 14, 1963, October 2, 1977; *New York Herald Tribune Book Review,* July 21, 1963; Roy Newquist, *Counterpoint,* Rand McNally, 1964; *Atlantic,* June, 1970; *Best Sellers,* February 1, 1971, September 15, 1972, January, 1979; *Choice,* July, 1971; *Time,* November 6, 1977; *Library Journal,* November 15, 1978; *Washington Post,* October 4, 1979.

—Sketch by Peter M. Gareffa

* * *

FAULKNER, John 1901-1963

PERSONAL: Born September 24, 1901, in Ripley, Miss.;

died March 28, 1963; son of Murry Cuthbert and Maud (Butler) Faulkner; married Lucille Ramey, 1922; children: James Murry, Murry Cuthbert II. *Education:* University of Mississippi, B.A., 1929. *Religion:* Episcopalian. *Residence:* Oxford, Miss. *Agent:* Scott Meredith Literary Agency, Inc., 845 Third Ave., New York, N.Y. 10022.

CAREER: Mississippi State Highway Department, project engineer, 1930-36; Mid-South Airways, Memphis, Tenn., pilot, 1936-37; farmer, Lafayette County, Miss., 1937-39; Works Project Administration, Lafayette County, engineer, 1937-39; writer, painter, speaker, 1940-63. *Military service:* Navy, 1942-46; became lieutenant commander. *Member:* Sigma Alpha Epsilon, Quiet Birdmen.

WRITINGS—All published by Gold Medal, except as indicated: *Men Working,* Harcourt, 1941, reprinted, Yoknapatawpha, 1975; *Dollar Cotton,* Harcourt, 1942, reprinted, Bantam, 1966; *Chooky,* Norton, 1948; *Cabin Road,* 1951, reprinted, Louisiana State University Press, 1969; *Uncle Good's Girls,* 1952; *Sin Shouter of Cabin Road,* 1954; *Ain't Gonna Rain No More,* 1957; *Uncle Good's Weekend Party,* 1959; *My Brother Bill: An Affectionate Remembrance,* Trident, 1963; *Just One Answer* (juvenile), Albert Whitman, 1967; *Judge Not* (juvenile), Albert Whitman, 1968. Contributor of stories to *Collier's* and other magazines.

SIDELIGHTS: John Faulkner was the younger brother of the late American novelist William Faulkner. His book, *My Brother Bill,* contains his memories of their childhood together. Some critics complained about the book's sometimes "clumsy" writing and the "gossipy" nature of its anecdotes. The reviewer for the *New York Times Book Review,* however, found the book "essential" for all those interested in William Faulkner and his work because "it provides much material from perhaps the closest source to William Faulkner."

BIOGRAPHICAL/CRITICAL SOURCES: *Time,* September 13, 1963; *Book Week,* September 15, 1963; *New York Times Book Review,* September 15, 1963; *Christian Science Monitor,* September 19, 1963; *Book World,* November 12, 1967; *South Atlantic Quarterly,* summer, 1969.†

* * *

FAYERWEATHER, John 1922-

PERSONAL: Born March 17, 1922, in Pittsfield, Mass.; son of Charles Swinburne and Margaret (Gardiner) Fayerweather; married Ruth Elizabeth Selina, 1947; children: John Charles, James George. *Education:* Princeton University, B.S. in geological engineering, 1943; Harvard University, M.B.A., 1948. *Home:* 64 Ferndale Dr., Hastings-on-Hudson, N.Y. *Office:* Graduate School of Business Administration, New York University, 100 Trinity Place, New York, N.Y.

CAREER: Harvard University, Graduate School of Business Administration, Boston, Mass., 1948-58, began as instructor, became assistant professor; Columbia University, Graduate School of Business, New York City, associate professor, 1958-60; *International Executive,* Hastings-on-Hudson, N.Y., managing editor, 1959—; New York University, Graduate School of Business Administration, New York City, professor, 1962—. Member of foreign commerce committee, U.S. Chamber of Commerce, 1956-62. Chairman of board of advisors for United States, Association Internationale des Etudiants en Sciences Economiques et Commerciales, 1962-63. *Military service:* U.S. Army, 1943-46; became first lieutenant; 1950-51, duty with Department of Defense Munitions Board. *Member:* Association for Education in International Business (president, 1960-61), International Academy of Management (fellow), American Economic Association, Phi Beta Kappa. *Awards, honors:* D.C.S. from Harvard University, 1954.

WRITINGS: *The Executive Overseas,* Syracuse University Press, 1959; *Management of International Operations,* McGraw, 1960; *Facts and Fallacies of International Business,* Holt, 1962; *International Marketing,* Prentice-Hall, 1965, 2nd edition, 1970; *International Business Management,* McGraw, 1969; *Foreign Investment in Canada: Prospects for National Policy,* Sharpe, 1973; (editor) *International Business-Government Affairs: Toward an Era of Accommodation,* Ballinger, 1973; *The Mercantile Bank Affair,* New York University Press, 1974; (with Ashok Kapoor) *Strategy and Negotiation for the International Corporation,* Ballinger, 1976; *International Business Strategy and Administration,* Ballinger, 1978. Contributor to business and educational journals.

AVOCATIONAL INTERESTS: Camping, photography.

* * *

FEHRENBACH, T(heodore) R(eed, Jr.) 1925-

PERSONAL: Born January 12, 1925, in San Benito, Tex.; son of Theodore Reed (a land developer) and Mardel (Wentz) Fehrenbach; married Lillian Breetz, August 22, 1951. *Education:* Princeton University, B.A., 1947. *Agent:* Richard Curtis, 156 East 52nd St., New York, N.Y. 10022.

CAREER: Self-employed as farmer, 1947-50, and insurance agent, 1954-69; president, Royal Poinciana Corp., 1971—. Free-lance writer, 1961—. *Military service:* U.S. Army, Infantry and Engineers, 1943-46, 1951-53; became major. U.S. Army Reserve, Civil Affairs Branch; retired as lieutenant colonel. *Member:* Authors Guild, Science Fiction Writers of America, Sons of the American Revolution, Sons of Republic of Texas, Conopus Club. *Awards, honors:* Freedoms Foundation Award, 1965; citations from Texas House of Representatives, 1969, 1973; distinguished service award from Texas State Historical Commission, 1970; citation from Texas legislature, 1977.

WRITINGS: *The Battle of Anzio,* Monarch Books, 1962; *U.S. Marines in Action,* Monarch Books, 1962; *The Crisis in Cuba,* Monarch Books, 1963; *This Kind of War,* Macmillan, 1963; *This Kind of Peace,* McKay, 1966; *The Swiss Banks,* McGraw, 1966; *Crossroads in Korea* (juvenile), Macmillan, 1966; *F.D.R.'s Undeclared War,* McKay, 1967; *Lone Star,* Macmillan, 1968; *Greatness to Spare,* Van Nostrand, 1968; *The U.N. in War and Peace,* Random House, 1968; *The Fight for Korea* (juvenile), Grosset, 1969; *Fire and Blood,* Macmillan, 1973; *Comanches: The Destruction of a People,* Knopf, 1974; *The San Antonio Story,* Continental Heritage, 1978. Contributor of stories and articles to *Argosy, Atlantic, Esquire, Saturday Evening Post,* and other periodicals both in America and Europe. Columnist and editorial writer, North San Antonio *Times.*

WORK IN PROGRESS: *The Anglos,* a novel; *World without End,* fiction; various articles.

SIDELIGHTS: Larry McMurtry writes: "[T. R. Fehrenbach] has mastered an extensive and complex subject" in *Comanches: The Destruction of a People;* "he is flexible, well-organized, and sensitive. Perhaps his most remarkable quality, however, is the balance of feeling that he brings to this story. . . . He describes the clash of two cultures—a clash broad events had rendered inevitable. . . . Fehrenbach's account of it is appropriately grave, but never lachrymose or petty. Indeed, he tells the story so well, as a historian, that he makes us wish the American frontier had had a Homer to tell it as a poet." McMurtry concludes: "Except for an occasional awkwardness of terminology . . . Fehrenbach handles his material admirably. He manages to make the constantly shifting governmental policies clear and his descriptions of battles and leaders are skillful. He tells a tragic story unsentimentally, with clarity and with a fine appreciation of the qualities that animated both peoples, victors and vanquished."

BIOGRAPHICAL/CRITICAL SOURCES: Virginia Quarterly Review, summer, 1969; *Washington Post,* December 9, 1974.

* * *

FEIRSTEIN, Frederick 1940-

PERSONAL: Born January 2, 1940, in New York, N.Y.; son of Arnold and Nettie (Schechter) Feirstein; married Linda Bergton (a psychotherapist), June 9, 1963; children: David Ben. *Education:* New York University, student, 1956-58, M.A., 1962; University of Buffalo, B.A., 1960; studied psychotherapy, National Psychological Association for Psychoanalysis, 1972-79. *Religion:* Jewish. *Home:* 355 East 86th St., New York, N.Y. 10028.

CAREER: Poet and dramatist. University of Wisconsin—Milwaukee, instructor in English, 1963-65; Temple University, Philadelphia, Pa., assistant professor of English, 1965-70; psychotherapist, Theodor Reik Consultation Center, 1975—. Private practice of psychotherapy, 1975—. Lecturer in theatre at New York University and New School for Social Research. *Member:* P.E.N., Poetry Society of America, Writers Guild, Dramatists Guild. *Awards, honors:* Second place, Audrey Wood Playwriting Award, for "Masquerade"; Guggenheim fellowship in poetry; Creative Artists Public Service Program award in poetry; John Masefield Prize, Poetry Society of America; Big Apple Poetry Contest award; Office for Advanced Drama research award in playwriting; *Survivors* was cited as an outstanding book of 1975-76 by the editors of *Choice.*

WRITINGS: "Simon" (play), produced at Chelsea Theater Center, 1966; "Harold" and "Sondra" (plays), produced at Provincetown Playhouse, 1967; "John Wayne Doesn't Hit Women" (play), produced in New York, N.Y., by New York Theater Ensemble, 1972; *The Family Circle,* Davis-Poynter, 1973; "Masquerade" (play), produced in Washington, D.C., by A.S.T.A., 1974; *Survivors* (poems), David Lewis, 1975; "The Children's Revolt" (play), produced in Milwaukee, Wis., by Theater X, 1976. Contributor of poems to *Quarterly Review of Literature, Shenandoah,* and other journals.

WORK IN PROGRESS: A book of poems; two plays.

SIDELIGHTS: Frederick Feirstein writes: "I'm interested in seeing that the current anti-intellectualism which, for instance, calls formal work bad names . . . ends. It's a tyranny as strangling as the one it rebelled against. The similarities between the revolutionary and the establishment he's overthrown are an important theme in my work."

* * *

FELDMAN, Irving (Mordecai) 1928-

PERSONAL: Born September 22, 1928, in Brooklyn, N.Y.; son of William and Anna (Goldberg) Feldman; married Carmen Alvarez, 1955; children: Fernando. *Education:* City College of New York (now City College of the City University of New York), B.S.S., 1950; Columbia University, M.A., 1953. *Office:* Department of English, State University of New York College, Buffalo, N.Y. 14260.

CAREER: University of Puerto Rico, Rio Piedras, teacher, 1954-56; Universite de Lyon, France, teacher, 1957-58; Kenyon College, Gambier, Ohio, assistant professor of English, 1958-64; State University of New York College at Buffalo, associate professor of English, 1964—. *Awards, honors:* Harry and Florence Kovner Memorial Award in English poetry, Jewish Book Council of America, 1962, for *Works and Days;* Ingram Merrill Foundation fellowship, 1963; Guggenheim fellowship, 1973; National Institute of Arts and Letters award, 1973.

WRITINGS—All poetry: *Works and Days,* Little, Brown, 1961; *The Pripet Marshes,* Viking, 1965; *Magic Papers,* Harper, 1970; *Lost Originals,* Holt, 1972; *Leaping Clear,* Viking, 1976; *New and Selected Poems,* Viking, 1979. Also author of *Beethoven's Bust,* Bellevue Press. Contributor to *New Yorker, Atlantic Monthly, Harper's Bazaar, Saturday Review, Nation,* and other magazines.

BIOGRAPHICAL/CRITICAL SOURCES: New York Times Book Review, August 15, 1965, November 22, 1970, September 19, 1976, March 9, 1980; *Virginia Quarterly Review,* spring, 1971, summer, 1977; *New York Review of Books,* October 14, 1976; *Contemporary Literary Criticism,* Volume VII, Gale, 1977; *Choice,* March, 1977.

* * *

FELLOWS, Otis (Edward) 1908-

PERSONAL: Born November 6, 1908, in Sprague, Conn.; son of James A. F. (an electrical engineer) and Elizabeth (Merritt) Fellows; married Frances E. Young, June 15, 1935; children: Jay F., Elisabeth M. (Mrs. Moulton Andrus). *Education:* Attended Amherst College, 1926-27; American University, A.B., 1930; University of Dijon, diplome superieur, 1930; Brown University, M.A., 1933, Ph.D., 1936. *Home:* 106 Morningside Dr., New York, N.Y. 10027. *Office:* Graduate School, Columbia University, New York, N.Y. 10027.

CAREER: Ecole Normale d'Instituteurs, Savenay, France, teacher of English, 1930-31; St. Dunstan's Choir School, Providence, R.I., instructor in French, 1931-32; Brown University, Providence, instructor in French, 1935-39; Columbia University, New York, N.Y., instructor, 1939-43, assistant professor, 1946-50, associate professor, 1950-58, professor of French literature, 1958-70, Avalon Foundation Professor of Humanities, 1970-76, professor emeritus, 1976—, chairman of department of Italian, 1963-66. Visiting professor, University of Pennsylvania, 1964 and 1969. Propaganda intelligence officer in Europe, U.S. Office of War Information, 1943-45; trustee, Horace Mann School, 1956-57. *Member:* Association Internationale des Etudes Francaises, Modern Language Association of America, American Association of University Professors, American Association of Teachers of French, Norwich Society of New York. *Awards, honors:* Medaille de la Quinzaine Anglo-Americaine, French Ministry of Education, 1944; American Philosophical Association research grants, 1955, 1957; Chevalier des Palmes Academiques (France), 1959; Guggenheim fellowship, 1959-60; Officier de l'Academie (France), 1965; Distinguished Alumni Award, American University, 1968.

WRITINGS: French Opinion of Moliere, Brown University Press, 1937; (with N. L. Torrey) *The Age of Enlightenment,* Crofts, 1942, 2nd edition, Appleton, 1971; *The Periodical Press in Liberated Paris,* Syracuse University Press, 1948; (editor) Simenon, *Tournants dangereux,* Appleton, 1953; *Look and Learn Italian,* Dell, 1966; *From Voltaire to "La*

Nouvelle Critique," Droz, 1970; (with S. Milliken) *Buffon,* Twayne, 1972; *Diderot,* Twayne, 1977. Founder of *Diderot Studies,* Volumes I and II, Syracuse University Press, 1949-52, Volumes III-XIX, Droz, 1961-78. Contributor to *Encyclopedia Americana* and *Encyclopedia of Philosophy;* contributor to periodicals including *Saturday Review* and *New Leader,* and to professional journals.

WORK IN PROGRESS: Alain-Rene LeSage, with Pamela Bevier.

SIDELIGHTS: Essays on Diderot and the Enlightenment in Honor of Otis Fellows, edited by John Pappas, was published by Droz in 1974.

* * *

FELSEN, Henry Gregor 1916-
(Henry Vicar, Angus Vicker)

PERSONAL: Born August 16, 1916, in Brooklyn, N.Y.; son of Harry and Sabina (Bedrick) Felsen; married Isabel Marie Vincent, 1937; children: Daniel, Holly. *Education:* Attended University of Iowa, two years.

CAREER: Free-lance writer. Des Moines Warriors Professional Football Club, Des Moines, Iowa, secretary; president, Future Professional Drivers Association, Inc. *Military service:* U.S. Marines, two and a half years; became sergeant.

WRITINGS—Published by Dutton, except as indicated: *Jungle Highway,* 1942; *Navy Diver,* 1942; *Submarine Sailor,* 1942; *Struggle Is Our Brother,* 1942; *He's in Submarines Now,* McBride, 1942; *He's in the Coast Guard Now,* McBride, 1942; (under pseudonym Henry Vicar) *The Company Owns the Tools,* Westminster, 1942; *Pilots All,* Harper, 1943; *Some Follow the Sea,* 1944; *Bertie Comes Through,* 1947; *Flying Correspondent,* 1947; *Bertie Takes Care,* 1948; *Bertie Makes a Break,* 1949.

Davey Logan, Intern, Dutton, 1950; *Hot Rod,* Dutton, 1950, reprinted, AMSCO School Publications, 1970; *Two and the Town,* Scribner, 1952; *Cub Scout at Last!,* Scribner, 1952; *Street Rod,* Random House, 1953; *Doctor, It Tickles!,* Prentice-Hall, 1953; *Anyone for Cub Scouts?,* Scribner, 1954; *The Cup of Fury,* Random House, 1954; (under pseudonym Angus Vicker) *Fever Heat,* Dell, 1954; *The Boy Who Discovered the Earth,* Scribner, 1955; *Crash Club,* Random House, 1958.

Boy Gets Car, Random House, 1960, published as *Road Rocket,* Bantam, 1963; *Letters to a Teen-Age Son,* Dodd, 1962; *To My Son, the Teen-Age Driver,* Dodd, 1964; *Here Is Your Hobby: Car Customizing,* Putnam, 1965; *A Teen-Ager's First Car,* Dodd, 1966; *Why Rustlers Never Win,* Scholastic Book Services, 1966; *To My Son in Uniform,* Dodd, 1967; *Living with Your First Motorcycle,* Putnam, 1976; *Can You Do It Until You Need Glasses?: A Different Drug Book,* Dodd, 1977. Also author of *Handbook for Teen-Age Drivers,* Benjamin Co.

WORK IN PROGRESS: A television show and feature film.

SIDELIGHTS: Henry Felsen's book *Fever Heat* was filmed by Paramount in 1968.†

* * *

FELTON, Harold William 1902-

PERSONAL: Born April 1, 1902, in Neola, Iowa; son of William Dennison and Vernie (Rishton) Felton; married Hildegarde Kessler, 1933. *Education:* University of Nebraska, A.B., 1925, LL.B., 1928. *Residence:* Falls Village, Conn.

CAREER: Lawyer in Omaha, Neb., 1928-33; U.S. Government, Internal Revenue Service, New York, N.Y., lawyer, 1933-70. *Member:* Federal Bar Association, American Folklore Society, Western Folklore Society, Nebraska Bar Association, New York Folklore Society, Alpha Sigma Phi.

WRITINGS—Published by Dodd, except as indicated: *Legends of Paul Bunyan,* Knopf, 1948; *Adventures of Pecos Bill,* Knopf, 1949; *John Henry and His Hammer,* Knopf, 1950; *Cowboy Jamboree,* Knopf, 1950; *Fire-Fightin' Mose,* Knopf, 1955; *Bowleg Bill,* Prentice-Hall, 1957; *New Tall Tales of Pecos Bill, Texas Cowpuncher,* Prentice-Hall, 1958; *Mike Fink,* 1960; *The World's Most Truthful Man,* 1961; *A Horse Named Justin Morgan,* 1962; *Sergeant O'Keefe and His Mule, Balaam,* 1962; *True Tall Tales of Stormalong,* Prentice-Hall, 1964; *Pecos Bill and the Mustang,* Prentice-Hall, 1965; *William Phips and the Treasure Ship,* 1965; *James P. Beckwourth, Negro Mountain Man,* 1966; *Edward Rose: Negro Trail Blazer,* 1967; *Nat Love: Negro Cowboy,* 1969; *Big Mose: Hero Fireman,* Garrard, 1969; *Mum Bet; The Story of Elizabeth Freeman,* 1970; *James Weldon Johnson,* 1971; *Gib Morgan: Oil Driller,* 1972; *Ely S. Parker: Spokesman for the Senecas,* 1973; *Nancy Ward: Cherokee,* 1975; *Deborah Sampson: Soldier of the Revolution,* 1976; *Uriah Phillips Levy,* 1978. Contributor to *Dictionary of American Negro Biography.* Contributor to *Morgan Horse* magazine and professional journals.

* * *

FENN, Dan H(untington), Jr. 1923-

PERSONAL: Born March 27, 1923, in Boston, Mass.; son of Dan Huntington and Anna (Yens) Fenn; married Nancy R. Ring, 1946 (divorced, 1965); children: Peter H., Ann H., David E., Thomas O. *Education:* Harvard University, A.B., 1946, M.A., 1972. *Politics:* Democrat. *Home:* 130 Worthen Rd., Lexington, Mass. 02173. *Office:* John F. Kennedy Library, 380 Trapelo Rd., Waltham, Mass. 02154; and Harvard Business School, Soldier's Field, Boston, Mass. 02163.

CAREER: Harvard University, Cambridge, Mass., assistant dean, 1946-49; World Affairs Council, Boston, Mass., executive director, 1949-54; Harvard Business School, Boston, faculty member and editor, *HBS Bulletin,* 1955-61; U.S. Government, Washington, D.C., staff assistant to the President, 1961-63; U.S. Tariff Commission, Washington, D.C., appointed commissioner, 1963, vice-chairman, 1964-67; Harvard Business School, lecturer, 1969—; John F. Kennedy Library, Waltham, Mass., director, 1971—. Advisor, U.S. delegation to GATT, July, 1965. Member of Lexington (Mass.) school committee, 1957-61; alternate delegate-at-large, Democratic national convention, 1960. *Military service:* U.S. Army Air Forces, 1943-45; became warrant officer junior grade. *Member:* Phi Beta Kappa. *Awards, honors:* Decorated by government of Morocco.

WRITINGS—All published by McGraw, except as indicated: (With E. C. Bursk) *Planning the Future Strategy of Your Business,* 1956; *Management Guide to Overseas Operations,* 1957; *Management in a Rapidly Changing Economy,* 1958; *Management's Mission in a New Society,* 1959; *Business Responsibility in Action,* 1960; *Managing America's Economic Explosion,* 1961; (with D. W. Ewing) *Incentives for Executives,* 1962; (with D. Frunewald and R. Katz) *Casebook in Business and Government,* Prentice-Hall, 1966; *Business Decision Making and Government Policy,* Prentice-Hall, 1966; (with R. A. Bauer) *The Corporate Social Audit,* Russell Sage, 1973.

FENNELL, John L(ister) I(llingworth) 1918-

PERSONAL: Born May 30, 1918, in Warrington, Lancashire, England; son of Charles and Sylvia (Mitchell) Fennell; married Marina Lopoukhin, 1947; children: Nicholas, Juliana. *Education:* Attended Radley College; Cambridge University, M.A., 1939, Ph.D., 1950. *Home:* 8 Canterbury Rd., Oxford, England.

CAREER: Cambridge University, Cambridge, England, assistant lecturer in Slavonic studies, 1947-52; University of Nottingham, University Park, England, reader in Russian and head of department of Slavonic languages, 1952-56; Oxford University, Oxford, England, lecturer in Russian, 1956-67, professor of Russian, 1967—, fellow and praelector in Russian, 1964-67. Visiting lecturer, Harvard University, and research associate in Russian Research Center, 1963-64; visiting professor at University of California, Berkeley, 1971, 1977, and University of Virginia, 1974. *Military service:* British Army, 1939-45; became captain.

WRITINGS: (Editor and translator) *Correspondence between Prince A. M. Kurbsky and Tsar Ivan IV of Russia, 1564-1579,* Cambridge University Press, 1955; (compiler) *The Penguin Russian Course,* Penguin, 1961; *Ivan the Great of Moscow,* Macmillan, 1961; (editor) *The Penguin Pushkin,* Penguin, 1964; (editor and translator) A. M. Kurbsky, *History of Ivan IV,* Cambridge University Press, 1965; *The Emergence of Moscow, 1304-1359,* University of California Press, 1968; *Nineteenth-Century Russian Literature,* University of California Press, 1973; *Early Russian Literature,* University of California Press, 1974; (editor with Robert Auty) *Oxford Slavonic Papers,* Oxford University Press, Volume IX, 1977, Volume X, 1977.

* * *

FERAVOLO, Rocco Vincent 1922-

PERSONAL: Born May 12, 1922, in Newark, N.J.; son of Michael R. and Angelina (DiCicco) Feravolor; children: Angela, Michael. *Education:* Attended Seton Hall University, 1941-43, and University of Michigan, 1943-44; Montclair State College, B.A., 1948, M.A., 1950; additional graduate study at Rutgers University. *Residence:* New Hope, Pa. *Office:* Morris School District, Morristown, N.J.

CAREER: Newark State College (now Kean College of New Jersey), Newark, N.J., fencing coach, 1942-43; Morris Plains Burough School, Morris Plains, N.J., teacher, 1948-52; George Washington School, Morristown, N.J., teacher, 1952-53, principal, 1954-68; Lafayette School, Morristown, principal, 1953-54; Morristown Public Schools, Morristown, assistant to superintendent, 1968-72, vice-principal of Morristown High School, 1972—; Morris School District, Morristown, secondary supervisor, 1972—. Fencing coach, Drew University, 1949-68; part-time instructor, Newark State College (now Kean College of New Jersey), 1956-64; instructor, Fairleigh Dickinson University, 1965-66. Educational consultant. *Military service:* U.S. Army, 1943-46; became sergeant.

MEMBER: National Education Association, National Elementary Principals Association, National Association for Supervision and Curriculum Development, Authors Guild, Authors League of America, National Fencing Coaches Association, Amateur Fencing League of America, National Association for the Advancement of Colored People, Aircraft Owners and Pilots Association, New Jersey Education Association, New Jersey Principals Association, New Jersey Science Teachers Association, New Jersey Association for Supervision and Curriculum Development, New Jersey Amateur Fencing League (member of executive council), Morris County Education Association (delegate chairman), Morris County Elementary Principals Association, Morris County Authors Association, Phi Lambda Pi, Kappa Mu Epsilon, Salle D'Armes Santelli (New York). *Awards, honors:* National Science Teachers award, 1956; New Jersey Teachers of English award, 1968, for *Around the World in Ninety Minutes.*

WRITINGS: Junior Science Book of Flying, Garrard, 1960; *Junior Science Book of Electricity,* Garrard, 1960; *Junior Science Book of Magnets,* Garrard, 1961; *Junior Science Book of Light,* Garrard, 1961; *Wonders of Sound,* Dodd, 1962; *Junior Science Book of Weather Experiments,* Garrard, 1963; *Wonders of Mathematics,* Dodd, 1963; *Junior Science Book of Heat,* Garrard, 1964; *Wonders of Gravity,* Dodd, 1965; *Junior Science Book of Water Experiments,* Garrard, 1965; *Third Grade Science Book,* Silver Burdett, 1965; *Easy Physics Projects,* Prentice-Hall, 1966; *Around the World in Ninety Minutes,* Lothrop, 1968; *Wonders beyond the Solar System,* Dodd, 1968; *More Easy Physics Projects,* Prentice-Hall, 1968; (co-author) *Practical Handbook of Professional Improvement Plans for the School Administrator,* F. L. Publications, 1980. Contributor to *New Jersey Education Review, Children's Digest,* and *Effective Reading.*

WORK IN PROGRESS: Where Has All the Fresh Air Gone?; Science Research Laboratory.

SIDELIGHTS: Rocco Feravolo fenced in the Aruba Sports Olympics in South America, 1960, and won a silver medal in sabre competition and a bronze medal in foil. He was a member of the National Interscholastic Fencing Championship Team and the Eastern Intercollegiate Fencing Championship Team. His original manuscripts were selected for inclusion in the deGrummond collection at the Southern Mississippi University library. Feravolo's book, *Wonders of Sound,* has been published in Portuguese and is being used in Brazil as part of a cultural exchange program.

AVOCATIONAL INTERESTS: Fencing (represents Salle D'Armes Santelli in competition), painting, landscape designing, flying (licensed private pilot).

BIOGRAPHICAL/CRITICAL SOURCES: Christian Science Monitor, November 29, 1968.

* * *

FILEP, Robert Thomas 1931-

PERSONAL: Surname sounds like "Philip"; born December 2, 1931, in New Brunswick, N.J.; son of John Michael and Irma (Mathis) Filep; married Marion Tudor Moxley (a college teacher), August 8, 1964; children: Felicia Allison, Ian Robert. *Education:* Rutgers University, B.S., 1953; Columbia University, M.A., 1957; University of Southern California, Ph.D., 1966. *Home:* 3104 Palos Verdes Dr. N., Palos Verdes Estates, Calif. 90274. *Office:* Communications 21 Corp., 1611 South Pacific Coast Hwy., Suite 206, Redondo Beach, Calif. 90277.

CAREER: Junior high school general science teacher in Teaneck, N.J., 1953-56; Rensselaer Polytechnic Institute, Troy, N.Y., assistant director of admissions, 1957-59; Mills College of Education, New York City, director of admissions and financial aid, 1959-61; Columbia University, Center for Programmed Instruction, New York City, secretary of the corporation and director of Information and Training Division, 1961-63; University of Southern California, Los Angeles, associate investigator of Cinema Research, 1963-

65; System Development Corp., Santa Monica, Calif., human factors scientist for Education Systems Project, 1965-67; Institute for Educational Development, El Segundo, Calif., vice-president and director of studies, 1967-72; U.S. Office of Education, Washington, D.C., associate commissioner for educational technology and director of National Center for Educational Technology, 1972-73; University of California, Los Angeles, professor of communications and instructional technology, and director of Learning Systems Center, 1973-79; Communications 21 Corp., Redondo Beach, Calif., president, 1979—. *Military service:* U.S. Air Force, 1953-55; became first lieutenant.

MEMBER: American Psychological Association, American Educational Research Association, National Society for Programmed Instruction (president, 1969), Association for Communications and Educational Technology, American Association for the Advancement of Science, Educational Media Council (president), Phi Delta Kappa. *Awards, honors:* Billings Bronze Award from American Medical Association, 1964, for best scientific exhibit.

WRITINGS: (Editor and contributor) *Prospectives in Programming,* Macmillan, 1963; (contributor) J. Koob, editor, *Catholic Education: Progress and Prospects,* National Catholic Education Association, 1963; (with others) *Biological Sciences: Patterns and Processes,* Holt, 1966; (contributor) Cuadra Carlos, editor, *Annual Review of Information Science and Technology 1967,* Wiley, 1968.

(With Wilbur Schramm) *A Study of the Impact of Research on Utilization of Media for Educational Purposes,* Institute for Educational Development, 1970; (contributor) K. Polcyn, *Satellites, U.S.A.,* Educational Technology Press, 1975; (with R. M. Gagliardi and McConaughy) *A Review of Economic and Technical Aspects of Documents Pertaining to the RCA Alaska Communications Plan,* RCA Communications, Inc., 1975; (contributor) *Public Broadcasting and Education,* Advisory Council of National Organizations, Corporation for Public Broadcasting, 1975; (with D. Wedmeyer) *An Analysis and Annotated Bibliography on Communication Satellites for Social Services: Focus on Users and Evaluation,* Annenberg School of Communications, University of Southern California, 1975; (contributor with S. Hague) M. Tehranian, editor, *Communications Policy for National Development: A Comparative Perspective,* Routledge & Kegan Paul, 1977; (with P. Johansen) *A Synthesis of the Final Reports and Evaluations of the ATS-6 Satellite Experiments in Education, Health, and Telecommunications* (monograph), Agency for International Development, 1977; (editor) *Social Research and Broadcasting,* Annenberg School of Communications, University of Southern California, 1977; (with Johansen) *Satellites and Public Service: An Annotated Bibliography and Analysis,* Systems 2000, 1978; (contributor) *A Critical Review of the State of Foreign Space Technology,* American Institute of Aeronautics and Astronautics, 1978; (contributor with R. Harvey) L. Grayson, editor, *Educational Applications of Communications Satellites,* IEEE Service Center, 1978.

Also author of papers presented to professional organizations. Contributor to proceedings and to *Teachers Encyclopedia.* Contributor to *New York Post* and education and programmed learning journals. Contributing editor of *AV Communications Review* and *Educational Technology,* 1968—.

* * *

FINE, Sidney 1920-

PERSONAL: Born October 11, 1920, in Cleveland, Ohio; son of Morris Louis (a teacher) and Gussie (Redalia) Fine; married Jean Schechter, December 5, 1942; children: Gail Judith, Deborah Ann. *Education:* Western Reserve University (now Case Western Reserve University), B.A. (summa cum laude), 1942; University of Michigan, M.A., 1944, Ph.D., 1948. *Religion:* Jewish. *Home:* 825 Russett Rd., Ann Arbor, Mich. 48103. *Office:* Department of History, University of Michigan, Ann Arbor, Mich. 48109.

CAREER: University of Michigan, Ann Arbor, instructor, 1948-51, assistant professor, 1951-55, associate professor, 1955-59, professor of history, 1959-74, Andrew Dickson White Professor of History, 1974—. Member of faculty, Salzburg Seminar in American Studies, Austria, 1959. *Military service:* U.S. Naval Reserve, 1942-46, became lieutenant junior grade. *Member:* American Historical Association, Organization of American Historians, Labor Historians (president, 1969-71), American Association of University Professors, University of Michigan Scientific Club, University of Michigan Research Club, Phi Beta Kappa, Phi Kappa Phi. *Awards, honors:* Rackham predoctoral fellow; Guggenheim fellow, University of Michigan Press book awards, 1964, for *The Automobile under the Blue Eagle,* and 1971, for *Sit-Down;* Distinguished Faculty Achievement Award, University of Michigan, 1969; Association of State and Local History award of merit; Historical Society of Michigan award of merit.

WRITINGS: Laissez Faire and the General-Welfare State, University of Michigan Press, 1956; (with Gerald Brown) *The American Past,* two volumes, Macmillan, 1961; *Recent America,* Macmillan, 1962, 2nd edition, 1967; *The Automobile under the Blue Eagle,* University of Michigan Press, 1963; *Sit-Down,* University of Michigan Press, 1969; *Frank Murphy: The Detroit Years,* University of Michigan Press, 1975; *Frank Murphy: The New Deal Years,* University of Chicago Press, 1979. Contributor to professional journals.

WORK IN PROGRESS: Frank Murphy: The Washington Years.

AVOCATIONAL INTERESTS: Opera, sports.

* * *

FINEGAN, Jack 1908-

PERSONAL: Born July 11, 1908, in Des Moines, Iowa; son of Henry M. and Clarissa (Chesnut) Finegan; married Mildred C. Meader, 1934; children: Jack Richard. *Education:* Drake University, B.A., 1928, M.A., 1929, B.D., 1930; Colgate-Rochester Divinity School, B.D., 1931, M.Th., 1932; University of Berlin, Lic. Theol., 1934. *Home:* 1116 Cragmont Ave., Berkeley, Calif. 94708.

CAREER: First Christian Church, Ames, Iowa, minister, 1934-39; Iowa State College of Agriculture and Mechanic Arts (now Iowa State University of Science and Technology), Ames, professor of religious education, 1939-46; Pacific School of Religion, Berkeley, Calif., professor of New Testament, 1946-75; University Christian Church, Berkeley, minister, 1949-74. *Member:* Society of Biblical Literature, Studiorum Novi Testamenti Societas, Phi Beta Kappa. *Awards, honors:* Fulbright research scholar in India, 1952-53; LL.D., Drake University, 1953; Litt.D., Chapman College, 1964.

WRITINGS: Die Ueberlieferung der Leidens-und Auferstehungs geschichte Jesu (Beiheft zur Zeitschrift fuer die neutestamentliche Wissenschaft, 15), Alfred Toepelman, 1934; *Light from the Ancient Past: The Archeological Background of the Hebrew-Christian Religion,* Princeton University

Press, 1946, revised edition, 1959; *Book of Student Prayers,* Association Press, 1946; *A Highway Shall Be There,* Bethany Press, 1946; *Youth Asks about Religion,* Association Press, 1949; *Like the Great Mountains,* Bethany Press, 1949; *The Archeology of World Religions,* Princeton University Press, 1952; *Rediscovering Jesus,* Association Press, 1952; *Clear of the Brooding Cloud,* Abingdon, 1953; *The Orbits of Life,* Bethany Press, 1954; *India Today!,* Bethany Press, 1955; *Beginnings in Theology,* Association Press, 1956; *Wanderer upon Earth,* Harper, 1956; *Christian Theology,* English Universities Press, 1957; *40 Questions and Answers on Religion,* Association Press, 1958; *Space, Atoms and God,* Bethany Press, 1959.

First Steps in Theology, Association Press, 1960; *In the Beginning,* Harper, 1962; *Let My People Go,* Harper, 1963; *At Wit's End,* John Knox, 1963; *The Three R's of Christianity,* John Knox, 1964; *Handbook of Biblical Chronology,* Princeton University Press, 1964; *Jesus, History, and You,* John Knox, 1964; *Hidden Records of the Life of Jesus,* Pilgrim Publications, 1969; *The Archeology of the New Testament,* Princeton University Press, 1969; *Mark of the Taw,* John Knox, 1972; *The Christian Church (Disciples of Christ),* Cathedral, 1973; *Encountering New Testament Manuscripts,* Eerdmans, 1974; *Archaeological History of the Ancient Middle East,* Westview, 1978.

Contributor to encyclopedias and scholarly journals. Former editorial associate, *Pulpit;* archeological editor, *Journal of Bible and Religion.*

WORK IN PROGRESS: Archaeological History of Indian Asia; Introduction to Israel, for Eerdmans; *The Mediterranean World of the Early Christian Apostles,* for Westview.

SIDELIGHTS: Several of Jack Finegan's books have been translated into foreign languages and recorded for the blind. *Avocational interests:* Flying, boating, mountain climbing.

* * *

FINNEY, Ben R(udolph) 1933-

PERSONAL: Born October 1, 1933, in San Diego, Calif.; son of Leon H. (a U.S. Navy career man) and Melba (Trefsger) Finney; married Ruth E. Sutherlin (a professor of human development), August 30, 1964; children: Sean, Gregory. *Education:* University of California, Berkeley, B.A., 1955; University of Hawaii, M.A., 1959; Harvard University, Ph.D., 1964. *Home:* 2467 Aha Aina Pl., Honolulu, Hawaii 96821. *Office:* Department of Anthropology, University of Hawaii, Honolulu, Hawaii 96822.

CAREER: University of California, Santa Barbara, assistant professor of anthropology, 1964-66; B. P. Bishop Museum, Honolulu, Hawaii, anthropologist, 1966; Australian National University, senior fellow in Pacific history, 1968-70; University of Hawaii, Honolulu, professor of anthropology, 1970—. Research associate at East-West Center, 1971-76, and Technology and Development Institute; senior fellow, Woods Hole Oceanographic Institute, 1979; visiting research associate in anthropology, Harvard University, 1979-80. *Military service:* U.S. Naval Reserve, active duty, 1957; became lieutenant junior grade. *Member:* American Association for the Advancement of Science, Australian Association of Social Anthropologists, Societe des Oceanistes, Papua New Guinea Society, Polynesian Voyaging Society (president, 1973—), Sigma Xi. *Awards, honors:* Fulbright research fellowship to Australia and New Guinea, 1967.

WRITINGS: Polynesian Peasants and Proletarians, Polynesian Society of New Zealand, 1965, revised edition, Schenkman, 1973; (with J. D. Houston) *Surfing: Sport of Hawaiian Kings,* Tuttle, 1966; *New Guinea Entrepreneurs,* Australian National University, 1969; (with Frank Margan) *A Pictorial History of Surfing,* Paul Hamlyn, 1970; *Big-Men and Business,* University Press of Hawaii, 1973; (with K. Watson) *A New Kind of Sugar: Tourism in the Pacific,* East-West Center, 1975; *Pacific Navigation and Voyaging* (monograph), Polynesian Society of New Zealand, 1976; *Hokule'a: The Way to Tahiti,* Dodd, 1979.

* * *

FISCHER, Edward (Adam) 1914-

PERSONAL: Born August 17, 1914, in Louisville, Ky.; son of Edward (a farmer) and Louise (Steinmetz) Fischer; married Mary Ewaniec (a television producer), April 10, 1939; children: John, Thomas. *Education:* University of Notre Dame, A.B., 1937, M.A., 1961. *Home:* 1006 St. Vincent, South Bend, Ind. 46617. *Office:* Department of Communication Arts, University of Notre Dame, Notre Dame, Ind. 46556.

CAREER: News Times, South Bend, Ind., reporter, 1936-38; *Herald Examiner,* Chicago, Ill., reporter, 1938-39; St. Joseph's College, Rensselaer, Ind., director of public relations, 1939-42; University of Notre Dame, Notre Dame, Ind., faculty member, 1947—, currently professor of communication arts. *Military service:* U.S. Army, Infantry, 1942-46, 1950-51; became captain. *Awards, honors:* Doctor of Letters (honoris causa), St. Joseph's College.

WRITINGS: The Screen Arts, Sheed, 1960; *Film as Insight,* Fides, 1971; *Why Americans Retire Abroad,* Sheed, 1973; *Light in the Far East,* Seabury, 1976; *Everybody Steals from God,* University of Notre Dame Press, 1977; *Mindanao Mission,* Seabury, 1978; *Mission Accomplished in Burma,* Seabury, 1980. Also author of films, "Shake Down the Thunder," 1953, "Life without Germs," 1956, "War on Gobbledygook," 1964, "Elements of the Film," 1965, "The Nature of the Film," 1965, "Visual Language of Film," 1965, "Film as Arts," 1965, and "Poetry of Polymers," 1967.

WORK IN PROGRESS: Fiji Revisited; Warm for December.

AVOCATIONAL INTERESTS: Horsemanship, painting.

* * *

FISHER, J(ohn) R(obert) 1943-

PERSONAL: Born January 6, 1943, in Barrow-in-Furness, England; son of John Robert (a carpenter) and Eleanor (Parker) Fisher; married Elizabeth Ann Postlethwaite, August 1, 1966; children: David John, Nicholas Stephen, Martin Joseph. *Education:* University College, London, B.A., 1964; University of London, M.Phil., 1967; University of Liverpool, Ph.D., 1973. *Religion:* Roman Catholic. *Home:* 27 Stapleton Ave., Greasby, Wirral, Merseyside L49 2QT, England. *Office:* Department of History, University of Liverpool, Liverpool L69 3BX, England.

CAREER: University of Liverpool, Liverpool, England, lecturer, 1967-75, senior lecturer in Latin American history, 1975—. *Member:* Society for Latin-American Studies (secretary, 1979—), Royal Historical Society (fellow). *Awards, honors:* Honorable mention, Bolton Prize, American Historical Association, 1971, for *Government and Society in Colonial Peru.*

WRITINGS: (Editor) *Arequipa 1796-1811: La relacion del gobierno del intendente Salamanca,* Universidad de San

Marcos, 1968; *Government and Society in Colonial Peru,* Athlone Press, 1970; *Latin America: From Conquest to Independence,* John Day, 1971; (editor) *Social and Economic Change in Modern Peru,* University of Liverpool, 1976; *Silver Mines and Silver Miners in Colonial Peru, 1776-1824,* University of Liverpool, 1977. Contributor to professional journals, including *Hispanic American Historical Review, Anvario de Estudios Americanos, History Today,* and *New Scholar.*

WORK IN PROGRESS: Enlightened Despotism in the Hispanic World: Charles III, 1751-1788.

* * *

FISKE, Marjorie
(Marjorie Fiske Lowenthal)

PERSONAL: Born in Attleboro, Mass.; daughter of Harold M. (a YMCA director) and Lena (Wells) Fiske; children: Carol (Mrs. Dennis Strong). *Education:* Mount Holyoke College, B.A., 1935; Columbia University, M.A., 1938; also attended Harvard University, summers, 1933-34. *Home:* 1100 Gough St., San Francisco, Calif. 94109. *Office:* Human Development and Aging Program, University of California, 745 Parnassus, San Francisco, Calif. 94143.

CAREER: Rockefeller Foundation, New York City, research assistant in Office of Radio Research, 1937-39; National Federation of Business and Professional Women, New York City, associate director of field service, 1939-41, research director, 1941-43; McCann Erikson, Inc., New York City, research psychologist, 1946-47; conducted research in Nuremburg, Germany, 1947-49; U.S. Department of State, International Broadcasting Service, New York City, deputy director of research, 1949-53; Ford Foundation, New York City, executive director of National Planning Committee on Media Research, 1953-54; Columbia University, New York City, research director, Bureau of Applied Social Research, 1953-55; University of California, Berkeley, lecturer in sociology, 1955-56, lecturer in social psychology and social research, 1956-57; University of California, San Francisco, lecturer, 1959-66, professor of social psychology, 1966—, chairman of Ph.D. program in human development and aging. Director of human development and aging research program, Langley Porter Neuropsychiatric Institute, 1958—. Consultant in adult development and aging.

MEMBER: American Psychological Association (fellow), American Sociological Association (fellow), American Gerontological Society (fellow), American Association for the Advancement of Science (fellow).

WRITINGS: (With Robert K. Merton and Alberta Curtis) *Mass Persuasion: The Social Psychology of a War Bond Drive,* Harper, 1946; (contributor) Albert Blankenship, editor, *How to Conduct Consumer and Opinion Research,* Harper, 1946; (with Merton and Patricia Kendall) *The Focused Interview,* Free Press, 1948; (contributor) Paul Lazarsfeld and Frank Stanton, editors, *Communications Research: 1948-1949,* Harper, 1949; *Book Selection and Censorship: A Study of School and Public Libraries in California,* University of California Press, 1959; (contributor) Mirra Komarovsky, editor, *Frontiers of the Social Sciences,* Free Press, 1957; (contributor) J. Periam Danton, editor, *The Climate of Book Selection,* School of Librarianship, University of California, 1959.

(Contributor) Leo Lowenthal, editor, *Literature, Popular Culture and Sociology,* Prentice-Hall, 1961; (contributor) Peter Ostwald, editor, *Communication and Human Interaction,* Grune, 1977; (contributor) Lissy Jarvik, editor, *Aging into the Twenty-First Century: Middle-Agers Today,* Gardner, 1978; *Middle Age: The Prime of Life?,* Harper, 1979; (contributor) James Birren and R. Bruce Sloane, editors, *Handbook of Mental Health and Aging,* Prentice-Hall, 1980; (contributor) Neil Smelser and Erik Erikson, editors, *Themes of Work and Love in Adulthood,* Harvard University Press, 1980.

Under name Marjorie Fiske Lowenthal: (Contributor) R. H. Williams, C. Tibbitts, and Wilma Donahue, editors, *Processes of Aging: Social and Psychological Perspectives,* Volume II, Atherton, 1963; *Lives in Distress: The Paths of the Elderly to the Psychiatric Ward,* Basic Books, 1964; (with Paul Berkman and others) *Aging and Mental Disorder in San Francisco: A Social Psychiatric Study,* Jossey-Bass, 1967; (contributor) S. Kirson Weinberg, editor, *The Sociology of Mental Disorders: Analyses and Readings in Psychiatric Sociology,* Aldine, 1967; (contributor) Bernice Neugarten, editor, *Middle Age and Aging: A Reader in Social Psychology,* University of Chicago Press, 1968; (contributor) Alexander Simon and L. J. Epstein, editors, *Aging in Modern Society,* American Psychiatric Association, 1968; (editor with Ario Zilli) *Interdisciplinary Topics in Gerontology: Colloquium on Health and Aging of the Population,* Volume III, S. Karger, 1969.

(With Alexander Simon and Leon Epstein) *Crisis and Intervention: The Fate of the Elderly Mental Patient,* Jossey-Bass, 1970; (contributor) Frances Carp, editor, *Retirement,* Behavioral Publications, 1972; (contributor) Carl Eisdorfer and M. P. Lawton, editors, *The Psychology of Adult Development and Aging,* American Psychological Association, 1973; (contributor) Irving Rosow, editor, *Socialization to Old Age,* University of California Press, 1974; (with Majda Thurnher, David Chiriboga, and others) *Four Stages of Life: A Comparative Study of Women and Men Facing Transitions,* Jossey-Bass, 1975; (contributor) Robert Binstock and Ethel Shanas, editors, *Handbook of Aging and the Social Sciences,* Van Nostrand, 1976; (contributor) James Birren and K. Warner Schaie, editors, *Handbook of the Psychology of Aging,* Van Nostrand, 1977.

Editor of a series in adult development and aging published by Jossey-Bass. Contributor to proceedings and archives. Contributor of numerous articles to journals in the behavioral sciences, including *Aging and Human Development, Journal of Geriatric Psychiatry, American Sociological Review, International Journal of Social Psychiatry, Journal of Gerontology,* and *Journal of Health and Human Behavior.*

WORK IN PROGRESS: An adult life course, "Impact of Social Change on Psychosocial Change."

* * *

FITZ GERALD, Gregory 1923-

PERSONAL: Born April 23, 1923, in New York, N.Y.; son of Benedict J. (a composer) and Erna (a poet; maiden name, von Scheuller) Fitz Gerald; married Barbara Farquhar, November 26, 1957 (divorced June 26, 1973); children: Geraldine Adare. *Education:* Boston University, A.B., 1946; Middlebury College, M.A., 1953; University of Iowa, Ph.D., 1967. *Home:* 32 Cherry Dr., Brockport, N.Y. 14420. *Office:* Department of English, State University of New York College, Brockport, N.Y. 14420.

CAREER: University of Iowa, Iowa City, instructor in English, 1954-55, 1956-61; Jackson Junior College, Jackson, Mich., instructor in English, 1961-62; Indiana State University, Terre Haute, assistant professor of English, 1962-65; Ithaca College, Ithaca, N.Y., associate professor of English,

1965-67; State University of New York College at Brockport, assistant professor, 1967-69, associate professor, 1969-73, professor of English, 1973—. Writers Forum, Brockport, founding director, 1967, director, 1967-71, 1979-80. Has hosted and participated in numerous radio and television programs. *Member:* Authors Guild, Authors League of America. *Awards, honors:* Smith-Mundt fellowship to Damascus, 1955-56; State University of New York Research Foundation grant-in-aid in satire, 1968-70, fellowship in criticism, 1969, fellowships in fiction, 1970, 1974.

WRITINGS: (Compiler) *Modern Satiric Stories: The Impropriety Principle,* Scott, Foresman, 1971; (with Jack Wolf) *Past, Present, and Future Perfect,* Fawcett, 1973; (with John Dillon) *The Late Great Future,* Fawcett, 1976; *Neutron Stars,* Fawcett, 1977. Contributor of 150 stories, poems, articles, interviews, and reviews to magazines, including *Modern Poetry Studies, Fiction International, Aspect, Southwest Review,* and *Cimarron Review.*

WORK IN PROGRESS: October Blood and Other Stories; a collection of poems, *Canal Songs; The Reef and Other Plays;* a novel, *Had He Not Resembled My Father.*

SIDELIGHTS: Gregory Fitz Gerald writes: "Though our society is doomed, I hubristically try, with infinitesimal effect, to retard its self-destruction. Science fiction is that literature which best clarifies our predicament, while satire illuminates our shortfall."

* * *

FITZGERALD, James A(ugustine) 1892-

PERSONAL: Born in 1892; son of Maurice A. and Helena G. (Farrell) Fitzgerald; married Patricia G. Geoghegan, 1935. *Education:* University of South Dakota, B.A., M.A.; University of Iowa, Ph.D. *Religion:* Catholic.

CAREER: Teacher and principal in public schools of South Dakota; Southern State Teachers College (now University of South Dakota at Springfield), associate professor; University of Iowa, Iowa City, research assistant; Loyola University, Chicago, Ill., associate professor and assistant dean; Fordham University, New York, N.Y., professor of education, 1939-58; University of Scranton, Scranton, Pa., professor of education, 1958-65. *Military service:* U.S. Army, Field Artillery, 1917-19. U.S. Army Reserve, 1921-35; became captain.

MEMBER: American Educational Research Association, American Association of School Administrators, American Association of University Professors, National Education Association, National Society for the Study of Education, International Reading Association, National Council of Teachers of English, National Conference on Research in English, National Catholic Educational Association, Phi Delta Kappa, Alpha Sigma Nu.

WRITINGS: (With Carl A. Hoffman and John R. Bayston) *Drive and Live,* Johnson Publishing, 1937; *A Basic Life Spelling Vocabulary,* Bruce, 1951; *The Teaching of Spelling,* Bruce, 1951; *For Fear of Little Men,* Exposition Press, 1977.

With wife, Patricia G. Fitzgerald; all published by Bruce: *Methods and Curricula in Elementary Education,* 1955; *Learning and Using Words: Advanced Spelling,* 1959; *Teaching Reading and the Language Arts,* 1965; *Fundamentals of Reading Instruction,* 1967.†

* * *

FITZGERALD, Robert (Stuart) 1910-

PERSONAL: Born October 12, 1910, in Geneva, N.Y.; son of Robert Emmet and Anne (Stuart) Fitzgerald; married Sarah Morgan, April 19, 1947 (separated, 1974); children: Hugh Linane, Benedict R.C., Maria Juliana, Michael A., Barnaby J. F., Caterina Maria Teresa. *Education:* Attended Trinity College, Cambridge University, 1932; Harvard University, B.A., 1933. *Religion:* Roman Catholic. *Office:* Warren House, Harvard University, Cambridge, Mass. 02138.

CAREER: New York Herald Tribune, New York City, reporter, 1933-35; *Time,* New York City, writer, 1936-49; Sarah Lawrence College, Bronxville, N.Y., teacher, 1946-53; Princeton University, Princeton, N.J., instructor, 1950-52; University of Notre Dame, South Bend, Ind., professor, 1957; University of Washington, Seattle, professor, 1961; Mt. Holyoke College, South Hadley, Mass., professor, 1964; Harvard University, Cambridge, Mass., Boylston Professor of Rhetoric, 1965—. *Military service:* U.S. Naval Reserve, 1943-46; became lieutenant. *Member:* American Institute of Arts and Letters, American Academy of Arts and Sciences, Academy of American Poets (chancellor), Indiana University School of Letters (fellow), Phi Beta Kappa (honorary member), Harvard Club (New York). *Awards, honors:* Midland Authors Prize from *Poetry* magazine, 1932; Guggenheim fellowships, 1952, 1972; Shelley Memorial Award from Poetry Society of America, 1956; National Institute of Arts and Letters award, 1957; Ford Foundation grant in creative writing, 1959; Bollingen Award for translation of poetry, 1961; Bollingen Foundation fellowship, 1965-66; National Endowment for the Humanities fellow, 1973; Ingram Merrill Foundation fellowship, 1974; Landon Award, 1976; Ingram Merrill Literary Award, 1978.

WRITINGS: Poems, Arrow Editions, 1935; *A Wreath for the Sea,* New Directions, 1943; *In the Rose of Time,* New Directions, 1956; *Spring Shade,* New Directions, 1972.

Editor: *The Collected Poems of James Agee,* Houghton, 1968; *The Collected Short Prose of James Agee,* Houghton, 1968; (with wife, Sally Fitzgerald) Flannery O'Connor, *Mystery and Manners,* Farrar, Straus, 1969.

Translator: (With Dudley Fitts) Euripides, *Alcestis,* Harcourt, 1936; (with Fitts) Sophocles, *Antigone,* Harcourt, 1939; Sophocles, *Oedipus at Colonus,* Harcourt, 1941; (with Fitts) Sophocles, *Oedipus Rex,* Harcourt, 1949; St. John Perse, *Chronique,* Pantheon, 1960; Homer, *The Odyssey,* Doubleday, 1961; St. John Perse, *Birds,* Pantheon, 1966; Homer, *The Iliad,* Doubleday, 1974.

* * *

FLACK, Naomi John White (Naomi Sellers)

PERSONAL: Born in Oklahoma; daughter of John Marion and Annie (Rice) White; married John Flack, 1976. *Education:* University of Oklahoma, B.A. and M.A. *Home:* 39 Erickson Rd., San Mateo, Calif. *Office:* Burlingame High School, Burlingame, Calif.

CAREER: Muskogee High School, Muskogee, Okla., teacher of English; Oklahoma Agricultural and Mechanical College (now Oklahoma State University), Stillwater, teacher of English; U.S. Navy, WAVES instructor, 1941-45; Burlingame High School, Burlingame, Calif., teacher of English. *Member:* Authors League of America, American Association of University Women, Delta Kappa Gamma, Phi Delta Theta, Alpha Chi Omega.

WRITINGS—All published under name Naomi Sellers, except as indicated: *Cross My Heart,* Doubleday, 1953; *The Little Elephant That Liked to Play,* Ginn, 1972; *Charley's*

Clan, Albert Whitman, 1973; (under name Naomi John White Flack) *Road Runner's Day,* Dutton, 1979. Contributor of about seventy short stories to *Ladies' Home Journal, Cosmopolitan,* and other magazines.

AVOCATIONAL INTERESTS: Music, travel.

* * *

FLANAGAN, John C(lemans) 1906-

PERSONAL: Born January 7, 1906, in Armour, S.D.; son of Charles Gibbons and Gertrude (Clemans) Flanagan; married Katherine Ross, January 18, 1930; married second wife, Ruth Colonna, June 21, 1962; children: (first marriage) J. Ross, Scott C. *Education:* University of Washington, B.S., 1929, M.A., 1932; Harvard University, Ph.D., 1934. *Religion:* Unitarian Universalist. *Home:* 1290 Sharon Park Dr., Menlo Park, Calif. 94025. *Office address:* American Institutes for Research, P.O. Box 1113, Palo Alto, Calif. 94302.

CAREER: High school math and science teacher in Renton, Wash., 1929-30, and in Seattle, Wash., 1930-32; Harvard University, Cambridge, Mass., assistant in education, 1934-35; American Council on Education, Cooperative Test Service, New York City, associate director, 1935-41; Columbia University, Teachers College, New York City, lecturer, 1936-41; University of Pittsburgh, Pittsburgh, Pa., professor of psychology, 1946-66; American Institute for Research, Pittsburgh, founder, president, 1946-73; American Institutes for Research, Palo Alto, Calif., chairman of board of directors, 1973—. Diplomate in industrial psychology, American Board for Examiners in Professional Psychology. Consultant to Agency for International Development, National Institutes of Health (accident prevention research study section), and to several foreign airlines. *Military service:* U.S. Army Air Forces, 1941-46, chief of Psychological Branch, Office of Air Surgeon; became colonel; received Legion of Merit.

MEMBER: American Association for Advancement of Science (vice-president, 1960), American Educational Research Association (member of executive committee, 1961-64), American Personnel and Guidance Association, American Psychological Association (president, division of measurement and evaluation, 1956; president, division of military psychology, 1962; president, division of general psychology, 1963), American Society of Training Directors, American Statistical Association, Human Factors Society, Institute of Management Science, Institute of Mathematical Statistics, Industrial Relations Research Association, National Council on Measurement in Education (director, 1961-63; president, 1965-66), Operations Research Society, Psychometric Society (president, 1952), Society for International Development, National Council on the Aging (director, 1963-66), New York Academy of Science, Sigma Xi.

AWARDS, HONORS: Raymond F. Longacre Award of Aero-Medical Association, 1954, for accomplishments in aviation medicine; Personnel and Industrial Relations Association award for contribution to utilization of high-talent manpower, 1958; Edward Lee Thorndike Award, 1972, and Distinguished Professional Contribution Award, 1976, both from American Psychological Association; Phi Delta Kappa award for outstanding contribution to evaluation, development, and research, 1977; Educational Testing Service award for distinguished service to measurement, 1978.

WRITINGS: Aviation Psychology Program in the Army Air Forces, U.S. Government Printing Office, 1948; *Aptitude Classification Tests,* Science Research Associates, 1953; (with R. B. Miller) *The Performance Record: The Critical Incident,* Science Research Associates, 1955; *Personal and Social Development Program,* Science Research Associates, 1956; *Tests of General Ability,* Science Research Associates, 1959; *Tapping Test,* Psychometric Techniques Associates, 1959; (with others) *Design for a Study of American Youth,* Houghton, 1962; *Industrial Tests,* Science Research Associates, 1964; *A Survey of the Educational Program of the Hicksville Public Schools,* American Institute for Research, 1966; (with others) *Project TALENT One Year Follow-up Studies,* University of Pittsburgh and American Institute for Research, 1966; (with D. Russ-Eft) *An Empirical Study to Aid in Formulating Educational Goals,* American Institutes for Research, 1975; *Perspectives on Improving Education: Project TALENT's Young Adults Look Back,* Praeger, 1978.

Contributor: *Handbook of Applied Psychology,* Henry Holt, 1950; *Educational Measurement,* American Council on Education, 1951; *Psychology in the World Emergency,* University of Pittsburgh Press, 1952; *Applications of Psychology,* Harper, 1952; *Social Welfare Administration,* Columbia University Press, 1961; *Leadership and Interpersonal Behavior,* Holt, 1961; *Developmental Efforts in Individualized Learning,* F. T. Peacock, 1971; *Systems of Individualized Education,* McCutchan, 1975; *Assessing Creative Growth: The Tests–Book One,* Creative Synergetic Associates, 1976. Contributor of over three hundred articles to professional journals.

* * *

FLEEGE, Urban H(erman) 1908-

PERSONAL: Born November 4, 1908, in Dubuque, Iowa; son of William B. (a life underwriter) and Dora K. (Kellner) Fleege; married Virginia B. Hansen (a Montessori school director), August 31, 1947; children: William, Kathleen, Richard, Robert, Maureen, Michael. *Education:* St. Louis University, B.A., 1932; University of Dayton, B.S., 1933; University of Chicago, graduate study, 1935-36; Catholic University of America, Ph.D., 1940. *Politics:* Democrat. *Religion:* Roman Catholic. *Home:* 1439 Monroe, River Forest, Ill. 60305. *Office:* Department of Education, DePaul University, 25 East Jackson Blvd., Chicago, Ill. 60604.

CAREER: St. Mary's University, San Antonio, Tex., assistant professor of educational psychology, 1940-41; principal of Cathedral High School, Belleville, Ill., 1941-43; Catholic University of America, Washington, D.C., associate professor of education, 1942-44, chairman of department, 1943-45; New Mexico Highlands University, Las Vegas, dean, 1945-46; Marquette University, Milwaukee, Wis., director of guidance clinic and coordinator of veteran affairs, 1946-47; U.S. State Department, Berlin, Nuernberg, and Frankfurt, Germany, chief of Cultural Affairs, 1947-50; National Catholic Education Association, Washington, D.C., secretary of College and University Division, 1950-52; chief of UNESCO for Southeast Asia, Manila, Philippines, 1952-55; DePaul University, Chicago, Ill., dean of School of Education, 1957-62, associate vice-president for planning and research, 1962-68, professor of child development, 1966—. President of Midwest Montessori Teacher Training Center, Chicago, Ill., 1965—; lecturer at George Washington University, 1952, and University of Maryland, 1953. *Member:* American Catholic Psychological Association, American Psychological Association, American Association for Higher Education, National Education Association, National Educational Research Association, National Catholic Education Association, American Association of University Professors, American Montessori Society, American Council of

Education, American Association of School Administrators, Delta Epsilon Psi, Knights of Columbus.

WRITINGS: Personal Problems of Modern Adolescents, Catholic University of America Press, 1942; *Self Revelation of the Adolescent Boy,* Bruce Publishing Co., 1945; (with Roy J. Defferari) *College Organization and Administration,* Catholic University of America Press, 1946; *Community School: Potentialities and Needs,* Philippine Government, 1954; *Problems in Education,* Philippine Government, 1955; *Mental Health for Teachers,* DePaul University Press, 1960; *Building the Foundations for Creative Learning,* American Montessori Society, 1965; *Montessori Pre-School Education,* U.S. Government, Department of Health, Education, and Welfare, 1967; *Issues,* Paulist/Newman, 1969; *Guidelines to Techniques for Early Child Development,* Success Research, Inc., 1975; *The Montessori System of Education,* F. T. Peacock, 1979. Contributor of over one hundred articles to professional journals.

WORK IN PROGRESS: A book, *Understanding the Behavior of Children;* field work on innovations in early education of children in the United States and in Europe.

* * *

FLEETWOOD, Frances 1902-
(Frank Fleetwood)

PERSONAL: Surname originally Buss; name legally changed; born May 24, 1902, in London, England; daughter of Francis Fleetwood (a professor) and Elsie (Hudson) Buss. *Education:* Sorbonne, University of Paris, certificat d'etudes francaises, 1922. *Politics:* "General skepticism." *Religion:* "Freethinker." *Home:* Via del Golfo 4, 04028 Scauri (Latina), Italy.

CAREER: Writer. Has worked at various times as secretary, language teacher, interpreter, stage manager and understudy in small club theatres, motion picture extra, and hostess-interpreter for a London tourist agency. Served with Civil Defense in London during World War II. *Awards, honors:* Civil Defense Medal, 1945; silver medal from Servizio Volontariato Giovanile, 1972, for work at Caserta Castle; honorable mention, Gradara (Italy) Literary Competition, 1973, for a short story in Italian; "Friends of Gradara" medal, 1972, for writing featuring that area.

WRITINGS—Published by W. H. Allen, except as indicated: (With Betty Conquest) *Conquest: The Story of a Theatre Family,* 1953; (translator from the French) Maurice Dekobra, *The Seventh Wife of Prince Hassan* (novel), 1961; (translator from the Italian) Umberto Nobile, *My Polar Flights,* Muller, 1961; (translator) Dekobra, *Double or Quits* (novel), 1962; *The Elephant and the Rose: Romance of the Malatesta Family of Rimini,* Ponticelli, 1968; *Concordia* (novel), 1971, St. Martin's, 1973; *Concordia Errant* (novel), 1973; *La Torre dei falchi* (history; title means "The Falcons' Tower"), Caramanica, 1973, 2nd edition, 1977; (with Vera Schuyler) *Beloved Upstart* (novel), 1974; *Controcorrente* (novel; title means "Upstream"), Russo, 1979.

Under pseudonym Frank Fleetwood: *The Threshold* (poems), Selwyn & Blount, 1925; (with George Cusack) *To What Purpose?* (novel), Stanley Paul, 1929; (translator from the Italian) Umberto Nobile, *With the "Italia" to the North Pole,* Allen & Unwin, 1930; (translator with Elizabeth Dithmer) Dithmer, *The Truth about Nobile,* Williams & Norgate, 1933; (translator from the German with Eric Reissner) Carl Schuett, *The Elements of Aeronautics,* Pitman & Sons, 1941.

Also ghost-writer of several books. Occasional contributor to *Times Educational Supplement* (London) and *La Pie* (Italian literary journal).

SIDELIGHTS: Frances Fleetwood describes her writing habits: "For a historical novel, I spend several months visiting research libraries and stocking-up relevant photocopies. Meanwhile, on long country walks or in bed at night, I compose (in my head) the general lines of the story, so that I have a clear idea of the beginning and the end, and some notion of the main incidents. Then I make a time-schedule of the actual historical dates and the way they fit in with the private lives of my characters. When I am ready to write, I start at Chapter I and work steadily through to the end (occasionally postponing a difficult chapter, or one for which I need further factual information). The first draft is handwritten in a copybook. Having accumulated several chapters, I type a rough draft, and at this stage the major corrections and alterations are made. At the end—several weeks or months later, by which time I can criticize my work impersonally—I type the fair copy and *never touch it again,* unless I discover an anachronism, a mistake in historical fact or a stylistic blunder. I abominate the type of writer who complains: 'I've written this chapter over and over again, and it *won't* come right!' My advice in this case is uncompromising: Leave the damned chapter as it stands, and finish the book. Then go back and see if it is really necessary to the plot; if not, scrap it entirely. If so, include the requisite information, casually, in some other chapter."

Fleetwood told *CA* that she wrote her first novel at the age of nine, but made no attempt to have it published. The book was entitled *The Suffragettes of the Twentieth Century.* At fifteen, she wrote a novel about the English Civil War ("strongly royalist") which was submitted to an agent who failed to place it with a publisher. Of her early interest in literature she writes: "My father had a complete collection of Walter Scott's novels, and as a child I read them all with enjoyment, but, frankly, have never opened one since! The writers who have influenced me most are (in time order) R. L. Stevenson, Rudyard Kipling and Lawrence of Arabia. All these combine pace and elegance with a love of sounding words and heroic deeds. *Puck of Pook's Hill* was the favourite book of my childhood, and I can read it today with the same thrill. In fact, I owe to it the 'time voyage' idea on which my latest novel is based.

"During the past twenty years, the work of filling wide gaps in my knowledge of Italian literature, classic and modern, has prevented my following contemporary developments in English-speaking countries. I recently discovered Thom Gunn and found his work exciting, especially the early verses, where he displays a profound European culture expressed in impeccable rhyme and rhythm schemes. As novelists I like Mary Renault, Mary Stewart and Lawrence Durrell; but to my mind the most absorbing book written in the last twenty-five years is Tolkien's *Lord of the Rings.* Irving Stone's biographical novels are all very fine, especially *The Greek Treasure.* I don't like modern drama, which is usually sordid, anti-heroic and taken up with dreary 'underdog' problems."

AVOCATIONAL INTERESTS: Gardening, weaving, cooking, swimming, long country walks, mediaeval history (especially Italian).

* * *

FLEMING, D(enna) F(rank) 1893-

PERSONAL: Born March 25, 1893, in Paris, Ill.; son of Albert (a farmer) and Eleanor (McCormick) Fleming; married

Doris S. Anundsen, June 29, 1929. *Education:* Eastern Illinois State College (now Eastern Illinois University), diploma, 1912; University of Illinois, A.B., 1916, A.M. 1920, Ph.D., 1928. *Politics:* Democrat. *Religion:* Methodist. *Home:* 4721 Sewanee Rd., Nashville, Tenn. 37220.

CAREER: Monmouth College, Monmouth, Ill., professor, 1922-28; Vanderbilt University, Nashville, Tenn., 1928-61, professor of international relations, 1938-61, professor emeritus, 1961—. Visiting professor at School of International Studies, New Delhi, India, 1959-60, University of Arizona, 1964, 1966, California State College (now University), Los Angeles, 1965, and Simon Fraser University, 1968-69. Radio commentator, station WSM, 1939-47. Member, Institute for Advanced Study, 1946, 1948-49; member of board of directors, Woodrow Wilson Foundation, 1950-55; member of National Citizens Committee for Woodrow Wilson Centennial, 1956. *Military service:* U.S. Army, World War I. *Member:* American Political Science Association (vice-president, 1943), American Association of University Professors (member of executive council, 1955-57), Southern Political Science Association (president, 1941), Phi Beta Kappa, Delta Sigma Rho, Kappa Delta Pi, Masons. *Awards, honors:* Penfield Traveling Scholar, University of Pennsylvania, 1932-33, 1938-39; Fulbright lecturer, Cambridge University, 1954; Fulbright lecturer, Indian School of International Studies, New Delhi, 1959-60; Pd.D., Eastern Illinois University, 1949.

WRITINGS: *The Treaty Veto of the American Senate,* Putnam, 1930, reprinted, AMS Press, 1968; *The United States and the League of Nations, 1918-1920,* Putnam, 1932, revised edition, Russell & Russell, 1968; *The United States and World Organization, 1920-33,* Columbia University Press, 1938, reprinted, AMS Press, 1968; *Can We Win the Peace?,* Broadman, 1943; *While America Slept,* Abingdon, 1944; *The United States and the World Court,* Doubleday, 1945, revised edition, Russell & Russell, 1968; *The Cold War and Its Origins, 1917-1960,* two volumes, Doubleday, 1961; *The Origins and Legacies of World War I,* Doubleday, 1968; *America's Role in Vietnam and Asia,* Funk, 1969; *Issues of Survival,* Doubleday, 1972.

Contributor: Reginald Trotter and Albert B. Corey, editors, *Conference on Canadian-American Affairs,* Ginn, 1941; Roy V. Peel and Joseph S. Roucek, editors, *Introduction to World Politics,* Crowell, 1941; Jesse D. Clarkson and Thomas Cochran, editors, *War as a Social Institution,* Columbia University Press, 1941; *Representative American Speeches, 1941-42,* Wilson, 1942; *Representative American Speeches, 1942-43,* Wilson, 1943; *Representative American Speeches, 1943-44,* Wilson, 1944; *Citizens for a New World,* National Council for the Social Studies, 1944; *The Winning of the Peace,* St. Louis Star-Times, 1944; Alan H. Monroe, editor, *Principles of Speech,* Scott, Foresman, 1945; *The National University Extension Association Debate Manual, 1953-54,* [Columbia, Mo.], 1953; William Appleman Williams, editor, *The Shaping of American Diplomacy,* Rand McNally, 1956; Hilman M. Bishop and Samuel Hendel, editors, *Basic Issues of American Democracy,* Appleton-Century-Crofts, 1956.

BIOGRAPHICAL/CRITICAL SOURCES: *Book World,* November 10, 1968; *New York Times Book Review,* December 8, 1968; *New York Review,* January 16, 1969; *Nation,* February 3, 1969.

* * *

FLITNER, David P(erkins), Jr. 1949-

PERSONAL: Born January 3, 1949, in Boston, Mass.; son of David Perkins (an engineer) and Mariam (Merrill) Flitner; married Emilie Munyan, December 15, 1973; children: Lisa Marie. *Education:* University of Maine, B.A., 1972; University of Cincinnati, M.A., 1975; Tufts University, Ph.D., 1979. *Politics:* Democrat. *Religion:* Protestant. *Home:* 26 Shipman Rd., Andover, Mass. 01810.

CAREER: Free-lance writer and composer. Has performed and recorded music alone and with various rock groups. Member of staff of Muskie presidential campaign, 1972.

WRITINGS: *Those People in Washington,* Childrens Press, 1973. Also author of *Those People in Watergate;* composer of numerous songs. Contributor to *Baltimore Sun* and *Boston Globe.*

WORK IN PROGRESS: *A Passing of Comets: The Politics of Presidential Commissions.*

SIDELIGHTS: David Flitner told *CA* that "*Those People in Washington* grew directly out of my attempts to explain American politics to my—at the time—little sister. Over the years my wife and I have become increasingly concerned about the low level of 'political intelligence' of many Americans. It seems to me that one way to have an impact on this situation is to stimulate, interest, and inform future participants in the political process. *Those People in Watergate* represents a further (although not universally welcomed) step in this direction, while *A Passing of Comets* will seek an older audience. I hope in the future to investigate for young readers areas, e.g., Cuba, the Arab world, which have been burdened with stereotypes and controversy in the minds of Americans. If we are to make rational judgements in a tense world, we must have rational facts upon which to base them.

"The Longer I have studied political science as an academic discipline the more convinced I have become that politics is better understood as an art than a science. To me, the novelist and the journalist—as well as the politician—are those most capable of showing us the motivations, passions, dilemmas, and very human complexities involved in the conduct of public affairs. I have been particularly influenced, in these feelings, by such writers as Philip Roth, Kurt Vonnegut, Gore Vidal, J. W. Fulbright, Michael Halberstam, and Les Whitten, all of whom have shed light on political and social life in a revealing, sympathetic and, ultimately, artistic way. My own efforts in writing for children and as a journalist have involved attempting to raise issues for discussion, to expand awareness and, fundamentally, to interest people in politics. It seems to me to be vital that we adults prepare our children to be informed, inquisitive, functioning members of society."

AVOCATIONAL INTERESTS: Travel (has visited Europe twice, Great Britain, and Morocco).

* * *

FLOUD, Roderick 1942-

PERSONAL: Surname is pronounced "flood"; born April 1, 1942, in London, England; son of Bernard and Ailsa (Craig) Floud; married Cynthia Smith (a justice of the peace), August 6, 1964; children: Lydia Jane, Sarah Katherine. *Education:* Wadham College, Oxford, B.A., 1964; Nuffield College, Oxford, D.Phil., 1970. *Politics:* Labour. *Religion:* None. *Home:* 21 Savernake Rd., London NW3 2JT, England. *Office:* Birkbeck College, University of London, Malet St., London WC1, England.

CAREER: University of London, University College, London, England, assistant lecturer in economic history, 1966-69; Cambridge University, Cambridge, England, assistant lecturer, 1969-73, lecturer in economic history, 1973-75; fellow and tutor at Emmanuel College, 1969-75; University of London, Birkbeck College, professor of modern history, 1975—. *Member:* Economic History Society (member of council), Economic History Association.

WRITINGS: *An Introduction to Quantitative Methods for Historians,* Princeton University Press, 1973; (editor) *Essays in Quantitative Economic History,* Clarendon Press, 1974; *The British Machine Tool Industry, 1850-1914,* Cambridge University Press, 1974; *The Economic History of Britain since 1700,* Cambridge University Press, 1980.

WORK IN PROGRESS: Research on human health and nutrition, 1750-1900.

* * *

FORCEY, Charles B(udd) 1925-

PERSONAL: Born January 14, 1925, in Sewickley, Pa.; son of Charles B. and Evelyn (Morsing) Forcey; married Pamela Cottier, 1949 (divorced, 1964); married Linda Rennie Nash, 1967; children: (first marriage) Blythe, Peter Cottier; (second marriage) Charles B. III; stepchildren: Sally M. Nash, Peter Adam Nash, Margaret Nash. *Education:* Princeton University, B.A., 1948; Columbia University, M.A., 1950; University of Wisconsin, Ph.D., 1954. *Home:* 125 R.D. 1, Nichols, N.Y. 13812. *Office:* Department of History, State University of New York, Binghamton, N.Y. 13901.

CAREER: University of Wisconsin Extension, Wausau, instructor, 1952-54; Miami University, Oxford, Ohio, assistant professor, 1954-56; Columbia University, New York, N.Y., assistant professor, 1956-61; Rutgers University, New Brunswick, N.J., associate professor of history, 1961-67; State University of New York at Binghamton, professor of history, 1967—. Fulbright lecturer, Xavier University (Philippines), 1964-65. *Military service:* U.S. Naval Reserve, 1943-46; became lieutenant. *Member:* American Historical Association, Organization of American Historians, American Civil Liberties Union, National Association for the Advancement of Colored People.

WRITINGS: *The Crossroads of Liberalism,* Oxford University Press, 1961; *A Strong and Free Nation,* Macmillan, 1971.

* * *

FORD, Jesse Hill (Jr.) 1928-

PERSONAL: Born 1928, in Troy, Ala.; son of Jesse Hill and Lucille (Musgrove) Ford; married Lillian Pellettieri, 1975; children: (previous marriage) Jesse Hill III, Charles Davis, Sarah Ann, Elizabeth Grimes. *Education:* Vanderbilt University, B.A., 1951; University of Florida, M.A., 1955; University of Oslo, Fulbright scholar, 1961. *Politics:* Democrat. *Religion:* Episcopalian. *Home:* Water Island, St. Thomas, Virgin Islands 00801. *Agent:* Dorothy Olding, Harold Ober Associates, Inc., 40 East 49th St., New York, N.Y. 10017.

CAREER: Tennessee Medical Association, Nashville, director of public service, 1955-56; American Medical Association, Chicago, Ill., assistant for public relations, 1956-57; free-lance writer, 1957—. *Military service:* U.S. Navy, 1951-52. *Member:* Overseas Press Club of America, American-Scandinavian Foundation. *Awards, honors:* *Atlantic Monthly* award, 1959, for "The Surest Thing in Show Business," grant, 1959, for *Mountains of Gilead;* honorable mention, Columbia Broadcasting System television network grants-in-aid, 1960; O. Henry Award, 1961, for "How the Mountains Are"; Edgar Award, Mystery Writers of America, 1975, for "The Jail."

WRITINGS—All published by Atlantic-Little, Brown, except as indicated: *Mountains of Gilead,* 1961; *The Conversion of Buster Drumwright,* Vanderbilt University Press, 1964; *The Liberation of Lord Byron Jones* (Book-of-the-Month Club selection), 1965; *Fishes, Birds, and Sons of Men* (stories), 1968; *The Feast of St. Barnabas,* 1969; *The Raider* (Book-of-the-Month Club alternate selection), 1975.

Screenplays: (With Stirling Silliphant) "The Liberation of L. B. Jones," Columbia, 1970.

WORK IN PROGRESS: A novel; a collection of short stories, for Putnam.

SIDELIGHTS: Jesse Hill Ford writes of the racial tensions of the South in a realistic style. He chose this particular topic because, he says in *Conversations:* "I found myself getting angrier and angrier about much of the fiction that touched on the racial issues. [The fiction was] either tracts barely disguised as novels . . . [or] slightly romantic novels in which a nice little kid or two brought a whole town to its senses. They ignored the fact that for over a century the average Southerner has been taught to believe that the Negro is an inferior person." Although Ford is optimistic about eventual integration in the South, he points out that "change is going to come slowly, with a lot of give and take, and it will be resisted all the way."

Ford's *The Conversion of Buster Drumwright* was made into a television play by CBS. *The Liberation of Lord Byron Jones* was filmed as "The Liberation of L. B. Jones" by Columbia in 1970.

BIOGRAPHICAL/CRITICAL SOURCES: *Atlantic,* May, 1959, August, 1965; Edward Weeks, *In Friendly Candor,* Atlantic-Little, Brown, 1960; Weeks, *Breaking Into Print,* Writer, Inc., 1962; Roy Newquist, *Conversations,* Rand McNally, 1967; *New York Times Book Review,* November 5, 1967, January 26, 1969, May 16, 1976; *National Observer,* November 13, 1967, March 10, 1969, February 15, 1971; *Listener,* April 18, 1968; *Best Sellers,* February 15, 1969; *Spectator,* April 18, 1969; *Punch,* April 23, 1969; *New York Times,* July 2, 1971, November 18, 1971, November 23, 1971; *Life,* October 29, 1971; *Today's Health,* December, 1971; *Virginia Quarterly Review,* autumn, 1976.

* * *

FORELL, George W. 1919-

PERSONAL: Born September 19, 1919, in Breslau, Germany; naturalized U.S. citizen in 1945; son of Frederick Joachim and Madeleine (Kretschmar) Forell; married Elizabeth Jean Rossing, 1945; children: Madeleine Helene (Mrs. Gary Marshall), Mary Elizabeth (Mrs. Christopher Davis). *Education:* Attended University of Vienna, 1937-38; Lutheran Theological Seminary, Philadelphia, B.D.; Princeton Theological Seminary, Th.M.; Union Theological Seminary, Th.D. *Politics:* Democrat. *Religion:* Lutheran. *Home:* 10 Bella Vista, Iowa City, Iowa 52240. *Office:* Department of Religion, University of Iowa, Iowa City, Iowa 52242.

CAREER: Minister in Lutheran churches in New Jersey and New York, 1941-47; Gustavus Adolphus College, St. Peter, Minn., associate professor of philosophy, 1947-54; University of Iowa, Iowa City, assistant professor, 1954-55, associate professor, 1955-58; professor at Chicago Lutheran Seminary, 1958-61; University of Iowa, professor of Protestant theology, 1961—, Carver Distinguished Professor, 1973—, director of School of Religion, 1966-71. Visiting professor, University of Hamburg, 1957-58, All-Africa Theological Seminar, 1960, Japan Lutheran College, 1968, and Gurukul Theological Research Institute, 1978. *Member:* American Society for Reformation Research (secretary-treasurer, 1946-56; president, 1959), American Philosophical Association, American Society of Church History, Society for Values in Higher Education (fellow), American Society for Christian Ethics.

WRITINGS: The Reality of the Church as the Communion of Saints, Wenonah, 1943; *Faith Active in Love,* Augsburg, 1954; *Ethics of Decision,* Muhlenberg Press, 1955; *What Is Your Gold?,* University of Alberta Press, 1956; (editor with Helmut T. Lehmann) Martin Luther, *Works,* Volume XXXII, Muhlenberg Press and Concordia, 1958; (contributor) W. Quanbeck, editor, *God and Caesar,* Augsburg, 1959; (with Grimm and Hoelthy-Nickel) *Luther and Culture,* Augsburg, 1960; *The Protestant Faith,* Prentice-Hall, 1960, revised edition, Fortress, 1975; (contributor) *The Place of Bonhoeffer,* Association Press, 1962; *The Christian Year,* Thomas Nelson, Volume I, 1964, Volume II, 1965; *Understanding the Nicene Creed,* Fortress, 1965; *Christian Social Teaching,* Doubleday, 1966; (with others) *The New American Revolution,* Lutheran Academy for Scholarship, 1968; *The Augsburg Confession: A Contemporary Commentary,* Augsburg, 1968; (contributor) *Reformation: 1517-1967,* [Berlin], 1968.

(Contributor) *All Things New,* Abingdon, 1972; (editor and translator) *Zinzendorf: Nine Public Lectures on Important Subjects in Religion,* University of Iowa Press, 1973; *The Proclamation of the Gospel in a Pluralistic World: Essays on Christianity and Culture,* Fortress, 1973; (contributor) Paul D. Opsahi and Marc H. Tannenbaum, editors, *Speaking of God Today: Jews and Lutherans in Conversation,* Fortress, 1974; *The Christian Lifestyle,* Fortress, 1975; *The Revolution at the Frontier: Reports from Moravian Missionaries among the American Indians, 1775-1781,* Moravian Archives, 1976; (contributor) *Against the World for the World: The Hartford Appeal and the Future of American Religion,* Seabury, 1976; *History of Christian Ethics,* Volume I: *From the New Testament to Augustine,* Augsburg, 1979. Also editor, with William H. Lazareth, of "Justice Books" series, Fortress, 1978—, including *God's Call to Public Responsibility,* 1978, *Crisis in Marriage,* 1978, *Human Rights: Rhetoric or Reality,* 1978, *Population Perils,* 1978, and *Work as Praise,* 1979. Contributor to religion journals. Advisor, *Encyclopaedia Britannica,* 1972—.

WORK IN PROGRESS: Volumes two and three of *History of Christian Ethics,* for Augsburg.

* * *

FORRESTER, Jay W(right) 1918-

PERSONAL: Born July 14, 1918, in Anselmo, Neb.; son of Marmaduke M. and Ethel (Wright) Forrester; married Susan Sweet, July 27, 1946; children: Judith, Nathan Blair, Ned Cromwell. *Education:* University of Nebraska, B.S., 1939; Massachusetts Institute of Technology, M.S., 1945. *Office:* Sloan School of Management, Massachusetts Institute of Technology, Cambridge, Mass. 02139.

CAREER: Massachusetts Institute of Technology, Cambridge, co-founder of Servomechanisms Laboratory, 1940, involved in developing servomechanisms for radar and gun mounts, 1940-46, director of Digital Computer Laboratory, 1946-51, head of Digital Computer Division, Lincoln Laboratory, 1952-56, professor of management, Alfred P. Sloan School of Management, 1956-72, Germeshausen Professor of Management, 1972—, director of Systems Dynamics Program. Holder of patents in servomechanism and digital computer fields.

MEMBER: National Academy of Engineering, Institute of Electrical and Electronics Engineers (fellow), American Academy of Arts and Sciences (fellow), Academy of Management (fellow), American Institute of Physics, Institute of Management Sciences, Sigma Xi, Eta Kappa Nu. *Awards, honors:* D. Eng., University of Nebraska, 1954, Newark College of Engineering, and University of Notre Dame; Inventor of the Year Award, George Washington University, 1968; D.Sc., Boston University, 1969, and Union College; Valdemar Poulsen Gold Medal of Danish Academy of Technical Sciences, 1969; New England Award, Engineering Societies of New England, 1972; Medal of Honor and Systems, Man, and Cybernetics Society Award for Outstanding Accomplishment, both from Institute of Electrical and Electronics Engineers, 1972; Benjamin Franklin fellow of Royal Society of Arts (London), 1972; Howard N. Potts Award, Franklin Institute, 1974; Harry Goode Memorial Award, American Federation of Information Processing Societies, 1977; inducted into the National Inventors Hall of Fame, 1979.

WRITINGS—All published by M.I.T. Press: *Industrial Dynamics,* 1961; *Principles of Systems,* 1968; *Urban Dynamics,* 1969; *World Dynamics,* 1971, 2nd edition, 1973; *Collected Papers,* 1975. Contributor of technical papers on digital computers and articles on industrial management to professional journals.

SIDELIGHTS: While he headed the Digital Computer Laboratory at Massachusetts Institute of Technology from 1946 to 1951, Jay W. Forrester was responsible for the design and construction of the Whirlwind I, one of the first high-speed computers. He invented, and holds the patent on, "random-access, coincident-current magnetic storage" which for many years was the standard memory device for digital computers. As head of the Digital Computer Division of M.I.T.'s Lincoln Laboratory, he guided the planning and technical design of the Air Force's Semi-Automatic Ground Environment (SAGE) system for continental air defense, the most extensive early application of digital computer technology. During his tenure at the Alfred P. Sloan School of Management, he applied his computer sciences and engineering background to the development of computer modeling and analysis of social systems; this led to a new field which is now called "system dynamics." Recently Forrester has been working on papers describing his early work in this field in which he and his associates developed a comprehensive simulation model for examining the forces underlying inflation, unemployment, energy shortage, foreign exchange rates, mobility of people, and tax policy. He feels that "by incorporating microeconomic structures at the level of industrial firms and macroeconomic structures at the national level, implications can be explored for the full range of policies that create behavior and cause difficulties in the socio-economic system."

* * *

FORSEE, (Frances) Aylesa

PERSONAL: Born in Kirksville, Mo.; daughter of Edward Wycliffe (a physician) and Lena (Moore) Forsee. *Education:* State College of Agriculture and Mechanic Arts (now South Dakota State University), B.S.; MacPhail College of Music, B.M.E., 1938; University of Colorado, M.A., 1939. *Home and office:* 1845 Bluebell Ave., Boulder, Colo. 80302.

CAREER: High school teacher, Two Harbors, Minn., 1937-39, and Rochester, Minn., 1939-45; University of Iowa, Iowa City, instructor in social science, 1945-46; University of

Denver, Denver, Colo., instructor in social science, 1946-49; Young Women's Christian Association, Denver, teacher of adult education classes, 1949-56; writer, 1956—. Member of Duluth Symphony while in Two Harbors, Minn., and Rochester Civic Symphony while in Rochester, Minn.; former member of Boulder Philharmonic Orchestra. *Member:* League of Women Voters. *Awards, honors:* Helen Dean Fish Award for *The Whirly Bird;* Top Hand Award from Colorado Authors' League, 1966, for *Pablo Casals: Cellist for Freedom,* and 1969, for *Famous Photographers;* National Writers Club Award, 1978.

WRITINGS: The Whirly Bird, Lippincott, 1955; *Miracle for Mingo,* Lippincott, 1956; *Too Much Dog,* Lippincott, 1957; *American Women Who Scored Firsts,* Macrae, 1958; *Louis Agassiz: Pied Piper of Science,* Viking, 1958; *Frank Lloyd Wright: Rebel in Concrete,* Macrae, 1959; *Women Who Reached for Tomorrow,* Macrae, 1960; *My Love and I Together,* Macrae, 1961; *Beneath Land and Sea,* Macrae, 1962; *Albert Einstein: Theoretical Physicist,* Macmillan, 1963; *William Henry Jackson: Pioneer Photographer of the West,* Viking, 1964; *Pablo Casals: Cellist for Freedom,* Crowell, 1965; *Men of Modern Architecture,* Macrae, 1966; *Headliners: Biographies of Famous American Journalists,* Macrae, 1967; *Famous Photographers,* Macrae, 1968; *Arthur Rubinstein: King of the Keyboard,* Crowell, 1969; *They Trusted God,* Christian Science Publishing Society, 1979. Also author of educational materials for Science Research Associates and Encyclopaedia Britannica Educational Corp. Contributor to *People's Almanac.* Contributor of numerous articles to juvenile and adult publications.

SIDELIGHTS: Aylesa Forsee told *CA:* "At one stage in her research, Marie Curie had a ton of pitchblende piled outside her leaky laboratory. Visitors, seeing the dull brown ore that would have to be subjected to analysis gram by gram, thought only of the drudgery involved. But for Marie Curie, stars lay hidden in the dust. She would find radium, she promised herself, even if she had to sift and test a mountain of pitchblende.

"It is the promise of stars in the dust that sustains the writer of biography during weeks and months of searching in documents, diaries, testaments, and tomes. I have had the additional motivation of knowing that in writing for young adults there is always the possibility that a book will set a dream in motion. Letters from readers indicate that a biography can help in choice of a life work, show *how* a person can succeed, or point to higher goals. Young readers gain insight and strength from seeing how others overcame handicaps, disappointments, [and] unhappy situations similar to their own."

Several of Forsee's books, including *American Women Who Scored Firsts,* have been selected by the United States Information Agency for translation into forty-eight foreign languages.

AVOCATIONAL INTERESTS: Reading, playing the violin, hiking, picnicking, camping, speaking to groups of children or teenagers.

BIOGRAPHICAL/CRITICAL SOURCES: Daily Camera, Boulder, Colo., January 22, 1928; *News-Press,* Santa Barbara, Calif., May 17, 1960.

* * *

FOULKE, Roy Anderson 1896-

PERSONAL: Born August 31, 1896, in New York, N.Y.; son of John Blackwell and Sarah Ann (Crozier) Foulke; married Mathilde F. Larsen, 1924; children: Sarah B., John H. *Education:* Bowdoin College, B.S., 1919. *Home:* 9 Midland Gardens, Bronxville, N.Y. 10708.

CAREER: Liberty National Bank, New York City, member of staff of credit department, 1919-22; National Credit Office, Inc., New York City, department manager, 1922-28; Paine Webber & Co., New York City, analyst, 1928-31; Dun & Bradstreet, Inc., New York City, vice-president, director, 1931-61. President of board of overseers, Bowdoin College; American Institute for Economic Research, president of board of trustees, honorary life chairman; trustee of Hebron Academy, Lincoln Foundation, and Robert Schalkenback Foundation; director, E-Z Mills, Inc. *Military service:* U.S. Army, Infantry, 1917-18; became second lieutenant. *Member:* Phi Beta Kappa, Zeta Psi; Union League Club, Players Club (all New York); Siwanoy Country Club (Bronxville). *Awards, honors:* Bowdoin College, M.A., 1939, LL.D., 1970.

WRITINGS: Commercial Paper Market, Bankers Publishing, 1932; (co-author) *Practical Bank Credit,* Prentice-Hall, 1939, 3rd edition, Harper, 1962; *Sinews of American Commerce,* Dun & Bradstreet, 1941; *Practical Finance Statement Analysis,* McGraw, 1945, 6th edition, 1968; *Behind Scenes of Business,* Dun & Bradstreet, 1957; *Foulke Family,* privately printed, 1974; *Crozier Family,* privately printed, 1976; *Larsen and Uggerby Families,* privately printed, 1978. Member of editorial advisory board, *American Journal of Economics and Sociology.*

SIDELIGHTS: Practical Finance Statement Analysis has been translated into Spanish.

* * *

FOWLER, Harry (Jr.) 1934-

PERSONAL: Born November 15, 1934, in Philadelphia, Pa.; son of Harry H. (a businessman) and Olga (Borowiec) Fowler; married Dolores E. Fraustro, September 13, 1956; children: Gregory Kenneth, Gary Keith, Geoffrey Kent. *Education:* University of Pennsylvania, B.A., 1956; Yale University, M.S., 1958, Ph.D., 1959. *Politics:* Democrat. *Religion:* Atheist. *Home:* 3212 Fox Run Rd., Allison Park, Pa. 15101. *Office:* Department of Psychology, University of Pittsburgh, Pittsburgh, Pa. 15260.

CAREER: U.S. Naval Air Development Center, Johnsville, Pa., experimental psychologist, 1956; Yale University, New Haven, Conn., assistant instructor in psychology, 1958-59; University of Pittsburgh, Pittsburgh, Pa., assistant professor, 1959-63, associate professor, 1963-68, professor of psychology, 1968—, head of learning program, 1968-71. Visiting associate professor of psychology, University of New Mexico, 1968; visiting professor of psychology, University of Sussex, England, 1974. Lecturer and participant at numerous professional conferences and colloquia. *Member:* Psychonomic Society, American Psychological Association (fellow), American Association for the Advancement of Science, Eastern Psychological Association, Midwestern Psychological Association, Phi Beta Kappa, Sigma Xi. *Awards, honors:* National Science Foundation grants, 1960-63, and 1970-74; National Institute of Health grants, 1961-63, 1964-68, 1964-72, and 1973-80; United Health Foundations grant, 1969-70; N.A.T.O. senior fellow in science, 1974.

WRITINGS: Curiosity and Exploratory Behavior, Macmillan, 1965; (editor with S. H. Hulse and W. K. Honig, and contributor) *Cognitive Processes in Animal Behavior,* Erlbaum, 1978.

Contributor: K. W. Spence and J. T. Spence, editors, *The Psychology of Learning and Motivation*, Academic Press, 1967; J. F. Hall, editor, *Readings in the Psychology of Learning*, Lippincott, 1967; E. E. Boe and R. M. Church, editors, *Punishment: Issues and Experiments*, Appleton, 1969; B. A. Campbell and R. M. Church, editors, *Punishment and Aversive Behavior*, Appleton, 1969; F. R. Brush, editor, *Aversive Conditioning and Learning*, Academic Press, 1971; Robert Glaser, editor, *The Nature of Reinforcement*, Academic Press, 1971; *Neal E. Miller: Selected Papers*, Aldine, 1971; G. R. Lafrancois, editor, *Child Development*, Wadsworth, 1973.

Contributor to *Encyclopedia of Education* and to proceedings of professional conferences. Contributor to professional journals, including *Journal of Psychology, Psychological Bulletin, Psychological Reports, Science, Journal of Comparative and Physiological Psychology, Canadian Journal of Psychology, Journal of Experimental Psychology, Psychonomic Science*, and *Learning and Motivation*.

WORK IN PROGRESS: Research and writing on signaling and affective properties of conditioned stimuli, on the nature of conditioned inhibitors, on blocking and "superconditioning" effects in Pavlovian and instrumental conditioning, and on discriminability functions of rewards and punishment.

SIDELIGHTS: Harry Fowler told *CA* that his "research has been concerned with fundamental principles and phenomena of conditioning and motivation, and therefore my writing has been directed primarily to professional audiences. Sometime in the not-too-distant future, I hope to be in a position where I can translate and apply this work to psychological topics of a more common interest."

* * *

FOWLER, William Morgan, Jr. 1944-

PERSONAL: Born July 25, 1944, in Clearwater, Fla.; son of William Morgan (a U.S. post office employee) and Eleanor (Brennan) Fowler; married Marilyn L. Noble (an elementary school teacher), August 11, 1968. *Education:* Northeastern University, B.A. (magna cum laude), 1967; University of Notre Dame, M.A., 1969, Ph.D., 1971. *Politics:* Democrat. *Religion:* Roman Catholic. *Home:* 323 Franklin St., Reading, Mass. 01867. *Office:* Department of History, Northeastern University, Boston, Mass. 02115.

CAREER: Northeastern University, Boston, Mass., assistant professor, 1971-77, associate professor of history, 1977—. *Military service:* U.S. Army Reserve, military intelligence, 1970—; present rank, first lieutenant. *Member:* North American Society of Oceanic Historians, Organization of American Historians, Society of American Archivists, American Association of University Professors (secretary of Northeastern University Chapter), New England Historic and Genealogical Society, Rhode Island Historical Society, Newport Historical Society, Reading Antiquarian Society (member of board of directors). *Awards, honors:* American Philosophical Society grant; National Endowment for the Humanities grant.

WRITINGS: William Ellery: A Rhode Island Politico and Lord of Admiralty, Scarecrow, 1973; *Rebels under Sail*, Scribner, 1976; (editor) *The American Revolution: A Retrospective*, Northeastern University Press, 1979; *The Baron of Beacon Hill: A Biography of John Hancock*, Houghton, 1980. Contributor to *Proceedings* of the United States Naval Institute. Contributor to professional journals, including *American Neptune, Pennsylvania Magazine of History and Biography, Rhode Island History, New York Historical Society Quarterly, Connecticut Historical Society Bulletin, Mariner's Mirror*, and *Harvard Magazine*.

WORK IN PROGRESS: American Naval History, 1783-1815.

AVOCATIONAL INTERESTS: Sailing, swimming, tennis.

BIOGRAPHICAL/CRITICAL SOURCES: Los Angeles Times, January 30, 1980.

* * *

FOX, Charles Philip 1913-

PERSONAL: Born May 27, 1913, in Milwaukee, Wis.; son of George William and Mary (Romadka) Fox; married Sophie Zore, 1942; children: Barbara, Peter. *Home:* 132 Grant Rd., Winter Haven, Fla. 33880.

CAREER: Circus World Museum, Baraboo, Wis., director, 1960-72; Ringling Brothers and Barnum & Bailey Circus, director of research and project development and circus historian, 1972—.

WRITINGS—Circus histories: *Circus Trains*, Kalmbach, 1948; *Circus Parades*, Century House, 1953; *A Ticket to the Circus*, Superior, 1960; *Pictorial History of Performing Horses*, Superior, 1961; *The Circus Comes to Town*, Inland Press, 1963; (with Tom Parkinson) *The Circus in America*, Country Beautiful Publishing Corp., 1969; *The Great Circus Street Parade*, Dover, 1978; *American Circus Posters*, Dover, 1978; (with Parkinson) *The Circus Moves by Rail*, Pruett, 1978; *Old Time Circus Cuts*, Dover, 1979. Also author of unpublished manuscripts "Circus Advertising" and, with Parkinson, of "Circus—America's Greatest Show."

Juveniles; all published by Reilly & Lee: *Frisky Try Again*, 1959; *Come to the Circus*, 1959; *A Fox in the House*, 1960; *Mr. Stripes the Gopher*, 1961; *When Winter Comes*, 1962; *Birds Will Come to You*, 1962; *Mr. Duck's Big Day*, 1963; *Snowball the Trick Pony*, 1963; *When Spring Comes*, 1964; *When Summer Comes*, 1966; *When Autumn Comes*, 1966; *Opie Possum's Trick*, 1968.

Photographic illustrator: Sam Campbell, *Sweet Sue's Adventures*, Bobbs-Merrill, 1959; Campbell, *Calamity Jane*, Bobbs-Merrill, 1962.

* * *

FOX, Robert J. 1927-

PERSONAL: Born December 24, 1927, in Watertown, S.D.; son of Aloysius John (a farmer) and Susie Emma (Lorentz) Fox. *Education:* Attended St. John's University, Collegeville, Minn., 1947-50; St. Paul Seminary, St. Paul, Minn., B.A. *Address:* Box 20, Redfield, S.D. 57469.

CAREER: Ordained Roman Catholic priest, 1955; pastor of churches in South Dakota, 1961-72; St. Bernard's Church, Redfield, S.D., pastor, 1972—. Chaplain to South Dakota State School and Hospital; national spiritual director of Cadets of Our Lady of Fatima.

WRITINGS—Published by Our Sunday Visitor, except as indicated: *Religious Education: Its Effects, Its Challenges Today*, Daughters of St. Paul, 1972; *The Catholic Prayerbook*, Apostolic Publishing Co., 1972, revised edition, Our Sunday Visitor, 1974; *Renewal for All God's People*, 1975; *Charity, Morality, Sex and Young People*, 1975; *The Marian Catechism*, 1976; *Saints and Heroes Speak*, 1977; *A Prayer Book for Young Catholics*, 1977; *Catholic Truth for Youth*, Ave Maria Press, 1978; *A World at Prayer*, 1979; *A Catechism of the Catholic Church: Two Thousand Years of Faith and Tradition,* Franciscan Herald, 1980. Also author of numerous pamphlets, booklets, and cassette recordings. Columnist, *National Catholic Register, Mini-Register, Twin Circle,* and *Soul.* Contributor to periodicals, including *Our Sunday Visitor* and *Priest.*

WORK IN PROGRESS: Fatima Today; The Call of Heaven: Life of Stigmatist of San Vittorino.

* * *

FOXX, Richard M(ichael) 1944-

PERSONAL: Born October 28, 1944, in Denver, Colo.; son of James Martin and Marie (Harris) Foxx; married Carolyn Crofutt, April 4, 1966; children: two. *Education:* University of California, Riverside, B.A., 1967; California State University, Fullerton, M.A., 1970; Southern Illinois University, Ph.D., 1971. *Agent:* Georges Borchardt, Inc., 136 East 57th St., New York, N.Y. 10022. *Office:* Department of Psychology, University of Maryland Baltimore County, 5401 Wilkens Ave., Baltimore, Md. 21228.

CAREER: Patton State Hospital, Patton, Calif., research assistant, 1968-69; California Department of Game and Fish, Los Angeles, researcher, 1968-70; research assistant, Pacific State Hospital, 1969-70; California State University, Fullerton, instructor in psychology, 1970; Anna State Hospital, Anna, Ill., research scientist in Behavior Research Laboratory, 1970-74; University of Maryland Baltimore County, Baltimore, assistant professor of psychology, 1974—, assistant professor in Medical School, 1975—. Private practice of psychology, 1975—. Adjunct assistant professor, Southern Illinois University, 1973-74. *Member:* American Psychological Association, American Association on Mental Deficiency, Association for the Advancement of Behavior Therapy, Behavior Research Society (fellow), Association of Behavior Analysis, National Society of Autistic Children, Psi Chi, Phi Kappa Phi.

WRITINGS—With Nathan H. Azrin: *Rapid Toilet Training of the Retarded: Day and Nighttime Independent Toileting,* Research Press, 1973; *Toilet Training in Less Than a Day,* Simon & Schuster, 1974; *Effective Behavioral and Educational Programming for the Retarded,* Research Press, in press. Contributor of articles to journals in the behavioral sciences.

WORK IN PROGRESS: A book on how to quit smoking; research on caffeinism, encopresis, and self-abusive behavior.

* * *

FRANCIS, Robert (Churchill) 1901-

PERSONAL: Born August 12, 1901, in Upland, Pa.; son of Ebenezer Fisher and Ida May (Allen) Francis. *Education:* Harvard University, A.B., 1923, Ed.M., 1926. *Home:* Fort Juniper, 170 Market Hill Rd., Amherst, Mass. 01002.

CAREER: Professional writer; taught at summer writers workshops and conferences and lectures at universities throughout the country. *Awards and honors:* Shelley Memorial Award, 1939; Golden Rose of New England Poetry Club, 1942-43, for a notable contribution to poetry; Phi Beta Kappa poet, Tufts University, 1955; Prix de Rome fellowship, American Academy of Arts and Letters, 1957-58; Phi Beta Kappa poet, Harvard University, 1960; Amy Lowell Traveling Scholar, 1967-68; L.H.D., University of Massachusetts, 1970; Brandeis University Creative Arts Award in Poetry, 1974.

WRITINGS—Poetry: *Stand with Me Here,* Macmillan, 1936; *Valhalla and Other Poems,* Macmillan, 1938; *The Sound I Listened For,* Macmillan, 1944; *The Face against the Glass,* privately printed, 1950; *The Orb Weaver,* Wesleyan University Press, 1960; *Come Out into the Sun: Poems New and Selected,* University of Massachusetts Press, 1965; *Like Ghosts of Eagles,* University of Massachusetts Press, 1974; *Robert Francis: Collected Poems, 1936-1976,* University of Massachusetts Press, 1976. Also author and performer of recording, *Robert Francis Reads His Poems,* Folkways, 1975.

Prose: *We Fly Away* (fiction), Swallow-Morrow, 1948; *The Satirical Rogue on Poetry* (essays), University of Massachusetts Press, 1968; *The Trouble with Francis* (autobiography), University of Massachusetts Press, 1971; *Frost, A Time to Talk: Conversations and Indiscretions Recorded by Robert Francis,* University of Massachusetts Press, 1972 (published in England as *Robert Frost: A Time to Talk,* Robson Books, 1973); Peter Kaplan, editor, *A Certain Distance* (sketches), Pourboire Press, 1976.

SIDELIGHTS: Robert Francis comments. "I live the year-round in my one-man house, Fort Juniper, in a wooded area on the outskirts of Amherst, Mass., where I devote myself to my writing and the ever-increasing involvements pertaining to it—this in spite of serious health handicaps.'' Collections of Robert Francis' papers are at the Syracuse University Library, the University of Massachusetts—Amherst library, and the Jones Library in Amherst. In 1974, the University of Massachusetts Press established the Juniper Prize in honor of Robert Francis.

BIOGRAPHICAL/CRITICAL SOURCES: Massachusetts Review, summer, 1960; *Horn Book,* February, 1966; *Antioch Review,* summer, 1966; *Chicago Review,* June, 1967; *Virginia Quarterly Review,* autumn, 1968, spring, 1977; *New Republic,* August 7, 1971; *Poetry,* November, 1972, November, 1977; *New York Times Book Review,* December 10, 1972; *Nation,* February 12, 1973; *Times Literary Supplement,* November 23, 1973; *Western Humanities Review,* summer, 1974; *Francis on the Spot* (interview), Tunnel Press, 1976; *Christian Science Monitor,* December 8, 1976; *Saturday Review,* January 8, 1977; *Hudson Review,* summer, 1977; *New England Quarterly,* June, 1977; *Sewanee Review,* July, 1977.

* * *

FRANK, Isaiah 1917-

PERSONAL: Born November 7, 1917, in New York, N.Y.; son of Henry and Rose (Isserles) Frank; married Ruth Hershfield, March 23, 1941; children: Robert, Kenneth. *Education:* City College (now City College of the City University of New York), B.A., 1936; Columbia University, M.A., 1938, Ph.D., 1960. *Home:* 3102 Hawthorne St. N.W., Washington, D.C. 20008. *Office:* School of Advanced International Studies, Johns Hopkins University, 1740 Massachusetts Ave. N.W., Washington, D.C. 20036.

CAREER: Amherst College, Amherst, Mass., instructor, 1939-41; War Production Board, Washington, D.C., economic consultant, 1942; Office of Strategic Services, Washington, D.C., senior economist, 1942-44; U.S. Department of State, Washington, D.C., 1945-63, posts include director of Office of International Trade Policy, director of Office of International Financial and Development Affairs, and deputy assistant secretary of state for economic affairs; Johns Hopkins University, School of Advanced International Studies, Washington, D.C., Clayton Professor of International Economics, 1963—. Executive director of President's

Commission on International Trade and Investment Policy, 1970-71; director of international economic studies, Committee for Economic Development, 1971—. Member of U.S. delegations to numerous international conferences on economic matters. Chairman of advisory committee on international investment, technology, and development, U.S. Department of State, 1975—; member of advisory committee, United Nations Trade and Development Board. *Military service:* U.S. Army, 1944-45; became first lieutenant. *Member:* American Economic Association, Council on Foreign Relations, Phi Beta Kappa, Cosmos Club (Washington, D.C.). *Awards, honors:* Carnegie fellow, National Bureau of Economic Research, 1941; Rockefeller Public Service Award, 1960; Ford Foundation research grant, 1964.

WRITINGS: The European Common Market: An Analysis of Commercial Policy, Praeger, 1961; (editor and contributor) *The Japanese Economy in International Perspective,* Johns Hopkins Press, 1975; (co-author) *The Implications of Managed Floating Exchange Rates for U.S. Trade Policy,* New York University, 1979. Contributor to professional journals.

WORK IN PROGRESS: Foreign Enterprise in Developing Countries.

* * *

FRANK, Joseph 1916-

PERSONAL: Born December 20, 1916, in Chicago, Ill.; son of A. Richard and Gertrude (Greenbaum) Frank; married first wife, Margery Goodkind, February 1, 1941; married second wife, Florence Stanton Clark Zartman, January 24, 1969; children: (first marriage) Thomas, Peter, Andrew. *Education:* Harvard University, B.A., 1939, M.A., 1948, Ph.D., 1953. *Politics:* Democrat. *Home:* 166 Lincoln Ave., Amherst, Mass. 01002. *Office:* Department of English, University of Massachusetts, Amherst, Mass. 01003.

CAREER: University of Rochester, Rochester, N.Y., instructor, 1948-53, assistant professor, 1953-58, associate professor, 1958-63, professor of English, 1963-67; University of New Mexico, Albuquerque, professor of English and chairman of department, 1967-69; University of Massachusetts—Amherst, professor of English, 1969—, chairman of department, 1969-75. Exchange professor, University of Kent, Canterbury, England, 1976-77. *Military service:* Served with British Army in North Africa, 1942, U.S. Army, 1943-45. *Member:* Modern Language Association of America, Renaissance Society, Milton Society, American Association of University Professors (president, Rochester chapter, 1957). *Awards, honors:* Huntington Library fellow, 1955-56; Guggenheim fellow, 1957-58, 1961; Folger Shakespeare Library fellow, 1961-62.

WRITINGS: The Levellers, Harvard University Press, 1955; *The Beginnings of the English Newspaper,* Harvard University Press, 1961; *Literature from the Bible,* Little, Brown, 1963; (editor) *Modern Essays in English,* Little, Brown, 1966; (editor) *The New Look in Politics: McCarthy's Campaign,* University of New Mexico Press, 1968; *Hobbled Pegasus: A Descriptive Bibliography of Minor English Poetry, 1641-1660,* University of New Mexico Press, 1968; (editor) *You,* Harcourt, 1972; (editor) *The Doomed Astronaut,* Winthrop Publishing, 1972; *Milton without Footnotes,* Harper, 1974. Associate editor, *Seventeenth-Century News.*

BIOGRAPHICAL/CRITICAL SOURCES: Times Literary Supplement, June 26, 1969.

FRANKLIN, John Hope 1915-

PERSONAL: Born January 2, 1915, in Rentiesville, Okla.; son of Buck C. and Mollie (Parker) Franklin; married Aurelia E. Whittington, 1940; children: John Whittington. *Education:* Fisk University, A.B., 1935; Harvard University, A.M., 1936, Ph.D., 1941. *Home:* 5805 South Blackstone Ave., Chicago, Ill. 60637. *Office:* Department of History, University of Chicago, Chicago, Ill. 60637.

CAREER: Fisk University, Nashville, Tenn., instructor, 1936-37; St. Augustine's College, Raleigh, N.C., professor, 1939-43; North Carolina College at Durham (now North Carolina Central University), professor, 1943-47; Howard University, Washington, D.C., professor, 1947-56; Brooklyn College (now Brooklyn College of the City University of New York), Brooklyn, N.Y., professor of history and chairman of department, 1956-64; University of Chicago, Chicago, Ill., professor of American history, 1964-69, John M. Manly Distinguished Service Professor of History, 1969—, chairman of department, 1967-70. Pitt Professor of American History and Institutions, Cambridge University, 1962-63. Member of boards of trustees, Fisk University, Museum of Science and History, and Chicago Symphony. Member of board of directors, Salzburg Seminar in American Studies. *Member:* American Historical Association (president, 1979), Organization of American Historians (president, 1974-75), Association for the Study of Negro Life and History, Southern Historical Association (president, 1969-70), Phi Beta Kappa. *Awards, honors:* Guggenheim grant; Social Science Research Council fellowship; Frederic Bancroft Prize for best article published in *Journal of Negro History,* 1945; honorary degrees from over sixty colleges and universities.

WRITINGS: The Free Negro in North Carolina, 1790-1860, University of North Carolina Press, 1943, reprinted, Russell, 1969; *From Slavery to Freedom,* Knopf, 1947, 5th edition, 1978; (editor) *The Civil War Diary of James T. Ayers,* Illinois State Historical Society, 1947; *The Militant South, 1800-1860,* Harvard University Press, 1956, reprinted, 1970; *Reconstruction after the Civil War,* University of Chicago Press, 1961; (editor) Albion Tourgee, *A Fool's Errand,* Harvard University Press, 1961; (editor) T. W. Higginson, *Army Life in a Black Regiment,* Beacon Press, 1962; *The Emancipation Proclamation,* Doubleday, 1963; (editor) *Three Negro Classics,* Avon, 1965; (co-author) *Land of the Free,* Benziger, 1966; (editor) *Reminiscences of an Active Life: The Autobiography of John R. Lynch,* University of Chicago Press, 1970; *Illustrated History of Black Americans,* Time-Life, 1970; (editor with Alfred Duster) *Crusade for Justice: The Autobiography of Ida B. Wells,* University of Chicago Press, 1972; (editor) Eugene Levy, *James Weldon Johnson: Black Leader, Black Voice,* University of Chicago Press, 1973; *A Southern Odyssey: Travelers in the Antebellum North,* Louisiana State University Press, 1976; *Racial Equality in America,* University of Chicago Press, 1976. Member of board of editors, *Journal of Negro History.*

* * *

FRANTZ, Joe B. 1917-

PERSONAL: Born January 16, 1917, in Dallas, Tex.; son of Ezra Allen (a manufacturer) and Mary (Buckley) Frantz; married Helen Boswell, September 3, 1939; children: Jolie, Lisa. *Education:* University of Texas, B.J., 1938, M.A., 1940, Ph.D., 1948; postdoctoral study at Harvard University, 1948-49. *Politics:* Democrat. *Religion:* Methodist. *Home:* 4301 Edgemont, Austin, Tex. 78731. *Office:* Department of History, University of Texas, Austin, Tex. 78712.

CAREER: San Jacinto Museum, Houston, Tex., acting director, 1942-43; University of Texas at Austin, assistant professor, 1949-53, associate professor, 1953-59, professor of history, 1959-77, Prescott Webb Professor of History, 1977—, chairman of department, 1961-65, director of research in Texas history, 1966—, director of Oral History Project, 1968—. Visiting professor at University of Chicago, 1962, Northwestern University, 1963, University of Chile, 1965, University of Colorado, 1966, University of San Marcos (Lima, Peru), 1967, University of Quito (Ecuador), 1969, and University of Guayaquil (Ecuador), 1969; lecturer, Law-Science Academy (Crested Butte, Colo.), 1963-64. Director of American Civilization by Its Interpreters Project, Texas Institute of Letters, 1963-65; member of National Historical Publications Commission and of National Parks Advisory Board. Consultant on history to the White House, 1968-69; consultant on films to U.S. Information Agency; consultant on maps to Rand-McNally Co.; historical consultant to Borden Co. *Military service:* U.S. Naval Reserve, 1943-46; became lieutenant.

MEMBER: American Historical Association, Organization of American Historians (member of executive council, 1962-64), Business History Foundation, Oral History Association, Committee on International Exchange of Persons, Southern Historical Association (member of executive council, 1960-63; president, 1978-79), Southwestern Social Science Association (president, 1963-64), Texas State Historical Association (member of executive council, 1959-66; director, 1966-77), Texas Institute of Letters (vice-president, 1965-67; president, 1967-69), Philosophical Society of Texas, Phi Alpha Theta (vice-president, 1960-62; president, 1962-64), Headliners Club (Austin). *Awards, honors:* Carr P. Collins Award, Texas Institute of Letters, 1951, for *Gail Borden, Dairyman to a Nation;* fellow of Ford Foundation and Social Science Research Council, 1953-54; Lemuel Scarborough Award for excellence in teaching, 1957; E. D. Farmer fellow, Mexico, 1958; Alumnus of the Year award, Phi Theta Kappa, 1971.

WRITINGS: Gail Borden, Dairyman to a Nation, University of Oklahoma Press, 1951; (co-author) *The American Cowboy: The Myth and the Reality,* University of Oklahoma Press, 1955; (editor) *An Honest Preface,* Houghton, 1959; (with Cordia S. Duke) *Six Thousand Miles of Fence,* University of Texas Press, 1961; (co-author) *The Heroes of Texas,* Texian Press, 1964; (editor) A. J. Sowell, *The Texas Rangers,* Argosy, 1964; (co-author) *Turner, Bolton and Webb,* University of Washington Press, 1965; (editor) J. Roy White, *A Hill Country Sketchbook,* Encino Press, 1968; *Houston,* Teachers College Press, 1971; *L.B.J.: Thirty-seven Years of Public Life,* Shoal Creek Publishers, 1974; *Aspects of the American West: Three Essays,* Texas A&M University Press, 1976; *Texas: A Bicentennial History,* Norton, 1976. Editor, *Southwestern Historical Quarterly,* 1966—; member of editorial boards, *American West, Montana, Arizona and the West,* and *Texana.*

* * *

FRASCONI, Antonio 1919-

PERSONAL: Born April 28, 1919, in Buenos Aires, Argentina; came to United States in 1945; son of Franco and Armida (Carbonai) Frasconi; married Leona Pierce, July 18, 1951; children: Pablo, Miguel. *Education:* Attended Circulo de Bellas Artes (Montevideo); studied at Art Students League (New York), 1944-46; studied mural painting at New School for Social Research, 1947-48. *Home and studio:* 26 Dock Rd., South Norwalk, Conn. 06854.

CAREER: Artist. Member of art faculty, New School for Social Research, New York, N.Y., 1951-57; artist-in-residence, University of Hawaii, Honolulu, 1964; member of art faculty, State University of New York College at Purchase, 1974—. Has had numerous one-man shows in the United States, Mexico, South America, and Europe; work represented in many permanent collections of museums and galleries, including Library of Congress, Museum of Modern Art (New York), Metropolitan Museum of Art (New York), Art Institute of Chicago, Detroit Institute of Arts, San Diego Museum of Arts, and Rhode Island School of Design.

AWARDS, HONORS: Purchase prize, Brooklyn Museum, 1946, and University of Nebraska, 1951; Philadelphia Print Club prize, 1951; Erickson Award, Society of American Graphic Artists, 1952; Yaddo scholarship, 1952; Guggenheim fellowship, 1952-53; National Institute of Arts and Letters grant, 1954; Grand Prix, Venice Film Festival, 1960, for film, "The Neighboring Shore"; American Library Association Notable Book Award, 1961, for *The Snow and the Sun;* Tamarind Lithograph grant, 1962; winner of competition to design postage stamp honoring National Academy of Science, 1963; Joseph H. Hirshorn Foundation Prize, Society of American Graphic Artists, 1963; W. H. Walker Prize, Philadelphia Print Club, 1964; prize of Second Biennale d'Art Graphique, Brno, Czechoslovakia, 1966; prize of Salon Nacional de Bellas Artes, Montevideo, 1967; Grand Premio, Exposition de la Habana, Cuba, 1968; prize of Ninth International Biennial of Arts, Tokyo, 1975.

WRITINGS—All self-illustrated: *12 Fables of Aesop,* Museum of Modern Art, 1954, revised edition, 1964; *See and Say: A Picture Book in Four Languages,* Harcourt, 1955; *Woodcuts by Antonio Frasconi,* E. Weyhe, 1957; *The House That Jack Built: A Picture Book in Two Languages,* Harcourt, 1958; *Birds from My Homeland,* privately printed, 1958; *The Face of Edgar Allan Poe,* privately printed, 1959; *A Whitman Portrait,* privately printed, 1960; *The Snow and the Sun: A South American Folk Rhyme in Two Languages,* Harcourt, 1961; *A Sunday in Monterey,* Harcourt, 1964; *See Again, Say Again,* Harcourt, 1964; *Kaleidoscope in Woodcuts,* Harcourt, 1968; (editor) *On the Slain Collegians,* Farrar, Straus, 1971; *Antonio Frasconi's World,* Macmillan, 1974; *Frasconi: Against the Grain,* Macmillan, 1975.

Illustrator: Ruth Krauss, *Cantilever Rainbow,* Pantheon, 1965; Pablo Neruda, *Bestiary/Bestiario* (verse), Harcourt, 1965; Louis Untermeyer, *Love Lyrics,* Odyssey, 1965; Walt Whitman, *Overheard the Sun,* Farrar, Straus, 1969; Mario Benedetti, editor, *Unstill Life,* Harcourt, 1969; Isaac B. Singer, *Elijah the Slave,* Farrar, Straus, 1970; Gabriela Mistral, *Crickets and Frogs: A Fable in Spanish and English,* translation by Doris Dana, Atheneum, 1972.

BIOGRAPHICAL/CRITICAL SOURCES: Print, winter, 1950; *Newsweek,* March 17, 1952, April 5, 1954; *Horizon,* March, 1961; *Time,* December 20, 1963; *New Republic,* February 29, 1964; *School Arts,* May, 1966; Diana Klemin, *The Art of Art for Children's Books,* C. N. Potter, 1966; Klemin, *The Illustrated Book,* C. N. Potter, 1970; *Graphis 155,* Volume 27, Graphis Press, 1971-72.

* * *

FRASER, Sylvia 1935-

PERSONAL: Born March 8, 1935, in Hamilton, Ontario, Canada; daughter of George Nicholas (a steel inspector) and Gladys (Wilson) Meyers; married Russell James Fraser (a lawyer), May 30, 1959 (divorced, 1977). *Education:* University of Western Ontario, B.A. (with honors), 1957. *Home:* 382 Brunswick Ave., Toronto, Ontario, Canada M5R 2Y9.

CAREER: Toronto Star Weekly, Toronto, Ontario, journalist, 1957-68; full-time novelist, 1968—. *Awards, honors:* Canadian Womens Press Club Awards, 1967 and 1968; President's Medal for Canadian Journalism from University of Western Ontario, 1969.

WRITINGS—All novels: *Pandora,* McClelland & Stewart, 1972, Little, Brown, 1973; *The Candy Factory,* Little, Brown, 1975; *A Casual Affair,* McClelland & Stewart, 1978, Macmillan, 1979.

WORK IN PROGRESS: A historical novel, *The Emperor's Women,* set in ancient Rome.

* * *

FRAZIER, Neta Lohnes

PERSONAL: Born in Owosso, Mich.; daughter of Emory Edward (an insurance agent) and Jennie (Osborn) Lohnes; married Earl Cooper Frazier (a teacher; deceased); children: Lesley (Mrs. Perry Thompson), Philip E., Richard B. *Education:* Whitman College, B.A. *Home and office:* South 1010 Rockwood Blvd., No. 403, Spokane, Wash. 99202.

CAREER: High school English teacher in Waitsburg, Wash.; substitute teacher in Spokane, Wash.; editor, *Spokane Valley Herald,* Opportunity, Wash.; professional writer, 1947—. *Member:* Authors Guild, Authors League of America, American Association of University Women (president, Spokane branch, 1951-53), Women in Communications, Pacific Northwest Writers Conference (member of board, 1969-71), Spokane Writers (president, 1969-70), Phi Beta Kappa, Kappa Kappa Gamma, Delta Kappa Gamma. *Awards, honors:* Named one of seven outstanding Kappa Kappa Gamma alumnae, 1960; Governor's Award for historical writing, 1968; Fort Wright College Award for historical studies, 1968; Women in Communications Award for Excellence, 1978.

WRITINGS: By-Line Dennie, Crowell, 1947; *My Love Is a Gypsy,* Longmans, Green, 1952; *Little Rhody,* McKay, 1953; *Somebody Special,* McKay, 1954; *Secret Friend,* Longmans, Green, 1956; *Young Bill Fargo,* Longmans, Green, 1956; *Rawhide Johnny,* McKay, 1957; *Magic Ring,* McKay, 1959; *Something of My Own,* McKay, 1960; (contributor) *Grandma Moses Storybook,* Random House, 1961; *One Long Picnic,* McKay, 1962; *Five Roads to the Pacific,* McKay, 1964; *The General's Boots,* McKay, 1965; *Eastern Washington State Historical Society: The First Half-Century* (monograph), Eastern Washington State Historical Society, 1966; *Sacajawea, the Girl Nobody Knows,* McKay, 1967; *Stouthearted Seven,* Harcourt, 1974.

WORK IN PROGRESS: Fiction and nonfiction about the early West.

SIDELIGHTS: Four of Neta Frazier's books have been Junior Literary Guild selections.

BIOGRAPHICAL/CRITICAL SOURCES: Spokane Daily Chronicle, April 5, 1962.

* * *

FREEBORN, Richard H. 1926-

PERSONAL: Born 1926, in Cardiff, Wales; son of Charles Fernandez and Alice P. (Smith) Freeborn; married Anne Verna Twentyman Davis, 1954; children: Rosalind, Elizabeth, Timothy, Caroline. *Education:* Oxford University, B.A., 1950, M.A., 1954, D.Phil., 1957. *Politics:* Conservative socialist. *Home:* Stowe House, 10 Portsmouth Ave., Thames Dilton, Surrey KT7 0RT, England. *Agent:* Rosalind Freeborn Battersby, c/o Hutchinson's, Fitzroy Sq., London W.1, England. *Office:* School of Slavonic and Eastern European Studies, University of London, Malet St., London WC1E 7HU, England.

CAREER: Attache of British Embassy, Moscow, U.S.S.R., 1952-54; Oxford University, Oxford, England, university lecturer, 1954-64; University of California, Los Angeles, visiting professor, 1964-65; University of Manchester, Manchester, England, Sir William Mather Professor of Russian, 1965-67; University of London, London, England, professor of Russian literature, 1967—. *Military service:* Royal Air Force, 1944-47; became sergeant. *Member:* Association of University Teachers, British Universities Association of Slavists, Association of Teachers of Russian.

WRITINGS: Turgenev, the Novelist's Novelist, Oxford University Press, 1960, reprinted, Greenwood Press, 1978; *Two Ways of Life,* Hodder & Stoughton, 1962; *The Emigration of Sergey Ivanovich,* Hodder & Stoughton, 1963, Morrow, 1965; *A Short History of Modern Russia,* Morrow, 1966; (translator) I. S. Turgenev, *Sketches from a Hunter's Album,* Penguin, 1967; (translator) Turgenev, *Home of the Gentry,* Penguin, 1970; *The Rise of the Russian Novel,* Cambridge University Press, 1973; (contributor) *The Age of Realism,* Penguin, 1974; (translator) Turgenev, *Rudin,* Penguin, 1975; (editor and contributor) *Russian Literary Attitudes from Pushkin to Solzhenitsyn,* Macmillan, 1976; (editor) *Russian and Slavic Literature,* Slavica, 1976; *Russian Roulette* (novel), Cassell, 1979.

* * *

FREEDBERG, Sydney Joseph 1914-

PERSONAL: Born November 11, 1914, in Boston, Mass.; married Anne Blake, 1942 (divorced, 1950); married Susan Pulitzer, 1954 (died, 1965); married Catherine Blanton, 1967; children: William Blake, Kate Pulitzer, Nathaniel Davis, Sydney Joseph, Jr. *Education:* Harvard University, A.B. (summa cum laude), 1936, A.M., 1939, Ph.D., 1940. *Home:* 5 Channing Place, Cambridge, Mass. *Office:* Department of Fine Arts, Fogg Art Museum, Harvard University, Cambridge, Mass. 02138.

CAREER: Harvard University, Cambridge, Mass., assistant and tutor, department of fine arts, 1938-40; Wellesley College, Wellesley, Mass., assistant professor, 1946-49, associate professor of art, 1950-54; Harvard University, visiting lecturer, 1953-54, associate professor, 1954-61, professor of art, 1961—, Arthur Kingsley Porter Professor of Fine Arts, 1979—, chairman of department of fine arts, 1959-63, member of faculty council, 1973-76, chairman of University Museums Council, 1977-80, acting director of Fogg Art Museum, 1978-79. National vice-chairman, Committee to Rescue Italian Art, 1966-74; member of board of directors, Save Venice, 1970—; member of Signet Associates. Member of advisory council, Guggenheim Foundation, 1976—. *Military service:* U.S. Army, 1942-46; received Order of the British Empire (military), 1946.

MEMBER: American Academy of Arts and Sciences (fellow), College Art Association of America (director, 1962-66), Phi Beta Kappa. *Awards, honors:* Faculty fellow, Wellesley College, 1949-50; Guggenheim fellow, 1949-50, 1954-55; American Council of Learned Societies fellow, 1958-59, 1966-67; Harvard Press Faculty Prize, 1961, for *Painting of the High Renaissance in Rome and Florence;* Morey Book Award of College Art Association, 1963, for *Andrea del Sarto;* named Grand Officer, Star of Italian Solidarity, 1968; National Endowment for the Humanities senior fellow, 1973-74; Walter Channing Cabot fellow, Harvard University, 1973-76.

WRITINGS: (With J. S. Plaut) *Sources of Modern Painting,* Institute of Modern Art (Boston), 1939; *Old Master Paintings,* Brandt Gallery, 1941; *New Masters from Old Holland: Less Known Painters of the Seventeenth Century,* Brandt Gallery, 1941; *Parmigianino: His Works in Painting,* Harvard University Press, 1950, reprinted, Greenwood Press, 1971; *Raphael, the Stanza della Segnatura in the Vatican,* Metropolitan Museum of Art (New York), 1953; *Painting of the High Renaissance in Rome and Florence,* two volumes, Harvard University Press, 1961; *Andrea del Sarto,* two volumes, Harvard University Press, 1963; *Painting in Italy, 1500-1600,* Penguin, 1971, 3rd edition, 1978.

Editor; all published by Garland: Katherine P. Erhart, *The Development of the Facing Head Motif on Greek Coins and Its Relationship to Classical Art,* 1979; Richard E. Lamoureux, *Alberti's Church of San Sebastiano in Mantua,* 1979; Sarah B. Landau, *Edward T. and William A. Potter, American Victorian Architects,* 1979; Sara Lichtenstein, *Delacroix and Raphael,* 1979; J. Russell Sale, *Filippino Lippi's Strozzi Chapel in Santa Maria Novella,* 1979; Charles Baudelaire, *Eugene Delacroix: His Life and Works,* 1979; Johann D. Passavant, *Raphael of Urbino and His Father Giovanni Santi,* 1979; John Ruskin, *The Stones of Venice,* 1979, Volume I: *The Foundation,* Volume II: *The Sea-Stories,* Volume III: *The Fall;* M. E. Chevreul, *The Principles of Harmony and Contrast of Colors and Their Applications to the Arts,* 1980; J. A. Crowe and G. B. Cavalcaselle, *New History of Painting in Italy from the Second to the Sixteenth Century,* three volumes, 1980; Eugene Delacroix, *The Journals of Eugene Delacroix,* 1980; A. C. De Quincy, *History of the Life and Works of Rafaello,* 1980; William Y. Ottley, *The Italian School of Design,* 1980. Contributor to *Encyclopedia of World Art* and to periodicals. Art exhibition reviewer, *Art News,* 1947-49.

* * *

FREEDMAN, David Noel 1922-

PERSONAL: Born May 12, 1922, in New York, N.Y.; son of David (a writer) and Beatrice (Goodman) Freedman; married Cornelia Anne Pryor, May 16, 1944; children: Meredith Anne, Nadezhda, David M., Jonathan P. *Education:* Attended City College (now City College of the City University of New York), 1935-38; University of California, Los Angeles, A.B., 1939; Princeton Theological Seminary, Th.B., 1944; Johns Hopkins University, Ph.D., 1948. *Home:* 1520 Broadway, Ann Arbor, Mich. 48105. *Office:* Studies in Religion, 1053 L.S.A. Bldg., University of Michigan, Ann Arbor, Mich. 48109.

CAREER: Ordained minister of Presbyterian Church, 1944; supply pastor in Acme, Wash. and Deming, Wash., 1944-45; Johns Hopkins University, Baltimore, Md., teaching fellow, 1946-47, assistant instructor, 1947-48; Western Theological Seminary, Pittsburgh, Pa., assistant professor, 1948-51, professor of Hebrew and Old Testament literature, 1951-60; Pittsburgh Theological Seminary, Pittsburgh, Pa., professor, 1960-62, James A. Kelso Professor of Hebrew and Old Testament Literature, 1962-64; San Francisco Theological Seminary, San Anselmo, Calif., professor of Old Testament, 1964-70, Gray Professor of Hebrew Exegesis, 1970-71, dean of faculty, 1966-70, acting dean of seminary, 1970-71; Graduate Theological Union, Berkeley, Calif., professor of Old Testament, 1964-71; University of Michigan, Ann Arbor, professor in department of Near Eastern studies and director of program on studies in religion, 1971—. Visiting professor, Hebrew University, Jerusalem, Israel, 1976-77. Director of Ashdod excavation project, 1962-64. Technical consultant, Milberg Productions, 1961—, including the films "Jacob and Joseph," 1974, and "King David," 1976.

MEMBER: Society of Biblical Literature (president, 1975-76), American Academy of Religion, Biblical Colloquium, Archaeological Institute of America, American Oriental Society, American Schools of Oriental Research (vice-president, 1970—; trustee, 1970—; director of publications, 1974—). *Awards, honors:* William H. Green fellow in Old Testament, 1944; William S. Rayner fellow, Johns Hopkins University, 1946-47; Guggenheim fellow, 1959; American Association of Theological Schools fellow, 1963; Carey-Thomas Award, *Publishers Weekly,* 1965, for "Anchor Bible" series; American Council of Learned Societies grant-in-aid, 1967; D.Litt., University of the Pacific, 1973; D.Sc., Davis and Elkins College, 1974; Johns Hopkins University Centennial Scholar, 1976; Laymen's National Bible Committee Annual Award, 1978.

WRITINGS: (With James D. Smart) *God Has Spoken,* Westminster, 1949; (with Frank M. Cross) *Early Hebrew Orthography,* American Oriental Society, 1952; (with J. M. Allegro) *The People of the Dead Sea Scrolls,* Doubleday, 1958; (with R. M. Grant) *The Secret Sayings of Jesus,* Doubleday, 1960; (editor with Edward F. Campbell) *The Biblical Archaeologist Reader,* Doubleday, Volume I, 1961, Volume II, 1964, Volume III, 1970; (contributor) G. Ernest Wright, editor, *The Bible and the Ancient Near East,* Doubleday, 1961; (contributor) L. J. Swidler, editor, *Scripture and Ecumenism,* Duquesne University Press, 1965; (with Moshe Dothan) *Ashdod I,* [Jerusalem], 1967; (with Jonas C. Greenfield) *New Directions in Biblical Archaeology,* Doubleday, 1969; (with Cross) *Scrolls from Qumran Cave I,* Albright Institute of Archaeological Research (Jerusalem), 1972; (with Cross) *Studies in Ancient Yahwistic Poetry,* Scholars Press, 1975; (editor) *The Published Works of W. F. Albright,* American Schools of Oriental Research, 1975; (with L. C. Running) *William F. Albright: Twentieth-Century Genius,* Two Continents Publishing, 1975; (with B. Mazar and Gaalyah Cornfeld) *The Mountain of the Lord,* Doubleday, 1975; (with W. Phillips) *An Explorer's Life of Jesus,* Two Continents Publishing, 1975; (with Cornfeld) *Archaeology of the Bible: Book by Book,* Harper, 1976. Also author of *Jesus: The Four Gospels,* 1973, and, with T. Kachel, of *Religion and the Academic Scene,* 1975.

"Anchor Bible" series, Doubleday, co-editor, 1956-71, editor, 1971—; editor, with J. A. Baird, "Computer Bible" series, Biblical Research Associates, 1971—. Consulting editor, *Interpreter's Dictionary of the Bible,* 1957-60; consultant, Confraternity of Christian Doctrine translation of the Bible, *Reader's Digest Atlas of the Bible,* 1979; editorial consultant to religious book departments, Doubleday & Co., 1959-70, and Macmillan & Co., 1961-66, and to Genesis Project, 1973. Contributor to professional journals. *Journal of Biblical Literature,* associate editor, 1952-54, editor, 1955-59; editor, *American Schools of Oriental Research Bulletin,* 1974-78, and *Biblical Archaeologist,* 1976—.

* * *

FREEDMAN, Leonard 1924-

PERSONAL: Born August 19, 1924, in London, England; married, 1973; wife's name Vivian. *Education:* London School of Economics and Political Science, B.Sc., 1950; University of California, Los Angeles, M.A., 1952, Ph.D., 1959. *Home:* 5322 Encino Ave., Encino, Calif. 91316. *Office:* Division of Continuing Education, University of California, Los Angeles, Calif. 90024.

CAREER: American Library Association, Chicago, Ill., field representative, adult education program, 1952-55; University of California Extension Service, Los Angeles, coordinator of discussion programs, 1955-57, head of department of liberal arts, 1957-60, head of department of social sciences, 1960-65, associate director, 1965—, professor of political science and dean of Division of Continuing Education, 1973—. *Military service:* British Army, 1944-47; became warrant officer, second class. *Member:* American Political Science Association, Adult Education Association, National University Extension Association (member of world affairs committee).

WRITINGS: (Editor with Cornelius P. Colter) *Issues of the Sixties,* Wadsworth, 1961, revised edition (sole editor), Wadsworth, 1965; (editor with Arthur C. Turner) *Tension Areas in World Affairs,* Wadsworth, 1964; *The Politics of Poverty,* Holt, 1969; (editor) *Issues of the Seventies,* Wadsworth, 1970; *Power and Politics in America,* Duxbury, 1971, 3rd edition, 1978.

* * *

FREEDMAN, Nancy 1920-

PERSONAL: Born July 4, 1920, in Chicago, Ill.; daughter of Hartley Farnham (a surgeon) and Brillianna Jellet (a newspaperwoman; maiden name, Hintermeister) Mars; married Benedict Freedman (a writer and professor of mathematics), June 29, 1941; children: Johanna (Mrs. Deane Shapiro, Jr.), Michael Hartley, Deborah. *Education:* Attended Chicago Art Institute, 1937-38, Los Angeles City College, 1938-39, and University of Southern California, 1939. *Agent:* Scott Meredith Literary Agency, Inc., 845 Third Ave., New York, N.Y. 10022.

CAREER: Writer. Actress; appeared on tour in Max Reinhardt's productions of "Faust," "The Miracle," and "Six Characters in Search of an Author"; played leading role in "Death Takes a Holiday"; worked in summer stock in Maine in 1937 and 1938.

WRITINGS—All novels: *Joshua, Son of None* (Literary Guild selection), Delacorte, 1973; *The Immortals,* St. Martin's, 1977; *Crescendo,* Morrow, 1980.

Novels; with husband, Benedict Freedman: *Back to the Sea,* Viking, 1942; *Mrs. Mike* (Literary Guild selection), Coward, 1947; *This and No More,* Harper, 1950; *The Spark and the Exodus,* Crown, 1954; *Lootville,* Holt, 1957; *Tresa,* Holt, 1958; *The Apprentice Bastard,* Simon & Schuster, 1966; *Cyclone of Silence,* Simon & Schuster, 1969.

WORK IN PROGRESS: A novel.

SIDELIGHTS: Nancy Freedman told *CA:* "I have kept house all over the world—in Spain, at a time when champagne was cheaper than water—we lived in North Africa, in Barbados, in Mexico, in Switzerland. As a novelist I am . . . particularly interested in the connective tissue of understanding and compassion and the demons of perversity that thwart our saner moments. . . . The contents of my notebooks and journals find their way into much of my backgrounds. . . . When I finish a novel I put it in a drawer under my underwear. I have one there now." *Mrs. Mike* has appeared in twenty-seven foreign editions and was produced as a motion picture in 1947. A Benedict and Nancy Freedman collection has been established at the Mugar Library of Boston University.

FREELING, Nicolas 1927-
(F.R.E. Nicolas)

PERSONAL: Born March 3, 1927, in London, England; married Cornelia Termes, 1954; children: four sons, one daughter, *Education:* Attended primary and secondary schools in England, Ireland, and France; attended University of Dublin. *Politics:* "Visionary." *Religion:* Catholic. *Home:* Grandfontaine, 67130 Schirmeck, Bas Rhin, France. *Agent:* James Brown Associates, Inc., 25 West 43rd St., New York, N.Y. 10036.

CAREER: Professional cook in hotels and restaurants throughout Europe, 1948-60; author and novelist, 1960—. *Military Service:* Royal Air Force, 1945-47. *Member:* Authors Guild. *Awards, honors:* Crime Writers Award, 1963, and Grand Prix de Roman Policier, 1965, for *Gun before Butter;* Mystery Writers of America Edgar Allen Poe Award, 1966, for *The King of the Rainy Country.*

WRITINGS—Novels: *Love in Amsterdam,* Gollancz, 1961, Harper, 1962; *Because of the Cats,* Gollancz, 1962, Harper, 1963; *Gun before Butter,* Gollancz, 1963, published as *Question of Loyalty,* Harper, 1964; (under pseudonym F.R.E. Nicolas) *Valparaiso,* Gollancz, 1964, published under name Nicolas Freeling, Harper, 1964; *Double Barrel,* Gollancz, 1964, Harper, 1965; *Criminal Conversation,* Gollancz, 1965, Harper, 1966; *The King of the Rainy Country,* Harper, 1966; *The Dresden Green,* Gollancz, 1966, Harper, 1967; *Strike Out Where Not Applicable,* Gollancz, 1967, Harper, 1968; *This Is the Castle,* Hamish Hamilton, 1968, Harper, 1969; *The Freeling Omnibus: Comprising Love in Amsterdam, Because of the Cats, Gun before Butter,* Gollancz, 1968; *Tsing-Boum,* Hamish Hamilton, 1969, Harper, 1970; *The Lovely Ladies,* Harper, 1970 (published in England as *Over the High Side,* Hamish Hamilton, 1970); *Aupres de ma Blonde,* Harper, 1971 (published in England as *A Long Silence,* Hamish Hamilton, 1971); *The Second Freeling Omnibus: Comprising Double Barrel, The King of the Rainy Country, The Dresden Green,* Gollancz, 1972; *Dressing of Diamond,* Harper, 1974; *The Bugles Blowing,* Harper, 1975 (published in England as *What Are the Bugles Blowing For?,* Heinemann, 1975); *Lake Isle,* Heinemann, 1976, published as *Sabine,* Harper, 1977; *Gadget,* Coward, 1977; *The Night Lords,* Pantheon, 1978; *The Widow,* Pantheon, 1979; *Castang's City,* Pantheon, 1980.

Nonfiction: *Kitchen Book,* Hamish Hamilton, 1972, condensed version published as *The Kitchen,* Harper, 1973; *Cook Book,* Hamish Hamilton, 1974.

WORK IN PROGRESS: Further novels on the "Widow" and "Castang" themes; several projects in both fiction and nonfiction.

SIDELIGHTS: Nicolas Freeling began writing when he was in his thirties "upon realising, tardily, that this was the work I was best suited for." As to the purpose behind his writing, he told *CA* that "Stendhal's prayer holds good: to have one reader a hundred years from now."

Freeling continues: "The crime novel is a plastic flower, an excrescence of the entertainment industry. That this must be so has been obstinately if not always ably held by most critics. I never have believed this and still don't. But it is peculiarly vulnerable to artificial convention, from the aristocrat amateur detective of the thirties to the naked raped girl (or boy) of the seventies. To attempt to match the originality of Stendhal, Dickens, Malraux or Chandler would be ridiculous, and anything less talented is a resounding crash between stools, which I have a gift for. When one looks at the admirable work done inside the convention by a writer as fine as Rex Stout it appears absurd to be dissatisfied. I am: and intend to go on being so.

"The first responsibility of the writer, perhaps, is to be a devoted and accurate witness to the thoughts and doings of his times. If, though, he is to be in any real sense creative he must make discoveries. It is sometimes valid to recall Ray Chandler's embittered remark that 'critics never discover anything: they explain it after it has become fashionable.' In general [reviews] are of no account. Humanly, one is gladdened by the good, and one learns to shrug at the bad. . . . A writer has to do better than stay abreast of his times: he must run a little in front of them.

"Since my vocation and profession is to write novels, I have refused all offers to write screenplays, adaptations, dialogue, etc. The reason for this is that I like to be sole author, and sole judge, of what I write. Disobeying this rule may make one rich, but will certainly make one miserable." Many of Freeling's novels have been made into films or television plays; of these adaptations into other mediums, Freeling comments that "the risk is that they get distorted out of recognition." He also has had "a great many foreign-language editions" of his books which he says "are rarely satisfactory, since translating is ill-paid and thus of generally poor quality."

AVOCATIONAL INTERESTS: Planting trees.

* * *

FREEMAN, Arthur 1938-

PERSONAL: Born July 31, 1938, in Cambridge, Mass.; son of Harold A. and Margaret (Zaroodny) Freeman. *Education:* Harvard University, A.B., 1959, Ph.D., 1965.

CAREER: Brown University, Providence, R.I., teaching assistant, 1960-61; Harvard University, Cambridge, Mass., teaching fellow, 1961-62, junior fellow in the Society of Fellows, 1962-65; Boston University, Boston, Mass., 1965-76, began as assistant professor, became professor of history. *Member:* Bibliographic Society. *Awards, honors:* National Endowment for the Humanities younger scholar fellow, 1969; American Council of Learned Societies fellow, 1971-72.

WRITINGS: *Izmir,* Identity Press, 1959; *Apollonian Poems,* Atheneum, 1961; *Estrangements,* Harcourt, 1966; *Thomas Kyd: Facts and Problems,* Clarendon Press, 1967; (editor) William Shakespeare, *Henry VI, Part Two,* New American Library, 1967; *Assays of Bias,* Godine, 1970; (editor) *Eighteenth Century Shakespeare,* thirty-one volumes, Frank Cass, 1971-74; (editor) *The English Stage: Attack and Defense,* fifty volumes, Garland, 1973-74; *Unworthies of England: Ten Brief Lives,* Garland, 1974; *Elizabeth's Misfits: Brief Lives of English Eccentrics, Exploiters, Rogues, and Failures, 1580-1660,* Garland, 1977. Contributor to *Atlantic Monthly, Paris Review, Journal of American Folklore, Poetry, New Yorker, Modern Language Review,* and to other periodicals. Former editor, *Audience.*

BIOGRAPHICAL/CRITICAL SOURCES: *Contemporary Literature,* Volume IX, number 1, winter, 1968.†

* * *

FRENCH, Charles E(zra) 1923-

PERSONAL: Born April 7, 1923, in Smithville, Mo.; son of Charley E. (a farmer) and Ruth (Downs) French; married Dolores Albers, August 31, 1947 (divorced February, 1976); married Jeanne Blair, June 2, 1979; children: (first marriage) Ned, Hugh, Sarasue; (second marriage) Judith. *Education:* University of Missouri, B.S. (with honors), 1948, A.M., 1949; Purdue University, Ph.D., 1951; also studied at Washington University, St. Louis, Mo., 1943, and University of California, Berkeley, 1947. *Politics:* Democrat. *Religion:* Protestant. *Home:* 9806 Fosbak Dr., Vienna, Va. 22180. *Office:* Agency for International Development, Rm. 309E RPC, Washington, D.C. 20523.

CAREER: Purdue University, West Lafayette, Ind., assistant professor, 1951-55, associate professor, 1955-58, professor of agricultural economics, 1958-77, head of department, 1966-73; U.S. State Department, Agency for International Development, Washington, D.C., 1977—, began as agricultural advisor-research, Development Support Bureau, now assistant agricultural development officer, Title XII Program. Assistant study director, World Food and Nutrition Study, National Academy of Sciences, 1975-77; study director, Food and Nutrition, President's Reorganization Project, Executive Offices of the President, 1978-79. Member of board of directors, Edward B. McClain Co.; member of agricultural board, National Academy of Sciences, and member of executive committee; participant in international conferences; has testified before U.S. Federal Trade Commission; consultant to U.S. government agencies and American business. *Military service:* U.S. Army Air Forces, fighter pilot, 1943-46; served in Mediterranean and European theaters; became captain.

MEMBER: International Association of Agricultural Economists, International Platform Association, American Agricultural Economics Association, American Economic Association, American Marketing Association, American Association for the Advancement of Science, Canadian Agricultural Economics Society, Western Agricultural Economics Association, Southern Agricultural Economics Association, Sigma XI, Alpha Gamma Sigma, Alpha Zeta, Phi Eta Sigma, Gamma Sigma Delta, Alpha Phi Zeta, Cosmos Club.

WRITINGS: (Contributor) C. J. Miller, editor, *Marketing and Economic Development,* University of Nebraska Press, 1967; (with David A. Vose, Sheldon W. Williams, Hugh L. Cook, and Alden C. Manchester) *Organization and Competition in the Midwest Dairy Industries,* Iowa State University Press, 1970; (with John C. Moore, Charles A. Kraenzle, and Kenneth F. Harling) *Survival Strategies for Agricultural Cooperatives,* Iowa State University Press, 1980. Contributor to *American Cooperation* (an annual publication). Contributor to proceedings, transactions, and annals, and to *World Book Encyclopedia.* Contributor of more than two hundred fifty articles to professional journals, including *News for Farmer Cooperatives, Cordially Yours, Indiana Agricultural News Digest, American Journal of Agricultural Economics, Journal of Farm Economics,* and *Journal of Operations Research.*

WORK IN PROGRESS: Further research on international economics, agricultural marketing and policy, and operations research applied to agriculture.

AVOCATIONAL INTERESTS: International travel, sports, fishing, hunting, church work.

* * *

FRENCH, Peter A(ndrew) 1942-

PERSONAL: Born March 19, 1942, in Newburgh, N.Y.; son of Ernest C. (a Lutheran minister) and Gretchen (Schillke) French; married Sandra Schall, June 1, 1961; children: Sean Trevor, Shannon Elizabeth. *Education:* Gettysburg College,

B.A., 1963; University of Southern California, M.A., 1965; University of Miami, Coral Gables, Fla., Ph.D., 1971. *Home:* 8 South Court, Morris, Minn. 56267. *Office:* Division of Humanities, University of Minnesota, 112 Humanities Building, Morris, Minn. 56267.

CAREER: Northern Arizona University, Flagstaff, assistant professor of philosophy, 1965-68; Miami-Dade Junior College, Miami, Fla., assistant professor of philosophy, 1968-71; University of Minnesota, Morris, associate professor, 1971-76, professor of philosophy, 1976—. Member of Minnesota Humanities Commission. *Member:* American Philosophical Association, Society for Philosophy and Public Affairs, Royal Institute of Philosophy, Minnesota Philosophical Society.

WRITINGS: Exploring Philosophy, Schenkman, 1970, revised edition, 1972; *Individual and Collective Responsibility: Massacre at My Lai,* Schenkman, 1972; *Conscientious Actions,* Schenkman, 1973; (contributor) Nagel, Held, and Morgenbesser, editors, *Philosophy, Morality, and International Affairs,* Oxford University Press, 1973; *Philosophical Explorations,* General Learning Corp., 1975; *Philosophers in Wonderland,* Llewellyn, 1975; *Contemporary Perspectives in the Philosophy of Language,* University of Minnesota Press, 1978; *The Scope of Morality,* University of Minnesota Press, 1979; *Ethics in Government,* Prentice-Hall, 1980. Contributor to philosophy journals, including *American Philosophical Quarterly, Philosophy,* and *Southern Journal of Philosophy.*

WORK IN PROGRESS: Foundations of Corporate Responsibility.

* * *

FRENCH, Warren G(raham) 1922-

PERSONAL: Born January 26, 1922, in Philadelphia, Pa.; son of Maurice Lester and Helen (Welsch) French. *Education:* University of Pennsylvania, B.A., 1943; University of Texas, M.A., 1948, Ph.D., 1954. *Religion:* Episcopalian. *Address:* P.O. Box 266, Cornish Flat, N.H. 03746. *Office:* Center for American Studies, Indiana University—Purdue University at Indianapolis, Indianapolis, Ind. 46202.

CAREER: University of Mississippi, Oxford, instructor, 1948-50; University of Kentucky, Lexington, instructor, 1954-56; Stetson University, Deland, Fla., assistant professor, 1956-58; University of Florida, Gainesville, assistant professor, 1958-62; Kansas State University, Manhattan, associate professor, 1962-65; University of Missouri—Kansas City, associate professor, 1965-66, professor of English and chairman of department, 1966-70, University of Missouri Press Committee, 1966-69, chairman, 1968-69; Indiana University—Purdue University at Indianapolis, professor of English, 1970—, chairman of department, 1970-73, director, Center for American Studies, 1977—. Member of Norman Foerster Award Committee, 1964. *Military service:* U.S. Army, 1943-46, became sergeant. U.S. Navy, 1951-53, became lieutenant junior grade. *Member:* American Association of University Professors, American Studies Association, Modern Language Association of America, International John Steinbeck Society (president), National Council of Teachers of English, Delta Chi.

WRITINGS: John Steinbeck, Twayne, 1961, revised edition, 1976; *Frank Norris,* Twayne, 1962; *J. D. Salinger,* Twayne, 1963; *A Companion to "The Grapes of Wrath,"* Viking, 1963; (contributor) Marshall Fishwick, editor, *American Studies in Transition,* University of Pennsylvania Press, 1964; *The Social Novel at the End of an Era,* Southern Illinois University Press, 1966; (editor) *The Thirties: Poetry, Prose, Drama,* Everett-Edwards, 1967; (editor with Walter Kidd) *American Winners of the Nobel Literary Prize,* University of Oklahoma Press, 1968; *The Forties: Fiction, Poetry, Drama,* Everett-Edwards, 1969; *The Fifties: Fiction, Poetry, Drama,* Everett-Edwards, 1971; *A Filmguide to "The Grapes of Wrath,"* Indiana University Press, 1973; *The Twenties: Fiction, Poetry, Drama,* Everett-Edwards, 1975.

Author of film scripts; all with H. Wayne Schuth: "Are Poets People?," 1968; "Three New Orleans," 1975; "Missions", 1977.

Editor, Twayne Theatrical Arts series, 1975—; field editor, Twayne United States Authors series, 1977—. Contributor to professional journals. Book reviewer, *Lexington Herald-Leader,* Lexington, Ky., 1954-56, *Kansas City Star,* 1964-69. Bibliographical editor, *Twentieth Century Literature,* 1958—; member of editorial board, *College Composition and Communication,* 1962-65, *Midcontinent American Studies Journal,* 1966—, *Western American Literature,* 1966—, *American Literature,* 1974-77, and *Twentieth Century Literature,* 1977—.

WORK IN PROGRESS: The Beat Generation and *Modernism in American Literature,* both for Twayne.

* * *

FREUND, Gerald 1930-

PERSONAL: Born October 14, 1930, in Berlin, Germany; came to United States in 1940, naturalized in 1946; son of Kurt and Annelise (Josephthal) Freund; married Jane Bicker Shaw Trask, September 29, 1956 (divorced September, 1970); married Peregrine Whittlesey; children: (first marriage) Jonathan G., Matthew T., Andrew J. *Education:* Haverford College, B.A., 1952; Oxford University, D.Phil., 1955. *Home:* 345 East 80th St., New York, N.Y. 10021. *Office:* 1000 Sunset Ridge Rd., Northbrook, Ill. 60062.

CAREER: Oxford University, St. Anthony's College, Oxford, England, research fellow, 1955-56; Institute for Advanced Study, Princeton, N.J., research associate, 1956-57; Council on Foreign Relations, New York City, Carnegie research fellow, 1957-58; Haverford College, Haverford, Pa., assistant professor, 1958-60; Rockefeller Foundation, New York City, consultant, 1960-61, assistant director of social sciences, 1961-64, associate director of humanities and social sciences, 1964-69, of arts, 1965-69, consultant to humanities, social sciences, and arts, 1969-70; Hunter College of the City University of New York, New York City, professor, dean of humanities and arts, and director of Arts Center, 1971-80; John D. and Catherine T. MacArthur Foundation, Chicago, Ill., vice-president, 1980—. Research associate, Washington Center of Foreign Policy Research, 1959-60; assistant to the president, Yale University, 1969-70. Member of board, Woodstock Country School (president), Institute of Current World Affairs, Manhattan Theatre Club, National Book Committee, Imagination Workshop (chairman), Foundation Advisory Services (secretary-treasurer), and Institute for the Study of World Politics. Consultant, New York State Council on the Arts, Institute des Hautes Etudes Musicales, Arts, Education, and Americans project, National Institute of Education, and MacArthur Foundation.

MEMBER: American Association of University Professors, Council on Foreign Relations, Film Society of Lincoln Center (executive vice-president, 1970-71), Phi Beta Kappa, Century Association, Lotos Club. *Awards, honors:* Fulbright fellowship, 1952-54; Carnegie fellowship, 1957-59; Rockefeller Foundation fellowships, 1956-57, 1959-60.

WRITINGS: *Unholy Alliance,* Harcourt, 1957; *Germany between Two Worlds,* Harcourt, 1961; (contributor) V. J. Esposito, editor, *A Concise History of World War I,* Praeger, 1964; (contributor) T. T. Hammond, editor, *Soviet Foreign Relations and World Communism,* Princeton University Press, 1965; *Performing Arts Programs Related to Schools,* New York State Council on Arts, 1974. Contributor to *Encyclopedia Americana* and *Encyclopedia of the Social Sciences;* contributor to professional journals and news magazines. Consultant, *Coming to Our Senses: The Significance of the Arts for American Education,* McGraw, 1977.

* * *

FRIEDMAN, Arnold P(hineas) 1909-

PERSONAL: Born August 25, 1909, in Portland, Ore.; son of Carl and Lena (Levy) Friedman; married Sara Fritz, July 10, 1939; children: Carol (Mrs. Eugene Ludwig). *Education:* University of Southern California, B.A., 1932, M.A., 1934; University of Oregon, M.D., 1939; Harvard University, postdoctoral study in neurology, 1943-44. *Home:* 3250 Sabino Vista Cir., Tucson, Ariz. 85715. *Office:* Neurological Associates, 5402 East Grant, Tucson, Ariz. 85712.

CAREER: Neurologist. Licensed to practice medicine in California, 1939, New York, 1944, and Connecticut, 1955; diplomate of American Board of Psychiatry and Neurology, 1945; qualified psychiatrist by State of New York, 1956; diplomate in neurology and psychiatry, Pan American Medical Association, 1972. Los Angeles County Hospital, Los Angeles, Calif., intern, 1939-40, resident in neurology, 1940-42; Boston Psychiatric Hospital, Boston, Mass., assistant physician, 1942-43; Boston City Hospital, Boston, resident in charge of head injury project in Office of Scientific Research and Development and research associate, 1943-44; Columbia University, College of Physicians and Surgeons, New York City, instructor in neurology, 1944-45, associate in neurology, 1946-49, assistant clinical professor, 1950-54, associate clinical professor, 1954-67, clinical professor of neurology, beginning 1967; currently consultant to Neurological Associates, Tucson, Ariz., and adjunct professor of neurology, Arizona Health Sciences Center, Tucson. Private practice in New York City, beginning 1946. Visiting neurologist, Cambridge Hospital, 1944; Division of Neurology, Montefiore Hospital and Medical Center, adjunct attending physician, 1944-47, associate attending physician, 1947-49, attending physician, beginning 1949, assistant in neuroentgenology, 1946, founder and physician in charge of Headache Clinic (now Headache Unit), beginning 1947; Neurological Institute, Presbyterian Hospital (New York City), assistant attending physician, 1948, associate attending physician, 1949-70, attending neurologist in Neurology Service, beginning 1971. Examiner in neurology and psychiatry for Induction Center (Boston), 1943-44; examiner in neuropsychiatry for veterans (New York City), 1945-46; certified examiner in mental hygiene, State of New York, 1946; American Board of Psychiatry and Neurology, associate examiner, 1946-49, member of board of directors, 1964, vice-president, 1970, president, 1971; neuropsychiatrist (intermediate grade), Veterans Administration (New York City), 1946-47. U.S. Pharmacopeia, member of scope panel on neuropsychiatry, 1960-70, member of advisory panel on neurological disease therapy, 1970-75; member of review panel on medical malpractice, Appellate Division, New York State Supreme Court, beginning 1971. Chairman of research group in headache and migraine, World Federation of Neurology, 1967—. Consultant to numerous groups. *Military service:* U.S. Naval Reserve, active duty, 1941-42; became lieutenant junior grade.

MEMBER: Internationale Collegium Allergilogicum, American Medical Association (fellow; former chairman of Section on Nervous and Mental Diseases), American College of Physicians (fellow), American Neurological Association (senior member), American Academy of Neurology (fellow; trustee, 1958, 1959), American Psychiatric Association (fellow; life member), Association for Research in Nervous and Mental Disease, National Migraine Foundation (member of board of directors), American Association for the Study of Headaches (president), American League against Epilepsy, New York Neurological Society, New York Academy of Medicine (fellow), New York State Medical Association, New York County Medical Association, Los Angeles County Society of Neurology and Psychiatry, Psi Chi, Harvard Club (New York, N.Y.).

AWARDS, HONORS: Honorary chief of Kiowa Indians in Oklahoma, 1958; Billings Silver Medal from American Medical Association, 1959, for "Facial Pain"; honorary surgeon, New York City Police Department, 1961; American Academy of General Practice Award from American Medical Association, 1968, and Rush Silver Medal from American Psychiatric Association, 1969, both for exhibit "Chronic Recurrent Headache: Aspects of Diagnosis and Differential Analysis"; Physician's Recognition Award in Continuing Medical Education from American Medical Association, 1969; certificate of merit from American Medical Association, 1972, for "Chronic Recurring Headache in Intracranial Disorders."

WRITINGS: *Modern Headache Therapy,* Mosby, 1951; (with H. H. Merritt) *Headache: Diagnosis and Treatment,* F. A. Davis, 1959; *Headache: Hope through Research,* Public Health Service, 1962, revised edition, 1971; (editor with E. Harms and contributor) *Headaches in Children,* C. C Thomas, 1967; *Drug Trials for Headache: Principles and Methods* (monograph), National Institute of Neurological Diseases and Blindness, National Institute of Mental Health, 1969; (with S. H. Frazier) *The Headache Book,* Dodd, 1973; (editor with others and contributor) *Research and Clinical Studies in Headache,* S. Karger (Basel), Volume V: *Epidemiology and Non-Drug Treatment of Head Pain,* 1978, Volume VI: *Headache Today: An Update by Twenty-one Experts,* 1978.

Contributor: M. Edward Davis and others, editors, *Current Therapy,* Saunders, 1950, revised edition, edited by H. F. Cohn, 1955; Francis M. Forster, editor, *Modern Therapy in Neurology,* Mosby, 1957; L. Schwartz, editor, *Disorders of the Temporomandibular Joint,* Saunders, 1959; J. G. Miller, editor, *The Pharmacology and Clinical Usefulness of Carisoprodol* (monograph), Wayne State University Press, 1959.

Paul David Cantor, editor-in-chief, *Traumatic Medicine and Surgery for the Attorney,* Butterworth, 1961; Earl A. Walker and S. Jablon, editors, *A Follow-up Study of Head Wounds in World War Two,* Veterans Administration Medical Monographs, 1961; Forster, editor, *Evaluation of Drug Therapy,* University of Wisconsin Press, 1961; J. H. Nodine and J. H. Moyer, editors, *Psychosomatic Medicine,* Lea & Febiger, 1962; A. M. Freedman and H. I. Kaplan, editors, *Comprehensive Textbook of Psychiatry,* William & Wilkins, 1967, 2nd edition, 1975; P. E. Siegler and J. H. Moyer, editors, *Animal and Clinical Pharmacologic Techniques in Drug Evaluation,* Volume II, Yearbook Medical Publishers, 1967; L. Schwartz, editor, *Facial Pain and Mandibular Dysfunction,* Saunders, 1968; P. J. Vinken and G. W. Bruyn, editors,

Handbook of Clinical Neurology, North-Holland Publishing, Volume V, 1968, Volume XXXVI, 1979; A. E. Walker, William F. Caveness, and M. Critchley, editors, *Late Effects of Head Injury,* C. C Thomas, 1969.

Current Pediatric Therapy, Saunders, Volume IV, 1970, Volume V, 1971; A. B. Baker, editor, *Clinical Neurology,* Volume II, Harper, 1971; Amilcare Capri, editor, *Pharmacology of the Cerebral Circulation,* Pergamon, 1972; *Advances in Neurology,* Raven Press, 1974; *Practice of Medicine,* Volume X: *Diseases of the Nervous System,* Harper, 1974; *Medical Thermography: Theory and Clinical Applications,* Brentwood Publishing, 1975; Pearce, editor, *Modern Topics in Migraine,* Heinemann, 1975; *Research and Clinical Studies in Headache,* Volume IV, S. Karger (Basel), 1976; Howard F. Conn, editor, *Current Therapy 1976,* Saunders, 1976; Raymond Greene, editor, *Current Concepts in Migraine Research,* Raven Press, 1978; H. H. Merritt, *Textbook of Neurology,* 6th edition, Lea & Febiger, 1979.

Contributor to transactions, archives, proceedings, reports, symposia, and yearbooks; also contributor to *Cyclopedia of Medicine, Surgery, Specialties, International Encyclopedia of Pharmacology and Therapeutics,* and *Encyclopedia of Mental Health.* Contributor of more than two hundred articles to medical journals, including *Postgraduate Medicine, Modern Medicine, Medical Clinics, Hospital Medicine, International Journal of Neurology,* and *Headache.* Editor-in-chief, *Research and Clinical Studies in Headache: An International Review,* 1963—; guest editor, *Modern Treatment,* 1964.

* * *

FRIEDMAN, Milton 1912-

PERSONAL: Born July 31, 1912, in New York, N.Y.; son of Jeno Saul and Sarah Ethel (Landau) Friedman; married Rose Director, June 25, 1938; children: Janet, David. *Education:* Rutgers University, A.B., 1932; University of Chicago, A.M., 1933; Columbia University, Ph.D., 1946. *Office:* Hoover Institution, Stanford, Calif. 94305.

CAREER: University of Chicago, Social Science Research Committee, Chicago, Ill., research assistant, 1934-35; National Resources Committee, Washington, D.C., associate economist, 1935-37; National Bureau of Economic Research, New York City, member of research staff, 1937-45, 1948—; U.S. Treasury Department, Division of Tax Research, Washington, D.C., principal economist, 1941-43; Columbia University, Division of War Research, New York City, associate director of statistical research group, 1943-45; University of Minnesota, Minneapolis, associate professor of economics and business administration, 1945-46; University of Chicago, associate professor, 1946-48, professor, 1948-62, Paul Snowden Russell Distinguished Service Professor of Economics, 1962—; Hoover Institution, Stanford, Calif., senior research fellow, 1977—. Columbia University, part-time lecturer, 1937-40, Wesley Clair Mitchell Research Professor of Economics, 1964-65. Visiting Fulbright lecturer, Cambridge University, 1953-54; visiting professor, University of California, Los Angeles, 1967, and University of Hawaii, 1972; visiting scholar, Federal Reserve Bank of San Francisco, 1977. Member of President's Commission on an All-Volunteer Armed Forces, 1969-70, President's Commission on White House Fellows, 1971-73, and Federal Reserve System advisory committee on monetary statistics, 1974. Host of ten-part television series, "Free to Choose," Public Broadcasting Service, 1980. Chief economic advisor to Senator Barry Goldwater, 1964. Consultant to Economic Cooperation Administration, Paris, 1950, and International Cooperation Administration, India, 1955.

MEMBER: National Academy of Sciences, American Statistical Association (fellow), American Economic Association (member of executive committee, 1955-57; president, 1967), Econometric Society (fellow), Institute of Mathematical Statistics (fellow), American Philosophical Society, Mont Pelerin Society (American secretary, 1957-62; member of council, 1962-65; vice-president, 1967-70, 1972—; president, 1970-72), American Enterprise Institute (member of council of academic advisors, 1956-78), Royal Economic Society, Philadelphia Society (member of board of trustees, 1965-67, 1970-72, 1976—), Quadrangle Club.

AWARDS, HONORS: John Bates Clark Medal, American Economic Association, 1951; Center for Advanced Study in the Behavioral Sciences fellow, 1957-78; Ford faculty research fellow, 1962-63; LL.D. from St. Paul's University, Tokyo, 1963, Kalamazoo College, 1968, Rutgers University, 1968, Lehigh University, 1969, Loyola University, 1971, University of New Hampshire, 1975, and Harvard University, 1979; L.H.D. from Rockford College, 1969, and Roosevelt University, 1975; D.Sc. from University of Rochester, 1971; named Chicagoan of the Year, Chicago Press Club, 1972; named Educator of the Year, Chicago United Jewish Fund, 1973; Nobel Prize for Economic Science, 1976; Scopus Award from American Friends of the Hebrew University, 1977; Ph.D. from Hebrew University of Jerusalem, 1977; D.C.S. from Francisco Marroquin University, 1978; Freedoms Foundation, Private Enterprise Exemplar Medal, 1978, Valley Forge Honor Certificate, 1978, for speech "The Future of Capitalism,"and George Washington Honor Medal, 1978, for television program "Open Mind" on WPIX, New York City; gold medal from National Institute of Social Sciences, 1978.

WRITINGS: (With Carl Shoup and Ruth P. Mack) *Taxing to Prevent Inflation,* Columbia University Press, 1943; (with Simon Kuznets) *Income from Independent Professional Practice,* National Bureau of Economic Research, 1946; (with H. A. Freeman, F. Mosteller, and W. Allen Wallis) *Sampling Inspection,* McGraw, 1948; *Essays in Positive Economics,* University of Chicago Press, 1953; (editor and contributor) *Studies in the Quantity Theory of Money,* University of Chicago Press, 1956; *A Theory of the Consumption Function,* Princeton University Press, 1957; *A Program for Monetary Stability,* Fordham University Press, 1959.

Price Theory: A Provisional Text, Aldine, 1962, revised edition, 1976; *Capitalism and Freedom,* University of Chicago Press, 1962; *Inflation: Causes and Consequences,* Asia Publishing House (Bombay), 1963; (with Anna J. Schwartz) *A Monetary History of the United States, 1867-1960,* Princeton University Press, 1963; (with Robert V. Roosa) *The Balance of Payments: Free Versus Fixed Exchange Rates,* American Enterprise Institute for Public Policy Research, 1967; *Dollars and Deficits: Inflation, Monetary Policy, and the Balance of Payments,* Prentice-Hall, 1968; *The Optimum Quantity of Money and Other Essays,* Aldine, 1969; (with Walter W. Heller) *Monetary Versus Fiscal Policy,* Norton, 1969; (with Schwartz) *Monetary Statistics of the United States,* Columbia University Press, 1970; (with Wilbur J. Cohen) *Social Security: Universal or Selective?,* American Enterprise Institute for Public Policy Research, 1972; *An Economist's Protest: Columns on Political Economy* (magazine column collection), Thomas Horton, 1972, 2nd edition, 1975, 2nd edition also published as *There Ain't No Such Thing as a Free Lunch,* Open Court, 1975; *Money and Economic Development,* Praeger, 1973; *Milton Friedman's*

Monetary Framework: A Debate with His Critics, edited by Robert J. Gordon, University of Chicago Press, 1974; (contributor) Frederick E. Webster, editor, *The Business System: A Bicentennial View,* University Press of New England, 1977; (with wife, Rose D. Friedman) *Free to Choose* (Book-of-the-Month Club alternate selection), Harcourt, 1980.

Also author of monographs, published speeches, and booklets. Columnist, *Newsweek,* 1966—. Contributor of articles and reviews to economic and statistics journals. Member of board of directors, Aldine Publishing Co., 1961-76. Member of board of editors, *American Economic Review,* 1951-53, and *Econometrica,* 1957-69. Member of advisory board, *Journal of Money, Credit, and Banking,* 1968—.

SIDELIGHTS: Milton Friedman is an influential conservative economist whose theories, sometimes called the "monetarist" or "Chicago" school, are highly regarded, although at variance with the dominant Keynesian school of economics.

Friedman's primary belief is that the quantity of money in circulation is of prime importance in determining a nation's economic health. In most instances, Friedman holds that the larger the supply of money in circulation, the healthier the economy. He has proposed increasing the nation's money supply at a fixed rate each year in order to insure a steady rate of growth. This idea is contrary to the Keynesian school which focuses more attention on how a nation's money is spent than on how much is in circulation.

Friedman has proposed a number of changes in the nation's economic policies, both in his books and speeches and while serving as a presidential advisor during the Nixon administration. These suggestions include instituting a guaranteed annual income, sometimes called a negative income tax, and the complete removal of the government from all aspects of the economy. As a believer in laissez faire capitalism, Friedman would like to see such social programs as welfare and social security abolished as well as the removal of government subsidies and tax breaks for business.

"One of the most profound intellectual changes in the last decade," writes H. Erich Heinemann in the *New York Times,* "has been the emergence of the monetarist school of economics, led by Professor Milton Friedman." One example of this change is the Federal Reserve System's decision to monitor the nation's money supply, as Friedman has suggested they do on several occasions.

Friedman's books have been published in Spanish, Japanese, Italian, French, German, and Portuguese.

BIOGRAPHICAL/CRITICAL SOURCES: Washington Post, November 24, 1963, February 1, 1980; *American Economic Review,* September, 1965; *U.S. News & World Report,* April 4, 1966, March 7, 1977; *Fortune,* June 1, 1967; *Wall Street Journal,* May 23, 1968, January 10, 1969; *Time,* January 10, 1969, December 19, 1969, February 1, 1971; *Commentary,* July, 1969; *Business Week,* July 19, 1969, November 1, 1976; *New York Times Magazine,* January 25, 1970; *Times Literary Supplement,* April 16, 1970; *New York Times,* July 12, 1970, January 14, 1980; *Esquire,* September, 1970; *Christian Century,* November 25, 1970; *National Review,* September 10, 1971, November 9, 1973, September 16, 1977; *Business History Review,* fall, 1971; *Newsweek,* January 31, 1972, October 25, 1976; *Economist,* July 1, 1972, October 9, 1976; *Commonweal,* February 23, 1973; *Listener,* September 26, 1974; *Journal of Economic Literature,* March, 1975; *Money,* September, 1976; *Science,* November 5, 1976; *New Republic,* November 6, 1976; *Nation,* November 20, 1976, January 22, 1977; *Scientific American,* December, 1976; *American Political Science Review,* March, 1977; *Saturday Evening Post,* May, 1977; *Christian Science Monitor,* February 11, 1980; *New York Times Book Review,* February 24, 1980.

* * *

FRIEDMAN, Norman 1925-

PERSONAL: Born April 10, 1925, in Boston, Mass.; son of Samuel and Eva (Nathanson) Friedman; married Zelda Nathanson, 1945; children: Michael, Janet. *Education:* Attended Brooklyn College (now Brooklyn College of the City University of New York), 1943, and Massachusetts Institute of Technology, 1943-44; Harvard University, A.B., 1948, A.M., 1949, Ph.D., 1952; Adelphi University, M.S.W., 1978; Gestalt Center for Psychotherapy and Training, certificate, 1978. *Home:* 33-54 164th St., Flushing, N.Y. 11358. *Office:* Department of English, Queens College of the City University of New York, Flushing, N.Y. 11367.

CAREER: Harvard University, Cambridge, Mass., teaching fellow, 1950-52; University of Connecticut, Storrs, instructor, 1952-57, assistant professor, 1957-61, associate professor of English, 1961-63; Queens College of the City University of New York, Flushing, N.Y., associate professor, 1963-67, professor of English, 1968—. Fulbright lecturer in France, 1966-67. Part-time private practice in Gestalt therapy, 1977—. *Military service:* U.S. Navy, 1943-46; became lieutenant junior grade. *Member:* American Association of University Professors, Modern Language Association of America, National Council of Teachers of English, National Association of Social Workers, New York State United Teachers, New York State Association of Practicing Psychotherapists, Phi Beta Kappa. *Awards, honors:* American Council of Learned Societies grants, summers, 1959, 1960; *Northwest Review* annual poetry prize, 1963; Borestone Mountain Poetry Award, 1964, third prize, 1967; winner of All-Nations Poetry Contest, 1977.

WRITINGS: E. E. Cummings: The Art of His Poetry, Johns Hopkins Press, 1960; (with C. A. McLaughlin) *Poetry: An Introduction to Its Form and Art,* Harper, 1961, revised edition, 1963; (with McLaughlin) *Logic, Rhetoric, and Style,* Little, Brown, 1963; *E. E. Cummings: The Growth of a Writer,* Southern Illinois University Press, 1964; (editor) *E. E. Cummings: A Collection of Critical Essays,* Prentice-Hall, 1972; *Form and Meaning in Fiction,* University of Georgia Press, 1975.

Contributor: Leonard F. Dean, editor, *Perspectives,* Harcourt, 1954; Lettis, McDonnell, and Morris, editors, *The Red Badge of Courage: Text and Criticism,* Harcourt, 1959; Robert Scholes, editor, *Approaches to the Novel,* Chandler Publishing, 1961; Rideout and Robinson, editors, *A College Book of Modern Fiction,* Row, Peterson, 1961; Kreuzer and Cogan, editors, *The Bobbs-Merrill Reader,* Bobbs-Merrill, 1962; Max Westbrook, editor, *The Modern American Novel,* Random House, 1966; Philip Stevick, editor, *The Theory of the Novel,* Macmillan, 1967; R. M. Davies, editor, *The Novel: Modern Essays in Criticism,* Prentice-Hall, 1969; Kakonis and Wilcox, editors, *Forms of Rhetoric,* McGraw, 1969; Jay Gellens, editor, *Twentieth Century Interpretations of "A Farewell to Arms,"* Prentice-Hall, 1970; Morris Beja, editor, *Virginia Woolf: "To the Lighthouse,"* Macmillan, 1970; M. Weiss, editor, *Kaleidoscope: Perspectives on Man,* Cummings, 1970; Rosalie Murphy, James Vinson, and D. L. Kirkpatrick, editors, *Contemporary Poets of the English Language,* St. Martin's, 1970, 2nd edition, 1975; Hans Burger, editor, *Die Amerikanische Short Story,* Wissenschaftliche Buchgesellschaft, 1972; Warren Shibles, editor, *Essays on Metaphor,* Language Press, 1972; John De Cecco, editor, *The Regeneration of the School,* Holt, 1972; C. E. May, editor, *Short Story Theories,* Ohio University Press, 1976; J. K. Robinson, editor, *Thomas Hardy, "The Mayor of Casterbridge": An Authoritative Text, Backgrounds, and Criticism,* Norton, 1977; Bruno Hillebrand, editor, *Zur Struktur des Romans,* Wissenschaftliche Buchgesellschaft, 1978.

Poetry represented in anthologies, including: *New Voices 2: American Writing Today,* Hendricks House, 1955; *The National Poetry Anthology 1958,* National Poetry Association, 1958; *Lyrics of Love: Best New Love Poems, 1963,* Young Publishers, 1963; *Best Poems of 1963: Borestone Mountain Poetry Awards, 1964,* Pacific Books, 1964; *Best Poems of 1966: Borestone Mountain Poetry Awards, 1967,* Pacific Books, 1967; *May My Words Feed Others,* A. S. Barnes, 1974; *Passage IV,* Triton College Press, 1978. Contributor to *Encyclopedia Americana* and *Encyclopedia of Poetry and Poetics.* Contributor to periodicals.

WORK IN PROGRESS: From Victorian to Modern; essays, poems, and stories.

SIDELIGHTS: Norman Friedman writes: "I write literary criticism in order to know and understand others, and I write poems and stories in order to know and understand myself. So you can see, I will stop at nothing, having gone to great lengths to receive formal education and training in order to become a psychotherapist, as well as a teacher and writer. I find that psychology helps deepen and extend my literary criticism, and also my poems and stories."

AVOCATIONAL INTERESTS: Music, jogging, motorcycling.

* * *

FRIERMOOD, Elisabeth Hamilton 1903-

PERSONAL: Born December 30, 1903, in Marion, Ind.; daughter of Burr and Etta (Hale) Hamilton; married Harold T. Friermood, 1928; children: Libby. *Education:* Attended Northwestern University, 1923-25, and University of Wisconsin, 1934-39. *Religion:* Baptist. *Home:* 3030 Park Ave., Bridgeport, Conn.

CAREER: Public Library, Marion, Ind., children's librarian, 1925-28; Public Library, Dayton, Ohio, children's librarian, 1930-42. Writer and storyteller. *Member:* Zeta Tau Alpha. *Awards, honors:* Indiana University Writers' Conference Award in children's literature, 1959; Ohioana Award, 1968, for *Focus the Bright Land.*

WRITINGS—Published by Doubleday, except as indicated: *The Wabash Knows the Secret,* 1951; *Geneva Summer,* 1952; *Hoosier Heritage,* 1954; *Candle in the Sun,* 1955; *That Jones Girl,* 1956; *Head High, Ellen Brody,* 1958; *Jo Allen's Predicament,* 1959; *Promises in the Attic,* 1960; *The Luck of Daphne Tolliver,* 1961; *Ballad of Calamity Creek,* 1962; *The Wild Donahues,* 1963; *Whispering Willows,* 1964; *Doc Dudley's Daughter,* 1965; *Molly's Double Rainbow,* 1966; *Focus the Bright Land,* 1967; *Circus Sequins,* 1968; *Pepper's Paradise,* 1969; *One of Fred's Girls,* 1970; *Frier and Elisabeth: Sportsman and Storyteller,* Vantage, 1979. Contributor to publications of Seashore Press. Contributor to periodicals.

* * *

FROMAN, Robert (Winslow) 1917-

PERSONAL: Born May 25, 1917, in Big Timber, Mont.; son of Harry Hunter and Muriel (Nolen) Froman; married Elizabeth Hull (a writer), 1942 (died January 11, 1975); married Katherine Cooper (a physical therapist), 1978. *Education:* Attended Reed College. *Residence:* Santa Cruz, Calif.

CAREER: Free-lance writer, 1945—.

WRITINGS: One Million Islands for Sale, Duell, 1953; *The Nerve of Some Animals,* Lippincott, 1961; *Man and the Grasses,* Lippincott, 1963; *Wanted: Amateur Scientists* (Junior Literary Guild selection for older members), McKay, 1963; *Quacko and the Elps* (Junior Literary Guild selection), McKay, 1964; *Faster and Faster* (Junior Literary Guild selection), Viking, 1965; *Our Fellow Immigrants,* McKay, 1965; *Spiders, Snakes, and Other Outcasts,* Lippincott, 1965; *The Human Senses,* Little, Brown, 1966; *Baseball-Istics,* Putnam, 1967; *Science of Salt,* McKay, 1967; *Billions of Years of You,* World Publications, 1967; *The Great Reaching Out: How Living Beings Communicate,* World Publications, 1968.

Science, Art and Visual Illusion, Simon & Schuster, 1970; *Hot and Cold and in Between,* Grosset, 1971; *Street Poems* (Junior Literary Guild selection), McCall, 1971; *Bigger and Smaller,* Crowell, 1971; *Mushrooms and Molds,* Crowell, 1972; *The Wild Orphan,* Scholastic Book Services, 1972; *Racism,* Delacorte, 1972; *Rubber Bands, Baseballs and Doughnuts,* Crowell, 1972; *Venn Diagrams,* Crowell, 1972; *Thomas the Tiger Teacher,* Scholastic Book Services, 1973; *Less Than Nothing Is Really Something,* Crowell, 1973; *Seeing Things: A Book of Poems,* Crowell, 1974; *A Game of Functions,* Crowell, 1974; *Arithmetic for Human Beings* (Book of the Month Club selection), Simon & Schuster, 1974; *Mr. Harry Know-It-All,* Macmillan, 1975; *The Stuff of You,* Macmillan, 1975; *Angles Are Easy as Pie,* Crowell, 1975; *The Greatest Guessing Game,* Crowell, 1977. Contributor of over two hundred articles to popular periodicals.

WORK IN PROGRESS: An autobiography, *Older Is Better; Mathematical Beauty;* a book with wife, Katherine Cooper Froman, on her experiences working with handicapped infants.

SIDELIGHTS: Robert Froman, who labels himself "self-educated," although he attended college, says: "I was an early victim of the college education craze. The kind of regimentation of the education process which a college inevitably enforces may be helpful to a small minority. For most of us it is debilitating. Usually it results in the victims' becoming convinced that the educational process is over for them, a conviction which amounts to a sort of resignation from life." As for his writing, he expects to "remain a free lance for the rest of my life."

Eight of Froman's books have been published in England. *Faster and Faster* has been translated into Japanese, and *The Human Senses* has been translated into French.

* * *

FROME, Michael 1920-

PERSONAL: Born May 25, 1920, in New York, N.Y.; son of William (a furrier) and Henrietta (Marks) Fromm; married Thelma Seymour, June 29, 1949; children: William Carroll, Michele Lloyd. *Education:* Attended City College (now City College of the City University of New York), 1936-39, and George Washington University, 1946. *Home and office:* 9426 Forest Haven Dr., Alexandria, Va. 22309.

CAREER: Main Line Times, Ardmore, Pa., managing editor, 1941-42; *Washington Post,* Washington, D.C., reporter, 1945-46; *Herald-Journal,* Spartanburg, S.C., managing editor, 1946; *Nashville Tennessean,* Nashville, Tenn., reporter,

1947; American Automobile Association, Washington, D.C., travel editor, 1947-57; free-lance writer, 1958—. Visiting professor of environmental studies, University of Vermont, 1978. *Military service:* U.S. Army Air Forces, Air Transport Command, 1942-45; served as navigator, became first lieutenant; awarded Air Medal. *Member:* American Society of Authors and Journalists, Society of American Travel Writers (vice-president, 1961-62; president, 1963-64), Defenders of Wildlife (vice-president, 1964-67), American Rivers Conservation Council (director), Environmental Policy Institute (director), Outdoor Writers Association of America, National Press Club, Cosmos Club.

WRITINGS: Better Vacations for Your Money, Doubleday, 1959, 2nd edition, 1960; *Washington: A Modern Guide to the Nation's Capital,* Doubleday, 1960; *Whose Woods These Are* (Literary Guild selection), Doubleday, 1962; *1001 Ways to Enjoy Your Car,* Popular Library, 1962; *Vacations, U.S.A.,* Kiplinger, 1966; *Strangers in High Places,* Doubleday, 1966, revised edition, University of Tennessee Press, 1980; (with Orville L. Freeman) *The National Forests of America,* Country Beautiful Corp., 1968; *The Forest Service,* Praeger, 1971; *Battle for the Wilderness,* Praeger, 1974. Author of annual *Rand McNally National Park Guide,* 1967—; also author of *The Varmints: Our Unwanted Wildlife,* 1969, and *The National Parks,* 1977. Columnist, *American Forests,* 1967-71; author of column, "Environmental Trails," in the *Los Angeles Times* and "Crusade for Wildlife," in *Defenders* magazine. Conservation editor and columnist, *Field and Stream,* 1968-74; contributing editor, *Changing Times;* contributing travel editor, *Woman's Day.*

SIDELIGHTS: Michael Frome gained widespread recognition in 1974 when he was fired from his position as conservation editor of *Field and Stream* because, as he says, he insisted on naming names in his column. He had, during the course of his employment with the magazine, come to be known as an ardent environmentalist who never hesitated to point out those individuals, corporations, or organizations whom he believed to be guilty of desecrating our natural resources. As a *Time* writer commented, Frome played it "tough and tendentious. He criticized timber companies, highway builders and strip miners. Frequently he used his column to lobby against legislation that might be potentially destructive to the environment. One of his notable victories came in 1970, when he helped defeat a bill which would have given timber cutting priority over recreational and other uses for national forests."

In 1972, Frome ran a "Rate Your Candidate" article in which Senators and Congressman were rated according to their attitudes and past records on conservation issues. In that article, Senator John Pastore of Rhode Island was rated as "marginal." Senator Pastore was chairman of the Subcommittee on Communications which had jurisdiction over broadcasting regulations and whose hearings had been known to be a thorn in the sides of industry executives. The Columbia Broadcasting System owns *Field and Stream* magazine and, according to Clare Dean Conley, who was editor at the time, "we got vibes from CBS that they didn't want trouble with Pastore." Frome says that it was soon after the article that he began getting pressure to "take it easy." He refused and eventually was removed from the editorial staff.

Michael Frome told *CA:* "My early interest in travel led me to the national parks, then to forests, wildlife, and to environmental issues in this country and abroad. I've been singularly fortunate in being able to take strong personal positions and still make it as a writing professional."

BIOGRAPHICAL/CRITICAL SOURCES: Northern Virginia Sun, September 15, 1960; *Leaders of American Conservation,* Ronald, 1971; *Time,* November 4, 1974; *Burlington Free Press,* March 21, 1978.

* * *

FROMM, Herbert 1905-

PERSONAL: Born February 23, 1905, in Kitzingen, Germany; son of Max (a merchant) and Mathilde (Maier) Fromm; married Leni Steinberg, January 22, 1942. *Education:* Attended Academy of Music, Munich, Germany, 1924-30. *Religion:* Jewish. *Home:* 100 Marion St., Brookline, Mass. 02146.

CAREER: Opera conductor in Wuerzburg, Germany, 1931-33; Temple Beth Zion, Buffalo, N.Y., music director and organist, 1937-41; Temple Israel, Boston, Mass., music director and organist, 1941-72, music director and organist emeritus, 1972—; composer. *Member:* American Guild of Organists. *Awards, honors:* D.H.L., Lesley College, 1966; Ernest Bloch Award for cantata, "Song of Miriam."

WRITINGS: The Key of See, Plowshare Press, 1967; (translator with Robert Lilienfeld from the German) Hans Kayser, *Akroasis: Theory of World Harmonics,* Plowshare Press, 1970; *Seven Pockets,* Dorrance, 1977; *On Jewish Music,* Bloch Publishing, 1978. Contributor of articles and essays to *American Choral Review, Liturgical Music Society, Cantors Voice,* and *Journal of Synagogue Music.*

* * *

FROST, Gavin 1930-

PERSONAL: Born November 20, 1930, in Staffordshire, England; naturalized U.S. citizen; son of Sidney and Dorothy Frost; married Yvonne Wilson (his partner in witchcraft), 1970; children: Bronwyn. *Education:* University of London, B.Sc. (cum laude), 1951. *Politics:* Republican. *Address:* Church of Wicca, Box 1502, New Bern, N.C. 28560.

CAREER: North American Rockwell, Anaheim, Calif., resident manager in Europe, 1964-68; Emerson Electric, St. Louis, Mo., director of international marketing, 1968-72; School of Wicca and Church of Wicca, New Bern, N.C., founder and operator (with wife), 1968—. Flamen (priest) of Church of Wicca and lecturer on witchcraft.

WRITINGS—All with wife, Yvonne Frost: *Witchcraft: The Way to Serenity,* Wicca, 1969; *The Witch's Bible: How to Practice the Oldest Religion,* Nash Publishing, 1973; *The Magic Power of Witchcraft,* Parker Publications, 1976; *Meta-Psychometry,* Parker Publications, 1978; *A Witch's Guide to Life,* Esoteric, 1978. Contributor to *Inland Psychic Review* and extrasensory perception publications.

WORK IN PROGRESS: The Shadow of the Ring.

SIDELIGHTS: Gavin and Yvonne Frost describe themselves as members of "a breed of contemporary middle-class witches who live in suburbia, practice in their living rooms, and maintain professional lives within the structure of Society." They founded the School of Wicca "in an attempt to correct . . . the fallacies and myths surrounding Witchcraft, Wicca Craeft (the Craft of the Wise), and the old religion to which most bona fide witches adhere." Both came to their new religion from conventional Christian backgrounds—Gavin from the Anglican faith and Yvonne from the Baptist.

They claim to have more than one thousand regular students

in their School of Wicca, enrolled from around the world. Their own publicist admits that "the source of the archaic knowledge which Gavin and Yvonne display and treat with familiarity remains somewhat mysterious." They tend to avoid questions on the subject, but will quote references.

BIOGRAPHICAL/CRITICAL SOURCES: St. Louis Post-Dispatch, May, 1972.

* * *

FRY, Alan 1931-

PERSONAL: Born April 21, 1931, in Lac la Hache, British Columbia, Canada; widowed; children: Margery, Lydia. *Education:* Attended University of British Columbia. *Residence:* Lives in a "bush camp in the Yukon Territory." *Mailing address:* Box 5373, Whitehorse, Yukon Territory, Canada Y1A 4Z2.

CAREER: Writer. Has worked as a ranch hand, sawmill laborer, and construction worker; district supervisor for Canadian Department of Indian Affairs and Northern Development, 1958-75; currently lives "off the land, common stock, debt securities and speculative mining ventures."

WRITINGS—All published by Doubleday: *Ranch on the Cariboo,* 1962; *How a People Die,* 1970; *Come a Long Journey,* 1971; *The Revenge of Annie Charlie,* 1973; *The Burden of Adrian Knowle,* 1974.

WORK IN PROGRESS: Go Well in the Bush.

* * *

FURNEAUX, Rupert 1908-

PERSONAL: Born June 29, 1908, in England. *Education:* Attended Eastbourne College. *Home:* Holine Farm House, Stanstead Park, Rowlands Castle, Hampshire, England.

CAREER: Writer, 1943—.

WRITINGS: The First War Correspondent (biography), Cassell, 1944; *The Other Side of the Story,* Cassell, 1953; *Fact, Fake or Fable,* Cassell, 1954; *The Man behind the Mask,* Cassell, 1954; *Famous Criminal Cases,* Volumes I-V, Wingate, 1954-59, Volume VI, Odhams, 1960, Volume VII, Odhams, 1962; *Myth and Mystery,* Wingate, 1956; *The Medical Murderer,* Elek, 1957; *The Siege of Plevna,* Blond, 1957, published as *The Breakfast War,* Crowell, 1958; *Legend and Reality,* Wingate, 1957; *Tried by Their Peers,* Cassell, 1958; *Tobias Furneaux, Circumnavigator* (biography), Cassell, 1959; *The Two Stranglers of Rillington Place,* Panther, 1961; *The World's Strangest Mysteries,* Odhams, 1961; *Courtroom U.S.A.,* Penguin, 1962; *The Zula War,* Lippincott, 1963; *The Mystery of the Empty Tomb,* Panther, 1963; *They Died by a Gun,* Jenkins, 1963; *Massacre at Amritsar,* Allen & Unwin, 1963; *What Happened on the Mary Celeste,* Parrish, 1964; *News of War,* Parrish, 1964; *Great Issues in Private Courts,* Kimber, 1964; *Krakatoa,* Prentice-Hall, 1964; *The World's Most Intriguing Mysteries,* Odhams, 1965; *Conquest, 1066,* Secker & Warburg, 1965, published as *Invasion 1066,* Prentice-Hall, 1966; *The Great Treasure Hunts,* Taplinger, 1969; *The Last Days of Marie Antoinette,* John Day, 1971; *Saratoga, Battle 1777,* Stein & Day, 1971; *The Money Pit Mystery,* Dodd, 1972, published as *Money Pit: The Mystery of Oak Island,* Collins, 1976; *Roman Siege of Jerusalem,* McKay, 1972; *The American Revolution,* Fergusson, 1973; *The Seven Years War,* Hart-Davis, 1973; *On Buried and Sunken Treasure,* Longman, 1973; *Volcanoes,* Penguin, 1974; *Primative Peoples,* David & Charles, 1975; *Ancient Mysteries,* McGraw, 1976; *The Tungus Event,* Nordon Publications, 1979.

"Crime Documentary" series, published by Sweet & Maxwell: *Guenther Podola,* 1960; *Robert Hoolhouse,* 1961; *The Murder of Lord Erroll,* 1961; *Michael John Davis,* 1962.

AVOCATIONAL INTERESTS: Golf.

BIOGRAPHICAL/CRITICAL SOURCES: Times Literary Supplement, July 13, 1967.

G

GAGLIANO, Frank 1931-

PERSONAL: Born November 18, 1931, in Brooklyn, N.Y.; son of Francis Paul and Nancy (La Barbera) Gagliano; married Sandra Gordon (an operatic soprano), January 18, 1958; children: Francis Enrico. *Education:* Attended Queens College of the City of New York (now Queens College of the City University of New York), 1949-53; University of Iowa, B.A., 1954; Columbia University, M.F.A., 1957. *Agent:* Gilbert Parker, Curtis Brown Ltd., 575 Madison Ave., New York, N.Y. 10022; and Michael Imison, Dr. Jan Van Loewen Ltd., 81-83 Shaftesbury Ave., London WIV 8BX, England. *Office:* Creative Arts Center, West Virginia University, Morgantown, W.Va. 26506.

CAREER: Royal Shakespeare Co., London, England, playwright-in-residence, 1967-69; Florida State University, Tallahassee, assistant professor of drama, playwright-in-residence, and director of Contemporary Playwright's Center, 1969-73; University of Texas at Austin, lecturer in playwriting and director of E. P. Conkle Workshop for Playwrights, 1973-74; West Virginia University, Morgantown, Benedum Professor of Theatre, 1974—. Distinguished Visiting Alumni Professor, University of Rhode Island, 1975. *Member:* Writers Guild of America East, Dramatists Guild, Actors Studio, American Theatre Association, New Dramatists Committee, Eugene O'Neill Theatre Center, American Association of University Professors. *Awards, honors:* Rockefeller Foundation grant, 1965-67; O'Neill Foundation-Wesleyan University fellowship in playwriting, 1967; National Endowment for the Arts fellowship in playwriting, 1973; Guggenheim fellowship, 1974.

WRITINGS—Plays: "The Library Raid" (three-act), first produced in Houston, Tex., at the Alley Theatre, October 12, 1961; *Conerico Was Here to Stay* (one-act; also see below; first produced off-Broadway at Village South Theatre, March 8, 1964), Samuel French, 1965; *Night of the Dunce* (full-length; first produced off-Broadway at Cherry Lane Theatre, December 28, 1966), Dramatists Play Service, 1967; *Father Uxbridge Wants to Marry* (full-length; first produced in Waterford, Conn., at Eugene O'Neill Theatre Centre; produced off-Broadway at American Place Theatre, October 12, 1967), Grove, 1969; *The Hide and Seek Odyssey of Madeline Gimple* (one-act children's play; first produced in Waterford, Conn., at Eugene O'Neill Theatre Centre and Project Create, November, 1967), Dramatists Play Service, 1970; *Frank Gagliano's City Scene* (includes two one-acts, "Paradise Gardens East" and "Conerico Was Here to Stay"; first produced off-Broadway at Fortune Theatre, March 10, 1969), Samuel French, 1965; *Big Sur* (one-act; first produced for television by NBC for "Experiment in Television," April 20, 1969; stage adaptation first produced at Florida State University, Tallahassee, April 19, 1970), Dramatists Play Service, 1971; "The Prince of Peasantmania" (two-act), first produced in Milwaukee, Wis., at Milwaukee Repertory Co., February 20, 1970, revised and produced at Florida State University, April 15, 1971; "In the Voodoo Parlour of Marie Laveau" [and] "The Commedia World of Lafcadio Beau," first produced in Waterford, Conn., at Eugene O'Neill Theatre Centre, produced off-Broadway at Phoenix Theatre, 1974; "The Resurrection of Jackie Cramer," music by Raymond Benson, first produced at the E. P. Conkle Workshop for Playwrights, 1974; "Congo Square," music by Claibe Richardson, first produced in Kingston, R.I., by University of Rhode Island's New Repertory Company, 1975.

Also author of "The Private Eye of Hiram Bodoni" (television play), 1971, "Quasimodo" (musical; music by Lionel Bart), 1971, "Anywhere the Wind Blows" (musical), 1972, and "The Total Immersion of Madeleine Favorini," 1979.

Represented in anthologies, including *Showcase 1,* edited by John Lahr, Grove, 1970, and *Scripts III,* Houghton. Contributor to *New York Times, Dramatists Guild Quarterly, Theatre Crafts,* and *Theatre Guild.*

WORK IN PROGRESS: A novel, *Georg;* a television movie, "Those Talented Ladies from Suicide Street"; a film, "The Bel Canto Gang"; a play for young spectators, "Humungus Toe Rides Again."

AVOCATIONAL INTERESTS: Reading and listening to music.

* * *

GAILEY, Harry A(lfred) 1926-

PERSONAL: Born December 4, 1926, in Kansas City, Mo.; son of Harry Alfred (a painting contractor) and Dora (Sons) Gailey; married Rosalie Joy Bray, June 17, 1951; children: Laurel, Karen, Nancy, Richard, Jennifer. *Education:* Attended Santa Ana Junior College, 1947-50; University of California, Los Angeles, A.B., 1953, M.A., 1955, Ph.D., 1958. *Politics:* Democrat. *Religion:* Protestant. *Home:* 134 Hollycrest Dr., Los Gatos, Calif. 95030. *Office:* Department of History, San Jose State University, San Jose, Calif. 95192.

CAREER: Mechanical and civil engineer in Santa Ana, Long Beach, and Los Angeles, Calif., 1946-52; Northwest Missouri State College (now University), Maryville, associate professor and chairman of humanities department, 1957-62; San Jose State University, San Jose, Calif., assistant professor, 1962-64, associate professor, 1964-68, professor of history, 1968—. *Military service:* U.S. Army Air Forces, 1945-46. U.S. Army Reserve, 1946-55; became first lieutenant. *Member:* African Studies Association, American Historical Association. *Awards, honors:* Ford Foundation research grant, 1960; Social Science Research Council grant, 1967; American Philosophical Society grant, 1971; San Jose State University, outstanding professor, 1971-72, president's scholar, 1979.

WRITINGS: *A History of the Gambia,* Routledge & Kegan Paul, 1964; *The History of Africa in Maps,* Denoyer-Geppert, 1967, 3rd edition, 1979; *History of Africa from Earliest Times to 1800,* Holt, 1970; *The Road to Aba,* New York University Press, 1970; *History of Africa from 1800 to Present,* Holt, 1972; *Sir Donald Cameron, Colonial Governor,* Hoover Institution, 1974; *Historical Dictionary of the Gambia,* Scarecrow, 1975; *Lugard and the Abeokuta Uprising,* Frank Cass, 1979. Contributor to *Journal of African History, Sierra Leone Studies,* and *College English.*

WORK IN PROGRESS: A biography of Sir Hugh Clifford; research on the military in Africa.

SIDELIGHTS: Harry A. Gailey is "concerned with in-depth investigations concerning British administrative policy in Africa during the twentieth century. [Recently] biographies of important British pro-consuls have seemed to be the most interesting way of approaching this problem."

* * *

GAL, Allon 1934-

PERSONAL: Born in 1934, in Israel; son of Lippa and Nesiah (Batt) Gal; married Snunit Zutra, 1954; children: Shahaf, Peleg, Keren. *Education:* Kibbutz Teachers' College, teacher's diploma, 1961; Hebrew University, B.A., 1968; Brandeis University, M.A., 1970, Ph.D., 1975. *Office:* Ben-Gurion Research Institute and Archives, Kiriat Sde-Boker, Israel.

CAREER: Agriculturist and high school teacher in Shaar Ha-Amakim, Israel, 1955-65; Hebrew College, Brookline, Mass., instructor in Near Eastern and Judaic Studies, 1969-75; currently research associate and lecturer, Ben-Gurion Research Institute and Archives, Kiriat Sde-Boker, Israel. *Military service:* Israeli Army, 1952-55. *Member:* Association for Jewish Studies, American Jewish Historical Society, Historical Society of Israel, Israeli. Association for American Studies, Brandeis University Alumni Association.

WRITINGS: *Socialist-Zionism: Theory and Issues in Contemporary Jewish Nationalism,* Schenkman, 1973; *Brandeis of Boston,* Harvard University Press, 1980. Contributor of articles to scholarly journals in the United States and Israel.

WORK IN PROGRESS: *Ben-Gurion and American Jewry, 1915-1943.*

* * *

GALLATI, Robert R. J. 1913-

PERSONAL: Born August 5, 1913, in New York, N.Y.; married Martha E. McNamee; children: Robert, Richard, Michele. *Education:* Fordham University, B.S., LL.B.; St. John's University, LL.M.; Brooklyn Law School, J.D. (summa cum laude); graduate of Federal Bureau of Investigation's National Academy; New York University, Ph.D. candidate. *Home:* 4 Teramar Way, White Plains, N.Y. 10605. *Office:* College of Criminal Justice, Northeastern University, Boston, Mass. 02115.

CAREER: Admitted to Bars of State of New York, U.S. Supreme Court, U.S. Court for the Southern District of New York, and General Courts Martial of the Armed Forces; New York Police Department, New York, N.Y., 1940-73, began as patrolman, became chief of department; Northeastern University, Boston, Mass., professor in College of Criminal Justice, 1974—. Director of New York State Identification and Intelligence System, Albany, 1964-73; chief of police, Brockton, Mass., and commissioner of police, Mt. Vernon, N.Y. Has worked with Federal Bureau of Investigation as confidential security investigator; commanding officer of New York City Police Academy, 1955-60; dean of police studies, Bernard M. Baruch School of Business and Public Administration (now Bernard M. Baruch College of the City University of New York), 1955-60. *Military service:* U.S. Naval Reserve, World War II, Korean Police Action; became captain.

MEMBER: International Association of Chiefs of Police, Police Association for Research (founding member), Academy of Police Science (member of board of governors; former president), National Sheriffs Association (life member), New York State Association of Chiefs of Police. *Awards, honors:* Achievement in Public Administration Award, New York Metropolitan Chapter, American Society for Public Administration, 1959; Mayor's Medal, New York City, 1964.

WRITINGS: *Introduction to Law Enforcement and Criminal Justice,* C. C Thomas, 1962; *Combating Organized Crime,* Allyn & Bacon, 1979; *Introduction to Security Management,* Prentice-Hall, 1979. Contributor to professional journals.

* * *

GALLIE, Menna (Patricia Humphreys) 1920-

PERSONAL: Born March 17, 1920, in Ystradgynlais, Swansea, South Wales; daughter of William Thomas and Elizabeth (Rhys-Williams) Humphreys; married W. Bryce Gallie (a professor of political science), 1940; children: Charles D. W., Edyth M. V. *Education:* Swansea University, B.A. (with honors), 1940. *Politics:* Labour Party. *Home:* Cilhendre, Newport, Pembrokeshire, Dyfed, South Wales.

CAREER: Ministries of Inland Revenue and Supply, civil servant, 1940-43; grammar school teacher, 1953-54. Tutor, Cambridge University. Cambridge Labour Party delegate. Committee member, Old People's Welfare; honorary treasurer, Care and After-Care Committee, County Down. *Member:* P.E.N. *Awards, honors:* Critics award, Crime Writers Association, 1959.

WRITINGS—Published by Harper: *Strike for a Kingdom,* 1960; *Man's Desiring,* 1960; *The Small Mine,* 1962; *Travels with a Duchess,* 1969; *You're Welcome to Ulster,* 1971. Also translator from the Welsh of *Full Moon,* Hodder & Stoughton.

WORK IN PROGRESS: A novel, *In These Promiscuous Parts.*

SIDELIGHTS: Although the reviewer for *Time* calls Menna Gallie's *You're Welcome to Ulster* "a beautifully written, cleanly unsentimental love story [which] skillfully use[s] as background the divided heart of present-day Northern Ireland," Stephen P. Ryan finds the love story to be "something less than successful." He does praise the novel's setting and the author's ability to depict the problems of life in

Northern Ireland. "Where Miss Gallie is at her very best," writes Ryan, "is in the scenes in which the whole problem of the North is discussed . . . by neighbors, and by the local townspeople. The author's sympathies are obviously with the Catholic minority, but what emerges is the strange spectrum of political beliefs which are to be found in Northern Ireland today. She makes it abundantly clear that the problems are largely due to fanaticism at the two extremes: the I.R.A. gunmen on the Republican left; and the Paisleyite rabble-rousers and Orange Order on the Unionist right. Between lies a vast population area of fundamental good will, baffled by bewilderment and fear. Miss Gallie's characters represent the interesting range of positions possible in Northern Ireland at the present moment."

AVOCATIONAL INTERESTS: Voluntary social work, Labour politics, education.

BIOGRAPHICAL/CRITICAL SOURCES: Listener, April 18, 1968; *New York Times Book Review,* April 21, 1968; *Books and Bookmen,* June, 1968; *Time,* May 3, 1971; *Best Sellers,* May 15, 1971.

* * *

GALVIN, Brendan 1938-

PERSONAL: Born October 20, 1938, in Everett, Mass.; son of James Russell (a letter carrier) and Rose (McLaughlin) Galvin; married Ellen Baer, August 1, 1968; children: Kim, Peter, Anne Maura. *Education:* Boston College, B.S., 1961; Northeastern University, M.A., 1964; University of Massachusetts, M.F.A., 1967, Ph.D., 1970. *Address:* Box 54, Durham, Conn. 06422. *Office:* Department of English, Central Connecticut State College, Stanley St., New Britain, Conn. 06050.

CAREER: Northeastern University, Boston, Mass., instructor in English, 1963-65; Slippery Rock State College, Slippery Rock, Pa., assistant professor of English, 1968-69; Central Connecticut State College, New Britain, assistant professor, 1969-74, associate professor of English, 1974—. Director of Connecticut Writers Conference; fellow of Fine Arts Work Center (Provincetown, Mass.), 1971-72; visiting writer, Connecticut College, 1975-76; affiliated with Wesleyan-Suffield Writer-Reader Conference, 1977, 1978. *Awards, honors:* National Endowment for the Arts creative writing fellow, 1974; Artists Foundation fellow, 1978.

WRITINGS: The Narrow Land, Northeastern University Press, 1971; *The Salt Farm,* Fiddlehead, 1972; *No Time for Good Reasons,* University of Pittsburgh Press, 1974; *The Minutes No One Owns,* University of Pittsburgh Press, 1977; *Atlantic Flyway,* University of Georgia Press, 1980. Contributor to *New Yorker, Poetry, Sewanee Review,* and other periodicals.

WORK IN PROGRESS: A book; poems.

SIDELIGHTS: Brendan Galvin writes: "I grew up on Cape Cod and in a suburb of Boston, and these two poles have affected my work strongly, in that my poems are full of imagery from the sea, the land, austere and muted, of the outer Cape, and the urban blight that infects humans who come in contact with it, especially through their work, most of which is unfulfilling and thus worthless."

* * *

GANN, Ernest Kellogg 1910-

PERSONAL: Born October 13, 1910, in Lincoln, Neb.; son of George Kellogg and Caroline (Kupper) Gann; married Eleanor Michaud, 1933 (divorced); married Dodie Post, 1966; children: (first marriage) George, Steven, Polly. *Education:* Attended Yale University, 1930-32. *Politics:* Republican. *Religion:* Protestant. *Residence:* San Juan Island, Wash. *Agent:* Scott Meredith Literary Agency, Inc., 845 Third Ave., New York, N.Y. 10022; and Adams, Ray & Rosenberg, 9220 Sunset Blvd., Penthouse 25, Los Angeles, Calif. 90069.

CAREER: Author and screen writer. *Military service:* U.S. Army Air Forces, Air Transport Command, 1942-46; became captain; received Distinguished Flying award. *Member:* Press Club (San Francisco), Quiet Birdmen. *Awards, honors:* National Association of Independent Schools Award for *The High and the Mighty,* 1954; award, Pacific Northwest Booksellers, 1973; Aviation Journalist of the Year, Ziff-Davis Publishing, 1975; Inspirational Award, Western Aerospace Association, 1977.

WRITINGS: Island in the Sky, Viking, 1944; *Blaze of Noon,* Holt, 1946; *Benjamin Lawless,* Sloane, 1948; *Fiddler's Green,* Sloane, 1950; *The High and the Mighty,* Sloane, 1952; *Soldier of Fortune,* Sloane, 1954; *Trouble with Lazy Ethel,* Sloane, 1957; *Twilight for the Gods,* Sloane, 1958; *Fate Is the Hunter,* Simon & Schuster, 1961; *Of Good and Evil,* Simon & Schuster, 1963; *In the Company of Eagles,* Simon & Schuster, 1966; *The Song of the Sirens,* Simon & Schuster, 1968; *The Antagonists,* Simon & Schuster, 1971; *Band of Brothers,* Simon & Schuster, 1973; *Ernest K. Gann's Flying Circus,* Macmillan, 1974; *A Hostage to Fortune* (autobiography), Knopf, 1978. Also author of *Brain 2000,* Doubleday.

Screenplays; all based on his novels: "The Raging Tide" (based on *Fiddler's Green*), Universal, 1951; "Island in the Sky," Warner Brothers, 1953; "The High and the Mighty," Warner Brothers, 1954; "Soldier of Fortune," Twentieth Century-Fox, 1955; "Twilight for the Gods," J. Arthur Rank, 1957.

WORK IN PROGRESS: The Encounter.

SIDELIGHTS: Ernest K. Gann's books about pilots and flying are highly popular with pilots around the world. His painstaking attention to aeronautical accuracy has been noted as one reason for this popularity. In his research for *Band of Brothers,* for instance, Gann interviewed pilots, airline officials, and traffic controllers in both Europe and Asia. "A lot of pilots read my stuff," he told the *Seattle Post-Intelligencer,* "and I knew it had to be absolutely as accurate as I could make it."

Gann's books have been translated into numerous languages and have been adapted for motion picture and television use. *The Antagonists* will appear as an eight-hour television special series in 1980.

BIOGRAPHICAL/CRITICAL SOURCES: World Journal Tribune, October 10, 1966; *New Yorker,* October 29, 1966; *Saturday Review,* December 24, 1966, April 29, 1972; *New York Times Book Review,* October 27, 1968, February 14, 1971; *New Statesman,* May 16, 1969; *Seattle Post-Intelligencer,* December 23, 1974; *Best Sellers,* January 1, 1974; *Flying,* April, 1974; *Christian Science Monitor,* January 30, 1975; *Spectator,* June 5, 1976; *Time,* September 25, 1978.

* * *

GARD, Richard A(bbott) 1914-

PERSONAL: Born May 29, 1914, in Vancouver, British Columbia, Canada; brought to United States in 1916; U.S. citizen; son of Charles N. and Clara (Abbott) Gard; married Tatiana Moravec, 1952; children: Alan M., Anita N. *Educa-*

tion: University of Washington, Seattle, B.A., 1937; graduate study on Buddhism in Japan, 1939-40, 1953-54; University of Hawaii, M.A., 1940; University of Pennsylvania, graduate study, 1945-47; Claremont College (now Claremont Graduate School), Ph.D., 1951. *Home:* Crane Neck Rd., Old Field, N.Y. 11733. *Office:* Institute for Advanced Studies of WorldReligions, Melville Memorial Library, State University of New York, Stony Brook, N.Y. 11794.

CAREER: University of Hawaii, Honolulu, teaching fellow in political science, 1936-47; University of Pennsylvania, Philadelphia, ASTP lecturer in Japanese studies, 1945-47; Johns Hopkins University, School of Advanced International Studies, Washington, D.C., lecturer in Far East affairs, 1952; visiting lecturer on Buddhism at universities in Japan, 1953-54, 1957-59, Thailand, 1956, Burma, 1957-58, and Korea, 1958; Asia Foundation, San Francisco, Calif., director of plans, 1954-56, special advisor on Buddhist affairs, 1956-59; visiting lecturer in Buddhist studies at Yale University, New Haven, Conn., 1959-63, Hartford Seminary Foundation, Hartford, Conn., 1961-62, and Center for Area and Country Studies, Foreign Service Institute, Department of State, Washington, D.C., 1968-76; reserve officer, U.S. Foreign Service, Department of State, 1963-70; State University of New York at Stony Brook, Institute for Advanced Studies of World Religions, director of institute services, 1971—. Visiting professor of Asian studies, Wittenberg University, 1970; adjunct professor of Asian studies, Center of Asian Studies, St. John's University, 1974-78; guest lecturer at universities elsewhere in the United States, Hong Kong, Malayasia, Singapore, Sri Lanka, and Vietnam. *Military service:* U.S. Marine Corps, 1941-46; retired as lieutenant colonel.

MEMBER: American Society for the Study of Religion, American Academy of Religion, Royal Asiatic Society, Mongolia Society, Pali Text Society, International Association of Buddhist Studies, North American Society for Buddhist Studies, Society for Asian and Comparative Philosophy, Society for the Study of Chinese Religions, Canada-Mongolia Society, Asiatic Society of Japan, Siam Society, Association for Asian Studies (Mid-Atlantic region president, 1974-75), World Fellowship of Buddhists (vice-president for U.S., 1961-64; assistant secretary-general, 1971-75), Buddhist Vihara Society (Washington, D.C.; member of board of directors, 1969), Tibet Society (member of board of directors, 1978-80). *Awards, honors:* Japanese Buddhist Jodo-shu Award, 1946; Japanese Buddhist Shingon-shu Award, 1950; Thai Buddhist Theravada Award, 1956; Burmese Buddhist Theravada Award, 1956; D.H.L. from Monmouth College, 1963.

WRITINGS: Studies in Oriental Philosophy, Kokusai Bunka Shinkokai (Tokyo), 1940; *A Comparative Study of Some Japanese and Wagnerian Aesthetic Principles,* Oriental Books, 1949; *Some Suggested Principles for the Reviewing of Scholarly Books,* Oriental Books, 1949; *Buddhist Influences on the Political Thought and Institutions of India and Japan,* Society for Oriental Studies (Claremont, Calif.), 1949; *Buddhist Political Thought,* Mahamakuta University (Bangkok), 1956; *Buddhism,* Braziller, 1961; *The Role of Thailand in World Buddhism,* World Fellowship of Buddhists, 1971.

Bibliographies: *Buddhist Political Thought: A Bibliography,* School of Advanced International Studies, Johns Hopkins University, 1952; *A Bibliography for the Study of Buddhism in Ceylon in Western Languages,* Asia Foundation (Berkeley), 1956, 2nd edition, 1957; *A Select Bibliography for the Study of Buddhism in Burma in Western Languages,* Asia Foundation (Tokyo), 1957; *A Select Bibliography for the Study of Buddhism in Thailand in Western Languages,* Asia Foundation (Berkeley), 1957; *A Guide to Non-Buddhist Materials in Western Languages for Buddhist Libraries in Asia,* Asia Foundation (Tokyo), 1957-58; *A Short Bibliography of Buddhist Jurisprudence and Legal Thought,* American Consulate General (Hong Kong), 1965; *Buddhist Text Information,* Institute for Advanced Studies of World Religions, State University of New York at Stony Brook, 1974—; *Buddhist Research Information,* Institute for Advanced Studies of World Religions, State University of New York at Stony Brook, 1979—; *Sikh Religious Studies Information,* Institute for Advanced Studies of World Religions, State University of New York at Stony Brook, 1979—.

Contributor: Philip W. Thayer, editor, *Southeast Asia in the Coming World,* Johns Hopkins University Press, 1953; Harold D. Lasswell and Harland Cleveland, editors, *The Ethic of Power: The Interplay of Religion, Philosophy, and Politics,* Conference on Science, Philosophy, and Religion, 1962; Charles J. Adams, editor, *A Reader's Guide to the Great Religions,* Free Press, 1965; Laurence G. Thompson, editor, *Studia Asiatica,* Chinese Materials Center (Taipei), 1976; O. H. De A. Wijesekera, editor, *Malalasekera Commemoration Volume,* Malalasekera Commemoration Volume Committee (Colombo), 1976; Ananda W. P. Guruge and D. C. Ahir, editors, *Buddhism's Contribution to the World Culture and Civilization,* Maha Bodhi Society of India (New Delhi), 1978; Piyadassi Mahathera, editor, *Narada Mahathera Felicitation Volume,* Buddhist Publication Society (Kandy, Sri Lanka), 1979.

General editor, "Great Religions of Modern Man" series, six volumes, Braziller, 1961. Contributor of articles on Buddhism to journals in the United States, Colombo, Japan, Vietnam, India, and South Korea.

WORK IN PROGRESS: A Political Study of Modern Buddhism in Viet-Nam; Buddhist Essays for Asian Students; Richard Wagner and Buddhism; Essentials of Buddhism; two books of poetry, *Cables from Bangkok* and *Leaves on the Snow.*

AVOCATIONAL INTERESTS: Chamber and symphonic music, mountain trekking, Japanese landscape gardening.

BIOGRAPHICAL/CRITICAL SOURCES: Dale Riepe, *The Philosophy of India and Its Impact on American Thought,* C. C Thomas, 1970; William Peiris, *The Western Contribution to Buddhism,* Motilal Banarsidass (Delhi), 1973.

* * *

GARDINER, C(linton) Harvey 1913-

PERSONAL: Born August 1, 1913, in Newport, Ky.; son of Clinton Fisk and Mabel (Henderson) Gardiner; married Katie Mae Nelson, 1937; children: Harvey Nelson. *Education:* West Kentucky State Teachers College (now Western Kentucky University), A.B., 1936; University of Kentucky, M.A., 1940; University of Michigan, Ph.D., 1945. *Home address:* The Oaks, R.R. 2, Box 365 A, Murphysboro, Ill.

CAREER: Covington, Ky., teacher in public school system, 1937-42; Washington University, St. Louis, Mo., associate professor, 1946-57; Southern Illinois University at Carbondale, professor, 1957-61, research professor, 1961-74, professor emeritus, 1974—. Fulbright lecturer at University of Bristol and University of Nottingham, 1962-63, University of Tokyo, Rikkyo University, and Seikei University, 1968. Visiting summer professor at University of Illinois, 1963, and University of Minnesota, 1965. *Military service:* U.S. Navy,

1942-46; became lieutenant. *Member:* American Historical Association, Conference on Latin American History, Academy of American Franciscan History. *Awards, honors:* Washington University research grants, 1949-55; American Philosophical Society research grants, 1950, 1956, and 1975; Guggenheim fellow, 1953-54; Robertson Prize, 1954; Folger Shakespeare Library fellow, 1956; Fulbright fellow, 1962-63; Newberry Library grant, 1964; Huntington Library grant, summer, 1967.

WRITINGS: Naval Power in the Conquest of Mexico, University of Texas Press, 1956; *Martin Lopez: Conquistador Citizen of Mexico,* University of Kentucky Press, 1958, reprinted, Greenwood Press, 1974; *William Hickling Prescott: An Annotated Bibliography,* Library of Congress, 1958; *Prescott and His Publishers,* Southern Illinois University Press, 1959; *Mexico: 1825-1828,* University of North Carolina Press, 1959; *William Hickling Prescott: A Memorial,* Duke University Press, 1959; *The Constant Captain: Gonzalo de Sandoval,* Southern Illinois University Press, 1961; *The Literary Memoranda of William Hickling Prescott,* two volumes, University of Oklahoma, 1961; *The History of the Reign of Ferdinand and Isabella,* Allen & Unwin, 1962; *The Japanese and Peru, 1873-1973,* University of New Mexico Press, 1975; *La politica de immigracion del dictador Trujillo: Estudio sobre la creacion de una imagen humanitaria,* Universidad Nacional de Pedro Henriquez Urena, 1980.

Editor: C. M. Flandrau, *Viva Mexico!,* University of Illinois Press, 1964; *The Papers of William Hickling Prescott,* University of Illinois Press, 1964; R. H. Dana, *To Cuba and Back,* Southern Illinois University Press, 1966; Henry Koster, *Travels in Brazil,* Southern Illinois University Press, 1966; F. C. Gooch, *Face to Face with the Mexicans,* Southern Illinois University Press, 1966; Merwin, *Three Years in Chile,* Southern Illinois University Press, 1966; W. H. Prescott, *History of the Conquest of Mexico,* University of Chicago Press, 1966; F. B. Head, *Journeys Across the Pampas and Among the Andes,* Southern Illinois University Press, 1967; F. Hassaurek, *Four Years Among the Ecuadorians,* Southern Illinois University Press, 1967; I. F. Holton, *New Granada,* Southern Illinois University Press, 1967; *A Study in Dissent: The Warren-Gerry Correspondence, 1776-1792,* Southern Illinois University Press, 1968. Contributor to journals in United States, Spain, Mexico, Ecuador, Chile, Peru, and Japan.

* * *

GARRETT, George (Palmer) 1929-

PERSONAL: Born June 11, 1929, in Orlando, Fla.; son of George Palmer (a lawyer) and Rosalie (Toomer) Garrett: married Susan Parrish Jackson (a musician), June 14, 1952; children: William Palmer, George Gorham, Alice. *Education:* Attended Columbia University, 1948-49; Princeton University, B.A., 1952, M.A., 1956. *Politics:* Democrat. *Religion:* Episcopalian. *Home and office address:* Box 264, York Harbor, Me. 03911. *Agent:* Curtis Brown, Ltd., 575 Madison Ave., New York, N.Y. 10022.

CAREER: Wesleyan University, Middletown, Conn., assistant professor, 1957-60; Rice University, Houston, Tex., visiting assistant professor, 1961-62; University of Virginia, Charlottesville, associate professor, 1962-67; Hollins College, Hollins College, Va., professor of English and director of graduate program, 1967-71; University of South Carolina, Columbia, professor and writer-in-residence, 1971-74; Princeton University, Princeton, N.J., senior fellow of the Council of Humanities, 1975-77; Columbia University, New York, N.Y., adjunct professor, 1977-78; University of Michigan, Ann Arbor, writer-in-residence, 1979. Writer-in-residence at Princeton University, 1964-65; visiting professor, Florida International University, 1974, and Bennington College, 1979-80. Has worked at various times at CBS Television and in Hollywood. *Military service:* U.S. Army, 1952-55. *Member:* Modern Language Association of America, Author's Guild, Writer's Guild, Southern Historical Association, Florida Historical Society, Princeton Tower Club. *Awards, honors: Sewanee Review* fellowship, 1958; Rome Prize of American Academy, 1958-59; Ford Foundation grant, 1961; National Endowment for the Arts sabbatical fellowship, 1966; *Contempora* writing award, 1971; Guggenheim fellowship, 1974-75.

WRITINGS: The Reverend Ghost: Poems, Scribner, 1957; *King of the Mountain* (short stories), Scribner, 1958; *The Sleeping Gypsy and Other Poems,* University of Texas Press, 1958; *The Finished Man* (novel), Scribner, 1960; *Which Ones Are the Enemy?* (novel), Little, Brown, 1961; *In the Briar Patch* (short stories), University of Texas Press, 1961; *Abraham's Knife and Other Poems,* University of North Carolina Press, 1961; *Sir Slob and the Princess* (play for children), Samuel French, 1962; *Cold Ground Was My Bed Last Night* (short stories), University of Missouri Press, 1964; *Do, Lord, Remember Me* (novel), Doubleday, 1965; *For a Bitter Season: New and Selected Poems,* University of Missouri Press, 1967; *A Wreath for Garibaldi and Other Stories,* Hart-Davis, 1969; *Death of the Fox* (novel), Doubleday, 1971; *The Magic Striptease,* (novel) Doubleday, 1973; *Welcome to the Medicine Show: Postcards/Flashcards/Snapshots,* Palaemon, 1978; *To Recollect a Cloud of Ghosts: Christmas in England, 1602-1603,* Palaemon, 1979; *Elizabeth and James* (novel), Doubleday, in press.

Editor: *New Writing from Virginia* (anthology), New Writing Association, 1964; *The Girl in the Black Raincoat* (anthology), Duell, 1966; (with W. R. Robinson) *Man and the Movies,* Louisiana State University Press, 1967; (with William Peden), *New Writing in South Carolina,* University of South Carolina Press, 1971; (with Jane Gelfman and O. B. Hardison, Jr.) *Film Scripts One,* Appleton, 1971; (with Gelfman and Hardison) *Film Scripts Two,* Appleton, 1971; (with R.H.W. Dillard and John Rees Moore) *The Sounder Few: Selected Essays from the "Hollins Critic,"* University of Georgia Press, 1971; (with Gelfman and Hardison) *Film Scripts Three,* Appleton, 1972; (with Gelfman and Hardison) *Film Scripts Four,* Appleton, 1972; (with John Graham) *Craft So Hard to Learn: Conversations with Poets and Novelists about the Teaching of Writing,* Morrow, 1972; (with Graham) *The Writer's Voice: Conversations with Contemporary Writers,* Morrow, 1973; (with Walton Beacham) *Intro 5,* University Press of Virginia, 1974; (with Katherine Garrison Biddle) *The Botteghe Obscure Reader,* Wesleyan University Press, 1974; *Intro 6: Life as We Know It,* Doubleday, 1974; (with James Whitehead and Miller Williams) *Intro 7: All of Us and None of You,* Doubleday, 1975; (with Stephen Kendrick) *Intro 8: The Liar's Craft,* Doubleday, 1977; (with Michael Mewshaw) *Intro 9: Close to Home,* Hendel & Reinke, 1978.

Author of produced motion picture scripts, "The Young Lovers," 1964, "The Playground," 1965, and (with others) "Frankenstein Meets the Space Monster," 1966. Writer for "Suspense" series, CBS-TV, 1958. Author of play, "Garden Spot, U.S.A.," produced in Houston at Alley Theatre, 1962. Editor of "Contemporary Poetry" series, University of North Carolina Press, 1962-68, and "Short Story" series, Louisiana State University Press, 1966-69. Poetry editor,

Transatlantic Review, 1958-71; *Hollins Critic*, contributing editor, 1965-67, co-editor, 1967-71; contributing editor, *Contempora*, 1969-73; assistant editor, *Film Journal*, 1970-74; consulting editor, *Kudzu*, 1978—; co-editor, *Poultry: A Magazine of Voice*, 1979—.

SIDELIGHTS: George Garrett told *CA:* "I have been writing all my life and publishing and calling myself a 'professional' for more than 25 years. And still I feel like a beginner. Which feeling is, I believe, accurate. Because one is always beginning, always challenged to learn newly. And what one learns is how you should have done the last book, the last story, the last poem. With that knowledge one commences the next and new ones with innocence rather than experience, with hope and faith and no security. Even habits, good or bad, aren't much help. This (to me) is the joy of the enterprise, always to be challenged, at hazard, working and living a quest without ending for as long as I may live. And for as long as I live I want to continue to try my all at doing it all—fiction, poetry, criticism, drama, films, etc. Treating each and every piece of work as first and last. 'Success' is mostly a matter of luck. But this joy, the joy of always beginning, making and doing, is a matter of faith and hope and love, given and received."

Reviewing *Death of the Fox,* Jean Stubbs calls Garrett "a born writer. I do not mean that words pour from him without effort on his part—though they sound as though they do—but his magical obsession with the beauty of language, with verbal impressions and images, is certainly a gift. No one can learn talent. One reads him as he must write, in thrall, in pursuit of something elusive and wholly absorbing. . . . A fine writer requires intellect and imagination, but of the two I place imagination higher. So, I think, does George Garrett, because he has pondered fancy quite as much as he has honoured and used it."

Death of the Fox, a historical novel about the life and death of Sir Walter Ralegh, received much praise from the critics. David R. Slavitt thought it "splendid, a magnificent book, and very probably one of the dozen best novels to have been written in my lifetime. Indeed, it is so extraordinary a work that it raises certain questions about the history and the future of the novel itself, about the relation of the novelist to his public, and about the ultimate mysteries of Fame and Fortune which lie not only at the heart of this novel but at the heart of the experience of all of us." John Carr writes that it is Garrett's "finest novel, the work in which his eschatological mode of thought, his mastery of his craft, and the results of his meditations upon history (and historians) find their highest expression." Carr echoes Slavitt's thoughts about the originality of the style of *Death of the Fox.* He writes: "Furthermore, it is a new *kind* of novel. And the vehicle for all of this is a style that will make mere novelists weep with envy. . . . It is a novel *from* History as well as *of* it. In other words, a dialogue between a poet of the twentieth century and a poet of the seventeenth century. . . . Ralegh stands within History and seeks to both live within it and rise out of it, and Garrett has caught this delicate balance in the man's character perfectly—in the way that the novel of the future must do it."

BIOGRAPHICAL/CRITICAL SOURCES: Seven Princeton Poets, Princeton University Library, 1963; *Mill Mountain Review,* Volume I, number 4, 1971; *Hollins Critic,* August, 1971; *Life,* September 24, 1971; *Time,* November 1, 1971; *Southern Review,* Volume VII, number 1, winter, 1971; *Books and Bookmen,* October, 1972; *Writer's Digest,* November, 1972; *Contemporary Literary Criticism,* Gale, Volume III, 1975, Volume XI, 1979.

GASH, Norman 1912-

PERSONAL: Born January 16, 1912, in Meerut, India; son of Frederick and Kate (Hunt) Gash; married Dorothy Whitehorn, 1935; children: Harriet, Sarah. *Education:* St. John's College, Oxford, B.A., B.Litt., 1934, M.A., 1938. *Home:* Gowrie Cottage, 73 Hepburn Gardens, St. Andrews Fife, Scotland. *Office:* Department of History, St. Salvator's College, University of St. Andrews, St. Andrews, Scotland.

CAREER: University of London, University College, London, England, assistant lecturer in modern history, 1936-40; University of St. Andrews, St. Salvator's College, St. Andrews, Scotland, lecturer in modern British and American history, 1946-53; University of Leeds, Yorkshire, England, professor of modern history, 1953-55; University of St. Andrews, St. Salvator's College, professor of history, 1955—, vice-principal, 1967-71, dean of Faculty of Arts, 1978—. Hinkley Visiting Professor in English History, Johns Hopkins University, 1962; Ford's Lecturer in English History, Oxford University, 1963-64. *Military serivce:* British Army, Intelligence, 1940-46; became major. *Member:* Royal Historical Society (fellow; member of council, 1961-64), Historical Association of Scotland (member of council, 1956-64; president, St. Andrews branch, 1955—), British Academy (fellow), Royal Society of Literature (fellow), Royal Society of Edinburgh (fellow).

WRITINGS: Politics in the Age of Peel, Longmans, Green, 1953, 2nd edition, Humanities, 1977; (contributor) *Essays Presented to Sir Lewis Namier,* Macmillan, 1956; *Mr. Secretary Peel,* Longmans, Green, 1961; *Reaction and Reconstruction in English Politics, 1832-52,* Clarendon Press, 1966; (editor) *Age of Peel,* Longmans, Green, 1968; *Sir Robert Peel,* Longman, 1973; (contributor) *The Conservative Leadership,* Macmillan, 1974; (contributor) *The Prime Ministers,* Volume I, Allen & Unwin, 1974; *Peel,* Longman, 1976; (contributor) *The Conservatives,* Allen & Unwin, 1977. Contributor of articles to professional journals.

WORK IN PROGRESS: Aristocracy and People: Britain 1815-65 in "New History of England,"for Edward Arnold; a life of the second Earl of Liverpool, for Weidenfeld & Nicolson.

* * *

GASTON, Jerry (Collins) 1940-

PERSONAL: Born October 16, 1940, in Trinidad, Tex.; son of James Elmore (a plant operator) and Alice (Airheart) Gaston; married Mary Frank Ballow (an antiques shop owner), September 16, 1961; children: Jeremy Jason. *Education:* Henderson County Junior College, A.A., 1960; East Texas State University, B.A., 1962, M.A., 1963; Yale University, M.Ph., 1967, Ph.D., 1969. *Home:* 411 North Ninth, Murphysboro, Ill. 62966. *Office:* Department of Sociology, Southern Illinois University, Carbondale, Ill. 62901.

CAREER: Southern Illinois University, Carbondale, assistant professor, 1969-72, associate professor, 1972-78, professor of sociology, 1978—. *Member:* International Sociological Association, American Sociological Association, American Association for the Advancement of Science, Midwest Sociological Society.

WRITINGS: Originality and Competition in Science, University of Chicago Press, 1973; (editor with Robert K. Merton) *The Sociology of Science in Europe,* Southern Illinois University Press, 1977; *The Reward System in British and American Science,* Wiley, 1978; (editor) *The Sociology of Science: Problems, Approaches, and Research,* Jossey-

Bass, 1979. Contributor to *American Sociological Review, Minerva, Irish Journal of Education, New Scientist, American Sociologist,* and *La Recherche.* Editor, *Sociological Quarterly,* 1978-81.

WORK IN PROGRESS: Research on the sociology of science, and on the sociology of paranormal beliefs.

BIOGRAPHICAL/CRITICAL SOURCES: Science, November 26, 1971.

* * *

GATES, Doris 1901-

PERSONAL: Born November 26, 1901, in Mountain View, Calif.; daughter of Charles Obed and Bessie Louise (Jones) Gates. *Education:* Attended Fresno State Teachers College (now California State University, Fresno), 1924-26, Los Angeles Library School, 1926-27, Western Reserve University (now Case Western Reserve University), 1929-30. *Home and office:* 159 Spindrift Rd., Carmel, Calif. 93923.

CAREER: Fresno County Free Library, Fresno, Calif., director, 1930-40; San Jose State College (now University), San Jose, Calif., instructor, 1940-43; visiting lecturer, University of California, Berkeley, 1943-45, University of Southern California, Los Angeles, 1947, and University of San Francisco, San Francisco, Calif., 1956-60. Advisory editor on book-length stories series, Ginn & Co., Boston, Mass. *Awards, honors:* William Allen White Award for *Little Vic.*

WRITINGS—All published by Viking: *Sarah's Idea,* 1938; *Blue Willow,* 1940; *Sensible Kate,* 1942; *Trouble for Jerry,* 1943; *North Fork,* 1945; *My Brother Mike,* 1948; *River Ranch,* 1949; *Little Vic,* 1951; *The Cat and Mrs. Cary,* 1962; *The Elderberry Bush,* 1967; *Lord of the Sky: Zues,* 1972; *The Warrior Goddess: Athena,* 1972; *The Golden God,* 1973; *Two Queens of Heaven,* 1974; *Mightiest of Mortals: Heracles,* 1975; *A Fair Wind for Troy,* 1976; *A Morgan for Melinda,* 1980.

All published by Ginn: *Becky and the Bandit,* 1952; (with David Russell and Constance McCullough) *Roads to Everywhere,* 1961; (with Russell and McCullough) *Trails to Treasure,* 1961; (with Russell and Mabel Snedaker) *Wings to Adventure,* 1961; (with Russell, and others) *Down Story Roads,* 1962; (with Russell, and others) *Along Story Trails,* 1962; (with Russell, and others) *On Story Wings,* 1962.

SIDELIGHTS: Doris Gates told *CA:* "That I was a trained children's librarian had much to do with my wanting to write for young people. And my wide experience as a storyteller groomed me in the craft. I decided early that what I might have wanted to say to adults had already been better said than I could say it, but I thought I had something special to say to young people.

"I would advise young writers to read widely and constantly and not just contemporary authors. Read the classics; know what has been done before."

Little Vic was adapted for television and broadcast by ABC in 1977.

AVOCATIONAL INTERESTS: Breeding Morgan horses.

* * *

GAULT, William Campbell 1910- (Will Duke, Roney Scott)

PERSONAL: Born March 9, 1910, in Milwaukee, Wis.; son of John H. and Ella (Hovde) Gault; married Virginia Kapreli-an, August 29, 1942; children: William Barry, Shelley Gault Amacher. *Education:* Attended University of Wisconsin, 1929. *Politics:* "Revolutionary Republican." *Religion:* "Faith in man." *Home and office:* 482 Vaquero Lane, Santa Barbara, Calif. 93111. *Agent:* Don Congdon, Harold Matson Co., Inc., 22 East 40th St., New York, N.Y. 10016.

CAREER: Free-lance writer. Has worked as waiter, busboy, shoe sole cutter, hotel manager, and mailman. Secretary, Channel Cities Funeral Society. *Military service:* U.S. Army, 1943-45. *Awards, honors:* Edgar Allan Poe Award from Mystery Writers of America, 1952, for *Don't Cry for Me;* award from Boys' Club of America, 1957, for *Speedway Challenge;* award from Southern California Council on Literature for Children and Young People, 1968.

WRITINGS—Mystery novels: *Don't Cry for Me,* Dutton, 1952; *The Bloody Bokhara,* Dutton, 1952; *The Canvas Coffin,* Dutton, 1953; *Blood on the Boards,* Dutton, 1953; *Run, Killer, Run,*, Dutton, 1954; *Ring around Rosa,* Dutton, 1955; *Day of the Ram,* Random House, 1956; *Square in the Middle,* Random House, 1956; *The Convertible Hearse,* Random House, 1957; *Night Lady,* Fawcett, 1958; (under pseudonym Will Duke) *Fair Prey,* Boardman, 1958; *Sweet Wild Wench,* Fawcett, 1959; *The Wayward Widow,* Fawcett, 1959; *Death out of Focus,* Random House, 1959; *Come Die with Me,* Random House, 1959; *Million Dollar Tramp,* Fawcett, 1960; *Vein of Violence,* Simon & Schuster, 1961; *The Hundred Dollar Girl,* Dutton, 1961; *County Kill,* Simon & Schuster, 1962; *Dead Hero,* Dutton, 1963; *The Bad Samaritan,* Harlequin, 1980.

Juveniles; all published by Dutton: *Thunder Road,* 1952; *Mr. Fullback,* 1953; *Gallant Colt,* 1954; *Mr. Quarterback,* 1955; *Speedway Challenge,* 1956; *Bruce Benedict, Halfback,* 1957; *Rough Road to Glory,* 1958; *Dim Thunder,* 1958; *Drag Strip,* 1959.

Dirt Track Summer, 1961; *Through the Line,* 1961; *Two Wheeled Thunder,* 1962; *Road Race Rookie,* 1962; *Wheels of Fortune: Four Racing Stories,* 1963; *Little Big Foot,* 1963; *The Checkered Flag,* 1964; *The Long Green,* 1965; *The Karters,* 1965; *Sunday's Dust,* 1966; *Backfield Challenge,* 1967; *The Lonely Mound,* 1967; *The Oval Playground,* 1968; *Stubborn Sam,* 1969.

Quarterback Gamble, 1970; *The Last Lap,* 1972; *Trouble at Second,* 1973; *Gasoline Cowboy,* 1974; *Wild Willie, Wide Receiver,* 1974; *The Underground Skipper,* 1975; *The Big Stick,* 1975; *Showboat in the Backcourt,* 1976; *Cut-Rate Quarterback,* 1977; *Thin Ice,* 1978.

Contributor of about three hundred short stories to magazines, including *Grit* and *Saturday Evening Post.*

WORK IN PROGRESS: The Cana Diversion, an adult mystery novel.

SIDELIGHTS: William Gault's mystery novels have been translated into fourteen languages.

* * *

GAUSTAD, Edwin Scott 1923-

PERSONAL: Born November 14, 1923, in Rowley, Iowa; son of Sverre and Norma (McEachron) Gaustad; married Virginia Morgan, December 19, 1946; children: Susan, Glen Scott, Peggy Lynn. *Education:* Baylor University, A.B., 1947; Brown University, A.M., 1948, Ph.D., 1951. *Home:* 650 West Sunset Dr., Redlands, Calif. *Office:* Department of History, University of California, Riverside, Calif.

CAREER: Brown University, Providence, R.I., instructor in religion, 1951-52; Shorter College, Rome, Ga., dean and professor of religion and philosophy, 1953-57; University of

Redlands, Redlands, Calif., associate professor of humanities, 1957-65; University of California, Riverside, associate professor, 1965-67, professor of history, 1967—. *Military service:* U.S. Army Air Forces, 1943-45; became first lieutenant; awarded Air Medal. *Member:* American Historical Association, American Society of Church History (president, 1978), Organization of American Historians, American Academy of Religion, Society for Values in Higher Education, Phi Beta Kappa. *Awards, honors:* American Council of Learned Societies scholar, 1952-53, grant, 1964-65.

WRITINGS: The Great Awakening in New England, Harper, 1957; (contributor) *Baptist Concepts of the Church,* Judson, 1959; *Historical Atlas of Religion in America,* Harper, 1962, revised edition, 1976; (contributor) *Recent Interpretations in American History,* Crowell, 1962; (contributor) *The Teacher's Yoke,* Baylor University Press, 1964; *A Religious History of America,* Harper, 1966, revised edition, 1974; *American Religious History,* Service Center for Teachers of History, 1967; *Dissent in American Religion,* University of Chicago Press, 1973; *Baptist Piety: The Last Will and Testimony of Obadiah Holmes,* Eerdmans, 1978; *George Berkeley in America,* Yale University Press, 1979.

Editor: *Religious Issues in American History,* Harper, 1968; (with R. A. Spivey and R. F. Allen) *Religious Issues in American Culture,* Addison-Wesley, 1972; (with Spivey and Allen) *Religious Issues in Western Civilization,* Addison-Wesley, 1973; *Rise of Adventism: Religion in Mid-Nineteenth Century America,* Harper, 1974; (with Spivey and Allen) *Religious Issues in World Cultures,* Addison-Wesley, 1976; H. W. Bowden, *Dictionary of American Religious Biography,* Greenwood Press, 1976; *Baptists: The Bible, Church Order and the Churches,* Arno, 1980. Contributor of reviews and articles to periodicals.

* * *

GAVIN, Catherine

PERSONAL: Born in Aberdeen, Scotland; daughter of James and Catherine (Irvine) Gavin; married John Ashcraft, 1948. *Education:* University of Aberdeen, M.A. (first class honors), 1928, Ph.D., 1931. *Home:* 1201 California St., San Francisco, Calif. 94109.

CAREER: University of Aberdeen, Aberdeen, Scotland, lecturer in history, 1932-34, 1941-43; University of Glasgow, Glasgow, Scotland, lecturer in history, 1934-36; Kemsley Newspapers, 1936-45, editorial writer in London, England, bureau chief in France, and leaderwriter and war correspondent; *London Daily Express,* London, foreign correspondent in Middle East and Ethiopia, 1945-47; *Time,* New York, N.Y., staff member, 1950-52. Active in Scottish politics in 1930's and was the Conservative candidate twice for Parliament. Public lecturer in United States, 1952-60.

WRITINGS: Louis Philippe, Methuen, 1933; *Clyde Valley* (novel), Arthur Barker, 1938; *The Hostile Shore* (novel), Methuen, 1940; *Britain and France,* J. Cape, 1941; *Edward the Seventh,* J. Cape, 1942; *The Black Milestone* (novel), Methuen, 1942; *The Mountain of Light* (novel), Methuen, 1944; *Liberated France,* J. Cape, 1954, St. Martin's, 1955; *Madeleine* (novel), St. Martin's, 1957.

The Cactus and the Crown (novel; Literary Guild selection), Doubleday, 1962; *The Fortress* (novel), Doubleday, 1964; *The Moon into Blood* (novel), Hodder & Stoughton, 1966; *The Devil in Harbour,* Morrow, 1968; *The House of War,* Morrow, 1970; *Give Me the Daggers,* Morrow, 1972; *Snow Mountain,* Hodder & Stoughton, 1973; *Traitors' Gate,* Hodder & Stoughton, 1976, St. Martin's, 1977; *None Dare Call It Treason,* St. Martin's, 1978; *How Sleep the Brave,* St. Martin's, 1980. Contributor to *Export Trade, New York Times Magazine, Holiday, Maclean's, Scottish Field,* and other magazines and newspapers.

SIDELIGHTS: Catherine Gavin speaks several foreign languages and travels extensively to do background research on her books. *Madeleine* and *The Cactus and the Crown* have both been translated into eight languages; *The Fortress* had simultaneous publication in the United States, London, Helsinki, and Stockholm.†

* * *

GELLMAN, Irwin F(rederick) 1942-

PERSONAL: Born September 3, 1942, in Philadelphia, Pa.; son of Albert A. and Mae (Rankin) Gellman; married Barbara Schwerin (an attorney), June 25, 1967; children: Susan Lynne, Scott Alexander, Charles Paul. *Education:* University of Maryland, B.A., 1964, M.A., 1966; Indiana University, Ph.D., 1970. *Office:* V.I.P. Properties, Inc., 260 Newport Center Dr., Suite 340, Newport Beach, Calif. 92660.

CAREER: Marion College, Marion, Ind., instructor in history, 1967; Morgan State College, Baltimore, Md., assistant professor, 1968-71, associate professor, 1971-75, professor of history, 1975-79, director of innovations in higher education, 1972-74, associate dean, 1974-75; currently affiliated with V.I.P. Properties, Inc., Newport Beach, Calif.

WRITINGS: Roosevelt and Battista: Good Neighbor Diplomacy in Cuba, 1933-1945, University of New Mexico Press, 1973; (contributor) Jules Davids, editor, *Perspectives in American Diplomacy,* Arno Press, 1976; *Good Neighbor Diplomacy: United States Policies in Latin America, 1933-1945,* Johns Hopkins University Press, 1979. Contributor to *Historian* and *American Jewish Historical Quarterly.*

* * *

GEORGAKAS, Dan 1938-

PERSONAL: Born March 1, 1938, in Detroit, Mich.; son of Xenophon and Sophia Georgakas. *Education:* Wayne State University, B.A., 1960; University of Michigan, M.A., 1961. *Politics:* Anarcho-communalist. *Religion:* Pantheist. *Address:* Box 1803-GPO, Brooklyn, N.Y. 11202. *Agent:* Rhoda Weyr, William Morris Agency, 1350 Sixth Ave., New York, N.Y. 10019.

CAREER: Teacher in public schools of Detroit, Mich., 1960-64 and in Overseas School of Rome, Italy, 1965; La Guardia Community College, Long Island City, N.Y., teacher, 1973—. *Awards, honors:* Fulbright research grant, Greece, 1963.

WRITINGS: Ombre Rosse (title means "Red Shadows"), Radio-Television Corp. of Italy, 1968; (editor) *Z Anthology of Poetry,* Smyrna Press, 1969; *And All Living Things Their Children* (poetry), Shameless Hussy Press, 1972; *Red Shadows* (history), Doubleday, 1973; *The Broken Hoop,* Doubleday, 1973; (with Marvin Surkin) *Detroit: I Do Mind Dying,* St. Martin's, 1975; (contributor) Alan Wells, editor, *Mass Media and Society,* Mayfield Press, 1975; (contributor) George Groman, editor, *The City Today,* Harper, 1978; (with Linda Blackaby, Barbara Margolis, and Affonso Beato) *In Focus,* Cine Information, 1980; *The Methuselah Factors,* Simon & Schuster, in press. Contributor of short stories and poetry to about 100 American and foreign publications. Member of editorial boards of *Cineaste,* 1968-80, and *Journal of the Hellenic Diaspora,* 1972-80.

WORK IN PROGRESS: Editing a book of interviews with

film personalities, tentatively entitled *Through Another Lens;* editing a book of interviews with surviving members of the I.W.W.

SIDELIGHTS: Dan Georgakas told *CA,* "I hope to use the decade of the eighties to take my crack at writing the great American novel."

* * *

GERBER, Sanford E(dwin) 1933-

PERSONAL: Born June 16, 1933, in Chicago, Ill.; son of Leon (an executive) and Rose (Ely) Gerber; married Leila B. Greenberg, June 28, 1953 (divorced, 1965); married Louise S. Borad, October 9, 1965; children: (first marriage) Howard M., Michael B.; (second marriage) Naomi R., Sharon S. *Education:* Lake Forest College, B.A., 1954; University of Illinois, M.S., 1956; University of Southern California, Ph.D., 1962. *Politics:* Democratic. *Religion:* Jewish. *Home:* 520 Barker Pass Rd., Santa Barbara, Calif. 93108. *Office:* Department of Speech, University of California, Santa Barbara, Calif. 93106.

CAREER: East Whittier city schools, Whittier, Calif., speech therapist, 1956-58; System Development Corp., Santa Monica, Calif., senior human factors specialist, 1958-60; Hughes Aircraft Co., Fullerton, Calif., head of speech and hearing research, 1960-65; University of California, Santa Barbara, assistant professor, 1965-69, associate professor, 1969-75, professor of audiology, 1975—, chairman of department of speech, 1979—. Consultant to U.S. Department of Defense and to Columbia Broadcasting System Technology Center.

MEMBER: International Society of Audiology, International Society of Phonetic Sciences, Acoustical Society of America, American Speech, Language, and Hearing Association, American Association of Phonetic Sciences, Society for Ear, Nose, and Throat Advances in Children, American Academy of Otolaryngology, Sigma Xi, Channel City Club.

WRITINGS: (Contributor) John A. R. Wilson, editor, *Diagnosis of Learning Difficulties,* McGraw, 1971; *Introductory Hearing Science,* Saunders, 1974; *Audiometry in Infancy,* Grune, 1977; *Early Diagnosis of Hearing Loss,* Grune, 1978; *Early Management of Hearing Loss,* Grune, 1980; *Auditory Dysfunction,* College Hill, 1980. Writer of speech and hearing research reports for System Development Corp. and Hughes Aircraft Co. Contributor of more than one hundred articles and reviews to journals, including *Journal of the Acoustical Society of America, Journal of Speech and Hearing Research,* and *Journal of American Auditory Society.*

* * *

GERBNER, George 1919-

PERSONAL: Born in August, 1919, in Budapest, Hungary; came to United States in 1939, naturalized in 1943; married Ilona Kutas (a lecturer), 1946; children: John C., Thomas J. *Education:* Studied at University of Budapest, 1938-39, and University of California, Los Angeles, 1940-41; University of California, Berkeley, B.A., 1942; University of Southern California, M.S., 1951, Ph.D., 1955. *Home:* 234 Golf View Rd., Ardmore, Pa. 19003. *Office:* Annenberg School of Communications, University of Pennsylvania, 3620 Walnut St., Philadelphia, Pa. 19104.

CAREER: *San Francisco Chronicle,* San Francisco, Calif., copy editor, reporter, feature writer, book reviewer, columnist, and assistant financial editor, 1942-43; U.S. Information Service, Vienna, Austria, editor, 1946-47; public relations representative and free-lance writer in Hollywood, Calif., 1947-48; John Muir College, Pasadena, Calif., instructor in journalism, English, and social science, 1948-51; El Camino College, Torrance, Calif., instructor in mass communications and reading development, 1952-56; University of Illinois at Urbana-Champaign, Institute of Communications Research, research assistant professor, 1956-59, research associate professor of mass communications, 1960-64; University of Pennsylvania, Annenberg School of Communications, Philadelphia, professor of mass communications and dean, 1964—. Lecturer at University of Southern California, 1954-56. *Military service:* U.S. Army, Parachute Infantry, editor of regimental newspaper and member of Office of Strategic Services, 1943-46; became first lieutenant; received Bronze Star award.

MEMBER: International Association for Mass Communication Research (member of board of directors, 1970), International Communication Association, American Sociological Association, American Association for Public Opinion Research, Association for Education in Journalism, American Academy of Political and Social Science. *Awards, honors:* Grant to study portrayal of mental illness in the mass media, 1959-61, grant to study institutional structure and decision-making on American television, 1971, and grants to measure trends in television content and effects, 1972, 1974, all from National Institute of Mental Health; U.S. Office of Education grant for cross-cultural study of mass communications and popular conceptions of education, 1960-64; grant for comparative study of films and the "film hero," 1964-68, and grant to study portrayal of scientists on television, 1980, both from National Science Foundation; National Commission on the Causes and Prevention of Violence grant to study violence in network television drama, 1968-69; Surgeon General's Scientific Advisory Committee on Television and Social Behavior grant to study violence in network television drama, 1969-70; International Research and Exchanges Board grant to study treatment of foreign news abroad, 1971-72; American Medical Association grant to study television violence, 1977-79.

WRITINGS: *Instructional Technology and the Press: A Case Study,* Technological Development Project, National Education Association, 1962; (editor with Ole R. Holsti, Klaus Krippendorff, William J. Paisley, and Philip J. Stone, and contributor) *The Analysis of Communication Content: Developments in Scientific Theories and Computer Techniques,* Wiley, 1969; (editor with Larry P. Gross and William H. Melody, and contributor) *Communication Technology and Social Policy,* Wiley, 1973; (editor) *Mass Media Policies in Changing Cultures,* Wiley, 1977; (editor with Katherine J. Ross and Edward Zigler, and contributor) *Child Abuse Reconsidered: An Analysis and Agenda for Action,* Oxford University Press, in press.

Contributor: John Ball and Francis Byrnes, editors, *Research, Principles, and Practices in Visual Communication,* National Project in Agricultural Communications, Michigan State University, 1960; Franklin Patterson and others, editors, *The Adolescent Citizen,* Free Press of Glencoe, 1960; Wilbur Schramm, editor, *Studies of Innovation and of Communication to the Public,* Institute for Communication Research, Stanford University, 1962; Louise M. Berman, editor, *The Nature of Teaching,* School of Education, University of Wisconsin—Milwaukee, 1963; L. A. Dexter and D. M. White, editors, *People, Society and Mass Communications,* Free Press of Glencoe, 1964; W. C. Meierhenry, editor, *Media and Educational Innovation,* University of Nebraska Press, 1964; Robert O. Hall, editor, *The Content and Pattern for the Professional Training of Audiovisual Communication Specialists,* Educational Media Branch, U.S. Office of Education, 1964.

Lee Thayer, editor, *Communication: Theory and Research,* C. C Thomas, 1966; Donald Ely, editor, *Technology and Education,* School of Education, Syracuse University, 1966; Frank E. X. Dance, editor, *Human Communication Theory: Original Essays,* Holt, 1967; Ronald T. Hyman, editor, *Teaching: Vantage Points for Study,* Lippincott, 1968; Paul Halmos, editor, *The Sociology of Mass-Media Communications* (monograph), University of Keele, 1969; Robert K. Baker and Sandra J. Ball, editors, *Violence and the Media,* U.S. Government Printing Office, 1969.

Giovanni Bechelloni, editor, *Politica Culturale? Studi, Materiali, Ipotesi,* Guaraldi Editore, 1970; *Communication: A "Scientific American" Book,* W. H. Freeman, 1972; Denis McQuail, editor, *Sociology of Mass Communications,* Penguin, 1972; G. A. Comstock and E. A. Rubinstein, editors, *Television and Social Behavior,* Volume I: *Content and Control,* U.S. Government Printing Office, 1972; David R. Olson, editor, *Media and Symbols: The Forms of Expression, Communication, and Education,* University of Chicago Press, 1974.

David Manning White and John Pendleton, editor, *Mirror of American Life,* Publishers, Inc. (Del Mar, Calif.), 1977; Judy Fireman, editor, *TV Book: The Ultimate Television Book,* Workman Publishing, 1977; *Popular Culture,* Publishers, Inc., 1977; Gaye Tuchman, Arlene Kaplan Daniels, and James Benet, editors, *Hearth and Home: Images of Women in the Mass Media,* Oxford University Press, 1978; Charles Winick, editor, *Deviance and Mass Media,* Sage Publications, 1978; W. Adams and F. Schreibman, editors, *Television News Archives: A Guide to Research,* George Washington University, 1978; Robert Atwin, Barry Orton, and William Vesterman, editors, *American Mass Media: Industry and Issues,* Random House, 1978; Horace Newcomb, editor, *Television: The Critical View,* Oxford University Press, 2nd edition, 1979; Edward L. Palmer and Aimee Dorr, editors, *Three Faces of Children's Television,* Academic Press, in press. Also contributor to *Writing the Research Paper,* edited by M. Cummins and C. Slade.

Contributor to technical reports, annals, yearbooks, and symposia, and to *Encyclopedia Americana.* Contributor to popular and academic journals, including *Scientific American, Saturday Review, American Scholar, Psychology Today, Journal of Communications, et cetera,* and *Human Behavior.* Book review editor, *Audio Visual Communication Review,* 1958-68; *Journal of Communication,* associate editor, 1966-68, editor, 1974—.

*　　*　　*

GERSCHENKRON, Alexander (Pavlovich) 1904-1978

PERSONAL: Born October 1, 1904, in Russia; emigrated to U.S. in 1938; naturalized, 1945; died October 26, 1978; son of Paul and Sophie (Kardow) Gerschenkron; married Erica Matschnigg, 1928; children: Helga-Susanna, Maria-Renate Gerschenkron Dawidoff. *Education:* University of Vienna, Doctor Rerum Politicarum, 1928. *Home:* 17 Robinson St., Cambridge, Mass. 02138.

CAREER: Research associate, Austrian Institute for Business Cycle Research, 1937-38; University of California (now University of California, Berkeley), research associate, 1938-42, lecturer in economics, 1942-44; Board of Governors of Federal Reserve System, staff member, 1944-48, chief of foreign areas section, 1946-48; Harvard University, Cambridge, Mass., associate professor, 1948-51, professor, 1951-55, Walter S. Barker Professor of Economics, 1955-75, director of economics projects at Russian Research Center, 1949-56, director of economic history workshop, beginning 1959, Frank W. Taussig research professor of economics, 1961-62. Ford research professor at University of California, Berkeley, 1958; visiting fellow at St. Catherine's College, Oxford University, 1962, and Princeton Institute for Advanced Study, 1968-69, 1971-72. *Member:* American Historical Association, American Economic Association (distinguished fellow), Economic History Association (president, 1966-68), American Philosophical Association, British Academy (corresponding fellow), Royal Swedish Academy, Phi Beta Kappa. *Awards, honors:* Guggenheim fellow, Oxford University, 1954-55; D.Litt., Oxford University, 1974; T.Dhc., University of Uppsala, 1978; Golden Doctorate, University of Vienna, 1978.

WRITINGS: Bread and Democracy in Germany, University of California Press, 1943, reprinted, Fertig, 1966; *Economic Relations with the U.S.S.R.,* [New York], 1945; (with Alexander Erlich) *A Dollar Index of Soviet Machinery Output, 1927-28 to 1937,* RAND Corp., 1951; (with Nancy Nimitz) *A Dollar Index of Soviet Petroleum Output, 1927-28 to 1937,* RAND Corp., 1952; (with Nimitz) *A Dollar Index of Soviet Iron and Steel Output, 1927/28-1937,* RAND Corp., 1953; *Soviet Heavy Industry: A Dollar Index of Output, 1927/28-1937,* RAND Corp., 1954; (with E. Marbury) *A Dollar Index of Soviet Electric Power Output,* RAND Corp., 1954; *Economic Backwardness in Historical Perspective: A Book of Essays,* Harvard University Press, 1962; *Continuity in History and Other Essays,* Harvard University Press, 1968; *Europe in the Russian Mirror: Four Lectures in Economic History,* Cambridge University Press, 1970; *Mercator Gloriosus,* Nederlandsche Boekhandel, 1973; *An Economic Spurt That Failed,* Princeton University Press, 1977. Contributor to scholarly journals.

BIOGRAPHICAL/CRITICAL SOURCES: Henry Rosovsky, editor, *Industrialization in Two Systems: Essays in Honor of Alexander Gerschenkron by a Group of His Students,* Wiley, 1966.†

*　　*　　*

GERSH, Harry 1912-

PERSONAL: Born December 1, 1912, in New York, N.Y.; son of Solomon and Dora (Lampert) Gersh; married Violet Eberil, October 21, 1939; children: John Raphael, Ruth Deborah. *Education:* Attended Drexel Institute of Technology (now Drexel University), 1931-34, New York University, 1936-37, University of Paris, 1938, and Harvard University, 1980. *Politics:* Democrat. *Religion:* Jewish. *Residence:* Menemsha, Mass. 02552.

CAREER: American Newspaper Guild, New York City, information director, 1952-53; Jewish Family Service, New York City, information director, 1953-57; information director, New York State Department of Labor, 1957-59; Martin E. Segal Co. (actuaries and consultants), New York City, information director, 1959-76. Former newspaperman for Philadelphia and New York dailies. *Military service:* U.S. Navy, chief radio technician, 1943-46. *Member:* Overseas Press Club, American Newspaper Guild.

WRITINGS: These Are My People, Behrman, 1959; *Minority Report,* Collier, 1961; *Women Who Made America Great,* Lippincott, 1962; *The Story of the Jew,* Behrman, 1964; *Sacred Books of the Jews,* Stein & Day, 1968; *When a Jew Cel-*

ebrates, Behrman, 1971. Contributor to magazines; radio script writer.

* * *

GEWEHR, Wolf M(ax) 1939-

PERSONAL: Born February 12, 1939, in Freiburg, Germany; son of Rudolf (a chemical engineer) and Ilse (Knecht) Gewehr; married Sieglinde Wegner (a teacher), August 15, 1969; children: Beate, Silvia. *Education:* Attended Freiburg University, 1961-63, and Colorado College, 1963-64; University of Colorado, M.A., 1965; University of Washington, Seattle, Ph.D., 1968. *Home:* Bogenstrasse 12, 4542 Tecklenburg, Germany. *Office:* Paedagogische Hochschule, Muenster, Germany.

CAREER: University of Utah, Salt Lake City, assistant professor of German, 1968-70; Paedagogische Hochschule, Muenster, Germany, professor of German and linguistics, 1970—.

WRITINGS: (With Wolff A. von Schmidt) *Reading German in the Natural Sciences*, Van Nostrand, 1972; (with von Schmidt) *Reading German in the Social Sciences*, Van Nostrand, 1972; (with von Schmidt) *Reading German in the Humanities*, Van Nostrand, 1972; (with von Schmidt) *German Review and Readings*, Holt, 1973; *Lexematische Strukturen*, Ehrenwirth, 1974; (contributor) D. Krywalski, editor, *Hand lexikon zur Literaturwissenschaft*, Ehrenwirth, 1974, 2nd edition, 1976; (with Helbling and von Schmidt) *First-Year German*, Holt, 1975, 2nd edition, 1979; *Hartmanns "Klage-Buechlein" im Lichte der Fruehscholastik*, Kuemmerle, 1975; (contributor) W. Pielow, editor, *Theorie und Praxis im Deutschunterricht*, Koesel, 1975; (with von Schmidt) *Grundprobleme der Poetick*, Ehrenwirth, 1976; (with von Schmidt) *Grundprobleme der Literaturtheorie im Zwanstiges Jahrhundert*, Ehrenwirth, 1977; (editor) *Sprachdidaktik*, Schwann, 1979; (with K.-P. Klein) *Grundprobleme der Linguistik*, Wilhelm Schneider, 1979. Contributor to *Zeitschrift fuer deutsche Philologie, Deutsche Vierteljahrsschrift, Muttersprache, Zeitschrift fuer Religions-und Geistesgeschichte*, and other publications.

* * *

GIBSON, (William) Walker 1919-

PERSONAL: Born January 19, 1919, in Jacksonville, Fla.; son of William Walker and Helen (Jones) Gibson; married Nancy Close, 1942; children: David, Susan, William W. III, John S. *Education:* Yale U., A.B., 1940; Harvard University, further study, 1940-41; University of Iowa, M.A., 1946. *Home:* Market Hill Rd., R.F.D., Amherst, Mass. 01002. *Office:* Department of English, University of Massachusetts, Amherst, Mass. 01003.

CAREER: Amherst College, Amherst, Mass., 1946-57, began as instructor, became associate professor; New York University, New York, N.Y., professor of English, 1957-67, director of freshman English, Washington Square College; University of Massachusetts—Amherst, professor of English, 1967—. Television teacher of course on modern literature, "Sunrise Semester," 1962-63, and "Studies in Style," CBS-TV, 1966-67. *Military service:* U.S. Army Air Forces, 1941-45; became first lieutenant. *Member:* Modern Language Association of America, National Council of Teachers of English (president, 1972-73), College English Association, Conference on College Composition and Communication. *Awards, honors:* Fund for Advancement of Education fellow, 1955-56; Guggenheim fellow, 1963-64, National Endowment for the Humanities grant, 1973-77.

WRITINGS: *The Reckless Spenders*, Indiana University Press, 1954; *Come As You Are*, Hastings House, 1958; *Seeing and Writing*, Longmans, Green, 1959, 2nd edition, 1974; (with J. M. Kierzek) *Macmillan Handbook of English*, Macmillan, 4th edition (Gibson was not associated with earlier editions), 1960, 5th edition, 1965; *The Limits of Language*, Hill & Wang, 1962; *Poems in the Making*, Houghton, 1963; *Tough, Sweet, and Stuffy: An Essay on Modern American Prose Style*, Indiana University Press, 1966; *Persona*, Random House, 1969; (editor) *New Students in Two Year Colleges*, National Council of Teachers of English, 1979. Contributor of poetry to periodicals.

WORK IN PROGRESS: An interdisciplinary book on creativity.

BIOGRAPHICAL/CRITICAL SOURCES: *New York Times Book Review*, January 9, 1955; *Saturday Review*, June 18, 1955.

* * *

GILBERT, Marilyn B(ender) 1926-
(Marilyn B. Ferster)

PERSONAL: Born January 26, 1926, in Newark, N.J.; daughter of Charles Henry and Rose (Schotland) Bender; married Charles B. Ferster, 1947 (divorced, 1964); married Thomas F. Gilbert, 1967; children: (first marriage) William Andrew, Andrea Carol, Samuel Kenneth, Warren Anthony; (second marriage) Robby Grodale, Eve Darling. *Education:* Montclair State Teachers College (now Montclair State College), B.A., 1946; Columbia University, M.A., 1951; Boston University, graduate study, 1951-53. *Home:* 5680 Winthrop Ave., Indianapolis, Ind.

CAREER: Jackson & Moorland Engineers, Boston, Mass., engineer writer, 1952-54; Arthur D. Little, Inc., Cambridge, Mass., technical editor, 1954-55; TOR Education, Inc., New York, N.Y., program writer, 1960-61; Indiana University, Indianapolis, lecturer, Downtown Center, beginning 1960. *Member:* Society of Technical Editors and Publishers, American Civil Liberties Union.

WRITINGS: (Under name Marilyn B. Ferster) *Arithmetic for Nurses*, Springer Publishing, 1961, 2nd edition, 1973; (under name Marilyn B. Ferster) *Programmed College Composition*, Prentice-Hall, 1962; *Clear Writing*, Wiley, 1972; *Communicating by Letter*, Wiley, 1973; (with husband, Thomas F. Gilbert) *Thinking Metric*, Wiley, 1973, 2nd edition, 1978. Assistant editor, *Journal of the Experimental Analysis of Behavior*, 1958-63.

WORK IN PROGRESS: *A Practical Guide to Performance Engineering*, with husband, Thomas F. Gilbert.

AVOCATIONAL INTERESTS: Piano.

* * *

GILBERT, Michael Francis 1912-

PERSONAL: Born July 17, 1912, in Billinghay, Lincolnshire, England; son of Bernard Samuel (a writer) and Berwyn Minna (Cuthbert) Gilbert; married Roberta Mary Marsden, July 28, 1947; children: Harriett Sarah, Victoria Mary, Olivia Margaret, Kate Alexandra, Richard Adam St. John, Laura Frances, Gerard Valentine Hugo. *Education:* University of London, LL.B., 1937. *Home:* Luddesdown Old Rectory, Cobham, Kent, England. *Agent:* Curtis Brown Ltd., 1 Craven Hill, London W2 3EW, England. *Office:* Trower, Still & Keeling, 5 New Square, Lincolns Inn, London, England.

CAREER: Ellis, Bickersteth, Aglionby & Hazel, London, England, articled clerk, 1938-39; Trower, Still & Keeling, London, solicitor, 1947-51, partner, 1952—. *Military service:* British Army, Royal Horse Artillery, 1939-45; served in North Africa and Italy; became major; mentioned in dispatches. *Member:* Law Society, Authors Guild, Society of Authors, Crime Writers Association (founder), Mystery Writers of America, British Film Association, Garrick Club.

WRITINGS: Close Quarters, Hodder & Stoughton, 1947, Walker, 1963; *He Didn't Mind Danger,* Harper, 1948 (published in England as *They Never Looked Inside,* Hodder & Stoughton, 1948); *The Doors Open,* Hodder & Stoughton, 1949, Walker, 1962; *Smallbone Deceased,* Harper, 1950, reprinted, Garland Publishing, 1976; *Death Has Deep Roots,* Hodder & Stoughton, 1951, reprinted, 1975, Harper, 1952; *The Danger Within,* Harper, 1952, reprinted, 1978 (published in England as *Death in Captivity,* Hodder & Stoughton, 1952); *Fear to Tread,* Harper, 1953, reprinted, 1978; *The Country-House Burglar,* Harper, 1955 (published in England as *Sky High,* Hodder & Stoughton, 1955); *Be Shot for Sixpence,* Harper, 1956; *The Claimant,* Constable, 1957; *Blood and Judgement,* Hodder & Stoughton, 1959, Harper, 1978; (editor) *Crime in Good Company* (essays), Constable, 1959; (editor, and author of introduction) A.A.G. Clark, *Best Detective Stories of Cyril Hare,* Faber, 1959.

A Clean Kill (play), Constable, 1960; *The Bargain* (play), Constable, 1961; *After the Fine Weather,* Harper, 1963; *Windfall* (play), Constable, 1963; *The Shot in Question* (play), Constable, 1963; *The Crack in the Teacup,* Harper, 1966; *The Dust and the Heat,* Hodder & Stoughton, 1967; *Overdrive,* Harper, 1968; *The Family Tomb,* Harper, 1969 (published in England as *The Etruscan Net,* Hodder & Stoughton, 1969).

Stay of Execution, Hodder & Stoughton, 1971; *The Body of a Girl,* Harper, 1972; *The Ninety-second Tiger,* Harper, 1973; *Sir Horace Rumbold,* Heinemann, 1973; *Flash Point,* Harper, 1974; *The Night of the Twelfth,* Harper, 1976; *The Law,* David & Charles, 1977; *Petrella at Q,* Harper, 1977; *The Empty House,* Harper, 1979; *The Killing of Katie Steelstock,* Harper, 1980. Also author of short stories.

WORK IN PROGRESS: Novels; short stories; television and radio scripts; plays.

AVOCATIONAL INTERESTS: Cricket, contract bridge.

* * *

GIST, Noel P(itts) 1899-

PERSONAL: Born June 17, 1899, in Hermitage, Mo.; son of Ruzan and Josephine (Pitts) Gist; married Mabel Wilks, 1923; children: Ronald Ralph, Patricia Jane. *Education:* Kansas State Teachers College (now Emporia State University), B.S., 1923; University of Kansas, A.M., 1929; University of Chicago, further study, 1929; Northwestern University, Ph.D., 1935. *Home:* 16 Springer Dr., Columbia, Mo. *Office:* Department of Sociology, University of Missouri, Columbia, Mo.

CAREER: University of Kansas, Lawrence, 1929-37, began as instructor, became assistant professor of sociology; University of Missouri—Columbia, 1937—, began as associate professor, became professor of sociology, professor emeritus, 1969—. Visiting lecturer, University of Wisconsin—Madison, 1944-45; research scholar in sociology for U.S. Educational Foundation, University of Mysore (India), 1951-52; lecturer in sociology, Sociologische Instituut (Netherlands), 1958-59; Fulbright lecturer, University of Calcutta (India), 1963-64; visiting summer professor at Washington University (St. Louis), Michigan State University, Northwestern University, and University of Hawaii. Senior specialist, East-West Center (Honolulu), 1968-69. *Military service:* U.S. Naval Reserve, 1918-19. *Member:* American Sociological Association (member of executive committee, 1945-48), American Association of University Professors, Midwest Sociological Society (president, 1938-39). *Awards, honors:* Distinguished Service Award, Emporia State University, 1973; Thomas Jefferson Award, University of Missouri, 1976.

WRITINGS: (With Sylvia F. Fava) *Urban Society,* Crowell, 1933, 6th edition, 1974; *Secret Societies,* University of Missouri Press, 1940; (with Pihlblad and Gregory) *Selective Factors in Migration and Occupation,* University of Missouri Press, 1943; (with A. G. Dworkin) *The Blending of the Races: Marginality and Identity in World Perspective,* Wiley, 1972; (with R. D. Wright) *Marginality and Identity: The Anglo-Indian Minority in India,* E. J. Brill (Leiden), 1973. Contributor to professional journals.

WORK IN PROGRESS: Research on Anglo-Indian minority group in India.

AVOCATIONAL INTERESTS: Travel.

* * *

GOCEK, Matilda A(rkenbout) 1923-

PERSONAL: Born February 18, 1923, in Hoboken, N.J.; daughter of Jacob Richard and Matilda (Meyer) Arkenbout; married H. F. Decker, May 15, 1939 (divorced, November, 1955); married John A. Gocek (an engineer), November 18, 1956; children: (first marriage) Ruth Ann (Mrs. Donald Case), Dianne Karen (Mrs. Ralph McKinstrie); (second marriage) John Jacob. *Education:* Orange County Community College, A.A., 1961; State University of New York at New Paltz, B.A. (with distinction), 1964; State University of New York at Albany, M.L.S., 1967. *Politics:* "Republican, but splits ticket." *Religion:* Presbyterian. *Home:* Dunderberg Rd., Monroe, N.Y. 10950. *Office:* Suffern Free Library, Suffern, N.Y. 10901.

CAREER: Monroe Free Library, Monroe, N.Y., librarian, 1958-61; Tuxedo Park Library, Tuxedo Park, N.Y., library director, 1963-76; Suffern Free Library, Suffern, N.Y., director, 1977—. Consultant, Tuxedo Union Free School, 1967-69; president of Orange-Sullivan Public Library Association, 1967-70; trustee, Tuxedo Park Day School, 1971—; secretary, Ramapo Catskill Library System Directors Association, 1973—. Member of South Eastern New York Library Resources Council, 1968-75, and Orange County Museums and Galleries Bicentennial Committee, 1972-76. President, Museum Village, 1979—. Official town historian in Tuxedo, 1973-76. *Member:* National Historical Society, American Library Association, Arnold Expedition Historical Society, New York Library Association, Association of Towns of New York State, Neversink Valley Area Museum (member of education committee), Library Association of Rockland County (member of indexing committee), Orange County Historical Society. *Awards, honors:* Idiom Poetry award, 1963; honorary doctorate, Colorado State Christian College, 1973.

WRITINGS: Tuxedo Park Library: Social Aspects of Growth, 1901-1940, Library Research Associates, 1968; *Library Service for Commuting Students: Study of Four South Eastern New York Counties,* South Eastern New York Library Resources Council, 1970; (author of introduction) Thomas Benton Brooks, *The Augusta Tract,* Library Research Association, 1972; *Benedict Arnold: Readers' Guide and Bibliography,* Library Research Associates, 1973; *Orange County, New York: Readers' Guide and Bibliography,* Library Research Associates, 1973; *Tuxedo's Green and Gold History,* Middletown Times Herald Record, 1976; *Love Is a Challenge: A Philosophy,* Library Research Associates, 1978. Contributor to *Unabashed Librarian.* Editor, *Dialogue,* 1969-76.

SIDELIGHTS: Matilda Gocek told *CA:* "I am what is known as a 'late bloomer.' As a child raised in the depression years, I learned early to live thriftily and to do the best with what I had, taught by a mother who appreciated the finer things in life. My love of the arts came from one grandfather who was a painter, and the other who sang in the Metropolitan Opera chorus. . . . The love of people, books and history has brought me to a career that I accept as a public service. Perhaps to inspire some other youngster to achieve a satisfaction he thinks is unattainable, perhaps to stimulate thought in an adult who thinks life has passed her by, perhaps to open a door to life anew—these are my goals, for the world is made of people and we have only each other."

* * *

GOCKEL, Herman W. 1906-

PERSONAL: Born October 11, 1906, in Cleveland, Ohio; son of Herman G. and Elise (Abe) Gockel; married Mildred C. Galen, October 10, 1931; children: Galen L., Greta Ann (Mrs. James T. Heinemeier). *Education:* Attended Concordia College, Fort Wayne, Ind., 1920-26; Concordia Seminary, B.D., 1931. *Home:* 5420 Jamieson, St. Louis, Mo. 63109.

CAREER: Ordained Lutheran minister, 1931; parish pastor in Anna, Ill., 1931-37, and Evansville, Ind., 1937-39; Lutheran Laymen's League, St. Louis, Mo., assistant executive secretary, 1940-42; Concordia Publishing House, St. Louis, advertising manager, 1941-45; editor, *Today* (professional journal for Lutheran clergy), 1945-51; "This Is the Life" (syndicated television program), St. Louis, program director and script editor, 1951-71; free-lance writer. Member of promotion department, "International Lutheran Hour" (radio program), 1939-42; co-founder, *St. Louis Lutheran,* 1945; assistant executive secretary, Board of Home Missions, Lutheran Church—Missouri Synod, 1946-51; director of four motion pictures for the Lutheran Church, 1947-55. *Awards, honors:* D.D., Concordia Seminary, 1956; L.H.D., Concordia College, 1971; inducted into National Religious Broadcasters Hall of Fame, 1979, for pioneering work in religious television drama.

WRITINGS—All published by Concordia: (With Theodore Hoyer) *The Devotional Bible,* 1947; *What Jesus Means to Me,* 1948; *The Cross and the Common Man,* 1955; *My Hand in His,* 1961; *Answer to Anxiety,* 1961; *My Father's World,* 1967; *Give Your Life a Lift,* 1968; *You Can Live above Your Circumstances,* 1973. Also author of numerous devotional booklets; author or editor of over 500 screenplays for "This Is the Life" television program; columnist for two Lutheran magazines. Author of over 200 syndicated newspaper articles. Member of editorial boards, *This Day,* 1949-60, and *American Lutheran.*

SIDELIGHTS: Herman W. Gockel told *CA:* "Having been a professional (clergy) writer for some forty years, I agree with the consensus of a group of writers who recently said, 'No one likes to write, but everyone likes to have written.' The price of good writing has always been, and will continue to be, very high. Few are willing to pay it. Besides the inevitable loneliness of marshalling thoughts in logical sequence there is the terrifying task of 'holding' them in sequence until one has found the proper and precise words to put them on the typewritten page.

"Speaking only for this writer, one of the greatest arts of the successful writer is the cultivation of empathy: a constant and ongoing identification of the writer with the reader. The writer dare never forget that he is the host and the reader is his guest. With this in mind he will do everything possible to make the reader comfortable in his presence. His is the task of creating and maintaining the proper rapport between himself and his reader so that the reader will enjoy his company as well as his 'conversation.'"

Gockel's works have been translated into a total of six foreign languages; some have been transcribed and recorded for the blind.

BIOGRAPHICAL/CRITICAL SOURCES: Saturday Evening Post, November 14, 1953; *Look,* December 14, 1954; *Concordia Historical Institute Quarterly,* spring, 1978.

* * *

GODWIN, John 1929-
(John Stark)

PERSONAL: Born November 23, 1929, in Melbourne, Australia; son of John and Gitta (May) Godwin. *Education:* Sydney University, graduate, 1949. *Home:* 1625 Leavenworth St., San Francisco, Calif. 94109. *Agent:* Don Congdon, Harold Matson Co., Inc., 22 East 40th St., New York, N.Y. 10016.

CAREER: Tempo Magazine, Sydney, Australia, reporter, 1950-51; *Daily Mirror,* Sydney, feature writer, 1951-53; *Daily Telegraph,* Sydney, feature writer and police reporter, 1953-55; free-lance writer in Europe, North Africa, Indonesia, Japan, the Middle East, Malaya, Australia, New Guinea, and Canada, 1955-60; *Everybody's Magazine,* Sydney, chief feature writer, 1961-62; free-lance writer in the United States, 1962—. *Member:* Authors Guild, Authors League of America, Magazine Writers Association (London; honorary secretary, 1960-61), Australian Journalists' Association, Media Alliance (San Francisco). *Awards, honors:* Mark Twain Society award, for *Alcatraz;* California District Attorneys Association Award, for *Murder, U.S.A.*

WRITINGS: Killers Unknown, Jenkins, 1960, Collier, 1962; *Killers in Paradise,* Jenkins, 1962, Hart Publishing, 1966; *Requiem for a Rat,* Jenkins, 1963; *Alcatraz,* Doubleday, 1963; *A Dollarwise Guide to Montreal and Quebec,* Frommer-Pasmantier, 1966; *This Baffling World,* Hart Publishing, 1967; *Happy Holland,* Frommer-Pasmantier, 1967.

Getaway Guide to San Francisco, Frommer-Pasmantier, 1970; *Getaway Guide to London,* Frommer-Pasmantier, 1971; *Getaway Guide to Paris,* Frommer-Pasmantier, 1971; *Occult America,* Doubleday, 1972; *The Mating Trade,* Doubleday, 1973; *Super Psychic,* Pocket Books, 1974; *Getaway Guide to Ireland,* Frommer-Pasmantier, 1974; *Getaway Guide to Phoenix,* Frommer-Pasmantier, 1975; *Unsolved: The World of the Unknown,* Doubleday, 1976; *Murder, U.S.A.: The Ways We Kill Each Other,* Ballantine, 1978; *Australia on $15 a Day,* Frommer-Pasmantier, 1978.

Contributor to periodicals, including *Saturday Evening Post, Cosmopolitan, Penthouse, Coronet,* and *Punch,* and to several dozen newspapers in the United States, Canada, England, Germany, France, Spain, Italy, and Japan.

WORK IN PROGRESS: A Guide to Canada, for Frommer-Pasmantier.

SIDELIGHTS: John Godwin told *CA:* "By and large I stick to the field I was trained for—investigative reporting in the broadest sense of the word. I include my travel paperbacks in this genre, since I nose into price ranges and accomodation quality like a bloodhound. No chamber of commerce handouts accepted. Four of my books dealt with occult matters. I found the theme somewhat frustrating—most of the phenomena involved depended on faith rather than facts. *This Baffling World* made the bestseller list, but that didn't lessen my frustration. With . . . *Murder, U.S.A.,* I'm back in familiar territory: investigating the whys and wherefores of people killing each other. Depressing, maybe, but also concrete enough not to evaporate when you shine a spotlight into a dark corner."

Some of Godwin's books have been translated into Spanish, French, German, Italian, and Japanese.

* * *

GOEDICKE, Hans 1926-

PERSONAL: Born August 7, 1926, in Vienna, Austria; son of Erich (an engineer) and Alice (von Schuller-Goetzburg) Goedicke; married Lucy McLaughlin, March 29, 1969. *Education:* University of Vienna, Ph.D., 1949. *Home:* 3959 Cloverhill Rd., Baltimore, Md. 21218. *Office:* Department of Near Eastern Studies, Johns Hopkins University, Baltimore, Md. 21218.

CAREER: Museum of Fine Arts, Vienna, Austria, assistant, 1949-51; Brown University, Providence, R.I., research associate, 1952-57; technical assistant in Egypt for UNESCO, 1957-58; University of Goettingen, Goettingen, Germany, assistant, 1958-60; Johns Hopkins University, Baltimore, Md., lecturer, 1960-62, assistant professor, 1962-66, associate professor, 1966-68, professor, 1968—, acting chairman, 1968-69, chairman of department of Near Eastern studies, 1970—. Governor of American Research Center in Egypt, 1970-77. Member of advisory board, Ecumenical Institute of Theology (Baltimore), 1971—. *Member:* German Archaeological Institute (corresponding member). *Awards, honors:* George and Eliza Gardner Howard Foundation fellowship, 1956-67; American Research Center in Egypt fellowship, 1964; Guggenheim fellowship, 1964; American Philosophical Society grant-in-aid, 1965.

WRITINGS: Die Stellung des Koenigs im Alten Reich, Harrassowitz, 1960; (with Edward F. Wente) *Ostraka Michaelides* (catalogue of Michaelides' collection), Harrassowitz, 1962; *Koenigliche Dokumente aus dem Alten Reich,* Harrassowitz, 1967; *The Report about the Dispute of a Man with His Ba,* Johns Hopkins Press, 1970; *Die Privaten Rechtsinschricten aus dem Alten Reich,* Verlag Notring, 1970; (editor) *Near Eastern Studies in Honor of William Foxwell Albright,* Johns Hopkins Press, 1971; (editor with Gertrud Thausing) *Nofretari: Eine Dokumentation der Wandgemaelde ihres Grabes* (title means "Queen Nefertiti: The Documentation of Her Tomb"), Druck & Verlagsanst, 1971; *Re-used Blocks from the Pyramid of Amenemhet I at Lisht,* Egyptian Expedition, Metropolitan Museum of Art (New York), 1971; *Die Gesichte des Schiffbruechigen,* Harrassowitz, 1974; (editor with J. M. Roberts) *Unity and Diversity: Essays in the History, Literature, and Religion of the Ancient Near East,* Johns Hopkins Press, 1975; *The Report of Wenamun,* Johns Hopkins Press, 1975; *The Protocol of Neferyt,* Johns Hopkins Press, 1977.

Review editor, *Journal of the American Research Center in Egypt,* 1968; editor-in-chief, *Records of the Ancient Near East* (Wiesbaden), 1970; editor, *Near Eastern Studies,* Johns Hopkins University, 1971.

WORK IN PROGRESS: Two books.

* * *

GOLAY, Frank H(indman) 1915-

PERSONAL: Born July 2, 1915, in Windsor, Mo.; son of Frank Leslie and Alice (Hindman) Golay; married Clara Wood, October 23, 1945; children: Frank, Jr., John Wood, David Clark, Jane White. *Education:* Central Missouri State Teachers College (now Central Missouri State University), B.S., 1936; University of Chicago, M.A., 1948, Ph.D., 1951. *Home:* 109 North Sunset Dr., Ithaca, N.Y. 14850. *Office:* Department of Economics, Cornell University, Ithaca, N.Y. 14850.

CAREER: Board of Governors of the Federal Reserve System, International Division, Washington, D.C., economist, 1950-52; Central Intelligence Agency, Washington, D.C., division chief, 1952-53; Cornell University, Ithaca, N.Y., assistant professor, 1953-58, associate professor, 1958-62, professor of economics and Asian studies, 1962—, chairman of department, 1963-70, Southeast Asia Program, associate director, 1961-70, director, 1970-76, Philippines Project, director, 1967-74, London-Cornell Project, director, 1968-70. Visiting professor at University of London, 1965-66, and University of Philippines, 1973-74. *Military service:* U.S. Naval Reserve, 1941-46; became lieutenant commander; received Silver and Bronze Stars. *Member:* National Academy of Sciences, Association for Asian Studies, American Economics Association. *Awards, honors:* Fulbright postdoctoral research grant, Philippines, 1955-56; Guggenheim Fellow, 1960-61; Social Science Research Council Fellow, 1960-61; LL.D., Ateneo de Manila University, 1966; National Endowment for the Humanities fellow, 1977-78.

WRITINGS: The Philippines: Public Policy and Economic Development, Cornell University Press, 1961; (editor) A.V.H. Hartendorp, *The Santo Tomas Story,* McGraw, 1964; (editor and contributor) *The United States and the Philippines,* Prentice-Hall, 1966; (with others) *Underdevelopment and Economic Nationalism in Southeast Asia,* Cornell University Press, 1969; (editor with Peggy Lush) *Director of the Cornell Southeast Asia Program, 1951-1976,* Southeast Asia Program, Cornell University, 1976; (with Marianne H. Hauswedell) *An Annotated Guide to Philippine Serials,* Southeast Asia Program, Cornell University, 1976.†

* * *

GOLDMAN, Alvin L. 1938-

PERSONAL: Born February 27, 1938, in New York, N.Y.; son of Joseph I. and Emma (Berger) Goldman; married Elisabeth C. Paris, November, 1956; children: Paula Kerry, Douglas Niles. *Education:* Columbia University, A.B., 1959; New York University, LL.B., 1962. *Politics:* Democratic. *Religion:* Jewish. *Home:* 2063 Bridgeport Dr., Lexington, Ky. 40502. *Office:* College of Law, University of Kentucky, Lexington, Ky. 40506.

CAREER: Admitted to the Bar of Kentucky and the Bar of New York State; Parker, Chapin & Flattau (law firm), New York, N.Y., attorney, 1962-65; University of Kentucky, Lexington, professor of labor and constitutional law, 1965—. Professor-in-residence, National Labor Relations Board, Washington, D.C., 1967-68; visiting professor, University of California, Davis, 1976-77. *Military service:* U.S. Army Reserve, 1956-66. *Member:* International Society for Labor Law and Social Legislation, Industrial Relations Research Association, Society of American Law Teachers, American Bar Association, Labor Law Group, Kentucky Bar Association.

WRITINGS: Processes for Conflict Resolution: Self-Help, Voting, Negotiation, and Arbitration, Bureau of National Affairs, 1972; *The Supreme Court and Labor-Management Relations Law,* Heath, 1976; *Labor Law and Industrial Relations in the U.S.A.,* Kluwer, 1979. Contributor to professional journals.

WORK IN PROGRESS: Employment Law: Cases and Materials.

* * *

GOLDMAN, James A. 1927-

PERSONAL: Born June 30, 1927, in Chicago, Ill.; son of Clarence (a businessman) and Marion (Weil) Goldman; married Marie McKeon, March 5, 1962 (divorced, 1972); married Barbara Deren (a producer), October 25, 1975; children: (first marriage) Julia, Matthew. *Education:* University of Chicago, Ph.B., 1947, M.A., 1950; Columbia University, graduate study, 1950-52. *Agent:* Sam Cohn, International Creative Management, 40 West 57th St., New York, N.Y. 10021.

CAREER: Playwright, screenwriter, novelist, and lyricist. *Military service:* U.S. Army, 1952-54. *Member:* Dramatists Guild (member of council, 1966—), Authors League of America (member of council, 1966—), Academy of Motion Picture Arts and Sciences, French Academy of Playwrights, National Academy of Recording Artists, P.E.N. *Awards, honors:* Academy Award (Oscar), 1968, American Screenwriters award, 1968, Writers Guild of Great Britain Zeta Plaque, 1969, and Writers Guild Award, 1969, all for screenplay, "The Lion in Winter"; Drama Critics Award for best musical, 1971, and Tony Award nomination, 1972, both for "Follies."

WRITINGS—Novels: *Waldorf,* Random House, 1965; *The Man from Greek and Roman,* Random House, 1973; *Myself as Witness,* Random House, 1980.

Plays: "They Might be Giants" (two-act), first produced in Stratford, England, at Theatre Royal, June 28, 1961; (with brother, William Goldman) *Blood, Sweat and Stanley Poole* (three-act; first produced on Broadway at Morosco Theatre, October 5, 1961), Dramatists Play Service, 1962; (author of lyrics and, with William Goldman, the book for musical) "A Family Affair" (two-act), music by John Kander, first produced on Broadway at Billy Rose Theatre, January 27, 1962; *The Lion in Winter* (two-act; first produced on Broadway at Ambassador Theatre, March 3, 1966), Random House, 1966; (author of book for musical) *Follies* (one-act; music and lyrics by Stephen Sondheim; first produced in Boston at Colonial Theatre, February 24, 1971; produced on Broadway at Winter Garden Theatre, April 4, 1971), Random House, 1971.

Screenplays: *The Lion in Winter,* Dell, 1968; *They Might Be Giants,* Lancer Books, 1970. Also author of screenplays "Nicholas and Alexandra," 1971, and "Robin and Marian," 1975. Author of a television musical, "Evening Primrose," 1967.

SIDELIGHTS: Judith Crist of *New York* calls James A. Goldman's award-winning film "The Lion in Winter" "as intellectually delicious as the stageplay and surpassing it in depth of characterization as well as in atmosphere and setting. . . . Once again we see Mr. Goldman's triumph in his twelfth-century talk, devoid of fake poetizing, sparked perpetually with idiom and wit. Add a charming John Barry score, and the excellence of 'The Lion in Winter' as a film concerned with characters in history—and not as a historical—is complete." Declaring it to be one of the ten best films of 1968, Crist concludes that Goldman's treatment of the story of Henry II of England and his queen, Eleanor of Aquitaine, successfully manages to convey "a universal and significant story of human relationships and the mark individuals make upon each other."

John Simon, writing in the *New Leader,* does not agree with Crist's assessment. He notes: "James Goldman's 'The Lion in Winter' was the kind of play to delight Walter Kerr: vaguely literate, somewhat historical yet saucily anachronistic, and as stuffed with suburbanly sub-urbane epigrams as a Victorian sofa with horsehair. Henry II of England, Eleanor of Aquitaine, and their three sons, using a French king and princess for pawns, wrangle over succession to the throne, power behind the throne, and disputed territories; this is presented as TV domestic comedy, dilutedly Freudian and Shavian, and concentratedly middle-class Jewish. The film version, from Goldman's own screenplay, sticks closely to the original and suffocatingly in our craw. The basic device, again, is the epigram, and a medieval royal family doggedly brandishing not broadswords but thin witticisms can be pretty funny—the wrong way."

Continues Simon: "If I make so much of the bad writing in 'The Lion in Winter,' it is because this kind of pseudoliterate hack work seems to be on the upswing. . . . [The inanities of this script] extend from such low-level nonsense as Henry's having his mutinous sons guarded by one solitary soldier when Eleanor and others of their faction are freely roaming the castle, to such advanced absurdities as having the cynical Henry overwhelmed by finding out about a homosexual liaison of an unfavorite son, or going to pieces over the discovery of his wife's long-past escapade with his late father. In terms of neither history nor plot nor character does this make sense—only a rather twisted twist of the plot."

Several critics, including Simon, detected similar weaknesses in Goldman's libretto for the highly successful stage play, "Follies." The story of a reunion of former Ziegfeld-type showgirls and performers in an old theater scheduled to be demolished, "'Follies' is a musical that must have sounded very good on paper," writes Simon in *New York.* "But on stage," he continues, "James Goldman's book whips up four interchangeable nonentities [the two main couples in the story]; turns them, by fascile diplography, into an octet; and proceeds to itemize their ins and outs and acrosses as if any of them were distinguishable from the other three or seven, and as if we would care a pin about which ends up with which. And all this in hackneyed language trying to act suave."

Walter Kerr of the *New York Times* observes that "'Follies' is intermissionless and exhausting, an extravaganza that becomes tedious for two simple reasons: Its extravagances have nothing to do with its pebble of a plot; and the plot, which could be wrapped up in approximately two songs, dawdles through twenty-two before it declares itself done. . . . James Goldman has done the libretto; everyone else is rather grimly attached to it. It is trivial and—for all the time it spends on its four fretting principals—unclear. . . . If they are not very interesting to follow, and difficult to feel for, it is because we never do—in two hours of searching—learn much that is private about them. . . . The body of the evening lies in these interlocked lives; the keys to the locks are lost in some other theater."

Clive Barnes, also commenting in the *New York Times,* feels that "Follies" "is the kind of musical that should have its original cast album out on 78's. It carries nostalgia to where sentiment finally engulfs it in its sickly maw. And yet—in part—it is stylish, innovative, it has some of the best lyrics I have ever encountered, and above all it is a serious attempt to deal with the musical form. . . . James Goldman's book is well enough written; indeed one of its problems is that the writing is far better than the shallow, narrow story, raising expectations that are never fulfilled. When, to give [his] all-too-eternal quadrilateral dramatic dimension, Mr. Goldman first has their lives intercut with the ghosts of their earlier selves, and finally puts all eight of them into an ironic Follies routine that is meant to comment on their personal and marital plights—by the faded beard of Pirandello he has gone too far."

The *New York Times'* Martin Gottfried does not, however, agree with his fellow critics' judgments. He writes: "I am convinced that 'Follies' is monumental theater. Not because I say so but because it is there for anybody to see. Moreover, its importance as a *kind* of theater transcends its interest as an example of a musical. . . . 'Follies' is not just another hit show. Had it not succeeded so tremendously at what it was trying to do, the attempt alone—the very idea—would have made it a landmark musical. . . . 'Follies' is a *concept musical,* a show whose music, lyrics, dance, stage movement and dialogue are woven through each other in the creation of a tapestry-like theme (rather than in support of a plot). . . . The concept behind 'Follies' is theater nostalgia, representing the rose-colored glasses through which we face the fact of age."

Despite this praise, though, Gottfried feels that "the book is weak. Admitted. James Goldman's device of a reunion of old Follies girls in a theater being torn down is a clumsy instigation for the action, and his comparative study of two soured marriages is awkward and trite. But Mr. Prince [Harold Prince, the director], who is heading toward the inevitable elimination of musical books, has stripped this story down, making the production itself the main event. So, Goldman's four unhappy people are haunted by memories—brought to life by four young actors as their ghosts."

Concludes Gottfried: "'Follies' has its imperfections. It seems overlong because of the lack of an intermission; this is an imposition on the audience and a pause would not have hurt the show's continuity anyhow. The story, though minimized by production, is undeniably simpleminded. Even so, 'Follies' is truly awesome and, if it is not consistently good, it is always great."

AVOCATIONAL INTERESTS: Tennis, music, reading.

BIOGRAPHICAL/CRITICAL SOURCES: Vogue, October 1, 1968; *New York,* November 4, 1968, January 6, 1969, March 19, 1971; *New York Times,* November 10, 1968, April 5, 1971, April 11, 1971, April 25, 1971; *New Leader,* November 18, 1968; *Variety,* March 3, 1971, April 7, 1971; *Cue,* April 10, 1971; *Newsweek,* April 12, 1971; *Life,* January 14, 1972; *Publishers Weekly,* February 8, 1980.

—*Sketch by Deborah A. Straub*

* * *

GOLDSTEIN, Nathan 1927-

PERSONAL: Born March 26, 1927, in Chicago, Ill.; son of Joseph (a factory worker) and Sarah (Commisarov) Goldstein; married Renee Rothbein (a painter), March 6, 1949; children: Sarah. *Education:* School of the Art Institute of Chicago, B.F.A., 1952, M.F.A., 1953; Art Students' League, graduate study, 1953-54. *Religion:* Hebrew. *Home:* 99 Pond Ave., Apt. D514, Brookline, Mass. 02146. *Office:* Art Institute of Boston, 700 Beacon St., Boston, Mass.

CAREER: Federal Civil Defense Administration Headquarters, Battle Creek, Mich., art director, 1956-57; Boston University, Boston, Mass., drawing instructor, 1960-78; De Cordova Museum, Lincoln, Mass., drawing and painting instructor, 1966-69; Art Institute of Boston, Boston, Mass., chairman of first year program of art study, 1972—. *Military service:* U.S. Navy, 1945-46.

WRITINGS: The Art of Responsive Drawing, Prentice-Hall, 1973; *Figure Drawing,* Prentice-Hall, 1975; *Visual and Technical Fundamentals,* Prentice-Hall, 1979. Illustrator of books for major publishing houses, 1949-67.

* * *

GOLV, Loyal E(ugene) 1926-
(Loyal E. Golf)

PERSONAL: Original name Loyal Eugene Golf; name legally changed in 1979; born May 31, 1926, in Chicago, Ill.; son of Ole and Olive (Kalvig) Golf; married Ruth Johnson, 1947; children: John, Naomi. *Education:* Attended Waldorf Junior College, 1946-48; Northwestern University, B.S., 1950; Luther Theological Seminary, B.Th., 1953, D.Min., 1978. *Home:* 1414 Fourth St., Brookings, S.D. *Office address:* First Lutheran Church, Box 300, Brookings, S.D. 57006.

CAREER: Wibaux-Carlyle parish, Wibaux, Mont., pastor, 1953-56; First Lutheran Church, Fargo, N.D., associate pastor, 1956-61; Bethel Lutheran Church, Wahpeton, N.D., pastor, 1961-65; St. John's Lutheran Church, Northfield, Minn., senior pastor, 1965-76; First Lutheran Church, Brookings, S.D., presiding minister, 1976—. *Military service:* U.S. Navy, 1944-46.

WRITINGS—Under name Loyal E. Golf: *The Cross and Crises,* Augsburg, 1961. Also author of *The Catechism and Creative Learning,* 1978.

* * *

GOODE, Erich 1938-

PERSONAL: Born September 21, 1938, in Austin, Tex.; son of William Josiah (a university professor) and Josephine (Cannizzo) Goode; married Roberta Buckingham, June 17, 1961 (divorced March 28, 1964); married Alice Neufold (a college instructor), December 28, 1968 (divorced February 9, 1977). *Education:* Oberlin College, A.B., 1960; Columbia University, Ph.D., 1966. *Home:* 108 Willis Ave., Port Jefferson, N.Y. 11777. *Office:* Department of Sociology, Social and Behavioral Sciences Building, State University of New York, Stony Brook, N.Y. 11794.

CAREER: New York University, Washington Square College, New York, N.Y., instructor, 1965-66, assistant professor of sociology, 1966-67; State University of New York at Stony Brook, assistant professor, 1967-70, associate professor of sociology, 1970—. Visiting associate professor at Florida Atlantic University, 1974, and University of North Carolina, 1977. Consultant to National Commission on Marijuana and Drug Abuse, 1971-72. *Member:* American Sociological Association, Society for the Study of Social Problems. *Awards, honors:* National Institute of Mental Health grant, 1968-69, 1976-78; grant from Research Foundation of State University of New York, summers, 1968, 1969, 1975, 1980; Guggenheim fellow, 1975-76.

WRITINGS: (Editor) *Marijuana,* Atherton, 1969; *The Marijuana Smokers,* Basic Books, 1970; *Drugs in American Society,* Knopf, 1972; *The Drug Phenomenon,* Bobbs-Merrill, 1973; (editor with Harvey A. Farberman) *Social Reality,*

Prentice-Hall, 1973; (editor with Richard R. Troiden) *Sexual Deviance and Sexual Deviants,* Morrow, 1974; *How Do You Know It's True?,* General Learning Press, 1974; *Deviant Behavior: An Interactionist Approach,* Prentice-Hall, 1978; *Social Class and Church Participation,* Arno, 1980. Contributor to *Social Problems, Journal of Health and Social Behavior, Psychiatry, American Journal of Psychiatry,* and other periodicals. Consulting editor, *American Journal of Sociology,* 1975-77; associate editor, *Journal of Health and Social Behavior,* 1977-79; member of editorial board, *Deviant Behavior: An Interdisciplinary Journal,* 1978-81.

* * *

GOODMAN, Norman 1934-

PERSONAL: Born February 19, 1934, in New York, N.Y.; son of Jack and Hannah (Hoffman) Goodman; married Marilyn Goldberg (a teacher), December 26, 1954; children: Jack, Susan Andrea, Carolyn Wendy. *Education:* Brooklyn College (now Brooklyn College of the City University of New York), B.A., 1955; New York University, M.A., 1961, Ph.D., 1963. *Home:* 4 Skylark Lane, Stony Brook, N.Y. 11790. *Office:* Department of Sociology, State University of New York at Stony Brook, Stony Brook, N.Y. 11794.

CAREER: New York Department of Welfare, New York City, social investigator, 1957-58; Russell Sage Foundation, New York City, research assistant, 1958-60; Association for the Aid of Crippled Children, New York City, research assistant, 1958-61; Columbia University, Teachers College, New York City, instructor in sociology, 1961-62; Queens College of the City University of New York, Flushing, N.Y., lecturer, 1962-63, assistant professor of sociology, 1963-64; State University of New York at Stony Brook, assistant professor, 1964-68, associate professor, 1968-73, professor of sociology and chairman of department, 1973—, assistant dean of Graduate School, 1966-67. *Military service:* U.S. Army, 1955-56. *Member:* American Association of University Professors, American Sociological Association, National Council on Family Relations, Society for Research in Child Development, Eastern Sociological Society, Alpha Kappa Delta. *Awards, honors:* Bobbs-Merrill Award in sociology from New York University, 1963; National Institute of Mental Health special research fellowship, 1970, to London School of Economics and Political Science.

WRITINGS: An Evaluation of the Eighth World Congress of the International Society for the Rehabilitation of the Disabled, International Society for the Rehabilitation of the Disabled, 1961; (with Orville G. Brim, Jr., David C. Glass, and David E. Lavin) *Personality and Decision Processes: Studies in the Social Psychology of Thinking,* Stanford University Press, 1962; (contributor) Helmut Strasser, editor, *Fortshritte der Heilpadagogik,* Carl Marhold, 1968, (contributor) Billy J. Franklin and Frank J. Kohout, editors, *Social Psychology and Everyday Life,* McKay, 1973; (contributor) Glen H. Elder, Jr. and Sigmund E. Dragastin, editors, *Adolescence in the Life Course,* Hemisphere Press, 1975; (editor with Gary T. Marx) *Sociology: Classic and Popular Approaches,* Random House, 1980; (with Gary S. Belkin) *Marriage, Family, and Intimate Relationships,* Rand McNally, 1980; (contributor) Harvey A. Farberman, editor, *Social Psychology: An Introduction to Symbolic Interaction,* Harper, in press. Contributor to journals.

WORK IN PROGRESS: Research in the effects of various educational programs in family day care.

GOUDIE, Andrew Shaw 1945-

PERSONAL: Born August 21, 1945, in Cheltenham, England; son of William (a pharmacist) and Mary (Pulman) Goudie. *Education:* Trinity Hall, Cambridge, B.A., 1970, Ph.D., 1971. *Religion:* Christian. *Home:* 9 Hayfield Rd., Oxford, England. *Office:* School of Geography, Oxford University, Mansfield Rd., Oxford, England.

CAREER: Oxford University, St. Edmund Hall and Hertford College, Oxford, England, lecturer and demonstrator in geography, 1970—. Honorary secretary, British Geomorphological Research Group. *Member:* Royal Geographical Society (fellow), Geographical Club, Institute of British Geographers.

WRITINGS: Duricrusts of Tropical and Sub-Tropical Landscapes, Clarendon Press, 1973; *Environmental Change,* Clarendon Press, 1977; *The Warm Desert Environment,* Cambridge University Press, 1977; *The Prehistory and Paleo-geography of the Great Indian Desert,* Academic Press, 1978. Also editor of *Theory and Practice in Geography.* Contributor to professional journals.

WORK IN PROGRESS: Research on the landforms and history of deserts; two books, *The Manual of Geomorphological Techniques* and *The Human Impact.*

* * *

GOURDIE, Thomas 1913-

PERSONAL: Born May 18, 1913, in Cowdenheath, Fife, Scotland; son of Thomas and Isabella (Galloway) Gourdie; married Lilias Boddie McKenzie Taylor, 1942; children: Lilias, Alison, Tommy. *Education:* Edinburgh College of Art, D.A., 1936. *Home:* 3 Douglas St., Kirkcaldy, Scotland.

CAREER: Teacher in Edinburgh, Scotland, 1939-40, and Banff, Scotland, 1945-46; Kirkcaldy High School, Kirkcaldy, Scotland, teacher, 1946-74; handwriting consultant and adviser on school handwriting, 1974—. Calligraphic adviser, E. S. Perry Ltd. (pen manufacturers), 1962—; adviser to Glasgow Education Committee and to Northern Ireland Ministry of Education. *Military service:* Royal Air Force, 1940-45. *Member:* Society of Scribes and Illuminators. *Awards, honors:* Member of Order of the British Empire, 1959.

WRITINGS: Italic Handwriting, Studio Books, 1955, revised edition, 1964; *Gourdei Italic Handwriting Method for Schools,* McDougall, 1956; *Pattern Making for Schools,* Studio Books, 1959; *Puffin Book of Lettering,* Penguin, 1961; *The Simple Modern Hand* (handwriting plan for schools), Collins, 1965; *Guide to Better Handwriting,* Studio Books, 1968; *The Ladybird Book of Handwriting,* Ladybird Books, 1968.

Handwriting for Today, Pitman, 1971; *Improve Your Handwriting,* Pitman, 1974; *I Can Write,* Macmillan, 1974; *Twenty Favourite Songs and Poems of Robert Burns,* Shepheard-Walwyn, 1978; *Calligraphic Styles,* Studio Books, 1978; *Calligraphy for the Beginner,* Taplinger, 1979; *Practice in Handwriting,* Macmillan, 1979. Also author, with Ronald Ridout, of Introductory Books 1 and 2 to *Write in English,* 1971.

WORK IN PROGRESS: The Puffin Book of Handwriting, for Penguin.

SIDELIGHTS: Thomas Gourdie told *CA:* "While I was trained as a calligrapher and thought to concentrate on formal calligraphy, in 1951 I decided to pursue the study of handwriting, in order to improve the standard of handwriting in schools. To this end I have produced methods for schools, books for children and for adults anxious to improve their writing, and have acted as adviser to Sweden and East Germany, where the systems of handwriting now being taught in the primary schools are based on my *Simple Modern Hand.* I have also been called upon to assist educationists in Australia and New Zealand to devise similar systems for their primary schools. At present I am assisting the Ministry of Education, Northern Ireland and also visiting America and Canada to lecture on my methods.

"According to Professor Albert Kapr (East Germany) I have enabled thousands upon thousands of children, the world over, to write better. This has been ample reward, as far as I am concerned, for all the work I have done in this field. My calligraphy books have mostly been written out in the Italic hand, thus dispensing with type and so saving in production costs. They have been devised by me from conception to the actual production and therefore I can claim that they are *my* books in the fullest sense of the word."

* * *

GRABER, Alexander 1914-
(Alexander Cordell)

PERSONAL: Born September 9, 1914, in Colombo, Ceylon (now Sri Lanka); son of Frank Alfred (an English soldier) and Amelia (Young) Graber; married Rosina Wells, 1937; children: Georgina Elizabeth. *Education:* By private tutors, at Marist Brothers' College. *Politics:* Active Socialist. *Religion:* Church of England. *Home:* 130 Friary, Ballabeg, Isle of Man, British Isles.

CAREER: Civil surveyor, Wales, 1936-39, 1945—. Began writing in 1950. *Military service:* British Army, sapper, 1932-36; Royal Engineers, 1939-45, became major. *Member:* Cardiff Writers' Circle (vice president), Leicester Literary Club.

WRITINGS—Under the pseudonym Alexander Cordell: *A Thought of Honour,* Museum Press, 1954; *The Race of the Tiger,* Doubleday, 1963; *The Sinews of Love,* Gollancz, 1965, Doubleday, 1966; *The Bright Cantonese,* Gollancz, 1967, published as *The Deadly Eurasian,* Weybridge, 1968; *The Traitor Within,* Brockhampton Press, 1971, Thomas Nelson, 1973; *The Fire People,* Hodder & Stoughton, 1972; *If You Believe the Soldiers,* Hodder & Stoughton, 1973, Doubleday, 1974; *The Dream and the Destiny,* Doubleday, 1975; *The Sweet and Bitter Earth,* St. Martin's, 1978; *Sea Urchin,* Collins, 1979; *Siesta without Sleep,* St. Martin's, in press.

The Welsh Trilogy: *The Rape of the Fair Country,* Doubleday, 1959; *Robe of Honour,* Doubleday, 1960 (published in England as *The Hosts of Rebecca,* Gollancz, 1960); *Song of the Earth,* Simon & Schuster, 1969, new edition, Coronet, 1976.

The White Cockade Trilogy for juveniles; published by Viking: *The White Cockade,* 1970; *Witches Sabbath,* 1970; *The Healing Blade,* 1971. Contributor of poems, short stories, and serials to magazines.

SIDELIGHTS: Alexander Graber told *CA* that he is "specifically interested in the advancement of Sino-British and Sino-American relations." He continued: "China, I believe, is the country of the future [and] at our peril we ignore her. Hitherto she has been the beaten child standing outside the door of the house of the world—now she has a house of her own and is inviting the world across its threshold. Let the old exploitations die and the terrors be forgotten in a new and vital relationship with the oldest civilisation in the world. My *Dream and the Destiny* was an attempt to bridge the gap of our un-understandings."

Graber was born to an English soldiering family and spent a great deal of his life traveling. He spent four years of his youth in North China and shorter periods of time in Egypt, Hong Kong, and Ceylon. He lists among his interests anti-blood sport movements.

BIOGRAPHICAL/CRITICAL SOURCES: Spectator, November 24, 1967, August 23, 1969; *Saturday Review,* December 28, 1968; *New York Times Book Review,* February 16, 1969; *New Yorker,* April 25, 1970; *Times Literary Supplement,* July 20, 1970.

* * *

GRABURN, Nelson H(ayes) H(enry) 1936-

PERSONAL: Surname is pronounced Gray-burn; born November 25, 1936, in London, England; son of Henry Long Kingsforth (with a tin mining company) and Cecily M. (Finch) Graburn; married Katherine Kazuko Yaguchi, June 25, 1966; children: Eva Mariko, Cecily Atsuko Ring. *Education:* Cambridge University, B.A., 1958; McGill University, M.A., 1960; University of Chicago, Ph.D., 1963. *Home:* 14 Wilson Circle, Berkeley, Calif. 94708. *Office:* Department of Anthropology, University of California, Berkeley, Calif. 94720.

CAREER: Government of Canada, Department of Northern Affairs, Ottawa, Ontario, research anthropologist, 1959-60; Northwestern University, Evanston, Ill., research anthropologist, 1963-64; University of California, Berkeley, assistant professor, 1964-70, associate professor, 1970-76, professor of anthropology, 1976—, fellow of Institute of International Studies, 1969-71. Guest researcher, National Museum of Ethnology, Osaka, Japan, 1979. *Member:* American Anthropological Association, Royal Anthropological Institute. *Awards, honors:* National Science Foundation research grants, 1967-69, and 1979-80.

WRITINGS: Taqagmiut Eskimo Kinship Terminology, Government of Canada, 1964; *Eskimos without Igloos: Social and Economic Change in Sugluk,* Little, Brown, 1969; (editor) *Readings in Kinship and Social Structure,* Harper, 1971; (with B. Stephen Strong) *Circumpolar Peoples: An Anthropological Perspective,* Goodyear Publishing, 1973; (co-author) *Traditions in Transition,* Lowie Museum, University of California, 1974; (editor) *Ethnic and Tourist Arts: Cultural Expressions from the Fourth World,* University of California Press, 1976. Contributor of articles and reviews to professional journals.

WORK IN PROGRESS: Art and Aesthetics of the Canadian Eskimos, for University of California Press.

SIDELIGHTS: Nelson H. H. Graburn lived with and studied Canadian Eskimos in 1959 and 1960. In 1963 and 1964 he worked on Northwestern University's Ethnocentrism Project, studying the inter-ethnic boundary of the Eskimos and Algonquian Indians of the Ungava Peninsula. He returned to the Canadian North to study soapstone carving and other Eskimo arts from 1967 to 1968 and in 1972 and 1976. Graburn has also lived in Japan and France and is particularly interested in contemporary tourism as a cultural phenomenon.

BIOGRAPHICAL/CRITICAL SOURCES: New York Times Book Review, October 7, 1979.

* * *

GRAFF, Henry F(ranklin) 1921-

PERSONAL: Born August 11, 1921, in New York, N.Y.;

son of Samuel F. and Florence (Morris) Graff; married Edith Krantz, 1946; children: Iris Joan (Mrs. Andrew R. Morse), Ellen Toby. *Education:* City College (now City College of the City University of New York), B.S. in S.S., 1941; Columbia University, A.M., 1942, Ph.D., 1949. *Home:* 47 Andrea Lane, Scarsdale, N.Y. 10583. *Office:* Fayerweather Hall, Columbia University, New York, N.Y. 10027.

CAREER: Columbia University, New York, N.Y., 1946—, began as instructor, professor of history, 1961—, chairman of department, 1961-64. Member, National Historical Publications Commission, 1965-71. *Military service:* U.S. Army, Security Agency, 1942-46; became lieutenant; received citation. *Member:* American Historical Association, Organization of American Historians, Society of American Historians, Society of Historians of American Foreign Relations, National Council for the Social Studies, Authors Guild, Authors League of America, P.E.N., American Council of Learned Societies (fellow), Phi Beta Kappa, Faculty House (Columbia University), Century Association (New York, N.Y.). *Awards, honors:* Townsend Harris Medal from City College of the City University of New York, 1966.

WRITINGS: *Bluejackets with Perry in Japan,* New York Public Library, 1952; (with Jacques Barzun) *The Modern Researcher,* Harcourt, 1957, 3rd edition, 1977; (with John A. Krout) *The Adventure of the American People,* Rand McNally, 1959, revised edition, 1973; (with Clifford Lord) *American Themes,* Columbia University Press, 1963; (contributor) John A. Garraty, editor, *Quarrels That Have Shaped the Constitution,* Harper, 1964; *Thomas Jefferson,* Silver, 1966; *The Free and the Brave,* Rand McNally, 1967, revised edition, 1980; *American Imperialism and the Philippine Insurrection,* Little, Brown, 1969; *The Tuesday Cabinet,* Prentice Hall, 1970; (with Paul J. Bohannan) *The Grand Experiment,* Rand McNally, Volume I: *The Call of Freedom,* 1978, Volume II: *The Promise of Democracy,* 1978. Contributor to *New York Times* and to popular and professional periodicals. Consulting editor, *Life's* "History of the United States" (book series), 1963-65.

WORK IN PROGRESS: Writing essays on the Presidency.

SIDELIGHTS: Henry F. Graff told *CA:* "The aim of good historical writing should be to orient the reader in his own time and thus to make him comfortable in the present. I would like to think that I am succeeding in this delicate and indispensable work."

* * *

GRANTHAM, Dewey Wesley 1921-

PERSONAL: Born March 16, 1921, in Manassas, Ga.; son of Dewey W. (a teacher) and Ellen (a teacher; maiden name, Holland) Grantham; married Virginia Burleson (a social worker), 1942; children: Wesley, Clinton, Lauren. *Education:* University of Georgia, A.B., 1942; University of North Carolina at Chapel Hill, M.A., 1947, Ph.D., 1949. *Politics:* Democrat. *Religion:* Unitarian Universalist. *Home:* 3510 Echo Hill Rd., Nashville, Tenn. 37215. *Office:* Department of History, Vanderbilt University, Nashville, Tenn. 37235.

CAREER: North Texas State College (now University), Denton, assistant professor, 1949-50; Woman's College of the University of North Carolina (now University of North Carolina at Greensboro), assistant professor, 1950-52; Vanderbilt University, Nashville, Tenn., assistant professor, 1952-55, associate professor, 1955-61, professor of history, 1961—, Holland N. McTyeire Professor of History, 1977—. *Military service:* U.S. Coast Guard, 1942-46; became lieutenant. *Member:* American Historical Association, Organization of American Historians, American Studies Association, American Association of University Professors, Southern Historical Association (president, 1966-67), Tennessee Council on Human Relations, Phi Beta Kappa, Pi Gamma Mu. *Awards, honors:* Sydnor Award from Southern Historical Association, for best book published on southern history, 1957-58; faculty fellow of Social Science Research Council, 1959; Guggenheim fellow, 1960; Henry E. Huntington Library and Art Gallery fellow, 1968-69; Fulbright-Hays lecturer, University of Aix-en-Provence, 1978-79.

WRITINGS: *Hoke Smith and Politics of the New South,* Louisiana State University Press, 1958; (contributor) *The Southerner as American,* University of North Carolina Press, 1960; *The Democratic South,* University of Georgia Press, 1963; (editor) R. S. Baker, *Following the Color Line,* Harper, 1964; (editor) *The South and the Sectional Image: The Sectional Theme Since Reconstruction,* Harper, 1967; (editor) *Theodore Roosevelt,* Prentice-Hall, 1971; (editor) *The Political Status of the Negro in the Age of FDR,* University of Chicago Press, 1973; *The United States since 1945: The Ordeal of Power,* McGraw, 1975; *The Regional Imagination: The South and Recent American History,* Vanderbilt University Press, 1979. General editor, "Twentieth-Century America" series, University of Tennessee Press, 1975—. Contributor to history journals.

* * *

GRATTAN, C(linton) Hartley 1902-1980

PERSONAL: Born October 19, 1902, in Wakefield, Mass.; son of Leonard E. and Laura (Campbell) Grattan; married Marjorie Campbell, 1939; children: Rosalind, Jacqueline, Jennifer, John. *Education:* Clark College, B.A., 1923. *Home:* 702 Spofford St., Austin, Tex. 78704.

CAREER: Free-lance writer in New York, N.Y., 1926-64; University of Texas at Austin, lecturer in history of Southwest Pacific, with rank of professor, and curator of Grattan Collection, 1964-74, professor emeritus, 1974-80. Trustee, Katonah Village Library. *Awards, honors:* D.Litt., Clark University, 1953; several grants from Carnegie Corp. for Australian studies; LL.D., Australian National University, 1977.

WRITINGS: *Why We Fought,* Vanguard, 1929, reprinted with afterword by author, Bobbs-Merrill, 1969; *Bitter Bierce,* Doubleday, 1929, reprinted, Cooper Square, 1967; *Australian Literature,* University of Washington Book Store, 1929, reprinted, Folcroft, 1977; *The Three Jameses,* Longmans, Green, 1932, reprinted, New York University Press, 1962; *Preface to Chaos,* Dodge, 1936; *Libraries: A Necessity for Democracy,* The Free Library Movement (Sydney, Australia), 1938; *The Deadly Parallel,* Stackpole, 1939; *Introducing Australia,* John Day, 1942, revised and enlarged edition, 1947; *Lands Down Under,* American Council, Institute of Pacific Relations, and Webster Publishing Co., 1943; *In Quest of Knowledge,* Association Press, 1955; *The United States and the Southwest Pacific,* Harvard University Press, 1961; *The Southwest Pacific to 1900,* University of Michigan Press, 1963; *The Southwest Pacific since 1900,* University of Michigan Press, 1963.

Editor: *A Bookman's Daybook,* Liveright, 1929; *The Critique of Humanism,* Harcourt, 1930, reprinted, Kennicat, 1968; *Recollections of the Last Ten Years,* Knopf, 1932; (with Sylvan Hoffman) *News of the Nation,* Garden City, 1941, revised edition, Prentice-Hall, 1952; *Australia,* University of California Press, 1947; (with Hoffman) *News of the World,* Garden City, 1953; *American Ideas about Adult*

Education, 1910-1951, Bureau of Publications, Teachers College, Columbia University, 1959.

Contributor: *Peerless Leader: William Jennings Bryan,* Farrar, Straus, 1929, reprinted with introduction by Charles A. Beard, finished by Grattan, Russell, 1973; *Such Is Life,* University of Chicago Press, 1948; F. P. King, editor, *Oceana and Beyond: Essays on the Pacific since 1945,* Greenwood Press, 1976; Louis and Livingston, editors, *The Southwest Pacific since World War I,* University of Texas Press, 1978. Contributor to numerous symposia on literature and public affairs, to anthologies and collections; contributor of more than two hundred articles to *American Mercury, Scribner's, Harper's,* and other magazines.

SIDELIGHTS: C. Hartley Grattan wrote as a literary critic, an economist, and a historical and social analyst. He was recognized as an expert on Australia and the Southwest Pacific. Grattan said that the greater part of his work dealt with American affairs, and that his "interest and status" in Australia and the Southwest Pacific were "superimposed on a fundamentally American preoccupation and career.

Grattan's first "professional publication" appeared in Mencken's *American Mercury* in May of 1924. In November of 1978, Grattan told *CA:* "Looking back . . . I suppose I am most impressed by the range and variety of my publications, but I am also pleased by the durability of so much that I have done. The core years of my career were 1926 to 1964, during which time I was a free-lance writer in New York, . . . a writer of 'think pieces' for the magazines, a book reviewer, and, occasionally, . . . a writer of books. My academic career (1964 to 1974) was a pendant to my career as a journalist. . . . I have consistently hewn to my self-chosen line, and the chips have fallen in strange places."

(Died June 25, 1980, in Austin, Tex.)

* * *

GREEN, Donald E(dward) 1936-

PERSONAL: Born April 15, 1936, in Wellington, Tex.; son of Lewis and Christene (Schoonover) Green; married Ozella M. Crawford (a teacher), September 7, 1956; children: Kelly Don, Kevin Dale. *Education:* Abilene Christian College (now University), B.A., 1958; Texas Technological College (now Texas Tech University), M.A., 1959; University of Oklahoma, Ph.D., 1969; additional study at University of Texas, Main University (now University of Texas at Austin), 1958, and University of California, Berkeley, 1960-61. *Politics:* Democrat. *Religion:* Christian. *Home:* 518 Ramblewood, Edmond, Okla. 73034. *Office:* Department of History, Central State University, Edmond, Okla. 73034.

CAREER: Oklahoma Christian College (now University), Oklahoma City, instructor, 1962-65, 1968-69; Central State University, Edmond, Okla., assistant professor, 1969-74, associate professor of history, 1974—, director of southwestern studies. *Military service:* U.S. Army Reserve, active duty, 1961-62. *Member:* Organization of American Historians, Agricultural History Society, Western History Association, Texas State Historical Association, Oklahoma Historical Society (member of board of directors).

WRITINGS: Land of the Underground Rain: Irrigation on the Texas High Plains, 1910-1970, University of Texas Press, 1973; *The Creek People,* Indian Tribal Series, 1973; (editor) *Rural Oklahoma,* Oklahoma Historical Society, 1977; *Fifty Years of Service to West Texas Agriculture: A History of Texas Tech University's College of Agricultural Sciences,* Texas Tech Press, 1977; *Panhandle Pioneer: Henry C. Hitch, His Ranch and His Family,* University of Oklahoma Press, 1979. Contributor to *Museum Journal, Drovers Journal, Irrigation Age,* and other professional journals.

* * *

GREEN, Margaret (Murphy) 1926-

PERSONAL: Born 1926, in Lawrence, Mass.; daughter of William Augustine and Margaret (Donovan) Murphy; married Francis J. Green, 1949; children: Ellen, Frank, William, Mary Leilani. *Education:* Attended Vesper George School of Art, 1943-44, Lowell State College (now University of Lowell), 1947-49, and University of Hawaii, 1958-59; American University, B.A., 1965. *Home:* 5100 Bradfield Ct., Anandale, Va.

CAREER: W. T. Woodson High School, Fairfax, Va., English teacher, beginning 1965.

WRITINGS: Defender of the Constitution: Andrew Johnson, Messner, 1962; *President of the Confederacy: Jefferson Davis,* Messner, 1963; *Paul Revere: The Man behind the Legend,* Messner, 1964; (editor) *The Big Book of Wild Animals,* F. Watts, 1964; (editor) *The Big Book of Animal Fables,* F. Watts, 1965; (editor) *The Big Book of Pets,* F. Watts, 1966; *Radical of the Revolution: Samuel Adams,* Messner, 1971.

AVOCATIONAL INTERESTS: Art, music, reading, and writing.

* * *

GREEN, Phyllis 1932-

PERSONAL: Born June 24, 1932, in Pittsburgh, Pa.; daughter of Victor Geyer (a plumbing contractor) and Phyllis (a teacher; maiden name, Sailer) Hartman; married Robert Bailey Green (an insurance executive), August 15, 1959; children: Sharon Ann, Bruce Robert. *Education:* Westminster College, New Wilmington, Pa., B.S. in Ed., 1953; University of Pittsburgh, M.Ed., 1955. *Residence:* Madison, Wis.

CAREER: Elementary and special education teacher in Dormont, Pa., and Newark and Wilmington, Del., 1953-59; free-lance writer, 1959—. Former band vocalist and actress in summer theater. *Member:* National League of American Pen Women, Society of Children's Book Writers, Detroit Women Writers.

WRITINGS: The Fastest Quitter in Town, Addison-Wesley, 1972; *Nantucket Summer,* Thomas Nelson, 1974; *Ice River,* Addison-Wesley, 1975; *Mildred Murphy, How Does Your Garden Grow?,* Addison-Wesley, 1977; *Grandmother Orphan,* Thomas Nelson, 1977; *Wild Violets,* Thomas Nelson, 1977; *Walkie-Talkie,* Addison-Wesley, 1978; *Nicky's Lopsided, Lumpy, but Delicious Orange,* Addison-Wesley, 1978; *The Empty Seat,* Elsevier-Nelson, 1979; *Gloomy Louie, the Doom King,* Albert Whitman, 1980; *Bagdad Ate It,* F. Watts, 1980. Also author of stage plays "Deer Season," produced off-Broadway at Theater at St. Clement's, January, 1980, and "By the Beautiful Sea"; author of radio plays "I'll Be Home for Christmas" and "Acapulco Holiday." Contributor of short stories, poems, and articles to national magazines.

WORK IN PROGRESS: A stage play and a novel for young people.

SIDELIGHTS: Reviewing Phyllis Green's play "Deer Season" for the *New York Times,* Michiko Kakutani writes: "The trouble with feminist plays, as with many dramas that take a political message as their raison d'etre, is that they all too often remain just that—narrowly focused works, which subordinate artistry and vision to a kind of self-conscious proselytizing. Such is the case with Phyllis Green's first play, 'Deer Season'.... Clearly the plight of the bored, unfulfilled housewife is an important one and one that is shared by many women today. And given sufficiently sensitive treatment, this subject, however familiar by now, might even provide some interesting dramatic material. As handled by Miss Green, though, it is neither interesting nor dramatic. Indeed, it trivializes the very women it attempts to ennoble."

BIOGRAPHICAL/CRITICAL SOURCES: New York Times, January 23, 1980.

* * *

GREEN, Stanley 1923-

PERSONAL: Born May 29, 1923, in New York, N.Y.; son of Rudy (a businessman) and Frances (Kuschner) Green; married Catherine Hunt, August 8, 1954; children: Susan Hunt, Rudy David. *Education:* Union College (now Union College and University), Schenectady, N.Y., B.A., 1943; University of Nebraska, Army Specialized Training Program, 1943-44.

CAREER: Writer. Lynn Farnol Group, New York City, account executive for American Society of Composers, Authors and Publishers, 1961-65; Radio station WBAI, New York City, music commentator, 1961-67. *Military service:* U.S. Army, 1943-46. *Member:* Players Club.

WRITINGS: The World of Musical Comedy, Ziff-Davis, 1960, revised edition, A. S. Barnes, 1980; *The Rodgers and Hammerstein Story,* John Day, 1963; *Ring Bells! Sing Songs!,* Arlington House, 1971; *Starring Fred Astaire,* Dodd, 1973; *Encyclopedia of the Musical Theatre,* Dodd, 1976, revised edition, Da Capo Press, 1980; *Broadway Musical Picture Book,* Dover, 1977; *Rodgers and Hammerstein Show by Show,* Lynn Farnol, 1980. Contributor to *Variety, Saturday Review, Atlantic Monthly, New York Times,* and other publications. Contributing editor, *Hi/Fi Stereo Review,* 1957-63; editor, *ASCAP Biographical Dictionary,* 1966.

WORK IN PROGRESS: Encyclopaedia of Film Musicals, for Oxford University Press.

BIOGRAPHICAL/CRITICAL SOURCES: Variety, February 26, 1969.

* * *

GREENE, Carla 1916-

PERSONAL: Born December 18, 1916, in Minneapolis, Minn.; daughter of William L. and Charlotte (Wunderman) Greene. *Education:* High school graduate. *Agent:* Toni Strassman, 138 East 18th St., 7-D, New York, N.Y. 10003.

CAREER: Started as secretary in Minneapolis, Minn.; worked as advertising writer for more than twenty years in department stores in Detroit, Mich., Chicago, Ill., and New York, N.Y.; writer of children's books, 1954—. Lecturer on travel and children's reading. Member, Reading Is Fundamental. *Member:* PEN International, Authors League of America, Southern California Council on Children's Literature, Los Angeles County Museum. *Awards, honors:* Outstanding Book Award from Junior Science Teachers of America, 1972, for *How Man Began.*

WRITINGS—"Travel" series; all published by Lantern Press, except as indicated: *A Hotel Holiday,* Melmont, 1954; *Holiday in a Trailer,* Melmont, 1955; *A Motor Holiday,* Melmont, 1956; *A Trip on a Train,* 1956; *A Trip on a Plane,* 1957; *A Trip on a Ship,* 1958; *A Trip to Hawaii,* 1959; *A Trip on a Jet,* 1960; *A Trip to the Zoo,* 1962; *A Trip on a Bus,* 1964; *A Trip to the Aquarium,* 1968.

"I Want to Be" series; all published by Children's Press: *I Want to Be an Animal Doctor,* 1956; *. . . a Baker,* 1956; *. . . a Train Engineer,* 1956; *. . . an Orange Grower,* 1956; *. . . a Coal Miner,* 1957; *. . . a Pilot,* 1957; *. . . a Teacher,* 1957; *. . . a Zoo-Keeper,* 1957; *. . . a Bus Driver,* 1957; *. . . a Dairy Farmer,* 1957; *. . . a Nurse,* 1957; *. . . a Fisherman,* 1957; *. . . a Doctor,* 1958; *. . . a News Reporter,* 1958; *. . . a Policeman,* 1958; *. . . a Postman,* 1958; *. . . a Road Builder,* 1958; *. . . a Storekeeper,* 1958; *. . . a Telephone Operator,* 1958; *. . . a Truck Driver,* 1958; *. . . a Mechanic,* 1959; *. . . a Restaurant Owner,* 1959; *. . . a Fireman,* 1959; *. . . a Carpenter,* 1959; *. . . a Ballet Dancer,* 1959; *. . . a Farmer,* 1959; *. . . a Cowboy,* 1960; *. . . a Dentist,* 1960; *. . . an Airplane Hostess,* 1960; *. . . a Librarian,* 1960; *. . . a Homemaker,* 1961; *. . . a Baseball Player,* 1961; *. . . a Scientist,* 1961; *. . . a Space Pilot,* 1961; *. . . a Musician,* 1962; *. . . a Ship Captain,* 1962.

"What Do They Do?" series; all published by Harper: *Policemen and Firemen,* 1962; *Doctors and Nurses,* 1963; *Soldiers and Sailors,* 1963; *Railroad Engineers and Airplane Pilots,* 1964; *Truck Drivers,* 1967; *Animal Doctors,* 1967; *Cowboys,* 1972.

"Let's Learn About" series; all published by Harvey House: *Where Does a Letter Go?,* 1965; *Let's Meet the Chemist,* 1966; *Let's Learn about the Orchestra,* 1967; *Moses: The Great Lawgiver,* 1968; *Let's Learn about Lighthouses,* 1969.

"Science and Natural History" series; all published by Bobbs-Merrill: *How to Know Dinosaurs,* 1966; *After the Dinosaurs,* 1968; *Before the Dinosaurs,* 1970; *How Man Began,* 1972; *Our Living Earth: Its Origin and Ecology,* 1974; *Man and Ancient Civilizations,* 1977.

Other: *Charles Darwin* (biography), Dial, 1968; *Gregor Mendel* (biography), Dial, 1969; *Manuel: Young Mexican-American,* Lantern Press, 1969.

SIDELIGHTS: Carla Greene told *CA:* "I believe that today's youngsters are much more eager, alert, and knowledgeable than former generations. Bearing this in mind, I try to bring them information about their world in a way that excites the young reader and leads him or her to further investigation on a subject. Without underestimating their intelligence or assaulting the reader with boring statistics or trite facts, I try to bring them insight into the world around them, both modern and ancient."

Some of Greene's books, intended for children at various interest and reading levels from ages five to twlceve, have reached the million mark in sales. Some are available in other countries, including England, Australia, and throughout the British Commonwealth. *Truck Drivers* has been translated into Spanish.

AVOCATIONAL INTERESTS: Painting, drama, ballet, music, attending lectures.

* * *

GREENFIELD, Eloise 1929-

PERSONAL: Born May 17, 1929, in Parmele, N.C.; daughter of Weston W. and Lessie (Jones) Little; married Robert J. Greenfield (a procurement specialist), April 29, 1950; children: Steven, Monica. *Education:* Attended Miner Teachers College, 1946-49. *Agent:* Curtis Brown Ltd., 575 Madison Ave., New York, N.Y. 10022.

CAREER: U.S. Patent Office, Washington, D.C., clerk-typist, 1949-56, supervisory patent assistant, 1956-60; worked as a secretary, case-control technician, and an administrative assistant in Washington D.C. from 1964-68. District of Columbia Black Writer's Workshop, co-director of adult fiction, 1971-73, director of children's literature, 1973-74; writer-in-residence with District of Columbia Commission on the Arts, 1973. *Awards, honors:* Carter G. Woodson Book Award, National Council for the Social Studies, 1974; Irma Simonton Black Award, Bank Street College of Education, 1974; Jane Addams Children's Book Award, Women's International League for Peace and Freedom, 1976; Coretta Scott King Award, 1978.

WRITINGS: (Contributor) Alma Murray and Robert Thomas, editors, *The Journey: Scholastic Black Literature,* Scholastic Book Services, 1970; (contributor) Karen S. Kleiman and Mel Cebulash, editors, *Double Action Short Stories,* Scholastic Book Services, 1973; *Sister* (novel), Crowell, 1974; *Honey, I Love* (poetry), Crowell, 1978; *Talk about a Family* (novel), Lippincott, 1978.

Picture books: *Bubbles,* Drum & Spear, 1972, published as *Good News,* Coward, 1977; *She Come Bringing Me That Little Baby Girl,* Lippincott, 1974; *Me and Neesie,* Crowell, 1975; *First Pink Light,* Crowell, 1976; *Africa Dream,* John Day, 1977; (with mother, Lessie Jones Little) *I Can Do It by Myself,* Crowell, 1978; *Grandmama's Joy,* Collins, in press.

Biographies; all published by Crowell: *Rosa Parks,* 1973; *Paul Robeson,* 1975; *Mary McLeod Bethune,* 1977; (with Little) *Childtimes: A Three Generation Memoir* (autobiography), 1979.

Contributor to *Black World, Ebony Jr!, Negro History Bulletin, Scholastic Scope,* and *Ms.*

SIDELIGHTS: Eloise Greenfield told *CA* that her goal in writing is "to give children words to love, to grow on."

BIOGRAPHICAL/CRITICAL SOURCES: Commonweal, February, 1976; *Book World,* September 12, 1976, May 1, 1977, January 13, 1980; *Christian Science Monitor,* November 3, 1976; *Negro History Bulletin,* January, 1978; *New York Times Book Review,* April 30, 1978.

* * *

GREENHALGH, P(eter) A(ndrew) L(ivsey) 1945-

PERSONAL: Surname is pronounced *Green*-halsh; born October 18, 1945, in Littleborough, Lancashire, England; son of Herbert Livsey (a draper) and Elsie (Wright) Greenhalgh; married Anna-Mary Beatrice Dixon (a solicitor), August 24, 1968; (children) Clare Elizabeth Jane. *Education:* King's College, Cambridge, B.A., 1967, M.A., 1970, Ph.D., 1971. *Home:* 81 Forest Glade, Tokai Cape 7945, South Africa. *Office:* Department of Classics, University of Cape Town, Rondebosch 7700, South Africa.

CAREER: Engaged in various business activities, 1970-72; Hill Samuel & Co., London, England, merchant banker, 1972-76; University of Cape Town, Rondebosch, South Africa, senior lecturer in classics, 1977—.

WRITINGS: Early Greek Warfare, Cambridge University Press, 1973; *The Year of the Four Emperors,* Weidenfeld & Nicolson, 1975; *Pompey: The Roman Alexander,* Weidenfeld & Nicolson, 1980; *Pompey: The Republican Prince,* Weidenfeld & Nicolson, in press. Contributor to classical journals, including *Greece and Rome* and *Historia.*

GREINER, Donald J(ames) 1940-

PERSONAL: Born June 10, 1940, in Baltimore, Md.; son of D. James (a physician) and Katherine (Murphy) Greiner; married Ellen Brunot, June 20, 1964; children: Kay, Jim. *Education:* Wofford College, B.A. (magna cum laude), 1962; University of Virginia, M.A., 1963, Ph.D., 1967. *Home:* 3833 Edinburgh Rd., Columbia, S.C. 29204. *Office:* Department of English, University of South Carolina, Columbia, S.C. 29208.

CAREER: University of South Carolina, Columbia, assistant professor, 1967-70, associate professor, 1970-74, professor of English, 1974—. *Member:* Modern Language Association of America, South Atlantic Modern Language Association, Phi Beta Kappa.

WRITINGS: (Editor with wife, Ellen Greiner) *The Notebook of Stephen Crane,* University Press of Virginia, 1969; *Guide to Robert Frost,* C. E. Merrill, 1969; *Checklist of Robert Frost,* C. E. Merrill, 1969; *Comic Terror: The Novels of John Hawkes,* Memphis State University Press, 1973, revised edition, 1978; *Robert Frost: The Poet and His Critics,* American Library Association, 1974; (editor) *Dictionary of Literary Biography: American Poets since World War II,* two volumes, Gale, 1980. Contributor to *Contemporary Literature, Critique, Studies in Modern Fiction, Southwest Review, English Journal, South Carolina Review,* and other professional journals.

WORK IN PROGRESS: The Other John Updike: Poems, Stories, Prose, and Play.

* * *

GRIBBIN, William James 1943-

PERSONAL: Born October 2, 1943, in Washington, D.C.; son of Walter James (an electrician) and Helena (Slechta) Gribbin. *Education:* Catholic University of America, B.A., 1965, M.A., 1966, Ph.D., 1968. *Politics:* Conservative. *Religion:* Roman Catholic. *Home:* 4744 Eastern Ave. N.E., Washington, D.C. 20017. *Office:* Senate Republican Policy Committee, U.S. Senate, 333 Old Senate Office Bldg., Washington, D.C. 20510.

CAREER: Virginia Union University, Richmond, assistant professor of history, 1968-71; District of Columbia Teachers College (now University of District of Columbia), Washington, D.C., assistant professor of history, 1973; legislative assistant to Senator James L. Buckley, 1974-77; U.S. Senate, Senate Republican Policy Committee, Washington, D.C., senior policy analyst, 1977—. Consultant, Office of Economic Opportunity, 1973. *Member:* Organization of American Historians, Phi Beta Kappa, Phi Alpha Theta. *Awards, honors:* Woodrow Wilson fellowship, 1965-66; Stephen Greene Press Award, 1974.

WRITINGS: The Churches Militant: The War of 1912 and American Religion, Yale University Press, 1973. Contributor to *New England Quarterly, Church History, Americas, Historian, Vermont History, South Atlantic Quarterly, Journal of Presbyterian History,* and many other periodicals.

SIDELIGHTS: William James Gribbin wrote *CA:* "My current writing concerns public policy and is of a political nature. Which is not to say that it is better or worse than the writing of history, just different."

* * *

GRIESE, Arnold A(lfred) 1921-

PERSONAL: Surname rhymes with "rice"; born April 13,

1921, in Lakota, Iowa; son of Helmut Adam (a farmer) and Augusta (Meltz) Griese; married Jane Warren (owner of modeling school), January 14, 1943; children: Warren, Cynthia (Mrs. Les Blakely). *Education:* Georgetown University, B.S., 1948; University of Miami, Coral Gables, Fla., M.Ed., 1957; University of Arizona, Ph.D., 1960. *Politics:* Independent. *Religion:* Episcopalian. *Home:* 3070 Riverview Dr., Fairbanks, Alaska 99701. *Office:* Department of Education, University of Alaska, Fairbanks, Alaska 99701.

CAREER: McGraw-Hill Publishing Co., New York, N.Y., sales representative in Colombia, South America, 1948-50; elementary school teacher in the public schools of Tanana, Alaska, 1951-56; University of Alaska, Fairbanks, assistant professor, 1960-65, associate professor, 1965-71, professor of education, 1971—. *Military service:* U.S. Army Air Forces, 1942-46; became captain. *Member:* National Council of Teachers of English, Alaska Council of Teachers of English, Delta Phi Epsilon, Phi Delta Kappa, Phi Kappa Phi.

WRITINGS: (Contributor) Miriam Hoffman, editor, *Authors and Illustrators of Children's Books,* Bowker, 1972; *At the Mouth of the Luckiest River* (juvenile), Crowell, 1973; *The Way of Our People* (juvenile), Crowell, 1975; *The Wind Is Not a River* (juvenile), Crowell, 1979; *Do You Read Me?* (textbook), Goodyear Publishing, 1976. Contributor to *Elementary English.*

WORK IN PROGRESS: A children's book of historical fiction on the Indians of Alaska, for Crowell; *Your Philosophy of Education: What Is It?,* for Goodyear Publishing.

SIDELIGHTS: Arnold Griese told *CA:* "As a writer I have a consuming interest in encouraging others to become writers. This leads me to suggest the following: Don't worry about being creative—we all are. The real concern is to develop that creativity through disciplined effort. This takes time (sometimes years) so be sure you have a job that provides you with your livelihood; but don't take one that occupies your mind after hours. During that time your mind needs to be free to incubate ideas so that when you finally sit down to write (this is in itself an act of discipline) there will be something to say and a feeling for how it should be said." *Avocational interests:* Flying his plane, chess, swimming, travel.

* * *

GRIESON, Ronald Edward 1943-

PERSONAL: Born March 8, 1943, in New York, N.Y.; son of Hans Willhelm (a manager) and Stella Grieson; married Barbara Anne Uchal, August 29, 1970. *Education:* Queens College of the City University of New York, B.A. (cum laude), 1964; University of Rochester, M.A., 1967, Ph.D., 1971. *Politics:* Independent. *Religion:* "Protestant by birth." *Home and office:* 8 College Rd., Princeton, N.J. 08540.

CAREER: University of Rochester, Rochester, N.Y., instructor in economics, 1968-69; Massachusetts Institute of Technology, Cambridge, assistant professor of economics, 1969-72; Queens College and Graduate Center of the City University of New York, New York City, associate professor of economics, 1972-74; Columbia University, New York City, associate professor of economics, 1974-79; Princeton University, Princeton, N.J., visiting associate professor, 1979—. Consultant to U.S. Economic Development Administration, Commonwealth of Massachusetts and City of New York. *Member:* American Economics Association, Econometric Society.

WRITINGS: (Editor) *Urban Economics: Readings and Analysis,* Little, Brown, 1973; (editor) *Public and Urban Economics,* Lexington Books, 1976. Contributor to *Journal of Urban Economics, American Economic Review, Journal of Public Economics, National Tax Journal,* and other publications.

WORK IN PROGRESS: Research in transportation, juvenile crime, the effect of taxes on location, the demand and supply of heroin, zoning, housing, and the effects of inflation on investments.

AVOCATIONAL INTERESTS: Fine arts, architecture, domestic and wild animals.

* * *

GRIFFIN, Arthur J. 1921-
(Lee Frank, Anne J. Griffin, Susan James)

PERSONAL: Born January 7, 1921, in Hartford, Conn.; married Jane Slattery; children: four. *Education:* Attended Hillyer College and Columbia University. *Home:* 46 Meadowood Lane, Old Saybrook, Conn. 06475. *Agent:* Chuck Neighbors, Waverly Pl., New York, N.Y.

CAREER: Worked in publishing and advertising in Massachusetts, New York, and Connecticut; currently employed as an advertising copywriter in Connecticut. *Military service:* U.S. Army Air Forces, 1942-45; became sergeant.

WRITINGS—Under pseudonym Lee Frank: *Kane,* Paperback Library, 1972; *Kane–and the Goldbar Killers,* Paperback Library, 1973; *Kane—and the Outlaw's Double-Cross,* Paperback Library, 1974; *Ocean of Fear,* Avon, 1975; *Spirit of Brynmaster Oaks,* Avon, 1975; *Hypnotist of Hilary Mansion,* Pocket Books, 1977. Also author of other novels under various pseudonyms.

WORK IN PROGRESS: Several novels.

* * *

GRIGSON, Jane 1928-

PERSONAL: Born March 13, 1928, in Gloucester, England; daughter of George Shipley (a town clerk) and Doris (Berkley) McIntire; children: Hester Sophia Frances. *Education:* Newnham College, Cambridge, B.A., 1949. *Home:* Broad Town Farm, Broad Town, Swindon, Wiltshire, England. *Agent:* Harold Ober Associates, Inc., 40 East 49th St., New York, N.Y. 10017; and David Higham Associates, 5-8 Lower John St., Golden Square, London W1R 3PE, England.

CAREER: Heffers Art Gallery, Cambridge, England, assistant, 1950-51; Walker's Art Gallery, London, England, assistant, 1952-53; George Rainbird Ltd. (publisher), London, assistant, 1953-54; Thames & Hudson Ltd. (publisher), London, assistant, 1954-55; editor, translator, writer. *Member:* Wine and Food Society. *Awards, honors:* John Florio Prize, 1965, for translation of *On Crimes and Punishments.*

WRITINGS: (Translator) Giovanni A. Cibotto, *Scano Boa,* Hodder & Stoughton, 1963; (translator) Cesare Beccaria, *On Crimes and Punishments,* Oxford University Press, 1964; (with Geoffrey Grigson) *Shapes and Stories,* Vanguard, 1965; (with Grigson) *More Shapes and Stories,* Vanguard, 1967; *Charcuterie & French Pork Cookery,* M. Joseph, 1967, published as *Art of Charcuterie,* Knopf, 1968; *Good Things,* Knopf, 1971; *Fish Cookery,* Wine and Fish Society, 1973; *The Mushroom Feast,* Knopf, 1975; *The Art of Making Sausage, Pates, and Other Charcuterie,* Knopf, 1976; *Jane Grigson's Vegetable Book,* Atheneum, 1979; *Food with the Famous,* Atheneum, 1980. Cookery correspondent, *Observer Colour Magazine,* 1968—.

WORK IN PROGRESS: Jane Grigson's Fruit Book; Observer Cookery School Anthology.

* * *

GRIMES, Alan P. 1919-

PERSONAL: Born February 3, 1919, in Staten Island, N.Y.; son of Willard Mudgette and Mildred (Staples) Grimes; married Margaret E. Whitehurst, 1942; children: Margaret G. Wallace, Alan P., Jr., Katherine Grimes Green, Peter E. *Education:* University of North Carolina, A.B., 1941, M.A., 1946, Ph.D., 1948. *Home:* 728 Lantern Hill Dr., East Lansing, Mich. *Office:* Department of Political Science, Michigan State University, East Lansing, Mich.

CAREER: University of North Carolina at Chapel Hill, instructor, 1946-48, assistant professor, 1948-49; Michigan State University, East Lansing, assistant professor, 1949-51, associate professor, 1951-57, professor of political science, 1957—. *Military service:* U.S. Navy, 1941-45; became lieutenant. *Member:* American Political Science Association. *Awards, honors:* Michigan State University Distinguished Faculty Award, 1969.

WRITINGS: The Political Liberalism of the New York Nation, 1865-1932, University of North Carolina Press, 1953; *American Political Thought,* Holt, 1955, revised edition, 1960; (with Robert Horwitz) *Modern Political Ideologies,* Oxford University Press, 1959; *Equality in America,* Oxford University Press, 1964; *The Puritan Ethic and Woman Suffrage,* Oxford University Press, 1967; (contributor) William C. Havard and Joseph L. Bernd, editors, *Two Hundred Years of the Republic in Retrospect,* University Press of Virginia, 1976; (contributor) John A. Garraty, editor, *Dictionary of American Biography: Supplement Five, 1951-55,* Scribner, 1977; *Democracy and the Amendments to the Constitution,* Heath, 1978. Contributor to professional journals.

SIDELIGHTS: Alan P. Grimes told *CA:* "My recent books have usually been a record of my thinking as I have attempted to understand a political question and explain a political settlement. *Equality in America* developed out of my effort to understand why Supreme Court decisions of the Warren court in religion, race, and representation favored the principle of equality. *The Puritan Ethic and Woman Suffrage* arose out of my curiosity as to why the woman suffrage movement in America achieved its early success in the West rather than the East. *Democracy and the Amendments to the Constitution* is my explanation for the success of the movement toward democratic equality in enacting amendments to the Constitution. In each instance the research and writing followed from curiosity as to why some pattern in politics had developed where it did, and when it did."

In his book, *The Puritan Ethic and Woman Suffrage,* Grimes attempts to disprove the widely-held belief that giving women the right to vote drastically changed the American political system. In truth, he claims, social and political leaders of the time who were in favor of the movement (including the suffragettes themselves) saw it as a way to double the voting power of the white Protestant ruling class and thus maintain the *status quo.* Milton Viorst of *Book Week* writes that "as a study of power, [*The Puritan Ethic and Woman Suffrage*] well deserves to be read. For Grimes challenges some of the mythology and shatters some of the complacency about the virtues of American society. He replaces a widely popular misconception with a glimmer of truth that gives us a sounder perspective on ourselves." Christopher Lasch of the *New York Review of Books* praises Grimes for writing "one of the few studies of women and woman suffrage that advances beyond guesswork and anecdote to real historical analysis."

BIOGRAPHICAL/CRITICAL SOURCES: Book Week, May 7, 1967; *New York Review of Books,* July 13, 1967.

* * *

GRIMES, Ronald L. 1943-

PERSONAL: Born May 19, 1943, in San Diego, Calif.; son of Milton L. and Joyce N. (Williams) Grimes; married Mary Judith Shown, May 31, 1964 (divorced); children: Trevor. *Education:* Kentucky Wesleyan College, B.A. (summa cum laude), 1964; Emory University, M.Div. (magna cum laude), 1967; Columbia University and Union Theological Seminary, Ph.D., 1970. *Religion:* Zen. *Home:* 81 Mount Hope St., Kitchener, Ontario, Canada N2G 2JS. *Office:* Religion and Culture Department, Wilfrid Laurier University, Waterloo, Ontario, Canada N2L 3C5.

CAREER: Columbia University, Barnard College, New York, N.Y., instructor in religion, 1970; Lawrence University, Appleton, Wis., assistant professor of religion, 1970-74; Wilfrid Laurier University, Waterloo, Ontario, associate professor of religion, 1974—. Guest scholar, University of Chicago, 1973-74. *Member:* American Academy of Religion, Theta Phi. *Awards, honors:* Younger Humanists grant from National Endowment for the Humanities, 1973-74, for field research in Santa Fe, N.M. and library research at the University of Chicago; Brown Memorial Award in Religion; Edward Arthur Mellinger Foundation Award.

WRITINGS: The Divine Imagination: William Blake's Major Prophetic Visions, Scarecrow, 1972; (contributor) Joseph A. Wittreich and Stuart Curran, editors, *Blake's Sublime Allegory,* University of Wisconsin Press, 1973; *Symbol and Conquest: Public Ritual and Drama in Santa Fe, New Mexico,* Cornell University Press, 1976. Contributor of numerous articles and reviews to academic journals, including *Face to Face, Christianity and Crisis, Classmate, Journal of the American Academy of Religion, Catholic World,* and *Union Seminary Quarterly Review.*

SIDELIGHTS: Ronald L. Grimes wrote *CA:* "The centre of my academic interests has been and remains the interpretation of symbolic forms. The problem of symbolization lies at the intersection of several sub-disciplines, religion and the arts, symbolic anthropology, and philosophy of religion, and it is the phenomenon of symbolization, rather than one of these sub-disciplines which constitutes my field. Because 'comparative symbology' (Victor Turner's term) is inter-disciplinary in nature, I spend much of my research teaching time dealing with methodological questions and pursuing phenomenological motifs.

"My understanding of both religion and art is strongly informed by William Blake. From him I learned what constitutes a symbol. I was also taught by him that generalizations are to be approached through the 'minute particulars.' Consequently, my work as a philosopher of religion usually occurs in the form of extended case studies of some rather carefully chosen and rigidly delimited data, for instance, a cycle of ritual and drama in Santa Fe or Blake's three major prophetic works. I think that philosophizing about religion should occur on the heels of field study, so I am more prone to search out religio-aesthetic performances than I am to read philosophical and theological texts as preludes to generalization. As a result, the metaphors which inform my method are dramatistic rather than linguistic; religion is 'performance' rather than 'text.' This is why I tend to emphasize ritual, storytelling, and meditational practice rather than ethics, theology, and poetry or novel."

* * *

GRONEMAN, Chris Harold 1906-

PERSONAL: Born May 29, 1906, in Newton, Kan.; son of Albert Christian and Kate (Launhart) Groneman; married Virginia Grace Krug, 1935. *Education:* Kansas State College of Pittsburg (now Pittsburg State University), B.S., 1931, M.S., 1935; attended University of Minnesota, 1939; Pennsylvania State University, D.Ed., 1950. *Religion:* Methodist. *Home:* 1501 Glade, College Station, Tex. *Office:* Texas A&M University, College Station, Tex. 77843.

CAREER: Mayetta High School, Mayetta, Kan., industrial arts teacher and coach, 1930-32; Plains High School, Plains, Kan., industrial arts teacher and coach, 1932-33; Woodward High School and Junior College, Woodward, Okla., assistant dean, 1933-37; East Texas State College (now University), Commerce, assistant professor, 1937-40; Texas A&M University, College Station, professor, 1940-67, acting head of industrial education department, 1943-49, head of department, 1949-67, chairman of athletic council, 1954-67, chairman of council on teacher education, 1954-67, coordinator of teacher education, 1956-67. Guest professor at University of Hawaii, 1967-68, and California State University, Fresno, 1968-75; summer professor at colleges in United States and Canada. Ford Motor Company National Industrial Arts Awards Program, judge, 1948-54, member of national advisory committee, 1949-53; member of industrial arts award committee, *Scholastic Magazine,* 1946-49.

MEMBER: American Council on Industrial Arts Teacher Education, American Industrial Arts Association (fellow), American Vocational Association (chairman of liaison committee with American Industrial Arts Association, 1951-53, chairman of industrial arts publications and research committee, 1953-56), National Association of Industrial Teacher Educators (vice-president, 1950-51), National Collegiate Athletic Association (vice-president and member of council, 1963-67), Southwest Athletic Conference (vice-president, 1961-63; president, 1963-65), Industrial Arts Conference of Mississippi Valley, Texas State Education Association, Texas Vocational Association (vice-president for industrial arts, 1945-46; vice-president-at-large, 1947-48; president, 1946-47), Texas Industrial Arts Association (life member), East Texas Industrial Arts Club, Phi Delta Kappa, Iota Lambda Sigma.

WRITINGS: General Bookbinding, McKnight & McKnight, 1941, revised edition, 1946; *Bent Tubular Furniture,* Bruce, 1941, revised edition, 1947; *Applied Leathercraft,* Bennett, 1942, revised edition, 1963; *Exploring the Industries* (worktext), Steck, 1944, revised edition, 1970, text, 1963, revised edition, 1971; (with Boehmer) *Making Things Is Fun,* Book I, Book II, and teachers' handbook, Steck, 1946; *Plastics Made Practical,* Bruce 1948; (with Rigsby) *Elementary and Applied Welding,* Bruce, 1948; *Organization, Management, and Planning for Industrial Arts,* Canvas Products Corp., 1948, revised edition, 1960; *Ornamental Tin Craft,* Bruce, 1950; *Leather Tooling and Carving,* Van Nostrand, 1950, reprinted, Dover, 1976; *Leather Tooling and Carving Patterns,* Van Nostrand, 1951; *General Woodworking,* McGraw, 1952, 6th edition, 1976; (with J. L. Feirer) *General Shop,* McGraw, 1954, 6th edition published as *General Industrial Education,'* 1979; (contributor) *Modern School Shop Planning,* Prakken, 1957; *Leathercraft,* Bennett, 1958, revised edition, 1963; (with E. R. Glazener) *Technical Woodworking,* McGraw, 1966; (with G. Grannis) *Plastics Learning Kit,* Broadhead-Garrett Co., 1979.

(With Feirer) "Getting Started" series, McGraw, 1979: *Getting Started in Drafting; . . . Woodworking; . . . Metalworking; . . . Electricity and Electronics.*

Consulting editor, McGraw publications in industrial education, 1949—. Contributor to *Encyclopedia Americana.* Contributor of over 144 articles to periodicals. Editorial chairman, *A Guide to Improving Instruction in Industrial Arts* (bulletin), American Vocational Association, 1953; editor, *School Shop Safety Newsletter,* National Safety Council, 1952-54; editorial board member, *School Shop Magazine,* 1954-59, and *Industrial Arts and Vocational Education Magazine,* 1961-67.

WORK IN PROGRESS: Book revisions, and articles for professional journals.

AVOCATIONAL INTERESTS: Furniture making, ranching.

* * *

GROOM, Arthur William 1898-1964 (Graham Adamson, George Anderson, Daphne du Blane, Gordon Grimsley, Bill Pembury, John Stanstead, Maurice Templar, Martin Toonder)

PERSONAL: Born 1898, in Hove, Sussex, England; died September, 1964; son of William Samuel and Emily Ann (Short) Groom; married Marjorie Helen Grimsley, 1928; children: Susan. *Education:* Attended schools in England. *Religion:* Church of England. *Home:* 3 Pembury Rd., Gloucester, England. *Agent:* A. M. Heath & Co. Ltd., 40-42 William IV St., London WC2N 4DD; and Howard Moorepark, 444 East 82nd St., New York, N.Y. 10028.

CAREER: Clerk, Bank of Scotland, England, 1916-19; Colonial Bank (now Barclay's), British West Indies and British Guiana, sub-manager, 1919-22; London's Underground Railways, London, England, editor of staff magazine, 1922-28; professional writer, 1928-64. Frequent lecturer. Vice-president, Gloucester branch, International Friendship League; vice-president, Gloucester branch, Y.M.C.A.; diocesan reader, Church of England, 1950-64. *Military service:* Pay Corps, 1940-45; became captain; awarded Certificate of Merit, made Birthday Honours List, 1945. *Member:* P.E.N., Society of Authors, Savage Club (London).

WRITINGS—Juvenile: *Merry Christmas,* Mills & Boon, 1930; *Collection of Tales for Children,* Birn, 1935; (with others) *Pamela's Pet* (stories), Birn, 1936; (with P. Megroz) *The Girls' Own Book,* Birn, 1936; *Our Friends Next Door,* Birn, 1947; *Tom Puss in Nursery Rhyme Land,* Marks & Spencer, 1948; *The Money Book,* Rockliff, 1948; *Farmyard Friends,* Birn, 1949; *Once Upon a Birthday,* Birn, 1950; *Around the Farm,* Birn, 1951; *The Book of Railways,* Birn, 1951; *The Boys' Book of Heroes,* Birn, 1951; *The Doll Dressing Books,* four volumes, Birn, 1951; *The Wild West Book,* Birn, 1952; (adapter) Charles Kingsley, *Water-Babies,* Birn, 1952; *The Girls' Book of Heroines,* Birn, 1952; *My Picture Book of Animals,* Dean, 1955; (adapter) Sir James Matthew Barrie, *Peter Pan and Wendy,* Birn, 1955; (adapter) *The Adventures of Robin Hood,* Dean, 1956; *My Picture Book of Trains,* Dean, 1956; *Marvell: The Amazing Magician,* George Newnes, 1956; *The Adventures of Dilly Duckling,* George Newnes, 1956; *Lone Ranger Adventure Stories,* Adprint, 1957; *Hopalong Cassidy Stories,* Adprint, 1957; *Champion: The Wonder Horse,* Daily Mirror, 1957; *Roy Rogers' Adventures,* Dean, Number 1, 1957, Number 2, 1958, Number 3, 1959; (adapter) Steve Frazee, *Zorro,* Daily Mirror, 1959; *Circus Boy,* Daily Mirror, 1959.

Also author of juvenile books, all published by Birn: *Little People of the Woods; Bedtime Stories; Tom Puss at the Panto; The Christmas Book; Leisure Hour Stories; School-Girl Stories; Wonders of the World.* Also author of juvenile books, all published by Dean: *Dilly Duckling Painting Book; Noah's Ark Story Book; Queen Elizabeth's Little House; Butterflies and Birds; The Four Seasons Country Book; Picture Book of Road Travel; Disneyland Pop-Up Book; Pussies and Puppies Book.* Adapter, from films by Walt Disney: *1001 Dalmations,* Dean, and *The Lady and the Tramp,* Dean.

Juvenile religious; all published by Wheaton Publishing: *The Man Who Loved God,* 1959; *The Coat of Many Colours,* 1959; *Jacob's Happy Day,* 1959; *The Baby in the Bulrushes,* 1959; *The Burning Bush,* 1959; *Moses and the Hidden Spring,* 1959; *The Promised Land,* 1959; *The Walls of Jerico,* 1959; *The Prodigal Son,* 1959; *The Child Jesus,* 1961. Also author of *My Picture Book of Prayers* (two volumes), *Dean's Picture Book of Prayers, Gold Medal Book about Jesus, My Picture Book about Jesus, Second Picture Book about Jesus.*

Junior novels: *The Kidnapped Form,* Juvenile Productions, 1938; *The Ghost of Gregory,* Lunn, 1946; *Lords of the Isle,* Art and Educational Publishers, 1947; (under pseudonym, Gordon Grimsley) *Champion,* Lunn, 1947; *The Bearded Stranger,* Lunn, 1947; *Ken of the "Courier,"* Art and Educational Publishers, 1947; *The Adventure at Marston Manor,* Lunn, 1947; *The First Term at Tenmeade,* Art and Educational Publishers, 1948; *Tenmeade and Western Priory,* Boardman, 1948; *The Scarlet Runner,* Jarrolds, 1948; *All Guns Ablaze!: A Story of Admiral Nelson,* Boardman, 1949; *The Smuggler's Secret: A Thrilling Tale of Cornwall in the Year 1870: With a Glimpse of the Days When Smugglers Held Sway,* Jarrolds, 1950; *The Phantom Frigate: A Story of the Year That Followed Trafalgar,* Boardman, 1950; *The Headland Mystery,* Collins, 1950; *John of the Fair,* Warne, 1950; *I, Elizabeth Tudor,* Burke Publishing, 1954; (adapter) *The Adventures of Sir Lancelot,* Adprint, 1958; *The Young David,* Roy, 1962.

Juvenile nonfiction: *Continent for Sale: A Story of the Louisiana Purchase,* Winston Press, 1953; *How Money Was Developed,* Routledge & Kegan Paul, 1958; *This Is the History of Money,* Archer Press, 1958; *Yellow Quiz Book,* Wheaton Publishing, 1960; *Red Quiz Book,* Wheaton Publishing, 1961; *How We Weigh and Measure,* Routledge & Kegan Paul, 1961; *Question and Answer Book,* Purnell Library Service, 1961; *Bible Quiz Book,* Pilgrim Publications, 1962; *Green Quiz Book,* Wheaton Publishing, 1962; *Blue Quiz Book,* Wheaton Publishing, 1962; *Quiz Book of Sport,* Wheaton Publishing, 1964; *How Law Is Kept,* Routledge & Kegan Paul, 1964; *One Mountain After Another,* Angus & Robertson, 1967. Also author of "Western Rangers" series, Progressive Press, 1949-64.

Adult novels; published by Progressive Press, except as indicated: The "Jack Broughton V. C." series, George Newnes, 1940; *Wheels on the Western Front,* George Newnes, 1940; *Montana Moon,* 1946; *Buck McHarty Rides Again,* 1946; *Ranch House Mystery,* 1946; *Vengeance Rides West,* 1946; *Death at the Crooked Y,* 1946; *The Grinning Skull,* 1946; *Ace High Jack,* 1946; *The Boss of the Double Diamond,* 1946; *The Sheriff of Angel County,* 1949; *The Sheriff's Badge,* Foley, 1949; (as ghost writer for Captain Freddie Guest) *Escape From the Blooded Sun,* Jarrolds, 1956.

Adult nonfiction: *Writing for Children,* A. & C. Black, 1929; (editor) Jasper Maskelyne, *Maskelyne's Book of Magic,* Harrap, 1936; *Edward the Eighth: Our King,* Allied Newspapers, 1937; *Etiquette for Everyone,* Southern Editorial Syndicate, 1946; *The Power of Public Speaking,* Vawser & Wiles, 1946; *Western Omnibus,* Coordination Press, 1949; *I Saw a Strange Land: Journeys in Central Australia,* Angus & Robertson, 1950; *His Late Majesty: King George VI,* Pitkin, 1952; (with Bella Austin) *Mother Christmas,* Parrish, 1961. Founder and author of *Buffalo Bill Wild West Annual,* 1946-51, and *Sunny Stories Annuals;* author of *Mickey Mouse Annual,* 1931-64, and *Sunny Stories Weekly Magazine,* 1953-55. Author of other annuals including *Donald Duck Annual, Gran'Pop's Annual, Pinky and Perky Annual, Bubble and Squeek Annual, Lenny the Lion Annual,* and *Brumas Annual.* Creator of Dilly and Dimple Duckling characters. Also editor of *Scouting in Europe,* George Newnes.

SIDELIGHTS: Arthur William Groom authored over four hundred books, many of which are not listed because "records of them were lost during bombing in World War II or subsequently" and because "it has been virtually impossible to keep a tag on all publications." He wrote original books based on TV Western programs, including "Range Rider," "Roy Rogers," "Cheyenne," "Circus Boy," "Frontier Circus," "Wagon Train," "Rawhide," "Champion the Wonder Horse," "Davy Crockett," "Hopalong Cassidy," "Gene Autry," "Lone Ranger," "Buffalo Bill," "Tenderfoot," "Laramie," "Klondike," "Royal Canadian Mounted Police," "Bonanza," and "Wells Fargo." He also wrote original books on the following children's literature: *Pinocchio, B'rer Rabbit, Gulliver's Travels, Water-Babies, Sleeping Beauty, Peter Pan, Snowwhite and the Seven Dwarfs, Robin Hood, Alice in Wonderland, 20,000 Leagues Under the Sea, Cinderella, Jack and the Beanstalk, The Toy Soldiers, Little Women, Sir Lancelot,* and *Sooty.* Several of his books have been adapted for television and screen.†

* * *

GROSS, Richard Edmund 1920-

PERSONAL: Born May 25, 1920, in Chicago, Ill.; son of Edmund Nicholas and Florence (Gallistel) Gross; married Jane Clare Hartl, May 25, 1943; children: Kathryn Ann, Elaine Clare, Edmund R., John R. *Education:* Attended Wright Branch of Chicago City College (now Wright College), 1938-40; University of Wisconsin, B.S., 1942, M.S., 1946; Stanford University, Ed.D., 1951. *Home:* 26304 Esperanza Dr., Los Altos Hills, Calif. 94022. *Office:* School of Education, Stanford University, Stanford, Calif. 94305.

CAREER: Central High School, Madison, Wis., teacher, 1943-48; Menlo College School of Business Administration, Menlo Park, Calif., instructor, 1948-51; Florida State University, Tallahassee, professor, 1951-55; Stanford University, Stanford, Calif., professor of education, 1955—. Lecturer, University of Wisconsin, summers, 1947 and 1955; Fulbright lecturer, University of Wales, 1961-62; visiting professor, University of Frankfurt, 1968-69, and Monash University, 1976. Curriculum consultant to school systems in eleven states and to the Ministry of Education, Santiago, Chile, 1973. Co-director, People Textual Program, Addison-Wesley Publishing Co., Inc., 1975—. *Member:* National Council for Social Studies (member of board of directors, 1957-59; vice-president, 1965; president, 1966-67), Association for Supervision and Curriculum Development, National Society for the Study of Education, American Academy of Political and Social Sciences, National Education Association, Educational Policies Commission (member of advisory board, 1961-64), Florida Council for Social Studies (founder), California Council for Social Studies (member of board of directors, 1961-67), Phi Delta Kappa, Phi Alpha Theta, Delta Tau Kappa.

WRITINGS: (With Myles Rodehaver and William Axtell) *The Sociology of the School,* Crowell, 1957; (with Lester B. Zeleny) *Educating Citizens for Democracy,* Oxford University Press, 1958; (editor) *Report of the State Central Committee on Social Studies,* California Department of Education, 1959; (editor with R. Muessig and G. Fersh and contributor) *The Problems Approach and the Social Studies,* revised edition (Gross was not associated with earlier editions), National Council for the Social Studies, 1960; (editor and contributor) *The Heritage of American Education,* Allyn & Bacon, 1962; (editor and contributor) *British Secondary Education,* Oxford University Press, 1965; (with V. Devereaux) *Civics in Action,* Harr Wagner, 1965; (with Frank McGraw) *Man's World: A Physical Geography,* Scholastic Book Services, 1966; (editor with W. McPhie and J. Fraenkel) *Teaching the Social Studies: What, Why and How,* International Textbook, 1969; (with J. Chapin and R. McHugh) *Quest for Liberty,* Field Educational Publications, 1971; (with Muessig) *Problem-Centered Social Studies Instruction,* National Council for the Social Studies, 1971; (with Chapin and M. S. Branson) *Teaching Social Studies Skills,* Little, Brown, 1971; (co-author) *The Human Experience,* Houghton, 1974; (with others) *Social Studies for Our Times,* Wiley, 1978; (co-author) *American Citizenship: How We Govern,* Addison-Wesley, 1979; (editor with David Dufty) *Learning to Live in Society: Toward a World View of the Social Studies,* Social Science Education Consortium, 1980.

Also author of numerous education pamphlets, charts, and transparencies. Editor and educational consultant, "World Affairs" multi-text series, twelve volumes, Scholastic Book Services, 1962-64. Contributor to *Encyclopedia Americana, International Encyclopedia,* and *World Book Encyclopedia of Educational Research.* Contributor of articles to professional journals, including *Social Studies, Social Education, School and Society, California Journal of Secondary Education,* and *Clearing House.* Editor, *California Social Science Review,* 1962-67.

WORK IN PROGRESS: A book comparing social studies and civic education in twenty countries.

* * *

GROSSMAN, Allen (R.) 1932-

PERSONAL: Born January 7, 1932, in Minneapolis, Minn.; son of Louis S. and Beatrice (Bernan) Grossman; children: Adam, Jonathan, Bathsheba, Lev, Austin. *Education:* Harvard University, B.A., 1955, M.A., 1957; Brandeis University, Ph.D., 1959. *Home:* 4 Jeffrey Terr., Lexington, Mass. *Office:* Department of English, Brandeis University, Waltham, Mass. 02154.

CAREER: Brandeis University, Waltham, Mass., 1967—, began as assistant professor, currently professor of English.

WRITINGS: A Harlot's Hire, Walker-de Berry, 1962; *The Recluse,* Pym-Randall, 1965; *Poetic Knowledge in the Early Yeats* (prose), University of Virginia Press, 1969; *And the Dew Lay All Night upon My Branch,* Aleph, 1973; *The Woman On the Bridge over the Chicago River,* New Directions, 1979.

BIOGRAPHICAL/CRITICAL SOURCES: Virginia Quarterly Review, autumn, 1969; *New Republic,* December, 1978.

* * *

GUEST, A(nthony) G(ordon) 1930-

PERSONAL: Born February 8, 1930, in Bristol, England; son of Gordon Walter Leslie and Marjorie (Hooper) Guest. *Education:* St. John's College, Oxford, B.A., 1954, M.A., 1957; Gray's Inn, Barrister-at-law, 1955, Bencher, 1978. *Politics:* Conservative. *Religion:* Roman Catholic. *Home:* 16 Trevor Pl., London S.W. 7, England. *Office:* King's College, University of London, Strand, London W.C.2, England.

CAREER: University College, Oxford, England, fellow and tutor, 1955-65; University of London, King's College, London, England, professor of English law, 1966—. Member of legal advisory committee, Hong Kong University, 1965; member of the Lord Chancellor's Law Reform Committee; delegate to United Nations Commission on International Trade Law. Sir Henry Strakosch Travelling Fellow to South Africa; governor of Rugby School. *Military service:* British Army, Royal Artillery, 1948-50; became lieutenant. *Member:* Garrick Club (London).

WRITINGS: (Editor) Anson, *Law of Contract,* 21st-25th editions, Oxford University Press, 1959-79; (general editor) *Oxford Essays in Jurisprudence,* Oxford University Press, 1961; (co-editor) *Chitty on Contract,* 21st-24th editions, Sweet & Maxwell, 1961-76; *The Law of Hire-Purchase,* Sweet & Maxwell, 1966; (co-editor) *Benjamin's Sale of Goods,* Sweet & Maxwell, 1974; (co-editor) *Encyclopedia of the Law of Credit and Security,* Sweet & Maxwell, 1975; (editor with Eva Lomnicka) *Introduction to the Law of Credit and Security,* Sweet & Maxwell, 1978.

* * *

GUPTA, Brijen Kishore 1929-

PERSONAL: Given name is pronounced Bri-jane; born September 17, 1929, in Ferozpur, India; son of Nawal Kishore (an engineer) and Susheela (Goyal) Gupta; married Virginia Martin (an art teacher), 1957; children: Martin, Sunita, Sheila. *Education:* Dayanand College, A.B., 1952; Yale University, A.M., 1954; University of Chicago, Ph.D., 1958. *Politics:* Independent. *Home:* 226 Idlewood Rd., Rochester, N.Y. 14618. *Office:* Council on International and Public Affairs, 60 East 42nd St., New York, N.Y. 10017.

CAREER: Southern Illinois University at Carbondale, assistant professor of Asian studies, 1958-60; Victoria University, Wellington, New Zealand, lecturer and director of program in Asian studies, 1960-63; Brooklyn College of the City University of New York, Brooklyn, N.Y., assistant professor, 1963-67, associate professor of history, 1967-70; University of Rochester, Rochester, N.Y., professor of history, 1970-76; State University of New York College at Brockport, professor of history, 1970-77; Council on International and Public Affairs, New York, N.Y., senior fellow and director of research and development, 1976—. Visiting professor at University of Cincinnati, summer, 1965, University of Hawaii, summer, 1967, Columbia University, 1968-69, and University of Rochester, 1969-70. Raja Ram Mohun Roy Lecturer, Yale University, 1975; National Endowment for the Humanities lecturer, University of Wisconsin, 1976.

AWARDS, HONORS: Overbrook fellow at Yale University, 1953-54; Foundation for World Government fellow, 1954-55; Asia Foundation fellow and University fellow at University of Chicago, 1955-58; Bharitya Itihas Parishad Prize, 1958-62, for best monograph on some aspect of eighteenth century history of India; Carnegie Fund research grant, 1961-62; Australian National University Institute of Advanced Studies, fellow, 1961-62; Sarkar Prize in Historiography of India, 1966; National Science Foundation grant, 1978-80.

WRITINGS: (Contributor) Robert K. Sakai, editor, *Studies on Asia, 1960,* University of Nebraska Press, 1960; *Sirajud-*

daullah and the East India Company, 1756-1757: Background to the Foundation of British Power in India, E. J. Brill, 1962, revised edition, 1966; (with Arjun P. Aggarwal) *Indian and American Labor Legislation and Practices: A Comparative Study,* Asia Publishing House, 1966; (editor) *India in English Fiction, 1800-1970: An Annotated Bibliography,* Scarecrow, 1973; (contributor) *Learning about India: An Annotated Guide for Nonspecialists,* New York State Education Department, 1977; (with Arthur Lopatin) *Small Business Developments in the Inner City Areas of Rochester,* Council on International and Public Affairs, 1978. Contributor, *Learning About India,* 1977. Contributor to numerous periodicals, including *Mankind, Journal of Asian Studies, English Historical Review, Middle East Journal, Journal of the National Academy of Administration, Journal of Indian History,* and *Man and World.*

WORK IN PROGRESS: Two books, *Science and Public Policy in India* (with Ward Morehouse) and *Sankara and Swedenborg: A Comparative Analysis.*

SIDELIGHTS: Brijen Kishore Gupta wrote *CA:* "All my publications examine the encounter between the West and the East (especially India). In *Sirajuddaullah,* I examined Indo-British diplomatic relations; in *Indian and American Labor Legislation,* the impact of American jurisprudence on the development of labor law in India; in *Sankara and Swedenborg,* the structure of intellectual presuppositions in Hindu and Christian theology; in *Science and Public Policy,* the transnational movement of science and technology from the United States to India; in *India in English Fiction,* the influence of a foreign language in the development of India's literary tradition. My basic thesis is that in spite of this massive encounter with the West, no convincing synthesis between the Eastern and the Western traditions has taken place, and no such synthesis seems viable."

* * *

GUTMANN, Joseph 1923-

PERSONAL: Born August 17, 1923, in Wuerzburg, Germany; came to U.S. in 1936; naturalized, 1943; son of Henry (a merchant) and Selma (Eisemann) Gutmann; married Marilyn B. Tuckman (a teacher of mathematics), October 8, 1953; children: David, Sharon. *Education:* Temple University, B.S., 1949; New York University, M.A., 1952; Hebrew Union College-Jewish Institute of Religion (Cincinnati), Ph.D., 1960. *Home:* 13151 Winchester, Huntington Woods, Mich. 48070. *Office:* Department of Art and Art History, Wayne State University, Detroit, Mich. 48202.

CAREER: Ordained rabbi, 1957. Hebrew Union College-Jewish Institute of Religion, Cincinnati, Ohio, assistant professor, 1960-65, associate professor of art history, 1965-69; Wayne State University, Detroit, Mich., professor of art and art history, 1969—. Adjunct professor, University of Cincinnati, 1961-68; Charles Friedman visiting lecturer, Antioch College, 1964. Member of board of advisors, Wayne State University Press, 1970—; adjunct curator, Detroit Institute of Arts, 1971—. Interim associate rabbi, Temple Beth El, Detroit, 1974; rabbi, Congregation Solel, Brighton, Mich., 1979—. *Military service:* U.S. Army Air Forces, 1943-46; interrogator and research analyst, U.S. Strategic Bombing Survey in Europe. *Member:* Society of Biblical Literature (chairman of art and Bible section, 1970—), World Union of Jewish Studies, Central Conference of American Rabbis, College Art Association of America, International Center of Medieval Art, Beta Gamma Sigma. *Awards, honors:* Henry Morgenthau fellowships to Israel, 1957, 1958; Memorial Foundation for Jewish Culture grants 1959, 1972; American Philosophical Society grant to Europe, 1965; Wayne State University faculty grants, 1971, 1973; American Council of Learned Societies grant, 1973.

WRITINGS: Juedische Zeremonialkunst, Ner-Tamid-Verlag, 1963, translation by Gutmann published as *Jewish Ceremonial Art,* T. Yoseloff, 1964, revised edition, 1968; *Images of the Jewish Past: An Introduction to Medieval Hebrew Miniatures,* Society of Jewish Bibliophiles, 1965; (editor and contributor) *Beauty in Holiness: Studies in Jewish Customs and Ceremonial Art,* Ktav, 1970; (editor and contributor) *No Graven Images: Studies in Art and the Hebrew Bible,* Ktav, 1971; (with Paul Pieper) *Die Darmstaedter Pessach-Haggadah,* Propylaen Verlag, 1972; (editor and contributor) *The Dura-Europos Synagogue: A Re-Evaluation,* Council on the Study of Religion, 1973; (with Stanley Chyet) *Moses Jacob Ezekiel: Memoirs from the Bath of Diocletian,* Wayne State University Press, 1975; (editor and contributor) *The Synagogue: Origins, Archaeology, and Architecture,* Ktav, 1975; (editor and contributor) *The Temple of Solomon: Archaeological Fact and Mediaeval Tradition in Christian, Islamic, and Jewish Art,* Scholars' Press, 1976; (editor and contributor) *The Image and the Word: Confrontations in Judaism, Christianity, and Islam,* Scholars' Press, 1977; *Hebrew Manuscript Painting,* Braziller, 1978; (contributor) *Danzig, 1939: Treasures of a Destroyed Community,* Wayne State University Press, 1980. Contributor of over one hundred and fifty articles, many reprinted separately, to scholarly journals.

WORK IN PROGRESS: Editing and contributing to *Ancient Synagogues: The State of Research,* for Scholars' Press.

AVOCATIONAL INTERESTS: Travel, photography, and reading.

* * *

GUTTMANN, Allen 1932-

PERSONAL: Born October 13, 1932, in Chicago, Ill.; son of Emile J. (clerk) and Jeanette (Krulewich) Guttmann; married Martha Britt Ellis, 1955 (divorced, 1972); married Doris Bargen, 1974; children: (first marriage) Johann F., Erika B. *Education:* University of Florida, B.A., 1953; Columbia University, M.A., 1956; University of Minnesota, Ph.D., 1961. *Home:* 22 Orchard St., Amherst, Mass. 01002. *Office:* Amherst College, Amherst, Mass. 01002.

CAREER: Amherst College, Amherst, Mass., instructor, 1959-62, assistant professor, 1962-66, associate professor, 1966—. *Military service:* U.S. Army, 1953-55. *Member:* American Studies Association, Modern Language Association of America, International Committee for Sport Sociology.

WRITINGS: The Wound in the Heart: America and the Spanish Civil War, Free Press, 1962; (editor with Louis Filler) *The Removal of the Cherokee Nation,* Heath, 1962; (editor) *American Neutrality and the Spanish Civil War,* Heath, 1963; (editor with Benjamin Ziegler) *Communism, the Constitution, and the Courts,* Heath, 1964; *The Conservative Tradition in America,* Oxford University Press, 1967; (contributor) Richard H. Brown and Van R. Halsey, editors, *Freedom and Authority in Puritan New England,* Addison-Wesley, 1970; *Jewish Writer in America: Assimilation and the Crisis of Identity,* Oxford University Press, 1971; (contributor) Brown and Halsey, editors, *God and Government: Problems of Church and State,* Addison-Wesley, 1972; (editor) *Korea: Cold War and Limited War,* Heath, 1972; *From Ritual to Record: The Nature of Modern Sport,* Columbia University Press, 1978.

WORK IN PROGRESS: A biography of Avery Brundage.

H

HACKER, Andrew 1929-

PERSONAL: Born August 30, 1929, in New York, N.Y.; son of Louis Morton (a professor) and Lillian (Lewis) Hacker; married Lois Wetherell (a librarian), June 17, 1955; children: Ann. *Education:* Amherst College, B.A., 1951; Oxford University, A.M., 1953; Princeton University, Ph.D., 1955. *Politics:* Republican. *Religion:* Jewish. *Home:* 20 West 64th St., New York, N.Y. 10023. *Office:* Department of Political Science, Queens College of the City University of New York, 65-30 Kissena Blvd., Flushing, N.Y. 11367.

CAREER: Cornell University, Ithaca, N.Y., instructor, 1955-56, assistant professor, 1956-61, associate professor, 1961-66, professor of government, 1966-71; Queens College of the City University of New York, Flushing, N.Y., professor, 1971—. Visiting professor, Salzburg Seminar in American Studies, Salzburg, Austria. Consultant to Fund for the Republic and National Industrial Conference Board. *Member:* American Political Science Association, American Society for Legal and Political Philosophy, Phi Beta Kappa. *Awards, honors:* Social Science Research Council fellowship, 1954-55; Ford Foundation fellowship, 1962-63.

WRITINGS: *Political Theory: Philosophy, Ideology, Science,* Macmillan, 1961; (co-author) *Social Theories of Talcott Parsons,* Prentice Hall, 1961; (co-author) *The Uses of Power,* Harcourt, 1962; *The Study of Politics,* McGraw, 1963; *Congressional Districting,* Brookings Institution, 1963; (editor) *The Corporation Take-Over,* Harper, 1964; (co-author) *Politics and Government in the United States,* Harcourt, 1965; *The End of the American Era,* Athenaeum, 1970; *The Study of Politics,* McGraw, 1973; *The New Yorkers,* Mason-Charter, 1975; *Free Enterprise in America,* Harcourt, 1977. Contributor to *Atlantic, Harper's, New York Review of Books, New York Times Magazine,* and other journals.

BIOGRAPHICAL/CRITICAL SOURCES: *New York Times Book Review,* April 19, 1964, May 31, 1970; *Commonweal,* May 29, 1964; *Time,* June 1, 1970; *Newsweek,* June 8, 1970; *National Review,* July 28, 1970; *Nation,* September 7, 1970; *Contemporary Sociology,* July, 1976.

*   *   *

HACKMAN, J(ohn) Richard 1940-

PERSONAL: Born June 14, 1940, in Joliet, Ill.; son of John E. (a pipe line engineer) and Helen (Davis) Hackman; married Mary Judith Dozier (a researcher), September 1, 1962; children: Julia Beth, Laura Diane. *Education:* MacMurray College, A.B., 1962; University of Illinois, M.A., 1965, Ph.D., 1966. *Religion:* Protestant. *Home:* Sperry Rd., Bethany, Conn. 06525. *Office:* 56 Hillhouse Ave., Yale University, New Haven, Conn. 06520.

CAREER: Yale University, New Haven, Conn., assistant professor, 1966-70, associate professor, 1971-78, professor of administrative sciences and psychology, 1978—. *Member:* American Psychological Association. *Awards, honors:* Creative Talent Award of American Institute for Research in the Behavioral Sciences, 1967; James McKeen Cattell Award of American Psychological Association, 1972.

WRITINGS: (With others) *Behavior in Organizations,* McGraw, 1974; *Perspectives on Behavior in Organizations,* McGraw, 1977; *Improving Life at Work,* Goodyear Publishing, 1977; *Managing Behavior in Organizations,* Little, Brown, 1979; *Work Redesign,* Addison-Wesley, 1980. Contributor of more than forty articles to journals.

WORK IN PROGRESS: book on the social psychology of organizations.

*   *   *

HAGEN, Everett E(inar) 1906-

PERSONAL: Born July 5, 1906, in Holloway, Minn.; son of John J. and Marthea (Moe) Hagen; married Ruth Alexander, June 4, 1937. *Education:* St. Olaf College, B.A., 1927; University of Wisconsin, M.A., 1932, Ph.D., 1941. *Residence:* Cataumet, Mass. 02534. *Office:* Center for International Studies, Massachusetts Institute of Technology, Cambridge, Mass. 02139.

CAREER: Teacher in high schools in Minnesota and Wisconsin, 1927-36; Michigan State College of Agriculture and Applied Science (now Michigan State University), East Lansing, instructor in economics, 1937-42; U.S. government, Washington, D.C., economist for National Resources Planning Board, 1942-43, Office of Strategic Services, 1943, and Federal Reserve System, 1943-45, economic adviser and chief of division of fiscal policy and program planning, Office of War Mobilization and Reconversion, 1945-46, chief fiscal analyst, Bureau of the Budget, 1946-48; University of Illinois at Urbana-Champaign, professor of economics, 1948-51; Government of Burma, Rangoon, economic adviser, 1951-

53; Massachusetts Institute of Technology, Center for International Studies, Cambridge, visiting professor, 1953-58, professor of economics, 1958-72, professor of political science, 1964-72, professor emeritus, 1972—, director of Center, 1971-72. Florence Purington Memorial Lecturer, Mt. Holyoke College, 1958-59. Economic advisor to governments of Japan, 1956, 1959-60, El Salvador, 1962-63, and Saudi Arabia, 1968—. Consultant to U.S. Council of International Chamber of Commerce, 1955. *Member:* American Economic Association, Royal Economic Society, American Academy of Arts and Sciences (fellow), Phi Beta Kappa. *Awards, honors:* Rockefeller Foundation grant, 1955-58; Guggenheim fellow, 1963-64; St. Olaf College distinguished alumni award, 1966; East-West Center fellow, 1972-73; LL.D. from University of Wisconsin, 1974.

WRITINGS: This Government of Ours, Broadway Press, 1934; *The Economic Development of Burma,* National Planning Association, 1956; *Handbook for Industry Studies,* Center for International Studies, Massachusetts Institute of Technology, 1956; (with others) *Kobe-Nagoya Expressway Survey,* Ministry of Construction, Government of Japan (Tokyo), 1956; *An Analytical Model of the Transition to Economic Growth,* Center for International Studies, Massachusetts Institute of Technology, 1957; (co-author) *The Emerging Nations,* Little, Brown, 1961; (co-author) *Development of Emerging Countries,* Brookings Institution, 1962; *On the Theory of Social Change: How Economic Growth Begins,* Dorsey, 1962; (editor) *Planning Economic Development,* Irwin, 1963; (with Stephanie T. W. White) *Great Britain: Quiet Revolution in Planning,* Syracuse University Press, 1966; *The Economics of Development,* Irwin, 1968, revised edition, 1975; (with Emile Benoit and Max F. Millikan) *Effect of Defense on Developing Economies,* Center for International Development, Massachusetts Institute of Technology, 1972. Contributor of articles to economics and social science journals.†

* * *

HAHN, Emily 1905-

PERSONAL: Born January 14, 1905, in St. Louis, Mo.; daughter of Isaac Newton and Hannah (Schoen) Hahn; married Charles Ralph Boxer, November 28, 1945; children: Carola Vecchio, Amanda. *Education:* University of Wisconsin, B.S., 1926; graduate study, Columbia University, 1928, and Oxford University, 1934-35. *Home and office:* Ringshall End, Little Gaddesden, Hertfordshire, England. *Agent:* Brandt & Brandt, 101 Park Ave., New York, N.Y. 10017.

CAREER: Deko Oil Co., St. Louis, Mo., mining engineer, 1926; courier in Santa Fe, N.M., 1927-28; Hunter College (now Hunter College of the City University of New York), New York City, instructor in geology, 1929-30; worked with Red Cross in Belgian Congo, 1930-31; writer of stories and scenarios in New York City and Hollywood, Calif. and correspondent in England, Europe, and North Africa for various newspapers, 1931-32; Customs College, Shanghai, China, instructor in English and writing, 1935-38; free-lance writer, 1938—. Instructor in English and writing, Customs College, Chungking, China, 1940; instructor, Customs University, Hong Kong, 1941. *Member:* Authors League, Overseas Press Club (New York), Womens Press Club (London), Cosmopolitan Club.

WRITINGS: Seductio ad Absurdum: The Principles and Practices of Seduction—A Beginner's Handbook, Brewer & Warren, 1930; *Beginner's Luck,* Brewer & Warren, 1931; *Congo Solo: Misadventures Two Degrees North,* Bobbs-Merrill, 1933; *With Naked Foot* (novel), Bobbs-Merrill, 1934; *Affair* (novel), Bobbs-Merrill, 1935; *Steps of the Sun* (novel), Dial, 1940; *The Soong Sisters* (biography), Doubleday, 1941, reprinted, Greenwood Press, 1970; *Mr. Pan* (short story collection), Doubleday, 1942; *China to Me: A Partial Autobiography,* Doubleday, 1944, reprinted, Da Capo Press, 1975; *Hong Kong Holiday* (autobiography), Doubleday, 1946; *Raffles of Singapore* (biography), Doubleday, 1946, reprinted, University of Malaya Press, 1968; *China A to Z* (juvenile), F. Watts, 1946; *The Picture Story of China* (juvenile), Reynal & Hitchcock, 1946; *Miss Jill* (novel), Doubleday, 1947, published as *House in Shanghai,* Fawcett, 1958; *England to Me* (autobiography), Doubleday, 1949.

A Degree of Prudery: A Biography of Fanny Burney, Doubleday, 1950; *Purple Passage* (novel), Doubleday, 1950; *Francie* (juvenile), F. Watts, 1951; *Love Conquers Nothing: A Glandular History of Civilization,* Doubleday, 1952 (published in England as *Love Conquers Nothing: A New Look at Old Romances,* Dobson, 1959), reprinted, Books for Libraries, 1971; *James Brooke of Sarawak* (biography), Arthur Barker, 1953; (with Charles Roetter and Harford Thomas) *Meet the British,* N. Neame, 1953; *Francie Again* (juvenile), F. Watts, 1953; *Mary, Queen of Scots* (juvenile), Random House, 1953.

Chiang Kai-shek: An Unauthorized Biography, Doubleday, 1955; *The First Book of India* (juvenile), F. Watts, 1955; (with Eric Hatch) *Spousery,* F. Watts, 1956; *Diamond: The Spectacular Story of Earth's Rarest Treasure and Man's Greatest Greed,* Doubleday, 1956; *Francie Comes Home* (juvenile), F. Watts, 1956; *Leonardo da Vinci* (juvenile), Random House, 1956; *Kissing Cousins* (autobiography), Doubleday, 1958; *The Tiger House Party: The Last Days of the Maharajas,* Doubleday, 1959; *Aboab: First Rabbi of the Americas* (juvenile), Farrar, Straus, 1959; *Around the World with Nellie Bly* (juvenile), Houghton, 1959.

June Finds a Way (juvenile), F. Watts, 1960; *China Only Yesterday, 1850-1950: A Century of Change,* Doubleday, 1963; *Indo,* Doubleday, 1963; *Africa to Me: Person to Person* (autobiography), Doubleday, 1964; *Romantic Rebels: An Informal History of Bohemianism in America,* Houghton, 1967; *Animal Gardens,* Doubleday, 1967 (published in England as *Zoos,* Secker & Warburg, 1968); *The Cooking of China,* Time-Life, 1968; *Recipes: Chinese Cooking,* Time-Life, 1968.

Times and Places (autobiography), Crowell, 1970; (with Barton Lidice) *Breath of God: A Book about Angels, Demons, Familiars, Elementals and Spirits,* Doubleday, 1971; *Fractured Emerald: Ireland,* Doubleday, 1971; *On the Side of the Apes,* Crowell, 1971; *Once upon a Pedestal: An Informal History of Women's Lib,* Crowell, 1974; *Lorenzo: D. H. Lawrence and the Women Who Loved Him* (biography), Lippincott, 1975; *Mabel: A Biography of Mabel Dodge Luhan,* Houghton, 1977; *Look Who's Talking! New Discoveries in Animal Communication,* Crowell, 1978. Contributor to *New Yorker* and other magazines.

SIDELIGHTS: "I have deliberately chosen the uncertain path whenever I had the chance," Emily Hahn once stated. This firm resolve to avoid the commonplace has rewarded her with what a *New York Times* interviewer characterizes as "a ground-breaking, breathtaking life in which she has thumbed her nose at convention all the way." Hahn's first run-in with convention came in the early 1920s at the University of Wisconsin, where the dean of the College of Engineering (as well as the all-male student body) strongly opposed her decision to seek a degree. In spite of such formidable obstacles, she became the first woman there to graduate as a mining engineer. Her actual career in engineering, however, was somewhat short-lived: "I worked for a firm in St. Louis and then got fed up with them. They wouldn't let me go out into the field."

Restless for a change, Hahn traveled and worked briefly in New Mexico and then headed for New York City and a teaching position at Hunter College. Still intending to be an engineer, she more or less backed into a writing career when, as she explains, "by accident I wrote a newspaper item for a reporter friend who hadn't the time. It was astonishingly easy, so I kept on writing little reportorial stories, until I sold not one, but three of them to the *New Yorker*. Even so, I thought of myself as an engineer, and continued to work at it with one hand, while writing with the other, until I suppose the balance simply shifted." Having managed to bank the $500 advance she received for her first novel (*Seductio ad Absurdum*), Hahn decided in 1930 that it was time to pursue a dream she had had for quite awhile—a trip to Africa. Arriving in the Belgian Congo, she worked in a hospital outpost for two years "to earn her keep" and lived with a tribe of Pygmies for a year.

In 1935, Hahn was hired as the *New Yorker*'s China Coast correspondent at a time when that country was suffering through the double effects of revolution and war with the Japanese. During her turbulent nine-year stay, she became a confidante of the Soong sisters (one married Sun Yat-sen, the other Chiang Kai-shek) and got to know such future notables as Mao Tse-tung, Chou En-lai, and Jomo Kenyatta. In addition, she found time for several much-talked about love affairs, including one with Sinmay Zau, an aristocratic Chinese intellectual who served as her first "cultural and political guide to China."

A subsequent liaison with Charles Boxer, a married British intelligence officer, produced a daughter, Carola. But when Hong Kong was captured by the Japanese, Boxer was imprisoned and Hahn, having avoided repatriation by claiming to be Eurasian, spent the next few years smuggling food into him and paying him "official" visits (that is, approved by the Japanese authorities) whenever she could, often accompanied by their daughter. Hahn and Carola eventually were repatriated to the United States in 1943; Boxer, on the other hand, was not released from prison until late 1945, several months after rumors of his execution had circulated in the American press—rumors which Hahn declared she did not intend to believe. Shortly after his release, while speaking to a reporter in Hong Kong, Boxer revealed that he intended to make an "honest woman" out of Hahn as soon as he returned to New York—"high time, don't you think?," he added (their daughter was then four years old). After encountering some license problems in New York State (due to the fact that Boxer had been divorced for adultery), they were married in New Haven, Conn., around Thanksgiving of 1945.

Looking back over her tumultous life, Hahn recalled the time in 1930 when she announced to an older, male teacher at Hunter College that she was resigning in order to travel and see the world. "'Be careful,' he said. I still don't know what he meant."

BIOGRAPHICAL/CRITICAL SOURCES: Book World, November 5, 1967; *New York Times Book Review*, November 19, 1967, September 21, 1975, July 16, 1978; *New York Times*, April 5, 1968, June 23, 1978; *Best Sellers*, July 1, 1971; *New Yorker*, September 29, 1975; *Saturday Review*, November 15, 1975; *Virginia Quarterly Review*, winter, 1976.

Autobiographies; all published by Doubleday, except as indicated: *China to Me: A Partial Autobiography*, 1944, reprinted, Da Capo Press, 1975; *Hong Kong Holiday*, 1946; *England to Me*, 1949; *Kissing Cousins*, 1958; *Africa to Me: Person to Person*, 1964; *Times and Places*, Crowell, 1970.

* * *

HAINING, Peter 1940-

PERSONAL: Born April 2, 1940, in Enfield, Middlesex, England; son of William (a manager) and Joan (Pattrick) Haining; married Philippa Waring, October 2, 1965; children: Richard, Sean, Gemma. *Education:* Educated in Buckhurst Hill, England. *Home:* Peyton House, Butcher's Lane, Boxford, Suffolk, England.

CAREER: Journalist and magazine writer, 1957-63; New English Library, London, England, 1963-72, began as editor, became senior editor, then editorial director; editorial consultant, writer, and anthologist, 1972—. *Member:* International P.E.N., British Film Institute.

WRITINGS: (With Arthur V. Sellwood) *Devil Worship in Britain*, Transworld Publishers, 1964; *Holiday Guide to the Channel Islands*, New English Library, 1966, revised edition, 1974; *Witchcraft and Black Magic*, Hamlyn, 1971, Ballantine, 1972; *The Warlock's Book: Secrets of Black Magic from the Ancient Grimoires*, University Books, 1972; *The Hero*, New English Library, 1973; *Ghosts: The Illustrated History*, Sidgwick & Jackson, 1974, Macmillan, 1975; *The Fortune Hunter's Guidebook*, Sidgwick & Jackson, 1975; *An Illustrated History of Witchcraft*, New English Library, 1975, Pyramid Books, 1976; *The Great English Earthquake*, R. Hale, 1976; *The Compleat Birdman: A History of Man-Powered Flight*, St. Martin's, 1976; *The Monster Trap and Other True Stories*, Armada Books, 1976; *Terror! A History of Horror Illustrations from the Pulp Magazines*, Souvenir Press, 1976; *Ancient Mysteries*, Taplinger, 1977; *The Legend and Bizarre Crimes of Spring Heeled Jack*, Muller, 1977; *The Restless Bones and Other True Mysteries*, Armada Books, 1978; *Mystery! An Illustrated History of Crime and Detective Fiction*, Souvenir Press, 1978; *The Mystery and Horrible Murders of Sweeney Todd*, Muller, 1978; *Movable Books: An Illustrated History*, New English Library, 1979.

Editor or compiler: *The Hell of Mirrors*, New English Library, 1964, published as *Everyman's Book of Classic Horror Stories*, Dutton, 1976; *Summoned from the Tomb*, Digit Books, 1966; *Beyond the Curtain of Dark*, New English Library, 1966, Pinnacle Books, 1972; *Where Nightmares Are*, Mayflower Books, 1966; *The Craft of Terror: Extracts from the Rare and Infamous Gothic 'Horror' Novels*, New English Library, 1966; (and author of introduction) *The Gentlewomen of Evil: An Anthology of Rare Supernatural Stories from the Pens of Victorian Ladies*, Taplinger, 1967; *The Evil People: Being Thirteen Strange and Terrible Accounts of Witchcraft, Black Magic and Voo-doo*, Frewin, 1968; *Dr. Caligari's Black Book: An Excursion into the Macabre, in Thirteen Acts*, W. H. Allen, 1968; *The Future Makers: A Selection of Science Fiction from Brian Aldiss [and Others]*, Sidgwick & Jackson, 1968; *The Midnight People: Being Eighteen Terrifying and Bizarre Tales of Vampires*, Frewin, 1968, published as *Vampires at Midnight: Seventeen Brilliant and Chilling Tales of the Ghastly Bloodsucking Undead*, Grosset, 1970; *The Witchcraft Reader*, Dobson, 1969, Doubleday, 1970; *The Satanists*, Neville Spearman, 1969, Taplinger, 1970; *The Unspeakable People: Being Twenty of the World's Most Horrible Horror Stories*, Frewin, 1969.

The Freak Show: Tales of Fantasy and Horror, Rapp & Whiting, 1970, published as *The Freak Show: Freaks, Monsters, Ghouls, Etc.,* Thomas Nelson, 1972; *The Hollywood Nightmare: Tales of Fantasy and Horror from the Film World,* Macdonald, 1970, Taplinger, 1971; *A Thousand Afternoons,* Cowles, 1970 (published in England with introduction and preface by Haining as *A Thousand Afternoons: An Anthology of Bullfighting,* P. Owen, 1970); *The Wild Night Company: Irish Stories of Fantasy and Horror,* Gollancz, 1970, Taplinger, 1971; *A Circle of Witches: An Anthology of Victorian Witchcraft Stories,* Taplinger, 1971; *The Clans of Darkness: Scottish Stories of Fantasy and Horror,* Taplinger, 1971; *The Ghouls,* Stein & Day, 1971; *The Necromancers: The Best of Black Magic and Witchcraft,* Hodder & Stoughton, 1971, Morrow, 1972; *Gothic Tales of Terror: Classic Horror Stories from Great Britain, Europe, and the United States, 1765-1840,* Taplinger, 1972 (published in England as *Great British Tales of Terror: Gothic Stories of Horror and Romance, 1765-1840,* Gollancz, 1972); *The Magicians: Occult Stories,* P. Owen, 1972, published as *The Magicians: The Occult in Fact and Fiction,* Taplinger, 1973; *The Lucifer Society: Macabre Tales by Great Modern Writers,* Taplinger, 1972 (published in England as *The Lucifer Society,* W. H. Allen, 1972); *The Anatomy of Witchcraft,* Taplinger, 1972; *The Dream Machines: An Eyewitness History of Ballooning,* New English Library, 1972, World Publishing, 1973; *Eurotunnel: An Illustrated History of the Channel Tunnel Scheme,* New English Library, 1972; *Nightfrights: Occult Stories for All Ages,* Gollancz, 1972, Taplinger, 1973; *The Nightmare Reader,* Doubleday, 1973; *The Graveyard Wit: The Humour of the Tombstone,* Frank Graham, 1973; *The Sherlock Holmes Scrapbook,* New English Library, 1973, Crown, 1974; *The Witchcraft Papers,* University Books, 1974; *The Magic Valley Travellers: Welsh Stories of Fantasy and Horror,* Taplinger, 1974; *The Monster Makers: Creators and Creations of Fantasy and Horror,* Taplinger, 1974; *Christopher Lee's New Chamber of Horrors,* Souvenir Press, 1974.

The Hashish Club: An Anthology of Drug Literature, Humanities, 1975, Volume I: *Founding of the Modern Tradition,* Volume II: *Psychedelic Era; The Ancient Mysteries Reader; The Penny Dreadful,* Gollancz, 1975; *The Fantastic Pulps,* Gollancz, 1975, St. Martin's, 1976; *The Ghost's Companion,* Gollancz, 1975, Taplinger, 1976; *The Black Magic Omnibus,* Robson Books, 1975, Taplinger, 1976; *Weird Tales: A Facsimile Edition,* Neville Spearman, 1976; *First Book of Unknown Tales of Horror,* Sidgwick & Jackson, 1976; *The Dracula Scrapbook,* Brandon House, 1976; *Peter Cushing's Tales of a Monster Hunter,* Arthur Barker, 1977; *Deadly Nightshade,* Gollancz, 1977, Taplinger, 1978; *The Edgar Allen Poe Scrapbook,* New English Library, 1977, Schocken, 1978; *Second Book of Unknown Tales of Horror,* Sidgwick & Jackson, 1978; *The H. G. Wells Scrapbook,* Crown, 1978; *The Jules Verne Companion,* Souvenir Press, 1978; *The Shilling Shockers: Stories of Terror from the Gothic Bluebooks,* Gollancz, 1978, St. Martin's, 1979; *Classic Horror Omnibus,* New English Library, 1979; *Third Book of Unknown Tales of Horror,* Sidgwick & Jackson, 1980.

WORK IN PROGRESS: Superstitions: An Illustrated History; Blood and Thunder: An Illustrated History of the First Superheroes; The Man Who Was Frankenstein, the story of an obscure Somerset scientist upon whom was based the literary character; further anthologies and stories of mystery.

SIDELIGHTS: Peter Haining told *CA:* "My interest in the macabre was prompted by seeing a television production of 'Dr. Jekyll and Mr. Hyde' when still a small child and being almost frightened to death! It also fired my interest in macabre fiction. As a journalist I came into contact with witchcraft and black magic, and this led to my first book, *Devil Worship in Britain.* Other books on the subject even resulted in my being 'cursed' by a group of Devil Worshippers in London. My ancestors lived in the lowlands of Scotland, and one of my works, *The Warlock's Book,* is based on records I discovered about a female ancestor who was burned at the stake for possessing a 'book of spells.' Over the years I have assembled a large library of books in both fact and fiction on all aspects of the supernatural and the occult and I draw on this in my work which has been published now in over a dozen languages."

AVOCATIONAL INTERESTS: Rare books, football.

* * *

HALE, Arlene 1924-
(Louise Christopher, Gail Everett, Will Kirkland, Mary Anne Tate, Lynn Williams)

PERSONAL: Born June 16, 1924, in New London, Iowa; daughter of Ira Tate and Florence (Hand) Hale. *Education:* Attended New London schools, and Burlington College of Commerce. *Religion:* Methodist. *Home and office:* 206 North Walnut, New London, Iowa. 52645.

CAREER: Silas Mason Co., Burlington, Iowa, typist, 1941-43; Burlington Instrument Company, Burlington, assembly, 1943-47; Iowa-Illinois Telephone Co., New London, Iowa, accounting clerk, 1947-52; Sylvania Electric Co., Burlington, office clerk, 1952-54; free-lance writer, 1954—. *Member:* Authors Guild, Authors League of America, Mystery Writers of America.

WRITINGS—All published by Bouregy, except as indicated: *The Reluctant Heart,* 1958; *Tender Harvest,* 1959; *Blossoms in the Wind,* Winston, 1959; *Reluctant Stranger,* 1960; *School Nurse,* 1960; *Be My Love,* 1961; *Dr. Myra Comes Home,* 1962; *Listen to Your Heart,* Messner, 1962; *Ghost Town's Secret,* Abelard, 1962; *The Hungry Heart,* 1962; *Wait for Love,* 1963; *The Girl from Sherman Oaks,* 1964; *Nurse Shelley Decides,* Pyramid, 1964; *Nothing but a Stranger,* Four Winds Press, 1966; *Stay with Me, Love,* Banner Books, 1967; *The Lady Is a Nurse,* 1967; *Private Nurse,* Belmont-Tower, 1968; *Nurse in Residence,* 1968; *The Bend of the River,* Banner Books, 1968; *Whistle Stop Nurse,* Lancer Books, 1968; *Stranger on the Beach,* 1969; *A Happy Ending,* 1969; *Nurse Rogers' Discovery,* 1969; *Share Your Heart,* 1970; (under pseudonym Will Kirkland) *Trouble on the Rimrock,* 1973.

All published by Ace: *Leave It to Nurse Kathy,* 1963; *Dude Ranch Nurse,* 1963; *Symptoms of Love,* 1964; *Nurse Marcie's Island,* 1964; *Nurse Connor Comes Home,* 1964; *Nurse on the Run,* 1965; *Disaster Area Nurse,* 1965; *Private Duty Nurse,* 1965; *Nurse on Leave,* 1965; *Chicago Nurse,* 1965; *Camp Nurse,* 1966; *Emergency for Nurse Selena,* 1966; *Mountain Nurse,* 1966; *Community Nurse,* 1967; *Nurse on the Beach,* 1967; *Lake Resort Nurse,* 1967; *Doctor's Daughter,* 1967; *University Nurse,* 1967; *Emergency Call,* 1968; *Doctor Barry's Nurse,* 1968; *Crossroads for Nurse Cathy,* 1969; *Nurse Jean's Strange Case,* 1970; *Walk Softly, Doctor,* 1971; *The Nurse from Mulberry Square,* 1972; *The Disobedient Nurse,* 1975; *Nurse from the Shadows,* 1975; *Frightened Nurse,* 1975; *Nurse Julia's Tangled Loves,* 1976; *Nurse Lora's Love,* 1977; *Nurse Jan's Troubled Loves,* 1978.

All published by Dell: (Under pseudonym Louise Christopher) *Robin West: Nurse's Aid,* 1963; (under pseudonym Louise Christopher) *Robin West: Freshman Nurse,* 1964; *A Nurse for Sand Castle,* 1969; *Private Hospital,* 1970; *Orphanage Nurse,* 1970; *Holiday to Fear,* 1970; *The New Nurses,* 1970; *Special Duty,* 1970; *Executive Nurse,* 1971; *The Secret Longing,* 1971; *Dark Flames,* 1971; *The Shining Mountain,* 1972; *The Reunion,* 1972; *Perilous Weekend,* 1975; *Dangerous Yesterdays,* 1975; *Midnight Nightmares,* 1975; *The Divided Heart,* 1975.

All published by Little, Brown: *When Love Returns,* 1970; *The Season of Love,* 1971; *The Runaway Heart,* 1971; *A Time for Us,* 1972; *Promise of Tomorrow,* 1972; *Goodbye to Yesterday,* 1973; *Where the Heart Is,* 1974; *Home to the Valley,* 1974; *A Glimpse of Paradise,* 1975; *One More Bridge to Cross,* 1975; *The Other Side of the World,* 1976; *The Winds of Summer,* 1976; *Island of Mystery,* 1977.

All published by New American Library: *The Heart Remembers,* 1975; *In Love's Own Fashion,* 1976; *The Stormy Sea of Love,* 1976; *Love's Destiny,* 1976; *Legacy of Love,* 1977; *A Vote for Love,* 1977; *Lovers' Reunion,* 1977; *Gateway to Love,* 1977.

Under pseudonym Gail Everett; all published by Bouregy, except as indicated: *Love Is the Winner,* 1960; *Love of Laura,* 1961; *Search for Love,* 1962; *Teach Me to Love,* 1962; *Designs on Love,* 1963; *Journey for a Nurse,* Ace, 1966; *When Summer Ends,* 1968; *My Favorite Nurse,* Ace, 1968; *The Way to the Heart,* 1970.

Under pseudonym Lynn Williams; all published by Dell: *Once upon a Nightmare,* 1971; *Lake of the Wind,* 1971; *Where Is Jane?,* 1972; *Shadows over Seascape,* 1972; *Picture Her Missing,* 1973; *Rendezvous with Danger,* 1973; *Secret of Hedges Hall,* 1973; *Threads of Intrigue,* 1973; *Medley of Mystery,* 1974; *Stranger at the Gate,* 1975; *Walk a Dark Road,* 1975.

SIDELIGHTS: Although traveling is one of her main interests, Arlene Hale has always lived in the rural community of New London, Iowa. Regarding her writing career, she told *CA,* "My interest in writing began with song lyrics, progressed to poetry, then to short stories, and finally to books." Hale has sold about 600 items, "mostly short stories slanted for the juvenile field." *Avocational interests:* Reading, fishing, movies, and music.

BIBLIOGRAPHICAL/CRITICAL SOURCES: Best Sellers, October 5, 1970.

* * *

HALL, James B(yron) 1918-

PERSONAL: Born July 21, 1918, in Midland, Ohio; son of Harry and Florence (Moon) Hall; married Elizabeth Cushman, February 14, 1946; children: Elinor, Prudence, Kathryn, Millicent, James M. *Education:* Attended Miami University, Oxford, Ohio, 1938-39, and University of Hawaii, 1938-40; University of Iowa, B.A., 1947, M.A., 1948, Ph.D., 1953; graduate study, Kenyon College, summers, 1948-49. *Politics:* Democrat. *Home:* 31 Hollins Dr., Santa Cruz, Calif. 95060. *Agent:* Gerard McCauley Agency, Inc., Suite I-E, 209 East 56th St., New York, N.Y. 10022. *Office:* Room 209, College V, University of California, Santa Cruz, Calif. 95060.

CAREER: Held various jobs, including a farm worker, merchant seaman, and soldier, 1936-45; Cornell University, Ithaca, N.Y., instructor, 1951-53; University of Oregon, Eugene, associate professor, 1953-60, professor of English, 1960-65; University of California, Irvine, professor of English, director of creative writing section, and chairman of creative writing committee, 1965-69; University of California, Santa Cruz, founding provost of arts college, 1969-75, professor of literature and writer-in-residence, 1975—. Visiting writer-in-residence, Miami University, 1948-49, Women's College of the University of North Carolina (now University of North Carolina at Greensboro), 1954, University of British Columbia, 1955, University of Colorado, 1963, and Kansas State University, 1978. University of Oregon Summer Academy of Contemporary Arts, founder, 1959, currently consultant; cultural specialist, U.S. Department of State, 1964. Editorial consultant, Doubleday & Co., Inc., 1962-65; president, Associated Writing Programs, 1975-76. *Military service:* U.S. Army, Parachute Infantry, Anti-Aircraft, and military government in Germany, 1941-46; became chief warrant officer. *Member:* Modern Language Association of America, American Association of University Professors, Pacific Coast Philological Society. *Awards, honors:* Octave Thanet Prize, 1950; writer-in-residence, Yaddo, 1952; Rockefeller grant, 1955; Oregon State Poetry Prize, 1957, for "The Tortoise"; Emily Clark Balch Fiction Prize, 1967; Chapelbrook Award, 1967.

WRITINGS: Not by the Door (novel), Random House, 1954; (editor with Joseph Langland) *The Short Story,* Macmillan, 1956; *TNT for Two* (novel), Ace, 1956; (with R. V. Cassill and Herbert Gold) *Fifteen by Three* (short stories), New Directions, 1957; *Racers to the Sun* (novel), Obolensky, 1960; *Us He Devours* (short stories), New Directions, 1964; (editor) *The Realm of Fiction: Sixty-One Short Stories,* McGraw, 1965, 3rd edition (with wife, Elizabeth C. Hall) published as *The Realm of Fiction: Seventy-Four Short Stories,* 1977; (editor with Barry Ulanov) *Modern Culture and the Arts,* McGraw, 1967, 2nd edition, 1972; *Mayo Sergeant* (novel), New American Library, 1967; *The Hunt Within* (poems), Louisiana State University Press, 1973; (with others) *Women: Portraits,* McGraw, 1976; *Minor Whites: Rites and Passages,* Aperture, 1978; *Her Name,* Pentagram, 1979.

Work represented in anthologies, including *Best American Short Stories,* edited by Martha Foley, Houghton, 1949, 1952, 1953, and 1954, *Poems from the Iowa Poetry Workshop,* Prairie Press, 1951, *Prize Stories: The O. Henry Awards,* Doubleday, 1951 and 1954, *Oregon Signatures,* edited by R. D. Brown, Binfords, 1959, *Midland Anthology,* edited by Paul Engle, Random House, 1961, and *A Country of the Mind,* edited by Ray B. West, Jr., Angel Island Publications, 1962. Contributor to *Collier's Encyclopedia.* Contributor of poems to journals, including *Sewanee Review, Poetry,* and *Western Review;* contributor of short stories and articles to *Esquire, Harper's Bazaar, Epoch, San Francisco Review, Los Angeles Times,* and other magazines, newspapers, and literary reviews. *Northwest Review,* co-founder, faculty advisor, 1957-60, advisory editor, 1965-69.

WORK IN PROGRESS: A novel.

SIDELIGHTS: Commenting on James B. Hall's novel, *Mayo Sergeant,* a reviewer in *Best Sellers* writes: "We have [here] an attempt to present a detailed character-study of a man without a conscience whose driving force is the desire for financial success and status. . . . [The author] writes of a milieu and people he appears to know well—the more or less idle rich of the American Far West. . . . In seeking to present a central character who lives and is fully believable, however, he succeeds less well. . . . All in all, [though,] this is a novel competently plotted and written that offers some interestingly ironic commentaries upon America past and present."

Wirt Williams of the *Kenyon Review* is somewhat more generous in his praise: "*Mayo Sergeant* is involved with a perdurable—the American dream—but James B. Hall has given it a sharp and shiny new minting. It is the Southern California dream now. . . . Deliberately, I think, the novel invokes *The Great Gatsby*, and sets itself up as a kind of counterpoint to it. . . . [It] is carefully planned, skilfully and passionately executed in both thematic and mythic aspects. However, one of its most impressive excellences is the detailed accuracy and richness of its naturalistic surfaces. . . . Beyond question, [Hall] is one of our really fine fiction writers."

A Virginia Quarterly Review critic, however, writes: "In treating seriously what is patently a comic matter [Hall] . . . has unintentionally travestied the gaudy, tinseled aspects of life in Southern California. . . . The novel itself, viewed objectively, is a competently organized, moderately interesting work, marred technically by unpredictable shifts in the point of view between narrator and the author himself." Martin Levin of the *New York Times Book Review* cites a lack of true drama and an inability to sympathize with the narrator ("a bitter Native Son" and "elegiac observer") against Mayo Sergeant ("a flint-hearted opportunist") as the book's major flaws. He concludes: "The blue-water environment Mr. Hall constructs is more commanding than the events that transpire there."

AVOCATIONAL INTERESTS: Golf.

BIOGRAPHICAL/CRITICAL SOURCES: New York Times Book Review, October 15, 1967; *Best Sellers*, November 11, 1967; *Virginia Quarterly Review*, winter, 1968; *Kenyon Review*, June 1, 1968.

* * *

HALL, R(obert) Cargill 1937-

PERSONAL: Born January 17, 1937, in Rochester, Minn.; son of Byron E. (a physician) and Elizabeth (Cargill) Hall; married Beverly Chichester, May 2, 1958; children: R. Cargill, Jr., Melanie Anne, Bradshaw Chichester. *Education:* Attended Escola Brasileira de Administracao Publica, 1957; Whitman College, B.A., 1959; San Jose State College (now University), M.A., 1966. *Politics:* Democrat. *Religion:* Roman Catholic. *Office:* Headquarters MAC(HO), Scott Air Force Base, Belleville, Ill. 62225.

CAREER: Lockheed Missiles and Space Co., Sunnyvale, Calif., assistant historian, 1960-66, historian, 1966-67; California Institute of Technology, Jet Propulsion Laboratory, Pasadena, historian, 1967-77; U.S. Air Force, Strategic Air Command Headquarters, Offutt Air Force Base, Omaha, Neb., historian, 1977-80; Military Airlift Command Headquarters, Scott Air Force Base, Belleville, Ill., historian, 1980—. *Member:* International Academy of Astronautics (corresponding member), American Institute of Aeronautics and Astronautics, International Institute of Space Law (member of executive committee, Association of U.S. Members of IISL), American Society of International Law. *Awards, honors:* Robert H. Goddard Historical Essay Trophy of National Space Club, 1962, 1963; named one of outstanding young men of America, U.S. Junior Chamber of Commerce, 1968.

WRITINGS: (Contributor) E. M. Emme, editor, *The History of Rocket Technology*, Wayne State University Press, 1964; *Project Ranger: A Chronology*, U.S. Government Printing Office, 1971; *Lunar Impact: A History of Project Ranger*, U.S. Government Printing Office, 1977; (editor) *Essays on the History of Rocketry and Astronautics*, U.S. Government Printing Office, 1977. Contributor to *American Journal of International Law, Airpower Historian, Air University Review*, and other journals.

WORK IN PROGRESS: A history of the first Air Force supersonic bombers, tentatively entitled *Hustler: A History of the B-58 Bomber*.

* * *

HALLIWELL, Leslie 1929-

PERSONAL: Born February 23, 1929, in Bolton, Lancashire, England; son of James and Lily (Haslam) Halliwell; married Ruth Porter, July 11, 1958. *Education:* St. Catharine's College, Cambridge, M.A., 1955. *Politics:* Conservative. *Religion:* Church of England. *Home:* 26 Atwood Ave., Richmond, Surrey, England. *Office:* Granada TV, 36 Golden Square, London W.1, England.

CAREER: Picturegoer, London, England, columnist, 1952; Rex (specialized movie theatre), Cambridge, England, manager, 1953-56; Rank Organization, London, film publicist, 1956-58; Granada TV, London, television film buyer, 1958—. Member of television and general selection committees, National Film Archive, 1967—; program buyer, ITV, 1968—.

WRITINGS: "Make Your Own Bed" (three-act play), first produced in Bolton, England at Hippodrome Theatre, 1957; "A Night on the Island" (three-act play), first produced in Bristol, England at Bristol Little Theatre, 1959; *The Filmgoers Companion*, with foreword by Alfred Hitchcock, MacGibbon, 1965, Hill & Wang, 1966, 6th revised edition, Hill & Wang, 1978; *The Filmgoers Book of Quotes*, Hart-Davis, 1973, Arlington House, 1974; *The Clapperboard Book of the Cinema*, Hart-Davis, 1974; *Mountain of Dreams: The Golden Years of Paramount Pictures*, Hart-Davis, 1977, Stonehill Publishing, 1978; *Halliwell's Film Guide*, Granada, 1977, Scribner, 1978, 2nd edition, Granada, 1979; *Halliwell's Movie Quiz*, Everest Books, 1977, Penguin, 1978; *Halliwell's Teleguide*, Granada, 1979. Also author of a play, "Let's Be Friends."

WORK IN PROGRESS: The Filmgoers Bedside Book; Supernatural, ghost stories; *Return to Shangri-la*, a novel; "Living on Velvet," a play; *Halliwell's Moving Picture Show*.

AVOCATIONAL INTERESTS: Driving in the countryside, especially in America, collecting buddhas.

* * *

HALPERIN, Samuel 1930-

PERSONAL: Born May 10, 1930, in Chicago, Ill.; son of Herman and Bertha (Kleban) Halperin; married Marlene Epstein, 1954; children: Elan, Deena. *Education:* Attended Illinois Institute of Technology, 1948-49; Washington University, St. Louis, Mo., A.B., A.M., Ph.D., 1956; Columbia University, graduate study, 1954. *Home:* 3041 Normanstone Ter. N.W., Washington, D.C. 20008. *Office:* Institute for Educational Leadership, George Washington University, 1001 Connecticut Ave. N.W., Washington, D.C. 20036.

CAREER: Wayne State University, Detroit, Mich., assistant professor of political science, 1956-60; U.S. Office of Education, Washington, D.C., legislative specialist, 1961-63, director of legislative services branch, 1963-64, assistant commissioner of education and director of Office of Legislation and Congressional Relations, 1964-66; U.S. Department of Health, Education, and Welfare, Washington, D.C., deputy assistant secretary for legislation, 1966-69; George Washington University, Washington, D.C., director of educational staff seminar, 1969-74, director of Institute for Educational Leadership, 1974—. Professorial lecturer, American University, 1962-63; adjunct professor, Teachers College, Columbia University, 1966-68; lecturer in educational policy, Institute of Policy Sciences and Public Affairs, Duke University, 1974-75; guest lecturer, Harvard University, University of California, Berkeley, Ohio State University, Claremont College, Yale University, Boston University, University of Nebraska, University of North Carolina, and Washington University. Research assistant to U.S. House of Representatives committee on education and labor, 1960-61; consultant, U.S. Senate subcommittee on education, 1961, and subcommittee on reorganization, research, and international organizations, 1970-73; consultant, Carnegie Commission on Higher Education, 1961, and White House Conference on Education, 1965. Member of review panels of various public and private educational research centers; member of national advisory boards of several organizations, including National Student Educational Fund, American Jewish Committee, National School Volunteer Program, and National Identification Program for the Advancement of Women in Higher Education Administration. Lecturer. *Military service:* U.S. Army, 1950.

MEMBER: American Political Science Association, Citizenship Clearing House, Western Political Science Association, Midwest Conference of Political Scientists, Phi Beta Kappa, Pi Sigma Alpha (president), Alpha Phi Omega, Pershing Rifles. *Awards, honors:* Weizmann Archives research fellow, 1958; AFL-CIO research award, 1960; American Political Science Association Congressional fellow, 1961-62; U.S. Department of Health, Education, and Welfare Superior Service Awards, 1964 and 1967, and Distinguished Service Award, 1968; National Association for Public School Adult Education Award of Merit, 1966; Alfred N. Whitehead fellow, Harvard University, 1969; National Association of State Boards of Education Distinguished Service Award, 1977.

WRITINGS: A University in the Web of Politics, Holt, 1960; *The Political World of American Zionism,* Wayne State University Press, 1961; *Essays on Federal Education Policy,* Institute for Educational Leadership, 1975; (co-editor and contributor) *Perspectives on Federal Educational Policy,* Institute for Educational Leadership, 1976; (co-editor and contributor) *Federalism at the Crossroads: Improving Educational Policymaking,* Institute for Educational Leadership, 1976. Contributor of chapters to books and of articles to encyclopedias; contributor of over seventy articles and reviews to education and political science journals. Consultant, *Change;* member of advisory board, *Journal of Multi-Cultural Education.*

* * *

HANCOCK, Edward L(eslie) 1930-

PERSONAL: Born May 26, 1930, in Reno, Nev.; son of John Leslie and Josephine (Rieman) Hancock; married Sheila Gibney (a teacher), June 25, 1967; children: Christopher, Garth, Leslie. *Education:* University of Nevada, B.A., 1954; University of Chicago, M.A., 1958. *Home:* 4830 Eisan Ave., Reno, Nev. 89506. *Office:* Department of English, Truckee Meadows Community College, Sun Valley, Nev.

CAREER: University of Nevada, Reno, instructor in English, 1965-74; Truckee Meadows Community College, Sun Valley, Nev., chairman of English department, 1974—. *Member:* American Association of University Professors. *Awards, honors:* National Endowment for the Humanities fellowship, 1976-77.

WRITINGS: Techniques for Understanding Literature: A Handbook for Readers and Writers, Wadsworth, 1972; *Connections,* Harcourt, 1974; *The New Student,* National Council of Teachers of English, 1979.

* * *

HANCOCK, Sibyl 1940-

PERSONAL: Born November 10, 1940, in Pasadena, Tex.; daughter of Briten E. (a department manager for Shell Oil Co.) and Floreine (Fisher) Norwood; married Thomas L. Hancock (a school administrator), August 21 1965; children: Kevin Thomas. *Education:* Attended Sam Houston State University, 1959-61, and University of Houston, 1963-65. *Religion:* Methodist. *Home:* 210 Coronation, Houston, Tex. 77034.

CAREER: Free-lance writer. Stenographer, Ellington Air Force Base, 1962. *Member:* National Writers Club, Society of Children's Book Writers (charter member), Associated Authors of Children's Literature (charter member), Pasadena Writers Club (president, 1966, 1973), Houston Writers Workshop, Friends of the Pasadena Public Library (vice-president, 1973). *Awards, honors:* First prize for best children's book, Texas Pen Women, 1970, for *Let's Learn Hawaiian.*

WRITINGS—Juveniles, except as indicated: (With Doris Sadler) *Let's Learn Hawaiian,* Tuttle, 1969; *Mario's Mystery Machine,* Putnam, 1972; *Mosshaven* (adult gothic novel), Beagle Books, 1973; *The Grizzly Bear,* Steck, 1974; *The Blazing Hills,* Putnam, 1975; *An Ark and a Rainbow,* Concordia, 1976; *Climbing Up to Nowhere,* Concordia, 1977; *Bill Pickett,* Harcourt, 1977; *Theodore Roosevelt,* Putnam, 1978; *Freaky Francie,* Prentice-Hall, 1979; *Famous Firsts of Black Americans,* Pelican, in press; *Old Blue,* Putnam, in press. Contributor to *Texas Star, Humpty Dumpty,* and *Kidstuff.* Juvenile book critic for *Houston Chronicle,* 1973-75, and for a Houston, Texas TV program, 1975—.

WORK IN PROGRESS: A picture book.

SIDELIGHTS: Sibyl Hancock told *CA:* "I find writing for children challenging. It is great fun to uncover interesting stories which have been almost overlooked by history and turn them into books for young readers." *Avocational interests:* Collecting old children's books, reading, astronomy.

* * *

HANEY, Lynn 1941-

PERSONAL: Born February 12, 1941; daughter of John J. (a civil servant) and Kay (a teacher) Haney. *Education:* University of Pittsburgh, B.A., 1963; Sorbonne, University of Paris, graduate study, 1963-64. *Politics:* Democrat. *Home:* 12 Trumbull St., Stonington, Conn. 06378. *Office:* P.O. Box 145, Stonington, Conn. 06378.

CAREER: Christian Dior (fashion design firm), Paris, France, interpreter, 1965-66; National Endowment for the Arts, Washington, D.C., member of public relations staff, 1966-68; *New York Times,* New York, N.Y., news assistant, 1969-73; writer, 1973—. *Member:* Authors Guild, Dramatists Guild, American Civil Liberties Union. *Awards, honors:* Publishers merit award from *New York Times,* for article on plastic surgery.

WRITINGS: The Lady Is a Jock, Dodd, 1973; (with Mason Reese) *The Memoirs of Mason Reese: In Cahoots with Lynn*

Haney, Dodd, 1974; *Ride'em Cowgirl!,* Putnam, 1975; *Chris Evert: The Young Champion,* Putnam, 1977; *Perfect Balance: The Story of an Elite Gymnast,* Putnam, 1979.

WORK IN PROGRESS: Naked at the Feast, a biography of Josephine Baker; *I Am a Dancer.*

AVOCATIONAL INTERESTS: Skiing, sailing, scuba diving.

* * *

HANLEY, Thomas O'Brien 1918-

PERSONAL: Born June 8, 1918, in Washington, D.C.; son of James Hugh and Mary J. (O'Brien) Hanley. *Education:* St. Louis University, A.B., 1941, S.T.B., 1954; Marquette University, M.A., 1955; Georgetown University, Ph.D., 1961. *Home:* 4501 North Charles, Baltimore, Md. 21210. *Office:* Department of History, Loyola College, Baltimore, Md. 21210.

CAREER: Historical Bulletin, St. Louis, Mo., business manager, 1944-46; St. Louis University High School, St. Louis, instructor, 1946-49; ordained Roman Catholic priest of Society of Jesus (Jesuits), 1952; Creighton University, lecturer in history, Omaha, Neb., 1955-56; Marquette University, Milwaukee, Wis., 1956-69, began as instructor, became associate professor of history; Catholic University of America, Washington, D.C., editor, John Carroll Papers, 1969-73; Loyola College, Baltimore, Md., adjunct professor of history, 1973—. Visiting associate professor, Loyola College, 1967-68, and Loyola University, Chicago, 1968-69; lecturer at Johns Hopkins University and St. Mary's Seminary and University. *Member:* American Historical Association, American Society of Church History, American Catholic Historical Association, Maryland Historical Society. *Awards, honors:* American Philosophical Society grants, 1963 and 1967; Good Citizen Medal, Sons of the American Revolution.

WRITINGS: Their Rights and Liberties, Newman, 1959; *Charles Carroll of Carrollton: The Making of a Revolutionary Gentleman,* Catholic University of America Press, 1970; (editor) *The Charles Carroll Papers,* Scholarly Resources, 1971; *The American Revolution and Religion,* Catholic University of American Press, 1972; (editor) *The John Carroll Papers,* three volumes, University of Notre Dame Press, 1976. Contributor to history and religion journals.

WORK IN PROGRESS: Charles Carroll of Carrollton, Volume II.

SIDELIGHTS: Thomas O'Brien Hanley's book, *Their Rights and Liberties,* was cited by the Supreme Court in 1961 in its decision against religious tests for office (*Torcaso v. Watkins*). *Avocational interests:* Writing (poetry and features), photography, tennis, opera.

* * *

HANNA, John Paul 1932-

PERSONAL: Born July 12, 1932, in New York, N.Y.; son of Paul Robert (an author and teacher) and Jean (Shuman) Hanna; married Joyce Adams, June 18, 1955; children: Kristine, Katherine. *Education:* Stanford University, B.A., 1954, J.D., 1959. *Politics:* Republican. *Religion:* Methodist. *Home:* 137 Atherton Ave., Atherton, Calif. 94025. *Office:* John Paul Hanna Professional Corp., 1400 Palo Alto Office Center, Palo Alto, Calif. 94301.

CAREER: Admitted to the Bar of California, 1959; Thoits, Lehman & Hanna (law firm), Palo Alto, Calif., partner, beginning 1960; currently president, John Paul Hanna Professional Corp., Palo Alto, Calif. Member of Peninsula Estate Planning Council, 1962-65, Santa Clara County Estate Planning Council, 1963-65, and Mayor's Committee for Planning in the Foothills, 1964—; member of Republican State Central Committee, 1971; trustee of Castilleja School. *Military service:* U.S. Army, 1954-56. U.S. Army Reserve, 1952-60; became captain. *Member:* American Bar Association, California Bar Association, Santa Clara County Bar Association, Palo Alto Bar Association, Palo Alto Chamber of Commerce, Delta Tau Delta, Phi Delta Phi, Benevolent and Protective Order of Elks, Kiwanis.

WRITINGS: (Editor and contributor) *Youth and the Law,* Palo Alto School District and Junior Chamber of Commerce, 1963; *Teenagers and the Law,* Ginn, 1967; *The Complete Layman's Guide to the Law,* Prentice-Hall, 1974; *California Condominium Handbook,* Bancroft-Whitney, 1975.

* * *

HANNA, Thomas 1928-

PERSONAL: Born November 21, 1928; son of John Dwight and Winifred (Beaumier) Hanna; married Susan Taff, 1950; children: Mary Alice, Michael John, Wendell France. *Education:* Texas Christian University, B.A., 1949; University of Chicago, B.D., 1954, Ph.D., 1958. *Home:* 455 Ridge Rd., Novato, Calif. 94947.

CAREER: Notre Maison Orphanage, Brussels, Belgium, assistant director, 1952-53; Hollins College, Roanoke, Va., associate professor of philosophy and religion and chairman of department of philosophy, 1958-64; University of North Carolina at Chapel Hill, and Duke University, Durham, N.C., resident writer in Cooperative Program in the Humanities, 1964-65; University of Florida, Gainesville, professor of philosophy and chairman of department, 1965-70; director of Humanistic Psychology Institute, 1973-76; Novato Institute for Somatic Research and Training, Novato, Calif., director, 1975—. Director of overseas study program, Paris, 1961-62. *Member:* International Association for Humanistic Psychology (member of executive board), Jean de Beauvais Refugee Club (Paris; director, 1951-52). *Awards, honors:* American Council of Learned Societies fellow.

WRITINGS: The Thought and Art of Albert Camus, Regnery, 1958; *The Lyrical Existentialists,* Atheneum, 1962; (co-author) *Camus,* Prentice-Hall, 1962; *The Bergsonian Heritage,* Columbia University Press, 1962; (co-author) *Existential Philosophy,* McGraw, 1967; (contributor) G. A. Panichas, editor, *Mansions of the Spirit,* Hawthorn, 1967; (contributor) James M. Edie, editor, *New Essays in Phenomenology: Studies in the Philosophy of Existence,* Quadrangle, 1969; *Bodies in Revolt: A Primer in Somatic Thinking,* Holt, 1970; *The End of Tyranny: An Essay on the Possibility of America,* Freeperson Press, 1976; *Explorers of Humankind,* Harper, 1979; *The Body of Life,* Knopf, 1980. Editor, *Somatics,* 1976—.

SIDELIGHTS: Bodies in Revolt has been translated into Spanish and Portuguese; *Explorers of Humankind* has been translated into Portuguese.

* * *

HARDING, Walter Roy 1917-

PERSONAL: Born April 20, 1917, in Bridgewater, Mass.; son of Roy V. (a farmer) and Mary Alice (MacDonald) Harding; married Marjorie Brook, June 7, 1947; children: David, Allen, Lawrence, Susan. *Education:* Bridgewater State

Teachers College (now Bridgewater State College), B.S. Ed., 1939; University of North Carolina, M.A., 1947; Rutgers University, Ph.D., 1950. *Religion:* Unitarian Universalist. *Address:* P.O. Box 115, Groveland, N.Y. 14462. *Office:* Department of English, State University of New York College, Geneseo, N.Y. 14454.

CAREER: Center School, Northfield, Mass., principal, 1939-41; Rutgers University, New Brunswick, N.J., instructor in English, 1947-51; University of Virginia, Charlottesville, assistant professor, 1951-56; State University of New York College at Geneseo, associate professor, 1956-59, professor of English and chairman of department, 1959-65, chairman of humanities division, 1965-66, university professor, 1966—. U.S. Department of State lecturer in Japan, 1964, and Europe, 1967. Director, Concord summer seminars, 1969—, and National Endowment for the Humanities summer seminars on transcendentalism, 1976-79. Member of board of directors, State University of New York Research Foundation, 1971—. *Member:* Thoreau Society (secretary, 1941—; president, 1963-64), Modern Language Association. *Awards, honors:* American Council of Learned Societies fellow, 1962.

WRITINGS: Thoreau's Library, University Press of Virginia, 1957; *A Thoreau Handbook,* New York University Press, 1959; *The Days of Henry Thoreau,* Knopf, 1965; *Emerson's Library,* University Press of Virginia, 1967.

Editor: *Thoreau: A Century of Criticism,* Southern Methodist University Press, 1954; (and author of introduction) Charles Mayo Ellis, *An Essay on Transcendentalism,* Scholars' Facsimiles & Reprints, 1954, reprinted, Greenwood Press, 1970; (with Carl Bode) *The Correspondence of Henry David Thoreau,* New York University Press, 1958, reprinted, Greenwood Press, 1974; *Thoreau: Man of Concord,* Holt, 1960; Amos Bronson Alcott, *Essays on Education,* Scholars' Facsimiles & Reprints, 1960; Henry David Thoreau, *The Variorum "Walden,"* Twayne, 1962; (with Milton Meltzer) *A Thoreau Profile,* Crowell, 1962; Thoreau, *A Week on the Concord and Merrimack Rivers,* Holt, 1963; Thoreau, *Journals,* Dover, 1963; Thoreau, *Anti-Slavery and Reform Papers,* Harvest Books, 1963; *The Thoreau Centennial,* State University of New York Press, 1964; William Ellery Channing, *The Collected Poems of William Ellery Channing, the Younger: 1817-1901,* Scholars' Facsimiles & Reprints, 1967; Thoreau, *The Variorum "Civil Disobedience,"* Twayne, 1967; *Henry David Thoreau: A Profile,* Hill & Wang, 1971; (with Jean C. Advena) *A Bibliography of the Thoreau Society Bulletin Bibliographies, 1941-1969: A Cumulation and Index,* Whitston Publishing, 1971; (with others) *Henry David Thoreau: Studies and Commentaries,* Fairleigh Dickinson University Press, 1972; (and author of introduction) *The Selected Works of Thoreau,* Houghton, 1975.

Editor, "Study Guides to American Literature," Shelley, beginning 1963; editor-in-chief, "The Writings of Henry D. Thoreau," Princeton University Press, 1965-74. Contributor to *Encyclopedia Americana.* Contributor of articles and book reviews to literary magazines and to the *Chicago Tribune, Library Journal,* and *American Literature.* Editor of Thoreau Society *Bulletin* and booklets, 1941—.

SIDELIGHTS: Though much has been written about Thoreau the author, much less has been written about Thoreau the man. In *The Days of Henry Thoreau,* Walter Roy Harding's goal is to portray Thoreau "as he really was" in order to dispel the image of him as an eccentric recluse scorned by society and the critics. Sterling North of *Saturday Review* calls the book "by far the most detailed report on the complete life of Thoreau from birth to death [which] has not missed, as far as I can see, a single fact, important or otherwise." Yet he feels that this "plethora of detail" tends to make the biography "a trifle tedious" and that Harding fails to "bring alive the active nature philosopher of Walden Pond."

A critic in *Book Week,* on the other hand, writes: "Mr. Harding's prose carries the reader effortlessly forward. The writing is transparent and simple—perhaps the best style in which to record the little adventures of a genius who traveled a great deal in Concord. . . . [The author] has written what looks like the definitive biography of the man, leaving to others, perhaps wisely, the rich and difficult problem of assessing Thoreau's 'philosophy' and his influence." Carl Bode of the *New York Times Book Review* acknowledges that Harding, "by instinct, perhaps, as well as design," avoids an in-depth examination of Thoreau the author and writes instead "out of [a] single-minded devotion." The result, he concludes, "is the best biography we have had. . . . There is [however] a trace of special pleading. Thoreau finishes by looking a trifle rosier than perhaps he should . . . but only a trifle."

Harding is the owner of one of the largest, if not *the* largest, collection of books, pamphlets, articles, and manuscripts by and about Henry David Thoreau.

AVOCATIONAL INTERESTS: Bird-watching.

BIOGRAPHICAL/CRITICAL SOURCES: Book Week, November 28, 1965; *New York Times Book Review,* December 26, 1965; *Saturday Review,* January 15, 1966.

* * *

HARRIS, Dorothy Joan 1931-

PERSONAL: Born February 14, 1931, in Kobe, Japan; daughter of Hubert and Alice (Gregory) Langley; married Alan Harris (a company secretary-treasurer), October 8, 1955; children: Kim, Douglas. *Education:* University of Toronto, B.A. (honors), 1952. *Politics:* None. *Religion:* Anglican. *Home:* 159 Brentwood Rd. N., Toronto, Ontario, Canada M8X 2C8. *Agent:* Dorothy Markinko, McIntosh & Otis, Inc., 475 Fifth Ave., New York, N.Y. 10017.

CAREER: Elementary school teacher in Kobe, Japan, 1954-55; editor for Copp Clark Publishing Co., 1955-60; writer of books for children.

WRITINGS: The House Mouse (juvenile), Warne, 1973; *The School Mouse* (juvenile), Warne, 1977; *The School Mouse and the Hamster* (juvenile), Warne, 1979.

SIDELIGHTS: Dorothy Joan Harris told *CA:* "My own children have often provided the story germ for my books. Although they are now almost grown-up, their childhood brought back my own childhood feelings and experiences vividly enough to stay with me still. I feel the best children's books are written out of the child the author once was." *Avocational interests:* Painting, music, cats.

* * *

HARRIS, Marshall (Dees) 1903-

PERSONAL: Born September 22, 1903, in Shelbyville, Ky.; son of Caleb D. and Anna Cora (Duvall) Harris; married Mary Katherine Franklin, 1934; children: John Wilton, David Marshall. *Education:* University of Kentucky, B.S., 1926; University of Illinois, M.S., 1932, Ph.D., 1942. *Religion:* Baptist. *Office:* Agricultural Law Center, College of Law, University of Iowa, Iowa City, Iowa 52240.

CAREER: University of Illinois, Urbana, research assistant, 1930-34; U.S. Department of Agriculture, Division of Land Economics, Washington, D.C., agricultural economist, 1934-54; University of Iowa, College of Law, Agricultural Law Center, Iowa City, research professor of agricultural law, beginning 1955. U.S. Department of Agriculture, agricultural research service, 1954-61, agricultural economist, beginning 1961. *Member:* American Farm Economics Association, Rural Sociological Society, Omicron Delta Epsilon, Alpha Zeta, Phi Delta Kappa, Gamma Sigma Delta, Sigma Xi. *Awards, honors:* Superior service award from U.S. Department of Agriculture.

WRITINGS: (Co-editor) *Family Farm Policy,* University of Chicago Press, 1947; (co-editor) *Agrarian Reform and Moral Responsibility,* Agricultural Missions, 1949; (contributor) O. B. Jesuess, editor, *Readings on Agricultural Policy,* Blakiston Co., 1950; *Origin of the Land Tenure System in the United States,* Iowa State College Press, 1953; (co-author) *Town and Country Churches and Family Farming,* Division of Home Missions, National Council of Churches of Christ in the U.S.A., 1956; (contributor and member of editorial committee) *Modern Land Policy,* University of Illinois Press, 1960; (co-editor) *Land Economics Research,* Johns Hopkins Press, 1962; (editor with N. William Hines) *Family Farm Corporations* (monograph), Agricultural Law Center, College of Law, University of Iowa, 1963; (with Hines) *Installment Land Contracts in Iowa* (monograph), Agricultural Law Center, College of Law, University of Iowa, 1965; (editor with Hines) *Methods for Legal-economic Research into Rural Problems* (monograph), Agricultural Law Center, College of Law, University of Iowa, 1966; (with Dean T. Massey) *Vertical Coordination via Contract Farming,* Natural Resource Economics Division, U.S. Department of Agriculture, 1968; *Entrepreneurship in Agriculture* (monograph), Agricultural Law Center, College of Law, University of Iowa, 1974; *Legal-economic Aspects of Waste Law as It Relates to Farming* (monograph), Agricultural Law Center, College of Law, University of Iowa, 1974.

Also author of numerous other monographs on agricultural topics including, with Hines and Charles Campbell, *Legal Aspects of the Small Watershed Program in Iowa,* Agricultural Law Center, College of Law, University of Iowa, 1965, and, with David D. Moyer, *Land Tenure in the United States: Development and Status,* Economic Research Service, U.S. Department of Agriculture, 1969. Contributor to books. Contributor to professional journals.

WORK IN PROGRESS: Locus of Entrepreneurship in American Agriculture.

AVOCATIONAL INTERESTS: Hunting, fishing, woodworking, gardening, and church work.†

* * *

HARRIS, R(obert) Laird 1911-

PERSONAL: Born March 10, 1911, in Brownsburg, Pa.; son of Walter William (a clergyman) and Pearl (Graves) Harris; married Elizabeth Nelson, September 11, 1937; children: Grace (Mrs. Richard D. Sears), Allegra (Mrs. Peter L. Smick), Robert Laird, Jr. *Education:* University of Delaware, B.S. in chemical engineering, 1931; Westminster Theological Seminary, Th.B., 1935, Th.M., 1937; University of Pennsylvania, M.A., 1941; Dropsie College of Hebrew and Cognate Learning (now Dropsie University), Ph.D., 1947. *Religion:* Evangelical Presbyterian. *Home:* 12304 Conway Rd., St. Louis, Mo. 63141. *Office:* Covenant Theological Seminary, 12330 Conway Rd., St. Louis, Mo. 63141.

CAREER: Faith Theological Seminary, Philadelphia, Pa., instructor and professor, 1937-56; Covenant Theological Seminary, St. Louis, Mo., professor of Old Testament, 1956—, dean of faculty, 1964-71. Special lecturer, Wheaton College, Wheaton, Ill., 1957-61; excavator and teacher, Near East School of Archaeology, Jerusalem, Hashemite Kingdom, Jordan, 1962. *Military service:* U.S. Army, Officers Reserve Corps; became first lieutenant. *Member:* Society of Biblical Literature, American Schools of Oriental Research, Evangelical Theological Society (president, 1960), American Institute of Archaeology (secretary of St. Louis chapter, 1971-73), Oriental Club of Philadelphia (secretary, 1945-50; president, 1954). *Awards, honors:* First prize, Zondervan Publishing Co. textbook contest, 1957.

WRITINGS: Introductory Hebrew Grammar, Eerdmans, 1950; *Inspiration and Canonicity of the Bible,* Zondervan, 1957; *Your Bible,* Evangelical Teachers Training Association, 1960, revised edition, 1976; (contributor) *Biblical Expositor,* A. J. Holman Co., 1960; (contributor) *Wycliffe Bible Commentary,* Moody, 1962; (contributor) *The Bible—Living Word of Revelation,* Zondervan, 1968; (contributor) *New Perspectives on the Old Testament,* Word Books, 1970; *Man—God's Eternal Creation,* Moody, 1971; (editor with others) *Theological Wordbook of the Old Testament,* Moody, 1980. Member of editorial board, *The Bible,* New International Version, Zondervan, 1978.

* * *

HART, James D(avid) 1911-

PERSONAL: Born April 18, 1911, in San Francisco, Calif.; son of Julien and Helen (Neustadter) Hart; married Ruth Arnstein, June 14, 1938; children: Carol Hart Field, Peter D. *Education:* Stanford University, A.B., 1932; Harvard University, M.A., 1933, Ph.D., 1936. *Home:* 740 San Luis Rd., Berkeley, Calif. 94707. *Office:* Bancroft Library, University of California, Berkeley, California 94720.

CAREER: University of California, Berkeley, instructor, 1936-41, assistant professor, 1941-47, associate professor, 1947-51, professor of English, 1951—, chairman of department, 1955-57, 1965-69, vice-chancellor of university, 1957-60, acting director of Bancroft Library, 1961-62, director, 1969—. Visiting professor, Harvard University, 1964; visiting Phi Beta Kappa scholar, 1980-81. Mills College, trustee, 1970-78, 1979—, president of board, 1973-76. *Military service:* Office of Strategic Services, World War II. *Member:* Modern Language Association of America, American Academy of Arts and Sciences, American Antiquarian Society, American Studies Association, Pacific Coast Philological Association, Book Club of California (president, 1956-58). *Awards, honors:* Commander of the Order of the British Empire; L.H.D., Mills College, 1978.

WRITINGS: Oxford Companion to American Literature, Oxford University Press, 1941, 4th edition, 1965; *The Popular Book: A History of America's Literary Taste,* Oxford University Press, 1950, reprinted, Greenwood Press, 1976; (with Clarence Gohdes) *America's Literature,* Holt, 1955; (editor) *My First Publication: Eleven California Authors Describe Their Earliest Appearances in Print,* Book Club of California, 1961; (editor) Robert Louis Stevenson, *From Scotland to Silverado: "The Amateur Emigrant: From the Clyde to Sandy Hook," "Across the Plains," "The Silverado Squatters" and "Four Essays on California,"* Harvard University Press, 1966; (editor) Frank Norris, *A Novelist in the Making: A Collection of Student Themes and the Novels "Blix" and "Vandover and the Brute,"* Harvard University

Press, 1970; *New Englanders in Nova Albion: Some Nineteenth-Century Views of California,* Boston Public Library, 1976; *A Companion to California,* Oxford University Press, 1978. Contributor to *American Heritage* and *American Literature.* Member of editorial board, *American Literature,* 1952-55, 1964-67.

AVOCATIONAL INTERESTS: Private handpress printing.

BIOGRAPHICAL/CRITICAL SOURCES: Los Angeles Times, Los Angeles, Calif., November 23, 1978.

* * *

HARTLEY, Lodwick (Charles) 1906-1979

PERSONAL: Born June 12, 1906, in Batesburg, S.C.; died July 2, 1979; son of Lodwick Chappell and Nannie (Kneece) Hartley. *Education:* Furman University, B.A., 1927; Columbia University, M.A., 1928; Princeton University, Ph.D., 1937. *Religion:* Episcopalian. *Home:* 812 Fairall Dr., Raleigh, N.C. 27607. *Office:* Department of English, North Carolina State University, Raleigh, N.C. 27607.

CAREER: Columbia (S.C.), High School, instructor, 1928-29; North Carolina State University at Raleigh, instructor, 1929-30, assistant professor, 1930-37, associate professor, 1937-40, professor of English, 1940-79, head of department, 1940-71. Visiting professor at University of North Carolina, 1940, 1950, University of Virginia, 1954, and Duke University, 1970, 1973; visiting scholar, University of Georgia, 1969. *Military service:* U.S. Naval Reserve, 1942-45; became lieutenant commander. *Member:* Modern Language Association of America, American Association of University Professors, College English Association, American Society of Engineering Education, South Atlantic Modern Language Association, North Carolina English Teachers Association, Blue Key, Phi Kappa Phi, Phi Beta Kappa. *Awards, honors:* Litt.D., Furman University, 1954.

WRITINGS: William Cowper, Humanitarian, University of North Carolina Press, 1938; *This Is Lorence: A Biography of the Reverend Laurence Sterne,* University of North Carolina Press, 1943; (with Arthur Ladu) *Patterns in Modern Drama,* Prentice-Hall, 1948; *William Cowper: The Continuing Revaluation,* University of North Carolina Press, 1960; *Laurence Sterne in the Twentieth Century: An Essay and a Bibliography of Sternean Studies,* University of North Carolina Press, 1966; (editor with George Core) *Katherine Anne Porter: A Critical Symposium,* University of Georgia Press, 1969; *Plum Tree Lane: A Fictional Memoir,* Sandlapper Store, 1975; (editor) *Laurence Sterne: An Annotated Bibliography,* G. K. Hall, 1978. Author of "Mr. Hennig's Wall," included in *O. Henry Memorial Prize Stories,* 1948. Contributor of articles, poems, short stories, and reviews to literary magazines.

* * *

HARTMANN, Frederick Howard 1922-

PERSONAL: Born July 6, 1922, in New York, N.Y.; son of Frederick H. and Grace (MacNamara) Hartmann; married Regina Lou Kiracofe, 1943; children: Lynne Merry, Vicky Carol, Peter Howard. *Education:* University of California, A.A., 1942, A.B., 1943; Princeton University, M.A., 1947, Ph.D., 1949; University of Geneva, graduate study, 1948. *Home:* 22 Chartier Cir., Newport, R.I. 02840. *Office:* Naval War College, Newport, R.I. 02840.

CAREER: Princeton University, Princeton, N.J., instructor, 1946-47; University of Florida, Gainesville, assistant professor, 1948-52, associate professor, 1952-56, professor of political science, 1956-66, director of Institute of International Relations, 1963-66; Naval War College, Newport, R.I., Alfred Thayer Mahan Professor of Maritime Strategy and special academic advisor to the president, 1966—. Occasional lecturer at Air War College, 1963—, and at Army War College, 1964, 1965, 1966, Naval War College, 1964, 1965, 1966, National War College, and Inter-American Defense College; visiting professor, Wheaton College, 1967-69, Brown University, 1968, University of Rhode Island, 1970, Texas Tech University, 1974-75, and University of California, Berkeley; visiting scholar, Hoover Institution, Stanford University, 1979-80. University of Florida, Fulbright advisor, 1950-53, secretary of Fulbright Committee, 1951-59, chairman, 1962-66; member of National Selection Committee for the Fulbright Program, 1954-56. Founding member and vice-president, Civic Action Association of Greater Gainesville, 1963-64. *Military service:* U.S. Naval Reserve, active duty, 1943-46; received seven battle stars; retired as captain.

MEMBER: International Studies Association (vice-president of New England division, 1970-71; president, 1971-72), Foreign Policy Association, American Political Science Association, American Association of University Professors (member of national council, 1963-66), Southern Political Science Association, Pi Sigma Alpha, Delta Phi Epsilon. *Awards, honors:* Fulbright research scholar at University of Bonn, Germany, 1953-54; Rockefeller grant for research in Germany on reunification, 1959; U.S. Naval War College Foundation research grant, 1973; Exxon Corporation research grant, 1973.

WRITINGS: (Editor) *Basic Documents of International Relations,* McGraw, 1951; (editor) *Readings in International Relations,* McGraw, 1952, revised edition published as *World in Crisis: Readings in International Relations,* Macmillan, 1967, 4th edition, 1973; *The Relations of Nations,* Macmillan, 1957, 5th edition, 1978; *The Swiss Press and Foreign Affairs in World War II* (monograph), University of Florida Press, 1960; *Germany between East and West: The Reunification Problem,* Prentice-Hall, 1965; *The New Age of American Foreign Policy,* Macmillan, 1970. Contributor of articles to professional journals.

WORK IN PROGRESS: The Conservation of Enemies.

* * *

HARTOCOLLIS, Peter 1922-
(Loizos Mandrepelias, Pitsa Palli)

PERSONAL: Born November 29, 1922, in Athens, Greece; son of Thomas (engaged in real estate) and Mary (Mandrapelias) Hartocollis; married Pitsa Palli (a psychologist), April 8, 1953; children: Anemona, Lina, Thomas. *Education:* Clark University, B.A., 1949; Michigan State University, M.A., 1951, Ph.D., 1954; University of Lausanne, M.D., 1955. *Religion:* Greek Orthodox. *Home:* 134 Woodlawn, Topeka, Kan. 66606. *Agent:* E. C. Casdaglis, 17 Cavalloti, Athens 402, Greece. *Office address:* Menninger Foundation, Box 829, Topeka, Kan. 66601.

CAREER: St. Mary's Hospital, Waterbury, Conn., intern, 1956-57; resident in psychiatry at Kansas University Medical Center, Kansas City, Kan., 1957, and Veterans Administration Hospital, Topeka, Kan., 1957-59; C. F. Menninger Memorial Hospital, Topeka, staff psychiatrist, 1960—, chief of clinical service, 1966-69, director of research, 1969—, director, 1973—, Menninger School of Psychiatry, professor, 1978—. Topeka Institute for Psychoanalysis, member of faculty, 1969—, training and supervising analyst, 1973—;

clinical professor of psychiatry, Kansas University Medical School, 1978—. Consultant to alcoholism program, Veterans Administration Hospital, Topeka, beginning 1963.

MEMBER: International Psychoanalytic Association, American Medical Association, American Psychiatric Association (fellow), American Psychological Association, American Psychoanalytic Association, American College of Psychoanalysts (fellow), Group for the Advancement of Psychiatry, American College of Physicians (fellow), American Association for the Advancement of Science, New York Academy of Sciences.

WRITINGS: La Psychopathologie du tremblement de terre (title means "The Psychopathology of Earthquakes"; monograph), Imprimeries Reunies, 1955; (contributor) Joseph Hirsh, editor, *Opportunities and Limitations in Treatment of Alcoholics,* C. C Thomas, 1967; *Idou o Nymphios Erchetai* (title means "Behold the Bridegroom Cometh"; short stories; many originally published in magazines, under pseudonyms Loizos Mandrepelias or Pitsa Palli), Kedros (Athens), 1971; (editor) *Borderline Personality Disorders,* International Universities Press, 1977; (contributor) G. U. Balis and others, editors, *The Behavioral and Social Sciences and the Practice of Medicine,* Butterworth, 1978; (contributor) L. Bellak, editor, *Psychiatric Aspects of Minimal Brain Dysfunction in Adults,* Grune, 1979; (contributor) W. E. Fann and others, editors, *Phenomenology and Treatment of Alcoholism,* SP Medical and Scientific Books, 1979; (contributor) E. M. Pattison and E. Kaufman, editors, *The American Handbook of Alcoholism,* Gardner Press, 1980. Contributor to *International Encyclopedia of Psychiatry, Psychology, Psychoanalysis and Neurology,* 1977. Contributor of about fifty articles to scientific journals and popular magazines.

WORK IN PROGRESS: A psycho-biography of Nikos Kazantzakis; a monograph on time and the self.

SIDELIGHTS: Peter Hartocollis told *CA:* "My psychiatric practice is geared toward scientific writing, which I try to combine with my literary interests. My wish is to engage more seriously in fiction writing, for which I have collected a great deal of personal material."

* * *

HASKINS, George Lee 1915-

PERSONAL: Born February 13, 1915, in Cambridge, Mass.; son of Charles Homer and Clare (Allen) Haskins; married Anstiss Crowinshield Boyden, July 15, 1944 (deceased); children: Harriet H. Nicol. *Education:* Harvard University, A.B. (summa cum laude), 1935, LL.B., 1942; Oxford University, graduate study, 1935-36. *Home address:* P.O. Box 760, Paoli, Pa. 19301. *Office:* 3400 Chestnut St., Philadelphia, Pa. 19104.

CAREER: Oxford University, Merton College, Oxford, England, Henry fellow, 1935-36; Harvard University, Cambridge, Mass., junior fellow of Society of Fellows, 1936-42; Herrick, Smith, Donald & Farley, Boston, Mass., associate, 1942; University of Pennsylvania, Philadelphia, assistant professor, 1946-48, associate professor, 1948-49, professor of law, 1949-74, Algernon Sydney Biddle Professor of Law, 1974—; Pennsylvania Railroad Co., Philadelphia, special attorney, 1951-54, consulting counsel, 1954-70. Admitted to bars of Massachusetts, 1942, Interstate Commerce Commission, 1951, Pennsylvania, 1952, United States Supreme Court, 1952, Federal Courts, 1953, 1954, and Maine, 1968. Member of United States delegation to United Nations Conference, San Francisco, 1945; member of staff of special assistant to Secretary of State James F. Byrnes, 1946; appointed member of Permanent Committee on Oliver Wendell Holmes Devise by President Eisenhower, 1956; assistant reporter, Supreme Court and Superior Courts of Pennsylvania, 1970-72; permanent member of Judicial Conference, U.S. Third Circuit. University seminar associate, Columbia University, 1971-73, 1977—. Director, Pennsylvania Mutual Funds, New York, 1961-68; member of humanities council, WHYY-TV, Philadelphia, Pa. and Wilmington, Del., 1976—. Appointed town official of Hancock, Me., for bicentennial and sesquicentennial, 1975-79. *Military service:* U.S. Army, General Staff Corps, 1942-46, became captain; received War Department Staff Citation with oak leaf clusters. U.S. Army Reserve, 1946-54; became major.

MEMBER: International Law Society, International Society of Comparative Law, International Commission for the History of Representative and Parliamentary Institutions (member of American Committee), Instituto Internacional para Unificacion de Derecho Publico (Madrid), Association Internationale pour l'Histoire du Droit (member of board of directors, 1975-80), American Bar Association, American Law Institute, Interstate Commerce Commission Practitioners Association, American Society for Legal History (president, 1970-74; member of board of directors, 1976-79), American Historical Association (member of Littleton-Griswold Fund committee), Mediaeval Academy of America (former councillor), Royal Historical Society (London; fellow), British Records Association, Massachusetts Bar Association, Pennsylvania Bar Association, Colonial Society of Pennsylvania, Colonial Society of Massachusetts, Seldon Society of Pennsylvania (overseas representative), Pennsylvania Society of Colonial Wars, Pennsylvania Society of the War of 1812, Philadelphia Bar Association, Association of the Bar of the City of New York; Juristic Society, Legal Club, Sharswood Law Club, and Swedish Colonial Society (all Philadelphia); Society of Mayflower Descendants and Sons of the Revolution (both New York); Phi Beta Kappa, Cum Laude Society, Order of the Coif.

AWARDS, HONORS: Demobilization award, Social Science Research Council, 1946; Guggenheim fellow, 1957; Award of Merit of the American Association for State and Local History, 1962, for *Law and Authority in Early Massachusetts;* M.A., University of Pennsylvania, 1972.

WRITINGS: The Statute of York, Harvard University Press, 1935, reprinted, Greenwood Press, 1977; *The Growth of English Representative Government,* University of Pennsylvania Press, 1948; (with others) *American Law of Property,* Little, Brown, 1952; (with M. P. Smith) *Pennsylvania Fiduciary Guide,* Little, Brown, 1956, revised edition, 1962; *Law and Authority in Early Massachusetts,* Macmillan, 1960; (editor and author of introduction) John Dickinson, *Death of a Republic,* Macmillan, 1963; (with others) *A History of the Town of Hancock, Maine, 1828-1978,* Downeast Graphics, 1978. Member of advisory board of editors, *The Papers of John Marshall.* Contributor to law and history journals in the United States and abroad.

WORK IN PROGRESS: Foundations of Power: John Marshall, Volume II of the Congressionally-authorized history of the U.S. Supreme Court; *Law and Society in Seventeenth-Century Massachusetts; Studies in the Law of Islam and the West.*

AVOCATIONAL INTERESTS: Farming.

* * *

HASSRICK, Peter H(eyl) 1941-

PERSONAL: Born April 27, 1941, in Philadelphia, Pa.; son

of Royal Brown (a writer) and Barbara (Morgan) Hassrick; married Elizabeth Drake, June 14, 1963; children: Philip Heyl, Charles Royal. *Education:* Attended Harvard University, 1962; University of Colorado, B.A., 1963; University of Denver, M.A., 1969. *Residence:* Cody, Wyo. *Office:* Buffalo Bill Historical Center, Cody, Wyo.

CAREER: Lone Star Ranch, Elizabeth, Colo., rancher and assistant foreman, summers, 1960-63; high school teacher of history, Spanish, and art history in Steamboat Springs, Colo., 1963-67; Amon Carter Museum, Fort Worth, Tex., curator of collections, beginning 1969; Buffalo Bill Historical Center, Cody, Wyo., currently director. Rancher in Colorado, summers, 1963-65. *Member:* American Association of Museums.

WRITINGS: Birger Sandzen, Amon Carter Museum, 1970; *Frederic Remington: An Essay and Catalogue to Accompany a Retrospective Exhibition,* Amon Carter Museum, 1972; *Frederick Remington: Paintings, Drawings, and Sculpture in the Amon Carter Museum and the Sid W. Richardson Foundation Collections,* Abrams, 1973; (editor) *Amon Carter Museum of Western Art: Catalogue of the Collection, 1972,* Amon Carter Museum, 1973; (with Ron Tyler) *The American West,* U.S. Information Agency, 1974; *The Way West,* Abrams, 1977. Contributor to *American Art Review, Southwestern Historical Quarterly, American Art Review, Antiques, American West,* and other periodicals.

* * *

HATHORN, Richmond Y(ancey) 1917-

PERSONAL: Born July 31, 1917, in Alexandria, La.; son of John Wesley and Aimee (Sleet) Hathorn; married Isabel Voelker, 1947; children: Isabel V., Richmond Y., Jr., Emily M. *Education:* Louisiana College, B.A., 1937; Louisiana State University, M.A., 1940; Columbia University, Ph.D., 1950. *Office:* Department of Classics, State University of New York, Stony Brook, N.Y. 11794.

CAREER: High school and college teacher, 1939-46; Columbia University, New York, N.Y., lecturer, 1947-53; Northwestern State College (now Northwestern State University of Louisiana), Natchitoches, professor, 1953-61; Louisiana State University, Baton Rouge, associate professor of classical languages, 1961-62; University of Kentucky, Lexington, chairman of department of classics, 1962-66; American University of Beirut, Beirut, Lebanon, professor of European languages and literature, 1966-69; State University of New York at Stony Brook, professor of classics and comparative literature, 1969—. Visiting professor, University of Michigan, 1959, and Columbia University, 1962 and 1965. *Member:* American Philological Association.

WRITINGS: Tragedy, Myth, and Mystery, Indiana University Press, 1962; *Crowell's Handbook of Classical Drama,* Crowell, 1967 (published in England as *The Handbook of Classical Drama,* Arthur Barker, 1967); *Greek Mythology,* American University of Beirut Press, 1977.

* * *

HAVIGHURST, Walter (Edwin) 1901-

PERSONAL: Born November 28, 1901, in Appleton, Wis.; son of Freeman Alfred and Winifred (Weter) Havighurst; married Marion Boyd (a writer), 1930 (died, 1974). *Education:* University of Denver, A.B., 1924; attended King's College, London, 1925-26; Columbia University, A.M., 1928. *Home:* Shadowy Hills, Oxford, Ohio. *Agent:* McIntosh and Otis, Inc., 475 Fifth Ave., New York, N.Y. *Office:* Department of English, Miami University, Oxford, Ohio.

CAREER: Miami University, Oxford, Ohio, assistant professor, 1928-35, associate professor, 1935-42, professor of English, 1942-49, research professor, 1949-68, Regents professor, 1968-69, research professor emeritus, 1969—. *Member:* Society of American Historians, Ohio Historical Society (member of board of editors, 1956—). *Awards, honors:* Ohioana Library Association Medal, 1946-50; Friends of American Writers Award, 1947, for *Land of Promise;* D.Litt., Lawrence College and Ohio Wesleyan University, both in 1947; Association for State and Local History Award, 1956, for *Wilderness for Sale;* L.H.D., Miami University, 1960, and Marietta College, 1961; History Prize, Society of Midland Authors, 1971, for *River to the West.*

WRITINGS: Pier 17, Macmillan, 1935; *The Quiet Shore,* Macmillan, 1937; *Upper Mississippi River,* Farrar, Rinehart, 1937, revised edition, 1944; (editor with H. L. Haley) *Designs for Writing,* Dryden, 1939; *The Winds of Spring,* Macmillan, 1940; *No Homeward Course,* Doubleday, 1941; *The Long Ships Passing,* Macmillan, 1942, revised and enlarged edition, 1975; (editor with R. F. Almy and J. M. Bachelor) *Approach to America,* Odyssey, 1942; (with wife, Marion Havighurst) *High Prairie,* Farrar, Rinehart, 1944; (editor) *Masters of the Modern Short Story,* Harcourt, 1945, 2nd edition, 1955; *Land of Promise,* Macmillan, 1946; *Signature of Time,* Macmillan, 1949; (with M. Havighurst) *Song of the Pines,* Winston, 1949.

Great Plains, Fideler, 1951, revised edition, 1967; *Midwest,* Fideler, 1951, revised edition, 1967; *Northeast,* Fideler, 1952, revised edition, 1967; *George Rogers Clark,* McGraw, 1952; (with M. Havighurst) *Climb a Lofty Ladder,* Winston, 1952; *Annie Oakley of the Wild West,* Macmillan, 1954; (co-editor) *Selection: A Reader for College Writing,* Dryden, 1955; *Wilderness for Sale,* Hastings House, 1956; *Buffalo Bill's Wild West Show,* Random House, 1957; *Vein of Iron,* World Publishing, 1958; *The Miami Years,* Putnam, 1958; *First Book of Pioneers,* F. Watts, 1959; *First Book of the Oregon Trail,* F. Watts, 1960; (editor) *Land of the Long Horizons,* Coward, 1960; *The Heartland,* Harper, 1962, revised edition, 1974; *First Book of the California Gold Rush,* F. Watts, 1962; *Voices on the River,* Macmillan, 1964; *Proud Prisoner,* Colonial Williamsburg, 1964; (editor) *The Great Lakes Reader,* Macmillan, 1966; *Three Flags at the Straits,* Prentice-Hall, 1966; *Alexander Spotswood,* Holt, 1967; *River to the West,* Putnam, 1970; *Ohio: A Bicentennial History,* Norton, 1976. Contributor to scholarly and popular magazines.

SIDELIGHTS: Although the majority of Walter Havighurst's books have focused on the "region between the Ohio River and the Great Lakes," his earlier works were drawn from his experiences as a merchant seaman in such diverse locations as London, Alaska, and Hong Kong. Havighurst attributes these earlier writings to the "groping" most authors undergo "before they find their essential material." Eventually, as he told *CA,* "I realized that my own background, of midland America, was for me the inexhaustible subject." Havighurst was born next to Wisconsin's Fox River, "where French explorers passed on their way to the Mississippi." This, according to the author, gave rise to a "dual curiosity, wanting to recall the Midwest of past times while trying to understand its ever-changing present. This is the background I am most at home with," he continued, "and toward which my writing seems to gravitate."

BIBLIOGRAPHICAL/CRITICAL SOURCES: Best Sellers, March 1, 1968, January 15, 1971.

HAVRAN, Martin J. 1929-

PERSONAL: Born November 12, 1929, in Windsor, Ontario, Canada; son of Joseph Havran; married, 1958; one child. *Education:* University of Detroit, Ph.B., 1951; Wayne University (now Wayne State University), M.A., 1953; Western Reserve University (now Case Western Reserve University), Ph.D., 1957. *Home:* 2206 Brandywine Dr., Charlottesville, Va. 22901. *Office:* Corcoran Department of History, Randall Hall, University of Virginia, Charlottesville, Va. 22903.

CAREER: Essex County Historical Association, Ontario, research associate, 1952-53; Kent State University, Kent, Ohio, instructor, 1957-60, assistant professor, 1960-64, associate professor of history, 1964-68; University of Virginia, Charlottesville, associate professor, 1968-72, professor of history, 1972—, chairman of Corcoran department of history, 1974-79. Visiting associate professor of history, University of Alberta, summer, 1965, and Northwestern University, 1967-68; member of board of overseers, Case Western Reserve University, 1976-79. *Member:* American Historical Association, American Catholic Historical Association, American Society for Eighteenth-Century Studies, The Historical Association, Association of Canadian Studies in the United States, Canadian Historical Association, Conference on British Studies (vice president, 1978-79; president, 1979-81), Royal Historical Society (fellow), Southern Historical Association. *Awards, honors:* Whittaker History Prize, 1953; Social Science Research Council fellowship, 1956-67, for study in England; Kent State University fellowship, 1962, for study in England; Distinguished Teacher Award, Kent State University, 1962 and 1964; University of Virginia sesquicentennial fellowship, 1974.

WRITINGS: (Contributor) Neil F. Morrison, *Garden Gateway to Canada: Windsor and Essex County, 1854-1954,* Ryerson, 1954; *The Catholics in Caroline England,* Stanford University Press, 1962; (editor with A. B. Erickson) *Readings in English History,* Scribner, 1967; (with Erickson) *England: Prehistory to the Present,* Doubleday, 1968; *Caroline Courtier: The Life of Lord Cottington,* Macmillan, 1973. Contributor to professional journals and encyclopedias.

* * *

HAZELTON, Roger 1909-

PERSONAL: Born November 11, 1909, in Chicago, Ill.; son of Purdy William and Esther (Palmer) Hazelton; married Bonnie Jean Hanvey; children: David Roger, Daniel Robert, Mark William. *Education:* Amherst College, A.B., 1931, D.D., 1951; University of Chicago, M.A., 1934, B.D., 1934; Yale University, Ph.D., 1937; Chicago Theological Seminary, D.D., 1960. *Religion:* United Church of Christ. *Home:* 99 Herrick Circle, Newton Centre, Mass. 02159. *Office:* 210 Herrick Rd., Newton Centre, Mass. 02159.

CAREER: Olivet College, Olivet, Mich., tutor in religion, 1936-39; Colorado College, Colorado Springs, dean of chapel, 1939-45; Andover Newton Theological School, Newton Centre, Mass., professor of theology, 1945-57; Pomona College and Claremont College (now Claremont Graduate School), Claremont, Calif., professor of religion and chairman of department, 1957-60; Oberlin College, Oberlin, Ohio, dean of Graduate School of Theology, 1960-65; Andover Newton Theological School, Abbot Professor of Christian Theology, 1965—. Fulbright research professor, University of Paris, 1951-52; visiting lecturer at Doshisha University (Japan), 1964, and Pontifical Gregorian University (Rome), 1971; visiting professor, Wake Forest University, 1978, and Berea College, 1979-80. Member of various commissions and committees of Congregational Christian Churches (now United Church of Christ). Delegate to assemblies of World Council of Churches in Netherlands, 1948, and India, 1961. *Member:* American Theological Society (secretary, 1961—), National Council on Religion in Higher Education. *Awards, honors:* Nietzsche-Archiv, Germany-study under a Carl Schurz scholarship, 1938; L.H.D., Findlay College, 1965; LL.D., Colorado College, 1974.

WRITINGS: The Root and Flower of Prayer, Macmillan, 1943; *The God We Worship,* Macmillan, 1946; *Renewing the Mind,* Macmillan, 1949; *On Proving God,* Harper, 1952; *God's Way with Man: Variations on the Theme of Providence,* Abingdon, 1956, published as *Providence: A Theme with Variations,* Student Christian Movement Press, 1958; *New Accents in Contemporary Theology,* Harper, 1960; *New Testament Heritage,* United Church Press, 1962; *Christ and Ourselves,* Harper, 1965; *Knowing the Living God,* American Baptist Publication Society, 1969; *Blaise Pascal: The Genius of His Thought,* Westminster, 1973; *Ascending Flame, Descending Dove,* Westminster, 1975.

Editor: David E. Roberts, *Existentialism and Religious Belief,* Oxford University Press, 1957; *Selected Writings of St. Augustine,* Meridian, 1962.

Contributor: *A Companion to the Study of St. Augustine,* Oxford University Press, 1955; *Wider Horizons in Christian Adult Education,* University of Pittsburgh Press, 1962; *New Frontiers of Christianity,* Association Press, 1962; *Best Sermons of 1962,* Van Nostrand, 1962; *The Heritage of Christian Thought,* Harper, 1965.

* * *

HEIDERSTADT, Dorothy 1907-

PERSONAL: Born October 8, 1907, in Geneva, Neb.; daughter of Charles Alden and Florence (Kilmer) Heiderstadt. *Education:* University of Kansas, A.B., 1936; Simmons College, B.S. in L.S., 1937. *Home:* 3028 Sheley Rd., Independence, Mo. 60452.

CAREER: Public library, Kansas City, Mo., children's librarian, 1930-36; Bethlehem Public Library System, Bethlehem, Pa., children's supervisor, 1937-42; Kansas City Public Library System, Kansas City, Mo., branch librarian, 1942-65, reference librarian, 1966-68, branch librarian, 1968-70. *Member:* American Library Association, Authors Guild, Oklahoma Historical Society, Phi Beta Kappa.

WRITINGS: A Book of Heroes, Bobbs-Merrill, 1954; *Indian Friends and Foes,* McKay, 1958; *To All Nations,* Thomas Nelson, 1959; *A Bow for Turtle,* McKay, 1960; *Knights and Champions,* Thomas Nelson, 1960; *Ten Torchbearers,* Thomas Nelson, 1961; *Frontier Leaders and Pioneers,* McKay, 1962; *Lois Says Aloha,* Thomas Nelson, 1963; *More Indian Friends and Foes,* McKay, 1963; *Marie Tanglehair,* McKay, 1965; *Stolen By the Indians,* McKay, 1967; *Painters of America,* McKay, 1970.

SIDELIGHTS: Dorothy Heiderstadt wrote *CA*: "I think you need to love to write, and you need to have special interests. You need to be able to work hard and be persistent. It isn't easy to sell a manuscript, but I think you can if you keep trying. After you sell the manuscript, there's a lot of hard work ahead. If you write mostly nonfiction, as I do, your facts must be right, your dates must be exact; your editor goes over them, and you have to go over them, too, and verify them. Sometimes your editor questions something you say, and you have to prove you are right by quoting the source of your information. Nobody takes your word for it, you have to prove it. All this is very character-building and teaches you to be patient and to get along with people, especially editors. I don't believe it would be possible to do it if you didn't have, down in your heart to buoy you up, the joy of writing!"

AVOCATIONAL INTERESTS: Travel, photography, reading.

* * *

HEILBRUN, Carolyn G(old) 1926-
(Amanda Cross)

PERSONAL: Born January 13, 1926, in East Orange, N.J.; daughter of Archibald (an accountant) and Estelle (Roemer) Gold; married James Heilbrun (a professor of economics), February 20, 1945; children: Emily, Margaret, Robert. *Education:* Wellesley College, B.A., 1947; Columbia University, M.A., 1951, Ph.D., 1959. *Home:* 151 Central Park W., New York, N.Y. 10023. *Agent:* Curtis Brown Ltd., 575 Madison Ave., New York, N.Y. 10022. *Office:* 613 Philosophy Hall, Columbia University, New York, N.Y. 10027.

CAREER: Brooklyn College of the City University of New York, Brooklyn, N.Y., instructor in English, 1959-60; Columbia University, New York, N.Y., instructor, 1960-62, assistant professor, 1962-67, associate professor, 1967-72, professor of English, 1972—. Visiting lecturer at Swarthmore College, Union Theological Seminary, and Yale University. Visiting professor at University of California, Santa Cruz. Member of policy advisory council, Danforth Foundation, 1978—. *Member:* American Association of University Professors, Modern Language Association of America (member of executive council, 1976-79), Authors' Guild. *Awards, honors:* Scroll from Mystery Writers of America, 1964, for *In the Last Analysis;* Guggenheim fellow, 1965-66; Rockefeller fellow; Radcliffe Institute fellow.

WRITINGS: The Garnett Family, Macmillan, 1960; *Christopher Isherwood,* Columbia University Press, 1970; *Toward a Recognition of Androgyny,* Knopf, 1973 (published in England as *Toward Androgyny,* Gollancz, 1973); (contributor) R. T. Francoeur and A. K. Francoeur, editors, *The Future of Sexual Relations,* Prentice-Hall, 1974; (contributor) T. Lewis, editor, *Essays on Virginia Woolf,* McGraw, 1975; (contributor) M. Springer, editor, *Portrayal of Women in British and American Literature,* Princeton University Press, 1975; (editor) *Lady Ottoline's Album,* Knopf, 1976; *Reinventing Womanhood,* W. W. Norton, 1979.

Under pseudonym Amanda Cross; all mystery novels: *In the Last Analysis,* Macmillan, 1964; *The James Joyce Murder,* Macmillan, 1967; *Poetic Justice,* Knopf, 1970; *The Theban Mysteries,* Knopf, 1972; *The Question of Max,* Knopf, 1976.

Work appears in anthologies. Contributor to *New York Times Book Review, Saturday Review, Texas Quarterly,* and other publications. Member of editorial board of *Virginia Woolf Newsletter,* 1971-72, *Virginia Woolf Quarterly,* 1971-73, *Twentieth Century Literature,* 1973—, and *Signs,* 1975—.

SIDELIGHTS: Carolyn Heilbrun writes both mystery novels and scholarly works. Under the pseudonym Amanda Cross, Heilbrun writes of Kate Fansler, a university professor and amateur detective. Her mystery writing has elicited favorable comment from several critics. A. J. Hubin, writing in the *New York Times Book Review,* says of *Poetic Justice* that "the mystery and detection here are almost incidental . . . to the dazzling display of elegance of language." Anthony Boucher describes *The James Joyce Murder* as "a highly attractive specimen of the leisurely and witty academic mystery novel." *Newsweek* reviewer Katrine Ames states that Heilbrun is "a smart, economical writer with a gift for creating quick, literate characters whom she can pin down in one sentence." Paul Pickrel of *Harper's* finds *The James Joyce Murder* so deftly complex that it "makes three-dimensional chess look like child's play."

Heilbrun's scholarly writings examine sex roles in modern society. Her *Reinventing Womanhood,* a study of the self-image of American women and its relationship to feminism, drew particular praise. Roberta Rubenstein writes in the *Chicago Tribune* that the book "forces one to re-examine a familiar issue from a fresh perspective, as it brings to light the hidden assumptions or unexplored implications of realities that daily stare one in the face." Rubenstein concludes that *Reinventing Womanhood* "is essential reading for anyone interested not only in the future of womanhood but in the stimulating possibilities for liberation of both sexes."

BIOGRAPHICAL/CRITICAL SOURCES: New York Times Book Review, May 24, 1964, March 19, 1967, June 21, 1970, October 3, 1976, January 8, 1978; *Book Week,* June 14, 1964; *Times Literary Supplement,* September 24, 1964, June 29, 1967; *Minnesota Review,* November, 1966; *Harper's,* April, 1967; *Modern Language Journal,* October, 1967; *Saturday Review,* June 27, 1970; *Christian Science Monitor,* September 15, 1976; *Newsweek,* October 4, 1976; *Listener,* November 25, 1976; *Spectator,* January 1, 1977; *Southwest Review,* autumn, 1977; *Book World,* April 22, 1979; *Chicago Tribune,* April 22, 1979.

* * *

HEIN, John 1921-

PERSONAL: Born March 1, 1921, in Freiburg, Germany; naturalized U.S. citizen in 1943; son of Siegfried (a physician) and Elisabeth (Dreifuss) Hein; married Jane Harmon (a music teacher), October 24, 1957; children: Jeremy, Simeon. *Education:* Columbia University, B.S., 1949, M.S., 1949, Ph.D., 1963. *Office:* Conference Board, 845 Third Ave., New York, N.Y. 10022.

CAREER: Federal Reserve Bank of New York, New York City, economist, 1953-61, chief of Foreign Research Division, 1962-64, special assistant, 1964-67; Conference Board, New York City, director of international economic research, 1967—. Visiting scholar, Economic Research Institute, Dublin, 1966. Consultant to Commission of Government Procurement, 1971. *Military service:* U.S. Army, 1943-45; received Purple Heart and Bronze Star. *Member:* American Economic Association, New York Association of Business Economists.

WRITINGS: Institutional Aspects of Commercial and Central Banking in Ireland, Economic Research Institute (Dublin), 1967; (with M. Ehrlich) *The Competitive Position of U.S. Exports,* Conference Board, 1968; *Understanding the Balance of Payments,* Conference Board, 1970; *Aspects of Incomes Policies Abroad,* Conference Board, 1972; *The World Economy in the 1970's: Trends and Issues,* Conference Board, 1973; *The Changing World Economy: Problems of Interdependence,* Conference Board, 1977; *United States Exports in World Markets,* Conference Board, 1978. Contributor to *Encyclopedia Americana, Conference Board Record, Journal of Finance, Economia Internazionale,* and *Canadian Banker.*

WORK IN PROGRESS: Interdependence and National Economic Policies.

AVOCATIONAL INTERESTS: Music, especially the flute and piano, and languages.

* * *

HEINLEIN, Robert A(nson) 1907-
(Anson MacDonald, Lyle Monroe, John Riverside, Caleb Saunders, Simon York)

PERSONAL: Surname rhymes with "Fine line"; born July 7, 1907, in Butler, Mo.; son of Rex Ivar and Bam (Lyle) Heinlein; married Virginia Gerstenfeld, October 21, 1948. *Education:* Graduate of U.S. Naval Academy, 1929; University of California, Los Angeles, graduate study, 1934. *Home:* 6000 Bonny Doon Rd., Santa Cruz, Calif. 95060.

CAREER: Commissioned lieutenant, U.S. Navy, 1929, retired 1934, because of physical disability in line of duty, aviation engineer, 1942-45. Free-lance writer, 1939—. Guest commentator during Apollo 11 flight, Columbia Broadcasting System, 1969. Forrestal Lecturer, United States Naval Academy, 1973. Owner of Shively & Sophie Lodes silver mine, 1934-35. *Member:* American Institute of Astronautics and Aeronautics, Authors' League of America, Navy League, Air Force Association, Air Power Council, Association of the Army of the United States, United States Naval Academy Alumni Association, American Association for the Advancement of Science. *Awards, honors:* Hugo Award, World Science Fiction Convention, 1956, for *Double Star,* 1960, for *Starship Troopers,* 1962, for *Stranger in a Strange Land,* and 1967, for *The Moon Is a Harsh Mistress;* Boys' Clubs of America Book Award, 1959; Sequoyah Children's Book Award of Oklahoma, Oklahoma Library Association, 1961, for *Have Space Suit, Will Travel;* Nebula Grand Master Award, Science Fiction Writers of America, 1974; National Rare Blood Club Humanitarian Award, 1974; Council of Community Blood Centers Award, 1977; American Association of Blood Banks Award, 1977; Inkpot Award, 1977.

WRITINGS—Science fiction novels: *Rocket Ship Galileo,* Scribner, 1947, reprinted, Ballantine, 1977; *Beyond This Horizon,* Fantasy Press, 1948, reprinted, New American Library, 1974; *Space Cadet,* Scribner, 1948, reprinted, Ballantine, 1978; *Red Planet,* Scribner, 1949, reprinted, Ballantine, 1977; *Sixth Column,* Gnome, 1949.

Farmer in the Sky, Scribner, 1950, reprinted, Ballantine, 1975; *Waldo* [and] *Magic, Inc.,* Doubleday, 1950; *Between Planets,* Scribner, 1951, reprinted, Ballantine, 1978; *Puppet Masters,* Doubleday, 1951; *Rolling Stones,* Scribner, 1952, reprinted, Ballantine, 1977 (published in England as *Space Family Stone,* Gollancz, 1969); *Revolt in 2100,* Shasta, 1953; *Starman Jones,* Scribner, 1953, revised edition, edited by Judy L. Del Rey, Ballantine, 1975; *Star Beast,* Scribner, 1954, reprinted, Ballantine, 1977; *Tunnel in the Sky,* Scribner, 1955, reprinted, Ballantine, 1977; *Double Star,* Doubleday, 1956, reprinted, Gregg, 1978; *Time for the Stars,* Scribner, 1956, reprinted, Ballantine, 1978; *Citizen of the Galaxy,* Scribner, 1957, reprinted, Ballantine, 1978; *Door into Summer,* Doubleday, 1957; (with others) *Famous Science Fiction Stories,* Random House, 1957; *Have Space Suit, Will Travel,* Scribner, 1958, reprinted, 1977; *Methusalah's Children,* Gnome Press, 1958; *Starship Troopers,* Putnam, 1959.

Stranger in a Strange Land, Putnam, 1961; *Glory Road,* Putnam, 1963; *Podkayne of Mars: Her Life and Times,* Putnam, 1963; *Orphans of the Sky,* Gollancz, 1963, Putnam, 1964; *Farnham's Freehold,* Putnam, 1964; *The Moon Is a Harsh Mistress,* Putnam, 1966; *I Will Fear No Evil,* Putnam, 1971; *Time Enough for Love: The Lives of Lazarus Long,* Putnam, 1973; *The Notebooks of Lazarus Long,* Putnam, 1978; *Expanded Universe,* Ace, 1980.

Omnibus volumes: *Three by Heinlein* (contains *The Puppet Masters, Waldo,* and *Magic, Inc.*), Doubleday, 1965 (published in England as *A Heinlein Triad,* Gollancz, 1966).

Short story collections: *The Man Who Sold the Moon,* Shasta, 1950, reprinted, New American Library, 1973; *The Green Hills of Earth,* Shasta, 1951, reprinted, Aeonian, 1976; (editor) *Tomorrow, the Stars,* Doubleday, 1952; *Assignment in Eternity,* Fantasy Press, 1953, reprinted, New American Library, 1970; *The Menace from Earth,* Gnome Press, 1959, reprinted, Aeonian, 1976; *The Unpleasant Profession of Jonathan Hoag,* Gnome Press, 1959, reprinted, Berkley, 1976, published as *6 x H,* Pyramid Publications, 1962; *The Worlds of Robert A. Heinlein,* Ace, 1966; *The Past through Tomorrow: Future History Stories,* Putnam, 1967; Angus Walls, editor, *Best of Robert Heinlein (1939-1959),* two volumes, Sidgwick & Jackson, 1973.

Nonfiction: (Contributor) Lloyd A. Eshbach, editor, *Of Worlds Beyond: The Science of Science Fiction,* Fantasy Press, 1947, reprinted, Dobson, 1967; (with others) *The Science Fiction Novel,* Advent, 1959.

Screenplays: "Destination Moon," Eagle Lion, 1950; "Project Moonbase," Lippert Productions, 1953.

Also author of engineering reports. Work appears in numerous anthologies. Contributor of over 150 short stories and articles, some under pseudonyms, to *Saturday Evening Post, Blue Book, Analog, Galaxy, Astounding Science Fiction,* and other magazines.

SIDELIGHTS: "The one author," Alfred Bester writes, "who has raised science fiction from the gutter of pulp space opera . . . to the altitude of original and breathtaking concepts is Robert A. Heinlein." Heinlein's influence in his field has been so great that Alexei Panshin states, "The last twenty-five years of science fiction may even be taken in large part as an exploration by many writers of the possibilities inherent in Heinlein's techniques."

Heinlein's influence is due primarily to his early fiction and, as Panshin points out, derives from his "narrative pace, wide range of materials, and thoroughly worked-out backgrounds, and most particularly his ability to inject detail into his stories without making them tedious." Reviewers believe that these techniques serve to make Heinlein's stories easily believable, even when they are most imaginative or unlikely. Other science fiction writers soon followed Heinlein's example in their own work. "Heinlein," Peter R. Weston states, "has been responsible for establishing the methods and techniques of modern speculative fiction." A poll taken by *Astounding Science Fiction* in 1953 found that eighteen of the top science fiction writers of the time counted Heinlein as their major influence.

Despite his great influence, Heinlein's explanations of his work seem to belie his importance. About his writing, he once told an interviewer, "I start out with some characters and get them into trouble and when they get themselves out of trouble the story's over." As for writing dialogue, he has said, "Once I hear the voices of my characters, I just take down what they're saying."

Throughout his career, Heinlein has displayed a continuing concern with the exploration and colonization of outer space. He wrote the screenplay and served as technical advisor to "Destination Moon," "the first serious *and* commercially successful space flight film," as Weston describes it, which also "helped to pave the way for . . . Apollo." Donald A. Wollheim notes that Heinlein "believes in the future of mankind and in the endless frontier of the galactic civilization that is to be.'' ''Heinlein assumes,'' Diane Parkin Speer writes, ''that technology will continue to develop, [that] the cosmos is infinite, [and that] with increased scientific knowledge man may roam the universe.''

Since the late 1950s, Heinlein's books have tended to deal with controversial subjects. *Starship Troopers,* for example, describes a society run by the military. *Stranger in a Strange Land* tells the story of a religious movement practicing free love and cannibalism. *The Moon Is a Harsh Mistress* depicts idealistic group marriages, while *Time Enough for Love* deals with incest. Heinlein has said that the reason he began to deal with sexual issues during the 1960s was ''because there was no market for sex in science fiction before then.''

Perhaps the most successful of Heinlein's more controversial novels has been *Stranger in a Strange Land.* A best-seller, the book won a Hugo Award, developed an intense cult following, and even inspired a real-life ''Church of All Worlds'' based upon the protagonist's church. Critics praised *Stranger's* satirical view of modern society. ''*Stranger,*'' Ronald Lee Cansler notes, ''takes a caustic look at everything from 'true confession' magazines to democracy, but in particular Heinlein is concerned with exposing and undermining stifling sexual mores and repressive religion.'' A reviewer for *Booklist* calls it ''severe social criticism conveyed through a blend of fantasy, satire, and science fiction.'' ''Heinlein,'' Willis E. McNelly writes, ''is almost Swiftian in his attack.''

Although several of these more controversial books have won major awards, some critics have expressed reservations about them. ''Instead of concerning himself with facts,'' Panshin says of several books from this period, Heinlein ''has treated his opinions as though they were facts. More than that, he has so concentrated on presenting his opinions with every narrative device he knows that he has neglected story construction, characterization, and plot.'' In reviewing the militaristic *Starship Troopers,* Robert McCary sees Heinlein as ''a peddler of dangerous ideologies'' who believes in ''the cult of violence.''

Despite some critical misgivings about his more recent work, Heinlein is generally acknowledged as a major stylistic innovator and holds a place of high esteem among science fiction writers. Daniel F. Galouye believes that if Heinlein wasn't ''voluntarily and enthusiastically involved in the restricted field of science fiction, [he] would certainly be one of today's literary giants.'' Adding to the praise, Panshin believes that ''Heinlein's reputation [will] come eventually to resemble that of Kipling. . . . I think English letters will grant both small, secure places [and that their] security will be increased by the fact that . . . both men will continue to be read.'' Summing up Heinlein's career and accomplishments, Harry Harrison states that ''as a seminal writer he shaped the future of the [science fiction] field. I tip my hat to him and suggest that a portrait bust of Robert Anson Heinlein be placed in the science fiction hall of fame, right next to that of Herbert George Wells.''

Heinlein told *CA:* ''I started writing for a reason many writers have had: I was in poor health and unable to work steadily. I continued because it turned out to be a gratifying way of supporting myself and my dependents. Most of my work has been fiction speculating about the future, with much of it concerned with space travel and the possibility of colonizing off Earth. My works show that I pioneered in anticipating the present ecological and population crises.''

Heinlein and his wife enjoy traveling, having visited some eighty countries and traveled over the North Pole. ''For many years,'' Heinlein told *CA,* ''my time has been about evenly divided between writing and travel. But for the past few years ill health has limited both.''

Television, radio, and film rights to many of Heinlein's works have been sold. A collection of his manuscripts and correspondence is housed at the University of California Library, Santa Cruz.

AVOCATIONAL INTERESTS: Stone masonry and sculpture, cats, ballistics, fiscal theory.

BIOGRAPHICAL/CRITICAL SOURCES: *Galaxy,* February, 1952, December, 1966; *Analog,* May, 1954, September, 1964; Damon Knight, *In Search of Wonder,* Advent, 1956, revised edition, 1967; *Magazine of Fantasy and Science Fiction,* June, 1956, November, 1961, March, 1971; *New York Times,* March 3, 1957, August 22, 1973; *Christian Science Monitor,* November 7, 1957; *Saturday Review,* November 1, 1958; *San Francisco Chronicle,* November 8, 1959.

New York Times Book Review, January 31, 1960, March 23, 1975; *American Mercury,* October, 1960; *Booklist,* July 15, 1961; *Chicago Tribune,* August 6, 1961; *New York Herald Tribune Book Review,* May 12, 1962; *New Worlds,* June, 1962; *Author and Journalist,* January, 1963; *National Review,* March 26, 1963, November 16, 1970; *New Statesman,* July 30, 1965; *Punch,* August 25, 1965, November 22, 1967; Sam Moskowitz, *Seekers of Tomorrow,* World Publishing, 1966; *Spectator,* June 3, 1966, July, 30, 1977; *Best Sellers,* June 15, 1966; Alexei Panshin, *Heinlein in Dimension,* Advent, 1968; *The CEA Critic,* March, 1968; *Speculation,* August, 1969; *Books & Bookmen,* October, 1969, March, 1972.

William Atheling, Jr., *More Issues at Hand,* Advent, 1970; Lois Rose and Stephen Rose, *The Shattered Ring: Science Fiction and the Quest for Meaning,* John Knox, 1970; *Science Fiction Review,* November, 1970; *National Observer,* November 16, 1970; *Extrapolation,* December, 1970; Donald A. Wollheim, *The Universe Makers,* Harper, 1971; *Times Literary Supplement,* April 2, 1971, June 14, 1974; *Worlds of If,* August, 1971, September/October, 1973; *Journal of Popular Culture,* spring, 1972; *Contemporary Literary Criticism,* Gale, Volume I, 1973, Volume III, 1975, Volume VIII, 1978; *Publisher's Weekly,* July 2, 1973; *Views and Reviews,* December, 1973; *Village Voice,* June 13, 1974; *New Yorker,* July 1, 1974; *Guardian Weekly,* August 24, 1974; *Book World,* May 11, 1975; *Commonweal,* August 1, 1975; George E. Slusser, *Robert A. Heinlein: Stranger in His Own Land,* Borgo Press, 1976; *Observer,* April 4, 1976; Slusser, *The Classic Years of Robert A. Heinlein,* Borgo Press, 1977; Joseph D. Olander and Martin H. Greenberg, editors, *Robert A. Heinlein,* Taplinger, 1978; James Gunn, *The Road to Science Fiction: From Heinlein to the Present,* New American Library, 1979.

—*Sketch by Thomas Wiloch*

* * *

HELCK, C. Peter 1893-

PERSONAL: Born June 17, 1893, in New York, N.Y.; son of Henry P. (a jeweller) and Clara L. (Brand) Helck; married Priscilla Edna Smith, September 30, 1922; children: Jerry Peter. *Education:* Studied art at Art Students League and in private classes in New York, N.Y. *Home and studio:* Boston Corners, R.D. 2, Millerton, N.Y. 12546.

CAREER: Free-lance artist, 1915—, whose work is a mixing of the fine and commercial arts. Advertising artist for the automotive and other industries, 1918—; illustrator for national magazines, 1925-60; both commercial and fine arts works have been exhibited in a dozen one-man shows since 1923, and are owned by Metropolitan Museum of Art, Philadelphia Museum of Fine Arts, Library of Congress, Carnegie Institute, New Britain Museum of American Art, Long Island Automotive Museum, Cunningham Automotive Museum, Montagu Museum, and Harrah Collection. Founding faculty member, Famous Artists Schools, Westport, Conn., 1948—.

MEMBER: National Academy of Design, American Watercolor Society, Allied Artists, Society of Illustrators (life member), Vintage Sports Car Club of America (honorary member), Salmagundi Club (honorary member), Society of Automotive Historians (honorary member). *Awards, honors:* Harvard Award, 1929; twenty art directors medals and awards since 1931 in New York, Philadelphia, Chicago, Detroit, and Cleveland; Salmagundi Club gold medal, 1961, Society of Illustrators gold medal, 1962, Thomas McKean Memorial Trophy, 1962, and Byrun Hull Cup, 1962, all for *The Checkered Flag;* elected to Society of Illustrators Hall of Fame, 1968; Byrun Hull Cup, 1976, for *Great Auto Races.*

WRITINGS: How I Make a Picture, Famous Artists School, 1949; *The Checkered Flag,* Scribner, 1961; *The Forgotten Briarcliff,* Antique Automobile, 1963; *Twenty-Four Hours to Go,* Automobile Quarterly, 1966; *Great Auto Races,* Abrams, 1976. Contributor of approximately forty articles on automotive history to the leading auto club journals. Editorial staff member of *Automobile Quarterly, Car Classics, Bulb Horn, Antique Automobile,* and *Automobilist.*

SIDELIGHTS: C. Peter Helck told *CA:* "My interest in autos dates from childhood. It's my good fortune to have personally known and ridden with such old time greats as 'Daredevil Joe' Tracy, Ralph DePalma, George Robertson, Louis Wagner, all of them winners in Vanderbilt Cup racing, 1906-1914. My own collection of elderly cars includes the first American winner, in 1908, of the Vanderbilt Cup, the 16.2 litre Locomobile widely known as 'Old 16.'

"Regarding my books, *The Checkered Flag* and *Great Auto Races,* both had been visualized as 'picture books' with but brief commentaries for each pictured subject. In each instance these commentaries became narratives, and eventually were expanded to fully developed text. I was now able to dispute that old cliche, 'One picture is equal to a thousand words.' Having witnessed racing since 1906 I found I could not say it all with paint and brushes. By this time the pleasure—and the anguish—derived from writing matched those in creating paintings. Such became my enthusiasm in the role of author-artist that my script for *Great Auto Races* had to be cut some 20,000 words to accommodate the prescribed 260 pages and the 220 illustrations, 90 in full color.

"The book was accorded favorable reviews here, in England, in Japan, the most amusing of which, in the *New York Times,* spoke highly of the writing but less so of the art." *Great Auto Races* was translated into Japanese.

BIOGRAPHICAL/CRITICAL SOURCES: Forty Illustrators and How They Work, Watson-Guptil, 1946; *Illustrating for the "Saturday Evening Post,"* Curtis, 1951; *Creative Perspective,* Watson-Guptil, 1952; *American Artist,* January, 1962, July, 1977; *Sports Car,* May, 1962; *Automobile Quarterly,* Volume III, number 1, 1964; *Antique Automobile,* May, 1964; *Twenty-Two Famous Artists and Illustrators,* McKay, 1964; *The Illustrator in America,* Reinhold, 1964; *Automobile Illustration,* Inomoto (Tokyo), 1970; *200 Years of American Illustration,* Random House, 1977; *Motor Trend,* February, 1977; *Autographics,* autumn, 1977; *Motor,* May, 1978; *Packard Cormorant,* summer, 1978.

HELD, Virginia (Potter) 1929-

PERSONAL: Born October 28, 1929, in Mendham, N.J.; daughter of John Howard Nott and Margaretta (Wood) Potter; married Hans W. Held, 1950 (separated, 1973); children: Julia, Philip. *Education:* Barnard College, B.A. (cum laude), 1950; attended University of Strasbourg and University of Paris; Columbia University, Ph.D., 1968. *Office:* Department of Philosophy, City University of New York, 33 West 42nd St., New York, N.Y. 10036.

CAREER: Columbia University, New York City, lecturer in philosophy, 1964-66; City University of New York, New York City, lecturer in philosophy, 1965-69, assistant professor, 1969-72, associate professor, 1973-77, professor of philosophy, 1977—. Visiting professor, Yale University, 1972. *Member:* American Philosophical Association, Society for Philosophy and Public Affairs (member of executive committee, 1970-73; chairperson, 1972; chairperson of program committee, 1976-77), International Association for Philosophy of Law and Social Philosophy (member of executive committee, 1978-80; vice-president, 1979-81), Society for Women in Philosophy. *Awards, honors:* Fulbright grant, 1950-51; Rockefeller Foundation Humanities fellowship, 1975-76.

WRITINGS: The Bewildered Age, C. N. Potter, 1962; *The Public Interest and Individual Interests,* Basic Books, 1970; (editor with Kai Nielsen and Charles Parsons) *Philosophy and Political Action,* Oxford University Press, 1972; (editor with Sidney Morgenbesser and Thomas Nagel) *Philosophy, Morality, and International Affairs,* Oxford University Press, 1974; (editor) *Property, Profits and Economic Justice,* Wadsworth, 1980. Contributor to *Reporter, New Leader, Nation, Social Research,* and other periodicals.

* * *

HEMLEY, Cecil Herbert 1914-1966

PERSONAL: Born July 21, 1914, in New York, N.Y.; died March 9, 1966, in Columbus, Ohio; buried in Alexander Cemetery, Athens, Ohio; son of Frederick and Sarah (Gottlieb) Hemley; married Kathryn Witherstine, May 29, 1945 (divorced); married Elaine Gottlieb (a novelist), July 3, 1952; children: (first marriage) Sara Elizabeth, Frederick; (second marriage) Jonathan, Robin, Nola (stepdaughter). *Education:* Amherst College, B.A., 1934; University of Chicago, M.A., 1950. *Office:* Ohio University Press, Athens, Ohio 45701.

CAREER: Noonday Press, Inc., New York City, co-founder, 1951, co-director, 1951-60; Farrar, Straus & Cudahy, Inc., New York City, editor-in-chief of Noonday Press, 1960-64; Ohio University Press, Athens, Ohio, director, 1964-66. Fellow, McDowell Colony, 1956. *Military service:* U.S. Army, Signal Corps, 1942-46; became first lieutenant. *Member:* P.E.N., Poetry Society of America (president, 1961-63).

WRITINGS: Porphyry's Journey (poetry), Noonday Press, 1951; *Twenty Poems,* Voyages Press, 1956; *In the Midnight Wood* (poetry), Noonday Press, 1958; *The Experience* (novel), Horizon, 1960; (editor) *Prison,* Twayne, 1962; (translator) Isaac Bashevis Singer, *The Slave,* Farrar, Straus, 1962; *Young Crankshaw* (novel), Harcourt, 1963; *Hemlock and the Cross* (poetry), Lippincott, 1963; *Dimensions of Midnight: Poetry and Prose,* edited by wife, Elaine Gottlieb, foreword by Mark Van Doren, Ohio University Press, 1967.

SIDELIGHTS: Reviewing *Dimensions of Midnight,* Chad Walsh wrote: "What the book reveals is a craftsman of a high order, but a writer to whom content and moral sensitivity are even more important than craft alone. [Cecil Hemley was] a civilized man, viewing a world of mixed comedy and tragedy and pathos, but gravely observing the brief players on the stage and giving them the same courteous due that he accorded himself as another player on the same stage.... Henley reveal[ed] himself most of all in his poetry. He wrote that kind of verse which is least in vogue today.... Hemley's poetry, in fact, stands in a perennial tradition of meditations upon the broken beauty, the mingled glory and pathos of the tangible world; the unbridgeable gap between that world and the world sensed by imagination or faith. Part of the power of his poetry is that he does not opt exclusively for one or the other; even while yearning for the unseen he celebrates the present world and its inhabitants in perceptive and loving verses."

BIOGRAPHICAL/CRITICAL SOURCES: New York Times Book Review, November 26, 1967.†

* * *

HEMPSTONE, Smith 1929-

PERSONAL: Born February 1, 1929, in Washington, D.C.; son of Smith (a naval officer) and Elizabeth (Noyes) Hempstone; married Kathaleen Fishback, January 30, 1954; children: Katherine Hope. *Education:* Attended George Washington University, 1946-47; University of the South, B.A., 1950; Harvard University, graduate study, 1964-65. *Politics:* "A conservative independent." *Religion:* Episcopalian. *Home and office:* 7611 Fairfax Rd., Bethesda, Md. 20014.

CAREER: Associated Press, Charlotte, N.C., radio rewrite, 1952; *Louisville Times,* Louisville, Ky., reporter, 1953; *National Geographic,* Washington, D.C., rewrite, 1954; *Washington Star,* Washington, D.C., reporter, 1955-56; Institute of Current World Affairs, fellow in Africa, 1956-60; *Chicago Daily News,* foreign correspondent in Africa, 1961-64, and Latin America, 1965; *Washington Star,* foreign correspondent in Latin America, 1966, and Europe, 1967-69, associate editor and editorial page director, 1970-75; author of syndicated twice-weekly column, "Our Times," 1975—. Trustee, University of the South, 1975-78; governor, Institute of Current World Affairs, 1975-78. *Military service:* U.S. Marines, 1950-52; became captain. *Member:* American Society of Newspaper Editors, National Conference of Editorial Writers, Chevy Chase Club, Metropolitan Club, Explorers Club. *Awards, honors:* Sigma Delta Chi Award for distinguished service in journalism (foreign correspondence), 1960; Nieman fellow, 1964-65; Overseas Press Club citations for excellence in foreign correspondence, 1968, 1974; honorary doctorate of letters from University of the South, 1968.

WRITINGS: Africa: Angry Young Giant, Praeger, 1961 (published in England as *The New Africa,* Faber, 1961); *Katanga Report,* Faber, 1962; *Rebels, Mercenaries and Dividends: The Katanga Story,* Praeger, 1962; *A Tract of Time* (novel), Houghton, 1966; *In the Midst of Lions* (novel), Harper, 1968. Contributor to *Saturday Evening Post, Atlantic, Reader's Digest, U.S. News & World Report,* and other magazines.

SIDELIGHTS: Smith Hempstone comments: "I try to place what I write in a historical perspective in the knowledge that there is, truly, nothing new under the sun. Because I do write from this perspective, my views in the main are conservative."

* * *

HENDEL, Samuel 1909-

PERSONAL: Born July 6, 1909, in New York, N.Y.; son of Judah and Leah (Gerber) Hendel; married Clara Hoch, May 14, 1932; children: Linda Susan, Stephen. *Education:* Brooklyn Law School, LL.B. (cum laude), 1930; City College (now City College of the City University of New York), B.S.S. (cum laude), 1936; Columbia University, Ph.D., 1948.

CAREER: Admitted to Bar of State of New York, 1931; Sharetts, Coe & Hillis, New York City, law clerk, 1926-31, attorney, 1931-34; private practice of law in New York City, 1934-41; City College of the City University of New York, New York City, 1941-70, professor of political science, 1957-70, chairman of department, 1957-62, chairman of Russian Area Graduate Program, 1960-70, ombudsman, 1969-70; Trinity College, Hartford, Conn., professor of political science, beginning 1970, chairman of department, 1970-73. Visiting professor of government, graduate faculty, Columbia University, 1958-60, summer, 1962; visiting professor of comparative government and international relations, Claremont Graduate School, spring, 1962; visiting professor, University of Connecticut Law School, fall, 1975. Legal consultant, 1941—. *Member:* American Political Science Association (member of executive council, 1965—), American Association for the Advancement of Slavic Studies, Far Western Slavic Association, American Association of University Professors, American Civil Liberties Union (chairman of Academic Freedom Committee, 1959-60, 1966-73; member of board of directors, 1967—; vice-chairman, 1974-76), American Jewish Congress (chairman of Committee on International Affairs, 1959-61), Phi Beta Kappa (president of Gamma Chapter, 1960-61). *Awards, honors:* Ford Faculty fellowship for study of Soviet affairs, 1953-54; Inter-University Committee on Travel Grants award to visit the Soviet Union, 1957.

WRITINGS: (Editor with Hillman M. Bishop) *Basic Issues of American Democracy,* Appleton, 1948, 7th edition (sole editor), published as *Bishop and Hendel's Basic Issues of American Democracy,* 1973, 8th edition, Prentice-Hall, 1976; *Charles Evans Hughes and the Supreme Court,* Columbia University Press, 1951, reprinted, Russell, 1968; (editor) *The Soviet Crucible: Soviet Government in Theory and Practice,* Van Nostrand, 1959, 4th edition, Duxbury, 1973; (contributor) William G. Andrews, editor, *European Politics,* Volume I, Van Nostrand, 1965; (contributor) Harry G. Shaffer, editor, *The Communist World: Marxist and Non-Marxist Views,* Appleton, 1967; (compiler) *The Politics of Confrontation,* Appleton, 1971.†

* * *

HENDERSON, Algo D(onmyer) 1897-

PERSONAL: Born April 26, 1897, in Solomon, Kan.; son of Calvert Columbus and Ella (Donmyer) Henderson; married Anne Cristy, 1923 (deceased); married Jean Glidden, 1963; children: (first marriage) Joanne Elizabeth Henderson Pratt, Philip Cristy. *Education:* Attended Georgetown University, 1917-18; University of Kansas, J.D., 1921, C.P.A., 1922; University of Chicago, graduate study, 1923; Harvard University, M.B.A., 1928. *Home:* 239 Glorietta Blvd., Orinda, Calif. 94563.

CAREER: University of Kansas, Lawrence, instructor in economics and commerce, 1920-24; Antioch College, Yellow Springs, Ohio, professor of business administration, 1925-48, dean, 1930-36, acting president, 1935-36, president, 1936-48; helped organize and administer State University of New York system, 1948-50; University of Michigan, Ann Arbor, professor of higher education, 1950-67, professor emeritus,

1967—, founder and director of Center for Study of Higher Education, 1957-66; University of California, Berkeley, research educator at Center for Research and Development in Higher Education, 1966-77. Member of President's Commission on Higher Education, 1946-48, Surgeon General's Committee on Medical School Grants and Financial Aids, 1949-50, and Michigan Commission on College Accreditation, 1950-64. *Military service:* U.S. Army, 1917-19; became second lieutenant. *Member:* American Society for Public Administration, Association for Higher Education. *Awards, honors:* Distinguished Alumnus Award, University of Kansas, 1948; LL.D. from Antioch College, 1948, Olivet College, 1959, Fenn College, 1963, and Cleveland State University, 1968; L.H.D. from Keuka College, 1950; Sesquicentennial Medal, University of Michigan, 1967; Distinguished Service Award, Higher Education Colloquium, 1971.

WRITINGS: *Vitalizing Liberal Education,* Harper, 1944; *Antioch College: Its Design for Liberal Education,* Harper, 1946; *Policies and Practices in Higher Education,* Harper, 1960; (editor) *Higher Education in Tomorrow's World,* University of Michigan, 1968; *The Innovative Spirit,* Jossey-Bass, 1970; (with wife, Jean G. Henderson) *Higher Education in America,* Jossey-Bass, 1974; (with J. G. Henderson) *Ms. Goes to College,* Southern Illinois University Press, 1975. Contributor to other books and to journals and proceedings. Editor, *Proceedings* of the Annual Conference on Higher Education, University of Michigan.

* * *

HENDERSON, Zenna (Chlarson) 1917-

PERSONAL: Born November 1, 1917, in Tucson, Ariz.; daughter of Louis Rudolph and Emily Vernell (Rowley) Chlarson; married, 1944. *Education:* Arizona State University, Tempe, B.A., 1940, M.A., 1954. *Religion:* Methodist. *Home:* 1111 North Ocotillo St., Eloy, Ariz. 85231. *Agent:* Curtis Brown, Ltd., 575 Madison Ave., New York, N.Y. 10022.

CAREER: Teacher in schools in Arizona, at U.S. Air Force dependents' school in France, and at The Seaside (a tuberculosis sanitorium for children), Waterford, Conn.; currently teaching in Eloy, Ariz. *Member:* National Education Association, Arizona Education Association, Science Fiction Writers of America, Society of Southwestern Authors. *Awards, honors:* Second prize, Ellery Queen Contest, 1954; American Library Association Notable Book Award, 1971, for *Holding Wonder.*

WRITINGS: *Pilgrimage: The Book of the People,* Doubleday, 1961; (contributor) Robert C. Pooley and others, editors, *Vanguard,* Scott Publishing, 1961; (contributor) Harold Wagenheim, editor, *This Is America,* Holt, 1963; *The Anything Box* (collected short stories), Doubleday, 1965; *The People: No Different Flesh,* Doubleday, 1966; *Holding Wonder,* Doubleday, 1971.

SIDELIGHTS: Zenna Henderson told *CA*: "I have had a large response, by fan letters, especially from the younger people, favorable to the presence of 'religion' in my stories. Each feels sure I must be a member of his particular persuasion. I feel that that is because of the underlying bond of faith and belief that binds us all together. I think it only proper, in my stories, to say a word for 'Our Sponsor.'" *Avocational interests:* Stamp collecting, languages, travel, needlework.

HENDRICH, Paula Griffith 1928-

PERSONAL: Born October 2, 1928, in Tulsa, Okla.; daughter of Floyd L. and Bernice (Ewert) Griffith; married Linvill L. Hendrich (manager, ARCO Petroleum Products), December 31, 1950; children: Suzanne, Melissa. *Education:* Central Missouri State College (now University), B.S. in Ed., 1950. *Politics:* Republican. *Religion:* Presbyterian. *Home:* 27915 Longhill Dr., Rancho Palos Verdes, Calif.

CAREER: High school teacher of speech and English in Clinton, Mo., 1952-53; Omaha Women's Job Corps, Omaha, Neb., substitute teacher, 1965-66; substitute teacher, Livonia, Mich., 1968-70.

WRITINGS—All published by Lothrop: *Trudy's First Day at Camp,* 1959; *Baby in the Schoolroom,* 1962; *Who Says So?,* 1972; *The Girl Who Slipped Through Time,* 1978; *The Birds Are in Their Hands,* 1980.

WORK IN PROGRESS: *The Hidden Face,* a science fiction book retelling the story of *The Beauty and the Beast; The Truth about CL 101,* another science fiction story concerning the attempt to eliminate clones from the earth.

* * *

HENDRICKSON, Robert 1933-

PERSONAL: Born August 24, 1933, in Far Rockaway, N.Y.; son of Oscar F. (a civil and electrical engineer) and Eunice (a teacher; maiden name, Tierney) Hendrickson; married Marilyn Maggio (a reading teacher), August 29, 1954; children: Robert Laurence, Brian, Karen, Lauren, Erik. *Education:* Adelphi University, A.B. (cum laude), 1957. *Politics:* Independent. *Home:* 2417 Cornaga Ave., Far Rockaway, N.Y. 11691.

CAREER: Free-lance writer. *Military service:* U.S. Army, 1952-54; served in Korea. *Member:* Phi Alpha Theta, Pi Gamma Mu. *Awards, honors:* Ford Foundation fellowship, 1958; Macdowell Colony fellowship, 1973.

WRITINGS: *Human Words,* Chilton, 1972; *Lewd Food,* Chilton, 1974, revised edition published as *Foods for Love,* Stein & Day, 1980; *Ripoffs,* Viking, 1975; *The Great American Chewing Gum Book,* Chilton, 1976; *The Great American Tomatoe Book,* Doubleday, 1977; *The Grand Emporium,* Stein & Day, 1979; *The Literary Life,* Viking, in press; *Animal Words,* Viking, in press; *The Berry Book,* Doubleday, in press. Also contributor to *New York Times Gardening Book, People's Almanac,* parts I and II, *Book of Lists,* parts I and II, and other books. Contributor of about one thousand articles, stories, and poems to literary quarterlies and general magazines.

WORK IN PROGRESS: A novel; a collection of short stories; a book of poems; *Word of Mouth,* for Viking; *More Cunning Than Man,* for Stein & Day; *The Ocean Almanac,* for Doubleday.

AVOCATIONAL INTERESTS: Gardening, philology, travel, ecology, running, distance swimming.

* * *

HENDRICKSON, Walter Brookfield, Jr. 1936-

PERSONAL: Born August 24, 1936, in Indianapolis, Ind.; son of Walter B. and M. Dorris (Walsh) Hendrickson. *Education:* Illinois College, B.A., 1958; special courses at MacMurray College, 1958-59; attended University of Illinois, 1959-61. *Religion:* Episcopalian. *Home and office:* 724 West State St., Jacksonville, Ill. 62650.

CAREER: Free-lance writer, 1958—. *Member:* American

Institute of Aeronautics and Astronautics, Aviation/Space Writers Association, Authors Guild, American Association for the Advancement of Science, American Civil Liberties Union, Jacksonville Junior Chamber of Commerce, Gamma Nu.

WRITINGS: Handbook for Space Travelers, Bobbs-Merrill, 1960; *Pioneering in Space,* Bobbs-Merrill, 1961; *The Study of Rockets, Missiles and Space Made Simple,* Doubleday, 1962; *Reach for the Moon,* Bobbs-Merrill, 1962; *Satellites and What They Do,* Bobbs-Merrill, 1963; *Winging Into Space,* Bobbs-Merrill, 1965; *What's Going On in Space?,* Harvey House, 1968; *Wild Wings,* Harvey House, 1969; *Apollo 11: Men to the Moon,* Harvey House, 1970; *Who Really Invented the Rocket?,* Putnam, 1974; *Manned Spacecraft to Mars and Venus: How They Work,* Putnam, 1975; (co-author) *Illinois: Its People and Culture,* Denison, 1975; *Class G-Zero,* Major Books, 1976. Contributor of articles to numerous periodicals including *Aviation Quarterly, Modern People, Analog, Popular Mechanics,* and *Better Homes and Gardens.*

WORK IN PROGRESS: Numerous other books.

SIDELIGHTS: Walter Hendrickson told *CA:* "When I first began writing, I was an undergraduate and I tried my hand at science fiction, but Sputnik had just caught the public's eye, so I changed to writing factual books on space exploration. Currently, with the hiatus in manned space shots, public interest has turned to science fiction so I have returned to my first love. My personal life is closely tied to my writing with much time at space conferences, visiting space centers, and reading in the aerospace field."

AVOCATIONAL INTERESTS: Painting, gardening, model railroading, photography, and astronomy.

* * *

HENEMAN, Herbert Gerhard, Jr. 1916-

PERSONAL: Born December 2, 1916, in Lester Prairie, Minn.; son of Herbert Gerhard and Alta (Beise) Heneman; married Jane L. Roberts, 1940; children: Alta, Herbert III, Robert. *Education:* University of Minnesota, B.B.A., 1938, M.A., 1943, Ph.D., 1948. *Home:* 1733 Blair Ave., St. Paul, Minn. *Office:* Industrial Relations Department, University of Minnesota, Minneapolis, Minn.

CAREER: Midland Cooperative Wholesale, Minneapolis, Minn., chief accountant,, 1938-40; Employment Stabilization Research Institute, Minneapolis, research associate, 1940-42; University of Minnesota, Minneapolis, instructor, 1942-44; Social Science Research Council, Minneapolis, research fellow, 1946-47; University of Minnesota, assistant director, Industrial Relations Center, 1947-49, associate professor, 1950-54, professor, 1954—, head of industrial relations department and director, Industrial Relations Center, 1961-73. Visiting professor, Stanford University, 1959, and University of Western Australia, 1973. University consultant, U.S. Bureau of Employment Security; chairman, St. Paul Fair Employment Practices Commission, 1956-61; chairman, Governor's Task Force on Labor Relations. Member of board of directors, American Society of Personnel Administration Accreditation Institute. Member of State of Minnesota Advisory Council on Employment Security. *Military service:* U.S. Naval Reserve, 1944-54; became lieutenant. *Member:* American Economic Association, American Society for Personnel Administration (honorary life member), American Association of University Professors, Industrial Relations Research Association, Iota Rho Chi, Alpha Kappa Psi, Beta Gamma Sigma, Campus Club (University of Minnesota). *Awards, honors:* Social Science Research Council fellowship.

WRITINGS: (Editor with John G. Turnbull) *Personnel Administration and Labor Relations,* Prentice-Hall, 1952; (with others) *Handbook of Personnel Management and Labor Relations,* McGraw, 1958; (with Dale Yoder) *Labor Economics,* South-Western, 1959, 2nd edition, 1965; (editor with others) *Employment Relations Research,* Harper, 1960; *The University as Usual in an Unusual World,* International Scholarly Book, 1974; (editor with Donald P. Schwab) *Perspectives on Personnel: Human Resource Management,* Irwin, 1978.

Editor with Yoder; all published by Bureau of National Affairs: *Staffing Policies and Strategies,* 1974; *Motivation and Commitment,* 1975; *Employee and Labor Relations,* 1976; *Planning and Auditing PAIR,* 1976; *Training and Development,* 1977; *Administration and Organization,* 1977; *PAIR Policy and Program Management,* 1978; *Professional PAIR,* 1979; *Handbook of Personnel Management and Industrial Relations,* 1979.

Author of column, "Research Round-up." Contributor of numerous articles to professional journals, most on industrial relations, economics, personnel management and labor relations. Book review editor, *Personnel Administration,* 1973—.

* * *

HENINGER, S(imeon) K(ahn), Jr. 1922-

PERSONAL: Born October 27, 1922, in Monroe, La.; son of Simeon Kahn and Elsye (Lieber) Heninger; married Irene Callen, 1957 (divorced); married Dorothy Langston, 1971; children: (first marriage) Polly Elizabeth, S. K. III; stepchildren: Dale Callen, Kathryn Leigh, Philip Ward. *Education:* Tulane University, B.S., 1943, B.A., 1947, M.A., 1949; Oxford University, B.Litt., 1952; Johns Hopkins University, Ph.D., 1955. *Home:* 6176 Alma St., Vancouver, British Columbia, Canada. *Office:* Department of English, University of British Columbia, Vancouver, British Columbia, Canada.

CAREER: Duke University, Durham, N.C., 1955-67, began as assistant professor, became professor of English; University of Wisconsin—Madison, professor of English, 1967-71, chairman of department, 1968-70; University of British Columbia, Vancouver, professor of English, 1971—. *Military service:* U.S. Army Air Forces, 1943-46; became captain. *Member:* Modern Language Association of America, Mediaeval Academy, Renaissance Society of America, Phi Beta Kappa. *Awards, honors:* Folger Library fellowship, 1961; Guggenheim fellowship, 1962-63; Huntington Library fellowship, 1970-71, 1980-81; Killam fellowship, 1975-76.

WRITINGS: A Handbook of Renaissance Meteorology, Duke University Press, 1960; (editor) *Selections from the Poetical Works of Edmund Spenser,* Houghton, 1970; *Touches of Sweet Harmony,* Henry E. Huntington, 1974; *The Cosmographical Glass,* Henry E. Huntington, 1977.

WORK IN PROGRESS: Sidney and Spenser: The Poet as Maker.

* * *

HERITEAU, Jacqueline 1925-

PERSONAL: Born October 12, 1925, in France; daughter of Marcel (a chef) and Piney (Sutherland) Heriteau; married H. A. Littledale, Jr., April 2, 1955 (divorced, 1961); married David M. Hunter, 1962; children: (first marriage) Krishnal; (second marriage) David S., Holly Brown. *Education:* Attended University of Montreal, 1944, and Sorbonne, University of Paris, 1948, 1950. *Religion:* Christian Science. *Home:* 1049 Park Ave., New York, N.Y. 10028.

CAREER: Free-lance writer. *Montreal Star,* Montreal, Quebec, member of staff, 1950-55.

WRITINGS: How to Grow and Cook It, Hawthorn, 1970; *Oriental Cooking the Fast Wok Way,* Hawthorn, 1972; *Potpourri and Other Fragrant Delights,* Simon & Schuster, 1973; *Easy Gardening Projects,* Popular Library, 1975; *Small Fruit and Vegetable Gardens,* Popular Library, 1975; (with Thalia Erath) *Preserving and Pickling: Putting Foods by in Small Batches,* Western Publishing, 1976; (editor) *Budget Recipes,* Winchester Press, 1976; *Hurry Up and Grow Gardens,* Popular Library, 1976; *Best of Electric Crockery Cooking,* Grosset, 1976; *The Office Gardener,* Hawthorn, 1977; *Small Flower Gardens,* Popular Library, 1977; *The Complete Book of Beans,* Hawthorn, 1978; *Hurry Up and Grow Plants and Gardens,* Popular Library, 1979.

General editor of "Family Creative Workshop" series, Time-Life, "The Good Housekeeping Illustrated Encyclopedia of Gardening," Hearst, and "Woman Alive," Doubleday. Contributor to *Family Circle* and other magazines.

SIDELIGHTS: Jacqueline Heriteau told *CA:* "I always found my joy in gardening and cooking. Arranging flowers in the garden and in the vases—making a warm and welcome table with food that delighted the palate and with flowers and candles and pretty things that delighted the eye—had a certain glory. All my books about gardening and cooking were written effortlessly and with remarkable speed because they'd been born in my most relaxed moments. So, when my children look puzzled at the many choices their talents and a contemporary world offer, I say 'follow your love' (quoting the philosopher/painter Earl Hubbard) because what I have loved most has sustained me in every way."

* * *

HERRICK, Marvin Theodore 1899-1966 (John Smith, a joint pseudonym)

PERSONAL: Born July 3, 1899, in Mocksville, N.C.; died January 22, 1966; buried in Urbana, Ill.; son of Glenn W. (a professor) and Nannie (Burke) Herrick; married Nigel Hill, February 5, 1929; children: Susan (Mrs. John Bosworth). *Education:* Cornell University, A.B., 1922, Ph.D., 1925; Harvard University, A.M., 1923. *Home:* 207 West Nevada, Urbana, Ill. 61801. *Office:* 207 English, University of Illinois, Urbana, Ill. 61801.

CAREER: Iowa State College of Agriculture and Mechanic Arts (now Iowa State University of Science and Technology), Ames, assistant professor, 1925-26; University of Illinois at Urbana-Champaign, assistant professor, 1926-27; University of Pittsburgh, Pittsburgh, Pa., 1927-34, began as assistant professor, became associate professor of English; George Washington University, Washington, D.C., associate professor, 1935-37; University of Illinois at Urbana-Champaign, 1937-66, began as assistant professor, professor of English, 1945-66, associate dean of liberal arts and sciences, 1942-45. Visiting professor at Swarthmore College, 1931-32, Princeton University, 1934, and Trinity College, Hartford, Conn., 1934-35. *Military service:* U.S. Navy, 1918-19. Illinois State Militia, 1943-44. *Member:* Modern Language Association of America, Renaissance Society, American Association of University Professors, Phi Beta Kappa.

WRITINGS: (With Hoyt Hudson, under joint pseudonym John Smith) *The Upper Forty* [and] *Out of the Night* (one-act plays), Samuel French, 1928; *The Poetics of Aristotle in England,* Yale University Press, 1930, reprinted, Phaeton Press, 1976; *The One-Act Play,* University of Pittsburgh, 1930; (with Charles G. Osgood) *Eleven British Writers,* Houghton, 1940; *The Fusion of Horation and Aristotelian Literary Criticism,* University of Illinois Press, 1946; *Comic Theory in the Sixteenth Century,* University of Illinois Press, 1950; *Tragicomedy: Its Origin and Development in Italy, France, and England,* University of Illinois Press, 1956; *Italian Comedy in the Renaissance,* University of Illinois Press, 1960; *Italian Tragedy in the Renaissance,* University of Illinois Press, 1965; (compiler) *Italian Plays, 1500-1700, in the University of Illinois Library,* University of Illinois Press, 1966; (editor) William Wycherley, *The Country Wife,* Barron's, 1967. Contributor to philology and literature journals.†

* * *

HIGHAM, Robin (David Stewart) 1925-

PERSONAL: Born June 20, 1925, in London, England; U.S. citizen; son of Frank David (an author's agent and novelist) and Anne (Stewart) Higham; married Barbara Davies, 1950; children: Susan, Martha, Carol. *Education:* Attended University of New Hampshire, 1947-48; Harvard University, A.B. (cum laude), 1950, Ph.D., 1957; Claremont College (now Claremont Graduate School), M.A., 1953. *Religion:* Presbyterian. *Home:* 2961 Nevada St., Manhattan, Kan. 66502. *Agent:* Harold Ober Associates, 40 East 49th St., New York, N.Y. 10017. *Office:* History Department, Kansas State University, Manhattan, Kan. 66516.

CAREER: Assistant and instructor at various institutions, 1950-57; University of North Carolina at Chapel Hill, assistant professor, 1957-63; Kansas State University, Manhattan, associate professor, 1963-66, professor of history, 1966—, graduate faculty lecturer, 1971. Historian, British Overseas Airways Corp., 1960-66, 1976—. Archivist, American Committee on the History of the Second World War, 1977—. Vice-chairman of editorial board, University Press of Kansas, 1967-71; military advisory editor, University Press of Kentucky, 1969-75; founder, director, and publisher, Sunflower University Press, 1978—. *Military service:* Royal Air Force, 1943-47; became flight sergeant pilot; received Burma Star. *Member:* American Historical Association, American Aviation Historical Society, U.S. Naval Institute, American Military Institute, Air Force Historical Foundation, Organization of American Historians, Aviation/Space Writers Association, Society for History of Technology, Conference on British Studies (member of publications committee, 1965—), Arnold Air Society (life member). *Awards, honors:* Social Science Research Council, National Security Policy Research Fellowship, 1960-61.

WRITINGS: Britain's Imperial Air Routes, 1918-1939, G. T. Foulis, 1960, Archon Books, 1961; *The British Rigid Airship, 1908-1931: A Study in Weapons Policy,* G. T. Foulis, 1961, Greenwood Press, 1976; *Armed Forces in Peacetime: Britain, 1918-1939,* G. T. Foulis, 1963; *The Military Intellectuals in Britain: 1918-1939,* Rutgers University Press, 1966; (with David H. Zook, Jr.) *A Short History of Warfare,* Twayne, 1966; *Air Power: A Concise History,* St. Martin's, 1972; *The Compleat Academic: Being an Informal Guide to the Ivory Tower,* St. Martin's, 1975.

Editor: *Bayonets in the Street,* University Press of Kansas, 1969, revised edition, Archon Books, 1975; *Official History: Essays in Historiography and Bibliographies of Official His-*

tories and of Service Historical Sections around the World, Kansas State University Library, 1970; *Civil Wars in the Twentieth Century,* University Press of Kentucky, 1972; *A Guide to the Sources of British Military History,* University of California Press, 1972; *Intervention or Abstention: The Dilemma of U.S. Foreign Policy,* University Press of Kentucky, 1975; *Flying Combat Aircraft of the USAAF-USAF,* Iowa State University Press, Volume I (with Abigail T. Siddall), 1975, Volume II (with Carol Williams), 1978; *Guide to the Sources of U.S. Military History,* Archon Books, 1975; (with Carol Brandt) *The U.S. Army in Peacetime: Essays in Honor of the Bicentennial,* Freedom Park Press, 1975; (with Jacob W. Kipp) *ACTA of the ICMH, Washington 1975,* Military Affairs/Aerospace Historian Publishing, 1976; (with Kipp) *Soviet Aviation and Air Power,* Westview Press, 1978.

Contributor: Joseph Dunner, editor, *Handbook of World History: Concepts and Issues,* Philosophical Library, 1967; William Geffen, *Command and Commanders in Modern Warfare,* U.S.A.F. Academy, 1970; *The Normandy Invasion in Retrospect,* University Press of Kansas, 1971; *Seemacht und Geschichte: Festschrift zum 80. Geburtstag von Friedrich Ruge,* Deutsches Marine Institut, 1974.

Editor with Jacob W. Kipp, "International Military History" series, Garland, 1978—. Contributor to *Encyclopaedia Britannica, U.S. Naval Institute Proceedings,* and *Proceedings* of the American Society of Mechanical Engineers and New York Academy of Sciences. Contributor to *Christian Science Monitor, American Neptune,* and to other history, business, and military journals. Advisory editor, *Technology and Culture,* 1967; editor of *Mandarin Memo,* 1974, and *Proceedings* of the International Commission of Military History, 1975; member of editorial board, *Revue Internationale d'Histoire Militaire,* 1976—; editor and co-publisher, *Journal of the West,* 1977—.

WORK IN PROGRESS: BOAC: Nationalization in Policy and Practice; Reasons in Writing, for Cornell University Press; *Production and Politics: The British Aircraft Industry;* editing *Military Frontiersmanship: World Wide Comparisons, Ending Enmities,* Sir Oswyn Murray's *The Admiralty,* John Greenwood's *American Defense Policy since 1945,* George Stewart's *Morning In Kansas: A Near-Frontier Boyhood,* and *Life, Death and Mystery.*

SIDELIGHTS: Robin Higham told *CA:* "Having grown up in Britain with a father who was an authors' agent and a mother with an interest in history and an uncle who wrote, I always had as a goal publication. My first published work was my honor's thesis from Harvard. I wish to preserve and explain historical phenomenon and help people use history to solve present problems rather than to repeat past mistakes.

"I have to do my work when I can grab the time. I consequently normally now have to write whenever there is a break of even a few minutes, but I prefer to be able to have four hours at a time. As I am usually working on several books at once, including also other people's, the circumstances behind any book are hard to define, but usually it is because I see an opportunity to answer a question that has not yet been dealt with. A number of my books have been published on both sides of the Atlantic in Britain and America; one is used as a text at the Royal Swedish Staff College in Stockholm, and [*A Short History of Warfare*] is being translated into Hebrew for the Israelis as their official text for the history of warfare. *The British Rigid Airship* was the basis for an English Granada-TV presentation some years ago.

"Young writers should not be afraid to put pen to paper. I have followed Nevil Shute's advice, get a typewriter that works—and use it constantly. I write 70 to 80 letters a week and also try to make my classroom work a careful selection of words. I started out being a Samuel Eliot Morison student at Harvard and I have always admired his breadth and readability."

BIOGRAPHICAL/CRITICAL SOURCES: Flying, February, 1976.

* * *

HIGHSMITH, (Mary) Patricia 1921-
(Claire Morgan)

PERSONAL: Born January 19, 1921, in Ft. Worth, Tex.; daughter of Jay Bernard Plangman and Mary (Coates) Plangman Highsmith. *Education:* Barnard College, B.A., 1942. *Home and office:* 21 Boissiere, 77 Moncourt, France. *Agent:* Patricia Schartle, McIntosh & Otis, 475 Fifth Ave., New York, N.Y. 10017.

CAREER: Writer. *Awards, honors:* Mystery Writers of America Scroll and Grand Prix de Litterature Policiere, 1957, both for *The Talented Mr. Ripley;* Crime Writers Association of England Award for best foreign crime novel of the year, 1964, for *The Two Faces of January.*

WRITINGS: (With Doris Sanders) *Miranda the Panda Is on the Veranda,* Coward, 1958; *The Cry of the Owl,* Harper, 1962; *The Two Faces of January,* Doubleday, 1964; *The Glass Cell,* Doubleday, 1964; *The Story-Teller,* Doubleday, 1965 (published in England as *A Suspension of Mercy,* Heinemann, 1965); *Plotting and Writing Suspense Fiction,* Writer, Inc., 1966, revised edition, 1972; *Those Who Walk Away,* Doubleday, 1967; *The Tremor of Forgery,* Doubleday, 1969; *The Snail-Watcher and Other Stories,* Doubleday, 1970 (published in England as *Eleven,* Heinemann, 1970); *Ripley under Ground,* Doubleday, 1970; *A Dog's Ransom,* Knopf, 1972; *Ripley's Game,* Knopf, 1974; *The Animal-Lovers Book of Beastly Murder* (short stories), Heinemann, 1975; *Edith's Diary,* Simon & Schuster, 1977; *Little Tales of Misogyny* (short stories), Heinemann, 1977; *Slowly, Slowly in the Wind* (short stories), Heinemann, 1979; *The Boy Who Followed Ripley,* Crowell, 1980.

Under pseudonym Claire Morgan: *Strangers on a Train,* Harper, 1949, reprinted under real name, Penguin, 1974; *The Price of Salt,* Coward, 1952, reprinted, Arno, 1975; *The Blunderer,* Coward, 1954; *The Talented Mr. Ripley,* Coward, 1955, reprinted under real name, Penguin, 1976; *Deep Water,* Harper, 1957, reprinted under real name, Penguin, 1974; *A Game for the Living,* Harper, 1958; *This Sweet Sickness,* Harper, 1960.

SIDELIGHTS: "Low-key is the word for Patricia Highsmith," writes J. M. Edelstein in the *New Republic.* "Low-key, subtle, and profound. It is amazing to me that she is not better known, for she is superb and is a master of the suspense novel. . . . Guilt is the theme of all Miss Highsmith's books, and she has consistently used the device of contrasting characters to express it, whether real or imagined." Noting that her books usually involve "a study of things moving out of control," Edelstein concludes that the source of terror in a Highsmith story "comes less from the performance of any particular catastrophic act than from the way in which it is being avoided—that is, from chance, coincidence, and stupid misunderstanding. . . . The psychological truth thus implied may be a greater horror than any climactic act of violence."

Brigid Brophy claims that Highsmith "writes not simply fiction about crime but, in the technical sense, crime fiction, instantly recognisable as such by addicts of the genre, which is by now thoroughly established as a distinct sub-compartment within the line of descent from Poe's invention, the detective story. Neither could an addict be disappointed in Miss Highsmith, who is a very good crime novelist. But there's the injustice. For as a novelist *tout court* she's excellent.... Highsmith and Simenon are alone in writing books which transcend the limits of the genre while staying strictly inside its rules: They alone have taken the crucial step from playing games to creating art."

Francis Wyndam agrees with Brophy's assessment: "Reviewers nearly always ... concede that her books are good novels as well as effective thrillers; but the essential distinction remains unmade. The point is, her writing is quite free from any element of fantasy.... Miss Highsmith writes murder stories which are literally that: stories about murder.... Her unemphatic style makes a highly effective medium for the unsettling view of life which she expresses." Commenting on the typical Highsmith plot, Wyndam notes that "it is rare for a death to occur ... until at least a third of the book is past; often it is reserved for the very end. When it takes place, her readers are made aware not only of the horror, but also of the *embarrassment* following an act of destructive violence; it is as if a person one knows quite well were suddenly killed by somebody else one knows quite well. And although Miss Highsmith makes the most scrupulous psychological preparation for her murders, so that their eruption is never unconvincing, yet the effect on her readers is shocking in the same kind of way as the experience of murder would be in life."

"For years I have been dinning it into people's heads that Miss Highsmith is in a class by herself as a writer of suspense novels," writes Maurice Richardson in the *Observer Review*. "Ever since her first success with *Strangers on a Train* ... she has been developing slowly but surely.... Miss Highsmith is a humanist with a distinct element of the scientist in her temperament. She sees the black side of life and writes about it in a way that probably relieves some inner tension." As for her style, a *Books and Bookmen* critic observes that it "is very appropriate to her theme and her kind of storytelling: colloquial, unadorned and well organised prose. No jargon, no padding and hardly any cliches." Janice Elliot writes that its "dry simplicity conceals a labyrinthine complexity it is a challenge and a pleasure to untangle." Richardson of the *Observer Review* simply calls it "austere, with all non-essentials left out."

Julian Symons of *London Magazine* identifies several specific qualities in Highsmith's work that make her, in his words, "such an interesting and unusual novelist." He writes: "First, no doubt, must come the power with which her male characters are realized.... [Secondly,] the investigation of what would seem to most people abnormal states of mind and ways of behaviour is carried through with a skill all the more impressive because she seems to understand criminal activity so well and to find it so natural.... The way in which all this is presented can be masterly in its choice of tone and phrase. Her opening sentences ... make a statement that is symbolically meaningful in relation to the whole book.... The setting is also chosen with great care.... [She seems to be saying that] in surroundings that are sufficiently strange, men become uncertain of their personalities and question the reason for their own conduct in society.... The quality that takes her books beyond the run of intelligent fiction is not, however, this professional ability to order a plot and create a significant environment, but rather the intensity of feeling that she brings to the problems of her central figures. The sparking point of a story may be merely sensational, but the development is something different. From original ideas that are sometimes far-fetched or even trivial she proceeds with an imaginative power that makes the whole thing terrifyingly real.... [Her work is] as serious in its implications and as subtle in its approach as anything being done in the novel today."

Finally, a *Times Literary Supplement* critic writes: "It is difficult to find ways of praising Patricia Highsmith that do not at the same time do something to diminish her. To say that among crime writers she is extraordinarily subtle, wise and complicated is by now a reviewer's commonplace. With each new book, she is ritually congratulated for outstripping the limitations of her genre, for being as much concerned with people and ideas as with manipulated incident, for attempting a more than superficial exploration of the psychopathology of her unpleasant heroes—for, in short, exhibiting some of the gifts and preoccupations which are elementarily demanded of competent straight novelists. She is the crime writer who comes closest to giving crime writing a good name."

Strangers on a Train was made into a film by Alfred Hitchcock for Warner Brothers in 1951; it also served as the basis for another Warner Brothers movie in 1969 entitled "Once You Kiss a Stranger." *The Talented Mr. Ripley* was filmed as "Purple Noon" by Times Film Corp. in 1961, and *The Blunderer* was filmed as "Enough Rope" by Artixo Productions in 1966.

BIOGRAPHICAL/CRITICAL SOURCES: New York Herald Tribune Books, February 7, 1960; *New Statesman,* May 31, 1963, February 26, 1965, October 29, 1965, January 24, 1969; *New York Times Book Review,* January 30, 1966, April 1, 1967, July 19, 1970, July 7, 1974; *Observer Review,* February 12, 1967, January 19, 1969, July 12, 1970; *New Republic,* May 20, 1967, June 29, 1974; *Times Literary Supplement,* June 1, 1967, September 24, 1971; *Punch,* January 29, 1969, March 10, 1971; *Spectator,* February 21, 1969; *London Magazine,* June, 1969; *Listener,* July 9, 1970; *Books and Bookmen,* March, 1971; *Contemporary Literary Criticism,* Gale, Volume II, 1974, Volume IV, 1975; *New Yorker,* May 27, 1974; *Newsweek,* July 4, 1977; *New York Review of Books,* September 15, 1977.

* * *

HILL, Margaret (Ohler) 1915-
(Meg Hill; pseudonyms: Rachel Bennett, Andrea Thomas)

PERSONAL: Born September 6, 1915, in Jefferson, Colo.; daughter of Thomas Randolph and Ruby (Hughes) Ohler; married Robert G. Hill (superintendent, Forest Products Treating Co.), February 28, 1942; children: Geraldine, Kathleen, Thomas, Christine. *Education:* Colorado State College (now University of Northern Colorado), B.A., 1962; University of Wyoming, M.Ed., 1966. *Religion:* Unitarian Universalist. *Home:* 2416 Hillside Dr., Laramie, Wyo.

CAREER: Teacher in public schools in Colorado, 1935-42; presently counseling at Laramie (Wyo.) Senior High School. *Member:* National Education Association, Wyoming Writers, Wyoming Personnel and Guidance Association, Wyoming Education Association, Albany County Education Association, Albany County Mental Health Association, Albany County Association for Retarded Children. *Awards, honors:* Wyoming Mental Health Award, for greatest contribution to mental health, 1962, for *The Extra Special Room;* received two first prizes, National Writers Club, for short stories, 1956, 1959; received twelve National Press Women awards between 1950 and 1963; Wyoming Writers award, 1978.

WRITINGS—All published by Little, Brown, except as indicated: *Goal in the Sky,* 1953; *Hostess in the Sky,* 1955; *Senior Hostess,* 1958; *Really, Miss Hillsbro!,* 1960; *The Extra Special Room,* 1962; *Time to Quit Running,* Messner, 1970; *Little White Lies,* Xerox Publishing, 1970. Also author of pamphlets, published by Public Affairs Committee, *The Retarded Child Gets Ready for School,* 1963, *Parents and Teenagers,* 1973, *Drugs: Use, Misuse, Abuse,* 1974, and *What to Expect from School Counselors.* Author of series of mental health radio scripts for audio-visual department of the University of Wyoming. Contributor of articles to national magazines and journals.

WORK IN PROGRESS: A home economics textbook for Harcourt.

SIDELIGHTS: Margaret Hill told *CA:* "The theme of all my writing is probably 'Let's get on with the business of living.' Sure, this is the way things are, but you, the reader, have the responsibility and the power to make life better. Thus, my motivation for writing is the need for material to help people to do a better job of living. . . . In my writing I hope to entertain and to help the reader, especially the young reader, to identify with the problems of others, and to gain insight into dealing with their own lives. My purpose in writing for teenagers is to help them to feel normal, but to recognize and deal with problems. I believe the secret of salability in writing is to have a specific message for a specific audience, to write it vividly and to exhaust market possibilities."

* * *

HILL, Pamela 1920-

PERSONAL: Born November 26, 1920, in Nairobi, Kenya; daughter of Harold John Edward (a mining engineer) and Jean Evelyn Napier (Davidson) Hill. *Education:* Glasgow School of Art, D.A., 1943; University of Glasgow, B.Sc. equiv., 1952. *Religion:* Catholic. *Residence:* Scotland. *Agent:* Winant, Towers Ltd., 14 Cliffords Inn, London EC4A 1DA, England.

CAREER: Has worked variously as a pottery and biology teacher in Glasgow and Edinburgh, Scotland and London, England, 1958-74, and as a mink farmer in Galloway, Scotland, 1965-70; novelist.

WRITINGS—Novels: *The King's Vixen,* Putnam, 1954 (published in England as *Flaming Janet: A Lady of Galloway,* Chatto & Windus, 1954, reprinted, Severn House, 1978); *The Crown and the Shadow: The Story of Francoise D'Aubigne, Marquise de Maintenon,* Putnam, 1955 (published in England as *Shadow of Palaces: The Story of Francoise d'Aubigne, Marquise de Maintenon,* Chatto & Windus, 1955); *Marjorie of Scotland,* Putnam, 1956, reprinted, Severn House, 1976; *Here Lies Margot,* Chatto & Windus, 1957, Putnam, 1958, reprinted, Severn House, 1976; *Maddalena,* Cassell, 1963; *Forget Not Ariadne,* Cassell, 1965; *Julia,* Cassell, 1967.

The Devil of Aske, St. Martin's, 1973; *The Malvie Inheritance,* St. Martin's, 1973; *The Incumbent,* Hodder & Stoughton, 1974, published as *The Heatherton Heritage,* St. Martin's, 1976; *Whitton's Folly,* St. Martin's, 1975; *Norah Stroyan,* Hodder & Stoughton, 1976, published as *Norah,* St. Martin's 1977; *Czar's Woman,* R. Hale, 1977; *The Green Salamander,* St. Martin's' 1977; *Stranger's Forest,* St. Martin's, 1978; *Daneclere,* R. Hale, 1978, St. Martin's, 1979; *Homage to a Rose,* R. Hale, 1979; *Daughter of Midnight,* R. Hale, 1980; *Fire Opal,* St. Martin's, 1980; *A Place of Ravens,* R. Hale, 1980.

* * *

HILL, Ralph Nading 1917-

PERSONAL: Born September 19, 1917, in Burlington, Vt.; son of Ralph N. and Marion A. (Clarkson) Hill. *Education:* Dartmouth College, B.A., 1939. *Home:* Oakledge, Burlington, Vt. *Office: Vermont Life* Magazine, Agency of Development and Community Affairs, 61 Elm St., Montpelier, Vt. 05602.

CAREER: Shelburne Steamboat Co., Inc., Burlington, Vt., president, 1950-53; *Vermont Life* magazine, Montpelier, senior editor, 1951—. Trustee, Shelburne Museum, Shelburne, Vt., beginning 1950, Vermont Historical Society, 1950-62, and Dartmouth Alumni Council, 1958-60. *Military service:* U.S. Army, Counter-Intelligence Corps, 1943-46; served with Ninth Infantry Division in four European Theatre Campaigns; became first lieutenant. *Awards, honors:* Litt.D., Dartmouth College, 1964.

WRITINGS: The Winooski: Heartway of Vermont, Rinehart, 1949; *Contrary Country: A Chronicle of Vermont,* Rinehart, 1950, 2nd edition, Stephen Greene Press, 1960; *Sidewheeler Saga: A Chronicle of Steamboating,* Rinehart, 1953, abridged edition published as *The Story of the Ticonderoga: A Chronicle of Steamboating,* Shelburne Museum, 1957; *Robert Fulton and the Steamboat,* Random House, 1954; (with Lilian Baker Carlisle) *The Story of the Shelburne Museum,* Shelburne Museum, 1955, 2nd edition, 1960; (co-editor) *A Treasury of Vermont Life,* A. S. Barnes, 1956; *Window in the Sea,* Rinehart, 1956; *The Doctors Who Conquered Yellow Fever,* Random House, 1957; *Yankee Kingdom: Vermont and New Hampshire,* Harper, 1960, revised edition, 1973; (co-editor) *Green Mountain Treasury,* Harper, 1960; (editor) *The College on the Hill: A Dartmouth Chronicle,* Dartmouth Publications, 1965; (compiler with Walter R. Hard, Jr. and Murray Hoyt) *Vermont,* Vermont Life Magazine, 1969; *The Voyages of Brian Seaworthy* (mystery), Vermont Life Magazine, 1971; (author of text) *Vermont Album: A Collection of Early Vermont Photographs,* Stephen Greene Press, 1974; *Lake Champlain—Key to Liberty,* Countryman Press, 1977. Contributor to *Atlantic Monthly, American Heritage,* and other periodicals.†

* * *

HILL, Richard 1901-

PERSONAL: Born February 18, 1901, in Ramsbury, Wiltshire, England; son of Richard Lansley and Margaret (Leslie) Hill; married Juliana Maria Sofia Cotton, 1937; children: Juliana and Elizabeth (twins), Margaret, Thirza. *Education:* Oxford University, B.A., 1925, B.Litt., 1928, M.A., 1945. *Home:* 47 Bainton Rd., Oxford OX2 7AG, England.

CAREER: Held various positions in the Sudan Civil Service, 1929-49; University of Durham, School of Oriental Studies, Durham, England, lecturer in Near Eastern modern history, 1949-66; University of California, Santa Barbara, visiting lecturer, 1966-67; Ahmadu Bello University, Abdullahi Bayero College, Kano, Nigeria, professor of history and dean of Islamic studies, 1968-69. Visiting professor, Simon Fraser University, 1967-68. *Military service:* Sudan Defense Force, 1939-41.

WRITINGS: (Compiler) *A Bibliography of the Anglo-Egyptian Sudan,* Oxford University Press, 1939; (compiler) *A Biographical Dictionary of the Anglo-Egyptian Sudan,* Clarendon Press, 1951; *Egypt in the Sudan, 1820-1881,* Oxford University Press, 1959; *Slatin Pasha,* Oxford University Press, 1965; *Sudan Transport: A History of Railway, Marine and River Services in the Republic of Sudan,* Oxford University Press, 1965; (editor) *On the Frontiers of Islam: Two Manuscripts Concerning the Sudan, 1822-1845,* Clarendon Press, 1970; (editor) *The Opening of the Nile Basin,* C. Hurst, 1974; (translator and editor with P. Santi) *The Europeans in the Sudan, 1834-1878,* Clarendon Press, 1979.

* * *

HILLERT, Margaret 1920-

PERSONAL: Born January 22, 1920, in Saginaw, Mich.; daughter of Edward Carl (a tool and die maker) and A. Ilva (Sproull) Hillert. *Education:* Bay City Junior College, A.A., 1941; University of Michigan, R.N., 1944; Wayne University (now Wayne State University), A.B., 1948. *Residence:* Birmingham, Mich. *Office:* Whittier School, 815 East Farnum, Royal Oak, Mich. 48067.

CAREER: Primary school teacher in public schools of Royal Oak, Mich., 1948—. Poet and writer of children's books. *Member:* International League of Children's Poets, Society of Children's Book Writers, Emily Dickinson Society, Poetry Society of Michigan, Detroit Women Writers. *Awards, honors:* Numerous awards for poems from Poetry Society of Michigan.

WRITINGS—Children's poetry: *Farther Than Far,* Follett, 1969; *I Like to Live in the City,* Golden Books, 1970; *Who Comes to Your House?,* Golden Books, 1973; *The Sleepy-time Book,* Golden Press, 1975; *Come Play with Me,* Follett, 1975; *What Is It?,* Follett, 1978; *I'm Special . . . So Are You!,* Hallmark, 1979; *Let's Take a Break,* Continental Press, 1980; *Action Verse for the Primary Classroom,* Denison, 1980.

Children's books; all published by Follett: *The Birthday Car,* 1966; *The Little Runaway,* 1966; *The Yellow Boat,* 1966; *The Snow Baby,* 1969; *Circus Fun,* 1969; *A House for Little Red,* 1970; *Little Puff,* 1973; *Happy Birthday, Dear Dragon,* 1977; *Play Ball,* 1978; *The Baby Bunny,* 1980; *What Am I?,* 1980; *Run to the Rainbow,* 1980; *I Love You, Dear Dragon,* 1980; *Happy Easter, Dear Dragon,* 1980; *Let's Go, Dear Dragon,* 1980.

Children's stories retold; all published by Follett: *The Funny Baby,* 1963; *The Three Little Pigs,* 1963; *The Three Bears,* 1963; *The Three Goats,* 1963; *The Magic Beans,* 1966; *Cinderella at the Ball,* 1970; *The Cookie House,* 1978; *The Golden Goose,* 1978; *Not I, Not I,* 1980; *The Little Cookie,* 1980; *Four Good Friends,* 1980.

Contributor of poems to *Horn Book, Christian Science Monitor, McCall's, Saturday Evening Post, Jack and Jill, Western Humanities Review, Poet Lore, Cricket,* and others.

WORK IN PROGRESS: Two collections of children's poetry and three of adult poetry; 21 juveniles.

SIDELIGHTS: In *Pass the Poetry, Please,* Margaret Hillert writes: "I can't give you a glib one-line definition of poetry such as many I have seen. Poetry has been an undefined but definite part of my life, and I don't think I chose to write it at all. I have been writing it ever since the first one I did when I was eight years old, which seems to indicate it has always been a part of my nature. I read widely, from the poetry stacks in the library when I was growing up—and still do to some extent. I'm not one of those people who can say, 'Today I'll write a poem.' I may go without writing anything for some time as a consequence, but once I get the grain of an idea, the thing must be worked through, sometimes for days, weeks, or months. Things don't usually come to me whole and full blown. It intrigues me to work generally, but not always, with traditional forms but in fresh ways."

BIOGRAPHICAL/CRITICAL SOURCES: J. R. LeMaster, editor, *Poets of the Midwest,* Young Publications, 1966; Lee B. Hopkins, *Pass the Poetry, Please,* Citation Press, 1972; *Authors in the News,* Volume I, Gale, 1976.

* * *

HILTNER, Seward 1909-

PERSONAL: Born November 26, 1909, in Tyrone, Pa.; son of Clement Seward and Charlotte (Porter) Hiltner; married Helen Margaret Johansen, May 29, 1936; children: James Seward (deceased), Anne Porter. *Education:* Lafayette College, A.B., 1931; University of Chicago, Ph.D., 1952. *Home:* 165 Ross Stevenson Cir., Princeton, N.J.

CAREER: Ordained minister, United Presbyterian Church, 1935; Council for Clinical Training, New York City, executive secretary, 1935-38; executive secretary, Department of Pastoral Services, Federal Council of Churches, 1938-50; Union Theological Seminary, New York City, lecturer, 1945-50; Yale Divinity School, New Haven, Conn., lecturer, 1945-50; University of Chicago, Chicago, Ill., professor of pastoral theology, 1950-61; Princeton Theological Seminary, Princeton, N.J., professor of theology and personality, 1961-80. Consultant, Menninger Foundation, Topeka, Kan., 1957-72, and Board of Missions, United Presbyterian Church, 1963-69; also consultant to Division of Family Study, University of Pennsylvania, 1964-68. *Member:* American Association of Theological Schools (chairman of commission on research and counsel, 1960-66), Association of Seminary Professors in the Practical Fields, American Orthopsychiatric Association (fellow), Orthopsychiatric Association. *Awards, honors:* D.D., Lafayette College; Academy of Religion and Mental Health annual award, 1966.

WRITINGS: *Religion and Health,* Macmillan, 1943; *Pastoral Counseling,* Abingdon, 1949; *Self-Understanding,* Scribner, 1951; *The Counselor in Counseling,* Abingdon, 1952; *Sex Ethics and the Kinsey Reports,* Association Press, 1953; *Sex and the Christian Life,* Association Press, 1957; *Preface to Pastoral Theology,* Abingdon, 1958; *The Christian Shepherd,* Abingdon, 1959; (with L. G. Colston) *The Context of Pastoral Counseling,* Abingdon, 1961; (with Karl Menninger) *Constructive Aspects of Anxiety,* Abingdon, 1963; (with J. L. Adams) *Pastoral Care in the Liberal Churches,* Abingdon, 1969; *Ferment in the Ministry,* Abingdon, 1970; *Theological Dynamics,* Abingdon, 1972; (editor) *Toward a Theology of Aging,* Human Sciences Press, 1976. Contributor of articles to popular and professional magazines, including *Journal of Religion, Psychoanalytic Quarterly, Mental Hygiene,* and *Ladies Home Journal.* Consultant, *Pastoral Psychology,* 1950-69. Member of editorial board, *Theology Today, Journal of Religion and Health, American Imago,* and *Quarterly Journal of Studies on Alcohol.*

* * *

HIMSTREET, William Charles 1923-

PERSONAL: Born January 10, 1923, in Milford, Utah; son of Thomas Charles and Marie (Edwards) Himstreet; married Maxine E. Toft, 1944; children: Sue Ann. *Education:* San

Jose State College (now University), A.B., 1947; Stanford University, M.A., 1950; University of Southern California, Ed.D., 1955. *Home:* 31328 Village 31, Camarillo, Calif. 93010. *Office:* University of Southern California, University Park, Los Angeles, Calif. 90007.

CAREER: Union Pacific Railroad, Salt Lake City, Utah, clerk, 1941-42; high school teacher in Petaluma, Calif., 1947-49; Humboldt State Teachers College (now Humboldt State University), Arcata, Calif., assistant professor, 1949-52; University of Southern California, Los Angeles, 1952—, professor of business administration, 1962—, associate dean, 1961-71, associate vice-president, 1971-75. Director of California Federal Savings and Loan Association. Member of board of directors, Interracial Council for Business Opportunity, 1964-70; director of Delta Pi Epsilon Research Foundation, 1979-81; president of Alpha Kappa Psi Foundation, 1979—. *Military service:* U.S. Navy, 1942-46; became lieutenant. *Member:* International Communication Association, United Business Education Association, American Business Communication Association (fellow), National Office Management Association (member of board of directors, 1960-62), Alpha Kappa Psi (vice-president, 1959-62; president, 1962-65), Delta Pi Epsilon, Beta Gamma Sigma, Phi Delta Kappa, Pi Omega Pi.

WRITINGS: Business Communications, Wadsworth, 1961, 5th edition, 1977; *Briefhand* (college edition), Allied, 1961; *Business English in Communication,* Prentice-Hall, 1964, 3rd edition, 1975; *Plaid for Business Communications,* Irwin, 1976; *Intercom: Communication for Management,* Wadsworth, in press. Also author of pamphlets and articles on business writing, consumer education, and business education. Editor, research summaries issues of the *National Business Education Quarterly,* 1955—; associate editor, *Delta Pi Epsilon Journal,* 1959-62.

* * *

HINDERER, Walter (Hermann) 1934-

PERSONAL: Born September 3, 1934, in Ulm, West Germany; came to United States, 1966; son of Ludwig (a manufacturer) and Anna (Dangel) Hinderer; married Dietlinde M. Reim, June 26, 1966. *Education:* Attended University of Tuebingen, 1954-55; University of Munich, Dr.Phil., 1960. *Religion:* Lutheran. *Home:* 17 Bayberry Rd., Princeton, N.J. 08540. *Office:* Department of German, Princeton University, Princeton, N.J. 08540.

CAREER: R. Piper & Co. Verlag, Munich, West Germany, director of Cultural-Scientific Division, 1961-66; Pennsylvania State University, University Park, assistant professor of German, 1966-69; University of Colorado, Boulder, associate professor of German, 1969-71; University of Maryland, College Park, professor of German, 1971-78; Princeton University, Princeton, N.J., professor of German, 1978—. Visiting professor at Stanford University, 1970-71. Fellow of Institute for Research in the Humanities, University of Wisconsin—Madison, 1976-77. *Member:* American Association of Teachers of German, Modern Language Association of America, Deutsche Schillergesellschaft, Lessing Society, International Association for German Studies, Buechuergesellschaft.

WRITINGS: Die "Todeserkenntnis" in Hermann Brochs "Tod des Vergil," Uni-Druck, 1961; (editor, and author of introduction and appendix) *Ludwig Boerne: Menzel der Franzosenfresser und andere Schriften,* Insel Verlag, 1969; (editor and contributor) *Christoph Martin Wieland: Hann und Gulpenheh, Schach Lolo,* Reclam Verlag, 1970; (editor with Joseph P. Strelka, and contributor) *Moderne amerikanische Literaturtheorien,* S. Fischer Verlag, 1970; (editor and contributor) *Deutsche Reden,* Reclam Verlag, 1973; (editor and contributor) *Sickingen-Debatte,* Luchterhand Verlag, 1974; *Elemente ser Literaturkritik,* Scriptor Verlag, 1976; *Buechner Kommentar zum dichterischen Werk,* Winkler Verlag, 1977; (editor) *Geschichte der politischen Lyrik in Deutschland,* Reclam Verlag, 1978; (editor) *Schillers Dramen: Neue Interpretationen,* Reclam Verlag, 1979; *Ueber deutsche Literatur und Rede: Historische Interpretationen,* Wilhelm Fink Verlag, 1980; *Der Mensch in der Geschichte: Eine Interpretation von Schillers "Wallenstein,"* Atheneum Verlag, 1980.

Contributor: Strelka, editor, *Perspective in Literary Symbolism,* Pennsylvania State University Press, 1968; Strelka, editor, *Problems of Literary Evaluation,* Pennsylvania State University Press, 1969; Manfred Durzak, editor, *Die deutsche Gegenwartsliteratur,* Reclam Verlag, 1971; Grimm Hermand, editor, *Die Deutsche Klassiklegende,* Athenaeum Verlag, 1971; Wolfgang Paulsen, editor, *Experiment und Revolte,* Lothar Stiehm Verlag, 1972; Durzak, editor, *Hermann Briochs Romane*, Wilhelm Fink Verlag, 1972; Wolfgang Kuttenkeuler, editor, *Poesie und Politik,* W. Kohlhammer Verlag, 1972; Peter Stein, editor, *Theorie der politischen Dichtung,* [Munich], 1973; Bauschinger, Denkler, and Malsch, editors, *Das Amerikabild in der deutschen Literatur,* Reclam Verlag, 1975; W. Hinck, editor, *Die deutsche Komoedie,* August Bagel Verlag, 1976; *Festschrift fuer Herman Meyer,* Niemeyer Verlag, 1976; K. O. Conrady, editor, *Deutsche Literatur zur Zeit der Klassik,* Reclam Verlag, 1977; B. V. Wiese, *Deutsche Dichter von der Aufklaerung bis zur Klassik,* Erich Schmidt Verlag, 1977. Contributor to *Jahrbuch der Deutschen Schillergesellschaft;* contributor of articles and reviews to books, German periodicals, and to *Die Zeit* and other newspapers.

WORK IN PROGRESS: Schiller, A Modern Biography.

* * *

HINE, (William) Daryl 1936-

PERSONAL: Born February 24, 1936, in New Westminster, British Columbia, Canada; son of Robert Fraser and Elsie (James) Hine. *Education:* Attended McGill University, 1954-58; University of Chicago, M.A., 1965, Ph.D., 1967. *Home:* 2740 Ridge Ave., Evanston, Ill. 60201.

CAREER: Poet and novelist. *Awards, honors:* Canadian Foundation fellowship, 1958; Canada Council grant, 1959; Ingram Merrill Award, 1961; Canada Council senior arts grant, 1979; Guggenheim fellowship, 1980.

WRITINGS—Poems, except as indicated: *Five Poems,* Emblem Books, 1955; *The Carnal and the Crane,* Contact Press, 1957; *The Devil's Picture Book,* Abelard, 1960; *The Prince of Darkness & Co.* (novel), Abelard, 1961; *Polish Subtitles* (travel), Abelard, 1962; *The Wooden Horse,* Atheneum, 1965; *Minutes,* Atheneum, 1968; (translator) *The Homeric Hymns,* Atheneum, 1972; *Resident Alien,* Atheneum, 1975; *In and Out,* privately printed, 1975; *Daylight Saving,* Atheneum, 1978; *Selected Poems,* Oxford University Press (Toronto), 1980, Atheneum, 1981. Contributor of poems to *New Yorker* and other magazines. Editor, *Poetry Magazine,* 1968-78.

WORK IN PROGRESS: More poems and translations.

BIOGRAPHICAL/CRITICAL SOURCES: Chicago Review, June, 1967; *Contemporary Literature,* spring, 1969; Richard Howard, *Alone with America,* Atheneum, 1969; *Georgia*

Review, winter, 1975; *Modern Poetry Studies*, spring, 1977; *New Leader*, May 22, 1978; *Poetry*, June, 1979; *Canto*, Volume 3, no. 1, 1979.

* * *

HINE, Robert Van Norden, Jr. 1921-

PERSONAL: Born April 26, 1921, in Los Angeles, Calif.; son of Robert V. and Betty (Bates) Hine; married Shirley McChord, June 24, 1949; children: Allison. *Education:* Pomona College, B.A., 1948; Yale University, M.A., 1949, Ph.D., 1952. *Religion:* Presbyterian. *Office:* Department of History, University of California, Riverside, Calif. 92521.

CAREER: Huntington Library, San Marino, Calif., research fellow, 1951-53; University of California, Riverside, instructor, 1954-55, assistant professor, 1955-61, associate professor, 1961-66, professor of history, 1966—. *Member:* American Historical Association, Western History Association, Beta Theta Pi. *Awards, honors:* Huntington Library fellowships, 1954, 1962; Pacific Coast Branch of American Historical Association award for best book of 1953, for *California's Utopian Colonies;* Guggenheim fellowships, 1957-58, 1968-69; Harbison Award, Danforth Foundation, 1967-68; National Endowment for the Humanities senior fellowship, 1976-77.

WRITINGS: California's Utopian Colonies, Huntington Library, 1953, reprinted, Norton, 1973; (editor) *William Andrew Spaulding: An Autobiographical Account,* Huntington Library, 1961; (editor and author of epilogue) *The Irvine Ranch,* Huntington Library, 1962; *Edward Kern and American Expansion,* Yale University Press, 1962; (author of foreword) *Sun Chief: The Autobiography of a Hopi Indian,* Yale University Press, 1963; (editor with Edwin R. Bingham) *The Frontier Experience: Readings in the Transmississippi West,* Wadsworth, 1963, revised edition published as *The American Frontier: Readings and Documents,* Little, Brown, 1972; *Bartlett's West: Drawing the Mexican Boundary,* Yale University Press, 1968; (editor with Savoie Lottinville) *Soldier in the West: Letters of Theodore Talbot during His Services in California, Mexico, and Oregon, 1845-53,* University of Oklahoma Press, 1972; *The American West: An Interpretive History,* Little, Brown, 1973; *Community on the American Frontier: Separate but Not Alone,* University of Oklahoma Press, 1980.

AVOCATIONAL INTERESTS: Music.

* * *

HINTZE, Naomi A. 1909-

PERSONAL: Born July 8, 1909, in Camden, Ill.; daughter of Jesse Estes (a clergyman) and Estella (Rang) Agans; married Harold Sanborn Hintze, April 19, 1930; children: Douglas, Jonathan, Elizabeth. *Education:* Attended Maryville College, Maryville, Tenn., 1927-29, and Ball State Teachers College (now Ball State University), 1929-30. *Politics:* Independent. *Religion:* Protestant. *Agent:* James O. Brown, 25 West 43rd St., New York, N.Y. 10036.

CAREER: Writer. *Member:* Authors Guild, Authors League of America. *Awards, honors:* Edgar Allan Poe special award from Mystery Writers of America, 1970, for *You'll Like My Mother.*

WRITINGS: Buried Treasure Waits for You, Bobbs-Merrill, 1962; *You'll Like My Mother,* Putnam, 1969; *The Stone Carnation,* Random House, 1971; *Aloha Means Goodbye,* Random House, 1972; *Listen, Please Listen,* Random House, 1974; *Cry Witch,* Random House, 1975; (with J. Gaither Pratt) *The Psychic Realm: What Can You Believe?,* Random House, 1975; (contributor) A. S. Burack, editor, *Writing Suspense and Mystery Fiction,* Writer, 1977; (with Peter van der Linde) *Time Bomb,* Doubleday, 1978. Contributor of more than a hundred short stories and articles to *Redbook, Ladies' Home Journal, Woman's Day, Good Housekeeping, McCalls',* and other magazines.

WORK IN PROGRESS: A mystery novel, tentatively entitled *The Ghost Child.*

SIDELIGHTS: You'll Like My Mother was made into a movie and released by Universal in 1973; *Aloha Means Goodbye* was made into a movie for television in 1974. *Avocational interests:* Travel, gardening.

* * *

HIRSCHMAN, Albert O. 1915-

PERSONAL: Born April 7, 1915, in Berlin, Germany; son of Carl and Hedwig (Marcuse) Hirschmann; married Sarah Chapiro, 1941; children: Catherine Jane, Elisabeth Nicole. *Education:* Sorbonne, Ecole des Hautes Etudes Commerciales, diploma, 1935; attended London School of Economics and Political Science, 1935-36; University of Trieste, Doctor Econ. Sci., 1938. *Office:* Institute for Advanced Study, Princeton, N.J.

CAREER: Federal Reserve Board, Washington, D.C., economist, 1946-52; financial adviser, National Planning Board, and private economic counselor in Bogota, Colombia, 1952-56; Yale University, New Haven, Conn., research professor, 1956-58; Columbia University, New York, N.Y., professor of international economic relations, 1958-64; Harvard University, Cambridge, Mass., professor, 1964-74; Institute for Advanced Study, Princeton, N.J., professor of social science, 1974—. Irving Fisher Research Professor, Yale University, 1956-57; visiting member, Institute for Advanced Study, 1972-73. Consultant to governmental agencies and foundations. *Military service:* Office of Strategic Services, 1943-45; became sergeant. *Member:* American Economic Association, American Philosophical Society, American Academy of Arts and Sciences, Council on Foreign Relations. *Awards, honors:* Rockefeller fellow, 1941-43; Ford Foundation faculty research fellow, 1964-65; Center for Advanced Study in the Behavioral Sciences fellow, 1968-69; honorary doctor of laws, Rutgers University, 1978; Frank E. Seidman Distinguished Award in Political Economy, 1980.

WRITINGS: National Power and the Structure of Foreign Trade, University of California Press, 1945, enlarged edition, 1980; *The Strategy of Economic Development,* Yale University Press, 1958, reprinted, Norton, 1978; (editor and contributor) *Latin American Issues,* Twentieth Century Fund, 1961; *Journeys toward Progress: Studies of Economic Policy-Making in Latin America,* Twentieth Century Fund, 1963; *Development Projects Observed,* Brookings Institution, 1967; *Exit, Voice, and Loyalty: Responses to Decline in Firms, Organizations and States,* Harvard University Press, 1970; *A Bias for Hope: Essays on Development and Latin America,* Yale University Press, 1971; *The Passions and the Interests: Political Arguments for Capitalism before Its Triumph,* Princeton University Press, 1977. Contributor of chapters to numerous books. Contributor to professional journals. Member of boards of editors of several journals.

* * *

HIRSH, Marilyn 1944-

PERSONAL: Born January 1, 1944, in Chicago, Ill.; daughter of Eugene (a meat-market owner) and Rose (Warshell) Hirsh; married James Harris, November 18, 1973. *Education:* Carnegie-Mellon University, B.F.A., 1965; New York University, M.A., 1974, currently doctoral candidate. *Religion:* Jewish. *Home:* 1580 Third Ave., Apt. 6, New York, N.Y. 10028. *Agent:* Florence Alexander, 50 East 42nd St., New York, N.Y. 10016.

CAREER: Peace Corps volunteer teaching English and art in Nasik, India, 1965-67; writer and illustrator for Children's Book Trust, New Delhi, India, 1967; writer and illustrator of children's books, New York, N.Y., 1968—. Part-time teacher of art and illustrator. *Awards, honors: The Pink Suit* was named to the Child Study Association's book list, 1970; Noma Concours for children's picture book illustrations, 1978, for *The Elephants and the Mice;* Asian Cultural Center for UNESCO prize, 1978.

WRITINGS—Self-illustrated: *The Elephants and the Mice: A Panchatantra Story* (Junior Literary Guild selection), Children's Book Trust (New Delhi), 1967, World Publishing, 1970; *Where Is Yonkela?,* Crown, 1969; *The Pink Suit,* Crown, 1970; (with Maya Narayan) *Leela and the Watermelon,* Crown, 1971; *How the World Got Its Color,* Crown, 1972; *George and the Goblins,* Crown, 1972; *Ben Goes into Business,* Holiday House, 1973; *Could Anything Be Worse?,* Holiday House, 1974; *The Rabbi and the 29 Witches,* Holiday House, 1976; *Captain Jiri and Rabbi Jacob,* Holiday House, 1976; *Deborah the Dybbick: A Ghost Story,* Holiday House, 1978; *The Hanukkah Story,* Bonim Books, 1978; *One Little Goat,* Holiday House, 1979; *Potato Pancakes All Around,* Bonim Books, 1979; *The Secret Dinosaur,* Holiday House, 1979.

Illustrator: Florence Adams, *Mushy Eggs,* Putnam, 1973; Tillie S. Pine and Joseph Levine, *The Polynesians Knew,* McGraw, 1974; David Adler, *The House on the Roof,* Bonim Books, 1977; Susan Saunders, *Wales' Tale* (Junior Literary Guild selection), Viking, 1980.

Also author and illustrator of filmstrips based on the books of the same titles, "Could Anything Be Worse?," Weston Woods, "Ben Goes into Business," Macmillan, and "The Rabbi and the 29 Witches," Encyclopaedia Britannica.

WORK IN PROGRESS: Joseph Who Loved the Sabbath, for Viking; *The Tower of Babel,* for Holiday House.

SIDELIGHTS: Marilyn Hirsh told *CA:* "During the last ten years I have explored my Jewish background through my books, first with two about my own father, *Where Is Yonkela?* and *The Pink Suit.* Then moving on cautiously to my editor and friend Eunice Holsaert's father in *Ben Goes into Business,* and then exploring folklore and finally attempting to write original works within the Jewish tradition. I feel that this will remain a theme in my books for some time—if not always. But I am looking forward to other types of projects like *Joseph Who Loved the Sabbath* which, though Jewish in content, will be illustrated in an Assyrian wall relief style and *The Tower of Babel* which will use a very different linear style with washes of color. At this time I feel very open to new material both in content and visual terms. I am also hoping to get back to Indian stories."

BIOGRAPHICAL/CRITICAL SOURCES: Christian Science Monitor, November 6, 1969; *Washington Post,* November 5, 1972.

* * *

HITCHCOCK, H(ugh) Wiley 1923-

PERSONAL: Born September 28, 1923; son of Hugh Wellman (in advertising) and Charlotte (Wiley) Hitchcock; married Janet Cox (a professor), May 22, 1965; children: (previous marriage) Susan Tyler, Hugh Jarvis. *Education:* Dartmouth College, B.A., 1944; University of Michigan, Ann Arbor, M.Mus., 1948, Ph.D., 1954. *Politics:* Independent. *Home:* 1192 Park Ave., New York, N.Y. *Office:* Department of Music, Brooklyn College of the City University of New York, Brooklyn, N.Y. 11210.

CAREER: University of Michigan, Ann Arbor, assistant professor, 1955-59, associate professor of music, 1959-61; Hunter College of the City University of New York, New York, N.Y., professor of music, 1961-71; Brooklyn College of the City University of New York, Brooklyn, N.Y., professor of music, 1971—, director of Institute for Studies in American Music. *Military service:* U.S. Army, 1943-46. *Member:* American Musicological Society, Society for Ethnomusicology, Societe de Musicologie, Music Library Association (president, 1966-67). *Awards, honors:* Fulbright senior research fellowships in Italy, 1954-55, and France, 1968-69; Guggenheim fellowship, 1968-69.

WRITINGS: "Judicium Salomonis" of Marc-Antoine Charpentier, A-R Editions, 1962; *Music in the United States: A Historical Introduction,* Prentice-Hall, 1969, 2nd edition, 1974; *"Le Nuove Musiche" of Giulio Caccini,* A-R Editions, 1970; *Ives,* Oxford University Press, 1977; (co-editor) *An Ives Celebration,* University of Illinois Press, 1977. Editor of "History of Music" series, eleven volumes, Prentice-Hall, 1965-74, and "Earlier American Music" series, Da Capo Press, 1972—. Area editor of *Grove's Dictionary of Music and Musicians,* 1970—.

WORK IN PROGRESS: A monograph on Giulio Caccini and an edition of his musical works.

* * *

HODDER-WILLIAMS, Christopher 1926-

PERSONAL: Born August 25, 1926, in London, England; son of Ralph (a publisher) and Marjorie (Glazebrook) Hodder-Williams; married Deirdre Matthew; children: Simon Glazebrook, Petra Louise. *Education:* Attended Eton College. *Politics:* "Horrified and disgusted by Right Wing politics and bored out of my mind by the extreme Left." *Home:* 18 Nevern Rd., London S.W.1., England.

CAREER: Writer and songwriter. Began his postwar career in Kenya with an abortive plan to set up long-distance bus service in Africa; ultimately directed an all-African dance band until he became property man and wardrobe supervisor for a Tarzan picture. Returning to England, he worked in a recording studio while writing musicals, then turned to composing music for commercial television, and to writing novels. *Military service:* Royal Signals, 1944-48; became lieutenant. *Member:* Songwriters' Guild (Britain).

WRITINGS: The Cummings Report, Hodder & Stoughton, 1958; *Chain Reaction,* Doubleday, 1959; *Final Approach,* Doubleday, 1960; *Turbulence,* Hodder & Stoughton, 1961; *The Higher They Fly,* Hodder & Stoughton, 1963, Putnam, 1964; *The Main Experiment,* Hodder & Stoughton, 1964, Putnam, 1965; *The Egg-Shaped Thing,* Putnam, 1967; *Fistful of Digits,* Hodder & Stoughton, 1968; *Ninety-Eight Point Six,* Hodder & Stoughton, 1969; *Panic O'Clock,* United Writers Publications, 1973; *Cowards Paradise,* United Writers Publications, 1974; *The Prayer Machine,* St. Martin's, 1977; *The Silent Voice,* Weidenfeld & Nicolson, 1977; *The Thinktank That Leaked,* United Writers Publications, 1979.

Television plays: "The Higher They Fly," "Voice in the

Sky," "Sister Ship," "Send a Telegram," "The Ship That Couldn't Stop."

WORK IN PROGRESS: The Chromosome Game.

SIDELIGHTS: Christopher Hodder-Williams, who built his own music recording studio, told *CA,* "all my books are primarily inspired by *music,* not literature." He is "crazy about Elgar, John Ireland, Brahms, Beethoven, ELO, Julie Covington, Vangelis, Mike Oldfield, Oscar Peterson, Garner, impressed by Easley Blackwood, stunned by Sir Adrian Boult, excited by Solti." Hodder-Williams has written the musical score for the play "A Nightingale in Bloomsbury Square" with Maureen Duffy. His books have been translated into German, French, and other languages.

AVOCATIONAL INTERESTS: Flying, playing the piano.

BIOGRAPHICAL/CRITICAL SOURCES: Fantasy and Science Fiction, November, 1965; *Times Literary Supplement,* March 23, 1967, November 9, 1973; *Books and Bookmen,* May, 1967; *Observer,* December 21, 1969, January 1, 1978; *New Statesman,* June 18, 1976.

* * *

HOEBEL, Edward Adamson 1906-

PERSONAL: Born November 16, 1906, in Madison, Wis.; son of Edward Charles (a businessman) and Katharine (Arnold) Hoebel; married Francis Elizabeth Gore, June 20, 1930 (died, July 21, 1962); married Irene H. Williams, August 26, 1963; children: Bartley Gore. *Education:* University of Wisconsin, B.A., 1928; Universitat Koeln, graduate study, 1928-29; New York University, M.A., 1930; Columbia University, Ph.D., 1934; University of California, Berkeley, postdoctoral fellow, 1940-41. *Home:* 2273 Folwell St., St. Paul, Minn. *Office:* 438 New Law Building, University of Minnesota, Minneapolis, Minn. 55455.

CAREER: New York University, New York, N.Y., 1929-48, began as instructor, became associate professor of sociology and anthropology; University of Utah, Salt Lake City, professor of anthropology and dean of University College, 1948-54; University of Minnesota, Minneapolis, professor of anthropology and chairman of department, 1954-68, Regents' Professor of Anthropology, 1966-72, Regents' Professor emeritus, 1972—, adjunct professor of law, 1968—. Fulbright professor, Oxford University, 1956-57; fellow, Center for Advanced Study in the Behavioral Sciences, 1960-61; senior specialist, Institute for Advanced Projects, Center for Cultural and Technical Interchange between East and West, 1964-65; visiting professor of law, Katholijke Universiteit, 1970, and University of Arizona, 1974-75; Andrew H. Mellon Distinguished Visiting Professor, Lehigh University, 1980. Community analyst, War Relocation Authority, 1943; special officer of Arms Control and Disarmament Agency, U.S. Department of State, 1968-71. *Member:* American Anthropological Association (president, 1956-57), American Ethnological Society (president, 1946-47), American Council of Learned Societies (member of board of directors, 1949), Social Science Research Council (member of board of directors, 1950-59), American Philosophical Society, American Judicature Society, Explorer's Club, Phi Kappa Phi. *Awards, honors:* Award of merit from Wisdom Society.

WRITINGS: (With K. Llewellyn) *The Cheyenne Way: Conflict and Case Law in Primitive Jurisprudence,* University of Oklahoma Press, 1941; *Man in the Primitive World,* McGraw, 1949, 2nd edition, 1958; (with Earnest Wallace) *The Comanches: Lords of the South Plains,* University of Oklahoma Press, 1953; *The Law of Primitive Man: A Study in Comparative Legal Dynamics,* Harvard University Press, 1954; (editor with others) *Readings in Anthropology,* McGraw, 1955: *The Cheyennes: Indians of the Great Plains,* Holt, 1961, 2nd edition, revised, 1978; (with K. Petersen) *A Cheyenne Sketchbook,* University of Oklahoma Press, 1964; *Anthropology: The Study of Man,* McGraw, 1966; *The Plains Indians: A Critical Bibliography,* Indiana University Press, 1978; (with Thomas Weaver) *Anthropology: The Human Experience,* McGraw, 1979.

* * *

HOEHLING, A(dolph) A. 1915-

PERSONAL: Born July 7, 1915; son of Adolph A. and Louise (Carrington) Hoehling; married Mary Duprey, 1936; children: Mrs. Richard Vinal, Patsy, Adolph A. Jr., Clara. *Education:* Trinity College, Hartford, Conn., B.A., 1936. *Home:* 7601 Hemlock St., Bethesda, Md. *Agent:* Blassingame, McCauley & Wood, 60 East 42nd St., New York, N.Y. 10017. *Office:* Congressional Research Service, U.S. Library of Congress, Washington, D.C. 20540.

CAREER: Reporter, *Washington Post, Washington Herald, Washington Star,* Washington, D.C., 1937-47; spent several years writing for magazines and editing in New York, N.Y., and as reporter for *Portland Telegram,* Portland, Me; Army Times Publishing Co., Washington, D.C., book editor, 1959-72; U.S. Library of Congress, Washington, D.C., editor, Congressional Research Service, 1972—. *Military service:* U.S. Navy, 1941-45, became lieutenant commander. *Member:* National Press Club (Washington).

WRITINGS: The Last Voyage of the Lusitania, Holt, 1956, reprinted, Dell, 1974; *A Whisper of Eternity,* Yoseloff, 1957; *Lonely Command,* Yoseloff, 1957; *Last Train from Atlanta,* Yoseloff, 1958; *They Sailed into Oblivion,* Yoseloff, 1959; *The Fierce Lambs,* Little, Brown, 1960; *The Great Epidemic,* Little, Brown, 1961; *Who Destroyed the Hindenburg?,* Little, Brown, 1962; *The Week before Pearl Harbor,* Norton, 1963; *The Great War at Sea: A History of Naval Action, 1914-1918,* Crowell, 1965; *Home Front, U.S.A.,* Crowell, 1966; *Women Who Spied,* Dodd, 1967; *Great Ship Disasters,* Contemporary Books, 1971; *Disaster: Major American Catastrophes,* Hawthorn, 1973; *Thunder at Hampton Roads,* Prentice-Hall, 1976; *Epics of the Sea,* Contemporary Books, 1977; *December 7, 1941: The Day the Admirals Slept Late,* Zebra Publications, 1978. Contributor of articles to national magazines.

* * *

HOFFMAN, Paul 1934-

PERSONAL: Born September 27, 1934, in Chicago, Ill.; son of William S. (a physician) and Miriam (Berliner) Hoffman; married Kathleen Scarlett, March 30, 1965 (deceased, 1978). *Education:* University of Chicago, A.B., 1957, A.M., 1958. *Home:* 205 West 10th St., New York, N.Y. 10014. *Agent:* Edward J. Acton, 17 Grove St., New York, N.Y. 10014.

CAREER: City News Bureau, Chicago, Ill., reporter, 1958-60; United Press International, Detroit, Mich., reporter, 1960-61; *Stars & Stripes,* New York City, reporter, 1962; *New York Post,* New York City, reporter, 1962-69; writer, 1969—. *Military service:* U.S. Army Reserve, 1958-64, active duty, 1958-59.

WRITINGS: Moratorium: An American Protest, Tower, 1970; *Lions in the Street,* Saturday Review Press, 1973; *Tiger in the Court,* Playboy Press, 1973; *What the Hell Is Justice?,* Playboy Press, 1974; *To Drop a Dime,* Putnam, 1976;

Courthouse, Hawthorn, 1979. Also author of *New Nixon,* Tower, and *Spiro,* Tower. Contributor to magazines, including *Saturday Review, Good Housekeeping, Nation,* and to New York area newspapers.

* * *

HOGAN, Inez 1895-

PERSONAL: Born August 5, 1895, in Washington, D.C.; daughter of John Edgar and Minnie (Holzer) Hogan. *Education:* Attended Teachers Training College, Washington, D.C., Berkshire Summer School of Arts, art school in Paris, 1917-19, Corcoran Art Gallery, 1920-21, National School of Fine and Applied Art, and George Washington University. *Politics:* Independent. *Religion:* Episcopalian. *Home:* 82 Commercial St., Provincetown, Mass.

CAREER: Writer, illustrator, lecturer. Supervisor of art for public schools, Washington, D.C., 1922-26, New York, N.Y., 1928-30. *Awards, honors:* Award for painting of Brittany peasant, Corcoran Art School.

WRITINGS—All self-illustrated juveniles; published by Dutton, except as indicated: *The Little Black and White Lamb,* Macrae, 1927; *Sandy, Skip and the Man in the Moon,* Macrae, 1928; *The Little Toy Airplane,* Macrae, 1930; *The White Kitten and the Blue Plate,* Macmillan, 1930; (editor with Mary Ellen Vorse) *Skinny Gets Fat,* Scott, 1940; *Bigger and Bigger,* Heath, 1942; *Listen Hitler! The Gremlins Are Coming,* 1943; *Read to Me about Nona, the Baby Elephant,* 1947; *Read to Me about Peter Platypus,* 1948; *World Round,* 1949; *Runaway Toys,* 1950; *Read to Me about Charlie,* 1950; *Read to Me about the Littlest Cowboy,* 1951; *A Party for Poodles,* 1952; *We Are a Family,* 1952; *A Bear Is a Bear,* 1953; *Me* (verse), 1954; *Upside Down Book, A Story for Little Girls,* 1955; *Upside Down Book, A Story for Little Boys,* 1955; *The Little Ones,* 1956; *The Big Ones,* 1957; *The Littlest Satellite,* 1958; *The Littlest Bear,* 1959; *Little Lost Bear,* 1960; *Monkey See, Monkey Do,* 1960; *The Lone Wolf,* 1961; *Cubby Bear and the Book,* 1961; *Fraidy Cat,* 1962; *Eager Beaver,* 1963; *A Dog for Danny,* Garrard, 1973.

"Nicodemus" series; all self-illustrated; all published by Dutton: *Nicodemus and His Little Sister,* 1932; *. . . and the Houn' Dog,* 1934; *. . . and His Gran'pappy,* 1936; *. . . and Petunia,* 1937; *. . . and His New Shoes,* 1938; *. . . and the Gang,* 1939; *. . . and the New Born Baby,* 1940; *. . . Laughs,* 1941; *. . . Runs Away,* 1942; *. . . Helps Uncle Sam,* 1943; *. . . and the Goose,* 1945.

"Twin" series; all self-illustrated; all published by Dutton: *Bear Twins,* 1935; *Elephant Twins,* 1936; *Twin Kids,* 1937; *Kangaroo Twins,* 1938; *Mule Twins,* 1939; *Twin Seals,* 1940; *Twin Deer,* 1941; *Monkey Twins,* 1943; *Twin Colts,* 1944; *Raccoon Twins,* 1946; *Giraffe Twins,* 1948; *Twin Lambs,* 1951; *Koala Bear Twins,* 1955; *Twin Kittens,* 1958; *Twin Puppies,* 1959; *Twin Otters and the Indians,* 1962; *Dinosaur Twins,* 1963; *Fox Twins,* 1964.

"Nappy" series; all self-illustrated; all published by Dutton: *Nappy Wanted a Dog,* 1942; *. . . Planted a Garden,* 1944; *. . . Chooses a Pet,* 1946; *. . . Has a New Friend,* 1947; *. . . Is a Cowboy,* 1949.

Illustrator: Lucy M. Cobb and M. A. Hicks, *Animal Tales from the Old North State,* Dutton, 1938; Erlin Hogan, *Four Funny Men,* Dutton, 1939; Mary Ellen Vorse, *Wakey Goes to Bed,* Scott, 1941.†

* * *

HOGAN, Robert (Goode) 1930-

PERSONAL: Born May 29, 1930, in Boonville, Mo.; son of Robert Goode and Helene (Sombart) Hogan; married Betty Matthews, December 1, 1950 (marriage dissolved, 1978); married Mary Rose Callaghan, December 21, 1979; children: (first marriage) Robert, Kathleen (Mrs. John McKenzie), Pamela, Sean, Shivaun. *Education:* University of Missouri, B.A., 1953, M.A., 1954, Ph.D., 1956. *Politics:* Shavian. *Religion:* Shavian. *Home:* 102 East Main, Newark, Del. 19711. *Office:* Department of English, University of Delaware, Newark, Del. 19711.

CAREER: University of Missouri—Columbia, instructor in English, 1954-56; Ohio University, Athens, instructor in English, 1956-58; Purdue University, Lafayette, Ind., assistant professor of English, 1958-66; University of California, Davis, associate professor of English, 1966-70; University of Delaware, Newark, professor of English, 1970—. Visiting professor, University of Rochester, Rochester, N.Y., 1962-63. Publisher, Proscenium Press, 1965—. *Military service:* U.S. Army, 1950-52. *Awards, honors:* Guggenheim fellowship for playwriting, 1961-62.

WRITINGS: The Experiments of Sean O'Casey, St. Martin's, 1960; (editor with Sven E. Molin) *Drama: The Major Genres,* Dodd, 1962; (editor) *Feathers from the Green Crow: Sean O'Casey, 1905-1925,* University of Missouri Press, 1962; *Arthur Miller,* University of Minnesota Press, 1964; *The Independence of Elmer Rice,* Southern Illinois University Press, 1965; (editor) Elmer Rice, *The Iron Cross,* Proscenium, 1965; *Saint Jane* (play), Proscenium, 1966; (editor with M. J. O'Neill) *Joseph Holloway's Abbey Theatre,* Southern Illinois University Press, 1967; *After the Irish Renaissance,* University of Minnesota Press, 1967; (editor) *Seven Irish Plays, 1946-1964,* University of Minnesota Press, 1967; (editor with H. Bogart) *The Plain Style,* American Book Co., 1967; (editor with O'Neill) *Joseph Holloway's Irish Theatre,* three volumes, Proscenium, 1968-70; *Betty and the Beast* (play), Proscenium, 1968; (editor) *The Crows of Mephistopheles and Other Stories by George Fitzmaurice,* Dolmen Press, 1968; *The Fan Club* (play; produced in New York at American Theatre Co., 1972), Proscenium, 1969; (editor) *Towards a National Theatre: The Theatrical Criticism of Frank J. Fay,* Dolmen Press, 1969; *Dion Boucicault,* Twayne, 1969.

(Editor with James Kilroy) *Lost Plays of the Irish Renaissance,* Proscenium, 1970; *Mervyn Wall,* Bucknell University Press, 1971; *Eimar O'Duffy,* Bucknell University Press, 1971; (with Kilroy) *The Modern Irish Drama: A Documentary History,* Dolman Press, Volume I: *The Irish Literary Theatre,* 1975, Volume II: *Laying the Foundations,* 1976, Volume III: *The Abbey Theatre, 1905-1909,* 1978, Volume IV (with others): *The Rise of the Realists, 1910-1915,* 1979; (editor) *Dictionary of Irish Literature,* Greenwood Press, 1979. Also editor, with Sven E. Molin, of *The Shanghrann, Volume I: The Early Years,* by Dion Boucicault, 1979.

Also author of plays, including: "The Old Man Says Yes!," produced in New York at Clark Center for the Performing Arts, 1971; "A Better Place," produced in New York at American Theatre Co., 1972; "An Unsocial Socialist," produced in Wilmington, Del. at Wilmington Drama League, 1973; "Happy Hour," produced in New York at Provincetown Playhouse, 1974; "Ever since Eden," produced in Los Angeles, Calif. at Advance Theatre Foundation; (with James Douglas) "The Painting of Babbi Joe," produced in New York at Nameless Theatre, 1978. Editor, *Journal of Irish Literature,* 1972—.

WORK IN PROGRESS: Further volumes of *The Modern Irish Drama: A Documentary History.*

HOIG, Stan(ley Warlick) 1924-

PERSONAL: Born June 24, 1924, in Duncan, Okla.; son of Melvin Erwin and Kathleen (Keever) Hoig; married Patricia Corbell, 1953; children: Melvin, Lisa, Brent. *Education:* Oklahoma State University, B.A., 1949; University of Oklahoma, M.A., 1964, Ph.D., 1971. *Office:* Department of Journalism, Central State University, Edmond, Okla. 73034.

CAREER: Douglas Aircraft Co., Tulsa, Okla., technical writer and handbook section head, 1953-56; National Lead Co., Baroid Division, Houston, Tex., editor, 1956-64; Central State University, Edmond, Okla., professor of journalism, 1964—. *Military service:* U.S. Army Air Forces, 1943-45; became sergeant. *Member:* Southeast Texas Industrial Editors (president, 1963).

WRITINGS: Humor of the American Cowboy, Caxton, 1958; *The Sand Creek Massacre,* University of Oklahoma Press, 1961; *The Western Odyssey of John Simpson Smith,* Arthur H. Clark, 1974; *The Battle of the Washita,* Doubleday, 1976; *The Peace Chiefs of the Cheyennes,* University of Oklahoma Press, 1979. Also author of book and lyrics, *Oklahoma, U.S.A.,* for Oklahoma Bicentennial Musical Pageant, 1976.

WORK IN PROGRESS: David L. Payne: The Oklahoma Boomer; another book.

* * *

HOLDEN, Jonathan 1941-

PERSONAL: Born July 18, 1941, in Morristown, N.J.; son of Alan Nordby (a physicist) and Jaynet (Conselyea) Holden; married Gretchen Weltzheimer, November 16, 1963. *Education:* Oberlin College, B.A., 1963; San Francisco State College (now University), M.A., 1970; University of Colorado, graduate study, beginning 1970. *Home:* 1731 Fairview, Manhattan, Kan. 66502. *Office:* Department of English, Kansas State University, Manhattan, Kan. 66506.

CAREER: Cambridge Book Co., Bronxville, N.J., editorial assistant, 1963-65; high school mathematics teacher in West Orange, N.J., 1965-68; University of Colorado, Boulder, teaching assistant in English, beginning 1970, editorial assistant for *English Language Notes,* beginning 1970; poet-in-residence, Stephens College, 1974-78, and Kansas State University, 1978—. *Awards, honors:* Devins Award for poetry, 1972, for *Design for a House;* National Endowment for the Humanities grant, 1974.

WRITINGS: Design for a House (poems), University of Missouri Press, 1972; *The Mark to Turn: A Reading of William Stafford's Poetry,* University Press of Kansas, 1976; *The Rhetoric of the Contemporary Lyric,* Indiana University Press, 1980. Contributor of poems to *Antioch Review, North American Review,* and other journals.

* * *

HOLLANDER, John 1929-

PERSONAL: Born October 28, 1929; son of Franklin (a physiologist) and Muriel (Kornfeld) Hollander; married Anne Loesser, June 15, 1953 (divorced, 1976); children: Martha, Elizabeth. *Education:* Columbia University, A.B., 1950, M.A., 1952; Indiana University, Ph.D., 1959. *Office:* Department of English, Yale University, New Haven, Conn. 06520.

CAREER: Harvard University, Cambridge, Mass., junior fellow, Society of Fellows, 1954-57; Connecticut College, New London, lecturer in English, 1957-59; Yale University, New Haven, Conn., instructor, 1959-61, assistant professor, 1961-63, associate professor of English, 1964-66; Hunter College of the City University of New York, New York, N.Y., professor of English, 1966-77; Yale University, professor of English, 1977—. Visiting professor, Salzburg Seminar in American Studies, 1965. Member of poetry board, Wesleyan University Press. *Member:* American Academy of Arts and Sciences (fellow), National Institute of Arts and Letters, Modern Language Association of America, English Institute. *Awards, honors:* Yale Younger Poets Award, 1958, for *A Crackling of Thorns;* Poetry Chap-Book Award, 1962, for *The Untuning of the Sky;* National Institute of Arts and Letters grant for creative work in literature, 1963; Levinson Prize, *Poetry* magazine, 1974; Guggenheim fellowship, 1979-80.

WRITINGS—All poetry: *A Crackling of Thorns,* Yale University Press, 1958, reprinted, AMS Press, 1973; *Movie Going and Other Poems,* Atheneum, 1962; *Various Owls,* Norton, 1963; *Visions from the Ramble,* Atheneum, 1965; *The Quest of the Gole,* Atheneum, 1966; *Types of Shape,* Atheneum, 1969; *The Night Mirror,* Atheneum, 1971; *Town and Country Matters,* David R. Godine, 1972; *Selected Poems,* Secker & Warburg, 1972; *The Head of the Bed,* David R. Godine, 1974; *Tales Told of the Fathers,* Atheneum, 1975; *Reflections on Espionage,* Atheneum, 1976; *Spectral Emanations,* Atheneum, 1978; *In Place,* Abattoir, 1978; *Blue Wine,* Johns Hopkins Press, 1979.

Other: *The Untuning of the Sky: Ideas of Music in English Poetry, 1500-1700,* Princeton University Press, 1961; *Images of Voice,* Chelsea House, 1969; *The Immense Parade on Supererogation Day,* Atheneum, 1972; *Vision and Resonance,* Oxford University Press, 1975; *The Figure of Echo,* University of California Press, 1981. Also author of play, "An Entertainment for Elizabeth, Being a Masque of the Seven Motions; or, Terpsichore Unchained," produced in New York, 1969.

Editor: (With Harold Bloom) *The Wind and the Rain,* Doubleday, 1961; (with Bloom) *Selected Poems of Ben Johnson,* Dell, 1961; (with Anthony Hecht) *Jiggery-Pockery,* Atheneum, 1966; *Poems of Our Moment,* Pegasus, 1968; *American Short Stories since 1945,* Harper, 1968; *Modern Poetry: Modern Essays in Criticism,* Oxford University Press, 1968; (with Frank Kermode) *The Oxford Anthology of English Literature,* Oxford University Press, 1973; (with Reuben Brower and Helen Vendler) *I. A. Richards: Essays in His Honor,* Oxford University Press, 1973.

Contributor of verse and prose to *New Yorker, Partisan Review, Kenyon Review, Paris Review, Esquire, Commentary,* and other popular and scholarly journals and magazines. Editorial associate for poetry, *Partisan Review,* 1959-64. Contributing editor, *Harper's,* 1970-71.

WORK IN PROGRESS: The Mingled Measure, a study of music and natural sound in romantic poetic tradition.

SIDELIGHTS: Labeled by some critics as a neo-Scholastic poet, John Hollander's earlier poetry reflected his belief in what he once termed "the modality of verse." Robert Alter explained that "the modality of verse" refers to "a poetry which avowedly elects long-established forms of expression works toward 'creating discourse in an ideal community, within which the literary dialect would be as speech.' Modern poets have often rejected all notions of the modality of verse, breaking down genre and decorum in the effort to forge a uniquely personal, purely *expressive* style. . . . [The] reaching for modality explains, I think, the strength, the limitations, and the peculiarity of John Hollander's own poetry.

It is heartening to discover in the scholarly analyst of prosody a poet who is himself a technical virtuoso."

As Daniel Hoffman wrote: "In a time when intelligence is so widely distrusted among poets and readers, John Hollander has never failed to engage his polymathic mind in the enterprise of his poetry. This makes for both the difficulties and the delights of reading his poems, which cunningly carry an overload of learning whatever their intrinsic forms. . . . Hollander's work results from the fusion of a curious, wide-ranging intelligence—equally a familiar of traditions in literature, philosophy, and myth, and of speculative psychology and science—with the skills of a virtuoso versemaker."

Marie Borroff agreed with Daniel Hoffman's assessment of Hollander's poetic ability and cited Hollander's *The Night Mirror* as a perfect example. Borroff wrote that the publication of "*The Night Mirror* shows him still an unexcelled virtuoso of the verbal keyboard, executing black-key glissandos, sweeping along in single-handed arpeggios, striking tenths, twelfths, fourteenths as single chords. Learned allusions, which the reader must grasp for himself, and intricate wit, involving words or images or both, enhance the pyrotechnics."

Recently, however, critics and readers have begun to view Hollander as a master of classical and English form. One such critic, Richard Poirier, writes in his review of *Spectral Emanations* that "[Hollander] can do a poem 'Fireworks' in strict Pindaric triads or a book length sequence like *Reflections on Espionage,* the unflaggingly brilliant and haunting book that preceded this one, in the hendecasyllabics favored by Catullus. He is forever playful about forms. There are included here six pieces from *Types of Shape*—one in the form of a car key, another of a light bulb—which are a delight to eye and ear. He is a formalist but a decidedly witty one. The changes that can be worked within form are made incumbent upon the discovery that any form is implicitly a substitute for or an interpretation of some other. Any form exists in the shadow of some other, and is on the verge sometimes of eliding into it; and the more you are aware—as Hollander asks you to be—of the form even of particular words, the more they are on the brink of those puns into which he sometimes lets them drop."

Just as form is an important part in Hollander's writing, music too plays an intricate role. Paul Auster writes in *Harper's* that "Hollander is unquestionably one of the most skillful versemakers around, and the qualities of his imagination are most evident at the verbal level. Music, in his work, is just as much an agent of meaning as discourse, and the sonorous textures of his poems compel us to read with our ears as well as our eyes. Intelligent to a fault, rational even in his darkest broodings, Hollander nevertheless achieves distinctive emotional effects through his subtle use of the technical resources at his command. Rhyme and meter, word play and allusion, a keen sense of the line: these are not ornaments in Hollander's poetry, but essential, binding forces, and they reveal to us that language is not merely a systematic organization of signs, but a magic soil in which the pre-history of the human unconscious can be traced."

BIOGRAPHICAL/CRITICAL SOURCES: Richard Howard, *Alone with America: Essays on the Art of Poetry in the United States since 1970,* Atheneum, 1969; *New York Times Book Review,* October 17, 1971, May 28, 1978; *Yale Review,* autumn, 1972; *Contemporary Literary Criticism,* Gale, Volume II, 1974, Volume V, 1976, Volume VIII, 1978; *Commentary,* September, 1975; *Harper's,* November, 1975; *Library Journal,* June 15, 1978; *Washington Post Book World,* December 17, 1978; Daniel Hoffman, editor, *Harvard's Guide to Contemporary American Writing,* Harvard University Press, 1979.

* * *

HOLLISTER, C. Warren 1930-

PERSONAL: Born November 2, 1930, in Los Angeles, Calif.; son of Nathan and Carrie (Cushman) Hollister; married Edith Elizabeth Muller, April 12, 1952; children: Charles Warren, Jr., Lawrence Gregory, Robert Cushman. *Education:* Harvard University, A.B., 1951; University of California, Los Angeles, M.A., 1957, Ph.D., 1958. *Home:* 4592 Via Clarice, Santa Barbara, Calif. 93111. *Office:* Department of History, University of California, Santa Barbara, Calif. 93106.

CAREER: University of California, Santa Barbara, 1958—, began as instructor, currently professor of history, chairman of department, 1967-70. Visiting assistant professor, Stanford University, 1962-63; visiting fellow, Merton College, Oxford University, 1965-66, and Australian National University, 1978. *Military service:* U.S. Air Force, 1951-53; became second lieutenant. *Member:* American Historical Association (vice-president, 1974-76), Royal Historical Society (fellow), Conference on British Studies, Mediaeval Academy of America, Pacific Coast Conference on British Studies. *Awards, honors:* Haynes Foundation fellowship, 1959; Social Science Research Council grant-in-aid, 1961; American Council of Learned Societies grant-in-aid, 1962-63, 1963-64; Triennial Book Prize, Conference on British Studies, 1963, for *Anglo-Saxon Military Institutions;* Guggenheim fellow, 1965-66; Fulbright research fellow, 1965-66; E. Harris Harbison Award for Distinguished Teaching, Danforth Foundation, 1966.

WRITINGS—All published by Wiley, except as indicated: *Anglo-Saxon Military Institutions,* Clarendon Press, 1962; *Medieval Europe: A Short History,* 1964, 4th edition, 1978; *The Military Organization of Norman England,* Clarendon Press, 1965; *The Making of England,* Heath, 1966, 3rd edition, 1976; *Roots of the Western Tradition,* 1966, 3rd edition, 1977; (with John Stipp and Alan Dirrum) *The Rise and Development of Western Civilization,* two volumes, 1967, 2nd edition, 1972; (editor) *Landmarks of the Western Civilization,* two volumes, 1967, 2nd edition, 1973; (editor) *The Impact of the Norman Conquest,* 1969; *Twelfth Century Renaissance,* 1969; (with Judith Pike) *The Moons of Meer* (children's fantasy), Walck, 1969; *Odysseus to Columbus: A Synopsis of Classical and Medieval History,* 1974; (with others) *River through Time: The Course of Western Civilization,* 1975. General editor, "Major Issues in World History," Wiley, 1968—. Contributor of articles to several professional journals. Associate editor, *Viator;* member of editorial board, *American Historical Review* and *Journal of Medieval History.*

WORK IN PROGRESS: King Henry I of England, for Eyre-Methuen.

* * *

HOLLY, Joan C(arol) 1932-
(Joan Hunter Holly)

PERSONAL: Born September 25, 1932, in Lansing, Mich.; daughter of Arthur Hunter and Hazel (Trumbo) Holly. *Education:* Michigan State University, B.A. (magna cum laude), 1954.

CAREER: Writer. Has worked as a teacher of creative writing. *Member:* Science Fiction Writers of America (treasurer, 1976-79), Academy of Science Fiction and Fantasy Films, Science Fiction Oral History Society, Authors Guild, Authors League of America, Count Dracula Society, Phi Kappa Phi, Psi Chi, Tau Sigma.

WRITINGS: Encounter, Bouregy, 1959; *The Green Planet,* Bouregy, 1960; *The Dark Planet,* Bouregy, 1962; *The Flying Eyes,* Monarch, 1962; *The Running Man,* Monarch, 1963; *The Gray Aliens,* Bouregy, 1963; *The Time Twisters,* Avon, 1964; *The Dark Enemy,* Bouregy, 1965; *The Mind Traders,* Bouregy, 1966; *The Assassination Affair,* Ace Books, 1967; *Keeper,* Lazer Books, 1976; *Shepherd,* Lazer Books, 1977; *The Death Dolls of Lyra,* Manor, 1977.

Contributor to science fiction anthologies, including *And Walk Now Gently through the Fire,* Chilton, 1973, *The Other Side of Tomorrow: Original Science Fiction Stories about Young People of the Future,* edited by Roger Elwood, Random House, 1973, *The Graduated Robot and Other Stories,* edited by Elwood, Lerner, 1974, and *Futurelove,* Bobbs-Merrill, 1977. Contributor to *Fantastic Magazine.*

WORK IN PROGRESS: Mind Sword, a science fiction novel; a vampire horror novel.

SIDELIGHTS: Joan Holly writes: "I only feel successful in my work when I manage to touch and move a reader's emotions and offer him a genuine 'experience' as he reads my stories. This, I believe, is the purpose of fiction. Even in the genre of science fiction, I think that the original ideas presented and explored must be clothed in a narrative full of believable and worthwhile characters, and that the reader is entitled to become involved with the plot and to immerse himself in its experience.

"During brief stints as a creative writing teacher, I've tried to impress my students with the fact that mastering the craft of writing is absolutely essential in providing them with the tools that enable them to tell their tales. Once learned, the basic skills allow a writer to expand and explore, but never learned, and the writer is strangled by his own inability to produce a coherent plot, living characters, and proper dialogue. Without these crucial ingredients, the writer is stifled, and no one will ever read his work."

"I follow a strict discipline in my writing time, working six to eight hours a day at the typewriter (often six days a week when the story gets 'hot'). Novels, of course, are constantly in charge of my mind even after the actual day's work is finished, and I fill scraps of paper and notebooks with myriad jottings and snatches of dialogue or action. I began writing when I was five years old when my mother actually wrote down my words for me as I composed them, since I was too young to be able to do it for myself. To me, writing is a joy, a terrifically hard job that gets harder with experience, and has a close resemblance to a non-curable disease. Once it begins to spread in you, there's no way to halt it."

All of Joan Holly's works have been translated into several languages, including German, Italian, French, Spanish, Japanese, and Swedish.

AVOCATIONAL INTERESTS: Psychology, anthropology, cats, gardening, American Indian history and lore, astronomy.

* * *

HOLMES, Joseph Everett 1922-
(Jay Holmes)

PERSONAL: Born January 18, 1922, in New York, N.Y.; son of Joseph Walter and Dorothy (Horton) Holmes; married Beatrice Hort, 1950; children: John, Dorothy, Olivia, Barbara. *Education:* Attended Stanford University, 1943-44, and University of Pennsylvania, 1945; Queens College (now Queens College of the City University of New York), B.A., 1949; Columbia University, certificate in advanced science writing program, 1959. *Politics:* Democratic. *Religion:* Unitarian Universalist. *Home:* 1948 Martha's Rd., Alexandria, Va. 22307. *Office:* Department of Energy, Office of Solar, Geothermal, Electric and Storage Systems, Washington, D.C. 20545.

CAREER: Greenwich Time, Greenwich, Conn., sports editor, 1949-50; *Elmira Advertiser,* Elmira, N.Y., reporter, 1950-51; Associated Press, newsman in Buffalo, N.Y., 1951-54, and Albany, N.Y., 1954-58; *Missiles and Rockets,* Washington, D.C., associate editor, 1959-61; affiliated with National Aeronautics and Space Administration, Washington, D.C., Office of Public Affairs, 1961-62, and Office of Manned Space Flight, 1962-72, Atomic Energy Commission, Washington, D.C., 1972, National Science Foundation, Washington, D.C., 1972-75, Energy Research and Development Administration, Division of Solar Energy, Washington, D.C., 1975-77, and U.S. Department of Energy, Washington, D.C., 1977—. Secretary of NASA Conference on Lunar Exploration and Science, summer, 1965. *Military service:* U.S. Army, four years; became staff sergeant. *Member:* National Association of Science Writers, American Society for Public Administration, Toastmasters International. *Awards, honors:* Sloan-Rockefeller fellowship in science writing, Columbia University, 1958-59; Special Achievement Award, Energy Research and Development Administration, 1976 and 1977.

WRITINGS—Under name Jay Holmes: *America on the Moon,* Lippincott, 1962 (published in England as *The Race for the Moon,* Gollancz, 1962); (editor) *Energy, Environment, Productivity,* National Science Foundation, 1974. Contributor to *World Book Encyclopedia Year Book,* 1962-73, *Science Year,* 1965, and *Britannica Yearbook of Science and the Future,* 1970.

* * *

HOLMES, Martin (Rivington) 1905-

PERSONAL: Born May 12, 1905, in London, England; son of Charles John (a landscape painter, writer on art, and gallery director) and Florence Hill (a violinist and composer; maiden name, Rivington) Holmes. *Education:* Attended Christ Church, Oxford, 1924-27, receiving second class honors in Classical Moderations, 1926. *Politics:* Conservative *Religion;* Church of England, *Home:* Castle Bank, Appleby, Westmorland CA16 6SN, England.

CAREER: London Museum, London, England, 1932-65, member of staff at Lancaster House, at St. James's, and at Kensington Palace; writer. Carl Rosa Trust, member, 1957-63, chairman 1963—. Occasional technical advisor for BBC educational television; honorary consultant, Bankside Theatre Museum. Appleby borough councillor, 1965-74, town councillor, 1974-75, town mayor, 1975-76; Eden district councillor, 1974-76. *Military service:* British Armed Forces, 1939-46; became major. *Member:* Society of Antiquaries (fellow).

WRITINGS: Medieval England, Methuen, 1934; *The Crown Jewels,* H.M.S.O., 1953, 3rd edition published as *The Crown Jewels in the Wakefield Tower of the Tower of London,* 1961; *Personalia,* Museums Association (London), 1957; *Arms and Armor in Tudor and Stuart London,* H.M.S.O., 1957, 2nd edition, 1970; *The London of Elizabeth I,* London Museums, 1959; *The London of Charles II,* H.M.S.O., 1960; *Shakespeare's Public: The Touchstone of His Genius,* Transatlantic, 1960, corrected edition, J. Murray, 1964; *Moorfields in 1559,* H.M.S.O., 1963; *The Guns of Elsinore,* Barnes & Noble, 1964; *The Parish Churches of Appleby,* privately printed, 1967; *Stage Costume and Accessories in the London Museum,* H.M.S.O., 1968; *Elizabethan London,* Praeger, 1969; *Shakespeare and His Players,* Scribner, 1972; (with H.D.W. Sitwell) *The English Regalia,* H.M.S.O., 1972; *Appleby and the Crown,* J. Whitehead & Son (Appleby), 1974; *Appleby Castle,* Ferguson Industrial Holdings, 1974; *Proud Northern Lady: Lady Anne Clifford,* Phillimore, 1975; *Shakespeare and Burbage,* Phillimore, 1978.

Plays: "Crichton the Scholar," first produced in London by Playwrights' Club, 1936; *The Road to Runnymede* (three-act; first produced in London by Goodrich Players, 1946), Samuel French, 1948; "From a Fair Lady," first produced by Goodrich Players, 1948, revived as "Dragon's Deathbed" in London at Gateway Theatre, 1955; "The Waiting Lady," first produced at Gateway Theatre, 1949; "Sword of Justice," first produced at Gateway Theatre, 1949; "The Last Burgundian," first produced at Gateway Theatre, 1949; "Fotheringhay," first produced at Gateway Theatre, 1950; "The Golden Unicorn," first produced at Gateway Theatre, 1951; "The Master of the Horse," first produced at Gateway Theatre, 1951; "King's Work," first produced at Gateway Theatre, 1952, revived as "Royal Portrait, 1666" in London at Toynbee Hall; "The Smiling Angel," first produced at Gateway Theatre, 1953; "They Call It Treason," first produced in London by Central Drama Group, 1959; "A Man Called Dante," first produced in London at Hovenden Theatre Club, 1961; "The Heavy Crown," first produced by Central Drama Group, 1961; "Duke of the English," first produced by Central Drama Group, 1966.

Contributor to *Encyclopedia Americana* and *Encyclopaedia Britannica;* contributor to journals and periodicals, including *Quarterly Review, Antiquaries Journal, Apollo, Connoisseur, Theatre Notebook, Illustrated London News, Drama, Listener,* and *London Times.*

WORK IN PROGRESS: Makers of Appleby; memoirs.

SIDELIGHTS: Martin Holmes studied voice and was a chorister in the last international opera season at Covent Garden in 1939; he is particularly interested in opera productions in London between 1920 and 1960. *Avocational interests:* Collecting arms and armour and 17th century history and travel books.

* * *

HONORE, Antony Maurice 1921-

PERSONAL: Born March 30, 1921, in London, England; son of Frederic Maurice and Marjorie (Gilbert) Honore; married former wife, Genouville Martine Marie-Odette, 1948; children: Veronique Martine, Frank Martin. *Education:* Attended University of Cape Town, 1939-40; University of South Africa, B.A., 1945; New College, Oxford, B.A. in Jurisprudence, 1947, B.C.L., 1948, M.A., 1952. *Politics:* Liberal. *Home and office:* All Souls College, Oxford University, Oxford, England.

CAREER: University of Nottingham, Nottingham, England, assistant lecturer, 1948-49; Oxford University, Oxford, England, fellow and praelector in law of Queen's College, 1949-64, fellow of New College, 1964-70, Regius Professor of Civil Law of All Souls College, 1971—, Rhodes reader in Roman-Dutch law, 1957-71. Visiting professor, McGill University, 1961, University of Cape Town, and University of Witwatersrand, 1964. *Military service:* Union Defence Force, five years; became lieutenant. *Member:* Society of Public Teachers of Law. *Awards, honors:* Rhodes Scholar, 1940; Honorary Bencher, Lincoln's Inn, 1971; Fellow of British Academy, 1972.

WRITINGS: (With R. W. Lee) *The South African Law of Obligations,* Butterworth, 1950; (with Lee) *The South African Law of Property, Family Relations and Succession,* Butterworth, 1954; (with H.L.A. Hart) *Causation in the Law,* Oxford University Press, 1959; *Gaius,* Oxford University Press, 1962; *The South African Law of Trusts,* Juta & Co., 1966, 2nd edition, 1976; *Triborian,* Duckworth, 1978; *Sex Law,* Duckworth, 1978.

* * *

HOOD, Hugh (John Blagdon) 1928-

PERSONAL: Born April 30, 1928, in Toronto, Canada; son of Alexander (a banker) and Marguerite (Blagdon) Hood; married Ruth Noreen Mallory (a painter and printmaker), April 22, 1957; children: Sarah Barbara, Dwight Alexander, John Arthur, Alexandra Mary. *Education:* University of Toronto, B.A., 1950, M.A., 1952, Ph.D., 1955. *Politics:* Radical socialist. *Religion:* Christian. *Home and office:* 4242 Hampton Ave., Montreal, Quebec, Canada H4A 2K9.

CAREER: University of Montreal, Montreal, Quebec, professor of English, 1961—; novelist.

WRITINGS: Flying a Red Kite (short stories), Ryerson, 1962; *White Figure, White Ground* (novel), Ryerson, 1964; *Around the Mountain* (short stories), Peter Martin Associates, 1967; *The Camera Always Lies* (novel), Harcourt, 1967; *Strength Down Centre: The Jean Beliveau Story,* Prentice-Hall, 1970; *A Game of Touch* (novel), Longmans, Green, 1970.

Published by Oberon Press, except as indicated: *The Fruit Man, the Meat Man and the Manager* (short stories), 1971; *You Can't Get There from Here* (novel), 1972; *The Governor's Bridge Is Closed* (essays), 1973; *The New Age/Le Nouveau Siecle,* Volume I: *The Swing in the Garden,* 1975, Volume II: *A New Athens,* 1977, Volume III: *Reservoir Ravine,* 1979; *Dark Glasses* (short stories), 1976; *Selected Stories,* 1978; (with Seymour Segal) *Scoring: The Art of Hockey* (art book), 1979; *None Genuine without This Signature* (short stories), ECW Press, 1980.

WORK IN PROGRESS: A collection of short stories; more volumes of *The New Age/Le Nouveau Siecle,* including Volume IV: *Black and White Keys.*

SIDELIGHTS: Hugh Hood told *CA:* "I consider my *roman-fleuve, The New Age/Le Nouveau Siecle,* to be the great, major work of my life. It should occupy me for a generation with the final volume appearing around the year 2000. Hence the title." Since writing those words, Hood has completed the opening trilogy of his saga. He now adds: "I have a very much clearer idea now than I did in the early 1970s of where I'm going with this work. I can now see what the proportions of the last six novels will be, and I am actively working on the second and third books in the second trilogy."

* * *

HOOPES, Robert (Griffith) 1920-

PERSONAL: Born March 29, 1920, in Chicago, Ill.; son of Ralph Griffith and Elsie (Lewey) Hoopes; married Margaret Payne, 1943; children: Kathy, Ralph. *Education:* Cornell College, Mount Vernon, Iowa, A.B., 1941; Boston University, A.M., 1942; Harvard University, A.M., 1948, Ph.D.,

1949. *Home:* 819 East Pleasant St., Amherst, Mass. 01002. *Office:* Department of English, University of Massachusetts, Amherst, Mass. 01003.

CAREER: Stanford University, Stanford, Calif., 1949-57, began as instructor, became assistant professor; American Council of Learned Societies, New York, N.Y., vice-president, 1957-59; Oakland University, Rochester, Mich., professor of English, 1959-70, chairman of department, 1962-70, dean of faculty, 1959-61, assistant to chancellor, 1961-62; University of Massachusetts—Amherst, professor of English, 1970—. Visiting professor at University of Berne, Berne, Switzerland, Yale University, 1954-55, and Boston University, 1965. *Military service:* U.S. Marine Air Corps, 1942-46; became captain; received Presidential Citation. *Member:* Modern Language Association of America, Renaissance Society of America, American Association of University Professors, Phi Beta Kappa. *Awards, honors:* Carnegie fellowship, 1954-55; Huntington Library grants, 1950, 1952; D.Litt., Cornell College, 1959.

WRITINGS: (Editor with others) *Prose of the English Renaissance,* Appleton, 1952; (editor with others) *Tudor Poetry and Prose,* Appleton, 1954; (editor with Wilfred Healey Stone) *Form and Thought in Prose,* Ronald, 1954, 4th edition, 1977; (with Hubert Marshall) *Undergraduate in the University,* Stanford University Press, 1957; *Right Reason in the English Renaissance,* Harvard University Press, 1962; *Science in the College Curriculum* (conference report), Oakland University, 1963; (with Stone and Nancy Huddleston Packer) *The Short Story: An Introduction,* McGraw, 1976. Contributor to literary journals.

WORK IN PROGRESS: Milton's "Better Teacher": The Ways of Literary Influence.

* * *

HOPKINS, Kenneth 1914-
(Christopher Adams, Anton Burney, Warwick Mannon, Paul Marsh, Edmund Marshall, Arnold Meredith)

PERSONAL: Born December 7, 1914, in Bournemouth, Hampshire, England; son of Reginald Marshall (a civil servant) and Elsa (Adams) Hopkins; married Elizabeth Coward, September 7, 1939; children: Edmund Marshall. *Education:* Attended school at St. Peter's, Bournemouth. *Home:* 12 New Rd., North Walsham, Norfolk NR28 9DF, England.

CAREER: Professional writer. Visiting lecturer in English, University of Texas, Main University (now University of Texas at Austin), 1961; visiting professor of English at Southern Illinois University, Carbondale, 1964-72, Carleton University, 1976-77, and Colgate University, 1978. Guest lecturer at St. Louis University, University of Tennessee, Colgate University, Boston College, Wake Forest College, and other schools. *Military service:* Royal Army Ordnance Corps, 1941-45. *Member:* Royal Society of Literature of the United Kingdom (fellow).

WRITINGS: Twelve Poems, privately printed, 1937; *Recent Poetry,* privately printed, 1937; *New Sonnets,* privately printed, 1938; *Six Sonnets,* privately printed, 1938; *The Younger Sister,* Grasshopper Press, 1944; *Love and Elizabeth* (poems), Sylvan Press, 1944; *Miscellany Poems,* Grasshopper Press, 1946; *Songs and Sonnets,* Grasshopper Press, 1947; *Poems on Several Occasions,* Grasshopper Press, 1948; *To a Green Lizard Called Ramorino,* Faun Press, 1949.

(Published anonymously) *Apes and Elderberries,* Grasshopper Press, 1950; *Walter De la Mare: A Study,* Longmans, Green, 1953, revised edition, 1957; *The Corruption of a Poet* (autobiography), Barrie & Rockliff, 1954; *The Poets Laureate,* Library Publishers, 1955, revised and augmented edition, Barnes & Noble, 1973; *The Girl Who Died* (detective novel), Macdonald, 1955; *Inca Adventure* (children's fiction), Chatto & Windus, 1956; *Great Moments in Exploration* (juvenile), Roy Publishers, 1956; *She Died Because* (detective novel), Macdonald, 1957, Holt, 1964; *The Forty-First Passenger* (detective novel), Macdonald, 1958; *Portraits in Satire,* Barnes & Noble, 1959.

Dead against My Principles (detective novel), Macdonald, 1960, Holt, 1962; *Pierce with a Pin* (detective novel), Macdonald, 1960; *Poor Heretic* (poems), University of Texas Press, 1961; *Foundlings and Fugitives* (poems), Brick Row Book Shop (Austin, Tex.), 1961; *Forty-Two Poems,* Putnam, 1961; *A Trip to Texas* (travel), Macdonald, 1962; *Body Blow* (detective novel), Macdonald, 1962, Holt, 1965; *English Poetry: A Short History,* Lippincott, 1963; *Campus Corpse,* Macdonald, 1963; *Collected Poems, 1935-1965,* Southern Illinois University Press, 1965; *The Powys Brothers,* Phoenix House, 1967, new edition, Warren House, 1972; *Poems English and American,* Brick Row Book Shop (Houston), 1968; *Slivers of Syntax: More Emanations from Emily,* Colgate University Press, 1969; *Bourbon and Branch: Poems,* Brick Row Book Shop, 1969.

Kickshaws and Carnishings (poems), Warren House, 1970; *American Poems and Others,* Rota, 1970; *The Enfant Terrible Again,* Warren House, 1974; *Mood, Comment and Occasion* (poems), Warren House, 1975; *Samuel Butler: Four Sonnets Concerning Miss Savage,* Warren House, 1976; *A Dull Head among Windy Spaces: The Eliot Cult,* Warren House, 1976; *By Invitation Only* (poems), Warren House, 1977; *Hal Trovillion and the Powys Brothers,* Warren House, 1978; *The Dead Slave and Other Poems,* Catalyst, 1978; *Collected Poems, 1966-1977,* Warren House, 1978; *Llewelyn Powys, an Essay,* Enitharmon, 1979.

Under pseudonym Christopher Adams: *Helen of Troy* (film story), Beverley Books, 1956; *English Literature for Fun,* Hutchinson, 1957; (author of introduction and notes) *The Worst English Poets,* Wingate, 1958; *Amateur Agent,* Boardman, 1964.

Under pseudonym Anton Burney: *The Liberace Story,* Beverley Books, 1957.

Under pseudonym Warwick Mannon; published by World Film Publications: *Vice Versa,* 1946; *Spring in Park Lane,* 1948; *Miranda,* 1948; *No Room at the Inn,* 1948; *Bond Street,* 1948.

Under pseudonym Paul Marsh: *Safari* (film story), Beverley Books, 1956.

Under pseudonym Edmund Marshall: *Tales of Ambledown Airport,* Hutchinson, Number 1: *Colin's Lucky Day,* 1960; *The Missing Viscount,* Hutchinson, 1960.

Under pseudonym Arnold Meredith: *The Guinea Pig,* World Film Publications, 1948.

Books edited, or with introduction, by Hopkins: *The English Lyric: A Selection,* De Visscher, 1945; *Edmund Blunden: A Selection of His Poetry and Prose,* Hart-Davis, 1950, Horizon, 1962; *Llewelyn Powys: A Selection from His Writings,* Macdonald, 1952, Horizon, 1961; *H. M. Tomlinson: A Selection from His Writings,* Hutchinson, 1953; *Walter De la Mare: A Selection from His Writings,* Faber, 1953; Guy de Maupassant, *Bel Ami,* Folio Society, 1954; Emily Eden, *The Semi-Attached Couple,* Folio Society, 1955; R. S. Surtees,

Hawbuck Grange, Folio Society, 1956; Walter De la Mare, *Ghost Stories,* Folio Society, 1956; Surtees, *Hillingdon Hill,* Folio Society, 1956; Henry Fielding, *Tom Jones,* Folio Society, 1959.

Daniel Defoe, *Journal of the Plague Year,* Folio Society, 1960; O. Henry, *Selected Stories,* Folio Society, 1960; Thomas Love Peacock, *Crotchet Castle,* Folio Society, 1963; *A Little Treasury of Familiar Verse,* John Baker, 1963; *A Little Treasury of Love Lyrics,* John Baker, 1963; *A Little Treasury of Familiar Prose,* John Baker, 1964; *A Little Treasury of Religious Verse,* John Baker, 1964; *John Cowper Powys: Selected Poems,* Macdonald, 1964, Colgate University Press, 1965; *The Search: Fourth Series,* Southern Illinois University Press, 1965; *Crusade against Crime,* Boardman, 1966; *Second Crime Crusade,* Boardman, 1966; *The Poetry of Railways,* Frewin, 1966; Louis Wilkinson, *Blasphemy and Religion,* Colgate University Press, 1969; Wilkinson, *Bumbore, a Romance,* Colgate University Press, 1969; William Allan, *Kit, the Courier,* Warren House, 1969.

Wilkinson, *Welsh Ambassadors,* Colgate University Press, 1971; Jacob Mountain, *Poetical Revieries 1977,* Warren House, 1977; Gamel Woolsey, *Twenty-Eight Sonnets,* Warren House, 1977; Woolsey, *The Last Leaf Falls,* Warren House, 1978; Frederick Locker-Lampson and A. E. Gathorne-Hardy, *An Exchange of Compliments,* Warren House, 1978.

Contributor: *For Those Who Are Alive,* Fortune Press, 1946; *Women, an Anthology,* Spottiswoode Ballantyne, 1947; *Holidays and Happy Days,* Phoenix House, 1948; *The Pick of "Punch" 1950,* Chatto & Windus, 1951; *The Pick of "Punch" 1951,* Chatto & Windus, 1952; *The Pleasure Ground,* Macdonald, 1952; *Considered Trifles,* Werner Laurie, 1955; *Peninsula, an Anthology of West Country Verse,* Macdonald, 1959; *Dawn and Dusk,* Brockhampton, 1962; *Theodore: Essays on T. F. Powys,* St. Albert's Press, 1964; *The Second Bed Post,* Macdonald, 1964; *Across a Crowded Room,* Frewin, 1965. Also contributor to *The Children's Book of Famous Lives,* Odhams, and to numerous other anthologies.

Contributor to *Encyclopaedia Britannica* and *Dictionary of National Biography;* contributor to *New Statesman, Punch, Spectator, Times Literary Supplement, Argosy,* and many other magazines and newspapers in the United States and England. Literary editor, *Everybody's,* 1949-54; editor, at various times, of *Literary Digest, Go, Preview,* and other journals.

WORK IN PROGRESS: Editing and writing memoir, *Collected Poems of Gamel Woolsey; Letters of Llewelyn Powys to Louis Wilkinson.*

SIDELIGHTS: The bulk of Kenneth Hopkins' manuscripts, a selection of his literary correspondence, and other material relating to his work is at the Humanities Research Center in the University of Texas.

BIOGRAPHICAL/CRITICAL SOURCES: Kenneth Hopkins, *The Corruption of a Poet* (autobiography), Barrie & Rockliff, 1954; *A Trip to Texas,* Macdonald, 1962; R. L. Blackmore, editor, *Advice to a Young Poet: The Correspondence of Llewelyn Powys and Kenneth Hopkins,* Farleigh Dickinson University Press, 1969.

* * *

HOSELITZ, Bert(hold) F(rank) 1913-

PERSONAL: Born May 27, 1913, in Vienna, Austria; son of Bela and Anna (Gross) Hoselitz; married Elin Gunhild Gustafson, 1945; children: David Carl, Ann Gunhild. *Education:* University of Vienna, Doctor Juris, 1936; University of Chicago, M.A., 1945. *Home:* 5318 Hyde Park Blvd., Chicago, Ill. 60615. *Office:* University of Chicago, 1126 East 59th St., Chicago, Ill. 60637.

CAREER: Manchester College, North Manchester, Ind., instructor, 1940-41; Yale University, New Haven, Conn., research assistant, 1943; University of Chicago, Chicago, Ill., assistant professor, 1945-47; Carnegie Institute of Technology (now Carnegie-Mellon University), Pittsburgh, Pa., associate professor, 1947-48; University of Chicago, professor of economics, 1948—. Member of United Nations Technical Assistance Mission to El Salvador, 1952, and Ford Foundation town planning advisory team to Government of India, 1957-58. *Member:* American Economic Association, Economic History Association, Royal Economic Society, Economic History Society, International Institute of Differing Civilizations. *Awards, honors:* Fellow, Center for Advanced Study in the Behavioral Sciences, 1955.

WRITINGS: (With Henry S. Bloch) *The Economics of Military Occupation,* University of Chicago Press, 1944; (editor) *Progress of Underdeveloped Areas,* University of Chicago Press, 1952; (editor and contributor) *A Reader's Guide to the Social Sciences,* Free Press, 1959, revised edition, 1970; *Sociological Aspects of Economic Growth,* Free Press, 1960; (editor with others) *Theories of Economic Growth,* Free Press, 1960; (editor with Richard D. Lambert) *The Role of Savings and Wealth in Southern Asia and the West,* Unesco, 1963; (with Mahinder D. Chaudhry) *State Income of Dehli State, 1951-52, 1955-56,* University of Chicago Press, 1963; (contributor) Raymond Firth and B. S. Young, editors, *Capital Saving and Credit in Peasant Societies,* Allen & Unwin, 1964; (editor) *Economics and the Idea of Mankind,* Columbia University Press, 1965; (contributor) William B. Hamilton, editor, *The Transfer of Institutions,* Duke University Press, 1965; (contributor) James S. Coleman, editor, *Education and Political Development,* Princeton University Press, 1965. Directed study of the role of small industry in the process of economic growth for Mouton, 1968. Editor, *Economic Development and Cultural Change,* 1954-59, 1965—.

SIDELIGHTS: Bert F. Hoselitz's economics books have been translated into twenty-five languages. *Avocational interests:* Classical music and art.

* * *

HOSTETTER, B(enjamin) Charles 1916-

PERSONAL: Born May 26, 1916, in Manheim, Pa.; son of Monroe and Kathryn (Charles) Hostetter; married Grace Brackbill, May 3, 1939; children: Miriam, Patsy, Douglas, Ronald, Darrell, Charles, Jr., Philip, Richard. *Education:* Eastern Mennonite College, graduated from junior college, 1937, A.B. in Bible, 1948; Eastern Baptist Theological Seminary, M.A. in Religion, 1968; additional graduate study at Eastern Mennonite College, Southern Baptist Seminary, and Goshen Biblical Seminary. *Home address:* Route 2, Box 870, Hickory, N.C. 28601.

CAREER: Ordained pastor in Mennonite Church, 1939; ordained bishop in Virginia Mennonite Conference, 1965; Manheim Mennonite Church, Manheim, Pa., pastor, 1939-45; Mennonite Central Committee, Akron, Pa., civilian public service pastor, 1945-46; Eastern Mennonite College, Harrisonburg, Va., faculty member, 1946-53; radio ministry, pastor and director of "The Mennonite Hour," 1952-66; missions representative, Mennonite Board of Missions and Charities, beginning 1966.

WRITINGS: Keep Yourself Pure, Moody, 1957; *How to Build a Happy Home,* Zondervan, 1960; *How to Grow in the Christian Life,* Moody, 1960; *How God Leads Us,* Herald Press, 1962; *How to Get Assurance,* Herald Press, 1963; *Life at Its Best,* Moody, 1966.

* * *

HOUSTON, Peyton (H.) 1910-

PERSONAL: First syllable of surname is pronounced "house"; born December 20, 1910, in Cincinnati, Ohio; son of George H. (an industrialist) and Mary S. (Hoge) Houston; married Priscilla Moore, November 26, 1942 (divorced, 1958); married Parrish Cummings Dobson, May 22, 1959; children: (stepchildren) Joseph P. Dobson, Michael Dobson, Laura Parrish Dobson. *Education:* Princeton University, A.B., 1932. *Home:* Indian Chase Dr., Greenwich, Conn. 06830. *Office:* Wheelabrator-Frye, Inc., Liberty Lane, Hampton, N.H. 03842.

CAREER: Wheelabrator-Frye, Inc. (formerly The Equity Corp.), Hampton, N.H., officer and director of various subsidiaries, 1950—, corporate secretary, 1971—. *Military service:* U.S. Army, 1943-46; became sergeant. *Member:* Princeton Club of New York, Phi Beta Kappa.

WRITINGS—All poetry: *Descent into the Dust,* Centaur Press, 1936; *Sonnet Variations,* Jonathan Williams, 1962; *Occasions in a World,* Jargon Society, 1969; *For the Remarkable Animals,* Burning Deck, 1970; *The Changes,* Open Places, 1977.

WORK IN PROGRESS: Arguments of Idea; Figures of the Musician; The Orders.

SIDELIGHTS: Peyton Houston told *CA:* "To me poetry is a way of using the imagination to think with, that is, to find the significant structures of experience. If one can find it for oneself, it may be that one finds it for another. The cognitional intellect cannot do this; it is too trapped by imperfect postulates and clumsy logics. But the imagination is the use of the whole mind and works with acute precisions."

BIOGRAPHICAL/CRITICAL SOURCES: Arts in Society, Volume VII, number 2, 1970.

* * *

HOVEY, E(lwyn) Paul 1908-

PERSONAL: Born February 24, 1908, in Minot, N.D.; son of Clark Samuel and Alice Maude (Hoopes) Hovey; married Barbara Brown, 1937; children: Roy Paul, Linda Nell. *Education:* Minot State Teachers College (now Minot State College), B.A., 1933; attended Chicago Theological Seminary, 1936; Presbyterian College of Christian Education, M.A., 1937; attended McCormick Seminary, 1943-45 and Garraret Biblical Institute, 1944. *Home:* 1712 Northeast 125th Ave., Portland, Ore. 97230.

CAREER: Central Presbyterian Church, Denver, Colo., director of Christian education, 1937-38; First Presbyterian Church, Amarillo, Tex., director of Christian education, 1938-43; Austin Presbyterian Church, Chicago, Ill., director of Christian education, 1943-45; United Churches, Hot Springs, S.D., minister, 1945-52; Congregational-Presbyterian Church, Lewiston, Idaho, minister, 1952-73; Lewis-Clark State College, Lewiston, member of faculty, 1967-73. Moderator, Synod of South Dakota, 1946-47, Black Hills Presbytery, and Northern Idaho Presbytery; Synod of Idaho, vice-moderator, 1961-62, moderator, 1964-65; member of faculty, Cascades Presbytery School, 1978; workshop leader, Christian writers conference, Warner Pacific College, 1980. Assistant chaplain, Veterans Hospital, Hot Springs, S.D., 1946-52. Member of school board advisory committee. *Member:* Idaho Council of Churches (vice-president, 1965-72), Inter-Agency Council, Idaho Writers League (member of Lewis-Clark chapter), Order of DeMolay (member of Legion of Honor), Lewiston Ministerial Association (president, 1954-56, 1964-65), Alpha Psi Omega, Mu Sigma Tau, Kiwanis (secretary, 1961-68), Outlook Club.

WRITINGS: The Man Who Entertained a King (play), International Council of Religious Education, 1946; *The Treasury of Inspirational Anecdotes, Quotations, and Illustrations,* Revell, 1959; *The Treasury for Special Days and Occasions,* Revell, 1961; *Presbyterian Yesterdays in Northern Idaho,* Palouse Press, 1964. Also author of *The Genuine Good News Today* and *One Gift That Is Often Unclaimed,* published by Upper Room.

Contributor: *Youth Work in the Church,* Abingdon, 1942; *The Society Kit,* Westminster, 1943-47; *Funeral Encyclopedia,* Harper, 1953; *Speaker's Illustrations for Special Days,* Abingdon, 1956; *The Treasury of Story Sermons for Children,* Harper, 1957; *Reader's Digest 40th Anniversary Treasury,* Reader's Digest Press, 1961; *Tsceminicum,* Printcraft, 1961; *Tarbell's Teacher's Guide,* Revell, 1962; *The Encyclopedia of Religious Quotations,* Revell, 1965; *Mark the Road,* Upper Room, 1973. Also contributor to *Christmas Ideals,* 1965, and *Ministers Manual,* 1969, 1970, 1971, 1975, 1977, 1978, 1979, and 1980.

Contributor to religion journals, newspapers, and popular magazines. Editorial associate, *Pulpit Preaching,* 1958-72; contributing editor, *Pulpit Digest,* 1972.

WORK IN PROGRESS: Christmas Stories in Biblical Settings to Read and Tell; A Christmas Treasury; A Pioneer Preacher in Idaho; Wisdom of Harry Emerson Fosdick; a history of the Presbyterian churches in the Pacific Northwest; a book of devotional messages; several articles.

* * *

HOWARD, Donald R(oy) 1927-

PERSONAL: Born September 18, 1927; son of Albert and Emily Louise (Johnson) Howard. *Education:* Tufts University, A.B. (summa cum laude), 1950; Rutgers University, M.A., 1951; University of Florida, Ph.D., 1954. *Office:* Department of English, Stanford University, Stanford, Calif. 94305.

CAREER: University of Florida, Gainesville, instructor, 1954-55; Ohio State University, Columbus, 1955-63, began as instructor, became associate professor of English; University of California, Riverside, associate professor of English, 1963-66; University of California, Los Angeles, associate professor of English, 1966-67; Johns Hopkins University, Baltimore, Md., professor of English, 1967-77, Caroline S. Donovan Professor of English, 1973-77; Stanford University, Stanford, Calif., professor of English, 1977—. *Military service:* United States Naval Reserve, one year. *Member:* Modern Language Association of America, Mediaeval Academy of America, Modern Humanities Research Association, Phi Beta Kappa, Phi Kappa Phi. *Awards, honors:* Fulbright research grant, 1959-60; American Council of Learned Societies research grant, 1964; American Philosophical Society research grant, 1964; Guggenheim fellowship, 1969-70; Melville Cane Award of the Poetry Society of America, 1977, for *The Idea of the Canterbury Tales;* National Endowment for the Humanities fellowship for independent study and research, 1978-79.

WRITINGS: College Workbook of Composition, Heath, 1960; *The Three Temptations: Medieval Man in Search of the World,* Princeton University Press, 1966; *The Idea of the Canterbury Tales,* University of California Press, 1976; *Writers and Pilgrims: Medieval Pilgrimage Narratives and Their Posterity,* University of California Press, 1980.

Editor: (With Christian K. Zacher, and contributor) *Critical Studies of Sir Gawain and the Green Knight,* University of Notre Dame Press, 1968; Lothario dei Segni (Pope Innocent III), *On the Misery of the Human Condition,* translation by M. Dietz, Bobbs-Merrill, 1969; Geoffrey Chaucer, *The Canterbury Tales: A Selection,* Signet, 1969; (with James Dean) Chaucer, *Troilus and Criseyde and Selected Short Poems,* Signet, 1976; (with M. Bloomfield and others) *Incipits of Latin Works on the Virtues and Vices, 1100-1500,* Mediaeval Academy of America, 1979.

Contributor: Allan H. Gilbert, editor, *Renaissance Papers,* University of South Carolina Press, 1954; R. J. Blanch, editor, *Sir Gawain and Pearl,* Indiana University Press, 1966; Dentox Fox, editor, *Twentieth-Century Interpretations of Sir Gawain and the Green Knight,* Prentice-Hall, 1968; Arthur Clare Cowley, editor, *Chaucer's Mind and Art,* Oliver & Boyd, 1969; Jerome Mandel and Bruce Rosenberg, editors, *Medieval Literature and Folklore Studies: Essays in Honor of Francis Lee Utley,* Rutgers University Press, 1970; J. Burke Severs, editor, *Recent Middle English Scholarship and Criticism: Survey and Desiderata,* Duquesne University Press, 1971; Howard D. Weinbrot, editor, *New Aspects of Lexicography: Literary Criticism, Intellectual History, Social Change,* Southern Illinois University Press, 1972; Robert S. Kinsman, editor, *The Darker Vision of the Renaissance: Beyond the Fields of Reason,* University of California Press, 1974; Joseph Anthony Wittreich, Jr., editor, *Milton and the Line of Vision,* University of Wisconsin Press, 1975; E. T. Donaldson, editor, *Essays and Studies,* Humanities Press, 1976.

Contributor of articles and reviews to scholarly journals. Member of editorial board of *ELH: Journal of English Literary History;* former member of editorial board of *Speculum* and advisory board of *PMLA.*

* * *

HOWARD, Joseph Leon 1917-

PERSONAL: Born December 21, 1917, in New Haven, Conn.; son of Benjamin Ely and Eva (Burban) Howard; married Irene Elizabeth Silver, October 17, 1942; children: Michael Edward, Kenneth Lee, John Wayne. *Education:* Attended San Diego State College (now University), 1935-38; University of California, Berkeley, A.B., 1940; graduate student, Naval War College, 1948-49, and Harvard Graduate School of Business Administration, 1963. *Home:* 2620 Second Ave., Apt. 11-A, San Diego, Calif. 92103. *Office:* 2357 State St., Suite C, San Diego, Calif.

CAREER: U.S. Navy, 1940-72; commissioned ensign in Supply Corps of Naval Reserve, 1940; transferred to Regular Navy, 1943; retired as rear admiral; full-time writer, 1972—. Served on West Coast and in Pacific during World War II; held various planning and operational positions in inventory management and depot operations, Department of the Navy, 1946-57, 1960-61; special assistant to chief of naval operations, 1957-59; executive officer, Naval Supply Center, San Diego, Calif., 1961-64; director of procurement, Office of the Assistant Secretary of the Navy, 1965-67; deputy chief of naval material, 1966-68; deputy director of defense supply agency, Defense Contract Administration Services, 1968-70; commanding officer, Naval Supply Center, Charleston, S.C., 1970-72. *Awards, honors*—Military: Legion of Merit with two gold stars; Bronze Star Medal with Combat V; Navy Commendation Medal. Civilian: Founder's medal from Society of Logistics Engineers, 1972.

WRITINGS: Our Modern Navy, Van Nostrand, 1961; *The Diamonite Conspiracy,* State Street Publications, 1980. Contributor to *Naval Institute Proceedings.* Also contributor of articles on supply, logistics and procurement to national magazines.

WORK IN PROGRESS: Several novels, *The Bellhop, Castles in Spain, La Madriguera, Anchors Awash, Rancho Machado.*

* * *

HOWARD, Robert West 1908-
(Michael Case)

PERSONAL: Born April 7, 1908, in Addison, N.Y.; son of Charles James (a minister) and Clara Jane (West) Howard; married Alice Harriet Barrett, 1938 (divorced, 1947); married Anna Margaret Taylor, 1947 (divorced, 1958); married Elizabeth Zimmermann, May 24, 1958; children: (first marriage) Elizabeth Barrett (Mrs. Edward Williams, Jr.), David James; (second marriage) Margaret Ann (Mrs. Donald Koller). *Education:* Attended Syracuse University, 1935-36, and Columbia University, 1947-49. *Politics:* "Independent, with Republican leanings." *Religion:* Congregationalist. *Home:* 11607 Vantage Hill Rd., Reston, Va. 22090.

CAREER: Copyboy and then reporter for daily newspapers in New York City and upstate New York, 1925-35; Works Progress Administration, Federal Writers Project, 1935-37, held various positions, finally became assistant state director for New York; Non-Sectarian Anti-Nazi League, New York City, public relations, 1937-38; *Farm Journal,* Philadelphia, Pa., 1938-43, began as assistant editor, became associate editor; *Pathfinder,* Washington, D.C., editor-in-chief, 1943-45; Lyme Foundation to Promote Social and Economic Decentralization, Hartford, Conn., vice-president, 1945-47; Antioch College, Yellow Springs, Ohio, vice-president for public relations, 1949-50; free-lance writer, and lecturer at Boston University Workshop, 1950-53; Adult Education Association of U.S.A., Chicago, Ill., coordinator of publications, 1953; American Meat Institute, Chicago, roving editor, 1954-59; free-lance writer of books, beginning 1959. *Member:* Westerners International (Chicago Corral), National Press Club (Washington, D.C.), Western Writers of America, New York State Historical Association. *Awards, honors:* Maggie Award, 1957, and Spur Award of Western Writers of America, 1958, both for *This Is the West;* Colonial Dames of America citation, 1977, for *The Dawnseekers.*

WRITINGS: Two Billion Acre Farm, Doubleday, 1945; *Real Book about Farms,* F. Watts, 1953; (with Paul Essert) *Educational Planning by Communities,* Teachers College, Columbia University, 1953; (contributor) *Wonderful World of Books,* Signet Books, 1953; (editor) *This Is the West,* Rand McNally, 1957; (editor) *This Is the South,* Rand McNally, 1959.

(Editor) *Hoofbeats of Destiny,* Signet Books, 1960; (editor) *The Bench Mark,* Church and Community Workshop, Emory University, 1960; (with Oren Arnold) *Rodeo—Last Frontier of the Old West,* Signet Books, 1961; *The Great Iron Trail,* Putnam, 1962; *The Race West: Boomtown to Ghost Town,* Signet Books, 1962; *The Wagonmen,* Putnam, 1964; *The Horse in America,* Follett, 1965; *The Flag of the Dreadful Bear,* Putnam, 1965; *The Boatmen,* Putnam, 1966;

South Pass, Putnam, 1966; *Eli Whitney,* Follett, 1966; *Thundergate: The Forts of Niagara,* Prentice-Hall, 1968; *The South Pass,* Putnam, 1968; *The First Book of Farms,* F. Watts, 1968; *The First Book of Niagara Falls,* F. Watts, 1969.

The Dawnseekers: The First History of American Paleontology, Harcourt, 1975; (contributor) *American Journeys,* Exxon Travel Club, 1975; (contributor) *Water Trails West,* Doubleday, 1978.

Contributor of several hundred articles to farm journals, newspapers, and popular magazines, including *Pageant, Reader's Digest, Christian Science Monitor, Nation's Business,* and *Better Homes and Gardens;* contributor of book reviews to *Saturday Review* and *Chicago Tribune.* Radio reviewer, *New York Telegram,* 1928-29; book editor, *Successful Farming,* 1951-53; writer for Educational Testing Service, 1951-52, Science Research Associates, 1961, *Encyclopaedia Britannica,* 1960-61, Field Enterprises, 1962, *Childcraft,* 1962-63, *World Book Encyclopedia,* 1964, and *Funk & Wagnalls Encyclopedia,* 1971. Editor, *N.Y. Westerners' Brand Book,* 1970-72.

WORK IN PROGRESS: Grandfather's Horses, a juvenile novel detailing the impact of the horsemen on the rise of Greek civilization, 3,000 through 300 B.C.; *The Trailmaker,* a biography of Jedediah Strong Smith; *Roots of the West,* a book on the origin places of the tools, animals, and folkways used to create and conquer the United States in 1600-1900.

SIDELIGHTS: Robert West Howard told *CA:* "I became a devotee of social-history during childhood and have stayed with it. Continental wanders as a roving editor for *Farm Journal* coupled with the causal-awareness and generosity of Wesley Hardenburgh, president of American Meat Institute, enabled my research into the socio-economic drives that created the West between 1770 and 1900.

"Thanks to my wife's expertise in the administration of American schools overseas, I have been able to expand this snoopery to Europe and most of Africa since 1970 [and] so intend to devote my 'golden years' to the commonalities of the family of man and the perils of insularism."

* * *

HOYT, Edwin P(almer), Jr. 1923-
(Cabot L. Forbes, Christopher Martin, C. Pritchard Smith, David Stuart)

PERSONAL: Born August 5, 1923, in Portland, Ore.; son of Edwin Palmer and Cecile (DeVore) Hoyt; married Olga Margaret Gruhzit, 1947; children: Diana, Helga, Christopher. *Education:* Attended University of Oregon, 1940-43, B.A., 1980. *Home:* 1010 Koloa St., Honolulu, Hawaii 96816.

CAREER: Office of War Information, member of psychological warfare and Assam-Burma Biological warfare team, 1943-45, assigned to China office, 1945; United Press, war correspondent in Formosa, Manchuria and China, covering the Indo-Chinese revolution, and in Korea, 1945-46; *Denver Post,* Denver, Colo., foreign correspondent in China, Malaya, Thailand, Burma, India, the Middle East, Europe, and North Africa, 1945; American Broadcasting Co., broadcaster from Czechoslovakia during the 1948 revolution, from Finland, Spain, and Italy, and from Arab-Israeli War; affiliated with *San Francisco Chronicle,* 1949; *Denver Post,* editor of editorial page, 1949-51; *Colorado Springs Free Press,* Colorado Springs, Colo., editor and publisher, 1951-55; *Collier's,* New York City, associate editor, 1955-56; television producer and writer-director, Columbia Broadcasting System, 1957; *American Heritage,* New York City, assistant publisher, 1958; full-time writer, 1958—; part-time lecturer, University of Hawaii, 1976-80. *Military service:* U.S. Army Air Forces.

WRITINGS—Nonfiction: *Jumbos and Jackasses,* Doubleday, 1960; *Whirly Birds,* Doubleday, 1961; *Lost Statesmen,* Reilly & Lee, 1961; *The Vanderbilts and Their Fortunes,* Doubleday, 1962; *Grover Cleveland,* Reilly & Lee, 1962; *The Supersalesmen,* World Publishing, 1962; *Commodore Vanderbilt,* Reilly & Lee, 1962; *The Tempering Years,* Scribner, 1963; *From the Turtle to the Nautilus: The Story of Submarines,* Atlantic Monthly Press, 1963; *Spectacular Rogue: Gaston B. Means,* Bobbs-Merrill, 1963; *Heroes of the Skies,* Doubleday, 1963; *John Quincy Adams,* Reilly & Lee, 1963; *Martin Van Buren,* Reilly & Lee, 1964; *James A. Garfield,* Reilly & Lee, 1964; *The Golden Rot: A Somewhat Opinionated View of America,* Bobbs-Merrill, 1964; *A Gentleman of Broadway: The Biography of Damon Runyon,* Little, Brown, 1964.

Andrew Johnson, Reilly & Lee, 1965; *A Short History of Science,* John Day, Volume I, 1965, Volume II, 1966; *Marilyn, the Tragic Venus,* Duell, Sloan & Pearce, 1965, revised edition, Chilton, 1973; *James Knox Polk,* Reilly & Lee, 1965; *One Penny Black: The Story of Stamp Collecting,* Duell, Sloan & Pearce, 1965; *Glorious Flattops,* Atlantic Monthly Press, 1965; *Zachary Taylor,* Reilly & Lee, 1966; *American Steamboat Stories,* Abelard, 1966; *The Idea Men,* Duell, Sloan & Pearce, 1966; *House of Morgan,* Dodd, 1966; *James Buchanan,* Reilly & Lee, 1966; *Teddy Roosevelt in Africa,* Duell, Sloan & Pearce, 1967; *Jewel Hunters,* Little, Brown, 1967; *Tragic Commodore: The Story of Oliver Hazard Perry,* Abelard, 1967; *William McKinley,* Reilly & Lee, 1967; *Alexander Woolcott: The Man Who Came to Dinner,* Abelard, 1967, 2nd edition, Chilton, 1974; *Leland Stanford,* Abelard, 1967; *The Guggenheims and the American Dream,* Funk, 1967; *Condition Critical: Our Hospital Crisis,* Holt, 1967; *The Germans Who Never Lost: The Story of the Koenigsberg,* Funk, 1967; *The Last Cruise of the Emden,* Macmillan, 1967, abridged edition published as *Swan of the East: The Life and Death of the German Cruiser Emden in World War I,* 1968; *The Army without a Country,* Macmillan, 1968; *The Goulds: A Social History,* Weybright, 1968; *Kreuzerkrieg,* World Publishing, 1968; *Deadly Craft: Fireships to PT Boats,* Little, Brown, 1968; *James Monroe,* Reilly & Lee, 1968; *The Peabody Influence: How a Great New England Family Helped to Build America,* Dodd, 1968; *The Typhoon that Stopped a War,* McKay, 1968; *Phantom Raider,* Crowell, 1969; *Raider 16,* World Publishing, 1969; *Paul Robeson: The American Othello,* World Publishing, 1969; *The Space Dealers: A Hard Look at the Role of American Business in Our Space Effort,* John Day, 1969; *Your Health Insurance: A Story of Failure,* John Day, 1969; *Count von Luckner: Knight of the Sea,* McKay, 1969; *The Defenders,* A. S. Barnes, 1969; *Destroyers: Foxes of the Sea,* Little, Brown, 1969; *He Freed the Minds of Men: Rene Descartes,* Messner, 1969; *John Tyler: The Tenth President of the United States,* Abelard, 1969; *The Palmer Raids, 1919-1920: An Attempt to Suppress Dissent,* Seabury, 1969; *That Wonderful A & P!,* Hawthorn, 1969; *The Zeppelins,* Lothrop, 1969; *The Last Explorer: The Adventures of Admiral Byrd,* John Day, 1969.

How They Won the War in the Pacific: Nimitz and His Admirals, Weybright, 1970; *The Elusive Seagull: The Adventures of a World War I German Minelayer, the Moewe,* Frewin, 1970; *Sea Eagle,* Wingate, 1970; *The Sea Wolves: Germany's Dreaded U-Boats of World War II,* Lancer Books, 1970;

(with wife, Olga Hoyt) *Censorship in America,* Seabury, 1970; *The American Attitude: The Story of the Making of Foreign Policy in the United States,* Abelard, 1970; *The Battle of Leyte Gulf: The Death Knell of the Japanese Fleet* (Military Book Club selection), Weybright, 1971; *The Nixons: An American Family,* Random House, 1971; *Leyte Gulf: The Death of the Princeton,* Lancer Books, 1972; *The Carrier War,* Lancer Books, 1972; *African Slavery,* Abelard, 1973; (with O. Hoyt) *Freedom of the News Media,* Seabury, 1973; *Asians in the West,* Thomas Nelson, 1974; *Ghost of the Atlantic: The Kronprinz Wilhelm, 1914-1919,* Barker, 1974; *Horatio's Boys: The Life and Works of Horatio Alger, Jr.,* Chilton, 1974; *Raider Wolf: The Voyage of Captain Nerger, 1916-1918,* Eriksson, 1974.

The Fall of Tsingtao, Barker, 1975; *Blue Skies and Blood: The Battle of the Coral Sea* (Military Book Club selection), Eriksson, 1975; *The Mutiny on the Globe,* Random House, 1975; *Arab Science: Discoveries and Contributions,* Thomas Nelson, 1975; *Disaster at Dardanelles, 1915,* Barker, 1976; *The Karlsruhe Affair,* Barker, 1976; *The Shah: The Glittering Story of Iran and Its People,* Eriksson, 1976; *The Damndest Yankees: Ethan Allen and His Clan,* Stephen Greene Press, 1976; *The Lonely Ships: The Life and Death of the U.S. Asiatic Fleet* (Military Book Club selection), McKay, 1976; *Alan Watts,* Chilton, 1976; *Coins, Collectors, and Counterfeiters,* Thomas Nelson, 1977; *H.M.S. Hood,* Barker, 1977, Stein & Day, 1980; *Sir Charlie* (biography of Charlie Chaplin), R. Hale, 1977; *Storm over the Gilberts* (Military Book Club selection), Van Nostrand, 1978; *War in the Deep,* Putnam, 1978; *Nantucket,* Stephen Greene Press, 1978; *U-Boats Offshore* (Military Book Club selection), Stein & Day, 1979; *Oliver Wendell Holmes,* Morrow, 1979; *After Thirty Years,* Muller, 1979; *Airborne,* Stein & Day, 1979; *Davies: A British-American Family,* Eriksson, 1979; *To the Marianas,* Van Nostrand, 1980; *Admiral von Spee,* R. Hale, 1980.

Novels: *A Matter of Conscience,* Duell, Sloan & Pearce, 1966; *The Voice of Allah,* John Day, 1968; *The Ghost Lane,* Luce, 1970; *Hellfire over Tripoli,* Pinnacle Books, 1973; *Against Cold Steel,* Pinnacle Books, 1974; *Decatur's Revenge,* Pinnacle Books, 1975; *The Tempting of Confucious,* Pinnacle Books, 1975.

Under pseudonym Christopher Martin: *The Wonders of Prehistoric Man,* Putnam, 1964; *Your National Parks: Great Smoky Mountains,* Putnam, 1965; *Your National Parks: Yellowstone,* Putnam, 1965; *The Russo-Japanese War,* Abelard, 1967; *The Boxer Rebellion,* Abelard, 1968; *Damn the Torpedos!: The Story of America's First Admiral, David Glasgow Farragut,* Little, Brown, 1968; *The Boer War,* Abelard, 1969; *The Amistad Affair,* Abelard, 1970.

Under pseudonym Cabot L. Forbes; "The Bradford Saga," Pinnacle Books: *Fourteen Washington Place,* 1976; *Two West Fifty-Seventh Street,* 1977; *Seven-Fifty Park Avenue,* 1977.

WORK IN PROGRESS: The Gambier Bay; Guadacanal; The Parkers: The Story of Hawaii's Fabled Family; Richard Harding Davis; The Fall of the Rising Sun; Red Sun, White Sun; a biography of Leland Stanford.

* * *

HOYT, Homer 1896-

PERSONAL: Born June 14, 1896, in St. Joseph, Mo.; son of Homer and Elizabeth (Vath) Hoyt; married Gertrude O'Neil, 1941; children: Michael Robert. *Education:* University of Kansas, A.B., 1913, A.M., 1913; University of Chicago, J.D., 1918, Ph.D. (economics), 1933; American Institute of Real Estate Appraisers, M.A.I., 1956. *Home and office:* 2939 Van Ness St. N.W., Washington, D.C. 20008.

CAREER: Beloit College, Beloit, Wis., instructor in economics, 1917-18; economist, War Trade Board, 1918-19; Delaware College (now University of Delaware), Newark, professor of economics, 1919-20; statistician, American Telephone & Telegraph Co., 1920-21; University of North Carolina at Chapel Hill, associate professor of economics, 1921-23; University of Missouri—Columbia, associate professor of economics, 1924-25; real estate broker and consultant in Chicago, Ill., 1925-34; principal housing economist, Federal Housing Administration, 1934-40; Chicago Plan Commission, Chicago, director of research, 1941-43; Regional Plan Association, New York City, director of economic studies, 1943-46; Homer Hoyt Associates (appraisers and consulting land economists), Washington, D.C., president, 1946—. Visiting professor at Massachusetts Institute of Technology and Columbia University, 1944-46. Chairman of the board, Homer Hoyt Institute. Member of the Bar, Supreme Court of Illinois, District of Columbia, and Supreme Court of the United States; member of American Institute of Real Estate Appraisers, Real Estate Board, Washington, D.C., and Metropolitan Washington Board of Trade. *Member:* American Historical Association, American Statistical Association, American Economic Association, National Association of Independent Fee Appraisers (honorary member). *Awards, honors:* Lambda Alpha, Urban Affairs Award, 1971, award for distinguished service, 1976; award for outstanding service in the general field of real estate, National Association of Independent Fee Appraisers, 1975; citation for distinguished service, University of Kansas, 1976; fellow, Institute for Real Estate and Applied Urban Economics, Indiana University, 1976.

WRITINGS: One Hundred Years of Land Values in Chicago, University of Chicago Press, 1933, reprinted, Arno, 1970; *Structure and Growth of Residential Neighborhoods in American Cities,* Federal Housing Administration, 1939, reprinted, Scholarly Press, 1972; (with Arthur M. Weimer) *Principles of Real Estate,* Ronald, 1939, 6th edition (with Weimer and George F. Bloom), 1972, 7th edition, 1978; *Master Plan of Residential Land Use of Chicago,* Chicago Plan Commission, 1943; *Economic Status of the New York Metropolitan Region in 1944,* Regional Plan Association of New York, 1944; *Economic Survey of the State of New Jersey; World Urbanization,* Urban Land Institute, 1962; *Where the Rich and Poor People Live,* Urban Land Institute, 1966; *According to Hoyt,* privately printed, 1966, revised edition, 1970; *The Location of Additional Retail Stores in the United States* (monograph), National Retail Merchants Association, 1969; *People, Profits, Places,* National Retail Merchants Association, 1969; (contributor) Maury Seldin, editor, *The Real Estate Handbook,* Dow Jones-Irwin, 1980.

"Land Appraisal" series; all published by Clearwater Publishing: *Kootenai Tribe Lands in Northern Idaho and Montana, 1859,* 1973; *Nez Perce Tribe Lands in Northern Idaho, 1894,* 1973; *Northern Paiute Nation: Appraisal of Lands in Nevada and California, 1853-1863,* two volumes, 1973; *Washoe Tribe of Indians: Appraisal of Lands in Nevada, 1862, and California, 1853,* 1973; *Cheyenne and Arapaho Lands in Colorado, Kansas, Wyoming, and Nebraska, 1865,* 1974; *Emigrant New York Lands in Illinois, 1832,* 1974; *Emigrant New York Lands in Northeastern Wisconsin and Northwestern Michigan,* 1974.

Also author of economic surveys, monographs, and booklets. Contributor to *Encyclopedia of Real Estate Appraising.*

Contributor to professional journals. Member of editorial board, *Land Economics*.

* * *

HOYT, Kenneth B(oyd) 1924-

PERSONAL: Born July 13, 1924, in Cherokee, Iowa; son of Paul Fuller and Mary Helen (Tinker) Hoyt; married Phyllis June Howland, May 25, 1946; children: Andrew Paul, Roger Alan, Elinore Jane. *Education:* University of Maryland, B.S., 1948; George Washington University, M.A., 1950; University of Minnesota, Ph.D., 1954. *Home:* 311 Colesville Manor Dr., Silver Spring, Md. 20904. *Office:* Office of Career Education, U.S. Office of Education, Washington, D.C.

CAREER: High school teacher and counselor in Maryland, 1948; director of guidance in high school in Maryland, 1949; University of Minnesota, Minneapolis, instructor in educational psychology, 1951-54; University of Iowa, Iowa City, assistant professor, 1954-57, associate professor, 1957-60, professor of education, 1961-69, head of Division of Counselor Education, 1966-69; University of Maryland, College Park, professor of education, 1969-74; U.S. Office of Education, Washington, D.C., director of Office of Career Education, 1974—. Member of faculty, national seminars on vocational aspects of counselor education, 1966-67; member of interim council on occupational and specialized education, National Commission on Accrediting, 1968-71; member of advisory committee of National Study of Innovative Practices in Career Education for the Center for Occupational Education, North Carolina State University, 1971-72; member of psycho-social study section of Rehabilitation Services Administration, U.S. Department of Health, Education, and Welfare, 1967-72; member of advisory task force on community involvement for National Advisory Commission on Criminal Justice, Standards, and Goals of Law Enforcement Assistance Administration, 1971—; chairman of ad hoc national advisory committee on residential vocational schools, U.S. Office of Education, 1971—, director of National Invitational Seminar on Career Education for the Gifted and Talented, 1972-73. Consultant to Ordnance Civilian Personnel Agency, Bureau of Indian Affairs (of U.S. Department of the Interior), U.S. Department of Labor, Veterans Administration, Brookings Institution, and Federal Trade Commission.

MEMBER: American Personnel and Guidance Association (life member; member of executive council, 1965-68, president of council, 1966-67; president, 1966-67), American Vocational Association (life member), American Psychological Association (fellow), Association for Counselor Education and Supervision, National Vocational Guidance Association, American School Counselors Association, American Educational Research Association, Phi Delta Kappa. *Awards, honors:* First distinguished service award, Association for Counselor Education and Supervision, 1965; professional recognition award, Iowa Personnel and Guidance Association, 1967.

WRITINGS: (With L. A. Van Dyke) *The Drop-Out Problem in Iowa High Schools*, University of Iowa Press, 1958; (with C. P. Froelich) *Guidance Testing*, Science Research Associates, 1959; (with others) *Selecting Employees for Development Opportunities*, Ordnance Civilian Personnel Agency, 1962; *An Introduction to the Specialty Oriented Student Research Program at the University of Iowa*, University of Iowa Press, 1962; (with others) *Guidance Services: Suggested Policies for Iowa Schools*, Iowa State Department of Public Instruction, 1963; *SOS Guidance Research Information Booklets*, Specialty Oriented Student Research Program, University of Maryland, Numbers 1-110, 1966-69, Numbers 111-414, 1969-72; *The Challenge of Guidance to Vocational Education*, American Vocational Association, 1966; *Vocational Aspects of Guidance: A Statement of Policy of the American Vocational Association*, American Vocational Association, 1968.

Vocational Educationism: A National Condition, American Vocational Association, 1970; (with G. Woolard) *Upper School Curriculum Guide* (monograph), National Center for Occupational Education, 1972; (with G. Mangum, R. Evans, and E. Mackin) *Career Education: What It Is and How to Do It*, Olympus Publishing, 1972; (with J. Hebeler) *Career Education for Gifted and Talented Students*, Olympus Publishing, 1973; (with D. Lawrence, Mangum, and N. Pinson) *Career Education in the Elementary School*, Olympus Publishing, 1973; (with Mangum and Evans) *Career Education in the Middle/Junior High School*, Olympus Publishing, 1974; *Career Education's Contribution to an Evolving Concept*, Olympus Publishing, 1975; (with Mangum and Evans) *Career Education in the Senior High School*, Olympus Publishing, 1976.

Contributor: James Adams, editor, *Counseling and Guidance: A Summary View*, Macmillan, 1965; Paul Torrence and Robert Strom, editors, *Mental Health and Achievement*, Wiley, 1965; Raymond Ehrle, editor, *Counseling in the Employment Service*, Leviathan, 1966; Thomas Sweeney, editor, *A Developmental Program for Vocational Counselors Directed toward Serving Disadvantaged Youth More Effectively*, University of South Carolina, 1966; Barrie Hopson and John Hayes, editors, *The Theory and Practice of Vocational Guidance: A Selection of Readings*, Pergamon, 1968; *Counseling: Challenge and Change*, Minnesota Counselors Association, 1968; W. H. Van Hoose and John J. Pietrofesa, editors, *Guidance and Counseling in the Twentieth Century: Reflections and Reformulations*, Houghton, 1970; Donald Dinkmeyer, editor, *Elementary School Guidance: Conceptual Beginnings and Initial Approaches*, American Personnel and Guidance Association, 1970; *Counseling Today and Tomorrow*, American Personnel and Guidance Association, 1972; *Educational Change: Implications for Measurement*, Educational Testing Service, 1972; *Career Education Resource Guide*, General Learning Corp., 1972.

Contributor to yearbooks and memorial volumes. Contributor of more than fifty articles to education journals, including *American Vocational Journal*, *Educational Technology*, *Counseling Interviewer*, *Vocational Guidance Quarterly*, and *Audio-Visual Instruction*. Member of editorial board, *Personnel and Guidance Journal*, 1960-63; editor, *Counselor Education and Supervision*, 1961-65.

* * *

HSU, Francis L(ang) K(wang) 1909-

PERSONAL: Born October 28, 1909, in Chuang-ho, China; son of Chung-ti and Li Hsu; married Vera Yi-nan Tung, 1943; children: Eileen Yi-nan, Penelope Se-Hwa. *Education:* University of Shanghai, B.A., 1933; University of London, Ph.D., 1940. *Home:* 61 Milland Dr., Mill Valley, Calif. 94941. *Office:* Center for Cultural Studies in Education, University of San Francisco, San Francisco, Calif. 94117.

CAREER: National Yunnan University, Kungming, China, 1941-44, began as assistant professor, became professor; Columbia University, New York, N.Y., lecturer, 1944-45; Cornell University, Ithaca, N.Y., assistant professor, 1945-47; Northwestern University, Evanston, Ill., 1947-78, began as assistant professor, became professor of anthropology, chairman of department, 1957-70; University of San Francisco, San Francisco, Calif., professor of anthropology and director of Center for Cultural Studies in Education, 1978—. Consultant, U.S. Department of Labor, 1945, Rockland State Hospital, Orangeburg, New York, 1951, Fort Meade, S.D., Veterans' Administration Hospital, 1957-58, and Veterans' Administration Research Hospital, Chicago, Ill., 1959-61. Frequent lecturer to academic audiences, parent-teacher associations, and business and religious groups. *Member:* American Anthropological Association (president, 1978-79). *Awards, honors:* Viking Fund fellowship, 1944-45; Wenner-Gren Foundation fellowship, 1949-50, 1955-57, and 1975-76; Social Science Research Council fellowship, 1949-50; Rockefeller Foundation fellowship, 1955-57; Carnegie Corp. research grant, 1964-1965; East-West Center fellowship, 1969-70, 1978-79.

WRITINGS: Under the Ancestor's Shadow, Columbia University Press, 1948, reprinted, Stanford University Press, 1971; *Religion, Science and Human Crisis,* Routledge & Kegan Paul, 1952; *Americans and Chinese,* Henry Schuman, 1953; (editor) *Aspects of Culture and Personality,* Abelard, 1954; (editor) *Psychological Anthropology,* Dorsey, 1961; *Clan, Caste, and Club,* Van Nostrand, 1963; *The Study of Literate Civilizations,* Holt, 1969; (with Eileen Hsu-Balzer and Richard Balzer) *China Day by Day,* Yale University Press, 1974; *Iemoto: The Heart of Japan,* Halsted, 1975; (co-editor) *Moving a Mountain: Culture Change in China,* University Press of Hawaii, 1979. Contributor to many scientific journals.

WORK IN PROGRESS: People without Each Other.

SIDELIGHTS: Francis Hsu told *CA* that he hopes "to improve human relations and reduce loneliness and violence in my adopted country." Hsu has traveled extensively in Europe and Asia. *Avocational interests:* Chinese, Hindu, and Western music, tennis, table tennis.

* * *

HUGHES, (James) Langston 1902-1967

PERSONAL: Born February 1, 1902, in Joplin, Mo.; died May 22, 1967 of congestive heart failure in New York, N.Y.; son of James Nathaniel (a businessman, lawyer, and rancher) and Carrie Mercer (a teacher; maiden name, Langston) Hughes. *Education:* Attended Columbia University, 1921-22; Lincoln University, A.B., 1929. *Home:* 20 East 127th St., New York, N.Y. *Agent:* Harold Ober Associates, Inc., 40 East 49th St., New York, N.Y. 10017.

CAREER: Poet, novelist, short story writer, playwright, song lyricist, radio writer, translator, author of juvenile books, and lecturer. In early years worked as assistant cook, launderer, busboy, and at other odd jobs; worked as seaman on voyages to Africa and Europe. Lived at various times in Mexico, France, Italy, Spain, and the Soviet Union. Madrid correspondent for *Baltimore Afro-American,* 1937; visiting professor in creative writing, Atlanta University, 1947; poet-in-residence, Laboratory School, University of Chicago, 1949. *Member:* Authors Guild, Dramatists Guild, American Society of Composers, Authors, and Publishers, P.E.N., National Institute of Arts and Letters, Omega Psi Phi. *Awards, honors: Opportunity* magazine literary contest, first prize in poetry, 1925; Witter Bynner undergraduate poetry prize contests, first prize, 1926; *Palms* magazine Intercollegiate Poetry Award, 1927; Harmon Gold Medal for Literature, 1931; Guggenheim fellowship for creative work, 1935; Rosenwald fellowship, 1941; Litt.D., Lincoln University, 1943; American Academy of Arts and Letters grant, 1947; Anisfeld-Wolfe Award for best book on racial relations, 1954; Spingarn Medal, National Association for the Advancement of Colored People, 1960.

WRITINGS—Poetry; published by Knopf, except as indicated: *The Weary Blues,* 1926; *Fine Clothes to the Jew,* 1927; *The Negro Mother and Other Dramatic Recitations,* Golden Stair Press, 1931; *Dear Lovely Death,* Troutbeck Press, 1931; *The Dream Keeper and Other Poems,* 1932; *Scottsboro Limited: Four Poems and a Play,* Golden Stair Press, 1932; *A New Song,* International Workers Order, 1938; (with Robert Glenn) *Shakespeare in Harlem,* 1942; *Jim Crow's Last Stand,* Negro Publication Society of America, 1943; *Freedom's Plow,* Musette Publishers, 1943; *Lament for Dark Peoples and Other Poems,* Holland, 1944; *Fields of Wonder,* 1947; *One-Way Ticket,* 1949; *Montage of a Dream Deferred,* Holt, 1951; *Ask Your Mama: 12 Moods for Jazz,* 1961; *The Panther and the Lash: Poems of Our Times,* 1967.

Novels: *Not without Laughter,* Knopf, 1930, reprinted, Macmillan, 1969; *Tambourines to Glory,* John Day, 1958, reprinted, Hill & Wang, 1970.

Short stories: *The Ways of White Folks,* Knopf, 1934, reprinted, 1963; *Simple Speaks His Mind,* Simon & Schuster, 1950; *Laughing to Keep from Crying,* Holt, 1952; *Simple Takes a Wife,* Simon & Schuster, 1953; *Simple Stakes a Claim,* Rinehart, 1957; *Something in Common and Other Stories,* Hill & Wang, 1963; *Simple's Uncle Sam,* Hill & Wang, 1965.

Autobiography: *The Big Sea: An Autobiography,* Knopf, 1940, reprinted, Hill & Wang, 1963; *I Wonder as I Wander: An Autobiographical Journey,* Rinehart, 1956.

Nonfiction: (With Roy De Carava) *The Sweet Flypaper of Life,* Simon & Schuster, 1955; (with Milton Meltzer) *A Pictorial History of the Negro in America,* Crown, 1956, 4th edition published as *A Pictorial History of Blackamericans,* 1973; *Fight for Freedom: The Story of the NAACP,* Norton, 1962; (with Meltzer) *Black Magic: A Pictorial History of the Negro in American Entertainment,* Prentice-Hall, 1967; *Black Misery,* Paul S. Erickson, 1969.

Juvenile: (With Arna Bontemps) *Popo and Fifina: Children of Haiti,* Macmillan, 1932; *The First Book of Negroes,* F. Watts, 1952; *The First Book of Rhythms,* F. Watts, 1954; *Famous American Negroes,* Dodd, 1954; *Famous Negro Music Makers,* Dodd, 1955; *The First Book of Jazz,* F. Watts, 1955, revised edition, 1976; *The First Book of the West Indies,* F. Watts, 1956 (published in England as *The First Book of the Caribbean,* E. Ward, 1965); *Famous Negro Heroes of America,* Dodd, 1958; *The First Book of Africa,* F. Watts, 1960, revised edition, 1964.

Editor: *Four Lincoln University Poets,* Lincoln University, 1930; (with Bontemps) *The Poetry of the Negro, 1746-1949,* Doubleday, 1949, revised edition published as *The Poetry of the Negro, 1746-1970,* 1970; (with Waring Cuney and Bruce M. Wright) *Lincoln University Poets,* Fine Editions, 1954; (with Bontemps) *The Book of Negro Folklore,* Dodd, 1958; *An African Treasury: Articles, Essays, Stories, Poems by Black Africans,* Crown, 1960; *Poems from Black Africa,* Indiana University Press, 1963; *New Negro Poets: U.S.,* foreword by Gwendolyn Brooks, Indiana University Press, 1964; *The Book of Negro Humor,* Dodd, 1966; *The Best Short Stories by Negro Writers: An Anthology from 1899 to the Present,* Little, Brown, 1967.

Translator: (With Mercer Cook) Jacques Roumain, *Masters of Dew,* Reynal & Hitchcock, 1947, second edition, Liberty Book Club, 1957; (with Frederic Carruthers) Nicolas Guillen, *Cuba Libre,* Ward Ritchie, 1948; *Selected Poems of Gabriel Mistral,* Indiana University Press, 1957.

Omnibus volumes: *Selected Poems,* Knopf, 1959, reprinted, Vintage Books, 1974; *The Best of Simple,* Hill & Wang, 1961; *Five Plays by Langston Hughes,* edited by Webster Smalley, Indiana University Press, 1963; *The Langston Hughes Reader,* Braziller, 1968; *Don't You Turn Back* (poems), edited by Lee Bennett Hopkins, Knopf, 1969; *Good Morning Revolution: The Uncollected Social Protest Writing of Langston Hughes,* edited by Faith Berry, Lawrence Hill, 1973.

Author of numerous plays (most have been produced), including "Little Ham," 1935, "Mulatto," 1935, "Emperor of Haiti," 1936, "Troubled Island," 1936, "When the Jack Hollers," 1936, "Front Porch," 1937, "Joy to My Soul," 1937, "Soul Gone Home," 1937, "Little Eva's End," 1938, "Limitations of Life," 1938, "The Em-Fuehrer Jones," 1938, "Don't You Want to Be Free," 1938, "The Organizer," 1939, "The Sun Do Move," 1942, "For This We Fight," 1943, "The Barrier," 1950, "Simply Heavenly," 1957, "Black Nativity," 1961, "Gospel Glory," 1962, "Jericho-Jim Crow," 1963, "The Prodigal," 1965, "Soul Yesterday and Today," "Angelo Herndon Jones," "Mother and Child," "Trouble with the Angels," and "Outshines the Sun."

Also author of screenplay, "Way Down South," 1942. Author of libretto for operas, "The Barrier," 1950, and "Troubled Island." Lyricist for "Just around the Corner," and for Kurt Weill's "Street Scene," 1948. Columnist for *Chicago Defender* and *New York Post.* Poetry, short stories, criticism, and plays have been included in numerous anthologies. Contributor to periodicals, including *Nation, African Forum, Black Drama, Players Magazine, Negro Digest, Black World, Freedomways, Harlem Quarterly, Phylon, Challenge, Negro Quarterly,* and *Negro Story.*

SIDELIGHTS: Langston Hughes was first recognized as an important literary figure during the 1920's, a period known as the "Harlem Renaissance" because of the number of emerging black writers. Du Bose Heyward wrote in 1926: "Langston Hughes, although only twenty-four years old, is already conspicuous in the group of Negro intellectuals who are dignifying Harlem with a genuine art life. . . . It is, however, as an individual poet, not as a member of a new and interesting literary group, or as a spokesman for a race that Langston Hughes must stand or fall. . . . Always intensely subjective, passionate, keenly sensitive to beauty and possessed of an unfaltering musical sense, Langston Hughes has given us a 'first book' that marks the opening of a career well worth watching."

Despite Heyward's statement, much of Hughes' early work was roundly criticized by many black intellectuals for portraying what they thought to be an unattractive view of black life. In his autobiographical *The Big Sea,* Hughes commented: "*Fine Clothes to the Jew* was well received by the literary magazines and the white press, but the Negro critics did not like it at all. The Pittsburgh *Courier* ran a big headline across the top of the page, *LANGSTON HUGHES' BOOK OF POEMS TRASH.* The headline in the New York *Amsterdam News* was *LANGSTON HUGHES—THE SEWER DWELLER.* The Chicago *Whip* characterized me as 'the poet low-rate of Harlem.' Others called the book a disgrace to the race, a return to the dialect tradition, and a parading of all our racial defects before the public. . . . The Negro critics and many of the intellectuals were very sensitive about their race in books. (And still are.) In anything that white people were likely to read, they wanted to put their best foot forward, their politely polished and cultural foot—and only that foot."

An example of the type of criticism of which Hughes was writing is Estace Gay's comments on *Fine Clothes to the Jew.* "It does not matter to me whether every poem in the book is true to life," Gay wrote. "Why should it be paraded before the American public by a Negro author as being typical or representative of the Negro? Bad enough to have white authors holding up our imperfections to public gaze. Our aim ought to be [to] present to the general public, already mis-informed both by well meaning and malicious writers, our higher aims and aspirations, and our better selves."

Commenting on reviewers like Gay, Hughes wrote: "I sympathized deeply with those critics and those intellectuals, and I saw clearly the need for some of the kinds of books they wanted. But I did not see how they could expect every Negro author to write such books. Certainly, I personally knew very few people anywhere who were wholly beautiful and wholly good. Besides I felt that the masses of our people had as much in their lives to put into books as did those more fortunate ones who had been born with some means and the ability to work up to a master's degree at a Northern college. Anyway, I didn't know the upper class Negroes well enough to write much about them. I knew only the people I had grown up with, and they weren't people whose shoes were always shined, who had been to Harvard, or who had heard of Bach. But they seemed to me good people, too."

Hoyt W. Fuller commented that Hughes "chose to identify with plain black people—not because it required less effort and sophistication, but precisely because he saw more truth and profound significance in doing so. Perhaps in this he was inversely influenced by his father—who, frustrated by being the object of scorn in his native land, rejected his own people. Perhaps the poet's reaction to his father's flight from the American racial reality drove him to embrace it with extra fervor." (Langston Hughes' parents separated shortly after his birth and his father moved to Mexico. The elder Hughes came to feel a deep dislike and revulsion for other American blacks.)

In Hughes' own words, his poetry is about "workers, roustabouts, and singers, and job hunters on Lenox Avenue in New York, or Seventh Street in Washington or South State in Chicago—people up today and down tomorrow, working this week and fired the next, beaten and baffled, but determined not to be wholly beaten, buying furniture on the installment plan, filling the house with roomers to help pay the rent, hoping to get a new suit for Easter—and pawning that suit before the Fourth of July." In fact, the title *Fine Clothes to the Jew,* which was misunderstood and disliked by many people, was derived from the Harlemites Hughes saw pawning their own clothing; most of the pawn shops and other stores in Harlem at that time were owned by Jewish people.

Lindsay Patterson, a novelist who served as Hughes' assistant, believed that Hughes was "critically, the most abused poet in America. . . . Serious white critics ignored him, less serious ones compared his poetry to Cassius Clay doggerel, and most black critics only grudgingly admired him. Some, like James Baldwin, were downright malicious about his poetic achievement. But long after Baldwin and the rest of us are gone, I suspect Hughes' poetry will be blatantly around growing in stature until it is recognized for its genius. Hughes' tragedy was double-edged: he was unashamedly black at a time when blackness was demode, and he didn't go much beyond one of his earliest themes, black *is* beautiful. He had the wit and intelligence to explore the black human condition in a variety of depths, but his tastes and selectivity were not always accurate, and pressures to survive as a black writer in a white society (and it was a miracle that he did for so long) extracted an enormous creative toll. Nevertheless, Hughes, more than any other black poet or writer, recorded faithfully the nuances of black life and its frustrations."

Although Hughes had trouble with both black and white critics, he was the first black American to earn his living solely from his writing and public lectures. Part of the reason he was able to do this was the phenomenal acceptance and love he received from average black people. A reviewer for *Black World* noted in 1970: "Those whose prerogative it is to determine the rank of writers have never rated him highly, but if the weight of public response is any gauge then Langston Hughes stands at the apex of literary relevance among Black people. The poet occupies such a position in the memory of his people precisely because he recognized that 'we possess within ourselves a great reservoir of physical and spiritual strength,' and because he used his artistry to reflect this back to the people. He used his poetry and prose to illustrate that 'there is no lack within the Negro people of beauty, strength and power,' and he chose to do so on their own level, on their own terms."

Hughes brought a varied and colorful background to his writing. Before he was twelve years old he had lived in six different American cities. When his first book was published, he had already been a truck farmer, cook, waiter, college graduate, sailor, and doorman at a nightclub in Paris, and had visited Mexico, West Africa, the Azores, the Canary Islands, Holland, France, and Italy. As David Littlejohn observed: "On the whole, Hughes' creative life [was] as full, as varied, and as original as Picasso's, a joyful, honest monument of a career. There [was] no noticeable sham in it, no pretension, no self-deceit; but a great, great deal of delight and smiling irresistible wit. If he seems for the moment upstaged by angrier men, by more complex artists, if 'different views engage' us, necessarily, at this trying stage of the race war, he may well outlive them all, and still be there when it's over. . . . Hughes' [greatness] seems to derive from his anonymous unity with his people. He *seems* to speak for millions, which is a tricky thing to do."

Hughes reached many people through his popular fictional character, Jesse B. Semple (shortened to Simple). Simple is a poor man who lives in Harlem, a kind of comic no-good, a stereotype Hughes turned to advantage. He tells his stories to Boyd, the foil in the stories who is a writer much like Hughes, in return for a drink. His tales of his troubles with work, women, money, and life in general often reveal, through their very simplicity, the problems of being a poor black man in a racist society. "White folks," Simple once commented, "is the cause of a lot of inconvenience in my life."

Donald C. Dickinson wrote that the "charm of Simple lies in his uninhibited pursuit of those two universal goals, understanding and security. As with most other humans, he usually fails to achieve either of these goals and sometimes once achieved they disappoint him. . . . Simple has a tough resilience, however, that won't allow him to brood over a failure very long. . . . Simple is a well-developed character, both believable and lovable. The situations he meets and discusses are so true to life everyone may enter the fun. This does not mean that Simple is in any way dull. He injects the ordinary with his own special insights. . . . Simple is a natural, unsophisticated man who never abandons his hope in tomorrow."

A reviewer for *Black World* commented on the popularity of Simple: "The people responded. Simple lived in a world they knew, suffered their pangs, experienced their joys, reasoned in their way, talked their talk, dreamed their dreams, laughed their laughs, voiced their fears—and all the while underneath, he affirmed the wisdom which anchored at the base of their lives. It was not that ideas and events and places and people beyond the limits of Harlem—all of the Harlems—did not concern him; these things, indeed, were a part of his consciousness; but Simple's rock-solid commonsense enabled him to deal with them with balance and intelligence. . . . Simple knows *who* he is and *what* he is, and he knows that the status of expatriate offers no solution, no balm. The struggle is here, and it can only be won here, and no constructive end is served through fantasies and illusions and false efforts at disguising a basic sense of inadequacy. Simple also knows that the strength, the tenacity, the commitment which are necessary to win the struggle also exist within the Black community."

Hoyt W. Fuller believed that, like Simple, "the key to Langston Hughes . . . was the poet's deceptive and *profound* simplicity. Profound because it was both willed and ineffable, because some intuitive sense even at the beginning of his adulthood taught him that humanity was of the essence and that it existed undiminished in all shapes, sizes, colors and conditions. Violations of that humanity offended his unshakable conviction that mankind is possessed of the divinity of God."

It was Hughes' belief in humanity and his hope for a world in which people could sanely and with understanding live together that led to his decline in popularity in the racially turbulent latter years of his life. Unlike younger and more militant writers, Hughes never lost his conviction that "*most* people are generally good, in every race and in every country where I have been." Reviewing *The Panther and the Lash: Poems of Our Times,* Laurence Lieberman recognized that Hughes' "sensibility [had] kept pace with the times," but he critized his lack of a personal political stance. "Regrettably, in different poems, he is fatally prone to sympathize with starkly antithetical politics of race," Lieberman commented. "A reader can appreciate his catholicity, his tolerance of all the rival—and mutually hostile—views of his outspoken compatriots, from Martin Luther King to Stokely Carmichael, but we are tempted to ask, what are Hughes' politics? And if he has none, why not? The age demands intellectual commitment from its spokesmen. A poetry whose chief claim on our attention is moral, rather than aesthetic, must take sides politically."

Despite some recent criticism, Langston Hughes' position in the American literary scene seems to be secure. David Littlejohn wrote that Hughes is "the one sure Negro classic, more certain of permanence than even Baldwin or Ellison or Wright. . . . His voice is as sure, his manner as original, his position as secure as, say Edwin Arlington Robinson's or Robinson Jeffers'. . . . By molding his verse always on the sounds of Negro talk, the rhythms of Negro music, by retaining his own keen honesty and directness, his poetic sense and ironic intelligence, he maintained through four decades a readable newness distinctly his own."

Hughes' poems have been translated into German, French, Spanish, Russian, Yiddish, and Czech; many of them have been set to music. Donald B. Gibson noted that Hughes "has perhaps the greatest reputation (worldwide) that any black writer has ever had. Hughes differed from most of his predecessors among black poets, and (until recently) from those who followed him as well, in that he addressed his poetry to the people, specifically to black people. During the twenties when most American poets were turning inward, writing obscure and esoteric poetry to an ever decreasing audience of readers, Hughes was turning outward, using language and themes, attitudes and ideas familiar to anyone who had the ability simply to read. He has been, unlike most nonblack poets other than Walt Whitman, Vachel Lindsay, and Carl Sandburg, a poet of the people. . . . Until the time of his death, he spread his message humorously—though always seriously—to audiences throughout the country, having read his poetry to more people (possibly) than any other American poet."

BIOGRAPHICAL/CRITICAL SOURCES—Books: W. Hart, editor, *American Writers' Congress,* International, 1935; Langston Hughes, *The Big Sea: An Autobiography,* Knopf, 1940; Hughes, *I Wonder as I Wander: An Autobiographical Journey,* Rinehart, 1956; Janheinz Jahn, *A Bibliography of Neo-African Literature from Africa, America and the Caribbean,* Praeger, 1965; Robert A. Bone, *The Negro Novel in America,* Yale University Press, 1965; Donald C. Dickinson, *A Bio-Bibliography of Langston Hughes, 1902-1967,* Archon Books, 1967; James Emanuel, *Langston Hughes,* Twayne, 1967; Milton Meltzer, *Langston Hughes: A Biography,* Crowell, 1968; Bernard Dekle, *Profiles of Modern American Authors,* Charles E. Tuttle, 1969; Donald B. Gibson, editor, *Five Black Writers,* New York University Press, 1970; Elizabeth P. Myers, *Langston Hughes: Poet of His People,* Garrard, 1970; Charlamae H. Rollins, *Black Troubador: Langston Hughes,* Rand McNally, 1970; Thermon B. O'Daniel, editor, *Langston Hughes: Black Genius, a Critical Evaluation,* Morrow, 1971; Houston A. Baker, Jr., *Black Literature in America,* McGraw, 1971; Arthur P. Davis and Saunders Redding, editors, *Cavalcade,* Houghton, 1971; *Contemporary Literary Criticism,* Gale, Volume I, 1973, Volume V, 1976, Volume X, 1979; Donald B. Gibson, editor and author of introduction, *Modern Black Poets: A Collection of Critical Essays,* Prentice-Hall, 1973; Blyden Jackson and Louis D. Rubin, Jr., *Black Poetry in America: Two Essays in Historical Interpretation,* Louisiana State University Press, 1974.

Periodicals: *New York Herald Tribune,* August 1, 1926; *Philadelphia Tribune,* February 5, 1927; *Ebony,* October, 1946; *Saturday Review,* November 22, 1958, September 29, 1962; *American Mercury,* January, 1959; *San Francisco Chronicle,* April 5, 1959; *Crisis,* August-September, 1960, June, 1967, February, 1969; *New York Herald Tribune Books,* November 26, 1961; *Life,* February 4, 1966; *New Leader,* April 10, 1967; *New York Times,* May 24, 1967, June 1, 1968, June 29, 1969, December 13, 1970; *Negro Digest,* September, 1967, November, 1967, April, 1969; *Nation,* December 4, 1967; *New Yorker,* December 30, 1967; *Poetry,* August, 1968; *New York Times Book Review,* November 3, 1968; *Book World,* February 2, 1969; *Black World,* June, 1970, September, 1972, September 1973; *Black Scholar,* June, 1971, July, 1976; *Negro American Literature Forum,* winter, 1971; *CLA Journal,* June, 1972; *New Republic,* January 14, 1974; *Booklist,* November 15, 1976; *English Journal,* March, 1977; *Washington Post,* November 13, 1978.†

—Sketch by Linda Metzger

* * *

HUGHES, Ted 1930-

PERSONAL: Full name, Edward J. Hughes; born August 17, 1930, in Mytholmroyd, Yorkshire, England; son of William Henry and Edith (Farrar) Hughes; married Sylvia Plath (an American poet), 1956 (died, 1963;) married Carol Orchard, 1970; children: (first marriage) Frieda Rebecca, Nicholas Farrar. *Education:* Pembroke College, Cambridge, B.A., 1954, M.A., 1959. *Home:* Court Green, North Tawton, Devonshire, England. *Office:* c/o Faber & Faber Ltd., 3 Queen's Square, London WC1N 3AU, England.

CAREER: Full-time writer. *Military service:* Royal Air Force, two years. *Awards, honors:* First prize, Young Men's and Young Women's Hebrew Association Poetry Center contest, 1957; first prize, Guinness Poetry Awards, 1958; Guggenheim fellow, 1959-60; Somerset Maugham Award, 1960; Hawthornden Prize, 1961; Abraham Wonsell Foundation awards, 1964-69; City of Florence International Poetry Prize, 1969; Taormina Prize, 1972; Queen's Medal for Poetry, 1974; Order of the British Empire, 1977.

WRITINGS—Verse, except as indicated: *The Hawk in the Rain,* Harper, 1957; *Lupercal,* Harper, 1960; (with Thom Gunn) *Selected Poems,* Faber, 1962; *The Burning of the Brothel,* Turret Books, 1966; *Recklings,* Turret Books, 1966; *Scapegoats and Rabies: A Poem in Five Parts,* Poet & Printer, 1967; *Animal Poems,* Gilbertson, 1967; *Wodwo* (miscellany), Harper, 1967; *Five Autumn Songs for Children's Voices,* Gilbertson, 1968; *The Martyrdom of Bishop Farrer,* Gilbertson, 1970; *A Crow Hymn,* Scepter Press, 1970; *A Few Crows,* Rougemont Press, 1970; *Crow: From the Life and Songs of the Crow,* Faber, 1970, revised edition, 1972, Harper, 1971; *Crow Wakes: Poems,* Poet & Printer, 1971; (with Ruth Fainlight and Alan Sillitoe) *Poems,* Rainbow Press, 1971; *Eat Crow,* Rainbow Press, 1972; *In the Little Girl's Angel Gaze,* Steam Press, 1972; *Selected Poems, 1957-1967,* Faber, 1972, Harper, 1973; *Gaudete,* Harper, 1977; *Cave Birds,* Faber, 1977, Viking, 1978; *Moortown,* Harper, 1980.

Juveniles: *Meet My Folks!,* Faber, 1961, Bobbs-Merrill, 1973; *The Earth-Owl and Other Moon-People,* Faber, 1963, Atheneum, 1964; *How the Whale Became,* Faber, 1963, Atheneum, 1964; *Nessie the Mannerless Monster,* Chilmark, 1964, published as *Nessie the Monster,* Bobbs-Merrill, 1974; *The Iron Giant: A Story in Five Parts,* Harper, 1968 (published in England as *The Iron Man: A Story in Five Parts,* Faber, 1968; also see below); *Poetry Is,* Doubleday, 1970; *Season Songs,* Faber, 1974, Viking, 1975; *Moon-Bells and Other Poems,* Chatto & Windus, 1978; *Remains of Elmet,* Harper, 1979.

Plays: "The Calm," first produced in Boston, Mass., 1961; (editor) *Seneca's Oedipus* (first produced in London, 1968), Faber, 1969, Doubleday, 1972; *The Coming of the King and Other Plays* (contains "Beauty and the Beast" [first televised in 1968; produced in London, 1971], "Sean, the Fool" [first produced in London, 1971], "The Devil and the Cats" [first produced in London, 1971], "The Coming of the King" [first televised in 1972], and "The Tiger's Bones"), Faber, 1970, revised edition (also contains "Orpheus") published as *The Tiger's Bones and Other Plays for Children,* Viking, 1975; "Orghast," first produced in Persepolis, Iran, 1971; *The Iron Man* (based on his juvenile book of the same title), Faber, 1973; "The Story of Vasco," first produced in London, 1974. Also author of radio plays, "The House of Aries," 1960, "A Houseful of Women," 1961, "The Wound," 1962, "Difficulties of a Bridegroom," 1963, and "Dogs," 1964.

Editor: (With Patricia Beer and Vernon Scannell) *New Poems 1962,* Hutchinson, 1962; (with Thom Gunn) *Five American Poets,* Faber, 1963; *Here Today,* Hutchinson,

1963; Keith Douglas, *Selected Poems,* Chilmark, 1964; *Poetry in the Making: An Anthology of Poems and Programmes for "Listening and Writing,"* Faber, 1967; Emily Dickinson, *A Choice of Emily Dickinson's Verse,* Faber, 1971; William Shakespeare, *Poems: With Fairest Flowers while Summer Lasts,* Doubleday, 1971 (published in England as *A Choice of Shakespeare's Verse,* Faber, 1971); Yehuda Amichai, *Selected Poems,* Penguin, 1971; Sylvia Plath, *Crossing the Water: Transitional Poems,* Harper, 1971 (published in England as *Crossing the Water,* Faber, 1971).

Contributor to anthologies, including *Corgi Modern Poets in Focus 1,* edited by Dannie Abse, Corgi Books, 1971. Contributor to numerous periodicals, including *New Yorker, Harper's, Atlantic, Nation, Vogue, Mademoiselle,* and *Spectator.* Co-editor, *Modern Poetry in Translation* (journal), 1965—.

SIDELIGHTS: M. L. Rosenthal calls Ted Hughes "the most striking single figure to emerge among the British poets since the last war"; A. Alvarez refers to him as "the most powerful and original poet now writing in this country." To read Hughes's poetry is to enter a world dominated by nature at its most brutal level. Alvarez calls it "a natural world of animals—farm, zoo, wild, domestic—all presented as though from the inside in their fierceness, animality and solitariness." Marjorie Perloff says that, "for Hughes, the violence of nature—what Yeats called its 'murderous innocence'—seems to be the essential and universal human condition. His poems are characterized by stark presentation, sharp definition, a peculiarly masculine energy. . . . [It] is often said that Hughes's violent nature imagery is symbolic of a dark descent to the depths of the unconscious, to a mysterious interior world of being. His animal poems—like 'Otter,' 'Horses,' and 'Pike'—are frequently called Laurentian. But there is, in fact, little resemblance between Lawrence's great poems of animistic projection like 'Bat' and 'Fish'—poems in which the self merges with an alien identity—and a Hughes poem like 'Hawk Roosting,' which . . . has no meaningful reference to any conceivable human situation."

Even though his animal poems may be said to have no direct correlation with the human world, there can be little doubt that Hughes, through his use of violence and animal imagery, is commenting on the human condition. Lawrence R. Ries writes: "In his continuing examination of violence and its role in the world, Hughes does not choose sides for or against the forces that are set in opposition to each other, except in a few particular situations. For the most part, violence is an accepted fact of life that exists as the connecting link between all creatures in the history of the earth from prehistoric times to contemporary England. . . . Again and again Hughes stresses the subtle connection in the primitive drives of the wind, the jaguar, the soldier, of all creation." Ries concludes that the "animal world is used by Hughes as a means of gaining greater insights into the human world."

Calvin Bedient calls Ted Hughes "our first poet of the will to live" and goes on to explain: "Lawrence wrote of animal joy, a lighter, perhaps more fanciful thing. Robinson Jeffers picked up the topic occasionally, a hawk on his wrist. . . . Hughes is its master and at the same time is mastered by it. The subject owns him, he is lord of the subject. The will to live might seem the first and healthiest of subjects, but in fact it is almost the last and most morbid. Men come to it after the other subjects have failed. It is the last stop, waterless and exposed, before nothingness." And yet Hughes, it would seem, finds hope at this "last stop." According to Bedient, it is as if, in discovering his own death, "Hughes concluded that the only thing that mattered was life. He became a worshipper of the claw. An animal's organs represent purely, with the logic of a geometrical proposition, what Schopenhauer called 'the will to live in [its] particular circumstances.' . . . To Hughes the human has nothing to recommend it; to be human is to start out *behind* the animals, like a one-legged man in a race. The human mind, for instance—what is it but a kind of missing leg, aching where the amputated part had once been? Not even in Lawrence does the intellect appear so repulsive as in 'Wings,' Hughes's poem on Sartre, Kafka, and Einstein." Ries says it is the intellect that, in Hughes's work, causes man to be excluded from the natural process of violence, "for his violence is no longer instinctual but planned. . . . Recognizing this rift between the two worlds of violence, Hughes in poem after poem sets out mental scouting parties that explore the forms of violence that still link man to the other world: birth, sex, war, and death. He sees these experiences as means for man to reestablish his connections with his primitive origins."

His apparent obsession with animals and nature has brought the wrath of more than one critic down upon Hughes. Colin Falck, for instance, writes that the "real limitation of Hughes's animal poems is precisely that they conjure emotions without bringing us any nearer to understanding them. They borrow their impact from a complex of emotions that they do nothing to define, and in the end tell us nothing about the urban civilised human world that we read the poems in. . . . Hughes's poetic world is really a prehistoric world of natural violence, where humanity has only the barest finger-hold: when the poems are not about animals they are often about inanimate nature ('October Dawn'), and they give no place to emotions and experience of an essentially human kind. In this sense Hughes is a nature poet, a kind of tough mid-century Blunden, . . . and makes no serious attempt to face the 'full range' of his experience: the experience and emotions that control his poems are frequently those that we share with animals, and these are evoked 'as in a dream' more often than they are explored. It would be one thing to write a single poem or two out of this idea, but to make it the dominant theme of an entire output is quite another." Graham Martin responds to the idea that Hughes is a "nature poet" by blaming critics for misinterpreting his work. Martin feels that "we still seem to suffer from a literalism not much different from the old Puritan argument that plays were lies because they clearly weren't true. With Ted Hughes, the argument is that because many poems describe animals and have animal titles (infallible sign!), animals is what he writes about. I don't see how else to explain how this original and distinguished poet could be landed with the reputation of a sort of Zoo Laureate. So perhaps it won't appear painfully simple-minded to insist that the animals aren't there for their own sake but as metaphors for a particular human vision, embodying either a sometimes active, sometimes baffled primal energy, or an unthinking predatory violence, awful in both senses, whose human application should need no spelling out."

Hughes's best-known and most intriguing creation is Crow, who began appearing in 1967 and eventually came to be the main character in several volumes of poetry. Keith Sagar notes that the raven, according to Eskimo legend, was the first creature on earth "and the world was, like him, black. Then came the owl and the world became white like him, with the whiteness of unending snow. Hughes's mythology of Crow is deeply rooted in such legends." But, ask several reviewers, why choose a crow for a protagonist? Sagar writes: "The prevalence of ravens and crows in folklore derives largely from the real bird's characteristics. The crow is the most intelligent of birds, the most widely distributed (being common on every continent), and the most omnivorous ('no carrion will kill a crow'). They are, of course, black all over, solitary, almost indestructible, and the largest and least musical of songbirds. It is to be expected that the Songs of the Crow will be harsh and grating. He kills a little himself, and, as carrion eater, is dependent on the killing of others and first on the scene at many disasters."

Christopher Porterfield says that Hughes "parcels out human history and legend in a succession of charnel-house episodes. The Garden of Eden, Oedipus, St. George, all our prototypes of beauty, heroism and love, are reduced to so much pulsing, thrashing sinew, murderously intent on survival. . . . To all the horror, Crow brings a note of jaunty irony, even whimsy, as the titles of his adventures show: 'Crow Tyrannosaurus,' 'Crow Improvises,' 'Crow's Last Stand.' Crow is a sort of cosmic Kilroy. Alternately a witness, a demon and a victim, he is in on everything from the creation to the ultimate nuclear holocaust. At various times he is minced, dismembered, rendered cataleptic, but always he bobs back. In his graceless, ignoble way, he is the lowest common denominator of the universal forces that obsess Hughes. He is a symbol of the essential survivor, of whatever endures, however battered." David Lodge sees Crow as "the beast of a very modern apocalypse, one in which images of global disaster and individual violence take absurd and grotesque and debased forms that derive quite as much from contemporary mass culture as from literary tradition." Sagar finds in Crow, an "Everyman who will not acknowlege that everything he most hates and fears—the Black Beast—is within himself. Crow's world is unredeemable. God made the Redeemer as a defeatist act of submission to Crow."

Jack Kroll, who calls the Crow sagas "those rare books of poetry that have the public impact of a major novel or a piece of super-journalism," summarizes the effect of the character: "The Crow, Ted Hughes has created one of the most powerful mythic presences in contemporary poetry. Crow is the blackness of all of us, including the whiteness that was. In these poems that hit like rocks and bite like beaks, Hughes speaks the ultimate prophecy: life will survive—in a terrain and continuum of destruction. It is a prophecy beyond hope and despair, made of its own black-blooded music. If our own organs—our brains, blood, hearts—could speak, this would be their language."

The word that arises most often in reviews of Hughes's work is "powerful." Critic Robert Pinsky accuses the poet of courting the adjective "with bloody persistence. His language and characters both resemble ponderous items of antique military engineering, futile rams and engines, so manically over-built for power that they cannot budge: fantastic artifacts of peacetime generals. Such writing is bad not because it tries to make violence seem erotic, stimulating, morally 'powerful,' but because it makes violence and eroticism both seem merely literary and boring. . . . For some readers the violence may be justified by deeper rewards; but as for me, I can't find anything under all that ketchup except baloney." On the other hand, Dabney Stuart feels that "the forms Ted Hughes has chosen . . . are grievous, possessed of an unremitting constancy, pursued as an obsession is pursued, or fled from in the same way. Hughes's poems are rare in this (as in other aspects, all excellent) that they perform their author's quest for terror and the center of terror as well as afford him the means by which to defend himself against it. . . . Hughes's poems sound inevitable, profoundly *necessary.*" Stuart concludes that his work "is astoundingly affirmative; what he has seen has not stopped him from speaking. His vision includes simultaneously his sense of the brutally animal center of all existence and the particularly human ability to make languages. I know of few other poets—Jeffers, Roethke, Muir—who have so insistently celebrated the mysterious mud we are made of, whose other name is darkness."

Vereen Bell offers a possible explanation for the polarity of Hughes's reviewers: "Hardly any of criticism's established systems of value, most of which are one way or the other neoplatonic, prove adequate for dealing with Ted Hughes's poetry, either as frames or as starting points. More obsessively than Lawrence, Hughes demands that we forget everything, moral value included (and moral and intellectual temporizing especially), in order to perceive the extent to which our assumptions about the nature of existence are crude illusions of perspective, innocent epistemologies based upon fastidiously selective habits of perception. Even to say that is to imply a conventional humanistic agenda which Hughes appears to have moved beyond. In fact he has divested romanticism of all its notions of sentimental humanistic utility, and it seems to me that this represents a quantuum progression even beyond Lawrence."

BIOGRAPHICAL/CRITICAL SOURCES—Periodicals: *Arizona Quarterly,* spring, 1967; *Observer Review,* May 21, 1967; *New Statesman,* June 16, 1967, January 5, 1979; *Times Literary Supplement,* July 6, 1967, July 1, 1977; *Books and Bookmen,* November, 1967, February, 1971; *Book World,* December 24, 1967, February 10, 1974; *New Yorker,* March 30, 1968; *Hudson Review,* spring, 1968; *Carleton Miscellany,* summer, 1968; *Drama,* summer, 1968; *Shenandoah,* summer, 1968, winter, 1972; *Virginia Quarterly Review,* summer, 1968, spring, 1974; *Listener,* August 1, 1968; *Comment,* September, 1968; *New York Review,* August 1, 1968; *New York Times Book Review,* November 3, 1968, January 13, 1974, December 25, 1977; *Young Readers Review,* February, 1969.

New York Times, March 18, 1971, July 19, 1978; *Critical Quarterly,* spring, 1971, summer, 1972; *Time,* April 5, 1971; *Newsweek,* April 12, 1971; *New York Review of Books,* July 22, 1971, March 7, 1974; *Mediterranean Review,* fall, 1971; *Commonweal,* September 17, 1971; *Saturday Review,* October 2, 1971; *Poetry,* February, 1972; *Prairie Schooner,* fall, 1972; *Contemporary Literature,* winter, 1973; *Salmagundi,* spring-summer, 1973; *Books Abroad,* winter, 1974; *New Republic,* February 16, 1974; *Nation,* March 16, 1974; *Midwest Quarterly,* summer, 1974; *Parnassus: Poetry in Review,* spring-summer, 1976; *Sewanee Review,* summer, 1976; *Encounter,* November, 1978.

Books: M. L. Rosenthal, *The New Poets: American and British Poetry since World War II,* Oxford University Press, 1967; Ian Hamilton, *The Modern Poet: Essays for "The Review,"* MacDonald & Co., 1968; Monroe K. Spears, *Dionysus and the City: Modernism in Twentieth-Century Poetry,* Oxford University Press, 1970; Keith Sagar, *Ted Hughes,* Longman, 1972; *Contemporary Literary Criticism,* Gale, Volume II, 1974, Volume IV, 1975, Volume IX, 1978; Lawrence R. Ries, *Wolf Masks: Violence in Contemporary Poetry,* Kennikat, 1977; *Children's Literature Review,* Volume III, Gale, 1978.†

—Sketch by Peter M. Gareffa

HUGHES, Walter (Llewellyn) 1910-
(Hugh Walters)

PERSONAL: Born June 15, 1910, in Bilston, Staffordshire, England; son of Walter Martin and Kate (Latham) Hughes; married Doris Higgins, 1933; married second wife, 1977; wife's name, Susan; children: (first marraige) Walter Fred, Gillian Doris Hughes Hudson. *Education:* Attended Wednesbury Technical College, 1928, and the Birmingham College of Advanced Technology. *Home:* The Bungalow, Elm Ave., Bilston, Staffordshire, England. *Agent:* Paul R. Reynolds, Inc., 12 East 41st St., New York, N.Y. 10017. *Office:* Bradsteds Ltd., Ash St., Bilston, Staffordshire, England.

CAREER: Bradsteds Ltd., Bilston, Staffordshire, England, managing director, 1938—. Justice of the Peace in Bilston, 1947—. *Member:* Institute of British Engineers, British Interplanetary Society, Ancient Order of Foresters (former high chief ranger), Bilston Rotary Club (former president).

WRITINGS—All juveniles under pseudonym Hugh Walters: *Blast-off at Woomera,* Faber, 1957, published as *Blast-off at 0300,* Criterion, 1958; *The Domes of Pico,* Faber, 1958; *Menace from the Moon,* Criterion, 1959; *First on the Moon,* Criterion, 1960; *Operation Columbus,* Faber, 1960; *Moon Base One,* Faber, 1961, published as *Outpost on the Moon,* Criterion, 1962; *Expedition Venus,* Faber, 1962, Criterion, 1963; *Destination Mars,* Faber, 1963, Criterion, 1964; *Terror by Satellite,* Criterion, 1964; *Journey to Jupiter,* Faber, 1965, Criterion, 1966; *Mission to Mercury,* Criterion, 1965; *Spaceship to Saturn,* Criterion, 1967; *The Mohole Mystery,* Faber, 1968, published as *The Mohole Menace,* Criterion, 1969; *Nearly Neptune,* Faber, 1969, published as *Neptune One Is Missing,* I. Washburn, 1969; *First Contact?,* Faber, 1971, Thomas Nelson, 1973; *Passage to Pluto,* Faber, 1973, Thomas Nelson, 1975; *Tony Hale, Space Detective,* Faber, 1973; *Murder on Mars,* Faber, 1975; *Boy Astronaut,* Abelard, 1977; *The Caves of Drach,* Faber, 1977.

WORK IN PROGRESS: The Blue Aura; First Family on the Moon; The Darit Triangle.

SIDELIGHTS: Walter Hughes told *CA* that he believes science fiction should "entertain, instruct, inspire. As all my books are for young people, they are as technically accurate as possible."

* * *

HULTMAN, Charles W(iliam) 1930-

PERSONAL: Born April 6, 1930, in Oelwein, Iowa; son of John William and Alma (Loeb) Hultman; married Irene Oliver, 1957; children: Susan Kay, Gregory John. *Education:* Upper Iowa University, B.A., 1952; Drake University, M.A., 1957; University of Iowa, Ph.D., 1960. *Home:* 3341 Crown Crest Rd., Lexington, Ky. *Office:* Office for Research, College of Business and Economics, University of Kentucky, Lexington, Ky. 40506.

CAREER: University of Iowa, Iowa City, instructor, 1957-60; University of Kentucky, Patterson School of Diplomacy, Lexington, assistant professor, 1960-64, associate professor, 1965-67, professor of economics, 1967—, chairman of department, 1969-71, associate dean for research, College of Business and Economics, 1976—. Visiting professor, University of California, 1964-65; Fulbright lecturer, National University (Cork, Ireland), 1967-68; chairman, Kentucky Council of Economic Advisors, 1976—. *Military service:* U.S. Army, three years; served with fiscal branch in Far East. *Member:* American Economic Association, Midwest Economic Association, Southern Economic Association.

WRITINGS: Modern International Economics, Simmons-Boardman, 1962; *International Finance,* Simmons-Boardman, 1963; *American Business and the European Common Market,* Simmons-Boardman, 1964; (co-editor) *Readings in Economic Development,* Heath, 1966; *Ireland in the World Economy,* Mercier Press, 1969; *Financing Unemployment Compensation in Kentucky,* Office of Business Development and Government Services, 1972; *Economic Implications of a Doubling of Kentucky Coal Production,* Office for Research, University of Kentucky, 1976; *Economic Implications of Low Btu Gas Production in Industrial Sites,* Office for Research, University of Kentucky, 1977.

WORK IN PROGRESS: Studies in energy.

* * *

HUMES, James C. 1934-

PERSONAL: Born October 31, 1934; son of Samuel Hamilton (a jurist) and Elenor (Graham) Humes; married Dianne Stuart (an editor), June 25, 1957; children: Mary Stuart, Rachel Bailey. *Education:* Attended Williams College; George Washington University, A.B. and J.D. *Religion:* Presbyterian. *Home:* 203 West Chestnut Hill Ave., Philadelphia, Pa. 19118. *Agent:* Theron Raines, Raines & Raines, 475 Fifth Ave., New York, N.Y. 10017. *Office:* 912 Western Savings Bldg., Philadelphia, Pa. 19107.

CAREER: Republican member of Pennsylvania House of Representatives, 1962-65; White House, Washington, D.C., special assistant to President, 1969-70; U.S. Department of State, Washington, D.C., director of Office of Policy and Plans, 1970-72; member of White House staff, 1976-77. Former executive director of Philadelphia Bar Association. Director of World Affairs Council. *Member:* American Bar Association, St. Andrew's Society, St. Nicholas Society, St. George's Society, War of 1812 Pennsylvania Society, Order of Magna Carta.

WRITINGS: Sweet Dream: Tale of a River City, Grit Publishing, 1966; *Instant Eloquence: A Lazy Man's Guide to Public Speaking,* Harper, 1973; *Podium Humor,* Harper, 1975; *Roles Speakers Play,* Harper, 1976; *How to Get Invited to the White House,* Crowell, 1976; *A Speaker's Treasury of Anecdotes,* Harper, 1977; *Churchill: Speaker of the Century,* Stein & Day, 1980.

WORK IN PROGRESS: How to Talk Your Way to the Top.

SIDELIGHTS: James C. Humes was the youngest member of the Pennsylvania legislature in 1962; he has worked as trial lawyer and public defender, and has written speeches for presidents Nixon and Ford. Humes has also done one-man shows imitating Winston Churchill. *Avocational interests:* Public speaking, humor (especially political humor).

BIOGRAPHICAL/CRITICAL SOURCES: Washington Post Book World, February 22, 1974.

* * *

HUNTINGTON, Samuel P(hillips) 1927-

PERSONAL: Born April 18, 1927, in New York, N.Y.; son of Richard Thomas and Dorothy (Phillips) Huntington; married Nancy Arkelyan, 1957; children: Timothy Mayo, Nicholas Phillips. *Education:* Yale University, B.A., 1946; University of Chicago, M.A., 1948; Harvard University, Ph.D., 1951. *Home:* 52 Brimmer St., Boston, Mass. 02108. *Office:* Center for International Affairs, Harvard University, 1737 Cambridge St., Cambridge, Mass. 02138.

CAREER: Harvard University, Cambridge, Mass., instructor, 1950-53, assistant professor of government, 1953-58; Brookings Institution, Washington, D.C., research associate, 1952-53; Columbia University, New York, N.Y., associate professor of government and associate director, Institute of War and Peace Studies, 1959-62; Harvard University, professor of government, 1962-67, Frank G. Thomson Professor of Government, 1967—, chairman of department, 1967-69, 1970-71, associate director of Center for International Affairs, 1973-77, director of center, 1978—. Coordinator of security planning, National Security Council, 1977-78. Visiting lecturer at University of Michigan, University of California, Dartmouth College, Ohio State University, Carnegie Institute of Technology (now Carnegie-Mellon University), Army War College, Air War College, National War College, and Industrial College of the Armed Forces. Faculty research fellow, Social Science Research Council, 1954-57; Ford research professor, Columbia University, 1960-61, 1962; visiting fellow, All Souls College, Oxford University, 1973. Consultant to Institute for Defense Analysis, 1961, Hudson Institute, 1962, U.S. Air Force Academy, 1962-64, Office of the Secretary of Defense, 1963-68, and National Security Council, 1977—. *Military service:* U.S. Army, 1946-47. *Member:* American Political Science Association (member of council, 1969-71), Institute of Strategic Studies, Council on Foreign Relations. *Awards, honors:* Center for Advanced Study in Behavioral Sciences fellow, 1969-70; Guggenheim fellow, 1972-73; American Academy of Arts and Sciences fellow.

WRITINGS: The Soldier and the State: The Theory and Politics of Civil-Military Relations, Harvard University Press, 1957; *The Common Defense: Strategic Programs in National Politics,* Columbia University Press, 1961; (editor) *Changing Patterns of Military Politics,* Free Press of Glencoe, 1962; (co-author) *Political Power: USA/USSR,* Viking, 1964; *Political Order in Changing Societies,* Yale University Press, 1968; (co-editor) *Authoritarian Politics in Modern Society: The Dynamics of Established One-Party Systems,* Basic Books, 1970; (co-author) *The Crisis of Democracy,* New York University Press, 1975; (co-author) *No Easy Choice: Political Participation in Developing Countries,* Harvard University Press, 1976. Contributor of over fifty articles to scholarly journals and periodicals including *Foreign Policy, Daedaus, World Politics, Foreign Affairs,* and *American Political Science Review.* Editor, *Foreign Policy,* 1970-77.

* * *

HUUS, Helen 1913-

PERSONAL: Born November 1, 1913, in Northwood, Iowa; daughter of Jacob H. and Mary Belle (Tiffany) Huus. *Education:* Iowa State Teachers College (now University of Northern Iowa), B.A., 1940; University of Chicago, M.A., 1941, Ph.D., 1944. *Religion:* Lutheran. *Home:* 208 North Ninth St., Northwood, Iowa 50459.

CAREER: Teacher in public schools in Worth County, Iowa, 1933-35, and Mediapolis, Iowa, 1936-38; Iowa State Teachers College (now University of Northern Iowa), Campus Demonstration School, Cedar Falls, teacher, 1938-40; Wayne University (now Wayne State University), Detroit, Mich., assistant professor of education, 1945-47; University of Pennsylvania, Philadelphia, 1947-67, began as assistant professor, became associate professor of education; University of Missouri—Kansas City, professor of education, 1967-78. Fulbright scholar, 1950-51. Member of education committee, Southeastern Pennsylvania League for Nursing; president, Women's evening group, Holy Communion Lutheran Church, 1958-59, 1961-63. Frequent speaker at reading conferences. *Military service:* U.S. Naval Reserve, 1944-45; became commander. *Member:* American Association of University Women, National Conference on Research in English (secretary-treasurer, 1964-66; president, 1966-67), National Council of Teachers of English, Comparative Education Society, International Reading Association (publicity chairman, 1955-57; member of board of directors, 1963-67; president, 1969-70), Kappa Delta Pi, Pi Lambda Theta. *Awards, honors:* Walgreen Foundation scholarship, 1941-43.

WRITINGS: Education of Children and Youth in Norway, University of Pittsburgh Press, 1960; *Children's Books to Enrich the Social Studies* (monograph), National Council for the Social Studies, 1961, revised edition, 1966.

Editor: *Education: Intellectual, Moral, Physical,* University of Pennsylvania Press, 1961; *Education and the National Purpose,* University of Pennsylvania Press, 1962; *Contemporary Issues Here and Aboard,* University of Pennsylvania Press, 1963; *Freedom and Education,* University of Pennsylvania Press, 1964; *Values for a Changing America,* University of Pennsylvania Press, 1966.

Contributor: *Children Learn to Read,* National Council of Teachers, 1949; *Good Education of Youth,* University of Pennsylvania Press, 1957; Alan Robinson, editor, *Reading and the Language Arts,* University of Chicago Press, 1963; Albert J. Mazurkiewics, editor, *New Perspectives in Reading,* Pitman, 1964; Helen M. Robinson, editor, *Innovation and Change in Reading Instruction,* University of Chicago Press, 1968. Contributor to reading monographs.

Co-author with Robert Whitehead and Henry Bamman of "Field Literature" series, Field Educational Publications, 1971. Author of column, "Cross Currents" for *Pi Lambda Theta Journal,* 1953-55. Contributor of articles on reading and children's literature to professional journals. Member of publications advisory committee, *Pi Lambda Theta Journal,* 1977—.

SIDELIGHTS: Helen Huus told *CA:* "I am interested in literature for children and in finding out the contribution reading literature of quality makes to their growth and development. [I am] also interested in comparative juvenile literature."

* * *

HYDE, Margaret Oldroyd 1917-

PERSONAL: Born February 18, 1917, in Philadelphia, Pa.; daughter of Gerald James and Helen (Lerch) Oldroyd; married Edwin Y. Hyde, Jr., 1941; children: Lawrence Edwin, Bruce Geoffrey. *Education:* Beaver College, A.B., 1938; Columbia University, M.A., 1939; Temple University, additional studies, 1942-43.

CAREER: Columbia University, Teachers College, New York, N.Y., science consultant, 1941-42; Shipley School, Bryn Mawr, Pa., teacher, 1942-48. Lecturer in elementary education, Temple University, Philadelphia, Pa., part-time and summers, 1942-43. Writer for young people. Member of board of directors, Northeast Mental Health Clinic. *Member:* Authors Guild. *Awards, honors:* Thomas Alva Edison Foundation National Mass Media Award, 1961, for best children's science book, *Animal Clocks and Compasses;* honorary doctor of letters from Beaver College, 1971.

WRITINGS—All published by McGraw, except as indicated: *Playtime for Nancy,* Grosset, 1941; (with G. S. Craig) *Our World of Science,* Ginn, 1947; (with F. W. Keene) *Hobby Fun Book,* 1952; *Flight Today and Tommorrow,*

1953, revised edition, 1962; *Driving Today and Tomorrow,* 1954, revised edition, 1965; *Atoms Today and Tomorrow,* 1955, 4th edition, 1970; (with husband, E. Y. Hyde) *Where Speed Is King,* 1955, revised edition, 1961; *Medicine in Action: Today and Tomorrow,* 1956, revised edition, 1964; *Exploring Earth and Space,* 1957, 5th edition, 1970; *From Submarines to Satellites,* 1958; *Off Into Space! Science for Young Space Travelers,* 1959, 3rd edition, 1969.

Plants Today and Tomorrow, 1960; *Animal Clocks and Compasses,* 1960; *This Crowded Planet,* 1961; *Animals in Science: Saving Lives through Research,* 1962, *Molecules Today and Tomorrow,* 1963; *Your Brain: Master Computer,* 1964; (with Edward Marks) *Psychology in Action,* 1967, 2nd edition, 1976; *Mind Drugs,* 1968, 3rd edition, 1974; *The Earth in Action,* 1969; *The Great Deserts,* 1969.

Know about Drugs, 1971, revised edition, 1979; *For Pollution Fighters Only,* 1971; *Your Skin,* 1972; (with others) *Mysteries of the Mind,* 1972; *VD: The Silent Epidemic,* 1972; *The New Genetics: Promises and Perils,* F. Watts, 1974; (with Elizabeth Forsyth) *What Have You Been Eating? Do You Really Know,* 1975; *Speak Out on Rape,* 1976; (with Forsyth) *Know Your Feelings,* F. Watts, 1976; *Alcohol: Drink or Drug,* 1976; *Juvenile Justice and Injustice,* F. Watts, 1977; *Fears and Phobias,* 1977; *Brainwashing and Other Forms of Mind Control,* 1977; *Know about Alcohol,* 1978; *Addictions: Smoking, Gambling, Cocaine Use and Others,* 1978; (with Forsyth) *Suicide: The Hidden Epidemic,* F. Watts, 1978; *Everyone's Trash Problem: Nuclear Wastes,* 1979; *My Friend Wants to Run Away,* 1979.

Crime and Justice in Our Time, F. Watts, 1980; *Cry Softly: The Story of Child Abuse,* Westminster, 1980; *Is the Cat Dreaming Your Dream?,* 1980. Also author of *Hotline,* 1976; author of two television scripts for "Animal Secrets," 1967.

SIDELIGHTS: Margaret Hyde told *CA:* "Writing is a wonderful way to learn more about the exciting world of science, for today one must contact people who are active in research to find out what is happening. Such people are most cooperative in talking about their projects and in checking material for accuracy. I gather material for several years from many sources and sometimes work on as many as four books at once."

HYMAN, Richard J(oseph) 1921-

PERSONAL: Born February 11, 1921, in Malden, Mass.; son of Myer (a cattle broker) and Ida (Orlove) Hyman. *Education:* Harvard University, A.B. (summa cum laude), 1942, M.B.A., 1948; Boston Hebrew Teachers College, B.J.L. (with honors), 1942; Columbia University, M.S., 1962, D.L.S., 1971. *Residence:* New York, N.Y. *Office:* Graduate School of Library and Information Studies, Queens College of the City University of New York, Flushing, N.Y. 11367.

CAREER: Ansco Camera and Film, New York City, market researcher, 1949-50; Dayton Rubber Company, New York City, sales administrator, 1950-51; Venus Pen and Pencil, New York City, assistant to vice-president, 1952-59; Wolf, Block, Schorr, Solis-Cohen (law office), Philadelphia, Pa., assistant to chairman, 1959-60; New York University Libraries, New York City, librarian, 1963-68; Queens College of the City University of New York, Flushing, N.Y., associate professor of library science, 1968—, chairperson of department, 1977—, director of Graduate School of Library and Information Studies, 1979—. *Military service:* U.S. Naval Reserve, 1942-46; became lieutenant. *Member:* American Library Association, Association of College and Research Libraries, Association of American Library Schools, New York Library Club, New York Technical Services Librarians (secretary-treasurer, 1969-70; president, 1972-73), Library Association of the City University of New York, Phi Beta Kappa, Archons of Colophon.

WRITINGS: (Editor with Maurice F. Tauber) *Use of Printed and Audio-Visual Materials for Instructional Purposes,* U.S. Department of Health, Education and Welfare, 1966; (with Lee Ash and V. R. Bruette) *Interlibrary Request and Loan Transactions among Medical Libraries of the Greater New York Area,* Medical Library Resources of Greater New York, 1966; *Access to Library Collections,* Scarecrow, 1972; *From Cutter to MARC: Access to the Unit Record,* Queens College Press, 1977; *Analytical Access: History, Resources, Needs,* Queens College Press, 1978; *Shelf Classification Research: Past, Present–Future?,* University of Illinois Press, 1980. Contributor of articles to *Library Resources and Technical Services, French Review, Library Journal, Bulletin of Medical Library Association, Bookmark, Iconoclast,* and *Christian Science Monitor.*

WORK IN PROGRESS: Shelf Arrangement Plans for Libraries.

I

ILCHMAN, Warren Frederick 1934-

PERSONAL: Born September 6, 1934, in Denver, Colo.; son of Frederick Warren and Imogene (Trovinger) Ilchman; married Alice Crawford Stone, 1960. *Education:* Brown University, A.B., 1955; Cambridge University, Ph.D., 1959. *Home:* 3105 Woodley Rd. N.W., Washington, D.C. 20008. *Office:* Ford Foundation, 320 East 43rd St., New York, N.Y. 10017.

CAREER: Cambridge University, Magdalene College, Cambridge, England, tutor, 1958-59; Williams College, Williamstown, Mass., instructor, 1959-62, assistant professor, 1962-65; University of California, Berkeley, 1965-73, began as assistant professor, became associate professor of political science; Harvard University, Cambridge, Mass., visiting professor, 1973-74; Boston University, Graduate School, Boston, Mass., dean of arts and sciences, 1974-76; Ford Foundation, New York, N.Y., program adviser, 1976—. *Member:* American Political Science Association, American Society for Public Administration, Royal Society for Public Administration.

WRITINGS: Professional Diplomacy in the United States, 1779-1939, University of Chicago Press, 1961; *New Men of Knowledge and Developing States,* University of California Press, 1965; *Agents of Change,* Praeger, 1969; (with Norman T. Uphoff) *The Political Economy of Change,* University of California Press, 1969; *Comparative Public Administration and "Conventional Wisdom,"* Sage Publications, Inc., 1971; (with Uphoff) *The Political Economy of Development,* University of California Press, 1971; (with others) *Policy Sciences and Population,* Heath, 1975; *Education and Employment,* Vikas (New Delhi), 1976.

* * *

INBAU, Fred E. 1909-

PERSONAL: Born March 27, 1909, in New Orleans, La.; son of Fred and Pauline (Boos) Inbau; married Ruth Major, September 21, 1935 (died, 1963); married Jane Hanchett Schoenewald, June 27, 1964; children: (first marriage) W. Robert, Louise. *Education:* Tulane University, B.S., 1930, LL.B., 1932; Northwestern University, LL.M., 1933. *Home:* 40 East Oak St., Chicago, Ill. 60611. *Office:* School of Law, Northwestern University, 357 East Chicago Ave., Chicago, Ill. 60611.

CAREER: Admitted to Louisiana State Bar, 1934, and Illinois State Bar, 1936; Northwestern University School of Law, Chicago, Ill., research assistant in legal psychology in scientific crime detection laboratory, 1933, instructor in police science, 1934-36, assistant professor of law, 1936-38; Chicago Police Scientific Crime Detection Laboratory, Chicago, director, 1938-41; Lord, Bissell & Kadyk, Chicago, attorney-at-law, 1941-45; Northwestern University School of Law, professor of law, 1945-77, John Henry Wigmore Professor of Law, 1974-77, professor emeritus, 1977—. Visiting consultant, public safety division, office of U.S. High Commissioner for Germany, 1951-52; consultant, American Bar Foundation survey of the administration of criminal justice in the United States, 1955-58; member, Chicago Crime Commission.

MEMBER: American Academy of Forensic Sciences (president, 1955-56), American Academy of Polygraph Examiners (president, 1954-56), American Bar Association, National District Attorneys Association (honorary member), American Society of Questioned Document Examiners (honorary member), Americans for Effective Law Enforcement (founder; president, 1966—), Illinois Academy of Criminology (president, 1951-52), Chicago Bar Association. *Awards, honors:* Furtherance of Justice Award, National District Attorneys Association, 1961; Outstanding Alumnus Award, Tulane University, 1978.

WRITINGS: Lie Detection and Criminal Interrogation, Williams & Wilkins, 1942, 3rd edition (with John Reid), 1953; *Self-Incrimination: What Can an Accused Person Be Compelled to Do?,* C. C Thomas, 1950; (with Claude R. Sowle) *Cases and Comments on Criminal Justice,* Foundation Press, 1960, 3rd edition (with Sowle and James R. Thompson) published in two volumes, 1968; (with Reid) *Criminal Interrogation and Confessions,* Williams & Wilkins, 1962, 2nd edition, 1967; (editor) *Conference on Prejudicial News Reporting in Criminal Cases: Papers and Proceedings,* Northwestern University School of Law, 1964, published as *Free Press-Fair Trial,* Da Capo Press, 1970; (with Yale Kamisar and Thurman Arnold) *Criminal Justice in Our Time,* University Press of Virginia, 1965; (with Reid) *Truth and Deception: The Polygraph (Lie Detector) Technique,* Williams & Wilkins, 1966, 2nd edition, 1977; (with Marvin E. Aspen) *Criminal Law for the Police,* Chilton, 1969; (with Aspen) *Criminal Law for the Layman,* Chilton, 1970, 2nd edition (with Aspen and Jeremy D. Margolis), 1977; (with Thompson) *Criminal Law and Its Administration,* Foundation Press, 1970, 2nd edition (with Thompson and James B. Zagel), 1974, supplement, 1976; (with Jon R. Waltz) *Medical Jurisprudence,* Macmillan, 1971; (with Andre A. Moenssens and Louis R. Vitullo) *Scientific Police Investigation,* Chilton, 1972; (with Aspen and Frank Carrington) *Evidence Law for the Police,* Chilton, 1972; (with Moenssens and Ray Edward Moses) *Scientific Evidence in Criminal Cases,* Foundation Press, 1973, 2nd edition (with Moenssens), 1978; (with Thompson and Moenssens) *Cases and Comments on Criminal Law,* Foundation Press, 1973; (with Thompson, Zagel, James B. Haddad, and Gary L. Starkman) *Cases and Comments on Criminal Procedure,* Foundation Press, 1974, supplements, 1975, 1976, 1977.

Contributor to legal and scientific journals. *Journal of Criminal Law, Criminology, and Police Science,* managing director, 1945-64, editor-in-chief, 1964-71; editor-in-chief, *Journal of Police Science and Administration,* 1973-78.

* * *

INGLIS, Ruth Langdon 1927-

PERSONAL: Born December 17, 1927, in China; daughter of William Russell (U.S. consul-general) and Laura (Filer) Langdon; divorced; children: Diana Eleanor, Neil Langdon. *Education:* Barnard College, B.A., 1949. *Politics:* Democrat. *Religion:* Episcopalian. *Home and office:* 40 Winchester St., London S.W.1, England. *Agents:* A.D. Peters & Co., Ltd., 10 Buckingham St., London WC2N 6BU England; and Helen Brann Agency, 14 Sutton Pl. S., New York, N.Y. 10022. *Office: Daily Express,* Standard House, 56 Farringdon St. London EC4A 4DY, England.

CAREER: Sarah Lawrence College, Bronxville, N.Y., news bureau director, 1957-58; *Daily Express,* London, England, feature writer, 1977—; free-lance writer and journalist, contributing especially to *Observer, Nova,* and *Good Housekeeping.*

WRITINGS: A Time to Learn, Dial, 1973; *Sins of the Fathers,* St. Martin's, 1978. Author of scripts for series "The Facts Are These," produced by Granada Television, London, England, 1968.

WORK IN PROGRESS: A book on the children of divorce, for Temple Smith.

SIDELIGHTS: Ruth Inglis writes: "London is alive with new experiments and findings in sociology (much of it pioneered at London University and the Institute of Psychiatry, South London) and so it is an exciting place for a London-American to be who is involved with new directions in child development and family relationships generally."

Inglis' book, *Sins of the Fathers,* is about physical and emotional abuse of children. The reviewer for *North Country Living* calls it a "compassionate study" which applies to "readers of *all* layers of society, and especially to those parents who consider themselves to be very good parents. . . . Once started, it is hard to put the book down. Written in simple language, true case histories, consultations with experts in the fields of social work, psychiatry and psychology, make up the body of the book. It is revealing that in many cases the abuse of children is the result of 'blindness' or 'inadequacies' of the 'fathers' or parents, and that this blindness is 'often transmitted from generation to generation, and is not visited upon the children in any conscious manner'. . . . If there was ever a how-to-understand-yourself book that should be on every family bookshelf, this is it."

BIOGRAPHICAL/CRITICAL SOURCES: North Country Living (San Diego, Calif.), January, 1979.

INKELES, Alex 1920-

PERSONAL: Born March 4, 1920, in Brooklyn, N.Y.; son of Meyer and Ray (Gewer) Inkeles; married Bernadette Mary Kane, 1942; children: Ann Elizabeth. *Education:* Cornell University, B.A., 1941, M.A., 1946; Columbia University, Ph.D., 1949. *Home:* 1101 Hamilton Ave., Palo Alto, Calif. 94301. *Office:* Hoover Institution on War, Revolution and Peace, Stanford University, Stanford, Calif. 94305.

CAREER: Cornell University, Ithaca, N.Y., teaching and research assistant, 1941-42; Harvard University, Cambridge, Mass., instructor in social relations, 1948, lecturer in social relations, 1948-56, professor of sociology, 1957-71, director of studies in social relations at Russian Research Center, 1950-71, research director of refugee interview project, 1950-55, acting director of regional studies program on the U.S.S.R., 1956-57, director of studies on non-economic aspects of development at Center for International Affairs; Stanford University, Stanford, Calif., Margaret Jacks Professor of Education, 1971-78, professor of sociology, 1971—, professor of education and senior fellow at Hoover Institution on War, Revolution and Peace, 1978—. Occasional lecturer at Army, Air, Naval, and National War Colleges, 1950-60; lecturer in sociology, Institute for the Study of the Soviet Union, University of Denver, summer, 1950; visiting professor, Facultad Latino-Americano de Ciencias Sociales, Santiago, Chile, 1963-64; occasional lecturer, Faculdade Candido Mendes, Rio de Janeiro, Brazil, 1964-69; lecturer, American Council of Life Insurance Arden House Conference on Freedom and Control in a Democratic Society, 1976; visiting scholar and lecturer, Royal Institute for International Affairs, London, England; visiting scholar, Institute for Social Research, Athens, Greece; lecturer and consultant at universities in India under sponsorship of Indian Social Science Research Council, 1977-78. Consultant to program evaluation branch, International Broadcasting Division, U.S. Department of State, 1949-51; consultant to UNESCO, 1950, 1978; Ford Foundation consultant for Latin America and Caribbean, 1967—; member of executive committee, behavioral science division, National Research Council, 1969-75; member of advisory committee on U.S.S.R. and Eastern Europe, National Academy of Sciences. Editor, Annual Reviews, Inc.; consulting editor for sociology, Little, Brown & Co. *Military service:* U.S. Army, 1943-46; research analyst in Division of U.S.S.R. Intelligence, Office of Strategic Services, 1943-45; assigned to Department of State, 1945-46; became sergeant.

MEMBER: World Association for Public Opinion Research, Society for the Study of Social Problems, Inter-American Society of Psychology, American Sociological Association (member of council and executive committee, 1960-63; president of section on social psychology, 1961; vice-president, 1975-76), Association for the Advancement of Slavic Studies (member of executive committee, 1961-63), American Psychological Association, American Association for Public Opinion Research, American Academy of Arts and Sciences (fellow), Eastern Sociological Society (member of executive committee, 1955-56; vice-president, 1958-59; president, 1960-61). *Awards, honors:* American Council of Learned Societies fellow, 1941-42; Social Science Research Council fellow, 1946-48, 1959-60; Kappa Tau Alpha Award, 1950, for *Public Opinion in Soviet Russia;* Grant Squires Prize for original investigation of a sociological nature, Columbia University, 1955; Center for Advanced Study in the Behavioral Sciences fellow, 1955-56; Foundations Fund for Research in Psychiatry fellow, 1957-60; Social Science Research Council Sociological Research fellow, 1959-60;

Russell Sage Foundation fellow, 1966; Hadley Cantril Award for *Becoming Modern;* Fulbright fellow, 1977; Guggenheim fellow, 1977-78.

WRITINGS: Public Opinion in Soviet Russia, Harvard University Press, 1950; (with Raymond B. Bauer and Clyde Kluckhohn) *How the Soviet System Works,* Harvard University Press, 1956; (with Bauer) *The Soviet Citizen: Daily Life in a Totalitarian Society,* Harvard University Press, 1959; (editor with H. Kent Geiger) *Soviet Society: A Book of Readings,* Houghton, 1961; *What Is Sociology?,* Prentice-Hall, 1964; (editor) *Readings in Modern Sociology,* Prentice-Hall, 1965; *Social Change in Soviet Russia,* Harvard University Press, 1968; (editor with Bernard Barber) *Stability and Social Change,* Little, Brown, 1971; (editor with Donald B. Holsinger) *Education and Individual Modernity in Developing Countries,* E. J. Brill, 1973; (with David H. Smith) *Becoming Modern: Individual Change in Six Developing Countries,* Harvard University Press, 1974; (editor with others) *Annual Review of Sociology,* Annual Reviews, Volume I, 1975, Volume II, 1976, Volume III, 1977, Volume V, 1979.

Contributor: *Communications Research 1948-49,* Harper, 1949; *Personality in Nature, Society, and Culture,* Knopf, 1953; *The World Influence of Communism,* University of Chicago Press, 1953; *Freedom and Control in Modern Society,* Van Nostrand, 1954; *Totalitarianism,* Harvard University Press, 1954; G. Lindzey, editor, *The Handbook of Social Psychology,* Addison-Wesley, Volume II, 1954, Volume III: *The Individual in a Social Context,* 2nd edition (Inkeles was not associated with earlier edition), 1969; *Psychoanalysis, Scientific Method and Philosophy,* New York University Press, 1959; *Sociology Today,* Basic Books, 1959; *The Transformation of Russian Society,* Harvard University Press, 1960; *Psychological Anthropology: Approaches to Culture and Personality,* Dorsey, 1961; Philip J. Allen, *Pitirim A. Sorokin in Review,* Duke University Press, 1963; Sigmund Koch, *Psychology: A Study of a Science,* McGraw, 1963; Myron Weiner, editor, *Modernization,* Basic Books, 1966; John Clausen, editor, *Socialization and Society,* Little, Brown, 1968; David A. Goslin, editor, *Handbook of Socialization Theory and Research,* Rand McNally, 1969.

J. C. McKinney and E. A. Tiryakian, editors, *Theoretical Sociology,* Appleton, 1970; A. R. Desai, editor, *Essays on Modernization of Underdeveloped Societies,* Volume II, Thacker, 1971; F.L.K. Hsu, editor, *Psychological Anthropology,* Schenkman, 1972; N. Hammon, editor, *Social Science and the New Societies: Problems in Cross-Cultural Research and Theory Building,* Michigan State University, 1973; C. S. Brembeck and T. J. Thompsin, editors, *New Strategies for Educational Development,* Heath, 1973; W. W. Taylor, J. L. Fisher, and E. Z. Vogt, *Culture and Life,* Southern Illinois University Press, 1973; Bertram S. Brown and E. Fuller Torrey, editors, *International Collaboration,* U.S. Government Printing Office, 1973; M. Kochen, editor, *Information for Action: From Knowledge to Wisdom,* Academic Press, 1975; George A. DeVos, editor, *Responses to Change,* D. Van Nostrand, 1976; Lewis Coser and Otto Larsen, editors, *The Uses of Controversy in Sociology,* Free Press, 1976; Mark G. Field, editor, *Social Consequences of Modernization in Communist Societies,* Johns Hopkins Press, 1976; G. C. Chu, S. A. Rahim, and D. L. Kincaid, editors, *Communication for Group Transformation in Development,* East-West Communication Institute, 1976; H. R. Bowen, editor, *Freedom and Control in a Democratic Society,* American Council on Life Insurance, 1977; Milton Yinger, editor, *Major Social Issues: A Multidisciplinary View,* Free Press, 1978.

Editor, "Foundations of Modern Sociology" series, Prentice-Hall. Contributor to professional journals and to *Atlantic, World Politics, New York Times Magazine,* and *Marriage and Family Living. Sociometry,* member of board of editors, 1955-61, associate editor, 1961-64; member of board of editors, *American Journal of Sociology,* 1956-59, and *Soviet Sociology,* 1962—; member of editorial committee, *Slavic Review,* 1961-73; member of board of consultants, *Psychoanalytic Review,* 1967-76.

* * *

IRWIN, John V(aleur) 1915-

PERSONAL: Born July 17, 1915, in Muskogee, Okla.; son of John Webb and Victoria (Vogel) Irwin; married Phyllis Stacy, January 15, 1944 (died December 3, 1975); married Evlyne Spears McDowell, January 15, 1977; children: (first marriage) John Owen, Nancy Ann. *Education:* Ohio Wesleyan University, B.A., 1937; Ohio State University, M.A., 1940; University of Wisconsin, Ph.D., 1947. *Home:* 4870 Briarcliff Ave., Memphis, Tenn. 38117. *Office:* Memphis Speech and Hearing Center, 807 Jefferson Ave., Memphis, Tenn. 38107.

CAREER: University of Washington, Seattle, associate speech pathologist, 1940-41; University of Minnesota, Minneapolis, assistant professor, 1947-49, associate professor of speech, 1949-50, director of speech science, 1947-50; University of Wisconsin—Madison, professor of speech and director of Speech Clinic, 1950-66; University of Kansas, Lawrence, Roy A. Roberts Professor of Speech Pathology and Audiology, 1966-70; Memphis State University, Memphis, Tenn., Pope M. Farrington Professor of Speech, 1970—. U.S. Office of Education, consultant, 1966—, member of Training Panel for Speech and Hearing, 1966-69, member of Early Education Panel, 1970; member, National Advisory Committee for the Handicapped, 1968-69; chairman of task force on three- and eight-year speech, language, and hearing, Colloborative Perinatal Project, National Institutes of Health, 1970-72. Member of board of directors, National Association of Hearing and Speech Agencies, 1962-67. *Military service:* U.S. Army Air Forces, 1942-46; became captain.

MEMBER: American Speech and Hearing Association (executive vice-president, 1963-66; president, 1968), American Academy of Aphasia, American Cleft Palate Association, Wisconsin Speech and Hearing Association (honorary life member). *Awards, honors:* Citation for distinguished service, Bureau of Education for the Handicapped, U.S. Office of Education, 1969; Honors of American Speech and Hearing Association, 1970.

WRITINGS: (With John Eisenson and Jeffrey J. Auer) *The Psychology of Communication,* Appleton, 1963; (with Marjorie Rosenberger) *Modern Speech,* Holt, 1961, revised edition, 1966.

(With Charles Van Riper) *Artikulationsstorungen Diagnose und Behandlung,* Carl Marhold Verlagsbuchhandlung, 1970; *Disorders of Articulation,* Bobbs-Merrill, 1972; (contributor) Alan J. Weston, editor, *Communicative Disorders: An Appraisal,* C. C Thomas, 1972; (editor with Michael Marge, and contributor) *Principles of Childhood Language Disabilities,* Appleton, 1972; (contributor) W. Dean Wolfe and Daniel J. Goulding, editors, *Articulation and Learning,* C. C Thomas, 1973, 2nd edition, in press; (contributor) Eldon Eagles, editor, *The Nervous System,* Volume III, Raven Press, 1975; (with A. J. Weston) *The Paired Stimuli Monograph,* Volume VI, Memphis State University, 1975; (editor with J. C. Kahane) *Proceedings of the Second Symposium on Auditory Processing and Learning Disabilities,* Volumes II and III, Memphis State University, 1975; (with M. Ward, C. Deen, and A. Greis) *The Lexington Developmental Scales,* revised edition, United Cerebral Palsy of the Bluegrass, 1977; (with M. Rosenberger and J. Sloan) *Speaking Effectively,* Holt, 1978; (contributor with M. Newhoff) Rolland Van Hattum, editor, *Introduction to Speech Pathology,* Macmillan, in press.

Conceived the idea, planned, and introduced each of eleven films in "Great Clinicians" series, University of Wisconsin, 1958-59. Contributor to *Encyclopedia of Education* and to journals in his field. Editor, *Acta Symbolica* (publication of International Association for Symbolic Analysis), 1972—.

WORK IN PROGRESS: With S. P. Wong, *Design and Analysis in Communication Disorders,* for Grune & Stratton; with Wong, *Phonological Development Monograph,* for Southern Illinois University Press; with M. Marge, revised edition of *Childhood Language Disabilities,* for Prentice-Hall.

* * *

IRWIN-WILLIAMS, Cynthia (Cora) 1936-
(Cynthia C. Irwin)

PERSONAL: Born April 14, 1936, in Denver, Colo.; daughter of Floyd William (a statistician) and Eleanor Cynthia (Evans) Irwin; married David C. Williams (a nuclear physicist), September 8, 1962. *Education:* Radcliffe College, B.A. (magna cum laude), 1957, M.A., 1958; Harvard University, Ph.D., 1963. *Home:* 1300 Espanola N.E., Albuquerque, N.M. 87110. *Office:* Department of Anthropology, Eastern New Mexico University, Portales, N.M. 88130.

CAREER: Hunter College of the City University of New York, New York, N.Y., lecturer in anthropology, 1963-64; Eastern New Mexico University, Portales, assistant professor, 1964-67, associate professor, 1967-73, professor, 1973-77, distinguished professor of anthropology, 1977—, director of Humanities Division, 1976-77. Has conducted research in central Mexico, Wyoming, Puebla (Mexico), New Mexico, and the San Juan Valley; delegate to international congresses.

MEMBER: American Anthropological Association (fellow), American Quaternary Association (member of council), Society for American Archaeology (member of executive committee), American Association for the Advancement of Science, American Association of University Professors, Rocky Mountain Association for the Advancement of Science, New Mexico Academy of Science, Phi Beta Kappa, Sigma Xi, Phi Kappa Phi. *Awards, honors:* Grants for research from American Philosophical Society, 1962-66, National Science Foundation, 1962-66, 1964-69, 1966-67, American Museum of Natural History, 1963-64, Wenner-Gren Foundation, 1968-71, National Geographic Society, 1971-73, and National Endowment for the Humanities, 1972-74.

WRITINGS—Published by Paleo-Indian Institute, Eastern New Mexico University, except as indicated: (With brother, Henry Irwin; under name, Cynthia C. Irwin) *Excavations at the LoDaiska Site,* Denver Museum of Natural History, 1959; (with H. Irwin) *Excavations at Magic Mountain,* Denver Museum of Natural History, 1966; (editor) *Early Man in Western North America,* 1968; (editor) *Contributions to Southwestern Prehistory,* Eastern New Mexico University Press, 1968; (with S. Tompkins) *Excavations at En Medio, Shelter, New Mexico,* 1968; (editor) *Archaic Prehistory in the Western United States,* 1968; (editor) *The Structure of Chacoan Society in the Northern Southwest,* 1972; *The Oshara Tradition: Origins of Anasazi Culture,* 1973; (with others) *Salmon Ruin Archeological Investigations,* Office of Archeology and Historic Preservation, National Park Service, Department of the Interior, 1975. Also author of *Preceramic and Early Ceramic Development in Central Mexico.*

Contributor to conferences, annals, symposia, and proceedings. Contributor of articles to anthropology and archeology journals, including *American Antiquity, National Geographic, Earth and Planetary Science Letters, Quaternary Research, Science,* and *Wyoming Archaeologist.* Editor of "Contributions in Anthropology" series, Eastern New Mexico University, 1968—, and *Newsletter* of the American Quaternary Association, 1969—.

WORK IN PROGRESS: The Growth of Theory in American Archaeology and *Directions in American Archaeology,* both for Random House.

* * *

ISBISTER, Jean Sinclair 1915-
(Clair Isbister)

PERSONAL: Born September 12, 1915, in Brisbane, Australia; daughter of Peter Sinclair and Hannah (Beet) Paton; married James Isbister, 1940; children: Peter, James, Helen, John. *Education:* University of Sydney, M.B., B.S., 1939, F.R.A.C.P., 1958, D.C.H. (London), 1949. *Religion:* Presbyterian. *Home:* 12 Wilona Ave., Wollstonecraft, Sydney, Australia. *Office:* North Shore Medical Center, 66 Pacific Highway, St. Leonards, Australia.

CAREER: Has practiced as specialist consultant pediatrician, 1949—; honorary pediatrician, Royal North Shore Hospital of Sydney; lecturer, Kindergarten Training College and University of Sydney. Honorary director, Child Care Center, Royal North Shore Hospital; member of advisory committee, International Childbirth Education Association and Nursing Mothers Association of Australia; member of Australian Government Committee of Non-Governmental Organizations for International Year of the Child, 1979. *Member:* Australian Pediatric Association, Medical Women's Society (committee member), National Council of Women (convenor, Health Australia and Health, Child and Family, New South Wales), Asthma Welfare Society of New South Wales (committee member). *Awards, honors:* Officer Order of the British Empire, 1969, for service to mothers and babies; Commander Order of the British Empire, 1977, for service to medicine.

WRITINGS—All under name Clair Isbister: *The A.B.C. of Motherhood,* Australian Broadcasting Commission, 1954; *What Is Your Problem, Mother?,* Angus & Robertson, 1958, C. C Thomas, 1960; *Preparing for Motherhood,* Angus & Robertson, 1963; *Birth, Infancy and Childhood: Parents' Guide to Child Care,* A. H. & A. W. Reed, 1965; *Living with Children,* Winchester, 1966; *Birth of a Family,* Thomas Nelson (Australia), 1977, Hawthorn, 1978; *Mommy, I Feel Sick,* Hawthorn, 1978. Contributor of articles on health to lay magazines and articles on technical topics to medical journals. Editor, *Asthma Welfare Society Journal.*

WORK IN PROGRESS: A book, *When Shall I Call the Doctor,* for Thomas Nelson; booklets for use by adolescents in Education for Living programs; articles to promote and strengthen family life for International Year of the Child, 1979.

SIDELIGHTS: Jean Sinclair Isbister told *CA:* "I write because of my firm conviction that children are primarily the responsibility of their parents, and parents will not only care for them better but enjoy them more if they know more about them. Thus, my books are aimed at helping parents, and so improving the lot of children. I also believe that governments should support the family system, and give priority to those men and women who commit themselves to the long term care of their children." In addition, Isbister says that parents should be willing to "accept the responsibility" for their children. She continues, "I believe that men and women have complementary roles in the family."

Isbister has appeared on several television and radio programs to discuss child care and controversial health, moral, and family issues.

* * *

ITSE, Elizabeth M(yers) 1930-

PERSONAL: Born September 28, 1930, in Washburn, Wis.; daughter of Laurence Cooley and Frances (Drescher) Myers; married Donald Otis Itse, January 22, 1955 (divorced, 1974); children: Daniel Christofferson, Karl Laurence. *Education:* Summer study at University of Iowa, 1951; Connecticut College for Women (now Connecticut College), B.A., 1952; Boston University, graduate study, 1967-69. *Home:* 43 Greenwood St., Sherborn, Mass. 01770. *Office:* Myers Associates, 5 Powderhouse Lane, Sherborn, Mass. 01770.

CAREER: Modern Handcraft, Inc., Sherborn, Mass., office manager, 1972-79; Myers Associates (advertising firm), Sherborn, president, 1979—. Secretary of Sherborn Yacht Club, Inc., 1971—.

WRITINGS: (Editor) *Hey Bug! And Other Poems about Little Things,* American Heritage Press, 1972; (illustrator) Stephen Falk, *Sailing Racing Rules the Easy Way,* St. Martin's, 1972, revised edition, 1973.

WORK IN PROGRESS: ZAT, a children's book.

SIDELIGHTS: Elizabeth M. Itse told *CA:* "Writing is a most important communication of the direct selling technique—in that if the copy is not read the product will not be sold." *Avocational interests:* Sailing, small boat racing.

* * *

IVRY, Alfred Lyon 1935-

PERSONAL: Born January 14, 1935, in Brooklyn, N.Y.; son of Morris (a businessman) and Belle (Malamud) Ivry; married Joann Saltzman (a social worker), June 15, 1958; children: Rebecca Ann, Jonathan, Sara Beth, Jessica. *Education:* Brooklyn College (now Brooklyn College of the City University of New York), B.A., 1957; Brandeis University, M.A., 1958, Ph.D., 1963; Oxford University, D.Phil., 1971. *Politics:* Democrat. *Religion:* Jewish. *Home:* 154 Randlett Park, Newton, Mass. 02165. *Office:* Department of Near Eastern and Judaic Studies, Brandeis University, Waltham, Mass.

CAREER: Cornell University, Ithaca, N.Y., assistant professor, 1967-71, associate professor of Arabic and Hebrew studies, 1971-74; Ohio State University, Columbus, professor of philosophy and Jewish studies, 1974-76; Brandeis University, Waltham, Mass., professor of Islamic and Jewish philosophy, 1976—. *Member:* Societe Internationale pour l'Etude de la Philosophie Medievale, American Oriental Society, Mediaeval Academy of America. *Awards, honors:* Fulbright research awards to England, 1963-65, and to Tunisia, 1972-73; National Endowment for the Humanities research awards, 1973 and 1979, and award for teaching summer seminar, 1976.

WRITINGS: (Author of introduction and commentary) *Al-Kindi's Metaphysics* (a translation of al-Kindi's treatise "On First Philosophy"), State University of New York Press, 1972; *Moses of Narbonne's "The Perfection of the Soul": A Critical Edition of the Hebrew Manuscript,* Israel Academy of Sciences (Jerusalem), 1977. Contributor to *Encyclopaedia Judaica* and to *Journal of the American Oriental Society, Philosophical Forum,* and *Jewish Quarterly Review.*

WORK IN PROGRESS: Translation of and commentary on Averroes' middle commentary on Aristotle's *De Anima.*

J

JACKINS, Harvey 1916-

PERSONAL: Born June 28, 1916, in Idaho; son of Harvey Wilson (a farmer) and Caroline (a teacher; maiden name, Moland) Jackins; married Dorothy Diehl, September 2, 1939; children: Gordon, Tim, Sarah, Chris. *Education:* University of Washington, Seattle, B.A., 1959. *Religion:* Methodist. *Home:* 719 2nd Ave. N., Seattle, Wash. 98109. *Office:* Personal Counselors, Inc., Seattle, Wash.

CAREER: Personal Counselors, Inc., Seattle, Wash., president, 1951—. International reference person for Reevaluation Counseling Communities, 1971—. *Member:* American Association for the Advancement of Science, American Mathematical Society, Mathematical Association of America, American Geophysical Union, Amonii Socii, Phi Beta Kappa, Phi Lambda Upsilon, Pi Mu Epsilon.

WRITINGS—All published by Rational Island: *The Human Side of Human Beings,* 1965; *The Meaningful Holiday,* 1970; *The Human Situation,* 1973; *Zest Is Best,* 1973; *Quotes,* 1975; *Rough Notes from Liberation I and II,* 1976; *The Upward Trend,* 1978; *Rough Notes from Buck Creek I,* 1979.

WORK IN PROGRESS: Questions and Answers on Reevaluation Counseling; The Benign Reality.

* * *

JACKMAN, Sydney W(ayne) 1925-

PERSONAL: Born March 25, 1925, in Fullerton, Calif.; son of Ensleigh Ellsworth and Dorothy (Anfield) Jackman. *Education:* University of Washington, B.S., 1946, M.A., 1947; Harvard University, A.M., 1948, Ph.D., 1953. *Religion:* Anglican. *Home:* 1065 Deal St., Victoria, British Columbia, Canada. *Office:* Clerihue Bldg., B218, University of Victoria, Victoria, British Columbia, Canada.

CAREER: Harvard University, Cambridge, Mass., tutor, 1949-52; Phillips Exeter Academy, Exeter, N.H., instructor in history, 1952-56; Bates College, Lewiston, Me., assistant professor, 1956-62, associate professor, 1962-64; University of Victoria, Victoria, British Columbia, associate professor, 1964-65, professor, 1965—. Clare College, Cambridge University, visiting scholar, 1961-62, member and associate of faculty board of history, 1971-72; visiting professor, University of Michigan, summer, 1965, and University of Tasmania, 1972; visiting fellow, Australian National University, 1975; visiting scholar, Trinity Hall, Cambridge University, 1978. *Military service:* U.S. Army. *Member:* Royal Historical Society (fellow), Society for Army Historical Research, Society for the Preservation of New England Antiquities, Authors Club (London), American Antiquarian Society, Massachusetts Historical Society, Colonial Society of Massachusetts. *Awards, honors:* Rockefeller reserach grant, 1961-62; American Philosophical Society research grant, 1965.

WRITINGS: Galloping Head, Phoenix, 1958; *A Diary in America,* Knopf, 1962; *March to Saratoga,* Macmillan (Canada), 1963; *Man of Mercury* (biography), Pall Mall, 1965; *English Reform Tradition,* Prentice-Hall, 1965; (editor) Henry St. John Bolingbroke, *Idea of a Patriot King,* Bobbs-Merrill, 1965; (editor with John F. Freeman) *American Voyageur: Journal of David Bates Douglass,* Marquette County Historical Society, 1969; (editor with Berangere Steel) *Romanov Relations,* Macmillan (London), 1969; *Portraits of the Premiers,* Gray's Publishing, 1969; *A Middle Passage,* Atheneum, 1970; *Vancouver Island,* David & Charles (England), 1972; *The Men at Cary Castle,* Morriss Printing, 1972; *Tasmania,* David & Charles, 1974; *Nicholas Cardinal Wiseman,* University Press of Virginia, 1977; (editor) *Acton in America: The American Journal of Sir John Acton, 1853,* Patmos Press, 1979. Also author of *A Slave to Duty: A Portrait Sketch of Sir John Arthur,* Hawthorn. Member of editorial advisory board, *American Neptune.* Contributor to historical journals.

WORK IN PROGRESS: Correspondence of Lady Malet; a study of women; an article on *Fraser's* magazine.

BIOGRAPHICAL/CRITICAL SOURCES: Times Literary Supplement, December 18, 1969.

* * *

JACKSON, Donald Dale 1935-

PERSONAL: Born July 18, 1935, in San Francisco, Calif.; son of Zalph Boone (an attorney) and Jean (Shuler) Jackson; married Joyce Darlene Hall, November 8, 1958; children: Dale Allen, Amy Lynn. *Education:* Attended Northwestern University, 1953-54; Stanford University, A.B., 1957; Columbia University, M.A., 1958. *Home address:* Saddle Ridge Rd., Route 4, Newtown, Conn. 06470. *Agent:* John Hawkins, Paul R. Reynolds, Inc., 12 East 41st St., New York, N.Y. 10017.

CAREER: United Press International, San Francisco, Calif., reporter, 1961-63; *Life* (magazine), New York, N.Y., reporter and staff writer, 1963-72; free-lance writer, 1972—. *Military service:* U.S. Army, Counter Intelligence Corps, 1958-60. *Awards, honors:* Nieman fellow, 1965-66; National Headliners Club award, 1969, for an article on the trial of Dr. Benjamin Spock.

WRITINGS: Judges, Atheneum, 1974; *Sagebrush Country,* Time-Life, 1974 (with Peter Wood) *The Sierra Madre,* Time-Life, 1975; *Gold Dust,* Knopf, 1980; *The Aeronauts,* Time-Life, 1980. Contributor to *Life, Readers Digest, Sports Illustrated, New Times, New West, American Heritage,* and other periodicals.

SIDELIGHTS: Donald Dale Jackson writes: "I have been writing for pay since I was thirteen, when the local newspaper gave me five cents an inch for covering high school tennis. I have always felt most alive, most pained, and most satisfied when writing. My father, a sportswriter in his youth, inspired in me a love of writing and language which I have retained. My book on U.S. judges grew out of a long fascination with the law and our system of justice in theory and practice. I am interested in many other aspects of contemporary American life—nature, the environment, sports and politics, to name a few. More broadly, I am interested in the individual and collective components of the American character."

AVOCATIONAL INTERESTS: Travel, sports, music.

BIOGRAPHICAL/CRITICAL SOURCES: Bridgeport Sunday Post, May 5, 1974.

* * *

JACKSON, W(illiam) T(homas) H(obdell) 1915-

PERSONAL: Born April 2, 1915, in Sheffield, England; came to United States, 1948, naturalized citizen, 1957; son of William Arthur and Harriet Sarah (Williams) Jackson; married Erika Anna Maria Noltemeyer, 1945; children: Thomas Christian Hobdell, Inge Anna Maria, Christopher Michael Peter. *Education:* Sheffield University, B.A., 1935, M.A., 1938; University of Washington, Ph.D., 1951. *Home:* 90 Morningside Dr., New York, N.Y. 10027. *Office:* Columbia University, West 116th St., New York, N.Y. 10027.

CAREER: University of Washington, Seattle, instructor in German, 1948-50; Coe College, Cedar Rapids, Iowa, assistant professor of German Classics, 1950-52; Columbia University, New York, N.Y., assistant professor of German, 1952-55, associate professor of German and comparative literature, 1955-58, professor, 1958-73, Villard Professor of German and Comparative Literature, 1973—, chairman of German department, 1961-67. Visiting professor at University of Chicago, 1955, Princeton University, 1957, Rutgers University, 1963, Duke University, 1965, Yale University, 1966, City University of New York, 1975-77, and Fordham University, 1977; Phi Beta Kappa Visiting Scholar, 1965-66. *Military service:* British Royal Artillery, 1940-46; became captain. *Member:* Modern Humanities Research Association, Mediaeval Academy (fellow). *Awards, honors:* Guggenheim fellow, 1958-59, and 1967-68; American Council of Learned Societies grants, 1968 and 1972.

WRITINGS: (Contributor) R. S. Loomis, editor, *Arthurian Literature in the Middle Ages,* Clarendon Press, 1959; *The Literature of the Middle Ages,* Columbia University Press, 1960; (editor) *Essential Works of Erasmus,* Bantam, 1965; *Medieval Literature: A History and Guide,* Collier Books, 1966; (contributor) John H. Fisher, editor, *The Medieval Literature of Western Europe,* Modern Language Association of America, 1966; *An Anthology of German Literature to 1750,* Prentice-Hall, 1967; (contributor) Fowkes and Sanders, editors, *Studies in Germanic Languages and Literature,* Adler, 1967; (contributor) F. X. Newman, editor, *The Meaning of Courtly Love,* State University of New York Press, 1968; (contributor) Stanley N. Werbow, editor, *Formal Aspects of Medieval German Poetry,* University of Texas Press, 1969; (contributor) *Festschrift for Francis Utley,* Rutgers University Press, 1970; *The Anatomy of Love: The Tristan of Gottfried von Strassburg,* Columbia University Press, 1971; (contributor) E. P. Mahoney, editor, *Philosophy and Humanism: Renaissance Essays in Honor of Paul Oskar Kristeller,* Columbia University Press, 1976; (author of introduction) H. Oskar Sommer, editor, *Vulgate Version of Arthurian Romances,* Volume I, AMS Press, 1978; *The Interpretation of Medieval Lyric,* Macmillan (London), 1979, Columbia University Press, 1980. Editor, Columbia University Press series, "Records of Civilization." Contributor of articles to professional publications in the United States and Germany.

WORK IN PROGRESS: A short book, *The Hero and the King—A Study of an Epic Theme; The Image of the Ruler.*

* * *

JACO, E(gbert) Gartly 1923-

PERSONAL: Born October 5, 1923, in Memphis, Tenn.; son of Oscar Hubert and Delzell (Simpson) Jaco; married Adele Marie Bolles, 1947; children: Linda Dell, Jerry Monroe, Andrew Richard, John Douglas. *Education:* University of Texas, B.A., 1949, M.A., 1950; University of Chicago, graduate study, 1951; Northwestern University, Ph.D., 1954. *Home:* 4519 Woodrow Ave., Galveston, Tex. 77550. *Office:* Preventive Medicine and Community Health, University of Texas Medical Branch, Galveston, Tex. 77550.

CAREER: University of Texas at Austin, instructor in sociology, 1952-55; University of Texas Medical Branch, Galveston, associate professor of medical sociology, 1955-59, director of Division of Medical Sociology, 1957-59; Western Reserve University (now Case Western Reserve University), Cleveland, Ohio, associate professor of sociology, 1959-62, research fellow in department of surgery, 1960-62, research associate in School of Dentistry, 1961-62; University of Minnesota, Minneapolis, 1962-66, began as associate professor, became professor of sociology, research director and director of doctoral program in School of Public Health; University of California, Riverside, professor of sociology, 1966-78, chairman of department, 1966-70; Trinity University, San Antonio, Tex., professor of sociology, 1976-78; University of Texas Medical Branch, Galveston, professor of preventive medicine and community health and director of Division of Health Behavior, 1978—. Visiting lecturer, Loma Linda University, 1966-75; visiting professor, University of California, Los Angeles, 1969-71, and University of California, Irvine, spring, 1974; adjunct professor, Health Science Center, University of Texas at San Antonio, 1976-78. Research consultant and director, Board of Texas State Hospitals and Special Schools, 1953-56; director, Laboratory of Socio-Environmental Studies, Cleveland Psychiatric Institute, 1959-61, and Special Aid to Dependent Children Project (Cleveland), 1961-62; research director, St. Luke's Hospital (St. Paul), 1964-66. Delegate to White House Conference on Aging (member of technical committee on health); member of research advisory committee, California State Department of Mental Hygiene. Consultant to several hospitals and health agencies; principle investigator of various health and research projects. Member of Citizens Advisory Council, California State Health Department. *Military:* U.S. Army Air Forces, 1943-46; became staff sargeant.

MEMBER: American Sociological Association (fellow; member of council, medical sociology section, 1969-72; visiting scientist, 1964-66), International Sociological Association, American Psychological Association, American Public Health Association (fellow), Conference on Social Sciences and Health (member of executive council, 1978—), American Orthopsychiatric Association (honorary fellow), American Hospital Association, Gerontological Society, American Association for the Advancement of Science, Royal Society of Health, Southwestern Sociological Association, Sigma Xi. *Awards, honors:* Russell Sage Foundation grant for project in social science and mental health, 1955-57; fellow, Summer Training Institute on Social Gerontology, University of Michigan and University of Connecticut, 1958; James A. Hamilton Book Award, American College of Hospital Administrators, 1974.

WRITINGS: (Editor and contributor) *Patients, Physicians and Illness: Sourcebook in Behavioral Science and Medicine,* Free Press, 1958, 3rd edition, 1979; *The Social Epidemiology of Mental Disorders: A Psychiatric Survey of Texas,* Russell Sage Foundation, 1960; (editor) *Cost Accountability for Health Services in the United States,* Center for Continuing Education in Health Administration, Trinity University Press, 1977; (editor) *Evolving National Health Policy: Effects on Institutional Providers,* Center for Professional Development in Health Administration, Trinity University Press, 1978. Also author of *Continuing Professional Education in Health Administration in the Southwest.*

Contributor: R. F. Winch, R. McGinnis, and H. Harrington, editors, *Selected Studies on Marriage and the Family,* Holt, 1953; (with I. C. Belknap) *The Epidemiology of Mental Disorders in a Political-Type City,* Milbank Memorial Fund, 1953; (with Belknap) M. B. Sussman, editor, *Sourcebook in Marriage and the Family,* Houghton, 1954; Sussman, editor, *Community Structure and Analysis,* Crowell, 1959; M. K. Opler, editor, *Culture and Mental Health,* Macmillan, 1959; *Causes of Mental Disorders: A Review of the Epidemiological Knowledge,* Milbank Memorial Fund, 1959; K. Young and R. Macks, editors, *Principles of Sociology,* American Book Co., 1960; L. J. DeGroot, editor, *Medical Care: Social and Organizational Aspects,* C. C Thomas, 1966; G. Gordon, editor, *Proceedings: Conference on Medical Sociology and Disease Control,* Health Information Foundation, 1966; S. Levine and N. Scotch, editors, *Social Stress,* Aldine, 1970; B. S. Georgopoulos and F. C. Mann, editors, *Organization Research on Health Institutions,* Institute for Social Research, University of Michigan Press, 1972. Also contributor to *Proceedings of the Invitational Conference on Research on Nurse Staffing in Hospitals,* 1973.

Contributor of numerous articles and book reviews to professional and medical health journals. Co-founder and editor-in-chief, *Journal of Health and Human Behavior,* 1960-66; member of editorial board, *Inquiry.*

* * *

JACOBS, Francine 1935-

PERSONAL: Born May 11, 1935, in New York, N.Y.; daughter of Louis (a glove manufacturer) and Ida (Schrag) Kaufman; married Jerome L. Jacobs (a psychiatrist), June 10, 1956; children: Laurie, Larry. *Education:* Queens College (now Queens College of the City University of New York), B.A., 1956. *Home:* 93 Old Farm Rd., Pleasantville, N.Y. 10570.

CAREER: Elementary school teacher in Rye, N.Y., 1956-58, and Chappaqua, N.Y., 1967-68. *Member:* Authors Guild. *Awards, honors:* Outstanding science book for children award from National Science Teachers Association and Children's Book Council, 1975, for *The Sargasso Sea.*

WRITINGS—Juvenile books; published by Morrow, except as indicated: *The Wisher's Handbook,* Funk, 1968; *The Legs of the Moon,* Coward, 1971; *The King's Ditch,* Coward, 1971; *Sea Turtles,* 1972; *The Freshwater Eel,* 1973; *Nature's Light: The Story of Bioluminescence,* 1974; *The Sargasso Sea: An Ocean Desert,* 1975; *A Secret Language of Animals: Communication by Pheromones,* 1976; *Sounds in the Sea,* 1977; *The Red Sea,* 1978; *Africa's Flamingo Lake,* 1979; *Sewer Sam,* Walker & Co., 1979; *Coral,* Putnam, 1980; *Fire Snake: The Railroad That Changed East Africa,* 1980.

WORK IN PROGRESS: A book on the Bermuda petrel, for Morrow; a book on the barracuda, for Walker & Co.; a dinosaur book, for Putnam.

SIDELIGHTS: Francine Jacobs writes: "Camping experiences with my family in shore and wilderness areas have stimulated my interest in ecology and nature science." *Avocational interests:* Travel, hiking, fishing, beachcombing, reading, cooking, gardening.

BIOGRAPHICAL/CRITICAL SOURCES: Washington Post Book World, January 13, 1980.

* * *

JACOBS, Louis 1920-

PERSONAL: Born July 17, 1920, in Manchester, England; son of Harry and Lena (Myerstone) Jacobs; married Shulamith Lisagorsky, 1944; children: Ivor, Naomi, David. *Education:* University College, London, B.A. (honors), 1946, Ph.D., 1952; Manchester Talmudical College, Rabbinical Diploma, 1941. *Home:* 37 Marlborough Hill, London N.W. 8, England.

CAREER: Central Synagogue, Manchester, England, rabbi, 1948-52; New West End Synagogue, London, England, rabbi, 1952-60; Jews' College, London, tutor, 1960-62; New London Synagogue, London, rabbi, 1964—.

WRITINGS: We Have Reason to Believe, Vallentine, Mitchell, 1959, 3rd edition, 1965; *Jewish Values,* Vallentine, Mitchell, 1960, 2nd edition, Hartmore, 1969; *Studies in Talmudic Logic,* Vallentine, Mitchell, 1962; (translator) Dobh Baer Schneor Zalman, *Tract on Ecstasy,* Vallentine, Mitchell, 1963; *Principles of the Jewish Faith,* Basic Books, 1964; *Seeker of Unity: The Life and Works of Aaron of Starosselje,* Basic Books, 1966; *Jewish Law,* Behrman, 1968; *Faith,* Basic Books, 1968; (editor) *Jewish Ethics, Philosophy and Mysticism,* Behrman, 1969; *Jewish Thought Today,* Behrman, 1970; *Hasidic Prayer,* Schocken, 1972; *What Does Judaism Say About . . .?,* Quadrangle, 1973; *Jewish Biblical Exegesis,* Behrman, 1973; *A Jewish Theology,* Behrman, 1973; *Theology in the Responsa,* Routledge & Kegan Paul, 1975; *Hasidic Thought,* Behrman, 1976; *Jewish Mystical Testimony,* Schocken, 1977. Contributor to theology publications.

WORK IN PROGRESS: Talmudic reasoning and literary analysis of the Talmud.

BIOGRAPHICAL/CRITICAL SOURCES: Times Literary Supplement, February 2, 1967.

* * *

JAFFE, Irma B(lumenthal)

PERSONAL: Born in New Orleans, La.; daughter of Harry

and Estelle (Blumenthal) Levy; married Samuel B. Jaffe; children: Yvonne Kovshak. *Education:* Columbia University, B.S., 1958, M.A., 1960, Ph.D., 1966. *Home:* 880 Fifth Ave., New York, N.Y. 10021. *Office:* Department of Fine Arts, Fordham University, Bronx, N.Y. 10458.

CAREER: Whitney Museum of American Art, New York, N.Y., research curator, 1964-66; Fordham University, Bronx, N.Y., assistant professor, 1966-68, associate professor, 1968-72, professor of art history, 1972—, chairman of department, 1966—. *Member:* American Studies Association, American Society for Eighteenth Century Studies, College Art Association, Phi Beta Kappa.

WRITINGS: Joseph Stella, Harvard University Press, 1970; (editor with Rudolf Wittkower) *Baroque Art: The Jesuit Contribution,* Fordham University Press, 1972; *"The Emergence of the Avant-Garde": The Genius of American Painting,* Weidenfeld & Nicholson, 1973; *John Trumbull: Patriot-Artist of the American Revolution,* New York Graphic Society, 1975; *Trumbull: The Declaration of Independence,* Penguin, 1976; *The Sculpture of Leonard Baskin,* Viking, 1980. Writer and narrator of television series, "Project Now: Introduction to Art History," WABC-TV (New York), 1969-70. Former art editor, *Main Currents in Modern Thought.*

SIDELIGHTS: Irma B. Jaffe wrote *CA:* "As an art historian, I like to write art historical biographies because in the process of studying an artist's life and his art, I learn something about the relationship between the creative personality and that strange phenomenon called style. Combining intellectual history and visual analysis, this kind of research makes the writer's life work a pleasure."

* * *

JAVITS, Jacob K(oppel) 1904-

PERSONAL: Born May 18, 1904, in New York, N.Y.; son of Morris and Ida (Littman) Javits; married Marion Ann Borris, 1947; children: Joy, Joshua, Carla. *Education:* Attended Columbia University; New York University, LL.B., 1926. *Politics:* Republican. *Religion:* Jewish. *Home:* 911 Park Ave., New York, N.Y. *Office:* 110 East 45th St., New York, N.Y. 10017; and 321 Russell Senate Office Building, Washington, D.C. 20510.

CAREER: Admitted to Bar of State of New York, 1927; member of law firm, Javits & Javits, New York City, 1927-54; began political career as active campaigner in reform movement of Mayor Fiorello La Guardia, New York City, 1937; elected to U.S. House of Representatives and served four terms as representative from Twenty-first Congressional District, 1946-54; attorney general of state of New York, 1954-56; U.S. senator from State of New York, 1956—; member of law firm, Javits, Trubin, Sillcocks & Edelman, New York City, 1958-71. Ranking minority member of Senate Foreign Relations Committee; member of Labor and Human Resources Committee, Government Affairs Committee, and Joint Economic Committee. Member of numerous Senate subcommittees, including European Affairs Subcommittee, Education, Arts, and Humanities Subcommittee, and International Economic Policy Subcommittee. Chairman of economic committee, Parliamentarian's Conference, North Atlantic Treaty Organization (NATO); U.S. delegate to United Nations General Assembly, 1970; member of National Commission on Marijuana and Drug Abuse, 1971-73. Special (civilian) assistant to chief of Chemical Warfare Service, U.S. Army, 1941-42. National vice-chairman, Anti-Defamation League of B'nai B'rith; member of board of directors, American Jewish Committee, Ballet Theatre Foundation, Negro Actor's Guild of America, and National Association for the Prevention of Addiction to Narcotics; trustee, Federation of Jewish Philanthropies, Freedom House, Jewish Theological Seminary, and American Israel Cultural Foundation; member of national council, Boy Scouts of America, Committee for the International University in America, Inc., and Paderewski Foundation. Lecturer on economic and political issues. Member of legislative advisory committee, Reserve Officers Association. *Military service:* U.S. Army, Chemical Warfare Service, 1942-45; served in European and Pacific Theaters; became lieutenant colonel; received Legion of Merit. New York National Guard, 1946-64; became colonel.

MEMBER: American Judicature Society, National Association for the Advancement of Colored People, American Legion, Veterans of Foreign Wars, Jewish War Veterans (honorary national commander), Republican Club (New York City), Capitol Hill Club (Washington), Army and Navy Club (Washington), City Athletic Club. *Awards, honors:* Has received honorary degrees from thirty-six colleges and universities, including New York University, Yeshiva University, Dartmouth College, Jewish Theological Seminary, and Colgate University.

WRITINGS: Discrimination, U.S.A., Harcourt, 1960; *Order of Battle: A Republican's Call to Reason,* Atheneum, 1964; (with Donald Kellerman) *Who Makes War: The President versus Congress,* Morrow, 1973. Contributor to periodicals, including *Reporter, Esquire, New York Times Sunday Magazine,* and *Look.*

WORK IN PROGRESS: An autobiography and collection of political memoirs, with Rafael Steinberg.

SIDELIGHTS: Jacob Javits's first book, *Discrimination, U.S.A.,* details the history—particularly the legal history—of racial prejudice in the United States and how it has affected a number of minority groups. A critic for *Kirkus Reviews* says that "the liberal Senior Senator from New York has written a forceful, hopeful book about discrimination and the changes which have taken place—certainly in the legal and statutory aspects—in the last twenty years." R. S. Derby calls the work "a serious book on a serious subject by a serious author. . . . It is, in fact, authoritative to the last degree." Anthony Lewis, however, found that despite Senator Javits's legal background, "there is almost a total lack of legal sophistication; the really hard questions that face legislators and judges in the civil-rights area are passed over in generalities. . . . He rightly rejects the theory that law is powerless to change patterns of society. It is somewhat astonishing therefore, to find him quoting with approval President Eisenhower's unfortunate bromide to the effect that law cannot change prejudice in the hearts of men."

A. H. Raskin says that Javits has spent much of his time in Congress explaining why he is a Republican when his political views are usually more closely aligned with the thinking of Democrats. In *Order of Battle: A Republican's Call to Reason,* the author outlines his political philosophy and tries to restate the principles upon which his party was built. W. D. Burnham calls it "a tract for the times, a book which is both a political *apologia pro vita sua* and a call to his party colleagues to return to the G.O.P.'s great liberal-national tradition. . . . The fact is that the tradition upon which Senator Javits relies has not really been a part of the mainstream of Republican thinking or voting since the Roosevelt Progressives, by bolting the G.O.P. in 1912, turned its organizational machinery over to its right wing. . . . What Senator Javits has to say in this book is well worth saying." Roscoe

Drummond feels that *Order of Battle* "is not just another political tract dispensing cliches and partisan eye-wash. It is written from the mind as well as from the heart; it is written from experience (Mr. Javits has experienced personal poverty and earned affluence) as well as from reason." W. A. Rusher calls Javits "one of the most accomplished practitioners of the religious bullet-vote that has ever graced the polyglot New York scene." But the reviewer believes that "such a man may be hard to beat, but he is not necessarily worth listening to." Rusher goes on to say that the book "is written in a kind of sly, all-things-to-all-men prose that makes of cogency just another outmoded eighteenth-century virtue." Raskin, however, disagrees; he writes: "Javits's views deserve much more respect than most Republican kingmakers ever accord them. He bespeaks the case of 'metropolitan man' in tones of sanity and sophistication."

Senator Javits's latest work, *Who Makes War: The President versus Congress,* traces the history of the power to commit the United States to a state of war from the beginning of the country to the present. The book also explains the rationale behind the War Powers Bill, sponsored by Javits, which was passed in 1973 over the veto of President Richard Nixon and which is designed to limit the power of a president to commit U.S. troops to combat without the approval of Congress. In a review of the book, Scott Wright says: "Stressing the role of such strong Presidential personalities as Washington, Jefferson, Polk, Lincoln, TR, Wilson, and FDR in establishing key precedents but treating as well many less dramatic instances of Presidential usurpation, this work is highly recommended for any reader wishing to know why some resurrection of the Congressional role in making war has become of vital importance for our future." P. B. Kurland finds that *Who Makes War* is "well written and makes for easy reading. Indeed, one hardly recognizes the polemic nature of the offering. With the result, perhaps, that the lesson it is intended to convey may not be received."

AVOCATIONAL INTERESTS: Tennis, squash, swimming.

BIOGRAPHICAL/CRITICAL SOURCES: Christian Science Monitor, October 10, 1960; *Kirkus Reviews,* August 15, 1960; *New York Herald Tribune Book Review,* October 2, 1960; *New York Times Book Review,* October 2, 1960, April 26, 1964, October 14, 1973; *Times Literary Supplement,* April 7, 1961; *Commonweal,* June 12, 1964; *National Review,* June 30, 1964; *Saturday Review,* May 23, 1964; *Library Journal,* August, 1973.

* * *

JENKINS, (John) Robin 1912-

PERSONAL: Born September 11, 1912, in Cambuslang, Lanarkshire, Scotland; son of James and Annie (Robin) Jenkins; married Mary McIntyre Wylie, 1937; children: Helen Jenkins White, Ann, Colin. *Education:* University of Glasgow, M.A. (honors), 1936.

CAREER: Ghazi College, Kabul, Afghanistan, teacher of English, 1957-59; Barcelona University, British Institute, Barcelona, Spain, lecturer in English, 1959-61; Gaya College, Sabah, Malaysia, lecturer in English, 1963-65; writer. *Member:* Society of Authors, Educational Institute of Scotland. *Awards, honors:* Frederick Niven Award for Scottish literature, 1955.

WRITINGS—Novels; published by Macdonald & Co., except as indicated: *Happy for the Child,* Lehmann, 1953; *The Thistle and the Grail,* 1954; *The Cone-gatherers,* 1955; *Guests of War,* 1956; *The Missionaries,* 1957; *The Changeling,* 1958; *Love Is a Fervent Fire,* 1959; *Some Kind of Grace,* 1960; *Dust on the Paw,* Putnam, 1961; *The Tiger of Gold,* 1962; *A Love of Innocence,* J. Cape, 1963; *The Sardana Dancers,* J. Cape, 1964; *Fergus Lamont,* Taplinger, 1979.

Published by Gollancz, except as indicated: *A Very Scotch Affair,* 1968; *The Holy Tree,* 1969; *The Expatriates,* 1971; *So Gaily Sings the Lark,* Cedric Chivers, 1971; *A Toast to the Lord,* 1972; *A Figure of Fun,* 1974; *A Would-Be Saint,* 1978.

Short stories: *A Far Cry from Bowmore, and Other Stories,* Gollancz, 1973.

AVOCATIONAL INTERESTS: Travel, golf.

BIOGRAPHICAL/CRITICAL SOURCES: New Saltire, spring, 1962.†

* * *

JENSEN, Virginia Allen 1927-

PERSONAL: Born September 21, 1927, in Des Moines, Iowa; daughter of Byron Gilchrist and Elsa (Erickson) Allen; married Flemming Jakob Jensen (a management consultant), March 21, 1953; children: Merete, Annette, Kirsten. *Education:* Bennington College, B.A., 1950; University of Minnesota, graduate study. *Home and office:* Kildeskovsvej 21, DK-2820 Gentofte, Denmark.

CAREER: International Children's Book Service, Gentofte, Denmark, director, 1960—. Member of board of directors of Danish section of International Board on Books for Young People, 1973-78. *Member:* Danish Authors' Union. *Awards, honors:* Honorable mention from Finnish Authors' Union, 1971, for *Lars Peter's Bicycle;* Nordic Cultural Fund grants, 1973 and 1974, for the promotion of Nordic children's literature; Margaret Batchelder Award runner-up, 1974, for *The Nisse from Timsgaard;* Danish Ministry of Cultural Affairs research grant, 1975; Premio Critici in Erba (Bologna), 1978, Deutscher Jugendbuchpreis, 1979, and Boeken Sleutel, 1979, all for *What's That?*

WRITINGS—Juvenile: *Lars Peter's Birthday,* Abingdon, 1959; *Hop Hans,* Gyldendal, 1966; *Lars Peters Cykel,* Gyldendal, 1968, published in England as *Lars Peter's Bicycle,* Angus & Robertson, 1970; *Sara and the Door,* Addison-Wesley, 1977; (with Dorcas Woodbury Haller) *What's That?,* Collins, 1979; *Red Thread Riddles,* UNESCO, 1979.

Translator from the Danish, except as indicated: Ib Spang Olsen, *The Marsh Crone's Brew,* Abingdon, 1960; Thea Bank Jensen, *Play with Paper,* Macmillan, 1962; Olsen, *The Boy in the Moon,* Abingdon, 1963, reprinted, Parents' Magazine Press, 1977; Susanne Palsbo, *Droll, Danish, and Delicious,* Hoest & Sons, 1966; Thoeger Birkeland, *When the Cock Crows,* Coward, 1968 (published in England as *The Wastelanders,* Angus & Robertson, 1972); Birkeland, *The Lemonade Murder,* Coward, 1971; Olsen, *Where Is Martin?,* Angus & Robertson, 1969, published as *Cat Alley,* Coward, 1971; Olsen, *Smoke,* Coward, 1972; Wilhelm Bergsoee, *The Nisse from Timsgaard,* Coward, 1972; Olsen, *The Little Switch Engine,* Coward, 1976; (translator from the Swedish) Sarah Catherine Martin, *Old Mother Hubbard and Her Dog* (translation from the original English by Lennart Hellsing), Coward, 1976.

SIDELIGHTS: Virginia Allen Jensen's book *What's That?* is illustrated in special raised print so that sight-handicapped as well as sighted children can follow the story in pictures. It has been published in ten countries.

BIOGRAPHICAL/CRITICAL SOURCES: New York Times Book Review, April 29, 1979.

JOHNSGARD, Paul A(ustin) 1931-

PERSONAL: Born June 28, 1931, in Fargo, N.D.; son of Alfred Bernard (a sanitarian) and Yvonne (Morgan) Johnsgard; married Lois Lampe, June 24, 1956; children: Jay, Scott, Ann, Karin. *Education:* North Dakota State University, B.S., 1953; Washington State University, M.S., 1956; Cornell University, Ph.D., 1959. *Home:* 7341 Holdrege, Lincoln, Neb. 68505. *Office:* Department of Zoology, University of Nebraska, Lincoln, Neb. 68508.

CAREER: University of Nebraska at Lincoln, instructor, 1961-62, assistant professor, 1962-64, associate professor, 1964-68, professor of zoology, 1968—. *Member:* American Ornithologists Union (fellow), Wilson Ornithological Society, Cooper Ornithological Society, Sigma Xi. *Awards, honors:* National Science Foundation fellow, University of Bristol, 1959-60; U.S. Public Health Service fellow, 1960-61; National Science Foundation research grant, 1963-66; top honor book award from Chicago Book Clinic, 1969, for *Waterfowl;* Guggenheim fellowship, 1971; outstanding book publication award from Wildlife Society, 1974, for *Grouse and Quails of North America.*

WRITINGS: Handbook of Waterfowl Behavior, Cornell University Press, 1965; *Animal Behavior,* W. C. Brown, 1967, 2nd edition, 1972; *Waterfowl: Their Biology and Natural History,* University of Nebraska Press, 1968; *Grouse and Quails of North America,* University of Nebraska Press, 1973; *Song of the North Wind: A Story of the Snow Goose,* Doubleday, 1974; *American Game Birds of Upland and Shoreline,* University of Nebraska Press, 1974; *Waterfowl of North America,* Indiana University Press, 1975; (editor) *The Bird Decoy: An American Art Form,* University of Nebraska Press, 1976; *Ducks, Geese, and Swans of the World,* University of Nebraska Press, 1978; *A Guide to North American Waterfowl,* Indiana University Press, 1979; *Birds of the Great Plains: Breeding Species and Their Distribution,* University of Nebraska Press, 1979; *Plovers, Sandpipers, and Snipes of the World,* University of Nebraska Press, in press.

WORK IN PROGRESS: Grouse of the World, for University of Nebraska Press; a book on the natural history of Jackson Hole.

SIDELIGHTS: Johnsgard has conducted field work in North and South America, Australia, and Europe. *Song of the North Wind* has been translated into Russian and Latvian. *Avocational interests:* Photography, art (especially line illustration).

* * *

JOHNSON, Irma Bolan 1903-

PERSONAL: Born April 19, 1903, in Gays, Ill.; daughter of John S. and Susie (Jeffries) Bolan; married Melvin H. Johnson, 1933; children: Fredric B., M. Herbert. *Education:* Attended Eastern Illinois State Teachers College (now Eastern Illinois University), 1921-24; Wayne University (now Wayne State University), B.S., 1951, graduate study, 1952-53. *Home:* 204 North State, Harrisville, Mich. 48740.

CAREER: Teacher in Bethany, Ill., 1921-24, Champaign, Ill., 1924-27, 1928-33, Riverside, Ill., 1927-28, and Pontiac, Mich., 1945-55; elementary school consultant, 1955-65. *Member:* Association for Childhood Education (president, 1955), Michigan Historical Society. Michigan Education Association, Pontiac Education Association, Order of Eastern Star. *Awards, honors:* Michigan Historical Society, certificate of honor, for *Three Feathers, the Story about Pontiac.*

WRITINGS: (With Mary Green) *Three Feathers, the Story about Pontiac,* Follett, 1960; *About Truck Farming,* Melmont, 1962; *The Goodenough Poultry Farm,* Elk Grove Press, 1967; *The March of the Harvest,* Elk Grove Press, 1968. Produced arithmetic strip film, "Primary Arithmetic," with Mary Green for Jam Handy Organization, 1960-61. Contributor of articles to education publications.

AVOCATIONAL INTERESTS: Writing, painting, crafts, reading, china, community work.

* * *

JOHNSON, Marilue Carolyn 1931-
(Marilue)

PERSONAL: Born February 3, 1931, in Grand Forks, N.D.; daughter of Obert Edwin (a telegrapher) and Ota (Grundman) Vig; married Harold Edward Johnson (a fashion buyer), December 31, 1959 (separated); children: Laurel Leif, Delph Lamberta. *Education:* Attended Walker Art School, Minneapolis, 1949-50. *Politics:* Republican. *Religion:* Lutheran. *Home and office address:* Box 252, Canyon, Tex. 79015.

CAREER: Commercial artist with various agencies in Minneapolis, Minn., 1950-56; Remington Rand Univac, Minneapolis, art director in Educational Division, 1959-60; Burgess Beckwith Publishing Co., Minneapolis, advertising art director, 1960-61; free-lance artist and designer, 1961—. Writer and illustrator of children's books; designer of sculpture jewelry, stationery, and greeting cards; lecturer to children and college students. *Member:* International Platform Association.

WRITINGS—Author and illustrator under name Marilue; all published by Oddo: *Bobby Bear's Red Raft,* 1972; *Bobby Bear's New Home,* 1972; *Bobby Bear's Thanksgiving,* 1973; *Bobby Bear's Christmas,* 1973; *Bobby Bear's Blizzard,* 1980; *Bobby Bear Finds Cousin Boo,* 1980; *Bobby Bear at the Beach,* 1980.

Illustrator under name Marilue; all published by Oddo: Marilyn O. Helmrath and Janet L. Bartlett, *Bobby Bear in the Spring,* 1964; Helmrath and Bartlett, *Bobby Bear and the Bees,* 1964; Helmrath and Bartlett, *Bobby Bear's Rocket Ride,* 1964; Helmrath and Bartlett, *Bobby Bear's Halloween,* 1964; Helmrath and Bartlett, *Bobby Bear Finds Maple Sugar,* 1964; Helmrath and Bartlett, *Bobby Bear Goes Fishing,* 1964; Rae Oetting, *When Jesus Was a Lad,* 1964; Oetting, *Prairie Dog Town,* 1965; Herbert Montgomery and Mary Montgomery, *Mongoose Magoo,* 1965; Dorothy Dowdell, *The Secrets of the A B C's,* 1967; Oetting, *The Orderly Cricket,* 1968.

WORK IN PROGRESS: Writing and illustrating books for pre-school children; a western mystery novel, *The Bloody Golden Spread.*

* * *

JOHNSON, Uwe 1934-

PERSONAL: First name is pronounced "Oo-veh"; born July 20, 1934, in Cammin, Germany; son of Erich and Erna (Straede) Johnson; married Elizabeth Schmidt, 1962; children: Katharina E. *Education:* Attended University of Rostock, two years; University of Leipzig, diploma in philology. *Home:* 26 Marine Parade, Sheerness, Kent ME12 2BB, England.

CAREER: Writer. Harcourt, Brace & World, New York, N.Y., full-time editor of new German writing, 1966-67. *Member:* P.E.N. (Federal Republic of Germany), Akademie

d. Kuenste (West Berlin), Deutsche Akademie (Darmstadt), Gruppe 47. *Awards, honors:* Fontane-Preis Westberlin, 1960; Prix International de la Litterature, 1962; Buechner-Preis, 1971; Raabe-Preis, 1975; Thomas Mann-Preis, 1978.

WRITINGS: Mutmassungen ueber Jakob, Suhrkamp Verlag, 1959, translation by Ursule Molinaro published as *Speculations about Jakob,* Grove, 1963; *Das dritte Buch ueber Achim,* Suhrkamp Verlag, 1961, translation by Molinaro published as *The Third Book about Achim,* Harper, 1967; *Zwei Ansichten,* Suhrkamp Verlag, 1965, translation by Richard Winston and Clara Winston published as *Two Views,* Harcourt, 1966; *Jahrestage I-III,* Suhrkamp Verlag, 1970-73, translation of Volume I by Leila Vennewitz published as *Anniversaries I,* Harcourt, 1975; *Eine Reise nach Klagenfurt,* Suhrkamp Verlag, 1974.

SIDELIGHTS: Webster Schott thinks that Uwe Johnson "writes like no one else anywhere. . . . Imagine the Faulkner style with Hemingway-like diction, and studded with Proustian minutiae. That is close but not quite it." John Fletcher notes that, for Johnson, "reality is not grasped by language, but created by it; language not only delimits the world . . . it also structures it. . . . [He] has siezed upon this essential truth, and explores it with dazzling virtuosity and invention." Fletcher finds Johnson's work "aesthetically the most accomplished to have come out of Germany in recent years." In it are present "the trauma of defeat and subsequent political division of his country, the need to recreate the literary tradition, and the problem of relating to a self-satisfied and philistine society."

The theme of divided Germany is at the center of all Johnson's work, even in *Anniversaries,* which is set in America. As E. R. von Freiburg writes, "[Johnson's] homeland is not merely divided but kaleidoscopically splintered. In novel after novel, with endless pains, he sweeps the glittering shards of his national identity together and tries to make them function, if not as what they were, then at least as what they are or might be, knowing from the start that even this melancholy compromise must fail."

Another characteristic of Johnson's writing is the controlled detachment with which he approaches his stories. As Joseph McElroy comments: "Even when we are closest to them, Johnson's people are frighteningly private. He has a way of retreating from scenes." A reviewer for the *Times Literary Supplement* puts this in another way: "[Johnson's] prose has an incisive, almost sullen reticence in which not a few Germans under forty will recognize their own voices—and silences. . . . He does not parade any sovereign knowledge of what is going on inside his characters' heads."

Richard Howard writes, "None of [Johnson's] earlier books . . . is much fun to read." But Howard finds *Anniversaries I* "a book so large in its aspirations, so fresh in its attitudes, so militant in its inventions, and so unmistakable in their realization that I must call it a masterpiece, even though it is not yet the entire work."

Johnson's prose "tends to bypass all the common abstractions which haunt German fiction," writes another reviewer. "Fictions, for him, are not devised to define some general truth behind the historical situation which he analyzes; they present rather the concrete infinitesimals of all the possibilities of what the truth might be to the characters within that situation. The situation is always Germany divided. The truth is always a scintillation given off, as actions and perceptions collide in the sensibilities of his characters: It is indefinable, in their nerves, like a solution that will not quite crystallize, or some sort of unlocalized ache in the midst of the German present."

BIOGRAPHICAL/CRITICAL SOURCES: Neue deutsche Hefte, 6, 1959/60; *Frankfurter Hefte,* 1960, 1961; *L'Express,* Paris, October 11, 1962; *Time,* January 4, 1963, April 12, 1963; *Nation,* April 6, 1963, February 13, 1967, September 4, 1967; *Saturday Review,* April 6, 1963, December 18, 1965; *New York Herald Tribune Books,* April 7, 1963; *New York Times Book Review,* April 14, 1963, November 20, 1966, April, 1967; *Commonweal,* April 26, 1963, April 14, 1967; *Atlantic,* May, 1963; *New Yorker,* May 18, 1963; *New Republic,* May 25, 1963; *New Statesman,* September 6, 1963; *Times Literary Supplement,* September 6, 1963, September 30, 1965; *Encounter,* January, 1964; D. Enright, *Conspirators and Poets,* Dufour, 1966; *New York Times,* December 4, 1966; *Christian Century,* March 1, 1967; *Christian Science Monitor,* April 27, 1967; *New Leader,* May 22, 1967; *Observer Review,* July 9, 1967, January 14, 1968; *Harper's,* August, 1967; *International Fiction Review,* July, 1974; *Contemporary Literary Criticism,* Gale, Volume V, 1976, Volume X, 1979.

* * *

JOHNSON, Wendell (Andrew Leroy) 1906-1965

PERSONAL: Born April 16, 1906, in Roxbury, Kan.; died August 29, 1965; buried in Oakland Cemetery, Iowa City, Iowa; son of Andrew R. (a farmer and cattleman) and Mary (Tarnstrom) Johnson; married Edna Bockwoldt, May 31, 1929; children: Nicholas, Katherine Louise. *Education:* Attended McPherson College, 1924-26; University of Iowa, B.A., 1928, M.A., 1929, Ph.D., 1931. *Religion:* Unitarian Universalist. *Home:* 508 Melrose Court, Iowa City, Iowa. *Office:* E-15, East Hall, University of Iowa, Iowa City, Iowa.

CAREER: University of Iowa, Iowa City, 1926-65, began as research assistant, professor of speech pathology and psychology, 1943-55, speech clinic director, 1943-55, chairman of council on speech pathology and audiology, 1951-55, chairman of council on rehabilitation, 1959-61, Louis W. Hills Research Professor, 1963-65. Visiting professor at University of Southern California, summer, 1948, University of Colorado, summer, 1956, and University of Hawaii, 1963. Iowa Remedial Education Program, technical director, 1939-42. Walter Reed Army Medical Center, consultant in speech pathology, 1954-61; U.S. Office of Vocational Rehabilitation, member, national advisory council on vocational rehabilitation, 1957-61; U.S. Office of Education, consultant, 1957-58, Division of Handicapped Children and Youth, member of committees on professional training and on research in speech and hearing, 1963-64; U.S. National Institute of Neurological Diseases and Blindness, consultant, 1957, member of committee on perinatal research, 1963-64; U.S. Veterans Administration, central office consultant in speech pathology, 1959-65; American Boards of Examiners in Speech Pathology and Audiology, member of board of directors, 1960-61; U.S. Public Health Service, Bureau of State Services, member of committee on nervous and sensory diseases, 1963-64; National Society for Crippled Children and Adults, member of professional advisory committee, 1963-65. American Board of Examiners in Professional Psychology, diplomate in clinical psychology. Presented approximately 400 lectures to radio, television, university and convention audiences.

MEMBER: American Speech and Hearing Association (fellow; president, 1950; member of executive council; chairman of publications board, 1957-61), American Speech and Hearing Foundation (founder, 1945; chairman, 1958-64), American Psychological Association (fellow), International

Society for General Semantics (president, 1945-47), Institute of General Semantics (fellow), Speech Association of America, National Society for the Study of Communication, National Rehabilitation Association, International Society for the Rehabilitation of the Disabled, American Association of Cleft Palate Rehabilitation, American Association for the Advancement of Science (fellow), American Association of University Professors, Midwestern Psychological Association, Central States Speech Association, Iowa Psychological Association, Iowa Speech and Hearing Association, Iowa Society for Crippled Children and Adults (vice-president, 1951-52; president, 1953-54), Iowa Association for Mental Health (member of professional advisory committee, 1954-65), Iowa Academy of Science (fellow), Sigma Xi, Phi Beta Kappa, Optimist International (president, Iowa City chapter, 1952-53), Cosmos Club (Washington, D.C.), Triangle Club, University Athletic Club (both Iowa City). *Awards, honors:* American Speech and Hearing Association, honors of the association award, 1946.

WRITINGS: Because I Stutter, Appleton, 1930; *People in Quandaries,* Harper, 1946; (co-author) *Speech Handicapped School Children,* Harper, 1948, third edition, 1967; (editor) Charles Gage Van Riper, *Stuttering,* National Society for Crippled Children and Adults, 1949; (co-author) *Diagnostic Manual in Speech Correction,* Harper, 1952; (editor and co-author) *Stuttering in Children and Adults: Thirty Years of Research at the University of Iowa,* University of Minnesota Press, 1955; *Your Most Enchanted Listener,* Harper, 1956, published as *Verbal Man: The Enchantment of Words,* Macmillan, 1965; *The Onset of Stuttering,* University of Minnesota Press, 1959; *Stuttering and What You Can Do about It,* University of Minnesota Press, 1961; (with Frederic L. Darley and D. C. Spriestersbach) *Diagnostic Methods in Speech Pathology,* Harper, 1963; (with Dorothy Moeller) *Self-Communication Factors in Clinical Counseling,* Department of Speech Pathology and Audiology, University of Iowa, 1967; *Living with Change: The Semantics of Coping,* edited by Moeller, Harper, 1972. Also author of *An Open Letter to the Mother of a Stuttering Child,* Interstate.

Contributed over 150 articles and over 100 book reviews to professional journals and commercial magazines. Editor, *Journal of Speech and Hearing Disorders,* 1943-48; member of editorial board, *ETC.: A Review of General Semantics,* 1943-58; associate editor, *Quarterly Journal of Speech,* 1950-56; member of international board of editors, section on rehabilitation, *Excerpta Medica,* 1958-65; co-founder, member of board of directors, 1960-63, Deafness Speech and Hearing Publications, Inc., publishers of an abstracting service in these fields.

SIDELIGHTS: Afflicted by severe stuttering until he was over forty, Wendell Johnson had an unusually close connection with the subject matter of his teaching and writing. As a researcher in the field of speech pathology, Johnson came to disagree strongly with traditional explanations of stuttering, which revolve around supposed organic or personality defects. He maintained that a stuttering problem usually arises when a teacher or parent is unduly critical of a child's fluency to the point of inhibiting further normal development. In treating stuttering cases, Johnson recommended educating parents as well as the child.

Johnson told *CA:* "If I may be said to have a hobby . . . it is the use of the tape recorder in the classroom and clinic. . . . I think the one thing that would go farthest to improve education . . . would be to place a tape recorder in front of every teacher and insure that at least once in a while the teacher would listen to what he or she has said and the tone and manner of speaking.

"I believe that symbolization and communication are to the social sciences what matter and energy are to the physical sciences. I take for granted that by all odds the most significant scientific advances of the future will occur in the social and behavioral sciences. If we don't bring off these advances in time we probably will not survive."

BIOGRAPHICAL/CRITICAL SOURCES: Saturday Evening Post, January 5, 1957; Ravina Gelfand and Letha Patterson, *They Wouldn't Quit,* Lerner, 1962; *New York Times,* August 31, 1965; *Time,* September 10, 1965.†

* * *

JOINER, Charles W(ycliffe) 1916-

PERSONAL: Born February 14, 1916, in Maquoketa, Iowa; son of Melvin William and Mary (von Schrader) Joiner; married Ann Martin, September 29, 1939; children: Charles W., Jr., Nancy C., Richard M. *Education:* University of Iowa, A.B., 1937, J.D., 1939. *Home:* 1345 Glendaloch Circle, Ann Arbor, Mich. *Office:* 251 Federal Court Bldg., Detroit, Mich. 48226.

CAREER: Miller, Huebner & Miller (law firm), Des Moines, Iowa, trial attorney and associate, 1939-47; University of Michigan, Law School, Ann Arbor, 1947-68, began as assistant professor, became professor of law, acting dean, 1965-66; Wayne State University, Law School, Detroit, Mich., dean, 1968-72; U.S. District Court, Detroit, judge, 1972—. Part-time lecturer, Des Moines College of Law, 1940-41. Member of Ann Arbor City Council, 1955-59; member of charter review committee, Ann Arbor Citizen's Council, 1959-62. *Military service:* U.S. Army Air Forces, 1943-45; became first lieutenant; received two Battle Stars.

MEMBER: American Bar Association (chairman, special committee on uniform rules of evidence for the federal courts; member, standing committee on professional ethics, 1961-70; member of several other committees), American Bar Foundation (chairman of fellows, 1978-79), American Law Institute, American Judicature Society, State Bar of Michigan (president, 1970-71), Michigan State Bar Foundation, Iowa State Bar Association, Rotary International, Scribes.

WRITINGS: (With E. B. Stason and William W. Blume) *Introduction to Civil Procedure,* Overbeck, 1949; (with Blume) *Jurisdiction and Judgments,* Prentice-Hall, 1953; *Trials and Appeals,* Prentice-Hall, 1957; *Civil Justice and the Jury,* Prentice-Hall, 1962; (with Delmar Karlen) *Trials and Appeals: Cases and Materials,* West Publishing, 1971. Contributor to professional journals.

* * *

JOLSON, Marvin A(rnold) 1922-

PERSONAL: Born June 7, 1922, in Chicago, Ill.; son of George and Bess (Sweetow) Jolson; married Betty Harris, July 8, 1944; children: Robert D., Nancy E. *Education:* George Washington University, B.E.E., 1949; University of Chicago, M.B.A., 1965; University of Maryland, D.B.A., 1969; also studied at University of Southern California, summer, 1967. *Home:* 7812 Ridge Ter., Pikesville, Md. 21208. *Office:* College of Business and Management, University of Maryland, Q-3114, College Park Md. 20742.

CAREER: Encyclopaedia Britannica, Inc., salesman in Baltimore, Md., 1946-49, sales manager 1950-52, district manager, 1952-58, division manager, 1959-60, Southeast zone manager in Washington, D.C., 1960-62, senior vice-president in Chicago, Ill., 1962-68; University of Maryland, College Park, lecturer, 1968-69, assistant professor, 1969-75, associate professor, 1975-79, professor of marketing, 1979—. Electrical engineer for Davies Laboratories, 1949-50. Lecturer at Roosevelt University, 1966; guest lecturer at DePaul University and University of Chicago, 1966; summer lecturer at Loyola College, Baltimore, 1971; visiting assistant professor at Johns Hopkins University, 1973. Member of board of directors of Crime Prevention Co. of America, Creative Chemical Co., and Public Telephone Telecommunications and Answering Service Co.; ad hoc advisor to Federal Trade Commission, 1972.

MEMBER: American Marketing Association, Association for Consumer Research, Southern Marketing Association, University of Chicago Executive Program Club, Delta Sigma Pi, Beta Gamma Sigma, Masons. *Awards, honors:* Winner of field sales management award from National Sales Executives Club, 1954.

WRITINGS: Consumer Attitudes Toward Direct-to-Home Marketing Systems, Dunellen, 1970; (with Richard T. Hise) *Quantitative Techniques for Marketing Decisions,* with instructor's manual, Macmillan, 1973; *Sales Management: A Technical Approach,* Van Nostrand, 1978; *Contemporary Readings in Sales Management,* Van Nostrand, 1978; *Marketing Management,* Macmillan, 1978. Contributor to proceedings. Contributor of about fifty-five articles and reviews to business journals. Associate editor of abstract review staff, *Journal of Marketing.*

WORK IN PROGRESS: Determinants of Sales Force Turnover: An Empirical Study; Profile of the Signature Goods Consumer.

BIOGRAPHICAL/CRITICAL SOURCES: New York Times, April 25, 1965; *Baltimore Morning Sun,* February 15, 1974.

* * *

JONES, Joseph Jay 1908-

PERSONAL: Born June 29, 1908, in Peru, Neb.; son of Clifford Weldon and Maude (Tubbs) Jones; married Johanna Zabel, 1935; children: David Clifford, Judith Ann Holden, Susan Sarrett. *Education:* University of Nebraska, B.Sc., 1930; Stanford University, M.A., 1931, Ph.D., 1934. *Religion:* Lutheran. *Home:* 2212 Longview St., Austin, Tex. 78705. *Office:* Department of English, University of Texas, Austin, Tex. 78712.

CAREER: Colorado State College (now University), Fort Collins, instructor, 1934; University of Texas at Austin, 1935—, began as instructor, professor of English, 1958-75, professor emeritus, 1975—. Visiting professor at University of Illinois and University of Minnesota; Fulbright lecturer in American literature in New Zealand, 1953, at University of Hong Kong, 1965; Smith-Mundt professor of American literature in South Africa, 1960. Field editor for new English literature, Twayne Publications, 1963-80. *Member:* Modern Language Association of America. *Awards, honors:* Warshaw Award of Western Humanities Research Association, 1952.

WRITINGS: (With Philip E. Graham) *A Concordance to Poems of Sidney Lanier,* University of Texas Press, 1939, reprinted, Johnson Reprint, 1969; (editor) *Meier's Thoughts on Jesting,* University of Texas Press, 1947; *Dryden Handbook of College Composition,* Dryden, 1949; *The Cradle of Erewhon: Samuel Butler in New Zealand,* University of Texas Press, 1959; (editor) *American Literary Manuscripts,* University of Texas Press, 1960; *Terranglia: The Case for English as World Literature,* Twayne, 1965; *Handful of Hong Kong* (poems), University of Hong Kong, 1966; *Radical Cousins: Nineteenth Century American and Australian Writers,* University of Queensland Press, 1976; (contributor) Hsia and Lai, editors, *Hong Kong: Images on Shifting Waters,* Kelly & Walsh, 1977; *Copernican English,* privately printed, 1978; (contributor) William S. Livingston and William Roger Louis, editors, *Australia, New Zealand and the Pacific Islands since the First World War,* University of Texas Press, 1979; (with wife, Johanna Jones) *Surveys of Canadian, Australian, and New Zealand Fiction,* Twayne, in press.

(With J. Jones) "Authors and Areas" series, Steck-Vaughn, 1970: *Authors and Areas of Australia; . . . of Canada; . . . of West Indies.* Also author of three collections of "seventeener" poems, published by Tardy Phoenix Press, 1971-72. Contributor to *American Literature* and other journals. Editor, *University of Texas Library Chronicle,* 1944-52, and *Newsletter* of Conference on British Commonwealth Literature, 1962-70.

WORK IN PROGRESS: Travel narratives; a critique of English methodology.

SIDELIGHTS: Joseph Jay Jones told *CA*: "In 1965, during my Fulbright lectureship in Hong Kong, I began writing free-style haiku verses which I named 'seventeeners,' and have continued to produce them, almost daily. I find that the discipline of this short-form has sharpened both my word-sense and my feeling for rhythm, such as they may be. Expecting to grow tired of so narrow a cage I seem to have found, instead, 'infinite riches in a little room': no two are ever quite alike, and they also work well in related clusters or sequences."

AVOCATIONAL INTERESTS: Handcraft, tool-collecting, travel.

* * *

JONES, Mervyn 1922-

PERSONAL: Born February 27, 1922, in London, England; son of Ernest (a psychoanalyst) and Katharine (Jokl) Jones; married Jeanne Urquhart, April 2, 1948; children: Jacqueline, Marian, Conrad. *Education:* Attended New York University, 1939-41. *Politics:* Socialist. *Religion:* None. *Home:* 10 Waterside Pl., London N.W.1, England. *Agent:* Richard Scott Simon, 32 College Cross, London N.1, England.

CAREER: Free-lance journalist and novelist, 1947—. *Military service:* British Army, 1942-47; became captain.

WRITINGS—Novels, except as indicated: *No Time to Be Young,* J. Cape, 1952; *The New Town,* J. Cape, 1953; *The Last Barricade,* J. Cape, 1953; *Helen Blake,* J. Cape, 1955; *On the Last Day,* J. Cape, 1958; *A Set of Wives,* J. Cape, 1965; *John and Mary,* J. Cape, 1966, Atheneum, 1967; *A Survivor,* Atheneum, 1968; *Joseph,* Atheneum, 1970; *Mr. Armitage Isn't Back Yet,* J. Cape, 1971; *Twilight of Our Day,* Simon & Schuster, 1973 (published in England as *Holding On,* Quartet, 1973); *The Revolving Door,* Quartet, 1973; *Strangers,* Quartet, 1974; *Lord Richard's Passion,* Knopf, 1974; *The Pursuit of Happiness,* Quartet, 1975, Mason/Charter, 1976; *Scenes from Bourgeois Life* (short story collection), Quartet, 1976; *Nobody's Fault,* Mason/Charter, 1977; *Today the Struggle,* Quartet, 1978; *The Beautiful Words,* Deutsch, 1979.

Nonfiction: (With Michael Foot) *Guilty Men,* Rinehart, 1957; *Potbank,* Secker & Warburg, 1961; *The Antagonists,*

C. N. Potter, 1962 (published in England as *Big Two: Life in America and Russia,* J. Cape, 1962); *Two Ears of Corn: Oxfam in Action,* Hodder & Stoughton, 1965, published as *In Famine's Shadow: A Private War on Hunger,* Beacon Press, 1967; (editor) *Kingsley Martin: Portrait and Self-Portrait,* Humanities, 1969; *Life on the Dole,* Davis-Poynter, 1972; (translator) K. S. Karol, *The Second Chinese Revolution,* Hill & Wang, 1974; (editor) *Privacy,* David & Charles, 1974; *The Oil Rush,* Quartet, 1976.

Contributor to newspapers and journals, including *London Tribune, Sunday Times, New Statesman,* and *Observer. London Tribune,* assistant editor, 1955-60, drama critic, 1958-67; assistant editor, *New Statesman,* 1966-68.

SIDELIGHTS: One of the most noticeable features of Mervyn Jones's novels, according to the critics, is a meticulous writing style combined with a decidedly leftist political or sociological approach to his subject matter. A typical Jones character, rather than being endowed by the author with a distinctly individual personality, usually serves as a representation or embodiment of a general human quality common to the setting in question. As a result of such preoccupations, some commentators criticize Jones for writing novels which seem "lifeless and contrived," as a *Times Literary Supplement* reviewer describes *Lord Richard's Passion.* Regarding this same book, a *Library Journal* critic notes that "the only reality is in the historical sidelights; Jones's people and places are cardboard creations."

The Pursuit of Happiness evokes a similar response in another *Times Literary Supplement* critic, Valentine Cunningham. After noting that the situations and characters are "unbelievably stereotyped," Cunningham concludes that the novel gives the overall impression of being "rigged for a script conference with some meat-headed film executive.... Even on the occasions when sentiments manage to be as laudable as they are credible, they are dwelt on ever so lengthily.... Not for a long time has the anti-Midas touch—at which everything that is not already dross turns into it before the reader's startled eyes—received such an orchestrating in a novel of allegedly serious pretensions."

Today the Struggle, a chronicle tracing the lives of several related English families from the 1930s to the 1970s, has also been criticized for its focus on causes and types rather than on "real" people. Paul Ableman of the *Spectator* writes: "The struggle referred to in [*Today the Struggle*] is, broadly speaking, the struggle to enlarge, or even merely to preserve, political decency in a world perpetually beseiged by barbarism.... Most of Mr. Jones's characters, throughout most of the book, are honourably engaged in resisting.... The trouble is that they are not free simply to resist and fade into history. Their fictional life must endure the length of the book. Thus while a few of them perish the rest get caught up in the most extraordinary web of coincidence. Selected initially to provide representative figures of the mid-twentieth century—idealistic working class, decaying aristocracy, culture-oriented bourgeoisie—they can only be penned into the same narrative by cavalier manipulation of the laws of probability."

Furthermore, notes Ableman, "apart from the coincidence-logged lives, necessary to preserve the appearance of unity in a work essentially devoid of it, the characters are pathetic. Not because of their innate nature—at least as conceived, if rarely achieved, by the author—but because they are swamped by History.... There are, in fact, two distinct sets of characters in the book: the fictitious and the real. These are juxtaposed but hardly ever interact, other than by report.... Here and there, Mr. Jones achieves an artistic evocation of scene and character.... [But in the end, he] hastily returns us to the world of the great causes and the plastic people."

Cunningham, this time commenting in *New Statesman,* disagrees with Ableman's assessment of *Today the Struggle.* Calling the book "so engrossing that it's hard to put down," he admits that "it's bound, of course, occasionally to seem a bit too schemed-for, too shrewdly schematising.... Inevitably, not all the events and characters are equally known to the author nor made equally knowable to us. There are some intriguing hops and yawns, and some blank spaces just tarted over with stereotypes; while items put in just for the record (journalist Sophie beds JFK; Mervyn Jones is mentioned) can seem sorely obtruded. But these are midget grouses. Many of the people are wonderfully believable in themselves ...; they are, what's more, placed most convincingly in their time."

Commenting on the author's work in general, an *Observer* critic states that "one thing that Mervyn Jones can certainly do is tell a story: his straightforward narrative technique looks simple, reads easily, and keeps you reading. At the same time, he has a good old-fashioned novelist's way with characters. There is no authorial presence, no overt trickery or tricksiness. And such things aren't unimportant to the ordinary reader."

Despite such praise, however, Alan Massie of the *Times Literary Supplement* summarizes the views of many of his fellow critics regarding Jones's work in his review of *Nobody's Fault.* In short, he concludes that "the central inescapable weakness" in Jones's novels is that "[his] characters, rather predictable at the start, never go on to surprise us.... Mr. Jones is always anxious to tell us; but he does not make us see or hear."

John and Mary was filmed by 20th Century-Fox Film Corp. in 1969.

BIOGRAPHICAL/CRITICAL SOURCES: Library Journal, April 15, 1974; *Times Literary Supplement,* October 25, 1974, November 7, 1975, August 19, 1977; *Listener,* December 11, 1975, July 12, 1979; *Spectator,* August 7, 1976, February 18, 1978; *New York Times Book Review,* October 16, 1977; *New Statesman,* February 17, 1978, July 13, 1979; *Contemporary Literary Criticism,* Volume X, Gale, 1979; *Observer,* July 22, 1979; *Books and Bookmen,* August, 1979.

—*Sketch by Deborah A. Straub*

* * *

JORDAN, Robert S(mith) 1929-

PERSONAL: Born June 11, 1929, in Los Angeles, Calif; married Sara Jane Hatch; children: Sara Jane, Mary Rebecca, Robert Hatch, David Thomas. *Education:* University of California, Los Angeles, A.B., 1951; University of Utah, M.S., 1955; Princeton University, M.A., 1957, Ph.D., 1960; Oxford University, D.Phil., 1960. *Office:* Department of Government and International Studies, Gambrell Hall, University of South Carolina, Columbia, S.C. 29208.

CAREER: U.S. Bureau of the Budget, Executive Office of the President, Washington, D.C., budget examiner, 1956; Princeton University, Princeton, N.J., instructor in politics, 1956-57; University of Pittsburgh, Pittsburgh, Pa., assistant professor of public and international affairs, 1959-60; George Washington University, Washington, D.C., associate professorial lecturer in Army and Air War College Programs, 1960-62, associate professor of political science and international affairs, 1962-70, assistant director of Army War College Center, 1960-61, director of Air University Center, 1961-62, assistant to president of university, 1962-64, senior research scientist in program of policy studies, 1964-65; State University of New York at Binghamton, professor of political science and chairman of department, 1970-74; director of research, United Nations Institute for Training and Research, 1974-79; University of South Carolina, Columbia, Dag Hammarskjoeld Professor, 1979—. Littauer Visiting Professor of Political Science and International Politics, dean of Faculty of Economic and Social Studies, and chairman of department of political science, University of Sierra Leone, 1965-67; visiting professor, Brigham Young University, summer, 1972. Lecturer at colleges and universities in the United States and abroad, and at British Imperial Defense College, National War College, Defense Intelligence School, Air Command and Staff College, Foreign Service Institute, Air War College, Army War College, Industrial College of the Armed Forces, U.S. Military Academy, and Washington International Center. Consultant to Battelle Memorial Institute, National Aeronautics and Space Administration, American Council on Education, Booneville Research Corp., and Ford Foundation. *Military service:* U.S. Air Force, personnel officer, 1951-53; became captain; received Bronze Star Medal.

MEMBER: International Studies Association (vice-president, 1979-80), International Institute for Strategic Studies, Committee on Atlantic Studies (former chairman of North American section), International Institute of Administrative Sciences, American Political Science Association, American Society for International Law, American Society for Public Administration, African Studies Association (fellow), American Association for the Advancement of Science, United Nations Association, Wilton Park Association, Cosmos Club (Washington, D.C.), Princeton Club (New York, N.Y.). *Awards, honors:* Fulbright scholarship, St. Antony's College, Oxford University, 1957-59; named distinguished alumnus, Hinckley Institute of Practical Politics, 1965; North Atlantic Treaty Organization (NATO) research fellowship, 1968-69.

WRITINGS: (Editor with Hubert Gibbs and Andrew Gyorgy and contributor) *Problems in International Relations,* 3rd edition (Jordan was not associated with earlier editions), Prentice-Hall, 1970; *The NATO International Staff/Secretariat, 1952-57: A Study in International Administration,* Oxford University Press, 1967; (with others) *Government and Power in West Africa,* Africana Publishing, 1969, 2nd edition, Ethiope Publishing Corp., 1979; (editor and contributor) *Europe and the Superpowers: Perceptions of European International Politics,* Allyn & Bacon, 1971; (editor and contributor) *International Administration: Its Evolution and Contemporary Applications,* Oxford University Press, 1971; (editor) *Multinational Cooperation: Economic, Social and Scientific Development,* Oxford University Press, 1972; (editor with Peter Toma and Gyorgy and contributor) *Basic Issues in International Relations,* 2nd edition (Jordan was not associated with first edition), Allyn & Bacon, 1974; (with Thomas Weiss) *The World Food Conference and Global Problem Solving,* Praeger, 1976; *Political Leadership in NATO: A Study in Multinational Diplomacy,* Westview Press, 1979.

Also author of monographs. Contributor of articles and reviews to *World Survey* and other professional journals. Member of editorial advisory board of *Atlantic Community Quarterly;* member of board of editors, *Public Administration Review.*

JORGENSEN, Mary Venn (Mary Adrian)

PERSONAL: Born in Sewickley, Pa.; daughter of George Charles and Claire (Adrian) Venn; married Henry G. Jorgensen, 1957. *Education:* Attended New York University, 1935-36. *Home:* 1000 South West Vista Ave., No. 817, Portland, Ore. 97205.

CAREER: *Vogue,* New York, N.Y., assistant to managing editor, 1929-45; novelist and nature writer, 1945—. *Member:* Authors League of America, Women's National Book Association, Ornithologists' Union, Audubon Society, National Wildlife Federation, Museum of American Natural History.

WRITINGS—Under pseudonym Mary Adrian; published by Hastings House, except as indicated: *Mystery Nature Stories,* Rinehart, 1948; *Firehouse Mystery,* Houghton, 1950; *Garden Spider,* Holiday, 1951; *Honey Bee,* Holiday, 1952; *Tugboat Mystery,* Houghton, 1952; *Fiddler Crab,* Holiday, 1953; *Hidden Spring Mystery,* Farrar, Straus, 1954; *Junior Sheriff Mystery,* Farrar, Straus, 1955; *Gray Squirrel,* Holiday, 1955; *Uranium Mystery,* 1956; *Refugee Hero,* 1957; *Jonathan Crow, Detective,* 1958; *Fox Hollow Mystery,* 1959.

Rare Stamp Mystery, 1960; *Mystery Night Explorers,* 1962; *American Eagle,* 1963; *Skin Diving Mystery,* 1964; *American Mustang,* 1964; *Mystery of the Dinosaur Bones,* 1965; *American Wolf,* 1965; *Indian Horse Mystery,* 1966; *North American Bighorn Sheep,* 1966; *The Lightship Mystery,* 1969.

A Day and a Night in the Arctic, 1970; *The Ghost Town Mystery,* 1971; *A Day and a Night in a Tide Pool,* 1972; *Secret Neighbors: Wildlife in a City Lot,* 1972; *Wildlife on the Watch: A Story of the Desert,* 1974; *The Fireball Mystery,* 1977; *Wildlife in the Antarctic,* Messner, 1978; *Wildlife on the African Grasslands,* Messner, 1979. Former author of a weekly nature column for *Boston Post.* Contributor of nature stories and articles to magazines for children and young people and to *Country Gentleman, Farm Journal,* and *Christian Science Monitor.*

WORK IN PROGRESS: Nature books and mysteries.

SIDELIGHTS: Mary Venn Jorgensen's mystery books are based on scientific facts, with information woven into the plot to educate the young reader. Her nature books are life-cycle stories. *Avocational interests:* All nature, bird watching, field trips.

* * *

JOYCE, R(oger) B(ilbrough) 1924-

PERSONAL: Born June 9, 1924, in Sydney, Australia; son of John (an accountant) and Jessie (Bilbrough) Joyce; married Elsbeth Whitehouse (a medical practitioner), August 26, 1950 (divorced August 26, 1977); married Barbara Nelson, April 22, 1978; children: (first marriage) David, Ralph, Timothy. *Education:* University of Sydney, B.A. (first class honors), 1948, LL.B., 1950; Cambridge University, M.Litt., 1952. *Home:* 50A Stawell St., Kew, Melbourne, Victoria 3101, Australia. *Office:* Department of History, La Trobe University, Bundoora, Melbourne, Victoria 3083, Australia.

CAREER: University of Queensland, Brisbane, Australia, lecturer, 1952-58, senior lecturer, 1959-66, reader in history, 1967-74; La Trobe University, Melbourne, Australia, professor of history, 1975—. Member of board of directors of Oxley Library; member of historical research subcommittee of National Trust; member of executive board of Australian Institute of International Affairs, 1956-69. *Military service:* Australian Imperial Force, 1942-45; became lieutenant. *Member:* Australian and New Zealand Association for the

Advancement of Science (president of history section, 1976), Australian Historical Association (president, 1976-77).

WRITINGS: (Contributor) Gordon Greenwood and Norman Harper, editors, *Australia in World Affairs: 1950-1955*, Cheshire, 1957; *New Guinea*, Oxford University Press, 1960; (editor) A.C.V. Melbourne, *Early Constitutional Development in Australia*, University of Queensland Press, 1963; (editor with Peter Edwards) Anthony Trollope, *Australia*, University of Queensland Press, 1968; (with Charles Grimshaw) *The Web of the World*, Jacaranda, 1968; (contributor) Graham Abbott and Bede Nairn, editors, *Economic Growth of Australia: 1788-1821*, Melbourne University Press, 1969; (editor with Denis Murphy and Colin Hughes) *Prelude to Power: The Rise of the Labor Party in Queensland: 1885-1915*, Jacaranda, 1970; *Sir William MacGregor*, Oxford University Press, 1971; (contributor) V. G. Venturini, editor, *Australia: A Survey*, Institute of Asian Affairs (Hamburg), 1971; (contributor) W. J. Hudson, editor, *Australia and Papua New Guinea*, Sydney University Press, 1971; (contributor) D. P. Crook, editor, *Questioning the Past*, University of Queensland Press, 1972; *Pathways from the Past*, McGraw, 1975; (contributor) Peter Loveday, Alan W. Martin, and R. S. Parker, editors, *The Emergence of the Australian Party System*, Hale & Iremonger, 1977; (editor with Murphy and contributor) *Queensland Political Portraits*, Queensland University Press, 1978; (editor with Murphy and Hughes) *Labor in Power*, Queensland University Press, 1980. Contributor to *Encyclopedia of Papua and New Guinea* and *Australian Dictionary of Biography*. Contributor of articles to *Historical Studies, Australian Journal of Politics and History, World Review, Fiji Society of Medicine Journal, Archives and Manuscripts, Queensland Heritage*, and other publications.

WORK IN PROGRESS: A biography of Sir Samuel Walker Griffith, first chief justice of Australia.

AVOCATIONAL INTERESTS: Travel (Europe, the U.S.S.R., and the United States), squash, volleyball.

* * *

JUSTICE, Blair 1927-

PERSONAL: Born July 2, 1927, in Dallas, Tex.; son of Sam Hugh (an auditor) and Lou Reine (Hunter) Justice; married Judy Frances Jackson, July 10, 1954 (divorced, 1972); married Rita Katherine Norwood (a psychologist), July 26, 1972; children: (first marriage) Cynthia Lou, David Blair, Jr., Elizabeth Ann. *Education:* University of Texas at Austin, B.A., 1948; Columbia University, M.S., 1949; Texas Christian University, M.A., 1963; Rice University, Ph.D., 1966. *Religion:* Episcopal. *Home:* 6331 Brompton Rd., Houston, Tex. 77005. *Office:* School of Public Health, University of Texas, 6905 Bertner, Houston, Tex. 77025.

CAREER: New York News, New York, N.Y., science feature writer, 1955-56; *Fort Worth Star-Telegram*, Fort Worth, Tex., columnist, 1956-73; *Houston Post*, Houston, Tex., columnist, 1964-73; University of Texas, School of Public Health, Houston, professor of social psychology, 1968—. Executive assistant to Mayor of Houston, 1966—; general chairman of Job Fair for Disadvantaged Youth, Houston, 1967-74; commissioner, Governor's Texas Urban Development Commission, 1970-71; director of UTSPH Project for the Early Prevention of Individual Violence, Houston, 1970-74, and of Houston Housing Development Corp., 1971—; chairman of Manpower Area Planning Council for Gulf Coast, 1971-74; member of Governor's Human Resources Council, 1972—; president of Houston Area Council on Sudden Infant Death Syndrome, 1978, and of Houston Youth Council, 1978. *Military service:* U.S. Navy, 1944-45. U.S. Air Force Reserve, 1950-51; became first lieutenant. *Member:* American Psychological Association, National Science Writers Association, New York Academy of Sciences, Houston Psychological Association, Phi Beta Kappa, Sigma Xi, Texas Gridiron Club (president, 1961-62). *Awards, honors:* Texas Writers Roundup Award, 1970, for best book in sociology written by a Texan; twenty-six awards for science news writing.

WRITINGS: Detection of Potential Community Violence, U.S. Government Printing Office, 1968; *Violence in the City*, Texas Christian University Press, 1969; (with wife, Rita Justice) *The Abusing Family*, Human Sciences Press, 1976; (with R. Justice) *The Broken Taboo: Sex in the Family*, Human Sciences Press, 1979. Also author of pamphlets and of numerous papers on physical and sexual abuse of children. Executive producer and editor of two films, "Square Up" and "I Ain't Goin' Back," Houston, 1972.

WORK IN PROGRESS: A book on successful families and one on stress management.

K

KAHANE, Howard 1928-

PERSONAL: Born April 19, 1928, in Cleveland, Ohio; son of Philip (a retail merchant) and Blanche (Landesman) Kahane; married Betsy Hyman, November 23, 1955 (divorced, December, 1964); married Judith McBride Weast, June, 1967 (divorced, 1973); children: Bonny Robin. *Education:* University of California, Los Angeles, B.A., 1954, M.A., 1958; University of Pennsylvania, Ph.D., 1962. *Politics:* "Liberal conservative (or vice versa)." *Religion:* "Agnostic (ethnic Jew)." *Office:* Department of Philosophy, University of Maryland Baltimore County, Baltimore, Md. 21228.

CAREER: Whitman College, Walla Walla, Wash., assistant professor of philosophy, 1962-64; University of Kansas, Lawrence, assistant professor, 1964-68, associate professor of philosophy, 1968-71; Bernard M. Baruch College of the City University of New York, New York, N.Y., assistant professor, 1971-73, associate professor of philosophy, 1974-76, chairman of department, 1972-73; University of Maryland Baltimore County, Baltimore, professor of philosophy, 1976—. *Military service:* U.S. Army, 1954-56. *Member:* American Philosophical Association. *Awards, honors:* Watkins summer fellowship, 1965; National Science Foundation grant, 1967-68.

WRITINGS: Logic and Philosophy: A Modern Introduction, Wadsworth, 1969, 3rd edition, 1978; *Logic and Contemporary Rhetoric: The Use of Reason in Everyday Life,* Wadsworth, 1971, 3rd edition, 1980. Contributor to *Journal of Philosophy, American Philosophical Quarterly, Review of Metaphysics, Nous, British Journal for the Philosophy of Science,* and *Philosophy of Science.*

* * *

KAISER, Ernest 1915-

PERSONAL: Born December 5, 1915, in Petersburg, Va.; son of Ernest Bascom (a railroad car cleaner) and Elnora (Ellis) Kaiser; married Mary Orford (an office manager and proof reader), 1949; children: Eric, Joan. *Education:* Attended City College (now City College of the City University of New York), 1935-38. *Home:* 31-37 95th St., East Elmhurst, N.Y. 11369. *Office:* Schomburg Center for Research in Black Culture, New York Public Library, 103 West 135th St., New York, N.Y. 10030.

CAREER: Erie Railroad, Jersey City, N.J., redcap, 1938-42; *Negro Quarterly,* New York City, member of editorial staff, 1943; Congress of Industrial Organizations, Political Action Committee, New York City, shipping clerk, 1944-45; New York Public Library, Schomburg Center for Research in Black Culture, New York City, member of staff, 1945—. Editor, reviewer, and consultant for Arno Press, Crowell-Collier, Beacon Press, McGraw—Hill Book Co., 1972—, and R. R. Bowker Co., 1974—. *Member:* American Institute for Marxist Studies.

WRITINGS: (Editor with Harry A. Ploski) *The Negro Almanac,* Bellwether, 1967, expanded and enlarged edition published as *Afro USA: A Reference Work on the Black Experience,* 1971, revised edition (with Ploski and Otto J. Lindenmeyer) published in five volumes as *Reference Library of Black America,* 1971; (editor with John H. Clarke, Esther Jackson, and J. H. O'Dell and contributor) *Black Titan: W.E.B. Du Bois,* Beacon Press, 1970; *In Defense of the People's Black and White History and Culture,* Freedomways, 1971; (editor with Stanton Biddle, Wendell Wray, and others) *No Crystal Stair: A Bibliography of Black Literature,* New York Public Library, 1971; (editor with Herbert Aptheker and Sidney Kaplan) *The Correspondence of W.E.B. Du Bois,* University of Massachusetts Press, Volume I: *Selections, 1877-1934,* 1973, Volume II: *Selections, 1934-1944,* 1976, Volume III: *Selections, 1944-1963,* 1978; (with Warren Halliburton) *Harlem: A History of Broken Dreams,* Doubleday, 1974; (editor and contributor) *A Freedomways Reader: Afro-America in the Seventies,* International Publishers, 1977; (editor with Clarke, Jackson, and O'Dell and contributor) *Paul Robeson: The Great Forerunner,* Dodd, 1978.

Contributor: John Henrik Clarke, editor, *Harlem: A Community in Transition,* Citadel, 1964; Clarke, editor, *William Styron's "Nat Turner": Ten Black Writers Respond,* Beacon Press, 1968; Patricia W. Romero, editor, *In Black America 1968: The Year of Awakening,* United Publishing, 1969; Addison Gayle, Jr., editor, *Black Expression: Essays by and about Black Americans in the Creative Arts,* Weybright, 1969; R. Baird Shuman, editor, *A Galaxy of Black Writing,* Moore Publishing, 1970; John M. Reilly, editor, *Twentieth Century Interpretations of "Invisible Man": A Collection of Critical Essays,* Prentice-Hall, 1970; Melvin J. Friedman and Irving Malin, editors, *William Styron's "The Confessions of Nat Turner": A Critical Handbook,* Wadsworth, 1970; Ruth Miller, editor, *Backgrounds to Blackamerican Literature,*

Chandler Publishing, 1971; Werner Sollers, editor, *A Bibliographic Guide to Afro-American Studies,* John F. Kennedy Institute (Berlin), 1972; Mabel M. Smythe, editor, *The American Negro Reference Book,* Prentice-Hall, 1974; Loften Mitchell, editor, *Voices of Black Theatre: Told in the Words of Its Pioneers,* James T. White, 1974; E. J. Josey and Ann Allen Schockley, editors, *Handbook of Black Librarianship,* Libraries Unlimited, 1977; Norman Rudich, editor, *Amerikanische Literatur-Kritik im Engagement,* Akademie-Verlag, 1978.

Author of introduction; all published by Arno, except as indicated: George W. Williams, *History of the Negro Race in America: 1619-1880,* 1968; William J. Simmons, *Men of Mark: Eminent, Progressive, and Rising,* 1968; Sojourner Truth, *Narrative of Sojourner Truth,* 1968; W.E.B. Du Bois, *The Atlanta University Publications,* Volume I, 1968, Volume II, 1969; George Edmund Haynes, *The Negro at Work in New York City,* 1968; James Weldon Johnson, *Black Manhattan,* 1968; I. Garland Penn, *The Afro-American Press and Its Editors,* 1969; D. W. Culp, editor, *Twentieth Century Negro Literature,* 1969; *The American Negro Academy Occasional Papers 1-22,* 1969; Mary Sagarin, *John Brown Russwurm,* Lothrop, 1970.

Author of bibliography; all published by U. N. Centre against Apartheid, except as indicated: Floyd B. Barbour, editor, *The Black Seventies,* Sargent, 1970; John H. Clarke, editor, *Pan-Africanism and the Liberation of Southern Africa: A Tribute to W.E.B. Du Bois,* 1978; Clarke, editor, *Dimensions of the Struggle against Apartheid: A Tribute to Paul Robeson,* 1979; *Frantz Fanon and the Fight for Freedom in Africa,* 1980. Also editor of and contributor to reprint series in Black studies, Bobbs-Merrill, 1970.

Contributor to *Encyclopedia of World Biography, Encyclopedia of Black America,* and *Dictionary of American Negro Biography.* Contributor to Black studies journals and literary publications, including *Science and Society, Black World, Journal of Negro Education, Phylon, Harlem Quarterly,* and *Masses and Mainstream.* Editor of *Dorie Miller Dispatch* (newspaper of Dorie Miller Cooperative), 1958-64; co-founder and associate editor, *Freedomways,* 1961—.

WORK IN PROGRESS: Bibliographical supplements to *Highlights of a Fighting History: Sixty Years of the Communist Party USA,* for the American Institute for Marxist Studies, and to Jean Corey Bond's *Lorraine Hansberry: Art of Thunder, Vision of Light;* contributing to *Research Guide to Central America and the Caribbean,* edited by Kenneth J. Grieb, for University of Wisconsin Press; collecting and revising his essays for publication in book form; an essay on the writings of Harold Cruse; a survey of recent books about Marcus Garvey; continued research on Marxist literary criticism.

SIDELIGHTS: Ernest Kaiser told *CA:* "I started out reading widely . . . with a view to becoming a writer. Then I focussed on trying to write literary criticism and I read as many books of literary criticism as I could find in public libraries or buy and borrow. . . . The Marxist writers, European and American, of the 1930s and 1940s seemed to place literature in a more meaningful context and perspective than the critics of any other literary school. They impressed me the most and I have been trying to write and publish Marxist social and literary criticism since the late 1940s. To agree with Kenneth Burke, it was my wide range of periodical reading over the years that shaped me. . . . I consider writing an important arm of the black liberation movement and of the struggles of all peoples for freedom."

Kaiser is regarded as one of today's foremost bibliographers in the area of Black life and history.

BIOGRAPHICAL/CRITICAL SOURCES: Peter M. Bergman, *The Chronological History of the Negro in America,* Bergman, 1969; John M. Bracey, Jr., August Meier, and Elliott Rudwick, editors, *Black Nationalism in America,* Bobbs-Merrill, 1970; Addison Gayle, Jr. editor, *The Black Aesthetic,* Doubleday, 1971; George A. Panichas, editor, *The Politics of Twentieth-Century Novelists,* Hawthorn, 1971; Richard K. Barksdale and Kenneth Kinnamon, editors, *Black Writers of America: A Comprehensive Anthology,* Macmillan, 1972; Jacqueline Covo, *The Blinking Eye: Ralph Waldo Ellison and His American, French, German and Italian Critics, 1952-1971,* Scarecrow, 1974.

* * *

KAMPEN, Irene Trepel 1922-

PERSONAL: Born April, 1922, in Brooklyn, N.Y.; daughter of Jack and Mary (Harris) Trepel; divorced; children: Christine. *Education:* University of Wisconsin, B.A., 1943. *Address:* P.O. Box 122, Ridgefield, Conn. 06877.

CAREER: Writer and lecturer.

WRITINGS: *Life without George,* Doubleday, 1961; *We That Are Left,* Doubleday, 1963; *The Ziegfelds' Girl,* Little, Brown, 1964; *Europe without George,* Norton, 1965; *Last Year at Sugarbush,* Norton, 1966; *Here Comes the Bride,* World Publishing, 1967; *Due to Lack of Interest Tomorrow Has Been Cancelled,* Doubleday, 1969; *Are You Carrying Any Gold or Living Relatives?,* Doubleday, 1970; *Nobody Calls at This House Just to Say Hello,* Doubleday, 1975; *Fear without Childbirth,* Lippincott, 1978. Contributor of stories and articles to *Ladies' Home Journal, McCall's, Redbook, Good Housekeeping, Woman's Day,* and other magazines.

BIOGRAPHICAL/CRITICAL SOURCES: *New York Times Book Review,* March 9, 1969, October 18, 1970; *Best Sellers,* April 1, 1969; *Saturday Review,* May 17, 1969; *Booklist,* January 15, 1976.

* * *

KARP, David 1922-
(Adam Singer, Wallace Ware)

PERSONAL: Born May 5, 1922, in New York, N.Y.; son of Abraham and Rebecca (Levin) Karp; married Lillian Klass, December 25, 1944; children: Ethan Ross, Andrew Gabriel. *Education:* City College (now City College of the City University of New York), B.S.S., 1948. *Politics:* "Independent-Democrat." *Home and office:* 1116 Corsica Dr., Pacific Palisades, Calif. 90272. *Agent:* Robinson/Weintraub Assos., Inc., 554 South San Vicente Blvd., Los Angeles, Calif. 90048.

CAREER: Free-lance writer and television and film producer, 1950—. Continuity director for radio station WNYC, 1948-49. President, Leda Productions, Inc., 1968—. *Military service:* U.S. Army, 1942-46; served with 81st Infantry Division in Philippines and Japan. *Member:* Writers Guild of America, West (council member, 1967-74; president, television branch, 1969-71), National Academy of Television Arts and Sciences, Academy of Motion Picture Arts and Sciences, Dramatists Guild, P.E.N. *Awards, honors:* Guggenheim fellowship in creative writing, 1956; Ohio State University award for best television show of the year, 1956; Robert E. Sherwood Award, 1956; American Library Association award for *All Honorable Men; Look* Award for best television script of 1958, for "The Plot to Kill Stalin," produced on "Playhouse 90" television series; "Edgar" award for best television script, Mystery Writers of America, 1960, for "The Empty Chair," produced on "The Untouchables" television series; Fund for the Republic award for "One," produced on "Kraft Television Theatre"; Emmy award, National Academy of Television Arts and Sciences, 1965, for "The 700 Year Old Gang," produced on "The Defenders" television series; Gavel award, American Bar Association, for "Charles Evans Hughes" and National Conference of Christians and Jews award for "Oscar W. Underwood," both produced on "Profiles in Courage" television series; National Academy of Television Arts and Sciences, best script nominations for "The Brotherhood of the Bell," 1970, and "Rally 'Round Your Flag," outstanding writing achievement in drama nomination for "Hawkins on Murder" (screenplay), 1972-73.

WRITINGS: *The Big Feeling,* Lion Books, 1952; *Hardman,* Lion Books, 1952; *Cry, Flesh,* Lion Books, 1952, published as *The Girl on Crown Street,* Banner Books, 1967; *The Brotherhood of Velvet,* Lion Books, 1953; (under pseudonym Adam Singer) *Platoon,* Lion Books, 1953; *One* (Book-of-the-Month Club alternate selection), Vanguard, 1953; (under pseudonym Wallace Ware) *The Charka Memorial,* Doubleday, 1954; *The Day of the Monkey,* Vanguard, 1955; *All Honorable Men,* Knopf, 1956; *Leave Me Alone,* Knopf, 1957; *Enter Sleeping,* Harcourt, 1960 (published in England as *The Sleepwalkers,* Gollancz, 1960); (with Murry D. Lincoln) *Vice President in Charge of Revolution,* McGraw, 1960; *The Last Believers,* Harcourt, 1964; (contributor) *Eight Courageous Americans,* Bantam, 1965; "Cafe Univers" (play), first produced Off-Broadway at The New Theatre, 1967; "Sol Madrid" (screenplay), Metro-Goldwyn-Mayer, 1968. Also author of screenplay, "Tender Loving Care."

Author of television scripts for network series, including "General Electric Theatre," "Playhouse 90," "The Defenders," "The Untouchables," "Profiles in Courage," and "I Spy." Also author of radio scripts for network radio shows, 1950-56. Contributor of short stories, articles, and reviews to newspapers and magazines, including *New York Times Magazine, New York Times Book Review, Esquire,* and *Nation.* Member of editorial board, *Television Quarterly,* 1965-71, 1972-78.

SIDELIGHTS: David Karp's manuscript collection is with the Mugar Collection at Boston University.

* * *

KASLOW, Florence Whiteman 1930-

PERSONAL: Born January 6, 1930, in Philadelphia, Pa.; daughter of Irving and Rose (Tarin) Whiteman; married Solis Kaslow (a stock broker), November 21, 1954; children: Nadine Joy, Howard Ian. *Education:* Temple University, A.B., 1952; Ohio State University, M.A.S.A., 1954; Bryn Mawr College, Ph.D., 1969. *Religion:* Jewish. *Home:* 807 Buckingham Rd., Rydal, Pa. 19046. *Office:* Department of Mental Health Sciences, Hahnemann Medical College, Basic Sciences Bldg., 15th and Vine St., Philadelphia, Pa.

CAREER: Temple University, Philadelphia, Pa., instructor in sociology, 1961-62; Pennsylvania State University, Ogontz Campus, Abington, instructor in sociology, 1962-65, 1968-69; University of Pennsylvania, Philadelphia, assistant professor of social work, 1969-72, associate in social work and psychiatry, 1972-73; Hahnemann Medical College, Department of Mental Health Sciences, Philadelphia, associate professor, 1973-78, professor, 1979—. Private practice in counseling in Rydal, Pa., 1964—. Supervisor of adoptive homes, Association for Jewish Children, Philadelphia, 1954. B'nai Brith Youth Organization, Philadelphia, assistant director, 1954-57, director of girls' division, 1959-60. Marriage and family counseling, Camden Family Counsel, Camden, N.J., 1958-59. Caseworker at Montgomery County Mental Health Clinics, summer, 1965 and Family Service of Montgomery County, summer, 1966. Member of faculty, Congregation Keneseth Israel, Elkins Park, 1967-68, 1969-70, 1972-73; Special lecturer in family therapy, Family Institute of Philadelphia, 1972—. Consultant in counseling at Leaves of Grass Nursery Schools, Philadelphia, 1970—, Therapeutic Creative Arts Unit at Lafayette School for Children with Learning Disabilities, Philadelphia, 1970-72, American Association of Psychiatric Services for Children, 1971-73, Prisoners Family Welfare Association, 1972, Management Counsellors Corp., 1972—, Pennsylvania Law and Justice Institute, 1973—, Neighborhood Center Board, 1972-78, Management Counselors, 1972-78, and Law and Justice Institute, 1973-75. Staff specialist at Abington Hospital Community Mental Health Center, 1972-73, Moss Rehabilitation Hospital Social Service Department, 1973, Catholic Social Services of Philadelphia, 1973, Jewish Y's and Centers of Philadelphia, 1973—; staff training specialist, Bureau of Corrections, Harrisburg, Pa., 1973-75. Member of board, Jewish Y's and Centers, Neighborhood Center Branch, 1972—; host family, International House for Foreign Students, Philadelphia, 1958—.

MEMBER: International Transactional Analysis Association, American Family Therapy Association, American Psychological Association, American Orthopsychiatric Association, American Association of Sex Educators, Counselors, and Therapists, American Association for Marital and Family Therapy (fellow), American Association of Marriage and Family Counselors, National Association of Social Workers (charter member, 1955), American Association of University Professors, American Psychology-Law Society (chairman of certification committee, 1977-78), Eastern Psychological Association, Pennsylvania Society for Clinical Social Workers (member of executive board, 1972—), Pennsylvania Association of Marriage and Family Counselors (treasurer, 1974-75; chairman of licensing committee, 1974-76; vice-president, 1976-77), Pennsylvania Psychological Association (fellow; chairman of awards committee, 1976; president of academic division, 1978-79), Philadelphia Society of Clinical Psychologists (fellow; program chairman, 1975-78; member of executive board, 1975-78), Family Institute of Philadelphia, Social Work Interfaculty Colloquium (chairman, 1970-72), Temple University Liberal Arts Alumni (president of board, 1960-62), Temple University Alumni Association (member of board, 1964; member of executive committee, 1971—), Phi Alpha Theta, Pi Gamma Mu.

WRITINGS: *Issues in Human Services: A Sourcebook in Supervisions and Staff Development,* Jossey-Bass, 1972; (with Lita L. Schwartz) *Personality* (instructors manual for test by Elaine Donelson), Appleton, 1973; (editor) *Supervision, Staff Training and Consultation in the Helping Professions,* Jossey-Bass, 1977.

Contributor: R. Hyatt and N. Rolnick, editors, *Teaching the Mentally Handicapped Child,* Behavioral Publications, 1974; Schwartz, editor, *Stress Their Abilities: A Primer in Special Education,* Wadsworth, 1975; P. Woods, editor, *Career Opportunities for Psychologists,* American Psychological Association, 1976; W. C. Adamson, editor, *Specific Learning Disorders: A Handbook for Bridging the Gap,*

Gardner Press, 1978; J. J. Platt and R. Wicks, editors, *The Psychologist as Consultant to the Court,* Grune, 1979; P. Sholevar, editor, *A Handbook of Marriage, Marital Therapy, and Divorce,* Spectrum, 1979; A. Gurman and D. Kniskern, editors, *Handbook of Family Therapy,* Brunner, 1980; G. Cooke, editor, *Readings in Forensic Psychology,* C. C Thomas, in press. Contributor of numerous articles and reviews to periodicals, including *Growth and Change, Academic Therapy Quarterly, Public Welfare,* and *Clinical Social Work Journal.* Consulting editor, *Clinical Social Work Journal,* 1972; editor, *Journal of Marital and Family Therapy,* 1976-81. Member of editorial boards, *Journal of Divorce, Marriage and Family Review,* and *Italian Journal of Family Therapy.*

* * *

KASTLE, Herbert D(avid) 1924- (Herbert d'H. Lee)

PERSONAL: Born July 11, 1924, in Brooklyn, N.Y.; son of Meyer and Eva Kastle; children: Rhona Deborah, Matthew Lloyd. *Education:* Washington Square College of Arts & Sciences, B.A., 1949; New York University, M.A., 1950. *Residence:* Los Angeles, Calif. *Agent:* Theron Raines, 475 Fifth Ave., New York, N.Y. 10017.

CAREER: Has worked as editor, advertising copywriter, and screenwriter. Full-time novelist, 1958—. *Military service:* U.S. Army Air Forces, three years, World War II. *Member:* Disabled American Veterans.

WRITINGS: One Thing on My Mind, Popular Library, 1957; *Koptic Court,* Simon & Schuster, 1958; *Camera,* Simon & Schuster, 1959; *Bachelor Summer,* Avon, 1959; *The World They Wanted,* St. Martin's, 1961; *Countdown to Murder,* Crest Books, 1961; *The Reassembled Man,* Gold Medal, 1965; *Hot Prowl,* Gold Medal, 1966; *The Movie Maker,* Geis, 1968; *Miami Golden Boy,* Geis, 1969; (under pseudonym Herbert d'H. Lee, with Valerie X. Scott) *Surrogate Wife,* Dell, 1971; *Millionaires,* Delacorte, 1972; *Ellie,* Delacorte, 1973; *Cross-Country,* Delacorte, 1975; *Edward Berner Is Alive Again!,* Prentice-Hall, 1975; *The Gang,* Dell, 1976; *Death Squad,* Dell, 1977; *Ladies of the Valley,* Arbor House, 1979; *Sunset People,* Jove, 1980.

WORK IN PROGRESS: A novel, *Death Dreams.*

SIDELIGHTS: Herbert Kastle told *CA,* "I write because I dislike, intensely, all other forms of making a living." His books have been published in England, France, Italy, Holland, Germany, Australia, and Japan.

BIOGRAPHICAL/CRITICAL SOURCES: Fantasy and Science Fiction, June, 1965; *New York Times Book Review,* December 29, 1968; *Books and Bookmen,* June, 1969; *Book World,* August 24, 1969; *Variety,* November 5, 1969; *Spectator,* September 1, 1973.

* * *

KATZ, Eve 1938-

PERSONAL: Born July 2, 1938, in Paris, France; naturalized U.S. citizen in 1943; daughter of Henry William and Friedel (Kramer) Katz. *Education:* Radcliffe College, B.A., 1959; University of California, Berkeley, M.A., 1960; Yale University, Ph.D., 1966. *Office:* Association of American Universities, One Dupont Cir. N.W., Washington, D.C. 20036.

CAREER: New York University, New York, N.Y., assistant professor, 1968-72, associate professor of French, 1972-75; director of undergraduate and graduate programs in France, Middlebury College, 1976-78; Association of American Universities, Washington, D.C., director of Federal Relations for Graduate Education, 1978—. *Awards, honors:* Woodrow Wilson grant, 1959; Fulbright grant, 1960.

WRITINGS—All published by Harper: (Editor with Donald R. Hall) Georges Simenon, *Le Chien jaune,* 1967; (with Hall) *Explicating French Texts: Poetry, Prose, Drama,* 1970; (editor) *La France en Metamorphose,* 1976. Contributor to *Yale French Studies, Studies on Voltaire and the Eighteenth Century,* and other journals.

* * *

KAUFELT, David Allan 1939-

PERSONAL: Born September 8, 1939, in Elizabeth, N.J.; son of Julius Louis (founder of supermarket chain) and Irene (Meyer) Kaufelt; married Lynn Higashi (a designer), 1974. *Education:* University of Pennsylvania, B.S.E., 1961; New York University, M.A., 1962. *Residence:* New York, N.Y.; Sag Harbor, N.Y.; and Key West, Fla. *Agent:* Dick Duane, Pinder Lane Productions, 159 West 53rd St., New York, N.Y. 10017.

CAREER: Advertising copywriter, 1965-75; director of public interest, Henry Street Settlement, 1975-77. Adjunct instructor of creative writing, Upsala College. *Military service:* U.S. Army, public information specialist, 1963-65.

WRITINGS: Six Months with an Older Woman, Putnam, 1973; *The Bradley Beach Rumba,* Putnam, 1974; *Spare Parts,* Warner Books, 1978; *Late Bloomer,* Harcourt, 1979; *Midnight Movies,* Delacorte, 1980.

WORK IN PROGRESS: Three Brothers, for Delacorte.

SIDELIGHTS: David Kaufelt wrote *CA:* "Writing is a craft that must be mastered and practiced before it can become art. I'm practicing as hard as I can."

* * *

KAUFFMAN, Joseph F(rank) 1921-

PERSONAL: Born December 2, 1921, in Providence, R.I.; son of Frank J. and Lena (Andelman) Kauffman; married Gladys Davidson, June 20, 1943; children: Marcia L. (Mrs. Willard Krasnow), Glenn Frank. *Education:* University of Denver, B.A., 1948; Northwestern University, M.A., 1951; Boston University, Ed.D., 1958. *Politics:* Democrat. *Religion:* Jewish. *Home:* 1426 Annen Lane, Madison, Wis. 53711. *Office:* Department of Educational Administration, University of Wisconsin, Madison, Wis. 53705.

CAREER: Brandeis University, Waltham, Mass., lecturer and assistant to president, 1952-56, dean of students, 1956-60; Jewish Theological Seminary of America, New York, N.Y., executive vice-president, 1960-61; Peace Corps, Washington, D.C., director of training, 1961-63; American Personnel and Guidance Association, Washington, D.C., director of higher education, 1963-65; University of Wisconsin—Madison, dean of student affairs and professor of counseling and behavioral science, 1965-68; Rhode Island College, Providence, president, 1968-73; University of Wisconsin—Madison, professor of educational administration, 1973—. Lecturer at University of Maryland, 1964-65, and Michigan State University, 1972. Chairman of national committee on student higher education, Edward W. Hazen Foundation, 1966—; member of national advisory council, Peace Corps, 1967-68; member of board of directors, American Council on Education, 1969-72. President of Rhode Island Council of Community Services, 1972. *Military service:* U.S. Army, Infantry, 1942-45; served in North Africa and Italy; became sergeant.

MEMBER: American Association for Higher Education, Association of Professors of Higher Education, American Sociological Association (fellow), American College Personnel Association, American Personnel and Guidance Association, Phi Beta Kappa.

WRITINGS: (Contributor) E. H. Erikson, editor, *Youth, Change and Challenge,* Basic Books, 1963; (editor with L. E. Dennis) *The College and the Student,* American Council on Education, 1966; *Education,* Potomac, 1966; (with others) *The Student in Higher Education,* Hazen Foundation, 1968; *The Selection of College and University Presidents,* Association of American Colleges, 1974; *At the Pleasure of the Board: The Service of the College and University President,* American Council on Education, 1980. Contributor to *Encyclopedia of Education* and educational journals.

* * *

KAUFMANN, Walter 1921-

PERSONAL: Born July 1, 1921, in Freiburg, Germany; son of Bruno and Edith (Seligsohn) Kaufmann; married Hazel Dennis, 1942; children: Dinah, David. *Education:* Williams College, B.A., 1941; Harvard University, A.M., 1942, Ph.D., 1947. *Office:* Department of Philosophy, Princeton University, Princeton, N.J. 08544.

CAREER: Princeton University, Princeton, N.J., instructor, 1947-50, assistant professor, 1950-54, associate professor, 1954-62, professor of philosophy, 1962—, Stuart Professor of Philosophy, 1979—. Fulbright professor at Heidelberg, Germany, 1955-56, and Jerusalem, Israel, 1962-63; Witherspoon Lecturer, Princeton University, 1962; visiting professor at Columbia University, Cornell University, New School for Social Research, University of Michigan, Purdue University, and University of Washington. Phi Beta Kappa visiting scholar, 1972; visiting fellow, Australian National University, 1974. Member of faculty, European Forum Alpbach, 1966, 1968, and 1976, and International University for Presidents, 1972, 1973. Committee for International Exchange of Persons, Department of State, advisor, 1957-61, chairman of screening committee for philosophy and religion, 1959-61. *Military service:* U.S. Army Air Forces and Military Intelligence Service, 1944-46. *Member:* American Philosophical Association, Interfuture (co-founder; chairman of board, 1969-70), Phi Beta Kappa. *Awards, honors:* International Leo Baeck Prize, 1961.

WRITINGS: Nietzsche, Princeton University Press, 1950, 4th edition, 1974; *Critique of Religion and Philosophy,* Harper, 1958, reprinted, Princeton University Press, 1978; *From Shakespeare to Existentialism,* Beacon Press, 1959, revised edition, Anchor Books, 1960, reprinted, Princeton University Press, 1980 (published in England as *The Owl and the Nightingale,* Faber, 1960); *The Faith of a Heretic,* Doubleday, 1961, reprinted, New American Library, 1978; *Cain and Other Poems,* Doubleday, 1962, 3rd edition, New American Library, 1975; *Hegel: Reinterpretation, Texts, and Commentary,* Doubleday, 1965; *Tragedy and Philosophy,* Doubleday, 1968, revised edition, Princeton University Press, 1979; *Without Guilt and Justice,* Peter H. Wyden, 1973; *Existentialism, Religion, and Death,* New American Library, 1976; *Religions in Four Dimensions,* Reader's Digest Press—McGraw, 1976; *The Future of the Humanities,* Reader's Digest Press—McGraw, 1977; *Man's Lot: A Trilogy* (includes *Life at the Limits, Time Is an Artist,* and *What Is Man?*), Reader's Digest Press—McGraw, 1978; *Goethe, Kant, and Hegel* (first volume in trilogy *Discovering the Mind*), McGraw, 1980.

Translator and editor: *The Portable Nietzsche,* Viking, 1954; *Existentialism from Dostoevsky to Sartre,* Meridian, 1956; *Judaism and Christianity: Essays by Leo Baeck,* Jewish Publication Society, 1958; *Goethe's Faust: A New (Verse) Translation,* Doubleday, 1961; *Philosophic Classics,* two volumes, *Thales to St. Thomas* and *Bacon to Kant,* Prentice-Hall, 1961; *Religion from Tolstoy to Camus,* Harper, 1961, revised edition, Torchbooks, 1964; *Twenty German Poets,* Random House, 1962, expanded edition published as *Twenty-Five German Poets,* Norton, 1975; Nietzsche, *Beyond Good and Evil,* Random House, 1966; Nietzsche, *The Will to Power,* Random House, 1967; Nietzsche, *Birth of Tragedy* [and] *The Case of Wagner,* Random House, 1967; Nietzsche, *On the Genealogy of Morals* [and] *Ecce Homo,* Random House, 1967; Martin Buber, *I and Thou,* Scribner, 1970; *Hegel's Political Philosophy,* Atherton, 1970; Nietzsche, *The Gay Science,* Random House, 1974.

Contributor: Ashley Montagu, *Toynbee and History,* Sargent, 1956; P. A. Schilpp, *The Philosophy of Karl Jaspers,* Tudor, 1957; Herman Feifel, *The Meaning of Death,* McGraw, 1959; (author of preface) Malcolm Hay, *Europe and the Jews,* Beacon Press, 1960; Wiener and Noland, *Ideas in Cultural Perspective,* Rutgers University Press, 1962; (author of preface) Kierkegaard, *The Present Age,* Torchbooks, 1962; Glikes and Schwaber, *Of Poetry and Power,* Basic Books, 1964; Sidney Hook, *Art and Philosophy,* New York University Press, 1966; George Barnett, *Philosophy and Educational Development,* 1966. Contributor to *Encyclopaedia Britannica, Chambers's Encyclopaedia, Encyclopedia Americana, Collier's Encyclopedia, Grolier's Encyclopedia, Encyclopedia of Morals, Encyclopedia of Philosophy,* and *The Concise Encyclopedia of Western Philosophy and Philosophers.* Contributor to journals.

WORK IN PROGRESS: Final two volumes of *Discovering the Mind* trilogy, for McGraw.

SIDELIGHTS: Walter Kaufmann told *CA:* "In *Religions in Four Dimensions* I made a first attempt to fuse philosophy and photography in a new way. The book contains over 180 of my own color photographs as well as more than 70 black and white photographs. The pictures are not mere illustrations, any more than the text is merely expanded captions. The trilogy *Man's Lot* carries this attempt further. The eighty pages of color [photographs] in the first volume, *Life at the Limits,* have no captions of any kind, and the sequence of images is conceived as an independent work of art that illuminates Life at the limits or *vita in extremis* in its own way as much as the text does in different ways. Each of the other two volumes of *Man's Lot* represents a new experiment in a similar vein.

"My other trilogy, *Discovering the Mind,* involves no photography but offers a new interpretation of German intellectual history since Kant. I am planning to continue my work in philosophy and scholarship of a more traditional kind while also publishing more books that involve visual images."

BIOGRAPHICAL/CRITICAL SOURCES: Scientific American, November, 1965; *Journal of the History of Ideas,* April-June, 1966; *Philosophical Review,* April, 1967; *Times Literary Supplement,* November 2, 1967; *Science and Society,* summer, 1969; *New York Review of Books,* November 20, 1969; *Journal of Aesthetics and Art Criticism,* spring, 1970; *Georgia Review,* spring, 1971; *New York Times,* April 7, 1973; *Review of Metaphysics,* December, 1973; *Journal of Asian Studies,* August, 1975; *Book World,* April 3, 1977; *Christian Science Monitor,* July 6, 1977; *New York Times*

Book Review, April 16, 1978; *South Atlantic Quarterly,* autumn, 1978.

* * *

KAZIN, Alfred 1915-

PERSONAL: Born June 5, 1915, in Brooklyn, N.Y.; son of Charles and Gita (Fagelman) Kazin; married Caroline Bookman, May 23, 1947 (divorced); married Ann Birstein (a writer), June 26, 1952; children: (first marriage) Michael; (second marriage) Cathrael. *Education:* College of the City of New York (now City College of the City University of New York), B.S.S., 1935; Columbia University, M.A., 1938. *Religion:* Jewish. *Office:* English Department, Hunter College of the City University of New York, 33 West 42nd St., New York, N.Y. 10036.

CAREER: College of the City of New York (now City College of the City University of New York), New York City, tutor in literature, 1937-42; *New Republic,* New York City, literary editor, 1942-43, contributing editor, 1943-45; *Fortune* magazine, New York City, associate editor, 1943-44; Harvard University, Cambridge, Mass., visiting lecturer, 1952; Smith College, Northampton, Mass., William Allan Neilson Research Professor, 1953-54; Amherst College, Amherst, Mass., professor of American studies, 1955-58; New York University, New York City, Berg Professor of Literature, 1957; University of Puerto Rico, Rio Piedras, Puerto Rico, visiting professor, 1959; Princeton University, Princeton, N.J., Christian Gauss Lecturer, 1961; City College of the City University of New York, Buell Gallagher Professor, 1962; University of California, Berkeley, Beckman Professor, 1963; State University of New York at Stony Brook, distinguished professor of English, 1963-73; Hunter College of the City University of New York, New York City, distinguished professor of English, 1973—. Visiting professor, University of Minnesota, summers, 1946, 1950; writer-in-residence, American Academy in Rome, 1975; William White Professor of English, University of Notre Dame, 1978-79. Visiting lecturer in English and general literature, New School for Social Research, 1941-42, 1948-49, 1951, 1952-53, and 1958-63; visiting lecturer, Black Mountain College, fall, 1944. Has also lectured in Germany, England, France, Sweden, and Norway.

MEMBER: National Institute of Arts and Letters, American Academy of Arts and Sciences, Phi Beta Kappa. *Awards, honors:* Guggenheim fellow, 1940, 1947; Rockefeller fellow in Britain, 1945; Fulbright lecturer, Cambridge University, 1952; recipient of George Polk Memorial Award for criticism, 1966; Brandeis University Creative Arts Award, 1973; Center for the Advanced Study of Behavioral Sciences fellow, 1977-78; National Endowment for the Humanities senior fellow, 1977-78; Townsend Harris medal from College of the City of New York Alumni; Litt.D., Adelphi University, 1964, and University of New Haven, 1974.

WRITINGS: On Native Grounds, Reynal, 1942; *A Walker in the City,* Harcourt, 1951; *The Inmost Leaf,* Harcourt, 1955; *Contemporaries,* Little, Brown, 1962; *Starting Out in the Thirties,* Little, Brown, 1965; *Bright Book of Life,* Little, Brown, 1973; *New York Jew,* Knopf, 1978.

Editor: *The Portable William Blake,* Viking, 1946; *F. Scott Fitzgerald: The Man and His Work,* World Publishing, 1951; (with Charles Shapiro) *The Stature of Theodore Dreiser,* Indiana University Press, 1955; Herman Melville, *Moby Dick,* Houghton, 1956; (with Daniel Aaron) *Ralph Waldo Emerson: A Modern Anthology,* Houghton, 1958; (with Ann Birstein) *The Works of Anne Frank,* Doubleday, 1959; Theodore Dreiser, *Sister Carrie,* Dell, 1960; Theodore Dreiser, *The Financier,* Dell, 1961; *The Open Form: Essays for Our Time,* Harcourt, 1961, revised edition, 1965; (author of introduction) *Selected Short Stories of Nathaniel Hawthorne,* Fawcett, 1966; *Writers at Work: The Paris Review Interviews, Third Series,* Viking, 1967; Henry James, *The Ambassadors,* Bantam, 1969.

Author of introduction to several editions of works by Dostoevsky, Sholom Aleichem, Theodore Dreiser, Henry James, H. G. Wells, D. H. Lawrence, and others. Contributor to *The New Republic, Atlantic Monthly,* and other periodicals.

SIDELIGHTS: Christopher Lehmann-Haupt writes: Alfred "Kazin's portraits of the many writers and intellectuals he knew . . . are distinctive because they are framed by ideas. He rarely allows people to emerge through anecdote. . . . Instead, he *explains* people." The reviewer continues: "The intellect is always at attention in these pages. But don't be fooled: Beneath the mind there is heart. It is evident in the passion of the prose when Mr. Kazin becomes excited about an idea."

John Gross writes: "Kazin is, I think, an excellent literary journalist: nimble, energetic, humane. He would rather get the best out of an author than get the better of him; his aim is to enlarge and exhilarate, and when he dislikes a book he manages to say so without doubling up in paroxysms of rage." R. D. Spector adds: "He has more to say about the meaning of literature than can be found in the crabbed notes of the symbol searchers and irony hunters. . . . He is never dull, and he is always personally involved."

BIOGRAPHICAL/CRITICAL SOURCES: New York Herald Tribune Books, April 22, 1962; *Atlantic,* May, 1962; *New Statesman,* February 8, 1963; *Encounter,* May, 1963; *Times Literary Supplement,* May 10, 1963; *Partisan Review,* Winter, 1966; *Book World,* August 4, 1968; *Commentary,* February, 1970; *New York Times Book Review,* May 7, 1978; *Publishers Weekly,* May 15, 1978.

* * *

KEANE, Patrick J(oseph) 1939-

PERSONAL: Born November 28, 1939, in New York, N.Y.; son of Joseph Patrick (an accountant for American Telephone and Telegraph) and Margaret (Fox) Keane; married Ann Knickerbocker. *Education:* Fordham University, B.S.S., 1961; New York University, M.A., 1969, Ph.D., 1971. *Home:* 306 Radcliffe Rd., Dewitt, N.Y. 13214. *Office:* Department of English, Le Moyne College, Syracuse, N.Y. 13214.

CAREER: Ronald Press, New York, N.Y., advertising copywriter, 1965-68; Skidmore College, Saratoga, N.Y., assistant professor of English, 1970-77; Le Moyne College, Syracuse, N.Y., associate professor of English, 1977—. *Military service:* U.S. Army, 1962-65. *Member:* Modern Language Association of America. *Awards, honors:* Summer seminar award, 1973, and College Teacher in Residence Award, 1977-78, both from National Endowment for the Humanities.

WRITINGS: (Editor and contributor) *William Butler Yeats: Contemporary Studies in Literature,* McGraw, 1973; *A Wild Civility: Interactions in the Poetry and Thought of Robert Graves,* University of Missouri Press, 1980. Contributor to periodicals, including *Salmagundi* and *New Republic.*

WORK IN PROGRESS: The Arch of Experience.

KEELEY, Edmund (Leroy) 1928-

PERSONAL: Born February 5, 1928, in Damascus, Syria; son of James Hugh and Mathilde (Vossler) Keeley; married Mary Stathatos-Kyris, 1951. *Education:* Princeton University, B.A., 1949; Oxford University, D.Phil., 1952. *Home:* 140 Littlebrook Rd., Princeton, N.J. *Agent:* Georges Borchardt, Inc., 136 East 57th St., New York, N.Y. 10022. *Office:* Creative Writing Program, Princeton University, 185 Nassau St., Princeton, N.J.

CAREER: American Farm School, Salonika, Greece, teacher, 1949-50; Brown University, Providence, R.I., instructor 1952-53; Salonika University, Salonika, professor of English and American literature and Fulbright lecturer, 1953-54; Princeton University, Princeton, N.J., instructor in English, 1954-57, assistant professor, 1957-62, associate professor, 1963-70, professor of English and creative writing, 1970—, co-director of comparative literature program, 1964-65, director of creative arts program, 1966-71, director of creative writing program, 1971—. Writer-in-residence, Knox College, 1963. Lecturer, U.S. Information Agency, in Greece, 1954, at Oxford University, 1960, at Writers Workshop, University of Iowa, 1962-63. Trustee, American Farm School; member of board of directors, Columbia University Translation Center. *Military service:* U.S. Navy, 1945-46. U.S. Air Force Reserve, 1952-56; became technical sergeant.

MEMBER: Comparative Literature Association, Modern Greek Studies Association (president, 1970-73, 1980—), Poetry Society of America (vice-president, 1977-79), P.E.N., Modern Language Association of America, Authors Guild, International Society of Neohellenic Studies, American Academy in Rome (fellow, 1959-60), Oxford Society, Phi Beta Kappa. *Awards, honors:* Council for the Humanities fellowship, 1956-57; Prix de Rome fellowship of American Academy of Arts and Letters, 1959; Guggenheim fellowship for fiction, 1959, for criticism, 1973; McCosh faculty fellow, 1969-70; P.E.N.-Columbia University Translation Center prize, 1975; Ingram Merrill Foundation grant, 1977-78; National Endowment for the Humanities grant, 1977-78; Harold Morton Laudon Translation Award, Academy of American Poets, 1980.

WRITINGS: The Libation, Scribner, 1958; *The Gold-Hatted Lover,* Little, Brown, 1961; *The Imposter,* Doubleday, 1970; *Voyage to a Dark Island,* Curtis, 1972; *Cavafy's Alexandria: Study of a Myth in Progress,* Harvard University Press, 1976.

Editor and translator: (With Philip Sherrard) *Six Poets of Modern Greece,* Thames & Hudson, 1960, Knopf, 1961; (with wife, Mary Keeley) Vassilis Vassilikos, *The Plant, The Well, The Angel: A Trilogy,* Knopf, 1964; (with Sherrard) *Four Greek Poets,* Penguin, 1965; (with Sherrard) George Seferis, *Collected Poems: 1924-1955,* Princeton University Press, 1967; (with George Savidis) C. P. Cavafy, *Passions and Ancient Days,* Dial, 1971; (with Peter Bien) *Modern Greek Writers,* Princeton University Press, 1972; (with Sherrard) Cavafy, *Selected Poems,* Princeton University Press, 1972; (with Savidis) Odysseus Elytis, *The Axion Esti,* Pittsburgh University Press, 1972; (with Sherrard and Savidis) Cavafy, *Collected Poems,* Princeton University Press, 1975; *Ritsos in Parentheses,* Princeton University Press, 1979; (with Sherrard) Angelos Sikelianos, *Selected Poems,* Princeton University Press, 1979.

WORK IN PROGRESS: A novel; *Odysseus Elytis: Selected Poems.*

AVOCATIONAL INTERESTS: Travel, rare books.

BIOGRAPHICAL/CRITICAL SOURCES: New York Herald Tribune, August 3, 1958; *Comparative Literature,* summer, 1973; *New York Times Book Review,* October 24, 1976; *New York Review of Books,* February 17, 1977; *Antioch Review,* spring, 1977; *Times Literary Supplement,* October 14, 1977.

* * *

KELLER, Beverly (Lou) (B. L. Harwick)

PERSONAL: Born in San Francisco, Calif.; daughter of Wearne E. and Ruth (Burke) Harwick; married William Jon Keller, June 18, 1949 (died, 1964); children: Lisa, Kristen, Michele. *Education:* University of California, Berkeley, B.A., 1950. *Residence:* Davis, Calif. *Agent:* Lurton Blassingame, 60 East 42nd St., New York, N.Y. 10017.

CAREER: Author, newspaper columnist, and feature writer.

WRITINGS: The Baghdad Defections (novel), Bobbs-Merrill, 1973.

Juvenile books; published by Coward, except as indicated: *Fiona's Bee,* 1975; *The Beetle Bush,* 1976; *Don't Throw Another One, Dover!,* 1976; (under name B. L. Harwick) *The Frog Prints,* Raintree Editions, 1976; *The Genuine, Ingenious Thrift Shop Genie, Clarissa Mae Bean and Me,* 1977; *Pimm's Place,* 1978; *The Sea Watch,* Four Winds Press, 1980; *Fiona's Flea,* 1981.

Work is anthologized in *The Best from Fantasy and Science Fiction,* edited by Edward Ferman, Doubleday, 1974. Contributor of short stories to *Atlantic Monthly, Iatros Djinn, Out of Sight, Fantasy and Science Fiction, Cosmopolitan,* and other magazines, and of articles and reviews to *San Francisco Chronicle, Atlantic, Women's News Service,* and Peninsula Newspapers, Inc.

WORK IN PROGRESS: A novel.

SIDELIGHTS: Beverly Keller lived in Baghdad, Beirut, and Rome. She drove from Beirut to Athens by way of Syria and Turkey, and has travelled throughout Europe. *Avocational interests:* Animals, politics.

* * *

KELLOGG, Steven 1941-

PERSONAL: Born October 26, 1941, in Norwalk, Conn.; son of Robert E. and Hilma Marie (Johnson) Kellogg; married Helen Hill, 1967; stepchildren: Pamela, Melanie, Kimberly, Laurie, Kevin, Colin. *Education:* Rhode Island School of Design, B.F.A., 1963; graduate study at American University. *Home:* Bennett's Bridge Rd., Sandy Hook, Conn. 06482. *Agent:* Sheldon Fogelman, 10 East 40th St., New York, N.Y. 10016.

CAREER: Author and illustrator of children's books; artist. Instructor in etching, American University, 1966; has taught printmaking and painting. Paintings and etchings have been shown at exhibitions. *Awards, honors:* "One of ten best picture-books" citation, *New York Times,* and ABC Award, Brooklyn Museum, both 1970, for *Matilda Who Told Lies and Was Burned to Death;* "one of best books of the year" citation, 1971, and Dutch Zilveren Griffel, 1974, both for *Can I Keep Him?;* "one of ten best picture-books" citation, *New York Times,* 1974, for *There Was an Old Woman; The Mystery of the Missing Red Mitten* chosen as Children's Book Showcase Title, 1974.

WRITINGS—Juvenile; self-illustrated; published by Dial, except as indicated: *The Wicked Kings of Bloon* (Junior Literary Guild selection), Prentice-Hall, 1970; *Can I Keep Him?* (Junior Literary Guild selection), 1971; *The Mystery Beast of Ostergeest*, 1971; *The Orchard Cat*, 1972; *Won't Somebody Play with Me?*, 1972; *The Island of the Skog*, 1973; *The Mystery of the Missing Red Mitten*, 1974; (adaptor) *There Was an Old Woman*, Parents' Magazine Press, 1974; *Much Bigger Than Martin*, 1976; *The Mysterious Tadpole*, 1977; *The Mystery of the Magic Green Ball*, 1979; *Pinkerton, Behave*, 1979; *The Mystery of the Flying Orange Pumpkin*, 1980.

Illustrator: George Mendoza, *Gwot! Horribly Funny Hairticklers*, Harper, 1967; James Copp, *Martha Matilda O'Toole*, Bradbury, 1969; Eleanor B. Heady, *Brave Johnny O'Hare*, Parents' Magazine Press, 1969; Mary Rodgers, *The Rotten Book*, Harper, 1969; Miriam Young, *Can't You Pretend?*, Putnam, 1970; Hilaire Bellock, *Matilda Who Told Lies and Was Burned to Death*, Dial, 1970; Ruth Loomis, *Mrs. Purdy's Children*, Dial, 1970; Fred Rogers, *Mister Rogers' Songbook*, Random House, 1970; Peggy Parish, *Granny and the Desperadoes*, Macmillan, 1970; Anne Mallett, *Here Comes Tagalong*, Parents' Magazine Press, 1971; Jan Wahl, *Crabapple Night*, Holt, 1971; Aileen Friedman, *The Castles of the Two Brothers*, Holt, 1972; Wahl, *The Very Peculiar Tunnel*, Putnam, 1972; Jeanette Franklin Caines, *Abby*, Harper, 1973; Joan M. Lexau, *Come Here, Cat*, Harper, 1973; Doris Herold Lund, *You Ought to See Herbert's House*, F. Watts, 1973; Liesel Moak Skorpen, *Kisses and Fishes*, Harper, 1974.

Jean Van Leeuwen, *The Great Christmas Kidnaping Caper*, Dial, 1975; Margaret Mahy, *The Boy Who Was Followed Home*, F. Watts, 1975; Cora Annett, *How the Witch Got Alf*, F. Watts, 1975; Alice Bach, *The Smartest Bear and His Brother Oliver*, Harper, 1975; Belloc, *Hilaire Belloc's "The Yak, the Python, the Frog"* (Junior Literary Guild selection), Parents' Magazine Press, 1975; Judith Chaote, *Awful Alexander*, Doubleday, 1976; Lou Ann Bigge Gaeddert, *Gustav the Gourmet Giant*, Dial, 1976; Edward Bangs, *Steven Kellogg's Yankee Doodle*, Parents' Magazine Press, 1976; Bach, *The Most Delicious Camping Trip Ever*, Harper, 1976; Bach, *Grouchy Uncle Otto*, Harper, 1977; Carol Chapman, *Barney Bipple's Magic Dandelions*, Dutton, 1977; Bach, *Millicent the Magnificent*, Harper, 1978; Mercer Mayer, *Appelard and Liverwurst*, Four Winds, 1978; Marilyn Singer, *Pickle Pan*, Dutton, 1978; Douglas Davis, *There's an Elephant in the Garage*, Dutton, 1979; William Sleator, *Once, Said Darlene*, Dutton, 1979; Susan Pearson, *Molly Moves Out*, Dial, 1979; Julia Castiglia, *Jill the Pill*, Atheneum, 1979; Jean Marzollo, *Uproar on Hollercat Hill*, Dial, 1980; Trinka Noble, *The Day Jimmy's Boa Ate the Wash*, Dial, 1980.

WORK IN PROGRESS: Illustrations for *Liverwurst Is Missing* by Mercer Mayer, for Four Winds; a picture-book version of Puccini's opera, "Gianni Schicchi."

SIDELIGHTS: Steven Kellogg told *CA:* "The more deeply involved I become in the creation of picture-books, the more fascinated I am by its limitless possibilities. The picture-book contains the characteristics of many diversified art forms; and I am intrigued and challenged by the fact that it introduces children to the world of art and that, at its best, can absorb and win them to a lifetime commitment to the world of art with all of its excitement and emotional fulfillment."

BIOGRAPHICAL/CRITICAL SOURCES: Times Literary Supplement, July 18, 1980.

KELLY, Frank K. 1914-

PERSONAL: Born June 12, 1914, in Kansas City, Mo.; son of Francis M. and Martha (King) Kelly; married Barbara Mandigo, 1941; children: Terence F., Stephen D. *Education:* University of Kansas City (now University of Missouri—Kansas City), A.B., 1937. *Politics:* Democrat. *Religion:* Roman Catholic. *Home and office:* 34 East Padre St., Santa Barbara, Calif. *Agent:* McIntosh & Otis, 475 Fifth Ave., New York, N.Y. 10017.

CAREER: Kansas City Star, Kansas City, Mo., reporter and editor, 1937-41; Associated Press, New York, N.Y., feature writer, 1941-46; Democratic National Committee, Washington, D.C., assistant research director, 1948; speech writer for President Harry S Truman, 1948; United States Senate, Washington, D.C., staff director of majority policy committee and assistant to Senate Majority Leader, 1949-52; U.S. director, International Press Institute Study of World News, 1952-53; special consultant, American Book Publishers Council, 1953-54; account executive and vice-president, Stephen Fitzgerald & Co. (public relations), 1954-56; Fund for the Republic, Inc., Santa Barbara, Calif., vice-president, 1956-75; Center for the Study of Democratic Institutions, Santa Barbara, director of Study of the Mass Media of Communication, 1957-75. Member of board of directors, Roosevelt House, Hunter College of the City University of New York, 1959-62, Catholic Welfare Bureau (Santa Barbara), 1962—, Santa Barbara Education Television, Inc., 1963—, Work Training Program, Inc., 1964—, Buffum Publishing Corp., 1964-69, and National Peace Academy Campaign, 1980—. *Military service:* U.S. Army, 1943-45, served as enlisted correspondent; awarded European Theater Citation, two Bronze Stars.

MEMBER: Overseas Press Club of America, Society of Nieman Fellows, Authors League of America. *Awards, honors:* Nieman fellow, Harvard University, 1942-43, 1946; Alumnus of the Year, University of Missouri—Kansas City, 1974.

WRITINGS: (Co-author) *Psychology for the Returning Serviceman*, Penguin, 1945; (co-author) *Your Newspaper*, Macmillan, 1947; (co-author) *Men Who Make Your World*, Dutton, 1949; *An Edge of Light* (novel), Little, Brown, 1949; *Reporters around the World*, Little, Brown, 1957; *The Fight for the White House*, Crowell, 1961; *Your Freedoms: The Bill of Rights*, Putnam, 1964; *The Martyred Presidents, and Their Successors*, Putnam, 1967; *Your Laws*, Putnam, 1970; *Star Ship Invincible* (science fiction), Capra, 1979. Also author of *Bold, Bright and Free*, 1979. Author of short stories anthologized in O'Brien's *Best American Short Stories* and other collections.

Contributor of stories and book reviews to national magazines, including *Atlantic Monthly*, *New Yorker*, and *Saturday Review*.

SIDELIGHTS: Frank Kelly told *CA* that his "principal concern" is to stop "the nuclear arms' race which threatens humanity." Kelly is currently working with World Peacemakers, Pax Christi, and "other groups advocating disarmament." *Avocational interests:* Music, theatre, and fine arts.

BIOGRAPHICAL/CRITICAL SOURCES: News Statesman, April 21, 1967; *Best Sellers*, November 15, 1970.

* * *

KEMP, Lysander (Schaffer, Jr.) 1920-

PERSONAL: Born November 13, 1920, in Randolph, Vt.; son of Lysander Schaffer (a physician) and Dorothy (Schontag) Kemp. *Education:* Bates College, B.A., 1942; Boston University, M.A., 1946. *Politics:* Democrat. *Religion:* None. *Address:* P.O. Box 608, South Harwich, Mass. 02661.

CAREER: Writer and translator. University of Buffalo (now State University of New York at Buffalo), instructor, 1946-50, assistant professor of English, 1950-53; University of Texas Press, Austin, head editor, 1966-75; University of Texas at Austin, Institute of Latin American Studies, publications coordinator, 1975-79. *Military service:* U.S. Army, Caribbean Defense Command, 1942-45. *Member:* Texas Institute of Letters. *Awards, honors:* First prize, Borestone Mountain Poetry Awards, 1958, for poem "Odysseus."

WRITINGS—Poems: *The Northern Stranger,* Random House, 1946; *The Conquest and Other Poems from Spanish America,* Humanities Research Center, University of Texas, 1970.

Translator from Spanish: Juan Rulfo, *Pedro Paramo,* Grove, 1959; Octavio Paz, *The Labyrinth of Solitude,* Grove, 1961; Ricardo Pozas, *Juan the Chamula,* University of California Press, 1962; Miguel Leon-Portilla, editor, *The Broken Spears: The Aztec Account of the Conquest of Mexico,* Beacon Press, 1962; Carlos Fuentos, *Aura,* Farrar, Straus, 1965; *Selected Poems of Ruben Dario,* University of Texas Press, 1965; Xavier Domingo, *The Dreams of Reason,* Braziller, 1966; Mario Vargas Llosa, *The Time of the Hero,* Grove, 1966; Paz, *The Other Mexico: Critique of the Pyramid,* Grove, 1972; (and editor) Paz, *The Siren and the Seashell: Selected Essays on Poets and Poetry,* University of Texas Press, 1977.

Poetry is represented in anthology, *Best Poems of 1957,* edited by Robert T. Moore, Stanford University Press, 1958.

WORK IN PROGRESS: A short novel; a book of essays on Mexico; a collection of poems.

* * *

KENNEDY, James William 1905-

PERSONAL: Born August 22, 1905, in Denison, Tex.; son of Sydney Carr and Addie (Francis) Kennedy; married Frances Pleasants Campbell, August 19, 1935; children: Stephen Campbell, Jane Pleasants. *Education:* Attended Agricultural and Mechanical College of Texas (now Texas A & M University), 1923-24, University of Colorado, 1927-29, and Northwestern University, 1929-32; Western Theological Seminary, S.T.B., 1932; Stephen F. Austin State Teachers College (now Stephen F. Austin State University), A.B., 1934; University of the South, S.T.M., 1946. *Home:* 1124 Fortview Pl., Cincinnati, Ohio 45202.

CAREER: Ordained clergyman of Episcopal Church, 1932; St. John's Church, Hartford, Conn., assistant rector, 1932-33; priest-in-charge of four missions in the Diocese of Texas, 1933-37; rector of Epiphany Church, Atlanta, Ga., 1937-39, All Saints Church, Richmond, Va., 1939-45, Christ Church, Lexington, Ky., 1945-55, and of Church of the Ascension, New York, N.Y., 1955-64; Forward Movement Publications, Cincinnati, Ohio, director and editor, beginning 1964. Episcopal Church, chairman of department of Christian social relations, Diocese of Atlanta, 1937-39, chairman of department of Christian education, Diocese of Virginia, 1943-45, and Diocese of Lexington, 1945-53, deputy to General Convention, 1946, 1949, and 1952, member of Joint Commission on Ecumenical Relations, 1949-76, secretary of Committee on Ecumenical Relations of the Executive Council; World Council of Churches, accredited visitor to first assembly, Amsterdam, Netherlands, 1948, delegate to assemblies in Evanston, Ill., 1954, New Delhi, India, 1961, and Uppsala, Sweden, 1968. Conducted several radio programs, 1940-50. *Member:* International Association of Torch Clubs (former president), Omicron Delta Kappa. *Awards, honors:* D.D., Seabury-Western Theological Seminary, 1948; Freedoms Foundation awards for sermons, 1950 and 1951.

WRITINGS: Haven, Whittet & Shepperson, 1942; *The Man Who Wanted to Know,* Morehouse, 1944; *Haven House,* John Knox, 1944; *Hey Buddy,* Cloister Press, 1946; *Advance into Light,* Cloister Press, 1947; *Parsons Sampler,* Pilgrim Publications, 1948; *A Lenten Query,* Church Congress, 1950; *Exploring Paths of Church Unity,* World Council of Churches, 1951; *He that Gathereth,* World Council of Churches, 1953; (editor) *Henry Drummond: An Anthology,* Harper, 1953; *Evanston Notebook,* Sowers, 1953; *Evanston Scrapbook,* Sowers, 1954; *Meditations in His Presence,* Seabury, 1954; *Empty Shoes,* National Council, Episcopal Church, 1956; *Holy Island,* Morehouse, 1958; *The Most Comfortable Sacrament,* Seabury, 1961; *No Darkness at All,* Bethany, 1962; *The Unknown Worshipper,* Morehouse, 1964; *Minister's Shop Talk,* Harper, 1965.

All published by Foreward Movement Publications: *Perspectives: Sacred and Secular,* two volumes, 1970; (with John A. Morgan) *Which Way Today?,* 1974; *Nairobi, 1975,* 1976; *Partners in Mission,* 1977; *Anglican Partners,* 1978.

* * *

KENNEDY, John Fitzgerald 1917-1963

PERSONAL: Born May 29, 1917, in Brookline, Mass.; assassinated November 22, 1963, in Dallas, Tex.; buried in Arlington National Cemetery, Arlington, Va.; son of Joseph P. and Rose (Fitzgerald) Kennedy; married Jacqueline Lee Bouvier, September 12, 1953; children: Caroline, John F., Jr., Patrick Bouvier (deceased). *Education:* Attended London School of Economics, 1935-36; Harvard University, B.A. (with honors), 1940; Stanford University, graduate study, 1940.

CAREER: Correspondent, *Chicago Herald-American* and International News Service, covering San Francisco United Nations Conference, Potsdam Conference, and British elections of 1945; U.S. House of Representatives, Washington, D.C., congressman from 11th Congressional District of Massachusetts, 1946-52; U.S. Senate, Washington, D.C., senator from Massachusetts, 1952-60; President of the United States, 1960-63. Member of various Senate committees, 1952-60, including Foreign Relations Committee, Labor and Public Welfare Committee, Joint Economic Committees, and Select Committee to Investigate Improper Activities in the Labor-Management Field; chairman, Subcommittee on Labor. Member of board of overseers, Harvard University, 1957. *Military service:* U.S. Navy, PT boat commander, 1941-45; became lieutenant; received Navy and Marine Corps Medal and Purple Heart.

AWARDS, HONORS: Received numerous honorary degrees, including LL.D. from University of Notre Dame, 1950, Tufts College, 1954, Boston University, 1955, Harvard University, 1956, Loras College, Rockhurst College, Boston College, and Northeastern University, and D.Sc. from Lowell Technological Institute, 1956; National Conference of Christians and Jews Annual Brotherhood Award; University of Notre Dame Patriotism Award, 1956; Italian Star of Solidarity of the First Order; "Grande Official" of the Italian government; Greek Cross of the Commander of the Royal Order of the Phoenix; Pulitzer Prize, 1956, American Library Association Notable Book Award, Christopher Book

Award, 1956, and Secondary Education Board Award, all for *Profiles in Courage*.

WRITINGS: *Why England Slept*, Funk, 1940; (editor and contributor) *As We Remember Joe*, privately printed, 1945; *Profiles in Courage*, Harper, 1956, inauguration edition, 1961, abridged edition for young readers, 1961, memorial edition, 1964, memorial edition for young readers, 1964; *A Nation of Immigrants*, Anti-Defamation League of B'nai B'rith, 1959, revised and enlarged edition, Harper, 1964; John W. Gardner, editor, *To Turn the Tide*, foreword by Carl Sandburg, Harper, 1962; (contributor) *Creative America*, Ridge Press, 1962; (contributor) Robert A. Goldwin, editor, *Why Foreign Aid?*, Rand McNally, 1963; *America, the Beautiful*, Country Beautiful Foundation, 1964; (with others) *Moral Crisis: The Case for Civil Rights*, Gilbert Publishing Co., 1964.

Author of preface, foreword, or introduction: *The American Heritage Book of Indians*, American Heritage Publishing, 1961; Robert Johns Bulkley, *At Close Quarters: PT Boats in the World War*, U.S. Government Printing Office, 1962; Adlai E. Stevenson, *Looking Outward: Years of Crisis at the United Nations*, Harper, 1963; Theodore C. Sorensen, *Decision-making in the White House*, Columbia University Press, 1963.

Speech collections: Allan Nevins, editor, *The Strategy of Peace*, Harper, 1960; *President Kennedy Speaks*, U.S. Information Service, 1961; *Speeches, Remarks, Press Conferences, and Statements: August 1 through November 7, 1960*, [Washington, D.C.], 1961; *John F. Kennedy*, three volumes, U.S. Government Printing Office, 1962-64; Sidney Kraus, editor, *The Great Debates*, Indiana University Press, 1962, reprinted, 1977; Gerald Gardner, editor, *The Quotable Mr. Kennedy*, Popular Library, 1963; Bill Adler, editor, *The Kennedy Wit*, Citadel, 1964; *Legacy of a President: The Memorable Words of John Fitzgerald Kennedy*, Indian Book Co. (Delhi), 1964; Gardner, editor, *The Shining Moments: The Words and Moods of John F. Kennedy*, Pocket Books, 1964; *Statements: July-November, 1963*, U.S. Information Service, 1964; Booton Herndon, editor, *The Humor of JFK*, Fawcett, 1964; Urs Schwarz, editor, *John F. Kennedy: 1917-1963*, P. Hamlyn, 1964; *John F. Kennedy and Poland: Selection of Documents, 1948-63*, Polish Institute of Arts and Sciences in America, 1964; *John Fitzgerald Kennedy: A Compilation of Statements and Speeches Made during His Service in the United States Senate and House of Representatives*, U.S. Government Printing Office, 1964; Ram Singh and M. K. Haldar, editors, *Kennedy through Indian Eyes*, Vir Publishing House (Delhi), 1964; Nevins, editor, *The Burden and the Glory*, Harper, 1964.

Harold W. Chase and Allen H. Lerman, editors, *Kennedy and the Press: The News Conferences*, Crowell, 1965; Maxwell Meyersohn, editor, *Memorable Quotations of John F. Kennedy*, Crowell, 1965; Adler, editor, *More Kennedy Wit*, Citadel, 1965; Alex J. Goldman, editor, *The Quotable Kennedy*, Citadel, 1965; T. S. Settel, editor, *The Wisdom of JFK*, Dutton, 1965; Settel, editor, *The Faith of JFK*, Dutton, 1965; *A John F. Kennedy Memorial Miniature*, four volumes, Random House, 1966; William T. O'Hara, editor, *John F. Kennedy on Education*, Teachers College Press, 1966; *Words to Remember*, foreword by Robert F. Kennedy, Hallmark Editions, 1967; Adler, editor, *The Complete Kennedy Wit*, Citadel, 1967; Jay David and Adler, editors, *The Kennedy Reader*, Bobbs-Merrill, 1967; Robert A. Marshall, editor, *Kennedy and Africa*, Pyramid Books, 1967; Nicholas Schneider and Nathalie S. Rockhill, *John F. Kennedy Talks to Young People*, Hawthorn, 1968; (contributor) William B. Thomas, editor, *Shall Not Perish: Nine Speeches by Three Great Americans*, Gyldendal, 1969; Arthur Luce Klein, editor, *Spoken Arts Treasury of John F. Kennedy Addresses*, Spoken Arts, 1972; Thomas J. McQuain, *An Analysis of the Inaugural Address of John F. Kennedy*, McClain Printing Co., 1977.

Also author of reports, speeches, addresses, and official papers and correspondence published by U.S. Government Printing Office and other publishers.

SIDELIGHTS: "For the brief time they were in power," states Midge Decter in *Commentary*, "John F. Kennedy and that circle of family, employees, political allies, and friends who after his death were to be dubbed the Court-in-Exile did a good deal more than constitute themselves a new administration. In fact, they swamped the national consciousness. Their arrival in the White House in January 1961 very quickly came to be seen as not a changeover but a breakthrough of some kind. Out of power, they succeeded in becoming a Sword of Damocles hanging over Washington. . . . Out of the mess of an assassination that might have been thought to spell the demise of much more than their now fallen leader, the Kennedy clan somehow managed to impose his two surviving brothers as a certain token of the future. . . . In a way, the Kennedy's peculiar hold over the times became all the more potent as it receded into the realm of the potential. Both remembered from the past and portending the future, they could serve as a general, highly flexible standard of invidiousness with the present."

Furthermore, notes Decter, "the first serious attempt to establish the Kennedy's as at once decisively influential and in the literal sense of the word inconsequential . . . was launched immediately after the death of JFK. In 1965 we were presented with two mammoth inside accounts of the Kennedy administration: Arthur Schlesinger, Jr.'s *A Thousand Days* and Theodore C. Sorensen's *Kennedy*, which invited us to believe that the United States under JFK had passed through three decisive years in which everything, and yet strangely enough, almost nothing happened. Both books frankly admitted to partisanship . . . and both, though in very different ways, set a pattern of apology that would prove of lasting value to the Kennedy movement in the years ahead. . . . To boil the proposition down to plain language, we were asked to judge Kennedy as President by his intentions rather than by his achievements."

This "pattern of apology" has only just begun to be challenged by revisionist historians who have discovered, in the words of a *Newsweek* critic, "that there was a good deal less to Camelot than met the eye." The result, it appears, is that "suddenly nothing seems too bad to say about the Kennedy's. Admirers have had their say—it takes a small library to accommodate it—but apparently there is a literary Newtonian law at work: every idolatrous book has an opposite revisionist work."

For the most part, criticism of John F. Kennedy centers around his basic political method—namely, an arrogance combined with a tendency to "manufacture" international crises situations which he could then appear to resolve, creating an illusion of power and competence in the process. As Decter notes: "Besides elegance and gaiety, that which preeminently characterized the New Frontier was a kind of swashbuckling, an arrogant lack of principle. . . . Kennedy and his 'best and brightest people in the country' swooped down on the White House and tackled its problems in the spirit of the belief that these problems continued to persist only because the 'right' people had never before been let loose on them. . . . Any possibility for a greatness of record, as distinguishable from high style and intention, Kennedy avoided. He took no real leadership except in foreign policy, and even there it was largely a matter of making a personal impression and establishing personal relations. . . . What the Kennedy administration wanted, then, what it sought to do, was to impose an image of itself on American society and American history; an image of itself as the rightful, by virtue of intrinsic superiority, American ruling class."

In his book *The Kennedy Promise: The Politics of Expectation,* Henry Fairlie contends that the Kennedy administration was obsessed with not only the politics of expectation but the "politics of confrontation" as well; in other words, the President and his advisors cultivated and enjoyed the prospects of putting rapid and clever counterinsurgency measures into effect whenever possible. Convinced that domestic problems were, for the most part, settled (or at least in the process of working themselves out), Kennedy focused his efforts on his real concern: "the exaltation of the power of the state." He was, in short, determined to restore the United States to "an elevated sense of national purpose," to help it regain its earlier confident lead over the Soviet Union in science, technology, and armaments. To achieve these goals, Fairlie continues, Kennedy used international crises as "a spectacular display of his power in a situation of maximum peril. . . . It was at one minute to midnight that the Administration believed the hands of the clock always stood, all over the globe; and they were driven by the fear that, if they did not act before the clock struck, they would all be pumpkins. They aspired to greatness not just occasionally, but all the time. . . . All over Washington men would rise early to answer the bidding to crisis and to greatness, and the still slumbering public would awake in the morning to find that they had been summoned to meet danger once more, and once more to be rescued from it. . . . [Kennedy's] legacy was that he had accustomed the American people to an atmosphere of crisis and taught them to seek confrontation, eyeball to eyeball, within it."

Concludes Fairlie: "One cannot study the Administration of John Kennedy, the men and the measures, without deciding that it was a last confident—almost braggart—assertion of the capacity of American positivism to fulfill the prophecy of American puritanism: that the city of man can be built in the image of the City of God on this earth, and that the response of the American people to this assertion was that of men who wished to believe it. When it failed, there was an assassination to blame; when it failed again, there was yet another assassination."

Arthur Schlesinger, Jr. disputes this view of the Kennedy administration. He writes: "It is true, of course, that Kennedy was by temperament an activist. . . . At the same time, [he] was far from incautious. 'Prudent' was a favorite adjective [of his]. . . . Far from believing that personal leadership was irresistible, Kennedy was by nature a conciliator, which meant among other things that he recognized the legitimacy, or at least the existence, of other points of view. . . . [He] simply did not believe there was an American solution to every world problem. On the contrary, he was keenly aware that nationalism was the strongest political emotion of the time, and his essential purpose in foreign affairs was to adjust American policy to what he called the 'revolution of national independence' he saw going on around the world." Yet this same president who was so "keenly aware" of the strong nationalistic forces of his time, according to David Halberstam in his book, *The Best and the Brightest,* once told James Reston that the Soviet Union's arrogance toward the administration meant that "now we have a problem of trying to make our power credible and Vietnam looks like the place."

James Q. Wilson also defends the Kennedy administration against Fairlie's claims of an imperial presidency. He notes: "Almost every Presidential candidate gives way to bombast and fantastical claims about what government can or should accomplish. . . . The 'imperial' rhetoric Kennedy employed was, substantively at least, very much in tune with the prevailing national concensus at the time. . . . When Kennedy spoke, he spoke for a generation that had been in the war, had shared and shaped that purpose, and that was in no mood to see this country once again turn its back on the world or on the possibility of agression." Nevertheless, Wilson concludes, "Kennedy was not only a poor, but a mischievous political executive, lacking in any experience in the management of large affairs, overly attentive to the verbal skills of 'gifted amateurs' and 'in-and-outers,' wrongly contemptuous of the federal bureaucracy (or at least contemptuous for the wrong reasons), and persistently inclined to attempt to govern by means of personal intervention and the waging of administrative guerrilla warfare on the slopes of a massive, complex, but not incompetent executive establishment. Kennedy not only sent a few thousand 'advisors' to Vietnam without much sense of what they were supposed to do, or how, or to what end; he also . . . sent them all over the globe and indeed into many parts of our own government."

In addition to condemning a political attitude which led to such confrontations as the Cuban Missile Crisis, critics have also questioned Kennedy's domestic record. Summarizes *Newsweek:* "Kennedy's crisis-mongering caused more than 75,000 bomb shelters to sprout up for 60 million Americans and occasioned such over-staged muscle-flexing as the price-rise showdown with U.S. Steel. . . . [His] impatience, [revisionists] say, betrayed him when it came to the long slog of getting legislation through Congress, and the nation's growing problems in housing, education and urban decay were either overlooked or let slide to the second term that never came. And Kennedy, despite his enormous popularity with black voters, gets only indifferent marks from the historians on the racial issue. His civil-rights bill plowed very shallow furrows, and the support he gave Martin Luther King's nonviolent activism was more cosmetic than substantive."

In another *Newsweek* article, Kenneth Auchincloss concludes that "disputes such as these are bootless and unreal. The Kennedy Administration simply didn't have time to be measured by achievements, real or putative. . . . 'He didn't leave much of a record,' Brandeis historian John Roche says. 'But his contribution was that he turned on a whole series of forces in American politics that had been latent. . . . He was responsible for bringing these forces front and center. After the parade come the street sweepers—they were Johnson.' . . . If the New Frontier was a parade, it was one conducted with high style and gusto, and that was hardly a trivial feature in those years. . . . For style is a crucial element in the U.S. Presidency: without the ability to lead, to inspire, to release potential energies and create a sense of hope, a President seems lacking in something vital to the office."

Finally, Tom Wicker, author of a 1964 book entitled *Kennedy without Tears,* reflects in a 1977 *Esquire* article that "even in 1964, I did not argue, in any case, that Kennedy was a great man or even a great President—only that we were going to treat him as if he had been. . . . We have, but not, I think, because of some mass American delusion that in a brief, unfinished term he managed to rank himself with

Washington, Jefferson, Lincoln, Roosevelt; rather, his murder was a disillusionment. Merely that he was cut down as he was, on a sunlit day, in the bloody mess of his mortality, might have been enough to establish him forever as the symbol of all our incompleted selves, spoiled dreams, blasted hopes. That, I believe, is the key to his meaning for us. Even Americans mindful of the limitations of John Kennedy's thousand days, and of the later revelations of his follies and fallibilities, look back upon him as to their own lost dreams. He is the most fascinating might-have-been in American history, not just for what he was in his time but for what we made of him—not because of what we were but because of what we thought we were, and know now we'll never be."

BIOGRAPHICAL/CRITICAL SOURCES—Books: Joseph Francis Dinneen, *The Kennedy Family,* Little, Brown, 1959; James MacGregor Burns, *John Kennedy: A Political Profile,* Harcourt, 1960; Joseph Weston McCarthy, *The Remarkable Kennedys,* Dial, 1960; Robert John Donovan, *PT-109: John F. Kennedy in World War II,* McGraw, 1961; Theodore White, *The Making of the President: 1960,* Atheneum, 1961; Jacques Lowe, *Portrait: The Emergence of John F. Kennedy,* McGraw, 1961; Richard Tregaskis, *John F. Kennedy and PT-109,* Random House, 1962; Alfred Kazin, *Contemporaries,* Little, Brown, 1962; Norman Mailer, *The Presidential Papers,* Putnam, 1963; Gene Schoor, *Young John Kennedy,* Harcourt, 1963; Benjamin Bradlee, *That Special Grace,* Lippincott, 1964; Jim Bishop, *A Day in the Life of President Kennedy,* Random House, 1964; T. G. Buchanan, *Who Killed Kennedy?,* Putnam, 1964; Tom Wicker, *Kennedy without Tears: The Man beneath the Myth,* Morrow, 1964; E. A. Glikes and P. Schwaber, editors, *Of Poetry and Power: Poems Occasioned by the Presidency and by the Death of John F. Kennedy,* Basic Books, 1964; *The Kennedy Years,* Viking, 1964; Charles J. Stewart and Bruce Kendall, editors, *A Man Named John F. Kennedy,* Paulist/Newman, 1964; *Homage to a Friend,* U.S. Committee for the United Nations, 1964; Arthur M. Schlesinger, Jr., *A Thousand Days,* Houghton, 1965; Theodore C. Sorensen, *Kennedy,* Harper, 1965; Goddard Lieberson, editor, *John Fitzgerald Kennedy . . . As We Remember Him,* Atheneum, 1965; Victor Lasky, *J.F.K.: The Man and the Myth,* Arlington House, 1966; William Manchester, *Death of a President,* Harper, 1967; Alfred Steinberg, *The Kennedy Brothers,* Putnam, 1969.

Janet Knight, editor, *Three Assassinations: The Deaths of John and Robert Kennedy and Martin Luther King,* Facts on File, 1971; Jim Bishop, *The Day Kennedy Was Shot,* 2nd edition, Crowell, 1972; Earl Latham, *J. F. Kennedy and Presidential Power,* Heath, 1972; Kenneth P. O'Donnell and David Powers, *Johnny, We Hardly Knew Ye: Memories of John Fitzgerald Kennedy,* Little, Brown, 1972; David Halberstam, *The Best and the Brightest,* Random House, 1972; Peter Noyes, *Legacy of Doubt,* Pinnacle Books, 1973; Henry Fairlie, *The Kennedy Promise: The Politics of Expectation,* Doubleday, 1973; Peter Schwab and J. Lee Shneidman, *John F. Kennedy,* Twayne, 1974; Benjamin Bradlee, *Conversations with Kennedy,* Norton, 1975; Bruce Miroff, *Pragmatic Illusions: The Presidential Politics of John F. Kennedy,* Longmans, 1976; Judith Exner, *My Story,* Grove, 1977; Carl M. Brauer, *John F. Kennedy and the Second Reconstruction,* Columbia University Press, 1977; Theodore White, *In Search of History: A Personal Adventure,* Harper, 1978; Vincent L. Toscano, *Since Dallas: Images of John F. Kennedy in Popular and Scholarly Literature, 1963-1973,* R & E Research Associates, 1978.

Periodicals: *New York Times,* January 1, 1956, January 31, 1969; *Christian Science Monitor,* January 5, 1956; *New York Herald Tribune Book Review,* January 15, 1956, July 23, 1961; *Saturday Review,* May 13, 1961; *New York Times Magazine,* June 16, 1968; *New York Times Book Review,* January 19, 1969; *Book World,* January 19, 1969; *New York Review of Books,* March 13, 1969; *New Republic,* July 5, 1969; *Commentary,* January, 1970, June, 1973; *Time,* February 1, 1971, January 8, 1973, July 3, 1978, September 18, 1978, November 27, 1978; *Newsweek,* February 1, 1971, February 12, 1973, November 19, 1973, December 6, 1976, September 18, 1978, October 9, 1978; *Harper's,* December, 1972, January, 1973; *Commonweal,* May 25, 1973; *Esquire,* June, 1977; *U.S. News and World Report,* July 23, 1979.†

—Sketch by Deborah A. Straub

* * *

KENNEDY, Kenneth A(drian) R(aine) 1930-

PERSONAL: Born June 26, 1930, in Oakland, Calif.; son of Walter Berkhart (a banker) and Margaret Mirium Kennedy; married Mary Caroline Marino (an anthropologist), August 5, 1961 (divorced, 1967); married Margaret Carrick Fairlie (a musician and filmmaker), August 10, 1969. *Education:* University of California, Berkeley, A.A., 1951, B.A., 1953, M.A., 1954, Ph.D., 1963. *Religion:* Episcopalian. *Home:* Hickory Circle, Hickory Highlands, Ithaca, N.Y. 14850. *Office:* Department of Anthropology, Cornell University, McGraw Hall, Ithaca, N.Y. 14850.

CAREER: Cornell University, Ithaca, N.Y., assistant professor, 1964-68, associate professor of anthropology, 1968—. Visiting professor at Deccan College, Poona, India, 1963-64, 1971-72. *Military service:* U.S. Army, Medical Service Corps, 1954-57; became sergeant. *Member:* American Anthropological Association (fellow), American Association of Physical Anthropologists, American Association for the Advancement of Science, Sigma Xi. *Awards, honors:* Received research grants from National Science Foundation, 1962-63, 1963-64, 1966, 1968-69, 1971-74, and American Institute of Pakistan Studies, 1976-77; Howard Foundation award, 1976.

WRITINGS: (Editor and contributor with Theodore D. McCown) *Climbing Man's Family Tree: A Collection of Major Writings on Human Phylogeny, 1699-1971,* Prentice-Hall, 1972; *Neanderthal Man,* Burgess, 1975; *Human Variation in Space and Time,* W. C. Brown, 1976. Writer of monographs. Contributor to professional journals.

WORK IN PROGRESS: Research in forensic anthropology.

SIDELIGHTS: Kenneth A. R. Kennedy wrote *CA,* "Good scientific writing is good literature also, or it may be if the investigator enjoys a firm control of his data."

Kennedy has made five research expeditions for collecting data and conducting archaeological excavations in South Asia (India and Ceylon) and has done research in libraries, museums, and laboratories in Germany, France, and England.

AVOCATIONAL INTERESTS: Playing violin (Mrs. Kennedy plays piano and her husband violin in a chamber music group).

* * *

KENNEDY, Robert F(rancis) 1925-1968

PERSONAL: Born November 20, 1925, in Boston, Mass.; assassinated June 6, 1968, in Los Angeles, Calif., while campaigning for the Democratic presidential nomination; buried in Arlington National Cemetery, Arlington, Va.; son of Joseph P. and Rose (Fitzgerald) Kennedy; married Ethel Skakel, June 17, 1950; children: Kathleen Hartington, Joseph Patrick, Robert Francis, David Anthony, Mary Courtney, Michael LeMoyne, Mary Kerry, Christopher, Matthew, Douglas Harriman, Rory. *Education:* Harvard University, B.A., 1948; University of Virginia, LL.B., 1951. *Politics:* Democrat. *Religion:* Roman Catholic. *Home:* Hickory Hill, McLean, Va.

CAREER: Admitted to Massachusetts State Bar, 1951, and to practice before United States Supreme Court, 1955; U.S. Department of Justice, Washington, D.C., attorney in Criminal Division, 1951-52; U.S. Senate, Washington, D.C., Permanent Subcommittee on Investigations, assistant counsel, 1953, chief counsel to minority, 1954, chief counsel and staff director, 1955, Select Committee to Investigate Improper Activities in the Labor-Management Field, chief counsel, 1957-60; Attorney General of the United States, 1960-64; United States Senator from New York, 1964-68. Assistant counsel, Hoover Commission, 1953. Manager of John F. Kennedy's campaigns for election to the U.S. Senate, 1952, and to the presidency of the United States, 1959-60. President, Joseph P. Kennedy, Jr. Foundation, and Foundation for All Africa. Member of advisory council, Law School, University of Notre Dame; member of board of visitors, Law School, University of Virginia. *Military service:* U.S. Naval Reserve, 1944-46. *Awards, honors:* Society of Professional Investigators Outstanding Investigator Award, 1957; LL.D., Assumption College, 1957, Mount St. Mary's College, 1958, Tufts University, 1958, Fordham University, 1961, Nihon University, 1962, and Manhattan College, 1962; University of Notre Dame Patriotism Award, 1958; Massachusetts State Council of Knights of Columbus Lantern Award, 1958; honorary degrees from University of the Philippines, Marquette University, and Free University of Berlin, 1964.

WRITINGS: The Enemy Within (memoir), Popular Library, 1960; *The Pursuit of Justice,* Harper, 1964; *America the Beautiful in the Words of Robert F. Kennedy,* Country Beautiful Foundation, 1968; *Thirteen Days: A Memoir of the Cuban Missile Crisis,* Norton, 1969, revised edition, edited by Richard Newstadt and Graham Allison, 1971.

Author of preface, foreword, or introduction: William D. Rogers, *The Twilight Struggle: The Alliance for Progress and the Politics of Development in Latin America,* Random House, 1967; Gerry Blumenfeld, *Everyman's Book of Catholic Humor,* World Publishing, 1967; William Crofut, *Troubadour: A Different Battlefield,* Dutton, 1968; Norman Dorsen, *Frontiers of Civil Liberties,* Pantheon, 1968.

Speech collections: *"We Must Meet Our Duty and Convince the World That We Are Just Friends and Brave Enemies,"* Popular Library, 1963; Thomas A. Hopkins, editor, *Rights for Americans: The Speeches of Robert F. Kennedy,* Bobbs-Merrill, 1964; Sue G. Hall, editor, *The Quotable Robert F. Kennedy* (also see below), Droke, 1967; *To Seek a Newer World,* Doubleday, 1967, revised edition, Bantam, 1968; Bill Adler, editor, *The Robert F. Kennedy Wit,* Berkley Publishing, 1968; Hall, editor, *Bobby Kennedy Off-guard* (includes excerpts from *The Quotable Robert F. Kennedy*), Grosset, 1968, published as *The Spirit of Robert F. Kennedy,* 1968; Adler, editor, *A New Day: Robert F. Kennedy,* New American Library, 1968; (contributor) William B. Thomas, editor, *Shall Not Perish: Nine Speeches by Three Great Americans,* Gyldendal, 1969; *Promises to Keep: Memorable Writings and Statements,* introduction by Edward M. Kennedy, Hallmark Editions, 1969.

Also author of reports, speeches, addresses, and official papers published by U.S. Government Printing Office and other publishers.

WORK IN PROGRESS: New Problems, New Proposals.

SIDELIGHTS: "Robert Kennedy died on June 6, 1968, at the age of forty-two—a decade ago as I write," notes Arthur Schlesinger, Jr. in his book, *Robert Kennedy and His Times.* "He lived through a time of unusual turbulence in American history; and he responded to that turbulence more directly and sensitively than any other political leader of the era. . . . History changed him, and, had time permitted, he might have changed history. . . . He never had the chance to fulfill his own possibilities, which is why his memory haunts so many of us now. Because he wanted to get things done, because he was often impatient and combative, because he felt simply and cared deeply, he made his share of mistakes, and enemies. He was a romantic and an idealist, and he was also prudent, expedient, demanding and ambitious. . . . Yet the insights he brought to politics—insights earned in a labor of self-education that only death could stop—led him to see power not as an end in itself but as the means of redeeming the powerless."

Continues Schlesinger: "It was not only that he deepened one's understanding of America, of its problems and possibilities, but that he was the occasion of such good and happy times. No one could be more fun than Robert Kennedy; no one more appealing, with those impulses of irony, bravado, gentleness and vulnerability so curiously intermingled in his vivid personality; no one in our politics, as I deeply believed, held out more promise for the future. I thought him the most creative man in American public life when he was killed. I am well aware that not everyone did. Some saw him as cold, vengeful, fanatical, 'ruthless.' But to adapt a phrase A.J.P. Taylor used in his life of Lord Beaverbrook, if it is necessary for a biographer of Robert Kennedy to regard him as evil, then I am not qualified to be his biographer."

In light of this particular assessment of the life and career of Robert Francis Kennedy, some revisionist historians would agree that Schlesinger is not qualified to be Kennedy's biographer. While they do not go so far as to claim that he was "evil," many feel that the time has come for a more realistic and less emotional appraisal of the man designated heir apparent to the family political fortune after the assassination of John F. Kennedy on November 22, 1963. As has been the case with the late President in recent years, historians are beginning to take a long, hard look at Robert in order to place his life and work in the proper perspective.

As a young man, for example, Kennedy acquired a reputation for ruthlessness that was to haunt him during his entire life. According to *Atlantic* commentator Robert Manning, he was "rude, brash, very rich, and oblivious to the needs of others. . . . He was like his father, a 'hater' and just as conservative in his politics (and that was conservative indeed), a mediocre student who preferred to hang out with the football jocks at Harvard, a fierce competitor on the field but not when it came to achieving grades at college or at the University of Virginia Law School. . . . In his first thirty-five years he was little aware of the problems plaguing millions of Americans, and may not have known personally more than one or two blacks." Even Theodore Sorensen, an eventual Kennedy confidant and enthusiastic supporter, described Robert in 1953 as "militant, aggressive, intolerant, opinionated, somewhat shallow in his convictions . . . more like his father than his brother."

Critics often point to his stint as a member of Senator Joseph

McCarthy's investigative subcommittee staff in the early 1950s as evidence enough of his true political leanings. A job obtained for him by his father, it involved little more than reporting on the status of trade in strategic materials between American allies and various Communist governments during the Korean War. After completing his report in mid-1953, the young attorney resigned from his post. But a *New York Review of Books* writer, admitting to the unlikelihood that Kennedy was involved in any of the more notorious McCarthy investigations, nevertheless wonders how, "even in that marginal collaboration, Kennedy could have remained insensate of that dark, dingy, buffoonish brutishness in McCarthy."

Walter Karp of *Harper's* speculates that there was another dimension to the situation not often taken into account when certain historians review Kennedy's early career. According to Karp, the same month that the late senator resigned from the subcommittee, "Democratic committee members began a six-month boycott of the committee, at the conclusion of which they rehired Kennedy as minority council. The connection is obvious.... Kennedy's 'inner standards' prompted him to resign just when Democratic party leaders decided to pull the rug out from under McCarthy.... [It was a case of] simple political calculation—keeping in step with the leaders of his party." Karp concludes that this particular move "was entirely characteristic of him. From the outset of his career to the end of his life, the fixed star of all Robert Kennedy's political calculations were the interests and opinions of Democratic party leaders."

Kennedy followed his stay on the McCarthy subcommittee as a Justice Department attorney working for the Senate Rackets Committee—a time he spent in "rabid" pursuit of Jimmy Hoffa. Driven by anger and a righteous conviction that the Teamsters' boss had betrayed the workers in his union, Kennedy interrogated Hoffa with such ferocity that Alexander Bickel was prompted to remark: "No one since the late Joseph R. McCarthy has done more than Mr. Kennedy to foster the impression that the plea of self-incrimination is tantamount to a confession of guilt.... He sees the public interest in terms of ends, with little appreciation of the significance of means." The *New York Review of Books* writer points to this incident as evidence of Kennedy's fundamental ignorance of or scorn for basic democratic processes. He writes: "It was part of Kennedy's sensibility as a partisan that he was never so enamored of the principles of the processes themselves as he was by effects. This was never so clear as in his application of extraordinary attentions and devices, improvisations of peripheral legal technicalities, in order to corner Hoffa. However authentically offensive Hoffa may have been, it yet indicated a certain defect in Kennedy's understanding about the far more crucial value of those elemental processes of a democracy under law which had seemed to frustrate him in this instance."

Kennedy's controversial term as Attorney General during his brother's presidency also contributed to his reputation for ruthlessness. During this period, his investigation of Hoffa continued, he authorized FBI surveillance of Martin Luther King, he helped plot the overthrow of Fidel Castro, he approved the appointments of openly racist judges to positions in the federal judiciary, and he concurred with his brother that the Vietnam War was a conflict that the United States had to become involved in—and win.

The wire-tapping of the civil rights leader, for example, was supposedly agreed to in order to placate J. Edgar Hoover (who was convinced that King was in league with Communists) and also as a means for the Kennedys to protect King, themselves, and the pending civil rights bill in the event some incriminating evidence *was* uncovered that might discredit the movement and, by extension, the administration. Despite these indications that it was perceived as a defensive maneuver, Karp of *Harper's* concludes that "such a vision reveals [Kennedy's] repugnance for democratic politics and [his] reckless disdain for the requirements of liberty." The *New York Review of Books* writer simply notes that "it is a rationale that leaves a tinge of brackishness lingering after it."

As for the Castro affair, even Schlesinger labels Kennedy's support of the various plots to overthrow the Cuban leader as his "most conspicuous folly." While there is no evidence to suggest that either Kennedy knew of the CIA's plans to *murder* Castro, they did fall victim to the blind hysteria generated by the agency after the revolution in Cuba that put Castro in power. Despite their basic distrust of the CIA, they agreed to its plans for an invasion of the island; shortly after, it was clear that the English language had acquired a new synonym for "debacle"—the Bay of Pigs. In the subsequent Cuban Missile Crisis, however, it was Robert who, according to *Newsweek*, "was probably responsible for turning the American reaction away from a military strike at Cuba and toward the blockade that resulted in a Russian retreat."

His clearances of appointments to the federal judiciary of judges (particularly Southern judges) who made no secret of their racism have been regarded by some critics as a major "failure of moral vision." Although the action was supposedly designed to curry favor with Southern committee chairmen in order to gain their support for the administration's civil rights bill, it basically reflected Kennedy's desire to preserve the federal balance in the face of requests by civil rights workers for government intervention to protect demonstrators. Karp believes that these decisions, along with the surveillance of King, constituted a deliberate effort "to impede, as far as he [Kennedy] could, one of the great grass-roots movements in our history."

As for the Vietnam War, in 1951 Kennedy expressed a belief that America should not get involved. By 1962, however, he was quoted as saying that "we are going to win in Vietnam. We will remain here until we do win." He and his brother were convinced that a withdrawal from the region would mean certain defeat for the Kennedys and a victory for Goldwater in the 1964 presidential election. In general, according to *Newsweek*, their attitude was that everything could be worked out after a second term had been won because, as "the good guys, [they] could afford to act shabbily, to do less than their best, just to keep the truly bad guys at bay."

While Schlesinger, among others, insists that Robert underwent a profound spiritual crisis after the death of his brother which resulted in an almost complete reversal of his earlier, more conservative politics, the *Harper's* critic feels that his "conversion" was a conveniently timed ploy designed to lead to an eventual Democratic presidential nomination. Kennedy knew that part of the backing for such a move was already there; he had, for example, considered forcing himself on the ticket as Johnson's running mate in 1964, but when Johnson flatly rejected the idea, Kennedy returned to New York and successfully captured a Senate seat with the help of the party faithful. He spent the next four years in an attempt to win over the distrustful liberals and reformers among the Democrats (who were suspicious of his past record) and building up a constituency through a process of "identifying" with the "outcasts" of American society—Chicanos, blacks, Indians—and, of course, with the youth of the country. "By mid-1967," Karp writes, "Kennedy had comfortably situated himself at the dead center of 'conventional politics.' A few painfully cautious criticisms of the Vietnam war had kept him from running too far afoul of the peace movement without forfeiting the trust of the Democratic syndicate.''

He still, however, had his sights on 1972 rather than 1968, for he hesitated to challenge Johnson and split the party, thus incurring the wrath of potential supporters. ''Unfortunately for Kennedy,'' Karp explains, ''in 1968 the 'professionals' had ceased to be what Kennedy had always regarded them as being: the only serious factor in the calculations of ambition. While he sat on his hands, countless rank-and-file Democrats were beginning to regard him with open scorn and contempt. . . . By March, 1968, Kennedy saw his long-sought objective—the Presidency in 1972—slipping out of his grasp.'' In the subsequent announcement of his candidacy, Kennedy informed fellow Democrats that he was entering the race because ''at stake is not simply the leadership of our party or even our country—it is our right to moral leadership on this planet.'' It was a message, according to Karp, that assured party leaders that ''he would never neglect those vast global duties and burdens'' of the type that had gotten America into the Vietnam War. It prompted Hubert Humphrey to remark: ''He's a party regular in spite of everything.''

Midge Decter of *Commentary* generally agrees with Karp's assessment of the state of Robert Kennedy's mind in 1968. Due to the new issues at stake that year—Vietnam, black militancy, urban decay, poverty, the growing military-industrial complex—there was, according to Decter, ''nowhere for Robert Kennedy to stand, or at least appear to stand, but to the Left of Lyndon Johnson. Which meant, since Johnson was already so busily and so successfully dispelling the myth of the powerless Presidency, two steps to the Left of his brother—and of his own former self. . . . History had blessed him, then, by presenting him with the need to move Left at precisely the moment when to do so would place him in a company highly congenial to his old contempt for liberals: the young, the militant, the righteous, and the generally restless.''

Furthermore, notes Decter, ''the 1968 campaign of Robert Kennedy served both him and his fellow New Frontiersmen as a means for dissociating themselves from the actual record of John Kennedy's administration (a) without experiencing any loss of the *mana* attached to it and everyone in it; and (b) without, by definition, being disloyal to it.'' Basically, this involved de-fusing the issue of Vietnam by insisting that ''under Jack, if he had lived, things would have been different.'' Explains Decter: ''As part of their sleight of hand, the Kennedyites have managed not only to lift any vestige of blame from themselves but to lay rather handsome portions of it elsewhere.'' As for their condemnation of the military-industrial complex, she continues, ''somehow the New Frontiersmen, in the vanguard of the movement to control the military, have been allowed to forego mention of the fact that in the years 1961-63, under the tutelage of none other than Robert S. McNamara, that same military-industrial complex enjoyed an enormous if not a geometric rate of growth . . . [due to] what was called the [administration's] '2½ war' strategy. This strategy called for a military establishment (and budget) adequate to the simultaneous waging of two major wars and one minor one.''

Yet despite all the criticisms of Robert Kennedy, it cannot be denied that in the last few years of his life he managed to arouse a tremendous amount of expectation and hope that Camelot *could* be revived and that things could finally be ''set right'' in America. Whether or not a Robert Kennedy in the White House would have made a difference is a question that, obviously, can never be answered. But at the very least, the *New York Review of Books* writer notes, ''after the Kennedys, American politics was permanently altered from largely a pedagogic commerce among principals who tended to evoke at the best sententious, vest-suited school superintendents . . . to an age, for better or worse, of sentiment and flourish, of matinee cavaliers. The current generation of politicians—Nixon and Ford having been the atavisms of the old—are surely all the children of the Kennedys, all striving to simulate some part of their look and casual flair, some hint of their glamor of urgency, their shirt-sleeved brio.'' And still others feel that the mere fact that Robert Kennedy ''was cut down in mid-struggle,'' as a *Time* commentator puts it, ''remains an abiding American tragedy.''

BIOGRAPHICAL/CRITICAL SOURCES—Books: Pierre Salinger and others, editors, *Honorable Profession: A Tribute to Robert F. Kennedy,* Doubleday, 1968; David Halberstam, *Unfinished Odyssey of Robert Kennedy,* Random House, 1969; Victor Lasky, *Robert F. Kennedy: They Myth and the Man,* Pocket Books, 1971; Janet Knight, editor, *Three Assassinations: The Deaths of John and Robert Kennedy and Martin Luther King,* Facts on File, 1971; Stuart G. Brown, *Presidency on Trial: Robert Kennedy's 1968 Campaign and Afterwards,* University Press of Hawaii, 1972; Henry Fairlie, *The Kennedy Promise: The Politics of Expectation,* Doubleday, 1973; Peter Noyes, *Legacy of Doubt,* Pinnacle Books, 1973; Victor S. Navasky, *Kennedy Justice,* Atheneum, 1977; Jack Newfield, *Robert F. Kennedy: A Memoir,* Berkeley Publishing, 1978; Arthur Schlesinger, Jr., *Robert Kennedy and His Times,* Houghton, 1978.

Periodicals: *Christian Science Monitor,* February 24, 1960, December 28, 1967, February 6, 1969, July 10, 1969; *Saturday Review,* February 27, 1960, February 8, 1969; *New York Times Book Review,* February 28, 1960, March 2, 1967, December 17, 1967, January 19, 1969, February 2, 1969; *New York Herald Tribune Book Review,* February 28, 1960; *Chicago Sunday Tribune,* February 28, 1960; *New Republic,* February 29, 1960, July 5, 1969; *Book World,* March 10, 1967, January 19, 1969, February 2, 1969; *Saturday Evening Post,* August 26, 1967; *New York Times,* September 23, 1967, March 18, 1968, January 31, 1969; *New Leader,* December 18, 1967, May 26, 1969; *Reporter,* April 4, 1968, May 30, 1968; *Listener,* April 11, 1968; *London Times,* June 7, 1968; *Time,* June 14, 1968, September 4, 1978, November 27, 1978; *New York Times Magazine,* June 16, 1968; *National Review,* July 2, 1968; *Christian Century,* July 10, 1968; *Life,* July 14, 1968, June 13, 1969; *New York Review of Books,* August 1, 1968, March 3, 1969, October 12, 1978; *Washington Post,* January 29, 1969, June 6, 1969; *Best Sellers,* March 1, 1969; *Atlantic,* July, 1969, October, 1978; *Commentary,* January, 1970; *National Observer,* March 16, 1970; *New York,* December 14, 1970; *Harper's,* December, 1972, January, 1973, September, 1978; *Newsweek,* February 12, 1973, September 4, 1978; *Esquire,* August 15, 1978; *Progressive,* November, 1978; *U.S. News and World Report,* July 23, 1979.†

—Sketch by Deborah A. Straub

* * *

KENNY, John Peter 1916-

PERSONAL: Born February 23, 1916, in Melbourne, Australia; son of Augustus Leo (a surgeon) and Olga Zichi (Woinarski) Kenny. *Education:* Attended Loyola College,

Watsonia, Victoria, 1936-39; University of Melbourne, M.A. (with honors), 1942; Canisius College, additional study, 1944-47; Pontifical Gregorian University, Rome, D.D., 1950; Tuebingen University, guest student, 1965-66. *Office:* Department of Theology, University of Otago, P.O.B. 56, Dunedin, New Zealand.

CAREER: Ordained Roman Catholic priest of Society of Jesus (Jesuit), 1947; lecturer in dogmatic theology at Jesuit theologate, Sydney, Australia, 1950-65, 1966-69; Corpus Christi College, Clayton, Victoria, Australia, lecturer in dogmatic theology, 1970-78; University of Otago, Dunedin, New Zealand, member of faculty of theology, 1978-80. Head of dogmatics department, Catholic Theological College, Clayton, 1973—. Guest lecturer, Corpus Christi College, 1960-69. Member of Board of Studies, Melbourne College of Divinity, 1973.

WRITINGS: Christ Outside Christianity, Spectrum, 1971; *The Supernatural: Medieval Theological Concepts to Modern,* Alba, 1972; *Roman Catholicism, Christianity and Anonymous Christianity: The Role of the Christian Today,* Mercier Press, 1977; *The Meaning of Mary for Modern Man,* Spectrum, 1980. Contributor of articles in dogmatic theology, liturgy, and religious art to journals in the United States, England, Australia, and Ireland.

WORK IN PROGRESS: An edition of *De institutione virginis* by St. Ambrose, with Latin text, English translation, and commentary.

SIDELIGHTS: Kenny reads Greek, Latin, German, French, and Italian. He has traveled in Jordan, Syria, and Israel, as well as Europe, Thailand and Nepal. *Avocational interests:* Eastern religions.

* * *

KENWORTHY, Leonard S. 1912-

PERSONAL: Born March 26, 1912; son of Murray S. and Lenora (Holloway) Kenworthy. *Education:* Earlham College, A.B., 1933; Columbia University, A.M., 1935, Ed.D., 1948. *Home:* 2676 Bedford Ave., Brooklyn, N.Y. *Office:* School of Education, Brooklyn College, Brooklyn, N.Y.

CAREER: Friends Select School, Philadelphia, Pa., assistant to headmaster, 1934-36; Brunswick School, Greenwich, Conn., social studies teacher, 1936-38; Friends Central School, Philadelphia, head of social studies department, 1938-42; Friends International Center, Berlin, Germany, director, 1940-41; secretariat, United Nations Educational, Scientific, and Cultural Organization, 1946-48; Brooklyn College of the City University of New York, Brooklyn, N.Y., 1949—, currently professor of education. Member of U.S. Committee for United Nations Children's Fund and U.S. Commission for UNESCO. *Member:* National Council for the Social Studies, Association for Supervision and Curriculum Development, Tau Kappa Alpha. *Awards, honors:* Van Loan Essay Contest, winner; Citizen of Paris Award.

WRITINGS: Introducing Children to the World, Harper, 1956; *Twelve Citizens of the World,* Doubleday, 1956; *Leaders of New Nations,* Doubleday, 1960; *Profile of Nigeria,* Doubleday, 1961; *Profile of Kenya,* Doubleday, 1962; *Guide to Social Studies Teaching,* Wadsworth, 1962, 4th edition, 1973; *Telling the U.N. Story: New Approaches to Teaching about the U.N. and Its Related Agencies,* Oceana, 1963; *Three Billion Neighbors,* Ginn, 1965; *Background Papers for Social Studies Teachers,* Wadsworth, 1966; *Social Studies for the Seventies: In Elementary and Middle Schools,* Blaisdell, 1968, 2nd edition, Xerox College Publishing, 1973; *The International Dimension of Education,* edited by Norman V. Overly, Association for Supervision & Curriculum Development, 1970; *Camels and Their Cousins,* Harvey House, 1975; (with Laurence Jaeger) *Soybeans: The Wonder Beans,* Messner, 1976; *Worldview: The Autobiography of a Social Studies Teacher and Quaker,* Friends United Press, 1977; *Hats, Caps and Crowns,* Messner, 1977; *The Story of Rice,* Messner, 1979; *Sixteen Quaker Leaders Speak,* Friends United Press, 1979. Also author of several titles in the "World Affairs Guides" series, published by Teachers College Press.

* * *

KENYON, F(rank) W(ilson) 1912-

PERSONAL: Born July 6, 1912, in Preston, England; son of Matthew Henry and Florence (Wilson) Kenyon; married Awdrey Mary Leathes, 1942; children: (previous marriage) Vivian Cook Foster. *Education:* Educated in England and New Zealand. *Agent:* Curtis Brown Ltd., 575 Madison Ave., New York, N.Y. 10022.

CAREER: Worked in department store in Auckland, New Zealand, for four years; traveled between New Zealand, Australia, and Europe; author.

WRITINGS—Historical novels, except as indicated: *The Emperor's Lady: A Novel Based on the Life of the Empress Josephine* (Literary Guild selection), Hutchinson, 1952, Crowell, 1953 (also published in England as *The Emperor's Lady: The Story of the Empress Josephine,* Hutchinson, 1972); *Royal Merry-Go-Round,* Crowell, 1954 (published in England as *Royal Merry-Go-Round: The Story of Louis XV,* Hutchinson, 1973); *Emma,* Crowell, 1955, published as *Emma: My Lord Admiral's Mistress,* Avon, 1955; *Marie Antoinette: A Novel,* Crowell, 1956; *Without Regret* (non-historical), Crowell, 1956; *Mary of Scotland,* Crowell, 1957; *Legacy of Hate: The Tragedy of Mary Stewart, Queen of Scotland and the Isles,* Hutchinson, 1957; *Never a Saint,* Hutchinson, 1958; *Shadow in the Sun: A Novel about the Virgin Queen, Elizabeth I,* Crowell, 1958 (published in England as *Shadow in the Sun: The Secret of Elizabeth I, the Virgin Queen,* Hutchinson, 1972); *The Golden Years: A Novel Based on the Life and Loves of Percy Bysshe Shelley,* Crowell, 1959 (published in England as *The Golden Years: The Life and Loves of Percy Bysshe Shelley,* Hutchinson, 1974).

Mistress Nell: Or, Restoration Divertimento, Appleton, 1961 (published in England as *Mrs. Nelly: Or, Restoration Divertimento,* Hutchinson, 1961, published as *Mrs. Nelly: The Life and Adventures of Nell Gwyn,* 1973); *The Seeds of Time,* Hutchinson, 1961, published as *The Seeds of Time: The Story of Arabella Churchill,* 1972; *I, Eugenie,* Hutchinson, 1962, also published in England as *I, Eugenie: The Memoirs of the Empress Eugenie,* Hutchinson, 1972, published as *That Spanish Woman,* Dodd, 1963, also published as *Eugenie: That Spanish Woman,* Belmont-Tower, 1978; *The Glory and the Dream,* Dodd, 1963 (published in England as *Glory and the Dream: The Story of John Churchill, 1st Duke of Marlborough,* Hutchinson, 1972); *The Questing Heart: A Romantic Novel about George Sand,* Dodd, 1964; *The Shadow and the Substance,* Hutchinson, 1965; *The Absorbing Fire: The Byron Legend,* Dodd, 1966; *Imperial Courtesan,* Dodd, 1967; *The Naked Sword: The Story of Lucrezia Borgia,* Dodd, 1968; *The Duke's Mistress: The Story of Mary Ann Clarke,* Dodd, 1969.

The Consuming Flame: The Story of George Eliot, Dodd, 1970; *My Brother Napoleon: The Confessions of Caroline*

Bonaparte, Dodd, 1971; *Passionate Rebel: The Story of Hector Berlioz,* Dodd, 1972; *Shadow of the Corsican,* Hutchinson, 1973; *Henry VIII's Secret Daughter: The Tragedy of Lady Jane Grey,* Hutchinson, 1974. Also author of short stories, radio plays, and radio serials.

SIDELIGHTS: F. W. Kenyon's books have been translated into eleven languages. *Avocational interests:* Golf, gardening, and swimming.

BIOGRAPHICAL/CRITICAL SOURCES: Best Sellers, October 15, 1968, September 1, 1969; *Christian Science Monitor,* December 15, 1970.†

* * *

KERMODE, (John) Frank 1919-

PERSONAL: Born November 29, 1919, in Douglas, Isle of Man, England; son of John Pritchard and Doris (Kennedy) Kermode; married Maureen Eccles, 1947 (divorced, 1970); married Anita Van Vactor, 1976; children: (first marriage) Mark, Deborah. *Education:* Liverpool University, B.A., 1940, M.A., 1947. *Office:* King's College, Cambridge University, Cambridge CB2 1ST, England.

CAREER: University of Durham, King's College, Newcastle upon Tyne, England, lecturer, 1947-49; University of Reading, Reading, Berkshire, England, lecturer, 1949-58; University of Manchester, Manchester, England, professor, 1958-65; University of Bristol, Bristol, England, Winterstoke Professor of English, 1965-67; University of London, University College, London, England, Lord Northcliffe Professor of Modern English Literature, 1967-74; Cambridge University, King's College, Cambridge, England, King Edward VII Professor of English Literature and fellow, 1974—. Visiting professor, Harvard University, summer, 1961; Warton Lecturer, British Academy, 1962; Wesleyan University fellow, Center for Advanced Studies, 1963-64, 1969-70; Mary Flexner Lecturer, Bryn Mawr College, 1965; lecturer, Princeton University, 1970; Charles Eliot Norton Professor, Harvard University, 1977-78. *Military service:* Royal Navy, 1940-46; became lieutenant. *Member:* Royal Society of Literature (fellow), British Academy (fellow), American Academy of Arts and Sciences (honorary member), Officier de l'Ordre des Arts et des Sciences (France).

WRITINGS—Criticism: *Romantic Image,* Routledge & Kegan Paul, 1957, Macmillan, 1958; *John Donne,* Longmans, Green, 1957; *Wallace Stevens,* Oliver & Boyd, 1960, Grove Press, 1961, revised edition, 1967; *Puzzles and Epiphanies: Essays and Reviews, 1958-1961,* Chilmark, 1962; *William Shakespeare: The Final Plays,* Longmans, Green, 1963; *The Patience of Shakespeare,* Harcourt, 1964; *On Shakespeare's Learning,* Wesleyan University Press, 1965; *The Sense of an Ending: Studies in the Theory of Fiction,* Oxford University Press, 1967; *Continuities,* Random House, 1968; *Modern Essays,* Collins, 1971; *Shakespeare, Spenser, Donne: Renaissance Essays,* Viking, 1971, published as *Renaissance Essays: Shakespeare, Spenser, Donne,* Fontana Books, 1973; *Novel and Narrative,* University of Glasgow Press, 1972; *D. H. Lawrence,* Viking, 1973; (contributor) Seymour Chatman, editor, *Approaches to Poetics,* Columbia University Press, 1973; *The Classic,* Viking, 1975; *How We Read Novels,* University of Southampton Press, 1975; *The Genesis of Secrecy,* Harvard University Press, 1979.

Editor: *English Pastoral Poetry: From the Beginnings to Marvell,* Barnes & Noble, 1952, reprinted, Norton, 1972; William Shakespeare, *The Tempest,* Metheun, 1954; *Seventeenth Century Songs,* Oxford University Press, 1956; *The Living Milton: Essays by Various Hands,* Routledge & Kegan Paul, 1960, Macmillan, 1961; *Discussions of John Donne,* Heath, 1962; *Spenser: Selections from the Minor Poems and the Fairie Queene,* Oxford University Press, 1965; *Four Centuries of Shakespearean Criticism,* Avon, 1965; *The Metaphysical Poets: Essays on Metaphysical Poetry,* Fawcett, 1969; *King Lear: A Casebook,* Macmillan, 1969; (with Richard Poirier) *The Oxford Reader: Varieties of Contemporary Discourse,* Oxford University Press, 1971; (with John Hollander and others) *The Oxford Anthology of English Literature,* two volumes, Oxford University Press, 1973; *Selected Prose of T. S. Eliot,* Harcourt, 1975.

General editor, "Modern Masters" series, Viking Press, 1970—. Contributor to *Encounter, New Statesman, Partisan Review, New York Review of Books,* and other periodicals. Co-editor, *Encounter,* 1966-67.

SIDELIGHTS: "Here is a temper to be trusted," James Gray writes of Frank Kermode. His is an "intelligence that one can respect without reserve." Gray continues: "Frank Kermode is a good critic because he envelopes his subject in a warm abundance of perceptivity.... The action of his sympathies is at once powerful and sensitive." Martin Price sees his writing as "exploratory rather than definitive.... What it can do extremely well is to relate elements in a complex and coherent pattern at once concrete and full of suggestion." Although Kermode has been called an academic "ritualist" whose "approach is essentially an external one," he is not associated with any particular school of criticism and varies his treatment according to his subject with admirable "intellectual flexibility." Gray gave this summary of Kermode's work, "He belongs as observer to the whole world of literature, and as critic only to himself."

AVOCATIONAL INTERESTS: Music.

BIOGRAPHICAL/CRITICAL SOURCES: Yale Review, June, 1958, autumn, 1967; *Spectator,* November 11, 1960; *Saturday Review,* March 2, 1963; *Listener,* June 29, 1967; *New Statesman,* August 4, 1967; *Kenyon Review,* September, 1967; *Commonweal,* December 1, 1967; *Partisan Review,* winter, 1968; *Hudson Review,* spring, 1968; *South Atlantic Quarterly,* summer, 1968; *Sewanee Review,* winter, 1969, January, 1975; *Book World,* February 23, 1969; *Times Literary Supplement,* March 13, 1969; *New York Times Book Review,* August 17, 1969; *Poetry,* December, 1969; *New York Review of Books,* March 12, 1970, October 5, 1972; *Books & Bookmen,* August, 1971, February, 1976; *New York Times,* October 1, 1971; *New Republic,* July 20, 1974; *New Yorker,* November 10, 1975; *American Scholar,* spring, 1976; *National Review,* April 2, 1976.

* * *

KERR, Clark 1911-

PERSONAL: Born May 17, 1911, in Stony Creek, Pa.; son of Samuel William (a farmer and teacher) and Caroline (Clark) Kerr; married Catherine Spaulding, December 25, 1934; children: Clark Edgar, Alexander William, Caroline Mary. *Education:* Swarthmore College, A.B., 1932; Stanford University, M.A., 1933; additional study at Institute of International Relations, Geneva, Switzerland, 1935-36, and London School of Economics and Political Science, 1936, 1939; University of California, Ph.D., 1939. *Politics:* Democrat. *Religion:* Society of Friends (Quaker). *Home:* 8300 Buckingham Dr., El Cerrito, Calif. 94530. *Office:* Carnegie Council on Higher Education, 2150 Shattuck Ave., Berkeley, Calif. 94704.

CAREER: Antioch College, Yellow Springs, Ohio, instructor in economics, 1936-37; Stanford University, Stanford, Calif., acting assistant professor of labor economics, 1939-40; University of Washington, Seattle, assistant professor of economics, 1940-45; University of California, Berkeley, 1945—, associate professor, 1945-67, professor of economics and industrial relations, beginning 1967, currently professor emeritus, director of Institute of Industrial Relations, 1945-52, chancellor of university, 1952-58, president of university, 1958-67. Chairman and executive director, Carnegie Commission on Higher Education, Berkeley, 1967-73; Carnegie Council on Policy Studies on Higher Education, Berkeley, chairman and staff director, 1974—. National War Labor Board, wage stabilization director of Tenth Region (San Francisco), 1942-43, vice-chairman of Twelfth Region (Seattle), 1943-45, chairman of Meat Packing Commission, 1945-47, public member and vice-chairman, 1950-51. Member of President Harry S Truman's Labor-Management Conference, 1945, President Dwight D. Eisenhower's Commission on Intergovernmental Relations, 1953-55, and Commission on National Goals, 1959-60, President John F. Kennedy's Committee on Labor Management Policy, 1961-63, and Railroad Emergency Board, 1963, and President Lyndon B. Johnson's Committee, 1963-65. Arbitrator for Armour Co. and United Packing House Workers, 1945-52, Waterfront Employer's Association and International Longshoremen's Union, 1946-47, and California Processors and Growers, Inc. and California State Council of Cannery Unions, 1953-58, and others. Chairman of board of Work in America Institute, 1975— and Global Perspectives in Education, 1976—. Member of board of directors, Center for Advanced Study in the Behavioral Sciences, 1953-61; member of university council, Chinese University of Hong Kong, 1964—; member of board of managers, Swarthmore College, 1968—. Member of board of trustees, Carnegie Foundation for Advancement of Teaching, 1958-60 and 1972—, Rockefeller Foundation, 1960-71, International Council for Economic Development, 1971, Council on Learning, 1975—, and Educational Testing Service, 1977-80.

MEMBER: American Economic Association, Industrial Relations Research Association (president, 1954-55), National Academy of Arbitrators (vice-president, 1947-48), American Association for the Advancement of Science, National Academy of Education (charter member), American Association of University Professors, Association of Governing Boards of Colleges and Universities (member of board of directors, 1977-80), Royal Economic Society, Phi Beta Kappa, Kappa Sigma, Bohemian Club, Century Association, Cosmos Club. *Awards, honors:* American Friends Service Committee traveling fellowship, 1935-36; Newton Booth fellowship, 1938-39; Alexander Meiklejohn award from American Association of University Professors, 1964, for contributions to academic freedom; Clark Kerr Award from University of California, Berkeley, 1968, for extraordinary and distinguished contributions to the advancement of higher education; College Board Medal, 1976, for distinguished service to education; received award from Academy for Educational Development, 1978, for distinctive contributions to the solution of critical problems in higher education; has also received over thirty-three honorary degrees, including degrees from Harvard University, Yale University, and University of Michigan.

WRITINGS: (With E. Wight Bakke and Charles Anrod) *Unions, Management and the Public,* Harcourt, 1948, 3rd edition, 1967; (with John T. Dunlop, Frederick H. Harbison, and Charles A. Myers) *Industrialism and Industrial Man: The Problems of Labor and Management in Economic Growth,* Harvard University Press, 1960, revised edition, 1975; *The Uses of the University,* Harvard University Press, 1964, revised edition, 1972; *Labor and Management in Industrial Society,* Doubleday, 1964; *Marshall, Marx, and Modern Times: The Multi-Dimensional Society,* Cambridge University Press, 1969; *Labor Markets and Wage Determination: The Balkanization of Labor Markets and Other Essays,* University of California Press, 1977; (editor with Jerome M. Rasow) *Work in America: The Decade Ahead,* Van Nostrand, 1979.

Contributor: *Migration to the Seattle Labor Market Area: 1940-42,* University of Washington Press, 1942, reprinted, Greenwood Press, in press; Richard Lester, editor, *Insights into Labor Issues,* Macmillan, 1948; Arthur Kornhauser, editor, *Industrial Conflict,* McGraw, 1954; Paul Webbink, editor, *Labor Mobility and Economic Opportunity,* Wiley, 1954; Clinton Golden, editor, *Causes of Industrial Peace,* Harper, 1955; Mirra Komarosky, editor, *Common Frontiers of the Social Sciences,* Free Press, 1957; Adolph Sturmthal, editor, *Contemporary Collective Bargaining,* Cornell University Press, 1957; George Taylor and Frank Pierson, editors, *New Concepts in Wage Determination,* McGraw, 1957; John Wilkes, editor, *Productivity and Progress,* Angus & Robertson, 1957; John Dunlop, editor, *Theory of Wage Determination,* Macmillan, 1957; Jack Steiber, editor, *U.S. Industrial Relations,* Michigan State University Press, 1958; Charles Myers, editor, *Wages, Prices, Profits and Productivity,* American Assembly, Columbia University, 1959.

Wilbert Moore, editor, *Labor Commitment and Social Change in Developing Areas,* Social Science Research Council, 1960; *Goals for Americans,* Prentice-Hall, 1960; Robert Morison, editor, *The Contemporary University: U.S.A.,* Houghton, 1966; (author of introduction) Abraham Flexner, *Universities,* Oxford University Press, 1968; Kermit Gordon, editor, *Agenda for the Nation,* Brookings Institution, 1968; George Z. F. Bereday, editor, *Essays on World Education: The Crisis of Supply and Demand,* Oxford University Press, 1969; Robert M. Hutchins and Mortimer J. Adler, editors-in-chief, *The Great Ideas Today,* Encyclopaedia Britannica, Inc., 1969; Peter A. Miescher, Carlo Henze, and Raeto Schett, editors, *The Modern University: Structure, Functions, and Its Role in the New Industrial State,* Georg Thieme, 1969; Stephen R. Graubard and Geno A. Ballotti, editors, *The Embattled University,* Braziller, 1970; David C. Nichols, editor, *Perspectives on Campus Tensions,* American Council on Education, 1970. Also contributor to numerous other books.

Contributor of numerous articles to economics, sociology, business, and other professional journals.

WORK IN PROGRESS: Education and National Development: Reflections from an American Perspective during a Period of Global Reassessment.

* * *

KERTZER, Morris Norman 1910-

PERSONAL: Born October 18, 1910, in Cochrane, Ontario, Canada; son of David Isaac (an insurance agent) and Pearl (Kroch) Kertzer; married Julia Hoffman, June 13, 1934; children: Ruth (Mrs. Aaron Seidman), David, Jonathan. *Education:* University of Toronto, B.A., 1930; University of Illinois, M.A., 1939; Jewish Theological Seminary, D.H. Lit., 1947. *Religion:* Jewish. *Home:* 7625 East Camel Back Rd., Scottsdale, Ariz. 85251.

CAREER: Became Jewish theological rabbi, 1934. University of Alabama, Tuscaloosa, instructor in philosophy, 1936-

39; University of Iowa, Iowa City, professor of religion, 1939-46; Park Avenue Synagogue, New York City, associate rabbi, 1946-49; American Jewish Committee, New York City, national director of interreligious affairs, 1949-60. Led delegation of rabbis to Soviet Union, 1956; has lectured in England, France, Italy, Israel, Japan, Brazil, India, and other nations. *Military service:* U.S. Army, 1943-46; became captain (chaplain); received Bronze Star Medal, battle stars for Anzio Beachhead, France, North Africa. *Member:* Central Conference of American Rabbis (member of executive committee), New York Board of Rabbis (secretary, 1952-54), Association of Jewish Military Chaplains (president, 1951-54), Rotary Club (past president). *Awards, honors:* George Washington Medal for series of articles on Soviet Russia in *New York Times* and other newspapers, 1957; Pro Deo Gold Medal (Rome, Italy); D.D., Hebrew Union College-Jewish Institute of Religion, 1965; Knight of Malta, 1970.

WRITINGS: *A Faith to Live By,* Jewish Welfare Board, 1944; *With an H on My Dog-Tag,* Behrman, 1947; *What Is a Jew?,* World Publishing, 1953, revised edition, Collier, 1978; *The Art of Being a Jew,* World Publishing, 1962; (editor) *The Rabbi and the Jewish Social Worker,* Federation of Jewish Philanthropies, Committee on Synagogue Relations, 1964; *Today's American Jew,* McGraw, 1967; *Tell Me Rabbi,* Macmillan, 1977. Contributor of articles to *Look, Reader's Digest, New York Times,* and *Guideposts.*

WORK IN PROGRESS: *Look Now Toward Heaven,* for Macmillan.

* * *

KESSEN, William 1925-

PERSONAL: Born January 18, 1925, in Key West, Fla.; son of Herman Lowery (a marine engineer) and Maria (Lord) Kessen; married Marion Lord, 1950; children: Judith, Deborah, Anne, Peter Christopher, Andrew Lord, John Michael. *Education:* University of Florida, B.S., 1948; Brown University, Sc.M., 1950; Yale University, Ph.D., 1952. *Home:* 30 Halstead Lane, Branford, Conn. *Office address:* Box 11A, Yale Station, New Haven, Conn.

CAREER: Yale University, New Haven, Conn., U.S. Public Health Service, postdoctoral fellow, 1952-54, assistant professor, 1954-60, associate professor, 1960-65, professor of psychology, 1965-78, Eugene Higgins Professor of Psychology and Professor of Pediatrics, 1978—. *Military service:* U.S. Army, 1943-46. *Member:* American Psychological Association, Society of Experimental Psychologists, Society for Research in Child Development, American Association for the Advancement of Science, Sigma Xi. *Awards, honors:* Auxiliary Research Award, Social Science Research Council, 1958; Center for Advanced Study of Behavorial Sciences, fellow, 1959-60; Guggenheim fellow, 1970-71.

WRITINGS: (With George Mandler) *The Language of Psychology,* Wiley, 1959; *The Child,* Wiley, 1965; *Childhood in China,* Yale University Press, 1975; (with Marc Bornstein) *Psychological Development from Infancy,* Erlbaum, 1979. Contributor of research papers to journals of the American Psychological Association and Society for Research in Child Development.

WORK IN PROGRESS: Continuing studies of human newborn behavior and of cognitive development; history of psychology.

KEY, Mary Ritchie 1924-

PERSONAL: Born March 19, 1924, in San Diego, Calif.; daughter of George Lawrence (an inventor) and Iris (a teacher; maiden name, Lyons) Ritchie; married Harold Hayden Key (marriage dissolved, 1968); married A. E. Patton; children: (first marriage) Mary Helen (Mrs. Keith Ellis), Harold Hayden, Jr., Thomas George. *Education:* University of Texas, M.A., 1960, Ph.D., 1963; also summer studies at University of Oklahoma, 1946 and 1949, University of Chicago, 1954, University of Michigan, 1959, and University of California, Los Angeles, 1966. *Office:* Program in Linguistics, University of California, Irvine, Calif. 92717.

CAREER: Chapman College, Orange, Calif., assistant professor of linguistics, 1963-66, bibliographer, Summer Institute of Linguistics, 1964-66; University of California, Irvine, assistant professor, 1966-71, associate professor, 1971-78, professor of English linguistics, descriptive linguistics, and sociolinguistics, 1978—. Has conducted field research on eight American English dialects and Spanish and American Indian languages; has studied in Mexico, Bolivia, and Chile. Lecturer in linguistics in Bolivia, 1956, and Kiel, Germany, 1968. Consultant to Center for Applied Linguistics (Washington, D.C.). *Member:* International Reading Association (member of board of directors of Orange County chapter, 1968-72), Delta Kappa Gamma (chapter president, 1974-76).

WRITINGS: (Editor with Harold Key) *Vocabulario Mejicano de la Sierra de Zacapoaxtla, Puebla,* Summer Institute of Linguistics, 1953; (editor) *Notas Linguisticas de Bolivia,* six volumes, Summer Institute of Linguistics, 1959-62; (editor) *Vocabularios Bolivianos,* five volumes, Summer Institute of Linguistics, 1962-66; (with H. Key) *Bolivian Indian Tribes: Classification, Bibliography, and Map of Present Language Distribution,* Summer Institute of Linguistics, 1967; (contributor) Robert R. Freeman and other editors, *Information in the Language Sciences,* American Elsevier, 1968; *Comparative Tacanan Phonology: With Cavinena Phonology and Notes on Pano-Tacanan Relationship,* Mouton, 1968; (editor with Adam Kendon and Richard M. Harris) *The Organization of Behavior in Face-to-Face Interaction,* Mouton, 1975; *Male/Female Language,* Scarecrow, 1975; *Paralanguage and Kinesics,* Scarecrow, 1975; *Nonverbal Communication: A Research Guide and Bibliography,* Scarecrow, 1977; *The Grouping of South American Indian Languages,* Gunter Narr, 1979; (editor) *The Relationship of Verbal and Nonverbal Communication,* Mouton, 1979. Contributor of over sixty articles and reviews to linguistic journals, including *International Journal of American Linguistics, Linguistics: An International Review, Elementary School Journal, Language, American Anthropologist,* and *Ethnomusicology.*

WORK IN PROGRESS: *Nonverbal Communication Today: Current Research; Sociolinguistic Variables.*

BIOGRAPHICAL/CRITICAL SOURCES: Robert E. Longacre, *Current Trends in Linguistics Four: Ibero-American and Caribbean Linguistics,* Mouton, 1968; *American Anthropologist,* August, 1969.

* * *

KIDD, David Lundy 1926-

PERSONAL: Born November 23, 1926, in Corbin, Ky. *Education:* University of Michigan, B.A.; attended Yenching University (Peking, China), two years. *Home:* 12-19 Kusunoki-Cho, Ashiya City, Japan. *Agent:* Kay Brown, International Creative Management, 40 West 57th St., New

York, N.Y. 10019. *Office:* Oomoto School of Traditional Japanese Arts, Kameoka City, Kyoto Pref., Japan.

CAREER: Yenching University, Peking, China, lecturer, 1946-48; Tsinghua University, Peking, lecturer, 1947-49; Asia Institute, New York, N.Y., lecturer, 1950-51; Kobe University, Kobe, Japan, lecturer, 1954-71; Oomoto School of Traditional Japanese Arts, Kameoka City, Kyoto, Japan, director and founder, 1976—.

WRITINGS: All the Emperor's Horses, Macmillan, 1960; (translator) *After Rain,* France-Asie, 1962. Contributor to *New Yorker,* Japanese magazines, and *Oriental Art* (London).

SIDELIGHTS: Several works by David Kidd have been adapted for the screen. He told *CA:* "Film options on *All the Emperor's Horses* were sold twice, first to David Susskind, and then to Sterling Silliphant. In both cases the problem was . . . to find a screenwriter who could create a scenario based on the book's exotic Chinese material. I even tried it myself, but discovered that short story writing and scenario writing are two different things, and being able to do one does not necessarily mean that one can do the other. Still, a movie possibility is not dead. The fall of the old China and the beginning of the new is now distant enough to be viewed as history, which should make the problem somewhat easier."

On the subject of contributing to various art history journals, he comments: "I have enjoyed writing articles for scholarly magazines. There is little pay, but much prestige. . . . Style in no way diminishes scholarship, and I am as pleased with my little stories on Tibetan art and Chinese portraiture as I am with those in the *New Yorker.*"

Kidd is currently the director of a school in Japan that teaches the traditional arts of that country. "One of the results of this venture," he says, "may well be a series of small books on the practice of these arts, rather than their history and theory."

AVOCATIONAL INTERESTS: Art, religion, and science.

* * *

KILPATRICK, James Jackson 1920-

PERSONAL: Born November 1, 1920, in Oklahoma City, Okla.; son of James Jackson (a timberman) and Alma Mia (Hawley) Kilpatrick; married Marie Pietri (a sculptor), September 21, 1942; children: Michael Sean, Christopher Hawley, Kevin Pietri. *Education:* University of Missouri, B.J., 1941. *Home:* White Walnut Hill, Woodville, Va. 22749. *Office:* Rudasill's Mill Rd., Scrabble, Va. 22749.

CAREER: Richmond News Leader, Richmond, Va., reporter, 1941-49, associate editor, 1949, editor, 1949-66; nationally syndicated columnist, Washington Star Syndicate, 1964—; commentator, "60 Minutes," CBS-TV, 1971-79. *Member:* National Conference of Editorial Writers (chairman, 1956-57), Gridiron Club (Washington, D.C.). *Awards, honors:* Medal of Honor for distinguished service to journalism, University of Missouri, 1953; Sigma Delta Chi, annual award for editorial writing, 1954, fellowship, 1975; elected to Oklahoma Hall of Fame, 1978; William Allen White Medallion, University of Kansas, 1979.

WRITINGS: The Sovereign States, Regnery, 1957; (co-editor) *The Lasting South,* Regnery, 1957; (editor) *We the States,* Commonwealth of Virginia, 1958; *The Smut Peddlers,* Doubleday, 1960; *The Case for Southern School Segregation,* Crowell-Collier, 1962; *The Foxes' Union,* EPM Publications, 1977; (with Eugene J. McCarthy) *A Political Bestiary,* McGraw, 1978.

SIDELIGHTS: Known for his conservative political views, James Jackson Kilpatrick commented in an interview with Mary Hoffelt on the dour reputation of most avowed conservatives: "Taking the conservative stance is saying 'no' more often than not. If you think of the body politic as a machine, the liberals' habit is to accelerate. The conservatives' function is to apply the brakes. Certain aspects of the conservative point of view are by nature solemn. But I don't take myself too seriously." Kilpatrick is often called upon to take a conservative stance in an advocate role. But he's honest about the pitfalls of being a "front office conservative." He notes that he "was once asked to take the side of 'The Conservative's View of Watergate.' And I asked myself, 'Just what is a conservative's view of burglary?'"

But Kilpatrick believes it important for the press to present a balanced view of the issues, especially in newspaper columns. He told an interviewer from *Quill:* "I think ours is one area where we must try with diligence to present the other side. It's only in this way that we can hope through our readers to arrive at some sort of political wisdom, some sort of knowledge, some kind of truth. We get at it by fighting it out, this side against that side with reasoned arguments, responsible presentations, a responsible kind of advocacy—and then let the people make up their own minds." Kilpatrick thinks that it is only through newspapers that people can have convenient access to conflicting points of view on the news. "They're not getting it from television, God knows," he comments. "Never are they going to get both sides fairly represented on television or radio."

Despite his conservative political stance, Kilpatrick's position on other issues is more libertarian. He believes that "private behavior shouldn't be punished unless it is proved to be socially damaging." This is not contradictory to his other positions because, as Kilpatrick comments, "most people think of a linear political spectrum from conservative to liberal. Actually political theory is a circle. As you head in opposite directions around the circle, you're bound to occasionally run into the other side."

BIOGRAPHICAL/CRITICAL SOURCES: Time, November 30, 1970; *Seattle Post-Intelligencer,* November 12, 1974; *Quill,* October, 1975; *Authors in the News,* Gale, Volume I, 1976, Volume II, 1976.

* * *

KIMBALL, Spencer L(evan) 1918-

PERSONAL: Born August 26, 1918, in Thatcher, Ariz.; son of Spencer Woolley and Camilla (Eyring) Kimball; married Kathryn Ann Murphy, 1939; children: Barbara, Judith, Kathleen, David, Kent, Tim. *Education:* University of Arizona, B.S., 1940; attended University of Utah, 1946-47; Oxford University, B.C.L., 1949; University of Wisconsin, S.J.D., 1958. *Residence:* Chicago, Ill. *Office:* University of Chicago Law School, Chicago, Ill.

CAREER: Affiliated with Hartford Accident & Indemnity Co., San Francisco, Calif., 1940-43; University of Utah, College of Law, Salt Lake City, 1949-57, began as associate professor, became professor, dean, 1950-54; University of Michigan, Law School, Ann Arbor, professor, 1957-68; University of Wisconsin—Madison, Law School, dean and professor, 1968-72; University of Chicago, Law School, Chicago, Ill., professor, 1972-78, Seymour Logan Professor of Law, 1978—. *Military service:* Served as Japanese linguist with U.S. Navy, Pacific Theatre, 1943-46, became lieutenant. *Member:* American Bar Association (Chicago, executive director, 1972-78). *Awards, honors:* Elizur Wright Award, 1960, for *Insurance and Public Policy.*

WRITINGS: *Insurance and Public Policy,* University of Wisconsin Press, 1960; *The Montana Insurance Commissioner,* University of Michigan Law School, 1960; *Historical Introduction to the Legal System: Cases and Materials,* Overbeck, 1961, revised edition, West Publishing, 1966; (contributor) *Festgabe Innami, der moderne Kapitalismus und Versicherung,* Hoken Kenkyujo, 1964; (contributor) Long and Gregg, editors, *Property and Liability Insurance Handbook,* Irwin, 1966; (editor with Herbert S. Denenberg, and contributor) *Insurance, Government and Social Policy,* Irwin, 1969; (with William C. Whitford) *Why Process Consumer Complaints?: A Case Study of the Office of the Commissioner of Insurance of Wisconsin,* American Bar Foundation, 1975; (editor with Werner Pfennigstorf, and contributor) *Legal Service Plans: Approaches to Regulations,* American Bar Foundation, 1977. Contributor of several articles and book reviews to legal publications.

WORK IN PROGRESS: Variety of projects relating to insurance law.

* * *

KING, Francis H(enry) 1923-
(Frank Cauldwell)

PERSONAL: Born March 4, 1923, in Adelboden, Switzerland; son of Eustace Arthur Cecil and Faith (Read) King. *Education:* Balliol College, Oxford, B.A., 1949, M.A., 1951. *Home:* 40-42 William IV St., London WC2N 4DD, England. *Agent:* A. M. Heath & Co., 19 Gordon Pl., London W8 4JE, England.

CAREER: British Council lecturer in Florence, Italy, 1949-50, Salonica, Greece, 1950-52, and Athens, Greece, 1953-57, assistant representative in Helsinki, Finland, 1957-58, regional director in Kyoto, Japan, 1959-63; *Sunday Telegraph,* London, England, literary critic, 1964—, drama critic, 1978—. *Member:* Royal Society of Literature (fellow), Society of Authors (England; chairman, 1975-77), P.E.N. (president of English center, 1978—). *Awards, honors:* Somerset Maugham Award, 1952; Katherine Mansfield Short Story Prize, 1965.

WRITINGS: *To the Dark Tower,* Home & Van Thal, 1946; *Never Again,* Home & Van Thal, 1947; *An Air That Kills,* Home & Van Thal, 1948; *The Dividing Stream,* Morrow, 1951; *Rod of Incantation* (poems), Longmans, Green, 1952; *The Dark Glasses,* Pantheon, 1954; (under pseudonym Frank Cauldwell) *The Firewalkers,* John Murray, 1955; (editor) *Introducing Greece,* Methuen, 1956, revised edition, 1968; *The Widow,* Longmans, Green, 1957; *The Man on the Rock,* Pantheon, 1957; *So Hurt and Humiliated* (short stories), Longmans, Green, 1959; *The Custom House,* Doubleday, 1961; *The Japanese Umbrella* (short stories), Longmans, Green, 1964; *The Last of the Pleasure Gardens,* Longmans, Green, 1965; *The Waves behind the Boat,* Longmans, Green, 1967; *The Brighton Belle* (short stories), Longmans, Green, 1968; *A Domestic Animal,* Longmans, Green, 1970; *Flights* (two short novels), Hutchinson, 1973; *A Game of Patience,* Hutchinson, 1974; *The Needle,* Mason/Charter, 1975; *Hard Feelings* (short stories), Hutchinson, 1976; *The Action,* Hutchinson, 1978; *E. M. Forster and His World,* Scribner, 1978.

SIDELIGHTS: A *New York Times* reviewer once referred to Francis King as a writer "with intensity of purpose skillfully concealed behind a facile style, swift-paced dialogue and a spoofing surface-irony." Others have used words such as "cold," "comfortless," and even "bloodless" to describe King's fiction, in which he grimly explores the "mad oddities of the human condition" in a very carefully composed and rather detached, yet completely gripping style. As a *Spectator* critic observes: "There has always been a dark side to Mr. King's novels, somewhat contradicting the conventional view of him as one of our more placid writers; although he is no Poe, and would not want to be, he is adept at casting various forms of terror and unease within his apparently calm, collected prose. . . . [He] never dabbles in overstatement. He is also too fastidious to bother with the throughly modern under-statement; he is, rather, a master of the precise statement—going very well with his constant effort to keep up appearances: the appearance of his characters, of his prose, and of the neatly but tightly formed shape of his narrative. But beneath this surface, some dark fantasies swoop and glitter. . . . [King's] darting imagination is only barely kept in check by the iron discipline he imposes upon his own writing."

A commentator in *Punch,* calling King "a master of the *frisson*" (literally, a shiver or shudder), notes that he has a "sure touch" in matters concerning "decadence and decay," or, as an *Observer Review* critic states, "murder, brutality and 'perversion' constantly appear in [King's stories in] the most surprising—and natural—way." A *Books and Bookmen* reviewer claims that readers "are at the mercy of whatever Mr. King chooses as his weapon: humour, wit, irony or compassion. His style is pared down to its lovely bones. His sentences lie in wait and blip you on the head, just as you were thinking how frank and nice they were. . . . His eye is wickedly sharp on detail, the eye of a painter, of a comedian. . . . [He] is fascinated by bizarre relationships. . . . [King writes] in gruesome but never tasteless detail. He is a fastidious, an elegant, a knowing writer."

Several critics, however, find his well-chilled plots to be "too perfectly made for [their] own good," in the words of a *Listener* critic. Noting King's reputation for cool detachment, the critic concludes that this tendency "is becoming a barrier—or an unwelcome filter through which only the perfect, clear, in its way romantic, essence of experience passes, leaving all the muddy sediment of life outside, unseen, unconsidered." A *London Magazine* reviewer, commenting on the short story collection *The Brighton Belle,* suggests that King's work is beginning to lose its "vitality and credibility," for the reader may well find it difficult "to feel any sympathy for the tired failures depicted with a corresponding tiredness of vision by their creator; they're moved, like pawns, from one rigged situation to another. King's Brighton is a fictional contrivance inhabited, in the main, by 'characters' instead of human beings."

Admitting that King has an "appallingly accurate ear, eye and nose for hypocrisy, and teeth to match," a *Spectator* critic is nevertheless disturbed to note that "there are alarming signs . . . that Francis King admires his own undeniable deftness and economy rather more than is good for his writing. At the end of several stories [in *Hard Feelings*], there is a suspicion of a faint sigh of self-satisfaction . . . which is unutterably irritating and, in fact, not always excused by the work's merit. Some of the plot devices creak with old age and over-use; sometimes the reader gets restless waiting for the smashing—and predictable—blow of dramatic irony."

Though commenting specifically on *The Action,* King's bitter examination of the effect of Britain's libel laws on novelists (inspired by personal experience), a *Books and Bookmen* critic offers this summary of the author's strengths and weaknesses: "I have long been an admirer of Francis King's work. At his best, he is perspicacious, shrewd, a very self-contained writer, good at revealing hidden truths, and at exposing sham and weakness beneath a variety of masks. But there are certain aspects of his technique and literary personality which are unattractive and occasionally even shabby. . . . [*The Action*] is a clever book, there are some sharp observations, but it is heartless, often unkind. . . . No, of course I am not asking for 'nice' characters. . . . [But] I do not feel that Mr. King is close to any of these people, or cares about them one jot, and therefore, they are not merely dislikeable but lifeless. . . . Not believing much in the people, I couldn't get very involved in what happens to them either. . . . Francis King has always succeeded brilliantly at the short-story; his talent is so concise and meticulous, yet his work within that exacting form never seems contrived or strained. When he has enough to say and complete conviction in, and commitment to, the saying of it, his novels are very good too. He owes it to himself not to give away to the impulses behind much of *The Action*."

BIOGRAPHICAL/CRITICAL SOURCES: New York Times, January 19, 1958; *Listener*, April 27, 1967, September 12, 1974, October 2, 1975, December 16, 1976, October 19, 1978; *Times Literary Supplement*, May 11, 1967, September 13, 1974, April 29, 1978; *New Statesman*, June 23, 1967, September 5, 1975; *Punch*, April 24, 1968; *Observer Review*, April 28, 1968; *London Magazine*, June, 1968; *Books and Bookmen*, June, 1968, December, 1975, November, 1978; *Spectator*, September 6, 1975, October 2, 1976; *Contemporary Literary Criticism*, Volume VIII, Gale, 1978.

—*Sketch by Deborah A. Straub*

* * *

KING, Richard L(ouis) 1937-

PERSONAL: Born May 21, 1937, in Portland, Ore.; son of Louis (a motion picture director) and Mary Elizabeth (White) King. *Education:* Sacramento State College (now California State University, Sacramento), B.A., 1964; University of California, Los Angeles, M.L.S., 1970. *Home:* 12614 East Park St., Cerritos, Calif. 90701.

CAREER: University of California, Los Angeles, Graduate School of Management Library, head of circulation department and acting curator of Gross Collection of Rare Books, 1966-70; California State University, Long Beach, head of Business and Economics Reference Library, 1971-77; consultant, teacher, and writer, 1978—. *Military service:* U.S. Air Force, 1960-64. *Member:* American Library Association, California Library Association.

WRITINGS: Airport Noise Pollution: A Bibliography of Its Effects on People and Property, Scarecrow, 1973; *Business Serials of the U.S. Government: A Selective, Annotated Checklist of Reference Titles*, American Library Association, 1978. Contributor of articles to *Journal of Industrial Archaeology, Special Libraries, Los Angeles Bar Bulletin, Business History*, and *Law Office Economics and Management*.

WORK IN PROGRESS: Ursprung und Ordnungen der Berwerke (Leipzig, H. Grossen, 1616), a collation and bibliographical treatise; compilation of a bibliography of corporate histories; a bibliographic and research guide to urban and occupational noise pollution; *Analytical Index to Business Reference Sources* (tentative title), for McFarland Publications.

* * *

KING, Roma Alvah, Jr. 1914-

PERSONAL: Born December 30, 1914, in Sanger, Tex.; son of Roma A. and Katie (Gentle) King; married Lucille Bailey, 1942; children: Anthony Louis, Gwendolyn Elayne, Dana Christopher. *Education:* University of Michigan, M.A., 1947, Ph.D., 1954. *Religion:* Episcopalian. *Home:* 9823 Twin Creek Dr., Dallas, Tex.

CAREER: University of Michigan, Ann Arbor, instructor, 1953-54; University of Kansas City (now University of Missouri—Kansas City), professor, 1954-63, chairman of department of English, 1956-63; Ohio University, Athens, professor of English, 1963-74, professor emeritus, 1974—; St. Luke's Episcopal Church, Marietta, Ohio, rector, 1973-79. *Military service:* U.S. Army, Signal Corps, 1941-46; became major; received Army Commendation Citation. *Member:* Modern Language Association of America.

WRITINGS: The Bow and the Lyre, University of Michigan Press, 1956; *Robert Browning's Finances*, Baylor University, 1957; (with Frederick McLeod) *Modern American Writer*, American Book Co., 1961; (editor with McLeod) *A Reader for Composition*, American Book Co., 1962; *The Focusing Artifice: The Poetry of Robert Browning*, Ohio University Press, 1969; (contributor) W. Paul Elledge and Richard L. Hoffman, editors, *Romantic and Victorian: Studies in Memory of William H. Marshall*, Fairleigh Dickinson University Press, 1971. General editor, "The Complete Works of Robert Browning," Ohio University Press, 1969—. Contributor to *Modern Fiction Study, Twentieth Century Literature*, and other journals. Associate editor, *Mundus Artium*, 1969—.

WORK IN PROGRESS: A literary study of Charles Williams; editing additional volumes of "The Complete Works of Robert Browning."

* * *

KING, Stephen (Edwin) 1947-

PERSONAL: Born September 21, 1947, in Portland, Me,; son of Donald (a sailor) and Ruth (Pillsbury) King; married Tabitha Spruce (a poet), January 2, 1971; children: Naomi, Joseph Hill, Owen. *Education:* University of Maine, B.Sc., 1970. *Politics:* Democrat.

CAREER: Writer. Has worked as a janitor, laundry worker, and in a knitting mill; Hampden Academy (high school), Hampden, Me., English teacher, 1971-73; University of Maine at Orono, writer-in-residence, 1978-79. *Member:* Authors Guild, Authors League of America. *Awards, honors:* Hugo Award nomination from World Science Fiction Convention, 1978, for *The Shining;* Balrog Awards, second place in best novel category for *The Stand*, and second place in best collection category for *Night Shift*, both 1979.

WRITINGS—Novels, except as indicated; published by Doubleday, except as indicated: *Carrie*, 1974, movie edition, New American Library, 1976; *Salem's Lot*, 1975, television edition, New American Library, 1979; *The Shining*, 1977, movie edition, New American Library, 1980; *The Stand*, 1978; *Night Shift* (short stories), 1978; *The Dead Zone*, Viking, 1979; *Firestarter*, Viking, 1980; *Stephen King's Danse Macabre* (nonfiction), Everest House, 1981. Author of numerous short stories; also author of screenplay "The Stand," based on his novel of the same title.

SIDELIGHTS: Stephen King is one of the most successful writers of modern horror fiction working in the genre today. His books have sold over ten million copies, and several of his novels have been produced as popular motion pictures. Judging by the widespread interest in these types of books and films, it is obvious that his fascination with the macabre is something that is shared by many others. As he told Mel Allen in a *Writer's Digest* interview, "people's appetites for terror seem insatiable." Readers have been revelling in his accounts of man-eating rats, gigantic worms, vampires, murder, revenge, and bloodletting since he first began writing as a student. Allen mentions that King is "amused that a classmate is still horrified by a short story [he] published in the student literary magazine. It was about a young man whose weapon of revenge is the nozzle of an air compressor which he sticks in his enemy's mouth."

Revenge is a subject that is central to King's first novel. *Carrie* is the story of an outcast high-school girl who is mercilessly tormented by her classmates. During the course of the action she discovers that she is the possessor of amazing telekinetic powers—that is, she can produce motion in objects through mind control—and is thus able to exact revenge. In a spectacular scene at the Spring Ball, she manages to do away with a good many of her persecutors by bringing about an explosion and uncontrollable fire which eventually destroys the better part of a small town. In a *Psychology Today* article, Elizabeth Hall says that *Carrie* "probably holds the record for the number of deaths perpetrated within its covers by a single adolescent." And Jane Belon Shaw, in a *Library Journal* review, calls the novel "a contender for the bloodiest book of the year—menstrual blood, blood of childbirth and miscarriage, blood of a whole town dying, and finally, the lifeblood of the heroine draining away." Newgate Callendar of the *New York Times Book Review* feels that "King does more than tell a story. . . . He gets into Carrie's mind as well as into the minds of her classmates." Echoing the sentiments of several critics, Callendar continues: "That this is a first novel is amazing. King writes with the kind of surety normally associated only with veteran writers."

Much of Carrie's trouble stems from her mother, a religious fanatic and stern disciplinarian who raises her daughter to fear and distrust people. As a result of her influence the girl is shy, unattractive, and all but mute. King's inspiration for these characters came to him while he was employed in a laundry. He told Allen: "There was a very strange woman working there with me. She was always quoting the Bible, and I thought, 'If she has children, I wonder what they're like.' That was when I got my idea for *Carrie*." He was moved to begin work on the book by a friend who challenged him to develop a plot centering on female characters, something he had previously been unable to do. After he had written a few pages, he decided that he could never write successfully about women and threw the work in the trash. But when he came home from his teaching job the next day, he found that his wife had retrieved the pages from the wastebasket; she was intrigued with the story and insisted that he continue.

King says that some elements of Carrie's character are based on incidents in his own childhood in which he, too, was the object of ridicule. "When I played baseball," he recalls, "I was always the kid who got picked last. 'Ha-ha, you got King,' the others would say." In a much more vicious manner Carrie, a seemingly-weak individual, is brutalized by her mother and her classmates. The twist is that she turns out to be the most powerful character in the book, and when she learns how to use her power she unleashes it on her tormentors much as King may have fantasized doing when he was a child. The moral of the story as he sees it: "Don't mess around with people. You never know who you may be tangling with."

In *Salem's Lot* King retells the legend of the vampire and updates it by bringing the action to a small town in modern-day Maine. Reviewers appear to have mixed feelings about the book. Walter Bobbie, for instance, in his *Best Sellers* article, praises it as "a novel of such chilling beginnings that we look forward to losing sleep over it. . . . It is the kind of goose bump fiction that makes grown men afraid of the dark." He is also impressed with King's characterization, saying that "it is here that the writer proves a master of this genre. He juggles character vignettes into a structural cross-fire that is hypnotic. A thousand detailed portraits become the broad canvas of *Salem's Lot*." But Bobbie feels that the book is somewhat disappointing in that the final confrontation between the vampire and his pursuers is "labored, obvious, and familiar. King adds nothing new to the legend." A *Publisher's Weekly* critic says that with *Salem's Lot* the author "has produced another tingling horror tale in which the sense of evil is almost palpable," but finds that "in doing so he has elongated his story unnecessarily, so that when the same ghastly, gruesome fate keeps on overtaking the Maine villagers . . . one does begin to wish things had been tightened up a bit." A *Fantasy Newsletter* writer goes so far as to name King "America's best contemporary writer of horror fiction," but then notes that "unfortunately, he doesn't seem to be aware that longer is not necessarily better."

King's next novel, *The Shining,* also met with mixed reviews. Jack Sullivan of the *New York Times Book Review* writes: "To say that Stephen King is not an elegant writer ('What had been left of the eight-nine people aboard hadn't looked much different from a Hamburger Helper casserole') is putting it mildly. But inelegance is not precisely the problem in *The Shining*. . . . [Here] memories and fantasies often find themselves pretentiously enclosed in parentheses. Sometimes non-punctuation or italics are used—quite arbitrarily—for gimmicky stream of consciousness effect. Occasionally we are subjected to all capitals in parentheses with triple exclamation points (!!!ON BOTH MARGINS!!!)! This is Mr. King's way of being climactic." Sullivan also criticizes the "derivative" nature of *The Shining*. He says that the author "lifts images and plot fragments from books (Poe, Blackwood, Lovecraft) and films ('Diabolique,' 'Psycho,' 'Village of the Damned')." Richard R. Lingeman of the *New York Times* refers to King as "a writer of fairly engaging and preposterous claptrap. . . . His long suit is an energetic and febrile imagination and a radar fix on the young people who probably make up the large hard core of the market. He is not up to [Ira] Levin and [Thomas] Tryon, however, because he lacks the sly craftsmanship of the former at his best, and the narrative strength of the latter. Still, like a fast short-order cook during the breakfast rush, he serves up the scary stuff with unremitting dexterity." Lingeman concludes that "Mr. King is a natural, but he lacks control; he simply rears back and lets fly with the fireball, and a lot of wild pitches result. That's a pity because his sheer rookie's energy is engaging."

In a *Nyclatops* article, Marc Laidlaw praises King's creation of atmosphere in *The Shining,* calling it "masterful—the first irrational hint I had that anything unusual might happen terrified me as fully as the later, more logically-constructed episodes. In fact, where the novel falls short is in the fact that the conclusion is not nearly as frightening as the mood that has been predicting it. King takes the stance that he should give the readers a hint of the ultimate horror early in the game, and then—when they're sure to be afraid that it's actually going to happen—give them exactly what they've been nervously waiting for. It's a technique that works rather well, though in this case the intimations of doom are more frightening than the doom itself." Frederick Patten, writing in *Delap's Fantasy and Science Fiction Review,* sums up: "When all's said, the novel *works!* It makes one tremble in anticipation of the day when King gets it all together and writes a 'perfect' book. . . . King's style . . . is his most obvious fault. It's all *good* writing, it's all pertinent, but it goes on and on. . . . Setting a realistic scene and creating believably complex characters are laudable traits, but King seriously overdoes it. . . . But it's still the goddamnedest best horror novel I've read in over two decades."

In *The Stand* King confronts a highly topical issue; a new strain of influenza virus, developed by the government for biological warfare, leaks out of its storage place in a cavern and spreads rapidly through the atmosphere, wiping out ninety-five per cent of the population of the United States (and probably the rest of the world) within a month. *Best Sellers* reviewer J. Justin Gustainis calls the book "something of a departure for [King]. This is not to suggest that it is not good, or, in its own way, scary." But Linda B. Osborne of the *Washington Post* does not believe this to be the case; she feels that "evil in *The Stand* is more a snicker than a shudder," and that "it's a kind of giant booby trap, the terror laced with adolescent giggles. People die 'slumped beside Hostess Twinkies'; a man with his face in a bowl of chunky sirloin soup. . . . Several characters wet their pants when they're scared, and draw attention to the trickle. Again and again there's a wisecrack to undercut the fear. It's difficult to take even the good guys seriously. . . . There's a gee-whiz air about the characters as they stumble through the heady questions of pride, free will, and survival, yet King certainly meant to include these as 'heavy issues.'" Osborne thinks that King could have written a better book—a "simple thriller"—if he had not attempted to deal with these issues. "King is best at dramatic action," she writes, "a page-turning briskness, and this book is certainly crammed with the trappings of fright. If *The Stand* had paid more attention to arousing terror than examining the nature of evil, one might be willing to turn more of its many pages."

Anne Collins of *Maclean's* also feels that *The Stand* is somewhat of a break from the more conventional horror stories in King's earlier fiction, and that, she says, "is why it ultimately bores. Horror lies in that area where known becomes unknown, where ordinary turns menacing. Too much of King's . . . book deals with a little leaguer's vision of American democracy somehow smiling through apocalypse; good and evil are set up like so many kindergarten blocks. Bad is Las Vegas where those survivors who sell their souls gather; good is Boulder, Colorado, and the American Constitution. Similar equations act like dry rot on the plot." A *New Yorker* critic, however, mentions that "Stephen King takes liberties permitted in science fiction and thrillers (the good guys share clairvoyant powers, and the plot often turns on lucky coincidences), but he grounds his apocalyptic vision of the blighted American vista, and he avoids the formulas of less talented popular novelists."

The Dead Zone is the story of John Smith, a young school teacher who emerges from a four-and-a-half-year coma with the ability to predict certain future events. John meets a New Hampshire congressman and envisions him eventually heading a fascist government in the United States and starting a nuclear war that wipes out all life on earth. Joseph McLellan of the *Washington Post* describes the main conflict in the book: "Do you kill a public servant because you have had a vision? How many men have become political assassins for reasons like that—and what is the world's judgment of them?"

In this novel, as in others, King is lauded for his skillful characterization. Christopher Lehmann-Haupt writes: "I believed in Johnny Smith. I believed in him because I wanted to believe in him, of course; because the fun of a certain kind of fiction is asking 'What if . . .?' and then playing with the possibilities. But I believed in him most of all because Stephen King, who specializes in such scary hypotheses . . . and who seems to be getting better at them all the time, Stephen King makes it easy and fun and, above all, frightening to believe in John Smith." Lehmann-Haupt also remarks that "the characters are straightforwardly and truly drawn, and Mr. King is capable of showing us their depths with a sort of simple eloquence that Thornton Wilder brought to Grover's Corners, N.H." In a *Detroit News* review, D. E. Wojack writes: "Throughout the novel, there is the unnerving feeling that this story is real. Though the characters are not complex, for the most part, they breathe a warmth and love of life it is easy to relate to. By creating a world so very close to our own existence, then disturbing it with a frightening supposition, King offers a horror no seven-foot green monster or fanged stalker ever can. After all, horror we can place in an isolation booth is one thing. Horror let loose in the real world is quite another."

King offered interviewer Paul Hendrickson of the *Washington Post* this analysis of horror fiction: "The reader comes to you and says, 'Scare me.' When he picks up your book at the counter and it says 'CHILLING' across the cover, what he says to himself, I think, is, 'Oh, yeah? Prove it.' It's sort of an arm-wrestle from then on." When asked why people so enjoy being scared, he replied: "Basically I think it's because the whole fright syndrome dredges up a lot of emotions we normally don't get to experience. The writer of the horror novel is asking: 'Do you want to risk getting scared? Come on, it may be good for you.' In a real way, the horror novelist is the agent of the norm. He's the Republican in a three-button suit. He's saying, 'Look at that over there—isn't it yeech?'" He also told Christine Winter, in a *Chicago Tribune* interview, that "there are some people whose lives are full of fears—that their marriage isn't working, that they aren't going to make it on the job, that society is crumbling all around them. But we're not really supposed to talk about things like that, and so they don't have any outlets for all those scary feelings. But the horror writer can give them a place to put their fears, and it's OK to be afraid then, because nothing is real, and you can blow it all away when it's over."

Winter notes that King is "amazingly good-natured about the fact that many of his most ardent fans suspect that he is probably a madman, or at least a firm believer in the psychic threads that run through all his novels." And Hendrickson lists a few of the author's unusual habits: "When he goes to bed at night, Stephen King makes sure both of his feet are under the blanket. No sense taking chances with that stuff. . . . He won't walk under ladders. 'It doesn't take that long to go around.' He never turns in without first checking on the children. 'I know there aren't really such things as bogeymen.' . . . When he's out driving and sees blackbirds, he just can't stop himself from poking the evil-eye sign at them so they won't fly through the grille and peck him to death. 'I mean, what does it hurt, right?'" Despite these few idiosyncrasies, Winter concludes that King is not the madman that some of his readers believe him to be. She writes: "The truth of the matter is that, no, Stephen King does not have any more nightmares than you and I; and no, Stephen King does not live in a haunted house; and no, Stephen King does not possess, or even particularly believe in supernatural experiences or the kind of darkly occult powers that make his novels so deeply horrifying. What he is committed to is good writing and offbeat ideas that 'just seem to spring from some place deep inside of me'—and just incidentally have the power to scare the life out of anyone who lives in a place where it gets dark at night.''

In regard to the horror genre and the development of his craft, King told Michael J. Bandler of the *Chicago Tribune Book World:* "[I] learned a lot about plotting and characterization from the books I read. Most of us learned pretty early on who the good guys are and who the bad guys are. But when I got into horror fiction, I discovered that in a lot of books by classic writers kids gravitate to—Poe, Lovecraft—there are no good guys, just people who are involved. There are no heroes, only anti-heroes; the writers want to set you up so when someone gets it in the end, you may be horrified, but won't really be sorry. It's entirely different from Ira Levin's *The Stepford Wives* or *Rosemary's Baby,* where you really care for those people because they seem to be good, and yet they go down anyway. I'm disturbed by that. I don't think good has to win over evil in a horror tale the way it does in a comic book—where nobody's hurt and you don't have to pay the price. At the same time, though, it's terrible that somebody like Rosemary has to struggle so hard to get out of her predicament—to no avail. That's an unnecessarily bleak view of how things turn out. . . . It's cynical, imbalanced. To put a character through the mill—the way Tom Tryon does in *Harvest Home*—isn't justified. Good shouldn't be allowed to win without paying some price, but there ought to be some hope at the end.''

When asked by Bandler to name the most frightening experience he ever encountered in a book, King cited William Golding's *Lord of the Flies.* "It was terrifying. That or Orwell's *1984*—probably *Lord of the Flies* for outright terror.'' He told Paul Hendrickson that he has only been scared once by his own writing. That was when he was doing a rewrite of a scene from *The Shining:* "Six weeks away from the scene,'' writes Hendrickson, "he began to get the light sweats. Then it was down to four days, three days, two days. The scene, he says, is of an old lady, dead ten or fifteen years, lying bloated and horrible in a bathtub. She comes alive, rises from the tub, while a child claws at the door to get out.'' Hendrickson asked what time of day he usually writes scenes like that. "Mornings,'' King replied, "always mornings. You think I want to write this stuff at night?''

MEDIA ADAPTATIONS: Carrie was filmed by United Artists in 1976, and *Salem's Lot* was produced as a television film by CBS in 1979. Stanley Kubrick's film version of *The Shining* was released by Warner Bros. in 1980. Jack Kroll of *Newsweek* says that Kubrick "has gone after the ultimate horror movie, something that will make 'The Exorcist' look like 'Abbott and Costello Meet Beelzebub.' The result is the first epic horror film, a movie that is to other horror movies what his '2001: A Space Odyssey' was to other space movies.'' And *Time*'s Richard Schickel calls it "a movie that will have to be reckoned with on the highest level.'' Stephen King's own screenplay adaption of *The Stand* is currently in production.

AVOCATIONAL INTERESTS: Reading (mostly fiction), jigsaw puzzles, playing the guitar ("I'm terrible and so try to bore no one but myself''), movies.

BIOGRAPHICAL/CRITICAL SOURCES: Kirkus Reviews, February 1, 1974, March 1, 1974, August 15, 1975, December 1, 1976, December 1, 1977, September 1, 1978, June 15, 1979; *Library Journal,* February 15, 1974, April 15, 1974, May 15, 1974, February 1, 1977, February 1, 1978; *Publisher's Weekly,* February 25, 1974, August 11, 1975, June 7, 1976, December 6, 1976, January 17, 1977, November 14, 1977, November 28, 1977; *New York Times Book Review,* May 16, 1974, February 20, 1977, March 26, 1978, February 4, 1979, September 23, 1979; *Psychology Today,* September, 1975; *School Library Journal,* December, 1975; *Best Sellers,* January, 1976, March, 1979, October, 1979; *New York Times,* March 1, 1977, August 17, 1979; *Delap's Fantasy and Science Fiction Review,* April, 1977; *Writer's Digest,* June, 1977.

Nyclatops, Volume I, number 7, 1978; *Horizon,* February, 1978; *Washington Post Book World,* October 1, 1978; *Washington Post,* November 23, 1978, August 30, 1979; *Maclean's,* December 18, 1978; *New Yorker,* January 15, 1979; *America,* February 17, 1979; *Los Angeles Times Book Review,* August 26, 1979; *Chicago Tribune,* September 18, 1979; *Detroit News,* September 26, 1979; *Rolling Stone,* December 27, 1979; *Fantasy Newsletter,* February, 1980; *Newsweek,* May 26, 1980; *Time,* June 2, 1980; *Chicago Tribune Book Review,* June 8, 1980; *Contemporary Literary Criticism,* Volume XII, Gale, 1980.

—Sketch by Peter M. Gareffa

* * *

KINKEAD, Eugene (Francis) 1906-

PERSONAL: Born September 18, 1906, in New York, N.Y.; married Katherine Jackson Theobald, 1937; children: Kathleen, Duncan, Maeve, Gwen. *Education:* University of Wisconsin, B.A., 1928. *Religion:* Episcopalian. *Residence:* Colebrook, Conn. 06021. *Office: New Yorker* Magazine, 25 West 43rd St., New York, N.Y. 10036.

CAREER: New Yorker, New York, N.Y., reporter, writer, and editor, 1932—. War correspondent, 1944-45, receiving U.S. Navy Commendation. *Member:* University Club (New York), Graduates Club (New Haven, Conn.), Cosmos Club (Washington, D.C.). *Awards, honors:* Benjamin Franklin Magazine Award, 1958, for *New Yorker* article, "Study of Something New in History''; Christopher Award, 1959, for *In Every War but One;* Westinghouse Science Writing Award, American Association for the Advancement of Science, 1972, for *New Yorker* article on bioluminescence.

WRITINGS: (With Russell Maloney) *Our Own Baedeker,* Simon & Schuster, 1950; *Spider, Egg & Microcosm,* Knopf, 1955; *In Every War but One,* Norton, 1959; *A Concrete Look at Nature,* Quadrangle, 1974; *Wildness Is All around Us,* Dutton, 1978.

AVOCATIONAL INTERESTS: Tennis, natural history.

BIOGRAPHICAL/CRITICAL SOURCES: New York Times Book Review, May 14, 1978.

* * *

KINNAIRD, Clark 1901-
(John Paul Adams, Edgar Poe Norris)

PERSONAL: Born May 4, 1901, in Louisville, Ky.; son of Charles Beck (an engineer) and Nellie (a teacher; maiden name, Wright) Kinnaird; married Marian Irene Gosnell, April 14, 1924; children: Kenneth D., Laird D. *Education:* Attended University of Kentucky. *Politics:* Republican. *Religion:* Protestant. *Home and office:* 76 Mine St., Flemington, N.J. 08822. *Agent:* Bertha Klausner International Literary Agency, Inc., 71 Park Ave., New York, N.Y. 10016.

CAREER: Reporter on daily newspapers in Kentucky and the Midwest, and correspondent in Europe, 1921-24; Central

Press Association, Cleveland Ohio and New York City, managing editor, 1924-28; *Edenton Daily News,* Edenton, N.C., publisher and editor, 1928-30; King Features Syndicate, New York City, associate editor, 1930-37, 1939-70, syndicated columnist, beginning 1949, author of numerous columns, including "The Best of Advice," "What's the Answer?," "Behind the Microphone," "My New York," "Your America Day-by-Day," "Centennial Scrapbook," "Daybook of America," and "Parade of Books," currently writing syndicated book reviews. WINS radio, New York City, general manager and associate director of Hearst Radio Service, arranged first U.S.-Soviet entertainment broadcast, 1931-32, and first transatlantic broadcast from the Vatican. Broadcaster-televiser on various local and national networks; conductor of weekly program, "Your America," on Armed Forces Radio and Television Network, for three years. Lecturer on journalism at Columbia University, New School for Social Research, New York University, Rider College, and Syracuse University. *Military service:* U.S. Navy, 1918-19. Kentucky National Guard, 1920-21; became second lieutenant; honorary colonel on governor's staff, 1933.

MEMBER: Kentucky Historical Society, New Jersey Historical Society, Dutch Treat Club (New York). *Awards, honors:* Freedoms Foundation Awards, 1949, 1950, 1953, 1962; President's Medal, National Society of the Children of the American Revolution, 1960; recipient of numerous other awards, including those from U.S. Department of Defense, 1966, American Legion, 1968, College of Journalism Honor Fraternity, 1973, U.S. Flag Foundation, 1977, and Pi Delta Epsilon.

WRITINGS: 500 Americans Who Made Us Great, Knickerbocker, 1941; (with Alan Roy Dafoe) *How to Raise Your Baby,* Bartholomew House, 1941; *Through Baby's First Years,* Brown & Bigelow, 1942; (under pseudonym John Paul Adams) *War Comes to Us,* Bartholomew House, 1942; *This Must Not Happen Again: The Black Book of Fascist Horror,* Howell, Soskin, 1945; *Wilton Caniff: Rembrandt of the Comic-Strips,* McKay, 1946; (with Murat "Chic" Young) *Blondie's Soups, Salads, Sandwiches Cook Book,* McKay, 1947; (with H. J. Heinz II and Josef Iorgy) *The Last Defense,* Duell, Sloan & Pearce, 1948; *50 Years of the Comics,* Knickerbocker, 1948; *Gangsters, Gun Molls and G-Men,* Avon, 1948; (with George McManus) *Fun for All,* World Publishing, 1948; *Big League Baseball,* Avon, 1951; *Puzzles for Everybody,* Avon, 1951; (with John K. Winkler) *William Randolph Hearst: A New Appraisal,* Hastings House, 1955; (under pseudonym John Paul Adams) *We Dare You to Solve This,* Berkley Publishing, 1957; (with Lawrence Langner, real name Alan Child) *The Importance of Wearing Clothes,* Hastings House, 1958; *First Century and After: A History of Military Order of the Loyal Legion,* Kingsport Press, 1966; *George Washington: The Pictorial Biography,* Hastings House, 1967.

Editor: *The Real F.D.R.,* Citadel, 1945; *Encyclopedia of Puzzles and Pastimes,* Citadel, 1946; *It Happened in 1945,* Duell, Sloan & Pearce, 1946; *It Happened in 1946,* Duell, Sloan & Pearce, 1947; (and author of notes) *Trials and Other Tribulations,* Lippincott, 1947; (and author of notes) Damon Runyon, *Poems for Men,* Duell, Sloan & Pearce, 1947; *Merry-Go-Round,* McKay, 1948; (and author of biography) Runyon, *Runyon First and Last,* Lippincott, 1949 (published in England with expanded biography as *All This and That,* Constable, 1950); (and author of notes) Runyon, *More Guys and Dolls,* Garden City Books, 1951; (and author of notes) *Various Temptations,* Avon, 1955; Runyon, *A Treasury of Runyon,* Modern Library, 1958, reprinted, Random House, 1979; (with Walter Howey) *Fighting Editions,* McKay, 1958; *Rube Goldberg vs. the Machine Age,* Hastings House, 1968.

Contributor: Harry C. McKown, *Home Room Guidance,* McGraw, 1934; *The College Anthology,* Scott, Foresman, 1949; *The Funnies: An American Idiom,* Macmillan, 1963; *From Source to Statement,* Houghton, 1968. Contributor to *Morrow's Almanack, For Loving a Book,* and other collections. Author of five serials published in periodicals under various pseudonyms, including Edgar Poe Norris. Contributor of non-fiction to *Liberty, Freeman, Argosy, Pictorial Review, American Weekly, American Mercury, New Yorker, Ken, Coronet, Saturday Review,* and other magazines.

WORK IN PROGRESS: A nonfiction book, *Women: Inevitable Warriors; Blythe Spirits;* a novel, under the working title, *The Suppressors.*

* * *

KINTNER, Earl W(ilson) 1912-

PERSONAL: Born November 6, 1912, in Corydon, Ind.; son of Jacob Leroy (a farmer) and Lillie F. (Chanley) Kintner; married second wife, Valerie Patricia Wildy, May 28, 1948; children: (first marriage) Anna Victoria, Jonathan M., Rosemary Jane (deceased); (second marriage) Christopher Earl Mackelean. *Education:* DePauw University, A.B., 1936; Indiana University, J.D., 1938. *Politics:* Republican. *Religion:* Episcopalian. *Home:* 5001 Van Ness St. N.W., Washington, D.C. 20016. *Office:* Arent, Fox, Kintner, Plotkin & Kahn, 1100 Federal Bar Building, 1815 H St. N.W., Washington, D.C. 20006.

CAREER: Admitted to Indiana Bar, 1938, U.S. Supreme Court Bar, 1945, and District of Columbia Bar, 1953; attorney-at-law in Princeton, Ind., 1938-44; United Nations War Crimes Commission, London, England, deputy U.S. commissioner and co-chairman of committee reviewing Allied war crime matters, 1945-48; Federal Trade Commission, Washington, D.C., senior trial attorney on antimonopoly cases, 1948-50, legal adviser, 1951-52, general counsel, 1953-59, commissioner and chairman, 1959-61; Arent, Fox, Kintner, Plotkin & Kahn, Washington, D.C., senior partner, 1961—. City attorney of Princeton, Ind., 1939-42; prosecuting attorney of 66th Indiana Judicial Circuit, 1943-44; delegate and chairman of committee on hearing officers, President's Conference on Administrative Procedure, 1953-54; member of executive committee of New York State Antitrust Law Section, 1957-60; adjunct professor at New York University, 1958; president of Federal Bar Building Corp, 1959—; member of Administrative Conference of the United States, and in charge of U.S. Patent Office management study, 1961-62; member of U.S. Department of Commerce panel on invention and innovation, 1965-66. *Military service:* U.S. Navy, Amphibious Forces, 1944-46; became lieutenant. *Awards, honors:* LL.B., DePauw University, 1970.

MEMBER: American Bar Association (member of house of delegates, 1957-58, 1959-60), Federal Bar Association (president, 1956-57, 1958-59; president of foundation, 1957—), American Judicature Society (member of board of directors, 1960-64), Inter-American Bar Association, National Lawyers Club (president, 1959—), National Press Club, Phi Delta Phi, Phi Sigma Alpha, Delta Sigma Rho, Sigma Delta Chi, American Legion, Disabled American Veterans (life member), Masons (past master; Shriner), Cosmos Club, Capitol Hill Club, Union League Club, Coral Beach Club, Tennis Club (Bermuda).

WRITINGS: (Editor) *The United Nations War Crimes*

Commission, H.M.S.O., 1948; (editor) *The Development of the Laws of War,* H.M.S.O., 1948; (editor) *The Hadamar Trial,* Hodge & Co., 1949; (editor) *Federal Trade Commission Manual for Attorneys,* Federal Trade Commission, 1952; *An Antitrust Primer: A Guide to Antitrust and Trade Regulation Laws for Businessmen,* Macmillan, 1964, 2nd edition, 1973; *A Robinson-Patman Primer,* Macmillan, 1969, 2nd edition, 1979; *A Primer on the Law of Deceptive Practices,* Macmillan, 1971, 2nd edition, 1978; *A Primer on the Law of Mergers,* Macmillan, 1973; *An International Antitrust Primer,* Macmillan, 1974; *An Intellectual Property Primer,* Macmillan, 1975; *The Legislative History of the Federal Antitrust Laws and Related Statutes,* Chelsea House, 1978; *A Treatise on the Antitrust Laws of the United States,* Anderson Publishing, 1979.

* * *

KIRCHNER, Walther 1905-

PERSONAL: Born May 18, 1905, in Berlin, Germany. *Education:* Franzoesisches Gymnasium, Germany, Abiturium, 1923; University of California, Los Angeles, A.B., 1941, M.A., 1942, Ph.D., 1944. *Religion:* Protestant. *Home:* 115 Lafayette Rd., Princeton, N.J. 08540.

CAREER: University of California, Los Angeles, lecturer, 1943-45; University of Delaware, Newark, assistant professor, 1945-48, associate professor, 1948-55, professor of history, 1955-65, H. Rodney Sharpe Professor, 1965-70. Fulbright professor, University of Copenhagen, 1952-53; member of Institute for Advanced Study, Princeton, N.J., 1955-56, and Max Planck Institut fuer Geschichte, Goettingen, Germany, 1961; visiting professor, University of Pennsylvania, 1946-50, University of Muenster, 1964, University of Muenchen, 1967, and University of Dusseldorf, 1979-80. *Member:* American Historical Association, American Society for Reformation Research (president, 1958), Hansischer Geschichtsverein, American Association for Advancement of Slavic Studies. *Awards, honors:* Distinguished scholarship award, American Association for the Advancement of Science, Southern Conference, 1977.

WRITINGS: History of Russia, Barnes & Noble, 1948, 6th edition, 1976; *Rise of the Baltic Question,* University of Delaware Press, 1954; *Eine Reise durch Sibirien im 18, Jahrhundert,* Gunther Olzog, 1954; *History of Western Civilization,* Barnes & Noble, Volume I: *Western Civilization to 1500,* 1958, Volume II: *Western Civilization since 1500,* 1960; *Alba, Spaniens Eiserner Herzog,* Musterschmidt, 1963; *Economic Relations between Russia and the West,* Indiana University Press, 1966; *A Siberian Journey: Journal of Hans Fries,* Frank Cass, International School Book Services, 1974; *Studies in Russian-American Commerce,* E. J. Brill, 1975. Contributor to *Journal of History of Ideas, American Slavic and East European Review,* and other journals. Editor, *Jahrbuecher fuer Geschichte Osteuropas.*

* * *

KIRK, Russell (Amos) 1918-

PERSONAL: Born October 19, 1918, in Plymouth, Mich.; son of Russell Andrew and Marjorie (Pierce) Kirk; married Annette Yvonne Cecile Courtemanche, September 19, 1964; children: Monica, Cecilia, Felicia, Andrea. *Education:* Michigan State College (now University), B.A., 1940; Duke University, M.A., 1941; St. Andrews University, D.Litt., 1952. *Politics:* Republican. *Home and office:* Piety Hill, Mecosta, Mich. 49332.

CAREER: Michigan State College (now University), East Lansing, assistant professor of the history of civilization, 1946-53; Long Island University, Greenvale, N.Y., research professor of politics at Merriweather Campus (now C.W. Post Center), 1957-61, university professor, 1958-61; writer and lecturer. Distinguished visiting professor at numerous colleges and universities, 1962—. President, Educational Reviewer (foundation), 1960—, and Marguerite Eyer Wilbur Foundation, 1979—. Director of social science program, Educational Research Council of America, 1979—. Justice of the peace, Morton Township, Mecosta County, Mich., 1961-64; *Military service:* U.S. Army, Chemical Warfare Service, 1941-45; became staff sergeant. *Awards, honors:* American Council of Learned Societies senior fellow, 1950-51; Guggenheim fellow, 1956; honorary degrees from Boston College, 1956, St. John's University, New York, N.Y., 1957, Le Moyne College, 1963, Park College, 1961, Loyola College, Baltimore, Md., Olivet College, Gannon College, and Niagara University; Ann Radcliffe Award for Gothic fiction, for *Old House of Fear* and *The Surly Sullen Bell;* Christopher Award, 1972, for *Eliot and His Age;* World Fantasy Award for short fiction, 1977, for "There's a Long, Long Trail a-Winding."

WRITINGS: Randolph of Roanoke, University of Chicago Press, 1951, enlarged edition published as *John Randolph of Roanoke,* Regnery, 1964, 3rd edition, Liberty Fund, 1978; *The Conservative Mind: From Burke to Santayana,* Regnery, 1953, 3rd revised edition published as *The Conservative Mind: From Burke to Eliot,* 1960, 6th revised edition, Gateway Editions, 1978; *St. Andrews,* Batsford, 1954; *A Program for Conservatives,* Regnery, 1954, abridged edition published as *Prospects for Conservatives,* 1956; *Academic Freedom,* Regnery, 1955, reprinted, Greenwood Press, 1977; *Beyond the Dreams of Avarice,* Regnery, 1956; *The Intelligent Woman's Guide to Conservatism,* Devin-Adair, 1957; *The American Cause,* Regnery, 1957, reprinted, Greenwood Press, 1975; *Old House of Fear* (novel), Fleet Press, 1961; *The Surly Sullen Bell* (short story collection), Fleet Press, 1962; *Confessions of a Bohemian Tory,* Fleet Press, 1963; *The Intemperate Professor and Other Cultural Splenetics,* Louisiana State University Press, 1965; *A Creature of the Twilight* (novel), Fleet Press, 1966; *Edmund Burke: A Genius Reconsidered,* Arlington House, 1967; (with James McClellan) *The Political Principles of Robert A. Taft,* Fleet Press, 1967; *Enemies of the Permanent Things: Observations of Abnormality in Literature and Politics,* Arlington House, 1969; *Eliot and His Age: T. S. Eliot's Moral Imagination in the Twentieth Century,* Random House, 1971; *The Roots of American Order,* Open Court, 1974; *Decadence and Renewal in the Higher Learning,* Regnery, 1978; *Lord of the Hollow Dark,* St. Martin's, 1979; *The Princess of All Lands* (short story collection), Arkham, 1979.

Also editor of books; contributor of introductions and articles to over forty-five books. Educational columnist, *National Review,* 1956—; author of syndicated newspaper column, "To the Point," 1962-75. Contributor to encyclopedias and dictionaries, including *Encyclopaedia Britannica, Collier's Encyclopedia, World Book Encyclopedia, Dictionary of Southern History,* and *Dictionary of Political Science.* Contributor of more than 500 articles, essays, and short stories to periodicals in the United States, Great Britain, Canada, Australia, Norway, Austria, Spain, Argentina, and Italy, including *Fortune, New York Times Magazine, Wall Street Journal, Journal of the History of Ideas, America, Commonweal,* and *Kenyon Review.* Founder and editor, *Modern Age,* 1957-59; editor, *University Bookman,* 1960—.

WORK IN PROGRESS: A memoir, *An Obscurant's History*

of His Own Time, for Gateway Editions; editing *The Viking Portable Conservative Tradition.*

SIDELIGHTS: "It is not merely an obvious affection for Edmund Burke that links Russell Kirk with the eighteenth century," writes Donald Atwell Zoll in the *Political Science Reviewer.* "His emergence in the arena of contemporary letters reveals the transmigration of an eighteenth century spirit, the revival of the literary grace and versatility of the century of the high baroque. He personifies the still lively *arete* of a more leisurely age, the urbane versatility of the literati of the era of Addison and Steel, Swift, Pope, Chesterfield, Johnson and Burke."

As the author of numerous books on American history and education, as well as several volumes of literary criticism and even a few Gothic novels and short story collections, Russell Kirk is indeed versatile. He is, however, best known for his writings on political theory, especially on what Zoll refers to as "aesthetic conservatism," which he defines as "a repudiation of vulgarity in terms of both life-style and the procedures of politics.... [Kirk's] is a visceral response—however expressed in genteel phraseology—to the demolition of gracefulness." Regarded as one of the country's leading conservative intellectuals, Kirk first became convinced in the early 1950's of the need for a new and comprehensive set of beliefs based on the heritage of British and American conservative thought. According to a *Chicago Sunday Tribune* reviewer, the result of Kirk's research—*The Conservative Mind*—"is in every respect a brilliant book. It is brilliant in its conception, brilliant in its avoidance of cliches, brilliant in its ability to relate a man to his landscape ... and brilliant in its choice of significant figures in the history of intellectual conservatism."

"Certainly the so-called 'new conservatism' of the postwar period takes on new substance and meaning with the publication of this splendid book," notes a critic in the *American Political Science Review.* A critic in the *New York Herald Tribune Book Review* writes: "To be a conservative in the United States has for so long been considered identical with being backward and even faintly alien, that Mr. Kirk's proud justification of the term is to be welcomed. His book is carefully wrought and honestly made. It embodies a point of view which deserves a hearing." The *New York Times* reviewer feels that *The Conservative Mind* shows Kirk to be "as relentless as his enemies, ... considerably more temperate and scholarly, and in passages of this very readable book, brilliant and even eloquent.... [The author] ... is amply familiar with the present need for a transvaluation of values."

Not everyone, however, agrees that *The Conservative Mind* advances the cause of conservatism. Peter Gay of *Political Science Quarterly,* for example, claims that "in thus attempting to prove the existence and the moral and intellectual respectability of a conservative ideology, Mr. Kirk has only succeeded in doing the opposite." A *Commonweal* reviewer admits that Kirk "has marshalled an impressive list of American and British conservative thinkers" in support of his views, yet "the question I would ask him and all conservatives is this: what is the key to the spirit conservatism is fighting? Unless that spirit be understood in its very essence, the fight is in vain. Until Mr. Kirk leads his investigation into this ground I am afraid his restoration of the conservative heritage will remain incomplete."

Writing from the vantage point of the 1970's (as opposed to the 1950's), Zoll, commenting once again in the *Political Science Reviewer,* feels that *The Conservative Mind* was at the very least noteworthy for its reintroduction of the "broken web of historical social conservatism by the deceptively simple device of describing it and declaring it to be yet lively." In addition, he continues, it may still have the potential to exert considerable influence on political thought. He concludes: "This feat [the reintroduction of historical social conservatism], no less of courage than of intellect, may have historic implications for the principal reason that it may yet be influential in channeling the resentment against the ideological drift of liberalism into forms both humane and restorative. Moreover, Kirk's brand of social conservatism provides an arresting contrast to the social Darwinistic tendencies of much contemporary Rightwing thought.... Kirk's social philosophy is ultimately a defense of simplicity, an ability to see the moral import in common experience, the final dignity, the joys of the elemental experiences that loom behind the 'winds of doctrine.'"

In a letter to *CA,* Kirk, citing Walter Scott, Edmund Burke, and T. S. Eliot as the writers who have most strongly influenced him, advises aspiring writers to "read much of the older great writers, keep journals and write long letters to their friends, take to heart Quiller-Couch's books *The Art of Writing* and *The Art of Reading,* and waste little time in courses in 'creative' and 'expository' writing, let alone courses in journalism." He does, however, recommend "good courses in critical writing and the history of criticism." Concludes Kirk: "The distinguishing quality of great writers ... is what Burke called 'the moral imagination.'"

Kirk has lived in Scotland and has traveled in Europe, Africa, and the Orient.

AVOCATIONAL INTERESTS: Telling ghost stories, "vigorous" walking, historic and architectural preservation.

BIOGRAPHICAL/CRITICAL SOURCES: Chicago Sunday Tribune, May 17, 1953; *New York Times,* May 17, 1953; *Commonweal,* June 19, 1953; *New York Herald Tribune Book Review,* August 2, 1953; *American Political Science Review,* September, 1953; *Political Science Quarterly,* December, 1953; *National Review,* September 19, 1967, April 9, 1968; *Times Literary Supplement,* February 22, 1968; *University Bookman,* spring, 1968, summer, 1968; *New Guard,* March, 1968; *Sewanee Review,* spring, 1970; *Detroit News,* May 7, 1972; *Political Science Reviewer,* fall, 1972; *Authors in the News,* Volume I, Gale, 1976; M. E. Bradford, *A Better Guide Than Reason: Studies in the American Revolution,* Sherwood Sugden & Co., 1979; *Michigan History,* September/October, 1979; *New York Times Book Review,* November 4, 1979.

—Sketch by Deborah A. Straub

* * *

KIRK, Samuel A(lexander) 1904-

PERSONAL: Born September 1, 1904, in Rugby, N.D.; son of Richard B. and Nellie (Boussard) Kirk; married Winifred Eloise Day (a psychologist), June 25, 1933; children: Jerome Richard, Lorraine (Mrs. Dale Fitzgerald). *Education:* University of Chicago, Ph.B., 1929, M.S., 1931; University of Michigan, Ph.D., 1935. *Politics:* Independent. *Religion:* Unitarian Universalist. *Home:* 9500 Morrill St., Tucson, Ariz. 85715. *Office:* Education Building, University of Arizona, Tucson, Ariz. 85721.

CAREER: Wayne County Training School, Northville, Mich., research psychologist, 1931-35; Milwaukee State Teachers College, Milwaukee, Wis., director of Division of Education for Exceptional Children, 1935-42, 1946-47; University of Illinois at Urbana-Champaign, professor of education and psychology, 1947-68, professor emeritus, 1968—, director of Institute for Research on Exceptional Children, 1952-68; University of Arizona, Tucson, professor of special education, 1968—. Consultant to U.S. High Commissioner for Germany, 1951, 1952; member of scientific mission to Soviet Union, 1962. Lecturer in Japan, 1965, and in other Asian and European countries. *Military service:* U.S. Army, 1942-46; became major.

MEMBER: Council for Exceptional Children (president, 1940-42), American Association on Mental Deficiency (vice-president, 1952-53), American Psychological Association (fellow), American Association for the Advancement of Science, British Association of Special Education (honorary vice-president), Sigma Xi. *Awards, honors:* Joseph P. Kennedy Foundation International Award in Mental Retardation, 1962; New York State Association for Retarded Children award, 1963; J. E. Wallace Wallin annual award, 1966; Association for Children with Learning Disabilities annual award, 1966; Caritas Society annual award, 1966; American Association on Mental Deficiency award, 1969; D.H.L., Lesley College, 1969; International Milestone Award from International Federation on Learning Disabilities, 1975; American Association on Speech and Hearing distinguished service award, 1976; University of Arizona Alumni Association distinguished citizen award, 1977.

WRITINGS: Teaching Reading to Slow-Learning Children, Houghton, 1940; (with G. O. Johnson) *Educating the Retarded Child,* Houghton, 1951; (with others) *You and Your Retarded Child,* Macmillan, 1955, 2nd edition, 1968; (with others) *Early Education of the Mentally Retarded: An Experimental Study,* University of Illinois Press, 1958.

Educating Exceptional Children, Houghton, 1962, 3rd edition (with S. S. Gallagher), 1979; (editor with B. B. Weiner) *Behavioral Research on Exceptional Children,* Council for Exceptional Children, 1963; (with Barbara D. Bateman) *Ten Years of Research at the Institute for Research on Exceptional Children,* Institute for Research on Exceptional Children, University of Illinois, 1963; *The Diagnosis and Remediation of Psycholinguistic Disabilities,* Institute for Research on Exceptional Children, University of Illinois, 1966; (with J. J. McCarthy and wife, Winifred D. Kirk) *The Illinois Test of Psycholinguistic Abilities,* University of Illinois Press, 1968; (with J. N. Paraskevopoulos) *The Development and Psychometric Characteristics of the Revised Illinois Test of Psycholinguistic Abilities,* University of Illinois Press, 1969.

(With W. D. Kirk) *Psycholinguistic Learning Disabilities: Diagnosis and Remediation,* University of Illinois Press, 1971; (with F. E. Lord) *Exceptional Children: Educational Resources and Perspectives,* Houghton, 1974; (contributor) J. M. Kauffman and D. P. Hallahan, editors, *Teaching Children with Learning Disabilities,* C. E. Merrill, 1976; (with McCarthy) *Learning Disabilities: Selected ACLD Papers,* Houghton, 1975; (with Kliebahn and Lerner) *Teaching Reading to Slow and Disabled Readers,* Houghton, 1978. Other publications include about 150 monographs and articles.

SIDELIGHTS: There have been numerous translations of Samuel A. Kirk's books: *Educating the Retarded Child* has been translated into German, Portuguese, and other languages; *You and Your Retarded Child* has been translated into Spanish, Swedish, and Portuguese; *The Illinois Test of Psycholinguistic Abilities* has been translated and standardized in Greek, German, Norwegian, Danish, Finnish, and Japanese; and *Educating Exceptional Children* has been translated into several languages, including German, Greek, Japanese, and Chinese.

* * *

KISH, George 1914-

PERSONAL: Born 1914, in Budapest, Hungary; son of Dezso and Ilonka (Vadnai) Kish; married Elvina Anger, 1949; children: Mary Susan. *Education:* Ecole des Sciences Politiques, A.B., 1935; University of Paris, M.A., 1937; University of Budapest, M.S., 1938, D.Sc., 1939; University of Michigan, Ph.D., 1945. *Home:* 3610 West Huron River Dr., Ann Arbor, Mich. *Office:* Department of Geography, University of Michigan, Ann Arbor, Mich. 48109.

CAREER: Association of Hungarian Textile Industries, Budapest, Hungary, assistant secretary, 1936-39; University of Michigan, Ann Arbor, member of faculty, 1940—, instructor in history, 1942, instructor in geography, 1943-46, assistant professor, 1946-50, associate professor, 1950-56, professor of geography, 1956—, former chairman of Committee on Russian Studies, and director of the Summer Institute of Russian Studies. James Ford Bell Lecturer, University of Minnesota, 1960; chairman, U.S. National Committee, International Geographical Union, 1965—; Eva G. R. Taylor Lecturer, Royal Geographical Society of London, 1968; Russell Lecturer, University of Michigan, 1975. Traveled extensively in Europe and the Soviet Union. *Military service:* Office of Strategic Services, World War II. *Member:* Association of American Geographers. *Awards, honors:* Star of Italian Solidarity, 1961; Linnaeus Medal, Swedish Academy of Sciences, 1973; Andree Medal, Swedish Society of Geography and Anthropology, 1973, for Arctic studies; Association of American Geographers award, 1979.

WRITINGS: Le Probleme de la Population au Japan, Riviere, 1936; *Introduction to World Regional Geography,* Prentice-Hall, 1956; *Economic Atlas of the Soviet Union,* University of Michigan Press, 1960, 2nd edition, 1971; *Italy,* Fideler, 1964; *Northeast Passage: The Life and Times of Adolf Erik Nordenskioeld,* Nico Israel (Amsterdam), 1973; *History of Cartography,* with 220 slides, Harper, 1974; *Sourcebook in Geography,* Harvard University Press, 1978; *Discovery and Settlement of North America, 1492-1865: A Cartographic Perspective,* Harper, 1978; *A Bibliography of International Geographical Congresses, 1871-1976,* G. K. Hall, 1979; *La Carte: Image, Illustration, Instrument,* Seuil (Paris), 1980. Author of more than 140 articles, monographs, and books (scientific and popular), published in the United States and abroad, since 1936.

WORK IN PROGRESS: A book, *Camel Bells: A Life of Sven Hedin.*

SIDELIGHTS: George Kish told *CA:* "My primary concern is with work in my own field, geography, as is reflected in the majority of articles and monographs of the last forty years. But I am equally interested in conveying to the general reader some of the excitement of discovery and exploration." This "interest" has resulted in six works, from his book on "one of the great explorers of the Arctic, Nordenskioeld," to *Sourcebook in Geography,* "an anthology of writings on geography, . . . as well as expository writings in geography," to his current project, *Camel Bells: A Life of Sven Hedin.* Hedin, says Kish, "was the last of the great explorers of Inner Asia, who led four major expeditions to Inner China, was one of the most prolific writers of his time, and an important figure in Swedish politics as well."

KITZINGER, U(we) W(ebster) 1928-

PERSONAL: Born April 12, 1928; married, 1952; wife's name, Sheila; children: Celia, Tessa, Elinor, Polly, Jenny. *Education:* New College, Oxford, B.A., 1951, M.A., 1953, B.Litt., 1956. *Home:* Standlake Manor, Witney, Oxfordshire, England. *Office:* INSEAD, Boulevard de Constance, 77305 Fontainebleau, France.

CAREER: Council of Europe, Strasbourg, France, secretary of Economic Division and Economic Committee, 1951-58; University of the Saar, Saarbrucken, West Germany, lecturer, 1955-56; Oxford University, Nuffield College, Oxford, England, research fellow, 1958-62, official fellow and investment bursar, 1964-76, emeritus fellow, 1976—; currently dean of European Institute of Business Administration (INSEAD), Fontainebleau, France. Lecturer in politics, Worcester College and Keble College, Oxford University, 1960-64; visiting professor of international relations, with research in eleven Latin American countries, University of West Indies, 1964-65.

WRITINGS: The Economics of the Saar Question, Nuffield College, 1958; *German Electoral Politics: A Study of the 1957 Campaign,* Clarendon Press, 1960; *The Challenge of the Common Market,* Basil Blackwell, 1961, revised edition published as *The Politics and Economics of European Integration,* Praeger, 1963; *Britain, Europe and Beyond: Essays in European Politics,* Sythoff, 1964; *The European Common Market and Community,* Barnes & Noble, 1967; *The Second Try,* Pergamon, 1968; *Diplomacy and Persuasion: How Britain Joined the Common Market,* Thames & Hudson, 1973; (with D. E. Butler) *The 1975 Referendum,* Macmillan (London), 1976. Also author of *The Background to Jamaica's Foreign Policy,* 1965, *Commitment and Identity,* 1968, and *Europe's Wider Horizons,* 1975. Contributor of articles to professional journals; contributor to *Encyclopaedia Britannica* and various books of symposia. Founding editor, *Journal of Common Market Studies.*

* * *

KLAMKIN, Marian 1926-

PERSONAL: Born December 29, 1926, in Providence, R.I.; daughter of Abraham and Goldie (Morrisson) Spungin; married Charles Klamkin (a writer-photographer), August 22, 1948; children: Joan, Lynn, Peter. *Education:* Clark University, B.A., 1948. *Home:* 141 Colonial Rd., Watertown, Conn. 06795. *Agent:* James Oliver Brown, James Brown Associates, Inc., 25 West 43rd St., New York, N.Y. 10036.

CAREER: University of Connecticut, Storrs, instructor in continuing education, 1971-73; writer. *Member:* Mattatuck Museum, Buten Museum.

WRITINGS: Flower Arrangements That Last, Macmillan, 1968; *Flower Arranging for Period Decoration,* Funk, 1968; *The Collector's Book of Boxes,* Dodd, 1970; *The Collector's Book of Art Nouveau,* Dodd, 1971; *The Collecter's Book of Wedgwood,* Dodd, 1971; *The Collector's Book of Bottles,* Dodd, 1971; *White House China,* Scribner, 1972; *Hands to Work: Shaker Folk Art and Industries,* Dodd, 1972; *American Patriotic and Political China,* Scribner, 1973; *The Collector's Guide to Depression Glass,* Hawthorn, 1973; *Picture Postcards,* Dodd, 1974; *Marine Antiques,* Dodd, 1974; *The Return of Lafayette (1824-1825),* Scribner, 1974; (with husband, Charles Klamkin) *Woodcarving: North American Folk Sculpture,* Hawthorn, 1974; *The Depression Glass Collector's Price Guide,* Hawthorn, 1974, revised edition, 1980; *Old Sheet Music,* Hawthorn, 1975; *Investing in Antiques and Popular Collectibles for Pleasure and Profit,* Funk, 1975; *Watertown, Then and Now,* Watertown (Conn.) Bicentennial Committee, 1976; *The Collector's Guide to Carnival Glass,* Hawthorn, 1976; *The Carnival Glass Collector's Price Guide,* Hawthorn, 1977; *American Antique Bottles,* Wallace-Homestead, 1977; *Made in Occupied Japan: A Collector's Guide,* Crown, 1977; *The Collector's Compendium,* Doubleday, 1980.

* * *

KLASSEN, Peter J(ames) 1930-

PERSONAL: Born December 18, 1930, in Alberta, Canada; son of John C. (a farmer) and Elizabeth (Martens) Klassen; married Nancy Jo Cooprider, August 1, 1959; children: Kenton, Kevin, Bryan. *Education:* University of British Columbia, B.A., 1955; Fuller Theological Seminary, graduate study, 1955-57; University of Southern California, A.M., 1958, Ph.D., 1962. *Politics:* Independent. *Religion:* Mennonite. *Home:* 1838 South Bundy, Fresno, Calif. 93727. *Office:* School of Social Sciences, California State University, Fresno, Calif. 93710.

CAREER: Principal of Fraser Lake School, British Columbia, 1953-54; University of Southern California, Los Angeles, lecturer in history, 1958-60, administrative supervisor of department of general studies, 1960-62; Pacific College, Fresno, Calif., assistant professor, 1962-63, associate professor, 1963-65, professor of history, 1965-66, head of department, 1962-66, curator of archives, 1962-67; California State University, Fresno, associate professor, 1968-70, professor of history, 1970—, head of department, 1969-74, dean of School of Social Sciences. *Member:* American Historical Association, America Society of Church History, Society for Reformation Research, Phi Alpha Theta.

WRITINGS: The Economics of Anabaptism, 1525-1560, Mouton, 1964; (contributor) Max Geiger, editor, *Gottesreich und Menschenreich,* Helbing und Lichtenhahn, 1970; *Church and State in Reformation Europe,* Forum Press, 1975; *Europe in the Reformation,* Prentice-Hall, 1979. Editor of *Journal of Church and Society,* 1966-70.

WORK IN PROGRESS: Research in the role of the masses in shaping the reformation.

* * *

KLEIN, David 1919-

PERSONAL: Born March 30, 1919, in New York, N.Y.; son of Solomon (a manufacturing jeweler) and Helen (Schoenberg) Klein; married Marymae Endsley (a textbook editor), December 6, 1942; children: Helen Leslie, Edith Sarah. *Education:* City College of New York (now City College of the City University of New York), B.A., 1940; Columbia University, M.A., 1941; attended New York University, 1962-65. *Politics:* Reform Democrat. *Religion:* Humanist. *Home:* 2032 Lagoon Dr., Okemos, Mich. 48864. *Agent:* Frances Collin, 156 East 52nd St., New York, N.Y. 10022. *Office:* Department of Social Science, Michigan State University, East Lansing, Mich. 48824.

CAREER: McGraw-Hill Book Co., New York City, technical editor, 1940-42; Henry Holt & Co., New York City, college textbook editor, 1946-48; Dryden Press, New York City, executive vice-president, 1948-56; Basic Books, Inc., New York City, vice-president, 1956-58; Association for the Aid of Crippled Children, New York City, director of publications, 1958-65; Michigan State University, East Lansing, associate professor, 1965-68, professor of social science, 1968—, professor of human development, 1970—. Instructor and lecturer in English and adult education, City College of New York (now City College of the City University of New York), 1946-56; exchange professor, University of Ryukyus (Okinawa), 1966; visiting professor, Hofstra University, 1970-71; senior lecturer, University of New South Wales, 1972-73. *Military service:* U.S. Army, 1942-46; became warrant officer junior grade. *Awards, honors:* Ford Foundation travel grant, 1966; certificate of recognition, National Safety Council, 1966; Fulbright grant, Australian-American Education Foundation, 1972, 1979.

WRITINGS: *The Army Writer,* Military Service Publishing Co., 1946; (with Mary Louise Johnson) *They Took to the Sea,* Rutgers University Press, 1948; *Your First Boat,* Funk, 1953; *Your Outboard Cruiser,* Norton, 1954; *Beginning with Boats,* Crowell, 1962; *Helping Your Teenager Choose a College,* Child Study Association, 1963; *Great Adventures in Small Boats,* Crowell-Collier, 1963; (with W. Haddon and E. A. Suchman) *Accident Research: Methods and Approaches,* Harper, 1964; (with S. A. Richardson and B. S. Dohrenwend) *Interviewing: Its Forms and Functions,* Basic Books, 1965; *When Your Teen-ager Starts to Drive,* Association for Aid of Crippled Children, 1965; *Yourself and Others,* McDougal, Littell, 1970; *Yourself Ten Years from Now,* Harcourt, 1977; *Supershopper,* Penguin, 1979; *More for Your Money,* Penguin, 1979. Contributor of articles on recreation, education, and consumer topics to *Consumer Reports, Ladies' Home Journal, Mademoiselle,* and other magazines.

WORK IN PROGRESS: Popular and professional writing on accidents and research methods in the social sciences.

AVOCATIONAL INTERESTS: Motorcycling, clock collecting. Interested in psychology, sociology, research on risk-taking, and consumer behavior.

* * *

KLEIN, Leonore (Glotzer) 1916-

PERSONAL: Born September 4, 1916, in New York, N.Y.; daughter of Isidor (a teacher) and Sadie (April) Glotzer; married Joseph M. Klein (chairman of a high school English department), April 1, 1939; children: Judith Anne, Robert Morris. *Education:* Barnard College, B.A.; Wellesley College, M.A.; Columbia University, M.S. in L.S., 1964. *Home:* 7 Barbara Lane, Hartsdale, N.Y. 10530.

CAREER: Long Island City High School, Long Island, N.Y., librarian, 1950-52; Bryant High School, Astoria, N.Y., librarian, 1952-54; Florida Southern College, Lakeland, reference librarian, 1954-59; public schools, Pleasantville, N.Y., librarian, 1959-62; public schools, White Plains, N.Y., librarian, 1962-76.

WRITINGS: *The Happy Surprise,* Grosset, 1952; *Guess What?,* Grosset, 1953; *Project Book for Boys and Girls,* Grosset, 1956; *What Would You Do If?,* Young Scott Books, 1956; *Brave Daniel* (Junior Literary Guild selection), Young Scott Books, 1958; *Arrow Book of Tricks and Projects,* Scholastic Book Services, 1960; *Mud, Mud, Mud,* Knopf, 1962; *Henri's Walk to Paris,* Young Scott Books, 1962; *Run Away John,* Knopf, 1963; *Tom and the Small Ant,* Knopf, 1965; *The Arrow Book of Project Fun,* Scholastic Book Services, 1965; *What Is an Inch?,* Harvey House, 1966; *Huit Enfants et un Bebe,* Abelard, 1966; *How Old Is Old?,* Harvey House, 1967; *Just Like You,* Harvey House, 1968; *Too Many Parents,* Knopf, 1968; *Silly Sam,* Scholastic Book Services, 1969; *Just a Minute,* Harvey House, 1969; *"D" Is for Rover,* Harvey House, 1970; *Only One Ant,* Hastings House, 1971; *Mazes and Mysteries,* Scholastic Book Services, 1975; *Picnics and Parades,* Knopf, 1976.

KLEIN, Philip Shriver 1909-

PERSONAL: Born June 10, 1909, in Allentown, Pa.; son of Harry Martin John (an historian) and Mary Winifred (Shriver) Klein; married Dorothy Grace Orr, August 30, 1946; children: John Douglass. *Education:* Franklin and Marshall College, A.B., 1929; University of Chicago, A.M., 1932; University of Pennsylvania, Ph.D., 1938. *Politics:* Republican. *Religion:* United Church of Christ. *Home:* 280 Nimitz Ave., State College, Pa. 16801. *Office:* Department of History, Pennsylvania State University, University Park, Pa. 16802.

CAREER: High school teacher in Pennsylvania, 1929-31; Franklin and Marshall College, Lancaster, Pa., assistant professor of history, 1938-41; Pennsylvania State University, University Park, assistant professor, 1941-42, associate professor, 1946-50, professor of American history, 1950-72, professor emeritus, 1972—, head of department, 1953-56. Member of Pennsylvania Historical and Museum Commission, 1974—. *Military service:* U.S. Naval Reserve, aviation training, 1942-45, Office of Naval History, 1945-46; became lieutenant commander. *Member:* American Historical Association, Organization of American Historians, Pennsylvania Historical Association (president, 1954-57; member of council, 1957—), Historical Society of Pennsylvania, Pennsylvania Federation of Historical Societies (vice-president, 1958—), Historical Foundation of Pennsylvania (president, 1976—). *Awards, honors:* Lewis H. Bell Memorial Award, 1962, for *President James Buchanan: A Biography;* Emeritus Distinction Award, Pennsylvania State University, 1978.

WRITINGS: *The Story of Wheatland,* Junior League (Lancaster, Pa), 1936; *Pennsylvania Politics, 1817-1832,* Historical Society of Pennsylvania, 1941; (with A. C. Bining) *History of the United States,* Scribner, 1950; (with H. S. Alshouse) *Pennsylvania Pioneers,* Penns Valley, 1951; (with Alshouse) *Pennsylvania Leaders,* Penns Valley, 1951; *President James Buchanan: A Biography,* Pennsylvania State University Press, 1962; (with Ari Hoogenboom) *A History of Pennsylvania,* McGraw, 1973; (co-editor) *Pennsylvania, 1776,* Pennsylvania State University Press, 1975.

AVOCATIONAL INTERESTS: Folk music, philately, and model railroading.

BIOGRAPHICAL/CRITICAL SOURCES: *Pittsburgh Press,* July 8, 1962.

* * *

KLINKOWITZ, Jerome 1943-

PERSONAL: Born December 24, 1943, in Milwaukee, Wis.; son of Jerome Francis (a sales manager) and Lucille (McNamara) Klinkowitz; married Elaine Ptaszynski, January 29, 1966 (divorced January 16, 1978); married Julie Huffman, May 27, 1978; children: (first marriage) Jonathan, Nina. *Education:* Marquette University, B.A., 1966, M.A., 1967; University of Wisconsin, Ph.D., 1969. *Home:* 1904 Clay St., Cedar Falls, Iowa 50613. *Office:* Department of English, University of Northern Iowa, Cedar Falls, Iowa 50613.

CAREER: Northern Illinois University, DeKalb, assistant professor of English, 1969-72; University of Northern Iowa, Cedar Falls, associate professor, 1972-76, professor of English, 1976—. Director of the Willard Motley Papers, 1971—. *Member:* Modern Language Association of America, Centre de Recherche sur la Litterature Americaine Contemporaine, Fiction Collective, Nathaniel Hawthorne Society, P.E.N./American Center.

WRITINGS: *Index to Willard Motley,* Northern Illinois University Library, 1972; (with John Somer) *Innovative Fiction,* Dell, 1972; (with Somer) *The Vonnegut Statement,* Delacorte, 1973; (with Asa Pieratt) *Kurt Vonnegut, Jr.,* Shoe String, 1974; *Literary Disruptions,* University of Illinois Press, 1975, revised edition, 1980; *The Life of Fiction,* University of Illinois Press, 1977; (with Donald Lawler) *Vonnegut in America,* Delacorte, 1977; (with Pieratt and Robert Murray Davis) *Donald Barthelme,* Shoe String, 1977; *Writing under Fire: Stories of the Vietnam War,* Dell, 1978; (editor) *The Diaries of Willard Motley,* Iowa State University Press, 1979; *Hawthorne's Day to the Present: The Practice of Fiction in America,* Iowa State University Press, 1980. Contributor of articles and reviews to *Village Voice, Chicago Sun-Times Book Week, Washington Post, Chicago Tribune, Nathaniel Hawthorne Journal, American Literature, Journal of English and Germanic Philology, North American Review, Partisan Review,* and other journals and periodicals. Critiques editor, *Fiction International.*

WORK IN PROGRESS: The American 1960's; The Self-Effacing Word; The Death of the Death of the Novel; The Short Season: April to August with the Class A Mason City Royals, a novel; *Listen: Gerry Mulligan.*

SIDELIGHTS: Jerome Klinkowitz told *CA:* "Although most of my work has involved the criticism and history of innovative American fiction, I've found lately that my real interest is *pure writing,* as a way of being in the world (*a la* Roland Barthes). Hence *The Life of Fiction,* which is simply a scrapbook of ten years' living in and around this literature. Hence *The Short Season,* the result of spending a summer knocking around with a minor league baseball club. And *Listen: Gerry Mulligan,* which is an autobiography of listening to all those jazz LP's, sixty of them, over twenty years. Writing is simply living with more consciousness and self-intent."

* * *

KLUG, Eugene F(rederick Adolf) 1917-

PERSONAL: Surname is pronounced "kloog"; born November 26, 1917, in Milwaukee, Wis.; son of Adolf O. M. (an insurance agent) and Eugenia (Albrecht) Klug; married Dorothy A. Bauch (a nurse), September 4, 1946; children: Charlotte, Christine (Mrs. Jon A. Ahoyt), Paul, Timothy. *Education:* Concordia College, Milwaukee, Wis., A.A., 1937; University of Chicago, M.A., 1941; Concordia Seminary, B.D., 1942; graduate study at University of Wisconsin, 1947-49, University of Illinois, Marquette University, Washington University, St. Louis, Mo., and Lutheran School of Theology; Free University of Amsterdam, D.Theol., 1971. *Office:* Department of Systematic Theology, Concordia Theological Seminary, 6600 North Clinton, Fort Wayne, Ind. 46825.

CAREER: Ordained minister of Lutheran Church-Missouri Synod, 1942; Concordia College, Milwaukee, Wis., assistant professor of religion, 1942-44; Calvary Lutheran University, Madison, Wis., campus pastor, 1947-49; Trinity Lutheran Church, Kalispell, Mont., pastor, 1949-55; University of Illinois at Urbana-Champaign, instructor in Lutheran Chair of Religion, 1955-60; Concordia Theological Seminary, Fort Wayne, Ind., assistant professor, 1960-65, associate professor, 1965-71, professor of systematic theology, 1971—, chairman of department, 1975—. Vice-president of Montana district, Lutheran Church-Missouri Synod, 1950-55. *Military service:* U.S. Navy, chaplain, 1944-46; became lieutenant senior grade. *Member:* Lutheran Academy for Scholarship, Concordia Historical Institute.

WRITINGS: (Contributor) A. G. Huegli, editor, *Church and State under God,* Concordia, 1964; *The Military Chaplaincy under the First Amendment,* U.S. Army Chaplain Board, 1967; *From Luther to Chemnitz on Scripture and the Word,* Eerdmans, 1971; (contributor) Ulrich Asendorf and Friedrich W. Kuenneth, editors, *Von der wahren Einheit der Kirche* (title means "Concerning the True Unity of the Church"), Verlag Die Spur Gmbh & Co., 1973; *Getting into the Formula of Concord,* Concordia, 1977; *A Study Guide of the Formula of Concord,* published with Leader's Manual, Concordia, 1977; (with others) *A Contemporary Look at the Formula of Concord,* Concordia, 1978. Contributor to *Dictionary of Christian Ethics* and religious journals, including *Christianity Today, Lutherischer Rundblick, Military Chaplain, Catholic Digest, Christian News, Lutheran Witness, Concordia Theological Quarterly, Balance, Affirm, Concordia Theological Monthly,* and *Springfielder.*

WORK IN PROGRESS: Research on Martin Luther's theology and on the post-Reformation era; *From Luther to Chemnitz on Church and Ministry.*

* * *

KNAPTON, Ernest John 1902-

PERSONAL: Born August 31, 1902, in Queensbury, Yorkshire, England; son of Ezra and Lavinia (Firth) Knapton; married Jocelyn Babbitt, 1928; children: Rosemary Knapton Currie, Christopher, David. *Education:* University of British Columbia, B.A., 1925; University of Oxford (Rhodes Scholar), B.A., 1928; Harvard University, A.M., 1931, Ph.D., 1934. *Home:* 779 Fox Hill Rd., Chatham, Mass. 02633.

CAREER: Wheaton College, Norton, Mass., 1931—, began as instructor, became professor of history, professor emeritus, 1969—. Member of Norton School Committee, 1941-49, Norton Library Board, and Norton District Health Association. *Member:* American Historical Association, American Association of University Professors, Society of French Historical Studies, Association of American Rhodes Scholars, Institut Napoleon, Societe d'Histoire Moderne, Societe des Etudes Staeliennes, Chatham Historical Society (vice-president), Friends of Monomy Theatre (Chatham; vice-president), Alpha Delta Phi. *Awards, honors:* Guggenheim fellowship, 1966-67; D.Litt., Wheaton College, 1972.

WRITINGS: The Lady of the Holy Alliance, Columbia University Press, 1939; *France since Versailles,* Holt, 1952; *Europe, 1450-1815,* Scribner, 1958; *Empress Josephine,* Harvard University Press, 1963; *Europe, 1815-1914,* Scribner, 1965; *Europe and the World since 1914,* Scribner, 1966; *France: An Interpretive History,* Scribner 1971; *Revolutionary and Imperial France,* Scribner, 1972; (contributor) Peter Gay, editor, *Eighteenth Century Studies: Presented to Arthur M. Wilson,* University Press of New England, 1972; *Chatham since the American Revolution,* Chatham Historical Society, 1976. Contributor to history journals and encyclopedias. Former associate editor, *American Oxonian.*

WORK IN PROGRESS: A study of Napoleon's rise to power in 1799.

AVOCATIONAL INTERESTS: Swimming, sailing, gardening.

* * *

KNEBEL, Fletcher 1911-

PERSONAL: Surname pronounced "Kuh-nabul"; born October 1, 1911, in Dayton, Ohio; son of A. G. (a Y.M.C.A. official) and Mary (Lewis) Knebel; married third wife, Laura Bergquist, 1965; children: (first marriage) Jack G., Mary L. Jecko. *Education:* Miami University, Oxford, Ohio, B.A.,

1934. *Politics:* Democrat. *Religion:* "Fallen-away Protestant." *Home and office:* 208 Edgerstoune Rd., Princeton, N.J. 08540.

CAREER: *Coatesville Record,* Coatesville, Pa., reporter, 1934; *Chattanooga News,* Chattanooga, Tenn., reporter, 1934-35; *Toledo News-Bee,* Toledo, Ohio, reporter, 1936; *Cleveland Plain Dealer,* Cleveland, Ohio, reporter, 1936, reporter with Washington Bureau, 1937-50; Cowles Publications (now Cowles Communications), Washington, D.C., author of syndicated column, "Potomac Fever," 1951-64; free-lance writer, 1964—. *Military service:* U.S. Navy, 1942-45; became lieutenant. *Member:* Authors Guild, Gridiron Club (president, 1964), Phi Beta Kappa, Sigma Chi. *Awards, honors:* Sigma Delta Chi award for best magazine reporting, 1955; D.L., Miami University, 1964; D.LL., Drake University, 1968.

WRITINGS: (Contributor) *Candidates 1960,* Basic Books, 1959; (with Charles W. Bailey) *No High Ground,* Harper, 1960; (with Bailey) *Seven Days in May,* Harper, 1962; (with Bailey) *Convention* (Literary Guild selection), Harper, 1964; *Night of Camp David* (Literary Guild selection), Harper, 1965; *Zinzin Road,* Doubleday, 1966; *Vanished,* Doubleday, 1968; *Trespass* (Literary Guild selection), Doubleday, 1969; *Dark Horse* (Literary Guild selection), Doubleday, 1972; *The Bottom Line,* Doubleday, 1974; *Dave Sulkin Cares!,* Doubleday, 1978. Contributor to *Look* and other periodicals.

SIDELIGHTS: Fletcher Knebel writes about political crises of the near-future, sometimes foreshadowing real-life events. His books have dealt with such topics as a presidential resignation, an attempted military takeover of the government, and the disappearance of a high government official. As Hal Burton points out, Knebel's work "makes you believe it could have happened. No novelist now writing has a greater capacity to make you believe the unbelievable or to accept the unacceptable." David Dempsey describes Knebel's writing as "craftsmanship of the highest order."

"You know," Knebel told an interviewer, "the interesting thing for me is exploring new things. Books are no longer a big part of my life." "In recent years," Knebel told *CA,* "under the influence of humanistic psychology and the human potential movement, my interests have shifted from politics to the inner being and to environmental concerns." This change can be seen in Knebel's more recent work, including *Dave Sulkin Cares!* in which an environmental group attempts to stop a housing development.

Knebel's books have sold over six million copies. Boston University houses a collection of his manuscripts.

BIOGRAPHICAL/CRITICAL SOURCES: *New York Herald Tribune Book Review,* June 5, 1960; *Chicago Tribune,* June 12, 1960; *New York Times Book Review,* January 3, 1965, January 21, 1968; *Book Week,* October 23, 1966; *National Observer,* October 31, 1966; *Christian Science Monitor,* November 23, 1966; *New Yorker,* November 26, 1966; *New York Times,* January 12, 1968, October 17, 1969; *Newsweek,* February 12, 1968; *Saturday Review,* March 2, 1968; *Books & Bookmen,* July, 1968; *Observer,* August 3, 1969; *Newsday,* October 11, 1969; *Negro Digest,* April, 1970; *Negro History Bulletin,* May, 1971; *National Review,* August 18, 1972; *Listener,* July 5, 1973; *Philadelphia Inquirer,* August 26, 1974; *New York Times Magazine,* September 15, 1974; *Akron Beacon-Journal,* October 27, 1974.

KNIGHT, Vick R(alph), Jr. 1928-
(J. H. Tweed)

PERSONAL: Born April 6, 1928, in Lakewood, Ohio; son of Vick R., Sr. (an advertising executive and composer) and Janice (Higgins) Knight; married Beverly Joyce McKeighan, April 14, 1949 (divorced, 1973); children: Stephen Foster, Mary Ann. *Education:* University of Southern California, B.S., 1952; Los Angeles State College of Applied Arts and Sciences (now California State University, Los Angeles), M.A., 1958; Whittier College, graduate study, 1959-61; Long Beach State College (now California State University, Long Beach), graduate study, 1960-61; California State College at Fullerton (now California State University, Fullerton), graduate study, 1961-64; Claremont Graduate School, graduate study, 1963-71. *Address:* P.O. Box 395, Placentia, Calif. 92670. *Office:* Children's Hospital of Orange County, P.O. Box 5700, Orange, Calif. 92667.

CAREER: Producer-director of "Here Comes Tom Harmon," radio series for American Broadcasting Co., 1947-50; school teacher and vice-principal in Pico Rivera, Calif., 1952-59; school principal in Placentia, Calif., 1959-64, assistant superintendent, 1965-71; Pepperdine College (now University), Los Angeles, Calif., coordinator of graduate education, 1968-70; National General West, Inc. (real estate investments), Fullerton, Calif., vice-president, 1971-74; Children's Hospital of Orange County, Orange, Calif., director of development and community relations, 1974—. Educational consultant, Key Records, 1960—; associate director of field services planning, La Verne College, 1970—; chairman of the board of William Claude Fields Foundation, 1972—. *Military service:* U.S. Navy (Armed Forces Radio Service), 1946-48.

MEMBER: International Wine and Food Society, International Platform Association, International Association of Business Communicators, American Society of Composers, Authors and Publishers, National Association for Hospital Development, Skull and Dagger, Turtles International Association, Society of Children's Book Writers, Escoffier Society, National School Public Relations Association, Audubon Society, Authors League, United States Junior Chamber of Commerce (director, 1958-59), National Education Association, W. C. Fields Fan Club of North America, Sierra Club, Western Society of Naturalists, California Junior Chamber of Commerce (vice-president, 1957-58), California Teachers Association, Nature Conservancy, Phi Sigma Kappa, Alpha Delta Sigma, Theta Nu Epsilon, Blue Key, West Atwood Yacht Club (commodore, 1971-72), Cardinal and Gold, Kiwanis (president of Placentia branch, 1960), Pico Rivera Junior Chamber of Commerce, Exhausted Roosters, Anti-Slubberdegulion Society. *Awards, honors:* Named one of California's five outstanding young men, California State Junior Chamber of Commerce, 1959; Distinguished Citizen Award, Whittier College, 1960; Educator of the Year award, Orange County Press Club, 1970; Author and Book Award, University of California, Irvine, 1973; Outstanding Service Award, Reading Educators Guild of California State University, Fullerton, 1979.

WRITINGS: (With John E. Moore) *It's Our World,* Charter, 1972; (with Moore) *It's Our Future,* Charter, 1972; (with Moore) *It's Our Choice,* Charter, 1972; (with Larry Harris) *Twilight of the Animal Kingdom,* Ritchie, 1972; *Snakes of Hawaii,* Nature Guides of the West, 1972; *Earle the Squirrel,* Ritchie, 1974; *The Night the Crayons Talked,* Ritchie, 1974; *Send for Haym Salomon!,* Borden, 1976. Author of "Nature Notebook," a syndicated newspaper column, 1954-62.

WORK IN PROGRESS: *My Word!,* a lexicon of favorite words of famous people; *A Tale of Twos,* the story of twins through the ages; *Honk if You're Horny,* a history of bumperstickers; *A Navel Salute,* a history of the omphalos; *Joby and the Wishing Well,* a children's story.

AVOCATIONAL INTERESTS: Herpetology, Greek history, environment.

* * *

KNOX, William 1928-
(Michael Kirk, Bill Knox, Robert MacLeod, Noah Webster)

PERSONAL: Born February 20, 1928, in Glasgow, Scotland; son of Robert (a journalist) and Rhoda (MacLeod) Knox; married Myra Ann McKill, March 31, 1950; children: Susan Elizabeth, Michael Craig, Marian Ailsa. *Education:* Attended schools in Scotland. *Religion:* Church of Scotland. *Home and office:* 55 Newtonlea Ave., Newton Mearns, Glasgow, Scotland.

CAREER: *Evening Citizen,* Glasgow, Scotland, copy boy, 1944-45; *Evening News,* Glasgow, reporter and deputy news editor, 1945-57; *Empire News,* London, England, Scottish news editor, 1957-59; Scottish Television, Glasgow, news editor, 1959-61; full-time writer and broadcaster, 1961—; host of "Crime Desk" weekly television program. *Member:* Mystery Writers of America, Crime Writers Association, Scottish Motoring Writers Association (past president), Royal Naval Volunteer Reserve Club (Scotland), Eastwood Rotary Club (past president).

WRITINGS—Fiction; under name Bill Knox: *Deadline for a Dream,* John Long, 1957, published as *In at the Kill,* Doubleday, 1961; *Cockatoo Crime,* John Long, 1958; *Death Department,* John Long, 1959; *Leave it to the Hangman,* John Long, 1960, Doubleday, 1961; *Death Calls the Shots,* John Long, 1961; *Die for Big Betsy,* John Long, 1961; *Little Drops of Blood,* Doubleday, 1962; *Sanctuary Isle,* John Long, 1962, published as *The Grey Sentinels,* Doubleday, 1963; *The Man in the Bottle,* John Long, 1963, published as *The Killing Game,* Doubleday, 1963; *The Drum of Ungara,* Doubleday, 1963 (published in England as *Drum of Power,* John Long, 1964); *The Scavengers,* John Long, 1964; *The Taste of Proof,* Doubleday, 1965; *Devilweed,* Doubleday, 1966; *The Ghost Car,* Doubleday, 1966 (published in England as *The Deep Fall,* John Long, 1966); *Blacklight,* Doubleday, 1967; *Justice on the Rocks,* John Long, 1967, Doubleday, 1968; *Figurehead,* Doubleday, 1968 (published in England as *The Klondyker,* John Long, 1968); *The Tallyman,* Doubleday, 1969; *Blueback,* Doubleday, 1969.

Who Shot the Bull?, Doubleday, 1970 (published in England as *Children of the Mist,* John Long, 1970); *Seafire,* Doubleday, 1970; *To Kill a Witch,* Doubleday, 1971; *Stormtide,* Doubleday, 1972; *Draw Batons,* Doubleday, 1973; (with Edward Boyd) *The View from Daniel Pike,* St. Martin's, 1974; *Whitewater,* Doubleday, 1974; *Rally to Kill,* John Long, 1975, Doubleday, 1976; *Hellspout,* Doubleday, 1975; *Pilot Error,* Doubleday, 1977; *Witchrock,* John Long, 1977, Doubleday, 1978; *Live Bate,* John Long, 1978, Doubleday, 1979; *Bomb Ship,* Doubleday, 1980.

Nonfiction; under name Bill Knox: (With Robert Colquhoun) *Life Begins at Midnight,* John Long, 1961; (with David Murray) *Ecurie Ecosse,* Stanley Paul, 1962; (with John Glaister) *Final Diagnosis,* Hutchinson, 1964; *Court of Murder,* Hutchinson, 1968; *The Thin Blue Line,* John Long, 1973.

Fiction; under pseudonym Robert MacLeod: *Cave of Bats,* John Long, 1964, Holt, 1966; *Lake of Fury,* John Long, 1966, Holt, 1968; *Isle of Dragons,* John Long, 1967; *Place of Mists,* John Long, 1969, McCall, 1970; *A Property in Cyprus,* John Long, 1970, published under pseudonym Noah Webster as *Flickering Death,* Doubleday, 1970; *Path of Ghosts,* John Long, 1971; *A Killing in Malta,* John Long, 1972, published under pseudonym Noah Webster, Doubleday, 1972; *Nest of Vultures,* John Long, 1973; *A Burial in Portugal,* John Long, 1973, published under pseudonym Noah Webster, Doubleday, 1974; *All Other Perils,* John Long, 1974, published under pseudonym Michael Kirk, Doubleday, 1974; *A Witchdance in Bavaria,* John Long, 1975, published under pseudonym Noah Webster, Doubleday, 1975; *Dragonship,* John Long, 1976, published under pseudonym Michael Kirk, Doubleday, 1977; *A Pay-Off in Switzerland,* John Long, 1977, published under pseudonym Noah Webster, Doubleday, 1977; *Salvage Job,* John Long, 1978, published under pseudonym Michael Kirk, Doubleday, 1979.

Author of television and radio scripts. Contributor of short stories to periodicals.

WORK IN PROGRESS: A documentary series on crime for British television; a novel on the work of the British fishery protection service.

SIDELIGHTS: Bill Knox explains to *CA* that "having a newspaper and TV background as a 'fact' man in crime and feature writing and as a TV presenter saves a lot of research time when it comes to novel writing. In fact, work is a circle pattern. Research for, say, a real-life TV piece has its spin-off in terms of ideas for a possible novel. The additional research to tidy the novel often sparks off a fresh, future 'real-life' piece.

"Again, any writer will agree it can be a pretty lonely business [but] the TV and media world is exactly the opposite and so one background compensates for the other. Not to mention that travel abroad as a journalist means someone else picks up the tab!"

Knox's books have been translated into German, French, Italian, Dutch, Portuguese, and other languages. A collection of his manuscripts was established at Boston University in 1969.

BIOGRAPHICAL/CRITICAL SOURCES: *Books & Bookmen,* February, 1968, July, 1973; *Saturday Review,* April 26, 1969; *Times Literary Supplement,* October 29, 1971; *Observer,* August 20, 1972; *New Yorker,* September 16, 1974; *New York Times Book Review,* October 24, 1976, January 1, 1978; *Book World,* February 20, 1977.

* * *

KOESTLER, Arthur 1905-

PERSONAL: Born September 5, 1905, in Budapest, Hungary; became a British subject after World War II; son of Hendrik (a promoter) and Adela (Jeiteles) Koestler; married Dorothy Asher, 1935 (divorced, 1950); married Mamaine Paget, 1950 (divorced, 1952); married Cynthia Jefferies, 1965. *Education:* Attended University of Vienna, 1922-26. *Agent:* A. D. Peters, 10 Buckingham St., Adelphi, London WC2N 6BU, England.

CAREER: Writer. Worked as a farmer in Palestine, an assistant to an Arabian architect, and an editor of a Cairo weekly, 1926-29; became foreign correspondent for Ullstein Publications, Germany, serving as Middle East correspondent, 1927-29, and as Paris correspondent, 1929-30; became science editor of *Vossische Zeitung* and foreign editor of *B.Z. am Mittag,* 1930; became member of Communist Party, 1931; was the only journalist taking part in the "Graf Zeppelin" Arctic expedition, 1931; in the thirties he traveled through Central Asia and spent one year in the U.S.S.R.; war correspondent in Spain for *News Chronicle,* 1936, captured by Fascists, 1937, sentenced to death, and released through the intervention of the British government; left Communist Party in 1938, at the time of the Moscow Trials; editor of *Zukunft,* 1938; in 1939, he was imprisoned in France after war was declared, released in 1940, and escaped to England; has since worked for the Ministry of Information, the British Broadcasting Corp., and as a night ambulance driver. *Military service:* French Foreign Legion, 1940; British Pioneer Corps, 1941-42. *Awards, honors:* Chubb fellow, Yale University, 1950; Royal Society of Literature fellow, 1958, named Companion of Literature, 1974; fellow, Center for Advanced Study in the Behavioral Sciences, 1964-65; Sonning Prize, University of Copenhagen, 1968; L.L.D., Queen's University, 1968; Commander of the Order of the British Empire, 1972; fellow, Royal Astronomical Society, 1976; D.Litt., Leeds University, 1977.

WRITINGS: Von Weissen Naechten und Roten Tagen, Ukranian State Publishers for National Minorities (Kharkov), 1933; *Menschenopfer Unerhoert,* Carrefour (Paris), 1937; *Spanish Testament* (autobiography), Gollancz, 1937, abridged edition published as *Dialogue with Death,* Macmillan, 1942, reprinted, Hutchinson, 1966; *Scum of the Earth* (autobiography), Macmillan, 1941, reprinted, 1968; *The Yogi and the Commissar and Other Essays,* Macmillan, 1945; (contributor) *The Challenge of Our Time,* P. Marshall, 1948; *Insight and Outlook: An Inquiry into the Common Foundations of Science, Art, and Social Ethics,* Macmillan, 1949; *Promise and Fulfillment: Palestine, 1917-1949* (history), Macmillan, 1949.

(Contributor) Richard Howard Stafford Crossman, editor, *The God that Failed: Six Studies in Communism,* Harper, 1950, reprinted, Arno, 1975; *Arrow in the Blue* (first part of autobiography), Macmillan, 1952; *The Invisible Writing* (second part of autobiography), Macmillan, 1954; *The Trail of the Dinosaur and Other Essays,* Macmillan, 1955; *Reflections on Hanging,* Gollancz, 1956, Macmillan, 1957; *The Sleepwalkers: A History of Man's Changing Vision of the Universe,* Macmillan, 1959, excerpt published as *The Watershed: A Biography of Johannes Kepler,* Anchor Books, 1960.

The Lotus and the Robot (nonfiction), Hutchinson, 1960, Macmillan, 1961; (with others) *Control of the Mind,* McGraw, 1961; (with C. H. Rolph) *Hanged by the Neck: An Exposure of Capital Punishment in England,* Penguin, 1961; (editor) *Suicide of a Nation?: An Enquiry into the State of Britain Today,* Hutchinson, 1963, Macmillan, 1964; *The Act of Creation* (nonfiction), Macmillan, 1964, new edition, Hutchinson, 1976; (with others) *Studies in Psychology,* University of London Press, 1965; (with others) *Celebration of the Bicentenary of John Smithson,* Smithsonian Institution Press, 1966; *The Ghost in the Machine* (nonfiction), Hutchinson, 1967, Macmillan, 1968; *Drinkers of Infinity: Essays, 1955-1967,* Hutchinson, 1968, Macmillan, 1969; (editor with J. R. Smythies) *Beyond Reductionism: New Perspectives in the Life Sciences,* Hutchinson, 1969, Macmillan, 1970, new edition, Hutchinson, 1972; (contributor) *The Ethics of Change,* Canadian Broadcasting Corp., 1969.

The Case of the Midwife Toad (nonfiction), Hutchinson, 1971, Random House, 1972; *The Roots of Coincidence* (nonfiction), Random House, 1972; *The Lion and the Ostrich* (lecture), Oxford University Press, 1973; (with Alister Hardy and Robert Harvie) *The Challenge of Chance: Experiments and Speculations,* Hutchinson, 1973, published as *The Challenge of Chance: A Mass Experiment in Telepathy and Its Unexpected Outcome,* Random House, 1974; *The Heel of Achilles: Essays, 1968-1973,* Hutchinson, 1974, Random House, 1975; *The Thirteenth Tribe: The Khazar Empire and Its Heritage,* Random House, 1976; (with Arnold Joseph Toynbee and others) *Life after Death,* McGraw, 1976; *Janus: A Summing Up,* Random House, 1978.

Novels: *The Gladiators,* Macmillan, 1939, 2nd edition, Graphic Books, 1956; *Darkness at Noon* (Book-of-the-Month Club selection), J. Cape, 1940, Macmillan, 1941, reprinted, Franklin Library, 1979; *Arrival and Departure,* Macmillan, 1943, revised edition, Hutchinson, 1966, Macmillan, 1967; *Thieves in the Night: Chronicle of an Experiment,* Macmillan, 1946, reprinted, 1967; *The Age of Longing,* Macmillan, 1951, reprinted, Hutchinson, 1970; *The Call-Girls,* Hutchinson, 1972, Random House, 1973.

Also author of screenplay "Lift Your Head, Comrade," 1944. Contributor to *Encyclopaedia Britannica, Encyclopaedia of Philosophy,* and *Encyclopaedia of Sexual Knowledge.* Contributor to periodicals.

WORK IN PROGRESS: Pilgrim's Regress.

SIDELIGHTS: Arthur Koestler gained international recognition with the publication of his novel *Darkness at Noon,* a fictionalized account of the Moscow Trials of 1938 in which many Bolshevik revolutionaries were put to death by the Soviet Government. "Koestler's object," a reviewer for *Encounter* notes, "was to expose the reality which lay behind the facade of the great Russian state trials of the 1930s, and he did it so effectively that to thousands, even millions, of people Communism, and the Communist party, . . . have never looked the same again." Peter Medawar observes that Koestler's novel "changed the direction of the flow of thought on political matters, and it is as such that he will live and continue to be read."

Darkness at Noon grew out of Koestler's own disillusionment with the Soviet Union and Communism after seven years of membership in the German Communist Party. He saw the Moscow Trials as both an abandonment of the Soviet Union's Communist ideals and as dangerously totalitarian in nature. "All the big shots, our heroes . . . were denounced, unmasked as British or American agents," Koestler says about the trials. "When most of my friends had been liquidated in the U.S.S.R., I sent my farewell letter to the German Communist Party." "I went to Communism as one goes to a spring of fresh water," Koestler states, "and I left Communism as one clambers out of a poisoned river strewn with the wreckage of flooded cities and the corpses of the drowned." As Jenni Calder observes, through his political writing Koestler presented "his life as an example that could teach and help the understanding of a certain period of history. He had made mistakes. These mistakes could be partially justified if they could be used to illustrate and interpret history."

Koestler's subsequent writings continued to examine the problems of political idealism and power. In such books as *The Yogi and the Commissar, Thieves in the Night,* and *Arrival and Departure,* he explored the problems involved in transforming one's ideals into political action. *The Yogi and the Commissar* contrasts the differences between religious and political ideals and methods of change. *Thieves in the Night* concerns the settlement of Israel by Jews who have long been victims and must now become rulers. *Arrival and*

Departure is about a young revolutionary who suffers a nervous breakdown.

By the 1950s, Koestler concentrated less attention on his political writing and eventually gave it up entirely. "There was a danger," Philip Toynbee writes, "that Koestler would remain in the constricting armour of his anti-Communism, . . . but Koestler saw the danger clearly enough [and] shed that armour." Speaking of his abandonment of political writing, Koestler states, "I have said all I have to say on these subjects which had occupied me for the best part of a quarter century; now the errors are atoned, the bitter passion has burnt itself out, Cassandra has gone hoarse—let others carry on."

Leaving politics behind him, Koestler devoted his energies to writing about scientific and philosophical matters. He has become, as Robert Boyers writes, "a learned and witty man who seems to enjoy writing about almost everything." Koestler has examined such topics as evolution, psychology, the history of science, capital punishment, and the nature of artistic creation. "Koestler's ideas," Lothar Kahn states, "probably range over a wider terrain than those of any other writer of our time. Few contemporaries have treated ideologies more analytically and in more original fashion." Medawar, admitting that Koestler "is not a scientist, though he has had some good ideas, . . . and he is not nearly critical or tough-minded enough to be a creative philosopher," believes that he is "an enormously intelligent man with a truly amazing power to apprehend knowledge and grasp the gist of quite difficult theories." P. Witonski disagrees. "Arthur Koestler's forays into the history of science," he writes, "have done little to enhance his reputation, save among those uneducated in science."

Koestler's most widely-known non-political work is *The Act of Creation,* a study of the creative process in many aspects of human behavior. The book received a mixed critical reaction. E. R. Hilgard believes that "reading the book is a rich experience, for the author wanders widely through science, art, and literature, uses charming and varied analogies, and says countless quotable things. If his book is not the last word on creativity, that is not much of a weakness. It is a serious work, immensely learned, and thoughtful." Anthony Lejeune, however, calls *The Act of Creation* "an unsatisfactory book," claiming that "Mr. Koestler had a worthwhile idea" that "would have made an admirable short essay." Elizabeth Janeway notes that "though I can't help but point out [Koestler's] short-comings [in writing about] the field I know most about, there is something here." She praises Koestler as a "master of the very difficult trade of synthesizing a mass of material [and] of serving up to the general reader facts that he would otherwise never know, and—most important—of explaining why they matter and how they relate to each other."

Koestler holds a distinctive place in contemporary thought and letters. "Koestler," a writer for *Time* states, "is a rare protean figure in modern intellectual life—a successful journalist, novelist, and popular philosopher. His concern for ultimate issues and his idealistic involvement lend weight to his fiction. His wit, clarity, and brilliance of exposition make his . . . volumes of political, scientific, and philosophical theory highly enjoyable as well as provocative." "To be the author," Alasdair MacIntyre states, "of one great novel and several good ones, to have written imaginatively on the history of science and polemically on the nature of the human mind, to have involved oneself continually in argument on politics and religion—each of these alone would make up an exceptional intellectual life. But Koestler's life embraces them all."

Darkness at Noon was made into a stage play by Sidney Kingsley and produced on Broadway in 1951. The book has also been translated into over thirty languages.

AVOCATIONAL INTERESTS: Chess, canoeing.

BIOGRAPHICAL/CRITICAL SOURCES—Books: Arthur Koestler, *Spanish Testament,* Gollancz, 1937, abridged edition published as *Dialogue with Death,* Macmillan, 1942; Koestler, *Scum of the Earth,* Macmillan, 1941; John Lewis and Reginald Bishop, *Philosophy of Betrayal,* Russia Today Society, 1945; Denys Val Baker, editor, *Writers of Today,* Sidgwick & Jackson, 1946; J. Nevada, *Arthur Koestler,* Robert Anscombe & Co., 1948; George Woodcock, *The Writer and Politics,* Porcupine Press, 1948; *The Crisis of the Human Person: Some Personalist Interpretations,* Longmans, Green, 1949; Koestler, *Arrow in the Blue,* Macmillan, 1952; *Books in General,* Chatto & Windus, 1953; Koestler, *The Invisible Writing,* Macmillan, 1954; George Orwell, *George Orwell: Critical Essays,* Secker & Warburg, 1954; Harvey Breit, *The Writer Observed,* World Publishing, 1956; John Atkins, *Arthur Koestler,* Neville Spearman, 1956, reprinted, Norwood, 1977.

Peter Alfred Huber, *Arthur Koestler: Das Literarische Werk,* Fretz & Wasmuth Verlag, 1962; Anthony Burgess, *The Novel Now: A Guide to Contemporary Fiction,* Norton, 1967; Burgess, *Urgent Copy: Literary Studies,* Norton, 1968; Lothar Kahn, *Mirrors of the Jewish Mind: A Gallery of Portraits of European Jewish Writers of Our Time,* A. S. Barnes, 1968; Jenni Calder, *Chronicles of Conscience: A Study of George Orwell and Arthur Koestler,* University of Pittsburgh Press, 1969; *Contemporary Literary Criticism,* Gale, Volume I, 1973, Volume III, 1975, Volume VI, 1976, Volume VIII, 1978; Wolfe Mays, *Arthur Koestler,* Judson, 1973; *Arthur Koestler,* Cahiers de l'Herne (Paris), 1975; Harold Harris, editor, *Astride the Two Cultures: Arthur Koestler at Seventy,* Random House, 1976; Reed B. Merrill and Thomas Frazier, editors, *Arthur Koestler: An International Bibliography,* Ardis, 1978; Sidney A Pearson, Jr., *Arthur Koestler,* Twayne, 1978; Murray Sperber, *Arthur Koestler: A Collection of Critical Essays,* Prentice-Hall, 1978.

Periodicals: *Cornhill,* autumn, 1946; *New Statesman,* July 3, 1954, October 1, 1971; *Nation,* July 3, 1954, November 20, 1976; *Encounter,* July, 1964, February, 1968, January, 1970; *Times Literary Supplement,* July 2, 1964, November 2, 1967, October 27, 1972, June 11, 1976; *Saturday Review,* October 17, 1964, March 6, 1976; *Commentary,* November, 1964; *National Review,* November 17, 1964, June 30, 1970, November 12, 1976; *New York Review of Books,* December 17, 1964, October 28, 1976; *Harper's,* January, 1965; *Science,* January 1, 1965, May 12, 1972; *Sewanee Review,* autumn, 1965; *Spectator,* October 1, 1965, April 27, 1974; *Observer,* October 15, 1967, September 8, 1968, October 5, 1969; *Time,* March 1, 1968, August 23, 1976; *Hudson Review,* summer, 1968; *Listener,* September 12, 1968, April 8, 1976; *Atlantic,* December, 1968, May, 1973; *Christian Science Monitor,* October 23, 1969, May 4, 1972; *New York Times,* June 23, 1970; *New York Times Magazine,* August 30, 1970; *Esquire,* March, 1972; *Detroit News,* April 2, 1972; *Natural History,* June, 1972; *Guardian Weekly,* October 28, 1972; *Books & Bookmen,* December, 1972, May, 1976; *Life,* December 29, 1972; *New Yorker,* April 21, 1973; *New Leader,* May 14, 1973; *Wall Street Journal,* July 26, 1973; *Psychology Today,* October, 1973, January, 1977; *Contemporary Review,* June,

1974; *Book World,* June 30, 1974; *New Republic,* February 1, 1975, May 13, 1978; *Christian Century,* February 26, 1975; *Ms.,* October, 1975; *Economist,* April 24, 1976; *Newsweek,* August 30, 1976; *America,* November 13, 1976; *Midstream,* February, 1977; *Commonweal,* March 4, 1977; *Critic,* August, 1978; *Virginia Quarterly Review,* autumn, 1978.

—Sketch by Thomas Wiloch

* * *

KOHNER, Frederick 1905-

PERSONAL: Born September 25, 1905, in Trnovany, Czechoslovakia; son of Julius and Helene (Beamt) Kohner; married Fritzie Klein, 1930; children: Ruth Kohner Drenick, Kathy Kohner Zuckerman. *Education:* Studied at Sorbonne; University of Vienna, Ph.D., 1929. *Home:* 12046 Coyne St., Los Angeles, Calif. *Agent:* William Morris Agency, 1350 Ave. of the Americas, New York, N.Y. 10019.

CAREER: Newspaper reporter, screenwriter, novelist, lecturer, playwright, since coming to United States in 1936; lecturer in film department at University of Southern California, 1961-63, and University of California, Los Angeles. *Member:* Writers Guild.

WRITINGS: *Gidget,* Putnam, 1957; *Cher Papa,* Putnam, 1959; *Gidget Goes Hawaiian,* Bantam, 1961; *The Continental Kick,* Bantam, 1962; *Mister, Will You Marry Me?,* New American Library, 1963; *Affairs of Gidget,* Bantam, 1963; *Gidget Goes to Rome,* Bantam, 1964; *Gidget in Love,* Dell, 1965; *The Gremmie,* New American Library, 1966; *Gidget Goes Parisienne,* Dell, 1966; *Kiki of Montparnasse,* Stein & Day, 1967; *Gidget Goes to New York,* Dell, 1968; *The Magician of Sunset Boulevard,* Morgan Press, 1975; *Amanda,* Droemer-Knaur, 1975; *Love in White,* Luebbe, 1976; *The Delights of Olding,* Morgan Press, 1979.

Plays: (With Albert Mannheimer) "The Bees and the Flowers," 1946; "Stalin Allee"; "The Woman of My Life." Author of about twenty screenplays for major producers, and "Gidget" series, ABC-TV, 1965.

SIDELIGHTS: "Gidget," a name Frederick Kohner coined from "girl" and "midget," has become popular with teenage readers. The Gidget books have been translated into ten languages.

* * *

KOHUT, Heinz 1913-

PERSONAL: Surname is pronounced *Ko*-hoot; born May 3, 1913, in Vienna, Austria; came to United States in 1940, naturalized in 1945; son of Felix and Else (Lampl) Kohut; married Elizabeth Meyer (a social worker), October 9, 1948; children: Thomas August. *Education:* Gymnasium XIX, Vienna, Matura, 1932; University of Vienna, M.D., 1938. *Home:* 5805 South Dorchester Ave., Chicago, Ill. 60637. *Office:* 180 North Michigan Ave., Chicago, Ill. 60601.

CAREER: University of Chicago Hospitals, Chicago, Ill., resident in neurology, 1941-42, instructor in neurology, 1943-44, instructor in neurology and psychiatry, 1944-47, assistant professor of psychiatry, 1947-50; University of Chicago, lecturer in School of Social Service Administration, 1952-53, professorial lecturer in department of psychiatry, 1954—; Institute for Psychoanalysis, Chicago, member of staff, 1953—. Freud Lecturer, State University of New York, 1968; Brill Lecturer, New York Psychoanalytic Society, 1972; visiting professor, University of Cincinnati, 1972—. Member of editorial board, American Psychoanalytic Association, 1955-58 and 1960-66. Diplomate, American Board of Psychiatry and Neurology.

MEMBER: International Psychoanalytic Association (vice-president, 1965-73), American Psychoanalytic Association (secretary, 1961-63; president, 1964-65), American Medical Association, American Psychiatric Association, Austrian Academy of Sciences, Chicago Psychoanalytic Society (president, 1963-64). *Awards, honors:* Doctor of Science, University of Cincinnati, 1973; Hartmann Prize, New York Psychoanalytic Society, 1972; Government of Austria Honor Cross for Science and Art, 1978.

WRITINGS: (Contributor) J. M. Wepman and R. W. Heine, editors, *Concepts of Personality,* Aldine, 1963; (contributor) H. M. Ruitenbeek, editor, *Psychoanalysis and Literature,* Dutton, 1964; *The Analysis of the Self: A Systematic Approach to the Psychoanalytic Treatment of Narcissistic Personality Disorders,* International Universities Press, 1971; (co-author) *The Psychology of the Self,* International Universities Press, 1978; *The Restoration of the Self,* International Universities Press, 1978; *The Search for the Self: Selected Essays of Heinz Kohut,* two volumes, International Universities Press, 1979. Contributor to medical and literary journals.

WORK IN PROGRESS: Further research on narcissism.

BIOGRAPHICAL/CRITICAL SOURCES: *New York Times,* May 2, 1964; *Medical Tribune,* December 21, 1964.

* * *

KOLDE, Endel Jakob 1917-

PERSONAL: Born March 9, 1917, in Virumaa, Estonia (now part of U.S.S.R.); son of Johannes E. (a farmer and businessman) and Elise (Wendt) Kolde; married second wife, Helga Rohe, October 14, 1968; children: (first marriage) Hubert, Annelise, Velle, Endel. *Education:* Tallin Technical University and National Military Academy, Estonia, B.S. equivalent, 1941; Stockholm School of Economics, D.H.S., 1947; University of Washington, Seattle, M.A., 1951, Ph.D., 1954; also attended Tartu University and University of Stockholm. *Home:* 5303 Northeast 178th St., Lake Forest Park, Wash. 98155. *Office:* Graduate School of Business Administration, University of Washington, Seattle, Wash. 98195.

CAREER: Junior executive in export and import business in Estonia, 1938-43, certified customhouse broker, 1940; Swedish Bureau of Census, Stockholm, statistician, 1944-45; *Balansboken* (financial handbook), Stockholm, financial editor, 1946-47; auditor and industrial analyst in Sweden for Bohlins Revionsbyra, 1947-48; University of Washington, Seattle, instructor and assistant director of Bureau of Business Research, 1951-54, assistant professor, 1954-56, associate professor, 1956-59, professor of international business, 1959—. Visiting professor, Harvard University, 1956, Management Development Institute, University of Lausanne, 1960-62, University of California, Berkeley, 1964-65, University of British Columbia, 1965-66, Kobe University of Commerce and Sophia University, 1968, and Cranfield Institute of Technology, England, 1973; guest lecturer or invited panelist at universities and seminars in more than twenty countries. Member of committee on exports, International Business Research Institute, Indiana University, 1968-70. Consultant to U.S. and foreign government agencies, international organizations, and aircraft, lumber, electro-chemical, maritime, and other industries. *Awards, honors:* Grants from Committee for Economic Development, 1953, Ford Foundation, 1956, and Small Business Administration, 1960; McKinsey Foundation for Management Research Award for outstanding contribution to management literature in 1965-

66; named honorary citizen and given key to the state, Hyogo Prefecture, Japan, for contributions to Japanese higher education, 1968.

WRITINGS: From Democracy to Communism: Sovietization of Estonia (first published as articles in *Pacific Northwest Industry*), three parts, U.S. Department of State, 1953; (with N. H. Engle) *An Economic Review of the Sources and of the Demand Pattern for Energy in the Pacific Northwest,* Canadian Atlantic Oil Co. (Edmonton), 1953; *Energy Base of the Pacific Northwest Economy: A Regional Analysis of Supply Utilization and Cost of Energy,* Committee for Economic Development, 1955; *From Mine to Market: A Study of Production, Marketing and Consumption of Coal in the Pacific Northwest,* Bureau of Business Research, University of Washington, 1956; *International Business Enterprise,* Prentice-Hall, 1968, 2nd edition, 1973; *Working Papers on the Organization and Behavior of the Multinational Firm,* Graduate School of Business Administration, University of Washington, 1970; *International Managerial Environments in Industrial Countries: Selected Lectures,* University of Washington, 1973; *The Multinational Company: Behavioral and Managerial Analysis,* Heath, 1974; *The Pacific Quest: The Concept and Scope of an Oceanic Community,* Heath, 1976.

Contributor: P. H. Nystrom and A. W. Frey, editors, *Marketing Handbook,* Ronald, 1965; *World Trade and the Citizen,* University of British Columbia, 1967; Walter Krause and F. J. Mathis, editors, *International Economies and Business,* Houghton, 1968; Richard N. Farmer, *International Management,* Dickenson, 1968; R. I. Hartman and others, editors, *Modern Business Administration,* Scott, Foresman, 1969; *Fifth Anniversary Review,* Graduate School of Business Administration, Seoul National University, 1971; Gordon E. Miracle and G. S. Albaum, editors, *International Marketing Management,* Irwin, 1970; Wholihan and Hartman, editors, *The Environment of Business,* Dickenson, 1972; Lee C. Nehrt, Gano S. Evans, and Lamp Li, *Managerial Policy, Strategy and Planning for Southeast Asia,* Chinese University of Hong Kong, 1976.

Also author of series of booklets for Management Development Institute, University of Lausanne, 1960-62, case studies for private firms, and business research studies. Contributor to proceedings and to the *International Encyclopedia of Higher Education.* Foreign correspondent, *Valis Eesti* (weekly newspaper), Sweden. Contributor to professional journals in the United States, France, Canada, Japan, China, Korea, and Estonia.

WORK IN PROGRESS: An international management primer; studies on American nationalism in world affairs, organization and behavior of multinational companies, managerial environments in industrial countries, and culture context of international organizations.

AVOCATIONAL INTERESTS: Long distance running, tennis, mountaineering, opera, travel.

* * *

KORN, Bertram Wallace 1918-1979

PERSONAL: Born October 6, 1918, in Philadelphia; Pa.; died December 11, 1979, in New Orleans, La.; son of Manuel and Blanche Korn; children: Judith Carole, Bertram Wallace, Jr. *Education:* University of Cincinnati, A.B. (with honors), 1939; Hebrew Union College, M.H.L., 1943, D.H.L., 1949. *Office:* Reform Congregation Keneseth Israel, Old York and Township Line Rds., Elkins Park, Philadelphia, Pa.

CAREER: Ordination as rabbi, 1943; rabbi in Mobile, Ala., 1943-44, Mansfield, Ohio, 1946-48; Hebrew Union College, Cincinnati, Ohio, professor of American Jewish history and assistant to the president, 1948-49; Reform Congregation Keneseth Israel, Elkins Park, Philadelphia, Pa., senior rabbi, 1949-79. Visiting professor, Hebrew Union College, 1962-79, and Dropsie University, 1974-79. Visiting preacher, Valley Forge Military Academy; member of President Nixon's Commission for the Observance of the 25th Anniversary of the United Nations. Board member, Hebrew Union College, Delaware Valley College, Gratz College, Museum of American Jewish History, and Federation of Jewish Agencies of Greater Philadelphia; member of advisory council of Civil War Centennial Commission of Federal Government, National Council of the Joint Defense Appeal, Friends of the Hebrew University (Philadelphia, Pa. branch), and Interfaith Commission of Central Conference of American Rabbis—Union of American Hebrew Congregations; member of commission on Jewish chaplaincy, Jewish Welfare Board, 1963-79. Past chaplain, Grand Lodge of Masons and American Legion (both of Pennsylvania). *Military service:* U.S. Navy, 1944-46, chaplain with service in Marine Corps in North China. U.S. Naval Reserve, Chaplain Corps, retired as rear admiral, 1978; received U.S. Navy Legion of Merit, 1978.

MEMBER: American Jewish Historical Society (president, 1959-61), Grand Lodge of B'nai B'rith, Jewish Publication Society of America, Central Conference of American Rabbis, American Section—Jewish Historical Society of Israel, Chapel of Four Chaplains (honorary life member), Alumni Association of Hebrew Union College (vice-president, 1963-65; president, 1965-79). *Awards, honors:* L.L.D., Temple University, 1957; Lee M. Friedman Award, American Jewish Historical Society, 1964; D. Litt., Delaware Valley College, 1967, and Dropsie University, 1976; D. D., Hebrew Union College, 1968; Merit Award, American Association for State and Local History, 1970, for *The Early Jews of New Orleans.*

WRITINGS: American Jewry and the Civil War, Jewish Publication Society, 1951; *Eventful Years and Experiences: Studies in Nineteenth Century American Jewish History,* American Jewish Archives, 1954; *The Centenary Edition of Solomon Nunes Carvalho's Incidents of Travel and Adventure in the Far West,* Jewish Publication Society, 1954; *The American Reaction to the Mortara Case,* American Jewish Archives, 1957; (co-editor) Baron Corvo (real name, Frederick Rolfe), *Letters to Leonard Moore,* Vane, 1960; (editor) *Retrospect and Prospect: Essays in Commemoration of the Seventy-Fifth Anniversary of the Central Conference of American Rabbis,* Central Conference of American Rabbis, 1965; *The Early Jews of New Orleans,* Jewish Publication Society, 1969; (editor) *Bicentennial Festschrift for Jacob Rader Marcus,* Ktav, 1976. Also author of *Naval Reserve Chaplains' Handbook,* 1959, revised edition, 1965, and *Benjamin Levy, New Orleans Printer and Publisher: Jews and Negro Slavery in the Old South,* 1961. Author of three filmstrips on American Jewish history for the Commission on Jewish Education of the Union of American Hebrew Congregations. Contributor to Jewish publications and history journals. Editor, *Yearbook* of the Central Conference of American Rabbis, 1952-53; contributing editor, *Jewish Exponent,* 1958-60; member of editorial advisory board, *Civil War History* (published by State University of Iowa), 1955-59, and *The Jewish Digest.*

KOSTYU, Frank A(lexander) 1919-

PERSONAL: Born August 3, 1919, in Lorain, Ohio; son of Frank Joseph (a steelworker) and Julia (Yager) Kostyu; married Marjorie Ann Butcher (a schoolteacher), June 11, 1944; children: Joel, Paul, Kathryn. *Education:* Heidelberg College, B.A., 1943; Eden Theological Seminary, B.D., 1945; Oberlin College, S.T.M., 1962; Vanderbilt University, D.Min., 1973. *Politics:* Independent. *Office:* Kinship Krafts, Inc., 174 Montclair Ave., Montclair, N.J. 07042.

CAREER: Ordained United Church of Christ minister, 1945; pastor in Dayton, Ohio, 1946-50, West Alexandria, Ohio, 1950-56, Alliance, Ohio, 1956-62, and Blue Island, Ill., 1962-64; *A.D. Magazine,* New York, N.Y., senior editor, 1964-77; currently president of Kinship Krafts, Inc., Montclair, N.J. *Awards, honors:* Freedoms Foundation awards, 1961 and 1962, for sermons; several exhibition awards for photographs; honorary Doctor of Divinity, Heidelberg College, 1980.

WRITINGS: Pathways to Personal Contentment, Prentice-Hall, 1960; *Power to Get What You Want out of Life,* Prentice-Hall, 1964; *Shadows in the Valley,* Doubleday, 1970; *How to Spark Your Marriage When the Kids Leave Home,* Pilgrim Press, 1972; *Sparks for Your Church Program,* Abingdon, 1974; *Healing Life's Sore Spots,* Hawthorn, 1976; *The Time of Your Life Is Now,* Seabury, 1977; (with son, Joel A. Kostyu) *Durham: A Pictorial History,* Donning, 1978; *Adventures in Faith and Freedom* (short history of the United Church of Christ), Kinship Krafts, 1979.

Photographic illustrator; all published by Seabury: Karl Rahner, *Watch and Pray with Me,* 1976; Fulton J. Sheen, *The World's Great Love,* 1978; Daniel Berrigan, *Beside the Sea of Glass,* 1978.

WORK IN PROGRESS: Loneliness and How to Cope with It, with son, Paul E. Kostyu; *History of the Hungarians in America,* photographs and text.

* * *

KRAFT, Charles H(oward) 1932-

PERSONAL: Born July 15, 1932, in Waterbury, Conn.; son of Howard R. (a manufacturer) and Marian (Northrup) Kraft; married Marguerite Gearhart (a professor), June 14, 1953; children: Cheryl E., Charles E., Richard L., Karen L. *Education:* Wheaton College, Wheaton, Ill., B.A., 1953; University of Oklahoma, graduate study, summer, 1954; Ashland Theological Seminary, B.D., 1960; Hartford Seminary Foundation, Ph.D., 1963. *Home:* 1200 Lyndon St., South Pasadena, Calif. 91030. *Office:* Fuller Theological Seminary, 135 North Oakland, Pasadena, Calif. 91101.

CAREER: Ordained minister of Brethren Church, 1955; Meadville Institute of Linguistics, Meadville, Pa., instructor in linguistics, summer, 1956; Church of the Brethren Mission, Michika and Mubi, Northern Nigeria, missionary and teacher of Hausa language to other missionaries, 1957-60; Toronto Institute of Linguistics, Toronto, Ontario, instructor in linguistics, summer, 1960; Meadville Institute of Linguistics, instructor in linguistics, summer, 1960; Syracuse University, Overseas Training Center, Syracuse, N.Y., instructor in Hausa, summer, 1961; Michigan State University, East Lansing, instructor in Hausa, summer, 1962, assistant professor of African languages, 1963-68, associate of African Studies Center, 1962-68, coordinator of African language instruction, 1964-66, language coordinator of Peace Corps training programs, summer and autumn, 1965; University of California, Los Angeles, visiting associate professor of linguistics and African languages, 1968-69; Fuller Theological Seminary, Pasadena, Calif., associate professor, 1969-77, professor of anthropology and African studies, 1977—. Lecturer, University of California, Los Angeles, 1969-73. External examiner for Hausa language degrees at Ahmadu Bello University, 1973. Field experience includes Nigeria, Senegal, Sierra Leone, Liberia, Ghana, Burundi, Tanzanai, Kenya, Cameroun, Niger, Korea, and Papua New Guinea.

MEMBER: African Studies Association (fellow), American Anthropological Association (fellow), American Scientific Affiliation (fellow). *Awards, honors:* U.S. Office of Education grant, 1963-66; U.S. Peace Corps grant for development of an introductory course in Pidgin English, 1966; grants for field study of Chadic languages from Social Science Research Council, 1966, and Fulbright-Hays Program, 1966-67.

WRITINGS: A Study of Hausa Syntax, three volumes, Hartford Seminary Foundation, 1963; *An Introduction to Spoken Hausa,* with workbook, African Studies Center, Michigan State University, 1965; *Cultural Materials in Hausa,* African Studies Center, Michigan State University, 1966; *Workbook in Intermediate and Advanced Hausa,* African Studies Center, Michigan State University, 1966; (with wife, Marguerite Kraft) *Where Do I Go From Here?: A Handbook for Continuing Language Study in the Field,* U.S. Peace Corps, 1966; (contributor) A. R. Tippett, editor, *God, Man, and Church Growth,* Eerdmans, 1973; (with M. Kraft) *Spoken Hausa: Introductory Course,* University of California Press, 1973; (with A.H.M. Kirk-Greene) *Teach Yourself Hausa,* English Universities Press, 1973; *Hausa Reader,* University of California Press, 1974; (contributor) Neil Warren, editor, *After Therapy What?: Lay Therapeutic Resources in Religious Perspective,* C. C Thomas, 1974; (contributor) Fred L. Casmir, editor, *International and Intercultural Communication,* University Press of America, 1978; *Christianity and Culture,* Orbis, 1979; *Communicating the Gospel God's Way,* Ashland Theological Seminary, 1979.

Contributor of about forty articles and reviews to theology, linguistics, and African studies journals, including *Evangelical Missions Quarterly, Theology, News, and Notes, Studies in African Linguistics, African Studies, Journal of African Languages,* and *Practical Anthropology.*

WORK IN PROGRESS: A popularization of *Christianity in Culture,* for Abingdon; *Intercultural Communication of Christianity.*

* * *

KRAFT, Ken(neth) 1907-

PERSONAL: Born November 16, 1907, in St. Louis, Mo.; son of Edward O. and Anne Elizabeth (Evans) Kraft; married Myrtle May (Pat) Gilmore (a writer), October 28, 1933. *Education:* Attended Washington University, St. Louis, Mo., 1926-28; University of Missouri, B.J., 1931.

CAREER: St. Louis Globe-Democrat, St. Louis, Mo., reporter, 1934-37; Southwestern Bell Telephone Co., St. Louis, writer and public relations man, 1937-42, 1946-49; American Telephone & Telegraph Co., New York, N.Y., writer and public relations man, 1942-43; free-lance writer, 1949—. *Military service:* U.S. Navy, Special Devices Division, writer, 1943-46. *Member:* Delta Sigma Phi (chapter president, 1930-31), Sigma Delta Chi.

WRITINGS: Land of Milk and Omelets, Appleton, 1959; *The Birds and the Beasts Were There,* Doubleday, 1961; *Give Father a Hard Knock,* Doubleday, 1962; *Garden to*

Order, introduction by Pearl S. Buck, Doubleday, 1963; *Gardener, Go Home,* Appleton, 1964; *Rainbow by the Bayou,* Chilton, 1965.

With wife, Pat Kraft: *Luther Burbank: The Wizard and the Man,* Meredith, 1967; *Fruits for the Home Garden,* Morrow, 1968; *The Home Garden Cookbook: From Seed to Plate,* Doubleday, 1970; *Growing Food the Natural Way,* Doubleday, 1973; *Grow Your Own Dwarf Fruit Trees,* Walker & Co., 1974; *The Best of American Gardening: Two Centuries of Fertile Ideas,* Walker & Co., 1975; *Exotic Vegetables: How to Grow and Cook Them,* Walker & Co., 1977. Also author of *Home Garden Cookbook: Delicious Natural Food Recipes,* Wilshire.

Contributor of articles, fiction, and humor to national magazines.†

* * *

KRAMER, Paul J(ackson) 1904-

PERSONAL: Born May 8, 1904, in Brookville, Ind.; son of LeRoy (a farmer) and Minnie (Jackson) Kramer; married Edith Vance, June 24, 1931; children: Jean Jackson (Mrs. Arthur F. Findeis), Richard. *Education:* Miami University, Oxford, Ohio, B.A., 1926; University of Idaho, graduate study, 1926-27; Ohio State University, M.S., 1929, Ph.D., 1931. *Religion:* Methodist. *Home:* 23 Stoneridge Cir., Durham, N.C. 27705. *Office:* Department of Botany, Duke University, Durham, N.C. 27706.

CAREER: Duke University, Durham, N.C., instructor, 1931-35, assistant professor, 1935-38, associate professor, 1938-45, professor of botany, 1945-54, James B. Duke Professor, 1954-74, professor emeritus, 1974—. Program director in regulatory biology, National Science Foundation, 1960-61. American Institute of Biological Sciences, member of governing board, 1955-65, 1967-71, president, 1964; member of agricultural board, National Research Council, 1958-60; member of visiting committee, department of biology, Harvard University, 1965-71; *Biological Abstracts,* member of board of trustees, 1966-71, president, 1971.

MEMBER: Botanical Society of America (vice-president, 1960; president, 1964), American Society of Plant Physiologists (vice-president, 1943; president, 1945), American Association for the Advancement of Science (vice-president and chairman of Section G, 1956), American Academy of Arts and Sciences, National Academy of Sciences, American Philosophical Society, North Carolina Academy of Sciences (president, 1961-62), Phi Beta Kappa, Sigma Xi. *Awards, honors:* Botanical Society of America Award of Merit, 1956; Society of American Foresters Award for contributing to advancement of forestry, 1961; D.Sc., University of North Carolina, 1966, and Ohio State University, 1972; D.Litt., Miami University, Oxford, Ohio, 1966; Docteur Honoris Causa, University of Paris VII, 1975; American Institute of Biological Sciences Distinguished Service Award, 1977.

WRITINGS: Plant and Soil Water Relationships, McGraw, 1949, 2nd edition, 1969; (with T. T. Kozlowski) *Physiology of Trees,* McGraw, 1960; (with Kozlowski) *Physiology of Woody Plants,* Academic Press, 1979. Contributor of chapters to about fifteen books. Contributor of about one hundred and fifty papers, many of them on research projects, to scientific journals. Associate editor, *Annual Review of Plant Physiology,* 1950-54.

WORK IN PROGRESS: Research on the effects of controlled environmental factors on plant growth.

SIDELIGHTS: Paul J. Kramer told *CA:* "My writing has been done for several reasons. Most of the short papers were written to make available to other scientists the results of various research projects. Publication of the results of research is as much a part of the research process as the experiments themselves. Several chapters in books were written to summarize the information available in certain fields of plant physiology. Review articles are important because I feel that progress in science is hampered as much by failure to use the information available as it is by lack of information. In a few instances I have written papers in order to publicize particular concepts which I felt were being neglected. . . . [My] books were written because of obvious lack of suitable texts and reference books in their fields. Both fields expanded so much that when revised versions were planned we ended up with completely new books rather than with revised editions. I have had the pleasure of seeing two fields, plant water relations and tree physiology, in which there was very limited activity when I started work, become large and active fields of research."

* * *

KRANTZ, Hazel Newman 1920-

PERSONAL: Born January 29, 1920, in Brooklyn, N.Y.; daughter of Louis John and Eva Newman; married Michael Krantz, 1942; children: Laurence Ira, Margaret Ann, Vincent. *Education:* New York University, B.S., 1942; Hofstra College (now University), M.S., 1959. *Home:* 875 Leeds Dr., North Bellmore, Long Island, N.Y..

CAREER: McGreevey, Werring & Howell, New York City, home-furnishings coordinator, 1942-43; Felix Lilienthal, New York City, fashion coordinator, 1944-45; elementary school teacher in public schools, Nassau County, N.Y., 1957-68; editor of *True Frontier* (magazine), 1970-72; copy editor of *db The Sound Engineering Magazine,* 1973-78; currently free-lance writer, specializing in educational materials. *Member:* National Council of Jewish Women, Society of Children's Book Writers, Authors Guild, New York State Teachers Association, Literacy Volunteers, Emissary Society.

WRITINGS—All published by Vanguard, except as indicated: *Hundred Pounds of Popcorn,* 1961; *Freestyle for Michael,* 1964; *The Secret Raft,* 1965; *Tippy,* 1968; *A Pad of Your Own,* Pyramid Publications, 1973; *Who's in Charge Here?,* Merit Publications, 1980.

AVOCATIONAL INTERESTS: Gardening, sewing, swimming, cooking, tennis, and tutoring reading.

BIOGRAPHICAL/CRITICAL SOURCES: Young Readers' Review, September, 1968.

* * *

KRAUSE, Walter 1917-

PERSONAL: Born 1917, in Canby, Ore. *Education:* University of Oregon, B.A., M.A.; Harvard University, A.M., Ph.D., 1945. *Office:* Department of Economics, University of Iowa, Iowa City, Iowa 52240.

CAREER: University of Texas, Main University (now University of Texas at Austin), assistant professor of economics, 1945-47; Dartmouth College, Hanover, N.H., assistant professor of economics, 1947-50; University of Utah, Salt Lake City, professor of economics, 1950-54; affiliated with U.S. Department of State, 1955-58; University of Iowa, Iowa City, professor of economics, 1958-68, John F. Murray Professor of Economics, 1968—. Visiting professor, University of California, Riverside, 1962-64. Member, U.S. Delegation to United Nations Conference on Economic Development, Bangkok, Thailand, 1955, and U.S. Delegation to Colombo Plan Conference, Saigon, South Viet Nam, 1957. Head of Survey Missions, Inter-American Development Bank and Pan-American Union, 1965. *Member:* American Economic Association, Society for International Development.

WRITINGS: Basic Data of the American Economy, Irwin, 1948; *The International Economy,* Houghton, 1955; *Economic Development,* Wadsworth, 1961; *International Economics,* Houghton, 1965; *The Economy of Latin America,* University of Iowa Press, 1966; *International Economics and Business,* Houghton, 1967; *Latin America and Economic Integration,* University of Iowa Press, 1970; (with others) *International Tourism and Latin American Development,* University of Texas, Bureau of Business Research, 1973.

WORK IN PROGRESS: Reflections on Economic Development.

* * *

KRAUSS, Ruth

PERSONAL: Born in Baltimore, Md.; daughter of Julius and Blanche (Rosenfeld) Krauss; married David Johnson Leisk (a writer and illustrator under pseudonym, Crockett Johnson), 1941 (died October, 1975). *Home:* 24 Owenoke, Westport, Conn.

CAREER: Author of books for children, and poems for adults. *Member:* Authors League of America, P.E.N.

WRITINGS—All juveniles; published by Harper, except as indicated: *A Good Man and His Good Wife,* 1944; *The Great Duffy,* 1945; *The Carrot Seed,* 1946, reprinted, 1971; *The Growing Story,* 1947; *Bears,* 1948, reprinted, 1970; *The Happy Day,* 1949; *The Backward Day,* 1950; *The Bundle Book,* 1951; *A Hole Is to Dig,* 1952; *I Can Fly,* Golden Press, 1952; *The Big World and the Little House,* 1952; *A Very Special House,* 1953; *I'll Be You and You Be Me,* 1954, reprinted, 1973; *The Birthday Party,* 1955; *Charlotte and the White Horse,* 1955; *How to Make an Earthquake,* 1956; *I Want to Paint My Bathroom Blue,* 1956; *Monkey Day,* 1957; (with husband, David J. Leisk) *Is This You?,* E. M. Hale, 1958; *Somebdy Else's Nut Tree,* 1959; *Open House for Butterflies,* 1960; *A Bouquet of Littles,* 1963; *Eye Nose Fingers Toes,* 1964; *The Cantilever Rainbow,* Pantheon, 1965; *The Little King,* 1967; *The Little Queen,* 1967; *The Little Monster,* Scholastic Book Services, 1967; *Everything under a Mushroom,* Scholastic Book Services, 1967; *This Thumbprint,* 1967; *What a Fine Day For,* Parents' Magazine Press, 1967; *I Write It,* 1969; *Little King, the Little Queen, the Little Monster, and Other Stories You Can Make Up Yourself,* Scholastic Book Services, 1969; *The Happy Egg,* O'Hare Books, 1972; *Monkey Day,* Bookstore Press, 1973; *Little Boat Lighter Than a Cork,* Magic Circle, 1976; *When I Walk I Change the Earth,* Burning Deck, 1978; *Somebody Spilled the Sky,* Morrow, 1979; *Poems for People,* Morrow, 1979.

Adult poetry: *If Only: A Theatre Poem,* Toad Press, 1969; *There's a Little Ambiguity Over There among the Bluebells: Theatre Poems,* Something Else, 1968; *This Breast Gothic,* Bookstore Press, 1973. Also author of *Under Twenty.* Also author of numerous verse plays, including "A Beautiful Day," produced at Judson Poets Theatre, "Re-examination of Freedom," produced at Boston University, and "If I Were Freedom," produced at Bard College. Contributor of adult poetry to *Harper's, New World Writing, Plumed Horn, Kulchur, Locus Solus,* and other publications.

KRAUTTER, Elisa (Bialk)
(Elisa Bialk)

PERSONAL: Born in Chicago, Ill.; daughter of John and Martha (Holcher) Bialk; married L. Martin Krautter, 1934; children: Elena (Mrs. Joseph E. Lonsdorf), Elisabeth (Mrs. Alexander F. Treadwell). *Education:* Attended Northwestern University School of Journalism. *Politics:* Republican. *Religion:* Episcopalian. *Home:* 6 Century Dr., Hilton Head Island, S.C. 29928.

CAREER: Began as newspaper reporter and columnist; after marriage she turned to short story and play writing, later concentrating on writing for young people. Publicity chairman, Lawrence Hall Home for Boys, 1948-52. *Member:* Authors Guild, Society of Midland Authors (member of board of directors; chairman of program committee), Arts Club of Chicago, Theta Sigmi Phi (associate; president of chapter, 1960-62), Skokie Country Club.

WRITINGS—Under name Elisa Bialk: *On What Strange Stuff,* Doubleday, 1935; *The Horse Called Pete,* Houghton, 1948; *Taffy's Foal,* Houghton, 1949; *Ride 'em Peggy,* Houghton, 1950; *Wild Horse Island,* Houghton, 1951; *Jill's Victory,* World Publishing, 1952; *The Colt of Cripple Creek,* World Publishing, 1952; *The Silver Purse,* World Publishing, 1952; *Marty,* World Publishing, 1953; *Giant of the Rockies,* World Publishing, 1954; *Marty Goes to Hollywood,* World Publishing, 1955; *Marty on the Campus,* World Publishing, 1956; *Passport Summer,* World Publishing, 1959; *Orville Mouse at the Opera House,* Albert Whitman, 1967.

"Tizz" series, published by Childrens Press: *Tizz,* 1955; *Tizz Takes a Trip,* 1956; *. . . Plays Santa Claus,* 1957; *. . . and Company,* 1958; *. . . Is a Cow Pony,* 1961; *. . . on a Pack Trip,* 1961; *. . . in Cactus Country,* 1964; *. . . on a Horse Farm,* 1964; *. . . on a Trail Ride,* 1966; *. . . in Texas,* 1966; *. . . at the Stampede,* 1968; *. . . in the Rockies,* 1968; *. . . at the Fiesta,* 1970; *. . . South of the Border,* 1970.

Also author of a play, "The Sainted Sisters." Contributor of approximately 200 short stories and articles to *Saturday Evening Post, McCall's,* and other publications.

WORK IN PROGRESS: A cookbook; a book on sculpture.

SIDELIGHTS: Elisa Krautter has been writing since high school, although her material, at that time, was aimed at a primarily adult audience. Her career as a children's author began with a request from her own children, who asked that she write something for them. In addition to her work in juvenile fiction, Krautter has written several articles and short stories for popular adult magazines. Her play, "The Sainted Sisters," was adapted as a film and released by Paramount Pictures in 1948.

AVOCATIONAL INTERESTS: Gourmet cooking, sculpture, and swimming.

* * *

KREPPS, Robert W(ilson) 1919-1980
(Beatrice Brandon; Jake Logan, a house pseudonym)

PERSONAL: Born December 11, 1919, in Pittsburgh, Pa.; died January 24, 1980; son of James Robert and Vera (Keebler) Krepps; married Nina Vaccaro, 1953 (deceased, 1969). *Education:* Westminster College, New Wilmington, Pa., A.B., 1941. *Home:* 501 38th Ave. N., St. Petersburg, Fla. 33704. *Agent:* Knox Burger Associates, 39½ Washington Sq. S., New York, N.Y. 10012.

CAREER: Westinghouse Electric Co., Pittsburgh, Pa., expediter, 1942-45; free-lance writer, 1946-59; U.S. Steel Corp., Monroeville, Pa., technical editor, 1959-61, administrative assistant, 1961-65, assistant to visual-aids chief, 1966-69; free-lance writer, 1969-80.

WRITINGS: The Field of Night, Rinehart, 1948; *The Courts of the Lion,* Rinehart, 1950; *Tell It on the Drums,* Macmillan, 1955; *Earthshaker,* Macmillan, 1958; *Gamble My Last Game,* Macmillan, 1958; *Baboon Rock,* Macmillan, 1959; *Fancy,* Little, Brown, 1969.

Novelizations of films; all published by Gold Medal: *The Big Gamble,* 1961; *El Cid,* 1961; *Boys' Night Out,* 1962; *Taras Bulba,* 1962; *Send Me No Flowers,* 1964; *Stagecoach,* 1966; *Hour of the Gun,* 1967.

With Barbara Van Tuyl: "The Bonnie Books for Girls of All Ages" series, published by Signet Books: *Sweet Running Filly,* 1971; *A Horse Called Bonnie,* 1971; *Sunbonnet: Filly of the Year,* 1973; *Bonnie and the Haunted Farm,* 1974; *The Betrayal of Bonnie,* 1975.

Under pseudonym Beatrice Brandon: *The Cliffs of Night,* Doubleday, 1974; *The Court of Silver Shadows,* Doubleday, 1980.

Under pseudonym Jake Logan: *Outlaw Blood,* Playboy Press, 1977.

Also author of more than four hundred short stories and novelettes published between 1942 and 1956 in *Saturday Evening Post, Collier's, Country Gentleman, Argosy,* and other magazines.

WORK IN PROGRESS: A novel of voodoo in modern Haiti, for Playboy Press; two books on the history of the Zulu nation; a book based on the old Norse religion and dealing with the various theories and concepts of time.

SIDELIGHTS: Robert Krepps told *CA:* "Advice to aspiring writers? I'm only competent to advise in my own field—go everywhere, listen intently, read your eyeballs crimson, and write of what you know, . . . and if you know it second hand, as I know nineteenth-century Africa, then research every bloody word you put on paper. Ignore what doesn't interest you, for you can't produce artificial zest that will stand scrutiny; there ought to be at least a thousand subjects you can write about with gusto. Oh, and learn grammar! Too many writers don't, but leave it to their editors to make corrections. That's flaccid and despicable. Hemingway knew grammar down to the ground and he did pretty well. . . . I'm proud to belong to the third oldest profession, that of storyteller. Humanity needs the entertainer as much as it needs the policeman, the farmer, and the builder. It sounds pompous, but it's true: we minister to the soul."

* * *

KRUGER, Arthur N(ewman) 1916-

PERSONAL: Born February 4, 1916, in Boston, Mass.; son of Samuel and Minnie (Meline) Kruger; married Eleanor Weisbrot, 1941; children: Robert S., Marylin J. *Education:* Attended City College of New York (now City College of the City University of New York), 1932-34; University of Alabama, A.B., 1936; Louisiana State University, Ph.D., 1941. *Home:* 28 Maytime Dr., Jericho, N.Y. *Office:* C. W. Post College, Long Island University, Greenvale, N.Y.

CAREER: Essex Junior College, Newark, N.J., instructor, 1940-41; North Carolina State University at Raleigh (now University of North Carolina), instructor, 1941-42; Empco, Atlantic City, N.J., vice-president, 1946-47; Wilkes College, Wilkes-Barre, Pa., assistant professor, 1947-54, associate professor, 1954-59, professor, 1959-62, director of forensics, 1947-62; Long Island University, C. W. Post College, Greenvale, N.Y., professor, 1962—, chairman of department of speech communication and director of forensics, 1962-76. Director of Eastern Debate Institute, 1965—. *Military service:* U.S. Army, Signal Corps, Signal Intelligence Service and Office of Strategic Services, 1942-46; became first lieutenant; received four battle stars, two Presidential Unit Citations. *Member:* American Association of University Professors (treasurer, C. W. Post College chapter, 1968-69), National Council of Teachers of English, College English Association, Speech Association of America, American Forensic Association, International Platform Association, Rhetoric Society of America, Speech Association of Eastern States, Debating Association of Pennsylvania Colleges (vice-president, 1955-56; president, 1956-57), Phi Delta Kappa (chapter president, 1947-48), Delta Sigma Rho-Tau Kappa Alpha.

WRITINGS: Modern Debate: Its Logic and Strategy, McGraw, 1960; (co-author) *Championship Debating,* J. Weston Walch, 1961; *A Classified Bibliography of Argumentation and Debate,* Scarecrow, 1964, revised edition published as *Argumentation and Debate: A Classified Bibliography,* 1974; *Counterpoint: Debates on Debate,* Scarecrow, 1966; (co-author) *Championship Debating II,* J. Weston Walch, 1966; (co-author) *Essentials of Logic,* American Book Co., 1968, revised edition published as *Logic: The Essentials,* McGraw, 1976; (co-author) *Workbook for Essentials of Logic,* American Book Co., 1968; (contributor) *The Rhetoric of Our Times,* Appleton-Century-Crofts, 1969; *Effective Speaking: A Complete Course,* Van Nostrand, 1970; (contributor) *The Comparative Advantage Case,* Championship Debate Enterprises, 1970; (contributor) *Ventures in Research,* C. W. Post Center, 1974. Contributor of over thrity-five articles to argumentation, speech communication, and philosophy journals. Editor, *Bulletin* of Debating Association of Pennsylvania Colleges.

WORK IN PROGRESS: Speech Communication: Principles and Practices; Selected Papers on Argumentation, 1952-1976.

SIDELIGHTS: Arthur Kruger told *CA:* "My primary objective both as a writer and as a teacher has been to inculcate in students a respect for reason—for critical thinking, for reasoned discourse, and for rational decision-making. Practically all of my published work deals with such concepts and disciplines, which I believe are often sadly neglected in formal education. I deplore the low regard which many students and instructors seem to have for scientific method and their uncritical acceptance of what often seem to be irrational doctrines. I believe that a liberal democracy can function effectively only when people cultivate what John Dewey once called 'deep-seated and effective habits of discriminating tested beliefs from mere assertions.'"

AVOCATIONAL INTERESTS: Reading, music art, bridge, and travelling.

BIOGRAPHICAL/CRITICAL SOURCES: Wilkes-Barre, Pa., Sunday *Independent,* January 30, 1955, December 1, 1957; Wilkes-Barre *Record,* June 2, 1960, April 24, 1961; Wilkes-Barre *Times-Leader,* June 3, 1960.

* * *

KULKARNI, Hemant B(alvantrao) 1916-

PERSONAL: Born November 25, 1916, in Kadapur, India; son of Balvantrao Kadapurkar (a revenue clerk) and Laxmi (Joshi) Kulkarni; married Yamuna Baji, June 17, 1941; children: Ravi, Teja (Mrs. L. G. Kuratti), Jayashri (Mrs. S. Desai), Pramod. *Education:* Bombay University, B.A., 1937, M.A., 1939; University of Utah, Ph.D., 1962. *Home:* 1510 East 1100 North, Logan, Utah 84321. *Office:* Department of English, Utah State University, Logan, Utah 84322.

CAREER: Osmania University, Hyderabad, India, reader in English, 1950-58, 1963-67; University of Utah, Salt Lake City, lecturer in English, 1961-63; Utah State University, Logan, assistant professor, 1967-69, associate professor of English, 1969—. *Member:* South Asian Literary Association (president, 1976—), London Poetry Society (president of Hyderabad chapter, 1964-66), Modern Language Association of America, Rocky Mountain Modern Language Association, Utah Academy of Arts, Letters and Sciences, Phi Kappa Phi. *Awards, honors:* League of Utah Writers second prize in poetry and first prize in article writing, both 1972; Utah State University College of Humanities, Arts, and Social Sciences Humanist of the Year Award, 1978.

WRITINGS: Stephen Spender: Poet in Crisis, Utah State University Press, 1970; *Moby-Dick: A Hindu Avatar,* Utah State University Press, 1970; *Exploring Roots* (poems), Omnipress, 1972; *In the Country of Black Mother* (poems), Prairie Poet Books, 1975; *Stephen Spender: Annotated Bibliography,* Garland Publishing, 1976; *Morning Dew* (poems), Creative Arts Enterprise, 1976; *Wedding Flame* (poems), Alliance for Varied Arts, 1977; *Driftwood from the Beach* (poems), United Writers (Calcutta), 1979; *The Flaming Sword* (poems), United Writers, 1979. Also author of a play, novels, and poetry in the Kannada language.

WORK IN PROGRESS: Two books of poems, *Tilted towards Dawn* and *Barbed Wire,* both for United Writers; *Oriental Perspectives on Literature: A Collection of Essays on American, English and Indian Literature.*

* * *

KUMIN, Maxine (Winokur) 1925-

PERSONAL: Born June 6, 1925, in Philadelphia, Pa.; daughter of Peter and Doll (Simon) Winokur; married Victor Montwid Kumin, June 29, 1946; children: Jane Simon, Judith Montwid, Daniel David. *Education:* Radcliffe College, A.B., 1946, A.M., 1948. *Residence:* Warner, N.H. 03278. *Agent:* Curtis Brown, 575 Madison Ave., New York, N.Y. 10022.

CAREER: Tufts University, Medford, Mass., instructor, 1958-61, lecturer in English, 1965-68; Radcliffe College, Cambridge, Mass., scholar of Radcliffe Institute for Independent Study, 1961-63; University of Massachusetts—Amherst, visiting lecturer in English, 1973; Columbia University, New York, N.Y., adjunct professor of writing, 1975; Brandeis University, Waltham, Mass., Fannie Hurst Professor of Literature, 1975; Princeton University, Princeton, N.J., visiting senior fellow and lecturer, 1977; Washington University, St. Louis, Mo., Fannie Hurst Professor of Literature, 1977; Randolph-Macon Woman's College, Lynchburg, Va., Carolyn Wilkerson Bell Visiting Scholar, 1978. Member of staff, Bread Loaf Writers' Conference, 1969-71, 1973, 1975, 1977. Poetry consultant to Library of Congress, 1981—. *Member:* Poetry Society of America, Radcliffe Alumnae Association. *Awards, honors:* Lowell Mason Palmer Award, 1960; National Endowment for the Arts grant, 1966; National Council on the Arts and Humanities fellow, 1967-68; William Marion Reedy Award, 1968; Eunice Tietjens Memorial Prize, *Poetry,* 1972; Pulitzer Prize for poetry, 1973, for *Up Country;* Borestone Mountain Award, 1976; D.Hum.Lett., Centre College, 1976, and Davis and Elkins College, 1977; Radcliffe College Alumnae Recognition Award, 1978.

WRITINGS—Poetry: *Halfway,* Holt, 1961; *The Privilege,* Harper, 1965; *The Nightmare Factory,* Harper, 1970; *Up Country,* Harper, 1972; *House, Bridge, Fountain, Gate,* Viking, 1975; *The Retrieval System,* Viking, 1978.

Novels: *Through Dreams of Love,* Harper, 1965 (published in England as *A Daughter and Her Loves,* Gollancz, 1965); *The Passions of Uxport,* Harper, 1968; *The Abduction,* Harper, 1971; *The Designated Heir,* Viking, 1974.

Juvenile; all published by Putnam, except as indicated: *Sebastian and the Dragon,* 1960; *Spring Things,* 1961; *A Summer Story,* 1961; *Follow the Fall,* 1961; *A Winter Friend,* 1961; *Mittens in May,* 1962; *No One Writes a Letter to the Snail,* 1962; (with Anne Sexton) *Eggs of Things,* 1963; *Archibald the Traveling Poodle,* 1963; (with Sexton) *More Eggs of Things,* 1964; *Speedy Digs Downside Up,* 1964; *The Beach before Breakfast,* 1964; *Paul Bunyan,* 1966; *Faraway Farm,* Norton, 1967; *The Wonderful Babies of 1809 and Other Years,* 1968; *When Grandmother Was Young,* 1969; *When Mother Was Young,* 1970; *When Great-Grandmother Was Young,* 1971; (with Sexton) *Joey and the Birthday Present,* McGraw, 1971; (with Sexton) *The Wizard's Tears,* McGraw, 1975; *What Color Is Caesar?,* McGraw, 1978.

Former columnist, *Writer.* Contributor of poetry to *New Yorker, Atlantic, Poetry, Saturday Review,* and other periodicals.

SIDELIGHTS: Maxine Kumin believes that a poet must be "terribly specific about naming things . . . bringing them back to the world's attention [and] dealing with things that are small and overlooked." Her Pulitzer Prizewinning poetry has won critical acclaim for doing just that. "Kumin doesn't miss a speck." Barbara Fialkowski writes in *Shenandoah,* "Her drive for detail and her compulsion to name recall Thoreau." Harvey Curtis Webster, writing in *Poetry,* praises her "accurate specificity" while a reviewer for *Choice* notes that Kumin's poetry possesses "a detailed knowledge of closely observed natural phenomena. Similarly, all of her imagery is clear, sharp, and concrete." Jane Howard adds that Kumin "brings tastes, sounds, textures, smells, and the look of things to vivid life." Reviewing her book *Up Country,* Ralph J. Mills, Jr. states that "she steeps herself . . . in the actualities of soil, pond, trees, . . . and so forth. As John Ciardi says of her accuracy with respect to the reality her poems render: 'She teaches me, by example, to use my own eyes. When she looks at something I have seen, she makes me see it better. When she looks at something I do not know, I therefore trust her.' "

BIOGRAPHICAL/CRITICAL SOURCES: Saturday Review, May 6, 1961, December 25, 1965, May 9, 1970; *Christian Science Monitor,* August 9, 1961, February 28, 1973; *Choice,* January, 1966; *New York Times Book Review,* May 5, 1968, November 19, 1972, June 23, 1974, April 23, 1978; *Book World,* May 5, 1968; *Yale Review,* autumn, 1968; *Writer,* April, 1970; *Virginia Quarterly Review,* spring, 1971; *Atlantic,* October, 1971; *New Yorker,* December 4, 1971; *New Leader,* January 22, 1973; *Parnassus,* spring/summer, 1973; *Sewanee Review,* spring, 1974; *New York Times,* June 26, 1974; *New Republic,* August 10, 1974; *Village Voice,* September 5, 1974; *Massachusetts Review,* spring, 1975; *Times Literary Supplement,* May 9, 1975; *Yankee,* December, 1975; *Contemporary Literary Criticism,* Gale, Volume V, 1976, Volume XIII, 1980; *Shenandoah,* spring, 1976; *American Poetry Review,* March, 1976, November, 1978; *Prairie Schooner,* spring, 1976; *Nation,* November 11, 1978; *Poetry,* January, 1979; *Washington Post,* May 6, 1980.

KUSLAN, Louis I(saac) 1922-

PERSONAL: Born February 14, 1922, in New Haven, Conn.; son of Joseph (a grocer) and Rebecca (Tucker) Kuslan; married Dorothy Jane Morris, June 22, 1947; children: James George, Richard David. *Education:* University of Connecticut, B.S., 1943; Yale University, M.A., 1947, Ph.D., 1954, postdoctoral fellow, 1966-67. *Religion:* Judaism. *Home:* 90 Robinwood Rd., Hamden, Conn. 06517. *Office:* Department of Chemistry, Southern Connecticut State College, New Haven, Conn. 06515.

CAREER: High school science teacher in Lebanon and Glastonbury, Conn., 1943-45; University of Connecticut, Waterbury, instructor in chemistry, 1945-47; Southern Connecticut State College, New Haven, instructor, 1950-54, assistant professor, 1954-57, associate professor, 1957-60, professor of chemistry, 1960-66, dean of arts and sciences, 1966-78, professor of chemistry, 1978—. Director of University Research Institute of Connecticut, 1968—, and of New Haven Institute of Allied Health Careers, 1971—. *Member:* American Association for the Advancement of Science (fellow), National Association for Research in Science Teaching, National Science Teachers Association, History of Science Society, Connecticut Science Teachers Association, Phi Delta Kappa.

WRITINGS: (With A. Harris Stone) *Teaching Children Science,* Wadsworth, 1968, 2nd edition, 1972; *Readings on Teaching Children Science,* Wadsworth, 1969; (with Stone) *Liebig: The Master Chemist,* Prentice-Hall, 1969; (with Stone) *Robert Boyle,* Prentice-Hall, 1970; (contributor) Leonard Wilson, editor, *Benjamin Silliman and His Circle,* Neale Watson, 1979; *Connecticut Science, Technology and Medicine in the Era of the American Revolution,* Connecticut Bicentennial Commission, 1979; *Projects in Physical Science,* Prentice-Hall, 1980. Contributor to proceedings and to *Science Teacher* and *Journal of the History of Medicine and Allied Sciences.*

* * *

KWITNY, Jonathan 1941-

PERSONAL: Born March 23, 1941, in Indianapolis, Ind.; son of I. J. (a physician) and Julia (Goldberger) Kwitny; married Martha Kaplan (a lawyer), June 2, 1968 (died June 19, 1978); children: Carolyn, Susanna. *Education:* University of Missouri, B.J., 1962; New York University, M.A., 1964. *Office: Wall Street Journal,* 22 Cortlandt St., New York, N.Y. 10007.

CAREER: Reporter, *News Tribune,* Perth Amboy, N.J., 1963-65 and 1967-69, *New York Post,* New York City, 1969, and *Wall Street Journal,* New York City, 1971—. U.S. Peace Corps volunteer in Benin City, Nigeria, 1965-66. *Awards, honors:* First prize from New Jersey Press Association, 1964 and 1967, for distinguished public service.

WRITINGS—All nonfiction, except as indicated: *The Fountain Pen Conspiracy,* Knopf, 1973; *The Mullendore Murder Case,* Farrar, Straus, 1974; *Shakedown* (novel), Putnam, 1977; *Vicious Circles: The Mafia in the Marketplace,* Norton, 1979.

SIDELIGHTS: "We ought to come away from reading Jonathan Kwitny's [*Vicious Circles*] in a state of shock and loathing," notes Christopher Lehmann-Haupt of the *New York Times.* A report on the pervasive presence of the Mafia in the American marketplace (including various food-processing industries, the Teamsters union, and banking and stockbrokering, to name only a few areas the book covers), *Vicious Circles* "presents a hellish view of American society, particularly life in New York City and environs," continues Lehmann-Haupt. "[Kwitny's] report begins and ends with meat. . . . It should all be quite enough to turn a red-blooded steak gnasher into a parsnip-guzzling vegetarian. . . . In between there is not a page that doesn't impress you with how energetically the author has pursued his prey, how deep he has dug for all his facts, and how much in the way of hard detail he has crammed into every bulging paragraph."

Nevertheless, reports the critic, "*Vicious Circles* is a snarl in both senses of the word. It is true that the author emerges now and then from his forest of facts to deliver a strong editorial opinion. . . . But such editorial comment, whatever its validity, gets lost in the storm of investigative detail, in a book that is badly organized, poorly edited and abysmally proofread. Where we ought to be impressed by the detail, we are simply numbed."

"Even worse," concludes Lehmann-Haupt, "all sense of proportion is lacking. . . . Mr. Kwitny, by omission, makes it look as if there are [no honest people or businesses in New York City]. . . . Is it actually possible to be boring on the subject of the Mafia? . . . Mr. Kwitny proves that it is. . . . One would almost prefer that the Mafia had been romanticized."

Thomas Powers of the *New York Times Book Review,* on the other hand, is glad that Kwitny does not try to romanticize the Mafia and its activities. After noting that "even the most jaded citizen is likely to come away from his meticulous book with an angry, helpless understanding of how the Mafia manages to shrug off the law and thrive," Powers writes: "Mr. Kwitny's Mafia does not sound much like Mario Puzo's or Gay Talese's. The names are mostly Italian, but there the likeness ends. Mr. Kwitny is not interested in Sicilian melodrama, blood oaths, territorial wars or the other staples of the movie Mafia, but in the hundred variations of the fix. His book has its failings. A chapter on a lunch-wagon racket in New York City's outer boroughs seems trivial. There is more on the Teamsters than a book about the Mafia strictly ought to have. The precise role of the Mafia in some of the frauds Mr. Kwitny describes is a bit tenuous. The factual details are a mighty ocean, the point at times a feeble stream. But every book has something wrong with it, and these are the faults, perhaps inevitable, of sobriety. Jonathan Kwitny intends to argue two related points, and he does so effectively. The first is that while the Mafia may kill one another, they certainly do not steal from one another. Their victims are ordinary people. . . . Mr. Kwitny's second point is that the Mafia gets away with it because we let them."

Robert Sherrill of the *Washington Post* also disagrees with Lehmann-Haupt's assessment of *Vicious Circles.* Admitting that "the sweep of Kwitny's presentation is so extensive . . . and the crimes are sometimes so intricate, and the hoodlum interrelationship so complex, that the effort to keep them all sorted out finally leaves the brain sodden," Sherrill concludes that "that reaction, in fact, simply proves the virtue of this book. It is a marvelous piece of grotesque art. It is like an enormous mural by Hieronymus Bosch in which hundreds of strange evil creatures perform their perversions against a background of tangled underbrush. One cannot grasp it all at one viewing, and one's stomach rebels at the thought of viewing it twice. So one comes away not so much with the memory of details as with a diffuse, unsettling, unforgettable impression. . . . In isolating details one actually loses the sense of *Vicious Circles.* Its emphasis is on the genre: the unconscionable corporation, the unreal judge, the hermaphroditic (ethically speaking) lawyer. Above all, *Vi-*

cious Circles addresses itself to the most pressing moral questions of our time.''

BIOGRAPHICAL/CRITICAL SOURCES: New York Times, April 5, 1979; *New York Times Book Review,* April 15, 1979; *America,* May 5, 1979; *Washington Post Book World,* May 13, 1979; *Los Angeles Times,* June 22, 1979; *Best Sellers,* July, 1979.

L

LACOSTE, Paul 1923-

PERSONAL: Born April 24, 1923, in Montreal, Quebec, Canada; son of Emile (a wing commander) and Juliette (Boucher) Lacoste; married Louise Mackay, June 19, 1948 (divorced, 1968); married Louise Marcel, August 31, 1973; children (previous marriage) Helene. *Education:* Universite de Montreal, B.A., 1943, M.A., 1944, L.Ph., 1946, LL.L., 1960; Universite de Paris, doctorate in philosophy, 1948. *Home:* 356 Woodlea Ave., Montreal, Quebec, Canada H3P 1R5. *Office address:* Rector, Universite de Montreal, P.O. Box 6128, Montreal, Quebec, Canada H3C 3J7.

CAREER: Universite de Montreal, Montreal, Quebec, professor of philosophy, 1946—, professor of law, 1960-68, vice-rector, 1966-68, executive vice-rector, 1968-75, rector, 1975—, guest professor on the faculty of law, 1962-70. Practicing attorney, 1964-66. President, Conference of Rectors and Principals of Quebec Universities, 1977-79. Member of board of governors, Clinical Research Institute of Montreal, Ecole polytechnique de Montreal, Fonds international de cooperation universitaire, and other institutions; member of Superior Council of Education, 1964-68, Quebec Education Council, 1964-68, Royal Commission on Bilingualism and Biculturalism, 1965-71, and Council of Quebec Universities, 1969-77; member of board of several public institutions; member of board of trustees, Canadian Human Rights Foundation, 1968—. Commentator and moderator, department of public affairs, CBC French language network, 1956-68. Member of Montreal City Council, 1970-74, and Montreal Urban Community, 1970-74.

MEMBER: Canadian Institute for Adult Education, Canadian Philosophical Association, Canadian Association of University Teachers, Association des universites partiellement ou entierement de langue francaise (president, 1978—), Association of Commonwealth Universities (member of board of governors), Association of Universities and Colleges of Canada (president, 1978-79), Canadian Bar Association, Canadian Association of Law Teachers, Association des Amis de L'Enfance (chairman of board, 1959-61), Montreal Bar Association, Montreal Museum of Fine Arts. *Awards, honors:* University of Chicago fellowship, 1946-47; Officer of the Order of Canada; LL.D. from McGill University and University of Toronto.

WRITINGS: (With others) *La crise de l'enseignement au Canada francais,* Editions du Jour, 1961; (with others) *Justice et Paix scolaire,* Editions du Jour, 1962; (with others) *A Place of Liberty,* Clarke, Irwin, 1964; (with others) *Le Canada au seuil du siecle de l'abondance,* HMH, 1969; (with others) *Education permanente et potentiel universitaire,* UNESCO-AIU, 1977. Contributor to *Encyclopedia Americana;* contributor of numerous articles on educational problems to professional journals.

*   *   *

LAKLAN, Carli 1907-
(John Clarke)

PERSONAL: Original name, Virginia Carli Laughlin; name legally changed; born 1907, in Paoli, Okla.; daughter of John Clarke and Elizabeth (Crawford) Laughlin; divorced; married James Aiello (an artist and writer), September 12, 1964. *Education:* Attended Stanford University; University of Washington, M.A., 1936; graduate study at Columbia University and New York University. *Home:* 14 Bay Ave., Sea Cliff, N.Y.

CAREER: Has worked as bank clerk, tax correspondent, dance instructor, and director of a stock company and little theater group; drama teacher at University of Washington; script writer for women's news feature and editorial program for radio station WOR, New York, N.Y., 1941-51; free-lance writer, 1951—. *Awards, honors:* Children's Book Committee Award, Child Study Association of America, 1972, for *Migrant Girl.*

WRITINGS: (With Frederick Thomas) *Gifts from Your Kitchen,* Barrows, 1955; *The Candlebook,* Barrows, 1956; *Nancy Kimball, Nurse's Aide* (juvenile), Doubleday, 1962; *Two Girls in New York* (juvenile), Doubleday, 1964; *Nancy Kimball, Nurse in Training* (juvenile), Doubleday, 1965; *Second Year Nurse,* Doubleday, 1965; *Competition Swimming,* Hawthorne, 1965; *Surf with Me* (juvenile), McGraw, 1967; *Olympic Champions: Why They Win,* Funk, 1968; *Migrant Girl* (juvenile), McGraw, 1970; *Serving in the Peace Corps,* Doubleday, 1970; *Ski Bum* (Junior Literary Guild selection), McGraw, 1973; (with Martin Chadzynski) *Runaway!,* McGraw, 1979; *Golden Girls: Stories about Women Stars of the Olympics,* McGraw, 1980.

Under pseudonym John Clarke: *High School Drop Out,* Doubleday, 1965; *Roar of Engines,* Doubleday, 1967; *Black Soldier,* Doubleday, 1968; *Sudden Iron,* McGraw, 1969.

WORK IN PROGRESS: *Golden Girls, Book II,* for McGraw.

LAKOFF, Sanford A(llan) 1931-

PERSONAL: Born May 12, 1931, in Bayonne, N.J.; son of Herman and Gertrude (Robins) Lakoff; married Evelyn Schleifer, 1961. *Education:* Brandeis University, B.A., 1953; Harvard University, Ph.D., 1959. *Home:* 3510 Dove Ct., San Diego, Calif. 92103. *Office:* Department of Political Science, University of California, San Diego, La Jolla, Calif. 92093.

CAREER: Harvard University, Cambridge, Mass., teaching fellow, 1954-56, instructor, 1958-61, assistant professor of government, 1961-65; State University of New York at Stony Brook, Long Island, associate professor of political science, 1965-67; University of Toronto, Toronto, Ontario, professor of political science, 1967-74; University of California, San Diego, La Jolla, professor of political science and chairman of department, 1975—. *Awards, honors:* Bowdoin Prize, 1955; Social Science Research Council fellow, 1957-58; Gardner fellowship, 1964; Woodrow Wilson International Center for Scholars fellow, 1973-74; Canada Council fellowship, 1973-74; National Humanities Center fellow, 1980-81.

WRITINGS: (With J. Stefan Dupre) *Science and the Nation: Policy and Politics,* Prentice-Hall, 1962; *Equality in Political Philosophy,* Harvard University Press, 1964; (editor) *Knowledge and Power,* Free Press, 1966; (editor with Maurice Cranston) *A Glossary of Political Ideas,* Basic Books, 1969; (editor with Daniel Rich) *Private Government: Introductory Readings,* Scott, Foresman, 1972; (editor) *Scientists and Ethical Responsibility,* Addison-Wesley, 1980. Contributor of chapters to several books.

* * *

LAMB, Hugh 1946-

PERSONAL: Born February 4, 1946, in Sutton, Surrey, England; son of Charles (a plumber) and Joyce (Russell) Lamb; married Susan Tadgell, September 30, 1967; children: Richard, Andrew. *Education:* Attended county school in Sutton, England. *Politics:* "Left wing but not avidly so." *Home:* 10 The Crescent, Westmead Rd., Sutton, Surrey, England.

CAREER: Journalist and editor; free-lance editor, beginning 1972.

WRITINGS—Editor; published by W. H. Allen, except as indicated: *A Tide of Terror,* 1972, Taplinger, 1973; *A Wave of Fear,* 1973, Taplinger, 1974; *Victorian Tales of Terror,* 1974, Taplinger, 1975; *Sixteen Grusel Stories,* Heyne, 1974; *The Thrill of Horror,* Taplinger, 1975; *Terror by Gaslight,* 1975, Taplinger, 1976; *The Star Book of Horror,* Star Books, Number I, 1975, Number II, 1976; *The Taste of Fear,* Taplinger, 1976; *Return from the Grave,* 1976, Taplinger, 1977; *Victorian Nightmares,* Taplinger, 1977; *Cold Fear,* 1977, Taplinger, 1978; *The Man Wolf and Other Horrors,* 1978; *Forgotten Tales of Terror,* Eyre Methuen, 1978; *Tales from a Gaslit Graveyard,* 1979; *New Tales of Terror,* Magnum Publications, 1980; *The Best Tales of Terror of Erckmann-Chatrain,* Millington Books, 1980. Also editor of *Strange Stories, And Midnight Never Came, Gaslit Nightmares,* and *The Best Tales of Terror of Bernard Capes.*

WORK IN PROGRESS: Researching old and new stories in the macabre vein by known and unknown authors, and preparing further anthologies.

* * *

LAMBERT, Gavin 1924-

PERSONAL: Born July 23, 1924, in Sussex, England; naturalized U.S. citizen, 1964; son of Mervyn and Vera (Pembroke) Lambert. *Education:* Attended Cheltenham College and Magdalen College, Oxford. *Residence:* Tangiers, Morocco. *Agent:* Harold Matson Co., Inc., 22 East 40th St., New York, N.Y. 10016.

CAREER: Wrote short stories for British magazines, London, England, 1947-50; edited film magazine, *Sight and Sound,* 1950-56; free-lance writer, 1957—. *Member:* Writers Guild of America West. *Awards, honors:* Thomas R. Coward Memorial Award, 1966, for *Norman's Letter.*

WRITINGS: *The Slide Area,* Viking, 1960; *Inside Daisy Clover,* Viking, 1963; *Norman's Letter,* Coward, 1966; *A Case for the Angels,* Dial, 1968; *The Goodbye People,* Simon & Schuster, 1971; *On Cukor,* W. H. Allen, 1972, Putnam, 1973; *GWTW: The Making of 'Gone with the Wind',* Little, Brown, 1973; *The Dangerous Edge,* Barrie & Jenkins, 1975, Viking, 1976; *In the Night All Cats Are Grey,* W. H. Allen, 1976.

Motion picture scripts: "Another Sky," 1956; "Bitter Victory," Columbia, 1958; "Sons and Lovers," Twentieth Century-Fox, 1960; "The Roman Spring of Mrs. Stone," Warner Brothers, 1961; "Inside Daisy Clover," Warner Brothers, 1965; "I Never Promised You a Rose Garden," 1978.

Contributor of articles to *New Statesman, Observer, Harper's Bazaar,* and other periodicals. Founder, *Sequence* (magazine).

WORK IN PROGRESS: A novel; a play.

SIDELIGHTS: Gavin Lambert wrote and directed the film "Another Sky" in Morocco in 1956. He has traveled in Europe and North Africa. *Avocational interests:* Reading, music, the beach.

BIOGRAPHICAL/CRITICAL SOURCES: *Times Literary Supplement,* June 30, 1966, September 7, 1973; *Atlantic,* August, 1966; *National Observer,* August 8, 1966; *Time,* August 19, 1966, October 29, 1973; *Harper's,* September, 1966; *Nation,* October 3, 1966; *Hudson Review,* winter, 1966-67; *New York Times Book Review,* April 14, 1968; *Book World,* May 5, 1968; *Punch,* August 7, 1968; *New Republic,* April 3, 1971, June 5, 1976; *America,* April 17, 1971; *New Statesman,* February 18, 1972; *Spectator,* February 26, 1972, June 28, 1978; *Saturday Review,* December 2, 1972; *Film Quarterly,* summer, 1973; *Books & Bookmen,* July, 1973; *New York Times,* November 17, 1973; *New York Review of Books,* November 29, 1973, April 29, 1976; *Listener,* May 27, 1976; *Twentieth Century Literature,* October, 1976; *Georgia Review,* summer, 1978.

* * *

LAMPE, David 1923-

PERSONAL: Born December 26, 1923, in Baltimore, Md.; son of David and Hattie (Singer) Lampe; married Patience Ann Saunders, 1958; children: David Samuel. *Education:* Attended Johns Hopkins University. *Address:* 40 Church Rd., Brightlingsea, Essex, England.

CAREER: David Lampe Advertising Co., Baltimore, Md., member of staff, 1946-50; free-lance writer, 1952—. *Military service:* U.S. Army, 1942-46. U.S. Air Force, 1950-52; became sergeant.

WRITINGS: *The Savage Canary: The Story of Resistance in Denmark,* Cassell, 1957, reprinted, Corgi Books, 1976, published as *The Danish Resistance,* Ballantine, 1960; *Pyke, The Unknown Genius,* Evans, 1959; (with Laszio Szenasi) *The*

Self-Made Villian: A Biography of I. T. Trebitsch-Lincoln, Cassell, 1961; *The Tunnel: The Story of the World's First Tunnel under a Navigable River Dug beneath the Thames, 1824-1842,* Harrap, 1963; *The Last Ditch,* Putnam, 1968. Contributor to British Broadcasting Corp. programs. Contributor to magazines and newspapers in North America, Europe, and Australia.

SIDELIGHTS: In *The Last Ditch* David Lampe details the little-known British plan for the organization of a resistance force to counter a possible German invasion during World War II. A reviewer for *Best Sellers* writes: "The lid has been removed from the story, kept tightly covered during World War II and even kept secret by many of its actors to this day, of the plans for fighting 'to the last ditch' should Hitler have ordered the invasion of Britain.... The fantastic story is told here—how the underground hideouts were made with such utter secrecy that people living in the vicinity were not aware of them, how resistance units trained at night and in all weathers to perfect skills in behind-the-enemy-line infiltration." Peter Fleming says that "this skeleton force, officially known as 'Auxiliary Units' was based on underground rural hideouts stocked with rations, weapons and demolition equipment. The nucleus of each unit consisted of one officer and a so-called 'striking force' of a dozen soldiers; to this nucleus were linked 'cells' of Home Guard personnel, covering a wide area and selected for their supposed suitability for guerrilla warfare.... As it happens, I was the first commander of the first Auxiliary Unit, and it goes against the grain to criticize a book in which I make frequent and creditable appearances as a sort of cross between Errol Flynn and Chingachgook.... But honesty compels me to warn Lampe's readers that accuracy is not his strong point." Fleming goes on to report that Lampe, "whose opinion of the military capabilities of Auxiliary Units is a great deal higher than any held at the time, nowhere gives an estimate of their operational value if the Germans had made a successful landing in September 1940.... My own guess is that we might, with luck, have justified our existence in the early stages but that reprisals against the civilian population would have put us out of business before long."

BIOGRAPHICAL/CRITICAL SOURCES: Observer Review, March 24, 1968; *Punch,* April 10, 1968; *Book World,* June 2, 1968; *Best Sellers,* June 15, 1968; *Listener,* December 19, 1968; *Spectator,* March 29, 1969.†

* * *

LANCIANO, Claude O(lwen), Jr. 1922-

PERSONAL: Born June 12, 1922, in Philadelphia, Pa.; son of Claude Olwen (an attorney) and Cathryn (Conte) Lanciano; married Arline Scheibel (a real estate broker), June 8, 1943; children: Claude Olwen III, Sheran (Mrs. John Hodges), Scott, Darwin. *Education:* Attended U.S. Naval Academy, 1940-43; American University, B.S. (with distinction), 1949; additional study at Case Institute of Technology (now Case Western Reserve University), College of William and Mary, Army Management School, and Industrial College of the Armed Forces. *Politics:* Independent. *Religion:* Agnostic. *Home and office address:* Lands End, Route 3, Box 370, Gloucester, Va. 23061.

CAREER: U.S. Department of Defense, Washington, D.C., and Ft. Eustis, Va., technical intelligence analyst, engineer, and research analyst, 1945-70. Director of Peoples National Bank of Gloucester (Va.), 1965-68. *Military service:* U.S. Navy, 1940-43. U.S. Maritime Service, 1943-45; retired as lieutenant commander.

WRITINGS: Radio Navigational Aids, Hydrographic Office, 1947; *Manual of Ice Seamanship,* Hydrographic Office, 1948; *Legends of Lands End,* Lands End Books, 1971; *Captain John Sinclair of Virginia,* Lands End Books, 1973; *Rosewell: Garland of Virginia,* Lands End Books, 1978; *Our Most Skillful Architect: Richard Taliaferro and Associated Colonial Virginia Constructions,* Lands End Books, 1980.

SIDELIGHTS: On the topic of Virginia's history, especially that of his home county, Gloucester, Claude O. Lanciano, Jr. writes: "I live in an area thrice wounded. Standing not far from Williamsburg and Yorktown in the state of Virginia, conceded to be [a] prime mover in the declaration of [the] Union, Gloucester was a leading county. Her first major injury was loss by fire of her colonial records in 1820. As a precaution, the surviving documents were sent to Richmond in 1860, only to be burned in that tragic conflagration. The third wound [the Civil War] was suffered by the full South as the general malaise of defeat requiring nearly a century for recovery.

"[These] three hurts contrast with a gallant but neglected and damaged pageant of events in Virginia in general, and Gloucester in particular. Addressing [these] voids is as satisfying as it is compelling."

* * *

LANGBAUM, Robert (Woodrow) 1924-

PERSONAL: Born February 23, 1924, in New York, N.Y.; son of Murray (a businessman) and Nettie (Moskowitz) Langbaum; married Francesca Levi Vidale, November 5, 1950; children: Donata Emily. *Education:* Cornell University, A.B., 1947; Columbia University, M.A., 1949, Ph.D., 1954. *Residence:* Charlottesville, Va. *Office:* Department of English, University of Virginia, Charlottesville, Va. 22901.

CAREER: Cornell University, Ithaca, N.Y., instructor, 1950-55, assistant professor of English, 1955-60; University of Virginia, Charlottesville, associate professor, 1960-63, professor, 1963-67, James Branch Cabell Professor of English and American Literature, 1967—. Visiting professor at Columbia University, 1965-66, and Harvard University, summer, 1965. *Military service:* U.S. Army, Military Intelligence Service, 1942-46; served as translator of Japanese; became first lieutenant. *Member:* Modern Language Association of America, American Association of University Professors. *Awards, honors:* Ford Foundation fellow, Center for Advanced Study, 1961-62; American Council of Learned Societies grants, 1961, 1975-76; Guggenheim fellowship, 1969-70; National Endowment for the Humanities senior fellow, 1972-73.

WRITINGS—Criticism, except as indicated: *The Poetry of Experience: The Dramatic Monologue in Modern Literary Tradition,* Random House, 1957, 2nd edition, Norton, 1971; *The Gayety of Vision: A Study of Isak Dinesen's Art,* Chatto & Windus, 1964, Random House, 1965, 2nd edition published as *Isak Dinesen's Art: The Gayety of Vision,* University of Chicago Press, 1975; (editor) William Shakespeare, *The Tempest* (play), New American Library, 1964; (editor) *The Victorian Age: Essays in History and in Social and Literary Criticism,* Fawcett, 1967; *The Modern Spirit: Essays on the Continuity of Nineteenth-and Twentieth-Century Literature,* Oxford University Press (New York), 1970; (contributor) *The Complete Signet Classic Shakespeare* (collection), Harcourt, 1972; (contributor) A. Walton Litz, editor, *Eliot in His Time,* Princeton University Press, 1973; (contributor) J. L. Altholz, editor, *The Mind and Art of Victorian England,* University of Minnesota Press, 1976; *The Myster-*

ies of Identity: A Theme in Modern Literature, Oxford University Press, 1977.

Contributor of articles and reviews to numerous literary journals, including *Commentary, American Scholar, Yale Review, PMLA, Partisan Review, Novel, Southern Review, Times Literary Supplement, New York Times Book Review,* and *American Poetry Review.* Member of editorial board, *Victorian Poetry,* 1963, *Style,* 1967, *New Literary History,* 1969, *Bulletin of Research in the Humanities,* 1977, *South Atlantic Bulletin,* 1978, *Studies in English Literature,* 1978, *Southern Humanities Review,* 1979, and *National Forum,* 1979.

SIDELIGHTS: Robert Langbaum is a highly regarded literary critic whose "continuing interest," notes a reviewer for the *Times Literary Supplement,* is "the preoccupation with myth, tradition, and identity, in literature from the Romantic period to the present day." Langbaum attained prominence with the publication of his first book, *The Poetry of Experience,* a critical essay that proposed a connection between the poetic themes of nineteenth- and twentieth-century authors, with a particular emphasis on the study of Robert Browning, Alfred Tennyson, and William Wordsworth. Langbaum's work drew scholarly attention for its innovative and provocative approach to the dramatic monologues of Browning and Tennyson. In *Books and Bookmen* Michael Mason writes: "Robert Langbaum became widely known in academic circles with his first book, *The Poetry of Experience*. . . . One thing which made this book impressive was that Langbaum wrote excitingly about the dramatic monologues of Browning and Tennyson—poems which had never attracted critical writing that seemed adequate to their virtuosity and newness. Indeed until Langbaum's contribution the standard books and articles on the subject formed one of the dreariest tracts in all English critical discourse." And the *Times'* critic maintains that "*The Poetry of Experience* . . . remains one of the finest studies of nineteenth-century English poetry yet written."

For the most part, Langbaum's subsequent works have been similarly acclaimed. James R. Kincaid of the *Virginia Quarterly Review* believes that Langbaum "is one of only a handful of critics capable of making [humanistic] claims explicit in a way so powerful as to give enormous support to an entire enterprise." Kincaid also provides an outline of three of Langbaum's works of criticism: "[*The Modern Spirit*] involves an investigation of the strategies Romantic and post-Romantic poets have employed to deal with the split between self and experience, between subject and object, created by the Enlightenment. *The Poetry of Experience,* an extraordinarily influential book, dealt with a genre, the dramatic monologue, formulated to recapture and revivify experience in a world where objectively verifiable meaning was problematic or nonexistent. In *The Mysteries of Identity* Langbaum turns to the even larger problem of being and to the ways artists have struggled to define and reinstitute valid identity."

Reviewers, such as Kincaid and Christopher Butler, contend that *The Mysteries of Identity* affirms Langbaum's position as an important critic. Butler praises the insight of this work and finds that Langbaum "not only states the problem of identity with admirable clarity, but also uses it to produce radical interpretations of [Matthew] Arnold, [D. H.] Lawrence, and in particular, [William Butler] Yeats, whose views in *A Vision* are given a dignity and coherence not often allowed them by critics." He calls *The Mysteries of Identity* "an important contribution to the history of ideas." Kincaid notes that "as well as being an important work of literary criticism, *The Mysteries of Identity* stands as a testament to the hope and courage still possible in this culture." And he adds, "Langbaum is clearly both a major critic and a major cultural historian."

AVOCATIONAL INTERESTS: European travel, spending summers at the country home of his wife's family near Florence, Italy.

BIOGRAPHICAL/CRITICAL SOURCES: *Yale Review,* December, 1970; *Times Literary Supplement,* July 30, 1971, August 18, 1978; *Virginia Quarterly Review,* winter, 1971, autumn, 1978; *New Statesman,* April 28, 1978; *Books and Bookmen,* August, 1978.

* * *

LANGONE, John (Michael) 1929-

PERSONAL: Surname is pronounced Lan-*goh*-neh; born December 23, 1929, in Cambridge, Mass.; son of Joseph (a furrier) and Josephine (Consolazio) Langone; married Dolores Nobrega (a health careers counselor), September 29, 1956; children: Matthew, Gia, Lisa. *Education:* Boston University, B.S., 1953; Harvard University, special student at School of Medicine, 1969. *Politics:* Democrat. *Religion:* Roman Catholic. *Home:* 28 Jarvis Ave., Hingham, Mass. 02043. *Office: Boston Herald-American,* 300 Harrison Ave., Boston, Mass. 02106.

CAREER: Worcester Gazette, Worcester, Mass., reporter, 1954-55; United Press (UP), Boston, Mass., reporter, 1955-56; *Worcester Telegram,* Worcester, reporter, 1956-57; United Press International (UPI), bureau chief, Providence, R.I., 1957-61, editor at national radio headquarters in Chicago, Ill., 1961-62; *Boston Herald-Traveler,* Boston, medical writer, 1962-66; *Psychiatric Opinion,* Framingham, Mass., editor, 1966-68; *Boston Herald-American,* Boston, editor of medical news and author of column "Medical Beat," 1968—. Member of ethics committee, Advisory Council, Radcliffe Programs in Health Care. Harvard University, lecturer in department of preventive and Social medicine, 1975—, instructor in journalism for University extension program, 1976—. Consulting science writer, Worcester Foundation for Experimental Biology, 1966-68. *Military Service:* U.S. Navy, 1948-49. U.S. Air Force Reserve, 1953-62; became first lieutenant.

MEMBER: National Association of Science Writers, American Public Health Association (fellow), Harvard Medical School Alumni Association (honorary associate member). *Awards, honors:* National journalism award, American Osteopathic Association, 1966, for series on osteopathy; citation for meritorious service, U.S. Veterans Administration, 1971, for series on Veterans Administration hospitals; Kennedy fellowship in medical ethics, Harvard University, 1974-75; Center for Advanced Study in the Behavioral Sciences fellowship in science writing, Stanford University, 1978-79.

WRITINGS—Published by Little, Brown, except as indicated: *Death Is a Noun,* 1972; *Goodbye to Bedlam,* 1974; *Vital Signs: The Way We Die in America,* 1974; *Bombed, Buzzed, Smashed or Sober,* 1976; *Life at the Bottom: The People of Antarctica,* 1978; *Long Life,* 1978; *Human Engineering,* 1978; *Love, Like, Lust,* 1980; *Women Who Drink,* Addison-Wesley, 1980. Executive editor of *Journal of Abdominal Surgery,* 1963—; member of editorial board of *American Journal of Public Health,* 1971—.

WORK IN PROGRESS: A book on ethical questions for teenagers, to be published by Little, Brown; a journalism textbook.

SIDELIGHTS: John Langone writes *CA:* "I am, I suppose, a compulsive writer who has been nurtured in the deadline world of daily newspaper and wire service reporting; and while I cannot honestly point to any special motivating factors and circumstances, I do know that I've wanted to be a journalist since my early high school days. My motivation to be a science journalist is a bit clearer: I grew up in a family with three scientist-members, and I used to spend a good deal of time during my adolescence playing in the biology and physiology laboratories at Harvard University where they worked. I'd wash bottles, get to talk to researchers, memorize the chemical formulas on the bottle labels. Eventually, I built my own home laboratory, which became a hobby I still pursue on occasion."

Thus far, Langone has published five books for teenagers, each of which concerns "a subject rarely discussed for this age group—death and dying, genetic manipulation, love and lust, mental illness, responsible drinking—and each raises ethical and moral questions which I feel have too long been neglected when dealing with junior and senior high school students." Langone continues: "I am committed to nonfiction of this genre for teenagers and am, frankly, quite impatient with the attention that fiction—which deals only obliquely, if at all, with these issues—receives. I write about the real world, and not about furry animals who talk. [My books concern such subjects as] violence and murder and euthanasia and suicide, pornography and prostitution, and recombinant DNA and the issue of science's responsibility.

"My adult books have attempted to deal with a variety of scientific and behavioral issues [, such as] the biology of aging and the prolongation of life, behavior in the isolation of Antarctica, the attitudes of dying patients and their caretakers, and medical ethics.

"When writing about purely scientific subjects, I try to translate as much as possible, always bearing in mind that the readers I am most interested in [reaching] are ordinary readers who have as much right to know about esoteric laboratory research as the scientists who do that research. Science writers who have forgotten their audience and write turgid prose in an attempt to impress their scientist-colleagues trouble me, just as do the scientists who refuse to discuss their work with a journalist on the grounds that it cannot be understood by an average reader.

"My writing biases are, obviously, the product of my years as a journalist, but I feel strongly about clarity and accuracy, about writing with one's senses, and am influenced, I will admit it, by the newspaper dictum, 'You cannot send your reader to the dictionary on a crowded bus.'"

Langone traveled with the National Science Foundation to Antarctica and the South Pole in 1972, and to Israel in 1973, to report on twenty-five years in the fields of science and medicine.

BIOGRAPHICAL/CRITICAL SOURCES: New England Journal of Medicine, April 9, 1970; *New York Times Book Review,* October 22, 1972, November 5, 1972, July 21, 1974; *Kirkus Reviews,* April 1, 1974, June 15, 1976; *Psychology Today,* February, 1979; *Choice,* April, 1979.

* * *

LANGTON, Jane (Gillson) 1922-

PERSONAL: Born December 30, 1922, in Boston, Mass.; daughter of Joseph Lincoln (a geologist) and Grace (Brown) Gillson; married William Langton (a physicist), 1943; children: Christopher, David, Andrew. *Education:* Attended Wellesley College, 1940-42; University of Michigan, B.S., 1944, M.A., 1945; Radcliffe College, M.A., 1948; Boston Museum School of Art, additional study, 1958-59. *Politics:* Democrat. *Home:* Concord Rd., Lincoln, Mass. 01773.

CAREER: Writer. Teacher of writing for children at Graduate Center for the Study of Children's Literature, Simmons College, 1979-80, and at Eastern Writer's Conference, Salem State College. Prepared art work and visual material for educational program in the natural sciences entitled "Discovery," WGBH, Channel 2, Boston, Mass., 1955-56. Volunteer worker for school and church. *Member:* Phi Beta Kappa.

WRITINGS—All juveniles, published by Harper, except as indicated: *The Majesty of Grace,* 1961, published as *Her Majesty, Grace Jones,* 1972; *The Diamond in the Window,* 1962; *The Transcendental Murder* (adult suspense novel), 1964, published as The *Minuteman Murder,* Dell, 1976; *The Swing in the Summerhouse,* 1967; *The Astonishing Stereoscope,* 1971; *The Boyhood of Grace Jones,* 1972; *Dark Nantucket Noon* (adult suspense novel), 1975; *Paper Chains,* 1977; *The Memorial Hall Murder* (adult suspense novel), 1978; *The Fledgling,* 1980. Children's book reviewer for *New York Times Book Review.*

SIDELIGHTS: Jane Langton told *CA:* "My books start with an interest in a place. This has been most often Concord, Massachusetts, with its several layers of history, both from revolutionary times and from nineteenth-century transcendental times. But it is the present time, littered about with the past, that I seem to want to write about. Putting real children (as real as I can make them) into a real setting (as real as I can copy it) and then pulling some sort of fantasy out of that litter of the past that lies around them—this is what particularly interests me.

"I am lucky in living in the town next to Concord. We go there very often for shopping, and walking or driving one is wading through air which to me seems thick with meaning. The thing I am most afraid of is making a muddle of too many things which are not pulled together into a single unit. But the thing I like best is taking a great many things and managing them all somehow in one fist like a complicated sort of cat's cradle."

BIOGRAPHICAL/CRITICAL SOURCES: New York Times Book Review, August 20, 1967; *Times Literary Supplement,* December 4, 1969, April 16, 1970; *New York Times,* May 21, 1978; *Booklist,* May 15, 1980.

* * *

LAPATI, Americo D. 1924-

PERSONAL: Born November 2, 1924, in Providence, R.I.; son of Antonio and Civita (Di Clementi) Lapati. *Education:* Attended Our Lady of Providence Seminary, 1942-44; St. Mary's Seminary, Baltimore, Md., A.B., 1945, S.T.B., 1947; Boston College, A.M., 1951, Ph.D., 1958. *Home:* 1525 Cranston St., Cranston, R.I. 02920.

CAREER: Ordained Roman Catholic priest, 1949. Our Lady of Grace Church, Johnston, R.I., assistant pastor, 1949-55; LaSalle Academy, Providence, R.I., instructor, 1951-52; Catholic Teachers College, Providence, lecturer, 1951-66; St. Xavier's Academy, Providence, instructor, 1952-55; Mt. St. Rita Novitiate, Cumberland, R.I., chaplain, 1955-70; St. Raphael's Academy, Pawtucket, R.I., instructor, 1958-62, guidance director, 1962-70; Catholic University of America, Washington, D.C., professor, 1970-76; St. Mary's Church, Cranston, R.I., pastor, 1976—. Visiting professor, University of Notre Dame, 1968, and Rhode Island College, 1969-70. Fulbright scholar, American Academy in Rome and Vergilian Classical School, Naples, 1964. *Member:* Catholic Teachers Institute of Rhode Island (president, 1965).

WRITINGS: A High School Curriculum for Leadership, Bookman Associates, 1961; *Orestes A. Brownson,* Twayne, 1965; *John H. Newman,* Twayne, 1972; *Education and Federal Government: A Historical Record,* Mason/Charter, 1975.

* * *

LAPP, Charles (Leon) 1914- (Chuck Lapp)

PERSONAL: Born November 26, 1914, in Liberal, Mo.; son of Garfield C. (a carpenter) and Grace (Cooley) Lapp; married Ruth Bradshaw (a social worker), September 1, 1945; children: Linda Sue Lapp Gravelle, Karen Lea Schneider. *Education:* Southwest Missouri State College (now University), A.B., 1936; Northwestern University, M.B.A., 1939; Ohio State University, Ph.D., 1950. *Home:* 116 Santa Clara, Irving, Tex. 75062. *Office:* Graduate School of Management, University of Dallas, Irving, Tex. 75061; and Graduate School of Business, Washington University, St. Louis, Mo. 63130.

CAREER: High school English teacher in Marshfield, Mo., 1936-38; high school social science teacher in Aurora, Mo., 1938-39; Drake University, Des Moines, Iowa, assistant professor of marketing, 1939-43, 1946-49; Ohio State University, Columbus, professor of sales, 1947-50; Washington University, St. Louis, Mo., professor of sales management, 1950-80, professor emeritus, 1980—; currently visiting professor at Graduate School of Management, University of Dallas, Irving, Tex. Visiting professor, Syracuse University, summers, 1952—; has taught at University of Missouri and University of Utah. Member of advisory board, Young Dental Manufacturing Co., 1970—, and Marketing 2000, 1971—. *Military service:* U.S. Army Air Forces, 1943-46; became sergeant. *Member:* American Marketing Association, Sales and Marketing Executives International, Beta Gamma Sigma, Eta Mu Pi, Alpha Kappa Psi.

WRITINGS: Personal Supervision of Outside Salesmen, Business Books, 1951; *Successful Selling Strategies,* McGraw, 1957; (with William W. Frank) *How to Outsell the Born Salesman,* Macmillan, 1959; *Training and Supervising Salesmen,* Prentice-Hall, 1960; (with Jack R. Dauner) *Conducting Sales Meetings,* Sales Success Unlimited, 1963; *Home Study Course in Salesmanship,* American Paper Merchant, 1967; *Add to Your Selling Know-How,* Farm and Power Equipment Association, 1968; (with Earle R. Conant) *Refresher Course in Salesmanship,* Sales and Marketing Executives International, 1970; (with Cliff Stevens) *Salesman's Reference Library,* Stevens & Associates, 1979; (with Joe Welch) *Basic Text in Sales Management,* South-Western, in press. Also editor-in-chief of selling and marketing management series, for Sales and Marketing Executives International.

Has also made numerous recordings, under name Chuck Lapp, including: "Planning: Foundation for Successful Selling"; "How to Let Your Wife Help You Succeed in Selling"; "How to Open and Close the Sale"; "How to Put Action into Your Sales."

WORK IN PROGRESS: A basic text for junior college courses in salesmanship; a book on selecting and keeping a job.

LARRABEE, Eric 1922-

PERSONAL: Born March 6, 1922, in Melrose, Mass.; son of Harold Atkins and Doris (Kennard) Larrabee; married Eleanor Barrows Doermann, 1944. *Education:* Harvard University, B.A., 1943. *Home:* 448 West 20th St., New York, N.Y. 10011; and 118 Summit Ave., Buffalo, N.Y. 14214.

CAREER: Harper's magazine, New York City, associate editor, 1946-58; *American Heritage,* New York City, executive editor, 1958-60, managing editor, 1960-61; *Horizon* magazine, New York City, managing editor, 1961-63; Doubleday & Co., Inc., New York City, editorial consultant, 1963-69; State University of New York at Buffalo, professor and provost, 1967-70; New York State Council on the Arts, New York City, executive director, 1970-75; president, National Research Center of the Arts, 1976-78. Member, New York Council for the Humanities, 1976—. Host on NETV program, "Past Imperfect," 1964, and on other television programs. Vice-president of board of directors, Greenwich Village Symphony, 1961-63. *Military service:* U.S. Army, three years; became first lieutenant; awarded Bronze Star and Army commendation ribbon. *Member:* New York State Historical Association (member of board of trustees, 1976—), Phi Beta Kappa, Century Club, Coffee House. *Awards, honors:* LL.D., Keuka College, 1961; National Arts Club medal of honor, 1971.

WRITINGS: (Editor) *American Panorama,* New York University Press, 1957; (editor) *Mass Leisure,* Free Press, 1958; *The Self-Conscious Society,* Doubleday, 1960; (co-editor) *American Perspectives,* Harvard University Press, 1961; (editor) *Museums and Education,* Smithsonian Institution, 1968; *The Benevolent and Necessary Institution,* Doubleday, 1971. Regular contributor, *Harper's,* 1948-67. Contributor of articles and reviews to national magazines.

* * *

LARRICK, Nancy 1910-

PERSONAL: Born December 28, 1910, in Winchester, Va.; daughter of Herbert S. (a lawyer) and Nancy (Nulton) Larrick; married Alexander L. Crosby (a writer), February 15, 1958. *Education:* Goucher College, A.B., 1930; Columbia University, M.A., 1937; New York University, Ed.D., 1955. *Politics:* "Liberal Democrat." *Religion:* Episcopalian. *Home:* Box 25, R.R. 4, Quakertown, Pa. 18951. *Agent:* Joan Daves, 59 East 54th St., New York, N.Y. 10022.

CAREER: Teacher in public schools, Winchester, Va., 1930-42; U.S. Treasury Department, War Bond Division, Washington, D.C., education director, 1942-45; *Young America Readers* (weekly news magazines), New York City, editor, 1946-51; Random House, Inc., New York City, education director in children's books department, 1952-59; Lehigh University, Bethlehem, Pa., adjunct professor of education, 1964-79. Has held teaching posts at New York University Graduate School of Education, Indiana University, and Bank Street College of Education; has lectured at University of Chicago, University of Montana, University of Texas, and at other universities. *Member:* International Reading Association (president, 1956-57), National Council of Teachers of English, National Conference on Research in English. *Awards, honors:* Founders Day Award, New York University, 1955; Edison Foundation Award, 1959; Carey-Thomas Award, 1959; LL.D., Goucher College, 1975; certificate of merit, International Reading Association, 1977; Drexel University certificate for contribution to children's literature, 1977; named to Reading Hall of Fame, 1977.

WRITINGS—Nonfiction: (With Daniel Melcher) *Printing and Promotion Handbook,* McGraw, 1949, 3rd edition, 1966; *See for Yourself,* Dutton, 1952; *A Parent's Guide to Children's Reading,* Doubleday, 1958, 4th edition, 1975; *Color ABC,* Platt, 1959; (with husband, Alexander L. Crosby) *Rockets Into Space,* Random House, 1959; *A Teacher's Guide to Children's Books,* Bobbs-Merrill, 1960; *Junior Science Book of Rain, Hail, Sleet, and Snow,* Garrard, 1961; *A Parent's Guide to Children's Education,* Trident, 1963.

Editor: *You Come Too: Poetry of Robert Frost,* Holt, 1959; *Piper, Pipe That Song Again,* Random House, 1965; *Poetry for Holidays,* Garrard, 1966; *Piping Down the Valleys Wild,* Dial, 1967; (with John A. Stoops) *What Is Reading Doing to the Child?,* Interstate, 1967; (with Charles J. Versacci) *Reading: Isn't It Really the Teacher?,* Interstate, 1968; *Green Is Like a Meadow of Grass,* Garrard, 1968; *On City Streets,* M. Evans, 1968; *I Heard a Scream in the Street,* M. Evans, 1970; (and contributor) *Somebody Turned On a Tap in These Kids,* Dell, 1971; *The Wheels of the Bus Go Round and Round,* Children's Press, 1972; *More Poetry for Holidays,* Garrard, 1973; (with Eve Merriam) *Male and Female under 18,* Avon, 1973; *Room for Me and a Mountain Lion,* M. Evans, 1974; *Crazy to Be Alive in Such a Strange World,* M. Evans, 1977; *Bring Me All of Your Dreams,* M. Evans, 1980.

Also editor of "Poetry Parade" recordings, Weston Woods Studios, 1967. Contributor of articles to *Saturday Review, Parents' Magazine, New York Times Book Review, Christian Science Monitor,* and other periodicals. *The Reading Teacher,* editor, 1950-54, editorial advisor, 1970-76; poetry editor, *English Journal,* 1974-76.

SIDELIGHTS: Nancy Larrick told *CA:* "I have edited eleven anthologies of poetry for young readers, and with each one I have turned to young readers for help in making selections. The first anthology I worked on was to be for second and third graders so I knew the poems had to be easy and interesting. At a school near Coopersburg, Pennsylvania, I borrowed groups of second and third graders whom I met twice a week for several months. 'Which poems can you read?,' I would ask them, and then 'Which of those poems would you like to have in a book of your own?.' The children were very selective, rejecting poems they found 'too sweet,' and recommending poems they called 'real.'

"The publisher had suggested what seemed to me to be a very dull title for the book. Before I made a counterproposal, I asked the children to select from several possibilities. 'Nobody would take it off the shelf with that title,' said one youngster of the publisher's suggestion. Their choice was taken from a poem by William Blake: 'Piper, Pipe That Song Again,' and the publisher honored their recommendation."

BIOGRAPHICAL/CRITICAL SOURCES: New York Times Book Review, May 9, 1965, November 19, 1972, May 1, 1977; *Grade Teacher,* November, 1965; *Book World,* November 3, 1968; *Saturday Review,* January 24, 1970, August 21, 1971; *Parents' Magazine,* May, 1970; *New Yorker,* December 2, 1972; *Instructor,* November, 1974; *Christian Science Monitor,* July 14, 1975; *Commonweal,* November 21, 1975; *Language Arts,* April, 1976.

* * *

LARSON, Arthur 1910-

PERSONAL: Born July 4, 1910, in Sioux Falls, S.D.; son of Lewis (a judge) and Anna Bertha (Huseboe) Larson; married Florence Faye Newcomb, June 30, 1935; children: Lex Kingsbury, Anna Barbara. *Education:* Augustana College (Sioux Falls, S.D.), A.B., 1931; University of South Dakota, additional study, 1931-32; Oxford University, B.A. Jurisprudence, 1935, M.A., 1938, D.C.L., 1957. *Politics:* Republican. *Religion:* Lutheran. *Office:* Rule of Law Research Center, Law School, Duke University, Durham, N.C.

CAREER: Quarles, Spence & Quarles, Milwaukee, Wis., practicing attorney, 1935-39; University of Tennessee, Law School, Knoxville, assistant professor, 1939-41; Office of Price Administration, Washington, D.C., division counsel of industrial materials division, 1941-44, acting price executive of lumber branch, 1944; Foreign Economic Administration, Washington, D.C., chief of Scandinavian branch, 1944-45; Cornell University, Law School, Ithaca, N.Y., associate professor, 1945-48, professor, 1948-53; University of Pittsburgh, School of Law, Pittsburgh, Pa., dean, 1953; U.S. Department of Labor, Washington, D.C., undersecretary of labor, 1954-56; U.S. Information Agency, Washington, D.C., director, 1956-57; special assistant to the President, 1957-58; Duke University, Law School, Durham, N.C., director, Rule of Law Research Center, 1958—. Special consultant to the President, Washington, D.C., 1958-61. Has served in executive and advisory capacities for Peace Research Institute, Institute for International Order, African Conference on Peace Through Law, Soviet-American Citizen's Conference, President's White House Conference on Aging, and Council of State Governments Advisory Council on Workmen's Compensation. Honorary fellow of Pembroke College, Oxford University. Professional lecturer.

MEMBER: American Association for the United Nations (member of national council), Phi Beta Kappa, Phi Delta Phi. *Awards, honors:* Rhodes scholar, Oxford University; Fulbright Advanced Research award, 1953; World Peace Award, American Freedom Association, 1960; Henderson Memorial Prize awarded by Harvard University for best book in field of administrative law during period of approximately five years, 1957, for *The Law of Workmen's Compensation;* received Order of the Coif. LL.D. from Augustana College, 1953, Thiel College, 1957, Valparaiso University, 1959, Lenoir-Rhyne College, Utah State University, 1967; L.H.D. from Coe College, 1960, University of South Dakota, 1965.

WRITINGS: (With R. S. Stevens) *Cases and Materials on the Law of Corporations,* West Publishing, 1947, 2nd edition, 1955; (co-author) *Towards World Prosperity,* Harper, 1947; *The Law of Workman's Compensation,* nine volumes, Matthew Bender, 1952; (co-author) *Economic Security for Americans,* American Assembly, 1953; *Know Your Social Security,* Harper, 1955, revised, 1959; *A Republican Looks at His Party,* Harper, 1956, reprinted, Greenwood Press, 1974; *What We Are For,* Harper, 1959; *Design for Research in International Rule of Law,* World Rule of Law Center, 1961; *When Nations Disagree: A Handbook on Peace through Law,* Louisiana State University Press, 1961; (with John B. Whitton) *Propaganda: Towards Disarmament in the War of Words,* Oceana, 1963; (editor and contributor) *Sovereignty within the Law,* Oceana, 1965; (with Donald R. Larson) *Vietnam and Beyond,* Rule of Law Research Center, Duke University, 1965; (co-editor and contributor) *Eisenhower: The President Nobody Knew,* Scribner, 1968; *Population and Law,* Sijthoff, 1971; (editor and contributor) *Injuries and Death,* two volumes, Matthew Bender, 1972; *The Law of Employment Discrimination,* four volumes, Matthew Bender, 1975.

Also editor and contributor with Arnold Toynbee, and others, *A Warless World.* Editor, "World Rule of Law" booklet series. Composer of works for organ, string quartet, and voice. Contributor of approximately 130 articles to professional, scholarly, and commercial journals. Member of board of editors, *Law and Contemporary Problems;* member of board of sponsors, *War/Peace Report.*

WORK IN PROGRESS: Several volumes of folk songs and transcriptions of Elizabethan songs from the tablature; *The Law of Housing Discrimination;* memoirs.

AVOCATIONAL INTERESTS: Music, particularly classical guitar, ancient instruments, and operatic singing.

BIOGRAPHICAL/CRITICAL SOURCES: Time, April 5, 1954; *U.S. News & World Report,* September 7, 1956; *Life,* January 21, 1957; *Newsweek,* October 28, 1957.

* * *

LASKER, Joe 1919-

PERSONAL: Born June 26, 1919, in Brooklyn, N.Y.; son of Isidore (a tailor) and Rachel (Strollowitz) Lasker; married Mildred Jaspen (a teacher), November 28, 1948; children: David, Laura, Evan. *Education:* Attended Cooper Union Art School, 1936-39. *Home and office:* 20 Dock Rd., Norwalk, Conn. 06854.

CAREER: Artist; author and illustrator of children's books. Oil paintings are part of permanent collections in various colleges, universities, and museums, including Whitney Museum, Philadelphia Museum, and Baltimore Museum. Art teacher, University of Illinois, 1953-54. *Military service:* U.S. Army, 1941-45.

MEMBER: National Academy of Design, Authors Guild, Authors League of America, Connecticut Association for Children with Learning Disabilities (president, 1964-65). *Awards, honors:* Abbey mural painting fellowships, 1947, 1948; several awards from National Academy of Design, including third Hallgarten prize, 1955, second Altman prize, 1958, Ranger Fund purchase award, 1966, Clark prize, 1969, and Isadore medal, 1972; Prix de Rome fellowship, 1950, 1951; Guggenheim fellowship, 1954; purchase award, Springfield Art Museum, 1964; Hassam Fund purchase awards, American Academy of Arts and Letters, 1965, 1968; National Institute of Arts and Letters grant, 1968; best illustrated children's book award, *New York Times,* 1976, outstanding children's book awards, *New York Times,* 1976, art books for children citation, Brooklyn Museum, 1976, and Brooklyn Library, 1979, and Notable Book of the Year Award, American Library Association, 1977, all for *Merry Ever After;* Notable Book of the Year Award, American Library Association, 1980, for *The Boy Who Loved Music.*

WRITINGS—Juvenile; self-illustrated: *Mothers Can Do Anything,* Albert Whitman, 1972; *He's My Brother,* Albert Whitman, 1974; *Tales of a Seadog Family,* Viking, 1974; *Merry Ever After: The Story of Two Medieval Weddings,* Viking, 1976; *The Strange Voyage of Neptune's Car,* Viking, 1977; *Lentil Soup,* Albert Whitman, 1977; *Nick Joins In,* Albert Whitman, 1980.

Illustrator; published by Albert Whitman, except as indicated: Miriam Schlein, *The Way Mothers Are,* 1963; Jean M. Craig, *Boxes,* Norton, 1964; Norma Simon, *Benjy's Bird,* 1965; Fern Brown and Andree Grabe, *When Grandpa Wore Knickers,* 1966; Simon, *What Do I Say?,* 1967; Simon, *See the First Star,* 1968; Simon, *What Do I Do?,* 1969 Simon, *How Do I Feel?,* 1970; Schlein, *My House,* 1971; Joel Rothman, *Night Lights,* 1972; Schlein, *Juju-Sheep and the Python Moonstone,* 1973; Joan Fassler, *Howie Helps Himself,* 1974; Judy Delton, *Carrot Cake,* Crown, 1975; Delton, *Rabbit Finds a Way,* Crown, 1975; Simon, *All Kinds of Families,* 1976; David Lasker, *The Boy Who Loved Music,* Viking, 1979.

WORK IN PROGRESS: Where Is Rubin?, for Viking.

SIDELIGHTS: Joe Lasker told *CA:* "Painting is my first love. I illustrate and write to support my habit and family. As it must to (practically) all illustrators of children's books, I too have become an 'author.'"

BIOGRAPHICAL/CRITICAL SOURCES: Life, March 20, 1950; Lloyd Goodrich and John Bauer, *American Art of Our Century,* Praeger, 1961; *Parade,* September 1, 1963; *New York Times Book Review,* October 20, 1974.

* * *

LATTIMORE, Richmond (Alexander) 1906-

PERSONAL: Born May 6, 1906, in Paotingfu, China; son of David (a professor) and Margaret (Barnes) Lattimore; married Alice Bockstahler (a dance teacher), August 31, 1935; children: Steven, Alexander. *Education:* Dartmouth College, A.B., 1926; University of Illinois, A.M., 1927, Ph.D., 1935; Christ Church, Oxford, B.A., 1932, M.A., 1964. *Home:* 123 Locust Grove Rd., Rosemont, Pa. 19010. *Office:* Bryn Mawr College, Bryn Mawr, Pa.

CAREER: Wabash College, Crawfordsville, Ind., assistant professor, 1928-29; Bryn Mawr College, Bryn Mawr, Pa., assistant professor, 1935-41, associate professor, 1945-48, professor of Greek, 1948-71, professor emeritus, 1971—. Senior fellow, Center for Hellenic Studies, Washington, D.C., 1960-65. Taft lecturer, University of Cincinnati, 1952; Turnbull Lecturer, Johns Hopkins University, 1957; Lord Northcliffe Lecturer, University College, University of London; Fulbright lecturer, Oxford University, 1963; Centennial Professor, University of Toronto, 1966; visiting professor, University of California, Los Angeles, 1974. *Military service:* U.S. Naval Reserve, 1943-46; became lieutenant.

MEMBER: American Philological Association, Archaeological Institute of America, American Philosophical Society, American Academy of Arts and Sciences, National Institute of Arts and Letters, P.E.N., Phi Beta Kappa, Merion Cricket Club. *Awards, honors:* Rhodes Scholar, Indiana, 1929; American Academy in Rome, fellow, 1935; Rockefeller post-war fellowship, 1946; Fulbright scholar to Greece, 1952; National Institute of Arts and Letters award, 1954; D. Let., Dartmouth College, 1958; American Council of Learned Societies award, 1959; Bollingen award, 1962, for verse translation of Aristophanes' *The Frogs* (shared with Robert Lowell).

WRITINGS: Themes in Greek and Latin Epitaphs, University of Illinois Press, 1942; *Poems,* University of Michigan Press, 1957; *The Poetry of Greek Tragedy,* Johns Hopkins Press, 1958; *Sestina for a Far-Off Summer,* University of Michigan Press, 1962; *Story Patterns in Greek Tragedy,* University of Michigan Press, 1964; *Selected Poems,* Harlequin Poets, Oxford, 1965; *The Stride of Time: New Poems and Translations,* University of Michigan Press, 1966; *Poems from Three Decades,* Scribner, 1972. Contributor to professional and literary journals.

Translator: M. McClure, *Early Philosophies of Greece,* Appleton, 1935; *Some Odes of Pindar,* New Directions, 1942; Pindar, *Odes,* University of Chicago Press, 1947; Homer, *The Iliad,* University of Chicago Press, 1951; *Greek Lyrics,* University of Chicago Press, 1956, 2nd edition, 1960; Hesiod, *Works and Days; Theogony;* [and] *The Shield of Herakles,* University of Michigan Press, 1959; Aristophanes, *The Frogs,* University of Michigan Press, 1962; *The Revelation of John,* Harcourt, 1962; Homer, *The Odyssey,* Harper, 1967; Euripides, *Iphigeneia in Tauris,* Oxford University

Press, 1973; *The Four Gospels and the Revelation,* Farrar, Straus, 1979.

Editor with David Grene: *Complete Greek Tragedies,* four volumes, University of Chicago Press, 1959, published in seven volumes, Modern Library, 1960. Translator in this series of Aeschylus', "Oresteia," and of four plays by Euripides, "Alcestis," "Helen," "The Trojan Women," and "Rhesus."

WORK IN PROGRESS: Poems.

SIDELIGHTS: Samuel French Morse writes that, whatever Richmond Lattimore does, "he does knowingly; and part of the pleasure his poems convey derives from the fact that they bear scrutiny from any perspective: they are technically inventive, their rhetoric is always under control, and form and matter cohere. He proves, too, that contemporary material lends itself to strict treatment."

Nevertheless, a critic from *Virginia Quarterly Review* points out that "a great deal of . . . Lattimore's best poetry is in his translations. . . . He is one of the rare translators who bring all their resources to bear on projects which too many writers regard as secondary to their own work." J. M. Brinnin agrees, because "when he translates, Lattimore jettisons much of the baggage of classical rhetoric. His renderings of the archaic show the bite and speed appropriate to the age of Pound. When he writes 'for himself,' whole carloads of that same baggage turn up on his doorstep." Joseph Bennett finds that "it is in the exquisiteness of his lyric translations that the tact and delicacy of Lattimore's poetic intelligence seem most communicable."

AVOCATIONAL INTERESTS: Sports, especially tennis and squash.

BIOGRAPHICAL/CRITICAL SOURCES: Poetry, March, 1967, May, 1969; *New York Times Book Review,* April, 1967, October 22, 1967, November 19, 1972, April 15, 1979; *Hudson Review,* winter, 1967-68, spring, 1973; *New Yorker,* March 30, 1968; *National Review,* April 23, 1968; *New York Review,* May 9, 1968; *Contemporary Literature,* winter, 1968; *Virginia Quarterly Review,* spring, 1973; *Contemporary Literary Criticism,* Volume III, Gale, 1975.

* * *

LAUTERBACH, Albert 1904-

PERSONAL: Born June 24, 1904, in Austria; came to United States, 1938, naturalized, 1944; son of Isidor and Augusta (Wiesenberg) Lauterbach; married Tilly Glauch, August 17, 1929. *Education:* Academy of Commerce, Vienna, diploma, 1923; University of Vienna, Dr.Rer.Pol., 1925. *Home:* Friedlgasse 25/14, A-1190, Vienna, Austria. *Office:* Department of Economics, Sarah Lawrence College, Bronxville, N.Y. 10708.

CAREER: Escompte-Gesellschaft, Vienna, Austria, member of staff, 1926-29; lecturer at extension colleges in Vienna, 1927-33; *Financial News,* London, England, Central European correspondent and feature writer, 1936-38; Institute for Social Research, New York, N.Y., research associate, 1939-40; Institute for Advanced Study, Princeton, N.J., research member, 1940-41; University of Denver, Denver, Colo., assistant professor of economics, 1941-42; Sarah Lawrence College, Bronxville, N.Y., 1943—, became professor of political economy, professor emeritus, 1972—, chairman of social science faculty, 1946-48, 1956-57, 1960-61, and 1966-67. Member of economics department, Brooklyn College (now Brooklyn College of the City University of New York), 1940, 1943, and 1946; visiting associate professor, New York University, 1947; Fulbright research professor, University of Chile, 1959-60; Rutgers University exchange professor in Bolivia, 1965; visiting professor, University of Wisconsin, 1966; also lecturer at colleges and universities in Columbia, Peru, Brazil, Bolivia, Uruguay, Venezuela, Argentina, Paraguay, Switzerland, and Austria. Researcher, Carnegie Endowment for International Peace, 1943-45; research fellow and consultant, Survey Research Center, University of Michigan, 1951-52 and 1956; Brookings Institution, research associate, 1955 and 1962, research professor, 1962-63. Head of Columbia University field training program in Colombia, 1965. Consultant, Committee for Economic Development, 1943-44; member of relief and education missions to France, Italy, and Austria, 1947-48; senior development economist, United Nations mission to Western Samoa, 1962; consultant, Organization of American States, 1963 and 1965; regional economic advisor for Latin America and the Caribbean, International Labour Office, United Nations, 1969-72. Public member, New York State Minimum Wage Board, 1956-57.

MEMBER: Society for International Development, Association for Comparative Economics (vice-president, 1966), Latin American Studies Association, American Economic Association, American Association of University Professors, American Association for the United Nations, Metropolitan Economic Association of New York (secretary, 1950-51). *Awards, honors:* Carnegie Corporation research grant, 1940; Social Science Research Council grants, 1954 and 1959-60; Smith-Mundt fellow in Chile, 1956; miembro academico, Catholic University of Chile, 1956; honorary member, Instituto de Economia, University of Chile, 1956.

WRITINGS: Economic Security and Individual Freedom: Can We Have Both?, Cornell University Press, 1948; *Man, Motives, and Money: Psychological Frontiers of Economics,* Cornell University Press, 1954, 2nd edition, 1959; *Increasing the Wealth of Nations: The Quest for Economic Development* (monograph), Public Affairs Press, 1957; *Managerial Attitudes in Chile* (monograph), Instituto de Economia, Universidad de Chile, 1961; *Psychologie des Wirtschaftslebens,* Rowohlt (Hamburg), 1962; *Kapitalismus und Sozialismus in neuer Sicht,* Rowohlt, 1963; (co-author) *Economic Survey and Proposed Development Measures for Western Samoa,* Department of Economic and Social Affairs, United Nations, 1963; *Enterprise in Latin America: Business Attitudes in a Developing Economy,* Cornell University Press, 1966; *Psychological Challenges to Modernization,* American Elsevier, 1974. Contributor to symposia; contributor to professional journals in the United States and abroad.

SIDELIGHTS: Some of Albert Lauterbach's books have been translated into Spanish, Portuguese, German, Dutch, and Italian.

* * *

LAWDER, Douglas W(ard) 1934-

PERSONAL: Born June 12, 1934, in New York, N.Y.; son of Douglas Ward and Janice (Chapman) Lawder; married Carvel Glidden (an artist), June 24, 1958 (divorced); children: Leland, Douglas. *Education:* Kenyon College, B.A., 1957; University of Oregon, M.F.A. (with honors), 1967. *Home:* 6379 East Reynolds Rd., Haslett, Mich. 48840. *Office:* Department of English, Morrill Hall, Michigan State University, East Lansing, Mich. 48823.

CAREER: J. Walter Thompson, New York, N.Y., copywriter trainee, 1957-58; teacher of Spanish, English, and horseback riding in Steamboat Springs, Colo., 1958-61; Wayland Academy, Beaver Dam, Wis., teacher of Spanish and chairman of department, 1961-63; University of Oregon, Eugene, managing editor of *Northwest Review* and associate editor of *Northwest Folklore,* 1964-67; Earlham College, Richmond, Ind., instructor in creative writing and chairman of department, 1968-70; Michigan State University, East Lansing, assistant professor, 1970-73, associate professor of literature and creative writing, 1973—. Writer-in-residence at Maine Writers' Workshop, Nathan Mayhew Seminars; fellow at MacDowell Colony and Yaddo. Has read poetry at numerous schools, colleges, and universities. *Awards, honors:* Grants from National Endowment for the Arts and Danforth Foundation, both 1968; Michigan State University summer writing grants, 1972, 1973, 1979.

WRITINGS: (With others) *Three Northwest Poets,* Quixote Press, 1970; *Trolling* (poems), Little, Brown, 1977. Contributor of poems, translations, and reviews to *Nation, Seventies,* and to literary journals, including *Poetry, Northwest Review, New York Quarterly,* and *Virginia Quarterly Review.*

WORK IN PROGRESS: A second volume of poems; translating work of South American poets.

SIDELIGHTS: "Perhaps not since the debut of James Dickey," remarks a *Choice* critic in a review of *Trolling,* "has an American poet published so remarkable a first collection. Lawder's poems at their frequent best are as crisply fresh as any verse in recent years. . . . This poet has simply vaulted past dozens of decently regarded academic poets and well beyond the status of promising."

BIOGRAPHICAL/CRITICAL SOURCES: Choice, October, 1977; *Virginia Quarterly Review,* winter, 1978.

* * *

LAZARETH, William Henry 1928-

PERSONAL: Born March 10, 1928, in New York, N.Y.; son of Otto W. and Marie (Muller) Lazareth; married Jacqueline Howell, 1955; children: Karen, Victoria, Paul. *Education:* Princeton University, B.A., 1948; attended Lund University, 1951; Philadelphia Lutheran Seminary, B.D., 1953; attended Tuebingen University, 1955; Columbia University, Ph.D., 1958; Muhlenberg College, D.D., 1966. *Office:* Faith and Order Commission, World Council of Churches, Geneva, Switzerland.

CAREER: Philadelphia Lutheran Seminary, Philadelphia, Pa., 1955-76, began as instructor, became professor of systematic theology, dean, 1965-76; Lutheran Church in America, Department of Church and Society, New York, N.Y., director of ethics, 1976-80; World Council of Churches, Faith and Order Commission, Geneva, Switzerland, director of secretariat, 1980—. Ordained clergyman of United Lutheran Church in America, 1956; area director, Lutheran World Federation, Service to Refugees, Germany, 1949-50; member of Board of Social Ministry, Lutheran Church in America, 1962; representative to Faith and Order Commission, World Council of Churches, 1962; member of commission on theological studies, Lutheran World Federation, 1978—. Passavant lecturer, 1962; fellow, University of Pennsylvania, 1966-67; lecturer, Princeton Theological Seminary, 1967-68. *Member:* American Society of Christian Social Ethics, American Theological Society. *Awards, honors:* L.L.D., Hartwick College, 1966; D.D., Muhlenberg College, 1966; L.H.D., Hamilton College, 1971; Franklin Clark Fry fellow, 1973-74.

WRITINGS—Published by Muhlenberg, except as indicated: *Luther on the Christian Home,* 1960; *A Theology of Politics,* 1960; *Man: In Whose Image,* 1961; *Helping Children Know Doctrine,* 1962; *Helping Youth and Adults Know Doctrine,* 1963; *Social Ministry: Biblical and Theological Perspectives,* 1966; *Exploration in Faith,* Fortress , 1973; *In, Not Of: Living Our Baptism in the World,* Fortress, 1974; (editor with others) *The Left Hand of God: Essays on Discipleship and Patriotism,* Fortress, 1976.

Contributor: H. Letts, editor, *Life in Community,* Muhlenberg, 1957; E. Pickhard, editor, *Every Tribe and Tongue,* Friendship, 1960; H. Lasswell, editor, *The Ethic of Power,* Harper, 1962; G. P. Butler, editor, *Best Sermons,* Van Nostrand, 1962; A. Motter, editor, *Preaching the Passion,* Fortress, 1963; W. Wolf, editor, *Protestant Churches and Reform Today,* Seabury, 1964: J. Bodensiech, editor, *The Encyclopedia of the Lutheran Church,* Augsburg, 1965; E. Steimle, editor, *Renewal in the Pulpit,* Fortress, 1966; (author of introduction) P. Athaus, *The Divine Command,* Fortress, 1966; (author of introduction) *Luther's Works,* Volume XLIV, Fortress, 1966; Paul Empie, editor, *Marburg Revisited,* Augsburg, 1966; J. Macquarrie, editor, *Dictionary of Christian Ethics,* Westminster, 1967; Trutz Rentdorff, editor, *Humane Gesellschaft,* Zwingli, 1971; I. Thomson, editor, *Word for the World,* British Bible Reading Fellowship, 1971; Carl Henry, editor, *Baker's Dictionary of Christian Ethics,* Baker Book, 1973. Member of editorial council, *Dialog.*

* * *

LEAF, Murray J(ohn) 1939-

PERSONAL: Born June 1, 1939, in New York, N.Y.; son of Julius (a retail merchant) and Jeannette (Kissel) Leaf; married Michelina Ruzzi (an editor), September, 1965. *Education:* Attended University of Arizona, 1958-59; Reed College, B.A., 1961; University of Chicago, Ph.D., 1966. *Residence:* Plano, Tex. *Office:* School of Social Science, University of Texas at Dallas, Richardson, Tex. 75080.

CAREER: Pomona College, Claremont, Calif., assistant professor of anthropology, 1966-67; University of California, Los Angeles, assistant professor of anthropology, 1967-75; University of Texas at Dallas, Richardson, associate professor of anthropology and political economy, 1975—. Honorary lecturer at Punjab University, 1964-65. *Military service:* U.S. Army Reserve, 1957-61. *Member:* American Anthropological Association (fellow), Royal Anthropological Society of Great Britain and Ireland (fellow), Association for Asian Studies, American Ethnological Society, Conference on Problems of Economic Change. *Awards, honors:* Social Science Research Council fellow, 1963; National Institute of Mental Health fellowship and research grants, 1963-66, 1979; grants from University of California Academic Sentate, 1968-74; Wenner Gren Foundation research grant, 1969.

WRITINGS: Information and Behavior in a Sikh Village: Social Organization Reconsidered, University of California Press, 1972; (contributor) Karigoudar Ishwaran, editor, *Contributions to Asian Studies,* Volume III, E. J. Brill, 1972; (editor with others) *Frontiers of Anthropology,* D. Van Nostrand, 1974; *Man, Mind and Science: A History of Anthropology,* Columbia University Press, 1979. Contributor to *Encyclopedia of Sikhism* and to anthropology journals.

WORK IN PROGRESS: A monograph, *The Green Revolution: A Panjab Village: 1964-1978.*

LEAVITT, Jerome E(dward) 1916-

PERSONAL: Born August 1, 1916, in Verona, N.J.; son of Thomas Edward (a painter) and Clara (Sonn) Leavitt. *Education:* Newark State Teachers College (now Kean College of New Jersey), B.S., 1938; Columbia University, graduate study, 1938-39; New York University, M.A., 1942; University of Colorado, graduate study, 1949-50; Northwestern University, Ed.D., 1952; University of Arizona, visiting scholar, 1959. *Home:* 1338 East Almendra Dr., Fresno, Calif. 93710. *Office:* School of Education, California State University, Fresno, Calif. 93740.

CAREER: Heights Elementary School, Roslyn Heights, N.Y., teacher, 1938-42; Sperry Gyroscope Co., Inc., Brooklyn, N.Y., instructor, 1942-45; Canyon Elementary School, Los Alamos, N.M., principal, 1945-49; Northwestern University, Evanston, Ill., instructor, 1950-52; Portland State University, Portland, Ore., assistant professor, 1952-55, associate professor, 1955-58, professor of education and executive assistant to the dean, School of Education, 1958-66; University of Arizona, Tucson, professor of education, 1966-69; California State University, Fresno, professor of education, 1969—. Research associate for evaluation of Arkansas experiment in teacher education; American specialist in education in Cyprus for U.S. State Department. *Member:* Association for Childhood Education, National Education Association, National Society of College Teachers of Education, Association for Supervision and Curriculum Development, California Teachers Association, Phi Delta Kappa, Kappa Delta Pi, Epsilon Pi Tau.

WRITINGS: Tools for Building, Childrens Press, 1955; (editor) *Nursery-Kindergarten Education,* McGraw, 1958; *Carpentry for Children,* Sterling, 1959; (with Huntsberger) *Terrariums and Aquariums,* Childrens Press, 1961; *America and Its Indians,* Childrens Press, 1961; (editor) *Readings in Elementary Education,* W. C. Brown, 1961; (with Salot) *The Beginning Kindergarten Teacher,* Burgess, 1965, revised edition, 1971; *The Complete Reference Handbook,* Stravon Education Press, 1966; *By Land, by Sea, by Air,* Putman, 1969; (editor) *The Battered Child: Selected Readings,* General Learning Press, 1974; *Herbert Sonn: Yosemite's Birdman,* privately printed, 1975. Contributor of over 100 articles to magazines and professional journals. General editor, "Twayne Juveniles" series, Twayne, 1971-76. *Education,* contributing editor, 1954-58, member of editorial board, 1973—; editor, *NSCTE Newsletter,* 1964-65; member of board of contributing editors, *Our World* (encyclopedia), Taylor Publishing, 1971; member of board of consultants, *Modern Century Illustrated Encyclopedia,* McGraw-Hill, 1972; editorial consultant, *Primaid,* 1972—; western regional coordinating news editor, *Education Professor,* 1975-77.

WORK IN PROGRESS: Child Abuse and Neglect, completion expected in 1981.

SIDELIGHTS: Jerome E. Leavitt told *CA:* "Most of my writing is a result of a felt need on my part. In some cases this is to provide informational material that is lacking, which was true in the case of *Nursery-Kindergarten Education.* With *America and Its Indians* the objective was to provide accurate up-to-date material for children on our Native Americans." *Avocational interests:* Gardening, remodeling houses, carpentry.

BIOGRAPHICAL/CRITICAL SOURCES: National Elementary Principal, June, 1949.

LEBRA, Joyce C(hapman)

PERSONAL: Daughter of Royal N. and Helen (Sanborn) Chapman. *Education:* University of Minnesota, B.A., 1947, M.A., 1949; Harvard University and Radcliffe College, Ph.D., 1958. *Office:* Department of History, University of Colorado, Boulder, Colo. 80302.

CAREER: Visiting lecturer in history, University of Texas, 1960-61; Rutgers University, New Brunswick, N.J., assistant professor, 1961-62; University of Colorado, Boulder, assistant professor, 1962-66, associate professor, 1966-69, professor of Japanese history, 1969—. *Member:* Association of Asian Studies, Asiatic Society of Japan, American Historical Association, American Association of University Women, Midwest Association of Asian Studies, Japan Society of New York. *Awards, honors:* Fulbright fellowships, 1955-57, 1965-66; American Association of University Women fellow, Japan, 1959-60; National Endowment for the Humanities fellowship, 1970-71; American Philosophical Society fellowship, 1970-71; Australian National University visiting fellowship, 1971.

WRITINGS: (Contributor) Robert K. Sakai, editor, *Studies on Asia,* University of Nebraska Press, 1967; *Chandora Bosu to Nihon* (title means "Chandra Bose and Japan"), Hara Shobo, 1968; *Jungle Alliance: Japan and the Indian National Army,* Asia Pacific Press, 1971; *Okuma Shigenobu: Statesman of Meiji Japan,* Australian National University Press, 1973; (editor) *Japan's Greater East Asia Co-Prosperity Sphere: Readings and Documents,* Oxford University Press, 1975; (editor) *Women in Changing Japan,* Westview Press, 1976; *Japanese-trained Armies in Southeast Asia: Independence and Volunteer Forces in World War II,* Columbia University Press, 1977; *Chinese Women in Southeast Asia,* Time Books International, 1979.

WORK IN PROGRESS: Women of Asia: Working Women in India, Tradition and Changes.

* * *

LEE, Sherman Emery 1918-

PERSONAL: Born April 19, 1918, in Seattle, Wash.; son of Emery H. I. and Adelia (Baker) Lee; married Ruth A. Ward, 1938; children: Katherine C., Margaret A., Elizabeth K., Thomas W. *Education:* American University, A.B., 1938, M.A., 1939; Western Reserve University (now Case Western Reserve University), Ph.D., 1941. *Home:* 2536 Norfolk Rd., Cleveland, Ohio. *Office:* Cleveland Museum of Art, 11150 East Blvd., Cleveland, Ohio.

CAREER: Detroit Institute of Art, Detroit, Mich., curator of Far Eastern art, 1941-46; Seattle Art Museum, Seattle, Wash., 1948-52, began as assistant director, became associate director; Cleveland Museum of Art, Cleveland, Ohio, curator of Oriental art, 1952—, assistant director, 1956-57, associate director, 1957-58, director, 1958—. *Military service:* U.S. Naval Reserve, 1944-46.

WRITINGS: Chinese Landscape Painting, Cleveland Museum of Art, 1954, revised edition, 1971; (with Wen Fong) *Streams and Mountains without End,* Ascona, 1955; *Japanese Decorative Style,* Cleveland Museum of Art, 1961; *Tea Taste in Japanese Art,* Arno, 1963; *History of Far Eastern Art,* Abrams, 1964, revised edition, 1974; (with W. K. Ho) *Chinese Art Under the Mongols,* Cleveland Museum of Art, 1968; *Ancient Cambodian Sculpture,* Interbook, 1970; *The Colors of Ink: Chinese Paintings and Related Ceramics from the Cleveland Museum of Art,* Arno, 1974; (editor) *On Understanding Art Museums,* Prentice-Hall, 1975.

WORK IN PROGRESS: Realism in Japanese Art.

LEE, William Storrs 1906-
(W. Storrs Lee)

PERSONAL: Born August 3, 1906, in Hanover, Conn.; son of William Storrs and Hettie-Belle (Chapman) Lee; married Mary Louise Minor (a teacher), December 26, 1932; children: William Storrs, Ralph Minor. *Education:* Middlebury College, A.B., 1928; attended Oxford University, 1928-29. *Politics:* Republican. *Religion:* Congregationalist. *Home:* Pemaquid Point, New Harbor, Me.; and Kihei, Maui, Hawaii.

CAREER: Norwich Free Academy, Norwich, Conn., English instructor, 1929-30; Middlebury College, Middlebury, Vt., English instructor and editor of Middlebury College Press, 1930-41, member of committee of three serving as acting president, 1941, dean of men, 1945-55; Hawaii Preparatory Academy, Kamuela, Hawaii, English instructor, 1962-63; writer. Sheldon Museum, Middlebury, Vt., trustee, 1932-56, president of board, 1946-56, honorary trustee, 1956—. *Military service:* U.S. Navy, Intelligence, 1941-45; became commander. *Member:* Society of American Historians, Phi Kappa Epsilon, Kappa Phi Kappa, Delta Upsilon. *Awards, honors:* Seattle Historical Society award, 1969, for *Washington State: A Literary Chronicle.*

WRITINGS: *Father Went to College,* Wilson-Erickson, 1936; (editor) *Bread Loaf Anthology,* Middlebury College Press, 1939; *Stage Coach North,* Macmillan, 1941; (editor) *Footpath in the Wilderness,* Middlebury College Press, 1942; *Town Father: A Biography of Gamaliel Painter,* Hastings House, 1952; *Green Mountains of Vermont,* Holt, 1955; *Yankees of Connecticut,* Holt, 1957; *The Strength to Move a Mountain,* Putnam, 1958; *God Bless Our Queer Old Dean,* Putnam, 1959; *Canal across a Continent,* Harrap, 1961; *The Sierra,* Putnam, 1962; *The Great California Deserts,* Putnam, 1963; (contributor) *A Vanishing America,* Holt, 1964; *The Islands,* Holt, 1966; (editor) *Partridge in a Swamp: Journals of Viola C. White,* Countryman Press, 1979.

Editor of "Literary Chronicle" series, published by Funk: *Hawaii: A Literary Chronicle,* 1967; *Maine: . . . ,* 1968; *California: . . . ,* 1968; *Washington State: . . . ,* 1969; *Colorado: . . . ,* 1970. Contributor of articles to newspapers and magazines. Song writer in collaboration with Jean Berger.

* * *

LEEDY, Paul D. 1908-

PERSONAL: Born March 4, 1908, in Harrisburg, Pa.; son of Charles Daniel and Mary (Dellinger) Leedy; married Irene Force, 1933; children: Thomas Force. *Education:* Dickinson College, A.B., 1930; University of Pennsylvania, M.A., 1938; New York University, Ph.D., 1958. *Politics:* Republican. *Home:* 407 Russell Ave., Apt. 805, Gaithersburg, Md. 20760. *Office:* School of Education, American University, Washington, D.C. 20016.

CAREER: Clergyman in Methodist Church, 1931-43; Dickinson College, Carlisle, Pa., instructor, 1943-44; New York University, New York, N.Y., instructor, 1944-46; Rutgers University, Newark, N.J., instructor, 1946-50; New York University, Reading Institute, senior specialist, 1950-61; American University, Washington, D.C., associate professor, 1961-64, professor, 1964-76, professor emeritus, 1976—. Editorial consultant to Abingdon-Cokesbury Press, Chilton Co., Harvard University Press, and McGraw-Hill Book Co., Inc. *Member:* International Reading Association, American Association of University Professors, National Education Association, Society for the Study of Education, College Reading Association (member of board of directors), Greater Washington Reading Council, Masons, Andiron Club (New York), Federal Schoolmen's Club (Washington, D.C.). *Awards, honors:* Founder's Day citation and award, New York University, 1958; Outstanding Educators of America citation, 1972; received men of achievement citation for distinguished achievement in education and authorship.

WRITINGS: (Co-author) *The Wonderful World of Books,* Houghton, 1952; *Reading Improvement for Adults,* McGraw, 1956, published as *Improve Your Reading,* McGraw, 1963; *Read with Speed and Precision,* McGraw, 1963; *Read—Like an Adult,* McGraw, 1967; *Key to Better Reading,* McGraw, 1968; *Practical Research: Planning & Design,* Macmillan, 1974, 2nd edition, 1980; *Practical Writing,* McGraw, 1980; *How to Read and Understand Research,* Macmillan, 1980. Editor of *Perspectives in Reading: College-Adult Reading Instruction* (yearbook of the International Reading Association), 1963.

SIDELIGHTS: Paul D. Leedy told *CA:* "Much publicity is given to the fact that we are a generation that can neither read nor write. Reading deficiencies, poor writing skill—these are phrases that claim the attention again and again. Why? Are we not looking at symptoms rather than causes? There's a reason for our deficiencies that lies below the manifest lack of communicational skills.

"Most of us think of writing as a ball point pen scurrying across a page. We think of it as a typewriter clicking out neat lines of printed communication. It is neither of these. In fact, these are not the first, but the last stages of the writing syndrome.

"Writing begins with thinking. We write the way we do, because we think the way we do. Split infinitives are not sins of writing; they are stupidities of thinking. Good writing is merely precise, sensitive thinking mirrored in carefully chosen words. . . . Writing and reading have always seemed to me to be opposite sides of the same coin. They both represent human thought in action. Think clearly and coherently and straight to the point and your words will take wings so that the reader may comprehend them with speed and precision. Those whose sentences lumber across the page do so because those who wrote them had a writing deficiency: a lumbering mind that we never taught to think.

"To write well is to think well, and to think well is the pinnacle of all human achievement. But when one reviews the products on our library shelves, what a dismal picture it gives of our lackluster use of the human mind."

AVOCATIONAL INTERESTS: Photography, music, horticulture, architecture (especially cathedral gothic), and travel.

* * *

LEFEVER, Ernest W(arren) 1919-

PERSONAL: Born November 12, 1919, in York, Pa.; son of Calvin Ashby and Katie (Roth) Lefever; married Margaret Briggs, 1951; children: David M., Bryce E. *Education:* Elizabethtown College, A.B., 1942; Yale University, B.D., 1945, Ph.D., 1956. *Home:* 7106 Beechwood Dr., Chevy Chase, Md. *Office:* Ethics and Public Policy Center, 1211 Connecticut Ave. N.W., Washington, D.C. 20036.

CAREER: National Council of Churches, New York, N.Y., international affairs specialist, 1952-54; Johns Hopkins University, Washington, D.C., research associate, School of Advanced International Studies, 1955-56; University of Maryland, College Park, Md., member of faculty, 1956-57;

Library of Congress, Washington, D.C., researcher and acting chief of Foreign Affairs Division, 1957-59; foreign relations specialist, Senator Hubert H. Humphrey, Washington, D.C., 1959-60; Johns Hopkins University, research associate, Washington Center for Foreign Policy Research, 1960-61; affiliated with Institute for Defense Analyses, Washington, D.C., 1962-64; Brookings Institution, Washington, D.C., member of senior staff of foreign policy studies division, 1964-76; Georgetown University, Washington, D.C., professorial lecturer in international relations, and faculty associate of center for Strategic and International Studies. Founder and president of Ethics and Public Policy Center, 1976—. Adjunct professor of international politics, American University; lecturer, Salzburg Seminar in American Studies, 1964, and National Defense College of Japan, 1968. Member of President John F. Kennedy's Task Force on Arms Control, 1961. Consultant to Council on Religion and International Affairs, 1958-64, to International Affairs Program of Ford Foundation, 1960, and to Institute for Defense Analyses.

MEMBER: International Institute for Strategic Studies, American Political Science Association, American Society of Christian Ethics, Society for Religion in Higher Education, Washington Institute of Foreign Affairs, Cosmos Club, Society of Scholars (Johns Hopkins University), Yale Club of Washington.

WRITINGS: Ethics and United States Foreign Policy, World Publishing, 1957; (editor) *The World Crisis and American Responsibility,* Association Press, 1958; (co-author) *Profile of American Politics,* Houghton, 1960; *Arms and Arms Control,* Praeger, 1962; *Crisis in the Congo,* Brookings Institution, 1965; *Uncertain Mandate: Politics of the U.N. Congo Operation,* Johns Hopkins Press, 1967; *Spear and Scepter: Army, Police, and Politics in Tropical Africa,* Brookings Institute, 1970; (editor) *Ethics and World Politics,* Johns Hopkins Press, 1972; *TV and National Defense: An Analysis of CBS News, 1972-1973,* Institute for American Strategy, 1974; *Nuclear Arms in the Third World,* Brookings Institution, 1979; *Amsterdam to Nairobi: The World Council of Churches and the Third World,* Ethics and Public Policy Center, 1979; (co-author) *The C.I.A. and the American Ethic,* Ethics and Public Policy Center, 1980. Contributor of chapters to other books; contributor of articles and book reviews to professional journals and other periodicals including *New York Times, Wall Street Journal, Washington Post,* and *Washington Star.* Member of editorial boards, *World Affairs* and *Policy Review.*

WORK IN PROGRESS: Editing a variety of studies published by the Ethics and Public Policy Center.

SIDELIGHTS: Ernest W. Lefever told *CA:* "Ethics and politics in our time are often seen as separate spheres which make contradictory claims on citizens and statesmen alike. To many persons the Judaeo-Christian heritage seems irrelevant to the clashing interests and compromises of political life. The coinage of political and moral discourse has been debased by this estrangement from our basic Western values, and we have become confused by cynical forebodings on the one hand and utopian expectations on the other."

* * *

LEFLER, Irene (Whitney) 1917-

PERSONAL: Born May 29, 1917, in Hominy Falls, W.Va.; daughter of Hughie Mac and Mary Magdalene (Whitney) Jamison; married James Cameron Lefler, December 2, 1939 (divorced, 1964); children: Mary Ellen (Mrs. Norman Wilson), James M., John G. *Education:* Oakland Community College, graduate, 1973. *Politics:* Democrat. *Religion:* Seventh-day Adventist. *Home and office:* 24 Jefferson St., Pontiac, Mich. 48058. *Agent:* Dorothy Markinko, McIntosh & Otis, Inc., 475 Fifth Ave., New York, N.Y. 10017.

CAREER: Free-lance writer, 1967—. Licensed practical nurse, 1965; Starr Commonwealth for Boys, Albion, Mich., housemother, 1965; Pontiac General Hospital, Pontiac, Mich., practical nurse, 1965-67; Pontiac State Hospital, Pontiac, practical nurse, 1968-71; Clinton Valley Center, Pontiac, practical nurse, 1969-72; Waterford School District, Media Materials Center, Waterford, Mich., technical assistant and educational puppeteer, 1977-79. Has conducted puppeteer's and writer's workshops. *Member:* Puppeteers of America, American Museum of Natural History, National Historical Society, National Geographic Society, Smithsonian Associates, St. Davids Christian Writers. *Awards, honors:* Special Recognition award, St. Davids Christian Writers Conference, 1972, for short story "Second Chance"; first place awards in two writer's workshops, 1972; Layman of the Year award, Michigan Conference of Seventh-day Adventists, 1976.

WRITINGS: Bessie Bee, Southern Publishing, 1972. Contributor of radio scripts, short stories, poetry, and articles to various publications, including *Guide, Primary Treasure, Our Little Friend, Teen Power, Stories for Children, Your Story Hour, The Secret Place,* and *Pontiac Times.*

WORK IN PROGRESS: Annie Ant for Southern Publishing; a complete nature series for Southern Publishing; *Buffalo Trail to Guyandotte; Balto; The Cracker Jack Teachers.*

SIDELIGHTS: Irene Lefler told *CA* that she "began writing by subscribing to writers' publications—*The Writer* and *Writer's Digest, The Writers' Yearbook* and *Writers' Market.* I checked out all books on creative writing I could find at my local library and studied them intently, taking notes and creating my own textbooks for reference to help me with the writing craft. I have created many helpful notebooks and charts, some suggested by other writers, and some original. At present, as I'm writing *Buffalo Trail to Guyandotte,* I'm creating a perpetual writer's calendar, which I'm filling with historical facts, nature information, and other information which will prove helpful to writers, and which I may also send to a publisher so other writers could benefit from it.

"Afternoons and nights are when I can write best. During the day I attend my chores and try to associate with friends while I have lunch in my favorite restaurant. Sometimes I work nights until two A.M. I enjoy the research most of all, and always file my research notes away for possible use later.

"I have to write my first drafts by pencil, and do a great deal of my editing as I go along. I keep writing one sentence over and over in various ways until it sounds right when I read it aloud, then I go on in the same way. This is a slow process, but I feel children deserve the best, and I continually strive for what should be perfect for a particular piece. Evidently this system pays off, for I did not have to do any revision after the complete manuscript of *Bessie Bee* was sent in.

"During the past four years I've been an educational puppeteer. I've conducted puppet workshops (and writer's workshops) in many schools, clubs, churches, etc. I hope to write a proposal so I can obtain a grant to enable me to use my Cracker Jack Puppets to encourage students in elementary schools not to use drugs, alcohol, or tobacco. I have several types and sizes of puppet stages, and my own recording equipment, special music and sound effect recordings. I do all the voices and record the special music and sound effects. Most of my programs are for one puppeteer. I write many of my own scripts. I may write a how-to book on puppetry and some scripts.''

To aspiring writers she writes: ''If I can do it, you can too. Lack of education is no excuse, if one really wants to write. When I wrote *Bessie Bee* and it was published in 1972, I had only a tenth-grade education. I kept educating myself, and have accumulated a personal reference library to be proud of. I did the latter by attending local book sales, going to flea markets, garage sales, and the Salvation Army store in search of informative books suitable for a reference library. In the same way I've furnished a nice study for myself. Decent bookcases, file cabinets, desks, sturdy three-ring notebooks (so very costly when new) all can be purchased from the places I mentioned.''

BIOGRAPHICAL/CRITICAL SOURCES: Pontiac Press, April 3, 1971; *Oakland Press,* April 3, 1971, September 6, 1972, December 19, 1973, September 9, 1974, August 21, 1976; *West Virginia Hillbilly,* spring, 1971; *Pontiac-Waterford Times,* March 15, 1979.

* * *

LEHMAN, Celia 1928-

PERSONAL: Born April 9, 1928, in Dalton, Ohio; daughter of Grover Cleveland (a farmer) and Fairy (Amstutz) Gerber; married Calvin R. Lehman (a farmer), March 30, 1968; children: Galen, Judith, Audrey, Ethan. *Education:* Goshen College, B.S., 1957; Kent State University, M.A., 1967. *Religion:* Mennonite. *Home:* 13170 Arnold Rd., Dalton, Ohio 44618.

CAREER: Employed as bookkeeper and telephone operator; elementary school teacher at public schools in Dalton, Ohio, 1957—; American School of Kinshasha, Kinshasa, Zaire, teacher, 1965-67; elementary school teacher at public schools in Kidron, Ohio, 1968—. *Member:* National Education Association, National Educators Fellowship.

WRITINGS: God Is My Best Friend, Standard Publishing, 1973; (co-author) *Wild West on the Range,* Standard Publishing, 1978. Also co-author of ''Unto These Hills,'' a sesquicentennial pageant, produced in Dalton, Ohio, 1972, and author of ''The Middle Man,'' a choric reading for the bicentennial celebration, produced in Ohio, 1976, and *I Felt Your Presence, Lord.* Contributor to *On the Line* and *Jet Cadets.*

WORK IN PROGRESS: ''The story of my mother's life in allegorical style.''

SIDELIGHTS: Celia Lehman told *CA* that her first book, *God Is My Best Friend,* ''came as a response to my fifth graders appeal, 'what will happen to us if there is a war?' It is an answer to that and other problems facing children.'' Her third book, *I Felt Your Presence, Lord* (as yet unpublished), ''uses vignettes and photographs of my diary while spending two years as a teacher in Africa.

''The book I am working on is in response to my mother's friend, [and] my college professor, who challenged me to write my mother's life story. I kept rolling the idea around. [Then] one night at 2:30 I awoke with such a burning desire to write that I jumped out of bed and ran for paper and pencil. By 6:00 a.m. that morning I had the complete story in allegorical style. As it turned out, I had placed my mother in an aquatic world. Her whole life fit into it beautifully. [As a result,] the words flowed.

''My advice to aspiring writers would be to keep ideas accumulating in your head. Eventually one of them 'pops' and you can no longer refrain from writing. Then writing is a cinch. There may be snags along the way, but you use these times for reflections and new insights. [Also,] keep researching, it helps ideas flow.''

* * *

LEHMAN, Chester K. 1895-1980

PERSONAL: Born November 5, 1895, in Millersville, Pa.; died March 2, 1980; son of Daniel N. and Magdalena (Kindig) Lehman; married Myra S. Kendig, 1921; children: Miriam Weaver, Esther, Dorothy Yoder, Robert. *Education:* Hesston College and Bible School, A.B., 1919; Princeton Theological Seminary, Th.B., 1921; Franklin and Marshall College, A.M., 1921; Union Theological Seminary, Th.M., 1935, Th.D., 1940. *Home and office:* 1033 College Ave., Harrisonburg, Va. 22801.

CAREER: Ordained minister in Mennonite church, 1929. Eastern Mennonite College, Harrisonburg, Va., professor of theology, 1921-66, professor emeritus, 1966-80, registrar, 1921-49, dean, 1924-56, dean emeritus, 1956-80. *Member:* Evangelical Theological Society.

WRITINGS—All published by Herald Press: *The Inadequacy of Evolution as a World View,* 1933; *New Testament Studies,* 1936; *Junior Catechism,* 1940; *The Fulfillment of Prophecy,* 1950, revised edition, 1971; *The Holy Spirit and the Holy Life,* 1959; *Biblical Theology,* Volume I: *Old Testament,* 1971, Volume II: *New Testament,* 1974. Compiler with others of ''Life Songs Number Two,'' and *The Mennonite Hymnal,* published by Herald Press.

AVOCATIONAL INTERESTS: Music.

* * *

LELCHUK, Alan 1938-

PERSONAL: Born September 15, 1938, in Brooklyn, N.Y.; son of Harry and Belle (Simon) Lelchuk. *Education:* Brooklyn College (now Brooklyn College of the City University of New York), B.A., 1960; Stanford University, M.A., 1963, Ph.D., 1965; University of London, graduate study, 1963-64. *Agent:* Georges Borchardt, Inc., 136 East 57th St., New York, N.Y. 10022. *Office:* Department of English, Brandeis University, Waltham, Mass. 02154.

CAREER: Brandeis University, Waltham, Mass., assistant professor of English, 1966-77, writer-in-residence, 1978—. *Member:* Authors Guild. *Awards, honors:* Received Yaddo fellowships, 1968-69, 1971, 1973; MacDowell Colony fellowship, 1969; Guggenheim fellow, 1976-77; Mishkenot Sha'Ananim fellow, 1976-77.

WRITINGS: American Mischief, Farrar, Straus, 1973; *Miriam at Thirty-Four,* Farrar, Straus, 1974; *Shrinking,* Atlantic, 1978; (contributor) A. Edelstein, editor, *Images and Ideas in American Culture,* Brandeis University Press, 1979. Contributor to periodicals, including *New American Review, Modern Occasions, Partisan Review, New York Review of Books, Dissent, Works in Progress, New Republic, New York Times Book Review,* and *Transatlantic Review.* Associate editor of *Modern Occasions,* 1970-72.

WORK IN PROGRESS: Editing, with Gershon Shaked, *Eight Great Hebrew Short Novels.*

SIDELIGHTS: Alan Lelchuk's first novel, *American Mischief,* achieved notoriety for its author even before its publication. The novel first received attention because Bantam Books reportedly paid more than $250,000 for the paperback rights—a very high figure for a first book, especially in 1972. Then Lelchuk collided with Norman Mailer over a scene in the novel in which a character named Norman Mailer is murdered in an ignominious manner. At a meeting with Lelchuk and Farrar, Straus & Giroux representatives, Mailer complained that the scene was libelous and degrading to his character. At one point in the discussion, which grew heated, Mailer remarked, "Lelchuk, I don't want ever to meet you in an alley, because if I do, you're going to be nothing but a hank of hair and some fillings." For his part, Lelchuk argued that the importance of the scene had been blown out of proportion. "The scene is four pages out of 500 pages," he said, "and it obviously plays a small part in the whole texture of the book." Eventually, Lelchuk made some changes in the scene, but he insisted that the alterations were minor.

Notwithstanding highly favorable advance comments from Philip Roth, *American Mischief* received many unfavorable reviews. A *Time* critic, for example, finds that "*American Mischief* is another exploitive, topical novel. Lelchuk romps through the confusions and contradictions of today's beleagured values . . . like a gratuitous looter in a cultural disaster area." Joseph Epstein, writing in the *Washington Post Book World,* believes that the novel is "as botched a piece of literature as has come along in some while. . . . Dialogue, plot and character are rudimentary. Everyone speaks exactly alike. . . . The plot itself, and especially the way the book ends, is slipshod and disappointing." In a *New York Times Book Review* critique, Alfred Kazin does find Lelchuk to be "a lively enough writer of narrative, entertaining above all in his provocativeness." Yet Kazin goes on to say that the novel is "too intellectual" and expresses "no point of view that gets to the reader." Eliot Fremont-Smith, in *Saturday Review,* also has a mixed response to the work. He considers the book "good and bad, immensely repetitive and boring," and "clever, funny, and fashionable."

Miriam at Thirty-Four, Lelchuk's second novel, also elicited some negative responses. In the *New York Times Book Review,* Sara Blackburn contends that Lelchuk's handling of female sexuality "leaves readers holding a bag of demonstration sex scenes and pretentious modern moralizing." In addition, Blackburn feels that the characters lack depth, and she concludes that "in presenting Miriam [the protaganist] and everyone in only one dimension—the sexual—Lelchuk has at once sensationalized and trivialized the culture and the character whose life he means to illuminate." On the other hand, William H. Pritchard notes in the *Hudson Review* that *Miriam at Thirty-Four* "is superb in its presentation of Greater Boston, particularly the 'accepted insanities' of Cambridge." But he finds this realistic presentation does not mesh well with the novel's "parables of self-destruction [or] self-fulfillment."

The mixed critical receptions continued with the publication of *Shrinking.* In *Saturday Review,* Robert Stephen Spitz comments that *Shrinking* "is a confusing, often brilliant work that is too grandiose in scope to command the force or focus necessary to substantiate any one of its many subplots." Robert Towers, writing in the *New York Times Book Review,* reacts more strongly. He objects that the book seems to plead for favorable treatment from critics, that it lacks wit, that "the writing is often slapdash," and that the book is a mixture of disparate elements, including "diatribes against critics and against stylistic distinction . . . , half-baked lectures on Melville and Babel, . . . transcripts of creative-writing classes, and remembered episodes from [the protaganist's] Brooklyn childhood." In contrast to this, Anthony R. Cannella, in *Best Sellers,* admires Lelchuk's ambition, integrity, and intelligence in tackling the "meaty topics" of "the relationships of life and art, literature and criticism, illusion and reality, genius and madness, psychiatry and religion, fiction and autobiography." And John Leonard of the *New York Times* discovers "fun and passion in *Shrinking,* as well as reasonably interesting counterpoint between the devices of art and psychiatry." Yet Leonard also finds "hundreds of pages of tedium," and he observes that "Mr. Lelchuk careens from a comedy of literary manners to a seriousness so nervous and defensive that you want to give him a calming lollipop."

BIOGRAPHICAL/CRITICAL SOURCES: New York Review of Books, February 8, 1973; *Washington Post Book World,* February 11, 1973; *New York Times Book Review,* February 11, 1973, November 17, 1974, May 21, 1978; *World,* February 13, 1973; *Saturday Review,* February 17, 1973, June 24, 1978; *Time,* February 26, 1973; *Ms.,* April, 1975; *Hudson Review,* Volume XXVIII, number 1, 1975; *Contemporary Literary Criticism,* Volume V, Gale, 1976; *New York Times,* May 8, 1978.

* * *

LEMAY, Harding 1922-

PERSONAL: Born March 16, 1922, in North Bangor, N.Y.; son of Henry James (a farmer) and Eva (Gorrow) Lemay; married Priscilla Amidon, September, 1947 (marriage dissolved, 1953); married Dorothy Shaw, September 19, 1953; children: (second marriage) Stephen, Susan. *Education:* Studied at Neighborhood Playhouse School of the Theatre, New York, N.Y., 1946-48. *Pllitics:* Registered Liberal. *Religion:* None. *Home and office:* 146 East 19th St., New York, N.Y. 10003. *Agent:* Harold Ober Associates, 40 East 49th St., New York, N.Y. 10017.

CAREER: New York Public Library, New York City, member of special assignments staff, 1952-56; American Book Publishers Council, New York City, member of television liaison staff, 1956-58; Alfred A. Knopf, Inc., New York City, publicity manager, 1958-61, assistant to chairman and to president, 1961-63, vice-president, 1963-67; free-lance writer, 1967—; National Broadcasting Corp. (NBC-TV), New York City, head writer for "Another World" television series, 1971—. Lecturer, Hunter College of the City University of New York, 1968-72. *Military service:* U.S. Army, 1943-46; became corporal. *Member:* P.E.N. American Center (vice-president, 1960-70), Dramatists Guild, New Dramatists Committee (member of executive board, 1965-71), The Players. *Awards, honors:* National Book Award nomination, 1972, for *Inside, Looking Out;* Emmy award, National Academy of Television Arts and Sciences, 1975, for "Another World" television series.

WRITINGS: Inside, Looking Out (autobiography), Harper's Magazine Press, 1971; (author of introduction) Arthur H. Bremer, *Introduction to an Assassin's Diary,* Harper's Magazine Press, 1973; *Only Make Believe,* Atheneum, 1980.

Plays—all first produced at New Dramatists Workshop, New York, N.Y.: "Look at Any Man," 1963; "The Little Birds Fly," 1965; "From a Dark Land," 1967; "Return Upriver," 1968; "The Death of Eagles," 1970; "The Joslyn Circle," 1971, also produced at Dublin Theatre Festival, 1973; "The Off Season," 1973; "How He Became a Writer," 1979.

Author of television scripts, including "They" (with Marya Mannes), produced by WNDT-TV, 1970, and "Whose Life?," produced by NBC-TV, 1970. Contributor to *Life, Washington Post, New Yorker* and *New York Herald Tribune Books.*

SIDELIGHTS: William McPherson, writing for the *Washington Post,* points out that in *Inside, Looking Out,* Harding Lemay attempts the formidable task of making sense "of an event as large, as formless and as perilous as a life." Yet according to McPherson, Lemay has "succeeded most beautifully, most movingly." *Inside, Looking Out,* McPherson continues, "is a remarkable odyssey of a man's drive to mine his memories and reconcile his tortured past to his present, to find a form to express the chaos of experience, to make sense of his life. He has succeeded." *New York Times* critic Christopher Lehmann-Haupt also finds that Harding has accomplished his goal, noting that *Inside, Looking Out* is "beautifully written, deeply felt, and structured with subtle craft yet seeming ease. . . . I suppose what it comes down to finally is Lemay's understated yet uncompromising eccentricity. The world went that way while he moved this way—a man with no credentials but his imagination and his soul, no expertise but his slowly dawning understanding of the past. And he arrived."

BIOGRAPHICAL/CRITICAL SOURCES: New York Times, April 14, 1971; *Washington Post,* April 15, 1971; *New York Times Book Review,* May 9, 1971; *Saturday Review,* June 5, 1971.

* * *

LENGYEL, Cornel Adam 1915-
(Cornel Adam)

PERSONAL: Born January 1, 1915, in Fairfield, Conn.; son of Elmer Alexander and Mary Elizabeth (Bismarck) Lengyel; married Teresa M. Delaney, 1933; children: Jerome, Paul, Cornelia, Michael Sebastian. *Home:* Adam's Acres West, El Dorado National Forest, Georgetown, Calif. 95634. *Office:* Department of English, California State University, Sacramento, Calif.

CAREER: Federal Writers' Project, editor, 1936-37; research project supervisor, San Francisco, Calif., 1938-41; Office of Censorship, San Francisco, censor, 1942; Kaiser Shipyards, Richmond, Calif., shipwright, personnel interviewer, 1943-44; Forty-Niner Theatre, Georgetown, Calif., manager, 1946-49; California State University, Sacramento, lecturer in English literature, 1962—. Writer-in-residence, Hamline University, 1968-69; guest lecturer, Massachusetts Institute of Technology, 1969; founder, Dragon's Teeth Press, 1970. Editorial consultant, U.S. Department of Health, Education, and Welfare. Educational director, International Ladies Garment Workers Union, Local 22. *Wartime service:* U.S. Merchant Marine, 1944-45. *Member:* Authors Guild, Poetry Society of America, American Historical Society, American Association of University Professors, P.E.N. American Center. *Awards, honors:* Albert M. Bender award in literature, 1945; first prize, Maxwell Anderson Awards for poetic drama, 1950; Huntington Hartford fellowship in literature, 1951, 1963; first prize, Poetry Society of Virginia, 1951; DiCastagnola Award, Poetry Society of America, 1971; National Endowment for the Arts award, 1976.

WRITINGS: American Testament: The Story of a Promised Land, Grace Books, 1956; *Four Days in July,* Doubleday, 1958, reprinted, Queen's House, 1976; *I, Benedict Arnold: The Anatomy of Treason,* Doubleday, 1960; *Presidents of the U.S.A.,* Bantam, 1961; *Ethan Allan and the Green Mountain Boys,* Doubleday, 1961; *The Declaration of Independence,* Grosset, 1969. Also editor of *History of Music in San Francisco,* 1942.

Poetry: *Thirty Pieces,* Hoffman, 1933; *First Psalms,* 1950; *Fifty Poems,* 1965; *The Lookout's Letter,* Dragon's Teeth, 1970; *The Creative Self,* Mouton, 1971; *Four Dozen Songs,* Blue Oak Press, 1976.

Plays: "The World's My Village," 1935; "Jonas Fugitive," 1936; "The Giant's Trap," 1938; *The Atom Clock* (produced in The Hague, Netherlands, 1954), Fantasy, 1951; "Eden, Inc.," 1954, produced under revised title, "Omega," 1963; "Will of Stratford," produced in 1964; *Three Plays,* Chandler Publishing, 1964; "The Case of Benedict Arnold," 1975; "Doctor Franklin," 1976; "The Shadow Trap," 1977; *The Master Plan,* Dragon's Teeth, 1978.

Contributor to anthologies, including: *The Golden Year,* Poetry Society of America, 1960, *The Britannica Library of Great American Writing,* edited by Louis Untermeyer, 1961, *The Menorah Treasury,* edited by Leo W. Schwarz, 1964, and *Interpretation in Our Time,* edited by Baxter Geeting, 1966. Contributor of poems, stories, and articles to magazines. Former music critic, *The Coast;* columnist, *Argonaut.*

WORK IN PROGRESS: A Book of 150 Fables.

SIDELIGHTS: Cornel Lengyel told *CA:* "To realize an enduring work of the mind, the creative man must practice more than ordinary virtues. The strength and dedication and discipline required, and the energy expended to accomplish his work, rivals the legendary labors of Hercules. The practice of a creative art is a private rite which starts with the taming of the ancestral ape in any man. Whatever the morality of the artist, a work of art represents virtue in action. In an age of mass values the practice of an art is one of the few ways left in which the individual may test his highest capacities, draw on all his inner resources, and expend himself freely in his full humanity."

* * *

LENS, Sidney 1912-

PERSONAL: Born Jan. 28, 1912, in Newark, N.J.; married Shirley Ruben, October, 1946. *Education:* Attended public schools in New York, N.Y. *Agent:* Blassingame, McCauley & Wood, 60 East 42nd St., New York, N.Y. 10017. *Office:* 127 North Dearborn St., Chicago, Ill. 60602.

CAREER: Writer. Active in labor unions for more than twenty-five years; United Service Employees Union, AFL-CIO, Local 329, Chicago, Ill., director, 1941-66. Lecturer at University of Chicago, Roosevelt University, University of Illinois, and other universities. Candidate for U.S. Congress from 2nd Illinois district, 1962; candidate for Illinois Legislature, 1964. *Member:* Institute of Social Studies (chairman), National Committee to End War in Vietnam (co-chairman), New Mobilization Committee to End War in Vietnam (co-chairman), Impeach Nixon Committee (chairman), Justice, Action, and Peace in Latin America (chairman), Mobilization for Survival (member of steering committee), Chicago Council on Foreign Relations (member of board of directors). *Awards, honors:* Patron Saints Award, Society of Midland Authors, 1970; Institute for Policy Studies fellow.

WRITINGS: Left, Right and Center, Regnery, 1949; *The Counterfeit Revolution,* Beacon Press, 1952; *A World in Revolution,* Praeger, 1956; *The Crisis of American Labor,* Sagamore Books, 1959; *Working Men,* Putnam, 1961; *Africa: Awakening Giant,* Putnam, 1962; *A Country Is Born,* Putnam, 1964; *The Futile Crusade,* Quadrangle, 1964; *Radicalism in America,* Crowell, 1966; *What Unions Do,* Putnam, 1968; *Poverty: Americans Enduring Paradox,* Crowell, 1969; *The Military Industrial Complex,* Pilgrim, 1970; *The Forging of the American Empire,* Crowell, 1972; *The Labor*

Wars, Doubleday, 1973; *Poverty, Yesterday and Today*, Crowell, 1973; *The Promise and Pitfalls of Revolution*, Pilgrim, 1974; *The Day before Doomsday: An Anatomy of the Nuclear Arms Race*, Beacon Press, 1978; *Unrepentent Radical: An American Activist's Account of His Five Turbulent Decades* (autobiography), Beacon Press, 1980. Columnist for *National Catholic Reporter*. Contributor of articles to magazines, including *Harper's*, *Harvard Business Review*, *Nation*, *Rotarian*, *Commonweal*, and many others. Editor, *Liberation;* contributing editor, *Progressive*.

SIDELIGHTS: Sidney Lens told *CA:* "As I view it, a writer must be (a) a nonconformist, (b) socially-conscious, and his works should be aimed at giving readers an insight beyond the mundane and conventional. It is no accident that most of the best-known writers in the country were at one time or another associated with radical causes, for it is only those who question that which is who can understand humankind's innermost strivings.

"I was born in what was then China-town Newark. My father died when I was three. My mother, a beautiful immigrant who worked for $2.50 a week—for seventy-two hours a week—when she first arrived here in 1907, never rose appreciably beyond the poverty level. During my formative years in the Great Depression, I had the same feelings of frustration that my mother probably did, but I can not say that I ever *felt* poor, even when I had only a dime in my pocket, which was more often than not. I became dedicated to causes. I organized unemployed, organized factory workers, led demonstrations and strikes, headed a crusade against gangsters in the Chicago union that I eventually led, participated in the Detroit sitdown strikes, then in the 1950's and 1960's became one of the leaders of the antiwar movement. I was co-chairman of the New Mobilization Committee to End the War in Vietnam, and Illinois chairman of the Impeach Nixon Committee—among many other things.

"My writings reflect these experiences, and while some people would argue that a writer should detach himself from his life and biases, I would counter-argue that first and foremost every writer is a proselytizer. And if he isn't, he is only a stylist, not a writer. In any case, I never have believed—though I've written seventeen books and hundreds of articles—that anyone should be a writer just to be a writer, acquiring hoped-for fame and fortune. He should be a writer to translate what he is doing in the world beyond, on paper."

BIOGRAPHICAL/CRITICAL SOURCES: Chicago Tribune, May 4, 1980; Sidney Lens, *Unrepentent Radical: An American Activist's Account of His Five Turbulent Decades*, Beacon Press, 1980.

* * *

LEON, Pierre R. 1926-

PERSONAL: Born March 12, 1926, in Ligre, France; son of Roger and Marie Louise (Cosson) Leon; married Monique Maury (a university professor), April 18, 1949; children: Francoise. *Education:* University of Paris, Licence es Lettres, 1951; University of Besancon, Doctorat, 1960, Doctorat es Lettres, 1972. *Home:* 150 Farnham Ave., No. 504, Toronto, Ontario, Canada M4V 1H5. *Office:* Department of French, University of Toronto, Toronto, Ontario, Canada M5S 1A8.

CAREER: University of Paris, Sorbonne, Paris, France, attache at Institute of Phonetics, 1950-58; Ohio State University, Columbus, assistant professor of French, 1958-60; University of Besancon, Besancon, France, director of language laboratory at Center for Applied Linguistics, 1960-63; Ohio State University, Columbus, associate professor of French, 1963-64; University of Toronto, Toronto, Ontario, associate professor, 1964-65, professor of French, 1965—, director of Experimental Phonetics Laboratory, 1966—. Maitre de conferences, Universite de Pau, 1978—. *Military service:* French Army, 1948-49, Reserve, 1949—; became lieutenant. *Member:* International Phonetic Association, Speech Association of America, Modern Language Association of America, Association Canadienne Francaise pour l'Avancement des Sciences, Societe Linguistique (Paris). *Awards, honors:* Prix of the French Academy, 1966, for *Introduction a la phonetique corrective;* Canada Council grants, 1965-74; Palmes academiques, 1978.

WRITINGS—Published by Didier, except as indicated: *Aide-memoire d'orthoepie*, 1961, new edition published as *Prononciation du francais standard: aide-memoire d'orthoepie*, 1966, 2nd edition, 1972; *Laboratoire de langues et correction phonetique: essai methodologique*, 1962, 2nd edition, 1967; (with wife, Monique Leon) *Introduction a la phonetique corrective a l'usage des professeurs de francais a l'etranger*, Hachette-Larousse, 1964, 4th edition, 1971; (contributor) *Recherches et techniques au service de l'enseignement*, Conseil de la Cooperation Culturelle (Strasbourg), 1964; (contributor) Albert Valdman, editor, *Trends in Language Teaching*, McGraw, 1966; (with others) *Le Francais international*, two volumes, Centre Educatif et Culturel (Montreal), 1967; (with Philippe Martin) *Prolegomenes a l'etude des structures intonatives*, 1970; *Essais de phonostylistique*, 1971; (with Allan Grundstrom) *Interrogation et intonation en francais standard et en francais canadien*, 1973; (editor with Henri Mitterand) *L'Analyse du discours*, Centre Educatif et Culturel, 1976; *Applied and Experimental Linguistics*, 1979; (with Martin) *Toronto English*, 1979; (with Ivan Fonagy) *L'Accent en francais contemporain*, 1980; *Animots croises*, Nathan (Paris), 1980.

Editor and contributor: *Applied Linguistics and the Teaching of French/Linguistique appliquee et enseignement du francais*, Centre Educatif et Culturel, 1967; *Recherches sur la structure phonique du francais canadien*, Didier, 1969; (with Georges Faure and Andre Rigault) *Prosodic Feature Analysis/Analyse des faits prosodiques*, Didier, 1970; (with others) *Problemes de l'analyse textuelle/Problems of Textual Analysis*, Didier, 1971; (with others) *Homages a Pierre Delattre*, Mouton, 1972; (with Henry Schogt and Edward Burstynsky) *La Phonologie*, Klincsieck (Paris), 1976.

WORK IN PROGRESS: Editing the "Studia Phonetica" series for Didier.

* * *

LEPROHON, Pierre 1903-
(Jean Valbonne)

PERSONAL: Born September 3, 1903, in Avesnes, Nord, France; son of Alain (a journalist) and Aline (Prunier) Leprohon. *Education:* Lycee de Lille, brevet elementaire, 1919. *Home:* 2 Square Francois Couperin, 92160 Antony, France.

CAREER: Film critic and historian, 1928—. *Le Rouge et le noir* (literary review), Paris, France, 1928-30, began as assistant editor, became editor; writer for literary and film journals, 1928-50; *Unifrance-Film* (official publication of Cinema Francais), Paris, editor-in-chief, 1950-58. *Member:* Societe des ecrivains de cinema (founding member and honorary copresident), Association des critiques de cinema, Societe des gens de lettres.

WRITINGS: Charlot: ou, La Naissance d'un myth (biography), Debresse, 1936, published as *Charles Chaplin,* J. Melot, 1946, 4th edition, Corymbe, 1970; *Le Cinema et la montagne,* J. Susse, 1944; *Les Mille et un metiers du cinema,* J. Melot, 1947; *La Hollande,* Documents d'Art (Monaco), 1951; *Cinquante ans de cinema francais, 1895-1945,* Cerf, 1954; *Presences contemporaines: Cinema,* Debresse, 1957; *Sahara horizon sud,* Gedalge, 1957.

Chasseurs d'images, A. Bonne, 1960; *Paul Cezanne* (biography), Editions et imprimeries du Sud-Est, 1961; *Michelangelo Antonioni,* Seghers, 1961, 4th edition, 1969, translation by Scott Sullivan published as *Michelangelo Antonioni: An Introduction,* Simon & Schuster, 1963; *Histoire du cinema,* two volumes, Cerf, 1961-63, Volume I: *Vie et mort du cinematographe (1895-1930),* Volume II: *L'Etape du film parlant (1927-1962);* (with Yvonne Deslandres and Henry Certigny) *La Vie des grands peintres impressionnistes et nabis,* Editions du Sud, 1964; *Tel fut Van Gogh* (biography), Editions de Sud, 1964, published as *Vincent Van Gogh,* Corymbe, 1972; *Jean Epstein,* Seghers, 1964.

Le Cinema italien, Seghers, 1966, translation by Roger Greaves and Oliver Stallybrass published as *The Italian Cinema,* Praeger, 1972; *Vittorio De Sica,* Seghers, 1966; *Hommes et cites du Val de Loire,* Editions de Sud and A. Michel, 1966; *Le Monde du cinema,* P. Waleffe, 1967; *Hommes et metiers de cinema,* A. Bonne, 1967; (with Arlette Marinie) *Les Grandes Hommes du Nord,* Editions du Sud and A. Michel, 1967; *Cote d'Azur,* Hermes, 1967; *Jean Renoir,* Seghers, 1967, translation by Brigid Elson published under same title, Crown, 1971; *Le Destin tragique de cavelier de La Salle* (biography), Debresse, 1969.

Published by Minerva (Geneva), except as indicated: *Le Cinema, cette aventure,* A. Bonne, 1970; *Francois d'Assise* (biography), Corymbe, 1972; *Toute la Grece,* 1974; *Toute la Yougoslavie,* 1975; *Tout Paris,* 1976; *Paul Gaugin,* Corymbe, 1976; *Tout Rome,* 1977; *Tout Florence,* 1978; *Tout Venise,* 1979; *Flora Tristan,* Corymbe, 1979.

Under pseudonym Jean Valbonne: *Villes de Provence et de Cote d'Azur,* A. Michel, 1966; *Toute l'Espagne,* Minerva (Geneva), 1972; *Toute l'Italie,* Minerva, 1972; *Toute la France,* Minerva, 1973.

Also author of *Toute la Hollande,* Minerva. Author of supplements to Anthologie du Cinema series, "L'Avant-scene du cinema": *Julien Duvivier, 1896-1967,* 1968; *Raimu, 1883-1946,* 1969; *Gerard Philipe, 1922-1959,* 1971. Author of weekly column for *L'Officiel des spectacles,* 1946-79. Contributor to *Encyclopaedia Britannica, L'Intran, L'Ami du peuple, La Liberte, L'Echo d'Oran, Le Journal, Varietes, Camping, La Grande Revue, Cinemonde, Pour Vous, Plaisir de lire,* and other publications.

SIDELIGHTS: Leprohon's works have been translated into twelve languages.

* * *

LEVENTMAN, Seymour 1930-

PERSONAL: Born June 9, 1930, in Brooklyn, N.Y.; son of Alex and Shirley (Sherman) Leventman; married Paula Goldman, 1961. *Education:* Washington State College, B.A., 1951; Indiana University, M.A., 1953; University of Minnesota, Ph.D., 1958. *Office:* Department of Sociology, Boston College, Chestnut Hill, Mass. 02160.

CAREER: Macalester College, St. Paul, Minn., instructor, 1957-58; Pennsylvania State University, State College, instructor, 1958-60; University of Pennsylvania, Philadelphia, assistant professor of sociology, 1960-68; Boston College, Chestnut Hill, Mass., associate professor of sociology, 1968—. Research consultant, Community Mental Health Center, 1966—. *Member:* American Sociological Association, American Association of University Professors, Society for Scientific Study of Social Problems, Eastern Sociological Society.

WRITINGS: (With Judith Rita Kramer) *Children of the Gilded Ghetto: Conflict Resolutions of Three Generations of American Jews,* Yale University Press, 1961; (with Charles R. Figley) *Strangers at Home: The Vietnam Veteran since the War,* Praeger, 1979.

WORK IN PROGRESS: The Black Ghetto in Transition.

AVOCATIONAL INTERESTS: Music, art, reading, sports.†

* * *

LEVIN, Alvin Irving 1921-

PERSONAL: Born December 22, 1921, in New York, N.Y.; son of David (a builder) and Frances (Schloss) Levin; married Beatrice Van Loon, June 5, 1976. *Education:* University of Miami, B.M., 1941; California State College (now University), Los Angeles, M.A., 1955; University of California, Los Angeles, Ed.D. (with honors), 1968. *Home and office:* 8612 Jellico Ave., Northridge, Calif. 91325.

CAREER: Allied Artists, Eagle-Lion Studios, Hollywood, Calif., composer-arranger for motion pictures, television, and theatre, 1945-65; Los Angeles Unified School District, Los Angeles, Calif., training and supervising teacher, 1957-65, adult education instructor, 1962-63, research specialist in the Office of the Superintendent, 1965-67; California State College (now University), Los Angeles, assistant professor of educational research, 1968-69; San Fernando Valley State College (now California State University), Northridge, assistant professor of elementary education, 1969-73; Alvin Irving Levin Philanthropic Foundation, Los Angeles, Calif., founder and president, 1973—; founder and president, Meet Your New Personality (mind expansion program), 1975-77; founder and president, Divine Love Church, 1977—; founder and president, Happy Land Complex (theme park), 1978. Ordained minister, 1975. Member of board of overseers, California School of Professional Psychology. Director, North Hollywood Chamber of Commerce. *Awards, honors:* Cited for outstanding achievement by California State Senate, 1977, and North Hollywood Chamber of Commerce, 1976, 1977.

WRITINGS: My Ivory Tower, House-Warren, 1950; *Symposium: Values in Kaleidoscope* (monograph), California State University Press, 1973. Also author of a musical drama, "Happy Land," 1971, and of videotape recordings and educational films. Contributor to U.S. Department of Education reports, 1966-67. Author of film scripts, "Main Street Symphony," 1960, "No Escape," 1961, "The Last Judgment," 1961.

WORK IN PROGRESS: Rendezvous with Humankind.

SIDELIGHTS: Alvin Levin told *CA:* "My writing career began in 1950 when, in having my first cosmic experience, I realized that the arts, sciences, and religions of our world, although diverse in expression, were saying 'the whole is far *greater* than the sum of its parts,' or 'there is unity in diversity.'" *Avocational interests:* Piano, recording, jogging, gym.

* * *

LEVINE, I(srael) E. 1923-

PERSONAL: Born August 30, 1923, in New York, N.Y.;

son of Albert E. and Sonia (Silver) Levine; married Joy Elaine Michael, 1946; children: David Myer, Carol Lynn. *Education:* City College (now City College of the City University of New York), B.S.S., 1946. *Home:* 140-41 69th Rd., Flushing, N.Y. *Office:* William H. White Publications, 322 West 57th St., New York, N.Y. 10019.

CAREER: City College of the City University of New York, New York City, publicity assistant, 1946-50, assistant director of public relations, 1950-54, director of public relations, 1954-77, assistant to the president, 1964-77; Gralla Publications, New York City, editor, *Health Care Week,* 1977-79; William H. White Publications, New York City, editor, 1979—. *Military service:* U.S. Army Air Forces, 1943-45; became second lieutenant; received Air Medal with four oak leaf clusters, Presidential Unit citation. *Member:* Authors Guild, Metropolitan College Public Relations Council (treasurer, 1959), American College Public Relations Association, American Alumni Council, City College Alumni Association, Queens Valley Home Owners Association.

WRITINGS: (Co-author) *Techniques of Supervision,* National Foremen's Institute, 1954.

Youth books; all published by Messner: *The Discovery of Insulin: Dr. Frederick Banting,* 1959; *Conqueror of Smallpox: Dr. Edward Jenner,* 1960; *Behind the Silken Curtain: Townsend Harris,* 1961; *Inventive Wizard: George Westinghouse,* 1962; *Champion of World Peace: Dag Hammarskjold,* 1962; *Miracle Man of Printing: Ottmar Mergenthaler,* 1963; *Electronics Pioneer: Lee DeForest,* 1964; *Young Man in the White House: John Fitzgerald Kennedy,* 1964; *Oliver Cromwell,* 1966; *Spokesman for the Free World,* 1967; *Lenin: The Man Who Made a Revolution,* 1969; *The Many Faces of Slavery,* 1975. Contributor of over 400 articles to periodicals including *This Week, Better Homes and Gardens, Writer's Digest, Nation's Business* and *Rotarian.* Executive editor, *City College Alumnus,* 1954-74.

SIDELIGHTS: I. E. Levine told *CA:* "I was born and brought up in New York City where I attended DeWitt Clinton High School and the City College of the City University of New York. Both schools have had a long tradition of educating future journalists and other professional writers. In college I majored in physics, but in my junior year, the writing bug infected me, and I changed my course of study to English and social science. However, I never regretted my science studies, for as it turned out a number of articles and books I have written have dealt with scientific subjects, within a biographical or historical framework.

"It seems to me that books of biography and history have a special importance for young people today. The world is complicated and uncertain. Youngsters are desperately searching for guideposts that will help them shape their aspirations and ideals and aid them in finding a way not only of making a living, but of making a life. Biography, which sets forth in an honest and realistic way the example of men and women who have tried to meet this challenge, and history, which places our life and times in a broader perspective, are sorely needed by modern youth. They offer truths that are timeless and universal.

"If the subject is interesting to me and to my own children, I feel it will be interesting to others as well.... My children have taught me that the greatest sin is to be patronizing, to write down. Youngsters today are astute enough to recognize ... a life story which the author has carefully filtered through rose-tinted lenses."

AVOCATIONAL INTERESTS: Golf, music, gardening.

BIOGRAPHICAL/CRITICAL SOURCES: Long Island Press, June 10, 1962; *The City College Alumnus,* December 1977.

* * *

LEVINSON, Harry 1922-

PERSONAL: Born January 16, 1922, in Port Jervis, N.Y.; son of David (a tailor) and Gussie (Nudell) Levinson; married Roberta Freiman, January 11, 1946 (divorced, 1970); children: Marc Richard, Kathy, Anne, Brian Thomas. *Education:* Kansas State Teachers College (now Emporia State University), B.S. in Ed., 1943, M.S., 1947; University of Kansas, Ph.D., 1952. *Religion:* Jewish. *Home:* 225 Brattle St., Cambridge, Mass. 02138. *Office address:* Levinson Institute, P.O. Box 95, Cambridge, Mass. 02138.

CAREER: Topeka Veterans Administration Hospital, Topeka, Kan., psychological intern, 1946-50; Topeka State Hospital, Topeka, coordinator of professional education, 1950-54; Menninger Foundation, Topeka, psychologist, 1954-55, director, division of industrial mental health, 1955-68; Levinson Institute, Cambridge, Mass., president, 1968—; Harvard University, Graduate School of Business, Boston, Mass., Thomas Henry Carroll-Ford Foundation Distinguished Visiting Professor, 1968-72; Boston University, College of Business Administration, Boston, adjunct professor, 1972-74; Harvard University, Medical School, Cambridge, lecturer, 1972—. Visiting professor, Sloan School of Management, Massachusetts Institute of Technology, 1961-62, and School of Business, University of Kansas, 1967; Visiting Centennial Professor, Texas A & M University, 1976; currently adjunct professor of advanced management, Pace University. Diplomate, American Board of Professional Examiners in Psychology; past president, American Board of Professional Psychology. Consultant to business and industry. *Military service:* U.S. Army, Field Artillery, 1943-46; became staff sergeant. *Member:* American Psychological Association (fellow; chairman of legislative committee), American Sociological Association, Industrial Relations Research Association, American Association for Advancement of Science, New York Academy of Science. *Awards, honors:* Distinguished service citation from Hadassah for contribution to public education in mental health; Distinguished Alumnus Award, Kansas State Teachers College, 1968.

WRITINGS: (With William C. Menninger) *Human Understanding in Industry,* Science Research Associates, 1956; (editor) *Toward Understanding Men,* Menninger Foundation, 1956; (with Charlton R. Price, Kenneth J. Munden, Harold J. Mandl, and Charles M. Solley) *Men, Management and Mental Health,* Harvard University Press, 1962; *Emotional Health in the World of Work,* Harper, 1964; *The Exceptional Executive,* New American Library, 1971; *Organizational Diagnosis,* Harvard University Press, 1972; *The Great Jackass Fallacy,* Harvard University Press, 1973; *Executive Stress,* New American Library, 1975; *Psychological Man,* Levinson Institute, 1976. Contributor to professional journals and popular periodicals.

WORK IN PROGRESS: Organizational Intervention; The Impact of CEO.

* * *

LEVY, Leonard Williams 1923-

PERSONAL: Born April 9, 1923, in Toronto, Ontario, Canada; U.S. citizen; son of Albert and Rae (Williams) Levy; married Elyse Gitlow, 1944; children: Wendy Ellen, Leslie

Anne. *Education:* Attended University of Michigan, 1940-43; Columbia University, B.S., 1947, M.A., 1948, Ph.D., 1951. *Religion:* Jewish. *Home:* 820 North Cambridge Ave., Claremont, Calif. 91711. *Office:* Department of History, Claremont Graduate School, Claremont, Calif.

CAREER: Columbia University, New York, N.Y., research assistant, 1950-51; Brandeis University, Waltham, Mass., 1951-70, began as instructor, became associate professor, Earl Warren Professor of American Constitutional History, 1958-70, dean of Graduate School of Arts and Sciences and associate dean of faculty, 1957-63, dean of arts and sciences faculty, 1963-66, chairman of graduate program in the history of American civilization, 1966-67, 1969-70, chairman of department of history, 1963-64, 1967-68; Claremont Graduate School, Claremont, Calif., William W. Clary Professor of History, 1970-74, Andrew W. Mellon All-Claremont Professor of Humanities, 1974—, chairman of graduate faculty of history, 1970—. Gaspar Bacon Lecturer, Boston University Law School, 1972; Sheldon Elliott Lecturer, University of Southern California Law School, 1972; Hugo L. Black Lecturer, University of Alabama, 1976. Member of U.S. Commission on the American Revolution Bicentennial, 1966-68; member of executive council, Institute for Early American History and Culture, 1970-73. Consultant to DaCapo Press, 1969-75. *Military service:* U.S. Army, 1943-46; became sergeant.

MEMBER: American Historical Association, American Studies Association, American Society for Legal History (member of board of directors, 1965-70), American Antiquarian Society (life member), Organization of American Historians, American Civil Liberties Union (member of national advisory council), Society of American Historians. *Awards, honors:* Columbia University fellow, 1949-50; Guggenheim fellowship, 1957-58; Sigma Delta Chi Prize, 1960; Frank Luther Mott Award for best research in journalism history, 1961; Harvard University Center for the Study of Liberty in America senior fellow, 1961-62; Pultizer Prize in history, 1969, for *Origins of the Fifth Amendment;* American Council of Learned Societies grant, 1973; American Bar Foundation Legal Merit fellow, 1973; National Endowment for the Humanitites senior fellow, 1974, research grant, 1979-82; Commonwealth Club prize for nonfiction, 1975.

WRITINGS: Law of the Commonwealth and Chief Justice Shaw, Harvard University Press, 1957; *Legacy of Suppression: Freedom of Speech and Press in Early American History,* Belknap, 1960; *Jefferson and Civil Liberties: The Darker Side,* Belknap, 1963; *Origins of the Fifth Amendment: The Right against Self-Incrimination,* Oxford University Press, 1968; *Judgments: Essays on Constitutional History,* Quadrangle Press, 1972; *Against the Law: The Nixon Court and Criminal Justice,* Harper, 1974; *Treason against God: A History of the Offense of Blasphemy,* Schocken, 1980.

Editor: (With Merrill D. Peterson, and contributor) *Major Crises in American History: Documentary Problems,* Harcourt, 1963; (with John P. Roche) *The American Political Process,* Braziller, 1963; (with Roche) *The Presidency,* Harcourt, 1964; (with Roche) *The Congress,* Harcourt, 1964; (with Roche) *The Judiciary,* Harcourt, 1964; (with Roche) *Political Parties and Pressure Groups,* Harcourt, 1964; (editor) *Freedom of the Press from Zenger to Jefferson,* Bobbs-Merrill, 1966; (editor) *American Constitutional Law,* Harper, 1966; *Judicial Review and the Supreme Court,* Harper, 1967; (with H. Hyman, and contributor) *Freedom and Reform,* Harper, 1967; (and contributor) *Essays on the Making of the Constitution,* Oxford University Press, 1969; (and contributor) *14th Amendment and the Bill of Rights,* DaCapo Press, 1971; (and contributor) *The Supreme Court under Warren,* Quadrangle Press, 1972; *Blasphemy in Massachusetts,* DaCapo Press, 1973; (co-editor, and contributor) *Jim Crow Education,* Da Capo Press, 1974; (co-editor) *Essays on the Early Republic,* Dryden, 1974.

Contributor: L. Weymouth, editor, *Thomas Jefferson,* Putnam, 1974; V. Hamilton, editor, *Bill of Rights and American Democracy,* University of Alabama, in press. Editor-in-chief: *The American Heritage Series: A Documentary History of the United States,* sixty volumes, Bobbs-Merrill; (with Eugene C. Black) *The Harper Documentary History of Western Civilization,* forty volumes, Harper; *Contemporary Essays,* twenty volumes, Harper; *Encyclopedia of the American Constitution,* four volumes, Macmillan. Consulting editor, U.S. constitutional history, Microbook Library of American Civilization. Member of advisory board, *The John Marshall Papers,* 1971—; member of editorial board, *Reviews in American History,* 1975—. Contributor to history journals and other periodicals.

BIOGRAPHICAL/CRITICAL SOURCES: New York Times Book Review, November 24, 1963; *Book Week,* December 22, 1963; *Journal of American History,* September, 1964; *Virginia Quarterly Review,* summer, 1968; *National Review,* March 11, 1969.

* * *

LEWIS, Arthur H. 1906-

PERSONAL: Born September 27, 1906, in Mahanoy City, Pa.; married Juliet Blum (an interior designer), October 5, 1930; children: Suzanne Lewis Olds. *Education:* Attended Franklin and Marshall College, one year, and Columbia University, two years. *Politics:* Republican. *Home:* 419 South Jessup St., Philadelphia, Pa. 19147. *Agent:* Julian Bach, 747 Third Ave., New York, N.Y. 10017.

CAREER: Philadelphia Inquirer, Phildelphia, Pa., reporter, 1927-38; Commonwealth of Pennsylvania, Harrisburg, press representative, 1939-52; free-lance writer, 1952—. Lecturer in journalism, University of Pittsburgh, 1945-50. *Member:* Authors Guild, Pen and Pencil Club, Philobiblon Club, Sons of the Copper Beeches, Philadelphia Art Alliance, Franklin Inn. *Awards, honors:* Edgar Allen Poe award, 1964, for *Lament for the Molly Maguires.*

WRITINGS—Published by Simon & Schuster, except as indicated: *The Aaronsburg Story,* Vanguard, 1956; *The Worlds of Chippy Patterson,* Harcourt, 1960; *The Day They Shook the Plum Tree,* Harcourt, 1963; *Lament for the Molly Maguires,* Harcourt, 1964; *La Belle Otero,* 1967; *Hex,* 1969; *Carnival,* 1970; *Copper Beeches,* 1971; *Children's Party,* 1972; *It Was Fun While It Lasted,* 1973; *Murder by Contract,* Macmillan, 1975; *Those Philadelphia Kellys with a Touch of Grace,* Morrow, 1977.

BIOGRAPHICAL/CRITICAL SOURCES: Best Sellers, October 1, 1967, March 15, 1969; Publishers Weekly, October 3, 1967; *New York Times Book Review,* October 29, 1967; *Washington Post,* April 11, 1970; *National Observer,* May 4, 1970.

* * *

LEWIS, Michael 1937-

PERSONAL: Born January 10, 1937, in New York, N.Y.; son of Bernard W. and Leah (Cohen) Lewis; married Rhoda Rosenzweig, August 18, 1962; children: Benjamin, Felicia. *Education:* University of Pennsylvania, B.A., 1958, Ph.D.,

1962. *Home:* 95 Linwood Circle, Princeton, N.J. 08540. *Office:* Educational Testing Service, Princeton, N.J. 08540.

CAREER: Fels Research Institute, Yellow Springs, Ohio, senior investigator, 1962-68; Educational Testing Service, Princeton, N.J., director of Infant Laboratory, 1968—. *Member:* American Psychological Association (fellow), Society for Research in Psychophysiology (fellow), American Association for the Advancement of Science (fellow), Society for Research in Child Development (fellow), Eastern Psychological Association (fellow), New York Academy of Science (fellow).

WRITINGS: (Contributor) Jerome Hellmuth, editor, *The Exceptional Infant,* Volume II, Brunner, 1971; (contributor) F. J. Monks, W. W. Hartup, and J. DeWit, editors, *Determinants of Behavioral Development,* Academic Press, 1972; (contributor) Patricia Pliner, Lester Krames, and Thomas Alloway, editors, *Communication and Effect: Language and Thought,* Academic Press, 1973; (editor with Leonard Rosenblum and contributor) *Origins of Behavior,* Wiley, 1973; (contributor) R. F. Thompson and M. M. Patterson, editors, *Methods in Physiological Psychology,* Volume I: *Bioelectric Recording Techniques,* Academic Press, 1974; (editor with Rosenblum) *Friendship and Peer Relations,* Wiley, 1975; (editor with Rosenblum) *Interaction, Conversation, and the Development of Language,* Wiley, 1977; (editor with Judith A. Lewis) *Community Counseling: A Human Services Approach,* Wiley, 1977; *The Culture of Inequality,* University of Massachusetts Press, 1978; (editor with Rosenblum) *The Development of Effect,* Plenum, 1978; (with J. Brooks-Gunn) *Social Cognition and the Acquisition of Self,* Plenum, 1979.

Contributor to symposia. Contributor to medical and behavioral science journals, including *Human Development, Journal of Experimental Child Psychology, Journal of Health, Physical Education, and Recreation, Science, Merrill-Palmer Quarterly of Behavior and Development,* and *Developmental Psychology.*

* * *

LIEBERSON, Stanley 1933-

PERSONAL: Born April 20, 1933, in Montreal, Quebec, Canada; son of Jack (a garment worker) and Ida (Cohen) Lieberson; married Patricia Beard, 1960; children: Rebecca, David, Miriam, Rachel. *Education:* Attended Brooklyn College (now Brooklyn College of the City University of New York), 1950-52; University of Chicago, M.A., 1958, Ph.D., 1960. *Home:* 3520 North Prescott Pl., Tucson, Ariz. 85715. *Office:* Department of Sociology, University of Arizona, Tucson, Ariz. 85721.

CAREER: State University of Iowa, Iowa City, 1959-61, began as instructor, became assistant professor of sociology; University of Wisconsin—Madison, assistant professor, 1961-63, associate professor, 1963-66, professor of sociology, 1966-67; University of Washington, Seattle, professor of sociology and director of Center for Demography and Ecology, 1967-71; University of Chicago, Chicago, Ill., professor of sociology and associate director of Population Research and Training Center, 1971-74; University of Arizona, Tucson, professor of sociology, 1974—. Associate director, Iowa Urban Community Research Center, 1959-61. Claude Bissell Visiting Professor, University of Toronto, 1979-80. *Member:* International Population Union, American Sociological Association, Population Association of America, Pacific Sociological Society.

WRITINGS: (With Otis Dudley Duncan, W. Richard Scott, Beverly Duncan, and Hal H. Winsborough) *Metropolis and Region,* Johns Hopkins Press, 1960; *Ethnic Patterns in American Cities,* Free Press of Glencoe, 1963; (editor) *Explorations in Sociolinguistics,* Indiana University Press, 1967; *Language and Ethnic Relations in Canada,* Wiley, 1970; (with Beverly Duncan) *Metropolis and Region in Transition,* Sage Publications, 1970.

WORK IN PROGRESS: A Piece of the Pie: Blacks and White Immigrants since 1880; Language Diversity and Language Contact.

* * *

LIGHT, James F. 1921-

PERSONAL: Born November 5, 1921, in Memphis, Tenn.; son of Luther and Lois (Billings) Light; married Norma Rowena Neal, 1948 (deceased); married Amy Marcella Wolf, 1959; children: (first marriage) Sheldon Neal, Matthew Forest, Jama Rowena. *Education:* University of Chicago, B.A., 1945, M.A., 1947; Syracuse University, Ph.D., 1953. *Office:* College of Liberal Arts, Southern Illinois University, Carbondale, Ill. 62901.

CAREER: University of Kentucky, Lexington, instructor, 1947-48; Syracuse University, Syracuse, N.Y., instructor, 1948-53; Radford College, Radford, Va., associate professor, 1953-56; Indiana State University, Terre Haute, 1956-65, began as assistant professor, became professor; University of Bridgeport, Bridgeport, Conn., Bernhard Professor of English and chairman of department, 1965-71; California State University, Fresno, dean of humanities, 1971-72; Herbert H. Lehman College of the City University of New York, Bronx, N.Y., dean of faculties, 1972-73, provost, 1973-79; Southern Illinois University, Carbondale, dean of College of Liberal Arts, 1979—. Has done public relations work in Washington, D.C. *Member:* American Association of University Professors, Modern Language Association of America, Indiana College English Association (president, 1962-63). *Awards, honors:* Fellow of Yaddo Artists Colony, 1959, 1962; named outstanding teacher, Indiana State University, 1961; Fulbright Award, England, 1963-64; named distinguished scholar, University of Bridgeport, 1971.

WRITINGS: (Contributor) E. Seaver, editor, *Cross Section—1945,* L. B. Fischer, 1945; *Nathanael West: An Interpretative Study,* Northwestern University Press, 1961, revised edition, 1971; (contributor) Carlos Baker, editor, *Ernest Hemingway: Critiques of Four Major Novels,* Scribner, 1962; (contributor) Malcolm Marsden, editor, *If You Really Want to Know: A Catcher Casebook,* Scott, Foresman, 1963; (contributor) H. P. Simonson and P. E. Hager, editors, *Salinger's "Catcher in the Rye": Clamor vs. Criticism,* Heath, 1963; *John William DeForest,* Twayne, 1965; *J. D. Salinger,* Barrister, 1967; (editor with Leonard Lief) *The Modern Age,* Holt, 1969, 4th edition, 1980; (editor) *Studies in "All the King's Men,"* C. E. Merrill, 1971. Contributor to *Encyclopaedia Britannica;* author of speeches for congressmen. Contributor to professional journals.

WORK IN PROGRESS: A novel.

SIDELIGHTS: James F. Light says of his writing: "I try for thoroughness and honesty, for I dislike facile generalizations and glib distortions. As an academic administrator, I find that I value simplicity and clarity in expressions, and I try to reflect these qualities in my own writing." *Avocational interests:* Music, gambling.

LIGHTNER, Robert P(aul) 1931-

PERSONAL: Born April 4, 1931, in Cleona, Pa.; son of Earnest A. and Edith (Miller) Lightner; married Pearl Hostetter, July 27, 1952; children: Nancy Kay, Nadine Pearl, Natalie Sue. *Education:* Baptist Bible Seminary, Johnson City, N.Y., Th.B., 1955; Dallas Theological Seminary, Th.M., 1959, Th.D., 1964; Southern Methodist University, M.L.A., 1972. *Politics:* Republican. *Home:* 2449 Wildoak Cir., Dallas, Tex. 75228. *Office:* Dallas Theological Seminary, 3909 Swiss Ave., Dallas, Tex. 75204.

CAREER: Ordained minister of Baptist Church, 1968; Grace Baptist Church, DeQueen, Ark., pastor, 1956-57; Baptist Bible Seminary, Johnson City, N. Y., instructor, 1959-61, assistant professor, 1964-66, associate professor of systematic theology, 1967-68, head of department, 1964-66; Dallas Theological Seminary, Dallas, Tex., assistant professor of systematic theology, 1969—. *Member:* Evangelical Theological Society, Near East Archaeological Society.

WRITINGS: Neo-Liberalism, Regular Baptist Press, 1959; *Neo-Evangelicalism,* Regular Baptist Press, 1959; *The Tongues Tide,* Empire State Baptist, 1964; *Speaking in Tongues and Divine Healing,* Regular Baptist Press, 1965; *The Saviour and the Scriptures,* Presbyterian & Reformed Publishing, 1966; *The Death Christ Died: A Case for Unlimited Atonement,* Regular Baptist Press, 1967; *Triumph through Tragedy,* Baker Press, 1969; *Church Union: A Layman's Guide,* Regular Baptist Press, 1971; *The First Fundamental: God,* Thomas Nelson, 1973; *Heaven for Those Who Can't Believe,* Regular Baptist Press, 1977; *Truth for the Good Life,* Accent Books, 1978; *Triumph through Tragedy,* Bible Memory Association, 1980.

WORK IN PROGRESS: Research on a comprehensive doctrine survey book.

* * *

LILIENFELD, Robert Henry 1927-

PERSONAL: Born February 24, 1927, in New York, N.Y.; son of Samuel and Sara (Barkan) Lilienfeld; married Louise Farrell, 1949; children: Kathryn, Hugo, Adam. *Education:* New York University, B.A., 1951, M.A., 1952; New School for Social Research, M.A., 1968, Ph.D., 1975. *Home:* 60 Hinckley Pl., Brooklyn, N.Y. 11218.

CAREER: Musician, sociologist, and writer. Associate professor of sociology, City College of the City University of New York; member of music faculty, New School for Social Research. Has worked as project director of City University of New York Population Health Survey and research director of New York University Neighborhood Youth Corps Study. Founder and director of Brooklyn Heights Chorus. Publisher of *New American Review. Military service:* U.S. Army, 1945-46.

WRITINGS: An Introduction to Music, Macmillan, 1962; (with Basil Cimino) *The Guitarist's Harmony,* Franco Colombo, 1965; *Learning to Read Music,* Funk, 1968, 2nd edition, Crowell, 1976; (editor with Edward Quinn and Rodman Hill) *Interdiscipline: An Introductory Reader in Psychology, Literature, and Sociology,* Free Press, 1972; (with Joseph Bensman) *Craft and Consciousness: Occupational Technique and the Development of World Images,* Wiley, 1973; *The Rise of Systems Theory: An Ideological Analysis,* Wiley, 1978; (with Bensman) *Between Public and Private: The Lost Boundaries of the Self,* Free Press, 1979. Contributor of articles and reviews to periodicals, including *Psychoanalytic Journal, Journal of Aesthetic Education, Diogenes,* and *Nation.*

WORK IN PROGRESS: Studies in the Sociology of Music, Intellectual Opportunism, The Social Critique of Jacques Ellul, New Forms of Social Thought.

* * *

LILLY, John C(unningham) 1915-

PERSONAL: Born January 6, 1915, in St. Paul, Minn.; son of Richard Coyle and Rachel (Cunningham) Lilly; married Antoinette Ficarotta, 1974; children: John C., Jr., Charles R., Pamela C., Cynthia, Nina. *Education:* California Institute of Technology, B.S., 1938; attended Dartmouth Medical School, 1938-40; University of Pennsylvania, M.D., 1942. *Agent:* Arthur Ceppos, 40 East Tenth St., New York, N.Y. *Office address:* Human Software, Inc., Human/Dolphin Foundation, Box 4172, Malibu, Calif. 90265.

CAREER: University of Pennsylvania, Philadelphia, Graduate and Medical Schools, fellow, 1942-46, assistant professor, 1946-49, associate professor of biophysics, 1949-52, of medical physics and experimental neurology, 1952-56; Communication Research Institute, Miami, Fla., and St. Thomas, U.S. Virgin Islands, founder, chairman of the board of trustees, 1959-60, director, 1959-68; chairman of neurological division, Maryland Psychiatric Research Center, 1968; treasurer, Human Software, Inc., 1974—; trustee, Human/Dolphin Foundation. 1976—. Reserved list of scientific personnel, War Manpower Commission, 1944; National Institute of Neurological Disease and Blindness, chief of cortical integration section, laboratory of neurophysiology, 1953-58; member of biosciences advisory panel, U.S. Air Force Office of Science Research, 1958-63. Hixon Lecturer, California Institute of Technology, 1952; Mayo Foundation lecturer, 1952; colloquium lecturer, Harvard University, 1954; John Kershman Memorial Lecturer, 1961. Visiting professor of medicine, University of Miami Medical School, 1960. Member of science advisory committee for graduate schools, National Institute of Health, 1954, member of fellowship board, National Institute of Mental Health, 1954-57.

MEMBER: American Physiological Society (member of steering committee on neurophysiology, 1953-56), American Association for Advancement of Science (fellow), American Electroencephalographic Society, Institute of Electrical and Electronics Engineers, Group for the Advancement of Psychiatry, Association for Research in Nervous and Mental Diseases, American Society for Cybernetics (charter member), Biophysical Society (charter member), Society for Experimental Biology and Medicine, Acoustical Society of America, International Brain Research Organization, Aerospace Medical Association, International Federation for Medical Electronics, Optical Society of America (associate), American Society of Mammalogists, Washington Academy of Sciences, New York Academy of Sciences (fellow), Philadelphia Association for Psychoanalysis, Sigma Xi, Alpha Mu Pi Omega, Order of the Dolphin. *Awards, honors:* John Clark Research Prize, University of Pennsylvania, 1942, for the development of the electrical capacitance manometer; effective service award, Committee on Medical Research, Office of Scientific Research and Development, 1945; research career award, National Institute of Mental Health, 1962-67; distinguished service award, American Medical Authors, 1964.

WRITINGS: Man and Dolphin, Doubleday, 1961; (with Ashley Montagu) *The Dolphin in History,* University of California Library, 1963; *The Mind of the Dolphin: A Non-Human Intelligence,* Doubleday, 1967; *Programming and Metaprogramming in the Human Biocomputer; Theory and Experi-*

ments, Communications Research Institute, 1967; *The Center of the Cyclone: An Autobiography of Inner Space,* Julian Press, 1972; *Lilly on Dolphins: The Humans of the Sea,* Anchor Books, 1975; *Simulations of God: The Science of Belief,* Simon & Schuster, 1975; (with wife, Antoinette Lilly) *The Dyadic Cyclone: The Autobiography of a Couple,* Simon & Schuster, 1976; *The Deep Self: Profound Relaxation and the Tank Isolation Technique,* Simon & Schuster, 1977; *The Scientist: A Novel Autobiography,* Lippincott, 1978; *Communication between Man and Dolphin; The Possibilities of Talking with Other Species,* Crown, 1978.

Contributor: *Handbook of Respiratory Data in Aviation,* National Research Council, 1944; J. H. Comroe, editor, *Methods in Medical Research,* Volume II, Year Book, 1950; O. Glasser, editor, *Medical Physics,* Volume II, Year Book, 1950; *The Biology of Mental Health and Disease,* Hoeber, 1952; *Biological and Biochemical Bases of Behavior,* University of Wisconsin Press, 1958; *The Central Nervous System and Behavior,* Macy Foundation, 1958; *The Central Nervous System and Behavior,* Macy Foundation and National Science Foundation, 1959; *Psychophysiological Aspects of Space Flight,* Columbia University Press, 1961; K. E. Schaefer, editor, *Man's Dependence on the Earthly Atmosphere,* Macmillan, 1962; Vernon Montcastle, editor, *Interhemispheric Relations and Cerebral Dominance,* Johns Hopkins Press, 1962; *Yearbook of Science and Technology,* McGraw, 1962; *Book of Knowledge Annual,* Grolier, 1962; *Handbook of Physiology: Adaptation to the Environment,* American Physiological Society, 1964; Charles T. Tart, editor, *Transpersonal Psychologies,* Harper, 1975.

SIDELIGHTS: John C. Lilly is noted for studies on the cerebral cortex, electrical studies of the brain, on human isolation and confinement, on methods of communication between man and other species, and on the psychology of man. He has discovered that the dolphin, if properly handled, will make definite attempts to imitate human conversational sounds.

Joseph McLellan writes: "John Lilly has been one of the most original and fascinating scientists of our time, when original, fascinating scientists are hardly a rarity. He is one of the pathbreaking explorers of that great terra incognita, the human brain." John Marks adds that, "in California, where reality is more widely perceived to have multiple levels, Lilly is a major culture hero."

Lilly's experiments have involved mind-altering drugs, the direct use of electrodes in the brain, and the effects of isolation and sensory deprivation in a water tank, in addition to his experiments with dolphins. These experiments were originally federally funded, but as McLellan explains, "despite Lilly's elaborate precautions, their possible applications for unconventional war were quickly seized upon. . . . When he saw the use to which the government work was being put, Lilly decided that further experiments would have to be done on his own. . . . They have also, as far as can be determined from [*The Scientist: A Novel Autobiography,* Lilly's] own account (but how much would he tell the world, after the perversion of his earlier work?), had much less spectacular results." The original dolphin project was conducted between 1955 and 1968. Resumption of active dolphin research occurred in 1976 with the founding of the non-profit Human/Dolphin Foundation. The program, called JANUS, is staffed by volunteers and supported by member contributions and by contributions of professional time by engineers and programmers. The first experiments with JANUS and the dolphins began in late 1979. According to Dr. Lilly, the researchers feel that "dolphins are intelligent, sentient moral beings." He adds: "We need to talk with them to know who we are from a non-human point of view fifteen million years older than we are. JANUS allows us to talk with them in their frequency range, ten times higher than human speech and hearings."

AVOCATIONAL INTERESTS: Computer programming, mountain climbing, skiing, writing, teaching, and learning.

BIOGRAPHICAL/CRITICAL SOURCES: Time, November 17, 1967; *Washington Post,* December 29, 1970, July 11, 1978; *New York Times Book Review,* June 3, 1979.

* * *

LIMMER, Ruth 1927-

PERSONAL: Born November 23, 1927, in New York, N.Y.; daughter of Kurt Alfred (a tool grinder) and Jennie (Levinson) Limmer. *Education:* Brooklyn College (now Brooklyn College of the City University of New York), A.B., 1948; Mills College, Oakland, Calif., M.A., 1950. *Religion:* Jewish. *Home:* 3014 Third Ave., Baltimore, Md. 21234. *Office:* Department of Housing and Urban Development, Washington, D.C. 20410.

CAREER: Manuscript editor at McGraw-Hill Book Co., New York City, 1952-54, and at *Horizon,* New York City, 1959-60; Western College, Oxford, Ohio, assistant professor, 1958-65, associate professor, 1965-71, professor of English, 1971-74; Goucher College, Baltimore, Md., chairman of English department, 1974-77; U.S. Department of Housing and Urban Development, Washington, D.C., writer-editor and program analyst, 1977—. *Member:* International Women Writers Guild, Modern Language Association of America.

WRITINGS: (Editor with Robert Phelps) *A Poet's Alphabet,* McGraw, 1970; (editor) *What the Woman Lived: Selected Letters of Louise Bogan: 1920-1970,* Harcourt, 1973; *How Well Are We Housed?* (six volumes), U.S. Government Printing Office, 1978-80; (editor) *Journey around My Room: The Autobiography of Louise Bogan,* Viking, 1980. Lyricist for *Four Songs for Literary Nay-Sayers,* by Richard Monaco, J. Fischer, 1968; also ghostwriter of articles and speeches.

* * *

LINCOLN, C(harles) Eric 1924-

PERSONAL: Born June 23, 1924, in Athens, Ala.; son of Less and Mattie (Sowell) Lincoln; married second wife, Lucy Cook (a teacher), July 1, 1961; children: (first marriage) Cecil Eric, Joyce Elaine; (second marriage) Hilary Anne, Less Charles II. *Education:* LeMoyne College, A.B., 1947; Fisk University, M.A., 1954; University of Chicago Divinity School, B.D., 1956; Boston University, M.Ed., 1960, Ph.D., 1960. *Office:* Department of Religion, Duke University, Durham, N.C. 27706.

CAREER: LeMoyne College, Memphis, Tenn., director of public relations, 1950-51; Fisk University, Nashville, Tenn., associate personnel dean, 1953-54; Clark College, Atlanta, Ga., assistant professor of religion and philosophy, 1954-57, associate professor of social philosophy, 1960-61, professor of social relations, 1961-65, administrative assistant to president, 1961-63, director of Institute for Social Relations, 1963-65; Portland State College (now University), Portland, Ore., professor of sociology, 1965-67; Union Theological Seminary, New York, N.Y., professor of sociology and religion, 1967-73; Fisk University, professor of religion and sociology and chairman of department of religious and philosophical studies, 1973-76; Duke University, Durham, N.C., professor of religion, 1976—. Boston University, Human Relations Center, director of Panel of Americans, 1958-60, adjunct professor, 1963-65; Dartmouth College, lecturer-in-residence, 1962, visiting professor, 1962-63; visiting professor, Spelman College, 1966; adjunct professor, San Francisco Theological Seminary, 1966-67, and Vassar College, 1969-70; director of African Studies Program, University of Ghana at Fordham, Fordham University, 1970; visiting professor, State University of New York at Albany, 1970-72, and Queens College of the City University of New York, 1972; adjunct professor of ethics and society, Vanderbilt University, 1973-76. Lecturer; has made numerous appearances on local and national television and on radio. Member of boards of directors or boards of trustees of several institutions, including Boston University, Jewish Theological Seminary, and Institute for Religious and Social Studies. Consultant in human relations. *Military service:* U.S. Navy, 1944-45.

MEMBER: American Academy of Arts and Sciences (fellow), American Sociological Association, Society for the Psychological Study of Social Issues, American Academy of Political and Social Science, Society for the Scientific Study of Religion, National Association of University Professors, National Education Association, Association for the Study of Negro Life and History, Black Academy of Arts and Letters (founding president; member of board of directors), American Association of Intergroup Relations Officials, Authors Guild, Authors League of America, National Geographic Society, Southern Sociological Society, New York Academy of Arts and Sciences, New York Academy of Sciences, Kappa Alpha Psi, Free and Accepted Masons, International Frontiers Club. *Awards, honors:* John Hay Whitney fellow, 1957; Crusade fellow, Methodist Church, 1958; Lilly Endowment fellow, 1959; human relations fellow, Boston University, 1959-60; L.L.D., Carleton College, 1968; Creative Communications Award, Art Institute of Boston, 1970; L.H.D., St. Michael's College, 1972; research grants from Society for the Psychological Study of Social Issues, Anti-Defamation League of B'nai B'rith, Fund for the Advancement of Education, Lilly Endowment, and Ford Foundation.

WRITINGS: The Black Muslims in America, Beacon Press, 1961, revised edition, 1972; *My Face Is Black,* Beacon Press, 1964; *Sounds of the Struggle,* Morrow, 1967; *The Negro Pilgrimage in America,* Bantam, 1967; *Is Anybody Listening?,* Seabury, 1968; (with Langston Hughes and Milton Meltzer) *A Pictorial History of the Negro in America,* Crown, 1968, revised edition, 1973; *A Profile of Martin Luther King, Jr.,* Hill & Wang, 1969; *The Blackamericans,* Bantam, 1969; *The Black Church since Frazier,* Schocken, 1974; (editor) *The Black Experience in Religion: A Book of Readings,* Doubleday, 1974.

Editor of "C. Eric Lincoln Series in Black Religion"; published by Doubleday, except as indicated: James H. Cone, *A Theology of Black Liberation,* Lippincott, 1970; Henry Mitchell, *Black Preaching,* Lippincott, 1970; Gayraud Wilmore, *Black Religion and Black Radicalism,* 1972; Joseph R. Washington, Jr., *Black Sects and Cults,* 1972; William R. Jones, *Is God a White Racist?,* 1973; Leonard E. Barrett, *Soul-Force,* 1973.

Contributor: Alice Horowitz, *The Outlook for Youth,* H. W. Wilson, 1962; Earl Raab, *New Frontiers in Race Relations,* Doubleday, 1962; Mulford Sibley, *The Quiet Battle,* Doubleday, 1963; Louis Lomax, *When the Word Is Given,* New American Library, 1963; Arnold Rose, editor, *Assuring Freedom to the Free,* Wayne State University Press, 1963; Rolf Italiander, editor, *Die Herasforderung des Islam,* Muster-Schmidt-Verlag (Gottingen), 1965; Gerald H. Anderson, *Sermons to Men of Other Faiths,* Abingdon, 1966; Arnold Rose and Caroline Rose, *Minority Problems,* Harper, 1965; John P. Davis, editor, *The American Negro Reference Book,* Prentice-Hall, 1966; Nils Petter Gleditsch, *Kamp Uten Vapen,* Eides Boktrykkeri (Bergen), 1966; Edgar A. Shuler and others, editors, *Readings in Sociology,* Crowell, 1967; William C. Kvaraceus and others, editors, *Poverty, Education and Race Relations,* Allen & Bacon, 1967; Milgon L. Barron, *Minorities in a Changing World,* Knopf, 1967; Bradford Chambers, *Chronicles of Negro Protest,* New American Library, 1968; Peter T. Rose, *Old Memories, New Moods,* Atherton Press, 1970; David Reimers, *The Black Man in America since Reconstruction,* Crowell, 1970; Benjamin Brawley, *A Social History of the American Negro,* Macmillan, 1970; George Ducas, *Great Documents in Black American History,* Praeger, 1970; Robert Weisbard and Arthur Stein, *The Bittersweet Encounter,* Negro Universities Press, 1970; Scott G. McNall, *The Sociological Perspective,* Little, Brown, 1971.

Contributor to *Encyclopaedia Britannica, Encyclopedia Americana, World Book Encyclopedia,* and *Encyclopedia of World Biography.* Contributor of articles, poetry, and reviews to numerous journals and popular periodicals.

* * *

LINDBLOM, Charles E(dward) 1917-

PERSONAL: Born March 21, 1917, in Turlock, Calif.; son of Charles August and Emma (Norman) Lindblom; married Rose Winther, 1942; children: Susan, Steven, Eric. *Education:* Stanford University, B.A., 1937; University of Chicago, Ph.D., 1945. *Home:* 9 Cooper Rd., North Haven, Conn. *Office:* Department of Economics and Political Science, Yale University, New Haven, Conn. 06520.

CAREER: University of Minnesota, Minneapolis, instructor, 1939-46; Yale University, New Haven, Conn., 1946—, began as assistant professor, currently professor of economics and political science. *Member:* American Economic Association, American Political Science Association (president-elect, 1980). *Awards, honors:* Guggenheim fellow, 1951; Center for Advanced Study in the Behavioral Sciences fellow, 1954-55.

WRITINGS: Unions and Capitalism, Yale University Press, 1949, reprinted, Shoe String, 1970; (with R. A. Dahl) *Politics, Economics, and Welfare,* Harper, 1953, reprinted, University of Chicago Press, 1976; (with D. Braybrooke) *A Strategy of Decision,* Free Press of Glencoe, 1963; *The Intelligence of Democracy,* Free Press of Glencoe, 1965; *The Policy-Making Process,* Prentice-Hall, 1968, revised edition, 1980; *Politics and Markets: The World's Political-Economic Systems,* Basic Books, 1977; (with Davis K. Cohen) *Usable Knowledge,* Yale University Press, 1979. Contributor to professional journals.

BIOGRAPHICAL/CRITICAL SOURCES: New York Times Book Review, July 29, 1979.

* * *

LINDE, Shirley Motter 1929-

PERSONAL: Surname is pronounced *Lind*-ee; born March 22, 1929 in Cincinnati, Ohio; daughter of Park Owen (a business consultant) and Helen (Eberhart) Motter: married D. W. Linde, 1954 (divorced, 1967); children: Scott, Robert. *Education:* University of Cincinnati, B.S., 1951; University of Michigan, M.S., 1953; also attended Northwestern University and New York University. *Home address:* Box 4196, Treasure Cay, Abaco, Bahamas.

CAREER: Author, editor, public relations consultant, and lecturer. Associate editor of *Together,* Methodist Publishing House, Chicago, Ill.; chief of information services, Northwestern University School of Medicine and Dentistry, Evanston, Ill.; medical copy editor, Yearbook Publishers, Chicago, Ill.; assistant editor, *Journal of International College of Surgeons,* Chicago, Ill.; Chicago Bureau chief of *Medical Tribune, Tele-Med,* and *Medical News,* Chicago, Ill.; editor of *Information, Inc.,* and *Medical Bulletin on Tobacco,* New York City; president, Pavilion Publishing Co., New York City, 1972—; president, Med-Assist, New York City, 1972—. Research chemist at Andrew Jergens Co., Cincinnati, Ohio. Director of Lake Lotawana Writer's Conference, Lee's Summit, Mo. Member of board of directors of Commando-Clean, Inc. *Member:* National Association of Science Writers (member of executive committee), American Medical Writers Association (secretary; vice president), Authors League of America, American Association for the Advancement of Science, Chicago Press Club. *Awards, honors:* American Medical Writers Association award, 1972, for outstanding service; National Youth Movement award, 1973, for community service and *Sickle Cell;* National Sickle Cell Disease Research Foundation award, 1973, for *Sickle Cell.*

WRITINGS: (Editor) *Radioactivity in Man,* C. C Thomas, 1961; *Total Rehabilitation of Epileptics,* U.S. Government Printing Office, 1962; (editor) *Science and the Public,* Northwestern University Press, 1962; *The Big Ditch: Story of the Suez Canal,* National Research Bureau, 1962; (editor) *Response of the Nervous System to Ionizing Radiation,* Academic Press, 1962; (editor) *Medical Science in the News,* Chicago Press Club, 1965; *Modern Woman's Medical Dictionary,* Bantam, 1968; *Airline Stewardess Handbook,* Careers Research Publishing, 1968.

Emergency Family First Aid Guide, Milton Cooper, 1971; *Cosmetic Surgery,* Award Books, 1971; (with Arthur Michele) *Orthotherapy,* M. Evans, 1971 (published in England as *You Don't Have to Ache: A Guide to Orthotherapy,* Souvenir Press, 1971); (with Howard Rapaport) *Complete Allergy Guide,* Simon & Schuster, 1971; *Sickle Cell: A Complete Guide to Prevention and Treatment,* Pavilion Publishing, 1972; (with Frank Finnerty) *High Blood Pressure,* McKay, 1973; *The Sleep Book,* Harper, 1974; (with Gideon Panter) *Now That You've Had Your Baby,* McKay, 1975; (with Robert Atkins) *Dr. Atkins Superenergy Diet,* Crown, 1977; *The Whole Health Catalogue,* Rawson-Wade, 1978; *How to Beat a Bad Back,* Rawson-Wade, 1980.

Contributor to annual reports and brochures. Contributor to medical journals, and to national periodicals, including *Good Housekeeping, McCall's, Reader's Digest, Today's Health, Better Homes and Gardens, Science and Mechanics, Coronet,* and *Science Digest.*

WORK IN PROGRESS: Two books.

AVOCATIONAL INTERESTS: Boating, visiting beaches, theater, jazz.

* * *

LINDGREN, Henry Clay 1914-

PERSONAL: Born April 12, 1914, in Sacramento, Calif.; son of Henry A. W. and Bertha (von Breymann) Lindgren; married Fredrica Lippman, 1935; children: Loretta Zoe. *Education:* Stanford University, A.B., 1934, A.M., 1935, Ph.D., 1942. *Religion:* Unitarian Universalist. *Home:* 120 Lansdale Ave., San Francisco, Calif. 94127. *Office:* Department of Psychology, San Francisco State University, San Francisco, Calif. 94132.

CAREER: Hilo Intermediate School, Hilo, Hawaii, teacher, 1935-37; T. K. Barker & Co., San Francisco, Calif., sales manager, 1937-40; San Francisco State University, San Francisco, professor of psychology, 1947—. Fulbright professor, University of Rome, Italy, 1956-57; expert in educational psychology for UNESCO, Sao Paulo, Brazil, 1962; visiting professor of psychology, American University of Beirut, 1964-65, 1968-70. *Military service:* U.S. Navy, 1942-46; became lieutenant commander. *Member:* American Association for the Advancement of Science (fellow), American Psychological Association (fellow).

WRITINGS: The Art of Human Relations, Thomas Nelson, 1953; *Effective Leadership in Human Relations,* Thomas Nelson, 1954; *Mental Health in Education,* Holt, 1954; *Meaning: Antidote to Anxiety,* Thomas Nelson, 1956; *Educational Psychology in the Classroom,* Wiley, 1956, 6th edition, Oxford University Press, 1980; *How to Live with Yourself and Like It,* Fawcett, 1960; *Psychology of Personal Development,* American Book Co., 1964, 3rd edition, Wiley, 1976; (with Donn Byrne and Lewis Petrinovich) *Psychology: Introduction to a Behavioral Science,* Wiley, 1966, 4th edition, 1975; *Introduction to Social Psychology,* Wiley, 1973; *Child Behavior,* Mayfield, 1975; (with P. Insel) *Too Close for Comfort,* Prentice-Hall, 1978; (with R. I. Watson) *Psychology of the Child and Adolescent,* Macmillan, 1979; *Great Expectations: The Psychology of Money,* William Kaufmann, 1980.

SIDELIGHTS: Some of Henry Lindgren's books have been translated into Polish, German, Italian, Spanish, Portuguese, and Hindi.

* * *

LINDSAY, Michael Francis Morris 1909-

PERSONAL: Born February 24, 1909, in London, England; son of Alexander Dunlop (a university teacher) and Erica Violet (Storr) Lindsay; married Li Hsiao-Li, June 25, 1941; children: Erica Susan, James Francis, Mary Muriel. *Education:* Balliol College, Oxford, B.A., 1931, M.A., 1935. *Politics:* British Labor Party. *Home:* 6812 Delaware St., Chevy Chase, Md. 20015.

CAREER: Assistant director, Industrial Survey of South Wales, 1935-36; Yenching University, Peiping, China, tutor in economics, 1937-41; University of Hull, University College, Hull, England, lecturer in economics, 1948-51; Australian National University, Canberra, reader in international relations, 1951-59; American University, Washington, D.C., professor of Far Eastern studies, 1959-74, professor emeritus, 1974—, chairman of East Asian Program, 1959-71. Visiting lecturer at Harvard University, 1946-47; visiting professor at Yale University, 1958, Ball State University, 1971-72, and Saint Olaf College and Carleton College, 1976. *Military service:* Chinese Eighteenth Group Army, technical adviser, 1942-45. *Member:* Royal Institute of International Affairs, American Association for Asian Studies.

WRITINGS: Educational Problems in Communist China, Institute for Pacific Relations, 1949; *China and the Cold War,* Melbourne University Press, 1955; *Is Peaceful Co-existence Possible?,* Michigan State University Press, 1960; (contributor) Yuan-li Wu, editor, *China: A Handbook,* Praeger, 1971; *The Unknown War: North China, 1937-1945,*

Bergstrom & Boyle, 1975; *Kung-chan-chu-i tso tsai na-li,* Line Ho Pao (Taipei), 1976. Contributor to *China Quarterly, Atlantic, Pacific Community,* and *Sckai Shuho.*

WORK IN PROGRESS: *Negative Education and Social Crisis.*

SIDELIGHTS: Michael Lindsay is Lord Lindsay of Birker, a member of the British House of Lords.

* * *

LININGTON, Elizabeth 1921-
(Anne Blaisdell, Lesley Egan, Egan O'Neill, Dell Shannon)

PERSONAL: Born March 11, 1921, in Aurora, Ill.; daughter of Byron G. (a musician) and Ruth (Biggam) Linington. *Education:* Glendale Junior College (now Glendale College), A.B., 1942. *Politics:* Republican. *Home:* 3284 South View Ave., Arroyo Grande, Calif. 93420. *Agent:* Barthold Fles Literary Agency, 501 Fifth Ave., Suite 707, New York, N.Y. 10017.

CAREER: Free-lance author of historical novels and mysteries. *Member:* John Birch Society (life member). *Awards, honors:* Gold medal for best historical novel by California author from California Commonwealth Club, 1956, for *The Long Watch;* runner-up award for best mystery from Mystery Writers of America, 1963, for *Knave of Hearts.*

WRITINGS: *The Proud Man* (historical novel), Viking, 1955; *The Long Watch,* (historical novel), Viking, 1956; (under pseudonym Egan O'Neill) *The Anglophile,* Messner, 1957; *Monsieur Janvier* (historical novel), Doubleday, 1957; *The Kingbreaker* (historical novel), Doubleday, 1958; (under pseudonym Anne Blaisdell) *Nightmare,* Harper, 1961; *Forging an Empire: Queen Elizabeth I* (historical novel), Kingston House, 1961; *Greenmask!,* Harper, 1964 (published in England under pseudonym Anne Blaisdell, Gollancz, 1965); *No Evil Angel,* Harper, 1964 (published in England under pseudonym Anne Blaisdell, Gollancz, 1965); *Come to Think of It,* Western Island Publishers, 1965; *Date with Death,* Harper, 1966; *Something Wrong,* Harper, 1967 (published in England under pseudonym Anne Blaisdell, Gollancz, 1968); *Policeman's Lot,* Harper, 1968; *Practice to Deceive,* Harper, 1971; *The Ringer,* Morrow, 1971, book club edition published under pseudonym Dell Shannon, 1971; *Crime by Chance,* Lippincott, 1973; *Perchance of Death,* Doubleday, 1977. Also author of *No Villain Need Be* and *Consequences of Crime.*

Under pseudonym Lesley Egan; all published by Harper, except as indicated: *A Case for Appeal,* 1961; *Against the Evidence* (Detective Book Club selection), 1962; *The Borrowed Alibi* (Detective Book Club selection), 1962; *Run to Evil* (Detective Book Club selection), 1963; *My Name Is Death,* 1964; *Detective's Due,* 1965; *Some Avenger, Rise!,* 1966; *The Nameless Ones,* 1967; *A Serious Investigation,* 1968; *The Wine of Violence,* 1969; *In the Death of a Man,* 1970; *Malicious Mischief,* 1971; *Paper Chase,* 1972; *Scenes of Crime,* Doubleday, 1976; *The Blind Search,* Doubleday, 1977; *A Dream Apart,* Doubleday, 1978; *Look Back on Death,* Doubleday, 1978. Also author of *The Hunters and the Hunted* and *Motive in Shadow.*

Under pseudonym Dell Shannon; all published by Morrow, except as indicated: *Case Pending,* Harper, 1960; *The Ace of Spades,* 1961; *Extra Kill,* 1962; *Knave of Hearts,* 1962; *Death of a Busybody,* 1963; *Double Bluff,* 1963; *The Deathbringers,* 1964; *Mark of Murder,* 1964; *Root of All Evil,* 1964; *Death by Inches,* 1965; *Coffin Corner,* 1966; *With a Vengeance,* 1966; *Chance to Kill,* 1967; *Rain with Violence,* 1967; *Kill with Kindness,* 1967; *Crime on Their Hands,* 1969; *Schooled to Kill,* 1969; *Unexpected Death,* 1970; *Whim to Kill,* 1971; *Murder with Love,* 1971; *With Intent to Kill,* 1972; *No Holiday for Crime,* 1973; *Spring of Violence,* 1973; *Crime File,* 1974; *Deuces Wild,* 1975; *Streets of Death,* 1976; *Appearances of Death,* 1977; *Cold Trail,* 1978. Also author of *Felony at Random.*

WORK IN PROGRESS: Additions to her crime-novel series.

SIDELIGHTS: Elizabeth Linington is the author of three crime-detective series that focus on the varied, yet interwoven, events of a police precinct and its members. Although her works offer a sizable dose of the violent and grotesque in life, they do so with a purpose. According to critic Anthony Boucher, Linington is "preoccupied with the terrifying theme of the stupidity of violence." The acts of violence and murder detailed in her novels closely resemble those in real life with what Boucher describes as their "stupidly inadequate, if not downright silly" pretexts. "Murder doesn't make much sense," he continues, "and Elizabeth Linington is almost the only novelist who knows it."

Yet Linington's chief concern seems to be in telling "exciting, suspenseful and plausible stories." In an article for the *Writer,* Linington says of her profession: "It is an emotional occupation, but it is also a very simple one. Some of the pundits and self-proclaimed intellectuals playing around at it today have tried to make it an esoteric mystique. They have lost sight of the realities of the job, and in so doing have lost touch with real life. Stories are told for one reason: to entertain the listener and the reader."

AVOCATIONAL INTERESTS: Archaeology, music, the occult, gemstones and jewelry, antique weapons, and languages.

BIOGRAPHICAL/CRITICAL SOURCES: *New York Times Book Review,* June 18, 1967, September 17, 1967, October 22, 1967, May 26, 1968, February 23, 1969; *Books and Bookmen,* July, 1968, July, 1969, December, 1969; *Spectator,* October 18, 1969; *Writer,* October, 1970; *Best Sellers,* January 15, 1971.

* * *

LINSENMEYER, Helen Walker 1906-

PERSONAL: Born March 3, 1906, in Energy, Ill.; daughter of Ben Fred (a farmer) and Nora (Poos) Walker; married Robert N. Linsenmeyer, October 18, 1943. *Education:* Attended Southern Illinois University, 1925, Santa Ana College, 1965-68, and California State University, Fullerton, 1967-70. *Politics:* Democrat. *Religion:* Roman Catholic. *Home:* 2107 Edith St., Murphysboro, Ill. 62966.

CAREER: W. N. Matthews Corp., St. Louis, Mo., secretary, 1930-40; McDonnell Aircraft Corp., St. Louis, secretary and supervisor, 1940-43; Topeka Chamber of Commerce, Topeka, Kans., office coordinator, 1947-48; Capper Publications, Topeka, secretary, 1950-54; Chicago Association of Commerce and Industry, Chicago, Ill., administrative assistant in Community Development Division, 1955-56; Capper Publications, secretary to manager of *Capper's Farmer,* 1956-58; McGraw-Hill, Inc., Chicago, secretary to district circulation manager, 1958-59; Chicago Archdiocese Catholic Cemeteries, Hillside, Ill., secretary to archdiocesan director, 1960-63; McGraw-Hill, Inc., New York, N.Y., field researcher in Orange County, Calif., 1964-65; Xerox Corp., Santa Ana, Calif., cataloger, 1965-70; Professional Cataloging Service, Costa Mesa, Calif., cataloger, 1972-73; affiliated with Sallie Logan Public Library, Murphysboro, Ill., 1976-78.

WRITINGS: From Fingers to Finger Bowls: A Sprightly History of California Cooking, Copley Press, 1972; *Cooking Plain,* Southern Illinois University Press, 1976.

WORK IN PROGRESS: An autobiography; research on history of fruits and vegetables and on cookstoves.

SIDELIGHTS: Helen Linsenmeyer told *CA:* "I began writing as soon as I could write; held the dream before me as I worked at a variety of jobs. California turned me on, and as I read more and more about that fabulous state I wondered about how the ethnic mix affected their eating habits. Hence, *From Fingers to Finger Bowls: A Sprightly History of California Cooking.* I wanted to pay homage to my ancestors at the time of the bicentennial, therefore *Cooking Plain* kept their spirit alive in the recipes which had been handed down through several generations. Our way of life is changing rapidly, and I wanted to leave some memories of how it was, and is, for the future.

"I do not read fiction, so know little of plots and situations as viewed by novelists. I gather that they portray a decadent society, more's the pity."

AVOCATIONAL INTERESTS: Traveling on back roads, exploring old towns and town sites, gardening, visiting historical and art museums, genealogy, local history.

* * *

LIPSCOMB, David M(ilton) 1935-

PERSONAL: Born August 4, 1935, in Morrill, Neb.; son of Roy Milton (a salesman) and Elsie (Schmidt) Lipscomb; married Gale F. Beck, December 13, 1978; children: (previous marriage) Scott David, Steven Roy, Shari Lea. *Education:* University of Redlands, B.A., 1957, M.A., 1959; University of Washington, Seattle, Ph.D., 1966; also studied at Purdue University, 1959-60, and University of Oregon, 1969. *Politics:* Democrat. *Religion:* Baptist. *Home:* 7200 Donna Lane, Knoxville, Tenn. 37920. *Office:* Department of Audiology, University of Tennessee, Knoxville, Tenn. 37916.

CAREER: West Texas State University, Canyon, assistant professor of speech, 1960-62; University of Tennessee, Knoxville, assistant professor of audiology and speech pathology, 1962-64; Veterans Administration Outpatient Clinic, Seattle, Wash., audiology graduate trainee, 1964-66; University of Tennessee, assistant professor, 1966-69, associate professor, 1969-73, professor of audiology and speech pathology, 1973—, director of audiology clinical services, 1966-69, director of Noise Research Laboratory, 1970—. Clinical audiologist for Amarillo Regional Hearing and Speech Foundation, 1960-62; instructor at University of Washington, Seattle, 1965. Vice-president of Industrial Noise Consultants, Inc., 1970—; member of research advisory board of Early Auditory Research (E.A.R.) Foundation, 1972—. Member of advisory board of Tennessee Board of Hearing Aid Dispensers, 1969-70; special adviser to Environmental Protection Agency's Office of Noise Abatement and Control, 1973—. Has made more than a hundred television and radio appearances. Film consultant to Public Broadcasting System; consultant to U.S. Army Medical Research Laboratory, 1971, and to industry.

MEMBER: American Acoustical Society, American Speech and Hearing Association (fellow; member of legislative council, 1972-74), Southern Audiological Society (member of executive board, 1972-73; president, 1974-75), Tennessee Hearing Aid Society (lifetime honorary member). *Awards, honors:* University of Tennessee alumni public service award, 1973.

WRITINGS: (Contributor) William A. Thomas, editor, *Indicators of Environmental Quality,* Plenum, 1972; *Noise: The Unwanted Sounds,* Nelson-Hall, 1974; *An Introduction to Laboratory Methods for the Study of the Ear,* C. C Thomas, 1974; (contributor) Jerry Northern, editor, *Communication Problems in Hearing Loss,* Little, Brown, 1974; (editor) *Noise and Audiology,* University Park Press, 1978; (editor) *Noise Control: Handbook of Principles and Practices,* Van Nostrand, 1978; (contributor) Larry Bradford and William Hardy, editors, *Hearing and Hearing Impairment,* Grune & Stratton, 1979; (contributor) Norman Lass and others, editors, *Speech, Language, and Hearing,* Saunders, 1980; (contributor) Ralph Rupp and Stockdell, editors, *Speech Protocols in Audiology,* Grune & Stratton, 1980; (contributor) Marc Krause and John Armbruster, editors, *Forensic Audiology,* University Park Press, 1981. Contributor to *World Book Encyclopedia.* Contributor of more than forty-five articles and reviews to professional journals, including *Journal of the Acoustical Society of America, Journal of Audiology Research, American Journal of Otolaryngology, Journal of the Tennessee Medical Association, Hearing and Speech News, Hearing Instruments,* and *Laryngoscope.* Member of editorial board of *Clinical Pediatrics,* 1969-79; member of editorial advisory board, *Journal of Speech and Hearing Disorders,* 1976—, and *American Journal of Otolaryngology,* 1979—.

WORK IN PROGRESS: The Ear as It Was Meant to Be Seen; research on the effects of noise on the ear and body.

BIOGRAPHICAL/CRITICAL SOURCES: National Geographic, June, 1973.

* * *

LIPSET, Seymour Martin 1922-

PERSONAL: Born March 18, 1922, in New York, N.Y.; son of Max (a printer) and Lena (Lippman) Lipset; married Elsie Braun, December 26, 1944; children: David, Daniel, Carola. *Education:* City College of New York (now City College of the City University of New York), B.S., 1943; Columbia University, Ph.D., 1949. *Religion:* Jewish. *Home:* 650 Gerona Rd., Stanford, Calif. 94305. *Office:* Herbert Hoover Memorial Bldg., Stanford University, Stanford, Calif. 94305.

CAREER: University of Toronto, Toronto, Ontario, lecturer in sociology, 1946-48; University of California, Berkeley, assistant professor, 1948-50; Columbia University, New York, N.Y., 1950-56, began as assistant professor, became associate professor, assistant director of Bureau of Applied Social Research, 1954-56; University of California, Berkeley, professor of sociology, 1956-66, director of Institute of International Studies, 1962-66; Harvard University, Cambridge, Mass., professor of government and social relations, 1966-75, George Markham Professor, 1974-75; Stanford University, Stanford, Calif., professor of political science and sociology, 1975—, senior fellow, Hoover Institution, 1975—. *Member:* American Sociological Association (member of council, 1958-61), International Sociological Association (chairman of committee on political sociology, 1959-71), International Society of Political Psychology (president, 1979-80), American Political Science Association (member of council, 1972-74), Sociological Research Association, American Academy of Arts and Sciences (fellow; vice-president, 1974-78), National Academy of Science, National Academy of Education, American Association for the Advancement of Science (fellow; chairman of section on economics and social sciences, 1975), Finnish Academy of Science, Institute of Political Studies (Spain; honorary member). *Awards, honors:* Fellow, Social Science Research Council, 1945-46; fellow, Center for Advanced Study in Behavioral Sciences, 1955, 1972; MacIver Award for outstanding work in sociology, 1962, for *Political Man;* M.A., Harvard University, 1966; Gunnar Myrdal prize, 1970, for *The Politics of Unreason;* Townsend Harris Medal, 1971; Guggenheim fellowship, 1972-73; 125th Anniversary Alumni Medal, City College of the City University of New York, 1973; L.L.D., Villanova University, 1973.

WRITINGS: Agrarian Socialism, University of California Press, 1950, revised edition, 1972; (editor with R. Bendix) *Class, Status, and Power,* Free Press, 1953; (with M. Trow and J. S. Coleman) *Union Democracy,* Free Press, 1956; (with R. Bendix) *Social Mobility in Industrial Society,* University of California Press, 1959, 2nd edition, 1966.

Political Man, Doubleday, 1960; (editor with W. Galenson) *Labor and Trade Unionism,* Wiley, 1960; (editor with L. Lowenthal) *Culture and Social Character,* Free Press, 1961; (editor with Neil Smelser) *Sociology: Progress of a Decade,* Prentice-Hall, 1961; (editor and author of introduction) Harriet Martineau, *Society in America,* Doubleday Anchor, 1962; *The First New Nation: The U.S. in Historical and Comparative Perspective,* Basic Books, 1963, 2nd edition, Norton, 1979; (editor) M. Ostrogorskii, *Democracy and the Organization of Political Parties,* Quadrangle, 1964; (editor with Sheldon Wolin) *The Berkeley Student Revolt,* Doubleday, 1965; (editor with Smelser) *Social Structure and Social Mobility in Economic Growth,* Aldine, 1966; (editor with Aldo Solari) *Elites in Latin America,* Oxford University Press, 1967; (with S. Rokkan) *Party Systems and Voter Alignments,* Free Press, 1967; (editor) *Student Politics,* Basic Books, 1968; (with Richard Hofstadter) *Turner and the Sociology of the Frontier,* Basic Books, 1968; *Revolution and Counterrevolution,* Basic Books, 1968; (contributor) Daniel Bell and Irving Kristol, editors, *Confrontation: The Student Rebellions and the Universities,* Basic Books, 1969; (editor) *Politics and the Social Sciences,* Oxford University Press, 1969; (editor with P. G. Altbach) *Students in Revolt,* Houghton, 1969.

(With Earl Raab) *The Politics of Unreason: Right Wing Extremism in America,* Harper, 1970, 2nd edition, University of Chicago Press, 1979; *Rebellion in the University: A History of Student Activism in America,* Little, Brown, 1972, 2nd edition, University of Chicago Press, 1976; (with Gerald M. Schaflander) *Passion and Politics,* Little, Brown, 1972; *Opportunity and Welfare in the First New Nation,* American Enterprise Institute for Public Policy Research, 1974; (with David Riesman) *Education and Politics at Harvard,* McGraw, 1975; (with Everett Carll Ladd, Jr.) *The Divided Academy: Professors and Politics,* Norton, 1976; (editor) *The Third Century: America As a Post-Industrial Society,* Hoover Institution, 1979; (editor) *Emerging Coalitions in American Politics,* Institute for Contemporary Study, 1979. Contributor to *Encounter, New Republic, Commentary, New York Times Magazine, Reporter,* and other periodicals. Co-editor, *Public Opinion,* 1978—.

BIOGRAPHICAL/CRITICAL SOURCES: New York Times, October 10, 1966; *New Leader,* December 4, 1967; *New Statesman,* December 22, 1967; *Christian Science Monitor,* August 22, 1968; *Times Literary Supplement,* August 29, 1969; *Washington Post,* October 7, 1970; *National Review,* February 23, 1971; *Detroit News,* February 6, 1972; *Quarterly Journal of Speech,* December, 1972; *Contemporary Sociology,* May, 1976; *New England Quarterly,* June, 1976; *New York Review of Books,* April 28, 1977.

* * *

LITTLE, Stuart W. 1921-

PERSONAL: Born December 19, 1921, in Hartford, Conn.; son of Mitchell Stuart (a manufacturer) and Elizabeth (Hapgood) Little; married Anastazia Raben-Levetzau, September 25, 1945; children: Caroline (Mrs. Jasper Larken), Christopher, Suzanne. *Education:* Yale University, B.A., 1944. *Home:* 131 Prince St., New York, N.Y. 10012.

CAREER: New York Herald Tribune, New York City, 1946-54, began as reporter, became assistant city editor; National Broadcasting Co., New York City, writer, 1954-58; *New York Herald Tribune,* theater news reporter, 1958-66; freelance writer, 1966—. Director of Theater Development Fund. *Military service:* U.S. Army Air Forces, 1943-45; assigned to Office of Strategic Services. *Member:* Century Club (New York).

WRITINGS: (With Arthur Cantor) *The Playmakers,* Norton, 1970; *Off-Broadway: The Prophetic Theater,* Coward, 1972; *Enter Joseph Papp,* Coward, 1974; *After the Fact,* Arno, 1975. Editor, *Authors Guild Bulletin.*

* * *

LITWACK, Leon F(rank) 1929-

PERSONAL: Born December 2, 1929, in Santa Barbara, Calif.; son of Julius and Minnie (Nitkin) Litwack; married Rhoda Lee Goldberg, 1952; children: John, Ann. *Education:* University of California, Berkeley, B.A., 1951, M.A., 1952, Ph.D., 1958. *Office:* History Department, University of California, Berkeley, Calif.

CAREER: University of Wisconsin—Madison, instructor, 1958-59, assistant professor, 1959-63, associate professor, 1963-65; University of California, Berkeley, assistant professor, summer, 1963, associate professor, 1965-72, professor, 1972—. *Military service:* U.S. Army, 1953-55. *Member:* American Historical Association, Organization of American Historians. *Awards, honors:* Social Science Research Council faculty fellow, 1961-62; Guggenheim fellowship, 1967-68; distinguished teaching award, University of California, Berkeley, 1971; Humanities research fellow, 1976; Pulitzer Prize in history, 1980, for *Been in the Storm So Long.*

WRITINGS: North of Slavery: The Negro in the Free States, 1790-1860, University of Chicago Press, 1961; (editor) *The American Labor Movement,* Prentice-Hall, 1962; (contributor) Martin Duberman, editor, *The Antislavery Vanguard,* Princeton University Press, 1965; (co-editor) *Reconstruction: An Anthology of Revisionist Writings,* Louisiana State University Press, 1969; (contributor) Tamara Herevan, editor, *Anonymous Americans: Explorations in Nineteenth Century Social History,* Prentice-Hall, 1971; *Been in the Storm So Long: The Aftermath of Slavery,* Knopf, 1979. Also co-author of *The United States: A World Power,* 1976. Author of a film, "To Look for America," 1971. Contributor to professional journals.

WORK IN PROGRESS: A biography of William D. Haywood; a book on the black South, 1868-1900.

SIDELIGHTS: Leon Litwack's Pulitzer Prize-winning *Been in the Storm So Long* is a study of the end of slavery in the American South. Peter H. Wood of *Book World* believes that "Litwack's painstaking and painful study of slavery's aftermath gives new insight into a crucial moment of social upheaval in America." David Herbert Donald of *New Republic* finds it the first "comprehensive account of the transition of blacks from slavery to freedom." Eugene D. Genovese, writing in the *New York Times Book Review*, judges that Litwack "renders intelligible the extraordinary efforts of the freedmen to build churches and schools, to maneuver desperately for a place in a modern economic system, and to consolidate their hard-won political rights."

A unique feature of the book is Litwack's extensive use of previously overlooked material, particularly the writings and recollections of former slaves. As Donald observes, Litwack "is the first historian to make use, in a general work on the Reconstruction era, of the thousands of slave narratives collected by interviewers from the Federal Writers' Project during the New Deal." These former slaves tell in their own words of the thoughts and feelings they had upon being set free at the end of the Civil War and of the problems they experienced in adjusting to American society as freedmen.

In addition to using the slaves' own accounts of the period, Litwack used many other contemporary sources as well. "Litwack," Genovese observes, "has returned to the sources and, indeed, done a good deal of new work." Donald notes that "it would be hard to think of a Southern manuscript collection, newspaper, or pertinent government document that Litwack . . . has not examined and used with discrimination and care."

Using these varied sources, Litwack "illustrates his social history with detailed anecdotes [and] shows the variety of responses on both sides to the changing conditions," Robert Kirsch writes in the *Los Angeles Times*. In using these anecdotes from the period, Genovese finds that Litwack "displays a keen sense of the revealing moment, expression, incident; a controlled passion against injustice and cruelty; and a grasp—not always in evidence these days—of the elements of genuine tragedy in the black-white confrontation that has shaped Southern history." David R. Roediger of the *Progressive*, although praising the book's "thorough research, encyclopedic detail, crisp writing, and attention to the variety and complexity of human behavior," nonetheless criticizes Litwack's tendency to leave "the reader wondering about where the weight of evidence lies and about how the stories [he] tells so well relate to larger themes in American history." In contrast, a reviewer for the *New Yorker* believes that "at the end [of *Been in the Storm So Long*] the reader feels that he himself has lived through this storm and can understand at least some of the sources of America's continuing difficulties with race."

Judging *Been in the Storm So Long* as a whole, Donald calls it "a long book, an important book, and a richly rewarding book [that] belongs on that short shelf of indispensable works on Southern history." Roediger adds to the praise by calling it "a triumph in liberal historiography" and "one of the finest books in the past decade on the postbellum South." Viewing Litwack's book in the context of the current position of black people in America, Genovese believes that it is "an honest and powerful history that carries a message of hope and of ultimate victory in the struggles that lie ahead."

BIOGRAPHICAL/CRITICAL SOURCES: New Republic, June 9, 1979; *New York Times Book Review*, June 10, 1979, November 25, 1979; *New Yorker*, June 25, 1979; *Book World*, July 8, 1979; *Christian Science Monitor*, July 9, 1979; *Wall Street Journal*, July 13, 1979; *Los Angeles Times*, August 15, 1979; *New York Review of Books*, August 16, 1979; *Progressive*, February, 1980; *New York Times*, April 15, 1980.

LIVINGSTON, Myra Cohn 1926-

PERSONAL: Born August 17, 1926, in Omaha, Neb.; daughter of Mayer Louis and Gertrude (Marks) Cohn; married Richard Roland Livingston, 1952; children: Joshua, Jonas Cohn, Jennie Marks. *Education:* Sarah Lawrence College, B.A., 1948. *Home:* 9308 Readcrest Dr., Beverly Hills, Calif. 90210. *Agent:* McIntosh and Otis, Inc., 475 Fifth Ave., New York, N.Y. 10017.

CAREER: Writer. Worked in personal public relations field for Hollywood personalities; poet-in-residence, Beverly Hills Unified School District, 1967—; senior extension teacher, University of California, Los Angeles. *Awards, honors:* Honor award, *New York Herald Tribune* Children's Spring Book Festival, 1958, for *Whispers and Other Poems;* Texas Institute of Letters award, 1962; Southern California Council on Books for Children award, 1968, 1972; Society of Children's Book Writers award, 1974, for *The Way Things Are;* National Council of Teachers of English award, 1980, for excellence in poetry.

WRITINGS—All published by Harcourt: *Whispers and Other Poems*, 1958; *Wide Awake and Other Poems*, 1959; *I'm Hiding*, 1961; *See What I Found*, 1962; *I Talk to Elephants*, 1962; *I'm Not Me*, 1963; *Happy Birthday*, 1964; *The Moon and a Star*, 1965; *I'm Waiting!*, 1966; *Old Mrs. Twindlytart, and Other Rhymes*, 1967; (editor) *A Tune Beyond Us: A Collection of Poetry*, 1968; *A Crazy Flight and Other Poems*, 1969; (editor) *Speak Roughly to Your Little Boy*, 1971; (editor) *Listen, Children, Listen*, 1972.

All published by Atheneum, except as indicated: *The Malibu and Other Poems*, 1972; (editor) *What a Wonderful Bird the Frog Are*, 1973; *The Poems of Lewis Carroll*, Crowell, 1973; *When You Are Alone—It Keeps You Capone: An Approach to Creative Writing with Children*, 1973; *Come Away*, 1974; *The Way Things Are and Other Poems*, 1974; (editor) *One Little Room: An Everywhere*, 1975; *Fourway Stop and Other Poems*, 1976; (editor) *O Frabjous Day: Poetry for Holidays, and Special Occasions*, 1977; *A Lollygag of Limericks*, 1978; *O Silver of Liver and Other Poems*, 1978; (editor) *Callooh! Callay!*, 1979; (editor) *Poems of Christmas*, in press; *No Way of Knowing: Dallas Poems*, in press.

WORK IN PROGRESS: Two books.

SIDELIGHTS: Myra Livingston told *CA:* "As it happens I work with children from kindergarten through high school; visits to schools and libraries throughout the country have convinced me that although the level of sophistication varies widely, the encounter with the cow in Kansas is still as important, in our total human framework, as with the subway of New York City. It is not the thing encountered that matters so much as the humanness with which we meet, apprehend, and possibly comprehend it. My husband and I are watching our three children grow up in a world that is essentially more difficult than was ours during our Nebraska and Indiana upbringing, but, in the world of the late 1950's in Texas and the 1960's in California, they have been geared to the world they will inherit.

"When *Whispers and Other Poems*, which I wrote as a college freshman, was published, one reviewer chided me for writing about 'simple things—merely everyday experiences.' Although intended as a rebuke, I accept it now as a compliment, for what more can one offer to the very young, for whom the poems were written, than a touchstone to deal with the early daily experiences of feelings, sights and sounds around them?"

LLOYD, Alan C(hester) 1915-

PERSONAL: Born May 3, 1915; son of Earl Leroy and Frances Ada (Gittins) Lloyd; married Helene McKenney, 1940; children: Richard. *Education:* University of Pittsburgh, A.B., 1936, Ed.M., 1939, Ph.D., 1951; attended University of Southern California, summer, 1940, and Harvard University, summer, 1941. *Religion:* Protestant. *Home:* 56 Second St., Garden City, N.Y. *Office:* Olsten Corp., 1 Merrick Rd., Westbury, N.Y. 11570.

CAREER: High school business teacher in Aliquippa, Pa., 1936-37; Woodlawn Junior High School, Munhall, Pa., business teacher, 1937-39; teacher in evening division, Robert Morris School of Business, 1937-42; Munhall Senior High School, teacher-counselor, 1939-42; McGraw-Hill Book Co., Gregg Publishing Division, New York, N.Y., book editor, 1945-47, magazine editor, 1947-56, executive editor of typewriting, 1956-78; Olsten Corp., Westbury, N.Y., director of testing, training, and career advancement, Office Temporaries Division, 1979—. Adjunct professor of business education, New York University, 1975—. *Military service:* U.S. Navy, 1942-45; became lieutenant commander. *Member:* National Business Education Association, Tri-State Business Education Association (vice-president, 1939-40), New York Academy of Public Education, Omicron Delta Kappa, Delta Delta Lambda (president, 1934-36), Phi Delta Kappa, Delti Pi Epsilon.

WRITINGS—All published by Gregg Publishing Division, McGraw-Hill: *Personal Typing,* 1946, 2nd edition (with Russell Hosler), 1959, 4th edition (with R. Hosler, Mary Margaret Hosler, and Rebecca Hall), 1979; (with Harold H. Smith) *College Typewriting Techniques,* 1952; (with John Rowe and Fred Winger) *Gregg Typewriting for Colleges,* 1957, 3rd edition published as *Typing 75,* 1970, 4th edition (with Rowe, Winger, Robert P. Poland, Robert N. Hanson, and Albert D. Rossetti), 1979; (with Rowe) *Gregg Typing,* 1953, 3rd edition (with Rowe and Winger), 1962, 5th edition published as *Typing 300,* 1972, 6th edition published in two volumes as *Typing 1* and *Typing 2,* 1977; (with Rowe and Winger) *Typing Power Drives,* 1956, 3rd edition, 1979; (with Nathan Krevolin) *You Learn to Type,* 1966, 2nd edition, 1979; *Gregg Typing Adult Text-Kits,* two volumes, 1970, 2nd edition (with Scott Ober and Jack Johnson), 1978. Contributor to professional journals. Founder, and editor, *Today's Secretary.*

WORK IN PROGRESS: Experimental editions of new testing/training materials "to ascertain employability and to remediate skills of office workers who almost meet employment requirements but need refresher and booster training"; "new-concept training aids for converting typists into word-processing equipment operators."

SIDELIGHTS: Alan Lloyd told *CA:* "I simply live and breathe typewriting. It may amuse you to think that a person could find his life absorbed by something that must seem narrow to you—typewriting. Yet when you think that more than five million persons a year learn to typewrite, that there is a great diversity of opinion concerning typewriting's role and instructional techniques, you begin to see that it really is something." More than two million copies of Lloyd's books, or the companion materials including workbooks, sets of transparencies or slides, are sold each year.

* * *

LLOYD, (Mary) Norris 1908-

PERSONAL: Born September 1, 1908, in Greenwood, S.C.; daughter of Robert Brown and Corrie (Van Diviere) Norris; married William Bross Lloyd, Jr., 1933; children: William B. III, Roberta Lloyd, Lola Lloyd Horwitz, Christopher. *Education:* Attended Barnard College and Anderson College; Antioch College, A.B.; additional study at University of Chicago. *Religion:* Religious Society of Friends. *Home:* 806 Rosewood Ave., Winnetka, Ill. 60093.

CAREER: Author. Former settlement house worker and teacher. Trustee, Community Music Center of North Shore, 1954-61, and Antioch College, 1960-62. *MKEMBER:* Authors Guild, Midland Authors. *Awards, honors:* Friends of Literature award for fiction, 1962; Midland Authors distinguished service award, 1973, for *Village That Allah Forgot.*

WRITINGS: Desperate Dragons, Hastings House, 1960; *A Dream of Mansions,* Random House, 1962; *Billy Hunts the Unicorn,* Hastings House, 1964; *Katie and the Catastrophe,* Reilly & Lee, 1968; *Village That Allah Forgot,* Hastings House, 1972. Also author of short stories and poems.

WORK IN PROGRESS: A novel and short stories.

SIDELIGHTS: Norris Lloyd wrote *CA:* "I often talk to young people who want to be writers. I say to them, keep a notebook; not a diary, but a big, cheap, lined notebook with space to write one line or six pages. Begin that notebook today with descriptions of faces, streets, flowers, animals. Write poems and read poems. Use your childhood. Sad, happy, or dull it is your own, unique to you. And finally I say, you can't dream a book; it has to be written. Writing requires discipline; a bell on the typewriter should ring for you to write at the same hour every morning."

AVOCATIONAL INTERESTS: Gardening.

* * *

LOCHHEAD, Douglas (Grant) 1922-

PERSONAL: Surname is pronounced *Lock*-heed; born March 25, 1922, in Guelph, Ontario, Canada; son of Allan Grant (a microbiologist) and Helen (Van Wart) Lochhead; married Jean Beckwith, September 17, 1949; children: Sara Louise, Mary Elizabeth. *Education:* McGill University, B.A., 1943, B.L.S., 1951; University of Toronto, M.A., 1947. *Religion:* Presbyterian. *Home address:* P.O. Box 1108, Sackville, New Brunswick, Canada E0A 3C0. *Office:* Centre for Canadian Studies, Mount Allison University, Sackville, New Brunswick, Canada E0A 3C0.

CAREER: University of Victoria, Victoria, British Columbia, chief librarian, 1951-52; Cornell University, Ithaca, N.Y., cataloguing librarian, 1952-53; Dalhousie University, Halifax, Nova Scotia, university librarian, 1953-60; York University, Toronto, Ontario, university librarian, 1960-63; Massey College, Toronto, Ontario, librarian and fellow, 1963-75; University of Toronto, Toronto, professor of English, 1965-75; Mount Allison University, Sackville, New Brunswick, Davidson Professor of Canadian Studies and director of Centre for Canadian Studies, 1975—. *Military service:* Canadian Army, Artillery and Infantry, 1943-45; became lieutenant. *Member:* League of Canadian Poets (vice-chairman, 1966-70), Bibliographical Society of Canada (president, 1974-76), Bibliographical Society of America. *Awards, honors:* Canada Council grants, 1967, 1978, 1979; fellow of Royal Society of Canada, 1976.

WRITINGS: The Heart Is Fire (poems), Ryerson, 1959; *Poems in Folio,* Three Fathom Press, Volume I, 1959, Volume II, 1963; *It Is All Around* (poems), Ryerson, 1960; *Poet Talking,* Apollo, 1964; *A&B&C&: An Alphabet,* Three Fathom Press, 1969; *Millwood Road Poems,* Roger Ascham Press, 1970; *Prayers in a Field* (poems), Aliquando Press,

1974; *The Full Furnace: Collected Poems,* McGraw, 1975; *High Marsh Road: Lines for a Diary* (poems), Anson-Cartwright Editions, 1979.

Editor: (With Northrop Frye and John A. Irving) Thomas McCullock, *The Stepsure Lectures,* McClelland & Stewart, 1960; A. G. Gilbert, *From Montreal to the Maritime Provinces and Back,* Bibliographical Society of Canada, 1967; (with Raymond Souster) *Made in Canada: An Anthology of Contemporary Canadian Poetry,* Oberon, 1970; *Bibliography of Canadian Bibliographies,* 2nd edition (Lochhead was not associated with earlier edition), University of Toronto Press, 1972; (with Souster) *One Hundred Poems of Nineteenth-Century Canada,* Macmillan (Canada), 1974; *Specimen of Printing Types and Ornaments, Lovell & Gibson, Montreal, 1846,* Bibliographical Society of Canada, 1975; Julia Catherine Beckwith, *St. Ursula's Convent,* R. P. Bell Library, Mount Allison University, 1978. General editor, "Literature of Canada" series, University of Toronto Press, 1971—, and "Toronto Reprint Library of Canadian Prose and Poetry," University of Toronto Press, 1973—.

WORK IN PROGRESS: Dictionary of Eighteenth-Century Canadian Printers' Ornaments and Illustrations; second edition of *Checklist of Nineteenth-Century Canadian Poetry in English.*

AVOCATIONAL INTERESTS: Hand press printing.

* * *

LOCKE, Duane

PERSONAL: Born in Vienna, Ga.; son of J. G. and Finis (Taylor) Locke; married Frances Combee (a school teacher), June 15, 1955. *Education:* University of Tampa, B.A., 1949; University of Florida, M.A., 1955, Ph.D., 1958. *Home:* 2716 Jefferson St., Tampa, Fla. 33602. *Office:* Department of English, University of Tampa, Tampa, Fla. 33606.

CAREER: University of Tampa, Tampa, Fla., instructor, 1958-60, assistant professor, 1960-66, associate professor, 1966-72, professor of English, 1972—, poet-in-residence, 1971—. *Member:* Committee of Small Magazine Editors and Publishers (past member of board of directors).

WRITINGS—All poetry: *From the Bottom of the Sea,* Black Sun, 1968; *Inland Oceans,* Cornish, 1968; *Dead Cities,* Gunrunner, 1969; *Light Bulbs: Lengthened Eyelashes,* Ghost Dance, 1969; *Rainbow under Boards,* Poetry Review, 1969; *Submerged Fern,* Ann Arbor Review Press, 1972; *Immanentist Sutras,* Ann Arbor Review Press, 1973; *Starfish Manuscript,* Ann Arbor Review Press, 1974; *The Word,* University of Tampa Press, 1975; *Various Light,* University of Tampa Press, 1976; *Foam on Gulf Shore,* University of Tampa Press, 1978. Editor of *University of Tampa Review,* 1964, *UT Review,* 1970.

WORK IN PROGRESS: A long poem in which "the poet writes as Adam naming for the first time what already exists. Through naming becomes involved with the thing named. The poet creates what already is, but was non-existent to the interior self"; a work of fiction which is a "juxtaposition of profane and sacred stories. Profane presenting the ugliness and brutality of commonplace life. Sacred, the mystic rapture of a non-egotistic love for another and things."

SIDELIGHTS: Duane Locke is the founder of the Immanentist school of poetry. He writes: "My poetry is based on altered state of consciousness that overcomes conceptualism and limited empirical observation. It is a type of psychedelic experience, self induced except for its source in the transforming experience of fused observations of herons, starfish, ferns, yuccas, and similar natural things found in Florida."

AVOCATIONAL INTERESTS: Yoga, nature photography, classical music.

* * *

LOCKWOOD, Theodore Davidge 1924-

PERSONAL: Born December 5, 1924, in Hanover, N.H.; son of Harold John (a professor) and Elizabeth (Van Campen) Lockwood; married Elizabeth A. White, 1944 (deceased); children: Tamara J. (Mrs. Warren Quinn), Richard D., Mavis F., Serena K. *Education:* Trinity College, Hartford, Conn., A.B., 1948; Princeton University, M.A., 1950, Ph.D., 1952. *Office:* Office of the President, Trinity College, Hartford, Conn.

CAREER: Trinity-Pawling School, New York, N.Y., member of faculty, 1951-52; Dartmouth College, Hanover, N.H., instructor, 1952-53; Juniata College, Huntingdon, Pa., assistant professor of history, 1953-55; Massachusetts Institute of Technology, Cambridge, assistant professor of history, 1955-60; Concord College, Athens, W.Va., associate dean, 1960-61, dean of faculty, 1961-64; Union College, Schenectady, N.Y., provost and dean of faculty, 1964-68; Trinity College, Hartford, Conn., president, 1968—. Visiting professor, Trinity College, 1950-60 (summers). Member of board of directors, Volunteers for International Technical Assistance, 1965—, chairman, 1966-71, Institute for Living, 1969, and Capital Higher Education Services, 1974; director, Connecticut General Insurance Corp., 1973—, American Council on Education, 1977-80, and Greater Hartford Chamber of Commerce, 1977—; member of board of trustees, Trinity College, 1964—, and Northwood School, 1969-78; member of advisory council, Commission for Higher Education, 1974—. Consultant on technical writing, Massachusetts Institute of Technology; coordinator of International Interinstitutional Affiliation Project, University of Dakar—Concord College, 1963-64. *Military service:* U.S. Army, 1943-45.

MEMBER: American Historical Association, Association of American Colleges (member of board of directors, 1973-78; chairman, 1976-77), Education Commission of the States, Connecticut Council for the Humanities, Greater Hartford Consortium for Higher Education (chairman, 1972—), Lexington Choral Society (member of board of directors), Phi Beta Kappa, Pi Gamma Mu, Rotary. *Awards, honors:* Terry fellow, Trinity College, Boudinot fellow, and Proctor senior fellow, all for study at Princeton University; Belgian-American Educational Foundation fellow; Union College Alumni Medal; New York Alumni Award; L.H.D., Concord College, Wesleyan University; LL. D., Union College, 1968, University of Hartford, 1969.

WRITINGS: Mountaineers, Artcraft, 1945; *Studies in European Socialism,* M.I.T. Press, 1960; *Our Mutual Concern: The Role of the Independent College,* Trinity College, 1968.

WORK IN PROGRESS: A History of the Belgian Labor Party, 1884-1914.

AVOCATIONAL INTERESTS: Mountain climbing (Lockwood has gone climbing in Nepal, 1971, 1974, 1976, and 1979, the Sahara, 1972, Kashmir, 1973, Patagonia, 1975, and India, 1979).

* * *

LOEFSTEDT, Bengt 1931-

PERSONAL: Born November 14, 1931, in Lund, Sweden; son of Ernst (a professor) and Sigrid (Johanson) Loefstedt; married Leena Kekomaeki, October 15, 1961; children:

Ragnar, Torsten, Ritva, Ingvar. *Education:* University of Uppsala, M.A., 1954; Phil.lic., 1957, Ph.D., 1961. *Religion:* Lutheran. *Office:* Department of Classics, University of California, Los Angeles, Calif. 90024.

CAREER: University of Uppsala, Uppsala, Sweden, assistant professor of Latin, 1962-67; University of California, Los Angeles, associate professor, 1967-68, professor of medieval Latin, 1968—. *Military service:* Swedish Army, 1960; became lieutenant. *Member:* Societe des Etudes Latines, Indogermanische Gesellschaft, American Philological Association. *Awards, honors:* Alexander von Humboldt-Stiftung fellow, 1961-62.

WRITINGS: Studien ueber die Sprache der langobardischen Gesetze, University of Uppsala, 1961; *Der hibernolateinische Grammatiker Malsachanus,* University of Uppsala, 1965; (editor) Zeno Veronensis, *Sermones,* Brepols (Turnhout, Belgium), 1971; (editor) Sedulius Scottus, *In Donati artem minorem, in Priscianum in Eutychem,* [Turnhout], 1977; (editor) Scottus, *In Donati artem maioren,* [Turnhout], 1977; (editor) *Ars Laureshamensis,* [Turnhout], 1977. Contributor of popular articles on classics and politics to *Fria Ord* and *Vaegen Framaat,* and scholarly articles to other journals.

WORK IN PROGRESS: Another edition of medieval Latin grammars.

SIDELIGHTS: Bengt Loefstedt speaks, reads, and writes German and French in addition to Swedish and English; he reads Finnish, ancient Greek, Latin, Spanish, and Italian.

* * *

LOGAN, Lillian M(ay) 1909-

PERSONAL: Born December 14, 1909, in Sykeston, N.D.; daughter of Adam Michael (a newspaper editor) and Minnie (Krieger) Stern; married Virgil G. Logan (a professor), September 30, 1946. *Education:* Eastern Michigan University, B.S., 1939; University of Wisconsin, M.S., 1950, Ph.D., 1953. *Religion:* Seventh-day Adventist. *Office:* Department of Education, Brandon University, Brandon, Manitoba, Canada.

CAREER: Teacher in public schools, Melvindale, Mich., 1936-46, and Madison, Wis., 1947-48; Union College, Lincoln, Neb., assistant professor, 1948-53, professor of education, 1953-54; Evansville College (now University of Evansville), Evansville, Ind., lecturer in education, 1954-65; Findlay College, Findlay, Ohio, professor of education, 1962-65; Brandon University, Brandon, Manitoba, associate professor of education, 1965—. Supervising teacher, Evansville public schools, 1954-65; lecturer at University of Alberta, summer, 1962, University of Calgary, summer, 1964, University of Victoria, summers, 1966-68, University of Prince Edward Island, summers, 1972, 1974, and University of Regina, summer, 1976. Member of U.S. National Committee for Childhood Education, 1953—. Lecturer to teachers' organizations, civic groups, and parent-teacher associations. *Member:* National Education Association, International Reading Association, Association for Supervision and Curriculum Development, Association for Childhood Education International (member of kindergarten committee, 1962-64), American Association for Educational Research, National Association for Education of Young Children, National Council for Social Studies (member of national advising curriculum committee, 1977—), Music Educators National Council, Soroptimist Club (national director, 1953), Tri-State Executive Club, Pi Lambda Theta (national vice-president, 1960-62), Delta Kappa Gamma. *Awards, honors:* Ella Victoria Dobbs Research Award, for Women in Education, 1953 and 1962, for kindergarten education in Mexico.

WRITINGS—All published by McGraw (Canada), except as indicated: *Teaching the Young Child,* Houghton, 1960; (with husband, Virgil G. Logan) *Teaching the Elementary School Child,* Houghton, 1961; (with V. G. Logan) *A Dynamic Approach to Language Arts,* 1967; (with G. Rimmington) *Social Studies: A Creative Direction,* 1969; (with V. G. Logan) *Design for Creative Teaching,* 1971; (with V. G. Logan and L. Paterson) *Creative Communications: Teaching the Language Arts,* 1972; (with V. G. Logan) *Educating Young Children,* 1974. Contributor to educational journals.

WORK IN PROGRESS: Teaching Reading: Beyond Literacy; Social Studies: A Global Approach.

SIDELIGHTS: Lillian M. Logan has been researching education in Mexico since 1948. *Avocational interests:* Music, gardening, travel, writing.

* * *

LOGAN, Rayford Whittingham 1897-

PERSONAL: Born January 7, 1897, in Washington, D.C.; son of Arthur C. and Martha (Whittingham) Logan; married Ruth Robinson, 1927 (died June 30, 1966). *Education:* Williams College, A.B., 1917; Harvard University, A.M., 1930, Ph.D., 1936. *Home:* 30001 Veazey Terrace N.W., Washington, D.C. 20008.

CAREER: Virginia Union University, Richmond, head of history department, 1925-30; Atlanta University, Atlanta, Ga., head of history department, 1933-38; Howard University, Washington, D.C., professor of history, 1938-69, 1971-74, distinguished professor emeritus, 1974—, head of department, 1942-64, historian of the university. *Military service:* U.S. Army, Infantry, 1917-19; became first lieutenant. *Member:* American Historical Association, Phi Beta Kappa, Alpha Phi Alpha, Epsilon Chapter, Sigma Pi Phi. *Awards, honors:* Commander of the National Order of Honor and Merit, Republic of Haiti; L.H.D., Williams College, 1965; L.L.D., Howard University, 1972.

WRITINGS: The Diplomatic Relations of the United States with Haiti, 1776-1891, University of North Carolina Press, 1941; *What the Negro Wants,* University of North Carolina Press, 1944; *The Negro in American Life and Thought: The Nadir, 1877-1901,* Dial, 1954; *The Negro in the United States: A Brief History,* Van Nostrand, 1957; *The Betrayal of the Negro: From Rutherford B. Hayes to Woodrow Wilson,* Macmillan, 1967; *Haiti and the Dominican Republic,* Oxford University Press, 1968; *Howard University: The First Hundred Years, 1867-1967,* New York University Press, 1969; *The Negro in the United States,* Van Nostrand, Volume I: *A History to 1945,* 1970, Volume II: (with Michael R. Winston) *Ordeal of Democracy,* 1971; (editor) *U. F. B. DuBois: A Profile,* Hill & Wang, 1971. Contributor of articles and reviews to professional journals.

WORK IN PROGRESS: Editing, with Michael R. Winston, *Dictionary of American Negro Biography,* for Norton; *The Struggle for Human Rights,* for Howard University Press; *Within and Without the Veil,* an autobiography.

AVOCATIONAL INTERESTS: Travel.

* * *

LOMASK, Milton (Nachman) 1909-

PERSONAL: Born June 26, 1909, in Fairmont, W.Va.; son

of Samuel Josiah and Clara (Reinheimer) Lomask. *Education:* University of Iowa, A.B., 1930; Northwestern University, A.M., 1941. *Religion:* Roman Catholic. *Home and office:* 6758 Towne Lane Rd., McLean, Va. 22101.

CAREER: Des Moines Register, Des Moines, Iowa, reporter, 1930-35; *St. Louis Star-Times,* St. Louis, Mo., copy editor, 1936-37; *New York Journal-American,* New York City, copy editor, 1938-39; Northwestern University, Evanston, Ill., assistant in speech, 1940-41; Nedick's, Inc., New York City, advertising manager, 1945-50; New York University, New York City, instructor, 1950-60. Lecturer at Catholic University of America, 1964—, and Georgetown University, 1964-70, and 1980. Consultant, National Science Foundation, 1971-72, and British Broadcasting Co., 1974. Participant in Suffield-Wesleyan Reader-Writer Conference, 1974-76. Free-lance writer, 1950—. *Military service:* U.S. Army, 1942-45; became captain. *Member:* Authors League, American Historical Association, Children's Book Guild of Washington, Washington Independent Writers, Georgetown University Library Associates.

WRITINGS—Adult: (With Leonard Hawkins) *The Man in the Iron Lung,* Doubleday, 1956; *Andrew Johnson: President on Trial,* Farrar, Straus, 1961; *Seed Money: The Guggenheim Story,* Farrar, Straus, 1964; (with Constance McLaughlin Green) *Vanguard, A History,* Smithsonain Institution Press, 1971; *A Minor Miracle: An Informal History of the National Science Foundation,* National Science Foundation, 1976; *Aaron Burr: The Years from Princeton to Vice President,* Farrar, Straus, 1979.

Juvenile: *St. Isaac and the Indians,* Vision Books, 1956; *John Carroll: Bishop and Patriot,* Vision Books, 1956; *My Eskimos,* Vision Books, 1957; *St. Augustine and His Search for Faith,* Vision Books, 1957; (with Brendan Larnen) *St. Thomas Aquinas and the Preaching Beggars,* Vision Books, 1957; *The Cure of Ars: The Priest Who Outtalked the Devil,* Vision Books, 1958; *The Secret of Grandfather's Diary,* Ariel Books, 1958; *The Secret of the Marmalade Cat,* Ariel Books, 1959; *Ship's Boy With Magellan,* Doubleday, 1959; *Charles Carroll and the American Revolution,* Kenedy, 1959.

General Phil Sheridan and the Union Cavalry, Kenedy, 1960; *The Secret of the One-Eyed Moose,* Ariel Books, 1960; *Andy Johnson: The Tailor Who Became President,* Ariel Books, 1961; *Cross Among the Tomahawks,* Doubleday, 1961; (with Ray Neville) *The Way We Worship,* Vision Books, 1961; *A Bird in the Hand,* Bruce, 1964; *John Quincy Adams: Son of the American Revolution,* Ariel Books, 1965; *Rochambeau and Our French Allies,* Kenedy, 1965; *Assignment to the Council,* Doubleday, 1966; *I Do Solemnly Swear,* Ariel Books, 1966; *This Slender Reed: A Life of James K. Polk,* Ariel Books, 1966; *Beauty and the Traitor: The Story of Mrs. Benedict Arnold,* Macrae Smith, 1967; *Odd Destiny: A Life of Alexander Hamilton,* Farrar, Straus, 1969; *Robert Goddard, Space Pioneer,* Girard, 1970; *The First American Revolution,* Farrar, Straus, 1974; *The Spirit of 1787: The Making of Our Nation,* Farrar, Straus, 1980. Contributor to *America, American Heritage, Better Homes and Gardens, Catholic Digest,* and other periodicals.

WORK IN PROGRESS: Aaron Burr: The Years of Exile, for Farrar, Straus.

BIOGRAPHICAL/CRITICAL SOURCES: Newsweek, July 23, 1979; *Washington Post,* August 7, 1979; *Chicago Tribune,* September 16, 1979; *New York Times Book Review,* September 23, 1979.

LOMAX, Alan 1915-

PERSONAL: Born January 31, 1915, in Austin, Texas; son of John Avery (a curator for the Library of Congress) and Bess (Brown) Lomax; married second wife, Antoinette Marchand, 1961; children: (first marriage) Anne L. *Education:* Attended Harvard College, 1931; University of Texas, B.A. (summa cum laude), 1936; Columbia University, graduate study, 1939. *Office:* 215 West 98th St., No. 12E, New York, N.Y. 10025. *Agent:* (Lectures) Keedick Lecture Bureau, 475 Fifth Ave., New York, N.Y.

CAREER: Library of Congress, Washington, D.C., assistant in charge of archives of American folk music, 1937-42; Columbia Broadcasting System, New York City, host of "Well-Springs of America" radio show, 1939-44; British Broadcasting Corp., London, England, producer and writer, 1950-58; Columbia Records, New York City, editor of World Library of Folk and Primitive Music, 1950-57; Columbia University, New York City, research associate in department of anthropology, 1961—. Lecturer. Member of board, Newport Folk Festival, 1958-60. *Military service:* U.S. Army. *Member:* International Folk Music Council, American Anthropological Association, Society of Ethnic Musicology (member of board, 1963 and 1979), American Association for the Advancement of Science (fellow), American Folklore Society, Texas Folklore Society, New York Academy of Science (fellow), Phi Beta Kappa. *Awards, honors:* American Council of Learned Societies grant, 1939, fellowship, 1960-61; Rockefeller Foundation research grant, 1962, 1976-79; National Institute of Mental Health grant, 1963-74; Wenner Gren Foundation grant, 1965; Ford Foundation grant, 1973; National Endowment for the Humanities grant, 1973-74, 1976, and 1980—; National Endowment for the Arts grant, 1975, 1979-80; Menil Foundation grant for filmmaking, 1976-77.

WRITINGS: (With father, John Avery Lomax) *American Ballads and Folk Songs,* Macmillan, 1934; (with J. Lomax) *Negro Folk Songs as Sung by Leadbelly,* Macmillan, 1936; (with J. Lomax) *Cowboy Songs,* Macmillan, 1937, revised edition, 1966; (with J. Lomax) *Our Singing Country,* Macmillan, 1938; (with J. Lomax) *Folk Song: USA,* Duell, 1946, reprinted, New American Library, 1975; *Mister Jelly Roll,* Duell, 1950, reprinted, University of California Press, 1973; *Harriet and Her Harmonium,* Faber, 1955, A. S. Barnes, 1959; *The Rainbow Sign,* Duell, 1959; *The Folk Songs of North America,* Cassell, 1959, Doubleday, 1960; (with Elizabeth Poston) *Penguin Book of American Folk Songs,* Penguin, 1961; (author of commentary) Pete Seeger, editor, *Hard-Hitting Songs for Hard-Hit People,* Oak Publications, 1967; *Folk Song Style and Culture,* American Association for the Advancement of Science, 1968; (editor with Raoul Abdul) *Three Thousand Years of Black Poetry,* Dodd, 1970; *Cantometrics,* with seven cassette recordings, Extension Media Center, University of California, 1977. Also author of numerous radio scripts and with J. Lomax of *Songs of the Cattle Camp and Cow Trail,* with Sidney R. Crowell of *American Folksong and Folklore: A Regional Bibliography,* and with R. T. Lomax of *Fourteen Traditional Songs from Texas.*

Recordings; compiler: "Columbia World Library of Folk and Primitive Music," eighteen volumes, Columbia Records, 1950-57; "Southern Journey," twelve volumes, Prestige Recording Co.; "Southern Folk Heritage," seven volumes, Atlantic Records; "Music and Interviews of Jelly Roll Morton," twelve volumes, Library of Congress; "Folk Songs of Spain," eleven volumes, Westminster; "Folk Songs of Great Britain," ten volumes, Caedmon.

Film scripts: (With Peter Kennedy and George Pickow) "Oss, Oss Wee Oss," English Folk Dance Society, 1951; (with Forrestine Paulay) "Dance and Human History," Extension Media Center, University of California, 1976; (with F. Paulay) "Step Style," Extension Media Center, University of California, 1979; (with F. Paulay) "Palm Play," Extension Media Center, University of California, 1979; "The Land Where the Blues Began," PBS-TV.

SIDELIGHTS: Alan Lomax became interested in the collecting and recording of folk songs through the work of his father, John Avery Lomax, a pioneer in the field. Over the years, Lomax has recorded folk songs in England, Scotland, Ireland, the Caribbean, Spain, and Italy as well as throughout the United States.

BIOGRAPHICAL/CRITICAL SOURCES: Southwest Review, winter, 1934, January, 1938; *Christian Science Monitor,* March 8, 1941, October 8, 1970; *Time,* November 26, 1945; *New York Times Book Review,* July 23, 1950, September 27, 1970; *Negro History Bulletin,* May, 1971; *Notes,* September, 1971; *Journal of American Folklore,* April, 1974.

* * *

LOMBARD, C(harles) M(orris) 1920-

PERSONAL: Born December 10, 1920, in Chicago, Ill.; son of Charles Morris and Elizabeth (Nolan) Lombard; married Louise Scherger (a pathologist), June, 1948; children: Elizabeth, Charles, Robert, James. *Education:* University of Wisconsin—Madison, Ph.D., 1953. *Politics:* Independent. *Religion:* Quaker. *Home:* 220 South Madison, Hinsdale, Ill. 60521. *Office:* Department of French, University of Illinois, Chicago, Ill. 60680.

CAREER: Villanova University, Villanova, Pa., assistant professor of French, 1950-56; Chicago Teachers College (now Chicago State University), Chicago, Ill., assistant professor, 1956-59, associate professor of French, 1960-62; Loyola University, Chicago, associate professor of French, 1962-66; University of Illinois at Chicago Circle, professor of French, 1966—.

WRITINGS—All published by Twayne, except as indicated: *French Romanticism on the Frontier,* Gredos, 1972; *Lamartine,* 1973; *Joseph de Maistre,* 1976; *Xavier de Maistre,* 1977; *Thomas H. Chivers,* 1978. Contributor to professional journals.

* * *

LONG, E(verette) B(each) 1919-

PERSONAL: Born October 24, 1919, in Whitehall, Wis.; son of Cecil Everette and Florence (Beach) Long; married Barbara Conzelman, 1942. *Education:* Attended Miami University, Oxford, Ohio, 1937-39, and Northwestern University, 1939-41. *Home:* 607 South 15th St., Laramie, Wyo. 82070. *Office:* Department of American Studies, University of Wyoming, Laramie, Wyo. 82070.

CAREER: Associated Press, Chicago, Ill., editor, 1944-52; Spencer Press, Chicago, associate editor, *American Peoples Encyclopedia,* 1952-55; director of research for Bruce Catton's "Centennial History of the Civil War" series (published by Doubleday), 1955-65; editorial assistant to Allan Nevins' *Ordeal of the Union,* a multi-volume work (published by Scribner), 1965-70; University of Wyoming, Laramie, associate professor, 1970-78, professor of American studies, 1978—. Visiting lecturer, University of California, Riverside, 1967-68, University of California, San Diego, 1968, and University of Illinois at Chicago Circle, 1968-69. *Member:* Chicago Civil War Round Table (president, 1955-56), Friends of the Chicago Public Library (president, 1960). *Awards, honors:* D.Litt., Lincoln College, 1961; Harry S Truman award for Civil War scholarship, 1964; award of merit, Illinois Civil War Centennial Commission, 1963, 1965; award of commendation, Oklahoma Civil War Centennial Commission, 1965; Huntington Library grant-in-aid, 1965; Centennial Medallion, U.S. Civil War Centennial Commission, 1966; Nevins-Freeman Award, 1979.

WRITINGS: (With Otto Eisenschiml) *As Luck Would Have It,* Bobbs-Merrill, 1948; (with Ralph Newman) *The Civil War: A Picture Chronicle,* Volume II (Long was not associated with earlier volume), Grossett, 1956; (editor with Newman) *The Civil War Digest,* Grosset, 1960; (contributor) *Lincoln for the Ages,* Doubleday, 1960; *The Civil War Day by Day,* Doubleday, 1971; *Saints and the Union: Utah Territory during the Civil War,* University of Illinois Press, 1980.

Author of introduction: (And editor) *Personal Memoirs of Ulysses S. Grant,* World Publishing, 1952; *The Post Reader of Civil War Stories,* edited by Gordon Carroll, Doubleday, 1958; (and editor) James Ford Rhodes, *History of the Civil War, 1861-1865,* Ungar, 1961; George F. R. Henderson, *Stonewall Jackson and the American Civil War,* Fawcett, 1962; Thomas Cooper De Leon, *Four Years in Rebel Capitals,* Collier Books, 1962; (and editor) *Selected Chapters: Allan Nevins' Ordeal of the Union,* Scribners, 1973. Member of editorial advisory board of *Civil War History;* member of bibliographical committee, *Lincoln Lore.*

WORK IN PROGRESS: Toward a Broader Approach to Civil War Strategy; Beyond the River: The Trans-Missouri in the Civil War.

SIDELIGHTS: In his research for Bruce Catton's "Centennial History of the Civil War" series, E. B. Long culled over nine million words of notes. Much of this material was obtained from original manuscripts, diaries, and records, and was gathered during trips throughout the country. Long visited over 150 libraries, universities, and archives and traveled over sixty thousand miles. In 1966, Doubleday presented his research notes to the Library of Congress. Long owns more than six thousand books, most of them about the Civil War and American history.

* * *

LONGAKER, Richard P(ancoast) 1924-

PERSONAL: Born July 1, 1924, in Philadelphia, Pa.; son of Edwin P. and Emily (Downs) Longaker; married Mollie M. Katz, January 25, 1964; children: Richard Pancoast II, Stephen Edwin, Sarah Ellen, Rachel Elise. *Education:* Swarthmore College, B.A., 1949; University of Wisconsin, M.A., 1950; Cornell University, Ph.D., 1954. *Office:* Office of the Provost, Johns Hopkins University, 34th and Charles Sts., Baltimore, Md. 21218.

CAREER: Kenyon College, Gambier, Ohio, assistant professor, 1953-54; University of California, Riverside, assistant professor, 1954-55; Kenyon College, associate professor, 1955-60; Cornell University, Ithaca, N.Y., visiting associate professor, 1960; University of California, Los Angeles, associate professor, 1961-62, professor of political science, 1963-67, chairman of department, 1965-76, dean of academic affairs, graduate division, 1970-71; Johns Hopkins University, Baltimore, Md., provost, 1976—. *Military service:* U.S. Army, 1943-45; became sergeant; awarded Bronze Star. *Member:* American Political Science Association.

WRITINGS: The Presidency and Individual Liberties, Cornell University Press, 1961; (with Charles Quigley) *Conflict, Politics, and Freedom,* Ginn, 1968; (editor and author of introductory note and additional text) Clinton L. Rossiter, *The Supreme Court and the Commander in Chief,* revised edition (Longaker was not associated with earlier editions), Cornell University Press, 1977.

* * *

LONGENECKER, Justin G. 1917-

PERSONAL: Born May 4, 1917, in Jackson County, Kan.; son of Irvin B. and Della (Gooderl) Longenecker; married Frances Pickering, 1942; children: Linda, Nancy, Jane. *Education:* Attended Central College, 1935-37; Seattle Pacific College (now University), B.A., 1939; Ohio State University, M.B.A., 1950; University of Washington, Ph.D., 1956. *Home:* 750 Arlington Dr., Waco, Tex. *Office:* Hankamer School of Business, Baylor University, Waco, Tex.

CAREER: U.S. Government Civil Service, Washington, D.C., and Dayton, Ohio, administrative officer, 1940-50; Western Washington College of Education (now Western Washington University), Bellingham, instructor, 1951-53; Baylor University, Waco, Tex., professor, 1955—, director of graduate studies in business, 1965-70, and 1971-72. *Member:* Academy of Management, American Association of University Professors, Southern Management Association, Waco Management and Personnel Association (president, 1962-63), Alpha Kappa Psi.

WRITINGS: (With H. N. Broom) *Small Business Management,* South-Western, 1961, 5th edition, 1979; *Principles of Management and Organizational Behavior,* C. E. Merrill, 1964, 4th edition, 1977; *Essentials of Management: A Behavioral Approach,* C. E. Merrill, 1977.

* * *

LOOVIS, David (Mactavish) 1926-

PERSONAL: Born April 20, 1926, in New York, N.Y.; son of Karl Solon and Marie (Mactavish) Loovis. *Education:* Colgate University, A.B., 1947. *Home and office:* 49 West 16th St., New York, N.Y. 10011.

CAREER: McGraw-Hill Publishing Co., New York City, sales representative, 1950-52; Brooks Brothers, New York City, salesman, 1953-60; J. Walter Thompson Co., New York City, copywriter, 1963-66; full-time writer, 1966—.

WRITINGS: Try for Elegance, Scribner, 1959; *The Last of the Southern Winds,* Scribner, 1961; *Gay Spirit: A Guide to Becoming a Sensuous Homosexual,* Grove Press, 1975; *Straight Answers about Homosexuality for Straight Readers,* Prentice-Hall, 1977. Contributor of short stories and articles to magazines.

WORK IN PROGRESS: A novel, tentatively entitled *Savage Mother of Desire.*

SIDELIGHTS: Try for Elegance has as part of its background an elegant Madison Avenue shop similar to Brooks Brothers. David Loovis was much celebrated as "that salesman who wrote the novel," and says it has taken him some years "to convince people that the truth was the other way around—I was a writer (since the age of sixteen) who happened to be a salesman."

Loovis states that *Gay Spirit* was "the first hardcover homosexual sex manual ever to be nationally advertised directly for the benefit of a homosexual reading audience." He told *CA* that in *Straight Answers,* he attempted to interpret homosexuality to heterosexual readers, emphasizing that everyone is potentially both homosexual and heterosexual. Loovis maintains that heterosexuals can best comprehend homosexuality by becoming aware of their own homosexual sensibility.

Commenting on the direction his future writing will take, Loovis said, "I consider myself essentially a novelist. Now that I have done my part for Gay Lib, I want to get back to fictional narrative. It is the art form to which I've devoted my life."

* * *

LOPEZ-MORILLAS, Juan 1913-

PERSONAL: Born August 11, 1913, in Jaen, Spain; naturalized U.S. citizen; son of Emilio and Teresa (Ortiz) Lopez-Morillas; married Frances Elinor Mapes, 1937; children: Martin, Maria-Consuelo, Julian. *Education:* University of Madrid, Bachelor of Letters, 1929, License in Law, 1934; University of Iowa, Ph.D., 1940. *Home:* 2200 Hartford Rd., Austin, Tex. 78703. *Office:* Batts 112, University of Texas, Austin, Tex. 78712.

CAREER: University of Iowa, Iowa City, instructor, 1939-41, assistant professor of Spanish, 1941-43; Brown University, Providence, R.I., assistant professor, 1943-47, associate professor, 1947-51, professor of Spanish, 1951-65, Alumni-Alumnae Professor, 1965-73, William R. Kenan, Jr. Professor of the Humanities, 1973-78, William R. Kenan, Jr. Professor Emeritus, 1978—, chairman of department of Spanish and Italian, 1960-67, chairman of department of comparative literature, 1967-71; University of Texas at Austin, professor of Spanish, 1978-79, Ashbel Smith Professor of Spanish, 1979—. Visiting lecturer, Harvard University, 1947, 1959; Phi Beta Kappa visiting scholar, 1966-67; visiting fellow, Trinity College, Oxford University, 1972; visiting Andrew W. Mellon Professor, University of Pittsburgh, 1974; visiting scholar, University Center in Virginia, 1976-77. *Member:* Modern Language Association of America, American Comparative Literature Association, American Association of University Professors (president, Brown University chapter, 1955-56), Hispanic Society of America, International Association of Hispanists (vice-president). *Awards, honors:* Guggenheim fellow, 1950-51, 1957-58; American Council of Learned Societies grants, 1954, 1960, and 1974; American Philosophical Society grant, 1954; Doctor of Humane Letters, Brown University, 1979.

WRITINGS: (With Erwin Kempton Mapes) *Y va de cuento,* Ginn, 1950; *El krausismo espanol,* Fondo de Cultura, 1956; *Intelectuales y espirituales,* Revista de Occidente, 1961; *F. Giner de los Rios: Ensayos,* Alianza, 1969; *Hacia el 98: Literatura, sociedad, ideologia,* Ariel, 1972; *Krausismo: Estetica y Literatura,* Labor, 1973. Contributor to professional journals in the United States and abroad.

WORK IN PROGRESS: Giner de los Rios: Conciencia de crisis, for Espasa-Calpe.

* * *

LOTH, David 1899-

PERSONAL: Born December 7, 1899, in St. Louis, Mo.; son of Albert and Fanny (Sunshine) Loth; married Helen J. Wilcox, 1942. *Education:* University of Missouri, B.J., 1920. *Home:* 2227 Canyon Blvd., Boulder, Colo. 80302. *Agent:* Shirley Collier, 1127 Stradella Rd., Los Angeles, Calif. 90024.

CAREER: The World, New York City, member of editorial

staff, 1920-31; *Daily Guardian,* Sydney, Australia, reporter, 1925; *Majorca Sun,* Palma, Spain, editor and publisher, 1931-34; *New York Times,* New York City, copy editor, 1934-41; Office of Inter-American Affairs, Washington, D.C., chief of publications, 1941-44; Press Research, Washington, D.C., managing editor, 1944; Surplus Property Board, Washington, D.C., director of information, 1945; Planned Parenthood Federation, New York City, director of information, 1946-51; Columbia University, New York City, director of bicentennial information, 1953-54; Finch College, New York City, director of information and lecturer in journalism, 1961-65. Consultant on editorial or information programs to Eisenhower Foundation, Rockefeller Brothers Fund, Office of War Mobilization, International Development Advisory Board; consultant to Psychological Corp., 1969-76. *Military service:* U.S. Army, 1918. *Member:* Mystery Writers of America, Society of American Historians, American Society of Journalists and Authors. *Awards, honors:* Associate Nieman fellow, Harvard University, 1957-58.

WRITINGS: The Brownings, A Victorian Idyll, Brentano, 1929; *Lorenzo the Magnificent,* Brentano, 1929; *Charles II, Ruler and Rake,* Brentano, 1930; *Philip II, Master of the Armada,* Brentano, 1932; *Public Plunder, A History of Graft,* Carrick & Evans, 1938; *Alexander Hamilton, Portrait of a Prodigy,* Carrick & Evans, 1939; *Woodrow Wilson: The Fifteenth Point,* Lippincott, 1941; *Chief Justice,* Norton, 1949; *The People's General,* Scribner, 1951; *The Marriage Counselor,* Greystone, 1952; *Gold Brick Cassie,* Gold Medal, 1953; *The Columbia Bicentennial,* Columbia University Press, 1955; *A Long Way Forward,* Longmans, Green, 1957; *Swope of G.E.,* Simon & Schuster, 1958; *The Erotic in Literature,* Messner, 1961; *Pencoyd and the Roberts Family,* privately printed, 1962; *Crime Lab,* Messner, 1964; *The City within a City,* Morrow, 1966; *Crime in the Suburbs,* Morrow, 1967; *The Taming of Technology,* Simon & Schuster, 1972; *Economic Miracle in Israel,* privately printed, 1974.

Co-author: *American Sexual Behavior and the Kinsey Report,* Greystone, 1948; *The People Know Best,* Public Affairs Press, 1949; *Voluntary Parenthood,* Random House, 1949; *For Better or Worse,* Harper, 1951; *Report on the American Communist,* Holt, 1952; *I Was a Drug Addict,* Random House, 1953; *Peter Freuchen's Book of the Seven Seas,* Messner, 1957; *The Frigid Wife,* Messner, 1962; *How High Is Up?,* Bobbs-Merrill, 1964; *The Emotional Sex,* Morrow, 1964; *Ivan Sanderson's Book of Great Jungles,* Messner, 1965.

Author and director of Northern section, *Integration North and South,* 1956; also author of *Colorado Model for Conservation Education,* 1980. Senior author and editor, *High School Geography Project,* 1967-68. Ghost-writer of six books in the fields of medicine, law, and public affairs.

* * *

LOUVISH, Misha 1909-
(Moshe Bar-Natan)

PERSONAL: Born July 5, 1909, in Kimpolung, Bukowina, Rumania; son of Nehemiah and Sarah (Goldschaeger) Louvish; married Eva Bersinski; children: David, Jonathan, Simon. *Education:* University of Glasgow, M.A. (honors in English language and literature), 1932. *Politics:* Labour-Socialist. *Religion:* Jewish. *Home:* 32a Bustanai St., Jerusalem 93 229, Israel.

CAREER: Teacher of English at Corporation of Glasgow Education Committee schools, Glasgow, Scotland, 1934-37, and at schools in Haifa and Tel Aviv, Palestine (now Israel), 1937-39; head of schools for evacuees, Skelmorlie, Scotland, 1940-42, and Glasgow, 1945-49; Jewish Agency, Jerusalem, Israel, editor, 1949-52; Government Information Services of Israel, Jerusalem, executive, 1952-54; *Jerusalem Post,* Jerusalem, labor correspondent, 1954-55; *Here and Now* (weekly), Jerusalem, managing editor, 1955-56; Israel Government Press Office, Jerusalem, editor of English publications, 1956-67; Keter Books, Jerusalem, editor and translator, 1967-74; free-lance writer, translator, and journalist, 1974—. *Military service:* British Army, Royal Artillery, 1942-45.

WRITINGS: (Editor) *Chanukah Highlights* (handbook for teachers and youth leaders), Youth Department, Jewish National Fund, 1953; (editor) *Flag of Freedom* (handbook), Youth Department, Jewish National Fund, 1955; *The Challenge of Israel,* Israel Universities Press, 1968, Ktav, 1969. Also author of *Jerusalem: Living City* and *The Facts about the Holocaust.*

Translator from the Hebrew: (With Mordekhai Nurock) David Ben-Gurion, editor, *Israel and Its Land,* Aldus Books, 1966; S. J. Agnon, *A Guest for the Night,* Schocken, 1968; Aharon Megged, *The Living on the Dead,* Saturday Review Press, 1971. Also translator of *We Built Jerusalem* by Arye Lifshitz.

Author of booklets, including *The Zionist Movement* and *How Israel's Democracy Works;* also author of speeches for Israeli prime ministers David Ben-Gurion, Moshe Sharett, Levi Eshkol, Golda Meir, Yitzhak Rabin, and Menachem Begin. Editor, *Facts about Israel* (annual), 1957-72; deputy editor, modern Israel section of *Encyclopaedia Judaica,* 1972. Contributor of articles on Israel, some under pseudonym Moshe Bar-Natan, to periodicals.

SIDELIGHTS: Misha Louvish told *CA:* "I regard myself first and foremost as an interpreter, whether I am translating a work of literature, commenting on recent developments in an article, or writing a book explaining the basic problems of my country. Since I settled in Israel in 1949, my principal goal has been to play my part in presenting the country's life and literature to those who are not familiar with the Hebrew language and the Israeli scene."

* * *

LOVASIK, Lawrence George 1913-

PERSONAL: Born June 22, 1913, in Tarentum, Pa.; son of Stephen Emery and Mary (Zalibera) Lovasik. *Education:* Divine Word Seminary, B.A.; additional study at Gregorian Papal University. *Home:* 207 Lytton Ave., Pittsburgh, Pa. 15213. *Office:* 211 West Seventh Ave., Tarentum, Pa. 15084.

CAREER: Ordained Roman Catholic priest, 1938, at Divine Word Seminary, Techny, Ill.; Divine Word Seminary, Epworth, Iowa, seminary professor, 1939-41; Divine Word Seminary, Girard, Pa., seminary professor, 1941-42; missionary work, preaching parish missions and retreats for lay and religious, 1942—. Founder, 1955, of Congregation of the Sisters of the Divine Spirit, a Roman Catholic religious order in modern habit, dedicated to teaching school, giving catechetical instructions, doing social work, and charitable activities; founder, 1967, of Family Service Corps, a lay institute to help the elderly; founder of Marian Action Publications (distributors).

WRITINGS: Stepping Stones to Sanctity, Macmillan, 1950; *Praying the Gospels,* Macmillan, 1952; *Mary My Hope,* Catholic Book Publishing, 1954; *Our Lady in Catholic Life,* Macmillan, 1956; *Catechism in Stories,* Bruce, 1956; *Catholic Picture Bible,* Catholic Book Publishing, 1958; *The Eu-*

charist in Catholic Life, Macmillan, 1960; *Treasury of Catechism Stories,* Marian Action, 1960; *Jesus My Life,* Catholic Book Publishing, 1960; *The Mass for Children,* Catholic Book Publishing, 1960; *St. Joseph Picture Prayerbook,* Catholic Book Publishing, 1960; *Our Lady's Knight,* Daughters of St. Paul, 1961; *Prayer in Catholic Life,* Macmillan, 1962; *Kindness,* Macmillan, 1962; *My Beloved Son,* Macmillan, 1962; *Catholic Marriage and Child Care,* Christopher, 1962; *Priestly Holiness,* Daughters of St. Paul, 1962; *Jesus Joy of the Suffering,* Daughters of St. Paul, 1962; *Lives of the Saints,* Catholic Book Publishing, 1962.

The Good News in Stories, Marian Action, 1965; *The Sister for Today,* Marian Action, 1965; *Treasury of Catechism Stories,* Marian Action, 1966; *Prayers for the People of God,* Catholic Book Publishing, 1966; *The Lord Jesus,* Catholic Book Publishing, 1969; *St. Dymphna,* Marian Action, 1971; *Catechism in Stories,* Marian Action, 1977; *St. Joseph New American Catechism,* Catholic Book Publishing, 1978; *Treasury of Prayers,* Marian Action, 1978; *Come Holy Spirit,* Marian Action, 1978; *The Bible Illustrated,* Marian Action, 1978.

St. Joseph Picture Books; all published by Catholic Book Publishing, 1962: *My Picture Missal; The Ten Commandments; Mary My Mother; Good Saint Joseph; I Believe in God; The Seven Sacraments; The Miracles of Jesus; The Angels; God Loves Us All; My Mass Book.*

Author of Divine Word Recordings (albums), produced by Marian Action, including "The Eucharistic Series," "The Prayerlife Series," "The Personality of Christ," "The Kindness Series," "The Virgin Mary Series," and "The Religious Life Series"; author of "Father Lovasik Meditations," a series of records and cassettes; also author of fifty devotional pamphlets.

AVOCATIONAL INTERESTS: Painting, poetry, music, dramatics, recordings of sermons.

* * *

LOW, Victor N. 1931-

PERSONAL: Born August 25, 1931, in New York, N.Y.; son of Sol (a business executive) Low and Rosamund (Trilling) Low Greenhill; married Helga L. B. Frentzel-Beyme, May 10, 1962; children: Joshua, Gideon. *Education:* University of Chicago, B.A., 1951; Columbia University, M.A., 1962; University of California, Los Angeles, Ph.D., 1967. *Politics:* Independent. *Religion:* Jewish. *Home address:* c/o Mr. and Mrs. Simon Greenhill, 1600 South Ocean Dr., Hollywood, Fla. 33019. *Office:* Harry S. Truman Institute for the Advancement of Peace, Hebrew University of Jerusalem, Jerusalem, Israel.

CAREER: Haile Selassie I University, Addis Ababa, Ethiopia, lecturer in Islamic history and institutions, 1967-69; Michigan State University, East Lansing, assistant professor of African and Middle East history, 1969-72; Hebrew University of Jerusalem, Jerusalem, Israel, visiting senior lecturer in West African history, 1972-73; Ahmadu Bello University, Zaria, Nigeria, senior lecturer in African history, 1973-75; University of Jos, Jos, Nigeria, senior lecturer and chairman of department of history, 1975-76; Michigan State University, visiting professor of African history, 1976-77; Hebrew University of Jerusalem, senior research fellow in African history and senior lecturer in modern Israeli history, 1978—. *Military service:* U.S. Army, 1952-54. *Member:* African Studies Association, American Historical Association, Middle East Studies Association, African Studies Association (United Kingdom). *Awards, honors:* Ford Foundation research fellow, 1963-65.

WRITINGS: Three Nigerian Emirates: A Study in Oral History, Northwestern University Press, 1972; (editor) *Africa to 1914: A Critical Survey of Relevant Books, with Special Reference to West Africa,* two volumes, F. Cass, 1979; (co-editor) *History of Modern Eretz Israel,* Akademon Press, 1980; (editor) *From West Africa: A Political and Social Record, 1917-1973,* four volumes, F. Cass, in press.

WORK IN PROGRESS: A Glossary of Names, Words and Terms Relevant to the History of Modern Eretz Israel; Israel and the Victorians: The Nineteenth Century Political, Religious and Intellectual Background to the Balfour Declaration.

* * *

LOWELL, Juliet 1901-

PERSONAL: Born August 7, 1901, in the lower berth of an American train; daughter of Max and Helen (Kohut) Loewenthal; married Leo Lowell (deceased); married Ben Lowell (deceased); children: Ross, Margot Lowell Einstein. *Education:* Vassar College, B.A., 1922. *Home and office:* The Hampton House, 28 East 70th St., Apt. 15-D, New York, N.Y. 10021.

CAREER: Writer and lecturer. Has made numerous radio and television appearances throughout the United States and Canada. Member of board, Heckscher Foundation for Children. *Member:* Authors League of America, New York-Tokyo Sister City Affiliation (chairman, book committee; vice-chairman, hospitality committee), Overseas Press Club.

WRITINGS—Published by Duell, except as indicated: *Dumb-Belles Lettres,* Simon & Schuster, 1933; *Dear Sir,* 1943; *Dear Sir or Madam,* 1945; *Dear Mr. Congressman,* 1948, 3rd edition, 1960; *Dear Hollywood,* 1950; *Dear Doctor,* Mill, 1955, revised edition, Funk, 1968; *Dear Justice,* Mill, 1957; *Dear Folks,* Harper, 1959; *Dear Man of Affairs,* Putnam, 1961; *Dear VIP,* Putnam, 1963; *Addled Ads and Typsy Typos,* Simon & Schuster, 1966; *Boners in the News,* Pocket Books, 1966; *Dear Candidate,* 1968; *Off-Color Good Humor Racy Tales for Adults and Adultresses,* 1969. Contributor to *Encyclopaedia Britannica.* Author of column, "Celebrity Letters," in *Family Weekly,* 1971-73. Contributor to *Reader's Digest, Coronet, Good Housekeeping, Collier's, Mademoiselle* and other popular magazines.

WORK IN PROGRESS: Laff with Lowell: Anecdotes about the Great, the Near Great, and Those Who Think It's Great to Laugh with Here and There a Thought or Gaffe; an autobiography, to be entitled *Me, Myself, and I: The Whole of Lowell.*

SIDELIGHTS: Juliet Lowell told *CA:* "I have a passion to make people laugh. Doing what I like to do has provided me with a living and kept me content sharing laughter with others. I have been able to find a bright spot in most situations. Naturally there have been problems and sorrows. The only way to entirely circumvent them is to be stillborn. I prefer to have been born alive and lively searching for fun in life." Three of Lowell's books have been produced as films.

AVOCATIONAL INTERESTS: Tennis, skiing, riding, dancing, swimming, climbing, ping pong.

* * *

LOWERY, Bruce Arlie 1931-

PERSONAL: Born February 17, 1931, in Reno, Nev.; son of Arlie Ross and Christine (Ver Steeg) Lowery. *Education:* Attended University of Wyoming; University of Denver, B.A., 1952; Universite de Clermont, diplome, 1953; Ecole de

Journalisme, diplome (with honorable mention), 1955; Sorbonne, Universite de Paris, licence-es-lettres (with honorable mention), 1955, doctorat (with very honorable mention), 1962. *Address:* 164 bis rue de l'Université, Paris 7, France; and 13021 West Ohio, Lakewood, Colo.

CAREER: Université de Paris, Paris, France, lecturer, 1958-59; Lycée Henry IV, Paris, assistant, 1959-62; Sorbonne, Universite de Paris, Ecole d'Interprètes, Paris, professor, 1962—. *Awards, honors:* Prix de l'Universalite de la Langue Francaise, 1961; Bourse de la Foundation del Duca, 1963; Prix Emile-Faguet de l'Academie Francaise, 1965.

WRITINGS: La Cicatrice (novel), Buchet-Chastel, 1960, translation by the author published as *Scarred,* Vanguard, 1961; *Porcepic,* Buchet-Chastel, 1963; *Marcel Proust et Henry James: Une Confrontation,* Plon, 1964; (translator) Pierre LeBailly, *Watch of Evil,* Exposition Press, 1965; (translator) Roger Peyrefitte, *The Jews,* Bobbs-Merrill, 1966; *Le Loup-garou,* Denoel, 1969, translation by the author published as *Werewolf,* Vanguard, 1969; *Revanches* (short stories), Denoel, 1970; *Le Philatosexual* (four novellas), Flammarion, 1977; *Qui Cherche le mal* (novel), Flammarion, 1978. Has made English translations of 160 full-length French and Italian films.

WORK IN PROGRESS: A book of short stories; a novel.

SIDELIGHTS: A Fulbright scholarship enabled Bruce Lowery to spend the first of his many years in France. His love for things European stems from the art and culture he discovered during his childhood in the Kansas City, Mo., museum.

Lowery often writes first in French and later translates into his native English. He states: "I feel I obtain, by writing in French, a greater detachment, rigor, and simplicity than I do when writing directly in English." He adds, "no one is a prophet in his own country."

AVOCATIONAL INTERESTS: Languages, painting, sculpture, architecture, the cinema.

BIOGRAPHICAL/CRITICAL SOURCES: Newsweek, June 12, 1961; *Realities* (English edition), June, 1961, August, 1965; *Detroit News,* February 13, 1972.

* * *

LOWRY, Bates 1923-

PERSONAL: Born 1923, in Cincinnati, Ohio; married Isabel Barrett, 1946; children: Anne, Patricia. *Education:* University of Chicago, Ph.B., M.A., Ph.D. *Office:* Department of Art, University of Massachusetts, Boston, Mass. 02125.

CAREER: University of Calfornia, Riverside, assistant professor, 1954-57; New York University, New York City, assistant professor, 1957-59; Pomona College, Claremont, Calif., professor of art and chairman of department, 1959-63; Brown University, Providence, R.I., professor of art, 1963-68; Museum of Modern Art, New York City, director, 1968-69; University of Massachusetts—Boston, professor of art and chairman of department, 1971—. Member of Institute for Advanced Study, 1971. *Military service:* U.S. Army. *Member:* College Art Association (editor, monograph series; member, board of directors), Society of Architectural Historians (member, board of directors), Renaissance Conference of Southern California (president, 1960-61).

WRITINGS: The Visual Experience: An Introduction to Art, Abrams, 1961, 2nd edition, Prentice-Hall, 1975; *Renaissance Architecture,* Braziller, 1962; *The Architecture of Washington, D.C.,* Dunlap Society, Volume I, 1977, Volume II, 1979. Contributor to art journals. Editor, *Art Bulletin,* 1965-68.

LUARD, (David) Evan (Trant) 1926-

PERSONAL: Born 1926, in Addington, Kent, England; son of Trant Bramston and Helen (Evans) Luard. *Education:* King's College, Cambridge, B.A., 1949. *Home and office:* St. Antony's College, Oxford University, Oxford England.

CAREER: Member of British Foreign Service staff, 1950-56; Oxford University, St. Antony's College, Oxford, England, research fellow, 1957—. City councillor, Oxford City Council, 1958-61.

WRITINGS: Economic Development of Communist China, Oxford University Press, 1959; *Britain and China,* Chatto & Windus, 1962; *Peace and Opinion,* Oxford University Press, 1962; *Nationality and Wealth,* Oxford University Press, 1964; (editor) *The Cold War,* Thames & Hudson, 1964; (editor) *First Steps to Disarmament,* Thames & Hudson, 1965; *Evolution of International Organizations,* Praeger, 1966; *International Protection of Human Rights,* Thames & Hudson, 1967; *Conflict and Peace in the International System,* Little, Brown, 1968; (editor) *International Regulation of Frontier Disputes,* Thames & Hudson, 1969; (editor) *International Regulation of Civil Wars,* Thames & Hudson, 1970; *The United Nations in a New Era,* Fabian Society, 1972; *The Control of the Seabed,* Heinemann, 1974; *Types of International Society,* Free Press, 1976; *International Agencies,* Macmillan, 1977; *The United Nations,* Macmillan, 1978.

* * *

LUDWIG, Jack 1922-

PERSONAL: Born August 30, 1922, in Winnipeg, Manitoba, Canada; son of Misha and Fanny (Dolgin) Ludwig; married Leya Lauer, 1946; children: Susan, Brina. *Education:* University of Manitoba, B.A., 1944; University of California, Los Angeles, Ph.D., 1953. *Address:* P.O. Box "A," Setauket, N.Y. 11733. *Office:* 268 Humanities Bldg., State University of New York, Stony Brook, N.Y. 11733.

CAREER: Williams College, Williamstown, Mass., instructor, 1949-53; Bard College, Annandale, N.Y., 1953-58, began as assistant professor, became associate professor and chairman of Division of Language and Literature; State University of New York at Stony Brook, professor of English, 1961—. Chairman of humanities group, Harvard International Seminar, Cambridge, Mass., summers, 1963-66. Writer-in-residence, University of Toronto, 1968-69; resident playwright, Stratford (Ontario) Shakespeare Festival, 1970; senior writer-in-residence, Banff Centre, 1974; visiting professor, University of California, Los Angeles, 1976. Consultant, Commission on College Physics film project, 1965-66, Canadian Broadcasting Corp. prison film, 1970, and Stratford Shakespeare Festival National Arts Centre theater project, 1970. *Awards, honors:* Longview Foundation fiction award, 1960; Atlantic First Award from *Atlantic Monthly,* 1960; Martha Foley Best American Short Story Award, 1961; O. Henry Short Story Award, 1961 and 1965; Canada Council Senior Arts Fellowship Awards in Fiction, 1962, 1967-68, and 1975-76.

WRITINGS: Recent American Novelists, University of Minnesota Press, 1962; *Confusions,* New York Graphic Society, 1963; *Above Ground,* Little, Brown, 1968; (contributor) James Baker and Thomas Staley, editors, *James Joyce's "Dubliners,"* Wadsworth, 1969; (editor with Andy Wainwright) *Soundings: New Canadian Poets,* Anansi, 1970; (contributor) William Kilbourn, editor, *Canada: A Guide to the Peaceable Kingdom,* St. Martin's, 1971; *Hockey Night in Moscow,* McClelland & Stewart, 1972, published as *The Great Hockey Thaw; or, the Russians Are Here!,* Doubleday, 1974; *A Woman of Her Age,* McClelland & Stewart, 1973; *Homage to Zolotova,* Banff Press, 1974; (contributor) George Woodcock, editor, *The Canadian Novel in the Twentieth Century,* McClelland & Stewart, 1975; (contributor) Terry Angus, editor, *The Prairie Experience,* Macmillan, 1975; *Games of Fear and Winning: Sports with an Inside View,* Doubleday, 1976; *The Great American Spectaculars: The Kentucky Derby, Mardi Gras, and Other Days of Celebration,* Doubleday, 1976; (contributor) Kilbourn, editor, *The Toronto Book,* Macmillan, 1976; *Five Ring Circus: The Montreal Olympics,* Doubleday, 1976. Also editor, with Richard Poirier, of *Stories: British and American.*

Adapter of several plays, including "The Alchemist," by Ben Jonson, for Stratford Shakespeare Festival, "Hedda Gabler," by Henrik Ibsen, for CBC-TV, and "Ubu Roi," by Alfred Jarry, for Stratford Workshop.

Work represented in anthologies, including *Best American Short Stories,* edited by Martha Foley and David Burnett, *Prize Stories: The O. Henry Awards,* edited by Richard Poirier, *Contemporary American Short Stories,* edited by Douglas and Sylvia Angus, *A Book of Canadian Stories,* edited by Desmond Pacey, *The Urban Experience,* edited by John Stevens, *The Canadian Century,* edited by A.J.M. Smith, and *Canadian Short Stories,* edited by Robert Weaver.

Contributor of several hundred short stories, articles, and reviews to magazines and newspapers in the United States, Canada, and Europe. Co-editor, *Noble Savage.*

WORK IN PROGRESS: Two novels, *The Rites of Leo Spring* and *The November May Day of Doba Montreal,* and a novella, *Meesh;* a play, "General Agamemnon"; a contemporary version of "Ubu Roi" entitled "Ubu Rex"; short stories for inclusion in a collection, tentatively entitled *Requiem for Bibul and Other Stories* in Canada and *Thoreau in California and Other Stories* in the United States and other countries; criticism on the novel of the 1960s and 1970s, on Joyce, Yeats, and the poetry of John Berryman, and on technology, values, and society.

SIDELIGHTS: Though better known for his short stories, Jack Ludwig has written several novels, one of which, *Above Ground,* is semi-autobiographical. In this particular story, according to a *Partisan Review* critic, "Jack Ludwig assumes the persona of an engaging narrator, Joshua, who again offers no more plot than the random events of his life sorted out in striking scenes.... This puts a great strain on Ludwig's performance and turns his novel into a concert program. We want to be held, not merely entertained, by his range and depth of feeling. Much of the time he can sustain it ... but when the novel depends on the purely random and sequential, even the vitality of Joshua cannot endow it with more than a surface excitement.... [Yet] if at times the material is weak, the performance in *Above Ground* is grand; the design enriches a mode which might be labeled American existential. The novel is immensely entertaining, never frivolous."

Other reviewers, however, do not find Ludwig's novel quite as enjoyable. Calling the book "exceedingly hard to get through and not yielding much pleasure," a *Kenyon Review* critic notes in his analysis of a particular section of the novel that "Ludwig has a good ear, the passage develops a rhythm, and some of the sensations are fine ... but the compound words [tarpaperpatched, springsprung, chalkygreen] signal a stylistic indulgence that permeates the whole book.... Too often the 'poetry' of his insistent voice overwhelms the possibilities for any modulation, variations of intensity.... Then there is the further problem of what, if anything, a series of lyric moments adds up to without the ordering principle of a story; for there is no story here, simply one damn' thing after another until suddenly it all ends."

"For a novel about survival, *Above Ground* has a curiously lifeless quality," writes a *New York Times Book Review* critic. "It is a book that yearns after a sense of language and, pursuing it, ends tangled in clumsy word constructions, strained metaphors, and images weighted with echoes from other, better writers.... [Furthermore,] it is hard to tell the characters apart.... The girls are all equally bosomy and equally addicted to literary allusions. If Joshua is finally their victim, he is drawn so abstractly that it is hard to care."

A reviewer in *Fiddlehead* writes: "Jack Ludwig's *Above Ground* is not a bad novel. There is a picaresque comic element about it which is often amusing. There are certain scenes which approach pathos." But he strongly criticizes Ludwig for limiting himself to the image of female breasts as a means of expressing his central theme—that of woman-as-wet-nurse who tends to man's needs with love in order to keep him alive (i.e., "above ground"). As a result of this preoccupation, "the characterization of the women had all the individuality of a Playboy fold-out.... And inasmuch as the novel appears to be very autobiographical, the result is embarrassing."

Finally, a *Canadian Forum* reviewer writes: "*Above Ground* bothers me ... [Ludwig] has a sensitivity to words, and a sophistication much too rare amidst the honest plodders of the standard Canadian novel. The qualities I admire are all there in *Above Ground,* yet the total impact is less than that of his best stories.... The feeling I'm finally left with is one of exposure to brilliant triviality.... In [the novel], Ludwig offers bits of learning, hints of mythic parallels, and a good deal of fugitive insight. But his central concern seems to me basically sentimental, in the sense that the world he offers us is not the one that exists, but the one that he wants to exist.... He has given us a novel that does not suggest as much about humanity and its situation as it does about the situation of the novelist himself."

AVOCATIONAL INTERESTS: Singing.

BIOGRAPHICAL/CRITICAL SOURCES: *Fiddlehead,* summer, 1968; *Virginia Quarterly Review,* summer, 1968; *New Yorker,* July 6, 1968; *National Observer,* July 15, 1968; *New York Times Book Review,* July 28, 1968; *Partisan Review,* fall, 1968; *Kenyon Review,* Number 5, 1968; *Canadian Forum,* January, 1969; Donald Cameron, *Conversations with Canadian Novelists,* two parts, Macmillan, 1973; Graeme Gibson, *Eleven Canadian Novelists,* Anansi, 1973.

* * *

LUGER, Harriett Mandelay 1914-

PERSONAL: Born July 21, 1914, in Vancouver, British Columbia, Canada; daughter of Leo Leon (a custom shirtmaker) and Mollie (Benjamin) Mandelay (both U.S. citizens); married Charles Luger (an instructor in botany), December 5, 1942; children: Carolyn (Mrs. Paul Slayback), Allen, Eleanor. *Education:* University of California, Los Angeles, B.A., 1936. *Home:* 3427 West 225th St., Torrance, Calif. 90505.

CAREER: Free-lance writer. *Member:* Authors Guild, Authors League of America, California Writers Guild.

WRITINGS—All young-adult books: *Bird of the Farallons,* Young, Scott, 1971; *The Last Stronghold,* Young, Scott, 1972; *Chasing Trouble,* Viking, 1976; *The Elephant Tree,* Viking, 1978; *Lauren,* Viking, 1979.

WORK IN PROGRESS: A young-adult novel; short stories, television scripts.

SIDELIGHTS: Harriett Luger began writing when her son, Allen, found an oil-soaked bird on the beach and brought it home. The experience inspired her first book, *Bird of the Farallons.* She told *CA:* "Practically right from the beginning I loved stories and wanted to make my own. As I read, I wrote, first for entertainment, then to live other lives than mine. Gradually I came to realize the possibilities of fiction. One might entertain, instruct, propagandize, illuminate the internal landscape, stimulate the intellect, or inspire—within the framework of a story. One could do one or several of these things, the one constant requirement being that the story must have a life of its own that draws the reader to participate in it from its beginning until it is finished. This means that it must be shaped and modelled and polished so that it has a shape which contains within it a smooth, logical progression from beginning to middle to end with characters who live and a problem that the reader wants solved.

"The action in all my books takes place in California. It is possible that sometime in the future I shall lay the scene elsewhere, but I doubt it. California contains almost the whole world within its boundaries. With the exception of the tropics, all the climates occur here, from glacial arctic cold to searing desert heat. It has old mountains and new, great plains in its inland valleys, a long seashore, hills. The social environment varies as much as the natural. Great cities, villages, wilderness each exerts its own pressures which pull and buffet the individual. The names, Los Angeles and San Francisco, have come to have special meanings which apply only to themselves—but they are also any metropolis where people crowd each other. Every spot on earth is unique and happens only once, but in my opinion the vigor and squalor of California cities and the various conditions of its varied landscape can be understood by people living almost anywhere on this planet."

* * *

LUKACS, John (Adalbert) 1923-

PERSONAL: Born 1923, in Budapest, Hungary; son of Paul (a doctor) and Magdalena (Gluck) Lukacs; married Helen Elizabeth Schofield, 1953 (died, 1970); married Stephanie Harvey, 1976; children: (first marriage) Paul, Annemarie. *Education:* Cambridge University, certificate of proficiency, 1939; Budapest University, Ph.D., 1946. *Home:* Williams' Corner, R.D. 2, Phoenixville, Pa. *Office:* Department of History, Chestnut Hill College, Philadelphia, Pa.

CAREER: Chestnut Hill College, Philadelphia, Pa., associate professor of history, 1947—; LaSalle College, Philadelphia, lecturer in history, 1949—. Visiting professor, Columbia University, 1954-55, University of Pennsylvania, 1964, School of Advanced International Studies, 1970-71, and Fletcher School of Law and Diplomacy, 1971, 1972; Fulbright professor, University of Toulouse, 1964-65. *Member:* American Catholic Historical Association (president, 1977).

WRITINGS—All published by Doubleday, except as indicated: *The Great Powers and Eastern Europe,* American Book Co., 1953; (editor and translator) Alexis de Tocqueville, *European Revolution* [and] *Correspondence with Gobineau,* 1959; *A History of the Cold War,* 1961, 3rd edition published as *A New History of the Cold War,* 1966; *Decline and Rise of Europe,* 1965; *Historical Consciousness,* Harper, 1968; *The Passing of the Modern Age,* Harper, 1970; *The Last European War, 1939-41,* 1976; *1945: Year Zero,* 1978. Also author of *A History of Chestnut Hill College, 1924-74,* 1975. Contributor to encyclopedias and periodicals.

BIOGRAPHICAL/CRITICAL SOURCES: National Review, November 5, 1968, October 20, 1970; *Book World,* November 10, 1968, November 15, 1970; *New Republic,* November 16, 1968, October 20, 1970, December 12, 1976; *Commonweal,* January 10, 1969; *Saturday Review,* March 1, 1969; *Best Sellers,* December 1, 1970; *Christian Science Monitor,* March 1, 1976; *New York Times Book Review,* March 21, 1976, April 23, 1978.

* * *

LUNDWALL, Sam J(errie) 1941-

PERSONAL: Born February 24, 1941, in Stockholm, Sweden; son of Thore (a master mechanic) and Sissi (Kuehn) Lundwall; married Ingrid Olofsdotter, June 16, 1972; children: Karin Beatrice Christina. *Education:* University of Stockholm, E.E., 1967. *Home:* Storskogsvaegen 19, S-161 39 Bromma, Sweden. *Agent:* Spectrum Literary Agency, 60 East 42nd St., New York, N.Y. 10017; and Goesta Dahl & Son AB, Aladdinsvaegen 14, S-161 38 Bromma, Sweden. *Office:* Delta Foerlags AB, Bromma, Sweden.

CAREER: SSTA (Stockholm Technical Night-School), Stockholm, Sweden, electronics engineer, 1956-60; University of Stockholm, Stockholm, professional photographer, 1964-67; Christer Christian Photographic School, Fox Amphoux, France, professional photographer, 1967-68; Swedish Broadcasting Corp., Stockholm, television producer, 1968-69; Askild & Kaernekull Foerlag AB (publishers), Stockholm, editor for science fiction and the occult, 1970-73; Delta Foerlags AB (publishers), Bromma, Sweden, president, 1973—. Judge, John W. Campbell Award, World Science Fiction Convention. Has directed television films; made short animated film based on his song "Waltz with Karin"; has recorded his own songs for Philips and Knaeppupp recording companies; has appeared on television, radio, and film as singer and artist throughout the Scandinavian countries. *Military service:* Swedish Air Force, 1960-61; electronics engineer. *Member:* Science Fiction Writers of America, World Science Fiction Society (secretary; member of board, European society). *Awards, honors:* "Waltz with Karin" was named Sweden's best short film, by Swedish Film Institute, 1967; Alvar award as Scandinavia's leading science fiction author, from Futura (science fiction organization), 1971.

WRITINGS: Bibliografi oever Science Fiction och Fantasy (title means "Bibliography of Science Fiction and Fantasy"), Fiktiva, 1964; *Visor i Vaar Tid* (title means "Songs of Our Times"), Sonora, 1965; *Science Fiction: Fraan Begynnelsen till vaara dagar* (title means "Science Fiction: From the Beginning to Our Days"), Sveriges Radio Foerlag, 1969.

Alice's World, Ace Books, 1971; *No Time for Heroes,* Ace Books, 1971; *Science Fiction: What It's All About,* Ace Books, 1971; *Gernhard the Conqueror,* Daw Books, 1973; *Den Fantastiska Romanen,* four volumes (textbooks on fantastic stories and novels), Gummessons Grafiska, 1973-74; *King Kong Blues,* Daw Books, 1974; *Bibliografi oever Science Fiction och Fantasy: 1741-1971,* Lindqvist Foerlag, 1974; *Wat Is Science Fiction?,* Meulenhoff, 1974; *Bernhards magiska sommar* (title means "Bernhard's Magic Summer"), Lindqvist, 1975; *Alltid lady MacBeth* (title means "Always Lady MacBeth"), Delta, 1975; *Moerkrets furste* (title means "The Prince of Darkness"), Delta, 1975.

Mardroemmen (title means "The Nightmare"), Lindqvist, 1976; *Gaest i Frankensteins hus* (title means "Guest in the House of Frankenstein"), Delta, 1976; *Utopia-Dystopia,* Delta, 1977; *Science fiction pa svenska* (title means "Science Fiction in Swedish"), Delta, 1977; *Science Fiction: An Illustrated History,* Grosset, 1978; *Faengelsestaden* (title means "The Prison City"), Norstedt, 1978; *Flicka i foenster vid vaerldens kant* (title means "Girl in Window at the Edge of the World"), Norstedt, 1980.

Editor of numerous science fiction anthologies and of collected works of Jules Verne; translator into Swedish of more than fifty novels and of poems by Francois Villon and George Brassens; author, producer, and director of television script from *The Hunting Season,* by Frank Robinson, and of other television films; author and composer of more than two hundred songs. Contributor of cartoons to Swedish edition of *Help!* and of articles to Swedish edition of *Popular Photography.* Editor-in-chief of *Jules Verne—Magasinet,* 1972—; editor, *Science Fiction-Serien,* 1973—.

WORK IN PROGRESS: Bristningen (title means "The Bursting"), a semi-biographical novel set in Sweden and France; *Marinette,* a novel.

* * *

LYNCH, Hollis Ralph 1935-

PERSONAL: Born April 21, 1935; divorced; children: Shola Ayn, Nnenna Jean, Ashale Herman. *Education:* University of British Columbia, B.A. (with honors), 1960, M.A., 1961, Ph.D., 1964. *Office:* Department of History, Columbia University, New York, N.Y. 10027.

CAREER: High school teacher of British and European history and English literature in Tobago, 1954-57; University of Ife, Ife, Nigeria, lecturer in West African and New World Negro history, 1964-66; Roosevelt University, Chicago, Ill., 1966-68, began as assistant professor, became associate professor of West African and Afro-American history; American University, Washington, D.C., lecturer and adviser to nationwide group of students in Accra, Ghana, summer, 1968; State University of New York at Buffalo, associate professor and director of black studies, 1968-69; Columbia University, New York, N.Y., professor of history, 1969—, director of Institute for African Studies, 1971-74. Visiting lecturer, Harvard University, summers, 1971 and 1973, and Emory University, summer, 1974; W. E. B. DuBois Visiting Research Scholar, University of California, Los Angeles, winter, 1976. Lecturer on Afro-American, Pan-African, West African, and Caribbean topics at more than two dozen colleges and universities, 1966—. Tutor and counselor, Outward Bound program, Chicago, 1967. Member of U.S. Archives advisory council for New England, New York, New Jersey, Puerto Rico, and the Virgin Islands.

MEMBER: American Historical Association (member of Committee of Committees, 1971-73), Organization of American Historians, African Studies Association, Association for the Study of Afro-American Life and History (member of executive committee, 1974—), Caribbean Studies Association. *Awards, honors:* Commonwealth scholar, University of London, 1961-64; Urban Center fellow, Columbia University, 1970-71; Hoover national fellow, Stanford University, 1973-74; American Council of Learned Societies summer fellow, 1975; American Comparative Literature Association research fellow, 1978-79.

WRITINGS: (Contributor) J. F. Ade Ajayi and Ian Espie, editors, *A Thousand Years of West African History,* Thomas Nelson, 1965; (contributor) Jeffrey Butler, editor, *Boston University Papers of Africa,* Volume II, Boston University Press, 1966; *Edward Wilmot Blyden, 1832-1912: Pan-Negro Patriot,* Oxford University Press, 1967; (author of introduction) John Mensah Sarbah, *Fanti Customary Law,* Frank Cass, 1968; (author of introduction) Sarbah, *Fanti National Constitution,* Frank Cass, 1968; (contributor) August Meier and E. M. Rudwick, editors, *The Making of Black America,* Volume I, Atheneum, 1969; (author of introduction) Marcus Garvey, *Philosophy and Opinions,* Atheneum, 1969.

(Author of introduction) Gustav Spiller, editor, *Papers of Inter-racial Problems,* Arno, 1970; (editor) *Black Spokesman: Selected Published Writings of Edward Wilmot Blyden,* Humanities, 1971; (editor) *Selected Letters and Unpublished Manuscripts of Edward Wilmot Blyden,* Frank Cass, 1973; *The Black Urban Condition, 1865-1971: A Documentary History,* Crowell, 1973; (editor) *Black Africa,* Arno, 1973; (editor) *Selected Letters of Edward Wilmot Blyden,* KTO Press, 1978. Also author of monographs.

Editor of series on African and Afro-American biographies, Oxford University Press, 1969-73; adviser to "Contributions in Afro-American and African Studies" series, Greenwood Press, 1974. Contributor to *Compton's Encyclopedia.* Contributor of articles and reviews to history journals, including *Journal of the Historical Society of Nigeria, Journal of African History, Pacific Historical Review, Presence Africaine, Nigeria, New Africa, Freedomways,* and *New World Quest.* Editor of *Journal of African Biography.*

WORK IN PROGRESS: Afro-Americans and Africa: A History of Their Interaction; Alexander Crummell: A Biography.

* * *

LYON, James K(arl) 1934-

PERSONAL: Born February 17, 1934, in Rotterdam, Netherlands; son of Thomas Edgar and Hermana (Forsberg) Lyon; married Dorothy Ann Burton; children: James, John, Elizabeth, Sally, Christina, Rebecca, Matthew. *Education:* University of Utah, B.A., 1958, M.A., 1959; Harvard University, Ph.D., 1962. *Politics:* Democrat. *Religion:* Church of Jesus Christ of Latter-day Saints (Mormon). *Home:* 13673 Boquita, Del Mar, Calif. 92014. *Office:* Department of Literature, University of California, San Diego, La Jolla, Calif. 92093.

CAREER: Harvard University, Cambridge, Mass., instructor, 1962-63, assistant professor of Germanic languages and literatures, 1966-71; University of Florida, Gainesville, associate professor, 1971-73, professor of German, 1973-74; University of California, San Diego, La Jolla, professor of German, 1974—, chairman of department of literature, 1978—, associate dean of Graduate School, 1977-78. *Military service:* U.S. Army, Intelligence Corps, 1963-66; became captain. *Member:* International Brecht Society, Modern Language Association of America, American Association of Teachers of German.

WRITINGS: Konkordanz zur Lyrik Gottfried Benns, Georg Olms, 1971; (with Craig Inglis and Hans Otto Horch) *Index zur Lyrik Gottfried Benns,* Athenaeum, 1971; *Bertolt Brecht and Rudyard Kipling: A Marxist's Imperialist Mentor* (monograph), Mouton, 1975; *Bertolt Brecht's American Cicerone,* Bouvier, 1976; *Bertolt Brecht's American Years,* Princeton University Press, 1980. Contributor of articles on modern German literature to professional journals.

SIDELIGHTS: James K. Lyon told *CA* that "among the documents used in my biography of Brecht in America are those in Brecht's FBI file, which still have not been fully analyzed." Lyon is acting as consultant to a film company which is producing a documentary on Brecht's American years. *Avocational interests:* Fishing, sailing, hiking, river running.

M

MacCANN, Donnarae 1931-

PERSONAL: Born October 24, 1931, in Culver City, Calif.; daughter of John Olson (a mechanic) and Charlotte (Purkey) Thompson; married Richard Dyer MacCann (a college professor), October 12, 1957. *Education:* Attended Santa Monica City College, 1949-51; University of California, Los Angeles, B.A., 1954; University of California, Berkeley, M.L.S., 1955. *Politics:* Democrat. *Religion:* Christian Scientist. *Home:* 115 Camelot Ct., Blacksburg, Va. 24060. *Office:* Department of English, Virginia Polytechnic Institute and State University, Blacksburg, Va. 24061.

CAREER: Los Angeles Public Library, Baldwin Hills Branch, Baldwin Hills, Calif., children's librarian, 1955-57; University of California, Los Angeles, head librarian at university elementary school, 1957-65, lecturer in arts and humanities in Extension Division, 1959-64, lecturer in English, fall, 1963; University of Kansas, Lawrence, lecturer in English, 1968-70; currently visiting associate professor of English, Virginia Polytechnic Institute and State University, Blacksburg. Member of board of directors of Children's Hour Nursery School and Head Start Program, 1966-70; coordinator for Senator McGovern's presidential campaign in Johnson County, Iowa, 1972. *Member:* American Library Association. *Awards, honors:* Dutton-Macrae Award of American Library Association, 1963, for advanced study in the field of library work for children and young people.

WRITINGS: The Child, the Artist, and the Book, Library, University of California, Los Angeles, 1963; (contributor) Sheila Egoff, editor, *Only Connect: Readings on Children's Literature,* Oxford University Press, 1969; (editor with Gloria Woodard) *The Black American in Books for Children: Readings in Racism,* Scarecrow, 1972; (with Olga Richard) *The Child's First Books: A Critical Study of Pictures and Texts,* Wilson, 1973; (editor with Woodard) *Cultural Conformity in Books for Children,* Scarecrow, 1977. Also contributor to *Twentieth-Century Children's Writers,* edited by D. L. Kirkpatrick. Contributor to library journals and newspapers, including *Wilson Library Bulletin, California Librarian, Los Angeles Times,* and *Christian Science Monitor.* Guest editor, *Wilson Library Bulletin,* December, 1969.

WORK IN PROGRESS: With Gloria Woodard, editing a new edition of *The Black American in Books for Children.*

MACDONALD, John (Barfoot) 1918-

PERSONAL: Born February 23, 1918, in Toronto, Ontario, Canada; son of Arthur Albert (a lawyer) and Gladys (Barfoot) Macdonald; married Beatrice Kathleen Darroch, June 5, 1942; married Liba Bockova, July 10, 1962; children: (first marriage) Kaaren (Mrs. David Bell), Grant, Scott; (second marriage) Vivian, Linda (stepchildren). *Education:* University of Toronto, D.D.S. (with honors), 1942; University of Illinois, M.S., 1948; Columbia University, Ph.D., 1953. *Home:* 39 Glenellen Dr. W., Toronto, Ontario, Canada M8Y 2H5. *Office:* Addiction Research Foundation, 33 Russell St., Toronto, Ontario, Canada M5S 2S1.

CAREER: University of Toronto, Toronto, Ontario, lecturer, 1942-44, instructor, 1946-47, assistant professor, 1949-53, associate professor, 1953-56, professor of bacteriology, 1956, chairman of Division of Dental Research, 1953-56; Harvard University, School of Dental Medicine, Boston, Mass., professor of microbiology and director of Forsyth Dental Infirmary, 1956-62; University of British Columbia, Vancouver, president, 1962-67; University of Toronto, professor of higher education, 1968—; Council of Ontario Universities, Toronto, executive director, 1968-76; Addiction Research Foundation, Toronto, president, 1976—. Chairman of the board, Banff School for Advanced Management, 1966-67, and Donwood Institute, 1972; review officer, Unicameral Experiment, University of Toronto, 1977. Consultant to Science Council of Canada and Canada Council on Support of Research in Canadian Universities, 1967-69, National Institutes of Health, 1968, Canadian International Development Agency, 1971, and other government agencies. *Military service:* Canadian Army, 1944-46; became captain.

MEMBER: International Association for Dental Research (president, 1968), International College of Dentists (honorary fellow), Canadian Mental Health Association (member of national scientific planning council, 1969), American Association for the Advancement of Science, American Society for Microbiology, Royal Society of Canada (fellow); honorary officer of a number of other Canadian societies. *Awards, honors:* A.M., Harvard University, 1956; LL.D., University of Manitoba, 1962, Simon Fraser University, 1965, and Wilfred Laurier University, 1976; D.Sc., University of British Columbia, 1967, and University of Windsor, 1977; L.D.D., University of Western Ontario, 1977.

WRITINGS: The Motile Non-Sporulating Anaerobic Rods

of the Oral Cavity, Faculty of Dentistry, University of Toronto, 1953; *A Prospectus on Dental Education for the University of British Columbia,* University of British Columbia, 1956; *Excellence and Responsibility* (inaugural address as fourth president of University of British Columbia), University of British Columbia, 1962; *Higher Education in British Columbia and a Plan for the Future,* University of British Columbia, 1962; (with others) *The Role of the Federal Government in Support of Research in Canadian Universities* (in English and French), Queen's Printer, 1969; *The Governing Council System of the University of Toronto, 1972-1977: A Review of the Unicameral Experiment,* University of Toronto, 1977.

Contributor: Reidar F. Sognnaes, editor, *Chemistry and Prevention of Dental Caries,* C. C Thomas, 1962; *Higher Education in a Changing Canada,* University of Toronto Press, for Royal Society of Canada, 1966; J. E. Hodgetts and Robin S. Harris, editors, *Changing Patterns of Higher Education in Canada,* University of Toronto Press, 1966; Robert F. Nixon, editor, *The Guelph Papers,* Peter Marten Associates, 1970; *Towards 2000: The Future of Post-Secondary Education in Ontario,* McClelland & Stewart, 1971; E. F. Sheffield, editor, *Agencies for Higher Education,* Ontario Institute for Studies in Education, 1974.

* * *

MacDONALD, John D(ann) 1916-
(John Wade Farrell, Robert Henry, John Lane, Scott O'Hara, Peter Reed, Henry Rieser)

PERSONAL: Born July 24, 1916, in Sharon, Pa.; son of Eugene Andrew and Marguerite Grace (Dann) MacDonald; married Dorothy Mary Prentiss, July 3, 1937; children: Maynard John Prentiss. *Education:* Attended University of Pennsylvania, 1934-35; Syracuse University, B.S., 1938; Harvard University, M.B.A., 1939.

CAREER: Author. Trustee, Ringling School of Art and New College Foundation. *Military service:* U.S. Army, 1940-46; became lieutenant colonel. *Member:* Mystery Writers of America (president, 1962), Authors Guild, P.E.N. *Awards, honors:* Benjamin Franklin Award, 1955, for best American short story; Gran Prix de Litterature Policiere, 1964, for French edition of *A Key to the Suite;* Pioneer Medal, Syracuse University, 1971; Grand Master Award, Mystery Writers of America, 1972; Doctor of Humane Letters, Hobart and William Smith Colleges, 1978; Popular Culture Association National Award for Excellence, 1978; American Book Award, 1980, for *The Green Ripper.*

WRITINGS—Mystery fiction: *The Brass Cupcake,* Fawcett, 1950, reprinted, 1977; *Murder for the Bride,* Fawcett, 1951, reprinted, 1978; *Judge Me Not,* Fawcett, 1951, reprinted, 1976; *Weep for Me,* Fawcett, 1951; *The Damned,* Fawcett, 1952, reprinted, 1978; *The Neon Jungle,* Fawcett, 1953, reprinted, 1978; *Dead Low Tide,* Fawcett, 1953, reprinted, 1977; *Cancel All Our Vows,* Appleton, 1953, reprinted, Fawcett, 1977; *All These Condemned,* Fawcett, 1954, reprinted, 1978; *Area of Suspicion,* Dell, 1954, reprinted, Fawcett, 1978; *Contrary Pleasure,* Appleton, 1954, reprinted, Fawcett, 1977; *A Bullet for Cinderella,* Dell, 1955, reprinted, Fawcett, 1977, published as *On the Make,* Dell, 1960; *Cry Hard, Cry Fast,* Popular Library, 1955, reprinted, Fawcett, 1978; *You Live Once,* Popular Library, 1955, reprinted, Fawcett, 1978.

April Evil, Dell, 1956, reprinted, Fawcett, 1977; *Border Town Girl,* Popular Library, 1956, reprinted, Fawcett, 1977; *Murder in the Wind,* Dell, 1956, reprinted, Fawcett, 1977; *Death Trap,* Dell, 1957, reprinted, Fawcett, 1978; *The Price of Murder,* Dell, 1957, reprinted, Fawcett, 1978; *The Empty Trap,* Popular Library, 1957, reprinted, Fawcett, 1977; *A Man of Affairs,* Dell, 1957, reprinted, Fawcett, 1978; *The Deceivers,* Dell, 1958, reprinted, Fawcett, 1978; *The Soft Touch,* Dell, 1958, reprinted, Fawcett, 1978; *The Executioners,* Simon & Schuster, 1958, reprinted, Fawcett, 1976, published as *Cape Fear,* Fawcett, 1962; *Clemmie,* Fawcett, 1958, reprinted, 1978; *Deadly Welcome,* Dell, 1959, reprinted, Fawcett, 1977; *Please Write for Details,* Simon & Schuster, 1959, reprinted, Fawcett, 1976; *The Crossroads,* Simon & Schuster, 1959, reprinted, Fawcett, 1978; *The Beach Girls,* Fawcett, 1959, reprinted, 1977; (editor) *Mystery Writers of America Anthology,* Dell, 1959.

Slam the Big Door, Fawcett, 1960, reprinted, 1977; *The End of the Night,* Simon & Schuster, 1960, reprinted, Fawcett, 1977; *The Only Girl in the Game,* Fawcett, 1960, reprinted, 1978; *Where Is Janice Gantry?,* Fawcett, 1961, reprinted, 1978; *One Monday We Killed Them All,* Fawcett, 1961, reprinted, 1978; *A Key to the Suite,* Fawcett, 1962, reprinted, 1978; *A Flash of Green,* Simon & Schuster, 1962, reprinted, Fawcett, 1977; *On the Run,* Fawcett, 1963, reprinted, 1978; *I Could Go On Singing,* Fawcett, 1963; *The Drowner,* Fawcett, 1963; (contributor) Roger Elwood and Samuel Moskowitz, editors, *Great Spy Novels and Stories,* Pyramid Publications, 1965; *End of the Tiger and Other Stories,* Fawcett, 1966; *The Last One Left,* Doubleday, 1967; *S*E*V*E*N* (short story collection), Fawcett, 1971.

"Travis McGee" mystery series; all published by Fawcett, except as indicated: *The Deep Blue Good-By,* 1964; *Nightmare in Pink,* 1964; *A Purple Place for Dying,* 1964; *The Quick Red Fox,* 1964; *A Deadly Shade of Gold,* 1965; *Bright Orange for the Shroud,* 1965; *Darker than Amber,* 1966; *One Fearful Yellow Eye,* 1966; *Pale Gray for Guilt,* 1968; *The Girl in the Plain Brown Wrapper,* 1968; *Three for McGee* (contains *The Deep Blue Good-By, Nightmare in Pink, A Purple Place for Dying*), Doubleday, 1968 (published in England as *McGee,* R. Hale, 1975); *Dress Her in Indigo,* 1969; *The Long Lavender Look,* 1970; *A Tan and Sandy Silence,* 1972; *The Scarlet Ruse,* 1973; *The Turquoise Lament,* Lippincott, 1973; *The Dreadful Lemon Sky,* Lippincott, 1975; *The Empty Copper Sea,* Lippincott, 1978; *The Green Ripper,* Lippincott, 1979.

Science fiction: *Wine of the Dreamers,* Greenberg, 1951, reprinted, Fawcett, 1977, published as *Planet of the Dreamers,* Pocket Library, 1953; *Ballroom of the Skies,* Greenberg, 1952, reprinted, Fawcett, 1977; *The Girl, the Gold Watch, and Everything,* Fawcett, 1962, reprinted, 1978; *Other Times, Other Worlds* (short story collection), Fawcett, 1978.

Other fiction: *Condominium,* Lippincott, 1977.

Nonfiction: *The House Guests,* Doubleday, 1965; *No Deadly Drug,* Doubleday, 1968.

Contributor of over five hundred short stories, some under house pseudonyms, to *Cosmopolitan, Collier's,* and other magazines.

WORK IN PROGRESS: When You and I Were Young, McGee; a nonfiction book, *Nothing Can Go Wrong.*

SIDELIGHTS: John D. MacDonald's character Travis McGee, a self-described "shabby knight errant," is one of the most successful series characters in the mystery field today. He is also, as Roger H. Smith has observed, "one of the most credible, most human of the paperback series heroes."

McGee lives an easy-going life aboard his boat "The Busted Flush," which he won in a card game. When the need arises, he will help the victim of a crime recover his stolen property—for a percentage of the return. McGee's adventures invariably concern a beautiful woman, large amounts of cash, and plenty of excitement. But MacDonald, as Jonathan Yardley points out, "is really more interested in characters and social situations, and uses his whodunit plots as convenient devices within which to explore them. A broad undercurrent of indignation runs through his work, focused in particular on the rape of the environment, slimy high-finance, and corrupt government."

For a time, MacDonald was wary of creating a series character. "I didn't want to do a series or be tied to a series character," he once observed; "the pressures are much greater." Why did he create Travis McGee? "The author of original paperbacks," MacDonald says, "is now in a real squeeze between pornography rising up from the bottom and reprints of block-buster best sellers coming down from the top. But a series is self-generating; new books in a series send readers back to the older ones."

Critics have compared MacDonald's writings with the best in American fiction. Macdonald's work "is actually better," writes Bruce Cook, "than about 90 per cent of the 'serious' fiction written today." Anthony Burgess observes that MacDonald is a master "in writing acutely plotted detective stories that are also considerable novels of the American scene."

MacDonald has described his books as "of the folk dance category, the steps and patterns traditionally imperative, the retributions obligatory. Within these limits I have struggled for freshness, for what insights I can muster, for validity of characterization and motivation, for the accuracies of method and environment which enhance any illusion of reality."

Over seventy million copies of MacDonald's books have been sold in numerous printings and editions throughout the world. Movie rights for six of his novels have been sold and twenty-seven stories have been adapted for television.

AVOCATIONAL INTERESTS: Playing and watching sports, poker, photography.

BIOGRAPHICAL/CRITICAL SOURCES: Amazing Science Fiction, January, 1952; *Galaxy,* June, 1953; *Analog,* October, 1953, May, 1979; *New Yorker,* June 22, 1963, April 7, 1975, December 13, 1976, November 6, 1978; *Publishers Weekly,* September 21, 1964, March 27, 1972; *New York Times Book Review,* October 24, 1965, March 3, 1968, September 22, 1968, June 10, 1973, April 9, 1978; *Fantasy & Science Fiction,* November, 1965; *Observer,* November 14, 1965, January 11, 1976; *Time,* February 17, 1967, December 3, 1973; D. Madden, editor, *Tough Guy Writers of the Thirties,* Southern Illinois University Press, 1968; *Army Times,* February 28, 1968; *Times Literary Supplement,* September 26, 1968, February 10, 1978; *Book World,* September 29, 1968, August 31, 1969, January 16, 1972, September 10, 1978; *Holiday,* November, 1968; *Saturday Review,* November 30, 1968, October 31, 1970; L. Moffat and J. Moffat, editors, *The JDM Master Checklist,* privately printed, 1969; *Booklist,* February 1, 1969; *Tampa Tribune,* April 6, 1969; *Chicago Daily News,* September 6, 1969, September 7, 1969.

Best Sellers, February 15, 1971; *Newsweek,* March 22, 1971, March 10, 1975; *National Review,* April 20, 1971; Julian Symons, *Mortal Consequences: A History from the Detective Story to the Crime Novel,* Harper, 1972; *New York Times,* January 1, 1974, April 5, 1977; *Critic,* March, 1974, fall, 1977; *Contemporary Literary Criticism,* Volume III, Gale, 1975; *Progressive,* June, 1975; *New Republic,* July 26, 1975; *Esquire,* August, 1975; *Journal of Popular Culture,* summer, 1976; *The Author Speaks,* Bowker, 1977; Frank D. Campbell, *John D. MacDonald and the Colorful World of Travis McGee,* Borgo Press, 1977; *Village Voice,* April 11, 1977; *Virginia Quarterly Review,* summer, 1977; *Books & Bookmen,* January, 1978; *Maclean's,* November 20, 1978.

* * *

MACGREGOR, Frances Cooke

PERSONAL: Born in Portland, Ore.; daughter of Charles Francis and Margaret (Spencer) Cooke. *Education:* University of California, B.A., 1927; University of Missouri, M.A., 1947; additional study at Columbia University. *Home:* 120 East 90th St., New York, N.Y. 10028. *Office:* Institute of Reconstructive Plastic Surgery, Medical Center, New York University, 560 First Ave., New York, N.Y. 10016.

CAREER: New York University, College of Medicine, New York City, research associate, 1949-52, Millbank fellow in research, 1952-54; Cornell University-New York Hospital School of Nursing, New York City, visiting assistant professor, 1954-57, visiting associate professor, 1957-60, associate professor, 1960-63, professor of social science, 1963-68; New York University, Medical Center, New York City, research scientist, Institute of Reconstructive Plastic Surgery, 1968—, clinical associate professor of surgery, 1970—. *Member:* American Sociological Society (fellow), American Anthropological Association (fellow), Society for Applied Anthropology (fellow), Eastern Sociological Society.

WRITINGS: Twentieth Century Indians, Putnam, 1941; (with Eleanor Roosevelt) *This Is America,* Putnam, 1942; (with Margaret Mead) *Growth and Culture: A Study of Balinese Childhood,* Putnam, 1951; *Facial Deformities and Plastic Surgery,* C. C Thomas, 1953; *Social Science in Nursing: Applications for the Improvement of Patient Care,* Russell Sage, 1960; *Transformation and Identify: The Face and Plastic Surgery,* Quadrangle, 1974; *After Plastic Surgery: Adaptations and Adjustments,* J. Bergin Publishers, 1979. Contributor of chapters to many medical books; also contributor of numerous articles to scientific and medical journals.

* * *

MACHAN, Tibor R(ichard) 1939- (Raymond Polony)

PERSONAL: Surname is pronounced McCann; born March 18, 1939, in Budapest, Hungary; son of Tibor G. Machan (a broadcaster) and Ingeborg Doczy-Guendish (a fencing master in Austria); married Marilynn H. Walther, December 23, 1965 (divorced, 1972); married Marty L. Zupan, May 5, 1973; children: Kate. *Education:* Claremont Men's College, B.A., 1965; New York University, M.A., 1966; University of California, Santa Barbara, Ph.D., 1971. *Politics:* "Libertarian." *Religion:* "Not a believer." *Home:* 625 Litchfield Lane, Santa Barbara, Calif. 93109. *Office:* Reason Foundation, 1129 State St., No. 4, Santa Barbara, Calif. 93101; and 3313 Phelps Hall, University of California, Santa Barbara, Calif. 93106.

CAREER: California State College, Bakersfield, assistant professor of philosophy and religious studies, 1970-72; State University of New York College at Fredonia, associate professor of philosophy, 1972— (on leave of absence); currently director of educational programs, Reason Foundation, Santa Barbara, Calif., and visiting lecturer in economics, University of California, Santa Barbara. Has worked as a draftsman; has appeared on radio and television programs and lecture circuits. Nonresident fellow, Institute for Human Studies, 1973. *Military service:* U.S. Air Force, 1958-62. *Member:* American Philosophical Association, Philadelphia Society, American Association for the Philosophic Study of Society. *Awards, honors:* National Endowment for the Humanities fellow, Hoover Institution, Stanford University, 1975-76.

WRITINGS: (Editor and contributor) *The Libertarian Alternative: Essays in Social and Political Philosophy,* Nelson-Hall, 1974; *The Pseudo-Science of B. F. Skinner,* Arlington House, 1974; *Human Rights and Human Liberties,* Nelson-Hall, 1975; *Introduction to Philosophical Inquiries,* Allyn & Bacon, 1977.

Contributor: J. Estrada, editor, *The University under Siege,* Nash Publishing, 1972; D. James, editor, *Outside Looking In,* Harper, 1972; Knorr and others, editors, *Determinants and Controls of Scientific Change,* D. Reidel, 1975; R. Cunningham, editor, *Law and Liberty: Essays on F. A. Hayek,* Texas A&M University Press, 1979. Contributor to periodicals, including *Personalist, Philosophia, Journal of Value Inquiry, American Philosophical Quarterly, Philosophical Studies, Modern Age, Folia Humanistica, Barron's, National Review, Humanist, New York Times,* and *Lugano Review.* Formerly newspaper columnist, *Santa Ana Register.* Senior editor, *Reason;* editor-in-chief, *Reason Papers;* associate editor, *Literature of Liberty.*

WORK IN PROGRESS: Individuals and Their Rights, for Johns Hopkins University Press; editing *Deregulation,* for University of Illinois Press; contributing to *Philosophers of Human Rights,* edited by A. Rosenberg, for Greenwood Press, and *Reason and Freedom: Essays on the Thought of Ayn Rand,* edited by D. Rasmussen and D. Den Uyl, for University of Illinois Press.

SIDELIGHTS: Tibor R. Machan told *CA:* "My main professional concern has been political theory, sparked by my early concerns about politics, including my escape from Communist Hungary in 1953. I have been influenced by Ayn Rand's writings, as well as by the ideas of the ancient Greek philosophers (mostly Aristotle) and such modern philosophers as J. L. Austin, Stephen Toulmin, A. R. Louch, David L. Norton. . . . I travel a lot and make presentations at scholarly meetings; speak German and Hungarian; write day in and out; delight in my family (with daughter Kate Machan a recent addition); despair of trends in American politics—the rejection of the principles of individual rights and private property."

* * *

MacINNES, Helen 1907-

PERSONAL: Born October 7, 1907, in Glasgow, Scotland; came to United States in 1937, naturalized in 1951; daughter of Donald and Jessica (McDiarmid) McInnes; married Gilbert Highet (a scholar and critic), 1932 (died January 20, 1978); children: Keith. *Education:* Glasgow University, M.A., 1928; University College, London, Diploma in Librarianship, 1931. *Religion:* Presbyterian. *Residence:* East Hampton, N.Y.

CAREER: Acted with Oxford University Dramatic Society and with the Experimental Theatre, both Oxford, England; writer, 1941—.

WRITINGS: (Translator with husband, Gilbert Highet) Otto Kiefer, *Sexual Life in Ancient Rome,* Routledge & Kegan Paul, 1934, Dutton, 1935; *Above Suspicion* (also see below), Little, Brown, 1941, reprinted, Fawcett, 1978; *Assignment in Brittany* (also see below), Little, Brown, 1942, reprinted, Fawcett, 1978; *While Still We Live,* Little, Brown, 1944 (published in England as *The Unconquerable,* Harrap, 1944), reprinted, Fawcett, 1964; *Horizon* (also see below), Harrap, 1945, Little, Brown, 1946, reprinted, Fawcett, 1979; *Friends and Lovers,* Little, Brown, 1947, reprinted, Fawcett, 1978; *Rest and Be Thankful,* Little, Brown, 1949, reprinted, Fawcett, 1978.

Neither Five Nor Three, Harcourt, 1951, reprinted, Fawcett, 1978; *I and My True Love,* Harcourt, 1953, reprinted, Fawcett, 1978; *Pray for a Brave Heart,* Harcourt, 1955, reprinted, Fawcett, 1979; *North from Rome* (also see below), Harcourt, 1958, reprinted, Fawcett, 1979; *Decision at Delphi,* Harcourt, 1960, reprinted, Fawcett, 1979; *Assignment: Suspense* (contains *Above Suspicion, Horizon,* and *Assignment in Brittany*), Harcourt, 1961; *The Venetian Affair,* Harcourt, 1963, reprinted, Fawcett, 1978; *Home Is the Hunter* (two-act play), Harcourt, 1964; *The Double Image* (also see below; Book-of-the-Month Club alternate selection), Harcourt, 1966; *The Salzburg Connection,* Harcourt, 1968; *Message from Malaga,* Harcourt, 1971; *Triple Threat* (contains *Above Suspicion, North from Rome,* and *The Double Image*), Harcourt, 1973; *Snare of the Hunter,* Harcourt, 1974; *Agent in Place,* Harcourt, 1976; *Prelude to Terror,* Harcourt, 1978.

WORK IN PROGRESS: A new novel.

SIDELIGHTS: Helen MacInnes' novels of international intrigue have long been regarded as among the most entertaining in the genre. As a *National Review* critic explains: "In the long ago, before Ian Fleming's sex 'n' sadists and John Le Carre's weary professionals took over the espionage field, a young English woman carved herself out a following. . . . [Her] formula, a quarter of a century later, remains much the same, a couple of non-professionals inveigled into taking a hand from—hold your breath—patriotic motives with the good guys against the bad [and] the adventure taking place in some attractive foreign part." A *Christian Science Monitor* reviewer notes: "Novels that blot out our environment can hardly be measured by those that reveal it, but they have their place all the same. There is nothing quite like 'a good read' to take us out of all our waiting-rooms. In her mysteries, Helen MacInnes has hit on just the formula, carefully combining a European countryside, much suspense, a little romance, and any number of likable, sensible characters."

As MacInnes herself comments: "I'm continually interested in the question of how an ordinary guy of intelligence and guts resists oppression. . . . My basic characters have a certain decency and honesty. They still believe in standards of human conduct, and they rise to the occasion without fear. . . . [In my stories,] suspense is not achieved by hiding things from the reader [who] . . . always would know who did it. The question is, when is the event going to take place and how can you stop it? A reader may know everything, but still be scared stiff by the situation."

All of her books are painstakingly researched, for she wants them to be as accurate—and as credible—as possible. A typical MacInnes novel, for example, begins with a kernel of truth, usually drawn from a brief newspaper clipping which has caught the author's eye and imagination. Around this seemingly insignificant fact, MacInnes builds her story, embellishing it with information discovered in the course of her extensive reading (which she insists is "the best training that there is" for a would-be-writer) or from personal experience and observation (she has visited and become thoroughly familiar with nearly every place she has ever written about). To add even more authenticity to her novels, she makes sure that such things as street names and directions are correct, though she may occasionally invent a town or a street for the purposes of her plot. "Underlying everything," MacInnes explains, "is the fact that I'm interested in international politics [and] in analyzing news, [for I try] to read newspapers both on and between the lines, to deduct and add, to utilize memory."

Some reviewers find the inclusion of such detail to be somewhat overwhelming at times; many of these same reviewers also criticize MacInnes for what they perceive as shallow and cliche-ridden characterization. Though admitting that she is probably "second to none in her power to evoke and employ a setting," a *National Observer* critic feels that her heroes and heroines "are rather flimsy stuff, curiously untouched by the deep drama in which the author involves them." In addition, he reports, "there is the matter of length, sometimes a difficulty with MacInnes books. [*The Salzburg Connection,* for example,] could well have been about 100 pages shorter. Not that it seems padded—merely overanalytical, a bit too discursive: The lady tells us perhaps a bit *too* much." A *Spectator* reviewer agrees with this evaluation: "[MacInnes'] plots are invariably as twisty and opaque as her heroes are broad-shouldered and thoroughly transparent. . . . After 380 pages the enemy are routed and [the hero] drives into the sun. . . . I found the novel far too long, but Miss MacInnes's fans will not be disappointed."

Anatole Broyard of the *New York Times* believes that, unlike "the new suspense movies, in which nothing is explained; in which there are no transitions and the actors never change expressions," in a MacInnes book, "everything is slow—talk, talk, talk,—and the burden of [interpretation] is on you too." In addition, he notes, "it would not be unreasonable to say that [she] . . . ought to avoid portraying desperate men who will stop at nothing. But her women are not much better. . . . [The author's] forte—her intimate evocation of the glamorous cities of Europe—is so overlaid with her characters' cliches that we see them as if through a chill rain. . . . Though [MacInnes] obviously knows these places well, we can't enjoy them in the company she has given us."

Joseph McLellan of *Book World,* however, is convinced that there is much more to admire in a Helen MacInnes novel than there is to criticize: He writes: "One reads Helen MacInnes for a good story well-told, of course, but also for reasurance that some things remain unchanged. . . . She has been writing her kind of novel for nearly 40 years, and her writing has reflected the realities of a changing world, but the basic approach has remained refreshingly the same. She writes of decent people in bad situations. There are certain truths to be learned, certain things awry to be set right, and her sympathetic characters go about what must be done, a bit clumsily and not without pain—but goodness wins out, and (a growing rarity in this kind of writing) it is recognizable as goodness. . . . Beyond the plot lie the values without which a good plot is merely a meaningless spinning of wheels. . . . [Her novels are] full of the things that make life worthwhile—not a perfectly mixed martini or an invigorating tumble in the hay, but works of art, dreams, the feelings of home, family, specially cherished places, friendship and (the only crime unthinkable in most suspense fiction) love. . . . Partly because she is a woman and much more because she is determinedly a bit old-fashioned, Helen MacInnes insists that [the good guys *do* differ from the bad guys] and that the difference is important."

MacInnes' books have sold over seventeen million copies in their various American editions and have been translated into more than twenty-two languages. Several have been made into films, including *Above Suspicion,* 1943, *Assignment in Brittany,* 1943, and *The Venetian Affair,* 1967, all by Metro-Goldwyn-Mayer, Inc., and *The Salzburg Connection,* 1972, by Twentieth Century-Fox Film Corp.

AVOCATIONAL INTERESTS: The American West, travel, music.

BIOGRAPHICAL/CRITICAL SOURCES: Harvey Breit, *The Writer Observed,* World Publishing, 1956; *New York Herald Tribune Books,* October 30, 1960; Roy Newquist, *Counterpoint,* Rand McNally, 1964; *New York Times,* January 8, 1966, September 16, 1971, August 13, 1976; *Writer's Yearbook,* Writer's Digest, 1967; *Cosmopolitan,* January, 1967; *Best Sellers,* September 13, 1968; *Christian Science Monitor,* October 3, 1968; *National Observer,* November 11, 1968; *Harper's,* December, 1968; *National Review,* January 14, 1969; *Washington Post,* February 9, 1969; *Spectator,* February 21, 1969; *Punch,* March 5, 1969; *Book World,* September 21, 1978; *New York Times Book Review,* December 17, 1978; *Chicago Tribune Magazine,* May 4, 1980.

—*Sketch by Deborah A. Straub*

* * *

MacKENDRICK, Paul Lachlan 1914-

PERSONAL: Born 1914, in Taunton, Mass.; son of Ralph Fulton and Sarah (Harvey) MacKendrick; married Dorothy Lau, 1945; children: Andrew, Sarah. *Education:* Harvard University, A.B. (summa cum laude), 1934, A.M., 1937, Ph.D., 1938; Balliol College, Oxford, additional study, 1934-36. *Politics:* Democrat. *Religion:* Unitarian Universalist. *Home:* 208 Bordner Dr., Madison, Wis. *Office:* 914 Van Hise Hall, University of Wisconsin, Madison, Wis. 53706.

CAREER: Phillips Academy, Andover, Mass., instructor in Latin, 1938-41; Harvard University, Cambridge, Mass., instructor in English, 1946; University of Wisconsin—Madison, assistant professor, 1946-48, associate professor, 1948-52, professor of classics, 1952-75, Lily Ross Taylor Professor, 1975—. American Academy in Rome, Rome, Italy, professor-in-charge, summer session, 1956-59, member of board of directors, 1964-72; professor-in-charge, Intercollegiate Center for Classical studies, 1973-74. Visiting professor, University of Ibadan, Nigeria, 1965-66. Member of Institute for Advanced Study, 1965. Lecturer on radio and television; consultant on Greek archaeology to National Broadcasting Co., on Roman archaeology to Time-Life, Inc. *Military service:* U.S. Naval Reserve, 1941-45; became lieutenant senior grade. *Member:* American Philological Association (president, 1972) Archaeological Institute of America, Classical Association of Middle West and South (former member of executive committee), American Council of Learned Societies (member of board of directors, 1956-63), Phi Beta Kappa. *Awards, honors:* Received Fulbright and Guggenheim fellowships; overseas fellow, Churchill College, Cambridge University.

WRITINGS: (With Herbert M. Howe) *Classics in Translation,* two volumes, University of Wisconsin Press, 1952; (with V. M. Scramuzza) *The Ancient World,* Holt, 1958; *The Roman Mind at Work,* Van Nostrand, 1958; *The Mute Stones Speak,* St. Martin's, 1960; *The Greek Stones Speak,* St. Martin's, 1962; *The Athenian Aristocracy,* Harvard University Press, 1968; (with others) *Greece and Rome: Builders of Our World,* National Geographic Society, 1968; *The Iberian Stones Speak,* Funk, 1969; *Romans on the Rhine,*

Funk, 1970; *Roman France,* St. Martin's, 1972; *The Dacian Stones Speak,* University of North Carolina Press, 1975. Contributor of articles and reviews to professional journals.

WORK IN PROGRESS: The North African Stones Speak, for University of North Carolina Press.

* * *

MacLYSAGHT, Edward Anthony 1887-

PERSONAL: Surname is anglicized form of the Gaelic, MacGiollaiasachta; born at sea, 1887; son of Seadna and Kathrine (Clarke) MacGiollaiasachta; married Mary Frances Cunneen, 1936; children: William Xavier, Patrick, Brian. *Education:* Attended Corpus Christi College, Oxford, 1908; National University of Ireland, M.A. *Home:* Raheen, Tuamgraney, County Clare, Ireland.

CAREER: Many-sided career, largely in farming and forestry in County Clare and County Cork, Ireland, 1910-35, in journalism in South Africa, 1938-39, and with Irish Manuscripts Commission and National Library of Ireland, 1939-55, became Keeper of Manuscripts, chairman of Manuscripts Commission, 1955-73. Member of Irish Senate, 1922-25; former university governor, nurseryman, and publisher. *Member:* Royal Irish Academy (member of council, 1952-55), United Arts Club (Dublin). *Awards, honors:* Litt.D., LL.D., both from National University of Ireland.

WRITINGS: The Gael, Maunsel, 1919; *Irish Eclogues and Relationships,* Maunsel, 1922; *Cursai Thomais,* Hodges Figgis, 1927, reprinted, 1969, translation by E. O'Cleary published as *The Small Fields of Carrig,* Heath Cranton, 1929; *Toil De,* An Gum, 1933; *Short Study of a Transplanted Family,* Browne & Nolan, 1935; *Irish Life in the Seventeenth Century,* University Press, 1939, revised edition, 1950, reprinted, Irish Academic Press, 1979; (editor) *Calendar of Orrery Papers,* Irish Manuscripts Commission, 1941; *The Kenmare Manuscripts,* Irish Manuscripts Commission, 1942; *An Aifric Theas,* An Gum, 1947; *East Clare: 1916-21,* C. Champion, 1954; *Irish Families: Their Names, Arms, and Origins,* Hodges Figgis, 1957, 4th edition, 1978; *More Irish Families,* O'Gorman, 1960, 2nd edition, 1979; *The Irish Hearth Money Rolls,* Irish Manuscript Commission, 1961; *Supplement to Irish Families,* Helicon, 1964; *Surnames of Ireland,* University Press, 1969, 3rd edition, 1978; *Changing Times: Ireland since 1898,* Colin Smythe, 1978, Humanities, 1979; *Leathanaigh om' Dhiallann,* Clodhanna, 1979; *The Families of Ireland,* Irish Academic Press, 1980. Also editor of *The Wardenship of Galway,* 1944, and of *Seventeenth-Century Hearth Money Rolls,* 1967. Contributor to *Studies, Catholic Bulletin, Journal of the Society of Antiquaries,* and other journals. Editor, *An Sguab,* 1922-25.

* * *

MACQUARRIE, John 1919-

PERSONAL: Born June 27, 1919, in Renfrew, Scotland; son of John and Robina (McInnes) Macquarrie; married Jenny Fallow Welsh, 1949; children: John Michael, Catherine Elizabeth, Alan Denis. *Education:* University of Glasgow, M.A., B.D., Ph.D., D.Litt. *Office:* Christ Church, Oxford OT1 1DP, England.

CAREER: Clergyman in Episcopal Church; St. Ninian's Church, Brechin, Scotland, minister, 1948-53; Glasgow University, Glasgow, Scotland, lecturer, 1953-62; Union Theological Seminary, New York, N.Y., professor of systematic theology, 1962-70; Oxford University, Oxford, England, Lady Margaret Professor of Divinity, 1970—. *Military service:* British Army, Chaplains Department, three years; became captain; Territorial Army, thirteen years. *Member:* Association of University Teachers.

WRITINGS: An Existentialist Theology, Macmillan, 1955, reprinted, Greenwood Press, 1979; *The Scope of Demythologizing,* Harper, 1960; (translator with Edward Robinson) Martin Heidegger, *Being and Time,* Harper, 1962; *Twentieth Century Religious Thought,* Harper, 1963, revised edition, Allenson, 1971; *Studies in Christian Existentialism,* McGill University Press, 1965; *Principles of Christian Theology,* Scribner, 1966, 2nd edition, 1977; (editor) *Dictionary of Christian Ethics,* Westminster, 1967; *God-Talk,* Harper, 1967; *God and Secularity,* Westminster, 1967; *Martin Heidegger,* John Knox, 1968; *Mysteries and Truth,* two volumes, Marquette University Press, 1969; *Three Issues in Ethics,* Harper, 1970; *Paths in Spirituality,* Harper, 1972; *Existentialism,* Westminster, 1972; *The Faith of the People of God,* Scribner, 1972; *The Concept of Peace,* Harper, 1973; *Thinking about God,* Harper, 1975; *Christian Unity and Christian Diversity,* Westminster, 1975; *The Humility of God,* Westminster, 1978; *Christian Hope,* Seabury, 1978. Contributor to professional journals.

BIOGRAPHICAL/CRITICAL SOURCES: New York Times Book Review, March 5, 1967, November 26, 1967; *Times Literary Supplement,* March 23, 1967, October 23, 1970, October 20, 1972; *Encounter,* summer, 1967, spring, 1969; *Christian Century,* November 15, 1967, March 20, 1968; *Commonweal,* January 12, 1968; *Book World,* July 7, 1968.

* * *

MADDEN, Edward H. 1925-

PERSONAL: Born May 18, 1925, in Gary, Ind.; son of Harry A. and Amelia (Schepper) Madden; married Marian C. Canaday, September 15, 1946; children: Kerry Arthur, Dennis William. *Education:* Oberlin College, A.B., 1946, A.M., 1947; University of Iowa, Ph.D., 1950. *Home:* 120 Brantwood, Snyder, N.Y. 14226. *Office:* Department of Philosophy, State University of New York, Buffalo, N.Y.

CAREER: University of Connecticut, Storrs, member of philosophy department staff, 1950-59; San Jose State College, (now University), San Jose, Calif., member of philosophy department staff, 1959-64; State University of New York at Buffalo, professor of philosophy, 1964—. Visiting professor, Brown University, 1954-55, Wesleyan University, summers, 1958 and 1959, Amherst College, 1962-63, University of Toronto, spring, 1967, and American University of Beirut, 1969-70; senior visiting research fellow, Linacre College, Oxford, 1978. *Military service:* U.S. Navy, 1943-45. *Member:* American Philosophical Association, Philosophy of Science Association, Charles S. Peirce Society, American Council of Learned Societies, American Association of University Professors, Phi Kappa Phi. *Awards, honors:* Research grants from University of Connecticut, 1956, American Philosophical Society, 1961, and State University of New York Research Foundation, 1973 and 1974; Fulbright-Hays Award, 1969-70; fellow, National Endowment for the Humanities, 1980-81.

WRITINGS: (Editor) *The Philosophical Writings of Chauncey Wright: Representative Selections,* Liberal Arts Press, 1958; (editor) *The Structure of Scientific Thought,* Houghton, 1960; (with R. M. Blake and C. J. Ducasse) *Theories of Scientific Method: The Renaissance through the Nineteenth Century,* University of Washington Press, 1960; *Philosophical Problems of Psychology,* Odyssey, 1962; *Chauncey Wright and the Foundations of Pragmatism,* University of

Washington Press, 1963; *Chauncey Wright,* Washington Square Press, 1964; (contributor) E. Moore and R. Robin, editors, *Studies in the Philosophy of Charles Sanders Peirce,* University of Massachusetts Press, 1964; (contributor) *Current Philosophical Issues,* C. C Thomas, 1966; (with Peter H. Hare) *Evil and the Concept of God,* C. C Thomas, 1968; (editor with Marvin Farber and Rollo Handy) *Philosophical Perspectives on Punishment,* C. C Thomas, 1968; *Civil Disobedience and Moral Law in Nineteenth-Century American Philosophy,* University of Washington Press, 1968; (editor with Farber and Handy) *The Idea of God: Philosophical Perspectives,* C. C Thomas, 1969; (with R. Harre) *Casual Powers,* Basil Blackwell, 1975; (with Hare) *Causing, Perceiving, and Believing,* D. Reidel, 1975. General editor, "Source Book Series in the History of Science," American Philosophical Association and Harvard University Press, 1960—; member of board of advisors, *The Works of C. S. Peirce;* member of editorial board, *The Works of William James,* American Council of Learned Societies and Harvard University Press. Member of editorial board, *Philosophy of Science,* 1960-76; consulting editor, *Journal of the History of Philosophy* and *Transactions of the C. S. Peirce Society.*

BIOGRAPHICAL/CRITICAL SOURCES: Criticism, winter, 1969; *Encounter,* winter, 1969.

* * *

MADISON, Charles A(llan) 1895-

PERSONAL: Born April 16, 1895, in Kiev, Russia; son of David (a tailor) and Bessie (Burakovsky) Madison; married Edith Hellman (an artist), July 1, 1924 (died August 5, 1970); children: Jeppy Yarensky. *Education:* University of Michigan, B.A., 1921; Harvard University, M.A., 1922. *Home:* 231 East 76th St., New York, N.Y. 10021; and 78 Mountain Rd., West Redding, Conn. 06896.

CAREER: Machinist in automobile factories, Detroit, Mich., 1909-16; American Book Co., New York City, editor, 1922-24; Holt, Rinehart & Winston, Inc., New York City, managing editor, 1924-62. Writer.

WRITINGS: Critics and Crusaders, Holt, 1947, 2nd edition, Ungar, 1959; *American Labor Leaders,* Harper, 1950, 2nd edition, Ungar, 1962; (contributor) *American Radicals,* Monthly Review Press, 1957; *Leaders and Liberals in 20th Century America,* Ungar, 1961; *Book Publishing in America,* McGraw, 1966; *The Owl among the Colophons: Henry Holt as Publisher and Editor,* Holt, 1966; *Yiddish Literature: Its Scope and Major Writers,* Ungar, 1968; *Eminent American Jews,* Ungar, 1970; *Irving to Irving: Author-Publisher Relations,* Bowker, 1974; *Jewish Publishing in America: The Impact of Jewish Writing on American Culture,* Sanhedrin Press, 1976. Contributor of literary and historical essays and book reviews to *Yale Review, Nation, Chicago Jewish Forum, Poet Lore,* and other journals.

AVOCATIONAL INTERESTS: Walking, gardening.

BIOGRAPHICAL/CRITICAL SOURCES: Books Abroad, winter, 1969; *Detroit Jewish News,* March 29, 1980.

* * *

MAGALANER, Marvin 1920-

PERSONAL: Born November 6, 1920, in New York, N.Y.; son of Benjamin and Sophie (Gribin) Magalaner; married Brenda Thea Plotkin, 1958; children: Seth, Jillian, Darcy. *Education:* City College (now City College of the City University of New York), A.B., 1942; Columbia University, A.M., 1947, Ph.D., 1951. *Home:* 505 LaGuardia Pl., New York, N.Y. 10012. *Office:* Department of English, John Jay College of Criminal Justice of the City University of New York, New York, N.Y. 10019.

CAREER: City University of New York, New York, N.Y., City College, 1946-75, began as assistant professor, became professor of English, Graduate Center, professor, 1962—, John Jay College of Criminal Justice, professor of English, 1975—. Lecturer, Columbia University, 1948 and 1954; Fulbright lecturer in Germany, 1965-66; visiting professor, University of Paris, 1974, and Institute of Modern Letters, University of Tulsa, 1978. *Military service:* U.S. Army Air Forces, 1942-46. *Member:* Modern Language Association of America, Phi Beta Kappa. *Awards, honors:* Ford Foundation and New York State Education Department grant, 1963-64.

WRITINGS: (With R. M. Kain) *Joyce: The Man, the Work, the Reputation,* New York University Press, 1956; (editor) *A James Joyce Miscellany,* first series, Gotham Book Mart, 1957, second series, Southern Illinois University Press, 1959, third series, Southern Illinois University Press, 1962; (with F. R. Karl) *A Reader's Guide to Great Twentieth Century English Novels,* Farrar, Straus, 1959; *Time of Apprenticeship: The Fiction of Young James Joyce,* Abelard, 1960; (editor with E. L. Volpe) *Twelve Short Stories,* Macmillan, first series, 1961, second series, 1969; (editor) *Critical Reviews of "A Portrait of the Artist as a Young Man,"* Selected Academic Readings, 1965; (editor with Volpe) *An Introduction to Literature: Drama,* Random House, 1967; (editor with Volpe) *An Introduction to Literature: Poetry,* Random House, 1967; *The Fiction of Katherine Mansfield,* Southern Illinois University Press, 1971. Contributor to literary journals.

* * *

MAGGIO, Joe 1938-

PERSONAL: Born March 19, 1938, in Atlantic City, N.J.; son of Peter (a businessman) and Marie (Rizzo) Maggio; married Barbara Levy, December 31, 1961; children: Dean, Bahama. *Address:* Dinner Key Marina, Coconut Grove, Fla. 33133.

CAREER: Central Intelligence Agency (CIA), agent in Cuba, Laos, and Vietnam, 1965-66; master of *Caribee,* a ninety-eight foot schooner, 1966-67; *Mainland Journal,* Pleasantville, N.J., columnist, 1968-69; master of *Polynesia,* a one hundred twenty-one foot schooner, 1969; *Miami Beach Sun,* Miami Beach, Fla., staff writer, 1970-71; free-lance writer, 1971—; master of schooner *William H. Atbury,* Abaco, Bahamas, 1976—. *Military service:* U.S. Marine Corps, 1959-61. U.S. Army, 1961-66; became sergeant. *Member:* Author's Guild, Authors League of America.

WRITINGS: Company Man, Putnam, 1972; *Scam,* Viking, 1980; *Days of Glory and Grieving,* Viking, 1981. Author of *Understanding American Fiction through History;* also author of plays "Circle Restep" and "Reflections upon an Uncle." Correspondent in Vietnam for *Mainland Journal* and free-lance stringer for *Tropic Magazine,* 1968, and for United Press International, Associated Press, and Reuters, 1968-69. Contributor to periodicals, including *Life, Newsweek, Boating,* and *Saga.*

WORK IN PROGRESS: Survive a Recent Sorrow, a novel.

SIDELIGHTS: Joe Maggio told *CA:* "I'm a writer. I have had no choice in that decision. It's simple: I write. Motivation came in the form of war. Vietnam. Early Vietnam before the escalation while I was under contract to the government running gunboats on the Mekong Delta. Those were the years that pushed through my first novel, a cleansing sort of work. . . . My work for the government was dirty and left its mark.

"I have been at sea a good part of my life. Not sea in the sense of merchant vessels hauling cargo . . . but rather in an anachronistic way in sailing many of the last old windjammers left afloat today. I crossed the Atlantic and Pacific under sail; have done the same in the Irish and North Seas, Bay of Biscay, Bahamas, West Indies, Virgin Islands. I've done charter and delivery work on many of the oldest schooners left today."

The schooner *William H. Atbury* which Maggio commands, represented the Bahamas in the Tall Ships race and Operation Sail in 1976. He plans to make a Cape Horn passage under sail and write a book about the experience.

* * *

MAHOLICK, Leonard T(homas) 1921-

PERSONAL: Born April 18, 1921, in Coaldale, Pa.; son of Peter and Mary (Gaydos) Maholick; married Ann Stanback, October 1, 1943; children: Leonard Thomas, Robert George, Kathleen Ann, Camille Louise, Regina Bayard. *Education:* Attended Franklin and Marshall College, 1939-41; University of Maryland, B.S., 1944, M.D., 1946; postgraduate study in logotherapy at University of Vienna, 1960; postgraduate study at Jung Institute, Zurich, 1965. *Home:* 1064 Clifton Rd. N.E., Atlanta, Ga. 30307. *Office:* Atlanta Psychiatric Clinic, 2905 Peachtree Rd. N.E., Atlanta, Ga. 30305.

CAREER: Emory University Hospital, Atlanta, Ga., intern, 1946-47; Lawson Veterans Administration Hospital and Emory University, both Atlanta, psychiatric resident, 1947-48; Oliver General Hospital, Augusta, Ga., assistant chief of neuropsychiatric services, 1948-50; Austin Riggs Foundation, Inc., Stockbridge, Mass., fellow, 1950; Savannah-Chatham County Mental Health Clinic, Savannah, Ga., director, 1951-52; private practice of psychiatry, Columbus, Ga., 1952—; Bradley Center, Inc., Columbus, director, 1955-73; Georgia State University, Atlanta, supervisor of psychotherapy in department of clinical psychology, 1973—. Consultant to numerous public and private health agencies, including Muscogee County Public Health Department, 1952-53, Georgia State Division of Vocational Rehabilitation, 1962—, National Institute of Mental Health, 1962-65, Alabama Baptist Children's Home, Troy, 1963-64, Sumter County Guidance Clinic, Americus, Ga., 1963-65, Wiregrass Mental Clinic, Dothan, Ala., 1964-70, Troup County Public Mental Health Clinic, 1966-70, Columbus Health Department Child Guidance Clinic, 1970-73, Georgia Association of Pastoral Care, 1973-75, and Houston County Public Health Department. *Military service:* U.S. Army, Medical Corps, 1948-50; became captain.

MEMBER: Royal Society of Health, American Group Psychotherapy Association, American Association for Psychotherapy, American Medical Association, American Psychiatric Association (fellow), American Society for Group Psychotherapy and Psychodrama, Psychotherapy Association, American Public Health Association (fellow), Medical Association of Georgia, Georgia Psychiatric Association (president, 1959-60), Atlanta Medical Society.

WRITINGS: (With David S. Shapiro) *Opening Doors for Troubled People,* C. C Thomas, 1963; (with others) *The Mental Health Counselor in the Community,* C. C Thomas, 1968; *The Conflicted Man,* Exposition Press, 1974; (contributor) Barbara Walton Spradley, editor, *Contemporary Community Nursing,* Little, Brown, 1975; (contributor) *Exploring Mental Health Parameters,* Clark College, Volume II, 1976, Volume III, 1980. Contributor of more than forty articles to professional journals.

AVOCATIONAL INTERESTS: Skiing, sailplaning, golf, travel, photography.

BIOGRAPHICAL/CRITICAL SOURCES: Sunday Ledger-Enquirer, Columbus, Ga., May 19, 1957.

* * *

MAIN, Jackson Turner 1917-

PERSONAL: Born August 6, 1917, in Chicago, Ill.; son of John Smith and Dorothy (Turner) Main; married Gloria Lund, 1957; children: Jackson Turner, Jr., Eifiona Llewelyn, Judson Kempton. *Education:* University of Wisconsin, B.A., M.A., Ph.D., 1949. *Home:* 3 Coraway Rd., Setauket, N.Y. 11733. *Office:* Department of History, State University of New York, Stony Brook, N.Y. 11794.

CAREER: Washington and Jefferson College, Washington, Pa., assistant professor, 1948-50; University of Maryland, College Park, assistant professor, 1949-51; San Jose State College (now University), San Jose, Calif., 1953-65, professor of history, 1959-65; University of Maryland, professor of history, 1965-66; State University of New York at Stony Brook, professor of history, 1966—, chairman of department, 1977-79, director, Institute for Colonial Studies, 1966-74. Visiting professor, Stanford University, 1958-59, and University of Maryland, 1965-66. *Military service:* U.S. Army Air Forces, four years; became technical sergeant. *Member:* American Historical Association, Organization of American Historians, Wisconsin Historical Society. *Awards, honors:* Institute of Early American History and Culture prize manuscript, 1958, for *The Antifederalists;* American Council of Learned Societies fellow, 1962-63; New York Sons of the Revolution prize, 1974, for *Political Parties before the Constitution.*

WRITINGS: The Antifederalists: Critics of the Constitution, 1781-1788, University of North Carolina Press, 1961; *The Social Structure of Revolutionary America,* Princeton University Press, 1965; *The Upper House in the Revolutionary Era, 1763-1788,* University of Wisconsin Press, 1967; *Political Parties before the Constitution,* University of North Carolina Press, 1973; *The Sovereign States 1775-1783,* F. Watts, 1973; (editor) *Connecticut Society in the Era of the American Revolution,* Connecticut Bicentennial Commission, 1978.

WORK IN PROGRESS: Essays in the Social History of Colonial Connecticut.

* * *

MALENBAUM, Wilfred 1913-

PERSONAL: Born January 26, 1913, in Boston, Mass.; son of Harry and Bertha (Brandwyn) Malenbaum; married Josephine Orenstein, February 26, 1950 (died, 1965); married Gloria B. Balaban, October 31, 1976; children: (first marriage) Bruce T., Roxanne F., Ronald G. *Education:* Harvard University, A.B., 1934, M.A., 1935, Ph.D., 1941; attended London School of Economics, 1937-38, and Institute of Economics, Oslo, Norway, 1937-38. *Religion:* Jewish. *Home:* 527 South 41st St., Philadelphia, Pa. 19104. *Office:* Faculty of Arts and Sciences, University of Pennsylvania, 387 McNeil, Philadelphia, Pa. 19104.

CAREER: Harvard University, Cambridge, Mass., instructor in economics, 1939-41; U.S. Government, Washington,

D.C., Office of Strategic Services, chief of agriculture and standard of living section, 1941-45, Department of State, special assistant to director of research and intelligence, 1945-46, chief of investment and economic development staff, 1948-52; Massachusetts Institute of Technology, Cambridge, visiting professor of economics and director of India project for Center for International Studies, 1953-59; University of Pennsylvania, Philadelphia, professor of economics, 1959—. Visiting professor, University of Hawaii, 1961, Vanderbilt University, Harvard University, 1964, and University of Heidelberg, 1966; U.S.I.S. guest lecturer in South Asia, summers, 1971 and 1972. Technical specialist with U.S. UNRRA delegation, 1944; advisor to U.S. delegations in Geneva, 1946-50; economic advisor, United Nations Economic Commission to Latin America, 1951; official U.S. representative, Consultative Committee for Far East, Karachi, Pakistan, 1952; U.S. delegate, SEATO Conference, Philippines, 1960. Consultant, National Labor Relations Board, SHAEF Agricultural Section, U.N. Food and Agriculture Organization, Delhi Urban Planning project, U.S. Department of State, 1961-66 and 1974, International Bank, 1963-64, UNESCO, 1965, and World Health Organization, 1976—. Member of board of governors, Davis Institute of Health Economics, 1967-70; member, External Advisory Group on Health, AID-TAB, 1970-73; and National Council for International Health, 1971-76. Cubmaster, Boy Scouts of America, 1959-60.

MEMBER: Society for International Development, Association for Asian Studies, American Economic Association, Phi Beta Kappa. *Awards, honors:* David A. Wells Prize, 1943; Ford Foundation faculty research fellow, 1964-65, health program development grant, summer, 1973; M.A., University of Pennsylvania, 1971; Smithsonian Institution senior fellow in India, 1977-78.

WRITINGS: The World Wheat Economy: 1885-1939, Harvard University Press, 1953; *India and China: Development Contrasts,* [New Delhi], 1956; *The East and West in India's Development,* National Planning Association, 1959; *Prospects for Indian Development,* Free Press of Glencoe, 1962; *Modern India's Economy,* Bobbs-Merrill, 1971; *Materials Requirements in the United States and Abroad in the Year 2000,* National Materials Policy Commission, 1973; *The World Demand for Raw Materials in 1985 and 2000,* McGraw, 1978.

Contributor: R. L. Parks and I. Tinker, editors, *Leadership and Political Institutions in India,* Princeton University Press, 1959; R. Braibanti and J. J. Spengler, editors, *Administration and Economic Development in India,* Duke University Press, 1963; B. N. Varma, *Contemporary India,* Asia Publishing, 1964; S. H. Robock and L. M. Solomon, editors, *International Development 1965,* Oceana, 1966; H. G. Shaffer and C. D. Pryblya, editors, *From Underdevelopment to Affluence,* Appleton, 1968; A. V. Bhuleshkar, editor, *Indian Economic Thought and Development,* [Bombay], 1969; H. E. Klarman, editor, *Empirical Studies in Health Economics,* Johns Hopkins Press, 1970; Kuan I. Chen and J. S. Uppal, *India and China: Studies in Comparative Development,* Free Press, 1971; *Nutrition, National Development, and Planning,* M.I.T. Press, 1973; Joseph di Bona, editor, *The Context of Education in Indian Development,* Duke University Press, 1974. Contributor of articles to professional journals.

* * *

MALESKA, Eugene Thomas 1916-

PERSONAL: Born January 6, 1916, in Jersey City, N.J.; son of Matthew Michael and Ellen (Kelly) Maleska; married Jean Merletto (a high school teacher), March 23, 1940; children: Merryl, Gary. *Education:* Montclair State Teachers College (now Montclair State College), A.B., 1937, A.M., 1940; Columbia University, graduate study, 1943-46; Harvard University, Ed.D., 1955 *Home:* Over Jordan, Wareham, Mass. *Agent:* Scott Meredith Literary Agency, Inc., 845 Third Ave., New York, N.Y. 10022.

CAREER: Junior high school teacher in Palisades Park, N.J., 1937-40; New York Public Schools, New York City, junior high school teacher, 1940-46, assistant to elementary school principal, 1946-52, elementary school principal, 1952-55, junior high school principal, 1955-58, coordinator of teacher recruitment, 1958-62, assistant superintendent in charge of teacher recruitment, 1962-64, assistant superintendent of schools in District 8, Bronx, 1964-66, associate program director for Center for Urban Education, 1966-70, assistant superintendent of schools in District 8, 1970-73; currently crossword puzzle editor for the *New York Times.* Instructor, Hunter College (now Hunter College of the City University of New York), 1947-51, and University of Vermont, summers, 1960-62; lecturer, City College of the City University of New York, 1952-62. Director, Washington Heights Play School, 1950. Formerly active on civic committees in Cresskill, N.J. *Member:* National Education Association, American Association of School Administrators, Poetry Society of America, Kappa Delta Pi, Phi Delta Kappa. *Awards, honors:* Spanish-American Council award in human relations, 1956; D.Litt., 1963, and Alumni Citation, 1979, both from Montclair State College.

WRITINGS: Sun and Shadow (poetry), Fine Editions, 1961; (with Carroll Atkinson) *Story of Education,* Chilton, 1962, revised edition, 1966; (editor) *Book of Cryptic Puzzles,* Simon & Schuster, 1980; *Take My Words,* Simon & Schuster, 1980. Editor, with Margaret Farrar, "Junior Crossword Puzzle Book" series, Simon & Schuster, beginning 1960; editor, "Educational Crosswords" series, Washington Square Press, includes *Fifty American Authors,* 1963, *The Fifty States,* 1966, and *Fifty Famous Americans,* 1966; editor, "Crossword Book of Quotations" series, Simon & Schuster, 1966—; editor, with Farrar, "Crossword Puzzle Book" series, Simon & Schuster, 1977—. Contributor to anthologies; contributor of articles to professional journals and poetry to newspapers and magazines, including the *New York Times, New York Herald Tribune,* and *Spirit.* Founding editor, *Intercom,* 1955-58.

BIOGRAPHICAL/CRITICAL SOURCES: Bergen Record, Bergen County, N.J., April 14, 1962.

* * *

MALGONKAR, Manohar (Dattatray) 1913-

PERSONAL: Born July 12, 1913, in Bombay, India; son of Dattatray Sakharam and Parvati (Walawalkar) Malgonkar; married, 1947; wife's name Manorama; children: Sunita. *Education:* Bombay University, B.A., 1936. *Home:* P.O. Jagalbet, Londa, R. Rly, Mysore, India.

CAREER: Big-game hunter in India, 1936-38; executive officer with Indian Government Service, 1938-43; proprietor of mining company in Mysore, India, 1952—. Independent candidate for the Indian Parliament. *Military service:* Indian Army Infantry, 1943-52; became lieutenant colonel.

WRITINGS: The Sea Hawk: Life and Battles of Kanhoji Angrey, Asia Publishing House, 1959, reprinted, Vision Books (New Delhi), 1978; *Distant Drum,* Asia Publishing House, 1961; *Combat of Shadows,* Hamish Hamilton, 1962,

Inter Culture Association, 1966; *The Puars of Dewas Senior,* Longmans, Green, 1963; *The Princes* (Literary Guild selection), Viking, 1963; *A Bend in the Ganges,* Hamish Hamilton, 1964, Viking, 1965; *Spy in Amber,* Orient (New Delhi), 1970; *Chhatrapatis of Kolhapur,* Popular Prakashan (Bombay), 1971; *The Devil's Wind,* Viking, 1972; *A Toast in Warm Wine* (short stories), Orient, 1973; (contributor) *John Kenneth Galbraith Introduces India,* Deutsch, 1973; *Bombay Beware* (short stories), Orient, 1975; *Rumble-Tumble* (short stories), Orient, 1977; *Line of Mars* (play), Hind, 1977; *Dead and Living Cities,* Hind, 1978; *Shalimar,* Viking, 1978; *The Men Who Killed Ghandi,* Macmillan (London), 1978; *The Garland Keepers,* Vision Books, 1979; *Cue from the Inner Voice: The Choice before Big Business,* Vikas (India), 1980.

WORK IN PROGRESS: Two novels, *Birds of Prey,* about the Indian takeover of Goa, and *Bandicoot Run,* about spying between India and Pakistan based on a real case; a book on the early life of Rudyard Kipling, entitled *Rudyard Baba.*

SIDELIGHTS: Manohar Malgonkar has spent most of his life in a village deep in the jungles of Canara, the site of his family's home for over one hundred years and where he currently operates manganese mines which he and a brother own. Though he once worked for several years as a professional big-game hunter, Malgonkar is now a wildlife conservationist. *Avocational interests:* Fishing, cooking, music.

BIOGRAPHICAL/CRITICAL SOURCES: Antioch Review, June, 1973.

* * *

MALHERBE, Abraham J(ohannes) 1930-

PERSONAL: Surname is accented on second syllable; born May 15, 1930, in Pretoria, South Africa; son of Abraham J. (an insurance agent) and Cornelia (Meyer) Malherbe; married Phyllis Melton, May 28, 1953; children: Selina, Cornelia, Abraham J. *Education:* Abilene Christian College (now University), B.A., 1954; Harvard University, S.T.B., 1957, Th.D., 1963; also studied at University of Utrecht, 1960-61. *Home:* 71 Spring Garden St., Hamden, Conn. 06517. *Office:* Divinity School, Yale University, 409 Prospect St., New Haven, Conn. 06510.

CAREER: Minister in Churches of Christ, 1953—; Abilene Christian College (now University), Abilene, Tex., assistant professor, 1963-64, associate professor of New Testament, 1964-69; Dartmouth College, Hanover, N.H., associate professor of New Testament, 1969-70; Yale University, New Haven, Conn., associate professor, 1970-78, professor of New Testament, 1978—. *Member:* American Academy of Religion, Society of Biblical Literature, Corpus Hellenisticum Novi Testamenti, Societas Novi Testamenti Studiorum, North American Patristic Society. *Awards, honors:* Christian Research Foundation award, 1967, for translation of *The Life of Moses.*

WRITINGS: (Editor and contributor) *The World of the New Testament,* R. B. Sweet, 1967; (contributor) Frank Magill, editor, *Current Events and Their Interpretations,* Salem Press, 1972; *Social Aspects of Early Christianity,* Louisiana State University Press, 1977; (editor and contributor) *The Cynic Epistles,* Scholars Press, 1977; (translator and author of notes with W. E. Ferguson) Gregory of Nyssa, *The Life of Moses,* Paulist Press, 1978. Contributor to honorary volumes. Contributor of articles and reviews to numerous journals, including *Journal of Biblical Literature, Novum Testamentum, Theologische Zeitschrift, Restoration Quarterly, Journal of Ecclesiastical History,* and *Vigiliae Christianae.*

WORK IN PROGRESS: Paul's Exhortation to the Greeks, a monograph.

* * *

MALLINSON, George Greisen 1918-

PERSONAL: Born July 4, 1918, in Troy, N.Y.; son of Cyrus J. and Mathilda (Greisen) Mallinson; married Jacqueline Vella Buck, 1954; children: Cyrus James, Virginia Alice, Charles Evans, Carolyn Louise. *Education:* New York State College for Teachers (now State University of New York at Albany), B.A., 1937, M.A., 1941; University of Michigan, Ph.D., 1948. *Politics:* Republican. *Religion:* Congregationalist. *Home:* 535 Kendall, Kalamazoo, Mich. 49007. *Office:* College of Education, 3409 Sangren Hall, Western Michigan University, Kalamazoo, Mich. 49008.

CAREER: High school teacher in Whitesboro, N.Y. and Eden, N.Y., 1937-42; Iowa State Teachers College (now University of Northern Iowa), Cedar Falls, director of science education, 1947-48; Western Michigan University, Kalamazoo, professor of science education, 1948-54, dean of Graduate College, 1955-77, distinguished professor of science education, 1977—. Summer session instructor in science at six universities, 1951-58. Director of over fifty National Science Foundation institutes. Adviser on development of science filmstrip and film program, Text-Film Division, McGraw-Hill Book Co.; adviser on science tests, Scholastic Testing Service. *Military service:* U.S. Army, Adjutant General's Office, Corps of Engineers, 1942-45; became sergeant.

MEMBER: National Association for Research in Science Teaching (president, 1953), American Association for the Advancement of Science, National Society for College Teachers of Education, School Science and Mathematics Association, American Educational Research Association, National Conference on the Administration of Research, Michigan Science Teachers Association (president, 1954), Sigma Lambda Sigma, Theta Chi Delta, Beta Beta Beta, Psi Kappa Psi, American Legion.

WRITINGS: Science in Daily Life, Ginn, 1953, 2nd edition, 1958; *General Physical Science,* McGraw, 1961; *Science in Modern Life,* Ginn, 1964, 2nd edition, 1969; *Science,* Books I-VI, Silver Burdett, 1965; *Science: Understanding Your Environment,* Books I-VI, Silver Burdett, 1972-78; *A Summary of Research in Science Education,* Wiley, 1977. Contributor of over five hundred articles to professional journals. Editor, *School, Science and Mathematics,* and *Blindness Annual.*

WORK IN PROGRESS Development of programmed learning materials for the adult blind; development of science activity materials for visually handicapped adolescents; research on the role of the blind in jazz and blues.

* * *

MALONE, Elmer Taylor, Jr. 1943-
(Ted Malone)

PERSONAL: Born December 18, 1943, in Wilson, N.C.; son of E. Taylor and Mildred (Winborne) Malone; married Lynda Cyrus, June 15, 1969; children: Anna Richard Malone. *Education:* Campbell College, B.S., 1967; University of Maryland graduate study in Europe, 1967-68; University of North Carolina, M.A., 1975. *Home:* 103 Carl Dr., Route 4, Chapel Hill, N.C. 27514. *Office:* Department of English, North Carolina Central University, Durham, N.C.

CAREER: Raleigh Times, Raleigh, N.C., reporter, 1969;

Dunn Dispatch, Dunn, N.C., editor, 1970; *Harnett County News,* Lillington, N.C., editor, 1972-74; U.S. Environmental Protection Agency, Technical Publications Division, Durham, N.C., member of staff, 1974; *Durham Sun,* Durham, assistant news editor and drama critic, 1974-77; North Carolina Central University, Durham, visiting lecturer in English, 1977—. *Military service:* U.S. Army, 1967-68. *Member:* North Carolina Folklore Society, North Carolina Literary and Historical Society, North Carolina Genealogy Society, Chapel Hill Historical Society.

WRITINGS—Poems; under name Ted Malone: *The Cleared Place of Tara,* Pope Printing, 1970; *The Tapestry Maker,* Blair, 1972. Work is represented in anthologies, including *Contemporary Poets of North Carolina,* edited by Guy Owen and Mary Williams, Blair, 1977. Contributor to *Journal of the American Medical Association, North Carolina Folklore Journal, Long View Journal, Crucible, Tar River Poets, Lyricist,* and numerous other periodicals.

WORK IN PROGRESS: Harnett County Historical Places; Edwin W. Fuller: His Life and Times; Pictures of Structures that Don't Exist; a book of poems; *In Search of Little C.D.: An Anecdotal Genealogy.*

SIDELIGHTS: Elmer Taylor Malone, Jr. wrote *CA:* "I am very much interested in the concept of 'sense of place' and, as a former archaeology student, how place and person shape one another. I see North Carolina as 'my place' and all its people, black and white, somehow part of my tribe." *Avocational interests:* The Irish dramatic movement and Irish history.

* * *

MANNING, Rosemary 1911-
(Mary Voyle)

PERSONAL: Born December 9, 1911, in Weymouth, England. *Education:* University of London, B.A. in classics, 1933. *Home:* 20 Lyndhurst Gardens, London N.W.3, England.

CAREER: Former teacher and business woman; writer.

WRITINGS: (Under pseudonym Mary Voyle) *Remaining a Stranger,* Heinemann, 1953; (under pseudonym Mary Voyle) *A Change of Direction,* Heinemann, 1955; *The Shape of Innocence,* Doubleday, 1960 (published in England as *Look, Stranger,* J. Cape, 1960); *The Chinese Garden,* J. Cape, 1962, Farrar, Straus, 1964; *Man on a Tower,* J. Cape, 1965.

Juvenile: *Green Smoke,* Doubleday, 1957; *Dragon in Danger,* Doubleday, 1959; *The Dragon's Quest,* Doubleday, 1961; *Arripay,* Constable, 1963, Farrar, Straus, 1964; *Heraldry,* A. & C. Black, 1966; (editor) William Blake, *A Grain of Sand,* F. Watts, 1967; *The Rocking Horse,* Hamish Hamilton, 1970; *Railways and Railwaymen,* Kestrel Books, 1977. Contributor of short stories to *Horizon, Cornhill, Cosmopolitan,* and *Mademoiselle.*

AVOCATIONAL INTERESTS: Music, books, the country.

* * *

MANUSHKIN, Fran 1942-

PERSONAL: Surname is pronounced Ma-*nush*-kin; born November 2, 1942, in Chicago, Ill.; daughter of Meyer (a furniture salesman) and Beatrice (Kessler) Manushkin. *Education:* Attended University of Illinois and Roosevelt University; Chicago Teachers College, North Campus (now Northeastern Illinois University), B.A., 1964. *Home:* 121 East 88th St., New York, N.Y. 10028. *Office:* Random House, Inc., 201 East 50th St., New York, N.Y. 10022.

CAREER: Elementary teacher in Chicago, Ill., 1964-65; worked at Doubleday Bookstore and as tour guide at Lincoln Center for Performing Arts, New York City, 1966; Holt, Rinehart & Winston, Inc., New York City, secretary to college psychology editor, 1967-68; Harper & Row Publishers, Inc., New York City, 1968-78, began as secretary, became associate editor of Harper Junior Books; Random House, Inc., New York City, editor of Clubhouse K-2 (student paperback book club), 1978—. *Member:* National Audubon Society. *Awards, honors:* Dutch Silver Pencil Award, 1972, for *Baby.*

WRITINGS—All juveniles, published by Harper: *Baby* (picturebook), illustrations by Ronald Himler, 1972; *Bubblebath!* (picturebook), illustrations by Himler, 1974; *Shirleybird,* 1975; *Swinging and Swinging* (picturebook), illustrations by Thomas DiGrazia, 1976; *The Perfect Christmas Picture,* in press.

AVOCATIONAL INTERESTS: Jogging, bird watching, cat watching, reading, book collecting.

* * *

MAPLE, Terry 1946-

PERSONAL: Born September 10, 1946, in Maywood, Calif.; son of Merrill (a truck driver) and Evelyn (Hayes) Maple. *Education:* University of the Pacific, A.B., 1968; University of Stockholm, additional study, 1971-72; University of California, Davis, M.A., 1971, Ph.D., 1974. *Office:* School of Psychology, Georgia Institute of Technology, Atlanta, Ga. 30332.

CAREER: University of California, Davis, research behavioral biologist, 1973-74, lecturer in comparative psychology, 1974-75; Emory University, Atlanta, Ga., assistant professor, 1975-78; Georgia Institute of Technology, Atlanta, associate professor, 1978—. *Member:* International Primatological Society, American Society of Primatologists, American Association for the Advancement of Science, American Association of University Professors, American Psychological Association, Animal Behavior Society, Sigma Xi.

WRITINGS: (Editor with D. W. Matheson) *Aggression, Hostility, and Violence,* Holt, 1973; (editor with J. Erwin and G. Mitchell) *Captivity and Behavior,* Van Nostrand, 1979; *Orangutan Behavior,* Van Nostrand, 1980; (with M. P. Hoff) *Gorilla Behavior,* Van Nostrand, in press. Contributor to *Primates, Archives of Sexual Behavior, Journal of Behavioural Science, International Journal of Psychobiology,* and other journals.

WORK IN PROGRESS: Research in interspecies social behavior, sexual behavior of macaques, human ethology, and aggression in animals and man.

AVOCATIONAL INTERESTS: Satirical cartooning, baseball, amateur drama productions.

* * *

MAPP, Alf J(ohnson), Jr. 1925-

PERSONAL: Born February 17, 1925, in Portsmouth, Va.; son of Alf Johnson (a school superintendent) and Lorraine (Carney) Mapp; married former wife, Hartley Lockhart, March 28, 1953; married Ramona Hartley (a college administrator), August 1, 1971; children: (first marriage) Alf Johnson III. *Education:* Attended College of William and Mary (Williamsburg, Va.); Norfolk College of William and Mary (now

Old Dominion University), A.B. (summa cum laude), 1961. *Politics:* Independent. *Religion:* Christian. *Home:* Willow Oaks, 2901 Tanbark Lane, Portsmouth, Va. 23703. *Office:* Department of English, Old Dominion University, Norfolk, Va. 23508.

CAREER: Portsmouth Star, Portsmouth, Va., editorial writer, 1945-46, associate editor, 1946-48, editorial chief, 1948-54; *The Virginian-Pilot,* Norfolk, Va., assistant city editor, assistant state editor, 1954-58; Old Dominion University, Norfolk, lecturer in English and history, 1961-62, instructor, 1962-67, assistant professor, 1967-73, associate professor, 1973-79, professor of English, journalism, and creative writing, 1979—. Professional lecturer, 1948—. Director, Virginia Y.M.C.A. Youth and Government Foundation, 1949-51; member of Virginia Committee for Library Development, 1949-50, and Virginia State Library Legislative Committee, 1950-51; member of board, Portsmouth Public Library, 1948-58; director, Portsmouth Area Community Chest, 1948-52; president, Portsmouth Inter-Club Council, 1951; member of advisory committee, Virginia Independence Bicentennial Commission, 1967—.

MEMBER: Modern Language Association of America, Authors Guild, Virginia Writers Club, Poetry Society of Virginia (president, 1974-75), Virginia Historical Society, Norfolk Historical Society (director), Portsmouth Historical Association, Jamestowne Society (chief historian, 1975-77; international secretary of state, 1977-78), Order of Cape Henry (international president, 1975-76). *Awards, honors:* Freedoms Foundation Honor Medal for editorials in an American newspaper, 1951; Pulitzer prize nomination, 1953; English award, Old Dominion College, 1961; Troubadour Great Teacher Award, 1969; Outstanding American Educator Award, 1972, 1974; Francais du Bicentenaire Medal (France), 1976; National Bicentennial Medal, American Revolution Bicentennial Administration, 1976.

WRITINGS: The Virginia Experiment: The Old Dominion's Role in the Making of America (1607-1781), Dietz, 1957, 2nd edition, Open Court, 1975; *Frock Coats and Epaulets: Character Studies of Six Confederate Leaders* (American History Publication Society selection), A. S. Barnes, 1963; *American Creates Its Own Literature,* Rand McNally, 1967; *Just One Man,* Dietz, 1968; *The Golden Dragon: Alfred the Great and His Times,* Open Court, 1975. Writer of scripts for WTAR-TV, Norfolk, and Voice of America. Contributor to *Saturday Review, New York Times, Virginia Quarterly Review,* and to specialized publications. Editorial consultant, *Encyclopaedia Britannica, World Book,*and *Worldmark Encyclopedia of the United States.* Member of editorial board, Jamestown Foundation, 1967—; member of publications committee, 350th Anniversary of Representative Government in the Western World, 1966-69.

SIDELIGHTS: Alf J. Mapp told *CA:* "My interest in writing was stimulated by home influences—my mother's skill as a reader, my father's ability to interpret literature in a way meaningful and exciting to a child, and my maternal grandmother's contagious enthusiasm for creative activity and considerable narrative talent. My fledgling efforts met with enthusiastic encouragement tempered by my father's judicious criticism. From the age of five onward I have always known that, whatever else I might be, I would be a writer.

"My interest in history and biography stemmed originally from family associations and historical artifacts in the home, all of which made historical personalities seem quite real and near. Uncensored access to a home library including quaint and curious volumes acquired over six generations of collecting helped to provide me with a nonstandard literary background. Nevertheless, the strongest influences on my writing style probably have been Chaucer, the King James version of the Bible, Shakespeare, Dickens, Mark Twain, William Faulkner, John Keats, and Sir Winston Churchill. An important part of my education was obtained as a correspondent covering Churchill, Eisenhower, Truman, Mackenzie King, and other international figures. I profited, too, from the advice and example of the late Douglas Southall Freeman.

"I find stimulus today in the acute questions of my students and my young son, and especially in the subtle and knowledgeable insights of my wife, Ramona."

AVOCATIONAL INTERESTS: "I enjoy good books, art, good music of almost all kinds (especially Beethoven and Mozart), good conversation, and walking through the fields and woods."

* * *

MARCUS, Adrianne 1935-

PERSONAL: Born March 7, 1935, in Everett, Mass.; daughter of George Z. (a lawyer) and Edith (Cohen) Stuhl; married Warren M. Marcus (owner of a men's store), June 13, 1954; children: Stacey Ann, Shelby Alice, Sarah Naomi. *Education:* Attended University of North Carolina at Greensboro, 1951-52, Campbell College, 1952, and Shorter College, 1952-53; University of California, San Francisco, A.B., 1955, M.A., 1963. *Politics:* Varied. *Religion:* Pagan. *Home and office:* 79 Twin Oaks, San Rafael, Calif. 94901.

CAREER: College of Marin, Kentfield, Calif., instructor in English, 1968-79; Indian Valley Colleges, Novato, Calif., instructor in English, 1972-74. *Member:* Poetry Society of America. *Awards, honors:* Borestone Mountain Poetry awards, 1968, 1971; National Endowment for the Arts grant, 1968.

WRITINGS: The Moon Is a Marrying Eye, Red Clay, 1972; *The Photojournalist: Mark and Leibovitz* (Book-of-the-Month Club alternate selection), Crowell, 1975; *Faced with Love* (poetry), Copper Beech Press, 1977; *The Chocolate Bible,* Putnam, 1978; *Child of Earthquake Country* (poetry), New World Press, 1980; *Gothic House World of Gifts,* St. Martin's, 1980; *What to Eat before the Earthquake Comes: Or, Eating to a Fault,* Presidio Press, 1980. Editor of poetry column in *Pacific Sun,* 1967-69.

WORK IN PROGRESS: The Last One (fiction) and *In Search of Three Men* (nonfiction).

SIDELIGHTS: Adrianne Marcus told *CA:* "I write poetry because I have to, nonfiction because I like to write about what others do, and fiction because it permits me to combine poetry and nonfiction in different ways to discover something about the world that I did not understand when I began the story. Writing always teaches me something; either about someone else's viewpoint or about some facet of my own that I hadn't expected to come upon. Writing is the only way I have of 'seeing' the world; I choose language because it is the form of communication which infers a whole range of circumstances from the smallest amount of information."

BIOGRAPHICAL/CRITICAL SOURCES: New York Times, May 16, 1979.

* * *

MARCUS, Rebecca B(rian) 1907-

PERSONAL: Born November 26, 1907, in New York, N.Y.;

daughter of William and Mary (Steinberg) Brian; married Abraham Marcus (a writer); children: Daniel, Judith. *Education:* Hunter College (now Hunter College of the City University of New York), A.B., 1928; attended City College (now City College of the City University of New York), and Columbia University, 1929-31. *Home:* 73-08 184th St., Flushing, N.Y.

CAREER: Junior high schools, New York, N.Y., teacher of science, 1934-54; professional writer, 1954—. *Member:* Federation of Science Teachers, Authors Guild.

WRITINGS—All published by F. Watts, except as indicated: *First Biography of Galileo,* 1960; *First Biography of Joseph Priestly,* 1961; *Science in the Bathtub,* 1961; *Science in the Garden,* 1961; *First Book of Glaciers,* 1962; *Immortals of Science: William Harvey,* 1962; *First Book of Volcanoes and Earthquakes,* 1963, revised, 1972; *Antoine Lavoisier and the Revolution in Chemistry,* 1964; *The First Book of the Cliff Dwellers,* 1968; *Prehistoric Cave Paintings,* 1968; *Moses Maimonides: Rabbi, Philosopher, and Physician,* 1969; (with Judith Marcus) *Fiesta Time in Mexico,* Garrard, 1974; *Survivors of the Stone Age: Nine Tribes Today,* Hastings House, 1975; *Being Blind: Seeing Without Eyes,* Hastings House, 1978. Associate science editor, *Book of Knowledge,* Grolier.

AVOCATIONAL INTERESTS: Traveling, camping, hiking, cooking, baking, reading.

* * *

MAREIN, Shirley 1926-

PERSONAL: Born January 20, 1926, in New York, N.Y.; daughter of Joseph (a typographer) and Celia (Breterman) Tobias; married Edmund Marein (a designer); children: Melissa Marein Cornfeld, Peter. *Education:* Cooper Union, B.F.A., 1946; Hofstra University, B.S., 1962; Hunter College of the City University of New York, M.A., 1966; Alfred University, graduate study in ceramics. *Home:* 2317 Cedar Swamp Rd., Brookville, N.Y. 11545. *Office:* New York Institute of Technology, Old Westbury, New York.

CAREER: New York Institute of Technology, Old Westbury, associate professor of design, 1967—. Part-time teacher at New School for Social Research and Brookfield Craft Center; has lectured and held demonstrations at Pratt Institute, Hofstra University, Museo de las Culturas, New York Guild of Handweavers, and New York University. Work has been exhibited at Museo de las Culturas, Maison de la Culture, Gobelin Museum, Musee des Beaux Arts (Lausanne), Princeton University, National Design Center, New York University, Almus Gallery, and in exhibition tours in the United States.

MEMBER: World Crafts Council, Archeology Society of America, American Craftsmen's Council, Archaeological Institute of America, Artist Craftsmen of New York (member of board of directors), Long Island Craftsmen's Guild, Kappa Delta Pi. *Awards, honors:* More than fifteen awards for artwork include first prize for wall hangings from Artist Craftsmen of New York, 1964; Long Island Craftsmen's annual awards, 1969, 1972; best in show prize from exhibition at Molloy College, 1970; National Endowment for the Arts grant, 1975.

WRITINGS: (Contributor) Ruth Lembach, *An Administrative Briefing in Art,* Croft Educational Services, 1968; (designer of frontispiece) Dona Meilach, *Making Contemporary Rugs and Wallhangings,* Abelard, 1970; (contributor of illustrations) Dona Meilach, *Macrame: Creative Design in Knotting,* Crown, 1971; (contributor of illustrations) Sarita Rainey, *Wall Hangings,* David Mass, 1971; *Off the Loom: Creating with Fiber,* Viking, 1972, 2nd edition, 1974; *Stitchery, Needlepoint, Applique, and Patchwork,* Viking, 1973; *Creating Rugs and Wall Hangings,* Viking, 1975; *The Flower in Design,* Viking, 1976; *Oriental Images,* Viking, 1978. Author of column, "New York/Fiber," *Crafts Horizons.* Contributor of articles and reviews to *Crafts Horizons.*

SIDELIGHTS: Shirley Marein told *CA:* "I am a true visual artist. I read, I write, I draw, I photograph. In these areas I am gifted, if that's what talented means, and am fortunate, if that's what education means. Therefore I teach because I want to do unto others and am published because I am God damned lucky."

* * *

MAREK, George R(ichard) 1902-

PERSONAL: Born July 13, 1902, in Austria; son of Martin (a physician) and Emily (Weisberger) Marek; married Muriel Hepner, August, 1925; children: Richard. *Education:* Attended Vienna College, 1916-20, and City College (now City College of the City University of New York), 1920-24. *Home:* 151 Central Park W., New York, N.Y. 10023. *Agent:* Phyllis Jackson, International Famous Agency, 1301 Avenue of the Americas, New York, N.Y. 10019.

CAREER: *Good Housekeeping* magazine, New York City, music editor, 1940-50; RCA Victor, New York City, vice-president and general manager, 1950-65. *Member:* Dutch Treat Club.

WRITINGS: *A Front Seat at the Opera,* Crown, 1948, reprinted, Greenwood Press, 1972; *Good Housekeeping Guide to Musical Enjoyment,* Rinehart, 1949; *Puccini: A Biography,* Simon & Schuster, 1951; (editor) *World Treasury of Grand Opera: Its Triumphs, Trials, and Great Personalities,* Harper, 1957, reprinted, Arno, 1978; *Opera as Theater,* Simon & Schuster, 1958, reprinted, Greenwood Press, 1977; *Richard Strauss: The Life of a Non-Hero,* Simon & Schuster, 1965; *Beethoven: The Story of a Genius,* Funk, 1970; *Mendelssohn: Gentle Genius,* Funk, 1972; *The Eagles Die,* Harper, 1974; *Toscanini,* Atheneum, 1975; *The Bed and the Throne: The Life of Isabella D'Este,* Harper, 1976; (with Maria Gordon-Smith) *Chopin,* Harper, 1978.

WORK IN PROGRESS: *Cosima Wagner,* a biography.

SIDELIGHTS: George Marek's biographies of composers have received considerable critical attention. One of the most controversial of these is *Richard Strauss: The Life of a Non-Hero,* which Ned Rorem of the *New York Times Book Review* calls an "interesting biography of a dull man." In a *Kenyon Review* article, Richard Freedman notes that Strauss "had few illusions about his ultimate place in the musical cosmos. At the end of his long life he said: 'After all, I may not be a first-rate composer, but I *am* a first-class second-rate composer.'" Freedman feels that Marek "takes Strauss all too readily at his own estimate" in his central contention that "Strauss failed in his later years." The critic says that this assessment is not a new one and that it raises "several questions which proliferate beyond the modest scope of this book and even beyond Strauss's own prodigious career." The most obvious of these questions is "did Strauss's genius indeed fail him about halfway through his life?" Freedman addresses this query: "How can we even begin to judge Strauss's late operas when we cannot see them on the stage, and when most of them are not even recorded? . . . As a high panjandrum of a record company [RCA Victor] whose assets compare favorably with those of the

Deity, Mr. Marek is to be held severely to blame for vouchsafing us no more than a ten-minute, mouth-watering excerpt from one of these late, allegedly problematical operas, *Die Aegyptische Helena.* This excerpt, Helen's rapturous aria, 'Aweite Brautnacht,' is so palpably Strauss at his absolute zenith that it not only belies Mr. Marek's argument that these works are arid, but also infuriates us the more at the niggardly policy of his company in recording them."

Strauss's attitude toward the Nazi regime is a subject that is mentioned by several reviewers. He continued to work—allegedly for the sake of his craft—even though many of his Jewish acquaintances, including his librettist Stefan Zweig, suffered humiliation at the hands of the Nazis. Winthrop Sargeant of the *New Yorker* writes that the composer's "continual shilly-shallying seemed an undignified tragicomic spectacle for such a respected figure. Strauss was, Mr. Marek makes evident, no hero. He was not exactly a villain, either. He took a position in between—one that made him merely weak, vacillating, and opportunistic." Sargeant notes that Strauss conducted in Berlin in place of Bruno Walter when Walter, a Jew, was threatened with a demonstration, and that he conducted in Bayreuth when Toscanini resigned in disapproval of the Nazi policies. The reviewer concludes, "the picture Mr. Marek draws is a slightly unpleasant one—an old man making peace with whatever powers there were, interested only in the furtherance of his own music, and just a shade sly and shifty."

Beethoven: The Story of a Genius, according to Donal Henahan of the *New York Times Book Review,* is "crammed with letters and other documentation, is promisingly heavy with scholarly apparatus. It even offers the ultimate in academic chic, the footnote within a footnote. But then most biographical scholarship, even the best, is merely gossip with footnotes. The questions are: How good is the gossip and how good the gossiper?" Henahan says there is a great need for a definitive new biography of the great composer. "But," he adds, "Marek's is not the awaited new book." He feels that Marek has failed to shed new light on Beethoven's life or his works, and that the author does little to clear up old questions. He writes, "there is, in fact, hardly a major issue in all of Beethoviana that this book does not forthrightly straddle." Henahan also objects to what he calls "an account of Beethoven's life and an appreciation of his achievements that contains not one paragraph of substantial discussion of his music, that finds it possible to handle the last three piano sonatas, Op. 109, 110, and 111, in fourteen fatuous lines. . . . In short, a Beethoven biography that you might safely give to Linus or possibly Lucy, but not, certainly, to Schroeder."

A *Best Sellers* reviewer, however, sees the book as "a superb biography . . . which is, thankfully, not a discussion of [Beethoven's] music . . . but a detailed and extraordinarily interesting inquest into the life and development of Beethoven as a man of music, the first such (and there is none such) biography in English in the last twenty-five years." A critic for the *Times Literary Supplement* agrees, calling the work "an important book. There have been countless specialized works on aspects of Beethoven's music, on his character and influence, and the bicentenary year [1970] has brought its own tributes. Straight biographies are rare, and an up-to-date one is overdue. . . . Mr. Marek's own Viennese origins give an added touch of authority to a scene set largely in Vienna. He has the gift of reliving the past, and his crisp narrative makes the book an ideal introduction to Beethoven as well as opening up some new lines of thought for hardened Beethoven readers."

In a review of *Chopin* for *Library Journal,* Beth Macleod says that Marek "skillfully intersperses his narrative with vivid passages from letters, diaries, and George Sand's novels. . . . This is a strictly biographical work—Marek does not discuss Chopin's compositions—but as such it is written with intelligence and integrity." But again some critics disagree with the author's insistence on sticking to the biographical facts with little interpretation of the subject's work. Harold C. Schonberg, for instance, asks "what is the point of a biography that does not put the subject into correct musical perspective?" Schonberg insists that a definitive biography of Chopin in English is desparately needed, but in his opinion Marek "was not really the man to write this book."

BIOGRAPHICAL/CRITICAL SOURCES: New Yorker, April 22, 1967; *New York Times Book Review,* April 23, 1967, November 6, 1969, November 26, 1978; *Time,* June 9, 1967; *Kenyon Review,* September, 1967; *Best Sellers,* December 1, 1969; *Times Literary Supplement,* June 4, 1970; *Library Journal,* September 15, 1978; *Washington Post Book World,* December 24, 1978.

—Sketch by Peter M. Gareffa

* * *

MARIEN, Michael 1938-

PERSONAL: Born March 27, 1938, in Washington, D.C.; son of Henry Matthew (a printer) and Ida (Silver) Marien; married Mary Lou Warner (an art historian), January 20, 1968. *Education:* Cornell University, B.S., 1959; University of California, Berkeley, M.B.A., 1964; Syracuse University, Ph.D., 1970. *Home:* Webster Rd., LaFayette, N.Y. 13084. *Office: Future Survey,* World Future Society, 4916 St. Elmo Ave., Washington, D.C. 20014.

CAREER: Educational Policy Research Center, Syracuse, N.Y., research fellow, 1968-72; World Institute Council, New York, N.Y., director of Information for Policy Design Project, 1972-78; World Future Society, Washington, D.C., editor of *Future Survey,* 1978—.

WRITINGS: Alternative Futures for Learning: An Annotated Bibliography of Trends, Forecasts, and Proposals, Educational Policy Research Center, 1971; *Beyond the Carnegie Commission: A Policy Study Guide to Space/Time/Credit-Preference Higher Learning,* Educational Policy Research Center, 1972; (editor with Warren L. Ziegler) *The Potential of Educational Futures,* Charles A. Jones Publishing, 1972; *Societal Directions and Alternatives: A Critical Guide to the Literature,* Information for Policy Design, 1976; *Future Survey Annual 1979: A Guide to Recent Literature of Trends, Forecasts, and Policy Proposals,* World Future Society, 1980.

WORK IN PROGRESS: The Two Visions of Post-Industrial Society, for Marion Boyars.

SIDELIGHTS: Michael Marien told *CA:* "A necessary global transformation is underway, toward more ecologically-oriented societies based on renewable resources, holistic thinking, and attention to the full range of human needs for the greatest number of people. Through my guidebooks to the diverse and voluminous literature, and my prose, I hope that others can better appreciate the complexity of our times and the many changes that we face."

* * *

MARK, Charles Christopher 1927-

PERSONAL: Born October 12, 1927, in Milwaukee, Wis.; son of Aloysius Leo and Gertrude (Wolf) Mark; married Alice Clair Resnick, June 13, 1954; children: Christopher Joshua, Hilary Beth. *Education:* University of Wisconsin, B.S., 1952, M.S., 1954. *Home:* 9214 Three Oaks Dr., Silver Spring, Md. 20901.

CAREER: Wisconsin Welfare Council, Madison, associate executive, 1954-56; Beloit United Givers Fund, Beloit, Wis., executive director, 1956-57; Winston-Salem Arts Council, Winston-Salem, N.C., executive director, 1957-60; Greater St. Louis Arts and Education Council, St. Louis, Mo., founder and executive director, 1961-64; National Council on the Arts, Washington, D.C., special consultant to White House cultural advisor, 1964-65; National Foundation on the Arts and Humanities, Washington, D.C., director of State and community operations, 1965-67; National Endowment for the Arts, Washington, D.C., director of planning analysis, 1967-69; Los Angeles Music Center, Performing Arts Council, Los Angeles, Calif., president, 1969; Arts Reporting Service, Washington, D.C., founder and publisher, beginning, 1970. Member of planning committee, Wisconsin Governor's Conference on Children and Youth, 1956. Senior lecturer, University of California, Los Angeles, 1969-70. Delegate consultant, UNESCO. *Military service:* U.S. Army Air Forces, 1946-47. *Member:* National Association of Social Workers, Community Arts Councils, Inc.

WRITINGS: *Run Away Home* (novel), Duell, Sloan & Pearce, 1960; *A Study of Cultural Policy in the United States,* UNESCO (Paris), 1969, Unipub, 1970; *The Mark Report: A Study and Evaluation of the Virginia Museum's Statewide Programs,* Virginia Museum (Richmond), 1974. Contributor of articles to numerous professional journals, including *Arts in Society* and *Dance.*

WORK IN PROGRESS: A novel, *And None Contented.*

AVOCATIONAL INTERESTS: Painting.†

* * *

MARK, Shelley M(uin) 1922-

PERSONAL: Born September 9, 1922, in China; came to United States in 1923, naturalized in 1944; son of Hing D. and S. (Wong) Mark; married Janet Chong, 1946 (died, 1977); married T. Chow, 1978; children: (first marriage) Philip, Diane, Paul, Peter, Steven. *Education:* University of Washington, Seattle, B.A., 1943, Ph.D., 1956; Columbia University, M.S., 1944; attended University of California, 1950, 1954, Harvard University, 1953, 1959-60, and Stanford University, 1958. *Home:* 2036 Keeaumoku St., Honolulu, Hawaii. *Office:* Department of Economics, University of Hawaii, Honolulu, Hawaii.

CAREER: University of Washington, Seattle, instructor, 1946-48; Arizona State University, Tempe, assistant professor, 1948-51; Office of Price Stabilization, Honolulu, Hawaii, chief economist, 1951-53; University of Hawaii, Honolulu, associate professor of economics, 1953-62, director of Economic Research Center, 1959-62; State of Hawaii, Department of Planning and Economic Development, director, 1962-74, state energy coordinator, 1973-74; U.S. Environmental Protection Agency, Office of Land Use Coordination, Washington, D.C., director, 1975-77; University of Hawaii, professor of economics, 1978—. Economic advisor to Hawaii legislature, 1954-62. Member of Hawaii Land Use Commission, 1962-74, Governor's Advisory Committee on Science and Technology, 1963-74, Oahu Transportation Policy Committee, 1964-74, Regional Export Expansion Council, 1964-74, Governor's Agriculture Coordinating Committee, 1969-74, Hawaii Foundation for History and Humanities, 1969-74, Hawaii Bicentennial Commission, 1971-74, Hawaii Transportation Control Commission, 1972-74, Governor's Ad Hoc Commission on Operations, Revenues, and Expenditures, 1973-74, Hawaii Manpower Council, 1974, and Federal Interagency Land Use-Environmental Planning Committee, 1975-79. Member of board of directors, University of Hawaii Research Corp., 1965-74. Council of State Planning Agencies, member of board of directors, president, 1973-74, honorary member, 1975—.

MEMBER: American Economic Association, Royal Economic Society, Econometric Society, Western Regional Science Association (president, 1974-75), Hawaii Economic Association (founder), Hawaiian Government Employees Association (director, 1958-59; president, university chapter, 1958-59), Phi Beta Kappa. *Awards, honors:* Sackett Memorial award, Columbia University, 1944; Ford research fellowships at Stanford University, 1958, and Institute of Basic Mathematics, Harvard University, 1959-60.

WRITINGS: *Economics in Action,* Wadsworth, 1959, 4th edition, 1969; (contributor) *The Property Tax and Its Administration,* University of Wisconsin Press, 1970; (contributor) *Sino-American Workshop on Land Use Planning,* U.S. National Academy of Science, 1978. Also author of *Input-Output Analysis of Hawaiian Economy.* Contributor to proceedings and professional journals.

WORK IN PROGRESS: A research project report on food production systems for the U.S. Department of Agriculture; a study of economic impact analysis for the U.S. Agency for International Development.

* * *

MARKSON, David M(errill) 1927-

PERSONAL: Born December 20, 1927, in Albany, N.Y.; son of Samuel A. (a newspaper editor) and Florence (a school teacher; maiden name, Stone) Markson; married Elaine Kretchmar (a literary agent), September 30, 1956; children: Johanna Lowry, Jed Matthew. *Education:* Union College, Schenectady, N.Y., B.A., 1950; Columbia University, M.A., 1952. *Politics:* Liberal Democrat. *Religion:* Jewish. *Home and office:* 39½ Washington Sq. S., New York, N.Y. 10012. *Agent:* Elaine Markson, 44 Greenwich Ave., New York, N.Y. 10011.

CAREER: *Albany Times-Union,* Albany, N.Y., staff writer, 1944-46, 1948-50; Weyerhauser Timber Co., Molalla, Ore., rigger, 1952; Dell Publishing Co., New York City, editor, 1953-54; Lion Books, New York City, editor, 1955-56; free-lance writer, 1956-64; Long Island University, Brooklyn Center, Brooklyn, N.Y., assistant professor of English, 1964-66; free-lance writer, 1966—. Part-time lecturer, Columbia University, 1977—. *Military service:* U.S. Army, 1946-48; became staff sergeant. *Member:* Louis Norman Newsom Memorial Society (executive secretary, 1973-80). *Awards, honors:* Fellow of Centro Mexicano de Escritores, 1960-61.

WRITINGS—Novels, except as indicated: (Editor) *Great Tales of Old Russia* (anthology), Pyramid Publications, 1956; *Epitaph for a Tramp,* Dell, 1959; *Epitaph for a Dead Beat,* Dell, 1961; *Miss Doll, Go Home,* Dell, 1965; *The Ballad of Dingus Magee,* Bobbs-Merrill, 1966; *Going Down,* Holt, 1970; *Springer's Progress,* Holt, 1977; *Malcolm Lowry's Volcano: Myth, Symbol, Meaning* (literary criticism), New York Times Co., 1978.

Also author of "Face to the Wind," a screenplay, Brut Productions, 1974. Contributor to magazines and newspapers, including *Saturday Evening Post, Nation, Atlantic,* and *Village Voice.*

WORK IN PROGRESS: A novel, as yet untitled; poetry.

SIDELIGHTS: David Markson achieved some notoriety with the publication of *The Ballad of Dingus Magee,* a parody of the Western novel complete with a ruthless young gunfighter, a corruptible sheriff, and a prosperous town bordello. According to a *Time* critic, the book "is stacked with enough sagebrush cliches to make it high Campfire. . . . Parts of the book are rollickingly funny parody, while other parts are slapstick." In a somewhat tongue-in-cheek review, Piers Brendon of *Books and Bookmen* writes: "Everyone has a cache of conviction inside him, however small, where to admit humour is to commit sacrilege. Personally, I can take jokes about the Virgin Mary, about disease, even about incest. But I do draw the line at laughing at the Wild West. . . . If God is dead one must have faith in something. I believe in John Wayne. However, Dingus Magee has shaken my simple faith. I feel rather like one of the Disciples who suddenly discovers that Christ has been secretly bottling the water which he has changed into wine and selling it at an exorbitant price." Dispelling his outrage, Brendon concludes that "there is plenty of action, plenty of bawdy and plenty of highly irreverent amusement in this novel." The book was filmed as "Dirty Dingus Magee" by M.G.M. in 1970, starring Frank Sinatra and George Kennedy.

In a review of *Going Down, Newsweek*'s S. K. Oberbeck writes: "A volcanic pretension bubbles at the bottom of the drama of a *menage a trois* of damaged U.S. expatriates nearing their doom in Mexico. It stumbles and stutters along in a dreamy barrage of elegant, unfinished sentences and unanswered rhetorical questions nipped at mid-phrase." Markson's unique style appears to be a favorite target for some critics who feel that it tends to detract from the underlying quality of his work. A *Virginia Quarterly Review* writer, for instance, calls him "an intelligent writer, often a humorous one, whose mannerisms tend to conceal his very solid attributes." But Christopher Lehmann-Haupt offers a possible explanation: "It may be that Mr. Markson is up to something here. On the other hand, it is equally possible that he is not. My reasoning runs as follows: If the prose style of fiction doesn't serve to illuminate the action it's describing, then it's either incompetent or it's meant to call attention to itself. . . . The prose of *Going Down* is by no means incompetent. It draws one's attention inexorably to the narrator, who turns out to be no one but the author himself." However, after arriving at this conclusion, Lehmann-Haupt decides that the illusion created by this method "is of a novelist, with nothing to say, trying to tell a story he doesn't believe for a minute."

David Markson was a close friend of author Malcolm Lowry. At various times he has lived in Mexico, Spain, Italy, and England.

BIOGRAPHICAL/CRITICAL SOURCES: Harvey Breit and Margerie Bonner Lowry, editors, *Selected Letters of Malcolm Lowry,* Lippincott, 1965; *Punch,* April 5, 1966; *Time,* April 22, 1966; *Books and Bookmen,* May, 1967; Leslie A. Fiedler, *The Return of the Vanishing American,* Stein & Day, 1968; *Newsweek,* April 6, 1970; *New York Times,* April 24, 1970; *Virginia Quarterly Review,* summer, 1970; *Union College Symposium,* winter, 1970-71; Douglas Day, *Malcolm Lowry,* Oxford University Press, 1974.

* * *

MARLOWE, Dan J(ames) 1914-

PERSONAL: Born July 10, 1914, in Lowell, Mass. *Education:* Studied business administration at Bentley School of Accounting and Finance. *Address:* P.O. Box 2590, Hollywood, Calif. 90028.

CAREER: Novelist. *Member:* Mystery Writers of America, British Crime Writers Association.

WRITINGS—Published by Gold Medal, except as indicated: *Doorway to Death,* Avon, 1959; *Killer with a Key,* Avon, 1959; *Doom Service,* Avon, 1960; *The Fatal Frails,* Avon, 1960; *Shake a Crooked Town,* Avon, 1961; *Backfire,* Berkley, 1961; *The Name of the Game Is Death,* 1962 (published in England as *Operation Overkill,* Coronet, 1973); *Strongarm,* 1963; *Never Live Twice,* 1964; *Death Deep Down,* 1965; (contributor) *Best Detective Stories of the Year,* Dutton, 1965; *The Vengeance Man,* 1966; *Nobody Laughs at Me,* 1966; *Four for the Money,* 1966; (with William Odell) *The Raven Is a Blood Red Bird,* 1967; *Route of the Red Gold,* 1967; *One Endless Hour,* 1969 (published in England as *Operation Endless Hour,* Coronet, 1975); *Operation Fireball,* 1969; *Flashpoint,* 1970, published as *Operation Flashpoint,* 1972; *Operation Breakthrough,* 1971; *Operation Checkmate,* 1972; *Operation Drumfire,* 1972; *Operation Stranglehold,* 1973; *Operation Whiplash,* 1973; *Operation Hammerlock,* 1974; *Operation Deathmaker,* 1975; *Operation Counterpunch,* 1976. Also contributor of 250 short stories and articles to mystery, suspense, adventure, and men's magazines.

WORK IN PROGRESS: Sachem, a humorous suspense novel.

SIDELIGHTS: Dan J. Marlowe's books have been translated into French, German, Italian, Swedish, Finnish, Danish, Norwegian, Japanese, Greek, Dutch, Afrikaans, Spanish, and Portuguese. *Avocational interests:* Sports, both active and spectator.

* * *

MARSH, John L(eslie) 1927-

PERSONAL: Born November 3, 1927, in Morristown, N.J.; son of Jack L. and Dorothy (Von Deilen) Marsh; married Charlotte Marie Anderson (a research associate), July 21, 1960; children: Arthur Andrew. *Education:* Syracuse University, B.A., 1950; University of Pennsylvania, M.A., 1953, Ph.D., 1959. *Politics:* Republican. *Religion:* Presbyterian. *Address:* P.O. Box 25, Edinboro, Pa. 16412. *Office:* Department of English, Edinboro State College, Edinboro, Pa. 16412.

CAREER: Edinboro State College, Edinboro, Pa., associate professor, 1960-66, professor of English, 1966—. *Military service:* U.S. Army Reserve, Military Intelligence, 1950-80; became colonel. *Member:* American Studies Association, Company of Military Historians, Popular Culture Association, American Society for Theatre Research, Theatre Historical Society, League of Historic Theatres.

WRITINGS: (With John Dove) *American Literature: A Televised Approach,* W. C. Brown, 1965, 2nd edition (with Charles Glendenning), 1968; (with Dove) *English Literature: A Televised Approach,* W. C. Brown, 1966, 2nd edition (with Glendenning), 1968; *A Student's Bibliography of American Literature,* Kendall/Hunt, 1971; *Of Prescriptions and Playbills: From the Diaries of Michael V. Ball* (monograph), Warren County Historical Society, 1973; *The Grandin Opera House, or Theatre on the Kerosene Circuit* (monograph), Warren County Historical Society, 1973; *Edinboro: A Dirt Street Town,* privately printed, 1976; *The Presbytery of Lake Erie: A Panorama,* Presbytery of Lake Erie, 1978.

WORK IN PROGRESS: A study of the theater of Opera House America, 1870-1914; a biography, *Colonel Fred E. Windsor: The Handsomest Man in the National Guard;* a monograph, *L. V. Kupper: A Dirt Street Town Photographer.*

* * *

MARSHALL, Sybil Mary (Edwards) 1913-

PERSONAL: Born November 26, 1913, in Ramsey, Huntingdon, England; daughter of William Henry (a farmer) and Kate (Papworth) Edwards; married Francis Marshall, August 27, 1939 (marriage dissolved, 1948); children: Prudence (Mrs. Anthony Atmore). *Education:* Exhall Training College, Ministry of Education teaching certificate, 1949; New Hall, Cambridge, Bachelor of Arts (English Honors), 1962, Master of Arts, 1967. *Religion:* Church of England. *Home:* 40, St. Mary's St., Ely, Cambridgeshire, England.

CAREER: Class teacher in Essex and Huntingdon schools, seven years; Kingston County Primary School, Cambridgeshire England, head teacher, eighteen years; University of Sheffield, Institute of Education, Sheffield, England, lecturer in primary education, five years; University of Sussex, Brighton, England, reader in primary education, ten years; full-time writer, 1976—. Lecturer on children's art, wit and humor, and subjects connected with English and literature to educational organizations, societies, and on the radio. Adviser for "Picture Box," Granada Television Ltd. *Member:* Independent Broadcasting Authority (member of school advisory committee).

WRITINGS: An Experiment in Education, Cambridge University Press, 1963; *Fenland Chronicle,* Cambridge University Press, 1966; *Adventure in Creative Education,* Pergamon, 1967; *Aspects of Art-Work,* Evans, 1969; *Expression,* six volumes, Hart-Davis, 1970; *Creative Writing,* Macmillan, 1974; (compiler) *Picture Box Companion,* Hart-Davis, 1974; *Polly at the Window,* Puffin, 1976; *Nicholas and Finnegan,* Puffin, 1977; *Once upon a Village,* Dent, 1979; *Tales the Greeks Told,* twelve volumes, Hart-Davis, 1979-80; *Everyman's Book of English Folk-Tales,* Dent, 1980; (with Anthony Atmore) *Living with Language,* Addison-Wesley, in press. Also author of "Lantern" series, Cambridge University Press, 1979—. Contributor to professional journals.

SIDELIGHTS: Sybil Mary Marshall told *CA:* "From the age of three, I prayed (literally) for a place 'to sit down and write.' I still find greater pleasure at my desk with a pen in my hand than anywhere else. I write now for my own pleasure, to continue to have some slight influence on the educational/literary scene, and for what little money it brings. I work at my desk about six hours a day, more if under pressure; but I give up and read for days on end.

"Since retirement I have (to my delight) been asked by publishers to write works other than those concerning education. I have found this entirely absorbing, and look forward to doing other books, including more books for children.

"My (very early) influence was the great English novelists, particularly Dickens, and the even greater American, Mark Twain. I believe I still look at life with a wryly humorous, though concerned, Dickensian/Twainish eye. It is probably reflected in my writing about English village life, and in my love of the tales of the folk. I view somewhat askance the contemporary inward-turning novel of psychological searching written in bald English and full of explicit sex/violence spattered with four-letter words. Though my own writing is often earthy, I'm content to be oldfashioned in this. Enough is as good as a feast—of sex and violence, better, I think."

MARSHALL, Tom 1938-

PERSONAL: Born April 9, 1938, in Niagara Falls, Ontario, Canada; son of Douglas Woodworth (a chemical engineer) and Helen (Kennedy) Marshall. *Education:* Queen's University, B.A., 1961, M.A., 1965. *Residence:* Kingston, Ontario, Canada. *Office:* Department of English, Queen's University, Kingston, Ontario, Canada.

CAREER: Queen's University, Kingston, Ontario, instructor, 1964-66, lecturer, 1966-69, assistant professor, 1969-73, associate professor of English, 1973—.

WRITINGS: (With Tom Eadie and Colin Norman) *The Beast with Three Backs* (poems), Quarry Press, 1965; *The Silences of Fire* (poems), Macmillan, 1969; *The Psychic Mariner* (critical study of poems by D. H. Lawrence), Viking, 1970; *A. M. Klein* (criticism), Ryerson, 1970; *Magic Water* (poems), Quarry Press, 1971; (editor with David Helwig) *Fourteen Stories High* (anthology), Oberon, 1971; *The Earth-Book* (poems), Oberon, 1974; *The White City* (poems), Oberon, 1976; *Rosemary Goal* (novel), Oberon, 1978; *Harsh and Lovely Land* (critical study), University of British Columbia Press, 1979; *The Elements* (poems), Oberon, 1980. Former chief editor of *Quarry;* poetry editor of *Canadian Forum.*

WORK IN PROGRESS: A book about Canadian fiction; several novels; a book of poems about people.

SIDELIGHTS: Tom Marshall wrote *CA:* "A poet attempts to make sense of the world, to discover what is real, for himself and others." He continues, "I am very concerned about Canada's national identity and the future of Canada, but more optimistic about it than some of my contemporaries seem to be. I am also interested in foreign countries and cultures, and enjoy travelling." With David Helwig, Gail Fox, and Stuart MacKinnon, he has made a sound recording of his own work, "Four Kingston Poets," Quarry Recordings, 1972.

* * *

MARTIN, Gerald Warren 1945- (Ged Martin)

PERSONAL: Born May 22, 1945, in Hornchurch, England; son of Percival Joseph Willing (a hospital administrator) and Edith Dorothy (Wheel) Martin; married Gillian Sanderson (a librarian), July 21, 1967. *Education:* Magdalene College, Cambridge, B.A. (first class honors), 1967, Ph.D., 1972. *Office:* Department of Modern History, University College, Cork, Ireland.

CAREER: Cambridge University, Magdalene College, Cambridge, England, Charles Kingsley Bye Fellow in History, 1969-70, research fellow, 1970-72; Australian National University, Canberra, Australia, research fellow in history, 1972-77; University College, Cork, Ireland, lecturer in modern history, 1977—. Has made broadcasts in Great Britain, North America, and New Zealand. *Member:* Historical Association (England), Australian Society for the Study of Labour History, Cambridge Historical Society. *Awards, honors:* M.A., Cambridge University, 1971.

WRITINGS—Under name Ged Martin: *A Visitor's Guide to Magdalene College, Cambridge,* Magdalene College, Cambridge University, 1971; *Durham Report and British Policy: A Critical Essay,* Cambridge University Press, 1972; (with Ronald Hyam) *Reappraisals in British Imperial History,* Macmillan, 1975; (editor) *The Founding of Australia,* Hale & Iremanger, 1978; *Episodes of Old Canberra,* Australian National University Press, 1978. Contributor to *Historical Journal, Journal of American Studies, Journal of Imperial and Commonwealth History, Albion, Irish Historical Studies, New Zealand Journal of History, Ontario History, Australian Economic History Review, Higher Education Review,* and *Sunday Times.*

WORK IN PROGRESS: Research on British attitudes to constitutional development in British North America between 1837 and 1867, and on British imperial history; a biography of Sir Francis Bond Mead.

* * *

MARTIN, Kenneth R(obert) 1938-

PERSONAL: Born February 12, 1938, in Upper Darby, Pa.; son of Kenneth Edward (a chemist) and Evelyn (Rankin) Martin; married Pamela Ann Miller (a college professor), December 19, 1968 (divorced, 1977). *Education:* Dickinson College, A.B., 1959; University of Pennsylvania, M.A., 1961, Ph.D., 1965. *Residence:* Walpole, Mass. *Office address:* Kendall Whaling Museum, P.O. Box 297, Sharon, Mass. 02067.

CAREER: Gettysburg College, Gettysburg, Pa., instructor, 1965-66, assistant professor of history, 1966-68; Slippery Rock State College, Slippery Rock, Pa., associate professor of history, 1968-74; Kendall Whaling Museum, Sharon, Mass., director, 1974—. Instructor at University of California Extension, Hawaii, 1976-78, and Nature Expeditions International, 1979—. Reviewer, National Endowment for the Humanities, 1979—. *Military service:* U.S. Army Reserve, 1959-67; became first lieutenant. *Member:* Pacific Historical Association. *Awards, honors:* Hagley Foundation research grant-in-aid, 1972.

WRITINGS: Delaware Goes Whaling, Eleutherian Mills-Hadley Foundation, 1973; *Whalemen and Whaleships of Maine,* Harpswell Press, 1975; (editor) *The Whaling Journal of John F. Martin,* David R. Godine, 1980; *Whalemen's Paintings and Drawings,* David R. Godine, in press. Editor, Kendall Whaling Museum series, 1977—. Contributor of articles and reviews to *Gettysburg Times, Historian, Mercer County History, National Antiques Review, Mankind, Victorian Studies, Down East, Magazine of Maine, Journal of Popular Culture, Wildlife News, Pennsylvania History, Delaware History, Oceans, Glimpses of Micronesia, Beaver, Hawaiian Journal of History,* and *Melville Society Extracts.* Editor, *Mercer County History,* 1970-72.

AVOCATIONAL INTERESTS: Travel, American primitive antiques and folk art, American jazz, and watercolorist.

* * *

MARTINSON, David (Keith) 1946-

PERSONAL: Born May 13, 1946, in San Diego, Calif.; son of Henry M. (an engineer) and Rosella (Olson) Martinson. *Education:* Moorhead State College, B.A., 1968; North Dakota State University, graduate study, 1969-72. *Home:* 404 18th Ave. S., Moorhead, Minn. 56560.

CAREER: Poet in the schools of Fargo, N.D., 1971-72, and St. Paul, Minn., 1972; resident poet in public school in Stillwater, Minn., 1972-73; Anishinabe Reading Materials, Duluth, Minn., director, 1975-78; Minnesota Chippewa Tribe, Cass Lake, writer-in-residence, 1978-79.

WRITINGS—Books of poems, except as indicated: *Three Pages,* privately printed, 1971; *Nineteen Sections from a Twenty Acre Poem,* Dakota Territory, 1973; (editor) *Moon of Many Bird Tails,* St. Paul Council of Arts and Sciences, 1973; *Bleeding the Radiator,* Territorial Press, 1974; *A Long Time Ago Is Just Like Today* (essays), Duluth Indian Education Advisory Committee, 1976; *A Cedar Grew from His Forehead* (essays), Meyer & Radosovitch, 1976; *Strips and Shavings,* Truck Press, 1978; (editor) *Time of the Indian: Angwamas Minosewag Anishinabeg,* Minnesota Chippewa Tribe, 1979.

Children's books; published by Anishinabe Reading Materials: *Real Wild Rice,* 1975; *Cheer Up Old Man,* 1975; *Manabozho and the Bullrushes,* 1976; *Shemay,* 1977; *Aseban,* 1978. Contributing editor, *Dakota Territory.*

WORK IN PROGRESS: A novel about the return of wild horses to these states, tentatively entitled *Postals;* daily meditations and concurrent poetics.

SIDELIGHTS: David Martinson once told *CA,* "I consider myself a poet of the land, and my poems are primarily overlays of the inevitable imagery of the soil and its precedence over 'the human' earth sciences, magic, and ecstasy." More recently he said that after more time in the world he would add "more emphasis on the human, on forgiveness and the need for relationship between peoples and their geographic connections."

* * *

MARTZ, John D(anhouse) 1934-

PERSONAL: Born July 8, 1934, in Latrobe, Pa.; son of John D. and Margaret (Sipe) Martz. *Education:* Harvard University, A.B. (magna cum laude), 1955; George Washington University, M.A., 1960; University of North Carolina, Ph.D., 1963. *Politics:* Democratic. *Home:* 2619 Acacia Dr., State College, Pa. 16801. *Office:* Department of Political Science, Pennsylvania State University, University Park, Pa. 16802.

CAREER: University of North Carolina at Chapel Hill, 1963-78, became professor of political science and chairman of department, assistant director of the Institute of Latin American Studies, 1966-78, director of graduate studies in political science, 1965-66, 1967-78; Pennsylvania State University, University Park, Pa., professor of political science and chairman of department, 1978—. Director of Latin American Summer Institute at Duke University and University of North Carolina, 1968. *Military service:* U.S. Army, 1957-59; became lieutenant. *Member:* American Political Science Association, Latin American Studies Association, Hispanic America Society, Southern Political Science Association, Southeastern Conference of Latin American Studies (president, 1972-73), Pi Sigma Mu, Pi Sigma Alpha. *Awards, honors:* Ford Foundation foreign area fellow, 1962-63; Guggenheim Foundation fellowship, 1966-67; National Science Foundation fellowship; Social Science Research Council fellowship.

WRITINGS: Colombia: A Contemporary Political Study, University of North Carolina Press, 1962; (editor) *Dynamics of Change in Latin American Politics,* Prentice-Hall, 1965, 2nd edition, 1971; *Accion Democratica: Evolution of a Modern Political Party in Venezuela,* Princeton University Press, 1966; *Central America: Crisis and Challenge,* University of North Carolina Press, 1969; (with Miguel Jorrin) *Latin American Political Thought,* University of North Carolina Press, 1970; *Ecuador: Conflicting Political Culture,* Allyn & Bacon, 1972; (with Enrique A. Baloyra) *Electoral Mobilization and Public Opinion: The Venezuelan Campaign of 1973,* University of North Carolina Press, 1976; (editor with David J. Myers) *Venezuela: The Democratic Experience,* Praeger, 1977; (with Baloyra) *Political Attitudes in Venezuela,* University of Texas Press, 1979. Contributor of monographs, book reviews, and articles to journals in his field.

WORK IN PROGRESS: Politics and Oil in Ecuador.

* * *

MASON, Douglas R(ankine) 1918-
(R. M. Douglas, John Rankine)

PERSONAL: Born September 26, 1918, in Hawarden, England; son of Russell (an engineer) and Bertha (Greenwood) Mason; married Norma Eveline Cooper (a social worker), May 26, 1945; children: Keith, Patricia (Mrs. Richard Morris), John, Elaine. *Education:* University of Manchester, B.A., 1947, teacher's diploma, 1948. *Politics:* "Liberal by inclination, Conservative sometimes by observation of policies." *Religion:* Methodist. *Home:* 16 Elleray Park Rd., Wallasey, Cheshire L45 OLH, England. *Agent:* E. J. Carnell, 17 Burwash Rd., Plumstead, London SE18 7QY, England.

CAREER: Taught in primary and secondary schools in Cheshire, England, 1950-67; St. George's Primary School, Wallasey, England, headmaster, 1967-78. *Military service:* British Army, Royal Signals Corps, 1939-46; served in Africa; became lieutenant. *Member:* National Association of Head Teachers, Wallasey Association of Head Teachers (president, 1973-74).

WRITINGS—Science fiction, published by R. Hale, except as indicated: *From Carthage Then I Came,* Doubleday, 1966, published as *Eight against Utopia,* Paperback Library, 1967; *Ring of Violence,* 1968, Avon, 1969; *Landfall Is a State of Mind,* 1968; *The Tower of Rizwan,* 1968; *The Janus Syndrome,* 1969; *Matrix,* Ballantine, 1970; *Satellite 54-0,* Ballantine, 1971; *Horizon Alpha,* Ballantine, 1971; *Dilation Effect,* Ballantine, 1971; *The Resurrection of Roger Diment,* Ballantine, 1972; *The Phaeton Condition,* Putnam, 1973; *The End Bringers,* Ballantine, 1973; *Pitman's Progress,* Elmfield Press, 1976; *The Omega Worm,* 1976; *Euphor Unfree,* 1977; *Mission to Pactolus R,* 1978. Also author of *Links over Space* and *The Vort Programme.*

Under pseudonym R. M. Douglas: *The Darkling Plain* (historical novel), 1979.

Under pseudonym John Rankine; published by Dobson, except as indicated: *The Blockade of Sinitron: Four Adventures of Dag Fletcher,* Thomas Nelson, 1964; *Interstellar Two Five,* 1966; *Never the Same Door,* 1967; *One Is One,* 1968; *Moons of Triopus,* 1968, Paperback Library, 1969; *Binary Z,* 1969; *The Weizman Experiment,* 1969; *The Plantos Affair,* 1971; *The Ring of Garamas,* 1972; *Operation Umanaq,* Ace Books, 1973; *The Bromius Phenomenon,* Ace Books, 1973; *The Fingalnan Conspiracy,* Sidgwick & Jackson, 1973; *Astral Quest,* Futura Publishing, 1975; *Moon Odyssey,* Futura Publishing, 1975; *Lunar Attack,* Futura Publishing, 1975; *Android Planet,* Futura Publishing, 1976; *The Thorburn Enterprise,* 1977; *The Star of Hesiock,* 1980.

WORK IN PROGRESS: A historical novel of the Saxon period, entitled *Sturmer;* science fiction novels.

* * *

MATENKO, Percy 1901-

PERSONAL: Born June 30, 1901, in Ekaterinoslav (now Dnepropetrovsk), Russia; naturalized U.S. citizen; son of Issac (founder and principal of first Yiddish school in Canada) and Helen (Moskowitch) Matenko; married Natalie Rubin, November 11, 1939; children: Anita Fay (Mrs. David Saunders). *Education:* University of Toronto, B.A., 1924, M.A., 1925; Columbia University, Ph.D., 1933. *Religion:* Jewish. *Home:* 2601 Glenwood Rd., Apt. 3J, Brooklyn, N.Y. 11210.

CAREER: Instructor in German in Extension Division, Columbia University, New York City, 1925-26, 1927-29, and at Hunter College (now Hunter College of the City University of New York), New York City, Evening School, 1928-35, Day Session, 1929-30; Brooklyn College of the City University of New York, Brooklyn, N.Y., instructor, 1930-37, assistant professor, 1937-52, associate professor, 1952-56, professor of German, 1956-65, professor emeritus, 1965—, adjunct professor of Yiddish, 1966-74. *Member:* Modern Language Association of America, American Association of Teachers of German, American Association of University Professors, American Association of Professors of Yiddish (president, 1973—), Association for Jewish Studies, Yiddish P.E.N., Leo Baeck Institute, Yivo Institute for Jewish Research, Verein der New Yorker Deutschlehrer. *Awards, honors:* Grants from Lucius N. Littauer Foundation, 1967, and Ingram Merrill Foundation, 1967, both for *Two Studies in Yiddish Culture,* and from Lucius N. Littauer Foundation, 1971, for *The Diary of the Vilna Ghetto.*

WRITINGS: (Author of introduction, commentary, and notes) *Tieck and Solger: The Complete Correspondence,* B. Westermann, 1933; (editor with Edwin H. Zeydel and Robert H. Fife) *Letters of Ludwig Tieck,* Modern Language Association of America, 1937; *Ludwig Tieck and America,* University of North Carolina Press, 1954; (editor with Zeydel and Bertha M. Masche) *Letters to and from Ludwig Tieck and His Circle,* University of North Carolina Press, 1967; *Two Studies in Yiddish Culture,* E. J. Brill, 1968, Part I: *The Aqedath Jishag* (author of introduction and notes with Samuel Sloan II), Part II: *Job and Faust* (translator and author of study); (contributor) Siegfried Mews, editor, *Studies in German Literature of the Nineteenth and Twentieth Centuries* (festschrift for Frederic E. Coenen), University of North Carolina Press, 1970; (translator and editor) *Yitskhok Rudashevski: The Diary of the Vilna Ghetto, June 1941-April 1943,* Ghetto Fighters' House (Israel), 1973; (contributor of translations) Saul L. Goodman, editor, *The Faith of Secular Jews,* Ktav Publishing, 1976. Contributor to *Encyclopedia of Literature, Encyclopedia Americana, Great Dictionary of the Yiddish Language,* and to yearbooks. Contributor of articles, original poetry, and poetry translations to *Poetry Workshop* (Brooklyn College), *Modern Language Quarterly, Jewish Frontier, Jewish Dialog, World of Yiddish, Dor le Dor,* and other language, literature, and history journals. Editorial consultant for work in German and Yiddish, *Britannica World Language Dictionary,* 2nd edition.

SIDELIGHTS: Percy Matenko comments: "My personal literary, as contrasted with my scholarly, endeavors were concentrated chiefly on the writing of original poetry and some prose in Yiddish, less so in English, and the translation of Yiddish poetry and prose into English. An essential element in this, as in all creative work, is obviously personal integrity and a striving formally, as far as the author is capable of doing so, for stylistic perfection."

* * *

MATHEWS, Richard (Barrett) 1944-

PERSONAL: Born November 16, 1944, in Washington, D.C.; son of James T., Jr. (a public relations representative) and Martha Anne (Moss) Mathews. *Education:* University of Florida, B.A., 1966; University of Heidelberg, graduate study, 1968-69; University of Virginia, Ph.D., 1973. *Home:* 5702 26th Ave. S., Gulfport, Fla. 33707. *Office address:* Konglomerati Press, P.O. Box 5001, Gulfport, Fla. 33737.

CAREER: Eckerd College, St. Petersburg, Fla., associate

professor of literature and poet-in-residence of writer's workshop, 1970-79; Konglomerati Press, Gulfport, Fla., founder, editor, publisher, and typesetter, 1971—. *Member:* Modern Language Association of America, College English Association, Committee of Small Magazine Editors and Publishers, American Civil Liberties Union, South Atlantic Modern Language Association, Florida College English Association, Phi Beta Kappa. *Awards, honors:* Woodrow Wilson fellowship, 1966-67; Academy of American Poets Prize, 1968, for "Pear Honey and Other Poems"; Rotary International foreign study fellowship, 1968-69; Inaugural Visiting fellow, William Morris Centre, 1975-76.

WRITINGS: *A Mummery* (poems), Konglomerati Press, 1971; *An Introductory Guide to the Utopian and Fantasy Writing of William Morris,* William Morris Centre (London), 1976; *Aldiss Unbound: The Science Fiction of Brian W. Aldiss,* Borgo Press, 1977; *Worlds beyond the World: The Fantastic Vision of William Morris,* Borgo Press, 1978; *Lightning from a Clear Sky: Tolkien, the Trilogy, and the Silmarillion,* Borgo Press, 1978; *The Clockwork Universe of Anthony Burgess,* Borgo Press, 1978.

Work represented in anthologies, including: *Adam among the Television Trees,* edited by Virginia Mollenkott, Word Books, 1971; *A Tumult for John Berryman,* edited by Marguerite Harris, Dryad Press, 1976; *A Geography of Poets,* edited by Edward Field, Bantam Books, 1979. Contributor to periodicals, including *Science Fiction and Fantasy Book Review, Louisville Review, Southern Poetry Review, Assembling, Apalachee Quarterly,* and *Small Press Review.* Founding editor, *Florida Quarterly,* 1967.

WORK IN PROGRESS: *The Magus and the Macroscope: The Science Fiction and Fantasy Writing of Piers Anthony; No Deposit: No Return,* a collection of poetry; *Emery Walker: An Eye for Detail,* a study of the "important and little-known Pre-Raphaelite photographer" to accompany a portfolio of his photographs.

SIDELIGHTS: Richard Mathews told *CA:* "My work as printer-publisher-editor at Konglomerati Press continues to occupy increasingly large portions of my time, and influences both my creative and critical writing. Work with letterpress typography has changed the shape of my poetry; and I find myself irresistibly drawn to write about types, book design, and fine printing. The disciplined work at the press has afforded closer coordination of hand, eye, heart and mind. I could hope for no more than the meeting of these in whatever work I do."

* * *

MAVES, Paul B(enjamin) 1913-

PERSONAL: Born April 21, 1913, in Burwell, Neb.; son of Benjamin C. and Ellen Alverda (Craun) Maves; married Mary Carolyn Hollman (a writer), September 10, 1939; children: Margaret Alverda Maves Hansell, David Hollman. *Education:* Nebraska Wesleyan University, A.B., 1936; Drew University, B.D., 1939, Ph.D., 1949; also studied at New York University, 1945-46, and Harvard University, 1957-58; Columbia University, visiting scholar, 1964-65. *Politics:* Democrat. *Home:* 10200 Edelweiss Cir., Merriam, Kans. 66203. *Office:* 5218 Oak St., Kansas City, Mo. 64112.

CAREER: Pastor of Methodist churches in Albany, N.Y., 1940-42, and Middlebury, Vt., 1942-45; New York University, New York City, instructor in education, 1945-46; Federal Council of Churches of Christ in America, research associate, 1946-48, acting executive secretary of department of pastoral services, 1948-49; Drew University, Madison, N.J., adjunct professor of human relations, 1948-49, assistant professor, 1949-51, associate professor, 1951-56, George T. Cobb Professor of Religious Education, 1956-67; National Council of Churches of Christ, New York City, associate executive director of department of educational development, 1967-70; St. Paul School of Theology, Kansas City, Mo., director of field education, 1970-75; Kingsley Manor, Los Angeles, Calif., administrator, 1975-78; National Shepherd's Center Development Project, Kansas City, Mo., director, 1978—. Staff associate, National Training Laboratories, Inc., 1960-70; delegate to White House Conference on Aging, 1961; member of board of directors, National Council on Aging, 1950-58; member of certification council, Board of Health and Welfare Ministries of United Methodist Church, 1964-72.

WRITINGS: (With J. Lennart Cedarleaf) *Older People and the Church* (Religious Book Club selection), Abingdon, 1949; *Christian Service to Older People* (pamphlet), Women's Division of Christian Services, Methodist Church, 1949; (editor) *The Practical Field in Theological Education* (pamphlet), Department of Pastoral Services, Federal Council of Churches of Christ in America, 1949; *The Christian Religious Education of Older People,* Department of Pastoral Services, Federal Council of Churches of Christ in America, 1950; (editor) *Anxiety in Religious Work and Medical Practice* (pamphlet), Clifton Springs Sanitarium, 1950; (contributor) J. Richard Spoon, editor, *Pastoral Care,* Abingdon, 1951; *They Shall Bring Forth Fruit in Age* (pamphlet), National Council of the Protestant Episcopal Church, 1951; *The Best Is Yet to Be,* Westminster, 1951; (editor) *The Church and Mental Health* (Religious Book Club selection), Scribner, 1953; *Understanding Ourselves as Adults,* Abingdon, 1959.

(Contributor) Marvin Taylor, editor, *Religious Education: A Comprehensive Survey,* Abingdon, 1960; (contributor) Clark Tibbitts, editor, *A Handbook of Social Gerontology,* University of Chicago Press, 1960; *On Becoming Yourself* (for seventh grade students), Graded Press, 1962; (with Charles Stewart) *Christian Faith and Emotional Health,* Abingdon, 1962; (with wife, Mary Carolyn Maves) *Finding Your Way through the Bible,* Graded Press and Abingdon, 1971; (with M. C. Maves) *Exploring How the Bible Came to Be,* Abingdon, 1973; (with M. C. Maves) *Discovering How the Bible Message Spread,* Abingdon, 1973; *A Faith for Growing: A Manual for Working with Older Volunteers,* Judson Press, 1980.

Author of curriculum materials for the Methodist church. Contributor to *Encyclopedia for Church Group Leaders.* Contributor of about fifty articles and reviews to church publications and theology and other journals, including *Church School, Child Guidance, Workers on Youth, Adult Teacher, Mature Years,* and *International Journal of Religious Education.* Guest editor, *Pastoral Psychology,* September, 1954.

WORK IN PROGRESS: A pastoral aid booklet dealing with need to change living arrangements in old age, for Augsburg Press.

AVOCATIONAL INTERESTS: Writing poetry.

* * *

MAYHALL, Mildred P(ickle) 1902-

PERSONAL: Born December 20, 1902, in Austin, Tex.; daughter of David J. (a lawyer) and Birdie Mildred (Givens) Pickle; married Temple B. Mayhall (an architect), September 12, 1925; children: David James, William Sherry. *Education:* University of Texas, B.A., 1924, M.A., 1926, Ph.D.,

1939; University of Chicago, postgraduate study, three summers. *Politics:* Democrat. *Religion:* Methodist. *Home and office:* 3308 Enfield Rd., Austin, Tex. 78703.

CAREER: University of Texas, Main University (now University of Texas at Austin), Austin, instructor in anthropology, 1927-45; Stephen F. Austin High School, Austin, teacher of social studies, 1956-64; currently full-time writer. *Member:* American Anthropological Association, Daughters of American Revolution, American Rose Society (consulting rosarian), Texas State Historical Association, Daughters of the Republic of Texas, Phi Beta Kappa, Chi Upsilon, Kappa Delta Pi, Pi Lambda Theta, Sigma Xi. *Awards, honors:* Award of merit from the American Association for State and Local History for filmstrip, "The Indians of Texas"; special citation for sponsorship of Junior Historians; Summerfield G. Roberts Award for best book on the Republic of Texas for 1972 from Sons of the Republic of Texas, 1973, for *Texas Wild Flowers*.

WRITINGS: The Kiowas, University of Oklahoma Press, 1962, 2nd edition, 1971; *Indian Wars of Texas,* Texian Press, 1965; (editor and contributor) Eliza Griffin Johnston, *Texas Wild Flowers,* Shoal Creek Publishers, 1972; (with others) *Texas and Its History,* Graphic Ideas, 1972, revised edition, Pepper, Jones, Martinez, 1978. Also co-editor of *This Is Austin* (guidebook), Austin Junior Historians, 1964. Author of filmscript, "The Indians of Texas," 1959. Contributor to *True West, Southwestern Heritage, American Rose,* and other periodicals; reviewer, Texas State Historical Association *Quarterly, West Texas Historical Association Year Book,* and *Austin American-Statesman.*

WORK IN PROGRESS: A historical novel about an Indian chief; research for a book on the Comanches; stories for a short story collection; *The Alabama-Coushatta Indians of the Big Thicket.*

SIDELIGHTS: Mildred P. Mayhall told *CA* about the difficulties she encountered in getting her first book published. "I was asked to write *The Kiowas* by a professor of history when I attended his seminar history course one summer," she writes. "He said he wanted history, not anthropology. . . . I wrote the manuscript as history alone, but wished I could add the fascinating anthropology. It took almost two years. . . . I thought my history professor was going to be delighted. But he wasn't. He said 'It's got too many anthropological words that nobody can understand.' He kept the manuscript a year. Then I decided to send my carbon copy to the University of Oklahoma Press. . . . They kept it a year!" After much waiting and offering the manuscript to another publishing house only to have it refused because it had already been offered, without a definite response, she gave the University of Oklahoma another chance. "They wanted it if I would add some anthropology to it. . . . I started over, delighted to rewrite my manuscript. . . . I had started it in 1956," and it was finally published in 1962.

AVOCATIONAL INTERESTS: Archeology, gardening (hybridizing of roses, iris), horseback riding.

* * *

MAYOR, A(lpheus) Hyatt 1901-1980

PERSONAL: Born June 28, 1901, in Gloucester, Mass.; died February 28, 1980, in New York, N.Y.; son of Alfred Goldsborough (a marine biologist) and Harriet (Hyatt) Mayor; married Virginia Sluder (an executive secretary), June 22, 1932; children: Alfred, Martha (Mrs. Joseph Yeardley Smith). *Education:* Princeton University, A.B., 1922; Oxford University, B.Litt., 1926; attended American School of Classical Studies, 1926-27. *Religion:* Episcopalian. *Home:* 51 East 97th St., New York, N.Y. 10029. *Office:* Hispanic Society of America, New York, N.Y. 10032; and Metropolitan Museum of Art, New York, N.Y.

CAREER: Taught art history at Vassar College, Poughkeepsie, N.Y. for one year; School of the American Laboratory Theatre, New York City, lecturer, 1928-32; Metropolitan Museum of Art, New York City, staff member of department of prints, 1932-66, curator of prints, 1946-66, curator emeritus, 1966-80; Hispanic Society of America, New York City, president, 1955-80. Trustee of Instituto de Valencia de Don Juan and of Sorolla Museum, both Madrid, Spain, and of Brookgreen Gardens, Georgetown, S.C. *Member:* American Federation of Arts (trustee), Real Academia de Bellas Artes (Madrid), Real Academia de Santa Isabel de Hungria (Seville), Grolier Club (New York), Century Club (New York). *Awards, honors:* Rhodes Scholar, Oxford University, 1926; Boston Museum Award, 1971; Majorie Peabody Waite Award from American Academy of Arts and Letters, 1973; American Federation of Arts Award, 1979; Mayor's Award of Honor for Arts and Culture, 1979.

WRITINGS: The Bibiena Family, Herbert Bittner, 1945; *Baroque and Romantic Stage Design,* Herbert Bittner, 1950; *Giovanni Battista Piranesi,* Herbert Bittner, 1952; *Venice: A City in Slippers,* Arts, 1961; *Prints and People : A Social History of Printed Pictures,* Metropolitan Museum of Art, 1971; *Popular Prints of the Americas,* Crown, 1973; *Goya: Sixty-Seven Drawings,* Metropolitan Museum of Art, 1974; *American Art at the Century,* Century Association, 1977; *Metropolitan Museum of Art Favorite Paintings,* Crown, 1979. Contributor to *Metropolitan Museum Bulletin* and other art magazines. Co-editor, *Hound and Horn,* 1929-32.

WORK IN PROGRESS: Illustrated festival books.

SIDELIGHTS: A. Hyatt Mayor spent much of his life involved with the print collection of the New York Metropolitan Museum of Art. His opinion of prints, as presented in his book *Prints and People,* was that they are primarily a form of communication. The fact that an unlimited number of prints can be produced thus distinguishes them from other forms of art in which there is only one original copy.

In a *Washington Post* obituary, J. Y. Smith noted that "items that Mr. Mayor added to the museum's engravings and woodblocks by such masters as Rembrandt and Durer, included wine labels, mail-order catalogues, which are useful as references on topics such as furniture, and one of the world's finest collections of cigarette insert-cards and similar emphemera. He thought the cards, once cheap and easy to come by and now expensive and rare, attractive as well as interesting."

BIOGRAPHICAL/CRITICAL SOURCES: New York Times, June 19, 1966; *Washington Post,* March 2, 1980.

* * *

McAFEE, (James) Thomas 1928-

PERSONAL: Born May 13, 1928. *Education:* University of Missouri, A.B., 1949, M.A., 1950. *Office:* Department of English, 231 A & S Building, University of Missouri, Columbia, Mo. 65211.

CAREER: University of Missouri—Columbia, currently professor of English. *Member:* Authors League, Authors Guild. *Awards, honors:* Pulitzer Prize nomination and William Faulkner Award nomination, both for *Rover Youngblood;* National Council on the Arts prize for short story, "Lady of the World"; National Endowment for the Arts creative writing fellowship grant, 1976-77.

WRITINGS: Poems and Stories, University of Missouri Press, 1960; *I'll Be Home Late Tonight* (poems), University of Missouri Press, 1967; (contributor) Charles Willig, editor, *Four Poets,* Central College (Pella, Iowa), 1967; *Rover Youngblood* (novel), Baron, 1969; *The Body and the Guest: New and Selected Poems,* Bookmark, 1975; *Time Now* (poems), Raindust Press, 1977; *The Tempo Changes. The Lights Go Up. The Partners Change.* (poems), Singing Wind Publications, 1978; *Whatever Isn't Glory* (short stories), Singing Wind Publications, 1979.

Work is represented in anthologies, including: *Modern Short Stories,* Grosset, 1961; James Moffett and Kenneth R. McElheny, editors, *Points of View,* Signet, 1966; George Garrett, editor, *The Girl in the Black Raincoat,* Duell, Sloan & Pearce, 1966; George Plimpton and Vance Bourjaily, editors, *American Literary Anthology,* Volume II, Random House, 1969; Wallace Kaufman and William Powers, editors, *The Writer's Mind,* Prentice-Hall, 1970; Louis M. Savary and Thomas J. O'Connor, editors, *Finding God, Finding Each Other,* Paulist/Newman, 1971; Charles Sanders, editor, *The Scope of Satire,* Scott, Foresman, 1971; John Bigby and Russell Hill, editors, *Language Is a Way of Saying,* Houghton, 1972; Bigby and Hill, editors, *Options: A Program for English,* Houghton, 1973; Per Engell Christensen, editor, *American Scenes,* Gyldendal, 1978.

Contributor of more than a hundred cartoons, poems, and stories to poetry magazines, literary journals, and other periodicals, including *Contempora, Inscape, Mill Mountain Review, Carleton Miscellany, Country Clothes, Perspective, Approach, Esquire, Contact, Sou'wester, Epoch, Prairie Schooner, Gambit, Blue Guitar,* and *Bard Review.*

SIDELIGHTS: Thomas McAfee told *CA:* "I have been writing for almost as long as I can remember. I write because I want to try to find out something about myself, because I love language, and because I'm fascinated by mystery (especially the mystery of the imagination)."

BIOGRAPHICAL/CRITICAL SOURCES: Virginia Quarterly Review, autumn, 1967; *Kenyon Review,* Volume XXXI, Number 3, 1969; *Best Sellers,* November 1, 1969.

* * *

McBRIDE, (Mary) Angela Barron 1941-

PERSONAL: Born January 16, 1941, in Baltimore, Md.; daughter of John Stanley (a police lieutenant) and Mary C. (a seamstress; maiden name, Szczepanski) Barron; married William Leon McBride (a philosophy professor), June 12, 1965; children: Catherine Alexandra, Kara Angela. *Education:* Georgetown University, B.S.N., 1962; Yale University, M.S.N., 1964; Purdue University, Ph.D., 1978. *Home:* 744 Cherokee Ave., Lafayette, Ind. 47905. *Office:* Department of Psychiatric/Mental Health Nursing, Indiana University School of Nursing, Indianapolis, Ind. 46223.

CAREER: Bon Secours Hospital, Baltimore, Md., practical nurse on Medical-Surgical Service, summer, 1960; St. Elizabeths Hospital, Washington, D.C., fellow in psychiatric nursing work-study program, summer, 1961; Johns Hopkins Hospital, Phipps Clinic, Baltimore, staff nurse, summer, 1962, evening charge nurse, summer, 1963; Connecticut Valley State Hospital, Middletown, Conn., director of psychiatric work-study program, summer, 1964; Yale University, School of Nursing, New Haven, Conn., instructor, 1964-67, lecturer, 1967-68, assistant professor of psychiatric/mental health nursing, 1968-73, coordinator of clinical experience for graduate students, 1965-67, research assistant, 1969-71, associate director of Program for Studying Psychiatric Nursing and Demands for Mental Health Care, 1969-72, director, 1972-73; Purdue University, West Lafayette, Ind., acting instructor in philosophy, 1974; Indiana University, School of Nursing, Indianapolis, associate professor in graduate program, 1978—, assistant chairperson of department of psychiatric/mental health nursing, 1979—. Adjunct professor, department of psychology, Indiana University-Purdue University at Indianapolis, 1980—. Lecturer to professional groups, workshops, and public service organizations; has appeared on radio and television programs. Consultant to Concept Media for two nursing films, 1970, National Institute of Mental Health, 1972, Children's Television Network, 1972 and 1973, Springer Publishing Co., 1974, John Wiley & Sons, 1976, Consortium on Parenthood Aptitude, 1977, and to Maternity League of Indiana, 1980—.

MEMBER: American Nurses Association (member of Council of Specialists in Psychiatric and Mental Health Nursing; member of Council of Nurse Researchers), American Psychological Association, National Council on Family Relations, Society for Research in Child Development, National Foundation for Women's Health, National Women's Health Network, Association for Women in Psychology, American Association for the Advancement of Science, Authors Guild, Authors League of America, National Organization for Women, American Civil Liberties Union, Yale University School of Nursing Alumnae Association (member of board of directors, 1967-69), Sigma Theta Tau. *Awards, honors: New York Times Book Review* and *American Journal of Nursing* cited *The Growth and Development of Mothers* as one of the best books of 1973; Distinguished Alumna Award, Yale University School of Nursing, 1978; American Nurses Foundation scholar, 1979.

WRITINGS: (Editor and author of preface, introduction, and epilogue) *Psychiatric Nursing and the Demand for Comprehensive Health Care* (monograph), Yale University Printing Office, 1972; *The Growth and Development of Mothers,* Harper, 1973; *A Married Feminist,* Harper, 1976, published as *Living with Contradictions: A Married Feminist,* Colophon Books, 1977; (contributor with V. Henderson) Henderson and G. Nite, editors, *The Principles and Practice of Nursing,* 6th edition (McBride was not associated with earlier editions), Macmillan, 1978; (contributor with husband, William L. McBride) B. Bandman and E. L. Bandman, editors, *Bioethics and Human Rights,* Little, Brown, 1978; (contributor) M. A. Kay, editor, *An Anthropology of Birth,* F. A. Davis, in press. Contributor of articles and reviews to professional journals and popular publications, including *American Journal of Nursing, Nursing Outlook, Glamour, Ms.,* and *New Woman.*

WORK IN PROGRESS: Research on the perceptions of new mothers; a book on the psychology of overweight.

SIDELIGHTS: In a *Library Journal* review of *The Growth and Development of Mothers,* Marian Petrow says that Angela Barron McBride "explores and explodes the 'motherhood mystique,' and offers viable options to the idealized mother role . . . so that women and men will be able to grow along with their children." Letty Cottin Pogrebin of the *New York Times Book Review* writes: "Here is a book that describes the very essence of motherhood with trenchant but loving honesty. It demonstrates the irony that courtship and the honeymoon, the most self-centered periods of life, should be followed by having babies." Pogrebin feels that "the first half of the book offers more incisive, practical advice for living hassle-free with kids than can be bought in a year's worth of family therapy. But it is the second half of this work that established Angela Barron McBride as a first-rate mind and a keen psycho-social theorist. . . . It is not too dramatic to say that if you have children the last sixty-five pages of this book can change your mind and your life."

In a review of *A Married Feminist*, a *Publisher's Weekly* writer states that "the author's writing is swift, entertaining and (above all) persuasive. . . . She has examined most of the literature which shows how women have been relegated to fill the roles of housekeeper, sex object, cook." And the *Washington Post Book World*'s Gabrielle Burton writes: "Angela Barron McBride is a married feminist—'a walking talking mass of contradictions'—who is striving for a rich relationship of equals which contains 'the best of the old and the best of the new.' After reading her book, my odds are that both she and her marriage will endure, for Barron McBride has integrity, pluck, humor and a sense of adventure. . . . With both relish and respect, she takes on a widely disparate crew of people who have influenced her—Freud, Florence Nightingale, Aquinas, Erikson, Erma Bombeck—but sometimes, as when she considers Sartre . . . with a kind of brooding awe, her interest and intensity do not compensate for the lengthy, often downright obscure, philosophical quotes. Sensing this possible flaw herself, she later says that her book 'has been rather heavy on academic references, perhaps more than were needed to make a particular point. I still can't believe that women have been held in so little regard and I keep having to quote chapter and verse to remind myself that whatever feelings of persecution I have are real.' "

Angela Barron McBride told *CA:* "Both my recent writings and my research in progress reflect an interest in the lived experience of women. I am particularly interested in criticizing the professional literature in light of women's everyday concerns."

BIOGRAPHICAL/CRITICAL SOURCES: Library Journal, April 15, 1973; *New York Times Book Review,* June 17, 1973; *Publisher's Weekly,* February 23, 1976; *Washington Post Book World,* July 2, 1976.

* * *

McCABE, John Charles III 1920-

PERSONAL: Born November 14, 1920, in Detroit, Mich.; son of Charles J. (an engineer) and Rosalie (Dropiewski) McCabe; married Vija Valda Zarina (a ballet teacher), October 19, 1958; children: Linard Peter, Sean Cahal, Deirdre Rose. *Education:* University of Detroit, Ph.B., 1947; Fordham University, M.F.A., 1948; Shakespeare Institute of University of Birmingham, Stratford-upon-Avon, England, Ph.D., 1954. *Politics:* Liberal Unionist. *Religion:* Roman Catholic. *Home:* Box 363, Mackinac Island, Mich. 49757. *Office:* 498 Sheridan Dr., Sault Ste. Marie, Mich. 49783.

CAREER: Wayne University (now Wayne State University), Detroit, Mich., instructor in theatre, 1948-51; City College of New York (now City College of the City University of New York), New York City, instructor in speech, 1955-56; New York University, New York City, assistant professor, 1956-58, associate professor, 1958-63, professor of theatre and chairman of department of dramatic art, 1963-67; Mackinac College, Mackinac Island, Mich., professor of theatre and chairman of department, 1967-70; Lake Superior State College, Sault Ste. Marie, Mich., author-in-residence, 1970—. Producer, writer, actor, and director of plays and films, 1943-62. *Military service:* U.S. Army Air Forces, 1943-45; became sergeant. *Member:* Actors Equity Association, Shakespeare Association of America, Catholic Actors Guild, Lambs, Players.

WRITINGS—All published by Doubleday, except as indicated: *Mr. Laurel and Mr. Hardy,* 1961, revised edition, Grosset, 1967; *George M. Cohan: The Man Who Owned Broadway,* 1973; *The Comedy World of Stan Laurel,* 1974; (with Al Kilgore and Dick Bann) *Laurel and Hardy,* Dutton, 1975; (with G. B. Harrison) *Proclaiming the Word,* Pueblo Press, 1976; *Charlie Chaplin,* 1978. Contributor to *Variety* and *Detroit News.* Consultant to James Cagney for *Cagney by Cagney* (autobiography), Doubleday, 1976.

WORK IN PROGRESS: A show business novel.

SIDELIGHTS: John McCabe told *CA:* "The theatre—into which I was born—became for me (perhaps inevitably) a paradigm of what life should be. As my years increased, I never saw essential reason to alter that view, and indeed in my maturity that opinion is constantly being reaffirmed. Our dear Will [Shakespeare] put life's outline clearly in the Seven Ages speech, and Christ set forth its best functional impulses in the Sermon on the Mount. Everything that I have experienced in life—both as a man and writer—reassures me that this pattern of life is not only drama unending but the deepest truth as well.

"The theatre—and in that I include film, radio, television, journalism, and all writing—when it does its job best both entertains and tells the truth. This is what I have tried to do as a writer.

"I love good wine, O. Henry, classic chili, the word 'grape,' blue, the songs of Noel Coward, Mackinac Island, water, the plays of Shaw, O'Casey, Shakespeare, and W. S. Gilbert, *The Tavern,* by George M. Cohan, 104 of the 105 films made by Laurel and Hardy, ["Twice Two" being the exception,] James Cagney, most Jesuits, London, potato salad, Stratford-upon-Avon, Mozart, draught beer, Dublin, God, and my family."

BIOGRAPHICAL/CRITICAL SOURCES: Variety, March 14, 1973; *New Yorker,* March 31, 1973; *New York Times Book Review,* May 14, 1978.

* * *

McCAIG, Robert Jesse 1907- (Edith Engren, a joint pseudonym)

PERSONAL: Born September 8, 1907, in Seattle, Wash.; son of Jesse Sefton and Lillian (McCabe) McCaig; married Edith V. Engren, 1953. *Education:* Attended public schools in Great Falls, Mont. *Home and office:* 2500 Fifth Ave. N., Great Falls, Mont. *Agent:* Lenniger Literary Agency, 250 West 57th St., New York, N.Y. 10019.

CAREER: Paris Dry Goods Company, Great Falls, Mont., receiving clerk, 1923-25; Montana Power Company, Great Falls, divisional assistant, 1925-63, division chief accountant, 1963-72. *Member:* Western Writers of America (director, 1961-62; president, 1975-76).

WRITINGS: Toll Mountain, Dodd, 1953; *Haywire Town,* Dodd, 1954; *Danger West!,* Dodd, 1954; *Ghost Town,* Collins, 1955; *Bronc Stomper,* Dodd, 1956; *Sun and the Dust,* Collins, 1957; *Snow on the Prairie,* Collins, 1958; *The Rangemaster,* Ace Books, 1958; *Wild Justice,* Macmillan, 1959; *Drowned Man's Lode,* Macmillan, 1960 (published in England as *Five Dead Men,* Collins, 1962); *The Burntwood Men,* Macmillan, 1961; *That Nester Kid* (juvenile), Scribner, 1961; *Crimson Creek,* Macmillan, 1963; *Electric Power in America,* Putnam, 1967; *The Gotherson Spread,* Berkley, 1967; *The Shadow Maker,* Ace Books, 1970; *The Danger Trail,* Doubleday, 1975; *Stoneman's Gap,* Ballantine, 1976; (with wife, Edith McCaig, under joint pseudonym Edith

Engren) *Marcy Tarrant*, Fawcett, 1978; (contributor) *Water Trails West*, Doubleday, 1978. Contributor of short stories to *Adventure, Blue Book*, and *Black Mask;* contributor to *Montana: The Magazine of Western History*.

AVOCATIONAL INTERESTS: Photography, history.

* * *

McCALL, John R(obert) 1920-

PERSONAL: Born August 3, 1920; son of John H. (a banker) and Mary (Walsh) McCall; married Mary Hanley, October 21, 1974. *Education:* St. Bernard's College, A.B., 1942; Boston College, M.A., 1947; Catholic University of America, M.A., 1949, Ph.D., 1955. *Home:* 4312 Lambeth Dr., Raleigh, N.C. 27609. *Office:* Director of Human Services, North Carolina Department of Correction, Raleigh, N.C. 27603.

CAREER: Fairfield University, Fairfield, Conn., professor of education and psychology, 1954-57, founder and director of guidance program; Boston College, Boston, Mass., professor of psychology, 1959-69, founder and director of Institute for the Study of Religious Education and Service, 1970-74; North Carolina Department of Correction, Raleigh, director of human services, 1975—. Adjunct professor of criminal justice, North Carolina State University at Raleigh, 1977—. *Member:* American Psychological Association, American Correctional Association (president of North Carolina chapter), Mental Health Association of North Carolina (president).

WRITINGS: Sex Differences in Intelligence: A Comparative Factor Study, Catholic University Press, 1955; *Playing It Straight with Youth*, Hi-Time Publishers, 1972; *Growing Up*, Paulist/Newman, 1972; *The Free and the Colonized Person*, Dimension Press, 1974; *Dimensions in Religious Education*, CIM Publishers, 1975.

* * *

McCALL, Thomas S(creven) 1936-

PERSONAL: Born September 1, 1936, in Dallas, Tex.; son of John Dean (an attorney) and Hazel (Bradfield) McCall; married Carolyn Sue Wilson (a registered nurse), August 2, 1958; children: Thomas Kevin, Carol Kathleen. *Education:* University of Texas, Main University (now University of Texas at Austin), B.A., 1957; Talbot Theological Seminary, B.D., 1961, Th.M., 1962; Dallas Theological Seminary, Th.D., 1965. *Home:* 6516 Aberdeen Ave., Dallas, Tex. 75230. *Office:* American Board of Mission to the Jews, Inc., 5324 West Northwest Highway, Dallas, Tex. 75220.

CAREER: Ordained Baptist minister, 1958; American Board of Missions to the Jews, missionary affiliated with Los Angeles, Calif. branch, 1958-62, missionary and national director, Dallas, Tex., 1962—. Visiting professor in Christian Ethics and Eschatology, Dallas Bible College, 1965-66; lecturer, Biola College, 1975. *Member:* Sons of American Revolution (former chaplain; president of Dallas chapter), Sons of Confederate Veterans (chaplain), Civitan International.

WRITINGS: (With Zola Levitt) *Satan in the Sanctuary*, Moody, 1973; (contributor) *When Is Jesus Coming Again?*, Creation House, 1974; (with Levitt) *The Coming Russian Invasion of Israel*, Moody, 1974; *Raptured*, Harvest House, 1975; (editor) *America in History and Bible Prophecy*, Moody, 1976; *Israel and Tomorrow's Temple*, Moody, 1977; *The Bible Jesus Read Is Exciting*, Doubleday, 1978; *Christ in the Passover*, McCall Books, 1978; *The Seven Feasts of Israel*, McCall Books, 1978. Contributor of articles to numerous periodicals, including *Bibleotheca Sacra, The Chosen People, Christian Life*, and *Bible Expositor and Illuminator*.

WORK IN PROGRESS: Biblical prophecy; studies in Old Testament sacrifices; archaeology.

* * *

McCALL, Virginia Nielsen 1909-
(Virginia Nielsen)

PERSONAL: Born June 14, 1909, in Idaho Falls, Idaho; daughter of Jesse Hans (a sheep rancher and teacher) and Florence (Kingston) Nielsen; married Robert M. Pressey, April 4, 1938 (deceased); married Joseph R. McCall (a park ranger), April 21, 1943. *Education:* Attended University of Idaho, 1927-29, and Utah State Agricultural College (now Utah State University), 1931. *Home and office:* 9028 Talisman Dr., Sacramento, Calif. 95826. *Agent:* Paul R. Reynolds, Inc., 12 East 41st St., New York, N.Y. 10017.

CAREER: Free-lance writer. Member of staff of writers' conferences in California, Utah, Washington, and Texas. *Member:* National League of American Penwomen, Inc., Authors Guild, Authors League of America, California Writers Club.

WRITINGS: Navy Nurse, Messner, 1968; (with husband, Joseph R. McCall) *Your Career in Parks and Recreation*, Messner, 1970, revised edition, 1974; (with J. R. McCall) *Outdoor Recreation, Forest, Park, and Wilderness*, Glencoe, 1977; *Civil Service Careers*, F. Watts, 1977.

Under name Virginia Nielsen: *Try to Forget Me*, Doubleday, 1942; *Cadet Widow*, Doubleday, 1942; *Bewildered Heart*, Arcadia House, 1946; *The Golden One*, Arcadia House, 1947; *Journey to Love*, Bouregy, 1959; *Remember Me*, Bouregy, 1960; *Dangerous Dream*, Bouregy, 1961; *The Road to the Valley*, McKay, 1961; *The Mystery of Fyfe House*, Bouregy, 1962; *The Whistling Winds*, McKay, 1964; *Keoni, My Brother*, McKay, 1965; *Kimo and Madame Pele*, McKay, 1966; *The Mystery of Secret Town*, McKay, 1969; *Adassa and Her Hen*, McKay, 1971; *Seven Tides*, Bantam Books, 1972; *Yankee Lover*, Doubleday, 1978; *The Marriage Contract*, Doubleday, 1980.

WORK IN PROGRESS: A Faraway Love, for Fawcett-Gold Medal.

AVOCATIONAL INTERESTS: Painting, crafts.

* * *

McCANDLESS, Perry 1917-

PERSONAL: Born December 9, 1917, in Lincoln, Mo.; son of William Albert (an auctioneer) and Edith (Graves) McCandless; married Opal Braland, July 5, 1947; children: Richard Lee, Anne Christine. *Education:* Central Missouri State College (now University), B.S., 1941; Southern Methodist University, M.A., 1948; University of Missouri, Ph.D., 1953. *Politics:* Democratic. *Religion:* Methodist. *Home:* 609 Christopher, Warrensburg, Mo. 64093. *Office:* Department of History, Central Missouri State University, Warrensburg, Mo. 64093.

CAREER: Central Missouri State University, Warrensburg, assistant professor, 1949-50 and 1953-56, associate professor, 1956-60, professor of history, 1960—. *Military service:* U.S. Army Air Forces, 1941-45; became master sergeant. *Member:* Organization of American Historians, State Historical Society of Missouri, Missouri State Teachers Association, Johnson County Historical Society.

WRITINGS: Constitutional Government in Missouri, Sernoll, 1971, 2nd edition, 1976; *The Missouri Story,* Sernoll, 1971, 2nd edition, 1978; *The Missouri Experience,* Sernoll, 1972; (with John Crockett) *A History of Missouri, 1820-1860,* University of Missouri Press, 1972; *Missouri: Then and Now,* Steck, 1976. Contributor to numerous encyclopedias, including *American Peoples Encyclopedia, Encyclopedia Americana,* and others; contributor of articles to *Missouri Historical Review* and other periodicals.

* * *

McCARTHY, Joseph Weston 1915-1980
(Joe McCarthy)

PERSONAL: Born March 6, 1915, in Cambridge, Mass.; died January 30, 1980, in Central Islip, Long Island, New York; son of Dennis F. and Elizabeth (Doyle) McCarthy; married Mary Dunn, December 21, 1941; children: Susan (Mrs. Michael Todd, Jr.), Elizabeth Doyle (Mrs. John Huckle), Dennis, Mary Dunn (Mrs. Richard Giza). *Education:* Boston College, A.B., 1939. *Politics:* Democrat. *Religion:* Roman Catholic. *Residence:* Blue Point, N.Y. 11715. *Agent:* Helen Strauss, William Morris Agency, 1350 Avenue of the Americas, New York, N.Y. 10019.

CAREER: Boston Post, Boston, Mass., reporter and sportswriter, 1936-40; radio and publicity writer, Boston, 1940-41; *Cosmopolitan,* articles editor, 1946-48; free lance writer, 1948-80. *Military service:* U.S. Army, 1941-45; became master sergeant; awarded Legion of Merit.

WRITINGS: The Remarkable Kennedys, Dial, 1960; *In One Ear,* Doubleday, 1962; (editor) *Fred Allen's Letters,* Doubleday, 1965; *Hurricane!,* American Heritage, 1970; (contributor) Kenneth P. O'Donnell and David F. Powers, *Johnny, We Hardly Knew Ye,* Little, Brown, 1972; *Days and Nights at Costello's* (memoirs), Little, Brown, 1980. Author of "Life World Library" book on Ireland, 1964. Contributor to national magazines such as *Life, Saturday Evening Post, Reader's Digest, This Week,* and *Holiday.* Author of weekly humor column for the *American Weekly,* 1959-63. *Yank: The Army Weekly,* sports editor, 1942, managing editor, 1942-45.†

* * *

McCLARY, Jane Stevenson 1919-
(Jane McIlvaine)

PERSONAL: Born February 19, 1919, in Pittsburgh, Pa.; daughter of William Cooper and Elizabeth (Walker) Stevenson; married second husband, Nelson Caldwell McClary, December 15, 1956; children: (first marriage) Stevenson McIlvaine, Mia McIlvaine; (second marriage) Christopher. *Education:* Attended Miss Porter's School, 1934-37. *Address:* P.O. Box 326, Middleburg, Va. 22117. *Agent:* Brandt & Brandt, 101 Park Ave., New York, N.Y. 10017.

CAREER: Chronicle, Middleburg, Va., correspondent, 1934—; *Washington Times-Herald,* Washington, D.C., columnist, 1939-42; *Fortune,* New York, N.Y., affiliated with "Letters" department, 1941-43; *Archive* (weekly newspaper), Downingtown, Pa., co-owner and editor, 1946-54. Lecturer. *Member:* Overseas Press Club. *Awards, honors:* Theta Sigma Phi award for outstanding achievement in field of journalism, 1952; named Woman of Achievement, Virginia Press Women, 1973.

WRITINGS—All Under name Jane McIlvaine; published by Macrae, except as indicated: *Front Page for Jennifer,* 1950; *Copper's Chance,* 1951; *It Happens Every Thursday,* 1951; *The Sea Sprite,* 1952; *Cintra's Challenge,* 1955; *Stardust for Jennifer,* 1956; (with Jennie Darlington) *My Antarctic Honeymoon,* Doubleday, 1956; *Cammie's Choice,* Bobbs-Merrill, 1961; *Cammie's Challenge,* Bobbs-Merrill, 1962; *Cammie's Cousin,* Bobbs-Merrill, 1963; *To Win the Hunt: A Virginia Foxhunter in Ireland,* Barre, 1966; *The Will to Win: The True Story of Tommy Smith and Jay Trump,* Doubleday, 1966; *A Portion for Foxes* (novel), Simon & Schuster, 1972. Contributor of articles to horse and ski magazines, *London Daily Express,* and International News Service.

WORK IN PROGRESS: More novels for Simon & Schuster.

AVOCATIONAL INTERESTS: Foxhunting, sailing, skiing, playing tennis and chess, and cooking.

* * *

McCLOSKEY, Mark 1938-

PERSONAL: Born February 1, 1938, in New York, N.Y.; son of John M. (a photographer) and Adele (Bernard) McCloskey; married Bernadette Maron, February 3, 1962 (divorced, 1973); children: Daria, Adrian. *Education:* Iona College, B.A., 1961; Ohio University, M.A., 1963. *Office:* Department of English, Occidental College, Los Angeles, Calif.

CAREER: Ohio University, Athens, instructor in English, 1963-64, assistant editor for Ohio University Press, 1963-66; State University of New York College at Cortland, assistant professor of English, 1966-70; University of Southern California, Los Angeles, assistant professor of English, 1970-73; California State University, Chico, lecturer in English, 1973-77; Occidental College, Los Angeles, visiting assistant professor of English and comparative literature, 1977-80. Writer-in-residence at Hollins College, 1970. *Awards, honors:* Brother Arthur A. Loftus Award in liberal arts, Iona College, 1970; Theodore Roethke Poetry Prize from *Poetry Northwest,* 1973.

WRITINGS: (Translator with Paul R. Murphy) *The Latin Poetry of George Herbert: A Bilingual Edition,* Ohio University Press, 1965; *Goodbye, but Listen: Poems,* Vanderbilt University Press, 1968; *The Sheen in Flywings Is What It Comes To: Poems,* Portfolio Press, 1972; *All That Mattered: Poems,* Greenfield Review Press, 1976; *The Secret Documents of America: Poems,* Red Hill Press, 1977. Contributor to newspapers and periodicals, including *Poetry, Quarterly Review of Literature, New Yorker, Commonweal, Saturday Review, Rolling Stone, Chelsea,* and *Reporter.*

WORK IN PROGRESS: Norman Pinto Invents Women; a book of verse, *Nursery Rhymes for Grown-ups;* a novel, *Loco the Grand: The Adventures of an Uninhibited Woman;* a play, *Possession;* a book of short stories.

* * *

McCORD, Arline F(ujii) 1934-

PERSONAL: Born May 16, 1934, in Nahcotta, Wash.; daughter of George S. (an exporter) and Mary (Murakami) Fujii; married Ted T. Sakuma, December 2, 1951 (divorced, 1971); married William M. McCord (a professor of sociology), May 8, 1971; children: (first marriage) Karen D., Ted D., Michael Jon; (second marriage) William Maxwell II, Elinor Mary. *Education:* University of Washington, Seattle, B.A., 1960, M.A., 1965, Ph.D., 1968. *Religion:* Protestant. *Home:* 1 Kingswood Dr., Orangeburg, N.Y. 10962. *Office:* Department of Sociology, Hunter College, 695 Park Ave., New York, N.Y. 10021.

CAREER: High school teacher of social studies in Seattle, Wash., 1961-63; California State College at Fullerton (now

California State University, Fullerton), assistant professor of sociology, 1967-68; Syracuse University, Syracuse, N.Y., assistant professor of sociology, 1968-71; Hunter College of the City University of New York, New York, N.Y., assistant professor, 1971-77, associate professor of sociology, 1977—. Consultant to Eisenhower Commission on Causes and Prevention of Violence. *Member:* American Sociological Association.

WRITINGS: (With Charles W. Willie) *Black Students at White Colleges,* Praeger, 1972; (contributor) Nelson Northrup Foote and others, editors, *Social Institutions: A Book of Readings,* Kendall/Hunt, 1974; (contributor) Morris Silver, editor, *Economics of Public Choice,* Columbia University Press, 1974; (contributor) Raymond Hall, editor, *Black Separatism,* New England University Press, 1976; (with husband, William McCord) *Urban Social Conflict,* Mosby, 1977; (with W. McCord) *American Social Problems,* Mosby, 1977; (with W. McCord) *Power and Equity,* Praeger, 1977; (contributor) Edward Sagarin, editor, *Basic Concepts in Sociology,* Praeger, 1977; (contributor) Hall, editor, *Comparative Study of Separatist Movements,* Pergamon, 1980. Also author of teacher's manual for *Sociology,* 4th edition, Harper, 1968.

WORK IN PROGRESS: A research project, with data from Ireland, on the democratization of industry.

* * *

McCORD, William Maxwell 1930-

PERSONAL: Born October 24, 1930, in St. Louis, Mo.; married Joan Fish, 1951; married second wife, Kirsten Christensen, 1965; married third wife, Arline Fujii, May 7, 1971; children: (first marriage) Geoffry Donald, Robert, Maxwell; (third marriage) William, Elinor Mary. *Education:* Stanford University, A.B., 1952; Harvard University, Ph.D., 1955. *Home:* 1 Kingswood Dr., Orangeburg, N.Y. 10962. *Office:* Department of Sociology, City College of the City University of New York, New York, N.Y. 10036.

CAREER: Harvard University, Cambridge, Mass., instructor, 1955-58; Stanford University, Stanford, Calif., assistant professor, 1958-60, associate professor of sociology, 1960-65, assistant dean, School of Humanities and Sciences, 1958-61; Rice University, Houston, Tex., Lena Gohlmon Fox Professor of Sociology, 1965-68; Syracuse University, Syracuse, N.Y., professor of sociology, 1968-71; City College of the City University of New York, New York, N.Y., professor of sociology, 1971—. Lecturer, Stanford-in-France, 1961; distinguished visiting professor, American University in Cairo, 1964; distinguished visiting scholar, Converse College, 1968; Fulbright professor, Trinity College, University of Dublin, 1977-78. Director of personality research project, National Institute of Mental Health, 1958-65; consultant to Office of Scientific Research, U.S. Air Force, 1957, and to Salvation Army, California Department of Mental Health, California Department of Public Health. *Member:* American Sociological Society, Pacific Sociological Society, Phi Beta Kappa. *Awards, honors:* Woodrow Wilson fellowship, 1952-53; Ford Foundation grant for political research in Ghana and Nigeria, 1961.

WRITINGS: (With Joan McCord) *Psychopathy and Delinquency,* Grune, 1956; (with J. McCord and Irving Zola) *Origins of Crime,* Columbia University Press, 1959; (with J. McCord and Jon Gudeman) *Origins of Alcoholism,* Stanford University Press, 1960; (with J. McCord) *The Psychopath,* Van Nostrand, 1964; *The Springtime of Freedom: Evolution of Developing Societies,* Oxford University Press, 1965; *Mississippi: The Long, Hot Summer,* Norton, 1965; (co-editor) *The Study of Personality,* Holt, 1968; (with John Howard, Bernard Friedberg, and Edwin Hardwood) *Life Styles in the Black Ghetto,* Norton, 1969; *Urban Social Conflict,* Mosby, 1977; (with wife, Arline McCord) *American Social Problems,* Mosby, 1977; *Power and Equity,* Praeger, 1977. Contributor of articles to professional journals.

WORK IN PROGRESS: A social history of the twentieth century.

BIOGRAPHICAL/CRITICAL SOURCES: New Leader, July 21, 1969.

* * *

McCORMICK, Wilfred 1903-
(Rand Allison, Lon Dunlap)

PERSONAL: Born February 8, 1903, in Newland, Ind.; son of Ivor B. and Nellie (Jordan) McCormick; married Eleanor Paddock, November 2, 1935 (died January, 1952); married Rebecca Flee, July 4, 1953 (died October, 1960); married Helene Adele Huff, August 1, 1962; children: (first marriage) Kathryn, Robert. *Education:* Attended University of Illinois, 1923-27, and Washington and Lee University, 1944-45. *Religious affiliation:* Christian Church. *Address:* Box 8857, Albuquerque, N.M. 87108.

CAREER: Writer and lecturer. President, Bronc Burnett Enterprises, Albuquerque, N.M., 1953—. Instructor in creative writing, University of New Mexico, extension division, 1949-76; lecturer, West Texas State University writing seminar, 1954; instructor, Glorietta Writers Assembly, 1955; staff member of Southwest Writers Conference, Corpus Christi, Tex., 1959-63; lecturer, National League of American Pen Women, 1959—. Member of armed forces advisory committee, Fourth Army Area, 1949—. Active in state and local civic organizations. *Military service:* U.S. Army, 1942-46; became lieutenant colonel. *Member:* International Institute of Letters, Arts, and Sciences (fellow), International Platform Association, Committee on Foreign Relations (past Albuquerque chairman), Retired Officers Association, American Legion, Rotary International (fellow; president of Albuquerque club, 1952-53; American delegate to international convention, 1952, 1967, and 1968; district governor, 1967-68; member of world consultative group, 1968-69), Wisdom Hall of Fame, Delta Sigma Tau, Delta Alpha Epsilon.

WRITINGS: First and Ten, Putnam, 1952; *The Starmaker,* Speller, 1963; *The Pro Toughback,* Duell, Sloan & Pearce, 1964; *Touchdown for the Enemy,* Putnam, 1965; *Rookie on First,* Putnam, 1967; *Fullback in the Rough,* Prentice-Hall, 1969.

"Bronc Burnett" series; published by Putnam, except as indicated: *The Three-Two Pitch,* 1948; *Legion Tourney,* 1948; *Fielder's Choice,* 1949; *Flying Tackle,* 1949; *Bases Loaded,* 1950; *Rambling Halfback,* 1950; *Grand-Slam Homer,* 1951; *Quick Kick,* 1951; *Eagle Scout,* 1952; *The Big Ninth,* 1958; *The Last Putout,* 1960; *One O'Clock Hitter,* McKay, 1960; *Stranger in the Backfield,* McKay, 1960; *The Bluffer,* McKay, 1961; *Man in Motion,* McKay, 1961; *Rebel with a Glove,* McKay, 1962; *Too Late to Quit,* McKay, 1962; *Once a Slugger,* McKay, 1963; *Rough Stuff,* McKay, 1963; *The Throwing Catcher,* McKay, 1964; *The Right-End Option,* McKay, 1964; *Seven in Front,* McKay, 1965; *The Go-ahead Runner,* McKay, 1965; *Tall at the Plate,* Bobbs-Merrill, 1966.

"Rocky McCune" series; published by McKay, except as

indicated: *The Man on the Bench,* 1955; *The Captive Coach,* 1956; *The Bigger Game,* 1958; *The Hot Corner,* 1958; *Five Yards to Glory,* 1959; *The Proud Champions,* 1959; *The Automatic Strike,* 1960; *Too Many Forwards,* 1960; *The Double Steal,* 1961; *The Play for One,* 1961; *Home-run Harvest,* 1962; *The Five Man Break,* 1962; *The Two-One-Two Attack,* 1963; *The Phantom Shortstop,* 1963; *The Long Pitcher,* Duell, Sloan & Pearce, 1964; *Wild on the Bases,* 1965.

"Bronc Burnett and Rocky McCune" series; published by Bobbs-Merrill: *No Place for Heroes,* 1966; *The Incomplete Pitcher,* 1967; *One Bounce Too Many,* 1967.

BIOGRAPHICAL/CRITICAL SOURCES: Albuquerque Journal, December 16, 1979.

* * *

McDONAGH, Don(ald Francis) 1932-

PERSONAL: Born February 6, 1932, in New York, N.Y.; son of Francis Frederick and Winifred (Tierney) McDonagh; married Jennifer Tobutt (a performing arts manager), November 16, 1957; children: Ann, Ruth, Rachel, Amy. *Education:* Fordham University, B.S., 1953. *Politics:* Democrat. *Religion:* Roman Catholic. *Home:* 150 Claremont Ave., New York, N.Y. 10027. *Agent:* Richard Boehm, 737 Park Ave., New York, N.Y. 10021. *Office: New York Post,* 210 South St., New York, N.Y. 10002.

CAREER: Benton & Bowles, Inc. (advertising agency), New York City, market research analyst, 1957-67; *New York Times,* New York City, dance reviewer, 1967-78; *New York Post,* New York City, dance reviewer, 1978—. Consultant to Schatz Research Associates (market research firm), 1967—. *Military service:* U.S. Army, 1953-55.

WRITINGS: (Contributor) Clement Crisp and Peter Brinson, editors, *Ballet for All,* Pan Books, 1970; *The Rise and Fall and Rise of Modern Dance,* Outerbridge & Dienstfrey, 1970; *Martha Graham: A Biography,* Praeger, 1973; *The Complete Guide to Modern Dance,* Doubleday, 1976; *How to Enjoy Ballet,* Doubleday, 1978; *Dance Fever,* Random House, 1979. Contributor of art column to *Financial Times,* 1968-73. Contributor of dance articles to *Time, New Republic, Hudson Review, Show, Dance,* and *Dance and Dancers.* Associate editor of *Ballet Review,* 1967—.

WORK IN PROGRESS: A monograph on choreographer George Balanchine.

SIDELIGHTS: Don McDonagh wrote *CA:* "Like every author I write the sort of books I like to read. This has inevitably led to producing books that I wanted in my library but no one had done before." *Avocational interests:* Following New York sports teams, playing stickball.

BIOGRAPHICAL/CRITICAL SOURCES: New York Times, November 7, 1970.

* * *

McGANN, Jerome J. 1937-

PERSONAL: Born July 22, 1937, in New York, N.Y.; son of John Joseph (a printer) and Marie V. (Lecouffe) McGann; married Anne Lanni (a teacher), August 20, 1960; children: Geoffrey, Christopher, Jennifer. *Education:* Le Moyne College, B.S., 1959; Syracuse University, M.A., 1962; Yale University, Ph.D., 1966. *Home:* 6 Longwood Rd., Baltimore, Md. 21210. *Office:* Department of English, Johns Hopkins University, Baltimore, Md. 21218.

CAREER: Member of faculty in department of English, University of Chicago, Chicago, Ill., 1966-75, and Johns Hopkins University, Baltimore, Md., 1975—. *Member:* Modern Language Association of America. *Awards, honors:* Fulbright fellowship, 1965; Guggenheim fellowships, 1970-71 and 1975-76; National Endowment for the Humanities fellowship, 1974-76.

WRITINGS: Fiery Dust: Byron's Poetic Development, University of Chicago Press, 1969; (editor) Edward Bulwer-Lytton, *Pelham,* University of Nebraska Press, 1972; *Swinburne: An Experiment in Criticism,* University of Chicago Press, 1972; *Don Juan in Context,* University of Chicago Press, 1976.

Plays: (Adapter) George Gordon Byron, "Cain," produced in Chicago, Ill., 1968; (adapter) William Blake, "Marriage of Heaven and Hell," produced in Chicago, 1970.

Poetry: *Air Heart Sermons,* Pasdeloup Press, 1975; (with Janet Kauffman) *Writing Home,* Coldwater Press, 1977; (with James Kahn) *Nerves in Patterns,* X Press, 1979.

WORK IN PROGRESS: A definitive edition of *Byron's Complete Poetical Works,* for Clarendon Press; analytic and historical studies of nineteenth-century literature and art.

* * *

McGARRITY, Mark 1943-
(Bartholomew Gill)

PERSONAL: Born July 22, 1943, in Holyoke, Mass.; son of Hugh F. and Cecilia (Gill) McGarrity; married Margaret Wellstood Dull (a photographer), October 10, 1966. *Education:* Brown University, B.A., 1966; Trinity College, Dublin, M.Litt., 1971. *Home and office:* 187 North Shore Rd., R.D. 3, Andover, N.J. 07821. *Agent:* Helen Brann, 14 Sutton Pl. S., New York, N.Y. 10022.

CAREER: Has worked as speech writer, public relations and annual report writer, financial reporter, and insurance man; free-lance writer, 1969—.

WRITINGS: Little Augie's Lament (novel), Grossman, 1973; *Lucky Shuffles* (novel), Grossman, 1973; *A Passing Advantage* (novel), Rawson, Wade, 1980; (contributor) Dilys Winn, *Murderess Ink,* Workman Publishing, 1980; *US #1* (nonfiction), photographs by wife, Margaret McGarrity, Boston Globe/Pequot Press, 1980.

Under pseudonym Bartholomew Gill; all novels; all published by Scribner: *McGarr and the Politician's Wife,* 1976; *McGarr and the Sienese Conspiracy,* 1977; *McGarr on the Cliffs of Moher,* 1978; *McGarr at the Dublin Horse Show,* 1980.

WORK IN PROGRESS: Lake House, a generational novel of an American family.

SIDELIGHTS: Under his pseudonym Bartholomew Gill, Mark McGarrity is the creator of a well-received addition to the world of international crime and mystery literature—Peter McGarr, chief inspector of detectives of the Irish police. Jean White of the *Washington Post Book World* assures readers that McGarr "is no imitation. [The author] has created a solid, original character." A *New York Times Book Review* critic agrees. Commenting on *McGarr and the Politician's Wife,* he writes that "there is no caricature or stage-Irishman stuff—Gill knows his people and treats them with dignity."

As for McGarrity's writing style, Newgate Callendar of the *New York Times Book Review* notes that "everything [in *McGarr and the Sienese Conspiracy*] is nicely relaxed. . . . Yet there is a great deal of tension, and also enough action to satisfy the reader who demands gore. McGarr . . . sort of ambles through everything. . . . There is never any feeling of heavy breathing. Gill paces everything beautifully. *McGarr and the Sienese Conspiracy* is very well plotted, very civilized and very, very good.''

McGarr on the Cliffs of Moher evokes a similar response in a *New Republic* reviewer. After admitting that McGarrity's novels ''grow upon one,'' he states that ''the pace is relaxed, the clues are planted with almost stodgy care, the author's intelligence is evident throughout, and Ireland comes alive, bit by bit. McGarr will not keep one up all night but he will not let one loose either. . . . Gill is a writer to watch.''

BIOGRAPHICAL/CRITICAL SOURCES: New York Times Book Review, April 8, 1973, May 1, 1977, February 12, 1978; *New Republic,* June 10, 1978; *Washington Post Book World,* August 20, 1978.

* * *

McGERR, Patricia 1917-

PERSONAL: Born December 26, 1917, in Falls City, Neb.; daughter of Patrick Thomas and Catherine (Dore) McGerr. *Education:* University of Nebraska, A.B., 1936; Columbia University, M.S., 1937. *Politics:* Democrat. *Religion:* Roman Catholic. *Home:* 5415 Connecticut Ave. N.W., Washington, D.C. 20015.

CAREER: American Road Builders' Association, Washington, D.C., publicity director, 1937-43; *Construction Methods* magazine, New York, N.Y., assistant editor, 1943-48; self-employed writer, 1948—. Lecturer and consultant, Georgetown University Writers' Conference, 1960—. *Member:* Mystery Writers of America (member of board of directors, 1959-62, 1965-69, 1977-81), Catholic Interracial Council of Washington (treasurer, 1950-60), Northwest Washington Fair Housing Association (treasurer, 1964-66). *Awards, honors:* First prize, Catholic Press Association short story contest, 1950; Grand Prix de Litterature Policiere, France, 1952; *Ellery Queen's Mystery Magazine,* short story contest, second prize, 1962, first prize, 1967.

WRITINGS—All published by Doubleday, except as indicated: *Pick Your Victim,* 1946; *The Seven Deadly Sisters,* 1947; *Catch Me If You Can,* 1948; *Save the Witness,* 1949; *Follow, As the Night,* 1950; *Death in a Million Living Rooms,* 1951; *The Missing Years,* 1953; *Fatal in My Fashion,* 1954; *Martha, Martha,* Kenedy, 1960; *My Brothers, Remember Monica,* Kenedy, 1964; *Is There a Traitor in the House?,* 1964; *Murder Is Absurd,* 1967; *Stranger with My Face,* Luce, 1968; *For Richer, for Poorer, til Death,* Luce, 1969; *Legacy of Danger,* Luce, 1970; *Daughter of Darkness,* Popular Library, 1974; *Dangerous Landing,* Dell, 1975. Contributor of short stories and book reviews to *This Week* and other magazines.

WORK IN PROGRESS: A Biblical novel.

SIDELIGHTS: Patricia McGerr's book *Follow, As the Night* was filmed in 1954 under title ''One Step to Eternity''; *The Missing Years* was dramatized on radio and television; *Fatal in My Fashion* has been televised; *Catch Me If You Can* has been presented on radio; a film based on her short story ''Johnny Lingo'' has won two national awards and has been dubbed in fourteen languages. All books have been published in England, and some in as many as twelve foreign countries.

BIOGRAPHICAL/CRITICAL SOURCES: Authors in the News, Volume I, Gale, 1976.

McGLOIN, Joseph Thaddeus 1917- (Thaddeus O'Finn)

PERSONAL: Born December 2, 1917, in Omaha, Neb.; son of Dennis J. (a railroad freight agent) and Clara (Finn) McGloin. *Education:* Attended Creighton University, 1935-36; St. Louis University, B.A., 1941, M.A., 1943, Ph.L., 1943; St. Mary's College (St. Mary's, Kan.), S.T.L., 1950. *Home and office:* Good Counsel Retreat House, Rt. 1, Box 110, Waverly, Neb. 68462.

CAREER: Entered Society of Jesus, Florissant, Mo., 1936; ordained to priesthood, 1949. St. John's College, Belize City, British Honduras, teacher, 1943-46; St. Joseph's Hall, Decatur, Ill., tertianship, 1950; St. Gabriel's Church, Prairie du Chien, Wis., assistant pastor, 1951; Regis High School, Denver, Colo., teacher, counselor, director of Sodalities, 1951-61; St. Margaret's Academy, Minneapolis, Minn., teacher and counselor, 1962-65; Marymount Military Academy, Tacoma, Wash., teacher and counselor, 1970-74; Sacred Heart church, Alturas, Calif., assistant pastor, 1974-75; Villa Nazareth (living center for teen girls), Fargo, N.D., chaplain and counselor, 1975-79; Good Counsel Retreat House, Waverly, Neb., chaplain and director of retreats, 1979—. Active in work with youth, including the formation of Sodality Council of Denver, 1954, the founding of *Sodality By-Line,* 1955, and Sodality conventions.

WRITINGS: (Under pseudonym Thaddeus O'Finn) *Happy Holiday!,* Rinehart, 1950; *I'll Die Laughing!,* Bruce, 1955; *Call Me Joe!,* Pageant, 1958; *Backstage Missionary* (biography of Dan Lord, S.J.), Pageant, 1958; *Smile at Your Own Risk!,* Bruce, 1959; *What to Do until the Psychiatrist Comes: A Handbook for the Parents of Teenagers,* Bruce, 1963; *Friends, Romans, Protestants,* Bruce, 1963; *That's the Old Spirit!,* Liguori, 1970; *Living to Beat Hell!,* Prentice-Hall, 1972; *The Solid Gold Crucifix,* Liguori, 1972; *How to Get More Out of the Mass,* Liguori, 1974; *Basic Truths of the Catholic Faith,* Liguori, 1976; *Hey, Why Don't We Try Christianity?,* Our Sunday Visitor, 1978; *Don't Panic!: A Handbook for Parents and Other Teachers,* Franciscan Herald Press, 1980.

''Love and Live'' series, published by Bruce: *Learn a Little! or, What's Life All About?, Yearn a Little! or, Why Did God Come Up with Two Sexes?,* and *Burn a Little! or, What's Love All About?,* all 1961.

''With Him, Through Him, To Him'' series (high school theology course), published by Bruce: *Living in God,* 1965; *Christ Lives On,* 1966; *Life of Man in Christ,* 1967; *Living in the Kingdom,* 1967.

''Called to Love, Called to Serve'' series, published by Benziger: *Alive in the Lord!, Faith to Share!, Christ with Us!,* and *Called to Love, Called to Serve!,* all 1979.

Shorter works; all published by Liguori, except as indicated: *Working to Beat Hell!,* Franciscan, 1965; *Getting a Kick Out of Life,* Franciscan, 1965; *Breaking the Maturity Barrier,* Franciscan, 1965; *Parents and Their Teenagers,* Franciscan, 1965; *Tricks That Trap Teens,* 1966; (with John L. Thomas) *Understanding Your Teenager,* 1966; *''Become Little Children'': Are You Kidding?,* 1968; *God Is No Blob,* 1969; *Sorry, Lucy, Happiness Is Not a Warm Puppy,* 1970. Also author of syndicated column, ''Working to Beat Hell!,'' 1963-66, and numerous pamphlets and plays. Contributor of short stories, under pseudonym Thaddeus O'Finn, to periodicals.

SIDELIGHTS: Joseph McGloin considers writing his main work within the priesthood but notes that his work with teenagers and their parents is his most interesting work. He insists that the key to most teenagers, for good or bad, is this: "*They hate mediocrity,* and simply are not moved by any mediocre 'challenge.' [They] simply look at you with a blank stare if you say, 'Let's go put a few nickels in the collection box, to help the poor.' But if you ask them to go out and help the poor face to face; say—laying linoleum, cooking meals for the poor, scrubbing floors, painting, and other tough jobs—they're with you in numbers." His works have had German and Italian editions.

* * *

McGURN, Barrett 1914-

PERSONAL: Born August 6, 1914, in New York, N.Y.; son of William Barrett and Alice Agnes (Schneider) McGurn; married Mary Elizabeth Johnson, May 30, 1942 (died, February 20, 1960); married Janice McLaughlin, June 19, 1962; children: (first marriage) William B., Betsy, Andrew; (second marriage) Martin, Lachie, Mark. *Education:* Fordham College, A.B., 1935. *Religion:* Roman Catholic. *Home:* 5229 Duvall Dr., Westmoreland Hills, Md. 20016. *Agent:* Curtis Brown Ltd., 575 Madison Ave., New York, N.Y. 10022; and W. Colston Leigh, Inc., 521 Fifth Ave., New York, N.Y. (lectures).

CAREER: New York Herald Tribune, staff reporter and foreign correspondent, 1936-66, covering assignments in twenty-five countries, bureau chief in Rome, Italy, 1946-52, in Paris, France, 1952-55, acting bureau chief in Moscow, U.S.S.R., 1958; U.S. Embassy, Rome, press attache, 1966-68; U.S. Embassy, Saigon, Viet Nam, counselor for press affairs, 1968-69; deputy spokesman, U.S. State Department, 1969-72; spokesman, U.S. Supreme Court, 1973—. Correspondent in Morocco, Algeria, Tunisia, Hungary, Egypt, Greece, French Equatorial Africa, Vatican City, and other countries. Representative of private industry on Fulbright fellowship selection committee in Italy, 1951-52; member of committee to choose winner of first World Press Achievement Award, American Newspaper Publishers Association, 1965. *Military service:* U.S. Army, 1943-45, writer and correspondent for *Yank;* became sergeant; received commendation medal and Purple Heart.

MEMBER: Stampa Estera (foreign correspondents association in Italy; vice-president, 1947-48; president, 1961-62), American Club of Rome, Italy, Overseas Press Club of New York (president, 1963-65), Authors Guild, American Newspaper Guild. *Awards, honors:* George Polk Memorial Award from Long Island University, 1956; Overseas Press Club award as best foreign correspondent of U.S. press, 1957; D. Litt., Fordham University, 1958; Christopher Award; chevalier officer, Italian Order of Merit, 1962; man of year of Catholic Institute of the Press, 1962; Fordham alumnus of year in communications field, 1963; co-winner of annual award for outstanding public service from New York Newspaper Reporters Association, 1965, for *New York Herald Tribune* series on "New York City in Crisis"; Page One Award from New York Newspaper Guild, as year's best foreign correspondent (for scoop on Pope Paul's plans to visit America and coverage of trip); other awards for initial story on Pope's trip.

WRITINGS: Decade in Europe, Dutton, 1959; *A Reporter Looks at the Vatican,* Coward, 1962; *A Reporter Looks at American Catholicism,* Hawthorn, 1967.

Contributor: *The Best from "Yank,"* Dutton, 1945; *Yank, the GI Story of the War,* World Publishing, 1946; *Combat,* Beacon, 1950; *Highlights from "Yank,"* Royal Books, 1953; *I Can Tell It Now,* Overseas Press Club, 1964; *How I Got That Story,* Overseas Press Club, 1967; *Heroes for Our Times,* Overseas Press Club, 1968; *Newsbreak,* Overseas Press Club, 1975; John Delaney, editor, *Saints for All Seasons,* Doubleday, 1978. Contributor to *American Peoples Encyclopedic Yearbook, Grolier Encyclopedic Yearbook,* and to magazines, including *Catholic Digest, Collier's, America, Reader's Digest, Mademoiselle,* and *Commonweal.*

SIDELIGHTS: Barrett McGurn told *CA:* "I became a news reporter in order to see life in its most vivid expressions, and also to become a writer. I have become fascinated with information and its role in democratic life. As a reporter I sought everything that was interesting or important, combining the two in the same article whenever I could; trusting that someone somewhere was putting everything together—the scoops, the plug stories, and the exposes—with the common interest in mind. As a government spokesman, I have been concerned with the consequences of disclosure, anxious that—so far as possible—the entertainment and education of the public enhance and not damage the common interest."

* * *

McILWAIN, William (Franklin, Jr.) 1925-

PERSONAL: Born December 15, 1925, in Lancaster, S.C.; son of William Franklin (in government Service) and Docia (a Latin teacher; maiden name, Higgins) McIlwain; married Anne Dalton, November 28, 1952 (divorced, 1971); married Kathleen Brelsford, 1978; children: (first marriage) Dalton (daughter), Nancy, William Franklin III. *Education:* Wake Forest College (now University), B.A., 1949; Harvard University, Nieman fellow, 1957-58. *Home:* 500 N St. S.W., Washington, D.C. *Office: Washington Star,* 225 Virginia Ave. S.E., Washington, D.C. 20003.

CAREER: Held various positions with *Wilmington (N.C.) Star,* 1943, *Charlotte (N.C.) Observer,* 1945, *Jacksonville (Fla.) Journal,* 1945, *Winston-Salem (N.C.) Journal-Sentinel,* 1949-52, and *Richmond (Va.) Times-Dispatch,* 1952-54; *Newsday,* Garden City, N.Y., chief copy editor, 1954-57, day news editor, 1957-60, city editor, 1960-64, managing editor, 1964-66, editor, 1967-70; Wake Forest University, Winston-Salem, N.C., writer-in-residence, 1970-71; *Toronto Star,* Toronto, Ontario, deputy managing editor, 1971-73; *Bergen Record,* Hackensack, N.J., managing editor, 1973-77; *Boston Herald American,* Boston, Mass., editor, 1977-79; *Washington Star,* Washington, D.C., deputy editor, 1979—. Dorm leader, Alcoholic Rehabilitation Center, Butner, N.C., 1971. Member of President Johnson's Commission on Civil Rights. *Military service:* U.S. Marine Corps Reserve, 1944. *Member:* American Society of Newspaper Editors, Society of Nieman Fellows, Delta Literary Club.

WRITINGS: (With Walter Friedenberg) *Legends of Baptist Hollow,* Delta, 1949; *The Glass Rooster,* Doubleday, 1960; (collaborator) *Naked Came the Stranger,* Lyle Stuart, 1969; *A Farewell to Alcohol,* Random House, 1972. Contributor to *Harper's, Atlantic Monthly, Esquire,* and *Reader's Digest.*

* * *

McKOWN, Robin ?-1976

PERSONAL: Born in Denver, Colo.; died, 1976; daughter of George S. and Anna Clason; married Dallas McKown (deceased). *Education:* University of Colorado, B.A.; additional study at University of Illinois and Northwestern University. *Home:* Dry Run Rd., Beaver Dams, N.Y. 14812. *Agent:* Curtis Brown Ltd., 1 Craven Hill, London W2 3EW, England.

CAREER: Writer, mainly of books for teen-agers. Worked in New York for several years doing sales promotion for a publicity concern and writing radio scripts and a column on books and authors for the Book-of-the-Month Club. Also worked as a literary agent. *Member:* Authors Guild. *Awards, honors:* Child Study Association Award, 1961, for *Janine*.

WRITINGS: Authors' Agent, Messner, 1957; *Painter of the Wild West—Frederic Remington,* Messner, 1959; *Marie Curie,* Putnam, 1959; *Publicity Girl,* Putnam, 1959; *Foreign Service Girl,* Putnam, 1959; *Janine* (Junior Literary Guild selection), Messner, 1960; *She Lived for Science—Irene Joliot-Curie,* Messner, 1961; *Pioneers of Mental Health* (adult book), Dodd, 1961; *Washington's America,* Grosset, 1961; *Thomas Paine,* Putnam, 1962; *The Fabulous Isotopes,* Holiday, 1962; *The Giant of the Atom* (story of Ernest Rutherford), Messner, 1962; *Roosevelt's America,* Grosset, 1962; *The Ordeal of Anne Devlin,* Messner, 1963; *Benjamin Franklin,* Putnam, 1963; *Seven Famous Trials in History,* Vanguard, 1963; *Patriot of the Underground,* Putnam, 1964; *Eleanor Roosevelt's World,* Grosset, 1964.

Mendeleyev and His Periodic Table, Messner, 1965; *Story of the Incas,* Putnam, 1966; *Heroic Nurses* (Junior Literary Guild selection), Putnam, 1966; *Rakoto and the Drongo Bird,* Lothrop, 1966; *The Boy Who Woke Up in Madagascar,* Putnam, 1967; *Girl of Madagascar,* Messner, 1968; *The Congo: River of Mystery,* McGraw, 1968; *Lumumba,* Doubleday, 1969; *The American Revolution: The French Allies,* McGraw, 1969; *Horatio Gates and Benedict Arnold: American Military Commanders,* McGraw, 1969; (with Mary Elting) *The Mongo Homecoming,* M. Evans, 1969; *Colonial Conquest of Africa,* F. Watts, 1971; *The World of Mary Cassatt,* Crowell, 1972; *The Republic of Zaire,* F. Watts, 1972; *Crisis in South Africa,* Putnam, 1972; *Nkrumah,* Doubleday, 1973; *The Execution of Maximilian: A Hapsburg Emperor Meets Disaster in the New World,* F. Watts, 1973; *The Image of Puerto Rico; Its History and Its People: On the Island — on the Mainland,* McGraw, 1973; *Mark Twain,* McGraw, 1974; *The Opium War in China, 1840-1842,* F. Watts, 1974; (editor) *The Resignation of Nixon: A Discredited President Gives up the Highest Office,* F. Watts, 1975.

SIDELIGHTS: Robin McKown's first literary success came at the University of Colorado where her one-act play, "The King's Enemy," won first prize and ran for three nights at the University little theatre. Later she did volunteer work for a New York committee that helped the widows and orphans of the French Resistance. In connection with this work, she made a six-week tour of France immediately after the war, visiting the families of men who had died in the Resistance.†

* * *

McNULTY, Faith 1918-

PERSONAL: Born November 28, 1918, in New York, N.Y.; daughter of Joseph Eugene (a judge) and Faith (Robinson) Corrigan; married John McNulty, 1945 (died, 1956); married Richard H. Martin, 1957; children: (first marriage) John Joseph. *Education:* Attended Barnard College, 1937-38. *Address:* Box 370, Wakefield, R.I. 02880. *Office: New Yorker,* 25 West 43rd St., New York, N.Y. 10036.

CAREER: New Yorker, New York, N.Y., staff writer, 1953—. *Awards, honors:* Dutton Animal Book Award, 1966, for *The Whooping Crane;* D.H.L., University of Rhode Island, 1977.

WRITINGS: (With Elisabeth Keiffer) *Wholly Cats,* Bobbs-Merrill, 1962; *The Whooping Crane: The Bird That Defies Extinction,* introduction by Stewart L. Udall, Dutton, 1966; *Must They Die?: The Strange Case of the Prairie Dog and the Black-Footed Ferret,* Doubleday, 1971; *The Great Whales,* Doubleday, 1974; *The Burning Bed,* Harcourt, 1980; *The Wildlife Stories of Faith McNulty,* Doubleday, 1980.

Juveniles: *The Funny Mixed-up Story,* Wonder Books, 1959; *Arty the Smarty,* Wonder Books, 1962; *When a Boy Gets Up in the Morning,* Knopf, 1962; *When a Boy Goes to Bed at Night,* Knopf, 1963; *Prairie Dog Summer,* Coward, 1972; *Woodchuck,* Harper, 1974; *Whales: Their Life in the Sea,* Harper, 1975; *Mouse and Tim,* Harper, 1978; *How to Dig a Hole to the Other Side of the World,* Harper, 1979; *The Elephant Who Couldn't Forget,* Harper, 1980.

* * *

MEADE, Marion 1934-

PERSONAL: Born January 7, 1934, in Pittsburgh, Pa.; daughter of Surain (a physicist) and Mary (Homeny) Sidhu; children: Alison Linkhorn. *Education:* Northwestern University, B.S., 1955; Columbia University, M.S., 1956. *Residence:* New York, N.Y. *Agent:* Julia Coopersmith Literary Agency, 10 West 15th St., New York, N.Y. 10011.

CAREER: Novelist; biographer.

WRITINGS: Bitching, Prentice-Hall, 1973; *Free Woman: The Life and Times of Victoria Woodhull,* Knopf, 1976; *Eleanor of Aquitaine,* Dutton, 1977; *Stealing Heaven: The Love Story of Heloise and Abelard,* Morrow, 1979; *Madame Blavatsky: The Woman behind the Myth,* Putnam, 1980.

WORK IN PROGRESS: Behold a Pale Horse, for Morrow; *Dorothy Parker: A Biography,* for Putnam.

SIDELIGHTS: Ms. Meade told *CA:* "I am a feminist and my writings reflect a feminist point of view."

* * *

MEGGED, Aharon 1920-
(A. M.)

PERSONAL: Name sometimes spelled Aron Meged or Aharon Meged; born August 10, 1920, in Wloclawcek, Poland; son of Moshe (a teacher) and Leah (Reichgot) Megged; married Eda Zirlin (a writer and painter), May 11, 1944; children: Eyal, Amos. *Education:* Attended high school in Palestine (now Israel), 1933-37. *Politics:* Labour Party. *Religion:* Jewish. *Home:* 26 Rupin St., Tel-Aviv, Israel. *Agent:* Gloria Stern Literary Agency, 1230 Park Ave., New York, N.Y. 10028. *Office: Davar,* Shenkin, Tel-Aviv, Israel.

CAREER: Member of a kibbutz in Sdot-Yam, Israel, 1938-50; *Massa* (bi-weekly newspaper), Tel-Aviv, Israel, editor, 1952-55; *Lamerchav* (daily newspaper), Tel-Aviv, literary editor, 1955-68; Israeli Embassy, London, England, cultural attache, 1968-71; *Davar* (daily newspaper), Tel-Aviv, columnist, 1971—. *Member:* International P.E.N., Israeli Writer's Association (member of central committee, 1954-60), National Arts Council (member of central committee, 1962-67), Hebrew Academy, Israeli Journalist's Association. *Awards, honors:* Ussishkin Prize, 1955, for *Hedva and I,* and 1966, for *Living on the Dead;* Brenner Prize, 1957, for *Israel Haverim;* Shlonsky Prize, 1963, for *ha-Brikha;* Bialik Prize, 1973, for *Makhbarot Evyatar* and *Al Etzim ve-avanim;* Fichman Prize, 1973, for *Asahel.*

WRITINGS: Ru'akh Yamin (title means "Spirit of the Seas"), Ha'kibutz Hame'uchad, 1950; *Harkhek ha-Arava* (title means "Far in the Wasteland"), Sifriat Po'alim, 1951; *Israel Haverim* (title means "Israeli Folk"), Ha'kibutz Hame'uchad, 1955; *Mikreh ha-kssil,* Ha'kubutz Hame'uchad, 1960, translation by Aubrey Hodes published as *Fortunes of a Fool,* Random House, 1963; *ha-Brikha* (title means "The Escape"), Ha'kibutz Hame'chad, 1962; *ha-Hai 'al ha-met,* Am Oved, 1965, translation by Misha Louvish published as *Living on the Dead,* McCall Publishing, 1970; *ha-Yom ha-Sheni* (title means "The Second Day"), Tarmil, 1967; *ha-Khayim ha-Ktzarim* (title means "The Short Life"), Ha'kibutz Hame'uchad, 1971, translation by Miriam Arad, Taplinger, in press; *Khatzot ha-Yom* (title means "Midday"), Ha'kubitz Hame'uchad, 1973; *Makhbarot Evyatar* (title means "Evyatar's Notebooks"), Ha'kibutz Hame'uchad, 1973; *Al Etzim ve-avanim* (title means "Of Trees and Stones"), Am Oved, 1973; *ha-Ataleph* (title means "The Bat"), Am Oved, 1975; *Heinz u'Vno ve Harnack ha'Raah* (title means "Heinz, His Son and the Evil Spirit"), Am Oved, 1976; *Asahel,* Am Oved, 1978, translation by R. Whitehill, Taplinger, in press.

Plays: "Incubator on the Rocks" (three-act), first produced in Tel-Aviv, at Ohel Theatre, 1950; *Hedvah ve-ani* (two-act; first produced in Tel-Aviv, at Habimah Theatre, 1955), Ha'kibutz Hame'uchad, 1954, translation published as *Hedva and I: A Play in Two Acts,* Youth and Hechalutz Department of the Zionist Organization, (Jerusalem), 1957; "The Way to Eylat" (two-act), first produced at Habimah Theatre, 1955; "I Like Mike" (three-act), first produced at Habimah Theatre, 1960; "Tit for Tat" (two-act), first produced at Ohel Theatre, 1960; *Hanna Senesh* (two-act; first produced at Habimah Theatre, 1962), Ha'kibutz Hame'uchad, 1954; "Genesis" (three-act), first produced at Habimah Theatre, 1965; *The High Season* (two-act; first produced at Habimah Theatre, 1968), Amikam, 1968.

Contributor to journals and newspapers, often under pseudonym A. M.

SIDELIGHTS: Jacob Kabakoff, in a *World Literature Today* review, calls Aharon Megged "one of the leading short story writers and novelists of the generation of Israel's War of Independence" and notes that the author has depicted "the varied aspects of life in the new state, from war themes to the kibbutz and urban life." In his novel *Living on the Dead,* Megged tells the story of a young Israeli writer who has signed a contract with a publishing house to write a biography of one of the country's Zionist pioneers. Even though he collects an advance from the publisher and receives monthly checks on which he is able to live and conduct research, the writer is unable to finish the project. Stephen G. Kellman of *Modern Fiction Studies* explains that "examples of necrophagia, of living on the dead, are scattered throughout this novel, from poets who seem to cultivate experiences in order to convert them into inert stanzas to a nation fond of worshipping its heroes dead. Jonas [the protagonist] is consumed by the realization that he himself is the most voracious necrophage in the drama. . . . [Like] those scholars who bide their time until such lives as Stravinsky, Pound, or Picasso are completed before rushing out with the definitive study, Jonas, beneficiary of the publisher's monthly check, is in a real sense feeding himself from a dead man."

Megged told *CA:* "Life in the country, first, in childhood, in a small village, and then in a Kibbutz, had a great effect on my work. In later years I traveled much in Europe in search of Jewish medieval mysticism, especially in Spain and France. European writers, such as Kafka, Svevo, Gogol, Chekhov, had influence on my work."

BIOGRAPHICAL/CRITICAL SOURCES: Commentary, August, 1972; *Modern Fiction Studies,* summer, 1976; *World Literature Today,* spring, 1977; *Contemporary Literary Criticism,* Volume IX, Gale, 1979.

MENDELSOHN, Jack 1918-

PERSONAL: Born July 22, 1918, in Cambridge, Mass.; son of Jack Mendelsohn; married December 26, 1949 (divorced, 1969); married Joan Silverstone Hall, August 3, 1969; children: (first marriage) Channing T., Deborah T., Kurt A.; (second marriage) Lisabeth Hall. *Education:* Boston University, B.A., 1939; Harvard University, S.T.B., 1945. *Home:* 5 Ledgewood, Bedford, Mass. 01730. *Office address:* First Parish, Box L, Bedford, Mass. 01730.

CAREER: Ordained Unitarian Universalist minister, 1945; minister in Rockford, Ill., 1947-54, and Indianapolis, Ind., 1954-59; Arlington Street Church, Boston, Mass., minister, 1959-69; First Unitarian Church, Chicago, Ill., senior minister, 1969-79; First Parish, Bedford, Mass., minister, 1979—. Member of adjunct faculty, Meadeville Theological School, University of Chicago, 1969—. Vice-president, Unitarian Universalist Service Committee,1963-67; president, Hyde Park-Kenwood Council of Churches and Synagogues (Chicago), 1974-76. President, Binder-Schweitzer Hospital Foundation (New York City), 1965—, Urban League of Greater Boston, 1966-68, Chicago Memorial Association, 1969—, and Abraham Lincoln Centre (Chicago), 1977-79; chairman, Alliance to End Repression (Chicago), 1970-76. Member of board of directors, World Affairs Council of Boston, 1962-66, and International Institute of Boston, 1962-68; member of advisory council, Comprehensive Health Planning (Chicago), 1969—. *Member:* National Association for the Advancement of Colored People, Massachusetts Civil Liberties Union, Harvard Club (Boston), Badminton and Tennis Club (Boston, Massachusetts). *Awards, honors:* D.D., Meadville Theological School, University of Chicago, 1962.

WRITINGS: Why I Am a Unitarian, Thomas Nelson, 1960, published as *Why I Am a Unitarian Universalist,* 1964; *God, Allah and Ju Ju,* Thomas Nelson, 1962; *The Forest Calls Back,* Little, Brown, 1965; *The Martyrs: Sixteen Who Gave Their Lives for Racial Justice,* Harper, 1966; *Channing, the Reluctant Radical,* Little, Brown, 1970. Contributor to magazines.

SIDELIGHTS: Jack Mendelsohn has traveled widely in Europe, the Middle East, Africa, and Latin America, to gain background for his writings.

* * *

MERRIAM, Alan P(arkhurst) 1923-1980

PERSONAL: Born November 1, 1923, in Missoula, Mont.; died March 14, 1980, in an air accident, over Warsaw, Poland; son of Harold Guy and Doris (Foote) Merriam; married Barbara Anne Williams, August 29, 1947 (divorced September 7, 1974); married Valerie A. Christian, May 6, 1977; children: (first marriage) Virginia Claire, Paige Alison, Cynthia Williams. *Education:* Montana State College (now University), B.A., 1947; Northwestern University, M.M., 1948, Ph.D., 1951. *Office:* Department of Anthropology, Indiana University, Bloomington, Ind. 47405.

CAREER: Northwestern University, Evanston, Ill, instructor, 1953-54, assistant professor, 1956-58, associate professor of anthropology, 1958-62; University of Wisconsin—Milwaukee, assistant professor of sociology and anthropology, 1954-56; Indiana University at Bloomington, professor of anthropology, 1962-80, chairman of department, 1966-69, associate chairman, 1978-80. Distinguished visiting professor, University of Montana, 1965; Fulbright professor, University of Sydney, 1976; visiting scholar, University of California, 1978. Member of committee on human resources in Central Africa, 1958; special consultant to U.S. government concerning the Congo, 1960; member of President Kennedy's Task Force for Africa, 1960; member of joint committee on African studies, Social Science Research Council and American Council of Learned Societies, 1960-80, chairman, 1962-65; member of advisory board, Inter-American Institute for Musical Research, 1961-80; U.S. delegate, First International Congress of Africanists, Ghana, 1962. *Military service:* U.S. Army Air Forces, served in Italy, 1943-45; became sergeant.

MEMBER: American Anthropological Association (fellow; member of editorial council, 1957-59), American Association for the Advancement of Science (fellow), Congress on Research in Dance, African Studies Association (founding fellow; chairman of committee of fine arts and humanities, 1960-62; member of board of directors, 1962-65), American Folklore Society, African Music Society, Society for Ethnomusicology (co-founder; member of the executive board, 1956-65; member of board of directors, 1969-72; member of council, 1958-80; vice-president, 1960-62; president, 1962-64; first vice-president, 1977-79), International Folk Music Council, Central States Anthropological Society (president, 1960-61), Sigma Xi.

WRITINGS: (With Robert J. Benford) *A Bibliography of Jazz,* American Folklore Society, 1954, reprinted, Da Capo Press, 1971; *Congo: Background of Conflict,* Northwestern University Press, 1961; *A Prologue to the Study of the African Arts,* Antioch Press, 1962; *The Anthropology of Music,* Northwestern University Press, 1964; (with Frank Gillis) *Ethnomusicology and Folk Music: An International Bibliography,* Wesleyan University Press, 1966; *Ethnomusicology of the Flathead Indians,* Aldine, 1967; *African Music on LP: An Annotated Discography,* Northwestern University Press, 1970; *The Arts and Humanities in African Studies,* African Studies Program, Indiana University, 1972; *An African World: The Basongye Village of Lupupa Ngye,* Indiana University Press, 1974; *Culture History of the Basongye,* African Studies Program, Indiana University, 1975. Author of monthly column on African music, *Africa Report,* 1962-80. *Ethnomusicology,* editor, 1953-58, member of editorial board, 1966-80; review editor, *Journal of American Folklore,* 1957-58.

WORK IN PROGRESS: Field research in ethnography and ethnomusicology of the Basongye, Kinshasha, Zaire.

SIDELIGHTS: Alan Merriam conducted ethnomusicological field research in Zaire and Ruanda-Urundi, Africa, and among the Flathead Indians of western Montana.

* * *

MERSAND, Joseph 1907-

PERSONAL: Born July 30, 1907, in Zbaraz, Austria-Hungary; son of Nathan and Mollie (Stein) Mersand; married Estelle Joy Himmelstein, 1950. *Education:* New York University, B.S., 1928, M.A., 1929, Ph.D., 1934. *Home:* Somerset 8-32, Century Village, West Palm Beach, Fla. 33409.

CAREER: Boys High School, Brooklyn, N.Y., instructor, 1931-43; Long Island City High School, Queens, N.Y., chairman of English and speech departments, 1943-53; Bureau of Curriculum Research, New York City, curriculum coordinator, 1953-54; James K. Paulding Junior High School, Bronx, N.Y., principal, 1954-55; supervisor of English for summer and evening high schools, New York City, 1947-52; Jamaica High School, Jamaica, Long Island, N.Y., chairman of English department, 1955-72; Fairleigh Dickinson University, Rutherford, N.J., instructor in education, 1972-73; York College of the City University of New York, New York City, 1973-77, began as assistant professor, became associate professor of education; affiliated with Institute of New Dimensions, Palm Beach Junior College, 1978—. Queens College of the City University of New York, Flushing, N.Y., instructor in School of General Studies, 1956-63; Yeshiva University, New York City, instructor in Graduate School of Education, 1959—; Hunter College of the City University of New York, New York City, instructor in School of General Studies, 1961-63. Visiting lecturer at summer sessions of various universities, 1955-62. *Military service:* Army Service Forces, 1943-45; became technical sergeant.

MEMBER: National Council of Teachers of English (president, 1958), New York State English Council (president, 1952-53), New York Society for the Experimental Study of Education (yearbook editor, 1953-63), New York City Association of Teachers of English (member of executive committee, 1957-61), Educators Square Club (New York).

WRITINGS: *Chaucer's Romance Vocabulary,* Comet Press Books, 1937, reprinted, Kennikat, 1968; *Traditions in American Literature,* Comet Press Books, 1939; *The American Drama since 1930,* Modern Chapbooks, 1949; *The Play's the Thing,* Modern Chapbooks, 1949, reprinted, Kennikat, 1968; *Grammar and Composition, Grade II,* Harcourt, 1958, revised edition, 1977; *Spelling Your Way to Success,* Barron, 1959, revised edition, 1974; *Attitudes toward English Teaching,* Chilton, 1961; *Guide to the Use of Bartlett's Familiar Quotations,* Little, Brown, 1962; *Index to Plays in Collections,* Scarecrow, 1966; *Teaching Drama in Secondary School,* Scarecrow, 1969; *The English Teacher: Basic Traditions and Successful Innovations,* Kennikat, 1977.

Editor; published by Pocket Books, except as indicated: (With F. J. Griffith) *One-Act Plays for Today,* Globe, 1945; (with F. J. Griffith) *Modern One-Act Plays,* Harcourt, 1950; Charles Dickens, *David Copperfield,* 1958; *Stories for Teen-Agers,* Globe, Volume I, 1959, Volume II, 1960; Dickens, *A Tale of Two Cities,* New American Library, 1960; Dickens, *The Pickwick Papers,* 1960; *Three Comedies of American Family Life,* 1961; *Three Plays about Doctors,* 1961; *Three Plays about American Idealism,* 1961; *Three Plays of American Realism,* 1961; *Three Plays about Marriage,* 1962; A. J. Cronin, *The Stars Look Down,* Little, Brown, 1963; *Studies in the Mass Media,* National Council of Teachers of English, 1964; *Three Plays about Business in America,* 1964; Elizabeth Barrett Browning, *Sonnets from the Portuguese,* Avon, 1966; A. E. Housman, *A Shropshire Lad,* Avon, 1966; *Great American Short Biographies,* Dell, 1966; *Great Narrative Essays,* 1968; *Three Dramas of American Individualism,* Washington Square Press, 1971; (with F. J. Griffith and Joseph B. Maggio) *One Act Plays for Our Times,* Popular Library, 1973; *Eight American Ethnic Plays,* Scribner, 1974. Also co-editor of *Guide to Play Selection,* Bowker. Advisory editor, "Literary Heritage" Series, Macmillan; general editor, *Spot Notes,* Dell. Consultant and editor, Educational Record Club. Contributor of more than two hundred articles to professional journals.

WORK IN PROGRESS: *Great Poems and Their Stories,* for Barron; *George S. Kaufman,* for Twayne; *Books for Retarded, Reluctant, and Remedial Readers; Index to Essays, with Suggestions for Teaching.*

SIDELIGHTS: Joseph Mersand told *CA:* "In my critical and educational writings, done while pursuing a heavy schedule of teaching, administration, and supervision, I have been able to express myself creatively and, at the same time, help my fellow teachers and supervisors on the basis of my own experience." *Avocational interests:* Folk dancing, book collecting, travel.

* * *

MESERVE, Walter Joseph, Jr. 1923-

PERSONAL: Born March 10, 1923, in Portland, Me.; son of Walter Joseph and Bessie (Bailey) Meserve; married, 1947 (divorced, 1967); married Ruth Ingeborg Vikdal, 1967; children: (first marriage) Gayle, Peter, Jo Alison, David. *Education:* Bates College, A.B., 1947; Boston University, M.A., 1948; University of Washington, Seattle, Ph.D., 1952. *Religion:* "Belief in a god." *Home address:* Box 31, R.R. 1, Nashville, Ind. 47448. *Office:* Department of Theatre and Drama, Indiana University, Bloomington, Ind. 47401.

CAREER: University of Kansas, Lawrence, instructor, 1951-53, assistant professor, 1953-58, associate professor, 1958-63, professor of English, 1963-67; Indiana University at Bloomington, professor of theatre and drama, 1968—. Lecturer in American literature, University of Manchester, 1959-60; visiting professor of dramatic art, University of California, Santa Barbara, 1967-68. *Military service:* U.S. Army Air Forces, 1943-46. *Member:* American Society for Theatre Research, American Theatre Association, Association for Asian Studies, Asia Society, Authors Guild. *Awards, honors:* American Philosophical Society grant, 1959-60; National Endowment for the Humanities fellowship, 1974-75; Rockefeller Foundation resident scholar, Bellagio, Italy, 1979.

WRITINGS: The Complete Plays of W. D. Howells, New York University Press, 1960; *An Outline History of American Drama,* Littlefield, 1965; (editor) *Discussions of Modern American Drama,* Heath, 1966; (editor with W. R. Reardon) *American Satiric Comedies,* Indiana University Press, 1969; *Robert E. Sherwood: Reluctant Moralist,* Bobbs-Merrill, 1970; (editor with wife, Ruth I. Meserve) *Modern Drama from Communist China,* New York University Press, 1970; (editor) W. D. Howell, *The Rise of Silas Lapham,* Indiana University Press, 1971; (editor) *Studies in "Death of a Salesman,"* C. E. Merrill, 1972; (editor with R. Meserve) *Modern Literature from China,* New York University Press, 1974; *An Emerging Entertainment: The Drama of the American People to 1828,* Indiana University Press, 1977; (with Travis Bogard and Richard Moody) *American Drama,* Methuen, 1977; *American Drama to 1900: An Information Guide,* Gale, 1980. Also contributor to *American Literary Scholarship* (annual), 1966-73. Member of editorial board, William Dean Howells, "Editions of American Authors" series, Modern Language Association of America, 1966-73. Contributor to *New England Quarterly, American Quarterly, Modern Drama,* and other periodicals. Member of editorial board, *Modern Drama,* 1960—.

WORK IN PROGRESS: Masks of a Developing Nation: The Drama of the American People, 1829-1889; Theatre for Utopia, a history of modern drama in China, with wife, Ruth I. Meserve.

SIDELIGHTS: Walter Meserve told *CA:* "I believe in Longfellow ('the love of learning, the sequestered nooks / and all the sweet serenity of books'), Emerson ('Self-Reliance'), Frost ('Mending Wall'), Unamuno ('The Tragic Sense of Life'), the Tao, and the necessity of understanding the people of our one world through their art and literature."

METCALF, Paul 1917-

PERSONAL: Born November 7, 1917, in East Milton, Mass.; son of Henry K. and Eleanor M. (Thomas) Metcalf; married Nancy Harman Blackford, May 31, 1942; children: Anne (Mrs. Gary Westmoreland), Adrienne (Mrs. Alan Weinman). *Education:* Attended Harvard University, 1936. *Home address:* R.F.D. 1, Box 26, Chester, Mass. 01011.

CAREER: Writer and teacher. Teacher of fiction workshop, Simon's Rock Early College, Great Barrington, Mass., 1973—. Has lectured at high schools, colleges, universities, and creative writing workshops, and has given public readings throughout the United States. Participant in creative arts festivals. Member of Hedgerow Theater; member of town planning board, Becket, Mass., 1969—. *Awards, honors:* Ford Foundation grants, 1970, 1971, for a stage adaptation of *Genoa* for use by National Theater of the Deaf.

WRITINGS: Will West, Jargon Press, 1956, Book Store Press, 1973; *Genoa,* Jargon Press, 1965; *Patagoni* (poem), Jargon Press, 1971; *Apalache* (poem), Turtle Island Foundation, 1976; *The Middle Passage* (poem), Jargon Press, 1976; *Willie's Throw* (poem), Five Trees Press, 1979; *Zip Odes* (poems), Tansy Press, 1979. Work is represented in the following anthologies: *The Moderns,* edited by LeRoi Jones, Corinth Books, 1963; *The American Equation: Literature in a Multi-Ethnic Culture,* edited by Katherine Newman, Allyn & Bacon, 1971; *A Berkshire Anthology,* edited by David Silverstein and Gerald Hausman, Book Store Press, 1972. Contributor of articles, poems, and reviews to literary magazines, including *Monk's Pond, Lillabulero, Isthmus, Toucan, Granite,* and *Io.*

WORK IN PROGRESS: 1-57, a poem, for Turtle Island Foundation; *Both,* for Jargon Press; *U.S. Department of the Interior,* a poem, for Gnomon Press; *The Assassination,* for Station Hill Press.

SIDELIGHTS: Paul Metcalf wrote *CA:* "Having been published for twenty-three years in small presses, I continue to write for this medium, and to believe that the best in both poetry and fiction will find its way to the public through these obscure, noncommercial outlets. What I take to be the 'great tradition in America' stems from Poe, Dickinson, Melville, Whitman, Dreiser, Anderson, Pound, and Williams. This tradition has been betrayed by the big commercial novelists, but its inheritors are very much alive, and may be found in the best of the small presses. . . . Success is not the criterion. It is well to remember that, at one time or another in their lives, Thoreau, Melville, and Whitman were self-published."

Metcalf is the great-grandson of Herman Melville; he has studies under Conrad Aiken and Charles Olson.

BIOGRAPHICAL/CRITICAL SOURCES: Lillabulero 12, winter, 1973, spring, 1973.

* * *

METZ, Leon C(laire) 1930-

PERSONAL: Born November 6, 1930, in Parkersburg, W.Va.; son of Leon (a union painter) and Velma (Balderson) Metz; married Mary Fitzgerald, October 4, 1950 (divorced, 1969); married Cheryl Schilling (a speech therapist in public schools), June 12, 1970; children: (first marriage) Velma Marlene, Leon Samuel, Matthew Claire; (second marriage) James David (stepson). *Education:* Attended University of Texas at El Paso, 1970. *Politics:* Independent. *Religion:* Protestant. *Home:* 4513 Cupid Dr., El Paso, Tex. 79924. *Office:* Office of the Mayor, City Hall, El Paso, Tex.

CAREER: Milkman and policeman in El Paso, Tex., 1953; Standard Oil Co. of Texas, El Paso, operator, 1953-67; University of Texas at El Paso, university archivist, 1967-79; executive assistant to mayor of El Paso, 1979—. *Military service:* U.S. Air Force, 1948-52; became staff sergeant. *Member:* Western Writers of America (vice-president, 1979-80; president, 1980-81), Society of American Archivists, Mission Heritage Association (president, 1976-80), El Paso Westerners Corral, El Paso County Historical Society (president, 1972-73), El Paso Council of Arts and Humanities (president, 1971-73), El Paso Society of Arts and Letters, El Paso Zoological Board (vice-president, 1973).

WRITINGS: John Selman: Texas Gunfighter, Hastings House, 1966; *Dallas Stoudenmire: El Paso Marshal,* Pemberton, 1969; *Pat Garrett: The Story of a Western Lawman,* University of Oklahoma Press, 1974; *The Shooters,* Mangan Books, 1976. Author of "Gunfighters of the Old West," a series published in *El Paso Times.* Contributor to *New York Westerners Brand Book* and *English Westerners Brand Book.* Contributor of articles and short stories to small western magazines and to *Arizona and the West, Montana, Password, Nova, Texas Military History, El Paso Herald-Post,* and *El Paso Times.*

WORK IN PROGRESS: The Mexican Border; El Paso: A History; History of Fort Bliss.

AVOCATIONAL INTERESTS: Hunting, hiking, fishing, motoring.

* * *

MEYER, Edith Patterson 1895-

PERSONAL: Born June 2, 1895, in Chatham, Mass.; daughter of John Nelson and Etta Mary (Briant) Patterson; married Shelby Rider Meyer, 1921 (died, 1943). *Education:* Attended Pratt Institute, 1915-16, Western Reserve University (now Case Western Reserve University), 1918-19, and University of Chicago, 1922, 1940. *Religion:* Congregationalist. *Home:* 83 Morgan St., Stamford, Conn. 06905.

CAREER: Public Library, Fond du Lac, Wis., first assistant librarian and children's librarian, 1916-18; public library, Cleveland, Ohio, children's librarian, 1918-21; American Library Association, Chicago, Ill., writer and editorial worker, 1922-24; Rand McNally & Co., Chicago, associate editor in children's department, 1924-44; Abingdon Press, New York, N.Y., editor of children's books, 1944-55. *Member:* American Library Association, Women's National Book Association, Stamford Forum for World Affairs. *Awards, honors:* Jane Addams Award, 1960, for *Champions of Peace.*

WRITINGS: Go It Alone, Lady! Harper, 1957; *Bible Stories for Young Readers,* Abingdon, 1958; *Dynamite and Peace: The Story of Alfred Nobel,* Little, Brown, 1958; *Champions of Peace: The Nobel Peace Prize Winners,* Little, Brown, 1959; *The Three Guardsmen and Other Stories,* Abingdon, 1960; *Pirate Queen,* Little, Brown, 1961; *The Friendly Frontier,* Little, Brown, 1962; *Meet the Future–Books and Ideas in Libraries of Today and Tomorrow,* Little, Brown, 1964; *Champions of the Four Freedoms,* Little, Brown, 1966; *That Remarkable Man: Justice Oliver Wendell Holmes,* Little, Brown, 1967; *First Lady of the Renaissance: Isabelle d'Este,* Little, Brown, 1970; *For Goodness Sake!, Growing Up in a New England Parsonage* (autobiography), Abingdon, 1973; *"Not Charity But Justice": The Story of Jacob A. Riis,* Vanguard, 1974; *Petticoat Patriots of the American Revolution,* Vanguard, 1976; *In Search of Peace: Nobel and the Nobel Peace Prize Winners,* Abingdon, 1978. Contributor to library and publishing journals and Methodist periodicals.

SIDELIGHTS: Edith Patterson Meyer told *CA* that most of her books are "biographical and required extensive research, some of it in foreign countries. My library training was helpful in this, as was my editorial experience in the writing and revising." Meyer believes that "a lifelong habit of reading good books is . . . the best preparation for writing." The underlying themes in her writing, she points out, are "peace and social betterment."

AVOCATIONAL INTERESTS: Travel, reading.

BIOGRAPHICAL/CRITICAL SOURCES: Young Readers' Review, January, 1967; *Book World,* April 7, 1968; *Best Sellers,* December 1, 1970; *America,* December 5, 1970; *West Coast Review of Books,* July, 1978.

* * *

MEYER, Karl E(rnest) 1928-

PERSONAL: Born May 22, 1928, in Madison, Wis.; son of Ernest L. and Dorothy (Narefsky) Meyer; married Sarah Neilson Peck, 1959; children: Ernest Leonard, Heather, Jonathan. *Education:* University of Wisconsin, B.S., 1951; Princeton University, Ph.D., 1956. *Home:* The Cherry Orchard, 96 Eleven O'Clock Rd., Weston, Conn. 06883.

CAREER: New York Times, New York City, general assignment reporter, 1952; *Washington Post,* Washington, D.C., member of editorial staff, 1956-64, London correspondent, beginning 1965, *Saturday Review,* New York City, senior editor, 1976-79; *New York Times,* member of editorial board, 1979—. Washington correspondent for *The New Statesman,* 1962-65. *Member:* American Newspaper Guild, Federal City Club. *Awards, honors:* Citation for excellence on Latin American reporting, Overseas Press Club; Sigma Delta Chi award, 1964.

WRITINGS: The New America, Basic Books, 1961; (with Tad Szulc) *The Cuban Invasion: The Chronicle of a Disaster,* Praeger, 1962; *Fulbright of Arkansas,* Robert B. Luce, 1963; *The Pleasures of Archaeology: A Visa to Yesterday,* Atheneum, 1970; *The Plundered Past,* Atheneum, 1973; *Teotihuacan,* Newsweek, 1973; *The Art Museum: Power, Money, and Ethics,* Morrow, 1979. Contributor to many magazines.

SIDELIGHTS: Karl Meyer has frequently been commended for bringing much-needed information on subjects of current interest to the attention of the general public. Richard Dudman finds *The Cuban Invasion* a "critical and circumstantial account [which] performs the role of the public inquiry that has never been made." Diana Loescher heralds *The Plundered Past* as a "finely documented, highly readable book, . . . the first major work on the illegal international traffic in works of art." "[Meyer] has obviously put an immense amount of energy into unraveling the antecedents of several important objects recently purchased by museums and private collections," explains Ian Graham; "all this he accomplished in urbane style and with sufficient detachment, even though an underlying sense of outrage is apparent."

Even Meyer's detractors are willing to make some concessions about his style. R. R. Brunn calls him a "clever phrasemaker" and admits that "often his judgments are accurate," although he warns that Meyer "is busy taking things apart and seldom stops to put things together again." In the same way, Charles Rolo's review of *The New America* calls it "cleverly packaged, eminently 'consumable'" and notes that it "has the appearance of seriousness," but he adds, "it really is quite lacking in ideas of any depth or originality." Hilton Kramer agrees that originality is a problem, noting that in *The Art Museum,* Meyer fails to "break new ground or, indeed, add anything to what has been conspicuously reported."

In spite of these complaints, Meyer's books serve a useful purpose. As a reviewer for *Newsweek* points out, in *The Pleasures of Archaeology* Meyer "is writing as a passionate hobbyist, genially, with love, and with much lively information," as opposed to making an attempt at a scholarly approach. Also in Meyer's defense, John Canaday answers Meyer's critics in a review of *The Art Museum*. "I never felt for a moment that Mr. Meyer's book was old news warmed over," he comments. "Rather, I found that half-faded events were freshened with details I had quite forgotten plus some that I had never managed to ferret out for myself."

AVOCATIONAL INTERESTS: Archaeology, music, and reading.

BIOGRAPHICAL/CRITICAL SOURCES: Atlantic, June 1961; *Christian Science Monitor,* June 14, 1961, November 28, 1973; *New York Times Book Review,* June 10, 1962, December 9, 1973, March 4, 1979; *New Republic,* May 21, 1967, March 3, 1979; *Natural History,* December, 1973; *Publishers Weekly,* December 11, 1978; *Washington Post Book World,* February 18, 1979.

* * *

MEYER, Thomas 1947-

PERSONAL: Born February 14, 1947, in Seattle, Washington; son of Edgar Adolph (a postman and policeman) and Bertha (a nurse; maiden name, Rinas) Meyer. *Education:* Bard College, A.B., 1969. *Home:* Highlands, N.C. 28741; and Corn Close, Dentdale, Sedbergh, Cumbria, England (summer). *Office:* Jargon Society, Book Organization, Elm St., Millerton, N.Y. 12546.

CAREER: Jargon Society, Penland, N.C., assistant to executive director, 1969—. Has given poetry readings in the United States, Canada, and England. *Awards, honors:* National Endowment for the Arts creative fellowship, 1980.

WRITINGS—Poetry: *The Bang Book,* Jargon Society, 1971; *Poikilos,* Finial Press, 1971; *O Nathan,* Finial Press, 1973; *The Umbrella of Aesculapius,* Jargon Society, 1975; (translator) Peter Jay, editor, *The Greek Anthology,* Oxford University Press, 1975; *Uranian Roses,* Catalyst Press, 1977; *Staves Calends Legends,* Jargon Society, 1979; (with John Furnival) *Blind Date,* Circle Press, 1979; *May,* Finial Press, 1980; *Beautiful Rivers,* Tansy Press, 1980; *Kittyhawk,* Sand Dollar Press, in press. Also translator of *Beowulf,* 1974, and of *Sappho,* with Sandra Fisher. Contributor to magazines, including *Prose, Caterpillar, Parnassus,* and *Aperture*.

SIDELIGHTS: Thomas Meyer writes: "The greatest field of influence on my own work lies—not in my involvement with Anglo-Saxon and Greek or in earlier skirmishes with Cabalism and Analytical Psychology—but in the art of cooking. As a result of careful and plodding study of culinary methods and techniques, there grew in me certain intimations about myself as a poet."

* * *

MICHELON, L. C. 1918-

PERSONAL: Born August 25, 1918, in Chicago, Ill.; married Margaret Mary Devereaux; children: Cecilia Marie. *Education:* DePaul University, Ph.B., 1939; Chicago Teachers College (now Chicago State University), M.E., 1940; University of Chicago, additional study, 1948. *Home:* 22307 Halburton Rd., Cleveland, Ohio 44122. *Office:* Retirement Investment Co., 1 Public Sq., Cleveland, Ohio 44113.

CAREER: Illinois Institute of Technology, Chicago, assistant professor, 1941-42; Purdue University, Lafayette, Ind., assistant professor, 1946-49; University of Chicago, Chicago, director of management services, 1949-53; Republic Steel Corp., Cleveland, Ohio, management consultant, 1957-58, coordinator of communication, 1958-60, director of public affairs and education, 1960—, vice-president, Republican Education Institute, 1967-72, president, Republic Education Institute, 1972—. Chairman, Retirement Investment Co. Vice-president, Center for Learning; adjunct professor, John Carroll University. *Military service:* U.S. Naval Reserve, active duty, 1942-46; became lieutenant. *Member:* American Political Science Association, Canterbury Club. *Awards, honors:* Gold Medal in management and behavioral sciences, Law-Science Academy, 1970.

WRITINGS: Industrial Inspection Methods, Republic Education Institute, 1942, revised edition, 1971; (with Ernest Dale) *Modern Management Methods,* World Publishing, 1967; (with Reuben Slesinger) *Understanding Basic Economics,* World Publishing, 1967; (with W. P. Irwin) *Understanding Politics,* World Publishing, 1968; (with Irwin) *Understanding Government,* World Publishing, 1968; *How to Be a Dynamic Conference Leader,* World Publishing, 1968; *Myths and Realities of Management,* Republic Education Institute, 1972; *The Art and Science of Professional Supervision,* Republic Education Institute, 1972; *Free Enterprise Economics,* Institute for Business and Economic Education, 1979.

* * *

MICHELSON, Peter 1937-

PERSONAL: Born December 23, 1937, in Chicago, Ill.; son of Paul Orne and Inez (Larson) Michelson; divorced; children: Kristen, Hilary. *Education:* Whitman College, B.A., 1958; University of Wyoming, M.A., 1959; University of Chicago, additional study, 1961-63. *Office:* English Department, University of Colorado, Boulder, Colo. 80302.

CAREER: Chicago Review, Chicago, Ill., associate editor, 1963, editor, 1964-65; University of Notre Dame, Notre Dame, Ind., instructor, 1965-67, assistant professor of English, 1967-68; University of Wyoming, Laramie, editor of *Purple Sage,* 1969-70; Northwestern University, Evanston, Ill., assistant professor of English, 1970-74; University of Colorado, Boulder, associate professor of English, 1974—.

WRITINGS: (Author of introduction) Eugene Wildman, editor, *Anthology of Concretism,* Swallow Press, 1967, 2nd edition, 1969; (contributor) Douglas A. Hughes, editor, *Perspectives on Pornography,* St. Martin's, 1970; *The Aesthetics of Pornography,* Herder & Herder, 1971; *The Eater* (poems), Swallow Press, 1972; *Pacific Plainsong I-XIII* (poems), Brillig Works Publications, 1978. Work represented in many anthologies, including: *The Young American Writers: Fiction, Poetry, Drama, and Criticism,* edited by Richard Kostelanetz, Funk, 1967; *New Poetry Anthology I,* edited by Michael Anania, Swallow Press, 1967; *Under Thirty: Fiction, Poetry and Criticism of the New American Writers,* edited by Charles Newman and William A. Henkin, Jr., Indiana University Press, 1968; *Heartland II,* edited by Lucien Stryk, Northern Illinois University Press, 1977. Poems have appeared in *Chicago Review, Prairie Schooner, North American Review, Tri-Quarterly, New Republic, Choice,* and others. Contributor of essays to *New Republic, Tri-Quarterly,* and other periodicals. Contributing editor, *Tri-Quarterly,* 1976—.

MICKEY, Paul A(lbert) 1937-

PERSONAL: Born May 13, 1937, in Amanda, Ohio; son of Martin E. (a clergyman) and Ellen (Koons) Mickey; married Jane E. Becker (an executive secretary), October 13, 1962; children: Bruce Jon, Sandra Lee. *Education:* Harvard University, B.A., 1963; Princeton Theological Seminary, B.D., 1966, Ph.D., 1970. *Home:* 2617 McDowell Rd., Durham, N.C. 27705. *Office:* School of Divinity, Duke University, 315 Divinity Bldg., Durham, N.C. 27706.

CAREER: Pastor of United Methodist churches in Cleveland, Ohio, 1966-67, and Bay Head, N.J., 1969-70; Duke University, Durham, N.C., associate professor of pastoral theology, 1970—. Member of board of directors of CONTACT-Teleministries, 1971-78, and of United Methodist Church organization, Good News, 1973—. *Military service:* U.S. Air Force, 1955-59; became staff sergeant. *Member:* American Academy of Religion, American Council on Pastoral Education, Association of Professional Educators for Ministry, Aircraft Owners and Pilots Association.

WRITINGS: (With Robert Wilson) *Conflict and Resolution,* Abingdon, 1973; (with Wilson) *What New Creation,* Abingdon, 1977, (with Gary Gamble) *Pastoral Assertiveness,* Abingdon, 1978; *Essentials of Wesleyan Theology,* Zondervan, 1980; (with Linda Hawkins) *Mary Magdalene: Exemplar for Ministry,* Seabury, 1981.

WORK IN PROGRESS: Another book.

AVOCATIONAL INTERESTS: The out-of-doors, flying (instrument flight instructor), farming, conservation work.

* * *

MILES, T(homas) R(ichard) 1923-

PERSONAL: Born March 11, 1923, in Sheffield, England; son of Richard (an engineer) and Alice (Miller) Miles; married Elaine Armstrong (a teacher of dyslexic children), August 21, 1951; children: P.J.R. *Education:* Magdalen College, Oxford, M.A., 1945, University College of North Wales, Ph.D., 1963. *Religion:* Society of Friends (Quaker). *Home:* Llys-y-Gwynt, Llandegfan, Menai Bridge, Gwynedd, Wales. *Office:* Department of Psychology, University College of North Wales, Bangor, Wales.

CAREER: University College of North Wales, Bangor, assistant lecturer, 1949-52, lecturer, 1952-63, professor of psychology, 1963—. Member of staff, Tavistock Clinic, 1953-54. *Member:* Royal Institute of Philosophy (member of council), British Psychological Society (fellow), British Dyslexia Association, Cheshire and North Wales Dyslexia Association (president).

WRITINGS: *Religion and the Scientific Outlook,* Allen & Unwin, 1959; *Eliminating the Unconscious,* Pergamon, 1966; *On Helping the Dyslexic Child,* Methuen, 1970; *Religious Experience,* Macmillan, 1972; *More Help for Dyslexic Children,* Methuen, 1975; *Understanding Dyslexia,* Hodder & Stoughton, 1978; (editor with G. Pavlidis) *Dyslexia Research and Its Application to Education,* Wiley, in press. Contributor to *Quarterly Journal of Experimental Psychology, Dyslexia Review, Mind, Philosophy, British Journal of Educational Psychology, British Journal for the Philosophy of Science,* and other professional journals.

WORK IN PROGRESS: Further research on dyslexia.

SIDELIGHTS: T. R. Miles wrote *CA:* "As a scientist researching into dyslexia I sometimes wonder if I should concern myself only with the disinterested pursuit of knowledge. When I see the hammering which some dyslexic children receive from the educational system, however, I find myself with no option but to campaign on their behalf. I do not think the roles of scientist and campaigner are incompatible." *Avocational interests:* Lawn tennis (former international and Wimbledon player), golf, playing the cello.

* * *

MILLER, Albert G(riffith) 1905-

PERSONAL: Born December 28, 1905, in Philadelphia, Pa.; son of Albert Griffith and Mabel (Morris) Miller; married Mary Susan Horney, 1928. *Education:* University of Pennsylvania, A.B., 1927. *Home:* 440 East 79th St., New York, N.Y. 10021.

CAREER: N. W. Ayer & Son, New York, N.Y., writer, 1928-33; free-lance writer, 1933—. Lecturer in dramatic writing for film and television, New York University. *Military service:* U.S. Navy; became lieutenant. *Member:* Writers Guild of America, Dramatists Guild, Authors League, Authors Guild.

WRITINGS: (Editor) Emidio Angelo, *The Infernal Revenue* (cartoons), Thomas Nelson, 1959; *Fury: Stallion of Broken Wheel Ranch,* Holt, 1959; *Fury and the Mustangs,* Holt, 1960; *Silver Chief's Big Game Trail,* Holt, 1961; *Fury and the White Mare,* Holt, 1962; *Fury,* adapted by Alice Thorne, Grosset, 1964; *Captain Whopper,* Astor-Honor, 1967; *More Captain Whopper Tales,* Astor-Honor, 1968; *A Friend for Shadow,* L. W. Singer, 1969; *Ring of Bright Water,* Golden Press, 1969; *King of the Grizzlies,* Golden Press, 1970; *Mark Twain in Love,* Harcourt, 1973.

All published by Random House: *The Wonderful Magic Motion Machine,* 1967; *The Magic Motion Martian Book,* 1967; *My Friend the Dragon,* 1967; *How Many Tadpoles?,* 1967; *A Magic-Scope Visit to Other Lands,* 1967; *Who Popped Out?,* 1967; *The Dog That Said Wow-Bow,* 1967; *The Clock Book,* 1968; *The Wishing Ring,* 1968; (adapter) Ian Fleming, *The Adventures of Chitty Chitty Bang Bang,* 1968; (adapter) Lyman Frank Baum, *The Wizard of Oz,* 1968; *Pinocchio,* 1968; (adapter) *Alice in Wonderland,* 1968; *Robin Hood,* 1968; (adapter) *20,000 Leagues under the Sea,* 1968; *The Book of Left and Right,* 1968; *Snow White and the Seven Dwarfs,* 1969; *The Birth of Jesus,* 1969; *Hansel and Gretel,* 1969; (adapter) *The Emperor's New Clothes,* 1969; *The Sesame Street Storybook,* 1972; *Walt Disney's Bambi Gets Lost,* 1972. Also Author of three "Talk-to-Me Books," *Clock Cleaners, Ghost Chasers,* and *Trucks.*

"Pop-up" series; published by Random House, except as indicated: *Pop-up Dr. Dolittle,* 1967; ... *Tournament of Magic,* 1967; ... *Color Book,* 1967; (editor) ... *Cinderella,* 1968; ... *Circus Book,* 1968; ... *Book of Flying Machines,* 1969; ... *Biggest Book,* 1969; ... *Book of Knock Knocks,* 1969; ... *Noah and the Ark,* 1969; ... *Story of the Nativity,* 1970; (editor) ... *Aladdin and the Wonderful Lamp,* 1970; ... *David and Goliath,* 1970; ... *Little Red Riding Hood,* 1970; ... *Three Little Pigs,* 1970; ... *Book of Boats,* 1972; ... *Book of Jokes: Pop Corn,* 1972; ... *The Black Hole,* Western Publishing, 1979.

"ABC Serendipity" series; published by Bowmar: *The ABC Dog Show,* 1974; *Backward Beasts from A to Z,* 1974; *Our Friends the ABC's,* 1974; *Talking Letters,* 1974; *26 Riddles from A to Z,* 1974; *Where Did That Word Come From,* 1974.

Also author of *Big Bird's Blunder Book,* Western Publishing, *Mickey Mouse and the Best Neighbor Contest,* Golden Press, *The Chimp Who Made Good,* Educational Challenges, Inc., "Little Boy Blue" (play), produced in Hollywood, Calif., and "Old Lady Robbins" (play). Author of two feature-length screen plays, "Spider's Web," based on the play by Agatha Christie, and "Around the World"; author of numerous television and radio scripts.

* * *

MILLER, Albert Jay 1928-

PERSONAL: Born December 7, 1928, in Beaver Falls, Pa.; son of Joseph Jefferson (a steel worker) and Alberta (Shaffer) Miller. *Education:* Geneva College, B.S., 1952; Rutgers University, M.S.L.S., 1958. *Religion:* Reformed Presbyterian Church of North America. *Home:* 417 Charles Ave., New Kensington, Pa. 15068. *Office:* Pennsylvania State University, New Kensington Campus, 3550 Seventh Street Rd., New Kensington, Pa. 15068.

CAREER: Librarian at West Allegheny Junior High School, Imperial, Pa., 1960-62, and Butler Area Senior High School, Butler, Pa., 1963-69; Pennsylvania State University, New Kensington Campus, librarian, 1969—. Water safety instructor for American Red Cross, 1970—. Member of board of directors, Butler County Mental Health Association, 1967-68, and Allegheny-Kiski Valley Senior Citizens Center. Member of Allegheny-Kiski Valley Human Relations Council, 1973—. Library consultant, Seattle World's Fair. Speaker for civil organizations. *Member:* American Library Association, American Society of Indexers, National Education Association (life member), Pennsylvania Library Association, Pennsylvania Education Association (life member), Westmoreland County Mental Health Association (member of board of directors, 1972-73).

WRITINGS: A Selective Bibliography of Existentialism in Education and Related Topics, Exposition, 1969; *Confrontation, Conflict, and Dissent: A Bibliography of a Decade of Controversy, 1960-1970,* Scarecrow, 1972; (with Michael J. Acri) *Death: A Bibliographical Guide,* Scarecrow, 1977. Contributor to *Pennsylvania School Journal, Aging in Pennsylvania, Library-College Omnibus, Learning Today,* and other periodicals. Book and media review editor, *Learning Today.*

WORK IN PROGRESS: "Research on bibliography"; a bio-bibliographical study of Joe Namath; a study of runaway youth.

SIDELIGHTS: Albert Jay Miller wrote *CA:* "My primary interest in higher education is to instill within learners the joy of life-long learning. I'm interested in building learning skills which will hopefully hold adult learners in good stead to solve their own problems regardless of what the problem may be, now and in the future.

"I have tremendous faith in young people and believe that they have initiative, talent, and an abundance of creative ability. They need our confidence and encouragement. They make worthy ambassadors for our state and country."

* * *

MILLER, George A(rmitage) 1920-

PERSONAL: Born February 3, 1920, in Charleston, W.Va.; son of George E. (an engineer) and Florence (Armitage) Miller; married Katherine James, November 29, 1939; children: Nancy Ruth, Donnally James. *Education:* University of Alabama, B.A., 1940, M.A., 1941; Harvard University, Ph.D., 1946. *Home:* 478 Lake Dr., Princeton, N.J. 08540. *Office:* Department of Psychology, Princeton University, Princeton, N.J. 08540.

CAREER: University of Alabama, Tuscaloosa, instructor in psychology, 1941-43; Harvard University, Cambridge, Mass., research fellow in psycho-acoustics, 1944-48, assistant professor, 1948-51; Massachusetts Institute of Technology, Cambridge, associate professor, 1951-55; Harvard University, Cambridge, associate professor, 1955-58, professor of psychology, 1958-68, chairman of department, 1964-67, co-director of Center for Cognitive Studies, 1960-67; Rockefeller University, New York, N.Y., professor of psychology, 1968-79, adjunct professor, 1979—; Princeton University, Princeton, N.J., professor of psychology, 1979—. Visiting professor, Rockefeller University, 1967-68, Massachusetts Institute of Technology, 1968-79; Institute for Advanced Study, member, 1950, 1970-72, visitor, 1972-76. Consultant at various times to Veterans Administration, Air Force, International Business Machines, Bell Telephone Laboratories, President's Scientific Advisory Council, National Institutes of Health.

MEMBER: American Psychological Association (president, 1968-69), American Philosophical Society, Society of Experimental Psychology, Acoustical Society of America, Linguistic Society of America, American Statistical Association, American Physiological Society, Psychometric Society, Psychonomic Society, American Association for the Advancement of Science, American Academy of Arts and Sciences, National Academy of Science, Eastern Psychological Association (president, 1961-62), Linguistic Circle of New York, Sigma Xi. *Awards, honors:* Doctorat Honoris Causa, Universite Catholique de Louvain, 1976; Doctor of Social Science, Yale University, 1979.

WRITINGS: Language and Communication, McGraw, 1951; (compiler) *Bibliography on Hearing,* Harvard University Press, 1955; (with Galanter and Pribam) *Plans and the Structure of Behavior,* Holt, 1960; *Psychology,* Harper, 1962; *Mathematics and Psychology,* Wiley, 1964; *Psychology of Communication,* Basic Books, 1967; (with Noam Chomsky) *Analyse formelle des langues naturelles,* Mouton, 1971; (with Buckhout) *Psychology: The Science of Mental Life,* Harper, 1973; *Communication, Language, and Meaning,* Basic Books, 1973; (with Johnson-Laird) *Language and Perception,* Harvard University Press, 1976; *Spontaneous Apprentices: Children and Language,* Seabury, 1977; (with Halle and Bresnan) *Linguistic Theory and Psychological Reality,* M.I.T. Press, 1978; (with Lenneberg) *Psychology and Biology of Language and Thought,* Academic Press, 1978. Contributor of chapters to books and articles to journals.

* * *

MILLER, James Edwin (Jr.) 1920-

PERSONAL: Born September 9, 1920, in Bartlesville, Okla.; son of James Edwin and Leona (Halsey) Miller; married Barbara Anderson, 1944; children: James Edwin III, Charlotte Ann. *Education:* University of Oklahoma, B.A., 1942; University of Chicago, M.A., 1947, Ph.D., 1949. *Home:* 5536 Blackstone Ave., Chicago, Ill. *Office:* Department of English, University of Chicago, Chicago, Ill.

CAREER: Roosevelt University, Chicago, Ill., lecturer in English, 1947-49; University of Michigan, Ann Arbor, instructor in English, 1949-50; University of Nebraska, Lincoln, 1953-62, became professor of English and chairman of department, Charles J. Mach Regents Professor of English, 1961; University of Chicago, Chicago, 1962—, currently professor of English and chairman of department. Fulbright lecturer in Italy, 1958-59, and Japan, 1968; participant in Kyoto (Japan) Seminar in American Studies, 1968. *Military service:*

U.S. Army, Signal Corps, 1942-46, 1950-52; became captain. *Member:* Modern Language Association of America, National Council of Teachers of English (president, 1970), American Association of University Professors, American Studies Association, Midwest Modern Language Association (president, 1961-62), Phi Beta Kappa. *Awards, honors:* Walt Whitman Award, Poetry Society of America, 1957, for *Critical Guide to "Leaves of Grass";* Poetry Chapbook Award, 1960, for *Start with the Sun;* Guggenheim fellowship, 1969-70; National Endowment for the Humanities fellowship, 1975; distinguished service award, National Councils of Teachers of English, 1975; Australian distinguished visitor grant, 1976.

WRITINGS: Fictional Technique of Scott Fitzgerald, Nijhoff, 1957, reprinted, Folcroft, 1976; *Critical Guide to "Leaves of Grass,"* University of Chicago Press, 1957; (editor) *Walt Whitman: Complete Poetry and Selected Prose,* Houghton, 1959; *Myth and Method: Modern Theories of Fiction,* University of Nebraska Press, 1960; (with Bernice Slote and Karl Shapiro) *Start with the Sun,* University of Nebraska Press, 1960; (with Slote) *Dimensions of Poetry,* Dodd, 1962; *A Reader's Guide to Herman Melville,* Noonday, 1962; *Walt Whitman,* Twayne, 1962; (contributor) *Eight American Writers,* Norton, 1963; (with Slote) *Dimensions of the Short Story,* Dodd, 1964; (editor) *Whitman's "Song of Myself": Origin, Growth, Meaning,* Dodd, 1964; *F. Scott Fitzgerald: His Art and His Technique,* New York University Press, 1964; *J. D. Salinger,* University of Minnesota Press, 1965; (with Blair, Hornberger, and Stewart) *Literature of the United States,* Scott, Foresman, 1966; (with Slote) *Dimensions of Literature,* Dodd, 1967; (editor with Paul Herring) *The Arts and the Public,* University of Chicago Press, 1967; *Quests Surd and Absurd: Essays in American Literature,* University of Chicago Press, 1967.

Word, Self, Reality: The Rhetoric of Imagination, Dodd, 1972; (editor) *Theory of Fiction: Henry James,* University of Nebraska Press, 1972; (with others) *England in Literature,* Scott, Foresman, 1973; (with others) *The United States in Literature,* Scott, Foresman, 1973; (with others) *The Human Condition,* Scott, Foresman, 1974; *T. S. Eliot's Personal Waste Land: Exorcism of the Demons,* Pennsylvania State University Press, 1977; *The American Quest for a Supreme Fiction: Whitman's Legacy in the Personal Epic,* University of Chicago Press, 1979.

Compiler; all with Robert O'Neal and Helen M. McDonnell; all published by Scott, Foresman, 1970: *Black African Voices; Of Time and Place: Comparative World Literature in Translation; The Human Condition: Literature Written in the English Language; Literature from Greek and Roman Antiquity; Russian and Eastern European Literature; Literature in the Eastern World; Translations from the French; Italian Literature in Translation; From Spain and the Americas: Literature in Translation; Teutonic Literature in English Translation.* Also author, with Stephen Judy, of *Writing in Reality,* Harper, and *American Literature: A Brief History,* 1974. Lecturer on three phonotapes, *The Catcher in the Rye,* by J. D. Salinger, Everett/Edwards, 1970, *The Great Gatsby,* by F. Scott Fitzgerald, Everett/Edwards, 1970, and *My Antonia,* by Willa Cather, Everett/Edwards, 1971. Editor, *College English,* 1960-66.

SIDELIGHTS: James Edwin Miller told *CA*: "If an English teacher can instill a passion for reading literature in students at an early age, it is likely that the students will come naturally to know, at conscious or unconscious levels, most of the elements fundamental to growth in language and composition. But they will also, through literature, come to know much more. What it is they come to know is not, except peripherally, about literature, but about life, reality, experience, themselves, and their society . . . . And what they know they will know in ways possible by no other means."

* * *

MILLER, Jim Wayne 1936-

PERSONAL: Born October 21, 1936, in Leicester, N.C.; son of James Woodrow (a service manager) and Edith (Smith) Miller; married Mary Ellen Yates (a teacher), August 17, 1958; children: James Yates, Fred Smith, Ruth Ratcliff. *Education:* Berea College, A.B., 1958; Vanderbilt University, Ph.D., 1965. *Politics:* Left-wing Democrat. *Religion:* "Not a member of any organized church." *Home:* 1512 Eastland Dr., Bowling Green, Ky. 42101. *Office:* Department of Foreign Languages, Western Kentucky University, Bowling Green, Ky. 42101.

CAREER: Western Kentucky University, Bowling Green, assistant professor, 1963-65, associate professor, 1966-70, professor of German, 1970—. Visiting professor, Appalachian Studies Workshop, Berea College, 1973—; invited reader, fiftieth anniversary meeting of South Atlantic Modern Language Association, 1978. Consultant to poetry workshops in Kentucky, Virginia, North Carolina, Tennessee, and West Virginia. *Member:* American Association of Teachers of German, American Association of University Professors. *Awards, honors:* Alice Lloyd Memorial Prize for Applachian Poetry from Alice Lloyd College, 1967, for poems in *Copperhead Cane;* Western Kentucky University faculty award for research and creativity, 1976.

WRITINGS: Copperhead Cane (poems), Robert Moore Allen, 1964; *The More Things Change, the More They Stay the Same* (ballads), Whippoorwill Press, 1971; *Dialogue with a Dead Man* (poems), University of Georgia Press, 1974; (translator) Enil Lerperger, *The Figure of Fulfillment* (poems), Green River Press, 1975; *The Mountains Have Come Closer* (poems), Appalachian Consortium Press, 1980; (editor) *I Have a Place* (poetry anthology), Appalachian Learning Laboratory, 1980.

Contributor: Sister Mary Carmel Browning, editor, *Kentucky Authors: A History of Kentucky Literature,* Keller-Crescent, 1968; Suzanne Crowell, editor, *Appalachian People's History Book,* Mountain Education Associates, 1971; *Appalachians Speak Up,* edited by Irmgard Best, [Berea, Ky.], 1972; *New Southern Poets,* edited by Guy Owen and Mary C. Williams, University of North Carolina Press, 1974; *The Wooden Tower: An Anthology of Appalachian Literature,* edited by Lorena Anderson, Marjorie Warner, and Barbara Yeager, Morris Harvey College Publications, 1975; *This Place Kentucky,* edited by Wade Hall, Data Courier, Inc., 1975; *An Anthology,* edited by Angus Wilson, Green River Press, 1975; *North Carolina Poetry: The Seventies,* edited by Owen and Williams, Southern Poetry Review Press, 1975; Bill Sullivan, Larry Benaquist, and Fred Moramarco, editors, *Contemporary American Poetry,* Professional Productivity Associates, 1975; *Voices from the Mountains,* edited by Guy Caraway and Candie Caraway, Knopf, 1975; *Voices from the Hills,* edited by Robert J. Higgs and Ambrose Manning, Ungar, 1975; Dorothy Townsend, editor, *Kentucky in American Letters,* Volume III, Georgetown College Press, 1976; *Newground: An Anthology of Appalachian Poetry,* edited by Donald Askins and David Morris, Southern Appalachian Writers Cooperative, 1977; *Contemporary Poetry of North Carolina,* edited by Owen and Williams, Blair, 1977; Higgs and Neil D. Isaacs, editors, *The*

Sporting Spirit: Athletes in Literature and Life, Harcourt, 1977; *Southern Poetry: The Seventies,* edited by Owen and Williams, Southern Poetry Review Press, 1977; *Contemporary Poets of the New South,* edited by Bob Millard, Project House Foundation, 1977; *Contemporary Southern Poetry,* edited by Owen and Williams, Louisiana State University Press, 1979; *The Kentucky Book,* edited by Hall, Courier Journal and Louisville Times Co., 1979; *A Geography of Poets,* edited by Edward Field, Bantam, 1979; *Anthology of Magazine Verse and Yearbook of American Poetry,* edited by Alan F. Pater, Monitor, 1980. Contributor to *Encyclopedia of Appalachia.* Contributor of short stories and poetry to literary magazines and of scholarly and critical essays to professional journals.

WORK IN PROGRESS: Translating contemporary German lyrics, a juvenile novel by a contemporary Austrian writer, and a nineteenth-century German treatise on rhyme; papers on Appalachian folklore and folklife; poems.

SIDELIGHTS: "Growing up in North Carolina," Jim Wayne Miller writes, "I was often amused, along with other natives, at tourists who fished the trout streams. The pools, so perfectly clear, had a deceptive depth. Fishermen unacquainted with them were forever stepping with hip waders into pools they judged to be knee-deep and going in up to their waists or even their armpits, sometimes being floated right off their feet. I try to make poems like those pools, so simple and clear their depth is deceiving. I want the writing to be so transparent that the reader forgets he is reading and is aware only that he is having an experience. He is suddenly plunged deeper than he expected and comes up shivering."

* * *

MILLER, Randolph Crump 1910-

PERSONAL: Born October 1, 1910, in Fresno, Calif.; son of Ray Oakley (a clergyman) and Laura (Crump) Miller; married Muriel Phyllis Hallett, 1938 (died, 1948); married Elizabeth Rives Williams Fowlkes, 1950; children: Barbara, Frank Fowlkes, Phyllis Symonds, Carol Rand, Rives Carroll, Muriel Leahy. *Education:* Pomona College, A.B., 1931; attended Episcopal Theological School, 1935-36; Yale University, Ph.D., 1936. *Home:* 15 Edgehill Rd., New Haven, Conn. 06511. *Office:* Yale Divinity School, Yale University, 409 Prospect St., New Haven, Conn. 06510.

CAREER: Ordained Protestant Episcopal priest, 1937; Church Divinity School of the Pacific, Berkeley, Calif., 1936-52, began as instructor, became professor of philosophy and religion; Yale University, Divinity School, New Haven, Conn., professor of Christian education, 1952-64, Horace Bushnell Professor of Christian Nurture, 1964—. Visiting professor at Harvard University and Episcopal Theological School, spring, 1954, Syracuse University, summers, 1956, 1957, 1958, Ecumenical Institute (Switzerland), fall, 1959, Andover Newton Theological School, spring, 1963, Garrett Theological Seminary, summer, 1963, Berkeley Divinity School, fall, 1964, Serampore College (India), fall, 1966, Divinity School, Drew University, fall, 1968, Pacific School of Religion, summer, 1972, and School of Theology, Claremont College, spring, 1976. Lecturer at Near East School of Theology (Beirut), winter, 1957, Trinity College (Singapore), summer, 1970, and Boston College, summer, 1973. Chaplain, Episcopal church at University of California, Berkeley, 1937-40; vicar, St. Alban's Church (Albany, Calif.), 1940-52; director of Christian education, Trinity Church (New Haven, Conn.), 1961-71. *Member:* Religious Education Association (chairman of the board, 1956-59). *Awards, honors:* S.T.D., Church Divinity School of the Pacific, 1952; D.D., Pacific School of Religion, 1952; D.D., Episcopal Theological School, 1961; William Rainey Harper Award, Religious Education Association, 1978.

WRITINGS: What We Can Believe, Scribner, 1941; *A Guide for Church School Teachers,* Cloister, 1943, revised edition, 1947; (co-editor) *Christianity and the Contemporary Scene,* Morehouse, 1943; (editor) *The Church and Organized Movements,* Harper, 1946; *Religion Makes Sense,* Seabury, 1950; *The Clue to Christian Education,* Scribner, 1950; *A Symphony of the Christian Year,* Seabury, 1954; *Education for Christian Living,* Prentice-Hall, 1956, revised edition, 1963; *Biblical Theology and Christian Education,* Scribner, 1956; *Be Not Anxious,* Seabury, 1957; *I Remember Jesus,* Seabury, 1958; (editor) *What Is the Nature of Man?,* United Church Press, 1959; *Christian Nurture and the Church,* Scribner, 1961; *Your Child's Religion,* Doubleday, 1962, 2nd edition, Hawthorn, 1975; *Youth Considers Parents as People,* Thomas Nelson, 1965; *The Language Gap and God,* Pilgrim Press, 1970; *Living with Anxiety,* Pilgrim Press, 1971; *Live until You Die,* Pilgrim Press, 1973; *The American Spirit in Theology,* Pilgrim Press, 1974; *This We Can Believe,* Seabury, 1976; *Theory of Christian Education: Practice,* Religious Education Press, 1980.

Contributor: T. Ferris, editor, *Episcopalians United,* Morehouse, 1947; S. Doniger, editor, *Religion and Human Behavior,* Association Press, 1954; Doniger, editor, *Human Nature,* Harper, 1961; R. Bretall, editor, *Empirical Theology of Henry Nelson Wieman,* Southern Illinois University Press, 1963; M. Taylor, editor, *Introduction to Christian Education,* Abingdon, 1966; K. Cully, editor, *The Episcopal Church and Education,* Morehouse, 1966; Cully, editor, *Does the Church Know How to Teach?,* Macmillan, 1970; J. Westerhoff, editor, *A Colloquy on Christian Education,* Pilgrim Press, 1972; J. M. Lee, editor, *The Religious Education We Need,* Religious Education Press, 1976; Gloria Durka and Joanmarie Smith, editors, *Aesthetic Dimensions of Religious Education,* Paulist/Newman, 1979. Author of pamphlets and a church school course. Contributor to religious periodicals. Editor, *Religious Education,* 1958-78.

BIOGRAPHICAL/CRITICAL SOURCES: K. Cully and I. Cully, editors, *Process and Relationship: Festschrift for Randolph Crump Miller,* Religious Education Press, 1978.

* * *

MILLER, Wayne Charles 1939-

PERSONAL: Born November 3, 1939, in New York, N.Y.; son of Charles Henry (a banker) and Florence (Keenan) Miller; married Carol DiGioia, December 1, 1962 (divorced, 1969); married Patricia Clemens, September 2, 1973; children: (first marriage) Alison Catherine, Heather Mary; (second marriage) W. Joshua. *Education:* St. John's University, Jamaica, N.Y., B.A., 1960; Columbia University, M.A., 1961; New York University, Ph.D., 1968. *Home:* 343 Compton Hills Dr., Cincinnati, Ohio 45215. *Office:* Department of English, University of Cincinnati, Cincinnati, Ohio 45221.

CAREER: Thomas Y. Crowell Publishers, New York, N.Y., staff writer, 1961-62; University of Colorado, Colorado Springs, lecturer in English, 1964-67; State University of New York College at Oneonta, associate professor of English, 1967-70; University of Cincinnati, Cincinnati, Ohio, professor of English, 1970—. *Military service:* U.S. Air Force, 1962-67; assistant professor of English at Air Force Academy, 1963-67; became captain. *Member:* American Academy of Political and Social Sciences, Modern Language

Association of America, Society for the Study of Multi-Ethnic Literature of the United States, Inter-University Seminar on the Armed Forces and Society. *Awards, honors:* Taft research fellowship, 1972; Ohio Program in the Humanities grants, 1973-77; National Endowment for the Humanities grants, 1976, 1977, and 1979.

WRITINGS—All published by New York University Press: *An Armed America—Its Face in Fiction: A History of the American Military Novel,* 1970; *Ghetto Writers: Irish, Italian, Jewish, Black, and Puerto Rican,* 1972; *A Comprehensive Bibliography for the Study of American Minorities,* two volumes, 1976; *A Handbook of American Minorities,* 1976. Also author of scripts for television. Contributor to scholarly journals.

WORK IN PROGRESS: A book on the fiction and film that have emerged from the war in Vietnam; a book on ethnic autobiography.

* * *

MILLER, William Alvin 1931-

PERSONAL: Born January 1, 1931, in Pittsburgh, Pa.; son of Christ William and Anna Ernestine (Wilhelm) Miller; married Marilyn Mae Miller, August 8, 1953; children: Mark William, Eric Michael. *Education:* Capital University, B.A., 1953; Lutheran Theological Seminary, Columbus, Ohio, M.Div., 1957; Andover Newton Theological School, M.S.T., 1958, D.Ministry, 1974. *Home:* 2005 Xanthus Lane, Plymouth, Minn. 55447. *Office:* Fairview Hospital, 2312 South Sixth St., Minneapolis, Minn. 55454.

CAREER: St. James Lutheran Church, Baltimore, Md., pastor, 1958-66; Fairview Hospital, Minneapolis, Minn., chaplain, 1966-73, director of department of religion and health, 1973—. Instructor at Fairview School of Nursing, 1967—, and Luther Theological Seminary (St. Paul, Minn.), 1973-74. President, Woodland Publishing Co., Inc., 1977—. Partner, Professional Pastoral Resources, 1978—. *Member:* Association for Clinical Pastoral Education (certified supervisor), American Protestant Hospital Association (fellow of College of Chaplains), Association of Mental Health Chaplains (fellow), National Council on Family Relations, Minnesota Council on Family Relations.

WRITINGS—Published by Augsburg: *Why Do Christians Break Down?,* 1973; *Big Kids' Mother Goose,* 1976; *When Going to Pieces Holds You Together,* 1976; *You Count, You Really Do,* 1976. Contributor to *Lutheran Standard, Contact, Covenant Companion,* and *Bond.*

WORK IN PROGRESS: Make Friends with Your Shadow, for Augsburg; *Mid-Life, New Life.*

AVOCATIONAL INTERESTS: Cabinetmaking, boating, skiing.

* * *

MINER, Earl (Roy) 1927-

PERSONAL: Born February 21, 1927, in Marshfield, Wis.; son of Roy J. and Marjorie (Plank) Miner; married Virginia Lane, 1950; children: Erik Earl, Lisa Lane. *Education:* University of Minnesota, B.A., 1949, M.A., 1951, Ph.D., 1955. *Home:* 62 Wheat Sheaf Lane, Princeton, N.J. 08540. *Office:* Department of Comparative Literature, 22 McCosh, Princeton University, Princeton, N.J. 08540.

CAREER: Williams College, Williamstown, Mass., instructor, 1953-55; University of California, Los Angeles, associate professor, 1955-64, professor, 1964-72, Clark Library Professor, 1971-72; Princeton University, Princeton, N.J., professor of English, 1972-75, Townsend Martin, Class of 1917, Professor of English and Comparative Literature, 1975—. Fulbright lecturer in Japan, 1960-61, and at Oxford University, 1966-67. General editor, Augustan Reprint Society. *Military service:* U.S. Army, 1944-47. *Member:* Modern Language Association of America, Association for Asian Studies, International Association of Professors of English, American Comparative Literature Association, International Comparative Literature Association, English Literary Society of Japan, Phi Beta Kappa. *Awards, honors:* American Council of Learned Societies fellowship, 1962-63; Guggenheim fellowship, 1977-78.

WRITINGS: The Japanese Tradition in British and American Literature, Princeton University Press, 1958, revised edition, 1966; (with Robert H. Brower) *Japanese Court Poetry,* Stanford University Press, 1961; *Nihon o Utsutsu Chiisana Kagami* (title means "A Little Mirror of Japan"), Chikuma Shobo, 1962; *Restoration Dramatists,* Prentice-Hall, 1966; *Dryden's Poetry,* Indiana University Press, 1967; (translator and author of introduction, with Brower) Fujiwara Teika, *Fujiwara Teika's Superior Poems of Our Time,* Stanford University Press, 1967; (with Brower) *An Introduction to Japanese Court Poetry,* Stanford University Press, 1968; *The Metaphysical Mode from Donne to Cowley,* Princeton University Press, 1969; *Seventeenth-Century Imagery: Essays on users of Figurative Language from Donne to Farquhar,* University of California Press, 1971; *The Cavalier Mode from Jonson to Cotton,* Princeton University Press, 1971; *The Restoration Mode from Milton to Dryden,* Princeton University Press, 1974; *Japanese Linked Poetry,* Princeton University Press, 1979.

Editor: "The Works of John Dryden," University of California Press, Volume VIII: *Plays: "The Wild Gallant," "The Rival Ladies," "The Indian Queen"* (associate editor), John Harrington Smith and Dougald Macmillan, editors, 1962, Volume III: *Poems: 1685-1692* (with Vinton A. Dearing), 1969, Volume XV: *Plays* (with others), 1976; John Ogilby, *The Fables of Aesop Paraphras'd in Verse,* Augustan Reprint Society, 1965; (compiler and translator) *Japanese Poetic Diaries,* University of California Press, 1969; (and author of introduction) *Selected Poetry and Prose of John Dryden,* Random House, 1969; (and author of introduction) *English Criticism in Japan,* Princeton University Press, 1972; *Stuart and Georgian Moments,* University of California Press, 1972; *Writers and Their Background: John Dryden,* Ohio University Press, 1973; *Illustrious Evidence: Approaches to English Literature of the Seventeenth Century,* University of California Press, 1975; *Literary Uses of Typology from the Late Middle Ages to the Present,* Princeton University Press, 1977. Associate general editor, "The Works of John Dryden," University of California Press, 1965-72.

WORK IN PROGRESS: A Guide to Classical Japanese Literature; The Monkey's Straw Raincoat and Other Haikai of the Basho School; Milton as Narrative Poet.

SIDELIGHTS: Earl Miner is the author of numerous scholarly works on Japanese fiction, and on the English poet, Dryden. Miner told *CA,* "All of us who aspire to be writers must deal with what is most important to us, for all the risks that may imply."

BIOGRAPHICAL/CRITICAL SOURCES: Prairie Schooner, fall, 1967; *Yale Review,* fall, 1967, June, 1970; *Village Voice,* March 21, 1968; *Criticism,* summer, 1968; *Poetry,* August, 1968, June, 1969; *Comparative Literature,* summer,

1969; *Books Abroad,* spring, 1970; *Times Literary Supplement,* June 2, 1972.

* * *

MINER, H. Craig 1944-

PERSONAL: Born October 12, 1944, in Evanston, Ill.; son of Stanley Cole (an attorney) and Marybel (Smith) Miner; married Susan E. Amstutz; children: Harold Thomas. *Education:* Wichita State University, B.A., 1966, M.A., 1967; University of Colorado, Ph.D., 1970. *Home:* 303 Circle Dr., Wichita, Kan. 67218. *Office:* Department of History, Wichita State University, Wichita, Kan. 67208.

CAREER: Wichita State University, Wichita, Kan., 1969—, began as instructor, associate professor of history, 1972—.

WRITINGS: The St. Louis-San Francisco Transcontinental Railroad: The Thirty-Fifth Parallel Project, 1853-1890, University Press of Kansas, 1972; *The Corporation and the Indian: Tribal Sovereignty and Industrial Civilization in Indian Territory, 1865-1907,* University of Missouri Press, 1976; (with William Unrau) *The End of Indian Kansas: A Study of Cultural Revolution, 1854-1871,* Regents Press of Kansas, 1978.

WORK IN PROGRESS: Wichita: The Frontier Years, 1865-1880; The Rebirth of the Missouri Pacific Railroad, 1933-1979.

SIDELIGHTS: H. Craig Miner wrote *CA:* "The primary source material for the economic history of the U.S. in the last century is so vast and the number of important topics remaining for treatment so significant that any author in this field has motivation in trying to develop the skill to do some of these justice. The fascination of history increases with its complexity to a certain point at which the reader's sense of being in the flux of events yields to confusion. The trick as a writer is to work to push that point closer to the feeling of past reality gained by the author as researcher without either author or reader losing control of the narrative."

* * *

MINES, Samuel 1909-

PERSONAL: Surname rhymes with "lines"; born October 4, 1909, in New York, N.Y.; married Susan Wanderman, August, 1936; children: Madeline. *Education:* Attended Columbia University. *Residence:* Southbury, Conn. *Agent:* Barbara Neilson, 677 Cherry Hill Rd., Princeton, N.J. 08540.

CAREER: Better Publications (distributers of science fiction), New York City, editor, 1942-55; *Collier's* magazine, New York City, editor, 1955-56; American Cyanamid Co., New York City, staff writer, 1956-61; Pfizer, Inc. (pharmaceutical firm), New York City, senior staff writer, 1961-75. *Member:* National Association of Science Writers, Sierra Club, Audubon Society, Wilderness Society, Nature Conservancy, American Forestry Association, National Parks Association, Save-the-Redwoods League, Association for Indian Affairs, Environmental Defense Fund.

WRITINGS: (Editor) *The Best from Startling Stories,* Morrow, 1952; *The Last Days of Mankind,* Simon & Schuster, 1971; *The Conquest of Pain,* Grosset, 1974, revised edition, 1979. Also author of *Pfizer: An Informal History,* 1978. Author of more than three hundred published short stories. Book reviewer for *Washington Post,* 1970-73; contributing editor, *Ecology Today,* 1971-73.

WORK IN PROGRESS: Are You Blue?, "a study of anxiety/depression."

SIDELIGHTS: Samuel Mines wrote *CA:* "[I] am presently best known, if at all, as a medical writer. Yet I began by writing short stories and I lament the presently deplorable state of short story writing and the lack of markets. Being now in a position to write as little or much as I please, I am again writing short stories, despite my agent's warning that there is almost no market for them. I write them in a mostly silent protest against the few short stories I occasionally see in print, which I find largely incomprehensible."

* * *

MINTZBERG, Henry 1939-

PERSONAL: Born September 2, 1939, in Montreal, Quebec, Canada; son of Myer (a manufacturer) and Irene (Wexler) Mintzberg; married Yvette Hoch (an educator and potter), May 12, 1963; children: Susan, Lisa. *Education:* McGill University, B.E., 1961; Sir George Williams University, B.A., 1962; Massachusetts Institute of Technology, S.M., 1965, Ph.D., 1968. *Religion:* Jewish. *Home:* 4208 Kindersley Pl., Montreal, Quebec, Canada H4P 1L1. *Office:* Faculty of Management, McGill University, Montreal, Quebec, Canada H3A 1G5.

CAREER: McGill University, Montreal, Quebec, assistant professor, 1968-70, associate professor, 1970-75, professor of management, 1975—. Visiting professor at Carnegie-Mellon University, spring, 1973, Universite d'Aix-Marseille, 1974-76, and Universite de Montreal, 1977-78; director, joint doctoral program in management of the four Montreal-area universities, 1977—; lecturer. Consultant to businesses and government agencies in Canada, United States, and Europe. *Member:* Canadian Operational Research Society, Institute of Management Sciences, Academy of Management, Administrative Sciences Association of Canada, Corporation of Engineers of Quebec. *Awards, honors:* Canada Council leave fellowship, 1974-75; McKinsey Award for best article in *Harvard Business Review,* 1975, for "The Manager's Job: Folklore and Fact"; Canadian Department of External Affairs travel grant, 1975-76.

WRITINGS: The Nature of Managerial Work, Harper, 1973; (with J. W. Lorsch, J. P. Baughman, and J. Reece) *Understanding Management,* Harper, 1978; *The Structuring of Organizations: A Synthesis of the Research,* Prentice-Hall, 1979; (contributor) Schendel and Hofer, editors, *Strategic Management,* Little, Brown, 1979. Also author of several monographs and of "Clues to Executive Time Control," AMACOM Cassette Program, 1978. Work represented in numerous anthologies, including: *Corporate Planning,* edited by B. W. Denning, McGraw, 1971; *Perspectives on Management and Organizations,* edited by Ponthieu and others, Random House, 1975; *Business Policy,* edited by W. F. Glueck, McGraw, 1976; *Readings in Managerial Psychology,* edited by Leavitt, Pondy, and Boje, University of Chicago Press, 1979. Contributor of more than 30 articles to journals, including *Harvard Business Review, Management Science,* and *Administrative Science Quarterly.* Member of editorial advisory board, *Journal of Management Studies, Journal of General Management,* and *La Revue Internationale de Gestion.*

WORK IN PROGRESS: Three books for Prentice-Hall, *Power in and around Organizations, The Making of Strategic Decisions,* and *The Formation of Organizational Strategies.*

SIDELIGHTS: Henry Mintzberg told *CA:* "My short term interests are to find out all I possibly can about how organizations function. My long term interests are to apply this knowledge to questions of effectiveness in organizations and government. I also have a parallel interest—kind of a hobby—in the contrast between analysis and intuition. *Avocational interests:* Mountain climbing, cross-country skiing, canoeing, bicycling.

BIOGRAPHICAL/CRITICAL SOURCES: New York Times, October 29, 1976; *Planning Review,* March, 1977; *Playboy,* June, 1977; *Fortune,* April, 1979.

* * *

MITCHELL, John J(oseph) 1941-

PERSONAL: Born October 15, 1941, in Corvallis, Oregon; son of Robert V. Mitchell (a teacher); married Anita Jenelle (a teacher); children: John Joseph. *Education:* University of Oregon, Ph.D., 1969. *Office:* Department of Educational Psychology, University of Alberta, Edmonton, Alberta, Canada.

CAREER: University of Alberta, Edmonton, professor of psychology, 1969—.

WRITINGS—Published by Holt (Toronto), except as indicated: *Adolescence: Some Critical Issues,* 1971; *Human Nature: Theories, Conjectures, and Descriptions,* Scarecrow, 1972; *Human Life: The First Ten Years,* 1973; *Human Life: The Early Adolescent Years,* 1974; *The Adolescent Predicament,* 1975; *Adolescent Psychology,* 1978; *Child Development,* 1979.

* * *

MITCHELL, Lee M(ark) 1943-

PERSONAL: Born April 16, 1943, in Albany, N.Y.; son of Maurice B. and Mildred R. Mitchell; married Barbara Anderson, August 27, 1966; children: Mitchell, Mark Robert, Matthew Lee. *Education:* Wesleyan University, A.B., 1965; University of Chicago, J.D., 1968. *Home:* 1323 Kirby Rd., McLean, Va. 22101. *Office:* Sidley & Austin, 1730 Pennsylvania Ave. N.W., Washington, D.C. 20006.

CAREER: Admitted to Bar of State of Illinois, 1968, Bar of District of Columbia, 1969, Bar of U.S. Court of Appeals for the District of Columbia, 1970, and Bar of U.S. Supreme Court, 1972; Leibman, Williams, Bennett, Baird & Minow (attorneys), Chicago, Ill. and Washington, D.C., attorney, 1968-72; Sidley & Austin, Washington, D.C., partner, 1972—. Co-director, Study of Political Access to Television, 1971-72; Twentieth Century Fund, rapporteur for Task Force on Political Public Affairs Broadcasting, 1974, and Task Force on Televised Presidential Debates, 1979; consultant to political candidates and organizations on regulation of political broadcasting. *Member:* Federal Communications Bar Association, Federal Bar Association, American Arbitration Association, National Press Club, National Lawyers Club, National Broadcasters Club, Chicago Bar Association.

WRITINGS: (Contributor) William L. Rivers and Michael J. Nyan, editors, *Aspen Notebook on Government and the Media,* Praeger, 1973; (with Newton N. Minow and John Bartlow Martin) *Presidential Television,* Basic Books, 1973; *Openly Arrived At,* Twentieth Century Fund, 1974; *With the Nation Watching,* Heath, 1979. Contributor to *Television Quarterly, Annals* of the American Academy of Political and Social Science, and *Journal of Communications.*

* * *

MITFORD, Jessica 1917-

PERSONAL: Born September 11, 1917, in Batsford, Gloucestershire, England; daughter of David (second baron of Redesdale) and Sydney (Bowles) Mitford; married Esmond Romilly, June, 1937 (killed in action, 1941); married Robert E. Treuhaft (a lawyer), June 21, 1943; children: (first marriage) Constancia Romilly; (second marriage) Benjamin. *Education:* Educated at home. *Home:* 6411 Regent St., Oakland, Calif. 94618. *Agent:* Scott Meredith Literary Agency, Inc., 845 Third Ave., New York, N.Y. 10022.

CAREER: J. Walter Thompson (advertising agency), London, England, market researcher, 1937-39; Roma Restaurant, Miami, Fla., bartender, 1939-40; Weinberger's Dress Shop, Washington, D.C., salesgirl, 1940-41; Office of Price Administration, Washington, D.C., investigator, 1941-43; Civil Rights Congress, Oakland, Calif., executive secretary, 1945-51; writer. Northern California representative, Southern Conference Educational Fund, 1961-62.

WRITINGS: Lifeitselfmanship, privately printed, 1956; *Daughters and Rebels* (autobiography), Houghton, 1960 (published in England as *Hons and Rebels,* Gollancz, 1960); *The American Way of Death,* Simon & Schuster, 1963; *The Trial of Dr. Spock, the Rev. William Sloane Coffin, Jr., Michael Ferber, Mitchell Goodman, and Marcus Raskin,* Knopf, 1969; *Kind and Usual Punishment: The Prison Business,* Knopf, 1973; *A Fine Old Conflict* (autobiography), Knopf, 1977; *Poison Penmanship: The Gentle Art of Muckraking,* Knopf, 1979. Contributor of articles to *Life, Esquire, Nation,* and *San Francisco Chronicle.*

SIDELIGHTS: Dubbed "Queen of the Muckrakers" by a *Time* magazine reviewer, Jessica Mitford has spent most of her writing career in search of worthy targets for exposes. Past subjects have included such diverse people and institutions as Bennett Cerf and other "faculty members" of the Famous Writers School, American funeral directors, television executives, a posh "fat farm" for wealthy women, and a snooty and overpriced New York City restaurant. "As her many admirers know," notes an *Esquire* critic, "she is past mistress of the neat skewer, the dry understatement, and the eliciting of utterly damning, freely offered quotes (her gifts in this area are positively magical).... [But] what makes Jessica Mitford's work stand out from the free-lance herd? Her legwork is tireless, her strategies simple but ingenious.... Her specialness lies ... in the character she projects in even the least of her writings: Behind these exposes of venal doings, we sense a woman who is jocular, common-sensical, forthright, self-reliant, amused, stout-hearted, opinionated, and utterly intoxicated with the chase."

Mitford did not begin her muckraking career until reaching the age of thirty-eight; her first major success came in 1963 with the publication of *The American Way of Death.* She was prompted to write this particular book after noting that the estates of many of her lawyer-husband's poorer clients were almost totally depleted after funeral costs had been deducted. The *New Yorker* praised Mitford for presenting "a brilliant journalistic case against the whole funeral industry." Francis Russell of the *National Review* wrote, "It is a book that deserves a place on the shelf between Evelyn Waugh's *The Loved One* and Aldous Huxley's *After Many a Summer [Dies the Swan].*" A *Time* critic, among several others, felt that the startling and well-documented work, while destroying the prevailing image of the funeral director as a "compassionate, reverent family-friend-in-need," went too far in the opposite direction and presented "an equally distorted picture of a hypocritical racketeer in black."

Though the demand for the services of funeral directors did not decrease as a result of the public outrage generated by the expose, the National Casket Company, according to Mitford, "was screaming that their gross had gone down by about 10 percent in the year after my book came out, at a time when all other manufactured goods were booming." In addition, there was at least one unexpected and amusing reaction to all the furor. As the author herself explains: "The best thing that happened was that a Middle Western manufacturer wrote to me and offered plans and specifications for a very cheap coffin, but he was proposing to market it as the Jessica Mitford Casket, so you can say:'I'm going to be buried in a Mitford.' I thought it was lovely—like Sandwich giving his name to two pieces of bread."

Poison Penmanship: The Gentle Art of Muckraking is an anthology of Mitford's articles covering a twenty-two-year span. As the *Chicago Tribune Book World* critic points out, it is "a virtual textbook on investigative reporting," for the author "offers commentary on how each article was conceived, the problems she confronted, her technique in getting the story, and its writing." He continues: "Mitford hates pomp and her prose is unpretentious. . . . In contrast to her subject matter, her range of ideas is narrow, but she is a witty writer with a gift for ingratiating rather than malicious irony, her workmanship grew increasingly resourceful under the space limitations imposed by magazine editors, and her many pages of advice to apprentice authors on how-to and how-not-to make a useful contribution to the craft."

Noting that "one muckrakes, as Miss Mitford cheerfully admits, because it is fun," the *Esquire* reviewer concludes that "you may not be able to change the world, but at least you can embarass the guilty. . . . [Mitford's] joy at running such foxes to earth glitters from every page in this collection and even gives a glint of jovial malice to four or five pieces that are really too dated and ephemeral to warrant enshrinement between hard covers. It's certainly a contagious sentiment. One closes *Poison Penmanship* exhilarated by Miss Mitford's example and itching to join the fray."

A *New York Times* critic, however, feels that Mitford occasionally attacks certain organizations without bothering to explore *why* they might be acting the way they do—in short, he concludes, she often "overestimate[s] the public's taste. It is possible that some of these victims ask for these organizations and invite their abuses. . . . Wouldn't there be less moral shoddiness, for example, if the consumer were not so eager to consume it? . . . [Mitford] is a very good writer and reporter, a valuable institution by now—and it's a pity to see our favorite muckraker inadvertantly stepping in the muck. . . . Miss Mitford's pen is mightier than the sword. That's why she cannot afford to be cavalier, why it is so important for her to get things exactly right."

Finally, a *New York Times Book Review* critic writes: "Any wayward industry fearing that sooner or later somebody may expose its defects should hire Jessica Mitford to do it first, because she would handle the chore with such deftness and charm. The industry might emerge from the experience with less money and credibility, but at least it would have attained a kind of immortality. . . . Even the crustiest of her old pieces still retain a touch of freshness. She has shown us here once again, as muckraker Carl Bernstein says in the afterword [of *Poison Penmanship*], that critical journalism need not always be mean but 'can be fun. Hallelujah.'"

Mitford is a member of a well-known British family that has made, according to Lynn Darling of the *Washington Post*, "one of the more stunning contributions to the lore of English upper-class eccentricity." Of the six Mitford sisters, Nancy was a respected novelist and biographer, "a card-carrying member of the Bright Young People of the post-World War I generation." Pamela lives in the country and tends her cows, chickens, and other assorted farm animals. Diana married Sir Oswald Mosley, a leader of the British fascists prior to World War II; their wedding guest list included the names of such notables as Adolf Hitler, Hermann Goering, and Joseph Goebbels. Unity, too, was a follower and companion of Hitler's; she was eventually "found in Paris with a bullet wound in her head, only to linger on in half life for many years." Deborah, "who always said she would grow up to be a duchess," is now the Duchess of Devonshire. The sole Mitford brother, Tom, was killed in World War II.

Jessica, whose political bent was exactly opposite that of her sisters Diana and Unity, ran away to Loyalist Spain during the Spanish Civil War and married a communist sympathizer (who, it so happens, was her second cousin and a nephew of Winston Churchill). Several years after he was killed in action during World War II, she married a labor lawyer she had met while working in Washington, D.C.; they soon moved to a racially integrated neighborhood in Oakland, Calif., and joined the Communist Party (from which they resigned in 1958). James Walt, describing Jessica Mitford in a *Washington Post* article, calls her "an older, more even-tempered, better read Jane Fonda who has maintained her activism long past middle age and carried on energetically in the face of increasing disillusion."

BIOGRAPHICAL/CRITICAL SOURCES: New Statesman, March 26, 1960, October 4, 1963; *Spectator,* April 1, 1960, February 14, 1970; *Times Literary Supplement,* April 1, 1960, October 4, 1963; *Saturday Review,* June 11, 1960, August 31, 1963, September 6, 1969; *New York Herald Tribune Book Review,* June 12, 1960, August 25, 1963; *Newsweek,* June 13, 1960, September 15, 1969, May 28, 1979; *Time,* June 20, 1960, September 20, 1963, October 3, 1969; *New York Times Book Review,* June 26, 1960, August 25, 1963, September 9, 1973, May 20, 1979; *New Yorker,* July 16, 1960, September 7, 1963; *Life,* July 18, 1960, September 12, 1969; Jessica Mitford, *Daughters and Rebels* (autobiography), Houghton, 1960; *New Republic,* August 31, 1963, September 13, 1969; *Christian Science Monitor,* September 18, 1963, October 22, 1969, September 19, 1973; *Reporter,* September 26, 1963; *National Review,* October 22, 1963; *Commonweal,* November 8, 1963; *Virginia Quarterly Review,* winter, 1964; Roy Newquist, editor, *Counterpoint,* Rand McNally, 1964; *Observer,* June 8, 1969, February 15, 1970; *New York Times,* August 6, 1969, September 8, 1977, May 16, 1979; *New York Post,* September 9, 1969; *Newsday,* September 13, 1969; *Harper's,* October, 1969; *Nation,* October 13, 1969; *Best Sellers,* October 15, 1969; *Christian Century,* October 22, 1969; *Commentary,* December, 1969; *Ramparts,* December, 1969; *Listener,* February 26, 1970, April 2, 1970; *Carlton Miscellany,* spring, 1970; *Books,* April, 1970; Mitford, *A Fine Old Conflict* (autobiography), Knopf, 1977; *Chicago Tribune Book World,* May 6, 1979; *Washington Post,* May 14, 1979, June 6, 1979; *Esquire,* May 22, 1979; *Los Angeles Times Book Review,* July 17, 1979.

—Sketch by Deborah A. Straub

* * *

MOHR, Nicholasa 1935-

PERSONAL: Born November 1, 1935, in New York, N.Y.; daughter of Pedro and Nicholasa (Rivera) Golpe; married Irwin Mohr (a clinical child psychologist), October 5, 1957; children: David, Jason. *Education:* Attended Art Students

League, 1953-56, Brooklyn Museum Art School, 1959-66, and Pratt Center for Contemporary Printmaking, 1966-69. *Home:* 727 President St., Brooklyn, N.Y. 11215.

CAREER: Fine arts painter in New York, California, Mexico, and Puerto Rico, 1952-62; printmaker in New York, Mexico, and Puerto Rico, 1963—; teacher in art schools in New York and New Jersey, 1967—; art instructor, Art Center of Northern New Jersey, 1971-73; MacDowell Colony, Peterborough, N.H., writer-in-residence, 1972, 1974, and 1976; artist-in-residence, New York City public schools, 1973-74; State University of New York at Stony Brook, lecturer in Puerto Rican studies, 1977. Visiting lecturer in creative writing for various educator, librarian, student, and community groups, including University of Illinois Educational Alliance Program (Chicago), 1977, Cedar Rapids community schools (Iowa), 1978, writers-in-residence seminar, University of Wisconsin—Oshkosh, 1978, and Bridgeport public schools (Conn.), 1978. Head creative writer and co-producer, "A Qui Ahora" (title means "Here and Now"). Member of council, New Jersey State Council on the Arts; member of board of trustees, and consultant, Young Filmakers Foundation. Consultant on bilingual media training, Young Filmakers/Video Arts.

MEMBER: Authors Guild, Authors League of America. *Awards, honors:* Outstanding book award in juvenile fiction, *New York Times,* 1973, best book award, School Library Journal, 1973, Jane Addams Children's Book Award, Jane Addams Peace Association, 1974, and citation of merit for book jacket of novel, Society of Illustrators, 1974, all for *Nilda;* outstanding book award in teenage fiction, *New York Times,* 1975, best book award, School Library Journal, 1975, and National Book Award finalist for "most distinguished book in children's literature," 1976, all for *El Bronx Remembered;* best book award, School Library Journal, best book award in young adult literature, American Library Association, and Notable Trade Book Award, National Conference of Social Studies, all 1977, for *In Nueva York;* Notable Trade Book Award, National Conference of Social Studies, 1980, for *Felita.*

WRITINGS—Juvenile: (Self-illustrated) *Nilda,* Harper, 1973; *El Bronx Remembered: A Novella and Stories,* Harper, 1975; *In Nueva York,* Dial, 1977; *Felita,* Dial, 1979. Contributor of stories to textbooks and to anthologies, including *The Ethnic American Woman: Problems, Protests, Lifestyles,* edited by Edith Blicksilver. Contributor of short stories to *Children's Digest, Scholastic Magazine,* and *Nuestro.* Member of board of contributing editors, *Nuestro.*

WORK IN PROGRESS: A book of short stories about Puerto Rican women in the United States.

SIDELIGHTS: Nicholasa Mohr is the author of young adult novels and short stories that offer what reviewers consider realistic and uncompromising portraits of life in New York's Puerto Rican barrio. In *Nilda,* a work that Ray Anthony Shepard calls "an outstanding first novel," Mohr traces a Puerto Rican girl's growth from childhood into adolescence, posing the question, "what does it feel like being poor and belonging to a despised minority?," according to Marilyn Sachs. She finds that although several books for young people have attempted to explore this condition, "few come up to 'Nilda' in describing the crushing humiliations of poverty and in peeling off the ethnic wrappings so that we can see the human child underneath." And a critic for the *New York Times Book Review* notes that *Nilda* "provides a sharp, candid portrayal of what it means to be poor and to be called 'spics,' 'animals,' 'you people'—and worse."

Mohr's subsequent works have afforded similar insight into this world. In *El Bronx Remembered* and *In Nueva York,* both of which are composed of collections of "stories tied together by their setting," according to the *English Journal*'s Aileen Pace Nilson, characters move in and out of the stories providing "an intimate look into the most interesting parts of several people's lives."

However some critics, such as Georgess McHargue and Irma Garcia, believe that Mohr creates contrived and stereotyped characters. In the *New York Times Book Review,* McHargue comments that *In Nueva York* appears "too obviously intended as slice-of-life fiction with the result that the characters are busier being Puerto Rican-Americans than being people." And Garcia finds similar fault with *El Bronx Remembered.* While she praises the stories for being "well-written and descriptive tales," she also states: "Despite some truths and sharp insights, these are not stories of change, struggle or love. Rather, they are negative stories which reinforce stereotypes."

Although these shortcomings have been noted, it is the realism and empathy in Mohr's work to which the critics most frequently refer. In a review of *In Nueva York,* a writer for *Kirkus Reviews* praises "the clarity, wry humor, genuine sympathy, and considerable success with which Mohr brings her neighborhood to life." And Sachs offers this assessment of *El Bronx Remembered:* "If there is any message at all in these stories, any underlying theme, it is that life goes on. But Nicholasa Mohr is more interested in people than in messages." She notes that the stories are without "complicated symbolism . . ., trendy obscurity of meaning, . . . hopeless despair or militant ethnicity. Her people endure because they are people," Sachs continues. "Some of them suffer, some of them die, a few of them fail, but most of the time they endure."

BIOGRAPHICAL/CRITICAL SOURCES: New York Times Book Review, November 4, 1973, November 10, 1974, November 16, 1975, May 22, 1977; Francelia Butler, editor, *Children's Literature: Annual of the Modern Language Association Seminar on Children's Literature and the Children's Literature Association,* Volume III, Temple University Press, 1974; *Newsweek,* March 4, 1974; *Bulletin of the Center for Children's Books,* June, 1976, July/August, 1977; *Interracial Books for Children Bulletin,* Volume VII, number 4, 1976; *Kirkus Reviews,* April 1, 1977; *Contemporary Literary Criticism,* Volume XII, Gale, 1980.

* * *

MOLETTE, Carlton W(oodard) II 1939-

PERSONAL: Born August 23, 1939, in Pine Bluff, Ark.; son of Carlton William (a college professor) and Evelyn Adelle (a college dean of women; maiden name, Richardson) Molette; married Barbara Jean Roseburr (a college instructor and costumer), June 15, 1960; children: Carla Evelyn, Andrea Rose. *Education:* Morehouse College, B.A., 1959; University of Iowa, M.A., 1962; Florida State University, Ph.D., 1968. *Home:* 8102 Braes View, Houston, Tex. 77071. *Office:* School of Communications, Texas Southern University, Houston, Tex. 77004.

CAREER: Tuskegee Institute, Tuskegee Institute, Ala., assistant director of Little Theatre, 1960-61; Des Moines Community Playhouse, Des Moines, Iowa, technical director, 1962-63; Howard University, Washington, D.C., assistant professor of drama, 1963-64; Florida Agricultural and Mechanical University, Tallahassee, assistant professor, 1964-66, associate professor of speech and drama, 1967-69;

Spelman College, Atlanta, Ga., associate professor of drama, 1969-75, chairman of department, 1971-73; Texas Southern University, School of Communications, Houston, dean, 1975—. Theatre consultant to colleges, festivals, and organizations. *Member:* International Council of Fine Arts Deans, Association for Communication Administration, Dramatists Guild, American Theatre Association, National Association of Dramatic and Speech Arts, United States Institute for Theatre Technology, Alpha Phi Alpha. *Awards, honors:* Ford Foundation scholarship, 1955-59; Carnegie Foundation grant, 1966-68; Atlanta University Center faculty research grant, 1970-71.

WRITINGS: "Doctor B. S. Black" (play), first produced in Atlanta, Ga. by Morehouse-Spelman Players, November 10, 1969, musical adaptation (with wife, Barbara Molette, and Charles Mann) produced in Atlanta at Atlanta University Summer Theatre, July 20, 1972; (with B. Molette) *Rosalee Pritchett* (play; first produced in Atlanta by Morehouse-Spelman Players, March 20, 1970; produced Off-Broadway at St. Mark's Playhouse, January 12, 1971), Dramatists Play Service, 1972; (with B. Molette) "Booji Wooji" (play), first produced at Atlanta University Summer Theatre, July 8, 1971; (contributor) Therman B. O'Daniel, editor, *James Baldwin: A Critical Evaluation,* Howard University Press, 1977. Also author with wife of screenplay of "Booji Wooji," a play, "Noah's Ark," and a filmstrip, "Stage Makeup for Black Actors," Alcone. Work appears in *Black Writers of America: A Comprehensive Anthology,* edited by Richard Barksdale and Kenneth Kinnamon, Macmillan, 1972. Contributor of articles and reviews to journals in his field. Editor, *Encore,* 1965-71; editorial consultant, *Southern Speech Journal,* 1966-68; member of advisory board, *Journal of Black Studies,* 1970-73.

WORK IN PROGRESS: A book, tentatively entitled *Black Theatre: Reflections of Afro-American Culture.*

* * *

MOLLOY, Julia Sale 1905-

PERSONAL: Born October 19, 1905, in La Grange, Ill.; daughter of William Benson and Dagmar (McKinley) Sale; married Francis H. Molloy, 1939; children: Francis H., Jr., Christopher Hugh. *Education:* University of Cincinnati, B.S., 1926; Harvard University, certificate in physical therapy, 1938; University of Wisconsin, graduate study, 1935-37; Northwestern University, M.A., 1950. *Home:* 910 Washington St., 4A, Evanston, Ill. 60202.

CAREER: Teacher in public schools for five years; Cook County Hospital, Levinson Foundation, Cook County, Ill., language pathologist, 1950-59; Orchard School for Special Education, Skokie, Ill., director, 1951-72. Visiting lecturer at National College of Education, Northwestern University, and University of Chicago; adjunct professor, University of San Diego, 1972—. Workshop participant for American Association on Mental Deficiency, National Association for Retarded Children, Ontario Association. Member of board of directors, Orchard School; member of council, Community Chest; member of executive board, Illinois Federation of the Council for Exceptional Children. *Member:* American Association on Mental Deficiency (fellow), American Speech and Hearing Association, National Association for Retarded Children, Mongoloid Development Council (advisory board member), American Association for the Severely Handicapped, Kappa Delta, Mortar Board, Northwestern Alumni Association, Cincinnati Alumni Association. *Awards, honors:* Skokie Chamber of Commerce, community service award; Jack Mabley Award.

WRITINGS—Published by John Day, except as indicated: *Teaching the Retarded Child to Talk,* 1961; *Trainable Children: Curriculum-Procedures,* 1963, revised edition, 1972; *Performance Goals Record,* 1972; (with Arlene Matkin) *Your Developmentally Retarded Child Can Communicate: A Guide for Parents and Teachers in Speech, Language, and Nonverbal Communication,* 1975; *Communication for the Severely/Profoundly Handicapped: A Manual for Paraprofessionals,* Love Publishing, 1978. Also author, with Janet Rowley, of *A Statistical Review of 1400 Cases of Retardation,* Cook County Hospital; contributor to *Mental Retardation in Infants and Children,* edited by Abraham Levinson and John A. Bigler. Author and director of films, "One Small Candle" and "And Crown Thy Good," both by Zenith Cinema Service, and "Are You Ready?," by LaRue Films.

WORK IN PROGRESS: Book on number concepts, book on handwriting, and a series of readers, all for retarded children.

AVOCATIONAL INTERESTS: Music, spectator sports, and the theater.

* * *

MONEY, John (William) 1921-

PERSONAL: Born July 8, 1921, in Morrinsville, New Zealand; son of Frank (a builder) and Ruth (Read) Money. *Education:* Victoria University of Wellington, M.A., 1943, Diploma of Honors, 1944; University of Pittsburgh, graduate study, 1947-48; Harvard University, Ph.D., 1952. *Home:* 2104 East Madison St., Baltimore, Md. 21205. *Office:* Johns Hopkins Hospital, Baltimore, Md. 21205.

CAREER: University of Otago, Dunedin, New Zealand, junior lecturer in philosophy and psychology, 1945-47; Johns Hopkins University, Baltimore, Md., instructor, 1951-55, assistant professor of medical psychology, 1955-57, assistant professor of medical psychology and pediatrics, 1957-59, associate professor of medical psychology, 1959-72, associate professor of pediatrics, 1959—, professor of medical psychology, 1972—, psychologist, Johns Hopkins Hospital, 1955—. Visiting professor at Albert Einstein College of Medicine, Yeshiva University, 1969, Harvard University, 1970, University of Nebraska, 1972, and University of Connecticut, 1975; visiting lecturer at Bryn Mawr College, 1952-53; Rachford lecturer at Children's Hospital, Cincinnati, 1969; American Urological Association Lecturer, 1975; Master Lecturer on Physiological Psychology, American Psychological Association, 1975; lecturer at hospitals and universities throughout the world. Member of board of directors of Sex Information and Education Council of the United States, 1965-68, Erickson Educational Foundation, 1967-77, and Neighborhood Family Planning Center, Inc., 1970—; member, National Institute of Mental Health Task Force on Homosexuality, 1967-69; member, Committee of Instruction for the Master of Mental Health, Johns Hopkins University, 1974—.

MEMBER: International Institute of Sex Identities (member of board of directors, 1973-76), International Academy of Sex Research (charter member), International Society of Psychoneuroendocrinology, Society for the Scientific Study of Sex (charter member; fellow; president-elect, 1972-74; president, 1974-76), Deutsche Gesellschaft fuer Sexualforschung, Royal Society of Medicine (England; affiliate member), Society for the Study of Reproduction (charter member), American Association of Sex Educators, Counselors, and Therapists (honorary member), American Psychiatric Association, European Society for Paediatric Endocrinology (corresponding member), Gesellschaft zur Forderung Sozialwissenschaftlicher Sexualforschuag, Czechoslovak Sexological Society (honorary member), Society for the Study of Social Biology, Centre for Human Freedom and Sexuality (honorary member), Colombian Sexological Society (honorary member), New Zealand Society on Sexology (honorary life member), Society of Pediatric Psychology, American Academy on Mental Retardation, Behavior Genetics Association (charter member), Maryland Society for Medical Research, Maryland Psychological Association, Sigma Xi. *Awards, honors:* Co-recipient of Hofheimer Prize, American Psychiatric Association, 1956; Gold Medal Award, Children's Hospital of Philadelphia, 1966; Society for the Scientific Study of Sex award, 1972; American Association for Sex Educators and Counselors award for pioneering research and distinguished service, 1976; Maryland Psychological Association award for outstanding contributions to psychology, 1976; honored by the Society for the Scientific Study of Sex for service, research, and education in the field of human sexuality, 1976; Harry Benjamin, M.D. Medal of Honor, Erickson Educational Foundation, 1976.

WRITINGS—Published by Johns Hopkins Press, except as indicated: *The Psychologic Study of Man,* C. C Thomas, 1957; (editor and contributor) *Reading Disability: Progress and Research Needs in Dyslexia,* 1962; (editor and contributor) *Sex Research: New Developments,* Holt, 1965; (with Duane Alexander and H. Thomas Walker, Jr.) *A Standardized Road-Map Test of Direction Sense,* 1965; (editor and contributor) *The Disabled Reader: Education of the Dyslexic Child,* 1966; (section editor and contributor) D. B. Cheek, editor, *Human Growth: Body Composition, Cell Growth, Energy and Intelligence,* Lea & Febiger, 1968; *Sex Errors of the Body: Dilemmas, Education and Counseling,* 1968; (editor with Richard Green and contributor) *Transsexualism and Sex Reassignment,* 1969.

(Editor and contributor) *Sexual Behavior—Readings V: Introduction to Psychiatry and the Behavioral Sciences,* School of Medicine, Johns Hopkins University, 1970; (with Anke A. Ehrhardt) *Man and Woman, Boy and Girl: Differentiation and Dimorphism of Gender Identity from Conception to Maturity,* 1972; (editor with Joseph Zubin and contributor) *Contemporary Sexual Behavior: Critical Issues in the 1970s,* 1973; (with P. Tucker) *Sexual Signatures,* Little, Brown, 1975; (editor with W. K. Anderson and G. McClearn) *Developmental Human Behavior Genetics,* Heath, 1975; (editor with H. Musaph) *Handbook of Sexology,* Excerpta Medica Foundation, 1977; *Love and Lovesickness: Sexology of Gender Differences and Pair-Bonding,* 1980; (editor with G. Williams) *Traumatic Abuse and Neglect of Children at Home,* in press.

Contributor: L. I. Gardner, editor, *Adrenal Function in Infants and Children,* Grune, 1956; Harold Michal-Smith, editor, *Management of the Handicapped Child,* Grune, 1957; J. Wortis, editor, *Recent Advances in Biological Psychiatry,* Grune, 1960; W. C. Young, editor, *Sex and Internal Secretions,* 3rd edition (Money did not contribute to earlier editions), Williams & Wilkins, 1961; S. M. Farber and R.H.L. Wilson, editors, *Man and Civilization: The Potential of Woman,* McGraw, 1963; George Winokur, editor, *Determinants of Human Sexual Behavior,* C. C Thomas, 1963; S. S. Gellis and B. M. Kagan, editors, *Current Pediatric Therapy,* Saunders, 1965.

Gellis and Sumner D. Liebman, editors, *The Pediatrician's Ophthalmology,* Mosby, 1966; K. L. Moore, editor, *The Sex Chromatin,* Saunders, 1966; C. W. Wahl, editor, *Sexual Problems: Diagnosis and Treatment in Medical Practice,* Free Press, 1967; Joseph Zubin, editor, *Psychopathology of Mental Development,* Grune, 1967; *Brennemann-Kelley Practice of Pediatrics,* Volume IV, Harper, 1967; J. J. Gold, editor, *Textbook of Gynecologic Endocrinology,* Harper, 1968; R. E. Cooke and Sidney Levin, editors, *The Biological Basis of Pediatric Practice,* McGraw, 1968; S. G. Vandenberg, editor, *Progress in Human Behavior Genetics,* Johns Hopkins Press, 1968; R. P. Michael, editor, *Endocrinology and Human Behavior,* Oxford University Press, 1968; J. G. Howells, editor, *Theory and Practice in Family Psychiatry,* Oliver & Boyd, 1968; Gardner, editor, *Endocrine and Genetic Diseases of Childhood,* Saunders, 1969, 2nd edition, 1975; P. J. Vinken and G. W. Bruyn, editors, *Handbook of Clinical Neurology,* Volume IV: *Disorders of Speech, Perception and Symbolic Behaviour,* North-Holland Publishing, 1969; C. B. Broderock, editor, *The Individual, Society and Sex: Background Readings for Sex Educators,* Johns Hopkins Press, 1969.

D. DeWeid and J.A.W.M. Weijnemen, editors, *Pituitary, Adrenal and the Brain,* Elsevier, 1970; Joseph Zubin and A. Freedman, editors, *Psychopathology of Adolescence,* Grune, 1970; H. C. Mack and A. E. Sherman, editors, *The Neuroendocrinology of Human Reproduction: Biological and Clinical Perspectives,* C. C Thomas, 1971; N. Kretchmer and D. N. Walcher, editors, *Environmental Influences on Genetic Expression,* U.S. Government Printing Office, 1971; V. W. Lippard, editor, *Macy Conference on Family Planning, Demography, and Human Sexuality in Medical Education,* Josiah Macy, Jr. Foundation, 1971; C. J. Sager and H. A. Kaplan, editors, *Progress in Family and Group Therapy,* Brunner, 1972; E. B. Astwood, editor, *Recent Progress in Hormone Research,* Academic Press, 1972; H.L.P. Resnik and M. E. Wolfgang, editors, *Treatment of the Sex Offender,* Little, Brown, 1972; C. H. Sawyer and R. A. Gorski, editors, *Steroid Hormones and Brain Function,* University of California Press, 1972; S. Arieti and E. B. Brady, editors, *American Handbook of Psychiatry,* Volume III, 2nd edition, Basic Books, 1974; S. Raiti, editor, *Advances in Human Growth Hormone Research,* U.S. Government Printing Office, 1974; R. Green, editor, *Human Sexuality: A Health Practitioner's Text,* Williams & Wilkins, 1975.

(With E. Higham) A. Davids, editor, *Child Personality and Psychopathology: Current Topics,* Volume III, Wiley, 1976; F. A. Beach, editor, *Human Sexuality in Four Perspectives,* Johns Hopkins Press, 1977; E. K. Oremland and J. D. Oremland, editors, *The Sexual and Gender Development of Young Children,* Ballinger, 1977; E. Sullerot, editor, *Le Fait Feminin,* Fayard (Paris), 1978; N. Rosenzweig and F. P. Pearsall, editors, *Sex Education for the Health Professional,* Grune, 1978; J. P. Brady and H.K.H. Brodie, editors, *Controversy in Psychiatry,* Saunders, 1978; (with D. Gain) E. Trimmer, editor, *Basic Sexual Medicine,* Heinemann, 1978; (with M. Schwartz) J. B. Hutchison, editor, *Biological Determinants of Sexual Behaviour,* Wiley, 1978.

Articles, reprints, and translations have been included in a number of other books. Contributor to *Technical Report of the Commission on Obscenity and Pornography,* Volume V, *Annual Review of Medicine, American Handbook of Psychiatry, Encyclopedia of Sexual Behavior, Encyclopedia of Mental Health, International Encyclopedia of the Social Sciences,* and *International Encyclopedia of Psychiatry, Psychology, Psychoanalysis and Neurology.* Contributor of more than 200 articles, reviews, abstracts, and editorials to medical journals and such periodicals as *Reading Teacher, Playboy, St. John's Law Review,* and *American Sociological Review.*

Member of editorial board, *Sexology,* 1961—, *Journal of Learning Disabilities,* 1970—, *Journal of Autism and Childhood Schizophrenia,* 1972—, *International Journal of Learning Disabilities,* 1974—, *Journal of Sex and Marital Therapy,* 1974—, *Behavioral Medicine,* 1974-76, *Psychoneuroendocrinology,* 1974—, *Signs: Journal of Women in Culture and Society,* 1974-78, *Journal of Homosexuality,* 1975-77, *Journal of Sexual Behavior and Identity,* 1975—, *Alternatives: Marriage, Family and Changing Life Styles,* 1977—, *British Journal of Sexual Medicine,* 1977—; associate editor, Archives of Sexual Behavior, 1970—; consulting editor, *Sexualmedezin,* 1972—, *Journal of the Psychology of Women,* 1975—, *Sexual Insight,* 1975—, *Sexuality and Disability,* 1977—.

WORK IN PROGRESS: Journal articles and a book of clinical reports on psychohormonal and sexological research.

AVOCATIONAL INTERESTS: Contemporary and ethnic art, especially improvisational art (three-dimensional and miniature graphics).

BIOGRAPHICAL/CRITICAL SOURCES: Edward M. Brecher, *The Sex Researchers,* Little, Brown, 1969, revised edition, Specific Press, 1979; James W. Kalat, *Biological Psychology,* Wadsworth, 1980.

* * *

MOODY, Joseph Nestor 1904-

PERSONAL: Born April 18, 1904, in New York, N.Y.; son of Hugh A. (an engineer) and Anne (Nolan) Moody. *Education:* St. Joseph's Seminary, Yonkers, N.Y., A.B., 1925; Fordham University, M.A., 1931, Ph.D., 1934; Columbia University, postdoctoral study, 1946-48. *Politics:* Democrat. *Home and office:* 127 Lake St., Brighton, Mass. 02135.

CAREER: Ordained Roman Catholic priest, 1929; College of New Rochelle, New Rochelle, N.Y., assistant professor of history, 1934-40; Notre Dame College (now Notre Dame College of St. Johns University), Staten Island, N.Y., assistant professor, 1936-46, associate professor, 1946-49, professor of history, 1949-58; Ladycliff College, Highland Falls, N.Y., professor of history, 1958-65, head of department, 1958-63; Catholic University of America, Washington, D.C., professor of French history, 1965-75; Boston College, Boston, Mass., professor of history, 1975—. *Military service:* U.S. Naval Reserve, 1940-46; became commander; received Presidential Citation. *Member:* Society for French Historical Studies (president, 1968-69; vice-president, 1950-51, 1964-65; member of executive board, 1969-75), American Historical Society, American Catholic Historical Association (president, 1978-79). *Awards, honors:* Human Rights Award from B'nai B'rith, 1938.

WRITINGS: (Editor with Edgar Alexander and others) *Church and Society: Catholic Social and Political Thought and Movements, 1789-1950,* New York Arts, 1953; (with Joseph F. X. McCarthy) *Man the Citizen: The Foundations of Civil Society,* Doubleday, 1957; (editor with Justus George Lawler) *The Challenge of Mater et Magistra,* Herder & Herder, 1963; (contributor) Evelyn M. Acomb and Marvin L. Brown, editors, *French Society and Culture since the Old Regime,* Holt, 1966; *The Church as Enemy: Anticlericalism in Nineteenth-Century French Literature,* Corpus Books, 1968; (contributor) Gaetano L. Vinctiorio, editor, *Crisis in the Great Republic,* Fordham University Press, 1969; *French Education since Napoleon,* Syracuse University Press, 1978. Also author of *The Third Republic and the Church,* 1980. Contributor to *Review of Politics* and *Bridge.* Associate editor of *Catholic Historical Review,* 1964—.

MOORE, Brian 1921-

PERSONAL: Born August 25, 1921, in Belfast, Northern Ireland; emigrated to Canada, 1948; Canadian citizen; son of James Brian and Eileen (McFadden) Moore. *Education:* Attended St. Malachy's College. *Agent:* Collins-Knowlton-Wing, Inc., 575 Madison Ave., New York, N.Y. 10022.

CAREER: Montreal Gazette, Montreal, Quebec, proofreader, reporter, and rewrite man, 1948-52; full-time writer, 1952—. *Military service:* Served with British Ministry of War Transport in North Africa, Italy, and France, World War II. *Awards, honors:* Author's Club first novel award, 1956; Governor General's Award for Fiction, 1960, for *The Luck of Ginger Coffey;* Quebec Literary Prize, 1958; Guggenheim fellowship, 1959; National Institute of Arts and Letters fiction grant, 1961; Canada Council fellowship for travel in Europe, 1962; W. H. Smith Prize, 1972; James Tait Black Memorial Award, 1975.

WRITINGS—Novels, except as indicated: *Judith Hearne,* Collins, 1955, published as *The Lonely Passion of Judith Hearne,* Little, Brown, 1956, reprinted, 1978; *The Feast of Lupercal,* Little, Brown, 1957; *The Luck of Ginger Coffey* (also see below), Little, Brown, 1960; *An Answer from Limbo* (also see below), Little, Brown, 1962; (with the editors of *Life*) *Canada* (travel book), Time-Life, 1963; *The Emperor of Ice-Cream,* Viking, 1965; *I Am Mary Dunne,* Viking, 1968; *Fergus,* Holt, 1970; *The Revolution Script* (nonfiction), Holt, 1971; *Catholics* (also see below), J. Cape, 1972, Harcourt, 1973; *The Great Victorian Collection,* Farrar, Straus, 1975; *The Doctor's Wife,* Farrar, Straus, 1976; *The Mangan Inheritance,* Farrar, Straus, 1979.

Screenplays: "The Luck of Ginger Coffey" (based on novel of same title; also see above), 1963; "Torn Curtain," 1966; "The Slave" (based on novel *An Answer from Limbo;* also see above), 1967; "Catholics" (based on novel of same title; also see above), 1973. Contributor of articles and short stories to *Spectator, Holiday, Atlantic,* and other periodicals.

SIDELIGHTS: Brian Moore's fiction most often concerns "the insignificant member of society who operates in an obscure segment of that society," as Hallvard Dahlie notes. Writing in a conventional style, Moore focuses attention on his characters' limited choices in the changing of their lives.

Christopher Ricks maintains that Moore is "a 'conventional' novelist quite without experimentalisms and gimmicks. In none of the novels is anything concealed except the art by which they transmute 'an ordinary sorrow of man's life' into something we care about. . . . [Moore] writes transparently, in a style which differs from ordinary speech only in being more tellingly economical, less muddled and less afraid."

Most of Moore's characters eventually fail at what they attempt to do. Moore once told an interviewer that "failure is a more interesting condition than success. Success changes people; it makes them something they were not and dehumanizes them in a way, whereas failure leaves you with a more intense distillation of that self you are." Moore's "focus is on suffering itself," Jack Ludwig writes. "His insignificant characters suffer much from contemplating their own insignificance." For Moore's characters, Ludwig believes, "awareness is paralysis. . . . The one thing impossible to contemplate is change. Every recognition, every epiphanic moment is confirmation of life's hopelessness."

Speaking of Moore's work as a whole, Bruce Cook holds that it is a "body of work of inestimably high quality that is unknown to the sort of large readership reached by many lesser writers." Josh Greenfeld, writing in *Time,* believes that "Moore is one of the last of a vanishing breed: the serious seeker who is also a consummate professional." Cook concludes that Moore "is the finest novelist writing in English today."

Film rights to *Judith Hearn* and *The Doctor's Wife* have been sold.

BIOGRAPHICAL/CRITICAL SOURCES: New York Herald Tribune Book Review, June 17, 1956; *Time,* June 18, 1956, June 21, 1968, October 12, 1970; *Atlantic,* May, 1957, July, 1968; *New Yorker,* May 11, 1957; *Catholic World,* July, 1957; *Commonweal,* July 12, 1957, September 27, 1968; *Canadian Literature,* winter, 1961, summer, 1971, winter, 1972; *Kenyon Review,* winter, 1961; *Tamarack Review,* spring, 1962; *Saturday Review,* October 13, 1962; *America,* October 27, 1962; *Encounter,* June, 1963; *Nation,* March 15, 1965, June 24, 1968, October 12, 1970; *Harper's,* October, 1965; *Critique,* Volume IX, number 1, 1966, Volume XIII, number 1, 1971; *Times Literary Supplement,* February 3, 1966, April 9, 1971, November 10, 1972; *New Statesman,* February 18, 1966; Jonathan Raban, *The Techniques of Modern Fiction,* Edward Arnold, 1968; *Christian Science Monitor,* June 27, 1968; *Life,* June 18, 1968, December 3, 1972; *New York Times Book Review,* June 28, 1968, March 18, 1973; *Book World,* July 7, 1968, April 8, 1973, June 1, 1975; *New Republic,* August 17, 1968; *Saturday Night,* September, 1968, November, 1970, July-August, 1975; *Eire,* Number 3, 1968; *Canadian Forum,* October, 1968; *Punch,* October 23, 1968; *Listener,* October 24, 1968; *Books & Bookmen,* December, 1968; Hallvard Dahlie, *Brian Moore,* Copp, 1969; *Yale Review,* spring, 1971; *Contemporary Literary Criticism,* Gale, Volume I, 1973, Volume III, 1975, Volume V, 1976, Volume VII, 1977, Volume VIII, 1978; *London Magazine,* February-March, 1973; Jeanne Flood, *Brian Moore,* Bucknell University Press, 1974; *New York Times,* October 1, 1976, September 12, 1979; *Detroit News,* October 14, 1979.

* * *

MOORE, Doris Langley

PERSONAL: Born in Liverpool, England; married Robin Sugden Moore, 1926 (divorced, 1942); children: Pandora. *Education:* Attended convent schools in South Africa; studied classical languages with a private tutor in England. *Home:* 5 Prince Albert Rd., London, England.

CAREER: Costume designer; author. Museum of Costumes, Assembly Rooms, Bath, England, founder and advisor, beginning 1955. Lecturer on the study of costume. *Awards, honors:* Officer, Order of the British Empire, 1971; Royal Society of Literature fellow, 1973; Rose Mary Crawshay Prize, British Academy, 1975.

WRITINGS: (Translator) *Anacreon: Twenty-Nine Odes Rendered into English Verse,* Gerald Howe, 1926; *The Technique of the Love Affair,* Simon & Schuster, 1928, revised and enlarged edition, Rich & Cowan, 1936, Knickerbocker Publishing Co., 1946; *Pandora's Letter Box,* Gerald Howe, 1929; (with June Moore) *Bride's Book,* Gerald Howe, 1932, revised edition published as *Our Loving Duty,* Rich & Cowan, 1936; *A Winter's Passion,* Heinemann, 1932; (editor) Edward de Pomiane, *Good Fare,* Gerald Howe, 1932; (with J. Moore) *The Pleasure of Your Company,* Gerald Howe, 1934, revised edition, Rich & Cowan, 1936; *Unknown Eros,* Secker & Warburg, 1935; *E. Nesbit: A Biography,* Benn, 1936, revised and enlarged edition, Chilton, 1966; *They Knew Her When: A Game of Snakes and Ladders,* Rich & Cowan, 1938, published as *A Game of Snakes and Ladders,* Cassell, 1955; *The Vulgar Heart,* Cassell, 1945; (translator) Serge Lifar, *Carlotta Grisi,* Lehmann, 1947; *Not at Home,* Cassell, 1948; *The Woman in Fashion,* Batsford, 1949; *All Done by Kindness,* Cassell, 1951, Lippincott, 1952; *Pleasure: A Discursive Guide Book,* Cassell, 1953; *The Child in Fashion,* Batsford, 1953; *My Caravaggio Style,* Lippincott, 1959; *Dancing Is for Dopes* (three-act play), Dramatic Publishing, 1960; *The Late Lord Byron,* Lippincott, 1961, reprinted, Harper, 1977; *Marie and the Duke of H.* (biography), Lippincott, 1966; *Fashion Through Fashion Plates, 1771-1970,* Ward, Lock, 1971, C. N. Potter, 1972; *Lord Byron: Accounts Rendered,* Harper, 1974; *Ada, Countess of Lovelace: Byron's Legitimate Daughter,* Harper, 1977. Also author of film scripts, including "The Diary."

SIDELIGHTS: Doris Langley Moore has written, as well as designed, for films, and several of her books have been about fashion. In addition to her work as designer, fashion writer, and screenwriter, Moore is also a novelist and biographer, chronicling the lives of such subjects as Edith Nesbit, Marie Bashkirsteff, and the poet, Byron. Her works on the latter appear to be among her most notable, prompting critic J.I.M. Stewart to write, "She has made the ground [covering Byron and 'his circle'] her own, and has established upon it a claim to be among the most accomplished biographers of her time."

Shortly after World War II, Moore began televising programs on costume, using pieces from her own, extensive collection. These programs, in addition to exhibitions, lectures, and books on the subject, led to the opening of the Museum of Costume, founded by the author in 1955.

AVOCATIONAL INTERESTS: Collecting Byroniana and documents relating to fashion.

BIOGRAPHICAL/CRITICAL SOURCES: New Yorker, October 8, 1966, January 16, 1978; *Times Literary Supplement,* February 2, 1967, October 14, 1977; *New York Times Book Review,* October 8, 1967, December 25, 1977; *Atlantic Monthly,* June, 1974, February, 1978; *New Statesman,* July 5, 1974; *New York Review of Books,* May 18, 1978.

* * *

MOOS, Rudolf H. 1934-

PERSONAL: Born September 10, 1934, in Berlin, Germany; naturalized U.S. citizen; son of Henry R. and Herta (Ehrlich) Moos; married Bernice Schradski, June 9, 1963; children: Karen, Kevin. *Education:* University of California, Berkeley, B.A., 1956, Ph.D., 1960. *Home:* 25661 Fremont Rd., Los Altos Hills, Calif. 94022. *Office:* School of Medicine, Stanford University, Stanford, Calif. 94305.

CAREER: University of California, Medical School, San Francisco, U.S. Public Health Service research fellow, 1960-62; Stanford University, School of Medicine, Stanford, Calif., assistant professor, 1962-67, associate professor, 1967-72, professor of psychiatry, 1972—, acting director of psychiatric residency program, 1967-68, director of Social Ecology Laboratory, 1967—; Veterans Administration Medical Center, Palo Alto, Calif., research fellow, 1962—, director of social ecology laboratory, 1967—, chief of research, 1975—. Visiting professor at Institute of Psychiatry, and Maudsley and Royal Bethlem Hospitals, London, 1969-70. Consultant, state of California, 1962-69, Youth and Adult Corrections Agency, 1967-68, National Council on Crime and Delinquency, 1968-70, and Mental Research Institute, 1968-71. Diplomate in clinical psychology, American Board of Professional Psychology. *Member:* American Psychological Association, American Psychosomatic Society, American Sociological Association, American Association for the Advancement of Science.

WRITINGS: (Editor with Paul M. Insel) *Issues in Social Ecology: Human Milieus,* National Press Books, 1974; *Evaluating Treatment Environments: A Social Ecological Approach,* Wiley, 1974; (editor) *Health and the Social Environment,* Heath, 1974; *Evaluating Correctional and Community Settings,* Wiley, 1975; *The Human Context: Environmental Determinants of Behavior,* Wiley, 1976; (editor) *Human Adaptation: Coping with Life Crises,* Heath, 1976; (editor) *Coping with Physical Illness,* Plenum, 1977; (with Robert Brownstein) *Environment and Utopia: A Synthesis,* Plenum, 1977; *Evaluating Educational Environments: Procedures, Methods, Findings and Policy Implications,* Jossey-Bass, 1979. Contributor of about 160 articles to professional journals. Member of editorial board, *Journal of Psychiatric Research,* 1966—, *Psychosomatic Medicine,* 1971—, *Journal of Educational Psychology,* 1978—, and *Evaluation and Program Planning,* 1978—.

WORK IN PROGRESS: Studies on evaluating residential settings for older people and the outcome of treatment for alcoholism.

* * *

MORA, George 1923-

PERSONAL: Born June 26, 1923, in Genoa, Italy; naturalized U.S. citizen; son of Ottorino and Teresita (Crovetto) Mora; married Marilyn Hall, May 3, 1958; children: Beth, John, Kate. *Education:* University of Genoa, M.D., 1947; further study at University of Zurich, 1949-50, and University of North Carolina, 1955-56. *Religion:* Roman Catholic. *Home:* 32 Slate Hill Dr., Poughkeepsie, N.Y. 12603. *Office:* Astor Home for Children, Mill St., Rhinebeck, N.Y. 12572.

CAREER: Resident at Thom Clinic for Children and Putnam Children's Center, Boston, Mass., 1951-52, and Butler Hospital, Providence, R.I., 1953-54; Bradley Hospital, Providence, director of outpatient department, 1956-60; Astor Home for Children, Rhinebeck, N.Y., medical director, 1961—. Research associate, Yale University, 1957—; lecturer in psychiatry at College of Physicians and Surgeons, Columbia University, 1964—; assistant clinical professor of psychiatry at New York Medical College, 1965—; associate clinical professor of psychiatry at Albany Medical College, 1967—. Diplomate in psychiatry, American Board of Psychiatry and Neurology, 1958, and diplomate in child psychiatry, 1960. Consultant to National Library of Medicine, 1970—.

MEMBER: American Medical Association, American Psychiatric Association (fellow; chairman of history committee, 1965-70), American Psychopathological Association, American Academy of Child Psychiatry, American Association for the History of Medicine (member of council, 1965-68), History of Science Society. *Awards, honors:* Rockefeller Foundation fellow, 1951-52.

WRITINGS: (Editor with Jeanne L. Brand) *Psychiatry and Its History: Methodological Problems in Research,* C. C Thomas, 1970; (editor) Karl Ludwig Kahlbaum, *Catatonia,* Johns Hopkins Press, 1974; (author of introduction) Johann Christian Heinroth, *Textbook on Mental Diseases,* Johns Hopkins Press, 1975; (editor) George Cabanis, *On the Relation between the Physical and Moral Aspects of the Mind,* Johns Hopkins Press, 1980. Regular contributor to *American Journal of Psychiatry.* Book review editor, *Journal of the History of the Behavioral Sciences,* 1966—.

WORK IN PROGRESS: *American Psychiatry: Recent Developments and Trends;* and *Attitudes Toward the Mentally Ill Throughout History.*

* * *

MOREMEN, Grace E(llen Partin) 1930-

PERSONAL: Born August 30, 1930, in Los Angeles, Calif.; daughter of John Leo (a civil engineer) and Agnes (Edwards) Partin; married William Moremen (a minister), September 5, 1953; children: Margaret Louise, John Frederic, Katherine Helen. *Education:* Pomona College, B.A., 1952; Oxford University, graduate study, 1955-56; University of Chicago, M.A., 1956; University of Southern California, teaching credential, 1970. *Politics:* Registered Democrat. *Religion:* Protestant. *Home:* 851 North Larrimore St., Arlington, Va. 22205.

CAREER: Teacher of English in adult education program, Los Angeles, Calif., 1970-71; National Gallery of Art, Washington, D.C., member of staff, 1974-77; member of staff, Alban Institute, 1977-79; free-lance writer, 1979—.

WRITINGS: *No, No, Natalie,* Childrens Press, 1973; *Touching Washington, D.C,* Moremen-Conklin, 1976; (contributor) *Women's Book of World Records and Achievements,* Doubleday, 1979; (contributor) *World of Surprises,* Harcourt, 1979. Contributor to *Parade, Working Woman,* and *Wilson Quarterly.*

WORK IN PROGRESS: Two children's books, *What Is a Mandala?* and *Let's Go, Goats!*

SIDELIGHTS: Grace E. Moremen told *CA:* "It was a white rabbit named Natalie that hooked me into writing my first book. As a child I loved photo stories, and Natalie's zany, real-life antics in a pre-school begged to be told in a photo book. Writing a satisfying photo or picture book is probably my favorite kind of work. I am influenced by authors Beatrix Potter, Wanda Gag, Marjorie Flack, Sid Fleischman, Maurice Sendak, among others, who, in very few words, can create an inviting world of caring relationships."

* * *

MORGAN, Al(bert Edward) 1920-

PERSONAL: Born January 16, 1920, in New York, N.Y.; son of Albert Edward (a businessman) and Julia (Britt) Morgan; married Martha Falconer Jones (an actress), December 19, 1945; children: Allen, Martha Jo, Amy Jane. *Education:* Attended New York University, 1937-41. *Home address:* RFD 2, Box 170, Putney, Vt. 05346. *Agent:* Roberta Pryor and Steve Sultan, International Creative Management, 40 West 57th St., New York, N.Y. 10019.

CAREER: Columbia Broadcasting System, Inc., New York City, writer and producer, 1941-53; National Broadcasting Corp. (NBC-TV), New York City, senior editor of "Home Show," 1954-56; Universal International, Hollywood, Calif., screenwriter, 1956; HMH Publishing Co., Chicago, Ill., editor of *Show Business Illustrated,* 1960-61; NBC-TV, New York City, producer of "Today Show," 1961-69; novelist and playwright, 1969—; Children's Television Workshop, New York City, producer, 1974-75. *Military service:* U.S. Army, Infantry, 1943-46; served in European theater; became sergeant; received Purple Heart, Silver Star, Bronze Star, and Croix de Guerre with palms (France). *Member:* Authors Guild of America, Dramatists Guild. *Awards, honors:* Ohio State Award for Journalism, 1953; Emmy Award for contribution to television programming, National Academy of Television Arts and Sciences, 1968, for "Today Show."

WRITINGS: The Great Man, Dutton, 1955; *Cast of Characters,* Dutton, 1957; (with Jose Ferrer) "Oh Captain" (musical comedy), first produced on Broadway at Alvin Theater, 1959; *One Star General,* Rinehart, 1959; *A Small Success,* Rinehart, 1960; *Minor Miracle,* Dodd, 1961; *The Six Eleven,* Morrow, 1963; *To Sit on a Horse,* Morrow, 1964; "Minor Miracle" (play), first produced on Broadway at Henry Miller Theatre, October 7, 1965; *The Whole World Is Watching,* Stein & Day, 1972; *Anchorwoman,* Stein & Day, 1974; *The Essential Man,* Playboy Press, 1977; *The Last Cavalier,* Richard Marek, 1980. Also author, with Joshua Logan, of book for musical comedy, "As the Lady Said to the Sailor." Contributor of articles and reviews to periodicals, including *New York Post, Saturday Review,* and *TV Guide.*

* * *

MORGAN, Alison Mary 1930-

PERSONAL: Born March 2, 1930, in Bexley, Kent, England; daughter of Geoffrey Taunton (an army officer) and Dorothy Wilson (Fox) Raikes; married John Morgan, April 23, 1960; children: Richard, Hugh. *Education:* Somerville College, Oxford, B.A. (second class honors), 1952; University of London, certificate in education, 1953. *Politics:* "Uncommitted." *Religion:* Anglican (Church of Wales). *Home:* Talcoed, Llanafan, Builth Wells, Breconshire, Wales. *Agent:* A. P. Watt & Son, 26/28 Bedford Row, London WC1R 4HL, England.

CAREER: Teacher of English in Great Malven, England, 1953-54, and Newtown, Wales, 1954-59. Justice of the Peace, 1964—. *Awards, honors:* Arts Council for Wales literary award, 1973, for *Pete.*

WRITINGS—All children's novels: *Fish,* Chatto & Windus, 1971, published as *A Boy Called Fish,* Harper, 1973; *Pete,* Chatto & Windus, 1972, Harper, 1973; *Ruth Crane,* Chatto & Windus, 1973, Harper, 1974; *River Song,* Harper, 1974; *At Willie Tucker's Place,* Chatto & Windus, 1975, Elsevier-Nelson, 1976; *Leaving Home,* Chatto & Windus, 1979; *All Sorts of Prickles,* Elsevier-Nelson, 1980. Also author of "Fire in the Forest," a radio play.

WORK IN PROGRESS: A sequel to *Leaving Home;* another children's novel.

SIDELIGHTS: "Writing in any form," Alison Morgan told *CA,* "I have always taken for granted as a form of self-expression essential to me, and always intended to take it up professionally when the opportunity arose. I think I moved from amateur to professional level with *Fish* because writing for children imposed a discipline my work had previously lacked. The best preparation was writing plays for local groups and producing them myself; I learned to prune ruthlessly. I write Welsh countryside books because that is where I live; I am tied domestically, so travel and access to literary material is limited, but staying still in one place one gets to know about people three-dimensionally."

* * *

MORGAN, Dewi (Lewis) 1916-

PERSONAL: Born February 5, 1916, in Wales; son of David and Anne (Lewis) Morgan; married 1942; wife's maiden name, Povey; children: Norna, Betty. *Education:* University of Wales, B.A., 1937; St. Michael's College (Llandaff, Wales), graduate study, 1937-39. *Home:* Rectory, Church of St. Bride, Fleet St., London E.C.4, England.

CAREER: Curate at various churches in Wales, 1939-50; Society for the Propagation of the Gospel, London, England, press officer, 1950-54, editorial and press secretary, 1954-62; Church of St. Bride, London, chaplain, 1953-62, rector, 1962—. Chaplain, Press Club, London, 1963—, and Institute of Journalists, London, 1963—. Prebendary, St. Paul's Cathedral, 1976. *Member:* Athenaeum Club, Press Club.

WRITINGS: Expanding Frontiers, Edinburgh House Press, 1957; *The Bishops Come to Lambeth,* Mowbray, 1957; *Lambeth Speaks,* Mowbray, 1958; (editor) *They Became Anglicans,* Mowbray, 1959; *The Undying Fire,* Mowbray, 1959; (contributor) *Twentieth Century Christianity,* Collins, 1961; *1662 and All That,* Mowbray, 1961; *But God Comes First,* Longmans, Green, 1962; *The Seeds of Peace,* Hodder & Stoughton, 1965; *They Became Christians,* Morehouse, 1965; (editor) *Arising from the Psalms,* Morehouse, 1965; (editor) *Faith in Fleet Street,* Mowbray, 1967; *God and Sons,* P. Davies, 1967; *The Church in Transition,* Charles Knight, 1970; *The Phoenix of Fleet Street: Two Thousand Years of St. Bride's,* Rowman & Littlefield, 1973. Also author of annual reports, Society for Propagation of the Gospel, 1954-63. Editor, *St. Martin's Review,* 1953-55, *Anglican Diocesan Information Digest,* 1963-67, *Quarterly Intercession Paper,* 1963—; associate editor, *Anglican World.*

SIDELIGHTS: The Church of St. Bride, where Dewi Morgan is rector, has been in existence since the sixth century. On the site of the present church are the ruins of seven previous churches along with a Roman building 1,800 years old.

Morgan has lectured and preached in Europe, the United States, and the Far East.

BIOGRAPHICAL/CRITICAL SOURCES: Contemporary Review, June, 1967; *Books and Bookmen,* August, 1970; *Times Literary Supplement,* September 25, 1970, January 4, 1974.

* * *

MORITA, Yuzo 1940-

PERSONAL: Born June 12, 1940, in Sukumo, Kochi, Japan; son of Ichio (an orchard owner) and Asae (Kuwahara) Morita. *Education:* Tokyo University of Agriculture, B.S., 1964. *Home:* 396-1 Tanoura, Sukumo, Kochi, Japan 788-02. *Office:* Youth Friendship Association, Room 401 Oshima Bldg., Daiichi Bekkan, 1-51-13 Higashinakano, Nakano-ku, Tokyo, Japan.

CAREER: Writer. Chairman, Youth Friendship Association. *Member:* Japan Youth Travel Club (president), Japan Ethnology Society, Japanese Society of Authors and Writers.

WRITINGS: Kore ga sekai no ningen da (title means "The People of the World"), Seichun Shuppan Sha, 1968; *Mohretsu na nippongin yaro* (title means "Adventurous Japanese"), Asahi Sonorama Sha, 1969; *Mirai no kuni Australia* (title means "Australia: The Hopeful Land"), Kodan Sha, 1970; *Yugoslavia,* Kodansha International, 1973; *In Pursuit of the Origin of the Japanese,* Kodan Sha, 1973; *Kilimanjaro no Yuki* (title means "Kilimanjaro, My Dream"), Eiko Shuppan Publishing, 1977; *Sekai Saihakken no Tabi* (essays; title means "Rediscovery of the World"), Ohbunsha, 1977; *Wagatomo Kibamin* (a study of a horseman tribe in Central Asia), Gakushukenkyusha, 1978; *Yagai Katsudo no Susume* (title means "Guide to Outdoor Group Activities"), Gakushukenkyusha, 1979. Contributor to *Sun, Heibonsha, Asahi-Graph,* and *Mainichi-Graph.*

WORK IN PROGRESS: A research project on primitive tribes in northern East Asia; research on the relations between Japanese ancestors and Mongoloid horseman tribes of the Mongolian Highlands.

SIDELIGHTS: Yuzo Morita has traveled around the world studying how modern civilization has permeated the underdeveloped and primitive societies and has caused the destruction of the primitive being of man. He told *CA:* "To recover the natural being of man in the highly-developed modern society is to experience the commutive life in the natural surroundings, away from the daily modern equipment. . . . I am organizing the movement to provide such opportunities for the modern Japanese, so that they would reorganize themselves for the true recovery of the natural man." Some of the activities of his Japan Youth Travel Club are forty-three-kilometer walking competition without food and drink, experimental tours into the farming lands outside Tokyo, overnight conference tours, and "year-end new-year courtesy calls" to local shrines.

* * *

MORRELL, William Parker 1899-

PERSONAL: Born November 20, 1899, in Auckland, New Zealand; son of William John and Agnes Mary (Tucker) Morrell; married Ethel Margaret Evans, 1940; children: William David, Judith Ann. *Education:* University of Otago, M.A., 1921; Balliol College, Oxford, D.Phil., 1927. *Home:* 20 Bedford St., St. Clair, Dunedin S.W.1, New Zealand. *Office:* University of Otago, Dunedin, New Zealand.

CAREER: Knox College, Dunedin, New Zealand, Ross fellow, 1921-22; Oxford University, Oxford, England, lecturer in colonial history, 1927-30; University of London, Birkbeck College, London, England, reader in history, 1930-46; University of Otago, Dunedin, professor of history, 1946-65, professorial fellow, 1965-68. Member, New Zealand Historic Places Trust. Chairman, Otago High Schools Board of Governors, 1961-74. *Military service:* Home Service, 1941-45. *Member:* Royal Historical Society (fellow; member of council, 1944-46), Royal Commonwealth Society (fellow; member of council and chairman of library committee, 1941-46), Hakluyt Society, Hudson's Bay Record Society, Van Riebeeck Society, Dunedin Club. *Awards, honors:* Hugh LeMay fellow, Rhodes University, Grahamstown, South Africa, 1951; Commander of the Order of the British Empire, 1978.

WRITINGS: (Editor with Kenneth N. Bell) *Select Documents on British Colonial Policy, 1830-60,* Clarendon Press, 1928, reprinted, 1968; *British Colonial Policy in the Age of Peel and Russell,* Clarendon Press, 1930, reprinted, Barnes & Noble, 1966; *The Provincial System in New Zealand, 1852-76,* Longmans, Green, 1932, 2nd edition, Whitcombe & Tombs, 1964; *New Zealand,* Benn, 1935; *The Gold Rushes,* A. & C. Black, 1940, 2nd edition, Dufour, 1968; (with D.O.W. Hall) *A History of New Zealand Life,* Whitcombe & Tombs, 1957; (editor) *Sir Joseph Banks in New Zealand: From His Journal,* A. H. & A. W. Reed, 1958; *Britain in the Pacific Islands,* Clarendon Press, 1960; (editor) Harriet Louisa Gore Browne, *Narrative of the Waitara Purchase and the Taranaki War,* University of Otago Press, 1965; *British Colonial Policy in the Mid-Victorian Age,* Clarendon Press, 1969; *The University of Otago: A Centennial History,* University of Otago Press, 1969; *The Anglican Church in New Zealand: A History,* John McIndoe, 1973; *Memoirs,* John McIndoe, 1979. Also author of historical pamphlets, including *Britain and New Zealand,* Longmans, Green, 1944.

WORK IN PROGRESS: A contribution to a volume commemorating Bishop G. A. Selwyn, for Auckland University Press.

BIOGRAPHICAL/CRITICAL SOURCES: Times Literary Supplement, February 12, 1970, August 21, 1970; *W. P. Morrell: A Tribute; Essays in Modern and Early Modern History Presented to William Parker Morrell,* University of Otago Press, 1973.

* * *

MORRIS, Edita (deToll)

PERSONAL: Born in Orebro, Sweden; daughter of Reinhold and Alma (Prom-Moller) deToll; married Ira Morris (an author); children: Ivan. *Education:* Attended Bromerska Skolan, Stockholm. *Address:* Nesles, par Rozay-en-Brie, France. *Agent:* Harold Ober Associates, 40 East 49th St., New York, N.Y. 10017.

CAREER: Writer. *Member:* P.E.N. (New York). *Awards, honors:* Albert Schweitzer Literary Prize, 1961, for *The Flowers of Hiroshima.*

WRITINGS: Birth of an Old Lady, Cassell, 1938; *My Darling from the Lions,* Viking, 1943, revised edition of part 1 published as *Life, Wonderful Life!,* Braziller, 1971; *Three Who Loved* (contains "Kullan," "The Melody," and "A Blade of Grass"), Viking, 1945; *Charade,* Viking, 1948; *The Flowers of Hiroshima,* Viking, 1959; *Echo in Asia: A Fictional Travelogue,* Dobson, 1961; *The Toil and the Deed,* Today & Tomorrow Publishers, 1964; *The Seeds of Hiroshima,* MacGibbon & Kee, 1965, Braziller, 1966; *Dear Me, and Other Tales from My Native Sweden* (contains stories from *Three Who Loved* and seven others), Braziller, 1967; *Love to Vietnam,* Monthly Review Press, 1968; *Straightjacket: Autobiography,* Crown, 1978. Contributor to stories to magazines in United States and Europe; six of her stories were anthologised in *The Best American Short Stories* annual collections.

WORK IN PROGRESS: A novel.

SIDELIGHTS: Edita Morris "has too much heart and too much talent to write a poor book, or even a novel no better than the average," claims Henry Bull in his review of *Charade.* Donald Barr describes the novel as "the sort of bold book which must either be a triumph or a fiasco. . . . Perhaps this is treating a charming and touching story with too much solemnity. But it is precisely because it is written with such rich and luminous simplicity, and because it does touch the center of [World War II,] the European tragedy . . . that it deserves not only the widest reading but the most serious thought." M. W. Stoer adds, "Ordinary literary standards will hardly suffice to judge this imaginative tale."

The qualities that set Morris's writing apart are the focus of many reviewers' analyses. Diana Trilling writes: "Mrs. Morris is one of those oh-the-aching-wonder-of-it-all literary women for whom a snowflake or a sausage is equal matter for ecstasy. Yet whatever my dislike of so much precosity, I have to admit Mrs. Morris's talent. Cumulatively, her sensibility . . . even begins to take effect; after the first hundred pages [of *My Darling from the Lions*], I found myself acutely aware of the charm of her village . . . almost as nostalgic for it as if I had experienced it myself." Later, Trilling comments in her review of *Three Who Loved:* "I have been wondering what accounts for Mrs. Morris's ability to involve and charm me against . . . my better judgment. . . . It must be simply—or not so simply—the communicating power of their creative intensity. But I think it is also in large measure the Swedish setting of her stories . . . an environment that is so lacking in the usual touchstones of sordid reality that it becomes a Never-Never Land of poetic possibility."

Eudora Welty does not find the "Never-Never Land" atmosphere a welcome addition to *Three Who Loved,* however. "We wish through the whole book for the flesh-and-blood gaiety that was in *My Darling,* the rambunctious energy and candid play, the imagination and the humor," she writes. "Here the glowing Scandinavian setting is muted, stylized, or symbolic. . . . All is still—fresh winds do not blow except when allowed by the author, for a specific hushed purpose."

Maxwell Geismar's review of *Dear Me and Other Tales from My Native Sweden* lends Morris more positive support. He comments: "I know her tormented and horrifying book, *Flowers of Hiroshima,* which has become an international classic. . . . But I did not know, I could never have guessed, how really talented she is just as a writer, as an artist. These stories . . . are delicate and light in texture; yet they are passionate, tragic, joyous, tormented, often utterly pagan and even savage in a way that is a pleasure to read. . . . Like the best tales of [Sherwood] Anderson, they can make you stop reading because you find yourself in tears—something that is rarely achieved in contemporary writing."

Charade was dramatized in an Off-Broadway production in 1961; *Flowers of Hiroshima* has been translated into twenty-six languages and was dramatized in East Berlin.

BIOGRAPHICAL/CRITICAL SOURCES: New York Times, June 6, 1943, February 18, 1945, October 10, 1948; *Nation,* June 12, 1943, February 24, 1945; *Saturday Review of Literature,* June 19, 1943, October 2, 1948; *Springfield Republican,* February 18, 1945; *New Yorker,* February 24, 1945; *Book Week,* March 11, 1945; *Christian Science Monitor,* September 30, 1948; *New York Herald Tribune Book Review,* October 11, 1959; *Ramparts,* March, 1968.†

* * *

MORRIS, Herbert 1928-

PERSONAL: Born July 28, 1928, in New York, N.Y.; son of Peter and Minnie (Miller) Morris; married Virginia Grenier, April 3, 1956 (divorced, 1977); children: Jacob Jeremy, Benjamin John. *Education:* University of California, Los Angeles, B.A., 1951; Yale University, LL.B., 1954; Oxford University, D. Phil., 1956. *Home:* 233 South Medio Dr., Los Angeles, Calif. 90049. *Office:* University of California Law School, Los Angeles, Calif. 90024.

CAREER: University of California, Los Angeles, assistant professor of philosophy, 1956-58; admitted to State Bar of California, 1958; Stanford University, Stanford, Calif., assistant professor, 1958-59; University of California, Los Angeles, assistant professor, 1959-61, associate professor, 1962-65, professor of philosophy and law, 1965—. *Member:* Phi Beta Kappa, Order of the Coif. *Awards, honors:* Fulbright scholar, 1954-56; Ford Foundation law faculty fellow, 1963-64; National Endowment for the Humanities senior fellow, 1970-71; Guggenheim fellowship, 1977-78.

WRITINGS: Freedom and Responsibility, Stanford University Press, 1961; *The Masked Citadel: The Significance of the Title of Stendhal's 'La Chartreuse de Parme,'* University of California Press, 1968; *Guilt and Shame,* Wadsworth, 1971; *On Guilt and Innocence,* University of California Press, 1976. Contributor to professional journals.

* * *

MORRIS, Jan 1926-
(James [Humphrey] Morris)

PERSONAL: Formerly James Humphrey Morris; name changed to Jan Morris after gender role change, 1972; born October 2, 1926, in Clevedon, Somerset, England; child of Walter and Enid (Payne) Morris; (divorced); five children. *Education:* Christ Church, Oxford, B.A. (second class honors), 1951, M.A., 1961. *Home:* Trefan Morys, Llanystumdwy, Gwynedd, Wales.

CAREER: Western Daily Press, Bristol, England, member of editorial staff, 1944; Arab News Agency, Cairo, Egypt, member of editorial staff, 1947-48; *Times,* London, England, member of editorial staff, 1951-56, and special correspondent in Egypt, Scandinavia, the Netherlands, India, and the United States; *Guardian,* Manchester, England, member of editorial staff, 1956-61; free-lance writer, 1961—. *Military service:* British Army, Ninth Lancers, 1943-47; became lieutenant. *Member:* Royal Society of Literature (fellow). *Awards, honors:* Commonwealth Fund fellow, 1953; Cafe Royal Prize, 1957, for *Coast to Coast;* George Polk Memorial Award, 1960; Heinemann Award, 1961, for *Venice.*

WRITINGS—Under name James Morris: *As I Saw the U.S.A.,* Pantheon, 1956 (published in England as *Coast to Coast,* Faber, 1956, 2nd edition, 1962); *Islam Inflamed: A Middle East Picture,* Pantheon, 1957 (published in England as *The Market of Seleukia,* Faber, 1957); *Sultan in Oman: Venture into the Middle East,* Pantheon, 1957; *Coronation Everest,* Dutton, 1958; *South African Winter,* Pantheon, 1958; *The Hashemite Kings,* Pantheon, 1959.

The World of Venice, Pantheon, 1960, revised edition, 1974 (published in England as *Venice,* Faber, 1960, revised edition, 1974); *The Upstairs Donkey, and Other Stolen Stories* (juvenile), Pantheon, 1961; *South America,* Manchester Guardian and Evening News Ltd., 1961; *The Road to Huddersfield: A Journey to Five Continents* (Book-of-the-Month Club selection), Pantheon, 1963 (published in England as *The World Bank: A Prospect,* Faber, 1963); *Cities,* Faber, 1963, Harcourt, 1964; *The Outriders: A Liberal View of Britain,* Faber, 1963; *The Presence of Spain,* Harcourt, 1964, published as *Spain,* Faber, 1970; *Oxford,* Harcourt, 1965, revised edition, Oxford University Press, 1978; *Pax Britannica: The Climax of an Empire* (first book of trilogy), Harcourt, 1968; *The Great Port: A Passage through New York,* Harcourt, 1969; (author of introduction) Roger Wood, *Persia,* Thames & Hudson, 1969, Universe Books, 1970.

Places, Faber, 1972, Harcourt, 1973; *Heaven's Command: An Imperial Progress* (second book of trilogy), Harcourt, 1973; *Farewell the Trumpets: An Imperial Retreat* (third book of trilogy), Harcourt, 1978.

Under name Jan Morris: *Conundrum* (autobiography), Harcourt, 1974; *Travels,* Harcourt, 1976; (editor) *The Oxford Book of Oxford,* Oxford University Press, 1978.

SIDELIGHTS: James Morris was considered to be one of Britain's leading journalists. He established his reputation at the age of 27, when, as a London *Times* reporter, he accompanied the 1953 Mt. Everest expedition to the 22,000 feet level; through an ingeniously organized communications system, he "scooped the world with the news of Hillary's and Tenzing's triumph," according to John Richardson. *Coronation Everest* is his book-length account of the event. In the years that followed Morris traveled the world reporting on wars and rebellions and wrote numerous history and travel books, establishing for himself a considerable reputation with the critics and public.

In the autobiographical *Conundrum,* Morris relates, "I was 3 or perhaps 4 years old when I realized that I had been born into the wrong body, and should really be a girl." In 1964, Morris began the transformation into the female Jan Morris by taking hormone pills; in 1972, the process was completed through surgery. A *Newsweek* writer calls *Conundrum* "certainly the best first-hand account ever written by a traveler across the boundaries of sex. That journey is perhaps the ultimate adventure for a human being, but although it has been the subject of myth and speculation since ancient times, it is an authentically modern experience." Jan Morris told Lorraine Kisly: "No one has ever been able to convince a real transsexual that his convictions about his true nature were wrong. No doctor or scientist can say where the conviction comes from, and for me it is a spiritual question, a matter of my soul, much deeper and broader than sexual preference or mode." The *Newsweek* writer concludes: "Morris can offer no real answer to the central mystery; neither she nor the scientists of this era can explain with any certainty why a transsexual's mind and body are at odds with each other. What Jan Morris does offer, through her life and her work, is a window on the wondrous possibilities of humankind."

BIOGRAPHICAL/CRITICAL SOURCES: Christian Science Monitor, October 13, 1959; *New Statesman,* December 5, 1959, October 25, 1968; Manchester *Guardian,* August 19, 1960; *Newsweek,* August 5, 1963, April 8, 1974; *Saturday Evening Post,* July 3, 1965; *Book World,* January 12, 1969; Jan Morris, *Conundrum,* Harcourt, 1974; *New York Times Magazine,* March 17, 1974; *New York Times Book Review,* April 14, 1974, November 19, 1978; *New York Review of Books,* May 2, 1974; *Harper's,* August, 1974.†

*   *   *

MORRIS, Richard (Ward) 1939-

PERSONAL: Born June 16, 1939, in Milwaukee, Wis.; son of Alvin Harry and Dorothy (Wissmueller) Morris. *Education:* University of Nevada, B.S., 1962, Ph.D., 1968; University of New Mexico, M.S., 1964. *Address:* P.O. Box 703, San Francisco, Calif. 94101.

CAREER: Committee of Small Magazine Editors and Publishers (COSMEP), San Francisco, Calif., coordinator, 1968—.

WRITINGS: Plays (poetry), Twowindows Press, 1974; *Poetry Is a Kind of Writing: Selected Poems,* Thorp Springs Press, 1975; *Light,* Bobbs-Merrill, 1979; *The End of the World,* Anchor Press, 1980. Editor of *Camels Coming,* 1965-68, and *COSMEP Newsletter.*

BIOGRAPHICAL/CRITICAL SOURCES: Hugh Fox, *The Living Underground: A Critical Overview,* Whitson, 1971.

*   *   *

MORRIS, Ruby Turner 1908-
(Ruby Turner Norris)

PERSONAL: Born April 28, 1908, in Pepperill, Mass.; daughter of George Freeman and Martha (Sibley) Turner; married second husband, Jack Gibbons Morris, May 14, 1946 (divorced, 1952). *Education:* Vassar College, A.B., 1929; Stanford University, M.A., 1930, Ph.D., 1937. *Home:* 56 Hawthorne Dr., Apt. 6, New London, Conn. *Office:* Department of Economics, Connecticut College, New London, Conn.

CAREER: Vassar College, Poughkeepsie, N.Y., 1933-52, began as instructor, became associate professor of economics; Office of Price Administration, Hawaii, grocery price administrator, 1941-45; Connecticut College, New London, professor of economics, 1952-75, currently professor emeritus, chairman of department, 1952-72. Exchange professor, University College for Women, Hyderabad, India, 1966-67. New London City Council, member, 1971-72, 1974-79, deputy mayor, 1972-73, mayor, 1976. *Member:* American Economic Association, American Association of University Professors, Phi Beta Kappa.

WRITINGS: (Under name Ruby Turner Norris) *The Theory of Consumer's Demand,* Yale University Press, 1941, revised edition, 1952, reprinted, Arno, 1976; *Fundamentals of Economics,* with workbook, Ronald, 1961; *Consumers Union: Methods, Implications, Weaknesses and Strengths,* [New London, Conn.], 1971. Contributor to *Reporter* and professional journals.

AVOCATIONAL INTERESTS: Sailing, painting.

*   *   *

MORRISON, Eleanor S(helton) 1921-

PERSONAL: Born May 21, 1921, in Stonega, Va.; daughter of Floyd Bunyan (a clergyman) and Nelle (Hines) Shelton; married Truman Aldrich Morrison, Jr. (a clergyman), August 22, 1942; children: Truman III, Melanie, Wendy, Stephanie. *Education:* Wesleyan College, B.A., 1941; Northwestern University, M.A., 1942. *Home:* 1400 Pershing Dr., Lansing, Mich. 48910. *Office:* College of Human Medicine, Michigan State University, East Lansing, Mich. 48824; and 469 North Hagadorn Rd., East Lansing, Mich. 48823.

CAREER: Michigan State University, East Lansing, instructor in department of family and child sciences, 1967-75, instructor in department of community medicine, College of Osteopathic Medicine, 1976-78, clinical instructor in department of psychiatry, College of Human Medicine, 1978—; ordained minister of United Church of Christ, 1976; Edgewood United Church, East Lansing, co-pastor (with husband), 1978—. Chairman of United Nations Day, 1964-66; staff counselor, Counselling Associates, East Lansing. *Member:* Young Women's Christian Association (member of board of directors of local chapter, 1960), League of Women Voters (member of board of directors of local chapter, 1955-65), Child Study Association, National Council of Family Relations, American Association of Sex Educators, Counsellors, and Therapists, Association for Creative Change in Religion and Other Systems, Michigan Personnel and Guidance Association, Michigan Group Work Specialists Association. *Awards, honors:* D.Litt., Chicago Theological Seminary, 1965.

WRITINGS: (With Virgil Foster) *Creative Teaching in the Church,* Prentice-Hall, 1963; (with husband, Truman Morrison) *Growing Up in the Family,* United Church Press, 1964; (editor) *Human Sexuality: Contemporary Perspectives,* National Press Books, 1973, 2nd edition, 1977; (with Mila Price) *Values in Sexuality,* Hart Publishing, 1974; *Growing Up Sexual,* Van Nostrand, 1980.

*   *   *

MORRISON, Theodore 1901-

PERSONAL: Born November 4, 1901, in Concord, N.H.; son of Henry Kent and Emma Marshall (Howard-Smith) Morrison; married Florence Kathleen Johnston, October 22, 1927; children: Robert Henry, Anne Guthrie Morrison Gentry. *Education:* Harvard University, A.B., 1923. *Home:* 164 Red Gate Lane, Amherst, Mass. 01002. *Office:* Department of English, Harvard University, Cambridge, Mass.

CAREER: Atlantic Monthly, Boston, Mass., member of editorial staff, 1925-30; Harvard University, Cambridge, Mass., instructor, 1931-37, assistant professor, 1937-39, lecturer, 1939-63, professor of English, beginning 1963, currently professor emeritus, director of English A, 1939-51. Director, Bread Loaf Writers' Conference, 1932-55. *Member:* American Academy of Arts and Sciences, Signet Society (Harvard). *Awards, honors:* Litt.D., Middlebury College, 1951.

WRITINGS: The Serpent in the Cloud (narrative poem), Houghton, 1931; *Notes of Death and Life* (poems), Crowell, 1935; (co-editor) *Five Kinds of Writing,* Little, Brown, 1939; *The Devious Way* (narrative poem), Viking, 1944; (translator and author of commentary and introduction) *The Portable Chaucer,* Viking, 1949, revised edition, 1977; *The Dream of Alcestis* (Narrative Poem), Viking, 1950; *The Stones of the House* (novel), Viking, 1953; *To Make a World* (novel), Viking, 1957; *The Whole Creation* (novel), Viking, 1961; *Chautauqua: A Center for Education, Religion and the Arts in America* (nonfiction), University of Chicago Press, 1974; *Bread Loaf Writers' Conference: The First Thirty Years, 1926-55* (nonfiction), Middlebury College Press, 1976. Contributor to *Harper's, Atlantic Monthly,* and professional journals.

SIDELIGHTS: Theodore Morrison began publishing as a poet and then, growing more interested in character and story, started writing novels. In *Chautauqua* and *Bread Loaf Writers' Conference,* however, Morrison turns to the history of two American cultural institutions. The former, the Chautauqua Institution, was founded in 1874 as a summer school for adults and continues to provide education today in the form of orchestra, opera, theater, and lectures. Concerning *Chautauqua,* Edward Weeks of the *Atlantic Monthly* comments, "The spirit of self-improvement, fundamental in the American character, can be overserious, and it is the grace of Mr. Morrison's history that he can equate so fairly the aspiration in Chautauqa with the amusing human behavior."

A stage version of *The Dream of Alcestis* was produced at the Very Little Theatre, Eugene, Ore.

BIOGRAPHICAL/CRITICAL SOURCES: New York Herald Tribune Book Review, March 1, 1953; *Atlantic Monthly,* July, 1974; *Choice,* December, 1974; *Journal of American History,* June, 1975.

* * *

MORRISON, Wilbur Howard 1915-

PERSONAL: Born June 21, 1915, in Plattsburgh, N.Y.; son of Martin William and Lucy (Watson) Morrison. *Education:* Attended public schools, Plattsburgh, N.Y. *Home:* 2036 East Alvarado St., Fallbrook, Calif. 92028. *Agent:* David Stewart Hull, James Brown Associates, Inc., 25 West 43rd St., New York, N.Y. 10036.

CAREER: Radio station WMFF, Plattsburgh, N.Y., announcer, 1935-37; radio station WOKO, Albany, N.Y., news commentator, 1937-38; radio station WGY, Schenectady, N.Y., announcer, 1938-41, 1946-48; radio station WRUN, Utica, N.Y., chief announcer, 1948-54; Douglas Aircraft Co., El Segundo and Long Beach, Calif., public relations representative, 1954-64; military publicity manager, Lockheed-California Co., 1965-70. *Military service:* U.S. Army Air Forces, 1942-46; became major; awarded Distinguished Flying Cross, Air Medal with three clusters, five battle stars, three Distinguished Unit citations. U.S. Air Force Reserve, 1954-75; became lieutenant colonel.

WRITINGS: Hellbirds, Duell, 1960, reprinted, Zenger, 1979; *The Incredible 305th,* Duell, 1962; *Wings over the Seven Seas,* A. S. Barnes, 1976; *Point of No Return: The Story of the Twentieth Air Force,* Times Books, 1979.

WORK IN PROGRESS: A Signal Victory, A Taste of Power, Sport, and *Life with Petey,* all for Times Books; *A Heart with Wings;* a children's book, *Mr. Peanut; Fortress without a Roof.*

SIDELIGHTS: As a bombardier-navigator, Wilbur Howard Morrison flew two combat tours totaling thirty-eight missions and 500 combat hours. *Avocational interests:* Hunting, fishing, gardening, and reading.

* * *

MORRISSEY, L(eroy) J(ohn) 1935-

PERSONAL: Born April 26, 1935, in Brainard, Neb.; son of Edward James and Edith (Stuchlick) Morrissey; married Alverta Strickland, July 11, 1959 (divorced, 1977); children: Timothy, Kathleen, Sean. *Education:* University of Nebraska, B.A., 1958; University of Chicago, M.A., 1959; University of Pennsylvania, Ph.D., 1964. *Home:* Apt. 8B, 305 26th St. E., Saskatoon, Saskatchewan, Canada. *Office:* Department of English, University of Saskatchewan, Saskatoon, Saskatchewan, Canada.

CAREER: Pennsylvania State University, University Park, instructor in English, 1959-60; Dickinson College, Carlisle, Pa., instructor in English, 1963-65; University of Western Ontario, London, assistant professor of English, 1965-69; University of Saskatchewan, Saskatoon, 1969—, began as associate professor, currently professor of Restoration and eighteenth-century literature. *Member:* Society for Eighteenth-Century Studies (Canada; member of executive board, 1971—), Society for Eighteenth-Century Studies (United States), Modern Language Association of America, Phi Beta Kappa.

WRITINGS: (Editor and author of notes) Henry Fielding, *Tom Thumb, or The Tragedy of Tragedies,* University of California Press, 1970; (editor and author of notes) Fielding, *Grub Street Opera,* Oliver & Boyd, 1974; *Gulliver's Progress,* Archon Books, 1978; *Henry Fielding: An Annotated Bibliography, 1755-1977,* G. K. Hall, 1980. Contributor to professional journals.

* * *

MOSS, Howard 1922-

PERSONAL: Born January 22, 1922, in New York, N.Y.; son of David Leonard and Sonya (Schrag) Moss. *Education:* Attended University of Michigan, 1939-40, and Harvard University, 1942; University of Wisconsin, B.A., 1943; Columbia University, graduate study. *Home:* 27 West 10th St., New York, N.Y. 10011. *Office: New Yorker,* 25 West 43rd St., New York, N.Y. 10036.

CAREER: Time, New York City, book reviewer, 1944; Vassar College, Poughkeepsie, N.Y., instructor, 1945-46; *New Yorker,* New York City, poetry editor, 1948—. Hurst Professor, Washington University, 1972; adjunct professor, Barnard College, 1976, Columbia University, 1977, University of California, Irvine, 1979, and University of Houston, 1980. *Member:* American Academy and Institute of Arts and Letters. *Awards, honors:* Janet Sewall Davis Award, *Poetry,* 1944; American Academy and Institute of Arts and Letters award, 1968; Ingram Merrill Foundation grant, 1972; National Book Award for poetry, 1972, for *Selected Poems.*

WRITINGS—Poems: *The Wound and the Weather,* Reynal, 1943; *The Toy Fair,* Scribner, 1954; *A Swimmer in the Air,* Scribner, 1957, reprinted, Greenwood, 1976; *A Winter Come, a Summer Gone: Poems 1946-1960,* Scribner, 1960; *Finding Them Lost,* Scribner, 1965; *Second Nature,* Atheneum, 1968; *Selected Poems,* Atheneum, 1971; *Buried City,* Atheneum, 1975; *A Swim Off the Rocks,* Atheneum, 1976; *Tigers and Other Lilies* (juvenile), Atheneum, 1977; *Notes from the Castle,* Atheneum, 1979.

Criticism: (Contributor) *A Casebook on Dylan Thomas*, Crowell, 1960; *The Magic Lantern of Marcel Proust*, Macmillan, 1962, reprinted, David R. Godine, 1979; *Writing against Time*, Morrow, 1969.

Editor: *Keats*, Dell, 1959; *The Nonsense Books of Edward Lear*, New American Library, 1964; *The Poet's Story*, Macmillan, 1973; *New York: Poems*, Avon, 1980.

Satire: *Instant Lives*, Dutton, 1974.

Plays: "The Folding Green" (also see below), produced by the Poets Theatre, Cambridge, Mass., 1958, Playwrights' Unit, 1964, and by Theatre, 1965; "Garden Music," produced by Theater Saint Paul, Saint Paul, Minn., 1966; "The Oedipus Mah-Jong Scandal," produced by the Cooperative Theatre Club, New York City, 1968; "The Palace at 4 A.M." (also see below), produced by the John Drew Theater, East Hampton, N.Y., 1972; *Two Plays: The Palace at 4 A.M.* [and] *The Folding Green*, Flying Point Press, 1980.

Poetry appears in several anthologies. Contributor to *New Yorker, Poetry, Harper's, Reporter, Nation, New Republic*, and other periodicals.

SIDELIGHTS: Howard Moss's poetry has been praised for its quiet, structured power. Laurence Lieberman writes that in the best of Moss's poems "a mellow calm quietly and slowly builds behind the elaborate structure and peaks in a final organ music, a beautiful sereneness, that is an unmistakable tonality of the earned purer mind." Howard Moss, Edmund White writes, "has [a] divine knack of arranging perfectly observed facts in a truthful way, a way that corresponds to the structure of our emotions, to their natural curvature."

Moss's wide-ranging criticism has also been well-received. His study of Marcel Proust, Arthur H. Beattie observes, "might well be viewed as the magic lantern of Howard Moss turned upon the world of Marcel Proust; as it illuminates that world, it suffuses it with colors which reveal the sensitive nature and keen mind of the critic."

The song cycle "King Midas" by Ned Rorem consists of ten poems by Moss. The Syracuse University Library houses a collection of Moss's manuscripts.

BIOGRAPHICAL/CRITICAL SOURCES: Atlantic, September, 1954; *Prairie Schooner*, fall, 1957, winter, 1976-77; *New York Herald Tribune Book Review*, April 17, 1960; *Yale Review*, September, 1960, autumn, 1971; *New York Times Book Review*, November 13, 1960, November 21, 1965, April 18, 1976, November 13, 1977, February 3, 1980; *Virginia Quarterly Review*, spring, 1963, fall, 1971, summer, 1976; *Arizona Quarterly*, spring, 1963; *New Yorker*, March 9, 1963, December 11, 1971; *Times Literary Supplement*, October 11, 1963, January 27, 1966, May 14, 1976; *Hudson Review*, autumn, 1965, autumn, 1971, summer, 1976; *Commonweal*, September 24, 1965, December 3, 1976; *Saturday Review*, October 9, 1965, March 15, 1969; *Holiday*, December, 1965; *Poetry*, March, 1966, August, 1969, March, 1974, August, 1978; Richard Howard, *Alone with America*, Atheneum, 1969.

Harper's, July, 1971; *Western Humanities Review*, autumn, 1972; *New York Review of Books*, December 13, 1973; *New Republic*, January 5, 1974, November 29, 1975; *Christian Science Monitor*, February 6, 1974; *Village Voice*, June 13, 1974; *Book World*, September 8, 1974, August 24, 1975; *Listener*, September 26, 1974; *American Scholar*, winter, 1974-75; *Observer*, January 12, 1975; *Georgia Review*, spring, 1976; *Nation*, October 9, 1976; Laurence Lieberman, *Unassigned Frequencies*, University of Illinois Press, 1977; *Contemporary Literary Criticism*, Volume VII, Gale, 1977; *Southwest Review*, summer, 1977; *Sewanee Review*, July, 1978.

* * *

MOWRER, O(rval) Hobart 1907-

PERSONAL: Born January 23, 1907, in Unionville, Mo.; son of John Andrew and Sallie Ann (Todd) Mowrer; married Willie Mae Cook (a child psychologist), September 9, 1931; children: Linda (Mrs. Peter K. Carlston), Kathryn (Mrs. David M. Philips), Todd. *Education:* University of Missouri, A.B., 1929; Johns Hopkins University, Ph.D., 1932. *Religion:* Protestant. *Home:* 610 West Vermont St., Urbana, Ill. 61801. *Office:* 725 Psychology Building, University of Illinois, Urbana, Ill. 61820.

CAREER: Northwestern University, Evanston, Ill., National Research fellow, 1932-33; Princeton University, Princeton, N.J., National Research fellow, 1933-34; Yale University, New Haven, Conn., Sterling fellow, 1934-36, instructor in psychology and member of research staff of Institute of Human Relations, 1936-40; Harvard University, Graduate School of Education, Cambridge, Mass., assistant professor, 1940-43, associate professor of education, 1943-48; University of Illinois at Urbana-Champaign, research professor of psychology, 1948-75, professor emeritus, 1975—. Diplomate, American Board of Examiners in Professional Psychology. Family Service Society, New York, consultant, 1942-44, member of board of directors, 1958-62; consultant to National Institute of Mental Health, 1951-54, and State Research Hospital, Galesburg, Ill.; lecturer at numerous theological seminaries. University of Illinois Young Men's Christian Association, member of board of directors, 1960-66, chairman, 1961-63. *Wartime service:* Office of Strategic Services, Assessment Psychologists, clinical psychologist, 1944-45. *Member:* American Psychological Association (fellow; member of board of directors, 1952-55; president, 1953-54), American Psychopathological Association, American Academy of Psychotherapists, Lambda Chi Alpha, Philosophy Club (University of Illinois). *Awards, honors:* M.A., Harvard University, 1946; certificate of merit, University of Missouri, 1956; Distinguished Contributions Award, Illinois Psychological Association, 1975.

WRITINGS: (Contributor) *Frustration and Aggression*, Yale University Press, 1939; (editor) *Patterns for Modern Living*, three volumes, Delphian Society, 1949, revised edition, 1955; *Learning Theory and Personality Dynamics*, Ronald, 1950; *Psychotherapy: Theory and Research*, Ronald, 1953; *Learning Theory and Behavior*, Wiley, 1960; *Learning Theory and the Symbolic Processes*, Wiley, 1960; *The Crisis in Psychiatry and Religion*, D. Van Nostrand, 1961; *The New Group Therapy*, D. Van Nostrand, 1964; (editor) *Morality and Mental Health*, Rand McNally, 1967; (with Ronald C. Johnson and Paul Dokecki) *Conscience, Contract and Social Reality*, Holt, 1972; *Psychology of Language and Learning*, Plenum, 1980. Editor, *Harvard Educational Review*, 1945-48.

AVOCATIONAL INTERESTS: Gardening and music.

BIOGRAPHICAL/CRITICAL SOURCES: Illinois Alumni News, April, 1961.

* * *

MOYNAHAN, Julian (Lane) 1925-

PERSONAL: Born May 21, 1925, in Cambridge, Mass.; son of Joseph Leo (a salesman) and Mary (Shea) Moynahan;

married Elizabeth Reilly (an architect), August 6, 1945; children: Catherine, Brigid, Mary Ellen. *Education:* Harvard University, A.B., 1947, A.M., 1951, Ph.D., 1957. *Politics:* Democrat. *Home:* 3439 Lawrenceville Rd., Princeton, N.J. *Office:* Department of English, Rutgers University, New Brunswick, N.J.

CAREER: Amherst College, Amherst, Mass., instructor in English, 1953-55; Princeton University, Princeton, N.J., assistant professor of English, 1955-63, bicentennial preceptor, 1960-63; University College, Dublin, Fulbright professor, 1963-64; Rutgers University, New Brunswick, N.J., associate professor, 1964-66, professor of English, 1966—. Visiting professor, University of Wyoming, summer, 1965, Harvard University, summer, 1967, and Breadloaf Graduate School, 1969. National Endowment for the Humanities Professor of Humanities, Manhattanville College, 1972; Christian Gauss Lecturer, Princeton University, 1975; visiting scholar, University of Utah, 1980. *Military service:* U.S. Army, 1943-44. *Member:* Modern Language Association of America, American Association of University Professors. *Awards, honors:* American Council of Learned Societies grant-in-aid, 1961; Fulbright-Hays Award, 1963-64; American Philosophical Society grant, 1964; National Endowment for the Arts sabbatical leave award, 1967-68; Rutgers Research Council faculty fellowship, 1967-68, 1971-72, 1975-76; Ingram-Merrill Foundation award, 1971; National Endowment for the Humanities award, 1975-76.

WRITINGS—Novels: *Sisters and Brothers,* Random House, 1960; *Pairing Off,* Morrow, 1969; *Garden State,* Little, Brown, 1973; *Where the Land and Water Meet,* Morrow, 1979.

Nonfiction: (Contributor) John Grass and Gabriel Pearson, editors, *Dickens and the Twentieth Century,* Routledge & Kegan Paul, 1962; *The Deed of Life: The Novels and Shorter Fiction of D. H. Lawrence,* Princeton University Press, 1963; (editor) D. H. Lawrence, *Sons and Lovers,* Viking, 1968; (author of preface) Lawrence, *A Modern Lover and Other Stories,* Ballantine, 1969; *Vladimir Nabokov,* University of Minnesota Press, 1971; (contributor) G. T. Wright, *Seven American Literary Stylists from Poe to Mailer,* University of Minnesota Press, 1973; (editor) *The Portable Thomas Hardy,* Viking, 1977; (contributor) Mark Spilka, editor, *Towards a Poetics of Fiction,* University of Indiana Press, 1978; (contributor) Anne Smith, editor, *Lawrence and Women,* Vision Press (London), 1978; (author of preface) Marina Turkevich Naumann, *Blue Evenings in Berlin: Nabokov's Short Stories of the 1920's,* New York University Press, 1978.

Contributor of articles and reviews to *Observer, New York Times Book Review, Book World,* and other periodicals.

SIDELIGHTS: Julian Moynahan stopped writing poetry in 1960 when he was asked to record some of his work for the Harvard Vocarium Archives of Contemporary Poets. He claims that he was so shocked at being taken seriously as a poet that he has never published another line. Moynahan's fiction and critical work have continued, however, and have met with critical success. Does this shock him? "I would record my fiction any day in the week," he states.

BIOGRAPHICAL/CRITICAL SOURCES: Canadian Forum, December, 1963; *Yale Review,* December, 1963, March, 1970; *Virginia Quarterly Review,* winter, 1964; *Saturday Review,* June 11, 1966, October 25, 1969; *Observer,* January 5, 1969; *New Statesman,* January 10, 1969; *Times Literary Supplement,* January 16, 1969; *Listener,* January 23, 1969; *New York Times,* August 15, 1969; *Newsweek,* August 18, 1969, July 30, 1973; *Time,* August 22, 1969, August 13, 1973; *Life,* August 22, 1969; *Book World,* August 24, 1969, August 26, 1973; *New York Times Book Review,* October 26, 1969, September 2, 1973, May 27, 1979; *Washington Post,* June 26, 1979, July 5, 1979.

* * *

MULLALLY, Frederic 1920-

PERSONAL: Born February 25, 1920, in London, England; son of Thomas and Margaret (Strutt) Mullally; married Suzanne Warner (divorced); married Rosemary Nichols (an actress and writer), September 27, 1971; children: (first marriage) Michael. *Education:* Attended St. Xavier College. *Home:* 9 Claridge House, Davies St., London W.1, England. *Agent:* John Farquharson, 15 Red Lion Sq., London WC1R 4QW, England.

CAREER: Financial News, London, England, sub-editor, 1940-43; *Tribune,* London, assistant editor, 1944-47; *Sunday Pictorial,* London, political editor, 1948-51; *Picture Post,* London, publicity director, 1956-58; full-time writer, 1958—. *Member:* Society of Authors (Great Britain), Authors Guild, Authors League of America.

WRITINGS: (With Fenner Brockway) *Death Pays a Dividend,* Gollancz, 1944; *Fascism inside England,* Claud Morris, 1946; *Danse Macabre,* Secker & Warburg, 1959, published as *Marianne,* Viking, 1960; *Man with Trumpet,* Barker, 1961, published as *Sara,* Dell, 1963; *Split Scene,* Barker, 1963, Dell, 1964; *The Assassins,* Barker, 1964, Walker, 1965; *No Other Hunger,* McKay, 1966; *The Prizewinner: A Diversion,* Barker, 1967; *The Munich Involvement,* Barker, 1968; *The Penthouse Sexicon,* New English Library, 1968; *Oh, Wicked Wanda!,* Sphere Books, 1969; *Clancy,* Hart-Davis, 1971, Morrow, 1972; *The Malta Conspiracy,* Hart-Davis, 1972; *Venus Afflicted,* Hart-Davis, 1974; *Hitler Has Won,* Simon & Schuster, 1975; *The Deadly Payoff,* W. H. Allen, 1978.†

* * *

MULLER, Herbert J(oseph) 1905-

PERSONAL: Born July 7, 1905, in Mamaroneck, N.Y.; son of Carl and Bess (Fay) Muller; married Janet Bailey, June 16, 1934; children: Richard Bailey, John Albert. *Education:* Cornell University, B.A., 1925, M.A., 1926, Ph.D., 1932. *Home:* 610 South Hawthorne Lane, Bloomington, Ind. 47401. *Office:* Department of English, Indiana University, Bloomington, Ind. 47401.

CAREER: Cornell University, Ithaca, N.Y., instructor, 1926-35; Purdue University, Lafayette, Ind., 1935-56, began as instructor, became professor of English; Indiana University at Bloomington, professor of English and government, 1956-59, Distinguished Service Professor, 1959-73, professor emeritus, 1973—. Visiting professor, Istanbul University (Turkey), 1946-47, and 1951-52, and Indiana University, 1953-54; Distinguished Visiting Professor, New York University, 1958; Sloan Visiting Professor, Menninger Foundation, 1963, and University of Alabama, 1967. Member of staff, Foreign Service Auxiliary, U.S. Department of State, Washington, D.C., 1943; editor, War Production Board, 1944.

MEMBER: World Academy of Arts and Sciences, American Academy of Arts and Sciences, American Association of University Professors, Phi Beta Kappa (senator, 1964). *Awards, honors:* Guggenheim fellow, 1939-40; Litt.D., Purdue University, 1960; Phi Beta Kappa award for most distinguished book in philosophy, religion, and history, 1961-62, for *Freedom in the Ancient World;* Frederic G. Melcher Book Award, 1964, for *Religion and Freedom in the Modern World;* Rockefeller Foundation grant.

WRITINGS: Modern Fiction: A Study of Values, Funk, 1937, reprinted, McGraw, 1964; *Science and Criticism: The Humanistic Tradition in Contemporary Thought,* Yale University Press, 1943, reprinted, Books for Libraries, 1971; *Thomas Wolfe,* New Directions, 1947, reprinted, Kraus Reprint, 1971; *The Uses of the Past: Profiles of Former Societies,* Oxford University Press, 1952, New American Library, 1959; *The Spirit of Tragedy,* Knopf, 1956; *The Loom of History,* Harper, 1958; *Issues of Freedom: Paradoxes and Promises,* Harper, 1960; *Freedom in the Ancient World,* Harper, 1961; *Freedom in the Western World, from the Dark Ages to the Rise of Democracy,* Harper, 1963; *Religion and Freedom in the Modern World,* University of Chicago Press, 1963; *The Individual in a Revolutionary World,* Ryerson Press, 1964; *Freedom in the Modern World,* Harper, 1966; *Adlai Stevenson: A Study in Values,* Harper, 1967; *The Uses of English: Guidelines for the Teaching of English from the Anglo-American Conferences at Dartmouth College,* Harper, 1967; *The Children of Frankenstein: A Primer on Modern Technology and Human Values,* Indiana University Press, 1970; *In Pursuit of Relevance,* Indiana University Press, 1971; (contributor) J. Laughlin, editor, *Surrealism Pro and Con,* Gotham Book Mart, 1973; *Uses of the Future,* Indiana University Press, 1974. Contributor of articles and book reviews to periodicals, including *Saturday Review, Yale Review, Virginia Quarterly Review, South Atlantic Quarterly,* and *American Scholar.*†

* * *

MUNGER, Frank James 1929-

PERSONAL: Born September 18, 1929, in Fort Worth, Tex.; son of Guy Elmer and Kathleen (Gallagher) Munger; married Rosemary B. Huppert, 1957. *Education:* Northwestern University, B.S., 1951; Harvard University, M.P.A., 1953, Ph.D., 1956. *Politics:* Carlist. *Home:* 814 Shadylawn Rd., Chapel Hill, N.C. 27514. *Office:* University of North Carolina, 02 Manning Hall, Chapel Hill, N.C. 27514.

CAREER: Syracuse University, Syracuse, N.Y., instructor, 1955-56, assistant professor, 1956-61, associate professor, 1961-65, professor of political science, 1965-70, chairman of department, 1962-65; University of Florida, Gainesville, professor of political science, 1970-71; University of North Carolina at Chapel Hill, professor of political science, 1971—, director of Institute for Research in Social Science, 1973—. Visiting professor, University of Rochester, 1967. *Member:* American Association for the Advancement of Science, Southern Political Science Association. *Awards, honors:* Social Science Research Council grant, 1956; Rockefeller Foundation grant, 1965-66; National Science Foundation research grants, 1967-69 and 1970-71.

WRITINGS: (With others) *River Basin Administration and the Delaware,* Syracuse University Press, 1960; (with Ralph Straetz) *New York Politics,* New York University Press, 1960; (with Roscoe C. Martin and others) *Decisions in Syracuse,* Indiana University Press, 1961; *The Struggle for Republican Leadership in Indiana, 1954,* McGraw, 1962; (with Richard Fenno) *National Politics and Federal Aid to Education,* Syracuse University Press, 1962; *American State Politics,* Crowell, 1967; *The Legitimacy of Opposition: The Change of Government in Ireland in 1932,* Sage Publications, 1975; (editor with James W. White) *Social Change and Community Politics in Urban Japan,* Institute for Research in Social Science, University of North Carolina, 1976.

WORK IN PROGRESS: Who Nominated Jimmy Carter?

* * *

MURPHY, Richard T. A. 1908-

PERSONAL: Born November 23, 1908, in Minneapolis, Minn.; son of William Bernard and Amelia (Heiker) Murphy. *Education:* Angelicum University, S.T.Lr., 1936, S.T.D., 1937; attended Ecole Biblique et Archeologique Francaise de Jerusalem, 1937-39; Pontifical Biblical Commission, Vatican City, Italy, S.S. Prolyta, 1939, S.S. Doctor, 1950; Dominican Order, S.T.M., 1960. *Home and office:* St. Dominic Priory, 775 Harrison Ave., New Orleans, La.

CAREER: Ordained in Order of Preachers (Dominican Order), 1935. Dominican House of Studies, Washington, D.C., professor of scripture, 1939-43; Dominican House of Studies, River Forest, Ill., professor, 1943-48; Aquinas Institute, Dubuque, Iowa, professor, 1951-66; Mount St. Bernard Seminary, Dubuque, professor, 1951-66; University of Western Ontario, London, Catholic chaplain, 1966-74. *Member:* Catholic Biblical Association.

WRITINGS: Commentary on the Psalms—The Little Office, Rosary Press, 1953, published as *The Little Office Companion,* Paluch, 1958; *The Sunday Gospels,* Bruce, 1960, 3rd edition, 1964; *The Sunday Epistles,* Bruce, 1961, 2nd edition, 1964; (author of introduction) Saint Thomas Aquinas, *Commentary on Saint Paul's Epistle to the Galatians,* Magi Books, 1966; (editor) *Lagrange and Biblical Renewal,* Priory, 1966; *Background to the Bible,* Servant Books, 1978; *Days of Glory,* Servant Books, 1980. Contributor to periodicals.

Translator: *Pere Lagrange and the Scriptures,* Bruce, 1946; Ricciotti, *History of Israel,* Bruce, 1955; Braun, *The Work of Pere Lagrange,* Bruce, 1963; *Summa: The Passion of Christ,* McGraw, 1966.

WORK IN PROGRESS: Prophets of Israel.

* * *

MURRA, John V(ictor) 1916-

PERSONAL: Born August 24, 1916, in Odessa, Russia; came to United States in 1934, naturalized, 1950. *Education:* University of Chicago, B.A., 1936, M.A., 1942, Ph.D., 1956. *Home:* 515 Dryden Rd., Ithaca, N.Y. 14850. *Office:* Department of Anthropology, Cornell University, Ithaca, N.Y. 14850.

CAREER: University of Chicago, Chicago, Ill., instructor in anthropology, 1943-47; University of Puerto Rico, Rio Piedras, 1947-50, began as assistant professor, became associate professor of anthropology; Vassar College, Poughkeepsie, N.Y., 1950-61, began as assistant professor, became professor of anthropology; Yale University, New Haven, Conn., visiting professor of anthropology, 1961-63; Institute of Andean Research, New York, N.Y., principal investigator of National Science Foundation-funded study of Inca life in Huanuco area, Peru, 1963-66; Smithsonian Institution, Washington, D.C., National Academy of Sciences postdoctoral associate, 1966-67; Cornell University, Ithaca, N.Y., professor of anthropology, 1968—. Area specialist, United Nations, 1951; visiting lecturer, Columbia University, spring, 1955; visiting professor at University of San Marcos, Lima, 1958, National School of Anthropology and History, Mexico, 1961, University of Chile, 1965, University of San Marcos, 1965-66, Yale University, 1970-71, Universite de

Paris-X, Nanterre, 1975-76, and Ecole des Hautes Etudes en Sciences Sociales, Paris, 1975-76. Did field work in southern Ecuador, 1941-42, Puerto Rico, 1947-48, Jamaica, 1953, Martinique, 1956, Peru, 1958, 1963-65, and 1973. Member of editorial board, Instituto Indigenista Interamericano, 1966-70. *Military service:* Spanish Republican Army, 15th International Brigade, 1937-39.

MEMBER: American Anthropological Association (fellow), American Ethnological Society (fellow; councilor, 1961-64; president, 1972-73), Society for American Archaeology (fellow), African Studies Association (fellow), American Society for Ethnohistory (member of board, 1967-69; president, 1970-71), Institute of Andean Research (vice-president, 1971; president, 1977—), Institute of Andean Studies (Berkeley), Societe des Americanistes (Paris), Instituto Indigenista Interamericano (Mexico), International African Institute (London), Instituto de Estudios Peruanos (founding member), Asociacion Peruana de Antropologos (founding member), Instituto Nacional de Antropologia e Historia (Ecuador; founding member), North Eastern Consortium for Andean Studies. *Awards, honors:* Honorary professor, University of San Marcos.

WRITINGS: (With Donald Collier) *Survey and Excavations in Southern Ecuador,* Field Museum of Natural History, 1943; (translator with Robert Hankin) *The Soviet Linguistic Controversy of 1950,* Queen's Crown Press, 1952; (editor) *Visita hecha a la provincia de Chucuito en 1567,* Casa de la Cultura del Peru, 1964; (editor) *Visita hecha de la provincia de Leon de Huanuco en 1562,* University of Huanuco, Volume I, 1967, Volume II, 1972; *Formaciones economicas y politicas del mundo andino* (essays), [Lima], 1975; *Organizacion economica del estado inca,* [Mexico], 1978, translation published as *Economic Organization of the Inca State,* Jai Press, 1980.

Contributor: Stanley Diamond, editor, *Culture in History: Essays in Honor of Paul Radin,* Columbia University Press, 1960; Anthony Leeds and A. P. Vayda, editors, *Man, Culture and Animals,* American Association for the Advancement of Science, 1965; Ronald Cohen and John Middleton, editors, *Comparative Political Systems,* Doubleday, 1967.

Contributor to *Handbook of Southamerican Indians; Handbook of Latin American Studies* (annual volume), 1967, 1970. Contributor of articles and reviews to *Nation, Natural History,* and to professional journals in United States, Mexico, Peru, Spain, France, and Argentina. Editor with N. Wachtel of special Andean issue of *Annales* (Paris), 1978.

WORK IN PROGRESS: Continuing studies on Andean ethnology.

SIDELIGHTS: John V. Murra told *CA:* "The public I am most eager to reach is the Andean reader. I think of my work as a contribution to the rewriting of Andean history. None of my work has yet been translated into Quecluca or Aymara, but I have not given up hope."

* * *

MURRAY, Edward (James, Jr.) 1928-

PERSONAL: Born April 8, 1928, in Brooklyn, N.Y.; son of Edward James and Catherine (Henn) Murray; married Margaret DeSantis, September 4, 1954 (died, 1974); children: Michael, Lisa, Stephen, Monica, Jeannette. *Education:* Studied at Television Workshop of New York, 1953-54; Youngstown University, B.A., 1962; University of Southern California, Ph.D., 1966. *Home:* 188 Hollybrook Rd., Brockport, N.Y. 14420. *Office:* State University of New York College at Brockport, Brockport, N.Y. 14420.

CAREER: Western Illinois University, Macomb, assistant professor, 1965-66, associate professor of English, 1967-68; State University of New York College at Brockport, assistant professor, 1968-70, associate professor, 1971-74, professor of English, 1974—. *Military service:* U.S. Army, Medical Corps, 1951-53; Became sergeant. *Awards, honors:* Woodrow Wilson fellowship, 1962.

WRITINGS—Published by Ungar, except as indicated: *Arthur Miller: Dramatist,* 1967; *Clifford Odets: The Thirties and After,* 1968; *The Cinematic Imagination: Writers and the Motion Pictures,* 1972; *Nine American Film Critics: A Study of Theory and Practice,* 1975; *Fellini the Artist,* 1976; *Ten Film Classics,* 1978; (contributor) Peter Bondanella, editor, *Federico Fellini: Essays in Criticism,* Oxford University Press, 1978. Contributor to *Literature/Film Quarterly* and *College Language Association Journal.*

WORK IN PROGRESS: Research on the work of individual film-makers, film theory, and film criticism.

* * *

MURRAY, James 1946-

PERSONAL: Born October 16, 1946, in New York, N.Y.; son of Eddie and Helena (Banks) Murray; married Mary Taylor, 1974; children: Sean Edward, Sherron Anita, Angela Dawn. *Education:* Syracuse University, A.B., 1968. *Home:* 5 Fieldstone Dr., Apt. 98, Hartsdale, N.Y. 10530. *Agent:* Charles Neighbors, 240 Waverly Pl., New York, N.Y. 10003. *Office:* NBC-TV, 30 Rockefeller Plaza, New York, N.Y. 10020.

CAREER: American Broadcasting Co., New York City, news trainee, 1970-71; Western Electric Co., New York City, public relations associate, 1971-72; *New York Amsterdam News,* New York City, arts and entertainment editor, 1972-75; National Broadcasting Co., New York City, publicity representative for NBC-TV, 1975—. *Military service:* U.S. Army, 1968-70; became first lieutenant; served in Vietnam; received Bronze Star Medal. *Member:* New York Film Critics Circle.

WRITINGS: To Find an Image: Black Films from Uncle Tom to Superfly, Bobbs-Merrill, 1974; (contributor) *Black Films and Film-Makers,* Dodd, 1974; (editor and contributor) *The Afro-American* (almanac), Bellwether Press, 1976.

* * *

MUSE, Benjamin 1898-

PERSONAL: Born 1898, in Durham, N.C.; son of William Henry and Elizabeth (Chadwick) Muse; married Beatriz de Regil, 1925; children: Benjamin, Jr., Katherine Furcron, Paul A., Philippa Millard, Carlota Rokita. *Education:* Attended Trinity College (now Duke University, Durham, N.C.), 1914-16, and George Washington University, 1919-20. *Politics:* Independent. *Religion:* Catholic. *Home:* 11442 Waterview Cluster, Reston, Va. 22090.

CAREER: U.S. State Department, Diplomatic Service, 1920-34, held posts of third, second and first secretary of embassy, counselor of the U.S. delegation to the Seventh International Conference of American States, 1933; Virginia State senator, 1936; Republican candidate for governor of Virginia, 1941; director, Southern Leadership Project of the Southern Region Council, 1959-64. Member, President's Committee on Equal Opportunity in the Armed Forces, 1962-64. *Military service:* British Army, Infantry, 1917-19; U.S. Army, General Staff Corps, 1942-44; became lieutenant colonel.

WRITINGS: Presidential Nominating Politics in 1952, Johns Hopkins Press, 1954; *Virginia's Massive Resistance,* Indiana University Press, 1961; *Ten Years of Prelude,* Viking, 1964; *The American Negro Revolution,* Indiana University Press, 1968. Contributor to numerous publications. Virginia affairs columnist, *Washington Post,* 1949-59.

WORK IN PROGRESS: The Twentieth Century as I Saw It.

AVOCATIONAL INTERESTS: Travel.

* * *

MYERS, Gail E(ldridge) 1923-

PERSONAL: Born March 1, 1923, in Clark, S.D.; son of Larry (a painter) and Pauline (Engen) Myers; married Catherine Bonette, March 17, 1947 (divorced September, 1967); married Michele Tolela (a communication consultant), December 20, 1968; children: (first marriage) Christopher, Kathleen Myers Simon; (second marriage) Erika, David. *Education:* Attended South Dakota College, 1941-42, and University of Oregon, 1942; University of Iowa, B.A., 1948, M.A., 1949; University of Denver, Ph.D., 1959. *Home:* 214 Stanford, San Antonio, Tex. 78212. *Office:* Department of Speech, Trinity University, San Antonio, Tex. 78212.

CAREER: Iowa State Teachers College (now University of Northern Iowa), Cedar Falls, instructor in journalism and television production, director of alumni, and director of publications, 1949-53; Colorado School of Mines, Golden, instructor in journalism, director of publications, and technical editor, 1953-59; Monticello College, Godfrey, Ill., vice-president, 1959-63; University of Denver, Denver, Colo., assistant professor of speech, 1963-66; Monticello College, president, 1966-71; Trinity University, San Antonio, Tex., professor of speech and journalism, 1971—, associate dean, 1971-72, dean of College of Arts and Sciences, 1972-76. President of Lewis and Clark Community College, 1970-71. Lecturer for organizations, businesses, seminars, workshops, and Peace Corps Communication Retreat. *Military service:* U.S. Army Air Forces, 1943-46; served in Pacific theater; became sergeant major. *Member:* International Communication Association, International Society for the Study of General Semantics, Speech Communication Association, Greater Alton Public Relations and Advertising Club (honorary life member), Sigma Delta Chi.

WRITINGS: (Editor with Johnnye Akin and others) *Language Behavior,* Mouton, 1970; *A Miracle Every March* (novel), Naylor, 1973; (with wife, Michele Myers) *Dynamics of Human Communication,* McGraw, 1973, 3rd edition, 1979; (with M. Myers) *Communicating When We Speak,* McGraw, 1974, 2nd edition, 1977; (with M. Myers) *Managing by Communication,* McGraw, 1980. Contributor to *Journal of Applied Behavioral Science* and *Junior College Journal.*

AVOCATIONAL INTERESTS: Photography, skiing, golf, music, writing.

* * *

MYERS, John Myers 1906-

PERSONAL: Born January 11, 1906, in Northport, N.Y.; son of John Caldwell and Alice (McCorry) Myers; married Charlotte Shanahan, 1943; children: Anne Caldwell, Celia. *Education:* Attended St. Stephen's College, Middlebury College, and University of New Mexico. *Home and office:* 6515 East Hermosa Vista Dr., Buckhorn District, Mesa, Ariz. *Agent:* Ned Brown, 315 South Beverly Dr., Beverly Hills, Calif.

CAREER: Free-lance writer. Worked as newspaperman, writer of advertising copy, and farmer. Special lecturer and writer's conference director, Arizona State University, two years; organized a collection of Western Americana for library, one year. *Military service:* U.S. Army, Armored Force, five years.

WRITINGS—Novels: *The Harp and the Blade,* Dutton, 1941; *Out on Any Limb,* Dutton, 1942; *The Wild Yazoo,* Dutton, 1947; *Dead Warrior,* Little, Brown, 1956; *I, Jack Swilling,* Hastings House, 1961.

Nonfiction: *The Alamo,* Dutton, 1948, reprinted, University of Nebraska Press, 1973; *The Last Chance: Tombstone's Early Years,* Dutton, 1950, reprinted, University of Nebraska Press, 1973; *Doc Holiday,* Little, Brown, 1955, reprinted, University of Nebraska Press, 1973; *The Deaths of the Bravos,* Little, Brown, 1962; *Pirate, Pawnee, and Mountain Man: The Saga of Hugh Glass,* Little, Brown, 1963, published as *The Saga of Hugh Glass: Pirate, Pawnee, and Mountain Man,* University of Nebraska Press, 1976; *San Francisco's Reign of Terror,* Doubleday, 1966.

Others: *Silverlock* (fantasy), Dutton, 1949, reprinted, Ace Books, 1979; *Maverick Zone* (narrative poems), Hastings House, 1961; *Print in a Wild Land,* Doubleday, 1967; (compiler) *The Westerner,* Prentice-Hall, 1969; *The Border Wardens,* Prentice-Hall, 1971. Also author of fantasy, *The Moon's Fire-eating Daughter.*

WORK IN PROGRESS: Plans to expand narrative poems in *Maverick Zone* into comprehensive verse coverage of frontier America, beginning with the settlement of the Atlantic seaboard.

SIDELIGHTS: John Myers Myers told *CA:* "When seeking a proper starting point for my series of narrative poems about America's frontiers, I came to realize that the primary frontier town was London, and that its skookum pioneer was Sir Walter Raleigh. But this place and person refused to accept the modest length limit established by previous poems of the series, so after working on the material [for] several years I had nothing but disjointed fragments to show. By then it was clear that I must forfeit the subject or invest the time and effort needed to produce a full scale epic—though I had never gone whale hunting before and understood epic requirements as little as anybody else whose acquaintance was limited to a reading knowledge of specimens."

Myers' book *Silverlock* enjoys a high place among contemporary fans of fantasy fiction. In his foreword to the Ace edition of the book, Poul Anderson writes that "*Silverlock* is . . . incomparable fun. There are few such glorious romps in all the world's literature, and surely none that surpass this one. A galloping narrative, endlessly inventive; people you must love or hate but can never be indifferent to; humor that ranges from the cat-subtle to the uproarious; discoveries, achievements, battles, feasts, drinking bouts, lovemaking, unabashed joy, celebration of life—what more do you want?" "*Silverlock* is not just a story," Anderson concludes, "it is an odyssey of the spirit" and is "among those books that become a part of people's lives."

BIOGRAPHICAL/CRITICAL SOURCES: New Worlds, October, 1966; *Pacific Historical Review,* November, 1966; *Atlantic,* May, 1967; *Time,* May 12, 1967; *Southwest Review,* spring, 1973; John Myers Myers, *Silverlock,* Ace Books, 1979.

* * *

MYERS, Norman 1934-

PERSONAL: Born August 24, 1934, in Whitewell, Yorkshire, England; naturalized citizen of Kenya; son of John and Gladys (Haworth) Myers; married Dorothy Mary Halliman, December 10, 1965; children: Malindi Elizabeth. *Education:* Oxford University, M.A., 1957, Diploma in Overseas Administration, 1958; University of California, Berkeley, Ph.D., 1973. *Address:* P.O. Box 48197, Nairobi, Kenya.

CAREER: H. M. Overseas Civil Service, Kenya, district officer, 1958-61; high school teacher in Nairobi, Kenya, 1961-65; free-lance writer, photographer, film-maker, and broadcaster on conservation of African wildlands, 1965-69; consultant in conservation ecology and land-use planning in Kenya, 1972—. Has conducted projects for numerous development organizations, research bodies, and government agencies, including Agency for International Development, Rockefeller Fund, National Academy of Sciences, and World Wildlife Fund. Lecturer on conservation in Africa on tours in Europe and United States, 1967—. Scientific editor, Garland Publishing, Inc. *Military service:* British Army, 1953.

MEMBER: International Association of Ecology, International Society of Tropical Ecology, International Society of Tropical Foresters, International Society of Social Economics, International Council for Environmental Law, International Lecturers Association, Institute for World Order, American Association of Environmental and Resource Economists, National Association of Science Writers, People/Natural Resources Research Council, Alternatives Society, National Audubon Society, Sierra Club.

WRITINGS: The Long African Day, Macmillan, 1972, 3rd edition, 1976; *Nairobi National Park: An Annotated Bibliography,* Office of Ecology, Smithsonian Institution, 1973; *The Sinking Ark,* Pergamon, 1979; *Survey of Conversion Rates in Tropical Moist Forests,* National Research Council, 1979; *The Role of Multinational Timber Corporations and Agro-Business in Depletion of Tropical Moist Forests,* Council for Economic Priorities, 1979. Also author of several technical papers and reports.

Contributor: R. L. Eaton, editor, *The World's Cats: Ecology and Conservation,* World Wildlife Society, 1973; N. Sitwell, editor, *Cats of the World,* Tom Stacey, 1973; Sitwell, editor, *The World Conservation Yearbook,* Danbury Press, 1973; C. Legum, editor, *A Traveller's Guide to Africa,* African Development and African Contemporary Record (London), 1974; *The World's Cats: Contributions on Status, Management and Conservation,* University of Washington, 1976; G. T. Prance, editor, *The Biological Model of Diversification in the Tropics,* Columbia University Press, 1979; F. B. Golley, editor, *Tropical Rain Forests: Structure and Function,* American Elsevier, 1979. Contributor to proceedings of professional organizations. Contributor to journals, including *International Wildlife, Animal Kingdom,* and *Africana.* Roving editor, *International Wildlife;* field editor, *Defender of Wildlife.*

WORK IN PROGRESS: Conservation and Development in Emergent Africa; The Leopard; The Contribution of Wild Species to Our Everyday Material Lives.

SIDELIGHTS: Norman Myers told *CA:* "I greatly enjoy writing, though I agree with those who say it is ninety-nine percent perspiration and one percent inspiration. After believing, from my time at Oxford University, that a writer is born and not made, I finally took a stab at it in the mid-1960s, and found that, in large measure, writing is a technique that can, through much agony, be learned. After publishing more than one million words, I still find it difficult to construct an English sentence. But I know of no other activity so satisfying as this, except running marathons."

Myers is fluent in Swahili and has moderate competence in German and French. He has been involved in field research in over seventy countries, including the People's Republic of China.

BIOGRAPHICAL/CRITICAL SOURCES: New York Times, January 1, 1980.

N

NAHAS, Gabriel G(eorges) 1920-

PERSONAL: Born March 4, 1920, in Alexandria, Egypt; came to United States in 1947, naturalized in 1962; son of Bishara and Gabrielle (Wolff) Nahas; married Marilyn Cashman, February 13, 1954; children: Michele, Anthony, Christiane. *Education:* University of Toulouse, B.A., 1937, M.D. (cum laude), 1944; University of Rochester, M.S., 1949; University of Minnesota, Ph.D., 1953. *Home:* 114 Chestnut St., Englewood, N.J. 07631. *Office:* 630 West 168th St., New York, N.Y. 10032.

CAREER: Hospital Marie Lannelongue, Paris, France, chief of laboratory of experimental surgery, 1954-55; University of Minnesota, Minneapolis, assistant professor of physiology, 1955-57; Walter Reed Army Institute of Research, Department of Cardiorespiratory Disease, Washington, D.C., chief of respiratory section, 1957-59; George Washington University Medical School, Washington, D.C., lecturer in physiology, 1957-59; Columbia University, College of Physicians and Surgeons, New York City, associate professor, 1959-62, professor of anesthesiology, 1962—, department director of research, 1959-62; Presbyterian Hospital, New York City, attending anesthesiologist, 1967—. Adjunct professor at Institute of Anesthesiology, University of Paris, 1968—. Member of advisory board of Council on Circulation and Basic Sciences, American Heart Association; vice-president of Foundation for Research in Biology and Medicine; active in World University Service and in Experiment in International Living; member of committee on trauma, National Research Council, 1963-66. Consultant to Oceanographic Institute of Monaco, 1964—. *Military service:* French Underground, special agent, 1941-44; French Army, Medical Corps, 1944-45; became first lieutenant; received Presidential Medal of Freedom with gold palm, Legion of Honor, and Croix de Guerre with three palms.

MEMBER: International Society of Hematology, Association des Physiologistes de Langue Francaise, American Physiological Society, American Heart Association (fellow), American Society for Pharmacology and Experimental Therapeutics, American Society of Clinical Pharmacology, Society for Artificial Internal Organs, American Association for the Advancement of Science (fellow), Undersea Medical Society, American Federation for Clinical Research, National Research Council, Harvey Society, New York Academy of Science (fellow), Sigma Xi. *Awards, honors:* Member of Order of Orange Nassau, 1947, and Order of the British Empire, 1948; Fulbright scholar, 1966; silver medal from City of Paris, 1972.

WRITINGS: (Editor) *In Vitro and In Vivo Effects of Amine Buffers,* Annals of New York Academy of Science, 1961; (editor) *Regulation of Respiration,* Annals of New York Academy of Science, 1963; (editor with D. V. Bates) *Respiratory Failure,* Annals of New York Academy of Science, 1965; (editor) *Current Concepts of Acid-Base Measurements,* Annals of New York Academy of Science, 1966; (editor with Charles Fox) *Body Fluid Replacement in the Surgical Patient,* Grune, 1970; (editor with Alan Robison and Lubos Triner) *Cyclic AMP and Cell Function,* Annals of New York Academy of Science, 1973; *Marihuana: Deceptive Weed,* Raven Press, 1973; (editor with Karl Schaeffer and Nicholas Chalazonitis) *CO2 and Metabolic Regulation,* Springer-Verlag, 1974; *Marihuana: Chemistry, Biochemistry, Cellular Effects,* Springer-Verlag, 1976; *Keep off the Grass,* Reader's Digest Press, 1976, revised edition, 1979; (editor with W. D. M. Paton) *Marihuana: Biological Effects,* Pergamon, 1979.

* * *

NAIPAUL, V(idiadhar) S(urajprasad) 1932-

PERSONAL: Born August 17, 1932, in Trinidad; married Patricia Ann Hale, 1955. *Education:* Attended Queen's Royal College, Trinidad and University College, Oxford. *Address:* c/o Andre Deutsch Ltd., 105 Great Russell St., London W.C.I., England.

CAREER: Free-lance broadcaster for the British Broadcasting Corp., two years; writer. *Member:* Society of Authors, Royal Society of Literature (fellow). *Awards, honors:* John Llewellyn Rhys Memorial Prize, 1958, for *The Mystic Masseur;* grant from government of Trinidad for travel in Caribbean, 1960-61; Somerset Maugham Award, 1961, for *Miguel Street;* Phoenix Trust Award, 1963; Hawthornden Prize, 1964, for *Mr. Stone and the Knights Companion;* W. H. Smith Award, 1968, for *The Mimic Men;* Booker Prize, 1971, for *In a Free State.*

WRITINGS: *The Mystic Masseur,* Deutsch, 1957, Vanguard, 1959, reprinted, Penguin, 1977; *The Suffrage of Elvira,* Deutsch, 1958; *Miguel Street,* Deutsch, 1959, Vanguard, 1960, reprinted, Penguin, 1977; *A House for Mr. Biswas,* Deutsch, 1961, McGraw, 1962; *The Middle Passage: Impressions of Five Societies—British, French and*

Dutch in the West Indies and South America (nonfiction), Deutsch, 1962, Macmillan, 1963, reprinted, Penguin, 1978; *Mr. Stone and the Knights Companion,* Deutsch, 1963, Macmillan, 1964; *An Area of Darkness* (nonfiction), Deutsch, 1964, Macmillan, 1965; *The Mimic Men,* Macmillan, 1967; *A Flag on the Island* (short story collection), Macmillan, 1967; *The Loss of El Dorado: A History* (nonfiction), Deutsch, 1969, Knopf, 1970; (contributor) Andrew Salkey, editor, *Island Voices: Stories from the West Indies,* new edition, Liveright, 1970; *In a Free State,* Knopf, 1971; *The Overcrowded Barracoon and Other Articles,* Deutsch, 1972, Knopf, 1973; *Guerrillas,* Knopf, 1975; *India: A Wounded Civilization* (nonfiction), Knopf, 1977; *A Bend in the River,* Knopf, 1979; *The Return of Eva Peron* (nonfiction), Knopf, 1980. Contributor to *New York Review of Books, New Statesman,* and other periodicals. Fiction reviewer, *New Statesman,* 1958-61.

SIDELIGHTS: Born in Trinidad to the descendants of Hindu immigrants from northern India and educated at England's Oxford University, V. S. Naipaul is considered to be one of the world's most gifted novelists. As a *New York Times Book Review* critic writes: "For sheer abundance of talent there can hardly be a writer alive who surpasses V. S. Naipaul. Whatever we may want in a novelist is to be found in his books: an almost Conradian gift for tensing a story, a serious involvement with human issues, a supple English prose, a hard-edged wit, a personal vision of things. Best of all, he is a novelist unafraid of using his brains. . . . His novels are packed with thought, not as lumps of abstraction but as one fictional element among others, fluid in the stream of narrative. . . . [He is] the world's writer, a master of language and perception, our sardonic blessing."

This ability to regard Naipaul as "the world's writer" is in large measure due to the author's self-proclaimed rootlessness. Unhappy with the cultural and spiritual poverty of Trinidad, distanced from India, and unable to relate to and share in the heritage of each country's former imperial ruler (England), Naipaul describes himself as "content to be a colonial, without a past, without ancestors." As a result of these strong feelings of nonattachment to any particular region or set of traditions, most of his work deals with people who, like himself, are estranged from the societies they are supposedly a part of and who are desperately seeking to find a way to belong or to "be someone." The locales Naipaul chooses for his stories represent an extension of this same theme, for most take place in emerging Third World countries in the throes of creating a new "national" identity from the tangled remnants of native and colonial cultures.

Naipaul's early work explored these themes via a West Indian variation of the comedy of manners—that is, an almost farcical portrayal of the comic aspects of an illiterate and divided society's shift from a colonial to an independent status, with an emphasis on multiracial misunderstandings and rivalries and the various ironies resulting from the sudden introduction of such democratic processes as elections. In *The Mystic Masseur, The Suffrage of Elvira,* and *Miguel Street,* Naipaul essentially holds a mirror up to Trinidadian society in order to expose its follies and absurdities; his tone is detached, yet sympathetic, as if he is looking back at a distant past of which he is no longer a part. The tragic aspects of the situation are not examined, nor is there any attempt to involve the reader in the plight of the characters. Michael Thorpe describes the prevailing tone of these early books as "that of the ironist who points up the comedy, futility and absurdity that fill the gap between aspiration and achievement, between the public image desired and the individual's inadequacies, to recognize which may be called the education of the narrator: 'I had grown up and looked critically at the people around me.'"

A House for Mr. Biswas marks an important turning point in Naipaul's work; his increasing attention to subject and theme via a blend of psychological and social realism and certain symbolic overtones foreshadows the intensive character studies of his later works. In addition, *A House for Mr. Biswas* has a universality of theme that the author's earlier books lacked for the most part due to their emphasis on strictly local-color elements. The cumulative effect of these "improvements" has led many critics to regard *A House for Mr. Biswas* as Naipaul's masterpiece. As Robert D. Hamner writes: "With the appearance in 1961 of *A House for Mr. Biswas,* Naipaul may have published his best fiction. It is even possible that this book is the best novel yet to emerge from the Caribbean. It is a vital embodiment of authentic West Indian life, but more than that, it transcends national boundaries and evokes universal human experiences. Mr. Biswas' desire to own his own house is essentially a struggle to assert personal identity and to attain security—thoroughly human needs."

The *New York Herald Tribune Books* reviewer notes that "Naipaul has a wry wit and an engaging sense of humor, as well as a delicate understanding of sadness and futility and a profound but unobtrusive sense of the tragi-comedy of ordinary living. . . . His style is precise and assured. In short, he gives every indication of being an important addition to the international literary scene. [*A House for Mr. Biswas*] is funny, it is compassionate. It has more than 500 pages and not one of them is superfluous."

Paul Theroux of the *New York Times Book Review* admits that "it is hard for the reviewer of a wonderful author to keep the obituarist's assured hyperbole in check, but let me say that if the stilting-up of the Thames coincided with a freak monsoon, causing massive flooding in all parts of South London, the first book I would rescue from my library would be *A House for Mr. Biswas.*"

Michael Thorpe agrees that the novel is "a work of rare distinction; . . . [it is] a 'novelist's novel,' a model work. . . . The book's popularity must be largely due to its universality of subject and theme, the struggle of one ordinary man to climb—or cling on to—the ladder of life; the ordinariness lies in his ambitions for home, security, status, his desire to live through his son, yet he remains an individual. . . . At first sight Mr. Biswas seems an abrupt departure from Naipaul's previous fiction: in its concentration upon the life history of a single protagonist it goes far deeper than *The Mystic Masseur* and the mood is predominantly 'serious,' the still pervasive comedy being subordinated to that mood. Yet on further consideration we can see *Mr. Biswas* as the natural and consummate development of themes that ran through the first three books: the perplexing relation of the individual to society, his struggle to impress himself upon it through achievement—or defy its pressures with a transforming fantasy that puts a gloss upon life and extracts order from the rude chaos of everyday existence. . . . We should not doubt that the narrative is to be heroic, the quest for the house—however flawed in its realization—a victory over the chaos and anonymity into which the hero was born. The novel is such a man's celebration, his witness, an answer to the dismal refrain, 'There was nothing to speak of him.'" In short, Thorpe concludes, "for West Indian literature *A House for Mr. Biswas* forged [the] connexion [between literature and life] with unbreakable strength and set up a model for emulation which no other 'Third World' literature in English has yet equalled.''

After his success with *A House for Mr. Biswas,* Naipaul turned away from exclusively West Indian locales in order to ''test'' his themes in a broader geographic and nationalistic landscape. At the same time, his earlier light-hearted tone gradually faded as he explored the more tragic consequences of alienation and rootlessness in the world at large through the eyes of various ''universal wanderers.'' As Thomas Lask reports in the *New York Times* on Naipaul's *In a Free State:* ''V. S. Naipaul's writings about his native Trinidad have often enough been touched with tolerant amusement. His is an attitude that is affectionate without being overly kind. . . . On his own, Mr. Naipaul [has] made no secret of his alienation from his native island. . . . [*In a Free State*] takes the story one step further. How does the expatriate fare after he leaves the island? . . . [The author] lifts the argument above and beyond material success and social position. These new stories focus on the failure of heart, on the animallike cruelty man exhibits to other men and on the avarice that . . . is the root of all evil. . . . What the author is saying is that neither customs nor color nor culture seems able to quiet that impulse to destruction, that murderous wantonness that is so much part of our make-up. . . . Mr. Naipaul's style in these stories seems leaner than in the past and much more somber. There is virtually none of the earlier playfulness. He appears to have settled for precision over abundance. Each detail and each incident is made to carry its weight in the narrative. The effect is not small-scaled, for in the title story he has created an entire country. He has not tidied up every loose strand. . . . But there is nothing unfinished in these polished novellas.''

Paul Theroux calls *In a Free State* ''Naipaul's most ambitious work, a story-sequence brilliant in conception, masterly in execution, and terrifying in effect—the chronicles of a half-a-dozen self-exiled people who have become lost souls. Having abandoned their own countries (countries they were scarcely aware of belonging to), they have found themselves in strange places, without friends, with few loyalties, and with the feeling that they are trespassing. Worse, their lives have been totally altered; for them there is no going back; they have fled, each to his separate limbo, and their existence is like that of souls in a classical underworld. . . . The subject of displacement is one few writers have touched upon. Camus has written of it. But Naipaul is much superior to Camus, and his achievement—a steady advance through eleven volumes—is as disturbing as it is original. *In a Free State* is a masterpiece in the fiction of rootlessness.''

Alfred Kazin of the *New York Review of Books* claims that ''Naipaul writes about the many psychic realities of exile in our contemporary world with far more bite and dramatic havoc than Joyce. . . . No one else around today, not even Nabokov, seems able to employ prose fiction so deeply as the very choice of exile. . . . What makes Naipaul hurt so much more than other novelists of contemporary exodus is his major image—the tenuousness of man's hold on the earth. The doubly unsettling effect he creates—for the prose is British-chatty, proper yet bitter—also comes from the many characters in a book like [*In a Free State*] who don't 'belong' in the countries they are touring or working in, who wouldn't 'belong' any longer in the countries they come from, and from the endless moving about of contemporary life have acquired a feeling of their own unreality in the 'free state' of endlessly moving about. . . . Naipaul has never encompassed so much, and with such brilliant economy, with such a patent though lighthanded ominousness of manner, as in [*In a Free State*]. The volume of detail is extraordinary. . . . I suppose one criticism of Naipaul might well be that he covers too much ground, has too many representative types, and that he has an obvious desolation about homelessness, migration, the final placelessness of those who have seen too much, which he tends to turn into a mysterious accusation. Though he is a marvelous technician, there is something finally modest, personal, openly committed about his fiction, a frankness of personal reference, that removes him from the godlike impersonality of the novelist. . . . Naipaul belongs to a different generation, to a more openly tragic outlook for humanity itself. He does not want to play God, even in a novel.''

A *New Statesman* critic, on the other hand, is not quite convinced that Naipaul's outlook is completely tragic. He writes: ''Each piece [of *In a Free State*] is a tour de force. . . . I don't know any writer since Conrad who's exposed the otherness of Africa so starkly, and Naipaul leaves his readers freer by his massacre of obstinate illusions. But his vision excludes elements of growth and hope which are, palpably, there. . . . Naipaulia remains a kingdom of cryptic anti-climax. I wonder, though, if the 'cryptic' final section is nudging away from pessimism.''

With the publication of *Guerrillas,* however, the first of Naipaul's novels to make his name widely known in the United States, more and more reviewers became convinced that his outlook is indeed grim. Notes Theroux: ''*Guerrillas* is a violent book in which little violence is explicit. . . . It is a novel, not of revolt, but of the play-acting that is frequently called revolt, that queer situation of scabrous glamour which Naipaul sees as a throw-back to the days of slavery. . . . *Guerrillas* is one of Naipaul's most complex books; it is certainly his most suspenseful, a series of shocks, like a shroud slowly unwound from a bloody corpse, showing the damaged—and familiar—face last. . . . This is a novel without a villain, and there is not a character for whom the reader does not at some point feel deep sympathy and keen understanding, no matter how villainous or futile he may seem. *Guerrillas* is a brilliant novel in every way, and it shimmers with artistic certainty. It is scarifying in the opposite way from a nightmare. One can shrug at fantasy, but *Guerrillas*—in a phrase Naipaul himself once used—is, like the finest novels, 'indistinguishable from truth.' ''

Paul Gray of *Time* believes that *Guerrillas* ''proves [Naipaul] the laureate of the West Indies. . . . [He] is a native expatriate with a fine distaste for patriotic rhetoric. . . . [The novel] is thus conspicuously short of heroes. . . . The native politicians are corrupt, the foreign businessmen avaricious, and the people either lethargic or criminal. When an uprising does flare, it is nasty and inept. Perhaps no one but Naipaul has the inside and outside knowledge to have turned such a dispirited tale into so gripping a book. His island is built entirely of vivid descriptions and offhand dialogue. At the end, it has assumed a political and economic history, a geography and a population of doomed, selfish souls. . . . *Guerrillas* is not a polemic (polemicists will be annoyed) but a Conradian vision of fallibility and frailty. With economy and compassion, Naipaul draws the heart of darkness from a sun-struck land.''

Noting that Naipaul takes a ''hackneyed'' theme (''incipient Black Power'') and manages to produce ''a more significant treatment of it than most of his contemporaries with similar concerns,'' Charles R. Larson of the *Nation* writes that *Guerrillas* ''builds so slowly and so skillfully that until the final scene bursts upon us, we are hardly aware of the necessary outcome of the events; it is only in retrospect that we see that the desultory action has in fact been charged with fate. . . . No one writes better about politics in the West Indies than V. S. Naipaul. Nor is there anyone who writes more profoundly about exiles, would-be revolutionaries and their assorted camp followers. Written in a deliberately flat style, *Guerrillas* is a deeply pessimistic novel, telling us that we have seen about as much political change in the West Indian island republics as we are likely to see."

In *A Bend in the River,* Naipaul returns to Africa as a locale (the scene of *In a Free State*), confirming his basic pessimism in the process. Comments John Leonard in the *New York Times:* "This is not an exotic Africa [in *A Bend in the River*]. . . . [The author] despises nostalgia for the colonial past, while at the same time heartlessly parodying . . . the African future. . . . *A Bend in the River* is a brilliant and depressing novel. It is no secret by now, certainly not since *Guerrillas* . . . , that V. S. Naipaul is one of the handful of living writers of whom the English language can be proud, if, still, profoundly uneasy. There is no consolation from him, any more than there is sentiment. His wit has grown hard and fierce; he isn't seeking to amuse, but to scourge."

John Updike, writing in the *New Yorker,* asserts that *A Bend in the River* "proves once more that Naipaul is incomparably well situated and equipped to bring us news of one of the contemporary world's great subjects—the mingling of its peoples. *A Bend in the River* struck me as an advance—broader, warmer, less jaded and kinky—over the much-praised *Guerrillas,* though not quite as vivid and revelatory as the fiction of *In a Free State. . . . A Bend in the River* is carved from the same territory [as *In a Free State*]—an Africa of withering colonial vestiges, terrifyingly murky politics, defeated pretensions omnivorous rot, and the implacable undermining of all that would sustain reason and safety. . . . Rage . . . is perhaps the deepest and darkest fact Naipaul has to report about the Third World, and in this novel his understanding of it goes beyond that shown in *Guerrillas. . . .* In *A Bend in the River,* the alien observer—white bureaucrat or Asian trader—is drawn closer into the rationale of the riots and wars that seethe in the slums or the bush beyond his enclave. The novel might be faulted for savoring a bit of the visiting journalist's worked-up notes: its episodes do not hang together with full organic snugness; there are a few too many clever geopolitical conversations and scenically detailed car rides. . . . [But] the author's embrace of his tangled and tragic African scene seems relatively hearty as well as immensely knowledgeable. Always a master of fictional landscape, Naipaul here shows, in his variety of human examples and in his search for underlying social causes, a Tolstoyan spirit, generous if not genial."

Walter Clemons of *Newsweek* calls *A Bend in the River* "a hurtful, claustrophobic novel, very hard on the nerves, played out under a vast African sky in an open space that is made to feel stifling. . . . Naipaul's is a political novel of a subtle and unusual kind. . . . [It] is about tremors of expectation, shifts in personal loyalty, manners in dire emergency. . . . As an evocation of place, [the novel] succeeds brilliantly. . . . *A Bend in the River* is by no means a perfected work. . . . But this imperfect, enormously disturbing book confirms Naipaul's position as one of the best writers now at work."

Finally, Irving Howe of the *New York Times Book Review* notes: "On the surface, *A Bend in the River* emerges mostly as a web of caustic observation, less exciting than its predecessor, *Guerrillas;* but it is a much better and deeper novel, for Naipaul has mastered the gift of creating an aura of psychic and moral tension even as, seemingly, very little happens. . . . [But in the end,] Naipaul offers no intimations of hope or signals of perspective. It may be that the reality he grapples with allows him nothing but grimness of voice. . . . A novelist has to be faithful to what he sees, and few see as well as Naipaul; yet one may wonder whether, in some final reckoning, a serious writer can simply allow the wretchedness of his depicted scene to become the limit of his vision. . . . Naipaul seems right now to be a writer beleaguered by his own truths, unable to get past them. That is surely an honorable difficulty, far better than indulging in sentimental or ideological uplift; but it exacts a price. . . . Perhaps we ought simply to be content that, in his austere and brilliant way, he holds fast to the bitterness before his eyes."

In his critical study of Naipaul, Michael Thorpe offers this overview of the novelist's accomplishments: "While Naipaul is by no means alone in coming from a makeshift colonial society and using the 'metropolitan' language with a native surety, these origins have helped him more than any of his contemporaries from the Commonwealth to develop an inclusive view of many facets of the larger world, a view focussed by his intense sense of displacement from society, race or creed. . . . He has gone beyond local conflicts, isolated instances of the colonial experience, to attempt something approaching a world view. . . . His insights and his manner of conveying them carry a persuasive truth."

As a result, continues Thorpe, "Naipaul has spoken from and to more points within that world [of imperial or social oppression] than any English writer—but his is not a comforting or hopeful voice. . . . Asked if he were an optimist [Naipaul] replied: 'I'm not sure. I think I do look for the seeds of regeneration in a situation; I long to find what is good and hopeful and really do hope that by the most brutal sort of analysis one is possibly opening up the situation to some sort of action; an action which is not based on self-deception.' . . . [But] he supplies none of the props even realists let us lean upon in the end: there are no consolations—no religious belief, no humanistic faith in man's future, not even the personal supports of friendship or love. . . . [Thus] Naipaul's is one of the bleakest visions any imaginative observer alive has given us. . . . [He] refuses to leap to positive attitudes he cannot justify. Naipaul would be the last to claim for his work that it represents a final or adequate vision; it is the record of one man's impressions of the world and it does not pretend to be the whole truth about it. . . . Yet Naipaul insists that he is hopeful: as one who has not flinched from harsh reality, he has earned the right to our reciprocal hope that he may yet find a way beyond despair."

BIOGRAPHICAL/CRITICAL SOURCES: Chicago Sunday Tribune, July 12, 1959; *Saturday Review,* July 2, 1960, October 23, 1971, November 15, 1975; *New York Herald Tribune Books,* June 24, 1962; *Christian Science Monitor,* July 19, 1962, March 29, 1968, May 28, 1970, March 14, 1973; *New Yorker,* August 4, 1962, August 8, 1970, June 6, 1977, May 21, 1979; *Times Literary Supplement,* May 31, 1963, April 27, 1967, September 14, 1967, December 25, 1969, July 30, 1971, November 17, 1972; *Observer Review,* April 30, 1967, September 10, 1967, October 26, 1969; *London Magazine,* May, 1967; *New Statesman,* May 5, 1967, September 15, 1967, November 7, 1969, October 8, 1971, June 17, 1977; *Punch,* May 10, 1967; *Illustrated London News,* May 20, 1967; *Listener,* May 25, 1967, September 28, 1967, May 23, 1968; *Spectator,* September 22, 1967, November 8, 1969; *Books and Bookmen,* October, 1967; *Nation,* October 9, 1967, October 5, 1970, December 13, 1975, July 2, 1977, June 30, 1979; *New York Times Book Review,* October 15, 1967, April 7, 1968, May 24, 1970, October 17, 1971, November 16,

1975, December 28, 1975, May 1, 1977, June 12, 1977, May 13, 1979; *New York Review of Books,* October 26, 1967, April 11, 1968, December 30, 1971, May 31, 1979; *Kenyon Review,* November, 1967; *New York Times,* December 16, 1967, December 25, 1971, August 17, 1977, May 14, 1979, March 13, 1980; *Best Sellers,* April 15, 1968; *Contemporary Literature,* winter, 1968; *Books Abroad,* winter, 1968, winter, 1969.

Washington Post Book World, April 19, 1970, December 5, 1971, November 28, 1976, June 19, 1977, July 1, 1979; *Atlantic,* May, 1970, January, 1976, July, 1977, June, 1979; *Time,* May 25, 1970, December 1, 1975, June 20, 1977, May 21, 1979; *National Review,* October 6, 1970; *Transition,* December, 1971; Robert D. Hamner, *V. S. Naipaul,* Twayne, 1973; *Choice,* June, 1973; *Contemporary Literary Criticism,* Gale, Volume IV, 1975, Volume VII, 1977, Volume IX, 1978, Volume XIII, 1980; *Newsweek,* December 1, 1975, June 6, 1977, May 21, 1979; Michael Thorpe, *V. S. Naipaul,* Longmans, 1976; *New Republic,* July 9, 1977, June 9, 1979; *Economist,* July 16, 1977; *Chicago Tribune Book World,* May 13, 1979, April 20, 1980; *Los Angeles Times Book Review,* June 24, 1979; *Los Angeles Times,* May 9, 1980.

—*Sketch by Deborah A. Straub*

* * *

NANCE, Joseph Milton 1913-

PERSONAL: Born September 18, 1913, in Kyle, Tex.; son of Jeremiah Milton and Mary Louise (Hutchison) Nance; married Eleanor Glenn Hanover (part-time illustrator), March 19, 1944; children: Jeremiah Milton III, Joseph Hanover, James Clifton. *Education:* University of Texas, Main University (now University of Texas at Austin), B.A. (magna cum laude), 1935, M.A., 1936, Ph.D., 1941. *Religion:* Episcopalian. *Home:* 1403 Post Oak Cir., College Station, Tex. 77840. *Office:* Department of History, Texas A & M University, College Station, Tex. 77843.

CAREER: Supervisor of American imprints, manuscripts, and newspaper inventories, state of Texas, 1938-40; U.S. Naval Training School, College Station, Tex., instructor, 1942-43; Texas A & M University, College Station, instructor, 1941-42, 1946-47, assistant professor, 1947-51, associate professor, 1951-57, professor of history, 1957—, head of department, 1958-73. Visiting professor of history, Southwest Texas State College (now University), summers, 1956, 1958. Vice-chairman, Brazos County Historical Commission, 1975—. *Military service:* U.S. Naval Reserve, Communications, 1943-46; became lieutenant junior grade. *Member:* American Historical Association, National Geographic Society, American Studies Association, Organization of American Historians, Western History Association, Southern Historical Association, Southwestern Social Science Association, Texas State Historical Association (fellow), Texas Institute of Letters, West Texas Historical Association (vice-president, 1978—), East Texas Historical Association, Phi Kappa Phi (chapter president, 1958-59), Phi Beta Kappa, Phi Alpha Theta. *Awards, honors:* Annual Writers Roundup Award, Theta Sigma Phi, 1963, and Texas Institute of Letters award, 1964, both for *After San Jacinto: The Texas-Mexican Frontier, 1836-1841;* Walter Prescott Webb Award, 1967, for *Attack and Counterattack: The Texas-Mexican Frontier, 1842;* AMOCO Award, 1979, for distinguished faculty achievement in research and publication.

WRITINGS: Checklist of Texas Newspapers, 1813-1939, San Jacinto Museum of History, 1941; (contributor) *The Handbook of Texas,* Texas State Historical Association, 1952; *The Early History of Bryan and the Surrounding Area,* Hood's Brigade-Bryan Centennial Celebration Committee, 1962; *After San Jacinto: The Texas-Mexican Frontier, 1836-1841,* University of Texas Press, 1963; *Attack and Counterattack: The Texas-Mexican Frontier, 1842,* University of Texas Press, 1964; (co-author) *Heroes of Texas,* Texian Press, 1964; (editor) *Some Reflections upon Modern America,* American Studies Association of Texas, 1969; (editor) *Mier Expedition Diary: A Texan Prisoner's Account,* University of Texas Press, 1978. Contributor to *Encyclopedia of Southern History, Handbook of Texas, Encyclopaedia Britannica,* and to professional journals.

WORK IN PROGRESS: Dare-Devils All: The Texan Mier Expedition of 1842; Stand-Off: The Texas-Mexican Frontier, 1843-1846; History of Brazos County.

AVOCATIONAL INTERESTS: Gardening, hunting, photography.

* * *

NARELL, Irena 1923-
(Irena Penzik)

PERSONAL: Born September 17, 1923, in Sanok, Poland; naturalized U.S. citizen; daughter of Abraham (a lawyer and Polish Socialist leader) and Antonina (Katz) Penzik; married Murray Narell (a social worker), June 29, 1945; children: Jeff, Andrew. *Education:* Columbia University, B.S. *Home:* 5949 Estates Dr., Oakland, Calif. 94611. *Agent:* Curtis Brown Ltd., 575 Madison Ave., New York, N.Y. 10022.

CAREER: United Nations, New York City, secretary to permanent representative of the Polish delegation, 1946-52; Art Originals Gallery, New York City, co-owner, 1958-60; manager with husband of The Steel Bandits (musical group), 1964-69; writer; lecturer. Project director, researcher, and writer, "Old Traditions on a New Frontier: The Jews of San Francisco" bicentennial exhibit, Judah L. Magnes Museum, Berkeley, Calif. *Member:* American Jewish Congress (president, local chapter). *Awards, honors:* Charles and Bertie G. Schwartz Juvenile Award, JWB Jewish Book Council, 1979, for *Joshua: Fighter for Bar Kochba.*

WRITINGS: (Under name Irena Penzik) *Ashes to the Taste* (autobiography), University Publishers, 1961; *The Invisible Passage* (short stories), Brook Press, 1969; *Old Traditions on a New Frontier: The Jews of San Francisco,* Judah L. Magnes Museum, 1977; *Joshua: Fighter for Bar Kochba* (juvenile), Akiba Press, 1978; *Syngar of Gaul,* Akiba Press, 1980; *Our City: The Jews of San Francisco,* Howell-North Books, 1980. Also author of *Syngar the Slave* and translator of *Holy Week* by Jerzy Andrzejewski and *Samson* by Kazimierz Brandys. Work appears in anthologies, including *Woman Who Lost Her Name,* edited by Julia Mazow, Harper, 1980. Contributor of articles and short stories to periodicals, including *Present Tense, Sh'ma, Hadassah,* and *Western States Jewish Historical Quarterly.* Member of editorial board, *Western States Jewish Historical Quarterly.*

WORK IN PROGRESS: A young adult novel on the zealot revolution, an adult novel, and a book on the author's childhood in Poland.

SIDELIGHTS: Irena Narell told *CA:* "The disillusionment with socialism which followed a 1951 trip to Poland was a central factor in my late twenties and made me wary of espousing any political doctrine. For a number of years since then, I have been immersed in the study of history, particularly Jewish history both ancient and modern. I have devoted the major amount of my time to research and writing on Jewish historical themes, in fiction and nonfiction. *Joshua* . . . holds the largest portion of my spiritual and emotional commitment as a Jew."

Concerning *Joshua,* Jacob Biely comments: "Although the historical narrative is intended for young people, it nevertheless will appeal to the general reader. . . . *Joshua* should be on the shelf of every Jewish school and library to remind the young and old about the heroism of their Israeli predecessors whose deeds and sacrifices extended over almost 2,000 years."

AVOCATIONAL INTERESTS: Reading, art history, art viewing and collecting, antique collecting, music, "particularly jazz played on steel drums by son Andy," swimming.

BIOGRAPHICAL/CRITICAL SOURCES: *Oakland Tribune,* June 23, 1976; *Bulletin,* December, 1978; *JWB Circle,* January, 1979; *Women's American ORT Reporter,* March/April, 1979; *Heritage,* September 21, 1979; *Israel Today,* December 20, 1979.

* * *

NATHAN, Hans 1910-

PERSONAL: Born August 5, 1910, in Berlin, Germany; naturalized U.S. citizen, 1944; son of Jacob and Lucie (Dobrin) Nathan; married Jael Wahlburg, 1937. *Education:* Private study of piano, conducting, orchestration, 1919-34; University of Berlin, Ph.D., 1934; Harvard University, additional study of musicology, 1936-38. *Home:* 699 Jaywood Dr., East Lansing, Mich. *Office:* Department of Music, Michigan State University, East Lansing, Mich.

CAREER: Music critic, Berlin, Germany, 1932-35; teacher and lecturer in Boston, Mass. and vicinity, 1939-45, including Boston Center for Adult Education and Cambridge Center for Adult Education; weekly radio lecturer under auspices of Boston Symphony Orchestra, WHDH, Boston, 1944-45; Michigan State University, East Lansing, assistant professor, department of literature and fine arts, 1946-51, associate professor, music department, 1951-64, professor, 1964—. Fulbright professor, University of Rome, 1952-53. Visiting professor, Tufts College (now University), 1945; visiting associate professor, Tulane University, fall, 1966. Member, Institute for Advanced Study, 1957-58, visitor, summer, 1979. *Member:* American Musicology Society (member of council, 1951-53, 1957-59, 1962-64, 1967-69). *Awards, honors:* McDowell and Yaddo residences, 1950 and 1955; Guggenheim fellowship, 1957-58; grants from Sonneck Memorial Fund at Library of Congress, 1959, American Philosophical Society, 1944, 1961, Italian government, 1961-62, Chapelbrook Foundation, 1969-70, and National Endowment for the Humanities, 1970.

WRITINGS: (Contributor) Denis Stevens, editor, *A History of Song,* Norton, 1961; (editor and author of introduction) William Billings, *The Continental Harmony,* Belknap Press, 1961; *Dan Emmett and the Rise of Early Negro Minstrelsy,* University of Oklahoma Press, 1962, revised edition, 1977; *William Billings: Data and Documents,* Information Coordinators, 1976; (editor) *The Complete Works of William Billings,* Volume II, American Musicological Society and Colonial Society of Massachusetts, 1977. Contributor to *Musik In Geschichte Und Gegenwark, Encyclopedia Americana,* and *Dictionary of Twentieth Century Music;* contributor of more than forty articles to music and folklore journals.

* * *

NATHAN, Norman 1915-

PERSONAL: Born November 19, 1915, in Brooklyn, N.Y.; son of Michael (a salesman) and Fannie (Levine) Nathan; married Frieda Agin (a part-time teacher), July 21, 1940; children: Linda, Michele, Lois. *Education:* New York University, A.B., 1936, A.M., 1938, Ph.D., 1947. *Home:* 1189 Southwest Tamarind Way, Boca Raton, Fla. 33432. *Office:* Department of English, Florida Atlantic University, Boca Raton, Fla. 33432.

CAREER: Western Electric Co., Jersey City, N.J., motion and time study engineer, 1943-45; City College (now City College of the City University of New York), New York, N.Y., instructor in English, 1946-49; Rutgers University, Newark Campus, lecturer in English, 1947-49; Syracuse University, Utica College, Utica, N.Y., assistant professor, 1949-52, associate professor, 1952-58, professor of English, 1958-68; Florida Atlantic University, Boca Raton, professor of English, 1968—. Visiting summer professor at University of Missouri—Kansas City, 1964, 1966, and University of Southern Nevada, 1968; visiting professor, College of the Virgin Islands, 1965-66. Public lecturer; radio lecturer on Shakespeare and on poetry, WKTV, in Utica, 1954-56, WPBT in Miami, Fla., 1971, and WEAT. *Member:* Modern Language Association of America, Shakespeare Association of America, National Council of Teachers of English, College English Association, American Association of University Professors, New York Council of Teachers of English.

WRITINGS: *Though Night Remain* (poems), Golden Quill, 1959; *Judging Poetry* (textbook), Putnam, 1961; *The Right Word* (vocabulary textbook), Houghton, 1962; *Writing Sentences* (textbook-workbook), Houghton, 1964; (compiler) *Short Stories: An Anthology,* Bobbs-Merrill, 1969; *Prince William B.: The Philosophical Conceptions of William Blake,* Mouton, 1975. Contributor of about four hundred articles, short stories, and poems to professional journals and literary magazines.

WORK IN PROGRESS: *I'm Not That Beast,* a collection of his poems.

SIDELIGHTS: Norman Nathan told *CA*: "My problems in publication, overcome partly by refusing to be disturbed by any number of rejection slips, occur often because my personality is antagonistic to the five or six fads that are current. Today, unfortunately, having an individual idiom means establishing an artificial and easily recognizable form. Just being yourself is usually too subtle." Nathan continues: "I feel that my writing makes me a better teacher, while my teaching indirectly gives me material to write about. My preference is toward poetry, but it is not in my nature to specialize."

AVOCATIONAL INTERESTS: Gardening, chess.

* * *

NAUHEIM, Ferd(inand Alan) 1909-

PERSONAL: Born November 3, 1909, in New York, N.Y.; son of Elias and Sadie (Rosenberger) Nauheim; married Beatrice Strasburger, August 23, 1934; children: Gail (Mrs. Carter S. Kaufmann), Stephen A. *Education:* Attended high school in New York, N.Y. *Politics:* "Variable." *Religion:* Jewish. *Home:* 4201 Cathedral Ave., Washington, D.C. 20016. *Office:* 1054 31st St. N.W., Washington, D.C. 20007.

CAREER: Continental Baking Company, New York, N.Y., assistant advertising manager, 1930-36; Plymouth Printing Co., Washington, D.C., owner, 1936-49; worked as a direct mail sales consultant in Washington, D.C., 1949-56; Kalb, Voorhis & Co., Washington, D.C., general partner, 1956-77; advertising, sales, and marketing consultant, 1977—. Member of advisory board, Salvation Army of Washington, 1959—; chairman of board of regents, College Financial Planning, 1971-72; vice-president of board of trustees, Columbia Lighthouse for the Blind, 1971—. Citizens Advisory Commission of Washington, and D.C. Bar Association, 1973. Professional lecturer, School of Business, American University, 1952-64. *Military service:* U.S. Army, 5th Armored Division, 1944-45. *Member:* International Society of Financial Planners (member of board of directors, 1973—), Direct Mail Advertising Association (member of board of governors, 1958-61), Sales and Marketing Executives of Washington (president, 1957-58), Mail Advertising Club of Washington. *Awards, honors:* Named Man of the Year by Sales and Marketing Executives of Washington, 1958, and by Mail Advertising Club of Washington, 1968.

WRITINGS: *Business Letters That Turn Inquiries into Sales,* Prentice-Hall, 1957; *Ferd Nauheim's Nine Day Sales Clinic,* Prentice-Hall, 1964; *Salesmen's Complete Model Letter Handbook,* Prentice-Hall, 1967; *Behold the Upright* (novel), Apollo Books, 1971; *Build Family Finances and Reduce Risk and Taxes,* Acropolis Books, 1973; (with Art Linkletter) *Two Hundred Ways to Save on Probate, Inflation, Taxes and Avoid the Financial Pit,* Acropolis Books, 1977. Also author of *Move Your Assets to Beat Inflation,* New York Institute of Finance. Author of business and industrial related material.

SIDELIGHTS: Ferd Nauheim told *CA:* "It is my conviction that the sole purpose of writing is to convey ideas and/or information. Because of that belief I have been drawn to the challenge of taking relatively technical subjects and presenting them in terms that invited reading and dispel needless complexity, mystery and fear. I deem this of particular importance in financial matters, for far too many people fail to do the things they should to protect themselves due to a lack of knowledge."

* * *

NAYLOR, James C(harles) 1932-

PERSONAL: Born February 8, 1932, in Chicago, Ill.; son of Joseph S. (a manufacturer) and Berniece (Berg) Naylor; married Georgia L. Mason, February 14, 1953; children: M. Denise, D. Darice, S. Dalice. *Education:* Purdue University, B.S. (with highest distinction), 1957, M.S., 1958, Ph.D., 1960. *Home:* 225 Pawnee, West Lafayette, Ind. 47906. *Office:* Department of Psychology, Purdue University, West Lafayette, Ind. 47907.

CAREER: Ohio State University, Columbus, assistant professor and research associate in Laboratory of Aviation Psychology, 1960-63, associate professor, 1963-67, professor of psychology, 1967-68; Purdue University, West Lafayette, Ind., professor of psychology, 1968—, chairman of department, 1968-79. Statistical consultant to U.S. Veterans Administration, 1962-68. *Military service:* U.S. Navy, 1950-54. *Member:* International Association of Applied Psychology, American Psychological Association (fellow), American Association for the Advancement of Science (fellow), Psychometric Society, Psychonomic Society, Society for Organizational Behavior (founder), Midwestern Psychological Association, Phi Beta Kappa, Phi Eta Sigma, Sigma Xi. *Awards, honors:* Grants for research from U.S. Navy, U.S. Air Force, and National Science Foundation; National Defense Education Act training grants, 1963-68; Fulbright research scholar, Umea University, Sweden, 1976.

WRITINGS: (Contributor) J. M. Champion and J. J. Bridges, editors, *Critical Incidents in Management,* Irwin, 1963; (with M. L. Blum) *Industrial Psychology: Its Theoretical and Social Foundation* (with instructor's guide), Harper, 1968; (with R. D. Pritchard and D. R. Ilgen) *A Theory of Behavior in Organizations,* Academic Press, 1980; (contributor) K. Duncan, M. Gruneberg, and D. Wallis, editors, *Changes in the Nature and Quality of Working Life,* Wiley, 1980. Author of papers presented to professional conferences; also author or co-author of technical reports. Contributor of articles and reviews to professional journals. Editor, *Organizational Behavior and Human Performance,* 1966—; consulting editor, *Professional Psychology,* 1969-76.

WORK IN PROGRESS: *Experimental and Statistical Procedures: An Introduction.*

SIDELIGHTS: James C. Naylor told *CA:* "There is a myth that scientific writing is devoid of the creativity found in fiction, poetry, and other writing forms. This is totally false. While scientific writing is bounded by the realities of data, observations, and real events, so are the biographical, documentary, historical, and newspaper writing forms. The facts are that most scientists today are more writers than scientists in the sense that they spend a much larger proportion of their time writing about their research than they spend actually doing it! I personally find writing the most difficult of activities to perform, but certainly one of the most rewarding experiences when completed. I must discipline myself severely to accomplish anything, and I set schedules for myself, such as two or three pages each day."

* * *

NEIGHBOUR, Ralph W(ebster) 1906-

PERSONAL: Born July 21, 1906, in Salisbury, N.C.; son of Robert Edward and Gertrude (Planck) Neighbour; married Ruth May Zimmerman, 1929; children: Ralph W., Jr., David Eugene, Carol Jane. *Education:* Wheaton College, Wheaton, Ill, B.A., 1927. *Home:* Twin Towers, 2020 North Atlantic Ave., Apt. 216N, Cocoa Beach, Fla. 32931.

CAREER: Pastor of several Baptist churches since 1929; former chaplain and associate director, federal prison Le Tourneau Evangelistic Center, Rockefeller Center, New York, N.Y.; former pastor and director, Fort Wayne Gospel Temple, Fort Wayne, Ind.; former pastor, Church of the Open Door, Elyria, Ohio; has broadcasted daily radio program, "The Morning Sunshine Program," over fifty radio stations, for twenty-nine years. Past president, Temple Missionary Training School. *Member:* National Religious Broadcasters (executive committee member; past vice-president), World Christian Crusade (president.)

WRITINGS—Published by Zondervan, except as indicated: *Dare to Decide,* 1938; *A Voice from Heaven,* 1958; *The Shining Light,* 1960; *Thine Enemy,* 1963; *The Searching Heart,* 1964; (editor) *Golden Nuggets,* Collins, 1969.

Also author of *The Dawn of Redemption, The God of Promise, Planet Earth on the Brink of Eternity, Health, Wealth, and Happiness, Ephesians for Everday Living, Colossians for Everyday Living, Philippians for Everyday Living, Hebrews for Everyday Living, Revelation for Everyday Living, 1 John, 2 John, 3 John, and Jude for Everyday Living, Matthew For Everyday Living, Titus for Everyday Living, Morning Sunshine, Morning Dawns,* and *1st and 2nd Timothy for Everyday Living.* Former Editor, *Baptist News* and *Christian Conservative.*

WORK IN PROGRESS: Writing on every book of the Bible under the title of *. . . for Everyday Living;* another novel; a devotional book which covers Psalms, Proverbs, Ecclesiastes, and Song of Solomon.

SIDELIGHTS: Ralph W. Neighbour told *CA:* "I am in the process of writing on every book of the Bible, completing the New Testament first, and later the Old Testament. It is my purpose to make the Bible clear and understandable to the average person, so it may be applied in daily life as a practical guide to successful living. I publish 5000 to 10,000 copies of each book as it is written, and give it free to radio listeners. Later all books will be published in one volume, entitled *The Bible for Everyday Living*.

"My first love is writing fiction, though I do enjoy writing study books. In fact, I enjoy juvenile fiction writing as much as adult fiction. I love to write short stories, and short short stories, but enter into a novel as if it were a living fact. I enjoy my characters.

"I am now living by the ocean, and find it most inspiring and relaxing for one who writes. The ocean has many moods, just as in life."

* * *

NELSON, Benjamin N(athaniel) 1935-

PERSONAL: Born November 3, 1935, in New York, N.Y.; son of Simon and Bertha (Rapkine) Nelson; married Miriam Sarah Jacobson, June, 1960. *Education:* Columbia University, B.A., 1957, M.F.A., 1959; graduate study at New York University. *Agent:* Sterling Lord Agency, Inc., 660 Madison Ave., New York, N.Y. 10021.

CAREER: Fairleigh Dickinson University, Rutherford, N.J., beginning 1962, began as instructor, became assistant professor.

WRITINGS: Tennessee Williams: The Man and His Work, Obolensky, 1961 (published in England as *Tennessee Williams: His Life and Work,* P. Owen, 1961); *Review Notes and Study Guide to the Major Plays of Tennessee Williams,* Monarch, 1966; *Arthur Miller: Portrait of a Playwright,* P. Owen, 1970.

SIDELIGHTS: George E. Wellwarth calls *Arthur Miller: Portrait of a Playwright* "a definitive study of Miller's works up to this point. Combining a biographical approach with a close analysis of the text, Nelson has come up with the best study of Miller's works to date." Irving Wardle, while admitting that the book "covers the subject more comprehensively than any other study I have come across," feels that it fails to "follow any continuous line of thought, or attempt to place Miller's very familiar plays in relation to their less familiar personal and public context. It takes the easiest critical position: that of simple reflex action to whatever stimulus the artist provides. Nelson himself gives the game away by acknowledging the help of Arthur Miller 'without whose plays (the book) would unquestionably never have been started.' The following chapters do rise above that level of rock-bottom naivety, but not all that much." Wardle goes on to say that "the biography seems scrambled together from old magazine articles and interviews. And Nelson falls into the usual trap of trying to compensate for insufficient information by over-writing what scraps he has got. Thus, seeking for some significant event in the playwright's childhood, he comes up with a story about Miller as a delivery boy, skidding off his bicycle and dropping his load of bagels on the ice. After archly spinning this out to a couple of pages, Nelson works himself up to the climax. Here we go. 'Thus the artist, as a young delivery boy, came face to face with the catastrophic potential in the human condition, and with the inexplicable buffetings which man can expect from an essentially alien universe.' Says you."

BIOGRAPHICAL/CRITICAL SOURCES: Plays and Players, May, 1970; *Books Abroad,* spring, 1971.†

* * *

NELSON, James B(ruce) 1930-

PERSONAL: Born May 28, 1930, in Windom, Minn.; married Wilys Claire Coulter, January 31, 1953; children: Stephen Joseph, Mary Elizabeth. *Education:* Macalester College, B.A. (summa cum laude), 1951; Yale University, B.D. (magna cum laude), 1957, M.A., 1959, Ph.D., 1962; Oxford University, postdoctoral study, 1969-70. *Office:* United Theological Seminary of the Twin Cities, 3000 Fifth St. N.W., Brighton, Minn. 55112.

CAREER: Ordained Congregational minister, 1958; minister in West Haven, Conn., 1957-59, and Vermillion, S.D., 1960-63; United Theological Seminary of the Twin Cities, New Brighton, Minn., associate professor, 1963-68, professor of Christian ethics, 1968—. Visiting lecturer at Luther Theological Seminary, fall, 1966, and Yale Divinity School, spring, 1969; visiting professor at St. John's University, fall, 1968. *Military service:* U.S. Army, 1952-54. *Member:* American Academy of Religion, American Society of Christian Ethics, Society for the Scientific Study of Religion, Society for Values in Higher Education, Phi Gamma Mu.

WRITINGS: (Contributor) Harvey Cox, editor, *The Situation Ethics Debate,* Westminster, 1968; *The Responsible Christian,* United Church Press, 1969; *Moral Nexus: Ethics of Christian Identity and Community,* Westminster, 1971; *Human Medicine: Ethical Perspectives on New Medical Issues,* Augsburg, 1973; *Rediscovering the Person in Medical Care,* Augsburg, 1976; (contributor) *Human Sexuality: A Preliminary Study,* United Church Press, 1977; *Embodiment: An Approach to Sexuality and Christian Theology,* Augsburg, 1978; *Quality or Sanctity* (booklet), Office for Church Life and Leadership, United Church of Christ, 1979. Contributor to *Encyclopedia of Bio-Ethics.* Contributor of numerous articles and reviews to *McCormick Quarterly, Journal of Ecumenical Studies, Theology Digest, Colloquy, Youth, Theological Markings, Theology and Life, Review of Religious Research, Religious Education, Journal of Religion,* and other journals.

* * *

NELSON, Mary Carroll 1929-

PERSONAL: Born April 24, 1929, in College Station, Tex.; daughter of James Vincent (an army officer) and Mary (Langton) Carroll; married Edwin Blakely Nelson (a retired Army officer; now research consultant), June 27, 1950; children: Patricia Ann, Edwin Blakely, Jr. *Education:* Barnard College, B.A., 1950; University of New Mexico, M.A., 1963, further graduate study, 1969-70. *Politics:* Republican. *Religion:* Catholic. *Home:* 1408 Georgia N.E., Albuquerque, N.M. 87110. *Office:* 3020 Morris St. N.E., Albuquerque, N.M. 87111.

CAREER: Teacher most of the time since 1957; currently art coordinator of Sunset Mesa School, Albuquerque, N.M. Professional artist. *Member:* National Writers Club, National League of American Pen Women (member of chapter board, 1970-74; member of state board, 1972-74), Rio Grande Writers Association, New Mexico Watercolor Society (member of board, 1970-73). *Awards, honors:* Various exhibition awards for paintings.

WRITINGS: Pablita Velarde, Dillon, 1971; *Maria Martinez,* Dillon, 1972, 2nd edition, 1974; *Annie Wauneka,* Dillon,

1972; (with Robert E. Wood) *Watercolor Workshop*, Watson-Guptill, 1974; *Michael Naranjo*, Dillon, 1975; *Robert Bennett*, Dillon, 1976; *Ramon Kelley Paints Portraits and Figures*, Watson-Guptill, 1977; (contributor) Susan E. Meyer, editor, *20 Landscape Painters and How They Work*, Watson-Guptill, 1977; (contributor) Meyer, editor, *20 Oil Painters and How They Work*, Watson-Guptill, 1978; Meyer, editor, *20 Figure Painters and How They Work*, Watson-Guptill, 1979; *The Legendary Artists of Taos*, Watson-Guptill, 1980. Contributor to art periodicals.

WORK IN PROGRESS: All Children Are Gifted, programs for kindergarten and first grade; *Painting and Drawing the West*, for Watson-Guptill.

SIDELIGHTS: Mary Carroll Nelson told *CA:* "I search for heroes. When I find one, he or she is usually an artist, a creative person in some field. Most of my writing is their stories, accurately and clearly stated as far as possible, told for future record and for today's readers. Creative people, who survive on the strength of their belief in themselves, are models of inspiration for others. I think of those others when I write."

* * *

NELSON, Raymond S(tanley) 1921-

PERSONAL: Born October 11, 1921, in Brooklyn, N.Y.; son of John R. (a contractor) and Gudrun (Andersen) Nelson; married K. Margaret Soderman, September 4, 1943; children: John, Fay (Mrs. Charles Smith), R. Stanley, Timothy. *Education:* Trinity Seminary and Bible College, B.Th., 1944; University of Minnesota, B.A., M.A., 1957; University of Nebraska, Ph.D., 1968. *Home:* 7301 Galoway, Wichita, Kan. 67212. *Office:* Friends University, Wichita, Kan. 67213.

CAREER: Christian minister of Covenant Church, 1944-57; Morningside College, Sioux City, Iowa, 1957-76, became professor of English, associate dean, 1970-72, academic dean, 1972-76; Friends University, Wichita, Kan., professor of English, 1976—, interim academic dean, 1978—. *Member:* Modern Language Association of America, American Association of Deans, American Association of University Professors, Phi Beta Kappa, Sigma Tau Delta.

WRITINGS: The Critical Research Essay, Morningside College, 1969; (editor and author of introduction) George Bernard Shaw, *Candida*, Bobbs-Merrill, 1972; *Hemingway: Expressionist Artist*, Iowa State University Press, 1979. Contributor to *Shaw Review, Modern Drama, Queen's Quarterly*, and other literary and education journals.

WORK IN PROGRESS: Creative Individualism; Ways of Thinking; Every Mark Has Meaning.

* * *

NELSON, Stanley 1933-

PERSONAL: Born June 9, 1933, in Brooklyn, N.Y.; son of Charles (a textile businessman) and Celia (Prager) Nelson; married Ellen Rice Beaty, March 10, 1957 (divorced December, 1965); married Betty Jean Minton Skrefstad (a medical writer/editor), June 26, 1966; children: (first marriage) Celia, Lycette. *Education:* University of Vermont, B.A., 1957. *Politics:* "I am essentially apolitical." *Religion:* Jewish. *Home:* 372 Pacific St., Brooklyn, N.Y. 11217.

CAREER: Teacher of retarded children in early years; *Medical World News*, New York City, news editor, 1963-65; *Roche Image*, New York City, senior writer, 1965-66; *Hospital Practice*, New York City, senior editor, 1966-69; poet and playwright. Editor, *Oncology News*, 1977—. Director of Generalist Association; member of board of directors, Theatre 77. *Member:* Poets and Writers, Dramatists Guild, P.E.N. *Awards, honors:* Thomas Wolfe Memorial Award for Poetry.

WRITINGS: Idlewild (poems), The Smith, 1969; *The Brooklyn Book of the Dead* (poems), The Smith, 1971; (editor with Harry Smith) *The Scene/1* (play anthology), New Egypt Publications, 1972; (editor with Smith) *The Scene/2*, New Egypt Publications, 1974; (editor) *The Scene/3*, New Egypt Publications, 1975; (editor) *The Scene/4*, New Egypt Publications, 1976; *Chirico Eyes* (poems), Midnight Sun Press, 1977; *The Travels of Ben Sira* (poems), The Smith/Horizon Press, 1978; *101 Fragments of a Prayer* (poems), Midnight Sun Press, 1979; *The Unknowable Light of the Alien* (stories), The Smith/Horizon Press, 1980.

Plays: "Emanons" (one-act), first produced in New York at Bastiano's Cellar Studio, April, 1968; "Shuffle-Off" (one-act), first produced at Bastiano's Cellar Studio, April, 1968; "Mr. Optometrist" (one-act), first produced at Bastiano's Cellar Studio, April, 1968; "The Harrison Progressive School" (one-act), first produced at Bastiano's Cellar Studio, October, 1968; "Mrs. Peacock" (one-act), first produced Off-Off-Broadway at Old Reliable Theatre, August, 1969, a two-act version produced Off-Off-Broadway at Omni Theatre Club, May, 1972; "The Examination" (one-act), produced Off-Off-Broadway by New York Theatre Ensemble, July, 1969; "The Plan," produced by New York Theatre Ensemble, January, 1970; "Ruth and the Rabbi" (one-act), produced at Omni Theatre Club, October, 1970; "Tsk, Mary, Tsk" (one-act), produced in New York at Stagelights Theatrical Club, April, 1970, produced under title, "The Mary Show," in New York at Stagelights II, April, 1971; "El Exejente" (one-act), first produced Off-Off-Broadway at Playhouse Theatre, September, 1971; "The Butler Carries the Sun Away" (one-act), first produced at Playhouse Theatre, 1971; "Rite of Spring" (two-act), first produced in New York at WPA Theatre, June, 1972; "The Master Psychoanalyst" (three-act), first produced at New Old Reliable Theatre, October, 1972; "The Poetry Reading" (one-act), first produced Off-Off-Broadway at Cubiculo Theatre, June, 1973; "No One Writes Drawing Room Comedies Anymore" (one-act), first produced in New York at Joseph Jefferson Theatre, August, 1973; "Poe: From His Life and Mind" (two-act), first produced in New York at Theatre 77, 1974.

Poetry represented in anthologies, including *The Living Underground*, Whitston Publishing, 1973. Contributor of plays to *Red Cedar Review* and *Scene*, poetry to about fifty periodicals, including *Beloit Poetry Journal, Kansas Quarterly, Caterpillar, Tri-Quarterly*, and *Confrontation*, and theatre and poetry criticism to literary journals.

WORK IN PROGRESS: NADA mit NADA, a novel.

AVOCATIONAL INTERESTS: Music (especially jazz), sports (especially pro football), the ancient world.

* * *

NELSON, Truman (John) 1911-

PERSONAL: Born February 18, 1911, in Lynn, Mass.; son of John Wilson and Ida (Seymour) Nelson; children: Garrison, Abigail. *Home and office:* 23 Olive St., Newburyport, Mass.

CAREER: Writer. Former actor with Shakespearean Repertory Companies, including Mercury Theatre. Worked at General Electric Co., Lynn, Mass., and served as chief union steward. Currently chairman of executive board, Community Action of Merrimack Valley. *Member:* Essex Institute, Thoreau Society, Emerson Society, Mark Twain Society, Society for the Preservation of Antiquities. *Awards, honors:* Rabinowitz fellowship in creative writing; Humanities award, Pan African Association, 1964; Citation, Second American Festival of Negro Arts, 1969.

WRITINGS: The Sin of the Prophet, Little, Brown, 1952; *Passion by the Brook,* Doubleday, 1953; *The Surveyor,* Doubleday, 1960; *The Torture of Mothers,* Garrison Press, 1965; *Documents of Upheaval: William Lloyd Garrison and the Rise and Fall of the Non-Violent, Passive-Resistant Movement,* Hill & Wang, 1966; *Abolitionism: The Right of Revolution,* Beacon Press, 1968; *The Old Man: John Brown at Harper's Ferry,* Holt, 1973.

Writing has appeared in anthologies, including *Thoreau in Our Time, The John Brown Reader, The Black Titan, The New Left, and Literature in Revolution.* Author of introductions to books, including *Negroes with Guns,* by Robert F. Williams and *The Souls of Black Folk* and *The Gift of Black Folk,* both by W.E.B. Du Bois. Author of motion pictures, "The Old Man," currently under option to B. & J. Films, and "The Torture of Mothers," being produced by Woody King Productions. Contributor to *Unitarian Historical Quarterly, Western Humanities Review, Massachusetts Review, Freedomways, Judaism,* and other journals, and to *Nation, Ramparts, Saturday Review, New York Times Book Review, Boston Globe Magazine,* and other national publications.

SIDELIGHTS: Truman Nelson once commented to *CA:* "My position is that man can, through knowledge and awareness brought on by communicative art, understand and perhaps control the physical and political facts of his existence, rather than submitting to them with a defeated whimper." Starting from this position, Nelson was writing what he then called "the novel of the organic event. By reconstructing the actual history, places, personalities and the physical and ideological motion of some turning and breaking point in history, deep psychological truth may be achieved."

More recently, Nelson told *CA* that he "had written three novels with this technique on the period from 1830 to 1860 with interconnected characters and intended to continue with a connected series of novels searching out those personalities, climaxes and crescendoes and those events which transform a people with their intensities and revelations . . . a sort of Balzacian Comedie Americaine. But I was never able to do this. In the fifties, possibly because of political reasons, the political-revolutionary-historical novel was phased out of the literary scene. No one pretended to take it seriously and it was not regarded in the realm of academia as containing any usable truths. So, no more advances were forthcoming and I turned to straight nonfiction for survival."

William Shafer, however, called Nelson's three novels "the most intelligent, meticulous and profoundly dramatic historical fiction in this century. They communicate the turmoil and intellectual ferment of America in the age of Emerson, Hawthorne, Melville, Thoreau, Garrison, Parker and John Brown. They also vivify the complex sociopolitical history of that period in dramatic characters. Nelson's achievement is major, but it has gone almost unacknowledged by critics and literary observers, probably because the historical novel is in bad repute with modern literary theorists and fiction-writers. The bad money of sleazy ante-bellum romances and potboilers built on tushery and pseudohistory has driven the good money of the traditional historical novel from our literary economy."

BIOGRAPHICAL/CRITICAL SOURCES: Nation, April 22, 1968; *Negro Digest,* August, 1968; *Minnesota Review,* fall, 1976.

* * *

NEMEROV, Howard 1920-

PERSONAL: Born March 1, 1920, in New York, N.Y.; son of David and Gertrude (Russek) Nemerov; married Margaret Russell, January 26, 1944; children: David, Alexander, Jeremy. *Education:* Harvard University, A.B., 1941. *Home:* 6970 Cornell Ave., St. Louis, Mo. 63130. *Office:* Department of English, Washington University, St. Louis, Mo. 63130.

CAREER: Hamilton College, Clinton, N.Y., instructor, 1946-48; Bennington College, Bennington, Vt., member of the faculty in literature, 1948-66; Brandeis University, Waltham, Mass., professor of English, 1966-68; Washington University, St. Louis, Mo., visiting Hurst Professor of English, 1969-70, professor of English, 1970-76, Edward Mallinckrodt Distinguished University Professor of English, 1976—. Visiting lecturer in English, University of Minnesota, 1958-59; writer-in-residence, Hollins College, 1962-63. Consultant in poetry, Library of Congress, 1963-64; chancellor, American Academy of Poets, beginning 1976. *Military service:* Royal Canadian Air Force, 1942-44; became flying officer; U.S. Army Air Forces, 1944-45; became first lieutenant.

MEMBER: National Institute of Arts and Letters, American Academy of Arts and Letters, American Academy of Arts and Sciences (fellow), Phi Beta Kappa (honorary member), Alpha of Massachusetts. *Awards, honors:* Bowdoin Prize, Harvard University, 1940; *Kenyon Review* fellowship in fiction, 1955; Blumenthal Prize, 1958, Harriet Monroe Memorial Prize, 1959, Frank O'Hara Memorial Prize, 1971, Levinson Prize, 1975, all from *Poetry* magazine; second prize, *Virginia Quarterly Review* short story competition, 1958; National Institute of Arts and Letters grant, 1961; New England Poetry Club Golden Rose, 1962; Brandeis Creative Arts Award, 1963; D.L., Lawrence University, 1964, and Tufts University, 1969; First Theodore Roethke Memorial Award, 1968, for *The Blue Swallows;* St. Botolph's Club (Boston) Prize for Poetry, 1968; Guggenheim fellow, 1969; Academy of American Poets fellowship, 1970; Pulitzer Prize and National Book Award, 1978, both for *The Collected Poems of Howard Nemerov;* honorary degree from Washington and Lee University.

WRITINGS: The Melodramatists (novel), Random House, 1949; *Federigo: Or the Power of Love* (novel), Little, Brown, 1954; *The Homecoming Game* (novel), Simon & Schuster, 1957; *A Commodity of Dreams and Other Stories,* Simon & Schuster, 1959; (editor and author of introduction) Henry Wadsworth Longfellow, *Longfellow: Selected Poetry,* Dell, 1959; *Poetry and Fiction: Essays,* Rutgers University Press, 1963; (author of commentary) William Shakespeare, *Two Gentlemen of Verona,* Dell, 1964; *Journal of the Fictive Life,* Rutgers University Press, 1965; (editor and contributor) *Poets on Poetry,* Basic Books, 1965; *Stories, Fables and Other Diversions,* David R. Godine, 1971; *Reflexions on Poetry and Poetics,* Rutgers University Press, 1972; *Figures of Thought: Speculations on the Meaning of Poetry and Other Essays,* David R. Godine, 1978.

Poetry; published by University of Chicago Press, except as indicated: *The Image and the Law,* Holt, 1947; *Guide to the Ruins,* Random House, 1950; *The Salt Garden,* Little, Brown, 1955; *Small Moment,* Ward Ritchie Press, 1957;

Mirrors and Windows, 1958; *New and Selected Poems,* 1960; *Endor: Drama in One Act* (verse play), Abingdon, 1961; *The Next Room of the Dream: Poems and Two Plays,* 1962; (contributor) Ted Hughes and Thom Gunn, editors, *Five American Poets,* Faber, 1963; *The Blue Swallows,* 1967; *The Winter Lightning: Selected Poems,* Rapp & Whiting, 1968; *The Painter Dreaming in the Scholar's House* (limited edition), Phoenix Book Shop, 1968; *Gnomes and Occasions,* 1973; *The Western Approaches: Poems, 1973-75,* 1975; *The Collected Poems of Howard Nemerov,* 1977.

Contributor of essays, poems, stories, and reviews to periodicals. Associate editor, *Furioso,* 1946-51.

SIDELIGHTS: Howard Nemerov is a highly acclaimed poet whom many readers find difficult to characterize. As Joyce Carol Oates remarks in *New Republic,* "Romantic, realist, comedian, satirist, relentless and indefatigable brooder upon the most ancient mysteries—Nemerov is not to be classified." Peter Meinke also discovers these contrasting qualities and believes that they are due to his "deeply divided personality." Meinke points out that Nemerov himself has spoken of a duality in his nature in *Journal of the Fictive Life* in which he says that "it has seemed to me that I must attempt to bring together the opposed elements of my character represented by poetry and fiction." Comments Meinke, "These 'opposed elements' in Howard Nemerov's character are reflected in his life and work: in the tensions between his romantic and realistic visions, his belief and unbelief, his heart and mind."

Nemerov's first book of poems, *The Image and the Law,* characteristically is based on opposed elements, on a duality of vision. As F. C. Golffing explains in *Poetry,* "Mr. Nemerov tells us that he dichotomizes the 'poetry of the eye' and the 'poetry of the mind,' and that he attempts to exhibit in his verse the 'ever-present dispute between two ways of looking at the world.'" Some reviewers find that this dichotomy leads to a lack of coherence in the verse. *New York Times* writer Milton Crane, for example, feels that the poems "unfortunately show no unity of conception such as their author attributes to them." The book was also criticized for being derivative of earlier modern poets such as T. S. Eliot, W. H. Auden, W. B. Yeats, and Wallace Stevens.

In *Guide to the Ruins,* Nemerov's second book of verse, at least one reviewer again found divergent qualities in his writing. In *Saturday Review,* I. L. Salomon asserts that Nemerov "suffers from a dichotomy of personality." The dichotomy, Salomon claims, is between Nemerov's "instinct for perfection" and unity and a modern "carelessness in expression." Yet Crane notices not so much modern "carelessness" as a praiseworthy modern sensibility; he believes that *Ruins* "is the work of an original and sensitive mind, alive to the thousand anxieties and agonies of our age." And Meinke contends that it is Nemerov's "modern awareness of contemporary man's alienation and fragmentation" combined with "a breadth of wit in the eighteenth century sense of the word" which "sets Nemerov's writing apart from other modern writers."

Ruins, like *Image and the Law,* was also criticized for being derivative. And the same charge was levied against *The Salt Garden.* "The accents of Auden and [John Crowe] Ransom," observes Louis Untermeyer, "occasionally twist his utterance into a curious poetic patois." Similarly, Randall Jarrell finds that "you can see where he found out how to do some of the things he does—he isn't, as yet, a very individual poet." Nemerov admits the influence of others on his work. When asked if his work had changed in character or style, he replied: "In style, . . . for I began and for a long time remained imitative, and poems in my first books . . . show more than traces of admired modern masters—Eliot, Auden, Stevens, [E. E.] Cummings, Yeats." Meinke, too, maintains that Nemerov in his early work was "writing Eliot, Yeats, and Stevens out of his system." Yet at the same time that Untermeyer and Jarrell fault Nemerov for his imitation, they, and other readers, are impressed by his growth as a poet. Jarrell comments that "as you read *The Salt Garden* you are impressed with how much the poet has learned, how well he has developed." While Hayden Carruth remarks, "Nemerov's new book is his third . . . and his best; steady improvement, I take it, is one sign of formidable ability."

The Salt Garden, many critics feel, marks the beginning of other changes in Nemerov's work as well. Meinke observes that in this volume "Nemerov has found his most characteristic voice: a quiet intelligent voice brooding lyrically on the strange beauty and tragic loneliness of life." In a review of *The Collected Poems of Howard Nemerov* (1977), Willard Spiegelman, like Meinke, discovers in the poems from *Salt Garden* "Nemerov's characteristic manner and tone." Spiegelman still finds opposed elements, but in balance; Nemerov's manner is "genuinely Horatian according to Auden's marvelous definition of looking at 'this world with a happy eye / but from a sober perspective.' Nemerov's *aurea mediocritas* [golden mean] sails between philosophical skepticism . . . and social satire on one side, and, on the other, an open-eyed, child-like appreciation of the world's miracles."

Another change which began with *Salt Garden* and continues in *Mirrors and Windows, The Next Room of the Dream,* and *The Blue Swallows* is Nemerov's growing concern with nature. In 1966, Nemerov wrote in *Poets on Poetry* of the impact of the natural world on his work: "During the war and since, I have lived in the country, chiefly in Vermont, and while my relation to the landscape has been contemplative rather than practical, the landscape nevertheless has in large part taken over my poetry." This interest in the landscape has led Chad Walsh to say of *Swallows* that "in its quiet lyricism and sensitivity to nature it suggests Robert Frost." The comparison to Frost, suggested by many other critics, is also made on the grounds that Nemerov, like Frost, brings philosophical issues into his poetry.

Yet, as was discussed earlier, the feature of Nemerov's writing which critics point to repeatedly is not primarily the use of nature but the dichotomy between a witty, ironic manner and a serious, perhaps pessimistic, philosophy. James Dickey observes the seriousness that underlies Nemerov's wit. Nemerov, Dickey maintains, "is one of the wittiest and funniest poets we have. . . . But the enveloping emotion that arises from his writing is helplessness: the helplessness we all feel in the face of the events of our time, and of life itself. . . . And beneath even this feeling is a sort of hopelessly involved acceptance and resignation which has in it more of the truly tragic than most poetry which deliberately sets out in quest of tragedy." At the same time, Julia Bartholomay detects a somewhat different dichotomy. She contends that in Nemerov's poetry there is a basic dualism that "underlies the two different . . . attitudes which appear consistently in the poet's work. On the one hand, he is very much the witty, sophisticated man of his time. . . . Nemerov often views life with a humorous but bitter irony. . . . On the other hand, the poet perceives the world ontologically. His experience may be philosophical, subjective, lyrical, or even mystical." Bartholomay argues that Nemerov's double view is expressed in his poetry through the use of paradox. The paradoxes reflect the "divisiveness, fragmentation, complexity, and absurdity of modern existence."

Not all critics applaud the tragic irony which Dickey and many others find. Carruth, for example, comments: "No one would deny that famous and marvelous poems have been written in the manner of poetic irony. . . . But today this manner is an exceedingly tired poetic attitude. . . . And Nemerov's tired attitude is revealed in tired poetry: spent meters, predictable rhymes, and metaphors haggard with use." *New York Times* critic Thomas Lask also objects to Nemerov's irony, but for different reasons. He believes that in *Blue Swallows* it has turned bitter, expressing "loathing and contempt for man and his work." In contrast to both these views, Laurence Lieberman, writing in *Yale Review*, feels that "Howard Nemerov has perfected the poem as an instrument for exercising brilliance of wit. Searching, discursive, clear-sighted, he has learned to make the poem serve his relaxed manner and humane insights so expertly, I can only admire the clean purposefulness of his statements, his thoughtful care, the measure and grace of his lines."

However strong his ironic voice, Nemerov has mellowed with age, according to many reviewers. Meinke claims that "Nemerov has progressed steadily in his poetry to a broader, more tolerant view, less bitter and more sad." Likewise, Harvey Gilman finds in a review of *Gnomes and Occasions* that "Nemerov's tone modulates as saving wit gives way to wistful contemplation, reminiscence, and prayer. The mask of irony is lowered and Nemerov writes a more sustained elegiac verse. . . . True, the epigrammatic manner remains in evidence . . . but the wit is here tinged with whimsy and warmth." Similarly, Spiegelman observes: "Nemerov, growing old, becomes younger as he adopts the manner of an ancient sage. Cynicism barely touches his voice; the occasional sardonic moments are offset by feeling and sympathy. . . . In the 40's and 50's Nemerov was rabbinically fixated on sin and redemption. What was, early on, a source of prophetic despair . . . , becomes in the poems of his middle age the cause of poetic variety and energy, metaphysical delight, and emotional equilibrium." And Helen Vendler discerns in a critique of *Collected Poems* that as "the echoes of the *grands maitres* fade, the poems get steadily better. The severity of attitude is itself chastened by a growing humanity, and the forms of the earth grow ever more distinct."

Nemerov's prose fiction has also been commended, especially for displaying an irony and wit similar to that of his poems. His novels, as Meinke remarks, "like his poems, . . . are basically pessimistic. The condition of man is not an enviable one: we act foolishly and understand imperfectly. Nemerov's dark viewpoint, which in his poetry is redeemed by beauty . . . , in his fiction is redeemed by humor." Meinke terms *The Melodramatists* "a highly successful first novel," and in *Nation* Diana Trilling seconds him, commenting that after a slow start, it is "a considerable first novel—literate and entertaining, with a nice satiric barb." *Federigo: Or the Power of Love* and *The Homecoming Game* were also well received. For example, Richard Sullivan calls the latter book a "beautifully controlled satire" with characters "rendered with authentic irony," and *Atlantic* reviewer C. J. Rolo finds that it has "wit, dash, and point."

On the other hand, some critics charge that Nemerov treats his characters coldly. Paul Pickrel, for instance, admires Nemerov's wit but argues that his characters "are always threatening to bore him. Only when he gets them under the scalpel is he completely at ease." Meinke answers the accusation by claiming that "the real problem is that readers do not know how to take Nemerov: Is he being funny, or what? Is he kidding us? The point is that Nemerov, like the 'Absurd' playwrights, is humorous and serious at the same time. One should not confuse seriousness with solemnity; Nemerov is never solemn but is always, even at his funniest, serious."

Like his poetry and fiction, Nemerov's essays have garnered considerable critical acclaim. *Figures of Thought: Speculation on the Meaning of Poetry and Other Essays* prompted Benjamin DeMott to respond: "Taken as a whole . . . these 'speculations' are uncommonly stimulating and persuasive. . . . [This book] communicates throughout a vivid sense of the possibility of a richer kind of knowing in all areas than we're in process of settling for. . . . Like the high art it salutes, it hums with the life of things." Moreover, Joyce Carol Oates adds: "The book is a marvelous one, rewarding not only for what it tells us about poetry in general . . . , but for what it tells us about the processes of the imagination. Nemerov is, quite simply, a brilliant mind."

The Homecoming Game was adapted as a play entitled "Tall Story" and filmed by Warner Bros. in 1959.

BIOGRAPHICAL/CRITICAL SOURCES: New York Times, August 1, 1947, May 21, 1950, March 3, 1957, March 30, 1968, April 28, 1968, December 26, 1978; *Poetry*, November, 1947, June, 1955, December, 1958, September, 1963, December, 1976; *New York Times Book Review*, April 3, 1949, May 21, 1950, July 17, 1955, February 8, 1959, March 1, 1959, January 8, 1961, July 21, 1963, March 29, 1964, April 28, 1968, January 14, 1978, April 16, 1978; *Nation*, May 7, 1949, August 16, 1958, January 21, 1961, July 13, 1963, November 8, 1975; *Saturday Review*, July 1, 1950, May 21, 1955, September 27, 1958, February 21, 1959, February 11, 1961, July 6, 1963; *Sewanee Review*, winter, 1952; *Atlantic*, November, 1954, May, 1957, November, 1961; *Yale Review*, autumn, 1954, autumn, 1955, autumn, 1968; *New Republic*, June 23, 1958, April 8, 1978; *Commonweal*, February 13, 1959; *New York Herald Tribune Book Review*, March 1, 1959, July 30, 1961; *New Yorker*, March 14, 1959, April 1, 1961.

Times Literary Supplement, February 19, 1960, June 11, 1976; *Harper's*, September, 1963; *Reporter*, September 12, 1963; *Christian Science Monitor*, January 29, 1964; *Prairie Schooner*, spring, 1965; *Partisan Review*, winter, 1965; M. L. Rosenthal, *The Modern Poets*, Oxford University Press, 1965; Howard Nemerov, *Poets on Poetry*, Basic Books, 1965; *Washington Post Book World*, December 24, 1967; Edward Hungerford, editor, *Poets in Progress*, Northwestern University Press, 1967; James Dickey, *Babel to Byzantium*, Farrar, Straus, 1968; Peter Meinke, *Howard Nemerov*, University of Minnesota Press, 1968; Julia A. Bartholomay, *The Shield of Perseus: The Vision and Imagination of Howard Nemerov*, University of Florida Press, 1972; *Chicago Review*, Volume XXV, number 1, 1973; *Contemporary Literary Criticism*, Gale, Volume II, 1974, Volume VI, 1976, Volume IX, 1978; *The Stillness in Moving Things*, Memphis State University Press, 1975; *Salmagundi*, fall, 1978; Ross Labrie, *Howard Nemerov*, Twayne, 1980.

—Sketch by David A. Guy

* * *

NETTELS, Curtis Putnam 1898-

PERSONAL: Born August 25, 1898, in Topeka, Kan.; son of Charles Henry and Nannie (Curtis) Nettels; married Elsie Patterson, December 21, 1923; children: Elsa. *Education:* University of Kansas, B.A., 1921; University of Wisconsin, M.A., 1922, Ph.D., 1925. *Home:* 303 Comstock Rd., Ithaca, N.Y. 14850.

CAREER: University of Wisconsin—Madison, instructor, 1924-26, assistant professor, 1926-31, associate professor, 1931-33, professor of history, 1933-44, chairman of department, 1939-40; Cornell University, Ithaca, N.Y., professor of American history, 1944-66, professor emeritus, 1966—. Lecturer at Harvard University, 1937-38, Columbia University, 1938, and Johns Hopkins University, 1941. *Member:* American Historical Association, Organization of American Historians, Massachusetts Historical Society, Colonial Society of Massachusetts, State Historical Society of Wisconsin (curator, 1943-44), Beta Theta Pi, Phi Beta Kappa, Phi Kappa Phi. *Awards, honors:* Guggenheim fellow, 1928; Social Science Research Council grant, 1933.

WRITINGS: The Money Supply of the American Colonies before 1720, University of Wisconsin Press, 1934, reprinted, Gordon Press, 1973; *The Roots of American Civilization,* Crofts, 1938, 2nd edition, Irvington Books, 1963; *George Washington and American Independence* (History Book Club selection), Little, Brown, 1951, reprinted, Greenwood, 1977; *The Emergence of a National Economy, 1775-1815,* Holt, 1962, reprinted, M. E. Sharpe, 1977. Work included in anthologies. Member of editorial board, *The Economic History of the United States,* eight volumes, 1945-62. Member of board of editors, *Journal of Economic History,* 1941-46, *William and Mary Quarterly,* 1943-46, *American Historical Review,* 1943-49, and *Presidential Studies Quarterly,* 1977—.

WORK IN PROGRESS: Studies and sketches in American biography.

SIDELIGHTS: Curtis P. Nettels told *CA:* "The interest that impelled me to write for publication was formed before 1915 in the period designated by Van Wyck Brooks as 'The Confident Years.' It was a time when Americans were imbued with feelings of optimism, pride in their achievements, and faith in the future. Sharing such feelings, I was moved to study and write about the American past and its relation to things present, hoping thereby to make some contribution to the welfare of the country and the betterment of mankind. The assumption was that knowledge and truth are better guides in public affairs than ignorance and falsehood."

AVOCATIONAL INTERESTS: Woodworking, gardening, music.

* * *

NEWLIN, Margaret Rudd 1925-
(Margaret Rudd)

PERSONAL: Born February 27, 1925, in New York, N.Y.; daughter of James H. and Marie (McLaughlin) Rudd; married Nicholas Newlin (a professor of English), April 2, 1956 (died July 16, 1976); children: James, David, Robin, Thomas. *Education:* Bryn Mawr College, B.A., 1947; University of Reading, Ph.D., 1951. *Home address:* Shipley Farm, Secane, Pa. 19018.

CAREER: Bryn Mawr College, Bryn Mawr, Pa., employed in office of admissions, 1948, instructor in English, 1953-54; Washington College, Chestertown, Md., instructor in English, 1955-56. Instructor in English at Harcum Junior College, 1953-54. *Member:* Poetry Society of America, Poetry Society (London, England). *Awards, honors:* International Greenwood Prize from London Poetry Society, 1969 and 1971; National Endowment for the Creative Arts fellowship, 1976-77; National Book Award nomination, 1977, for *The Snow Falls Upward;* D.Litt., Washington College, 1980.

WRITINGS—Under name Margaret Rudd: *Divided Image: A Study of Yeats and Blake,* Routledge & Kegan Paul, 1953, Haskell House, 1970; *Organiz'd Innocence: The Story of Blake's Prophetic Books,* Routledge & Kegan Paul, 1956, Greenwood Press, 1973.

Under name Margaret Newlin; poetry: *The Fragile Immigrants,* Carcanet, 1971; *Day of Sirens,* Carcanet, 1973; *The Snow Falls Upward: Collected Poems,* Ardis, 1976; *The Book of Mourning,* Ardis, 1980. Work represented in *A Galaxy of Verse,* edited by Louis Untermeyer, M. Evans, 1978. Contributor to *Critical Quarterly, Essays in Criticism,* and *Southern Review.*

WORK IN PROGRESS: A study of chief women poets from the time of Sappho to the present.

SIDELIGHTS: Margaret Rudd Newlin told *CA:* "Most serious poets, if they are honest, write in an effort to praise and capture what they love in life before it vanishes, and to frame, distance, and in some way come to terms with, that which is painful and difficult. 'It is a fearful thing to love / What death can touch,' lines which Josephine Jacobsen found on a tombstone, seem to express the impetus behind much poetry. The poet loves and names what he loves—people, nature, his own vivid sense of how it feels to be alive—in an effort to communicate across time to those who will be living when he and what he loves are gone. What matters is a sort of cry across the centuries, and the hope, vain and foolish as it may be, that in readers yet unborn, he will evoke the gut response of the tingling scalp, Emily Dickinson's 'that desirable gooseflesh,' and the shock of recognition.

"A poem must begin, as Robert Frost said, with 'a lump in the throat,' not as some would-be game with ideas and words. And, as [W. B.] Yeats warned, it will be hard work with few to recognize it as such: 'A line will take us hours maybe; / Yet if it does not seem a moment's thought, / Our stitching and unstitching has been naught.' Any poet's life is, on the whole, a solitary one, and he would be unwise to expect rewards in terms of money or instant fame. The only reason to write is because you are unable *not* to write. 'Even tomorrow,' said Montale, 'the important voices will be those of artists who, from their own isolation, echo the fatal isolation of each one of us.'"

* * *

NICOL, Eric (Patrick) 1919-
(Jabez)

PERSONAL: Born December 28, 1919, in Kingston, Ontario, Canada; son of William (an accountant) and Amelia (Mannock) Nicol; married Myrl Mary Helen Heselton (a nurse), September 13, 1955; children: Catherine, Claire, Christopher. *Education:* University of British Columbia, B.A., 1941, M.A., 1948; attended Sorbonne, University of Paris, 1949-50. *Politics:* "Anarchist, in theory; liberal, in practice." *Religion:* No church affiliation. *Home and office:* 3993 West 36th Ave., Vancouver, British Columbia, Canada V6N 2S7.

CAREER: Free-lance writer for radio and television in London, England, 1949-51; *Province* (newspaper), Vancouver, British Columbia, syndicated columnist, 1951—. *Military service:* Royal Canadian Air Force, 1942-45. *Awards, honors:* Stephen Leacock Medal for Humour, 1951, for *The Roving I,* 1956, for *Shall We Join the Ladies?,* and 1958, for *Girdle Me a Globe.*

WRITINGS: (Under pseudonym Jabez) *Sense and Nonsense,* Ryerson, 1948; (under pseudonym Jabez) *The Roving*

I, Ryerson, 1950; *Twice Over Lightly*, Ryerson, 1953; *Girdle Me a Globe*, Ryerson, 1957; *Shall We Join the Ladies?*, Ryerson, 1958; *In Darkest Domestica*, Ryerson, 1959; *An Uninhibited History of Canada*, D. Hackett, 1959, 5th edition, Musson, 1965; (with Peter Whalley) *Say Uncle: A Completely Uncalled-for History of the U.S.*, Harper, 1961; *A Herd of Yaks: The Best of Eric Nicol*, Ryerson, 1962; (with Whalley) *Russia, Anyone? A Completely Uncalled-for History of the USSR*, Harper, 1963; *Space Age, Go Home!*, Ryerson, 1964; (with Whalley) *100 Years of What?*, Ryerson, 1966; *A Scar Is Born*, Ryerson, 1968; *Vancouver*, Doubleday, 1970; *Don't Move! Renovate Your House & Make Social Contracts*, McClellan & Stewart, 1971; *Still a Nicol*, McGraw-Ryerson, 1972; *Letters to My Son*, Macmillan, 1974; *There's a Lot of It Going Around*, Doubleday, 1975; *Canada Cancelled Because of Lack of Interest*, Hurtig, 1977; (with David More) *The Joy of Hockey*, Hurtig, 1978.

Plays: "Like Father, Like Fun" (three-act), first produced in Vancouver, B.C., at Playhouse Theatre, 1966, produced as "A Minor Adjustment" on Broadway at Brooks Atkinson Theatre, October 6, 1967; "Beware the Quickly Who" (two-act children's play) first produced in Vancouver at Metro Theatre (now Holiday Theatre), 1967; "The Clam Who Made a Face" (one-act children's play) first produced in Vancouver at Holiday Theatre, 1968; "The Fourth Monkey" (three-act), first produced in Vancouver at Playhouse Theatre, 1969; "Pillar of Sand" (two-act), first produced in Ottawa, Ont., at National Theatre, 1973; "Free at Last," first produced in Vancouver at New Play Centre, 1979. Also author of three-act play, "Regulus," first produced in Vancouver at Peretz Theatre.

Television plays: "The Bathroom," 1963; "The Man from Inner Space," 1974. Also author of several dozen radio plays. Contributor to radio revue, "Inside from the Outside" (CBS), 1970—. Contributor to *Maclean's* and *Saturday Night*.

WORK IN PROGRESS: A stage play.

AVOCATIONAL INTERESTS: Tennis, badminton, gardening.

* * *

NIDA, Eugene A(lbert) 1914-

PERSONAL: Born November 11, 1914, in Oklahoma City, Okla.; son of Richard Eugene (a chiropractor) and Alma Ruth (McCullough) Nida; married Althea Lucille Sprague, 1943. *Education:* University of California, Los Angeles, A.B., 1936; University of Southern California, M.A., 1939; University of Michigan, Ph.D., 1943. *Home:* 33 Husted Lane, Greenwich, Conn. *Office:* American Bible Society, 1865 Broadway, New York, N.Y. 10023.

CAREER: Ordained Baptist minister, 1943. University of Oklahoma, Summer Institute of Linguistics, Norman, professor of linguistics, 1937-53; American Bible Society, New York City, executive secretary for translations, 1943—; United Bible Societies, New York City, translations research coordinator, 1972-79. *Member:* Linguistic Society of America (vice president, 1960), American Anthropological Association, Society of New Testament Studies, Society of Biblical Literature, Linguistic Circle of New York, Phi Beta Kappa, Pi Gamma Mu. *Awards, honors:* D.D., Eastern Baptist Seminary, 1956, and Southern California Baptist Seminary, 1959.

WRITINGS: Bible Translating, American Bible Society, 1947, 2nd edition, United Bible Societies, 1961; *Linguistic Interludes*, Summer Institute of Linguistics of University of Oklahoma, 1947; *Morphology: The Descriptive Analysis of Words*, University of Michigan Press, 1949; *Learning a Foreign Language*, Friendship, 1950; *God's Word in Man's Language*, Harper, 1952; *Customs and Cultures*, Harper, 1954, reprinted, William Carey Library, 1975; (with William A. Smalley) *Introducing Animism*, Friendship, 1959; *Message and Mission*, Harper, 1960; *A Synopsis of English Syntax*, Summer Institute of Linguistics of University of Oklahoma, 1960; (with Robert G. Bratcher) *A Translator's Handbook on Mark*, E. J. Brill, 1961; *Toward a Science of Translating*, E. J. Brill, 1964; *Religions across Cultures*, American Bible Society, 1968; (editor with Charles R. Taber) *The Theory and Practice of Translation*, E. J. Brill, 1969; *Understanding Latin Americans*, William Carey Library, 1973; *Translator's Notes on Literacy Selections*, two parts, American Bible Society, 1974; *Componential Analysis of Meaning*, [The Hague], 1975; *Exploring Semantic Structures*, [Munchen], 1975; *Language Structure and Translation: Essays by Eugene A. Nida*, Stanford University Press, 1975; *Good News for Everyone*, Word Books, 1977. Also author of *A Book of a Thousand Tongues*.

Published by United Bible Societies: (With B. M. Newman, Jr.) *Translator's Handbook on the Acts of the Apostles*, 1972; (with Newman) *Translator's Handbook on Paul's Letter to the Romans*, 1973; (with J. De Waard) *Translator's Handbook on the Book of Ruth*, 1973; (with P. Ellingworth) *Translator's Handbook on Paul's Letter to the Thessalonians*, 1975; (with D. C. Arichea, Jr.) *Translator's Handbook on Paul's Letter to the Galatians*, 1976; (with I. Loh) *Translator's Handbook on Paul's Letter to the Philippians*, 1977. Contributor of more than twenty articles to professional journals. Former editor, *The Bible Translator*; associate editor, *Practical Anthropology*.

WORK IN PROGRESS: Communicating to the Latin Mind; with Robert Bratcher, a translator's wordbook of New Testament vocabulary.

SIDELIGHTS: Eugene A. Nida has travelled in more than sixty countries doing linguistic work and checking translations in more than 200 languages. *Avocational interests:* Wood sculpturing, designing and making furniture, gardening, hiking.

* * *

NIELSEN, Helen Berniece 1918-
(Kris Giles)

PERSONAL: Born 1918, in Roseville, Ill.; daughter of Niels C. and May (Christensen) Nielsen. *Education:* Took extension course in journalism, attended Chicago Art Institute, and took U.S. defense course in aeronautical drafting. *Home:* 2622 Victoria Dr., Laguna Beach, Calif. 92651. *Agent:* Ann Elmo, 545 Fifth Ave., New York, N.Y.

CAREER: Old Globe Theatre Productions, Chicago, Ill., costumer, 1934-35; free-lance newspaper and commercial artist,, 1937-41; Air Associates, Inglewood, Calif., draftsman, 1942-43; Interstate Aircraft, Los Angeles, Calif., draftsman, 1943-44; Van Tuyl Engineering, Los Angeles, loftsman, 1945. Member of California Democratic Council, 1956-66. *Member:* Authors Guild, Hollywood Highlands Democratic Club, Adlai Stevenson Democratic Club (secretary, 1954-55; president, 1956-57).

WRITINGS—All published by Morrow, except as indicated: *The Kind Man*, Washburn, 1951; *Gold Coast Nocturne*, Washburn, 1952; *Obit Delayed*, Washburn, 1953; *Detour*, Washburn, 1953; *The Woman on the Roof*, Washburn, 1954;

Stranger in the Dark, Washburn, 1955; *Borrow the Night,* 1956; *The Crime Is Murder,* 1957; *False Witness,* Washburn, 1959; *The Fifth Caller,* 1959; *Sing Me a Murder,* 1960; *Verdict Suspended,* 1964; *After Midnight,* 1965; *A Killer in the Street,* 1967; *Darkest Hour,* 1969; *Shot on Location,* 1971; *The Severed Key,* 1973; *The Brink of Murder,* 1976. Work appears in anthologies, including *Best Detective Stories,* 1955, 1959, *Alfred Hitchcock's Hangman's Dozen,* 1962, *Ellery Queen's Double Dozen,* 1964, and *Best Legal Stories,* 1970.

WORK IN PROGRESS: Teleplays.

SIDELIGHTS: Several of Helen Nielsen's works have been filmed. *Gold Coast Nocturne* was filmed under the title "Blackout," while *The Fifth Caller* and several of her short stories and original teleplays have been presented on television. *Avocational interests:* Politics, Norwegian elkhounds.

BIOGRAPHICAL/CRITICAL SOURCES: Saturday Review, October 25, 1969, September 25, 1971; *Observer,* December 14, 1969; *New York Times Book Review,* September 12, 1971; *Spectator,* August 18, 1973.

* * *

NOBLE, David Watson 1925-

PERSONAL: Born March 17, 1925, in Princeton, N.J.; son of Charles John (an attorney) and Agnes (Konow) Noble; married Lois Keller, August 2, 1944; children: David, Jr., Jeffrey, Douglas, Patricia. *Education:* Princeton University, B.A., 1948; University of Wisconsin, M.A., 1949, Ph.D., 1952. *Religion:* Episcopalian. *Home:* 2089 Commonwealth Ave., St. Paul, Minn. 55108. *Office:* 723 Social Science, University of Minnesota, Minneapolis, Minn. 55455.

CAREER: University of Minnesota, Minneapolis, instructor, 1952-55, assistant professor, 1955-58, associate professor, 1958-65, professor of American history, 1965—. *Military service:* U.S. Army, 1943-44. *Member:* American Studies Association.

WRITINGS: The Paradox of Progressive Thought, University of Minnesota Press, 1958; *Historians against History,* University of Minnesota Press, 1965; *The Eternal Adam and the New World Garden,* Braziller, 1968; *The Progressive Mind,* Rand McNally, 1970, 2nd edition, 1980; (with Peter Carroll) *The Restless Centuries: A History of the American People,* Burgess, 1973, 2nd edition, 1979; (with Carroll) *The Free and the Unfree: A New History of the United States,* Penguin, 1977; (with Carroll and David Horowitz) *Twentieth Century Limited,* Houghton, 1980.

WORK IN PROGRESS: Negative Revolution: The Failure of the American Political Imagination.

* * *

NOBLE, John (Appelbe) 1914- (Jan, Lookout)

PERSONAL: Born January 27, 1914, in Hull, England; son of William (a railroad station master) and Georgina (Appelbe) Noble; married Marjorie Nelligan, July 20, 1940; children: Ian Appelbe, Cynthia Marjorie (Mrs. David O'Keefe). *Education:* Attended Graham Sea Training School, Scarborough, England, 1925-28; received Second Mate's Certificate, 1933, First Mate's Certificate, 1936, and Master's Certificate, 1940. *Home:* 8 Agnes Ave., North Balwyn, Melbourne, Victoria 3104, Australia. *Office:* 596 High St., East Kew, Victoria 3102, Australia.

CAREER: Bank Line Ltd., London, England, 1929-36, began as apprentice, became junior ship's officer; Union Steamship Co. of New Zealand Ltd., Wellington, ship's officer, 1936-58, ship's master, 1951-58; Port Phillip Pilots, Williamstown, Victoria, Australia, sea pilot, 1959-79; Great Circle Services Pty. Ltd., East Kew, Victoria, Australia, managing director, 1979—. *Wartime service:* Officer on merchant ships, including troopship "Wahine," 1939-45. *Member:* Company of Master Mariners of Australia, Australian Naval Institute, Royal Historical Society of Victoria, Australian Society of Authors, Returned Services League.

WRITINGS: Australian Lighthouses, Doubleday, 1966; *Hazards of the Sea: Three Centuries of Challenge in Southern Waters,* Verry, 1970; *Port Phillip: Pilots and Defences,* Hawthorn Press (Melbourne), 1973; *Port Phillip Panorama,* Hawthorn Press (Melbourne), 1975. Revised "Shipwrecks" section of *Australian Encyclopaedia,* Grolier, 1977. Contributor of articles to *Weekly News* (Auckland) under pseudonym Jan, 1957-58, and to *Sydney Bulletin* under pseudonym Lookout, 1958-59. Editor, *Journal of the Company of Master Mariners of Australia,* 1965-71.

SIDELIGHTS: John Noble told *CA:* "I started writing magazine articles to occupy time on ocean voyages as a ship's master in 1956. After becoming a pilot at Melbourne in 1959, and six years experience as editor of the *Journal of the Company of Master Mariners,* I was asked to submit a short work on Australian lighthouses. Shipwrecks are prominent in the history of lighthouses and the editor suggested a longer work on Australian shipwrecks. *Hazards of the Sea* was the result. Meanwhile the history of the Port Phillip pilots needed to be written, also other aspects of the port's maritime history. *Port Phillip: Pilots and Defences* and *Port Phillip Panorama* materialised.

"After retiring from the Pilot Service early in 1979, occupation of time again became a problem, solved by founding Great Circle Services Pty. Ltd., a company involved in the maritime industry. If this founders, or gets too big for its founder to handle, there is still a wealth of experience gleaned from a lifetime afloat to keep more volumes flowing."

* * *

NOLAN, William F(rancis) 1928- (Frank Anmar, F. E. Edwards, Michael Phillips)

PERSONAL: Born March 6, 1928, in Kansas City, Mo.; son of Michael Cahill (an insurance adjuster) and Bernadette M. (Kelly) Nolan; married Marilyn Seal, 1970. *Education:* Attended Kansas City Art Institute, 1946-47, San Diego State College (now University), 1947-48, Los Angeles City College, 1953. *Politics:* Independent. *Religion:* None. *Home:* 22720 Cavalier St., Woodland Hills, Calif.

CAREER: Has worked as a greeting card cartoonist, office clerk, aircraft inspector, retail clerk, employment agency interviewer, and motion picture actor. Exhibited art in one-man show at Spanish Village Art Center, 1949. Free-lance writer, 1956—; free-lance book and magazine editor, 1963-70. Co-chairman, Western Science Fiction Convention, 1952.

MEMBER: Allied Artists Council, Studio Art Guild, Young Painters' Workshop (treasurer, 1949), Authors Guild, Mystery Writers of America (chairman, motion picture award committee, 1970), Science Fiction Writers of America, Writers Guild of America West, Writers Guild Film Society, San Diego Fine Arts Society, San Diego Science-Fantasy Society, Dashiell Hammett Society of San Francisco (co-founder, 1977). *Awards, honors:* American Library Association selection, 1960, for *Adventures on Wheels;* Edgar Allan Poe Award, Mystery Writers of America, 1970, for *Dashiell Hammett: A Casebook,* 1972, for *Space for Hire;* doctorate in science fiction, American River College, 1975.

WRITINGS—Science fiction: *Impact 20,* Paperback Library, 1963; (editor) *Man against Tomorrow,* Avon, 1965; (editor) *The Pseudo-People,* Sherbourne, 1965; (with George Clayton Johnson) *Logan's Run,* Dial, 1967; (editor) *Three to the Highest Power,* Avon, 1968; (editor) *A Wilderness of Stars,* Sherbourne, 1969; (editor) *A Sea of Space,* Bantam, 1970; (editor) *The Future Is Now,* Sherbourne, 1970; (editor) *The Human Equation,* Sherbourne, 1971; *Alien Horizons,* Pocket Books, 1974; *Wonderworlds,* Gollancz, 1977; *Logan's World,* Bantam, 1977; *Logan's Search,* Bantam, 1980; (editor) *Science Fiction Origins,* Popular Library, 1980.

Nonfiction: (Editor) *Ray Bradbury Review* (bibliography), privately printed, 1952; (contributor) *Max Brand: The Man and His Work,* Fantasy Publishing, 1952; (editor with Charles Beaumont) *Omnibus of Speed,* Putnam, 1958; (with John Fitch) *Adventures on Wheels,* Putnam, 1959; *Barney Oldfeld,* Putnam, 1961; *Phil Hill: Yankee Champion,* Putnam, 1962; *Men of Thunder,* Putnam, 1964, revised edition published as *Selections from Men of Thunder,* Bantam, 1966; (editor with Beaumont) *When Engines Roar,* Bantam, 1964; *John Huston: King Rebel,* Sherbourne, 1965; *Sinners and Supermen,* All Star, 1965; *Dashiell Hammett: A Casebook* (biography), McNally & Loftin, 1969; *Steve McQueen: Star on Wheels,* Putnam, 1972; *Carnival of Speed,* Putnam, 1973; *Hemingway: Last Days of the Lion,* Capra Press, 1974; (editor) *The Ray Bradbury Companion,* Gale, 1975.

Mystery fiction: *Death Is for Losers,* Sherbourne, 1967; *The White Cad Cross-Up,* Sherbourne, 1969; *Space for Hire,* Lancer Books, 1971.

Also author of twenty television scripts and five motion picture scripts. Work appears in 100 anthologies and textbooks including *Adventures for Americans.* Columnist, *Badge Bar Journal,* 1956-58. Contributor of articles, short stories, and reviews to over 150 periodicals including *Sports Illustrated, Playboy, Road and Track, Prairie Schooner, Mickey Mouse Comics,* and *Armchair Detective.* Book reviewer, *Los Angeles Times,* 1964—. Contributing editor, *Rhodomagnetic Digest;* managing editor, *Gamma,* 1963; West Coast editor, *Auto,* 1964; associate editor, *Motor Sport Illustrated,* 1964; contributing editor, *Chase,* 1964. Member of advisory board, *First Printings of American Authors,* Volume I, Gale, 1977.

WORK IN PROGRESS: A chronological checklist of Ernest Hemingway's writings, with William White; a sequel to *Space for Hire; The Eyes of Night,* a collection of suspense stories; several motion picture and television projects.

SIDELIGHTS: To beginning writers, William Nolan emphatically advises, "Writers shouldn't give up!" He recalls that he began to write in lined nickel notebooks in school when he was ten years old and calculates that he wrote more than 100,000 words before submitting anything for publication. He sold only eleven items in his first four years of writing, and when he quit his job in 1956 to write full time he had made only sixteen sales; now his sales total over seven hundred.

On a more personal aspect of writing, Nolan observes: "I've never met a 'normal' writer—I mean a full time professional. If you write day in and day out for many years it means you are *driven* to do it. A strange inner chemistry demands the kind of creative release found only in written words. Sure, you do it for money—and for ego-boost—but you really do it because writing is the center of yourself and you have no choice in the matter. To write is to breathe. And, yes, it's agony part of the time, and it's hard work (all of the time) and it's frustrating and demanding—but it's also sheer joy and triumph mixed with a deep sense of personal satisfaction. The writing is *you.* If you've been born to write, no one can keep you from it: the words, the images, the people, are all inside, crying out for release. And if you *do* write, and you *do* get published, and reach those millions of minds out there in the world, then, by God, it's the greatest reward any man or woman could ask for, and nothing else you do can touch it."

Logan's Run was filmed in 1976 and was named Best Science Fiction Film of the Year by the Academy of Science Fiction and Fantasy.

BIOGRAPHICAL/CRITICAL SOURCES: Motoracing, January 6, 1961; *Automobile Quarterly,* Number 1, 1962; *Magazine of Fantasy and Science Fiction,* May, 1962, February, 1968; *Negro Digest,* December, 1965; *Books & Bookmen,* April, 1966; *Amazing Science Fiction,* August, 1966; *New York Times Book Review,* September 17, 1967, July 27, 1969; *Punch,* August 7, 1968; *Saturday Review,* June 28, 1969; *Writer's Digest,* December, 1970; *Los Angeles Times,* December 6, 1974; *American Reference Books Annual,* 1976; *Cinefantastique,* fall, 1976; *Observer,* May 8, 1977; *Times Literary Supplement,* July 8, 1977; *Future,* August, 1978.

* * *

NORBECK, Edward 1915-

PERSONAL: Born March 18, 1915, in Prince Albert, Saskatchewan, Canada; son of Gabriel and Hannah (Norman) Norbeck; married Jeanne Lewellen, 1940 (died, 1944); married Margaret Roberta Field, 1950 (divorced, 1976); married Katherine Clarke Shannon, 1977; children: (second marriage) Hannah Field, Edward Crosby, Seth Peter. *Education:* University of Michigan, B.A., 1948, M.A., 1949, Ph.D., 1952. *Home:* 3656 Overbrook, Houston, Tex. *Office:* Department of Anthropology, Rice University, Houston, Tex. 77001.

CAREER: University of Utah, Salt Lake City, 1952-54, began as instructor, became assistant professor of anthropology; University of California, Berkeley, assistant professor of anthropology, 1954-60; Rice University, Houston, Tex., associate professor, 1960-62, professor of anthropology, 1962—, chairman of anthropology and sociology department, 1960-71, dean of humanities, 1966-68. Conducted research in Japan, 1950-51, 1958-59, 1964-65, 1966, and 1974, and in Hawaii 1956. Visiting lecturer, National Science Foundation, 1962-66; Rice University, director of symposia, "Prehistoric Man in the New World," 1962, and "The Study of Personality," 1966. *Military service:* U.S. Army, Military Intelligence, 1943-47; became second lieutenant. *Member:* American Association for the Advancement of Science (fellow), Asia Society (member of advisory council), Japan America Society (member of board of directors), American Anthropological Association (fellow; program director of annual meeting, 1977), American Ethnological Society (president, 1977), Association for Asian Studies, Japanese Society for Ethnology, Society for the Scientific Study of Religion, Association for the Anthropological Study of Play, Houston Archaeological Society, Phi Beta Kappa, Phi Kappa Phi, Sigma Xi. *Awards, honors:* National Science Foundation senior post-doctoral fellow, 1958-59; research awards from National Science Foundation, Ford Foundation, Social Science Research Council, and Wenner-Gren

Foundation for Anthropological Research; Piper Foundation Award, 1972, for excellence in teaching and scholarship.

WRITINGS: Takashima, a Japanese Fishing Community, University of Utah Press, 1954; *Pineapple Town—Hawaii,* University of California Press, 1959; *Religion in Primitive Society,* Harper, 1961; (co-editor) *Prehistoric Man in the New World,* University of Chicago Press, 1964; *Changing Japan,* Holt, 1965, 2nd edition, 1976; *The Study of Personality: An Interdisciplinary Approach,* Holt, 1968; *Religion and Society in Modern Japan,* Tourmaline Press, 1970; *The Study of Japan in the Behavioral Sciences,* Rice University Studies, 1970; *Religion in Human Life: Anthropological Views,* Holt, 1974; *The Anthropological Study of Human Play,* Rice University Studies, 1974; *Ideas of Culture: Sources and Uses,* Holt, 1976; *Country to City: The Urbanization of a Japanese Hamlet,* University of Utah Press, 1978; *Forms of Play of Native North Americans,* American Ethnological Society, 1979.

Contributor: D. G. Haring, editor, *Personal Character and Cultural Milieu,* Syracuse University Press, 1956; Robert Carneiro and Gertrude E. Dole, editors, *Essays in the Science of Culture,* Crowell, 1960; F.L.K. Hsu, editor, *Psychological Anthropology: Approaches to Culture and Personality,* Dorsey, 1961, revised edition, 1972; R. J. Smith and R. K. Beardsley, editors, *Japanese Culture: Its Development and Characteristics,* Aldine, 1962; *Horizons of Anthropology,* Aldine, 1964, revised edition, 1977; G. A. DeVos, editor, *Japan's Invisible Race,* University of California Press, 1966; R. P. Dore, editor, *Aspects of Social Change in Modern Japan,* Princeton University Press, 1967; J. C. Feaver and W. Horosz, editors, *Religion in Philosophical and Cultural Perspective,* Van Nostrand, 1967; W. A. Glaser and D. L. Sills, editors, *The Government of Associations: Selections from the Behavioral Sciences,* Bedminster, 1967; J. Middleton, editor, *Gods and Rituals: Readings in Religious Beliefs and Practices,* American Museum of Natural History, 1967; L. Plotnicov and A. Tuden, editors, *Essays in Comparative Social Stratification,* University of Pittsburgh Press, 1970; *Anthropology Today,* CRM Books, 1971; A. Bharati, editor, *World Anthropology: The Realm of the Extra-Human,* Aldine, 1976; R. D. Fogelson and R. N. Adams, editors, *The Anthropology of Power,* Academic Press, 1977. Editor, *Rice University Studies* (journal), 1962—. Contributor to professional journals.

* * *

NORMAN, Donald A(rthur) 1935-

PERSONAL: Born December 25, 1935, in New York, N.Y.; son of Noah N. (with U.S. Public Health Service) and Miriam (Friedman) Norman; married Julia Lustig; children: Cynthia, Michael, Eric. *Education:* Massachusetts Institute of Technology, B.S.E.E., 1957; University of Pennsylvania, M.S.E.E., 1959, Ph.D., 1962. *Office:* Department of Psychology, San Diego State University, La Jolla, Calif. 92093.

CAREER: Harvard University, Cambridge, Mass., lecturer in psychology, 1964-66; San Diego State University, La Jolla, Calif., associate professor, 1966-69, professor of psychology, 1969—, chairman of department, 1974-78, director of program in cognitive science, 1977—. Visiting professor, University of Hawaii, 1977; fellow, Center for Advanced Study in the Behavioral Sciences, 1973-74. *Member:* American Psychological Association (fellow), Association for Computing Machinery, American Association for the Advancement of Science (fellow), Psychonomic Society, American Association for Artificial Intelligence, Cognitive Science Society (secretary-treasurer, 1979—), Human Factors Society, Society for Experimental Psychologists, Society of Laboratory Users of Computers in Psychology (member of steering committee, 1974-78), Society for Mathematical Psychology. *Awards, honors:* National Science Foundation postdoctoral fellow at Harvard University, 1962-65.

WRITINGS: Memory and Attention: An Introduction to Human Information Processing, Wiley, 1968, 2nd edition, 1976; (editor) *Models of Human Memory,* Academic Press, 1970; (with Peter Lindsay) *Human Information Processing,* Academic Press, 1972, 2nd edition, 1977; (with D. E. Rumelhart) *Explorations in Cognition,* W. H. Freeman, 1975; *Human Learning and Memory,* Scientific American Books, 1980; (editor) *Perspectives on Cognitive Science,* Erlbaum, 1980.

Contributor: (With W. D. Larkin) R. C. Atkinson, editor, *Studies in Mathematical Psychology,* Stanford University Press, 1964; (with G. A. Miller and A. S. Bregman) B. Waxman and R. W. Stacy, editors, *Computers in Biomedical Research,* Academic Press, 1965; A. Sanders, editor, *Attention and Performance I,* North-Holland, 1967; A. Sanders, editor, *Attention and Performance III,* North-Holland, 1970; *Psychology Today: An Introduction,* CRM Books, 1970; (with E. C. Carterette) E. F. Bechenbach and C. B. Tompkins, editors, *Concepts of Communication,* Wiley, 1971; J. F. Kavanagh and E. G. Mattingly, editors, *Language by Ear and by Eye: The Relationships between Speech and Reading,* MIT Press, 1972; S. Kornblum, editor, *Attention and Performance IV,* Academic Press, 1973; J. A. Deutsch, editor, *Psychological Basis of Memory,* Academic Press, 1973; F. Klix, editor, *Organismische Informationsverarbeitung: Zeichenerkennung-Begriffsbildung-Problemloesen,* Akademie-Verlag, 1974; P. Rabbitt and S. Dornic, editors, *Attention and Performance V,* Academic Press, 1974; (with A. Stevens and D. Gentner) D. Klahr, editor, *Cognition and Instruction,* Halsted, 1976; C. N. Cofer, editor, *The Structure of Human Memory,* W. H. Freeman, 1976.

Member of editorial board, Harvard University Press Cognitive Science Series and Lawrence Erlbaum Associates Cognitive Sciences Series. Contributor to *Encylopaedia of Linguistics, Information and Control.* Contributor of articles to numerous professional journals, including *American Journal of Psychology, Journal of Experimental Psychology, Contemporary Psychology,* and *Psychonomic Science.* Member of editorial board, *Cognitive Psychology, Journal of Experimental Psychology,* and *Cognitive Science.*

* * *

NORMAN, Lilith 1927-

PERSONAL: Given name is pronounced *Lie*-lith; born November 27, 1927, in Sydney, New South Wales, Australia. *Education:* Studied with Library Association of Australia. *Politics:* "Small 'l' liberal, left of centre." *Religion:* None. *Home:* 21 Rhodes Ave., Naremburn, New South Wales, 2065, Australia. *Agent address:* Curtis Brown Pty. Ltd., P.O. Box 19, Paddington, Sydney, New South Wales 2021, Australia.

CAREER: Newtown Municipal Library, Sydney, Australia, library assistant, 1947-49; Bonnington Hotel, London, England, telephonist, 1950-51; Angus & Robertson, Ltd., Sydney, bookshop assistant, 1951-53; Balmain District Hospital, Sydney, nursing trainee, 1953-56; City of Sydney Public Library, Sydney, 1956-70, began as research librarian, became children's librarian; New South Wales Department of Education, *School* Magazine, Sydney, member of editorial staff, 1970-78, editor, 1975-78; full-time writer, 1978—. *Member:* Library Association of Australia (president of Children's Libraries Section, New South Wales Division, 1969-71; branch councillor, 1969-70), Australian Society of Authors, Children's Book Council of New South Wales (treasurer, 1968-70). *Awards, honors:* Commendation from Children's Book Council Australian Book Awards, 1971, for *Climb a Lonely Hill;* Queen's Silver Jubilee Medal, 1977.

WRITINGS—All juveniles; published by Collins, except as indicated: *Climb a Lonely Hill,* 1970, Walck, 1972; *The Shape of Three,* 1971; *The Flame Takers,* 1973; *Mockingbird Man,* Hodder & Stoughton, 1977; *A Dream of Seas,* 1978; *My Simple Little Brother,* 1979. Author of a series of local histories, *Kings Cross, Paddington, Newtown,* and *The Glebe,* 1958-64, all published by the Council of City of Sydney; also author of episode for television series "Catch Kandy," 1972. Contributor to *Reading Time.* Editor, *Felis,* journal of Siamese Cat Society of New South Wales, 1965-69.

SIDELIGHTS: Lilith Norman writes: "I wonder why there is this passionate interest in writers. Writers are not special. Why not *Contemporary Plumbers*? How I took up plumbing; my philosophy of plumbing; why I plumb; plumbing the depths!. . . . It's all very odd. I know why I say I write books. I can analyse my books and pick out the reasons for this bit or that, and find reflections of my own life. But that is afterwards. It's a far more complex and subconscious process while it is actually going on, and I don't think these later rationalisations are helpful or even particularly accurate. Except, perhaps, to provide easy material for the tertiary industry that has spread like a fungus over all literature. It seems to me that a book should speak directly to the reader. If I have anything worth saying it is there, in my books, in a far more entertaining and accessible (I hope) way than a pretentious self-analysis would provide."

AVOCATIONAL INTERESTS: Animals, films, opera, conservation, reading, food, and "what makes people tick."

BIOGRAPHICAL/CRITICAL SOURCES: *Australian Women's Weekly,* December 2, 1970; *Reading Time,* December, 1970, October, 1971; H. M. Saxby, *A History of Australian Children's Literature, 1941-70,* Wentworth Books, 1971.

* * *

NOVAK, Michael 1933-

PERSONAL: Born September 9, 1933, in Johnstown, Pa.; son of Michael John and Irene Louise (Sakmar) Novak; married Karen Laub (a painter and printmaker), June 29, 1963; children: Richard, Tanya, Jana. *Education:* Stonehill College, A.B. (summa cum laude), 1956; Gregorian University (Rome, Italy), B.T. (cum laude), 1958; attended Catholic University, 1958-60; Harvard University, M.A., 1965. *Agent:* Donald Cutler, Sterling Lord Agency, Inc., 660 Madison Ave., New York, N.Y. 10021.

CAREER: Stanford University, Palo Alto, Calif., assistant professor of humanities, 1965-68; State University of New York, Old Westbury, associate professor of philosophy and religious studies, 1968-73, provost, Disciplines College, 1969-71; Rockefeller Foundation, New York, N.Y., associate director of humanities, 1973-74; Syracuse University, Syracuse, N.Y., Watson-Ledden Professor of Religious Studies, 1977-79; American Enterprise Institute, Washington, D.C., resident scholar, 1978—. Visiting professor at Union Theological Seminary, 1966, Carleton College, 1970, Immaculate Heart College, Hollywood, Calif., 1971, and University of California, Santa Barbara, 1972. Senior policy advisor to R. Sargent Shriver, 1970; speechwriter for R. Sargent Shriver, 1970, 1972, and for Edmund Muskie, 1971; member of staff, George McGovern's presidential campaign, 1972. Fellow of Institute for Society, Ethics, and the Life Sciences, 1969—. Advisor on programs in medicine and ethics, Joseph P. Kennedy, Jr. Foundation, 1971. Founder and member of board of directors, Ethnic Millions Political Action Committee.

MEMBER: Society for Values in Higher Education (member of central committee, 1969-72), American Academy of Religion (program director, 1968-72), Council on Foreign Relations, Council on Religion and International Affairs. *Awards, honors:* LL.D., Keuka College, 1970, LeMoyne College, 1976; L.H.D., Davis and Elkins College, 1971, Stonehill College, 1977; Doctor of Literature, Sacred Heart College, 1977, Muhlenberg College, 1979.

WRITINGS—All published by Macmillan, except as indicated: *The Tiber Was Silver,* Doubleday, 1961; *A New Generation: American and Catholic,* Herder & Herder, 1964; *The Open Church: Vatican II: Act II,* 1964; (editor) *The Experience of Marriage,* 1964; *Belief and Unbelief,* 1965; *A Time to Build,* 1967; (editor) *American Philosophy and the Future,* Scribner, 1968; *A Theology for Radical Politics,* Herder & Herder, 1969; *Naked I Leave* (novel), 1970; *The Experience of Nothingness,* Harper, 1970; *Ascent of the Mountain, Flight of the Dove: An Invitation to Religious Studies,* Harper, 1971, revised edition, 1978; *Politics: Realism and Imagination,* Herder & Herder, 1971; *The Rise of the Unmeltable Ethnics: Politics and Culture in the Seventies,* 1972; (with wife, Karen Laub-Novak) *A Book of Elements,* Herder & Herder, 1972; *Choosing Our King: Powerful Symbols in Presidential Politics,* 1974; *The Joy of Sports: End Zones, Bases, Baskets, Balls, and the Consecration of the American Spirit,* Basic Books, 1976; *The Guns of Lattimer,* Basic Books, 1978; (editor) *Capitalism and Socialism: A Theological Inquiry,* American Enterprise Institute for Public Policy Research, 1979. Also author of *The American Vision: An Essay on the Future of Democratic Capitalism,* 1978, and several monographs.

Contributor: Leonard Liek and David Hawke, editors, *American Colloquy,* Bobbs-Merrill, 1963; Edward Schillebeck, editor, *Concilium Dogma,* Volume I: *The Church and Mankind,* Paulist Press, 1964; William Birmingham, editor, *What Catholics Think about Birth Control,* Sheed & Ward, 1965; Daniel Callahan, editor, *Generation of the Third Eye,* Sheed & Ward, 1965; *Voluntary associations: A Study of Groups in Free Societies,* John Knox Press, 1966; Mitchell Cohen and Dennis Hale, editors, *The New Student Left: An Anthology,* Beacon Press, 1966; Elwyn A. Smith, editor, *Church-State Relations in Ecumenical Perspective,* Duquesne University Press, 1966; Sister M. Charles Borromeo, editor, *The New Nuns,* New American Library, 1967; Bernard Murchland, editor, *The Meaning of the Death of God,* Random House, 1967; *Conspiracy,* Harper, 1973; H. Wheeler, editor, *Beyond the Punitive Society,* W. H. Freeman, 1973; *Television as a Social Force,* Praeger, 1975; Marvin Barrett, editor, *The Fifth Alfred I. DuPont-Columbia University Survey of Broadcast Journalism,* Crowell, 1975.

Contributor to scholarly and general publications, including *Commentary, Harper's, New Republic,* and *Commonweal.* Associate editor, *Commonweal,* 1966-69; contributing editor, *Christian Century,* 1967—, *Christianity and Crisis,* 1968-74; member of editorial board, *Motive,* 1966-68, *Journal of*

Ecumenical Studies, 1967—, *Worldview,* 1971; member of board of advisors, *American Report,* 1970.

SIDELIGHTS: D. W. Ferm claims "anything that Michael Novak writes is bound to stimulate and provoke." Having established a reputation as an articulate religious philosopher, educator, and activist, Novak has had ample opportunity to do both. His books have explored individual and organized religion, the need for renewal and reform in religious, political, and social philosophies, the secular "religions" of politics and sports, and the many aspects of Catholic life. *Commonweal* reviewer R. A. Schroth feels that Novak is most effective as a religious journalist, in his interpretations and criticisms of "other more detached scholars' discoveries." "Novak has . . . become a severe critic of the hollowness of American culture, its invisible civic religions, its evasive amoral dessicated intellectuals and its flabby counterculture," Schroth continues in his review of *All the Catholic People.* "He offers little evidence for some of his assertions other than his own intuition and experience. But . . . he has helped transform the church."

Many reviewers seem uncertain as to how Novak's work should be received. In his *Book Week* review of *The Open Church,* Wilfred Sheed notes that Novak "goes to some pains to be charitable to his opponents" but adds that this is done "in a style just patronizing enough to infuriate them." On the other hand, F. R. McManus feels that Novak is being "most fair and indeed generous" in his treatment of the more conservative arguments and personalities of Vatican II. The transition from essay to book chapter that much of Novak's writing undergoes is also perceived as having varied effectiveness. Although Philip Deasy of *Commonweal* declares himself impressed by the breadth of Novak's interests and the quality of his perceptions in *A New Generation,* and though he believes the articles contained therein revealed a "first rate mind" and a "most refreshing candor" when originally published, he finds that "inconsistencies and even contradictions become apparent" when the articles become chapters of a book. W. E. May's review of *Belief and Unbelief* catalogues the conflicting responses that Novak's work frequently receives. He calls the book "simultaneously promising and discouraging, stimulating and frustrating, deep and shallow. Its promise, its stimulation, [and] its depth spring from its purpose . . . as well as from its substance. . . . Its discouragement, its frustration, [and] its shallowness stem from the author's bias."

Some critics offer another interpretation for this sense of conflict: that Novak intentionally draws no real conclusions, thus enabling the reader to reach his own informed decisions. Novak "has at least taken the trouble to reflect on where one must stand in deciding about intelligent belief," notes P. M. Van Buren in *Christian Century.* Mary Daly praises Novak for being "a thinker who doesn't make a cult of change but accepts it and subjects it to analysis." Yet Novak is not always engaged in such tactics. In his analysis of *The Experience of Nothingness,* J. F. Drane comments that "no symbol or institution escapes Novak's criticism. He offers helpful explanations for the widespread disillusionment among the young and is at his best interpreting today's cultural revolution." *Book World* reviewer Charles Frankel calls Novak "a philosopher of the rising generation. . . . He is passionate; he is unbending in his scorn for what exists; he wants to recover individuality, human warmth, and a sense of purpose in life." This wide-scale support of individuality is reflected in a *Saturday Review/World* reviewer's opinion that "what is best about Mr. Novak is . . . his capacity to communicate an impassioned sense of American diversity."

As a "philosopher of the rising generation" in the seventies, Novak changes his focus from theology to politics. Although his ostensible reason for writing in this period may be to extol the virtues of ethnic identity, the significance of our leader-selection processes, or the cathartic necessity of sports, reviewers have often commented on the political slant these books have taken in their approach to such diverse subjects. *Newsweek*'s Arthur Cooper and *Book World*'s B. A. Weisberger have both granted that Novak deserves to be read carefully, but Weisberger cautions that some skepticism should be exercised. Novak's analyses of given situations frequently evolve into attacks against existing powers or against those who espouse points of view contrary to his own.

New York Times Book Review critic Garry Wills sees such a slanted point of view in a serious light. "There is something dismaying about an immoral book written by a very moral man," he writes in his review of *The Rise of the Unmeltable Ethnics.* "Novak must . . . huff and puff to prove his own ethnicity, merrily inventing angers as he goes, . . . working his gentle soul into Zorba-the-Greek exhibitionism. Nothing is quite so strange as a naturally pleasant person who feels it is his duty to be unpleasant, to call civility an Anglo-Saxon deceit." The emphasis of the book shifts from a championship of ethnic identity to an effort to coalesce the varied ethnic factions in support of Edmund Muskie in the 1972 presidential election. A later book about the massacre of a group of striking Slovak miners, *The Guns of Lattimer,* approaches the subject of downtrodden ethnic minorities with more singularity of purpose. Richard Kluger notes that for Novak, *The Guns of Lattimer* is "an act of overdue ancestral homage. . . . His book, modest but insistent in its claims for his ethnic forbears, serves as an antidote of sorts to the long-running epidemic of Polish jokes, which, considered in the context offered here, are not harmless leftovers of the great American melting pot but still virulent strains in a heritage of hatred."

The Guns of Lattimer can be classed along with *The Rise of the Unmeltable Ethnics* as part of what Wills refers to as "a rapidly growing literature on the social uses of hatred." As Novak suggests in the latter book, "The enemy is educated, wealthy, powerful—and sometimes wears liberal, sometimes radical, sometimes conservative, disguise. The enemy is concentrated power. Lower-class ethnics and blacks, who lack that power, are allies." This definition of the "enemy" evidently finds its way into other books. In *The Joy of Sports,* in which Novak celebrates the existence of sports as "the highest products of civilization and the most accessible, lived, experiential sources of the civilizing spirit," John Leonard sees "one more broadside against work, rationalism, secularism, politics, science, the dreary Protestants, and reason itself." However, G. F. Gilder of *National Review* finds that it is "a brave and truthful book" that casts "rare and penetrating light on the entire crisis of Western culture and politics." In much the same way, Novak's *Choosing Our King* is commended by Dorothy Rabinowitz for being timely, thoughtful, and informing. But once again, the "enemy" reappears, this time in Novak's view of the political process, which he sees as "disproportionately masculine, WASPish, inbred and often superficial", according to John Deedy.

In these critics' opinions, Novak often "takes each of his good ideas and overworks it," as E. J. Cripps wrote of *The Joy of Sports.* In spite of his passionate biases, however, Novak still attempts to act as he recommended others to in

The Rise of the Unmeltable Ethnics: as "an intellectual who tries to give voice to [his] instincts."

BIOGRAPHICAL/CRITICAL SOURCES: America, March 14, 1964, November 6, 1965, May 3, 1969, September 12, 1970; *Commonweal,* March 20, 1964, August 21, 1964, September 6, 1968, February 18, 1972; *Library Journal,* June 1, 1964; *Book Week,* June 28, 1964; *Critic,* October, 1964; *Christian Century,* January 12, 1966, March 12, 1969, April 11, 1973; *Saturday Review,* January 6, 1968; *Book World,* May 31, 1970; *Nation,* November 9, 1970; *Best Sellers,* July 1, 1971; *New York Times Book Review,* April 23, 1972, June 13, 1976; *Newsweek,* April 24, 1972; *New York Times,* April 29, 1972; *Time,* May 8, 1972; *American Scholar,* winter, 1972-73; *Saturday Review/World,* March 23, 1974; *New Republic,* May 30, 1974.

* * *

NOWELL, Elizabeth Cameron (Elizabeth Cameron; pseudonym: Elizabeth Clemons)

PERSONAL: Daughter of Alfred George and Edith (Catton) Cameron; married Arthur Granville Robinson (a vice admiral), 1961 (died January 31, 1967); married Nelson T. Nowell, February 15, 1969 (died September 24, 1973). *Education:* San Jose State College (now University), A.B., 1928; Stanford University, M.A., 1937; additional study at Columbia University, University of Minnesota, Oxford University, and University of Pennsylvania. *Address:* P.O. Box 686, Carmel, Calif. 93921. *Agent:* Dorothy Markinko, McIntosh & Otis, Inc., 475 Fifth Ave., New York, N.Y. 10017.

CAREER: San Jose State College (now University), San Jose, Calif., member of staff, education department, 1928-39; member of staff, extension division, University of California, 1939-42; elementary editor, John C. Winston Co., 1942-43, Silver Burdett Co., 1943-44, and D. C. Heath & Co., 1944-46; University of Minnesota, Minneapolis, member of staff, English department, 1947; writer and editor, General Mills Corp, 1947; free-lance writer, 1950—. Partner, Needlework Studio, 1977-78. Member of board of directors, Community Hospital Auxiliary, 1962; member of board of directors, Visiting Nurse Association, 1965. Reading consultant, Monterey City Schools, 1959-62. Judge of needlework exhibitions, Good Samaritan Hospital Auxiliary, Los Angeles, 1977 and 1979, Phoenix Needlework Guild, 1978, Scripps Memorial Hospital Auxiliary, La Jolla, Calif., 1980, and Montalvo Center for the Arts, Saratoga, Calif., 1980. *Member:* National League of American Penwomen, League of Women Voters, International Platform Association, Soroptomist International, Pi Lambda Theta, Delta Phi Upsilon, Kappa Delta Pi, Delta Kappa Gamma, Kappa Alpha Theta, Republican Club, Woman's City Club, Embroiderers' Guild of America (member of certification board, 1975—; president, Monterey Peninsula chapter, 1977-78; member of national board, 1979—).

WRITINGS—Under name Elizabeth Cameron; all published by Grosset: *Away I Go,* 1956; *All About Baby,* 1956; *I Live on a Farm,* 1956; *A Wish for Billy,* 1956; *The Big Book of Real Fire Engines,* 1958; *The Big Book of Real Trains,* 1958; *The Big Book of Real Trucks,* 1958.

Under pseudonym Elizabeth Clemons: *The Pixie Dictionary,* John C. Winston, 1953, revised edition, 1965; *The Catholic Child's First Dictionary,* John C. Winston, 1954; *The Winston Dictionary for Canadian School Children,* John C. Winston, 1955; *Wings, Wheels and Motors,* Grosset, 1957; *Rodeo Days,* Lane, 1960; *Shells Are Where You Find Them,* Knopf, 1960; *Rocks and the World Around You,* Coward, 1960; *Big and Little,* Holt, 1961; *Tide Pools and Beaches,* Knopf, 1964; *Waves, Tides, and Currents,* Knopf, 1967; *The Seven Seas,* Knopf, 1971; *The Friendly Frog,* Harcourt, 1971; *What I Like,* Harcourt, 1971. Contributor of articles to *Better Homes and Gardens, American Home,* and other national magazines. California editor, *American Home,* 1965-70.

SIDELIGHTS: Elizabeth C. Nowell wrote *CA:* "The books I have written have all been about things in which I am interested—animals, rodeos, seas and beaches, rocks, transportation, travel, stories of people in other lands, and canvas work embroidery (more commonly called needlepoint in the United States). Most of my books are factual but I have written a few simple fiction books for young people.

"I wrote *Shells Are Where You Find Them* because there was no authentic book on shells that elementary school boys and girls could read to help them accurately identify the shells they collected. The book is simply written, but it is used by many adults because the information is arranged with scientific names as well as the more common names for easy reference. This is true of *Tide Pools and Beaches* as well.

"*Waves, Tides, and Currents* was begun after a trip to the beach with several young friends. When one of the boys asked me what caused the waves to roll in, I found that I could not explain in simple terms . . . and he told me he could not understand the information he had found in books. The book took four years to write, and I hope it is a good introduction for anyone who wants to understand the mysteries and wonders of the sea."

AVOCATIONAL INTERESTS: Shell collecting, travel, and canvas embroidery.

* * *

NOYES, Stanley 1924-

PERSONAL: Born April 7, 1924, in San Francisco, Calif.; son of James Goodman (a lumber merchant) and Winnifred (Tinning) Noyes; married Nancy Black, March 12, 1949; children: Frank, Charles, Julie. *Education:* University of California, Berkeley, A.B., 1950, M.A., 1951. *Home:* 634 East Garcia, Santa Fe, N.M. 87501. *Agent:* A. L. Hart, The Fox Chase Agency, Inc., 419 East 57th St., New York, N.Y. 10022.

CAREER: California College of Arts and Crafts, Oakland, assistant professor of humanities and dean of men, 1954-61; College of Santa Fe, Santa Fe, N.M., lecturer in humanities, 1965-71; coordinator for "Poetry in the Schools" program and other literature programs, New Mexico Arts Division, 1972—. Visiting lecturer in writing program, University of New Mexico, fall, 1976. *Military service:* U.S. Army, cavalry reconnaissance, 1943-46; received Bronze Star Medal. *Member:* P.E.N. American Center, American Civil Liberties Union (member of board of directors of northern New Mexico chapter, 1972-75), St. John's College Library Associates Committee, Rio Grande Writers Association (member of board of directors, 1976-78).

WRITINGS: No Flowers for a Clown (novel), Macmillan, 1961; (contributor) Olga Carlisle, *Poets on Street Corners,* Random House, 1969; *Shadowbox* (novel), Macmillan, 1970; *Faces and Spirits* (poems), Sunstone Press, 1974; (editor with Gene Frumkin) *The Indian Rio Grande: Recent Poems from Three Cultures,* San Marcos Press, 1977; *Beyond the Mountains beyond the Mountains* (poems), Solo Press, 1979.

Contributor to anthologies, including: *Poems Southwest,* edited by A. Wilber Stevens, Prescott College Press, 1968; *Voices from the Rio Grande,* Rio Grande Writers Association Press, 1976; *Southwest: A Contemporary Anthology,* edited by Karl Kopp and Jane Kopp, Red Earth Press, 1977; *The Poetry of Horses,* edited by William Cole, Scribner, in press. Contributor to literary journals, including *Trace, Quetzal, Desert Review, Pembroke Magazine, New Mexico Quarterly,* and *Sumac.* Poetry editor of *New Mexico,* 1973-77.

WORK IN PROGRESS: A novel, *The Truchas County War.*

SIDELIGHTS: Stanley Noyes told *CA:* "Where I live has always been important to me. I grew up in northern California, lived in Berkeley for years. For a total of almost five years I lived in France. I detest cities, except for visiting. For the last fifteen years I have lived in New Mexico, and seem to have found a place where I feel at home. There is perhaps a strange hiatus here for an American writer. Except for a short stay at the MacDowell Colony in 1976, I have never lived in the east. I have no wish to live in America east of the Missouri River.

"I think and see and feel as a Westerner, and I write because I have to. People mean a great deal to me—good friends, family. They nourish my life, which nourishes my work. But writing has never been easy, nor has publishing. A lot of stories and poems, a couple of novels, have been turned down. It would be a lie to say these experiences have been encouraging. Yet I keep on scribbling—and skiing in the mountains in the winter and walking in the mountains in the summer—and I write out of where I live, and I write what I want."

* * *

NUECHTERLEIN, Donald Edwin 1925-

PERSONAL: Born June 20, 1925, in Saginaw, Mich.; son of Edwin William and Laura Anna (Kreutzer) Nuechterlein; married Mildred Virginia Usak, 1948; children: Jan, Jill, Jeffrey, Jonathan. *Education:* University of Michigan, A.B., 1948, M.A., 1949, Ph.D., 1959; attended University of Copenhagen, 1949-50 and Oxford University, 1950. *Home:* 124 Falcon Dr., Charlottesville, Va. *Office:* Federal Executive Institute, Charlottesville, Va.

CAREER: U.S. Government, assistant reports officer in Berlin, Germany, 1946-47; U.S. Department of State, Washington, D.C., research analyst, 1952-54; U.S. Information Service, press attache, U.S. Embassy in Reykjavik, Iceland, 1954-56, desk officer in Washington, D.C., 1957-60, cultural attache, U.S. Embassy in Bangkok, Thailand, 1960-63; U.S. Department of Defense, Washington, D.C., senior staff officer, 1964-68; U.S. Office of Personnel Management, Charlottesville, Va., professor of international relations, Federal Executive Institute, 1968—. Associate lecturer, George Washington University, 1966-68; senior lecturer, University of Virginia, 1969—; Fulbright-Hayes Lecturer, University College of Wales, 1975-76. *Military service:* U.S. Navy, 1943-46. U.S. Naval Reserve, 1946-68; retired as lieutenant commander. *Member:* Council on Foreign Relations, British International Studies, Southern Political Science Association. *Awards, honors:* Rockefeller Foundation fellow, 1963-64.

WRITINGS: God's Own Country and Mine, Nyt Nordisk, 1951; *Iceland: Reluctant Ally,* Cornell University Press, 1961; *Thailand and the Struggle for Southeast Asia,* Cornell University Press, 1965; *U.S. National Interests in a Changing World,* University Press of Kentucky, 1973; *National Interests and Presidential Leadership: The Setting of Priorities,* Westview Press, 1978; (co-author) *Inside the Bureaucracy: The View from the Assistant Secretary's Desk,* Westview Press, 1978.

AVOCATIONAL INTERESTS: Sports, travel, music.

* * *

NUNN, William Curtis 1908- (Will Curtis, Ananias Twist)

PERSONAL: Born June 2, 1908, in Georgetown, Tex.; son of W. H. and Mattie E. Nunn; married Thelma Inez Petsick, June 25, 1940; children: Charles Franklin, Nancy Carolyn. *Education:* Southwestern University, B.A., 1928; University of Texas, M.A., 1931, Ph.D., 1938. *Religion:* Baptist. *Home and office:* 3801 South Dr., Fort Worth, Tex.

CAREER: Southwest Texas State Teachers College (now Southwest Texas State University), San Marcos, associate professor, 1941-44; University of Houston, Houston, Tex., associate professor, 1945-46; Texas Christian University, Fort Worth, associate professor, 1946-51, professor of history, 1951-76, professor emeritus, 1976—. Summer professor, Mexico City College, 1951, and Monterrey Technical College, 1957. Vice-president, Fort Worth Good Neighbor Council, 1958-59. *Military service:* U.S. Navy, 1944. *Member:* American Historical Association, Sons of the American Revolution, Southern Historical Association, Texas State Historical Association, Sigma Phi Epsilon, Phi Alpha Theta, Masons. *Awards, honors:* Carnegie grant for the advancement of teaching, 1950; Earl R. Davis Award, 1978, for contribution to Texas confederate history; Hillcrest Foundation grant, 1978.

WRITINGS: (Co-author) *Texas: Story of the Lone Star State,* Holt, 1948, 2nd edition, 1954; *Escape from Reconstruction,* Leo Potishman Foundation, 1956, reprinted, Greenwood Press, 1974; (co-author, under pseudonym Ananias Twist) *Snide Lights* (farce), Naylor, 1959; *Texas under the Carpetbaggers,* University of Texas Press, 1962; (editor) *Ten Texans in Gray,* Hill Junior College Press, 1968; (under pseudonym Will Curtis) *Peace Unto You,* Grosset, 1970; (co-author) *Frontier Forts of Texas,* Hill Junior College Press, 1970; (co-author) *Indians of Texas,* Hill Junior College Press, 1971; (co-author) *Women of Texas,* Hill Junior College Press, 1972; *Somervell: Story of a Texas County,* Texas Christian University Press, 1975. Author of newspaper feature, "Be Still," under pseudonym Will Curtis.

WORK IN PROGRESS: Editing, *They Too Wore the Gray,* for Hill Junior College Press; a biography of Marguerite Clark for Hillcrest Foundation.

SIDELIGHTS: William Nunn told *CA:* "I have found writing to be the most attractive hobby one can have. Still it is a discipline and should not be neglected a single day, for life is short—even if one lives to hundred and two and then is shot by an angry husband. There are so many things to be written about—particularly in history—and really there is time enough to do it too if one plans it. Yet one should write for a reader and not for oneself if there is a desire to sell the material, but to find out what that reader wants is something else again."

* * *

NYE, Robert Evans 1911-

PERSONAL: Born February 18, 1911, in Viroqua, Wis.; son of Evans McGregor and Minnie Adelle (Hermann) Nye; married Vernice Trousdale, 1954. *Education:* Milwaukee

State Teachers College, B.E., 1932; University of Wisconsin, M.A., 1942, Ph.D., 1949. *Religion:* Methodist. *Home:* 2510 Woodland Dr., Eugene, Ore. 97403.

CAREER: Teacher in public schools in Wisconsin and Illinois, 1932-48; Florence State Teachers College (now University of North Alabama), Florence, Ala., professor of music, 1949-50; University of Oregon, Eugene, professor of music education, 1950-76. *Military service:* U.S. Army, 1942-45; became sergeant. *Member:* American Federation of Musicians.

WRITINGS: (With Bjornar Bergethon) *Basic Music for Classroom Teachers,* Prentice-Hall, 1954, 5th edition, 1981; (with wife, Vernice Nye) *Music in the Elementary School,* Prentice-Hall, 1957, 4th edition, 1977; (with V. Nye, Neva Aubin, and George Kyme) *Singing with Children,* Wadsworth, 1962, 2nd edition, 1970; (with William R. Sur and others) *This Is Music,* four volumes, Allyn & Bacon, 1963; *Music for Elementary School Children* (monograph), Center for Applied Research in Education, 1963; (with V. Nye) *Exploring Music with Children,* Wadsworth, 1966; (with V. Nye and H. Virginia Nye) *Toward World Understanding with Song,* Wadsworth, 1966; (with Meg Peterson) *Teaching Music with the Autoharp,* Music Education Group, 1973; (with Ian Johnstone) *Learning Music with the Recorder,* Prentice-Hall, 1979. Contributor to professional journals.

Contributor: *Providing for Individual Differences in the Elementary School,* Prentice-Hall, 1960; *Music Education in Action,* Allyn & Bacon, 1960.

NYE, Vernice Trousdale 1913-

PERSONAL: Born December 20, 1913, in Florence, Ala.; daughter of Emmett Arthur and Minnie Pearl (Thomas) Trousdale; married Robert Evans Nye, 1954. *Education:* Florence State Teachers College (now University of North Alabama), B.S., 1945; George Peabody College for Teachers, M.A., 1948. *Home:* 2510 Woodland Dr., Eugene, Ore. 97403.

CAREER: Teacher in elementary schools in Lauderdale County, Ala., 1936-41; Central Elementary School, Florence, Ala., principal, 1941-43, teacher, 1943-48; Florence State Teachers College (now University of North Alabama), Florence, member of staff, 1948-53; George Peabody College for Teachers, Nashville, Tenn., instructor, 1953-54; worked in the public school system in Eugene, Ore., 1954-56; University of Oregon, Eugene, 1956-79, began as associate professor, became professor of education. *Member:* National Education Association, Association for Supervision and Curriculum Development, Delta Kappa Gamma.

WRITINGS: (With husband, Robert E. Nye) *Music in the Elementary School,* Prentice-Hall, 1957, 4th edition, 1977; (contributor) *Providing for Individual Differences in the Elementary School,* Prentice-Hall, 1960; (with R. E. Nye, Neva Aubin, and George Kyme) *Singing with Children,* Wadsworth, 1962, 2nd edition, 1970; (with R. E. Nye) *Exploring Music with Children,* Wadsworth, 1966; (with R. E. Nye and H. Virginia Nye) *Toward World Understanding with Song,* Wadsworth, 1966; *Essentials of Teaching Elementary School Music,* Prentice-Hall, 1974; *Music for Young Children,* W. C. Brown, 1975, revised edition, 1979.

O

OBREGON, Mauricio 1921-

PERSONAL: Born January 24, 1921, in Barcelona, Spain; son of Mauricio and Madronita (Andreu) Obregon; married Cristina Matinez-Irujo, 1952; children: Sancho, Javier, Santiago, Ines, Ana, Beltran. *Education:* Attended Stonyhurst College, 1939, Oxford University, 1939-40, and Massachusetts Institute of Technology, 1940-41; Harvard University, B.A., 1943. *Religion:* Roman Catholic. *Home:* Villa Leticia, Carretera a Suba, Bogota, Colombia. *Office:* Apartado Aereo 3529, Bogota, Colombia.

CAREER: Grumman Aircraft Engineering Corp., Bethpage, N.Y., engineering test captain, 1944-45; LANSA Airlines, Bogota, Colombia, founder and technical vice-president, 1945-47; Government of Colombia, Bogota, director general of civil aviation, 1947-48, negotiator of Bilateral Air Agreements, 1948-60, coordinator of economic planning, 1951, ambassador to Venezuela, 1955-58, and to Organization of American States (OAS), 1958-63; historian, navigator, engineer, and lecturer. Chairman, Hotel del Prado and Obregon Textile Mill, beginning 1950; chairman of board of directors, Accion Cultural Popular Colombia (educational radio and publishing network), 1965-73, and Bogota Planetarium, 1970; Avianca Airlines, member of board of directors, 1965-73, chairman, beginning 1975; president, Choco Development and Interoceanic Canal Corp., 1969-71; member of board of directors, Energy Fund (New York), 1970-73, and Colombian Tourism Corp., 1971-73. International Civil Aviation Organization, member of first council, 1948, president, beginning 1964; University of the Andes, vice-rector, beginning 1948, rector, beginning 1979. Visiting lecturer, Harvard University, 1972. *Military service:* British Army, 1938; Colombian Air Force, 1948-58; became captain. *Member:* Federation Aeronautique Internationale (honorary president), Colombian Aeroclub (honorary president), Colombian Society of Engineers, Colombian Geographic Society, Colonial Society of Massachusetts, Club of Odd Volumes (Boston), Jockey and Country Club (Bogota). *Awards, honors:* Chevalier de la Legion d'Honneur, from French government; Gran Cordon del Orden del Libertador, from Venezuelan government; Cruz del Merito Aeronautico, from Colombian government.

WRITINGS: Colombian Manual of Air Regulations and Aviation Law, Government of Colombia, 1947; (with Samual Eliot Morison) *The Caribbean As Columbus Saw It,* Little, Brown, 1964; *Ulysses Airborne,* Harper, 1971; *De los argonautas a los astronautas,* Argos Vergara (Barcelona), 1977, translation published as *Argonauts to Astronauts: An Unconventional History of Discovery,* Harper, 1980. Contributor of articles to Colombian and American periodicals. Editor and publisher, *Semana* (Bogota), 1955—.

SIDELIGHTS: Mauricio Obregon set the world lightplane speed record in 1966.

BIOGRAPHICAL/CRITICAL SOURCES: New York Times, November 4, 1971.

* * *

O'BRIEN, John Anthony 1893-1980

PERSONAL: Born January 20, 1893, in Peoria, Ill.; died April 18, 1980, in South Bend, Ind.; son of John Francis and Elizabeth T. (Powers) O'Brien. *Education:* St. Viator College, B.A., 1913, M.A., 1914; graduate study at University of Chicago, 1915, Catholic University of America, 1916-17, and University of Mexico; University of Illinois, Ph.D., 1920; Oxford University, postdoctoral study, 1939-40. *Home:* Holy Cross House, Notre Dame, Ind.

CAREER: Roman Catholic priest; University of Illinois at Urbana-Champaign, 1917-39, became Catholic chaplain and teacher of the philosophy of religion, founder of Newman Foundation, 1920; University of Notre Dame, Notre Dame, Ind., research professor of theology and author-in-residence, 1940-75. Diocesan superintendent of parochial schools, Peoria, Ill., 1924-30. Has appeared on television, including documentary report for Columbia Broadcasting System network, "Birth Control and the Law." *Member:* National Conference of Christians and Jews (co-chairman of commission on religious organizations, beginning 1950). *Awards, honors:* Freedoms Foundation George Washington Honor Medal, 1952, for best magazine article of the year interpreting American life and ideals; University of Notre Dame Laetare Medal, 1973.

WRITINGS: Silent Reading, Macmillan, 1921; *Reading: Its Psychology and Pedagogy,* Century Co., 1926; *Evolution and Religion,* Century Co., 1931, revised edition published as *God and Evolution,* University of Notre Dame Press, 1961; *The Church and Marriage,* Courtney, 1934; *Legitimate Birth Control,* Our Sunday Visitor, 1934, revised edition published as *Lawful Birth Control,* Courtney, 1934, 3rd edition published as *Natural Birth Control without Contraceptives,* Newman, 1938; *The Priesthood in a Changing World,*

Kenedy, 1936, revised edition, St. Anthony Guild Press, 1943; *The Faith of Millions,* Our Sunday Visitor, 1938, latest edition, 1974; *Religion in a Changing World,* Our Sunday Visitor, 1938; *The Power of Love,* Paulist Press, 1938; *Pathways to Happiness,* Our Sunday Visitor, 1940; *Thunder from the Left,* Our Sunday Visitor, 1941; *Discovering Mexico,* Our Sunday Visitor, 1943; *Truths to Live By,* Macmillan, 1946; *Courtship and Marriage: Happiness in the Home,* St. Anthony Guild Press, 1949.

What's the Truth about Catholics?, Our Sunday Visitor, 1950; *The Art of Courageous Living,* McMullen Books, 1950; *The American Martyrs,* Appleton, 1953, published as *First Martyrs of North America,* University of Notre Dame Press, 1960; *The Open Door,* Our Sunday Visitor, 1953; *Understanding the Catholic Faith,* Ave Maria Press, 1955; *Happy Marriage: Guidance before and After,* Hanover House, 1956; *The Life of Christ,* John Crawley, 1957; *Giants of the Faith,* Hanover House, *Twenty-Five Questions Non-Catholics Ask,* Our Sunday Visitor, 1958; *The Early Public Life of Jesus,* Catholic Know-Your-Bible Program, 1961; *Jesus Spreads His Gospel,* Catholic Know-Your-Bible Program, 1962; *The Catholic Way of Life,* Prentice-Hall, 1962; *Eternal Answers for an Anxious Age,* Prentice-Hall, 1962; *One Hundred Common Questions about Catholic Faith,* Our Sunday Visitor, 1962; *Catching up with the Church: Catholic Faith and Practice Today,* Herder, 1967; *The Inquisition: A Tragic Mistake,* Macmillan, 1973.

Editor: *Catholics and Scholarship,* Our Sunday Visitor, 1939; *Winning Converts,* Kenedy, 1948; *The Road to Damascus,* Doubleday, 1949 (published in England with *Where I Found Christ* [also see below] as *Road to Damascus Omnibus,* W. H. Allen, 1951); *Where I Found Christ,* Doubleday, 1950; *Sharing the Faith,* Our Sunday Visitor, 1951; *Sex-Character Education,* Macmillan, 1952; *Paths to Christ,* Our Sunday Visitor, 1952; *The Conquest of Life,* St. Anthony's Guild Press, 1952; *The Way to Emmaus,* McGraw, 1953 (published in England as *Road to Damascus,* Volume III, W. H. Allen, 1954), excerpts published as *Why I Became a Catholic,* Notre Dame Books, 1958; *The Vanishing Irish: The Enigma of the Modern World,* McGraw, 1953; *Roads to Rome,* Macmillan, 1954 (published in England as *Road to Damascus,* Volume IV, W. H. Allen, 1955); *Bringing Souls to Christ,* Hanover House, 1955; *Where Dwellest Thou?,* Gilbert Press, 1956 (published in England as *Road to Damascus,* Volume V, W. H. Allen, 1956); (and contributor) *Steps to Christian Unity,* Doubleday, 1964; *Family Planning in an Exploding Population,* Hawthorn, 1968; *Why Priests Leave: The Intimate Stories of Twelve Who Did,* Hawthorn, 1969; *A Treasury of Great Thoughts from Ancient to Modern Times,* Fell, 1973. Also editor of eighteen books in "Cathedral Basic Readers" series, Scott, Foresman, 1946-58.

Contributor: Ei-ichiro Nagasawa, *Contemporary American Writers,* Nan-un-do, 1950; Rawley Myers, *The Greatest Calling,* McMullen Books, 1951; *Thirtieth Anniversary Reader's Digest Reader,* Reader's Digest Association, 1951; George L. Kane, *Why I Became a Priest,* Newman, 1952; H. E. Bates, *Reader's Digest Omnibus,* Deutsch, 1952; Louis J. Putz, *The Catholic Church Today,* Fides, 1956; Philip Friedman, *Their Brothers' Keepers,* Crown, 1957.

Contributor of articles to scholarly journals and to *Saturday Evening Post, Look, Reader's Digest, Ladies' Home Journal,* and *Pageant;* contributor of newspaper features to North American Newspaper Alliance and King Features Syndicate.

WORK IN PROGRESS: The Church in a Changing World, for Hawthorn.

SIDELIGHTS: John Anthony O'Brien's *The Faith of Millions* has sold over 800,000 copies. It has been translated into ten languages, including Hungarian, Malayan, and Korean. Other books of his have appeared in ten foreign editions.

BIOGRAPHICAL/CRITICAL SOURCES: Best Sellers, July 15, 1969; *Commonweal,* August 22, 1969; *Christian Century,* April 8, 1970, July 8, 1970.†

* * *

OCKENGA, Harold John 1905-

PERSONAL: Born July 6, 1905, in Chicago, Ill.; son of Herman (employed by a railroad) and Angelina (Tetzlaff) Ockenga; married Audrey L. Williamson, August 6, 1935; children: Audrey Ockenga Oury, Aldryth Ockenga Molyneux, Harold John, Jr. *Education:* Taylor University, A.B., 1927; Westminster Theological Seminary, Th.B., 1930; University of Pittsburgh, M.A., 1934, Ph.D., 1939. *Politics:* Republican. *Religion:* Protestant. *Home:* 624 Bay Rd., Hamilton, Mass. 01936. *Office:* Gordon-Conwell Theological Seminary, South Hamilton, Mass. 01982; and Gordon College, Wenham, Mass. 01984.

CAREER: Ordained minister of Presbyterian Church, 1931; First Presbyterian Church, Pittsburgh, Pa., assistant, 1930-31; Point Breeze Presbyterian Church, Pittsburgh, pastor, 1931-36; Park Street Church, Boston, Mass., pastor, 1936-69; president of Gordon-Conwell Theological Seminary, South Hamilton, Mass., and Gordon College, Wenham, Mass., 1969—. Fuller Theological Seminary, Pasadena, Calif., president, 1947-54, 1959-63, trustee. Director, Christian Freedom Foundation. Member of President Truman's Clergymen's Mission to Europe, 1947. *Military service:* U.S. Navy Reserve, 1933-39, became lieutenant. *Member:* Academy of Political Science, National Association of Evangelicals (founder; first president, 1942-44; past chairman of international commission), World Evangelical Fellowship (president), Rotary Club and Union Club (both Boston, Mass.). *Awards, honors:* D.D. from Taylor University, 1937, Wheaton College, 1960, Fuller Theological Seminary, 1963, and Gordon College, 1968; Litt.D. from Suffolk University, 1939, Norwich University, 1962, Seattle Pacific College, 1963, and Chungang University, 1975; Hum.D. from Bob Jones College, 1944; LL.D. from Houghton College, 1946.

WRITINGS: These Religious Affections, Zondervan, 1937; *Our Protestant Heritage,* Zondervan, 1938; *Have You Met These Women?,* Zondervan, 1940; *Everyone That Believeth,* Revell, 1942; *The Comfort of God,* Revell, 1944; *Our Evangelical Faith,* Revell, 1946; *The Spirit of the Living God,* Revell, 1947; *Faithful in Christ Jesus,* Revell, 1948; *The Church in God,* Revell, 1955; *Protestant Preaching in Lent,* Eerdmans, 1956; *Power through Pentecost,* Eerdmanns, 1956; *Women Who Made Bible History,* Zondervan, 1961; *Preaching in Thessalonians,* Baker Book, 1962; *A Christian Primer,* Zondervan, 1966; *No Other Lord,* Independent School Press, 1969; (contributor) C.F.H. Henry, editor, *Prophecy in the Making,* Creation House, 1971; (contributor) David F. Wells and Clark H. Pinnock, editors, *Toward a Theology for the Future,* Creation House, 1971. Also author of *Faith in a Troubled World,* 1972. Contributor to periodicals. Chairman of board, *Christianity Today,* 1956—.

SIDELIGHTS: As an evangelical Bible teacher, Harold John Ockenga has led tours to the Holy Land on several occasions. He has also conducted missionary journeys to Asia, Africa, and Latin America and preached in Australia, New Zealand, Africa, the Orient, and Europe. *Avocational interests:* Skiing, golf, swimming.

O'CONNOR, William Van 1915-1966

PERSONAL: Born January 10, 1915, in Syracuse, N.Y.; died September 26, 1966; buried in Davis, Calif.; son of Patrick Sarsfield and Violet B. (McKnight) O'Connor; married Mary Allen, January 23, 1942; children: Willa Van, Ellen Lee, Jewett Marion. *Education:* Syracuse University, B.A., 1936, M.A., 1937; Columbia University, Ph.D., 1947. *Home:* 32 Oakside Drive, RFD 1, Davis, Calif.

CAREER: Louisiana State University, Baton Rouge, instructor, 1941-42; University of Minnesota, Minneapolis, assistant professor, 1946-55, professor of English, 1955-61; University of California, Davis, professor of English and chairman of department, 1961-66. Visiting lecturer, University of Liege, 1953-54; Berg Professor of English and American Literature, New York University, 1958; Fulbright lecturer in England, 1964-65. *Military service:* U.S. Army, Signal Corps, 1942-46; served in New Guinea and the Philippines; became staff sergeant. *Member:* Modern Language Association of America, American Association of University Professors. *Awards, honors:* Rockefeller Foundation humanities fellow, 1946-47.

WRITINGS: The New Woman of the Renaissance (literary history), Field, 1942; (with wife, Mary Allen O'Connor) *Climates of Tragedy* (literary criticism), Louisiana State University Press, 1943, reprinted, Russell, 1965; *Sense and Sensibility in Modern Poetry,* University of Chicago Press, 1948, reprinted, Gordian, 1973; *Forms of Modern Fiction: Essays Collected in Honor of Joseph Warren Beach,* University of Minnesota Press, 1948; *The Shaping Spirit: A Study of Wallace Stevens,* Regnery, 1950; *An Age of Criticism: 1900-1950* (Volume V of "Twentieth-Century Literature in America" series; see below), Regnery, 1952; (editor with Leonard Unger) *Poems for Study: A Critical and Historical Introduction,* Rinehart, 1953; *The Tangled Fire of William Faulkner* (literary criticism), University of Minnesota Press, 1954; (editor) *History of the Arts in Minnesota,* University of Minnesota Press, 1958; *Campus on the River* (short stories), Crowell, 1959; (editor) *Modern Prose: Form and Style,* Crowell, 1959; *William Faulkner* (pamphlet; Volume III of "Pamphlets on American Writers" series; see below), University of Minnesota Press, 1959, revised edition, 1965; (editor with Edward Stone) *A Casebook on Ezra Pound,* Crowell, 1959; (editor) Joseph Warren Beach, *Obsessive Images,* University of Minnesota Press, 1960; *A Key to American Literature* (volume VI of "Reader's Bookshelf of American Literature" series; see below), Crowell, 1962, special edition published separately, 1965; *The Grotesque: An American Genre,* Southern Illinois University Press, 1962; *The New University Wits and the End of Modernism,* Southern Illinois University Press, 1963; *Ezra Pound* (pamphlet; Volume XXVI of "Pamphlets on American Writers" series; see below), University of Minnesota Press, 1963; *High Meadow* (poems), Everett Edwards Press, 1964; (editor) *Seven Modern American Novelists: An Introduction,* University of Minnesota Press, 1964; *Joyce Cary* (pamphlet), Columbia University Press, 1966; *In the Cage* (play), Proscenium, 1967.

General editor: (With Frederick J. Hoffman) "Twentieth-Century Literature in America" series, six volumes, Regnery, 1951-52; (with Allen Tate, Robert Penn Warren, and J. L. Unger) "Pamphlets on American Writers" series, University of Minnesota Press, beginning 1959; "American Literary Forms" series, five volumes, Crowell, 1960, published as "Reader's Bookshelf of American Literature" series, six volumes, 1962. Contributor to *Encyclopaedia Britannica, World Book Encyclopedia,* and *Collier's Encyclopedia;* also contributor of poetry, articles, and reviews to *College English, Poetry, New York Times Book Review, Saturday Review, Story, Kenyon Review,* and *Sewanee Review.* Executive editor, *American Quarterly,* 1949-51.

WORK IN PROGRESS: Co-editing *Religion and American Literature.*†

* * *

ODDO, Gilbert L. 1922-

PERSONAL: Born February 18, 1922, in New York, N.Y.; son of Gilbert A. and Jane (Brancato) Oddo; married Marian Solberg, 1950; children: Kristine, Cathleen, David, James, Stephen. *Education:* Union College, B.A., 1948; Georgetown University, M.A., 1950, Ph.D., 1952. *Office:* Department of Political Science, University of San Diego, Alcala Park, San Diego, Calif. 92110.

CAREER: Mount St. Mary's College, Emmitsburg, Md., assistant professor, 1952-58; St. Joseph College, Emmitsburg, associate professor, 1958-62, professor of social studies, 1962-66, chairman of department, 1958-66; University of San Diego, San Diego, Calif., professor of political science, 1966—. Institute of Technology (ITESO), Guadalajara, Mexico, executive assistant to president, 1963-64, founder and director of Summer School for U.S. college students, 1964, Fulbright lecturer, 1965. *Military service:* U.S. Navy, four years, served in Pacific Theater; received three battle stars. *Member:* American Political Science Association, Catholic Association for International Peace, Association for Asian Studies. *Awards, honors:* Ford Foundation grant for Far Eastern studies, 1962; Fulbright award, 1965.

WRITINGS: These Came Home, Bruce Books, 1954; *Slovakia and Its People,* Speller, 1960; *Freedom and Equality,* Goodyear Publishing, 1979; *American Constitutional Law,* Goodyear Publishing, in press.

WORK IN PROGRESS: Rise to World Power: U.S. Foreign Policy in the 20th Century; a novel, *A String of Pearls.*

* * *

ODIORNE, George Stanley 1920-

PERSONAL: Born November 4, 1920, in Merrimac, Mass.; son of Charles Thomas and Katherine (Hosford) Odiorne; married Margaret Janet Hanna, 1943; children: Robert. *Education:* Rutgers University, B.S., 1948; New York University, Ph.D., 1957. *Religion:* Presbyterian. *Office:* School of Business, University of Massachusetts, Amherst, Mass. 01002.

CAREER: Affiliated with American Can Co., 1938-52; Rutgers University, New Brunswick, N.J., head of department of management, 1952-56; American Management Association, New York, N.Y., manager, 1956-58; General Mills, Inc., Minneapolis, Minn., personnel manager, 1958-59; University of Michigan, Ann Arbor, professor and director of Bureau of Industrial Relations, 1959-68; University of Utah, College of Business, Salt Lake City, dean, 1969-74; University of Massachusetts—Amherst, School of Business, dean, 1974-78, professor of management, 1978—. Committeeman, Bridgewater Township, N.J., and member of Township Board of Health, 1957-58. Lectures to about eighty groups annually. *Military service:* U.S. Army, 1942-46; became captain. *Member:* American Economic Association, Academy of Management, Academy of Political Science.

WRITINGS: How Managers Make Things Happen, Prentice-Hall, 1961; *Effective College Recruiting,* Bureau of

Industrial Relations, University of Michigan, 1961; *Executive Skills,* Prentice-Hall, 1962; *Personnel Policy,* C. E. Merrill, 1962; *Management by Objectives: A System of Managerial Leadership,* Pitman, 1965; *Management Decisions by Objectives,* Prentice-Hall, 1969; *Green Power: The Corporation and the Urban Crisis,* Pitman, 1969; *Training by Objectives: An Economic Approach to Management Training,* Macmillan, 1970; *Personnel Administration by Objectives,* Irwin, 1971; *Management and the Activity Trap,* Harper, 1974; *Management Objectives II: A System of Managerial Leadership for the 80's,* Pitman, 1979. Also author of *Effectiveness,* 1967. Contributor of about two hundred articles to *Nation's Business, Harper's, Factory,* and to personnel and other professional journals.

* * *

O'DONNELL, Thomas Francis 1915-

PERSONAL: Born June 2, 1915, in Oneida, N.Y.; son of Thomas F. and Ellen (Pardee) O'Donnell; married Gertrude M. Delaney, 1940; children: Noel O'Donnell Taylor, Thomas F., Jr. *Education:* Hamilton College, A.B., 1942; Syracuse University, M.A., 1947, Ph.D., 1957. *Home:* 38 Meadow Farm N., North Chili, N.Y. *Office:* Department of English, State University of New York College, Brockport, N.Y. 14420.

CAREER: Instructor in English at Hamilton College, Clinton, N.Y., 1942-44, and at Syracuse University, Syracuse, N.Y., 1945-49; Syracuse University, Utica College, Utica, N.Y., 1949-70, began as instructor, professor of English, 1965-70, chairman of Division of Languages, 1962-70; State University of New York College at Brockport, professor of English, 1970—. *Member:* Modern Language Association of America (American literature group), Phi Beta Kappa.

WRITINGS: (With Hoyt C. Franchere) *Harold Frederic,* Twayne, 1961; (with Harry F. Jackson) *Back Home in Oneida,* Syracuse University Press, 1965; (editor) Harold Frederic, *Stories of York State,* Syracuse University Press, 1966; (editor) J. K. Paulding, *The Dutchman's Fireside,* College and University Press, 1966; (editor) Adriaen Van der Donck, *A Description of the New Netherlands,* Syracuse University Press, 1968; (with Stanton Garner and Robert Woodward) *A Bibliography of Writings by and about Harold Frederick,* G. K. Hall, 1975. Contributor of articles to *American Literature.*

WORK IN PROGRESS: Collected poems of William Dean Howells.

* * *

OFFIT, Sidney 1928-

PERSONAL: Born October 13, 1928, in Baltimore, Md.; son of Barney and Lillian (Cohen) Offit; married Avodah Crindell Komito (a psychiatrist and writer), August 8, 1952; children: Kenneth, Michael Robert. *Education:* Johns Hopkins University, B.A., 1950. *Politics:* Democrat. *Religion:* Jewish. *Home:* 23 East 69th St., New York, N.Y. 10021.

CAREER: Mercury Publications, New York City, member of editorial staff, 1952-53; Macfadden Publications, New York City, member of editorial staff, 1954; free-lance writer, 1954—. Adjunct professor, New York University, 1964—; member of creative writing faculty, New School for Social Research, 1964—. Political commentator, WNEW-TV, 1975—. Curator, George Polk, Awards for distinguished achievement in journalism, 1977—. Assistant manager, Aladdin Hotel, Woodbourne, N.Y., summers, 1953-62. Chairman, 19th Precinct Community Council, 1964-80; member of New York County Committee, 1966—. *Military service:* U.S. Army Reserve, 1950-52; became captain. *Member:* P.E.N. (vice-president, 1970-74; member of executive committee, 1970—), Authors Guild (member of executive council, 1971-77, 1979—), Authors League (member of national council, 1975-78), Century Association, Reserve Officers Association. *Awards, honors:* Distinguished alumni award from Valley Forge Military Academy, 1961, for achievement in letters.

WRITINGS: (Compiler) *The Best of Baseball,* Putnam, 1956; *He Had It Made,* Crown, 1959; *The Boy Who Won the World Series,* Lothrop, 1960; *Cadet Quarterback,* St. Martin's, 1961; *The Other Side of the Street,* Crown, 1962; *Cadet Command,* St. Martin's, 1962; *Soupbone,* St. Martin's, 1963; *Cadet Attack,* St. Martin's, 1964; *Topsy Turvy,* St. Martin's, 1965; *The Adventures of Homer Fink,* St. Martin's, 1966; *The Boy Who Made a Million,* St. Martin's, 1968; *Not All Girls Have Million Dollar Smiles,* Coward, 1971; *Only a Girl Like You,* Coward, 1972; *What Kind of a Guy Do You Think I Am?,* Lippincott, 1977. Contributor to western pulp magazines, 1950-53; contributor of short stories and articles to *Saturday Evening Post, Columbia Journalism Review, New Leader, Publishers Weekly, Harpers,* and other publications. Contributing editor, *Baseball Magazine,* 1955-58; *Intellectual Digest,* associate editor, 1971-72, senior editor, 1972-74; book editor, *Politics Today,* 1978-80.

WORK IN PROGRESS: An untitled novel; a satiric treatment of man's role in "modern" marriage.

SIDELIGHTS: Sidney Offit told *CA* that when his two sons were children, "I wrote stories for the boys. My early books trace aspects of their fantasies and interests—sports, the classics, poetry, pets, friendships and first love. Ken and Mike continue to be my best friends, but they are no longer my severest critics. I have been promising to put aside teaching, editing, the other occupational vices by which I earn my way and write a novel dealing with the realities of my life at fifty. It would more than likely involve the same elements as my fiction for young readers. I wonder, I wonder."

BIOGRAPHICAL/CRITICAL SOURCES: New York Times, August 30, 1959, November 12, 1972; *Baltimore News-Post,* December 28, 1962; *Saturday Review,* January 19, 1964; *Baltimore Sun,* February 21, 1965.

* * *

OLDERMAN, Murray 1922-

PERSONAL: Born March 27, 1922, in New York, N.Y.; son of Max and Jennie (Sternberg) Olderman; married Nancy Jo Calhoun, February 28, 1945; children: Lorraine, Marcia, Mark. *Education:* University of Missouri, B.J., 1943; Stanford University, B.A., 1944; Northwestern University, M.S., 1947. *Politics:* Democrat. *Home and office:* 1740 Broadway, San Francisco, Calif. 94109.

CAREER: McClatchy Newspapers, Sacramento, Calif., cartoonist and writer, 1947-51; *Minneapolis Star,* Minneapolis, Minn., cartoonist and writer, 1951-52; Newspaper Enterprise Association, New York, N.Y., executive editor, 1952-71, editor in San Francisco, Calif., 1971—. Assistant professor, San Francisco State University, 1973-78. *Military service:* U.S. Army, Military Intelligence, 1943-46; became first lieutenant. *Member:* Football Writers Association of America (president), Phi Beta Kappa, Sigma Delta Chi. *Awards, honors:* Professional Football Writers of America Dick McCann Award, 1978.

WRITINGS: (Self-illustrated) *Nelson's Twentieth Century Encyclopedia of Baseball,* Nelson, 1962; *The Pro Quarterback,* Prentice-Hall, 1966; *The Running Backs,* Prentice-Hall, 1969; *The Defenders,* Prentice-Hall, 1973; *Tennis Clinic,* Hawthorn Books, 1976; *The Warrior Way,* California Living Books, 1976. Writer for American Broadcasting Co. radio network. Editor of "Golden Year" series, Prentice-Hall.

* * *

OLDS, Sally Wendkos 1933-

PERSONAL: Born September 20, 1933, in Philadelphia, Pa.; daughter of Samuel and Leah (Waxman) Wendkos; married Mark Olds (a radio executive), December 18, 1955; children: Nancy, Jenny, Dorri. *Education:* University of Pennsylvania, B.A. (summa cum laude), 1956. *Politics:* Democrat. *Religion:* Jewish. *Home:* 25 North Washington St., Port Washington, N.Y. 11050. *Agent:* Julian Bach Literary Agency, Inc., 747 Third Ave., New York, N.Y. 10017.

CAREER: Writer. Has worked in public relations for social agencies and business firms; has appeared on radio and television programs; teaches an adult education course on writing and selling magazine articles. *Member:* International Childbirth Education Association, American Society of Journalists and Authors, National Association of Science Writers, Association for Maternal and Child Health, National Organization for Women, Phi Beta Kappa. *Awards, honors:* First place media award from Family Service Association of America, 1973, for *Raising a Hyperactive Child.*

WRITINGS: (With Marvin S. Eiger) *The Complete Book of Breastfeeding,* Workman Publishing, 1972; (with Mark A. Stewart) *Raising a Hyperactive Child,* Harper, 1973; (with Diane Papalia) *A Child's World: Infancy through Adolescence,* McGraw, 1975, 2nd edition, 1979; *The Mother Who Works outside the Home,* Child Study Press, 1975; (with Sidney B. Simon) *Helping Your Child Learn Right from Wrong: A Guide to Values Clarification,* Simon & Schuster, 1976; (with Papalia) *Human Development,* McGraw, 1978, 2nd edition, 1980. Contributor of more than two hundred articles to national magazines, including *McCall's, Ladies' Home Journal, Family Health, Seventeen, Redbook, Ms, Parents' Magazine, Today's Health, Good Housekeeping,* and the *New York Times Magazine.*

WORK IN PROGRESS: A book about working parents, for Bantam.

* * *

OLEKSY, Walter 1930-

PERSONAL: Born June 24, 1930, in Chicago, Ill.; son of John Joseph (an elevated motorman) and Pauline (Standacher) Oleksy. *Education:* Michigan State University of Agriculture and Applied Sciences (now Michigan State University), B.A., 1955. *Politics:* Independent. *Religion:* Roman Catholic. *Home and office:* 2106 Maple Ave., Evanston, Ill. 60201. *Agent:* Adele Leone, 52 Riverside Dr., Apt. 6-A, New York, N.Y. 10024.

CAREER: City News Bureau, Chicago, Ill., reporter and rewriter, 1958; *Chicago Tribune,* Chicago, reporter, writer, and editor, 1958-65; Geyer, Oswald (advertising agency), Chicago, editor and writer, 1965-67; *Chicago Land* (magazine), Chicago, editor, 1968; Allstate Insurance Co., Northbrook, Ill., editor of *Discovery* (motor club travel magazine), 1968-71; free-lance writer, 1971—. *Military service:* U.S. Army, 1955-57; served in Germany.

WRITINGS: *One Thousand Tested Money-Making Markets for Writers,* Parker Publishing, 1973; *The Old Country Cook Book,* Nelson-Hall, 1974; *Laugh, Clown, Cry: The Story of Charlie Chaplin,* Raintree, 1976; *If I'm Lost, How Come I Found You?* (novel), McGraw, 1978; *Visitors from Outer Space,* Putnam, 1978; *Careers in the Animal Kingdom,* Messner, 1979; *Clones,* Putnam, 1979; *It's Women's Work, Too,* Messner, 1980. Former managing editor of Third Armored Division newspaper; former editor of *Progress.*

WORK IN PROGRESS: *Magic Dimes-to-Dollars Wealth Secrets,* for Parker Publishing; a sequel to *If I'm Lost, How Come I Found You?,* for McGraw.

AVOCATIONAL INTERESTS: Photography and microphotography, music, gardening, cooking, home improvement projects, dinners with friends, swimming, tennis, wilderness canoe trips, long walks.

* * *

OLIVER, Paul (Hereford) 1927-

PERSONAL: Born May 25, 1927, in Nottingham, England; son of William Norman (an architect) and Dorothy (Edmunds) Oliver; married Valerie Coxon (an artist), August 19, 1950. *Education:* Attended Harrow School of Art and Craft; Goldsmiths' College, Art Teacher's Diploma, 1948. *Home:* 12, St. Margaret's Rd., Oxford OX2 6RU, England. *Office:* Department of Architecture, Oxford Polytechnic, Headington, Oxford OX3 0BP, England.

CAREER: County Grammar School, Harrow, Middlesex, England, senior art master, 1949-61; Harrow Technical College, Harrow, part-time lecturer in music appreciation, 1949-61; Architectural Association, School of Architecture, London, England, senior lecturer in art and history of art, 1961-65, head of department of arts and history, 1965-70, head of Graduate School, 1970-73; Dartington College of Arts, Dartington Hall, Devon, England, head of department of art and design, 1973-78; Oxford Polytechnic, Headington, Oxford, England, associate head of department of architecture, 1978—. Public lecturer in art at National Gallery and Tate Gallery, London, 1955-58; visiting lecturer, Kwame Nkrumah University of Science and Technology, Ghana, and at University of Ghana, 1964; lecturer on art and folk music at English universities; illustrator and graphic designer for publishers and recording firms. Broadcasts for British Broadcasting Corp., including series, "Conversation with the Blues." Compiler and designer, U.S. Embassy, London exhibition, 1964; compiler, Arts Council of Great Britain exhibitions, 1975-76, 1979. *Member:* Architectural Association, Royal Anthropological Institute (fellow), Royal Geographical Society (fellow). *Awards, honors:* Scholarship to study American art and mass media, Salzburg Seminar in American Studies, 1955; U.S. Department of State foreign specialist's research grant to do field research on the blues, 1960; Prix d'Etranger, 1962.

WRITINGS: *Bessie Smith,* Cassell, 1959, A. S. Barnes, 1961; *Blues Fell This Morning,* Cassell, 1960, Horizon, 1962, published as *Meaning of the Blues,* Collier, 1963; *Conversation with the Blues,* Horizon, 1965; *Il Jazz,* ten volumes, Fratelli Fabbri Editori, 1965-70; *Screening the Blues,* Cassell, 1968, published as *Aspects of the Blues Tradition,* Oak Publications, 1970; *Savannah Syncopators: African Retentions in the Blues,* Stein & Day, 1969; *The Story of the Blues,* Chilton, 1969; (editor) *Shelter and Society,* Praeger, 1970; (editor) *Shelter in Africa,* Barrie & Jenkins, 1971, Praeger, 1972; (with others) *Jazz on Record,* Hanover Books, 1971; (editor) *Shelter, Sign and Symbol,* Barrie & Jenkins, 1975, Overlook Press, 1977.

Contributor: P. Gammond, editor, *The Decca Book of Jazz,* Muller, 1958; Martin Williams, editor, *The Art of Jazz,* Oxford University Press (New York), 1959; Hentoff and McCarthy, editors, *Jazz—New Perspectives,* Rinehart, 1959; Dennis Sharp, editor, *Planning and Architecture,* Barrie & Rockliff, 1967; David Warren Piper, editor, *Readings in Art and Design Education,* Davis-Poynter, 1973; C.W.E. Bigsby, editor, *Superculture,* Paul Elek, 1975; James Gowan, editor, *A Continuing Experiment,* Architectural Press, 1975; Bigsby, editor, *Aspects of Popular Culture,* Edward Arnold, 1975.

Also editor of *Shelter in Greece,* 1974. Editor, "Blues Paperbacks" series, Studio Vista, 1970-72. Contributor to *Grove's Dictionary of Music and Musicians,* 1980, and to art, architecture, jazz, and folk music publications. Editor, *Architectural Association Journal,* 1961-63.

WORK IN PROGRESS: With Ali Bakhtiar and John Donat, *The Bazaar at Isfahan, Architecture and Organization;* with Ian Davis and Ian Bentley, *Dunroamin—Conflicts of Values in the Suburb; Essays on African Shelter and Settlement.*

SIDELIGHTS: Searching out vernacular architecture and folk music, Paul Oliver has traveled throughout Europe and the United States and in many countries in Africa and the Middle East. His books have been translated into five languages. About his work, he writes: "My principal concern is with the function of the artist and builder within his society. . . . I have found that this is often best understood in terms of folk communities and I have a special interest in vernacular art forms."

* * *

OLSEN, Tillie 1913-

PERSONAL: Born January 14, 1913, in Omaha, Neb.; married Jack Olsen (a printer), 1936; children: Karla Olsen Lutz, Julie Olsen Edwards, Katherine Jo, Laurie. *Education:* High school graduate. *Home:* 1435 Laguna, #6, San Francisco, Calif. 94115. *Agent:* Elaine Markson Literary Agency, 44 Greenwich Ave., New York, N.Y. 10011.

CAREER: Worked in industry and as typist-transcriber. Visiting professor, Amherst College, 1969-70, and University of Massachusetts, 1974; visiting instructor, Stanford University, 1971; writer-in-residence, Massachusetts Institute of Technology, 1973; Regents Lecturer, University of California, 1978. *Awards, honors:* Stanford University creative writing fellowship, 1956-57; Ford grant in literature, 1959; O. Henry Award for best American short story, 1961, for "Tell Me a Riddle"; fellowship, Radcliffe Institute for Independent Study, 1962-64; National Endowment for the Arts grant, 1968; Guggenheim fellowship, 1975-76; award in literature, American Academy and National Institute of Arts and Letters, 1975; University of Nebraska, Doctor of Arts and Letters, 1979; Ministry to Women Award, Unitarian Women's Federation, 1980.

WRITINGS: Tell Me a Riddle (story collection), Lippincott, 1961, reprinted, Delacorte, 1978; (author of biographical interpretation) Rebecca Harding Davis, *Life in the Iron Mills* (nonfiction), Feminist Press, 1972; *Yonnondio: From the Thirties* (novel), Delacorte, 1974; *Silences* (nonfiction), Delacorte, 1978. Short stories appear in over fifty anthologies, including *Best American Short Stories,* 1957, 1961, and 1971, *Fifty Best American Stories, 1915-1965, Prize Stories: The O. Henry Awards, 1961, Norton Introduction to Literature,* 1977, *Elements of Literature,* 1978, and *The Modern Tradition,* 1979. Contributor to *Ms., Harper's, College English,* and *Trellis.*

WORK IN PROGRESS: Books.

SIDELIGHTS: Tillie Olsen writes about those people who, because of their class, sex, or race, have been denied the opportunity to express and develop themselves. In a strongly emotional style, she tells of their dreams and failures, of what she calls "the unnatural thwarting of what struggles to come into being but cannot."

Olsen has published relatively little, citing her own life circumstances as the cause. She was forced to delay her writing for some twenty years while working at a number of jobs and raising four children. Her novel *Yonnondio* was begun during the depression but not finished until the early seventies. As Margaret Atwood writes in the *New York Times Book Review,* "few writers have gained such wide respect on such a small body of published work. . . . Among women writers in the United States, 'respect' is too pale a word: 'reverence' is more like it. This is presumably because women writers, even more than their male counterparts, recognize what a heroic feat it is to have held down a job, raised four children, and still somehow managed to become and to remain a writer."

Olsen's prose has been praised by a number of critics. A reviewer for the *New Yorker* writes that "the strength of Mrs. Olsen's writing is remarkable." Speaking of *Tell Me a Riddle,* R. M. Elman of *Commonweal* states that "there are stories in this collection which are perfectly realized works of art." Jack Salzman of *Book World* believes that "Tillie Olsen is one of the greatest prose stylists now writing" and calls her *Yonnondio* "a magnificent novel" and "the best novel to come out of the so-called proletarian movement of the '30s."

Olsen's stories have been recorded by WBAI radio in New York City and by the Lamont Poetry Room at Harvard University. Some stories have been adapted for theatrical presentation. A collection of Olsen's manuscripts is housed in the Berg Collection at the New York Public Library.

BIOGRAPHICAL/CRITICAL SOURCES: Time, October 27, 1961; *Chicago Tribune,* October 29, 1961; *Christian Science Monitor,* November 9, 1961, September 18, 1978; *New York Times Book Review,* November 12, 1961, March 31, 1974, July 30, 1978; *New Republic,* November 13, 1961, March 30, 1974, December 6, 1975, July 29, 1978; *Commonweal,* December 8, 1961; *New York Herald Tribune Books,* December 17, 1961; *Story,* Volume I, number 1, 1964; *Nation,* April 10, 1972; *New Yorker,* March 25, 1974; *Book World,* April 7, 1974; *Village Voice,* May 23, 1974, August 7, 1978; *Ms.,* September, 1974; *Virginia Quarterly Review,* fall, 1974; *Contemporary Literary Criticism,* Gale, Volume IV, 1975, Volume XIII, 1980; Sara Ruddick and Pamela Daniels, editors, *Working It Out,* Pantheon, 1977; Tillie Olsen, *Silences,* Delacorte, 1978; *New Leader,* May 22, 1978; *New York Times,* July 31, 1978; *Atlantic,* September, 1978; *Washington Post,* September 11, 1978, March 30, 1980; *Antioch Review,* fall, 1978; *Yale Review,* winter, 1979; *American Poetry Review,* May/June, 1979.

* * *

OLSON, Harvey S(tuart) 1908-

PERSONAL: Born February 28, 1908, in Chicago, Ill; son of Nils and Hildur (Lind) Olson. *Education:* Purdue University, B.S., 1929. *Home:* 2707 Marlborough Dr., San Antonio, Tex. *Office:* 8848 Tradeway, San Antonio, Tex. 78217.

CAREER: Olson's Campus Tours, Inc., Chicago, Ill., founder and past president, 1930—; Olson Travel Organization,

Chicago, Ill., president, 1949—; Olson's Travelworld Organization, Los Angeles, Calif., founder and consultant, 1975—. Has appeared on radio and television programs. *Military service:* U.S. Navy, 1942-45; became lieutenant commander; awarded Commendation ribbon for activities in amphibious air liason in Sicily and Normandy. *Member:* Phi Kappa Sigma, Executives Club of Chicago (member of board of directors, 1962-64; president, 1964-65), Club International (Chicago), Purdue Club of Chicago (past-president), Sunset Ridge Country Club (Winnetka, Ill.). *Awards, honors:* Decorated by French government, 1960, Officer of the French Order of Touristic Merit.

WRITINGS: Aboard and Abroad (annual), Lippincott, 1953—; *Olson's Orient Guide,* Lippincott, 1962; *Olson's Hotel, Restaurant, and Shopping Guide to Europe* (annual), Lippincott, 1963—; *Olson's Complete Motoring Guide to France, Switzerland and Italy,* Lippincott, 1967; *Olson's Complete Motoring Guide to the British Isles,* Lippincott, 1967; *Olson's Complete Motoring Guide to Germany, Austria, and the Benelux Countries,* Lippincott, 1968.

SIDELIGHTS: Harvey S. Olson abandoned an engineering career to become a professional traveler after his first visit to Europe in 1929. Since then he has spent a combined total of thirteen years in Europe, crossing the Atlantic more than one hundred times. He has also traveled extensively in the Far East.

AVOCATIONAL INTERESTS: Golf.

* * *

OLSON, Sigurd F(erdinand) 1899-

PERSONAL: Born April 4, 1899, in Chicago, Ill.; son of Lawrence J. and Ida May (Cedarholm) Olson; married Elizabeth Dorothy Uhrenholdt, August 8, 1921; children: Sigurd Thorn, Robert Keith. *Education:* Attended Northland College, 1916-18; University of Wisconsin, B.Sc., 1920; University of Illinois, M.S., 1931. *Home:* 106 Wilson E., Ely, Minn. 55731. *Agent:* Marie Rodell-Frances Collin Literary Agency, 141 East 55th St., New York, N.Y. 10022.

CAREER: Ely Junior College, Ely, Minn., chairman of biology department, 1922-35, dean, 1936-45; affiliated with department of zoology, American Army University, Shrivenham, England, 1945; employed by Information and Education Division, U.S. Army, European Theater of Operations, 1945-46; free-lance writer and lecturer. Consultant to U.S. Department of Interior, beginning 1962, President's Quetico-Superior Committee, Izaak Walton League of America, Time-Life Books, National Geographic Books, Readers Digest publications, and Kodansha-International/U.S.A. Ltd. *Military service:* U.S. Army, 1918. *Member:* National Parks Association (president, 1954-60), Ecological Society of America, American Association for the Advancement of Science, Nature Conservancy, Wilderness Society (member of executive committee; president, 1968-71), Association of Interpretive Naturalists (fellow), Cosmos Club (Washington, D.C.), Explorers Club, Sierra Club. *Awards, honors: The Singing Wilderness,* chosen as one of forty-two significant books of 1956 by the American Library Association, and as one of ten books of the century by a native Minnesotan during Minnesota Centennial of 1957; Pi Delta Epsilon journalism award, 1959; L.H.D., Hamline University, 1960; D.Sc. from Northland College, 1961, Macalester College, 1963, and Carleton College, 1965; University of Wisconsin—Green Bay faculty award; Silver Antelope award, Boy Scouts of America, 1963; Isaak Walton League of America, named to Hall of Fame and received Founders Award, 1963; H. M. Albright Medal, American Scenic and Historical Preservation Society, 1963; John Muir Award, Sierra Club, 1967; Dimock Award, ACA, 1969; distinguished service award, Upper Mississippi Basin Commission, 1975.

WRITINGS—Published by Knopf, except as indicated: *The Singing Wilderness,* 1956; *Listening Point,* 1958; *The Lonely Land,* 1961; *Runes of the North,* 1963; *The Hidden Forest,* Viking, 1969; *Open Horizons* (autobiography), 1969; *Sigurd F. Olson's Wilderness Days,* 1972; *Reflections from the North Country,* 1976. Contributor of articles to newspapers and magazines.

WORK IN PROGRESS: Echo Trail.

SIDELIGHTS: Sigurd F. Olson has explored by canoe much of the wilderness country of the North from the Canadian border known as the Quetico-Superior to the Arctic Coast. Olson's explorations provide the material for his books. Concerning *Open Horizons,* David McCord comments: "What Mr. Olson has done is to give us in tremendous drama on a wilderness stage the substance of a sentence he has quoted from Archibald MacLeish: 'The task of a man is not to discover new worlds, but to discover his own world in terms of human comprehension and beauty.' . . . I have never read anything quite like [*Open Horizons*], anything that testifies so eloquently to the value of the wilderness or pleads so profoundly the cause of conservation."

BIOGRAPHICAL/CRITICAL SOURCES: Life, March, 1962; *Atlantic,* June, 1969; *Harper's,* June, 1969; *Christian Science Monitor,* June 20, 1969, November 28, 1969; *New York Times Book Review,* September 28, 1969.

* * *

OPOTOWSKY, Stan 1923-

PERSONAL: Born April 13, 1923, in New Orleans, La.; son of Soloman and Fannie (Latter) Opotowsky; married Martha Anne Coble; children: Scott Peter, Anne Amanda. *Education:* Attended Tulane University. *Office:* American Broadcasting Co., 1330 Avenue of the Americas, New York, N.Y. 10019.

CAREER: Times-Picayune, New Orleans, La., writer, 1938-42; United Press International (UPI), writer in New Orleans, Denver, Colo., and New York City, 1946-50; *Sea Coast Echo,* Bay St. Louis, Miss., publisher, 1950-52; *New York Post,* New York City, writer and editor, beginning 1952; American Broadcasting Co., New York City, began as assignment editor for ABC-TV News, named assistant assignment manager, director of operations for television news documentaries, 1974-75, director of television news coverage, 1975—. Cinematographer and film editor. *Military service:* U.S. Marine Corps, combat correspondent, 1942-45. *Member:* National Press Club (Washington, D.C.).

WRITINGS: The Longs of Louisiana, Dutton, 1960; *TV: The Big Picture,* Dutton, 1961, revised edition, Collier, 1962; *The Kennedy Government,* Dutton, 1961; *Men behind Bars,* Pinnacle Books, 1972.†

* * *

O'ROURKE, William (Andrew) 1945-

PERSONAL: Born December 4, 1945, in Chicago, Ill.; son of William Andrew (a general manager) and Elizabeth (Kompare) O'Rourke. *Education:* University of Missouri—Kansas City, B.A., 1968; Columbia University, M.F.A., 1970. *Home:* 8 Park St., South Hadley, Mass. 01075. *Office:* Department of English, Mount Holyoke College, South Hadley, Mass. 01075.

CAREER: Kean College of New Jersey, Union, instructor in journalism, 1973-75; Rutgers University, New Brunswick, N.J., assistant professor of English, 1975-78; Mount Holyoke College, South Hadley, Mass., assistant professor of English, 1978—. *Awards, honors:* Creative Artists Public Service Award, New York State Council on the Arts, 1975.

WRITINGS: The Harrisburg 7 and the New Catholic Left, Crowell, 1972; *The Meekness of Isaac,* Crowell, 1974; (editor) *On the Job: Fiction About Work by Contemporary American Writers,* Random House, 1977.

WORK IN PROGRESS: Idle Hands, to be published by Delacorte.

* * *

ORZECK, Arthur Z(alman) 1921-

PERSONAL: Born November 23, 1921, in Atoka, Okla.; son of Michael (an insurance agent) and Beatrice (Byers) Orzeck; married Marilyn Adelman, September 15, 1956 (divorced, 1965); children: Elise, Toren. *Education:* University of Southern California, A.B., 1951; University of Texas, Ph.D., 1954. *Office:* Veterans Administration Hospital, Sepulveda, Calif. 91343.

CAREER: Veterans Administration Hospital, Sepulveda, Calif., coordinator of Admissions Testing Program, 1960—; El Tory Publishing Co., Simi Valley, Calif., co-owner, 1972—; University of Southern California, Los Angeles, clinical associate professor, 1973-74. *Military service:* U.S. Army, 1943-45; received two battle stars. *Member:* American Society of Clinical Hypnosis (fellow).

WRITINGS—All with Al Hendrickson: *Guitar Melody Playing,* Carl Fischer, 1948; *Duets for Classical Guitar,* Carl Fischer, 1965; *The Fretted Bass,* El Tory, 1972; *Fretted Bass Arpeggios,* El Tory, 1973; *Deluxe Encyclopedia of Electric Bass Chords, Arpeggios and Scales,* Mel Bay, 1974; *Deluxe Guitar Arpeggio Studies,* Mel Bay, 1975; *Guitar Duets on Great Classic Themes,* Mel Bay, 1975; *Jazz Guitar Duets,* Mel Bay, 1976; *Chord Symbol Standardization,* Ernie Ball Publishing, 1980. Contributor to *American Journal of Psychiatry, Journal of Pastoral Care,* and *American Journal of Clinical Hypnosis.*

WORK IN PROGRESS: Sex, the Intimate Fraud: Do You Get What You Come For? and *The Zap Trance,* both with Jody Milligan.

* * *

OSBORNE, Cecil G. 1904-

PERSONAL: Born December 10, 1904, in Oklahoma City, Okla.; son of Schuyler Colfax (a real estate broker) and Harriet (Gillette) Osborne; married Isobel Herbert Virgin, December 3, 1926; children: Michael Bruce, Sherilyn. *Education:* Studied at Baylor University, 1922-23, Columbia University, 1924-25, and City College (now City College of the City University of New York), 1926; Southern Baptist Theological Seminary, Th.B., 1929. *Politics:* Independent. *Home:* 58 North El Camino Real, San Mateo, Calif. 94401. *Office:* 19 Park Rd., Burlingame, Calif. 90410.

CAREER: Baptist minister in Chicago, Ill., 1929-36, and of First Baptist Church, Burlingame, Calif., 1936-70. Founder and director, Burlingame Counseling Center. Served on general council of the American Baptist Convention. *Member:* California Association of Marriage and Family Counselors, Yokefellows, Inc. (president and director of local group). *Awards, honors:* D.D., University of Redlands, 1948.

WRITINGS: The Art of Understanding Yourself, Zondervan, 1967; *The Art of Understanding Your Mate,* Zondervan, 1970; *You're In Charge,* Word Books, 1972; *The Art of Learning to Love Yourself,* Word Books, 1976; *The Art of Becoming a Whole Person,* Zondervan, 1978; *The Art of Getting Along with People,* Zondervan, 1980; *Primal Integration,* Word Books, 1980.

AVOCATIONAL INTERESTS: Collecting archaeological artifacts, especially Roman glassware of the pre-Christian era.

* * *

OSIPOW, Samuel H(erman) 1934-

PERSONAL: Born April 18, 1934, in Allentown, Pa.; son of Louis M. (a businessman) and Tillie (Wolfe) Osipow; married Sondra Feinstein, August 26, 1956; children: Randall, Jay, Reva, David. *Education:* Lafayette College, B.A., 1954; Columbia University, M.A., 1955; Syracuse University, Ph.D., 1959. *Home:* 575 Enfield Rd., Columbus, Ohio 43209. *Office:* Department of Psychology, Ohio State University, 1945 North High St., Columbus, Ohio 43210.

CAREER: University of Wisconsin—Madison, lecturer in education, 1961; Pennsylvania State University, University Park, assistant professor of psychology and counselor, 1961-67; Ohio State University, Columbus, associate professor, 1967-69, professor of psychology, 1969—, chairperson of department, 1973—. Research associate in education at Harvard University, 1965; visiting professor at Tel-Aviv University, 1972. *Military service:* U.S. Army Reserve, 1954-63, active duty, 1959-60; became captain. *Member:* American Psychological Association (fellow).

WRITINGS: Theories of Career Development, Appleton, 1968, 2nd edition, 1973; (with W. B. Walsh) *Strategies in Counseling for Behavior Change,* Appleton, 1970; (editor with Walsh) *Behavior Change in Counseling,* Appleton, 1970; (editor) *Emerging Woman: Career Analysis and Outlook,* C. E. Merrill, 1975; (with Tiedeman, Katz, and Miller-Tiedeman) *The Cross-sectional Story of Early Career Development,* American Personnel and Guidance Association, 1978; (with Walsh and Tosi) *A Survey of Counseling Methods,* Dorsey, 1980. Contributor to counseling, personnel, and psychology journals. Editor, *Journal of Vocational Behavior,* 1970-75, and *Journal of Counseling Psychology,* 1975-81.

WORK IN PROGRESS: Further research on vocational counseling and on occupational stress.

* * *

OTT, William Griffith 1909-

PERSONAL: Born February 21, 1909, in Wilmington, Del.; son of David Lewis and Greta (Griffith) Ott; married, 1961; children: (previous marriage) Nancy, William G., Jr., David C. *Education:* University of Delaware, B.A., 1932; LaSalle Extension University, LL.B., 1948. *Home:* 508 Milltown Rd., Wilmington, Del. 19808. *Office:* Goldey Beacom College, Wilmington, Del. 19808.

CAREER: Worked as program director and announcer for radio station WDEL, Wilmington, Del.; affiliated with American Bridge Co., New York, N.Y., 1934; W. H. Neal & Sons, Hurlock, Md., canning plant manager, 1935-36; *Dorchester News,* Hurlock, editor and business manager, 1935-37; Goldey Beacom College, Wilmington, director of law and assistant director of administration, 1938-78, currently president. Consultant to Delaware Credit Union

League. *Member:* Eastern Business Teachers Association, Delaware State Business Teachers Association, New Castle County (Del.) Legal Secretaries Association (honorary member), Kappa Alpha.

WRITINGS: Credit World—The Phantom Profession, Retail Credit Men's Association, 1948; (with R. Robert Rosenberg) *College Business Law,* with instructor's manual, McGraw, 1961, 5th edition, edited by Edward E. Byers, 1978; (with Rosenberg) *Business and the Law,* with instructor's manual, McGraw, 1975; (with Rosenberg) *Schaum's Outline of College Business Law,* McGraw, 1977. Contributor to periodicals.

WORK IN PROGRESS: A short course in practical application of credit theory for use by the average consumer; a consumer's guide to consumer rights and obligations.

SIDELIGHTS: In order to gather material for his feature stories, William Ott has taken trips into the Atlantic with commercial fishing fleets and gone to islands in the Chesapeake Bay area for stories of people and their accomplishments. Former students of his law classes in a tri-state area formed the W. G. Ott Law Association in 1952. The association now has a membership of nearly one thousand men and women who are interested in the law, although not necessarily lawyers. Ott told *CA:* "Success in writing and teaching comes from one's wide and variegated experiences that open avenues of communication to all levels and sectors of our society."

AVOCATIONAL INTERESTS: Gardening, camping, work with young people.

* * *

OTTO, Herbert Arthur 1922-

PERSONAL: Born May 19, 1922, in Berlin, Germany; son of Arthur Curt (a businessman) and Frieda (Franck) Otto; married Sarah Thorpe, May 15, 1952 (divorced April, 1967); married Roberta Aikman (a group facilitator), December 30, 1968 (divorced September, 1979); children: (first marriage) Frieda, Curt, Sally. *Education:* University of Michigan, A.B., 1946; Tulane University, M.S.W., 1950; Harvard University, M.Sc., 1955; Florida State University, Ph.D., 1956. *Home:* 1006 South Marjan St., Anaheim, Calif. 92806. *Office:* National Center for the Exploration of Human Potential, San Diego, Calif.

CAREER: University of Georgia, Athens, assistant professor of mental health education, 1952-60; University of Utah, Salt Lake City, associate professor of social work, 1960-67; Stone Foundation, Chicago, Ill., director of research, 1967-69; National Center for the Exploration of Human Potential, San Diego, Calif., president, 1969—. Professor at San Diego State University, 1971—. President of Utah State Conference on Public Welfare; member of board of directors, National Conference on Family Relations, 1970-73. Consultant to Achievement Motivation Systems. *Military service:* U.S. Army, 1942-44. *Member:* American Academy of Social Workers, American Society for Group Psychotherapy and Psychodrama, American Association of Marriage and Family Counselors (fellow), National Council on Family Therapists (member of board of directors).

WRITINGS: The Otto Pre-Marital Schedules: Three Educational Instruments for Use in Pre-Marital Counseling, Consulting Psychologists Prèss, 1961; *Manual for Pre-Marital Counseling,* Consulting Psychologists Press, 1961; (with Nina Garton) *The Development of Theory and Practice in Social Casework,* C. C Thomas, 1964; (contributor) Richard H. Klemer, editor, *Counseling in Marital and Sexual Problems: A Physician's Handbook,* Williams & Wilkins, 1965; (editor) *Explorations in Human Potentialities,* C. C Thomas, 1966; *Guide to Developing Your Potential,* Scribner, 1967; (editor with John Mann) *Ways of Growth,* Grossman, 1968; (editor) *Human Potentialities: The Challenge and the Promise,* Warren Green, 1968; *More Joy in Your Marriage,* Hawthorn, 1969.

(Editor) *The Family in Search of a Future,* Appleton, 1970; *Group Methods to Actualize Human Potential: A Handbook,* Holistic Press, 1970, 3rd revised edition, 1973; *The Family Cluster: A Multi-Base Alternative* (monograph), Holistic Press, 1971; (editor) *The New Sexuality,* Science & Behavior Books, 1971; (editor) *Love Today: A New Exploration,* Association Press, 1972; (with Roberta Otto) *Total Sex: Developing Sexual Potential,* Peter H. Wyden, 1972; *Fantasy Encounter Games,* Nash Publishing, 1972; *Marriage and Family Enrichment: New Perspectives and Programs,* Abingdon, 1976; *The New Sex Education,* Association Press, 1978; (editor with James W. Knight) *Dimensions in Wholistic Healing: New Frontiers in the Treatment of the Whole Person,* Nelson-Hall, 1979. Contributor to professional journals, including *Journal of Human Relations, Family Life Coordinator, Christian Century, Group Psychotherapy,* and *Educational Record.*

WORK IN PROGRESS: Research on human potential, humanistic psychology, expanding awareness, and on pleasure, divorce, and the function of society, with books expected to result.

SIDELIGHTS: Herbert Arthur Otto wrote *CA:* "I was a clinician and therapist when I discovered the implications of the human potential hypothesis. Since then I have been more and more convinced that the social matrix is the prime determinant in the unfoldment of human possibilities. Most of my work is directed toward this end."

* * *

OUTLER, Albert C(ook) 1908-

PERSONAL: Born November 17, 1908, in Thomasville, Ga.; son of John Morgan and Gertrude (Dewberry) Outler; married Carlotta Smith; children: Frances Outler Allsop, David Stevens. *Education:* Wofford College, A.B., 1928; Emory University, B.D., 1933; Yale University, Ph.D., 1938. *Religion:* Methodist. *Home:* 6019 Lakehurst, Dallas, Tex. 75230. *Office:* Perkins School of Theology, Southern Methodist University, Dallas, Tex. 75275.

CAREER: Duke University, Durham, N.C., professor, 1938-45; Yale University, New Haven, Conn., professor, 1945-51; Southern Methodist University, Perkins School of Theology, Dallas, Tex., professor, 1951-79. Official observer, *Vaticanum Secundum,* Rome, Italy, 1962-65. Summer professorships at various universities, including the Ecumenical Institute, Bossey, Switzerland; lecturer at 36 universities. Delegate, First North American Conference on Faith and Order, Oberlin, Ohio, 1957, Third World Conference on Faith and Order, Lund, Sweden, 1952, General Conference of the Methodist Church, 1960, 1964, World Council of Churches, New Delhi, India, 1961, and General Conference of the United Methodist Church, 1968, 1970, 1972, 1976; delegate and vice-chairman, Fourth World Conference on Faith and Order, Montreal, 1963.

MEMBER: American Society of Church History (vice-president, 1962-63; president, 1963-64), American Theological Society (president, 1960-61; secretary, 1961-62), World Council of Churches (member of working committee, Faith and Order Commission, 1954—; chairman, Theological Study Commission, North American section, 1954-63), National Council of Religion in Higher Education, National Association of Biblical Instructors, Duodecim Theological Discussion Group, Professional Discussion Group, North Texas Conference (member, Board of Evangelism), Phi Beta Kappa (past president, Texas Gamma), Town and Gown Club, The Elizabeth Club (New Haven, Conn.). *Awards, honors:* D.D., Wofford College, 1953, Kalamazoo College, 1962; Southern Methodist University Alumni Award, 1961; L.H.D., Lycoming College, 1964, Ohio Wesleyan University, 1967, Duke University, 1974, Loyola University of the South, 1978, Catholic University of America, 1979; LL.D., University of Notre Dame, 1966; S.T.D., General Theological Seminary, 1967; Litt.D., Emory University, 1968, Southwestern University, 1975; American Academy of Arts and Sciences fellow.

WRITINGS: Psychotherapy and the Christian Message, Harper, 1954; *St. Augustine: Confessions and Enchiridion,* Westminster, 1955; *The Christian Tradition and the Unity We Seek,* Oxford University Press, 1957; (author of preface) *The Crucial Task of Theology,* John Knox, 1958; (author of foreword) *Protestant Patriarch,* John Knox, 1961; (editor and contributor) *John Wesley,* Oxford University Press, 1964; *Methodist Observer at Vatican II,* Paulist/Newman, 1967; *Who Trusts in God,* Oxford University Press, 1968; *Evangelism in the Wesleyan Spirit,* Tidings, 1972; *Theology in the Wesleyan Spirit,* Tidings, 1975.

Contributor: *The Vitality of the Christian Tradition,* Harper, 1944; *A Companion to the Study of St. Augustine,* Oxford University Press, 1955; *Natural Law and Natural Rights,* Southern Methodist University Press, 1955; *The Tragic Vision and the Christian Faith,* Association Press, 1957; *The Nature of the Unity We Seek,* Bethany, 1958; *How My Mind Has Changed in the Last Ten Years,* Meridian, 1961; *That the World Might Believe,* Woman's Society of Christian Service of the Methodist Church, 1966. Contributor to religious and professional publications. Member of editorial committee, "Library of Protestant Thought."

WORK IN PROGRESS: Editing four volumes of John Wesley's sermons, for Clarendon Press.

AVOCATIONAL INTERESTS: Gardening, photography, stamp collecting, hi-fi.

* * *

OXNARD, Charles (Ernest) 1933-

PERSONAL: Born September 9, 1933, in Durham, England; son of Charles (an engineer) and Frances Anne (Golightly) Oxnard; married Eleanor Mary Arthur, February 2, 1959; children: Hugh Charles Neville, David Charles Guy. *Education:* University of Birmingham, B.Sc. (first class honors), 1955, M.B., and Ch.B., 1958, Ph.D., 1962. *Home:* 820 Oak Knoll Cir., Pasadena, Calif. 91106. *Office:* Graduate School, University of Southern California, Los Angeles, Calif. 90007.

CAREER: Queen Elizabeth Hospital, Birmingham, England, house physician, 1958-59, house surgeon, 1959; University of Birmingham, Birmingham, research fellow, 1959-62, lecturer, 1962-65, senior lecturer in anatomy, 1965-66; University of Chicago, Chicago, Ill., associate professor, 1966-70, professor of anatomy, anthropology, and evolutionary biology, 1970-78, faculty associate of Center for Graduate Studies, 1969-78, master of Biology Collegiate Division and associate dean of Biological Sciences Graduate Division and Pritzker School of Medicine, 1972-73, dean of Biological Sciences Graduate Division, 1973-78; University of Southern California, Los Angeles, professor and dean of graduate school, 1978—. Research associate, Field Museum, 1968—; overseas associate, University of Birmingham, 1970—.

MEMBER: Society for Study of Human Biology (treasurer, 1962-66), American Society of Biomechanics (president, 1979—), American Society of Zoologists, American Association for the Advancement of Science, Anatomical Society of Great Britain and Ireland (councillor, 1972—), and other scientific, anatomical, zoological, evolutionary, and human biology societies; Phi Beta Kappa, Sigma Xi. *Awards, honors:* Research grants from U.S. Department of Health, Education, and Welfare, 1963-66 and 1967-70, U.S. Public Health Service, 1967-70, and National Science Foundation, 1971, 1974, and 1977; D.Sc., University of Birmingham, 1975; named honorary professor, University of Hong Kong, 1977.

WRITINGS: Form and Pattern in Human Evolution, University of Chicago Press, 1973; (with J. T. Stern, Jr.) *Primate Locomotion: Some Links with Evolution and Morphology,* Albert J. Phiebig, 1973; *Uniqueness and Diversity in Human Evolution: Morphometric Studies of Australopithecines,* University of Chicago Press, 1975; *Human Fossils: The New Revolution,* Encyclopaedia Britannica, 1977. Also author of over one hundred published scientific papers in the area of morphology and human evolution, and about twenty in the area of primate diseases, especially vitamin deficiency. Member of editorial board, *American Journal of Anatomy,* 1972—, *Annals of Human Biology,* 1973—, and *American Journal of Physical Anthropology,* 1974—.

WORK IN PROGRESS: A book, *The Order of Man;* other studies in primate and human evolution and in the biomechanics of animal form.

P

PACE, R(alph) Wayne 1931-

PERSONAL: Born May 15, 1931, in Wanship, Utah; son of Ralph W. (a retailer and wholesaler) and Elda (Fernelius) Pace; married Gae Tueller, March 19, 1953; children: Michael, Rebecca, Lucinda, Gregory, Angela, Lavinia. *Education:* University of Utah, B.S., 1953; Brigham Young University, M.S., 1957; Purdue University, Ph.D., 1960. *Politics:* Republican. *Religion:* Church of Jesus Christ of Latter-day Saints (Mormon). *Home:* 95 North Paradise Dr., Orem, Utah 84057. *Office:* Department of Communication, Brigham Young University, Provo, Utah 84602.

CAREER: Parsons College, Fairfield, Iowa, associate professor of speech and drama, beginning 1960, head of department, 1961-62; Fresno State College (now California State University, Fresno), assistant professor of public address and communication, 1962-66, head of area, 1962-66; University of Montana, Missoula, professor of speech communication and head of department, 1966-72; University of New Mexico, Albuquerque, professor of speech communication and chairman of department, 1972-78; Brigham Young University, Provo, Utah, professor of communication, 1978—. Director, lecturer, and small-group leader of communication workshops for church leaders, school personnel, and community development programs. Executive director, Organizational Associates (consultants), 1971—. *Military service:* U.S. Army, 1953-55.

MEMBER: International Communication Association (president, 1970-71), Speech Communication Association of America, American Business Communication Association, American Association for the Advancement of Science (fellow), Western Speech Communication Association (president, 1978-79).

WRITINGS: (Editor with Brent D. Peterson and Terrence R. Radcliffe) *Communicating Interpersonally: A Reader,* C. E. Merrill, 1973; (with Robert R. Boren) *The Human Transaction: Facets, Functions, and Forms of Interpersonal Communication,* Scott, Foresman, 1973; (with Peterson and Gerald M. Goldhaber) *Communication Probes,* Science Research Associates, 1974, 2nd edition, 1977; (with Boren and Peterson) *Communication Behavior and Experiments: A Scientific Approach,* Wadsworth, 1975; (with Peterson and M. Dallas Burnett) *Techniques for Effective Communication,* Addison-Wesley, 1979. Contributor to numerous journals, including *Journal of Applied Psychology, Personnel Journal, Improvement Era, Instructor, Journal of Business Communication, Communication Education,* and *Journal of Western Speech Communication.*

* * *

PACKER, J(ames) I(nnell) 1926-

PERSONAL: Born July 22, 1926, in Twyning, Gloucestershire, England; son of James Percy (a clerk) and Dorothy (Harris) Packer; married Ethel Mullett; children: Ruth, Naomi, Martin. *Education:* Corpus Christi College, Oxford, B.A., 1948, M.A. and D.Phil., both 1954; also attended Wycliffe Hall, Oxford, 1949-52. *Politics:* "Eclectic." *Religion:* Anglican. *Office:* Regent College, 2130 Wesbrook Mall, Vancouver, British Columbia, Canada V6T 1W6.

CAREER: Anglican clergyman; assistant curate in Birmingham, England, 1952-54; Tyndale Hall, Bristol, England, tutor, 1955-61; Latimer House, Oxford, England, librarian, 1961-64, warden, 1964-69; Tyndale Hall, principal, 1970-71; Trinity College, Bristol, associate principal, 1971-79; Regent College, Vancouver, British Columbia, professor of historical and systematic theology, 1979—. Visiting professor at Westminster Theological Seminary, 1968; adjunct professor, Gordon-Conwell Seminary, 1975—. *Member:* Society for the Study of Theology, Tyndale Fellowship for Biblical Research.

WRITINGS: "Fundamentalism" and the Word of God, Eerdmans, 1958; (translator and editor with O. R. Johnston) *Luther's Bondage of the Will,* Revell, 1958; *Evangelism and the Sovereignty of God,* Inter-Varsity Press, 1961; *God Has Spoken,* Westminster, 1965, 2nd edition, Inter-Varsity Press, 1980; (with A. M. Stibbs) *The Spirit within You,* Hodder & Stoughton, 1967; *Knowing God,* Inter-Varsity Press, 1973; *I Want to Be a Christian,* Tyndale House, 1977; *Knowing Man,* Cornerstone, 1979; *Beyond the Battle for the Bible,* Cornerstone, 1980.

WORK IN PROGRESS: The Refining Fire, a history of the Puritans; *The Way of Salvation;* research on biblical, historical, and systematic theology.

AVOCATIONAL INTERESTS: Music (Western classical and early American jazz), cricket, railroads.

* * *

PALMER, Dave Richard 1934-

PERSONAL: Born May 31, 1934, in Ada, Okla.; son of William Turner (stepfather) and Lorena (Clardy) Glover; married Ludelia Clemmer, April 13, 1957; children: Allison, Kersten. *Education:* U.S. Military Academy, B.S., 1956; Duke University, M.A., 1966; attended Army War College, 1972-73. *Religion:* Protestant. *Home:* 2636 South Lynn St., Arlington, Va. 22202. *Office:* Organization of the Joint Chiefs of Staff, Pentagon, Washington, D.C.

CAREER: U.S. Army, armor service, career officer, 1956—, currently brigadier general; U.S. Military Academy, West Point, N.Y., professor of military history, 1966-69; overseas duty in Germany, 1957-60 and 1969-71, combat in Vietnam, 1967, and 1971-72; assigned to Office of Chief of Staff, Washington, D.C., 1973-76; assigned to Fort Hood, Tex., 1976-79; assigned to Joint Chiefs of Staff, Washington, D.C., 1979—. *Member:* Association of the U.S. Army, Armor Association. *Awards, honors*—Military: Legion of Merit, Bronze Star, and Air Medal.

WRITINGS: The River and the Rock: The History of Fortress West Point, 1775-1783, Greenwood Press, 1969; (with A. Sidney Britt) *The Art of War in the 17th and 18th Centuries,* West Point Press, 1969; *Readings in Current Military History,* West Point Press, 1969; *The Way of the Fox: American Strategy in the American War, 1775-1783,* Greenwood Press, 1975; *The Summons of the Trumpet: America-Vietnam in Perspective,* Presidio Press, 1978.

WORK IN PROGRESS: A book on change in the 19th century and its impact on warfare.

SIDELIGHTS: Dave Palmer told *CA:* "Being a serious student of military history adds a degree of perspective that augments significantly my efforts to be a truly professional soldier. And publishing some of the results of my studies may help others in their own efforts to be or to understand professional soldiers."

* * *

PALMER, Richard Edward 1933-

PERSONAL: Born November 6, 1933, in Phoenix, Ariz.; son of Edward Y. and Agnes Mae (Smith) Palmer; married Bette Louise Wheaton, September 15, 1956; children: Kay, Kent, Scott. *Education:* Phoenix College, A.A., 1953; University of Redlands, B.A. (magna cum laude), 1955; Claremont Graduate School (in conjunction with University of Redlands), M.A., 1955, Ph.D., 1959. *Politics:* Democrat. *Religion:* Society of Friends (Quaker). *Home:* 866 Grove, Jacksonville, Ill. 62650. *Office:* MacMurray College, Jacksonville, Ill. 62650.

CAREER: MacMurray College, Jacksonville, Ill., assistant professor of English and humanities, 1959-64, associate professor of humanities and world literature, 1964-69, professor of philosophy and world literature, beginning 1969, professor of philosophy and English, 1976—, director of humanities core literature program, 1972-76. Research fellow, Institute of Hermeneutics, University of Zurich, 1964-65, and University of Heidelberg, summer, 1965; guest researcher, University of Heidelberg, 1971-72; visiting professor of humanities, University of Minnesota, spring, 1976. Guest lecturer and speaker on hermeneutics at several universities, colleges, conferences, and workshops in the United States and Germany. *Member:* Modern Language Association of America, Society for Phenomenology and Existential Philosophy, Hegel Society of America, Heidegger Conference of Scholars, American Comparative Literature Association, Society for Values in Higher Education. *Awards, honors:* American Council of Learned Societies fellowship in Switzerland and Germany, 1964-65; National Endowment for the Humanities fellowship in Germany, 1971-72, summer fellowships, 1977, 1978.

WRITINGS: (Contributor) Richard Bender, editor, *The Teacher in the University,* National Council of Churches (Nashville), 1967; *Hermeneutics: Interpretation Theory in Schleiermacher, Dilthey, Heidegger, and Gadamer,* Northwestern University Press, 1969; (contributor) Harald Weinrich, editor, *Positionen der Negativitaet,* Fink, 1975; (contributor) Michel Benamou and Charles Caramello, editors, *Performance in Postmodern Culture,* Coda Press, 1978; (contributor) William V. Spanes, editor, *Heidegger and the Idea of Literature,* Indiana University Press, 1979; (contributor) Peter McCormick and Stephen Kresic, editors, *Modern Hermeneutics and Classical Authors,* Ottawa University Press, 1980; (contributor) Guttorm Floistad, editor, *Philosophy of Science,* Nijhoff, 1980; (translator with Thomas Sheehan) Edmund Husserl, *The Brittanica Article and the Amsterdam Lectures,* Nijhoff, 1980.

Contributor of translations: Husserl, *Phenomenology and Existentialism,* edited by Don Ihde and Richard Zaner, Capricorn Books, 1974; Hans-Georg Gadamer, *Philosophical Hermeneutics,* edited by David Linge, University of California Press, 1976; (with Jim Morgan) Dieter Heinrich, *New Perspectives in German Literary Criticism,* edited by Richard E. Amacher and Victor Lange, Princeton University Press, 1979. Contributor of articles, reviews, and translations to numerous professional publications, including *Modern Drama, Cultural Hermeneutics, Journal of Religion, Boundary 2,* and *Eros.*

WORK IN PROGRESS: A six volume historical anthology of hermeneutics, *A Hermeneutics Compendium; A Hermeneutics Reader: Essays in Philosophical Hermeneutics; On the Hermeneutical Matrix: The Phenomenology of Textual Encounter; Nietzsche and the Postmodern Turn in Hermeneutics; A Short History of Hermeneutics.*

SIDELIGHTS: Richard E. Palmer's interest is hermeneutics, the study of the principles of interpretation. He told *CA:* "Martin Heidegger has said, 'a thinker thinks one thought.' That is, beneath the varied output of every thinker can be found a guiding question that is the key to his thought.

"I do not consider myself a thinker in Heidegger's sense of the word, but rather an interpreter of thinkers. Yet I do find a guiding question in my own endeavors: What would a postmodern philosophy of text interpretation be like? It is evident that down through history there have been a variety of modes of text interpretation. These modes reflect certain assumptions about language, history, metaphysics, the sacred, the function [and reading] of texts, and of human beings in the world. There is a marked contrast in the character of these assumptions in premodern times (antiquity and the middle ages) and in modern times (since the Renaissance and Reformation)."

Palmer continues: "The lively hermeneutical ferment of the past decades can be deepened, I believe, by a study of the history of text interpretation. It is a great step to bring philosophy, expecially contemporary phenomenology, into conjunction with the problem of text interpretation. It will also be a major step to bring into this conjunction an awareness of the historical development of philosophies of interpretation. This will enable us to perceive the contrasts and relative strengths of premodern, modern, and postmodern philosophies of interpretation."

PANGLE, Thomas L(ee) 1944-

PERSONAL: Surname rhymes with "angle"; born November 29, 1944, in Gouverneur, N. Y.; son of James Lee (an attorney) and Helen (a teacher; maiden name, Carey) Pangle. *Education:* Attended Yale University, 1962-64; Cornell University, A.B., 1966; University of Chicago, Ph.D., 1972. *Religion:* Episcopalian. *Home:* 8 Linden St., Toronto, Ontario, Canada M4Y 1V6. *Office:* Department of Political Economy, University of Toronto, Toronto, Ontario, Canada M5S 1A1.

CAREER: Yale University, New Haven, Conn., 1971-79, began as assistant professor, became associate professor of political philosophy; University of Toronto, Toronto, Ontario, associate professor of political philosophy, 1979—. *Member:* American Political Science Association, Canadian Political Science Association, Northeastern Political Science Association, Boston Area Conference for the Study of Political Thought, Phi Beta Kappa. *Awards, honors:* Woodrow Wilson fellow, 1966-67; National Security Education Seminar fellow, 1973; National Endowment for the Humanities fellow, 1975-76.

WRITINGS: Montesquieu's Philosophy of Liberalism: A Commentary on the Spirit of the Laws, University of Chicago Press, 1972; *The Laws of Plato,* Basic Books, 1980. Also author, with Klaus Knorr and others, of *Historical Dimensions of National Security Problems.* Contributor to *American Political Science Review, Essays in Arts and Sciences, Thomist,* and *Yale Review.*

WORK IN PROGRESS: The Moral and Political Philosophy of Nietzsche.

* * *

PAPANEK, Gustav F(ritz) 1926-

PERSONAL: Born July 12, 1926, in Vienna, Austria; son of Ernst (an educator) and Helene (a physician; maiden name, Goldstern) Papanek; married Hanna Kaiser (a sociologist), June 13, 1947; children: Thomas H., Joanne R. *Education:* Cornell University, B.S., 1947; Harvard University, A.M., 1949, Ph.D., 1951. *Home:* 2 Mason St., Lexington, Mass. 02173. *Office:* Department of Economics, Boston University, 705 Commonwealth Ave., Boston, Mass. 02215.

CAREER: Harvard University, Cambridge, Mass., research associate, 1949-51; U.S. Government, Washington, D.C., Department of Agriculture, economist, 1951, Department of State, Technical Cooperation Administration, deputy chief of program planning for South and Southeast Asia, 1951-53; Harvard University, lecturer in department of economics, 1958-74, consultant on taxation and development to Harvard Law School, 1953-54, adviser on economics and acting project director, Harvard Advisory Group to Pakistan, 1954-58, member of staff of Harvard Development Advisory Service, Center for International Affairs, 1958-71, deputy director, 1958-65, and director, 1966-70, director of Harvard Advisory Group to Indonesia, 1971-74; Boston University, Boston, Mass., professor of economics and chairman of department, 1974—, interim director of Center for Asian Development Studies, 1977—. Consultant to United Nations, Ford Foundation, and Agency for International Development. *Military service:* U.S. Army, 1944-46.

MEMBER: Society for International Development (member of council, 1970-72), Association for Comparative Economic Studies (member of executive committee, 1969-72), American Economic Association, American Agricultural Economics Association, Association for Asian Studies.

WRITINGS: A Plan for Planning: The Need for a Better Method of Assisting Underdeveloped Countries on Their Economic Policies, Center for International Affairs, Harvard University, 1961; *Pakistan's Development: Social Goals and Private Incentives,* Harvard University Press, 1967; (editor and contributor) *Development Policy: Theory and Practice,* Harvard University Press, 1968; (editor with Jesse W. Markham) *Industrial Organization and Economic Development: In Honor of E. S. Mason,* Houghton, 1970; (with others) *Decision Making for Economic Development: Text and Cases,* Houghton, 1971; (editor with Walter P. Falcon, and contributor) *Development Policy II: The Pakistan Experience,* Harvard University Press, 1971; (editor and contributor) *The Indonesian Economy,* Praeger, 1980.

Contributor: *International Conciliation,* Carnegie Endowment for International Peace, 1960; *Organization, Planning and Programming for Economic Development,* U.S. Government Printing Office, 1963; Guy Benveniste and Warren F. Ilchman, editors, *Agents of Change: Professionals in Developing Countries,* Praeger, 1969; Colin Legum, editor, *The First UN Development Decade: Lessons for the 1970's,* Praeger, 1970; Dudley Sears and Michael Faber, editors, *The Crisis in Planning,* Chatto & Windus, 1972. Contributor to *Public Policy* (yearbook); contributor of monographs, articles, reviews, and notes to professional publications.

WORK IN PROGRESS: Comparative Development Strategies: Japan, China, India and Pakistan.

* * *

PAPER, Herbert H(arry) 1925-

PERSONAL: Born January 11, 1925, in Baltimore, Md.; son of Solomon and Rose (Greenberg) Paper; married Bess G. Brandwein, August 29, 1949; children: Susan R., James J. *Education:* Attended Yeshiva College (now University), 1940-41; University of Colorado, B.A., 1943; University of California, Berkeley, graduate study, 1944; University of Chicago, M.A., 1948, Ph.D., 1951. *Religion:* Jewish. *Home:* 3172 South Farmcrest, Cincinnati, Ohio 45213. *Office:* School of Graduate Studies, Hebrew Union College, 3101 Clifton Ave., Cincinnati, Ohio 45220.

CAREER: Cornell University, Ithaca, N.Y., research associate in division of modern languages, 1952-53; University of Michigan, Ann Arbor, Mich., assistant professor, 1953-57, associate professor, 1957-62, professor in department of Near Eastern studies, 1962-77, professor of linguistics and chairman of department, 1963-77; Hebrew Union College, Cincinnati, Ohio, professor and dean of school of graduate studies, 1977—. Member of board of trustees, Center for Applied Linguistics (Arlington, Va.). *Military service:* U.S. Army, 1943-46; became technical sergeant. *Member:* Linguistic Society of America, American Oriental Society, American Association of Jewish Studies. *Awards, honors:* Fulbright fellowship to Iran, 1951-52.

WRITINGS: (With M. A. Jazayery) *The Writing System of Modern Persian,* American Council of Learned Societies, 1955; *The Phonology and Morphology of Royal Achaemenid Elamite,* University of Michigan Press, 1955; (with Jazayery and others) *English for Iranians,* American Council of Learned Societies, 1955; (with Jazayery) *Modern Persian Reader,* Volume I (with M. Farzan): *Elementary,* Volume II: *Intermediate,* Volume III (with P. Avery): *Advanced,* University of Michigan Press, 1963; (editor of translation) V. S. Rastorgueva, *A Short Sketch of the Grammar of Persian,* Research Center in Anthropology, Folklore, and Linguistics, Indiana University, 1964; (editor of translation) D. A.

Shafeev, *A Short Grammatical Outline of Pashto,* Research Center in Anthropology, Folklore, and Linguistics, Indiana University, 1964; (editor of translation) V. I. Abaev, *A Grammatical Sketch of Ossetic,* Research Center in Anthropology, Folklore, and Linguistics, Indiana University, 1964; (editor with T. A. Sebeok, C. A. Ferguson, and C. T. Hodge) *Linguistics in Southwest Asia and North Africa,* Mouton & Co., 1970; (contributor of translation) Irving Howe and Eliezer Greenberg, editors, *Voices from the Yiddish,* University of Michigan Press, 1972; (contributor of translations) Carol Saivetz and Sheila Woods, editors, *August 12, 1952: The Night of the Murdered Poets,* American Conference on Soviet Jews, 1972; *Hatorah beparsityehudit* (title means "A Judeo-Persian Pentateuch"), Ben-Zvi Institute, Hebrew University, 1972; (editor) *Language and Texts: The Nature of Linguistic Evidence,* Center for Coordination of Ancient and Modern Studies, University of Michigan, 1975; *A Judeo-Persian Book of Job,* Israel Academy of Sciences and Humanities, 1976; (with Jes P. Asmussen) *The Song of Songs in Judeo-Persian,* Historical-Philosophical Section, Royal Danish Academy (Copenhagen), 1977; (editor) *Jewish Languages: Theme and Variations,* Association for Jewish Studies, 1978.

Contributor to *Encyclopaedia Judaica.* Contributor and translator of more than fifty articles, reviews, and translations to academic journals, including *Language, Judaism, Language Sciences, Source, Current Anthropology, Studies in Bibliography and Booklore,* and *Journal of the American Oriental Society.*

SIDELIGHTS: Herbert Paper has lived in England, Denmark, India, Iran, and Israel. He reads more than a dozen languages and speaks French, German, Hebrew, Persian, and Yiddish.

* * *

PARKE, Ross D(uke) 1938-

PERSONAL: Born December 17, 1938, in Huntsville, Ontario, Canada. *Education:* University of Toronto, B.A., 1962, M.A., 1963; University of Waterloo, Ph.D., 1965. *Office:* Department of Psychology, University of Illinois, Urbana, Ill. 61820.

CAREER: University of Wisconsin—Madison, assistant professor, 1965-68, associate professor, 1968-70, professor of psychology, 1970-72; Fels Research Institute, Yellow Springs, Ohio, chief of social development section, 1972-75; University of Illinois at Urbana-Champaign, professor of psychology, 1975—. Fels Clinical Professor of Research Pediatrics at University of Cincinnati, 1972. *Awards, honors:* Research grants from National Institute of Mental Health, 1965-66, National Science Foundation, 1967-69, 1970-75, and National Institute of Child Health and Human Development, 1978-81.

WRITINGS: (Editor) *Readings in Social Development,* Holt, 1969; (editor) *Recent Trends in Social Learning Theory,* Academic Press, 1972; (with E. M. Hetherington) *Child Psychology,* McGraw, 1975, 2nd edition, 1979. Member of editorial board, *Child Development, Journal of Experimental Child Psychology,* and *Human Development.*

* * *

PARKER, Nancy Winslow 1930-

PERSONAL: Born October 18, 1930, in Maplewood, N.J.; daughter of Winslow Aurelius (a textile executive) and Beatrice (Gaunt) Parker. *Education:* Mills College, B.A., 1952; additional study at Art Students League, 1956, 1957, and School of Visual Arts, 1966-67. *Home:* 51 East 74th St., New York, N.Y. 10021.

CAREER: National Broadcasting Co., Inc. (NBC), New York City, sales promoter, 1956-60; New York Soccer Club, New York City, sports promoter, 1961-63; Radio Corp. of America (RCA), New York City, sales promoter, 1964-67; Appleton-Century-Crofts, Inc. (publishers), New York City, art director, 1968-70; Holt, Rinehart & Winston, Inc. (publishers), New York City, graphic designer, 1970-72; freelance writer and illustrator of children's books, 1972—. *Member:* Society of Illustrators, Bichon Frise Club of America (past member of board of directors), Mills College Club of New York. *Awards, honors:* Jane Tinkham Broughton fellowship in writing for children, Bread Loaf Writers Conference, 1975; Notable Children's Book in the field of social studies, 1975, for *Warm as Wool, Cool as Cotton; The Goat in the Rug* cited as "best of the season" in children's books, *Saturday Review,* 1976; *Willy Bear* received "year's best children's book" citation, *Philadelphia Inquirer,* and Christopher Award, both 1976.

WRITINGS—Juvenile; self-illustrated; published by Dodd, except as indicated: *The Man with the Take-Apart Head,* 1974; *The Party at the Old Farm,* Atheneum, 1975; *Mrs. Wilson Wanders Off,* 1976; *Love from Uncle Clyde* (Junior Literary Guild selection), 1977; *The Crocodile under Louis Finneberg's Bed,* 1978; *The President's Cabinet* (nonfiction; Junior Literary Guild selection), Parents' Magazine Press, 1978; *The Ordeal of Byron B. Blackbear,* 1979; *Puddums, the Cathcarts' Orange Cat,* Atheneum, 1980; *Poofy Loves Company* (Junior Literary Guild selection), 1980; *The Spotted Dog,* 1980.

Illustrator: John Langstaff, *Oh, A-Hunting We Will Go!* (songbook; Junior Literary Guild selection), Atheneum, 1974; Carter Hauck, *Warm as Wool, Cool as Cotton: The Story of Natural Fibers,* Seabury, 1975; Blood and Link, *The Goat in the Rug,* Parents' Magazine Press, 1976; Kantrowitz, *Willy Bear* (Book-of-the-Month Club selection), Parents' Magazine Press, 1976; Langstaff, *Sweetly Sings the Donkey* (songbook), Atheneum, 1976; Lawler, *The Substitute,* Parents' Magazine Press, 1977; Langstaff, *Hot Cross Buns and Other Old Street Cries* (songbook), Atheneum, 1978; Yolen, *No Bath Tonight* (Junior Literary Guild selection), Crowell, 1978.

WORK IN PROGRESS: A book on American presidential history for children; several fictional works for children; making wood constructions combining oils, wood carving, and electric lights.

SIDELIGHTS: Nancy Winslow Parker writes: "I cannot remember when I have not been interested in children's literature. As a writer, the field has limitless potential for fantasy and the joy of creation. As an illustrator, the opportunity to let yourself go in wild interpretation is an artist's dream come true."

AVOCATIONAL INTERESTS: Travel (Hawaii, West Indies, France), all things French (history, theater, literature, language, painting, architecture), carpentry, squash, tennis, gardening.

* * *

PARKER, Robert B(rown) 1932-

PERSONAL: Born September 17, 1932, in Springfield, Mass.; son of Carroll Snow (a telephone company executive) and Mary Pauline (Murphy) Parker; married Joan Hall (an education specialist), August 26, 1956; children: David F., Daniel T. *Education:* Colby College, B.A., 1954; Boston University, M.A., 1957, Ph.D., 1970. *Residence:* Lynnfield, Mass. *Agent:* The Helen Brann Agency, Inc., 14 Sutton Place S., New York, N.Y. 10022.

CAREER: Curtiss-Wright Co., Woodridge, N.J., management trainee, 1957; Raytheon Co., Andover, Mass., technical writer, 1957-59; Prudential Insurance Co., Boston, Mass., advertising writer, 1959-62; Boston University, Boston, lecturer in English, 1962-64; Massachusetts State College at Lowell (now University of Lowell), instructor in English, 1964-66; Massachusetts State College at Bridgewater, instructor in English, 1966-68; Northeastern University, Boston, assistant professor, 1968-74, associate professor, 1974-76, professor of English, 1976-79. Lecturer, Suffolk University, 1965-66. Co-chairman, Parker-Farman Co. (advertising agency), 1960-62. Film consultant to Arthur D. Little, 1962-64. *Military service:* U.S. Army, 1954-56.

WRITINGS—Published by Houghton, except as indicated: (With others) *The Personal Response to Literature,* 1970; (with Peter L. Sandberg) *Order and Diversity: The Craft of Prose,* Wiley, 1973; (with John R. Marsh) *Sports Illustrated Weight Training,* Lippincott, 1974; *The Godwulf Manuscript* (fiction), 1974; *God Save the Child* (fiction), 1974; *Mortal Stakes,* 1975; *Promised Land,* 1976; *The Judas Goat,* 1978; (with wife, Joan Parker) *Three Weeks in Spring,* 1978; *Wilderness,* Delacorte, 1979; *Looking for Rachel Wallace,* Delacorte, 1980. Contributor to *Lock Haven Review* and *Revue des Langes Vivantes.*

WORK IN PROGRESS: Love and Glory, fiction; *Early Autumn* and *Tinsel Town,* both for Delacorte.

* * *

PARKINSON, Ethelyn M(inerva) 1906-

PERSONAL: Born September 13, 1906, in Oconto County, Wis.; daughter of James Nelson (a salesman) and Ethel (a teacher; maiden name, Bigelow) Parkinson. *Education:* Oconto County Normal School, first grade teaching certificate, 1923; Bellin Memorial Hospital School of Nursing, R.N., 1928. *Religion:* Presbyterian. *Residence:* Green Bay, Wis.

CAREER: Has taught in elementary school and practiced private nursing; writer. *Awards, honors:* First place in playwriting from Wisconsin Dramatic Society, 1933, for "Shepherd's Queen"; first place for children's short fiction from Scholastic Book Services, 1957, for "A Man or a Mouse"; Abingdon Press Award, 1970, for *Never Go Anywhere with Digby;* Wisconsin Historical Society Award of Merit, 1971, for *Higgins of the Railroad Museum.*

WRITINGS—All juveniles; all published by Abingdon, except as indicated: *Double Trouble for Rupert,* Scholastic Book Services, 1958; *Triple Trouble for Rupert,* Scholastic Book Services, 1960; *Good Old Archibald,* 1960; *The Merry Mad Bachelors,* 1962; *The Terrible Troubles of Rupert Piper,* 1963; *The Operation That Happened to Rupert Piper,* 1966; *Today I Am a Ham,* 1968; *Higgins of the Railroad Museum,* 1970; *Elf King Joe,* 1970; *Never Go Anywhere with Digby,* 1971; *Rupert Piper and Megan, the Valuable Girl,* 1972; *Rupert Piper and the Dear, Dear Birds* (Junior Literary Guild selection), 1976; *Rupert Piper and the Boy Who Could Knit,* 1979. Also author of play, "Shepherd's Queen," and of short juvenile fiction.

SIDELIGHTS: "I grew up in the country, in northern Wisconsin," reports Ethelyn Parkinson. "Summers were heavenly. We weren't farmers, but we had one of everything. . . . I spent my summers on a horse's back—when I hadn't sneaked a book outdoors, or wasn't practicing my music lesson. Always, I wrote. My poems and stories went into a notebook which looked something like granite. Nobody ever saw what I wrote.

"I wrote throughout my school life, including the years in the school of nursing. There I was with girls of my own age for the first time in my life, and there I had a wonderful time. However, there was the writing. When I completed my nursing education, and got my R.N., I knew that my career would be writing, not nursing. I have a profound respect and true affection for that profession, and the happiest memories of the school life, but I had to be a writer.

"Poetry and plays came first. Then I had a go at syndicated newspaper fiction. I learned to cram a strong plot with a surprise ending, a good background, great characters, and terrific dialog into one thousand words—for from five to twenty dollars.

"When I had had enough of that, a conversation with a thirteen-year-old girl did something for me. I wrote a new kind of story for a new market. I was doing a great deal of youth work with boys and girls of this age. Why not tell their stories the way they told them, using their language? I knew it well. I had found part of my field.

"A few dozen stories later a thought came home to me that since there is nothing more alive, more interesting, more appealing, more lovable and delightful—albeit more maddening—than an eleven-year-old boy, I should be writing about one and for one. I should be telling it the way it is, in the boy's own language.

"Sometimes I have a feeling about my writing—a feeling that I haven't done things, but rather that things have happened to me. Perhaps that's because people—children included—have helped me all the way. Nieces and nephews and their friends have been an inexhaustible source of inspiration. I am thankful.

"My books are funny. I'm dedicated to giving as much happiness as I can to children through my writing, and in other ways."

* * *

PARSONS, Howard L(ee) 1918-

PERSONAL: Born July 9, 1918, in Jacksonville, Fla.; son of Howard Lee and Edna (Powell) Parsons; married Helen Brummall (a psychiatric social worker), March 31, 1946; children: Deborah, Margaret, Susan. *Education:* Attended University of Missouri, 1936-39, 1940-41; University of Chicago, B.A., 1942, Ph.D., 1946. *Office:* Department of Philosophy, University of Bridgeport, Bridgeport, Conn. 06602.

CAREER: University of Southern California, Los Angeles, visiting assistant professor of philosophy of religion, 1946-47; University of Illinois, Galesburg Campus, instructor in philosophy, 1947-49; University of Tennessee, Knoxville, assistant professor of philosophy, 1949-57; Coe College, Cedar Rapids, Iowa, associate professor, 1957-60, professor of philosophy, 1960-65, chairman of department of philosophy and religion, 1959-65; University of Bridgeport, Bridgeport, Conn., Bernhard Professor of Philosophy and chairman of department, 1965—. Member of advisory board, Center for Creative Exchange.

MEMBER: World Federation of Scientific Workers, World Peace Council (member of presidential committee), International Institute for Peace (member of scientific council),

American Philosophical Association, Society for Values in Higher Education, Society for the Philosophical Study of Dialectical Materialism (president, 1962-63; vice-president, 1963), American Institute for Marxist Studies (founding sponsor; member of board, 1964—), Societe Europeenne de Culture, American Association of University Professors, Iowa Philosophical Society (president, 1964-65). *Awards, honors:* Wenner-Gren Foundation grant, 1956; Kavir Institute grant, 1963-64; American Council of Learned Societies travel grant, 1975-76.

WRITINGS: Ethics in the Soviet Union Today, American Institute for Marxist Studies, 1967; *Humanistic Philosophy in Poland and Yugoslavia,* American Institute for Marxist Studies, 1968; *Humanism and Marx's Thought,* C. C Thomas, 1971; *Man East and West,* B. R. Gruener (Amsterdam), 1973; *Man Today,* B. R. Gruener, 1973; (editor with John Somerville) *Dialogues on the Philosophy of Marxism,* Greenwood Press, 1974; (editor with Somerville) *Marxism, Revolution, and Peace,* B. R. Gruener, 1974; *Self, Global Issues, and Ethics,* B. R. Gruener, 1977; *Marx and Engels on Ecology,* Greenwood Press, 1977. Contributor to *Praxis, Comprendre, Voprosy Filosofii,* and other philosophy journals.

WORK IN PROGRESS: Creativity.

* * *

PARTRIDGE, William L(ee) 1944-

PERSONAL: Born December 1, 1944, in Miami, Fla.; son of William Edward and Bernice (Rust) Partridge; married Kitty Kannette, September, 1965 (divorced, March, 1968); married Antoinette Brown, April, 1976; children: (first marriage) Denise Lee; (second marriage) Christopher Michael, Michelle Bernice-Helene. *Education:* University of Florida, B.A., 1966, M.A., 1969, Ph.D., 1974. *Office:* Department of Anthropology, University of Southern California, Los Angeles, Calif. 90007.

CAREER: University of Florida, Gainesville, instructor in social science, 1968-71; University of Southern California, Los Angeles, Calif., assistant professor of anthropology, 1974—; Harza Engineering Co., Chicago, Ill., senior anthropologist, 1978-79. Conducted field research in Colombia, 1972-74, and in southern Mexico, 1977-78. *Member:* American Anthropological Association, American Ethnological Society, Society for Applied Anthropology, Council on Anthropology and Education, Southern Anthropological Society, Royal Anthropological Institute. *Awards, honors:* National Institute of Mental Health fellowship, 1972-74.

WRITINGS: The Hippie Ghetto: The Natural History of a Subculture, Holt, 1973; (editor with E. M. Eddy) *Applied Anthropology in America,* Columbia University Press, 1978; (with S. T. Kimball) *The Craft of Community Study: Fieldwork Dialogues,* University of Florida Press, 1979. Contributor to several books and to *Current Anthropology, American Ethnologist,* and *Florida Anthropologist.*

SIDELIGHTS: William Partridge writes that he is motivated by "a strong dedication to the unpopular idea that there must be a working relationship between policy and social reality; an intellectual interest in the nature of social groupings, the relationship between belief and behavior."

* * *

PASSIN, Herbert 1916-

PERSONAL: Born December 16, 1916, in Chicago, Ill.; son of Hyman and Edith (Block) Passin; married Helen Wood Latham, December 18, 1964; children: Thomas B. *Education:* Attended University of Illinois, 1935-36; University of Chicago, B.A., 1940, M.A., 1941. *Home:* 25 Claremont Ave., New York, N.Y. *Office:* Department of Sociology, Columbia University, Broadway and West 116th St., New York, N.Y. 10027.

CAREER: Northwestern University, Evanston, Ill., instructor in anthropology, 1941-42; U.S. Department of Agriculture, Division of Program Surveys, Washington, D.C., social science researcher, 1942-43; Office of War Information, Bureau of Opinion Research, Washington, D.C., social science researcher, 1943; War Relocation Office, Detroit, Mich., relocation officer, 1943-44; Supreme Commander of the Allied Powers in Japan, Tokyo, deputy chief of Public Opinion and Sociological Research Division, 1947-51; University of California, Berkeley, lecturer in anthropology, 1952; researcher, Social Science Research Council, Japan, 1952-53; Ohio State University, Columbus, research associate, 1953-54; *Encounter* magazine, Tokyo, Far Eastern representative, 1954-57; Congress for Cultural Freedom, Paris, France, director of international seminar program, 1957-59; University of Washington, Seattle, visiting professor, 1959-62, professor of Far Eastern studies, 1962; Columbia University, New York, N.Y., professor of sociology, 1962—, executive director of United States-Japan parliamentary exchange program for School of International Affairs, 1967—, chairman of department of sociology, 1973-77. Chairman of board of editorial advisors, TBS Britanika Co., Japan, 1969-71. Field research includes studies of the Chicago Negro community and of Tarahumara Indians. Consultant to Ford Foundation, RAND Corp., Hudson Institute, Salk Institute for Biological Studies, Aspen Institute for Humanistic Studies, and International Council on Educational Development. *Military service:* U.S. Army, Japanese language officer, 1944-47; served in Tokyo; became first lieutenant. *Member:* Sigma Xi. *Awards, honors:* Research fellowship from Social Science Research Council, 1952-53, to study foreign-educated students in Japan.

WRITINGS: (With Arthur F. Raper and others) *The Japanese Village in Transition,* Supreme Commander of the Allied Powers in Japan, 1951; (editor and contributor) *Cultural Freedom in Asia,* Tuttle, 1956; (with J. W. Bennett and R. K. McKnight) *In Search of Identity,* University of Minnesota Press, 1958; *China's Cultural Diplomacy,* Praeger, 1963; (with K. A. B. Jones-Quartey) *Africa: Dynamics of Change,* Ibadan University Press, 1964; *Society and Education in Japan,* Teachers College Press, 1965; (editor and contributor) *The United States and Japan,* Prentice-Hall, 1966; (editor with Kinhide Mushakoji, and contributor) *Nichibei Kankei no Tembo* (title means "The Prospects of Japanese-American Relations"), Simul, 1967; (editor and contributor) *Nihon to Amerika* (title means "Japan and America"), Nanundo, 1967; *Nihon Kindaika to Kyoiku* (title means "Modernization and Education in Japan"), Simul, 1969.

(With Edward Seidensticker) *The United States and Japan,* Nanundo, 1970; *Japanese Education: A Bibliography of Materials in the English Language,* Teachers College Press, 1970; *Japanese and the Japanese,* Kinseido, 1978; *Enryo to Donyoku* (title means "Reserve and Greediness"), Shodensha, 1978; (editor and contributor) *Encounter at Shimoda,* Westview Press, 1979; (editor and contributor) *A Season of Voting: The 1976 House of Representatives Elections and the 1977 House of Councillors Elections in Japan,* American Enterprise Institute for Public Policy Research, 1979; (editor) *Indo o Sukuu Michi—Narayan no Gokuchuki* (title means "India's Road to Salvation—Jayaprakash Narayan's

Prison Diary"), Simul, 1979; (with H. Kase and K. Takemura) *Nihonjin no Hasso, Amerikajin no Hasso* (title means "The Way Japanese Think, the Way Americans Think"), Tokuma Shobo, 1979.

Nihon to no Deai (title means "Encounter with Japan"), TBS Britanika Co., 1980; *Japanese Culture Seen through the Japanese Language,* Kinseido, 1980; *Language and Culture in Japan,* Tuttle, 1980; *The Outlook of Intellectuals in Japan,* East Asian Institute Occasional Papers, Columbia University, 1980.

Contributor: Elizabeth Velan and Victor Velan, editors, *The New Japan,* H. W. Wilson, 1958; Hinetoshi Kato, editor, *Japanese Popular Culture,* Tuttle, 1959; Morton Kaplan, editor, *The Revolution of Our Times,* Wiley, 1963; Lucien Pye, editor, *Communications and Political Development,* Princeton University Press, 1963; Marius Jansen, editor, *The Modernization of Japan,* Princeton University Press, 1965; C. Arnold Anderson and M. J. Bowman, editors, *Education and Economic Development,* Aldine, 1965; Alan Dundes, editor, *Study of Folklore,* Prentice-Hall, 1965; Jansen, editor, *Nihon ni okeru Kindaika no Mondai* (title means "Problems of Modernization in Japan"), Iwanami, 1968; M. Tanaka and S. Kaizuka, editors, *Taiwa: Nihon no Kadai* (title means "Dialogue: The Agenda for Japan"), Chuko Shinsho, 1968; Joseph A. Kahl, editor, *Comparative Perspectives on Stratification: Mexico, Great Britain, Japan,* Little, Brown, 1968; J. A. Fishman, C. A. Ferguson, and J. Das Gupta, editors, *Language Problems of Developing Nations,* Wiley, 1968; Pye, editor, *Masu-media to Kokka no Kindaika* (title means "Mass Media and the Modernization of Nations"), NHK Broadcasting Research Institute, 1968; Gerald Curtis and Fuji Kamiya, editors, *Okinawa igo no Nichibei Kankei* (title means "Japanese-American Relations after Okinawa"), Simul, 1970; James A. Perkins and Barbara B. Israel, editors, *Higher Education: From Autonomy to Systems,* International Council for Educational Development, 1972; J.A.A. Stockwin, editor, *Japan and Australia in the Seventies,* Angus & Robertson, 1972.

Also author of research reports. Contributor to annals and conferences, and to *International Encyclopedia of the Social Sciences.* Contributor to professional journals in the United States and abroad, including *Discover Japan, Reporter, Comparative Education Review, American Anthropologist, New Japan, Rural Sociology, American Sociological Review, Man, Acta Americana, Social Forces,* and *American Political Science Review.*

* * *

PATERSON, Thomas G(raham) 1941-

PERSONAL: Born March 4, 1941, in Oregon City, Ore.; son of Thomas (a plastics plant foreman) and Suzanne Virginia Paterson. *Education:* University of New Hampshire, B.A., 1963; University of California, Berkeley, M.A., 1964, Ph.D., 1968. *Home:* 571 Gurleyville Rd., Storrs, Conn. 06268. *Office:* Department of History, University of Connecticut, Storrs, Conn. 06268.

CAREER: University of Connecticut, Storrs, assistant professor, 1967-70, associate professor, 1970-73, professor of history, 1973—. Director, National Endowment for the Humanities summer seminar, 1980. *Member:* American Historical Association, Organization of American Historians, Society for Historians of American Foreign Relations, American Association of University Professors, Phi Beta Kappa, Phi Kappa Phi, Pi Sigma Alpha, Pi Gamma Nu. *Awards, honors:* Harry S Truman Institute grants-in-aid, 1967, 1968, 1972, and 1975; Rabinowitz Foundation research grant, 1972; American Philosophical Society grant, 1972; Eleanor Roosevelt Institute grant-in-aid, 1975; National Endowment for the Humanities fellowship, 1976-77.

WRITINGS: (Editor and author of introduction) *The Origins of the Cold War,* Heath, 1970, 2nd edition, 1974; (editor and contributor) *Cold War Critics: Alternatives to American Foreign Policy in the Truman Years,* Quadrangle, 1971; (editor) *American Imperialism and Anti-Imperialism,* Crowell, 1973; (editor) *Containment and the Cold War: American Foreign Policy since 1945,* Addison-Wesley, 1973; *Soviet-American Confrontation: Postwar Reconstruction and the Origins of the Cold War,* Johns Hopkins Press, 1973; (with others) *American Foreign Policy: A History,* Heath, 1977; (editor) *Problems in American Foreign Policy,* two volumes, Heath, 1978; *On Every Front: The Making of the Cold War,* Norton, 1979.

Contributor to numerous books, including: Barton J. Berstein, editor, *Politics and Policies of the Truman Administration,* Quadrangle, 1970; James V. Compton, editor, *America and the Origins of the Cold War,* Houghton, 1972; John Hennessy and John Gimbel, editors, *From Coalition to Confrontation: Readings on Cold War Origins,* Wadsworth, 1972; Gary R. Hess, editor, *America and Russia: From Cold War Confrontation to Coexistence,* Crowell, 1973; Frank Merli and Theodore Wilson, editors, *Makers of American Diplomacy,* Scribner, 1974; *International Encyclopedia of the Social Sciences: Biographical Supplement,* Free Press, 1979. Contributor of about fifty articles and reviews to newspapers and various journals, including *Nation, Journal of American History, Washington Post, Diplomatic History, Historian, American Historical Review,* and *Business History Review.*

WORK IN PROGRESS: The Truman Doctrine and the Containment Principle: 1945-1975; American History (textbook), for Houghton.

AVOCATIONAL INTERESTS: Travel, sports, New England inns.

* * *

PATRICK, Robert 1937-

PERSONAL: Born September 27, 1937, in Kilgore, Tex. *Education:* Attended Eastern New Mexico University, three years. *Home:* c/o La Mama, 74A East Fourth St., New York, N.Y. 10003.

CAREER: Playwright, actor, director, and songwriter. Worked as dishwasher, autopsy typist, accounts receivable correspondent, astrologer, and reporter. Caffe Cino, New York City, waiter, doorman, and stage manager, 1961-63; Old Reliable Theatre Tavern, New York City, playwright-in-residence, 1967-71. *Member:* New York Theatre Strategy, Playwrights Cooperative, Actors Studio. *Awards, honors:* *Show Business* best Off-Off Broadway playwright award, 1968-69, for "Joyce Dynel," "Fog," and "Salvation Army"; nominated for *Village Voice* "Obie" award, 1973; Glasgow Citizens' Theatre International play contest, first prize, 1973, for "Kennedy's Children"; Rockefeller Foundation playwright-in-residence grant, 1973; Creative Artists Public Service grant, 1976.

WRITINGS—Plays; first produced Off-Off-Broadway, except as indicated: "The Haunted Host" (also see below), first produced at Caffe Cino, November 29, 1964; "Mirage" (also see below), first produced at La Mama, July 8, 1965; "The Sleeping Bag," first produced at Playwrights' Workshop, June, 1966; "Indecent Exposure," first produced at Caffe Cino, September 27, 1966; "Halloween Hermit," first produced at Caffe Cino, October 31, 1966; "Cheesecake" (also see below), first produced at Caffe Cino, 1966; "Sketches," first produced in 1966; "Lights, Camera, Action" (also see below), first produced at Caffe Cino, June 8, 1967; "The Warhol Machine," first produced at Playbox Studio, July 18, 1967; "Still-Love," first produced at Playbox Studio, July 18, 1967; "Cornered" (also see below), first produced at Theatre Gallery, January 26, 1968; "Un Bel Di," first produced at Theatre Gallery, January 26, 1968; "Help, I Am" (also see below), first produced at Theatre Gallery, January 26, 1968; "Camera Obscura," first produced at Caffe Cino; produced Off-Broadway at Cafe au Go Go, May 8, 1968; "The Arnold Bliss Show" (also see below), first produced by New York Theatre Ensemble, April 1, 1969; "Silver Skies," produced in 1969; "Tarquin Truthbeauty," produced in 1969; "The Actor and the Invader," produced in 1969.

"A Bad Place to Get Your Head," first produced at St. Peters Church, July 14, 1970; "Bread-Tangle," first produced at St. Peters Church, July 14, 1970; "Picture Wire," first produced at St. Peters Church, August 13, 1970; "I Am Trying to Tell You Something," first produced at The Open Space, August, 1970; "Shelter," first produced at Playbox Studio, November, 1970; "The Richest Girl in the World Finds Happiness" (also see below), first produced at La Mama, December 24, 1970; "Hymen and Carbuncle" (also see below), produced by the Dove Company, 1970; "La Repetition," produced in 1970; "Sketches and Songs," produced in 1970; "A Christmas Carol," first produced at La Mama, December 22, 1971; "Youth Rebellion," first produced at Sammy's Bowery Follies, February, 1972; *Play by Play* (first produced at La Mama, December 20, 1972), Samuel French, 1975; "Songs," produced in 1972; "Something Else" (also see below), first produced by New York Theatre Ensemble, January, 1973; "Ludwig and Wagner" (also see below), first produced at La Mama, February, 1973; "Mercy Drop" (also see below), first produced at W.P.A. Theatre, March, 1973; "Simultaneous Transmissions," first produced at Kranny's Nook, March 1, 1973; "The Track of the Narwhal," first produced in Boston, Mass. at Boston Conservatory, April 28, 1973; *Kennedy's Children* (first produced at Clark Center, May 30, 1973; produced on the West End at Arts Theatre Club, May, 1975; produced on Broadway at Golden Theatre, November 3, 1975), Samuel French (London), 1975, Random House, 1976; "Cleaning House" (also see below), first produced at W.P.A. Theatre, June 27, 1973; "Hippy as a Lark," first produced at Stagelights II, June, 1973; "The Golden Circle," first produced by Spring Street Company, September 26, 1973; "Imp-Prisonment," produced in 1973; "The Twisted Root," produced in 1973; "Love Lace" (also see below), first produced at Pico Playhouse, 1974; "How I Came to Be Here Tonite," first produced at La Mama Hollywood, Hollywood, Calif., March 21, 1974; "Orpheus and Amerika," first produced in Los Angeles, Calif. at Odyssey Theatre, April, 1974.

"Fred and Harold, and One Person," first produced in London, England, 1976; "My Dear It Doesn't Mean a Thing," first produced in London, 1976; *My Cup Ranneth Over* (first produced in Brooklyn, N.Y. at Everyman Theatre, November 3, 1977), Dramatists Play Service, 1979; "Judas," first produced in Santa Maria, Calif., April, 1978; "T-Shirts," first produced in Minneapolis, Minn. at Out-and-About Theatre, October 19, 1978; *Mutual Benefit Life* (full-length; first produced by Production Company, October, 1978), Dramatists Play Service, 1979; "Bank Street Breakfast" (also see below), first produced by the Fourth E, February, 1979; "Communication Gap," first produced in Greensboro, N.C., 1979; "The Family Bar" (also see below), first produced in Hollywood, at Deja Vu, 1979.

All first produced Off-Off-Broadway at Old Reliable Theatre Tavern: "See Other Side," produced April 1, 1968; "Absolute Power over Movie Stars," produced May 13, 1968; "Preggin and Liss" (also see below), produced June 17, 1968; "The Overseers," produced July 1, 1968; "Angels in Agony," produced July 1, 1968; "Salvation Army," produced September 23, 1968; "Dynel," produced December 16, 1968; "Fog," produced January 20, 1969; "I Came to New York to Write" (full-length; also see below), produced March 24, 1969; "Joyce Dynel" (full-length; also see below) produced April 7, 1969; "The Young Aquarius," produced April 28, 1969; "Oooooooops!," produced May 12, 1969; "Lily of the Valley of the Dolls," produced June 30, 1969; "One Person" (also see below), produced August 29, 1969; "Angel, Honey, Baby, Darling, Dear," produced July 20, 1970; "The Golden Animal," produced July 20, 1970.

Collections: *Robert Patrick's Cheep Theatricks!* (contains "I Came to New York to Write," "The Haunted Host," "Joyce Dynel," "Cornered," "Still-Love," "Lights, Camera, Action," "Help, I Am," "The Arnold Bliss Show," "One Person," "Preggin and Liss," and "The Richest Girl in the World Finds Happiness"), edited by Michael Feingold, Winter House, 1972; *One Man, One Woman* (contains "Mirage," "Cleaning House," "Cheesecake," "Something Else," "Love Lace," and "Bank Street Breakfast"), Samuel French, 1975; *Mercy Drop and Other Plays* (contains "Mercy Drop," "Ludwig and Wagner," "Diaghilev and Nijinsky," "Hymen and Carbuncle," and "The Family Bar"), Calamus Books, 1980.

Work represented in numerous anthologies, including: *Collision Course,* edited by Ed Parone, Random House, 1968; *New American Plays 3,* edited by William M. Hoffman, Hill & Wang, 1970; *The Off-Off-Broadway Book,* edited by Albert Poland and Bruce Mailman, Bobbs-Merrill, 1972; *The Scene/2: Plays from Off-Off-Broadway,* edited by Stanley Nelson, The Smith, 1974; *Homosexual Acts,* Inter-Action Imprint (London), 1976; *Gay Plays: The First Collection,* edited by Hoffman, Avon, 1979; *West Coast Plays #5,* Berkley Publishing, 1980.

Also author of two screenplays, "The Haunted Host" (based on the play of the same title), 1969 and "The Credit Game," 1972 and numerous one-act plays, including "Love: A Game of Any Length," 1972 and "Let Me Tell It to You, Dr. Paroo," 1978. Columnist, *Proscenium,* 1972—. Contributor of articles and plays to numerous periodicals, including *Saturday Review, Astrology Today, Off-Off, Playbill, Gaysweek, New York,* and *Dramatics.*

WORK IN PROGRESS: An autobiography, *The Thing from the Planet Earth.*

SIDELIGHTS: Although Robert Patrick has been termed Off-Off-Broadway's most prolific and most produced playwright, he is best known for *Kennedy's Children,* a play which achieved success on both the West End and Broadway. The play depicts the barroom confessions of five representative figures from the sixties, yet according to Patrick, the play is not primarily concerned with the sixties. He told Robert Berkvist of the *New York Times* that "the play's theme is the loss of heroes. And it's not about the sixties, it's about now, about why we have become what we are." As Patrick was writing the play, he found that the characters "were each a different aspect of the lost-hero theme: one had killed his hero, another had seen his hero betrayed, another had tried to be a hero."

Whether it focuses on the sixties or lost heroes or both, *Kennedy's Children* has been acclaimed by many critics. *Newsweek* reviewer Jack Kroll, for example, comments that it "is a work of genuine power, an elegy for lost hopes, illusory goals, aborted energies, an outburst of anger, desperation and bitter humor about the most shock- and shlock-filled ten years in America's history." Similarly, T. E. Kalem writes in *Time* that the play "is an incisive portrait of that sadly lost generation's wistful hopes and bewildered and embittered disenchantment." In addition, *New York Times* critic Clive Barnes praises "Mr. Patrick's uncanny ear for the way people talk, and his equally uncanny ability to transmute that into the small yet totally convincing traffic of the stage."

One of the play's characters, an actor, describes his ideal experience of Off-Off-Broadway: "We did plays without worrying whether we were going to be a hit, or get a review, or become a star, or take it to Broadway." Patrick told *CA* of a similar ideal: "Off-Off-Broadway was a completely new idea. Never before had there been a theatre of any scope in space or time where plays were produced without academic, legal, financial, popular, critical, religious, governmental, police, military or esthetic pressures to conform to. In other words, with Off-Off-Broadway, theatre became for the first time an area of free expression on a level with the other arts. This great break has created the theatre of the present and of the future."

Patrick also told *CA:* "A play is primarily a shared experience which exists only in performance. Its immediacy is its special quality. Unlike films and literature, which record experiences that once happened, a play presents an event. Its *reality* makes it a powerful moral and psychological tool. Theatrical artists who do not communicate consciously communicate helplessly and unconsciously."

"Lily of the Valley of the Dolls" and "The Arnold Bliss Show" were produced at the Edinburgh Arts Festival in 1972. "Camera Obscura" has been presented on television and in over 500 productions throughout North America and Europe. "My Cup Ranneth Over" was produced by PBS-TV. *Kennedy's Children* has been published in over 40 languages and produced in over 60 countries, on television in many. Festivals of Patrick's work have been held in Minneapolis, Minn., San Francisco, Calif., and Phoenix, Ariz.

BIOGRAPHICAL/CRITICAL SOURCES: Albert Poland and Bruce Mailman, editors, *The Off-Off-Broadway Book,* Bobbs-Merrill, 1972; Michael Feingold, editor, *Robert Patrick's Cheep Theatricks!,* Winter House, 1972; *New York Times,* May 4, 1975, September 3, 1975, November 9, 1975, June 23, 1978; *Newsweek,* November 17, 1975; *Time,* November 17, 1975; *Authors in the News,* Volume II, Gale, 1976.

* * *

PATTON, Bobby R(ay) 1935-

PERSONAL: Born December 18, 1935, in Fort Worth, Tex.; son of Elton Guy (a shopkeeper) and Violet (Daniels) Patton; married Bonnie Ritter (a government executive), June 1, 1958 (divorced, 1976); married Eleanor Nyquist (a theatre costumer), July 4, 1978. *Education:* Texas Christian University, B.F.A. (magna cum laude), 1958; University of Kansas, M.A., 1962, Ph.D., 1966. *Politics:* Democrat. *Religion:* Unitarian Universalist. *Home:* 2608 West 24th Ter., Lawrence, Kan. 66046. *Office:* Department of Speech and Drama, 356 Murphy Hall, University of Kansas, Lawrence, Kan. 66045.

CAREER: High school teacher of speech in Hutchinson, Kan., 1958-61; Wichita State University, Wichita, Kan., instructor, 1961-62, assistant professor of speech, 1962-65; University of Kansas, Lawrence, assistant professor, 1966-69, associate professor, 1969-74, professor of speech, 1974—, chairman of department of speech and drama, 1972—. *Member:* International Communication Association, Speech Communication Association, Kansas Speech Association (president, 1961-63). *Awards, honors:* Named outstanding college speech teacher in the state, Kansas Speech Association, 1968.

WRITINGS—All with Kim Giffin, except as indicated; published by Harper, except as indicated: *Fundamentals of Interpersonal Communication,* 1971, 2nd edition, 1976; (editor) *Basic Readings in Interpersonal Communication: Theory and Application,* 1971, 2nd edition, 1976; *Problem-Solving Group Interaction,* 1973, 2nd edition published as *Decision-Making Group Interaction,* 1978; *Interpersonal Communication,* 1974; *Personal Communication in Human Relations,* C. E. Merrill, 1974; (with Bonnie Ritter) *Living Together: Female-Male Communication,* C. E. Merrill, 1976; (sole author) *Interpersonal Communication in Action,* 1977, 2nd edition, 1980.

WORK IN PROGRESS: Authentic Communication between Speakers and Audiences, for Scott, Foresman; with Giffin and Paul Friedman, *The A-Frame: Achieving Authentic Communication,* for Harper; with Giffin and Bonnie Grant, *Interpersonal Communication in Humanistic Nursing,* for F. A. Davis; with Giffin, *Experiences in Speech Communication,* for Harper.

* * *

PAUKER, Guy J(ean) 1916-

PERSONAL: Born September 15, 1916, in Bucharest, Rumania; came to United States, 1948, naturalized in 1954; married Ewa Teresa Toczylowska. *Education:* University of Bucharest, licence es lettres, 1938, licence en droit, 1938, Dr. Political and Economic Science, 1946; Harvard University, M.A., 1950, Ph.D., 1952. *Home:* 21423 Colina Dr., Topanga, Calif. 90290.

CAREER: Jurnalul, Bucharest, Rumania, editorial writer on foreign affairs, 1936-40, 1944-47; admitted to Bucharest Bar, 1946; Harvard University, Cambridge, Mass., instructor, 1952-54, lecturer in government, 1954-56; University of California, Berkeley, assistant professor, 1956-59, associate professor of political science, 1959-60, chairman of Center for Southeast Asian Studies, 1956-60; RAND Corp., Santa Monica, Calif., head of Asia section in social science department, 1960-65, senior staff member in social science department, 1965—. Research associate at Center for International Affairs, Massachusetts Institute of Technology, 1953-56; faculty research associate in Environmental Quality Laboratory, California Institute of Technology, 1970-73; research associate, Resource Systems Institute, East-West Center, 1979—. Secretary general, Rumanian Institute of International Affairs, 1945-47; member of committee on comparative politics, Social Science Research Council, 1954-58; executive secretary, Asia-Pacific Energy Studies Consultative Group, 1979—. Consultant to U.S. Government and American businesses.

WRITINGS: (Contributor) Robert R. Bowie and Carl J. Friedrich, editors, *Studies in Federalism,* Little, Brown, 1954; *The Bandung Conference,* Center for International

Studies, Massachusetts Institute of Technology, 1955; *Bandung in Perspective,* Center for International Studies, Massachusetts Institute of Technology, 1956; *Human Values in Social Change in South and Southeast Asia and in the United States,* U.S. Department of State for U.S. National Commission for UNESCO, 1956; *1956 Perspectives on Indonesian Politics and Economic Development,* National Planning Association, 1956.

(Contributor) J. J. Johnson, editor, *The Role of the Military in Underdeveloped Countries,* Princeton University Press, 1962; (contributor) R. A. Scalapino, editor, *The Communist Revolution in Asia,* Prentice-Hall, 1965, 2nd edition, 1969; (contributor) E. Z. Vogt and E. M. Albert, editors, *People of Rimrock: A Study of Values in Five Cultures,* Harvard University Press, 1966; (contributor) Anthony Pascal, editor, *Thinking about Cities: New Perspectives on Urban Problems,* Dickinson, 1969.

(With Lester Lees, Mahlon Easterling, Burton Klein and others) *Smog: A Report to the People,* Ward-Ritchie, 1972; (with Frank H. Golay and Cynthia H. Enloe) *Diversity and Development in Southeast Asia: The Coming Decade,* McGraw-Hill, 1977; *Military Implications of a Possible World Order Crisis in the 1980's,* RAND Corporation, 1977. Author of research reports. Contributor to yearbooks and proceedings and to *Encyclopaedia Britannica.* Contributor of more than sixty articles to American and foreign journals including *Asian Survey, Foreign Affairs, Pacific Affairs,* and *World Politics.*

* * *

PAYES, Rachel C(osgrove) 1922-
(E. L. Arch, Rachel Cosgrove)

PERSONAL: Born December 11, 1922, in Westernport, Md.; daughter of Jacob A. (a mine superintendent) and Martha (Brake) Cosgrove; married Norman M. Payes (a senior laboratory specialist with IBM), September 12, 1954; children: Robert, Ruth. *Education:* West Virginia Wesleyan College, B.Sc., 1943. *Politics:* Republican. *Religion:* United Methodist. *Home:* 3589 Frost Rd., Shrub Oak, N.Y. 10588.

CAREER: Registered medical technologist; American Cyanamid, Research Division, Pearl River, N.Y., research associate, 1945-57; novelist. *Member:* Science Fiction Writers of America.

WRITINGS—Mystery novels; all published by Bouregy, except as indicated: *Forsythia Finds Murder,* 1960; *Death Sleeps Lightly,* 1960; *Shadow of Fear,* 1961; *Curiosity Killed Kitty,* 1962; *Memoirs of Murder,* 1964; *Mystery of Echo Caverns,* 1966; *O Charitable Death,* Doubleday Crime Club, 1968.

Gothic novels: *The Silent Place,* Ace Books, 1969; *Malverne Hall,* Ace Books, 1970; *Forbidden Island,* Berkley Publishing, 1973; *Devil's Court,* Berkley Publishing, 1974; *House of Tarot,* Berkley Publishing, 1975; *The Black Swan,* Berkley Publishing, 1975; *The Sapphire Legacy,* Berkley Publishing, 1976.

Romance novels: *Peace Corps Nurse,* Bouregy, 1967; *Moment of Desire,* Playboy Press, 1978; *Coach to Hell,* Playboy Press, 1979; *Bride of Fury,* Playboy Press, 1980; *Satan's Mistress,* Playboy Press, 1980.

Under name Rachel Cosgrove; novels; all published by Bouregy, except as indicated: *Hidden Valley of Oz,* Reilly & Lee, 1951; *Marjory Thurman, Lab Technician,* 1960; *Long Journey Home,* 1962; *Not for Glory,* 1963; *The Candystripers,* 1964; *Ann Gordon of the Peace Corps,* 1965; *Linda's Gifts,* 1966; *Designs for Love,* 1966.

Under pseudonym E. L. Arch; science fiction; all published by Bouregy: *Bridge to Yesterday,* 1963; *Planet of Death,* 1964; *The Deathstones,* 1964; *The First Immortals,* 1965; *The Double-Minded Man,* 1966; *The Man with Three Eyes,* 1967.

Science fiction is represented in the following anthologies: *And Walk Now Gently through the Fire,* edited by Roger Elwood, Chilton, 1972; *Children of Infinity,* edited by Elwood, Watts, 1973; *Androids, Time Machines and Blue Giraffes,* edited by Elwood and Vic Ghidalia, Follett, 1973; *Alien Condition,* edited by Stephen Goldin, Ballantine, 1973; *Cooking Out of This World,* edited by Anne McCaffrey, Ballantine, 1973; *Strange Gods,* edited by Elwood, Pocket Books, 1974; *Dystopian Visions,* edited by Elwood, Prentice-Hall, 1975; *Quest,* edited by David Bischoff, Raintree, 1977.

Contributor of articles and stories to *Analog, Magazine of Fantasy & Science Fiction, Magazine of Horror, Writer, Straight, Worlds of If, Worlds of Tomorrow, Amazing,* and *Vertex;* contributor of fillers and puzzles to magazines and newspapers, including *Herald Tribune, Weekday,* and *New York Journal American.* Writer of verse for Buzzo Cardoza and Barker greeting card companies

WORK IN PROGRESS: Five romance novels.

SIDELIGHTS: Rachel Payes told *CA* that aspiring writers should "quit talking about it and WRITE." She began her own writing career with a novel set in L. Frank Baum's Land of Oz because, she notes, "I was raised on Oz." Her books have been translated into Spanish, Italian, French, German, Swedish, and Danish.

* * *

PECKHAM, Morse 1914-

PERSONAL: Born August 17, 1914, in Yonkers, N.Y.; son of Ray Morse and Edith (Roake) Peckham. *Education:* University of Rochester, B.A., 1935; Princeton University, M.A., 1938, Ph.D., 1947. *Home:* 6478 Bridgewood Rd., Columbia, S.C. 29206. *Office:* Department of English, University of South Carolina, Columbia, S.C. 29208.

CAREER: The Citadel, Charleston, S.C., assistant professor of English, 1938-41; Rutgers University, New Brunswick, N.J., instructor, 1946-47, assistant professor of English, 1947-49; University of Pennsylvania, Philadelphia, assistant professor, 1949-52, associate professor, 1952-61, professor of English, 1961-67, director of Institute of Humanistic Studies, 1953-54, director of University of Pennsylvania Press, 1953-55; University of South Carolina, Columbia, Distinguished Professor of English and Comparative Literature, 1967-80, professor emeritus, 1980—. *Military service:* U.S. Army Air Forces, 1941-46; became first lieutenant; received Bronze Star Medal. *Member:* Society of Architectural Historians, Modern Language Association of America, American Association for Aesthetics, Art Alliance (Philadelphia).

WRITINGS: A Humanistic Re-education for the Corporation Executive, Fund for Adult Education, 1957; *Humanistic Education for Business Executives: An Essay in General Education,* University of Pennsylvania Press, 1960; *Beyond the Tragic Vision: The Quest for Identity in the Nineteenth Century,* Braziller, 1962; *Man's Rage for Chaos: Biology, Behavior, and the Arts,* Chilton, 1965; *Art and Pornography: An Experiment in Explanation,* Basic Books, 1969; *Victorian Revolutionaries: Speculation on Some Heroes of a Culture Crisis,* Braziller, 1970; *The Triumph of Romanticism: Collected Essays,* University of South Carolina Press, 1970;

Romanticism and Behavior: Collected Essays II, University of South Carolina Press, 1976; *Explanation and Power: The Control of Human Behavior,* Seabury, 1979.

Editor: Charles Darwin, *On the Origin of Species: A Variorum Text,* University of Pennsylvania Press, 1959; *Word, Meaning, Poem: An Anthology of Poetry,* Crowell, 1961; *Romanticism: The Culture of the Nineteenth Century,* Braziller, 1965; Robert Browning, *Paracelsus,* Ohio State University Press, 1969; (with P. J. McFarland) *Perceptions in Literature,* Houghton, 1972.

Contributor of chapters to several books. Contributor to professional journals and other periodicals, including *Studies in Romanticism, Magazine of Art,* and *Saturday Review.*

WORK IN PROGRESS: Cultural History of Romanticism in the Nineteenth Century.

SIDELIGHTS: A *New Republic* critic refers to Morse Peckham's most widely-reviewed book, *Art and Pornography: An Experiment in Explanation,* as "a high level, one-man bull session about human behavior. Professor Peckham mixes psychology, philosophy, aesthetics, semantics, history and whatnot into a grand paste before displaying his grand theme about pornography. . . . If the book were not so eccentrically spacious, and if Peckham did not rattle on interminably, in sentences of Faulknerian length, it might fare better among those who most chiefly worry the issue of the culture's 'tolerance for innovation,' namely our judges." In another review, Eric Moon criticizes the author for his "whirlpool of never-ending definition," and he mentions the fact that Peckham himself admits to "dreary repetition." Moon continues: "There is no doubt about the author's scholarship in a variety of areas (though it is doubtful whether pornography is one of them). . . . An experiment, to quote the subtitle, it may well be; an explanation, never."

Peckham told *CA:* "Virtually all my writings have developed from an effort to develop a theory of Romanticism. To do this I have found it necessary to develop theories (satisfactory to me) of knowledge, art, criticism, cultural history, science, human behavior. Yet almost everything I have done has been written at the request of someone else. To my surprise, I have become a kind of professional author, since all my original books have been done for trade publishers, except for my collected essays."

AVOCATIONAL INTERESTS: Music, architecture, art.

BIOGRAPHICAL/CRITICAL SOURCES: Washington Post, November 21, 1969; *New Republic,* November 29, 1969; *Antioch Review,* winter, 1969-70; *Library Journal,* February 1, 1970; *Nation,* March 2, 1970; *Saturday Review,* April 18, 1970; *Choice,* September, 1970; *American Historical Review,* December, 1970; *New York Review of Books,* May 20, 1971; *Yale Review,* winter, 1971.

* * *

PELIKAN, Jaroslav Jan 1923-

PERSONAL: Born December 17, 1923, in Akron, Ohio; son of Jaroslav Jan, Sr. (a minister) and Anna (Buzek) Pelikan; married Sylvia Burica, 1946; children: Martin John, Michael Paul, Miriam Ruth. *Education:* Concordia Junior College, diploma (summa cum laude), 1942; Concordia Seminary, B.D., 1946; University of Chicago, Ph.D., 1946. *Home:* 156 Chestnut Lane, Hamden, Conn. 06518. *Office:* Department of History, Yale University, New Haven, Conn. 06520.

CAREER: Ordained minister of the Lutheran Church. Valparaiso University, Valparaiso, Ind., professor, 1946-49; Concordia Seminary, St. Louis, Mo., professor, 1949-53; University of Chicago, Ill., professor, 1953-62; Yale University, New Haven, Conn., Titus Street Professor of Ecclesiastical History, 1962-72, Sterling Professor of History and Religious Studies, 1972—, acting dean of Graduate School, 1973-74, dean, 1975-78. President, Fourth International Congress for Luther Research, 1971; president, New England Conference on Graduate Education, 1976-77. Member of commission on faith and order, World Council of Churches. *Member:* American Society for Reformation Research, American Society of Church History (member of council, 1961—; president, 1965), American Academy of Arts and Sciences (fellow; councillor, 1974—; vice-president, 1976—), Mediaeval Academy of America (fellow), Americans for Democratic Action, National Academic Council of Valparaiso University (president, 1963—), Phi Beta Kappa. *Awards, honors:* Abingdon Award, 1959, for *The Riddle of Roman Catholicism;* Pax Christi Award, Saint John's University, 1966; National Endowment for the Humanities senior fellow, 1967-68; John Gilmary Shea Prize, American Catholic Historical Association, 1971; National Award, World Slovak Congress, 1973; Religious Book Award, Catholic Press Association, 1974; Christian Unity Award, Atonement Friars, 1975; American Philosophical Society at Philadelphia award, 1978. Also has received various honorary degrees from seventeen colleges and universities, 1960-78.

WRITINGS: From Luther to Kierkegaard, Concordia, 1950; *Fools for Christ,* Muhlenberg, 1955; *The Riddle of Roman Catholicism,* Abingdon, 1959; *Luther the Expositor,* Concordia, 1959; *The Shape of Death: Life, Death, and Immortality in the Early Fathers,* Abingdon, 1961; *The Light of the World: A Basic Image in Early Christian Thought,* Harper, 1962; *Obedient Rebels: Catholic Substance and Protestant Principle in Luther's Reformation,* Harper, 1964; *The Finality of Jesus Christ in an Age of Universal History: A Dilemma of the Third Century,* Lutterworth, 1965; *The Christian Intellectual,* Harper, 1966; *Spirit Versus Structure: Luther and the Institutions of the Church,* Harper, 1968; *Development of Christian Doctrine: Some Historical Prolegomena,* Yale University Press, 1969; *Historical Theology: Continuity and Change in Christian Doctrine,* Westminster, 1971. Also author of *The Christian Tradition: A History of the Development of Doctrine,* University of Chicago Press, 1971—.

Editor: (With others) Theodore Tappert, *Book of Concord: The Confessions of the Evangelical Lutheran Church,* Fortress, 1959; *The Preaching of Chrysostom: Homilies on the Sermon on the Mount,* Fortress, 1967; *Interpreters of Luther: Essays in Honor of Wilhelm Pauck,* Fortress, 1968; *Twentieth Century Theology in the Making,* Collins, Volume I: *Themes of Biblical Theology,* 1969, Volume II: *The Theological Dialogue: Issues and Resources,* 1970, Volume III: *Ecumenicity and Renewal,* 1971; *The Preaching of Augustine: Our Lord's Sermon of the Mount,* Fortress, 1973. Editor of *Luther's Works,* twenty-two volumes, 1955-70; also editor of *Makers of Modern Theology,* five volumes, 1966-68; occasional departmental editor for religion, *Encyclopaedia Britannica.*

SIDELIGHTS: Clark M. Williamson calls *The Christian Intellectual* "another in a list of highly instructive books which [Jaroslav Pelikan] has written for the theological public. Professor Pelikan long ago demonstrated his ability to bring his rich knowledge of the history of Christian thought decisively to bear on the issues and problems facing people in their immediate situations. . . . *The Christian Intellectual* brings the same helpful and resourceful approach to a new problem, the one stated in the title." Williamson concludes that the book, "is written in an inviting style, and quietly stresses the importance of a grasp of the history of Christian thought if one is properly to comprehend what is involved in speaking meaningfully to the contemporary world."

In *Spirit Versus Structure,* Pelikan deals with the issue of institutional structure and the problems which faced Martin Luther, who, according to Thomas Tredway, during the heat of the early Reformation, "tended to view the extant institutions of the church as inhibiting grace. But in the crises of the 1520s and '30s he came increasingly to realize the inevitability of structure and even to admit with characteristic candor that the institutions being erected in the name of Reformation were not necessarily better than those of the Roman church which they replaced." However Tredway finds that, "a cursory reading of this book may . . . produce impatience and even disappointment in some quarters, for Pelikan is as cautious as Luther himself. Those wanting a moratorium on criticism of the church will find little comfort in Luther's commitment to *ecclesia semper reformanda.* And those wanting to wipe clean the churchly slate and start all over will be equally frustrated by the respect which he considered the extant institutions of Christianity."

In a review of *The Christian Tradition,* Robert L. Wilken says that Jaroslav Pelikan "stands in a grand line extending back to the great period of Christian historiography in nineteenth-century Germany, the time of Ferdinand Christian Baur, Albrecht Ritschl, and Adolf von Harnack. As such, his work can and should be seen as the first major attempt by an American historian to answer the chief question that has dominated the study of early Christian thought, namely the problem of 'hellenization' of the gospel. How did a movement which began with the preaching of a Jewish rabbi in Palestine become the dogmatic religion that we know from Christian history? . . . Though this inquiry is historical in its conception and execution, it clearly bears a message for contemporary Christian thinkers. The author has no patience with those shrill voices that, proclaiming their liberation from the past, despise the Christian intellectual tradition in the name of modernity. Indeed, he is convinced that the Christian intellectual tradition is worth taking seriously even—perhaps particularly—in the late twentieth century."

BIOGRAPHICAL/CRITICAL SOURCES: Encounter, winter, 1967; *Times Literary Supplement,* October 12, 1967; *Christian Century,* November 6, 1968, July 16, 1969; *Yale Review,* spring, 1969; *Saturday Review,* August 7, 1971.

* * *

PERCY, Walker 1916-

PERSONAL: Born May 28, 1916, in Birmingham, Ala.; son of Leroy Pratt and Martha (Phinizy) Percy; married Mary Bernice Townsend; children: Ann Boyd, Mary Pratt. *Education:* University of North Carolina, B.A., 1937; Columbia University, M.D., 1941. *Home:* Old Landing Rd., Covington, La. 70433. *Agent:* McIntosh & Otis, Inc., 475 Fifth Ave., New York, N.Y. 10017.

CAREER: Author. *Member:* American Academy of Arts and Sciences (fellow), National Institute of Arts and Letters. *Awards, honors:* National Book Award for fiction, 1962, for *The Moviegoer;* National Institute of Arts and Letters grant, 1967; National Catholic Book Award, 1971, for *Love in the Ruins,*

WRITINGS—All published by Farrar, Straus, except as indicated: *The Moviegoer,* Knopf, 1961, reprinted, Avon, 1980; *The Last Gentleman,* 1966; *Love in the Ruins,* 1971; *The Message in the Bottle,* 1975; *Lancelot,* 1977; *The Second Coming,* 1980. Contributor of numerous philosophical, critical, and medical articles to journals and magazines.

WORK IN PROGRESS: Another novel.

SIDELIGHTS: Upon graduation from Columbia University's Medical School, Walker Percy began serving his internship at Bellevue Hospital in New York City. As a result of performing autopsies on derelicts, Percy contracted pulmonary tuberculosis. During the following two years he was confined to his bed with reading being his main activity. Percy suffered a relapse when he attempted to return to medicine as an instructor of pathology. After another lengthy recovery period, which included more philosophical reading, Percy decided to give up his medical career in favor of a writing career.

Discussing this switch from the scientific to the literary, Percy told an interviewer for *Bookweek:* "If the first great intellectual discovery of my life was the beauty of the scientific method, surely the second was the discovery of the singular predicament of man in the very world which has been transformed by this science. An extraordinary paradox became clear: that the more science progressed and even as it benefited man, the less it said about what it is like to be a man living in the world." Several critics have written that through his writings, Percy is searching for a solution to this paradox.

For example, while reviewing Percy's *The Message in the Bottle,* Martin Kirby suggests that Percy "writes in a quasi-scientific style; he seems to be trying to persuade logically, but his insights are essentially emotional, even poetic; and the whole effort seems to be directed toward opening a line of thought leading toward a Christian concept of human existence."

Jonathan Culler writes: "Percy offers a forceful, if unnecessarily repetitive, critique of behaviorism, but he is not always aware of the implications of his own insights and formulations, and this can lead to a measure of confusion. Thus, the central fact on which he insists is that man lives in a symbolic universe, and that therefore his experience is mediated by symbolic structures and systems of names. The varieties of symbolic mediation are what explain man's paradoxical behavior: the bored commuter on his evening train becomes less bored by reading a book about bored commuters sitting on trains. And Mr. Percy's superb discussion of the 'dialectic of sightseeing' (the way in which symbolic representations of frameworks alter the character of perception) is based on his awareness of mediation. . . . The impossibility of direct, unmediated experiences is the basis of this dialectic."

In a review for *South Atlantic Quarterly,* John M. Bradbury discusses the concept of Walker Percy as a Southern writer. Bradbury explains that "John Barth and Walker Percy, [are] the most gifted of recent Southern novelists. The premises for them all can only be termed 'existential': that is, the world in which they live is to them radically absurd, disburdened of intrinsic values. Their individual freedom to exist without reference to prefabricated patterns of behavior, or essences, is only too available and operative. They inherit only sensitivities, no moral or religious codes, though Ebenezer (who after all lived in the seventeenth and early eighteenth centuries) may be regarded as purveyor of no heritage rather than as an inheritor of none. Regardless of chronological age, in any event, these are all quite modernly alienated young men."

Joan Bischoff feels that while Percy is very much a Southern author, "[he] is not a typical Southern writer in the sense that he does not ape Faulknerian mannerisms or utilize Southern local color; indeed, he had declared that he thinks the age of Southern writing is over. Percy epitomizes the new Southern writer, both a descendant of the past and a man of the present. In any case, Percy specifically disavows any legacy from Southern literary tradition; rather, he declares his indebtedness to philosophers and to French and Russian novelists."

However Richard Lehan sees similarities between Faulkner and Percy. Lehan writes: "As in Faulkner's novels, Percy's fiction takes place in a prolapsed world, often cut off from the ordinary workaday world, where characters are haunted by the past and bound by the absurdity of their situation. To this, Percy adds two states of narrative consciousness—one of perception and another of reflection—and also a sense of the grotesque. Percy's strength as a novelist—his brilliant sense of the grotesque, his ability to depict the estranged mind, his sense of coincidence—is also the source of his weakness because it leads at times to far-fetched situations, especially in *The Last Gentleman*. . . . Percy puts a great burden upon his abundant stylistic ability, and when the style breaks down he is in serious narrative trouble."

BIOGRAPHICAL/CRITICAL SOURCES: Time, May 19, 1961, February 1, 1963; *New York Times Book Review,* May 28, 1961, June 26, 1966; *New Yorker,* July 22, 1961; *Partisan Review,* summer, 1966; *Bookweek,* December 25, 1966; *Southern Review,* spring, 1968; *South Atlantic Quarterly,* summer, 1969; *Contemporary Literary Criticism,* Gale, Volume II, 1974, Volume III, 1975, Volume VI, 1976, Volume VIII, 1978; *Yale Review,* winter, 1976; *Carleton Miscellany,* Volume XVI, 1976-77; *Dictionary of Literary Biography,* Volume II, Gale, 1978.

—Sketch by Margaret Mazurkiewicz

* * *

PERHAM, Margery (Freda) 1895-

PERSONAL: Born September 6, 1895, in Bury, Lancashire, England; daughter of Frederick and Marion (Needell) Perham. *Education:* St. Hugh's College, Oxford, B.A. and M.A., 1919. *Religion:* Church of England. *Home:* 5 Rawlinson Rd., Oxford, England. *Agent:* A. P. Watt & Son, 26/28 Bedford Row, London WC1R 4HL, England.

CAREER: Assistant lecturer in history, University of Sheffield, Sheffield, England; Oxford University, St. Hugh's College, Oxford, England, fellow and tutor in modern history, 1924-29, research fellow, 1930-39; Rhodes travelling fellow in North America, Polynesia, Australia, and Africa, 1929-32; Rockefeller travelling fellow in East Africa and Sudan, 1932; Oxford University, research lecturer in colonial administration, 1935-39, reader in colonial administration, 1939-48, fellow of Nuffield College, 1939-63, honorary fellow of Nuffield College, 1963—, vice-chairman of Summer School of Colonial Administration, 1937-38, director of Institute of Colonial Studies, 1945-48, chairman of Colonial Records Research Project, 1963-73. Member of Higher Education Commission and West Indies Higher Education Committee, 1944; member of executive committee, Inter-University Council on Higher Education Overseas, 1946-67; member of Colonial Social Science Research Council, 1947-61; president of Universities' Mission to Central Africa, 1963-64. Reith Lecturer, British Broadcasting Corp., 1961. Member of advisory Committee on Education in the Colonies, 1939-45.

MEMBER: British Academy (fellow), Royal Commonwealth Society, American Academy of Arts and Sciences (fellow).

Awards, honors: Commander, Order of the British Empire, 1948; commander, Order of St. Michael and St. George, 1965; Gold Wellcome Medal, Royal African Society. D.C.L., University of Southampton, 1962; LL.D., University of St. Andrews, 1962, University of London, 1964, and University of Birmingham, 1969; L.H.D., Cambridge University, 1966, and Oxford University.

WRITINGS: Major Dane's Garden, Hutchinson, 1925, reprinted, Africana Publishing, 1970; *The Protectorate of South Africa: The Question of Their Transfer to the Union,* Oxford University Press, 1935; *Native Administration in Nigeria,* Oxford University Press, 1937; *Africans and British Rule,* Oxford University Press, 1941; *The Government of Ethiopia,* Faber, 1948, revised edition, Northwestern University Press, 1969; (with Elspeth Huxley) *Race and Politics in Kenya,* Faber, 1956, revised edition, Greenwood Press, 1975; *Lugard,* Collins, Volume I: *The Years of Adventure, 1858-1898,* 1956, Volume II: *The Years of Authority, 1898-1945,* 1960; *The Colonial Reckoning,* Collins, 1961, Knopf, 1962, reprinted, Greenwood Press, 1976, revised edition, Collins, 1963; *African Outline,* Oxford University Press, 1966; *Colonial Sequence, 1930-1949,* Barnes & Noble, 1967; *Colonial Sequence, 1949-1969,* Methuen, 1970; *African Apprenticeship: An Autobiographical Journey in South Africa, 1929,* Africana Publishing, 1974; *East African Journey: Kenya and Tanganyika, 1929-1930,* Faber, 1976. Also author of *Tribes of the Niger Delta: Their Religion and Customs.*

Editor: *Ten Africans,* Faber, 1936, 2nd edition, Northwestern University Press, 1964; (with J. Simmons) *African Discovery: An Anthology of Exploration,* Faber, 1942, 2nd edition, 1957, Northwestern University Press, 1963; *The Economics of Tropical Dependency,* Faber, Volume I: *The Native Economics of Nigeria,* 1946, Volume II: *Mining, Commerce, and Finance in Nigeria,* 1948; J. W. Davidson, *Northern Rhodesian Legislative Council,* Faber, 1948; *Colonial Government,* Oxford University Press, 1950; *The Diaries of Lord Lugard,* Northwestern University Press, 1959-63, Volume I: *East Africa, November, 1889 to December, 1890,* Volume II: *East Africa, December, 1890 to December, 1891,* Volume III: *East Africa, January, 1892 to August, 1892,* Volume IV: *Nigeria, 1894-95 and 1898;* Kenneth Robinson, *Essays in Imperial Government,* Basil Blackwell, 1963.

Contributor to periodicals, including London *Times.*

AVOCATIONAL INTERESTS: Gardening, animal welfare.

BIOGRAPHICAL/CRITICAL SOURCES: Observer, November 26, 1961; *Times Literary Supplement,* November 2, 1967.†

* * *

PERREAULT, John 1937-

PERSONAL: Born August 26, 1937, in New York, N.Y.; son of Jean Baptiste and Mary (Urzendowski) Perreault. *Education:* Attended Montclair State College, New School for Social Research, and City College (now City College of the City University of New York). *Home:* 54 East Seventh St., New York, N.Y. 10003.

CAREER: Art News, New York City, associate editor, 1964-68; *Village Voice,* New York City, art critic, 1966-74; New York correspondent for *Le Monde* and *Art International,* 1970; U.S. Commissioner, Tokyo Biennale of Figurative Art, 1974; host, "John Perreault . . . Talking about Art,"

WBAI-FM, 1975; *Soho Weekly News,* New York City, senior art critic, 1975—. Editor, *Elephant* (magazine), New York City. Instructor of yearly seminars, School of Visual Arts, New York City, 1966-69; distinguished professor of art, University of Arizona, 1979. Participant in numerous poetry events, including "Balloon," "The Fashion Show Poetry Event," and "The Fashion Show Poetry Event No. 2," all held in New York City, and "Alternatives," held in New York City and Ann Arbor, Mich. Has made two 8 mm. films, "Film Poem" and "TV Set." *Member:* International Association of Art Critics (president, American section, 1979-81). *Awards, honors:* National Association for Education fellowships, 1973 and 1979, for art criticism; Dylan Thomas Award; National Council on the Arts award; two Poets Foundation awards.

WRITINGS—Poetry: *Camouflage,* Lines Press, 1966; *Luck,* Kulchur Press, 1969; *Harry,* Coach House Press, 1974. Work represented in anthologies, including *The American Writers,* edited by Richard Kostelanetz, Funk & Wagnalls, 1967, *Under Thirty,* Indiana University Press, *Minimal Art,* Dutton, *Conceptual Art,* Dutton, and *Idea Art,* Dutton. Work appears in several art exhibition catalogs, including *Beyond Literalism,* Moore College of Art, *The Thickening Surface,* University of Florida, and *Outside the City Limits,* New York Gallery Association. Contributor of poetry, short stories, and articles to *Sun and Moon, Arts, Art News, Art in America, Vogue, Portfolio, New York Magazine,* and other publications. Co-editor, *Anti-Object Art,* winter, 1975.

WORK IN PROGRESS: A collection of short stories; a novel, tentatively entitled *The Art World Murders; Collected Art Criticism;* a book about pattern painting.

SIDELIGHTS: John Perreault writes: "I see no conflict among my various careers: poetry, fiction, art criticism, and, sometimes, art. You only live once. Each career feeds the other." Perreault notes that "time is the only problem." He continues: "Certainly I would like more time for my poetry and fiction, but I consider it a great honor to be recognized as an art critic. In this regard, newspaper art criticism excites me the most. I am able to write about art as it happens, and it has always seemed to me that writing for [the] general public is a very important and valuable thing to do. Art is for everyone."

In 1975, a special "John Perreault" issue of *Serif,* the Kent State Libraries quarterly, was published.

* * *

PERRY, Lewis (Curtis) 1938-

PERSONAL: Born November 21, 1938, in Somerville, Mass.; son of Albert Quillen (a Universalist minister) and Irene (Lewis) Perry; married Ruth Opler, June 5, 1962 (divorced, 1970); married Elisabeth Israels (a university teacher), November 26, 1970; children: (first marriage) Curtis Allen; (second marriage) Susanna Irene, David Mordecai. *Education:* Oberlin College, B.A., 1960; Cornell University, M.S., 1964, Ph.D., 1967. *Home:* 1212 Pickwick Place, Bloomington, Ind. 47401. *Office:* Department of History, Indiana University, Bloomington, Ind. 47405.

CAREER: New Freedom, Ithaca, N.Y., co-editor, 1961-62; State University of New York at Buffalo, lecturer, 1966-67, assistant professor, 1967-72, associate professor of history, 1972-78; currently professor of history, Indiana University at Bloomington. *Member:* American Historical Association, Organization of American Historians, American Studies Association, Phi Kappa Phi. *Awards, honors:* American Council of Learned Societies fellow, 1972-73; State University of New York Research Foundation summer fellow, 1968, 1972, and 1974; National Humanities Institute fellow, 1975-76; National Endowment for the Humanities demonstration grant, 1976-78.

WRITINGS: (Editor with Leonard Krimerman) *Patterns of Anarchy,* Doubleday, 1966; *Radical Abolitionism: Anarchy and the Government of God in Antislavery Thought,* Cornell University Press, 1973; (editor with Michael Fellman) *Antislavery Reconsidered,* Louisiana State University Press, 1979; *Childhood, Marriage, and Reform: Henry Clarke Wright, 1797-1870,* University of Chicago Press, 1980. Contributor to journals. Editor, *Journal of American History.*

WORK IN PROGRESS: American Theatre in the 19th Century; A Survey of American Thought and Culture.

* * *

PERRY, Ritchie (John Allen) 1942- (John Allen)

PERSONAL: Born January 7, 1942, in King's Lynn, Norfolk, England; son of Hubert John (a teacher) and Ella (Allen) Perry; married Lynn Mary Charlotte Barton, November 23, 1976; children: Tina Elizabeth, Sara Charlotte. *Education:* St. John's College, Oxford, B.A. (honors), 1964. *Home:* 4 The Close, Limbury, Luton, Bedfordshire, England. *Agent:* A. D. Peters, 10 Buckingham St., London WC2N 6BU, England.

CAREER: Bank of London & South America Ltd., Brazil, managerial trainee, 1964-66; assistant teacher in Norfolk, England, 1966-74, and in Luton, England, 1975—. *Member:* Crime Writers Association.

WRITINGS—Mysteries, except as indicated: *The Fall Guy,* Collins, 1972, Houghton, 1973; *A Hard Man to Kill,* Houghton, 1973 (published in England as *Nowhere Man,* Collins, 1973); *Ticket to Ride,* Collins, 1973, Houghton, 1974; *Holiday with a Vengeance,* Collins, 1974, Houghton, 1975; *Your Money and Your Wife,* Collins, 1975, Houghton, 1976; *One Good Death Deserves Another,* Collins, 1976, Houghton, 1977; *Dead End,* Collins, 1977; *Brazil* (juvenile), Macdonald Educational, 1977; *Dutch Courage,* Collins, 1978; (under pseudonym John Allen) *Copacabana Stud,* R. Hale, 1978; *Bishop's Pawn,* Collins, 1979, Pantheon, 1979; *Up Tight,* R. Hale, 1979; *Grand Slam,* Collins, 1980.

WORK IN PROGRESS: Two mysteries; a children's book, *George H. Ghastly, Esquire;* a book of test records for cricket.

* * *

PETERSON, Hans 1922-

PERSONAL: Born October 26, 1922, in Varing, Sweden; son of Emil G. (an electrician) and Hilda (Peterson) Peterson; married Anne Marie Nordstrand (a photographer), June 17, 1958; children: Lena, Jan. *Education:* Attended public schools in Sweden. *Home:* Marstrandsgatan 21, Gothenburg, Sweden 41724.

CAREER: Has worked at various jobs, including lift-boy, factory worker, and electrician; author, 1947—. *Awards, honors:* Nils Holgersson prize, 1958, for *Magnus and the Van Horse;* German young-books prize, 1959, for *Magnus and the Squirrel; Liselott and the Goloff* included in Hans Christian Andersen Honor List, 1964; received several Swedish State and Gothenburg town prizes for collected work.

WRITINGS: Den uppdaemda ravinen: Roman (novel),

Bonnier (Stockholm), 1949; *Flicken och sommaren* (title means "The Girl and the Summer"), Tidens forlag (Stockholm), 1950; *Laerkorna* (title means "The Larks"), Tidens forlag, 1952; *Hejda solnedgaangen* (title means "Stop the Sunset"), Tidens forlag, 1955; *Kvinnors Kaerlek: Noveller* (novel; title means "Women's Love"), Norstedt (Stockholm), 1956; *Skaadespelaren* (title means "The Actor"), Norstedt, 1957; *Aelskarinnan* (title means "The Mistress"), Norstedt, 1959; *Resebidrag* (title means "Traveling Letters"), Norstedt, 1961; *Kvinnorna: Tre beraettelser* (short stories; title means "The Women: Three Stories"), Norstedt, 1962; *Historien om en by: Roman* (novel; title means "A Story about a Village"), Norstedt, 1963; *Aelskaren* (novel; title means "The Lover"), Norstedt, 1966; *Elise och Rickard* (novel; title means "Elise and Richard"), Gebers, 1971; *Elise ensam* (novel; title means "Elise Alone"), Gebers, 1972; *Elise och de andra* (novel; title means "Elise and the Others"), Gebers, 1973; *Frm dagari november* (novel; title means "Five days in November"), Gebers, 1977.

Children's books; all Swedish editions published by Raben & Sjoegren (Stockholm), except as indicated: *Magnus och ekorrungen* (also see below), 1956, translation by Madeleine Hamilton published as *Magnus and the Squirrel,* Viking, 1959; *Magnus, Mattias och Mari* (also see below), 1958, translation by Marianne Turner published in England as *Magnus and the Van Horse,* Burke, 1961, published as *Magnus and the Wagon Horse,* Pantheon, 1966; *Magnus i hamn* (also see below), 1958, translation by Turner published as *Magnus in the Harbor,* Pantheon, 1966; *Naer vi snoeade inne,* 1959, translation by Irene Morris published as *The Day It Snowed,* Burke, 1969; *Magnus i fara* (also see below), 1959, translation by Turner published as *Magnus in Danger,* Pantheon, 1967; *Petter Joensson hade en gitarr,* 1959, adaptation by Kay Ware and Lucille Sutherland published as *Peter Johnson and His Guitar,* Webster, 1961, stage adaptation by Turner, Burke, 1965.

Naer vi regnade inne (title means "The Day It Rained"), 1960; *Gubben och Kanariefaageln,* 1960, adaptation by Ware and Sutherland published as *The Old Man and the Bird,* Webster, 1964, stage adaptation by Marianne Helweg, Burke, 1966; *Maens och mia,* 1960, translation published as *Tom and Tabby,* Lothrop, 1965; *Magnus och skeppshunden Jack,* 1961, translation by Turner published as *Magnus and the Ships Mascot,* Burke, 1964; *Lille-Olle och sommardagen,* 1962, adaptation by Ware and Sutherland published as *Benjamin Has a Birthday,* Webster, 1964; *Liselott och Garaffen,* 1962, translation by Annabelle Macmillan published as *Liselott and the Goloff,* Coward, 1964; *Det nya huset,* 1962, adaptation by Ware and Sutherland published as *The New House,* Webster, 1964, stage adaptation by Helweg, Burke, 1966; *Mick och Malin,* 1962, translation published as *Mickey and Molly,* Lothrop, 1964; *Boken om Magnus* (title means "A Book about Magnus"; includes *Magnus och ekorrungen, Magnus, Mattias och Mari, Magnus i hamn, Magnus i fara*), 1963; *Haer Kommer Petter,* 1963, translation by Turner published as *Here Comes Peter,* Burke, 1965; *Hunden Buster,* 1963, translation published as *Brownie,* Lothrop, 1965; *Stina och Lars rymmer,* 1964, translation by Patricia Crampton published as *Stina and Lars in the Mountains,* Burke, 1970; *Petter kommer igen,* 1964, translation by Turner published as *Peter Comes Back,* Burke, 1966; *Naer hoensen blaaste bort,* 1964, translation by Morris published as *The Day the Chickens Blew Away,* Burke, 1970.

Liselott och de andra, 1965, translation by Morris published as *Lisa Settles In,* Burke, 1967; *Den nya vaegen,* 1965, translation by Morris published as *The New Road,* Burke, 1967; *Petter klarar allt,* 1966, translation by Evelyn Ramsden published as *Peter Makes His Way,* Burke, 1968; *Bara Liselott,* 1967, translation by Morris published as *Just Lisa,* Burke, 1969; *Den nya bron,* 1967, translation by Morris published as *The New Bridge,* Burke, 1969; *Sara och sommerhuset,* 1967, translation by Morris published as *Sara in Summer-time,* Burke, 1973; *Expedition Snoestorm* (title means "Expedition Snowstorm"), 1968; *Jag vill inte, sa Sara,* 1968, translation by Morris published as *I Don't Want to, Said Sara,* Burke, 1969; *Lill-Anna, Johan och den vilda bjoernen* (title means "Lill-Anna, Johan and the Wild Bear"), Gebers (Stockholm), 1968; *Magnus Lindberg och haesten Mari,* 1968, adaptation by Christine Hyatt published as *Eric and the Christmas Horse,* Burke, 1969, Lothrop, 1970; (with Harald Wiberg) *Naer Per gick vilse i skogen,* 1969, translation published as *When Peter Was Lost in the Forest,* Coward, 1970.

Franssonsbarna i Faagelhult (title means "These Children in Bird-Cottage"), Gebers, 1970; *Aake gaar till sjoess* (title means "Aake Goes on Board"), Gebers, 1970; *Ett lejon i huset* (title means "A Lion in the House"), 1970; *Pelle Jansson, en kille med tur,* 1970, translation by Hanne Barnes published as *Pelle Jansson,* Burke, 1974; *Sara och Lillebror,* 1970, translation by Morris published as *Sara and Her Brother,* Burke, 1973; *Pelle Jansson, en kille mitt i stan,* 1971, translation by Barnes published as *Pelle in the Big City,* Burke, 1974; *Radovan och Ritva* (title means "Radovan and Ritva"), 1971; *Pelle Jansson, en kille som inte ger sig,* 1972, translation by Barnes published as *Pelle in Trouble,* Burke, 1976; *Rut och Rickard* (title means "Rut and Richard"), 1972; *Var kommer bullen ifraan?* (title means "From Where Comes the Roll?"), 1972; *Dagen naer allting haende* (title means "The Day Everything Happens"), 1973; *Den nya bilen* (title means "The New Car"), 1974; *Lantgaarden* (title means "The Modern Farm"), 1974; *Vilse i fjaellen* (title means "Lost in the Mountains"), 1974.

Den stora snoestormen, 1975, translation by Barnes published as *The Big Snowstorm,* Burke, 1976; *Jakten paa Janne* (title means "The Hunt for Johnny"), 1975; *Malin paa en oede oe* (title means "Malin on the Waste Island"), 1975; *Veckan Anna och Vlasto foersvann* (title means "The Week Anna and Vlast Escaped"), 1975; *Varfoer blir det saa* (title means "Why Does That Go So?"), 1975; *Maja-Lena gaar till morfar* (title means Maja-Lena Going to Grandfather"), 1975; *Faagelpojken* (title means "The Birdboy"), 1976; *Dagen innan vintern kom* (title means "The Day before Winter Comes"), 1976; *De fyra hemloesa* (title means "The Four Homeless"), 1977; *Dagen naer Simon flyttade* (title means "The Day Simon Removed"), 1977; *Malin har en hemlighet* (title means "Malin Has a Secret"), 1977; *Kaera Alberta* (title means "Dear Alberta"), 1977; *Huset* (title means "The House"), 1977; *Resan* (title means "The Trip"), 1977; *Aron heter jag* (title means "My Name Is Aron"), 1978; *Malin aer indian* (title means "Malin Is an Indian"), 1978; *Jag, Alberta* (title means, "I, Alberta"), 1978; *Aentigen Alberta* (title means "At Last, Alberta"), 1979; *Dagen naer Simon strejkade* (title means "The Day Simon Goes on Strike"), 1979; *Vilhelmina, den ensamma hunden* (title means Vilhelmina, the Lonely Dog"), 1980; *Ni faar inte skiljas* (title means "You Must Not Divorce"), 1980; *Christer som Aelskar* (title means "Christer Who Loves"), 1980.

Also author of two novels, *The Tale about Elin,* 1973 and *Helge and Annie,* 1974.

WORK IN PROGRESS: Novels, short stories, children's books, picture books.

SIDELIGHTS: Hans Peterson has written novels for adults with seeing and hearing difficulties and intends to write more. His books have been published in countries all over the world, including Austria, Japan, Canada, France, and South Africa. *Avocational interests:* Traveling, working at his summer house, meeting friends, living.

* * *

PETERSON, Roger Tory 1908-

PERSONAL: Born August 28, 1908, in Jamestown, N.Y.; son of Charles Gustav and Henrietta (Bader) Peterson; married Mildred Washington, 1936 (divorced); married Barbara Coulter, 1943 (divorced); married Virginia Westervelt, 1976; children: (second marriage) Tory Coulter, Lee Allen. *Education:* Attended Art Student's League, 1927-28, and National Academy of Design, 1929-31. *Home and office:* 125 Neck Rd., Old Lyme, Conn. 06371.

CAREER: Rivers School, Brookline, Mass., instructor in science and art, 1931-34; National Audubon Society, New York, N.Y., administrative staff, educational director, 1934-43, screen tour lecturer, 1946-72, member of board of directors, 1958-60, 1965-67, 1968-70, secretary, 1960-64, special consultant, 1970—; Houghton-Mifflin Co., Boston, Mass., editor of "Field Guide" series of nature handbooks, 1946—; National Wildlife Federation, Washington, D.C., art director, 1946-75. Member of council, Cornell University Laboratory of Ornithology. Fellow, Davenport College, Yale University, 1966—, and Rochester Museum and Science Center, 1972—. Member of board of directors, Baharini Foundation (Kenya), 1970—. Public lecturer on natural history subjects. Has done commissioned art work for *Life*, 1938-45, National Wildlife Federation, 1940-60, Quaker State Publishing Co., 1940-45, Mill Pond Press, Inc., 1973—, and Morell and Co. Work has been exhibited in numerous one-man shows and in public collections. *Military service:* U.S. Army Air Forces, and U.S. Army, Corps of Engineers, 1943-45.

MEMBER: Society of Wildlife Artists (vice-president), Society of Animal Artists, World Wildlife Fund (member of board of directors, 1962-76), National Parks Association, American Nature Study Society (president, 1952-53), Association of Interpretive Naturalists, American Ornithologists Union (fellow; first vice-president, 1962-63), American Association for the Advancement of Science (fellow), Audubon Naturalist Society (honorary vice-president), Biologists Field Club, Wilson Ornithological Society (president, 1964-65), Baird Club, Brooks Bird Club, Cooper Ornithological Society, Wilderness Society, Wildfowl Trust, Linnaean Society (fellow), East African Wild Life Society, British Trust for Ornithology, Severn Waterfowl Trust (England), British Ornithologists's Union (honorary member), Zoological Society of London (honorary fellow), Spanish Ornithological Society (honorary member), British Ornithological Society (corresponding fellow), Wildlife Protective Society of South Africa, German Ornithological Society, Hawk Mountain Sanctuary Association (member of board of directors, 1962-67; member of board of sponsors, 1967-74), Pacific Northwest Bird Banding Society, New York Zoological Society (fellow), Maryland Ornithological Society, South Dakota Ornithologists' Union, New Jersey Audubon Society (honorary vice-president, 1970-71), Massachusetts Audubon Society (honorary vice-president), Texas Ornithological Society (honorary fellow), Audubon Society of District of Columbia (honorary vice-president), Rhode Island Audubon Society (honorary vice-president), Hartford Audubon Society, Nuttall Club (Cambridge, Mass.), Intrepids Club (president, 1974-79), Explorers Club, Savile Club (London), Cosmos Club (Washington, D.C.), Century Club (New York, N.Y.).

AWARDS, HONORS: William Brewster Award, American Ornithologists Union, 1944, for 2nd edition of *A Field Guide to the Birds;* John Burroughs Medal, John Burroughs Memorial Association, 1950, for *Birds over America;* Certificate of Recognition, American Nature Study Society, 1953; Geoffrey St. Hilaire Gold Medal, Societe Nationale de Acclimation de France, 1958, for *A Field Guide to the Birds of Britain and Europe;* Carey-Thomas Award honorable mention, 1959, for *A Field Guide to the Birds;* Gold Medal, New York Zoological Society, 1961; Certificate of Recognition, Wisconsin Society of Ornithology, 1964; Arthur A. Allen Award, Cornell Laboratory of Ornithology, 1967; Gold Medal, Safari Club, 1968; Conservation Award, White Memorial Foundation, 1968; Paul Bartsch Award, 1969, and Oak Leaf Cluster Award, 1974, both from Audubon Naturalist Society; Frances K. Hutchinson Medal, Garden Club of America, 1970; Gold Medal, Garden Club of New Jersey, 1970; Audubon Medal, National Audubon Society, 1971; Gold Medal, World Wildlife Fund, 1972; Joseph Wood Krutch Medal, Humane Society, 1973; Distinguished Public Service Award, Connecticut Bar Association, 1974; Golden Key Award as Outstanding Teacher of the Year, 1974; Explorers Club Medal, 1974; Conservation Achievement Award, National Wildlife Federation, 1975; Linnaeus Gold Medal, Swedish Academy of Sciences, 1976; Green World Award, New York Botanical Society, 1976; Cosmos Club Award, 1976; Sarah Josepha Hale Award, Richards Library, 1977; Horatio Alger Award, 1977; Officier of Order of the Golden Ark (Netherlands), 1978; Master Artist Medal, Leigh Yawkey Museum, 1978; Gold Medal, Holland Society of New York, 1979; Medal of Freedom from U.S. Government, presented by President Carter, 1980; Ludlow Griscom Medal, American Birding Association, 1980. D.Sc. from Franklin and Marshall College, 1952, Ohio State University, 1962, Fairfield University, 1967, Allegheny College, 1967, Wesleyan University, 1970, Colby College, 1974, and Gustavas Adolphus College, 1978; D.H., Hamilton College, 1976; D.H.L., Amherst College, 1977.

WRITINGS—Published by Houghton, except as indicated: *A Field Guide to the Birds,* 1934, 3rd edition, 1947; *The Junior Book of Birds,* 1939; *A Field Guide to Western Birds,* 1941, 2nd edition, 1961; (with John Baker) *The Audubon Guide to Attracting Birds,* Doubleday, 1941; *Birds over Americe,* Dodd, 1948, revised edition, 1964; *How to Know the Birds,* 1949, 3rd edition, 1962; *Wildlife in Color,* 1951; (with Guy Montfort and P.A.D. Hollom) *A Field Guide to the Birds of Britain and Europe,* 1954, revised edition, 1959; (with James Fisher) *Wild America,* 1955; *The Bird Watcher's Anthology,* Harcourt, 1957; *A Field Guide to the Birds of Texas and Adjacent States,* 1960, revised edition, 1963; *The Birds,* Life Nature Books, 1963, 2nd edition, 1968; (with Fisher) *The World of Birds,* Doubleday, 1964; (with Margaret McKenny) *A Field Guide to Wildflowers (Northeastern and North-Central North America),* 1968; (with Edward L. Chalif) *A Field Guide to Mexican Birds,* 1973; *Birds of America,* Audubon Society, 1978; *Penguins,* 1979.

Editor; published by Houghton: Percy A. Morris, *A Field Guide to Shells of the Atlantic and Gulf Coasts and the West Indies,* 1947, 3rd edition, 1973; Alexander B. Klots, *A Field Guide to the Butterflies,* 1951; William H. Burt and Richard P. Grossenheider, *A Field Guide to the Mammals,* 1952; Morris, *A Field Guide to Pacific Coast Shells,* 1952, 2nd edition, 1966; Frederick H. Pough, *A Field Guide to Rocks and Minerals,* 1953, 3rd edition, 1960; Olaus J. Murie, *A Field*

Guide to Animal Tracks, 1954; Boughton Cobb, *A Field Guide to the Ferns and Their Related Families,* 1956; George A. Petrides, *A Field Guide to Trees and Shrubs,* 1958; Roger Conant, *A Field Guide to Reptiles and Amphibians,* 1958; John J. Craighead, Frank C. Craighead, Jr., and Ray J. Davis, *A Field Guide to Rocky Mountain Wildflowers,* 1963; Donald H. Menzel, *A Field Guide to the Stars and Planets,* 1964; (with John A. Livingston) Maurice Brooks, *The Appalachians,* 1965; Robert O. Stebbins, *A Field Guide to Western Reptiles and Amphibians,* 1966; F. H. van der Brink, *A Field Guide to the Mammals of Britain and Europe,* 1968; Donald J. Borror and Richard E. White, *A Field Guide to the Insects,* 1970; (with Livingston) Verna R. Johnston, *Sierra Nevada,* 1970; (with Livingston) Ruth Kirk, *Desert,* 1973; Hal H. Harrison, *A Field Guide to Birds' Nests (Found East of Mississippi River),* 1975; (with Livingston) Betty Flanders Thompson, *Shaping America's Heartland,* 1977; Theodore F. Niehaus and Charles L. Ripper, *A Field Guide to Pacific States Wildflowers,* 1976; Kenneth L. Gosner, *A Field Guide to the Atlantic Seashore,* 1978; Lee Peterson (son), *A Field Guide to Edible Wild Plants,* 1978; Hal H. Harrison, *A Field Guide to Western Bird Nests,* 1979.

Contributor of introductions, prefaces, and art work to numerous books. Author of educational leaflets for National Audubon Society and "Bird Study Merit Badge" booklet for Boy Scouts of America. Columnist for *Audubon.* Contributor of articles on birds, natural history, and conservation to nature publications and popular magazines. Art editor, *Audubon,* 1934-43. Roving reporter, *International Wildlife,* 1970—.

WORK IN PROGRESS: A complete revision of *A Field Guide to the Birds;* a limited edition of bird prints, for Mill Pond Press (Venice, Fla.); several books on birds and natural history.

AVOCATIONAL INTERESTS: Photography (black and white, still, and movies) and travel.

BIOGRAPHICAL/CRITICAL SOURCES: Audubon, November, 1961; *Life,* December 22, 1961; *Reader's Digest,* January, 1962; *Maclean's Magazine,* January, 1962; John Devlin and Grace Naismith, *The World of Roger Tory Peterson,* Times Books, 1977; *New York Times,* November 6, 1979; *People,* March 17, 1980.

* * *

PETROCELLI, Orlando R(alph) 1930-
(Brian Dyer)

PERSONAL: Born October 10, 1930, in New York, N.Y.; son of Lucio (a foundry worker) and Carmela (Carrione) Petrocelli; married Kathleen Fontana, October 23, 1960; children: Lucio, Joseph, Neil. *Education:* Attended Brooklyn College (now Brooklyn College of the City University of New York), 1948-50. *Politics:* Republican. *Religion:* Roman Catholic. *Home:* 174 Brookstone Dr., Princeton, N.J. 08540. *Office:* Petrocelli Books, Inc., 1101 State Rd., Princeton, N.J. 08540.

CAREER: D. Van Nostrand Co., Inc., New York City, business manager, 1948-67; Stein & Day (publishers), New York City, comptroller, 1967-69; Auerbach Publishers, Philadelphia, Pa., vice-president and publisher, 1969-73; Mason & Lipscomb Publishers, New York City, publisher and executive vice-president, 1973-76; Petrocelli Books, Inc., Princeton, N.J., president, 1976—. *Member:* American Booksellers Association, Association of American Publishers, Authors' Guild, Players Club.

WRITINGS: (Editor) *Best Computer Papers 1971,* Auerbach, 1971; *The Pact* (novel; also see below), Dodd, 1973; *Olympia's Inheritance* (novel; sequel to *The Pact*), Dodd, 1974; (with Brian Rothery, under joint pseudonym Brian Dyer) *Saga of Celtic Queen,* Mason & Lipscomb, 1974; (under pseudonym Brian Dyer) *Without Regrets,* Mason & Lipscomb, 1975; *Match Set,* Pinnacle Books, 1977; (under pseudonym Brian Dyer) *A Woman's Story,* Mason & Lipscomb, 1977; *Five Days to Paradise,* Manor, 1978; (under pseudonym Brian Dyer) *The Wayward Heart,* Manor, 1978.

WORK IN PROGRESS: The Carlona Legacy.

* * *

PETTINGILL, Olin Sewall, Jr. 1907-

PERSONAL: Born October 30, 1907, in Belgrade, Me.; son of Olin Sewall (a physician) and Marion Bradbury (Groves) Pettingill; married Eleanor Rice (a writer), December 31, 1932 (died March 3, 1977); children: Polly-Ann (Mrs. Philip N. Losito), Mary-Ann (Mrs. Jack Vondra). *Education:* Bowdoin College, A.B., 1930; Cornell University, Ph.D., 1933. *Residence:* Wayne, Me. 04284.

CAREER: Instructor, lecturer, photographer, and author on subject of ornithology and other wildlife. New Hampshire Nature Camp, Lost River, instructor in ornithology, summers, 1934, 1936; Westbrook Junior College, Portland, Me., instructor in biology, 1935-36; Carleton College, Northfield, Minn., instructor, 1936-41, assistant professor, 1941-45, associate professor of zoology, 1946-54; University of Michigan Biological Station, Pellston, instructor in ornithology, summers, 1938-45, 1947-57, 1959-74; Cornell University, Ithaca, N.Y., director of Laboratory of Ornithology, 1960-73. Research associate of Cranbrook Institute of Science, 1940-45. Visiting professor of biology, Virginia Polytechnic Institute and State University, Blacksburg, 1978. Photographer, Carnegie Museum expedition to Hudson Bay, 1931; co-leader, Cornell-Carleton Ornithological Expedition to Mexico, 1941; director, Whooping Crane project, sponsored by National Audubon Society and U.S. Fish and Wildlife Service, 1945. Has lectured and shown his films of birds and other wildlife in the United States, Canada, Great Britain, and the Caribbean islands, 1939—; photographer-lecturer, National Audubon Society's annual "Screen Tours" series, 1943—. Narrator, "The Films of Olin Sewall Pettingill," WCBB-TV (Maine), 1978. Delegate to Twelfth International Ornithological Congress (Helsinki, Finland), 1958, and Fourteenth International Ornithological Congress (Oxford, England), 1966. Consultant on life sciences, *The American Heritage Dictionary of the English Language,* 1969. Trustee, Kents Hill School, 1975—.

MEMBER: American Ornithologists' Union (secretary, 1946-51; life member), National Wildlife Federation (life member), National Audubon Society (member of board of directors, 1955-66, 1967-75; secretary, 1957-59, 1963-66), Wilson Ornithological Society (secretary, 1937-41; vice-president, 1942-47; president, 1948-50), British Ornithologists' Union (life member), Wildlife Society (life member), Ornithological Society of New Zealand (life member), Maine Audubon Society (president, 1959-60), Nebraska Ornithologists' Union (honorary member), South Dakota Ornithologists' Union (honorary member), New Hampshire Audubon Society (honorary vice-president), Delmarva Ornithological Society (honorary member), Sigma Xi. *Awards, honors:* D.Sc., Bowdoin College, 1956, and Colby College, 1979; Detroit Audubon Society Award for distinguished contributions to ornithology and conservation, 1964, Arthur A. Allen Award, Cornell University, 1974.

WRITINGS: Laboratory and Field Manual of Ornithology, Burgess, 1939, 4th revised edition published as *Ornithology in Laboratory and Field,* 1970; *A Guide to Bird Finding East of the Mississippi,* Oxford University Press, 1951, 2nd edition, 1977; *A Guide to Bird Finding West of the Mississippi,* Oxford University Press, 1953, revised edition, in press; (editor) *Enjoying Maine Birds,* Maine Audubon Society, 1960; (contributor of photographs) Eleanor Rice Pettingill, *Penguin Summer,* C. N. Potter, 1960; (with S. F. Hoyt) *Enjoying Birds in Upstate New York,* Laboratory of Ornithology, Cornell University, 1963; (with N. R. Whitney, Jr.) *Birds of the Black Hills,* Laboratory of Ornithology, Cornell University, 1965; (editor) *The Bird Watcher's America,* McGraw, 1965; (editor-in-chief) Edgar M. Reilly, *The Audubon Illustrated Handbook of American Birds,* McGraw, 1968; *Another Penguin Summer,* Scribner, 1975.

Also script writer and photographer for ten films on birds, produced by Coronet Instructional Films. Advisory editor, "Our Living World of Nature" series, McGraw, 1963-68.

Compiler of section on birds of prey for *World Book Encyclopedia,* and author of introduction to section on birds in *Book of Knowledge.* Columnist, *Audubon Magazine,* 1957-68. Editor of bird section, *Biological Abstracts,* 1942-53; review editor, *Wilson Bulletin,* 1959-69; *Living Bird,* editor, 1962-64, co-editor, 1965-72; contributing editor, *Audubon Magazine,* 1962—; advisory editor, *American Birds,* 1962—.

WORK IN PROGRESS: "Many projects."

SIDELIGHTS: Olin Sewall Pettingill, Jr. told *CA* that his "research interests center on the distribution, ecology, breeding biology, and behavior of birds." On the Whooping Crane project in 1945, Pettingill followed the cranes by car, boat, and plane from the Gulf Coast to their breeding grounds in the Canadian wilds and back again—a study designed to help save the dwindling species from extinction. In 1953-54, Pettingill spent about six months in the Falkland Islands, filming penguins and other wildlife. The story of that expedition was published in *National Geographic* and was also the subject of a book, *Penguin Summer,* written by his wife, Eleanor. Some of the film from this study was later included in the movie "Islands of the Sea," produced by Walt Disney, and on several Disney television programs. In addition, three other films by Walt Disney Productions—"Nature's Half Acre," "Water Birds," and "Vanishing Prairie"—contain Pettingill's footage. Pettingill has also produced wildlife films in Iceland, 1958, on Midway Atoll, 1963, and in New Zealand, 1965-66. Early in 1970, he was the naturalist and lecturer on a Linblad Tour to the Antarctic.

Bob Niss of the *Maine Sunday Telegram* believes that Pettingill is "perhaps America's second-ranking ornithologist." Moreover, he praises Pettingill's lectures and discussions on the subject for their "concise, easygoing and often humorous" style. Niss adds: "He makes no attempt to lecture. He entertains."

BIOGRAPHICAL/CRITICAL SOURCES: National Geographic, March, 1956; Eleanor Rice Pettingill, *Penguin Summer,* C. N. Potter, 1960; Olin Sewall Pettingill, Jr., *Another Penguin Summer,* Scribner, 1975; *Maine Sunday Telegram,* April 30, 1978.

* * *

PFAHL, John K(erch) 1927-

PERSONAL: Born January 17, 1927, in Akron, Ohio; son of Charles A. and Hazel (Kerch) Pfahl; married Floradelle Atwater, 1948; children: Jay Charles, John Christopher, Susan Kay. *Education:* Pennsylvania State University, B.A., 1947; Ohio State University, M.B.A., 1949, Ph.D., 1953. *Home:* 2610 Charing Rd., Columbus, Ohio 43221. *Office:* 1085 Fishinger Rd., Columbus, Ohio 43220.

CAREER: Ohio State University, Columbus, instructor, 1949-53, assistant professor, 1953-57, associate professor, 1957-63, professor of finance, 1963-70; executive vice-president, Management Horizons, 1970-75; John K. Pfahl, Inc., Columbus, president, 1975—. State finance chairman, United Cerebral Palsy, 1961-70. *Member:* Society of Financial Analysts, Financial Management Association (former president), Financial Executives Institute, American Finance Association, American Economic Association, American Marketing Association, Columbus Chamber of Commerce, Phi Sigma Kappa. *Awards, honors:* Outstanding Young Men of Columbus, 1960; Wasserman Award from United Cerebral Palsy, 1970.

WRITINGS: Profitable Service Management, General Electric Co., 1960; (with E. F. Donaldson) *Personal Finance,* Ronald, 1961, 7th edition, 1980; (with Donaldson) *Corporate Finance,* Ronald, 1963, 4th edition, 1975; (contributor) *The Financial Handbook,* Ronald, 1964. Contributor to *Encyclopaedia Britannica Yearbook* and to journals.

* * *

PHILLIPS, Almarin 1925-

PERSONAL: Born March 13, 1925, in Port Jervis, N.Y.; son of Wendell Edgar and Hazel (Billett) Phillips; married Dorothy K. Burns, June 14, 1947 (divorced, 1976); married Carole C. Greenberg, December 19, 1976; children: (first marriage) A. Paul, F. Peter, Thomas R., David J., Elizabeth L., Charles S. *Education:* University of Pennsylvania, B.S., 1948, M.A., 1949; Harvard University, Ph.D., 1953. *Home:* 1115 Remington Rd., Wynnewood, Pa. 19096. *Office:* Department of Economics, University of Pennsylvania, Philadelphia, Pa.

CAREER: University of Pennsylvania, Philadelphia, instructor, 1948-50, 1951-53, assistant professor of economics, 1953-56; University of Virginia, Charlottesville, associate professor, 1956-61, professor, 1961-63; University of Pennsylvania, professor of economics and law, 1963—, chairman of department of economics, 1968-71, 1972-73, associate dean of Wharton School of Finance and Commerce, 1973-74, dean of School of Public and Urban Policy, 1974-77. Visiting professor, University of Hawaii at Honolulu, summer, 1968, University of Warwick, spring, 1972, London Graduate School of Business Studies, summer, 1972; Everett D. Reese Visiting Professor, Ohio State University, summer, 1972. Member of Virginia State Milk Commission, beginning 1958, President's Commission on Financial Structure and Regulation, 1970-71, and National Commission on Electronic Fund Transfers, 1976-77. Consultant, Bureau of the Budget, 1955, Board of Governors, Federal Reserve System, 1962-73, Rand Corp., 1964—, and Pennsylvania Commission on Banking Law, 1965-66. *Military service:* U.S. Army, 1943-45.

MEMBER: American Statistical Association (fellow), American Association for the Advancement of Science (fellow), American Economic Association, Econometric Society, Southern Economic Association. *Awards, honors:* Ford Foundation faculty research fellowship, 1967-68; Brookings Institution senior fellow, 1970-75.

WRITINGS: (With Cabell) *Problems in Basic Operation Research for Management,* Wiley, 1961; *Market Structure, Organization and Performance,* Harvard University Press,

1962; (editor) *Perspectives on Antitrust Policy,* Princeton University Press, 1965; (editor with O. E. Williamson) *Prices: Issues in Theory, Practice, and Public Policy,* University of Pennsylvania Press, 1968; *Technology and Market Structure,* Heath Lexington, 1971; (editor) *Promoting Competition in Regulated Markets,* Brookings Institution, 1975. *American Statistician,* editor, 1953-56, associate editor, 1956-70, acting editor, 1959-60; editor, *Southern Economic Journal,* 1963-65, and *Journal of Industrial Economics,* 1974—.†

* * *

PHILLIPS, Gene D(aniel) 1935-

PERSONAL: Born March 3, 1935, in Springfield, Ohio; son of Ira Granville (a factory foreman) and Johanna (Davoran) Phillips. *Education:* Loyola University, Chicago, Ill., A.B., 1957, M.A., 1959; West Baden College, Ph.L., 1959; Bellarmine School of Theology, S.T.L., 1966; Fordham University, Ph.D., 1970. *Home:* Faculty Residence, Loyola University, 6525 North Sheridan Rd., Chicago, Ill. 60626. *Office:* Department of English, Loyola University, Chicago, Ill. 60626.

CAREER: Entered Society of Jesus (Jesuits), 1952, ordained priest, 1965; Loyola University, Chicago, Ill., 1970—, began as assistant professor, associate professor of film history, fiction, and drama, 1975—. Trustee of Film Archive, Art Institute of Chicago. *Member:* Society for Cinema Studies, Modern Language Association of America. *Awards, honors:* American Philosophical Society grant, 1971; named Teacher of the Year, Loyola University, 1979.

WRITINGS: *The Movie Makers: Artists in an Industry,* Nelson-Hall, 1973; *Graham Greene: The Films of His Fiction,* Teachers College Press, 1974; *Stanley Kubrick: A Film Odyssey,* Popular Library, 1975, enlarged edition, 1977; *Evelyn Waugh's Officers, Gentlemen, and Rogues: The Fact behind His Fiction,* Nelson-Hall, 1975; *Ken Russell,* Twayne, 1979; *The Films of Tennessee Williams,* Associated University Presses, 1980; *Hemingway and Film,* Ungar, 1980.

Contributor: Samuel Hynes, editor, *Graham Greene: A Collection of Critical Essays,* Prentice-Hall, 1973; Thomas Atkins, editor, *Sexuality in the Movies,* Indiana University Press, 1975; Stuart Kaminsky, editor, *Ingmar Bergman: Essays in Criticism,* Oxford University Press, 1975; Atkins, editor, *Science Fiction Films,* Simon & Schuster, 1976; Atkins, editor, *Ken Russell,* Simon & Schuster, 1976; Frank Magill, editor, *Contemporary Literary Scene II,* Salem Press, 1979. Contributor to *Focus on Film* (England), *America, Cinema, Sequences* (Canada), and other journals.

WORK IN PROGRESS: *John Schlesinger,* for Twayne.

SIDELIGHTS: Gene D. Phillips comments: "Interviews both here and in England, with directors ranging from Cukor and Kubrick to Losey and Schlesinger, enabled me to write my first book, [*The Movie Makers,*] about the difficulty of an artist functioning in an industry. (I have since developed the chapters on Kubrick, Russell, and Schlesinger into separate books.) Graham Greene's personal cooperation was most helpful in my doing the book on his fiction and films. The publication of Waugh's diaries, and interviews with his family, sparked the book, [*Evelyn Waugh's Officers, Gentlemen, and Rogues*]."

PHILLIPS-BIRT, Douglas Hextall Chedzey 1920-1977
(Argus, David Hextall, Douglas Hogarth)

PERSONAL: Born May 18, 1920, in England; died April, 1977; son of Raymond and Enid (Rowe) Phillips-Birt. *Education:* Attended Devitt and Moore Nautical College, Pangbourne, 1936; University of Southampton, degree as naval architect, 1948.

CAREER: Worked for a time as a naval architect with John I. Thornicroft, Hampshire, England; writer. *Military service:* British Army, Royal Artillery, 1939-45; became captain. *Member:* Royal Institution of Naval Architects, Royal Southern Yacht Club, Royal Ocean Racing Club.

WRITINGS: *Sailing Yacht Design,* Adlard Coles, 1951, 3rd edition, 1976, Scribner, 1979; *Power Yacht Design,* Adlard Coles, 1953; *Motor Yacht and Boat Design,* John DeGraff, 1953, 2nd edition, 1966; (with Kaines Adlard Coles) *Yachts and Their Recognition,* John DeGraff, 1953; *The Rigs and Rigging of Yachts,* John DeGraff, 1954; *An Eye for a Yacht,* Barnes & Noble, 1955; *The Naval Architecture of Small Craft,* Hutchinson, 1957, Philosophical Library, 1958; *Famous Speed Boats of the World,* Muller, 1959, St. Martin's, 1960; *British Ocean Racing,* John DeGraff, 1960; *Finding Out about the Vikings,* Muller, 1962; *Fore and Aft Sailing Craft,* John DeGraff, 1962; *Finding Out about the Phoenicians,* Muller, 1964; *The Nature of Ship Design,* Studio Vista, 1966; *Ships and Boats: The Nature of Their Design,* Reinhold, 1966; *Waters of Wight,* Cassell, 1967; *Reflections in the Sea,* Harrap, 1969; *Reflections on Yachts,* Harrap, 1969; *The Future of Ships,* Imray, Laurie, Norie & Wilson, 1970; *Ship Model Testing,* International Textbook, 1970; *A History of Seamanship,* Allen & Unwin, 1971; *When Luxury Went to Sea,* David & Charles, 1971; *The History of Yachting,* Stein & Day, 1974; *The Love of Sailing,* Octopus Books, 1976; *The Building of Boats,* Norton, 1980.

Contributor to *Encyclopaedia Britannica.* Contributor to *Country Life, New Scientist, Sydney Daily Telegraph, Weekly Times, Far and Wide, Times,* and to yachting magazines. Editor, *Yachting World Annual,* St. Martin's, 1956-77; editor and adviser, *The Yachtman's Week End Book;* advisory editor, *The Wonder Book of Ships.*

AVOCATIONAL INTERESTS: Old furniture, painting, literature.†

* * *

PICHASKE, David Richard 1943-

PERSONAL: Surname is pronounced Pick-*ask*-ee; born September 2, 1943; son of Donald Richard (a clergyman) and Martha (Schisa) Pichaske; married Elaine Ezekian, August, 1968; children: Stephen Geoffrey, Kristin Diane. *Education:* Wittenberg University, B.A., 1965; Ohio University, Ph.D., 1969. *Politics:* "Clean." *Religious affiliation:* Christian. *Home:* 2724 N. North St., Peoria, Ill. 61604. *Office:* Department of English, Bradley University, Peoria, Ill. 61606.

CAREER: Currently member of faculty of English, Bradley University, Peoria, Ill. *Member:* Early English Text Society.

WRITINGS: *Beowulf to Beatles: Approaches to Poetry,* Free Press, 1972; *Writing Sense: A Handbook of Composition* (textbook), Free Press, 1975; *Movement in the Canterbury Tales: Chaucer's Literary Pilgrimage* (literary criticism), Folcroft, 1978; *A Generation in Motion: Popular Music and Culture in the 1960's,* Schirmer Books, 1979; *Beowulf to Beatles and Beyond,* Macmillan, 1980. Contributor to poems and essays to periodicals. Editor, *Spoon River Quarterly,* 1977—.

WORK IN PROGRESS: "Investigations into American dream," tentatively entitled *Peoria, U.S.A.*, completion expected in 1984; a novel, *Heading Home; The Poetry of Rock—The Sixties*.

* * *

PIERRE, Andrew J. 1934-

PERSONAL: Born June 13, 1934, in Vienna, Austria; son of Leo J. (a banker) and Nina (Hutter) Pierre; married Clara Grossman (a writer), July 5, 1969. *Education:* Amherst College, B.A., 1955; Institut d'Etudes Politiques, University of Paris, C.E.P., 1956; Columbia University, M.I.A., 1957, Ph.D., 1968. *Religion:* Protestant. *Home:* 697 West End Ave., Apt. 11E, New York, N.Y. 10025. *Office:* Council on Foreign Relations, 58 East 68 St., New York, N.Y. 10021.

CAREER: Brookings Institution, Washington, D.C., research assistant, 1960-61; U.S. Department of State, foreign service officer in London and Washington, D.C., 1962-64; Hudson Institute, Croton-on-Hudson, N.Y., research associate, 1966-69; Columbia University, New York City, lecturer in political science, 1968-69; Council on Foreign Relations, New York City, research fellow, 1969—. Consultant to Office of International Security Affairs, U.S. Department of Defense, 1967, and Stanford Research Institute. *Military service:* U.S. Army, 1957-59. *Member:* International Studies Association, International Institute for Strategic Studies, American Political Science Association, Federation of American Scientists, Arms Control Association, American Friends of Wilton Park.

WRITINGS: (Contributor) I. William Zartman, editor, *Czechoslovakia: Intervention and Impact*, New York University Press, 1970; (contributor) Steven Warnecke, editor, *The European Community in the 1970's*, Praeger, 1972; *Nuclear Politics: The British Experience with an Independent Strategic Force, 1939-1970*, Oxford University Press, 1972; (contributor) William T. R. Fox and Warner Schilling, editors, *European Security and the Atlantic System*, Columbia University Press, 1973; (contributor) James Chace and Earl C. Ravenal, editors, *Atlantis Lost: U.S.-European Relations after the Cold War*, New York University Press, 1976; (with C. W. Moyne) *Nuclear Proliferation: A Strategy for Control*, Foreign Policy Association, 1976; (contributor) John D. Elliott and Leslie K. Gibson, editors, *Contemporary Terrorism*, International Association of Chiefs of Police, 1978; (editor) *Arms Transfer and American Foreign Policy*, New York University Press, 1979. Contributor to professional journals.

WORK IN PROGRESS: The Global Politics of Arms Sales.

* * *

PIHERA, Larry 1933-

PERSONAL: Born January 9, 1933, in Cleveland, Ohio; son of Charles and Dorothy Pihera; married Patricia Dunn (an advertising agent), August 22, 1954; children: Lauren, Scott. *Education:* Attended Cooper Union and University of Hawaii. *Home:* 1605 Ambridge Rd., Dayton, Ohio 45459. *Office:* Pihera Advertising Associates, Dayton, Ohio.

CAREER: Johnson Rubber Co., Middlefield, Ohio, advertising manager, 1956-60; G. W. Young Public Relations, Dayton, Ohio, creative director, 1960-70; Pihera Advertising Associates, Dayton, president, 1970—. Member of board of directors, Centerville, Ohio Chamber of Commerce; member of Centerville Arts Commission. *Member:* American Society of Management Consultants, American Businessmen's Club, Dayton Advertising Club, Art Center (Dayton). *Awards, honors:* Received first place awards for advertising writing for television, 1974, and newspaper, 1978.

WRITINGS: The Making of a Winner: Porsche 917, Lippincott, 1972; *19 Slices of Life with Mustard* (poetry), Carillon Communications, 1979. Architectural columnist, *Institutional Management*. Contributor of articles to numerous periodicals, including *Today's Motorsports, Dayton U.S.A., Reader's Digest, Spirit, Now*, and *American School & University*.

WORK IN PROGRESS: A book on auto racing; a humorous novel; a book on ESP.

SIDELIGHTS: Larry Pihera told *CA:* "Inner resolve fascinates me. As a result I am intrigued by auto racers, long distance runners, and novelists who achieve success after age 50. Young writers should learn to write at any time, in any place—airports at midnight, Central Park at noon, a motel room at 10 p.m. This is a mark of professionalism. A writer must *produce*, or look for another job." *Avocational interests:* Sailing, mountains, sunsets, good conversation, travel.

* * *

PIXLEY, Jorge V. 1937-

PERSONAL: Born March 29, 1937, in Chicago, Ill.; son of John Stage (a physician) and Phebe (Rice) Pixley; married Janyce Irene Babcock, June 14, 1958; children: Rebecca Ray, Kevin Vail, Mark Christian. *Education:* Attended Wheaton College, Wheaton, Ill., 1955-56; Kalamazoo College, B.A., 1958; University of Chicago, M.A., 1962, Ph.D., 1968. *Home and office:* Seminario Bautista de Mexico, San Jeronimo 111, Mexico 20, D.F., Mexico.

CAREER: Baptist clergyman, ordained in 1963; Evangelical Seminary of Puerto Rico, Rio Piedras, professor of Old Testament, 1963-75; Seminario Bautista de Mexico, San Jeronimo, professor of Old Testament, 1975—. Visiting professor at Evangelical Faculty of Theology, Buenos Aires, 1969-70. *Member:* Society of Biblical Literature, Society for Values in Higher Education, American Academy of Religion, Sociedad Argentina de Profesores de Sagrada Escritura.

WRITINGS: Pluralismo de tradiciones en la religion biblica, Editorial La Aurora (Buenos Aires), 1971; *Reine de Dios*, Editorial La Aurora, 1977. Contributor to *Lutheran Quarterly, Revista Biblica, Process Studies, Servir, Christus, Taller de Teologia*, and *Cuadernos de Teologia*.

WORK IN PROGRESS: Commentaries on the books of Job and Exodus.

SIDELIGHTS: Jorge V. Pixley told *CA* that his "literary activity has been almost entirely in Spanish, and much of it is only intelligible within the Latin American context in which I have lived most of my life."

* * *

PLACE, Irene Magdaline (Glazik) 1912-

PERSONAL: Born January 27, 1912, in Omaha, Neb.; daughter of Paul A. and Magdaline (Krance) Glazik; married Darold Place, August 11, 1940. *Education:* University of Nebraska, A.B., 1932; Columbia University, M.A., 1933; New York University, Ed.D., 1946. *Home:* 13550 Southwest Berthold St., Beaverton, Ore. 97005. *Office:* School of Business Administration, Portland State University, Portland, Ore. 97207.

CAREER: Briarcliff Junior College (now Briarcliff College), Briarcliff Manor, N.Y., instructor and acting dean of prep school, 1933-36; Marshall College (now University), Huntington, W.Va., instructor, 1936-37; University of Toledo, Toledo, Ohio, assistant professor, 1937-43; University of Michigan, Ann Arbor, School of Business Administration, associate professor, 1943-66; Portland State University, Portland, Ore., professor of business education, 1966—. Visiting summer instructor at University of Omaha, 1939, University of Oregon, 1960, New York University, 1965, and California State University, 1974. Frequently conducts seminars for businesswomen. Member of board of presidents, Council of Portland, 1972-74. *Member:* Systems and Procedures Association, National Office Management Association (chairman of education committee, 1953-55, of program services committee, 1955-57), American Records Management Association (honorary member of Oregon chapter), National Secretaries Association (honorary member), Zonta, Y.W.C.A., Delta Pi Epsilon (national vice-president, 1961-63), Kappa Delta, Phi Lambda Theta, Phi Chi Theta, Alpha Sigma Alpha. *Awards, honors:* University of Michigan research grant, 1956; Rackham faculty fellow, University of Michigan, 1962; Ford Foundation fellowship, 1965; distinguished service award, Systems and Procedures Association, 1967; Oregon educational research grant, 1970-72; annual achievement award, Alpha Beta chapter of Delta Pi Epsilon, 1975.

WRITINGS: (With Charles B. Hicks) *College Secretarial Procedures,* McGraw, 1952, 4th edition (with Hicks and Edward E. Byers), 1972; (with Madeline S. Strony) *The Road to Secretarial Success,* McGraw, 1954; (with Hicks) *Office Management,* Allyn & Bacon, 1956, 3rd edition (with Hicks and Robin Wilkinson), 1971; *Administrative Systems Analysis,* Bureau of Business Research, School of Business Administration, University of Michigan, 1957; (with Hicks) *Opportunities in Office Management,* Vocational Guidance Manuals, 1959; *Medical Office Management,* [Ann Arbor, Mich.], 1960; (with Estelle Popham) *Filing and Records Management,* Prentice-Hall, 1966; (with Leonard Robertson) *Opportunities in Management Careers,* Vocational Guidance Manuals, 1969, revised edition, 1979; (with Harry Fujita and Popham) *Fundamental Filing Practice,* Prentice-Hall, 1973; (with Alice Armstrong) *Management Careers for Women,* Vocational Guidance Manuals, 1975; (with Byers and Elaine Uthe) *Administrative Secretarial Procedures,* McGraw, 1980; (with Sylvia Plummer) *Women in Management,* Vocational Guidance Manuals, 1980.

Contributor; all published by National Business Education Association, except as indicated: *Business Theory for Secretaries,* Masterco Press, 1951; *Perspectives in Education for Business,* 1963; *Recent and Projected Developments Affecting Business Education,* 1964; *Ideas for Management,* International Systems and Procedures Association, 1964; *Business Education Now and in the 1970's,* New York Business Education Association, 1964; *Cost Control and the Supervisor,* American Management Association, 1966; *Business and Office Education,* Center for Vocational and Technical Education, Ohio State University, 1966; *Suggested Curricula Guide,* Office of Education, U.S. Department of Health, Education, and Welfare, 1967; *Selected Readings in Business and Office Occupations,* 1967; *A Taxonomy of Office Activities for Business and Office Education,* Center for Vocational and Technical Education, Ohio State University, 1968; *Business Education: An Evaluative Inventory,* 1968; *Criteria for Evaluating Business and Office Education,* 1969; *The Emerging Content and Structure of Business Education,* 1970. Also contributor to *American Business Education Yearbook.* Author of brochures on office management and secretarial procedures; contributor of numerous articles to professional publications. Editor, *Systems and Procedures Journal,* 1958-61, and *Delta Pi Epsilon Journal,* 1966-69.

SIDELIGHTS: Irene Magdaline Place told *CA:* "I believe that when one devotes a lifetime to a special subject area, especially if it is part of higher education curricula, that person should, toward the end of his/her career, take time to write as much as possible. Writings remain available in libraries long after one is gone. They are a way of sharing and continuing to communicate with current generations. It seems to me that this is particularly important for experienced authors who have seen textbooks through four or five revisions, because this may be their last chance to pull together and preserve content from their years of experience, observation, research and thought."

BIOGRAPHICAL/CRITICAL SOURCES: Business Education Forum, May, 1961; *Supervisory Management,* November, 1961.

* * *

POLK, Kenneth 1935-

PERSONAL: Born March 28, 1935, in San Diego, Calif.; son of Keith Vivien and Bertha Polk; married Joan Rae, 1958; children: Benjamin Kenneth, Sarah McCormick. *Education:* Attended Arizona State College (now University) 1952-53; San Diego State College (now University), B.A., 1956; Northwestern University, M.A., 1957; University of California, Los Angeles, Ph.D., 1961. *Office:* Department of Sociology, Boston College, Chestnut Hill, Mass. 02167.

CAREER: System Development Corp., Santa Monica, Calif., social scientist, 1958; University of Oregon, Eugene, instructor, 1960-61, assistant professor, 1961-66, associate professor of sociology, 1966-70; Boston College, Chestnut Hill, Mass., associate professor of sociology, 1970—. Research director, Lane County Youth Project, 1962-67; director, Marion County Youth Project, 1966—. Consultant, President's Crime Commission, 1966, Joint Commission for Correctional Manpower and Training, 1966-67, Office of Economic Opportunity, 1966-67, and Office of Juvenile Delinquency and Youth Development, 1967. *Military service:* U.S. Air Force Reserve; became first lieutenant. *Member:* American Sociological Association, National Council on Crime and Delinquency.

WRITINGS: (With Joseph W. Eaton) *Measuring Delinquency,* University of Pittsburgh Press, 1961; (with Walter E. Schafer) *Schools and Delinquency,* Prentice-Hall, 1972.†

* * *

POLLINI, Francis 1930-

PERSONAL: Born September 9, 1930, in West Wyoming, Pa.; son of Sem and Assunta (Ciani) Pollini; married Gloria Ann Swann, 1959. *Education:* Pennsylvania State University, B.A., 1951. *Address:* 41 Sunningdale, Norwich, England.

CAREER: Writer. *Military service:* U.S. Air Force, 1952-57; became first lieutenant.

WRITINGS—Novels, except as indicated: *Night,* Olympia (Paris), 1960, Houghton, 1962; *Glover,* Spearman, 1964, Putnam, 1965; *Excursion,* Spearman, 1965, Putnam, 1966; *The Crown,* Putnam, 1967; *Three Plays* (play collection), Spearman, 1967; *Pretty Maids All in a Row,* Delacorte, 1968; *Dubonnet,* Quartet, 1975; *The Hall,* Quartet, 1976.

WORK IN PROGRESS: Novels; plays.

SIDELIGHTS: Francis Pollini's novels are either hailed as the work of a "subtle" and "sensitive" writer, a "rare and fascinating" talent, or they are brutally panned as the ravings of a "simple-minded" pornographer. For instance, in a review of *Glover,* Martin Greenburg writes: "I suppose it's possible to be stupid in any literary style, but some styles encourage stupidity more than others. . . . The current style of the grotesque, of which *Glover* is a horrible example, is one of the latest encouragements to mindlessness. Apparently, the irresistible message that it whispers is: thinking isn't so important, just be outrageous." Greenburg finally comes to the conclusion that the novel "isn't worth discussing." And Kenneth Lamott, in another critical article, warns that "a writer who chooses to work in a medium at the level of a comic strip has to be very clever indeed to escape the inference that the comic strip is his natural mode of expression." However, Julian Gloag finds that *Glover* is "a satirical novel that can be favorably compared with James Purdy's *Cabot Wright Begins.* . . . Francis Pollini has fashioned a staccato, shorthand style that admirably fits Glover's fierce, inarticulate concentration on his succession of sexual exploits." Gloag decides that *Glover* "is lifted far above the ruck of novels by the power and unity of an original mind and by the vigor and invention of a style which catches the mechanical, ritual cadences of obscenity and pomposity and which rises sometimes to an incantatory rhythm of brutal glee. Joe Glover himself rings dead true."

The Crown, which details the exploits of a boxer on his way to the middleweight and then light-heavyweight championships, brought similarly polarized reaction. On the plus side, Webster Schott writes: "In its ripping, gutty way, *The Crown* escapes its machine-gun dialogue and monorail narrative. It becomes simultaneously a case history of an undiagnosed psychosis and a ritual of human defeat. . . . Tight as a wire, it is drawn from a steely despair. Within its own terms, it absolutely convinces. This negatively charged vision of a warped and busted soul affirms the capacity of art to wound and inform. And, in the occult act of creation, it relieves the pain of hearing our secret truths repeated." Schott says that "Pollini mangles the emotions. Traveling with him is like joyriding with a calculating maniac frozen to the wheel. Hands wet, shaking, you stumble away from the smashing finish wondering what you hit." On the other hand, a *Publishers Weekly* reviewer calls *The Crown* "a strikingly unoriginal novel. . . . Except for three fights, described round by round, and the sexual encounters, also described round by round, there is very little action here. . . . [The author] isn't even very interesting in his sex scenes; there's nothing much here we haven't read, better written, hundreds of times before."

Even Pollini's best-known work, *Pretty Maids All in a Row,* which was made into a film starring such popular screen personages as Rock Hudson, Angie Dickinson, and Telly Savalas, failed to escape the critics' barbs. Raymond Sokolov proclaims: "Pornography is a difficult art—and, with all the competition in today's free market, it isn't getting any easier. . . . These days, the self-respecting pornographer has to make fun of his genre, or at least pretend to put it on. Francis Pollini has tried this gambit, but without much success. As a put-on artist, he is suicidal, while his sex scenes begin in cliche and end in boredom, with scarcely an instant of erotic invention in between. . . . Real pornography takes itself seriously, and never consciously plays for laughs at its own expense. Parodies of pornography, on the other hand, are clearly that and never approach the real thing closely enough to risk confusion with it. Pollini is trying to have it both ways. He has almost written a routine dirty book, but he can't stop smirking at the whole business. As a tactic, that's fatal, like an actor giggling in the middle of a farce." Fred Rotondaro, who apparently appreciates Pollini's earlier work, has some misgivings about *Pretty Maids.* He calls Pollini "the talented and experienced author of such works as *Night* and *Glover.* His way with words and plot development marks him as one of the major young talents of the period. And yet *Pretty Maids All in a Row* fails as art and fails as a reflection of reality." Of the element of satire in the book, Rotondaro says, "perhaps there is some genuine satiric talent in this latest Pollini work but it is so totally covered by [the main character's] sexual adventures that neither it, nor very much else emerges clearly from the novel." A writer for *Publishers Weekly,* however, is less reserved, commenting that "it's almost as hard to describe this novel as it is to put it down. Try calling it a dirty black comedy-mystery. . . . A marvelously macabre tale, with some horrendously hilarious situations and sharp swings from the giggly to the grotesque, this has some of the same shock effect as Mr. Pollini's [earlier] novel, *Glover,* but is funnier."

BIOGRAPHICAL/CRITICAL SOURCES: New York Times Book Review, October 31, 1965, August 28, 1966, July 9, 1967, October 20, 1968; *Saturday Review,* November 27, 1965, August 20, 1966; *Kirkus Reviews,* January 15, 1966, April 1, 1967; *New York Times,* August 12, 1966; *Kenyon Review,* September, 1966; *Publishers Weekly,* April 3, 1967, June 17, 1968, March 3, 1969; *Book World,* May 18, 1969; *Spectator,* August 4, 1969; *Books and Bookmen,* August, 1970; *Best Sellers,* September 15, 1970.

—Sketch by Peter M. Gareffa

* * *

POMEROY, Wardell B. 1913-

PERSONAL: Born December 6, 1913, in Kalamazoo, Mich.; son of Percy and Mary (Baxter) Pomeroy; married Martha Catherine Sindlinger, 1937; children: David, John, Mary Lynne. *Education:* Indiana University, A.B., 1935, M.A., 1941; Columbia University, Ph.D., 1952. *Home:* 1611 Vallejo St., Apt. 301, San Francisco, Calif. 94123. *Office:* Institute for the Advanced Study of Human Sexuality, 1523 Franklin St., San Francisco, Calif. 94109.

CAREER: Department of Public Welfare, South Bend, Ind., psychologist, 1939-43; Indiana University at Bloomington, Institute for Sex Research, research associate and director of field research, 1943-63; private practice as marriage counselor in New York, N.Y., 1963-76; Institute for the Advanced Study of Human Sexuality, San Francisco, Calif., academic dean, 1976—. Diplomate, American Board of Examiners of Professional Psychologists. *Member:* American Psychological Association (fellow), American Association of Marriage Counselors.

WRITINGS: (With Alfred Charles Kinsey and others) *Sexual Behavior in the Human Male,* Saunders, 1948; (with Kinsey and others) *Sexual Behavior in the Human Female,* Saunders, 1953; (co-author) *Pregnancy, Birth and Abortion,* Harper, 1958; (co-author) *Sex Offenders,* Harper, 1965; *Boys and Sex,* Delacorte, 1968; *Girls and Sex,* Delacorte, 1969; *Dr. Kinsey and the Institute for Sex Research,* Harper, 1972; *Your Child and Sex,* Delacorte, 1974.

WORK IN PROGRESS: Taking a Sex History.

SIDELIGHTS: Wardell B. Pomeroy was an important collaborator on *Sexual Behavior in the Human Male* and *Sexual Behavior in the Human Female,* the revolutionary studies pioneered by Alfred Kinsey. Since Kinsey's death in 1956, Pomeroy has continued to research sexual attitudes and behavior and has published several books on the subject.

Pomeroy told *CA:* "Hendrick van Loon, the portly Dutch geographer, met a friend one day on the street. Van Loon was asked if he would give a speech that night at the friend's club. He sadly shook his head, patted his paunch and said, 'I can't. I am with book.' This is much the way I feel. The fetus stirs, nags me, causes labor pains, and eventually I give birth. I can never write at the suggestion of others, but only when I worry and ponder an idea over and over again until I become too uncomfortable *not* to write it.

"My life is governed by what I call the principle of subgoals. I can never write an entire book, not even an entire chapter. But I can write a paragraph, and then another, and another. Until, finally, a book is written."

AVOCATIONAL INTERESTS: Herpetology, chess, and billiards.

BIOGRAPHICAL/CRITICAL SOURCES: Best Sellers, April 15, 1968; *Saturday Review,* July, 1968, March 25, 1972; *New York Times,* March 4, 1972; *Washington Post,* March 8, 1972; *Newsweek,* March 13, 1972; *New York Times Book Review,* March 26, 1972; *Atlantic Monthly,* May, 1972.

* * *

POND, Alonzo W(illiam) 1894-

PERSONAL: Born June 18, 1894, in Janesville, Wis.; son of William Samuel (a merchant and salesman) and Marie (Olson) Pond; married Dorothy Helen Long (the chief guide at Wisconsin Gardens), July 20, 1926; children: Chomingwen D., Arthur A. *Education:* Beloit College, B.S., 1918, 1920; University of Chicago, M.A., 1928; attended American School in Europe for Prehistoric Studies and University of Paris, 1921-22; University of Chicago, graduate study, 1931-32; American University of Beirut, certificate, 1951. *Politics:* Republican. *Home and office:* Wisconsin Gardens, 8953 Minch Dr., Minocqua, Wis. 54548. *Agent:* Lurton Blassingame and Larry Sternig, Larry Sternig Literary Agency, 742 Robertson St., Milwaukee, Wis. 53213.

CAREER: Beloit College, Beloit, Wis., Logan Museum, assistant curator, 1924-31; U.S. National Park Service, archaeologist at Mammoth Cave, Ky., 1934-35, superintendent of Civilian Conservation Corps Camp, St. Croix Falls, Wis., 1936-37; Cave of the Mounds, Blue Mounds, Wis., manager, 1940-45; free-lance lecturer on travel and archaeology, 1946-49; U.S. Air Force, Maxwell Air Force Base, Ala., chief of desert branch of Arctic-Desert-Tropic Information Center of Research Studies Institute, 1949-58; Wisconsin Gardens, Minocqua, Wis., manager, 1958-68. *Military service:* U.S. Army, 1917-19, served as ambulance driver attached to French Army. *Member:* Nature Conservancy, American Legion, Northland Historical Society, Explorers Club (New York), Wisconsin Phenological Society, Sigma Xi. *Awards, honors:* Distinguished service citation award, Beloit College, 1978.

WRITINGS: (Contributor) *Explorers Club Tales,* Dodd, 1936; (contributor) *Practices in Reading and Thinking,* Macmillan, 1940; (with Paul H. Nesbitt and William H. Allen) *The Survival Book,* Van Nostrand, 1959, published as *The Pilot's Survival Manual,* Norton, 1978; *The Desert World,* Thomas Nelson, 1962; *Deserts,* Norton, 1965; *Caverns of the World,* Norton, 1969; *Survival in Sun and Sand,* Norton, 1969; (contributor) *Explorers Club Cookbook,* Caxton, 1971; *Andrews, Gobi Explorer,* Grosset, 1972. Also author of two books for the U.S. Air Force, *Afoot in the Desert: A Contribution to Basic Survival,* 1951, and *Climate and Weather in the Central Gobi of Mongolia,* 1951. Author of script for educational film, "Limestone Caverns," produced by Coronet Productions, and "Sun, Sand, and Survival," a film for the U.S. Air Force. Author of bulletins and guides for museums and parks; contributor to scientific publications.

WORK IN PROGRESS: Paul Bunyan's Cookbook; Torchlight on Cold Trails; a travel book, as yet untitled.

SIDELIGHTS: Alonzo W. Pond told *CA:* "The results of exploration and scientific research are of little value until they are available and understood by people. Reporting exactly what one sees or hears is not always a truthful account of an event. A trained observer sees beyond the obvious."

"I write," he continued, "to be understood and to share experience. My writings are based on my pragmatic observations, but I have found it valuable to back-up my own experience with studies of what others have done."

Experience, coupled with enthusiasm, is a key aspect of Pond's life. "'Never lose your enthusiasm,' John D. Rockefeller said to the explorer, Roy Chapman Andrews, 'it's your greatest asset.' Henry Luce (the Time-Life publisher) once said that a man . . . should change his center of interest at least every seven years, . . . because experience is priceless. My wife, Dorothy, and I have followed the advice of both men."

Pond is the author of several books on exploration and survival for children and adults. "When I find something I have written twenty or forty years ago included in an anthology or reprinted on a list of 'distinctive' books for libraries to buy," he concluded, "it makes me think that my time of writing and digging up the facts has not been wasted."

* * *

PONDER, Catherine 1927-

PERSONAL: Born February 14, 1927, in Hartsville, S.C.; daughter of Roy Charles (an electrical engineer) and Kathleen (Parrish) Cook; married Robert Stearns (a chiropractor), June 19, 1970; children: (previous marriage) Richard. *Education:* Attended University of North Carolina, 1946; Worth Business College, graduate, 1948; Unity School of Christianity, Ministerial School, B.S., 1956. *Agent:* Bertha Klausner, International Literary Agency, 71 Park Ave., New York, N.Y. 10016. *Office address:* P.O. Drawer 1278, Palm Desert, Calif. 92260.

CAREER: Licensed into Unity ministry, 1957; ordained, 1958. Federal Bureau of Investigation, Washington, D.C., staff member of Identification Division, 1944-46; worked as private secretary in Fayetteville, N.C., 1948-56; minister of Unity churches in Birmingham, Ala., 1956-61, Austin, Tex., 1961-70, and San Antonio, Tex., 1969-73; founder-minister of Unity Church Worldwide, Palm Desert, Calif., 1973—. *Member:* International New Thought Alliance, International Platform Association, Unity Ministers' Association, Los Angeles Club, Bermuda Dunes Country Club, Palm Springs Racquet Club, Palm Springs Tennis Club.

WRITINGS: The Dynamic Laws of Prosperity, Prentice-Hall, 1962; *The Prosperity Secret of the Ages,* Prentice-Hall, 1964; *The Dynamic Laws of Healing,* Parker Publishing, 1966; *Prospering Power of Love,* Unity Books, 1966; *The Healing Secret of the Ages,* Parker Publishing, 1967; *Secret of Unlimited Supply,* Unity Books, 1967; *Pray and Grow Rich,* Parker Publishing, 1968; *Open Your Mind to Prosperity,* Unity Books, 1971; *The Millionaires of Genesis,* De Vorss, 1976; *The Millionaire Moses,* De Vorss, 1977; *The Millionaire Joshua,* De Vorss, 1978; *The Millionaire from Nazareth,* De Vorss, 1979. Contributor to professional journals, including Unity publications and *New Thought* magazine.

* * *

POPE-HENNESSY, John W(yndham) 1913-

PERSONAL: Born December 13, 1913, in London, England; son of L.H.R. and Una (a writer) Pope-Hennessy. *Education:* Balliol College, Oxford, M.A., 1935. *Religion:* Roman Catholic. *Home:* 1130 Park Ave., New York, N.Y. 10028. *Office:* Department of European Paintings, Metropolitan Museum of Art, New York, N.Y.

CAREER: Victoria and Albert Museum, London, England, member of staff, 1938-73, keeper of the department of architecture and sculpture, 1954-66, director and secretary, 1967-73; British Museum, London, director, 1974-76; Metropolitan Museum of Art, New York, N.Y., consultative chairman of the department of European paintings, 1977—. Slade Professor of Fine Art at Oxford University, 1956-57, and Cambridge University, 1964-65; Robert Sterling Clark Professor of Art, Williams College, 1961-62; Mellon Lecturer, National Gallery of Art, 1963; New York University, lecturer, 1965, professor, Institute of Fine Arts, 1977—. *Member:* British Academy (fellow), Society of Antiquaries (fellow), Royal Society of Literature (fellow), Accademia Fiorentina delle Arti del Disegno (honorary academician), Accademia Senese Degli Intronati, Bayerische Akademie der Wissenschaften, American Philosophical Society. *Awards, honors:* Commander, Order of the British Empire, 1959; Serena Medal from British Academy for Italian Studies, 1961; New York University Medal, 1965; knighted by Queen Elizabeth, 1971; LL.D from Aberdeen University, 1972, and Loyola University, Chicago, Ill., 1979; Torch of Learning Medal, 1977.

WRITINGS: *Giovanni di Paolo,* Chatto & Windus, 1937; *Sassetta,* Chatto & Windus, 1939; *Sienese Quattrocento Painting,* Phaidon Press, 1947; *A Sienese Codex of the "Divine Comedy,"* Phaidon Press, 1947; *The Drawings of Domeninchino at Windsor Castle,* Phaidon Press, 1948; *Donatello's Ascension,* H.M.S.O., 1949; *The Virgin with the Laughing Child,* H.M.S.O., 1949; (editor) *Autobiography of Benvenuto Cellini,* Phaidon Press, 1949; *Nicholas Hilliard,* Home & van Thal, 1949.

Paolo Uccello, Phaidon Press, 1950, revised edition, 1969; *Italian Gothic Sculpture in the Victoria and Albert Museum,* H.M.S.O., 1952; *Fra Angelico,* Phaidon Press, 1952, revised edition, Cornell University Press, 1974; *Italian Gothic Sculpture,* Phaidon Press, 1955, 2nd edition, Dutton, 1972; *Italian Renaissance Sculpture,* Phaidon Press, 1958, 2nd edition, Dutton, 1971; *Italian High Renaissance and Baroque Sculpture,* Phaidon Press, 1963, Dutton, 1970; *Catalogue of Italian Sculpture in the Victoria and Albert Museum,* H.M.S.O., 1964; *Renaissance Bronzes in the Kress Collection,* Phaidon Press, 1965; *The Portrait in the Renaissance,* Bollingen Foundation, 1966; *Essays on Italian Sculpture,* Phaidon Press, 1968.

The Frick Collection: Catalogue of Sculpture, Princeton University Press, 1970; *Raphael,* New York University Press, 1970; *An Introduction to Italian Sculpture,* three volumes, Phaidon Press, 1970-72; *Luca Della Robbia,* Cornell University Press, 1980.

SIDELIGHTS: *The Portrait in the Renaissance,* according to David Piper, "will remain for a long time the standard account of the aesthetic development of the Renaissance portrait. . . . Its weight of scholarship is supported by references of awe-inspiring density." John Hale agrees, calling the book "densely pondered, deftly informative, always lucid and a pleasure to read for insight and wit." The *Virginia Quarterly Review* writer praises the book's "infinite attention to detail . . . [which] is used to smooth and strengthen the path of the reader until he reaches an amplitude of knowledge almost as full as that of the author himself. But only [Pope-Hennessy] could have achieved the remarkable unity found in the book."

BIOGRAPHICAL/CRITICAL SOURCES: *Yale Review,* summer, 1967; *Observer Review,* August 6, 1967; *New York Review of Books,* September 28, 1967; *Virginia Quarterly Review,* autumn, 1967; *Statesman,* September 13, 1968.

* * *

POPESCU, Julian John Hunter 1928-

PERSONAL: Born July 4, 1928, in Oxford, England; son of Vintila (a professor of theology) and Gladys (a teacher; maiden name, Hunter) Popescu; married Christine Pullein-Thompson (a writer of children's books), 1956; children: Philip, Charlotte, Mark, Lucy. *Education:* Institute of Italian Culture, Bucharest, Italian certificate, 1947; University of London (external student), B. Com (2nd class honours), 1953; University of Reading, Diploma in Education, 1963. *Politics:* Conservative. *Religion:* Church of England. *Home:* The Old Parsonage, Mellis Eye, Suffolk, England.

CAREER: Northern Assurance Co. Ltd., London, England, clerk, 1948-51; language monitor, British Broadcasting Corp., 1951-79; free-lance writer, 1979—. *Member:* British Broadcasting Corporation Club, Phyllis Court Club (Henley-on-Thames).

WRITINGS: *An Elementary Italian Grammar,* Macmillan, 1961; *The Danube,* Oxford University Press, 1961; *The Volga,* Oxford University Press, 1962; *The Po,* Oxford University Press, 1962; *Italian for Commerce,* Pergamon, 1965; *Let's Visit the U.S.S.R.,* Burke, 1967, published as *Let's Visit Russia,* John Day, 1968; *Let's Visit Yugoslavia,* Burke, 1968; *Let's Visit Romania,* Burke, 1969; *Let's Visit Czechoslovakia,* Burke, 1970; *Read about France,* Wheaton Publishing, 1970; *Russian Space Exploration,* Gothard House, 1979. Also author of scripts for school broadcasts.

WORK IN PROGRESS: Studying audiovisual aids in education, and linguistic theories about the origin of language; researching Russian polar exploration.

SIDELIGHTS: Julian Popescu has traveled extensively in Italy and Sicily, noting dialectal differences. *Avocational interests:* Gardening and beekeeping.

BIOGRAPHICAL/CRITICAL SOURCES: *Henley Standard,* June 23, 1961.

* * *

PORTER, Katherine Anne 1890-

PERSONAL: Born May 15, 1890, in Indian Creek, Tex.; daughter of Harrison Boone and Mary Alice (Jones) Porter; first married at sixteen; married second husband, Eugene Dove Pressly, 1933 (divorced April 19, 1938); married Albert Russel Erskine, Jr. (a professor of English), 1938 (divorced, 1942). *Education:* Educated at home and in Southern girls' schools.

CAREER: Professional writer. Lecturer and teacher at writers' conferences; speaker at more than 200 universities and colleges in the United States and Europe. Writer-in-residence, or member of the faculties of English, at Olivet College, Olivet, Mich., 1940, Stanford University, Stanford, Calif., 1948-49, University of Michigan, Ann Arbor, 1953-54,

University of Virginia, Charlottesville, 1958, and Washington and Lee University, Lexington, Va., where she was first woman faculty member in the school's history, 1959. Ewing Lecturer, University of California, Los Angeles, 1959; first Regents Lecturer, University of California, Riverside, 1961. Member, President Johnson's Committee on Presidential Scholars.

MEMBER: National Institute of Arts and Letters (vice-president, 1950-52), American Academy of Arts and Letters. *Awards, honors:* Guggenheim fellowship for literature, 1931, 1938; Society of the Libraries of New York University first annual gold medal, 1940, for *Pale Horse, Pale Rider;* fellow of the Library of Congress in regional American literature, 1944; chosen one of six representatives of American literature at International Expositions of the Arts in Paris, France, 1952; Ford Foundation grant, 1959-61; State Department grant for international exchange of persons to Mexico, 1960, 1964; first prize, O. Henry Memorial Award, 1962, for "Holiday"; Emerson-Thoreau Bronze Medal for Literature of American Academy of Arts and Sciences, 1962; Pulitzer Prize, 1966, and National Book Award, 1966, both for *The Collected Stories of Katherine Anne Porter;* National Institute of Arts and Letters gold medal, 1967. Honorary degrees include D.Litt. from University of North Carolina, 1949, Smith College, 1958, and Wheaton College; D.H.L. from University of Michigan, 1954, and University of Maryland, 1966; D.F.A. from LaSalle College.

WRITINGS: My Chinese Marriage, Duffield, 1921; *Outline of Mexican Popular Arts and Crafts,* Young & McCallister, 1922; *What Price Marriage,* Sears, 1927; *Flowering Judas* (Book-of-the-Month Club selection), Harcourt, 1930, 2nd edition with added stories published as *Flowering Judas and Other Stories,* 1935; (translator and compiler) *Katherine Anne Porter's French Songbook,* Harrison Co., 1933; *Hacienda: A Story of Mexico,* Harrison Co., 1934; *Noon Wine,* Schuman's, 1937; *Pale Horse, Pale Rider* (three novelettes), Harcourt, 1939; (translator) Fernandez de Lizardi, *The Itching Parrot,* Doubleday, 1942; (author of preface) Flores and Poore, *Fiesta in November,* Houghton, 1942; *The Leaning Tower, and Other Stories,* Harcourt, 1944; *The Days Before: Collected Essays and Occasional Writings,* Harcourt, 1952, revised and enlarged edition published as *The Collected Essays and Occasional Writings of Katherine Anne Porter,* Delacorte, 1970; *Old Order: Stories of the South,* Harcourt, 1955; *Fiction and Criticism of Katherine Anne Porter,* University of Pittsburgh Press, 1957, revised edition, 1962; *Ship of Fools* (novel; Book-of-the-Month Club selection), Little, Brown, 1962; *The Collected Stories of Katherine Anne Porter,* Harcourt, 1965; *A Christmas Story,* illustrations by Ben Shahn, Dial, 1967; *The Never Ending Wrong,* Little, Brown, 1977. Contributor to numerous magazines.

SIDELIGHTS: "My whole attempt," writes Katherine Anne Porter, "has been to discover and understand human motives, human feeling, to make a distillation of what human relations and experiences my mind has been able to absorb. I have never known an uninteresting human being, and I have never known two alike; there are broad classifications and deep similarities, but I am interested in the thumbprint. I am passionately involved with these individuals who populate all these enormous migrations, calamities; these beings without which, one by one, all the 'broad movements of history' could never take place. One by one—as they were born."

These feelings for humanity are reflected in her writings, George Hendrick believes. He wrote in his book, *Katherine Anne Porter:* "Over the last four decades, Miss Porter's short stories have been marked by a mastery of technique, by honesty, and by a desire to explore the human heart and mind and society itself, without lapsing into popular cliches. No matter whether she has written about Mexicans, Texans, Irishmen, or Germans, one feels that she knows the people and their backgrounds perfectly; she has lived and relived the experiences and emotions so thoroughly that she has often written her stories and short novels in a matter of hours or days."

Although she considers herself primarily a writer, Porter has had to adopt sidelines to make a living. At 21, she worked for a newspaper in Chicago and later played bit parts in movies. In 1921, she went to Mexico to study Aztec and Mayan art designs and became involved in the Obregon Revolution. All the while she continued to write, burning 'trunksful' of manuscripts. She told a *Paris Review* interviewer: "I practiced writing in every possible way that I could. . . . This has been the intact line of my life which directs my actions, determines my point of view, profoundly affects my character and personality, my social beliefs and economic status and the kind of friendships I form. . . . I made no attempt to publish anything until I was thirty, but I have written and destroyed manuscripts quite literally by the trunkful. I spent fifteen years wandering about, weighted horribly with masses of paper and little else. Yet for this vocation I was and am willing to live and die, and I consider very few other things of the slightest importance."

James William Johnson feels that "had Miss Porter left those trunksful of manuscripts unburned, the objection [some critics have] based on volume could have been met. Yet this very act of selectivity is an indication of the guiding principle which has made her unique. Her critical judgment, as accurate and impartial as a carpenter's level, has limited her artistry in several ways. It has not permitted her to universalize but has confined her to being a 'witness to life.' Consequently, her fiction has been closely tied to what she herself has experienced firsthand. The fact that Miss Porter's essays parallel her stories in theme—love, marriage, alien cultures—is significant in this light. Her artistic preoccupation with 'truth' has prevented the fictional generalizations often thought of as scope."

Christopher Isherwood agrees and introduces this reservation: "She is grave, she is delicate, she is just—but she lacks altogether, for me personally, the vulgar appeal. I cannot imagine that she would ever make me cry, or laugh aloud."

But Miss Porter has stern words for much of the "vulgar appeal" of some contemporary literature: "We are being sluiced at present with a plague of filth in words and in acts, almost unbelievable abominations, a love of foulness for its own sake, with not a trace of wit or low comedy to clear the fetid air. There is a stylish mob with headquarters in New York that is gulping down the wretched stuff spilled by William Burroughs and Norman Mailer and John Hawkes—the sort of revolting upchuck that makes the old or Paris-days Henry Miller's work look like plain, rather tepid, but clean and well-boiled tripe." As a retort to those who consider contemporary life to be alienated and meaningless, she says: "But I tell you, nothing is pointless, and nothing is meaningless if the artist will face it. And it's his business to face it. He hasn't got the right to sidestep it like that. Human life itself may be almost pure chaos, but the work of the artist—the only thing he's good for—is to take these handfuls of confusion and disparate things, things that seem to be irreconcilable, and put them together in a frame to give them some kind of shape and meaning."

Ship of Fools was filmed by Columbia in 1965. *Noon Wine*

was dramatized and filmed for the television stage, "ABC Stage 67" in 1967. The movie rights to *Pale Horse, Pale Rider* were sold in 1970.

AVOCATIONAL INTERESTS: Outdoor life (she is the great-great-great granddaughter of Jonathan Boone, the younger brother of Daniel Boone), old music, medieval history, reading, cookery, gardening.

BIOGRAPHICAL/CRITICAL SOURCES: New Republic, April 19, 1939, December 4, 1965; Edmund Wilson, *Classics and Commercials,* Farrar, Straus, 1950; *Virginia Quarterly Review,* autumn, 1960; *New York Times Book Review,* April 1, 1962; Harry John Mooney, editor, *The Fiction and Criticism of Katherine Anne Porter,* University of Pittsburgh Press, 1962; Ray B. West, Jr., *Katherine Anne Porter* (pamphlet), University of Minnesota Press, 1963; *Paris Review,* Number 29, 1963-64; William L. Nance, *Katherine Anne Porter and the Art of Rejection,* University of North Carolina Press, 1964; George Hendrick, *Katherine Anne Porter,* Twayne, 1965; *Harper's,* September, 1965; *New York Times,* March 16, 1966; John W. Aldridge, *Time to Murder and Create,* McKay, 1966; *Partisan Review,* spring, 1966; *Twentieth Century Literature,* April, 1967; L. C. Hartley and G. Core, editors, *Katherine Anne Porter,* University of Georgia Press, 1969; *Washington Post,* May 15, 1970; J. E. Hardy, *Katherine Anne Porter,* Ungar, 1973; *Contemporary Literary Criticism,* Gale, Volume I, 1973, Volume III, 1975, Volume VII, 1977, Volume X, 1979, Volume XIII, 1980; *Sewanee Review,* spring, 1974; *Washington Star,* May 11, 1975; *Authors in the News,* Volume II, Gale, 1976.†

* * *

PORTIS, Charles (McColl) 1933-

PERSONAL: Born December 28, 1933, in El Dorado, Ark.; son of Samuel Palmer (a school superintendent) and Alice (Waddell) Portis. *Education:* University of Arkansas, B.A., 1958. *Religion:* Presbyterian. *Home:* 7417 Kingwood, Little Rock, Ark. 72207. *Agent:* Lynn Nesbit, International Creative Management, 40 West 57th St., New York, N.Y. 10019.

CAREER: Commercial Appeal, Memphis, Tenn., reporter, 1958; *Arkansas Gazette,* Little Rock, reporter, 1959-60; *New York Herald Tribune,* New York, N.Y., reporter and London correspondent, 1960-64; full-time writer, 1964—. *Military service:* U.S. Marine Corps, 1952-55; became sergeant.

WRITINGS—Novels: *Norwood,* Simon & Schuster, 1966; *True Grit* (Literary Guild Selection), Simon & Schuster, 1968; *The Dog of the South* (Book-of-the-Month Club alternate selection), Knopf, 1979.

SIDELIGHTS: Charles Portis is perhaps best known for *True Grit,* a novel which was praised by many critics and whose movie incarnation, produced by Paramount in 1969, met with box-office success. (John Wayne won an Oscar for his portrayal of Rooster Cogburn, a tough U.S. Marshal.) Portis's later novel, *The Dog of the South,* has, however, encountered mixed criticism. On the one hand, *Los Angeles Times* reviewer Ralph B. Sipper remarks, "We are dealing here with a main character who is about as exciting as a lukewarm bath." Sipper finds that only the minor characters are interesting; they make the novel "intermittently" amusing. Larry L. King, writing in the *New York Times Book Review,* also feels that the work is tedious. Like Sipper, King believes that only the secondary figures are "engaging," and he wants to see more of one, Dr. Symes, "because he is the only character in the book capable of sustaining passion and zeal."

On the other hand, Joseph McLellan of the *Washington Post* comments that *The Dog of the South* "is a story of lost souls, hardships, constant misunderstanding and suffering, trickery and violence. If it weren't so darned funny, it would be a tragedy." McLellan is particularly impressed by Portis's dialogue in which "he has caught to perfection the special intonations of American vocal cords, the motley concerns—ranging from eternal salvation to a quick buck—that occupy the American soul." In the *Chicago Tribune Book World,* Larry McMurty seeks a middle critical ground. He notes that the novel is a picaresque, subject to the strengths and weaknesses of the genre. McMurty observes that "as with many another picaresque, it is difficult to decide if the page-by-page charm of the novel is exceeded by the sum of its parts. The story has an exceptional amount of drift . . . but it does not become boring." He finds that the minor characters allay any monotony that the narrator "might have dropped into." Overall, McMurty concludes "drift is more or less its point. Its appeal is to be found in anecdote, dialog, observation, and characterization. Charles Portis has had the good sense to vary his tone often enough to keep these elements in balance; the tone, like the narrator, is slightly off-key, but it works."

BIOGRAPHICAL/CRITICAL SOURCES: Saturday Review, June 29, 1968; *New York Times Book Review,* July 7, 1968, July 29, 1979; *Nation,* August 5, 1968; *New York Times,* June 22, 1979; *Los Angeles Times,* July 6, 1979; *Chicago Tribune,* July 8, 1979; *Washington Post Book World,* August 3, 1979.

* * *

POTTER, Marian 1915-

PERSONAL: Born January 9, 1915, in Blackwell, Mo.; daughter of Samuel and Flora (Bookstaver) McKinstry; married David Potter, October 18, 1943; children: Andrew, Pamela, Rebecca. *Education:* University of Missouri, B.J., 1939. *Politics:* Democrat. *Religion:* Presbyterian. *Home:* 124 Beaty St., Warren, Pa. 16365.

CAREER: Elementary school teacher in Jefferson and Monroe countries, Mo., 1932-35; *Monroe City News,* Monroe City, Mo., reporter, 1939; University of Missouri—Columbia, editor, 1940-41; *St. Louis Globe-Democrat,* St. Louis, Mo., copy-reader, 1942-43; United Nations Information Office, New York, N.Y., assistant press officer, 1944; WNAE and WRRN (radio stations), Warren, Pa., editorial writer, 1962-74. Member of board of directors of Northern Allegheny Broadcasting Co., 1965-74. *Awards, honors:* Received award for outstanding contribution to children's literature, Central Missouri State College, 1971.

WRITINGS: The Little Red Caboose, Golden Press, 1953; *Milepost 67,* Follett, 1965; *Copperfield Summer,* Follett, 1967; *The Shared Room,* Morrow, 1979; *Blather Skite,* Morrow, 1980.

SIDELIGHTS: Marian Potter told *CA:* "My father was a railroad station agent in rural Missouri when even the smallest village had a depot. The railroad was an exciting part of my childhood. I worked as a journalist and did not consider writing for children until I had children of my own. For little ones I wrote a story about a freight train. *The Little Red Caboose* is now read by a second generation. In *Milepost 67* and *Copperfield Summer* I hoped to share with children some events of a childhood lived close to the rails and close to the country. *The Shared Room* is a three-generation family story that tells of recent changes in the treatment of mental illness. I believe I have chosen to write for children because they are so interesting."

AVOCATIONAL INTERESTS: Gardening, travel, painting.

* * *

POTTER, Robert Alonzo 1934-

PERSONAL: Born December 28, 1934, in New York, N.Y.; son of Henry C. (a stage and film director) and Lucilla (Wylie) Potter; married Sally Alabaster, December 20, 1958 (divorced May 15, 1977); married Nancy Collinge, September 17, 1977; children: (first marriage) Lucilla, Daniel, Jane, Maria; (second marriage) Bryn. *Education:* Pomona College, B.A., 1956; Claremont Graduate School, M.A., 1963, Ph.D., 1965. *Politics:* Democrat. *Office:* Department of Dramatic Art, University of California, Santa Barbara, Calif. 93106.

CAREER: Harvey Mudd College, Claremont, Calif., instructor in humanities, 1965; University of California, Santa Barbara, assistant professor of English, 1965-72, lecturer in dramatic art, 1972-75, associate professor of dramatic art, 1975—. Directed plays at Bristol Shakespeare Festival, 1964, and in Santa Barbara, 1966. Member of Santa Barbara County Democratic Central Committee, 1968-76. *Military service:* U.S. Army Reserve, 1957-63. *Member:* Modern Language Association of America, American Theatre Association, Medieval Association of the Pacific. *Awards, honors:* Fulbright scholarship, University of Bristol, 1963-64; fellowship from University of California's Institute for Creative Arts, 1967-69; Harold J. Plous Memorial Award, for teaching and community service, 1971-72.

WRITINGS: (With Brooke Whiting) *Lawrence Durrell: A Checklist,* University of California Library, 1961; (with James Sullivan) *The Campus by the Sea Where the Bank Burned Down* (Report to the Presidential Commission on Campus Unrest), Faculty Clergy Observers Program, 1970; *The English Morality Play: Origins, History, and Influence of a Dramatic Tradition,* Routledge & Kegan Paul, 1975.

Plays: (Adapter and translator) Moliere, "The Miser," first produced in Claremont, Calif., 1965; "Where Is Sicily?," first produced by Institute of Creative Arts, Santa Barbara, Calif., 1969; "In a Pig's Eye," first produced in Philadelphia, Pa., 1974; (adapter and translator with Richard Exner) Thomas Mann, "Fiorenza," produced in Santa Barbara, 1975; "Queen Margaret of England" (based on William Shakespeare's *The Three Parts of Henry VI*), first produced at Temple University, Philadelphia, 1977; "Fifteen Signs of the Apocalypse," with music by Marc Ream, first produced at Santa Barbara Contemporary Music Festival, Santa Barbara, 1978; (adapter with Tom Markus) Ben Jonson, "Volpone," first produced by Virginia Museum Theatre, Richmond, Va., 1978; (adapter) Bertolt Brecht, "Mother Courage," first produced by Virginia Museum Theatre, Richmond, 1979; "The Vision of Children," first produced by Department of Dramatic Art, University of California, Santa Barbara, 1980.

Contributor of articles and reviews to *Quarterly Journal of Speech, Callboard, New Theatre, Claremont Quarterly,* and *Research Opportunities in Renaissance Drama.*

SIDELIGHTS: Robert Potter told *CA:* "My career as a playwright is somewhat unusual, because it has come about as an extension of my career as a literary scholar. During a year in England as a Fulbright scholar at the University of Bristol, completing research for my doctoral dissertation, I got involved with practical theatre, through an assignment to direct the first modern revival of Bale's *King John,* the earliest English History Play. In scholarly terms this led on to research and publications in the field of early English drama; in theatrical terms it has involved me in writing new plays of a historical sort: 'Where Is Sicily?,' about the Peloponnesian War (with glances at Vietnam), 'In a Pig's Eye,' about student-police confrontations in the '60s, 'Fifteen Signs of the Apocalypse,' about the end of the world, and 'The Vision of Children,' set in the Middle Ages. I've always attempted to find a comic as well as a serious texture for these plays.

"I've also done a series of adaptations/translations, ranging from a fairly conventional Moliere 'Miser' to an abbreviation of Thomas Mann's Renaissance epic, 'Fiorenza,' and three projects with Tom Markus as director of which I'm particularly proud: 'Queen Margaret of England,' focusing on that fascinating character, a streamlined and stealthily rewritten 'Volpone,' and an American version of Brecht's 'Mother Courage,' transposed to the circumstances of the Civil War. It is my firm conviction that none of the above-mentioned authors is spinning in his grave over what I have done (with the exception of Ben Jonson, who never let the opportunity for a quarrel go untried) since my research informs me that all of the above gentlemen dealt freely with, and in many cases improved on, the work of their predecessors. So much for the liberating qualities of scholarship.

"Having begun to learn something about writing plays, through these means and by running a playwriting program, and in the process moving my academic address from English to Drama, I'm looking forward to writing more and better of them."

* * *

POUND, Omar S(hakespear) 1926-

PERSONAL: Born September 10, 1926, in Paris, France; son of Ezra Loomis (the poet) and Dorothy (Shakespear) Pound; married Elizabeth Parkin, May 14, 1955; children: Katherine, Oriana. *Education:* Hamilton College, A.B., 1951; McGill University, M.A., 1958. *Politics:* "Nil." *Religion:* "Nil." *Address:* c/o E. Parker Hayden, P.O. Box 417, Princeton, N.J. 08540.

CAREER: Roxbury Latin School, Boston, Mass., member of faculty, 1957-62; American School of Tangier, Tangier, Morocco, headmaster, 1962-65; Cambridgeshire College of Arts and Technology, Cambridge, England, lecturer, 1967-80. *Military service:* U.S. Army, 1945-46; served in Germany.

WRITINGS: (Translator) *Arabic and Persian Poems,* New Directions, 1970; (translator) Nizam al-Din 'Ubayd Zakani, *Gorby and the Rats,* New Directions, 1972, 2nd edition, Migrant Press, 1979; (contributor) *New Poetry,* Arts Council of Great Britain, 1975; (contributor) Elizabeth W. Fernea and Basima Q. Bezirgan, editors, *Middle Eastern Muslim Women Speak,* University of Texas Press, 1977; (with Philip Grover) *Wyndham Lewis: A Descriptive Bibliography,* Dawson/Archon, 1978; (author of foreword) *Catalogue of Wyndham Lewis Retrospective Exhibition,* Manchester City Art Gallery, 1980. Contributor to *Montemora.*

AVOCATIONAL INTERESTS: Anything Islamic, choral music.

* * *

POWELL, Anthony (Dymoke) 1905-

PERSONAL: Surname rhymes with "Lowell"; born December 21, 1905, in London, England; son of Philip Lionel William (an Army officer) and Maude Mary (Wells-Dymoke) Powell; married Lady Violet Pakenham, daughter of fifth Earl of Longford, 1934; children: Tristram, John. *Education:*

Balliol College, Oxford, M.A., 1926. *Home:* The Chantry, near Frome, Somerset, England.

CAREER: Affiliated with Duckworth & Co. Ltd (publisher), London, England, 1926-35; scriptwriter, Warner Brothers of Great Britain, 1936; reviewer for the *Daily Telegraph, Times Literary Supplement,* and other London papers, beginning 1936; *Punch,* London, literary editor, 1953-58; writer. Trustee, National Portrait Gallery, London, 1962-76. *Military service:* Welch Regiment, Infantry, 1939-41, Intelligence Corps, 1941-45, serving as liaison officer at War Office; became major. *Member:* American Academy of Arts and Letters (honorary member), Travellers' Club (London). *Awards, honors:* Order of the White Lion, Czechoslovakia; Order of Leopold II, Belgium; Oaken Crown and Croix de Guerre, Luxembourg, 1945; commander, Order of the British Empire, 1956; James Tait Black Memorial Prize, 1958, for *At Lady Molly's;* D.Litt from University of Sussex, 1971, University of Leicester, 1976, and University of Kent, 1976; W. H. Smith Fiction Award, 1974, for *Temporary Kings.*

WRITINGS: Afternoon Men (novel), Duckworth, 1931, Holt, 1932, reprinted, Popular Library, 1978; *Venusberg* (novel; also see below), Duckworth, 1932, Popular Library, 1978; *From a View to a Death* (novel), Duckworth, 1933, reprinted, Popular Library, 1978, published as *Mr. Zouch, Superman: From a View to a Death,* Vanguard, 1934; *Agents and Patients* (novel; also see below), Duckworth, 1936, Popular Library, 1978; *What's Become of Waring?* (novel), Cassell, 1939, Little, Brown, 1963, reprinted, Popular Library, 1978; (editor and author of introduction) *Novels of High Society from the Victorian Age,* Pilot Press, 1947; *John Aubrey and His Friends,* Scribner, 1948, revised edition, Barnes & Noble, 1963; (editor and author of introduction) John Aubrey, *Brief Lives and Other Selected Writings,* Scribner, 1949; *Two Novels: Venusberg* [and] *Agents and Patients,* Periscope-Holliday, 1952; *Two Plays: The Garden God* [and] *The Rest I'll Whistle,* Heinemann, 1971, Little, Brown, 1972; (contributor of a memoir) Richard Shead, *Constance Lambert,* Simon Publications, 1973; *To Keep the Ball Rolling: The Memoirs of Anthony Powell,* Volume I: *Infants of the Spring,* Heinemann, 1976, published as *Infants of the Spring: The Memoirs of Anthony Powell,* Holt, 1977; *Messengers of Day: The Memoirs of Anthony Powell,* Holt, 1978 (published in England as *To Keep the Ball Rolling: The Memoirs of Anthony Powell,* Volume II: *Messengers of Day,* Heinemann, 1978).

"A Dance to the Music of Time" series: *A Question of Upbringing,* Scribner, 1951, reprinted, Popular Library, 1976; *A Buyer's Market,* Heinemann, 1952, Scribner, 1953, reprinted, Popular Library, 1976; *The Acceptance World,* Heinemann, 1955, Farrar, Straus, 1956, reprinted, Popular Library, 1976; *At Lady Molly's,* Heinemann, 1957, Little, Brown, 1958, reprinted, Popular Library, 1976; *Casanova's Chinese Restaurant,* Little, Brown, 1960; *The Kindly Ones,* Little, Brown, 1962; *The Valley of Bones,* Little, Brown, 1964; *The Soldier's Art,* Little, Brown, 1966; *The Military Philosophers,* Heinemann, 1968, Little, Brown, 1969; *Books Do Furnish a Room,* Little, Brown, 1971; *Temporary Kings,* Little, Brown, 1973; *Hearing Secret Harmonies,* Heinemann, 1975, Little, Brown, 1976.

"A Dance to the Music of Time" omnibus volumes; all published by Little, Brown: *A Dance to the Music of Time: First Movement* (contains *A Question of Upbringing, A Buyer's Market,* and *The Acceptance World*), 1963; ... *Second Movement* (contains *At Lady Molly's, Casanova's Chinese Restaurant,* and *The Kindly Ones*), 1964; ... *Third Movement* (contains *The Valley of Bones, The Soldier's Art,* and *The Military Philosophers*), 1971; ... *Fourth Movement* (contains *Books Do Furnish a Room, Temporary Kings,* and *Hearing Secret Harmonies*), 1976.

SIDELIGHTS: As Bernard Bergonzi notes, some novelists become famous with the publication of their first book. Anthony Powell's reputation, however, "has developed in quite the opposite way, in a slow and deliberate fashion over forty years, from fairly obscure beginnings to a point where he is now widely regarded as one of the finest living English novelists." Powell's renown grew as each volume of his highly acclaimed "A Dance to the Music of Time" series appeared.

Powell's career as a novelist began long before the appearance of the first volume of "Music of Time" in 1951. Before World War II, Powell had written five novels, which Charles Shapiro terms "finger exercises for his later, larger efforts." The prewar novels, Shapiro continues, are "extremely funny" but limited by a "vagueness of focus which prevents the entertainment from becoming serious criticism." Although he echoes Shapiro's assessment in general, Bergonzi singles out *Afternoon Men* "as one of the few outstanding first novels to appear in England during the twenties and thirties.... It is a comic masterpiece."

Bergonzi contends that Powell's last prewar novel, *What's Become of Waring?,* clearly anticipates "Music of Time" in both style and subject and that Powell seemed ready to begin a work such as "Music of Time," but the Second World War began, and Powell's military duty prevented him from writing. In an interview in *Summary,* Powell discusses the difficulty he foresaw in returning to fiction after the interruption of the war: "I thought that I wouldn't be able to write a novel immediately after the war if I survived, and therefore did start making notes on John Aubrey, the seventeenth-century antiquary, with the idea of writing a book on Aubrey.... At the end of the war I produced this book which was simply a question of plugging away at a lot of historical material—and then I found that somehow did the trick, and one was in a mood to write a novel again."

In the same interview, Powell says that after the war he thought a great deal about writing novels, and he decided to write a series, rather than independent novels, for "if you wrote a lot more novels, each one separate, you would be losing a lot from the ideas you put into them by not connecting those ideas, if you see what I mean. And therefore I thought one would do best to settle down to write one really long novel. I hadn't then decided that it would necessarily be twelve volumes, but I did think it would be a great number of volumes, and that one would, so to speak, pick up in that way all you lose by ending a book and starting again with a lot of entirely new characters." In fact, the resultant series, which chronicles a segment of upper-class and upper-middle-class English society from the twenties to the seventies, is so tightly knit together that Bergonzi finds that "the separate volumes are by now quite unintelligible without a good knowledge of the previous volumes."

One of the ways in which "A Dance to the Music of Time" achieves its unity is through the controlling metaphor of the series' title. At the beginning of *A Question of Upbringing,* Nicholas Jenkins, the narrator, sees a group of workmen in a London street and is reminded of a painting by Nicolas Poussin called "A Dance to the Music of Time" in which "the Seasons, hand in hand and facing outward, tread in rhythm to the notes of the lyre that the winged and naked greybeard plays. The image of Time brought thoughts of mortality: of human beings, facing outward like the Seasons, moving hand in hand in intricate measure: stepping slowly, methodically, sometimes a trifle awkwardly, in evolutions that take recognisable shape: or breaking into seemingly meaningless gyrations, while partners disappear only to reappear again, once more giving pattern to the spectacle: unable to control the melody, unable, perhaps, to control the steps of the dance."

Many critics find that the image evoked by this painting accurately describes the complex interrelationships of the characters and the manner in which they appear, disappear, and reappear throughout the series. Arthur Mizener, for example, comments that the description of the painting "tells us all we need to know about the design of 'The Music of Time.' It proposes that we contemplate the interaction of these brief lives as constituting a loosely woven pattern within which parallels, contrasts, repetitions will occasionally occur. . . . Its emphasis is on the relations of the dancers to the dance, and what it finds important is not what abstract meanings may be ascribed to the dance or to the melody by which the winged and naked greybeard guides it, but what response of the order evoked by Poussin it arrouses." Similarly, Michael Wood contends that the dance-like structure is more important than the account of English social life upon which many critics concentrate. Wood remarks that "although it looks like a chronicle, 'The Music of Time' is really a set of strictly selected, highly focused scenes, spots of time rather than chunks or stretches of it. The scenes serve to underscore myths, point up patterns, connect characters, sever identities, and only incidentally, it seems to me, record anything much about the history of England. That is to say that the books offer the pleasures primarily of formal design, or more precisely of designs forming and unforming and reforming, like figures in a dance."

At the same time, James Tucker argues that the dance metaphor has negative implications which are borne out in the course of the action. According to Tucker, Powell's use of the word "dance" in the title is ironic; it suggests not gaiety, harmony, and freedom but their opposites: "People behave as if they can play fresh, original parts in life, whereas really the lines have been laid down from far back, and all the moves are inflexibly formalised, limited, repetitive. . . . Patterns exist but they may be utterly destructive of those which people would wish for themselves. . . . The contrast between how people might want to behave—or might have been expected to in view of upbringing and background—and the actual performance imposed as time calls the tune is a main theme."

In contrast to this, many reviewers emphasize the comedy in "Music of Time." Shapiro feels that "Powell very well might be England's best comic writer since Charles Dickens." Similarly, Richard McLaughlin believes that "his ambitiously scaled series of novels show him to be a master of social comedy, with few, if any, rivals." "There is no other living British novelist," adds Julian Symons, "whose sense of social nuance . . . is so delicate or so subtle, or whose comic range is so wide, and none except Mr. [Evelyn] Waugh whose power of comic characterization is so great."

On the other hand, John S. Monagan, like Tucker, sees a sober side to the work, "Powell has often been called a comic writer and it is true that he has created numerous memorable scenes of high comedy, but he has always been a more serious commentator than at first he seems, and his insights, however jocular the context, are basically serious." Robert Towers discerns an even darker facet to the work: "It is by now a cliche to insist upon the melancholy and often the horror that underlie so much good comedy. Cliche or not, Powell's world—droll as it is—is shot through with pain. . . . Personal wretchedness of one sort or another is everywhere present and makes itself felt, despite the detachment, even flippancy, with which it is often presented. The inhabitants of Powell's world, whatever their age or sex, often give the impression of being lost or abandoned children putting on a funny or a brave or a goblin face in a dance that allows much display but only the briefest gratification." Moreover, Mizener confirms, even extends, Towers' contentions, arguing that Powell finds men, underneath their masks of socially governed behavior, demented and driven. Yet, Mizener continues, Powell's horrifying vision is mitigated by his humor. His characters, however terrifying, "are also ridiculous, 'to reason most absurd,' an endless source of comic enchantment."

Not all critics concentrate on uncovering the tragedy beneath the comedy. Max Egremont, for example, praises the realism of "Music of Time": "So complete has been [Powell's] creation that it is hard not to feel as one lays the [final] book down that a whole world is being abandoned, a world whose characters and landscapes attain an almost tangible degree of reality. In this respect Powell has achieved what must surely be one of the criteria of a great, perhaps even epic, work of fiction—the ability to take the reader, for an instant, entirely out of himself into a set of situations and circumstances created for him by the novelist." Bergonzi, too, focuses less on the possibly somber implications of Powell's vision, concluding that he "is unlike other twentieth-century novelists in having a general affection for all his characters. . . . We are all sinners, he seems to imply, and should not judge one another, and although Powell displays a quintessentially secular caste of mind he regards his creations with an exemplary religious compassion. Underlying the marvellously observed and recorded social comedy of a particular culture and phase of history, there is something more fundamental; the basic human comedy where, as in Chaucer and Rabelais and Shakespeare, folly and weakness and vice are transformed into an unending comic dance."

BIOGRAPHICAL/CRITICAL SOURCES—Periodicals: *Time,* August 11, 1958, March 3, 1967, March 28, 1969; *Commonweal,* July 31, 1959, May 12, 1967; *Spectator,* June 24, 1960, September 16, 1966, October 18, 1968; *New Statesman,* June 25, 1960, July 6, 1962; *Christian Science Monitor,* October 6, 1960, January 25, 1967, March 16, 1967; *Kenyon Review,* winter, 1960; *New York Times Book Review,* January 21, 1962, September 30, 1962, March 19, 1967, March 9, 1969, November 1, 1973, April 11, 1976; *New York Herald Tribune Books,* February 11, 1962; *Atlantic,* March, 1962; *New Republic,* September 24, 1962, April 22, 1967; *Critique,* spring, 1964; *New Yorker,* July 3, 1965, June 3, 1967; *Saturday Review,* March 18, 1967, March 8, 1969, April 17, 1976; *Book Week,* April 9, 1967; *New York Review of Books,* May 18, 1967; *Nation,* May 29, 1967; *Hudson Review,* summer, 1967; *Observer Review,* October 10, 1967, October 13, 1968, February 14, 1971; *New York Times,* March 14, 1968, March 13, 1969, September 8, 1971, February 17, 1972; *Listener,* October 14, 1968; *Times Literary Supplement,* October 17, 1968; *London Magazine,* January, 1969; *Best Sellers,* March 15, 1969; *Newsweek,* March 24, 1969; *Books & Bookmen,* April, 1971, March, 1976; *Washington Post Book World,* April 4, 1976; *Publishers Weekly,* April 5, 1976.

Books: Anthony Powell, *A Question of Upbringing,* Scribner, 1951; Frederick R. Karl, *The Contemporary English Novel,* Farrar, Straus, 1962; James Hall, *The Tragic Comedians,* Indiana University Press, 1963; Arthur Mizener, *The Sense of Life in the Modern Novel,* Houghton, 1964; Walter

Allen, *The Modern Novel,* Dutton, 1965; Charles Shapiro, *Contemporary British Novelists,* Southern Illinois University Press, 1965; Julian Symons, *Critical Occasions,* Hamish Hamilton, 1966; Robert K. Morris, *The Novels of Anthony Powell,* University of Pittsburgh Press, 1968; Bernard Bergonzi, *The Situation of the Novel,* University of Pittsburgh Press, 1970; Bergonzi, *Anthony Powell,* Longman, 1971; *Contemporary Literary Criticism,* Gale, Volume I, 1973, Volume III, 1975, Volume VII, 1977, Volume IX, 1978, Volume X, 1979; James Tucker, *The Novels of Anthony Powell,* Columbia University Press, 1976.

—*Sketch by David A. Guy*

* * *

**POYER, Joseph John (Jr.) 1939-
(Joe Poyer)**

PERSONAL: Born November 30, 1939, in Battle Creek, Mich.; son of Joseph John (a salesman) and Eileen (Powell) Poyer; married Susan Pilmore; children: Joseph John III, Geoffrey. *Education:* Kellogg Community College, A.A., 1959; Michigan State University, B.A., 1961. *Politics:* Independent. *Religion:* None. *Residence:* Orange, Calif. *Agent:* Wallace & Sheil Associates, 177 East 70th St., New York, N.Y. 10021; and Anthony Sheil Associates Ltd., 2-3 Morewell St., London WC1B 3AR, England.

CAREER: Michigan Tuberculosis and Respiratory Disease Association, Lansing, assistant director of public information, 1961-62; Pratt & Whitney Aircraft, East Hartford, Conn., proposals writer, 1963-65; Beckman Instruments, Fullerton, Calif., proposals writer, 1965-67; Bioscience Planning, Anaheim, Calif., manager of interdisciplinary communications, 1967-68; Allergan Pharmaceuticals, Irvine, Calif., senior project manager, 1968-77; full-time novelist, 1977—. Teacher of writing course at Golden West College, 1974-76.

WRITINGS—All under name Joe Poyer; all novels: *Operation Malacca,* Doubleday, 1968; *North Cape* (Book-of-the-Month Club selection in England), Doubleday, 1969; *The Balkan Assignment,* Doubleday, 1971; *The Chinese Agenda* (Junior Literary Guild selection; Book-of-the-Month Club selection in Sweden), Doubleday, 1972; *The Shooting of the Green,* Doubleday, 1973; *Day of Reckoning,* Weidenfeld & Nicolson, 1976; *The Contract,* Atheneum, 1978; *Tunnel War,* Atheneum, 1979; *Vengeance 10,* Atheneum, 1980.

Editor: *Instrumentation Methods for Predictive Medicine,* Instrument Society of America, 1966; *Biomedical Sciences Instrumentation,* Plenum, 1967.

Contributor of about a dozen short stories and articles to magazines.

WORK IN PROGRESS: A four volume novel on World War II; a novel about the escape of the Princess Tatiana from a massacre.

AVOCATIONAL INTERESTS: Travel, photography, karate, antique firearms.

BIOGRAPHICAL/CRITICAL SOURCES: Spectator, February 28, 1970; *Washington Post,* November 30, 1979; *Los Angeles Times Book Review,* December 9, 1979.

* * *

PRASSEL, Frank Richard 1937-

PERSONAL: Born October 5, 1937, in San Antonio, Tex.; son of Frank Gustav (a manufacturer) and Julie (Oge) Prassel; married Ann Hetherington (a librarian), July 30, 1966. *Education:* Trinity University, San Antonio, B.A., 1959, M.A., 1961; University of Texas, LL.B. (since converted to J.D.), 1965, Ph.D., 1970. *Religion:* Lutheran. *Address:* P.O. Box 957, San Antonio, Tex. 78294. *Office:* Law Enforcement Training Center, University of Arkansas, Fayetteville, Ark.

CAREER: Admitted to Texas Bar, 1965; San Antonio College, San Antonio, Tex., assistant professor and director of law enforcement, 1966-70; Sacramento State College (now California State University, Sacramento), Sacramento, Calif., associate professor of police science, 1970-71; Fulbright professor of law in Taiwan, 1971-72; Stephen F. Austin State University, Nacogdoches, Tex., associate professor and coordinator of criminal justice, 1972-78; University of Arkansas, Law Enforcement Training Center, Fayetteville, director, 1978-80. *Military service:* U.S. Army Reserve, 1959-73; became captain. *Member:* Texas Bar Association.

WRITINGS: The Western Police Officer: A Legacy of Law and Order, University of Oklahoma Press, 1972; *Introduction to American Criminal Justice,* Harper, 1975; *Criminal Law, Justice and Society,* Goodyear Publishing, 1979.

WORK IN PROGRESS: Writing on criminal justice and retirement planning.

* * *

**PRATT, John 1931-
(John Winton)**

PERSONAL: Born May 3, 1931, in Hampstead, London; son of John and Margaret Young (Stuart Winton) Pratt; married Sally Elizabeth Wild, 1960; children: Elizabeth Alice, Adam John Winton. *Education:* Attended Royal Naval College, one year; Royal Naval Engineering College, B.S.C.

CAREER: Royal Navy, 1949-63; retired as lieutenant commander. Served on H.M.S. *Birmingham,* 1952-53, H.M.S. *Eagle,* 1955-56, and in submarines *Springer, Acheron,* and *Explorer,* 1957-62. *Member:* P.E.N., Society of Authors.

WRITINGS—All under pseudonym John Winton; all published by M. Joseph, except as indicated: *We Joined the Navy,* St. Martin's, 1959; *We Saw the Sea,* St. Martin's, 1960; *Down the Hatch,* 1961, St. Martin's, 1962; *Never Go to Sea,* St. Martin's, 1963; *All the Nice Girls,* 1964; *H.M.S. "Leviathan,"* Coward, 1967; (editor) *The War at Sea, 1939-1945,* introduction by Earl Mountbatten, Hutchinson, 1967, published as *The War at Sea: The British Navy in World War II,* Morrow, 1968; *The Forgotten Fleet,* 1969, published as *The Forgotten Fleet: The British Navy in the Pacific, 1944-1945,* Crown, 1970; *The Fighting Temeraire,* Coward, 1971; *One of Our Warships,* 1975; *The Little Wonder: The Story of the Festiniog Railway,* 1975; *Sir Walter Ralegh,* Coward, 1975; *Air Power at Sea, 1939-45,* Sidgwick & Jackson, 1976, Crowell, 1977; *Good Enough for Nelson,* 1977; *Hurrah for the Life of a Sailor! Life on the Lower-deck of the Victorian Navy,* 1977; *The Victoria Cross at Sea,* 1978; *War in the Pacific: Pearl Harbor to Tokyo Bar,* Sidgwick & Jackson, 1978.

BIOGRAPHICAL/CRITICAL SOURCES: Books and Bookmen, February, 1968.†

* * *

PREIL, Gabriel 1911-

PERSONAL: Surname rhymes with "file"; born August 21, 1911, in Dorpat, Estonia; came to United States in 1922, naturalized in 1928; son of Elias and Clara (Matzkel) Preil. *Education:* Attended Rabbi Isaac Elchanan Theological Seminary, 1923-24, Teachers' Institute (now part of Yeshivah

University), 1924-26. *Religion:* Jewish. *Home and office:* 1011 Walton Ave., Bronx, N.Y. 10452.

CAREER: In early youth, did occasional work of great variety, manual as well as intellectual; free-lance writer, translator, and editor of Hebrew, Yiddish, and English prose and poetry, 1935—. Member of Israeli delegation to World P.E.N. Congress, New York, N.Y., 1966. *Awards, honors:* Louis La Med award for Hebrew literature, 1942; Kovner Memorial Hebrew Poetry Prize, Jewish Book Council of America, 1955, 1961; Bitzaron award for Hebrew poetry, 1960; Congress of Jewish Culture grant, 1965; D.H.L., Hebrew Union College-Jewish Institute of Religion, 1972; Irving and Bertha Neuman Literary Award, New York University, 1974.

WRITINGS—Hebrew poetry, except as indicated: *Nofshemesh ukhfor* (title means "Landscape of Sun and Frost"), Ohel Publishing, 1944; *Ner mul kohavim* (title means "Candle against Stars"), Bialik Institute (Jerusalem), 1954; *Hebrew Poetry in Peace and War* (essays), Herzl Press, 1959; *Mapat erev* (title means "Map of Evening"), Dvir (Tel Aviv), 1961; *Gabriel Prail Mivhar Shirim Udevarim al Yezirato* (title means "Gabriel Preil: A Selection of Poems and a Study of His Poetry"), Mahbarot Leshira (Tel Aviv), 1965; *Lider* (poems in Yiddish), Yiddish P.E.N. Club (New York), 1966; *Haesh vehademama* (title means "Fire and Silence"), Israeli Writers' Association (Tel Aviv), 1968; *Mitoch zeman vanof* (title means "Of Time and Place"), Bialik Institute, 1973; *Shirim Mishnai Hakzavot,* Schocken (Tel Aviv), 1976; *Yalkut Shirim,* Nechdav Writers' Association, 1978; *Autumn Music* (poems in English translation), edited by Howard Schwartz, Cauldron Press, 1979.

Work represented in anthologies, including: *The Modern Hebrew Poem Itself: From the Beginnings to the Present,* edited by Ezra Spicehandler, Stanley Burnshaw, and others, Holt, 1965; *Anthology of Modern Hebrew Poetry,* Volume II, edited by S. Y. Penueli and Azriel Ukhmani, Institute of Translation of Hebrew Literature (Tel Aviv), 1966; *Antologia Poesia Hebrea Moderna,* Aguilar (Madrid), 1971; *Contemporary Israeli Literature,* edited by Elliott Anderson, Jewish Publication Society, 1977; *Penguin Book of Hebrew Verse,* edited by T. Carmi, Penguin, 1980; *Voices Within the Ark: The Modern Jewish Poets,* edited by Schwartz, Avon, 1980.

Also translator of poems of Robert Frost, Carl Sandburg, and Robinson Jeffers. Contributor to periodicals. Editor, *Niv,* 1937-39, and *Bitzaron,* 1969—.

WORK IN PROGRESS: A new volume of poems.

SIDELIGHTS: Gabriel Preil told *CA* he is an anomaly, "a Hebrew poet living in the U.S., considered among the better practitioners of the art, well-known in Israel. Invited by the City of Haifa in Israel to accept residence there for life (1953), guest of Jerusalem Municipality and of President Shazar (1968), I am yet unable to leave the U.S. Family reasons—yet they are more intricate than that. In any case, here I work in isolation, rooted in Israeli literature, affected by English and American influences."

AVOCATIONAL INTERESTS: Art, music.

BIOGRAPHICAL/CRITICAL SOURCES: Meyer Waxman, editor, *A History of Jewish Literature,* Yoseloff, 1960; *Judaism,* spring, 1966; Eisig Silberschlag, editor, *From Renaissance to Renaissance: Hebrew Literature 1492-1967,* Ktav, 1972.

PRICE, Jacob M(yron) 1925-

PERSONAL: Born November 8, 1925, in Worcester, Mass.; son of Abraham Oscar and Alice (Pike) Price. *Education:* Harvard University, A.B., 1947, A.M., 1948, Ph.D., 1954; Oxford University, graduate study, 1949-50; London School of Economics and Political Science, University of London, graduate study, 1950-51. *Religion:* Jewish. *Home:* 1050 Wall St., Apt. 4-D, Ann Arbor, Mich. 48105. *Office:* Department of History, University of Michigan, Ann Arbor, Mich. 48109.

CAREER: Smith College, Northampton, Mass., instructor in history, 1954-56; University of Michigan, Ann Arbor, instructor, 1956-58, assistant professor, 1958-61, associate professor, 1961-64, professor of history, 1964—. *Military service:* U.S. Army Air Forces, 1944-46; became staff sergeant. *Member:* American Historical Association, Conference on Early American History, Economic History Society, Conference on British Studies. *Awards, honors:* Fulbright fellow, Oxford University, 1949-50; Guggenheim fellow, 1958-59, 1965-66; Social Science Research Council fellowship, 1962-63; American Council of Learned Societies fellowship, 1972-73; National Endowment for the Humanities fellow, 1977-78.

WRITINGS: (Editor) *Reading for Life: Developing the College Student's Lifetime Reading Interest,* University of Michigan Press, 1959; *The Tobacco Adventure to Russia,* American Philosophical Society, 1961; (editor with V. R. Lorwin) *The Dimensions of the Past: Materials, Problems and Opportunities for Quantitative Work in History,* Yale University Press, 1972; *France and the Chesapeake,* University of Michigan Press, 1973; (contributor) Ann Whiteman and others, editors, *Statesmen, Scholars and Merchants: Essays in Eighteenth Century History,* Clarendon Press, 1973; (contributor) Aubrey C. Land and others, editors, *Law, Society and Politics in Early Maryland,* Johns Hopkins Press, 1977; (editor) *Joshua Johnson's Letterbook, 1771-1774,* London Record Society, 1979. Contributor to *International Encyclopedia of Social Sciences* and to journals, including *Economic History Review, William and Mary Quarterly, Journal of British Studies, New Cambridge Modern History,* and *Journal of Economic History.*

WORK IN PROGRESS: Research in 18th-century British and American economic history, particularly international trade and finance.

* * *

PRICE, (Edward) Reynolds 1933-

PERSONAL: Born February 1, 1933, in Macon, N.C.; son of William Solomon and Elizabeth (Rodwell) Price. *Education:* Duke University, A.B. (summa cum laude), 1955; Merton College, Oxford, B.Litt., 1958. *Home:* 4813 Duke Station, Durham, N.C. 27706. *Agent:* Harriet Wasserman, Russell & Volkening, Inc., 551 Fifth Ave., New York, N.Y. 10017. *Office:* Department of English, Duke University, Durham, N.C.

CAREER: Duke University, Durham, N.C., instructor, 1958-61, assistant professor, 1961-68, associate professor, 1968-72, professor of English, 1972-77, James B. Duke Professor of English, 1977—. Writer-in-residence at University of North Carolina at Chapel Hill, spring, 1965, University of Kansas, 1967, 1969, and University of North Carolina at Greensboro, 1971; Glasgow Professor, Washington and Lee University, 1971; faculty member, Salzburg Seminar, Salzburg, Austria, 1977. National Endowment for the Arts, Literature Advisory Panel, member, 1973-77, chairman, 1976.

Member: Phi Beta Kappa. *Awards, honors:* Rhodes Scholar, 1955-58; William Faulkner Foundation Award for notable first novel and Sir Walter Raleigh Award, both 1962, for *A Long and Happy Life;* Guggenheim fellow, 1964-65; National Association of Independent Schools Award, 1964; National Endowment for the Arts fellow, 1967-68; National Institute of Arts and Letters award, 1971; Bellamann Foundation Award, 1972; Lillian Smith Award, 1976, for *The Surface of Earth;* Sir Walter Raleigh Award, 1976; North Carolina Award, 1977; National Book Award nomination for translation, 1979, for *A Palpable God;* D.Litt. from St. Andrew's Presbyterian College and Wake Forest University.

WRITINGS—Published by Atheneum, except as indicated: *A Long and Happy Life* (novel), 1962; *The Names and Faces of Heroes* (stories), 1963; *A Generous Man* (novel), 1966; (contributor) *The Arts and the Public,* University of Chicago Press, 1967; *Love and Work* (novel), 1968; *Late Warning: Four Poems,* Albondocani, 1968; *Permanent Errors* (stories), 1970; (author of introduction) Henry James, *The Wings of the Dove,* C. E. Merrill, 1970; *Things Themselves: Essays and Scenes,* 1972; *The Surface of Earth* (novel), 1975; *Early Dark: A Play* (three act; adapted from *A Long and Happy Life;* first produced Off-Off-Broadway at WPA Theater, April, 1978), 1977; *Lessons Learned: Seven Poems,* Albondocani, 1977; (contributor) *Symbolism and Modern Literature: Studies in Honor of Wallace Fowlie,* Duke University Press, 1978; *A Palpable God: Thirty Stories Translated from the Bible with an Essay on the Origins and Life of Narrative,* 1978; *Nine Mysteries* (poems), Palacmon, 1979. Contributor of poetry, reviews, and articles to newspapers and magazines, including *Time, Harper's, Southern Review, Esquire, Saturday Review, Washington Post,* and *New York Times Book Review.* Editor, *The Archive,* 1954-55; advisory editor, *Shenandoah,* 1964—.

SIDELIGHTS: Reynolds Price's first novel, *A Long and Happy Life,* received much critical praise, especially for its style and characters. Richard Sullivan remarks: "The writing is beautiful. There's not a wasted word. The characters . . . all jump with vitality." Gene Baro adds: "Mr. Price's gifts are many. His observations are vivid and acute. His dialogue is colorful and real. . . . And he passes that ultimate test of the novelist: he has the ability to create character that is memorable." Julian Mitchell hails the novel as "a work of art, without question."

In contrast to the acclaim garnered by *A Long and Happy Life,* Price's second novel, *A Generous Man,* generated critical controversy. On the one hand, Granville Hicks finds that *A Generous Man* demonstrates the same gifts of "lyric power" and vigorous prose as *A Long and Happy Life,* but the style is varied more to suit the more complicated experiences related in the second novel. Hicks also praises Price's "impressive" insight into his characters. Overall, he considers the novel "rich, original, and profound."

Robert Drake, on the other hand, feels that *A Generous Man* is thematically confusing and stylistically inferior. He argues that the theme of the novel, a young man's coming of age, "often appears confused because, in speaking of love, [Price] frequently seems to be dealing with sex. . . . [It's] all mixed up with some sort of 'meaningful' chase after 'Death' [the name of an escaped circus snake], and daughters and mothers and sons and lovers all being reunited and understanding each other. What to make of it all remains finally . . . something of a mystery." Moreover, Drake continues, "Price's style, which seemed so powerful and moving in his first novel . . . seems to have degenerated here into a *manner.* His prose has become more modish, as his theme has become more muddled." In addition, the central character, comments Drake, speaks and acts more like "a suburbanite Ivy Leaguer than a country boy whose folks raise tobacco."

A *Times Literary Supplement* reviewer, who terms Price "a most talented writer," is also disappointed with *A Generous Man,* for Price's style, "at its best conveying a Miranda-ish wonder at all the sensuous marvels of the world, has none the less developed mannerisms; and both characters and fable have had loaded on to them a greater weight of significance than they are able to bear."

In reviews of *Love and Work,* Price's third novel, critics once again praise his prose style. A *New Statesman* critic comments: "Price's prose is a delicately fashioned but steely instrument, sharp enough to cut through the fatty tissue of appearance and falsehood to the nerve and bone of truth; time and energy are not wasted by graceful or vigorous flourishes in the air, with the result that the language reverberates in the imagination in a way that rhapsodic, 'poetic' writing rarely, if ever, manages to do." Thomas Lask deems the prose "a pleasure to read, pliant, capable of fine gradations of mood and atmosphere and especially effective in building up the interior weather of every act and scene."

Yet the overall reception of the novel is mixed, some reviewers finding it powerfully real and others artificial. Peter Wolfe remarks: "Without knowing what is happening to them, his characters explode suddenly into love and hatred. The sudden occurrences of these white-hot peaks of emotion rouse in the reader the same highly charged response that appears on the page. Price makes you feel that you are living through an experience, not reading a book."

William Kennedy, however, contends that although "the novel is a neat work of literary architecture, a short and perfect display of Mr. Price's considerable talent for plot, language, literary form," it is too "cerebral"; the main character is a "dullard" who only generates a slight and intellectual interest on the part of the reader. Katherine Gauss Jackson agrees; she considers the novel "earnestly and carefully done, the ideas meticulously worked out," but "rather academic." John Wain also thinks that the story is so neatly constructed that "the total effect is lacking in spontaneity," but he concludes that "the book is worth persevering with, for Mr. Price has important things to say."

The critical debates about Price's work continue with his fourth novel, *The Surface of Earth.* Richard Gilman argues that the book, a Southern gothic, is an anachronism, which "comes to us like a great lumbering archaic beast, taking its place among our literary fauna with the stiff queer presence of the representative of a species thought to be extinct." Gilman regards the novel as "a narrative of astonishingly fierce, parochial single-mindedness, whose narrow thematic range and indifference to nearly everything but its central obsession leave it largely bereft of dramatic incident, intellectual complication or any sense of full destiny." Gilman continues: "As I read on I was continually assailed by an awareness of everything that isn't present, all the wit and humor we have been accustomed to in recent fiction." He also misses "that acute contemporary insight into the chasms that accompany changing moral systems and that lie in fact behind all values at any time."

In response to Gilman's contentions, Eudora Welty, a highly regarded Southern writer, asserts that Gilman "has kept himself removed from the *life* of this book. . . . He sees it, from off, as 'largely bereft of dramatic incident, intellectual complication or any sense of full destiny.' But seen in its own terms, this long, complicated, evolving novel has embraced a theme no less than the continuity of human experience." For Welty, *The Surface of Earth* is a novel for all "readers who are able to accept the reality of other people, living or dead, who have spoken and acted and dreamed out of their own lifetimes, to ask for and to give and to receive and to generate, as they can, affirmation and love."

Several other critics who admire *The Surface of Earth* express reservations about it. Peter S. Prescott praises "the complexity of its characters" and finds the work "impressive," but he discovers "a cumulative overbearingness to the whole that makes it finally difficult to finish." Similarly, Stephen Koch respects the power of the book, for its images "obsess the mind after one reads it." Yet he discerns long moments of "rather empty mellifluousness." Finally, James Ross concludes: "Price is concerned with the difficulty of finding and giving love or even recognizing it when it is offered. His success in dealing with the two themes of love and destiny is considerable. But I left the book with the feeling that somehow it ought to have been better—and about 150 pages shorter."

In *A Palpable God,* Price presents a forty-six page study of narrative, an essay on translation, and thirty translated selections from the Bible. Like his other works, *A Palpable God* divides critics. P. A. Reilly comments, "Readers attracted to this book because of their esteem for Price . . . will find herein the admirable artistic unity and vision of the author applied to the serious subject of Biblical studies." In contrast to this, a *Critic* reviewer believes that "the key to the book—Price's translation and the Biblical excerpts chosen—doesn't really impress as fresh, strikingly different or particularly meaningful." Anthony Burgess, however, admires Price's attempts "to recapture the physicality—palpability, or feelability, is the right word—of the ancient narratives," and he thinks that "Mr. Price's long introductory essay [on narrative] . . . from now on must be required reading in creative-writing courses."

BIOGRAPHICAL/CRITICAL SOURCES: New York Times Book Review, March 18, 1962, June 30, 1963, May 29, 1966, June 30, 1968, January 29, 1975, July 20, 1975, March 12, 1978; *Chicago Sunday Tribune,* March 18, 1962; *New York Herald Tribune Books,* March 18, 1962, June 23, 1963; *Spectator,* March 23, 1962; *Times Literary Supplement,* March 23, 1962, September 27, 1963, January 19, 1967; *Time,* March 23, 1962, October 26, 1970; *New Statesman,* March 23, 1962, November, 1968; *Atlantic,* April, 1962, July, 1963; *New Yorker,* April 7, 1962, May 7, 1966; *Commonweal,* April 27, 1962, September 20, 1963; *Christian Century,* June 27, 1962; *Harper's,* August, 1963, June, 1968; *Saturday Review,* March 26, 1966, July 26, 1975; *Southern Review,* winter, 1967; *National Observer,* June 10, 1968; *New Leader,* June 17, 1968; *Book World,* June 23, 1968; *New York Times,* July 13, 1968, April 26, 1978; *New York Review of Books,* August 22, 1968; *Hudson Review,* autumn, 1968; *Virginia Quarterly Review,* autumn, 1968; *Nation,* November 2, 1970, September 27, 1975; *Twentieth Century Literature,* January, 1971; *Contemporary Literary Criticism,* Gale, Volume III, 1975, Volume VI, 1976, Volume XIII, 1980; *Newsweek,* July 7, 1975; *Publishers Weekly,* August 4, 1975; *Best Sellers,* April, 1978; *Critic,* summer, 1978.

—Sketch by David A. Guy

* * *

PRICE, Steven D(avid) 1940-

PERSONAL: Born April 17, 1940, in Brooklyn, N.Y.; son of Martin and Rose (Myiofis) Price; married Jenene C. Levy, August 18, 1968 (divorced, 1972); married Anne London Wolf, 1978. *Education:* University of Rochester, B.A., 1962; Yale University, LL.B., 1965. *Home:* 510 East 85th St., New York, N.Y. 10028.

CAREER: Lawyer, subsidiary rights director, and editor in publishing field in New York, N.Y., 1965-71; free-lance writer, 1971—. Literary agent, 1978-80.

WRITINGS: Teaching Riding at Summer Camps, Stephen Greene Press, 1971; *Panorama of American Horses,* Westover Publishing, 1972; *Get a Horse!: Basics of Back-yard Horsekeeping,* Viking, 1974; *Take Me Home,* Praeger, 1974; (with William J. Goode) *The Second-Time-Single Man's Survival Handbook,* Praeger, 1974; *Horseback Vacation Guide,* Stephen Greene Press, 1975; *Old As the Hills: The Story of Bluegrass Music,* Viking, 1976; (with Anthony D'Ambrosio, Jr.) *Schooling to Show: Basics of Hunter-Jumper Training,* Viking, 1976; (editor) *The Whole Horse Catalog,* Simon & Schuster, 1977. Contributor to *Classic, Horse Lover's National, Practical Horseman, Better Homes and Gardens,* and *Village Voice.*

SIDELIGHTS: Steven D. Price told *CA:* "Literary aspirations notwithstanding, specialization is essential if the nonfiction writer is to survive financially. In my case, books and articles about horses in general have been narrowed to hunter-jumper subjects. Such focusing permits greater depth and the development of a reputation."

* * *

PRICE, Willard 1887-

PERSONAL: Born July 28, 1887, in Peterborough, Ontario, Canada; came to United States in 1901; son of Albert Melancthon and Stella (Martin) Price; married Jean Reeve, August 4, 1914 (died, 1929); married Mary Virginia Selden, May 28, 1932; children: (first marriage) Robert. *Education:* Western Reserve University (now Case Western Reserve University), B.A., 1909; graduate study at New York University; Columbia University, M.A., 1914. *Home:* 814-N, Via Alhambra, Laguna Hills, Calif. 92653.

CAREER: Explorer; naturalist; writer. Member of editorial staff, *Survey,* 1912-13; Methodist Episcopal Church, editorial secretary, Board of Foreign Missions, 1915-19, editor of *World Outlook,* 1915-20; worked as foreign affairs correspondent, 1933-37; director of periodicals department, Interchurch World Movement; supervising editor of various travel publications. Has traveled to over 140 countries, particularly on expeditions for National Geographic Society and American Museum of Natural History, 1920-67. *Awards, honors:* Litt. D., Columbia University, 1930.

WRITINGS—Published by John Day, except as indicated: *Ancient Peoples at New Tasks,* Interchurch, 1918; *The Negro around the World,* Doran, 1925; *Pacific Adventure,* 1936; *Children of the Rising Sun,* 1938; *Barbarian,* 1941; *Japan Rides the Tiger,* 1942; *Japan's Islands of Mystery,* 1944; *Japan and the Son of Heaven,* Duell, Sloan & Pearce, 1945; *Key to Japan,* 1946; *Roving South,* 1948; *I Cannot Rest from Travel,* 1951; *The Amazing Amazon,* 1952; *Journey by Junk,* 1953; *Adventures in Paradise,* 1955; *Roaming Britain,* 1958; *Incredible Africa,* 1962; *The Amazing Mississippi,* Heinemann, 1962, John Day, 1963; *Rivers I Have Known,* 1965; *America's Paradise Lost,* 1965.

Juveniles; all published by John Day: *Amazon Adventure,* 1949; *South Sea Adventure,* 1954; *Underwater Adventure,* 1954; *Volcano Adventure,* 1956; *Whale Adventure,* 1960; *African Adventure,* 1963; *Elephant Adventure,* 1964; *Safari*

Adventure, 1966; *Lion Adventure*, 1967; *Gorilla Adventure*, 1968; *Diving Adventure*, 1969; *Cannibal Adventure*, 1970; *Tiger Adventure*, 1979; *Arctic Adventure*, 1980.

Contributor to *Encyclopaedia Britannica*. Contributor to national periodicals.

SIDELIGHTS: Willard Price's books have been published in twenty-five languages.

* * *

PROFFER, Ellendea 1944-

PERSONAL: Born November 24, 1944, in Philadelphia, Pa.; daughter of Joseph and Helen (Jardine) McInnes; married Carl R. Proffer (a professor), October 28, 1967; children: Andrew A., Christopher L., Ian G., Arabella M. *Education:* University of Maryland, B.A. (cum laude), 1966; Indiana University, M.A., 1968, Ph.D., 1970. *Home:* 2901 Heatherway, Ann Arbor, Mich. 48104. *Office:* Ardis Publishers, Ann Arbor, Mich. 48104.

CAREER: Wayne State University, Detroit, Mich., instructor in Russian, 1970-71; Ardis Publishers, Ann Arbor, Mich., editor, 1971—.

WRITINGS—Published by Ardis, except as indicated: (Contributor) Alfred Appel, Jr. and Charles Newman, editors, *Nabokov*, Northwestern University Press, 1970; (editor) Mikhail Bulgakov, *Zoikina Kvartira*, 1971; (editor with husband, Carl R. Proffer) Bulgakov, *Diaboliad and Other Stories*, Indiana University Press, 1972; (editor and translator with C. R. Proffer) *The Early Plays of Mikhail Bulgakov*, Indiana University Press, 1972; (contributor) Edward J. Brown, editor, *Major Soviet Writers: Essays in Criticism*, new edition, Oxford University Press, 1973; (editor with C. R. Proffer) *The Ardis Anthology of Recent Russian Literature*, 1975; (editor with C. R. Proffer) *The Silver Age of Russian Culture*, 1975; (editor) *Ann Akhmatova: Ikonografia*, 1977; (compiler) *Bulgakov: An International Bibliography*, 1977; *Regency Miss* (novel), Fawcett, 1978; (translator) Iurii V. Trifonov, *The Long Goodbye: Three Novellas*, Harper, 1978; (editor) *The Ardis Anthology of Russian Futurism*, 1979; (translator) Kozhevnikov, *Metropol*, Norton, 1980. Contributor to *The Modern Encyclopedia of Russian and Soviet Literature*, *Dictionnaire des litteratures etrangeres contemporaines*, *Books Abroad*, and Slavic journals. Co-editor, *Russian Literature Triquarterly*.

WORK IN PROGRESS: A book on the life and works of Mikhail Bulgakov; a novel set in America in the 1930s.

* * *

PRONKO, Leonard Cabell 1927-

PERSONAL: Born October 3, 1927, in Cebu, Philippine Islands; son of Stephen Michael Pronko and Alice Lee Ludwell Beal. *Education:* Drury College, B.A., 1947; Washington University, M.A., 1950; Tulane University, Ph.D., 1957. *Home:* 1543 Bates Pl., Claremont, Calif. *Office:* Pomona College, Claremont, Calif. 91711.

CAREER: Lake Erie College, Painesville, Ohio, instructor, 1954-56; Pomona College, Claremont, Calif., assistant professor, 1957-63, associate professor, 1963-69, professor, 1969—. Director and actor with Valley Community Theatre; first American to participate in Kabuki Training Program, National Theatre of Japan, 1970-71; has directed numerous English language kabuki productions; founder of Kabuki West, a touring group; frequent lecturer and demonstrator of kabuki. *Awards, honors:* French government grant, Ecole Dullin, 1956-57; Guggenheim fellowship, 1963-64; Japan Foundation grant, 1977; Los Angeles Drama Critics Award for "bringing kabuki to America and sharing it."

WRITINGS: *The World of Jean Anouilh*, University of California Press, 1961; (author of introduction) Alfred de Musset, *Camille and Perdican*, Chandler Publishing, 1961; *Avant-Garde: The Experimental Theatre in France*, University of California Press, 1962; (contributor of translation) *New Theatre of Europe*, Volume I, Dell, 1962; *Eugene Ionesco*, Columbia University Press, 1965; (editor) *Three Modern French Plays of the Imagination*, Dell, 1966; *Theatre East and West*, University of California Press, 1967; *Guide to Japanese Drama*, G. K. Hall, 1973; *Georges Feydeau*, Ungar, 1975. Contributor to *Tulane Drama Review*, *Modern Drama*, *French Review*, *Theatre Arts*, and other journals.

WORK IN PROGRESS: Writings on Japanese theatre and dance; a study of bourgeois French comedy in the nineteenth century; texts of kabuki on western themes.

SIDELIGHTS: In a review of *Theatre East and West*, Michael Smith finds that the book "explores the Oriental theater from a curiously European point of view. It discusses the influence of Balinese theater on Artaud; of Chinese Noh on Jacques Copeau, Charles Dullin, Paul Claudel, Jean-Louis Barrault, Beckett and Benjamin Britten; of Kabuki on Max Rinhardt and Vsevolod Meyerhold. It's a pity Mr. Pronko doesn't look closer to home, or to the more immediate present." Smith also feels that the author "has a disappointing tendency to support himself on established opinion rather than venturing any but the most general opinions of his own. The strongest parts of the book are his descriptions of the direct experience of attending these Oriental performances, especially the Balinese. When it comes to what these experiences have to teach, he prefers to quote."

John Rees Moore, however, sees the book as "only one of many signs of a growing desire to carry on a dialogue with the Orient about matters philosophical and aesthetic, to enlarge our perspectives in the hope of recovering a lost wholeness. . . . Pronko does not suggest that we can successfully imitate what is culturally foreign to us—in fact, his evidence argues that Westerners, even men of genius like Yeats and Brecht, have sometimes misappropriated techniques without understanding—but that a new vision of 'total' theater may emerge once we are able to experience fully now forgotten, or never known, possibilities." Moore concludes, "Whether or not he has brought the day of 'total theater' closer, Pronko makes us feel that until we know the Oriental theater we won't know what theater is all about."

AVOCATIONAL INTERESTS: Music (vocal, classical), ceramics, wood cuts, folk arts, archeology, travel.

BIOGRAPHICAL/CRITICAL SOURCES: *New York Times Book Review*, November 5, 1967; *Village Voice*, March 21, 1968; *Kenyon Review*, Volume III, Issue 3, 1968.

* * *

PRONZINI, Bill 1943-
(Jack Foxx, Alex Saxon)

PERSONAL: Born April 13, 1943, in Petaluma, Calif.; son of Joseph (a farm worker) and Helene (Guder) Pronzini; married Laura Patricia Adolphson, May 15, 1965 (divorced, 1967); married Brunhilde Schier, July 28, 1972. *Politics:* Liberal Democrat. *Home and office:* 40 San Jacinto Way, San Francisco, Calif. 94127. *Agent:* Henry Morrison, Inc., 58 West 10th St., New York, N.Y. 10011.

CAREER: *Petaluma Argus-Courier*, Petaluma, Calif., reporter, 1957-60; writer, 1969—. *Member:* Authors Guild, Mystery Writers of America, Science Fiction Writers of America, Western Writers of America, Writers Guild of America, West.

WRITINGS—Published by Random House, except as indicated: *The Stalker*, 1971; *The Snatch*, 1971; *Panic!*, 1972; (under pseudonym Alex Saxon) *A Run in Diamonds*, Pocket Books, 1973; *The Vanished*, 1973; *Undercurrent*, 1973; *Snowbound*, Putnam, 1974; (with Barry N. Malzberg) *The Running of Beasts*, Putnam, 1976; *Games*, Putnam, 1976; *Blowback*, 1977; (with Malzberg) *Acts of Mercy*, Putnam, 1977; (with Collin Wilcox) *Twospot*, Putnam, 1978; (with Malzberg) *Night Screams*, Playboy Press, 1979; *Labyrinth*, St. Martin's Press, 1980; (with Malzberg) *Prose Bowl*, St. Martin's Press, 1980; (with Jack Anderson) *The Cambodian File*, Doubleday, 1980.

Under pseudonym Jack Foxx; all published by Bobbs-Merrill: *The Jade Figurine*, 1972; *Dead Runnjl 1975; Freebooty*, 1976; *Wildfire*, 1978.

Editor: (With Joe Gores) *Tricks or Treats*, Doubleday, 1976; *Midnight Specials*, Bobbs-Merrill, 1977; (with Malzberg) *Dark Sins, Dark Dreams*, Doubleday, 1978; *Werewolf!*, Arbor House, 1979; (with Malzberg) *The End of Summer*, Ace Books, 1979; (with Malzberg) *Shared Tomorrows*, St. Martin's Press, 1979; (with Malzberg) *Bug-Eyed Monsters*, Harcourt, 1980; *The Edgar Winners*, Random House, 1980; *Voodoo!*, Arbor House, 1980; *Mummy!*, Arbor House, 1980. Work appears in anthologies. Contributor of over two hundred short stories and articles to magazines, including *Argosy*, *Ellery Queen's Mystery Magazine*, and *Magazine of Fantasy and Science Fiction*.

WORK IN PROGRESS: Hoodwink, a novel for St. Martin's Press.

SIDELIGHTS: Bill Pronzini's books have been translated into nine languages and published in fifteen countries. The film option for *The Jade Figurine* has been sold. *Avocational interests:* Sports, old movies and radio shows.

BIOGRAPHICAL/CRITICAL SOURCES: Book World, March 21, 1976; *New York Times Book Review*, May 15, 1977, January 1, 1978; *Observer*, October 22, 1978.

* * *

PROPES, Stephen Charles 1942-
(Steve Propes)

PERSONAL: Born July 21, 1942, in Berkeley, Calif.; son of Clarence Bernard (a writer) and Aileen (a writer; maiden name, Williams) Propes; married Sylvia Theresa Liebi (a free-lance artist), September 11, 1965; children: Heather, Shea. *Education:* Long Beach State College (now California State University, Long Beach), B.A., 1965. *Politics:* Democratic. *Home:* 5338 Hanbury St., Long Beach, Calif. 90808.

CAREER: Free-lance writer; children's services worker for Los Angeles County.

WRITINGS—Under name Steve Propes: *Those Oldies but Goodies: A Guide to 50's Record Collecting*, Macmillan, 1973; *Golden Oldies: A Guide to 60's Record Collecting*, Chilton, 1974; *Golden Goodies: A Guide to 50's and 60's Rock & Roll Record Collecting*, Chilton, 1975. Also author of *The County Kid*, *Whatever's Right*, and *The Elvis Connection*, all unpublished novels.

WORK IN PROGRESS: The Million Dollar Giveaway, a novel.

SIDELIGHTS: Stephen Propes writes: "What started as an innocent enough hobby in the early sixties—collecting rock and roll/rhythm and blues records of the fifties—soon developed into an unmanageable and mysterious avocation. Mysterious only because no authoritative work had ever been written as a guide for this sort of collecting—the way numerous guides had been written about collecting everything else, from matchbook covers to Model T's. But nothing on rock and roll record collecting. Nothing. Now that made collecting doubly hard. So in the early seventies, after making the startling discovery that there were thousands of other vinyl fanatics who had also been collecting these 45 RPM discs for years, I set about collecting research data and then wrote *Those Oldies but Goodies* with angry persistence. The influence of this first book continues to be felt. By now, the ranks of the dedicated record collector have multiplied, while the recordings themselves have become even more scarce, thus doubling or tripling in value. Records which cost one buck new now fetch from five to five hundred dollars. And teenagers who weren't even around prior to 1962 now actively seek out the rarest record from 1954. But collecting has expanded well past the fifties to the British Invasion of the early sixties, covered in *Golden Oldies;* post-Beatles; seventies music and beyond. Others might collect only records which hit the charts, basically covered in *Golden Goodies*."

Propes calls his first book sale an "over-the-transom affair. Several phone calls with the people at Macmillan and a quick contract—no doubt for a much smaller advance than a good agent could have secured. Reviews were mainly favorable for *Those Oldies but Goodies*. Then my editor went to Chilton and I found out how fluid the employment roster of a big-name publishing house could get. Two more sales (still without the benefit of an agent) and two more nonfiction books were published by Chilton. . . . And as I commuted to and from my eight-to-five job, I began wondering: what's all this nonsense about a self-sustaining writing career?

"Maybe the key is fiction. Well, heck, I work with foster children in a really fascinating job. I know my way around the bureaucracy and inside my files are dozens of good stories. I could write the next *New Centurians* about the strange high-pressure life of a children's services worker in an L.A. area government agency. So I wrote.

"I called it *The County Kid*. A solid idea led to a straightforward manuscript. I'm pleased to report that these pages still provide enjoyment to many of my colleagues who ask to read it. Apparently there was little enjoyment for agents or publishers. Then I wrote *Whatever's Right*, about a social worker who establishes a relationship with a drug-sodden girl he meets at juvenile hall. A local fledgling agent took a flyer at it. The agent is now teaching school, her agency operations are suspended. I refuse to believe that representing my novel was to blame for the demise of the agency. Perhaps books on social work are too hopeless, too grim. Maybe it was too difficult to love the characters and their universe where heroes are hard to find.

"I was contacted by someone who's read my books on record collecting. This person had connections with an ultra-secret Elvis Presley fan club, and he invited me to view some Presley home movies. Though sworn to secrecy about the membership of this club, I was still anxious to document what I'd viewed. People in the club had well-founded suspicions about the death of The King of Rock and Roll and the movies were convincing. What I discovered inspired the writing of *The Elvis Connection*, a fictionalized account of my findings."

Q

QUARLES, Benjamin 1904-

PERSONAL: Born January 23, 1904, in Boston, Mass.; son of Arthur Benedict (a waiter) and Margaret (O'Brien) Quarles; married Ruth Brett, December 21, 1952; children: (first marriage) Roberta; (second marriage) Pamela. *Education:* Shaw University, B.A., 1931; University of Wisconsin, M.A., 1933, Ph.D., 1940. *Home:* 2205 Southern Ave., Baltimore, Md. 21214. *Office:* Morgan State University, Baltimore, Md. 21239.

CAREER: Shaw University, Raleigh, N.C., instructor in history, 1934-38; Dillard University, New Orleans, La., professor of history, 1938-46, dean, 1946-53; Morgan State University, Baltimore, Md., professor of history and chairman of department, 1953-69, professor emeritus, 1969—. Member of national council, Frederick Douglass Museum of African Art; member of Project Advisory Committee on Black Congressmembers, Joint Center for Political Studies; chairman, Maryland State Commission on Negro History and Culture, 1969-71; member of fellowship selection committee, American Council of Learned Societies, 1976-78. Member of building committee, Amiştad Research Center. *Member:* Association for the Study of Afro-American Life and History (vice-president), American Antiquarian Society, Maryland Historical Society (member of committee on publications). *Awards, honors:* Guggenheim fellow, 1958-59; honorary consultant in United States history, Library of Congress, 1970-71. Thirteen honorary degrees from universities and colleges in the United States, including University of Maryland, Colby College, Kent State University, and Rutgers University.

WRITINGS: *Frederick Douglass,* Associated Publishers, 1948; *The Negro in the Civil War,* Little, Brown, 1953, reprinted, Russell, 1968; *The Negro in the American Revolution,* University of North Carolina Press, 1961; *Lincoln and the Negro,* Oxford University Press, 1962; *The Negro in the Making of America,* Collier, 1964, revised edition, 1971; (with Dorothy Sterling) *Lift Every Voice: The Lives of Booker T. Washington, W.E.B. DuBois, Mary Church Terrell, and James Weldon Johnson,* Doubleday, 1965; (editor with Leslie H. Fishel) *The Negro American: A Documentary History,* Scott, Foresman, 1967, hardcover edition, Morrow, 1968, 3rd edition published as *The Black American: A Documentary History,* Scott, Foresman, 1976; (editor) *Frederick Douglass,* Prentice-Hall, 1968; *Black Abolitionists,* Oxford University Press, 1969; (editor) *Blacks on John Brown,* University of Illinois Press, 1972; *Allies for Freedom: Blacks and John Brown,* Oxford University Press, 1974. Also author of chapters in books and contributor of articles and reviews to journals. Member of editorial board, Frederick Douglass Papers Project; member of advisory board, The Correspondence of Lydia Maria Child and *American History and Life.*

SIDELIGHTS: Benjamin Quarles, a historian of black culture, stated in a lecture at Howard University, as reported by the *Washington Post,* that "'for the black rank-and-file, the man in the street, . . . black history's main objective is to create a sense of pride and personal worth.'" For the white reader, on the other hand, its purpose "is to eradicate the American myth of liberty and justice for all and illustrate the centrality of blacks in this country's experience."

Quarles has been accused of being overly optimistic in his accounts of recent black history. In reviews of *The Negro American,* Howard N. Meyer in the *Nation* and Eliot Fremont-Smith in the *New York Times* criticize Quarles and co-editor Fishel for ignoring the frustrations of blacks evidenced by the riots and demonstrations of the late 60's. Yet, overall, Quarles' work has been consistently praised as an important contribution to black history.

BIOGRAPHICAL/CRITICAL SOURCES: *New York Times,* February 27, 1968, December 12, 1968; *Nation,* June 3, 1968; *Times Literary Supplement,* August 7, 1969; *Journal of American History,* December, 1969, March, 1975; *Virginia Quarterly Review,* spring, 1970; *Washington Post,* May 5, 1971.

* * *

QUESNELL, John G(eorge) 1936-

PERSONAL: Surname is pronounced Kwe-*nell;* born September 19, 1936, in Thief River Falls, Minn.; son of Lloyd W. (a railroad brakeman) and Fern (Collins) Quesnell; married Alice Lehar, June 6, 1959; children: Catherine, Michael, Timothy. *Education:* St. John's University, Collegeville, Minn., B.A., 1959; University of Minnesota, M.S. Social Work, 1961, further graduate study, 1964-65. *Religion:* Roman Catholic. *Home:* 3429 Stinson Blvd., Minneapolis, Minn. 55418. *Office:* 1653 Medical Arts Bldg., Minneapolis, Minn. 55402.

CAREER: Probation officer in Minneapolis, Minn., 1961; Minneapolis Catholic Welfare Services, Minneapolis, director of family services department, 1965-69; private practice as marriage and family counselor, 1969—. Professor at St. Paul Seminary; lecturer and consultant; member of Pro-Life Movement. *Military service:* U.S. Air Force, 1961-64; psychiatric social worker; became first lieutenant. *Member:* American Association of Marriage and Family Counselors (past president of Minnesota chapter), National Association of Social Workers (past member of board of directors of Minnesota chapter), National Council on Family Relations, Serra International, Minnesota Council on Family Relations, Minnesota Citizens Concerned for Life.

WRITINGS: (Contributor) Clayton C. Barbeau, editor, *Future of the Family,* Bruce, 1971; (contributor) Hirsch Lazaar Silverman, editor, *Marital Therapy,* C. C Thomas, 1972; *Marriage: A Discovery Together,* Fides, 1973; *The Family Planning Dilemma Revisited,* Franciscan Herald, 1975; *The Message of Christ and the Counselor,* Franciscan Herald, 1975; *Holy Terrors and Holy Parents,* Franciscan Herald, 1976; *Three to Get Ready: A Guide for the Engaged,* Liturgical Press, in press. Contributor to professional journals and popular magazines, including *Catholic Charities Review, Corrective Psychiatry and Journal of Social Therapy, American Journal of Correction,* and *Our Family.*

WORK IN PROGRESS: The Christian Teenager and Sexuality.

* * *

QUINE, Willard Van Orman 1908-

PERSONAL: Born June 25, 1908, in Akron, Ohio; son of Cloyd Robert and Harriet (Van Orman) Quine; married 1948; wife's name, Marjorie; children: Elizabeth Quine Roberts, Norma, Douglas, Margaret. *Education:* Oberlin College, A.B., 1930; Harvard University, A.M., 1931, Ph.D., 1932; Oxford University, M.A., 1953. *Home:* 38 Chestnut St., Boston, Mass. 02108. *Office:* Department of Philosophy, Harvard University, Cambridge, Mass. 02138.

CAREER: Harvard University, Cambridge, Mass., Sheldon traveling fellow to Vienna, Austria, Prague, Czechoslovakia, and Warsaw, Poland, 1932-33, junior fellow, Society of Fellows, 1933-36, instructor, 1936-41, associate professor, 1941-48, professor of philosophy, 1948-56, Pierce Professor of Philosophy, 1956-78, Pierce Professor of Philosophy emeritus, 1978—. Visiting professor at University of San Paulo, 1942, Tokyo University, 1959, Rockefeller University, 1968, and College of France, 1969; Eastman Visiting Professor, Oxford University, 1953-54; Hagerstrom Lecturer, Uppsala University, 1973. Consultant, Rand Corp., 1949; member, Institute for Advanced Study, 1956-57. *Member:* American Academy of Arts and Sciences, National Academy of Sciences, American Philosophical Society, American Philosophical Association (president of eastern division, 1957), Institut de France, Association for Symbolic Logic (president, 1953-56), British Academy. *Awards, honors:* Litt.D. from Oberlin College, 1955, University of Akron, 1965, Washington University, 1966, Temple University, 1970, Oxford University, 1970, and Cambridge University, 1978; Doctorat, University of Lille, 1956, and University of Uppsala, 1980; L.L.D., Ohio State University, 1957, and Howard University, 1979; Center for Advanced Study in the Behavioral Sciences fellow, 1958-59; Center for Advanced Studies fellow, Wesleyan University, 1965; L.H.D., University of Chicago, 1967; Nicholas M. Butler Gold Medal, Columbia University, 1970; Sir Henry Saville fellow, Merton College, Oxford University, 1973-74.

WRITINGS: A System of Logistic, Harvard University Press, 1934; *Mathematical Logic,* Norton, 1940, revised edition, Harvard University Press, 1951; *Elementary Logic,* Ginn, 1941, revised edition, Harper, 1965; *O Sentido da Nova Logica,* Martins, 1944; *Methods of Logic,* Holt, 1950; *From a Logical Point of View,* Harvard University Press, 1953; *Word and Object,* M.I.T. Press, 1960; *Set Theory and Its Logic,* Harvard University Press, 1963; *The Ways of Paradox,* Random House, 1966, revised edition, 1976; *Selected Logic Papers,* Random House, 1966; *Ontological Relativity and Other Essays,* Columbia University Press, 1969; (with J. S. Ullian) *The Web of Belief,* Random House, 1970; *Philosophy of Logic,* Prentice-Hall, 1970; *The Roots of Reference,* Open Court, 1974. Contributor of articles to mathematics and philosophy journals. Consulting editor, *Journal of Symbolic Logic,* 1936-52.

SIDELIGHTS: Willard Quine, a specialist in symbolic logic, is highly esteemed in the field of philosophy. The reviewer in the *Times Literary Supplement* notes: "The death of Bertrand Russell has deprived the philosophical world of its greatest contemporary figure. Of those who remain perhaps no one has a higher professional reputation than the American philosopher, Willard Van Orman Quine." Yet Quine, who taught logic at Harvard University for over forty years, does not consider logic to be of paramount importance. As he remarked to a *New York Times* interviewer: "I think this would be an awful world if everyone made a point of trying to be logical and acted according to his conclusions. There's so much chance of error along the way. And it's conceivable that there are some illusions without which people would be less happy."

Quine's books have been translated into eight foreign languages.

BIOGRAPHICAL/CRITICAL SOURCES: New York Times, November 9, 1969; *Times Literary Supplement,* October 9, 1970.

* * *

QUITSLUND, Sonya A(ntoinette) 1935-

PERSONAL: Born March 8, 1935, in Portland, Ore.; daughter of Phelps Garney (a businessman and engineer) and Leona Agnes (Ederer) Quitslund. *Education:* Attended Duchesne College, 1953-54; Seattle University, A.B. (magna cum laude), 1958; further study at University of Clermont-Ferrand, 1959-60, and Sorbonne, University of Paris, 1960-61; Catholic University of America, M.A., 1964, Ph.D., 1967. *Religion:* Roman Catholic. *Office:* Department of Religion, George Washington University, Washington, D.C. 20052.

CAREER: Teacher in private school in Seattle, Wash., 1956-57, and in public schools in Edmonds, Wash., 1958-59, 1961-63; Catholic University of America, Washington, D.C., instructor in religion, 1964-67; George Washington University, Washington, D.C., assistant professor of religion, 1967—. Member of advisory board on religious education, Catholic Archdiocese of Washington, D.C., 1967-71; member of task force on the liturgy, National Council of Catholic Women, 1969—; member of governing board, Priests for Equality, 1975-77; member, Women's Ordination Conference Core Commission, 1976-78; member of board, National Catholic Conference for Interracial Justice, 1978—; member of subcommittee on discriminatory language, International Commission on English in the Liturgy, 1978—.

MEMBER: Catholic Biblical Association of America, American Academy of Religion, Catholic Theology Society of America (member of regional board of directors, 1973-77;

chairperson, 1974-76; member of national board, 1977-79), American Association of University Professors, Women for the Unborn. *Awards, honors:* Fulbright scholar in France, 1959-60; College Theology Society book of the year award, 1973, for *Beauduin: A Prophet Vindicated;* Underwood fellowship, Danforth Foundation, 1974-75; Year of the Woman Award, Institute of Women Today, 1975.

WRITINGS: Beauduin: A Prophet Vindicated, Paulist/Newman, 1973; (contributor) T. M. McFadden, editor, *Theology Confronts a Changing World,* Twenty-Third Publications, 1977; (contributor) Len Swidler and Arlene Swidler, editors, *In the Image of Christ,* Paulist/Newman, 1977. Contributor of articles and about sixty reviews to Catholic and other periodicals.

WORK IN PROGRESS: Research on church involvement in providing housing for the elderly.

SIDELIGHTS: Sonya A. Quitslund told *CA:* "I began my writing career in high school and won two $25 awards. I have always enjoyed writing but need quiet and a good block of time. Because the latter is hard to come by due to personal and professional demands, pressure builds up as deadlines for reviews or articles approach. Once the task is begun I can work straight through fourteen or more hours with hardly a break, but it is very exhausting mentally. Only a drastic change in my lifestyle would make another book feasible. In the meantime I'll probably continue to address timely issues that arouse my interest or concern. Most of my articles, however, were written at the invitation of editors, so I've been spared the disappointment of not having my 'gems' published."

R

RABE, Berniece (Louise) 1928-

PERSONAL: Surname rhymes with "Abe"; born January 11, 1928, in Parma, Mo.; daughter of Grover Cleveland (a farmer) and Martha (Green) Bagby; married Walter Henry Rabe (vice-president of Precision Diamond Tool Co.), July 30, 1946; children: Alan Walter, Brian Cleve, Clay Victor, Dara Mari. *Education:* National College of Education, B.A., 1963; graduate study at Northern Illinois University and at Roosevelt University. *Religion:* Church of Jesus Christ of Latter-Day Saints (Mormon). *Home:* 860 Willow Lane, Sleepy Hollow, Ill. 60118. *Agent:* McIntosh & Otis, Inc., 475 Fifth Ave., New York, N.Y. 10017.

CAREER: Model with Patricia Stevens Model Agency, Chicago, Ill., 1945-46; teacher and tutor in special education classes, Elgin, Ill., 1963-67. Teacher-trainer with Chicago Stake of Church of Jesus Christ of Latter-Day Saints. *Member:* Fox Valley Writers (member of executive board), Off-Campus Writers (member of executive board). *Awards, honors:* Novel awards at Indiana University Writers' Conference and Judson Writers' Conference for manuscript of *Rass;* a chapter of *Rass* received first prize for short story in Chicago Fine Arts competition; *Naomi* named best book of the decade by *School Library Journal;* Golden Kite awards, Society of Children's Books, for *Naomi* and *The Girl Who Had No Name; The Orphans* named best book of the year by Society of Midland Authors.

WRITINGS—All juveniles: *Rass,* Thomas Nelson, 1973; *Naomi,* Thomas Nelson, 1975; *The Girl Who Had No Name,* Dutton, 1977; *The Orphans,* Dutton, 1978; *Who's Afraid?,* Dutton, 1980; *The Balancing Girl* (picture book), Dutton, 1980. Contributor of stories to children's magazines.

WORK IN PROGRESS: Two juvenile novels for Dutton, *Joey Caruba Superkid* and *The Dance of the Clowns.*

BIOGRAPHICAL/CRITICAL SOURCES: Chicago Tribune, December 9, 1974.

* * *

RAFFERTY, Max 1917-

PERSONAL: Born May 7, 1917, in New Orleans, La.; son of Maxwell Lewis and DeEtta (Cox) Rafferty; married Frances Luella Longman, 1944; children: Kathleen, Dennis, Eileen. *Education:* University of California, Los Angeles, B.A., 1938, M.A., 1949; University of Southern California, Ed.D., 1955. *Politics:* Republican. *Religion:* Episcopalian. *Office:* School of Education, Troy State University, Troy, Ala. 36081.

CAREER: Elementary and high schools in California, teacher and principal, 1940-51, district superintendent, 1951-61; La Canada Unified School District, La Canada, Calif., superintendent, 1961-63; superintendent of public instruction, state of California, 1963-71; Troy State University, Troy, Ala., dean of School of Education, 1971—. Made unsuccessful bid for office of U.S. Senator from California, 1968. *Member:* American Association of School Administrators, National Education Association, California Association of School Administrators, California Teachers Association, Phi Delta Kappa, Rotary Club (president, local chapter), Lions Club (secretary, local chapter). *Awards, honors:* Shankland Memorial Award, American Association of School Administrators, 1955; George Washington Gold Medal Awards, Freedom Foundation, 1962, 1963, 1965; American Educators Medal, 1964; honorary degrees from Brigham Young University and Lincoln University.

WRITINGS: About Our Schools, California Education Press, 1955; *Practices and Trends in School Administration,* Ginn, 1960; *Home Discipline,* Economics Press, 1961; *Suffer, Little Children: Reflections on American Education,* Devin-Adair, 1962; *What They Are Doing to Your Children,* New American Library, 1964; *Max Rafferty on Education,* Devin-Adair, 1968; *Classroom Countdown: Education at the Crossroads,* Hawthorn, 1971; *Handbook of Educational Administration,* Allyn & Bacon, 1975. Contributor to professional journals and popular periodicals.

SIDELIGHTS: Max Rafferty first achieved national recognition when, upon being hired as superintendent of the La Canada Unified School District in 1961, he delivered a speech entitled "The Passing of the Patriot" at a public school board meeting. In the speech Rafferty criticized his own generation of educators for having been "so busy educating for 'life adjustment' that we forgot that the first duty of a nation's schools is to preserve the nation. . . . The results are plain for all to see: The worst of our youngsters growing up to become booted, sideburned, ducktailed, unwashed, leather-jacketed slobs, whose favorite sport is ravaging little girls and stomping polio victims to death. . . ." In the end he pledged to return patriotism to education and to make "our young people informed and disciplined and alert—militant for freedom, clear-eyed to the filthy menace of Communist corruption . . . [and] happy in their love of country." Response to the speech was swift and hotly polarized. Conservatives welcomed his plan to return to the basics in education, the "three Rs"; right-wing groups distributed copies of the speech and touted Rafferty as the man who would clean the Communists out of the progressive educational system. Liberal educators, on the other hand, saw the new superintendent as a threat to the accomplishments of thirty years of progressivism. As it turned out, Rafferty's campaign to restructure educational priorities was just beginning.

In 1962, Rafferty was urged by the conservative Citizen's Advisory Committee on Education to run for California state superintendent of public instruction opposite Ralph Richardson, a professor at the University of California who enjoyed the support of most of the state's educators. Rafferty's backers included a collection of right-wing organizations as well as the conservative business establishment. In public debate Rafferty's flamboyant elocution weighed heavily in his favor and he defeated Richardson by almost 222,000 votes. His program of "Education in Depth" became the official policy of California's school system; this policy, according to Rafferty, "intends to regard the individual as the be-all and end-all of the educative process . . . regards reading and recitative discussion as still the most effective and economic method of instruction." During his tenure as superintendent of public instruction, Rafferty succeeded in returning grammar texts to the elementary schools, adopting music books containing patriotic songs, and returning to such terms as "English," "history," and "geography" as opposed to the progressives' "language arts" and "social studies." In apparent approval of these and other changes made under Rafferty, the voters of California returned him to office for a second term in 1966 by a record landslide of 3,000,000 ballots.

The success of Rafferty's "Education in Depth" policy was, however, somewhat blunted due to the structure of California's educational hierarchy. His position as superintendent allowed him to preside over a ten-member Board of Education who collectively established policy for the state schools. He was not able to dominate the state's educational decisions because of the liberal nature of this board. (Rafferty was to gain further attention by several highly-publicized feuds with board members.) Another factor which served to diminish his authority was the considerable autonomy with which individual school districts operated in California. These districts, for the most part, remained under the influence of liberal directors.

In 1967, Max Rafferty was convinced by a group of conservative Republicans to run for the Senate seat then occupied by Thomas H. Kuchel, a liberal. In an interview with the *New York Times,* Rafferty explained his decision to run: "One, as a Republican, I felt my opponent wasn't in the mainstream of the Republican party. Two, as an educator, I was appalled by the waste of Federal money and the ratholes down which it was being poured. Three, as a father whose only son is in the Air Force and is scheduled to go to Vietnam, I knew we had to clean up that mess somehow." Rafferty succeeded in unseating Kuchel in the primary, and ran in the general election against Democrat Alan Cranston. In his campaign, Rafferty ran on a strict law and order platform in which he blamed much of the social upheaval of the time on the members of a permissive Supreme Court whom he called "a bunch of political hacks, ideological reformers, poker-playing cronies of the President, and child-marrying mountain climbers." According to *Newsweek,* he also favored "shooting looters, summary street courts-martial for other rioters, more capital punishment, abolishing most foreign aid, and escalating the Vietnam war (perhaps with nuclear weapons)." Much of the latter part of his campaign was occupied by his attempts to qualify these early statements, and some observers felt that he mellowed considerably as the election drew near. In the 1968 election, Rafferty lost to Cranston by almost 400,000 votes.

In a review of *What They Are Doing to Your Children,* J. A. Fitzgerald says that the book "is severely critical of many practices in our schools. It is challenging, but controversial. Some of Dr. Rafferty's statements are justified, but others will require further substantiation as is evidenced by a careful reading of the eighteen chapters. . . . Perhaps one of the deficiencies of the book is that the reader is left with uncertainty about the author's understanding of the term 'progressive education.'" In a highly critical article, R. F. Butts writes: "Those who are easily persuaded by a simplistic view of history and of education and who want to thrill again to the black-and-white drama of the morality play (western style) may find that this book serves their purposes. . . . Mr. Rafferty's writing abounds with florid passages, bristles with caustic condemnation, and introduces comic relief by means of chatty, slangy, folksy anecdotes." Butts concludes that "his book does not provide a fruitful medium for the rational discussion of public education. Mr. Rafferty's excursions into the history of philosophy of education are so lacking in substance as to be thoroughly misleading."

In *Max Rafferty on Education,* which critic Paul Woodring calls "a loose collection of anecdotes, aphorisms, opinions and prejudices, with a few facts thrown in for good measure," the author continues to voice his conservative philosophy. Considering the fact that the book was released at the time that he was engaged in his Senate campaign, it is not surprising that much of Rafferty's invective is political in nature. Throughout the book he remains, much to the delight of reviewers and the news media, highly quotable. On the subject of the demonstrators of 1968, he says, "Every news photo and television show I've seen of the continuing collegiate demonstrations and protest marches features a cast of characters who appear to have taken a common lifelong vow against bathing. . . . Why don't we give the male hippies a shave, a shower and a fast ship to Vietnam?" Speaking of the college administrators of the time, he writes that "most of them are trained and experienced negotiators and moderators, skilled in the subtle techniques of mediation, and dedicated worshipers at the shrine of compromise. They shrink in almost physical revulsion from the merest suggestion that sometimes in dealing with the young, the immature and the cocky it's necessary to lower the boom."

Reviewing *Max Rafferty on Education,* Woodring writes: "When he is on the attack, which is most of the time, he strikes at so many diverse targets that he cannot fail to hit some vulnerable ones: excessive permissiveness in school and home, the softness and confusion that beset our affluent nation, and the reluctance of teachers and parents to make moral judgments or to take a firm stand on anything. But in this volume, as in his previous writings, Rafferty also lashes out at such thoroughly battered victims of the critics as life-adjustment education, professional courses for teachers, Dick and Jane, and John Dewey (whose views he persistently misrepresents). Lest his favorite target escape him, he makes a vigorous effort to prove that Progressive Education has not really faded away but has only gone underground and taken on various pseudonyms." A *Saturday Review* critic sees the book as a list of Rafferty's likes and dislikes; on the minus side: Dewey, teacher strikes, Dick and Jane, federal control, published professors, and the Supreme Court; the plusses: "Education in Depth," Munchkins, Robin Hood, Alice, patriotism, and homework. The reviewer says of the book: "Here is a veritable roller coaster of a polemic. It swoops upon purported evils, skirts sophistication, and zooms once again to unnerving heights of 'should' and 'ought.' It bursts with alliterative assurances, verbless periods, and rustic expletives. 'Bunk, rot, horsefeathers,' exclaims Rafferty. Indeed!"

BIOGRAPHICAL/CRITICAL SOURCES: Christian Science Monitor, May, 1961; *New York Times,* May 20, 1962, September 1, 1968; *Nation,* January 27, 1964; *Best Sellers,* April 1, 1964; *Reporter,* April 9, 1964; *National Observer,* April 13, 1964; *Book Week,* April 19, 1964; *Atlantic,* December, 1967; *Time,* March 1, 1968, May 24, 1968, November 2, 1970; *New Republic,* March 9, 1968; *Newsweek,* June 17, 1968, September 30, 1968, November 16, 1970; *New York Times Magazine,* September 1, 1968, September 22, 1968; *Congressional Quarterly,* October 18, 1968; *Saturday Evening Post,* October 19, 1968; *New York Times Book Review,* October 20, 1968; *National Review,* October 22, 1968, December 3, 1968, January 12, 1971; *Reader's Digest,* November, 1968; *Saturday Review,* November 16, 1968.

—*Sketch by Peter M. Gareffa*

* * *

RAINWATER, Dorothy T(hornton) 1918-

PERSONAL: Born September 14, 1918, in Ardmore, Okla.; daughter of Verne Ashley (a tool designer) and Grace (Jones) Thornton; married H. Ivan Rainwater (an agriculturalist for U.S. Department of Agriculture), April 20, 1940. *Education:* University of Oklahoma, A.B., 1941; also studied art at St. Louis University, University of Hawaii, and Honolulu Academy of Arts. *Religion:* Methodist. *Home and office:* 2805 Liberty Pl., Bowie, Md. 20715.

CAREER: Bernice P. Bishop Museum, Honolulu, Hawaii, scientific illustrator and designer of exhibits, 1953-63. Illustrator for Hawaiian archaeological expeditions; lecturer on American silver at antiques forums; former chairman of exhibits for Hawaiian State Science Fair; former member of National Science Fair International Council. *Member:* American Association of University Women (past member of executive board), Hawaiian Academy of Sciences, Phi Sigma, Eta Sigma Phi, Kappa Phi.

WRITINGS: American Silver Manufacturers, Everybodys Press, 1966; (senior author with Donna H. Felger) *American Spoons: Souvenir and Historical,* Wallace-Homestead, 1968; (senior author with husband, H. Ivan Rainwater) *American Silverplate,* Everybodys Press, 1972; (editor and author of introduction) *Sterling Silver Holloware,* Pyne Press, 1973; *Encyclopedia of American Silver Manufacturers: Their Marks, Trademarks, and History,* Crown, 1975; (with Felger) *A Collector's Guide to Spoons around the World,* Everybodys Press, 1976; *American Jewelry Manufacturers,* Everybodys Press, in press. Contributor to journals and newspapers, including *Spinning Wheel, Antiques, Western Collector, Silver, Antiques Journal, Antiques Trader,* and *Jewelers' Circular-Keystone.*

AVOCATIONAL INTERESTS: Travel, gardening, playing the organ, genealogy.

* * *

RAMSEY, (R.) Paul 1913-

PERSONAL: Born December 10, 1913, in Mendenhall, Miss.; son of John William and Mamie (McCay) Ramsey; married Effie Register, June 23, 1937; children: Marcia, Jenifer, Janet. *Education:* Millsaps College, B.S., 1935; Yale University, B.D., 1940, Ph.D., 1943. *Religion:* Methodist. *Home:* 152 Cedar Lane, Princeton, N.J. *Office:* 613 Seventy Nine Hall, Princeton University, Princeton, N.J. 08544.

CAREER: Millsaps College, Jackson, Miss., instructor in history and social science, 1937-39; Garrett Biblical Institute (now Garrett Theological Seminary), Evanston, Ill., assistant professor of Christian ethics, 1942-44; Princeton University, Princeton, N.J., assistant professor, 1944-47, associate professor, 1947-54, professor, 1954—, Harrington Spear Paine Professor of Religion, 1957—, chairman of department of religion, 1959-63. Visiting professor at Colgate University, Pacific School of Religion, Union Theological Seminary, and other theological schools.

MEMBER: American Theological Society (Eastern division; vice-president, 1959-60; president, 1964-65), American Society of Christian Ethics (president, 1962-63), Institute of Medicine (National Academy of Sciences). *Awards, honors:* Council of the Humanities senior fellow, Princeton University, 1958-59; McCosh faculty fellow, Princeton University, 1965-66; National Endowment for the Humanities senior fellow, 1973-74; Guggenheim fellow, 1978. Academic: Litt.D. from Marquette University, 1968; Sc.D. from Worcester Polytechnic Institute, 1972; H.L.D. from Rockford College, 1973, Millsaps College, 1974, Fairfield University, and Monmouth College, 1980; D.D. from St. Anselm's College, 1978.

WRITINGS: Basic Christian Ethics, Scribner, 1950; *War and the Christian Conscience,* Duke University Press, 1961; *Christian Ethics and the Sit-In,* Association Press, 1961; *Nine Modern Moralists,* Prentice-Hall, 1962; *Deeds and Rules in Christian Ethics,* Scribner, 1966; *Who Speaks for the Church?,* Abingdon, 1967; (contributor) *Life or Death: Ethics and Options,* University of Washington Press, 1968; *The Just War,* Scribner, 1968; *Fabricated Man,* Yale University Press, 1970; *The Patient as Person,* Yale University Press, 1971; *Ethics of Fetal Research,* Yale University Press, 1975; *Ethics at the Edges of Life,* Yale University Press, 1978.

Editor: Jonathon Edwards, *Freedom of the Will,* Yale University Press, 1957; *Faith and Ethics: The Theology of H. Richard Niebuhr,* Harper, 1957; *Religion, The Princeton Studies: Humanistic Scholarship in America,* Prentice-Hall, 1965; (with Gene Outka) *Norm and Context in Christian Ethics,* Scribner, 1968; *Doing Evil to Achieve Good,* Loyola University Press, 1978. Also member of editorial board, "Works of Jonathon Edwards" series, Yale University Press. Member of editorial board, *Theology Today* and *Worldview.*

WORK IN PROGRESS: The Ethical Writings of Jonathan Edwards.

BIOGRAPHICAL/CRITICAL SOURCES: Commonweal, August 25, 1967, October 4, 1968, April 4, 1969; *Christian Century,* September 6, 1967, December 25, 1968, May 21, 1969, November 11, 1970; *New York Times Book Review,* September 17, 1967; *Reporter,* January 11, 1968.

* * *

RANDALL, John Herman, Jr. 1899-

PERSONAL: Born February 14, 1899, in Grand Rapids, Mich.; son of John Herman (a minister) and Minerva I. (Ballard) Randall; married Mercedes Irene Moritz (a writer),

1922; children: John Herman, III, Francis Ballard. *Education:* Columbia University, B.A., 1918, M.A., 1919, Ph.D., 1922. *Politics:* Socialist. *Religion:* "Ethical Culture." *Home:* 15 Claremont Ave., New York, N.Y. 10027; and Peacham, Vt. (summer residence).

CAREER: Columbia University, New York, N.Y., instructor, 1920-25, assistant professor, 1925-31, associate professor, 1931-35, professor of philosophy, 1935-51, F.J.E. Woodbridge Professor of Philosophy, 1951-67, Woodbridge Professor Emeritus, 1967—. *Member:* American Philosophical Association (president, eastern division, 1956), Renaissance Society of America (president, 1956-57), American Academy of Arts and Sciences (fellow), Phi Beta Kappa, Alpha Delta Phi, Men's Faculty Club (Columbia University). *Awards, honors:* Butler Medal; Litt.D., Ohio Wesleyan University, 1961; Ralph Waldo Emerson Award, Phi Beta Kappa, 1966, for *The Career of Philosophy;* Ph.D.,University of Padua (Italy), 1967; L.H.D., Columbia University, 1968; LL.D., Temple University, 1968; L.H.D., Bard College, 1972.

WRITINGS: Introduction to Contemporary Civilization: A Syllabus, Columbia University Press, 1925; *The Making of the Modern Mind,* Houghton, 1926, revised edition, 1940, reprinted, Columbia University Press, 1976; *Our Changing Civilization,* Stokes, 1929; (with father, John Herman Randall, Sr.) *Religion and the Modern World,* Stokes, 1929; (with Justus Buchler) *Philosophy: An Introduction,* Barnes & Noble, 1942, revised edition, 1971; (with H. S. Thayer), *Newton's Philosophy of Nature,* Hafner, 1953; *The Role of Knowledge in Western Religion,* Beacon Press, 1958; *Nature and Historical Experience,* Columbia University Press, 1958; *Aristotle,* Columbia University Press, 1960; *The School of Padua and the Emergence of Modern Science,* Antenore, 1961; *The Career of Philosophy in Modern Times,* Columbia University Press, Volume I, 1962, Volume II, 1965; *How Philosophy Uses Its Past,* Columbia University Press, 1963; *The Meaning of Religion for Man,* Harper, 1968; *Plato: Dramatist of the Life of Reason,* Columbia University Press, 1970; *Hellenistic Ways of Deliverance and the Making of the Christian Synthesis,* Columbia University Press, 1970; *Philosophy after Darwin,* Columbia University Press, 1977. Also author of *The Problem of Group Responsibility,* 1922.

Contributor: *Studies in the History of Ideas,* Columbia University Press, 1925; *American Philosophy Today and Tomorrow,* Lee Furman, 1935; *Studies in Civilization,* University of Pennsylvania Press, 1941; *Philosophical Essays in Honor of E. A. Singer, Jr.,* University of Pennsylvania Press, 1942; *Theory and Practice in Historical Study,* New York Social Science Research Council, 1943; *Preface to Philosophy,* Macmillan, 1946; *Freedom and Experience,* Cornell University Press, 1947; *Organized Religion in the United States,* American Academy of Political and Social Science, 1948; *Wellsprings and the American Spirit,* Harper, 1948; *The Renaissance Philosophy of Man,* University of Chicago Press, 1948; *The Philosophy of Ernst Cassirer,* Library of Living Philosophers, 1949; *Freedom and Reason,* Free Press, 1951; *The Theology of Paul Tillich,* Macmillan, 1952; *The Unity of Knowledge,* Doubleday, 1955; *A History of the Faculty of Philosophy, Columbia University,* Columbia University Press, 1957; *Patterns of Faith,* Harper, 1957. Also contributor to *The Philosophy of John Dewey,* Northwestern University Press.

Joint editor, *Journal of Philosophy,* 1937—; chairman of editorial committee, *Journal of the History of Ideas,* 1941-55.

SIDELIGHTS: Many of John Herman Randall, Jr.'s works have been translated into foreign languages, including Spanish, German, and Arabic.

BIOGRAPHICAL/CRITICAL SOURCES: John P. Anton, editor, *Naturalism and Historical Understanding: Essays on the Philosophy of John Herman Randall, Jr.,* [Albany], 1957.

* * *

RANKIN, Hugh F(ranklin) 1913-

PERSONAL: Born June 17, 1913, in Washington, D.C.; son of Hugh Patrick and Dixie (Hall) Rankin; married Betty Jean Bursley, 1943; children: Patrick Allyn, John Bursley, Wade Dillard. *Education:* Attended Virginia Agricultural and Mechanical College and Polytechnic Institute (now Virginia Polytechnic Institute and State University), 1931-35; Elon College, A.B., 1949; University of North Carolina, M.A., 1951, Ph.D., 1959. *Religion:* Presbyterian. *Home:* 6325 Freret St., New Orleans, La. 70118. *Office:* Department of History, Tulane University, New Orleans, La. 70118.

CAREER: Worked as foreman, assistant superintendent, and superintendent for construction companies in North Carolina and South Carolina, 1936-41; Colonial Williamsburg, Inc., Williamsburg, Va., research associate, 1955-57; Tulane University, New Orleans, La., 1957—, began as instructor, associate professor, 1961-64, professor of history, 1964—. Bingham Professor, University of Louisville, fall, 1978. *Military service:* U.S. Army, Engineers, 1941-45; became first lieutenant. *Member:* American Historical Association, Organization of American Historians, Company of Military Collectors and Historians (fellow), Authors League of America, Southern Historical Association, North Carolina Literary and Historical Association. *Awards, honors:* R.D.W. Connor prize, 1953 and 1954, for best article in *North Carolina Historical Review;* Guggenheim fellow, 1962-63.

WRITINGS: (With George F. Scheer) *Rebels and Redcoats,* World Publishing Co., 1957; *North Carolina in the American Revolution,* North Carolina Division of Archives and History, 1959; *The Pirates of Colonial North Carolina,* North Carolina Division of Archives and History, 1960; (editor) *The Battle of New Orleans: A British View,* Hauser, 1961; *Upheaval in Albemarle: The Story of Culpeper's Rebellion,* North Carolina Tercentenary Commission, 1962; *The American Revolution,* Putnam, 1964; (contributor) George A. Billias, editor, *George Washington's Generals,* Morrow, 1964; (contributor) *Writing Southern History: Essays in Honor of Fletcher M. Green,* Louisiana State University Press, 1965; *The Theatre in Colonial America,* University of North Carolina Press, 1965; *Criminal Trial Proceedings in the General Court of Colonial Virginia,* University of Virginia Press, 1965; *The Golden Age of Piracy,* Colonial Williamsburg, 1969; *The North Carolina Continentals,* University of North Carolina Press, 1971; *Francis Marion: The Swamp Fox,* Crowell, 1973; (with W. P. Cumming) *The Fate of a Nation,* Phaidon, 1975; *George Rogers Clark and the Winning of the West,* Virginia Bicentennial Commission, 1976; *Greene and Cornwallis: The Campaign in the Carolinas,* North Carolina Division of Archives and History, 1976; *The North Carolina Continental Line in the American Revolution,* North Carolina Division of Archives and History, 1977; (contributor) Howard Peelchum, editor, *Sources of American Independence,* University of Chicago Press, 1978; *The War of the Revolution in Virginia,* Virginia Bicentennial Commission, 1979. Contributor of articles and reviews to professional journals.

WORK IN PROGRESS: *British Strategy and American Revolution;* a biography of Nathaniel Greene.

AVOCATIONAL INTERESTS: Woodworking, high-fidelity music, fishing.

* * *

RAPHAEL, Frederic (Michael) 1931-
(Mark Caine, a joint pseudonym)

PERSONAL: Born August 14, 1931, in Chicago, Ill; son of Cedric Michael and Irene (Mauser) Raphael; married Sylvia Betty Glatt, 1955; children: Paul Simon, Sarah Natasha. *Education:* St. John's College, Cambridge, M.A. (honors), 1954. *Home:* The Wick, Langham, Essex, England; Lagardelle, St. Laurent la Vallee, 24170 Balves, France; Ios, Cyclades, Greece. *Agent:* Hilary Rubinstein, A. P. Watt & Son, 26 Bedford Row, London WC1, England.

CAREER: Writer. *Member:* Royal Society of Literature (fellow), P.E.N. *Awards, honors:* Lippincott Prize, 1961; British Screenwriters' award for best comedy screenplay, 1964, for "Nothing but the Best"; British Screenwriters' award for best original screenplay of 1965, British Film Academy award for best screenplay of 1965, and Oscar Award of Academy of Motion Picture Arts and Sciences (United States) for best original screenplay of 1965, all for "Darling"; received Oscar Award nomination, 1966, for "Two for the Road"; named Writer of the Year, Royal Television Society, 1976.

WRITINGS: *Obbligato,* Macmillan (London), 1956; *The Earlsdon Way,* Cassell, 1958; *The Limits of Love,* Cassell, 1960, Lippincott, 1961; *A Wild Surmise,* Cassell, 1961, Lippincott, 1962; (with Tom Maschler, under joint pseudonym Mark Caine) *The S-Man: A Grammar of Success,* Houghton, 1961; *The Graduate Wife,* Cassell, 1962; *The Trouble with England,* Cassell, 1962; *Lindmann,* Cassell, 1963, Holt, 1964; (contributor) James Turner, editor, *The Neighbour's Wife,* Cassell, 1964; (contributor) *New World Writing 22,* Lippincott, 1964; (contributor) Michael Ratcliffe, editor, *Voices 2,* M. Joseph, 1965; *Darling* (also see below), New American Library, 1965; *Two for the Road* (also see below), Holt, 1967; *Orchestra and Beginners,* J. Cape, 1967, Viking, 1968; *Like Men Betrayed,* J. Cape, 1969, Viking, 1970.

Who Were You with Last Night?, J. Cape, 1971; *April, June and November,* J. Cape, 1972, Houghton, 1976; *Richard's Things,* J. Cape, 1973, Houghton, 1976; (editor) *Bookmarks,* J. Cape, 1974; *California Time,* J. Cape, 1975, Houghton, 1976; *Somerset Maugham and His World,* Scribner, 1977; *The Glittering Prizes,* Penguin, 1977, St. Martin's, 1978; (translator with Kenneth McLeish) *The Poems of Catullus,* J. Cape, 1978, David R. Godine, 1979; (translator) *The Oresteia of Aeschylus,* Cambridge University Press, 1979; *For and Against,* W. H. Allen, 1979; *Sleeps Six* (short story collection), J. Cape, 1979.

Film scripts: "Nothing But the Best," 1964; "Darling," 1965; "Two for the Road," 1966; "Far from the Madding Crowd," 1967; "A Severed Head," 1971; "How About Us?," 1971; "Daisy Miller," 1973; "Rogue Male," 1976; "Something's Wrong," 1978; "Roses, Roses ...," 1978; "School Play," 1979.

Plays: (With Lucienne Hill) "Lady at the Wheel," produced in London, England, 1958; "A Man on the Bridge," produced in Hornchurch, England, 1961; "An Early Life," 1979; "From the Greek," 1979.

Also author of plays for Independent Television Network and of radio plays for British Broadcasting Corp. Contributor to periodicals. Critic, *Sunday Times.*

WORK IN PROGRESS: A novel, *Final Demands;* a screenplay, "A New Wife"; translations of "Medea" and "Bacchae" by Euripides; *Byron: A Personal Documentary.*

SIDELIGHTS: Frederic Raphael writes both highly-regarded novels and film scripts. Of his novels, Frederick P. W. McDowell writes: "In England, if we are to credit reviews, Frederic Raphael is regarded as one of the most talented of emerging novelists. In protesting against the strength of outmoded conventions he is similar to writers like Kingsley Amis, John Braine, and Alan Sillitoe who since the middle 1950's have been criticizing the Establishment. But unlike these novelists he is little interested in the clash between the classes or in the life of the working-class. He has instead focused upon the English middle class, . . . and he frequently, but not exclusively, writes about Jewish people. . . . Although he has written well and extensively, no one of his novels, except possibly . . . *Lindmann,* has received the acclaim from intelligent readers that is Raphael's due. . . .

"Because of the variety of his abilities and his use of techniques ranging from Wellsian naturalism in *The Limits of Love* to dissolving montage in *A Wild Surmise* to Joycean experimentalism in *Lindmann,* Raphael's books have not been unified in subject and approach. . . . What his novels do possess in common are varied and authentic aesthetic excellences. Raphael reveals an inclusive and ranging imagination. . . . He is sensitive, moreover, to the quirks of personality which make an individual different from his fellows. He is a novelist who is, accordingly, much preoccupied with the analysis of the motives and internal states of his characters. . . . [And] of all novelists now writing in England, Raphael seems to me to have the sharpest ear for all the varieties of speech and the greatest ability to reproduce them with effectiveness in his fiction."

Raphael's filmscripts have been as well-received as his novels. His prize-winning "Darling," for example, a spirited look at contemporary married life, is considered "one of the key works in the evolution of the swinging cinema" by Andrew Sarris.

BIOGRAPHICAL/CRITICAL SOURCES: *New Statesman,* June 28, 1963, November 3, 1967; *Book Week,* March 29, 1964; *Critique,* fall, 1965; Anthony Burgess, *The Novel Now: A Guide to Contemporary Fiction,* Norton, 1967; *New York Times,* April 28, 1967, October 19, 1967, February 17, 1978; *Spectator,* September 8, 1967; *Listener,* October 12, 1967, November 12, 1970; *Punch,* October 18, 1967; *Times Literary Supplement,* October 19, 1967, November 12, 1971; *Time,* October 27, 1967; Andrew Sarris, *The American Cinema,* Dutton, 1968; *Saturday Review,* March 23, 1968; *New York Times Book Review,* March 31, 1968, October 26, 1975; *New York Review of Books,* April 11, 1968; *Jewish Quarterly,* autumn, 1968, autumn, 1972; *Christian Science Monitor,* March 18, 1971; *Book World,* May 30, 1971; *Books & Bookmen,* March, 1973; *Observer,* November 4, 1973; *Contemporary Literary Criticism,* Volume II, Gale, 1974; *Contemporary Review,* January, 1974; *Economist,* March 8, 1975; *New Yorker,* April 18, 1977; *Hudson Review,* summer, 1978.

* * *

RATLIFF, Charles Edward, Jr. 1926-

PERSONAL: Born October 13, 1926, in Morven, N.C.; son of Charles Edward (a merchant and farmer) and Mary Katherine (Liles) Ratliff; married Mary Virginia Heilig, December 8, 1945; children: Alice Ann, Katherine Virginia, John Charles. *Education:* Davidson College, B.S., 1947; Duke

University, A.M., 1951, Ph.D., 1955. *Politics:* Democrat. *Religion:* Methodist. *Home:* 301 Pinecrest St., Davidson, N.C. *Office:* Department of Economics, Davidson College, Davidson, N.C. 28036.

CAREER: Davidson College, Davidson, N.C., instructor, 1947-48, assistant professor, 1948-49, 1951-54, associate professor, 1954-60, professor of economics, 1960-67, Charles A. Dana Professor of Economics, 1967-77, William R. Kenan Professor of Economics, 1977—. Visiting summer professor, Charlotte College (now University of North Carolina at Charlotte), 1958 and 1960, and Appalachian State Teachers College (now Appalachian State University), 1962; visiting professor, University of Punjab, 1963-64, and Kinnaird College, 1965; professor of economics, Forman Christian College, Lahore, Pakistan, 1963-66, and 1969-70; member of faculty, National Defense Education Act Institute in Asian History, summer, 1968; U.S. Cultural Affairs Lecturer, East and West Pakistan, 1969-70; director of Fulbright-Hays Group Project Abroad, summer, 1973. United Methodist Church, lay speaker, service with Board of Missions, 1963-66, and 1969-70. Member of Conference Board of Missions, 1968-72, Conference Priorities Committee, 1972-74, and Conference Planning and Research Committee, 1974—. Chairman of Committee on Interstate Allocation and Apportionment of Business Income, 1972-74; Mayor's Committee on Community Relations, Davidson, N.C., member, 1973—, chairman, 1973-78; member of Mecklenburg County Housing and Economic Development Committee, 1975—; member of national board of directors, Rural Advancement Fund of the National Sharecroppers Fund, Inc., 1978—. *Military service:* U.S. Navy, Supply Corps, 1944-46; became reserve commander.

MEMBER: National Tax Association, American Economic Association, Association for Asian Studies, American Association of University Professors, Lahore American Society (secretary of board of directors, 1965-66), Southern Economic Association (member of executive committee, 1961-63; vice-president, 1975-76), Phi Beta Kappa, Omicron Delta Kappa, Old Catawba Society. *Awards, honors:* Inter-University Committee for Economic Research on the South research fellow, 1960-61; award of appreciation from Davidson College Alumni Association, 1970; named Outstanding Educator of America, 1971; Thomas Jefferson Award, Davidson College, 1972; Love Servant Award, 1979.

WRITINGS: (Co-author) *Public Finance,* Pitman, 1959; *Interstate Apportionment of Business Income for State Income Tax Purposes,* University of North Carolina Press, 1962; (contributor) Julius Gould and W. L. Kolb, editors, *A Dictionary of the Social Sciences,* Free Press of Glencoe, 1964; (contributor) Max K. Lowdermilk, editor, *Economic and Community Development Seminar,* [Khanewal (West Pakistan)], 1966; (contributor) *The Administration of Government Education in West Pakistan,* Institute of Education and Research, University of Punjab, 1966; (co-author) *Rural Development in Pakistan,* Carolina Academic Press, in press. Author of several economic reports for the United Methodist Church; also author of tapes, "Christian Involvement," 1967, "The Christian Mission and a Pushbutton World," 1971, and "Reaching Out in Love," 1972; contributor to *Proceedings* of National Tax Association, 1962 and 1974. Contributor of articles and reviews to professional journals, including *National Tax Journal, Southern Economic Journal,* and *Pakistan Economist.*

RAUNER, Robert M(cKenzie) 1925-

PERSONAL: Born January 25, 1925, in Walden, N.Y.; son of Maurice Francis and Helen (Miller) Rauner; married Brenda B. Knight, September 7, 1951; children: Peter, Catherine, Margaret, Thomas. *Education:* Middlebury College, A.B., 1950; London School of Economics and Political Science, Ph.D., 1956. *Home:* 5909 Kingswood Rd., Bethesda, Md. 20014. *Office:* RMC, Inc., 7910 Woodmont Ave., Bethesda, Md. 20014.

CAREER: Trinity College, Hartford, Conn., assistant professor, 1954-57; RAND Corp., Santa Monica, Calif., economist, 1957-65; Department of Commerce, Economic Development Administration, Washington, D.C., director of Office of Program Evaluation, 1965-68; REDI, Inc., Washington, D.C., president, 1968-69; RMC, Inc., Bethesda, Md., vice-president, 1969—. *Military service:* U.S. Marine Corps Reserve, 1943-46. *Member:* American Economic Association, Institute of Management Science.

WRITINGS: *Laboratory Evaluation of Supply and Procurement Policies: The First Experiment of the Logistics Systems Laboratory,* RAND Corp., 1958; *Samuel Bailey and the Classical Theory of Value,* Harvard University Press, 1961. Contributor to professional journals.†

* * *

READ, Donald 1930-

PERSONAL: Born July 31, 1930, in Manchester, England; son of Charles Stanley and Furness (Harbottle) Read; married Joyce Mary Curran, 1955; children: Martin John, Andrew Fergus. *Education:* University College, Oxford, M.A., 1955, B.Litt., 1955; University of Hull, postgraduate study, 1954-55; University of Sheffield, Ph.D., 1955-56. *Home:* 64 Beaconsfield Rd., Canterbury, Kent, England. *Office:* Darwin College, University of Kent, Canterbury, Kent, England.

CAREER: University of Sheffield, Sheffield, England, research fellow, 1955-56; University of Leeds, Leeds, England, lecturer in modern history, 1956-65; University of Kent, Canterbury, Kent, England, senior lecturer in history, 1965-68, reader, 1969-73, professor of modern history, 1974—. *Member:* Royal Historical Society (fellow), Historical Association.

WRITINGS: *Peterloo: The Massacre and Its Background,* Manchester University Press, 1958; (contributor) *Chartist Studies,* Macmillan, 1959; *Press and People, 1790-1850,* St. Martin's, 1961; (with Eric Glasgow) *Feargus O'Connor: Irishman and Chartist,* Edward Arnold, 1961; *The English Provinces, 1760-1960: A Study in Influence,* Edward Arnold, 1964, St. Martin's, 1965; *Cobden and Bright: A Victorian Political Partnership,* Edward Arnold, 1967; *Edwardian England,* Harrap, 1972; *Documents from Edwardian England,* Harrap, 1973; *England 1868-1914: The Age of Urban Democracy,* Longman, 1979. Contributor of articles to professional journals.

WORK IN PROGRESS: A book on nineteenth-century British prime ministers and their public image.

* * *

REED, Lillian Craig 1932-
(Kit Reed)

PERSONAL: Born June 7, 1932, in San Diego, Calif.; daughter of John Rich (a lieutenant commander in U.S. Navy) and Lillian (Hyde) Craig; married Joseph Wayne Reed, Jr. (a professor), December 10, 1955; children: Joseph McKean,

John Craig, Katherine Hyde. *Education:* College of Notre Dame of Maryland, B.A., 1954. *Home:* 45 Lawn Ave., Middletown, Conn. *Agent:* Brandt & Brandt, 1501 Broadway, New York, N.Y. 10036.

CAREER: St. Petersburg Times, St. Petersburg, Fla., reporter and television editor, 1954-55; *New Haven Register,* New Haven, Conn., reporter, 1956-59; free-lance author of fiction. Visiting professor of English, Wesleyan University, 1974—. Visiting writer in India, 1974. *Awards, honors:* Named New England Newspaper Woman of the Year, New England Women's Press Association, 1958, 1959; Abraham Woursell Foundation literary grant, 1965-70; Guggenheim fellowships, 1964-65, 1968; Best Catholic Short Story of the Year Award, Catholic Press Association.

WRITINGS—Under name Kit Reed: *Mother Isn't Dead, She's Only Sleeping,* Houghton, 1961; *At War as Children,* Farrar, Straus, 1964; *When We Dream,* Hawthorne, 1966; *The Better Part,* Farrar, Straus, 1967; *Mister Da V. and Other Stories,* Faber, 1967, Berkeley Publishing, 1973; *Armed Camps,* Faber, 1969, Dutton, 1970; *Cry of the Daughter,* Dutton, 1971; *Tiger Rag,* Dutton, 1973; (compiler) *Fat* (anthology), Bobbs-Merrill, 1974; *Captain Grown-up,* Dutton, 1976; *The Killer Mice,* Gollancz, 1976; *The Ballad of T. Rantula,* Little, Brown, 1979; *Magic Time,* Putnam, 1980. Works represented in several anthologies, including *Winter's Tales,* Macmillan. Author of a radio play, "The Bathyscaphe," 1979. Contributor of short stories and articles to *Transatlantic Review, Cosmopolitan, Ladies' Home Journal, Magazine of Fantasy and Science Fiction, Argosy, Writer,* and other publications.

BIOGRAPHICAL/CRITICAL SOURCES: New York Times Book Review, March 8, 1964, June 17, 1979; *Books and Bookmen,* March, 1968; *Best Sellers,* July 1, 1970, April 1, 1971.

* * *

REES, Jean A(nglin) 1912-

PERSONAL: Born November 11, 1912, in Newcastle upon Tyne, England; daughter of John and Esther (Anglin) Sinclair; married Thomas Rees, 1936 (died, 1970); children: Jennifer Rees Larcombe, Justyn. *Education:* Attended local schools.

CAREER: Author of novels, biographies, and children's books, 1947—. Founder, with husband, of Hildenborough Hall, Kent, England, 1945; founder of Christian Homes and Christian Lunch and Dinner Clubs.

WRITINGS—Published by Pickering & Inglis, except as indicated: *Carol & Co.,* 1947; *The Conways of Chelwood House,* 1951; *Penelope and Jane,* 1952; *Junior Detectives Ltd.,* 1954; *The Lady with the Sun Lamp,* Oliphants, 1954; *The Isle of Auchencreel,* 1955; *Madame Estelle,* 1956; *Not in Our Stars,* 1956; *Wife of Hamish,* 1957; *Wedding Presents,* Lutterworth, 1957; *Antonia,* Oliphants, 1957; *Mrs. Brown of the Corner Shop,* Oliphants, 1958; *He Dared to Believe,* Victory Press, 1958; *Singing the Story,* Lutterworth, 1958; *Junior Detectives Work Again,* 1958; *Carol and Nicola,* 1958; *Danger, Saints at Work,* Victory Press, 1958.

Apron Strings, Lutterworth, 1961; *Road to Sodom,* Random House, 1961; *Jacob Have I Loved,* P. Davies, 1962, Eerdmans, 1963; *Iron on the Anvil,* 1962; *Rose among Thistles,* Zondervan, 1963; *Danger, Devils at Work,* Victory Press, 1966; *Challenge to Pray,* Oliphants, 1966, Zondervan, 1967; *God Wondered,* Oliphants, 1967; *Embarrassing Relations,* Walter, 1967; *Back to Balcromie,* 1969; *Great Promises,* Oliphants, 1969; *His Name Was Tom: The Biography of Tom Rees,* Hodder & Stoughton, 1971; *What Jesus Said,* Pickering & Inglis, 1978; *What Jesus Did,* Pickering & Inglis, 1978.

WORK IN PROGRESS: Her autobiography; booklets on daily meditation.

AVOCATIONAL INTERESTS: Art and handicrafts.

* * *

REID, Loren (Dudley) 1905-

PERSONAL: Born August 26, 1905, in Gilman City, Mo.; son of Dudley and Josephine (Tarwater) Reid; married Augusta Towner, 1930; children: Mrs. Joel Gold, John, Stephen, Tony. *Education:* Grinnell College, A.B., 1927; University of Iowa, M.A., 1930, Ph.D., 1932. *Religion:* Episcopalian. *Home:* 200 East Brandon Rd., Columbia, Mo. 65201. *Office:* 115 Switzler Hall, University of Missouri, Columbia, Mo. 65205.

CAREER: Vermillion High School, Vermillion, S.D., teacher, 1927-29; University of Iowa, Iowa City, instructor, 1930-33; Westport High School, Kansas City, Mo., instructor, 1933-35; University of Missouri—Columbia, instructor, 1935-37, assistant professor, 1937-39; Syracuse University, Syracuse, N.Y., associate professor of speech and education, 1939-44; University of Missouri—Columbia, professor of speech, 1944-75, professor emeritus, 1975—. University of Maryland, visiting professor of German and English, 1952-53 and 1960-61, visiting professor of English, 1955; Carnegie Visiting Professor, University of Hawaii, 1957. Trustee, Daniel Boone Regional Library, 1958-60. *Member:* Speech Association of America (vice-president, 1956; president, 1957), American Association of University Professors, Royal Historical Society (fellow), Central States Speech Association (executive secretary, 1937-39), Hansard Society (London), University Club (president, 1947). *Awards, honors:* Alumni achievement award, Grinnell College, 1962; special award for outstanding service, New York Speech Association, 1967; James A. Winans Award, 1969, for distinguished research; award for distinguished book, Speech Communication Association, 1970; University of Missouri, award for distinguished service, 1970, distinguished teaching award, 1971; Missouri Library Association literary award, 1979; Missouri Writers Guild literary award, 1979; distinguished service award, Central States Speech Association, 1979.

WRITINGS: Charles James Fox, privately printed, 1932; (contributor) *Fundamentals of Speaking,* Macmillan, 1951; *Teaching of Speech,* 3rd edition, Artcraft, 1960, 4th edition, McGraw, 1971; *First Principles of Public Speaking,* Artcraft, 1960, 2nd edition, 1962; (editor) *American Public Address: Studies in Honor of Albert Craig Baird,* University of Missouri Press, 1961; *Speaking Well,* Artcraft, 1962, 4th edition, McGraw, 1981; *Charles James Fox: A Man for the People,* University of Missouri Press, 1969; *Hurry Home Wednesday,* University of Missouri Press, 1978. Contributor of articles to speech and education journals.

WORK IN PROGRESS: Hurry Home Wednesday II; a history of British public address, completion expected in 1983.

* * *

REID, W(illiam) Stanford 1913-

PERSONAL: Born September 13, 1913, in Montreal, Quebec, Canada; son of William Dunn (a Presbyterian clergyman) and Daisy (Stanford) Reid; married Priscilla Lee, August 24, 1940. *Education:* McGill University, B.A., 1934,

M.A., 1935; Westminster Theological Seminary, Th.B. and Th.M., 1938; University of Pennsylvania, Ph.D., 1941. *Politics:* Independent liberal. *Home:* 120 Edinburgh Rd., Guelph, Ontario, Canada N1G 2Y6. *Office:* Department of History, University of Guelph, Guelph, Ontario, Canada.

CAREER: McGill University, Montreal, Quebec, lecturer, 1941-44, assistant professor, 1944-51, associate professor, 1951-63, professor of history, 1963-65, director of men's residences, 1951-65; University of Guelph, Guelph, Ontario, professor of history, 1965-79, professor emeritus, 1979—, chairman of department, 1965-70. Presbyterian clergyman in Montreal, Quebec, 1941-51. Visiting lecturer at Oxford University, 1959, and University of West Indies, 1962. Member of board of managers, Presbyterian Theological College of Montreal, 1943-45; trustee, Westminster Theological Seminary, 1944—. *Member:* Canadian Historical Association (member of council), American Historical Association, Conference on Scottish Studies (president), American Society of Church History (member of council), American Association for Reformation Research (member of council), Royal Historical Society (fellow), Economic History Society, Conference on British Studies, Conference on Faith and History, American Scientific Affiliation, P.E.N., Scottish Church History Society, The History Association (London), Society for Netherlandic Studies, Mediaeval Academy of America, Montreal Historical Society (president). *Awards, honors:* Research grants from American Philosophical Association, 1949 and 1951, Nuffield Foundation, 1962, British Council, 1963, Canada Council, 1960-74, Government of France, 1971, and Institute for Advanced Christian Studies, 1972-74; L.H.D., Wheaton College, Wheaton, Ill., 1975; D.D., Presbyterian College, 1979.

WRITINGS: The Church of Scotland in Lower Canada: Its Struggle for Establishment, Thorn Press, 1936; *Economic History of Great Britain,* Ronald, 1954; *Skipper from Leith: The History of Robert Barton of Over Barnton,* University of Pennsylvania Press, 1962; *The Protestant Reformation: Revival or Revolution?,* Holt, 1970; *Trumpeter of God: A Biography of John Knox,* Scribner, 1974; (editor and contributor) *The Scottish Tradition in Canada,* McClelland & Stuart, 1976; (editor) *Called to Witness: Presbyterian Biographies,* Volume I, Presbyterian Publications, 1976, Volume II, Porcupine Press, 1980; *A Century and a Half of Service: The History of St. Andrews Presbyterian Church, Guelph, Ontario,* Moyers & Smart, 1980. Contributor to history and theology journals, including *Catholic Historical Review, Church History, Canadian Historical Review, Juridical Review, Mariner's Mirror, Scottish Historical Review,* and *Westminster Theological Journal.*

WORK IN PROGRESS: Research on the social and economic background of the Reformation, especially in Scotland, France, and the Netherlands.

SIDELIGHTS: W. Stanford Reid told *CA:* "While I have moved back to a certain extent into Canadian ecclesiastical history as a result of special demands for help in this field, my interest is still basically in the 16th century European scene. I am carrying on the laborious work of research in the background of the Reformation, seeking to relate the religious aspects to the social, economic and political developments of the time. My feeling is that most writers on the Protestant Reformation tend to ignore the influence which the economic and social changes had on the religious movement which in some regards explain the pattern the movement took in different lands."

REINHARDT, Kurt F(rank) 1896-

PERSONAL: Born November 2, 1896, in Munich, Germany; son of Siegfried and Julie (Schwab) Reinhardt; married Bertha Bollinger, 1926 (died, 1967). *Education:* Attended University of Munich, 1916-18, and University of Heidelberg, 1919-20; University of Freiburg, Ph.D. (magna cum laude), 1922. *Politics:* Democrat. *Religion:* Roman Catholic. *Home:* Channing House, 850 Webster St., Apt. 322, Palo Alto, Calif. 94301.

CAREER: Herder Publishing Co., Freiburg, Germany, editor, 1922-25; *Der Feuerreiter,* Zurich, Switzerland, editor-in-chief, 1925-27; foreign correspondent in Winnipeg, Manitoba, 1927-28; University of Oregon, Eugene, assistant professor of German and lecturer in School of Architecture and Allied Arts, 1928-30; Stanford University, Stanford, Calif., professor of Germanic languages, 1930-62, professor emeritus, 1962—; affiliated with St. Patrick's Seminary, Menlo Park, Calif., 1962-66, and with Newman Center, Palo Alto, Calif., 1967—. Conductor of courses at University of California Adult Education Center, San Francisco. *Member:* American Philosophical Association, American Association of University Professors, Catholic Association for Intellectual and Cultural Affairs. *Awards, honors:* Moraga Crest, St. Mary's College, California, 1938; Order of Civil Merit, awarded by Spain for the promotion of Spanish culture in the United States, 1960; Officers' Cross First Class of Order of Merit, Federal Republic of Germany, 1962.

WRITINGS: Mystik and Pietismus, Theatiner Verlag, 1925; *The Commonwealth of Nations and the Papacy,* Bruce, 1943; *A Realistic Philosophy: The Perennial Principles of Thought and Action in a Changing World,* Bruce, 1944, 2nd edition, 1961; *Germany: 2000 Years,* two volumes, Bruce, 1950, 2nd edition, 1960; *The Existentialist Revolt: The Main Themes and Phases of Existentialism,* Bruce, 1952, 3rd edition, Ungar, 1972; (contributor) *Saints for Now,* edited by Clare Boothe Luce, Sheed, 1952; (author of introduction) Nietzsche, *Joyful Wisdom,* Ungar, 1960; (contributor) *Sources of Existentialism: A Symposium,* edited by Arthur Burton, Ungar, 1966; *Theological Novel of Modern Europe: An Analysis of Masterpieces by Eight Authors,* Ungar, 1969.

Translator: Oswaldo Robles, *The Main Problems of Philosophy,* Bruce, 1946; St. John of the Cross, *The Dark Night of the Soul,* Ungar, 1957; Miguel De Unamuno, *The Agony of Christianity,* Ungar, 1960; Wilfred Daim, *Depth Psychology and Salvation,* Ungar, 1963; Ludwig Landgrebe, *Main Problems of Contemporary European Philosophy: From Dilthey to Heidegger,* Ungar, 1965.

SIDELIGHTS: Kurt Reinhardt's fields of interest include philosophy, theology, philosophy of medicine, and existentialism, particularly existential psychology and psychiatry. He is competent in German, English, French, Spanish, Latin.

* * *

RENICK, Marion (Lewis) 1905-

PERSONAL: Born March 9, 1905, in Springfield, Ohio; daughter of Bertram Charles (a U.S. Government employee) and Anna (a public school teacher; maiden name, Washway) Lewis; married James L. Renick (a sports writer), September 3, 1930 (divorced, 1945). *Education:* Wittenberg University, A.B., 1926. *Home:* 267 East Longview Ave., Columbus, Ohio 43202.

CAREER: The News, Springfield, Ohio, reporter, 1924-27; American Education Press, Columbus, Ohio, editor of *My*

Weekly Reader, 1945-51; Ohio State University, Bureau of Educational Research, Columbus, editor of teachers manuals and script supervisor and broadcaster for educational radio and television, 1952-61, teacher in department of journalism, 1956-57; free-lance writer of youth books in Columbus, 1961—. *Member:* Women in Communications, National League of American Pen Women, Authors League of America, Theta Sigma Phi, Chi Omega. *Awards, honors:* Boys' Clubs of America Medal, 1951; Headliner Award, Women in Communications, 1956; Ohiona Library Medal for Nonfiction, 1971, for *Ohio;* honorary doctor of letters, Wittenberg University, 1972.

WRITINGS—All juveniles; published by Scribner, except as indicated: (With husband, James L. Renick; see *Sidelights* below) *Tommy Carries the Ball,* 1940; (with J. L. Renick) *David Cheers the Team,* 1941; (with J. L. Renick) *Steady,* 1942; *Champion Caddy,* 1943; *Skating Today,* 1945; *Swimming Fever,* 1947; *A Touchdown for Doc,* 1948; *The Dooleys Play Ball,* 1950; *The Shining Shooter,* 1951; *Nicky's Football Team,* 1952; *Pete's Home Run,* 1953; *Jimmy's Own Basketball,* 1953; *The Heart for Baseball,* 1953; *John's Back Yard Camp,* 1954; *Todd's Snow Patrol,* 1955; *Seven Simpsons on Six Bikes,* 1956; *Bats and Gloves of Glory,* 1956; *Young Mr. Football,* 1957; *The Tail of the Terrible Tiger,* 1959.

Boy at Bat, 1961; *Steve Marches with the General,* 1962; *The Big Basketball Prize,* 1963; *Roger the Crow,* American Book Co., 1964; *The Secret Halfback,* American Book Co., 1964; *Watch Those Red Wheels Roll,* 1965; *Ricky in the World of Sport,* Seabury, 1967; *Football Boys,* 1967; *Little Fish Hard to Catch,* Random House, 1969; *Ohio,* Coward, 1970; *Take a Long Jump,* 1971; *Five Points for Hockey,* 1973; *Sam Discovers Soccer,* 1975; *The Famous Forward Pass Pair,* 1977.

SIDELIGHTS: Marion Renick told *CA:* "For a person who was to write sports stories later, my growing-up years were ideal. Behind our house was an undeveloped area of the Wittenberg College campus with fields for games and sprawly old apple trees for climbing. The college tennis courts were only a lob away, and other athletic opportunities abounded on the football field, the baseball diamond and the basketball court, although this latter, being indoors, took some conniving to get into. Around the neighborhood were fraternity houses with spacious lawns where the brothers tried out all sorts of athletic feats and seemed to enjoy giving instruction to us small fry hanging around.

"Naturally I thought I was qualified to write sports when, after finishing college, I got a job on a newspaper. The editor thought differently. But I married a sports writer and for fifteen years helped 'cover' sports around the country, meeting outstanding athletes, coaches, trainers and sports writers and, far more important, listening to them talk shop. How I wished I could share that with my long-ago neighborhood pals! I decided the next best thing was to share it with new generations of young sports enthusiasts. I began writing books combining sports fundamentals with a story. The story was essential because I believe the real heart of a book is its story. The story is what keeps a reader interested to the end, and if good enough can prove to a child that the effort of learning to read is indeed worthwhile. More than anything else I am concerned that children should know not only how to read but how to enjoy books, learning all kinds of helpful things from them including how to laugh and how to understand themselves as well as how to kick a soccer ball or catch a forward pass.

"Because I am an honest writer, I take great care to put into my books only what is true, at least to my knowledge. This has made problems for me, like the time I wanted the boy in *Take a Long Jump* to do a science experiment on the praying mantis. I wasn't satisfied just to read up on the insect. To be authentic I felt I had to do the experiment myself. I bought a praying mantis egg cocoon and waited for the hatching. I found the books were correct. Several hundred baby mantises do come out in the spring. Unfortunately they hatched in my workroom. Building a Soap Box car for *Watch Those Red Wheels Roll* was far less disastrous, although I hope no kids who build their own racers have as much trouble as I did to make the brake work."

The first three books in Marion Renick's bibliography carry her ex-husband's name, James L. Renick, as co-author. However, as Marion Renick explained to *CA:* "Actually, Scribner's used [my husband's] name as co-author at first because they said 'nobody would buy a sports book written by a woman.'" Renick continued: "After my first three books did well, my editor decided to give me an honest by-line, but I am still stuck with being catalogued on those first three as a sort of helpful assistant to James L. Renick who, as a matter of fact, had previously disclaimed to the publishers any part in writing them."

Twenty of Marion Renick's books were adapted for television and presented by National Educational Television as the series "Sport Studio" in 1959. The stories are still broadcast at three-year intervals in an effort "to advance the planning and production of TV programs for children which deal with ethics in a way to hold interest and have meaning."

* * *

REPS, John W(illiam) 1921-

PERSONAL: Born November 25, 1921, in St. Louis, Mo. *Education:* Dartmouth College, A.B. (summa cum laude), 1943; Cornell University, M. Regional Planning, 1947; further graduate study at University of Liverpool, 1947, and London School of Economics and Political Science, 1950-51. *Home:* 102 Needham Pl., Ithaca, N.Y. *Office:* Department of City and Regional Planning, Cornell University, Ithaca, N.Y. 14850.

CAREER: Cornell University, Ithaca, N.Y., lecturer, 1948-50, associate professor, 1952-60, professor of city and regional planning, 1960-70, 1971—, chairman of department, 1952-64, research associate at Center for Housing and Environmental Studies, 1951. Visiting scholar, University of California, Berkeley, fall, 1958; visiting professor, Institute of Social Studies (The Hague), 1965-66. Has lectured at many colleges and universities in the United States and abroad. Planning aide, U.S. Natural Resources Planning Board, 1942; planning director, Broome County, N.Y., 1947-50; member of Greater Ithaca Regional Planning Board, 1957-58; member of Ithaca Planning Board, 1956-58, 1968-70, vice-chairman, 1956-57, 1968-69, chairman, 1958; member of board of directors, McGraw Housing Corp., 1970-74. *Military service:* U.S. Army Air Forces, 1943-46; became sergeant.

MEMBER: American Planning Association, American Society of Planning Officials (member of board of directors, 1966-69), Society of Architectural Historians, Phi Beta Kappa. *Awards, honors:* Fulbright scholarship, 1950-51, research fellowship in Netherlands, 1965-66; Guggenheim fellowship, 1958; Eisenhower exchange fellowship, 1959; Ford Foundation travel grant to England, Netherlands, Soviet Union, and Yugoslavia, 1964; American Institute of Architects Foundation scholarship, 1965; American Institute of Planners award, 1968; National Endowment for the Humanities, 1973-74.

WRITINGS: Legal Aspects of Municipal Control of Land Subdivision: A Bibliography, Department of City and Regional Planning, Cornell University, 1957; (contributor) Jones and Kelly, editors, *Long Range Needs and Opportunities in New York State: A Series of Working Papers,* Center for Housing and Environmental Studies, Cornell University, 1962; *The Making of Urban America: A History of City Planning in the United States,* Princeton University Press, 1965; *Monumental Washington: The Planning and Development of the Capitol Center,* Princeton University Press, 1967; *Town Planning in Frontier America,* Princeton University Press, 1969; *Checklists and Catalogs of Map and Print Collections Containing North American Town Plans and Views: A Bibliography of Guides to the Location of Graphic Records of Urban Development Prior to 1900,* Department of City and Regional Planning, College of Architecture, Art, and Planning, Cornell University, 1970, revised edition, 1978; (contributor) Walter Whitehill and Sinclair Hitchings, editors, *Boston Print Makers of the Pre-Revolutionary Period,* University Press of Virginia, 1972; *Tidewater Towns: City Planning in Colonial Virginia and Maryland,* University Press of Virginia, 1972; *Cities on Stone: Nineteenth Century Lithograph Images of the Urban West,* Amon Carter Museum of Western Art, 1976; *Cities of the American West: A History of Frontier Urban Planning,* Princeton University Press, 1979; *The Forgotten Frontier: Urban Planning in the American West Before 1890,* Braziller, 1980.

Author of about thirty research reports. Contributor to proceedings and to *Encyclopaedia Britannica.* Contributor of about forty articles and reviews to planning, history, and law journals. Member of editorial advisory board, *Zoning Digest,* 1959-67.

* * *

REYBURN, Wallace (Macdonald) 1913-

PERSONAL: Born July 3, 1913, in Auckland, New Zealand; son of William Robert (a dentist) and Florence (Fisher) Reyburn; married Lucille Peart, February 7, 1941 (divorced November 6, 1946); married Elizabeth Munro (a magazine editor), November 21, 1946; children: (second marriage) Ross Macdonald, Lorna Robin (Mrs. Steven Bicknell), William Scott. *Education:* Attended school in England. *Politics:* Conservative. *Religion:* Church of England. *Home and office:* 16 Harley Rd., London N.W.3, England. *Agent:* Curtis Brown Ltd., 575 Madison Ave., New York, N.Y. 10022.

CAREER: Reporter and assistant editor for newspapers in New Zealand, 1931-34, and their correspondent in London, England, 1935-36; assistant editor, then editor, of Canadian magazines in Toronto and Montreal, 1937-40, 1946-50; assistant and features editor of magazines in London, 1950-53; *Toronto Telegram,* Toronto, Ontario, daily columnist in London, 1954-64; *Queen Magazine,* London, deputy editor, 1965-66; writer, 1966—. *Wartime service:* War correspondent for *Montreal Standard,* 1941-45. *Awards, honors:* Order of the British Empire.

WRITINGS: Rehearsal for Invasion, Harrap, 1943; *Glorious Chapter,* Oxford University Press, 1943; *Some of It Was Fun,* Thomas Nelson (Toronto), 1948; *Follow a Shadow* (novel), Cassell, 1956; *Port of Call* (novel), Cassell, 1957; *The Street That Died* (Novel), Cassell, 1958; *Three Women* (novel), Cassell, 1959.

Good and Evil (novel), Cassell, 1960; *Getting the Boy* (novel), Elek, 1965; *The World of Rugby,* Elek, 1966; *The Lions,* Stanley Paul, 1967; *The Unsmiling Giants,* Stanley Paul, 1968; *Frost: Anatomy of a Success,* Macdonald & Co., 1968; (editor) *Best Rugby Stories,* Faber, 1969; *The Rugby Companion,* Stanley Paul, 1969; *Flushed with Pride: The Story of Thomas Crapper,* Macdonald & Co., 1969, Prentice-Hall, 1970.

There Was Also Some Rugby, Stanley Paul, 1970; *Bust Up: The Story of Otto Titzling,* Macdonald & Co., 1971, Prentice-Hall, 1972; *A History of Rugby,* Arthur Barker, 1972; *Bridge across the Atlantic,* Harrap, 1973; *The Inferior Sex,* Prentice-Hall, 1973; *The Winter Men,* Stanley Paul, 1973; *Twickenham: The Story of a Rugby Ground,* Allen & Unwin, 1976; *All about Rugby,* W. H. Allen, 1976; *Mourie's Men,* Cassell, 1979; (with Reginald Bosanquet) *Let's Get Through Wednesday,* M. Joseph, 1980.

Contributor to *New Yorker, Life, Reader's Digest,* and other magazines. Editor of *New Liberty* (a Canadian journal).

SIDELIGHTS: Reyburn told *CA:* "I have been writing since I was eight, because I have a nagging desire to do so. I think self-discipline is the most important attribute for an author. Not without reason has it been said that the longest trip in the world is from the armchair to the typewriter."

* * *

RHODES, Richard (Lee) 1937-

PERSONAL: Born July 4, 1937, in Kansas City, Kan.; son of Arthur (a laborer) and Georgia (Collier) Rhodes; married Linda biredell Hampton, August 29, 1960 (divorced April 27, 1974); married Mary Magdalene Evans, November 26, 1976; children: (first marriage) Timothy James, Katherine Hampton. *Education:* Yale University, B.A. (cum laude), 1959. *Agent:* John Cushman, John Cushman Associates, Inc., Suite 1401, 200 West 57th St., New York, N.Y. 10019. *Office: Playboy,* 919 North Michigan Ave., Chicago, Ill. 60611.

CAREER: Newsweek, New York City, writer trainee, 1959; Radio Free Europe, New York City, staff assistant, 1960; Westminster College, Fulton, Mo., instructor in English, 1960-61; Hallmark Cards, Inc., Kansas City, Mo., book editing manager, 1962-70; *Harper's,* New York City, contributing editor, 1970-74; *Playboy,* Chicago, Ill., contributing editor, 1974—. Writer-in-residence, Kansas City Regional Council for Higher Education, 1972. *Military service:* U.S. Air Force Reserve, 1960-65; surgical technician. *Awards, honors: Playboy* editorial award, 1972; Guggenheim fellowship, 1974-75; National Endowment for the Arts grant in writing, 1978.

WRITINGS: The Inland Ground: An Evocation of the American Middle West, Atheneum, 1970; *The Ungodly: A Novel of the Donner Party,* Charterhouse, 1973; *The Ozarks,* Time-Life, 1974; *Holy Secrets* (novel), Doubleday, 1978; *Looking for America: A Writer's Odyssey,* Doubleday, 1979; *The Last Safari* (novel), Doubleday, 1980; *Sons of Earth* (novel), Coward, in press. Author of "The Loss of Innocence," produced on National Educational Television, 1965. Contributor of about fifty articles to popular magazines, including *Harper's, Redbook, Esquire, Playboy, Audience,* and *Reader's Digest,* and of book reviews to *New York Times Book Review, National Observer,* and *Chicago Tribune Book World,* 1965—.

SIDELIGHTS: Richard Rhodes has been referred to by several critics as one of the few good Midwestern writers of this generation. For example, Bill Greer of the *Washington Post* writes that "speaking straight from the heartland, Rhodes attempts in [*The Inland Ground*] to do for the Middle West what Willie Morris has done for the deeply misunderstood South." Mark Neyman writes in *Library Journal* that

"Rhodes has attempted to capture the spirit of the American heartland. . . . He skillfully avoids sentimentality, but the essays do reflect a certain melancholy over the passing of the frontier identity."

In his *Chicago Tribune* review of *The Last Safari,* Peter Collier compares Rhodes to Ernest Hemingway. Collier writes that in Rhodes' fiction, his "characters occasionally attitudinize as Hemingway's sometimes did, nattering about their fate. . . . Yet as with Hemingway, there is a vigor here, a conviction so strong that it forces the action along and the reader with it. There is also the ability to write splendidly for long stretches, descriptions that give something like a general social and natural science course on life in the savannahs and mountain ranges of eastern Africa. Damn fine, as Papa himself might have said."

BIOGRAPHICAL/CRITICAL SOURCES: Library Journal, November 15, 1970; *Washington Post,* November 21, 1970; *New York Times Book Review,* January 21, 1979, March 9, 1980; *New York Times,* January 24, 1980; *Chicago Tribune,* February 17, 1980.

* * *

RICE, Charles E. 1931-

PERSONAL: Born August 7, 1931, in New York, N.Y.; son of Laurence J. (a building contractor) and Mary (Convey) Rice; married Mary E. Mannix, 1956; children: John, Mary, Anne, Joseph, Charles, Jeanne, Theresa, Kathleen, Ellen, Patricia. *Education:* College of the Holy Cross, A.B., 1953; Boston College, LL.B., 1959, J.S.D., 1962. *Religion:* Roman Catholic. *Home:* 59800 Tyholland Lane, Mishawaka, Ind. 46544. *Office:* School of Law, University of Notre Dame, Notre Dame, Ind. 46556.

CAREER: Admitted to bar, 1957; C. W. Post College (now Center), Brookville, N.Y., lecturer in history and political science, 1958-61; New York University, School of Law, New York City, lecturer, 1958-60; Fordham University, School of Law, New York City, 1960-69, became professor of constitutional law; University of Notre Dame, School of Law, Notre Dame, Ind., 1969—, currently professor of law. State vice-chairman, New York Conservative Party, 1962-69. *Military service:* U.S. Marine Corps, 1956-58. U.S. Marine Corps Reserve, 1958—; present rank lieutenant colonel.

WRITINGS: Freedom of Association, New York University Press, 1962; *The Supreme Court and Public Prayer,* Fordham University Press, 1964; *The Vanishing Right to Live,* Doubleday, 1969; *Authority and Rebellion: The Case for Orthodoxy in the Catholic Church,* Doubleday, 1971; *Beyond Abortion: The Theory and Practice of the Secular State,* Franciscan Herald, 1979; *Fifty Questions on Abortion,* Cashel Institute, 1979. Contributor of articles and reviews to periodicals.

* * *

RICE, Edward E. 1918-

PERSONAL: Born in 1918; son of Edward and Elizabeth Rice; children: Edward III, Christopher. *Education:* Attended Columbia College. *Home address:* Box 381, N.Y. 11962.

CAREER: Writer, artist, photographer.

WRITINGS: The Man in the Sycamore Tree: The Good Times and Hard Life of Thomas Merton, Doubleday, 1970; *Mother India's Children: Meeting Today's Generation in India,* Pantheon, 1971; (editor) Pagal Baba, *Temple of the Phallic King,* Simon & Schuster, 1973; *The Five Great Religions,* Four Winds Press, 1973; *John Frum He Come: A Polemical Work about a Black Tragedy,* Doubleday, 1974; *The Ganges: A Personal Encounter,* Four Winds Press, 1974; *Journey to Upolu: Robert Louis Stevenson, Victorian Rebel,* Dodd, 1974; *Marx, Engels and the Workers of the World,* Four Winds Press, 1977; *Eastern Definitions,* Doubleday, 1978; *Ten Religions of the East,* Four Winds Press, 1978; *Babylon, Next to Nineveh,* Four Winds Press, 1979; *Margaret Mead: A Portrait,* Harper, 1979. Also author of *Cities of the Sacred Unicorn.*

* * *

RICHARDS, Cara E(lizabeth) 1927-

PERSONAL: Born January 13, 1927, in Bayonne, N.J.; daughter of Vere S. (a teacher of singing) and Virginia M. (Tyler) Richards; married Henry F. Dobyns, September 11, 1958 (divorced, 1968); children: York H. Dobyns. *Education:* Queens College of the City of New York (now Queens College of the City University of New York), A.B., 1952; Columbia University, graduate study, 1952-53; Cornell University, Ph.D., 1957. *Residence:* Lexington, Ky. *Office:* Division of Social Sciences, Transylvania University, Lexington, Ky. 40508.

CAREER: Cornell University, Ithaca, N.Y., curatorial assistant in primitive art, White Art Museum, 1956-57, resident at Many Farms Navajo-Cornell Experimental Field Health Clinic in Arizona, 1958-59, field director of family life study in Peru, 1960-61; Escuela de Servicio Social del Peru, Lima, professor of anthropology, 1961, 1962; area studies coordinator for Peace Corps training programs for South America at University of Washington, Seattle, and Springfield College, Springfield, Mass., 1963; Cornell University, lecturer in anthropology, 1963-64; Ithaca College, Ithaca, associate professor of anthropology, 1964-67; Transylvania University, Lexington, Ky., associate professor, 1967-75, professor of sociology, 1975—, program director of sociology and anthropology. Lecturer, Cornell University, summers, 1963, 1965-68.

MEMBER: American Anthropological Association (director of visiting lecturer program, 1963-69), Society for Applied Anthropology, American Association for the Advancement of Science, American Ethnological Society, American Society for Ethnohistory, American Association of University Professors, Central States Anthropological Association, Anthropologists and Sociologists of Kentucky (president, 1973-74), Phi Beta Kappa, Phi Alpha Theta. *Awards, honors:* American Association of University Women fellow, 1957-58; Russell Sage Foundation fellow, 1958-59.

WRITINGS: (Contributor) Elisabeth Tooker, editor, *Iroquois Culture, History and Prehistory,* New York State Museum and Science Service, 1967; *Man in Perspective: An Introduction to Cultural Anthropology,* Random House, 1971, 2nd edition published as *People in Perspective,* 1977; (contributor) Carol J. Matthiason, editor, *Many Sisters: Women in Cross-Cultural Perspective,* Free Press, 1974; *The Oneida People,* Indian Tribal Series, 1974. Contributor to *Human Organization* and anthropology journals.

WORK IN PROGRESS: Research on the role of women, and history of the Onondaga Indians.

SIDELIGHTS: Cara E. Richards comments: "I have always enjoyed writing, but sort of backed into becoming a published author. A friend dragooned me into collaborating with what became my first journal article, and another bullied me into writing my first book. The main reason for the reluctance was that I was so busy as a student, or, later, as a teacher, that I could never find the time to write. That problem persists, but grows more irksome with the passage of time and the increasing sense of urgency currently afflicting me. The frustration of not being able to find time to do what I am more and more determined to do will probably lead to some career changes in the near future. At least, I hope so."

AVOCATIONAL INTERESTS: Reading science fiction, swimming, playing basketball.

* * *

RICHARDSON, W(alter) C(ecil) 1902-

PERSONAL: Born 1902, in Spurgeon, Ind.; son of William G. and Emma (Chancellor) Richardson; married Griselda Silvanus, 1952; children: Anna Reeve (stepdaughter). *Education:* Oakland City College (now Laney College), B.A., 1925; University of Michigan, M.A., 1926, Ph.D., 1936. *Home:* 4263 Sweetbriar St., Baton Rouge, La. 70808. *Office:* Department of History, Louisiana State University, Baton Rouge, La.

CAREER: Taught in secondary schools in Indiana for four years and in Holland, Mich., 1926-27; Ironwood Junior College (now Gogebic Community College), Ironwood, Mich., instructor, 1934-37; Ohio University, Athens, assistant professor, 1937-40; Louisiana State University, Baton Rouge, 1940—, began as assistant professor, became professor, 1951, Boyd Professor of History, 1954, currently Boyd Professor Emeritus. *Member:* American Historical Association, Economic History Association, Royal Historical Society (fellow), South-Central Renaissance Conference (president, 1962-63), Southern Historical Society. *Awards, honors:* Herbert Baxter Adams Prize from American Historical Association for best book in European history, 1954, for *Tudor Chamber Administration;* alumnus of the year award from Oakland City College, 1967; presentation of a festschrift, *Tudor Men and Institutions,* 1973; DD.L. from Laney College, 1975; LL.D., Oakland City College, 1975.

WRITINGS: Tudor Chamber Administration, 1485-1547, Louisiana State University Press, 1952; *Stephen Vaughan,* Louisiana State University Press, 1953; *History of the Court of Augmentations, 1536-1554,* Louisiana State University Press, 1961; *Mary Tudor: The White Queen,* University of Washington Press, 1970; (editor) *Royal Commission Report of 1552,* West Virginia University Library, 1974; *History of the Inns of Court,* Claitors, 1977. Also author of *Tudor First Fruits.* Contributor of articles, essays, and reviews to scholarly journals. Member of editorial board, *Journal of Modern History.*

WORK IN PROGRESS: Tudor First Fruits and Tenths.

BIOGRAPHICAL/CRITICAL SOURCES: Spectator, January 31, 1970; *Books and Bookmen,* March, 1970; Arthur J. Slavin, editor, *Tudor Men and Institutions: Studies in English Law and Government,* Louisiana State University Press, 1972.

* * *

RICKELS, Karl 1924-

PERSONAL: Born August 17, 1924, in Wilhelmshaven, Germany; son of Karl E. and Stephanie (Roehrhoff) Rickels; married Christa Loessin (deceased); married Rosalind Wilson, June 27, 1964; children: (first marriage) Laurence A.; (second marriage) Stephen W., Michael R. *Education:* University of Muenster, M.D., 1951; postdoctoral study at University of Erlangen and University of Frankfurt, 1952-54. *Religion:* Catholic. *Home:* 1518 Sweetbriar Rd., Gladwyne, Pa. 19035. *Office:* 203 Piersol Building, Hospital of the University of Pennsylvania, 3400 Spruce St., Philadelphia, Pa. 19104.

CAREER: Dortmund Hospital, Dortmund, Germany, intern in internal medicine, microbiology, and radiology, 1951-52; Mental Health Institute, Cherokee, Iowa, resident in psychiatry, 1954-55; University of Pennsylvania, Philadelphia, resident in psychiatry in University Hospital, 1955-57, instructor, 1957-59, associate, 1959-60, assistant professor, 1960-64, associate professor, 1964-69, professor of psychiatry, 1969—, Stuart and Emily B. H. Mudd Professor of Human Behavior and Reproduction, 1977—, director of psychopharmacology, 1964—. Licensed to practice in West Germany and Pennsylvania. Member of panel on psychiatric drugs, participating in drug efficacy study, National Research Council and National Academy of Sciences, 1966-68; chairman of Food and Drug Administration's advisory review panel on OTC daytime and nighttime sedatives and stimulant products, 1972-75. Consultant to West German consulate, American Medical Association Council on New Drugs, and National Institutes of Mental Health.

MEMBER: American Medical Association, American Psychiatric Association (fellow), Academy of Psychosomatic Medicine (fellow), American Association for the Advancement of Science, American College of Clinical Pharmacology (fellow), American Society for Psychosomatic Obstetrics and Gynecology, American College of Neuropsychopharmacology (charter fellow), American Psychopathological Association, American Psychosomatic Society, American Society for Clinical Pharmacology and Therapeutics, American Society for Pharmacology and Experimental Therapeutics, Collegium Internationale Neuro-Psychopharmacologicum (fellow), Royal Society of Medicine (fellow), Society of Biological Psychiatry, Psychiatric Research Society, John Morgan Society, Pennsylvania Psychiatric Society, Pennsylvania Medical Society, Philadelphia Medical Society, College of Physicians of Philadelphia (fellow), Philadelphia Psychiatric Society, Philadelphia Country Club, Faculty Club of the University of Pennsylvania. *Awards, honors:* U.S. Public Health Service grants to study psychopharmacology, 1959—; M.A., University of Pennsylvania, 1971.

WRITINGS: (Editor and contributor) *Non-Specific Factors in Drug Therapy,* C. C Thomas, 1968; (editor with F. Kagan, T. Harwood, A. Rudzik, and H. Sorer, and contributor) *Hypnotics: Methods of Development and Evaluation,* Spectrum, 1975.

Contributor: D. M. Rogers, editor, *Depression and Antidepressant Drugs,* Massachusetts Department of Mental Health, 1960; Philip Solomon, editor, *Psychiatric Drugs,* Grune, 1966; J. H. Masserman, editor, *Current Psychiatric Therapies,* Grune, 1967; D. H. Efron, J. O. Cole, J. Levine, and J. R. Wittenborn, editors, *Psychopharmacology: A Review of Progress, 1957-1967,* U.S. Public Health Service, 1968; P.R.A. May and Wittenborn, editors, *Psychotropic Drug Response: Advances in Prediction,* C. C Thomas, 1969; Cole and Wittenborn, editors, *Drug Abuse: Social and Psychopharmacological Aspects,* C. C Thomas, 1969.

Wittenborn, May, and S. C. Goldberg, editors, *Psychopharmacology and the Individual Patient,* Raven Press, 1970; Levine, B. C. Schiele, and L. Bouthilet, editors, *Principles and Problems in Establishing the Efficacy of Psychotropic Agents,* U.S. Public Health Service, 1971; P. Kielholz, editor, *Relaxation Therapy for Psychosomatic Disorders,* Ciba-Geigy, 1971; O. Vinar, Z. Votava, and P. B. Bradley, editors, *Advances in Neuro-Psychopharmacology,* North-Holland, 1971; S. Garattini, E. Mussini, and L. O. Randall, editors, *The Benzodiazepines,* Raven Press, 1973; P. Kielholz, editor, *Depressive Illness: Diagnosis, Assessment, Treatment,* Hans Huber, 1972; L. E. Hollister, editor, *Anxiety: The Ubiquitous Symptom,* MEDCOM, 1972; L. Lasagna, editor, *The Use and Regulation of Combination Drugs,* Stratton Intercontinental Medical Book Corp., 1975; F. Gilbert McMahon, editor, *Principles and Techniques of Human Research and Therapeutics,* Futura Publishing, 1975.

L. A. Gottschalk and S. Merlis, editors, *Pharmacokinetics of Psychoactive Drugs: Blood Levels and Clinical Response,* Spectrum, 1976; Gottschalk, editor, *The Content Analysis of Verbal Behavior: Further Studies,* Spectrum, 1976; S. Kulber and J. Berger, editors, *Klinisch-statistiche Forschung,* F. K. Schattauer, 1976; J. P. Brady, J. Mendels, M. T. Orne, and W. Rieger, editors, *Psychiatry: Areas of Promise and Advancement,* Spectrum, 1976; M. E. Jarvik, editor, *Psycho-Pharmacology in the Practice of Medicine,* Appleton-Century-Crofts, 1977; A. Frazer and A. Winokur, editors, *Biological Bases of Psychiatric Disorders,* Spectrum, 1977; M. A. Lipton, A. DiMascio, and K. F. Killam, editors, *Psychopharmacology: A Generation of Progress,* Raven Press, 1978; L. L. Iversen and S. D. Iversen, editors, *Handbook of Psychopharmacology,* Volume XIII, Plenum, 1978; H. Helmchen and B. Mueller-Oerlinghausen, editors, *Psychiatrische Therapie-Forschung, Ethische und juristische Probleme,* Springer-Verlag, 1978; P. Deniker, C. Radouco-Thomas, and A. Villeneuve, editors, *Neuro-Psychopharmacology,* Volume I: *Proceedings of the 10th Congress of the Collegium International Neuro-Psychopharmacologicum (CINP),* Pergamon, 1978; W. G. Clark and J. del Fiordice, editors, *Principles of Psychopharmacology,* 2nd edition, Academic Press, 1978; G. Morozav, J. Saarma, and B. Silvestrini, editors, *Depression and the Role of Trazodone in Antidepressant Therapy,* Edizioni Luigi Pozzi, 1978; B. S. Brown, editor, *Clinical Anxiety/Tension in Primary Medicine: Proceedings of a Colloquium,* Excerpta Medica, 1979.

Author of research reports. Contributor to *Cyclopedia of Medicine, Surgery, Specialties,* and to symposia and proceedings. Contributor of more than 260 articles to medical journals, including *Psychopharmacology, Clinical Medicine, American Journal of Psychiatry, Archives of General Psychiatry, Journal of Clinical Pharmacology, Journal of Nervous and Mental Diseases,* and *Current Therapeutic Research.* Advisory editor in psychiatry and psychopharmacology, *Psychosomatic,* 1966-71; member of advisory board, *Psychopharmacology,* 1966-78; member of editorial board, *International Pharmacopsychiatry,* 1967—, and *Current Therapeutic Research,* 1978—; member of international editorial board, *Journal of International Medical Research,* 1972—; editor, *Pharmakopsychiatrie-Neuropsychopharmakologie,* 1973—; member of board of editorial advisors, *Annual Review of Psychiatric Drug Treatment,* 1974—, and *Progress in Neuro-Psychopharmacology,* 1977—.

*   *   *

RIDGWAY, Brunilde Sismondo 1929-

PERSONAL: Born November 14, 1929, in Chieti, Italy; came to United States in 1953; naturalized in 1963; daughter of Giuseppe G. and Maria (Lombardo) Sismondo; married Henry W. Ridgway, Jr. (a physical therapist), September 6, 1958; children: Conrad W., Eric R., Kevin P., Christopher L. *Education:* University of Messina, Laurea in Lettere Classiche, 1953; Bryn Mawr College, M.A., 1954, Ph.D., 1958; American School of Classical Studies, additional study, 1955-57. *Religion:* Roman Catholic. *Home:* 225 North Roberts Rd., Bryn Mawr, Pa. 19010. *Office:* Department of Archaeology, Bryn Mawr College, Bryn Mawr, Pa. 19010.

CAREER: Bryn Mawr College, Bryn Mawr, Pa., instructor in archaeology, 1957-60; Hollins College, Hollins College, Va., assistant professor and head of department of classics, 1960-61; Bryn Mawr College, assistant professor, 1961-67, associate professor, 1967-70, professor of archaeology, 1970—, Rhys Carpenter Professor, 1977—. Mellon visiting professor in fine arts, University of Pittsburgh, 1978. Director of summer school program at American School of Classical Studies, Athens, Greece, 1967, 1971. Member, Institute for Advanced Study, 1967-68. *Member:* International Association for Classical Archaeology, Archaeological Institute of America (life member), German Archaeological Institute. *Awards, honors:* American Council of Learned Societies grants, 1965, 1973; Philosophical Society grants, 1965, 1969; National Endowment for the Humanities grant, 1969; Guggenheim fellow, 1974-75.

WRITINGS: (Contributor) W. H. Schuchhardt, editor, *Antike Plastik 7,* German Archaeological Institute, 1967; (contributor) Carl Roebuck, editor, *The Muses at Work,* M.I.T. Press, 1969; *The Severe Style in Greek Sculpture,* Princeton University Press, 1970; *Classical Sculpture* (catalogue of the classical collection), Museum of Art, Rhode Island School of Design, 1972; *The Archaic Style in Greek Sculpture,* Princeton University Press, 1977; *Fifth Century Styles in Greek Sculpture,* Princeton University Press, in press. Also editor with W.G.F. Pinney, *Aspects of Ancient Greece,* 1979. Contributor to American and foreign archaeological journals. Editor-in-chief, *American Journal of Archaeology,* 1977—.

SIDELIGHTS: Brunilde Sismondo Ridgway wrote *CA:* "I write to ask new questions to old problems, to show that the old answers are often in need of revision. I may suggest some answers of my own, but my main purpose is to make my readers think anew."

*   *   *

RIEDMAN, Sarah R(egal) 1902-
(Sarah R. Gustafson)

PERSONAL: Born April 20, 1902, in Kishinev, Rumania; became U.S. citizen, 1918; daughter of Benjamin and Hilda (Gdansky) Regal; married Maurice F. Riedman, June 26, 1921; married second husband, Elton T. Gustafson, December 8, 1953 (died, 1969); children: (first marriage) Olin, Eric. *Education:* Hunter College (now Hunter College of the City University of New York), B.A., 1926; New York University, M.S., 1928; Columbia University, Ph.D., 1935. *Home:* 7 Palmetto Way, Jensen Beach, Fla. 33457.

CAREER: Hunter College (now Hunter College of the City University of New York), New York, N.Y., instructor, 1926-30; Brooklyn College (now Brooklyn College of the City University of New York), Brooklyn, 1930-52, began as instructor, became assistant professor of biology; free-lance scientific writer, 1952-58; Hoffmann-LaRoche, Inc., Nutley, N.J., director of medical literature, 1958-67, consultant, 1967—. Lecturer on science for young people. *Member:* American Association for Advancement of Science, Authors League, American Medical Writers Association (fellow), New York Academy of Sciences, Sigma Xi.

WRITINGS: *How Man Discovered His Body,* Young World Books, 1947, revised edition, Abelard, 1966; *The Physiology of Work and Play,* Dryden, 1950; *Water for People,* H. Schuman, 1951, revised edition, Abelard, 1961; *Grass, Our*

Greatest Crop, Thomas Nelson, 1952; *Your Blood and You,* H. Schuman, 1952, revised edition published as *Your Blood and You: The Story of Circulation,* Abelard, 1963; (with Albert Schatz) *The Story of Microbes,* Harper, 1952; *Food for People,* Abelard, 1954, 2nd revised edition, 1976; *The World through Your Senses,* Abelard, 1954, revised edition, 1962; *Let's Take a Trip to a Skyscraper,* Abelard, 1955; *Let's Take a Trip to a Fishery,* Abelard, 1956; *Our Hormones and How They Work,* Abelard, 1956, revised edition published as *Hormones: How They Work,* 1973; *Antoine Lavoisier: Scientist and Citizen,* Thomas Nelson, 1957, revised edition, Abelard, 1967; *Men and Women behind the Atom,* Abelard, 1958; *Let's Take a Trip to a Cement Plant,* Abelard, 1959; *Charles Darwin,* Holt, 1959.

Shots without Guns: The Story of Vaccination, Rand McNally, 1960, published as *The Story of Vaccination,* Bailey Bros. & Swinfen, 1974; *Trailblazer of American Science,* Rand McNally, 1961; *Masters of the Scalpel,* Rand McNally, 1962; *World Provider: The Story of Grass,* Abelard, 1962; *Naming Living Things: The Grouping of Plants and Animals,* Rand McNally, 1963; (with husband, Elton T. Gustafson) *Portraits of Nobel Laureates in Medicine and Physiology,* Abelard, 1963; *Clang, Clang: The Story of Trolleys,* Rand McNally, 1964; (with Clarence C. Green) *Benjamin Rush: Physician, Patriot, Founding Father,* Abelard, 1964; (with Charles H. Carter) *Drugs in Neurospastic Disorders,* C. C Thomas, 1965; (with E. T. Gustafson) *Home Is the Sea: For Whales,* Rand McNally, 1966; (editor) Suzanne Loebl, *Fighting the Unseen: The Story of Viruses,* Abelard, 1967; (editor) Loebl, *Exploring the Mind,* Abelard, 1968; (with E. T. Gustafson) *Focus on Sharks,* Abelard, 1969.

(Editor) Matt Warner, *Your World—Your Survival,* Abelard, 1970; *Heart,* Western Publishing, 1974; *Trees Alive,* Lothrop, 1974; (with Ross Witham) *Turtles: Extinction or Survival?,* Abelard, 1974; *How Wildlife Survives Natural Disasters,* McKay, 1977; *Sharks,* F. Watts, 1977; *Allergies,* F. Watts, 1978; *Gardening without Soil,* F. Watts, 1978; *Have You Ever Seen a Shell Walking?,* McKay, 1978; *Spiders,* F. Watts, 1979; *Diabetes,* F. Watts, 1980; *Odd Habitats of Land Animals,* McKay, 1980. Coordinating editor, under name Sarah R. Gustafson, "The Pediatric Patient," Lippincott, beginning 1963. Contributor to *World Encyclopedia, Book of Knowledge, Basic Everyday Encyclopedia,* and to magazines.

WORK IN PROGRESS: Biological Rhythms, for Crowell.

SIDELIGHTS: Sarah R. Riedman told *CA* that, as a child, "I loved to write about anything, but I never dreamed of being an author. I was much too interested in becoming a teacher of the subject I chose for my major—physiology." However, "after a number of years of teaching," Riedman continued, "I was bothered by the lack of course time available for the exciting material on the history of science. I wrote an outline for a book, which was accepted and became my first, *How Man Discovered His Body.* It was then that I was bitten by the writing bug." Riedman writes with the conviction that "science *can* be made meaningful and alive to all people—young and old." Her books have been translated into a number of languages, including Japanese, Hungarian, and Bengali.

AVOCATIONAL INTERESTS: Travel, singing, arts and crafts, gardening hiking, and sightseeing.

RIFKIN, Shepard 1918-
(Dale Michaels; Jake Logan, a house pseudonym)

PERSONAL: Born September 14, 1918, in New York, N.Y.; son of David and Bessie (Cooper) Rifkin. *Education:* City College (now City College of the City University of New York), 1936-38. *Home:* 105 Charles St., New York, N.Y. 10014. *Agent:* Knox Burger Associates Ltd., 39½ Washington Sq. S., New York, N.Y. 10012.

CAREER: Writer. Except for a period with the Merchant Marine, Rifkin summarizes his career as "too many jobs in too many places over too many years." He has held jobs as cab-driver, ambulance driver, gardener, editor, cocktail lounge manager, cook, tugboatman, and manager of the first paperback bookstore in the United States. *Wartime service:* Merchant Marine, 1942-45. *Awards, honors:* Writing fellowships to McDowell Colony, 1959, 1974, and Yaddo, 1962.

WRITINGS: Texas: Blood Red, Dell, 1956; *Desire Island,* Ace Books, 1960; *What Ship? Where Bound?* Knopf, 1961; *The Warring Breed,* Gold Medal, 1961; *King Fisher's Road,* Gold Medal, 1963; (editor) *The Savage Years,* Gold Medal, 1967; *Ladyfingers,* Gold Medal, 1969; *The Murderer Vine,* Dodd, 1970; *McQuaid,* Putnam, 1974; *The Snow Rattlers,* Putnam, 1977; *McQuaid in August,* Doubleday, 1979.

Under pseudonym Jake Logan; all published by Playboy Press: *Across the Rio Grande,* 1975; *Slocum's Woman,* 1976; *Slocum's Rage,* 1979.

WORK IN PROGRESS: A Company of Rivers, for Random House.

SIDELIGHTS: Shepard Rifkin told *CA:* "I wrote my first novel while I was driving an ambulance in East Harlem. I worked twelve hours a night, six nights a week, for forty-two dollars a week. Since [my novel] was set in Texas in the 1870's, I arrived for my research at the American history room at the New York Public Library promptly at nine a.m. every morning, spent four hours reading and making notes. Then I went home, typed up my notes, wrote, and got in a few hours of sleep before I went to work again behind the wheel of 'ambulance 27.' Whenever I meet people who put in forty hours a week at some well-paying job who'd tell me it's hard to write I am intolerant.

"Of course it's hard. I find, like most other writers, that my brain switches off after four hours. Four hours every twenty-four hours, that's all it will work. It's far more exhausting writing than moving furniture up and down five flights—and I've done that, too. I was even a foreman and driver for a moving company.

"Going to writing school is easy. It costs nothing except a library card. I admire Chekhov for two reasons, for instance: He taught me how to lure the reader into a story with his first sentence, and I learned how to emulate his superb economy in choosing images to set a scene; Dostoevsky for his magisterial handling of intense psychological analyses of people in severe stress; Conrad for his cool, imperial evasion of that dangerous malady which infects so many American writers: a passion for over-obvious symbolism. Most people think that Conrad wrote about the sea. He did not. He wrote about people who worked out their fears and manhood against the backdrop of the oceans. His sensitive yet powerful treatment of the typhoons, calms and fires which intermeshed so intimately with his captains and mates is without equal."

AVOCATIONAL INTERESTS: Travel, collecting Americana.

**RINGI, Kjell (Arne Soerensen) 1939-
(Kjell S-Ringi)**

PERSONAL: Born February 3, 1939, in Gothenburg, Sweden; son of Arne (a sales director) and Ingrid (Adolfsson) Soerensen Ringi. *Education:* Attended Sloejdfoereningen, Gothenburg, Sweden, 1955-56 and Berghs Reklamskola, Stockholm, Sweden, 1957-58. *Religion:* Protestant. *Home:* Storgatan 41-41138, Gothenburg, Sweden.

CAREER: Affiliated with Gumaelius (advertising firm), Sweden, 1960-62; author and illustrator of comic strip, "The Mirrors," for Swedish television and magazines, 1962—; painter, 1962—; illustrator-author, 1967—. Author and illustrator of comic strip, "Corks Crew." Has had exhibitions in Stockholm, Gothenburg, Amsterdam, Frankfurt, Norrkoeping, Copenhagen, New York, Chicago, Seattle, San Francisco, Dallas, Los Angeles, San Diego, and other cities in the United States and Europe. Work represented in museums and collections in the United States and Europe. *Military service:* Swedish Army, 1959-60. *Awards, honors:* Sloejdfoereningen award, 1956; Berghs Reklamskola award, 1958; citation of merit, Society of Illustrators Annual National Exhibition, 1970, for *The Winner,* and 1977, for cover illustration.

WRITINGS—Juvenile; all self-illustrated: *The Magic Stick* (also see below), Harper, 1968; *The Stranger* (Junior Literary Guild selection), Random House, 1968; *The Winner* (also see below), Harper, 1969; *The Sun and the Cloud,* Harper, 1971.

Illustrator: Adelaide Holl, *The Man Who Had No Dream,* Random House, 1969; Holl, *My Father and I* (also see below), F. Watts, 1972; Holl, *The Parade* (also see below), F. Watts, 1975.

Television films: "Pappa och Jag" (based on Ringi's and Holl's book, *My Father and I*), produced in Sweden, 1971; "Paraden" (based on Ringi's and Holl's book, *Parade*), produced in Sweden, 1971; "Parts of Ringi" (about his art), produced in Sweden, 1978. Also author of films based on *The Magic Stick* and *The Winner* and of other films based on his books, and produced by Swedish television. Contributor of illustrations to magazines in the United States and Sweden.

WORK IN PROGRESS: Continuing work on the comic strips, "The Mirror" and "Corks Crew"; picture books for children; various ideas for books and television films; paintings for exhibition in New York and elsewhere; working with tapestries and printed editions for American publishers; planning a new film about his work.

SIDELIGHTS: Author, illustrator, and painter Kjell Ringi told *CA* that since he has entered "the exciting field of children's books," he sometimes finds it difficult to decide whether to concentrate on painting or the creation of picture books for children. "I always show my books at the European and American art galleries where [my paintings are exhibited]," Ringi notes, "and I am glad to say [that my books] seem to be appreciated even by the more sophisticated and grown-up [members of] the audience." He adds, "The picture book has one big advantage [when] compared to the painting, it can be seen by many more people."

"I have worked for children in other fields, too," Ringi continues. "During the last years, I have produced several television films for children." In addition, several Swedish schools have commissioned Ringi to paint large works which are "placed in the refectories and entrances" of the buildings. "I am very happy and proud," he comments, "that they have not yet been destroyed by sandwiches and balls!"

Ringi concludes: "I think children's books can mean a lot in a person's life. [I remember] the picture books I read as a child . . . better than books I read two weeks ago. . . . I use, in my books and television films, just a few or no words to get the children to see as many things as possible in the pictures. If the parents who buy my books are also amused while looking through them with their children, I think I have succeeded. I am happy if I can give a human message through my books. I don't want to do it with grand airs or mastering manners—just with a discreet tap on the shoulder. As a matter of fact, I am a little bashful with children and, therefore, I am glad and grateful to be able to speak to them through my books."

* * *

**RIPPER, Charles L(ewis) 1929-
(Chuck Ripper)**

PERSONAL: Born October 28, 1929, in Pittsburgh, Pa.; son of Arthur Daniel (an ornamental iron worker) and Hazel Mae (an art teacher; maiden name, Porter) Ripper; married Virginia S. Ogle, August 1, 1953; children: Elisabeth Anne, Janet Gail and Joy Lee (twins). *Education:* Attended Institute of Pittsburgh. *Religion:* Presbyterian. *Home and office:* 3525 Brandon Rd., Huntington, W.Va. 25704.

CAREER: Staff illustrator, Carnegie Museum, Pittsburgh, Pa.; Standard Printing & Publishing Co., Huntington, W.Va., art director, for twelve years; currently full-time free-lance artist and illustrator of books and magazines. *Military service:* U.S. Army, Corps of Engineers, served as map draftsman, 1951-53; became sergeant. *Member:* National Audubon Society, National Wildlife Federation, National Geographic Society. *Awards, honors:* Award from West Library Association, 1957, for outstanding contributions to literature.

WRITINGS—All self-illustrated; all published by Morrow, except as indicated: *Bats,* 1954; *Hawks,* 1956; *Moles and Shrews,* 1958; *The Weasel Family,* 1959; *Ground Birds,* 1960; *Foxes and Wolves,* 1961; *Woodchucks and Their Kin,* 1963; *Swallows,* 1964; *Trout,* 1966; *Diving Birds,* 1967; *Mosquitoes,* 1969; (illustrator; under name Chuck Ripper) Dion Henderson, *A Season of Birds,* Tamarack Press, 1976; (illustrator) Theodore F. Niehaus, *A Field Guide to Pacific States Wildflowers,* Houghton, 1976.

SIDELIGHTS: Several hundred paintings by Charles L. Ripper have been sold to the National Wildlife Federation for use on conservation stamps. Ripper, who has been drawing most of his life, calls himself a realist in all forms of art. He told *CA* that he has little time for "this 'modern school' of art, which . . . dominates most of today's exhibitions and fine art galleries."

BIOGRAPHICAL/CRITICAL SOURCES: New York Times Book Review, May 4, 1969.

* * *

RIPPON, Marion E(dith) 1921-

PERSONAL: Born October 24, 1921, in Drumheller, Alberta, Canada; daughter of Arthur W. and Louise (Brownell) Simpson; married Clive Langley Rippon (a military judge in the Canadian Armed Forces), February 25, 1944; children: Michelle, David, Thomas. *Education:* University of Alberta, B.S.C., 1940; Holy Cross Hospital School of Nursing, R.N., 1943. *Home:* 849 Pemberton Rd., Victoria, British Columbia, Canada V8S 3R5.

CAREER: Victoria General Hospital, Halifax, Nova Scotia,

night supervisor, 1950; Rockcliffe Hospital, Ottawa, Ontario, night supervisor, 1951-54; Stadacona Hospital, Halifax, psychiatric nurse, 1961-63; Correspondence Branch of the Department of Education, Victoria, British Columbia, instructor in creative writing, 1971-74; University of Victoria, Victoria, lecturer in creative writing, 1974—. *Member:* American Author's Association, Mystery Writers of America.

WRITINGS—Novels: *The Hand of Solange,* Doubleday, 1969; *Behold, the Druid Weeps,* Doubleday, 1970; *The Ninth Tentacle,* Doubleday, 1974; *Ahmi,* Sono Nis Press, 1978; *Lucien's Tombs,* Doubleday, 1978. Contributor to *Writer.*

SIDELIGHTS: "I started writing a book because I wanted an electric dishwasher," Marion Rippon asserts in *Writer.* At least that is what she told her family. Her real reasons, however, were less mercenary. Rippon explains: "The desire to create had been with me as long as I could remember: to create even one fictional character so real that he would become immortal. . . . Added to this was the growing obsession that I felt I needed to prove to my family that I wasn't about to become a candidate for a senior citizens' home."

She studied best seller lists, read reviews of current work, and tried to discover what she could write about that would sell. Eventually Rippon recognized that due to her experience as a psychiatric nurse, she knew the workings of troubled minds. With that clue she began a mystery novel about Solange, the dangerously ill owner of a cafe. Rippon spent months writing, often staying up until 3 or 4 a.m. Perhaps to cure her seeming obsession, her sons chipped in and bought her that coveted dishwasher; but she was hooked, and in spite of frustration and numerous dead ends, she kept writing.

Upon finishing, Rippon "put the manuscript on a shelf in the bedroom under an old hatbox where it remained for about a month." She feared rejection and also did not know where to send it, but her husband encouraged her and then mailed the manuscript to the Doubleday Crime Club. Unsolicited manuscripts are rarely accepted, but the editors at Doubleday were impressed with Rippon's work—especially with her characterization—and in October, 1968, they accepted *The Hand of Solange* for publication.

BIOGRAPHICAL/CRITICAL SOURCES: Writer, March, 1970.

* * *

ROARK, Garland 1904-
(George Garland)

PERSONAL: Born July 26, 1904, in Groesbeck, Tex.; son of James H. and Mona Lee (Davidson) Roark; married Leola Elizabeth Burke, September 14, 1939; children: Sharon Leigh (Mrs. David Garland), Wanda Louise (Mrs. James G. Ledbetter). *Education:* Attended West Texas State Normal College (now West Texas State University), 1920. *Politics:* Republican. *Religion:* Presbyterian. *Home and office:* 1323 North Fredonia, Nacogdoches, Tex. 75961. *Agent:* Paul R. Reynolds, 12 East 41st St., New York, N.Y. 10017.

CAREER: Skillern Drug Stores, Dallas, Tex., advertising manager, 1924-28; Courthouse Pharmacies, Houston, Tex., advertising and sales manager, 1929; Walgreen Drugstores, Chicago, Ill., assistant advertising manager, 1929; Sommers Drugstores, San Antonio, Tex., advertising sales manager, 1930-33; Henke and Pillot Supermarket, Houston, member of advertising sales staff, 1933-39; Gordon Jewelry Stores, Houston, advertising director, 1941-46; novelist, 1946—. Director, Houston Heart Association, 1950-53. *Member:* Texas Institute of Letters, Colorado Authors League, East Texas Historical Association. *Awards, honors:* Western Writers of America Spur Award, 1966, for *Hellfire Jackson.*

WRITINGS—All published by Doubleday, except as indicated: *Wake of the Red Witch* (Literary Guild selection), Little, Brown, 1946, reprinted, Award Books, 1971; *Fair Wind to Java,* 1948; *Rainbow in the Royals,* 1950; *Slant of the Wild Wind,* 1952; *The Wreck of the Running Gale,* 1953; *Star in the Rigging,* 1954; *The Outlawed Banner,* 1956; *The Cruel Cocks,* 1957; *The Lady and the Deep Blue Sea,* 1958; *Captain Thomas Fenlon,* Messner, 1958; *Tales of the Caribbean,* 1959; *Should the Wind Be Fair,* 1960; *The Witch of Manga Reva,* 1962; *The Coin of Contraband,* 1964; *Bay of Traitors,* 1966; (with Charles Thomas) *Hellfire Jackson,* 1966; *Angels in Exile,* 1967 (published in England as *Sinner in the Sun,* Cassell, 1968); *Drill a Crooked Hole,* 1968.

Under pseudonym George Garland: *Doubtful Valley,* Houghton, 1951; *The Big Dry,* Houghton, 1953; *Apache Warpath,* New American Library, 1961; *Bugles and Brass,* Doubleday, 1964; *The Eye of the Needle,* Doubleday, 1970; *Slow Wind in the West,* Doubleday, 1973. Historical feature writer and columnist, *Houston Chronicle,* 1960-63.

WORK IN PROGRESS: A novel.

SIDELIGHTS: Some of Garland Roark's oil paintings form part of a permanent collection in the Sam Houston Room in Nacogdoches, Tex. Two of his books have been made into films by Republic—*Wake of the Red Witch* in 1948 and *Fair Wind to Java* in 1953. *Avocational interests:* Portrait and landscape painting.

BIOGRAPHICAL/CRITICAL SOURCES: Best Sellers, November 15, 1967, October 1, 1968.†

* * *

ROBERTS, Walter R(onald) 1916-

PERSONAL: Born August 26, 1916, in Waltendorf, Austria; came to United States in 1939, naturalized in 1944; son of Ignatius R. (an editor and writer) and Elisabeth (Diamant) Roberts; married Gisela K. Schmarak, August 22, 1939; children: William M., Charles E., Lawrence H. *Education:* Cambridge University, M.Litt., 1940, Ph.D., 1980. *Home:* 4449 Sedgwick St., N.W., Washington, D.C. 20016. *Office:* Board for International Broadcasting, 1030 15th St. N.W., Washington, D.C. 20005.

CAREER: Harvard University, Law School, Cambridge, Mass., research assistant, 1940-42; U.S. Office of War Information, Voice of America, New York, N.Y., writer and editor, 1942-49; U.S. Department of State, Washington, D.C., foreign affairs officer, 1950-53; U.S. Information Agency, Washington, D.C., deputy assistant director, 1954-60; counselor for public affairs at U.S. Embassy in Belgrade, Yugoslavia, 1960-66; counselor to U.S. Mission to International Organizations, Geneva, Switzerland, 1967-69; U.S. Information Agency, deputy associate director, 1969-71, associate director, 1971-74; Georgetown University, Washington, D.C., director of diplomatic studies at the Center for Strategic and International Studies, 1974-75; Board for International Broadcasting, Washington, D.C., executive director, 1975—. Press officer, U.S. Delegation to Austrian Treaty Talks, 1949, 1955. Diplomat in residence, Brown University, 1966-67. *Awards, honors:* Distinguished honor award, U.S. Information Agency, 1974.

WRITINGS: Tito, Mihailovic and the Allies, 1941-1945, Rutgers University Press, 1973; (with Terry Deibel) *Culture and*

Information: Two Foreign Policy Functions, Sage Publications, Inc., 1976. Contributor to *Slavic Review.*

* * *

ROBINSON, Anthony (Christopher) 1931-

PERSONAL: Born March 10, 1931, in Hindenburg, Germany; son of Henry Morton and Gertrude (Ludwig) Robinson (U.S. citizens); married Mary Chika, 1957 (died, 1976); children: Jennifer, Henry. *Education:* Columbia University, B.A., 1953, M.A., 1960. *Politics:* Democrat. *Religion:* Roman Catholic. *Home:* 153 Huguenot St., New Paltz, N.Y. 12561. *Office:* Department of English, State University of New York College, New Paltz, N.Y. 12561.

CAREER: State University of New York College at New Paltz, 1964—, began as instructor, currently associate professor of English. *Military service:* U.S. Navy, 1953-56; became lieutenant junior grade. *Member:* United University Professions, Alpha Delta Phi. *Awards, honors:* Fletcher Pratt Memorial fellowship, Bread Loaf Writers' Conference, 1960; State University of New York faculty fellowship, 1966, 1970, and 1971.

WRITINGS: A Departure from the Rules, Putnam, 1960; *The Easy Way,* Simon & Schuster, 1963; *Home Again, Home Again,* Morrow, 1969. Work anthologized in *Best American Short Stories, 1957.*

WORK IN PROGRESS: A novel, tentatively entitled *Life and Life Only;* short stories.

SIDELIGHTS: Anthony Robinson told *CA:* "Since *Home Again, Home Again* [was published in] 1969, I have written two full-length novels, both of which were rejected by publishers. It's enough to make a writer lay down his pen. One thing I know, writing doesn't become easier. But now I've started a new novel and again I feel hopeful; it must be the process." *Avocational interests:* Dry fly fishing, small game hunting, and golf.

BIOGRAPHICAL/CRITICAL SOURCES: New York Times Book Review, January 19, 1969; *Best Sellers,* February 1, 1969.

* * *

ROBINSON, Roland Inwood 1907-

PERSONAL: Born August 24, 1907, in Pellston, Mich.; son of James Inwood and Florence (Barnard) Robinson; married Lucy Domboorajian, 1933; children: Beth Watson, Rucha Evalyn. *Education:* Western State Teachers College (now Western Michigan University), B.A., 1927; University of Michigan, Ph.D., 1937. *Home:* 4345 Wausau Rd., Okemos, Mich. 48864.

CAREER: Public schools, Oscoda, Mich., mathematics and physics teacher, 1927-28; University of Michigan, Ann Arbor, junior instructor, 1929-34; Federal Reserve Board, Washington, D.C., research associate and economist, 1934-46, adviser, Division of Research and Statistics, 1956-61; National Association of Mutual Savings Banks, New York City, economist, 1946-47; Northwestern University, Evanston, Ill., professor of banking, 1947-56; National Bureau of Economic Research, New York City, staff member of postwar capital markets project, 1955-56; Michigan State University, East Lansing, professor of financial administration and economics, 1961-74. Lecturer, Central States School of Banking, 1949-56; consultant on public debt management, U.S. Treasury Department, 1951-52; U.S. representative at conference of Economic Commission for Europe on saving, Geneva, 1957; lecturer, SEANZA School of Central Banking, Sydney, Australia, 1958. *Member:* American Finance Association (vice-president, 1951-53; president, 1953-54), American Economic Association, Phi Beta Kappa, Cosmos Club (Washington, D.C.). *Awards, honors:* Ford Foundation fellowship, 1962.

WRITINGS: (Contributor) *Banking Studies,* Federal Reserve System, 1943; (contributor) *American Fiscal Policy,* Prentice-Hall, 1951; (editor) *Financial Institutions,* Irwin, 1951, 3rd edition, 1960; *Management of Bank Funds,* McGraw, 1951, 2nd edition, 1962; *Market for State and Local Government Securities,* Princeton University Press, 1960; *Money and Capital Markets,* McGraw, 1964, revised edition (with Dwayne Wrightsman) published as *Financial Markets: The Accumulation and Allocation of Wealth,* McGraw, 1974, 2nd edition, 1980; (with Robert W. Johnson) *Self-Correcting Problems in Finance,* Allyn & Bacon, 1967, 3rd edition, 1976. Contributor to scholarly and financial publications.

WORK IN PROGRESS: Small Business Finance, with emphasis on technologically-based enterprises.

SIDELIGHTS: Roland Robinson wrote *CA:* "Textbook writing, which started out as a sideline, became my major occupation. My goal has been to bring originality and vitality to what is too often an exercise in slavish recasting of other textbooks." *Avocational interests:* Playing with chamber music groups.

* * *

ROGERS, Carl R(ansom) 1902-

PERSONAL: Born January 8, 1902, in Oak Park, Ill.; son of Walter Alexander and Julia (Cushing) Rogers; married Helen Elliott, 1928 (died March 29, 1979); children: David E., Natalie. *Education:* University of Wisconsin, B.A., 1924; Columbia University, M.A., 1928, Ph.D., 1931; attended Union Theological Seminary, New York, N.Y., 1924-26. *Home:* 2311 Via Siena, La Jolla, Calif.

CAREER: Institute for Child Guidance, New York, N.Y., fellow in psychology, 1927-28; Society for the Prevention of Cruelty to Children, Rochester, N.Y., psychologist, 1928-30, director of child study department, 1930-38; Rochester Guidance Center, Rochester, director, 1939; Ohio State University, Columbus, professor of psychology, 1940-45; University of Chicago, Chicago, Ill., professor of psychology and executive secretary, Counseling Center, 1945-57; University of Wisconsin—Madison, professor in departments of psychology and psychiatry, 1957-63; Western Behavioral Sciences Institute, La Jolla, Calif., resident fellow, 1964-68; Center for Studies of the Person, La Jolla, resident fellow, 1968—. Visiting professor at Columbia University, University of California, Los Angeles, Harvard University, and other colleges, 1935-54. Lecturer, University of Rochester, 1935-40; psychological consultant to Army Air Forces, 1944; director of counseling services of United Service Organizations, 1944-45; member of executive committee, Wisconsin Psychiatric Institute, University of Wisconsin, 1960-63. Fellow, Center for Advanced Study in the Behavorial Sciences, 1962-63.

MEMBER: American Association for Applied Psychology (charter member; fellow; chairman of clinical section, 1942-44; president, 1944-45), American Orthopsychiatric Association (fellow; vice-president, 1941-42), American Psychological Association (fellow; president, 1946-47; president of division of clinical and abnormal psychology, 1949-50), American Academy of Psychotherapists (charter member; president, 1956-58), American Academy of Arts and Sciences (fellow), Phi Beta Kappa, Phi Kappa Alpha. *Awards, honors:* Nicholas Murray Butler Silver Medal from Columbia University, 1955; special contribution award, American Psychological Association, 1956, for research in the field of psychotherapy; Knapp Professorship (honorary) at University of Wisconsin, 1957; selected as humanist of the year, American Humanist Association, 1964; distinguished contribution award, American Pastoral Counselors Association, 1967; American Psychological Association, distinguished professional contribution award, 1972, and distinguished professional psychologist award from Division of Psychotherapy, 1972. D.H.L. from Lawrence College (now University), 1956, and University of Santa Clara, 1971; honorary doctorate from Gonzaga University, 1968; D.Sc. from University of Cincinnati, 1974, and Northwestern University, 1978; D.Ph. from University of Hamburg, 1975; DS.Sc. from University of Leiden, 1975.

WRITINGS: Measuring Personality Adjustment in Children Nine to Thirteen Years of Age, Teachers College, Columbia University, 1931; *The Clinical Treatment of the Problem Child,* Houghton, 1939; *Counseling and Psychotherapy,* Houghton, 1942; (co-author) *Counseling with Returned Servicemen,* McGraw, 1946; *Client-Centered Therapy: Its Current Practice, Implications, and Theory,* Houghton, 1951; (editor with Rosalind F. Dymond) *Psychotherapy and Personality Change,* University of Chicago Press, 1954; *On Becoming a Person,* Houghton, 1961; (editor and co-author) *The Therapeutic Relationship with Schizophrenics,* University of Wisconsin Press, 1967; *Person to Person: The Problem of Being Human,* Real People Press, 1967; (editor with William R. Coulson) *Man and the Science of Man,* C. E. Merrill, 1968; *Freedom to Learn: A View of What Education Might Become,* C. E. Merrill, 1969; *Carl Rogers on Encounter Groups,* Harper, 1970; *Becoming Partners: Marriage and Its Alternatives,* Delacorte, 1972; *Carl Rogers on Personal Power,* Delacorte, 1977. Contributor of many articles in psychological, psychiatric, and educational journals.

* * *

ROGERS, (Grenville) Cedric (Harry) 1915-

PERSONAL: Born May 29, 1915, in Schenectady, N.Y.; son of Stanley Reginald Harry and Frances (Clare) Rogers; married Victoria Walden Bergman, 1946; children: Adam, Christina, Simon. *Education:* Attended Dulwich College and Goldsmith's School of Art. *Agent address:* Evelyn Singer Agency, Inc., Box 163, Briarcliff Manor, N.Y. 10510.

CAREER: Illustrator, cartoonist, portrait painter, and author. *Military service:* Royal Air Force, 1940-45; became flight lieutenant. *Member:* Chelsea Arts Club (London).

WRITINGS: (Self-illustrated) *Rags, Bottles, and Bones: Paul's Amazing Collection,* McKay, 1962; *A Collectors Guide to Minerals, Rocks and Gemstones in Cornwall and Devon,* D. Bradford Barton, 1968; *Finding Britain's Gems,* Lapidary, 1972; *Pebble Polishing and Pebble Jewellery,* Hamlyn, 1973; *Rocks and Minerals,* Triune Books, 1973; *How to Buy a Camera,* Lapidary, 1977. Contributor of cartoons to *Punch.*

AVOCATIONAL INTERESTS: Photography, mineralogy.†

* * *

ROGERS, Dorothy 1914-

PERSONAL: Born May 31, 1914, in Ashburn, Ga.; daughter of Edwin A. and Ella Mae (Evans) Rogers. *Education:* University of Georgia, A.B., 1934, M.A., 1936; Duke University, Ph.D., 1947. *Home:* Franklin Street, Oswego, N.Y. 13126. *Office:* Department of Psychology, State University of New York College, Oswego, N.Y. 13126.

CAREER: Public school teacher in Sumner, Ga., 1934-35, and Birmingham, Ala., 1935-44; State University of New York College at Oswego, instructor, 1946-48, assistant professor, 1948-50, professor of psychology, 1950—. *Member:* American Association of University Professors, American Psychological Association, New York State Psychological Association, Phi Beta Kappa, Phi Kappa Phi, Kappa Delta Pi. *Awards, honors:* Educator's Award, Delta Kappa Gamma International Society, 1958.

WRITINGS: Mental Hygiene in Elementary Education, Houghton, 1957; *Jeopardy and a Jeep: Africa Conquered by Two Women Professors,* Richard Smith, 1957; *Oswego: Fountainhead of Teacher Education,* Appleton, 1961; *The Psychology of Adolescence,* Appleton, 1962, 3rd edition, Prentice-Hall, 1977; *Highways across the Horizon,* R. Hale, 1966; *Child Psychology,* Brooks/Cole, 1969, 2nd edition, 1977; (compiler) *Issues in Adolescent Psychology,* Appleton, 1969, 3rd edition, Prentice-Hall, 1977; (compiler) *Issues in Child Psychology,* Brooks/Cole, 1969, 2nd edition, 1977; (compiler) *Readings in Child Psychology,* Brooks/Cole, 1969; *Adolescence: A Psychological Perspective,* Brooks/Cole, 1972, 2nd edition, 1978; *The Adult Years: An Introduction to Aging,* Prentice-Hall, 1979; *Issues in Adult Development,* Brooks/Cole, 1980; *Issues in Lifespan Human Development,* Brooks/Cole, 1980. Contributor of chapters to books and of more than twenty articles to periodicals.†

* * *

ROGERS, Francis M(illet) 1914-

PERSONAL: Born November 26, 1914, in New Bedford, Mass.; son of Frank Leo and Laura Sylvia Rogers; married Nathalie Mary Esselborn, July 25, 1942 (died, 1968); married Elsie Bann La Carrubba, October 24, 1970; children: (first marriage) Sheila Mary. *Education:* Cornell University, A.B., 1936; Harvard University, A.M., 1937, Ph.D., 1940. *Home:* 202 Grove St., Belmont, Mass. 02178. *Office:* Widener Library, Harvard University, Cambridge, Mass. 02138.

CAREER: Harvard University, Cambridge, Mass., Society of Fellows, junior fellow, 1940-41, instructor, 1945-46, associate professor, 1946-52, professor of Romance languages and literatures, 1952-77, Nancy Clark Smith Professor of the Language and Literature of Portugal, 1977—, chairman of department, 1947-49, 1961-66, dean of Graduate School of Arts and Sciences, 1949-55. Member of administrative board, International Association of Universities, 1950-55. Advisor, Institute of International Education, committee on graduate studies, 1949-56, Emmanuel College, Boston, Mass., 1956—, and Assumption College, Worcester, Mass., 1958—. Honorary professor, University of San Marcos, Lima, Peru, 1961. Trustee, St. John's Seminary, 1968-76, and Old Dartmouth Historical Society and Whaling Museum, 1970-73. *Military service:* U.S. Marine Corps, on active duty, 1941-45, serving in Morocco, Sicily, and at Salerno Bay; became lieutenant colonel; awarded Silver Star, and Chevalier of the Legion of Honor (France). U.S. Marine Corps Reserve, 1946—.

MEMBER: American Association of Teachers of Spanish and Portuguese, Society for the History of Discoveries (president, 1968-69), Hispanic Society of America, Phi Beta Kappa, Phi Kappa Phi, Pi Delta Phi, Delta Phi Alpha, Delta Epsilon Sigma (honorary), Pi Lambda Beta, Portuguese Educational Society (honorary member), Hakluyt Society (London), International Academy of Portuguese Culture (Lisbon; corresponding member).

AWARDS, HONORS: Litt.D., Loyola University, Chicago, Ill., 1952; L.H.D., Duquesne University, 1953, Assumption College, 1960, New Bedford Institute of Technology, 1963, and Georgetown University, 1966; LL.D., Miami University, Oxford, Ohio, 1953, Stonehill College, 1957, Providence College, 1960; DR, Universidade da Bahia, Brazil, 1959; Camoes Prize (Portugal), 1961, for *The Travels of the Infante Dom Pedro of Portugal,* and 1962, for *The Quest for Eastern Christians.*

WRITINGS: (Contributor) *The Preparation of College Teachers,* American Council Studies, 1950; *Higher Education in the United States: A Summary View,* Harvard University Press, 1952, 3rd edition, 1960; (contributor) *Yearbook of Comparative and General Literature IV,* University of North Carolina Press, 1955; *The Obedience of a King of Portugal,* University of Minnesota Press, 1958; *List of Editions of the Libro del Infante don Pedro of Portugal,* [Lisbon], 1959; *The Travels of the Infante Dom Pedro of Portugal,* Harvard University Press, 1961; *The University of San Marcos in Lima, Peru,* University of San Marcos Press, 1961; *The Quest for Eastern Christians: Travels and Rumor in the Age of Discovery,* University of Minnesota Press, 1962; (with David T. Haberly) *Brazil, Portugal, and Other Portuguese-Speaking Lands,* Harvard University Press, 1968; *Precision Astrolabe: Portuguese Navigators and Trans-Oceanic Aviation,* Academia Internacional da Cultura Portuguesa (Lisbon), 1971; *Americans of Portuguese Descent: A Lesson in Differentiation,* Sage Publications, Inc., 1974; *The Portuguese Heritage of John Dos Passos,* Portuguese Continental Union of the United States of America (Boston), 1976; *Atlantic Islanders of the Azores and Madeiras,* Christopher, 1979.

Contributor to *Encyclopaedia Britannica.* Contributor of articles and reviews to professional journals in Portugal, Peru, and the United States. Member of advisory committee, *International Bulletin of Luso-Brazilian Bibliography,* 1959-73.

SIDELIGHTS: Francis M. Rogers has traveled extensively throughout Portugal and its colonies. His *Higher Education in the United States* has been translated into thirteen languages.

* * *

ROGERS, George Calvin, Jr. 1922-

PERSONAL: Born June 15, 1922, in Charleston, S.C.; son of George Calvin (a school superintendent) and Helen (Bean) Rogers. *Education:* College of Charleston, B.A., 1943; University of Chicago, M.A., 1948, Ph.D., 1953; University of Edinburgh, additional study, 1949-50. *Politics:* Democrat. *Religion:* Episcopalian. *Home:* 1819 Seneca Ave., Columbia, S.C. 29205. *Office:* Department of History, University of South Carolina, Columbia, S.C. 29208.

CAREER: University of Pennsylvania, Philadelphia, instructor, 1953-56; Hunter College (now Hunter College of the City University of New York), New York, N.Y., instructor, 1956-57; Emory University, Atlanta, Ga., assistant professor, 1957-58; University of South Carolina, Columbia, assistant professor, 1958-63, associate professor of history, 1963-66, professor, 1966-72, Yates Snowden Professor of History, 1972—. Chairman of Committee on Scholarly Activities, South Carolina Tricentennial Commission, 1967-71. Visiting research fellow, Merton College, Oxford University, 1975. *Military service:* U.S. Army Air Forces, 1943-46; became first lieutenant. *Member:* American Historical Association, American Antiquarian Society, Southern Historical Association, Organization of American Historians, South Carolina Historical Society (president, 1978-80). *Awards, honors:* Award of merit, American Association for State and Local History, 1963, and Russell Award for creative research, University of South Carolina, both for *Evolution of a Federalist: William Loughton Smith of Charleston, 1758-1812;* alumnus of the year, College of Charleston, 1979.

WRITINGS—All published by University of South Carolina Press, except as indicated: *Evolution of a Federalist: William Loughton Smith of Charleston, 1758-1812,* 1962; (editor) *The Papers of Henry Laurens,* Volume I (with Philip Hamer), 1968, Volume II, 1970, Volume III, 1972, Volume IV (with David Chesnutt), 1974, Volume V, 1976, Volume VI (with others), 1978, Volume VII, 1979, Volume VIII, 1980; *Charleston in the Age of the Pinckneys,* University of Oklahoma Press, 1969; *The History of Georgetown County, South Carolina,* 1970. Also author, *A South Carolina Chronology, 1497-1970.* Editor, *South Carolina Historical Magazine,* 1964-70. Member of board of editors, *Journal of Southern History.*

* * *

ROGERS, George W(illiam) 1917-

PERSONAL: Born April 15, 1917, in San Francisco, Calif.; son of George Arthur and Mary Jane (Smith) Rogers; married Jean M. Clark, 1942; children: Shelley M., Goeffrey W., Sidney M., Gavin W., Sabrina M., Garth W. *Education:* University of California, Berkeley, B.A., 1942, M.A., 1943; Harvard University, Ph.D., 1950. *Home:* 1790 Evergreen Ave., Juneau, Alaska. *Office:* Department of Economics, University of Alaska, Juneau, Alaska.

CAREER: Standard Oil Company, San Francisco, Calif., statistical clerk, 1934-39; University of California, Berkeley, research assistant, 1942-43; Office of Price Administration, San Francisco, Calif., and Juneau, Alaska, economist and price executive, 1943-45; Office of the Governor, Juneau, economic advisor, 1946-47; U.S. Department of the Interior, Juneau, economist and chairman of Alaska Field Commission, 1950-56; Arctic Institute of North America, Juneau, staff social scientist, 1956-60; University of Alaska, Juneau, professor of economics, 1961—. Visiting fellow, Cambridge University, 1967-78. Member, City Council, Juneau, 1956-57, and City and Borough Assembly, 1970-74. *Member:* American Economic Association, Arctic Institute of North America.

WRITINGS: Alaska in Transition: The Southeast Region, Johns Hopkins Press, 1960, revised edition, 1967; *Alaska's Future: The Economic Consequences of Statehood,* Johns Hopkins Press, 1962, revised edition, 1970; (with R. A. Cooley) *Alaska's Population and Economy, 1950-1980,* two volumes, University of Alaska Press, 1963; (contributor) St. J. Macdonald, editor, *The Arctic Frontier,* University of Toronto Press, 1966; (editor) *Change in Alaska: People, Petroleum and Politics,* University of Washington Press, 1970; (with W. J. Mead) *Transporting Gas from the Arctic,* American Enterprise Institute, 1977; (with D. Kresge and T. Morehouse) *Issues in Alaska Development,* University of Washington Press, 1978; (with T. Armstrong and G. Rowley) *The Circumpolar North: An Economic Geography,* Methuen, 1978.

* * *

ROGERS, Michael 1950-

PERSONAL: Born November 29, 1950, in Santa Monica, Calif.; son of Don Easterday (an engineer) and Mary (Gilbertson) Rogers; married Janet Hopson, October 23, 1976.

Education: Stanford University, B.A., 1972. *Agent:* Elizabeth McKee, Harold Matson Co., 22 East 40th St., New York, N.Y. 10016.

CAREER: Rolling Stone, New York, N.Y., contributing editor, 1973—; founding editor, *Outside* Magazine, 1975-77. *Member:* Authors Guild. *Awards, honors:* American Association for the Advancement of Science—Westinghouse award for distinguished science writing, 1974.

WRITINGS: Mindfogger, Knopf, 1973; *Biohazard,* Knopf, 1977; *Do Not Worry About the Bear* (short stories), Knopf, 1979. Books columnist, *Rolling Stone,* 1973-74. Contributor of short fiction to *Playboy, Esquire,* and *Rolling Stone.*

WORK IN PROGRESS: A novel about the computer industry, for Simon & Schuster.

SIDELIGHTS: Michael Rogers told *CA:* "I write journalism to support my fiction habit. If I wasn't a writer, I'd like to be a forest ranger, a doctor, a rural mailman, or a photographer." *Avocational interests:* Fly-fishing, skiing, travel.

BIOGRAPHICAL/CRITICAL SOURCES: Chicago Tribune, March 11, 1979; *Nation,* April 7, 1979; *Washington Post Book World,* April 12, 1979.

* * *

ROGERS, Timothy (John Godfrey) 1927-

PERSONAL: Born April 24, 1927, in Birkenhead, England; son of John Douglas Wales (a captain in the Royal Navy) and Marjorie Leslie (Scholfield) Rogers; married Eva Schack (a cultural correspondent for a Danish newspaper), July 20, 1951; children: Jennifer, Jonathan, Nicola. *Education:* King's College, Cambridge, B.A., 1951, M.A., 1955. *Politics:* Radical. *Religion:* Church of England. *Home:* Broad Meadow, 9 Leicester Lane, Desford, Leicester LE9 9JJ, England. *Office:* Bosworth College, Desford, Leicester, LE9 9JL, England.

CAREER: Leighton Park School, Reading, Berkshire, England, assistant teacher, 1952-56; Pocklington School, East Riding, Yorkshire, England, head of English, 1956-64; Dixie Grammar School (now reorganized into Bosworth College), Market Bosworth, England, headmaster, 1965-69; Bosworth College, Desford, Leicester, England, principal of upper school and community college, 1969—. *Military service:* British Army, Royal Tank Regiment, 1945-48; became lieutenant.

WRITINGS—All published by Routledge & Kegan Paul: *Rupert Brooke: A Reappraisal and Selection from His Writings, Some Hitherto Unpublished,* 1971; *School for the Community: A Grammar School Reorganizes,* 1971; *Georgian Poetry: 1911-1922,* 1977; *Those First Affections: An Anthology of Poems Composed between the Ages of Two and Eight,* 1979. Contributor to *Times Literary Supplement* and *English.*

SIDELIGHTS: Timothy Rogers wrote *CA* that he is "particularly interested in the Powys family: John Cowper, Theodore Francis, and Llewelyn; but especially in Littleton Powys, A. R. Powys (architect and writer), Philippa Powys (novelist and poet), Marion Powys (lacemaker), and Gertrude Powys (painter)—yes, they were all siblings!"

* * *

ROGOW, Arnold Austin 1924-

PERSONAL: Born August 10, 1924, in Harrisburg, Pa.; son of Morris and Mary (Hilelson) Rogow; children: Jennifer, Jeanne. *Education:* University of Wisconsin, A.B., 1947; Princeton University, A.M., 1950, Ph.D., 1953. *Agent:* James Brown Associates, 25 West 43rd St., New York, N.Y. *Office:* 1100 Madison Ave., New York, N.Y. 10028.

CAREER: University of Iowa, Iowa City, instructor, 1952-54, assistant professor, 1955-57; Haverford College, Haverford, Pa., assistant professor, 1958-59; Stanford University, Stanford, Calif., associate professor, 1959-64, professor of political science, 1964-66; City College of the City University of New York, New York, N.Y., professor of political science, 1966—. *Military service:* U.S. Army, Infantry, 1943-46; awarded Purple Heart. *Member:* American Political Science Association, American Psychoanalytic Association, Authors Guild, P.E.N. *Awards, honors:* Social Science Research Council fellow, 1951-52; Center for Advanced Study in the Behavioral Sciences fellow, 1954-55; Guggenheim fellowship, 1965-66; research grants from Ford Foundation and Fund for the Republic.

WRITINGS: The Labour Government and British Industry, 1945-51, Basil Blackwell, 1955, Cornell University Press, 1956; (editor) *Government and Politics: A Reader,* Crowell, 1961; (editor) *The Jew in a Gentile World: An Anthology of Writings about Jews, by non-Jews,* Macmillan, 1961; (with Harold Lasswell) *Power, Corruption and Rectitude,* Prentice-Hall, 1963; *James Forrestal: A Study of Personality, Politics and Policy,* Macmillan, 1964; (editor) *Politics, Personality and Social Science in the Twentieth Century,* University of Chicago Press, 1969; *The Psychiatrists,* Putnam, 1970; *The Dying of the Light: A Searching Look at America Today,* Putnam, 1975. Contributor to *Nouvel Observateur, New Statesman, Book Week,* and other publications.

AVOCATIONAL INTERESTS: Collecting antiquities.

* * *

ROHRBACH, Peter Thomas 1926-
(James P. Cody)

PERSONAL: Born February 27, 1926, in New York, N.Y.; son of James Peter and Kathryn (Foley) Rohrbach; married Shiela Sheehan, September 21, 1970; children: Sarah Catherine. *Education:* Catholic University of America, A.B., 1951, M.A., 1953. *Home and office:* 9609 Barkston Ct., Potomac, Md. 20854.

CAREER: Former Roman Catholic priest, served as superior of the Discalced Carmelite Monastery, Washington, D.C.; currently free-lance author and editorial consultant. Member of summer faculty, Georgetown University, 1961-70. *Member:* Authors Guild, P.E.N., International Association of Writers.

WRITINGS: Conversation With Christ, Fides, 1956; *A Girl and Her Teens,* Bruce Publishing, 1959, 7th edition, 1965; *A Gentle Fury,* Doubleday, 1959; *Bold Encounter,* Bruce Publishing, 1960; *The Search for St. Therese,* Doubleday, 1961; *The Photo Album of St. Therese,* Kenedy, 1962; *The Art of Dynamic Preaching,* Doubleday, 1965; *Journey to Carith,* Doubleday, 1966; *The Disillusioned,* Doubleday, 1968; (under pseudonym James P. Cody) *The French Killing,* Berkeley Publishing, 1975. Also author, under pseudonym James P. Cody, of *Top Secret Kill,* 1974, *Search and Destroy,* 1974, *Your Daughter Will Die,* 1975, and *The D.C. Man.* Author of several television and film scripts, including "Flying the Seasons," 1974, and "Safe Flight," for the Federal Aviation Administration, 1976. Contributor of numerous articles to encyclopedias, magazines, and newspapers. Editor, *Avtech,* 1977—.

BIOGRAPHICAL/CRITICAL SOURCES: Best Sellers, October 15, 1968.

* * *

ROHRBERGER, Mary 1929-

PERSONAL: Born January 22, 1929, in New Orleans, La.; daughter of Adolph (a manufacturer) and Flora (Ketry) Rohrberger. *Education:* Tulane University, B.A., 1950, M.A., 1952, Ph.D., 1962. *Residence:* Perkins, Okla. *Office:* Department of English, Oklahoma State University, Stillwater, Okla. 74074.

CAREER: Oklahoma State University, Stillwater, assistant professor, 1962-66, associate professor, 1966-72, professor of English, 1972—. Conducts graduate seminars and workshops around the country. *Member:* Modern Language Association of America, National Council of Teachers of English, American Association of University Professors, South Central Modern Language Association, Phi Beta Kappa.

WRITINGS: Hawthorne and the Modern Short Story, Mouton, 1966; (with Samuel H. Woods, Jr. and Bernard Dukore) *An Introduction to Literature,* Random House, 1968; (with Woods) *Reading and Writing about Literature,* Random House, 1970; *The Art of Katherine Mansfield,* University of Microfilms, 1977; *Story to Anti-story,* Houghton, 1979. Contributor of articles and reviews to literature journals. Fiction editor, *Cimarron Review.*

WORK IN PROGRESS: Surrealism in British and American Fiction.

SIDELIGHTS: Mary Rohrberger told *CA* that she is "maintaining a continuing interest in the Socratic Dialogue as a teaching strategy."

* * *

ROLL, Charles W(eissert), Jr. 1928-

PERSONAL: Born July 26, 1928, in Trenton, N.J.; son of Charles W. (a dentist) and Katherine (Horn) Roll. *Education:* Princeton University, A.B., 1950; Columbia University, M.A., 1953. *Home:* 2797 Main St., Lawrenceville, N.J. 08648. *Office:* Advocacy Management, Inc., 1525 New Hampshire N.W., Washington, D.C.

CAREER: Gallup Organization, Princeton, N.J., study director, 1958-77; Advocacy Management, Inc., Washington, D.C., vice-president of research, 1979—. President, Political Surveys & Analyses, Inc., 1971-75. Founder and president of Polls, Inc., 1974—. Consultant to Turkish Airlines. *Military service:* U.S. Army, 1954-56.

WRITINGS: (With A. H. Cantril) *Hopes and Fears of the American People,* Universe Books, 1971; (with Cantril) *Polls: Their Use and Misuse in Politics,* Basic Books, 1972. Contributor to *Journal of American History* and *Public Opinion Quarterly.*

SIDELIGHTS: Charles W. Roll wrote *CA:* "My interest in writing has centered around that which I feel I know best, my work. My motivation has been to translate an unnecessarily arcane profession into simple guidelines that will enable the layman to understand survey research and, if he or she is sufficiently sensitive and sophisticated, to do it—thanks to me."

* * *

ROLT, L(ionel) T(homas) C(aswall) 1910-1974

PERSONAL: Born February 11, 1910, in Chester, England; died May 9, 1974; son of Lionel Caswall and Jemima Alice (Timperley) Rolt; married Sonia Mary South; children: Two sons. *Education:* Attended Cheltenham College. *Home:* Stanley Pontlarge, Winchcombe, Gloucestershire GL54 5HD, England. *Agent:* A. P. Watt & Son, 26/28 Bedford Row, London WC1R 4HL, England.

CAREER: Served apprenticeship as mechanical engineer for steam and diesel locomotives, 1926-31; Sentinel Wagon Works Ltd., Shrewsbury, England, fitter, 1932; John I. Thornycroft & Co. Ltd., Basingstroke, England, fitter, 1933; Phoenix Green Garage, Hartley Row, England, partner, 1934-39; Ministry of Supply, London, England, technical assistant, 1941-45; writer, 1944-74. Talyllyn Railway Co., general manager, 1951-52, superintendent of line, beginning 1955, chairman, 1963-68. Member of Inland Waterways Development Advisory Committee, 1959-62, Science Museum Advisory Council, beginning 1964, and York Railway Museum Committee, beginning 1973. Occasional lecturer and broadcaster. *Member:* Inland Waterways Association (co-founder and secretary, 1946-51), Royal Society of Literature (fellow), Society for the History of Technology (member of advisory council, 1964-69; member of executive committee, beginning 1969), Newcomen Society (member of council, beginning 1958; vice-president, 1965), Talyllyn Railway Preservation Society (founder, 1951; vice-president, 1955), Vintage Sports Car Club (honorary founder), Bugatti Owners Club (honorary member; member of competitions committee, beginning 1959). *Awards, honors:* M.A., University of Newcastle, 1965; M.Sc., University of Bath, 1973.

WRITINGS: Narrow Boat (travel diary), Eyre & Spottiswoode, 1944, 2nd revised edition, 1978; *High Horse Riderless* (nonfiction), Allen & Unwin, 1946; *Sleep No More: Twelve Stories of the Supernatural,* Constable, 1948, published as *Sleep No More: Railway, Canal and Other Stories of the Supernatural,* Harvester Press, 1974; *Worcestershire* (nonfiction), R. Hale, 1949; *Green and Silver* (nonfiction), Allen & Unwin, 1949; *The Inland Waterways of England* (nonfiction), Allen & Unwin, 1950, reprinted, 1979; *Horseless Carriage: The Motor-Car in England* (nonfiction), Constable, 1950; *The Thames from Mouth to Source* (nonfiction), Batsford, 1951; *Lines of Character* (nonfiction), Constable, 1952, 2nd edition, Harvester Press, 1975; *Railway Adventure* (nonfiction), Constable, 1953, new edition, David & Charles, 1961, reprinted, 1977; *Winterstroke* (fiction), Constable, 1954; *The Clouded Mirror* (nonfiction), Bodley Head, 1955; *Red for Danger: A History of Railway Accidents and Railway Safety Precautions,* Bodley Head, 1955, 3rd edition, David & Charles, 1977; *A Picture History of Motoring,* Macmillan, 1956; *Isambard Kingdom Brunel* (biography), Longmans, Green, 1957, St. Martin's, 1959; *Motor Cars* (juvenile nonfiction), Educational Supply Association (London), 1957; *Canals* (juvenile nonfiction), Educational Supply Association, 1958; *Thomas Telford* (biography), Longmans, Green, 1958; *Look at Railways* (juvenile nonfiction), Hamish Hamilton, 1959.

The Cornish Giant: The Story of Richard Trevithick, Father of the Steam Locomotive (juvenile biography), Lutterworth, 1960, St. Martin's, 1962; *George and Robert Stephenson: The Railway Revolution* (biography), Longmans, Green, 1960, reprinted, Greenwood Press, 1977, published as *The Railway Revolution: George and Robert Stephenson,* St. Martin's, 1962; *Look at Canals* (juvenile nonfiction), Hamish Hamilton, 1962; *Great Engineers* (nonfiction), G. Bell, 1962, St. Martin's, 1963; *James Watt* (biography), Batsford, 1962, Arco, 1963; *Thomas Newcomen: The Prehistory of the Steam Engine* (biography), David & Charles, 1963; *Alec's Adventures in Railwayland,* I. Allan, 1964; *A Hunslet*

Hundred: One Hundred Years of Locomotive Building by the Hunslet Engine Company (nonfiction), David & Charles, 1964; *Inside a Motor Car* (juvenile nonfiction), I. Allan, 1964; *Motoring History*, Studio Vista, 1964; *Patrick Stirling's Locomotives* (nonfiction), Hamish Hamilton, 1965; *Tools for the Job: A Short History of Machine Tools*, Batsford, 1965, published as *A Short History of Machine Tools*, M.I.T. Press, 1965; (editor) *Talyllyn Century: The Talyllyn Railway, 1865-1965*, David & Charles, 1965; *The Story of Brunel* (biography), Methuen, 1965, Abelard-Schuman, 1968; *The Aeronauts: A History of Ballooning, 1783-1903*, Walker, 1966; *Transport and Communications*, Methuen, 1967; *The Mechanicals*, Heinemann, 1967; *Railway Engineering*, Macmillan, 1968; *Navigable Waterways*, Longmans, Green, 1969; *Waterloo Ironworks: A History of Taskers at Andover, 1809-1968*, Augusta M. Kelley, 1969; (editor and author of introduction) *Best Railway Stories*, Faber, 1969.

Victorian Engineering, Allen Lane, 1970; (author of introduction) Samuel Smiles, *Industrial Biography*, David & Charles, 1970; *Landscape with Machines* (autobiography), Longman, 1970; *The Making of a Railway*, H. Evelyn, 1971; *From Sea to Sea: The Canal du Midi*, Allen Lane, 1973, Ohio University Press, 1974; *The Potters' Field: A History of the South Devon Ball Clay Industry*, David & Charles, 1974; (with J. S. Allen) *The Steam Engine of Thomas Newcomen*, Science History Publications, 1977; *Landscape with Canals* (autobiography), Allen Lane, 1977. General editor, "Industrial Archaeology" series, Longman. Contributor to various papers and magazines.

SIDELIGHTS: L.T.C. Rolt's chief interest was the history of technology, particularly developments in the field of transportation. He once lived on a canal boat for twelve years, traveling on most of the inland waterways of England and Ireland (his experiences are described in the book, *Narrow Boat*). An old car enthusiast as well, Rolt often used vintage cars for everyday travel and was the organizer of the first Anglo-American vintage car rally in Britain in 1954.

In 1951, Rolt founded the Talyllyn Railway Preservation Society in an attempt to keep the Talyllyn Railway in business. Established in 1865, the railway was one of the very few British public railway companies not nationalized after World War II. It has since been run by the Society on a semi-volunteer basis with enough success to inspire the formation of similar organizations throughout Britain and elsewhere. Rolt's book *Railway Adventure* recounts the story of this preservation effort.

L.T.C. Rolt served as technical advisor to Ealing Studios for the 1944 film "Painted Boats."

BIOGRAPHICAL/CRITICAL SOURCES: L.T.C. Rolt, *Landscape with Machines* (autobiography), Longman, 1970; *London Times*, May 11, 1974; Rolt, *Landscape with Canals* (autobiography), Allen Lane, 1977.†

* * *

ROMAN, Eric 1926-

PERSONAL: Name legally changed in 1959; born March 26, 1926, in Bekescsaba, Hungary; became U.S. citizen in 1959; son of Henry (a lawyer and military defense attorney) and Margaret (Frank) Herzog; married Eva Fazekas, 1953; children: Lynda, Ronald. *Education:* Rudolf Real Gymnasium, Matura, 1943; Hunter College (now Hunter College of the City University of New York), B.A., 1958; New York University, M.A., 1959, Ph.D., 1965. *Home:* 24 Grand Pl., Newton, Conn. 06470. *Office:* Department of History, Western Connecticut State College, Danbury, Conn. 06810.

CAREER: Variously employed in Hungary, France, Brazil, and Canada; affiliated with U.S. Treasury Department, New York, N.Y., 1959-65; Western Connecticut State College, Danbury, 1965—, began as instructor, currently professor of history and political science. *Military service:* Served in Hungarian army, 1943-45. *Awards, honors:* Americanism Medal from National Daughters of the American Revolution, 1970.

WRITINGS: The Best Shall Die, Prentice-Hall, 1961; *After the Trial*, Citadel, 1968; *A Year as a Lion*, Stein & Day, 1978. Contributor to *East European Quarterly* and *Journal of Philosophy*.

SIDELIGHTS: Eric Roman told *CA:* "For so long I've believed that it was the intensity of experience during the first 25 years of my life that turned me to writing: persecution in my youth, the war, being under a death sentence as a deserter and, later, an inmate in a concentration camp, a two-year odyssey through Europe and parts of the Americas, the struggle to build a livelihood in a strange land. But the impulse to write persisted long after the experiences became mere memories. Life to me is an inexhaustible font of potential literary themes. But I cannot think of writing as a full-time occupation unless it involves extensive and demanding research. Full-time writers tend to become either narcissistic or opportunistic. I paraphrase Kierkegaard when I say, 'Do your writing in the arena!'

"Existentialist thinking has strongly influenced my literary imagination. I regard the positing of a situation in which the fictional character faces an authentic choice, without a guideline for proper action, the most effective literary device. It is a measure of the writer's skill to what extent he can make such a situation, even if the dilemma is superficially minor, so genuine that even the most passive reader feels compelled to choose for the hero, or to agree or disagree with his choice."

In 1974, Roman's book, *After the Trial*, was made into a motion picture by Twentieth Century-Fox.

* * *

RONNE, Finn 1899-1980

PERSONAL: Born December 20, 1899, in Horten, Norway; came to United States in 1923; naturalized citizen in 1929; died January 12, 1980, in Bethesda, Md.; son of Martin Richard and Maren Gurine (Gulliksen) Ronne; married Edith Maslin, March 18, 1944; children: Karen. *Education:* Horten Technical College, degree in naval architecture and marine engineering, 1922. *Home:* 6323 Wiscassett Rd. N.W., Washington, D.C. 20016.

CAREER: Fred-Olsen Shipping Co., Oslo, Norway, engineering assistant, 1922-23; Bethlehem Ship Building Co., Elizabeth, N.J., engineer, 1923; Westinghouse Electric Corp., Pittsburgh, Pa., engineer, 1923-33, 1935-39; ski expert, Second Byrd Antarctic Expedition, 1933-35; second in command, East Base, U.S. Antarctic Service Expedition, 1939-41; leader and commander, Ronne Antarctic Research Expedition, 1946-48; member of Antarctic expedition with the Argentine Navy, 1958-59; leader of Arctic expedition to Spitsbergen, 1962-63. Appointed first American postmaster of Antarctica, Oleana Base, 1946. Commanding officer and science director of Weddell Sea Station, Ellsworth Base, and Edith Ronne Land (Antarctica). Consultant to U.S. Department of Defense. *Military service:* U.S. Navy, 1941-61; on active duty as captain, 1958; received three special congressional gold medals, 1938, 1943, and 1958, and U.S. Congressional Gold Medal, 1967. *Member:* American Geophysical

Union (life member), Arctic Institute (member of board, 1949-52), American Polar Society (honorary member; vice president), American Antarctic Association (chairman), Trimetrogon Engineering Society, American Geographical Society (fellow), Explorers Club (life member), Arktisk Club (Norway; honorary member), Adventure Club (New York), Gibson Island Club, Masonic Lodge. *Awards, honors:* Explorers Club citation of merit, 1963, gold medal, 1965; President's Legion of Merit Award, 1964; Knight of the Royal Order of St. Olav (Norway), 1965; Elish-Kent-Kane gold medal of the Geographical Society of Philadelphia, 1966; decoration from the government of Argentina, 1967.

WRITINGS: Antarctic Conquest, Putnam, 1949; *Antarctic Command,* Bobbs-Merrill, 1961; *The Ronne Expedition to Antarctica,* Messner, 1971; *Antarctica—My Destiny,* Hastings House, 1979. Contributor to *Encyclopedia Americana, Encyclopaedia Britannica,* and to numerous journals, including *Geographical Review, Scientific Monthly,* and *Explorers Journal.*

WORK IN PROGRESS: Keeno, a book about sledge-dog experiences; *Antarctic Picture Album,* the history of the Antarctic in pictures with short chapters of explanation; *A Life-Span in Exploration,* his autobiography.

SIDELIGHTS: Finn Ronne's interest in Antarctic exploration came at a young age. His father, a polar explorer, had been a member of Roald Amundsen's expedition to the South Pole upon its discovery in 1911. This early exposure inspired Ronne to further explore the Antarctic, first with Admiral Byrd and, later, as the leader of his own expeditions.

Ronne's third trip, the privately financed Ronne Antarctic Research Expedition, occurred in 1946 and resulted in the photographed exploration of the world's last uncharted coastline—a 450 mile stretch from Palmer Land to Coast Land at the edge of the Weddell Sea. In addition, over 250,000 square miles of land were discovered and claimed, including Edith Ronne Land, named for the explorer's wife, the first woman to set foot in Antarctica. In all, 134 new place names were added, and detailed investigations in eleven branches of science were conducted.

Ronne's Antarctic expedition, according to George Goodman, Jr. of the *New York Times* "was notable, too, as the first occasion of its kind to include the participation of women as scientific researchers, one of whom was ... Ronne's wife, Edith. The other scientist was Jenny Darlington."

Ronne's was the last private expedition to venture to the Antarctic continent. He told *CA:* "As a result of the present day onslaught, the aroma of polar exploration and its adventure has faded away. Where only a handful of men struggled independently to solve the mysteries looming over the horizon, now, every year, thousands of men are in action."

Ronne also spent two seasons in the Canadian arctic and Greenland. He made several television appearances and was a frequent lecturer in the United States and abroad.

AVOCATIONAL INTERESTS: Skiing, photography, and stamp collecting.

BIOGRAPHICAL/CRITICAL SOURCES: Congressional Record, May 10, 1949, February 9, 1960; *New York Times,* January 14, 1980.

* * *

ROSENBAUM, Veryl 1936-

PERSONAL: Born October 6, 1936, in Windsor, Ontario, Canada; daughter of Archibald Henry (a bookkeeper) and Edith (Bernard) Ellis; married Jean Rosenbaum (a physician, psychoanalyst, writer, and composer), February 14, 1962; children: Ronnie, Marc. *Education:* Attended University of Michigan; Wayne State University, B.A., 1960; attended New Mexico Psychoanalytic Institute, 1969. *Politics:* None. *Religion:* None. *Home address:* Route 2, P.O. Box 115N, Durango, Colo. 87501.

CAREER: Catholic Maternity Institute, Santa Fe, N.M., family counselor, 1964-67; psychoanalyst in private practice, 1965—. *Member:* National Association for Accreditation in Psychoanalysis, Southwest Association for Psychoanalysis (president, 1973—), New Mexico Association for Psychoanalysis (secretary, 1971-73).

WRITINGS: Long Way from Home (poems), American Poet Press, 1965; *Being Female: Understanding and Enjoying Your Physical, Sexual, and Emotional Nature,* Prentice-Hall, 1973; *Mother, Daughter, Self,* Tower, 1979.

With husband, Jean Rosenbaum: *The Psychiatrists' Cookbook,* Sunstone Press, 1972; *Conquering Loneliness,* Hawthorn, 1973; *Dental Psychology,* Dental Economics Press, 1974; *Stepparenting,* Chandler & Sharp, 1979; *How to Avoid Divorce,* Harper, 1980; *Living with Teenagers,* Stein & Day, 1980. Also author with J. Rosenbaum of *Preparing for Retirement* and *Lifemanship.*

Author of column, "Emotionally Speaking," *Coronet,* 1972-73. Contributor to magazines, including *Prism, Parents' Magazine, New Ingenue, Dental Economics,* and *Dynamic Maturity.*

WORK IN PROGRESS: A novel, *My Sister Pamela;* two screenplays, "The Bond" and "The Children of Cerenon."

SIDELIGHTS: Veryl Rosenbaum told *CA:* "Writers stay forever young. I am a beginning novelist and screenplay writer. All writers belong to a special family of gifted people, and we should always lend each other emotional support and advice. Armor yourself against rejection, present your work with professional excellence, and develop patience. Have a good love life to keep your spirits high and your priorities straight." *Avocational interests:* Wood gathering for survival, meditation, fishing.

* * *

ROSSI, Alice S(chaerr) 1922-

PERSONAL: Born September 24, 1922, in New York, N.Y., daughter of William A. (an experimental machinist) and Emma Clara (Winkler) Schaerr; married second husband, Peter Henry Rossi, September 29, 1951; children: (second marriage) Peter Eric, Kristin Alice, Nina Alexis. *Education:* Brooklyn College (now Brooklyn College of the City University of New York), B.A., 1947; Columbia University, Ph.D., 1957. *Politics:* Independent. *Religion:* None. *Home:* 34 Stagecoach Rd., Amherst, Mass. 01002. *Office:* Department of Sociology, University of Massachusetts, Amherst, Mass. 01003.

CAREER: Cornell University, Ithaca, N.Y., research associate in sociology and anthropology, 1951-52; Harvard University, Cambridge, Mass., research associate at Russian Research Center, 1952-54, research associate in Graduate School of Education, 1954-55; University of Chicago, Chicago, Ill., lecturer in sociology, 1959-61, research associate in anthropology, 1961-62, research associate in sociology, 1963-64, research associate at National Opinion Research Center, 1964, research associate for Committee on Human Development, 1964-67; Johns Hopkins University, Baltimore, Md., research associate in social relations, 1967-69; Goucher College, Towson, Md., associate professor, 1969-71, professor of sociology and anthropology, 1971-74; University of Massachusetts—Amherst, professor, 1974—. Worked for War Manpower Commission, Lend Lease, and municipal nursery and day care center, 1942-46. Social Science Research Council, member of board of directors, 1971, chairman of board of directors, 1976-78; member of board of directors, Schlesinger Library (of Harvard University), 1972-75. Member of task force, Citizens Council on Status of Women, Family Law and Policy, 1967-68; member of advisory council of fellowship program for married women, Danforth Foundation, 1967-69; member of advisory board of committee on marriage and divorce, National Conference of Commissioners on Uniform State Laws, 1968-71; member of academic advisory council, Kirkland College, 1968-71; member of National Commission for the Observance of International Women's Year, 1977-78.

MEMBER: American Sociological Association (vice-president, 1974-76), Sociologists for Women in Society (president pro tempore, 1971-72), American Council on Education, American Association of University Professors (vice-president, 1974-76), National Academy of Sciences (member of committee on ability testing, 1978-80), National Association for Repeal of Abortion Laws (member of board of directors, 1969-72), National Organization for Women (member of governing board, 1966-70), Eastern Sociological Society (president-elect, 1972-73; president, 1973-74), Washington Opportunities for Women (member of board of directors, 1971—). *Awards, honors:* Career development awards, National Institute of Mental Health, 1965-67, 1967-69; D.H.L. from Towson State College, 1973; Dr. Sci. from Rutgers University, 1975; Dr. L.L. from Simmons College, 1977.

WRITINGS: (Contributor) Robert K. Mertman and Paul F. Lazarsfeld, editors, *Continuities in Social Research,* Free Press, 1950; (contributor) Robert Lifton, editor, *The Woman in America,* Beacon Press, 1965; (contributor) Jacquelyn A. Mattfeld and Carol G. Van Aken, editors, *Women and the Scientific Professions,* M.I.T. Press, 1965; (contributor) Robert Hall, editor, *Abortion in a Changing World,* Volume I, Columbia University Press, 1970; (editor and contributor) John Stuart Mill and Harriet Taylor Mill, *Essays on Sex Equality,* University of Chicago Press, 1970; (contributor) Joseph Zubin and John Money, editors, *Critical Issues in Contemporary Sexual Behavior,* Johns Hopkins Press, 1972; (editor) *The Feminist Papers: From Adams to de Beauvoir,* Columbia University Press, 1973; (editor with Ann Calderwood) *Academic Women on the Move,* Russell Sage, 1973; (editor with J. Kogan and T. Hareven) *The Family,* Norton, 1978.

Contributor to symposia. Contributor of about twenty-five articles to journals, including *American Journal of Psychiatry, Psychology Today, Dissent, Atlantic Monthly, American Sociologist,* and *Humanist.* Member of editorial board, *American Sociological Review,* 1969-72.

* * *

ROSSNER, Robert 1932-
(Ivan T. Ross)

PERSONAL: Born March 25, 1932, in New York, N.Y.; married Judith Perelman (a writer), June 13, 1954 (divorced); married Leah Goldschmidt, 1975; children: (first marriage) Jean, Daniel; (second marriage) Talya. *Education:* City College of New York (now City College of the City University of New York), B.A., 1953, post-graduate study, 1956-58; Hunter College (now Hunter College of the City University of New York), graduate study, 1956-58. *Agent:* Raines & Raines, 475 Fifth Ave., New York, N.Y. 10017.

CAREER: Board of Education, New York, N.Y., high school English teacher, 1957-71; magazine editor, 1972—.

WRITINGS: Year without an Autumn: Portrait of a School in Crisis, Baron, 1969; *A Hero like Me; A Hero like You,* Saturday Review Press, 1972; *The End of Someone Else's Rainbow,* Saturday Review Press, 1974.

Under pseudonym Ivan T. Ross; all mysteries: *Murder Out of School,* Simon & Schuster, 1960; *Requiem for a Schoolgirl,* Simon & Schuster, 1961; *Old Students Never Die,* Doubleday, 1962; *The Man Who Would Do Anything,* Doubleday, 1963; *Teacher's Blood,* Doubleday, 1964.

AVOCATIONAL INTERESTS: Travel, gardening.

* * *

ROTH, Philip (Milton) 1933-

PERSONAL: Born March 19, 1933, in Newark, N.J.; son of Herman and Bess (Finkel) Roth; married Margaret Martinson, February 22, 1959 (died, 1968). *Education:* Attended Rutgers University, 1950-51; Bucknell University, A.B., 1954; University of Chicago, M.A., 1955, additional study, 1956-57.

CAREER: Novelist and short story writer. Instructor, University of Chicago, Chicago, Ill., 1956-58; visiting lecturer, University of Iowa, Iowa City, 1960-62. Writer-in-residence, Princeton University, 1962-64, and University of Pennsylvania, 1965-80. *Military service:* U.S. Army, 1955-56. *Member:* National Institute of Arts and Letters, Phi Beta Kappa. *Awards, honors:* Aga Khan Award, *Paris Review,* 1958; Houghton-Mifflin literary fellowship, 1959; National Institute of Arts and Letters grant, 1959; National Book Award for fiction, 1960, and Daroff Award, Jewish Book Council of America, both 1960, for *Goodbye, Columbus, and Five Short Stories;* Guggenheim fellowship, 1960; received O. Henry second prize award, 1960; Ford Foundation grant in playwrighting, 1965; American Book Award nomination (declined), 1980, for *The Ghost Writer.*

WRITINGS—Novels: *Letting Go,* Random House, 1962; *When She Was Good,* Random House, 1967; *Portnoy's Complaint,* Random House, 1969; *The Breast,* Holt, 1972; *The Great American Novel,* Holt, 1973; *My Life as a Man,* Holt, 1974; *The Professor of Desire,* Farrar, Straus, 1977; *The Ghost Writer,* Farrar, Straus, 1979.

Short stories: *Goodbye, Columbus, and Five Short Stories* (novella and short stories), Houghton, 1959; *On the Air,* New American Library, 1969.

Other: *Our Gang (Starring Tricky and His Friends),* Random House, 1971; *Reading Myself and Others,* Farrar, Straus, 1975; *The Philip Roth Reader,* Farrar, Straus, in press. Short stories have been published in *Best American Short Stories,* edited by Martha Foley, Houghton, 1955, 1959, and 1960, *The American Judaism Reader,* edited by Paul Krish, Abelard, 1967, and *Penguin Modern Stories,* Penguin, 1969. Contributor of reviews to *New Republic;* contributor to many periodicals including *Esquire, Harper's, New Yorker, Commentary,* and *Paris Review.*

SIDELIGHTS: The publication of *Portnoy's Complaint* in 1969 established Philip Roth, in the eyes of many critics, as one of the few novelists who successfully explore the problems of contemporary Jewish life and family. Discussing the writings of Roth and the "Jewish Renaissance" of the 1950's and 1960's in an article in *Saturday Night,* Robert Fulford feels that "one of the great events of the culture of this period is the development of Jewish-American fiction. Nothing that has happened in literature in North America since 1945 is so impressive as the wave of Jewish writing. A minority that was culturally underprivileged only a few decades ago now finds itself dominating serious literature. . . . My guess is that it amounts to a kind of historical coincidence: the Jew as writer has arrived on the scene at the moment when he happened to be needed, and when his special abilities could be most usefully employed."

One thing that may set Roth apart from the other talented writers in this genre, *Judaism* critic Joel Grossman believes, is the fact that "Philip Roth may well be, as one looks over his works, the inventor of the Jewish novel of manners. . . . Roth concerns himself with what Lionel Trilling calls 'that part of a culture which is made up of half-uttered or unutterable expressions of value.' . . . It is in this way that Roth can be seen as a 'Jewish' novelist—he sets out to define what the manners of American Jews are; not what they believe, but how they act. . . . [Maybe] the great contribution of the Jewish novelists as a group and of Roth specifically, their close analysis of 'manners as the indication of the direction of man's soul,' may, in the end, serve to tell us not only what Jews in America were like at a specific moment, but, also what the culture they separated themselves from was like."

Often described by critics as a Jewish writer writing Jewish novels, Roth has been both criticized and praised for his depictions of Jewish life. Much of the criticism is based on Roth's satirical portrayal of his characters. These critics feel Roth's characterizations are not accurate. Peter Shaw writes in *Commentary* that he believes "Roth's insistence that he is a friend to the Jews can only theoretically be squared with the loathing for them that he displays in his work. . . . The real message here, or rather the real aspiration, is not to sweep away anti-Semitism, but to transcend being Jewish. If only you try hard enough, Roth's books tell us, it can be done. This is a message that will not do the Jews any more damage than other specious advice that they have received from time to time, so that one has to agree with Roth that his books are not harmful as charged. But if he has not been bad *for* the Jews, he had decidedly been bad *to* them—and at the expense of his art. . . . Roth has been a positive enemy to his own work, while for the Jews he has been a friend to the proverbial sort that makes enemies unnecessary."

However, many critics seem to disagree with Shaw. One of these reviewers, *New York Times* critic Christopher Lehmann-Haupt, feels *Portnoy's Complaint* is "a technical masterpiece that succeeds in 274 pages in bringing the genre of the so-called Jewish novel (whose various practitioners have more or less dominated the literary scene for the last two decades) to an end on a new point of departure."

While acknowledging that some readers may be led to believe that Roth's writings are anti-Semitic, Irving Howe feels there is more to Roth's writing and offers *Portnoy's Complaint* as an example. Howe writes in *Commentary* that "*Portnoy's Complaint* is not, as enraged critics have charged, an anti-Semitic book, though it contains plenty of contempt for Jewish life. Nor does Roth write out of traditional Jewish self-hatred. . . . What the book speaks for is a yearning to undo the fate of birth; there is no wish to do the Jews any harm . . . nor any desire to engage with them as a fevered antagonist: Portnoy is simply crying out to be left alone, to be released from the claims of distinctiveness and the burdens of the past, so that, out of his own nothingness, he may create himself as a 'human being.' Who, born a Jew in the 20th century, has been so lofty in spirit never to have shared this fantasy? But who, born a Jew in the 20th century, has been so foolish in mind as to dally with it for more than a moment?"

In answer to the charges that he has no respect for his Jewish heritage, Roth told George Plimpton in an interview in the *New York Times Book Review:* "I myself have always been far more pleased by my good fortune in being born a Jew than any of my critics may begin to imagine. It's a complicated, interesting, orally demanding and very singular experience, and I like that. There is no question but that it has enriched my life. . . . I find myself in the historic predicament of being Jewish, with all its implications. Who could ask for more?"

Humor is another vital factor in Roth's writings. Albert Goldman writes in *Life* that Roth "had learned to be funny when he was a child, probably on those walks from [his] grade school in the Weequahic section of Newark to the little Hebrew school fifteen minutes away. In that precious quarter of an hour those highly regimented Jewish kids could blow off steam and subject the pyramided pieties of their world to a healthy dose of desecratory humor. For a few minutes they could afford to be bad. Being bad and being funny were much the same thing in Roth's mind."

In his review of *The Breast* in the *New York Times Book Review,* John Gardner addresses the subject of Roth's humor. He writes: "Sensibly, casually, Roth plays the existentialist jive for laughs. . . . The humor and pathos come from his solid grasp of how life is, his firm knowledge of the importance of strength of character and the will to live. . . . The trick which is the heart of the book is brilliant: to celebrate the ordinary, the silly, the banal."

However, Stanley Cooperman does not appreciate Roth's humor. As he comments in *Twentieth Century Literature:* "Roth's laughter too often becomes thin-souled, a kind of simpering posture directed against human potential for significant pain or joy. This lack of significance shapes the essential *reductive* quality of Roth's work; in many of his short stories and novels, with the exception of *Letting Go,* whether writing of a Jewish milieu or (less convincingly) of a Gentile one, whether writing of sex, politics, marriage, religion, ambition, or motherhood, Roth reduces human beings to carnival snap-shots of themselves—sometimes comic, sometimes ugly, sometimes wistful, but always without that strength of existence, that awareness of moral truth which (even when attenuated) redeems our temporal grotesqueries into the possibility of significant human action."

Roth's comic humor is often compared to that of the late Lenny Bruce. A reviewer for *Time* points out that "although the literary qualities of *Portnoy's Complaint* are uniquely Roth's, the monologue technique is pure show biz. The similarities between Portnoy's delivery and that of the late Satirist Lenny Bruce are readily apparent. While Bruce used scatology in his nightclub performances as a tool, primarily to uncover social hypocrisies, his savage humor also gained its neurotic style from conflicts about appearance and reality." The reviewer completes the comparison by informing the readers that "although sex, psycholanalysis and Jewishness form the content of [*Portnoy's Complaint*], they are not its subject. The book is about absurdity—the absurdity of a man who knows all about the ethnic, sociological and Freudian hang-ups."

However, when asked if Bruce was a great influence on his writings, Roth told an interviewer for the *New York Times Book Review:* "Not really, I would say I was somewhat more strongly influenced . . . by a sit-down comic named Franz Kafka and a very funny bit he does called *The Metamorphosis*. . . . I never saw Bruce work, by the way, though I've heard tapes and records, and since his death I've watched a movie of one of his performances and read a collection of his routines. I recognize and admire in him what I used to admire in the "Second City Company" at it's best, that joining of precise social observation with extravagant and dream-like fantasy."

Although many critics recognize and compliment Roth on his writing style and seeming overabundance of talent, a number of critics can not overlook what they feel is unnecessarily explicit sex and the frequent use of obscene language. In 1970, the government of Australia banned *Portnoy's Complaint*, calling the book "obscene." Gerda Charles writes in the *Jewish Quarterly* that "*Portnoy's Complaint* could conceivably . . . be the pornographic novel to end all contemporary pornography. . . . Mr. Roth fails just as badly as other writers of erotica in portraying either the pleasure or—and this is the really astonishing omission in a writer of his large and melancholy talent—the famous *post coitus* sadness of sex."

According to a reviewer for *Time:* "No one has written so amusingly and yet crassly about sex since Henry Miller. It is no secret that laughter is one of man's best defenses against those things that embarrass and terrorize him. Neither is it a secret that those who can make us laugh the loudest are often the most embarrassed and terrorized."

Saul Maloff seems to sum up the feelings of several critics in his review in *Commonweal*. He writes: "Although there are 'redeeming social values' in generous profusion—of narrative drive and comic vitality, of lunatic wit and that murderous precision of social observation that has always been Roth's birthright—let's not distract ourselves with apologetic cant. *Portnoy's Complaint* is a desperately dirty novel; and that, like it or not, is its chief joy and aesthetic principle. In order to impart some sense of its central and pervasive quality, one would have to scald this page with an assaultive spilling-out of all the famous words and phrases which—despite all fatuous (and disingenuous) disclaimers about how 'boring' they are in their insane and brutal repetitiveness—have never lost their ancient power to shock and appall, repel and magnetize, disgust and delight, disclose and illuminate, for better or worse; which is to say they have never, in the hands of a master, lost any of their old power to perform the full work of a literary language."

However, Roth feels that he uses certain words and sets his characters in specific scenes for a purpose. As he tells George Plimpton: "Obscenity as a usable and valuable vocabulary, and sexuality as a subject, have been available to us since Joyce, and I don't think there's a serious American writer in his thirties who has felt restricted by the times particularly, or suddenly now feels liberated because these have been advertised as 'the swinging sixties.' In my writing lifetime, the use of obscenity has by and large been governed by one's literary taste and tact and not by the mores of the audience."

Roth continues: "My . . . book, *Portnoy's Complaint*, is full of dirty words and dirty scenes; my . . . book, *When She Was Good*, had none. Why is that? Because I've suddenly become 'a swinger'? Because I'm no longer 'uptight'? But then I was apparently 'swinging' all the way back in 1957, with 'Epstein'. And what about all those dirty words in *Letting Go*? No, no. The reason there is no obscenity, or blatant sexuality either, in *When She Was Good* is because it would have been beside the point, gratuitous, ridiculous—above all, destructive of what I was up to. *When She Was Good* takes place among very conventional and upright small town Middle Westerners; their uprightness and conventionality shaped not only their own language, but my own. In order to create a certain moral susceptibility in the reader (and in myself) to these plain people, I tried in my prose to come up with a slightly heightened version of their own rare language, for instance to employ their cliches and banalities in the narration itself. Not to satirize then, you see, but to communicate as fully as I could their way of seeing and judging; it occurs to me that I was trying to create a certain *respect* for them in their ordinariness."

In addition to the criticism of Roth's treatment of sex in his books, a number of reviewers have objected to Roth's characterization of women, specifically that he fails to make the women in his novels three-dimensional. Robert Towers remarks in the *New York Times Book Review* that "Roth who writes so obsessively about sexuality, fails to create convincing and unsentimentalized young female characters and the deficiency is serious, amounting to what is finally a structural defect. It is as though one half of his equation is missing. All we are left with is the self-preoccupied young man and the various phantasms with which—like St. Anthony in the desert—he must contend." Towers continues his observation, illustrating what he regards as flaws in Roth's writing: "The attitudes toward women, toward sexuality, toward what is likeable or contemptible in his male characters, toward psychoanalytical interpretations—these are all inconsistent enough to suggest a lack of steady authorial control, a tendency to grasp at whatever seems cleverest or most astonishing or most intense at the moment. The resultant myopia, confusion of affect, and lapses into sentimentality are, however, much less obvious than they would be in a writer whose intelligence and stylistic resources were inferior to Roth's."

And finally, Marya Mannes writes in *Saturday Review* that she believes that "the sexual exploits of Portnoy the man are one more noxious instance of the writer-intellectual being 'with it.' . . . Roth's way is in making Portnoy an intellectual-liberal public servant crying his heart out to his unseen analyst about the terrible obsession that ultimately ruins his life. . . . Again, as in most of the new 'culture,' woman gets the short end of the stick even if she gets the long end of the antihero. Her use, and her interest, reside in one place only, and that place is certainly not mind or spirit. As on today's stage she is stripped naked, not merely of clothes . . . but of every quality that makes a whole woman."

Geoffrey Wolff writes in *Newsweek* that he feels that *Portnoy's Complaint* is "a refreshing change, this is a controversial novel that seems to have been read by almost as many people as have expressed their opinions of it. At this late time there is little left to say except to remind those who have not read it that *Portnoy's Complaint* is a landmark in America fiction. Too much has been said about Portnoy's sexuality, and about his Jewishness, and about his mother. The most astonishing thing about Philip Roth's novel is its language. Within the limits of a monologue, and restricting his character to rage and self-contempt, Roth manages to ring virtuoso changes in mood and expression. The funniest novel I have ever read."

Goodbye, Columbus was filmed by Paramount in 1969; *Letting Go* was filmed by Leon Mirell Productions, Inc. and Noblelight Productions in 1969; *Portnoy's Complaint* was filmed by Warner Bros. in 1972. Three of Roth's short stories have been dramatized for the theatre by Larry Arrick and produced under the title "Unlikely Heroes."

BIOGRAPHICAL/CRITICAL SOURCES: Saturday Review, April 11, 1959, May 16, 1959, June 16, 1962; *Time,* May 11, 1959, June 15, 1962, February 1, 1963, February 21, 1969; *New York Herald Tribune Book Review,* May 17, 1959, June 17, 1962; *New York Times Book Review,* May 17, 1959, June 17, 1962, February 23, 1969, November 7, 1971, September 17, 1972, May 6, 1973, September 18, 1977, September 2, 1979; *New Republic,* June 15, 1959; *New Yorker,* June 20, 1959; *Spectator,* October 23, 1959; *New Statesman,* October 31, 1959, November 30, 1962; *Times Literary Supplement,* November 13, 1959, November 23, 1962.

Atlantic, July, 1962, December, 1971; Alfred Kazin, *Contemporaries,* Little, Brown, 1962; Irving Malin and Irwin Stark, editors, *Breakthrough,* McGraw, 1964; Richard Kostelanetz, editor, *On Contemporary Literature,* Avon, 1964; *Life,* February 7, 1969, April 25, 1969; *New York Times,* February 18, 1969, February 21, 1969, September 4, 1979, April 16, 1980; *Newsweek,* February 24, 1969, December 22, 1969, Augusm 3, 1970; *New York Review,* February 27, 1969; *Commonweal,* March 21, 1969; *Cue,* March 29, 1969; *Saturday Night,* April, 1969; *Commentary,* May, 1969, December, 1972, September, 1974; *New York,* May 12, 1969; *Jewish Quarterly,* summer, 1969.

Esquire, May, 1970; Solotaroff, *The Red Hot Vacuum,* Atheneum, 1970; *Variety,* November 10, 1971; *Library Journal,* May 1, 1973; *Twentieth Century Literature,* July, 1973; *Contemporary Literary Criticism,* Gale, Volume I, 1973, Volume II, 1974, Volume III, 1975, Volume IV, 1975, Volume VI, 1976, Volume IX, 1978; *The Critical Point,* Horizon, 1973; *Harper's,* July, 1974; J. N. McDaniel, editor, *The Fiction of Philip Roth,* Haddonfield, 1974; B. F. Rodgers, *Philip Roth,* Scarecrow, 1974; Philip Roth, *Reading Myself and Others,* Farrar, Straus, 1975; *Judaism,* winter, 1977; *New York Review of Books,* October 27, 1977; *Detroit News,* November 13, 1977; *Washington Post Book World,* September 2, 1979; *Chicago Tribune Book World,* September 9, 1979.

—*Sketch by Margaret Mazurkiewicz*

* * *

ROTHENBERG, Jerome 1931-

PERSONAL: Born December 11, 1931, in New York, N.Y.; son of Morris and Esther (Lichtenstein) Rothenberg; married Diane Brodatz, December 25, 1952; children: Matthew. *Education:* College of the City of New York (now City College of the City University of New York), B.A., 1952; University of Michigan, M.A., 1953. *Home addresses:* 1026 San Abella, Encinitas, Calif. 92024; and Box 433, Salamanca, N.Y. 14779. *Office:* c/o New Directions, 80 Eighth Ave., New York, N.Y. 10011.

CAREER: Poet, teacher, and translator; Hawk's Well Press and *Poems from the Floating World,* New York City, founder, publisher, and editor, 1959-64; Mannes College of Music, New York City, instructor in English, 1961-70; *Some/Thing,* New York City, co-editor, 1965-69; *Alcheringa: A First Magazine of Ethnopoetics,* New York City, coeditor, 1970-76; editor, *New Wilderness Letter,* 1976—. University of California, San Diego, Regents professor, 1971, professor of visual arts, 1977-79; visiting research professor, University of Wisconsin—Milwaukee, 1974-75; visiting professor at San Diego State University, 1976-77, and University of California, Riverside, 1980. *Military service:* U.S. Army, 1953-55. *Awards, honors:* Longview Foundation Award for Poetry, 1961; Wenner-Gren Foundation for Anthropological Research grant, 1968, for experiments in the translation of American Indian poetry; Guggenheim Foundation fellowship for poetry, 1974; National Endowment for the Arts fellowship in creative writing, 1976.

WRITINGS—Poems: *White Sun Black Sun,* Hawk's Well Press, 1960; *The Seven Hells of the Jigoku Zoshi,* Trobar, 1962; *Sightings I-IX,* Hawk's Well Press, 1964; *The Gorky Poems,* El Corno Emplumado, 1966; *Between: 1960-1963,* Fulcrum Press, 1967; *Conversations,* Black Sparrow Press, 1968; *Poems 1964-1967,* Black Sparrow Press, 1968; *Sightings I-IX* [and] *Red Easy a Color,* Circle Press, 1968; *Poland/1931,* Part I, Unicorn Press, 1969.

Poems for the Game of Silence, 1960-1970, Dial Press, 1971; *A Book of Testimony,* Tree Books, 1971; *Esther K. Comes to America,* Unicorn Press, 1973; *Seneca Journal 1: A Poem of Beavers,* Perishable Press, 1973; *Poland/1931* (complete), New Directions, 1974; *The Cards,* Black Sparrow Press, 1974; *The Pirke and the Pearl,* Tree Books, 1975; *Seneca Journal: Midwinter,* Singing Bone Press, 1975; *A Poem to Celebrate the Spring and Diane Rothenberg's Birthday,* Perishable Press, 1975; *The Notebooks,* Membrane Press, 1976; *Narratives and Realtheater Pieces,* Braad Editions, 1978; *Seneca Journal: The Serpent,* Singing Bone Press, 1978; *A Seneca Journal* (complete), New Directions, 1978; (with Ian Tyson) *Poems for the Society of the Mystic Animals,* Tetrad Press, 1979; *Abulafia's Circles,* Membrane Press, 1979; *B.R.M.Tz.V.H.,* Perishable Press, 1979.

Numbers and Letters, Salient Seedling Press, 1980; *Vienna Blood,* New Directions, 1980; *Pre-Faces and Other Writings,* New Directions, in press; *Altar Piece,* Station Hill Press, in press.

Other: (Editor and translator) *New Young German Poets,* City Lights, 1959; (adaptor of American activing version) Rolf Hochhuth, *The Deputy* (produced in New York, 1964), Samuel French, 1965; (editor) *Ritual: A Book of Primitive Rites and Events* (anthology), Something Else Press, 1966; (translator) Angel Maria Gariboy, *The Flight of Quetzalcoatl,* Unicorn Bookshop, 1967; (translator with Michael Hamburger) Hans Magnus Enzenberger, *Poems for People Who Don't Read Poems,* Atheneum, 1967; (editor) *Technicians of the Sacred: A Range of Poetries from Africa, America, Asia, and Oceania,* Doubleday, 1968; (translator) Eugen Gomringer, *The Book of Hours and Constellations,* Something Else Press, 1968; (translator with Hamburger) Enzenberger, *Selected Poems,* Penguin, 1968.

(Translator) *The Seventeen Horse Songs of Frank Mitchell, Nos. X-XIII,* Tetrad Press, 1970; (editor) *Shaking the Pumpkin: Traditional Poetry of the Indian North Americans,* Doubleday, 1972; (editor with George Quasha) *America a Prophecy: A New Reading of American Poetry from Pre-Columbian Times to the Present,* Random House, 1973; (editor) *Revolution of the Word: A New Gathering of American Avant Garde Poetry 1914-1945,* Seabury-Continuum Books, 1974; (editor with Michel Benamov) *Ethnopoetics: A First International Symposium,* Alcheringa, 1976; (translator with Harris Lenowitz) *Gematria 27,* Membrane Press, 1977; (editor) *A Big Jewish Book: Poems and Other Visions of the Jews from Tribal Times to Present,* Doubleday, 1978; (with Diane Rothenberg) *An Ethnopoetics Reader,* University of California Press, in press.

Poetry represented in anthologies, including: *A Controversy of Poets,* edited by Paris Leary and Robert Kelly, Doubleday-Anchor, 1965; *New Modern Poetry,* edited by M. L. Rosenthal, Macmillan, 1967; *Where Is Vietnam?,* edited by Walter Lowenfels, Doubleday-Anchor, 1967; *Nota-*

tions, edited by John Cage, Something Else Press, 1969; *Caterpillar Anthology,* edited by Clayton Eshleman, Doubleday-Anchor, 1971; *Open Poetry,* edited by George Quasha and others, Simon & Schuster, 1972; *East Side Scene,* edited by Allen DeLoach, Doubleday-Anchor, 1972; *New Directions Annual,* edited by James Laughlin, New Directions, 1973, 1975, 1976, 1978, 1980; *Preferences,* edited by Richard Howard, Viking, 1974; *The New Naked Poetry,* edited by Stephen Berg and Robert Mezey, Bobbs-Merrill, 1976; *Performance in Postmodern Culture,* edited by Michel Benamou, Coda Press, 1977; *Sound Poetry,* edited by Steve McCaffery and B. P. Nichol, Underwhich Editions, 1978; *Talking Poetics at Naropa,* edited by Anne Waldman and Marilyn Webb, Shambala Books, 1978; *Esthetics Contemporary,* edited by Richard Kostelanetz, Prometheus Books, 1979; *The New American Poetry,* edited by Donald M. Allen and George Butterick, Grove Press, 1980.

Contributor to numerous journals, including *Caterpillar, Trobar, Kulchur, El Corno Emplumado, Action Poetique, American Book Review, American Poetry Review, Contact II, Boundary 2, Change, Dialectical Anthropology, Io, l-a-n-g-u-a-g-e, Partisan Review, Poetry Review, River Styx,* and *Vort.* Ethnopoetics editor, *Stony Brook,* 1968-71. Arranger with David Antin, Jackson Maclow, and Rochelle Owens, of "Origins and Meanings," and "From a Shaman's Notebook," both part of a series of primitive and archaic poetry, both recorded by Broadside, 1968. Recorded poetry includes "Horse Songs and Other Soundings," S-Press, 1975, and "6 Horse Songs for 4 Voices," New Wilderness Audiographics, 1978.

SIDELIGHTS: Jerome Rothenberg has identified with both the twentieth century avant garde and with "a range of tribal and subterranean poetries" that can provide "a poetics big enough to account for human creativity, human language-making, over the broadest span available." Of his poetry and his experimental "anthology-assemblages," he writes: "My process has been like what Samuel Makidemewabe (per Howard Norman) said of the Cree Indian Trickster: 'to walk forward while looking backward.' With past and future up for grabs, the possibility opened up—by the late 1950s—to make a near-total change in poetry, perception, language, etc., tied up with earlier twentieth century 'revolutions of the word'.... My own contributions (nomenclature and praxis) have included 'deep image,' ethnopoetics, 'total translation,' poetics of performance, and assorted attempts 'to reinterpret the poetic past from the point of view of the present.'"

Rothenberg has been particularly interested in the poetry of the North American Indians, both verbal and non-verbal: a poetry which can often be expressed, according to Rothenberg, in "music, non-verbal phonetic sounds, dance, gesture and event, game, dream, etc." It is, he explains, "a high poetry and art, which only a colonialist ideology could have blinded us into labeling 'primitive' or 'savage.'" At the same time, he writes, "I have been exploring ancestral sources of my own in the world of Jewish mystics, thieves and madmen," the latter resulting in works like *Poland/1931* and *A Big Jewish Book.*

Writing in *Vort,* Kenneth Rexroth describes Rothenberg and his poetry in the following way: "Jerome Rothenberg is one of the truly contemporary American poets who has returned U.S. poetry to the mainstream of international modern literature. At the same time, he is a true autochthon. Only here and now could have produced him—a swinging orgy of Martin Buber, Marcel Duchamp, Gertrude Stein, and Sitting Bull. No one writing poetry today has dug deeper into the roots of poetry."

BIOGRAPHICAL/CRITICAL SOURCES: David Ossman, editor, *The Sullen Art,* Cornith Books, 1963; *New York Quarterly,* winter, 1970; William Packard, editor, *The Craft of Poetry,* Doubleday, 1974; *Boundary 2,* Volume III, number 3, April 1975; *Vort,* Volume III, number 1, 1975; *Contemporary Literary Criticism,* Volume VI, Gale, 1976; Richard Kostelanetz, editor, *Twenties in the Sixties,* Greenwood Press, 1979.

* * *

ROTHENSTEIN, John K(newstub) M(aurice) 1901-

PERSONAL: Born July 11, 1901, in London, England; son of Sir William and Alice Mary (Knewstub) Rothenstein; married Elizabeth Kennard Smith, 1929; children: Lucy (Lady Dynevor). *Education:* Worcester College, Oxford, M.A.; University College, London, Ph.D. *Religion:* Roman Catholic. *Home:* Beauforest House, Newington, Dorchester-on-Thames, Oxfordshire, England; and 8 Tryon St., Chelsea, London SW3 3LH, England.

CAREER: University of Kentucky, Lexington, assistant professor of art history, 1927-28; University of Pittsburgh, Pittsburgh, Pa., assistant professor, 1928-29; City Art Gallery, Leeds, England, director, 1932-34; City Art Galleries and Ruskin Museum, Sheffield, England, director, 1933-38; Tate Gallery, London, England, director, 1938-64; University of St. Andrews, St. Andrews, Scotland, rector, 1964-67; Fordham University, Bronx, New York, visiting professor, 1967-68; Agnes Scott College, Decatur, Ga., visiting professor of art history, 1969-70; Brooklyn College of the City University of New York, Brooklyn, N.Y., distinguished professor, 1971, 1972; University of California, Irvine, Regents Lecturer, 1973. Fellow of University College, University of London, 1976. *Member:* Chelsea Arts Club, Athenaeum Club. *Awards, honors:* Commander, Order of the British Empire; Knight-Commander, Mexican Order of the Aztec Eagle; LL.D., University of New Brunswick, 1961, and University of St. Andrews, 1965; honorary fellow, Worcester College, Oxford University, 1963; Knight-Commander, Order of St. Gregory the Great.

WRITINGS: The Artists of the 1890's, Routledge & Sons, 1928, published as *A Pot of Paint: The Artists of the 1890's,* Covici Friede, 1929, reprinted, Books for Libraries, 1970; *Morning Sorrow* (novel), Constable, 1930; (editor) Oscar Wilde, *Sixteen Letters,* Coward, 1930, reprinted, Folcroft Press, 1969; *British Artists and the War,* P. Davies, 1931; *Nineteenth-Century Painting,* John Lane, 1932, reprinted, Books for Libraries, 1967; *An Introduction to English Painting,* Cassell, 1933, 5th edition, 1965, Norton, 1967; *The Life and Death of Conder,* Dent, 1938; *Augustus John,* Phaidon, 1944, reprinted, AMS Press, 1976, revised edition, Oldbourne, 1962; *Edward Burra,* Penguin, 1945, reprinted, Tate Gallery, 1973; (author of introduction) *Manet,* Faber, 1945, Pitman, 1949; (author of introduction and notes) *Turner,* Faber, 1949, Abrams, 1960, published as *Joseph Mallard William Turner,* 1971.

(Editor with Vincent Turner) *London's River,* Faber, 1951; *Modern English Painters,* Volume I: *Sickert to Smith,* Macmillan, 1952, Volume II: *Lewis to Moore,* Macmillan, 1956, published in one volume as *Modern English Painters: Sickert to Moore,* Eyre & Spottiswoode, 1957, Volume III: *Wood to Hockney,* St. Martin's, 1974, revised editions of Volumes I and II, St. Martin's, 1976, revised editions of Volumes I, II, and III, Macdonald & Janes, 1976; *The Mod-*

erns and Their World, Phoenix House, 1957, Philosophical Library, 1958; *The Tate Gallery,* Abrams, 1958; *Sickert,* Oldbourne, 1962; *British Art since 1900,* New York Graphic Society, 1962; *Matthew Smith,* Oldbourne, 1963; *Paul Nash,* Oldbourne, 1963; (with Ronald Alley) *Francis Bacon,* Thames & Hudson, 1964; (with Martin Butlin) *Turner,* Braziller, 1964; *The World of Camera,* Doubleday, 1964; *Masterpieces of the Tate and National Galleries,* Heron Books, 1964; (editor) *Great Paintings of All Time: One Hundred Masterpieces,* Simon & Schuster, 1965; *Summer's Lease* (autobiography), Hamish Hamilton, 1965, Holt, 1966; *Brave Day, Hideous Night* (autobiography), Hamish Hamilton, 1966, Holt, 1967; *Time's Thievish Progress* (autobiography), Cassell, 1970; *Victor Hammer: Artist and Craftsman,* Godine, 1978; *Stanley Spencer the Man: Correspondence and Reminiscences,* Elek, 1979. Also author of *The Houthuesens: Albert and Catherine* and *Walter Greaves: Victim of Whistler.* Honorary editor, *Museums Journal,* 1959-61; editor, *The Masters,* 1965-67.

SIDELIGHTS: When John Rothenstein assumed the directorship of the Tate Gallery in 1938, he found the situation there to be almost hopeless. There was no filing system, the collection was poorly catalogued and badly hung, and the staff was lethargic. Worst of all, the storage of unhung paintings included thirty-four Turners covered with dust, the best of them unstretched. According to Edward Weeks, "Sir John assumed office with two working principles: first, that the aura of the French Impressionists had unfairly depreciated the respect for British painting, and he meant to right this balance; second, that the enthusiasm for modern art was too often accompanied by a superficial acceptance." At this time, the Tate Gallery was dependent on the National Gallery for funding; its total allotment for purchases of new art for a year totalled two thousand dollars. With this sum the gallery was expected to assemble the national collection of British painting of all periods as well as modern foreign painting and all modern sculpture. Under Rothenstein's direction in the years prior to World War II, the gallery came to boast of a concentrated exhibition of such British painters as Sickert, Wyndham Lewis, Matthew Smith, and thirty-four previously hidden works by Turner.

Rothenstein knew that the rapidly-approaching war would seriously threaten the valuable works with which he had been entrusted. In his autobiographical *Brave Day, Hideous Night,* he describes the "brave days" when he sought refuge for his charges in country homes, castles, and other shelters where the conditions necessary for safe storage of the paintings could be accomplished. His foresight proved itself, for in the early days of the *blitzkrieg* the Tate Gallery sustained severe bomb damage but the irreplaceable works of art survived.

Shortly after the war, Rothenstein encountered the "hideous nights" to which he refers in this same book. In 1948 he met a personable South African museum director named Leroux Smith Leroux whom he persuaded to come to London and accept a temporary position at the Tate. It quickly became apparent that Leroux was less a gentleman than Rothenstein had initially been led to believe. The newcomer used a scandal-hungry British press to accuse the director of such transgressions as brutalizing his staff, mishandling of purchase funds, having poor taste, and buying the wrong works at inflated prices. Since the Tate Gallery depended on public funds for financing, the staff members were all civil servants and as such were barred from commenting on these matters. Rothenstein, therefore, was unable to defend himself in the face of these charges. A special inquiry was convened and the committee found the director innocent of all charges, but by then the hysteria surrounding "The Tate Affair" was at a peak and several trustees took the matter to Parliament and questioned the appropriate minister. Unfortunately he declined to answer either in support or opposition to the administration of the gallery. As a result, Rothenstein suffered the stigma of the investigation for several years as the air slowly cleared.

Many times Rothenstein came to the brink of resigning so as to be allowed the chance to speak in his own defense; but each time his dedication to art and to the work he had begun won out. At one point, he punched critic Douglas Cooper, a supporter of Leroux, on the nose in public. Eventually Leroux was dismissed from his position at the gallery; he went on to become involved in an incident of fraud against Lord Beaverbrook involving thousands of dollars and died a presumed suicide. *Brave Day, Hideous Night* is the author's first attempt to tell the story from his point of view and, as Alan Pryce-Jones says, "the length at which all this is expounded is perhaps excessive. As the victim himself says, it was all really about nothing. Still, he writes, luckily, with such clarity and grace that he is never for a moment boring."

BIOGRAPHICAL/CRITICAL SOURCES: *Book Week,* April 30, 1967; *Best Sellers,* May, 1967; *New Yorker,* May 20, 1967; *New York Times Book Review,* June 18, 1967; *Atlantic,* July, 1967; *Bookseller,* September 5, 1970; *Listener,* September 24, 1970; *Books,* October, 1970.

* * *

ROTHERY, Brian 1934-
(Brian Dyer, a joint pseudonym)

PERSONAL: Born January 23, 1934, in Dublin, Ireland; son of Thomas (an entrepreneur) and Mary (Gaffney) Rothery; married Mary Cullen, June 29, 1957; children: Sean-Paul; Grainne (an adopted daughter). *Education:* Completed secondary school in Dublin, Ireland; additional study in correspondence accounting courses. *Home:* 12 Green Rd. Blackrock, Dublin, Ireland. *Agent:* Laurence Pollinger, 18 Maddox, London W1R 0EU, England. *Office:* Institute for Industrial Research and Standards, Dublin, Ireland.

CAREER: Bell Telephone Co., Montreal, Quebec, analyst, 1957-63; International Business Machines Corp., Dublin, Ireland, computer systems engineer, 1963-66; Irish Transport Co., Dublin, manager, 1966-75; affiliated with Institute for Industrial Research and Standards, Dublin, 1975—. Outside examiner, Ulster College. *Member:* European Union of Science Journalists, Author's Guild (United States).

WRITINGS: *Installing and Managing a Computer,* Business Books, 1968, Brandon/Systems, 1969; (with Alan Mullally and Brendan Byrne, and editor) *The Art of Systems Analysis,* Business Books, 1969, Prentice-Hall, 1971; (with Mullally) *The Practice of Systems Analysis,* Business Books, 1970; *The Crossing* (novel), Constable, 1970, Lippincott, 1971; *The Myth of the Computer,* three volumes, Business Books, 1971; (editor) *A Computel-Constable Course,* Constable, 1971; *The Storm* (novel), Constable, 1972; *Survival by Competence,* Business Books, 1972, Petrocelli Books, 1973; *How to Organize Your Time and Resources,* Business Books, 1972; (with Orlando R. Petrocelli under joint pseudonym, Brian Dyer) *Saga of the Celtic Queen* (novel), Mason & Libscomb, 1974; *Men of Enterprise,* Institute for Industrial Research and Standards, 1977.

WORK IN PROGRESS: Research in future society, in power-politics, and in frustration and achievement; historical research.

AVOCATIONAL INTERESTS: Mountain exploring (Arctic, Rockies, Alps), collecting and restoring late-nineteenth century landscape oil paintings.

* * *

ROUECHE, Berton 1911-

PERSONAL: Surname is pronounced Roo-*shay;* born April 16, 1911, in Kansas City, Mo.; son of Clarence Berton (a business executive) and Nana Marie (Mossman) Roueche; married Katherine Eisenhower, October 28, 1936; children: Bradford. *Education:* University of Missouri, B.J., 1933. *Home:* Stony Hill Rd., Amagansett, N.Y. 11930. *Agent:* Harold Ober Associates, 40 East 49th St., New York, N.Y. 10017. *Office: New Yorker,* 25 West 43rd St., New York, N.Y. 10036.

CAREER: Kansas City Star, Kansas City, Mo., reporter, 1934-41; *St. Louis Globe-Democrat,* St. Louis, Mo., reporter, 1941-42; *St. Louis Post-Dispatch,* St. Louis, reporter, 1942-44; *New Yorker,* New York, N.Y., staff writer, 1944—, originator and sole proprietor of "Annals of Medicine" department. Faculty member, Bread Loaf Writers' Conference, Middlebury, Vt., 1958, and Indiana University Writers' Conference, Bloomington, 1962. Trustee of Guild Hall, East Hampton, N.Y., 1960-76, and National Foundation for Infectious Diseases, 1976—; member of executive committee, Health Research Council, New York, N.Y., 1966-72. *Member:* American Epidemiological Society (honorary member), Kansas City Academy of Medicine (fellow), Preservation Society of the East End (president, 1971—), Sigma Alpha Epsilon, Devon Yacht Club (Amagansett, N.Y.), Coffee House Club (New York, N.Y.). *Awards, honors:* Albert Lasker Medical Journalism Award, 1950, for "The Fog," and 1960, for *The Neutral Spirit*; Mystery Writers of America award, 1954; National Council of Infant and Child Care annual award, 1956; American Medical Writers Association annual award, 1963 and 1978; American Medical Association Annual Journalism Award, 1970; William E. Leidt Award for Religious Reporting, Episcopal Church, 1973; J. C. Penney-University of Missouri Annual Journalism Award, 1978.

WRITINGS—Published by Little, Brown, except as indicated; nonfiction, except as indicated: *Black Weather* (novel), Reynal, 1945; *Eleven Blue Men,* 1953; *The Last Enemy* (novel), Grove, 1956; *The Incurable Wound,* 1958; *The Delectable Mountains,* 1959; *The Neutral Spirit,* 1960; (editor) *Curiosities of Medicine,* 1963; *A Man Named Hoffman,* 1965; *Annals of Epidemiology,* 1967; *Field Guide to Disease,* 1967; *What's Left: Reports on a Diminishing America,* 1969; *The Orange Man and Other Narratives of Medical Detection,* 1971; *Feral* (novel), Harper, 1974; *Fago* (novel), Harper, 1977; *The River World and Other Explorations,* Harper, 1978; *The Medical Detectives,* Times Books, 1980.

* * *

ROWSE, A(lfred) L(eslie) 1903-

PERSONAL: Born December 4, 1903, in St. Austell, Cornwall, England; son of Richard and Ann (Vanson) Rowse. *Education:* Christ Church, Oxford, M.A., 1929, D.Litt., 1953. *Home and office:* Trenarren House, St. Austell, Cornwall, England. *Agent:* Curtis Brown Ltd., 575 Madison Ave., New York, N.Y. 10022.

CAREER: Oxford University, All Souls College, Oxford, England, fellow, 1925-74, emeritus fellow, 1974—. Senior research associate, Huntington Library, San Marino, Calif., 1962-69. George A. Millar Visiting Professor, University of Illinois, 1952-53; Raleigh Lecturer, British Academy, 1957; visiting professor, University of Wisconsin, 1957-58; Trevelyan Lecturer, Cambridge University, 1958; Beatty Memorial Lecturer, McGill University, 1963. *Member:* British Academy (fellow), Royal Society of Literature (fellow), English Association (president, 1952-53), Shakespeare Club (president, 1970-71). *Awards, honors:* D.Litt., University of Exeter, 1960; D.C.L., University of New Brunswick, 1960.

WRITINGS: On History: A Study of the Present Tendencies, K. Paul, Trench, Trubner, 1927, reprinted, Folcroft Library Editions, 1975; *Science and History: A New View of History,* Norton, 1928; *Politics and the Younger Generation,* Faber, 1931; (with George B. Harrison) *Queen Elizabeth and Her Subjects,* Allen & Unwin, 1935, reprinted, Books for Libraries, 1970; (co-editor) Charles Anderson, *Essays in Cornish History,* Oxford University Press, 1935, reprinted, D. B. Barton, 1963; *Mr. Keynes and the Labor Movement,* Macmillan (London), 1936; *Sir Richard Grenville of the Revenge: An Elizabethan Hero,* Houghton, 1937, reprinted, J. Cape, 1962.

Tudor Cornwall: Portrait of a Society, J. Cape, 1941, reprinted, 1957; *Poems of a Decade: 1931-1941,* Faber, 1941; *A Cornish Childhood: Autobiography of a Cornishman,* J. Cape, 1942, Macmillan, 1947; *The Spirit of English History,* Longmans, Green, 1943, Oxford University Press (New York), 1945; *Poems Chiefly Cornish,* Faber, 1944; *The English Spirit: Essays in History and Literature,* Macmillan (London), 1944, 2nd revised edition published as *The English Spirit: Essays in Literature and History,* 1966, Funk, 1967; *West Country Stories,* Macmillan (London), 1945; *The Use of History,* Hodder & Stoughton, 1946, Macmillan, 1948, revised edition, P. Collier, 1963; *Poems of Deliverance,* Faber, 1946; *The End of an Epoch: Reflections on Contemporary History,* Macmillan (London), 1947; (editor) *The West in English History,* Hodder & Stoughton, 1949.

The Elizabethan Age, Volume I: *The England of Elizabeth: The Structure of Society,* Macmillan (London), 1950, Macmillan (New York), 1951, reprinted, P. Collier, 1966, Volume II: *The Expansion of Elizabethan England,* St. Martin's, 1955, reprinted, Scribner, 1972, Volume III: *The Elizabethan Renaissance,* Part I: *The Life of the Society,* Macmillan (London), 1971, Scribner, 1972, Part II: *The Cultural Achievement,* Scribner, 1972; *The English Past: Evocations of Places and Persons,* Macmillan (London), 1951, Macmillan (New York), 1952, revised edition published as *Times, Persons, Places,* Macmillan (London), 1965; (editor and translator) Lucien Romier, *A History of France,* St. Martin's, 1953; *Royal Homes Illustrated,* Odhams, 1953; *An Elizabethan Garland,* St. Martin's, 1953, reprinted, AMS Press, 1972; *The Early Churchills* (also see below), Harper, 1956, reprinted, Greenwood Press, 1974; *The Churchills: From the Death of Marlborough to the Present* (also see below), Harper, 1958 (published in England as *The Later Churchills,* Macmillan, 1958, reprinted, Penguin, 1971); *Poems Partly American,* Faber, 1959; *The Elizabethans and America,* Harper, 1959, reprinted, Greenwood Press, 1978.

St. Austell: Church, Town, Parish, H. E. Warne, 1960; *Appeasement: A Study in Political Decline, 1933-1939,* Norton, 1961, published as *All Souls and Appeasement: A Contribution to Contemporary History,* St. Martin's, 1961; *Sir Walter Raleigh: His Family and Private Life,* Harper, 1962 (published in England as *Ralegh and the Throckmortons,* Macmillan, 1962); *William Shakespeare: A Biography,* Harper, 1963; (editor and author of introduction and notes) William Shakespeare, *Sonnets,* Harper, 1964, 2nd edition published as *Shakespeare's Sonnets: The Problems Solved,* 1973; *Christopher Marlowe: A Biography,* Macmillan (London),

1964, published as *Christopher Marlowe: His Life and Work*, Harper, 1965; *A Cornishman at Oxford: The Education of a Cornishman* (autobiography), J. Cape, 1965; *Shakespeare's Southampton: Patron of Virginia*, Harper, 1965; *Bosworth Field: From Medieval to Tudor England*, Doubleday, 1966 (published in England as *Bosworth Field and the Wars of the Roses*, Macmillan, 1966); *The Churchills: The Story of a Family* (contains *The Early Churchills* and *The Churchills: From the Death of Marlborough to the Present*), Harper, 1966; *Cornish Stories*, Macmillan (London), 1967; *Poems of Cornwall and America*, Faber, 1967; (editor) *A Cornish Anthology*, Macmillan (London), 1968; *The Cousin Jacks: The Cornish in America*, Scribner, 1969 (published in England as *The Cornish in America*, Macmillan, 1969); (editor and author of foreword) James Anthony Froude, *The Two Chiefs of Dunboy: A Story of Eighteenth-Century Ireland*, Chatto & Windus, 1969.

Strange Encounter (poems), J. Cape, 1972; *The Tower of London in the History of England*, Putnam, 1972 (published in England as *The Tower of London in the History of the Nation*, Weidenfeld & Nicolson, 1972); *Westminster Abbey in the History of the Nation*, Weidenfeld & Nicolson, 1972; (contributor) Goldwin Albert Smith, editor, *The Professor and the Public: The Role of the Scholar in the Modern World*, Wayne State University Press, 1972; *Shakespeare the Man*, Harper, 1973; *Peter, the White Cat of Trenarren*, M. Joseph, 1974; *Sex and Society in Shakespeare's Age: Simon Forman the Astrologer*, Scribner, 1974 (published in England as *Simon Forman: Sex and Society in Shakespeare's Age*, Weidenfeld & Nicolson, 1974); *Windsor Castle in the History of England*, Putnam, 1974 (published in England as *Windsor Castle in the History of the Nation*, Weidenfeld & Nicolson, 1974).

Jonathan Swift, Scribner, 1975 (published in England as *Jonathan Swift: Major Prophet*, Thames & Hudson, 1975); *Oxford in the History of England*, Putnam, 1975 (published in England as *Oxford In the History of the Nation*, Weidenfeld & Nicolson, 1975); *Discoveries and Reviews: From Renaissance to Restoration*, Barnes & Noble, 1975; *Matthew Arnold: Poet and Prophet*, Thames & Hudson, 1976; *Brown Buck: A Californian Fantasy*, M. Joseph, 1976; *A Cornishman Abroad*, J. Cape, 1976; *Homosexuals in History: A Study of Ambivalence in Society, Literature, and the Arts*, Macmillan, 1977; *Shakespeare the Elizabethan*, Putnam, 1977; *Milton the Puritan: Portrait of a Mind*, Macmillan (London), 1977; *The Heritage of Britain*, Putnam, 1977; *The Road to Oxford* (poems), J. Cape, 1978; (editor) *The Poems of Shakespeare's Dark Lady*, J. Cape, 1978; (editor and author of notes) *The Annotated Shakespeare*, C. N. Potter, 1978, Volume I: *The Comedies*, Volume II: *The Histories, Sonnets and Other Poems*, Volume III: *The Tragedies and Romances; The Byrons and the Trevanions*, St. Martin's, 1979; *A Man of the Thirties*, Weidenfeld & Nicolson, 1979; *Portraits and Views: Literary and Historical*, Macmillan, 1979; *The Story of Britain*, St. Michael's Press, 1979; *Three Cornish Cats*, Weidenfeld & Nicolson, 1979; (editor) *Roper's Life of Sir Thomas More*, Folio Society, 1980. Editor, "Men and Their Times" series, Hodder & Stoughton, beginning 1947.

SIDELIGHTS: "If it is something about the Elizabethan Age, you would do well to ask me," A. L. Rowse once wrote to a critic. Indeed, most scholars would agree that Rowse is one of the foremost contemporary authorities on seventeenth-century England. As a *Newsweek* reviewer comments: "No sexual custom, no oddity of language or quirk of lore seems to have escaped his attention." He has, however, been subjected to a great deal of criticism throughout his long career, primarily for his arrogance, his intensely personal interpretations of history and literature, and his occasionally haphazard application of the rules of traditional historical scholarship.

At no time does this uproar become more pronounced than when the subject in question is William Shakespeare. In his 1963 biography of the playwright, Rowse claimed to have solved several mysteries concerning the sonnets, including the time period during which they were written and to whom they were addressed. Commenting on Rowse's methods, Hugh MacLean of *Canadian Forum* wrote: "It is not only that Professor Rowse is much less inclined to untie scholarly knots than to take a cutlass to them, nor even that his daredevil and headlong application of 'proper historical method' to Shakespeare will certainly raise every hair on most critics' heads. What is especially insidious and deadly is the author's determination to make the poetry point at something else, and to read it primarily, sometimes exclusively, as a transcript of Shakespeare's experience."

Some reviewers found Rowse's tone, rather than his methods, to be the book's single greatest flaw. As the *Economist* critic noted: "There is so much to be said against Dr. Rowse's book that it is only just to admit, at the outset, that it draws on a formidable stock of knowledge about social and political life in Elizabethan England and that it is written with immense gusto. . . . [But] the coarseness of the writing is all of a piece with the arrogance exhibited throughout the book. . . . The main defect of [the biography,] which is full of interesting suggestions and illuminating background information, is its authoritarian tone." Christopher Sykes of *Nation* observed this and other problems: "[The] pace-making criticism [of this biography] came out on October 10 in the B.B.C.'s weekly magazine, the *Listener*. It was by Christopher Ricks, and it was short, hostile, deadly. It emphasized what Dr. Rowse had not made plain to the general reader: that many of his discoveries were in fact theories of long standing. . . . Few critics could quite forgive the historian's arrogant and bullying tone. . . . [Yet] Dr. Rowse has written a fascinating book. After reading it, the lover of Shakespeare can approach nearer to the prin3e of poets. . . . If only [Rowse] hadn't ordered us about so unnecessarily, and sometimes so offensively, we should have all followed him like lambs."

A *Book Week* reviewer also criticized several aspects of the biography, but concluded that it was worth reading. "In spite of Rowse's self-congratulation," he wrote, "there is little in his book which is altogether new, [since] most of the discoveries that he claims as his own have been in print for more than 30 years. And the scholar may well complain that if this is an example of 'historical method,' then historical method is far laxer than literary scholarship. Again and again Rowse makes confident statements for which there is no verifiable evidence. . . . Nor does [he] hesitate to suppress inconvenient evidence. . . . Nevertheless, in spite of scholarly and human shortcomings, Dr. Rowse's biography is the liveliest and most elaborate account of Shakespeare in his age that has yet been written. . . . All in all, [he] has written a memorable book, more important as a sensitive work of art and imagination than as definitive historical biography."

Rowse's massive, three-volume illustrated edition of Shakespeare's complete plays and sonnets—*The Annotated Shakespeare*—has given rise to even more criticism of the author's methods and intentions. Nona Balakian of the *New Republic* writes: "Every now and then, as if to redeem itself, commercial publishing will lavish its superior resources on an ambitious and worthy project with what can only be described as inspired beneficence (no irony meant). *The Annotated Shakespeare* . . . is plainly such an endeavor. . . . At first sight, the choice of A. L. Rowse as guide would seem to be exactly right. . . . [But as a result of this choice the book] might more accurately have been titled *The Annotated Shakespeare of A. L. Rowse,* for it is Rowse's Shakespeare as it has never been the Shakespeare of other annotators. . . . As a Shakespearean critic Rowse is no match for a Harry Levin or a Jan Kott . . . but neither critic commands Rowse's familiarity with the bric-a-brac of Shakespeare's world or is so zealously proprietary of the bard. . . . As a biographer of Shakespeare, Rowse has bouncing confidence in his facts but little subtlety in his interpretation of them. . . . At all times, Shakespeare is clear-cut to Rowse."

But while she praises his familiarity with the Elizabethan Age and Shakespeare's life, Balakian finds that Rowse's critical interpretations of the various plays are, at best, inadequate. She admits that he has "no trouble distinguishing between the various types of Shakespearean comedy, . . . but he might as well be a cataloguer for all the clues he gives readers of their relative merit as dramatic art." Noting that he has "no ear for poetry [and] no heart for pathos," Balakian claims that it is in his section on the tragedies that "Rowse's inadequacy as a critic of Shakespeare becomes an embarrassment." To do justice to a study of Shakespeare, Balakian concludes, "we must first see him as an artist. And that is something quite different from seeing him—as Rowse does—first as a man."

Other critics are far less kind in their appraisal of *The Annotated Shakespeare.* A *Book World* reviewer, for example, declares that "the volumes are shoddily produced, sketchily annotated, and shockingly illustrated. . . . [Rowse] has lately made a career of popularized, nonscholarly publication. He will make money off this set of Shakespeare, but his reputation as an historian will continue to sink lower and lower." In addition, the critic continues, "just looking at *The Annotated Shakespeare* will give most readers a nice headache. The 4,200 illustrations are thrown in helter-skelter. . . . [But as] bad as the illustrations are, the text is worse. Rowse has taken a 1900 Globe edition, first edited in 1864 by Clark and Wright at Cambridge, and cut it up and blown it up. . . . [But] printing a text now 100 years old allows Rowse to ignore decades of scholarly work. . . . [As a result, he] hasn't done Shakespeare or the reading public a service with *The Annotated Shakespeare.* For shame, Mr. Rowse, for shame."

A *New Leader* critic writes: "Compared to [other annotated editions of Shakespeare], the new entry is a poor job indeed. A. L. Rowse's commentary is just plain inadequate. Better it were called *The Unannotated Shakespeare.* . . . [His] glossing contents itself with explaining a few words or short phrases, ignoring many larger phrases or references that are often difficult to follow. . . . Even when [he] lets himself go occasionally on long notes, he is apt to be chasing a pet theory about contemporary allusions in Shakespeare. . . . [The text itself] is an old critical version of Shakespeare that for many reasons ought to be retired from view."

Rowse dismisses all his critics with a characteristic response: "They are not entitled to an opinion." He does admit, however, that "writing about Shakespeare is like putting your head in a hornet's nest," as he once told a *Chicago Tribune* interviewer. "But to a historian, plain common sense is plain common sense. My approach to Shakespeare is direct and simple, not the bloody rubbish the third-rate literary scholars think up. Literary folk without knowledge of history are hobbling on one leg. You must remember that most people are very third-rate. They're not first-rate. They don't know what they're talking about. They don't like me. After all, I'm not arguing these matters with them. I'm telling them. This is authoritative. There's no answering it."

In an interview with Auberon Waugh, Rowse explained why he is so confident that his interpretations are correct. "Of course I have opinions about the Elizabethan Age because I know a great deal about it. If my opinions weren't a damn sight more valuable than anyone else's, I wouldn't be worth my keep. Democratic society supposes all opinions are equally valuable. Bloody humbug and nonsense. . . . Don't you think, my dear, there's something paradoxical here, that I'm far more popular with the people than any of these second-rate buggers and middle-class intellectuals? Four of my books have sold over 300,000 copies, and they go on selling. Nobody reads these people. Nobody."

BIOGRAPHICAL/CRITICAL SOURCES: A. L. Rowse, *A Cornish Childhood* (autobiography), J. Cape, 1942, Macmillan, 1947; *Economist,* October 19, 1963; *New Yorker,* October 19, 1963, April 6, 1968; *Book Week,* January 5, 1964; *Newsweek,* January 6, 1964; *Best Sellers,* January 15, 1964, June 15, 1967; *Nation,* January 27, 1964; *Atlantic,* February, 1964, February, 1979; *Canadian Forum,* February, 1964; *New Statesman,* August 4, 1964; Rowse, *A Cornishman at Oxford* (autobiography), J. Cape, 1965; *Kenyon Review,* November, 1966; *Books and Bookmen,* May, 1967; *Times Literary Supplement,* June 22, 1967; *Punch,* June 25, 1969; *Listener,* September 10, 1970; *Detroit News,* May 14, 1972; *New York Times Book Review,* June 26, 1977, February 4, 1979; *Time,* November 13, 1978; *Book World,* Novemer 26, 1978; *Washington Post,* November 24, 1978; *New Leader,* December 4, 1978; *Chicago Tribune,* December 6, 1978; *New Republic,* January 13, 1979.

—*Sketch by Deborah A. Straub*

* * *

RUBIN, Michael 1935-

PERSONAL: Born February 17, 1935, in New York, N.Y.; son of Henry and Charlotte (Portnoy) Rubin. *Education:* Bard College, B.A., 1956; attended University of Melbourne, 1957; Columbia University, M.A. (English), 1959; Lone Mountain College, M.A. (clinical psychology), 1973. *Home:* 610 Clipper St., No. 8, San Francisco, Calif. 94114. *Agent:* Curtis Brown Ltd., 575 Madison Ave., New York, N.Y. 10022.

CAREER: Gorton High School, Yonkers, N.Y., teacher, 1959-62; Woodlands High School, Hartsdale, N.Y., teacher, 1963-68; University of California, Berkeley, conductor of writing workshops, 1972—; San Jose State University, San Jose, Calif., instructor in creative writing, 1975-77; San Francisco State University, San Francisco, Calif., lecturer in creative writing, 1978—. Counseling intern, Marin Center for Intensive Therapy, 1972-74. *Awards, honors:* Fulbright grant, 1957; Curtis Brown fellowship, 1962; National Endowment for the Arts grant, 1978.

WRITINGS: A Trip into Town, Harper, 1961; *Whistle Me Home,* McGraw, 1967; *In a Cold Country,* McGraw, 1971; *An Absence of Bells,* McGraw, 1972; *In the Middle of Things: An Experience with Primal Theory,* Putnam, 1973; *Unfinished Business,* Putnam, 1975; (editor) *Men without Masks: The Emotional Lives of Modern Men,* Addison-Wesley, 1980. Contributor of short stories and articles to *Cosmopolitan, Redbook, Family Circle, Bay Guardian,* and other publications. Assistant editor, *Parachutist,* 1958-59; participating editor, "Readers' Enrichment" series, Washington Square Press, 1965.

AVOCATIONAL INTERESTS: The theater.

* * *

RUBIN, Zick 1944-

PERSONAL: Born April 29, 1944, in New York, N.Y.; son of Eli H. (a physician) and Adena (a teacher; maiden name, Lipschitz) Rubin; married Carol Moses (a psychiatric social worker), June 21, 1969; children: Elihu James. *Education:* Yale University, B.A., 1965; University of Michigan, Ph.D., 1969. *Office:* Department of Psychology, Brandeis University, Waltham, Mass. 02254.

CAREER: Harvard University, Cambridge, Mass., 1969-76, began as instructor, became associate professor of psychology; Brandeis University, Waltham, Mass., Louis and Frances Salvage Professor of Social Psychology, 1976—. *Member:* American Psychological Association, Society for the Pscyhological Study of Social Issues, Phi Beta Kappa, Sigma Xi. *Awards, honors:* Socio-Psychological prize, American Association for the Advancement of Science, 1969, for research on social psychology of romantic love.

WRITINGS: Liking and Loving: An Invitation to Social Psychology, Holt, 1973; (editor) *Doing unto Others: Joining, Molding, Conforming, Helping, Loving,* Prentice-Hall, 1974; (with Elton B. McNeil) *The Psychology of Being Human,* 2nd edition, Harper, 1977; *Children's Friendships,* Harvard University Press, 1980. Editor of "Patterns of Social Behavior," series, Prentice-Hall.

* * *

RUE, Leonard Lee III 1926-

PERSONAL: Born February 20, 1926, in Paterson, N.J.; son of Leonard Lee (a marine engineer) and Mae (Sellner) Rue; married Beth Castner, May 6, 1945 (divorced, 1976); children: Leonard Lee IV, Tim Lewis, James Keith. *Education:* Educated in Belvidere, N.J. *Religion:* Methodist. *Home and office:* RD3, Box 31, Blairstown, N.J. 07825.

CAREER: Free-lance writer and photographer. Summer guide for canoe trips in Canada, gamekeeper for hunt club, teacher of outdoor subjects, lecturer, photographer, former camp ranger. *Member:* Society of American Mammalogists, National Parks Society, Wilderness Society, National Wildlife Federation, Audubon Society, Wildlife Society, Masons. *Awards, honors:* Received eleven book awards from New Jersey State Association of English; New Jersey Institute of Technology golden award, 1979; inducted to New Jersey Literary Hall of Fame, 1979.

WRITINGS: Animals in Motion, Doubleday, 1956; *Tracks and Tracking,* Doubleday, 1958; *The World of the White-Tailed Deer,* Lippincott, 1962; *The World Picture Guide to American Animals,* Arco, 1962; (with Dorothy Knight) *The World of the Beaver,* Lippincott, 1963; *The World of the Raccoon,* Lippincott, 1964; *New Jersey Out-of-Doors,* privately printed, 1964; (illustrator) *American Animals,* Ridge Press, 1965; *Cottontail,* Crowell, 1965; *Pictorial Guide to the Mammals of North America,* Crowell, 1967; *Sportsman's Guide to Game Animals,* Outdoor Life, 1968; *The World of the Red Fox,* Lippincott, 1969; *Pictorial Guide to Birds,* Crowell, 1970; *The World of the Ruffed Grouse,* Lippincott, 1973; *Game Birds of North America,* Outdoor Life, 1973; *The Deer of North America,* Outdoor Life, 1978; *Furbearing Animals of North America,* Crown, 1981. Contributor of monthly nature columns to *American Hunter* and *Trailer Travel Magazine;* also contributor of articles and photographs to more than a thousand publications in thirty-three countries.

RUSSELL, Don(ald Bert) 1899-

PERSONAL: Born 1899, in Huntington, Ind.; son of Oscar Elwood and Ethel (Bert) Russell; married Ruth Holsenbeck, 1922; children: Elaine Canfield Jones, John Robert, Martha-Jane Bissell. *Education:* Attended Northwestern University, 1916-17, 1919; University of Michigan, B.A., 1921. *Home:* 191 Clinton Ave., Elmhurst, Ill. 60126.

CAREER: Newspaperman in Chicago, Ill., from 1923-50, on *Chicago Journal,* copy reader, 1923-25, *Chicago Daily News,* editorial writer, 1925-46, *Chicago Tribune,* makeup editor, 1947-50; *New Standard Encyclopedia,* Chicago, senior associate editor, 1950-53, 1956-67. *Military service:* U.S. Army, Infantry, two years in World War I; became sergeant. U.S. Army Reserve, 1925-41, became first lieutenant. *Member:* American Historical Association, American Military Institute, Western History Association (honorary life member), The Westerners, Society of Midland Authors, English Westerners' Society (honorary president), Illinois State Historical Society, Kansas State Historical Society (life member). *Awards, honors:* Friends of Literature, Chicago, best book award, 1961; received honorable mention, Society of Midland Authors; Spur Award for nonfiction, Western Writers of America, 1962.

WRITINGS: One Hundred and Three Fights and Scrimmages, U.S. Cavalry Association, 1936; *Invincible Ike,* Successful Living, Inc., 1952; *The Lives and Legends of Buffalo Bill,* University of Oklahoma Press, 1960; *Sioux Buffalo Hunters,* Encyclopaedia Britannica, 1962; (author of introduction) Charles King, *Campaigning with Crook,* University of Oklahoma Press, 1964; (editor and author of introduction and notes) Percival G. Lowe, *Five Years a Dragoon,* University of Oklahoma Press, 1965; *Custer's Last,* Amon Carter Museum of Western Art, 1968; (compiler) *Custer's List: A Checklist of Pictures,* Amon Carter Museum of Western Art, 1969.

The Wild West: A History of the Wild West Shows, Amon Carter Museum of Western Art, 1970; (author of introduction) *Medicine Lodge,* Swallow Press, 1970; (author of introduction) Robert J. Ege, *Strike Them Hard,* Old Army Press, 1970; (author of introduction) Tal Luther, *Custer High Spots,* Old Army Press, 1972; (editor with Nancy Alpert Mowrer) Francios des Montaignes, *The Plains,* University of Oklahoma Press, 1972; (editor) John E. Cox, *Five Years in the Army,* Sol Lewis, 1973; (editor) *Trails of the Iron Horse,* Doubleday, 1975; (contributor) *The Cowboy: Six Shooters, Songs, and Sex,* University of Oklahoma Press, 1976; (editor) Ernest L. Reedstrom, *Bugles, Banners, and War Bonnets,* Caxton, 1977; *Elmhurst: Trails from Yesterday,* Elmhurst Bicentennial Commission, 1977; (author of introduction) John Gibbon, *Personal Recollections of the Civil War,* Morningside Bookshop, 1978; (author of introduction) *The Life of William F. Cody, Known as Buffalo Bill: An Autobiography,* University of Nebraska Press, 1978. Also author, "Adam Bradford: Cowboy" series, Benefic, 1970. Contributor to military and history journals. Editor, *Westerns Brand Book,* 1946—; member of editorial board, *The American West,* 1964-79.

* * *

RUSTOW, Dankwart A(lexander) 1924-

PERSONAL: Born December 21, 1924, in Berlin, Germany; naturalized U.S. citizen; son of Alexander and Anna (Bresser) Rustow; children: Stephen Lowe, Janet Susan, Timothy. *Education:* Attended University of Istanbul, 1943-45; Queens College, B.A., 1947; Yale University, M.A., 1949,

Ph.D., 1951. *Home:* 239 Central Park West, New York, N.Y. *Office:* Graduate School, City University of New York, 33 West 42nd St., New York, N.Y. 10036.

CAREER: Oglethorpe University, Atlanta, Ga., associate professor of political science, 1950-52; Princeton University, Princeton, N.J., assistant professor, 1952-57, associate professor of politics, 1957-59, staff member, Near Eastern Studies Program, 1952-59, research associate, Center of International Studies, 1955-59, field researcher in Turkey and other Near Eastern countries, 1953-54, 1958-59; Columbia University, New York City, associate professor, 1959-63, professor of international social forces, 1963-70; City University of New York, New York City, distinguished professor of political science, 1970—. Senior staff member, Brookings Institution, Division of Foreign Policy Research, Washington, D.C., 1961-63. Consultant to the U.S. Department of State, 1962—, and RAND Corp., 1963—. Visiting lecturer or professor at Hunter College (now Hunter College of the City University of New York), 1955-56, Columbia University, 1956-57, Yale University, 1961, University of Heidelberg, 1961, School of Advanced International Studies, 1964, and London School of Economics and Political Science, 1965. Lecturer at many universities; conducted lecture tour for American Association of Middle East Studies, spring of 1961. Delegate, 25th International Congress of Orientalists, Moscow, 1960, and 26th Congress, New Delhi, 1964. Conducted research in Sweden, 1949-50 and 1958.

MEMBER: American Political Science Association, Middle East Institute (member of board of governors, 1963—), Council on Foreign Relations (research secretary, study group on defense of the Near East, 1954-55), Society for International Development, Social Science Research Council (secretary, committee on Near and Middle East, 1955-58; member of joint committee on Near and Middle East of the Council and American Council of Learned Societies, 1959-62), Institute of Current World Affairs. *Awards, honors:* Social Science Research Council fellow, 1949-50; Fund for the Advancement of Education fellow, 1951-52; Guggenheim fellowship, 1965-66.

WRITINGS: The Politics of Compromise: A Study of Parties and Cabinet Government in Sweden, Princeton University Press, 1955, reprinted, Greenwood Press, 1969; *Politics and Westernization in the Near East,* Princeton Center of International Studies, 1956; (editor with Robert E. Ward) *Political Modernization in Japan and Turkey,* Princeton University Press, 1964; *Succession in the Twentieth Century,* School of International Affairs, Columbia University, 1964; *Modernization and Political Leadership,* Brookings Institution, 1967; *A World of Nations: Problems of Political Modernization,* Brookings Institution, 1967; (editor) *Philosophers and Kings: Studies in Leadership,* Braziller, 1970; *Middle Eastern Political Systems,* Prentice-Hall, 1971; (editor with M. Donald Hancock) *American Foreign Policy,* Prentice-Hall, 1971; (with John F. Mugno) *OPEC: Success and Prospects,* New York University Press, 1976; (editor with Ernst-Otto Czempiel) *The Euro-American System: Economic and Political Relations between North America and Western Europe,* Westview, 1976.

Contributor: *Modern Political Parties,* University of Chicago Press, 1956; *Islam and the West,* Mouton, 1957; *Foreign Policy in World Politics,* Prentice-Hall, 1958; *The Politics of Developing Areas,* Princeton University Press, 1960; *Modern Political Systems,* Prentice-Hall, 1963; *The Military in the Middle East,* Ohio State University Press, 1963; *Islam and International Relations,* Praeger, 1965; *Political Culture and Political Development,* Princeton University Press, 1965; *Political Parties and Political Development,* Princeton University Press, 1966.

Also author of *Freedom and Domination: A Historical Critique of Civilization,* Princeton University Press; editor of "America's Role in World Affairs" series, Prentice-Hall. Contributor to *Americana Annual, Encyclopaedia of Islam,* and to professional journals.

WORK IN PROGRESS: Comparative Politics.

SIDELIGHTS: Dankwart Rustow is fluent in English, German, Turkish, French, and Swedish and knows some Arabic, Danish, Norwegian, Spanish, and Italian.†

* * *

RUTSTRUM, Calvin 1895-

PERSONAL: Name legally changed; born October 26, 1895, in Hobart, Ind.; son of Tiofil and Emily (Carlson) Rudstrom; married Florence M. Merth. *Education:* Attended public schools of Minneapolis, Minn., to seventh grade. *Home:* South Wedge Hills, Marine-on-St. Croix, Minn.

CAREER: Worked in Minneapolis, Minn., 1908-10; cowboy in Montana, 1911-13; baker in Minneapolis until World War I; after the war, sold real estate and automobiles; for fifteen years worked as crime investigator in the United States and Canada; began youth conservation work in 1945, sending numerous canoe trips into Canada; after researching wilderness equipment and living methods, set up wilderness trips and organized expeditions; bought and sold real estate water frontage in Minnesota and developed subdivisions; established a canoe outfitting and trading post and a resort which he subsequently sold to their respective managers before becoming a full-time writer. Lecturer and guest on radio and television programs. *Military service:* U.S. Navy, Medical Corps, World War I. *Member:* National Geographic Society, Explorers Club.

WRITINGS—Published by Macmillan, except as indicated: *Way of the Wilderness,* Burgess, 1946; *Memoranda for Canoe Country* (booklet), Burgess, 1947; *The New Way of the Wilderness,* 1958; *The Wilderness Cabin,* 1961; *North American Canoe Country,* 1964; *The Wilderness Route Finder,* 1967; *Paradise below Zero,* 1968; *Once upon a Wilderness,* 1973; *The Wilderness Life,* 1975; *Chips from a Wilderness Log,* Stein & Day, 1978; *Greenhorns in the Southwest,* University of New Mexico Press, 1979; *Here's Cal Rutstrum* (collection of newspaper columns), Nodin, 1980. Author of column, "The Outpost," in *Post Messenger* (Stillwater, Minn.), 1949-50, and of column, "Here's Cal Rutstrum," in *Osceola Sun.* Contributor to *American Annual of Photography,* 1934-45, and to magazines concerned with nature and outdoor life.

WORK IN PROGRESS: Back Country.

SIDELIGHTS: Calvin Rutstrum told *CA:* "The aspiring writer must want to write with passionate zeal . . . for earliest success. He will be reading every day, writing every day; and seeking some pertinent, vital experience every day, with an urgency that time is his greatest poverty. [He] will read voraciously on as many subjects as possible—even at times making himself read palling and painfully diverting subject matter to get contrary viewpoints. Specialization is largely a squeezing from many subjects the juices and essences which pertain to a specialized subject. . . .

"My opinion . . . is that the aspiring writer will show further wisdom if he avoids . . . the growing cult of rapid reading. You do not study the finer and most significant points of botany in the forest below from the height of a jet plane in flight. . . . Rapid-reader converts tell us that we should read rapidly for one particular purpose, then slower for another purpose. But . . . we are habit-forming animals, subject to the shackling enslavement of our reflexes. . . .

"The position of the writer . . . is to give expression to unexpressed knowledge and ideas. . . . His most important role is to give new expression to basic life, no matter how well it has been treated by past writers, and no matter how durable these writings continue to be. We live with concepts that seem infallible until they are subsequently reviewed and revised by a greater mind or a more knowledgeable one. Most of man's human problems remain unsolved—a condition which should be an inspiring source of satisfaction to those who think that all has been said, that all has been documented.

"The writer who determines his course strictly on intellectual appeal, will, I am afraid, suffer the fatal consequence—unassimilated acceptance by too many readers. Thinking is hard work for most. You might better, for the most part, appeal to their emotions. The iconoclast and satirical writer has perhaps the most effective appeal. He accomplishes his end result by ridicule. . . . No one wants to appear ridiculous. . . ."

Because of Rutstrum's avid interest in natural phenomena and wilderness activity, new acquaintances visiting his home for the first time are generally surprised to find an absence of a simulated, small Disneyland, or a collection of stuffed animal heads and draped skins on the walls. When they find a diversified collection of books that might suggest an evening around the fireside, on art, music, science, literature, politics, or possibly some new approach to the Freudian theory, they register both surprise and a seeming disappointment. Many of his avocational and personal interests, however, have stemmed from his interest in nature. He has at one time or another extensively studied position-finding and navigation and built some instruments of his own. He has built many cabins and even his own permanent home. He has studied photography and developed military field equipment. He feels that "no life is psychologically or physically complete or satisfying without some kind of home craft or manual pursuit."

* * *

RYAN, John (Gerald Christopher) 1921-

PERSONAL: Born March 4, 1921, in Edinburgh, Scotland; son of Andrew and Ruth (van Millingon) Ryan; married Priscilla Ann Blomfield, January 1, 1950; children: Marianne, Christopher, Isabel. *Education:* Attended school in England. *Home and office:* 12 Airlie Gardens, London W8, England.

CAREER: Artist, illustrator, and maker of films for children. *Military service:* British Army, 1941-45; became captain.

WRITINGS—All self-illustrated; all juveniles: *Captain Pugwash,* Bodley Head, 1955; *Pugwash Aloft,* Bodley Head, 1957; *Pugwash and the Ghostship,* Bodley Head, 1962, S. G. Phillips, 1968; *Pugwash in the Pacific,* S. G. Phillips, 1973; *Dodo's Delight,* Deutsch, 1977; *Doodle's Homework,* Deutsch, 1978; *The Adventures of Tiger-pig,* Hamlyn, 1978; *Tiger-pig at the Circus,* Hamlyn, 1979.

Author and producer of films for BBC-Television: "Captain Pugwash" series, 1958-68; "Mary Mungo and Midge," 1969; "Sir Prancelot," 1972; "Captain Pugwash" series II, 1976-77.

WORK IN PROGRESS: A series of twelve children's books about Noah's Ark, for Hamlyn.

* * *

RYMER, Alta May 1925-

PERSONAL: Born June 20, 1925, in San Diego, Calif.; daughter of Rendal H. and Rachel Marie (Worden) Bickford; married Keith C. Rymer (a former employee of North Island), May 27, 1943; children: Sharon (deceased), Timothy, Rebecca, Tracy. *Education:* Attended Grossmont Community College, 1971. *Home and office address:* P.O. Box 104, Tollhouse, Calif. 93667.

CAREER: Standard Parachute Co., San Diego, Calif., trimmer and thread supplier, 1943-44; Ryan Aeronautical Co., San Diego, cadmium plater, 1944-45; Rymer Books, Tollhouse, Calif., publisher, editor, and publicity manager, 1972—; free lance writer. Lecturer in schools.

WRITINGS: "Tales of Planet Artembo" series; all self-illustrated; all juveniles: *Beep-Bap-Zap-Jack,* Bordeaux Press, 1972, 2nd edition, Rymer Books, 1974; *Captain Zomo,* Rymer Books, 1980; *Chambo Returns,* Rymer Books, 1980.

WORK IN PROGRESS: More of "Tales of Planet Artembo" series, *Oopletrumps Odyssey, Exony's Excursion,* and *Hobart and Humbert Gruzzy;* more self-illustrated juveniles, *Up from Uzam, Visit from Voltassia, Princess Sugarfoot, Rosiepola Tickletoes, Tharma Lo, The Strange Solution to the King's Dilemma,* and *Ippy from Tron.*

SIDELIGHTS: Alta May Rymer told *CA:* "A great deal of joy and wonder and love are bound up in my children's stories. They are part of me when I was a child, part of me today. I wrote first for my own children.

"The characters in my books are purely inspired, brought forth into being immediately upon their conception, laid down just as they came to me upon the first dawning—dancing out of my head in jolly fashion, delighting me as they appeared. They were created through a process I shall never quite fathom. Is there some joyful little invisible being from somewhere else guiding my hand, or somehow creating invisible pictures for me? The stories also were inspiration; they were written *after* the characters were drawn.

"I hope to have added a new dimension to the thinking of every person who reads my work. I also hope to teach as well as to entertain them. I hope to give a little joy."

AVOCATIONAL INTERESTS: Painting, lettering, photography, clothes designing, rock collecting, ecology, printing with a press.

S

SAALMAN, Howard 1928-

PERSONAL: Born February 17, 1928, in Stettin, Germany; son of Walter G. and Gertrude (Robert) Saalman; married Jeanne Farr, 1954; children: Daphne Lydia. *Education:* City College (now City College of the City University of New York), A.B., 1949; New York University, M.A., 1955, Ph.D., 1960. *Office:* Department of Architecture, Carnegie-Mellon University, Pittsburgh, Pa. 15213.

CAREER: Carnegie-Mellon University, Pittsburgh, Pa., 1958—, currently Andrew Mellon Professor of Architecture. Excavations at Santa Trinita, Florence, Italy, 1957-58. *Member:* College Art Association, Society of Architectural Historians. *Awards, honors:* Fulbright fellow; American Council of Learned Societies fellow, 1961, 1963-64; Kress fellow in Florence, Italy, 1964-65; National Endowment for the Humanities fellow, 1973-74.

WRITINGS: *Medieval Architecture,* Braziller, 1962; *The Church of Santa Trinita in Florence,* Archaeological Institute of America and College Art Association, 1965; *Medieval Cities,* Braziller, 1968; *The Bigallo: The Oratory and Residence of the Compagnia del Bigallo e della Misoricordia in Florence,* Archaeological Institute of America and College Art Association, 1969; (editor and author of introduction and notes) *The Life of Brunelleschi by Antonio Manetti,* translation by Catherine Engass, Pennsylvania State University Press, 1970; *G. E. Haussmann: Paris Transformed,* Braziller, 1971; *Filippo Brunelleschi: The Cupola of Santa Maria del Fiore,* [London], 1980. Contributor to *Encyclopaedia Britannica.* Contributor of articles and reviews to professional journals.

WORK IN PROGRESS: *Filippo Brunelleschi: The Buildings; The City in the Renaissance; The Cupola of Saint Peter's.*

* * *

SAFA, Helen Icken 1930-

PERSONAL: Surname is accented on second syllable; born December 4, 1930, in Brooklyn, N.Y.; daughter of Gustav F. (self-employed) and Erna (Keune) Icken; married Manouchehr Safa-Isfahani (with United Nations), December 23, 1962; children: Mitra; stepchildren: Kaveh, Arya. *Education:* Cornell University, B.A., 1952; Columbia University, M.A., 1958, Ph.D., 1962. *Politics:* Democrat. *Religion:* Protestant. *Home:* 42 Gloucester Ct., East Brunswick, N.J. 08816. *Office:* Department of Anthropology, Rutgers University, New Brunswick, N.J. 08903.

CAREER: New York City Board of Education, New York, N.Y., research assistant, 1954; training and evaluation officer, Puerto Rican Department of State, Technical Cooperation Administration, 1954-55; information analyst, Commonwealth of Puerto Rico, Social Programs Administration, 1955-56; Syracuse University, Syracuse, N.Y., assistant professor of anthropology and senior research associate of Youth Development Center, 1962-67; Rutgers University, New Brunswick, N.J., associate professor, 1967-72, professor of anthropology, 1972—, associate director of Latin American Institute, 1967-70, New Brunswick Chairperson of Anthropology, 1974—. Member of advisory screening committee, Fulbright program, 1974-77; member of Smithsonian Institution foreign currency program, 1978. *Member:* International Congress of Americanists, American Anthropological Association (fellow), Society for Applied Anthropology (fellow), Latin American Studies Association (member of executive committee, 1974-77), American Ethnological Society, Social Science Research Council, National Organization for Women, Women's Equity Action League, American Civil Liberties Union, Phi Beta Kappa. *Awards, honors:* National Institute of Mental Health grants, 1963, 1969-70; U.S. Office of Education grant, 1966-67.

WRITINGS: *The Socio-Economic Conditions of Parceleros Resettled by the Social Programs Administration,* Agricultural Extension Service (Puerto Rico), 1956; *A Study of Aged Ineligible Applicants for Public Housing in New York City,* New York State Division of Housing, 1957; *Profiles in Poverty: An Analysis of Social Mobility in Low-Income Families,* Youth Development Center, Syracuse University, 1966; (contributor) Irwin Deutscher and E. Thompson, editors, *Among the People: Encounters with the Urban Poor,* Basic Books, 1968; (contributor) Peter Orleans and Russell Ellis, editors, *Urban Affairs Annual Review,* Volume V, Sage Publications, Inc., 1971; (contributor) Charles O. Crawford, editor, *The Family: Structure and Function in Health Crises,* Macmillan, 1971; *The Urban Poor of Puerto Rico,* Holt, 1972; (contributor) *Family and Social Change in the Caribbean,* Institute of Caribbean Studies, University of Puerto Rico, 1973; *Social Problems in Corporate America,* Harper, 1975; (editor with Brian M. Du Toit) *Migration and Development,* Mouton, 1975; (editor with J. Nash) *Sex and Class in Latin America,* Praeger, 1976. Also contributor to

Anthropological Perspectives on Education, edited by Murray Wax, *Perspectives on Latin America*, for Bobbs-Merrill, and to *Proceedings* of the thirty-sixth International Congress of Americanists. Contributor to numerous publications, including *Caribbean Studies, Human Organization, Urban Affairs Quarterly, Anuario Indegenista, Psychology Today, American Society for Public Administration, American Anthropologist, Hispanic American Historical Review*, and *American Behavioral Scientist*.

WORK IN PROGRESS: A comparative study of women factory workers in Brazil and the United States; editing *Urbanization in Developing Countries*, for Oxford University Press.

* * *

SAMETZ, Arnold W(illiam) 1919-

PERSONAL: Born December 4, 1919, in Brooklyn, N.Y.; son of Milton W. (a lawyer) and Natalie (Holland) Sametz; married Agnes Baroth, November 23, 1956; children: Margaret Baroth, Laura Holland. *Education:* Brooklyn College (now Brooklyn College of the City University of New York), A.B., 1940; Princeton University, A.M., 1942, Ph.D., 1951. *Home:* 37 Washington Square West, New York, N.Y. 10011. *Office:* Graduate School of Business Administration, New York University, 90 Trinity Pl., New York, N.Y. 10006.

CAREER: Princeton University, Princeton, N.J., instructor, 1948-51, assistant professor of economics, 1951-56; New York University, New York, N.Y., associate professor of banking, 1957-62, professor of economics and finance, 1962—, research director of Institute of Finance, beginning 1965, director of Salomon Brothers Center for the Study of Financial Institutions, 1975—. Lecturer for business firms. Bank trustee. *Military service:* U.S. Navy, 1942-46; became lieutenant. *Member:* American Economic Association, American Finance Association, Royal Economic Society, Metropolitan Economics Association (president, 1962-63), New York City Council for Economic Education (vice-chairman, 1960-65), Princeton Graduate Alumni Association (member of board of governors, 1959-62), Phi Beta Kappa, Phi Alpha Kappa. *Awards, honors:* Social Science Research Council fellow, 1946; Princeton University fellow, 1947, bicentennial preceptorship, 1951-54.

WRITINGS: (With Paul T. Homan and Albert Gailord Hart) *The Economic Order*, Harcourt, 1958; (with Robert Lindsay) *Financial Management: An Analytical Approach*, Irwin, 1963, 2nd edition, 1966; (editor and contributor) *Cyclical and Growth Problems Facing the Savings and Loan Industry*, Graduate School of Business Administration, New York University, 1968; (editor and contributor) *Financial Development and Economic Growth: Underdeveloped Capital Markets*, New York University Press, 1972; (contributor) *The Modern Economy in Action: An Analytic Approach*, 2nd edition, Pitman, 1973; (with E. Bloch) *A Modest Proposal for a National Market System and Its Governance* (monograph), Graduate School of Business Administration, New York University, 1977; (with E. Altman) *Financial Crises: Institutions and Markets in a Fragile Environment*, Wiley, 1977; (with P. Wachtel) *The Financial Environment, 1975-1985*, Heath Lexington, 1977; *Prospects for Capital Formation and Capital Markets: Financial Requirements Over the Next Decade*, Heath Lexington, 1978; (contributor) M. Polakoff, editor, *Financial Institutions and Markets*, Houghton, 1980; (editor), *Securities Activities of Commercial Banks*, Heath Lexington, 1980. Contributor of articles to professional journals. Associate editor, *Journal of Banking and Finance*, 1977—.

WORK IN PROGRESS: Financing Business Investment in a Fragile Financial Environment of High Investment and Rising Prices; Backcasting: What Can Go Wrong with Long Term Financial Forecasts; Bond Markets: Trading and Portfolio Patterns and Strategies.

* * *

SAMPSON, Roy J(ohnson) 1919-

PERSONAL: Born March 3, 1919, in Elmwood, Tenn.; son of B. V. and Lizzie (Farley) Sampson; married Rosetta Pannier, 1942; children: Donald, Stuart, Carole, Linda. *Education:* Tennessee Polytechnic Institute (now Tennessee Technological University), B.S., 1946; University of California, Berkeley, M.B.A., 1948, Ph.D., 1951. *Home:* 38730 Dexter Rd., Dexter, Ore. 97431. *Office:* School of Business Administration, University of Oregon, Eugene, Ore. 97403.

CAREER: University of Utah, Salt Lake City, instructor in management, 1950-51; Office of Price Stabilization, Seattle, Wash. and Portland, Ore., economist, 1951-53; Pacific University, Forest Grove, Ore., 1953-55, began as assistant professor, became associate professor of business administration; Texas Technological College (now Texas Tech University), Lubbock, 1955-59, began as assistant professor, became associate professor of economics; University of Oregon, Eugene, 1959—, began as assistant professor, professor of transportation economics, 1965—. President, Pacific Northwest Advisory Board. *Military service:* U.S. Navy, 1942-45; became petty officer. *Member:* American Economic Association, American Society of Traffic and Transportation, American Transportation Research Forum, Western Economic Association, Delta Nu Alpha (member of national educational committee), Traffic Club and Chamber of Commerce (both Eugene). *Awards, honors:* Foundation for Economic Education fellowship, 1956-57; Ford Foundation fellowship, University of California, Berkeley, 1959, and Cornell University, 1960.

WRITINGS: (With others) *Principles of Economics*, Pitman, 1959; *Obstacles to Railroad Unification* (monograph), Bureau of Business Research, University of Oregon, 1960; *Railroad Shipments and Rates from the Pacific Northwest* (monograph), Bureau of Business Research, University of Oregon, 1961; (with L. S. Levy) *American Economic Development*, Allyn & Bacon, 1962; *Railroad Shipments and Rates into the Pacific Northwest* (monograph), Bureau of Business Research, University of Oregon, 1963; (with W. P. Mortenson and D. T. Krider) *Understanding Our Economy*, Houghton, 1964; *Oregon Rail and Water Commodity-Flow Trends* (monograph), Bureau of Business and Economic Research, University of Oregon, 1965; *Transportation Trends in the State of Washington* (monograph), Bureau of Economic and Business Research, Washington State University, 1965; (with M. T. Farris) *Domestic Transportation: Practice, Theory and Policy*, Houghton, 1966, 4th edition, 1979; (with Mortenson and I. Marienhoff) *The American Economy*, Houghton, 1972, 2nd edition, 1975; (with Farris) *Public Utilities: Regulation, Management, and Ownership*, Houghton, 1973; (with T. W. Calmus) *Economics: Concepts, Applications, Analysis*, Houghton, 1974. Contributor of articles and reviews to professional journals and business magazines.

SIDELIGHTS: Roy Sampson told *CA:* "One cannot aspire higher than that the world be a little better place for one's having been here. Parents, teachers, and writers have the greatest opportunities for making the world better. I have always known that I was going to teach and write and actually started writing for local publications at the age of eleven. I have also been blessed by parenthood and by years of university teaching. . . . When I finish the race, I hope that I can say, like St. Paul, that 'I have fought the good fight . . . I have kept the faith.'" *Avocational interests:* Fishing, camping.

* * *

SANBORN, Duane 1914-
(Duane Bradley)

PERSONAL: Born June 13, 1914, in Clarinda, Iowa; daughter of Clifford Cleveland (a minister) and Nellie Anne (Harryman) Cox; married George Andrews Sanborn; children: Louis, Marilyn (Mrs. James Bowie), Anne (Mrs. Nicholas Rowe), Hugh. *Education:* Educated in public schools. *Religion:* Congregational Church. *Home:* Warner Rd., Henniker, N.H.

CAREER: Has worked in newspaper, publicity, and public relations fields. Writer for young people. *Awards, honors: Meeting with a Stranger* selected by Library of Congress as one of the outstanding juvenile books of 1964; Jane Addams Children's Book Award, 1965.

WRITINGS—All under name Duane Bradley; all published by Lippincott, except as indicated: *Cappy and the Jet Engine,* 1957; *Engineers Did It!,* 1958; (with Eugene Lord) *Our World of Science,* 1959; *Time for You,* 1960; *Mystery at the Shoals,* 1962; (with Lord) *Here's How It Works,* 1962; *Electing a President,* Van Nostrand, 1963; *Meeting with a Stranger,* 1964; *The Newspaper: Its Place in a Democracy,* Van Nostrand, 1965; *Sew It and Wear It,* Crowell, 1966; *Count Rumford,* Van Nostrand, 1967; *Practical and Pretty Fashions from Simple Shapes Sewing,* C. R. Gibson, 1975; *Design It, Sew It, and Wear It: How to Make Yourself a Super Wardrobe without Commercial Patterns,* Crowell, 1979. Contributor of articles and stories to magazines.

WORK IN PROGRESS: A series of books on design and sewing.

SIDELIGHTS: Duane Sanborn's book, *Engineers Did It!* has been published in Persian and Arabic. The U.S. Information Agency has published a Korean edition of *Electing a President* and a French edition of *The Newspaper: Its Place in a Democracy.*†

* * *

SANDEEN, Ernest Robert 1931-

PERSONAL: Born March 27, 1931, in Oak Park, Ill.; son of Ernest T. (a corporation executive) and Evelyn (Beguelin) Sandeen; married Eunice Fechner (an arts administrator), 1952; children: Jill Marjorie, Judith Heldt. *Education:* Wheaton College, Wheaton, Ill., B.A., 1953; University of Chicago, M.A., 1955, Ph.D., 1959. *Home:* 826 Goodrich Ave., St. Paul, Minn. 55105. *Office:* Department of History, Macalester College, St. Paul, Minn. 55105.

CAREER: North Park College, Chicago, Ill., assistant professor of history, 1959-63; Macalester College, St. Paul, Minn., assistant professor, 1963-68, associate professor, 1968-71, professor of history, beginning 1971, currently James Wallace Professor of History. *Member:* Society of Architectural Historians, American Society of Church History, American Studies Association. *Awards, honors:* English-Speaking Union scholar in England, 1957-58; Ford Foundation humanities grant, 1969-70.

WRITINGS: Roots of Fundamentalism: British and American Millenarianism, 1800-1930, University of Chicago Press, 1970; (editor with Frederick Hale) *American Religion and Philosophy: A Guide to Information Sources,* Gale, 1978; *St. Paul's Historic Summit Avenue,* Living Historical Museum, 1978; (with David Lanegran) *The Lake District of Minneapolis: A History of the Calhoun-Isles Community,* Living Historical Museum, 1979.

* * *

SANGUINETTI, Elise Ayers 1926-

PERSONAL: Born January 26, 1926, in Anniston, Ala.; daughter of Harry Mell (a newspaper publisher and editor) and Edel (Ytterboe) Ayers; married Phillip A. Sanguinetti (a newspaper editor), 1950. *Education:* Attended St. Olaf College, one year, and University of Oslo, summer session; University of Alabama, A.B. *Religion:* Episcopalian. *Home:* 818 Glenwood Ter., Anniston, Ala. *Agent:* McIntosh & Otis, 475 Fifth Ave., New York, N.Y. 10017.

CAREER: Anniston Star, Anniston, Ala., reporter and feature writer, four years.

WRITINGS: The Last of the Whitfields, McGraw, 1962; *The New Girl,* McGraw, 1964; *The Dowager,* Scribner, 1968; *McBee's Station,* Holt, 1971. Contributor of short stories to *Mademoiselle* and other periodicals.

WORK IN PROGRESS: A novel.

BIOGRAPHICAL/CRITICAL SOURCES: New York Times Book Review, October 3, 1968; *Virginia Quarterly Review,* winter, 1969; *Best Sellers,* June 6, 1971.

* * *

SAPP, Phyllis Woodruff 1908-

PERSONAL: Born October 21, 1908, in Oklahoma City, Okla; daughter of John A. and Maude (Laws) Woodruff; married J. D. Sapp, June 5, 1930; children: Kathryn Sapp Malthaner, John Davis, Phillip Woodruff. *Education:* Oklahoma University, A.B., 1930; graduate work in writing and counseling, 1948, 1950. *Religion:* Baptist. *Home:* 7100 South Kentucky, Oklahoma City, Okla.

CAREER: Organizer and director of first children's theater in Oklahoma City, Okla., 1930-35; Oklahoma City Theatre Guild, Oklahoma City, director, 1940-42; speech teacher in public high school, Pensacola, Fla., 1944-45; Jackson Junior High School, Oklahoma City, speech teacher, 1946-48, counselor, 1948-50; free-lance writer, 1951—. Real estate broker, 1969—, currently secretary-treasurer, Sapp Realty, Inc. Conducted workshop for persons interested in religious writing, University of Oklahoma, 1954, 1962, on teaching staff, 1965. YWCA, Oklahoma City chapter, member of executive board, 1973—, president, 1976-79, member of national board, 1979—. *Member:* International Platform Association, National League of American Pen Women (Oklahoma City branch, vice-president, 1962-63, president, 1968-70, 1976-78, treasurer, 1973-75; national vice-president, 1970-72; chairman of national letters board, 1972-74; national chaplain, 1974-76), Oklahoma Heritage Association, Pi Kappa Delta, Alpha Phi. *Awards, honors:* First prize, Christian Fiction Contest, Zondervan Publishers, 1957.

WRITINGS—Published by Home Mission Board, Southern Baptist Convention, except as indicated: *The Ice Cutter: The Life of J. B. Rounds, Missionary to the Indians,* 1948; *Accidental Hero* (three-act comedy), Eldridge Entertainment House, 1950; *Whispers Out of the Dust,* 1951; *For Such a Time* (biography), 1953; *Living for Jesus Every Day* (vacation Bible school text), Convention Press, 1957; *Small Giant* (novel), Zondervan, 1957; *The Long Bridge,* 1957; *Working*

Together in Our Church, 1959; *Life at Its Best,* Broadman, 1963; (editor and contributor) *Lighthouse on the Corner: A History of the First Baptist Church, Oklahoma City, Oklahoma,* Century Press, 1964; *Creative Teaching in the Church School,* Broadman, 1967; *Teaching Guide for Youth Sunday School Work,* Convention Press, 1969; *59 Programs for Pre-Teens,* Broadman, 1969; *Jeff the Baptist,* 1972; *The Very Best Plan,* 1978. Author of church school texts and curriculum materials published by Southern Baptist Sunday School Board. Also author of *Children of Men,* 1968, *Real Estate Workbook,* 1972, and *Very Best Friend,* 1976. Contributor of articles and stories to church publications.

WORK IN PROGRESS: High on a Hill, for Century Press; a novel about race relations.

SIDELIGHTS: Phyllis Woodruff Sapp told *CA:* "My book, *The Long Bridge,* . . . was the first book published by Southern Baptists about the denomination's work with Negroes. It caused a furor [and] was banned by the Home Mission Board who had contracted with me for its writing. Then, surprisingly, the 'grass roots' of the denomination rose up and demanded the right to read the book. It finally led the way for numerous publications on the same subject. It led me into strange and circuitous paths for a mature, upper middle class white woman: invitations to write for *Ebony,* to a racial confrontation in San Francisco, to be a facilitator in racial seminars, and now to a position on the National Board of the YWCA. . . . The YWCA's One Imperative, adopted at [the] National Convention in 1973, is the elimination of racism by whatever means possible."

* * *

SARTON, (Eleanor) May 1912-

PERSONAL: Born May 3, 1912, in Wondelgem, Belgium; brought to United States, 1916; became naturalized U.S. citizen, 1924; daughter of George A. L. (historian of science) and Eleanor Mabel (Elwes) Sarton. *Politics:* Democrat. *Religion:* Unitarian Universalist. *Residence:* York, Me. *Agent:* Russell & Volkening, Inc., 551 Fifth Ave., New York, N.Y. 10017. *Office:* Academy of American Poets, 1030 Fifth Ave., New York, N.Y.

CAREER: Eva Le Gallienne's Civic Repertory Theatre, New York City, apprentice, 1929-34; Associated Actors Theatre, New York City, founder, director, 1934-37; Overseas Film Unit, New York City, script writer, 1941-52; Harvard University, Cambridge, Mass., Briggs-Copeland Instructor in English Composition, 1949-52; Bread Loaf Writer's Conference, Middlebury, Vt., lecturer, 1951-53; Boulder Writers' Conference, Boulder, Colo., lecturer, 1954; Wellesley College, Wellesley, Mass., lecturer in creative writing, 1960-64; Lindenwood College, St. Charles, Mo., poet-in-residence, 1965. Danforth visiting lecturer, Arts Program, 1959; Phi Beta Kappa visiting scholar, 1960; visiting lecturer, Agnes Scott College, 1972. *Member:* Poetry Society of America, New England Poetry Society, American Academy of Arts and Sciences (fellow). *Awards, honors:* Golden Rose Award, New England Poetry Society, 1945; Bland Memorial Prize, *Poetry,* 1945; Reynolds Lyric Award, Poetry Society of America, 1952; Lucy Martin Donnelly fellowship, Bryn Mawr College, 1953-54; Guggenheim fellow in poetry, 1954-55; Litt.D., Russell Sage College, 1958; Johns Hopkins University Poetry Festival Award, 1961; Emily Clark Balch Prize, 1966; National Endowment for the Arts grant, 1966; Litt.D., New England College, 1971; Sarah Josepha Hale Award, 1972; doctorate degrees from Bates College, 1974, Colby College, 1974, University of New Hampshire, 1974, Clark University, 1975, Thomas Starr King School of Religious Leadership, 1976, and Nassa College, 1980.

WRITINGS—Poetry; published by Norton, except as indicated: *Encounter in April,* Houghton, 1937; *Inner Landscape,* Houghton, 1939; *The Lion and the Rose,* Rinehart, 1948; *The Land of Silence,* Rinehart, 1953; *In Time Like Air,* Rinehart, 1957; *Cloud, Stone, Sun, Vine,* 1961; *A Private Mythology,* 1966; *As Does New Hampshire,* Richard R. Smith, 1967; *A Grain of Mustard Seed,* 1971; *A Durable Fire,* 1972; *Collected Poems: 1930-1973,* 1974; *Selected Poems,* 1978; *Hellway to Silence,* 1980.

Fiction; published by Norton, except as indicated: *The Single Hound,* Houghton, 1938; *The Bridge of Years,* Doubleday, 1946; *Underground River* (play), Play Club, 1947; *Shadow of a Man,* Rinehart, 1950; *A Shower of Summer Days,* Rinehart, 1952, reprinted, Norton, 1970; *Faithful Are the Wounds,* Rinehart, 1955, reprinted, Norton, 1972; *The Birth of a Grandfather,* Rinehart, 1957; *The Small Room,* 1961; *Joanna and Ulysses,* 1963; *Mrs. Stevens Hears the Mermaids Singing,* 1965, revised edition, 1974; *Miss Pickthorn and Mr. Hare* (fable), 1966; *The Poet and the Donkey,* 1969; *Kinds of Love,* 1970; *As We Are Now,* 1973; *Punch's Secret* (juvenile), Harper, 1974; *Crucial Conversations,* 1975; *A Walk through the Woods* (juvenile), Harper, 1976; *A Reckoning,* 1978.

Nonfiction; published by Norton, except as indicated: *I Knew a Phoenix: Sketches for an Autobiography,* Rinehart, 1959; (contributor) *The Movement of Poetry,* Johns Hopkins Press, 1962; *Plant Dreaming Deep* (autobiography), 1968; *Journal of a Solitude,* 1973; *A World of Light: Portraits and Celebrations,* 1976; *The House by the Sea,* 1977.

Also author of the screenplays "Toscanini: The Hymn of Nations," 1944, and "Valley of the Tennessee," 1944. Contributor of poetry, short stories, and essays to periodicals.

SIDELIGHTS: "Examined as a whole," Lenora P. Blouin writes, "the body of May Sarton's writing is almost overwhelming. It reveals an artist who has not remained stagnant or afraid of change. 'Truth,' especially the truth within herself, has been her life-long quest." "May Sarton," Victor Howes states, "is the kind of writer whom fans and admirers write letters to, or cross the continent to consult, or just visit. Reading her poems, one comes to see why."

Sarton's poetry is calm, cultured, and urbane. A reviewer for *Poetry* describes it as "fluent, fluid, humble with a humility not entirely false, cultivated rather than worldly, tasteful, civilized, and accomplished." James Dickey believes that Sarton "attains a delicate simplicity as quickeningly direct as it is deeply given, and does so with the courteous serenity, the clear, caring, intelligent and human calm of the queen of a small, well-ordered country." "In her most perfect poems," a reviewer for *Choice* writes, ". . . the fusion of passion and discipline is marvelously realized." Reviewing *Collected Poems,* Elizabeth Knies avows that it is "intelligently conceived and finely wrought" and calls it "the consummation of a distinguished career and a major achievement in its own right."

Other critics, however, find less to admire in Sarton's poetry. James McMichael writes that Sarton's poetry "is too self-conscious, . . . the products are dull too much of the time [and] the writing is quaint but accurate." Rosellen Brown, reviewing *Durable Fire,* comments that it contains "many brief evocations of an actual rural world, but it is, every bit of it, . . . *used* and directed."

Critical commentary about Sarton's fiction has been generally favorable. Among her harsher critics, R. L. Brown finds that Sarton's writing is "sensitive to the point of fussiness and totally without humor." Lore Dickstein criticizes Sarton's style, "which tends toward the ready cliche and occasionally teeters on the edge of sentimentality," while noting that "Sarton is best at evoking the private sensibility of one person." R. P. Corsini, however, finds that "the music of Miss Sarton's prose leaves compelling echoes in one's mind." "Sarton," Beverly Grunwald writes, "knows how to be tender and romantic, melancholy and amusing, all at once." Cade Ware notes that "Sarton is particularly adept at presenting intelligent women intelligently.... She is famous, too, for catching the flavor of background.... She is an aristocrat whose patent is clarity of mind."

"It is my hope," Sarton has written, "that all [my work] may come to be seen as a whole, the communication of a vision of life that is unsentimental, humorous, passionate, and, in the end, timeless."

BIOGRAPHICAL/CRITICAL SOURCES: *Saturday Review,* March 27, 1937, October 23, 1965; *Poetry,* July, 1937, April, 1968; *Time,* March 21, 1938, October 1, 1965; *New York Times Book Review,* March 15, 1939, September 8, 1957, November 24, 1963, October 24, 1965, November 12, 1978; *Christian Science Monitor,* April 8, 1939, June 10, 1950, November 13, 1978; *Chicago Tribune,* May 7, 1950; *Boston Globe,* May 14, 1950; *Atlantic,* January, 1953, June, 1975; *Yale Review,* winter, 1954; *New Yorker,* February 27, 1954; *New Leader,* March 28, 1955; *Los Angeles Times,* March 16, 1957; *Sewanee Review,* spring, 1958; May Sarton, *I Knew a Phoenix: Sketches for an Autobiography,* Rinehart, 1959.

Harpers, September, 1961; John O. Lyons, *The College Novel in America,* Southern Illinois University Press, 1962; *Arizona Quarterly,* winter, 1962; *Virginia Quarterly Review,* spring, 1962; *Punch,* April 11, 1962; *Book Week,* December 29, 1963; Joseph Blotner, *The Modern American Political Novel: 1900-1960,* University of Texas Press, 1966; *San Francisco Chronicle,* June 19, 1966; Joseph Henderson, *Thresholds of Initiation,* Wesleyan University Press, 1967; *Denver Quarterly,* winter, 1967; *Southern Review,* spring, 1967; *Hudson Review,* summer, 1967; *Massachusetts Review,* summer, 1967; James Dickey, *Babel to Byzantium,* Farrar, Straus, 1968; Sarton, *Plant Dreaming Deep,* Norton, 1968.

Western Humanities Review, autumn, 1971; Susan K. Cornillon, *Images of Women in Fiction,* Bowling Green University Press, 1972; Agnes Silbey, *May Sarton,* Twayne, 1972; *Contempora,* spring, 1972; *Parnassus,* spring/summer, 1973; *New Republic,* June 8, 1974; *Village Voice,* June 13, 1974; *Publishers Weekly,* June 24, 1974; *Contemporary Literary Criticism,* Volume IV, Gale, 1975; Jane Rule, *Lesbian Images,* Doubleday, 1975; *Chrysallis Journal,* summer, 1975; *Green River Review,* summer, 1975; *Maine Times,* June 20, 1975; *Commonweal,* July 4, 1975; Sarton, *A World of Light: Portraits and Celebrations,* Norton, 1976; *San Francisco Examiner,* November 29, 1976; Lenora Blouin, *May Sarton: A Biography,* Scarecrow, 1978; *Choice,* January, 1979.

* * *

SASEK, Lawrence A(nton) 1923-

PERSONAL: Born March 22, 1923, in Glen Carbon, Ill.; son of Frank and Rose Mary (Chaloupka) Sasek; married Gloria Theresa Burns, 1960. *Education:* University of Illinois at Urbana-Champaign, B.A., 1947, M.A., 1948; Harvard University, Ph.D., 1953. *Home:* 1458 Kenilworth Pkwy., Baton Rouge, La. 70808. *Office:* Department of English, Louisiana State University, Baton Rouge, La. 70803.

CAREER: Louisiana State University, Baton Rouge, instructor, 1953-56, assistant professor, 1956-61, associate professor, 1961-69, professor of English, 1969—. *Military service:* U.S. Army Air Forces, 1943-46. *Member:* American Association of University Professors, Modern Language Association of America, National Council of Teachers of English, College English Association, Renaissance Society of America, Phi Beta Kappa.

WRITINGS: *The Literary Temper of the English Puritans,* Louisiana State University Press, 1961; (contributor) Waldo F. McNeir, editor, *Studies in English Renaissance Literature,* Louisiana State University Press, 1962; (editor and author of introduction) *The Poems of William Smith,* Louisiana State University Press, 1970. Also author of *The Drama of Paradise Lost, XI-XII,* 1962.

WORK IN PROGRESS: A study of English puritanism, completion expected in 1981.

* * *

SAVAGE, Elizabeth Fitzgerald 1918-

PERSONAL: Born 1918, in Hingham, Mass.; daughter of Robert Brassil and Mildred (Ridlon) Fitzgerald; married Thomas Savage (a writer), 1939; children: Robert, Russell, Elizabeth. *Education:* Colby College, B.A., 1940. *Home:* Georgetown, Me. 04548. *Agent:* Blanche Gregory, 2 Tudor City Pl., New York, N.Y. 10017.

CAREER: Free-lance writer. *Member:* Phi Beta Kappa.

WRITINGS—All published by Little, Brown: *Summer of Pride,* 1961; *But Not for Love,* 1970; *A Fall of Angels,* 1971; *Happy Ending,* 1972; *The Last Night at the Ritz,* 1973; *A Good Confession,* 1975; *The Girls from the Five Great Valleys,* 1977; *Willowwood,* 1978; *Toward the End,* 1980. Contributor of short stories to *Saturday Evening Post, Cosmopolitan, Paris Review,* and other magazines.

WORK IN PROGRESS: *I Am Innocent.*

* * *

SAVITT, Sam

PERSONAL: Born March 22, in Wilkes-Barre, Pa.; son of Hyman (a salesman) and Rose (Eskowitz) Savitt; married Bette Orkin, March 28, 1946; children: Dara Vickery, Roger Scott. *Education:* Pratt Institute, graduate, 1941; attended Art Students League, 1950-51. *Home:* One-Horse Farm, North Salem, N.Y.

CAREER: Free-lance writer and illustrator. Has served as official artist for United States equestrian team. *Military service:* U.S. Army, 1942-46; served in China-Burma-India Theater; became first lieutenant. *Member:* Society of Illustrators, Authors Guild, Authors League of America, Graphic Artists Guild. *Awards, honors:* Boys' Clubs of America junior book award, 1958, for *Midnight.*

WRITINGS: *Step-A-Bit,* Dutton, 1956; *Midnight,* Dutton, 1958; *There Was a Horse,* Dial, 1960; *Around the World with Horses,* Dial, 1962; *Rodeo: Cowboys, Bulls, and Broncos,* Doubleday, 1963; *Sam Savitt Guide to Horses,* Black Horse Press, 1963; *Vicki and the Black Horse,* Doubleday, 1964; *Day at the LBJ Ranch,* Random House, 1965; *America's Horses,* Doubleday, 1966; *Equestrian Olympic Sketchbook,* A. S. Barnes, 1968; *Sam Savitt's True Horse Stories,* Dodd, 1971; *Wild Horse Running* (Junior Literary Guild selection),

Dodd, 1973; (with Suzanne Wilding) *Ups and Downs,* St. Martin's, 1973; (with Herb Marlin) *How to Take Care of Your Horse until the Vet Comes,* Dodd, 1975; *Vicki and the Brown Mare,* Dodd, 1976; (with William Steinkraus) *Great Horses of the United States Equestrian Team,* Dodd, 1977; *The Dingle Ridge Fox and Other Stories,* Dodd, 1978; *Draw Horses with Sam Savitt,* Viking, in press. Contributor of articles to magazines, including *Western Horseman* and *Equus.*

Illustrator: *Bold Passage,* Simon & Schuster, 1950; *Learning to Ride and Hunt,* Doubleday, 1950; *Tiger Roan,* Pocket Books, 1950; *Trailing Trouble,* Holiday House, 1952; *Desert Dog,* Holiday House, 1956; *Wildlife Cameraman,* Holiday House, 1957; *Horsemanship,* A. S. Barnes, 1958, *Black Beauty,* Scholastic Book Services, 1958; *Gimmery,* Dodd, 1958; *Wild Horse Tamer,* Scholastic Book Services, 1958; *Witch's Colt,* Dodd, 1958; *Dark Colt, Light Filly,* Scholastic Book Services, 1959; *Fury,* F. Watts, 1959; *Long Trail Drive,* Scholastic Book Services, 1959; *Mountain Pony,* Scholastic Book Services, 1959; *Shasta and Gimmery,* Dodd, 1959; *A Saddlebag of Tales,* Dodd, 1959; *Blizzard Rescue,* F. Watts, 1959; *Born to Race,* St. Martin's, 1959; *Challenger,* Coward, 1959; *Pets at the White House,* Dutton, 1959; *The Torch Bearer,* F. Watts, 1959.

Up and Away, Harcourt, 1960; *The Top Hand of Lone Tree Ranch,* Crowell, 1960; *Johnny's Island Ark,* F. Watts, 1960; *Diving Horse,* Coward, 1960; *Fury and the Mustangs,* Holt, 1960; *Horse in Her Heart,* Coward, 1960; *Horseback Riding,* Lippincott, 1960; *Daughter of the Silver Brumby,* Dutton, 1960; *Gun Law at Laramie,* Pocket Books, 1960; *Spook the Mustang,* Lippincott, 1960; *Wild Horses of Tuscanny,* F. Watts, 1960; *Alcatraz the Wild Stallion,* Pocket Books, 1961; *Animal Anthology,* Scholastic Book Services, 1961; *Training Your Dog,* Doubleday, 1961; *White Fang,* Scholastic Book Services, 1961; *Little Smoke,* Coward, 1961; *Loco the Bronc,* Coward, 1961; *The Snow Filly,* Dutton, 1961; *Thudding Hoofs,* St. Martin's, 1961; *Wilderness Renegade,* F. Watts, 1962; *The Horse Trap,* Coward, 1962; *Teddy Koala,* Dodd, 1962; *Lad, a Dog,* Dutton, 1962; *Fawn in the Forest,* Dodd, 1962; *Dream Pony for Robin,* St. Martin's, 1962; *Dinny and the Dreamdust,* Doubleday, 1962; *Buffalo Bill,* Garrard, 1962; *American Girl Book of Horse Stories,* Random House, 1963; *Boy's Life Book of Horse Stories,* Random House, 1963; *Care and Training of Dogs,* Random House, 1963; *Forever the Wild Mare,* Dodd, 1963; *Horse of Your Own,* Doubleday, 1963; *No Love for Schnitzle,* St. Martin's, 1963; *Patrick Visits the Zoo,* Dodd, 1963; *Show Ring Rouge,* Coward, 1963; *Wild Heart,* Doubleday, 1963; *Two Dogs and a Horse,* Dodd, 1964; *Old Quarry Fox Hunt,* Washburn, 1964; *Horse in the House,* Coward, 1964; *Big Book of Favorite Horse Stories,* Platt, 1965; *Big Jump for Robin,* St. Martin's 1965; *Ghost Hound of Thunder Valley,* Dodd, 1965; *Redhead and the Roan,* Van Nostrand, 1965; *Christy Finds a Rider,* Norton, 1965; *Star Bright,* Norton, 1965; *Encyclopedia of Horses,* Crowell, 1966; *Star Lost,* Norton, 1966; *If You Want a Horse,* Coward, 1966; *Dave and His Dog Mulligan,* Dodd, 1966; *Star, the Sea Horse,* Norton, 1968; *Golden Book of Horses,* Golden Press, 1968; *The Pony that Didn't Grow,* Washburn, 1968; *The Lord Mayor's Horse Show,* Doubleday, 1969; *Great Stories for Young Readers,* Reader's Digest Press, 1969; *Harlequin Horse,* Van Nostrand, 1969; *Horses,* Golden Press, 1969; *Ride, Gaucho,* World Publishing, 1969.

Sky Rocket, Dodd, 1970; *Horses, Horses, Horses,* Van Nostrand, 1970; *Elementary Dressage,* A. S. Barnes, 1970; *Horseman's Almanac,* Agway, 1971; *Wild Animal Rescue,* Dodd, 1971; *Hundred Horse Farm,* St. Martin's, 1972; *Horses in Action,* St. Martin's, 1972; *How to Bring Up Your Pet Dog,* Dodd, 1973; *Gift of Gold,* Dodd, 1973; *Summer Pony,* Macmillan, 1973; *The Art of Painting Horses,* Grumbacher Library, 1973; *A Boy and a Pig, But Mostly Horses,* Dodd, 1974; *Gallant Grey Trotter,* Dodd, 1974; *Grand Prix Jumping,* Aberdeen Press, 1974; *Backyard Pony,* F. Watts, 1975; *Horses: A First Book,* F. Watts, 1975; *Riding Teachers Manual,* Doubleday, 1975; *Horse Tales,* St. Martin's, 1976; *The Tale of the Horse,* Walter Field, 1976; *Springfellow,* Windmill Books, 1977; *Pluto,* Garrard, 1978; *My Mane Catches the Wind,* Harcourt, 1979; *Run Hiboy Run,* Garrard, 1980.

WORK IN PROGRESS: A book on endurance riding for Dodd.

AVOCATIONAL INTERESTS: Sculpture, fox hunting with golden bridge hounds, schooling horses, swimming, hiking.

BIOGRAPHICAL/CRITICAL SOURCES: *Polo Magazine,* XXVI, 7, 1960; *Sunday Independence* (Wilkes Barre, Pa.), January 17, 1960; *The Sun* (Baltimore, Md.), July 17, 1962; *Western Horseman,* April, 1973; *Palm Beach Daily News,* February 7, 1974; *Sun Sentinel* (Pompano Beach, Fla.), February 14, 1974; *Reporter Dispatch* (White Plains, N.Y.), April 1, 1974; *Horse Play,* April, 1974; *Lead Line* (Bedford, N.Y.), March, 1978.

* * *

SAYLES, Leonard Robert 1926-

PERSONAL: Born April 30, 1926, in Rochester, N.Y.; son of Robert (a merchant) and Rose (Sklof) Sayles; children: Robert, Emily. *Education:* University of Rochester, B.A. (with highest honors), 1956; Massachusetts Institute of Technology, Ph.D., 1950. *Home:* 19 Birch Lane, Dobbs Ferry, N.Y. 10522. *Office:* Graduate School of Business, Columbia University, New York, N.Y. 10027.

CAREER: Cornell University, Ithaca, N.Y., assistant professor of industrial relations,, 1950-53; University of Michigan, Ann Arbor, assistant professor of business administration, 1953-56; Columbia University, Graduate School of Business, New York, N.Y., associate professor, 1956-60, professor of business administration, 1960—, head of Industrial Relations and Organizational Behavior Division. Consultant to numerous private and public organizations. *Member:* Society for Applied Anthropology (member of executive committee, 1959-62), Bureau of Applied Social Research (member of board of governors, 1960—), Industrial Relations Research Association (member of executive board, 1970-73), National Academy of Public Administration (fellow), Phi Beta Kappa. *Awards, honors:* Society for the Psychological Study of Social Issues award for most outstanding book on industrial relations, 1953, for *The Local Union;* McKinsey Award, 1964, for *Individualism and Big Business;* Organization Development Council publication award, 1965, for *Managerial Behavior;* recipient of several faculty research fellowships and awards from Ford Foundation as well as various annual research and publication awards from professional organizations.

WRITINGS: (With G. Strauss) *The Local Union,* Harper, 1953; (contributor) *Money and Motivation,* Harper, 1955; *Behaviour of Industrial Work Groups,* Wiley, 1958, reprinted, Arno, 1977; (with Strauss) *Personnel,* Prentice-Hall, 1960, 3rd edition, 1972; (with E. Chapple) *The Measure of Management,* Macmillan, 1961; (with M. Chandler) *Contracting-Out* (monograph), Graduate School of Business, Columbia University, 1961; *Individualism and Big Business,*

McGraw, 1963; *Managerial Behavior,* McGraw, 1964, 2nd edition, Krieger, 1979; (with Strauss) *Human Behavior in Organizations,* Prentice-Hall, 1966; (with W. Dowling) *How Managers Motivate,* McGraw, 1971; (with Chandler) *Managing Large Systems,* Harper, 1971; (with R. Wegner) *Cases in Organizational and Administrative Behavior,* Prentice-Hall, 1972; *Leadership,* McGraw, 1979. Contributor to professional journals.

* * *

SCHAAF, Martha Eckert 1911-

PERSONAL: Born September 21, 1911, in Madison, Ind.; daughter of Frederick William and Julia (Richert) Eckert; married Clarence William Schaaf (a colonel in the U.S. Army), 1941; children: Susan Elizabeth. *Education:* Indiana University, A.B. (with distinction), 1933; Columbia University, M.S., 1945. *Home:* 51 South West Tenth Ter., Boca Raton, Fla. 33432.

CAREER: Grade school and high school teacher in Crothersville, Ind., 1936-38, Angola, Ind., 1938-39, and Indianapolis, Ind., 1939-41; high school librarian in Evansville, Ind., 1942; Library, Columbus, Ga., county supervisor, 1943; Camp Van Dorn Hospital, Camp Van Dorn, Miss., librarian, 1944; Bulova Watch Co., Long Island, N.Y., librarian, 1944-45; Eli Lilly & Co., Indianapolis, business librarian, 1946-50; Indiana Historical Society Library, Indianapolis, cataloger of Lew Wallace Collection, 1958-61; David-Stewart Publishing Co., Indianapolis, member of staff, 1963-67; Pompano Beach Public Library, Pompano Beach, Fla., member of staff, 1967-72; free-lance author, musician, lecturer, 1973—. *Member:* National League of American Pen Women, National Federation of Music Clubs, Phi Beta Kappa, Pi Lambda Theta Chi Omega, Mortar Board (president, 1933).

WRITINGS: *Lew Wallace: Boy Writer,* Bobbs-Merrill, 1962; (contributor) *War Paint and Wagon Wheels,* David-Stewart, 1968; *Duke Ellington: Young Music Maker,* Bobbs-Merrill, 1975. Also author of *The Greatest of These* (poetry), 1976. Also contributor to McGraw's "Reading Incentive" series, 1968. Contributor of articles to professional journals.

AVOCATIONAL INTERESTS: Music composition, playing piano.

* * *

SCHAFER, Edward Hetzel 1913-

PERSONAL: Born August 23, 1913, in Seattle, Wash.; son of Edward H. and Lillian (Moorehead) Schafer; married Donna Deering, 1942 (divorced, 1970); married Phyllis Brooks, 1971; children: (first marriage) Tamlyn, Julian, Kevin. *Education:* Attended University of California, Los Angeles, 1934-37; University of California, Berkeley, A.B., 1938, Ph.D., 1947; University of Hawaii, M.A., 1940; Harvard University, graduate study, 1940-41. *Home:* 60 Avis Rd., Berkeley, Calif. 94707. *Office:* Department of Oriental Languages, 104 Durant Hall, University of California, Berkeley, Calif. 94720.

CAREER: University of California, Berkeley, lecturer, 1947, assistant professor, 1947-53, associate professor, 1953-58, professor of oriental languages, 1958-70, Agassiz Professor of Oriental Languages and Literature, 1970—. *Military service:* U.S. Navy, 1941-46; became lieutenant commander. *Member:* American Oriental Society (secretary of Western branch, 1951-59; member of executive committee, 1958—; president of Western branch, 1959-60; vice-president, 1973-74; president, 1974-75). *Awards, honors:* Guggenheim fellowship, 1953-54, and 1968-69; American Council of Learned Societies grant, 1960-61.

WRITINGS: *The Empire of Min,* Tuttle, 1954; *Tu Wan's Stone Catalogue of Cloudy Forest: A Commentary and Synopsis,* University of California Press, 1961; *The Golden Peaches of Samarkand: A Study of T'ang Exotics,* University of California Press, 1963; *The Vermilion Bird,* University of California Press, 1967; *Ancient China,* Time-Life, 1967; *Shore of Pearls: Hainan Island in Early Times,* University of California Press, 1970; *The Divine Woman: Dragon Ladies and Rain Maidens in T'ang Literature,* University of California Press, 1973; *Pacing the Void: T'ang Approaches to the Stars,* University of California Press, 1977. Compiler, *Index to the Journal of the American Oriental Society,* Volumes 21-60. *Journal of the American Oriental Society,* associate editor, 1955-58, editor, 1958-68.

* * *

SCHALEBEN, Arville Orman 1907-

PERSONAL: Born January 25, 1907, in Brown County, Minn.; son of Wilhelm (a realtor) and Lina (Helling) Schaleben; married Ida Androvandi, September 14, 1935; children: Joy (Mrs. Robert Lewis), Susan (Mrs. T. W. Wilson), Mary (Mrs. Tony Totero), Will. *Education:* University of Minnesota, B.S., 1929. *Politics:* Independent. *Religion:* Congregationalist. *Home:* 8254 North Gray Log Lane, Milwaukee, Wis. 53217. *Office:* School of Journalism, University of Wisconsin, Madison, Wis. 53706.

CAREER: *Milwaukee Journal,* Milwaukee, Wis., 1929-72, began as reporter, became associate editor and vice-president of Journal Co.; University of Wisconsin-Madison, editor-in-residence, 1972—. Held Riley Chair in Journalism, Indiana University, 1972; visiting professor, Medill School of Journalism, Northwestern University, 1973-74; lecturer at more than fifty colleges and universities. *Member:* International Platform Association, American Society of Newspaper Editors, Associated Press Managing Editors Association (director; chairman of news research; regent, 1970—), Society of the South Pole, Antarctic Society, Sigma Delta Chi (president of Milwaukee chapter, 1953-54; state chairman, 1957), Milwaukee Press Club, University of Minnesota Alumni Association, Ozaukee Country Club. *Awards, honors:* Award of Merit for the decade 1962-1972, from North American Society of Venezuela; Knight of the Golden Quill, Milwaukee Press Club, 1973; named Wisconsin Journalist of the Year by Society of Professional Journalists, 1974; shared Pulitzer Prize for series of articles on clean water appearing in the *Milwaukee Journal.*

WRITINGS: *Will Rogers Said,* New York Press, 1935; (contributor) *Best News Stories of 1935,* University of Iowa Press, 1936; (contributor) *Headlining America,* University of Iowa Press, 1937; *Your Future in Journalism,* Richards Rosen, 1961, revised edition, 1966; (contributor) *The Citizen and the News,* Marquette University Press, 1962; (contributor) *The American Dream,* Doubleday, 1964. Also author of material for radio and television broadcasts. Contributor to periodicals.

WORK IN PROGRESS: Editing *Chew More—Eat Less,* for Thomas Nelson.

SIDELIGHTS: Arville Schaleben has photographed and reported news from every continent of the world except Australia; this includes several reports from Antarctica and from the South Pole itself for the National Science Foundation. He is credited with the last interview with Will Rogers, only a few hours before the fatal crash of Rogers and Wiley

Post in Alaska. In 1935, Schaleben lived for five months with the Matanuska Valley colonists; this was the first United States colony ever established. Schaleben told *CA* that he helped solve the largest mass murder in U.S. history (at that time—1935), and that his part in the proceedings was dramatized on both radio and national television.

* * *

SCHARY, Dore 1905-1980

PERSONAL: Original name Isadore Schary; born August 31, 1905, in Newark, N.J.; son of Herman Hugo and Belle (Drachler) Schary; married Miriam Svet (an artist), March 5, 1932; children: Jill Zimmer, Joy Stashower, Jeb. *Education:* Attended public schools, Newark, N.J. *Politics:* Democrat. *Religion:* Jewish.

CAREER: Playwright, director, producer. Engaged in amateur theatricals, entertainment for summer hotels, publicity work, and newspaper writing, 1926-32; screenwriter for Columbia, Paramount, and Warner Brothers Studios, Hollywood, Calif., 1932-37; Metro-Goldwyn-Mayer Studios, Culver City, Calif., writer, 1938-40, executive producer, 1940-43; Selznick International Studio, Culver City, executive producer, 1943-46; executive vice-president in charge of production, RKO Studios, 1947-48; executive vice-president in charge of production and studio operations, MGM Studios, 1948-56; independent producer, 1956-80; president of Schary Productions, 1959-80; president and chief executive officer, Theatrevision, Inc., and Telepremiere International, 1972-75. Producer of over 350 films, including "Boys' Town," 1938, "Lassie Come Home," 1943, "Bataan," 1943, "The Spiral Staircase," 1946, "The Farmer's Daughter," 1947, "Crossfire," 1947, "Mr. Blandings Builds His Dream House," 1948, "Father of the Bride," 1950, "American in Paris," 1951; "Lili," 1953; "Seven Brides for Seven Brothers," 1954, "Bad Day at Black Rock," 1954, "The Blackboard Jungle," 1955, "Designing Woman," 1957, and "Sunrise at Campobello," 1960. Producer and director of plays, including "A Majority of One," "The Devil's Advocate," and "The Unsinkable Molly Brown." Frequent lecturer. Commissioner of Cultural Affairs of the City of New York, 1970-71. Member of advisory council, U.S. Committee for the United Nations; member of board of directors, Interracial Council for Business Opportunities, Jewish Theological Seminary of America, and Brandeis Camp; trustee, Eleanor Roosevelt Memorial Foundation and Brandeis University; founding member and member of national board, Eleanor Roosevelt Institute for Cancer Research; member of President's Committee on Employment of the Handicapped, National Citizens Committees for Farm Labor and Immigration Reform, national committee of Citizens Crusade against Poverty, national honorary board of *Encyclopedia Judaica,* Adolph Ullman Creative Arts Commission of Brandeis University, and Musical Theatre Academy of New York.

MEMBER: Anti-Defamation League of B'nai B'rith (national chairman, 1963-69; honorary chairman beginning 1969), United World Federalists (honorary vice-president), Hollywood Museum Associates (founding member), Dramatists Guild, Authors League (member of board of directors), Screen Writers Guild, Screen Producers Guild, Academy of Motion Picture Arts and Sciences, United Nations Association, National Association for the Advancement of Colored People (life member), League of New York Theatres, New Jersey State Council on the Arts. *Awards, honors:* Academy Award for best screenplay, 1938, for "Boys' Town"; two Antoinette Perry Awards, 1958, for "Sunrise at Campobello"; National Association of Independent Schools Award, 1959; Valentine Davies Award from Writers Guild, 1969; Barney Balaban Human Relations Award from B'nai B'rith Anti-Defamation League, 1971; D.H.L., College of the Pacific and Wilberforce University, both 1951; D.F.A., Lincoln College, 1960; recipient of more than 150 awards from various charitable, community, and professional groups.

WRITINGS: Hanukkah Home Service (booklet), United Synagogues of America, 1950; *Case History of a Movie,* as told to Charles Palmer, Random House, 1950, new edition edited by Bruce S. Kupelnick, Garland Publishing, 1978; *For Special Occasions* (autobiography), Random House, 1962; *Heyday: An Autobiography,* Little, Brown, 1980.

Plays: *Sunrise at Campobello* (first produced on Broadway at Cort Theatre, January 30, 1958), Random House, 1958; *The Highest Tree* (first produced on Broadway at Longacre Theatre, November 4, 1959), Random House, 1960; (adaptor from the novel by Morris L. West) *The Devil's Advocate* (first produced on Broadway at Billy Rose Theatre, March 9, 1961), Morrow, 1961; "Banderol," first produced in New York City, 1963; "One By One," first produced on Broadway at Belasco Theatre, December 1, 1964; "Brightower," first produced on Broadway at John Golden Theatre, January 28, 1970; "Antiques," first produced in New York City at Mercer-O'Casey Theatre, June 19, 1973; (co-author) "Herzl," first produced on Broadway, 1976.

Screenplays: "Fury of the Jungle," Columbia, 1933; (with Ethel Hill) "Fog," Columbia, 1933; (with Hill) "Most Precious Thing in Life," Columbia, 1934; "He Couldn't Take It," Monogram, 1934; "Young and Beautiful," Mascot, 1934; "Let's Talk It Over," Universal, 1934; (with Roy Chanslor) "Murder in the Clouds," First National, 1934; "Chinatown Squad," Universal, 1935; (with Lou Breslow and Edward Elison) "Silk Hat Kid," Twentieth Century-Fox, 1935; (adaptor) "Your Uncle Dudley," Twentieth Century-Fox, 1935; (with Gilbert W. Pratt and Virginia Van Upp) "Timothy's Quest," Paramount, 1936; (with Harry Sauber) "Her Master's Voice," 1936; "Mind Your Own Business," Paramount, 1936; (with Doris Anderson) "The Girl from Scotland Yard," Paramount, 1937; (with others) "Big City," MGM, 1937; "Too Many Heroes," 1937; (with others) "Boys' Town," Loew's, 1938; "The Right Way," Vitaphone, 1939; (with Hugh Butler) "Edison the Man," Loew's, 1940; (with Butler and Bradbury Foote) "Young Tom Edison," Loew's, 1940; "Broadway Melody of 1940," 1940; "Married Bachelor," Loew's, 1941; (with Allen Rivkin) "Behind the News," Republic, 1940; "It's a Big Country," 1952; "Battle of Gettysburg," 1956; (adaptor from the novel by Nathaniel West and the play by Howard Teichmann) "Lonelyhearts," 1959; "Sunrise at Campobello," Warner Brothers, 1960; "Act One," Warner Brothers, 1963; (with Sinclair Lewis) *Storm in the West,* Stein & Day, 1964.

SIDELIGHTS: Dave Zurawik finds that Dore Schary's *Heyday: An Autobiography* "feels like a weekend in the country with a friendly storyteller who just happens to have a wallet full of snapshots and all the time in the world to remember." The reviewer summarizes Schary's contributions to the entertainment industry when he writes, "he had a solid, if not distinguished, screenwriting career and then went on to head the achetypical Hollywood studio during the days when the studio meant everything. As head of MGM . . . he brought us everything from 'Easter Parade' to 'Blackboard Jungle,' oversaw the careers of everyone from Judy Garland to Spencer Tracy. When people speak of the studio system, they are speaking of Dore Schary as much as anyone else."

Schary discussed the studio system and his years at MGM in

an interview with Charles Champlin of the *Los Angeles Times.* "There were things that were wrong," he conceded. "It could be tough and cruel and the system could come to quixotic decisions, to say the least. But at least it was *contained.* You could really experiment, you could create relationships and an area of trust. And always at Metro you had the feeling of being around the very best. . . . Compare the best of the rest with the Metro musicals and I will immodestly say that nobody else made 'em like that. There was a magnificent bunch of talent there."

Unfortunately, critics such as Clancy Sigal feel that this "magnificent bunch of talent" was not put to its best possible use during Schary's producing career. "Schary substituted good intentions for good movies," claims Sigal. His films "ushered in a bland, timid post-World War II era of prestigiously empty movies that helped kill the Golden Age" instead of prolong it as Schary's words might have one think. As the former producer commented in the *Los Angeles Times* interview, today "everyone seems to be interested in the mechanics of money, and not enough people are in love with the medium. We were. And that helped make it the time it was."

Sigal sees *Heyday* as romanticized hindsight. He condemns the book as evasive, "so full of self-praise and so devoid of blunt facts," although he finds this "rewriting of Hollywood's political history and his role in it . . . consistent with the type of . . . movies [Schary] made." Sigal explains: "Schary shrewdly understood that audiences wanted more challenging fare—but he had neither the talent nor the imagination to really buck the system that had made him rich. . . . He was the perfect Man in the Gray Flannel Suit who made gray flannel movies for a Hollywood more anxious to submit its non-controversial credentials (to the House UnAmerican Activities Committee . . . etc.) than to create films of substance."

AVOCATIONAL INTERESTS: Walking and tennis.

BIOGRAPHICAL/CRITICAL SOURCES: Time, October 20, 1947, July 12, 1948; *Newsweek,* July 12, 1948, May 29, 1950; *New York Times Magazine,* February 6, 1949; *Collier's,* November 19, 1949; *Theatre Arts,* May, 1952; *Look,* June 15, 1954, April 1, 1958; *Men in the News, 1958,* Lippincott, 1959; G. Weales, *American Drama since World War II,* Harcourt, 1962; Jill Zimmer, *With a Cast of Thousands,* Stein & Day, 1963; B. Rosenberg and H. Silverstein, *Real Tinsel,* Macmillan, 1970; *New York Times,* January 29, 1970, February 25, 1970, May 2, 1976, December 1, 1976; *Variety,* February 4, 1970; *New Yorker,* February 7, 1970; Dore Schary, *Heydey: An Autobiography,* Little, Brown, 1980; *Detroit Free Press,* February 3, 1980; *New York Times Book Review,* February 17, 1980; *Los Angeles Times,* March 7, 1980; *Chicago Tribune Book World,* March 30, 1980.

(Died of cancer, July 7, 1980, in New York, N.Y.)

* * *

SCHECHNER, Richard 1934-

PERSONAL: Born August 23, 1934, in Newark, N.J.; son of Sheridan and Selma (Schwarz) Schechner; married Joan MacIntosh (a performer); children: Samuel MacIntosh. *Education:* Cornell University, B.A., 1956; Johns Hopkins University, graduate study, 1956-57; Iowa State University, M.A., 1958; Tulane University, Ph.D., 1962. *Office:* Department of Drama, Graduate, New York University, 300 South Bldg., Washington Sq., New York, N.Y. 10003; and The Performance Group, P.O. Box 654, Canal St. Station, New York, N.Y. 10013.

CAREER: Tulane University, New Orleans, La., assistant professor, 1962-65, associate professor of drama, 1965-67; New York University, New York, N.Y., professor of drama, 1967—. Director of plays for the East End Players, Provincetown, Mass., 1958 and 1961, and of one play at Tulane University, 1963; co-producing director, Free Southern Theatre, 1964-65; co-director, New Orleans Group, 1965-67; founder and director, Performance Group, 1967—. *Military service:* U.S. Army, 1958-60. *Member:* American Theater Association, American Association of University Professors, American Association for the Advancement of Science. *Awards, honors:* Guggenheim fellow, 1976; Fulbright senior fellow, 1976; Indo-American fellow, 1978.

WRITINGS: "Blessing of the Fleet" (play), first produced in Provincetown, Mass. by East End Players, 1958; "Briseis and the Sergeant" (play), first produced in New Orleans, La. at Tulane University, 1962; *Public Domain,* Bobbs-Merrill, 1968; (editor with Gilbert Moses and Tom C. Dent) *Free Southern Theater,* Bobbs-Merrill, 1969; (editor) *Dionysus in Sixty Nine,* Farrar, Straus, 1970; *Environmental Theater,* Hawthorn, 1973; (with Brooks McNamara and others) *Theatres, Spaces and Environments: Eighteen Projects,* Drama Book Specialists, 1975; *Essays on Performance Theory, 1970-1976,* Drama Book Specialists, 1976; (editor with Mady Schuman) *Ritual, Play and Performance: Readings in the Social Sciences—Theatre,* Seabury, 1976. Contributor to periodicals, including *Educational Theatre Journal, Yale French Studies,* and *Salmagundi.* Editor, *Tulane Drama Review,* 1962-67; contributing editor, *Drama Review,* 1969—.

* * *

SCHEFFLER, Israel 1923-

PERSONAL: Born November 25, 1923, in New York, N.Y.; son of Leon and Ethel (Grunberg) Scheffler; married Rosalind Zuckerbrod, 1949; children: Samuel, Laurie. *Education:* Brooklyn College (now Brooklyn College of the City University of New York), A.B., 1945, A.M., 1948; University of Pennsylvania, Ph.D., 1952. *Office:* Emerson Hall, Harvard University, Cambridge, Mass. 02138.

CAREER: Harvard University, Cambridge, Mass., instructor, 1952-54, assistant professor, 1954-57, lecturer, 1957-59, associate professor, 1959-60, professor of education, 1961-62, professor of education and philosophy, 1962-64, Victor S. Thomas Professor of Education and Philosophy, 1964—. Mead-Swing Lecturer, Oberlin College, 1965. Chairman of General Problems Section, International Congress of Logic, Methodology, and Philosophy of Science, 1964; director of professional seminars for school administrators, National Endowment for the Humanities, 1976, 1977, and 1978. *Member:* American Philosophical Association, Philosophy of Education Society, Philosophy of Science Association (past president), National Academy of Education (founding member), American Academy of Arts and Sciences, Aristotelian Society. *Awards, honors:* Ford Foundation fellow, 1951-52; Guggenheim fellow, 1958-59 and 1972-73; A.M., Harvard University, 1960; National Science Foundation grants, 1962 and 1965; Alumni Award of Merit, Brooklyn College of the City University of New York, 1967; Center for Advanced Study in the Behavioral Sciences fellow, 1972-73; Distinguished Service Medal from Columbia University Teachers College, 1980.

WRITINGS: (Editor) *Philosophy and Education,* Allyn & Bacon, 1958, revised edition, 1966; *The Language of Education,* C. C Thomas, 1960; *The Anatomy of Inquiry,* Knopf, 1963; *Conditions of Knowledge,* Scott, Foresman, 1965; *Sci-*

ence and Subjectivity, Bobbs-Merrill, 1967; (contributor) L. J. Cronbach and P. Suppes, editors, *Research for Tomorrow's Schools,* National Academy of Education, 1969; (editor with Richard S. Rudner) *Logic and Art,* Bobbs-Merrill, 1972; *Reason and Teaching,* Bobbs-Merrill, 1973; *Four Pragmatists,* Routledge & Kegan Paul, 1974; *Beyond the Letter,* Routledge & Kegan Paul, 1979. Contributor to professional journals.

* * *

SCHEIBER, Harry N(oel) 1935-

PERSONAL: Born in 1935, in New York, N.Y. *Education:* Columbia University, A.B., 1955; Cornell University, M.A., 1957, Ph.D., 1961. *Office:* Department of History, University of California, San Diego, La Jolla, Calif. 92093.

CAREER: Dartmouth College, Hanover, N.H., 1960-71, began as instructor, became professor of history, director of Center for the Study of Social Change, 1968-70; University of California, San Diego, La Jolla, professor of history, 1971—. Director of seminars for public administrators, National Endowment for the Humanities, 1978 and 1979. *Member:* American Historical Association (chairman of Beveridge Prize Committee, 1971-74), Organization of American Historians, Agricultural History Society (member of executive committee, 1965-68; president, 1977-78), Economic History Association (trustee, 1967—), Economic History Society (Great Britain), American Society for Legal History (member of nominations committee, 1978), Law and Society Association (trustee, 1977—), Phi Kappa Phi. *Awards, honors:* Social Science Research Council fellow, 1959-60; Resources for the Future staff grant, 1963; American Council of Learned Societies fellow, 1966-67; Center for Advanced Study in the Behavioral Sciences resident fellow, 1966-67; Ohio University Press award, 1967-70; Guggenheim fellow, 1970-71; National Science Foundation research grant, 1978; Rockefeller Foundation fellowship, 1979-80; Project '87 grant, 1979-80; University of California Teaching Excellence Award.

WRITINGS: The Wilson Administration and Civil Liberties, 1917-1921, Cornell University Press, 1960; (editor) *United States Economic History: Selected Readings,* Knopf, 1964; (contributor) G. M. Lyons, editor, *America: Purpose and Power,* Quadrangle, 1965; *Ohio Canal Era: A Case Study of Government and the Economy,* Ohio University Press, 1969; (editor) *The Old Northwest,* University of Nebraska Press, 1969; (contributor) *Law in American Society,* Little, Brown, 1972; (contributor) Thomas Lyons, editor, *The Supreme Court and Individual Liberties,* Addison-Wesley, 1975; (co-author) *American Economic History,* Harper, 1976; (co-editor) *American Law and the Constitutional Order,* Harvard University Press, 1978. Contributor of articles and reviews to professional journals.

WORK IN PROGRESS: Studies in American legal history; a book on the history of American federalism and the economic order.

* * *

SCHEICK, William J(oseph) 1941-

PERSONAL: Born July 15, 1941, in Newark, N.J.; son of Joseph Edward (an engineer) and Irene (Corvi) Scheick; married Marion Ruth Voorhees, August 3, 1963 (divorced February 29, 1980); children: Jessica Holly, Nathan Andrew. *Education:* Montclair State College, B.A., 1963; University of Illinois, M.A., 1965, Ph.D., 1969. *Home:* 1901 East Anderson Lane No. 245, Austin, Tex. 78752. *Office:* Parlin Hall, University of Texas, Austin, Tex. 78712.

CAREER: University of Texas at Austin, assistant professor, 1969-74, associate professor, 1974-79, professor of English, 1979—.

WRITINGS: The Will and the Word: The Poetry of Edward Taylor, University of Georgia Press, 1974; (editor and author of introduction) Increase Mather, *The Life and Death of That Reverend Man of God, Mr. Richard Mather,* York Mail-Print, Inc., 1974; *The Writings of Jonathan Edwards: Theme, Motif, and Style,* Texas A & M University Press, 1975; *Seventeenth-Century American Poetry,* G. K. Hall, 1977; *The Slender Human Word: Emerson's Artistry in Prose,* University of Tennessee Press, 1978; *The Half-Blood: A Cultural Symbol in Nineteenth-Century American Fiction,* University Press of Kentucky, 1979; (editor) *Critical Essays on Jonathan Edwards,* G. K. Hall, 1980. Contributor of over seventy-five articles and book reviews to academic and literary journals. Member of editorial board of *English Literature in Transition,* 1970—. Editor of *Texas Studies in Literature and Languages,* 1975—.

WORK IN PROGRESS: The Splintering Fame: H. G. Wells and the Transition from Victorian to Modern Fiction.

* * *

SCHEMM, Mildred Walker 1905-
(Mildred Walker)

PERSONAL: Born May 2, 1905, in Philadelphia, Pa.; daughter of Walter M. (a minister) and Harriet (Merrifield) Walker; married Ferdinand Ripley Schemm (a cardiologist), October 25, 1927 (died, 1955); children: Margaret Ripley Hansen, George W., Christopher M. *Education:* Wells College, B.A., 1926; University of Michigan, M.A., 1934. *Politics:* Democrat. *Religion:* Protestant. *Agent:* James Brown Associates, Inc., 25 West 43rd St., New York, N.Y. 10031.

CAREER: Writer. John Wanamaker Co., Philadelphia, Pa., advertising copy writer, 1926-27; Wells College, Aurora, N.Y., professor of English literature, 1955-68. Fulbright lecturer in Kyoto, Japan, 1959-60. Member of staff of Breadloaf Writers Conference, Middlebury, Vt., 1956 and 1957, and of writers conference in Boulder, Colo., 1959 and 1961. *Member:* American Association of University Professors, Phi Beta Kappa. *Awards, honors:* Avery Hopwood Award, University of Michigan, for *Fireweed.*

WRITINGS—Published by Harcourt, except as indicated: *Fireweed,* 1934; *Light from the Arcturus,* 1935; *Dr. Norton's Wife,* 1938; *The Brewers' Big Horses,* 1940; *Unless the Wind Turns,* 1941; *Winter Wheat,* 1944; *The Quarry,* 1947; *Medical Meeting,* 1949; *The Southwest Corner,* 1951; *The Curlew's Cry,* 1955; *The Body of a Young Man,* 1960; *If a Lion Could Talk,* 1970; *A Piece of the World,* Atheneum, 1972.

SIDELIGHTS: Mildred Walker Schemm told *CA:* "I began writing in my early teens and by now it has become a way of life. Growing up in a parsonage, surrounded by books (and sermons) made me aware of the excitement and power of words and drew me inevitably toward writing. . . . Some inborn sense of 'place' moved me to try to show, in narrative form, the effect of the natural world on human beings." The issues she feels are vital include "the necessity for World peace, the protection and reverence for the natural world if we are to survive and the generations after us. I feel strongly about the need to oppose materialism in both our national and individual life—the importance of the freedom of *every* individual, but the need for a better understanding of the nature of freedom—the need to dethrone success as the American ideal and substitute for it a creative quality in our daily living. These are too big and too general to be meaningful set down this way—but how else, except in a novel?"

* * *

SCHICKEL, Richard (Warren) 1933-

PERSONAL: Born February 10, 1933, in Milwaukee, Wis.; son of Edward John and Helen (Hendricks) Schickel; married Julia Carroll Whedon, March 11, 1960 (divorced); children: Erika, Jessica. *Education:* University of Wisconsin, B.S., 1956, graduate study, 1956-57. *Home:* 311 East 83rd St., New York, N.Y. 10028. *Agent:* Sterling Lord Agency, 660 Madison Ave., New York, N.Y. 10021. *Office: Time* Magazine, Rockefeller Center, New York, N.Y. 10020.

CAREER: Sports Illustrated, New York City, reporter, 1956-57; *Look,* New York City, senior editor, 1957-60; *Show,* New York City, senior editor, 1960-62, book columnist, 1963-64; book critic for "Sunday," NBC-TV, 1963-64; Rockefeller Brothers Fund, New York City, consultant, 1963-65; Rockefeller Foundation, New York City, consultant, 1965; *Life* Magazine, New York City, film reviewer, 1965-72; *Time* Magazine, New York City, film reviewer, 1972—. *Member:* National Society of Film Critics, Writers Guild of America, Directors Guild of America, New York Film Critics. *Awards, honors: New Republic* Young Writer Award, 1959; Guggenheim fellowship, 1964-65.

WRITINGS: The World of Carnegie Hall, Messner, 1960; *The Stars,* Dial, 1962; *Movies: The History of an Art and an Institution,* Basic Books, 1964; *The Gentle Knight* (juvenile), Abelard, 1964; (with Lena Horne) *Lena,* Doubleday, 1965; *The World of Goya,* Time-Life, 1968; (editor with John Simon) *Film 67/68,* Simon & Schuster, 1968; *The Disney Version: The Life, Times, Art, and Commerce of Walt Disney,* Simon & Schuster, 1968; *Second Sight: Notes on Some Movies* (collection of film criticism), Simon & Schuster, 1972; *His Picture in the Papers,* Charterhouse, 1973; *Harold Lloyd: The Shape of Laughter,* New York Graphic Society, 1974; (with Bob Willoughby) *The Platinum Years,* Random House, 1974; *The Men Who Made the Movies,* Atheneum, 1975; *The World of Tennis,* Random House, 1975; (with Douglas Fairbanks, Jr.) *The Fairbanks Album,* New York Graphic Society, 1976; *Another I, Another You: A Love Story for the Once Married,* Harper, 1978.

Television scripts; all for Public Broadcasting Service, except as indicated: "The Film Generation," 1969; "The Movie-Crazy Years," 1971; (also producer) "Hollywood: You Must Remember This," 1972; (also producer and director) "The Men Who Made the Movies" (eight-part series), 1973; (also producer) "Life Goes to the Movies," National Broadcasting Co., 1976; (also producer and director) "Into the Morning: Willa Cather's America," 1978; (also producer and director) "Funny Business," Columbia Broadcasting System, 1978; (also producer and director) "The Horror Show," Columbia Broadcasting System, 1979. Also author of syndicated television series "The Coral Jungle," 1976. Contributor to magazines.

WORK IN PROGRESS: A biography of D. W. Griffith; a novel.

SIDELIGHTS: Richard Schickel's *The Disney Version,* a study of animator Walt Disney and his place in American popular culture, has received high critical praise. Bernard Wolfe calls it a "carefully researched, intelligently organized, [and] expertly written study." Katherine Gauss Jackson, writing in *Harper's,* describes it as a "discerning biography" which is "a thoroughly satisfying and most informative discussion of all aspects of the Disney legend." Edmund Carpenter of the *New York Times Book Review* concludes that "Schickel has written an important book."

Schickel's first novel, *Another I, Another You,* has also been well-received. Joseph McLellan sees it as "a blending of new subject matter with an older kind of style" producing "a Dickens-Thackeray sort of feeling to some of [Schickel's] social observations. . . . Unfortunately," McLellan continues, "there is also a 19th-century flavor in the treatment of secondary characters . . . who are simplified almost to the point of abstraction." McLellan concludes, however, that the book contains "some moments of grown-up tenderness described with uncommon skill and delicacy." Writing in the *New York Times Book Review,* Richard Freedman states that "rarely has the pathos of the detritus of divorce been more skillfully rendered," and describes the book as "one of those rarities of current storytelling, a genuinely nice—but unsticky—novel."

Schickel told *CA:* "I think—I hope—I'm belatedly making a transition from nonfiction, mostly critical in nature, to fiction, which I find seductively interesting and instructive to do. But I hope I'll always continue to do some journalism [and] some TV production, just because I like to balance self-expression with group creation."

BIOGRAPHICAL/CRITICAL SOURCES: Playboy, January, 1965; *Science & Society,* fall, 1965; *Times Literary Supplement,* December 16, 1965, July 2, 1976; *Book World,* April 28, 1968; *Time,* May 3, 1968, May 1, 1978; *New York Times Book Review,* May 5, 1968, April 9, 1978; *Wall Street Journal,* May 22, 1968, June 5, 1978; *Film Quarterly,* summer, 1968; *Harper's,* June, 1968; *New Republic,* July 6, 1968; *Commentary,* September, 1968; *Milwaukee Journal,* March 3, 1974; *New Statesman,* February 25, 1977; *Washington Post,* June 12, 1978.

* * *

SCHILLING, S. Paul 1904-

PERSONAL: Born February 7, 1904, in Cumberland, Md.; son of Sylvester (a postal clerk) and Ida C. (Weber) Schilling; married Mary Elizabeth Albright, June 18, 1930; children: Robert, Paula (Mrs. Bruce E. Foreman). *Education:* St. John's College, Annapolis, Md., B.S., 1923; Boston University, A.M., 1927, S.T.B., 1929, Ph.D., 1934; additional graduate study at Harvard University, 1929-30, and University of Berlin, 1930-31. *Politics:* Democrat. *Home:* 219 Holly Point Rd., Centerville, Mass. 02632.

CAREER: Ordained minister of Methodist Episcopal Church, 1930; Mt. Vernon Place Methodist Church, Baltimore, Md., associate pastor, 1933-36; Methodist Church, Prince Frederick, Md., pastor, 1936-40; Brookland Methodist Church, Washington, D.C., pastor, 1940-45; Westminster Theological Seminary, Westminster, Md., professor of systematic theology and philosophy of religion, 1945-53; Boston University, Boston, Mass., professor of systematic theology, 1953-69, professor emeritus, 1969—, chairman of Division of Theological Studies, Graduate School, 1954-69. Research at University of Heidelberg, 1959-60 and at University of Tuebingen, 1966-67; theological lecturer, Lowell Institute, 1968; visiting professor of systematic theology, Union Theological Seminary, Manila, Philippines, 1969-70, Garrett Evangelical Theological Seminary, 1974, and Andover-Newton Theological School, 1978-80; visiting professor of philosophical theology, Wesley Theological Seminary, 1970-73. Chairman of Commission on a Just and Durable Peace, Washington Federation of Churches, 1942-45; president of Baltimore Conference Board of Education, Methodist Church, 1948-53.

MEMBER: American Theological Society (president, 1968-69), American Academy of Religion, American Association of University Professors, American Philosophical Association, Fellowship of Reconciliation, American Civil Liberties Union, National Association for the Advancement of Colored People (member of executive board, Cape Cod Branch), Cape Cod Council of Churches. *Awards, honors:* Society for Religion in Higher Education fellow, 1929; Frank D. Howard fellow, Boston University School of Theology, 1929-30; American Association of Theological Schools faculty fellow, 1959-60.

WRITINGS: (Contributor) *Church and Social Responsibility,* Abingdon, 1953; *Isaiah Speaks,* Methodist Publishing House, 1958, revised edition, Crowell, 1959; *Methodism and Society in Theological Perspective,* Abingdon, 1960; *Contemporary Continental Theologians,* Abingdon, 1966; (contributor) *Christian Mission in Theological Perspective,* Abingdon, 1967; *God in an Age of Atheism,* Abingdon, 1969; (contributor) *Theological Perspectives of Stewardship,* United Methodist Board of Laity, 1969; (contributor) *Dynamic Interpersonalism for Ministry,* Abingdon, 1973; *God Incognito,* Abingdon, 1974; *God and Human Anguish,* Abingdon, 1977. Contributor to religion journals.

WORK IN PROGRESS: Research and writing on theology in Christian hymnody.

AVOCATIONAL INTERESTS: Photography, gardening.

* * *

SCHLESINGER, Arthur (Meier), Jr. 1917-

PERSONAL: Born October 15, 1917, in Columbus, Ohio; son of Arthur M. (a historian) and Elizabeth (Bancroft) Schlesinger; married Marian Cannon (an author and artist), August 10, 1940 (divorced, 1970); married Alexandra Emmet, July 9, 1971; children: (first marriage) Stephen Cannon and Katharine Bancroft (twins), Christina, Andrew Bancroft, (second marriage) Robert Emmet Kennedy. *Education:* Harvard University, A.B. (summa cum laude), 1938. *Politics:* Democrat. *Religion:* Unitarian. *Office:* Graduate Center, City University of New York, 33 West 42nd St., New York, N.Y. 10036.

CAREER: Affiliated with Office of War Information, Washington, D.C., 1942-43, and with Office of Strategic Services, Washington, D.C., London, England, and Paris, France, 1943-45; free-lance writer, Washington, D.C., 1945-46; Harvard University, Cambridge, Mass., associate professor, 1946-54, professor of history, 1954-62; special assistant to President John F. Kennedy, 1961-63, and to President Lyndon Johnson, 1963-64; City University of New York, New York City, Albert Schweitzer Professor of Humanities, 1966—. Member, Adlai Stevenson presidential staff, 1952, 1956. Trustee of John F. Kennedy Center for the Performing Arts, Robert F. Kennedy Memorial, American National Theatre and Academy, Recorded Anthology of American Music, and Twentieth Century Fund. Director of Harry S Truman Library Institute, John Fitzgerald Kennedy Library, and Ralph Bunche Institute. Advisor, Arthur and Elizabeth Schlesinger Library on the History of Women in America. Consultant, Economic Cooperation Administration, 1948, and Mutual Security Administration, 1951-52. *Military service:* U.S. Army, 1945; served in Europe.

MEMBER: American Historical Association, Association for the Study of Afro-American Life and History, Organization of American Historians, Society for Historians of American Foreign Relations, National Institute of Arts and Letters, Center for Inter-American Relations, Council on Foreign Relations, Americans for Democratic Action (national chairman, 1953-54), American Civil Liberties Union (member of national council), Massachusetts Historical Society, Colonial Society of Massachusetts. *Awards, honors:* Henry Fellow, 1938-39; Harvard Fellow, 1939-42; Pulitzer Prize for history, 1946, for *The Age of Jackson,* and for biography, 1966, for *A Thousand Days;* Guggenheim fellow, 1946; American Academy of Arts and Letters grant, 1946; Francis Parkman Prize, 1957; Bancroft Prize, 1958; National Book Award, 1966, for *A Thousand Days,* 1979, for *Robert Kennedy and His Times;* gold medal, National Institute of Arts and Letters, 1967; Ohio Governor's Award for history, 1973; Sidney Hillman Foundation Award, 1973; Eugene V. Debs Award in education, 1974. Honorary degrees from Muhlenberg College, 1950, Bethany College, 1956, University of New Brunswick, 1960, New School for Social Research, 1966, Tusculum College, 1966, Rhode Island College, 1969, Aquinas College, 1971, Western New England College, 1974, Ripon College, 1976, Iona College, 1977, Utah State University, 1978, and University of Louisville, 1978.

WRITINGS: Orestes A. Brownson: A Pilgrim's Progress (Catholic Book Club selection), Little, Brown, 1939, published as *A Pilgrim's Progress: Orestes A. Brownson,* 1966; *The Age of Jackson,* Little, Brown, 1945; *The Vital Center: The Politics of Freedom,* Houghton, 1949 (published in England as *The Politics of Freedom,* Heinemann, 1950).

What about Communism?, Public Affairs Committee, 1950; (with Richard H. Rovere) *The General and the President and the Future of American Foreign Policy,* Farrar, Straus, 1951, revised edition published as *The MacArthur Controversy and American Foreign Policy,* 1965; (co-editor) *Harvard Guide to American History,* Harvard University Press, 1954; (editor with Quincy Howe) *Guide to Politics,* Dial, 1954; *The Age of Roosevelt,* Volume I: *The Crises of the Old Order, 1919-1933* (Book-of-the-Month-Club selection), Houghton, 1957, Volume II: *The Coming of the New Deal* (Book-of-the-Month-Club selection), Houghton, 1959, Volume III: *The Politics of Upheaval* (Book-of-the-Month-Club selection), Houghton, 1960.

Kennedy or Nixon: Does It Make Any Difference?, Macmillan, 1960; *The Politics of Hope* (essay collection), Houghton, 1963; (contributor) *Four Portraits and One Subject: Bernard DeVoto,* Houghton, 1963; (editor with Morton White) *Paths of American Thought,* Houghton, 1963; *A Thousand Days: John F. Kennedy in the White House,* Houghton, 1965; *The Bitter Heritage: Vietnam and American Democracy, 1941-1966,* Houghton, 1967; (editor) Herbert Croly, *The Promise of American Life,* Belknap, 1967; (with Alfred De Grazia) *Congress and the Presidency: Their Role in Modern Times,* American Enterprise Institute for Public Policy Research, 1967; *Violence: America in the Sixties,* New American Library, 1968; *The Crisis of Confidence: Ideas, Power, and Violence in America,* Houghton, 1969.

(With Lloyd C. Gardner and Hans J. Morgenthau) *The Origins of the Cold War,* Ginn-Blaisdell, 1970; (editor) Edwin O'Connor, *The Best and the Last of Edwin O'Connor,* Little, Brown, 1970; (editor) *The Coming to Power: Critical Presidential Elections in American History,* Chelsea House, 1972; (editor) *The Dynamics of World Power: A Documentary History of United States Foreign Policy, 1945-1973,* five volumes, Chelsea House, 1973; (editor) *History of U. S. Political Parties,* Chelsea House, 1973, Volume I: *From Factions to Parties: 1789-1860,* Volume II: *1860-1910: The Gilded Age of Politics,* Volume III: *1910-1945: From Square Deal to New Deal,* Volume IV: *1945-1972: The Politics of Change; The Imperial Presidency,* Houghton, 1973; (editor with

Roger Bruns) *Congress Investigates: A Documented History, 1792-1974,* five volumes, Chelsea House, 1975; *Robert Kennedy and His Times,* Houghton, 1978.

Also author of television screenplay "The Journey of Robert F. Kennedy." Author of pamphlets on political subjects. Speechwriter for Adlai Stevenson, John F. Kennedy, Robert F. Kennedy, George McGovern, and Edward Kennedy. Movie reviewer for *Show* and *Vogue*. Contributor to magazines.

SIDELIGHTS: A distinguished historian and liberal political advisor, Arthur Schlesinger has played an influential role in American politics. His work with a number of political figures has served to promote and implement wide-sweeping social reform while his historical studies have won major awards and become best-sellers.

Schlesinger's political involvement first began when he served as advisor and speechwriter to Democratic presidential candidate Adlai Stevenson. In 1956, Schlesinger again worked for the Stevenson campaign. In subsequent elections, Schlesinger has worked for other liberal Democratic candidates—in 1960 for John F. Kennedy, in 1968 for Robert F. Kennedy, in 1972 for George McGovern, and in 1980 for Edward Kennedy.

After John F. Kennedy won his presidential bid in 1960, Schlesinger was appointed to his most influential political position—Special Assistant to the President. Under both Presidents Kennedy and Lyndon Johnson, Schlesinger helped to formulate first the "New Frontier" and then the "Great Society"—two programs of reform that resulted in much of the social legislation of the 1960s including Medicare and the Civil Rights Act.

In his book *A Thousand Days,* Schlesinger tells of his role in the Kennedy Administration. "I felt I owed it," Schlesinger says of his reasons for writing the book, "both to the memory of the President and the profession to put it all down." The book is not so much a history of the Kennedy Administration as it is a description of its deliberations and decisions as Schlesinger remembers them. Because of this, Schlesinger found himself attacked by some historians who expected a more evaluative and scholarly treatment. Responding to this attack, John P. Roche asked that the book "be treated as the raw material of history, not as historical commentary." Speaking to Alvin Toffler, Schlesinger defended his work: "If the participants didn't make records of sorts, how would anyone ever know how decisions were made?"

Schlesinger's more scholarly works of contemporary history have been highly-regarded. *The Age of Roosevelt,* for example, is judged by R. C. Woodward of *Library Journal* to be "the fullest and best treatment of the Roosevelt era [and] the finest kind of history." R. E. Burke writes in *American Historical Review* that the book is Schlesinger's "magnum opus" and "a major work of recent history." Other Schlesinger books have won major literary awards including the Pulitzer Prize and the National Book Award.

Schlesinger holds a distinguished position in the field of history. As Christopher Sharp notes in an article for the *Akron Beacon Journal,* Schlesinger's "stylistic superiority over contemporary historians leaves him in a class by himself, almost in regal solitude." R. L. Strout writes in *New Republic* that "Schlesinger is the greatest historical marathoner America has produced."

BIOGRAPHICAL/CRITICAL SOURCES: Saturday Review, March 2, 1957, September 18, 1971; *New Republic,* October 27, 1958, November 10, 1958, January 12, 1959, September 26, 1960; *New York Times Book Review,* January 4, 1959, April 7, 1963, January 7, 1979; *Nation,* January 31, 1959, November 12, 1960; *Commonweal,* February 27, 1959; *American Historical Review,* October, 1959; *New Yorker,* September 10, 1960, December 10, 1973; *New York Herald Tribune Book Review,* September 11, 1960; *Library Journal,* November 15, 1960; Deane Heller and David Heller, *Kennedy Cabinet,* Monarch, 1961; *New York Post,* April 3, 1961; *New Statesman,* May 26, 1961; *Life,* July 16, 1965; *Playboy,* May, 1966; *Atlantic,* March, 1967; *New Leader,* May 8, 1967; *Christian Century,* May 14, 1969; *Book World,* June 29, 1969; *Economist,* October 18, 1969; *Washington Post,* February 18, 1970; *American Political Science Review,* December, 1972; *America,* October 6, 1973; *Newsweek,* November 19, 1973; *Progressive,* December, 1973; *Village Voice,* December 20, 1973; *Akron Beacon Journal,* December 30, 1973; *Modern Age,* winter, 1975; *Authors in the News,* Volume I, Gale, 1976; *Harper's,* September, 1978; *Time,* September 4, 1978; *Wall Street Journal,* September 8, 1978; *Maclean's,* September 18, 1978; *Esquire,* September 26, 1978; *American Heritage,* October, 1978; *New York Review of Books,* October 12, 1978; *Christian Science Monitor,* October 23, 1978; *National Review,* October 27, 1978; *Los Angeles Times,* March 22, 1979; *Virginia Quarterly Review,* spring, 1979; *Political Science Quarterly,* summer, 1979.

* * *

SCHMIDHAUSER, John R(ichard) 1922-

PERSONAL: Born January 3, 1922, in New York, N.Y.; son of Richard John and Gertrude (Grabinger) Schmidhauser; married Thelma L. Ficker, June 9, 1951; children: Steven, Paul, Thomas, John Christopher, Martha, Sarah, Susan. *Education:* University of Delaware, B.A., 1949; University of Virginia, M.A., 1952, Ph.D., 1954. *Politics:* Democrat. *Religion:* Unitarian Universalist. *Home:* 136 West 64th Pl., Inglewood, Calif. 90302. *Office:* Department of Political Science, University of Southern California, Los Angeles, Calif. 90007.

CAREER: University of Virginia, Charlottesville, instructor in political science, 1952-54; University of Iowa, Iowa City, instructor, 1954-56, assistant professor, 1956-60, associate professor, 1960-61, professor of political science, 1961-65; U.S. House of Representatives, Washington, D.C., congressman from 1st District of Iowa, 1965-67; University of Iowa, professor of political science, 1967-73; University of Southern California, Los Angeles, professor of political science, 1973—. Member of board of directors and board of trustees, Citizen's Research Foundation. *Military service:* U.S. Navy, 1941-45. *Member:* American Political Science Association, American Association of University Professors, International Political Science Association, Phi Beta Kappa, Phi Kappa Phi, Raven Society. *Awards, honors:* Senior research fellow in law and behavioral sciences at University of Chicago, 1959-60.

WRITINGS: The Supreme Court as Arbiter in Federal State Relations, 1789-1957, University of North Carolina Press, 1958, published as *The Supreme Court as Final Arbiter in Federal-State Relations, 1789-1957,* Greenwood Press, 1973; *The Supreme Court: Its Politics, Personalities and Procedures,* Holt, 1960; *Constitutional Law in the Political Process,* Rand McNally, 1963; *Iowa's Campaign for a Constitutional Convention in 1960* (monograph), McGraw, for Eagleton Institute of Rutgers University, 1963; (with Larry Berg) *The Supreme Court and Congress: Conflict and Interaction, 1945-1970,* Free Press, 1972; (with Berg and Hahn) *Political Corruption,* General Learning Corp., 1976; (with

Totten) *Whaling in Japan: United States Relations,* Westview Press, 1978; *Judges and Justices: The Federal Appellate Judiciary,* Little, Brown, 1979. Contributor to law reviews, political science journals, *Reporter, Saturday Review, Gerontologist,* and other periodicals.

WORK IN PROGRESS: Books on congressional politics, on campaign finance, and on environmental issues.

* * *

SCHMIDT, Alvin J(ohn) 1932-

PERSONAL: Born September, 1932, in Waldersee, Manitoba, Canada; son of John (a farmer) and Lydia (Dreger) Schmidt; married Carol Dorothy Gross, August 15, 1964; children: Timothy John, Mark Alvin. *Education:* Valparaiso University, B.A., 1962; Concordia Theological Seminary, B.D., 1964; University of Nebraska, M.A., 1967, Ph.D., 1969. *Politics:* Republican. *Home:* 10614 Alderwood Lane, Fort Wayne, Ind. 46825. *Office:* Department of Sociology, Concordia Seminary, Fort Wayne, Ind. 46825.

CAREER: Member, Royal Canadian Mounted Police, 1951-52; ordained Lutheran clergyman, 1963; Concordia Teachers College, Seward, Neb., instructor, 1963-67, assistant professor, 1967-70, associate professor of sociology, 1970-73; Lenoir Rhyne College, Hickory, N.C., associate professor of sociology, 1973-75; Concordia Seminary, Fort Wayne, Ind., professor of sociology, 1975—. Guest lecturer, University of Manitoba, 1968; visiting professor, University of Nebraska, 1969-70. *Member:* American Sociological Association, Association for the Sociology of Religion, Society for the Scientific Study of Religion, Society for the Study of Social Problems, Evangelical Theological Society, Association of Voluntary Action Scholars, Midwest Sociological Society.

WRITINGS: Oligarchy in Fraternal Organizations: Study in Organizational Leadership, Gale, 1973; (contributor) David H. Smith and others, editors, *Voluntary Action Research,* Lexington Books, 1973; *Fraternal Organizations,* Greenwood Press, 1980. Contributor to journals.

WORK IN PROGRESS: Two books, *Sociology: A Christian Perspective* and *A Sociology of the Lutheran Church—Missouri Synod;* an article on religious and fraternal affiliation of state legislators; a chapter for a book edited by L. D. Nelson.

AVOCATIONAL INTERESTS: Hunting, fishing, gardening, and camping.

* * *

SCHMIDT, James Norman 1912- (James Norman)

PERSONAL: Born 1912, in Chicago, Ill.; son of Hugo and Laura (Blais) Schmidt; married Margaret Fox, 1961; children: Paul, Melissa Thompson (stepdaughter). *Education:* Loyola University of Chicago, B.A., 1932; Ecole des Beaux Arts (France), certificat, 1934; attended Centro Universitario Mexico, 1953-54; Instituto Allende, Mexico, M.A., 1967. *Residence:* Athens, Ohio.

CAREER: Chicago Tribune and United Press, Paris, France, reporter, 1933-36; free-lance writer, 1936—. Lecturer on Mexican history and customs, Academia Hispano-Americana, Mexico; writer-in-residence, Hanover College, spring, 1965; Ohio University, lecturer in English, 1965-66, professor of creative writing, 1967-79. *Military service:* U.S. Army, three years; became first lieutenant; awarded Bronze Star. *Member:* Phi Beta Kappa (honorary member). *Awards, honors:* Silver Pen Award from Mexican government, 1977, for "The Tarahumaras," and 1978, for "The Huichols—Mexico's People of Myth and Magic," both articles in *National Geographic.*

WRITINGS—Under name James Norman: *Little Bosses,* Ziff-Davis, 1934; *Murder Chop Chop,* Morrow, 1941; *An Inch of Time,* Morrow, 1942; *The Nightwalkers,* Ziff-Davis, 1946; *A Little North of Everywhere,* Pellegrini & Cudahy, 1950; *Father Juniper and the General,* Morrow, 1953; *In Mexico,* Morrow, 1956, revised edition, Doubleday, 1965; *The Fell of Dark,* Lippincott, 1960; *Terry's Guide to Mexico,* Doubleday, 1962, revised edition, 1972; *The Valley of Lotus House,* P. Davies, 1962; *Navy That Crossed Mountains,* Putnam, 1964; *The Forgotten Empire,* Putnam, 1965; *Wonders of the Reptile World,* Putnam, 1965; *The Young Generals,* Putnam, 1968; *Riddle of the Incas,* Hawthorn, 1968; *Charro,* Putnam, 1969; *Kearny Rode West,* Putnam, 1971; (with wife, Margaret Fox Schmidt) *A Shopper's Guide to Mexico,* Doubleday, 1973; *Ancestral Voices,* Four Winds, 1975; *The Obsidian Mirror,* Carpenter Press, 1977. Television writer; contributor to *Saturday Evening Post, Cosmopolitan, Holiday,* and other journals.

WORK IN PROGRESS: A biography of Cassius M. Clay, Lincoln's minister to Russia.

SIDELIGHTS: James Schmidt told *CA:* "A good high school teacher aroused my interest in literature, but my writing career began as a fluke. I was studying sculpture in Paris, ran out of money, then landed a job with the Paris edition of the *Chicago Tribune.* Joyce's agent, William Aspenwall Bradley, took an interest in short stories I had begun writing—so off I went. In novels my hope is to involve readers in a mood and in people, extraordinary ones. In non-fiction books my object is to share experiences and interests.

"As a teacher I am expected to advise aspiring writers. This boils down to: read widely and carefully, write even when you don't feel in the mood, and be prepared for hard times."

* * *

SCHMIDT, Paul Frederic 1925-

PERSONAL: Born September 14, 1925, in Rochester, N.Y.; son of Carl Frederic and Ann (Crecely) Schmidt; married Rebecca Jane Kennedy, April 7, 1947 (divorced January, 1964); married Gail Ann Baker, August 1, 1964; children: (first marriage) Lawrence, Eric, Karl, Allen. *Education:* University of Rochester, A.B., 1947; Yale University, Ph.D., 1951. *Office:* Department of Philosophy, University of New Mexico, Albuquerque, N.M. 87106.

CAREER: Oberlin College, Oberlin, Ohio, 1951-65, began as instructor, became associate professor of philosophy, acting chairman of department, 1957-58 and 1964-65; University of New Mexico, Albuquerque, professor of philosophy and chairman of department, 1965—. Visited India under U.S. Department of State auspices, 1957. *Military service:* U.S. Air Force. *Member:* American Philosophical Association, American Association of University Professors, Phi Beta Kappa.

WRITINGS: Religious Knowledge, Free Press, 1961; *Perception and Cosmology in Whitehead's Philosophy,* Rutgers University Press, 1967; *Rebelling, Loving, and Liberation,* Hummingbird Press, 1970; *Temple Reflections: Japan, Java, India, Iran, and Greece,* Hummingbird Press, 1980. Contributor to *American Journal of Physics, Humanist, Journal of Philosophy,* and other periodicals.

WORK IN PROGRESS: The Aesthetics of Existing.

SCHMIDT, Warren H(arry) 1920-

PERSONAL: Born November 10, 1920, in Detroit, Mich.; son of Henry W. (a businessman) and Lillian (Kath) Schmidt; married Amanda Regelean, September 25, 1945; children: Jacqueline Ann, Barbara Jean, Nancy Marie, Ronald Henry. *Education:* Wayne University (now Wayne State University), B.A., 1942; Concordia Theological Seminary, B.D., 1945; Washington University, Ph.D., 1950. *Politics:* Democrat. *Home:* 9238 Petit Ave., Sepulveda, Calif. 91343. *Office:* School of Public Administration, University of Southern California, University Park, Los Angeles, Calif. 90007.

CAREER: Ordained Lutheran minister, 1945; pastor in Glendale, Mo., 1945-47; Washington University, St. Louis, Mo., instructor in psychology, 1948-49; University of Missouri, Columbia, instructor in psychology, 1949-50; Union College, Schenectady, N.Y., assistant professor of psychology, 1950-51; Springfield College, Springfield, Mass., assistant professor of psychology, 1951-53; Adult Education Association of the U.S.A., Washington, D.C., project coordinator, 1953-55; University of California, Los Angeles, lecturer in psychology, 1955-59, lecturer, 1965-68, senior lecturer in behavioral sciences, 1969-77, director of statewide conferences and community services, 1959-61, director of M.B.A. program, 1965-68, assistant dean, 1969-73; University of Southern California, University Park, Los Angeles, professor of public administration, 1977—. Senior vice-president, Leadership Resources, Inc., Washington, D.C., 1960-68. Consultant to airlines, National Council of Churches, and to other organizations, business firms, government agencies, and film production companies.

MEMBER: American Psychological Association, International Association of Applied Social Scientists, California Psychological Association, Sigma Xi, Beta Gamma Sigma. *Awards, honors:* Academy of Motion Picture Arts and Sciences Award (Oscar) for best animated short subject, 1970, for film script, "Is It Always Right to Be Right?"

WRITINGS: *Techniques That Produce Teamwork,* Croft Educational, 1954; *Looking into Leadership,* Leadership Resources, 1962; *Organizational Frontiers and Human Values,* Wadsworth, 1970; *Is It Always Right to Be Right?* (adapted from film script of same title; also see below), Wadsworth, 1970.

Film scripts; all animated: "Freedom River," Stephen Bosustow Productions, 1971; "The Hand-off," Salenger Educational Media, 1979; "Creative Problem Solving," CRM, 1979. Also author of "Is It Always Right to Be Right?," 1970. Contributor to adult education, business, and management journals.

WORK IN PROGRESS: A series of short animated films dealing with purpose, power, and prospective, all for Stephen Bosustow Productions; a book on management and conflict resolution.

* * *

SCHOCHET, J(acob) Immanuel 1935-

PERSONAL: Born August 27, 1935, in Basel, Switzerland; son of Dov Yehudah and Sarah (Musenson) Schochet; married Yettie-Rachel Elzas, June 5, 1962; children: Yehudith Oryah, Yitzchak Yehonathan, Chanah Sharonne, Yisrael Ovadyah. *Education:* Tomchei Temimim Lubavitch, Brooklyn, N.Y., rabbi, 1957; University of Windsor, B.A., 1964; McMaster University, M.A. (philosophy), 1965, M.A. (religion), 1966; University of Waterloo, Ph.D., 1973. *Home:* 55 Charleswood Dr., Downsview, Ontario, Canada. *Office:* Humber College, Humber College Blvd., Rexdale, Ontario, Canada.

CAREER: Rabbi in Toronto, Ontario, 1959; history teacher, chairman of department, and assistant principal of high school in Willowdale, Ontario, 1966-70; Humber College, Rexdale, Ontario, professor of philosophy and religion, 1971—. Visiting professor of philosophy and dean of graduate studies, Maimonides College, Toronto, 1975—. Member of executive board, Rabbinical Alliance of America; member of board of various cultural and educational institutions.

MEMBER: Academy of Religion, Philosophical Society, Canadian Jewish Congress (member of executive board), Rabbinical Council of Ontario. *Awards, honors:* Canada Council fellowships, 1969-70, 1970-71; National Foundation for Jewish Culture research fellowship, 1972.

WRITINGS: *Rabbi Israel Baal Shen Tov,* Lieberman's, 1961; *Arrest and Liberation of Schneur Zalman of Liadi,* Kehot, 1964; *Tzitzith,* Kehot, 1967, 7th edition, 1979; (translator and author of notes) *Igereth Hakodesh,* two volumes, Kehot, 1968, revised edition, Soncino, 1972; *Gemiluth Chassadim: Performance of Loving-Kindness,* Kehot, 1968, 6th edition, 1979; *Kibbud Av Vaem,* Kehot, 1968, 6th edition, 1979; *Mystical Concepts in Hassidism,* Soncino, 1972, revised edition, Kehot, 1979; *The Great Maggid,* Kehot, 1974; *Tzavaat Rivash,* Kehot, 1975; *Mafteichot I: Rivash,* Kehot, 1978; *Mafteichot II: Maggid,* Kehot, 1979; (translator and author of introduction and notes) *Likulei Sichot,* Volume I, Kehot, 1979. Also author, with Vallentine Mitchell and others, of *Challenge,* 1970. Contributor to numerous publications, including *Response, Judaism, Di Yiddishe Heim, Bitaon Chabad, Toronto Hebrew Journal, Tradition, Canadian Jewish News,* and *Hapardess,* and to newspapers in the United States and Canada.

WORK IN PROGRESS: *Historical and Philosophical Foundations of Hassidism,* Volume II: *The Philosophy of the Maggid of Mezeritch;* revising *Rabbi Israel Baal Shem Tov; Studia Chassidiana,* a collection of studies and monographs.

SIDELIGHTS: J. Immanuel Schochet comments: "I believe that when one feels he has something to contribute in word or writing which may enlighten and thus better humanity, one has an obligation to do so. I generally write and lecture only on [those] topics which I feel will contribute something positive and inspiring, or will urge the reader to pursue such subjects."

Schochet has traveled and lectured in Israel, western Europe, and the United States.

* * *

SCHODER, Raymond Victor 1916-

PERSONAL: Born April 11, 1916, in Battle Creek, Mich.; son of Harold Maurice and Hildred (Baird) Schoder. *Education:* Xavier University, A.B., 1938; Loyola University of Chicago, M.A., 1940; St. Louis University, Ph.D., 1944; West Baden College, S.T.L., 1948. *Religion:* Roman Catholic. *Office:* Department of Classical Studies, Loyola University of Chicago, 6525 Sheridan Rd., Chicago, Ill. 60626.

CAREER: Joined Jesuit order, 1933; University of Detroit High School, Detroit, Mich., teacher of Latin, Greek, and English, 1943-44; West Baden College, West Baden, Ind., assistant professor of Latin and Greek, 1950-59; University of Detroit, Colombiere College, professor of classical literature and archaeology, 1959; Loyola University of Chicago, Chicago, Ill., professor of Greek and Latin literature and art,

1960—. American School of Classical Studies, Athens, Greece, member of managing committee, 1953—, visiting professor, 1961-62; director, summer course in classical archaeology for teachers at Vergilian Society of America's School, Cumae, Italy, 1953-57, 1961, and 1965; Fulbright professor of Greek art and archaeology, University of Nijmegen, Netherlands, 1956-57; lecturer, art program, Association of American Colleges, 1958-60; Rojtman Foundation lecturer in classical art, Milwaukee, Wis., 1962-63; visiting professor, Sophia University, Tokyo, Japan, summer, 1964. Lecturer throughout the United States and Europe. *Member:* American Philological Association, Archaeological Institute of America. *Awards, honors:* Award for best illustrated book of 1975, Associated Church Press and Catholic Press Association, for *Landscape and Inscape*.

WRITINGS: (With V. C. Horrigan) *A Reading Course in Homeric Greek,* three volumes, Loyola University Press, 1947; (editor with others) *Immortal Diamond: Studies in G. M. Hopkins,* Sheed, 1948; *Masterpieces of Greek Art,* New York Graphic Society, 1960, 3rd edition, Ares Publishers, 1975; *Italian Is Easy—If You Know Latin,* American Classical League, 1960; (editor and author of introduction) Sellers, *The Elder Pliny's Chapters on Art,* Argonaut, 1966; *Ancient Greece from the Air,* Oxford University Press, 1974; (illustrator) Peter Milward, *Landscape and Inscape,* Eerdmans, 1975; (co-editor and contributor) *Readings of the Wreck,* Loyola University Press, 1976. Contributor of articles and book reviews to professional journals; poet and poetry translator. Supplies photographic documentation on art and archaeology for others' books, including "Great Ages of Man" series, Time-Life.

WORK IN PROGRESS: Books of color photos and commentary on archeological sites of the ancient classical world; running vocabulary to Greek text of Homer's *Iliad;* college edition of Plato in Greek.

SIDELIGHTS: Raymond Schoder's published works have been translated into eight languages. *Avocational interests:* Color photography, archaeological travel.

* * *

SCHRAFF, Anne E(laine) 1939-

PERSONAL: Born September 21, 1939, in Cleveland, Ohio; daughter of Frank C. and Helen (Benninger) Schraff. *Education:* Pierce Junior College, A.A., 1964; San Fernando Valley State College (now California State University, Northridge), B.A., 1966, M.A., 1967. *Politics:* Republican. *Religion:* Roman Catholic. *Address:* P.O. Box 1345, Spring Valley, Calif. 92077.

CAREER: Academy of Our Lady of Peace, San Diego, Calif., teacher of social studies, 1967—. *Member:* California Social Studies Council.

WRITINGS: (With brother, Francis N. Schraff) *Jesus Our Brother* (children's book), Liguori Publications, 1968; *Black Courage: Sagas of Pioneers, Sailors, Explorers, Miners, Cowboys—21 Heros of the American West* (nonfiction), Macrae, 1969; *North Star* (novel), Macrae, 1972; *The Day the World Went Away* (novel), Doubleday, 1973; *Faith of the Presidents* (nonfiction), Concordia, 1978; (with F. N. Schraff) *The Adventures of Peter and Paul: Acts of the Apostles for the Young,* Liguori Publications, 1978; *Tecumseh: The Story of an American Indian,* Dillon, 1979; *Christians Courageous* (nonfiction), Concordia, 1980; *You Can't Stop Me, So Don't Even Try* (novel), Perfection Form Co., 1980.

"Passages Reading Program" series; juvenile novels; published by Perfection Form Co.: *Don't Blame the Children,* with workbook, 1978; *Please Don't Ask Me to Love You,* with workbook, 1978; *An Alien Spring,* with workbook, 1978; *The Vandal,* with workbook, 1978; *The Ghost Boy,* with workbook, 1978; *Haunting of Hawthorne,* with workbook, 1978. Contributor of reviews to *Scholastic Teacher*.

WORK IN PROGRESS: Several young adult novels, as yet untitled.

SIDELIGHTS: Anne E. Schraff writes *CA:* "I've been motivated by a powerful desire to write that made it impossible to do otherwise. I began my writing career at [the age of] eight when I wrote a love story for the *Saturday Evening Post* titled, "Orchids for Linda." I told all my friends it would soon be published and thus learned very early not to count chickens yet unhatched. I sold my first story, *Stage to Hell,* while a college freshman. It sold to *Ranch Romances,* and constituted one of the rare truly glorious experiences available to people.

"In my books, chiefly for young people, I hope to enable my readers to share the magic and adventure of life [that] I enjoyed in the books I devoured as a child. I also hope to convey the powerful beliefs that life is worth living and goodness is worth achieving.

"I wrote the 'Passages' novels to create exciting stories to interest reluctant teenaged readers who usually didn't read. Some letters from kids have told me my books were the first they ever read straight through. That pleased me greatly."

AVOCATIONAL INTERESTS: Music, hiking.

* * *

SCHRAG, Calvin Orville 1928-

PERSONAL: Born May 4, 1928, in Marion, S.D.; son of John A. and Katherine (Miller) Schrag. *Education:* Bethel College, North Newton, Kan., B.A., 1950; Yale University, B.D., 1953; Oxford University, graduate study, 1955; Harvard University, Ph.D., 1957. *Home:* 1315 North Grant St., West Lafayette, Ind. *Office:* Department of Philosophy, Purdue University, West Lafayette, Ind. 47907.

CAREER: Purdue University, West Lafayette, Ind., assistant professor, 1957-59, associate professor, 1960-64, professor of philosophy, 1964—, interim chairman of department, 1972-73. Visiting lecturer, University of Illinois at Urbana-Champaign, 1959-60; visiting associate professor, Northwestern University, 1963-64. *Member:* American Philosophical Association, Metaphysical Society of America, American Association of University Professors, Society for Phenomenology and Existential Philosophy, Indiana Philosophical Society, Phi Beta Kappa (foundation member of Purdue chapter, 1971). *Awards, honors:* Fulbright fellow, Heidelberg University, 1954-55; Purdue grant for research and writing at University of Paris, 1961; Eli Lilly postdoctoral award, 1962; Guggenheim fellowship for study and writing at University of Freiburg, 1965-66; National Foundation on the Arts and Humanities fellowship, 1967-68; American Council of Learned Societies grant-in-aid, 1974; National Endowment for the Humanities grant for summer seminar for college teachers in philosophy, 1978 and 1980.

WRITINGS: (Contributor) *Phenomenology: The Philosophy of Edmund Husserl and Its Interpretation,* Doubleday, 1957; *Existence and Freedom,* Northwestern University Press, 1961; (contributor) Frank Magill, editor, *Masterpieces of World Philosophy,* Salem Press, 1961; (contributor) Magill, editor, *Masterpieces of Christian Literature,* Salem Press,

1963; (contributor) M. S. Frings, editor, *Heidegger and the Quest for Truth,* Quadrangle, 1968; *Experience and Being,* Northwestern University Press, 1969; (with J. Edie and F. Parker) *Patterns of the Life-World,* Northwestern University Press, 1970; *Radical Reflection and the Origin of the Human Sciences,* Purdue University Press, 1980. Consulting editor, "Studies in Phenomenology and Existential Philosophy," Indiana University Press, and *Journal of Existential Psychiatry;* editor, *Man and World: An International Philosophical Review.*

WORK IN PROGRESS: Philosophy of the Human Sciences.

AVOCATIONAL INTERESTS: Modern art, fishing, and golf.

* * *

SCHUERER, Ernst 1933-

PERSONAL: Born September 13, 1933, in Germany; naturalized U.S. citizen, 1961; son of Josef (a craftsman) and Hermine (Ahlbrink) Schuerer; married Margarete Richter, June 20, 1964; children: Frank, Norbert, Anne. *Education:* University of Texas, B.A., 1960; Yale University, M.A., 1962, Ph.D., 1965. *Politics:* Democratic. *Home:* 705 East Foster Ave., State College, Pa. 16801. *Office:* Department of German, Pennsylvania State University, S-323 Burrowes Bldg., University Park, Pa. 16802.

CAREER: Yale University, New Haven, Conn., instructor, 1965-67, assistant professor, 1967-70, associate professor of German, 1970-73, director of undergraduate studies, 1969-71, director of graduate studies, 1971-73; University of Florida, Gainesville, professor of German, 1973-78, chairman of department, 1977-78; Pennsylvania State University, University Park, professor of German and head of department, 1978—. *Member:* Modern Language Association of America, American Association of Teachers of German, American Comparative Literature Association, American Association of Teachers of Foreign Languages, Phi Beta Kappa. *Awards, honors:* Woodrow Wilson fellowship, 1960-61; Morse fellowship, Yale University, 1968-69; Alexander von Humboldt fellowship, 1973.

WRITINGS: (Editor) *Lebendige Form,* Wilhelm Fink, 1970; *Georg Kaiser,* Twayne, 1971; *Georg Kaiser und Bertolt Brecht,* Atheneum, 1971; *Georg Kaiser: Nebeneinander,* Reclam (Stuttgart), 1978; *Carl Sternheim: Tabula rasa,* Reclam, 1978. Contributor to anthologies. Contributor to *Monatshefte, Books Abroad, Journal of English and German,* and *Philology.*

WORK IN PROGRESS: Research on Post-Expressionistic drama, German literature in exile, and imagery in Expressionist drama.

AVOCATIONAL INTERESTS: Philosophy and archeology.

* * *

SCHULTZ, Dodi 1930-

PERSONAL: Born August 21, 1930, in Lancaster, Pa.; married Ed Schultz (a film producer-director), December 23, 1955. *Education:* Attended Goucher College, 1947-50. *Politics:* Democrat. *Home and office address:* 152 West 77th St., New York, N.Y. 10024.

CAREER: Free-lance writer, 1964—. *Member:* American Society of Journalists and Authors (vice-president, 1979-80), Authors Guild, Authors League of America, American Association for the Advancement of Science, Environmental Defense Fund, National Organization for Women, American Civil Liberties Union, National Audubon Society, American Museum of Natural History, New York Botanical Garden, Sierra Club. *Awards, honors:* Certificate of commendation, American Academy of Family Physicians, 1974; National Journalism Award, Epilepsy Foundation of America, 1975; National Journalism Awards, American Academy of Family Physicians, second place, 1976, honorable mention, 1979.

WRITINGS: The Busy Cook's Look-It-Up Book, New American Library, 1969; *Slimming with Yoga,* Dell, 1969; *ABC's of Skin Care,* Bantam, 1969; *Have Your Baby—and Your Figure, Too,* Hawthorn, 1970; (with Virginia E. Pomeranz) *The Mothers' Medical Encyclopedia,* New American Library, 1972; (with husband, Ed Schultz) *How to Make Exciting Home Movies and Stop Boring Your Friends and Relatives,* Doubleday, 1972; (with Arnold P. Friedman and Shervert H. Frazier) *The Headache Book,* Dodd, 1973; (with Seth F. Abramson) *Home and Family Medical Emergencies,* Meredith, 1973; (with Pomeranz) *The First Five Years: A Relaxed Approach to Child Care,* Doubleday, 1973; (with Sheldon Paul Blau) *Arthritis,* Doubleday, 1974; (with Pomeranz) *The Mothers' and Fathers' Medical Encyclopedia,* Little, Brown, 1977; (with Blau) *Lupus: The Body against Itself,* Doubleday, 1977; (with James T. Howard, Jr.) *We Want to Have a Baby,* Dutton, 1979. Columnist, *Viva.* Contributor to *Cosmopolitan, Family Circle, New York Times Magazine, Parade, Science Digest, Self,* and other publications. Contributing editor, *Girl Talk,* beginning 1972, *Viva,* 1977-78, and *Parents,* 1979—.

AVOCATIONAL INTERESTS: Conchology, painting, and gardening.

* * *

SCHULTZ, Edward W(illiam) 1936-

PERSONAL: Born November 16, 1936, in Buffalo, N.Y.; son of Edward J. and Julia (Bender) Schultz; married Patricia Riley (a nurse), September 29, 1961; children: Kirsten, Erich. *Education:* State University of New York College at Buffalo, B.S., 1960; Syracuse University, M.S., 1964, Ph.D., 1969. *Home address:* Box 52, New Sharon, Me. 04955. *Office:* Program in Special Education and Rehabilitation, University of Maine, 86 Main St., Farmington, Me. 04938.

CAREER: Methodist Home for Children, Williamsville, N.Y., child care worker, 1958-63, director of education, 1964-66; teacher at public schools in Kenmore, N.Y., 1960-61, and Williamsville, 1961, 1962-63; University of Illinois at Urbana-Champaign, assistant professor of special education and director of program for educating emotionally disturbed children, 1969-72; University of Maine, Farmington, associate professor of special education and director of program for educating emotionally disturbed children, 1972-74; U.S. Office of Education, Bureau of Education for the Handicapped, education program specialist to Division of Personnel Preparation, 1974-75; University of Maine, associate professor, 1975-76, professor of special education and rehabilitation, 1977—, director of program for educating emotionally disturbed children, 1975—, chairperson of program in special education and rehabilitation, 1976-78. Lecturer and consultant, State University of New York College at Buffalo, 1964-66. Educational coordinator, Ramapo-Anchorage Camp, Rhinebeck, N.Y., 1964, 1965. *Military service:* U.S. Air Force, 1961-62, served in National Guard. *Member:* Council for Children with Behavioral Disorders (president, 1964-66), Council for Exceptional Children, Teacher Educators for Children with Behavioral Disorders, Phi Delta Kappa.

WRITINGS: (With A. Hirshoren, A. B. Manton, and R. A. Henderson) *A Survey of Public School Special Education Programs for Emotionally Disturbed Children* (monograph), Educational Resources Information Center, 1971; (with M. E. Brown and R. Cohn) *Educational Services for Emotionally Handicapped Children in Illinois Residential Centers* (monograph), Educational Resources Information Center, 1972; (with C. Heuchert and S. M. Stampf) *Pain and Joy in School,* Research Press, 1973; *The Affective Development of Children and Teachers in School,* Sigma Information, Inc., 1974.

Contributor: L. Marcus, editor, *The Role of the Classroom Teacher of the Emotionally Disturbed,* Association of New York State Educators of Emotionally Disturbed Children, 1967; F. Eugene Thomure, editor, *Improving Supervisory Behavior in Programs for Auditorily Impaired Children,* Volume I, Memphis State University Press, 1972, Volume II, Gallaudet College, 1973; S. A. Kirk and F. E. Lord, editors, *Exceptional Children: Educational Resources and Perspectives,* Houghton, 1974; J. Gilmore, editor, *CBTE: Human Teaching for Human Learning,* Division of Handicapped Children, New York State Education Department, 1974; L. M. Bullock, editor, *Teacher Educators for Children with Behavior Disorders: Proceedings of the Annual Fall Conference,* [Gainesville, Fla.], 1974; (with L. C. Burrello and M. L. Tracy) Grace J. Warfield, editor, *Mainstream Currents,* Council for Exceptional Children, 1974; J. J. Creamer and Gilmore, editors, *Design for Competence Based Education in Special Education,* Division of Special Education and Rehabilitation, Syracuse University, 1974; Henry Dupont, editor, *Educating Emotionally Disturbed Children,* 2nd edition (Schultz was not associated with earlier edition), Holt, 1975; (with R. Barnes) K. Beeler and Thayer, editors, *Activities and Exercises for Affective Education,* American Educational Research Association, 1975; Thayer, editor, *Affective Education,* University Associates, 1976; Beeler and Thayer, editors, *Affective Education: Innovations for Learning,* American Educational Research Association, 1977.

Contributor to numerous professional publications, including *Exceptional Children, Newsletter: Council for Children with Behavior Disorders, Journal for Research in Mathematics Education, Psychology in the Schools, Illinois School Research, Psychological Reports,* and *Journal of Abnormal Child Psychology.*

* * *

SCHULTZ, Pearle Henriksen 1918- (Marie Pershing)

PERSONAL: Born September 10, 1918, in Havre, Mont.; daughter of Louis G. (an architect) and Anne (Jacobson) Henriksen; married Harry Pershing Schultz (a professor of chemistry), September 25, 1943; children: Stephanie, Tor and Alison (twins). *Education:* University of Wisconsin, B.S., 1939; University of Miami, Coral Gables, Fla., M.Ed., 1951. *Politics:* Republican. *Religion:* Protestant. *Home:* 5835 Southwest 81st St., South Miami, Fla. 33143. *Agent:* McIntosh & Otis, Inc., 475 Fifth Ave., New York, N.Y. 10017.

CAREER: Teacher of English and history and guidance counselor in Racine, Wis., Middleton, Wis., Rahway, N.J., and Dade County, Fla., 1940-51; Cutler Cove Preparatory School, Miami, Fla., principal, 1956-63; Dade County Public Schools, Miami, supervisor of curriculum publications, 1963-72; full-time writer in South Miami, Fla., 1972—. Director, Florida Independent School Council, 1961-63.

WRITINGS: Sir Walter Scott: Wizard of the North, Vanguard, 1968; (with husband, Harry P. Schultz) *Isaac Newton: Scientific Genius,* Garrard, 1972; *Paul Laurence Dunbar: Black Poet Laureate,* Garrard, 1974; *Generous Strangers: Six Heroes of the American Revolution,* Vanguard 1976; (under pseudonym Marie Pershing) *First a Dream,* Dell, 1979; (under pseudonym Marie Pershing) *Maybe Tomorrow,* Dell, 1980; (under pseudonym Marie Pershing) *Bid Time Return,* Dell, 1980.

WORK IN PROGRESS: Under pseudonym Marie Pershing, *Handful of Stars,* completion expection in 1981; a fictional portrayal of large public school systems, *A Reverse of Bugles,* completion expected in 1982.

BIOGRAPHICAL/CRITICAL SOURCES: Science Books, September, 1972.

* * *

SCHWAB, George 1931-

PERSONAL: Born November 25, 1931; son of Arkady (a medical doctor) and Klara (Jacobson) Schwab; married Eleonora Storch, February 27, 1965; children: Clarence Boris, Claude Arkady, Solan Bernhard. *Education:* City College (now City College of the City University of New York), B.A., 1954; Columbia University, M.A., 1955, Ph.D., 1968. *Home:* 140 Riverside Dr., New York, N.Y. 10024. *Office:* Department of History, City College of the City University of New York, 138th St. and Convent Ave., New York, N.Y. 10031; and Graduate School and University Center, City University of New York, 33 West 42nd St., New York, N.Y. 10036.

CAREER: Columbia University, New York City, lecturer in political science, 1959; City College of the City University of New York, New York City, lecturer, 1960-68, assistant professor, 1968-72, associate professor of history, 1973—; currently affiliated with Graduate School and University Center, City University of New York, New York City. *Member:* American Historical Association, American Political Science Association, International Platform Association, Phi Alpha Theta. *Awards, honors:* City University of New York Research Foundation grants, 1970, 1972; Volkswagen Foundation grant, 1978.

WRITINGS: Dayez: Beyond Abstract Art, L'Edition d'Art H. Piazza (Paris), 1967; *The Challenge of the Exception: An Introduction to the Political Ideas of Carl Schmitt between 1921 and 1936,* Duncker & Humblot (Berlin), 1970; (editor with Henry Friedlander, and contributor) *Detente in Historical Perspective,* Cyrco Press, 1975; (translator and author of introduction and notes) Carl Schmitt, *The Concept of the Political,* Rutgers University Press, 1976.

Contributor: *Ideology and Foreign Policy,* Cyrco Press, 1978; *Germany in World Politics,* Cyrco Press, 1979; *Nationalism: Essays in Honor of Louis L. Snyder,* Ark House, 1980; *Innenund Aussenpolitik,* Paul Haupt, 1980. Contributor to *Encyclopedia Judaica,* and to numerous journals, including *Orbis, Interpretation,* and *Canadian Journal of Political and Social Theory.*

AVOCATIONAL INTERESTS: Art collecting (primarily contemporary French, German, and American abstract art, Yugoslavian native art, and stage designs by Russian and French artists).

* * *

SCHWARTZ, Anne Powers 1913- (Anne Powers)

PERSONAL: Born May 7, 1913, in Cloquet, Minn.; daughter of John P. and Maud (Lynch) Powers; married Harold A. Schwartz, 1938; children: Weldon, Lynn. *Education:* Attended University of Minnesota and Miss Brown's School of Business. *Religion:* Roman Catholic. *Home:* 3800 North Newhall St., Milwaukee, Wis. *Agent:* Larry Sternig Literary Agency, 742 Robertson St., Milwaukee, Wis. 53213.

CAREER: Author. Instructor at summer workshop sponsored by University of Wisconsin at Rhinelander, 1964; lecturer in free-lance writing, College of Journalism, Marquette University, 1967—. *Member:* Bookfellows of Milwaukee, Allied Authors, Fictioneers. *Awards, honors:* Fiction award, National Federation of Press Women, 1946, for *The Gallant Years;* Theta Sigma Nu award.

WRITINGS—Under name Anne Powers: *The Gallant Years,* Bobbs-Merrill, 1946; *Ride East! Ride West!,* Bobbs-Merrill, 1947, young people's edition published as *Ride with Danger,* 1959; *No Wall So High,* Bobbs-Merrill, 1949, published as *Royal Bondage,* Pinnacle Books, 1977; *The Ironmaster,* Bobbs-Merrill, 1951, paperback edition published as *The Delaware River Man,* Pinnacle Books, 1978; *The Only Sin,* Bobbs-Merrill, 1953; *The Thousand Fires,* Bobbs-Merrill, 1957; *No King but Caesar,* Doubleday, 1960, paperback edition published as *The Promise and the Passion,* Pinnacle Books, 1977; *Rachel,* Pinnacle Books, 1972; *The Four Queens,* R. Hale, 1977; *Royal Consorts,* Pinnacle Books, 1978; *Young Empress,* Pinnacle Books, 1979; *Possession,* Major Books, 1979; *To Follow the Passionate Heart,* R. Hale, 1980.

SIDELIGHTS: Anne Schwartz researched two of her books in Europe. Most of them have appeared in foreign editions and in paperback.

* * *

SCHWEID, Eliezer 1929-

PERSONAL: Born September 7, 1929, in Jerusalem, Israel; son of Zevi Israel and Osnath (Rosin) Schweid; married Sabina Fuchs (a teacher), October 14, 1953; children: Michal, Jacob, Rachel. *Education:* Hebrew University, B.A., 1956, M.A., 1958, Ph.D., 1961. *Home:* 11 Yishay, Jerusalem, Israel 93-544. *Office:* Department of Jewish Philosophy, Hebrew University, Jerusalem, Israel.

CAREER: University of Haifa, Haifa, Israel, lecturer in Hebrew literature, 1962-67; Hebrew University, Jerusalem, Israel, associate professor of Jewish philosophy, 1964—. Senior lecturer in Jewish philosophy, University of Beersheba, Beersheba, Israel, 1968-71. Adviser to Israeli Ministry of Education, 1967-73. *Military service:* Israeli Defence Army, 1948-49. *Member:* Society international pour l'etude de la philosophie medievale, Association for Jewish-Humanistic Education (president, 1973), Israeli Philosophical Society, Israeli Authors Corp., Zionists Conference in Israel, Israel Interfaith Community. *Awards, honors:* Valenrod Award, Hebrew Writers Association, 1968.

WRITINGS: Shalosh ashmorot (title means "Three Generations in Modern Hebrew Literature"), Am Oved, 1964; *Toldot ha-filosofyah ha-yehudith* (title means "History of Jewish Philosophy"), Akdamon, 1967; (editor and author of introduction) Joseph Albo, *Sefer Haikarim* (title means "Book of Principles"), Bialik Institute, 1967; *Ha-'Ergah li-mele ut ha-havayah* (title means "Striving for Full Existence"), Bialik Institute, 1968; *Ad mashber,* 1969, translation by Alton M. Winters published as *Israel at the Crossroads,* Jewish Publication Society, 1973; *Ta-am va-hakasheh* (title means "Experience and Reason—Studies in Medieval Jewish Philosophy"), Massadah, 1970; *Haphilosophia hadathit shel Rabbi Chrisdai Crescas* (title means "The Theology of Rabbi Chrisdai Crescas"), Makor, 1970; *Hayahid—Oamo shel A. D. Gordon* (title means "The World of A. D. Gordon"), Am Oved, 1970; *Leumiyuth Yehudith* (title means "Jewish Nationhood"), Zack, 1972; *Emunath Am Yisrael we-thazbutho* (title means "The Faith of the Jewish People and Its Culture"), Zack, 1976; *Tholdoth Hehaguth Hayehudith Baeth Hahadashah* (title means "History of Modern Jewish Thought"), Kether, 1977; *Democrathia we halachah* (title means "Democracy and the Law"), Ragnes Press, 1978; *Moledeth we-Srez Yeudah* (title means "Homeland and a Land of Promise"), Am Oved, 1979.

Also author of *Iyunim Bishmonah perakim larambam* (title means "Studies in Maimonides's 'Eight Chapters'"), 1965, and of a booket on modern Hebrew literature and contemporary Jewish thought. Contributor to *Encyclopedia Judaica* and *Hebrew Encyclopedia,* and to periodicals. Member of editorial board, *Petahim,* 1967.

WORK IN PROGRESS: A book on the problem of Jewish identity in our age; a history of modern Jewish philosophy; a project on Jewish-humanistic education in Israel.

* * *

SCOBEY, Mary-Margaret 1915-

PERSONAL: Born September 30, 1915, in San Francisco, Calif.; daughter of Marshall Louis and Susan (Thompson) Scobey. *Education:* San Francisco State College (now University), A.B., 1937; Columbia University, M.A., 1947; Stanford University, Ed.D., 1952. *Home:* 1617 Skycrest Dr., No. 21, Walnut Creek, Calif. 94595.

CAREER: Public school elementary teacher, California, 1937-43; Merced County, Calif., general supervisor of schools, 1946-50; Syracuse University, Syracuse, N.Y., assistant professor of education, 1952-54; San Francisco State University, San Francisco, Calif., assistant professor, 1954-58, associate professor, 1958-63, professor of education, 1963-72, professor emeritus, 1972—. Summer teacher, Fresno State College (now California State University, Fresno), 1948, Southern Illinois University, Utica College, and Western Washington State University; visiting assistant professor, Stanford University, 1954; visiting associate professor, University of Oregon, 1963. Has conducted workshops in elementary school industrial arts. Breeder of champion French bulldogs. Consultant, American International School, Vienna, Austria, 1972-73. *Military service:* U.S. Naval Reserve, 1943-46. *Member:* Association for Supervision and Curriculum Development, American Industrial Arts Association, California Teachers Association, California Association of Leadership and Curriculum Development (director, 1966-71), Kappa Delta Pi, Pi Lambda Theta, Epsilon Pi Tau, *Awards, honors:* Laureate Citation from Epsilon Pi Tau, 1970.

WRITINGS: (With G. Wesley Sowards) *The Changing Curriculum and the Elementary Teacher,* Wadsworth, 1961, revised edition, 1968; (with others) *Teaching Elementary School Subjects,* Ronald, 1961, 3rd edition published as *Teaching in Elementary School,* 1965; *Teaching Children about Technology,* McKnight & McKnight, 1968; (editor) *Rebellion: Today's Dilemma: Watch, Join, Squelch, or Lead?,* California Association for Supervision and Curriculum Development, 1969; (editor) *To Nurture Humaneness: Commitment for the 70's,* Association for Supervision and Curriculum Development, 1970; (editor with John A. Fiorino) *Differentiated Staffing,* Association for Supervision and Curriculum Development, 1973. Contributor to professional journals. Editor, *California Journal for Instructional Improvement*, 1967-71.

WORK IN PROGRESS: A book on elementary school industrial arts; *For Every Human Being: Potentiality in the School.*

AVOCATIONAL INTERESTS: Photography, travel, writing.

* * *

SCOTT, Robert E(dwin) 1923-

PERSONAL: Born April 27, 1923, in Chicago, Ill.; son of Jules F. and Helen (Kasmar) Scott. *Education:* Northwestern University, B.A., 1945, M.A., 1946; University of Wisconsin, Ph.D., 1949. *Home:* 2010 Bruce Dr., Urbana, Ill. *Office:* Department of Political Science, 403 Lincoln Hall, University of Illinois, Urbana, Ill. 61801.

CAREER: University of Illinois at Urbana-Champaign, instructor, 1949-50, assistant professor, 1950-58, associate professor, 1958-61, professor of political science, 1961—. Visiting professor, Yale University, 1962; senior staff member, Brookings Institution, 1963-64. Consultant, Public Administration Services, 1950; consultant to Episcopal Church in Central America, 1957, Mexico, 1958, and Venezuela, 1966. *Member:* American Political Science Association, Association for Latin American Studies, Midwest Conference of Political Scientists, University Club (Urbana).

WRITINGS: Mexican Government in Transition, University of Illinois Press, 1959, revised edition, 1964; (editor) *Latin American Modernization Problems: Case Studies in the Crises of Change,* University of Illinois Press, 1973.

Contributor: H. Davis, editor, *Government and Politics in Latin America,* Ronald, 1958; K. Deutsch and W. Foltz, editors, *Nation Building,* Atherton, 1963; S. Verba and L. Pye, editors, *Political Culture and Political Development,* Princeton University Press, 1965; J. G. LaPalombara and M. Weiner, editors, *Political Parties and Development,* Princeton University Press, 1966; S. M. Lipset and A. E. Solari, editors, *Elites in Latin America,* Oxford University Press, 1967.

WORK IN PROGRESS: Research on Latin American politics, especially those of Peru.

AVOCATIONAL INTERESTS: Sailing, travel.†

* * *

SCOTT, Roy Vernon 1927-

PERSONAL: Born December 26, 1927, in Wrights, Ill.; son of Roy J. and Edna (Dodson) Scott; married Jane A. Brayford, July 9, 1959; children: John D., Elizabeth M., Sarah Ann. *Education:* Iowa State College of Agriculture and Mechanic Arts (now Iowa State University of Science and Technology), B.S., 1952; University of Illinois, M.A., 1953, Ph.D., 1957. *Home:* 207 Seville Pl., Starkville, Miss. 39759. *Office:* Department of History, Mississippi State University, Mississippi State, Miss. 39762.

CAREER: University of Southwestern Louisiana, Lafayette, assistant professor, 1957-58; Business History Foundation, St. Paul, Minn., research associate, 1958-59; University of Missouri—Columbia, assistant professor, 1959-60; Mississippi State University, Mississippi State, assistant professor, 1960-62, associate professor, 1962-64, professor of American history, 1964—, distinguished professor, 1979—. Visiting summer lecturer, University of Illinois at Urbana-Champaign, 1961. Associate, Business History Foundation, 1963-64. *Military service:* U.S. Air Force, 1946-48; became sergeant. *Member:* Agricultural History Society (member of executive committee, 1974-77; vice-president, 1977-78; president, 1978-79), Organization of American Historians, American Historical Association, American Association of University Professors, Economic History Association, Southern Historical Association, Phi Kappa Phi, Phi Alpha Theta. *Awards, honors:* E. E. Edwards Award in agricultural history, 1958; American Philosophical Society grants, 1962, 1969, 1970, and 1976; American Association of State and Local History certificate of commendation, 1977.

WRITINGS: The Agrarian Movement in Illinois, 1880-1896, University of Illinois Press, 1962; *The Reluctant Farmer: The Rise of Agricultural Extension to 1914,* University of Illinois Press, 1970; (with J. G. Shoalmire) *The Public Career of Cully A. Cobb: A Study in Agricultural Leadership,* University and College Press of Mississippi, 1973. Contributor of numerous articles and book reviews to journals in his field and encyclopedias.

WORK IN PROGRESS: Economic Development and Freight Traffic Generation: A Study of American Railroad Development Programs; A History of the Great Northern Railway Company; Change in America's Heartland: Farming and Farm Life in the Middle West, 1900-1975.

* * *

SEE, Ruth Douglas 1910-

PERSONAL: Born March 16, 1910, in Baltimore, Md.; daughter of Robert Gamble and Louisa (Spear) See. *Education:* Mary Baldwin College, A.B., 1931; Biblical Seminary in New York (now New York Theological Seminary), M.R.E., 1934; New York University, Ph.D., 1953. *Address:* P.O. Box 386, Montreat, N.C. 28757. *Office:* Department of History, Virginia Commonwealth University, 901 West Franklin St., Richmond, Va. 23284.

CAREER: First Presbyterian Church, Baton Rouge, La., student worker, 1935-36; Stillman College, Tuscaloosa, Ala., instructor in Bible and English, 1938-45; First Presbyterian Church, New Bern, N.C., director of Christian education, 1945-46; Biblical Seminary in New York (now New York Theological Seminary), New York, N.Y., assistant supervisor of field work, 1946-49; Presbyterian Board of Christian Education, Richmond, Va., editor of youth materials, 1949-67; Virginia Commonwealth University, Richmond, assistant professor of history, 1967—. Visiting English teacher and director of Presbyterian student center, Taiwan National University, Taipei, 1956-57. Member of Richmond Council on Human Relations. *Member:* Religious Education Association, American Association of University Professors, Zonta Club, Mary Baldwin Honor Society. *Awards, honors:* Emily Smith Award of Mary Baldwin College, 1965.

WRITINGS: What Can We Do?, Friendship, 1957, revised edition, 1965; *Make the Bible Your Own,* John Knox, 1961; (with Howard G. Hageman) *That the World May Know,* published with *Leader's Guide,* CLC Press, 1965; (compiler) *Historical Foundation Holdings of Eighteenth-Century American Publications,* Historical Foundation of the Presbyterian and Reformed Churches, 1976.

AVOCATIONAL INTERESTS: Music, choral work.†

* * *

SEGAL, Martin

PERSONAL: Born in Warsaw, Poland; married Ruth Berkowicz; children: Naomi Jane, Jonathan Henry. *Education:* Queens College (now Queens College of the City University of New York), B.A., 1948; Harvard University, M.A., 1950, Ph.D., 1953. *Home:* 5 Fairview Ave., Hanover, N.H. 03755. *Office:* Department of Economics, Dartmouth College, Hanover, N.H. 03755.

CAREER: Harvard University, Cambridge, Mass., instructor, 1953-56; economist, New York Metropolitan Region Study, 1956-57; Williams College, Williamstown, Mass., assistant professor, 1957-58; Dartmouth College, Hanover, N.H., associate professor, 1958-65, professor, 1965—. Research associate, Harvard University, 1965; senior staff economist, Council of Economic Advisers, Washington, D.C., 1966; economist, International Labor Office, 1968-69. *Military service:* U.S. Army, 1942-46. *Member:* American Economic Association, Industrial Research Association, Phi Beta Kappa. *Awards, honors:* Alumnus of the Year, Queens College of the City University of New York, 1962.

WRITINGS: Wages in the Metropolis, Harvard University Press, 1961; *Population, Labor Force and Unemployment in Chronically Depressed Areas,* U.S. Department of Commerce, 1964; *The Rise of the United Association,* Harvard University Press, 1970; *Government Pay Policy in Ceylon,* International Labor Office, 1971. Contributor to professional journals.

* * *

SELLMAN, Roger R(aymond) 1915-

PERSONAL: Born September 24, 1915, in London, England; married Minnie Coutts, 1938. *Education:* University of Oxford, M.A. (honors), 1941; University of Exeter, Ph.D., 1974. *Home:* Pound Down Corner, Whitestone, Exeter, Devonshire EX4 2HP, England.

CAREER: History specialist in three grammar schools in England, 1938-52; history lecturer in two teacher's colleges, 1952-60; county inspector of schools, Devonshire, England, 1960-69; free-lance author, 1969—. Extramural lecturer in local history.

WRITINGS—All published by Edward Arnold: *Modern British Economic History,* 1947, 3rd edition, 1972; *Modern European History,* 1949, 3rd edition, 1974; *Survey of British History,* Volume I, 1949, 2nd edition, 1964; *Student's Atlas of Modern History,* 1952, revised edition, 1972; *Outline Atlas of Eastern History,* 1954; *Historical Atlas, 1789-1962,* 1963; *Modern World History,* 1972; *Modern British History, 1815-1970,* 1976.

All published by Methuen, except as indicated: *Castles and Fortresses,* 1954, 2nd edition, 1962; *The Crusades,* 1955; *Roman Britain,* 1956, 4th edition, Roy Publishers, 1974; *English Churches,* 1956; *The Vikings,* 1957; *Elizabethan Seamen,* 1957; *Prehistoric Britain,* 1958; *The Anglo-Saxons,* 1959; *Norman England,* 1959; *Medieval English Warfare,* 1960; *Illustrations of Dorset History,* 1960; *The First World War,* 1961, revised edition, Criterion, 1962; *Illustrations of Devon History,* 1962; *The Second World War,* 1964; *Devon Village Schools in the Nineteenth Century,* Augustus M. Kelley, 1968; *Outline Atlas of World History,* St. Martin's, 1970; *Bismarck and the Unification of Germany,* 1973; *Garibaldi and the Unification of Italy,* 1973. Also author of "Brief Lives" series, five volumes, 1971-73.

WORK IN PROGRESS: A chapter on schools for *The Victorian Countryside.*

SIDELIGHTS: Roger Sellman told *CA:* "My list of publications may appear diffuse; but since giving up full-time employment I have at last had the opportunity for specialized research, not only in my own subject of rural education (which arose out of my time as inspector of schools in Devon) but also in the raw material of local social history to be found in parish records—fleshing out, and sometimes modifying or correcting, the generalizations of secondary works. My lifelong and almost passionate interest in the past has been enhanced by its having become a welcome refuge from an increasingly uncomfortable present and clouded future."

* * *

SERLING, Robert J(erome) 1918-

PERSONAL: Born March 28, 1918, in Cortland, N.Y.; son of Samuel Lawrence and Esther Lillian (Cooper) Serling; married Patricia Huntley, June, 1948 (divorced, 1958); married Priscilla Arone, September 5, 1968; children: (second marriage) Jennifer Ann, Jeffrey Lawrence. *Education:* Antioch College, B.A., 1942. *Home and office:* 10038 Carmelita Dr., Potomac, Md. 20854.

CAREER: United Press International, Washington, D.C., reporter and manager of Radio News Division, 1945-60, aviation editor, 1960-66; air safety lecturer and consultant, 1966—. *Military service:* U.S. Army, 1942-44, served as instructor in aircraft identification. *Member:* Society of Air Safety Investigators, Aviation/Space Writers Association. *Awards, honors:* Trans-World Airlines, seven awards, 1958-65, for aviation news reporting, Strebig-Dobben Memorial Award, 1960; special citations from Sherman Fairchild Foundation, 1963, Flight Safety Foundation, 1970, and Airline Pilots Association, 1970; Aviation/Space Writers Association, James Trebig Memorial Award, 1964, special citation, 1967, award in fiction, 1966, for *The Left Seat,* and in nonfiction, 1969, for *Loud and Clear.*

WRITINGS—Published by Doubleday, except as indicated: *The Probable Cause,* 1960; *The Electra Story,* 1962; *The Left Seat* (novel), 1964; *The President's Plane Is Missing* (novel), 1967; *The Newsman and Air Accidents,* Aviation/Space Writers Association, 1967; *Loud and Clear,* 1969; *She'll Never Get Off the Ground* (novel), 1971; *Ceiling Unlimited,* Wadsworth, 1973; *Maverick,* 1974; *The Only Way to Fly,* 1976; *Wings* (novel), Dial, 1978; *From the Captain to the Colonel,* Dial, 1980.

WORK IN PROGRESS: Coffee, Tea, or Murder, a mystery; *The Old Man,* a novel.

SIDELIGHTS: The President's Plane Is Missing has been adapted for television. *Avocational interests:* Collecting commercial airline models (owns more than four hundred) and material on aviation research.

BIOGRAPHICAL/CRITICAL SOURCES: Books and Bookmen, August, 1968; *Best Sellers,* February 15, 1969, February 1, 1971; *Washington Post,* August 25, 1978.

* * *

SERRAILLIER, Ian (Lucien) 1912-

PERSONAL: Born September 24, 1912, in London, England; son of Lucien and Mary (Rodger) Serraillier; married Anne Margaret Rogers, 1944; children: Helen, Jane, Christine Anne, Andrew. *Education:* St. Edmund Hall, Oxford, M.A., 1935. *Home:* Singleton, Chichester PO18 OHA, Sussex, England.

CAREER: Wycliffe College, Stonehouse, Gloucestershire, England, schoolmaster, 1936-39; Dudley Grammar School, Dudley, Worcestershire, England, teacher, 1939-46; Midhurst Grammar School, Midhurst, Sussex, England, teacher, 1946-61. *Awards, honors:* Boys' Clubs of America Junior Book Award, 1960, for *The Silver Sword.*

WRITINGS: (Contributor) *Three New Poets: Roy McFadden, Alex Comfort, Ian Serraillier,* Grey Walls Press, 1942; *The Weaver Birds* (poems), Macmillan, 1944; *Thomas and the Sparrow* (poems), Oxford University Press, 1946; *They Raced for Treasure,* J. Cape, 1946, simplified educational edition published as *Treasure Ahead,* Heinemann, 1954; *Flight to Adventure,* J. Cape, 1947, simplified educational edition published as *Mountain Rescue,* Heinemann, 1955; *Captain Bounsaboard and the Pirates,* J. Cape, 1949.

The Monster Horse (poems), Oxford University Press, 1950; *There's No Escape,* J. Cape, 1950, educational edition, Heinemann, 1952; *The Ballad of Kon-Tiki,* Oxford University Press, 1952; *Belinda and the Swans,* J. Cape, 1952; (translator with wife, Anne Serraillier) S. Chonz, *Florina and the Wild Bird,* Oxford University Press, 1952; (translator) *Beowulf the Warrior,* Oxford University Press, 1954, Walck, 1961; *Everest Climbed* (poem), Oxford University Press, 1955; *The Silver Sword,* J. Cape, 1956, educational edition, Heinemann, 1957, Criterion, 1958, published as *Escape from Warsaw,* Scholastic, 1963; *Poems and Pictures,* Heinemann, 1958; (contributor) Eleanor Graham, editor, *A Puffin Quartet of Poets: Eleanor Farjeon, James Reeves, E. V. Rieu, Ian Serraillier,* Penguin, 1958, revised edition, 1964.

The Ivory Horn (adaptation of *The Song of Roland,* an early 12th century *chanson de geste* sometimes attributed to Turoldus), Oxford University Press, 1960, educational edition, Heinemann, 1962; *The Gorgon's Head: The Story of Perseus* (also see below), Oxford University Press, 1961, Walck, 1962; *The Way of Danger: The Story of Theseus* (also see below), Oxford University Press, 1962, Walck, 1963; *The Windmill Book of Ballads,* Heinemann, 1962; *Happily Ever After: Poems for Children,* Oxford University Press, 1963; *The Clashing Rocks: The Story of Jason,* Oxford University Press, 1963, Walck, 1964; *The Midnight Thief: A Musical Story,* music by Richard Rodney Bennett, BBC Publications, 1963; *The Enchanted Island: Stories from Shakespeare,* Walck, 1964, educational edition, Heinemann, 1966; *Ahmet the Woodseller: A Musical Story,* music by Gordon Crosse, Oxford University Press, 1965; *A Fall from the Sky,* Walck, 1966; *The Challenge of the Green Knight,* Walck, 1966; *Robin in the Greenwood,* Oxford University Press, 1967, Walck, 1968; *Chaucer and His World* (non-fiction), Lutterworth, 1967, Walck, 1968; *The Turtle Drum* (musical story), music by Malcolm Arnold, BBC Publications, 1967; *Havelok the Dane,* Walck, 1967 (published in England as *Havelok the Warrior,* Hamish Hamilton, 1968); *Robin and His Merry Men,* Oxford University Press, 1969, Walck, 1970.

The Tale of Three Landlubbers, Hamish Hamilton, 1970, Coward, 1971; *Heracles the Strong,* Walck, 1970; *The Ballad of St. Simeon,* F. Watts, 1970; *A Pride of Lions* (musical story), music by Phyllis Tate, Oxford University Press, 1971; *The Bishop and the Devil,* F. Watts, 1971; *Have You Got Your Ticket?,* Longman, 1972; *Marko's Wedding,* Deutsch, 1972; *I'll Tell You a Tale,* Longman, 1973, revised edition, Kestrel Books, 1976; *Pop Festival,* Longman, 1973; *Suppose You Met a Witch,* Little, Brown, 1973; *The Robin and the Wren,* Longman, 1974; *How Happily She Laughs,* Longman, 1976; *The Sun Goes Free,* Longman, 1977; *The Road to Canterbury,* Kestrel Books, 1979.

(With Ronald Ridout) *Wide Horizon Reading Scheme,* Heinemann, fifteen volumes, including: *Jungle Adventure,* 1953; *The Adventures of Dick Varley,* 1954; *Making Good,* 1955; *Guns in the Wild,* 1956; *Katy at Home,* 1957; *Katy at School,* 1959; *The Cave of Death,* 1965; *Fight for Freedom,* 1965.

Founder and editor with A. Serraillier, "New Windmill" series of contemporary literature, published by Heinemann.

Omnibus volumes: *The Way of Danger* [and] *The Gorgon's Head,* educational edition, Heinemann, 1965.

SIDELIGHTS: Ian Serraillier is a poet with a passion for old balladry and legends. Many of his original works have received less acclaim than those in which he retells classic tales. As a reviewer for *Times Literary Supplement* comments: "To venture on the story of Beowulf in verse, whether for children or adults, is a deed with its own kind of heroism. . . . There must be a hundred ways of failing; Mr. Serraillier has hit on one of the ways to succeed." The reviewer further commends Serraillier in that he has "preserved the note of royal breeding, of steadfast endeavor, and heroic resignation, which is so pronounced in the original poem."

In *The Challenge of the Green Knight,* "as usual, and . . . most wisely, Mr. Serraillier does not attempt a translation or a paraphrase," writes a *Junior Bookshelf* reviewer. "Instead, he has written an original poem out of the roots of the remote masterpiece." In this case, again, "he keeps something of the mediaeval formality and mannerisms, preserving the grave courtliness in which this startlingly brutal tale [Sir Gawain and the Green Knight] is dressed. The result is a slow, powerful, occasionally beautiful poem, the weaknesses of which are built into the theme." Paul Heins agrees, noting that Serraillier's version "preserves the subtlety as well as the proportions of the original. . . . But beyond fantasy of event and realism of detail, the poet has caught Gawain's sensitive reactions to the testing of his character."

Brian Alderson writes: "It is not surprising to find Ian Serraillier turning to an adaptation of the ballads [about Robin Hood]. . . . It has been a characteristic of Serraillier's own poetry and of his previous adaptations that the words sound better off the tongue than they look on the page. . . . The Robin Hood ballads would seem to offer an even richer fund of material." Serraillier's versions "could only have been made by someone who loves the whole body of early ballad, carol, and lay, and knows it intimately," notes a reviewer for *Times Literary Supplement,* who adds his own praise for Serraillier's "very skillfull" success "in preserving color, rhythm, and phrase while presenting a more immediately comprehensible language." In fact, one reviewer comments that "it takes some research to discover how much of this is Mr. Serraillier and how much the mediaeval balladeer. The modern poet has matched the old anonymous material with extraordinary skill." However, he points out that, "while all this is extremely well done . . . readers who know Mr. Serraillier as . . . our finest poet writing for the young may feel that this is not the best use of his great talents." That sentiment is echoed in other reviews.

A book in which Serraillier achieves less success is *The Enchanted Island.* In it, writes Aileen Peppett, he "attempts to lure children to enjoy Shakespeare on their own level of understanding. His method is to stress the humor, by-pass the romance, and simplify the action as much as possible." A *Junior Bookshelf* reviewer suggests that "maybe the author tries too hard. This is a book mainly for children who don't know Shakespeare, to be read for its own sake. The child who meets Shakespeare for the first time here will take away the impression of fun, romance, heroism—all conveyed in simple words. . . . If *The Enchanted Island* does not quite succeed, this is because it attempts the impossible."

Perhaps the comments that Serraillier could do better result from the fact that his award-winning novel, *The Silver*

Sword, was published more than twenty years ago. In comparison, many of his more recent works may be found lacking. Marcus Crouch writes that, in *The Silver Sword,* "Serraillier brought a poet's sensibility to a true story. . . . The story was written without heroics, but the heroism and endurance of the [characters] shone brightly in [his] unobtrusively lovely prose." Crouch also has noted that "it is a book which one cannot read without profound emotional response and personal involvement. . . . Serraillier tells the story straight, never overstating the suffering, never adding his personal comment." As a reviewer for *Junior Bookshelf* says, the book is "touched with greatness. . . . It is obviously the work of a poet, who values words and uses them with restraint and economy, who never overplays a scene or overworks an emotion." He concludes: "It is sometimes said that children should be shielded from the harsh realities of life. . . . A book like *The Silver Sword* . . . can only enrich and ennoble the reader."

BIOGRAPHICAL/CRITICAL SOURCES: Times Literary Supplement, November 19, 1954, November 28, 1963, November 24, 1966, November 30, 1967, July 2, 1971; *Junior Bookshelf,* December, 1956, July, 1964, February, 1967, December, 1967, December, 1968, August, 1971; Marcus Crouch, *Treasure Seekers and Borrowers: Children's Books in Britain, 1900-1960,* Library Association, 1962; *New York Times Book Review,* September 20, 1964, December 10, 1967; *Christian Science Monitor,* November 5, 1964; *Horn Book,* August, 1967, June, 1968; *School Library Journal,* September, 1971; Marcus Crouch, *The Nesbit Tradition: The Children's Novel in England,* Benn, 1972; John Rowe Townsend, *Written for Children: An Outline of English-Language Children's Literature,* revised edition, Lippincott, 1974; *Children's Literature Review,* Volume II, Gale, 1976.

* * *

SEVERN, William Irving 1914-
(Bill Severn)

PERSONAL: Born May 11, 1914, in Brooklyn, N.Y.; son of William E(llwood) and Margaret (Stone) Severn; married Sue Schulz (production manager, *Portfolio*), July 4, 1936; children: Ellen Sue (Mrs. James Coulter). *Education:* Attended public schools in Montclair, N.J. *Politics:* "Vote for candidate, never party." *Religion:* Episcopalian. *Home:* Maple Ave., Great Barrington, Mass. *Agent:* John K. Payne, August Lenninger Agency, 250 West 57th St., New York, N.Y. 10107.

CAREER: Farmingdale Post, Farmingdale, N.Y., editor, 1933; Radio station WFBR, Baltimore, Md., news editor, 1935-36; Transradio Press Service, San Francisco, Calif., west coast news director, 1936-37; Radio station WCAU, Philadelphia, Pa., news editor; *Buffalo Evening News,* Buffalo, N.Y., editor of radio news for paper-owned stations; Associated Press, New York, N.Y., news editor, 1940-45; free-lance writer, 1945—. Advertising manager, *Lakeville Journal,* Lakeville, Conn., 1961-63. *Member:* Authors League, International Brotherhood of Magicians, Society of American Magicians, Magic Circle (London).

WRITINGS—All under name Bill Severn: (With wife, Sue Severn) *Let's Give a Show,* Knopf, 1956; (with S. Severn) *How to Earn Money,* Prentice-Hall, 1957; (with S. Severn) *Highways to Tomorrow,* Prentice-Hall, 1959; (with S. Severn) *The State Makers,* Putnam, 1963; *Free but Not Equal,* Messner, 1967; *The End of the Roaring Twenties: Prohibition and Repeal* (Junior Literary Guild selection), Messner, 1969; *Ellis Island, the Immigrant Years,* Messner, 1971; *Magic in Mind,* Walck, 1974; *Democracy's Messengers, the Capitol Pages* (Junior Literary Guild selection), Hawthorn, 1975; *Bill Severn's Magic Workshop,* Walck, 1976; *Frances Perkins, a Member of the Cabinet,* Hawthorn, 1976.

All published by McKay: *Magic Wherever You Are,* 1957; *Magic and Magicians* (Junior Literary Guild selection), 1958; *Shadow Magic,* 1959; *Rope Roundup,* 1960, published as *The Book of Ropes and Knots,* 1976; *The Story of the Human Voice,* 1961; *You and Your Shadow,* 1961; *Magic with Paper,* 1962; *Here's Your Hat,* 1963; *Magic in Your Pockets,* 1964; *If the Shoe Fits,* 1964; *Magic Shows You Can Give,* 1965; *Hand in Glove,* 1965; *Adlai Stevenson, Citizen of the World* (Junior Literary Guild selection), 1966; *Packs of Fun,* 1967; *Mr. Chief Justice: Earl Warren,* 1968; *Magic Comedy,* 1968; *John Marshall, The Man Who Made the Court Supreme* (Junior Literary Guild selection), 1969; *William Howard Taft, The President Who Became Chief Justice* (Junior Literary Guild selection), 1970; *The Long and Short of It: Five Thousand Years of Fun and Fury over Hair* (Junior Literary Guild selection), 1971; *Magic across the Table,* 1972; *Bill Severn's Big Book of Magic,* 1973; *A Carnival of Sports,* 1974; *Bill Severn's Magic Trunk,* 1974; *Magic with Coins and Bills,* 1977; *Fifty Ways to Have Fun with Old Newspapers,* 1978; *Bill Severn's Big Book of Close-up Magic,* 1978.

All published by Washburn: *Teacher, Soldier, President: The Life of James A. Garfield,* 1964; *Frontier President: The Life of James K. Polk* (Junior Literary Guild selection), 1965; *In Lincoln's Footsteps: The Life of Andrew Johnson,* 1966; *People Words,* 1966; *Toward One World: The Life of Wendell Willkie* (Junior Literary Guild selection), 1967; *Samuel J. Tilden and the Stolen Election,* 1968; *Place Words,* 1969; *Irish Statesman and Rebel, The Two Lives of Eamon De Valera,* 1970; *The Right to Vote* (Junior Literary Guild selection), 1972; *The Right to Privacy,* 1973.

WORK IN PROGRESS: Bill Severn's Guide to Magic as a Hobby; More Magic in Your Pockets.

AVOCATIONAL INTERESTS: Magic, American history, book collecting.

* * *

SEWALL, Marcia 1935-

PERSONAL: Born November 5, 1935, in Providence, R.I.; daughter of Edgar Knight and Hilda (Osgood) Sewall. *Education:* Pembroke College, B.A., 1957; Tufts University, M.Ed., 1958. *Religion:* Unitarian Universalist. *Residence:* Boston, Mass.

CAREER: Children's Museum, Boston, Mass., staff artist, 1961-63; teacher of art in Winchester, Mass., 1967-75. Participant in Boston adult literacy program. *Awards, honors: Come Again in the Spring* named one of "Outstanding Books of the Year," *New York Times,* 1976; notable book citation, American Library Association, 1978, for *Little Things; The Nutcrackers and the Sugar-Tongs* named one of best picture books, *New York Times,* 1978.

WRITINGS: Master of All Masters, Little, Brown, 1972; (self-illustrated) *The Wee, Wee Mannie and the Big, Big Coo,* Atlantic-Little, Brown, 1979; (self-illustrated) *The Little Wee Tyke,* Atheneum, 1979.

Illustrator; text by Richard Kennedy: *The Parrot and the Thief,* Atlantic-Little, Brown, 1974; *The Porcelain Man,* Atlantic-Little, Brown, 1976; *Come Again in the Spring,* Harper, 1976; *The Rise and Fall of Ben Gizzard,* Atlantic-Little, Brown, 1978; *The Leprechaun's Story,* Dutton, 1979; *Crazy in Love,* Dutton, 1980.

P. C. Asbjornsen, *The Squire's Bride,* Atheneum, 1975; Joseph Jacobs, *Coo-My-Dove, My Dear,* Atheneum, 1976; Anne Laurin, *Little Things,* Atheneum, 1978; Edward Lear, *The Nutcrackers and the Sugar-Tongs,* Atlantic-Little, Brown, 1978; Anne Elito Crompton, *The Lifting Stone,* Holiday House, 1978; Paul Fleischman, *The Birthday Tree,* Harper, 1979; Phyllis Krasilovsky, *The Man Who Tried to Save Time,* Doubleday, 1979; John Reynolds Gardiner, *Stone Fox,* Crowell, 1980.

* * *

SHAPIRO, David S(idney) 1923-

PERSONAL: Born December 4, 1923, in New York, N.Y.; son of Abraham (a laborer) and Dora (Robins) Shapiro; married Elaine Sharff (a teacher), March 28, 1948; children: Judith Deborah, Jonathan Aaron. *Education:* Brooklyn College (now Brooklyn College of the City University of New York), A.B., 1948; Columbia University, Ph.D., 1956. *Religion:* Jewish.

CAREER: Connecticut State Hospital, Middletown, psychology intern, 1951-52; Hunter College (now Hunter College of the City University of New York), New York, N.Y., research assistant, 1952-53; Tompkins County Mental Health Clinic, Ithaca, N.Y., clinical psychologist, 1953-56; Bradley Center, Columbus, Ga., chief clinical psychologist, 1956-63, director of training and education, 1963-66; Harvard University, School of Public Health, Cambridge, Mass., lecturer in social psychiatry, beginning 1966. *Military service:* U.S. Army, 1943-46; became technician, fifth grade. *Member:* American Psychological Association, American Association for the Advancement of Science, American Public Health Association, Georgia Psychological Association.

WRITINGS: (With Leonard T. Maholick) *Opening Doors for Troubled People,* C. C Thomas, 1963; *Neurotic Styles,* Basic Books, 1965; (with others) *The Mental Health Counselor in the Community: Training of Physicians and Ministers,* C. C Thomas, 1968. Contributor to *Medical Times* and to psychology and psychiatry journals.

SIDELIGHTS: David S. Shapiro told *CA* that throughout his career as a clinical psychologist, "I have been concerned about the vast number of troubled people who never get help at all, or receive help only after long years of suffering. Because of this, I have focused upon developing methods and procedures for training non-psychiatric professional people in methods of detecting early, and treating, individuals with emotional and social problems."

In line with this interest, he and Leonard T. Maholick directed a three-year demonstration project (supported by the National Institute of Mental Health) devoted to methods of training physicians and ministers for mental health work.†

* * *

SHAPIRO, Karl (Jay) 1913-

PERSONAL: Born November 10, 1913, in Baltimore, Md.; son of Joseph and Sarah (Omansky) Shapiro; married Evalyn Katz (a literary agent), March 25, 1945 (divorced, January, 1967); married Teri Kovach, July 31, 1967; children: (first marriage) Katharine, John Jacob, Elizabeth. *Education:* Attended University of Virginia, 1932-33, Johns Hopkins University, 1937-39, and Enoch Pratt Library School, 1940. *Politics:* None. *Religion:* None. *Home:* 2223 Amador Ave., Davis, Calif. 95616. *Office:* Sproul Hall, University of California, Davis, Calif. 95616.

CAREER: Library of Congress, Washington, D.C., consultant in poetry, 1947-48; Johns Hopkins University, Baltimore, Md., associate professor of writing, 1948-50; *Poetry,* Chicago, Ill., editor, 1950-56; University of Nebraska, Lincoln, professor of English, 1956-66; University of Illinois at Chicago Circle, professor of English, 1966-68; University of California, Davis, professor of English, 1968—. Lecturer in India, summer of 1955, for U.S. Department of State. Visiting professor or lecturer at University of Wisconsin, 1948, Loyola University, 1951-52, Salzburg Seminar in American Studies, 1952, University of California, 1955-56, and University of Indiana, 1956-57. Member, Bollingen Prize Committee, 1949. *Military service:* U.S. Army, 1941-45.

MEMBER: National Institute of Arts and Letters, Phi Beta Kappa. *Awards, honors:* Fellow in American Letters, Library of Congress; Jeanette S. Davis Prize and Levinson prize, both from *Poetry* in 1942; *Contemporary Poetry* prize, 1943; American Academy of Arts and Letters grant, 1944; Pulitzer Prize in poetry, 1945, for *V-Letter and Other Poems;* Shelley Memorial Prize, 1946; Guggenheim Foundation fellowships, 1944, 1953; Kenyon School of Letters fellowship, 1956-57; Eunice Tietjens Memorial Prize, 1961; Oscar Blumenthal Prize, *Poetry,* 1963; Bollingen Prize, 1968.

WRITINGS: English Prosody and Modern Poetry, Johns Hopkins Press, 1947, reprinted, Folcroft Library Editions, 1975; *A Bibliography of Modern Prosody,* Johns Hopkins Press, 1948, reprinted, Folcroft Library Editions, 1976; (editor with Louis Untermeyer and Richard Wilbur) *Modern American and Modern British Poetry,* Harcourt, 1955; (author of libretto) *The Tenor* (opera; music by Hugo Weisgall), Merion Music, 1956; (editor) *American Poetry* (anthology), Crowell, 1960; (editor) *Prose Keys to Modern Poetry,* Harper, 1962; (with Robert Beum) *Prosody Handbook,* Harper, 1965; *Edsel* (novel), Geis, 1970.

Poetry; published by Random House, except as indicated: *Poems,* Waverly, 1935; (contributor) *Five Young American Poets,* New Directions, 1941; *Person, Place, and Thing,* Reynal, 1942; *The Place of Love,* Comment Press, 1942; *V-Letter and Other Poems,* Reynal, 1944; *Essay on Rime,* Secker & Warburg, 1945; *Trial of a Poet and Other Poems,* Reynal, 1947; (contributor) *Poets at Work,* Harcourt, 1948; *Poems: 1940-1953,* 1953; *The House,* privately printed, 1957; *Poems of a Jew,* 1958; *The Bourgeois Poet,* 1964; *Selected Poems,* 1968; *White-Haired Lover,* 1968; *Adult Book Store,* 1976; *Collected Poems: 1948-1978,* 1978.

Literary criticism: *Beyond Criticism,* University of Nebraska Press, 1953, published as *A Primer for Poets,* 1965; *In Defense of Ignorance,* Random House, 1960; (with James E. Miller, Jr. and Beatrice Slote) *Start with the Sun: Studies in Cosmic Poetry,* University of Nebraska Press, 1960; (with Ralph Ellison) *The Writer's Experience,* Library of Congress, 1964; *Randall Jarrell,* Library of Congress, 1967; *To Abolish Children and Other Essays,* Quadrangle Books, 1968; *The Poetry Wreck: Selected Essays, 1950-1970,* Random House, 1975.

Author of introduction: Pawel Majewski, editor, *Czas Niepokoju* (anthology; title means "Time of Unrest"), Criterion, 1958; Jack Hirschman, *A Correspondence of Americans,* Indiana University Press, 1960; Bruce Cutler, *The Year of the Green Wave,* University of Nebraska Press, 1960.

Also author of screenplay "Karl Shapiro's America," 1976. Work appears in anthologies. Contributor of articles, poetry, and reviews to *Partisan Review, Poetry, Nation, Saturday Review,* and other periodicals. Editor, *Newberry Library Bulletin,* 1953-55, and *Prairie Schooner,* 1956-63.

SIDELIGHTS: Karl Shapiro's poetry received early recognition, winning a number of major poetry awards during the 1940's. Strongly influenced by the traditionalist poetry of W. H. Auden, Shapiro's early work is "striking for its concrete but detached insights," Alfred Kazin writes. "It is witty and exact in the way it catches the poet's subtle and guarded impressions, and it is a poetry full of clever and unexpected verbal conceits. It is a very professional poetry—supple [and] adaptable." Stephen Stepanchev notes that Shapiro's poems "found impetus and subject matter in the public crises of the 1940's [and all] have their social meaning."

Although his early traditionalist poetry was successful, Shapiro doubted the value and honesty of that kind of poetry. In many of his critical essays, he attacked the assumptions of traditionalist poetry as stifling to the poet's creativity. "What he wants," Paul Fussell, Jr. maintains, "is a turning from received and thus discredited English and European techniques of focus in favor of honest encounters with the stuff of local experience."

In the poetry of both Walt Whitman and the Beat poets, Shapiro found a confirmation of his own idea of feeling over form. In his collection *The Bourgeois Poet,* Shapiro broke with his traditional poetic forms in favor of the free verse of Whitman and the Beats. Hayden Carruth sees these poems as bearing "little resemblance to [Shapiro's] previous work. Blocky, free, prose-like, iconoclastic, touched with apocalyptic insight, they seemed, coming from Shapiro, actually shocking. Today their shock is gone; yet they remain fresh, shrewd poems." Hyatt H. Waggoner finds *The Bourgeois Poet* "a work of greater poetic integrity than any of Shapiro's earlier volumes."

Examining Shapiro's career as a whole, Laurence Leiberman sees him as one of "a generation of poets who . . . wrote a disproportionate number of superbly good poems in early career, became decorated overnight with honors . . . and spent the next twenty-odd years trying to outpace a growing critical notice of decline." Leiberman judges *The Bourgeois Poet* to be Shapiro's attempt to "recast the poetic instrument to embody formerly intractable large sectors of [his life]" and to win "a precious freedom to extend the limits of [his art]." Leiberman sees the two styles in Shapiro's poetry, the traditionalist and free verse, enhancing each other. He believes that Shapiro's "future work stands an excellent chance of merging the superior qualities of two opposite modes: the expressiveness of candid personal confession and the durability of significant form."

BIOGRAPHICAL/CRITICAL SOURCES—Periodicals: *Kenyon Review,* winter, 1946; *College English,* February, 1946; *Yale Review,* winter, 1954, June, 1975; *Western Review,* spring, 1954; *Nation,* July 5, 1958, September 24, 1960, August 24, 1964, November 11, 1978; *New York Times Book Review,* September 7, 1958, May 8, 1960, July 14, 1968, July 25, 1976; *Commonweal,* September 19, 1958, January 20, 1960; *Saturday Review,* September 27, 1958, April 15, 1978; *New Republic,* November 24, 1958; *New York Herald Tribune Book Review,* May 8, 1960; *Books,* March, 1964; *Harper's,* August, 1964; *Book Week,* August 2, 1964; *New Yorker,* November 7, 1964; *Hollins Critic,* December, 1964; *Prairie Schooner,* winter, 1965; *Sewanee Review,* winter, 1965; *Carleton Miscellany,* spring, 1965; *Poetry,* June, 1965, April, 1969, July, 1969; *Literary Times,* June, 1967; *Esquire,* April, 1968; *Christian Science Monitor,* July 3, 1968; *Los Angeles Times,* July 7, 1968; *Book World,* July 28, 1968; *New York Times,* July 29, 1968, January 6, 1969, October 4, 1971; *Time,* August 2, 1968; *Partisan Review,* winter, 1969; *Virginia Quarterly Review,* winter, 1969; *Antioch Review,* Volume XXXI, Number 3, 1971; *Southern Review,* winter, 1973; *Hudson Review,* autumn, 1975; *Village Voice,* March 29, 1976; *Wall Street Journal,* July 7, 1976; *Washington Post,* January 4, 1980.

Books: William White, *Karl Shapiro: A Bibliography,* Wayne State University Press, 1960; M. L. Rosenthal, *The Modern Poets: A Critical Introduction,* Oxford University Press, 1960; Alfred Kazin, *Contemporaries,* Little, Brown, 1962; Howard Nemerov, *Poetry and Fiction,* Rutgers University Press, 1963; Stephen Stepanchev, *American Poetry since 1945; A Critical Survey,* Harper, 1965; Hyatt H. Waggoner, *American Poets from the Puritans to the Present,* Houghton, 1968; Randall Jarrell, *The Third Book of Criticism,* Farrar, Straus, 1969; Monroe K. Spears, *Dionysus and the City,* Oxford University Press, 1970; *Contemporary Literary Criticism,* Gale, Volume IV, 1975, Volume VIII, 1978; Vernon Scannell, *Not without Glory,* Woburn Press, 1976; Lee Bartlett, *Karl Shapiro: A Descriptive Bibliography,* Garland Publishing, 1979.

* * *

SHAPIRO, Samuel 1927-
(Richard Falcon)

PERSONAL: Born August 23, 1927, in Ellenville, N.Y.; son of Abraham and Ethel (Victor) Shapiro; married Gloria Joan Kaufman, 1959; children: Isabel, David. *Education:* City College of New York (now City College of the City University of New York), B.S., 1948; Columbia University, M.A., 1949, Ph.D., 1958. *Home:* 305 Wakewa, South Bend, Ind. *Office:* Department of History, University of Notre Dame, Notre Dame, Ind.

CAREER: Teacher in secondary schools, New York, N.Y., 1949-57; Brandeis University, Waltham, Mass., instructor in history, 1957-59; Oberlin College, Oberlin, Ohio, assistant professor of history, 1960; Oakland University, Rochester, Mich., assistant professor of history, 1960-63; University of Notre Dame, Notre Dame, Ind., assistant professor, 1963-64, associate professor of history, 1964—. Fulbright professor of American history, Universities of Tucuman and Buenos Aires, Argentina, 1959; director, National Defense Education Act Institutes, University of Notre Dame, 1967, and Innsbruck University, 1968. *Military service:* U.S. Army Air Forces, 1945-47.

WRITINGS: Richard Henry Dana, Jr., Michigan State University Press, 1961; *Invisible Latin America,* Beacon Press, 1963; (editor) *Integration of Man and Society in Latin America,* University of Notre Dame, 1968; *Cultural Factors in Inter-American Relations,* University of Notre Dame Press, 1968. Contributor to *New Republic, Reporter, Commentary.*

WORK IN PROGRESS: Black Women and Music.

SIDELIGHTS: Samuel Shapiro has travelled to Japan, Mexico, Guatemala, Europe, and South America.

* * *

SHARPES, Donald K(enneth) 1934-

PERSONAL: Born November 16, 1934, in Yakima, Wash.; son of Kenneth and Lillian Violette Sharpes; married Linda Bamberg, June 27, 1964; children: Michael Joseph, Mary Melissa. *Education:* Gonzaga University, B.A. (with honors), 1959, M.A. (English), 1961; Stanford University, M.A. (education), 1967; Arizona State University, Ph.D., 1968. *Home:* 4245 Edgehill Dr., Ogden, Utah 84403. *Office:* School of Education, Weber State College, Ogden, Utah 84408.

CAREER: Gonzaga Preparatory School, Spokane, Wash., English teacher and chairman of department, 1960-63; Yamato Dependents School, Tokyo, Japan, academic dean, 1964-66; U.S. Office of Education, Washington, D.C., senior program officer and program manager and director of Technical Division of Office of the Deputy Commissioner, 1968-73; senior Fulbright researcher, Malaysian Ministry of Education, 1973-78; Virginia Polytechnic Institute and State University, Blacksburg, associate professor of education, 1976-77; currently professor, and director of combined teacher education graduate program at Weber State College, Ogden, Utah and Utah State University, Logan. Professor at National Academy of School Executives, American Association of School Administrators. Chairman of board, Rocky Mountain Symphony Orchestra, 1979—.

MEMBER: American Educational Research Association, American Association for the Advancement of Science, National Association of Secondary School Principals. *Awards, honors:* Charles F. Kettering Foundation grant, 1970; American Federation of Teachers grant, 1971; received Cortez faculty award in poetry.

WRITINGS: (Contributor) Ed Buffie and James L. Olivero, editors, *Educational Manpower,* Indiana University Press, 1970; *The Community and School: Participation, Partnership, and Control,* Charles F. Kettering Foundation, 1970; (contributor) James Cooper, editor, *Differentiated Staffing,* Saunders, 1972; (with Fenwick W. English) *Strategies for Differentiated Staffing,* McCutchan, 1972; *Differentiated Staffing: A State of the Art Report,* U.S. Government Printing Office, 1973; *Flexible Staffing: An Administrator's Guide to Staff Development,* American Association for School Administrators, 1973. Also author of *Education and the Federal Government* and *Education and Malaysian Government,* and of poems *This Island, Love* and *The Prau and Other Poems of Southeast Asia.*

Monographs: *An Introduction to Modular Scheduling: With the Stanford School Scheduling Service,* School of Education, Stanford University, 1967; *Differentiated Salaries for Teachers: An Economic Analysis and Survey,* American Federation of Teachers, 1971; (with Michael DeBloois) *A Conceptual Model of School Personnel Utilization: A Developmental Spectrum for Evaluation Purposes,* American Educational Research Association, 1971; *Teaching a Philosophy of Education,* National Center for Educational Systems, U.S. Office of Education, 1972; *Impressions of Soviet Teacher Education,* U.S. Office of Education, 1973; *A Report on Two Year Colleges,* Bureau of Higher Education, U.S. Office of Education, 1973; *Administering Federal Educational Policy,* American Educational Research Association, 1973; *Graduate Programs and Policies for Minority Group Students,* American Association for the Advancement of Science, 1973.

Author of reports. Contributor to *America, Clearing House, American School Board Journal, Journal of American Indian Education,* and other publications.

AVOCATIONAL INTERESTS: Sports, especially tennis, flying (Sharpes holds a private pilot's license).

* * *

SHAW, Arnold 1909-

PERSONAL: Born June 28, 1909, in New York, N.Y.; married Ghita Milgrom; children: (previous marriage) Elizabeth Hilda; (current marriage) Mindy Sura. *Education:* Columbia University, M.A., 1931. *Home:* 2288 Gabriel Dr., Las Vegas, Nev. 89109.

CAREER: Robbins Music Corp., New York City, advertising and publicity manager, 1944-45; *Swank* magazine, New York City, editor, 1945; Leeds Music Corp., New York City, advertising and publicity director, 1945-49; Duchess Music Corp., New York City, vice-president and general professional manager, 1950-53; Hill & Range Songs, New York City, vice-president and general professional manager, 1953-55; Edward B. Marks Music Corp., New York City, vice-president and general professional manager, 1955-66. Lecturer, Juilliard School of Music, 1945, Fairleigh Dickinson University, 1964-65, University of Oklahoma, 1971, University of Nevada, 1977—. Member of national advisory board, Fisk University Institute for Research in Black American Music; chairman, Bolognini Scholarship Fund, 1976-80. *Member:* American Society of Composers, Authors, and Publishers, Authors Guild, American Musicological Society, American Guild of Authors and Composers, National Academy of Recording Arts and Sciences, Las Vegas Music Teachers Association (president, 1975-77), University Musical Society (president), Sonneck Society. *Awards, honors:* Deems Taylor Award, American Society of Composers, Authors, and Publishers, 1968 and 1979; named Nevada Composer of the Year, 1973-74.

WRITINGS: (Co-editor) *Schillinger System of Musical Composition,* Carl Fischer, 1946; (editor) *Mathematical Basis of the Arts,* Philosophical Library, 1948; *Lingo of Tin Pan Alley,* Broadcast Music, 1950; *The Money Song,* Random House, 1953; *Belafonte,* Chilton, 1960; *Sinatra: Twentieth Century Romantic,* Holt, 1968; *The Rock Revolution: What's Happening in Today's Music,* Crowell-Collier, 1969; *The World of Soul: Black America's Contribution to Pop Music,* Cowles, 1970; *The Street That Never Slept: New York's Fabled 52nd Street,* Coward, 1970, published as *52nd Street: The Street of Jazz,* Da Capo, 1977; *The Rockin' 50's: The Decade That Transformed the Pop Music Scene,* Hawthorn, 1974; *Honkers and Shouters: The Golden Years of Rhythm and Blues,* Macmillan, 1978.

Composer; all published by Surosalida Music: *Mobiles: Ten Graphic Impressions for Piano,* 1966; *Stabiles: 12 Images for Piano,* 1968; *Plabiles: 12 Songs without Words for Piano,* 1971; *A Whirl of Waltzes for Piano,* 1974; *The Mod Moppet: 7 Nursery Rip-Offs for Piano,* 1974; *The Bubble-Gum Waltzes,* 1977; *The Lights of Christmas/Chanukah,* 1980; *Felicidad,* 1980.

Also composer of "Sing a Song of Americans" with lyrics by Rosemary Benet and Stephen Vincent Benet, 1941, and of "They Had a Dream," 1976. Producer, narrator, and writer of "Curtain Time" television series; co-producer, narrator, and writer of "Window on the Arts" television series. Contributor of articles and book reviews to magazines and newspapers. Author of liner notes for jazz, pop, and rock recordings.

WORK IN PROGRESS: The Sound and Fury of the 1960's; A Black History of American Popular Music; Arnold Shaw's Rocktionary.

SIDELIGHTS: While working in the music business in the 1950's, Arnold Shaw was involved in the discovery, publishing, recording, or promoting of a number of hit songs. He was especially active in the then-growing market for both rhythm and blues and rock and roll music, buying the rights to or arranging the recording of such popular songs as "Sh-boom," "Lollipop," and "What a Difference a Day Makes."

Shaw also played an instrumental role in promoting Elvis Presley. Presley's early records were popular in the South but unknown elsewhere until Shaw persuaded a Cleveland radio station to put them on the air. The resulting clamor for Presley's music attracted the attention of RCA Records, who signed Presley and promoted him nationally.

Shaw's book *The Street That Never Slept,* a history of New York City's 52nd Street and its jazz clubs, inspired a number of people to work for the street's preservation as a historical landmark. In 1978, after years of effort, the street was officially designated a landmark. Imbedded in its sidewalk, renamed "Jazzwalk," are plaques bearing the names of famous jazz performers who once worked in the 52nd Street clubs. Shaw was a featured speaker at the dedication ceremony.

BIOGRAPHICAL/CRITICAL SOURCES: Observer, June 9, 1968; *Listener,* June 27, 1968; *Punch,* July 3, 1968; *New York Times Book Review,* November 3, 1968; *New York Times,* November 27, 1968, January 19, 1979; *Playboy,* December, 1968; *Best Sellers,* December 15, 1968; *Hollywood Reporter,* May 9, 1969; *Harper's,* September, 1969; *Saturday Review,* September 13, 1969; *New Yorker,* December 13, 1969; *Variety,* February 4, 1970; *Saturday Night,* March, 1970; *Top of the News,* April, 1971; *Detroit News,* November 14, 1971; *American Bookman,* December 13, 1971; *Music Educators Journal,* March, 1972; Arnold Shaw, *The Rockin' Fifties: The Decade That Transformed the Pop Music Scene,* Hawthorn, 1974; *Nevadan,* June 4, 1978; *Las Vegas Review-Journal,* June 14, 1978; *Book World,* July 30, 1978; *Hi Fidelity,* November, 1978; *Rolling Stone,* December 28, 1978.

* * *

SHAW, Bob 1931-

PERSONAL: Born December 31, 1931, in Belfast, Northern Ireland; son of Robert William (a policeman) and Elizabeth (Megaw) Shaw; married Sarah Gourley, July 3, 1954; children: Alisa Claire, Robert Ian, Elizabeth Denise. *Education:* Attended a technical high school in Belfast, 1945-47. *Politics:* None. *Religion:* None. *Home:* 3 Braddyll Terrace, Ulverston, Cumbria, England. *Agent:* E. J. Carnell Literary Agency, Rowneybury Bungalow, Sawbridge, near Old Harlow, Essex CM20 2EX, England.

CAREER: Short Brothers & Harland Ltd. (aircraft manufacturers), Belfast, Northern Ireland, public relations officer, 1960-66; Belfast Telegraph Newspapers Ltd., Belfast, Northern Ireland, journalist, 1966-69; free-lance writer in Belfast, Northern Ireland, 1969-70; Short Brothers & Harland Ltd., public relations officer, 1970-73; Vickers Shipbuilding Group, Barrow-in-Furness, England, public relations officer, 1973-75; free-lance writer, 1975—. *Member:* Science Fiction Writers of America. *Awards, honors:* Hugo Award, 1979, for best fantasy writer.

WRITINGS—All novels, except as indicated: *Night Walk,* Avon, 1967; *The Two-Timers,* Ace Books, 1968; *The Palace of Eternity,* Ace Books, 1969; *The Shadow of Heaven,* Avon, 1969; *One Million Tomorrows,* Ace Books, 1971; *The Ground Zero Man,* Avon, 1971; *Other Days, Other Eyes,* Ace Books, 1972; *Tomorrow Lies in Ambush* (short stories), Ace Books, 1973; *Orbitsville,* Ace Books, 1975; *A Wreath of Stars,* Doubleday, 1977; *Cosmic Kaleidoscope* (short stories), Doubleday, 1977; *Who Goes Here?,* Ace Books, 1978; *Medusa's Children,* Doubleday, 1979; *Ship of Strangers,* Ace Books, 1979; *Vertigo,* Ace Books, 1979; *Dagger of the Mind,* Gollancz, 1979. Contributor of over fifty short stories to American and British science fiction magazines.

WORK IN PROGRESS: Several novels, as yet untitled.

SHAW, Frederick 1912-

PERSONAL: Born September 24, 1912, in New York, N.Y.; son of Theodore and Hermina (Farkas) Shaw; married Daisy Katz (director of guidance for New York City Board of Education), November, 1940; children: Richard M., Ellen. *Education:* City College (now City College of the City University of New York), B.A., 1932; Columbia University, M.A., 1933, Ph.D., 1950; also attended Oxford University, 1937, New School for Social Research, 1939-40, New York University, 1939-40, 1954-56, and Cornell University, 1961. *Home:* 41 Henry St., Brooklyn, N.Y. 11201.

CAREER: High school social studies teacher in New York City, 1935-43, 1946-53; Board of Education, New York City, research associate at Research Bureau, 1953-64; City College of the City University of New York, New York City, visiting assistant professor of political science, 1964-66; Board of Education, New York City, research associate at Research Bureau, 1966-67, coordinator of federal programs, 1967, director of Bureau of Educational Program Research, 1967-75, director of research in Office of Bilingual Education, 1975-78; educational consultant, 1975—. Special examiner, New York City Department of Personnel; trustee, Payne Educational Sociology Foundation of New York University; delegate to New York State Special Task Force on Equity and Excellence in Education. *Military service:* U.S. Army, 1943-46; served as counselor and head of counselor research and training at Separation Centers in Florida and North Carolina; became technical sergeant.

MEMBER: Academy of Political Science, American Academy of Political and Social Science, American Educational Research Association, American Association of School Administrators, National Municipal League, Authors Guild, Authors League of America, Mensa, New York Academy of Public Education, Doctorate Association of New York Educators (past president), Phi Delta Kappa (president of New York University chapter), New York Schoolmasters Club, City Club of New York (chairman of education committee), Citizens Union of New York.

WRITINGS: The American City, Oxford Book Co., 1953; *The History of the New York City Legislature,* Columbia University Press, 1953; *A Major Urban Problem: Educating the Disadvantaged Child,* Institute for Child Study, University of Maryland, 1962; *Urban Affairs,* Oxford Book Co., 1962; (with Howard Hurwitz) *Economics in a Free Society,* Oxford Book Co., 1962; (with Hurwitz) *Mastering Basic Economics,* Oxford Book Co., 1962. Author, with Hurwitz and Jacob Irgang, of *Using Economics: Principles, Institutions, Issues,* 1975. Also author of monographs and special reports for Bureau of Educational Program Research, New York City Board of Education.

Contributor: Wallace Sayre and Herbert Kaufman, *Governing New York City: Politics in the Metropolis,* Russell Sage, 1960, revised edition, Norton, 1965; Leo Doherty, editor, *Educational Theory: Research and Practice,* State University of New York Press, 1964; Robert Schasre and Jo Wallach, editors, *Readings in Dropouts and Training,* Delinquency Training Project, Youth Studies Center, University of Southern California, 1965; J. L. Frost and Glenn R. Hawkes, editors, *The Disadvantaged Child: Issues and Innovations,* Houghton, 1966; August Kerber and Barbara Bommarito, editors, *The Schools and the Urban Crisis,* Holt, 1966; Joe A. Apple, editor, *Readings in Educating the Disadvantaged,* Selected Academic Readings, 1967; William M. Alexander, editor, *The Changing Secondary School Curriculum,* Holt, 1967; J. T. Kelley and T. Darwin Milligan, editors, *Teaching in Public Schools,* Selected Academic Readings, 1968; John R. Shaffer, editor, *Current Issues in Secondary Education,* MSS Educational Publishing, 1969.

Leonard Golubchick and Barry Persky, editors, *Urban, Social and Educational Issues,* Kendall/Hunt, 1974; Golubchick, Persky, and Hernan Lafontaine, editors, *Bilingual Education,* Avery, 1978. Also contributor to *Fact Book: New York Metropolitan Region* (annual publication), edited by Albert Alexander, New York City Council on Economic Education, 1970-81; contributor to yearbooks and proceedings of professional organizations and to *Cowles Comprehensive Encyclopedia* and *Book of Knowledge.* Contributor of more than one hundred articles and reviews to professional journals and other publications, including *Public Personnel Review, Action for Safety, National Civic Review,* and *American Economic Review.* Guest editor, *Phi Delta Kappan,* September, 1964.

WORK IN PROGRESS: Ethnic America: A Spectrum of Cultures; revising *Using Economics.*

AVOCATIONAL INTERESTS: Municipal affairs.

* * *

SHAW, Malcolm Edwin 1926-

PERSONAL: Born November 3, 1926, in Holyoke, Mass.; son of Marcus Albert and Marjorie (Malcolm) Shaw; married Jean Tench, 1946. *Education:* Rutgers University, B.Sc. in Business Administration, 1949. *Home:* 2 East End Ave., New York, N.Y. 10021. *Office:* Educational Systems and Designs, Inc., 21 Charles, Westport, Conn. 06880.

CAREER: Radio Corporation of America, Harrison, N.J., training manager, 1951-55; American Management Association, New York City, conference director, 1955-57; *Cincinnati Enquirer,* Cincinnati, Ohio, vice-president of personnel, 1957-59; Cornell University, School of Industrial and Labor Relations, New York City, visiting lecturer, 1959-60; Leadership Development Associates, New York City, vice-president, 1960-66; Educational Systems and Designs, Inc., Westport, Conn., president, 1966—. Former director, National Network for Educational Reform, U.S. Office of Education; former commissioner, Study Commission on Undergraduate Education and the Education of Teachers. Former member, Westport (Conn.) Board of Education. *Military service:* U.S. Coast Guard, 1944-46; became musician third class.

WRITINGS: (With Raymond Corsini and Robert Blake) *Role Playing in Business and Industry,* Free Press of Glencoe, 1960, revised edition (with Corsini, Blake, and Jane Mouton), published as *Role Playing: A Practical Manual for Group Facilitators,* University Associates, 1979; *Scales for the Measurement of Attitudes,* McGraw, 1967; *Assertive-Responsive Management: A Personal Handbook,* Addison-Wesley, 1979; (with Emmett Wallace and Frances Labella) *Making It Assertively,* Prentice-Hall, 1980. Contributor to various journals, including the *Journal of Group Psychotherapy, Public Administration Review,* and *American Society of Training and Development Journal.*

* * *

SHEEHY, Gail

PERSONAL: Daughter of Harold Merritt and Lillian (Rainey) Henion; married Albert Sheehy (an internist), August 20, 1960 (divorced, 1968); children: Maura. *Education:* University of Vermont, B.S., 1958; Columbia University, graduate study, 1970. *Residence:* New York, N.Y. *Agent:* Paul R. Reynolds, Inc., 12 East 41st St., New York, N.Y. 10017. *Office:* c/o William Morrow & Co., 105 Madison Ave., New York, N.Y. 10016.

CAREER: Democrat and Chronicle, Rochester, N.Y., fashion editor, 1961-63; *New York Herald Tribune,* New York City, feature writer, 1963-66; *New York* magazine, New York City, contributing editor, 1968-77; free-lance writer. Has worked as a traveling home economist. *Member:* Author's Guild, Authors League of America, P.E.N. American Center (member of national advisory board), Common Cause, National Organization for Women, Cambodian Crisis Committee, Girls Clubs of America, Newswomen's Club of New York. *Awards, honors:* Front Page award from Newswomen's Club of New York, 1964, for most distinguished feature of interest to women, and 1973, for best magazine feature; National Magazine award, 1972, for reporting excellence; Alicia Patterson Foundation fellowship, 1974.

WRITINGS: Lovesounds, Random House, 1970; *Panthermania: The Clash of Black against Black in One American City,* Harper, 1971; *Speed Is of the Essence,* Pocket Books, 1971; *Hustling: Prostitution in Our Wide Open Society,* Delacorte, 1973; *Passages: Predictable Crises of Adult Life,* Dutton, 1976. Contributor to *Cosmopolitan, McCall's, Glamour, Good Housekeeping, London Sunday Telegraph, Paris Match,* and *New York Times Magazine.*

WORK IN PROGRESS: A book dealing with "high well-being people who have negotiated successful 'passages.'"

SIDELIGHTS: Gail Sheehy's first book, *Lovesounds,* deals with the breakup of a marriage. But, as Judith Martin of the *Washington Post* points out, it may be a disappointment to "devotees of the genre, who know how to enjoy first her side, then his side, and then the counselor's view showing that they both had faults but could learn to correct them and have another baby." In this book there are no major faults in the characters. Sheehy has created a good wife and a good husband, both of whom love their child and have rewarding careers, but who are nonetheless getting a divorce. Martin says that "it would seem to be a step backwards in novel writing because we have all been brought up to believe that everything in books, if not in life, happens for a reason." Here, this is clearly not the case, but "once you accept the fact that the marriage was a good one, and that its dissolution is something that neither husband nor wife wished and for which neither was deliberately responsible, you find a good study of the pure emotions involved."

Israel Horovitz states that with *Lovesounds* "Gail Sheehy has written the most brutal indictment of hypocrisy in marriage, the most incisive analysis of the daily experience, the most hearty yet subtle feminist line since that Friday morning in July when Anton Chekhov died in Olga Knipper's arms. She has written a truly pop novel: a book that reads as easily as any of R. Art Crumb's comix, yet stays as firmly lodged in your stomach as Grandma's kreplach. *Lovesounds* is a fine, fine piece of writing that should be read by anyone who is married, was married, or will be married." But Paul D. Zimmerman, in a *Newsweek* review, insists that the book is a failure. His explanation: "Imprisoned in nearly every journalist lives a captive novelist struggling to get out. . . . But the rules of the novel are different. The subject stands inside the characters, not across the table taking notes, and the language that serves so well to capture the surface tensions of a tow-away depot or the anxieties of a student revolutionary cannot necessarily handle the swollen emotions of inner life bursting apart." Zimmerman concludes that "Gail Sheehy has broken out as a novelist all right. But this book at least makes it doubtful that it was worth the struggle."

Sheehy's best-known work is probably *Passages: The Predictable Crises of Adult Life.* The theme of the book, as Jill Tweedie puts it in a *Saturday Review* article, is that "not only are there crises in every life, not only do they occur with reasonable predictability, but they are (cheeringly) entirely natural—comparable, say, to the seasons of the year or to the germination of a seed." Sheehy contends that there are four main "passages" in life; she terms them "Pulling up Roots," "The Trying Twenties," "Passage to the Thirties," and "The Deadline Decade: Setting off on the Midlife Passage." She feels that everyone must confront each of these milestones and must pass through each in order to advance to the next.

Reviewing the book for *Ms.,* Patricia O'Brien writes: "I barely made it past the Introduction to *Passages* before I found myself underlining passages—not because I was learning startling new facts, but because finally somebody was putting universal human fears and uncertainties about change and growing old into a manageable perspective. On the whole, *Passages* succeeds most when it is defining these fears, and not when Sheehy is presenting her numerous case histories." O'Brien calls it "a book that gives us the chance to track ourselves. Sheehy particularly makes it easier for us to understand the lonely polarization that may occur between men and women by pointing out that the sexes are rarely in the same identity and career questions at the same time."

Maurice Hart of *Best Sellers* says that the writing in *Passages* "is basically journalistic in style, and the arguments are not as clearly and precisely stated as they should be in a scholarly presentation. Consequently, for a definitive work on the stages of adult life one will have to look elsewhere—possibly to one of Ms. Sheehy's sources." Around those sources centers a noteworthy controversy. In researching this subject Sheehy talked with such experts as Yale psychologist Daniel Levinson, Harvard psychiatrist George Vaillant, and U.C.L.A. psychiatrist Roger Gould. She also attributes some of her information to Erik Erikson, Else Frenkel-Brunswick, Margaret Hennig, and Margaret Mead. When the book first appeared, *Time* noted that Levinson "outlined the 'mentor phenomenon'—that in middle age a man feels the need to promote the fortunes of a younger worker," and that Hennig "reported on the importance of mentors to women in corporate life" in 1970.

Levin was somewhat perturbed at Sheehy's allegedly unauthorized use of his research, saying "she is incomplete, to put it mildly, in acknowledging her use of my published and unpublished material." But Hennig, according to *Time,* had no complaints. "She used my stuff," she said, "but this is real life and I'm not upset about it. She gave me credit." Roger Gould, however, was furious. A *Time* writer said that he "filed a plagiarism suit against Sheehy and Dutton [her publisher]. The case was settled out of court: Gould received $10,000 and 10% of the book's royalties." Gould contended that he was under the impression that he was to be a collaborator on the book, but after he had discussed his research with Sheehy, found that she considered him a paid consultant. She claimed that it was made clear from the beginning that Gould was not to be a co-author.

In defense of Sheehy, Roderick MacLeish of the *Washington Post* emphasises that "by her own assertion, Gail Sheehy is not the central theorist of her work. . . . What Sheehy has done is to gather together the materials of the relatively new social science of adult development, codify it into skillfully popularized form, invest it with the classy, vernacular prose style for which she is justifiably admired and arrive at a generalist's conclusions—there's more hope in the aging process than you've been led to believe." And, as MacLeish goes on to conclude, "I'm sure that specialists will quarrel with what she has done. That's what specialists are for. But the hope, wit and de-mythification of adulthood that permeates Sheehy's book make *Passages* a work of revelation for the layman as he tries to understand the inevitable movement of his life. It is a stunning accomplishment."

BIOGRAPHICAL/CRITICAL SOURCES: New York, July 21, 1969, August 3, 1970; *McCall's,* August, 1970; *Newsweek,* August 10, 1970, August 30, 1973; *Village Voice,* August 20, 1970; *Washington Post,* August 29, 1970; *Saturday Review,* July 24, 1971, May 15, 1976; *Best Sellers,* August 1, 1971, September, 1976; *New York Times Book Review,* September 5, 1971; *Washington Post Book World,* March 23, 1976; *Time,* May 10, 1976; *Ms.,* August, 1976; *New York Times,* August 16, 1976; *New York Review of Books,* October 28, 1976.

—Sketch by Peter M. Gareffa

* * *

SHEPPARD, Harold L(loyd) 1922-

PERSONAL: Born April 1, 1922, in Baltimore, Md.; married Inge-Lise Graf; children: Mark, Jenny Ann. *Education:* University of Chicago, M.A., 1945; University of Wisconsin, Ph.D., 1948. *Home:* 6311 Herkos Ct., Bethesda, Md. 20034. *Office:* American Institute for Research, 1055 Thomas Jefferson St. N.W., Washington, D.C. 20007.

CAREER: Wayne State University, Detroit, Mich., instructor, 1947-53, associate professor of sociology, 1953-59; U.S. Senate Committee on Aging, Washington, D.C., research director, 1959-60, staff director, 1960-61; U.S. Department of Commerce, Area Redevelopment Administration, Washington, D.C., deputy assistant administrator, 1961-62, assistant administrator for operations, 1962-63; W. E. Upjohn Institute for Employment Research, Washington, D.C., staff social scientist, 1963-75; American Institute for Research, Washington, D.C., senior research fellow, 1975—. Member of staff, Institute of Industrial and Labor Relations, University of Michigan and Wayne State University, 1947-59; visiting lecturer, University of California, Los Angeles, 1948; visiting assistant professor, University of Michigan, 1956. President's coordinator of federal government activities in South Bend, Ind., 1963-64; chairman of task force on poverty and the older American, Office of Economic Opportunity, 1965-68; member of President's task force on economic security and welfare, White House Conference on Civil Rights, 1966; member of advisory committee on older Americans, Administration on Aging, 1966-67; member of task force on environmental health and related problems for John Gardner, then Secretary of Health, Education, and Welfare, 1966-67; member of technical committee on employment and retirement, White House Conference on Aging, 1971-72; chairman of advisory council, U.S. Senate Committee on Aging, 1971-72; member of action committee on aging, Maryland Commission on Aging, 1972. Consultant to U.S. Senate subcommittee on manpower, employment, and poverty, 1967, Organization for Economic Cooperation and Development, 1971—, U.S. Congress, and several organizations. Lecturer in the United States and abroad.

MEMBER: American Sociological Association, Industrial Relations Research Association, National Economists Club, Gerontological Society, National Council on the Aging (member of board of directors), Eastern Sociological Society. *Awards, honors:* Fulbright senior research scholarship in France, 1957-58.

WRITINGS: (Editor and translator) Georges Friedmann, *Industrial Society,* Free Press of Glencoe, 1955; (with Arthur Kornhauser) *When Labor Votes: A Study of Auto Workers,* University Books, 1956; *Too Old to Work, Too Young to Retire,* Committee on Unemployment Problems, U.S. Senate, 1959; (with Sar Levitan) *Impact of Technological Change upon Communities and Public Policy,* Harper, 1964; (with A. Harvey Belitsky) *The Job Hunt: Job-seeking Behavior of Unemployed Workers in a Local Economy,* Johns Hopkins Press, 1966; (with Herbert Striner) *Civil Rights, Employment, and the Social Status of American Negroes,* Upjohn Institute, 1966; *Effects of Family Planning on Poverty in the United States,* Upjohn Institute, 1967; (with Belitsky) *Promoting Job-finding Success for the Unemployed,* Upjohn Institute, 1968; (with Michael Aiken and Louis Ferman) *Economic Failure, Alienation, and Extremism,* University of Michigan Press, 1968; *Employment Aspects of the Economics of Aging,* Special Committee on Aging, U.S. Senate, 1969; *The Nature of the Job Problem and the Role of New Public Service Employment,* Upjohn Institute, 1969; (editor and author of introduction) *Poverty and Wealth in America,* Quadrangle, 1970; (editor and contributor) *Towards an Industrial Gerontology: An Introduction to a New Field of Applied Research and Services,* Schenkman, 1970; (with Neal Q. Herrick) *Where Have All the Robots Gone?,* Free Press, 1972; *The Graying of Working America,* Free Press, 1979.

Contributor: *The Requirements of Automated Jobs,* Organization for Economic Cooperation and Development, 1965; Juanita Kreps, editor, *Technology, Manpower, and Retirement Policy,* World Publishing, 1966; Levitan and Irving Siegel, editors, *Dimensions of Manpower Policy: Programs and Research,* Johns Hopkins Press, 1966; Carter Clarke Osterbind, editor, *Income in Retirement: The Need and Society's Responsibility,* University of Florida Press, 1967; Edward Jakubauskas and Phillip Baumel, editors, *Human Resources Development,* Iowa State University Press, 1967; Arthur Field, editor, *Urbanization and Work in Modernizing Societies: A Working Paper,* Glengary Press, 1967; Paul Lazarsfeld, Harold Wilensky, and William Sewell, editors, *The Uses of Sociology,* Basic Books, 1967; Matilda Riley, John Riley, and Marilyn Johnson, editors, *Aging and Society,* Volume II, Russell Sage, 1969; Robert Binstoch and Ethel Shanas, editors, *Handbook on Social Sciences and Aging,* Van Nostrand, 1977. Contributor to *Social Problems* and *American Behavioral Scientist.*

WORK IN PROGRESS: "A study of the retirement age issue from the standpoint of the political, economic, and social consequences of a growing older population."

SIDELIGHTS: In 1966 Harold L. Sheppard, an industrial sociologist, and his colleagues visited Moscow. Since that time, Sheppard's activities in this field have taken him to Kiev, Tokyo, Jerusalem, and to several European capitals. He told *CA* that he hopes his research results in "readable books and articles for the educated general public, and for policy-makers."

* * *

SHMUELI, Adi 1941-

PERSONAL: Born July 16, 1941, in Bagdad, Iraq; became Israeli citizen; son of Oved (an accountant) and Naima (Soffer) Shmueli. *Education:* Tel-Aviv University, M.A., 1965; Soeren Kierkegaard Society, postgraduate study, 1965-66; University of Tours, Ph.D., 1968; University of Rochester, Ph.D., 1973, post-doctoral study in clinical psychology, 1973—. *Religion:* Jewish. *Home:* 8406 North Brook Lane, Bethesda, Md. 20014.

CAREER: Tel-Aviv University, Tel-Aviv, Israel, assistant professor of philosophy, 1968-70; Genesee Hospital, Department of Psychology, Rochester, N.Y., clinical psychologist, 1973-76; Professional Associates, Washington, D.C., clinical psychologist, 1976—.

WRITINGS: Kierkegaard and Consciousness, Princeton University Press, 1971; *The Tower of Babel: Identity and Sanity,* Humanities, 1978.

WORK IN PROGRESS: Research on personality and communication as reflected in a therapeutic milieu.

* * *

SHOCKLEY, Ann Allen 1927-

PERSONAL: Born June 21, 1927, in Louisville, Ky.; daughter of Henry (a social worker) and Bessie (a social worker; maiden name, Lucas) Allen; divorced; children: William Leslie Shockley, Jr., Tamara Ann Shockley. *Education:* Fisk University, B.A., 1948; Western Reserve University (now Case Western Reserve University), M.S.L.S., 1959. *Politics:* Independent. *Home:* 1809 Morena St., Apt. G-4, Nashville, Tenn. 37203. *Office:* Fisk University Library, Nashville, Tenn. 37203.

CAREER: Delaware State College, Dover, Del., assistant librarian, 1959-60; Maryland State College (now University of Maryland Eastern Shore), Princess Anne, assistant librarian, 1960-66, associate librarian, 1966-69; Fisk University, Nashville, Tenn., associate librarian and head of special collections, 1969-75, associate librarian for public services, 1975—, associate professor of library science. Lecturer at University of Maryland, 1968, Vanderbilt University, and Jackson State College, 1973; free-lance writer. *Member:* Association for Study of Afro-American Life and History, Modern Language Association of America, Oral History Association, Society of American Archivists, National Women's Studies Association, American Library Association Black Caucus, Tennessee Archivists, Tennessee Literary Arts Association. *Awards, honors:* American Association of University Women short story award, 1962; Fisk University faculty research grant, 1970; University of Maryland Library Administrators Development Institute fellowship, 1974; American Library Association Black Caucus award, 1975, for editorship of Black Caucus Newsletter.

WRITINGS: A History of Public Library Services to Negroes in the South, 1900-1955 (monograph), Delaware State College, 1960; *The Administration of Special Negro Collections,* Fisk University Library, 1970, 3rd edition published as *The Administration of Special Black Collections,* 1974; (contributor) E. J. Josey, editor, *Black Librarian in America,* Scarecrow, 1970; *A Manual for the Black Oral History Program,* Fisk University Library, 1971; (editor with Sue P. Chandler) *Living Black American Authors: A Bibliographical Directory,* Bowker, 1973; *Loving Her* (novel), Bobbs-Merrill, 1974; (contributor) Bill Katz and Robert Burgess, editors, *Library Lit. 5,* Scarecrow, 1975; (editor with Josey, and contributor) *A Handbook on Black Librarianship,* Libraries Unlimited, 1977; *The Black and White of It* (short stories), Naiad Press, 1980; *Say Jesus and Come to Me* (novel), Avon, 1980.

Work represented in anthologies, including: *Impressions in Asphalt,* edited by Ruthe T. Sheffey and Eugnia Collier, Scribner, 1969; *Out of Our Lives: A Selection of Contemporary Black Fiction,* edited by Quandra Prettyman Stadler,

Howard University Press, 1975; *True to Life Adventure Stories*, edited by Judy Graham, Diana Press, 1978; *Afro-American Writers*, New Life (Berlin), 1980.

Contributor of short stories and articles to magazines, newspapers, and professional journals, including *Negro Digest, Umbra, Black World, College and Research Libraries, Negro History Bulletin*, and *American Libraries*. Editor of American Library Association Black Caucus Newsletter.

WORK IN PROGRESS: A collection of short stories.

* * *

SHOESMITH, Kathleen A(nne) 1938-

PERSONAL: Born July 17, 1938, in Keighley, Yorkshire, England; daughter of Roy and Lilian Shoesmith. *Education:* Avery Hill Teachers' Training College, Diploma, 1956. *Home:* 351 Fell Lane, Keighley BD22 6DB, Yorkshire, England.

CAREER: Teacher in Keighley, Yorkshire, England, 1958—, at Lees County Primary School, 1973—.

WRITINGS—Historical romances; published by R. Hale, except as indicated: *Jack O'Lantern*, 1969, Ace Books, 1973; *Cloud over Calderwood*, 1969, Ace Books, 1973; *The Tides of Tremannion*, 1970, Ace Books, 1973; *Mallory's Luck*, 1971, Ace Books, 1974; *Return of the Royalist*, 1971; *The Reluctant Puritan*, 1972, Ace Books, 1973; *The Highwayman's Daughter*, 1972, Ace Books, 1974; *Belltower*, 1973, Ace Books, 1974; *The Black Domino*, 1975; *Elusive Legacy*, 1976; *The Miser's Ward*, 1977; *Smugglers' Haunt*, 1978; *Guardian at the Gate*, 1979; *Brackenthorpe*, 1980.

Juvenile series: "Playtime Stories," six books, E. J. Arnold, 1966; "Judy Stories," four books, Charles & Son, 1968; "Easy to Read," six books, Charles & Son, 1968; "How Do They Grow?," four books, Charles & Son, 1969; "Do You Know About?," sixteen books, Burke Publishing, 1970-75; "Use Your Senses," five books, Burke Publishing, 1973.

WORK IN PROGRESS: A historical romance set in Yorkshire in 1843.

SIDELIGHTS: Most of Kathleen Shoesmith's historical romances have been published in paperback in France, Italy, and the Netherlands, as well as in America. *Avocational interests:* Sewing, reading, and touring by car in the Yorkshire countryside.

* * *

SHRIVER, Donald W(oods), Jr. 1927-

PERSONAL: Born December 20, 1927, in Norfolk, Va.; son of Donald W. (an attorney) and Gladys (Roberts) Shriver; married Peggy Ann Leu, August 9, 1953; children: Gregory, Margaret, Timothy. *Education:* Davidson College, A.B. (summa cum laude), 1951; Union Theological Seminary, Richmond, Va., B.D., 1955; Yale University, S.T.M., 1957; Harvard University, Ph.D., 1963. *Office:* Office of the President, Union Theological Seminary, 3041 Broadway, New York, N.Y. 10027.

CAREER: Ordained Presbyterian minister; minister of Presbyterian church in Gastonia, N.C., 1956-59; Cambridge Center for Adult Education, Cambridge, Mass., instructor in Western ethics, 1962; North Carolina State University at Raleigh, instructor in social studies, 1963-64, 1966-67, adjunct assistant professor of religion, 1965-68, visiting associate professor of religion, 1968-72; Emory University, Atlanta, Ga., professor of ethics and society and director of doctor of ministry program, 1972-75; Union Theological Seminary, New York, N.Y., William E. Dodge Professor of Applied Christianity and president of the faculty, 1975—. Duke University, visiting assistant professor of religion, 1964-65, alumni lecturer at Divinity School, 1965-66; visiting associate professor of church and society, Union Theological Seminary, 1967-68; Luther A. Weigle Visiting Lecturer, Yale University, spring, 1969; Chaffee-Grissom Lecturer, Purdue University, 1972. National chairman, United Christian Youth Movement, 1951-53; member of board of national ministries of Presbyterian Church of the United States, 1966-72; delegate to international church conferences. Delegate to Democratic National Convention, 1968; member of board of directors, Complex, Inc. (Ministry to the Systems of the Research Triangle), 1969-72; vice president, Fellowship for Racial and Economic Equality, 1969-74; member of North Carolina Council on Human Relations. Member of Atlanta Chamber of Commerce. *Military service:* U.S. Army, Signal Corps, 1946-47.

MEMBER: American Society for Christian Ethics, Society for the Scientific Study of Religion, Society for Values in Higher Education, Religious Research Association, American Academy of Religion, Institute for Theological Encounter with Science and Technology, National Council of Churches, American Association for Higher Education, American Sociological Association, American Society of Engineering Education, European Society of Culture, American Association for the Advancement of Science, American Association of University Professors, American Civil Liberties Union, Common Cause, Housing Opportunity Made Equal, Phi Beta Kappa, Omicron Delta Kappa, Sigma Upsilon, Golden Chain, L.C.Q. Lamar Society, Friends of the Earth. *Awards, honors:* L.H.D., Central College, 1970; National Institute of Mental Health grant to study information, values, and urban policy formation, 1971-73; D.D., Wagner College, 1978.

WRITINGS: (Editor) *The Unsilent South: Prophetic Preaching in Racial Crisis*, John Knox, 1965; *How Do You Do—And Why?: An Introduction to Christian Ethics for Young People*, John Knox, 1966; (editor with Rolf Buchdahl) *A Guide to Dialogue between Science and Religion*, Experimental Study of Religion and Society, North Carolina State University, 1967; *Rich Man, Poor Man: Moral Issues in American Economic Life*, John Knox, 1972; (with John Earle and Dean Knudson) *Spindles and Spires: A Restudy of Religion and Social Change in Gastonia*, John Knox, 1976; (with Karl Ostrom) *Is There Hope for the City?*, Westminster, 1977; (editor) *Medicine and Religion: Strategies of Care*, University of Pittsburgh Press, 1980; *The Social Ethics of the Lord's Prayer*, Mar Thoma Press (Kottayam, South India), 1980. Author of research reports; contributor to conference reports. Contributor of about fifty articles to theology and social science journals, including *Technology and Culture: Journal of the International Society for the History of Technology, Religion in Life, Soundings, New South, Presbyterian Outlook, Theology Today*, and *Harvard Business Review*.

BIOGRAPHICAL/CRITICAL SOURCES: *Raleigh News and Observer*, May 4, 1964; *Christian Century*, October 18, 1967; Joseph Axelrod, *Case Studies in the Campus Ministry*, Church Society for College Work, 1968; Kenneth Underwood, *The Church, the University, and Social Policy*, Wesleyan University Press, 1969; *First Source*, June 8, 1970; Henry B. Clark, *Ministries of Dialogue*, Association Press, 1971; *Review of Religious Research*, fall, 1971; *Religious Studies Review*, January, 1978.

SHULL, Fremont Adam, Jr. 1924-

PERSONAL: Born April 28, 1924, in Findlay, Ohio; son of Fremont Adam and Pearl (Walcutt) Shull; married Dorothy Siddaway, August 31, 1947; children: Scott Alden, Marcy Lee. *Education:* Ohio State University, B.S., 1948, M.B.A., 1949; Michigan State University, Ph.D., 1958. *Office:* Department of Management, University of Georgia, Athens, Ga. 30602.

CAREER: Drake University, Des Moines, Iowa, instructor, 1949-51; Michigan State University of Agriculture and Applied Science (now Michigan State University), East Lansing, instructor, 1951-56; Indiana University at Bloomington, assistant professor, 1956-63; Southern Illinois University, Carbondale, associate professor, 1963-66, professor of management, 1966-67, chairman of department, 1965-66; University of Georgia, Athens, research professor of management, 1969—. Visiting professor at University of Wisconsin and University of Kentucky. Member of board of directors, Thomas J. Bronson Foundation. Consultant, Anaconda Aluminum Co., Louisville, Ky., 1960-62. *Military service:* U.S. Army Air Forces, 1942-45; received two Purple Hearts, three Bronze Stars, and an Air Medal. *Member:* Academy of Management (fellow; president of midwest division), American Sociological Association, American Psychological Association, Society for General Systems Research (regional chairman), Beta Gamma Sigma, Sigma Iota Epsilon, Alpha Kappa Psi, Alpha Delta Sigma. *Awards, honors:* Beta Gamma Sigma National Distinguished Scholar.

WRITINGS: (Editor) *Selected Readings in Management,* Irwin, Volume I, 1958, Volume II, 1962; *Matrix Structure and Project Authority for Optimizing Organization Capacity* (monograph), Business Research Bureau, Southern Illinois University, 1965; (with others) *Organizational Decision Making,* McGraw, 1970. Also co-author of *Matrix Organizational Design,* 1978. Contributor to *Administrative Science Quarterly, Academy of Management Journal, Advanced Management,* and other professional publications. Co-editor, *Proceedings,* Midwest Academy of Management.

WORK IN PROGRESS: Analysis of Managerial Attitudes of Nursing Home Administrators.†

* * *

SIEGMEISTER, Elie 1909-

PERSONAL: Born January 15, 1909, in New York, N.Y.; son of William and Bessie (Gitler) Siegmeister; married Hannah L. Mersel, January 15, 1930; children: Willa, Miriam Koren, Nancy Mandel. *Education:* Columbia College, B.A., 1927; Ecole Normale de Musique, diploma, 1931; Julliard Graduate School, diploma, 1938. *Home:* 56 Fairview Ave., Great Neck, N.Y. 11023.

CAREER: Free-lance composer, conductor, author, 1932—; founder, American Composers Alliance, 1938; founder and director, American Ballad Singers, 1940-47; Hofstra University, Hempstead, Long Island, N.Y., professor of music, 1949-76, Hofstra Symphony Orchestra, conductor, 1950-65; Pro Arte Symphony Orchestra, conductor, 1965-66, composer in residence, 1966-76. *Member:* American Music Center (vice-president, 1964-67), Composers and Lyricists Guild (vice-president, 1965-68), American Society of Composers, Authors, and Publishers, Council of Creative Artists, Libraries, and Museums (board member and chairman). *Awards, honors:* American Academy of Arts and Letters award, 1978; Guggenheim fellowship, 1978-79.

WRITINGS—Books: *Music and Society,* Critics Group Press, 1938, reprinted, Haskell House, 1974; (editor with Olin Downes) *A Treasury of American Song,* Knopf, 1940; *The Music Lover's Handbook* (Book of the Month Club selection), Morrow, 1944, revised edition published as *The New Music Lover's Handbook,* Harvey House, 1973; *Work and Sing,* W. R. Scott, 1944; *Invitation to Music,* Harvey House, 1961; *Harmony and Melody,* Wadsworth, Volume I: *The Diatonic Style,* 1965, Volume II: *Modulation, Chromatic and Modern Styles,* 1966. Also editor of *The Joan Baez Songbook* by Joan Baez, Music Sales Corp.

Theatrical works: *Doodle Dandy of the U.S.A.* (play; based on book by Saul Lancourt), Composers Facsimile Edition, 1942; *Sing Out, Sweet Land* (musical; based on book by Walter Kerr; first produced on Broadway by the Theatre Guild, 1944), MCA Music Corp., 1944; *Darling Corie* (one-act opera), libretto by Lewis Allen, Chappell, 1952; *Miranda and the Dark Young Man* (one-act opera), libretto by Edward Eager, Shawnee Press, 1955; *The Mermaid in Lock No. 7* (one-act opera), libretto by Edward Mabley, Henmar Press, 1958; *The Plough and the Stars* (opera; based on play by Sean O'Casey; first produced in St. Louis, Mo., May 15, 1963), libretto by Mabley, MCA Music Corp., 1963; "Night of the Moonspell" (opera; based on *Midsummer Night's Dream*), libretto by Mabley, first produced in Shreveport, La., 1976; "Julietta" (opera; based on *The Marquise of O* by Heinrich von Kleist), libretto by Norman Rosten, 1980.

Composer of film score for "They Came to Cordura," Columbia, 1959, and of other film scores for films and television programs. Composer of symphonies, choral music, sonatas, and other musical works.

SIDELIGHTS: Elie Siegmeister incorporates elements of American folk songs, spirituals, and jazz into his musical works, seeking to create a distinctly American music. His works have been performed by symphony orchestras throughout the United States and Europe under such conductors as Toscanini, Mitropoulos, Stokowski, and Maazel.

Siegmeister told *CA:* "I am quite disturbed over the domination of our culture by Madison Avenue, the multinational conglomerates, and their values. I see little hope for us unless some deep American traditions—of individual independence, of healthy contempt for bigness and material affluence . . .—are revived once more. When that happens, I see lots of hope."

BIOGRAPHICAL/CRITICAL SOURCES: John Tasker Howard, *Our American Music,* Crowell, 3rd edition, 1946; David Ewen, *World of Twentieth Century Music,* Prentice-Hall, 1968; *Music Journal,* January, 1973.

* * *

SILBERSCHLAG, Eisig 1903-

PERSONAL: Born 1903, in Styrj, Austria; son of David and Blume (Pomeranz) Silberschlag; married Milka Antler, 1938. *Education:* University of Vienna, Ph.D., 1926. *Home:* 1801 Lavaca, Austin, Tex. *Office:* Center for Middle Eastern Studies, University of Texas, Austin, Tex. 78712.

CAREER: Author, educator, and lecturer; Jewish Theological Seminary, Teachers' Institute, New York, N.Y., instructor in Jewish history, 1930-31; Hebrew College, Brookline, Mass., instructor, 1932-44, professor of Hebrew literature, 1944—, dean, 1947-68, president, 1968-70; University of Texas at Austin, visiting Gale Professor of Judaic Studies, 1973-77, visiting professor of comparative studies, 1977—. Visiting professor, Emmanuel College, 1970-73. Visiting scholar, Oxford University, 1978-79. Chairman of sessions,

World Congress of Jewish Studies, 1977. Trustee, Hebrew College, Boston. *Member:* Middle East Studies Association (fellow), American Academy for Jewish Research (fellow), National Association of Professors of Hebrew (president), P.E.N. *Awards, honors:* Lamed Prize, 1943; Saul Tschernichowsky Prize, Municipality of Tel Aviv, 1951; Florence and Harry Kovner Memorial Award, 1960, 1972; golden doctorate, University of Vienna, 1976; Doctor of Humane Letters, Hebrew Union College—Jewish Institute of Religion, 1977.

WRITINGS—Books in English: *Hebrew Literature: An Evaluation,* Herzl Institute, 1959; (contributor) Alexander Altmann, editor, *Studies and Texts,* Harvard University Press, 1965; *Saul Tschernichowsky: Poet of Revolt,* Cornell University Press, 1968; *From Renaissance to Renaissance: Hebrew Literature from 1492-1967,* Ktav, 1972; *An Exhibition of Judaica and Hebraica,* University of Texas Humanities Research Center, 1973; *Hebrew Literature in the Land of Israel, 1870-1970,* Ktav, 1977.

Books in Hebrew: *Bi-Shebilim Bodedim* (poetry; title means "In Lonely Paths"), Ogen, 1931; *Tehiyah u-Tehiyah be-Shirah* (title means "Revolt and Revival in Poetry"), Abraham Joseph Stybel, 1938; *Ale Olam be-Shir* (poetry; title means "Arise, Oh World, in Song"), Ogen, 1946; *Kimron Yamai* (poetry; title means "Dome of Days"), Kiryat Sefer, 1959. Also author of *Bi-Yeme Isabella* (play; title means "In the Days of Isabella"), [New York], 1939, *Sheva Panim le-Havah* (play; title means "Eve Has Seven Faces"), [Tel Aviv], 1942, *Iggerotai El Dorot Aherim* (title means "Letters to Other Generations"), [Jerusalem], 1971, and *Yesh Reshit Le-Kol Aharit* (title means "Each End Has a Beginning"), [Jerusalem], 1976. Also translator of *Poems of Love* by Paulus Silentiarius, [New York], 1945, [Tel Aviv], 1962, *Berenice: A Tragedy in Five Acts* by Carl de Hass, [New York], 1947, and *The Eleven Comedies of Aristophanes,* [Tel Aviv], 1967. Also co-editor of *Sefer Touroff* (title means "Touroff Book"), [Boston], 1938, and *Hatekufah,* Volumes 30-31, 32-33, [New York], 1946-47.

Contributor to *Encyclopedia of Poetry and Poetics*. Contributor to proceedings of the American Academy for Jewish Research. Contributor of articles to *Commentary, Judaism, World Literature Today,* and other journals. Editor, *Poet Lore,* 1939.

BIOGRAPHICAL/CRITICAL SOURCES: Bulletin of the School of Oriental and African Studies (London), Volume 23, part 1, 1960; *South African Jewish Times,* July 19, 1963; *Barkai,* December 16, 1963; *Maariv Literary Supplement,* March 10, 1965.

* * *

SILVERBERG, Robert 1935-
(Walker Chapman, Walter Drummond, Ivar Jorgenson, Calvin M. Knox, David Osborne, Lee Sebastian; Robert Randall, a joint pseudonym)

PERSONAL: Born January 15, 1935, in New York, N.Y.; son of Michael and Helen (Baim) Silverberg; married Barbara H. Brown (an engineer), August 26, 1956. *Education:* Columbia University, A.B., 1956. *Address:* Box 13160, Station E, Oakland, Calif. 94661. *Agent:* Scott Meredith Literary Agency, Inc., 845 Third Ave., New York, N.Y. 10022.

CAREER: Writer. *Member:* Science Fiction Writers of America (president, 1967-68), Hydra Club (chairman, 1958-61). *Awards, honors:* World Science Fiction Society Hugo Award, 1956, as most promising new author, and 1969, for *Nightwings; Lost Race of Mars* selected by *New York Times* as one of the best one hundred children's books of the year, 1960; Nebula Award, 1970, for "Passengers," 1972, for *A Time of Changes* and "Good News from the Vatican," and 1975, for *Born with the Dead;* Jupiter Award, 1974, for *The Feast of St. Dionysus.*

WRITINGS—Science fiction: *Revolt on Alpha C* (Teenage Book Club selection), Crowell, 1955; *Master of Life and Death,* Ace Books, 1957, reprinted, Sidgwick & Jackson, 1977; (with Randall Garrett under joint pseudonym Robert Randall) *The Shrouded Planet,* Gnome Press, 1957; *The Thirteenth Immortal* (bound with *This Fortress World* by J. E. Gunn), Ace Books, 1957; (under pseudonym David Osborne) *Aliens from Space,* Avalon, 1958; *Invaders from Earth* (bound with *Across Time* by D. Grinnell), Ace Books, 1958, published separately, Avon, 1968, published as *We, the Marauders* (bound with *Giants in the Earth* by James Blish; published under joint title *A Pair from Space*), Belmont Books, 1965; (under pseudonym David Osborne) *Invisible Barriers,* Avalon, 1958; (under pseudonym Ivar Jorgenson) *Starhaven,* Avalon, 1958; *Starman's Quest,* Gnome Press, 1958, 2nd edition, Meredith Press, 1969; (under pseudonym Calvin M. Knox) *Lest We Forget Thee, Earth,* Ace Books, 1958; *Stepsons of Terra* (bound with *A Man Called Destiny* by L. Wright), Ace Books, 1958, published separately, 1977; (with Randall Garrett under joint pseudonym Robert Randall) *The Dawning Light,* Gnome Press, 1959; *The Planet Killers* (bound with *We Claim These Stars!* by Poul Anderson), Ace Books, 1959; (under pseudonym Calvin M. Knox) *The Plot against Earth,* Ace Books, 1959.

Lost Race of Mars, Winston, 1960; *Collision Course,* Avalon, 1961, reprinted, Ace Books, 1977; *Next Stop the Stars* [and] *The Seed of Earth,* Ace Books, 1962, each published separately, 1977; *Recalled to Life,* Lancer Books, 1962, reprinted, Ace Books, 1977; *The Silent Invaders* (bound with *Battle on Venus* by William F. Temple), Ace Books, 1963, published separately, 1973; *Godling, Go Home!,* Belmont Books, 1964; *Regan's Planet,* Pyramid Books, 1964; (under pseudonym Calvin M. Knox) *One of Our Asteroids Is Missing,* Ace Books, 1964; *Time of the Great Freeze,* Holt, 1964.

Conquerors from the Darkness, Holt, 1965; *To Worlds Beyond: Stories of Science Fiction,* Chilton, 1965; *Needle in a Timestack,* Ballantine, 1966; *The Gate of Worlds,* Holt, 1967; *Planet of Death,* Holt, 1967; *Those Who Watch,* New American Library, 1967; *The Time-Hoppers,* Doubleday, 1967; *To Open the Sky,* Ballantine, 1967; *Hawksbill Station,* Doubleday, 1968 (published in England as *The Anvil of Time,* Sidgwick & Jackson, 1968); *The Masks of Time,* Ballantine, 1968; *Across a Billion Years,* Dial, 1969; *The Calibrated Alligator and Other Science Fiction Stories,* Holt, 1969; *Dimension Thirteen,* Ballantine, 1969; *The Man in the Maze,* Avon, 1969; *Thorns,* Walker, 1969; (contributor) *Three for Tomorrow: Three Original Novellas of Science Fiction,* Meredith Press, 1969; *Three Survived,* Holt, 1969; *To Live Again,* Doubleday, 1969; *Up the Line,* Ballantine, 1969.

The Cube Root of Uncertainty (short story collection), Macmillan, 1970; *Downward to the Earth,* Doubleday, 1970; *Great Short Novels of Science Fiction,* Ballantine, 1970; *Nightwings,* Walker, 1970; *Parsecs and Parables: Ten Science Fiction Stories,* Doubleday, 1970; *The Pueblo Revolt,* Weybright, 1970; *A Robert Silverberg Omnibus,* Sidgwick & Jackson, 1970; *Tower of Glass,* Scribner, 1970; *Vornan-19,* Sidgwick & Jackson, 1970; *World's Fair, 1992,* Follett, 1970; *Moonferns and Starsongs,* Ballantine, 1971; *Son of Man,* Ballantine, 1971; *A Time of Changes,* Doubleday, 1971; *The World Inside,* Doubleday, 1971; *The Book of Skulls,* Scribner, 1972; *Dying Inside,* Scribner, 1972; *Thomas the Proclai-*

mer (bound with *A Chapter of Revelation* by Poul Anderson and *Things Which Are Caesar's* by Gordon Dickson; published under joint title *The Day the Sun Stood Still: Three Original Novellas of Science Fiction*), Thomas Nelson, 1972; *The Reality Trip and Other Implausibilities,* Ballantine, 1972; *The Second Trip,* Doubleday, 1972; *Earth's Other Shadow: Nine Science Fiction Stories by Robert Silverberg,* New American Library, 1973; (contributor) *An Exaltation of Stars: Transcendental Adventures in Science Fiction,* Simon & Schuster, 1973; *This Is the Road* (bound with *The Winds at Starmont* by Terry Carr and *The Partridge Project* by R. A. Lupoff; published under joint title *No Mind of Man: Three Original Novellas of Science Fiction*), Hawthorn, 1973; *Unfamiliar Territory* (short story collection), Scribner, 1973; *Valley beyond Time,* Dell, 1973; *Born with the Dead: Three Novellas about the Spirit of Man,* Random House, 1974; *Sundance and Other Science Fiction Stories,* Thomas Nelson, 1974.

The Feast of St. Dionysus: Five Science Fiction Stories, Scribner, 1975; *The Stochastic Man,* Harper, 1975; *Sunrise on Mercury and Other Science Fiction Stories,* Thomas Nelson, 1975; *The Best of Robert Silverberg,* Pocket Books, 1976; *Capricorn Games,* Random House, 1976; *Shadrach in the Furnace,* Bobbs-Merrill, 1976; *The Shores of Tomorrow* (short story collection), Thomas Nelson, 1976; *The Best of Robert Silverberg,* two volumes, Gregg Press, 1978; *Lord Valentine's Castle,* Harper, 1980.

Nonfiction: (With Arthur C. Clarke) *Going into Space,* Harper, 1954 (published in England as *The Young Traveller in Space,* Phoenix House, 1954), revised edition, 1971; *Treasures beneath the Sea,* Whitman Publishing, 1960; *First American into Space,* Monarch Books, 1961; *Lost Cities and Vanished Civilizations* (Literary Guild Young Adult selection), Chilton, 1962; *Empires in the Dust: Ancient Civilizations Brought to Light,* Chilton, 1963; *The Fabulous Rockefellers: A Compelling, Personalized Account of One of America's First Families,* Monarch Books, 1963; *Fifteen Battles That Changed the World,* Putnam, 1963; *Home of the Red Man: Indian North America before Columbus,* New York Graphic Society, 1963; *Sunken History: The Story of Underwater Archaeology* (Literary Guild Young Adults selection), Chilton, 1963; *Akhnaten: The Rebel Pharaoh,* Chilton, 1964; *The Great Doctors,* Putnam, 1964; (under pseudonym Walker Chapman) *The Loneliest Continent: The Story of Antarctic Discovery,* New York Graphic Society, 1964; *Man before Adam: The Story of Man in Search of His Origins,* Macrae, 1964; *The Man Who Found Nineveh: The Story of Austen Henry Layard,* Holt, 1964.

The Great Wall of China, Chilton, 1965, published as *The Long Rampart: The Story of the Great Wall of China,* 1966; *The Mask of Akhnaten,* Macmillan, 1965; *Men Who Mastered the Atom,* Putnam, 1965; *Niels Bohr: The Man Who Mapped the Atom,* Macrae, 1965; *The Old Ones: Indians of the American Southwest,* New York Graphic Society, 1965; *Scientists and Scoundrels: A Book of Hoaxes,* Crowell, 1965; *Socrates,* Putnam, 1965; *The World of Coral,* Duell, 1965; *Bridges,* Macrae, 1966; *Frontiers in Archeology,* Chilton, 1966; *Forgotten by Time: A Book of Living Fossils,* Crowell, 1966; (under pseudonym Walker Chapman) *Kublai Khan: Lord of Xanadu,* Bobbs-Merrill, 1966; (under pseudonym Lee Sebastian) *Rivers,* Holt, 1966; *To the Rock of Darius: The Story of Henry Rawlinson,* Holt, 1966; *The Adventures of Nat Palmer: Antarctic Explorer and Clipper Ship Pioneer,* McGraw, 1967; *The Auk, the Dodo, and the Oryx: Vanished and Vanishing Creatures,* Crowell, 1967; *The Dawn of Medicine,* Putnam, 1967; (under pseudonym Walker Chapman) *The Golden Dream: Seekers of El Dorado,* Bobbs-Merrill, 1967, published as *The Search for El Dorado,* 1967; *Light for the World: Edison and the Power Industry,* Van Nostrand, 1967; *Men against Time: Salvage Archaeology in the United States,* Macmillan, 1967; *The Morning of Mankind: Prehistoric Man in Europe,* New York Graphic Society, 1967; *The World of the Rain Forest,* Meredith Press, 1967; *Four Men Who Changed the Universe,* Putnam, 1968; *Ghost Towns of the American West,* Crowell, 1968; *Mound Builders of Ancient America: The Archaeology of a Myth,* New York Graphic Society, 1968, abridged edition published as *The Mound Builders,* 1970; (under pseudonym Lee Sebastian) *The South Pole,* Holt, 1968; *Stormy Voyager: The Story of Charles Wilkes,* Lippincott, 1968; *The World of the Ocean Depths,* Meredith Press, 1968; *Bruce of the Blue Nile,* Holt, 1969; *The Challenge of Climate: Man and His Environment,* Meredith Press, 1969; *Vanishing Giants: The Story of the Sequoias,* Simon & Schuster, 1969; *Wonders of Ancient Chinese Science,* Hawthorn, 1969; *The World of Space,* Meredith Press, 1969.

If I Forget Thee, O Jerusalem: American Jews and the State of Israel, Morrow, 1970; *Mammoths, Mastodons and Man,* McGraw, 1970; *The Seven Wonders of the Ancient World,* Crowell-Collier, 1970; *Before the Sphinx: Early Egypt,* Thomas Nelson, 1971; *Clocks for the Ages: How Scientists Date the Past,* Macmillan, 1971; *To the Western Shore: Growth of the United States, 1776-1853,* Doubleday, 1971; *The Realm of Prester John,* Doubleday, 1972; *John Muir: Prophet among the Glaciers,* Putnam, 1972; *The Longest Voyage: Circumnavigators in the Age of Discovery,* Bobbs-Merrill, 1972; *The World within the Ocean Wave,* Weybright, 1972; *The World within the Tide Pool,* Weybright, 1972.

Editor: *Great Adventures in Archaeology,* Dial, 1964; (under pseudonym Walker Chapman) *Antarctic Conquest: The Great Explorers in Their Own Words,* Bobbs-Merrill, 1966; *Earthmen and Strangers: Nine Stories of Science Fiction,* Duell, 1966; *Voyagers in Time: Twelve Stories of Science Fiction,* Meredith Press, 1967; *Men and Machines: Ten Stories of Science Fiction,* Meredith Press, 1968; *Dark Stars,* Ballantine, 1969; *Tomorrow's Worlds: Ten Stories of Science Fiction,* Meredith Press, 1969.

The Ends of Time: Eight Stories of Science Fiction, Hawthorn, 1970; *The Mirror of Infinity: A Critics' Anthology of Science Fiction,* Harper, 1970; *Science Fiction Hall of Fame,* Volume I, Doubleday, 1970; *Worlds of Maybe: Seven Stories of Science Fiction,* Thomas Nelson, 1970; *Mind to Mind: Nine Stories of Science Fiction,* Thomas Nelson, 1971; *The Science Fiction Bestiary: Nine Stories of Science Fiction,* Thomas Nelson, 1971; *To the Stars: Eight Stories of Science Fiction,* Hawthorn, 1971; *Beyond Control: Seven Stories of Science Fiction,* Thomas Nelson, 1972; *Invaders from Space: Ten Stories of Science Fiction,* Hawthorn, 1972; *Deep Space: Eight Stories of Science Fiction,* Thomas Nelson, 1973; *Other Dimensions: Ten Stories of Science Fiction,* Hawthorn, 1973; (and author of introduction) George Alec Effinger, Gardner R. Dozois, and Gordon Ecklund, *Chains of the Sea,* Dell, 1974; *Infinite Jests: The Lighter Side of Science Fiction,* Chilton, 1974; *Mutants: Eleven Stories of Science Fiction,* Thomas Nelson, 1974; (and author of introduction) *Threads of Time: Three Original Novellas of Science Fiction,* Thomas Nelson, 1974; *Windows into Tomorrow: Nine Stories of Science Fiction,* Hawthorn, 1974.

(With Roger Elwood) *Epoch,* Putnam, 1975; (and author of introduction) *Explorers of Space: Eight Stories of Science Fiction,* Thomas Nelson, 1975; *Strange Gifts: Eight Stories of Science Fiction,* Thomas Nelson, 1975; *The Aliens: Seven Stories of Science Fiction,* Thomas Nelson, 1976; (and author of introduction) *The Crystal Ship: Three Original Novellas of Science Fiction,* Thomas Nelson, 1976; *The New Atlantis and Other Novellas of Science Fiction,* Warner Books, 1976; *Earth Is the Strangest Planet: Ten Stories of Science Fiction,* Thomas Nelson, 1977; (and author of introduction) *Galactic Dreamers: Science Fiction as Visionary Literature,* Random House, 1977; *The Infinite Web: Eight Stories of Science Fiction,* Dial, 1977; *Triax,* Pinnacle Books, 1977; *Trips in Time: Nine Stories of Science Fiction,* Thomas Nelson, 1977; *Lost Worlds, Unknown Horizons: Nine Stories of Science Fiction,* Thomas Nelson, 1978; *The Androids Are Coming: Seven Stories of Science Fiction,* American Elsevier-Thomas Nelson, 1979; (with Martin H. Greenberg) *Car Sinister,* Avon, 1979; (with others) *Dawn of Time: Prehistory through Science Fiction,* American Elsevier-Thomas Nelson, 1979.

Editor of "Alpha" series: *Alpha One,* Ballantine, 1970; . . . *Two,* Ballantine, 1971; . . . *Three,* Ballantine, 1972; . . . *Four,* Ballantine, 1973; . . . *Five,* Ballantine, 1974; . . . *Six,* Berkley Publishing, 1976; . . . *Seven,* Berkley Publishing, 1977; . . . *Eight,* Berkley Publishing, 1977; . . . *Nine,* Berkley Publishing, 1978.

Editor of "New Dimensions: Science Fiction" series: *New Dimensions: Science Fiction No. 1,* Doubleday, 1971; . . . *No. 2,* Doubleday, 1972; . . . *No. 3,* New American Library, 1974; . . . *No. 4,* New American Library, 1974; . . . *No. 5,* Harper, 1975; . . . *No. 6,* Harper, 1976; . . . *No. 7,* Harper, 1977; . . . *No. 8,* Harper, 1977; . . . *No. 9,* Harper, 1979; . . . *No. 10,* Harper, 1980; *Best of New Dimensions* (includes stories from No. 1-No. 9), Pocket Books, 1979.

SIDELIGHTS: Despite the fact that a substantial portion of his work consists of nonfiction books and articles on topics ranging from archaeology to zoology, in addition to numerous biographies of people as diverse as the Egyptian pharaoh Akhnaten and inventor Thomas Edison, Robert Silverberg is probably best known to his readers as a science fiction writer and anthologist. In a critical study of his work, Thomas D. Clareson writes that Silverberg "has always been a first-rate storyteller, even while dealing with a tired plot. . . . His artistry has grown, of course, as he has become a less hurried, more experienced writer, and half the fun of reading any of his stories is to observe his increasing skill as he experiments with such technical matters of language and form. . . . The most obvious change in Silverberg . . . lies in the absence of the complex, melodramatic plot action of his earlier works." After noting that Silverberg also avoids writing "the same story over and over again," Clareson concludes that "time and time again he has expanded that parameters of science fiction. . . . He exemplifies the conscious artist, making decisions to increase the effectiveness of his stories. . . . [This] awareness . . . is one significant mark of his growth during his career."

Although she is rather critical of some aspects of his writing style, Joanna Russ agrees that Silverberg's writing has improved through the years. In her review of his short story collection, *The Cube Root of Uncertainty,* Russ claims that "New Silverberg [post-1967] is something else: a highly colored, gloomy, melodramatic, morally allegorical writer who luxuriates in lush description and has a real love of calamity. . . . I don't like his feverishness or his intense, mad romanticism, and I suspect Mr. Silverberg . . . needs some time to get out of his system all the sophomoric dark doom that most of us—far less technically expert—dealt with during our apprenticeships." Nevertheless, she concludes, the best story in the collection "achieves a playing with reality that is often aimed at in science fiction but seldom realized. Mr. Silverberg gets better and better."

A "typical" Silverberg theme, according to Clareson, concerns "the dilemma of man isolated amid the fragmenting cultures of the contemporary world. . . . He employs man's encounter with nonhuman intelligence, be it alien or android, to search for values which he and his readers may accept. . . . His use of such familiar devices as telepathy, multiple personalities fused within a single consciousness, and time travel—as well as the theme of immortality—simply provide him a wider range of plot materials to work with as he seeks for those moments which transcend man's loneliness, man's separateness. . . . [His alien characters] are *people;* they provide a perspective from which to measure the conduct and nature of man; and they can teach him what he has ignored or forgotten." In short, Clareson writes, Silverberg's writings reflect his "concern for transcendence and the unity of all sentient beings."

In his introduction to *The Infinite Web: Eight Stories of Science Fiction,* Silverberg comments on what he believes the purpose of science fiction should be: "The trouble with a lot of the 'ecological' science fiction of recent years is that the authors, intent on warning us about present and future evils, neglect their function as storytellers. They give us neither plot nor theme, really, but only somber vignettes of civilizations buried in beer cans or drowning in sewage. Such aspects of fiction as characterization, style, conflict, and revelation are overlooked in the author's haste to tell us things we already know. I believe that the writer's job is to tell the reader things he *doesn't* already know, which means creating art rather than assembling harangues."

AVOCATIONAL INTERESTS: Travel, collecting rare books, gardening, contemporary music and literature.

BIOGRAPHICAL/CRITICAL SOURCES: New York Times Book Review, May 9, 1965, November 3, 1968; *Best Sellers,* February 1, 1968, December 1, 1969, January 1, 1970, December 15, 1971; *Young Readers' Review,* April, 1968; *Books and Bookmen,* February, 1969; *Book World,* February 9, 1969, July 6, 1969; *Times Literary Supplement,* June 12, 1969; *National Review,* November 3, 1970; *Magazine of Fantasy and Science Fiction,* April, 1971, April, 1974; *Variety,* April 7, 1971; *Books,* October, 1971; *Contemporary Literary Criticism,* Volume VII, Gale, 1977; *Writer,* November, 1977.

* * *

SIMAK, Clifford D(onald) 1904-

PERSONAL: Born August 3, 1904, in Millville, Wis.; son of John Lewis and Margaret (Wiseman) Simak; married Agnes Kuchenberg, April 13, 1929; children: Scott, Shelley. *Education:* Attended University of Wisconsin. *Residence:* Minnetonka, Minn. *Agent:* Blassingame, McCauley, & Wood, 60 East 42nd St., New York, N.Y. 10017.

CAREER: Worked with various newspapers in Midwest during 1930's; *Minneapolis Star and Tribune,* Minneapolis, Minn., 1939-76, news editor of *Minneapolis Star,* beginning 1949, co-ordinator of *Minneapolis Tribune*'s Science Reading Series, beginning 1961. *Member:* Sigma Delta Chi. *Awards, honors:* International Fantasy Award for best science fiction novel, 1953, for *City;* Hugo Award for best science fiction novelette, 1958, for "The Big Front Yard," and for best science fiction novel, 1963, for *Way Station;* Minnesota Academy of Science Award, 1967, for distinguished service to science; Juniper Award for best novel, Instructors of Science Fiction in Higher Education, 1977, for *A Heritage of Stars;* First Fandom Hall of Fame Award, 1973; Jupiter Award, 1979, for *A Heritage of Stars;* Grand Master Award, Science Fiction Writers of America, for lifetime achievement.

WRITINGS—All science fiction and fantasy: *The Creator* (novelette), Crawford, 1946; *Cosmic Engineers,* Gnome Press, 1950, reprinted, Paperback Library, 1970; *Empire,* Galaxy, 1951; *Time and Again,* Simon & Schuster, 1951, reprinted, Ace, 1976, published as *First He Died,* Dell, 1952; *City,* Gnome Press, 1952, reprinted, Ace, 1976; *Ring around the Sun,* Simon & Schuster, 1953; *Time Is the Simplest Thing,* Ace, 1961, reprinted, Nordon Publications, 1977; *The Trouble with Tycho,* Ace, 1961; *They Walked Like Men,* Doubleday, 1962, reprinted, Avon, 1979; *Way Station,* Doubleday, 1963, reprinted, Bentley, 1980; *All Flesh Is Grass,* Doubleday, 1965; *Why Call Them Back from Heaven?,* Doubleday, 1967; *The Werewolf Principle,* Putnam, 1967; *The Goblin Reservation,* Putnam, 1968; *Out of Their Minds,* Putnam, 1970; *Destiny Doll,* Putnam, 1971; *A Choice of Gods,* Putnam, 1972; *Cemetery World,* Putnam, 1973; *Our Children's Children,* Putnam, 1974; *Enchanted Pilgrimage,* Berkley, 1975; *Shakespeare's Planet,* Berkley, 1976; *A Heritage of Stars,* Berkley, 1977; *The Fellowship of the Talisman,* Ballantine, 1978; *Mastodonia,* Ballantine, 1978; *The Visitors,* Ballantine, 1980.

Short story collections: *Strangers in the Universe,* Simon & Schuster, 1956; *The Worlds of Clifford Simak,* Simon & Schuster, 1960 (published in England as *Aliens for Neighbours,* Faber, 1961); *All the Traps of Earth and Other Stories,* Doubleday, 1962, reprinted, Avon, 1979, published as *The Night of the Puudly,* Four Square, 1964; *Other Worlds of Clifford Simak,* Doubleday, 1962; *Worlds without End,* Belmont Books, 1964; *Best Science Fiction Stories of Clifford Simak,* Faber 1967, Doubleday, 1971; *So Bright the Vision,* Ace, 1968; (editor) *Nebula Award Stories #6,* Doubleday, 1971; *The Best of Clifford D. Simak,* Sidgwick & Jackson, 1975; *Skirmish: The Great Short Fiction of Clifford D. Simak,* Berkley, 1977.

Nonfiction: *The Solar System: Our New Front Yard,* St. Martin's, 1962; *Trilobite, Dinosaur, and Man: The Earth's Story,* St. Martin's, 1965; (editor) *From Atoms to Infinity: Readings in Modern Science,* Harper, 1965; *Wonder and Glory: The Story of the Universe,* St. Martin's, 1969; *Prehistoric Man: The Story of Man's Rise to Civilization,* St. Martin's, 1971; (editor) *The March of Science,* Harper, 1971.

Work has been anthologized. Author of columns "Science in the News," *Minneapolis Star*, and "Medical News," *Minneapolis Tribune*. Contributor of two hundred short stories to science fiction magazines.

SIDELIGHTS: Clifford D. Simak's best-known work is *City,* a future history of mankind and its eventual destruction through the misuse of technology. "Once Simak had written *City* . . . ," Thomas D. Clareson believes, "American science fiction could never again be what it had been. . . . [No] one, so thoroughly as Simak, had condemned man's surrender to that technology which led him to Hiroshima and the Moon." Clareson concludes that Simak "did more, perhaps, than any of his contemporaries to free science fiction from its established patterns and to create credible, imaginary worlds better able to sustain metaphors of the condition of man. As few other writers before him, he gave the genre a moral stature."

Simak's own view of *City* differs from that of the critics. He told *CA* that, although the book "is used in the classroom, . . . perhaps is my best-known work, [and] did have some impact on the field, . . . that doesn't make it my major work. I still hope to write the major work."

Simak's story "How-2" has been adapted as a musical. His books have been translated into numerous languages including French, Russian, Italian, and Hebrew.

BIOGRAPHICAL/CRITICAL SOURCES: *Galaxy,* October, 1952, June, 1967, July, 1971; L. Sprague De Camp, *Science Fiction Handbook,* Hermitage, 1953; *Analog,* April, 1954, July, 1969, December, 1971, January, 1977; *Magazine of Fantasy and Science Fiction,* October, 1960, March, 1966, February, 1969; Kingsley Amis, *New Maps of Hell,* Harcourt, 1960; *Amazing Stories,* December, 1961, June, 1965, June, 1973; Samuel Moskowitz, *Seekers of Tomorrow,* World Publishing, 1966; *Science Books,* March, 1966; *Times Literary Supplement,* March 24, 1966, August 8, 1975; *Natural History,* November, 1966; *New Statesman,* February 3, 1967; *Punch,* April 3, 1968; *Observer,* April 14, 1968; *Books & Bookmen,* June, 1968; *Sky & Telescope,* October, 1970; Donald A. Wollheim, *The Universe Makers,* Harper, 1971; *Saturday Review,* May 15, 1971; *Contemporary Literary Criticism,* Volume I, Gale, 1973; Thomas D. Clareson, editor, *Voices for the Future,* Volume I, Bowling Green University Press, 1976; *New York Times Book Review,* June 26, 1977; *Spectator,* July 30, 1977; *Books West,* October, 1977.

* * *

SIMBARI, Nicola 1927-

PERSONAL: Born July 13, 1927, in St. Lucido, Calabria, Italy; son of Carmine (a constructor) and Clorinda (Sangineto) Simbari; married Elfrida Kerbey (an actress and singer), October 1, 1957. *Education:* Degree from Accademia di Belle Arti, 1944. *Religion:* Roman Catholic. *Home:* Via Sant'Andrea 13, Grottaferrata, Rome, Italy 00046.

CAREER: Artist and author in Rome, Italy. Has worked at film and stage set designing; art director in Italy and England. Paintings have been exhibited in Europe and the United States. *Military service:* Italian Air Force.

WRITINGS: (Self-illustrated) *Gennarino* (children's book), Lippincott, 1962; *Nicola Simbari* (collection of paintings), texts by Sergio Barletta, Herve Bazin, Genevieve Breerette, and Sterling McIlbany, Editoriale Grafica (Rome), 1972; *Simbari* (collection of paintings), commentary by Stuart Preston, Simon & Schuster, 1975; *Crazy Horse Saloon vu par Simbari* (about women in art), Wally Findlay Galleries International (Paris), 1976.†

* * *

SIMON, Shirley (Schwartz) 1921-

PERSONAL: Born March 21, 1921, in Cleveland, Ohio; daughter of Bernard H. and Sylvia (Silverman) Schwartz; married Edgar H. Simon (an interior designer), March 1, 1942; children: Allen H., Ruth Esther. *Education:* Attended Spencerian Business College, 1938-40 and Western Reserve University (now Case Western Reserve University), 1940-43; Goddard College, B.A., 1973. *Religion:* Jewish. *Home:* 3630 Cedarbrook Rd., Cleveland, Ohio. *Agent:* McIntosh & Otis, 475 Fifth Ave., New York, N.Y. 10017.

CAREER: Secretary to vice-president of aluminum smelting plant in Cleveland, Ohio, 1943-46; free-lance writer, 1950—; Case Western Reserve University, General Studies Division, Cleveland, lecturer and instructor, 1965-67; John Carroll University, Cleveland, lecturer and instructor, 1969-76; Educational Dimensions, Inc., Cleveland, writer and researcher, 1969-72; Ohio University, Athens, instructor, 1972-74; Glen Oak School, Gates Mills, Ohio, instructor, 1973—, chairperson of English department, 1978—. *Member:* Authors Guild, National League of American Pen Women, Pioneer Women. *Awards, honors: Cousins at Camm Corners* named one of the one hundred outstanding 1963 books for young readers by the *New York Times*.

WRITINGS—All juveniles; all published by Lothrop, except as indicated: *Molly's Cottage,* 1959; *Molly and the Rooftop Mystery,* 1961; *Cousins at Camm Corners,* 1963; *Best Friend,* 1964; *Libby's Step-Family,* 1966; (with Bea Stadtler) *Once Upon a Jewish Holiday,* Ktav, 1966.

Work appears in anthologies and textbooks, including: Sylvia Kamerman, editor, *Children's Plays from Favorite Stories,* Plays, 1959; Kamerman, editor, *Fifty Plays for Junior Actors,* Plays, 1966; Paul S. Anderson, *The Young America Basic Reading Program, Level 12,* Lyons & Carnahan, 1972. Contributor of stories, plays, and articles to *Jack and Jill, Calling All Girls, Plays, Grade Teacher, Child Life,* and *Instructor*.

WORK IN PROGRESS: A junior novel set in Cleveland in the 1950s.

SIDELIGHTS: Shirley Simon told *CA:* "I have always loved children's stories. My mother read to me endlessly. At age eight I was writing (bad) poetry. My mother gathered up some of my 'poems' and shipped them off to the editor of the local newspaper, along with a letter submitting them for publication. The editor returned my poems with a very kind letter. He explained that newspapers seldom buy poetry, almost never from eight-year-old girls. He picked out the least bad poem and declared that to be his favorite of the group. He advised me to keep on writing—and to read poetry and novels. I did all of these. About thirty years later I began to sell what I wrote.

"As I grew into adulthood I never lost my passion for children's books. I still read them. All of my novels are about my childhood—or that of my children, friends' children, or children's friends. I receive many letters from readers all over the country. Most of them ask whether Marcy (or Molly or Jenny) is a real person. The answer is 'Not really,' but many of the things that happen in my books happened to our family or to our friends or neighbors. *Best Friend* is based on my own experiences and feelings when I was Jenny's age. I had a friend very much like Dot, who was delightful and fickle, and I learned that I needed more than one friend.

"When my husband was a boy about Sandy's age, he and his friends built a raft like the one in *Cousins at Camm Corners,* and it did not stay afloat, either. We once saw a talking crow at school (just like the crow in *Cousins*) that kept saying 'What is Charles going outside for?' Imogene is exactly like a poodle that belonged to one of our neighbors, and a boy who lived next door had a catfish like Louis Cats. We even listened to the same records that Molly enjoyed.

"One of the greatest joys of writing . . . for me . . . is receiving the letters from girls who read my books. Readers send snapshots, tell me about themselves and their families and friends. The largest number of letters are about *Best Friend.* I can't tell you how many girls have written to say they have had the same experience that Jenny had and experienced the same pain and frustration that Jenny felt.

"My interest in children's literature had led me into two second careers—writing and adapting material for classroom use, designing course material, and most recently, teaching children's literature and other English courses in an independent high school for girls.

"I am particularly interested in the ways in which books for very young children depict girls and women, and I enjoy helping my students to understand the ways in which their early conditioning affects their values and expectations as young women. The most recent books for children are very different in the way they show girls . . . and very exciting."

AVOCATIONAL INTERESTS: "When I am not working, my husband and I enjoy all kinds of travel . . . from trailering in New England to visits to London and Tel Aviv. We enjoy visiting our son and daughter, who live in New Hampshire and Georgia, respectively. We love music . . . classical music, folk music, and Dixieland Jazz."

BIOGRAPHICAL/CRITICAL SOURCES: Young Readers Review, January, 1965; *Books Today,* January 17, 1965; *Parents,* July, 1965; *Christian Science Monitor,* November 3, 1966.

* * *

SIMPSON, Howard Russell 1925-

PERSONAL: Born April 27, 1925, in Alameda, Calif.; son of Howard and Columbia (Profumo) Simpson; married Mary Alice Turner, 1954; children: Shawn Louise, Lisa Ann, Kathleen Marie, Margaret Alice. *Education:* Attended City College of San Francisco, California School of Fine Arts, and Academie Julian. *Agent:* John Schaffner Literary Agency, 425 East 51st St., New York, N.Y. 10022. *Office:* American Embassy, Paris, France.

CAREER: San Francisco Call-Bulletin, San Francisco, Calif., staff artist, 1950-51; *San Francisco Chronicle,* San Francisco, artist and writer, 1956; U.S. Information Agency, press officer, Saigon, Vietnam, 1951-55, information officer and consul, Lagos, Nigeria, 1957-59, Marseille, France, 1959-61, 1962-64, press officer and attache, Paris, France, 1961-62, press adviser, Saigon, 1964-66, information attache, American Embassy, Paris, 1966-68; Naval War College, Newport, R.I., faculty advisor, 1968-69; American Embassy, Canberra, Australia, counselor, 1969-71; Swiss Embassy, Algiers, Algeria, first secretary for U.S. Interests Section, 1971-74; consul general, Marseille, France, 1974-77; American Embassy, Paris, deputy public affairs officer, 1977—. Press adviser, UNESCO Conference, Paris, 1960; U.S. delegate to International Film Festival, Cannes, 1960-66. *Military service:* U.S. Army, 1943-45; became sergeant. *Member:* San Francisco Press and Union League Club, Anglo-American Press Association. *Awards, honors:* Distinguished service award, U.S. Information Agency, 1955, for "covering [as correspondent] seven major campaigns involving Vietnamese troops" at considerable risk and personal danger; Order of French Military Engineers, rosette d'officier, 1968, cravate de commandeer, 1973; medal for civilian service in Vietnam, 1968.

WRITINGS: To a Silent Valley, Knopf, 1961; *Assignment for a Mercenary,* Harper, 1965; *The Three Day Alliance,* Doubleday, 1971; *Rendezvous Off Newport,* Curtis Books, 1973. Contributor of articles and fiction to magazines and newspapers. Cartoonist, *Foreign Service Journal*.

* * *

SIMPSON, Louis (Aston Marantz) 1923-

PERSONAL: Born March 27, 1923, in Kingston, Jamaica, British West Indies; son of Aston and Rosalind (Marantz) Simpson; married Jeanne Rogers, 1949 (divorced, 1953); married Dorothy Roochvarg, 1955 (divorced, 1979); children: (first marriage) Matthew; (second marriage) Anne,

Anthony. *Education:* Columbia University, B.S., 1948, M.A., 1950, Ph.D., 1959. *Home:* 1 Highview Ave., East Setauket, N.Y. *Office:* Department of English, State University of New York, Stony Brook, N.Y. 11794.

CAREER: Bobbs-Merrill Publishing Co., New York City, editor, 1950-55; Columbia University, New York City, instructor in English, 1955-59; University of California, Berkeley, 1959-67, began as assistant professor, became professor of English; State University of New York at Stony Brook, professor of English and comparative literature, 1967—. Has given poetry readings at colleges and poetry centers throughout the United States and Europe and on television and radio programs in New York, San Francisco, and London. *Military service:* U.S. Army, 1943-46; became sergeant; awarded Bronze Star with oak leaf cluster, Purple Heart (twice), Presidential Unit Citation. *Awards, honors:* Fellowship in literature (Prix de Rome) at American Academy in Rome, 1957; *Hudson Review* fellowship, 1957; Columbia University, distinguished alumni award, 1960, Medal for Excellence, 1965; Edna St. Vincent Millay Award, 1960; Guggenheim fellowship, 1962, 1970; American Council of Learned Societies grant, 1963; Pulitzer Prize for poetry, 1964, for *At the End of the Open Road;* American Academy of Arts and Letters award in literature, 1976; D.H.L., Eastern Michigan University, 1977.

WRITINGS: The Arrivistes: Poems, 1940-49, Fine Editions, 1949; *Good News of Death and Other Poems,* Scribner, 1955; (editor with Donald Hall and Robert Pack) *New Poets of England and America,* Meridian, 1957; *A Dream of Governors* (poems), Wesleyan University Press, 1959; *Riverside Drive* (novel), Atheneum, 1962; *James Hogg: A Critical Study,* St. Martin's, 1962, reprinted, Arden Library, 1977; *At the End of the Open Road* (poems), Wesleyan University Press, 1963; (contributor) Thom Gunn and Ted Hughes, editors, *Five American Poets,* Faber, 1963; *Selected Poems,* Harcourt, 1965; (editor) *An Introduction to Poetry,* St. Martin's, 1967, 2nd edition, 1972; *Adventures of the Letter I* (poems), Harper, 1972; *North of Jamaica* (autobiography), Harper, 1972 (published in England as *Air with Armed Men,* London Magazine Editions, 1972); *Three on the Tower: The Lives and Works of Ezra Pound, T. S. Eliot and William Carlos Williams,* Morrow, 1975; *Searching for the Ox* (poems), Morrow, 1976; *A Revolution in Taste: Studies of Dylan Thomas, Allen Ginsberg, Syliva Plath and Robert Lowell,* Macmillan, 1978. Contributor of poems, plays, and articles to literary periodicals, including *American Poetry Review, Listener, Hudson Review, Paris Review,* and *Critical Quarterly.*

SIDELIGHTS: In a discussion of Louis Simpson's early poetry, Yohma Gray comments that he "never departs from traditional form and structure and yet he never departs from contemporary themes and concerns." Gray describes one poem, for example, in which Simpson "handles a modern psychological situation in the delicate cadence of seventeenth century verse." Ronald Moran makes a similar comment in regard to *The Arrivistes,* Simpson's first book. Moran finds that Simpson often sounds "like an Elizabethan song-maker or like a Cavalier poet." Gray argues that this juxtaposition of traditional form (ordered meter and rhyme) and modern subjects emphasizes, particularly in the poems about the world wars, the chaotic quality and the tensions of contemporary life. Gray finds that Simpson neither complains nor moralizes about modern problems; rather he clarifies difficulties and presents rational insights.

Gray also praises Simpson for his ability to make his readers heed that which usually passes undiscerned. As Gray remarks: "Even in the most mundane experience there is a vast area of unperceived reality and it is Louis Simpson's kind of poetry which brings it to our notice. It enables us to see things which are ordinarily all about us but which we do not ordinarily see; it adds a new dimension to our sensational perception, making us hear with our eyes and see with our ears." In addition, Gray contends that Simpson's art "imposes order from within on chaos without, gives meaning to the apparently meaningless, suggests fresh vantage points from which to probe experience." Gray comments in conclusion that poetry seeks the same goal as religious belief, "to formulate a coherent and significant meaning for life. The poetry of Louis Simpson offers us that meaning."

After 1959, the publication date of *A Dream of Governors,* Simpson's work changed, and Stephen Stepanchev contends that it changed for the better. Notes Stepanchev: "The prosaism of his early work—which required metrics and rhyme in order to give it character as verse—now gave way to rich, fresh, haunting imagery. His philosophical and political speculations achieved a distinction and brilliance that they had lacked before." A *Chicago Review* critic also remarks on the shift in Simpson's poetry, "*A Dream of Governors* has wit, sophistication, perceptiveness, intelligence, variety, and knowingness, but it comes perilously close to being a poetry of chic." The reviewer goes on to say that this early work lacks a depth of feeling. However, he continues, "*At the End of the Open Road* (1963) . . . is a different story entirely. Simpson has found the secret of releasing the meaning and power of his themes. . . . It is not that his stanzas . . . are becoming more flexible and experimental: this in itself does not mean very much. . . . What is more fundamental, it seems to me, is that greater stylistic flexibility should be the sign of growth in the character and thought of the speaker. Simpson is becoming more able to be a part of what he writes about, and to make what he writes about more a part of him."

Not all critics appreciate the change in Simpson's verse. In a review of *Selected Poems,* which contains twelve new poems in addition to selections of earlier work, Harry Morris states that "Mr. Simpson's first three volumes are better" than his new poetry. Morris believes that Simpson's "new freedoms" have not helped him convey his themes more effectively. T. O'Hara, in a critique of *Adventures of the Letter I,* also questions Simpson's new manner: "What has happened to Louis Simpson's energy? . . . It almost appears that success has mellowed the tough poetic instinct that once propelled him, for this present collection barely flexes a muscle." Yet Marie Borroff, speaking of the same book, avows that "when the remaining decades of the twentieth century have passed ignominiously into history along with the 1960's, these stanzas and other gifts will remain to us." And Christopher Hope deems *Adventures* "a work of pure, brilliant invention."

Critical dissent continues in reviews of *Searching for the Ox.* Derwent May finds the quiet, reflective mood of the poems attractive. Nikki Stiller, on the other hand, feels that "Louis Simpson's work now suggest too much comfort: emotional, physical, intellectual. He has stopped struggling, it seems, for words, for rhythms, for his own deepest self." Yet in contrast to this, Peter Stitt remarks that *Searching for the Ox* "is a tremendously refreshing book. . . . The style in which [the poems] are written presents us with no barriers—it is plain, direct and relaxed. Moreover, the poems tell a story, or stories, in which we can take a real interest."

Simpson has also ventured into other genres: novel, autobiography, and literary critical study. Robert Massie writes in the *New York Times Book Review:* "Into fragments of dialogue, [Simpson] packs more meaning and drama than many novelists can bring off in a chapter. . . . As novels go, *Riverside Drive* is not a tragedy to shake the Gods—but it should stir most of its readers. From the first chapter to the last, it has the ring of truth." William Cole calls Simpson's autobiography, *North of Jamaica,* "magnificent." Concerning *A Revolution in Taste,* a literary critical study, Paul Zweig comments: "[Simpson] has provided a series of engaging portraits of poets whom he presents less as cultural exemplars than as individuals struggling, as Baudelaire wrote, to absolve the pain of their lives with the grace of an enduring poem. It is the life narrowing intensely and heatedly into the act of writing that interests Simpson, the life pared to the poem. And this has enabled him to write a series of compact literary biographies that have the pithiness of a 17th-century 'character' and a literary good sense that reminds me of [Samuel] Johnson's 'Lives of the Poets.'"

Recordings of Louis Simpson reading his poetry are available in "Spoken Arts Treasury of 100 Modern American Poets Reading Their Poems," Volume XV, Spoken Arts, "Today's Poets," Volume I, Scholastic Magazine, and "Yale Series of Recorded Poets," Carillon. In addition, the Poetry Center of San Francisco State University and the State University of New York at Stony Brook have videotapes of his readings.

BIOGRAPHICAL/CRITICAL SOURCES: New York Times Book Review, September 27, 1959, May 13, 1962, May 9, 1976, December 17, 1978; *New York Herald Tribune Book Review,* November 15, 1959, May 13, 1962; *Poetry,* April, 1960; *Saturday Review,* May 21, 1960; *Time,* May 18, 1962; *New Statesman,* January 31, 1964; *Yale Review,* March, 1964, October, 1972; *New York Times Magazine,* May 2, 1965; *Harper's,* October, 1965; Stephen Stepanchev, *American Poetry Since 1945,* Harper, 1965; *Times Literary Supplement,* June 9, 1966, January 4, 1980; *Chicago Review,* Volume XIX, number 1, 1966; Edward Hungerford, editor, *Poets in Progress: Critical Prefaces to Thirteen Modern American Poets,* Northwestern University Press, 1967; *Sewanee Review,* spring, 1969; Ronald Moran, *Louis Simpson,* Twayne, 1972; *Best Sellers,* June 15, 1972; *Contemporary Literary Criticism,* Gale, Volume IV, 1975, Volume VII, 1977, Volume IX, 1978; George S. Lensing and Ronald Moran, *Four Poets and the Emotive Imagination,* Louisiana State University Press, 1976; *Saturday Review/World,* April 3, 1976; *The Listener,* November 25, 1976; *Midstream,* December, 1976; *London Magazine,* February-March, 1977; *American Poetry Review,* January-February, 1979.

—Sketch by David A. Guy

* * *

SIMPSON, Ruth Mary Rasey 1902-
(Ruth M. Rasey)

PERSONAL: Born January 21, 1902, in Rupert, Vt.; daughter of Henry Lee (a farmer) and Hattie (Harwood) Rasey; married E. Wilbur Simpson (an industrial chemist), September 22, 1968. *Education:* New York State College for Teachers (now State University of New York College at Buffalo), B.S., 1932; graduate study at Cornell University, University of Buffalo (now State University of New York at Buffalo), University of New Hampshire, and State University of New York at Albany. *Politics:* "Liberal thinker." *Religion:* "Ecumenical." *Home and office:* 286 Goundry St., North Tonawanda, N.Y. 14120.

CAREER: Elementary school teacher in Salem, N.Y., 1921-24, Cambridge, N.Y., 1924-25, and Valley Falls, N.Y., 1925-27; Felton Junior High School, North Tonawanda, N.Y., English teacher, 1929-57; private tutor, 1957-68. Writer, 1938—. Chairman of youth committee, Y.W.C.A., 1946-49; chairman of festivals committee, Bicentennial Commission of North Tonawanda, 1975-77. *Member:* National League of American Pen Women (Western New York branch; secretary, 1950-52; president, 1958-60; chairman of writers' workshop, 1962-64), New York Retired Teachers Association, Vermont Historical Society, Bennington Museum Association, Alpha Delta Kappa (honorary life member). *Awards, honors:* Named woman of the year by Business and Professional Women of the Tonawandas, 1963; named one of ten outstanding women of North Tonawanda, 1976; received several awards from National League of American Pen Women for verse and nonfiction.

WRITINGS—Under name Ruth M. Rasey: *Out of the Saltbox,* Rand McNally, 1962, revised edition, Academy Books, 1975; *Mountain Fortitude* (poetry), Windy Row Press, 1969; *Hand-Hewn in Old Vermont,* Poly Two Press, 1979. Contributor of articles and poetry to periodicals, including *Nature, Vermont Life, Catholic Digest, Woman, National Parent Teacher,* and *Hospital Review.* Editor of National League of American Pen Women *Bulletin,* 1952-54; regional editor of *Pen Woman,* 1970-72.

WORK IN PROGRESS: Early New England Remedies.

SIDELIGHTS: Ruth Simpson told *CA:* "My chief motivation has been my love of nature and interest in natural history and early Americana, influenced by living in a fourth-generation Vermont home surrounded by family memorabilia. I am also greatly interested in activities promoting national and world peace, aid to those in need, basics in education, ecumenical religious development, and solar energy. I feel that much of the current writing is shallow and erroneous in content due to insufficient research or to a desire to sensationalize. It ignores sound values, also." *Avocational interests:* Travel, nature hikes, berry expeditions, bridge, reading (biography and Americana), rug-making, cooking, picnicking.

BIOGRAPHICAL/CRITICAL SOURCES: Manchester Journal (Manchester, Vt.), April 20, 1959; *Buffalo Evening News,* March 30, 1960; *Buffalo Courier Express,* November 17, 1961; *Tonawanda News* (North Tonawanda, N.Y.), October 16, 1964, October 22, 1964, October 15, 1976; *Kappan,* spring, 1966; *Buffalo Courier Express,* August 7, 1979; *Buffalo News,* November 25, 1979.

* * *

SINCLAIR, Bennie Lee 1939-

PERSONAL: Born April 15, 1939, in Greenville, S.C.; daughter of Waldo Graham (an engraver) and Bennie Lee (Ward) Sinclair; married Don Lewis (a potter), August 1, 1958. *Education:* Furman University, B.A., 1961. *Address:* Wildernesse, P.O. Box 345, Cleveland, S.C. 29635.

CAREER: Poet; poet-in-the-schools for South Carolina, 1972-73, 1973-74, under program sponsored by National Endowment for the Arts and South Carolina Arts Commission; Furman University, Greenville, S.C., instructor in creative writing, 1977-80; Fine Arts Center, Greenville, writer-in-residence, 1979-80. Conducts poetry readings in colleges and universities. *Awards, honors:* Stephen Vincent Benet Award for narrative poem from *Poet Lore,* 1970, for *David, the Grit Salesman;* citation, Best American Short Stories, 1972; Excellence in Writing Award in poetry, Winthrop College, 1978, for *The Arrowhead Scholar; South Carolina Re-*

view poetry award, 1972; awards for individual poems from state poetry societies of Pennsylvania, South Carolina, and Kentucky, and from Poets Club of Chicago.

WRITINGS: Little Chicago Suite (poems), Drummer Press, 1971, 2nd edition, Wildernesse Books, 1978; (editor) *Taproots: A Study in Cultural Exploration,* South Carolina Arts Commission, 1975; *The Arrowhead Scholar* (poems), Wildernesse Books, 1978; (editor) *The Fine Arts Center Story: A Living History,* [Greenville, S.C.], 1980. Also author of *The Conditions.* Work included in anthologies. Contributor of poems and short stories to literary magazines, including *Foxfire, South Carolina Review,* and *Human Voice.* Advisory and contributing editor, *Appalachian Heritage,* 1973—.

WORK IN PROGRESS: A collection of poems, *Light: For Pernecy and Ben;* a novel, *A Lynching in the Town.*

SIDELIGHTS: Bennie Lee Sinclair told *CA:* "I write because of the incurable disease 'cacoethis scribindi'—the insatiable urge to write. I write poetry, fiction, nonfiction, and aspire to drama.

"My home, Wildernesse, is a 135 acre wildlife and wild-plant sanctuary in the southern Appalachian mountains of South Carolina. Remote and beautiful, it affects my life and work strongly. I hope to spend the 1980's here, writing. My husband, Don Lewis, is a potter and builder who also affects my life and work strongly. His training by a Bauhaus master has led me to appreciate simplicity and directness of statement."

BIOGRAPHICAL/CRITICAL SOURCES: Furman Magazine (publication of Furman University), summer, 1973; *Auntie Bellum,* Volume I, number 3, 1977; *North Carolina Arts Journal,* Volume IV, number 12, 1979.

* * *

SINGER, Isaac Bashevis 1904-
(Isaac Bashevis, Isaac Singer; pseudonym: Isaac Warshofsky)

PERSONAL: Born July 14, 1904, in Radzymin, Poland; came to United States in 1935, naturalized in 1943; son of Pinchos Menachem (a rabbi and author) and Bathsheba (Zylberman) Singer; married first wife, Rachel (divorced); married Alma Haimann, February 14, 1940; children: (first marriage) Israel. *Education:* Attended Tachkemoni Rabbinical Seminary, 1920-27. *Religion:* Jewish. *Home:* 209 West 86th St., New York, N.Y. 10024.

CAREER: Novelist, short story writer, children's author, and translator. Worked in Poland for the Yiddish and Hebrew press, 1923-35; *Literarishe Bletter,* Warsaw, Poland, proofreader and translator, 1923-33; *Globus,* Warsaw, co-editor, 1932; *Jewish Daily Forward,* New York, N.Y., member of staff, 1935—. *Member:* Jewish Academy of Arts and Sciences (fellow), National Institute of Arts and Letters (fellow), Polish Institute of Arts and Sciences in America (fellow), American Academy of Arts and Sciences, P.E.N. *Awards, honors:* Louis Lamed Prize, 1950, for *The Family Moskat,* 1956, for *Satan in Goray;* National Institute of Arts and Letters and American Academy award in literature, 1959; Harry and Ethel Daroff Memorial Fiction Award, Jewish Book Council of America, 1963, for *The Slave;* D.H.L., Hebrew Union College, Los Angeles, Calif., 1963; National Council on the Arts grant, 1966; National Endowment for the Arts grant, 1966-67; *Playboy* magazine award for best fiction, 1967; Newbery Honor Book Award, 1967, for *Zlateh the Goat and Other Stories,* 1968, for *The Fearsome Inn;* Bancarella Prize, 1968, for Italian translation of *The Family Moskat;* Brandeis University Creative Arts Medal for Poetry-Fiction, 1970; National Book Award, for children's literature, 1970, for *A Day of Pleasure,* for fiction, 1974, for *A Crown of Feathers and Other Stories;* D.Litt. from Texas Christian University, 1972, and Colgate University, 1972; Ph.D., Hebrew University, Jerusalem, 1973; Litt.D., Bard College, 1974; Agnon Gold Medal, 1975; Nobel Prize for Literature, 1978.

WRITINGS—All writings originally in Yiddish; novels: *Der Satan in Gorey,* [Warsaw], 1935, translation by Jacob Sloan published as *Satan in Goray,* Noonday, 1955, reprinted, Farrar, Straus, 1979; (under name Isaac Bashevis) *Di Familie Mushkat,* two volumes, [New York], 1950, translation by A. H. Gross published under name Isaac Bashevis Singer as *The Family Moskat,* Knopf, 1950, reprinted, Fawcett, 1975; *The Magician of Lublin,* translation by Elaine Gottlieb and Joseph Singer, Noonday, 1960, reprinted, Fawcett, 1979; *The Slave,* translation by author and Cecil Hemley, Farrar, Straus, 1962, reprinted, Fawcett, 1980; *The Manor,* translation by Gottlieb and J. Singer, Farrar, Straus, 1967; *The Estate,* translation by Gottlieb, J. Singer, and Elizabeth Shub, Farrar, Straus, 1969; *Enemies: A Love Story* (first published in *Jewish Daily Forward* under title "Sonim, di Geshichte fun a Liebe," 1966), translation by Aliza Shevrin and Shub, Farrar, Straus, 1972; *Shosha,* Farrar, Straus, 1978.

Short story collections; published by Farrar, Straus, except as indicated: *Gimpel the Fool and Other Stories,* translation by Saul Bellow and others, Noonday, 1957, reprinted, Fawcett, 1980; *The Spinoza of Market Street and Other Stories,* translation by Gottlieb and others, 1961, reprinted, Fawcett, 1980; *Short Friday and Other Stories,* translation by Ruth Whitman and others, 1964; *Selected Short Stories,* edited by Irving Howe, Modern Library, 1966; *The Seance and Other Stories,* translation by Whitman, Roger H. Klein, and others, 1968; *A Friend of Kafka and Other Stories,* 1970; *An Isaac Bashevis Singer Reader,* 1971; *A Crown of Feathers and Other Stories,* 1973; *Passions and Other Stories,* 1975; *Old Love,* 1979.

Juvenile books; fiction, except as indicated; translations by author and Elizabeth Shub; published by Farrar, Straus, except as indicated: *Mazel and Schlimazel; or, The Milk of a Lioness,* Harper, 1966; *Zlateh the Goat and Other Stories,* Harper, 1966; *The Fearsome Inn,* Scribner, 1967; *When Schlemiel Went to Warsaw and Other Stories,* 1968; *Elijah the Slave: A Hebrew Legend Retold* (nonfiction), 1970; *Joseph and Koza; or, The Sacrifice to the Vistula,* 1970; *Alone in the Wild Forest,* 1971; *The Topsy-Turvy Emperor of China,* Harper, 1971; *The Wicked City* (nonfiction), 1972; *The Fools of Chelm and Their History,* 1973; *Why Noah Chose the Dove* (nonfiction), 1974; *A Tale of Three Wishes,* 1975; *Naftali the Storyteller and His Horse, Sus, and Other Stories,* 1976.

Autobiography: (Under pseudonym Isaac Warshofsky) *Mayn Tatn's Bes-din Shtub,* [New York], 1956, translation by Channah Kleinerman-Goldstein published under name Isaac Bashevis Singer as *In My Father's Court,* Farrar, Straus, 1966; *A Day of Pleasure: Stories of a Boy Growing Up in Warsaw* (juvenile), translation by author and Shub, Farrar, Straus, 1969; *A Little Boy in Search of God: Mysticism in a Personal Light,* Doubleday, 1976; *A Young Man in Search of Love,* Doubleday, 1978.

Plays: "The Mirror," produced in New Haven, Conn., 1973; (with Leah Napolin) *Yentle, the Yeshiva Boy* (produced on Broadway at Atkinson Theatre, 1974), Samuel French, 1978; "Schlemiel the First," produced in New Haven, Conn., 1974; (with Eve Friedman) "Teibele and Her Demon," first produced in Minneapolis at Guthrie Theatre, 1978, produced on Broadway at Atkinson Theatre, December 16, 1979.

Translator into Yiddish: Knut Hamsen, *Pan,* Wilno (Warsaw), 1928; Erich Maria Remarque, *All Quiet on the Western Front,* Wilno, 1930; Thomas Mann, *The Magic Mountain,* four volumes, Wilno, 1930; Remarque, *The Road Back,* Wilno, 1930; Leon S. Glaser, *From Moscow to Jerusalem,* privately printed, 1938.

Other books: (Editor with Elaine Gottlieb) *Prism 2,* Twayne, 1965; (contributor) Anatol Filmus, *Tully Filmus,* Jewish Publication Society of America, 1971; (with Ira Moscowitz) *The Hasidim: Paintings, Drawings, and Etchings,* Crown, 1973; *Nobel Lecture,* Farrar, Straus, 1979; *Isaac Bashevis Singer on Literature and Life,* University of Arizona Press, 1979.

Contributor of stories and articles to periodicals in the United States and Poland, including *Die Yiddische Welt, Commentary, Esquire, New Yorker, Globus, Literarishe Bletter, Harper's,* and *Partisan Review.*

SIDELIGHTS: Widely proclaimed to be the foremost living writer of Yiddish literature, Isaac Bashevis Singer stands clearly outside the mainstream and basic traditions of both Yiddish and American literature. Singer's writing has proven difficult to categorize, with critics attaching to him various and sometimes contradictory labels in an attempt to elucidate his work. He has been called a modernist, although he personally dislikes most contemporary fiction, and he has also been accused of being captivated by the past, of writing in a dying language despite his English fluency, of setting his fiction in a world that no longer exists, the *shtetls* (Jewish ghettos) of Eastern Europe which were obliterated by Hitler's campaign against the Jews. Despite the attention called to the mysticism, the prolific presence of the supernatural, and the profoundly religious nature of his writing, he has been called both a realist and a pessimist. Undeniably a difficult author to place in critical perspective, Singer addresses himself to the problems of labeling his work in an interview with Cyrena N. Pondrom: "People always need a name for things, so whatever you will write or whatever you will do, they like to put you into a certain category. Even if you would be new, they would like to feel that a name is already prepared for you in advance. . . . I hope that one day somebody will find a new name for me, not use the old ones."

Commenting on the paradoxical nature of Isaac Singer and his work, Irving Howe states: "Singer writes in Yiddish, a language that no amount of energy or affection seems likely to save from extinction. He writes about a world that is gone, destroyed with a brutality beyond historical comparison. He writes within a culture, the remnant of Yiddish in the Western world, that is more than a little dubious about his purpose and stress. . . . And he does all this without a sigh or apology, without so much as a Jewish groan. It strikes one as a kind of inspired madness: here is a man living in New York City, a sophisticated and clever writer, who composes stories about places like Frampol, Bilgoray, Kreshev, *as if they were still there.*"

More than most writers, the key to Singer's work lies in his background, in his roots in the Polish Yiddish-speaking Jewish ghettos. "I was born with the feeling that I am part of an unlikely adventure, something that couldn't have happened, but happened just the same," Singer once remarked to a *Book Week* interviewer. Born in a small Polish town, his father was a Hassidic rabbi and both his grandfathers were also rabbis. Visiting his maternal grandfather in Bilgoray as a young boy, Singer learned of life in the *shtetl,* which would become the setting of much of his later work. The young Singer received a basic Jewish education preparing him to follow his father and grandfathers' steps into the rabbinical vocation; he studied the Torah, the Talmud, the Cabala, and other sacred Jewish books. An even stronger influence than his education and his parents' orthodoxy was his older brother, the novelist I. J. Singer, who broke with the family's orthodoxy and began to write secular stories. Attempting to overcome the influence of his brother's rationalism and to strengthen the cause of religion, his parents told him stories of *dybbuks* (wandering souls in Jewish folklore believed to enter a human body and control its actions), possessions, and other spiritual mysteries. Singer has commented that he was equally fascinated by his parents' mysticism and his brother's rationalism. Although he was eventually to break from both traditions, this dualism characterizes his writing.

His desire to become a secular writer caused a painful conflict within Singer and with his family; it represented a break from traditional ways. Aaron, the writer-protagonist of *Shosha* "senses that the literary vocation cannot provide a substitute for the life-giving bread of the Jewish religion from which he has separated himself," according to Edward Alexander. Both *Shosha* and *Young Man in Search of Love,* Alexander further elaborates, "dwell on the special difficulties of the Yiddish writer, who felt isolated and frustrated not only because his choice of such a vocation made him a *meshumad* (apostate) in the eyes of the religious, but, also, because he was 'stuck with a language and culture no one recognized outside a small circle of Yiddishists and radicals.' Here was a sort of double exile." Reviewing the autobiographical *In My Father's Court,* Herbert Leibowitz comments: "What Singer writes of his brother becomes true of himself later: 'he had deserted the old, but there was nothing in the new that he could call his own.' The two brothers became that familiar figure in the modern landscape (and in Singer's fiction): the spiritual outlander, the man whose soul is the battleground for a war between the sacred and the profane, the erotic and the ascetic."

Eventually, Singer rejected his parents' orthodoxy, although not their faith in God. He joined his brother in Warsaw and began working for the Hebrew and Yiddish press and also began to publish stories. At first he wrote in Hebrew but switched to Yiddish because he felt that Hebrew was a dead language (this was before its revival as the national language of Israel). Feeling that the Nazis would certainly invade Poland, Singer followed his brother to the United States where he began to write for the *Jewish Daily Forward.* Here he wrote fiction under the name Isaac Bashevis and nonfiction under the pseudonym Isaac Warshofsky. Most of Singer's stories appeared first in the *Jewish Daily Forward* in their original Yiddish; the novels appeared in serialized form.

Singer still does all of his writing in Yiddish, and much of his large body of writing remains untranslated. Before he felt sufficiently fluent in English, Singer had to rely on other people to do the translations; his nephew Joseph Singer was responsible for much of it. Now, Singer usually does a rough translation into English himself and has someone help him polish the English version and work on the idioms. The English translations are often a "second original," according to Singer, differing structurally from the Yiddish. "I used to play with the idea [of writing in English]," Singer has admitted, "but never seriously. Never. I always knew that a writer has to write in his own language or not at all." Inevitably, much of Singer's fine style is lost in translation. Although some Yiddish critics have accused him of stylistic ineptitude in Yiddish, Irving Howe believes that "no translation . . . could possibly suggest the full idiomatic richness and syntactical verve of Singer's Yiddish. Singer has left behind the oratorical sententiousness to which Yiddish literature is prone, he has abandoned its leisurely meandering pace, which might be called the *shtetl* rhythm, and has developed a style that is both swift and dense, nervous and thick. His sentences are short and abrupt; his rhythms coiled, intense, short-breathed."

Lance Morrow defines Yiddish as "that subtle, rich, vital, and probably doomed tongue. . . . Yiddish, based originally on a Middle High German dialect, developed in the tenth century and eventually became a wonderfully supple international language with borrowings from almost every Indo-European language. Among Jews, Hebrew was the language of piety; Yiddish, quivering with life and idiom, was the medium of the street. Before World War II it was the principal language of some eleven million people; now it is spoken by four million and fading yearly." More optimistic than Morrow about the fate of the Yiddish language, Singer calls Yiddish in his Nobel lecture "a language of exile, without a land, without frontiers, not supported by any government, a language which possesses no words for weapons, ammunition, military exercises, war tactics; a language that was despised by both gentiles and emancipated Jews. . . . Yiddish has not yet said its last word. It contains treasures that have not been revealed to the eyes of the world. It was the tongue of martyrs and saints, of dreamers and cabalists—rich in humor and in memories that mankind may never forget. In a figurative way, Yiddish is the wise and humble language of us all, the idiom of the frightened and hopeful humanity."

Yet Singer is realistic about the fate of Yiddish. Morrow quotes him as saying that the language "is a tragedy and a responsibility." Singer has commented on the dwindling Yiddish-reading audience: "You don't feel very happy about writing in a language when you know it dies from day to day. . . . The only thing is, I don't have this feeling while I write; I don't choose to remember it. . . . When I sit down to write I have a feeling that I'm talking maybe to millions or maybe to nobody." In a lighter vein, Singer told Morrow that one of the reasons he writes in Yiddish is that "I like to write ghost stories and nothing fits a ghost better than a dying language. The deader the language, the more alive is the ghost. Ghosts love Yiddish, and as far as I know, they all speak it."

Awarding him the Nobel Prize for Literature in 1978, the Swedish Academy cited Singer for "his impassioned narrative art which, with roots in a Polish-Jewish cultural tradition, brings universal human conditions to life." In his acceptance speech, Singer said that "the high honor bestowed upon me by the Swedish Academy is also a recognition of the Yiddish language." Yet Singer's sternest detractors are other Yiddish writers and American Yiddishists. Besides the charge of stylistic ineptitude, Yiddish critics, according to Lothar Kahn, have accused Singer of "deliberately misrepresenting life in the *shtetls* and city ghettos of Poland. . . . He has been faulted for a morbid fascination with animal slaughter, blood, demons . . . and with the dominant presence of sex and fantasy. . . . His critics have also been visibly disturbed by the fact that Singer has not sentimentalized Jewish life in a world that is no more, and whose inhabitants were ruthlessly slain."

Singer has deliberately disassociated himself from the American Yiddishists. He said in the interview with Pondrom: "Yiddish culture and I are two different things. Though I love Yiddish, I'm not a Yiddishist, because these people really want to create a movement. They always talk about a movement—the Jewish literature, the Jewish theater, or the Yiddish theater. I'm not a man of movements at all. . . . I know that movements and mediocrity always go together. Whatever becomes a mass movement . . . would be bad. . . . Also, these people were all on the socialistic side. They always thought about creating a better world. And, because of this, they were sentimental, which is not my way; I would also like to see a better world, but I don't think, really, that men can create it." Kahn points out that Singer believes "what human contentment is attainable can be found on the individual, not the social level, in the moral and spiritual and not the sociopolitical sphere, in man's quest for self-improvement more than in dicta and programs from above and for all. . . . Singer thus cannot be expected to please progressives, socialists, utopians or those preaching a politically committed literature. He might faintly suggest that the artist more than the statesman can achieve progress and human satisfaction." According to Howe, Singer is not caught up in the Enlightenment as most Yiddish writers are. He "shares very little in the collective sensibility . . . of the Yiddish masters; he does not unambiguously celebrate in the common man as a paragon of goodness; he is impatient with the sensual deprivation implicit in the value of *edelkeit* (refinement, nobility); and above all he moves away from a central assumption of both Yiddish literature in particular and the 19th century in general, the assumption of an imanent fate or end in human existence."

The criticism of the Yiddishists that Singer's work is saturated with sex has some validity. Stefan Kanfer believes Singer to be "one of the least explicit but most sexually charged of modern writers." Singer himself told Kenneth Turan: "I like to write about sex and love, which is not kosher to the orthodox people. I believe in God, but I don't believe that God wants man to run away completely from pleasure. If he has created men and women with a great desire to love and be loved, there must be something in it; it can't be all bad. Love and sex are the things that give life some value, some zest. Miserable as flesh and blood is, it is still the best you can get."

Although his preoccupation with sex links him to much of twentieth-century literature, Singer dislikes modern fiction which focuses on the writer revealing his inner self and complaining about his problems and complexes. Singer commented to Edith Gold, "There is more art, more challenge in writing a real story than in just sitting there and complaining." He also denigrates the tendency for the writer to take on a cause, to be not motivated by art for its own sake but by political, sociological, or psychological postures. Singer told Harold Flender that one of the things he learned from his brother was that "while facts never become obsolete or stale, commentaries *always* do. . . . Imagine Homer explaining the deeds of his heroes according to the old Greek philosophy, or the psychology of his time. Why nobody would read Homer! Fortunately, Homer just gives us the images and the facts; and because of this the *Iliad* and the *Odyssey* are fresh in our time."

Singer believes that the only role of fiction is entertainment. As he comments to Sanford Pinsker: "I never thought that my fiction—my kind of writing—had any other purpose than to be read and enjoyed by the reader. I never sit down to write a novel to make a better world or to create good feelings towards the Jews or for any other purpose. I knew this from the very beginning, that writing fiction has no other purpose than to give enjoyment to a reader. . . . I consider myself an entertainer. . . . I mean an entertainer of good people, of intellectual people who cannot be entertained by cheap stuff. And I think this is true about fiction in all times. . . . Whatever other good things come out from fiction are to say sheer profit." He reiterated this theory of the function of literature to Pondrom: "Literature is a force without direction. . . . Literature stirs the mind; it makes you think about a million things, but it does not lead you." He told Alexandra Johnson, "Whenever a writer tries to be more than a storyteller, he becomes less."

Singer is the ultimate storyteller; according to Gold, "for Singer . . . literature means storytelling." Considered to be a master of the short story, it is his most effective and favorite genre because, as he has explained, it is more possible to be perfect in the short story than in a longer work. Also Singer doesn't think that the supernatural, which is his element, lends itself well to longer, novelistic writing. Singer's style in the short story is simple, spare, in the tradition of the spoken tale. Paddy Chayefsky writes: "There is none of the cumbersome complexity of modern writing, no obsession with the externals of relationships, no fumbling about for profundity beneath the civilized sigh." In a *Commentary* interview, Singer remarked: "When I tell a story, I tell a story. I don't try to discuss, criticize, or analyze my characters." Irving Howe calls him "above and beyond everything else . . . a great performer in ways that remind one of Twain, Dickens, Sholom Aleichem," and in another writing states that Singer "simply as a literary performer has few peers among living writers." Maureen Howard says that in his short stories Singer "writes as if words themselves were not questioned in high literary circles, as if we had been lectured and analyzed quite enough, as if, given the possibility of thorough destruction, stories still matter." Singer borrows from everyday life in order to produce his stories; he told Gold, "every encounter with a human being is for me a potential story." Moreover, Singer feels that it is the writer's responsibility to find the stories which best fit him. "Every human being—not only every writer—has stories which only he can tell," he commented in an interview with Alexandra Johnson. "These are *his* stories. The important thing for a writer is to find and trust these stories."

For Singer, his special stories, the ones that belong to him, are placed for the most part in the nineteenth- and early twentieth-century *shtetl*. He has been criticized for his overuse of this setting, with some critics suggesting that he is not effective in any other surrounding. Singer told Morrow: "I prefer to write about the world which I knew, which I know, best. This is Bilgoray, Lublin, the Jews of Kreshev. This is enough for me. I can get from these people art. I don't need to go to the North Pole and write a novel about the Eskimos who live in that neighborhood. I write about the things where I grew up, and where I feel completely at home." Ruth R. Wisse believes that the *shtetl* stories "vivify a world whose beatific fictional existence is set into fiercely tragic perspective by its historical extinction. Most of Singer's stories inspire a fresh awareness of human malignancy and remorseless fate." Morrow calls Singer's world "a pure act of devotional memory, protected and elaborated, made to move, brought alive by a tender and sinister imagination. . . . By writing about a lost world, he achieves an eerie distancing effect, an undertone something like what Hawthorne accomplished in his demon-ridden tales of earliest Puritan New England."

Jacob Sonntag notes that even in those stories which take place in a modern setting, such as *Enemies: A Love Story* which has modern-day New York City as its background, "the people we encounter are the same we have met before in Warsaw or Tzvikev and other *shtetls* and villages in prewar Poland. It is as if Singer was looking for them among the new arrivals, those who have survived the ghettos, concentration camps, and the deportations to Siberia and, after the war, had found their way to the New World; and having found them, had made them once again the vehicle of his imagery and morbid philosophy." Singer's new settings follow the classical pattern of the European Jewish emigre—from East European ghetto to New York or Miami. A *Virginia Quarterly Review* writer believes that "Singer, like Nabokov, is a great spanner of widely different cultures—and this makes him very modern and very American." Michael Wood points out that more than half the stories in *A Crown of Feathers and Other Stories* deal with immigrants to the New World. "Singer is thus forced to find in isolated individuals what he formerly found in the re-created memories of small East European communities: an image of the ongoing Jewish enterprise, a mark of the indefatigable persistence of the past."

Wisse makes another connection to the *shtetl* setting and the use of Old World characters, linking them to Singer's use of Yiddish. According to Wisse, Singer wrote an essay in 1943 which complained that Yiddish in America was in a serious decline. There were no new expressions to match the modern experience of Jews in America. "This explains," wrote Singer, "why the best Yiddish prose writers consciously or unconsciously avoid writing about American life. They don't want to fake the dialogue, and they are fed up with describing yet again the narrow circle of coarse aging immigrants. . . . The prose writer, who must develop a broad cast of characters, has to yield to linguistic pressure, recognizing that he is a slave to the past, where Yiddish was thoroughly at home." According to Wisse, Singer "plucks Yiddish prose out of the 20th century to move it back to its roots, to a culture ruled by the impulses of evil and good rather than by the id and superego, or fascism and democracy. . . . His analysis serves as a kind of justification for returning artistically to a world he had abandoned in fact. . . . Others have justified Singer's method, noting that in these traditional Jewish settings, the demonic still retains the power to anger and shock . . . [and the *shtetl*] provided him with the only convincing medium for the representation of sin on a still-human scale."

Singer is preoccupied with the problem of sin, with man's capacity to know God, but because he does not insert philosophy or commentary directly into his work, the characters must speak for him. William Peden calls his characters "prodigious, insatiable, indomitable talkers; one has the feeling that if the hydrogen bomb is finally dropped, the last sound on earth will be that of one of Singer's wonderful people, relating a tale of love, lust, betrayal, passion, demonic possession, madness, success, frustration, suicide, life." Maureen Howard also finds the Singerian characters delightful and links them to the folktale-like quality of his work. "These inspired characters, rabbis, charlatans, whores, so good, so evil, are out of a world that can never be parochial, a world out of our childhood legends, out of medieval romance, out of episodic sagas," Howard writes. "These are the stories that were once told to sustain life and community of an evening in any house, any town. But being at least partially literary in origin, Singer's tales are also more sophisticated than we first imagine. . . . In Singer's balance of innocence and sophistication is really where his magic lies."

The word magic is not missplaced, for Singer uses the irrational—the world of ghosts, possessions, *dybbuks*, magicians, seances, religious fanaticism, sexual perversion, pacts with the devil—prolifically in his stories. A *Virginia Quar-*

terly Review writer comments that one of Singer's aims is "to present the irrational in the clearest and most disciplined of styles." A *Times Literary Supplement* reviewer writes: "What gives his stories their undoubted strength is a quality common to all folk literature: an exact literalness about the visible combined with an unquestioned acceptance of the invisible." In his tales, replete with mysticism, imps, and ghosts, it is not unusual to see the dead move and dance among the living. Reviewing *The Slave,* David Boroff writes: "Few writers since Shakespeare have been able to evoke so harrowingly the nightmare world of savage animals . . . and of man's kinship with them." Singer believes in the possibility that the supernatural entities of which he writes are real. As he told Gold, "there are many things we do not yet understand. We are surrounded by secrets and entities of which we have no inkling. These things may all exist, just as electricity existed before Franklin discovered it." Singer uses the electricity analogy often, commenting that a pre-Franklin man probably thought that the sparks which emanated from his wool sweater on a dark night were of supernatural origin. "We also see sparks," notes Singer, "but we ignore them." He told Pinsker that he writes about *dybbuks* and devils "because these facts express the subconscious better than any other events a writer can write about. The story of the *dybbuk* is always the story of a suppressed human spirit. . . . I think all my heroes are possessed people—possessed by a mania, by a fixed idea, by a strange level of fear or passion." Yet Singer makes clear that his demonic possessions are not merely Freudian appelations. "I believe that there may be such a thing as possession, I actually believe that there are powers in this world of which we have no inkling, but which have an influence on our lives and on our way of thinking. . . . I personally believe in God and in spirits and in many things about which other men think are only superstition and folklore."

Singer's personal belief in God permeates his work, making him, as Donald Phelps says, "a pre-eminently religious writer." He commented to Pinsker that "by losing religion we have lost a lot of our spirit, a lot of what sustained us and kept us alive. It is true that I am a Jewish writer, but I am also, in a way, a philosophic writer. My philosophy is expressed not in philosophical terms but in events, in stories. But the eternal questions bother me all my life. . . . What is expressed in my stories is the doubt about realities, the question of the problem of human suffering and so on and so on. But even though it is Jewish, it is also universal because these are the questions which all men ask in all times and in all places." Indeed, Linda G. Zatlin believes that Singer's obsession with "the individual's struggle to find a viable faith in an age possessed by this very problem" places him in some perspective as far as being a twentieth-century writer. According to Zatlin, although most of his stories are placed in nineteenth-century Eastern Europe and appear on the surface to be simple folk tales, they portray the dilemma of modern man. "Specifically Singer predicates his fiction on the idea that the presence or absence of human faith in God is an eternal, omnipresent dilemma which the individual must resolve for himself, and he consistently shows that man's fate . . . is directly correlated to his degree of faith in God." Zatlin views Singer's characters as allegorical representations of three postures of individual belief. She outlines these categories of Singerian characters as the "God-chooser; he directs his energy toward living consistently within His laws; . . . the God-denier; he has already submitted to the forces of evil by embracing Satan; . . . the doubter; he ruminates at length about God's existence but utilizes his drives in resolving his conflict and arrives ultimately at complete faith in or denial of Him. This last group illustrates most clearly the dilemma of modern man."

Yet Singer allows himself a healthy skepticism; he has been called, despite his deep faith in God, a profoundly pessimistic writer. Phelps comments that "by the token of Singer's faith, skepticism is not a self-protective distrust of any certainty, but a recognition of reality's rich elusiveness." Kahn also calls attention to Singer's skeptical and doubting nature, calling him "both a skeptic and a pessimist. He is dubious about human nature which can so quickly succumb to lusts and savagery. He is even more dubious about men's ability to know God or the ultimate secrets of the universe. . . . He is attracted to a past world which never doubted the moral importance of life, but he knows the clock cannot be turned back." Compared by an interviewer to other Yiddish masters, Singer commented: "I consider myself—in spite of all my beliefs—a modern man, more free to think, more free to doubt." That he doubts about man's future is clear in his comments to Harold Flender. "Nothing will save us," says Singer. "We will make a lot of progress, but we will keep on suffering, and there will never be an end to it. We will always invent new sources of pain. . . . Being a pessimist to me means to be a realist."

Ted Hughes summarizes Singer's extraordinary talent: "No psychological terminology or current literary method has succeeded in rendering such a profound, unified and fully apprehended account of the Divine, the Infernal, and the suffering space of self-determination between, all so convincingly interconnected, and fascinatingly peopled. . . . [To] isolate his decisive virtue: whatever region his writing inhabits, it is blazing with life and actuality. His powerful, wise, deep, full-face paragraphs make almost every other modern fiction seem by comparison labored, shallow, overloaded with alien and undigested junk, too fancy, fuddled, not quite squared up to life."

BIOGRAPHICAL/CRITICAL SOURCES—Books: Alfred Kazin, *Contemporaries,* Atlantic Monthly Press, 1962; Richard Kostelanetz, editor, *On Contemporary Literature,* Avon, 1964; Stanley Edgar Hyman, *Standards: A Chronicle of Books for Our Time,* Horizon Press, 1966; Isaac Bashevis Singer, *Selected Short Stories,* introduction by Irving Howe, Modern Library, 1966; Singer, *In My Father's Court,* Farrar, Straus, 1966; Marcia Allentuck, editor, *The Achievement of Isaac Bashevis Singer,* Southern Illinois University Press, 1967; Irving H. Buchen, *Isaac Bashevis Singer and the Eternal Past,* New York University Press, 1968; Charles A. Madison, *Yiddish Literature: Its Scope and Major Writers,* Ungar, 1968; Irving Malin, editor, *Critical Views of Isaac Bashevis Singer,* New York University Press, 1969; Donald Phelps, *Covering Ground,* Ascot Press, 1969; Singer, *A Day of Pleasure: Stories of a Boy Growing Up in Warsaw,* Farrar, Straus, 1969.

William H. Gass, *Fiction and the Figures of Life,* Knopf, 1970; Sanford Pinsker, *The Schlemiel as Metaphor: Studies in the Yiddish and American Jewish Novel,* Southern Illinois University Press, 1971; Irving Malin, *Isaac Bashevis Singer,* Ungar, 1972; *Contemporary Literary Criticism,* Gale, Volume I, 1973, Volume III, 1975, Volume VI, 1976, Volume IX, 1978, Volume XI, 1979; Alfred Kazin, *Bright Book of Life: American Novelists and Storytellers from Hemingway to Mailer,* Atlantic Monthly Press, 1973; *Children's Literature Review,* Volume I, Gale, 1976; *Authors in the News,* Gale, Volume I, 1976, Volume II, 1976; Singer, *A Little Boy in Search of God: Mysticism in a Personal Light,* Doubleday, 1976; Singer, *A Young Man in Search of Love,* Doubleday, 1978; Paul Kresh, *Isaac Bashevis Singer: The Magician of West 86th Street,* Dial, 1979.

Periodicals: *New York Times Book Review,* December 29, 1957, June 26, 1960, October 22, 1961, June 17, 1962, November 15, 1964, October 8, 1967, June 25, 1972, November 4, 1973, November 2, 1975, April 30, 1978, July 23, 1978, October 28, 1979; *Saturday Review,* January 25, 1958, November 25, 1961, June 16, 1962, November 21, 1964, September 19, 1970, July 22, 1972, July 8, 1978; *Spectator,* October 17, 1958, September 15, 1961, May 11, 1962, June 10, 1966; *Commentary,* November, 1958, October, 1960, November, 1963, February, 1965, February, 1979; *New Republic,* November 24, 1958, January 2, 1961, November 13, 1961, June 18, 1962, November 3, 1973, October 25, 1975, September 16, 1978, October 21, 1978; *Times Literary Supplement,* January 2, 1959, May 4, 1962.

Atlantic, August, 1962, January, 1965, July, 1970, January, 1979; *Judaism,* fall, 1962, winter, 1974, winter, 1979; *Jewish Currents,* November, 1962; *Wilson Library Bulletin,* December, 1962; *Criticism,* fall, 1963; *Kenyon Review,* spring, 1964; *Reporter,* April 22, 1965; *New York Review of Books,* April 22, 1965, February 7, 1974, December 7, 1978; *Book Week,* July 4, 1965; *Harper's,* October, 1965, September, 1978; *Encounter,* March, 1966; *New York Times,* October 30, 1966, January 29, 1967, July 10, 1978, July 22, 1978, December 9, 1978, October 17, 1979, December 5, 1979, December 16, 1979, December 17, 1979, April 19, 1980; *Hudson Review,* Volume XIX, number 4, winter, 1966-67, Volume XXVII, number 1, spring, 1974; *Jewish Quarterly,* winter, 1966-67, autumn, 1972; *Minnesota Review,* Volume VII, number 3, 1967; *Midstream,* March, 1967; *Illustrated London News,* March 9, 1967; *Punch,* April 5, 1967; *Time,* October 20, 1967, September 21, 1970, October 27, 1975, November 3, 1975; *Christian Science Monitor,* October 28, 1967, September 5, 1978, September 18, 1978; *Book World,* October 29, 1967, March 3, 1968, September 1, 1968, November 25, 1979; *Paris Review,* fall, 1968; *Critique,* Volume XI, number 2, 1969, Volume XIV, number 2, 1972; *Contemporary Literature,* Volume X, number 1, winter, 1969.

Best Sellers, October 1, 1970; *Southern Review,* spring, 1972, spring, 1973; *Newsweek,* June 26, 1972, November 12, 1973; *Books and Bookmen,* October, 1973, December, 1974; *Studies in Short Fiction,* summer, 1974, fall, 1976; *Sewanee Review,* fall, 1974; *Village Voice,* February 2, 1976; *Critical Quarterly,* spring, 1976; *Virginia Quarterly Review,* spring, 1976; *New Review,* June, 1976; *New Leader,* August 14, 1978; *Washington Post,* October 6, 1978, October 16, 1979, October 26, 1979; *Detroit Free Press,* October 6, 1978, October 24, 1979; *Los Angeles Times,* November 8, 1978; *People,* December 11, 1978; *Vogue,* April, 1979; *Christian Century,* May 16, 1979; *World Literature Today,* spring, 1979.

—*Sketch by Linda Metzger*

* * *

SIRACUSA, Joseph 1929-

PERSONAL: Born July 30, 1929, in Siculiana, Italy; naturalized U.S. citizen; son of Cristoforo (a post office employee) and Cristina (Piro) Siracusa. *Education:* Attended University of Palermo, 1948-49; University of Rochester, B.A., 1958; University of Illinois, M.A., 1959, Ph.D., 1962. *Politics:* Independent. *Religion:* Roman Catholic. *Home:* 35 Kernwood Dr., Rochester, N.Y. 14624. *Office:* Department of Modern Languages, State University of New York College, Brockport, N.Y. 14420.

CAREER: Rice University, Houston, Tex., assistant professor of Spanish and Italian, 1962-65; Del Mar College, Corpus Christi, Tex., associate professor of modern languages, 1965-67; State University of New York College at Brockport, 1967—, began as associate professor, currently professor of Spanish and Italian. Visiting professor of Italian linguistics at Central Connecticut State College, summer, 1960; visiting professor of Spanish linguistics at Knox College, summer, 1961 and 1962, University of North Carolina at Chapel Hill, summer, 1963, and at Universidad Maria Cristina, San Lorenzo del Escorial, Spain, summer, 1966, all under auspices of National Defense Education Act. Associate director of National Defense Education Act Institute, Rice University, summer, 1965. *Military service:* U.S. Army Reserve, 1959. *Member:* American Association of Teachers of Spanish and Portuguese, Phi Beta Kappa. *Awards, honors:* Woodrow Wilson national fellowship, 1958.

WRITINGS: (With Joseph L. Laurenti) *Literary Relations between Spain and Italy: A Bibliographic Survey of Comparative Literature/Relaciones literarias entre Espana e Italia: Ensayo de una bibliografia de literatura comparada,* G. K. Hall, 1972; *Federico Garcia Lorca y su mundo: Ensayo de una bibliografia general,* Scarecrow, 1974. Contributor to periodicals, including *Books Abroad, World Literature Today, Modern Language Journal,* and *Lingua Nostra.*

* * *

SKAGGS, Jimmy M(arion) 1940-

PERSONAL: Born June 13, 1940, in Gorman, Tex.; son of Clarence Elijah and Bessie (Martin) Skaggs; married Janette Johnson, March 30, 1961 (divorced, 1976); children: Janeen, Jessica, Joy Dale. *Education:* Attended Odessa College, 1958-60; Sul Ross State College (now University), B.S. (cum laude), 1962; Texas Tech University, M.A., 1965, Ph.D., 1970. *Politics:* Democrat. *Religion:* None. *Home:* 2323 North Woodlawn, No. 423, Wichita, Kan. 67220. *Office:* Department of American Studies, Wichita State University, Wichita, Kan. 67208.

CAREER: Teacher in public schools in Lubbock, Tex., 1962-65; Texas Tech University, Lubbock, instructor in history and deputy archivist of Southwest Collection, 1968-70; Wichita State University, Wichita, Kan., assistant professor, 1970-73, associate professor of economics, 1973-75, associate professor of American studies, 1975-76, professor of economics and American studies, 1976—, chairman of department of American studies, 1975—. Historical consultant, Philips Petroleum Co., 1979—. *Member* Southwest Social Science Association, Texas State Historical Association.

WRITINGS: (With David B. Gracy II and Roy Sylvan Dunn) *Irrigation in the Southwest: A Center for Historical Research in the Southwest Collection,* Texas Technological College, 1968; (editor) J. L. Hill, *The End of the Cattle Trail,* Pemberton, 1969; (contributor) Wilson M. Hudson, editor, *Hunters and Healers,* Encino Press, 1971; (editor with Fane Downs and Winifred Vigness) *Chronicles of the Yaqui Expedition,* West Texas Museum Association, 1972; *Wichita, Kansas: Economic Origins of Metropolitan Growth, 1870-1960,* Center for Business and Economic Research, Wichita State University, 1972; *The Cattle-Trailing Industry: Between Supply and Demand, 1866-1890,* University Press of Kansas, 1973; *An Interpretive History of the American Economy,* Grid Publishing, 1975; (with Seymour V. Connor) *Broadcloth and Britches: The Santa Fe Trade,* Texas A&M University Press, 1977; (editor with Glenn W. Miller) *Metropolitan Wichita: Past Present and Future,* Regents Press of

Kansas, 1978; (editor) *The Ranch and Range in Oklahoma,* Oklahoma Historical Society, 1978.

Contributor to yearbooks and to *Handbook of Texas.* Contributor of more than forty articles and reviews to professional journals and regional periodicals, including *Kansas Economic Indicators, Great Plains Journal, Museum Journal, Business Journal, Rocky Mountain Social Science Journal, Arizona and the West, Southwestern Historical Quarterly,* and *True West. Military History of Texas and the Southwest,* associate editor, 1968—, book review editor, 1970—; member of editorial board, *Great Plains Journal,* 1972—.

WORK IN PROGRESS: Cornicks of Texas: The Biography of an American Family.

BIOGRAPHICAL/CRITICAL SOURCES: Arizona and the West, spring and summer, 1972.

* * *

SKELTON, Eugene (Lamar) 1914-

PERSONAL: Born October 29, 1914, in McKinney, Tex.; son of William Argyle and Geneva (Watts) Skelton; married Ann Thomas, November 16, 1940; children: Henry Thomas, Laura Ann (Mrs. Clint Guthrie), William Eugene, Martha Ellen. *Education:* Baylor University, B.A., 1939; Southwestern Baptist Theological Seminary, Th.M., 1946, Th.D., 1952. *Home:* 240 Blackman Rd., Nashville, Tenn. 37211. *Office:* Sunday School Board of the Southern Baptist Convention, 127 Ninth Ave. North, Nashville, Tenn. 37234.

CAREER: Ordained minister of Southern Baptist Church, 1935; minister in Pascagoula, Miss., 1956-60, Phoenix, Ariz., 1960-65, and Topeka, Kan., 1965-69; Baptist Sunday School Board, Nashville, Tenn., consultant in Sunday School Department, 1969—. *Military service:* U.S. Army, chaplain, 1941-46.

WRITINGS: Meet the Prophets, Broadman, 1972; *Committed to Reach People,* Convention Press, 1973; *Ten Fastest Growing Southern Baptists Sunday Schools,* Broadman, 1974; *Involving People in Reaching People,* Convention Press, 1974; (with Andy Anderson) *Where Action Is,* Broadman, 1976; *A Walk in the Light,* Skipworth Press, 1980.

WORK IN PROGRESS: Willie Huckstep and the Travelling Church, a story of a church that migrated from Virginia to Kentucky in 1781.

* * *

SKELTON, Geoffrey (David) 1916-

PERSONAL: Born May 11, 1916, in Springs, South Africa; son of Richard Hugh (a mining engineer) and Saizy (Watson) Skelton; married Gertrude Klebac, September 4, 1947; children: Stephen, Robert Piers. *Education:* Attended schools in England and Hong Kong. *Home:* 49 Downside, Shoreham, Sussex BN4 6HF, England.

CAREER: Reporter and sub-editor for various newspapers and periodicals, 1935-38; free-lance writer and journalist, 1938-40; sub-editor, *Sussex Daily News,* 1946-48; Press Association, London, England, sub-editor, 1948-49; British Information Services, Foreign Office in Germany, controller on *Die Welt* in Hamburg, 1949, information officer in Dortmund and Hamburg, 1950-56; British Broadcasting Corp., London, sub-editor in External Services News Department, 1956-58, program assistant in BBC German Service, 1958-66, program organizer, 1966-67; full-time writer and translator, 1967—. *Wartime service:* Conscientious objector; served in British Army Medical Corps, 1940-46. *Member:* Radiowriters Association (member of executive committee, 1969-72), Translators Association (member of executive committee, 1972—, chairman, 1974, 1979—). *Awards, honors:* American P.E.N. Club translation award, 1965, for *The Persecution and Assassination of Jean-Paul Marat as Performed by the Inmates of the Asylum of Charenton under the Direction of the Marquis de Sade;* Schlegel-Tieck Translation Prize, 1973, for *Frieda Lawrence: The Story of Frieda von Richthofen and D. H. Lawrence; Yorkshire Post* Music Award, 1975, for *Paul Hindemith: The Man behind the Music.*

WRITINGS: Wagner at Bayreuth: Experiment and Tradition, Barrie & Rockliff, 1965, Braziller, 1966, 2nd edition, White Lion Publishers, 1976; *Wieland Wagner: The Positive Sceptic* (biography), St. Martin's, 1971; (editor with Robert L. Jacobs) *Wagner Writes from Paris,* John Day, 1973; *Paul Hindemith: The Man behind the Music,* Crescendo Book, 1975; (contributor) Peter Burbridge and Richard Sutton, editors, *The Wagner Companion,* Faber, 1979.

Plays; all one-act: *Flowers for the Leader,* Samuel French, 1939; "Summer Night," published in *Twelve One-Acts,* edited by Elizabeth Everard, Allen & Unwin, 1939; *Have You Seen My Lady?,* Muller, 1948; "Memories for Sale," published in *Twenty Minute Theatre,* J. Garnet Miller, 1955.

Translations from the German: Theodor Storm, *The White Horseman* (short stories), New English Library, 1962; Guenter Herburger, *A Monotonous Landscape* (short stories), Harcourt, 1968; Friedrich Heer, *God's First Love: Christians and Jews over 2000 Years,* Weidenfeld & Nicolson, 1970, Weybright, 1971; Robert Lucas, *Frieda Lawrence: The Story of Frieda von Richthofen and D. H. Lawrence,* Viking, 1973; Max Frisch, *Sketchbook, 1966-1971,* Harcourt, 1974; Frisch, *Montauk,* Harcourt, 1976; Frisch, *Sketchbook, 1946-1949,* Harcourt, 1977; (and author of introduction and notes) *Cosima Wagner's Diaries,* Harcourt, Volume I, 1978, Volume II, 1980; Frisch, *Man in the Holocene,* Harcourt, 1980.

Plays translated from the German: (With Adrian Mitchell) Peter Weiss, *The Persecution and Assassination of Marat as Performed by the Inmates of the Asylum of Charenton under the Direction of the Marquis de Sade* (English version by Skelton, verse adaptation by Mitchell; first produced by Royal Shakespeare Company on West End at Aldwych Theatre, August 20, 1964; produced on Broadway at Martin Beck Theatre, 1966), Calder & Boyars, 1965, 4th edition, 1969, published as *The Persecution and Assassination of Jean-Paul Marat . . . ,* Atheneum, 1966; Erich Fried, *Arden Must Die* (opera; music by Alexander Goehr; first produced in London, England, at Sadler's Wells Theatre, April 17, 1974), Schott, 1967; Bertolt Brecht, *Lesson on Consent* (cantata; music by Paul Hindemith; first produced in Brighton, England, at Brighton Festival, May 5, 1968), Schott, 1968; Weiss, *Discourse on the Progress of the Prolonged War of Liberation in Viet Nam,* published with *Song of the Lusitanian Bogey* as *Two Plays,* Atheneum, 1970 (published in England as *Discourse on Vietnam,* Calder & Boyars, 1970); Weiss, *Trotsky in Exile* (broadcast by BBC Radio Three, November, 1970), Methuen, 1971, Atheneum, 1972. Also author of unpublished translation of "The Mountain King," by Ferdinand Raimund, first produced in Nottingham, England, at Nottingham Theatre, 1968.

Radio scripts, all produced by BBC: (With Christopher Sykes) "Return to the Shrine," 1961; (with Sykes) "Bayreuth Backstage I," 1962, ". . . II," 1963, ". . . III," 1965; "Pleasant Are the Tears Which Music Weeps," 1965; "Wagner's Comic Masterpiece: *Die Meistersinger,*" 1968; "Music from the Dead Composers," 1969; "Winifred Wagner Remembers" (interview), 1969; "Rossini and Wagner," 1970; "Wagner's Problem Child: *Tannhaeuser*," 1972; "The Art of Wagnerian Singing," 1974; "Preserving Wagner's Heritage," 1974; "How Wagner Wrote and Produced *The Ring*," 1976.

Contributor of short stories to periodicals, including *New Writing, Penguin Parade, English Story, Bugle Blast, Adelphi,* and *London Magazine,* and of articles on music and theatre to *World Review, Musical Times, Musical Opinion, Music and Musicians, Plays and Players,* and other publications.

WORK IN PROGRESS: Richard and Cosima Wagner: Biography of a Marriage, for Houghton; translating Max Frisch's play, "Triptychon," for Harcourt, and Gyoergy Ligeti's opera, *Le Grand Macabre,* for Schott.

AVOCATIONAL INTERESTS: "Enthusiastic piano player for own private amusement (serious music only)."

* * *

SLESAR, Henry 1927-
(O. H. Leslie; Jay Street)

PERSONAL: Born June 12, 1927, in Brooklyn, N.Y.; son of Benjamin and Sophie (Motlin) Slesar; married Oehone Scott, August 3, 1952 (divorced, 1969); married Jan Maakestao, December 12, 1970 (divorced, 1974); married Manuela Jone, June 1, 1975; children: Leslie Ann. *Education:* Attended School of Industrial Art, New York, N.Y. *Agent:* Theron W. Raines, Raines & Raines, 475 Fifth Ave., New York, N.Y. 10017; and Jerome S. Siegel, 8733 Sunset Blvd., Hollywood, Calif. 90069.

CAREER: Young & Rubicam, Inc. (advertising agency), New York City, copywriter, 1945-49; Robert W. Orr & Associates, Inc. (advertising agency), New York City, creative director, 1949-57; Fuller & Smith & Ross, Inc. (advertising agency), New York City, creative director, 1957-60; Donahue & Coe, Inc. (advertising agency), New York City, creative director, 1960-64; Slesar & Kanzer, Inc., New York City, president, beginning 1964; headwriter of daytime serials "The Edge of Night," 1968—, and "Somerset," 1971-73. *Military service:* U.S. Army, 1946-47. *Member:* Mystery Writers of America, Science Fiction Writers of America, National Academy of Television Arts and Sciences, Authors League. *Awards, honors:* Edgar Award, Mystery Writers of America, 1959, for best first mystery novel.

WRITINGS: The Gray Flannel Shroud, Random House, 1959; *Enter Murderers,* Random House, 1960; *Clean Crimes and Neat Murders,* introduction by Alfred Hitchcock, Avon, 1961; *A Crime for Mothers and Others,* Avon, 1962; *The Bridge of Lions,* Macmillan, 1963; *The Right Kind of House* (one-act play), Dramatic Publishing, 1963; *The Seventh Mask,* Ace Books, 1969; *The Thing at the Door,* Pocket Books, 1974.

Screenplays: "Two on a Guillotine," Warner Bros., 1968; "Murders in the Rue Morgue," American International. Author of numerous television scripts for various television series including over sixty scripts for "Alfred Hitchcock Presents"; also author of twenty-eight radio scripts for "CBS Radio Mystery Theatre." Work is represented in over eighty-five anthologies. Contributor of over 500 short stories and novelettes to various magazines.

WORK IN PROGRESS: Various television and motion picture assignments.

AVOCATIONAL INTERESTS: Music, both jazz and classical.†

SLOBODKINA, Esphyr 1908-

PERSONAL: Born 1908, in Siberia, Russia; daughter of Solomon A. and Itta (Agranovich) Slobodkina; married Ilya Bolotowsky (a painter), 1933 (divorced, 1936); married William Lester Urquhart, 1960 (died, 1963). *Education:* Attended National Academy of Design. *Home:* 20 West Terrace Rd., Great Neck, N.Y. 11021; and 1420 Atlantic Shores Blvd., Apt. 329, Hallandale, Fla. 33009.

CAREER: Painter, writer, sculptor, interior decorator, and illustrator. *Member:* American Abstract Artists (charter member; secretary, 1945-46, 1949-53; vice-president and treasurer, 1960-62; president, 1963-65), Federation of Modern Artists and Sculptors (charter member).

WRITINGS: Billie, Lothrop, 1959; *Boris and His Balalaika,* Abelard, 1964; *Notes for a Biographer* (autobiography), privately printed, Volume I, 1977, Volume II, 1979; *American Abstract Artists: Its Publications, Catalogs and Membership,* privately printed, 1979.

Author and illustrator: *Caps for Sale,* W. R. Scott, 1940, revised edition, 1947; *The Wonderful Feast,* Lothrop, 1955; *Little Dog Lost, Little Dog Found,* Abelard, 1956; *The Clock,* Abelard, 1956; *Behind the Dark Window Shade,* Lothrop, 1958; *Little Dinghy,* Abelard, 1958; *Pinky and the Petunias* (based on a story by Tamara Schildkraut), Abelard, 1959; *Moving Day for the Middlemans,* Abelard, 1960; *Jack and Jim,* Abelard, 1961; *The Long Island Ducklings,* Lantern Press, 1961; *Pezzo the Peddler and the Circus Elephant,* Abelard, 1968; *The Flame, the Breeze and the Shadow,* Rand McNally, 1969; *Pezzo the Peddler and the Thirteen Silly Thieves,* Abelard, 1970; *Billy, the Condominium Cat,* Addison-Wesley, 1980.

Illustrator: Margaret Wise Brown, *The Little Fireman,* W. R. Scott, 1938, revised edition, 1952; Louise Woodcock, *Hiding Places,* W. R. Scott, 1943; Brown, *The Little Cowboy,* W. R. Scott, 1948; Brown, *Sleepy ABC,* Lothrop, 1953.

SIDELIGHTS: Esphyr Slobodkina told *CA* that through her children's books she hopes to "provide *parents* with readable, amusing reading matter which is not embarrassing in its inanity." In addition, she seeks to "teach children basic examples of good taste in art, and amuse without corrupting their moral sense."

Slobodkina's paintings are represented in various museums and private collections.

* * *

SMALLEY, William A. 1923-

PERSONAL: Born April 4, 1923, in Jerusalem, Palestine; U.S. citizen; son of William F. and Dorothy L. (Allen) Smalley; married Jane Adams (a secretary), June 17, 1946; children: Carol Jane, William Allen, Stephen David. *Education:* Houghton College, A.B., 1945; Columbia University, Ph.D., 1956; Yale University, postdoctoral fellow, 1967-69 and 1974-75. *Religion:* Christian. *Home:* 6946 Knollwood Dr., Minneapolis, Minn. 55432. *Office:* Bethel College, St. Paul, Minn. 55112.

CAREER: Christian and Missionary Alliance, missionary linguist in Laos and Vietnam, 1950-54; American Bible Society, New York, N.Y., research associate, 1954-56, associate secretary for translations, 1956-62, linguistic and translations consultant, 1962-77, research consultant, 1972-77; Bethel College, St. Paul, Minn., instructor, 1977-78, professor of linguistics and anthropology, 1978—. Nyack Missionary College, instructor in English literature, 1946-49, assistant professor of anthropology, 1955-60, associate professor of anthropology, 1960-62; United Bible Societies, lecturer at month-long translators' institutes, 1958-77, translations consultant, 1967-77, Asia-Pacific regional translations coordinator, 1969-72; principal, Toronto Institute of Linguistics, 1956-62. *Member:* Linguistic Society of America, American Anthropological Association (fellow), Linguistic Association of Canada and the United States, American Association of Applied Linguistics, American Society for Missiology, Siam Society.

WRITINGS: (With Eugene A. Nida) *Introducing Animism,* Friendship, 1959; *Manual of Articulatory Phonetics,* with tape recordings, Division of Foreign Missions of National Council of Churches of Christ and Practical Anthropology, Part I, 1961, Part II, 1962, revised edition published in one volume, William Carey Library, 1963; *Outline of Khmu Structure* (booklet), American Oriental Society, 1961; (editor and contributor) *Orthography Studies: Articles on New Writing Systems,* United Bible Societies, 1964; (contributor) *Felicitation Volumes of Southeast-Asian Studies Presented to His Highness Prince Dhaninivat Kromamun Bidyalabh Bridhyakorn,* Volume I, Siam Society, 1965; (editor and contributor) *Readings in Missionary Anthropology,* William Carey Library, 1967, enlarged edition, 1978; (author of introduction) Ernest E. Heimbach, *White Meo-English Dictionary,* Southeast Asia Program, Cornell University, 1969; (with Donald N. Larson) *Becoming Bilingual: A Guide for Language Learners,* William Carey Library, 1972; *Phonemes and Orthography: Language Planning in Ten Minority Languages of Thailand,* Department of Linguistics, Australian National University, 1976; (with Jan de Waard) *Translators Handbook on Amos,* United Bible Societies, 1979.

Also author with Nguyen-van-Van of five-volume mimeographed course in Vietnamese for missionaries, Imprimerie Evangelique (Dalat, Vietnam), 1954. Contributor to *Dictionary of Christian Ethics* and *Concise Dictionary of the Christian World Mission;* contributor of more than sixty articles and reviews to linguistic, anthropology, and missionary journals. Editor, *Practical Anthropology,* 1955-68; associate editor, *Bible Translator,* 1957-59; associate, *Current Anthropology.*

WORK IN PROGRESS: Two books, *Linguistic Diversity and National Unity in Thailand: A Sociolinguistic Analysis* and *Ethnolinguistic Presuppositions of Bible Translation;* an ethnolinguistic survey of Khmer speakers in Northeast Thailand; work on a global theory of discourse structure.

SIDELIGHTS: William A. Smalley has done linguistic field work in Comanche, Sre, Khmu, Hmong (Meo), Vietnamese, Thai, Northern Khmer, and consultant work in several other Southeast Asian and African languages. In addition to his residence in Laos and Vietnam in 1950-54, he spent 1962-67 and 1969-72 in Thailand as a United Bible Societies' translations consultant.

* * *

SMITH, Bernard (William) 1916-

PERSONAL: Born October 3, 1916, in Sydney, New South Wales, Australia; son of Charles and Rose (Tierney) Smith; married Kate Beatrice Hartley Challis, 1941; children: Elizabeth, John. *Education:* Attended Warburg Institute, London, 1949-50; University of Sydney, B.A., 1952; Australian National University, Ph.D., 1957. *Office:* Australian Academy of the Humanities, 168 Nicholson, St. Fitzroy, Victoria, Australia.

CAREER: National Art Gallery of New South Wales, Sydney, Australia, education officer, 1945-48, 1951-52; University of Melbourne, Melbourne, Australia, senior lecturer in department of fine arts, 1957-63, reader, beginning 1964; University of Sydney, Sydney, professor of contemporary art, 1967-77; Australian Academy of the Humanities, St. Fitzroy, president, 1977—. Member of Humanities Research Council. *Member:* Society of Antiquaries of London (fellow), Hakluyt Society (London).

WRITINGS: Place, Taste and Tradition: A Study of Australian Art since 1788, Ure Smith, 1945; *A Catalogue of Australian Oil Paintings in the National Gallery of New South Wales,* National Gallery of New South Wales, 1953; (editor) *Education through Art in Australia,* Melbourne University Press, 1958; *European Vision and the South Pacific, 1768-1850,* Oxford University Press, 1960; *Australian Painting, 1788 to 1960,* Oxford University Press, 1962, 2nd edition published as *Australian Painting, 1788-1970,* 1972; (with wife, Kate Smith) *The Architectural Character of Glebe, Sydney,* University Co-operative Bookshop (Sydney), 1973; (editor) *Concerning Contemporary Art: The Power Lectures, 1968-1973,* Clarendon Press, 1975; (editor) *Documents on Art and Taste in Australia: The Colonial Period, 1770-1914,* Oxford University Press, 1975; *The Antipodean Manifesto: Essays in Art and History,* Oxford University Press, 1976. Contributor to professional journals.

* * *

SMITH, David (Jeddie) 1942-
(Smith Cornwell, Dave Smith)

PERSONAL: Born December 19, 1942, in Portsmouth, Va.; son of Ralph Gerald (a naval engineer) and Catherine (Cornwell) Smith; married second wife, Deloras Mae Weaver, March 31, 1966; children: (second marriage) David Jeddie, Jr., Lael Cornwell, Mary Margaret. *Education:* University of Virginia, B.A. (with highest distinction), 1965; College of William and Mary, graduate study, 1966; Southern Illinois University, M.A., 1969; Ohio University, Ph.D., 1976. *Home:* 3740 East Yosemite Dr., Salt Lake City, Utah 84109. *Office:* Department of English, University of Utah, Salt Lake City, Utah 84112.

CAREER: High school teacher of French and English, and football coach, in Poquoson, Va., 1965-67; instructor at Night School Divisions, College of William and Mary, Williamsburg, Va., Christopher Newport College, Newport News, Va., and Thomas Nelson Community College, Hampton, Va., all 1969-72; Western Michigan University, Kalamazoo, instructor, 1973-74, assistant professor of English, 1974-75; University of Utah, Salt Lake City, associate professor of English, 1976—. Visiting professor of English, State University of New York at Binghamton, 1980—; instructor in English, Cottey College, Nevada, Mo. Has conducted poetry readings at colleges and universities. *Military service:* U.S. Air Force, 1969-72; became staff sergeant. *Member:* American Association of University Professors, Rocky Mountain Modern Language Association, Escondidos, Phi Delta Theta. *Awards, honors:* Fiction prize, *Miscellany,* 1972; Breadloaf Writer's Conference scholarship, summer, 1973; poetry prize, *Sou'wester,* 1973; National Endowment for the Arts fellowship in poetry, 1976; Academy-Institute Award, American Academy and Institute of Arts and Letters, 1979; David P. Gardner Award, 1979.

WRITINGS—Poems: *Bull Island,* Back Door Press, 1970; *Mean Rufus Throw Down,* Basilisk Press, 1973; (under name Dave Smith) *The Fisherman's Whore,* Ohio University Press, 1974; *Cumberland Station,* University of Illinois

Press, 1977; *In Dark, Sudden with Light,* Croissant & Co., 1977; *Goshawk, Antelope,* University of Illinois Press, 1979.

Poems represented in many anthologies, including *I Love You All Day: It Is That Simple,* edited by Philip Dacey and Gerald Knoll, Abbey Press, 1970, *Yearbook of Modern Poetry,* edited by Jeanne Hollyfield, Young Publications, 1971, *New Voices in American Poetry,* edited by Dave Allen Evans, Winthrop, 1973, *Heartland II,* edited by Lucien Stryk, Northern Illinois University Press, 1975, and *American Poets in 1976,* edited by William Heyen, Bobbs-Merrill, 1976. Poetry columnist, *American Poetry Review,* 1978—.

Contributor, sometimes under pseudonym Smith Cornwell, of short stories, poems, articles, and reviews to numerous popular and poetry magazines, including *Nation, Southern Review, Shenandoah, Poetry Northwest, Prairie Schooner,* and *Open Places.* Editor, founder, and publisher, *Back Door;* editor, *Sou'wester,* 1967-68.

WORK IN PROGRESS: Two poems, *Sister Celia,* for University of Illinois Press, and *Homage to Edgar Allan Poe,* for Louisiana State University Press; a novel, tentatively entitled *Onliness;* an essay on contemporary poetry, *Against Minimalism;* editing a collection of essays, *James Wright: The Pure, Clear Word,* for University of Illinois Press; a study, *The Art of John Gardner;* various essays.

SIDELIGHTS: David Smith, according to Calvin Bedient in the *Chicago Review,* is a "poet threatening greatness." In his review of *Cumberland Station*—a work which Bedient finds flawed in some respects—he writes, "Astonishing all the same that a potentiality for greatness booms like a waterfall at the back of these poems." He explains: "Smith's sensibility, Whitmanian in its ardor, has a fact-gathering, fact-hurtling force. It is excited and chiefly what excites it is the painful evidence of life's wreckage. Smith is one of those—like James Agee and Philip Levine—who recognize (in Agee's words) 'the ultimately mortal wound which is living' and who venerate 'the indignant strength not to perish.'"

Smith told *CA:* "Writing is, as many have said, an act of exploration, and that definition means that whatever one says about his writing is necessarily the residue of what has already been done, though it may also reflect one's hopes for future accomplishment. I have written poems which were essentially narrative, elegaic, and Aristotelian in form. These poems seem to me to celebrate fundamental human, perhaps heroic, virtues such as courage, love, pride, passion, hate, joy, and, before all, some kind of belief. They all appear to devolve to the theme of obligation. [That is,] given a crisis of some sort, given stories which will initially evoke our interest, my poems appear to want to discover in the crisis story what action or character deserves and receives our faith, our love, our pity.

"Many of my poems have evolved from a sense of place, the way in which a specific landscape becomes a symbolic, affective, and even psychological text. Curiously, my books describe a trail of movement from the Atlantic coast of Virginia, where I was born, across the country to Utah. This travel has been a passage from poems rooted in, but not faithful to, autobiographical experience to poems of entire invention, [such as those] in *Goshawk, Antelope.*

"Since completing this voyage within language, I have finished two manuscripts which will soon be published. Both of them represent, in different ways, returns to origins. *Sister Celia* is a collection of longish narrative and lyrical poems which return to the Atlantic coast and conclude on the Pacific coast. *Homage to Edgar Allan Poe,* which may be viewed as an extension of *Sister Celia,* returns to the traditional forms of English poetry. I view both manuscripts as being a point of rest before the beginning of another kind of poetry. Whatever I write in the future, and that is certainly not to be predicted, will have to conform to two principles: I want poetry whose clarity is pronounced and resonant and I want poetry whose validity will be proved to the extent the poems embody the true, durable, and felt experience of emotional life."

BIOGRAPHICAL/CRITICAL SOURCES: Sou'wester, spring, 1974; *Hudson Review,* winter, 1974-75; *Three Rivers Poetry Journal,* spring, 1977; *Chicago Review,* autumn, 1977; *American Poetry Review,* January/February, 1978; Helen Vendler, *Part of Nature, Part of Us,* Harvard University Press, 1980, *Georgia Review,* spring, 1980.

* * *

SMITH, Frances C(hristine) 1904-
(Jean Smith)

PERSONAL: Born September 6, 1904, in Washington, Kan.; daughter of Henry D. (a physician) and Marjorie (a teacher; maiden name, Whittet) Smith. *Education:* Attended Rockford College, 1923-24; University of Kansas, A.B., 1926; Columbia University, M.A., 1936. *Politics:* Democrat. *Religion:* Presbyterian. *Residence:* Santa Fe, N.M. 87501. *Agent:* Lurton Blassingame, Blassingame, McCauley, & Wood, 60 East 42nd St., New York, N.Y. 10017.

CAREER: Teacher of English and history in Kansas and Missouri schools, 1927-30; Jones Oil Co., New York City, member of publications department, 1931; Columbia University, Teachers College, New York City, staff member, 1932-43; *Boys' Life* magazine, New Brunswick, N.J., associate editor, 1944-70; free-lance writer, 1970—. Instructor in writers' workshops; occasional lecturer to university classes. Member of board of trustees, Public Library, Cranbury, N.J. *Member:* Authors Guild, Authors League of America, Women's National Book Association, Society of American Travel Writers, Western Writers of America, American Polar Society, Appalachian Mountain Club, Sierra Club.

WRITINGS: First Book of Conservation, F. Watts, 1954, revised edition, 1973; *First Book of Water,* F. Watts, 1959; (under pseudonym Jean Smith) *Find a Career in Conservation,* Putnam, 1959; *The World of the Artic,* Lippincott, 1960; *Find a Career in Education,* Putnam, 1960; *First Book of Mountains,* F. Watts, 1964; *Men at Work in Alaska,* Putnam, 1967; *First Book of Swamps and Marshes,* F. Watts, 1969. Contributor of articles and stories for adults to various magazines.

WORK IN PROGRESS: Log of a Loner.

SIDELIGHTS: Frances C. Smith is interested in study of natural science, geography, the inter-relationships of peoples of the world, and their natural environments. Travels have taken her to Europe, Mexico, the Arctic, Australia, New Zealand, the South Pacific Island, and to all the states in the Union and the provinces of Canada. *Avocational interests:* Nature study, hiking, canoeing, and "non-technical" mountain climbing.

* * *

SMITH, Ken(neth Danforth) 1902-

PERSONAL: Born January 8, 1902, in Danbury, Conn.; son of William Clark (a factory executive) and Marion Grace (Quien) Smith; married Emilie Idell Bolen, February 11, 1932. *Education:* Attended Trinity College, Hartford, Conn., 1922-25. *Home:* Knollcrest, New Fairfield, Conn. 06810.

CAREER: *New York Evening Mail,* New York City, copy boy and cub reporter, 1920-22; *Hartford Courant,* Hartford, Conn., reporter of state news and sports, 1922-25; *New York Graphic,* New York City, baseball writer, 1925-30; *New York Mirror,* New York City, baseball writer, 1931-63; National Baseball Hall of Fame and Museum, Cooperstown, N.Y., director, 1964-76, public relations director, 1977-78, director emeritus, 1979—. *Member:* Baseball Writers Association of America (secretary-treasurer, 1939-57), Professional Football Writers Association of America (president, 1940), Phi Delta Gamma. *Awards, honors:* Gold Key Award from Connecticut Sports Alliance, 1947; citation for sports writing from Trinity College, 1955.

WRITINGS: *Baseball's Hall of Fame,* A. S. Barnes, 1947, revised edition, with foreword by Ford Frick, 1952, 9th edition, Grosset, 1979; *The Willie Mays Story,* with foreword by Leo Durocher, Greenberg, 1954; (author of foreword) *Guide to Baseball Literature,* Gale, 1975. Contributor to *Street & Smith Baseball Year Book.* Contributor to periodicals, including *Esquire, Liberty,* and *Baseball Quarterly.*

SIDELIGHTS: Ken Smith began writing in high school where he published and circulated his own newspaper; he notes that he was "even granted space for bulletins on the home room blackboard." Three months after graduation, he was working on a New York paper with such notable personalities as Ed Sullivan, Mary Margaret McBride, and Rube Goldberg. He told *CA* that he went on to develop "lifetime associations with Damon Runyon, Grantland Rice, Jack Lait, Bob Considine, Heywood Broun, Dan Parker, and Emile Gauvreau."

During his career as a sports writer Smith covered thirty-eight World Series and covered Eastern League baseball during the time Lou Gehrig and Leo Durocher played for Hartford. From 1927 to 1963 he traveled with the New York Giants and New York Yankees.

* * *

SMITH, Myron J(ohn), Jr. 1944-

PERSONAL: Born May 3, 1944, in Toledo, Ohio; son of Myron J. and Marion (Herbert) Smith; married Susan Ballou, June 15, 1968; children: Myron J. III. *Education:* Ashland College, A.B., 1966; Western Michigan University, M.L.S., 1967; Shippensburg State College, M.A., 1969. *Office:* Department of History, Salem College, Salem, W.Va. 26426.

CAREER: Mystic Seaport Library, Mystic, Conn., research librarian, 1967-68; Western Maryland College, Westminster, assistant librarian, 1969-72; Huntington Public Library, Huntington, Ind., director, 1972-76; Salem College, Salem, W.Va., associate professor of history and library science, director of libraries, and associate director of career aviation program, 1976—. R.O.T.C. liason, Salem College, 1976—. *Member:* American Library Association, U.S. Naval Institute, U.S. Military Institute, American Committee on the History of the Second World War, American Committee for the Bibliography of History, Civil Air Patrol (aerospace education director of West Virginia Wing), West Virginia Library Association, Beta Phi Mu, Phi Alpha Theta. *Awards, honors:* Named honorary admiral in Texas Navy for work on bibliography of Texas State Navy.

WRITINGS: *An Indiana Sailor Scuttles Morgan's Raid,* Fort Wayne Public Library, 1972; *Sophisticated Lady: The Battleship "Indiana" in World War II,* Fort Wayne Public Library, 1973; (editor) *Huntington Historical Handbook,* Our Sunday Visitor, 1973; *Cloak-and-Dagger Bibliography,* Scarecrow, 1975; *The Sea Fiction Guide,* Scarecrow, 1976; *World War II at Sea,* Scarecrow, 1976; *World War I in the Air,* Scarecrow, 1977; *The Soviet Navy,* American Bibliographic Center-Clio Press, 1979; *Air War Southeast Asia,* Scarecrow, 1979; *War Stories Guide,* Scarecrow, 1980; *The Secret Wars: A Guide to the Literature of Intelligence, Espionage, Covert Operations, and International Terrorism,* American Bibliographic Center-Clio Press, 1980.

Series: "American Naval Bibliography" series, Scarecrow, 1972-74; "Air War Bibliography" series, *Military Affairs/Aerospace Historian,* 1977—; "Air War Chronology" series, *Military Affairs/Aerospace Historian,* 1977—.

Author of regular column, "HPL: The World of Books," in *Huntington Herald Press,* 1972-76. Contributor of articles and reviews to periodicals, including *Library Journal, Military Affairs, Aerospace Historian, Log of Mystic Seaport,* and *Civil War History.* Contributing editor, *Military Journal.*

WORK IN PROGRESS: *The Soviet Air and Strategic Rocket Forces; The Soviet Red Army; Secret Wars: The Fiction Guide;* research on the history of the Maryland State Navy during the Revolutionary War.

* * *

SMITH, Ralph Lee 1927-

PERSONAL: Born November 6, 1927, in Philadelphia, Pa.; son of Hugh Harold and Barbara (Schatkin) Smith; married Betty Handy, October, 1954 (divorced January, 1963); married Mary Louise Hollowell (a writer), November 13, 1971; married third wife, Shizuko Maruyama; children: (first marriage) David, Robert; (present marriage) Lisa. *Education:* Swarthmore College, B.A., 1951. *Politics:* Democrat. *Home:* 1662 Chimney House Rd., Reston, Va. 22090. *Office:* Technology & Economics, Inc., 204 G St. N.E., Washington, D.C. 20002.

CAREER: National Better Business Bureau, New York, N.Y., publications editor, 1954-58; free-lance writer and consultant, 1959-71; Howard University, School of Communications, Washington, D.C., associate professor, 1972-76; Berner & Smith Associates, Washington, D.C., partner, 1977-79; Technology & Economics, Inc., Washington, D.C., director of communications programs, 1979—. Senior staff assistant, Sloan Commission on Cable Communications, 1970-71; writer and researcher, MITRE Corp., 1972. *Military service:* U.S. Air Force, 1952-53; became sergeant. *Member:* Overseas Press Club. *Awards, honors:* Russell L. Cecil Distinguished Medical Writing Award, Arthritis Foundation, 1963; Medical Journalism Award, American Medical Association, 1965; Fletcher Pratt fellow in nonfiction writing, Bread Loaf Writers Conference, 1965; Business and Financial Writing Award, University of Missouri, 1971; National Magazine Award for public service, Columbia University, 1971; Nelson Poynter fellow in modern journalism, Yale University, 1972.

WRITINGS: *The Health Hucksters,* Crowell, 1960; (with John W. O'Daniel) *The Challenge of the New Vietnam,* Coward, 1960, revised edition, 1962; (with Owen D. Pelt) *The Story of the National Baptists,* Vantage, 1960; (contributor) *The Story of Our Time,* Grolier, 1960; *The Bargain Hucksters,* Crowell, 1963; *Getting to Know the World Health Organization* (juvenile), Coward, 1963; (with Ben Wattenberg) *The New Nations of Africa,* Hart Publishing, 1963; *The Grim Truth about Mutual Funds,* Putnam, 1963; *The Tarnished Badge,* Crowell, 1965; (contributor) Jean Wilkinson and Muriel Blatt, editors, *A Various Collection: Essays, Stories, and Poems,* Aegeus, 1966; (contributor)

Manpower and Natural Resources, Science Research Associates, 1966; *At Your Own Risk,* Trident, 1969; *The Wired Nation,* Harper, 1972. Contributor to magazines.

* * *

SMITH, Robert Freeman 1930-

PERSONAL: Born May 13, 1930, in Little Rock, Ark.; son of Robert Freeman and Emma (Buerkle) Smith; married Alberta Vester, 1951; children: Robin Ann, Robert F. III. *Education:* University of Arkansas, B.A., 1952, M.A., 1953; University of Wisconsin, Ph.D., 1958. *Home:* 2256 Barrington Dr., Toledo, Ohio. *Office:* Department of History, University of Toledo, Toledo, Ohio 43606.

CAREER: Texas Lutheran College, Seguin, associate professor, 1958-62; University of Rhode Island, Kingston, assistant professor, 1962-64, associate professor of history, 1964-66; visiting professor, University of Wisconsin, 1966-67; University of Connecticut, Storrs, associate professor, 1967-69; University of Toledo, Toledo, Ohio, professor of history, 1969—. *Military service:* U.S. Army Reserve, Signal Corps, 1953-61; active duty, 1953-55; became first lieutenant. *Member:* Organization of American Historians, Society for Historians of American Foreign Relations, Conference on Latin American History, Southern Historical Association, Phi Beta Kappa, Phi Alpha Theta, Lambda Tau, Masons. *Awards, honors:* Texas Writer's Round-up Award, 1961, for one of twenty best books of year; Ohio Academy of History book award, 1973, for *The United States and Revolutionary Nationalism in Mexico;* Tom L. Evans Research Award from Harry S. Truman Library Institute, 1976-77.

WRITINGS: The United States and Cuba: Business and Diplomacy, 1917-1960, College & University Press, 1960; *What Happened in Cuba?,* Twayne, 1963; (editor) *Background to Revolution: The Development of Modern Cuba,* Knopf, 1966, revised edition, Robert E. Krieger, 1979; (contributor) Bayless Manning, editor, *The United States and Cuba: Long-Range Perspectives,* Brookings Institution, 1966; (contributor) Marvin Bernstein, editor, *Foreign Investment in Latin America,* Knopf, 1966; *The United States and Revolutionary Nationalism in Mexico,* University of Chicago Press, 1972; (contributor) Jules Davids, editor, *Perspectives in American Diplomacy,* Arno, 1976. Also contributor to *Encyclopedia of American Foreign Policy,* 1978. Contributor to history journals.

WORK IN PROGRESS: The United States and the Latin American Sphere of Influence, for Robert E. Krieger.

SIDELIGHTS: Robert Smith told *CA:* "My interest in Cuba and Latin America goes back to 1948 when I visited Cuba as a seaman in the U.S. Naval Reserve. In Santiago de Cuba I saw Cuban life in the raw, and narrowly missed being seized by an anti-American mob. Thus, I experienced the idea of 'Yankee No' long before Fidel Castro came to power."

BIOGRAPHICAL/CRITICAL SOURCES: Arkansas Democrat, February 12, 1961; *Austin Statesman,* October 19, 1961.

* * *

SMOLANSKY, Oles M. 1930-

PERSONAL: Born May 2, 1930, in Ukraine, U.S.S.R.; naturalized U.S. citizen, 1955; son of Nicholas (an economist) and Irene (Pliuto) Smolansky; married Bettie Moretz (a professor), December 29, 1966; children: Alexandra, Nicholas. *Education:* New York University, B.A., 1953; Columbia University, M.A., 1955, Ph.D., 1959. *Politics:* Democrat. *Religion:* Greek Orthodox. *Home:* 3665 Walt Whitman Lane, Bethlehem, Pa. 18017. *Office:* Department of International Relations, Lehigh University, Bethlehem, Pa. 18015.

CAREER: University of California, Los Angeles, instructor in political science, 1960-62; Lehigh University, Bethlehem, Pa., assistant professor, 1963-66, associate professor, 1966-70, professor of international relations, 1970—, chairman of department, 1975—. Visiting professor of international relations, University of Pennsylvania, 1970, 1971. *Member:* International Studies Association, Middle East Studies Association, Middle East Institute, American Association for the Advancement of Slavic Studies, American Political Science Association. *Awards, honors:* Senior Lindback Distinguished Teacher Award, 1979.

WRITINGS: The Soviet Union and the Arab East under Krushchev, Bucknell University Press, 1974.

Contributor: A. J. Cottrell and R. M. Burrell, editors, *The Indian Ocean: Its Political, Economic, and Military Importance,* Praeger, 1972; Alvin Z. Rubinstein, editor, *Soviet and Chinese Influence in the Third World,* Praeger, 1975; Michael McGuire, Ken Booth, and John McDonnell, editors, *Soviet Naval Policy: Objectives and Constraints,* Praeger, 1975; William E. Griffith, editor, *The Soviet Empire: Expansion and Detente,* Heath, 1976; McGuire and McDonnell, editors, *Soviet Naval Influence: Domestic and Foreign Dimensions,* Praeger, 1977; Anne Sinai and Allen Pollock, editors, *The Hashemite Kingdom of Jordan and the West Bank,* American Academic Association for Peace in the Middle East, 1977; Grayson Kirk and Mils H. Wessel, editors, *The Soviet Threat: Myths and Realities,* Academy of Political Science, 1978. Contributor to professional journals, including *Political Science Quarterly, Slavic Review, Journal of International Affairs, Middle East Forum,* and *Current History.*

WORK IN PROGRESS: Soviet-Iraqi Relations.

* * *

SMOOT, Dan 1913-

PERSONAL: Born October 5, 1913, near East Prairie, Mo.; son of a farmer. *Education:* Southern Methodist University, B.A., 1938, M.A., 1940; Harvard University, additional study, 1941-42. *Home address:* Route 1, Box 121 D, Big Sandy, Tex. 75755.

CAREER: Itinerant worker in teens until 1931 when he started to work for Ben E. Keith Co. (wholesale produce firm), Dallas, Tex.; Federal Bureau of Investigation, Washington, D.C., agent with assignments in Portland, Ore., San Francisco, Calif., Dallas, Cleveland, Ohio, and Washington, D.C., 1942-51; Facts Forum, Dallas, radio and television commentator, 1951-55; Dan Smoot Report, Inc., Dallas, editor, publisher, and radio and television commentator, 1955-71; free-lance writer, 1971-78.

WRITINGS: The Hope of the World, Newman-Miller, 1958; *America's Promise,* Dan Smoot Report, Inc., 1960; *Invisible Government,* Dan Smoot Report, Inc., 1962; *The Business End of Government,* Western Islands, 1973.

* * *

SNYDER, (Donald) Paul 1933-

PERSONAL: Born June 17, 1933, in Jersey City, N.J.; son of William Ludwig Henry (a steel plant manager) and Margaret (Emley) Snyder. *Education:* Wagner College, A.B. (magna cum laude), 1956; Duke University, Ph.D., 1964. *Politics:* "Leftish Democrat." *Religion:* "Lutheran-Catholic background; no present affiliation (Latter-day Humanist, perhaps)." *Home:* 6 Ferry St., Lambertville, N.J. 08530. *Office:* Department of Philosophy, Temple University, Philadelphia, Pa. 19122.

CAREER: Worked as a singer in New York, N.Y. and Montreal, Quebec, 1950-53; high school teacher in Fairfax, Va., 1958-60; Purdue University, West Lafayette, Ind., assistant professor of philosophy, 1964-65; Temple University, Philadelphia, Pa., assistant professor, 1965-69, associate professor of philosophy, 1969—. *Member:* American Philosophical Association, Philosophy of Science Association, American Association for the Advancement of Science, American Association of University Professors.

WRITINGS: Modal Logic and Its Applications, Van Nostrand, 1971; *Toward One Science: The Convergence of Tradition,* St. Martin's, 1978; *Health and Human Nature: The Holistic Revolution in Modern Medicine,* Chilton, 1980. Contributor of articles and reviews to philosophy, logic, and biology journals.

WORK IN PROGRESS: The Grain of Truth: A Sympathetic Look at Pseudo-science; a novel.

SIDELIGHTS: Paul Snyder told *CA:* "I'm trying to make a transition from writing for a professional, academic audience to writing for the general public. It's not as easy a transition as I thought it would be. Right now I'm in the middle of a four-book scheme to teach myself a whole new way of writing. What is important to people whose profession is the history and philosophy of science is different from what is important to people who simply want to understand what's going on in the world, and to make sense of the new way of approaching human problems that seems to be catching hold in the sciences.

"Making the transition to fiction is even more difficult. In between a technical book on logic and a book on the convergence of Eastern and Western scientific thought, I spent a couple of years working on a novel. It was awful. I've got three hundred pages of manuscript that just isn't good enough to show to anybody, and that is much too tightly focused on unresolved issues in my own life to do anybody else any good. You really have to get yourself out of your system, and establish some distance between yourself and your characters, in order to turn out a decent piece of fiction. I was pleased to find out that I can write good dialogue, at least. I expect to try writing fiction again after the next two projects. There are insights that just can't be passed along in any form other than the novel. But for me, at least, it requires some effort to get the necessary skills, the discipline to keep believing in a project for as long as it takes to complete it, and the self-confidence to put a slice of my mind out there where everybody can see it."

AVOCATIONAL INTERESTS: Working with stained glass.

* * *

SOBOL, Donald J. 1924-

PERSONAL: Born October 4, 1924, in New York, N.Y.; son of Ira J. and Ida (Gelula) Sobol; married Rose Tiplitz, 1955; children: Diane, Glenn, Eric, John. *Education:* Oberlin College, B.A., 1948. *Residence:* Miami, Fla. *Agent:* McIntosh & Otis, Inc., 475 Fifth Ave., New York, N.Y. 10017.

CAREER: New York Sun, New York City, member of editorial staff, 1948; *Long Island Daily Press,* New York City, member of editorial staff, 1949-51; R. H. Macy, New York City, worked in merchandising, 1953-54; free-lance writer, 1954—. *Military service:* U.S. Army, Combat Engineers, World War II; served in Pacific Theater. *Member:* Authors Guild, Authors League of America.

WRITINGS: The Double Quest, F. Watts, 1957; *The Lost Dispatch,* F. Watts, 1958; *First Book of Medieval Man,* F. Watts, 1959; *Two Flags Flying,* Platt, 1960; *The Wright Brothers at Kitty Hawk,* Thomas Nelson, 1961; *A Civil War Sampler,* F. Watts, 1961; *The First Book of the Barbarian Invaders,* F. Watts, 1962; (with wife, Rose Sobol) *Stocks and Bonds,* F. Watts, 1963; *Encyclopedia Brown, Boy Detective,* Thomas Nelson, 1963; *Lock, Stock, and Barrel,* Westminster, 1963; *An American Revolutionary War Reader,* F. Watts, 1964.

Encyclopedia Brown and the Case of the Secret Pitch, Thomas Nelson, 1965; *Encyclopedia Brown Finds the Clues,* Thomas Nelson, 1966; *Secret Agents Four,* Four Winds, 1967; *The Strongest Man in the World,* Westminster, 1967; *Encyclopedia Brown Solves Them All,* Thomas Nelson, 1968; *Encyclopedia Brown Keeps the Peace,* Thomas Nelson, 1969; *Two-Minute Mysteries,* Scholastic Book Services, 1970; *Greta the Strong,* Follet, 1970; *Encyclopedia Brown Saves the Day,* Thomas Nelson, 1970; *More Two-Minute Mysteries,* Scholastic Book Services, 1971; *Milton, the Model A,* Harvey House, 1971; *Encyclopedia Brown Tracks Them Down,* Thomas Nelson, 1971; *The Amazons of Greek Mythology,* A. S. Barnes, 1972; *Encyclopedia Brown Shows the Way,* Thomas Nelson, 1972; *Encyclopedia Brown Takes the Case,* Thomas Nelson, 1973; *Encyclopedia Brown Lends a Hand,* Thomas Nelson, 1974; *Encyclopedia Brown and the Case of the Dead Eagles,* Thomas Nelson, 1975; *Still More Two-Minute Mysteries,* Scholastic Book Services, 1975; *True Sea Adventures,* Thomas Nelson, 1975; *Encyclopedia Brown Gets His Man,* Thomas Nelson, 1976; *Encyclopedia Brown and the Case of the Midnight Visitor,* Thomas Nelson, 1977; *Disaster,* Archway, 1979; *Encyclopedia Brown's Record Book of Weird and Wonderful Facts,* Delacorte, 1979; *Encyclopedia Brown Carries On,* Four Winds, 1980.

Author of syndicated column, "Two Minute Mysteries." Contributor of stories and articles, some under a variety of pseudonyms, to national magazines.

WORK IN PROGRESS: A juvenile mystery novel featuring a girl detective.

SIDELIGHTS: The Encyclopedia Brown character appears in a syndicated newspaper comic strip. *Avocational interests:* Travel, gardening, tennis.

* * *

SOCOLOFSKY, Homer E(dward) 1922-

PERSONAL: Born May 20, 1922, in Tampa, Kan.; son of Abraham L. (a salesman) and Mary Belle (a teacher; maiden name, Reneau) Socolofsky; married Helen Margot Wright (a registered nurse), November 23, 1946; children: Robert M., Mary Jennifer Sims, Thomas C., Edward T., Theodore J., Elizabeth. *Education:* Attended Bowling Green State University, 1943; Kansas State University, B.S., 1944, M.S., 1947; University of Missouri, Ph.D., 1954. *Politics:* Republican. *Religion:* Methodist. *Home:* 1314 Fremont St., Manhattan, Kan. 66502. *Office:* Department of History, Eisenhower Hall, Kansas State University, Manhattan, Kan. 66506.

CAREER: Kansas State University, Manhattan, 1947—, began as instructor, professor of history, 1963—, acting head of department, 1964-65. Visiting assistant professor of history, Yale University, New Haven, Conn., 1954-55; consultant, University of Mid-America, 1975-77. Member, Kansas State University-Newton Cooperative Curriculum Study;

advancement chairman, Pawnee District Boy Scouts 1962-64; member, Kansas Centennial Commission, 1957-61; member of faculty senate, Kansas State University, 1961-64; member of Professional Standards Board, Kansas State Board of Education, 1974-79; member of Kansas American Revolution Bicentennial Commission, 1975-76; member of board of trustees, Riley County Historical Museum. Consultant to Mid-Continent Regional Educational Laboratory, 1965-67, and to Columbia Broadcasting System (CBS) News, 1974. *Military service:* U.S. Marine Corps Reserve, 1943-46, became captain. *Member:* Organization of American Historians, Agricultural History Society (president, 1968-69), Great Plains Historical Association, Western Historical Association (member of executive council, 1978-81), Kansas Historical Society (member of board of directors, 1960—; president, 1975-76; member of executive committee, 1979), Kansas Association of Teachers of History and Social Science (vice-president, 1957-58, president, 1958-59, member of executive committee, 1959-60), Phi Alpha Theta, Phi Kappa Phi, Kiwanis. *Awards, honors:* Woods fellowship, Nebraska Historical Society, 1961; Award of Merit, Association for State and Local History, 1963, for *Arthur Capper;* Co-Founders Award, Westerners International, 1973.

WRITINGS: (Contributor) *Marketing Kansas Wheat,* Kansas State Board of Agriculture, 1959; *Arthur Capper: Publisher, Politician, and Philanthropist,* University of Kansas Press, 1962; *The Cimarron Valley,* Teachers College Press, 1969; (with Huber Self) *The Historical Atlas of Kansas,* University of Oklahoma Press, 1972; *Landlord William Scully,* Regents Press of Kansas, 1979. Contributor to *Kansas, the First Century,* 1956; editor of *Kansas History in Graduate Study,* 1959; also contributor to *Readers Encyclopedia of the American West* and to *Biographical Dictionary of the Governors of the United States, 1789-1978.* Contributor to history journals. Editor of Great Plains issue of *Journal of the West,* 1967, 1976, and 1977; editor of history issues of *Kansas Quarterly.*

WORK IN PROGRESS: The Presidency of Benjamin Harrison; Sorghum Sugar; Kansas History.

AVOCATIONAL INTERESTS: Reading, family history, volleyball.

* * *

SOKOL, David M(artin) 1942-

PERSONAL: Born November 3, 1942, in New York, N.Y.; son of Harry (a businessman) and Ruth (Waldman) Sokol; married Sandra Schorr, June 15, 1963; children: Adam, Andrew. *Education:* Hunter College of the City University of New York, A.B., 1963; New York University, A.M., 1966, Ph.D., 1971. *Politics:* Independent. *Religion:* Jewish. *Home:* 330 South Taylor Ave., Oak Park, Ill. 60302. *Office:* History of Architecture and Art Department, University of Illinois, Chicago, Ill. 60680.

CAREER: City University of New York, New York, N.Y., lecturer in art at Bronx Community College, Bronx, N.Y., 1965-66, instructor in art at Kingsborough Community College, Brooklyn, N.Y., 1966-68; Western Illinois University, Macomb, assistant professor of art, 1968-71; University of Illinois at Chicago Circle, associate professor of art history, 1971—, chairman of department, 1977—. *Member:* American Association of University Professors, College Art Association, American Society for Aesthetics, American Studies Association.

WRITINGS: John Quidor: Painter of American Legend, Wichita Art Museum, 1973; *American Architecture and Art,* Gale, 1976; *Otto Neumann 1895-1975: A Retrospective Exhibition,* Goethe Institute, 1979; (co-author) *American Art,* Abrams, 1979; *American Decorative Arts and Old World Influences,* Gale, 1980. Contributor of articles and book reviews to *American Art Journal, Journal of Aesthetics and Art Criticism, Antiques, Art Journal,* and *American Art Review.*

* * *

SOLDOFSKY, Robert Melvin 1920-

PERSONAL: Born August 12, 1920, in St. Louis, Mo.; son of Abraham Lincoln and Thelma (Darrish) Soldofsky; married Marcella Portnoy, 1947; children: Alan D., Sue Anne. *Education:* St. Louis University, B.S., 1942; Washington University, St. Louis, Mo., M.A., 1948, Ph.D., 1953. *Home:* 229 Lowell, Iowa City, Iowa. *Office:* Department of Finance, University of Iowa, Iowa City, Iowa 52240.

CAREER: University of Arkansas, Fayetteville, instructor in economics, 1948-51; U.S. Government, Ninth Regional Wage Stabilization Board, Kansas City, Mo., industrial relations analyst supervisor, 1951-53; aircraft plant cost and financial analyst in Kansas City, 1953-54; University of Iowa, Iowa City, assistant professor, 1954-58, associate professor 1959-63, professor of finance, 1964—. Visiting summer professor, University of California, Los Angeles, 1960; visiting professor, University of South Carolina, 1972. Consultant to U.S. Senate Subcommittee on Reports, Accounting, and Management. *Military service:* U.S. Army, economist; retired as lieutenant colonel. *Member:* American Finance Association, Financial Management Association, American Association of University Professors, Midwest Finance Association (president, 1967).

WRITINGS: Lectures in Financial Management, 3rd edition, Lucas Brothers, 1961; *Financial Management: A Workbook of Core Problems,* 2nd edition, W. C. Brown, 1961; (with J. T. Murphy) *Growth Yields on Common Stocks: Theory and Practice,* State University of Iowa, 1964; *College and University Retirement Programs,* University of Iowa, 1966; *Institutional Holdings of Common Stock, 1900-2000,* University of Michigan, 1971; (with Garnet Olive) *Financial Management,* South-Western, 1974, 2nd edition (with Serraino and Singhvi) published as *Frontiers of Financial Management,* 1976, 3rd edition, 1980; (with Dale Max) *Holding Period Yields and Risk-Premium Curves for Long-Term Marketable Securities,* New York University, 1978. Also author of *Capital Budgeting Practices in Small Manufacturing Companies in Iowa,* 1963. Contributor to accounting, financial, and public utilities journals.

* * *

SOLO, Robert A(lexander) 1916-

PERSONAL: Born August 2, 1916, in Philadelphia, Pa.; son of Louis (a merchant) and Rebecca (Muchnick) Solo; married Carolyn Shaw Bell, June, 1942 (divorced, 1949); married Roselyn Starr (a university teacher), August, 1958; children: (first marriage) Tova. *Education:* Harvard University, B.S. (magna cum laude), 1938; American University, M.A., 1941; Cornell University, Ph.D., 1953; also attended London School of Economics and Political Science. *Politics:* "Democratic Left." *Religion:* Jewish. *Office:* Department of Economics, Michigan State University, East Lansing, Mich. 48823.

CAREER: Economist in U.S. Government agencies, Washington, D.C., 1939-41; WCAU-Television (Columbia Broadcasting System affiliate), Philadelphia, Pa., writer and script chief, 1948-49; Rutgers University, New Brunswick, N.J., instructor, 1952-54, assistant professor of economics, 1954-55; McGill University, Montreal, Quebec, visiting lecturer in economics, 1955-56; City College (now City College of the City University of New York), New York, N.Y., assistant professor of economics, 1956-59; Economic Development Administration of Commonwealth of Puerto Rico, San Juan, consultant, 1959-61; National Planning Association, Washington, D.C., project director, 1961-63; Organization for Economic Cooperation and Development, Paris, France, consultant to directorate of scientific affairs, 1963-64; Sorbonne, University of Paris, Paris, France, lecturer in economics, 1964-65; National Academy of Sciences and National Research Council, Washington, D.C., special associate to foreign secretary, 1965; Princeton University, Princeton, N.J., senior research economist, 1965-66; Michigan State University, East Lansing, professor of economics and management, 1966—, director of Institute of International Business and Economic Development Studies, 1966-68. Visiting lecturer, University of Michigan, summer, 1955; professeur associe, University of Paris, 1971; Fulbright lecturer, University of Grenoble, 1972-73. Consultant to U.S. Senate subcommittee on patents, trademarks, and copyrights, 1956-58, to National Aeronautics and Space Administration (NASA), 1965-67, and to National Conference Board, 1970-72. *Military service:* U.S. Navy, 1941-46.

WRITINGS: Industrial Capacity in the United States, Office of Price Administration and Civilian Supply, 1941; (with Georges Agadjanian) *La Vallee des Ombres* (novel), Editions de la Maison Francaise, 1941; (editor and contributor) *Economics and the Public Interest,* Rutgers University Press, 1955; *Synthetic Rubber: A Case Study in Technological Development under Government Direction,* U.S. Government Printing Office (for U.S. Senate Committee on the Judiciary), 1959.

Essai su l'Amerique, Editions de la Diaspora Francaise, 1960; *Journal,* Editions de la Diaspora Francaise, 1961; *Economic Organizations and Social Systems,* Bobbs-Merrill, 1967; (editor with Everett Rogers, and contributor) *Inducing Technological Advance in Economic Growth and Development,* Michigan State University Press, 1973; *Organizing Science for Technology Transfer in Economic Development,* Michigan State University Press, 1975.

Contributor: Nathan Rosenberg, editor, *The Economics of Technological Change,* Penguin, 1971; *Does Economics Ignore You?,* Committee on Economic Development, 1972; Martin Pfaff, editor, *Frontiers of Social Thought,* North-Holland Publishing, 1975; Lindberg, Alford, Crouch, and Offe, editors, *Stress and Contradiction in Modern Capitalism,* Lexington Books, 1976; Pfaff, editor, *Grants and Exchange,* North-Holland Publishing, 1976. Also contributor to *America's World Role for the Next Twenty-five Years,* proceedings of a professional conference in Taiwan, 1976.

Contributor of about fifty articles and reviews to economics journals and other publications, including *Saturday Review, Technology and Culture, Current, Looking Ahead, Challenge, Canadian Bar Review, Journal of Philosophy,* and *Social Science.*

SIDELIGHTS: In a *Science* review, Kenneth E. Boulding calls *Economic Organizations and Social Systems* "an important work, a milestone on the long and difficult road toward the development of an adequate theory of the dynamics of the world social system." He notes that although the book is somewhat uneven in style "with some long, textbookish passages of rather dull though usually accurate and insightful analysis of social systems," these are interspersed with "passages that are on fire with intellectual and humane passion, and historical vignettes which are masterpieces of condensation and insight with not a word wasted." Boulding concludes that "if this is a work of insight rather than of science it is because of the absence of an adequate system of social instrumentation.... The cognitive theory of social change, which Solo is propounding, will remain in the realm of insight until we develop an adequate information system for what might be called a mass cognitive structure. This we do not now have, and in its absence we have to rely on illustration rather than demonstration."

Robert A. Solo writes: "I sometimes wonder why many who are so beautifully articulate verbally, cannot write effectively. I think it has something to do with the need for an audience. Writing is a kind of talking to yourself, listening to yourself, evaluating yourself by yourself, a solitary business in a way, not for the one geared into and needing the active interplay of conversation and the immediacy of discourse. Before the writer is the dreamer, and for both there is a closed world, a space of rich solitude, for them a haven and the vital source."

BIOGRAPHICAL/CRITICAL SOURCES: Science, September, 1967.

* * *

SOMERS, Herman Miles 1911-

PERSONAL: Born April 11, 1911, in Brooklyn, N.Y.; son of Morris and Edna (Chalfonte) Somers; married Anne M. Ramsay (a medical school professor), August 31, 1946; children: Sara Ramsay, Margaret Ramsay. *Education:* University of Wisconsin, B.S., 1933, Ph.M., 1934; Harvard University, M.A., 1944, Ph.D., 1947. *Office:* Woodrow Wilson School of Public and International Affairs, Princeton University, Princeton, N.J. 08540.

CAREER: Wisconsin Public Welfare Department, Madison, director of research and statistics, 1934-39; U.S. Government, National Resources Planning Board, Washington, D.C., senior economist, 1940-42, Office of War Mobilization and Reconversion, Washington, D.C., economist, 1946-47; Harvard University, Cambridge, Mass., lecturer in government, 1947-48; Haverford College, Haverford, Pa., professor of political science, 1948-63; Princeton University, Woodrow Wilson School of Public and International Affairs, Princeton, N.J., professor of politics and public affairs, 1963—. Visiting professor at several colleges and universities, including University of California. Member of President Kennedy's Task Force on Health and Social Security, 1960-61; counsellor, International Labor Office, Geneva, Switzerland, 1962-63; member of Advisory Council on Social Security, Washington, D.C., 1962-64, and President Johnson's Task Force on Health Legislation, 1964; chairman of New Jersey Employment Security Council, 1964-67; trustee of Blue Cross of New Jersey, 1968—, and College of Medicine and Dentistry of New Jersey, 1970-76; member of board of managers, Haverford College, 1970-76. Consultant to various state and federal agencies. *Military service:* U.S. Army, 1942-46; became lieutenant colonel; received Commendation Medal.

MEMBER: Institute of Medicine, National Academy of Sciences, Industrial Relations Research Association (member of executive board, 1958-61), American Society for Public Administration, Royal Society for Public Administration (Great Britain), Phi Beta Kappa (honorary), Cosmos Club (Washington, D.C.). *Awards, honors:* Toppan Prize, Harvard University, 1947; senior research fellow, Social Science Research Council; Fulbright fellow to United Kingdom; Elizur Wright Award, American Risk and Insurance Association, 1962, for *Doctors, Patients, and Health Insurance;* Ford Research Professor in Government Affairs, 1966-67; Justin Ford Kimball Award, American Hospital Association, 1973; Norman Welch Award, National Association of Blue Shield Plans, for *Health and Health Care.*

WRITINGS: Presidential Agency, Harvard University Press, 1950; (co-author) *Workmen's Compensation,* Wiley, 1954; (with wife, Anne R. Somers) *Doctors, Patients, and Health Insurance,* Brookings Institution, 1961; (contributor) Wallace S. Sayre, *The Federal Government Service,* Prentice-Hall, 1965; (contributor) Stephen K. Bailey, *American Politics and Government,* Basic Books, 1965; (contributor) D. E. Haight and L. D. Johnston, *The President: Roles and Powers,* Rand McNally, 1965; (contributor) John H. Knowles, *Hospitals, Doctors, and the Public Interest,* Harvard University Press, 1965; (contributor) Margaret S. Gordon, *Poverty in America,* Chandler Publishing, 1965; (co-author) *Medicare and the Hospitals,* Brookings Institution, 1967; (with A. Somers) *Health and Health Care: Policies in Perspective,* Aspen Systems Corp., 1977. Contributor to *Encyclopaedia Britannica* and to *International Encyclopedia of the Social Sciences.* Contributor of more than fifty articles to professional journals.

* * *

SOMMER, Richard J(erome) 1934-

PERSONAL: Born August 27, 1934, in St. Paul, Minn.; son of Henning V. and Ida (Jerome) Sommer; married Gillian Taylor, June 17, 1961 (divorced, 1969); married Victoria Tansey (a dancer and teacher), May 1, 1969; children: (second marriage) Jonathan, Anna. *Education:* University of Minnesota, B.A. (summa cum laude), 1956; Harvard University, A.M., 1957, Ph.D., 1962. *Religion:* Buddhist. *Home:* Pinnacle Mt. Rd., Abercorn, Quebec, Canada. *Office:* Department of English, Sir George Williams Campus, Concordia University, Montreal, Quebec, Canada H3G 1M8.

CAREER: Worked as an electric meter reader and a dance company stage manager; Concordia University, Sir George Williams Campus, Montreal, Quebec, assistant professor, 1962-67, associate professor of English, 1967—. *Awards, honors:* American-Scandinavian Foundation fellowship for research in Norway, 1958-59.

WRITINGS: The Odyssey and Primitive Religion, Norwegian Universities Press, 1962; (with Georg Roppen) *Strangers and Pilgrims: An Essay on the Metaphor of Journey,* Norwegian Universities Press, 1964.

Poetry; all published by Delta Canada: *Homage to Mr. MacMullin,* 1969; *The Blue Sky Notebook,* 1972; *Milareba,* 1976; *Left Hand Mind,* 1976; *The Other Side of Games,* 1977.

WORK IN PROGRESS: Research on the Aesthetics of improvisation in poetry, sound poetry, music, and movement art.

* * *

SONTAG, Frederick (Earl) 1924-

PERSONAL: Born October 2, 1924, in Long Beach, Calif.; son of M. Burnett and Matilda (Nicholson) Sontag; married Carol Ann Furth, June 10, 1950; children: Grant Furth, Ann Burnett. *Education:* Stanford University, B.A. (with great distinction), 1949; Yale University, M.A., 1951, Ph.D., 1952. *Office:* Department of Philosophy, Pomona College, Claremont, Calif. 91711.

CAREER: Yale University, New Haven, Conn., instructor in philosophy, 1951-52; Pomona College, Claremont, Calif., Robert C. Denison Professor of Philosophy, 1952—, chairman of department, 1960-67 and 1976-77, chairman of Committee on Honors Study, 1961-70. Visiting professor, Union Theological Seminary, 1959-60, Collegio di Sant'Anselmo (Rome), 1966-67, University of Copenhagen, 1972, University of Kyoto (Japan), 1974, and East-West Center (Honolulu), 1974; theologian-in-residence, American Church in Paris, 1973; Fulbright Regional American Professor, East Asian and Pacific Area, 1977-78. President of board of directors, Claremont Family Service, 1960-64; member of coordinating committee in philosophy, Claremont Graduate School and University Center, 1962-65; member of board of trustees, Coro Foundation, 1967-71; member of board of directors and chairman of Ways and Means Committee, Pilgrim Place, 1970—. Member of national advisory board, Kent Fellowship Program of the Danforth Foundation, 1965-66. *Military service:* U.S. Army, 1943-46; became sergeant. *Member:* American Philosophical Association, National Council on Religion in Higher Education (fellow), American Academy of Religion, Metaphysical Society of America, Phi Beta Kappa. *Awards, honors:* Wig Distinguished Professor Award, 1970 and 1976; LL.D., College of Idaho, 1971.

WRITINGS: Divine Perfection, Harper, 1962; (author of critical introduction) Kierkegaard, *Authority and Revelation,* Harper, 1966; *The Existentialist Prolegomena: To a Future Metaphysics,* University of Chicago Press, 1969; *The Future of Theology: A Philosophical Basis for Contemporary Protestant Theology,* Westminster, 1969; *The Crisis of Faith: A Protestant Witness in Rome,* Doubleday, 1969; *The God of Evil: An Argument from the Existence of the Devil,* Harper, 1970; *God, Why Did You Do That?,* Westminster, 1970; *The Problems of Metaphysics,* Chandler Publishing (San Francisco), 1970; *How Philosophy Shapes Theology: Problems in the Philosophy of Religion,* Harper, 1971; (with John K. Roth) *The American Religious Experience: The Roots, Trends, and the Future of American Theology,* Harper, 1972; *Love Beyond Pain: Mysticism within Christianity,* Paulist/Newman, 1977; *Sun Myung Moon and the Unification Church,* Abingdon, 1977; (with Roth) *God and America's Future,* Consortium, 1977; *What Can God Do?,* Abingdon, 1979; *A Kierkegaard Handbook,* John Knox, 1980. Also author of *The Anatomy of Philosophy: Understanding Understanding* and of *The Sound of Silence: Speaking for God.*

Contributor: McGill, editor, *Masterpieces of World Philosophy,* two volumes, Salem Press, 1961; *Library of Philosophy and Theology,* S.C.M. Press, 1962; (with Jones, Bechner, and Fogelin) *Approaches to Ethics,* McGraw, 1962, 3rd edition, 1977; McGill, editor, *Masterpieces of Christian Literature,* two volumes, Salem Press, 1963; J. H. Gill, editor, *Essays on Kierkegaard,* Burgess, 1970; James William McClendon, Jr., editor, *Philosophy of Religion and Theology: 1974,* Scholars' Press, 1974; Peter Slater, editor, *Philosophy of Religion and Theology: 1976,* Scholars' Press, 1976. Contributor to proceedings of numerous conferences and to *Encyclopaedia of Morals.* Contributor of articles and reviews to philosophy and religion journals.

SIDELIGHTS: In a review of *The Existentialist Prolegomena: To a Future Metaphysics,* Erazim V. Kohak writes that Frederick Sontag's thesis in the book "is not only that human existence is real, but that human reality is *knowable and intelligible.* He argues that the traditional fortes of existentialism, philosophical psychology and literature, reveal not simply reality, but an order—eidetic structures of human being-in-the-world which can serve as categories of radically new metaphysics. Sontag proposes no less than to use them in precisely that way." But the problem with this book, according to Kohak, is that "Sontag works in an intellectual isolation unusual even for an existentialist. Not only does he ignore the large body of material in related areas, but he chooses rather narrowly even among the existentialists. The description of existence with which he works is derived entirely from the work, quarter of a century old, of two war-time existentialists, Heidegger and Sartre." In the end, the reviewer concludes that "Sontag is ultimately so entirely right. A radically new metaphysics will have to be based on experience, concrete, immediate human living-in and dealing-with the world, not on metaphysical abstractions of another era, including the titantic abstractions of war-time existentialism. The proposal Sontag makes in *The Existentialist Prolegomena* is significant—the failure, though unfortunate, is incidental."

Robert L. Perkins calls *The God of Evil: An Argument from the Existence of the Devil* "exciting for the novel insights which [Sontag] brings to the task of the philosophical analysis of theology and the theological analysis of philosophy." He feels that the author's conclusions are significant because "he restores some of the complexity of the idea of God which has been lacking in much recent philosophical speculation and theology, which is the result of modern man's search for simplicity and certainty." But Charles E. Winquist finds Sontag's arguments "disarmingly casual. There is a need for a more rigorous method in constructing the metaphysical structures which he claims are necessary for a revitalized theism in a philosophical climate which has rejected metaphysics. Methodological problems are also present in his theological claims. The arguments relating to the denial of the existence of God do not explain the positive attributes which Sontag ascribes to God."

BIOGRAPHICAL/CRITICAL SOURCES: *Commonweal,* October 10, 1969; *Library Journal,* July, 1970; *Christian Century,* October 21, 1970.

* * *

SORDEN, L(eland) G(eorge) 1898-

PERSONAL: Born May 23, 1898, in Webster, Iowa; son of George A. and Mary Jane Sorden; married Ruth Bartholomew, 1926; children: Dale L., Sue L., James L. *Education:* Iowa State College of Agriculture and Mechanic Arts (now Iowa State University of Science and Technology), B.S., 1923; also attended University of Wisconsin. *Home:* 212 North Allen, Madison, Wis.

CAREER: County agricultural agent in Atlantic, Iowa, 1923-27, and Rhinelander, Wis., 1928-34; U.S. Department of Agriculture, agricultural agent in Rhinelander, and Madison, Wis., 1934-41; University of Wisconsin—Madison, member of staff of Cooperative Extension Service, 1941-65. *Military service;* Students' Army Training Corps, 1917. *Member:* Wisconsin Forest History Association, Epsilon Sigma Phi, Phi Mu Alpha, Rotary Club, Lions Club.

WRITINGS: (With Robert Gard) *Wisconsin Lore,* Duell, Sloane & Pearce, 1962; (with Gard) *The Romance of Wisconsin Place Names,* October House, 1968; (with E. Louise Miller) *I Am the Mississippi,* Stanton & Lee, 1974. Also author of *Loggers Words of Yesteryear,* 1956, *Family Records,* 1960, and *Lumberjack Lingo,* 1966.

SIDELIGHTS: Considered an authority on the folklore and tools of agriculture, past and present, L. G. Sorden is interested in logging history, the Rhinelander, Wisc. Museum, and Wisconsin stories and people.

* * *

SOUTHERN, Terry 1926- (Maxwell Kenton, a joint pseudonym)

PERSONAL: Born May 1, 1926, in Alvarado, Tex.; son of T. M. (a pharmacist) and Helen (Simonds) Southern; married Carol Kauffman, 1956; children: Nile (son). *Education:* Attended Southern Methodist University and University of Chicago; Northwestern University, B.A., 1948. *Home address:* R.F.D., East Canaan, Conn.

CAREER: Writer. *Military service:* U.S. Army, 1943-45. *Awards, honors:* British Screen Writers Award, 1964, for "Dr. Strangelove."

WRITINGS: *Flash and Filigree,* Coward, 1958; (with Mason Hoffenberg under joint pseudonym Maxwell Kenton) *Candy,* Olympia Press (Paris), 1958, published under names Terry Southern and Mason Hoffenberg, Putnam, 1964, published as *Lollipop,* Olympia Press (Paris), 1962; *The Magic Christian* (also see below), Deutsch, 1959, Random House, 1960; *The Journal of "The Loved One": The Production Log of a Motion Picture,* Random House, 1965; *Red-Dirt Marijuana and Other Tastes* (short story collection), New American Library, 1967; (contributor) *Pardon Me, Sir, But Is My Eye Hurting Your Elbow?,* Geis, 1968; (with Peter Fonda and Dennis Hopper) *Easy Rider* (text of screenplay; also see below), New American Library, 1969; *Blue Movie,* World Publishing, 1970.

Screenplays: (With David Burnett) "Candy Kisses," 1955; (with Stanley Kubrick and Peter George) "Dr. Strangelove or; How I Learned to Stop Worrying and Love the Bomb," Columbia, 1964; (with Christopher Isherwood) "The Loved One," Metro-Goldwyn-Meyer, 1965; (with Ring Lardner, Jr.) "The Cincinnati Kid," Metro-Goldwyn-Meyer, 1965; (with Roger Vadim) "Barbarella," Paramount, 1968; (with Peter Fonda and Dennis Hopper) "Easy Rider," Columbia, 1969; (with Aram Avakian) "The End of the Road," Allied Artists, 1969; (with Peter Sellers and Joseph McGrath) "The Magic Christian" (based on novel of same title), Commonwealth United, 1969. Also author of "The Private War of Wolsey Fickett." Contributor to *Paris Review, Esquire, Argosy, Playboy, Nation,* and other periodicals. Advisory editor, *Best American Short Stories,* 1955-56.

SIDELIGHTS: A satirical writer of both novels and screenplays, Terry Southern once explained that "the important thing in writing is the capacity to astonish. Not shock—shock is a worn-out word—but astonish. The world has no grounds whatever for complacency. The *Titanic* couldn't sink, but it did. Where you find smugness you find something worth blasting. I want to blast it."

Southern's *Candy* appeared on the bestseller lists only after overcoming several obstacles. A spoof of pornography, *Candy* was banned by the French government as indecent after its original publication in Paris, and the French publisher had to change the title of the book to *Lollipop* before continuing publication. In America, publishers waited several years before printing the book, fearful that in satirizing pornography the book itself was pornographic and subject to legal action. In England only a shorter version was published, with certain questionable passages removed from the text.

Despite *Candy*'s scandalous reputation, William Styron

maintains that "much of the book is not about sex at all" and "in its best scenes [it] is wickedly funny to read and morally bracing as only good satire can be." Alfred Chester writes that, as satire, *Candy* "is very safe satire indeed. It abuses only those who are quite used to abuse from the popular press and from popular prejudices. . . . One can come away from this book with all one's provincialism and narrow-mindedness intact."

Southern's screenplays have met with an intensely divided reaction. Many critics find the satire in films like "The Magic Christian," and "The End of the Road" to be overdone. Judith Christ, in a review of "The End of the Road," describes Southern as a member of "the Screw-You-and-Everything-Else-in-the-Vicinity School of Screenwriting." When his work is more serious, however, or the satire more firmly in control, the critical reaction can be very favorable. Speaking of "Easy Rider," for example, Joseph Morgenstern states that "the movie reached out and profoundly shook me." Anthony West judges "Rider" to be "one of the most effective and memorable films that has so far been produced in the United States."

Speaking with Paul Krassner about his youth and early writing, Southern once said: "I was pretty much a regular guy in most respects . . . just a good, ordinary Texas boy. But there was this wild story by [Edgar Allan] Poe—"The Narrative of A. Gordon Pym." I used to rewrite this story and try to make it wilder. And then once I showed it to my friend Big Lawrence. 'God-damn, you must be crazy,' he said. I think that's when we began to drift apart—I mean, Texas and me."

The Magic Christian and *Candy* have been filmed. Film rights to *Flash and Filigree* have been sold.

AVOCATIONAL INTERESTS: Animals and hunting.

BIOGRAPHICAL/CRITICAL SOURCES: *New York Times Book Review,* September 28, 1958, September 13, 1970; *Time,* September 29, 1958, June 12, 1964, February 23, 1970, August 24, 1970; *Spectator,* July 3, 1959, September 13, 1968; *New Statesman,* July 4, 1959; *Times Literary Supplement,* July 17, 1959; *Nation,* February 27, 1960, May 18, 1964; *Commonweal,* April 29, 1960; *New York Review of Books,* May 14, 1964; *Newsweek,* June 22, 1964, July 21, 1969; *New Republic,* July 11, 1964; *Life,* August 21, 1964; *Realist,* Number 50; *Books,* June, 1965; *Holiday,* June, 1965; *New York Times Magazine,* January 16, 1966; Robert Scholes, *The Fabulators,* Oxford University Press, 1967; *National Observer,* January 8, 1968; *Hudson Review,* spring, 1968; *Listener,* September 12, 1968; *Punch,* September 18, 1968; *Vogue,* August 1, 1969; *New York Times,* February 11, 1970; *New York,* February 16, 1970; *Village Voice,* February 26, 1970; *Washington Post,* March 6, 1970; *Saturday Review,* October 31, 1970; *Books and Bookmen,* September, 1973; *Chicago Tribune Book Week,* May 17, 1974; *Contemporary Literary Criticism,* Volume VII, Gale, 1977.†

* * *

SPACKS, Patricia Meyer 1929-

PERSONAL: Born November 17, 1929, in San Francisco, Calif.; daughter of Norman Bernhardt and Lillian (Talcott) Meyer; married Barry B. Spacks, 1955; children: Judith Elizabeth. *Education:* Rollins College, B.A. (summa cum laude), 1949; Yale University, M.A., 1950; University of California, Ph.D., 1955. *Home:* 16 Abbott St., Wellesley, Mass. *Office:* Department of English, Wellesley College, Wellesley, Mass. 02181.

CAREER: Indiana University at Bloomington, instructor, 1954-56; University of Florida, Gainesville, instructor, 1958-59; Wellesley College, Wellesley, Mass., 1959—, began as instructor, currently professor of English. *Member:* Modern Language Association of America, American Society for Eighteenth-Century Studies. *Awards, honors:* Shirley Farr fellowship of American Association of University Women, 1962-63; Guggenheim fellowship, 1969-70; National Endowment for the Humanities senior fellowship, 1974; National Humanities Institute fellowship, 1976-77; D.H.L., Rollins College, 1976; American Council of Learned Societies fellowship, 1978-79.

WRITINGS: *The Varied God: A Critical Study of Thomson's "The Seasons,"* University of California Press, 1959; *The Insistence of Horror: Aspects of the Supernatural in Eighteenth-Century Poetry,* Harvard University Press, 1962; (editor) *Eighteenth-Century Poetry,* Prentice-Hall, 1964; *John Gay,* Twayne, 1965; *The Poetry of Vision,* Harvard University Press, 1967; (editor) *Late Augustan Prose,* Prentice-Hall, 1971; *An Argument of Images,* Harvard University Press, 1971; (editor) *Late Augustan Poetry,* Prentice-Hall, 1973; *The Female Imagination,* Knopf, 1975; *Imagining a Self,* Harvard University Press, 1976; (editor) *Contemporary Woman Novelists,* Prentice-Hall, 1977. Contributor to drama and language journals.

WORK IN PROGRESS: A study of adolescent fantasies about adolescence from the eighteenth century to the present.

* * *

SPERRY, (Sally) Baxter 1914-
(S.S.E.)

PERSONAL: Born July 10, 1914, in Wurzburg, Germany; daughter of John Augustus (a physician) and Lillian (Mason) Sperry; married Sterling Robert Newman, March 16, 1934 (divorced, 1941). *Education:* Attended Saline-Johnstone Business College, 1931-32, and University of California, Berkeley, 1943; San Francisco College for Women (now Lone Mountain College), B.A., 1956; San Francisco State College (now University), M.A., 1958; Washington State University, additional graduate study, 1960-62. *Residence:* Galt, Calif. *Office address:* Laurel Hill Press, P.O. Box 202, Galt, Calif. 95632.

CAREER: *Utah Magazine,* Salt Lake City, Utah, women's editor, 1937-38; U.S. Army, Okinawa, teacher, 1951, writer, 1952-53; U.S. Navy, Philippine Islands, teacher, 1956; teacher in Sacramento County, Calif., 1958-59; California Redwood Association, San Francisco, editorial writer and assistant director of public relations, 1963; California Department of Rehabilitation, Los Angeles, counselor, 1966-67; Laurel Hill Press and Covenant Press, Galt, Calif., publisher, 1968—. Director of Galt Bicentennial Commission. *Member:* National Trust for Historic Preservation, Archives Associates, American Biographical Institute Research Association, American Security Council, California Teachers Association, San Joaquin County Historical Association, Dry Creek Antiquarian Association (secretary, 1968—), Sacramento County Property Owners Association (chairman of Galt chapter, 1969—), Psi Chi. *Awards, honors:* Third prize from San Francisco Browning Society, 1968, for dramatic monologue, *Nikita, Prophet;* Literary Achievement Award, Sacramento Arts Council, 1974; commendation and gold medal for history from State of California, 1976; plaque and commendation from city of Galt, 1976; National Trust for Historic Preservation grant, 1978; National Endowment for the Humanities grant, 1978.

WRITINGS: (Under initials S. S. E.) *Mad Dog Daze,* privately printed, 1951; *Long Remember,* privately printed, 1957.

Published by Covenant Press, except as indicated: *Cruachan,* Peach Pit Press, 1966; *Ne Obliviscaris,* privately printed, 1967; *Nikita, Prophet,* 1968; *Senator Joe McCarthy, Martyr,* 1968; *This King, No Crown in Heaven,* 1968; *For Our Long Future's Sake,* 1969; *Death is a Moment's Wonder,* 1969; *Dramatic Monologues,* Laurel Hill Press, 1969.

All published by Laurel Hill Press: *Old Buildings, Sacramento, etc.,* 1970; *The City of Galt,* 1970; *Recollections of Joe Woodard,* 1971; *Recollections of Maude Quiggle Proctor,* 1971; *Recollections of Jim Sawyer,* 1972; *Reincarnation,* 1974; *Recollections of Eloisa Del Castillo Sifers,* 1974; *Engravings of Galt,* 1974; *The Ninth Earl of Argyll,* 1974; *The Chabolla Land Grant,* 1975; *Mexican Land Grants* (five volumes), 1976; *Almanac, 1833,* 1977; *Liberty City,* 1978; *Arroyo Seco Grant, Del Paso Grant, San Juan Grant,* 1980; *Jackson Burke and the Printing Arts,* 1980.

"Star Storm" sonnet series: *Spring,* Covenant Press, 1968; *Summer,* Laurel Hill Press, 1971; *Autumn,* Laurel Hill Press, 1977.

WORK IN PROGRESS: Decorative Capitals.

SIDELIGHTS: Baxter Sperry told *CA:* "English is my third language, and as a small child in school I had trouble with spoken English. I suppose this is one element in my taking the direction of a writer. I have six teaching fields, and when I find difficulty in finding materials during research, I put everything I find together into a short book, with conclusions. In actually doing the work, I research my subject, sometimes over several years, and then write my piece all at once, working eight or ten hours a day, then rewrite, or edit immediately. I do not write legibly by hand, and do all my writing on a typewriter.

"In my series of 855 sonnets I was naturally influenced by Shakespeare and Petrarch and Spenser. Their thought systems are different from contemporary American thought, and I tried to express the upheavals of our century and the very complex American philosophy. I wrote one sonnet a night for 855 nights."

BIOGRAPHICAL/CRITICAL SOURCES: California Librarian, April, 1972; *American Book Collector,* May-June, 1973.

* * *

SPIRO, Melford E(lliot) 1920-

PERSONAL: Born April 26, 1920, in Cleveland, Ohio; son of Wilbert I. (a businessman) and Sophie (Goodman) Spiro; married Audrey Goldman, May 29, 1950; children: Michael, Jonathan. *Education:* University of Minnesota, B.A., 1941; Northwestern University, Ph.D., 1950. *Home:* 2500 Torrey Pines Rd., La Jolla, Calif. 92037. *Office:* Department of Anthropology, University of California, San Diego, La Jolla, Calif. 92037.

CAREER: Washington University, St. Louis, Mo., assistant professor of anthropology, 1948-52; University of Connecticut, Storrs, associate professor of anthropology, 1952-57; University of Washington, Seattle, professor of anthropology, 1957-64; University of Chicago, Chicago, Ill., professor of anthropology, 1964-68; University of California, San Diego, La Jolla, professor of anthropology, 1968—. Member of board of directors, Social Science Research Council, 1960-62.

MEMBER: American Anthropological Association, American Ethnological Society (president, 1967-68), American Association for the Advancement of Science, American Academy of Religion, Association for Asian Studies. *Awards, honors:* Social Science Research Council fellow, 1951-52 (in Israel), 1955-57; Center for Advanced Study in the Behavioral Sciences fellow, 1958-59; National Science Foundation grant for research in Burma, 1961-62; National Institute of Child Health and Human Development grant for research in Burma and Israel, 1968-72; American Academy of Arts and Sciences fellow, 1975—; Guggenheim fellow, 1976-77.

WRITINGS: (With E. G. Burrows) *An Atoll Culture,* Human Relations Area File Press, 1953; *Kibbutz: Venture in Utopia,* Harvard University Press, 1956, revised edition, Schocken, 1971; *Children of the Kibbutz: A Study in Child Training and Personality,* Harvard University Press, 1958; (editor) *Context and Meaning in Cultural Anthropology,* Free Press, 1965; *Burmese Supernaturalism: A Study in the Explanation and Reduction of Suffering,* Prentice-Hall, 1967; *Buddhism and Society,* Harper, 1971; *Kinship and Marriage in Burma,* University of California Press, 1977; *Gender and Culture,* Duke University Press, 1979. Associate editor, *American Anthropologist,* 1962-64, *Philosophy of Science,* 1964-75, and *Ethos,* 1971—.

WORK IN PROGRESS: Cultural Systems and Symbolic Analysis.

* * *

SPOLSKY, Bernard 1932-

PERSONAL: Born February 11, 1932, in Wellington, New Zealand; son of Choony Aby (an accountant) and Ellen K. (Green) Spolsky; married Ellen Schaps (an associate professor of English), December 22, 1962; children: Avram, Ruth. *Education:* Victoria University of Wellington, B.A., 1951, M.A., 1953; University of Montreal, Ph.D., 1966. *Religion:* Jewish. *Home:* 2317 Camino de los Artesanos N.W., Albuquerque, N.M. 87107. *Office:* Department of Linguistics, University of New Mexico, Albuquerque, N.M. 87131.

CAREER: Assistant master at schools in New Zealand and Australia, 1954-58; Hebrew University of Jerusalem, Jerusalem, Israel, instructor in English, 1958-61; McGill University, Montreal, Quebec, assistant professor of education, 1961-64; Indiana University at Bloomington, assistant professor of linguistics, 1964-68; University of New Mexico, Albuquerque, associate professor, 1968-72, professor of linguistics, elementary education, and anthropology, 1972—, graduate dean, 1974—. Visiting professor at University of Montreal, 1962-64; Hebrew University of Jerusalem, visiting lecturer, 1968, Lady Davis Visiting Professor, 1979. Member of board of trustees, Center for Applied Linguistics, 1978-80. Consultant to Ford Foundation in Thailand, 1967, U.S. Department of State in Poland, 1968, Bureau of Indian Affairs, 1969, Trust Territory of Pacific Islands, 1973-74, and government of American Samoa, 1979. *Military service:* Israel Defence Forces, 1959-60.

MEMBER: American Association for Applied Linguistics (secretary-treasurer, 1978-80), Linguistic Society of America, Modern Language Association of America, American Anthropological Association, Teachers of English to Speakers of Other Languages (president, 1978-79). *Awards, honors:* Guggenheim fellowship, 1971.

WRITINGS: Educational Linguistics: An Introduction, Newbury House Publishers, 1978.

Editor: (With Paul Garvin) *Computation in Linguistics: A Case Book,* Indiana University Press, 1966; *The Language Education of Minority Children: Selected Readings,* Newbury House Publishers, 1972; (with Leslie Palmer) *Papers in Language Testing, 1967-1974,* TESOL, 1975; (with Randall L. Jones) *Testing Language Proficiency,* Center for Applied Linguistics, 1975; (with Robert L. Cooper) *Frontiers of Bilingual Education,* Newbury House Publishers, 1977; (with Cooper) *Case Studies in Bilingual Education,* Newbury House Publishers, 1978; *Advances in Language Testing: Series 2,* Center for Applied Linguistics, 1978; *Advances in Language Testing: Series 1,* Center for Applied Linguistics, 1979.

Contributor to professional journals, including *Language Learning, International Review of Education,* and *Behavioral Science.* Editor, *Applied Linguistics.*

WORK IN PROGRESS: Studies of sociolinguistics of literacy, bilingualism, and educational linguistics.

* * *

SPOTTE, Stephen 1942-

PERSONAL: Born March 16, 1942, in Wheeling, W.Va.; son of Adler E. (an engineer) and Helen (Hancock) Spotte; married Carol Daniels, July 22, 1971 (divorced September 1, 1978); children: Sara Lynn, Michael. *Education:* Marshall University, B.S., 1965. *Home address:* P.O. Box 173, North Stonington, Conn. 06359. *Office:* Sea Research Foundation, Inc., Mystic Marinelife Aquarium, Mystic, Conn. 06355.

CAREER: Aquarium of Niagara Falls, Niagara Falls, N.Y., curator of exhibits, 1965-67, general curator, 1967-70, director, 1970-72; New York Aquarium, Brooklyn, N.Y., curator, 1972-73; Aquarium Systems, Inc., Eastlake, Ohio, director of aquariums, 1973-77; Mystic Marinelife Aquarium, Sea Research Foundation, Inc., Mystic, Conn. director of aquariums, 1977—. Scuba diver and underwater photographer.

WRITINGS: Fish and Invertebrate Culture, Wiley, 1970, 2nd edition, 1979; *Marine Aquarium Keeping,* Wiley, 1973; *Secrets of the Deep,* Scribner, 1976; *Seawater Aquariums,* Wiley, 1979. Contributor of scientific articles to professional journals; contributor of photographs and articles on natural history to popular periodicals.

* * *

SPRAGUE, Marshall 1909-

PERSONAL: Born March 14, 1909, in Newark, Ohio; son of Joseph Taylor and Della Grace (Cochran) Sprague; married Edna Jane Ailes, February 14, 1939; children: Joseph Taylor, Stephen John Eugene, Sharon Huff. *Education:* Princeton University, B.S., 1930. *Home:* 1523 Wood Ave., Colorado Springs, Colo. 80907.

CAREER: Women's Wear Daily, New York, N.Y., reporter, 1931; *North China Star,* Tientsin, China, reporter, 1933-34; member of Paris staff, *New York Herald-Tribune,* 1934-35; feature writer and book reviewer, *New York Times,* 1936—. Director of nonfiction workshop, Annual Writer's Conference, University of Colorado, 1965. *Awards, honors:* Top Hands Award, Colorado Authors League, 1957, for *Massacre: The Tragedy at White River;* Benjamin McKie Rastall Award, Colorado College, 1959, for "distinguished cultural service to Colorado"; D.H.L., University of Colorado, 1978.

WRITINGS: The Business of Getting Well, Crowell, 1943; *Money Mountain: The Story of Cripple Creek Gold,* Little, Brown, 1953, reprinted, University of Nebraska Press, 1979; *This Is Central City,* Central City Opera House Association, 1955; *Massacre: The Tragedy at White River,* Little, Brown, 1957, reprinted, University of Nebraska Press, 1980; (contributor) *Great Pioneer Heroes,* Bartholomew House, 1958; *Newport in the Rockies,* Sage Books, 1961, revised edition, Ohio University Press, 1980; *The Great Gates,* Little, Brown, 1964, reprinted, University of Nebraska Press, 1980; *A Gallery of Dudes,* Little, Brown, 1967, reprinted, University of Nebraska Press, 1979; *The Mountain States,* Time-Life, 1967; *One Hundred Plus,* Colorado Springs Centennial, 1971; *So Vast So Beautiful a Land,* Little, Brown, 1974; *Colorado: A Bicentennial History,* Norton, 1976; *El Paso Club: A Century of Friendship,* Colorado Springs Centennial, 1977. Contributor of articles to popular magazines.

WORK IN PROGRESS: A study of mountain men.

SIDELIGHTS: When asked what advice he would give to aspiring authors, Marshall Sprague told *CA:* "You learn to write by writing. There is no other way."

BIOGRAPHICAL/CRITICAL SOURCES: Saturday Review, August 22, 1953; *Territorial Enterprise and Virginia City News,* June 2, 1961; *New York Times Book Review,* February 5, 1967; *Christian Science Monitor,* August 3, 1967; *Denver Post,* September 26, 1976.

* * *

SPURLING, John 1936-

PERSONAL: Born July 17, 1936, in Kisumu, Kenya; son of Anthony Cuthbert (a barrister) and Elizabeth (Stobart) Spurling; married Hilary Forrest (a writer), April 4, 1961; children: Amy Maria, Nathaniel Stobart, Gilbert Alexander. *Education:* St. John's College, Oxford, B.A. 1960. *Residence:* London, England. *Agent:* MLR Ltd., 194 Old Brompton Rd., London SW5 OA5, England.

CAREER: Playwright. British Government, Kumba, Southern Cameroons, plebiscite officer, 1960-61; British Broadcasting Corp., London, England, announcer, 1963-66. *Military service:* British Army, Royal Artillery, 1955-57; became second lieutenant. *Awards, honors:* Henfield writing fellowship, University of East Anglia, 1973.

WRITINGS: (With John Fletcher) *Beckett: A Study of His Plays,* Hill & Wang, 1972; (contributor) *Best Plays of 1969-70,* edited by Otis Guernsey, Jr., Dodd, 1970; (contributor) *Best Plays of 1971-72,* edited by Guernsey, Dodd, 1972.

Plays: "Char," first produced in Oxford, England, 1959; *MacRune's Guevara (as Realised by Edward Hotel)* (first produced in London at Jeanette Cochrane Theatre, February 8, 1969; first produced in New York, 1975), Calder & Boyars, 1969; *In the Heart of the British Museum* (first produced in Edinburgh, Scotland, at Traverse Theatre, August 5, 1971), Calder & Boyars, 1971; "Romance" (musical), music and lyrics by Charles Ross, first produced on the West End, at Duke of York's Theatre, September 28, 1971; "Peace in Our Time," first produced in Sheffield, England, at Crucible Theatre, November 16, 1972; "McGonagall and the Murderer," first produced in Edinburgh, August, 1974; "On a Clear Day You Can See Marlowe," first produced in London, 1974; *Shades of Heathcliff* [and] *Death of Captain Doughty* (contains "Shades of Heathcliff" [first produced in Sheffield, at Lucky's, December 8, 1971] and "Death of Captain Doughty" [television play; first broadcast in 1973]), Calder & Boyars, 1975; "While Rome Burns," first produced in Canterbury, England, at Marlowe Theatre, 1976; "Antigone through the Looking Glass," first produced in London, at King's Head Theatre, September, 1979; "The

British Empire, Part One,'' first produced in Birmingham, England, February, 1980.

Also author of television plays, "Hope," 1970, "Faith," 1971, and "Silver," 1973. Art critic for *New Statesman.* Contributor to periodicals.

SIDELIGHTS: Martin Seymour-Smith, in a *Spectator* review, calls *MacRune's Guevara* "consistently intelligent . . . and entertaining." He goes on to say that comparison of the play to "a many-layered cake is tempting but misleading. It is primarily an intellectual play, a witty double-barrelled discharge at abstractionism and uninformed political passion; but the author allows his own passionate emotional involvement with South America to be reflected in a structure that much more resembles a delicately constructed mathematical model than an object with simple layers." Seymour-Smith also notes that "Mr. Spurling has made use of techniques employed by Shaw, Pirandello and—I would suggest—such experimental plays of Eugene O'Neill as *The Great God Brown;* he has also drawn upon the available literature on the Bolivian campaign. The author's originality is apparent in his savage and subtle exploitation of cliche, his rueful but satirical recognition of the power of theatrical rhetoric, and the bad effect it may have—and, most strikingly, in the dazzling manner in which he counterpoints his characters against one another to raise truly Borgesian . . . issues about identity."

BIOGRAPHICAL/CRITICAL SOURCES: Spectator, February 28, 1969; *Stage,* July 9, 1970, December 30, 1971.

* * *

STAAR, Richard F(elix) 1923-

PERSONAL: Born January 10, 1923, in Warsaw, Poland; son of American parents; married Jadwiga Maria Ochota, March 28, 1950; children: Monica Gloria, Christina Marie. *Education:* Dickinson College, A.B., 1948; Yale University, A.M., 1949; University of Michigan, Ph.D., 1954. *Politics:* Republican. *Religion:* Methodist. *Home:* 38 Pearce Mitchell Pl., Stanford, Calif. 94305. *Office:* Hoover Institution on War, Revolution, and Peace, Stanford University, Stanford, Calif. 94305.

CAREER: U.S. Government, Washington, D.C., research specialist, 1949-54; Harding College, Searcy, Ark., professor of political science, 1954-57; Arkansas State College (now University), Jonesboro, professor, 1957-58; University of Maryland in Germany, lecturer in government, 1958-59; Emory University, Atlanta, Ga., professor of political science, 1959-67, chairman of department, 1966-67; National War College, Washington, D.C., professor of foreign affairs, 1967-69; Stanford University, Hoover Institution on War, Revolution, and Peace, Stanford, Calif., associate director, 1969—. Fleet Admiral Nimitz Professor of Social and Political Philosophy, U.S. Naval War College, Newport, R.I., 1963-64. Assistant district commissioner, Quapaw Area Council, Boy Scouts of America, 1955-57; speaker, "Voice of America" radio, 1957—; lecturer in Strasbourg, France, 1958. *Military service:* U.S. Marine Corps Reserve; present rank, colonel. *Member:* American Political Science Association, Navy League, Marine Corps Reserve Officers Association, World Affairs Council of Northern California, Phi Beta Kappa, Phi Kappa Phi, Pi Gamma Mu, Pi Sigma Alpha, Kappa Sigma, Bohemian Club, Cosmos Club.

WRITINGS: Poland, 1944-62: Sovietization of a Captive People, Louisiana State University Press, 1962: *Communist Regimes in Eastern Europe.* Hoover Institution Press, 1967, 3rd edition, 1977; (editor) *Aspects of Modern Communism,* University of South Carolina Press, 1968. Editor of *Yearbook on International Communist Affairs,* Hoover Institution Press, 1969—. Contributor of articles to professional journals in the United States and Europe.

WORK IN PROGRESS: U.S.-Soviet Relations.

SIDELIGHTS: Richard F. Staar speaks or reads Czech, Slovak, French, German, Polish, Bulgarian, Ukrainian, and Russian. He has translated four books and many articles from German, Polish, and Russian.

* * *

STACKPOLE, Edouard Alexander 1903-

PERSONAL: Born December 7, 1903, in Nantucket, Mass.; son of Charles Henry and Therese (Mauduit) Stackpole; married second wife, Florence T. Brown, November 20, 1945; children: (first marriage) Eugenie A., Renny A.; (second marriage) Christopher E. and Matthew P. (twins), Anita L. (stepdaughter). *Education:* Roxbury Latin School, diploma, 1924; University of Massachusetts, special course, 1925-26. *Politics:* Republican. *Religion:* Roman Catholic. *Home:* 84 Main St., Nantucket, Mass. 02554. *Office:* Peter Foulger Museum, Nantucket, Mass.

CAREER: Inquirer and Mirror (weekly newspaper), Nantucket, Mass., reporter, linotype operator, pressman, 1925-45, associate editor, 1945-51, consulting editor, 1957—; Nantucket Historical Association, Nantucket, Mass., librarian and curator, 1951-52; Marine Historical Association, Mystic, Conn., curator, 1953-66; Peter Foulger Museum, Nantucket, director, 1971—. Director of Frank C. Munson Institute of American Maritime History, 1955-66; president of Coffin School Association. *Member:* Sons of the American Revolution, Nantucket Historical Association (president, 1938-52, 1968-71), Winter Club (Nantucket; secretary, 1947-52), Cornet Club. *Awards, honors:* Guggenheim fellow, 1951-52, 1963-64; M.A., Yale University, 1964, and University of Massachusetts, 1979.

WRITINGS: Smuggler's Luck, Morrow, 1931; *You Fight for Treasure,* Morrow, 1933; *Madagascar Jack,* Morrow, 1935; *Privateer Ahoy!,* Morrow, 1937; *Mutiny at Midnight,* Morrow, 1941; *Rambling through the Streets and Lanes of Nantucket,* Inquirer and Mirror Press, 1947, 2nd edition, 1951; *The Sea Hunters,* Lippincott, 1953, reprinted, Greenwood Press, 1973; *Captain Prescott and the Opium Smugglers,* Marine Historical Association, 1954; *Scrimshaw at Mystic Seaport,* Marine Historical Association, 1955; *Voyage of the "Huron" and the "Huntress,"* Marine Historical Association, 1956; *Small Craft at Mystic Seaport,* Marine Historical Association, 1957; *Dead Man's Gold,* Washburn, 1958; (co-author) *The Story of Yankee Whaling,* American Heritage Press, 1960; *Those in Peril on the Sea,* Dial, 1962; *Nantucket Rebel,* Washburn, 1963; *Figureheads and Ship Carvings at Mystic Seaport,* Marine Historical Association, 1964; *The Charles W. Morgan: The Last Wooden Whaleship,* Meredith, 1967; *Whales and Destiny: The Rivalry between America, France, and Great Britain for Control of the Southern Whale Fishery, 1785-1825,* University of Massachusetts Press, 1972; (with Melvin B. Summerfield) *Nantucket Doorways,* Hastings House, 1974; (with Peter Dreyer) *Nantucket in Color,* Hastings House, 1974.

Editor: *Wreck of the "San Francisco,"* Marine Historical Association, 1958; Robert S. Burns, *Ships and Shipping,* World Book Encyclopedia, 1960.

Author of introduction: Prescott, *Rough Passage,* Caxton, 1958; Russell, *The Wreck of the Grosvenor,* Dodd, 1959; *A Conrad Anthology,* Dodd, 1963; *The Globe Mutiny,* Corinth

Books, 1963. Also author of introduction for seven publications of Marine Historical Association.

Author of *Nantucket in the American Revolution,* 1976, and of *The Loss of the Essex,* 1977; also author of three booklets on Nantucket history and events; contributor to *The Concise Encyclopedia of American Antiques, The Concise Encyclopedia of Firearms,* and to *Grolier Encyclopedia.* Contributor of several hundred articles to newspapers, magazines, and history journals; contributor of poetry to *Yankee.* Editor of *Log of Mystic Seaport,* 1960-66, and of *Historic Nantucket* (quarterly of Nantucket Historical Association), 1970—.

WORK IN PROGRESS: A second volume of *The Sea Hunter.*

SIDELIGHTS: Edouard Stackpole has made several television appearances, including two on Columbia Broadcasting System's "Adventure" series. *Avocational interests:* Sailing, working on small craft.

* * *

STAGG, Frank 1911-

PERSONAL: Born October 20, 1911, in Eunice, La.; son of Paul (a rice grower) and Della Edith (Hammers) Stagg; married Evelyn Owen (a public school teacher), August 19, 1935; children: Theodore Owen, Robert Hammers, Virginia. *Education:* Louisiana College, B.A., 1934; Southern Baptist Theological Seminary, Th.M., 1938, Ph.D., 1943; also attended New College, Edinburgh, Scotland, University of Basel, 1953-54, and University of Tuebingen, 1967-68. *Home:* 5610 Ahuawa Pl., Bay St. Louis, Miss. 39520. *Office:* Department of New Testament, Southern Baptist Theological Seminary, 2825 Lexington Rd., Louisville, Ky. 40206.

CAREER: First Baptist Church, De Ridder, La., pastor, 1941-44; New Orleans Baptist Theological Seminary, professor of New Testament and Greek, 1945-64; Southern Baptist Theological Seminary, Louisville, Ky., James Buchanan Harrison Professor of New Testament Interpretation, 1964-76, senior professor of New Testament interpretation, 1976—. *Awards, honors:* LL.D., Louisiana College, 1955.

WRITINGS: The Book of Acts: The Early Struggle for an Unhindered Gospel, Broadman, 1955; *Exploring the New Testament,* Convention Press, 1961; *New Testament Theology,* Broadman, 1962; *Matthew,* Broadman, 1969; *Philippians,* Broadman, 1971; *Polarities of Man's Existence in Biblical Perspective,* Westminster, 1973; *The Holy Spirit Today,* Broadman, 1973; (with wife, Evelyn Stagg) *Woman in the World of Jesus,* Westminster, 1978. Contributor to professional journals.

WORK IN PROGRESS: Galatians/Romans, for John Knox.

* * *

STANKIEWICZ, W(ladyslaw) J(ozef) 1922-

PERSONAL: Born May 6, 1922, in Warsaw, Poland; son of Jozef Edmund (a geographer) and Helena (Pawlowicz) Stankiewicz. *Education:* University of St. Andrews, M.A., 1944; London School of Economics and Political Science, Ph.D., 1952. *Religion:* Roman Catholic. *Office:* Department of Political Science, University of British Columbia, Vancouver, British Columbia, Canada V6T 1W5.

CAREER: Polish University College, London, England, lecturer in political science, 1947-52; Mid-European Studies Center, New York, N.Y., research associate, 1952-54; University of British Columbia, Vancouver, assistant professor, 1957-61, associate professor, 1961-65, professor of political science, 1965—. Government of Ontario, economist, 1956-57, senior economist, summers, 1958-59. Has lectured at over forty universities in Europe, North America, New Zealand, Australia, and Southern Africa. *Military service:* Served with Polish Army in exile, 1940-46; on active service with British Liberation Army, 1944-45, in Europe.

MEMBER: Canadian Political Science Association (member of executive council, 1960-62), American Political Science Association, American Society for Political and Legal Philosophy, Institute for Social Philosophy (associate member), Polish Historical Institute (Rome; member of executive council, 1967—), Polish Society of Arts and Science (London), Societe Historique et Litteraire Polonaise (Paris), Institut International de Philosophie Politique. *Awards, honors:* Postdoctoral visiting fellowship at Center of International Studies, Princeton University, 1954-55; Canada Council leave fellowship, 1968-69, 1974-75; Killam senior fellowship, I. W. Killam Memorial Fund, 1969-70, 1971-72, 1977-78; Social Sciences and Humanities Research Council of Canada leave fellowship, 1979-80.

WRITINGS: (With John Michael Montias) *Institutional Changes in the Postwar Economy of Poland,* Mid-European Studies Center, 1955; *Politics and Religion in Seventeenth-Century France,* University of California Press, 1960, reprinted, Greenwood Press, 1976; (editor) *Political Thought Since World War II,* Free Press of Glencoe, 1964; (editor and contributor) *The Living Name,* University of Toronto Press, 1964; (editor) *Crisis in the British Government,* Collier-Macmillan, 1967; (editor and contributor) *In Defense of Sovereignty,* Oxford University Press, 1969; *What Is Behavioralism?,* Girs Press, 1971; *Relativism: Thoughts and Aphorisms,* Girs Press, 1972; *Canada-U.S. Relations and Canadian Foreign Policy,* Girs Press, 1973; (editor) *British Government in an Era of Reform,* Collier-Macmillan, 1976; *Aspects of Political Theory: Classical Concepts in an Age of Relativism,* Collier-Macmillan, 1976; *A Guide to Democratic Jargon,* Oficyna S. Gliwa, 1976; *Normandia 1944,* Oficyna S. Gliwa, 1977; *Approaches to Democracy: Philosophy of Government at the Close of the Twentieth Century,* Edward Arnold, 1980. Contributor to *Encyclopaedia Britannica, Dictionary of Political Science, Encyclopedic Dictionary of Religion, Corpus Dictionary of Western Churches,* and *New Catholic Encyclopedia.* Contributor to *Proceedings of the American Philosophical Society, Political Science Quarterly, Canadian Slavonic Papers, Political Science* (Wellington), *Political Studies, Politikon,* and other professional journals. Contributor to periodicals, including *Canadian Forum* and *Contemporary Review.* Editor, *Soldier's Daily,* 1945; member of editorial board, *Canadian Forum,* 1958-70.

WORK IN PROGRESS: Further books on relativism in politics.

* * *

STANLEY, William O(liver), Jr. 1902-

PERSONAL: Born October 26, 1902, in Sedalia, Mo.; son of William Oliver and Minnie Dee (Raymond) Stanley; married Lola L. Sizemore, 1933; children: William Oliver III. *Education:* Baker University, A.B., 1926; University of Chicago, graduate study, 1928-29; Columbia University, A.M., 1936, Ph.D., 1954. *Home:* The Bluffs, 708 Grovewood Lane, Largo, Fla. 33540. *Office:* College of Education, University of Illinois, Urbana, Ill.

CAREER: High school history teacher in Goodland, Kan., Rocky Ford, Colo., and Elmhurst, Ill., 1926-35; Columbia University, Teachers College, New York, N.Y., assistant instructor, 1935-39; Madison College (now James Madison University), Harrisonburg, Va., assistant professor of education, 1939-42; University of Illinois at Urbana-Champaign, 1942—, associate professor, 1951-54, professor of the philosophy of education, 1954-71, professor emeritus, 1971—, chairman of Division of Social Foundations of Education, 1954-63, chairman of department of history and the philosophy of education, 1963-65. Lecturer at Seminar on American Studies, Kyoto University and Dosisha University (Japan), 1952; professor of education, University of South Florida, 1971-73. *Member:* John Dewey Society (vice-president, 1956), Philosophy of Education Society (secretary-treasurer, 1947-50; president, 1954-55), National Society of College Teachers of Education (vice-president, 1958-59; president, 1959-60), Comparative Education Society, History of Education Society, American Philosophical Association, American Sociological Society, American Association of University Professors.

WRITINGS: (Editor) *Essays for John Dewey's Ninetieth Birthday,* Bureau of Research and Services, University of Illinois, 1949; (with others) *Social Diagnosis for Education,* World Publishing, 1950; (with others) *Fundamentals of Curriculum Development,* Harcourt, 1950, 2nd edition, 1957; (with others) *Social Aspects of Education,* Interstate, 1951; *Education and Social Integration,* Bureau of Publications, Teachers College, Columbia University, 1953; (with others) *Social Foundations of Education,* Holt, 1956; (editor with Harry S. Broudy and R. Will Burnett) *Improving Science Programs in Illinois Schools: Analysis and Recommendations,* University of Illinois, 1958; (with others) *Outlines and Selected Readings: Social Foundations of Education,* Interstate, 1962. Editor, *Educational Theory,* 1965-71. Contributor to professional publications.

* * *

STARKEY, Marion L(ena) 1901-

PERSONAL: Born April 13, 1901, in Worcester, Mass.; daughter of Arthur E. (a printer and publisher) and Alice T. (Gray) Starkey. *Education:* Boston University, B.S., 1922, M.A., 1935; Harvard University, graduate study, 1946. *Home:* 7 Stocker St., Saugus, Mass. 01906. *Agent:* Curtis Brown, Ltd., 575 Madison Ave., New York, N.Y. 10022.

CAREER: Saugus Herald, Saugus, Mass., editor, 1924-29; Hampton Institute, Hampton, Va., associate professor of English, 1930-43; University of Connecticut extension, assistant professor of English at New London, 1946-50, and Hartford, 1950-61; full-time writer, 1961—. *Military service:* Women's Army Corps, 1943-45, translator and editor for Office of Strategic Services in Algiers, Bari, Caserta, and Paris. *Member:* League of Women Voters, Lynn Historical Society, Saugus Historical Society, First Saugus Ironworks Association, Phi Beta Kappa (honorary member). *Awards, honors:* Guggenheim fellow, 1953, 1958.

WRITINGS: The First Plantation: A History of Hampton and Elizabeth City County, Va., 1607-1887, privately printed, 1936; *The Cherokee Nation,* Knopf, 1946, reprinted, Russell, 1972; *The Devil in Massachusetts: A Modern Enquiry into the Salem Witch Trials,* Knopf, 1949; *A Little Rebellion,* Knopf, 1955; *Land Where Our Fathers Died: The Settling of the Eastern Shores, 1607-1735,* Doubleday, 1962; *Striving to Make It My Home: The Story of Americans from Africa,* Norton, 1964; *The Congregational Way: The Role of the Pilgrims and Their Heirs in Shaping America,* Doubleday, 1966; *Lace Cuffs and Leather Aprons: Popular Struggles in the Federalist Era, 1738-1800,* Knopf, 1972; *The Visionary Girls: Witchcraft in Salem Village* (juvenile), Little, Brown, 1973; *The Tall Man from Boston,* Crown, 1975. Contributor to encyclopedias, magazines, and newspapers.

WORK IN PROGRESS: Home Is Where the Cat Is.

SIDELIGHTS: Now that she has left the teaching field, Marion L. Starkey finds that she misses her students but "not the grading of papers." Starkey terms herself a maverick in the academic field, explaining that "while I taught English, what I wrote was history. I'm also interested in psychology, approached the theme of *The Devil in Massachusetts* from that viewpoint, and was proud that the Library of Congress classified it as psychology." Her travels have included West Africa, the West Indies, Peru, Greece, and Israel. She also enjoys exploring the Saugus marshes.

* * *

STARR, Chester G. 1914-

PERSONAL: Born October 5, 1914, in Centralia, Ill.; son of Chester Gibbs and Nettie (Glore) Starr; married Gretchen T. Daub, July 15, 1940; children: Jennifer, Deborah, Richard, Thomas. *Education:* University of Missouri, A.B. (with distinction), 1934, M.A., 1935; Cornell University, Ph.D., 1938. *Home:* 2301 Blueberry Lane, Ann Arbor, Mich. 48103. *Office:* 4629 Haven Hall, University of Michigan, Ann Arbor, Mich. 48109.

CAREER: University of Illinois at Urbana-Champaign, 1940-70, began as instructor, became professor of ancient history; University of Michigan, Ann Arbor, currently Bentley Professor of History. Visiting professor at University of Michigan, summer, 1950, and University of Washington, 1963-64; Walker-Ames Lecturer, University of Washington, 1979. Consultant to *Encyclopedia Americana* and to *World Book.* Director, Champaign, (Ill.) Public Library, 1955-58. *Military service:* U.S. Army, Infantry, 1942-46; became lieutenant colonel; awarded Bronze Star, Italian Bronze Cross. *Member:* American Association of University Professors (Urbana chapter, president, 1956-57), American Historical Association, Archaeological Institute of America, Society for Promotion of Roman Studies, Association of Ancient Historians (first president, 1974-78). *Awards, honors:* American Academy in Rome fellow, 1938-40; Guggenheim fellow, 1950-51, 1958-59; received certificate of merit, University of Missouri, 1963.

WRITINGS: Roman Imperial Navy, 30 B.C.-A.D. 324, Cornell University Press, 1941, 2nd edition, Barnes & Noble, 1960; *From Salerno to the Alps, 1943-45,* Infantry Journal Press, 1948; *Emergence of Rome as Ruler of the Western World,* Cornell University Press, 1950; *Civilization and the Caesars,* Cornell University Press, 1954; (editor) *Intellectual Heritage of the Early Middle Ages,* Cornell University Press, 1957; (contributor) *History of the World,* two volumes, Rand McNally, 1960; *Origins of Greek Civilization,* Knopf, 1961; *History of the Ancient World,* Oxford University Press, 1965, 2nd edition, 1974; *Rise and Fall of the Ancient World,* Rand McNally, 1965; *Awakening of the Greek Historical Spirit,* Knopf, 1968; *Athenian Coinage, 480-449 B.C.,* Clarendon Press, 1970; *Ancient Greeks,* Oxford University Press, 1971; *Ancient Romans,* Oxford University Press, 1971; *Early Man,* Oxford University Press, 1973; *Political Intelligence in Classical Greece,* E. J. Brill, 1974; *Greeks and Persians in the Fourth Century,* Iranica Antiqua, 1976; *Economic and Social Growth of Early Greece,* Oxford University Press, 1977; *Essays on Ancient History,* E. J. Brill, 1979; *The Beginnings of Imperial Rome,* University of Michigan Press, 1980.

SIDELIGHTS: "My interests," Chester G. Starr told *CA*, "have centered more and more upon the course of ancient civilization, seen as a coherent unit of human history; from studying its decline I was led back to a consideration of its origins, and am now surveying the entire course. Here, alone in history, one can view an entire cycle of civilization."

* * *

STEEDMAN, Marguerite Couturier 1908-

PERSONAL: Born January 4, 1908, in Atlanta, Ga.; daughter of William Kelsey and Lillie Mae (Stevens) Steedman. *Education:* Attended schools in Atlanta, Ga. *Politics:* Conservative. *Religion:* Anglican. *Residence:* Mount Pleasant, S.C.

CAREER: *Atlanta Journal Sunday Magazine,* Atlanta, Ga., staff feature writer, 1933-45; Emory University, Atlanta, teacher of courses in feature writing, 1945-46; *Charleston News and Courier,* Charleston, S.C., columnist, for a period in the 1950s; *Atlanta Times,* Atlanta, book editor, 1964-65. Teacher of official guides of the city of Charleston, 1973. *Member:* Daughters of the American Revolution, United Daughters of the Confederacy, Huguenot Society of South Carolina, South Carolina Historical Society. *Awards, honors:* Literary Achievement Award, Georgia Writers Association, 1962, for *Refuge in Avalon.*

WRITINGS: *But You'll Be Back,* Houghton, 1942; *Refuge in Avalon,* Doubleday, 1962; *Charles Town's Forgotten Tea Party,* University of Georgia Press, 1967; *A Short History of the French Protestant (Huguenot) Church of South Carolina,* privately printed, 1970; *The South Carolina Colony,* Crowell-Collier, 1970. Contributor of articles to magazines and newspapers. Assistant editor of *Charleston Magazine,* 1976-77.

WORK IN PROGRESS: A novel set in Revolutionary Charleston.

AVOCATIONAL INTERESTS: Doing French and Latin translations, wood-carving, leather work.

* * *

STEFANILE, Felix 1920-

PERSONAL: Surname is pronounced Stef-a-*nee*-lee; born April 13, 1920, in New York, N.Y.; son of Frank (a shopkeeper) and Genevieve (Lauri) Stefanile; married Selma Epstein, January 17, 1953. *Education:* City College (now City College of the City University of New York), B.A., 1944. *Politics:* Independent. *Religion:* Roman Catholic. *Home:* 103 Waldron St., West Lafayette, Ind. 47906. *Office:* Heavilon Hall, Purdue University, West Lafayette, Ind. 47906.

CAREER: New York State Department of Labor, New York, senior claims examiner, 1950-61; Purdue University, West Lafayette, Ind., visiting professor and lecturer, 1961-62, assistant professor, 1962-64, associate professor, 1965-69, professor of English, 1969—. Publisher and editor of *Sparrow* and *Black Rooster. Military service:* U.S. Army, 1942-46. *Member:* Poetry Society of America, American Literary Translator Association, Coordinating Council of Literary Magazines. *Awards, honors:* National Endowment for the Arts Awards, 1967, for essay, "The Imagination of the Amateur"; Emily Clark Balch Price, *Virginia Quarterly Review,* 1972, for poetry; Standard Oil of Indiana Foundation "Best Teacher" award, 1972.

WRITINGS: *Nine by Three* (poems), Hearse Chap Books, 1960; *The Patience That Befell* (poems), Goosetree, 1964; *A Fig Tree in America* (poems), Elizabeth Press, 1970; *East River Noctune* (poems), Elizabeth Press, 1976; (translator) *Umberto Saba: 31 Poems,* Elizabeth Press, 1978; (contributor) Bill Henderson, editor, *The Art of Literary Publishing: Editors on Their Craft,* Pushcart Press, 1980. Work represented in *American Literary Anthology,* edited by George Plimpton and Peter Ardery, Farrar, Strauss, 1968. Contributor of articles and poems to national publications, including *Poetry, Saturday Review, Harper's, Perspective* and *New York Times Book Review.*

SIDELIGHTS: Felix Stefanile told *CA:* "Poems have always done a good part of my thinking for me, and I have always equated writing poems with staying alive, believing as I do that the only consciousness that counts—for all of us, not only poets—is, as Erich Auerbach would have referred to it, our figurative consciousness, which, by a process of selection, rejects the random and the personal in favor of the timeless. To me the poem is this kind of time, or timeless machine. Art shapes life into form, in understandable and useable relation to spirit—again, the only life that counts—'criticism of life.' It is in the sense of ever-recurrent life that I see a poem as an interpretation of 'what happens,' a commemoration, a remembering-together, 'a stay against confusion.'"

BIOGRAPHICAL/CRITICAL SOURCES: *Serials Librarian,* spring, 1977; *New York Times,* June 5, 1977; *Prairie Schooner,* summer, 1977.

* * *

STEGNER, Wallace E(arle) 1909-

PERSONAL: Born February 18, 1909, in Lake Mills, Iowa; son of George H. and Hilda (Paulson) Stegner; married Mary Stuart Page, September 1, 1934; children: Stuart Page. *Education:* University of Utah, B.A., 1930; additional study at University of California, 1932-33; State University of Iowa, M.A., 1932, Ph.D., 1935. *Home:* 13456 South Fork Lane, Los Altos Hills, Calif. 94022. *Agent:* Brandt & Brandt, 101 Park Ave., New York, N.Y. *Office:* Department of English, Stanford University, Stanford, Calif.

CAREER: University of Utah, Salt Lake City, instructor, 1934-37; University of Wisconsin—Madison, instructor, 1937-39; Harvard University, Cambridge, Mass., Briggs-Copeland Instructor of Composition, 1939-45; Stanford University, Stanford, Calif., professor of English, 1945-71, director of creative writing program, 1946-71. Phi Beta Kappa visiting scholar, 1960-61; writer-in-residence, American Academy in Rome, 1960. Assistant to the Secretary of Interior, 1961; member of National Parks Advisory Board, 1962.

MEMBER: American Association of University Professors, American Academy of Arts and Sciences, National Institute and Academy of Arts and Letters, Phi Beta Kappa. *Awards, honors:* Little, Brown Novelette Prize, 1937, for *Remembering Laughter;* O. Henry Award, 1942, 1950, 1954; Houghton-Mifflin Life-in-America Award, 1945, and Ainsfield-Wolfe Award, 1945, both for *One Nation;* Guggenheim fellowship, 1950, 1959; Rockefeller fellowship, 1950-51, to conduct seminars with writers throughout the Far East; Wenner-Gren Foundation grant, 1953; Center for Advanced Studies in the Behavioral Sciences fellow, 1955-56; D.Litt., University of Utah, 1968; D.F.A., University of Colorado, 1969; D.F.A., Utah State University, 1972; National Endowment for the Humanities senior fellowship, 1972; Pulitzer Prize, 1972, for *Angle of Repose;* D.L., University of Saskatchewan, 1973; National Book Award for Fiction, 1977, for *The Spectator Bird;* has also received four Commonwealth Club medals.

WRITINGS: Mormon Country, Duell, 1941; (with the editors of *Look*) *One Nation,* Houghton, 1945; (with others) *Look at America: The Central Northwest,* Houghton, 1947; *The Women on the Wall* (short story collection), Houghton, 1948; *The Writer in America,* Perkins & Hutchins, 1953, reprinted, Haskell House, 1977; *Beyond the Hundredth Meridian: John Wesley Powell and the Second Opening of the West,* Houghton, 1954; *The City of the Living and Other Stories,* Houghton, 1956; *The Papers of Bernard DeVoto: A Description and a Checklist of His Work,* Taylor & Taylor, 1960; *Wolf Willow: A History, a Story, and a Memory of the Last Plains Frontier,* Viking, 1962, reprinted, University of Nebraska Press, 1980; *The Gathering of Zion: The Story of the Mormon Trail,* McGraw, 1964; *The Sound of Mountain Water* (essay collection), Doubleday, 1969; *Discovery!: The Search for Arabian Oil,* Middle East Export Press, 1971; *Variations on a Theme of Discontent,* Utah State University Press, 1972; *Robert Frost and Bernard DeVoto,* Association of the Stanford University Libraries, 1974; *The Uneasy Chair: A Biography of Bernard DeVoto,* Doubleday, 1974; *Ansel Adams: Images, 1923-1974,* New York Graphic Society, 1974.

Novels: *Remembering Laughter,* Little, Brown, 1937; *The Potter's House,* Prairie Press, 1938; *On a Darkling Plain,* Harcourt, 1940; *Fire and Ice,* Duell, 1941; *The Big Rock Candy Mountain,* Duell, 1943, reprinted, Pocket Books, 1977; *Second Growth,* Houghton, 1947; *The Preacher and the Slave,* Houghton, 1950, published as *Joe Hill: A Biographical Novel,* Doubleday, 1969; *A Shooting Star,* Viking, 1961; *All the Little Live Things,* Viking, 1967; *Angle of Repose,* Doubleday, 1971; *The Spectator Bird,* Doubleday, 1976; *Recapitulation,* Doubleday, 1979.

Editor: (With others) *An Exposition Workshop: Readings in Modern Controversy,* Little, Brown, 1939; (with others) *Readings for Citizens at War,* Harper, 1941; (with Richard Scowcraft and Boris Ilyin) *The Writer's Art: A Collection of Short Stories,* Heath, 1950, reprinted, Greenwood Press, 1972; *This Is Dinosaur: The Echo Park Country and Its Magic River,* Knopf, 1955; J. W. Powell, *The Exploration of the Colorado River of the West,* University of Chicago Press, 1957; (with wife, Mary Stegner) *Great American Short Stories,* Dell, 1957; *Selected American Prose: The Realistic Movement,* Rinehart, 1958; Samuel Clemens, *The Adventures of Huckleberry Finn,* Dell, 1960; Bret Harte, *The Outcasts of Poker Flat,* New American Library, 1961; Powell, *Report on the Lands of the Arid Region of the United States,* Harvard University Press, 1962; (with others) *Modern Composition,* four volumes, Holt, 1964; *The American Novel: From Cooper to Faulkner,* Basic Books, 1965; A. B. Guthrie, Jr., *The Big Sky,* Houghton, 1965; (with others) *Twenty Years of Stanford Short Stories,* Stanford University Press, 1966; Nathaniel Hawthorne, *Twice-Told Tales,* Heritage Press, 1967; *The Letters of Bernard DeVoto,* Doubleday, 1975.

Editor of *Stanford Short Stories* annual, 1946—. Contributor of short stories and book reviews to *New York Times Book Review, Saturday Review, Esquire, Harper's,* and other periodicals. West Coast editor, Houghton-Mifflin Co., 1945-53; former editor-in-chief, *American West Magazine.*

SIDELIGHTS: Wallace Stegner's work is concerned with the problem of human ethics. Kerry Aheam believes that "what has fascinated Stegner from the beginning is the most earnest theme of all, the way to live—how shall a good man conduct himself."

Often using the background of the American West, Stegner explores this question in both historical works and novels. In their book-length study of Stegner's work, Forrest Robinson and Margaret Robinson emphasize the importance of the West in Stegner's writing. "The defining characteristics of Stegner's art," they state, "are neither stylistic . . . nor philosophical. . . . Rather, it is a region and personal experience within that region that have been the crucial determinants in the development of his art."

Stegner's traditional and realistic style of writing has been highly praised. "Stegner," Rachel Trickett writes, "is a writer of professional skill, capable of carrying on a narrative and sensitively responsive to climate, atmosphere, and appearances." Paul Pickrel believes Stegner "shows a fine ability to look at things with clear eyes and describe them in clear prose." B. A. Young simply states that "Stegner can write like an angel."

All the Little Live Things, Angle of Repose, and *The Spectator Bird* are three of Stegner's more successful novels. A reviewer for *Virginia Quarterly Review* calls *All the Little Live Things* "a great novel of our generation" while Edward Weeks considers it "one of the very best books [Stegner] has written." William Abrahams describes *Angle of Repose,* winner of a Pulitzer Prize, as "a superb novel, with an amplitude of scale and richness of detail altogether uncommon in contemporary fiction." Writing of the National Book Award-winning *The Spectator Bird,* P. L. Adams praises it as "consistently elegant and entertaining reading, with every scene adroitly staged and each effect precisely accomplished."

BIOGRAPHICAL/CRITICAL SOURCES: Writer, February, 1940; *New York Herald Tribune Book Review,* October 8, 1950; *Saturday Review,* May 20, 1961, December 1, 1962, January 16, 1965, March 20, 1971; *New Statesman,* May 26, 1961; *Sewanee Review,* winter, 1962; Chester E. Eisinger, *Fiction of the Forties,* University of Chicago Press, 1963; *Times Literary Supplement,* April 26, 1963; *Book Week,* January 10, 1965; *Dialogue: A Journal of Mormon Thought,* winter, 1966; *New York Times,* July 27, 1967, March 24, 1971, February 24, 1979; *Christian Science Monitor,* November 16, 1967, February 12, 1979; *Yale Review,* spring, 1968; *Per Se,* fall, 1968; *Book World,* June 1, 1969, March 11, 1979; *Western American Literature,* summer, 1970; *Life,* March 26, 1971; *South Dakota Review,* spring, 1971; *Atlantic,* April, 1971; Merrill Lewis and Lorene Lewis, *Wallace Stegner,* Boise State College, 1972; *Southern Review,* autumn, 1973; *Courier-Journal & Times* (Louisville, Ky.), July 28, 1974; *Authors in the News,* Volume I, Gale, 1976; Forrest Robinson and Margaret Robinson, *Wallace Stegner,* Twayne, 1977; *Southwest Review,* spring, 1977; *Western Humanities Review,* spring, 1977; *Contemporary Literary Criticism,* Volume IX, Gale, 1978; *Los Angeles Times Book Review,* March 25, 1979.

* * *

STEIN, Morris I(saac) 1921-

PERSONAL: Born June 11, 1921, in New York, N.Y.; son of Sam and Lena (Citron) Stein. *Education:* City College (now City College of the City University of New York), B.S., 1940, M.S., 1942; Harvard University, M.A., 1943, Ph.D., 1949. *Home:* 7 Washington Mews, New York, N.Y. 10003. *Office:* Department of Psychology, New York University, New York, N.Y. 10003.

CAREER: Harvard University, Cambridge, Mass., research associate, 1943-44; Wheaton College, Wheaton, Ill., instructor, 1947-48; Veterans Administration, Boston, Mass., staff psychologist, 1947-48; University of Chicago, department of psychology, Chicago, Ill., research associate, 1948-51, assistant professor, 1951-54, associate professor, 1954-60; New York University, New York, N.Y., professor of psychology, 1960—, director, Research Center for Human Relations, 1960-62, 1966-67. Diplomate in clinical psychology, 1953. Lecturer in neurology and psychiatry, Northwestern University Medical School, 1956-60. *Military service:* U.S. Army, Office of Strategic Services, 1944-46; became sergeant. *Member:* American Psychological Association (fellow), American Association for the Advancement of Science, Sigma Xi. *Awards, honors:* Center for Advanced Study in the Behavioral Sciences fellow, 1955-56; National Institute of Mental Health award, 1962—.

WRITINGS: The Thematic Apperception Test: A Manual for Its Clinical Use with Adult Males, Addison-Wesley, 1948; (with Stern and Bloom) *Methods in Personality Assessment,* Free Press, 1956; (with Heinze) *Creativity and the Individual: Summaries of Selected Writings in the Psychological and Psychiatric Literature,* Free Press, 1960; (editor) *Contemporary Psychotherapies,* Free Press, 1961; *Personality Measures in Admissions,* College Entrance Examination Board, 1963; *Volunteers for Peace,* Wiley, 1966; *Stimulating Creativity,* Academic Press, Volume I: *Individual Procedures,* 1974, Volume II: *Group Procedures,* 1975. Also author of monograph, *Creativity: The Process and Its Stimulation,* 1975.

WORK IN PROGRESS: Explorations in Typology and Creativity: Its Social Context and Administration.

SIDELIGHTS: Morris Stein has traveled and lectured in Western Europe, South America, and Israel.

* * *

STEINBECK, John (Ernst) 1902-1968 (Amnesia Glasscock)

PERSONAL: Born February 27, 1902, in Salinas, Calif.; died December 20, 1968 of heart disease, in New York, N.Y.; buried in Salinas, Calif.; son of John Ernst (a county treasurer) and Olive (a schoolteacher; maiden name, Hamilton) Steinbeck; married Carol Henning, 1930 (divorced, 1943); married Gwyn Conger (a writer, singer, and composer), March 29, 1943 (divorced, 1948); married Elaine Scott, December 29, 1950; children: (second marriage) Tom, John. *Education:* Stanford University, special student, 1919-25. *Residence:* New York, N.Y. *Agent:* McIntosh & Otis, Inc., 475 Fifth Ave., New York, N.Y. 10017.

CAREER: Variously employed as hod-carrier, fruit-picker, apprentice painter, laboratory assistant, caretaker, surveyor, and reporter; writer. Foreign correspondent in North Africa and Italy for *New York Herald Tribune,* 1943; correspondent in Vietnam for *Newsday,* 1966-67. Special writer for U.S. Army Air Forces, during World War II. *Awards, honors:* General Literature Gold Medal, Commonwealth Club of California, 1936, for *Tortilla Flat,* 1937, for *Of Mice and Men,* and 1940, for *The Grapes of Wrath;* New York Drama Critics Circle Award, 1938, for play, "Of Mice and Men"; Pulitzer Prize in novel, 1940, for *The Grapes of Wrath;* Academy Award (Oscar) nomination for best original story, Academy of Motion Picture Arts and Sciences, 1944, for "Lifeboat," and 1945, for "A Medal for Benny"; Nobel Prize for literature, 1962; Paperback of the Year Award, *Best Sellers,* 1964, for *Travels with Charley: In Search of America.*

WRITINGS—Novels; published by Viking, except as indicated: *Cup of Gold: A Life of Henry Morgan, Buccaneer,* Robert McBride, 1929, reprinted, Penguin, 1976; *The Pastures of Heaven,* 1932, new edition, 1963; *To a God Unknown,* 1933, reprinted, Heinemann, 1970; *Tortilla Flat,* 1935, illustrated edition, 1947, reprinted, Penguin, 1977; *In Dubious Battle,* 1936, new edition, 1971; *Of Mice and Men* (also see below; Book-of-the-Month Club selection), 1937, reprinted, Bantam, 1970; *The Red Pony* (also see below), Covici, Friede, 1937, reprinted, Heinemann Educational Books, 1972; *The Grapes of Wrath,* 1939, reprinted, Franklin Library (Franklin Center, Pa.), 1978, published with introduction by Carl Van Doren, World Publishing, 1947, revised edition, edited by Peter Lisca, 1972.

The Forgotten Village (also see below), 1941; *The Moon Is Down* (also see below), 1942, reprinted, 1974; *Cannery Row,* 1945, new edition, 1963, published with manuscript, corrected typescript, corrected galleys, and first edition, Stanford Publications Service, 1975; *The Wayward Bus* (Book-of-the-Month Club selection), 1947, reprinted, Penguin, 1979; *The Pearl* (also see below), 1947, reprinted, 1966; *Burning Bright: A Play in Story Form* (also see below), 1950, reprinted, Penguin, 1979; *East of Eden,* 1952, reprinted, Penguin, 1979; *Sweet Thursday,* 1954, reprinted, Penguin, 1979; *The Short Reign of Pippin IV: A Fabrication* (Book-of-the-Month Club selection), 1957, reprinted, Penguin, 1977; *The Winter of Our Discontent,* 1961.

Short stories: *Saint Katy the Virgin* (also see below), Covici, Friede, 1936; *Nothing So Monstrous,* Pynson Printers, 1936, reprinted, Porter, 1979; *The Long Valley* (contains fourteen short stories, including "The Red Pony," "Saint Katy the Virgin," "Johnny Bear," and "The Harness"), Viking, 1938, reprinted, Bantam, 1970, published as *Thirteen Great Short Stories from the Long Valley,* Avon, 1943, published as *Fourteen Great Short Stories from the Long Valley,* Avon, 1947; *How Edith McGillicuddy Met R.L.S.,* Rowfant Club (Cleveland), 1943; *The Crapshooter,* Mercury Publications (New York), 1957.

Plays: (With George S. Kaufman) *Of Mice and Men: A Play in Three Acts* (based on novel of same title; first produced on Broadway at The Music Box Theatre, November 23, 1937), Viking, 1937, reprinted, Dramatist's Play Service, 1964; *The Moon Is Down: Play in Two Parts* (based on novel of same title; first produced on Broadway at Martin Beck Theatre, April 7, 1942), Dramatist's Play Service, 1942; *Burning Bright: Play in Three Acts* (based on novel of same title; first produced on Broadway at Broadhurst Theatre, October 18, 1950), acting edition, Dramatist's Play Service, 1951, reprinted, Penguin, 1979.

Screenplays: "Forgotten Village" (based on novel of same title), independently produced, 1939; "Lifeboat," Twentieth Century-Fox Film Corp., 1944; "A Medal for Benny," Paramount, 1945 (published in *Best Film Plays—1945,* edited by John Gassner and Dudley Nichols, Crown, 1946); "The Pearl" (based on novel of same title), RKO, 1948; "The Red Pony" (based on novel of same title), Republic, 1949; *Viva Zapata!* (produced by Twentieth Century-Fox Film Corp., 1952), edited by Robert E. Morsberger, Viking, 1975.

Other works: *"Their Blood Is Strong"* (factual story of migratory workers), Simon J. Lubin Society of California, 1938; *A Letter to the Friends of Democracy,* Overbrook Press, 1940; (with Edward F. Ricketts) *Sea of Cortez* (description of expedition to Gulf of California), Viking, 1941, published as *Sea of Cortez: A Leisurely Journal of Travel and Research,* Appel, 1971, revised edition published as *The Log from the "Sea of Cortez": The Narrative Portion of the Book, "Sea of Cortez,"* Viking, 1951, reprinted, Penguin,

1976; *Bombs Away: The Story of a Bomber Team* (account of life and training in U.S. Army Air Forces), Viking, 1942; *A Russian Journal* (description of tour to Russia), photographs by Robert Capa, Viking, 1948; *Once There Was a War* (collection of dispatches and anecdotes from World War II), Viking, 1958, reprinted, Penguin, 1977; *Travels with Charley: In Search of America,* Viking, 1962, reprinted, Penguin, 1980; *Letters to Alicia* (collection of newspaper columns written as a correspondent in Vietnam), [Garden City, N.J.], 1965; *America and Americans* (description of travels in United States), Viking, 1966; *Journal of a Novel: The "East of Eden" Letters,* Viking, 1969.

Steinbeck: A Life in Letters (collection of correspondence), edited by Elaine Steinbeck and Robert Wallsten, Viking, 1975; *The Acts of King Arthur and His Noble Knights: From the Winchester Manuscripts of Thomas Malory and Other Sources,* edited by Chase Horton, Farrar, Straus, 1976; *The Collected Poems of Amnesia Glasscock* (poems published by Steinbeck under pseudonym Amnesia Glasscock in *Monterey Beacon,* January-February, 1935), Manroot Books (San Francisco), 1976; *Letters to Elizabeth: A Selection of Letters from John Steinbeck to Elizabeth Otis,* edited by Florian J. Shasky and Susan F. Riggs, Book Club of California (San Francisco), 1978.

Omnibus volumes: Pascal Covici, editor, *Steinbeck,* Viking, 1943, enlarged edition published as *The Portable Steinbeck,* 1946, revised edition, 1971 (published in Australia as *Steinbeck Omnibus,* Oxford University Press, 1946); *Short Novels: Tortilla Flat, The Red Pony, Of Mice and Men, The Moon Is Down, Cannery Row, The Pearl,* Viking, 1953, new edition, 1963; *East of Eden* [and] *The Wayward Bus,* Viking, 1962; *The Red Pony, Part I: The Gift* [and] *The Pearl,* Macmillan (Toronto), 1963; *The Pearl* [and] *The Red Pony,* Viking, 1967; *Cannery Row* [and] *Sweet Thursday,* Heron Books, 1971; *To a God Unknown* [and] *The Pearl,* Heron Books, 1971; *Of Mice and Men* [and] *Cannery Row,* Penguin (Harmondsworth, England), 1973, Penguin (New York), 1978; *The Grapes of Wrath* [and] *The Moon Is Down* [and] *Cannery Row* [and] *East of Eden* [and] *Of Mice and Men,* Heinemann, 1976; *John Steinbeck, 1902-1968* (contains "Tortilla Flat," "Of Mice and Men," and "Cannery Row"), limited edition, Franklin Library, 1977.

Short stories and short novels have appeared in numerous anthologies. Author of syndicated column written during tour of Vietnam, 1966-67. Contributor of numerous short stories, essays, and articles to popular magazines and periodicals.

SIDELIGHTS: Throughout his long and controversial career, John Steinbeck extolled the virtues of the American dream while he warned against what he believed to be the evils of an increasingly materialistic American society. Although his subject and style varied with each book, the themes of human dignity and compassion, and the sense of what a *Time* critic called, "Steinbeck's vision of America," remained constant. Steinbeck was a uniquely American novelist, the critics contended, whose distrust and anger at society was offset by his faith and love for the land and its people. Of his seventeen novels, *The Grapes of Wrath* is perhaps the best example of Steinbeck's philosophy, perception, and impact. It is Steinbeck's "strongest and most durable novel," the *Time* reviewer commented, "a concentration of Steinbeck's artistic and moral vision."

Published in 1939, *The Grapes of Wrath* is a novel of social protest that caused a furor of both praise and denunciation. Although many protest novels appeared during the 1930s, none was as widely read nor as effective as Steinbeck's. According to Daniel Aaron, Steinbeck possessed a "special combination of marketable literary talent, sense of historical timing, eye for the significant subject, and power of identification," that made the book "the first of the Thirties protest novels to be read on a comparable scale with . . . best-selling novels." Peter Lisca recalled the impact of this combination: "*The Grapes of Wrath* was a phenomenon on the scale of a national event. It was publicly banned and burned by citizens; it was debated on national radio hook-ups; but above all was read."

Written during the Depression, *The Grapes of Wrath* concerns the Joad family and their forced migration from the Dust Bowl of Oklahoma to what they had been told was "the land of promise," California. What they find, however, is a land of waste, corruption, and poverty. Expecting to find work, decent wages, and a chance to someday acquire their own land, they are instead introduced to a system of degrading migrant labor camps, menial wages, and near starvation. F. W. Watt commented: "The Paradise in front of them is a fallen world, . . . the place they have reached is as filled with suffering as the place from which they have fled. The subtle but relentless stages by which the realisation comes makes the irony all the more intense—to hear and gradually understand the term 'Okies' and to know that they are Okies; to realise that 'Hooverville'—any and every rough camp on a town's outskirts or garbage dump, named as an ironical tribute to the President who saw prosperity just around the corner—Hooverville was their home; to discover that the rich lands all around them are owned and controlled by large impersonal companies; to be hired for daily wages that barely cover the day's food, then to have those wages cut, and finally to be beaten and driven off at a sign of protest."

The Grapes of Wrath was Steinbeck's second attempt at gaining support and sympathy for the migrants' condition. The first, *L'Affaire Lettuceberg,* had been a satire that Steinbeck destroyed because he felt that it failed to promote understanding and came dangerously close to ridiculing the very people he wanted to help. In 1937, shortly after the publication of his first major success, *Of Mice and Men,* Steinbeck left for Oklahoma. There he joined a group of farmers embarking for California. For two years Steinbeck lived and worked with the migrants, seeking to lend authenticity to his account and to deepen his understanding of their plight. "To make their story convincing, he had to report their lives with fidelity," Aaron explained, and Watt noted that Steinbeck's "personal involvement was intimate and his sympathies were strongly aroused by the suffering and injustice he saw at first hand." Critics contended that this combination of concern, first-hand knowledge, and commitment produced what a reviewer for the *London Times* termed "one of the most arresting [novels] of its time."

One of the most prevalent themes in *The Grapes of Wrath* is the misuse and waste of lives and land. "The real power of *The Grapes of Wrath* is the savage anger at the impersonal process that uproots men from the land and rapes it, substituting rattletraps and highways for place and kindred," Nancy L. McWilliams and Wilson C. McWilliams wrote. Steinbeck was appalled at an economic system that, having collapsed, bankrupted and forced thousands of farmers from work on their own land to work on massive and impersonal farms concerned only with profit. On these highly productive "agricultural 'factories,'" Aaron contended, the migrants "slaved and starved." Watt elaborated: "Here the land is not sick, but the system that is supposed to distribute the land's fruitfulness has broken down, and so in the midst of plenty men are starving: produce is being destroyed because it will not fetch the price of marketing, while the starving watch."

Steinbeck saw this "large-scale commercial and industrial exploitation of the land" as the end of "pioneer ideals," Watt commented. He opposed the continued growth of powerful private interest groups, such as "the growers and their . . . financial allies," Aaron explained, at the expense of individual rights and dignity. "The Okies have had their ramshackle but cherished homes snatched away from them by the insatiable behemoth of big-scale agriculture," John S. Kennedy wrote. "What is wrong with this, it is suggested, is not the pooling of hundreds of family-farms, but the fact of the alien ownership of the amalgam." Steinbeck advocated what Aaron described as a "cooperative commonwealth" attitude, a return to "neighborly interdependence."

Certain groups, however, misinterpreted this message and charged Steinbeck with writing a Communist tract. "Publicists for the big California growers and the right-wing press denounced [*The Grapes of Wrath*] as a pack of lies," Aaron reported. "Spokesmen for the Association Farmers, incorporated in 1934 to combat unionism and other 'subversive activities,' accused Steinbeck of writing a brief for Communism."

In reality, Steinbeck "was a conservative, a man who valued and even clung to the old America," McWilliams and McWilliams noted. What he wrote, Aaron remarked, was "the insider's plea to the popular conscience, not a call for revolution." While Steinbeck criticized what he believed were evil and immoral institutions, he offered what critics contended was an optimistic picture of the American ideal. He presented the migrants as the "preservers of the old American verities, innocent of bourgeois proprieties, perhaps, but courteous, trusting, friendly, and generous," Aaron commented. "What preserved them in the end, and what would preserve all America, was a recovery of a neighborly interdependence that an acquistive society had almost destroyed." Although Steinbeck recorded "the symptoms of his sick society," Aaron continued, "[he] did not regard himself as one of its gravediggers."

In *The Grapes of Wrath,* as well as in his other novels, Steinbeck took a "biological view" towards man. He did not look for the causes or motives behind a given situation. Instead, he sought to objectively observe the actuality of a situation rather than what that situation could or should have been. Frederick Bracher described this as "a way of looking at things characteristic of a biologist."

Because he held a biological view of man, Steinbeck believed that the evolutionary concepts of adaption and "survival of the fittest" applied to men as well as animals. "The ability to adapt to new conditions is one of man's most valuable biological attributes, and the loss of it might well lead to man's extinction," is an important concept in Steinbeck's work, according to Bracher. Although Steinbeck is sympathetic toward the migrants in *The Grapes of Wrath,* "he is not blind to [their] defects," Warren French noted. "He shows clearly that he writes about a group of thoughtless, impetuous, suspicious, ignorant people." As such, French suggested, they too are bound by the laws of nature and "must also change if they are to survive." Thus, French described the book as "a *dynamic* novel about people who learn that survival depends upon their adaptability to new conditions." Jackson L. Benson noticed an example of this evolutionary concept in *Of Mice and Men,* a short novel concerning two itinerant farm hands, George and Lennie. George, the "fittest" of the two, is compelled to shoot the strong but feeble-minded Lennie after the latter inadvertently kills their employer's daughter-in-law: "Lennie kills without malice—animals and people die simply because of his strength. Lennie himself must die simply because within the society of man he is an anomaly and weak."

The concept of "group-man" was another aspect of Steinbeck's biological view. This idea was later outlined in *Sea of Cortez,* Steinbeck's and marine biologist Ed Ricketts' account of their expedition to the Gulf of California. According to Peter Shaw: "The book . . . took each day's observations of sea life as an occasion for the drawing of biological parallels with human society. The most striking parallel for Steinbeck was the seeming existence of a group instinct in man similar to that found in schools of fish and colonies of marine fauna. Man, Steinbeck suggested,. . .could be regarded as a group phenomenon as well as an individual one. Accordingly, it might be possible to discover more about an individual by studying his behavior as it related to the group than by studying him in isolation." Steinbeck took this premise one step further by suggesting that man as an individual has no identity and that mankind as a whole is the only reality. This idea is expressed by Doc Burton in Steinbeck's novel about a fruit picker's strike, *In Dubious Battle:* "I want to watch these group men, for they seem to me to be a new individual, not at all like single men. A man in a group isn't himself at all; he's a cell in an organism that isn't like him any more than the cells in your body are like you." Kennedy found the concept of group-man to be "the central point in Steinbeck's concept of life." He added: "Permeating his works is this idea, which is the very heart of his philosophy of life: that the concrete person is in himself virtually nothing, whereas the abstraction 'humanity' is all."

Throughout his work, Steinbeck maintains what R.W.B. Lewis called, "a celebrational sense of *life*." This quality, critics have remarked, set him apart from his contemporaries and accounted for much of his popular appeal. "He has a generous indignation at the spectacle of human suffering," Walter Allen noted. "But apart from this, he is the celebrant of life, any kind of life, just because it is life." Alfred Kazin claimed that while other Depression era authors "saw life as one vast Chicago slaughterhouse, a guerrilla war, a perpetual bomb raid," Steinbeck displayed "a refreshing belief in human fellowship and courage; he had learned to accept the rhythm of life." This is not to suggest, however, that Steinbeck held any unrealistically optimistic illusions. Kennedy noted: "He depicts human existence as conflict, unremitting and often savage battle. But he suggests that life is worth living, flagellant and baffling though it may be. . . . In a time when the prevalent note in creative literature is that of despondency and abandonment to malign fate, . . . Steinbeck's assertion of the resiliency and tough durability of life has set him off from the generality."

Although Steinbeck possessed a "moving approach to human life," as Kazin described it, he was generally unsuccessful at bringing his characters to life. Reviewers frequently criticized his people for appearing to be manipulated, stage-like creations. "Nothing in his books is so dim, significantly enough, as the human beings who live in them," Kazin wrote, "and few of them are intensely imagined as human beings at all." Edmund Wilson found that the characters in *The Grapes of Wrath* "are animated and put through their paces rather than brought to life." He added: "They are like excellent character actors giving very conscientious performances in a fairly well-written play.

Their dialect is well managed, but they always sound a little stagy."

Steinbeck's descriptive ability, on the other hand, has been widely praised. The *Time* critic contended that Steinbeck wrote with "cinematic clarity." Aaron compared the effects of the images and descriptions in *The Grapes of Wrath* to those rendered by a "camera eye." He found that the novel "unfolds cinematically almost as if Steinbeck had conceived of it as a documentary film."

Critics have suggested that Steinbeck's best novels are those set in his birthplace, northern California's Salinas Valley. "He was a Californian," McWilliams and McWilliams remarked, "and his writings never succeeded very well when he tried to walk alien soil." They defined his California as "a very special one, . . . sleepy California that time passed by." Bruce Cook noted that while Steinbeck was "a writer of international reputation, he was almost a regionalist in his close concentration on the 50 miles or so of California that surrounded his birthplace. The farming towns up and down the Salinas Valley," Cook continued, "and the commercial fishing port of Monterey just a few miles across the mountains provided the settings for most of his best books."

Steinbeck often used this setting to stress his theme of the importance of the "relationship between man and his environment," Shaw claimed. "The features of the valley at once determined the physical fate of his characters and made symbolic comment on them." Moreover, while Steinbeck dwelled on the beauty and "fruitfulness" of the valley, he "did not make it a fanciful Eden," Shaw commented. "The river brought destructive floods as well as fertility, and the summer wind could blow hot for months without let-up." Thus, "Man struggled within a closed system that both formed and limited him; there he was responsible for his acts and yet unable to control the larger forces."

After *The Grapes of Wrath,* Steinbeck's reputation as a novelist began to decline. Although his later works, such as *The Moon Is Down, East of Eden,* and *The Winter of Our Discontent,* have been public favorites and best sellers, they have also been considered critical disappointments. Too often, the reviewers contended, Steinbeck's later work is flawed by sentimentality, obvious symbolism, and the inability to achieve the power and statement of *The Grapes of Wrath.*

The first such novel to have provoked critical attack is *The Moon Is Down.* Published in 1942, it deals with a mythical European town and its invasion by what Watt described as a "totalitarian and inhumane power which arouses, instead of crushing, the desire of the conquered for freedom." The novel, most critics have agreed, is a thinly disguised account of Germany's occupation of Norway. It was written, according to Watt, "in the interest of the Office of Strategic Services in helping resistance movements in Occupied Europe." Steinbeck wrote the novel with the same sense of objectivity that had characterized his earlier work. He tried to present the Nazi-like characters as fully as possible; they are good as well as evil, strong as well as weak. In this instance, however, Steinbeck's objectivity worked against him. Kennedy explained: "His Nazi characters emerged as something like human beings, by no means admirable, but by no means demoniac either. For not making them intrinsically and uniformly monstrous, at a time when some of our most celebrated writers were trying to whip Americans up to a frenzy of indiscriminate hatred, Steinbeck was pilloried." Although at the novel's end the Europeans triumph over their enemy, Steinbeck was nevertheless accused, as French recalled, of being "soft toward the Nazis." Later critics, however, detached from the immediate tensions aroused by the war, found more serious fault with what French regarded as the novel's "artificiality."

East of Eden and *The Winter of Our Discontent* similarly fell short of critical expectations. The former, a biblical allegory of the Cain and Abel story, is considered Steinbeck's most ambitious novel. Yet the *Time* critic claimed that "the Biblical parallels of Cain and Abel are so relentlessly stenciled upon the plot that symbolized meaning threatens to overwhelm the narrative surface." *The Winter of Our Discontent,* Steinbeck's last novel, "is spoilt by sentimentality and the consequent evasion of the moral issues raised," the reviewer for the *London Times* remarked. "Steinbeck was unable in any of his later work to master the problems he seems to have set himself, and though several of his books were widely popular, they appeared too small an achievement to be worthy of the author of *The Grapes of Wrath.*" Max Westbrook echoed this claim when he wrote: "The general feeling is that novels like *East of Eden* . . . and *The Winter of Our Discontent* . . . ought to be like *The Grapes of Wrath* but are not. . . . Neither novel comes to grips with the problems handled so courageously in *The Grapes of Wrath.*"

French blamed these later failures on the popular and critical reaction to *Cannary Row.* Written after the war, the novel is a satire "on contemporary American life with its commercialised values, its ruthless creed of property and status, and its relentlessly accelerating pace," according to Watt. For the most part, however, the novel has been misread as light-hearted, escapist fare. French commented: "Another letter of advice to an erring world; but, as had happened before, the advice went not only unheeded but unperceived. After this, Steinbeck was to strain to make his points clear to the reader; and as he belabored his points, the quality of his fiction suffered."

In 1962, Steinbeck was awarded the Nobel Prize, an honor that many believed "had been earned by his early work," noted the *London Times'* critic, rather than for his later efforts. Several reviewers, however, thought this attitude was unjust. Watt, for example, offered this assessment: "Like America itself, his work is a vast, fascinating, paradoxical universe: a brash experiment in democracy; a naive quest for understanding at the level of the common man; a celebration of goodness and innocence; a display of chaos, violence, corruption and decadence. It is no neatly-shaped and carefully-cultivated garden of artistic perfections, but a sprawling continent of discordant extremes." Shaw was seemingly in agreement when he wrote: "When one begins to talk about the shape of a career rather than about single books, one is talking about a major writer. Steinbeck used to complain that reviewers said each new book of his showed a falling-off from his previous one, yet they never specified the height from which his apparently steady decline had begun. What he was noticing was the special kind of concern for a grand design that readers feel when they pick up the book of a writer whose career seems in itself to be a comment on the times."

In addition to numerous translations, several of Steinbeck's works have been adapted for films, the stage, and television. *The Grapes of Wrath,* with Henry Fonda, was filmed by Twentieth Century-Fox Film Corp. in 1940. *Of Mice and Men,* starring Burgess Meredith and Lon Chaney, was produced by United Artists in 1939 and, in 1970, premiered as an opera, adapted by Carlisle Floyd, at the Seattle Opera House. *Tortilla Flat,* featuring Spencer Tracy, was filmed by Metro-Goldwyn-Mayer in 1942. *The Moon Is Down,* produced by Twentieth Century-Fox Film Corp. in 1943, starred

Sir Cedric Hardwicke and Lee J. Cobb. *East of Eden,* with James Dean and Jo Van Fleet, who won an Oscar for her performance, was filmed by Warner Bros. in 1954; it was later adapted into a musical, "Here's Where I Belong," which opened at the Billy Rose Theatre in 1968. "Pipe Dream," a 1955 musical adapted by Oscar Hammerstein II, with music by Richard Rogers, was based on Steinbeck's *Sweet Thursday.* Twentieth Century-Fox Film Corp. produced *The Wayward Bus* in 1957. The National Broadcasting Co. has produced the following works for television: *America and Americans,* 1967, and *Travels with Charley,* 1968, both narrated by Henry Fonda; "The Harness," a story from *The Pastures of Heaven,* was televised in 1971 and featured Lorne Greene; *The Red Pony,* starring Henry Fonda and Maureen O'Hara, was shown in 1973.

BIOGRAPHICAL/CRITICAL SOURCES—Books: John Steinbeck, *In Dubious Battle,* Viking, 1936, new edition, 1971; Harry Thornton Moore, *The Novels of John Steinbeck: A First Critical Study,* Normandie House, 1939; Edmund Wilson, *The Boys in the Back Room,* Colt Press, 1941; Maxwell Geismar, *Writers in Crisis,* Houghton, 1942; Alfred Kazin, *On Native Grounds: An Interpretation of Modern American Prose Literature,* Harcourt, 1942; George Snell, *The Shapers of American Fiction: 1798-1947,* Dutton, 1947; W.M. Frohock, *The Novel of Violence in America,* University Press in Dallas, 1950, revised edition, Southern Methodist University Press, 1957; Wilson, *Classics and Commercials: A Literary Chronicle of the Forties,* Noonday Press, 1950; Harold C. Gardiner, editor, *Fifty Years of the American Novel,* Scribner, 1951; E. W. Tedlock, Jr. and C. V. Wicker, editors, *Steinbeck and His Critics: A Record of Twenty-Five Years,* University of New Mexico Press, 1957; Peter Lisca, *The Wide World of John Steinbeck,* Rutgers University Press, 1958; Carl Bode, editor, *The Young Rebel in American Literature,* Heinemann, 1959.

Joseph Warren Beach, *American Fiction: 1920-1940,* Russell & Russell, 1960; Warren French, *John Steinbeck,* Twayne, 1961; F. W. Watt, *John Steinbeck,* Grove, 1962 (published in England as *Steinbeck,* Oliver & Boyd, 1962); Joseph Fontenrose, *John Steinbeck,* Barnes & Noble, 1963; Walter Allen, *The Modern Novel,* Dutton, 1965; Max Westbrook, editor, *The Modern American Novel: Essays in Criticism,* Random House, 1966; *William Faulkner, Eugene O'Neill, John Steinbeck* (Nobel Prize presentation addresses and acceptance speeches), Gregory, 1971; Robert Murray Davis, editor, *Steinbeck: A Collection of Critical Essays,* Prentice-Hall, 1972; *Contemporary Literary Criticism,* Gale, Volume I, 1973, Volume V, 1976, Volume IX, 1978, Volume XIII, 1980; Tetsumaro Hayashi, editor, *John Steinbeck: A Dictionary of His Fictional Characters,* Scarecrow, 1976; Joel W. Hedgpeth, editor, *The Outer Shores,* Mad River Press, 1978.

Periodicals: *Pacific Spectator,* winter, 1948; *Saturday Review,* November 1, 1958, September 28, 1968, February 8, 1969; *New York Times Book Review,* November 16, 1958, June 25, 1961; *New Statesman,* June 30, 1961; *Times Literary Supplement,* July 7, 1961; *New Republic,* August 21, 1961; *Yale Review,* December, 1961; *Life,* November 2, 1962; *Newsweek,* November 5, 1962, January 30, 1967; *Detroit Free Press,* January 9, 1967; *Antioch Review,* spring, 1967; *Ramparts,* July, 1967; *Washington Post,* December 21, 1968, December 23, 1969; *Observer,* December 22, 1968; *National Observer,* December 23, 1968; *Time,* December 27, 1968; *Commonweal,* May 9, 1969; *New York Times,* June 2, 1969; *Esquire,* November, 1969; *Novel: A Forum on Fiction,* spring, 1977.†

—Sketch by Denise Gottis

STEINBERG, Leo 1920-

PERSONAL: Born July 7, 1920, in Moscow, Russia; son of Isaac N. and Nehama (Esselson) Steinberg. *Education:* Slade School, London, fine arts diploma, 1940; New York University, B.S., 1954, Ph.D., 1960. *Residence:* New York, N.Y. *Office:* Department of Art History, University of Pennsylvania, G-29 Fine Arts Bldg., Philadelphia, Pa. 19174.

CAREER: Hunter College of the City University of New York, New York, N.Y., associate professor, 1962-67, professor of art history, 1967-75; University of Pennsylvania, Philadelphia, Benjamin Franklin Professor and University Professor of the History of Art, 1975—. *Member:* American Academy of Arts and Sciences (fellow).

WRITINGS: Jasper Johns, Wittenborn, 1963; (contributor) Theodore R. Bowie and Cornelia V. Christenson, editors, *Studies in Erotic Art,* Basic Books, 1970; *Other Criteria,* Oxford University Press, 1972; *Michelangelo's Last Paintings,* Oxford University Press, 1975; *Borromini's San Carlo alle Quattro Fontane: A Study in Multiple Form and Architectural Symposium,* Garland Publishing, 1977. Columnist, *Arts,* 1955-56. Contributor to *Art Bulletin, Art News, Art Quarterly, Art in America, Critical Inquiry,* and *Daedalus.*

* * *

STEINBERGH, Judith W(olinsky) 1943-

PERSONAL: Born October 18, 1943, in Louisville, Ky.; daughter of Mayer (a real estate agent) and Rosalyn (Levin) Wolinsky; married Alex M. Steinbergh (a management consultant), September 5, 1965 (divorced, 1978); children: Shauna, David. *Education:* Wellesley College, B.A., 1965.

CAREER: McKinsey & Co., Cleveland, Ohio, manager of research department, 1965-71; Cambridge Research Institute, Cambridge, Mass., research associate, 1971-72; Calliope Children's Theatre, Brookline, Mass., educational director, 1972—. Teacher of poetry writing, Poets in School Program, 1972—. *Member:* Ohio Poets' Association.

WRITINGS: Marshmallow Worlds, Grosset, 1972; *Lillian Bloom: A Separation,* Wampeter Press, 1980; *Beyond Words,* North Shore Teachers' Association, 1980. Contributor of poems to *Prairie Schooner, Andover Review, Dark Horse,* and other periodicals; also contributor of articles to *Boston Sunday Globe, Ms., Poemmakers, Teachers and Writers,* and other periodicals.

WORK IN PROGRESS: Earth and the Great Weather Move Me; writing exercises for an Eskimo curriculum; children's stories; a new collection of poems; short stories.

SIDELIGHTS: Judith W. Steinbergh wrote *CA:* "The subjects of my poems and stories come from the issues of my life as a woman in this society; raising children alone, being allowed into their profound discussions, teaching children with joy and humanity, maintaining a household and relationships, dealing with separation, too many demands, a parent's death, and making a space for my writing, the core, the only hope for keeping the rest of it together. Writing under these conditions is not uncommon particularly for mothers, single fathers, people with financial insecurity as Tillie Olsen says so well in *Silences.* Poems and stories written beside a sick child, or in the midst of bedlam or commuting to work each day is a reality and from it emerges strong and important voices."

* * *

STEINBRUNNER, (Peter) Chris(tian) 1933-
(Peter Christian)

PERSONAL: Born December 25, 1933, in New York, N.Y.;

son of Josef and Maria Steinbrunner. *Education:* Fordham University, M.A. *Religion:* Roman Catholic. *Home:* 6252 82nd St., Middle Village, N.Y. 11379.

CAREER: Film manager and producer of "Journey to Adventure" (syndicated travel show), RKO General Television, New York City; co-editor and co-publisher, Centaur Books, Inc., New York City; writer. *Member:* Mystery Writers of America (vice-president), Science Fiction Writers of America, Baker Street Irregulars, Sons of the Desert, Fantasy Film Club, Knights of Columbus. *Awards, honors:* Edgar Allan Poe Award, 1977, for *The Encyclopedia of Mystery and Detection.*

WRITINGS: (Contributor) Dick Lupoff and Don Thompson, editors, *All in Color for a Dime,* Ace Books, 1971; (with Burt Goldblatt) *The Cinema of the Fantastic,* Saturday Review Press, 1972; (editor with Otto Penzler) *The Encyclopedia of Mystery and Detection,* McGraw, 1977; *The Films of Sherlock Holmes,* Citadel, 1978; (author of introduction) *The Shadow Scrapbook,* Harcourt, 1979.

Also author of television pilot script, "Lights Out," Twentieth Century-Fox, 1977, and of introductions to first six reprints of the Philo Vance murder novels, Gregg, 1980; also editor of *The Detectionary,* and contributor to *The Comic Book Book.* Author of columns, "Cinema Fantastic," for *Science Fiction Chronicle,* "Crime on Screen," under name Peter Christian, for *Alfred Hitchcock's Mystery Magazine,* and "Bloody Visions," for *Ellery Queen's Mystery Magazine.* Editor, *Third Degree* (newsletter of Mystery Writers of America); co-editor, *Baker Street Journal.*

* * *

STEINER, Stan(ley) 1925-

PERSONAL: Born January 1, 1925, in Brooklyn, N.Y.; son of Bernard (a designer) and Regina (Storch) Steiner; married Veronka Polgar (a university professor); children: Suki, Sanyi, Paul. *Education:* Attended University of Wisconsin for five months. *Politics:* "As little as possible." *Religion:* "Tribal." *Home and office:* 1000 Camino Rancheros, Santa Fe, N.M. 87501.

CAREER: "None that I know of, or wish. Writing is not a career, it is a religion." Lecturer at Colorado College, 1974, University of New Mexico, 1974-79, College of Idaho, 1976, University of California, Berkeley, 1977, and University of Nebraska, 1979; guest professor of year, University of Paris, 1975-76. *Member:* American Indian Historical Society, Western Writers of America, National Congress of American Indians, National Indian Youth Council, Chinese Historical Society of America, National Association for Lawmen and Outlaw History (founding member), Northern Plains Resource Council, Western History Association. *Awards, honors:* Anisfield-Wolf Award from *Saturday Review,* 1971, for *La Raza;* Golden Spur Award from Western Writers of America, 1973, for *The Tiguas,* 1977, for *The Vanishing White Man.*

WRITINGS: The Last Horse, Macmillan, 1961; *The New Indians,* Harper, 1968; *La Raza: The Mexican Americans,* Harper, 1969; *George Washington: The Indian Influence,* Putnam, 1970; *The Tiguas: Lost Tribe of City Indians,* Macmillan, 1972; *The Islands: The Worlds of the Puerto Ricans,* Harper, 1974; *The Vanishing White Man,* Harper, 1976; *The Mexican Americans,* Minority Rights Group (London), 1978; *Fusang: The Chinese Who Built America,* Harper, 1979; *In Search of the Jaguar: The Paradox of Development in Venezuela,* New York Times Books, 1979; *The Spirit Woman,* Harper, 1980; *The Ranchers: A Book of Generations,* Knopf, 1980.

Editor: (With Shirley Hill Witt) *The Way: An Anthology of American Indian Literature,* Knopf, 1972; (with Luis Valdez) *Aztlan: An Anthology of Mexican American Literature,* Knopf, 1972; (with Maria Teresa Babin) *Borinquen: An Anthology of Puerto Rican Literature,* Knopf, 1974.

Filmscripts: "The Water Was So Clear the Blind Could See," NET-TV, 1970; "The American Indian Speaks," Encyclopaedia Britannica, 1973; "Black Coal, Red Power," NET-TV, 1973; "Our Public Lands," NET-TV, 1977.

Work represented in more than fifty university textbooks and scholarly anthologies, 1968-78. General editor, "American Indian Tribes Today" series, Crowell, 1968-72. Contributor to *Grolier Encyclopedia* and *Encyclopedia of the West.* Contributor to periodicals, including *New York Times, Washington Post, New Republic, Nation, Current Anthropology, Harper's, Warpath, Navajo Times, Phylic,* and *Natural History.* Member of board of contributors, *Nuestro: The Magazine for Latinos,* 1977-78.

WORK IN PROGRESS: The Dark and Dashing Horsemen, for Harper; a novel, *The Flesh Country.*

SIDELIGHTS: "One's admiration for Stan Steiner's work does not come easily," writes F. W. Turner in *Nation.* "Rather it is like one's stubborn assent to Dreiser whose sheer integrity and blood experience eventually must triumph over the false attitudinizing, the sentimentalism, and the soft stretches of his prose. Such is the case with Steiner. [However] Steiner is one of our better authors. This is because he is a gifted listener. . . . In his travels across the country he has discovered the quality that makes America the strange psychological environment it is: our loneliness which comes from our historical alienation from the land."

In *The Vanishing White Man,* Steiner suggests that white men, not Indians, will disappear one day from the American West because of their lack of regard for the land and environment. Writing in the *New York Times Book Review,* Vine Deloria calls the work "a tough, honest and incisive book, which brings a sense of realism to an otherwise exotic subject. It is without a doubt Steiner's finest effort, . . . a book that may bring a needed sobriety to the problem of Indian-white relations." A *Publishers Weekly* reviewer believes that Steiner "portrays with rare empathy the Indians' way of life and their desparate efforts to preserve it. Many of the Indians with whom Steiner spoke seem convinced that the white man has doomed himself by his attempt to lord it over nature and his reckless plunder of the environment. . . . Partly a paean to the beauty of the American West, the narrative also interweaves a penetrating psychohistory of the white's relationship with the Indian. Powerful, eloquent, heartrending."

Steiner told *CA:* "The roots of America, which are its true heritage and will be its only salvation, are what I seek in my work. For these are my roots. And in seeking and finding them there is joy and peace. There is no other."

BIOGRAPHICAL/CRITICAL SOURCES: Publishers Weekly, June 21, 1976; *New York Times Book Review,* September 12, 1976; *Nation,* October 2, 1976, May 12, 1979; *America,* November 13, 1976; *New Republic,* March 24, 1979.

* * *

STEINHAUER, Harry 1905-

PERSONAL: Born June 11, 1905, in Cracow, Poland; son of Abraham and Anna (Klagsbrun) Steinhauer; married Minnie Singer, 1932; children: Judith Ann, Esther Joan Battle. *Education:* University of Toronto, B.A. (with honors), 1927, M.A., 1928, Ph.D., 1937.

CAREER: University of Saskatchewan, Saskatoon, 1929-43, began as instructor, professor of German and French, 1936-43; University of Manitoba, Winnipeg, head of German department, 1943-50; Antioch College, Yellow Springs, Ohio, professor of German, 1951-62; Western Reserve University (now Case Western Reserve University), Cleveland, Ohio, head of German department, 1962-63; University of California, Santa Barbara, professor of German, 1964-71, chairman of department of German, Russian, and Eastern languages, 1964-69. Visiting and summer professor at other schools. *Member:* Modern Language Association of America (secretary of Germanic section, 1962; chairman, 1964), American Society of Aesthetics, American Association of University Professors, American Association of Teachers of German, American Civil Liberties Union.

WRITINGS: *An Elementary German Grammar,* Ryerson, 1932; *Die Deutsche Novelle 1880-1933,* Norton, 1936, expanded edition, 1958; (translator with Helen Jessiman) *Modern German Short Stories,* Oxford University Press, 1938; *Das Deutsche Drama 1880-1933,* two volumes, Norton, 1938; *Deutsche Kultur: Ein Lesebuch,* Oxford University Press, 1939, revised edition, 1962; (with Felix Walter) *An Omnibus of French Literature,* two volumes, Macmillan, 1941; (with William Sundermeyer) *An Introduction to German,* Macmillan, 1950, revised edition, 1956; (with Ernst Feise) *German Literature since Goethe,* two volumes, Houghton, 1958, 1959; *Kulturlesbuch fuer Anfanger,* Macmillan, 1961; (editor) *German Stories,* Bantam, 1961; *Goethe's Werther,* Bantam, 1962; (editor) *A First German Reader,* Bantam, 1964; (editor) *German Short Novels,* Bantam, 1965; (editor) *Read, Write, Speak German,* Bantam, 1965; *Ten German Novellas,* Doubleday-Anchor, 1969; (with Roselinde Konrad) *Stilvolles Deutsch,* Prentice-Hall, 1970; *Goethe's Werther,* Norton, 1971; *Twelve German Novellas,* University of California Press, 1977. Contributor of numerous articles to professional journals.

* * *

STEPHENS, William N(ewton) 1927-

PERSONAL: Born February 3, 1927, in Evansville, Ind.; son of Olen C. and Charlotte (Wheeler) Stephens; married Judith Wilson, 1947 (divorced, 1967); married Carolyn Thomson, 1969; children: (first marriage) Mark Newton; (second marriage) Kenneth Michael. *Education:* University of Colorado, B.A., 1955; Boston University, M.A., 1956; Harvard University, Ed.D., 1959, postdoctoral study, 1959-61. *Office:* Department of Sociology and Anthropology, Dalhousie University, Halifax, Nova Scotia, Canada.

CAREER: University of Kansas, Lawrence, assistant professor of sociology and anthropology and research associate in Bureau of Child Research, 1961-65; Florida Atlantic University, Boca Raton, associate professor of sociology, 1965-69; Dalhousie University, Halifax, Nova Scotia, professor of sociology and anthropology, 1969—. Visiting professor, Florida State University, 1976-77, 1980. *Military service:* U.S. Army, 1945-47. *Member:* National Council on Family Relations.

WRITINGS: *The Oedipus Complex: Cross-Cultural Evidence,* Free Press of Glencoe, 1962; *The Family in Cross-Cultural Perspective,* Holt, 1963; (contributor) Neil Joseph Smelser, editor, *Sociology: An Introduction,* Wiley, 1967; *Hypothesis and Evidence,* Crowell, 1968; (editor) *Reflections on Marriage,* Crowell, 1968; *Our Children Should Be Working,* C. C Thomas, 1979. Contributor to professional journals.

WORK IN PROGRESS: *Activities for Teenagers.*

STERN, Fritz 1926-

PERSONAL: Born February 2, 1926, in Breslau, Germany; son of Rudolf A. and Catherine (Brieger) Stern; married Margaret J. Bassett, 1947; children: Frederick Preston, Katherine Bassett. *Education:* Columbia University, B.A., 1946; M.A., 1948, Ph.D., 1953. *Home:* 15 Claremont Ave., New York, N.Y. 10027. *Office:* Department of History, Columbia University, New York, N.Y. 10027.

CAREER: Columbia University, New York, N.Y., instructor, 1949-51; Cornell University, Ithaca, N.Y., acting assistant professor of history, 1951-53; Columbia University, assistant professor, 1953-57, associate professor, 1957-63, professor of history, 1963-67, Seth Low Professor of History, 1967—. Visiting professor at Yale University, 1964-65, and Free University of Berlin; appointed permanent visiting professor, University of Konstanz (Germany), 1967; Elie Halevy Professor, University of Paris, spring, 1979. Member of OECD examination panel for West German education, 1971-72; member of visiting board, department of German, Princeton University, 1972—. Consultant to U.S. Department of State, 1966-67; editorial consultant, International Archive for the Social History of German Literature, 1974—.

MEMBER: American Historical Association, American Academy of Arts and Sciences, Council on Foreign Relations, Phi Beta Kappa. *Awards, honors:* Fellowships from Stanford University, 1957-58, Social Science Research Council, 1960-61, American Council of Learned Societies, 1966-67, Oxford University, 1966-67, Guggenheim Foundation, 1969-70, Princeton University, 1969-70, and Ford Foundation, 1976-77; Great Teachers award from Society of Older Graduates of Columbia University, 1975; Officer's Cross of the Order of Merit from the Federal Republic of Germany, 1976; Lionel Trilling award from Columbia University, 1977, and National Book award nomination, 1978, both for *Gold and Iron.*

WRITINGS: (Editor) *The Varieties of History: From Voltaire to the Present,* Meridian, 1956, 2nd edition, Vintage Books, 1973; *The Politics of Cultural Despair: A Study in the Rise of the Germanic Ideology,* University of California Press, 1961, 2nd edition, 1974; (editor with Leonard Krieger) *The Responsibility of Power: Historical Essays in Honor of Hajo Holborn,* Doubleday, 1967; *The Failure of Illiberalism: Essays on the Political Culture of Modern Germany,* Knopf, 1972; *Gold and Iron: Bismarck, Bleichroeder and the Building of the German Empire,* Knopf, 1977.

Contributor: Thomas Green, editor, *Educational Planning in Perspective, Forecasting, and Policy-Making,* Guilford Press, 1971; Dora B. Weiner and William R. Keylor, editors, *From Parnassus: Essays in Honor of Jacques Barzun,* Harper, 1976; Quentin Anderson, Stephan Donadio, and Steven Marcus, editors, *Art, Politics, and Will* (essays), Basic Books, 1977; D. Spring, editor, *European Landed Elites in the Nineteenth Century,* Johns Hopkins University Press, 1977. Also contributor to *Chapters in Western Civilization,* Volume II, 3rd edition (Stern was not associated with earlier editions), 1962, and *Columbia History of the World.* Contributor of reviews to *Foreign Affairs,* 1962—; contributor of articles to journals. Member of board of editors, *American Historical Review,* 1974-77, and *Foreign Affairs,* 1978—.

WORK IN PROGRESS: A book on contemporary Europe.

BIOGRAPHICAL/CRITICAL SOURCES: *New York Times,* February 20, 1977, March 19, 1977; *Washington Post,* April 3, 1977.

STERN, Richard G(ustave) 1928-

PERSONAL: Born February 25, 1928, in New York, N.Y.; son of Henry George (a dentist) and Marion (Veit) Stern; married Gay Clark, March 14, 1950 (divorced, February, 1972); children: Christopher, Kate, Andrew, Nicholas. *Education:* University of North Carolina, B.A., 1947; Harvard University, M.A., 1949; University of Iowa, Ph.D., 1954. *Office:* Department of English, University of Chicago, 1050 East 59th St., Chicago, Ill. 60637.

CAREER: Jules Ferry College, Versailles, France, lecturer, 1949-50; University of Heidelberg, Heidelberg, Germany, lektor, 1950-51; educational advisor, U.S. Army, 1951-52; Connecticut College, New London, instructor, 1954-55; University of Chicago, Chicago, Ill., assistant professor, 1956-61, associate professor, 1962-64, professor of English, 1965—. Visiting lecturer, University of Venice, 1962-63, University of California, Santa Barbara, 1964, 1968, State University of New York at Buffalo, 1966, Harvard University, 1969, University of Nice, 1970, University of Urbino, 1977. *Member:* Philological Society (University of Chicago), Phi Beta Kappa. *Awards, honors:* Longwood Award, 1960; Friends of Literature Award; Rockefeller grant, 1965; National Institute of Arts and Letters grant, 1968; Guggenheim fellowship, 1973-74; Carl Sandburg Award, Friends of the Chicago Public Library, 1979, for *Natural Shocks.*

WRITINGS—Novels: *Golk,* Criterion, 1960; *Europe; or Up and Down with Schreiber and Baggish,* McGraw, 1961 (published in England as *Europe; or Up and Down with Baggish and Schreiber,* MacGibbon & Kee, 1962); *In Any Case,* McGraw, 1963; *Stitch,* Harper, 1965; *Other Men's Daughters,* Dutton, 1973; *Natural Shocks,* Coward, 1978.

Other: *Teeth, Dying, and Other Matters, and The Gamesman's Island: A Play* (short story collection), Harper, 1964; (editor) *Honey and Wax: Pleasures and Powers of Narrative,* University of Chicago Press, 1966; *1968: A Short Novel, An Urban Idyll, Five Stories, and Two Trade Notes,* Holt, 1970; *The Books in Fred Hampton's Apartment* (essay collection), Dutton, 1973; *Packages,* Coward, 1980.

Work appears in anthologies. Contributor to *Encyclopaedia Britannica.* Contributor to *Partisan Review, New York Times,* and other periodicals.

SIDELIGHTS: "Celebrations are due many a good writer languishing under an excess of obscurity," writes Peter Straub in *New Statesman,* "but few deserve them as much as Richard Stern. Stern has been . . . getting stronger and more audacious with each new novel, inventing a distinctive and mature narrative style, and always following his own elegant hard-won line." Christopher Lehmann-Haupt calls Stern "a craftsman par excellence" and "a writer's writer" whose work, although admired by Saul Bellow, John Cheever, and others, "is not as well known as it ought to be."

One reason for Stern's relatively low profile is his preference for the psychological exploration of his characters. "Many French and American writers are bored with psychology," Stern told an interviewer. "They prefer novelistic virtuosity to individual histories. I don't believe we've come close to exploring what Augustine calls the 'abysses of human consciousness.'"

Another reason for Stern's anonymity is his decision not to live in the literary center of New York. "I'm glad Chicago is my place," he has said, "for the reasons that discourage other writers: its nonliterariness and commercialism. These help preserve the anonymity of its writers. It may infuriate his vanity, but it allows him to spend less time playing 'writer' and more [time on] his writing."

A collection of Stern's manuscripts is housed at the Regenstein Library at the University of Chicago.

BIOGRAPHICAL/CRITICAL SOURCES: Chicago Tribune, April 24, 1960, May 6, 1979; *Commonweal,* May 13, 1960; *Saturday Review,* July 23, 1960, January 21, 1978; *Book Week,* October 25, 1964; *Harper's,* April, 1965; *Time,* November 5, 1965; *Newsweek,* November 22, 1965; *Christian Science Monitor,* December 9, 1965; *New York Review of Books,* December 9, 1965, August 13, 1970; *New York Times,* December 15, 1965, January 9, 1978; *Chicago Review,* summer, 1966; *Prairie Schooner,* summer, 1966; *National Review,* December 27, 1966; *Punch,* May 3, 1967; *Times Literary Supplement,* May 4, 1967; *New York Times Book Review,* July 12, 1970; *Partisan Review,* winter, 1971; *New Statesman,* March 19, 1971, May 10, 1974; *Book World,* October 28, 1973; *New Yorker,* November 19, 1973; *Atlantic,* December, 1973, March, 1978; *Ms,* March, 1974; *Listener,* May 16, 1974; *Yale Review,* June, 1974; *London Magazine,* August/September, 1974; *Contemporary Literary Criticism,* Volume IV, Gale, 1975; *Nation,* February 11, 1978; *West Coast Review of Books,* March, 1978; *Hudson Review,* summer, 1978; *Chicago Review,* winter, 1980.

* * *

STEVENS, Robert Warren 1918-

PERSONAL: Born June 29, 1918, in Columbus, Ohio; son of Warren Aden (an accountant) and Hazel (Bryan) Stevens; married Elizabeth Cole, December 15, 1944 (divorced, 1966); married Dorothy Drexler, November, 1972; children: (first marriage) Carolyn, Douglas. *Education:* Ohio Wesleyan University, B.A., 1940; University of Michigan, M.A., 1942, Ph.D., 1949. *Politics:* Democrat. *Religion:* Unitarian-Universalist. *Home:* 835 Judson, Evanston, Ill. 60202. *Office:* Department of Economics, Roosevelt University, Chicago, Ill. 60605.

CAREER: University of Michigan, Ann Arbor, instructor in money and banking and principles of economics, 1948-49; U.S. Embassy, London, England, economist and financial attache for Marshall Plan, Mission to United Kingdom, 1950-55; Standard Oil Co., New York, N.Y., senior economist, 1955-66; Indiana University at Bloomington, associate professor of business economics and international business, 1966-71; Indiana University Northwest, Gary, professor of business administration and director of graduate program, 1971-74; Roosevelt University, Chicago, Ill., professor of economics and chairman of department, 1974—. Lecturer, City College of the City University of New York, 1958-61, 1964-65; visiting associate professor, New School for Social Research, 1968-69. Has testified before U.S. Congressional committees.

MEMBER: American Economic Association, National Foreign Trade Council, Society for International Development, American Association of University Professors, New York International Economists Club (co-founder), Phi Beta Kappa, Omicron Delta Kappa, Beta Gamma Sigma. *Awards, honors:* Two research awards from International Business Research Institute, Indiana University.

WRITINGS: (Contributor) Harrop Freeman, editor, *Peace Is the Victory,* Harper, 1944; (contributor) John M. Cassels, editor, *The Sterling Area: An American Analysis,* U.S. Economic Cooperation Administration Mission to the United Kingdom, 1951; (contributor) William Allen and Clark Lee Allen, editors, *Foreign Trade and Finance,* Macmillan, 1959; (contributor) Emile Benoit and Kenneth Boulding, editors, *Disarmament and the Economy,* Harper, 1963; (contributor) L. H. Officer and T. D. Willett, editors, *The International Monetary System: Problems and Proposals,* Prentice-Hall, 1969; (editor with Richard Farmer and Hans Schollhammer) *Readings in International Business,* Dickenson, 1972; *The Dollar in the World Economy,* Random House, 1972; *Vain Hopes, Grim Realities: Economic Consequences of the Vietnam War,* F. Watts, 1976.

Contributor to *Encyclopedia Americana.* Contributor of articles and reviews to business and economics journals, including *American Economic Review, New Republic, Social Research, Journal of Commerce, Nation,* and *Business Horizons.*

WORK IN PROGRESS: Research on the relationship between multi-national corporations and economic development; *U.S. International Monetary Policy and General Foreign Policy.*

* * *

STEVENSON, Dwight E(shelman) 1906-

PERSONAL: Born March 6, 1906, in Cuba, Ill.; son of Luther and Mabel (Eshelman) Stevenson; married Deloris Ray, 1928; children: Virginia Stevenson Bryant, Dwight Ward. *Education:* Bethany College, A.B. (summa cum laude), 1929; Yale University, B.D., 1933; *Home:* 592 Bellcastle Rd., Lexington, Ky.

CAREER: Bethany Memorial Church, Bethany, W.Va., minister, 1933-44; Bethany College, Bethany, instructor, 1935-44, professor, 1944-47; Lexington Theological Seminary, Lexington, Ky., professor of homiletics, 1947-74, interim president, 1964 and 1974, dean, 1969-74. Visiting professor, Union Theological Seminary, Philippines, 1953-54; honorary lecturer, American School of Oriental Research, Palestine, 1960-61; adjunct professor of religion and chaplain, Around the World Semester, Chapman College of the Seven Seas, 1965-66; visiting professor, School of Theology at Claremont, 1968. Coordinator, Theological Education Association of Mid-America, 1974—. *Member:* Association of Theological Professors in the Practical Fields. *Awards, honors:* D.D., Bethany College, 1947.

WRITINGS: Faiths That Compete for My Loyalty, Bethany Press, 1945, revised edition, 1953; *Walter Scott: Voice of the Golden Oracle: A Biography,* Bethany Press, 1946; (with Goodnight) *Home to Bethphage: A Biography of Robert Richardson,* Bethany Press, 1949; *Strong Son of God,* Bethany Press, 1949; *Beginning at Jerusalem,* Bethany Press, 1950; *The Fourth Witness,* Bethany Press, 1954; *Faith Take a Name,* Harper, 1954; *Christianity in the Philippines,* College of the Bible, 1955; *Preaching on the Books of the New Testament,* Harper, 1956; (with Charles F. Diehl) *Reaching People from the Pulpit,* Harper, 1958; *The Church after Paul,* Bethany Press, 1959; *Your Face in This Mirror,* Bethany Press, 1959.

Preaching on the Books of the Old Testament, Harper, 1961; *The Church—What and Why,* Bethany Press, 1962; *The Bacon College Story,* College of the Bible, 1962; *On Holy Ground,* Bethany Press, 1963; *Lexington Theological Seminary: The College of the Bible Century, 1865-1965,* Bethany Press, 1964; *The False Prophet,* Abingdon, 1965; *In the Biblical Preacher's Workshop,* Abingdon, 1967; *A Way in the Wilderness,* Bethany Press, 1968; *Disciple Preaching in the First Generation,* Disciples of Christ Historical Society, 1969; *Monday's God,* Bethany Press, 1976.

SIDELIGHTS: Dwight Stevenson has traveled around the world twice. He has also followed the path of the Apostle Paul through the Middle East and the northern Mediterranean.

* * *

STEVENSON, Robert (Murrell) 1916-

PERSONAL: Born July 3, 1916; son of Robert Emory (a minister) and Ada (Ross) Stevenson. *Education:* Attended Juilliard Graduate School of Music, 1934-38; University of Texas, A.B., 1936; Yale University, M. Mus., 1939; University of Rochester, Ph.D., 1942; Harvard University, S.T.B. (cum laude), 1943; Princeton Theological Seminary, Th.M.; Oxford University, B. Litt. *Office:* Department of Music, University of California, Los Angeles, Calif. 90024.

CAREER: University of Texas at Austin, instructor, 1941-43, 1946; Westminster Choir College, Princeton, N.J., faculty member, 1946-49; University of California, Los Angeles, 1949—, began as instructor, currently professor of music. Visiting professor at Columbia University, 1955-56, Indiana University, 1959-60, University of Maryland, 1961, University of Chile, 1965-66, and Northwestern University, 1976; Louis C. Elson Lecturer, Library of Congress; Faculty Research Lecturer, University of California, Los Angeles, 1981. Consultant to UNESCO, 1977. *Military service:* U.S. Army, Chaplain Corps, 1943-46; became captain.

MEMBER: Hispanic Society of America, Centro de Estudios Folkloricos y Musicales (Bogota), Real Academia de San Fernando de Bellas Artes, Plainsong and Mediaeval Music Society. *Awards, honors:* Charles Ditson traveling fellowship, Yale University; Joseph Bearns and Victor Baier Awards, Columbia University; Buenos Aires Convention award, Mexico; Del Amo fellowship, Spain; Carnegie Foundation award; three Fulbright research awards; fellowships from American Philosophical Society, Ford Foundation, Pan American Organization of American States, Guggenheim Foundation, Calouste Gulbenkian Foundation, Institute of Creative Arts (University of California), and National Endowment for the Humanities.

WRITINGS: Music in Mexico: A Historical Survey, Crowell, 1952; *Patterns of Protestant Church Music,* Duke University Press, 1953; *La Musica en la Catedral de Sevilla: 1478-1606,* Raul Espinosa, 1954; *Music before the Classic Era,* Macmillan, 1955, 2nd edition, 1958; *Shakespeare's Religious Frontier,* Nijhoff, 1958; *Juan Sebastian Bach: Su Ambiente y Su Obra,* Pacific Press Publishing Association, 1959; *Cathedral Music in Colonial Peru,* Pacific Press Publishing Association, 1959.

The Music of Peru: Aboriginal and Viceroyal Epochs, Pan American, 1960; *Juan Bermudo,* Nijhoff, 1960; *Spanish Music in the Age of Columbus,* Nijhoff, 1960; *Spanish Cathedral Music in the Golden Age,* University of California Press, 1961; *La Musica Colonial en Columbia,* Instituto Popular de Cultura de Cali, 1964; *Protestant Church Music in America,* Norton, 1966; *Music in Aztec and Inca Territory,* University of California Press, 1968.

Renaissance and Baroque Musical Sources in the Americas, Organization of American States, 1970; *Christmas Music from Baroque Mexico,* University of California Press, 1974; *Latin American Colonial Music,* Organization of American States, 1975; *Tomas de Torrejon La Purpura de la Rosa,* Instituto Nacional de Cultura (Lima), 1976; *Vilancicos Portugueses,* Fundacao Calouste Guibenkien (Lisbon), 1976. Also author of *Seventeenth-Century Villancicos,* 1974, *Foundations of New World Opera,* 1974, and *A Guide to Caribbean Music,* 1975. Contributor to *Grove's Dictionary of Music and Musicians, The New Grove's Dictionary of*

Music and Musicians, Die Musik in Geschichte und Gegenwart, Enciclopedia della Musica Ricordi, Encyclopedie des musiques sacres, Enciclopedia della Musica Rizzoli, and *New Catholic Encyclopedia*. Contributor of articles to music, theology, folklore, and language journals. Contributing editor, *Handbook of Latin American Studies,* 1976—; editor, *Inter-American Music Review,* 1978—.

* * *

STEWART, Mary (Florence Elinor) 1916-

PERSONAL: Born September 17, 1916, in Sunderland, Durham, England; daughter of Frederick Albert (a Church of England clergyman) and Mary Edith (Matthews) Rainbow; married Frederick Henry Stewart, 1945. *Education:* University of Durham, B.A. (first class honours), 1938, M.A., 1941. *Address:* c/o William Morrow & Co., 105 Madison Ave., New York, N.Y. 10016.

CAREER: University of Durham, Durham, England, lecturer, 1941-45, part-time lecturer, 1948-55; writer, 1954—. *Military service:* Royal Observer Corps, World War II. *Member:* Royal Society of Arts (fellow). *Awards, honors:* British Crime Writers Association Award, 1960, for *My Brother Michael;* Mystery Writers of America award, 1964, for *This Rough Magic;* Frederick Niven Award, 1971, for *The Crystal Cave;* Scottish Arts Council Award, 1974, for *Ludo and the Star Horse.*

WRITINGS: Madam, Will You Talk? (also see below), Hodder & Stoughton, 1955, Mill, 1956; *Wildfire at Midnight* (also see below), Appleton, 1956; *Thunder on the Right,* Hodder & Stoughton, 1957, Mill, 1958; *Nine Coaches Waiting* (also see below), Hodder & Stoughton, 1958, Mill, 1959; *My Brother Michael* (also see below), Hodder & Stoughton, 1959, Mill, 1960; *The Ivy Tree* (also see below), Mill, 1961; *The Moon-Spinners* (also see below), Hodder & Stoughton, 1962, Mill, 1963; *Three Novels of Suspense* (contains *Madam, Will You Talk?, Nine Coaches Waiting,* and *My Brother Michael*), Mill, 1963; *This Rough Magic* (Literary Guild selection; also see below), Mill, 1964; *Airs above the Ground* (also see below), Mill, 1965; *The Gabriel Hounds* (Doubleday Book Club selection; *Reader's Digest* Condensed Book Club selection; Literary Guild alternate selection), Mill, 1967; *The Crystal Cave* (Literary Guild selection; also see below), Morrow, 1970; *The Little Broomstick* (juvenile), Brockhampton Press, 1971, Morrow, 1972; *The Wind Off the Small Isles,* Hodder & Stoughton, 1968; *The Spell of Mary Stewart* (contains *This Rough Magic, The Ivy Tree,* and *Wildfire at Midnight*), Doubleday, 1968; *Mary Stewart Omnibus* (contains *Madam, Will You Talk?, Wildfire at Midnight,* and *Nine Coaches Waiting*), Hodder & Stoughton, 1969; *The Hollow Hills* (also see below), Morrow, 1973; *Ludo and the Star Horse* (juvenile), Brockhampton Press, 1974, Morrow, 1975; *Touch Not the Cat,* Morrow, 1976; *Triple Jeopardy* (contains *My Brother Michael, The Moon-Spinners,* and *This Rough Magic*), Hodder & Stoughton, 1978; *Selected Works* (contains *The Crystal Cave, The Hollow Hills, Wildfire at Midnight,* and *Airs above the Ground*), Heinemann, 1978; *The Last Enchantment* (Literary Guild selection), Morrow, 1979. Also author of four short plays, produced on the British Broadcasting Corp. network, 1958.

WORK IN PROGRESS: A third children's book.

SIDELIGHTS: Ever since the publication of her first book, *Madam, Will You Talk?,* Mary Stewart has impressed readers and critics alike with her "labyrinthine" modern-Gothic thrillers, told "for the sheer joy of telling," in the words of a *National Observer* critic. "Like a magician," the critic continues, "she conjures exotic moods and mysteries from mere words, her only aim to entertain."

While "predictability" is not a quality most authors would strive for, a *Christian Science Monitor* reviewer feels that this very trait is more likely the secret of Stewart's success. Prior to 1970, for example, her plots followed a fairly consistent pattern of romance and suspense set in vividly depicted locales such as Provence, the Isle of Skye, the Pyrenees, Delphi, and Lebanon. Furthermore, notes the *Christian Science Monitor* reviewer, "Mrs. Stewart doesn't pull any tricks or introduce uncomfortable issues. Attractive, well-brought-up girls pair off with clean, confident young men, always on the side of the angels. And when the villains are finally rounded up, no doubts disturb us—it is clear that the best men have won again." The heroine of these stories is always "a girl displaying just the right combination of strengths and weaknesses. She may blunder into traps and misread most of the signals, but she will—feminine intuition being what it is—stumble onto something important. She will also need rescuing in a cliff-hanging finale." In short, the reviewer concludes, "it all makes excellent escape fiction."

Anthony Boucher of the *New York Times* writes: "A backward glance will reveal so many whopping coincidences and inadequate or inconsistent motivations that you can't believe a word of it; but so unusually skillful is this young Englishwoman in her first novel that you really don't care. You've had too enjoyable a time . . . to worry about trifles like plausibility." James Sandoe of the *New York Herald Tribune Book Review* agrees. He calls *Madam, Will You Talk?* "a distinctly charming, romantic thriller . . . [that is] intelligently soft-boiled, pittypat and a good deal of fun."

Stewart's subsequent novels have also received similar words of praise, especially from Boucher, who notes: "That special sub-species of mystery one might call the Cinderella-suspense novel is designed by feminine authors for feminine readers; yet a male can relish such highpoints as *Jane Eyre* or *Rebecca*. Of current practitioners, I can't think of anyone (aside from du Maurier herself) who tells such stories quite as well as Mary Stewart, and *Nine Coaches Waiting* is her longest and probably her best to date." The *New York Herald Tribune Book Review* critic simply states: "For any one even half-heartedly inclined toward romance and adventure, *Nine Coaches Waiting* is a novel that will not easily be laid down."

My Brother Michael, according to Frances Iles of the *Guardian,* is "the contemporary thriller at its very best." Christopher Pym of the *Spectator* comments: "Mary Stewart gives each of her admirable novels an exotically handsome (if somewhat rather travel-folderish) setting. . . . This [is] by a long chalk the best of them. . . . The Greek landscape and—much more subtle—the Greek character are splendidly done, in a long, charmingly written, highly evocative, imperative piece of required reading for an Hellenic cruise." Boucher, too, finds the book worthy of praise: "If the delightfully entertaining novels of Mary Stewart . . . have had a fault, it is that their plots are (in James Sandoe's useful term) Eurydicean—they cannot survive a backward glance. But in *My Brother Michael* even this flaw vanishes. . . . This detective adventure, rich in action and suspense, is seen through the eyes of a characteristic Stewart heroine; and surely there are few more attractive young women in today's popular fiction. . . . These girls are as far removed as you can imagine from the Idiot Heroine who disfigures (at least for men) so much romantic fiction."

After commenting on Stewart's overall accomplishments,

F.W.J. Hemmings concludes that it is "no wonder that Mary Stewart should be accounted 'very successful.' It is success well-earned, for there is nothing cheap in the writing and nothing machine-made in the devising.... Of course, the books do not pretend to offer anything but delight.... But they are the genuine triumphs of a minor art."

In 1970, Stewart deviated from her usual modern-Gothic thrillers and turned to historical fiction instead. The main focus of this new interest was Arthurian England, especially as seen through the eyes of Merlin the magician. Unlike most other authors who have written about the legends of Camelot in terms of the Middle Ages, Stewart places her story in more historically accurate fifth-century Britain. Reviewing *The Crystal Cave,* the first of three books on Merlin, a *Best Sellers* critic writes: "Fifth century Britain and Brittany come to life in Miss Stewart's vigorous imagination.... Those who have read and enjoyed the many novels of Mary Stewart will not need to be told this is an expertly fashioned continually absorbing story, with a facile imagination fleshing out the legend of the parentage of the future King Arthur—and, too, of Merlin himself. There is, besides, a fine feeling for the waters and mountains, the moods and mystery of its pre-historic Welsh setting." A *Books and Bookmen* critic calls it "a highly plotted and rattling good yarn. Mary Stewart's evocation of an era of magic, as well as of blood-letting, is magnificently done. Her writing is virile, and of a very high quality indeed. Her descriptions of the countryside are often moving, also poetical. I cannot recommend the book highly enough."

Martin Levin of the *New York Times Book Review,* after reminding readers that little is actually known of Merlin's life, notes that "the author obligingly expands [Merlin's] myth into a first person history.... Cheerfully disclaiming authenticity, Miss Stewart ... lightens the Dark Ages with legend, pure invention and a lively sense of history." A *Christian Science Monitor* reviewer, however, finds this type of "history" to be somewhat compromised by the author's emphasis on Merlin's magical powers. "There really is little 'magic' in the story," the reviewer begins, "and what there is rarely exceeds the familiar 'knowing before the event.' But the very uncertainty of its inclusion lends a certain falseness to an otherwise absorbing story, which has been carefully researched historically so that it is peripherally authentic." At any rate, the reviewer concludes, "*The Crystal Cave* evokes an England long gone and could prove an interesting guidebook to some of the less touristy attractions of the Cornish and Welsh countryside."

The Hollow Hills, a continuation of Merlin's story, was also fairly well-received. *Publisher's Weekly* calls it "romantic, refreshing and most pleasant reading.... Mrs. Stewart has steeped herself well in the folklore and known history of fifth century Britain and she makes of her feuding, fighting warlords lively and intriguing subjects." A *Best Sellers* critic writes: "All in all, this makes a smashing good tale. The suspense is superb and the reader is kept involved in the unwinding of the plot. Miss Stewart has taken the main lines of the Arthurian legend and has developed the basic elements in a plausible way. She gives one a feeling for the century about which she writes." Finally, a *Library Journal* reviewer notes: "Not the caricature, mystic or eccentric of other Arthurian novels, Merlin is human and readers will understand, sympathize with, and like him."

Joseph McLellan of the *Washington Post Book World* finds the third Merlin book, *The Last Enchantment,* to be somewhat of an anti-climax. "Having used two long, exciting novels to get Arthur on the throne," he writes, "Miss Stewart has reached the final volume of her trilogy and we can settle back expecting to hear the old stories told again with her unique touch. There is only one trouble with this expectation: Mary Stewart does not fulfill it, and she quite clearly never had any intentions of fulfilling it. Her story is not strictly about Arthur but about Merlin.... Strictly speaking, once Arthur is safely on the throne ... Merlin's life work is over. He spends most of *The Last Enchantment* fading away as gracefully as he can manage.... [As a result of this shift in emphasis,] the role of Arthur in this volume is fitful and erratic; he is a powerful presence but not the central character."

Very much aware of the difficulties involved in gathering and making sense out of the confusing source material available on Merlin's life, McLellan praises Stewart for "the ingenuity of [her] effort," though he feels that the story's ultimate plausibility is somewhat in doubt. "She gives us ... traditional materials," he notes, "but the treatment is her own, the emphasis shifted for her purpose, which is not simply to recast old material but to bring alive a long-dead historical epoch—not the Middle Ages of Malory but the Dark Ages of the original Arthur. This she does splendidly. Fifth-century Britain is caught in these pages, and while it may lack some of the exotic glitter of the imaginary 12th-century Britain that Arthur usually inhabits, it is a fascinating place."

Explaining her decision to switch from writing modern-Gothic thrillers to historical fiction, Mary Stewart told *CA:* "I always planned that some day I would write a historical novel, and I intended to use Roman Britain as the setting. This is a period that I have studied over many years. But then, quite by chance, I came across a passage in Geoffrey of Monmouth's *History of the Kings of Britain,* which described the first appearance of Merlin, the Arthurian 'enchanter.' Here was a new story, offering a new approach to a dark and difficult period, with nothing known about the 'hero' except scraps of legend. The story would have to come purely from imagination, pitched somewhere between legend and truth and fairy-tale and known history. The setting would be imaginary, too, a Dark Age Britain in the unrecorded aftermath of the Roman withdrawal. I had originally no intention of writing more than one volume, but the story seized my imagination.... It has been a tough job and a rewarding one. I have learned a lot, not least that the powerful themes of the Arthurian 'Matter of Britain' are as cogent and real today as they were fourteen centuries ago. And Merlin's story has allowed me to return to my first avocation of all, that of poet."

Elsewhere, Mary Stewart has written: "I believe that it is not enough to produce what one sees as 'plain reality,' to hold up a mirror to the ordinary, and nothing else. If the writers of an age settle for the mediocre, or even the plain nasty as the norm of an age, then imperceptibly but definitely that does become the norm of the age.... It is my view that the things we would like to see have as much of a place in fiction as the things we do see. The novel should strike a medium between the true and the longed-for; it should move between the two poles, as indeed life moves. If we live in an age which is scared of excellence, and which devalues the human individual, the novelist has all the more responsibility laid on him to create a world where the individual is still seen to matter, and where right is still paramount. It is not enough faithfully to reflect the chaos and unease which we feel in the world; a sense of helplessness and futility will not confine itself in the necessary disciplines of art, and art without discipline conveys nothing. The novelist, like the poet, is a maker. Let him make."

Mary Stewart's books have been translated into sixteen languages. *The Moon-Spinners* was made into a Walt Disney movie starring Hayley Mills.

AVOCATIONAL INTERESTS: Music, painting, the theatre, gardening.

BIOGRAPHICAL/CRITICAL SOURCES: New York Times, March 18, 1956, September 9, 1956, May 18, 1958, January 18, 1959; *New York Herald Tribune Book Review,* May 27, 1956, October 5, 1958, March 8, 1959, March 4, 1962; *San Francisco Chronicle,* October 21, 1956, May 22, 1960; *Guardian,* February 26, 1960; *New York Times Book Review,* April 10, 1960, January 7, 1962, October 24, 1965, October 15, 1967, August 9, 1970, July 29, 1973, September 2, 1979; Roy Newquist, *Counterpoint,* Rand McNally, 1964; *New Statesman,* November 5, 1965; *Book Week,* November 21, 1965; *Christian Science Monitor,* September 28, 1967, September 3, 1970; *Best Sellers,* October 1, 1967, July 15, 1970, July 15, 1973; *National Observer,* October 23, 1967; *Time,* January 5, 1968; *Washington Post Book World,* March 31, 1968, September 15, 1976, July 22, 1979; *Writer,* May, 1970; *Books and Bookmen,* August, 1970; *Harper's,* September, 1970; *Library Journal,* June 15, 1973; *Sunday Times Colour Supplement,* June 13, 1976; *Contemporary Literary Criticism,* Volume VII, 1977.

—Sketch by Deborah A. Straub

* * *

STEWART, Randall 1896-1964

PERSONAL: Born July 25, 1896, in Fayetteville, Tenn.; died June 17, 1964; son of William Jesse and Fannie K. (Chestnut) Stewart; married Cleone Odell, December 29, 1920; children: Ann Odell Stewart Orth. *Education:* Vanderbilt University, B.S., 1917; Harvard University, M.A., 1921; Yale University, Ph.D., 1930. *Home:* 506 Lynwood Blvd., Nashville, Tenn. *Office:* Department of English, Vanderbilt University, Nashville, Tenn. 37203.

CAREER: University of Oklahoma, Norman, instructor in English, 1917-20, 1922-23; U.S. Naval Academy, Annapolis, Md., instructor in English, 1921-22; University of Idaho, Moscow, assistant professor, 1923-25; Yale University, New Haven, Conn., instructor, 1927-31, assistant professor, 1931-34; Vanderbilt University, Nashville, Tenn., professor, 1934-37; Brown University, Providence, R.I., professor, 1937-55, chairman of English department, 1955; Vanderbilt University, professor of English and head of department, 1955-64. Visiting professor, Yale University, 1947-48, University of Washington, 1957, and State University of Iowa. *Member:* Modern Language Association of America (chairman, American literature section, 1951), Elizabethan Club (Yale), Coffee House (Nashville), Phi Beta Kappa, Omicron Delta Pi. *Awards, honors:* Guggenheim fellow, 1943.

WRITINGS: (Editor) Nathaniel Hawthorne, *American Notebooks,* Yale University Press, 1932, reprinted, Folcroft, 1970; (editor) Hawthorne, *English Notebooks,* Modern Language Association, 1941, reprinted, Russell, 1962; *Nathaniel Hawthorne: A Biography,* Yale University Press, 1948, reprinted, Archon Books, 1970; *American Literature and Christian Doctrine,* Louisiana State University Press, 1958; (editor) *American Poetry,* Scott, Foresman, 1964; *Regionalism and Beyond* (a collection of essays), edited by George Core, Vanderbilt University Press, 1968. Contributor to literary journals.†

STILL, Richard R(alph) 1921-

PERSONAL: Born April 19, 1921, in Nampa, Idaho; son of Ralph Essick (a grocer), and Helen E. (Casey) Still; married Mary C. Austin, December 21, 1946; children: Roberta F. Still Holland. *Education:* University of Idaho, B.A., 1942; Stanford University, M.B.A., 1949; University of Washington, Seattle, Ph.D., 1953. *Politics:* Democrat. *Religion:* Presbyterian. *Home:* 190 Ravenswood Ct., Athens, Ga. 30605. *Office:* College of Business Administration, University of Georgia, Athens, Ga. 30602.

CAREER: Eastern Washington College of Education (now Eastern Washington State University), Cheney, instructor, 1946-47; University of Washington, Seattle, instructor in marketing, 1950-53; University of Rochester, Rochester, N.Y., assistant professor of marketing, 1953-55; Syracuse University, Syracuse, N.Y., professor of marketing, 1955-68, chairman of department of marketing and transportation, 1959-68; University of Georgia, Athens, professor of marketing and international business, 1968—. Consultant to government of Spain, 1958, and to industry. *Military service:* U.S. Army, Field Artillery, 1942-46; served in Pacific and Asiatic Theatres; became first lieutenant; received six battle stars. *Member:* Academy of International Business, Sales and Marketing Executives International, American Marketing Association, American Association of University Professors, Delta Tau Delta, Beta Sigma Gamma, American Institute of Decision Sciences.

WRITINGS: Sales Management, Prentice-Hall, 1958, 3rd edition, 1976; *Industrial Distribution,* Syracuse University Press, 1961; *Basic Marketing: Concepts, Environment and Decisions,* Prentice-Hall, 1964; *Essentials of Marketing,* Prentice-Hall, 1972; (with Clyde E. Harris, Jr.) *Cases in Marketing,* Prentice-Hall, 1972; *Fundamentals of Modern Marketing,* Prentice-Hall, 1974, 3rd edition, 1980. Contributor to professional journals.

WORK IN PROGRESS: A revision of *Sales Management,* for Prentice-Hall.

AVOCATIONAL INTERESTS: Philately, gardening.

* * *

STILLINGER, Jack 1931-

PERSONAL: Born 1931, in Chicago, Ill.; son of Clifford Benjamin and Ruth (Hertzler) Stillinger; married Shirley Van Wormer, 1952 (divorced January, 1971); married Nina Zippin Baym, May 21, 1971; children: (first marriage) Thomas, Robert, Susan, Mary. *Education:* University of Texas, B.A., 1953; Northwestern University, M.A., 1954; Harvard University, Ph.D., 1958. *Home:* 806 West Indiana, Urbana, Ill. *Office:* University of Illinois, 100 English Building, Urbana, Ill. 61801.

CAREER: Harvard University, Cambridge, Mass., teaching fellow, 1955-58; University of Illinois at Urbana-Champaign, assistant professor, 1958-61, associate professor, 1961-64, professor of English, 1964—, permanent member of Center for Advanced Study, 1970—. *Member:* Modern Language Association of America, Byron Society, Keats-Shelley Association, Phi Beta Kappa. *Awards, honors:* Guggenheim fellowship, 1964-65.

WRITINGS: The Early Draft of John Stuart Mill's "Autobiography," University of Illinois Press, 1961; (editor) A. Munday, *Zelauto,* Southern Illinois University Press, 1963; (editor) William Wordsworth, *Poems and Prefaces,* Houghton, 1965; (editor) *The Letters of Charles Armitage Brown,* Harvard University Press, 1966; (editor) *Twentieth Century*

Interpretations of Keats's Odes, Prentice-Hall, 1968; (editor) John Stuart Mill, *Autobiography and Other Writings,* Houghton, 1969; *The Hoodwinking of Madeline and Other Essays on Keats's Poems,* University of Illinois Press, 1971; *The Texts of Keats's Poems,* Harvard University Press, 1974; (editor) *The Poems of John Keats,* Harvard University Press, 1978.

* * *

STITSKIN, Leon D. 1910-1978

PERSONAL: Born July 2, 1910, in Cracow, Poland; naturalized U.S. citizen; died November 3, 1978; son of Samuel and Anna (Zisner) Stitskin; married Dorothy Gerston, July 2, 1933; children: Rochelle Dicker, Debbi Roth, Miriam Krater. *Education:* Hiram College, B.A., 1935; Yeshiva University, Ph.D., 1956. Attended Rabbi Isaac Elchanan Theological Seminary, three years, Dropsie College, two years, and Hebrew University, Jerusalem, one year. *Home:* 1440 54th St., Brooklyn, N.Y. 11219. *Office:* Bernard Revel Graduate School, Yeshiva University, New York, N.Y. 10033.

CAREER: Beth Israel, Warren, Ohio, rabbi, 1932-42; Beth Joseph, Rochester, New York, rabbi, 1942-50; Yeshiva University, New York, N.Y., professor of philosophy in Bernard Revel Graduate School, beginning 1952, dean of West Coast Division, beginning 1963, editor in department of special publications, beginning 1969. Serves on New York State Board of Equality in Education. *Member:* Rabbinical Council of America (treasurer, 1949; secretary, 1952-54), Zionist Organization of America, American Academy for Research, Mizrach, B'nai B'rith, Jewish Congress, New York Board of Rabbis, Yeshiva University Alumni Association. *Awards, honors:* Received Jewish War Veterans Award, 1952; D.D., West Coast Teachers College, 1977.

WRITINGS: Judaism as a Religion, Bloch, 1937; *Judaism as a Philosophy: The Philosophy of Abraham Bar Hiyya, 1065-1143,* Bloch, 1960; (editor) *Studies in Torah Judaism,* Yeshiva University Press, 1969; (editor with Sidney B. Hoenig) *Joshua Finkel Festschrift: In Honor of Joshua Finkel,* Yeshiva University Press, 1974; (editor) *Studies in Judaica: In Honor of Dr. Samuel Belkin as Scholar and Educator,* Ktav, 1974; *Jewish Philosophy: A Study in Personalism,* Yeshiva University Press, 1976. Contributor to *Spectator, National Jewish Monthly,* and other periodicals. Editor of *Sermon Manual* of Rabbinical Council of America, 1948-56, and *Tradition.*†

* * *

STODDARD, Ellwyn R(eed) 1927-

PERSONAL: Born February 16, 1927, in Garland, Utah; son of Roscoe and Mary (Redford) Stoddard; married Elaine Kirby; children: Ellwyn R., Jr., Michael V., Dawn D., Jared Evan, Sunday, Summer; stepchildren: Laura Jane Packham, George H. Packham, R. Kirby Packham. *Education:* Utah State University, B.S., 1952; Brigham Young University, M.S., 1955; Michigan State University, Ph.D., 1961. *Religion:* Church of Jesus Christ of Latter-Day Saints (Mormon). *Home:* 747 Camino Real, El Paso, Tex. 79922. *Office:* University of Texas, El Paso, Tex. 79968.

CAREER: Drake University, Des Moines, Iowa, assistant professor, 1959-63, associate professor of sociology, 1963-65; University of Texas at El Paso, associate professor, 1965-70, professor of sociology and anthropology, 1970—. National Institute of Health Lecturer, College of Osteopathic Medicine and Surgery, 1963-64; New Mexico State University, National Endowment for the Humanities Lecturer, 1969-70, National Institute of Mental Health Lecturer, 1972. Sociological researcher, 1955—. Consultant to over forty research and action projects involving civil defense, disaster relief, racial awareness, organizational functioning, health and social services delivery systems, and other subjects. Presenter and panelist at numerous professional conferences and workshops. *Military service:* U.S. Coast Guard, Amphibious Corps, 1944-46; served as radioman. U.S. Army, Artillery Corps, 1952-53; served as battalion communications officer.

MEMBER: American Sociological Association, Association of Borderland Scholars (founder), Inter-University Seminar on Armed Forces and Society, International Rural Sociological Society, Rural Sociological Society, Pacific Sociological Association, Western Social Science Association, Southwestern Anthropological Association, Southwestern Social Science Association, Southwestern Sociological Association, Rocky Mountain Conference for Latin American Studies (member of executive council, 1970-73), Phi Kappa Phi, Delta Tau Kappa International Social Science Honor Society (life member).

WRITINGS: Mexican Americans, Random House, 1973. Also editor, with R. Nostrand and J. West, of *Borderlands Sourcebook,* 1980.

Contributor: Norman Johnston, Leonard Savitz, and Marvin E. Wolfgang, editors, *The Sociology of Punishment and Correction,* Wiley, 2nd edition (Stoddard was not associated with earlier edition), 1970; Clifton D. Bryant, editor, *Social Problems Today,* Lippincott, 1971; Bryant, editor, *The Social Dimensions of Work,* Prentice-Hall, 1972; Arthur Shostak, editor, *Putting Sociology to Work,* McKay, 1974; Jerome H. Skolnick and Thomas C. Gray, editors, *Police in America,* Little, Brown, 1974; Bryant, editor, *Deviant Behavior: Occupational and Organizational Bases,* Rand McNally, 1974; Lawrence W. Sherman, editor, *Police Corruption: A Sociological Perspective,* Doubleday, 1974; (with C. Cabanillas) Nancy L. Goldman and David R. Segal, editors, *The Social Psychology of Military Service,* Sage Publications Inc., 1976; Edna J. Hunter and D. Stephen Nice, editors, *Military Families: Adaptation to Change,* Praeger, 1978; *Academic American Encyclopedia,* Arete Publishing, 1979; Richard Lundman, editor, *Police Behavior: A Sociological Perspective,* Oxford University Press (New York), 1979.

Also author of numerous booklets and reports, including: *Conceptual Models of Human Behavior in Disaster,* Texas Western Press, 1968; *Patterns of Poverty along the U.S.-Mexico Border,* Center for Inter-American Studies, University of Texas at El Paso, 1978; (with Miguel Angel Martinez and O. J. Martinez) *El Paso-Ciudad Juarez Relations and the "Tortilla Curtain": A Study of Local Adaptation to Federal Border Policies,* University of Texas at El Paso, 1979.

Contributor to proceedings. Contributor of articles and reviews to sociology journals, including *Social Science Quarterly, Rocky Mountain Social Science Journal, Summation, Trans-Action, Human Organization, Journal of Inter-American Studies,* and *American Sociologist.*

WORK IN PROGRESS: Multidisciplinary Coordination of U.S.-Mexico Border Research; an encyclopedic volume of biographical summaries on borderlands topics.

* * *

STOGDILL, Ralph M(elvin) 1904-

PERSONAL: Born August 29, 1904, in Convoy, Ohio; son of

John Le Roy and Pearl (Foley) Stogdill; married Zoe Emily Leatherman, March 29, 1928; children: Robert Edmund. *Education:* Attended Ohio Wesleyan University, 1923-25; Ohio State University, B.A., 1928, M.A., 1930, Ph.D., 1934. *Home:* 3658 Olentangy Blvd., Columbus, Ohio 43214.

CAREER: Ohio Bureau of Juvenile Research, Columbus, psychologist, 1936-42; Ohio State University, Columbus, associate director of Leadership Studies, 1946-53, research associate, 1954-59, Bureau of Business Research, professor of management science, beginning 1950. *Wartime services:* U.S. Maritime Service, lieutenant commander, 1942-45. *Member:* American Psychological Association, Psychonomic Society, Institute of Management Sciences, American Association for the Advancement of Science. *Awards, honors:* Cattell Award from American Psychological Association.

WRITINGS: Individual Behavior and Group Achievement, Oxford University Press, 1959; (with Walter R. Bailey) *Changing the Response of Vocational Students to Supervision* (monograph), Center for Vocational and Technical Education, Ohio State University, 1969; (with Nicholas P. Coady and Adele Zimmer) *Response of Vocational Students to Supervision* (monograph), Center for Vocational and Technical Education, Ohio State University, 1970; (editor) *The Process of Model-Building in the Behavioral Sciences,* Ohio State University Press, 1970; (with Lorane C. Kruse) *The Leadership Role of the Nurse* (monograph), U.S. Department of Health, Education, and Welfare, 1973; *Handbook of Leadership: A Survey of Theory and Research,* Free Press, 1974.

Monographs—All published by Bureau of Business Research, College of Administrative Science, Ohio State University: (With Carroll L. Shartle) *Methods in the Study of Administrative Leadership,* 1955; (with Shartle and others) *Patterns of Administrative Performance,* 1956; (with others) *A Predictive Study of Administrative Work Patterns,* 1956; (with E. L. Scott and W. E. Jaynes) *Leadership and Role Expectations,* 1956; *Leadership and Structures of Personal Interaction,* 1957; (with Shartle) *Methods in the Study of Administrative Leadership,* 1957; (editor with Alvin E. Coons) *Leader Behavior: Its Description and Measurement,* 1957; *Team Achievement Under High Motivation,* 1963; *Manager-Employee Behavior and Organizational Performance,* 1965; *Managers, Employees, Organizations,* 1966; *Leadership Abstracts and Bibliography, 1904-1974,* 1977.

Contributor: H. Guetzkow, editor, *Groups, Leadership and Men,* Carnegie Press, 1951; Robert K. Merton, editor, *Reader in Bureaucracy,* Free Press, 1952; J. E. Hulett, Jr. and Ross Stagner, editors, *Problems in Social Psychology,* University of Illinois Press, 1952; J. L. Moreno, editor, *Sociometry and the Science of Man,* Beacon House, 1956; M. Sherif, editor, *Intergroup Relations and Leadership,* Wiley, 1962; J. A. Culbertson and S. P. Heneley, editors, *Educational Research: New Perspectives,* Interstate, 1963; S. B. Sells, editor, *Stimulus Determinants of Behavior,* Ronald, 1963; J. D. Thompson, editor, *Approaches to Organizational Design,* University of Pittsburgh Press, 1966; R. E. Campbell, editor, *Guidance in Vocational Education,* Center for Vocational and Technical Education, Ohio State University, 1966; *Leadership in the Post-70's,* U.S. Military Academy, 1970. Contributor to journals.†

* * *

STOKES, Donald Elkinton 1927-

PERSONAL: Born April 1, 1927, in Philadelphia, Pa.; son of Joseph and Frances (Elkinton) Stokes; married Sybil Langbaum, 1955; children: Elizabeth Ann, Susan Carol. *Education:* Princeton University, B.A., 1951; Yale University, Ph.D., 1958. *Religion:* Religious Society of Friends (Quakers). *Home:* 150 Fitzrandolph Rd., Princeton, N.J. 08540. *Office:* Woodrow Wilson School of Public and International Affairs, Princeton University, Princeton, N.J. 08544.

CAREER: Yale University, New Haven, Conn., instructor, 1952-54; Social Science Research Council fellow, 1955-57; University of Michigan, Ann Arbor, 1958-74, began as assistant professor, became professor of political science and chairman of department, dean of Graduate School, 1971-74, senior study director and program director of Survey Research Center, 1958-74; Princeton University, Princeton, N.J., professor of politics and public affairs and dean of Woodrow Wilson School of Public and International Affairs, 1974—. *Member:* American Political Science Association, American Statistical Association, American Association for Public Opinion Research, Phi Beta Kappa. *Awards, honors:* Fulbright research scholar, 1962-63; Guggenheim fellow; Woodrow Wilson Prize for best work published in American political science, 1970, for *Political Change in Britain.*

WRITINGS: (With others) *The American Voter,* Wiley, 1960; *Elections and the Political Order,* Wiley, 1966; (with David E. Butler) *Political Change in Britain: Forces Shaping Electoral Choice,* St. Martin's, 1969, revised edition published as *Political Change in Britain: The Evolution of Electoral Choice,* 1976; *The Federal Investment in Knowledge of Social Problems,* National Academy of Sciences, 1978.

* * *

STONE, Gregory P(rentice) 1921-

PERSONAL: Born October 28, 1921, in Olean, N.Y.; son of Horace P. (a commercial artist) and Grace (Emerson) Stone; married Margaret Renee Cuthbertson, July, 1944 (deceased); married Gladys Ishida (a sociologist), June, 1962; children: (first marriage) Mead Meredith, Susan Lea. *Education:* Hobart College, B.A., 1942; Princeton University, certificate in Turkish studies, 1944; University of Chicago, M.A., 1952, Ph.D., 1959. *Politics:* Democratic Liberal. *Religion:* "Atheist Episcopalian." *Home:* St. Croix Cove, Route 3, Hudson, Wis. 54016. *Office:* Department of Sociology, University of Minnesota, Minneapolis, Minn. 55455.

CAREER: Michigan State University, East Lansing, assistant professor, 1949-55; University of Minnesota, Minneapolis, instructor in sociology, 1955-58; University of Missouri—Columbia, lecturer, 1958-59; Washington University, St. Louis, Mo., assistant professor, 1959-61; University of Minnesota, associate professor, 1961-64, professor of sociology, 1964—, professor of American studies, 1964-78, professor of textiles and clothing, 1978—, member of board of trustees of University Episcopal Center, 1971-74. Consultant to the mass media, urban planners, the U.S. Government, and to *Sports Illustrated. Military service:* U.S. Army, Infantry, 1943-45; received three battle stars and presidential citation. *Member:* International Sociological Association, International Committee for the Sociology of Sport, International Platform Association, American Sociological Association, Society for the Study of Social Problems, American Association for the Advancement of Science, American Civil Liberties Union, World Future Society, Society for the Study of Symbolic Interaction (founder and co-chairman; president, 1976-77), Midwest Sociological Association. *Awards, honors:* Recognition from University of Minnesota Pan Hellenic Society, 1967; award for research design in television, 1970.

WRITINGS: (With William H. Form and others) *Community in Disaster,* Harper, 1958; (editor with Harvey A. Farberman) *Social Psychology through Symbolic Interaction,* Xerox College Publishing, 1970; (editor) *Games, Sport, and Power,* Transaction Books, 1972; (with David A. Karp and William C. Yoels) *Being Urban: A Social Psychological View of City Life,* Heath, 1977; (editor with Gunther Luschen) Herman Schmalenbach, *Herman Schmalenbach on Society and Experience,* University of Chicago Press, 1978.

Monographs: (With Form) *The Social Significance of Clothing in Occupational Life,* Michigan Agricultural Experiment Station, 1955; (with Form) *Clothing Inventories and Preferences among Rural and Urban Families,* Michigan Agricultural Experiment Station, 1955; (with Form) *The Local Community Clothing Market: A Study of the Social and Social Psychological Contexts of Shopping,* Michigan Agricultural Experiment Station, 1957.

Contributor: Eric Larrabee and Rolf Meyerson, editors, *Mass Leisure,* Free Press, 1958; Talcott Parsons and others, editors, *Theories of Society,* Volume I, Free Press, 1961; Jack P. Gibbs, editor, *Urban Research Methods,* Van Nostrand, 1961; Charles R. Snyder and David Pittman, editors, *Society, Culture, and Drinking Patterns,* Wiley, 1962; Arnold M. Rose, editor, *Human Behavior and Social Processes,* Houghton, 1962; Alvin W. Gouldner and others, editors, *Modern Sociology,* Harcourt, 1963; (with Robert P. Scheurell and Ethan Z. Kaplan) *The Future of Outdoor Recreation in Metropolitan Regions of the United States,* U.S. Government Printing Office, 1963; Richard L. Simpson and Ida Harper, editors, *Social Organization and Behavior,* Wiley, 1964; Ralph Slovenko and James A. Knight, editors, *Motivations in Play, Games, and Sport,* C. C Thomas, 1967; Gerald S. Kenyon, editor, *Sociology of Sport,* Athletic Institute, 1969.

Robert Gutman and David Popenoe, editors, *Neighborhood, City, and Metropolis,* Random House, 1970; David J. Rachman, editor, *Retail Management Strategy,* Prentice-Hall, 1970; Eric Dunning, editor, *Sport and Society,* Cass, 1971; Alfred R. Lindesmith and others, editors, *Readings in Social Psychology,* Dryden, 1975; Daniel M. Landers, editor, *Social Problems in Athletics,* University of Illinois Press, 1976; Manfred Auwarter and others, editors, *Kommunikation, Interaktion, Identitaet,* Suhrkamp Verlag, 1976; March Krotee, editor, *The Dimensions of Sport,* Leisure Press, 1979.

Contributor to *Encyclopedia International.* Contributor of numerous articles to professional journals.

WORK IN PROGRESS: Sport, Play, and Leisure; Symbolic Interaction as Social Psychology; research on honesty in social circles, "the philosophy of the act," hustling as a way of life, the professionalization of sport, play among the Sanema Indians of Venezuela, and on interpersonal relations and social structure.

SIDELIGHTS: Gregory P. Stone told *CA:* "The strange and confused manner in which we are 'meeting' the energy crisis has little to do with the intrinsic nature of our resources (in particular the sun), but very much to do with the meanings we attach to fossil fuels; or the meaning we attach to work in our society seems to blind us to the importance of planning for our society in which distribution, rather than production, is the most fundamental socio-political-economic problem. Nor do we seem ever to grasp the meaning of our activities in the larger context of socio-economic history."

AVOCATIONAL INTERESTS: Symphonic music (especially contemporary), paintings, sculpture.

STONE, Irving 1903-

PERSONAL: Name legally changed; born July 14, 1903, in San Francisco, Calif.; son of Charles Tennenbaum and Pauline (Rosenberg) Tennenbaum Stone; married Jean Factor (his editor since 1933), February 11, 1934; children: Paula Stone Hubbell, Kenneth. *Education:* University of California, Berkeley, B.A., 1923, post-graduate study, 1924-26; University of Southern California, M.A., 1924. *Politics:* Independent. *Religion:* Jewish. *Address:* c/o Doubleday & Co., 501 Franklin Ave., New York, N.Y. 11530.

CAREER: University of Southern California, Los Angeles, instructor in economics, 1923-24; University of California, Berkeley, instructor in economics, 1924-26; writer, 1926—. Visiting professor of creative writing, University of Indiana, 1948, and University of Washington, 1961; lecturer, University of Southern California and California State Colleges, 1966; contributing member, American School of Classical Studies, Athens, Greece, 1965—; specialist on cultural exchange for U.S. State Department to Soviet Union, Poland, and Yugoslavia, 1962. Member of advisory board, University of California Institute for Creative Arts, 1963—; founder, California State Colleges Committee for the Arts, 1967; member of California Civil War Centennial Commission, 1961-65, California Citizens' Committee for Higher Education, 1964, and California State Committee on Public Education, 1966-67. Member of Eleanor Roosevelt Memorial Foundation, 1963; vice-president, Eugene V. Debs Foundation, 1963—; trustee, Douglass House Foundation, 1967-74; chairman, Allan Nevins Memorial Fund, Huntington Library, 1972—. Member of American Assembly, Columbia University, 1963-67; president, Beverly Hills Improvement Association, 1964-65. Founder with wife, Jean Stone, of two annual $1000 awards for the best biographical and historical novels published.

MEMBER: Authors League of America, P.E.N., Society of American Historians, National Society of Arts and Letters (member of advisory council, 1976—), Academy of American Motion Picture Arts and Sciences, Academy of Political Science, Academy of American Poets (founder), Western Writers of America, Renaissance Society of America, California Writers Guild (president, 1960-61), California Writers Club (honorary member), Historical Society of Southern California, Fellows for Schweitzer (founder and president, 1955—), Berkeley Fellows (charter member), Los Angeles Dante Alighieri Society (president, 1968-69). *Awards, honors:* Christopher Award, and Silver Spur Award from Western Writers of America, both 1957, for *Men to Match My Mountains;* Golden Lily of Florence, Rupert Hughes Award, Gold Medal from Council of American Artist Societies, and Gold Medal from Commonwealth Club of California, all for *The Agony and the Ecstasy;* named commendatore of Republic of Italy; American Revolution Round Table Award and Literary Father of the Year Award, both 1966, for *Those Who Love;* Gold Trophy from American Women in Radio and Television, 1968; Herbert Adams Memorial Medal from National Sculpture Society, 1970; Golden Plate Award from American Academy of Achievement, 1971; Alumnus of the Year from University of California, Berkeley, 1971; honorary citizen of Athens, Greece, 1972; Corpus Litterarum Award from Friends of the Libraries, University of California, Irvine, 1975; Distinguished Alumni Award from Los Angeles Unified School District, 1976; Author of the Year Award from Book Bank USA, 1976. D.L. from University of Southern California, 1965; D.Litt. from Coe College, 1967, and California State Colleges, 1971; LL.D. from University of California, Berkeley, 1968; H.H.D. from Hebrew Union College, 1978.

WRITINGS—All published by Doubleday, except as indicated: *Pageant of Youth,* A. H. King, 1933; *Lust for Life* (about Van Gogh), 1934, reprinted, Grosset, 1961, published with reader's supplement, Washington Square Press, 1967; (editor) *Dear Theo* (autobiography of Van Gogh), 1937, reprinted, 1957; *Sailor on Horseback* (about Jack London), 1938, published as *Jack London, Sailor on Horseback,* Pocket Books, 1966, published with twenty-eight London stories as *Jack London, His Life, Sailor on Horseback,* Doubleday, 1977; *False Witness,* 1940; *Clarence Darrow for the Defense,* 1941, reprinted, New American Library, 1971; *They Also Ran: The Story of the Men Who Were Defeated for the Presidency,* 1943, reprinted, New American Library, 1968; *Immortal Wife* (about Jessie B. Fremont), 1944; *Adversary in the House* (about Eugene V. Debs), 1947, reprinted, New American Library, 1972; *Earl Warren,* 1948; *The Passionate Journey,* 1949, reprinted, New American Library, 1972.

We Speak for Ourselves, 1950; *The President's Lady* (about Rachel Jackson), 1951, reprinted, New American Library, 1968; *Love Is Eternal* (about Mary Todd Lincoln), 1954, reprinted, New American Library, 1972; *Men to Match My Mountains: The Opening of the Far West, 1840-1900,* 1956; *The Agony and the Ecstasy* (about Michelangelo), 1961, abridged juvenile edition published as *The Great Adventure of Michelangelo,* 1965; (author of introduction) *The Drawings of Michelangelo,* Borden Publishing, 1962; (editor with wife, Jean Stone) *I, Michelangelo, Sculptor* (letters), translated by Charles Speroni, 1962; (editor with Allan Nevins) *Lincoln: A Contemporary Portrait,* 1962; *The Irving Stone Reader,* 1963; *The Story of Michelangelo's Pieta,* 1964; *Those Who Love* (about Abigail Adams), 1965; (editor and author of introduction) *There Was Light: Autobiography of a University: Berkeley, 1868-1968,* 1970; *The Passions of the Mind* (about Sigmund Freud), 1971; *The Greek Treasure* (about Henry and Sophia Schliemann), 1975; *The Origin* (about Charles Darwin), 1980.

Author of plays, "The Dark Mirror," 1928, "The White Life" (on Spinoza), 1929, and "Truly Valiant," 1936, all produced in New York. Also author of screenplay for "Magnificent Doll," 1946.

Contributor: *The People's Reader,* Consolidated, 1949; Isabel Leighton, editor, *The Aspirin Age,* Simon & Schuster, 1949; Rudolf Flesch, editor, *Best Articles, 1953,* Hermitage House, 1953; *American Panorama: West of the Mississippi,* Doubleday, 1960; *The Good Housekeeping Treasury,* Simon & Schuster, 1960; Bucklin Moon, editor, *A Doubleday Anthology,* Doubleday, 1962; Donald C. Rehkoff, editor, *Portraits in Words,* Odyssey, 1962; Roy Newquist, editor, *Counterpoint,* Rand McNally, 1964; *My Most Inspiring Moment,* Doubleday, 1965; Bromberg and Greene, editors, *Biography for Youth,* Globe, 1965; Tanner and Vittetoe, editors, *A Guide for Objective Writing,* Ginn, 1968. Also contributor to *Fourteen Radio Plays,* edited by Arch Oboler, Random House, and *Three Views of the Novel,* 1957.

SIDELIGHTS: Irving Stone is best known for his large, extensively researched works of "bio-history." He defined the term for Roy Newquist as "bringing history to life in terms of the tremendous human stories that have made history." Stone believes that "with the exception of isolated predecessors, *Lust for Life* [Stone's 1934 bio-history of Van Gogh] was the first work in a new art form." He told Newquist, "I guess one might say that in 1934, when *Lust for Life* was published, the contemporary biographical novel came into a new life of its own."

Joseph Henry Jackson traces the development of Stone's writing style in his introduction to *The Irving Stone Reader.* He notes: "A writer is peculiarly fortunate when he discovers, reasonably early, both a principle and a pattern to which he may hew. Irving Stone made that happy discovery before he was thirty.... Still better, ... he had become accustomed to the practice of a relentless, unflagging industry. And it was automatic with him never to be wholly satisfied with what he had done." Jackson continues: "Working on detective stories ... [taught Stone] the necessity of careful plotting, the trick of keeping a narrative on the move, the techniques of construction.... His attempts in the field [of the creative novel taught him that] any fiction of quality depends largely upon people, upon character seen in the round and presented in the process of growth and development and change under stress."

In *Lust for Life* Jackson claims Stone found "the kind of spark that would fire his imagination. That spark was character-ready-made, the story of someone who had lived, whose acts could be found in the record and whose motives might be traced by patient, careful, sympathetic investigation." What spurs Stone to bring a given character to life is "any suspicion that such a character had been misunderstood, perhaps even misrepresented through historical accident or through an early biographer's prejudice."

Perhaps because of his efforts to champion the underdog and to set the historical records straight, Stone is aware of his responsibility to accurate representation in his work and has done extensive research for each book. During the preparation of *The Agony and the Ecstasy* (which required four and a half years), he engaged the founder of the Italian Department of University of California, Los Angeles to translate Michelangelo's letters into English for the first time. But he told Newquist: "Even if there is endless documentation it would be impossible to know what a man thought inside his own mind.... This is where the novelist's creative imagination has to take over, and this raises the great question: Do you push your character around, and distort history, or do you study [him] so carefully, identify with him so totally and with such honesty, that when you come to the point where documentation leaves off, and you must put yourself inside the heart and mind of this man or woman, can you think and feel as he (or she) would have, in the given circumstances? This is the creative part of the book, and if you are honest, if you are sincere, if you have worked hard, if you are determined to be true and to achieve exact identity and to plumb the depths of a man's feelings, I think you have a good chance of doing the job proudly."

Stone described one aspect of his investigative technique to Susan Forrest: "I live with the character. I must. And I have to feel myself inside the character's skin, head, mind, and brain. I live where he lived, eat what he ate, go among his people. During this time, I don't do anything else. There is no other way to write a biographical novel." As a result, many reviewers have commented on the extent of Stone's sympathy with and loyalty to his subjects, even though some decry his idealization of them and his subjective attempts at interpreting their lives and motivations through "becoming" the character. As Hassoldt Davis writes of *Sailor on Horseback:* "Jack London would have applauded the skill and honesty with which his biographer has portrayed him. This is a portrait in full relief, a biography as brave as the life of the man, even though the author has minimized his defects." Nevertheless, "there are many paragraphs that are substantially London's own and so dexterously insinuated without quotation marks or admission of origin that it is hard to tell whether biographer or subject is speaking. . . . But it is an excellent job of biography, regardless of who wrote what."

Although Stone is best known for his novels, critics seem to agree that he is better suited to historical and biographical nonfiction. Despite its large sales, many critics cite *The Agony and the Ecstasy,* Stone's 664-page fictionalized biography of Michelangelo, as simply a bad novel. Richard Winston, however, distinguishes between Stone's weaknesses and his obvious talent. "This biographical novel," he writes, "is at its best as biography, at its worst as fiction. . . . How elegant and convincing one of Mr. Stone's shrewd guesses and fictional insights might have been in a straight biography—whereas here they are so often embarrassing and give rise to uneasiness and dissatisfaction." Phoebe Adams believes that the novel "contains a number of things that never happened, is dry as marble dust all the way, and never for one second suggests Michelangelo or any other working artist." Winston apparently disagrees. "Mr. Stone has . . . perhaps gone beyond the call of duty in apprenticing himself to a sculptor in order to learn what the sculptor feels as he works," he writes. "This direct experience has resulted in some of the best passages in an uneven book." A reviewer for the *Boston Transcript* noted in his defense of *Lust for Life:* "Irving Stone did not need to call this fiction. Many biographers have taken more liberties with less results. There is reality here, pathos, humor, a knowledge of art and artists, and a delightful, nonchalant style which keeps us fascinated . . . to the end."

Stone's patient and careful researching has brought much previously unpublished and important information into print. In addition to Michelangelo's letters, he has had access to Van Gogh's letters and Freud's papers, as well as having access to friends and relatives of his more current subjects. Though some critics may scoff at the possibility of such determined research ("Come on, Irving," writes Robert F. Jones, "don't kid us that you've read all those books"), most save their highest praise for the amount of work that goes into each book. Edwin Fadiman calls *Passions of the Mind* "a stunning job of research. . . . The author's integrity is revealed in every line. But it is precisely this . . . earnestness, this obsession with detail that make [this book] praiseworthy yet dull. . . . [Stone's] exposition of the facts is remarkable indeed." Still, a *Times Literary Supplement* reviewer notes, "He has an abundant bibliography but perhaps not an adequately critical one."

Stone admits that as a writer he may be "overblown" or long-winded. His wife edits all his work, routinely cutting about ten per cent of it before a finished product is achieved, a finished product which some reviewers may claim is still too long. Yet Peter Andrews speculates: "The secret of the popularity of Irving Stone's novels may very well lie in their unreadability. . . . Getting through an Irving Stone bio[e]pic gives one a sense of accomplishment." But there is more to his popularity than that. As Allan Nevins states in the case of *Immortal Wife,* "It is safe to say that most of those who take up this book will find their attention gripped to the end, that they will rise from it both instructed and charmed, and that they will carry away an enduring impression of one of the most remarkable stories in our national record." And as Marcus Cunliffe notes in his review of *Those Who Love,* "It should please those members of the public who like to have their history . . . [to use John Adams's phrase], 'a little embellished with fiction.'"

False Witness was filmed by Republic in 1941; *The President's Lady* was filmed by Twentieth Century-Fox in 1953; *Lust for Life* was filmed by Metro-Goldwyn-Mayer in 1956; *The Agony and the Ecstasy* was filmed by Twentieth Century-Fox in 1965. "Lust for Life" starred Kirk Douglas; "The Agony and the Ecstasy" starred Charleton Heston.

AVOCATIONAL INTERESTS: Collecting art.

BIOGRAPHICAL/CRITICAL SOURCES: New York Herald Tribune, September 26, 1934; *Boston Transcript,* September 26, 1934; *Books,* September 30, 1934, October 19, 1941; *New York Times,* September 30, 1934, September 18, 1938, April 14, 1940, November 9, 1941, October 1, 1944, March 27, 1971; *Christian Science Monitor,* October 17, 1934, September 27, 1951, October 14, 1954, August 30, 1962; *Nation,* November 7, 1934; *Time,* September 19, 1938, November 5, 1965, April 5, 1971, September 15, 1975; *New Republic,* September 21, 1938; *Forum,* October, 1938; *Saturday Review of Literature,* September 30, 1944, September 29, 1951; *New York Herald Tribune Book Review,* September 28, 1947, August 22, 1954, September 30, 1956; *San Francisco Chronicle,* October 7, 1951, September 23, 1956, March 17, 1961; *Saturday Review,* August 21, 1954, March 18, 1961, May 15, 1965, November 20, 1965, April 10, 1971; *Kirkus Service,* July 15, 1956; *Springfield Republican,* September 30, 1956, August 19, 1962; *New York Times Book Review,* March 19, 1961, August 26, 1962, March 14, 1965, November 7, 1965, October 12, 1975; *New York Herald Tribune Lively Arts,* March 19, 1961; *Chicago Sunday Tribune,* March 26, 1961; *Atlantic Monthly,* May, 1961, April, 1971; *Catholic World,* August, 1961; *The Irving Stone Reader,* Doubleday, 1963; Roy Newquist, *Counterpoint,* Rand McNally, 1964; *Newsweek,* November 1, 1965; *Times Literary Supplement,* July 13, 1967, January 2, 1976; *Washington Post,* April 2, 1971; *Fort Lauderdale News,* January 10, 1975; *Authors in the News,* Volume I, Gale, 1976; *Contemporary Literary Criticism,* Volume VII, Gale, 1977.

—Sketch by Penelope S. Gordon

* * *

STOOPS, Emery 1902-

PERSONAL: Born December 13, 1902, in Pratt, Kan., son of Eli and Marry Elizabeth (Bruhaker) Stoops; married Evelyn R. FitzSimmons, 1929 (died, 1937); married Maude F. FitzSimmons, 1937 (died, 1967); married Joyce B. King, 1968; children: Emelyn Ruth Jackson, Emerson F., Eileen C. *Education:* University of Colorado, A.B., 1930; University of Southern California, M.A. in Ed., 1934, Ed.D., 1941. *Home:* 10736 Le Conte Ave., Los Angeles, Calif. 90024. *Office:* University of Southern California, Los Angeles, Calif. 90007.

CAREER: Superintendent of schools in Richfield, Kan., 1932-33; teacher and principal in Whittier, Beverly Hills, and Los Angeles, (all Calif.), 1934-45; Office of County Superintendent of Schools, Los Angeles, administrative assistant, 1945-53; University of Southern California, Los Angeles, 1953—, professor emeritus, 1970—.

MEMBER: American Educational Research Association, National Education Association, National Vocational Guidance Association, American Association of School Administrators, National Conference of Professors of Educational Administration, California Teachers Association, Phi Delta Kappa (international president, 1953-55), American Quill, Adelphi, Delta Epsilon, Kiwanis International.

WRITINGS: Principles and Practices in Guidance, McGraw, 1958; *Guidance Service: Organization and Administration,* McGraw, 1959; *Classroom Discipline,* Economics

Press, 1959; *Practices and Trends in School Administration*, Ginn, 1961; *Classroom Personalities*, Economics Press, 1961; *Home Discipline*, Economics Press, 1962; *Just a Minute, Junior*, Economics Press, 1964; *Problems with Parents*, Economics Press, 1964; *Elementary School Supervision*, Allyn & Bacon, 1965; *How Johnny Learns*, Economics Press, 1966; *Elementary School Education*, McGraw, 1969; *Handbook of Educational Supervision*, Allyn & Bacon, 1971, revised edition, 1978; *Discipline or Disaster*, Phi Delta Kappa, 1972; *Handbook of Educational Administration*, Allyn & Bacon, 1975, revised edition, 1981. Author of six educational monographs; also author of "Discipline Service" (bi-weekly letter), Economics Press, 1962—; contributor of chapters to school surveys. Contributor of articles to professional journals.

WORK IN PROGRESS: Handbook for School Secretaries; Psychology of Success; Prairie Pioneers, a novel.

AVOCATIONAL INTERESTS: Travel, agriculture, real estate.

* * *

STOREY, Margaret 1926-

PERSONAL: Born June 27, 1926, in London, England; daughter of Harold (an editor) and Lyn (a chemist; maiden name, Bramwell) Storey. *Education:* Girton College, Cambridge, B.A., 1948, M.A., 1953.

CAREER: Teacher of English language and literature in London, England, 1957—. Has also done secretarial and publicity work. *Member:* Institute for Comparative Study of History, Philosophy, and the Sciences.

WRITINGS—All juveniles; published by Faber, except as indicated: *Kate and the Family Tree*, Bodley Head, 1965, published as *The Family Tree*, Nelson, 1973; *Pauline*, 1965, Doubleday, 1967; *Timothy and Two Witches*, 1966, Dell, 1974; *The Smallest Doll*, 1966; *The Smallest Bridesmaid*, 1966; *The Stone Sorcerer*, 1967; *The Dragon's Sister, and, Timothy Travels*, 1967, Dell, 1974; *A Quarrel of Witches*, 1970; *The Sleeping Witch*, 1971; *The Mollyday Holiday*, 1971; *Wrong Gear*, 1973; *Keep Running*, 1974, published as *Ask Me No Questions*, Dutton, 1975; *A War of Wizards*, 1977; *The Double Wizard*, 1978.

WORK IN PROGRESS: More books for children.

SIDELIGHTS: Margaret Storey told *CA:* "I like writing for children because they are nice people. For the same reason I enjoy teaching. I'm not interesting otherwise. . . . It's hard to take myself seriously as an Author." She lists R. M. Peyton and William Mayne as her favorite children's book authors and advises aspiring writers "to do that most difficult thing: write, just write and keep writing."

* * *

STOTTS, Herbert Edward 1916-

PERSONAL: Born December 22, 1916, in Clinton, Mo.; son of Fred Hargrove and Jessie (McClelland) Stotts; married Gwendolyn Ricklefs, 1938 (died, 1975); married N. Carolyn (Hitchcock) Berger, 1976; children: (first marriage) Mary, Michael, Martha. *Education:* Baker University, A.B., 1938; Southern Methodist University, B.D., 1941; University of Denver, Ph.D., 1950. *Home:* 10 Kepner St., Buckhannon, W.Va. 26201. *Office:* West Virginia Wesleyan College, Buckhannon, W.Va. 26201.

CAREER: Minister of Methodist churches in California, 1941-48; Iliff School of Theology, Denver, Colo., professor, 1948-55; Boston University School of Theology, Boston, Mass., professor, 1955-75; West Virginia Wesleyan College, Buckhannon, coordinator of Advanced Institutional Development Program (AIDP), 1975—. Visiting professor at Isabella Thoburn College, Lucknow, India, 1962-63; affiliated with Greek Orthodox International Center, Xania, 1970. *Awards, honors:* D.D., Baker University, 1960; Fulbright award, 1962-63.

WRITINGS: Church Inventory Handbook, Addison-Wesley, 1953; *Sociology of Religion*, Addison-Wesley, 1961; (with Paul Deats, Jr.) *Methodism and Society: Guidelines for Strategy*, Abingdon, 1962; *The Passionists*, Passionist Press, Volume I: *The Religious*, 1975, Volume II: *A Social System*, 1975.

* * *

STOVER, John F(ord) 1912-

PERSONAL: Born May 16, 1912, in Manhattan, Kan.; son of John W. and Maud (Ford) Stover; married Marjorie E. Filley, 1937; children: John Clyde, Robert Vernon, Charry Ellen. *Education:* University of Nebraska, A.B., 1934, M.A., 1937; University of Wisconsin, Ph.D., 1951. *Politics:* Republican. *Religion:* Methodist. *Home:* 615 Carrolton Blvd., West Lafayette, Ind. *Office:* Department of History, Purdue University, West Lafayette, Ind. 47907.

CAREER: Instructor at schools in Nebraska and New Jersey, 1936-41; Purdue University, West Lafayette, Ind., 1947—, began as instructor, professor of history, 1959-78, professor emeritus, 1978—. Honorary member of Indiana American Revolution Bicentennial Commission, 1972—. *Military service:* U.S. Army Air Forces, 1942-46; became captain. *Member:* American Historical Association, Organization of American Historians, Society of American Historians (fellow), American Association of University Professors (chapter vice-chairman, 1954-56; treasurer, 1957-59), Southern Historical Association, Indiana Historical Society, Indiana History Teachers Association (president, 1958-59), Indiana Sesquicentennial Commission (chairman, committee on education), Indiana Academy of Social Sciences (member of board of directors, 1964-66), Lexington Group, Phi Beta Kappa, Delta Sigma Rho, Phi Alpha Theta, Kiwanis, Torch Club, Sagamore of the Wabash. *Awards, honors:* Purdue Research Foundation XLGrants, 1957, 1959; fellowship in College-Business Exchange Program (Illinois Central Railroad), 1962.

WRITINGS: The Railroads of the South, 1865-1900, University of North Carolina Press, 1955; *American Railroads*, University of Chicago Press, 1961; (contributor) *Mississippi in the Confederacy*, Louisiana State University Press, 1961; *A History of America's Railroads*, Rand McNally, 1967; *Turnpikes, Canals, and Steamboats*, Rand McNally, 1969; *The Life and Decline of the American Railroad*, Oxford University Press, 1970; *History of the Illinois Central Railroad*, Macmillan, 1975; *Iron Road to the West: American Railroads in the 1850s*, Columbia University Press, 1978. Also author of *Transportation in American History*, 1970. Contributor to professional journals.

WORK IN PROGRESS: Work on late nineteenth-century American railroading; a history of the B & O Railroad.

AVOCATIONAL INTERESTS: Stamp collecting, model railroading, golf.

* * *

STRAUSS, Richard L(ehman) 1933-

PERSONAL: Born May 4, 1933, in Philadelphia, Pa.; son of

Lehman (a clergyman) and Elsie (Hannah) Strauss; married Mary Getz, June 19, 1954; children: Stephen, Michael, Mark, Timothy. *Education:* Wheaton College, Wheaton, Ill., A.B., 1954; Dallas Theological Seminary, Th.M., 1958, Th.D., 1962. *Home:* 410 Mira Loma Lane, Escondido, Calif. 92025. *Office:* Emmanuel Faith Community Church, 639 East Felicita, Escondido, Calif. 92025.

CAREER: Ordained Baptist minister, 1958; minister in Fort Worth,Tex., 1958-64, Huntsville, Ala., 1964-72; Emmanuel Faith Community Church, Escondido, Calif., clergyman, 1972—.

WRITINGS—All published by Tyndale, except as indicated: *Marriage Is for Love,* 1973; *Confident Children and How They Grow,* 1975; *Living in Love: Secrets from Bible Marriages,* 1978; *Decisions! Decisions! How God Shows the Way,* 1979; *Win the Battle for Your Mind,* Victor Books, 1980.

* * *

STRENG, William D(ietrich) 1909-

PERSONAL: Born March 22, 1909, in Auburn, Neb.; son of Theodore J. and Wilhelmina (Schmidt) Streng; married Helen Conklen, 1936; children: William P., Marcus S., Kristine H., Joel A. *Education:* Wartburg College, A.B., 1930; Wartburg Theological Seminary, B.D., 1933; Chicago Divinity School, graduate study, 1944; Trinity Seminary, D.D., 1957; Union Theological Seminary, post-doctoral study, 1959. *Home:* 2070 Simpson St., Dubuque, Iowa. *Office:* Wartburg Theological Seminary, Dubuque, Iowa.

CAREER: Immanuel Lutheran Church, Rock Falls, Ill., pastor, 1933-47; St. John Lutheran Church, Ft. Wayne, Ind., pastor, 1947-51; Wartburg Theological Seminary, Dubuque, Iowa, professor of Christian education and dean of Luther Academy, 1951-65, dean of students, 1966—. *Member:* Torch Club. *Awards, honors:* Fredrik Schiotz Award, 1974.

WRITINGS—All published by Augsburg, except as indicated: *Altars that Alter,* Ernst Kaufman, 1949; *What Language Shall I Borrow?,* 1962; *The Faith We Teach,* 1962; *Toward Meaning in Worship,* 1964; *Will He Find Faith?,* 1966; *In Search of Ultimates,* 1969; *Be Alive!,* 1972; *Faith for Today: A Brief Outline of Christian Thought,* 1975. Contributor to religious periodicals.

SIDELIGHTS: William D. Streng told *CA:* "Since ninety-nine percent of the Church consists of lay people, my writings have more and more been directed toward them. They seem to appreciate any effort which enables them to discover what the new theologies are all about, and how these can be absorbed into the basics."

* * *

STRONG, Roy (Colin) 1935-

PERSONAL: Born August 23, 1935, in London, England; son of George Edward Clement (a businessman) and Mabel Ada (Smart) Strong; married Julia Trevelyan Oman (a designer), October 9, 1971. *Education:* Queen Mary College, London, B.A. (with honors), 1956; Warburg Institute, London, Ph.D., 1959. *Office:* Victoria and Albert Museum, South Kensington, London S.W.7, England.

CAREER: National Portrait Gallery, London, England, assistant keeper, 1959-67, director, 1967-73; Victoria and Albert Museum, London, director, 1974—. *Member:* Society of Antiquaries, Royal Archaeological Institute, Beefsteak, Garrick, Grillions.

WRITINGS: Portraits of Queen Elizabeth I, Clarendon Press, 1963; (with J. A. van Dorsten) *Leicester's Triumph,* Sir Thomas Browne Institute, University of Leiden, 1964; *Holbein and Henry VIII,* Pantheon, 1967; *The House of Tudor,* Pendragon House, 1967; (editor) *Festival Designs by Inigo Jones* (exhibition catalog), University Press of Virginia, 1967; *The Elizabethan Image: Painting in England, 1540-1620* (exhibition catalog), Arno, 1969; *The English Icon: Elizabethan and Jacobean Portraiture,* Routledge & Kegan Paul, for Paul Mellon Foundation for British Art, 1969, Yale University Press, 1970; *Tudor and Jacobean Portraits,* two volumes, Pendragon House, 1969.

(With wife, Julia Trevelyan Oman) *Elizabeth R,* Secker & Warburg, 1971, Stein & Day, 1972; (with Oman) *Mary Queen of Scots,* Secker & Warburg, 1972, Stein & Day, 1973; *Van Dyck: "Charles I on Horseback,"* Viking, 1972; *Splendour at Court: Renaissance Spectacle and the Theatre of Power,* Houghton, 1973; (with Stephen Orgel) *Inigo Jones: The Theatre of the Stuart Court,* two volumes, University of California Press, 1973; (editor with Colin Ford) *An Early Victorian Album: The Hill-Adamson Collection,* J. Cape, 1974; *Nicholas Hilliard,* M. Joseph, 1975; *Cult of Elizabeth: Elizabethan Portraiture and Pagentry,* Thames & Hudson, 1977; *Recreating the Past and British History and the Victorian Painters,* Norton, 1978 (published in England as *And When Did You Last See Your Father,* Thames & Hudson, 1978); *The Renaissance Garden in England,* Thames & Hudson, 1979; *Britannia Triumphans,* Thames & Hudson, 1980.

Author of numerous exhibition catalogs; writer of television scripts. Contributor of articles and reviews to scholarly journals and popular periodicals.

SIDELIGHTS: Of *Tudor and Jacobean Portraits,* a *Spectator* reviewer wrote: "For students of the period, it is as though a new gold mine had been thrown open, not only without restrictions, but with the addition of the most comprehensive system of signposts, and notices. . . . Dr. Strong says of his own work that 'it is intended primarily as a working tool for students of the period regardless of the field in which they are active.' He has certainly provided an instrument which will cut the corners of many a future historian's task."

BIOGRAPHICAL/CRITICAL SOURCES: Spectator, November 1, 1969.

* * *

STRONGIN, Lynn 1939-
(Lynn Michaels)

PERSONAL: Born February 27, 1939, in New York, N.Y.; daughter of Edward Israel (a psychologist) and Marguerite (an artist; maiden name, Rosenblum) Strongin. *Education:* Attended Manhattan School of Music, 1956-59; Hunter College of the City University of New York, B.A. (cum laude), 1963; Stanford University, M.A., 1965; University of New Mexico, graduate study, 1971—. *Home:* 825 Cook St., Apt. 3, Victoria, British Columbia, Canada V8V 3Z1.

CAREER: Long Island University, C. W. Post College, Long Island, N.Y., instructor in English, 1965-66; Merritt College, Oakland, Calif., instructor in English, 1967-68; Mills College, Oakland, instructor in English, 1968-69; Anna Head School, Oakland, instructor in English, 1970; University of New Mexico, Albuquerque, teaching assistant, 1971-75. *Member:* American Association of University Professors, Alumnae Association of Hunter College. *Awards, honors:* Woodrow Wilson fellow, 1963-64; P.E.N. research grant, 1971; creative writing fellowship from National Endowment for the Arts, 1972-73; American Association of University Women grant, 1975-76.

WRITINGS—All poetry, except as indicated: *The Dwarf Cycle,* Thorp Springs Press, 1972; *Shrift: A Winter Sequence,* Thorp Springs Press, 1975; *Paschal Poem,* Sun Ring Press, 1976; *Toccata of the Disturbed Child,* Fallen Angel Press, 1977; *A Hacksaw Brightness,* Ironwood Press, 1977; *Nightmare of Mouse,* L'Epervier Press, 1977; *Countrywoman/Surgeon,* L'Epervier Press, 1979; *Railway Child and Money-Chains* (novel), Spinster's Ink, 1980.

Poetry is represented in the following anthologies: *Thirty-One New American Poets,* edited by Ron Schrieber, Hill & Wang, 1969; *Green Flag,* edited by Schreiber, City Lights, 1969; *Sisterhood Is Powerful,* edited by Robin Morgan, Random House, 1970; *American Literary Anthology 3,* edited by George Plimpton, Viking, 1970; *Mark in Time: Portraits and Poets of San Francisco,* edited by Nick Harvey, Glide, 1971; *The San Francisco Bark,* edited by Christa Fleischman and Harvey, Thorp Springs Press, 1972; *Probes: An Introduction to Poetry,* edited by William K. Harlan, Macmillan, 1973; *Rising Tides: Contemporary American Women Poets,* edited by Laura Chester and Sharon Barba, Simon & Schuster, 1973; *"No More Masks!,"* edited by Ellen Bass, Doubleday, 1973.

Author of verse play, "Nocturne," produced by KPFA, Berkeley, Calif., 1969. Contributor of short stories, under pseudonym Lynn Michaels, to *Ladder;* contributor of poetry to over thirty-five magazines, including *Poetry, Sumac, New York Quarterly, Trace,* and *Painted Bride Quarterly.*

WORK IN PROGRESS: A book of poems; *Emma's Book,* a novel.

SIDELIGHTS: In a letter to *CA,* Lynn Strongin writes: "I began my writing career by writing music on an old, broken-down, two-octave piano under the stairs during World War II. I began my college career majoring in musical composition. It seemed a natural thing to branch off into poetry as I read more poetry and felt it more deeply; musical composition with its rhythms and melody found a counterpart in poetry. I felt, besides, the need for words rather than notes to express what I saw and felt about me." Two of Strongin's poems were set to music and performed in "Premiere Concert" at Studio 58 in New York City in 1972. Five other poems were set to dance and performed in "Four Premieres: Four Women Choreographers" at Barnard College's Dance Uptown Concert Series in 1973.

BIOGRAPHICAL/CRITICAL SOURCES: Shocks, summer, 1973; *Bartleby's Review,* winter, 1974; *Man-Root,* spring, 1974; Roberta Berke, *Bounds Out of Bounds: A Compass for Recent Poetry,* Oxford University Press, 1981.

* * *

STRUNK, Orlo, Jr. 1925-

PERSONAL: Born April 14, 1925, in Pen Argyl, Pa.; son of Orlo Christopher and Katherine Elizabeth (Glasser) Strunk; married Mary Louise Reynolds, July 3, 1947; children: Laura Louise, John Christoper. *Education:* West Virginia Wesleyan College, A.B., 1953; Boston University, S.T.B. (cum laude), 1955, Ph.D., 1957. *Home:* 15 Stearns Rd., Scituate, Mass. 02066. *Office:* Division of Theological and Religious Studies, Boston University, 705 Commonwealth Ave., Boston, Mass. 02215.

CAREER: Ordained minister, Methodist Church. Institute of Pastoral Care, Boston, Mass., executive secretary, 1955-57; West Virginia Wesleyan College, Buckhannon, associate professor of psychology, 1957-59, dean, 1959-69; Boston University, Boston, Mass., professor of psychology of religion, 1969—. Staff psychologist, Ecumenical Counseling Service. Summer instructor, Boston University, 1958, 1964. Leadership training project associate, North Central Association of Colleges and Secondary Schools, 1960-61. *Military service:* U.S. Army Air Forces, 1943-46; became technical sergeant; awarded Air Medal with three oak leaf clusters. *Member:* National Education Association, American Psychological Association, Society for the Scientific Study of Religion.

WRITINGS—Published by Abingdon: (Editor) *Readings in the Psychology of Religion,* 1950; *Religion: A Psychological Interpretation,* 1962; *Mature Religion: A Psychological Study,* 1965; *The Choice Called Atheism,* 1968; *The Psychology of Religion,* 1971; (editor) *Dynamic Interpersonalism for Ministry,* 1973; *The Secret Self,* 1976. Contributes to professional journals. Managing editor, *Journal of Pastoral Care.*

WORK IN PROGRESS: Personal Religious Values: Anatomy of a Concept.

SIDELIGHTS: Orlo Strunk told *CA:* "I began writing at the age of twelve—air war stories for the old pulp magazines (none were accepted!). My first published piece was a poem written while in basic training during World War Two and accepted by the old *Southern Literary Messenger.* I have been writing ever since. Perhaps the greatest 'breakthrough' as a writer was getting over the notion that one is never really a writer until he or she is able to write short stories and/or novels for a living. Now I know that an authentic writer is anyone who takes seriously the idea of writing well anything and everything he or she is called upon to write."

* * *

SURET-CANALE, Jean 1921-

PERSONAL: Born April 27, 1921, in Paris, France. *Education:* French Ministry of Education, Professeur Agrege de l'Universite, 1946; Institute of Africa, Academy of Sciences of the U.S.S.R., Docteur es sciences historiques, 1963; University of Paris, Docteur de 3e cycle, 1969. *Home:* 3 Rue des Arts, 92100 Boulogne—Billancourt, France. *Office:* University of Paris VII, 2 Place Jussier, Paris, France.

CAREER: Professor at lycees in France and Senegal, 1946-59; Lycee de Conakry, Conakry, Guinea, principal, 1959-61; Institut National de Recherches, Conakry, director, 1960-62; Ecole Normale Superieure, Kindia, Guinea, director, 1962-63; Centre d'Etudes et de Recherches Marxistes, Paris, France, deputy director, 1963-79; Centre National de la Recherche Scientifique, Section de Geographie, Paris, France, attache de recherches, 1966-68, charge de recherches, 1968-74; University of Oran, Institute of Geography, Oran, Algeria, maitre-assistant, 1974-78; currently affiliated with University of Paris VII, Paris, France. *Wartime service:* French Resistance, 1940-44.

WRITINGS: Afrique noire, occidentale et centrale, Editions Sociales (Paris), Volume I, 1958, 3rd revised and updated edition, 1968, Volume II, 1964, Volume III, 1972, translation of Volume II by Till Gottheiner published as *French Colonialism in Tropical Africa, 1900-1945,* Pica Press, 1971; (with Djibril T. Niane) *Histoire de l'Afrique occidentale,* Presence Africaine, 1961; *La Naissance des dieux,* Editions de l'Union Rationaliste, 1966; *La Republique de Guinee,* Editions Sociales, 1970; (with Emma Maquet and Ibrahima Baba Kake) *Histoire de l'Afrique centrale,* Presence Africaine, 1972; (with Jean-Emil Vidal) *La Coree populaire,* Editions Sociales, 1973; (with J. C. Mouchel) *La faim dans le Monde*, Editions Sociales, 1975; *Essais d'histoire africaine*, Editions Sociales, 1980. Also author of other historical and economic studies.

* * *

SUSSER, Mervyn (Wilfred) 1921-

PERSONAL: Born September 26, 1921, in Johannesburg, South Africa; came to United States, 1965; son of Solomon and Ida Rose (Son) Susser; married Zena Athene Stein (a professor of epidemiology), March 28, 1949; children: Ida, Ezra, Ruth. *Education:* University of the Witwatersrand, B.Ch. and M.B., 1950; Diploma in Public Health (London), 1960. *Home:* 21 Oakdale Dr., Hastings-on-Hudson, N.Y. 10706. *Office:* School of Public Health, Columbia University, 600 West 168th St., New York, N.Y. 10032.

CAREER: Alexandra Health Centre and University Clinic, Johannesburg, South Africa, 1951-55, began as medical officer, became superintendent; Willesden Chest Clinic, London, England, and Central Middlesex Hospital, London, medical registrar, 1956; University of Manchester, Manchester, England, lecturer, 1957-59, senior lecturer, 1960-64, reader in department of social and preventive medicine, 1964-65; Columbia University, School of Public Health, New York, N.Y., professor of epidemiology, 1966—, Gertrude H. Sergievsky Professor of Epidemiology, 1977—, head of Division of Epidemiology, 1966-78, director, Gertrude H. Sergievsky Center, 1977—. Medical officer in charge of mental health services, Salford, England, 1957-64. World Health Organization visiting professor at G.S.V.M. Medical College, Kapur, India, 1962. *Military service:* South African Army, 1940-45.

MEMBER: Royal College of Physicians (Edinburgh; fellow), American Heart Association (fellow), American Public Health Association (fellow). *Awards, honors:* Milbank Memorial Fund travel grant, 1965, for study of teaching of social medicine in United States and Canada; Belding Scholar, Association for the Aid of Crippled Children, 1965-66; Guggenheim fellow, 1972-73.

WRITINGS: (With William Watson) *Sociology in Medicine*, Oxford University Press (London), 1962, 2nd edition, 1971; *Community Psychiatry: Epidemiologic and Social Themes*, Random House, 1968; (editor with others, and contributor) *Sociological Studies in Medicine*, Book & Knowledge, 1968; *Causal Thinking in the Health Sciences: Concepts and Strategies in Epidemiology*, Oxford University Press (New York), 1973; (with wife, Zena A. Stein, Gerhard Saenger, and Frank Marolla) *Famine and Human Development: Studies of the Dutch Hunger Winters of 1944/45*, Oxford University Press, 1975; (with David Rush and Stein) *Diet in Pregnancy: A Randomized Controlled Trial of Prenatal Nutritional Supplementation*, Alan Liss, 1979.

Contributor to numerous books, including: A. T. Welford and others, editors, *Society: Problems and Methods of Study*, Routledge & Kegan Paul, 1962; Paul Halmos, editor, *Sociology and Medicine*, University of Keele, 1962; Julian Huxley, Jacob Bronowski, and Gerald Berry, editors, *Health and Wealth*, Macmillan, 1965; George A. Jervis, editor, *Expanding Concepts in Mental Retardation*, C. C Thomas, 1967; Hugh Freeman and James Farndale, editors, *New Aspects of the Mental Health Services*, Pergamon, 1967; M. W. Riley, J. W. Riley, and M. E. Johnson, editors, *Aging and the Practicing Professions*, Russell Sage, 1968; G. T. Stewart, editor, *Trends in Epidemiology: Application to Health Service Research and Training*, C. C Thomas, 1972; E. Struening and M. Guttentag, editors, *Handbook of Evaluation Research*, Sage Publications, Inc., 1975; B. H. Kaplan, R. N. Wilson, and A. H. Leighton, editors, *Further Explorations in Social Psychiatry*, Basic Books, 1976; M. Sokolowska, J. Holowska, and A. Ostrowska, editors, *Health, Medicine, Society*, Polish Scientific Publishers, 1977; (with M. Alavanja and I. Goldstein) *Water Chlorination: Environmental Impact and Health Effects*, Ann Arbor Science Publishers, 1978; W. Kruskal and J. Tanur, editors, *Statistics: A Volume Compiled from the International Encyclopedia of the Social Sciences*, 3rd edition (Susser was not associated with earlier editions), Free Press, 1979.

Contributor with Stein: J. G. Howells, editor, *Theory and Practice of Family Psychiatry*, Oliver & Boyd, 1968; Frederick Ledlich, editor, *Social Psychiatry*, Volume XLVII, Williams & Wilkins, 1968; J. Hellmuth, editor, *Studies in Abnormalities*, Brunner, 1971; S. Chess and A. Thomas, editors, *Annual Progress in Child Psychiatry and Child Development*, Brunner, 1971; (and Rush and G. Christakis) M. Winick, editor, *Proceedings of the Symposium on Nutrition and Fetal Development*, Wiley, 1972; S. Arieti, editor, *Child and Adolescent Psychology*, Basic Books, 1974; M. J. Begab and S. A. Richardson, editors, *The Mentally Retarded and Society: A Social Perspective*, University Park Press, 1975; Lloyd-Still, editor, *Nutrition and Mental Development* (monograph), Medical & Technical Publishers, 1976; E. B. Hook, editor, *Birth Defects: Risks and Consequences*, Academic Press, 1976; (and J. Kline and D. Warburton) *Population Cytogenetics: Studies in Humans*, Academic Press, 1977; D. M. Reed and F. J. Stanley, editors, *The Epidemiology of Prematurity*, Urgan & Schwarzenberg, 1977; (and Rush) P. Mittler, editor, *Research to Practice in Mental Retardation: Biomedical Aspects*, Volume III, International Association for the Scientific Study of Mental Deficiency, 1977; (and M. Mittelman and L. Belmont) *Cognitive Defects in the Development of Mental Illness*, Brunner, 1977; W. H. Mosley, editor, *Nutrition and Human Reproduction*, Plenum, 1978; N. E. Morton and C. S. Chung, editors, *Genetic Epidemiology*, Academic Press, 1978; (and Ostrowska, Sokolowska, A. Firkowska-Mankiewicz, and M. Czarkowski) Sokolowska, editor, *Health and Society*, Polish Academy of Sciences Institute of Philosophy and Sociology, 1978; J. Last, editor, *Preventive Medicine and Public Health*, 11th edition (Susser and Stein were not associated with earlier editions), Appleton, in press; D. Clark and B. MacMahon, editors, *Preventive Medicine*, 2nd edition (Susser and Stein were not associated with earlier edition), Little, Brown, in press.

Also author of reports on mental health services. Contributor of over eighty-five papers and articles to medical and public health journals. Guest editor, *International Journal of Health Services* and *International Journal of Mental Health*.

* * *

SWARTHOUT, Glendon (Fred) 1918-

PERSONAL: Born April 8, 1918, in Pinckney, Mich.; son of Fred H. and Lila (Chubb) Swarthout; married Kathryn Vaughn, 1940; children: Miles. *Education:* University of Michigan, A.B., 1939, A.M., 1946; Michigan State University, Ph.D., 1955. *Home:* 5045 Tamanar Way, Scottsdale, Ariz. 85253. *Agent:* William Morris Agency, 1350 Avenue of the Americas, New York, N.Y. 10019.

CAREER: University of Michigan, Ann Arbor, teaching fellow, 1946-48; University of Maryland, College Park, instructor, 1948-51; Michigan State University, East Lansing, associate professor of English, 1951-59; Arizona State University, Tempe, lecturer in English, 1959-63. Writer. *Military service:* U.S. Army, Infantry, 1943-45; became sergeant; awarded two battle stars. *Awards, honors:* Theatre Guild Playwriting Award, 1947; Hopwood Award in Fiction, 1948; O. Henry Prize Short Story, 1960; National Society of Arts and Letters Gold Medal, 1972; Spur Award from Western Writers of America for best novel, 1975.

WRITINGS: *Willow Run,* Crowell, 1943; *The Eagle and the Iron Cross,* New American Library, 1966.

All published by Random House: *They Came to Cordura,* 1958; *Where the Boys Are,* 1960; *Welcome to Thebes,* 1962; (with wife, Kathryn Swarthout) *The Ghost and the Magic Saber,* 1963; *The Cadillac Cowboys,* 1964; (with K. Swarthout) *Whichaway,* 1966.

All published by Doubleday: *Loveland,* 1968; (with K. Swarthout) *The Button Boat,* 1969; *Bless the Beasts and Children,* 1970; *The Tin Lizzie Troop,* 1972; (with K. Swarthout) *T. V. Thompson,* 1972; *Luck and Pluck,* 1973; *The Shootist,* 1975; (with K. Swarthout) *Whales to See The,* 1975; *The Melodeon,* 1977; *Skeletons,* 1979. Contributor of stories to *Cosmopolitan, Collier's, New World Writing, Esquire,* and *Saturday Evening Post.*

SIDELIGHTS: Richard Schickel, in his review of *Bless the Beasts and Children* writes: "Glendon Swarthout had the misfortune of selling a couple of his early books to the movies and since his sensibility seems to lead him naturally toward the linear adventure story, no one takes him very seriously. But he is a good, entertaining writer—exuberant, optimistic, maybe a little childlike (in a nice way) in his love of archetypal characters and situations, but always intelligent and alive." Peter Corodimas seems to appreciate Swarthout's optimism. "At a time when many novelists are preoccupied with themes of absurdity and alienation," he explains, "it is enjoyable, not to say helpful to one's sanity, to read a novel about life which sees life the way novelists used to see it: at least as partly intelligible—which may in itself be a wrong view, but comforting nonetheless."

Despite Swarthout's "honesty, idealism, and vitality," his first novel, *Willow Run,* suffers from "unreal people who talk all wrong and act like idiot children," writes a reviewer for *Commonweal.* As Rose Feld comments, "One is left with the impression that he has fine material for a good novel but that he hasn't sufficiently absorbed or developed it." Even so, notes a *New York Herald Tribune* reviewer, "the author . . . is an arresting writer . . . who [shows] real power in his first book. . . . But his talent deserves better things to work with" than the material available in a later book, *Welcome to Thebes.* David Dempsey agrees. He writes: "When he is at his best, which is about [fifty] percent of the time, Glendon Swarthout is a skillful, even a brilliant writer. The book throbs with a blistering vitality. . . . [It] is a tour de force of a high order, endowed with a literary dimension which the material really doesn't deserve."

Such strong words have been applied to some of Swarthout's other books as well. Taliaferro Boatwright calls *They Came to Cordura* "a vivid and bruising story." Walter Havighurst calls *Where the Boys Are* "very funny and very grim." Boatwright's review continues, "Its dramatic impact is immediate but beyond this it conveys a concept of heroism and of life as triumph through and over suffering that is both profound and thought-provoking." However, Martin Levin finds that *Where the Boys Are* leaves room for improvement: "Without an arresting narrative, Mr. Swarthout's comic novel is a series of random explosions instead of the humorous chain reaction it might have been." Nevertheless, as Schickel concludes: "He never falls into limp banalities. He is a stylist who also entertains and instructs and I say good for him. It is not as easy as it sounds."

They Came to Cordura was produced as a motion picture by Columbia in 1959, *Where the Boys Are* was produced by Metro-Goldwyn-Mayer in 1960, and *Bless the Beasts and Children* was produced by Columbia in 1971. *The Shootist* was produced by Paramount in 1976 and starred John Wayne and Lauren Bacall.

BIOGRAPHICAL/CRITICAL SOURCES: *New York Times,* May 30, 1943, February 9, 1958; *Commonweal,* June 18, 1943; *Saturday Review,* February 8, 1958, January 23, 1960; *New York Herald Tribune Book Review,* February 9, 1958; *Chicago Sunday Tribune,* January 17, 1960; *Time,* January 18, 1960; *New York Times Book Review,* February 7, 1960, June 17, 1962, October 5, 1969; *New York Herald Tribune Books,* July 1, 1962; *Best Sellers,* October 1, 1968; *Harper's,* April, 1970.

* * *

SWORTZELL, Lowell (Stanley) 1930-

PERSONAL: Born August 5, 1930, in Washington, D.C.; son of Stanley and Ora (Van Pelt) Swortzell; married Nancy Ellen Foell (an associate professor of educational theater at New York University), September 14, 1959. *Education:* George Washington University, B.A., 1952, M.A., 1953; New York University, Ph.D., 1963. *Home:* 76 Washington Pl., New York, N.Y. 10011. *Office:* Program in Educational Theatre, 733 Shimkin Hall, New York University, Washington Sq., New York, N.Y. 10003.

CAREER: Yale University, New Haven, Conn., assistant in playwriting and theater history, 1958-59; Tufts University, Medford, Mass., assistant professor of speech and drama, 1959-60; New York University, New York City, assistant professor of dramatic art, 1960-65; University of Wisconsin—Madison, associate professor of speech and education, 1965-66; New York University, associate professor, 1966-70, professor of educational theatre, 1970—. Trustee of Children's Museum, Washington, D.C., 1960—. *Military service:* U.S. Army, 1954-56. *Member:* American Theatre Association, Children's Theatre Association, American Society for Theatre Research, Speech Communication Association.

WRITINGS: *A Partridge in a Pear Tree* (one-act play), Samuel French, 1967; (editor) *All the World's a Stage: Modern Plays for Young People,* Delacorte, 1972; *Here Come the Clowns: A Cavalcade of Comedy from Antiquity to the Present,* Viking, 1978; *The Arabian Nights* (play), Dramatic Publishing, 1978. Also author of three one-act plays, "Praises to the Peacock," "London Bridge," and "The Fisherman and His Wife" and a dramatic adaptation of Geoffrey Chaucer's *Canterbury Tales.* Contributor to *Reader's Encyclopedia of World Drama,* Crowell, 1969.

WORK IN PROGRESS: *Theatre-in-Education,* with wife, Nancy Foell Swortzell, for Longman; editing *The Seeds of Drama: Plays for, by and about Young People,* for Delacorte.

SIDELIGHTS: Lowell Swortzell believes that theater producers must be more eager to fail. That is, they must be more willing to risk failure in the pursuit of better drama, especially in children's theater in which new plays are rare. In *News and Notes,* a publication of New Plays, Inc., Swortzell writes: "In the theatre, how can we experience, analyze and question unless we fail as well as succeed? The margin for error must exist here too if we are to develop a dramatic literature for young people that is also a genuine art form." Swortzell is not talking about minor failures. "I am talking about important failures," he continues, "those that make possible later significant successes. I am talking about exciting failures, failures that sometimes even win prizes, because although we have reservations about their total achievement, their aims have been so high we must applaud them, we must recognize their colossal effort to move the theatre forward in forms, content, uses of space, view points, and concepts."

BIOGRAPHICAL/CRITICAL SOURCES: News and Notes, November, 1979.

* * *

SYNGE, (Phyllis) Ursula 1930-

PERSONAL: Surname rhymes with "bring"; born April 8, 1930, in Minehead, Somerset, England; daughter of Walter John Reginald (a chartered accountant) and Kathleen Phyllis (Vowles) Synge; married Bernard Perrin (an artist), 1950; children: Jonathan, Abigail. *Education:* Attended West of England College of Art, 1944-46; University of Bristol, B.A., 1979. *Politics:* "Totally a-political." *Religion:* "I subscribe to all religious beliefs without preference for any particular one." *Home:* 10 Highbury Villas, St. Michael's Hill, Bristol, England.

CAREER: Author, and bookseller specializing in books and art books for young people, 1957—. Has worked as bookseller's assistant, photographer's assistant, manager of a village shop in rural England, and accounts clerk.

WRITINGS—Juveniles: *Weland: Smith of the Gods,* Bodley Head, 1972, S. G. Phillips, 1973; *The People and the Promise,* Bodley Head, 1974, S. G. Phillips, 1975; *Audun and the Bear,* Bodley Head, 1975; *Kalevala,* Bodley Head, 1977; *Margaret McElderry,* Atheneum, 1978; *The Giant at the Ford,* Bodley Head, 1980. Editor of quarterly news-sheet for Bristol branch of Society for Mentally Handicapped Children, 1958-61.

WORK IN PROGRESS: A novel-length fairy tale; research on medieval and ancient history, on folk-lore and legends, and on mythology.

SIDELIGHTS: Ursula Synge wrote *CA:* "Reading has always been my ruling passion and as a child I read widely and omnivorously but, in those days, I never thought of writing as a possible career. I wanted to be an artist—there was no question of any other life. So, when I left school I went to art college and it was there I started writing. Very seriously. But I could never finish anything. Circumstances changed—I married, had children and read—but put my writing away. Reading aloud those stories that I had most enjoyed, I began to think again of writing, and this time, after so long an interval, it went well. I was no longer trying to write the definitive twentieth-century novel, but had returned to my earliest influences—mythology, legend, the folk-tale. These stories are recreated for each generation and contain, I believe, important truths that we would be foolish to ignore."

AVOCATIONAL INTERESTS: Walking, "unspoiled" country, English villages and small country towns.

BIOGRAPHICAL/CRITICAL SOURCES: New York Times Book Review, April 27, 1980.

* * *

SZPORLUK, Roman 1933-

PERSONAL: Born September 8, 1933, in Grzymalow, Tarnopol, Poland (now Ukrainian Soviet Socialist Republic); son of Basil (a lawyer) and Maria (Michenko) Szporluk; married Mary Ann Bridley, December 21, 1963; children: Benjamin, Larisa, Michael-Andrei. *Education:* Lublin State University, LL.M., 1955; Oxford University, B.Litt., 1961; Stanford University, Ph.D., 1965. *Home:* 1820 Hanover Rd., Ann Arbor, Mich. 48103. *Office:* Department of History, University of Michigan, Ann Arbor, Mich. 48109.

CAREER: University of Michigan, Ann Arbor, assistant professor, 1965-70, associate professor, 1970-75, professor of history, 1975—. Harvard University, research associate in Ukrainian studies and associate of Russian Research Center, 1972-73, associate chairman of department of history, 1973-75. *Member:* American Association for the Advancement of Slavic Studies.

WRITINGS: (Translator with wife, Mary Ann Szporluk, and editor and author of introduction) M. N. Pokrovskii, *Russia in World History: Selected Essays,* University of Michigan Press, 1970; (contributor) Zev Katz, editor, *Handbook of Major Soviet Nationalities,* Free Press, 1975; (contributor) Peter J. Potichnyj, editor, *Ukraine in the Seventies,* Mosiac Press, 1975; (editor) *The Influence of Eastern Europe and the Soviet West on the U.S.S.R.,* Praeger, 1976; (contributor) Raymond Grew, editor, *Crises of Political Development in Europe and the United States,* Princeton University Press, 1978; *Ukraine: A Brief History,* Ukrainian Festival Committee (Detroit), 1979; (contributor) Edward Allworth, editor, *Ethnic Russia in the U.S.S.R.: The Dilemma of Dominance,* Pergamon, 1980.

WORK IN PROGRESS: T. G. Masaryk's Political Thought; Nationalism in East Europe and the U.S.S.R.

* * *

SZUMIGALSKI, Anne 1926-

PERSONAL: Born January 3, 1926, in London, England; daughter of Herbert E. (an army officer and chartered accountant) and Mary (Winder-Allen) Davis; married Jan Szumigalski (a land surveyor), March, 1945; children: Katharine Szumigalski Bitney, Elizabeth Szumigalski Carrier, Anthony, Mark. *Education:* Privately educated. *Home:* 9 Connaught Pl., Saskatoon, Saskatchewan, Canada.

CAREER: Teacher of creative writing in poetry in Saskatoon, Saskatchewan, elementary and secondary schools, 1971—. Instructor in poetry at Saskatchewan Summer School of the Arts, 1971—; founder and coordinator of Saskatoon Poets, a cooperative group of working poets. *Wartime service:* British Red Cross and Friends Ambulance Unit, civilian relief worker, 1943-46. *Awards, honors:* Canada Council Grant, 1976; Saskatchewan Poetry Prize, 1977-78.

WRITINGS: Woman Reading in Bath, Doubleday, 1974; (with Terrence Heath) *Wild Man's Butte,* Coteau Books, 1979; *A Game of Angels* (poems), Turnstone Press, 1980. Also translator, *The Invisible Ladder,* 1976. Also author of verse dramas for Canadian Broadcasting Corp., with Heath, "The Eyes of the Fishes," 1973, "The Exile's Catalogue," 1977, "The Chrome Parts," 1978, and others. Contributor of poetry and line drawings to literary magazines. Associate editor of *Grain.*

WORK IN PROGRESS: Doctrine of Signatures, a collection of poems; "Stories from the Shell," a series of books for children with Eileen Aubert; *Risks,* a collection of short prose.

SIDELIGHTS: Anne Szumigalski wrote *CA:* "The first and

abiding devotion must be to language, especially its sound and ceremonial; after that it's the quirks and absurdities of human nature that I love the most. Can anything be truly serious, if it's not at the same time funny, ridiculous, absurd?''

T

TAGGART, (Paul) John 1942-

PERSONAL: Born October 5, 1942, in Guthrie Center, Iowa; son of D. F. (a clergyman) and Pauline (Farwell) Taggart; married Jennifer James, December 13, 1967; children: Sarah, Holly. *Education:* Earlham College, B.A., 1965; University of Chicago, M.A., 1966; Syracuse University, Ph.D., 1974. *Religion:* Society of Friends (Quakers). *Home:* 210 South Washington, Shippensburg, Pa. 17257. *Office:* Shippensburg State College, Shippensburg, Pa. 17257.

CAREER: Shippensburg State College, Shippensburg, Pa., assistant professor of English, 1969—. *Member:* Coordinating Council of Literary Magazines, Committee of Small Magazine Editors and Publishers. *Awards, honors:* Ford Foundation fellowship, 1965; National Endowment for the Arts grant, 1976; received distinguished academic service award, 1976.

WRITINGS: To Construct a Clock, Elizabeth Press, 1971; *Pyramid Canon,* Burning Deck Press, 1973; *The Pyramid Is a Pure Crystal,* Elizabeth Press, 1974; *Prism and the Pine Twig,* Elizabeth Press, 1977; *Dodeka,* Membrane Press, 1979. Editor of *Maps,* an independent magazine of contemporary American poetry.

WORK IN PROGRESS: Peace on Earth, a poetry collection.

SIDELIGHTS: John Taggart told *CA,* "Writing poems is an exercise in heuristic; it can be more than that, but I see it as essentially 'algebra,' one man's algebra, which is also a music."

* * *

TANHAM, George K(ilpatrick) 1922-

PERSONAL: Born February 23, 1922, in Englewood, N.J.; son of Thomas Francis and Irene (Kilpatrick) Tanham; married Barbara Hunt. *Education:* Princeton University, B.A., 1943; Stanford University, M.A., 1947, Ph.D., 1951. *Home:* Idlewild Farm, Middleburg, Va. 22117. *Office:* RAND Corp., 2100 M St. N.W., Washington, D.C. 20032.

CAREER: California Institute of Technology, Pasadena, associate professor of history, 1947-55; RAND Corp., Santa Monica, Calif., staff member, 1955-59, Washington, D.C., deputy to vice-president, 1959-64, 1965-68, vice-president and trustee, 1970—. Member of U.S. Department of Defense task force, Vietnam, 1961; U.S. representative, Southeast Asia Treaty Organization expert study group on countersubversion, Thailand, 1961 and 1969; associate director, Agency for International Development mission to Vietnam, 1964; special assistant for counter-insurgency (with rank of minister), U.S. Embassy, Bangkok, Thailand, 1968-70. *Military service:* U.S. Army, 1943-46; became captain; awarded Silver Star with oak leaf cluster, Air Medal, Purple Heart, French Croix de Guerre with silver star. *Member:* Council on Foreign Relations (New York), Institute for Strategic Studies (London). *Awards, honors:* Belgium-American Educational Foundation fellow, 1950; Ford Foundation fellow, 1952-53; Social Science Research Council grants, 1955-57; Knight Commander, Order of the White Elephant (Thailand), 1970.

WRITINGS: Communist Revolutionary Warfare: The Vietminh in Indochina, Praeger, 1961, revised edition, 1967; *War without Guns: American Civilians in Rural Vietnam,* Praeger, 1966; *Contribution a l'histoire de la resistance belge,* University of Brussels Press, 1971; *Trial in Thailand,* Crane, Russak & Co., 1974. Contributor to military and historical journals.

AVOCATIONAL INTERESTS: Sports, music, and travel.

* * *

TATE, Joan 1922-

PERSONAL: Born in 1922; married; three children. *Home:* 32 Kennedy Rd., Shrewsbury SY3 7AB, England.

CAREER: Writer. *Member:* Society of Authors, PEN International, Translators Association, Amnesty International.

WRITINGS—All juvenile or young adult: *Sam and Me,* Macmillan, 1968; *Whizz Kid,* Macmillan, 1969; *The Nest,* Macmillan, 1969; *The Cheapjack Man,* Macmillan, 1969; *The Gobbleydock,* Macmillan, 1969; *The Tree House,* Macmillan, 1969; *The Ball,* Macmillan, 1969; *Gramp,* Chatto & Windus, 1971; *Your Town,* David & Charles, 1972; *Ben and Annie,* Doubleday, 1972; *Jack and the Rock Cakes,* Brockhampton, 1972; *Grandpa and My Little Sister,* Brockhampton, 1972; *Taxi!,* Schoeningh, 1973; *How Do You Do?,* Schoeningh, 1974; *The World of the River,* Dent, 1974; *You Can't Explain Everything,* Longman, 1976; *Billoggs,* Pelham Books, 1976; *See You,* Longman, 1977; *On Your Own I,* Wheaton, 1977; *On Your Own II,* Wheaton, 1978; *The House That Jack Built,* Pelham Books, 1978; *See How They Run,* Pelham Books, 1979; *Cat Country,* Ram Publishing, 1979;

Turn Again Whittington, Pelham Books, 1980; *Helter Skelter,* Pelham Books, 1980.

All published by Heinemann: *Jenny,* 1964; *The Crane,* 1964; *The Rabbit Boy,* 1964; *Coal Hoppy,* 1964; *The Silver Grill,* 1965; *The Next Doors,* 1965; *Picture Charlie,* 1965; *Lucy,* 1965; *The Tree,* 1966, published as *Tina and David,* Nelson, 1973; *The Holiday,* 1966; *Tad,* 1966; *Bill,* 1966; *Mrs. Jenny,* 1966; *Bits and Pieces,* 1968; *The Circus and Other Stories,* 1968; *Letters to Chris,* 1968; *The Crow,* 1968; *Luke's Garden,* 1968; *Jenny and Mrs. Jenny,* 1968, published as *Out of the Sun,* 1968; *Clipper,* 1969, published as *Ring on My Finger,* 1971; *The Long Road Home,* 1971; *Wump Day,* 1972; *Dad's Camel,* 1972.

All published by Almqvist & Wiksell: *The Lollipop Man,* 1967, Macmillan, 1969; *The Wild Boy,* 1967, Harper, 1973, published as *Wild Martin,* Heinemann, 1968; *The Train,* 1967; *The New House,* 1968; *The Soap Box Car,* 1968; *Polly,* 1969; *The Great Birds,* 1969; *The Old Car,* 1969; (with Sven Johansson and Bengt Astrom) *Going Up One* (language text), with workbook, 1969; *The Letter and Other Stories,* 1969; *Puddle's Tiger,* 1969; *The Caravan,* 1969; *Edward and the Uncles,* 1969; *The Secret,* 1969; *The Runners,* 1969; (with Johansson and Astrom) *Going Up Two* (language text), with workbook, 1970; *Night Out and Other Stories,* 1970; *The Match and Other Stories,* 1970; *Dinah,* 1970; *The Man Who Rang the Bell,* 1970; *Ginger Mick,* 1970; *Journal for One,* 1970.

Translator: John Einar Aberg, *Do You Believe in Angels,* Hutchinson, 1963; Dagmar Edqvist, *Black Sister,* Doubleday, 1963; Maertha Buren, *A Need to Love,* Dodd, 1964; Berndt Olsson, *Noah,* Hutchinson, 1964; Buren, *Camilla,* Dodd, 1965; Per Wahloo, *The Assignment,* Knopf, 1965; Ralph Herrmanns, *River Boy: Adventures on the Amazon,* Harcourt, 1965; Mika Waltari, *The Roman,* Putnam, 1966; Folke Henschen, *History of Diseases,* Longmans, Green, 1966, published as *The History and Geography of Diseases,* Dial, 1967; Nan Inger, *Katrin,* Hamish Hamilton, 1966; Maria Lang, *Wreath for the Bride,* Hodder & Stoughton, 1966; Lang, *No More Murders,* Hodder & Stoughton, 1967; Lang, *Death Awaits Thee,* Hodder & Stoughton, 1967; Sven Gillsaeter, *From Island to Island,* Allen & Unwin, 1968; Wahloo, *A Necessary Action,* Pantheon, 1968 (published in England as *The Lorry,* M. Joseph); Margit Fjellman, *Queen Louise of Sweden,* Allen & Unwin, 1968; Wahloo and Maj Sjoewall, *The Man Who Went Up in Smoke,* Pantheon, 1969; Carl Nylander, *The Deep Well,* Allen & Unwin, 1969; Hans Heiberg, *Ibsen,* Allen & Unwin, 1969.

Wahloo, *The Steel Spring,* Knopf, 1970; Goeran Bergman, *Why Does Your Dog Do That?,* Hutchinson, 1970; Anders Bodelsen, *Freezing Point,* Knopf, 1970; Wahloo and Sjoewall, *The Fire-Engine That Vanished,* Pantheon, 1970; Gunnel Beckman, *Admission to the Feast,* Macmillan, 1971; Doris Dahlin, *The Sit-In Game,* Viking, 1972; Beckman, *A Room of His Own,* Viking, 1972; Wahloo, *The Generals,* Pantheon, 1973; Beckman, *Mia,* Bodley Head, 1974; Astrid Lindgren, *That Emil,* Brockhampton, 1974; Barbro Lindgren, *Alban,* A. & C. Black, 1974; Olle Hoegstrand, *The Debt,* Pantheon, 1974; Astrid Lindgren, *The Lionheart Brothers,* Brockhampton, 1974; Lennart Frick, *The Threat,* Brockhampton, 1974; Wahloo, *The Generals,* M. Joseph, 1974.

Beckman, *The Loneliness of Mia,* Viking, 1975; Bodelsen, *Operation Cobra,* Pelham Books, 1975; Bjorn Borg, *The Bjorn Borg Story,* Pelham Books, 1975; Thomas Dineson, *My Sister, Isak Dineson,* M. Joseph, 1975; Ole Lund, *Otto Is a Rhino,* Pelham Books, 1975; Merete Kruuse, *Scatty Ricky,* Pelham Books, 1975; Lief Esper Anderson, *Witch Fever,* Pelham Books, 1976; Kare Holt, *The Race,* M. Joseph, 1976; Lindgren, *Emil and the Bad Tooth,* Hodder & Stoughton, 1976; Max Lundgren, *Summer Girl,* Macmillan, 1976; Irmelin Sandman Lilius, *Gold Crown Lane,* Oxford University Press, 1976; Maj Sjowall and Wahloo, *The Terrorists,* Random House, 1976; Gun Bjork and Ingvar Bjork, *Shrews,* Pelham Books, 1977; Bjork and Bjork, *Bees,* Pelham Books, 1977; Hans-Erik Hellberg, *Follow My Leader,* Macmillan, 1977; Lundgren, *For the Love of Lisa,* Macmillan, 1977; Svend Otto, *Jasper the Taxi Dog,* Pelham Books, 1977; Otto, *Tim and Trisha,* Pelham Books, 1977; Lilius, *The Goldmaker's House,* Oxford University Press, 1977; Stig Weimar, *Denmark Is Like This,* Kaye & Ward, 1977; Eva Bexell, *The Minister's Naughty Grandchildren,* Bodley Head, 1978; Bjork and Bjork, *Ants,* Pelham Books, 1978; Bjork and Bjork, *Frogs,* Pelham Books, 1978; Anne Bulow-Olsen, *Plant Communities,* Penguin, 1978; Gunnel Linde, *I Am a Werewolf Cub,* Dent, 1978; Otto, *A Christmas Book,* Pelham Books, 1978; Martha Sandwall-Bergstrom, *Anna Keeps Her Promise,* Blackie, 1978; Sandwall-Bergstrom, *Anna All Alone,* Blackie, 1978; Sandwall-Bergstrom, *Anna at Bloom Farm,* Blackie, 1978; Bexell, *Christmas with Grandfather,* Bodley Head, 1979; Arne Blom, *The Limits of Pain,* Ram Publishing, 1979; Eva Eriksson, *Hocus Pocus,* Methuen, 1979; Eriksson, *Sometimes Never,* Methuen, 1979; Robert Fisher, *Sparrow Falls Out of the Nest,* Pelham Books, 1979; Eigel Holm, *The Biology of Flowers,* Penguin, 1979; Ulf Malmgren, *When the Leaves Begin to Fall,* Oxford University Press, 1979; Jan Martensson, *Death Calls on the Witches,* Ram Publishing, 1979; Otto, *Inuk and His Sledge-Dog,* Pelham Books, 1979; Otto, *Karen and the Space Machine,* Pelham Books, 1979; Sandwall-Bergstrom, *Anna Wins Through,* Blackie, 1979; Sandwall-Bergstrom, *Anna at the Manor House,* Blackie, 1979; Sandwall-Bergstrom, *Anna Solves the Mystery,* Blackie, 1979; Lilius, *Horses of the Night,* Oxford University Press, 1979; Elisabeth Soderstrom, *In My Own Key,* Hamish Hamilton, 1979; Sven Krister Swahn, *The Twilight Visitors,* Methuen, 1980; Lilius, *King Tulle,* Pelham Books, 1980; Allen Rune Pettersson, *Frankenstein's Aunt,* Hodder, 1980.

* * *

TAVARD, George H(enry) 1922-

PERSONAL: Born February 6, 1922, in Nancy, France; son of Henri Ernest and Marguerite (Wasser) Tavard. *Education:* Major Seminary, B. Scolastic Philosophy, 1942; Facultes Catholiques, S.T.D., 1949. *Home:* 2151 Waldorf Rd., Columbus, Ohio 43229. *Office:* Methodist Theological School, Delaware, Ohio 43015.

CAREER: Ordained Roman Catholic priest of Assumptionist Order, 1947; Capenor House, Surrey, England, lecturer, 1948-50; *Documentation Catholique,* Paris, France, assistant editor, 1950-51; Assumption College, Worcester, Mass., lecturer, 1958-59; Mount Mercy College (now Carlow College), Pittsburgh, Pa., chairman of department of theology, 1960-67; Pennsylvania State University, College Park, professor, 1967-69; Methodist Theological School in Ohio, Delaware, professor, 1970—. Expert, Second Vatican Council; Catholic observer-consultant to Consultation on Church Union. *Member:* Catholic Theological Society of America, American Society of Church History, Catholic Historical Association, Society for Reformation Research, Delta Epsilon Sigma.

WRITINGS: The Catholic Approach to Protestantism, Harper, 1955; *The Church, the Layman, and the Modern World,* Macmillan, 1959; *Protestantism,* Hawthorn, 1959; *Protestant Hopes and the Catholic Responsibility,* Fides, 1960, revised edition, 1964; *Two Centuries of Ecumenism,* Fides, 1960; *Holy Writ or Holy Church,* Harper, 1960; *Paul Tillich and the Christian Message,* Scribner, 1962; *Quest for Catholicity: The Development of High Church Anglicanism,* Herder, 1964; *The Church Tomorrow,* Herder, 1965; *Woman in Christian Tradition,* University of Notre Dame Press, 1973; *The Inner Life,* Paulist/Newman, 1976; *A Way of Love,* Orbis, 1977; *Song for Avalokita* (poems), Dorrance, 1979.

* * *

TAYLOR, Jerome 1918-

PERSONAL: His name was originally Jerome Krejci; born November 21, 1918, in Chicago, Ill.; son of Louis J. and Rose (Dvorak) Krejci; married Carol Duthie, 1946; children: Jane, Edward, Lucy, Marie, Peter, Stephen, Thomas, Patrick, Celia. *Education:* Catholic University of America, A.B., 1942; University of Chicago, M.A., 1945, Ph.D., 1959. *Home:* Sunny Hollow Farm, Route 1, Rock Springs, Wis. *Office:* Room 6131, White Hall, University of Wisconsin, 600 North Park St., Madison, Wis. 53706.

CAREER: University of Chicago, Chicago, Ill., instructor, 1946-48; Dartmouth College, Hanover, N.H., instructor, 1948-52, assistant professor, 1952-53; University of Notre Dame, Notre Dame, Ind., assistant professor, 1953-59, associate professor, 1959-62; University of Chicago, associate professor, 1962-67, professor of English, 1967-70, associate chairman, department of English, 1963-64, chairman, committee on medieval studies, 1966-70; University of Wisconsin—Madison, professor of English, 1970—. *Member:* Mediaeval Academy of America, Modern Language Association of America, National Council of Teachers of English, Catholic Commission of Intellectual and Cultural Affairs, New Chaucer Society. *Awards, honors:* American Council of Learned Societies, fellow, 1952-53, and research grant, 1973; Danforth Foundation study grant, 1958-59, and special fellowship, 1960-61; E. Harris Harbison award for distinguished teaching, 1964; Guggenheim fellowship, 1965; American Philosophical Society research grant, 1973; Institute for Research in the Humanities fellow, 1973-74; National Endowment for the Humanities senior fellowship, 1974-75.

WRITINGS: (Editor with R. J. Schoeck) *Chaucer Criticism: The Canterbury Tales,* University of Notre Dame Press, 1960; (editor with Schoeck) *Chaucer Criticism: The Troilus and Minor Works,* University of Notre Dame Press, 1961; *The Didascalicon of Hugh of St. Victor: A Medieval Guide to the Arts,* Columbia University Press, 1961; (contributor) *Literature and Society,* University of Nebraska Press, 1964; (editor and translator) *Nature, Man, and Society in the Twelfth Century,* University of Chicago Press, 1968; (author and editor with Alan H. Nelson) *Medieval English Drama: Essays Critical and Contextual,* University of Chicago Press, 1972. Contributor to numerous periodicals including *Commonweal, America,* and *Comparative Drama.*

WORK IN PROGRESS: The first critical edition of Geoffrey Chaucer's *Boece* and his first Middle English translation of Boethius, *De consolatione Philosophiae.*

SIDELIGHTS: Jerome Taylor told *CA:* "I am interested both in the internal form and depth and in the external outreach or personal and social effect of a work of literary art. The first of these interests relates to formal or textual criticism; the second, to contextual interpretation and evaluation. The first is best associated with the analytic method of Aristotle and his successors in art and criticism; the second, with Plato, Neoplatonists, and Platonizers of variegated stripe throughout the ages. Intextual and contextual concerns, whether in reading or in writing, involve three liberal or personally and intellectually liberating arts: the art of perception (seeing every detail in all its fullness), the art of interpretation (classifying, defining, expositing the significance of what one has perceived), and the art of evaluation (assessing the truth of intrinsic consistency, and the truth of external correspondences, regarding what one has perceived and interpreted).

"Whether working at poetry, at the medieval origins of modern theater, at historical fiction, at literary criticism, or even at the mystery story, these are the three arts I seek both to practice and to inculcate in those with whom I am working. They are like three activating light-beams which give life and shape and moving substance to the human works one seeks to create. But the source of these light-beams, the Light and Radiance given to any and all of us without skill or merit of our own—that is something else, and for it one lays oneself open, humbly and with deep thanks, like warming earth under the Sun in spring."

* * *

TAYLOR, John Laverack 1937-

PERSONAL: Born 1937, in Yorkshire, England; son of Donald J. (a shipping agent) and Ivy L. (Laverack) Taylor; married Dorothy Annette King (a university lecturer in music), December 24, 1960; children: Alison, Caroline, Mark. *Education:* Leeds School of Architecture and Town Planning, diploma in architecture, 1960; Columbia University, M.Sc., 1964; University of Sheffield, Ph.D., 1970. *Home:* Lytleheyfilde, Hall Lane, Ingatestone, Essex CM4 9NN, England. *Office:* North East London Polytechnic, Forest Rd., London E17 4JB, England.

CAREER: University of Sheffield, Sheffield, England, senior lecturer in town and regional planning, 1970-75; head of Trent Department of Town and Country Planning, Nottingham, England, 1975-79; North East London Polytechnic, London, England, assistant director and dean of environmental studies, 1979—. Director of Sheffield Centre for Environmental Research, 1972-76. *Member:* Royal Institute of British Architects, Royal Town Planning Institute, English Speaking Union (fellow). *Awards, honors:* Royal Institute of British Architects Certificate of Merit, 1960; Fulbright fellow, 1962-64; Salzburg fellow, 1965; Nuffield Foundation fellow, 1970-74.

WRITINGS: (With Robert Armstrong) *Instructional Simulation Systems in Higher Education,* Cambridge Institute, 1970; *Instructional Planning Systems,* Cambridge University Press, 1971; (editor with Armstrong) *Feedback on Instructional Simulation,* Cambridge Institute, 1971; (with Rex Walford) *Simulation in the Classroom,* Penguin, 1972; (editor) *Planning for Urban Growth,* Praeger, 1972; (with Walford) *Learning and the Simulation Game,* Holt, 1979.

* * *

TEMKO, Florence

PERSONAL: Married second husband, Henry Petzal; children: (first marriage) Joan Temko, Ronald Temko, Stephen Temko. *Education:* Attended Wycombe Abbey, London School of Economics and Political Science, and New School for Social Research. *Home and office:* 2 Plunkett St., Lenox, Mass. 01240.

CAREER: Berkshire Museum, Pittsfield, Mass., currently assistant to the director. *Member:* American Craftsman, Authors Guild, National League of American Pen Women, Artist-Craftsmen of New York.

WRITINGS: Kirigami: The Creative Art of Papercutting, Platt, 1962; *Party Fun with Origami,* Platt, 1963; *Paperfolding to Begin With,* Bobbs-Merrill, 1968; *Papercutting,* Doubleday, 1973; *Feltcraft,* Doubleday, 1974; *Paper: Folded, Cut, Sculpted,* Macmillan, 1974; *Paper Capers,* Scholastic Book Service, 1974; *Self-Stick Craft,* Doubleday, 1975; *Decoupage Crafts,* Doubleday, 1976; *Folk Crafts for World Friendship,* Doubleday, 1976; (contributor) *The Golden Happy Birthday Book,* Golden Press, 1976; *The Big Felt Burger and 27 Other Craft Projects to Relish,* Doubleday, 1977; *The Magic of Kirigami,* Japan Publications, 1978; *Paperworks,* Bobbs-Merrill, 1979. Also contributor to *National Camp Directors Guide,* 1974. Author of weekly column, "Things to Make," in *Berkshire Eagle* and other newspapers. Contributor to magazines and newspapers, including *Grade Teacher, New York Times, Berkshire Eagle,* and *Boston Globe.*

WORK IN PROGRESS: Elementary Games and Puzzles: An Arts and Crafts Approach for Teachers, for Parker Publishing Co.; a traveling exhibition of "Paperarts" with a catalogue of the exhibit.

SIDELIGHTS: Florence Temko told *CA:* "Crafting with paper is my specialty, and I love origami (paper folding) and Kirigami (paper cutting) for the wonderful ways in which paper can be turned into holiday decorations or works of art. I felt that a book could spread my enthusiasm to a large number of people and was very surprised that not one of fifteen New York publishers agreed with me. Finally my first book did make it and once you are in print, it is easier to do again. But I never thought I would end up writing [so many] books. One of my editors discovered I could write clear instructions that readers could follow easily, a writing talent I did not know I possessed."

* * *

TEMPLE, Wayne C(alhoun) 1924-

PERSONAL: Born February 5, 1924, near Richwood, Ohio; son of Howard Milton and Ruby March (Calhoun) Temple; married Lois Marjorie Bridges, September 22, 1956 (died April 21, 1978); married Sunderine Wilson Mohn, April 9, 1979. *Education:* University of Illinois, A.B. (cum laude), 1949, A.M., 1951, Ph.D., 1956. *Religion:* Presbyterian. *Home:* 1121 South Fourth Street Ct., Springfield, Ill. 62756. *Office:* Illinois State Archives, Springfield, Ill. 62756.

CAREER: University of Illinois at Urbana-Champaign, Urbana, research assistant, 1949-53, teaching assistant, 1953-54; Illinois State Museum, Springfield, curator of ethnohistory, 1954-58; Lincoln Memorial University, Harrogate, Tenn., associate professor of American history, 1958, John Wingate Weeks Professor of History and director of department of Lincolniana, 1958-64, chairman of department of history, 1959-62; Illinois State Archives, Springfield, archivist, 1964-77, deputy director, 1977—. Member of advisory council, U.S. Civil War Centennial Commission, 1960-65; secretary-treasurer, National Lincoln Civil War Council. Assistant district commissioner, Boy Scouts of America, 1958-60. Regent, Lincoln Academy of Illinois. Member of board of governors, Shriners Hospitals for Crippled Children. *Military service:* U.S. Army, 1943-46; received two commendations for action under fire in European Theater; lieutenant general in militia.

MEMBER: Royal Society of Arts (London; life fellow), Civil War Press Corps (major), Lincoln Group of District of Columbia (honorary), Sigma Tau Delta, Delta Sigma Rho, Phi Alpha Theta, Chi Gamma Iota, Tau Kappa Alpha, Alpha Psi Omega, Sigma Pi Beta (headmaster), Order of the Arrow. *Awards, honors:* Lincoln Medallion of Lincoln Sesquicentennial Commission, 1960; Scouter's Award, Boy Scouts of America, 1960; Lincoln Diploma of Honor, Lincoln Memorial University, 1963; award of achievement, U.S. Civil War Centennial commission, 1965; distinguished service awards, Illinois State Historical Library, 1969 and 1977; received honorary degree from the International Supreme Council for the Order of De Molay, 1972.

WRITINGS: Indian Villages of the Illinois Country: Historic Tribes, Illinois State Museum, 1958, revised edition, 1977; (editor) *Campaigning with Grant,* Indiana University Press, 1961; (editor) *The Civil War Letters of Henry C. Bear,* Lincoln Memorial University Press, 1961; *Lincoln the Railsplitter,* Willow House, 1961; *Lincoln As Seen by C. C. Brown,* Crabgrass, 1963; *Abraham Lincoln and Others at the St. Nicholas,* St. Nicholas Hotel, 1968; *Alexander Williamson: Tutor to the Lincoln Boys,* Lincoln Fellowship of Wisconsin, 1971; *First Steps to Victory: Grant's March to Naples,* Seventh Cavalry, 1977; *Indian Villages of the Illinois Country,* Illinois State Museum, 1975. Co-author of play, "Abe Lincoln Takes a Wife."

Contributor to *A Civil War Cook Book, Mountain Life and Work,* and *Lincoln Day by Day.* Also contributor to *World Book Encyclopedia* and to magazines. Editor of scripts for radio series, "A. Lincoln, 1809-1959," for Broadcast Music. *Lincoln Herald,* editor-in-chief, 1958-73, associate editor, 1973—.

WORK IN PROGRESS: Mrs. Lincoln's Cookbook; writing about Lincoln and his father as farmers, and Lincoln in Sangamon County.

BIOGRAPHICAL/CRITICAL SOURCES: Journal of the Illinois State Historical Society, summer, 1958; *Louisville Courier-Journal,* February 8, 1962; *Knoxville Journal,* February 12, 1962.

* * *

TENENBAUM, Shea 1910-

PERSONAL: Born April 14, 1910, in Ireno, Poland; came to United States in 1934; son of Abraham Motek (a watchmaker) and Rachel Leah (Grossman) Tenenbaum. *Education:* Privately educated. *Religion:* Jewish. *Home:* 45-35 44th St., Long Island City, N.Y. 11104.

CAREER: Writer, novelist, and printer. *Member:* Yiddish P.E.N., Jewish National Workers Alliance. *Awards, honors:* American Committee for Emigree Scholars, Writers, and Artists fellowship, 1947, for *The Writing on the Horizon;* Zvi Kessel Prize for Jewish Literature, 1951, for *In the Image of God;* Congress for Jewish Culture and Yiddish P.E.N. Karl Rotman Stipendium, 1967, for *Job of Lemberg;* Congress for Yiddish Culture Award, 1980, for outstanding total output.

WRITINGS: Euphorion, [Antwerp], 1931; *Bei der welt zugast* (title means "A Visitor to the World"), [Warsaw], 1937; *Der sfinks* (title means "The Sphinx"), Chicago Courier, 1938; *Kinder fun der zun* (title means "Children of the Sun"), Voice (Mexico), 1942; *Gold un zhaver* (novel; title means "Gold and Rust"), Voice, 1943; *Di schrift oifn horizont* (title means "The Writing on the Horizon"), [New York], 1947; *Shnit fun mayn feld* (title means "Harvest"), [New York], 1949; *In Got's geshtalt* (title means "In the

Image of God"), [New York], 1951; *A hant farshraybt* (title means "A Hand Is Writing"), [New York], 1953; *Dikhter un doyres* (title means "Poets and Generations"), [New York], 1955; *Un di erd bashteyt oyf eybik* (title means "And the Earth Remains Forever"), [New York], 1957; *Ana Frank, du vos host getrunken fun gots hant* (title means "Anna Frank Who Hast Drunk from the Hand of God"), [New York], 1958; *Der emes zol zayn dayn shtern* (autobiography; title means "The Truth Should Be Your Star"), [New York], 1960; *Der sar fun lebn* (title means "The Angel of Life"), [New York], 1963; (contributor) Joseph Leftwich, editor, *Yisroel: First Jewish Omnibus,* Yoseloff, 1963; *Ayzik Ashmeday* (title means "Isaac Ashmedai"), Central Yiddish Culture Organization, 1965; *Iyev fun Lemberg* (title means "Job of Lemberg"), Central Yiddish Culture Organization, 1967; *Geshtaltn baym shrayb'tish* (title means "Personalities by My Desk"), Central Yiddish Culture Organization, 1969; *Hunger tsum vort* (title means "Hunger for the Word"), Central Yiddish Culture Organization, 1972; *Der letzter eides* (title means "The Last Witness"), Central Yiddish Culture Organization, 1972; *In der keiserlicher Weinshenk* (title means "In the Royal Tavern"), Central Yiddish Culture Organization, 1973; *Otzrot in der finsternish* (title means "Treasures in the Darkness"), [New York], 1974; *De suda fun wort* (title means "Feast of the Word"), [New York], 1976; *A lok fun Maidaneck* (title means "A Lock of Hair from Maidaneck"), [New York], 1978; *Er vet tzurikcomen fun Auschwitz* (title means "Return from Auschwitz"), Cyco Publishing House, 1980.

Contributor to *Memorial Book of Korif* and to periodicals, including *Chicago Courier, Dorem Afrike, Forois, Haint,* and *Israel-Stimme.*

WORK IN PROGRESS: Evenings with Writers; a new edition of *The Truth Should Be Your Star.*

SIDELIGHTS: Shea Tenenbaum told *CA:* "English is not my language; I write in Yiddish. Therefore, I feel inadequate to touch vital problems of literature in a language in which I am limited. I don't dare to give advice to writers. Personally, I have been writing over half a century, having written thousands of prose-pages. Still I am struggling hard with the technique of writing, which is one of the most difficult of art-forms. Each writer must go through his own purgatory in the art of writing. It is also a matter of the writer's soul, character, temperament, experiences, talent, power of expression, and mastery of form.

"Yes, I have been influenced by other writers, especially by Walt Whitman with his eternal spring and summer, and by Edgar Allan Poe with his sadness and melody of crying winds in perpetual fall. In addition to having had twenty-four books published I have had published in the Jewish press of the world more than ten thousand stories and essays. In recent years it has been my special purpose to put down my remembrances of the Jewish writers and painters I have known, also of my family, and of the Jewish life in Eastern Europe which is no more. However I feel I am still at the beginning and still holding my pen on the first line. The writing of literature is like the living of life, an endless attempt at perfection."

BIOGRAPHICAL/CRITICAL SOURCES: Isaac Liebman, *Builders and Creators of My Generation,* [New York], 1953; Mordecai Yardeini, *Interviews with Jewish Writers,* [New York], 1955; Joseph Hillel Levy, *Collected Writings,* Volume II, [London], 1958; Benjamin Skuditsky, *Of a Whole Life,* [Buenos Aires], 1958; Yeheskel Brownstein, *People Whom I Have Known,* [Los Angeles], 1962; Yossel Cohen, *At the Edge of the Beginning,* [New York], 1963; Schloime Bickel, *Writers of My Generation,* Volume III, [Tel Aviv], 1970; Rebecca Kope, *Authors, Books, Opinions,* [Paris], 1973.

* * *

TESSLER, Mark A(rnold) 1941-

PERSONAL: Born July 25, 1941, in Youngstown, Ohio; son of Sidney L. and Louise (Kirtz) Tessler; married Patricia Mayerson, June 12, 1966; children: Joelle. *Education:* Attended Hebrew University, Jerusalem, Israel, 1961-62; Case Western Reserve University, B.A., 1963; University of Tunis, certificat, 1965; Northwestern University, Ph.D., 1969; also studied at Institute of World Affairs, Salisbury, Conn. *Home:* 4671 North Woodburn, Milwaukee, Wis. 53211. *Office:* Department of Political Science, University of Wisconsin, Milwaukee, Wis. 53211.

CAREER: University of Wisconsin—Milwaukee, instructor, 1968-69, assistant professor, 1969-74, associate professor, 1974-76, professor of political science, 1976—, chairman of department, 1976-79, director of political research laboratory, 1970-71, director of graduate studies, 1973-76. Director of Wisconsin Universities United Nations Summer Seminars, 1969, 1970, and 1975, and Institute of World Affairs Summer Institute, 1971. *Member:* Social Science Research Council, American Political Science Association, African Studies Association, Middle East Studies Associations. *Awards, honors:* Grants from Social Science Research Council, 1972-73, American Philosophical Society, 1972 and 1974, International Communication Agency, 1978-79, and National Endowment for the Humanities, 1979; Fulbright-Hays fellowships, 1976 and 1980.

WRITINGS: (Editor and contributor) *A New Look at the Middle East,* Institute of World Affairs, University of Wisconsin—Milwaukee, 1971; (editor with William O'Barr and David Spain, and contributor) *Survey Research in Africa: Its Applications and Limits,* Northwestern University Press, 1973; (with O'Barr and Spain) *Tradition and Identity in Changing Africa,* Harper, 1973; (editor with Naiem Sherbiny, and contributor) *Arab Oil: Impact on the Arab Countries and Global Implications,* Praeger, 1976.

Contributor: Russell Stone and John Simmons, editors, *Change in Tunisia: Essays in the Social Sciences,* State University of New York Press, 1976; James Allman, editor, *Women's Status and Fertility in the Muslim World,* Praeger, 1978; *Women in the Muslim World,* Harvard University Press, 1978; R. D. McLaurin, editor, *The Political Role of Minorities in the Middle East,* Praeger, 1979; R. Wirsing, editor, *The Protection of Minorities,* Pergamon, 1980; Charles Keyes, editor, *Ethnic Change,* University of Washington Press, 1981. Contributor of numerous articles and reviews to national magazines and to political science and social science journals, including *New Republic, World Affairs, Journal of Social Psychology, Social Science Quarterly, Comparative Political Studies, International Journal of Middle East Studies, Journal of Modern African Studies,* and *Social Science Information.*

WORK IN PROGRESS: Three books, tentatively entitled *Three Non-Assimilating Minorities: Jews in Tunisia and Morocco and Arabs in Israel, Political Elites in Five Arab Countries,* and *The Political Economy of Attitude Change in Developing Countries.*

THOMAS, Ernest Lewys 1904-
(Richard Vaughan)

PERSONAL: Born July 19, 1904, in Wales; son of Thomas and Raddie (Lewis) Thomas; married, 1937. *Education:* Attended West Monmouth School and Trent Park College, England. *Religion:* Anglican. *Agent:* Curtis Brown Ltd., 1 Craven Hill, London W2 3EW, England.

CAREER: Tollington Grammar School, London, England, English master, 1950-63; author; journalist; radio and television script writer. *Military service:* British Army, Royal Artillery, 1942-46.

WRITINGS—All published under pseudonym Richard Vaughan: *Moulded in Earth,* Dutton, 1951; *Who Rideth So Wild?,* Dutton, 1952; *Son of Justin,* Dutton, 1955, reprinted, Chivers, 1974; *All through the Night,* Dutton, 1957; *There Is a River* (autobiography), Dutton, 1961; *All the Moon Long,* Christopher Davies, 1974; *Dewin y Daran* (play; written in Welsh), Christopher Davies, 1974, translation by T. J. Jones published under same title, 1974. Contributor of short stories to periodicals.

WORK IN PROGRESS: Two novels, *Benighted in Eden,* and *Silent in Askelon,* and a play, "Dark Wanes the Moon."

AVOCATIONAL INTERESTS: Literature and music.†

* * *

THOMAS, Jack W(illiam) 1930-

PERSONAL: Born October 24, 1930, in Seattle, Wash.; son of Edward Moore (a photographer) and Margaret (Walker) Thomas; married Cathleen F. Cagney, February 17, 1962; children: Verney Lee, Christina May. *Education:* University of Arizona, B.A., 1957. *Home and office:* 1961 Lookout Dr., Agoura, Calif. 91301. *Agent:* James Fox, 2195 Roberto Dr., Palm Springs, Calif. 92262.

CAREER: Free-lance writer for motion pictures, 1959-62; Los Angeles County Probation Department, Los Angeles, Calif., probation officer, 1964-70; writer, 1970—. *Military service:* U.S. Navy, 1950-54. *Member:* Writers Guild of America West, Authors Guild.

WRITINGS—All published by Bantam: *Turn Me On,* 1969; *Reds,* 1971; *Bikers,* 1972; *Girls Farm,* 1974; *The Fear Dealers,* 1975; *Heavy Number,* 1976; *High School Pusher,* 1977; *Burnout,* 1979.

Screenplays; produced by Twentieth Century-Fox, except as indicated: "Lone Texan," 1959; "Thirteen Fighting Men," 1960; "20,000 Eyes," 1961; "Francis of Assisi," 1961; "We'll Bury You," Columbia, 1962; "Embryo," 1976. Also author of script for documentary, "Nine Bows to Conquer," 1964.

SIDELIGHTS: Jack Thomas told *CA:* "My experience as a probation officer made me aware of the abuse of drugs in many young people's lives. I try to inject anti-drug themes into my books without making it propaganda." Thomas spent 1958 travelling in Europe and Mexico and lived in Egypt for nine months in 1964.

* * *

THOMAS, Lee 1918-

PERSONAL: Born May 10, 1918, in Paul's Valley, Okla.; son of Steine Jesse and Flora (Harris) Thomas; married Jeanne Wylie, 1946; children: Suzanne Carrol. *Education:* Attended University of Southern California, 1938-39, U.S. Armed Forces Institute, 1940-42, L.I.F.E. Bible College, 1945-48, and Pioneer Theological Seminary, 1951-52. *Home:* West Covina, Calif. *Office:* South Hills Baptist Church, 17250 Francisquito Ave., West Covina, Calif.

CAREER: Evangelist in Western United States and foreign countries, Youth for Christ International, 1948-57; South Hills Baptist Church, West Covina, Calif., pastor, 1957—, administrator of South Hills Academy, 1957-80. Writer for Sunday school board on writing curriculum, Sunday school committee, Southern Baptist General Convention, 1970—; member of executive board, World Opportunities International; executive director, Park Pacific Towers (apartment project for senior citizens). Member of board, San Gabriel Valley Association. *Military service:* U.S. Army Air Forces, 1940-45; became staff sergeant; awarded Purple Heart, American Defense and Asiatic-Pacific service medals. *Member:* Southern Baptist Convention (Los Angeles Association, member of board of directors), Baptist Foundation, Baptist Teachers Association, Veterans of Foreign Wars, Epsilon Delta Chi, Delta Chapter Alumni Society, Lions Club. *Awards, honors:* "Streets of the Walking Dead," a television film based on Thomas's book of the same title, received first place honors at the Religious Film Festival, 1959; Doctor of Divinity degree, Linda Vista Baptist Theological Seminary, 1960; recipient of certificate of appreciation, World Opportunities International; recipient of certificate of management for the elderly, National Center for Housing Management, Inc.

WRITINGS: *Streets of the Walking Dead,* International Gospel League, 1959; *The Billy Sunday Story* (biography), Zondervan, 1961; *Sunday,* Bible Voice, 1976. Also author of *God in the Coliseum,* for Billy Graham Evangelist Association, 1963. Contributor of numerous articles to magazines and newspapers.

WORK IN PROGRESS: A book on China, *Trend or Trick.*

SIDELIGHTS: As an evangelist for Youth for Christ International, Lee Thomas conducted revival services in thirty-two foreign countries. In addition to his writings, Thomas told *CA* that he has been "involved in extensive radio and television work. The major motivating factor of my career," he continued, "is to propogate the message of Jesus Christ through writings, television, radio, speaking, and motion pictures."

Thomas's book, *Sunday,* is being developed for the stage and television by Danny Thomas Production Co.

* * *

THOMPSON, Bard 1925-

PERSONAL: Born June 18, 1925, in Waynesboro, Pa.; son of Charles H. and Frances (Beard) Thompson; married Bertha Denning, September 1, 1951; children: Andrew Bard, Frances Rutledge. *Education:* Haverford College, A.B., 1947; Union Theological Seminary, New York, N.Y., B.D., 1949; Columbia University, Ph.D., 1953. *Office:* Graduate School, Drew University, Madison, N.J. 07940.

CAREER: Emory University, Atlanta, Ga., assistant professor, 1951-55; Vanderbilt University, Nashville, Tenn., associate professor, 1955-59, Buffington Professor of Church History, 1959-61; Lancaster Theological Seminary, Lancaster, Pa., professor of church history, 1961-64; Drew University, Madison, N.J., professor of church history, 1964—, dean of Graduate School, 1969—. Official Protestant observer, Vatican Council II, 1964. *Member:* American Society of Church History.

WRITINGS: *Liturgies of the Western Church,* Meridian, 1962; (with R. Howard Paine) *Book of Prayers for Church and Home,* United Church Press, 1962; (with Hendrikus Berkhof, Eduard Schweizer, and Howard G. Hageman) *Essays on the Heidelberg Catechism,* United Church Press, 1963; (editor with George H. Bricker) Philip Schaff, *The Principle of Protestantism,* United Church Press, 1964; (editor with Bricker) John W. Nevin, *The Mystical Presence,* United Church Press, 1965.

* * *

THOMPSON, Leonard Monteath 1916-

PERSONAL: Born March 6, 1916, in Cranborne, Dorset, England; son of Gerald Monteath (a clergyman) and Rhoda E. (Collins) Thompson; married Evelyne Betty White, February 9, 1940; children: Caroline Thompson Hickey, Jacqueline Thompson Sitterle. *Education:* Rhodes University, B.A., 1935, M.A., 1938; Oxford University, Rhodes Scholar, 1937, B.A., 1939, M.A., 1944. *Home:* 92 Northrop Rd., Woodbridge, Conn. 06525. *Office:* Department of History, Yale University, New Haven, Conn. 06520.

CAREER: University of Cape Town, Cape Town, South Africa, senior lecturer, 1946-54, associate professor, 1954-58, King George V Professor and head of department of history, 1958-61; University of California, Los Angeles, professor of history, 1961-68; Yale University, New Haven, Conn., professor of history, 1968—, director of Yale-Wesleyan Southern African Research Program, 1977—. Visiting Commonwealth Professor, Duke University, spring, 1961; Leverhulme visiting fellow, University of Sussex, 1968-69; visiting fellow, All Souls College, Oxford, 1978; Walter Prescott Webb Memorial Lecturer, University of Texas at Arlington, 1979. Consultant, Foreign Area Fellowship Program, 1962-64, 1966-67, and National Endowment for the Humanities, 1977—. *Military service:* Royal Navy, 1939-46; became lieutenant. *Member:* American Historical Association, African Studies Association (U.S.A.), African Studies Association (U.K.), South African Institute of Race Relations, American Academy of Political and Social Science. *Awards, honors:* D.Litt., Rhodes University, 1961; Fulbright-Hays fellow, 1964-65; Ford Foundation grant, 1974; Rockefeller Foundation fellow, 1979.

WRITINGS: The Cape Coloured Franchise, South African Institute of Race Relations, 1949; *Democracy in Multi-Racial Societies,* South African Institute of Race Relations, 1949; (editor with Albert Centlivres) *The Open Universities in South Africa,* Witwaterstand University Press, 1957; *The Unification of South Africa, 1902-1910,* Clarendon Press, 1960; *Politics in the Republic of South Africa,* Little, Brown, 1966; (editor) *African Societies in Southern Africa: Historical Studies,* Praeger, 1969; (editor with Monica Wilson) *The Oxford History of South Africa,* Oxford University Press, Volume I, 1969, Volume II, 1971; (editor with Richard Elphick and Inez Jarrick) *Southern African History before 1900: A Select Bibliography of Articles,* Hoover Institution, 1971; *Survival in Two Worlds: Moshoeshoe of Lesotho, 1786-1870,* Clarendon Press, 1975; (editor with Jeffrey Butler) *Change in Contemporary South Africa,* University of California Press, 1975; (with P. Curtin, S. Feierman, and J. Vansina) *African History,* Little, Brown, 1978; (editor with Howard Lamar) *The Frontier in History: North American and South African Comparisons,* Yale University Press, in press.

Contributor: Sydney Bailey, editor, *Parliamentary Government in the Commonwealth,* Hansard Society, 1951; Coenraad Beyers and others, editors, *Archives Year Book for South African History,* Government Printer, 1952; Louis Hartz, editor, *The Founding of New Societies,* Harcourt, 1964; Robin Winks, editor, *The Historiography of the British Empire-Commonwealth,* Duke University Press, 1966; Leo Kuper and M. G. Smith, editors, *Pluralism in Africa,* University of California Press, 1969; Prosser Gifford and William Roger Louis, editors, *France and Britain in Africa,* Yale University Press, 1971; H. W. van der Merwe and David Welsh, editors, *The Future of the University in Southern Africa,* David Philip, 1977; Gifford and Louis, editors, *The Transfer of Power in Africa,* Yale University Press, in press. Contributor to professional journals.

SIDELIGHTS: Leonard Thompson told *CA:* "I am partly an insider and partly an outsider in South Africa, having lived there for 25 years, but having spent my childhood in Great Britain, my war years in the Royal Navy, and my recent professional life in the United States. South Africa is a microcosm of humanity: with immense potential, but also a terrible burden of injustice and inequality. I hope my writings may contribute to knowledge of what South Africa is like and how it came that way."

* * *

THOMPSON, Vivian L(aubach) 1911-

PERSONAL: Born 1911, in Jersey City, N.J.; daughter of Harry J. and Letty B. (Lendrum) Laubach; married Daniel Thompson, 1951. *Education:* Columbia University, B.S., 1939, M.A., 1943; attended Maren Elwood School of Professional Writing, 1948; private study with Odessa Davenport in juvenile fiction, 1948-49. *Religion:* Episcopalian. *Home:* 936 Kumukoa St., Hilo, Hawaii 96720.

CAREER: Teacher in public schools of Nutley, N.J., Millburn, N.J., and Union, N.J., 1930-37, Ossining, N.Y., 1937-43, 1946-47, La Jolla, Calif., 1945-46, 1947-49, Paauilo, Hawaii, and Honolulu, Hawaii, 1949-51; free-lance writer, 1951—. Member of Library Advisory Commission (Hawaii); affiliated with Hawaii Island Girl Scout Council, 1951-61. *Military service:* U.S. Marine Corps, Women's Reserve, 1943-45, became second lieutenant. *Awards, honors:* Community Service award, Paauilo, Hawaii, 1961; received citation from New Jersey Association of Teachers of English, 1963, for *Sad Day, Glad Day;* received honorable mention, Hilo Community Players playwriting contest, 1979-80, for children's play "IWA the Crafty One."

WRITINGS: Camp-in-the-Yard (Junior Literary Guild selection), Holiday House, 1961; *The Horse That Liked Sandwiches,* Putnam, 1962; *Sad Day, Glad Day,* Holiday House, 1962; *Kimo Makes Music,* Golden Gate Junior Books, 1962; *Faraway Friends,* Holiday House, 1963; *Ah See and the Spooky House,* Golden Gate Junior Books, 1963; *George Washington,* Putnam, 1964; *Hawaiian Myths of Earth, Sea, and Sky,* Holiday House, 1966; *Keola's Hawaiian Donkey,* Golden Gate Junior Books, 1966; *Meet the Hawaiian Menehunes,* Petroglyph, 1967; *Hawaiian Legends of Tricksters and Riddlers,* Holiday House, 1969; *Maui-Full-of-Tricks,* Golden Gate Junior Books, 1970; *Hawaiian Tales of Heroes and Champions,* Holiday House, 1971; *Aukele the Fearless,* Golden Gate Junior Books, 1972. Also author of children's play "IWA the Crafty One." Contributor of short stories to children's magazines.

WORK IN PROGRESS: "Several upcoming titles in Houghton's Minibooks."

SIDELIGHTS: Vivian L. Thompson and her husband are the godparents of eight Oriental children, two of whom, Daniel and David Kim of Paauilo, inspired the plot of Mrs. Thompson's book, *Camp-in-the-Yard.* Thompson told *CA* that her book about moving, *Sad Day, Glad Day,* "has brought more letters from young readers than any of my other books. Moving day, apparently, is a universal bittersweet experience."

BIOGRAPHICAL/CRITICAL SOURCES: Hilo Tribune-Herald, August 13, 1961, September 10, 1970; *West Hawaii Today,* March 11, 1971.

* * *

THORNDIKE, Robert Ladd 1910-

PERSONAL: Born September 22, 1910, in Montrose, N.Y.; son of Edward Lee and Elizabeth (Moulton) Thorndike; married Dorothy Vernon Mann, 1933; children: Nancy Lee, Robert Mann, Virginia Vernon. *Education:* Wesleyan University, B.A., 1931; Columbia University, M.A., 1932, Ph.D., 1935. *Home:* Travis Lane, Montrose, N.Y. *Office:* 525 West 120th St., New York, N.Y.

CAREER: George Washington University, Washington, D.C., instructor, 1934-35, assistant professor, 1935-36; Columbia University, Teachers College, New York, N.Y., assistant professor, 1936-40, associate professor, 1940-48, professor of education, beginning 1948, professor emeritus, 1976—. *Military service:* U.S. Army Air Forces, 1942-46; became major. *Member:* American Psychological Association, American Statistical Association, Psychometric Society, Phi Beta Kappa, Sigma Xi.

WRITINGS: (Editor) *Research Problems and Techniques,* U.S. Government Printing Office, 1947; *Personnel Selection,* Wiley, 1949; (with Hagen) *Measurement and Evaluation in Psychology and Education,* Wiley, 1955, 4th edition, 1977; (with Hagen) *Ten Thousand Careers,* Wiley, 1959; (with Hagen) *Characteristics of Men Who Remained in and Left Teaching,* Teachers College, Columbia University, 1961; (with Richard Rowe) *Virgin Islands Intelligence Testing Survey,* Teachers College, Columbia University, 1963; *The Concepts of Over- and Underachievement,* Bureau of Publications, Teachers College, Columbia University, 1963; (editor) William H. Angoff and others, *Educational Measurement,* 2nd edition (Thorndike was not associated with earlier edition), American Council on Education, 1971; *Reading Comprehension in Fifteen Countries: An Empirical Study,* Wiley, 1973. Also author of *The Human Factor in Accidents,* 1951. Contributor of articles and reviews to education and psychology journals.

* * *

THORNE, Jim 1922-

PERSONAL: Born 1922, in Milwaukee, Wisconsin; divorced; children: Jeffrey, Gary, Marc. *Education:* University of California, Los Angeles, special courses in creative writing and drama.

CAREER: Newspaper reporter in California; pilot and executive pilot with Civil Air Patrol, Palm Springs, Calif.; motion picture actor, with roles in such films as "Beware My Lovely," "Letter from Home," and "Day before Tomorrow"; radio commercial announcer; founder and president, Adventure, Inc. (underwater film production company), 1957—; oceanographer and lecturer, 1972—. Has acted in many industrial films and short subjects and has appeared on television programs, including "Jack Paar Show," "Captain Kangaroo," and "Merv Griffin"; skin diver and underwater photographer; toured the United States lecturing and showing two of his films. *Military service:* U.S. Army Reserve, World War II; became major. *Member:* Adventurers Club.

WRITINGS: Occupation: Adventure (Literary Guild selection for young adults), Doubleday, 1962; *Adventures Undersea,* Walker & Co., 1965; *2000 Years under the Sea,* Walker & Co., 1965; *Red Road through Africa,* Putnam, 1966; *Guide to Adventure,* Crowell, 1966; *The Underwater World,* Crowell, 1969; *Adventurer's Guide to North America,* Bobbs-Merrill, 1974; *The White Hand of Athene* (novel), Pinnacle Books, 1974. Contributor of adventure stories to magazines.

WORK IN PROGRESS: Ghost Ships.

SIDELIGHTS: Jim Thorne was part of a South Pole expedition in 1961 when he made an historic dive under the Antarctic ice as part of Operation Deepfreeze. Since then, he has taken part in diving expeditions to Greece and Puerto Rico. He is the discoverer of the underwater city of Emporium off the Greek island of Melos. Thorne was the first non-Mexican to successfully accomplish the 136-foot dive from the famous diving cliff at Acapulco, Mexico, in February, 1965. *Avocational interests:* Judo (holds brown belt), yoga, fencing.

* * *

THORNTON, James W., Jr. 1908-

PERSONAL: Born April 23, 1908, in Ackley, Iowa; son of James William and Anna Marcia (Harney) Thornton; married Cyrilla Dolan, 1933; children: James William III. *Education:* Stanford University, A.B., 1930, M.A., 1934, Ph.D., 1941. *Home:* 283 Del Mesa Carmel, Carmel, Calif. 93921.

CAREER: Teacher in California, 1933-38; University of Minnesota, General College, Minneapolis, acting assistant director, 1938-40; Sequoia Union High School, Redwood City, Calif., assistant superintendent, 1940-47; Orange Coast College, Costa Mesa, Calif., vice-president, 1947-57; Florida State University, Tallahassee, professor, 1957-58; San Jose State College (now University), San Jose, Calif., professor, 1958-70; Honolulu Community College, Honolulu, Hawaii, provost, 1970-72. Chairman of Redwood City Chapter of American Red Cross, 1942-45. *Member:* Association for Higher Education, American Association of Junior Colleges, National Education Association, Phi Delta Kappa, Kiwanis Club (Newport Harbor; president, 1950-52).

WRITINGS: The Community Junior College, Wiley, 1960, 3rd edition, 1972; (with James W. Brown) *New Media in Higher Education,* National Education Association, 1963; (with Brown) *College Teaching,* McGraw, 1964, 2nd edition, 1971; (with John T. Wahlquist) *State Colleges and Universities,* Library for Applied Research in Education, 1964; (editor with John Wright) *Secondary School Curriculum,* C. E. Merrill, 1964; (with Brown) *Going to College in California,* Fearon, 1965; (with Brown) *New Media and College Teaching,* National Education Association, 1968. Contributor to education journals.

* * *

THORWALD, Juergen 1916-
(Heinz Bongartz)

PERSONAL: Original name, Heinz Bongartz, pseudonym, Juergen Thorwald, adopted as name, 1949; born October 28, 1916, in Solingen, Germany; son of Jakob (a schoolteacher) and Auguste (Hartmann) Bongartz; married Hanna Seen, April 12, 1942 (divorced, 1948); married Inge Wetzel (a physical therapist), October 4, 1955; children: (first marriage) Brigitte; (second marriage) Robert Kim. *Education:* Attended University of Cologne, 1935-40. *Politics:* None. *Religion:* Protestant. *Home:* Casa California, Via Bellavista 8, CH 6977 Suvigliana, Switzerland; and 24380 Mulholland Highway, Calabasas, Calif. 91302.

CAREER: *Christ und Welt* (a weekly newspaper), Stuttgart, Germany, editor, 1947-52; author, 1952—. *Military service:* German Navy, 1940. *Member:* P.E.N. (Club Fuerstentum Liechtenstein). *Awards, honors:* Edgar Allan Poe special award, 1966; award from the International Organization in Forensic Medicine, 1979.

WRITINGS: *Es begann an der Weichsel* (also see below), Steingrueben, 1950; *Das Ende an der Elbe* (also see below), Steingrueben, 1950; *Flight in the Winter: Russia Conquers* (one volume condensation and translation of *Es begann an der Weichsel* and *Das Ende an der Elbe* by Fred Wieck), Pantheon, 1951, published as *Defeat in the East: Russia Conquers, January to May 1945,* Ballantine, 1959; *Die grosse Flucht* (one volume edition of *Es begann an der Weichsel* and *Das Ende an der Elbe*), Steingrueben, 1962, revised edition, Droemer, 1979; *Die ungeklaerten Faelle,* Steingrueben, 1950; *Wen sie verderben wollen: Bericht des grossen Verrats,* Steingrueben, 1952, revised edition published as *Die Illusion,* Droemer, 1973, translation by Richard Winston and Clara Winston published as *The Illusion: Soviet Soldiers in Hitler's Armies,* Harcourt, 1974; *Das Jahrhundert der Chirurgen: Nach den Papieren meines Grossvaters, des Chirurgen H. St. Hartmann* (also see below), Steingrueben, 1956, translation published as *The Century of the Surgeon* (*Reader's Digest* Condensed Book), Pantheon, 1957; *Das Weltreich der Chirurgen: Nach den Papieren meines Grossvaters, des Chirurgen P. St. Hartmann* (also see below), Steingrueben, 1958, translation by R. Winston and C. Winston published as *The Triumph of Surgery* (*Reader's Digest* Condensed Book), Pantheon, 1960.

Die Entlassung: Das Ende des Chirurgen Ferdinand Sauerbruch, Droemer, 1960, translation by R. Winston and C. Winston published as *The Dismissal: The Last Days of Ferdinand Sauerbruch, Surgeon,* Thames & Hudson, 1961, published as *The Dismissal: The Last Days of Ferdinand Sauerbruch,* Pantheon, 1962; *Macht und Geheimnis der fruehen Aerzte: Aegypten, Babylonien, Indien, China, Mexiko, Peru,* translation by R. Winston and C. Winston published as *Science and Secrets of Early Medicine: Egypt, Mesopotamia, India, China, Mexico, Peru,* Thames & Hudson, 1962, Harcourt, 1963; *Das Jahrhundert der Detektive: Weg und Abenteuer der Kriminalistik,* Droemer, 1964, translation by R. Winston and C. Winston published as *The Century of the Detective* (*Reader's Digest* Condensed Book), Harcourt, 1965 (translation published in England in three parts by Thames & Hudson as *The Marks of Cain,* 1965, *Dead Men Tell Tales,* 1966, and *Proof of Poison,* 1966); *Die Geschichte der Chirurgie* (one volume edition of *Das Jahrhundert der Chirurgen* and *Das Weltreich der Chirurgen*), Steingrueben, 1965; *Die Stunde der Detektive: Werden und Welten der Kriminalistik,* Droemer, 1966, translation by R. Winston and C. Winston published as *Crime and Science: The New Frontier in Criminology,* Harcourt, 1967; *Die Traum-Oase (Beverly Hills),* Droemer, 1968.

Die Patienten, Droemer, 1971, translation by R. Winston and C. Winston published as *The Patients,* Harcourt, 1972; *Das Gewuerz: Die Saga der Juden in Amerika, Teil I,* Droemer, 1978; *Der Mann auf dem Kliff* (novel), Droemer, 1980.

Under name Heinz Bongartz: *Luftkrieg im Westen: Fluege, Kaempfe, Siege deutscher Flieger,* W. Kohler, 1940; *Luftmacht Deutschland: Aufstieg, kanpf und sieg,* Essener verlaganstalt, 1941; *Seemacht Deutschland: Wiederaufstieg. Kampf und Sieg,* Essener verlaganstalt, 1941.

Contributor to *Speigel, Stern, Zeit, Weltwoche,* and *Reader's Digest.*

WORK IN PROGRESS: A translation of *Die grosse Flucht;* the second volume of *Das Gewuerz: Die Saga der Juden in Amerika,* entitled *Die Wenigen und die Maechtigen: Die Saga der Juden in Amerika, Teil II;* a history of gynecology, *Die Frauenaerzte;* a personal history of the author's generation in Germany and Europe during the time of Hitler and after and the problem of human and intellectual liberation, *Jahrgang 1916* (title means "Generation of 1916").

SIDELIGHTS: Juergen Thorwald told *CA* that he adopted his pseudonym for the first volume of *Es begann an der Weichsel* (*Flight in the Winter*) in order to avoid harassment in Soviet occupied Germany while doing research for the second volume (*Das Ende an der Elbe*) and *Wen sie Verderben wollen.* The popularity of the first books written under that pseudonym led him to use it as a legal name for himself and his second family. They moved to Switzerland for the first time in 1955, and then after some visits to the United States, they moved to California. While his wife and son choose California as their permanent residence, Thorwald has shifted between California and his studio in Switzerland ever since.

* * *

THURMAN, Judith 1946-

PERSONAL: Born October 28, 1946, in New York, N.Y.; daughter of William A. (a lawyer) and Alice (a teacher; maiden name, Meisner) Thurman; married Jonathan David (a cinematographer). *Education:* Brandeis University, A.B., 1967. *Residence:* New York, N.Y.

CAREER: Writer and poet in New York, N.Y., 1972—. Adjunct lecturer at Brooklyn College of the City University of New York, 1973—. *Awards, honors:* National Endowment for the Humanities fellow, 1980.

WRITINGS: *Putting My Coat On* (poems), Covent Garden Press (London), 1972; (editor with Lilian Moore) *To See the World Afresh,* Atheneum, 1974; *I Became Alone* (essays), Atheneum, 1975; *Flashlight* (poems), Atheneum, 1976; *Lost and Found* (juvenile), Atheneum, 1978; *The Magic Lantern: How Movies Got to Move,* Atheneum, 1979; (contributor of translations) *Penguin Women Poets,* Penguin, 1979. Poems represented in anthologies, including *The New York Times Book of Poems,* edited by Thomas Lask, Macmillan, 1970, and *The Logic of Poetry,* edited by Briggs and Monaco, McGraw, 1974. Contributor to *Ms, New York Times,* and *Shenandoah.*

WORK IN PROGRESS: A biography of Isak Dinesen, for St. Martin's.

SIDELIGHTS: Judith Thurman told *CA:* "My energy as a writer is 'feminist,' but my poetry has no consistent bias. Poems are occasions—I think they exist as much outside as inside a poet." Thurman speaks four languages.

* * *

THYGERSON, Alton L(uie) 1940-

PERSONAL: Surname is pronounced *Thur*-ger-son; born April 23, 1940, in Pampa, Tex.; son of Luie Snow (an electrician) and Callie (Spradlin) Thygerson; married Ardith Moss, December 26, 1964; children: Alton Scott, Michael Snow, Steven Moss, Whitney, Matthew Luie, Justin S. *Education:* Brigham Young University, B.S., 1962, M.H.Ed., 1965, Ed.D., 1969; graduate study at San Jose State College (now University), 1965, California State College (now University), Hayward, 1966, and University of Utah, 1976. *Religion:* Church of Jesus Christ of Latter-day Saints. *Home:* 3300 Mohican Lane, Provo, Utah 84601. *Office:* Department of

Health and Safety, 229-J Richards Bldg., Brigham Young University, Provo, Utah 84602.

CAREER: High School teacher of health and safety in San Jose, Calif., 1963-65; Chabot College, Hayward, Calif., instructor in health, 1965-67; Brigham Young University, Provo, Utah, instructor, 1967-69, assistant professor, 1969-71, associate professor, 1971-76, professor of health and safety, 1976—. *Member:* National Safety Council, American Driver and Traffic Safety Association, American Association for Health, Physical Education and Recreation, American Academy of Safety Education (fellow). *Awards, honors:* Radio and Television Annual Safety Award from KSL, 1972.

WRITINGS: Student Manual on Utah Driving Rules and Regulations, Brigham Young University Press, 1968; (editor with Brent Hafen and Ray Petersen) *First Aid: Contemporary Practices and Principles,* Burgess, 1972; *Safety: Principles, Instruction, and Readings,* Prentice-Hall, 1972, 2nd edition, 1976; *Accidents and Disasters: Causes and Countermeasures,* Prentice-Hall, 1977; *Study Guide for First Aid Practices,* Prentice-Hall, 1978; *Disaster Survival Handbook,* Brigham Young University Press, 1979; *First Aid and Medical Self-Help,* Prentice-Hall, 1980. Author of weekly column, "The Safe Life." Contributor to *Journal of Traffic Safety Education, Journal of Safety Research, Health Education,* and *Improving University and College Teaching.*

AVOCATIONAL INTERESTS: Birding, reading, racketball, jogging, and spectator sports.

* * *

TIFFT, Ellen

PERSONAL: Born in Elmira, N.Y.; daughter of Halsey and Julia (Day) Sayles; married Bela Tifft (a lawyer), July 16, 1938; children: Wilton, John, Nicol. *Education:* Attended Elmira College, 1936-38. *Politics:* Democrat. *Religion:* Society of Friends (Quakers). *Home address:* Box 312, R.D. 3, East Hill, Elmira, N.Y. 14901.

CAREER: Poet and writer. *Member:* Poetry Society of America.

WRITINGS—Poems: *A Door in a Wall,* Hors Commerce Press, 1966; *The Kissed Cold Kite,* Hors Commerce Press, 1968; *The Live-Long Day,* Charas Press, 1972. Work is included in anthologies, including *The Best Poems of 1941,* edited by Thomas Moult, Harcourt, 1942, *Abraxas 5 Anthology,* edited by James Bertolino, 1973, *Women Writing about the Creativity of Life,* edited by Toni Ortner-Zimmerman, Connections, 1979, and *Christmas in Texas,* edited by H. Williams and V. Abercrombie, Brown Rabbit Press. Contributor of poems and short stories to literature journals, including *Western Review, Transatlantic Review, Saturday Evening Post,* and *New Yorker.*

WORK IN PROGRESS: The Platform, a novel.

SIDELIGHTS: Ellen Tifft wrote to *CA:* "Poems, short stories, and novels have been my greatest joys in life. The great writers have helped me discover myself and others around me. Long ago I decided writing was for me. I work at it six days a week. I hope I can spark some inner feeling in someone so that he or she can do more of what he or she wants and needs to do. My work is a reaching out and a paying back." Tifft has made a television film reading from her own work.

* * *

TILMAN, Robert O(liver) 1929-

PERSONAL: Born July 21, 1929, in Caruthersville, Mo.; son of Alfred O. and Jeanette (Powell) Tilman; married Jo Huddleston, December 19, 1954. *Education:* Memphis State University, B.S., 1957; Duke University, M.A., 1959, Ph.D., 1961. *Home:* 2800 Wycliff Rd., Raleigh, N.C. 27607. *Office:* 3136 D. H. Hill Library, North Carolina State University, Raleigh, N.C. 27650.

CAREER: National Security Agency, Washington, D.C., intelligence research analyst, 1954-56; Duke University, Commonwealth Studies Center, Durham, N.C., executive secretary, 1960-62; Tulane University, New Orleans, La., assistant professor of political science, 1962-65; Yale University, New Haven, Conn., assistant professor, 1965-67, associate professor of political science, 1967-70; Columbia University, New York, N.Y., senior research associate, 1970-71; North Carolina State University at Raleigh, professor of political science and dean of School of Humanities and Social Sciences, 1971—. Visiting research professor of politics, University of the Philippines, 1969-70; visiting fellow, Institute of Southeast Asian Studies, Singapore, 1970. Member of executive committee, Southeast Asia Development Advisory Group, Agency for International Development, U.S. Department of State, 1965-68; member of joint committee on Asia, American Council of Learned Societies, 1968-69; member of political science advisory panel, National Science Foundation, 1971-73; Southeast Asia team leader, Goals for Mankind Project, Club of Rome, 1974-77. *Military service:* U.S. Army, 1951-54; became sergeant.

MEMBER: Association for Asian Studies (member of Southeast Asia regional council, 1971-74; vice-president, 1972-73; president of Southeastern Regional Conference, 1973-74), Asia Society (chairman of Malaysia council, 1968-69), Southern Political Science Association, Phi Beta Kappa, Phi Kappa Phi. *Awards, honors:* American Society of International Law fellowship, 1963; American Council of Learned Societies fellowship, 1964; National Science Foundation senior fellowship, 1969-70; Yale University senior faculty fellowship, 1969-70; senior scholar fellowship, Columbia University Southern Asian Institute, 1970-71; American Philosophical Society fellowship, 1974.

WRITINGS: (Editor with Taylor Cole) *The Nigerian Political Scene,* Duke University Press, 1962; *Bureaucratic Transition in Malaya,* Duke University Press, 1964; (compiler) *International Biographical Directory of Southeast Asia Specialists,* Interuniversity Southeast Asia Committee, Association for Asian Studies, 1969; *Malaysian Foreign Policy,* Research Analysis Corp., 1969; (editor and contributor) *Man, State, and Society in Contemporary Southeast Asia,* Praeger, 1969; *In Quest of Unity: The Centralization Theme in Malaysian Federal-State Relations, 1957-75,* Institute of Southeast Asian Studies, 1976.

Contributor: Ralph Braibanti and J. J. Spengler, editors, *Administration and Economic Development in India,* Duke University Press, 1963; Wang Gungwu, editor, *Malaysia,* Praeger, 1964; Braibanti, editor, *Bureaucratic Systems Emergent from the British Imperial Tradition,* Duke University Press, 1966; Ludo Rocher, editor, *Education et developpement dans le sud-est de l'Asie,* Free University of Brussels, 1967; John D. Montgomery and Albert O. Hirschman, editors, *Public Policy,* Volume XVI, Harvard University Press, 1967; Robert I. Crane, editor, *Southern Asia,* Southern Regional Educational Board, 1968; Wayne Wilcox, Leo Rose, and Gavin Boyd, editors, *Asia and the International System,* Winthrop, 1972; Ervin Laszlo and others, editors, *Goals for Mankind: A Report to the Club of Rome,* Dutton, 1977; Laszlo and others, editors, *Goals in a Global Society,* Volume II, Pergamon, 1977.

Contributor to *American Political Science Review, Journal of Asian Studies,* and other professional journals. Member of international editorial advisory board, *Southeast Asia,* 1970—, and *Asian Survey,* 1979—.

WORK IN PROGRESS: Research on problems of political leadership succession in the Association of South East Asian Nations (ASEAN) region in the 1980s.

* * *

TOBE, John Harold 1907-1979

PERSONAL: Born January 18, 1907, in Toronto, Ontario, Canada; son of Solomon and Eva Rosa (Moscna) Tobe; married Rose Bolter, 1929 (deceased); married Adele Lockstein, November 16, 1968; children: (first marriage) Estelle Sharp, Allen, Victoria Wright, Stephen. *Politics:* Liberal. *Home:* R.R.1, Rice Rd., Duncan, British Columbia, Canada V9L 1M3. *Office:* Provoker Press, Lakeshore Rd., St. Catherines, Ontario, Canada L2R 7C9.

CAREER: Nurseryman and seedman, Tobe's Seeds Ltd., St. Catherines, Ontario; publisher of *The Provoker* and of books on natural health, Provoker Press, St. Catherines. Lecturer on horticulture, travel, and health. *Member:* Canadian Authors Association, Royal Horticultural Society (fellow), Garden Writers Association of America, Lions Club (past president, local club).

WRITINGS: Growing Flowers, MacLeod, 1956; *Garden Glimpses,* Thorsons, 1957; *Romance in the Garden,* MacLeod, 1958; *Hunza: Adventures in a Land of Paradise,* Rodale, 1960.

All published by Provoker Press: *Your Prostate,* 1967; *Proven Herbal Remedies,* 1969; *The "No Cook" Book,* 1969; *I Found Shangri-La,* 1970; *Security from Five Acres,* 1971; *The Golden Treasury of Natural Health,* 1973; *Cataract, Glaucoma, and Other Eye Disorders,* 1973; *How to Prevent and Gain Remission from Cancer,* 1975; *How to Conquer Arthritis,* 1976; *The Miracles of Live Juices and Raw Foods,* 1977; *Constipation: Its Causes, Control, and Treatment,* 1979.

Also author of several monographs. Contributor of articles to periodicals.

SIDELIGHTS: John Tobe told *CA:* "My chief interests are the land, books, and the laws of natural living. I have traveled around the world but have not seen all of it, so I am going to keep going. I try to map out a new course of adventure every year. I am a true maverick. I have never been branded and I never intend to allow myself to be branded."

* * *

TOBIN, Richard Lardner 1910-

PERSONAL: Born August 9, 1910, in Chicago, Ill.; son of Richard Griswold and Anna (Lardner) Tobin; married Sylvia Cleveland, 1937; children: Mark Cleveland. *Education:* University of Michigan, B.A., 1932. *Politics:* Republican. *Religion:* Episcopalian. *Home:* 935-A, Heritage Village, Southbury, Conn. 06488. *Office:* Department of Journalism, Ernie Pyle Bldg., Indiana University, Bloomington, Ind. 47401.

CAREER: Reporter in Niles, Mich., and South Bend, Ind., 1927-28; *New York Herald Tribune,* New York City, reporter, 1932-36, assistant city editor, 1936-1942, director of radio news broadcasting, 1942-44, war correspondent, 1944-45, radio-television news director, 1946-53; director of news, American Broadcasting Co., 1945-46; national public relations director, Citizens for Eisenhower, 1955-56; Campbell Soup Co., Camden, N.J., assistant to president, 1956-58; *Saturday Review,* New York City, communications editor, 1960-71, managing editor, 1961-68, associate publisher, 1968-71, executive editor, 1971-77; Indiana University at Bloomington, Riley Professor of Journalism, 1978—. Assistant professor at Pulitzer School of Journalism, Columbia University, 1940-52. Public lecturer on current events.

WRITINGS: Invasion Journal, Dutton, 1944; *Golden Opinions,* Dutton, 1948; *The Center of the World,* Dutton, 1951; *Decisions of Destiny,* World Publishing, 1961. Editor, *The Golden Age: Saturday Review's Fiftieth Anniversary Reader,* 1974. Contributor of articles to national magazines, including *Reader's Digest, Coronet, New Yorker,* and *Saturday Review.*

* * *

TODD, Janet M(argaret) 1942-

PERSONAL: Born September 10, 1942, in Wales; daughter of George and Elizabeth (Jones) Dakin; married Aaron R. Todd (a professor of mathematics), December 21, 1966; children: Julian, Clara. *Education:* Cambridge University, B.A., 1964; University of Leeds, diploma, 1968; University of Florida, Ph.D., 1971. *Office:* Department of English, Douglass College, Rutgers University, New Brunswick, N.J. 08903.

CAREER: School teacher in Cape Coast, Ghana, 1964-65; University College of Cape Coast, Cape Coast, Ghana, lecturer in English, 1965-66; English teacher in Bawku, Ghana, 1966-67; University of Puerto Rico, Mayaguez, assistant professor of English, 1972-74; Rutgers University, Douglass College, New Brunswick, N.J., assistant professor, 1974-78, associate professor of English, 1978—. *Member:* Modern Language Association of America, Women's Caucus of Modern Languages, American Society of Eighteenth Century Studies, Jane Austen Society.

WRITINGS: In Adam's Garden: A Study of John Clare's Pre-Asylum Poetry, University of Florida Press, 1973; *Mary Wollstonecraft: An Annotated Bibliography,* Garland Publishing, 1976; (editor) *A Wollstonecraft Anthology,* Indiana University Press, 1977; *Women's Friendship in Literature,* Columbia University Press, 1980. Contributor to *Philological Quarterly, Phylon, Atenea,* and *British Studies Monitor.* Editor, *Women and Literature;* former editor, *Mary Wollstonecraft Journal.*

WORK IN PROGRESS: Mary Wollstonecraft, a biography; a study of the vampire in literature; a critical study of women novelists of the late eighteenth century.

SIDELIGHTS: Janet Todd told *CA:* "I am concerned with bringing women writers into the mainstream of English literary history and of reevaluating established literature according to a feminist perspective. I am especially interested in the late eighteenth and early nineteenth century because so many of our cultural attitudes were then being formed."

BIOGRAPHICAL/CRITICAL SOURCES: Times Literary Supplement, June 20, 1980.

* * *

TOMASSON, Richard F(inn) 1928-

PERSONAL: Born May 28, 1928, in Brooklyn, N.Y.; son of Solfest (comptroller of U.S. Lines) and Sigrun (Egge) Tomasson; married Nancy Lensen, August 16, 1958 (divorced, 1972); children: Lars, Leif, Christopher. *Education:* Gettysburg College, B.A., 1949; University of Illinois, M.A., 1953; University of Pennsylvania, Ph.D., 1960. *Politics:* Democrat. *Religion:* None. *Home:* 1602 Sigma Chi Rd. N.E., Albuquerque, N.M. 87106. *Office:* Department of Sociology, University of New Mexico, Albuquerque, N.M. 87131.

CAREER: Gettysburg College, Gettysburg, Pa., instructor in sociology, 1952-53; University of Pennsylvania, Philadelphia, instructor in sociology, 1955-58; Butler University, Indianapolis, Ind., instructor in sociology, 1958-59; Miami University, Scripps Foundation for Research in Population Problems, Oxford, Ohio, research assistant, 1959-61; University of Illinois at Urbana—Champaign, 1961-67, began as assistant professor, became associate professor of sociology; University of New Mexico, Albuquerque, 1967—, began as associate professor, currently professor of sociology, chairman of department, 1967-73. Visiting instructor in sociology, Princeton University, spring, 1958; Fulbright lecturer in sociology, Uppsala University, 1963-64. *Military service:* U.S. Army, Army Security Agency, 1953-55; became lieutenant.

MEMBER: International Union for the Scientific Study of Population, American Sociological Association, Population Association of America, Society for the Advancement of Scandinavian Study (president, 1977-79), Comparative Interdisciplinary Studies Society (chairman, 1980-81). *Awards, honors:* Grant from Population Council of New York, N.Y., 1962, for study of factors associated with family size; Fulbright research scholar, Sweden, 1964-65, Iceland, summer, 1969; National Endowment for the Humanities senior fellowship, 1970-71.

WRITINGS: (Contributor) Bernard Farber, editor, *Kinship and Family Organization,* Wiley, 1966; (contributor) Edgar A. Schuler and others, editors, *Readings in Sociology,* Crowell, 1967; (contributor) Seymour M. Lipset and Philip G. Altbach, editors, *Students in Revolt,* Houghton, 1969; *Sweden: Prototype of Modern Society,* Random House, 1970; (contributor) Robert Hybels, editor, *Social Problems,* Holbrook Press, 1970; (translator from the Swedish with Greta Frankel, and contributor) Herbert Tingsten, *The Swedish Social Democrats,* Bedminster, 1973; (contributor) Lewis Bowman and G. E. Boynton, editors, *Political Behavior and Public Opinion,* Prentice-Hall, 1974; (editor) *Comparative Social Research* (annual), JAI Press, 1978—; *Iceland: The First New Society,* University of Minnesota Press, 1979. Contributor to conferences. Contributor of more than seventy-five articles and reviews in sociology to journals and magazines in the United States and abroad, including *Harper's, Journal of Politics, Daedalus, Social Compass, Sociology of Education, Comparative Studies in Society and History, Social Biology, Scandinavian Studies,* and *Social Forces.*

WORK IN PROGRESS: A study of the making of social policy in Sweden; a study of the comparative method of James Bryce.

* * *

TRASK, David F(rederic) 1929-

PERSONAL: Born May 15, 1929, in Erie, Pa.; son of Hugh Archie and Ruth (Miller) Trask; married Roberta Kirsch, 1959 (divorced July, 1964); married Elizabeth Marie Brooks, February 6, 1965; children: (first marriage) Noel Hugh, Amanda Ruth. *Education:* Wesleyan University, B.A., 1951; Harvard University, A.M., 1952, Ph.D., 1958. *Home:* 3100 Connecticut Ave. N.W., Apt. 307, Washington, D.C. 20008. *Office:* Office of the Historian, U.S. State Department, Washington, D.C.

CAREER: Boston University, Boston, Mass., instructor in political economy, 1955-58; Wesleyan University, Middletown, Conn., 1958-62, began as instructor, became assistant professor of history; University of Nebraska at Lincoln, assistant professor, 1962-63, associate professor of history, 1963-66; State University of New York at Stony Brook, Long Island, N.Y., 1966-76, began as associate professor, became professor of history, chairman of department, 1969-74; U.S. State Department, Office of the Historian, Washington, D.C., director, 1976—. Visiting professor, Naval War College, 1974-75. Member, National Historic Publications and Records Commission, 1976—. *Military service:* U.S. Army, Infantry, 1952-54; became lieutenant. *Member:* American Historical Association, Organization of American Historians, Society of Historians of American Foreign Relations (member of board of directors, 1973-75), National Association for the Advancement of Colored People (president, Portland-Middletown branch, 1960-61), United Nations Association of the United States of America (president, Lincoln, Neb. branch, 1965), Phi Beta Kappa, Phi Alpha Theta. *Awards, honors:* Ford Foundation grant; Danforth Foundation faculty research grant; University of Nebraska faculty summer grant.

WRITINGS: (Compiler with John C. Rule and others) *A Select Bibliography for Students of History,* [Cambridge], 1958; *The United States in the Supreme War Council: American War Aims and Inter-Allied Strategy, 1917-1918,* Wesleyan University Press, 1961, reprinted, Greenwood Press, 1978; *General Tasker Howard Bliss and the "Sessions of the World," 1919,* American Philosophical Society, 1966; (compiler with Michael C. Meyer and Roger R. Trask) *A Bibliography of United States-Latin American Relations since 1810,* University of Nebraska Press, 1968; *Victory without Peace: American Foreign Relations in the Twentieth Century,* Wiley, 1968; (editor) *World War I at Home: Readings on American Life, 1914-1920,* Wiley, 1969; *Captains and Cabinets: Anglo-American Naval Relations, 1917-1918,* University of Missouri Press, 1972; (with Samuel F. Wells, Jr. and Robert H. Ferrell) *The Ordeal of World Power: American Diplomacy since 1909,* Little, Brown, 1975. Author of "American History, 1900-1961," in *Collier's Encyclopedia,* 1962; contributor to *Encyclopaedia Britannica* and professional journals. Member of editorial board, *Journal of American History,* 1973-76.

* * *

TRESSELT, Alvin 1916-

PERSONAL: Surname is pronounced *Treh*-selt; born September 30, 1916, in Passaic, N.J.; son of Alvin and Elizabeth Ellen (Thaller) Tresselt; married Blossom Budney (a writer of children's books), April 9, 1949; children: Ellen Victoria, India Rachel. *Education:* Graduate of high school in Passaic. *Politics:* Democrat. *Home:* R.D. 3, West Redding Conn. 06896.

CAREER: Held a variety of jobs, including working in a defense plant in Connecticut, 1934-46; B. Altman & Co., New York City, 1946-52, began as interior display designer, became advertising copywriter; *Humpty Dumpty's Magazine,* New York City, editor, 1952-65; Parents' Magazine Press, New York City, editor, 1966-67, executive editor and vice-president, 1967-74; free-lance writer and editor, 1974—; Institute of children's Literature, Redding Ridge, Conn., currently instructor. *Awards, honors:* Caldecott Medal, American Library Association, 1948, for *White Snow, Bright Snow;* first prize in picture-book division, *New York Herald Tribune* Children's Spring Book Festival, 1949, for *Bonnie*

Bess, the Weathervane Horse; Irma Simonton Black Award, Bank Street College of Education, 1973, for *The Dead Tree.*

WRITINGS—All juveniles: *The Wind and Peter,* Oxford University Press, 1948; *Little Lost Squirrel,* Grosset, 1950; *The Smallest Elephant in the World,* Knopf, 1959; *An Elephant Is Not a Cat,* Parents' Magazine Press, 1962; *How Far Is Far?,* Parents' Magazine Press, 1964; *A Thousand Lights and Fireflies,* Parents' Magazine Press, 1965; *The Old Man and the Tiger,* Grosset, 1967; *The Fox Who Traveled,* Grosset, 1968; *Stories from the Bible,* Coward, 1971; *The Dead Tree,* Parents' Magazine Press, 1972.

All published by Lothrop: *Rain Drop Splash,* 1946; *Johnny Maple Leaf,* 1948; *White Snow, Bright Snow,* 1948; *Bonnie Bess, the Weathervane Horse,* 1949, reprinted, Parents' Magazine Press, 1970; *Sun Up,* 1949; *Follow the Wind,* 1950; *Hi, Mister Robin,* 1950; *Autumn Harvest,* 1951; *The Rabbit Story,* 1952; *Follow the Road,* 1953; *A Day with Daddy,* 1953; *I Saw the Sea Come In,* 1954; *Wake Up, Farm!,* 1955; *Wake Up, City!,* 1956; *The Frog in the Well,* 1958; *Timothy Robbins Climbs the Mountain,* 1960; *Under the Trees and Through the Grass,* 1962; *Hide and Seek Fog,* 1965; *The World in the Candy Egg,* 1967; *It's Time Now!,* 1969; *The Beaver Pond,* 1970; *What Did You Leave Behind?,* 1978.

Adaptor; all based on folktales; all published by Parents' Magazine Press: *The Mitten: An Old Ukranian Folktale,* 1964; *The Tears of the Dragon,* 1967; (with Nancy Cleaver) *Legend of the Willow Plate,* 1968; *The Crane Maiden,* 1968; *Helpful Mr. Bear,* 1968; *Ma Lien and the Magic Brush,* 1968; *The Witch's Magic Cloth,* 1969; *How Rabbit Tricked His Friends,* 1969; *The Rolling Rice Ball,* 1969; *The Fisherman under the Sea,* 1969; *Eleven Hungry Cats,* 1970; *A Sparrow's Magic,* 1970; *Gengorah and the Thunder God,* 1970; *The Land of Lost Buttons,* 1970; *The Hare and the Bear and Other Stories,* 1971; *Ogre and the Bride,* 1971; *Lum Fu and the Golden Mountain,* 1971; *The Little Mouse Who Tarried,* 1971; *Wonder Fish from the Sea,* 1971; *The Little Green Man,* 1972; *The Nutcracker,* 1974.

SIDELIGHTS: Alvin Tresselt's books have sold over one million copies. A collection of his original manuscripts form a part of the Kerlan Collection at the University of Minnesota. *Avocational interests:* Antiques, architecture, organic gardening, music, ecology, travel.

BIOGRAPHICAL/CRITICAL SOURCES: Saturday Review, February 18, 1967; *Christian Science Monitor,* May 4, 1967; *New York Times Book Review,* April 14, 1968, May 7, 1972; *Book World,* May 5, 1968; Lee Bennett Hopkins, *Books Are by People,* Citation, 1969.

* * *

TREVOR, (Lucy) Meriol 1919-

PERSONAL: Born April 15, 1919, in London, England; daughter of Arthur Prescott and Lucy (Dimmock) Trevor. *Education:* St. Hugh's College, Oxford, B.A., 1942. *Religion:* Roman Catholic. *Home:* 70 Pulteney St., Bath BA2 4DL, England. *Agent:* Harold Ober Associates, Inc., 40 East 49th St., New York, N.Y. 10017.

CAREER: Author. Relief worker, United Nations Relief and Rehabilitation Administration, Italy, 1946-47.

WRITINGS—Novels, except as indicated: *The Last of Britain,* Macmillan (London), 1956; *The New People,* Macmillan, 1957; *Midsummer, Midwinter* (poem), Hand and Flower Press, 1957; *A Narrow Place,* Macmillan, 1958; *Shadows and Images,* Macmillan, 1960, McKay, 1962; *The City of the World,* Dent, 1970; *The Holy Images,* Dent, 1971; *The Two Kingdoms,* Constable, 1973; *The Fortunate Marriage,* Dutton, 1976; *The Civil Prisoners,* Dutton, 1977; *The Wanton Fires,* Dutton, 1979.

Published by Hodder & Stoughton: *The Fugitives,* 1973; *The Marked Man,* 1974; *The Enemy at Home,* 1974; *The Forgotten Country,* 1975; *The Treacherous Paths,* 1976; *The Fortunes of Peace,* 1978.

Biographies: *Newman: The Pillar of the Cloud* (also see below), Doubleday, 1962; *Newman: Light in Winter* (also see below), Macmillan (London), 1962, Doubleday, 1963; *Apostle of Rome,* Macmillan, 1966; *Pope John in His Time,* Doubleday, 1967; *Prophets and Guardians,* Doubleday, 1969; *The Arnolds,* Scribner, 1973; *Newman's Journey* (contains abridged editions of *Newman: The Pillar of the Cloud* and *Newman: Light in Winter),* Collins, 1974.

Children's books: *Forest and the Kingdom,* Faber, 1949; *Hunt the King, Hide the Fox,* Faber, 1950; *Fires and the Stars,* Faber, 1951; *Sun Faster, Sun Slower,* Collins (Toronto), 1955; *The Other Side of the Moon,* Collins, 1956; *Merlin's Ring,* Collins, 1957; *The Treasure Hunt,* Hamish Hamilton, 1957; *Four Odd Ones,* Collins, 1958; *The Sparrow Child,* Collins, 1958; *The Caravan War,* Hamish Hamilton, 1963; *The Rose Round,* Hamish Hamilton, 1963, Dutton, 1964; *William's Wild Day Out,* Hamish Hamilton, 1963; *Lights in a Dark Town,* Macmillan (London), 1964; *The Midsummer Maze,* Macmillan, 1964; *The King of the Castle,* Macmillan, 1966.

AVOCATIONAL INTERESTS: Looking at buildings, old and new, at pictures, old and new, and listening to music.

BIOGRAPHICAL/CRITICAL SOURCES: Listener, July 7, 1967; *Books and Bookmen,* August, 1967, September, 1973; *Times Literary Supplement,* October 5, 1967, April 27, 1973; *Best Sellers,* November 15, 1967; *Commonweal,* February 27, 1970; *Kirkus Reviews,* August 15, 1977; *America,* January 29, 1977.

* * *

TROTTER, Grace V(iolet) 1900- (Nancy Paschal)

PERSONAL: Born November 23, 1900, in Dallas, Tex.; daughter of William Daniel and Nancy (Paschal) Trotter. *Education:* Attended public and private schools in Dallas. *Religion:* Christian Church. *Home:* 2028 Whitedove Dr., Dallas, Tex. 75224.

CAREER: Writer; speaker on creative writing. *Member:* Dallas Story League.

WRITINGS—All junior novels; all under pseudonym Nancy Paschal: *Clover Creek* (Junior Literary Guild selection), Thomas Nelson, 1946; *Magnolia Heights* (Junior Literary Guild selection), Thomas Nelson, 1947; *Sylvan City,* Viking, 1950; *Spring in the Air,* Viking, 1953; *Promise of June* (Junior Literary Guild selection), Thomas Nelson, 1955; *Someone to Care,* Westminister, 1957; *Portrait by Sheryl,* Westminster, 1958; *Name the Day,* Westminster, 1959; *Prescription for Two,* Westminster, 1960; *Song of the Heart,* Westminster, 1961; *No More Good-Bys,* Westminster, 1962; *Make Way for Lauren,* Westminster, 1963; *Hillview House,* Westminster, 1963; *Emeralds on Her Hand,* Farrar, Straus, 1965. Contributor of short stories to periodicals.

WORK IN PROGRESS: "Books for six-to-nine-year-olds"; song lyrics.

SIDELIGHTS: "Since my mother's death in late 1965," Grace Trotter told *CA,* "I have become very much interested in the occult, because my mother appeared to me twice after her passing. I wrote to Hans Holzer, the parapsychologist, about it, and he wrote of my experience . . . in his book *The Phantoms of Dixie.*"

Trotter notes that she has received numerous letters from young admirers of her books, all of which she has "carefully stored in boxes" and ranks as her "most prized possessions."

AVOCATIONAL INTERESTS: Gardening (has made a study of the flowers of Texas), pets, bird lore, poetry, painting, "the study of personality."

BIOGRAPHICAL/CRITICAL SOURCES: Texas Week Newsmagazine, January 18, 1947; *Dallas Times Herald,* October 5, 1947, September 24, 1950; Hans Holzer, *The Phantoms of Dixie,* Bobbs-Merrill, 1972.

* * *

TUFTE, Edward R(olf) 1942-

PERSONAL: Born March 14, 1942, in Kansas City, Mo.; son of Edward E. and Virginia (James) Tufte. *Education:* Stanford University, B.S., 1963, M.S., 1964; Yale University, Ph.D., 1968. *Office:* Department of Political Science, Yale University, New Haven, Conn. 06520.

CAREER: Princeton University, Princeton, N.J., assistant professor, 1968-71, associate professor, 1971-74, professor of politics and public affairs, 1974-77; Yale University, New Haven, Conn., professor of political science and statistics, 1977—. *Awards, honors:* Fellow, Center for Advanced Study in the Behavioral Sciences, 1973-74; Guggenheim fellow, 1977; Gladys M. Kammerer Award, American Political Science Association, 1978, for best book on U.S. national policy.

WRITINGS: (Editor) *The Quantitative Analysis of Social Problems,* Addison-Wesley, 1970; (with Robert A. Dahl) *Size and Democracy,* Stanford University Press, 1973; *Data Analysis for Politics and Policy,* Prentice-Hall, 1974; *Political Control of the Economy,* Princeton University Press, 1978.

WORK IN PROGRESS: A book on statistical graphics and visual display of quantitative information; a book on political economy.

* * *

TURNER, Alberta Tucker 1919-

PERSONAL: Born October 22, 1919, in New York, N.Y.; daughter of Albert Chester (a financier) and Marion (Fellows) Tucker; married William Arthur Turner (a college professor), April 9, 1943; children: Prudence Mab (Mrs. Sidney D. Comings), Arthur Brenton. *Education:* Hunter College (now Hunter College of the City University of New York), B.A., 1940; Wellesley College, M.A., 1941; Ohio State University, Ph.D., 1946. *Politics:* None. *Religion:* Protestant. *Home:* 482 Caskey Ct., Oberlin, Ohio 44074. *Office:* Department of English, Cleveland State University, Euclid at 24th St., Cleveland, Ohio 44115.

CAREER: Oberlin College, Oberlin, Ohio, lecturer in English literature, 1947-50, 1951-69; Cleveland State University, Cleveland, Ohio, lecturer, 1964-69, assistant professor, 1969-73, associate professor, 1973-78, professor of English literature, 1978—, director of Poetry Center, 1964—. *Member:* Milton Society of America, P.E.N., Midwest Modern Language Association.

WRITINGS: North (poems), Triskelion Press, 1970; *Need* (poems), Ashland Poetry Press, 1971; *Learning to Count* (poems) University of Pittsburgh Press, 1974; *Lid and Spoon* (poems), University of Pittsburgh Press, 1977; (editor) *50 Contemporary Poets: The Creative Process,* McKay, 1977; (editor) *Poets Teaching: The Creative Process,* Longman, 1980. Associate editor, *Field: Contemporary Poetry and Poetics,* 1969—.

WORK IN PROGRESS: Criticism of contemporary poetry and poetics; poems.

AVOCATIONAL INTERESTS: Collecting islands.

* * *

TURNER, Robert (Harry) 1915-
(Eric Calhoun, K. K. Klein, Steve Lawson, Parker Lee, Robert Morgan, Ken Murray, Lisa Roberts, Don Romano, Mark Savoy)

PERSONAL: Born April 28, 1915, in Jamaica, N.Y.; son of Harry (an employment manager) and Agnes (Phillips) Turner; married Jessie P. Anderson (an associate buyer), December 24, 1933; children: Judith (Mrs. Irving Kerzner), Laura, Timothy. *Education:* Attended schools in New York and Connecticut. *Politics:* Independent. *Religion:* Protestant. *Residence:* Hollywood, Calif. *Agent:* M. J. Hamilburg Agency, 1105 Glendon, Los Angeles, Calif. 90024.

CAREER: Writer. New York University, New York City, supervisor of messenger service, 1929-39; Ace Magazines, Inc., New York City, editor, 1939-40; Popular Publications, Inc., New York City, editor, 1943; Author's Agency (literary agency), New York City, owner, 1946; public relations director, Weeki Wachee Spring, 1958. *Military service:* U.S. Naval Reserve, 1944-46. *Member:* Mystery Writers of America (regional vice president, 1967-68; regional director of southern California chapter, 1969-71).

WRITINGS: Pulp Fiction, Quality House, 1948; *She Devil,* Rainbow Press, 1952; (under pseudonym Ken Murray) *Feud in Piney Flats,* Ace Books, 1953; (under pseudonym Ken Murray) *Hellion's Hole,* Ace Books, 1953; *The Tobacco Auction Murders,* Ace Books, 1954; *The Girl in the Cop's Pocket,* Ace Books, 1956; *The Lonely Man,* Avon, 1957; *Wagonmaster,* Pocket Books, 1958; *The Scout,* Pocket Books, 1958; *Wagons West,* Pocket Books, 1958; *Gunsmoke,* Whitman Publishing, 1958.

The Night Is for Screaming, Pyramid Publications, 1960; *Cheater,* Beacon Books, 1961; *Woman Chaser,* Beacon Books, 1962; *Strange Sisters,* Beacon Books, 1962; (under pseudonym Lisa Roberts) *A Dream to Share,* Lancer Books, 1965; (under pseudonym Mark Savoy) *Teen Age Runaways,* Viceroy Books, 1967; (under pseudonym Eric Calhoun) *Sex and the Southern Girl,* Viceroy Books, 1967; (under pseudonym Parker Lee) *Lollypop,* All Star Books, 1967; *Pretty Thing,* Olympia Press, 1968; (under pseudonym K. K. Klein) *Sex of Angels,* Olympia Press, 1969.

Shroud 9 (short stories), Powell Publications, 1970; *Some of My Best Friends Are Writers but I Wouldn't Want My Daughter to Marry One,* Sherbourne, 1970; (under pseudonym Don Romano) *Mafia: Operation Porno,* Pyramid Publications, 1973; (under pseudonym Don Romano) *Mafia: Operation Hit Man,* Pyramid Publications, 1974; (under pseudonym Don Romano) *Mafia: Operation Cocaine,* Pyramid Publications, 1974; (under pseudonym Robert Morgan) *The Golden Hoard,* Pinnacle Books, 1975; (under pseudonym Steve Lawson) *Scorpio,* Pyramid Publications, 1976.

Work appears in anthology *A Choice of Murders,* edited by Dorothy S. Davis, Scribner, 1958. Author of scripts for television series, including "Mike Hammer," "Johnny Midnight," "Miami Undercover," "Coronado 9," "Tombstone Territory," and "Shotgun Slade." Contributor of short stories to magazines.

WORK IN PROGRESS: Short stories and plays.

SIDELIGHTS: Robert Turner advises young writers that "unless you can write fast and glibly, can latch on to at least one highly exploitable, promotable novel gimmick or write self-help books, choose another profession. Forget about short stories because there is comparatively no market." Some of Turner's stories have been adapted for the television programs "Alfred Hitchcock Presents," "Pepsi Cola Playhouse," "City Detective," and "Suspense." His books have been published in Europe, South America, and the Far East.

AVOCATIONAL INTERESTS: Fishing, horse racing, playing Quinto.

* * *

TUTE, Warren (Stanley) 1914-
(Andrew Warren, a joint pseudonym)

PERSONAL: Born February 22, 1914, in West Hartlepool, County Durham, England; son of Stanley Harries and Laura Edith (Thompson) Tute; married Annette Elizabeth Neil, 1944 (divorced, 1955); married Evelyn Mary Dalley, 1958; children: Katharine Maria, Sophie Lucinda Jane. *Education:* Attended Dragon School, Oxford, 1925-28, and Wrekin College, Shropshire, 1928-31. *Home:* 54 Rosemont Rd., Richmond, Surrey TW10 6QL, England; and The Old Stables, 13 St. Anne Junction, Mosta, Malta. *Agent:* June Hak, 15 Brownlow Ct., Brownlow Rd., London N11 2BH, England.

CAREER: Royal Navy, 1932-46, retired as lieutenant commander; radio script writer for Ted Kavanagh Associated, 1946-47; director, Random Film Productions Ltd., 1947-52; made films and trained Greek scriptwriters for U.S. Mutual Security Agency (Marshall Plan), 1952-54; director, Theatrework Ltd., London, beginning 1960, and Kenway Theatre Co. Ltd., beginning 1960. During World War II, took part in North African, Sicilian, and Normandy landings; mentioned in dispatches, 1944. Head of scripts, London Weekend TV, 1968-69. Consultant, Capital Radio, 1978—. Archivist, Worshipful Company of Cordwainers.

WRITINGS—Novels: *The Felthams,* Cassell, 1950; *Lady in Thin Armour,* Cassell, 1951; *The Younger Felthams,* Cassell, 1952; *Gentlemen in Pink Uniform,* Cassell, 1953; *Girl in the Limelight,* Cassell, 1954; *The Cruiser,* Cassell, 1955, Ballantine, 1957, reprinted, Hutchinson, 1973; *The Rock,* Cassell, 1957, Sloane, 1959, reprinted, Panther Books, 1976; *Leviathan,* Cassell, 1959, Little, Brown, 1960, reprinted, Panther Books, 1975; *The Golden Greek,* Cassell, 1960, Knopf, 1961, reprinted, Panther Books, 1976; *A Matter of Diplomacy,* Dent, 1969, Coward, 1970; *The Powder Train,* Dent, 1970; (with Andrew Rosenthal under pseudonym Andrew Warren) *This Time Next October,* Dent, 1971; *The Tarnham Connection,* Dent, 1971; *The Resident,* Constable, 1973; (adapter) Ennio de Concini, Maria Pia Fusco, and Wolfgang Reinhardt, *Hitler: The Last Ten Days* (novelization of screenplay), Fontana, 1973; *Next Saturday in Milan,* Constable, 1975; *Honours of War and Peace,* Constable, 1976; *The Cairo Sleeper,* Constable, 1977.

Nonfiction: (With Felix Fonteyn) *Chico,* Cassell, 1950; (with Fonteyn) *Life of a Circus Bear,* Cassell, 1952; *Cockney Cats,* Museum Press, 1953; *The Grey Top Hat: The Story of Moss Bros. of Covent Garden,* Cassell, 1961; *Atlantic Conquest,* Little, Brown, 1962; *The Admiral,* Cassell, 1963; *Cochrane: A Life of Admiral the Earl of Dundonald,* Cassell, 1965; *Escape Route Green,* Dent, 1971; *The Deadly Stroke,* Coward, 1973; (with John Costello and Terry Hughes) *D-Day,* Macmillan, 1974, revised edition, Pan Books, 1975; *The North African War,* Sidgwick & Jackson, 1976.

Plays: (Translator) Andre Obey, *Frost at Midnight,* Samuel French, 1957; *A Time to Be Born,* Evans, 1958; *Jessica,* Samuel French, 1959; "A Few Days in Greece," first produced in Dallas, Tex., at Margo Jones Theater, 1959; (translator) Marc Camoletti, "Quartet for Five," first produced in London at Arts Theatre, 1960; (translator) Jean Nohain and F. Caradec, *Le Petomane,* Souvernir Press, 1968. Also translator of "A Family Affair," by Constance Coline, as yet neither published nor produced.

AVOCATIONAL INTERESTS: People, cats, and wine.

U

UDALL, Morris K(ing) 1922-

PERSONAL: Born June 15, 1922, in St. Johns, Ariz.; son of Levi Stewart (a chief justice of Arizona Supreme Court) and Louise (Lee) Udall; married Patricia Emery, 1949 (divorced, 1966); married Ella Royston, 1968; children: (first marriage) Mark, Randolph, Judith, Anne, Bradley, Katherine. *Education:* University of Arizona, LL.B. (with distinction), 1949. *Politics:* Democrat. *Religion:* Church of Jesus Christ of Latter-day Saints (Mormon). *Office:* House Office Bldg., Washington, D.C. 20515.

CAREER: Denver Nuggets (basketball team), Denver, Colo., basketball player, 1948-49; admitted to Bar of Arizona, 1949; Udall & Udall (law firm), Tucson, Ariz., partner, 1949-61; U.S. House of Representatives, Washington, D.C., representative from second district, Arizona, 1961—, chairman of House Interior and Insular Affairs Committee and Office of Technology Assessment, vice-chairman of House Post Office and Civil Service Committee. Candidate for Democratic presidential nomination, 1976. Chief deputy county attorney, Pima County, Ariz., 1950-52, county attorney, 1953-54. Lecturer in labor law, University of Arizona, Tucson, 1955-56. Delegate to Democratic National Convention, 1956. Co-founder and former director, Bank of Tucson and Catalina Savings and Loan Association; legal counsel and member of board of directors, Tucson Better Business Bureau; member of board of directors, Tucson Metropolitan Young Men's Christian Association (Y.M.C.A.); trustee, Arizona-Sonora Desert Museum; president, Tucson Boys Band. *Military service:* U.S. Army Air Forces, 1942-46; became captain. *Member:* American Bar Association, American Judicature Society, Arizona Bar Association (past vice-president), Pima County Bar Association, Phi Kappa Phi, Phi Delta Phi, American Legion.

WRITINGS: Arizona Law of Evidence, West Publishing, 1960; (with Donald G. Tacheron) *The Job of the Congressman,* Bobbs-Merrill, 1966, 2nd edition, 1970; (contributor) Lester Thonssen, editor, *Representative American Speeches, 1967-1968,* H. W. Wilson, 1968; *The Education of a Congressman,* edited by Robert L. Peabody, Bobbs-Merrill, 1972. Contributor to *Reader's Digest, Progressive, New Republic,* and *Playboy.*

SIDELIGHTS: When his brother, Stewart L. Udall, left his position as a U.S. Representative to become Secretary of the Interior, Mo Udall ran for the vacant congressional seat and won it in 1961. "Like all freshman congressmen," Arthur Hadley writes in *Atlantic,* "Udall bumbled and stumbled trying to learn [during his first term in office]. The next term he organized a school that taught the ropes so the newcomers would not have to grope as he had [done]." Out of this experience came Udall's book *The Job of the Congressman* which, Hadley states, is "still the bible for new members [of Congress]."

During his years in the House of Representatives, Udall has become known as an environmentalist and a reformer. A writer for *Time* notes that Udall is "the principal author of a host of bills to protect and restore the air, earth, and water," including bills concerned with land-use planning and strip-mining. Udall's work for political reform resulted in the campaign finance law of 1974 that established a campaign spending limit as well as the public funding of presidential elections.

In 1974, Udall was approached by several other congressmen who suggested that he try for the Democratic presidential nomination in 1976. After gaining the support of some forty members of the House, Udall took the plunge and announced his candidacy. Although he was not taken too seriously when he began his campaign, being a relatively unknown figure from a small state, he had the advantage of being, as Leslie Bennetts points out in the *Philadelphia Bulletin,* "a liberal congressman elected for 13 years from a very conservative state [whose] career has been an ongoing triumph of personal popularity over formidable obstacles."

Throughout 1974 and 1975, Udall appeared at numerous Democratic fund raising events around the country, helping fellow Democrats in their campaign efforts as well as making himself better known among the party leadership. Compared by observers to both Abraham Lincoln, for his six-foot-five-inch frame, and to Will Rogers, for his story-telling abilities, Udall fared well in his campaigning efforts. By the end of 1975 he was perceived as one of a handful of candidates who had a good chance of winning the Democratic nomination. A reporter for *Time* notes that Udall's "unflagging drive and shrewd campaigning attracted a good volunteer organization, the backing of Democratic intellectuals like Harvard Professor John Kenneth Galbraith, and many of the old McGovern-McCarthy liberal legions."

With the support of many moderate and liberal Democrats, Udall did well in the 1976 primaries. In New Hampshire and Massachusetts, two early races, he had strong second-place showings, beating such liberal rivals as Senator Birch Bayh, Sargent Shriver, and Fred Harris, and establishing himself, a writer for *Time* states, as "the clear favorite among the liberals."

Udall's platform concentrated on what he called "the three E's"—energy, environment, and the economy. To lower the cost of oil, Udall believed that the large, monopolistic oil companies should be broken up into smaller, more competitive companies. He also advocated that a crash program be instituted to develop other energy sources. On environmental issues Udall, quite expectedly, called for a careful and planned use of natural resources. "We have come to the end of an era," Robert S. Boyd of the *Detroit Free Press* quotes Udall as saying, "the era of cheap, abundant land, oil, timber, minerals, food, and water. The age of unlimited growth is over." To strengthen the nation's economy, Udall proposed a government-guaranteed full employment program, a cut in the defense budget, and the federalization of the welfare system. Udall also supported the Equal Rights Amendment and a national health insurance plan. As Larry L. King writes in *New Times,* Udall was "the only candidate . . . to pledge to be an activist president, the only one to address himself to using the government as an instrument for social good."

Despite Udall's early primary strength and his support from the liberal wing of the Democratic party, he was never able to win a primary victory. In several states he came agonizingly close—in Connecticut by two percent of the vote and in Michigan and Wisconsin by less than one percent. Udall came in second in so many primaries that he jokingly took to calling himself "ol' second-place Mo." King writes in *New Times* that "there's much that's sad, if brave, in Udall's futile campaign to awaken a people determined to play Rip Van Winkle."

After losing the Ohio primary on June 9, 1976, Udall ended his campaign. "I'm a realist," *Time* quoted him as saying, "and I can count and I know the difference between a fighter and a winner and a long shot and a no-shot." Udall's campaign had taken him a long way: from a "dark horse" candidate in 1974 to a nationally-known political figure. He had garnered more votes and delegates than several of his more widely-recognized opponents and finished second in a race that had seen some ten candidates in the running. Udall found, however, that a presidential campaign "tests your marriage, your sanity, your digestion, your sense of humor, and just about everything else."

AVOCATIONAL INTERESTS: Golf, hiking, mountain climbing.

BIOGRAPHICAL/CRITICAL SOURCES: Daily Citizen (Tucson, Ariz.), October 29, 1968; *Newsweek,* January 6, 1969, December 8, 1975, January 12, 1976, April 5, 1976, May 3, 1976, June 7, 1976, June 21, 1976; *Washington Star-News,* October 2, 1974; *Detroit Free Press,* October 13, 1974; *Atlantic,* December, 1974; *Nation,* February 15, 1975; *Philadelphia Bulletin,* April 10, 1975; *U.S. News & World Report,* August 18, 1975; *Time,* August 25, 1975, March 15, 1976, April 12, 1976, April 26, 1976; *New Republic,* August 30, 1975; *Progressive,* December, 1975; *New York Times Magazine,* February 1, 1976; *New Times,* April 16, 1976, May 28, 1976; *Publishers Weekly,* May 9, 1977; *Business Week,* December 25, 1978.

—Sketch by Thomas Wiloch

UDELL, Jon G(erald) 1935-

PERSONAL: Born June 22, 1935, in Columbus, Wis.; son of Roy Grant and Jessie (Foster) Udell; married Susan Smykla, May 16, 1960; children: Jon G., Jr., Roy Steven, Susan E., Bruce F., Alan J., Kenneth G. *Education:* University of Wisconsin, B.B.A., 1957, M.B.A., 1958, Ph.D., 1961; University of California, Berkeley, postdoctoral study, summer, 1963. *Politics:* Independent. *Religion:* Presbyterian. *Home:* 5210 Barton Rd., Madison, Wis. 53711. *Office:* Graduate School of Business, University of Wisconsin, Madison, Wis. 53706.

CAREER: University of Wisconsin—Madison, instructor, 1959-61, assistant professor, 1961-65, associate professor, 1965-68, professor of business, 1968—, assistant director of Bureau of Business Research and Service, 1959-63, associate director, 1963-66, director, 1967-74. Visiting associate professor at Cornell University, 1966-67. Public interest director of Federal Home Loan Bank of Chicago; member of board of directors, United Banks of Wisconsin, Research Products Corp., and Wisconsin Electric Power Co.; trustee, Greater Wisconsin Foundation. Service to State of Wisconsin includes director of State Chamber of Commerce, member of governor's council for economic development, chairman of governor's conference on mergers and acquisitions, co-chairman of governor's executive conference on marketing and research and development, member of governor's committee on commerce and industry, member, vice-president, and president of consumer advisory council of Department of Agriculture, chairman of economic mission for the seventies, and trustee and vice-president of Wonderful Wisconsin Foundation. Local service includes member of employment and economic development committee of Madison, director of Greater Madison Chamber of Commerce, director of Central Madison Mall Committee, and chairman of Business-Education Coordinating Council. Corporate member and adviser, Man-Environment Communications Center; technical adviser to advisory committee of Project Sanguine; member of advisory committee, Educational Satellite Telecommunications Center; consultant to American Newspaper Publishers Association and Mosinee Paper Co.

MEMBER: American Marketing Association, Phi Beta Kappa, Beta Gamma Sigma, Phi Kappa Phi, Phi Eta Sigma. *Awards, honors:* Citations from the governor of Wisconsin, 1970, for contribution to state's economic development, and 1971, for service to the state; Sidney S. Goldish Award from International Newspaper Promotion Association, for contribution to newspaper research; Marketer of the Year Award from Wisconsin Chapter of American Marketing Association, 1976.

WRITINGS: Tabulation of Retail Trade Survey Questionnaires, University of Wisconsin, 1959.

The Second Midwest Newsprint Survey, Bureau of Business Research and Service, University of Wisconsin, and Inland Daily Press Association, 1960; *An Analysis of Midwest Newsprint Consumption,* University of Wisconsin and Inland Daily Press Association, 1961; *A New Analysis of Midwest Newsprint Supply and Demand,* University of Wisconsin and Inland Daily Press Association, 1962; *A Model of Non-Price Competitive Strategy,* Bureau of Business Research and Service, University of Wisconsin, 1963; *An Analysis of National and Regional Newsprint Trends,* American Newspaper Publishers Association, 1964; *The Economic Future of the Newspaper Business,* American Newspaper Publishers Association, 1965; *1975 U.S. Newsprint Consumption: An Economic Analysis of Consumption Trends with Projections for the Next Decade,* American Newspaper Publishers Association, 1965.

The Growth of Newsprint Consumption by United States Newspapers, American Newspaper Publishers Association, 1966; *The Growth of Newspapers and Newsprint Consumption in the Midwest,* Inland Daily Press Association, 1967; (with William Strang) *Consumer Attitudes and Shopping Behavior in the South Wood County Area: An Attempt to Develop New Methodology for Retail Trade Analysis,* University of Wisconsin, 1967; *Newsprint Consumption in the United States: 1956-1966, and the Current Outlook,* American Newspaper Publishers Association, 1967; (contributor) Reed Mayer and Stanley C. Hollander, editors, *Markets and Marketing in Developing Economies,* Irwin, 1968; (with Strang and Gene Gohlke) *Wisconsin's Economy in 1975: Wisconsin's Economic Growth since World War II and Projections for 1975,* Bureau of Business Research and Service, University of Wisconsin, and University of Wisconsin Foundation, 1968; (contributor) *The Lakes and Seas: New Frontiers for Industry,* University of Wisconsin Extension, 1968; *U.S. Newspaper Growth and Newsprint Consumption,* American Newspaper Publishers Association, 1968; *Social and Economic Consequences of the Merger Movement in Wisconsin,* Division of Economic Development, State of Wisconsin, 1969; *Economic Growth and Newsprint Consumption of Midwest Newspapers Projected through 1975,* Inland Daily Press Association, 1969; *U.S. Newsprint Consumption and Economic Growth, 1958-1968, and the Current Outlook,* American Newspaper Publishers Association, 1969.

(Editor with Linda Kohl and contributor) *Marketing and Research and Development,* Division of Economic Development, State of Wisconsin, 1970; (with Strang, William P. Glade, and James E. Littlefield) *Marketing in a Developing Nation,* Heath, 1970; *Future Newsprint Demand: 1970-1980,* American Newspaper Publishers Association, 1970; (with Strang) *Perceptions of Wisconsin: A Study of the Strengths and Weaknesses of Wisconsin as Seen by Manufacturing Executives,* Journal Co. and Bureau of Business Research and Service, University of Wisconsin, 1972; (with Strang) *Importance of Location Decisions Factors as Seen by Southeastern Wisconsin Industry,* Journal Co. and Bureau of Business Research and Service, University of Wisconsin, 1972; *Taxation and Changes of Residency,* Journal Co. and Bureau of Business Research and Service, University of Wisconsin, 1972; (with Strang) *Importance of Location Decision Factors as Seen by Wisconsin Manufacturers in a Sixty-Five County Area,* Journal Co. and Bureau of Business Research and Service, University of Wisconsin, 1972; *Research and Development in Wisconsin Industry: An Analysis of Current Programs and Future Research and Development Needs of Wisconsin Manufacturers,* Bureau of Business Research and Service, University of Wisconsin, 1972; *Perceptions of Wisconsin: The State as Seen by the Leaders of Organized Labor,* Journal Co. and Bureau of Business Research and Service, University of Wisconsin, 1972; *The State as Seen by Rank and File Delegates to the American Federation of Labor-Congress of Industrial Organizations Biennial Convention,* Journal Co. and Bureau of Business Research and Service, University of Wisconsin, 1972; *Successful Marketing Strategies in American Industry,* Mimir Publishers, 1972; *The Economic Impact of Man-Made Lakes on Area Businesses,* Bureau of Business Research and Service, University of Wisconsin, 1973; *Expenditures and Perceptions of Property Owners at Lakes Sherwood and Camelot,* Bureau of Business Research and Service, University of Wisconsin, 1973; *The Supply and Demand for Newsprint in the United States, 1962-1973,* American Newspaper Publishers Association, 1974; *The U.S. Economy and Newspaper Growth,* American Newspaper Publishers Association, 1974.

Dynamics of U.S. Daily Newspapers and Newsprint Consumption, American Newspaper Publishers Association, 1976; *U.S. Economic Growth and Newsprint Consumption,* American Newspaper Publishers Association, 1977; (with William Strang and E. Lauck Parke) *Skilled Labor in the Milwaukee Area: The Supply, Education, Problems and Opportunities,* Graduate School of Business, University of Wisconsin—Madison, 1977; *The Impact of Recent Legislation on Wisconsin Manufacturers and Employment Growth,* Graduate School of Business, University of Wisconsin—Madison, 1977; *The Economics of the American Newspaper,* Hastings House, 1978; *Future Newspaper and Newsprint Growth: 1977-1985,* American Newspaper Publishers Association, 1978; *Rockford Illinois* (five economic studies), Rock Valley College, 1978; *Executive Evaluations of National Tax Proposals,* Wisconsin Association of Manufacturers and Commerce, 1978; *Toward Economic Development in Illinois through Better Understanding and Cooperation by Industry, Labor, Government and Education,* Community College Board of the State of Illinois, 1978; (contributor) *Small Business and the Quality of American Life,* U.S. Government Printing Office, 1978; *Wisconsin's Taxation of Capital Gains: Fair? Progressive? Competitive?,* Public Expenditure Survey of Wisconsin, 1979.

Also author of research reports; contributor to conference reports and proceedings. Contributor of over seventy-five articles to professional journals, including *Journal of Marketing, Management Science, Community, Mergers and Acquisitions,* and *Administrative Science Quarterly.*

WORK IN PROGRESS: A marketing textbook; a textbook on business and economic reporting, for Prentice-Hall; studies on consumer purchasing, after-sales services, inflation, and business organization; a research monograph on death taxes.

* * *

UMPHLETT, Wiley Lee 1931-

PERSONAL: Born October 25, 1931, in Norfolk, Va.; son of James Vernon (a plumber) and Dollie Virginia (Woolard) Umphlett; married Joyce Estelle Campbell (a travel agent), April 23, 1966; children: Reginald, Donald, Edward (stepsons). *Education:* Southwestern at Memphis, B.A., 1954; Columbia University, M.A., 1960; Florida State University, Ph.D., 1967. *Home:* 7246B Dogwood Ter., Pensacola, Fla. 32504. *Office:* University of West Florida, Pensacola, Fla. 32504.

CAREER: Public school teacher in Norfolk, Va., 1958-61; Longwood College, Farmville, Va., instructor in English, 1962-64; Florida State University, Tallahassee, director of off-campus program, 1967-68; University of West Florida, Pensacola, director of continuing education, 1969—. *Military service:* U.S. Army, 1954-57; served in Germany. *Member:* National University Extension Association, Benevolent and Protective Order of Elks.

WRITINGS: The Sporting Myth and the American Experience, Bucknell University Press, 1974; *Mythmakers of the American Dream: The Nostalgic Vision in Popular Culture,* A. S. Barnes, 1980.

WORK IN PROGRESS: The Movies Go to College: The College-life Film in America; editing *The Humanistic Role of Sports in Modern Society.*

SIDELIGHTS: Wiley Lee Umphlett told *CA:* "I always wanted to be a fiction writer until I discovered the wealth of nonfiction subject areas as an outlet for my creative energies. In fact, I now have so many ideas for writing projects that I find it very difficult in deciding which ones to pursue."

* * *

UPPAL, Jogindar S. 1927-

PERSONAL: Born January 16, 1927, in Lahore, India (now in Pakistan); son of Dhian S. (a teacher) and Durga (Devi) Uppal; married Pritam K. Uppal, May, 1945; children: Paul, Jack, Inni. *Education:* Punjab University, B.A., 1950, M.A. (with first class honors), 1952; University of Minnesota, M.A., 1961, Ph.D., 1965. *Religion:* Sikh. *Home:* 5 Hollow Rd., Newtonville, N.Y. 12128. *Office:* Department of Economics, State University of New York at Albany, Albany, N.Y. 12222.

CAREER: Punjab University, Punjab, India, lecturer in economics, 1952-59; University of Minnesota, Minneapolis, instructor in economics and social science, 1959-64; University of Hawaii, Honolulu, assistant professor of economics and Asian studies, 1964-65; Michigan State University, East Lansing, assistant professor of economic and social science, 1965-67; State University of New York at Albany, associate professor, 1967-71, professor of economics, 1971—. Visiting Fulbright professor at Gokhale Institute of Politics and Economics, India, 1976. Director of Capital District Inter-Collegiate Seminar on Asia, 1968-69; frequent lecturer to various groups. Economic researcher, Bemis Bag Co., summers, 1961-64, Department of Planning and Development (Honolulu), 1964-65, New York Conference of Mayors and Municipal Affairs, 1969-70, New York State Commission on State and Local Finances, 1974—, and New York Institute for Public Policy Alternatives.

MEMBER: American Economic Association, Association of Asian Studies, Indian Economic Studies Association (member of executive committee), Indian Society of Agricultural Economics. *Awards, honors:* Institute of International Education fellowship, 1960; Ford Foundation grants, India, 1966 and 1970; State University of New York Research Foundation grants, 1973 and 1974; Institute for Public Policy Alternatives grant, 1974.

WRITINGS: (Editor with Kuan-I Chen) *Comparative Development of India and China,* Free Press, 1971; *Nature and Measurement of Disguised Unemployment in an Underdeveloped Economy,* Asia Publishing House, 1972; (editor with Louis Salkevey) *Africa: Problems in Economic Development,* Free Press, 1972; (with Robert B. Pettengill) *Can Cities Survive?: The Fiscal Plight of American Cities,* St. Martin's, 1974; (editor) *India's Economic Problems: An Analytical Approach,* McGraw, 1975, revised edition, 1978; *Economic Development of South Asia,* St. Martin's, 1977. Also author of monographs and research reports. Contributor of articles and reviews to international studies, economics, and education journals, including *Journal of Asian and African Studies, Oxford Economic Papers, Canadian Journal of Economics, Education Quarterly, Economic Affairs, Asian Economic Review, Economica Internationale,* and *Journal of Developing Areas.*

WORK IN PROGRESS: Economic Planning: The Indian Experience; Backward Regions and Economic Development: The Indian Case.

URIS, Leon (Marcus) 1924-

PERSONAL: Born August 3, 1924, in Baltimore, Md.; son of Wolf William and Anna (Blumberg) Uris; married Betty Katherine Beck, 1945 (divorced January, 1968); married Margery Edwards, September 8, 1968 (died February 20, 1969); married Jill Peabody, February 15, 1970; children: (first marriage) Karen Lynn, Mark Jay, Michael Cady. *Education:* Attended public schools in Baltimore, Md. *Residence:* Aspen, Colo. *Agent:* Willis Kingsley Wing, 24 East 38th St., New York, N.Y. 10016.

CAREER: Former newspaper driver, *San Francisco Call-Bulletin,* San Francisco, Calif. Full-time writer, 1950—. *Military service:* U.S. Marine Corps, 1942-45. *Member:* Writers League, Screenwriters Guild. *Awards, honors:* Daroff Memorial Award, 1959; National Institute of Arts and Letters grant, 1959.

WRITINGS—All published by Doubleday, except as indicated: *Battle Cry,* Putnam, 1953; *The Angry Hills,* Random House, 1955, reprinted, Bantam, 1972; *Exodus,* 1957 (also see below), reprinted, Bantam, 1975; (with Dimitrios Haussiadis) *Exodus Revisited* (photo-essay), 1959 (published in England as *In the Steps of Exodus,* Heinemann, 1962); *Mila 18,* 1960; *Armageddon,* 1964; *The Third Temple,* published with *Strike Zion* by William Stevenson, Bantam, 1967; *Topaz,* McGraw, 1967; *QB VII,* 1970; (with Walt Smith) "Ari" (musical version of his novel, *Exodus*), first produced on Broadway at the Mark Hellinger Theater, January 15, 1971; (with wife, Jill Uris) *Ireland, a Terrible Beauty: The Story of Ireland Today,* 1975; *Trinity,* 1976.

Screenplays: "Battle Cry," 1955; "Gunfight at the O.K. Corral," 1957.

SIDELIGHTS: Kathy Hacker writes: "Through the years, [Leon] Uris has taken considerable guff from critics who've accused him of myriad literary vices, from simplistic writing to crass commercialism." One of those critics, Anthony Boucher, claims that Uris "is flagrantly unable to construct a plot, a character, a novel, or a sentence in the English langauge." Nevertheless, Hacker notes that "Uris has proved himself to be one of the few long-distance runners in the race to the cash register and high-volume book sales." But Midge Decter adds, "Mr. Uris . . . has done a great deal more than merely wax rich and famous—possibilities, after all, open to any American whose commodity finds its proper market. He has become the master chronicler and ambassador of Jewish aspiration not only to the Gentiles but to the Jews themselves. His commodity has, in fact, found a market far out of proportion, numerically and sociologically, to its special quality."

"It is a simple thing to point out that Uris often writes crudely, that his dialogue can be wooden, that his structure occasionally groans under the excess baggage of exposition and information," concedes Pete Hamill. "Simple, but irrelevent. None of that matters as you are swept along in the narrative. Uris is certainly not as good a writer as Pynchon or Barthelme or Nabokov; but he is a better storyteller." In the case of *Exodus,* writes Dan Wakefield, "the plot is so exciting that the characters become exciting too; not because of their individuality or depth, but because of the historic drama they are involved in." He continues, "The real achievement . . . lies not so much in its virtues as a novel as in its skillful rendering of the furiously complex history of modern Israel in a palatable, popular form that is usually faithful to the spirit of the complicated realities."

Decter notes, "There remains the riddle of why these books by themselves have seemed to accomplish what years of persuasion, arguments, appeals, and knowledge of the events have failed to do—why people have claimed to be converted . . . uplifted, thrilled, [and] enthralled by them."

In order to write *Exodus,* Uris read about 300 books, traveled 12,000 miles inside Israel, and interviewed more than 1,200 people; similar efforts went into his other books. The results have alternately been called "non-fiction" novels, "propaganda" novels, and just plain "journalism." As a reviewer for *Christian Science Monitor* comments, "Few readers are expert enough to be 100 percent certain where Mr. Uris's imagination has taken over the record." Nevertheless, Maxwell Geismar points out: "If Mr. Uris sometimes lacks tone as a novelist, if his central figures are social types rather than individual portraits, there is also a kind of 'underground power' in his writing. No other novel I have read recently has had the same capacity [as *Exodus*] to refresh our memory, inform our intelligence, and to stir the heart." In the same vein, Pete Hamill writes of *Trinity:* "The novel sprawls, occasionally bores, meanders like a river. . . . But when the story is finished the reader has been to places where he or she has never been before. The news items . . . will never seem quite the same again."

AVOCATIONAL INTERESTS: Skiing, bowling, and tennis.

BIOGRAPHICAL/CRITICAL SOURCES: Saturday Review, September 27, 1958; *New York Herald Tribune Book Review,* September 28, 1958; *Christian Science Monitor,* December 4, 1958, November 16, 1967; *Nation,* April 11, 1959; *Commentary,* October, 1961; *New York Review of Books,* April 16, 1964; *New York Times Book Review,* June 28, 1964, October 15, 1967, March 14, 1976; *Atlantic,* July, 1964; *Philadelphia Bulletin,* March 31, 1976; *Authors in the News,* Volume II, Gale, 1976; *Contemporary Literary Criticism,* Volume VII, Gale, 1977.†

* * *

UTTON, Albert Edgar 1931-

PERSONAL: Born July 6, 1931, in Aztec, N.M.; son of Charles Herbert and Alta (Wood) Utton; married Mary Lodge, June 28, 1958; children: Jennifer, John. *Education:* University of New Mexico, B.A., 1953; Oxford University, B.A., 1956, M.A. (Juris), 1959; studied at University of London, 1957-58, and Yale University, 1958-59. *Politics:* Democrat. *Religion:* Episcopalian. *Home:* 3400 Grande Vista Pl. N.W., Albuquerque, N.M. 87120. *Office:* School of Law, University of New Mexico, 1117 Stanford N.E., Albuquerque, N.M. 87131.

CAREER: Attorney with law firm in Albuquerque, N.M., 1959-61; University of New Mexico, School of Law, Albuquerque, assistant professor, 1961-65, associate professor, 1965-68, professor of law, 1968—. *Military service:* U.S. Air Force, 1956-58; became captain. *Member:* American Bar Association, International Law Association, Universities Council on Water Resources, New Mexico Bar Association, Albuquerque Committee on Foreign Relations.

WRITINGS: (With Robert Emmet Clark) *Water and Water Rights,* Volume II, Allen Smith, 1967; (editor) *National Petroleum Policy: A Critical Review,* University of New Mexico Press, 1970; (editor with Daniel H. Henning) *Environmental Policy: Concepts and International Implications,* Praeger, 1973; (editor and author of introduction) *Pollution and International Boundaries: United States-Mexican Environmental Problems,* University of New Mexico Press, 1973; (editor and contributor) *Interdisciplinary Environmental Approaches,* Educational Media Press, 1974; (editor with Ludwik Teclaff, and contributor) *International Environmental Law,* Praeger, 1974; (editor with W.R.D. Sewell and T. O'Riordan) *Natural Resources for a Democratic Society,* Westview Press, 1976; (editor with Teclaff) *Water Resources Management in a Changing World,* Westview Press, 1977; (editor with Walter Mead) *U.S. Energy Policy: Errors of the Past, Proposals for the Future,* Ballinger, 1978. Contributor to law reviews and to journals dealing with water and other natural resources. Editor, *Natural Resources Journal,* 1962—.

V

VACCA, Roberto 1927-

PERSONAL: Born May 31, 1927, in Rome, Italy; son of Giovanni (a mathematician and sinologist) and Virginia (an Arabic scholar and fiction writer; maiden name, De Bosis) Vacca; married Stefania Piscini (a psychotherapist), February 25, 1954; children: Giovanni. *Education:* University of Rome, doctorate in electrical engineering, 1951, libera docenza, 1960. *Religion:* None. *Home:* 3 Via Oddone di Cluny, Rome, Italy.

CAREER: Engineer in Italy, designing and building electric power transmission lines, 1951-55; National Research Council of Italy, Rome, researcher in digital computers, 1955-62; University of Rome, Rome, professor of digital computers, 1960-66; Compagnia Generale Automazione, Rome, technical manager, 1962-64, general manger, 1964-75; consultant in systems engineering, energy, communication, and transportation systems. UNESCO visiting fellow at Cambridge University and Harvard University, both 1961. *Member:* Institute of Electrical and Electronics Engineers, Institute of Traffic Engineers, Club of Rome.

WRITINGS: *Il robot e il minotauro* (science fiction stories and essays; title means "The Robot and the Minotaur"), Rizzoli, 1963; *Esempi de avvenire* (science fiction stories and essays; title means "Examples of the Future"), Rizzoli, 1965; *Il medioevo prossimo venturo,* Mondadori, 1971, translation by J. S. Whale published as *The Coming Dark Age,* Doubleday, 1973; *La morte di megalopoli* (novel; title means "The Death of Megalopolis"), Mondadori, 1974; *Handbook for an Improbable Salvation,* Mondadori, 1974; *Greggio e Pericoloso* (novel; title means "Crude and Evil"), Mondadori, 1976; *Perengana* (novel), Rizzoli, 1977; *Tecniche modeste per un mondo complicato,* Rizzoli, 1978, translation by author published as *Modest Technologies for a Complicated World,* Pergamon, 1980; *Le 99 scale* (title means "The 99 Staircases"), Mondadori, 1980; *Croce Bianca in Campo Russo* (novel; title means "A White Cross in a Russian Field"), Sugar, 1980. Contributor to *Traffic Quarterly, Mathematics of Computation, Playmen, Playboy, Il Mondo, L'Espresso,* and *Il Messaggero.*

SIDELIGHTS: Roberto Vacca told *CA:* "In my essays I try as hard as I can to be reasonable. Probably this is why these essays have such a scarce impact. Many people quote from them (especially in Italy), but nobody—or hardly anybody—has been getting the message that the contemporary complex world requires that each of us learns more and more. My message is that it is possible to learn just about anything for just about anybody. 'There are 99 staircases to go up to Heaven: 99 for intelligent people and one for all the rest': this Arabic saying gives the title to my 1980 book in which I recount how I managed to learn about physics, math, administration and management, engineering, systems, writing, speaking in public, eight languages, etc. My novels are intended to amuse myself and—hopefully—my readers, but using complicated ideas. *Croce Bianca in Campo Russo* gives the real story behind the Russian revolution—it is an economic-fiction story, although sometimes I feel tempted to believe that by sheer serendipity I managed to get at the improbable truth."

* * *

VACCARO, Louis C(harles) 1930-

PERSONAL: Born July 25, 1930, in Los Angeles, Calif.; son of Louis C. and Louise M. (Vincequerra) Vaccaro; married Jean Mae Hudak, January 29, 1955; children: Mary Lou, Theresa Jean, Vicki Ann, Frances Paula, Michelle Marie, Justin Louis. *Education:* Los Angeles Valley College, A.A., 1954; University of Southern California, A.B., 1957, M.Ed., 1961; San Fernando Valley State College (now California State University, Northridge), M.A., 1960; Michigan State University, Ed.D., 1963; postdoctoral study at University of Oregon, 1966, and University of Michigan, 1970. *Religion:* Roman Catholic. *Home:* 3910 Birnwick, Adrian, Mich. 49221. *Office:* Sienna Heights College, Adrian, Mich.

CAREER: Los Angeles Department of Recreation and Parks, Los Angeles, Calif., assistant recreation director, 1949-51; *Los Angeles Times,* Los Angeles, wholesale and promotional agent, 1950-51, 1953-57; Pacific Telephone & Telegraph Co., Los Angeles, sales representative and plant staff assistant, 1957-58, junior accountant and business office manager, 1958-59, plant engineer, 1959-60; San Fernando Valley State College (now California State University), Northridge, Calif., assistant instructor in education, 1960-61; St. Mary's College, Notre Dame, Ind., instructor in education and geography, 1961-62; Marquette University, Milwaukee, Wis., assistant professor of higher education, and assistant to vice-president for academic affairs, 1963-66; University of Portland, Portland, Ore., vice-president for academic affairs, 1967-70; Marycrest College, Davenport, Iowa, president, 1970-72; Colby-Sawyer College, New London, N.H., president, 1972-77; Sienna Heights College, Adrian, Mich., president, 1977—. Instructor in personnel management, adult schools of Los Angeles, Calif., 1960-61. Visiting professor at University of Colorado, University of Michigan, University of Pittsburgh, University of Notre Dame, University of Toronto, and several universities in Brazil. *Military service:* U.S. Air Force, personnel specialist, 1951-53.

MEMBER: Association of Governing Boards of Colleges and Universities, Association of American Colleges, American Association for Higher Education, American Educational Research Association, American Council on Education, American Association for the Advancement of Science, National Catholic Educational Association (member of executive committee, 1970-72), United Community Service, Iowa College Foundation, New Hampshire College and University Council (vice-chairman, 1975-77), Center for Constructive Change (Durham, N.H.; member of board of directors, 1974—), South Eastern Michigan Telecommunications Educational Consortium (SEMTEC; vice-chairman), Delta Epsilon Sigma. *Awards, honors:* Postdoctoral research fellowship, Center for the Advanced Study of Educational Administration, Institute for Community Studies, University of Oregon, 1966-67; Litt.D., St. Martin's College, 1969; L.H.D., Vermont College of Norwich University, 1978.

WRITINGS: (Editor) *Toward New Dimensions of Catholic Higher Education,* Education Research Associates, 1967; (editor and contributor) *Student Freedom in American Higher Education,* Teachers College Press, 1969; (editor) *Reshaping American Higher Education,* AMI Press, 1975; *Notes from a College President: Issues in American Higher Education,* Beacon Hill Press, 1976; *Planning in Small Colleges,* Blissfield Press, 1979. Author of research reports and monographs for U.S. Office of Education and other government agencies. Contributor of articles and reviews to professional journals, including *Junior College Journal, Personnel Administrator, American Interprofessional Quarterly, Adult Leadership, Journal of Higher Education,* and *Improving College and University Teaching.* Member of editorial advisory board, *Child and Family Journal.*

WORK IN PROGRESS: Education and Human Development: Focus on Brazil.

AVOCATIONAL INTERESTS: Writing fiction and poetry.

* * *

Van ATTA, Winfred 1910-

PERSONAL: Born October 18, 1910, in Hidalgo, Ill.; son of William I. and Mae (Spraggins) Van Atta; married Frieda E. Anderson, 1939; children: Mary Lynne, Gretchen. *Education:* Attended school in Newton, Ill. *Home and office:* 10 Glorybower Court, The Woodlands, Tex. 77380. *Agent:* Blassingame, McCauley & Wood, 60 East 42nd St., New York, N.Y. 10017.

CAREER: Attendant and staff secretary, Elgin State Hospital, Elgin, Ill., for five years; promotion writer, Diversey Corp., Chicago, Ill., for five years; copy chief of book clubs, Doubleday & Co., Inc., for eight years; managing director of book clubs, Sears, Roebuck & Co., New York City, for eight years; *Newsweek,* New York City, copy chief for circulation, 1959-61; free-lance writer, 1961-62, 1964-65; senior medical writer-editor, Smith, Kline & French Laboratories, 1962-63; director, Office of Public Interest, Columbia-Presbyterian Medical Center, 1966-78. *Member:* Authors League of America, Mystery Writers of America, New York Advertising Club. *Awards, honors:* Received special Edgar Allan Poe award for best first suspense novel, 1961, for *Shock Treatment.*

WRITINGS—All published by Doubleday, except as indicated: *Shock Treatment* (Mystery Guild Book Club selection), 1961; *Nicky,* Hill & Wang, 1965; *Hatchet Man* (Mystery Guild Book Club selection), 1965; *A Good Place to Work and Die,* 1966; *The Adam Sleep,* 1979. Contributor, *Good Housekeeping Family Medical Guide,* Hearst Books, 1979. Also contributor on health and medical topics to popular magazines; contributor of over 300 short stories and articles to popular publications.

WORK IN PROGRESS: A novel, *No Room at the Inn.*

SIDELIGHTS: Winfred Van Atta told *CA:* "Except for two years as a free-lance writer, I have worked at a full-time job, writing as an avocation. After retiring from Columbia-Presbyterian Medical Center and moving here to Texas, near Houston, I have finally been able to write at my own leisure and pace. I look back on my thirteen years as public relations director at the world's first and largest voluntary medical center and my five years at a large state hospital as the most interesting and rewarding of my life, providing enough material and inspiration for a dozen books, if one only had years enough to write them. At 69, it's comforting to look ahead with knowledge that P. G. Wodehouse did his last Bertie and Jeeves book at ninety-two."

* * *

Van DEUSEN, Glyndon Garlock 1897-

PERSONAL: Born September 22, 1897, in Clifton Springs, N.Y.; son of Frank F. and Jennie May (Garlock) Van Deusen; married Ruth Naomi Litteer, 1931; children: Nicholas, Nancy. *Education:* University of Rochester, B.A., 1925; Amherst College, M.A., 1926; Columbia University, Ph.D., 1932. *Home:* 10 Manhattan Sq., Apt. 3G, Rochester, N.Y. 14607.

CAREER: University of Rochester, Rochester, N.Y., instructor, 1930-33, assistant professor, 1933-42, associate professor, 1942-47, professor of history, 1947-62, chairman of department, 1954-62, research professor emeritus, 1962—. Teacher, Salzburg Seminar in American Studies, Salzburg, Austria, summers, 1950, and 1952. Fulbright lecturer in American history, University of New Zealand, Dunedin, 1951-52. *Member:* American Historical Association, Society of American Historians, Organization of American Historians, Rochester Association for the United Nations (president, 1953-54), Phi Beta Kappa. *Awards, honors:* Albert J. Beveridge Award, 1950, for manuscript of *Horace Greeley: Nineteenth-Century Crusader;* Fletcher Pratt Award, 1967.

WRITINGS: Sieyes: His Life and His Nationalism, Columbia University Press, 1932; *The Life of Henry Clay,* Little, Brown, 1937, reprinted, Greenwood Press, 1979; *Thurlow Weed: Wizard of the Lobby,* Little, Brown, 1947, reprinted, Da Capo Press, 1969; *Horace Greeley: Nineteenth-Century Crusader,* University of Pennsylvania Press, 1953; *The Jacksonian Era: 1828-1848,* Harper, 1959; (with Dexter Perkins) *The United States of America: A History,* two volumes, Macmillan, 1962, 2nd edition, 1968; (editor with Herbert Bass) *Readings in American History,* two volumes, Macmillan, 1962; (with Dexter Perkins) *The American Democracy: Its Rise to Power,* Macmillan, 1964; *William Henry Seward,* Oxford University Press, 1967; *The Rise and Decline of Jacksonian Democracy,* Robert E. Krieger, 1979. Contributor to history journals. Member of editorial board, *Mississippi Valley Historical Review,* 1958-61.

AVOCATIONAL INTERESTS: Gardening, travel.

* * *

van ITALLIE, Jean-Claude 1936-

PERSONAL: Born May 25, 1936, in Brussels, Belgium; came to United States in 1940, naturalized in 1952; son of Hugo Ferdinand (an investment banker) and Marthe (Levy) van Itallie. *Education:* Harvard University, B.A., 1958; graduate study, New York University, 1959. *Religion:* Buddhist (Vajrayana). *Address:* Box 7, Charlemont, Mass. 01339; and 463 West St., New York, N.Y. 10014. *Agent:* Janet Roberts, William Morris Agency, 1350 Avenue of the Americas, New York, N.Y. 10019.

CAREER: Playwright; *Transatlantic Review,* New York City, associate editor, 1959-61; Columbia Broadcasting System, New York City, researcher, 1962; Open Theatre, New York City, playwright-in-residence, 1963-68; New School for Social Research, New York City, instructor in playwriting, 1968 and 1972; Yale University, Drama School, New Haven, Conn., instructor in playwriting, 1969; Princeton University, Princeton, N.J., lecturer, 1972—. Teacher of playwriting, Naropa Institute, Boulder, Colo., 1974-78; visiting Mellon Professor, Amherst College, 1976. Member of Theater Advisory Panel, National Council of the Arts, 1971-73. *Awards, honors:* Rockefeller Foundation grant, 1962-63; Guggenheim fellow, 1963-64; Vernon Rice Drama Desk Award, Outer Circle Critics Award, and Jersey Journal Award, all in 1967, all for "America Hurrah"; Off-Broadway Award (Obie), 1969, for "The Serpent"; Creative Artists Public Service grant, 1975; Ph.D., Kent State University, 1977.

WRITINGS: (Contributor) Joseph F. McCrindle, editor, *Stories from the "Transatlantic Review,"* Holt, 1970; (author of introduction, and contributor) McCrindle, editor, *Behind the Scenes: Theatre and Film Interviews from the "Transatlantic Review,"* Holt, 1971; (contributor) *The American Theatre, 1970-1971,* International Theatre Institute of the United States, and Scribner, 1972. Also author of unpublished book, *To India: A Journal.*

Plays: *America Hurrah* (three one-acts; contains "Interview" [previously performed as "Pavane" Off-Off-Broadway at Cafe La Mama, April, 1965], "TV," and "Motel" [previously performed as "America Hurrah" Off-Off-Broadway at Cafe La Mama, April, 1965]; first produced Off-Broadway at Pocket Theatre, November 6, 1966; produced in London at Royal Court Theatre, June, 1967), Coward, 1967 (British publication under same title also contains "War" [also see below] and "Almost Like Being" [also see below], Penguin, 1967); *War and Four Other Plays* (contains "War" [one-act; first performed by Barr-Wilder-Albee Playwrights Unit Off-Off-Broadway at Vandam Theatre, December 22, 1963; produced Off-Broadway at Martinique Theatre, April 11, 1966], "I'm Really Here" [one-act; first produced by Barr-Wilder-Albee Playwrights Unit Off-Off-Broadway at Vandam Theatre, February, 1965], "Almost Like Being" [one-act; first produced by Barr-Wilder-Albee Playwrights Unit Off-Off-Broadway at Vandam Theatre, February, 1965; published in *Tulane Drama Review,* summer, 1965], "Where Is de Queen?" [one-act; first produced under title "Dream" by the Open Theatre Off-Off-Broadway at Cafe La Mama, December, 1965; produced as "Where Is de Queen?" in Minneapolis, Minn. at Firehouse Theatre, March, 1966], and "The Hunter and the Bird" [one-act; first produced by the Open Theater Off-Broadway at Sheridan Square Playhouse, 1965]), Dramatists Play Service, 1967; (with Sharon Thie) "Thoughts on the Instant of Greeting a Friend on the Street" (one-act; also see below; first produced with other plays under title "Collision Course" Off-Broadway at Cafe au Go Go, May 8, 1968), published in *Collision Course* (also see below), edited by Edward Parone, Random House, 1968; (in collaboration with players of the Open Theatre, under direction of Joseph Chaikin) *The Serpent: A Ceremony* (one-act; first produced by Open Theatre in Rome at Teatro degli Arte, 1968; produced in Cambridge, Mass. at Loeb Drama Center, January 10, 1969; produced by Open Theatre Off-Broadway at Public Theatre, May 16, 1969), Atheneum, 1969.

Mystery Play (two-act; produced Off-Broadway at Cherry Lane Theatre, January 3, 1973), Dramatists Play Service, 1973, revised version published and produced as *The King of the United States* (produced in Westbeth, N.Y. at Theatre for the New City, May, 1973), Dramatists Play Service, 1975; *Seven Short and Very Short Plays* (contains "Eat Cake" [produced in Denver, Colo., 1971], "Take a Deep Breath" [one-act; first produced in New York by the D.M.Z. political cabaret, 1969], "Photographs: Mary and Howard" [produced in Los Angeles, 1969], "Harold," "Thoughts on the Instant of Greeting a Friend in the Street," "The Naked Nun," and "The Girl and the Soldier" [produced in Los Angeles, 1967]), Dramatists Play Service, 1973; (adapter) Anton Chekhov, *The Seagull* (first produced in Princeton, N.J. at McCarter Theatre, October, 1973; produced in New York at Manhattan Theater Club, 1975), Dramatists Play Service, 1974; *A Fable* (produced in New York at Lenox Arts Center, 1975), Dramatists Play Service, 1976; (adapter) Chekhov, *The Cherry Orchard* (produced in New York at Lincoln Center for the Performing Arts, 1977), Grove, 1977.

Other plays: "Children on the Shore," 1959; "From an Odets Kitchen," first produced by the Open Theatre Off-Broadway at Sheridan Square Playhouse, December, 1963; "The Murdered Woman," first produced by the Open Theatre Off-Broadway at Martinique Theatre, April, 1964; "The First Fool," 1964; (with Megan Terry and Sam Shepard) "Nightwalk," produced in New York by the Open Theatre, 1973; (adapter) Euripides, "Medea," first produced in Kent, Ohio by Kent State University student group, 1979; (adapter) Chekhov, "Three Sisters," first produced in New York by River Arts Productions, 1979; "Bag Lady," first produced in New York at Theatre for the New City, November, 1979. Also author of "The Airplane," "Picnic in Spring," "Simple Simon," "The Worlds of Rip Van Winkle," and "Naropa."

Television scripts for CBS series, "Look Up and Live": "The Stepinac Case," 1963; "New Church Architecture, I," 1964; "New Church Architecture, II," 1964; "The Sounds of Courage," 1965; "Hobbies, or Things Are All Right with the Forbushers," 1967; "Take a Deep Breath," 1969. Also writer of eleven adaptations for the series, 1964-66.

Screenplay adaptations: "Three Lives for Mississippi" (based on the novel by William Bradford Huie), Cinema Center Films, 1971; (author of first draft) "Follies" (based on the musical by William Goldman), 20th Century-Fox, 1973. Also wrote and produced a 20-minute film, "The Box Is Empty," screened with other experimental films at Cinematheque, New York, N.Y., March, 1965.

Plays are represented in anthologies, including: *Eight Plays from Off-Off-Broadway,* edited by Nick Orzel and Michael Smith, Bobbs-Merrill, 1966; *Playwrights for Tomorrow,* Volume III, edited by Arthur H. Ballet, University of Minnesota Press, 1967; *The Off-Off-Broadway Book: The Plays,*

People, Theaters, edited by Albert Poland, Bobbs-Merrill, 1972. Contributor to *New York Times, Village Voice, Transatlantic Review,* and other publications.

WORK IN PROGRESS: Adapting Anton Chekhov's "Uncle Vanya."

SIDELIGHTS: "The first of the Off-Off-Broadway playwrights to attract considerable attention was Jean-Claude van Itallie," writes Mardi Valgemae. Identified with the Open Theatre group which is directed by Joseph Chaikin, van Itallie's plays explore the sources and dimensions of unhappiness and violence in American life; the inability to cope with the disparity between remembered, mythical ideals and present realities, the sentimental longing for the old, personal alienation, self-repression, and fear are shown to culminate in either violent behavior or withdrawal from the world. Phyllis Wagner writes, however, that these themes are underlined by a belief that "it is possible for human beings to expand beyond the cultural and personal limits they have imposed on themselves." In an interview with Wagner, van Itallie discusses the difficulty in confronting an audience with these issues, given the ritualistic nature of the theater: "You go, and you discuss certain things during intermission and you go away and you've had a certain amount of pleasure. The playwright who is working seriously very much needs to get to the audience more directly. . . . He's got to use seduction, he's got to use shock, he's got to use different forms of theater." Robert Pasolli assesses this objective, which van Itallie shares with the Open Theater, as "an effort to make visible in acting and staging those untidy masses of emotional and psychic experience which the Absurdists, Pinter, and the new American writers have tapped, to mine aspects of human experience which naturalism, realism, and what has been called 'the narrative fix' obscure."

While noting that "you can't transgress the boundaries of reality. Reality is everything . . . ," van Itallie states that "you can transgress what you *think* are reality's boundaries. . . . You can certainly push beyond what you thought was allowable, what you thought was the shape of things." The extension of reality to include the realm of dreams is based on the idea that "reality is disguised and revealed in our dreams as a metaphor. If the metaphor a playwright chooses comes from deep enough within him, then he must have faith that, with the application of some craft, it will induce recognition in the audience of its own dream, conveying and revealing a share of the public unconscious . . . a private dream reshaped and publicly revealed to be everyone's." Although non-verbal communication is a major device in van Itallie's exploration of inner reality, language, when juxtaposed to dramatic action, provides an otherwise unobtainable focus and helps to elicit from the audience the desired shock of recognition—in the playwright's words, the "Ah, Yes!" experience. He feels it necessary, however, to move away from the conventional use of dialogue, to counteract the "understandable, but frightening mistrust of words everywhere, because they are used as the lying tools of the power forces. . . . One has to find a new way to use language . . . where each word is chosen with care for its importance in juxtaposition with the other words and in juxtaposition with the action that's going on on stage—so that the total *play* comes out being a new language."

Robert Brustein believes that van Itallie has "discovered the truest poetic function of the theatre, which is to . . . invent metaphors which can poignantly suggest a nation's nightmares and afflictions. These metaphors solve nothing, change nothing, transform nothing, but they do manage to relax frustration and assuage loneliness by showing that it is still possible for men to share a common humanity." In "Bag Lady" van Itallie selects as metaphor one of those women seen in many urban areas who live on the street and carry all of their belongings with them in shopping bags. "There is something primordial about the arrangement: life is reduced to necessities," comments Mel Gussow. "The play is less a search for psychological motivations, for literal behavior patterns, than it is an attempt to give the character a kind of mythic stature. . . . Even after the play ends, we are not sure who she is and where she is from. She may even be an avatar. . . . The play is not, as one might expect, a literal transcription from the street, but a poetic interpretation by a discerning playwright."

Van Itallie told *CA:* "[I] speak French, hate cities especially New York City where I live half the time because it's stimulating, love New England where I live on a farm the other part of the time when I'm not traveling which I like to do, don't eat meat much or drink coffee, prefer herb teas and fresh fruit, worry about air pollution, the insanity of governments generally and ours in specific, protest whenever possible against war, do a lot of yoga and exercise, practice Buddhism, [and] treasure my good friends."

Several of van Itallie's plays have been produced on television, including "Pavane" and "Thoughts on the Instant of Greeting a Friend on the Street," both NET, 1969, and "America Hurrah" and "Take a Deep Breath," both New York Television Theater, 1969. His papers have been collected at Kent State University.

BIOGRAPHICAL/CRITICAL SOURCES: Tulane Drama Review, summer, 1966; *Newsday,* November 23, 1966; *New York Times,* November 27, 1966, December 11, 1966, November 7, 1967, November 27, 1979; Robert Brustein, *The Third Theatre,* Knopf, 1969; Robert Pasolli, *A Book on the Open Theater,* Bobbs-Merrill, 1970; *Theatre 2: American Theatre, 1968-69,* International Theatre Institute, 1970; John Lahr, *Up Against the Fourth Wall: Essays on Modern Theatre,* Grove, 1970; *Twentieth Century Literature,* October, 1971; *Serif* (entire issue), winter, 1972; *Contemporary Literary Criticism,* Volume III, Gale, 1975.

* * *

VELIE, Alan R. 1937-

PERSONAL: Born November 16, 1937, in New York, N.Y.; son of Lester (a writer) and Frances (Rockmore) Velie; married Sue Thompson (a teacher), June 23, 1962; children: Jonathan Thompson, William Place. *Education:* Harvard University, B.A., 1959; Stanford University, M.A. and Ph.D. *Politics:* Democrat. *Home:* 1178 Merrymen Green, Norman, Okla. 73069. *Office:* Department of English, University of Oklahoma, Norman, Okla. 73069.

CAREER: University of Oklahoma, Norman, member of faculty teaching English and American Indian literature, 1967—, chairman of English department, 1978—. *Military service:* U.S. Marine Corps, 1959-62; became first lieutenant. *Awards, honors:* National Endowment for the Humanities fellowship, 1973.

WRITINGS: Shakespeare's Repentance Plays, Fairleigh Dickinson University Press, 1972; *Blood and Knavery,* Fairleigh Dickinson University Press, 1973; *Man and Nature in Literature,* Goodyear Publishing, 1974; *American Indian Literature: An Anthology,* University of Oklahoma Press, 1979.

VIERECK, Peter (Robert Edwin) 1916-

PERSONAL: Born August 5, 1916, in New York, N.Y.; son of George Sylvester (a poet) and Margaret (Hein) Viereck; married Anya de Markov, June, 1945 (divorced May, 1970); married Betty Martin Falkenberg, August 30, 1972; children: (first marriage) John-Alexis, Valerie Edwina (Mrs. John Gibbs). *Education:* Harvard University, B.S. (summa cum laude), 1937, M.A., 1939, Ph.D., 1942; Christ Church, Oxford, graduate study, 1937-38. *Home:* 12 Silver St., South Hadley, Mass. 01075. *Office:* Mount Holyoke College, South Hadley, Mass.

CAREER: Harvard University, Cambridge, Mass., instructor in German literature, tutor in history and literature departments, 1946-47; Smith College, Northampton, Mass., assistant professor of history, 1947-48, visiting lecturer in Russian history, 1948-49; Mount Holyoke College, South Hadley, Mass., associate professor, 1948-55, professor of modern European and Russian history, 1955-65, holds Mt. Holyoke Alumnae Foundation Chair of Interpretive Studies, 1965—. Visiting lecturer on American culture at Oxford University, 1953; Whittal Lecturer in Poetry, Library of Congress, 1954, 1963; Fulbright professor in American poetry and civilization, University of Florence, 1955; Elliston Chair, poetry lecturer, University of Cincinnati, 1956; visiting lecturer, University of California, Berkeley, 1957, 1964, and City College of the City University of New York, 1964; director of poetry workshop, New York Writers Conference, 1965-67. Speaker at numerous universities. Participated in cultural exchange mission to Russia for U.S. State Department, 1961; visiting research scholar in Russia for Twentieth Century Fund, 1962-63. *Military service:* U.S. Army, Psychological Warfare, 1943-45; awarded two battle stars; taught history at U.S. Army University, Florence, Italy, 1945.

MEMBER: American Committee for Cultural Freedom (member of executive committee), Committee for Basic Education (charter member), American Historical Association, Oxford Society, Poetry Society of America, P.E.N., Phi Beta Kappa, Harvard Club (New York City), Harvard Club of London, Bryce Club (Oxford, England). *Awards, honors:* Tietjens Prize for poetry, 1948; Pulitzer Prize for poetry, 1949, for *Terror and Decorum;* Guggenheim fellowship, Rome, 1949-50; Rockefeller Foundation researcher in history, Germany, summer, 1958; most distinguished alumnus award, Horace Mann School for Boys, 1958; honorary L.H.D. from Olivet College, 1959; National Endowment for the Humanities senior research fellow, 1969.

WRITINGS—All published by Scribner, except as indicated: *Metapolitics: From the Romantics to Hitler,* 1941, revised edition published as *Metapolitics: The Roots of the Nazi Mind,* Capricorn Books, 1961, 2nd revised edition, 1965; *Terror and Decorum: Poems, 1940-1948,* 1948, reprinted, Greenwood Press, 1972; *Conservatism Revisited: The Revolt against Revolt, 1815-1949,* 1949, 2nd edition published as *Conservatism Revisited, and the New Conservatism: What Went Wrong?,* 1962, 3rd edition, 1972; *Strike through the Mask: New Lyrical Poems,* 1950, reprinted, Greenwood Press, 1972; *The First Morning: New Poems,* 1952, reprinted Greenwood Press, 1972; *Shame and Glory of the Intellectuals: Babbitt, Jr. vs. the Rediscovery of Values,* Beacon Press, 1953, reprinted, Greenwood Press, 1978; *Dream and Responsibility: The Tension between Poetry and Society,* University Press of Washington, D.C., 1953, reprinted, 1972; *The Unadjusted Man: A New Hero for Americans,* Beacon Press, 1956, reprinted, Greenwood Press, 1973; *Conservatism: From John Adams to Churchill,* Van Nostrand, 1956, revised edition, 1962, reprinted, Greenwood Press, 1978; *The Persimmon Tree* (poems), 1956; *Inner Liberty: The Stubborn Grit in the Machine,* Pendle Hill, 1957; *The Tree Witch: A Poem and a Play (First of All a Poem),* 1961; *New and Selected Poems, 1932-1967,* Bobbs-Merrill, 1967.

Contributor: *Mid-Century American Poets,* Twayne, 1950; *Arts in Renewal,* University of Pennsylvania Press, 1951; *The New American Right,* Criterion, 1955; *Education in a Free Society,* University of Pittsburgh Press, 1958; *The Radical Right,* Doubleday, 1963; P. H. Juviler and H. W. Morton, editors, *Soviet Policy Making,* Burns & McEachern, 1967; D. B. James, editor, *Outside Looking In,* Harper, 1972; Louis Filler, editor, *A Question of Quality,* Bowling Green University Popular Press, 1976. Contributor of monographs, essays, reviews, and poems to popular magazines and professional journals.

WORK IN PROGRESS: A book on his experience with Soviet poets and intellectuals, tentatively entitled *A New Russian Revolution.*

SIDELIGHTS: Peter Viereck's first book seems to have made a strong impression on reviewers. For example, John Barnes calls *Metapolitics* "a corrosive analysis of some of the ideas of National Socialism. . . . It does as much as any book since the war began to define the specifically German elements of what Mr. Viereck calls 'the theology of nightmare.'" A reviewer for *Christian Science Monitor* finds it "an extremely important book, notable because it makes it possible for the normal western mind to understand at least partially the disease which has warped the thinking of the German people. This is no easy task because no German has ever been able to explain it intelligently." Crane Brinton writes in *Saturday Review of Literature:* "This is the best account of the intellectual origins of Nazism available to the general reader. It is a controversial book, packed with points worth disputing."

Catholic World's Erik von Kuehnelt-Leddihn expresses a similar opinion of Viereck's later nonfiction book, *Shame and Glory of the Intellectuals.* He comments: "In this . . . internally cohesive and brilliant statement of a young conservative spokesman, the reader will be intellectually stimulated by a scintillating wealth of ideas. He will also be introduced to the indignation of a true American idealist and forced to shake with laughter at the salty humor of a highly amusing author." Elmer Davis adds, "He has a good many things of importance to say and we had better listen to him."

While reviewers are generally favorable toward Viereck's nonfiction work, critics frequently comment on the time it has taken him to mature as a poet. Although Chad Walsh's 1956 review of *The Persimmon Tree* describes Viereck as "the lyricist who is now coming into his own," this maturation process has been a long one for him. The early reviews of *Terror and Decorum* reflect this. In *Nation,* Rolfe Humphries points out that "Mr. Viereck has . . . a good deal to learn," and David Daiches notes that while there was great promise evident in Viereck's earlier work, "much in this volume is still promise." Though Selden Rodman acknowledges that "his book as a whole is so rich in experimental vigor, so full of new poetic attitudes toward civilization and its discontents, so fresh and earthy in its reanimation of the American spirit, that it seems to offer endless possibilities of development—both for Viereck himself, and for other young poets," he also writes that Viereck's "style is much less finished." Other reviewers of the prize-winning book found faults besides Viereck's lack of maturity. Robert Fitzgerald notes that "the poems are lively and a few of them sustain a neat, coarse clarity and a satiric turn of fancy that is not disagreeable. However, he has a warm, breezy, familiar way of being acutely embarrassing." He continues, "The favorable reception of this patter may be significant, but I judge it to be momentary, for Viereck has as yet written very little to which one could wish to return often or with serious interest." Paul Goodman agrees in a *Poetry* review, saying "it is hard to read these verses seriously because, though Viereck has many lively talents, he seems to have no personal language."

James Reaney echoes Goodman's opinion when he writes in *Canadian Forum:* "Peter Viereck's poems, for the most part ... are the results of forced fancy, of imagination overdriven by a sort of imagery-engine.... At their best these poems describe a horrifying, harsh world not even our own but always five centuries ahead.... His poems ... are a perfect illustration of the proverb: One may be a visionary and a visionary with all the correct myths, symbols, and assorted gobbets of erudition on their right places and still not be a poet."

Viereck's collection *Strike through the Mask,* published in 1950, generated comments as to his classification as a lyric poet. While *New York Times* reviewer W. C. Williams feels that "Viereck's talent is ... in the purest sense lyrical, sensitive, [and] distinguished in feeling," Selden Rodman disagrees, explaining "the real trouble [with *Strike through the Mask*], is that Viereck is not a lyric poet at all.... His great gifts are in the realm of the didactic, the meditative and perhaps the pastoral. And if he exercises them in these fields with restraint, he can well become the universal catalyst he aspires to be." But Anne Freemantle's review of *First Morning* in *Commonweal* still reflects the early complaints of Viereck's maturity as a poet: 'Dr. Viereck is staying young too long. His 'new poems' are still full of promise; but by now, in his thirties, he should have backed them up with performance."

Since the publication of *The Persimmon Tree* in 1956, critics have apparently sensed a difference in Viereck's tone. The book is lauded by L. B. Drake, who notes in *Atlantic,* "Gone is that vague unease, that preoccupation with nightmare and fugue that haunted his earlier work," while Hayden Carruth finds "the new poems offer a gentler flow, an easier tone of voice." Walsh believes that "underneath the technical fireworks and plain vitality was a quieter, more tranquil Viereck, the lyricist gravely recording the eternal flow of life and experience."

A decade later, Viereck's publication of *New and Selected Poems* prompts Andrew Glaze to write: "It is hard to imagine a poet more out of style at this moment than Peter Viereck," and yet, "he goes on in his baroque way, turning out complicated, interesting and old-fashioned pieces in the midst of triumphant, new alien styles.... He has always been unpredictable and difficult. He has never made points with moderation and safety.... No one has created more wonderful poems out of near-doggerel rhythms and unlikely rhymes, as though from the pure pleasure of barely skirting disaster.... Even when his poems fail, they are rarely as dull as the poetry we have had to grow accustomed to. In an era overpowered with self-revelation and interiorness, Viereck's fascination with ideas and the *fun* of ideas is blessed. Never have we needed relief more from skilled heartfelt dreariness and fervent amateurism."

In addition, Ernest Kroll notes that "it isn't easy ... to mistake a poem by Peter Viereck. Impulse in the saddle, with unbounded energy raring to take on any subject, is the outstanding impression one gets from his work.... He frequently takes his reader for a wild ride from which he alone, the poet, returns.... There is fortunately, however, another Viereck, the memorable one, who can and does rein his mount in tightly after the wilder rides." According to *Shenandoah*'s Lisel Mueller, Viereck "believes that poetry must communicate and that it must celebrate the emotional life, the life of meaning rather than gesture." She continues, "He writes for the intelligent common reader, in the traditional forms he is intent on preserving. He writes with wit, spirit, conviction and a great understanding of history and modern western culture."

Thus, after many years of slow development and disappointment, the promise so hopefully anticipated in 1948 is finally regarded as fulfilled in many critics' eyes. As one of those critics, Andrew Glaze, concludes, "Wouldn't it be pleasant if [Viereck] were recognized right now for what he is: one of our greatest living poets?"

BIOGRAPHICAL/CRITICAL SOURCES: Saturday Review of Literature, October 4, 1941, October 9, 1948; *Books,* October 5, 1941; *Nation,* October 11, 1941, November 13, 1948; *Christian Science Monitor,* November 7, 1941, December 24, 1953, October 11, 1956; *New York Herald Tribune Weekly Book Review,* November 21, 1948, October 9, 1949; *New York Times,* November 21, 1948, March 12, 1950, March 15, 1953, October 28, 1956; *Poetry,* February, 1949, February, 1957; *Canadian Forum,* April, 1949; *Commonweal,* August 5, 1949, October 24, 1952; *New Republic,* August 8, 1949, April 24, 1950, March 16, 1953; *New York Herald Tribune Book Review,* March 26, 1950, March 22, 1953; *New Yorker,* January 31, 1953, March 21, 1953, March 24, 1962; *Saturday Review,* February 28, 1953, July 22, 1961, October 14, 1967; *Catholic World,* July, 1953; *Atlantic,* June, 1957; *Kirkus,* January 15, 1961; *Library Journal,* April 1, 1961; Paul Engle and Joseph Langland, editors, *Poet's Choice,* Dial Press, 1962; Howard Nemerov, *Poetry and Fiction,* Rutgers University Press, 1963; Marie Henault, *Peter Viereck, Poet and Historian,* Twayne, 1966; *New York Times Book Review,* August 6, 1967; *Shenandoah,* spring, 1968; *New Leader,* April 8, 1969; *Michigan Quarterly Review,* summer, 1969; *Contemporary Literary Criticism,* Volume IV, Gale, 1975.†

—Sketch by Penelope S. Gordon

* * *

VILLANUEVA, Tino 1941-

PERSONAL: Born December 11, 1941, in San Marcos, Tex.; son of Lino B. and Leonor (Rios) Villanueva. *Education:* Southwest Texas State University, B.A., 1969; State University of New York at Buffalo, M.A., 1971. *Address:* P.O. Box 450-316 Scott St., San Marcos, Tex. 78666; and 879 Beacon St., Apt. 4, Boston, Mass. 02215. *Agent:* Odon Betanzos, 125 Queen St., Staten Island, N.Y. 10314. *Office:* Department of Spanish, Wellesley College, Wellesley, Mass. 02181.

CAREER: State University of New York at Buffalo, instructor in Spanish, 1969-71; Boston University, Boston, Mass., lecturer in Spanish, 1971-1976; Wellesley College, Wellesley, Mass., instructor in Spanish, 1974—. Locutor and program director for "La Hora Hispana," broadcast for the Spanish-speaking community by Harvard University radio station WHRB. *Military service:* U.S. Army, 1964-66. *Member:* American Association of Teachers of Spanish and Portuguese. *Awards, honors:* Ford Foundation fellowship, 1978-79.

WRITINGS: (Contributor) O. Romano and H. Rios, editors, *El Espejo/The Mirror: Selected Chicano Literature,* Quinto Sol Publications, 1972; *Hay Otra Voz Poems* (title means "There Is Another Voice Poems"), Editorial Mensaje, 1972, 3rd edition, 1979; (with others) *Literatura Chicana: Texto Y Contexto* (title means "Chicano Literature: Text and Context"), Prentice-Hall, 1973; (contributor) Philip D. Ortego, editor, *We Are Chicanos: An Anthology of Mexican-American Literature,* Washington Square Press; 1974; *Chicanos: Antologia de ensayos y literatura* (title means "Chicanos: Anthology of Essays and Literature"), Fondo de Cultura Economica, 1979. Contributor of poetry to *San Antonio Express/News, Persona, El Grito, Entre Nosotros, Caribbean Review, Hispamerica: Revista De Literatura, Revista Chicano-Riquena, Poema Convidado,* and *Texas Quarterly;* contributor of essays to *Cuadernos Hispanoamericanos, Papeles de Son Armadans,* and *Journal of Spanish Studies: Twentieth Century.*

WORK IN PROGRESS: A book, *Tres poetas de la Oposicion: Celaya, Gonzalez y Caballero Bonald (Estudio y entrevistas).*

* * *

VILLIERS, Alan (John) 1903-

PERSONAL: Born September 23, 1903, in Melbourne, Australia; son of Leon Joseph (a poet) and Anastasia (Hayes) Villiers; married Daphne Kay Harris, 1924 (divorced, 1936); married Nancie Wills, December 24, 1940; children: (second marriage) Christopher Alan, Katherine Lisbeth, Peter John. *Education:* Attended state schools and Essendon High School in Melbourne, Australia. *Home:* 1-A Lucerne Rd., Oxford OX2 7QB, England. *Agent:* A. Watkins, Inc., 77 Park Ave., New York, N.Y. 10016.

CAREER: Author, photographer, adventurer, and sailor; sailing ship apprentice, 1919; sailed with pioneer whaling ship, *Sir James Clark Ross,* Ross Sea, Antarctica, 1923-24; *Hobart Mercury,* Hobart, Tasmania, journalist, 1925-27; free-lance writer and photographer, 1929—. In command of ship, *Joseph Conrad,* 1934-36; sailed with Arab dhows in Persian Gulf and Red Sea, 1938-39, Portuguese dory-fishing schooner, *Argus,* 1950, *Mayflower II,* 1957, and nuclear ship, *Savannah,* 1962; master of training ship, *Warspite,* Outward Bound Sea School, Aberdovey, North Wales, 1949. President, vice-president, Society for Nautical Research; trustee, National Maritime Museum, 1948-74. Nautical advisor to films "Moby Dick," 1955, "John Paul Jones," 1958, "Billy Budd," 1961, and "Hawaii," 1965. *Military service:* Royal Navy Reserve, 1940-44; became commander; received Distinguished Service Cross. *Member:* Royal Geographical Society (fellow), Circumnavigators Club (New York), Cosmos Club (Washington, D.C.). *Awards, honors:* Camoes Prize for literature (Portugal), for *Quest of the Schooner Argus;* commendador, Order of St. James of the Sword (Portugal).

WRITINGS: Whaling in the Frozen South, Bobbs-Merrill, 1925; *Falmouth for Orders,* Scribner, 1929, reprinted, Patrick Stephens, 1976; *By Way of Cape Horn,* Scribner, 1930; *Vanished Fleets,* Holt, 1930, reprinted, Scribner, 1974; *The Sea in Ships* (pictures), Morrow, 1932; *Grain Race,* Scribner, 1934; *Cruise of the Conrad,* Scribner, 1934; *Last of the Wind Ships* (pictures), Morrow, 1934; *Making of a Sailor* (pictures), Morrow, 1938; (self-illustrated) *Sons of Sinbad,* Scribner, 1940, reprinted, 1969; *The Set of the Sails* (autobiography), Scribner, 1949, reprinted, White Lion Publishers, 1974; *The Coral Sea,* McGraw, 1950; *Quest of the Schooner Argus,* Scribner, 1951; *Monsoon Seas,* McGraw, 1952; (self-illustrated) *The Way of a Ship,* Scribner, 1954, reprinted, 1975; *Posted Missing,* Scribner, 1956; *Sailing Eagle* (pictures), Scribner, 1956; *Wild Ocean,* McGraw, 1957; *The Western Ocean: The Story of the North Atlantic,* Museum Press, 1957; *The Navigators and the Merchant Navy,* Brown, Son & Ferguson, 1957; *Give Me a Ship to Sail,* Scribner, 1958; (editor and author of introduction) *Great Sea Stories,* Dell, 1959.

(With others) *Men, Ships and the Sea,* National Geographic Society, 1962, new edition, 1973; *The "Cutty Sark": Last of a Glorious Era,* Hodder & Stoughton, 1963; *Captain James Cook,* Scribner, 1967 (published in England as *Captain Cook, the Seaman's Seaman: A Study of the Great Discoverer,* Hodder & Stoughton, 1967); *The Deep Sea Fishermen,* Hodder & Stoughton, 1970; *The War with Cape Horn,* Scribner, 1971; (with Henri Picard) *The Bounty Ships of France: The Story of the French Cape Horn Sailing Ships,* Patrick Stephens, 1972, Scribner, 1973; *My Favourite Sea Stories,* Lutterworth, 1972; *Voyaging with the Wind: An Introduction to Sailing Large Square-Rigged Ships,* H.M.S.O., 1975; (with Basil Bathe) *The Visual Encyclopedia of Nautical Terms under Sail,* Crown, 1978.

Juvenile books: *Whalers of the Midnight Sun,* Scribner, 1934; *Joey Goes to Sea,* McGraw, 1952; *And Not to Yield,* Scribner, 1953; *Pilot Pete,* Museum Press, 1953; *Stormalong,* Routledge & Kegan Paul, 1958; *The New Mayflower,* Scribner, 1959; (compiler) *Of Ships and Men: A Personal Anthology,* George Newnes, 1962, Arco, 1964; *The Ocean: Man's Conquest of the Sea,* Dutton, 1963 (published in England as *Oceans of the World: Man's Conquest of the Sea,* Museum Press, 1963); *Battle of Trafalgar,* Macmillan, 1965. Contributor to *National Geographic.*

SIDELIGHTS: Alan Villiers' career as sailor and adventurer has been quite varied. He ran away to sea at the age of fifteen. Since that time, writes Harry Gordon, "he has been criss-crossing the world's oceans, fascinated always by the problems that confronted men like Magellan, Tasman, Dampier and Cook." In 1957, Villiers sailed the *Mayflower II* (a replica of the 1620 sailing vessel) over the same course taken by the original *Mayflower.* The voyage was fifty-four days in progress. In his own ship, the *Joseph Conrad,* Villiers sailed some 58,000 miles around the world. Villiers also sailed with the nuclear ship *Savannah* when, as he states in his preface to *Oceans of the World,* "she made history by being the first cargo and passenger merchantman to go to sea under nuclear power."

In a review of Villiers' biography of James Cook, Gordon comments: "Alan Villiers is one of those men who seem to have been dealt the wrong century. It would be wrong to call them historical misfits, but they do give the impression that they would have fitted in admirably at some other moment in history. . . . In Villiers' case the 18th century, a vintage one for explorers, would have suited well; his passion is for old sailing ships, and he has dedicated most of his life to the study and handling of them. He has a deep nostalgia for a time he never knew."

BIOGRAPHICAL/CRITICAL SOURCES: Newsweek, January 10, 1949; *Scholastic,* April 12, 1957; *U.S. News and World Report,* June 21, 1957; Alan Villiers, *Oceans of the World: Man's Conquest of the Sea,* Museum Press, 1963; *New York Times Book Review,* November 26, 1967, November 11, 1969, February 20, 1972; *New York Times,* November 27, 1967; *Times Literary Supplement,* February 4, 1972, December 8, 1972; *Booklist,* November 1, 1974; *Books and Bookmen,* September, 1978.

* * *

VOLPE, Edmond L(oris) 1922-

PERSONAL: Born November 16, 1922, in New Haven, Conn.; son of Joseph D. and Rose (Maisano) Volpe; married Rose M. Conte, 1950; children: Rosalind, Lisa. *Education:* University of Michigan, A.B., 1943; Columbia University, A.M., 1947, Ph.D., 1954. *Home:* 56 Howard Ave., Staten Island, N.Y. 10301. *Office:* Office of the President, College of Staten Island of the City University of New York, Staten Island, N.Y. 10301.

CAREER: New York University, New York City, instructor, 1949-54; City University of New York, professor of English and chairman of department, City College, New York City, 1954-74, president, College of Staten Island, Staten Island, N.Y., 1974—. Fulbright professor of American literature, in France, 1960-61. *Military service:* U.S. Army, Infantry, 1943-46; became staff sergeant. *Member:* Modern Language Association of America, American Studies Association, American Association of University Professors, Andiron Club (New York; president, 1972—).

WRITINGS: (Co-editor) *Ten Modern Short Novels,* Putnam, 1958; (co-author) *Grammar in Context,* Putnam, 1959; (co-editor) *Nobel Prize Stories,* Noonday, 1959; (co-editor) *Essays of Our Time,* McGraw, 1960; (co-editor) *Nobel Prize Essays,* Noonday, 1960; (co-editor) *Twelve Short Stories,* Macmillan, 1961; (co-editor) *Seven Short Novel Masterpieces,* Popular Library, 1961; (co-editor) *Pulitzer Prize Reader,* Popular Library, 1961; (co-editor) *Reading and Rhetoric from Harper's,* Harper, 1962; (co-editor) *Essays of Our Time II,* McGraw, 1962; *A Reader's Guide to William Faulkner,* Farrar, Straus, 1964; (contributor) Harry T. Moore, editor, *Contemporary American Authors,* University of Southern Illinois Press, 1964; (with Marvin Magalaner) *Poetry: An Introduction to Literature,* Philadelphia Book Co., 1967.

SIDELIGHTS: Edmond L. Volpe told *CA:* "I'm delighted to be labeled a contemporary author. I think of myself, however, primarily as an academic, spinning around in that academic dynamo with its multiple magnets: the class room, administration, educational theory, research, travel, textbook editing and writing, studying, pleasure reading, and, of course, writing."

* * *

VONNEGUT, Kurt, Jr. 1922-

PERSONAL: Born November 11, 1922, in Indianapolis, Ind.; son of Kurt (an architect) and Edith (Lieber) Vonnegut; married Jane Marie Cox, September 1, 1945 (divorced, 1979); married Jill Krementz (a photographer), November 24, 1979; children: (first marriage) Mark, Edith, Nanette; (adopted deceased sister's children) James, Steven, and Kurt Adams. *Education:* Attended Cornell University, 1940-42, and Carnegie Institute of Technology (now Carnegie-Mellon University), 1943; University of Chicago, student, 1945-47, M.A., 1971. *Residence:* New York, N.Y. *Agent:* Donald C. Farber, 600 Madison Ave., New York, N.Y. 10022.

CAREER: Chicago City News Bureau, Chicago, Ill., police reporter, 1947; General Electric Co., Schenectady, N.Y., public relations, 1947-50; free-lance writer, 1950—. Teacher at Hopefield School, Sandwich, Mass., 1965—; lecturer at University of Iowa Writers Workshop, 1965-67, and at Harvard University, 1970-71; distinguished professor at City College of the City University of New York, 1973-74. *Military service:* U.S. Army, Infantry, 1942-45; received Purple Heart. *Member:* Authors League of America, P.E.N. (American Center; vice-president, 1974—), National Institute of Arts and Letters, Delta Upsilon, Barnstable Yacht Club, Barnstable Comedy Club. *Awards, honors:* Guggenheim fellow, Germany, 1967; National Institute of Arts and Letters grant, 1970; Litt.D., Hobart and William Smith Colleges, 1974.

WRITINGS—Novels; published by Delacorte, except as indicated: *Player Piano,* Scribner, 1952, reprinted, Dell, 1974; *The Sirens of Titan,* Dell, 1959; *Canary in a Cathouse* (short stories), Fawcett, 1961; *Mother Night,* Fawcett, 1962; *Cat's Cradle,* Holt, 1963; *God Bless You, Mr. Rosewater, or Pearls before Swine,* Holt, 1965; *Welcome to the Monkey House: A Collection of Short Works,* 1968; *Slaughterhouse Five, or the Children's Crusade: A Duty-Dance with Death, by Kurt Vonnegut, Jr., a Fourth-Generation German-American Now Living in Easy Circumstances on Cape Cod (and Smoking Too Much) Who, as an American Infantry Scout Hors de Combat, as a Prisoner of War, Witnessed the Fire-Bombing of Dresden, Germany, the Florence of the Elbe, a Long Time Ago, and Survived to Tell the Tale: This Is a Novel Somewhat in the Telegraphic Schizophrenic Manner of Tales of the Planet Tralfamadore, Where the Flying Saucers Come From,* 1969; *Breakfast of Champions, or Goodbye Blue Monday,* 1973; *Wampeters, Foma and Granfalloons: Opinions* (essays), 1974; *Slapstick, or Lonesome No More,* 1976; *Jailbird,* 1979; (with Ivan Chermayeff) *Sun Moon Star,* Harper, 1980.

Plays: "Penelope," first produced on Cape Cod, Mass., 1960, revised version published as *Happy Birthday, Wanda June* (first produced Off-Broadway at the Theater De Lys, October 7, 1970), Delacorte, 1971, revised edition, S. French, 1971; *Between Time and Timbuktu, or Prometheus Five: A Space Fantasy* (television play; first produced on National Educational Television Network, 1972), Delacorte, 1972. Also author of "Something Borrowed," 1958, "The Very First Christmas Morning," 1962, "EPICAC," 1963, "My Name Is Everyone," 1964, and "Fortitude," 1968, all produced Off-Broadway or in summer stock.

Contributor of fiction to numerous publications, including *Saturday Evening Post, Cosmopolitan, McCall's, Playboy,* and *Ladies' Home Journal.*

SIDELIGHTS: Although he is now one of America's most widely-read and well-respected novelists, Kurt Vonnegut, Jr. was virtually ignored by critics from the beginning of his writing career until the 1963 publication of *Cat's Cradle.* While this may have been the result of his early classification as a science fiction writer, and it is true that technology and the future have played an important part in much of his work, it is generally agreed that his books go far beyond the realm of most pure science fiction. Ernest W. Ranly explains: "Vonnegut at times adds fantasy to his stories, whereas pure sci-fi permits only what is possible within a given scientific hypothesis. Vonnegut adds humor, a wild black humor, while most sci-fi is serious to the point of boredom. Vonnegut, generally, adds a distinctive sense and literary class. And, finally, Vonnegut seems pre-occupied with genuine human questions, about war, peace, technology, human happiness. He is even bitterly anti-machine, anti-technology, anti-science." According to Leslie A. Fiedler, the early lack of recognition may have had a profound underlying effect on Vonnegut's development as a writer and on his later work. Fiedler says: "To writers like Vonnegut, on the border between New Pop and Old High Art, their initial invisibility is a torment which leaves scars, if not disabling traumas." Fiedler finds that to "discover that from 1952 to 1963 no book of Vonnegut's is recorded as having appeared or been reviewed is to understand the persistent defensiveness which underlies his playful-bitter references to his status as 'a writer of science fiction.' . . . A writer, however much a pro, lives only days by what his stories earn him, [but he] must get through his nights on remembering what the critics say." Whether or not Vonnegut was traumatized by lack of critical recognition is debatable. What is clear is that any reviews of his early novels must be understood to have been written by critics analyzing the developmental work of one of the country's outstanding novelists. The benefit of hindsight, along with the knowledge that Vonnegut has now gained general and academic acceptance, may have an influence on reviewers' opinions and analyses of second or third reprints of his first few books.

The science fiction aspect of Vonnegut's work is explored by Karen and Charles Wood who refer to *Player Piano* as "one of the best science fiction novels ever written," but point out that "it rests uneasily in the science fiction genre precisely because it is such a good novel—a novel, that is, in the Jamesian sense, a detailed examination of human experience. The devotee of science fiction comes away from *Player Piano* with the uneasy feeling that somehow this isn't science fiction at all, that there is something wrong here. What is wrong here is that someone finally wrote a science fiction novel that puts the emphasis on characters—upon human experience and actions." According to the Woods, Vonnegut admits that "science exists and has become vastly important to our lives. The communication of such an idea would not be easy to accomplish without the techniques of science fiction. Therefore Vonnegut both philosophizes and characterizes, and when a statement is made, it draws as much importance from who says it, and how, as from the idea itself."

Peter J. Reed, who sees *Player Piano* as an important social commentary, finds that it is the most difficult of Vonnegut's novels to analyze. He writes: "Initially it may strike us as another socio-moral analysis of the present through the future in the tradition of *The Time Machine, Brave New World,* or *1984*. But then the resemblance shows shifts in the direction of the more immediate kinds of social criticism, like *Babbit, Main Street,* or even *The Grapes of Wrath*. Furthermore, comic episodes become frequent, sometimes roughly in the social-satiric vein of Aldous Huxley or Evelyn Waugh, sometimes as pure slapstick, sometimes almost of the comic strip guffaw-inducing variety. These references to other works and writers should not be taken to imply that Vonnegut is highly derivative, but simply to suggest the mixture present in the novel." The satiric and humorous qualities which Reed mentions are significant in that they are common to much of Vonnegut's work. Like many writers, he uses satire as a means of emphasizing serious points. However Vonnegut has the ability to temper biting satire with warmth and concern for his characters and to direct much of the humor toward himself. The result is that Vonnegut, even when he is at his most critical and fatalistic, does not tend to alienate readers; we are able to identify with the writer because he is just as much the object of satire as the rest of society. As Reed concludes, "the attacks on social ills obviously grow out of a deep compassion, and we sense the gentleness of this writer who so often portrays violence."

The Sirens of Titan is sometimes lumped together with *Player Piano* and several short stories as Vonnegut's "science fiction period." G. K. Wolfe, however, argues that *Sirens* is more closely related, thematically and stylistically, to his later fiction; Wolfe calls the book the "seminal work" in Vonnegut's development as a writer. He writes: "It is not possible to read *Sirens* as mere escapist fiction, for we are consistently drawn back to the individual human element and the harsh realities of meaningless cruelty and death, whether on Mars, Titan, Mercury, or earth. Vonnegut suggests that these realities will follow man wherever he goes, whatever he does, not because of a failure in man's vision of himself (though this is certainly involved), but because, fortunately or unfortunately, they are a part of what makes him human." *Sirens* marks the introduction of several themes that continue throughout much of Vonnegut's later work: the futility of trying to change the world and, as a result, the necessity of change within the individual; the fatality of searching for meaning outside of the self when the answer is really a part of human nature; and the elevation of the main character to new levels of understanding through his quest for meaning in human existence.

Stylistically, too, *Sirens* may be closely linked with Vonnegut's more recent work. Reed finds that "there are far fewer digressions, subplots, and simultaneous developments to keep track of than in *Player Piano,* a fact which helps to make the second novel smoother reading." He also sees other qualities which separate *Sirens* from the first book: "*The Sirens of Titan,* for all its wanderings, futurity, and concern with larger, abstract questions, transmits a greater sense of direction and concreteness. Rather surprising, too, is the fact that this novel with its science fiction orientation, with its robots and near-robot humans, and with its several central characters who are intentionally presented as being rather cold-hearted, generates more human warmth than *Player Piano* which is directly concerned with the agonies of exploring and following conscience, emotion, and love."

Mother Night, Vonnegut's third novel, is the story of Howard W. Campbell, Jr., an American playwright living in Germany at the outbreak of World War II, who is persuaded by the Allies to remain in Germany as a spy while posing as a radio propagandist. After the war he fades into obscurity in the United States until, with his wartime cover still intact, he is kidnapped by Israeli agents to stand trial for his crime. Eventually Campbell's American bosses reveal his true identity, but before he can be released he commits suicide in an Israeli jail cell. Henry Tube calls the book "remarkable for the . . . simplicity of its content, the classical economy of its presentation, and the almost unruffled humour of its tone of voice." And Roger Baker says that "Vonnegut's approach is bracing yet thoughtful; there are passages of detached wit, some moments of splendid drama. One feels sympathy for Campbell, not simply because he is surrounded by American fascists and avenging Israelis, but because he is trying to be true to himself against overwhelming odds."

Mother Night may be considered important for a number of reasons. It is, for instance, Vonnegut's first novel to be written with a first-person narrator. It is also the first in which technology and the future play no significant part; for this reason it is seen by many people as a "transitional" novel between Vonnegut's early and later work. It is the first book in which the author's incidental comments (an "introduction" and "editor's note") play an important part. In the introduction, Vonnegut sets forth the moral of the story: "We are what we pretend to be, so we must be careful about what we pretend to be." Perhaps most obvious, in comparison with the first two novels, *Mother Night* relies very little on time shifts, resulting in a more unified or "conventional" book. Reed sees it as "Vonnegut's most traditional novel in form. Paradoxically, perhaps, that also accounts for the relative weaknesses of the book. For *Mother Night* lacks some of the excitement and verve of *The Sirens of Titan,* for example, and it is sometimes less likely to carry its reader along than that earlier, more wandering fantasy."

Cat's Cradle, published in hardcover in 1963, marked what many critics believe to be the beginning of a turn-around in Vonnegut's career. Although some see the book as *the* point at which his work gained acceptance, it might more properly be viewed as the first in a series of books through which Vonnegut came to the attention of the general public. However, if one single point must be chosen for the transition of Vonnegut from "cult figure" to "popular author" it would most probably be a statement by Graham Greene calling *Cat's Cradle* "one of the three best novels of the year by one of the most able living writers." The book is held in high regard by most critics, including Robert Scholes who writes: "The life of [*Cat's Cradle*] is in its movement, the turns of plot, of character, and of phrase which give it vitality. Vonnegut's prose has the same virtues as his characterization and plotting. It is deceptively simple, suggestive of the ordinary, but capable of startling and illuminating twists and turns. He uses the rhetorical potential of the short sentence and short paragraph better than anyone now writing, often getting a rich comic or dramatic effect by isolating a single sentence in a separate paragraph or excerpting a phrase from context for a bizarre chapter-heading. The apparent simplicity and ordinariness of his writing masks its efficient power, so that we are often startled when Vonnegut pounces on a tired platitude or cliche like a benevolent mongoose and shakes new life into it."

Peter J. Reed believes that *Cat's Cradle* may be the novel that best exemplifies Vonnegut's style. He says that the book "illustrates almost every device, technique, attitude, and subject we encounter in Vonnegut, and is filled with particulars which echo other novels." As an example, *Cat's Cradle* is as autobiographical as any of his work up to that time. The Hoenikker family of the novel closely parallels Vonnegut's own family, consisting of an elder son who is a scientist, a tall middle daughter, and a younger son who joins Delta Upsilon. The narrator is again a writer who, in this case, is working on a book called *The Day the World Ended,* about the bombing of Hiroshima. (This may be the beginning of Vonnegut's preoccupation with apocalyptic endings or an early attempt to deal with the bombing of Dresden later detailed in *Slaughterhouse Five.*) And once again, as in *Mother Night,* Vonnegut introduces the idea that writers are deceivers whose fictional worlds are false depictions of reality.

Since its publication, *Cat's Cradle* has consistently appeared on high school and college reading lists; Reed says that it might be the most widely-read of Vonnegut's novels among young people. He explains that "to the 'counter-culture' it should appeal as a book which counters almost every aspect of the culture of our society. To a generation which delights in the 'put on,' parody and artifice, often as the most meaningful expressions of deeply held convictions in a world which they see as prone to distortion, *Cat's Cradle*'s play with language, symbol and artifice should find some accord."

In *God Bless You, Mr. Rosewater, or Pearls before Swine* we see the introduction of a theme which crops up repeatedly in the later novels and which many believe to be the essence of all of Vonnegut's writing. It is expressed by the main character, Eliot Rosewater, in the motto "Goddamn it, you've got to be kind." John R. May calls the book "Kurt Vonnegut's finest novel to date," and says that it is the author's "most positive and humane work. . . . We may not be able, Vonnegut is saying, to undo the harm that has been done, but we can certainly love, simply because there are people, those who have been made useless by our past stupidity and greed, our previous crimes against our brothers. And if that seems insane, then the better the world for such folly." Daniel Talbot writes: "It's a tribute to Kurt Vonnegut, Jr. that he has covered such a large territory of human follies in so short a book. . . . Using a reasonably popular fictional hero, an eccentric boozing multi-millionaire who shakes up the establishment . . . the author has literally taken on the late Norbert Wiener's book title—*The Human Use of Human Beings*—and fashioned a black satire out of its implications. His technique of presenting this material is fascinating. . . . The net effect is at once explosively funny and agonizing."

In addition to the familiar theme of human frailty as man's greatest asset, another attempt to deal with the Dresden experience (this time the protagonist hallucinates that Indianapolis is engulfed in a firestorm), and a satire on writers in the character of Kilgore Trout, Vonnegut once again suggests the inability of the individual to conquer his environment. As Raymond M. Olderman sees it: "Although Vonnegut's tone, spirit, and overall response to man are very different from Jonathan Swift's, his idea of the universe and man's role in it is somewhat Swiftian, for he pictures us as modern Lilliputians, claiming big things for ourselves in a universe too immense to be anything but indifferent. . . . [According to Vonnegut] men are 'the listless playthings of enormous forces.'" Rosewater's struggle for kindness in an unkind world and the difficulty he experiences in attempting to realize his motto illustrate what Robert W. Uphaus calls "individual action reduced to sham theatricality—to gestures without ultimate significance." However, as Uphaus points out, even though individual action may be of little consequence to the universe as a whole, it is still "desperately laden with personal meaning." And it is toward this personal meaning that much of Vonnegut's prose is directed.

In *Slaughterhouse Five,* after touching on the subject in several earlier works, Vonnegut finally delivers a complete treatise on Dresden. The main character, Billy Pilgrim, is a very young infantry scout who is captured in the Battle of the Bulge and quartered in a Dresden slaughterhouse where he and other prisoners are employed in the production of a vitamin supplement for pregnant women. During the February 13, 1945 firebombing by Allied aircraft, the prisoners take shelter in an underground meat locker. When they emerge, the city has been levelled and they are forced to dig corpses out of the rubble. The story of Billy Pilgrim is the story of Kurt Vonnegut who was captured and survived the firestorm in which 135,000 German civilians perished, more than the number of deaths in the bombings of Hiroshima and Nagasaki combined. Robert Scholes says that "for twenty years Vonnegut has been trying to do fictional justice to that historical event. Now he has finished, and he calls his book a failure. Speaking of the Biblical destruction of Sodom and Gomorrah (like Dresden, subjected to a firestorm), Vonnegut writes: 'Those were vile people in both of those cities, as is well known. The world is better off without them. And Lot's wife, of course, was told not to look back where all those people and their homes had been. But she looked back, and I love her for that, because it was so human. So she was turned to a pillar of salt. So it goes. People aren't supposed to look back. I'm certainly not going to do it any more. I've finished my war book now. The next one I write is going to be fun. This one is a failure, and had to be, since it was written by a pillar of salt.' "

Scholes sums up the theme of *Slaughterhouse Five:* "Be kind. Don't hurt. Death is coming for all of us anyway, and it is better to be Lot's wife looking back through salty eyes than the Deity that destroyed those cities of the plain in order to save them." The reviewer concludes that "far from being a 'failure,' *Slaughterhouse Five* is an extraordinary success. It is a book we need to read, and to reread. It has the same virtues as Vonnegut's best previous work."

If *Cat's Cradle* is viewed as the beginning of a process through which Vonnegut moved into the realm of general acceptance, then *Slaughterhouse Five,* his greatest commercial success and best-known work, may be described as the culmination of that process. The book's popularity is due, in part, to its timeliness; it deals with many issues that were vital to the late sixties: war, ecology, overpopulation, and consumerism. Reed says that in this book Vonnegut "brings together many of the other things he has talked about in his first five novels. The numerous recapitulations of previous themes, resurrections of characters who have appeared before, and recollections of earlier mentioned incidents in this novel are not just self-parody as they might be in *Cat's Cradle,* nor are they simply the development of a kind of extended in-joke as they might be in the intervening novels. Rather they represent an attempt at integration, an effort to bring together all that Vonnegut has been saying about the human condition and contemporary American society, and to relate those broad commentaries to the central traumatic, revelatory and symbolic moment of the destruction of Dresden."

In *Slaughterhouse Five* Vonnegut once again relies heavily on elements of science and technology. Billy Pilgrim is able to travel through time and space; he masters the art of taking "time trips" from the present into the past and the future, and he is kidnapped to the planet Tralfamadore (a hold-over from other novels). Jerome Klinkowitz feels that "science fiction time-travel is [Vonnegut's] metaphor, but behind this device stands man's greatest power, what separates him from other living creatures—the ability to imagine that anything, even he himself, is different from what is. Turn things around, make them different. Overcome the trouble, in one's mind to start with, but, when you have the technology, that way too. The horrors of war, our complex machines of destruction: why not reinvent them as they would be reinvented when we take a war movie and run it backwards?" (Indeed, at one point in the book bombs are sucked back up into the airplanes which then fly backwards to their bases; the bombs are then shipped back to factories where, on backward-moving disassembly lines, they are reduced to harmless minerals which are then redeposited into the earth.) Donald J. Greiner believes that science fiction, in this novel, is used as a distancing technique by the author. He writes that "Vonnegut's juggling of Billy Pilgrim's imaginary adventures with a dispassionate account of his personal experiences at Dresden is a way of balancing his efforts to maintain an objective view of the atrocity. . . . Successfully handling a complex technique, Vonnegut creates in *Slaughterhouse Five* a novel that clearly surpasses his earlier work."

Wayne D. McGinnis says that in this book Vonnegut "avoids *framing* his story in linear narration, choosing a circular structure. Such a view of the art of the novel has much to do with the protagonist . . . Billy Pilgrim, an optometrist who provides corrective lenses for Earthlings. For Pilgrim, who learns of a new view of life as he becomes 'unstuck in time,' the lenses are corrective metaphorically as well as physically. Quite early in the exploration of Billy's life the reader learns that 'frames are where the money is.' . . . Historical events like the bombing of Dresden are usually 'read' in the framework of moral and historical interpretation." McGinnis feels that the novel's cyclical nature is inextricably bound up with its major themes which he identifies as "time, death, and renewal." And he goes on to say that "the most important function of 'so it goes' [a phrase that recurs at each death in the book] . . . , is its imparting a cyclical quality to the novel, both in form and content. Paradoxically, the expression of fatalism serves as a source of renewal, a situation typical of Vonnegut's works, for it enables the novel to *go on* despite—even because of—the proliferation of deaths." The phrase "so it goes" is an illustration of the Tralfamadorian view of death which Vonnegut adopts as his own. Since the people of Tralfamadore see all time at once, they feel that good and bad moments coexist. As Billy Pilgrim explains: "When a Tralfamadorian sees a corpse, all he thinks is that the dead person is in bad condition at that particular moment, but that the same person is just fine in plenty of other moments. Now, when I myself hear that somebody is dead, I simply shrug and say what the Tralfamadorians say about dead people, which is 'So it goes.' "

After the publication of *Slaughterhouse Five,* Vonnegut entered a period of depression during which he vowed, at one point, never to write another novel. He concentrated, instead, on lecturing, teaching, and finishing a play, "Happy Birthday, Wanda June," that he had begun several years earlier. The play, which ran Off-Broadway from October, 1970 to March, 1971, received mixed reviews. Jack Kroll wrote that "almost every time an American novelist writes a play he shows up most of our thumb-tongued playwrights, who lack the melody of mind, the wit, dash and accuracy of Saul Bellow and Bruce Jay Friedman. And the same thing must be said of the writing in 'Happy Birthday, Wanda June,'. . . . Vonnegut's dialogue is not only fast and funny, with a palpable taste and crackle, but it also means something. And his comic sense is a superior one; 'Wanda June' has as many laughs as anything by Neil Simon." On the other hand, Stanley Kauffmann called it "a disaster, full of callow wit, rheumatic invention, and dormitory profundity. . . . The height of its imagination is exemplified by a scene in Heaven between a golden-haired little girl and a Nazi *Gauleiter* in which they discuss the way Jesus plays shuffleboard." Whether or not the play was totally successful, however, is less important than the opportunity it gave the author to create solid characters portrayed by real people, a quality which he felt was lacking in the novel.

There are several factors which could be interpreted as the cause of Vonnegut's period of depression, including, as he has admitted, the approach of his fiftieth birthday and the fact that his children had begun to leave home. Many critics believe that, having at last come to terms with Dresden, he lost the major impetus for much of his work; others feel that *Slaughterhouse Five* may have been the single great novel that Vonnegut was capable of writing. Whatever the cause, *Breakfast of Champions* marked the end of his depression and a return to the novel. In honor of this event, Vonnegut subtitled the work, *Goodbye Blue Monday.* S. K. Oberbeck calls the book "the author's fiftieth birthday present to his swollen ego. . . . From its pop cartoons [Vonnegut includes drawings or doodles on almost every page] . . . to its blithe Radiclib (or 'Radglib,' a word coined by one of those big, black useless machines), the book is Lit-Pop politics, as if Richard Brautigan were feyly fictionalizing Tom Hayden and wife Jane. From capitalism, imperialism, racism, ecology, overpopulation and Fem Lib to hand-guns and Holiday Inns, Vonnegut doesn't miss touching a base.'' Nora Sayre writes that ''in this novel Vonnegut is treating himself to a giant brain-flush, clearing his head by throwing out acquired ideas, and also liberating some of the characters from his previous books. Thus, he has celebrated his fiftieth birthday in the same spirit that made Tolstoy release his serfs and Thomas Jefferson free his slaves. Once again, we're back on the people-grid; major and minor personae from other novels resurface in this one, their lives ridiculously entangled. . . . This explosive meditation ranks with Vonnegut's best.''

In *Breakfast of Champions,* as in most of Vonnegut's work, there are very clear autobiographical tendencies. In this novel, however, the author seems to be even more wrapped up in his characters than usual. He appears as Philboyd Sludge, the writer of the book which stars Dwayne Hoover, a Pontiac dealer (Vonnegut once ran a SAAB dealership) who goes berserk after reading a novel by Kilgore Trout, who also represents Vonnegut. Toward the end of the book, Vonnegut arranges a meeting between himself and Trout, who Robert Merrill calls his ''most famous creation,'' in which he casts the character loose forever; by this time the previously unsuccessful Trout has become rich and famous and is finally able to stand on his own. Merrill says that Vonnegut ''insists on his role as master puppeteer. . . . [The author] allows no pretense about the status of his fictional creations; toward the end, Vonnegut even seats himself at the same bar with his characters. While sipping his favorite drink, he proceeds to explain why he has decided to have these characters act as they do.'' The result, according to Merrill, is the emphasis of the fact that the novel really has only one character: Vonnegut himself. The reviewer concludes that *Breakfast of Champions* ''is about its author's triumph over a great temptation. Saint Anthony's temptation was of the flesh, and Vonnegut's is of the spirit; we should know by now that the spirit both kills and dies. At the end of the novel, Vonnegut's spirit refuses to die. . . . His hope is that we might all become 'better'; his message is that to become so we must resist the seductions of fatalism.''

With his next book, *Slapstick,* Vonnegut undertakes the theme that the wane of the extended family has caused loneliness for most Americans, and he proposes a system for providing everyone with such a family (hence the subtitle, *Lonesome No More*). Charles Nicol notes that the first sentence of the book is, ''This is the closest I will ever come to writing an autobiography,'' and says that ''we are then supposed to extrapolate from a few family reminiscences to the action of the novel and marvel at something or other.'' Vonnegut's sister, Alice, died of cancer at the age of forty-one; she described her impending death as ''soap opera'' and ''slapstick.'' As Nicol puts it, ''a Vonnegut through and through. So *Slapstick* is 'really' about Kurt and Alice. . . . Alice's husband died in a grotesque accident two days before she did; he was a passenger on 'the only train in American railroading history to hurl itself off an open drawbridge.' Consequently *Slapstick* is 'grotesque, situational poetry'; it is supposedly about 'what life *feels* like' to Vonnegut.'' Nicol goes on to say that the idea of giving everyone an extended family ''was supposed to be earthshakingly delightful, the hopeful vision of *Slapstick,* but it doesn't work. . . . What's gone wrong? Simply, as Vonnegut rather circumspectly admits, he has lost the inspiration of the Muse. His sister 'was the person I had always written for.' He felt her 'presence' for a number of years after she died, 'but then she began to fade away, perhaps because she had more important business elsewhere.' Now Vonnegut is without his own 'audience of one,' and it shows. This grotesque tribute to their growing up together hasn't brought back his sister's presence, and *Slapstick* is dedicated not to her, but to Laurel and Hardy. It doesn't live up to their memory, or Vonnegut's either.''

Jerome Klinkowitz calls *Slapstick* a ''deceptively short and simple book'' which, he says, ''returns to the greatest strength of this writer's art: the ability to project the big and little concerns of his own life into the field of imaginary action.'' Klinkowitz also believes that the novel represents something of a departure for Vonnegut in that it contains no old characters or familiar themes. Roger Sale disagrees; he writes: ''*Slapstick* opens with a typical Vonnegut cynicism about America having become a place of interchangeable parts, so that Indianapolis, which 'once had a way of speaking all its own,' now is 'just another someplace where automobiles live.' I can't speak about Indianapolis, but one thing I resist in Vonnegut's books is that they seem formulaic, made of interchangeable parts, though this is one quality which may endear him to others. Once Vonnegut finds what he takes to be a successful character, motif or phrase, he can't bear to give it up, and so he carries it around from novel to novel. . . . The story in *Slapstick* is part *Cat's Cradle,* part *God Bless You, Mr. Rosewater,* part Kilgore Trout and part Thomas Pynchon.'' But, Sale continues, ''where Pynchon's mania leads him into huge soaring flights of paranoic fantasy he calls the history of our century, Vonnegut's easy, sentimental cynicism leads him into endless parading of the dumb notion that life isn't much good in America because we're all stupid, unloving or both. It takes stamina, determination and crazy intelligence to read Pynchon's two enormous novels; it takes nothing more than a few idle hours to turn the pages of *Slapstick.*'' Klinkowitz, however, rejoins that the book's ''readability should not distract one from the fact that Vonnegut has found a fictional situation which considers serious human problems. . . . Against the insipid madness of life . . . [the author] chooses to be unalienated, self-effacing, funny and comforting.''

Reviewing *Jailbird,* John Leonard says that in previous novels Vonnegut has told us ''that he believed in the Bill of Rights, Robert's Rules of Order and the principles of Alcoholics Anonymous. In his new novel, *Jailbird*—his best in my opinion since *Mother Night* and *Cat's Cradle*—he adds another sacred document. It is the Sermon on the Mount.'' In this novel the main character, Walter F. Starbuck, is asked by Congressman Richard M. Nixon at a 1949 hearing why he has joined the Communist Party; Starbuck replies: ''Why? The Sermon on the Mount, sir.'' And Leonard says, ''When you think about it, the Sermon on the Mount *is* a radical document, promising that the meek shall inherit the earth. Shall they, indeed? Mr. Vonnegut has his doubts.'' Jean Strouse agrees that this is his best book ''since *Cat's Cradle.* Using the laid-back, ironic voice that has become his trademark, Vonnegut this time combines fiction and fact to construct an ingenious, wry morality play about the capitalist U.S. of A. . . . Vonnegut makes it delightful not to wonder what is really going on.''

Leonard perceives Vonnegut's obsessions in *Jailbird* to be ''Harvard and Mr. Nixon, the Holocaust and Watergate, Sacco and Vanzetti, Alger Hiss and Whittaker Chambers, trade unionism and conglomerate capitalism, not to mention Roy M. Cohn.'' The reviewer finds that ''not once in *Jailbird* does Mr. Vonnegut nod off, go vague. His people bite into their lives. Kindnesses, as inexplicable as history, are collected, like saving remnants. New York, with catacombs under Grand Central Terminal and harps on top of the Chrysler Building, is wonderfully evoked. The prose has sinew. Mr. Nixon's 'unhappy little smile,' for instance 'looked to me like a rosebud that had just been smashed by a hammer.' Or: 'There was a withered old man . . . hunched over his food, hiding it with his arms. Sarah whispered that he ate as though his meal were a royal flush.' "

Even though Leonard makes a point of identifying *Jailbird* as a "fable of evil and inadvertence," Michael Wood criticizes Vonnegut for his inability to "see evil at all. He sees only weakness, and in these long, flattened perspectives, everything—Watergate, Auschwitz, Goering and yesterday's news—comes to belong simply to a blurred, generalized representation of damage and error. There is a real subject here, and it is one of Vonnegut's subjects: What are we to do when we cannot perceive the reality of evil, or distinguish it from other forms of human failure?" Wood arrives at the conclusion that "Vonnegut's work is so likable that its shallowness may seem to be a part of its appeal." John Leonard's opinion on this is that "it is the fashion these days . . . to dismiss Mr. Vonnegut as simplistic. He is insufficiently obscure; he is not loud enough about the ambiguities. Well, as he would say, listen. The simple—courtesy and decency—is hardest."

Kurt Vonnegut's work has been likened to that of numerous literary figures; he has, for instance, been compared to Dickens, Swift, Orwell, Huxley, Richard Sterne, Bruce Jay Friedman, Thomas Pynchon, Joseph Heller, and John Barthelme, to name only a few. With so many critics arguing for their personal favorites, it is difficult to decide exactly who has influenced whom. What is more important, and more realistic, is to analyze Vonnegut's style, his recurring themes, and, ultimately, his impact on contemporary literature. Charles Thomas Samuels says that Vonnegut "absorbed what preceded him. Like most advanced novelists in the modern period, Vonnegut deemphasizes plot and character while working for effects of emotional contradiction and intellectual ambiguity. He borrows the debased formulas of science fiction and comic books as a serious travesty of our present condition, whose silliness is also represented by one-dimensional grotesques impersonating people. Random structure facilitates digressions, which also preclude the emotional satisfactions of climax, denouement and uniformity of tone. As in his forebears, such technical features express a conviction: the world is incoherent and therefore can't be imitated through closed or univocal forms. Nothing so declares the modernity of Vonnegut as the shortness of his books, chapters and sentences. Jabs to the intellectual and emotional solar plexus are intended; if we judge by his admirers, the intention is achieved." Samuels mentions that Vonnegut's admirers include young people, which "isn't difficult to understand. His own spiritual age is late adolescence. . . . That Vonnegut is beloved by critics (and presumably adult readers) is more disconcerting. For them, he provides an easy bridge from an age of skepticism and baffled hope to one of faith in any nostrum that bears the certifications of novelty and youth."

Vonnegut commented on the shortness of his books in an interview with Joe David Bellamy and John Casey; he said that "this is what a novel should be right now," and explained that the reason "novels were so thick for so long was that people had so much time to kill. I do not furnish transportation for my characters; I do not move them from one room to another; I do not send them up the stairs; they do not get dressed in the mornings; they do not put the ignition key in the lock, and turn on the engine, and let it warm up and look at all the gauges, and put the car in reverse, and back out, and drive to the filling station, and ask the guy there about the weather. You can fill up a good-sized book with this connective tissue. People would be satisfied, too."

The way Peter J. Reed sees it, Vonnegut "can be viewed as putting the traditional American novel in contemporary dress." Reed feels that Vonnegut's detractors "evidently feel the contemporary techniques are slick and superficial, the substance a thin caricature of the tradition. Others find the techniques revitalize old forms and make possible a return to traditions lost or observed earlier in the century. Although the wide readership Vonnegut has enjoyed in recent years demonstrates the appeal of his technique to contemporary audiences, obviously that contemporaneity could prove a limitation in the long run. . . . On the other hand, the basic questions Vonnegut's novels explore are timeless, even if the form in which they are pursued remains closely tied to a period. The breadth of Vonnegut's readership may indicate that as his appeal to youth as a peculiarly contemporary and relevant writer fades, his stature with older generations as a 'serious' writer will grow; in fact, the indications are strong that this process has already begun. Clearly, Vonnegut is peculiarly in tune with the mood of America in recent years, and has found a style which effectively expresses that mood."

Vonnegut has stated that the two main themes of all his work were best expressed by his brother, who soon after the birth of his first child, wrote, "Here I am cleaning shit off of practically everything," and by his sister, whose last words were, "no pain." J. Michael Crichton calls this analysis "as true as anything a writer has said of his work." Crichton thinks that Vonnegut's novels "have attacked our deepest fears of automation and the bomb, our deepest political guilts, our fiercest hatreds and loves. Nobody else writes books on these subjects; they are inaccessible to normal novelistic approaches. But Vonnegut, armed with his schizophrenia, takes an absurd, distorted, wildly funny framework which is ultimately anaesthetic. . . . And as he proceeds, from his anaesthetic framework, to clean the shit off, we are able to cheer him on—at least for a while. But eventually we stop cheering and stop laughing." Crichton calls this "a classic sequence of reactions to any Vonnegut book. One begins smugly, enjoying the sharp wit of a compatriot as he carves up Common Foes. But the sharp wit does not stop, and sooner or later it is directed against the Wrong Targets. . . . He becomes an offensive writer, because he will not choose sides, ascribing blame and penalty, identifying good guys and bad." This same idea is expressed by Vonnegut himself when, in *Slaughterhouse Five,* he quotes his father saying to him, "you know—you never wrote a story with a villain in it." Likewise, as numerous critics have pointed out, he has never created a hero.

The recurrence of characters, themes, and phrases throughout Vonnegut's novels has led reviewers to offer various interpretations of his work and numerous explanations for the emphasis he places on certain points. Kindness, for example, is one overriding theme; "Goddamn it, you've got to be kind" is a catch-phrase that many critics adopt as a convenient means of summarizing Vonnegut's "message." The struggle of the individual against a hostile universe is the main conflict in all of his novels, and the universe remains consistently hostile while the characters are forced to adapt.

In the final analysis, perhaps it is best to look to Vonnegut's first novel, *Player Piano* in which he creates a world where machines not only do manual labor, but also do all of man's thinking; in protest, a renegade group called the Ghost Shirt Society is formed to sabotage all machines. The credo of the group, as Ernest W. Ranly says, can be taken to be Vonnegut's own: "That there must be virtue in imperfection, for Man is imperfect, and Man is a creation of God. That there must be virtue in frailty, for Man is frail and Man is a creation of God. That there must be virtue in inefficiency, for Man is inefficient and Man is a creation of God. That there must be virtue in brilliance followed by stupidity, for Man is alternately brilliant and stupid and Man is a creation of God." Ranly concludes that Vonnegut embraces the principles of the religion of Bokonism in *Cat's Cradle,* namely that "the one thing sacred is not the mountain, is not the ocean, is not the sun, is not even God. The one thing sacred is man. That's all. Just man. Man is that lucky mud from among all the mud which can sit up and see what a nice job God has done."

Vonnegut's works, which have sold in the millions of copies and appeared in numerous foreign editions, have also been adapted for the stage and screen. *Slaughterhouse Five* was produced as a film by Universal in 1972. *God Bless You, Mr. Rosewater* was adapted for the stage by Howard Ashman and produced by Vonnegut's daughter, Edith, in 1979; *Player Piano, The Sirens of Titan,* and *Cat's Cradle* have also been produced as plays.

AVOCATIONAL INTERESTS: Painting, wood carving, welded sculpture.

BIOGRAPHICAL/CRITICAL SOURCES—Periodicals: *New York Times Book Review,* June 2, 1963, April 25, 1965, August 6, 1967, September 1, 1968, April 6, 1969, February 4, 1973, October 3, 1976, September 9, 1979; *Saturday Review,* April 3, 1965, March 29, 1969, February 6, 1971, May 1, 1971; *Book Week,* April 11, 1965; *Christian Science Monitor,* May 9, 1965, December 5, 1968, September 10, 1979; *New Yorker,* May 15, 1965, May 17, 1969; *Times Literary Supplement,* November 11, 1965, December, 12, 1968, July 17, 1969; *Commonweal,* September 16, 1966, June 6, 1969, November 27, 1970, May 7, 1971, December 7, 1973; *Esquire,* June, 1968, September, 1970; *Life,* August 16, 1968, September 12, 1969, November 20, 1970; *Book World,* August 18, 1968, March 2, 1975, September 2, 1979; *Newsweek,* August 19, 1968, March 3, 1969, April 14, 1969, October 19, 1970, December 20, 1971, May 14, 1973, October 1, 1979; *New York Times,* August 19, 1968, September 13, 1969, October 6, 1970, October 8, 1970, October 18, 1970, November 18, 1970, May 27, 1971, May 13, 1973, September 7, 1979, October 15, 1979; *Time,* August 30, 1968, April 11, 1969, June 29, 1970, June 3, 1974; *Atlantic,* September, 1968, May, 1973; *Nation,* September 23, 1968, June 9, 1969; *Spectator,* November 29, 1968; *Punch,* December 4, 1968; *Books and Bookmen,* February, 1969, February, 1973, November, 1973; *Best Sellers,* April 15, 1969, November, 1979; *New Republic,* April 26, 1969, November 7, 1970, June 12, 1971, May 12, 1973, September 28, 1973, June 1, 1974, July 5, 1974, September 25, 1976, November 26, 1976; *Christian Century,* August 13, 1969; *Hudson Review,* autumn, 1969.

Partisan Review, number 1, 1970, number 2, 1974; *Observer Review,* March 15, 1970; *Observer,* March 22, 1970; *New York Review of Books,* July 2, 1970, May 31, 1973, November 25, 1976, November 22, 1979; *America,* September 5, 1970; *Washington Post,* October 12, 1970, May 13, 1973; *New York Times Magazine,* January 24, 1971; *New York,* December 13, 1971; *Critique: Studies in Modern Fiction,* Volume XII, number 3, 1971, Volume XIV, number 2, 1973, Volume XV, number 2, 1973, Volume XVII, number 1, 1975, Volume XVIII, number 3, 1977; *Southwest Review,* winter, 1971; *Twentieth Century Literature,* January, 1972; *Detroit News,* June 18, 1972, September 16, 1979; *American Poetry Review,* January-February, 1973; *Modern Fiction Studies,* spring, 1973, summer, 1975; *Library Journal,* April 15, 1973; *Harper's,* May, 1973, July, 1974; *World,* June 19, 1973; *Critic,* September-October, 1973; *Journal of Popular Culture,* winter, 1973; *Encounter,* February, 1974; *American Literature,* May, 1974; *National Observer,* June 29, 1974; *Western Humanities Review,* summer, 1974; *Commentary,* July, 1974, November, 1975; *Cleveland Press,* July 10, 1974, July 12, 1974; *New Statesman,* April 4, 1975; *Novel: A Forum on Fiction,* winter, 1975; *Detroit Free Press,* November 14, 1976; *Antioch Review,* Volume XXXVII, number 1, 1979; *Los Angeles Times Book Review,* September 23, 1979.

Books: Jerry H. Bryant, *The Open Decision,* Free Press, 1970; R.H.W. Dillard, George Garrett, and John Rees Moore, editors, *The Sounder Few: Essays from the "Hollins Critic,"* University of Georgia Press, 1971; Tony Tanner, *City of Words: American Fiction 1950-1970,* Harper, 1971; Donald A. Wolheim, *The Universe Makers,* Harper, 1971; David H. Goldsmith, *Kurt Vonnegut: Fantasist of Fire and Ice,* Bowling Green University Popular Press, 1972; Gilbert A. Harrison, editor, *The Critic as Artist: Essays on Books, 1920-1970,* Liveright, 1972; Peter J. Reed, *Kurt Vonnegut, Jr.,* Warner Paperback, 1972; Betty Lenhardt Hudgens, *Kurt Vonnegut, Jr.: A Checklist,* Gale, 1972; Jerome Klinkowitz and John Somer, editors, *The Vonnegut Statement,* Delacorte, 1973; Alfred Kazin, *Bright Book of Life: American Novelists and Storytellers from Hemingway to Mailer,* Little, Brown, 1973; Raymond M. Olderman, *Beyond the Waste Land: A Study of the American Novel in the Nineteen-Sixties,* Yale University Press, 1973; Ihab Hassan, *Contemporary American Literature, 1942-1972,* Ungar, 1973; Thomas R. Holland, *Vonnegut's Major Works,* Cliff's Notes, 1973; *Contemporary Literary Criticism,* Gale, Volume I, 1973, Volume II, 1974, Volume III, 1975, Volume IV, 1975, Volume V, 1976, Volume VIII, 1978, Volume XII, 1980.

Jerome Klinkowitz and Asa B. Pieratt, *Kurt Vonnegut, Jr.: A Descriptive Bibliography and Secondary Checklist,* Shoe String, 1974; Kurt Vonnegut, Jr., *Wampeters, Foma, and Granfalloons,* Delacorte, 1974; David Joe Bellamy, editor, *The New Fiction: Interviews with Innovative American Writers,* University of Illinois Press, 1974; Jean E. Kennard, *Number and Nightmare: Forms of Fantasy in Contemporary Fiction,* Archon Books, 1975; Stanley Schatt, *Kurt Vonnegut,* Twayne, 1976; John W. Tilton, *Cosmic Satire in the Contemporary Novel,* Bucknell University Press, 1977; Clark Mayo, *Kurt Vonnegut: The Gospel from Outer Space, or Yes We Have No Nirvanas,* Borgo Press, 1977; Richard Giannone, *Vonnegut: A Preface to His Novels,* Kennikat, 1977; Jerome Klinkowitz and Donald L. Lawler, editors, *Vonnegut in America: An Introduction to the Life and Work of Kurt Vonnegut,* Delacorte, 1977; Michael Chernuchin, editor, *Vonnegut Talks!,* Pylon, 1977.

—Sketch by Peter M. Gareffa

W

WAGENER, Hans 1940-

PERSONAL: Born July 27, 1940, in Lagel Lippe, Germany; son of Rudolf Albrecht (a printer) and Johanne (Geller) Wagener; married Marlene Winders, December 26, 1969; children: Matthias, Christopher, Natasha. *Education:* University of Freiburg, B.A., 1963; University of California, Los Angeles, M.A., 1965, Ph.D., 1967. *Religion:* Protestant. *Home:* 16922 Escalon Dr., Encino, Calif. 91436. *Office:* Department of Germanic Languages, University of Southern California, Los Angeles, Calif. 90007.

CAREER: University of Southern California, Los Angeles, assistant professor of German, 1967-68; University of California, Los Angeles, assistant professor of German, 1968-71; University of Southern California, associate professor, 1971-75, professor of German, 1975—.

WRITINGS: Die Komposition der Romane Christian Friedrich Hunolds, University of California Press, 1969; (with Theo Vennemann) *Die Anredeformen in den Dramen des Andreas Gryphius,* Wilhelm Fink (Munich), 1970; *The German Baroque Novel,* Twayne, 1973; *Erich Kaestner,* Colloquium Verlag (Berlin), 1973; *Stephan Andres,* Colloquium Verlag (Berlin), 1974; *Siegfried Lenz,* C. H. Beck (Munich), 1976; *Frank Wedekind,* Colloquium Verlag (Berlin), 1979.

WORK IN PROGRESS: Carl Zuckmayer, for publication by C. H. Beck.

* * *

WAHL, Robert (Charles) 1948-

PERSONAL: Born May 24, 1948, in Toledo, Ohio; son of Russell Rothenberger (a physician) and Nina Marie (Boyer) Wahl. *Education:* Attended Ohio State University, 1966-67, and University of Toledo, 1967-73. *Politics:* Independent. *Home:* 433 East Ave., North Augusta, S.C. 29841.

CAREER: Parks developer in Toledo, Ohio, 1966-67; Lasalle, Inc., Toledo, Ohio, clothing salesman, 1969; Augusta National Golf Club, Augusta, Ga., assistant maintenance supervisor, 1973; WRDW-TV, Augusta, Ga., news reporter and assignment editor, 1976—.

WRITINGS: What Will You Do Today, Little Russell?, Putnam, 1972.

WORK IN PROGRESS: Ride the Giant Wolf; Old Swayback; Scarleaf.

SIDELIGHTS: Robert Wahl told *CA:* "My writing is at its best when I suddenly realize looking at the clock that four or five hours have actually passed since I began with a blank sheet of paper, when in my mind it seemed that only one hour transpired. Then I know my concentration was extraordinary and my scope had narrowed to nothing more than me, my typewriter, and ideas. I also know that experience is the best of highs.

"Since I am a mood writer, I have to do everything I can to enhance the working atmosphere around me, even going so far as to put up pictures of the type of subjects I am writing about, keeping an array of reference materials within arm's reach, a big picture window to gaze out of, and usually some type of mood music playing subliminally in the background."

AVOCATIONAL INTERESTS: Target shooting (named professional rifle marksman at National Target Shoot, 1959-60); early American lifestyles, especially Indian; woodcarving; wine collecting; tennis; golf; skiing.

* * *

WAKELYN, Jon L(ouis) 1938-

PERSONAL: Born August 19, 1938; son of Arthur Thomas and Elsa (Koch) Wakelyn; married Catherine Marcia Carl, August 1, 1964; children: David, Meredith Elizabeth. *Education:* Long Island University, B.A., 1962; Rice University, Ph.D., 1966. *Politics:* Democrat. *Religion:* Protestant. *Home:* 7218 Holly Ave., Takoma Park, Md. *Office:* Department of History, Catholic University of America, Washington, D.C. 20017.

CAREER: Long Island University, Greenvale, N.Y., instructor in history, 1965; Washington College, Chestertown, Md., assistant professor, 1966-69, associate professor of history, 1970; Catholic University of America, Washington, D.C., assistant professor, 1970-72, associate professor, 1972-77, professor of history, 1977—, associate dean of school of arts and sciences, 1974-76. Visiting professor, University of Maryland, 1973-74. *Member:* Organization of American Historians, American Studies Association, Southern Historical Association. *Awards, honors:* National Foundation for the Humanities grant, 1968; *Biographical Dictionary of the Confederacy* was named an outstanding reference book by the American Library Association, 1978.

WRITINGS: The Politics of a Literary Man: William Gilmore Simms, Greenwood Press, 1973; *Biographical Dictio-*

nary of the Confederacy, Greenwood Press, 1977; (editor) *The Common People of the Nineteenth Century South,* Greenwood Press, 1980. Editor, "Contributions in American History" series, Greenwood Press, 1972—. Contributor to academic journals.

WORK IN PROGRESS: The Antebellum South; Literacy, Learning, and Knowledge in the Nineteenth Century South.

* * *

WAKEMAN, Frederic (Evans), Jr. 1937-

PERSONAL: Born December 12, 1937, in Kansas City, Kan.; son of Frederic Evans (an author) and Margaret (Keyes) Wakeman; married Nancy Schuster, December 28, 1957 (divorced January, 1974); married Carolyn Huntley, December 31, 1974; children: Frederic Evans III, Matthew Clark. *Education:* Harvard University, A.B., 1959; Institut d'Etudes Politiques, graduate study, 1959-60; University of California, Berkeley, M.A., 1962, Ph.D., 1965. *Home:* 56 Arlington Ct., Kensington, Calif. 94704. *Office:* Center for Chinese Studies, University of California, Berkeley, Calif. 94720.

CAREER: University of California, Berkeley, assistant professor of Chinese history, 1965-67; Inter-University Program for Chinese Language Studies, Taipei, Taiwan, director, 1967-68; University of California, Berkeley, associate professor, 1968-70, professor of Chinese history, 1971-79, currently chairman of Center for Chinese Studies. Visiting scholar at Corpus Christi College, Cambridge University, and Beijing University. *Member:* American Historical Association, Association for Asian Studies, Society for Ch'ing Studies. *Awards, honors:* Guggenheim fellowship, 1973-74; National Book Award nomination, 1974, for *History and Will: Philosophical Perspectives of the Thought of Mao Tse-tung;* National Research Council fellow.

WRITINGS: Seventeen Royal Palms Drive (novel), New American Library, 1962; *Strangers at the Gate: Social Disorder in South China, 1839-1861,* University of California Press, 1966; *Nothing Concealed: Essays in Honor of Liu Yu-yun,* Chinese Materials and Research Aids Service Center, 1970; (with Thomas Metcalf and Edward Tannenbaum) *A World History,* Wiley, 1973; *History and Will: Philosophical Perspectives of the Thought of Mao Tse-tung,* University of California Press, 1973; (editor) *Conflict and Control in Late Imperial China,* University of California Press, 1975; *The Fall of Imperial China,* Free Press, 1975; (contributor) Jonathon Spence and John Wills, editors, *From Ming to Ch'ing,* Yale University Press, 1979; (contributor) John K. Fairbank, editor, *The Cambridge History of China,* Volume X, Cambridge University Press, 1979. Contributor of articles and reviews to scholarly journals.

WORK IN PROGRESS: A book on the Manchu conquest of China in the seventeenth century; a book on the Taiping occupation of Suzhou.

SIDELIGHTS: Frederic Wakeman, Jr., according to a reviewer in the *Times Literary Supplement,* "is one of the brightest of the middle generation of American historians of China." He praises Wakeman's first study of the Chinese, *Strangers at the Gate,* for being "one of the few Western studies of nineteenth-century Chinese history that can be recommended . . . to readers not accustomed to . . . sinological writing." Wakeman's subsequent work has been similarly praised.

History and Will, which was nominated for the 1974 National Book Award, is Wakeman's analysis of the influence of various Chinese and European political, philosophical, and cultural traditions on Mao Tse-tung's thought. The *Library Journal*'s Leo Oufan Lee comments that *History and Will* "presents a mosaic of documentation, insights, and reflections on a variety of historical and philosophical subjects . . . which provide the intellectual background of Maoism." Although the *Times Literary Supplement* critic points to certain structural and thematic flaws and suggests that Wakeman may have "tried to cover too much ground," he considers the book a "bold effort" and concludes: "The faults of this interesting book do not cancel out its achievements, which are considerable. Dr. Wakeman has opened up new perspectives on modern Chinese intellectual history and sown some ideas that will yield fruit in the future. It is not often that a book on China makes one think hard, and so long as *History and Will* is treated neither as a textbook nor as an authoritative work it is to be welcomed."

BIOGRAPHICAL/CRITICAL SOURCES: Library Journal, April 15, 1973; *Choice,* January, 1974; *Journal of Asian Studies,* February, 1974; *Times Literary Supplement,* March 15, 1974, May 21, 1976.

* * *

WALD, Malvin (Daniel) 1917-

PERSONAL: Born August 8, 1917, in New York, N.Y.; son of Rudolph and Bella (Danglo) Wald; married Sylvia B. Fish (a nursery school teacher), June, 1946; children: Alan Russel, Jenifer Diane. *Education:* Brooklyn College (now Brooklyn College of the City University of New York), B.A., 1936; University of Southern California, graduate study, 1960-64; Woodland University, J.D., 1976. *Home:* 4525 Greenbush Ave., Sherman Oaks, Calif. 91423.

CAREER: University of Southern California, Los Angeles, lecturer, 1949-67, adjunct professor of cinema, 1967-79; executive producer for Twentieth Century-Fox Television, 1962-63; writer producer for U.S. Information Agency, 1964-65, and for Ivan Tors Films, 1966-72. *Military service:* U.S. Army Air Forces, member of first motion picture unit, 1942-45; became technical sergeant. *Member:* Academy of Motion Picture Arts and Sciences, Writers Guild of America (former member of board of directors). *Awards, honors:* "The Naked City" received Writers Guild award nomination and Academy Award nomination for best story, 1949; White House Commendation for "An Answer"; Gold Medal Award, Venice Children's Film Festival, for "The Boy Who Owned a Melephant"; Locarno Critics award for "Al Capone."

WRITINGS: (Editor with Michael Werner) *Three Major Screenplays,* Globe Book, 1972; (with Albert Maltz) *The Naked City* (screenplay; also see below), Southern Illinois University Press, 1979; (contributor) *Close-Ups,* Workman Press, 1979.

Filmscripts: "Two in a Taxi," Columbia, 1941; "Ten Gentlemen from West Point," Fox, 1942; "The Powers Girl," United Artists, 1943; "The Underdog," PRC, 1943; "Jive Junction," PRC, 1943; (with Albert Maltz) "The Naked City," Universal, 1948; "Behind Locked Doors," Eagle Lion, 1948; "The Undercover Man," Columbia, 1949; "The Dark Past," Columbia, 1949; "Not Wanted," Film Classics, 1949; "Outrage," RKO, 1951; "Battle Taxi," United Artists, 1955; "Man on Fire," MGM, 1957; "Al Capone," Allied Artists, 1959; "The Steel Claw," Warner Bros., 1961; "In Search of Historic Jesus," 1979; "The Legend of Sleepy Hollow," 1979. Also author of "This Is Freedom," "An Answer" (U.S. Navy documentary), "Employees Only" (industrial film), "An Afternoon with Hans Christian Andersen," "The Boy Who Owned a Melephant" (theatrical short), and "Biography of a Rookie" (sports documentary). Television scripts: "D-Day," "Hollywood: The Golden Years," "The Rafer Johnson Story," and "Around the World of Mike Todd." Author of scripts for "Life and Times of Grizzly Adams," "Mark Twain's America," and "Greatest Heroes of the Bible."

SIDELIGHTS: Malvin Wald was the author of five of the twenty American entries at the Monte Carlo TV Film Festival in 1962.

* * *

WALKER, David Harry 1911-

PERSONAL: Born February 9, 1911, in Dundee, Scotland; son of Harry Giles and Elizabeth Bewley (Newsom) Walker; married Willa Magee, 1939; children: Allan Giles, Barclay James, David Clibborn, Julian Harry. *Education:* Attended Royal Military College at Sandhurst, 1929-30. *Religion:* Presbyterian. *Home:* Strathcroix, St. Andrews, New Brunswick, Canada. *Agent:* Russell & Volkening, Inc., 551 Fifth Ave., New York, N.Y. 10017.

CAREER: British Army, the Black Watch, 1931-47; served in India, 1932-36, Sudan, 1936-38; aide-de-camp to Governor General of Canada, 1938-39; captured in France with Highland Division in 1940 and held prisoner of war until 1945; instructor at Staff College, Camberley, 1945-46; comptroller to Viceroy of India, 1946-47; retired with rank of major, 1947. Professional writer, 1947—. Member, Canada Council, 1957-61; Roosevelt International Campobello Commission, Canadian commissioner, 1965, chairman, 1970-72. *Member:* Royal Society of Literature (fellow), Royal and Ancient Golf Club, St. Andrews (Scotland). *Awards, honors:* Member of the Order of the British Empire (military), 1946; D.Litt., University of New Brunswick; Governor General's prize, 1952, for *The Pillar,* and, 1953, for *Digby.*

WRITINGS—All published by Houghton, except as indicated: *The Storm and the Silence,* 1949; *Geordie,* 1950; *The Pillar,* 1952; *Digby,* 1953; *Harry Black,* 1956; *Sandy Was a Soldier's Boy,* 1957; *Where the High Winds Blow,* 1960; *Storms of Our Journey, and Other Stories,* 1962; *Dragon Hill* (juvenile), 1962; *Winter of Madness,* 1964; *Mallabec,* 1965; *Come Back, Geordie,* 1966; *Cab-Intersec,* 1968 (published in England as *Devil's Plunge,* Collins, 1968); *Pirate Rock,* 1969; *Big Ben* (juvenile), 1970; *The Lords Pink Ocean,* 1972; *Black Dougal,* 1973; *Ash,* 1976; *Pot of Gold,* Collins, 1977. Contributor to *Saturday Evening Post, Atlantic,* and other magazines.

SIDELIGHTS: David Harry Walker's book *Geordie* was filmed with title "Wee Geordie," by George K. Arthur in 1956, and *Harry Black* was made into film with title, "Harry Black and the Tiger," by Twentieth Century-Fox in 1958. *Avocational interests:* Skiing, bird watching.

BIOGRAPHICAL/CRITICAL SOURCES: New York Times Book Review, March 17, 1968.

* * *

WALLACE, Irving 1916-

PERSONAL: Born March 19, 1916, in Chicago, Ill.; son of Alexander and Bessie (Liss) Wallace; married Sylvia Kahn (formerly Hollywood editor of *Modern Screen* and of *Photoplay;* author); children: David, Amy Deborah. *Education:* Attended Williams Institute, Berkeley, Calif., and Los Angeles City College. *Address:* Box 49699, Los Angeles, Calif. 90049.

CAREER: Author. Sold his first story for five dollars to *Horse and Jockey* magazine at the age of fifteen and has been a free-lance writer ever since. He has worked as a writer on newspapers and magazines, and as a screenwriter for every major film company in Hollywood. His articles and short stories number over 500, and his magazine assignments took him all over the world. Since 1957, he has devoted all of his time to writing books. He covered the Democratic and Republican National Conventions for the Chicago Sun-Times/Daily News Wire Service, 1972. *Military service:* U.S. Army Air Forces, writer in the First Motion Picture Unit, 1942-46; became staff sergeant. *Member:* Authors Guild, Authors League of America, P.E.N., Writers Guild of America, Manuscript Society, Society of Authors (London). *Awards, honors:* Supreme Award of Merit and honorary fellowship from George Washington Carver Memorial Institute, 1964, for writing *The Man,* and contributing "to the betterment of race relations and human welfare"; received silver medal from Commonwealth Club, 1965; received award from *Bestsellers* magazine, 1965, for *The Man;* Paperback of the Year award, National Bestsellers Institute, 1970, for *The Seven Minutes;* Popular Culture Association award of excellence, 1974, for distinguished achievements in the popular arts; Venice Rosa d'Oro Award, 1975, for contributions to American letters.

WRITINGS: The Fabulous Originals, Knopf, 1955, Kraus Reprint, 1972; *The Square Pegs,* Knopf, 1957; *The Fabulous Showman: The Life and Times of P. T. Barnum* (Literary Guild selection), Knopf, 1959; *The Twenty-Seventh Wife* (biography), Simon & Schuster, 1961; *The Sunday Gentleman* (collected writings), Simon & Schuster, 1965; *The Writing of One Novel,* Simon & Schuster, 1968; *The Nympho and Other Maniacs* (Literary Guild alternate selection), Simon & Schuster, 1971; (compiler with son, David Wallechinsky) *The People's Almanac* (Literary Guild special selection), Doubleday, 1975; (compiler with Wallechinsky and daughter, Amy Wallace) *The Book of Lists* (Book-of-the-Month club special selection), Morrow, 1977; (with Wallechinsky) *The People's Almanac #2* (Literary Guild special selection), Morrow, 1978; (with Amy Wallace) *The Two* (biography; Literary Guild special selection), Simon & Schuster, 1978; (with Wallechinsky, Amy Wallace, and wife, Sylvia Wallace) *The Book of Lists #2* (Literary Guild special selection), Morrow, 1980.

All novels; all published by Simon & Schuster, except as indicated: *The Sins of Philip Fleming,* Fell, 1959, new edition, 1968; *The Chapman Report,* 1960; *The Prize* (Book-of-the-Month Club special selection), 1962; *The Three Sirens* (Mid-Century Society Book Club selection), 1963; *The Man* (*Reader's Digest* Book Club selection; Book-of-the-Month Club alternate selection), 1964; *The Plot* (Book-of-the-Month Club alternate selection), 1967; *The Seven Minutes* (Literary Guild alternate selection), 1969; *The Word* (Book-of-the-Month Club selection), 1972; *The Fan Club* (Literary Guild alternate selection), 1974; *The R Document* (*Reader's Digest* Book Club selection; Literary Guild alternate selection), 1976; *The Pigeon Project* (Literary Guild selection), 1979; *The Second Lady,* New American Library, 1980.

Screenplays: (With John Monks, Jr. and Charles Hoffman) "The West Point Story," Warner Bros., 1950; "Meet Me at the Fair," Universal, 1953; (with Lewis Meltzer) "Desert Legion," Universal, 1953; (with William Bowers) "Split Second," RKO, 1953; (with Roy Huggins) "Gun Fury," Columbia, 1953; (with Horace McCoy) "Bad for Each Other," Columbia, 1954; (with Gerald Adams) "The Gambler from Natches," Twentieth Century-Fox, 1954; "Jump into

Hell," Warner Bros., 1955; "Sincerely Yours," Warner Bros., 1955; "The Burning Hills," United Artists, 1956; "Bombers B-52," Warner Bros., 1957; (with Irwin Allen and Charles Bennett) "The Big Circus," Allied Artists, 1959.

Also author of plays: "And Then Goodnight," "Because of Sex," "Hotel Behemoth," "Speak of the Devil," "Murder by Morning," and (with Jerome Weidman) "Pantheon." Also author of biographies of P. T. Barnum for *Collier's Encyclopedia,* 1960, *American Oxford Encyclopedia,* and *Encyclopaedia Britannica.* Contributor of over 500 articles and short stories to magazines, including *Saturday Evening Post, Reader's Digest, Esquire, Collier's,* and many others.

WORK IN PROGRESS: The Intimate Sex Lives of Famous People, "a family collaboration," for Delacorte; with Wallechinsky, *The People's Almanac #3,* for Morrow; another novel.

SIDELIGHTS: Despite the fact that Irving Wallace has sold more than 132,000,000 copies of his books and is believed to have an estimated worldwide readership of more than 6,000,000,000 persons, a number of literary critics continue to criticize certain aspects of his writings. While the criticism ranges from John Leonard of the *New York Times* writing that "Mr. Wallace has a tin ear. Yes, [*The Seven Minutes*] is unconscionably padded," and Maynard Pont of the *San Francisco Chronicle* reviewing *The Chapman Report* as "sophomoric" with a story line that is "outrageously contrived," to Peter Share describing *The Fan Club* as "tasteless," usually, at one point in their reviews, the critics praise Wallace for his research, attention to details and great storytelling ability.

Reviewing Wallace's *The Seven Minutes,* Alan Branigan, for example, points out that "there is a brash, journalistic jazziness to much of Wallace's writing. But there is also a sympathy for people caught in an inevitable clash between ideologies. Above all, the book has a stinging pace and more excitement than one has any right to expect as the author's author's vision takes him farther and farther into the background of the involved personalities."

Lawrence Lafore agrees with Branigan's assessment and sees merit in Wallace's writing. Lafore explains that "Wallace is a leading figure in what might be regarded as a new branch of American literature, the novel based on subjects of topical interest and universal appeal. The conversion of current events into fiction is not new, but Mr. Wallace . . . has developed a theme into a form. His novels, particularly *The Chapman Report* and *The Prize,* which dealt respectively with a Kinsey-type survey and the selection of Nobel Prize winners, have been hugely popular, in both senses of the word. They skillfully combine the most alluring features of the headline, the expose, the editorial and the mystery story."

Louise Hackett seems to sum up the feelings of many readers when she writes: "From time to time there have been critics who have belittled Wallace's talent, suggesting that he has achieved a commercial success based solely on lurid subject matter designed to titilate the masses. I have come to suspect that this brand of snobbish criticism may be at least partially based upon an envious unwillingness to admit that literature can be both popular and good. This attitude seems to me to be that only those works which are appreciated by an initiated few (including, of course, the critics themselves) can be considered to be art. They either neglect—or refuse—to consider the fact that most of the classical authors of the past, who may appeal to only a few scholarly types today, wrote the popular 'bestsellers' of their times. If this weren't true, their work would not have survived to the present." And the *New York Times* critic Leonard wonders: "Is [Wallace] so wrong? And although we may lounge about wishing that Irving Wallace weren't the only novelist millions of people read, is it permissible in any court of critical opinion to sneer at his introduction of ideas and convictions into a commercial work of fiction? I think not."

Wallace believes one reason for his lack of popularity with some critics is his enormous success in marketing his work. He told John Leverence and Sam Grogg, Jr. during an interview: "The critics who read these stories well, as I've said before, they equated money with dishonesty. That's the important thing I learned. If an author is earning a lot of money, that means he is catering to the public. If he's catering to the public, he's not being true to himself and he's not being honest. And once this starts, there's no stopping it. Say what you will about your real reasons for writing, and the critics still will not believe it. Yet, I can't see how a creative person can just write for money, mainly write out of desire for money, and make it. Maybe a few writers do that successfully, but I can't imagine how, and I've never met one, not one."

Wallace feels some critics do not only review the book but they also review the author. As he explains to H. T. Anderson: "A good book review should not contain anything about the author's domestic or social behavior, income tax bracket, or supposed motivations for writing his work. . . . Only the product of the author's pen should be of the concern of a good review." Discussing the same topic with Haskel Frankel of *National Observer,* Wallace comments: "I'll pick up one of the news magazines when I've got a new book out. I'm eager to know if they read my book and what they thought of it. But I don't find out. They tell me why I wrote my book and how. I want to know if this book I sat along with is good or bad, and they're telling me why I wrote it."

As if to disregard the complaints of Wallace's critics, publishers and filmmakers consider Wallace's novels guaranteed bestsellers. Joyce Haber explains: "Wallace is one of the two authors in the world who needs only to speak the phrase 'I have an idea' to find himself signing contracts assuring him of zillions of dollars for life." And *Variety* reported on July 12, 1972, that "Wallace . . . once got $1,000,000 from Twentieth Century-Fox for the screen rights to two sight-unseen, not-yet written novels."

The key to Wallace's success with his readers might be found in his philosophy of writing. He wrote *CA:* "I believe in telling a story as stories were told in wayside inns or around fires before men could read or had bound books. You tell a tale to adults as you might tell a different one to your child curled in bed at night, so that the listener or reader will exclaim, 'But what happened next?' or 'What happened to her?'"

He continued: "If I have to write a book because I love it, to satisfy my own curiosity in the characters or its subject, then perhaps thousands of other people, too wise to live by dreams, but with the same common interests I have, may want to buy or borrow some of my make-believe."

If there is one area for which Wallace seems generally well respected, it is for his apparent dedication to details and authenticity. As a reviewer for *Ladies' Home Journal* explains: "While it may take Wallace only four to six months to complete the actual writing of one of his long, thematic novels (most of them run to a thousand pages), his books are many years in gestation, research, rewriting and editing. A meticulous craftsman, Wallace not only rewrites pages as he goes along, but also produces numerous drafts. *The Word* required five separate drafts before he was satisfied with it. Since he began working on *The Word* in 1961, when he submitted an outline to his publisher, Simon & Schuster, the novel was ten years in the making." Agreeing with this observation P. J. Earl writes in his review of *The Nympho and Other Maniacs* that this book "is a full-fledged history book and a rather well documented and researched history."

John Barkham feels that Wallace does a service to his readers besides providing entertaining novels. Barkham writes: "His novels have probably taught readers more about the awarding of Nobel Prizes and the legal intricacies of censorship than they could learn anywhere else. With each novel, too, he becomes more expert in the blending of fact and fiction, never permitting one to overwhelm the other."

In an interview with Kirk Polkiny in *Writer's Yearbook,* Wallace admits that he works hard at his writing: "As a writer, any modest success I've had has not been entirely accidental. I've never ceased trying to improve. I'm always studying books by other authors, often with admiration at how they achieve their effects and with dismay at my own shortcomings. I've never stopped reading books about writing. Since the day I was born, it sometimes seems, I've been reading."

Another popular addition to Wallace's bibliography is the nonfiction work he writes and compiles with his family. The first such venture was *The People's Almanac.* As Wallace explains to Isobel Silden of *Family Weekly:* "It was my son David's idea. He'd collected almanacs from an early age, but he found that brevity distorted facts and that many governments take prepared material. He wanted to be able to learn and have pleasure while doing it. He worked on it for two and a half years alone, when he was living in Berkeley. . . . I offered to help him, but I knew that in order for us to collaborate, we had to stop being father and son. I treated him as a person I like. Because of his own two published books, he had no trouble putting his ego aside. We wanted to do a reference book to be read for fun. We also ended up with a closer relationship than ever before."

The People's Almanac has sold more than a million copies. Wallace has since collaborated with his wife, Sylvia, son David, and daughter Amy on several additional books, including another bestseller, *The Book of Lists.*

Many readers have wondered how Wallace can alternate between writing fiction and nonfiction. In an interview published in *Writer's Yearbook,* Kirk Polking asked Wallace about his ability to write in both forms. Wallace remarked: "In nonfiction, I enjoy the detective work involved in research, and the challenge of trying to transform cold facts, which are so limiting, into an exciting true story. In fiction, I enjoy the even greater challenge of letting my imagination soar, and then trying to harness it and bring it down to the corral that white paper, with its boundaries, represents. Actually, I enjoy my greatest satisfaction in attempting to merge fiction with nonfiction."

Almost all of Wallace's novels have been acquired by motion picture studios and filmed, including: *The Fabulous Showman* was purchased by Columbia; *The Three Sirens* was purchased by Brenco Pictures; *The Chapman Report* was filmed Warner Bros. in 1962; *The Prize* was filmed by Metro-Goldwyn-Mayer in 1963; *The Seven Minutes* was filmed by Twentieth Century-Fox in 1971; *The Man* was filmed by ABC Circle Films and distributed by Paramount in 1972; *The Plot* was purchased by Twentieth Century-Fox; *The Fan Club* was purchased by Columbia; *The R Document* was purchased by United Artists; *The Word* was filmed by Columbia Broadcasting Co. and networked in 1978.

Most of Wallace's books have been published worldwide. Two primary collections of Wallace's manuscripts and research papers are located at University of Wyoming and University of Texas at Austin.

AVOCATIONAL INTERESTS: Travel, collecting autographed letters, inscribed first edition books, and impressionist paintings.

BIOGRAPHICAL/CRITICAL SOURCES: San Francisco Chronicle, June 5, 1960, April 29, 1971; *New York Times Book Review,* September 22, 1963, October 2, 1969, March 19, 1972; *Life,* July 31, 1964; *Best Sellers,* September 15, 1964, October 1, 1969; *Writer,* January, 1965, November, 1968; Irving Wallace, *The Sunday Gentleman,* Simon & Schuster, 1965; *Writer's Yearbook,* Number 37, 1966; Roy Newquist, *Conversations,* Rand McNally, 1967; Irving Wallace, *The Writing of One Novel,* Simon & Schuster, 1967; *Friends,* October, 1968; *National Observer,* November 25, 1968; *Newark Sunday Times,* October 5, 1969; *Censorship Today,* October/November, 1969; *Variety,* November 5, 1969, July 12, 1972.

Ladies' Home Journal, March, 1972; *New York Post,* March 9, 1972; *Columbus Enquirer,* July 31, 1972; *Ramparts,* February, 1973; *Journal of Popular Culture,* summer, 1973; *Los Angeles Times,* February 17, 1974; John Leverence, *Irving Wallace: A Writer's Profile,* Popular Press, 1974; John G. Cawelti, *Adventure, Mystery, and Romance,* University of Chicago Press, 1976; *Authors in the News,* Volume I, Gale, 1976; *New West,* January 17, 1977; *Wall Street Journal,* May 3, 1977; *Los Angeles Times Book Review,* May 15, 1977; *Phoenix Gazette,* May 27, 1977; *Bookviews,* October, 1977; *Book Digest,* November, 1977; *Contemporary Literary Criticism,* Gale, Volume VII, 1977, Volume XIII, 1980; *Family Weekly,* February 18, 1979; *Chicago Tribune Book World,* April 29, 1979; *Washington Post,* February 28, 1980.

—Sketch by Margaret Mazurkiewicz

* * *

WALVIN, James 1942-

PERSONAL: Born February 1, 1942, in Manchester, England; son of James (an engineer) and Emma (Wood) Walvin. *Education:* University of Keele, B.A. (first class honors), 1964; McMaster University, M.A. (first class honors), 1965; University of York, Ph.D., 1970. *Office:* Department of History, University of York, York, England.

CAREER: University of York, York, England, currently member of faculty in department of history.

WRITINGS: (With M. J. Craton) *A Jamaican Plantation,* University of Toronto Press, 1970; *The Black Presence,* Orbach & Chambers, 1971, Schocken, 1972; *Black and White: The Negro and English Society, 1555-1945,* Allen Lane, 1972; *The People's Game: A Social History of British Football,* Allen Lane, 1975; (editor with Craton) *Slavery, Abolition and Emancipation,* Longman, 1976; *Beside the Seaside: A Social History of the Popular Seaside Holiday,* Allen Lane, 1978; *Leisure and Society, 1830-1950,* Longman, 1978; (editor with D. Eltis) *The Slave Trade and Abolition,* University of Wisconsin Press, in press; *Seen and Heard: Children in Britain,* Penguin, in press.

* * *

WARREN, Donald Irwin 1935-

PERSONAL: Born May 24, 1935, in Detroit, Mich.; son of

Joseph (a businessman) and Anne (Marks) Warren; married Rachelle Barcus (a social psychologist), June 5, 1960; children: Dianna Michele, Lisa Nicole. *Education:* Wayne State University, B.A., 1957, M.A. (political science), 1959; University of Michigan, M.A. (sociology), 1961, Ph.D., 1964. *Home:* 2233 Delaware, Ann Arbor, Mich. 48103.

CAREER: Wayne State University, Detroit, Mich., associate professor of sociology and anthropology, 1965-68; University of Michigan, Ann Arbor, associate professor in School of Social Work, 1969-72, senior research scientist in Institute of Labor and Industrial Relations, beginning 1973; Oakland University, Rochester, Mich., currently chairperson of department of sociology and anthropology. Oakland University, visiting lecturer, 1964, 1965, visiting professor, 1970, 1974. Project director of Ford Foundation studies and of U.S. Department of Health, Education, and Welfare studies. Consultant to NASA, 1966, to Teachers College of Columbia University, 1970, to Johnson, Johnson & Roy (planning architects), 1973, and to Detroit Urban League, New Detroit, and Equal Justice Council. *Military service:* U.S. Air Force Reserve, 1959-65. *Member:* American Sociological Association, Society for the Study of Social Problems, Archaeological Institute of America, American Civil Liberties Union.

WRITINGS: Black Neighborhoods: An Assessment of Community Power, University of Michigan Press, 1974; *The Radical Center: Middle Americans and the Politics of Alienation,* University of Notre Dame Press, 1976; (with wife, Rachelle Warren) *The Neighborhood Organizer's Handbook,* University of Notre Dame Press, 1977.

WORK IN PROGRESS: Research on ethnicity and urban life, on status inconsistency and social behavior, and on neighborhood structure and urban social structure.

AVOCATIONAL INTERESTS: Classical archaeology (Roman urban life).

* * *

WARREN, (Francis) Eugene 1941-

PERSONAL: Born October 3, 1941, in Craig, Colo.; son of George William (a farmer) and Elizabeth (Wilson) Warren; married Rosalee Cecelia Bazil, January 19, 1963; children: Cynthia, Matthew, Timothy, Jennifer. *Education:* Attended College of Emporia, 1959-62; Kansas State Teachers College (now Emporia State University), B.A., 1966, M.A., 1967. *Politics:* "Radical Christian." *Religion:* Christian. *Home:* 300 West Third, Rolla, Mo. 65401. *Office:* Department of Humanities, University of Missouri, Rolla, Mo. 65401.

CAREER: Has worked as farmhand, grocery clerk, orderly, truck driver, cable television lineman, and janitor; University of Missouri—Rolla, instructor, 1967-73, assistant professor, 1973-79, associate professor of English, 1979—. *Member:* Conference on Christianity and Literature, New York C. S. Lewis Society, Fine Arts Fellowship. *Awards, honors:* Evangelical Press Association first prize for poem, 1974, for "A Conversion 1741."

WRITINGS—All poetry: *Christographia,* Ktaadn Poetry Press, 1973; *Rumors of Light,* Grafiktrakts, 1974; *Christographia 1-32,* Cauldron Press, 1977; *Fishing at Easter,* BkMk Press, 1980; *Eden of Stone, Eden of Light,* Eden, 1980.

Work is represented in anthologies, including *Adam among the Television Trees,* edited by Virginia Mollenkott, Word Books, 1971, *The Risk of Birth,* edited by Luci Shaw, Shaw, 1974, *Your Own Poets,* edited by Phil Silva, Praise the Lord Press, 1977, *The Country of the Risen King,* edited by Merle Meeter, Baker Book, 1978, and *Anthology of Magazine Verse and Yearbook of American Poetry,* edited by Alan F. Pater, Monitor, 1980.

Editor of "Grafiktrakts" series of pamphlets, 1974—. Contributor of poems and articles to professional journals. Contributing editor, *Post-American,* 1973-76, and *For the Time Being,* 1974—; poetry editor, *Christianity and Literature,* 1975—; correspondent, *Sojourners,* 1976—.

WORK IN PROGRESS: A creative writing textbook; a collection of essays, *Poetry and Discipleship;* a long poem, *The Similitudes.*

SIDELIGHTS: Eugene Warren told *CA:* "Raised on a farm, southwest of Topeka, Kan., the rhythms and creature of that area are a part of who I am, how I sound. Organic view of verse, life, kosmos. More or less deliberate Christian since 1963—theology Anabaptist—Mennonite heritage. Large interest in apocalypse, visionary image. Happily married seventeen years, four children. Ideas of poetry influenced by Pound, William Carlos Williams, Gerard Manley Hopkins, David the king [psalms]."

Reflecting on these earlier comments, Warren adds: "I've found myself moving continuously, if slowly, in the direction I indicated. I'm especially interested now in the interflow of self and world, the imagination and language as shaping our experience and persons. I'm seeking a poetry in which body and spirit and intellect are fused in clear, calm joy. I'm seeking that Logos who informs every instant of our lives, that Word who is flesh in Jesus of Nazareth."

* * *

WARREN, Patricia Nell 1936-
(Patricia Kilina)

PERSONAL: Born June 15, 1936; daughter of Conrad K. (a rancher) and Nellie Bradford (Flinn) Warren; married George O. Tarnawsky (an electrical engineer and writer), June 21, 1957 (divorced, 1973). *Education:* Stephens College, A.A., 1955; Manhattanville College of the Sacred Heart (now Manhattanville College), B.A., 1957. *Politics:* Liberal. *Religion:* None. *Agent:* Paul R. Reynolds, Inc., 12 East 41st St., New York, N.Y. 10017. *Office: Reader's Digest,* Pleasantville, N.Y. 10570

CAREER: Reader's Digest, Pleasantville, N.Y., associate book editor, 1959—. *Member:* Dignity International, International Somali Cat Club, Mariposa Foundation, Empire Cat Club, Walk on the Wild Side Cat Club. *Awards, honors:* First prize for short story in *Atlantic* college fiction contest, 1954; Walt Whitman Award for Excellence in Gay Literature, 1978.

WRITINGS: (Under pseudonym Patricia Kilina) *The Last Centennial* (novel), Dial, 1971; *The Front Runner* (novel), Morrow, 1974; *The Fancy Dancer* (novel), Morrow, 1976; *The Beauty Queen* (novel), Morrow, 1978; (translator with George O. Tarnawsky) *Ukrainskiy Dumy* (poetry), Harvard University Press, 1979. Also author of three books of poetry, in Ukrainian, under pseudonym Patricia Kilina. Contributor of articles on cats to periodicals, including *Cats* Magazine, *All Cats,* and *Cat World.*

WORK IN PROGRESS: Two novels, *Billy's Boy* and *Jump the Moon.*

SIDELIGHTS: Patricia Warren told *CA* that her pseudonym, Kilina, is an ancient Slavic woman's name derived from the Ukrainian word "kalyna," which means holly tree. "In Ukrainian folklore," wrote Warren, "the holly tree symbolizes woman." *Avocational interests:* Wildlife conservation, gardening, gourmet cooking, antiques, showing horses, and breeding and showing fancy cats.

* * *

WASSERMAN, Paul 1924-

PERSONAL: Born January 8, 1924, in Newark, N.J.; son of Joe and Sadie (Ringelescu) Wasserman; married Krystyna Ostrowska, 1973; children: (previous marriage) Jacqueline R., Steven R. *Education:* City College (now City College of the City University of New York), B.B.A., 1948; Columbia University, M.S. in library science, 1949, M.S. in economics, 1950; University of Michigan, Ph.D. in library administration, 1960; Western Reserve University (now Case Western Reserve University), postdoctoral study in data processing and information retrieval, 1963-64. *Home:* 3501 Duke St., College Park Woods, Md. *Office:* Undergraduate Library, University of Maryland, College Park, Md. 20742.

CAREER: Brooklyn Public Library, Brooklyn, N.Y., assistant to business librarian, 1949-51, chief of science and industry, 1951-53; Cornell University, Graduate School of Business and Public Administration, Ithaca, N.Y., assistant professor, 1953-56, associate professor, 1956-62, professor, 1962-65, librarian, 1953-65; University of Maryland, College Park, dean of Graduate School of Library and Information Services, 1965-70, professor in College of Library and Information Services, 1970—. Lecturer, American Management Association seminars, New York, 1956-58; Isabel Nichol Lecturer, Graduate School of Librarianship, University of Denver, 1968; tutor on inventing and designing information products and services, American Society for Information Science conference, Denver, 1971; lecturer, Louisiana State University Library series, 1972; Perrie Jones Lecturer, St. Paul Public Library, 1973; international lecturer, European Summer School, Liverpool Polytechnic, 1973; lecturer, workshop planner, and consultant, United Board for College Development, Atlanta, 1975-77; lecturer, University of Mexico, 1976. Research director, Library Manpower Research Study, sponsored by U.S. Office of Education, National Library of Medicine, and National Science Foundation, 1967-70; director, Institute on Comparative and International Librarianship and Information Science, 1972; chairman of committee working group on establishment of international summer school in librarianship and information science, Federation Internationale de Documentation, 1972-75; seminar director, Program for Officials, Economists, and Librarians, Brazil Institute of Space Research, 1975; co-director, International Seminar for Library Administrator Development, Mexico, 1975, and Philippines, 1976; seminar director, Organization of American States program for national information for industry personnel, Central America, 1976; director of development of a library in administration, Middle East Technical University, Ankara, Turkey. U.S. national representative, Committee in Education and Training, Federation Internationale de Documentation, 1969—; member of executive board, Documentation Abstracts, Inc., 1970-73; member of planning committee, Institute on Educational Problems in Information Science, Hungary, 1972; member of U.S.-Mexico Bilateral Committee on Scientific Information Relations and Exchange and chairman of Sub-Committee on Education and Training, 1976. Researcher and editorial consultant, Gale Research Co., 1959-60, 1963-64, and Indiana University School of Business, 1961-63; consultant to Special Libraries Association, 1961-69, Public Health Service, 1966-69, Ohio State Board of Regents, 1969, Redgrave Information Resources, Inc., 1972-75, and to Organization of American States, 1976—; consultant to various UNESCO programs, 1973-78. *Military service:* U.S. Army, 1943-46; received Bronze Star Medal and Purple Heart.

MEMBER: American Library Association (chairman of business and technology committee, 1952-53; member of new reference tools committee, 1964-69; member of research committee, 1965-70; member of statistics committee, 1965-70), Special Libraries Association (chairman of business division, 1952-53; member of committee on standards, 1960-62; member of finance committee, 1960-63), Library Public Relations Council, American Association of University Professors, Maryland Library Association. *Awards, honors:* Tangley Oaks fellow, United Educators, Inc., 1963-64.

WRITINGS: The Librarian and the Machine: Observations on the Applications of Machines in the Administration of College and University Libraries, Gale, 1965; *The New Librarianship: A Challenge for Change,* Bowker, 1972; (with Rizzo) *Outline for a Course in Administration for Managers of Information Services and Centers,* Universal System for Information in Science and Technology (UNISIST), 1977.

Editor: *Directory of University Research Bureaus and Institutes,* Gale, 1960; (co-editor) *Directory of Health Organizations: National, State, and Regional,* Graduate School of Business and Public Administration, Cornell University, 1961, 2nd edition, 1965; (co-editor) *Statistics Sources,* Gale, 1962, 6th edition, 1980; (editor with Mary Lee Bundy) *Reader in Library Administration,* Microcard Editions, 1968; (editor with Bundy) *Reader in Research Methods in Librarianship,* Microcard Editions, 1970; *Learning Independently,* Gale, 1979.

Managing editor; published by Gale, except as indicated: *Sources of Commodity Prices,* Special Libraries Association, 1960, 2nd edition (with Diane Kemmerling) published as *Commodity Prices: A Source Book and Index,* Gale, 1974; *Consultants and Consulting Organizations,* Graduate School of Business and Public Administration, Cornell University, 1966, 2nd edition, Gale, 1973, 4th edition, 1979; *Who's Who in Consulting,* Graduate School of Business and Public Administration, Cornell University, 1968, 2nd edition, Gale, 1973; *Readers in Librarianship and Information Science,* Information Handling Services, 1968—; *Awards, Honors and Prizes: A Sourcebook and Directory,* 1969, 2nd edition, 1973, 3rd edition published as *Awards, Honors and Prizes,* Volume I: *United States and Canada,* Volume II: *International and Foreign,* 1975, 4th edition, 1978; *Contributions in Librarianship and Information Science,* Greenwood Press, 1969—; *List: Library and Information Science Today,* Science Associates International, 1970-73, Gale, 1974-75; *Encyclopedia of Business Information Sources,* two volumes, 1970, 3rd edition of Volume I, 1976, 3rd edition of Volume II, 1978; *New Consultants: A Periodic Supplement to "Consultants and Consulting Organizations,"* 1973-78, 4th edition, 1979; *Museum Media,* 1973, 2nd edition published as *Catalog of Museum Publications and Media,* 1980; *Consumer Sourcebook,* 1974, 2nd edition, 1978; *Library Bibliographies and Indexes,* 1975; (with Esther Herman) *Festivals Sourcebook,* 1976; *Ethnic Information Sources in the United States,* 1976; *Training and Development Organizations,* 1978, 2nd edition, 1980; *Speakers and Lecturers: How to Find Them,* 1979. Also coordinating managing editor of Gale's "Information Guide Library" series, 1971—.

Monographs; published by Graduate School of Business and Public Administration, Cornell University, except as indicated: *Information for Administrators,* Cornell University Press, 1956; *Basic Library in Public Administration,* 1957;

(co-author) *Decision-Making: An Annotated Bibliography,* 1958, *Supplement, 1958-1963,* 1964; *Measurement and Evaluation of Organizational Performance: An Annotated Bibliography,* 1959; *Sources for Hospital Administrators,* 1961.

Also author of numerous technical papers and reports. Contributor to *Proceedings* of various organizations. Contributor of articles to professional journals. Book review editor, *Administrative Science Quarterly,* 1951-59, 1960-61; member of editorial advisory boards, *Social Sciences Citation Index,* 1972—, and *American Society for Information Science Bulletin,* 1977—.

* * *

WATKINS, John G(oodrich) 1913-

PERSONAL: Born March 17, 1913, in Salmon, Idaho; son of John Thomas and Ethel (Goodrich) Watkins; married Helen Huth, 1971; children: (previous marriage) John Dean, Jonette Alison, Richard Douglas, Gregory Keith, Rodney Phillip; (present marriage) Marvin Huth, Karen Eiblmayr. *Education:* Attended College of Idaho, 1929-30, 1931-32; University of Idaho, B.S., 1932, M.S., 1936; Columbia University, Ph.D., 1941. *Politics:* Democrat. *Religion:* Unitarian Universalist. *Home:* 413 Evans St., Missoula, Mont. *Office:* Department of Psychology, University of Montanta, Missoula, Mont. 59801.

CAREER: High school teacher in Homedale, Rupert, and Mountain Home (all Idaho), 1933-39; Columbia University, New York, N.Y., assistant, 1940; Ithaca College, Ithaca, N.Y., assistant professor, 1940-41; Alabama Polytechnic Institute (now Auburn University), Auburn, professor, 1941-43; Washington State College (now University), Pullman, associate professor, 1946-49; Veterans Administration Hospital, American Lake, Wash., clinical psychologist, 1949-50; Veterans Administration Mental Hygiene Clinic, Chicago, Ill., chief clinical psychologist, 1950-53; Veterans Administration Hospital, Portland, Ore., chief clinical psychologist, 1953-64; University of Montana, Missoula, professor of psychology and director of clinical training, 1964—. Diplomate in clinical psychology, American Board of Examiners in Professional Psychology; part-time practice in psychotherapy and psychological consultation. Lecturer, University of Washington, University of Portland, Northwestern University, Portland State College (now University), and Florida Institute of Technology; visiting professor, University of California, Los Angeles, and State University of New York at Binghamton; director of planning and development, International Graduate University, Switzerland, 1974-77. Acting chief of training in clinical psychology for Illinois Region of Veterans Administration, 1950-51; president, American Board of Examiners in Psychological Hypnosis, 1959-62. Public speaker and workshop lecturer. Consulting psychologist, Dammasch State Hospital, Oregon, 1961-64, and V.A. Hospitals and Montana State Prison, 1965—. *Military service:* U.S. Army, Quartermaster Corps, 1943-46; served as chief clinical psychologist at Welch Convalescent Hospital, Daytona Beach, Fla.; became first lieutenant.

MEMBER: International Society for Clinical and Experimental Hypnosis (executive secretary, 1958-62; president-elect, 1962-64; president, 1965-67), American Psychological Association (president of Division 30, 1975-76), Society for Clinical and Experimental Hypnosis (president, 1969-71), American Academy of Psychotherapists, Montana Psychological Association, Phi Delta Kappa, Kappa Delta Pi, Phi Mu Alpha.

WRITINGS: *Objective Measurement of Instrumental Performance,* Columbia University Press, 1942; *Hypnotherapy of War Neuroses,* Ronald, 1949; *General Psychotherapy,* C. C Thomas, 1960; *The Therapeutic Self,* Human Sciences Press, 1978.

Contributor: B. B. Wolman, editor, *Handbook of Clinical Psychology,* McGraw, 1965; I. A. Berg and L. A. Pennington, editors, *Introduction to Clinical Psychology,* Ronald, 1966; H. L. Collier, editor, *What's Psychotherapy and Who Needs It?,* O'Sullivan Woodside, 1976. Also contributor of chapters to several other books, including, *Medical Hypnosis,* edited by Jerome Schneck, *Hypnosis throughout the World,* edited by Fred Marcuse, *Taboo Topics,* edited by Norman L. Farberow, *Short Term Approaches to Psychotherapy,* edited by H. Grayson, and *Therapy in Psychosomatic Medicine,* edited by F. Antonelli. Contributor of over ninety articles and reviews to professional journals. Member of editorial boards of four journals.

WORK IN PROGRESS: Working in areas of hypnoanalysis, psychosomatic medicine, psychological theory and psychotherapy.

SIDELIGHTS: John G. Watkins told *CA:* "As a psychologist I am continually trying to understand human behavior, both in myself and others. As a writer I transmit the results of this search with the hope of promoting the betterment of mankind. I am conceited enough to think that my writings do make a contribution, and trust that when it seems to be otherwise I will have the good sense to stop writing. I read voraciously and am willing to borrow or steal from any source which might improve my contributions—but expect to give proper credit to those whose ideas I have purloined.

"I am also lazy, with islands of intense productivity occasionally looming out of an ocean of non-creative hours. When the time, the place and the feelings bloom simultaneously inspirations spring forth, alive with near-ripened fruit. When not, the land is a desert. The hardest job is to sit down and start writing; after that it's easy."

AVOCATIONAL INTERESTS: Music, boating, public speaking.

* * *

WATTLES, Santha Rama Rau 1923-
(Santha Rama Rau)

PERSONAL: Born January 24, 1923, in Madras, India; came to United States in 1941; daughter of Benegal and Dhanvanthi (Handoo) Rama Rau; married Faubion Bowers, 1952 (divorced); married Gurdon W. Wattles, 1970; children: (first marriage) Jai Peter. *Education:* Wellesley College, B.A. (with honors), 1944. *Home:* 522 East 89th St., New York, N.Y. 10028; and Leedsville Rd., Amenia, N.Y. 12501. *Agent:* Owen Laster, William Morris Agency, 1350 Avenue of the Americas, New York, N.Y. 10019.

CAREER: Free-lance writer. Instructor, Sarah Lawrence College. Lecturer on tours, 1961, 1962. *Member:* P.E.N., Phi Beta Kappa. *Awards, honors:* Harper Book Find, 1945; *Mademoiselle* Award, 1947; National Association of Independent Schools Award, 1960, for *My Russian Journey;* D.Litt. from Bates College, 1961, Roosevelt College (now University), 1962, Brandeis University, 1963, and Bard College, 1964.

WRITINGS—All under name Santha Rama Rau; all published by Harper, except as indicated: *Home to India,* 1945; *East of Home,* 1950; *This Is India,* 1953; *Remember the House,* 1956; *View to the Southeast,* 1957; *My Russian Journey,* 1959; *Gifts of Passage,* 1961; (adapter) *A Passage to*

India (play adaptation of E. M. Forster's novel; first produced in London, England, 1960, produced on Broadway, 1961), Harcourt, 1961; *The Cooking of India,* Time-Life, 1970; *The Adventures,* 1970; (with Gayatri Devi) *A Princess Remembers: The Memoirs of the Maharani of Jaipur,* Lippincott, 1974. Contributor of articles to *New Yorker, Holiday, Harper's, Saturday Review,* and *Vogue.*

WORK IN PROGRESS: A novel.

SIDELIGHTS: The unusual success of Rama Rau's travel books is often attributed to her gift for "transcribing life to paper in terms of people, their talk, their manners and customs." She is said to possess an "acute sense of membership in the family of man" which is evidenced in the perceptive and sensitive accounts of her travels."

BIOGRAPHICAL/CRITICAL SOURCES: New York Herald Tribune Book Review, March 1, 1959; *Springfield Republican,* April 5, 1959; *New Statesman,* November 28, 1959; *Christian Science Monitor,* May 11, 1961; *Book World,* August 9, 1970; *New York Times Book Review,* March 13, 1977.

* * *

WATTS, William 1930-

PERSONAL: Born May 30, 1930, in New York, N.Y.; son of Bigelow and Helen (Spader) Watts; divorced; children: Evelyn G., Shelby S., Heidi H. *Education:* Attended Yale University, 1948-51; Syracuse University, B.A., 1953; Harvard University, M.A., 1956. *Residence:* Washington, D.C. *Office:* Potomac Associates, 1740 Massachusetts Ave. N.W., Washington, D.C. 20036.

CAREER: U.S. Department of State, U.S. Foreign Service, Washington, D.C., foreign service officer in Korea, Germany, and the Soviet Union, 1956-65; Ford Foundation, New York City, program officer, 1965-68; New York State Government, New York City, director of Office for Urban Innovation, 1968-69; National Security Council, Washington, D.C., staff secretary, 1969-70; Potomac Associates, Washington, D.C., president, 1970—. Memer of board of trustees, Prescott College; member of advisory council, School for Advanced International Studies; member of national advisory council of the Monterey Institute of International Studies. *Member:* Council on Foreign Relations. *Military service:* U.S. Air Force, Intelligence Division, 1951-55; became staff sergeant.

WRITINGS: (With Lloyd A. Free) *State of the Nation,* Potomac Associates, 1973; (with Robert W. Tucker) *Beyond Containment: U.S. Foreign Policy in Transition,* Potomac Associates, 1973; (with Free) *State of the Nation, 1974,* Basic Books, 1974; (with Free) *State of the Nation III,* Lexington Books, 1978; (with George R. Packard, Ralph N. Clough, and Robert B. Oxnam) *Japan, Korea, and China: American Perceptions and Policies,* Lexington Books, 1979.

* * *

WAUGH, Dorothy

PERSONAL: Born in Burlington, Vt.; daughter of Frank Albert and (Mary) Alice (Vail) Waugh. *Education:* Attended University of Massachusetts, Massachusetts School of Art, and Museum School of the Cleveland Museum of Art; graduate of Art Institute of Chicago. *Home address:* P.O. Box 130, Murray Hill Station, New York, N.Y. 10156.

CAREER: Writer, commercial artist, illustrator, decorator, and designer. Teacher, Parsons School of Design and Cooper Union Art School, both New York, N.Y.; former director of public relations, Montclair Library, Montclair, N.J.; public relations assistant to mayor of Montclair. Conducted a commentary and interview program on WVNJ Radio for seven years. Designer of posters and book jackets; illustrator of juvenile and adult books and publications of National Park Service; manager of children's book department, Alfred A. Knopf, Inc., 1937-40.

WRITINGS: (Self-illustrated) *Among the Leaves and Grasses,* Holt, 1931; (contributor) Shuler, Knight, and Fuller, editors, *Lady Editor,* Dutton, 1941; (self-illustrated) *Warm Earth,* Oxford University Press, 1943; (self-illustrated) *Muriel Saves String,* McKay, 1956; (self-illustrated) *A Handbook of Christmas Decoration,* Macmillan, 1958; (self-illustrated) *Festive Decoration the Year Round,* Macmillan, 1962; *Emily Dickinson's Beloved, a Surmise,* Vantage, 1976. Contributor of poetry to periodicals.

Illustrator: Frances Frost, *Innocent Summer,* Farrar, Straus, 1936; Inglis and Stewart, *Adventures in World Literature,* Harcourt, 1936; Van der Veer, *The River Pasture,* Longmans, Green, 1936; Van der Veer, *Brown Hills,* Longmans, Green, 1938; Dunham, *What's in the Sky,* Oxford University Press, 1941. Also illustrator of books and articles by her father, Frank Albert Waugh. Contributor of designs to *Family Circle, House Beautiful, Horticulture, Popular Gardening,* and *Flower Grower.*

WORK IN PROGRESS: Work on Emily Dickinson's setting and her writings.

SIDELIGHTS: Dorothy Waugh told *CA:* "Because I grew up at Amherst, where Emily Dickinson spent her entire life, and because I am an admirer of her poetry, I have long been collecting data on her life and studying her writings. Most that is published about her today fails to take into consideration the vast differences in viewpoint, habits, surroundings between her environment and ours. It is a fad today to 'interpret' the poetry; and the 'interpretations' show great lack of knowledge of what she could, in her day, have been thinking. For instance, today's excessive fascination with sex results in many of the poems being interpreted as having sexual significance where there is not the faintest probability that the poet had the subject in mind; the many fine nature poems are not as intimately appreciated by today's largely urban readers as they must have been in her day; Dickinson poems once labelled sacreligious are accepted at face value by a generation more candid."

BIOGRAPHICAL/CRITICAL SOURCES: Times (Montclair, N.J.), April 8, 1965; *Burlington Free Press* (Vermont), July 21, 1977.

* * *

WEBER, Marc 1950-

PERSONAL: Born November 26, 1950; son of Frank John and Pauline Weber; married, September 21, 1973. *Education:* University of Colorado, B.A. and M.A., 1971.

CAREER: Poet; has taught writing at University of Colorado, Bernard M. Baruch College of the City University of New York, and other schools. *Awards, honors:* U.S.A. Award, International Poetry Forum, 1972.

WRITINGS: Forty-Eight Small Poems, University of Pittsburgh Press, 1973; *Circle of Light,* San Marcos Press, 1976. Contributor to *Eureka Review, Poetry Now, People and Policy,* and other magazines.

WORK IN PROGRESS: The Earth Is Afloat, a collection of poems; *Yoga,* a book length poem.

SIDELIGHTS: Marc Weber told *CA:* "Recently I was asked

about 'exercises' for poets and I recommended the following: First write a haiku or tanka and then start to write a longer poem on the same subject. When it seems appropriate include the haiku or tanka as a stanza in its own right. You may also try to insert it after completing the longer poem, although I find it most interesting to keep it in mind as I compose the longer poem as it seems that it makes a neater 'envelope'. As far as the forms of the longer poem—that is completely open, but I do suggest that you not make the other stanzas resemble the shorter form of the haiku or tanka.

"The longer poem should expand the mood of the haiku; it seems that this expansion occurs in a way similar to the meeting of two poets in a collaborative poem or the meeting of a clear Zen mind with a discursive Western one or simply the abstract with the personal (at times). In any case, you should think of the haiku or tanka as the seed for a flourishing growth.

"These considerations aside, I have found that the exercise makes you more aware of what type of self-editing you as a writer are doing unconsciously as you write. The form of the haiku or tanka should change your language, to some extent it should make you speak a different language. By limiting both poems to the same subject you may become aware of what habits or poetic taste for certain words or phrasings you have acquired. Dichotomies, of course, always heighten consciousness. To quote Gregory Bateson, whose book *Mind and Nature* contains enough insights to jog the poetic spirit of any potential writer: 'to produce news of difference, i.e. information, there must be two entities.' This exercise has been meaningful for me, and I think it can be for anyone because of the stereoscopic depth which accrues from the process of double description."

* * *

WEIDMAN, Jerome 1913-

PERSONAL: Born April 4, 1913, in New York, N.Y.; son of Joseph and Annie (Falkovitz) Weidman; married Elizabeth Ann Payne (a writer), 1943; children: Jeffrey, John Whitney. *Education:* Attended City College (now City College of the City University of New York), 1931-33, Washington Square College, 1933-34, and New York University Law School, 1934-37. *Agent:* Brandt & Brandt, 1501 Broadway, New York, N.Y. 10036.

CAREER: Worked as clerk in New York, N.Y. during 1930's; novelist, playwright, short story writer, and essayist. *Wartime service:* U.S. Office of War Information, 1942-45. *Member:* Authors Guild and Dramatists Guild of Authors League of America (president, 1969-74), Writers Guild of America East. *Awards, honors:* Co-winner of Pulitzer Prize in drama, New York Drama Critics Circle Award, and Antoinette Perry Award, 1960, all for "Fiorello!"

WRITINGS: *Letter of Credit* (travel), Simon & Schuster, 1940; (editor) *A Somerset Maugham Sampler,* Garden City Books, 1943; (editor) *Traveler's Cheque* (travel), Doubleday, 1954; (editor with others) *The First College Bowl Question Book,* Random House, 1961; *Back Talk* (essays), Random House, 1963.

Novels: *I Can Get It for You Wholesale* (also see below), Simon & Schuster, 1937, reprinted, Modern Library, 1959; *What's in It for Me?,* Simon & Schuster, 1938, reprinted, Pocket Books, 1963; *I'll Never Go There Anymore,* Simon & Schuster, 1941; *The Lights around the Shore,* Simon & Schuster, 1943; *Too Early to Tell,* Reynal & Hitchcock, 1946; *The Price Is Right,* Harcourt, 1949, reprinted, Manor, 1976; *The Hand of the Hunter,* Harcourt, 1951, reprinted, Avon, 1968; *Give Me Your Love,* Eton Books, 1952; *The Third Angel,* Doubleday, 1953; *Your Daughter Iris,* Doubleday, 1955; *The Enemy Camp,* Random House, 1958.

Published by Random House, except as indicated: *Before You Go,* 1960, reprinted, Pinnacle Books, 1976; *The Sound of Bow Bells,* 1962; *Word of Mouth,* 1964; *Other People's Money,* 1967; *The Center of the Action,* 1969; *Fourth Street East: A Novel of How It Was,* 1970; *Last Respects,* 1972; *Tiffany Street,* 1974; *The Temple,* Simon & Schuster, 1975; *A Family Fortune,* Simon & Schuster, 1978; *Counselors-at-Law,* Doubleday, 1980.

Short stories: *The Horse That Could Whistle "Dixie" and Other Stories,* Simon & Schuster, 1939; *The Captain's Tiger,* Reynal & Hitchcock, 1947, reprinted, Macfadden-Bartell, 1964; *A Dime a Throw,* Doubleday, 1957; *My Father Sits in the Dark and Other Selected Stories,* Random House, 1961; *Where the Sun Never Sets and Other Stories,* Heinemann, 1964; *The Death of Dickie Draper and Nine Other Stories,* Random House, 1965.

Plays: (With George Abbott) *Fiorello!* (musical; first produced on Broadway at Broadhurst Theatre, November 23, 1959), Random House, 1960; (with Abbott) *Tenderloin* (musical; produced in New York City, 1960), Random House, 1961; *I Can Get It for You Wholesale* (musical based on the novel of the same title; first produced on Broadway at Shubert Theatre, March, 22, 1962), Random House, 1963; "Cool Off!," produced in Philadelphia, Pa., 1964; "Pousse Cafe," produced on Broadway at Forty-Sixth Street Theatre, March 18, 1966; (with James Yaffe) *Ivory Tower* (three act; produced in Ann Arbor, Mich., 1968), Dramatists Play Service, 1969; "The Mother Lover," first produced on Broadway at Booth Theatre, January 30, 1969; *Asterisk! A Comedy of Terrors* (produced in New York City, 1969), Dramatists Play Service, 1969.

Screenplays: "The Damned Don't Cry," Warner Bros., 1950; "The Eddie Cantor Story," Warner Bros., 1953; "Slander," Metro-Goldwyn-Mayer, 1957. Also author of "The Reporter" television series, 1964.

Contributor of many short stories and essays to numerous periodicals, including *New Yorker, Harper's, Esquire,* and *Punch.*

SIDELIGHTS: Jerome Weidman graduated from high school at the height of the depression, which made his life, he told *Miami Herald* writer Caroline Heck, quite simple, "There was only one problem, and that was to eat." Using the clerical skills he had acquired in high school, he landed an office job in the New York City garment district that paid $11 per week. Weidman read for recreation, and feeling that he could do better himself, he wrote a short story based on an account of a New Year's Eve episode that he had overheard in his office. He sent the piece off to a magazine; much to his surprise, it was accepted. The $10 he received for the story spurred him to write more, which kept him very busy since he was working days and attending college and then law school nights. After hearing about a novel contest at Doubleday, Weidman began his first novel. He wrote a chapter each night upon returning from school, finishing the book in thirty days. Although it did not win, Doubleday expressed an interest in the novel. Eventually, it was published by Simon & Schuster, and Weidman has been a full time freelance writer ever since.

I Can Get It for You Wholesale, his first novel, was praised highly by the critics. Otis Ferguson, writing in *New Republic,* comments, "This is a novel, hard, wise, slangy, written with such unseen dramatic discipline and such a fine spare working style, that for once you can believe the blurb writers." Adds Charles Poore, "Mr. Weidman's novel ... is racy, fresh, and continuously interesting." And George Stevens finds it "a tough, vigorous, ironic story of an individual poisoned by ambition."

Yet many of Weidman's subsequent efforts have met a less sympathetic response from some critics. A *Time* reviewer believes that "Jerome Weidman comes close to being a really good short story writer; his ear is accurate, and he presents the nubs of his stories, neatly wrapped, for his readers to carry away. The trouble is that while there is always something in the package, there is never much. One smiles at a character's small defeat . . . and then passes on untroubled to another story equally expert and forgettable." In a review of *The Death of Dickie Draper,* Chad Walsh, on the other hand, remarks, "at times the stories become just a shade slick and gimmicky . . . , but taking the collection as a whole, Mr. Weidman shows an impressive ability to create real plots, real characters, and to dramatize those rare moments when the self reveals itself with fearful clarity."

Weidman's novels have also received a mixed critical response. *Other People's Money,* for instance, is called "a long, turgid pot-boiler" by a *Times Literary Supplement* reviewer. Yet Bruce Cook believes that "Jerome Weidman is about as consistent and competently professional as any novelist in America. . . . We can expect a well-made job with more than enough in the way of character, incident, and factual background to keep us reading with pleasure to the last page. And this, with a few incidental ammendments, is what we get in *Other People's Money.*"

The reviews of *A Family Fortune* provide another example of the critical conflict over Weidman's work. "*A Family Fortune,*" notes *New York Times* reviewer Thomas Lask, "is not unlike that whipped cream spewed out by a pressurized container. It is pleasant enough going down, but it doesn't take long to realize that the product is all air and no substance." In contrast to this, Frederic Morton finds that "*A Family Fortune* dramatizes an episodic numbness. Too many of us can no longer respond to smallness and simplicity. . . . Only the jackpot, the billion dollars, the star-treatment—only everything is something. I didn't believe any one incident in this book. I was appalled by its truth." A *New Yorker* reviewer finds both strength and weakness, "Mr. Weidman's novel . . . can bear very little scrutiny, and it is burdened by annoying anachronisms . . . , but this has nothing to do with its narrative strength and its non-stop flight into high-voltage entertainment."

In an interview with Richard F. Shepard, Weidman expressed his reaction to criticism: "I don't think that I'm as bad as some people may feel. I don't think I'm a genius. I have the confidence of my own experience in a number of things. I know to handle my bag of tools. I can write a story about anything under the sun. . . . I am not one of those people who say that they can learn something even from bad reviews. It's a funny thing that the writer has about reviewers, and it has to do with your own emotions and with selling books. I am crazy about favorable reviews even if they're written by Jack the Ripper, and I hate a bad review, even if it comes from Edmund Wilson. It's a psychic blow, no matter how thick a writer's skin is."

Rather than trying to produce infrequent and spectacular "James Joycean" books, Weidman told Heck, "I have always felt that . . . the primary mission of the writer of fiction is to entertain." He's not aiming for guffaws, he continued, but the type of entertainment that will "take the reader out of the chair he's in and take him to another world. . . . I am essentially a natural born storyteller, writing of commonplace rather than heroic events. If you portray real people, they are entertaining in and of themselves."

Two of Weidman's plays enjoyed notable success on Broadway. The award-winning *Fiorello!* ran for 795 nights, while the musical version of *I Can Get It for You Wholesale* played for 300 nights. *Wholesale* was also made into a feature-length film by Twentieth Century-Fox in 1951. *House of Strangers* was filmed by Twentieth Century-Fox in 1949, and "Invitation," a movie based on one of his short stories, was produced by Metro-Goldwyn-Mayer in 1952.

BIOGRAPHICAL/CRITICAL SOURCES: Saturday Review of Literature, May 15, 1937; *New York Times,* May 16, 1937, February 3, 1969, July 16, 1969, July 25, 1969, July 6, 1978; *New Republic,* June 9, 1937; *Time,* July 7, 1961, May 19, 1967; *Chicago Tribune Book Week,* May 30, 1965; *National Observer,* May 29, 1967, August 4, 1969; *Best Sellers,* June 1, 1967; *Times Literary Supplement,* November 9, 1967; *New Yorker,* February 8, 1969, October 18, 1969, June 5, 1978; *Book World,* June 29, 1969; *Books,* April, 1970; *Saturday Review,* January 9, 1971; *New Republic,* January 30, 1971; *Books and Bookmen,* June, 1971; *Detroit News,* January 2, 1972; *Miami Herald,* February 9, 1976; *New York Times Book Review,* February 22, 1976, May 28, 1978; *Authors in the News,* Volume II, Gale, 1976; *Contemporary Literary Criticism,* Volume VII, Gale, 1977; *Washington Post,* July 1, 1978.

—Sketch by David A. Guy

* * *

WEINBERG, Samuel Kirson 1912-

PERSONAL: Born October 10, 1912, in Chicago, Ill.; son of Herman Yoel and Rebecca (Kirson) Weinberg; married Rita Mohr (a psychologist), September 15, 1946; children: Carol Rebecca, Roger Maynard, Douglas Daniel. *Education:* University of Chicago, A.B., 1934, A.M., 1935, Ph.D., 1942. *Politics:* Liberal Democrat. *Religion:* Jewish. *Home and Office:* 255 Vernon Ave., Glencoe, Ill. 60022.

CAREER: Mental Hygiene Association, Columbus, Ohio, co-director, study of mental hospitals, 1945-46; Whitman College, Walla Walla, Wash., assistant professor, 1946-47; Roosevelt University, Chicago, Ill., 1952-68, began as assistant professor, became professor of sociology and chairman of department of sociology and anthropology; Loyola University, Chicago, professor of sociology, beginning 1969; currently president of Sociological and Psychological Associates, Glencoe, Ill. Visiting professor at University of Minnesota, 1951-52, University of Ghana, Accra, Africa, 1961, University of California, Berkeley, summer, 1963, and Portland State University, 1966-68. Research sociologist, department of psychiatry, Northwestern University Medical School, 1964-65; trained parole officers and Peace Corps students in seminars. Visiting scientist, American Sociological Association. Research consultant, Osawatomie State Hospital, Osawatomie, Kan., 1964-65. *Military service:* U.S. Army, 1942-45; served as clinical psychologist, research psychologist; became lieutenent. *Member:* American Sociological Association (fellow), American Psychological Association, Society for the Study of Social Problems (chairman of committee on psychiatric sociology, 1961-65), Midwest Sociological Society (chairman of session on primary group, 1963, 1964); Illinois Academy of Criminology (vice-president, 1960-61). *Awards, honors:* Roosevelt University faculty research fellow; cited as "outstanding member of the profession" by American Sociological Association.

WRITINGS: Society and Personality Disorders, Prentice-Hall, 1952; *Incest Behavior,* Citadel, 1955; *Culture and Personality,* Public Affairs Press, 1958; *Social Problems in Our Time,* Prentice-Hall, 1960; (co-author) *Culture of the State Mental Hospital,* Wayne State University Press, 1960; *The Sociology of Mental Disorders,* Aldine, 1966; *Social Problems in Modern Urban Society,* Prentice-Hall, 1970; *Deviant Behavior and Social Control,* W. C. Brown, 1974. Also contributor to *Criminology: A Book of Readings,* edited by Robert Clark, Clyde Vedder and Samuel Koenig, *Mental Health and Mental Disorder,* edited by Arnold M. Rose, *UNESCO Dictionary of the Social Sciences,* 1964, *Human Nature and Collective Behavior,* edited by Tamolgu Shibutani, 1970, *Crime and Delinquency,* edited by James Short, 1973, and to other books. Contributor to professional journals.

WORK IN PROGRESS: Research on the nature, formation and development of closest friendship among adolescents of the same sex; *The Age-Role Theory of Personality Development; Social World of the Stock Investor; Closest Friendship among Students.*

AVOCATIONAL INTERESTS: Baseball, football, basketball, swimming, drama, magazines.

* * *

WEISBROD, Burton Allen 1931-

PERSONAL: Born February 13, 1931, in Chicago, Ill.; son of Leon Harold (a businessman) and Idelle (Chernoff) Weisbrod; married Shirley Lindsay, December 23, 1951; children: Glen Elliot, Linda Jill. *Education:* University of Illinois, B.S., 1951; Northwestern University, M.A., 1952, Ph.D., 1958. *Home:* 3696 Lake Mendata Dr., Madison, Wis. 53705. *Office:* 6422 Social Science Building, University of Wisconsin, Madison, Wis. 53706.

CAREER: Northwestern University, Evanston, Ill., lecturer in economics, 1954-55; Carleton College, Northfield, Minn., instructor in economics, 1955-57; Washington University, St. Louis, Mo., instructor, 1957-58, assistant professor, 1958-62, associate professor of economics, 1962-64; University of Wisconsin—Madison, associate professor, 1964-66, professor of economics, 1966—, member of staff of Institute for Research on Poverty and member of Health Economics Research Center. Visiting lecturer at Princeton University, 1962-63; senior Fulbright lecturer at Universidad Autonoma de Madrid, summer, 1970; visiting professor at Yale University, 1976-77. U.S. delegate to United Nations World Population Conference (Belgrade), 1965; member of panel on federal use of health manpower of National Advisory Commission on Health Manpower, 1966-68; member of ad hoc advisory committee to U.S. Surgeon General on regional medical program, 1966-67; member of research advisory committee of Economic Development Administration (of U.S. Department of Commerce), 1967-69; member of research training grants review committee of National Center for Health Services Research and Development, 1969-71; member of advisory committee on medical care and medical economics to Third National Cancer Survey, 1969—; member of internal advisory committee of Health Technical Assistant Bureau (of U.S. Agency for International Development), 1971—; co-chairman of committee on economics and finance of National Academy of Education, 1971-73. Consultant to Economic Council of Canada, 1969, 1971, U.S. Bureau of the Budget, 1966-68, U.S. Council of Economic Advisers, 1964-68, U.S. Office of Economic Opportunity, 1965-67, Department of Defense, 1964-65, Urban Institute, 1970—, and others. *Member:* American Association of University Professors (member of executive committee of Washington University chapter, 1961-62), American Economic Association (member of executive committee, 1975-78), Midwest Economic Association (president-elect, 1979). *Awards, honors:* Guggenheim fellowship, 1969-70; Ford faculty fellowship, 1971-72.

WRITINGS: Economics of Public Health, University of Pennsylvania Press, 1961; *External Benefits of Public Education,* Industrial Relations Section, Princeton University, 1964; (editor and contributor) *The Economics of Poverty,* Prentice-Hall, 1965; (with W. Lee Hansen) *Benefits, Costs, and Finance of Public Higher Education,* Markham, 1969; *The Private Nonprofit Sector,* D. C. Heath, 1978; (co-author) *Public Interest Law,* University of California Press, 1978.

Contributor: *Public Finances: Needs, Sources, and Utilization,* National Bureau of Economic Research, Princeton University Press, 1961; *Student Financial Aid and National Purpose,* College Entrance Examination Board, 1962; Robert Dorfman, editor, *Measuring Benefits of Government Investments,* Brookings Institution, 1965; Julius Margolis, editor, *The Public Economy of Urban Communities,* Resources for the Future, 1965; *The Theory and Empirical Analysis of Production,* National Bureau of Economic Research, 1967; R. A. Gordon, editor, *Toward a Manpower Policy,* Wiley, 1967; R. Pavalko, editor, *Sociology of Education,* F. E. Peacock, 1968; Samuel Chase, Jr., editor, *Problems in Public Expenditure Analysis,* Brookings Institution, 1968; S. Kannappan, editor, *Manpower Problems in Economic Development,* Macmillan (London), 1969; *Higher Education in the United States: Structure, Growth and Financing,* U.S. Government Printing Office, 1969; *The Analysis and Evaluation of Public Expenditures: The PPB System,* U.S. Government Printing Office, 1969.

G. C. Somers and W. D. Wood, editors, *Cost-Benefit Analysis of Manpower Policies,* Queen's University (Kingston, Ontario), 1970; B. F. Kiker, editor, *Investment in Human Capital,* University of South Carolina Press, 1971; R. Wykstra, editor, *Human Capital Formation and Manpower Development,* Free Press, 1971; Wanderer and Mercer, editors, *A Reader for the Study of Society,* Wadsworth, 1971; Mel Orwig, editor, *Financing Higher Education,* American College Testing Program, 1971. Also contributor to *Education and Distribution of Income,* 1971.

Contributor to proceedings and annals. Contributor of about fifty articles to professional journals, including *Journal of Business, Review of Economics and Statistics, Public Health Report, Journal of Political Economy, Quarterly Journal of Economics, Monthly Labor Review, American Economic Review, New Republic, Policy Analysis, Challenge,* and *National Tax Journal.* Member of editorial board, *Journal of Human Resources,* 1966—, and *Public Finance Quarterly,* 1971—; associate editor, *Journal of Public Economics,* 1971—.

* * *

WEISMAN, John 1942-

PERSONAL: Born August 1, 1942, in New York, N.Y.; son of Abner I. and Syde (Lubowe) Weisman. *Education:* Bard College, A.B., 1964; University of California, Los Angeles, graduate study, 1965-67. *Religion:* Jewish. *Residence:* Chevy Chase, Md. *Agent:* Lucy Kroll Agency, 390 West End Ave., New York, N.Y. 10024. *Office: TV Guide,* 605 National Press Bldg., Washington, D.C. 20045.

CAREER: Stage manager for repertory companies, including New York Shakespeare Festival, 1964-69; *Coast* (magazine), Beverly Hills, Calif., managing editor, 1969-71; *Rolling Stone* (magazine), San Francisco, Calif., film critic, 1971; *Detroit Free Press,* Detroit, Mich., assistant to the entertainment editor, 1971-73; *TV Guide,* Radnor, Pa., associate editor, 1973-76, chief of Washington bureau, 1977—. *Member:* National Press Club, Washington Press Club, Federal City Club, Players (New York City).

WRITINGS: Guerrilla Theater, Doubleday, 1973; (with Brian Boyer) *Heroin Triple Cross,* Pinnacle Books, 1974; *Evidence,* Viking, 1980.

BIOGRAPHICAL/CRITICAL SOURCES: Los Angeles Times, July 15, 1973.

* * *

WEISMILLER, Edward Ronald 1915-

PERSONAL: Born August 3, 1915, in Monticello, Wis.; son of Jacob and Georgia (Wilson) Weismiller; married Frances Merewether Power, 1941 (divorced, 1963); children: Mariana (Mrs. Kenneth Chaffee), Georgia (Mrs. Emmet R. Sargeant, Jr.), Peter, Charles, Merie. *Education:* Attended Swarthmore College, 1931-32; Cornell College, B.A., 1938; Harvard University, M.A., 1942; Oxford University, D.Phil., 1950. *Home:* 2400 Virginia Ave. N.W., Apt. C-1120, Washington, D.C. 20037. *Office:* Department of English, George Washington University, Washington, D.C. 20052.

CAREER: Pomona College, Claremont, Calif., assistant professor, 1950-52, associate professor, 1952-58, professor of English, 1958-68; George Washington University, Washington, D.C., professor of English, 1968-80, professor emeritus, 1981—. Fulbright professor of English literature, University of Leiden, Netherlands, 1957-58. Member, Council for International Exchange of Scholars, 1976-79. *Military service:* U.S. Marine Corps Reserve, 1943-46; became first lieutenant; served in European Theater; awarded Bronze Star and Medaille de la Reconnaissance Francaise. *Member:* Phi Beta Kappa. *Awards, honors:* Midland Authors' Prize, *Poetry* magazine, 1935; Rhodes scholar, Merton College, Oxford University, 1938-39 and 1948-50; Commonwealth Club of California silver medal for poetry, 1947; Guggenheim fellowships, 1946-47 and 1947-48; Ford Foundation education fellowship, 1953-54; D.Litt., Cornell College, 1953; American Council of Learned Societies grants, 1963, 1966, and 1969; Folger Library study grant, 1965, senior fellowship, 1972-73; Rockefeller Foundation grant, 1965-66; American Philosophical Society grants, 1966, 1969; Center for Advanced Studies, Wesleyan University, senior fellowship, 1967-68; Fairfield Foundation grant, 1968; Huntington Library summer grants, 1970, 1971, 1974, and 1980; National Endowment for the Humanities research grants, 1972-73 and 1977-82.

WRITINGS: The Deer Come Down (poetry), Yale Series of Younger Poets, 1936, reprinted, AMS Press, 1971; (translator) Makhali-Phal, *Young Concubine,* Random House, 1942; *The Faultless Shore* (poetry), Houghton, 1946; *The Serpent Sleeping* (novel), Putnam, 1962; (contributor) *The Lyric and Dramatic Milton: Selected Papers from the English Institute,* Columbia University Press, 1965; (contributor) *A Milton Encyclopedia,* Bucknell University Press, 1978—; *The Branch of Fire* (poetry), Word Works, 1979. Contributing editor, *A Variorum Commentary on the Poems of John Milton,* six volumes, Columbia University Press, 1970—. Contributor of poems, articles, and reviews to national magazines, including *New Republic, Nation, Atlantic Monthly, Harper's, Saturday Review, New Yorker,* and to literary journals and reviews.

WORK IN PROGRESS: Fourth book of poems; additional essays and notes on the prosody of Milton's English poems for *A Variorum Commentary on the Poems of John Milton.*

SIDELIGHTS: Edward Weismiller started writing poetry in the early thirties while spending two years on a farm near Brattleboro, Vt.

* * *

WEISS, Ann E(dwards) 1943-

PERSONAL: Born March 21, 1943, in Newton, Mass.; daughter of Donald Loring (a teacher) and Dorothy (a teacher; maiden name, Poole) Charlton; married Malcolm E. Weiss (a writer), January 31, 1966; children: Margot Elizabeth, Rebecca Bates. *Education:* Brown University, A.B., 1965. *Residence:* Whitefield, Me. 04362. *Agent:* Marilyn Marlow, Curtis, Brown Ltd., 575 Madison Ave., New York, N.Y. 10022.

CAREER: Scholastic Magazines, Inc., New York, N.Y., writer and assistant editor, 1965-69, associate editor, 1969-72. *Awards, honors:* Christopher Award, 1975.

WRITINGS—Children's books; all published by Messner: *Five Roads to the White House,* 1970; *We Will Be Heard: Dissent in the United States,* 1972; *Save the Mustangs: How a Federal Law Is Passed,* 1974; *The American Presidency,* 1976; *The American Congress,* 1977; (with husband, Malcolm E. Weiss) *The Vitamin Puzzle,* 1976.

Other: *News or Not?,* Dutton, 1977; *Polls and Surveys,* F. Watts, 1979; *The School on Madison Avenue* (Junior Literary Guild selection), Dutton, 1980; *What's That You Said?,* Harcourt, 1980.

* * *

WEITZ, Raanan 1913-

PERSONAL: Born July 27, 1913, in Rehovot, Palestine (now Israel); son of Joseph and Ruchama (Altschuler) Weitz; married Rifka Schechtman; children: Ruth, Yechiam. *Education:* Attended Hebrew University of Jerusalem; University of Florence, Ph.D., 1937. *Home:* Moshav Ora, Hare Yehuda Mobile P.O., Israel. *Office:* Settlement Study Centre, P.O.B. 555, Rehovot, Israel.

CAREER: Jewish Agency, Land Settlement Department, Israel, village and regional instructor, 1938-42, secretary of settlement planning committee, 1946-48, secretary-general, 1949-52, director-general, 1952-62, head of Department, 1963—. Chairman of National and University Institute of Agriculture, Rehovot, Israel, 1960-66; head of Settlement Study Centre, Rehovot, 1963—, lecturer, 1965—. Lecturer at University of the Philippines, 1961; professor of regional development theory at University of Haifa, 1973-78, and Bar Ilan University, 1978—. Consultant to organizations or participant in seminars in United States, Burma, Thailand, Philippines, Crete, Venezuela, Puerto Rico, Brazil, Turkey, and Ceylon, at various times, 1960-79, and to United Nations Economic and Social Council, 1971. Member of board of governors, Hebrew University (Jerusalem), Israel Institute of Technology, Haifa University, and University of the Negev; member of steering committee, University of Ceara, Brazil. Member of World Executive of the Jewish Agency; chairman, Agriculture and Rural Settlement Planning and Authority, Israel. Former member, Haganah. *Military service:* British Army, Intelligence Corps, 1942-45. Israel Defence Forces, 1947-48. *Member:* Society for International Development (SID: chairman of Israeli chapter, 1964-67), American Agricultural Association.

WRITINGS: Agriculture and Settlement in Israel, Am Oved (Tel Aviv), 1958; (with Avshalom Rokach) *Agriculture and Rural Development in Israel: Projection and Planning,* National and University Institute of Agriculture, 1963; *Rural Planning in Developing Countries* (report from 1963 Rehovoth Conference), Routledge & Kegan Paul, 1965; *Rural Development in the Technological Era: The Israeli Case,* Am Oved, 1967; (with Rokach) *Agricultural Development: Planning and Implementation,* Praeger, 1968; (editor with Yehuda H. Landau, and contributor) *Rural Development in a Changing World,* MIT Press, 1971; (with Levia Applebaum) *From Peasant to Farmer: A Revolutionary Strategy for Development,* Columbia University Press, 1971; (with David Pelley and Applebaum) *Employment and Income Generation in New Settlement Projects,* ILO (Geneva), 1978; *Integrated Rural Development: The Rehovot Approach,* Settlement Study Centre, 1979. Contributor to proceedings and transactions; author of numerous papers submitted to conferences in Israel, the United States, and Europe. Contributor to *Engineering Review, Economic Quarterly, Agriculture in Israel, Molad,* and *Ha-Sadeh* (all Israel), *Indian Journal of Agricultural Economics, Economie Rurale,* and other publications.

WORK IN PROGRESS: Research on changes in the structure and ideology of the Moshar (small-holder's cooperative); study of development planning, sponsored by Twentieth-Century Fund.

*   *   *

WELBURN, Ron(ald Garfield) 1944-

PERSONAL: Born April 30, 1944, in Bryn Mawr, Pa.; stepson of Howard (a welder) and Jessie W. Watson; married Eileen D. Millett, August 21, 1971. *Education:* Lincoln University, Lincoln University, Pa., B.A., 1968; University of Arizona, M.A., 1970. *Address:* Box 244, Vanderveer Sta., Brooklyn, N.Y. 11210. *Office:* Institute of Jazz Studies, Rutgers University, Newark, N.J. 08903.

CAREER: File clerk in New York, N.Y., and Philadelphia, Pa., 1962-64; Lincoln University, Lincoln University, Pa., instructor in English, spring, 1968; Syracuse University, Syracuse, N.Y., assistant professor of English, 1970-75; currently affiliated with Institute for Jazz Studies, Rutgers University. Visiting lecturer, Auburn Correctional Facility, 1972; writer-in-residence, Lincoln University, 1973-74. *Awards, honors:* Silvera Award for poetry from Lincoln University, 1967, 1968; fellow, Smithsonian Institute and Music Critics Association, 1975.

WRITINGS: Peripheries: Selected Poems, 1966-1968, Greenfield Review Press, 1972; *Brownup: Selected Poems,* Greenfield Review Press, 1977. Contributor of poetry to *Black World, Black Fire, Journal of Black Poetry, You Better Believe It, New Black Poetry, Greenfield Review, Intro,* and other periodicals. Co-founding editor, *Grackle,* 1976.

WORK IN PROGRESS: Heartland, for Lotus Press; *The Jackals; Saguaro Sections; Devon-Hill: Tales of a Hoodoo-Gothic.*

SIDELIGHTS: Ron Welburn told *CA* that his "books have been and will be a combination of statement and affirmation of my existence, exorcism of demons of the psyche, and a means to fulfill a musicianship beyond my limited instrumental training and experience." He sees the current literary scene as much the same as it has always been. "There are still publishers, and there are various degrees of sharecroppers, brokers, henchmen and women, hit men and women, left- and right-wing secret societies and meetings. I do feel that the small presses are continuing to put out the best writing in America. I'm partial to Greenfield Review Press."

AVOCATIONAL INTERESTS: Musical composition, chess, bird-watching, squash, hiking.

*   *   *

WESKER, Arnold 1932-

PERSONAL: Born May 24, 1932, in London, England; son of Joseph (a tailor) and Leah (Perlmutter) Wesker; married Doreen Cecile Bicker, November 14, 1958; children: Lindsay Joe, Tanya Jo, Daniel. *Education:* Attended London School of Film Technique, 1955-56. *Politics:* Humanist. *Religion:* Jewish. *Home:* 27 Bishops Road, London N6 4HR, England.

CAREER: Started working at sixteen as furniture maker's apprentice and tried half-a-dozen jobs, mainly along manual lines, before receiving Arts Council of Great Britain grant in 1958. Worked as carpenter's mate, bookseller's assistant, plumber's mate, seed sorter, kitchen porter, 1948-50, 1952-54, and as pastry cook in Norwich and London, England, and in Paris, France, 1954-58; playwright, 1958—; director, 1968—. Co-founder and artistic director, Centre 42 Ltd., London, 1961-70. *Military service:* Royal Air Force, 1950-52. *Awards, honors:* Arts Council of Great Britain grant, 1958; *Evening Standard* award as most promising British playwright, 1959; co-winner of *Encyclopaedia Britannica* play prize, 1959, for "Chicken Soup with Barley"; Premio Marzotto, 1964, for "Their Very Own and Golden City"; Public and Critic's Gold Medal Award, 1973, for "The Kitchen."

WRITINGS—Plays: *Chicken Soup with Barley* (first play of trilogy; first produced in Coventry, England at Belgrade Theatre, July 7, 1958, produced in London at Royal Court Theatre, July 14, 1968, produced in Cleveland, Ohio, 1962), published in *New English Dramatists,* Penguin, 1959, published separately, Evans Brothers, 1961; *Roots* (second play of trilogy; first produced in Coventry, England at Belgrade Theatre, May 25, 1959, produced in London at Royal Court Theatre, June 30, 1959, produced off-Broadway at Mayfair Theater, March 6, 1961), Penguin, 1959, published with introduction and notes by A.H.M. Best and Mark Cohen, Longmans, Green, 1967; *I'm Talking about Jerusalem* (third play of trilogy; first produced in Coventry, England at Belgrade Theatre, March 28, 1960, produced in London at Royal Court Theatre, July 27, 1960), Penguin, 1960.

The Kitchen (first produced in London at Royal Court Theatre, September 6, 1959, expanded version produced in London at Royal Court Theatre, 1961, produced off-Broadway at Eighty-First Street Theatre, June 13, 1966), published in *New English Dramatists 2,* Penguin, 1960, expanded version published separately, J. Cape, 1961, Random House, 1962; *Chips with Everything* (first produced in London at Royal Court Theatre, April 27, 1962, produced on the West End at Vaudeville Theatre, 1962, produced on Broadway at Plymouth Theatre, October 1, 1963), J. Cape, 1962, Random House, 1963, critical edition edited by Michael Marland, published with introduction by Wesker, Blackie, 1966; *Their Very Own and Golden City* (first produced in Brussels at Belgium National Theater, 1964, produced in London at Royal Court Theatre, May 19, 1966),J. Cape, 1966; *The Four Seasons* (first produced in Coventry, England at Belgrade Theatre, 1965, produced on the West End at Saville Theatre, September 21, 1965, produced off-Broadway at Theatre Four, March 14, 1968), J. Cape, 1966.

The Friends (first produced in Stockholm at Stadsteatern,

January, 1970, produced in London at Roundhouse, May 19, 1970), J. Cape, 1970; "The Nottingham Captain: A Moral for Narrator, Voices and Orchestra" (first produced in Wellingborough, England at Centre 42 Trades Union Festival, 1962), published in *Six Sundays in January* (also see below), J. Cape, 1971; *The Old Ones* (first produced in London at Royal Court Theatre, August 8, 1972, produced in New York at Theatre at the Lambs Club, December 6, 1974), J. Cape, 1973, revised version edited by Michael Marland, Blackie, 1974; *The Journalists* (produced in Highgate, North London at Jackson's Lane Community Centre, July, 1975), Writer and Readers Publishing Cooperative, 1975.

Unpublished plays: "The Wedding Feast" (adapted from short story by Dostoyevsky), produced in Stockholm, 1974; "The Merchant" (based on Shakespeare's "The Merchant of Venice"), produced in Stockholm, 1976, produced on Broadway at Plymouth Theatre, November 16, 1977; "Love Letters on Blue Paper" (adapted from short story by Wesker; also see below), produced in London by National Theatre Company, 1978, produced in Washington, D.C. at Folger Theatre, February 9, 1980.

Television plays: "Menace" (produced on "First Night" series, BBC-TV, December 8, 1963), published in *The Plays of Arnold Wesker,* Volume II (also see below), Harper, 1978; "Love Letters on Blue Paper" (adapted from short story by Wesker; also see below), produced on BBC-TV, 1976.

Collected plays: *The Wesker Trilogy* (contains "Chicken Soup with Barley," "Roots," and "I'm Talking about Jerusalem"), J. Cape, 1960, Random House, 1961, published with introduction and notes by A.H.M. Best and Mark Cohen, Longmans, Green, 1965; *Three Plays* (contains "The Kitchen," "The Four Seasons," and "Their Very Own and Golden City"), Penguin, 1976; *The Plays of Arnold Wesker,* Harper, Volume I (contains "The Kitchen," "Chicken Soup with Barley," "Roots," "I'm Talking about Jerusalem," and "Chips with Everything"), 1976, Volume II (contains "The Four Seasons," "Their Very Own and Golden City," "Menace," "The Friends," and "The Old Ones"), 1977.

Other books: *Labour and the Arts: II, or What, Then, Is to Be Done?,* Gemini, 1960; *The Modern Playwright; or, "O Mother, Is It Worth It?,"* Gemini, 1961; (author of introduction) Roger Frith, *The Serving Boy,* Colchester, 1968; *Fears of Fragmentation* (essays), J. Cape, 1970; *Six Sundays in January* (short stories and television play), J. Cape, 1971; *Love Letters on Blue Paper* (short stories), J. Cape, 1974, Harper, 1975; (with John Allin) *Say Goodbye, You May Never See Them Again: Scenes from Two East-End Backgrounds,* text by Wesker, paintings by Allin, J. Cape, 1974; *Words as Definitions of Experience,* Writers and Readers Publishing Cooperative, 1977; *Fatlips: A Story for Children,* Harper, 1978; *Journey into Journalism: A Very Personal Account in Four Parts,* Writers and Readers Publishing Cooperative, 1978; *Said the Old Man to the Young Man* (short stories), J. Cape, 1978.

Author of screenplay, "The Kitchen" (adapted from Wesker's play), produced by Kingsley, 1962. Also author of unpublished and unproduced plays, "Master," 1966, "The New Play," 1969, and "Stand Up, Stand Up" and of unproduced filmscript, "Madame Solario," 1968.

SIDELIGHTS: Arnold Wesker's original reknown came from his trilogy of plays ("Chicken Soup with Barley," "Roots," and "I'm Talking about Jerusalem") which traces the attitudes of a family of Jewish Socialist intellectuals from 1936 through 1959. Geoffrey Grigson calls it "a Forsyte Saga of the Left." Wesker, describing his trilogy, writes: "A number of themes bind the trilogy together. Basically it is [about] a family; on another level it is a play about human relationships; and on a third, and most important level, it is a story of people moved by political ideas in a particular social time. There are many theories about Socialism. 'Chicken Soup with Barley' handles the Communist aspect. 'Roots' handles the personal aspect. . . . 'I'm Talking about Jerusalem' is a sort of study in a William Morris kind of Socialism."

Wesker has been described as a "committed" playwright and in his early plays embraced the ideals of Socialism. He was identified with a group of English playwrights who emerged after the dramatic revival in England in 1956 and who were dubbed "the angry young men." A writer for the *Christian Science Monitor* comments that of this group, which included among others John Osborne, Brendan Behan, and David Storey, "Wesker is certainly—and this is something to admire when most people are busy keeping up their defenses in all directions—the most unafraid, the most naive, the most vulnerable. He is the least technically expert, the most self-indulgent. . . . Yet . . . in all his plays he has striven not to exploit the disintegration of individuals and society, but the possibility of their self-redemption—and this again is not ignoble when the opposite is the fashion, and artists in every medium go all out for easy hysteria."

Beginning with "Chips with Everything," Wesker's work during the 1960s "became less documentary and immediate in impact," according to Glenda Leeming. His more recent plays are not as didactic or political in tone as his earlier Socialist realism. Disillusioned with his earlier political beliefs, Wesker told Richard Skloot that the paradox of Socialism "is that it is producing people who are socially selfish and indifferent. The State has taken on all responsibility and people don't care about each other and they don't care about what happens outside their own country, outside their own community. There's this terrible social listlessness that has been created." Turning from socialistic didacticism in "The Four Seasons," which depicts the allegorical seasons of a love affair from its spring budding through its winter disintegration, Wesker begins to explore what he has called the theme of "private pain." With this play and "The Friends" Wesker is, according to Leeming, "breaking new ground, not in techniques of presentation, but in his increasingly introspective subject matter."

The critical reception to "The Friends" was, for the most part, unfavorable. Benedict Nightingale finds that it "isn't a very good play. The characters, though naturalistically presented, have little objective, individual life. Except when they drop into north-country dialect, they speak much the same ardent, lilting prose. They speak a great deal, too. . . . They don't define themselves by action. . . . One misses, as always in Wesker, any sense of the obstinacy of unreason and the destructive power of human evil." A *Plays and Players* reviewer writes: "The fault of 'The Friends' is that Mr. Wesker is like a man who does not know when to stop. The play is the verbal vomit of his ideas, as if he is suffering from some kind of literary indigestion." Ronald Bryden calls the play "a kind of secular Yom Kippur for his generation of the fifties. In it their faults are confessed, their insincerities admitted, their frittered and waning energies rededicated to the achievement of social justice. . . . I wish I could say the play was as impressive as the intention which churns woolilly behind its almost total lack of action. . . . [Wesker's] real betrayal has been to abandon the role of our most precise social realist for that of a cloudy prophet of uplift."

Michael Kustow believes that Wesker "has suffered unduly

from the weight of an undeserved legend [that of a leftist crusader], which has led to superficial readings of his plays, obscuring their real advances of technique and content. The sense of suspension and withdrawal, of inward-turning, in his latest plays and stories is both the natural reassessment of a writer in mid-route, and the enforced defensiveness . . . of a playwright who seems to have been left out by a headstrong and often mindless theatre, and also made a scapegoat for its unfulfilled promise.'' Wesker addresses himself to the criticism of his abandonment of his original themes: ''There's an argument which says that individual or private pain can have no relevance in a society where man's real tragedies abound inextricably with his social environment. . . . To which I make this reply: if compassion and teaching the possibility of change are two of the many effects of art, a third is this. To remind and reassure people that they're not alone. Not only in their attempt to make a better world, but in their private pains and confusions also.''

Several reviewers expressed ambivalent feelings about ''The Old Ones,'' Wesker's play about aging Jewish pensioners. J. W. Lambert writes that the play ''has like its predecessor 'The Friends' been given a pretty rough reception, in tones varying from weary contempt to stertorous irritation—and despite all its shortcomings, its loose ends, its repeated losses of dramatic focus, I can't really see why this should have been so. . . . Wesker has written scenes of humanity and understanding I should think any playgoer would be grateful for.'' Jacob Sonntag believes that ''Wesker's achievement is that his characters are accepted, not as some eccentrics arousing one's curiousity, but as real people—unusual perhaps, but real nevertheless. . . . Some critics may find faults in the play's construction, others may consider it too sentimental and vague. . . . Wesker retains his fine sense of dialogue, his compassion, his social involvement, adding to it a newly acquired insight into Jewishness.''

Wesker wrote ''The Merchant'' because he was dissatisfied with the blatant anti-Semitism and what he feels was the unrealistic character portrayal of the original Shakespearean play. ''The Merchant'' received reviews which ranged from very positive to absolute pans. Colin Chambers calls the play ''quite out of character with most contemporary drama but full of the dense argumentation inspired by a critical caring love of people, of their knowledge and of their language.'' Brendan Gill finds it ''an ambitious and very intelligent play.'' Clive Barnes thinks it is ''perhaps Wesker's finest play. . . . Most of the writing is brilliant, with masterly sensibility. . . . The play raises issues and risks arguments and it teems with life as a consequence.'' Conversely, Martin Gottfried calls it ''a theoretical and argumentative play with little life force of its own. Its own definitions of anti-Semitism are superficial. Its characters and events exist only to disagree with Shakespeare.'' John Simon is even more sharp in his attack on the play: '' 'The Merchant,' I am afraid, is to 'The Merchant of Venice' what lumpfish is to caviar, or a hot-water bottle to the Gulf Stream.'' Richard Eder feels comparison of Wesker's play to the original Shakespeare to be invalid. ''Wesker has used the same rough elements of plot and the same principal characters—all of them with a widely different human weight and meaning—for a totally original play,'' Eder writes. He describes his mixed reaction to the play: ''It is provocative, generally intelligent and sometimes strained or confused. Its writing has moments of ferocious brilliance and wit; on the other hand, its dramatic structure is weak and its dramatic impact fitful and uncertain. It starts and stops; it repeatedly takes off with a thrill and repeatedly disappears into a cloud bank. There is a general effect of a vision that aims for more than it achieves.''

Despite so much negative criticism to Wesker's plays, Leeming feels that he is still developing as a playwright, growing in scope, and she is confident that eventually the critical reception will be favorable. ''Unlike many of his erratic contemporaries, Wesker has steadily improved his mastery of theme and techniques, as the brightness of the early plays give way to a more subtle shading of richer colours,'' Leeming writes. ''The very steadiness of his development so far suggests that he will not waste energy on uncharacteristic dead-end experiments, but will evolve within his own line of continuity. He has always had an ear for dialogue and an assured sense of form; this has been reinforced by a new dramatic poetry while the more awkward moments of exposition and occasional didacticism of the trilogy have been eliminated. The level of simple social dramatist that was initially hung like a millstone round Wesker's neck has necessarily hindered assessment of his far-from-simple plays, but . . . the sheer persuasive quality of his writing must elicit recognition of his stature as dramatist.''

The stage play and television versions of ''Love Letters on Blue Paper'' drew the favorable reviews that Leeming feels Wesker deserves. Jack Tinker calls the play ''a towering love story'' and Micheline Victor comments that ''Wesker is remarkably, and un-Englishably daring [in] his representation of emotion.'' Michael Billington wrote that ''what is interesting is the way the emotion of the play bursts through with this very tight rigid form. It's a play, simply, it seems to me, about a kind of human desperation. . . . I thought the pulse and intensity of that emotion worked against the artificiality of the form in a very moving way.'' Alan Hulme comments that ''plays as intensely moving as Arnold Wesker's 'Love Letters on Blue Paper' are very rare. . . . It is a play you will have to learn to live with because once experienced it won't go away.'' Stephen Biscoe goes even further in his praise of the play: ''Apart from anything else 'Love Letters on Blue Paper' proved that great plays are still being written; the quality of a masterpiece was unmistakeable. . . . His play was profound and very moving and set a standard that one hopes other playwrights will attempt to emulate if they can.''

BIOGRAPHICAL/CRITICAL SOURCES: Laurence Kitchin, *Mid-Century Drama,* Faber, 1960; *Spectator,* October 21, 1960, August 10, 1962, August 24, 1974; *Nation,* November 19, 1960; *Times Literary Supplement,* November 25, 1960; *Twentieth Century,* February, 1961; *Canadian Forum,* July, 1961; James Gindin, *Postwar British Fiction,* University of California Press, 1962; John Russell Taylor, *Anger and After,* Methuen, 1962; *Contemporary Theatre,* Edward Arnold, 1962; W. A. Armstrong, editor, *Experimental Drama,* G. Bell, 1963; A. C. Ward, *Twentieth-Century English Literature, 1901-1960,* Methuen, 1964; *Antioch Review,* winter, 1964-65; G. Wellworth, *Theatre of Protest and Paradox,* New York University Press, 1965; *New Statesman,* August 6, 1965, September 17, 1965, May 29, 1970, August 30, 1974; Harold U. Ribalow, *Arnold Wesker,* Twayne, 1966; Walter Wager, editor, *The Playwrights Speak,* Delacorte, 1967; Frederick Lumley, *New Trends in Twentieth Century Drama,* Oxford University Press, 1967; *Village Voice,* March 21, 1968; *Time,* March 22, 1968; *Christian Science Monitor,* March 22, 1968, June 6, 1970; *New Yorker,* March 23, 1968, June 9, 1975, November 14, 1977.

Plays and Players, May, 1970, July, 1970, August, 1970, October, 1973, February, 1977, December, 1978; *New York Times,* May 22, 1970, July 14, 1970, August 20, 1970, August

26, 1972, November 8, 1977, November 17, 1977; *Observer Review*, May 24, 1970; *Listener*, May 28, 1970; Glenda Leeming and Simon Trussler, *The Plays of Arnold Wesker*, Gollancz, 1971; Leeming, *Arnold Wesker*, Longman, 1972; *Variety*, August 23, 1972, November 23, 1977; *Jewish Quarterly*, autumn, 1972; *Drama*, winter, 1972; *Contemporary Literary Criticism*, Gale, Volume III, 1975, Volume V, 1976; *New Review*, March, 1975; *Saturday Review*, May 17, 1975; *Washington Post*, June 1, 1975; *Yorkshire Post*, March 3, 1976; *BBC Kaleidoscope*, March 3, 1976; *Theatre Quarterly*, Volume VII, number 28, 1977; *New York Post*, November 17, 1977; London *Times*, December 3, 1977, October 17, 1978; *New York*, December 5, 1977; *Daily Mail*, February 16, 1978; *Time Out*, March 3, 1978; *Jewish Chronicle*, October 20, 1978; *Times Educational Supplement*, October 20, 1978; *Morning Star*, October 20, 1978; *Performing Arts Journal*, Volume II, number 3, winter, 1978; *Manchester Evening News*, December 6, 1978; *Los Angeles Times*, January 28, 1979; *Washington Post*, February 11, 1980.

—*Sketch by Linda Metzger*

* * *

WESTERHOFF, John H(enry) III 1933-

PERSONAL: Born June 28, 1933, in Paterson, N.J.; son of John Henry, Jr. and Nona C. Westerhoff; married Alberta Barnhart, December 27, 1955; children: Jill, Jack, Beth. *Education:* Ursinus College, B.S., 1955; Harvard University, M.Div., 1958; Columbia University, Ed.D., 1959. *Home:* 3510 Racine St., Durham, N.C. 27707. *Office:* Divinity School, Duke University, Durham, N.C. 27706.

CAREER: Ordained minister of United Church of Christ, 1958; ordained priest of Episcopal Church. Minister in Presque Isle, Me., 1958-60, Needham, Mass., 1960-64, and Williamstown, Mass., 1964-66; United Church Board for Homeland Ministries, Philadelphia, Pa., staff member in Division of Christian Education, 1966-74; Duke University, Divinity School, Durham, N.C., associate professor, 1974, professor of religion and education, 1974—. Visiting lecturer at Union Theological Seminary (New York), 1970-71, Harvard Divinity School, 1972-73, Andover Newton Theological Seminary, 1972-73, University of Toronto, summer, 1973, and Fordham University, summer, 1973. Associate, T.D.R. Associates (educational consultant firm), Newton, Mass., 1970-73; reporter for Religious News Service, 1969-70; director of United Ministries in Public Education, Washington, D.C., 1970-73. *Member:* Association of Supervision and Curriculum Development, National Education Association, Council on Education and Anthropology, Religious Education Association, Society for the Scientific Study of Religion, Associated Church Press, Harvard Divinity School Alumni Association.

WRITINGS: *Values for Tomorrow's Children*, Pilgrim Press, 1970; (contributor) George Devone, editor, *Theology in Revolution*, Alba, 1970; (contributor) Gerson Meyer, editor, *Encuentro*, World Council of Churches, 1971; (editor) *A Colloquy on Christian Education*, Pilgrim Press, 1972; *Liberation Letters*, United Church Press, 1972; (with Joseph Williamson) *Learning to Be Free*, United Church Press, 1972; (with Gwen K. Neville) *Generation to Generation*, Pilgrim Press, 1974; *Tomorrow's Church: A Community of Change*, Word Books, 1976; *Will Our Children Have Faith?*, Seabury, 1976; (with Neville) *Learning through Liturgy*, Seabury, 1978; *Who Are We? The Quest for a Religious Education*, Religious Education Press, 1978; *McGuffey and His Readers: Piety, Morality and Education in Nineteenth-Century America*, Abindgon, 1978; (with Urban T. Holms) *Christian Believing*, Seabury, 1979; *Inner Growth-Outer Change: An Educational Guide to Church Renewal*, Seabury, 1979; *Bringing Up Children in Christian Faith*, Winston Press, 1980. Also author of several booklets. Contributor to journals including *Vanguard*, *AAUW Journal*, *Catechist*, *New Jersey Law Review*, *Perspectives on Education*, *Religious Education*, *Andover Newton Quarterly*, and *Colloquy*. Editor, *Colloquy*, 1966-74.

* * *

WESTON, J(ohn) Fred(erick) 1916-

PERSONAL: Born February 6, 1916, in Ft. Wayne, Ind.; son of David Thomas and Bertha (Schwartz) Weston; married June Mildred Sherman, May 16, 1942; children: Kenneth F., Byron L., Ellen J. *Education:* University of Chicago, B.A., 1937, M.B.A., 1942, Ph.D., 1948. *Home:* 258 Tavistock Ave., Los Angeles, Calif. 90049. *Office:* Graduate School of Management, University of California, 405 Hilgard Ave., Los Angeles, Calif. 90024.

CAREER: General Electric Co., Schenectady, N.Y., management trainee, 1937-39; University of Chicago, Chicago, Ill., instructor in business, 1939-42; American Bankers Association, Chicago, economic consultant to the president, 1945-46; University of Chicago, assistant professor of business, 1946-49; University of California, Los Angeles, professor of management, 1949—. Has lectured at University of Oklahoma, University of Utah, and Michigan State University. Consultant to business firms; member of the Committee on Analysis of Economic Census Data of the Social Science Research Council. Director, California Teachers Fund. *Military service:* U.S. Army, Ordnance, Signal Corps, 1943-45; became chief warrant officer. *Member:* American Economic Association, American Finance Association (director of business finance, 1960-62; vice-president, 1965), American Statistical Association, Institute for Management Sciences, Econometric Society, Western Economic Association (president, 1959-60). *Awards, honors:* Ford Foundation faculty research fellowship, 1961-62; McKinsey Foundation grant, 1965-68; General Electric Company grant, 1969-72.

WRITINGS: *Competitive Bidding*, University of Chicago Press, 1943; *The Role of Mergers in the Growth of Large Firms*, University of California Press, 1953, reprinted, Greenwood Press, 1976; (with Eugene F. Brigham) *Managerial Finance*, Holt, 1961, 6th edition, Dryden Press, 1978; (editor and contributor) *Procurement and Profit Renegotiation*, Wadsworth, 1961; *Influences of Stages of Development on Growth Rates*, Bureau of Business and Economic Research, University of California, 1962; *The Timing of Financial Policy*, Bureau of Business and Economic Research, University of California, 1962; *The Measurement of Cost of Capital*, Bureau of Business and Economic Research, University of California, 1963; *A Test of Cost of Capital Propositions*, Bureau of Business and Economic Research, University of California, 1963; *Economic Problems in Lieu of Taxation of Banks*, Bureau of Business and Economic Research, University of California, 1963; (with Peter Duncan) *Economic Development Patterns*, Stanford Research Institute, 1963; (editor) *Defence-Space Market Research*, M.I.T. Press, 1964; *Scope and Methodology of Finance*, Prentice-Hall, 1966; (editor with Donald H. Woods) *Basic Financial Management*, Wadsworth, 1967; (editor with Woods) *Theory of Business Finance*, Wadsworth, 1967; *Public Policy toward Mergers*, Bureau of Business and Economic Research, University of California, 1968; (with Brigham) *Essentials of Managerial Finance*, Holt, 1968, 5th edition,

Dryden Press, 1979; (with Brigham) *Study Guide to Essentials of Managerial Finance,* Holt, 1968, 4th edition, Dryden Press, 1977.

(With Bart W. Sorge) *International Managerial Finance,* R. D. Irwin, 1972; (editor with Stanley I. Ornstein) *The Impact of Large Firms on the U.S. Economy,* Lexington Books, 1973; (editor with Harvey J. Goldschmid and H. Michael Mann) *Industrial Concentration: The New Learning,* Little, Brown, 1974; (editor) *Large Corporations in a Changing Society,* New York University Press, 1974; *Programmed Learning Aid for Financial Management,* edited by Roger H. Hermanson, Learning Systems Co., 1975; (editor with Maurice B. Goudzwaard) *The Treasurer's Handbook,* Dow Jones-Irwin, 1976; (contributor) Carl H. Madden, editor, *The Case for the Multinational Corporation,* Praeger, 1977; (with Sorge) *Guide to International Financial Management,* McGraw, 1977. Contributor of numerous articles to professional journals. Associate editor, *Journal of Finance,* 1948-55.

* * *

WHEELER, (John) Harvey 1918-

PERSONAL: Born October 17, 1918, in Waco, Tex.; married Norene Burleigh (a psychiatric counselor), March 26, 1971; children: (first marriage) David Carroll, John Harvey III, Mark Jefferson. *Education:* Attended Wabash College; Indiana University, B.A., 1946, M.A., 1947; Harvard University, Ph.D., 1950. *Home:* 7200 Casitas Pass Rd., Carpinteria, Calif. 93013. *Agent:* Zeigler, Diskant, Inc., 9255 Sunset Blvd., Hollywood, Calif. 90069. *Office:* Institute for Higher Studies, Box 704, Carpinteria, Calif. 93013.

CAREER: Johns Hopkins University, Baltimore, Md., assistant professor of political science, 1950-54; Washington and Lee University, Lexington, Va., associate professor, 1954-56, professor of political science, 1956-60; Center for the Study of Democratic Institutions, Santa Barbara, Calif., senior fellow-in-residence, 1960-75, visiting scholar, 1961-63, program director, 1969-72 and 1974-75; Institute for Higher Studies, Carpinteria, Calif., founder, and president, 1975—. Consultant, Fund for the Republic (which established Center for the Study of Democratic Institutions), 1958—. *Military service:* U.S. Army, 1941-46. *Member:* American Political Science Association, Pi Sigma Alpha.

WRITINGS: (Editor with George Boas) *Lattimore: The Scholar,* [Baltimore], 1950; *The Conservative Crisis,* Public Affairs Press, 1956; (with Eugene Burdick) *Fail-Safe,* McGraw, 1962, new edition, edited by Virginia P. Allen, Falcon Books, 1967; (with others) *Natural Law and Modern Society,* World Publishing, for Center for the Study of Democratic Institutions, 1963; *Democracy in a Revolutionary Era,* Praeger, 1968; *Politics of Revolution,* Glendessary, 1971; (editor) *Beyond the Punitive Society: Operant Conditioning, Social & Political Aspects,* W. H. Freeman, 1973.

Contributor: Larry Ng, editor, *Alternatives to Violence,* Time-Life, 1968; *Anti-Ballistic Missile: Yes or No?,* Hill & Wang, for Center for the Study of Democratic Institutions, 1968; Nigel Calder, editor, *Unless Peace Comes,* Viking, 1968; *Asian Dilemma: United States, Japan and China,* Valley Publishing, for Center for the Study of Democratic Institutions, 1969. Contributor to other symposia published by Center for the Study of Democratic Institutions and author of a number of the Center's "Occasional Papers." Contributor of about thirty articles to *Saturday Review, Nation, Center Magazine, Astronautics & Aeronautics, Conflict Resolution, Reporter,* and other journals. Co-founder and chief editor, *Journal of Social and Biological Structures.*

WORK IN PROGRESS: With E. M. Nathanson, *The Rise of the Elders.*

SIDELIGHTS: Harvey Wheeler wrote *CA:* "Since I was a kid I've been interested in model societies the way most kids are interested in model airplanes or race cars. World War II and the bomb gave me a presentiment of impending catastrophe; I studied political science out of both infleunces: to try to understand why everything went wrong and what might be done to make things better. . . . My fiction has been a spin-off from my academic work. When I thought I had run into something important that people in general ought to know about I chose fiction as the medium for communicating that message. Some people go into politics; I went into novels."

Fail-Safe was made into a movie by Columbia in 1964.

BIOGRAPHICAL/CRITICAL SOURCES: Saturday Review, October 20, 1962.

* * *

WHITE, Robb 1909-

PERSONAL: Born June 20, 1909, in the Philippine Islands; son of Robb and Placidia (Bridgers) White; married Rosalie Mason, 1937 (divorced, 1964); married Joan Gibbs; children: Robb, Barbara, June. *Education:* U.S. Naval Academy, B.S., 1931. *Home:* 1780 Glen Oaks Dr., Montecito, Calif.

CAREER: Writer. Has held positions as book clerk, draftsman, construction engineer, deck hand on a sailboat. *Military service:* U.S. Navy, 1941-45; became ensign; recalled to active duty, 1947-48, served in aviation administration and public information; became captain.

WRITINGS: The Nub, Little, Brown, 1935; *Smuggler's Sloop,* Little, Brown, 1937; *Midshipman Lee,* Little, Brown, 1938; *Run Masked,* Knopf, 1938; *In Privateer's Bay,* Harper, 1939; *Three against the Sea,* Harper, 1940; *Sailor in the Sun,* Harper, 1941; *Midshipman Lee of the Naval Academy,* Random House, 1954.

All published by Doubleday: *The Lion's Paw,* 1946; *Secret Sea,* 1947; *Sail Away,* 1948; *Candy,* 1949; *The Haunted Hound,* 1950; *Deep Danger,* 1952; *Our Virgin Island,* 1953; *Up Periscope,* 1956; *Flight Deck,* 1961; *Torpedo Run,* 1962; *The Survivor,* 1964; *Surrender,* 1966; *Silent Ship, Silent Sea,* 1967; *No Man's Land,* 1969; *Deathwatch,* 1972; *The Frogmen,* 1973; *The Long Way Down,* 1977; *Fire Storm,* 1979.

Screenplays: "Macabre," "House on Haunted Hill," "13 Ghosts," "The Tingler," "Homicidal."

Also author of scripts for "Silent Service," "Perry Mason," "Men of Annapolis," and other television programs.

SIDELIGHTS: Robb White never went to school (there weren't any in the area where his father was a missionary in the Philippines) until he attended high school in Virginia. White resigned his Navy commission, on graduation from Annapolis; held various jobs, wrote, and went back to sea in 1941 after joining the Navy.

BIOGRAPHICAL/CRITICAL SOURCES: Children's Literature Review, Volume III, Gale, 1978.

* * *

WHITE, William F(rancis) 1928-

PERSONAL: Born June 26, 1928, in Syracuse, N.Y.; son of John J. and Helen (Markel) White; married Gail D. Eisensohn; children: Kevin, Brian. *Education:* St. Bernard's College, Rochester, N.Y., B.A., 1946; State University of New York at Buffalo, Ed.M., 1962, Ph.D., 1964. *Home:* Plum

Nelly-Holiday Estates, Morehead, Ky. 40351. *Office:* Morehead State University, Morehead, Ky. 40351.

CAREER: California State College (now University), Long Beach, assistant professor of educational psychology, summer, 1964; University of Georgia, Athens, assistant professor, 1964-67, associate professor, 1967-70, professor of educational psychology, 1970-76; dean of education, West Chester State College, West Chester, Pa.; currently vice-president for academic affairs, Morehead State University, Morehead, Ky. *Member:* American Psychological Association (fellow), American Educational Research Association, Southeastern Psychological Association, Georgia Psychological Association. *Awards, honors:* Danforth fellowship, 1967-69; U.S. Office of Education grants, 1969, 1970, 1971, 1972, 1979; U.S. Department of Housing and Urban Development grant, 1971.

WRITINGS: (With Fred Schab and James Wash) *Exercises in Adolescent Psychology* (monograph), Edwards Brothers, 1966; (with Schab, Wash, and Albert Kingston) *A Study Guide for Educational Psychology,* Edwards Brothers, 1966; (editor with Therry Deal) *World of the Young Child,* Journal of Research and Development in Education, 1968; *Psychosocial Principles Applied to Classroom Teaching,* McGraw, 1969; (with E. Paul Torrance) *Issues and Advances in Educational Psychology,* F. E. Peacock, 1969; (contributor) R. L. Jones, editor, *Psychology and Education of Exceptional Children: Current Issues and Problems,* Houghton, 1970; *Tactics for Teaching the Disadvantaged,* McGraw, 1971; (with Torrance) *Issues and Advances: 1974,* F. E. Peacock, 1974; (with A. J. Kingston) *Human Learning,* Harcourt, 1975; *Intelligence and Cognitive Processes,* Journal of Research and Development in Education, 1979.

Contributor of about sixty articles to psychology and education journals, including *Journal of Educational Psychology, Journal of Clinical Psychology, Perceptual and Motor Skills, Journal of Negro Education, Measurement and Evaluation in Guidance, Journal of Educational Research, Psychological Reports, Journal of Reading Behavior,* and *Educational and Psychological Measurement.*

* * *

WIERSMA, William, Jr. 1931-

PERSONAL: Born June 22, 1931, in Wisconsin; married Joan E. McCoy; children: Susan, Lisa. *Education:* Wisconsin State College, B.S., 1953; University of Wisconsin, M.S., 1957, Ph.D., 1962. *Religion:* Protestant. *Home:* 3525 Orchard Trail, Toledo, Ohio 43606. *Office:* University of Toledo, Toledo, Ohio 43606.

CAREER: University of Wisconsin—Madison, instructor in education, 1962-63; University of Toledo, Toledo, Ohio, assistant professor, 1963-65, associate professor, 1965-67, professor of education, 1967—. Fellow, Educational Testing Service, 1969-70; consultant to Associated Colleges of the Midwest. *Military service:* U.S. Army, 1953-55. *Member:* American Educational Research Association, National Council on Measurement in Education, Phi Delta Kappa.

WRITINGS: *Handbook of Research Methodology for Teachers in R. and I. Units,* University of Toledo, 1967; *Research Methods in Education: An Introduction,* Lippincott, 1969, 3rd edition, F. E. Peacock, 1980; (contributor) *A Reader's Guide to the Comprehensive Models for Preparing Elementary Teachers,* American Association of Colleges for Teacher Education and Eric Clearinghouse on Teacher Education, 1969; (contributor) V. DeValut, D. Anderson, and G. E. Dickson, editors, *Competency Based Teacher Education: Book I,* McCutchan, 1973; *Student Teachers in the MUS: A Study of Attitudes,* University of Toledo, 1973; (contributor) Dickson and R. Saxe, editors, *Partners for Educational Reform and Renewal,* McCutchan, 1973; (with Elmer A. Lemke) *Principles of Psychological Measurement,* Rand McNally, 1976; (with Stephen G. Jurs) *Evaluation of Instruction in Individually Guided Education,* Addison-Wesley, 1976; (with Edward Nussel and Joan Inglis) *The Teacher and Individually Guided Education,* Addison-Wesley, 1976. Also author with Jurs and Dennis Hinkle, *Applied Statistics for the Behavioral Sciences,* 1979.

Contributor to yearbooks. Contributor of about twenty-five articles to education, language, and psychology journals, including *Journal of Educational Measurement, Journal of Teacher Education, Science Education, Modern Language Journal, Psychological Reports,* and *Journal of Experimental Education.*

WORK IN PROGRESS: Co-authoring, with Hinkle and Jurs, *Elementary Statistics;* research on the evaluation of teacher performance.

SIDELIGHTS: William Wiersma has conducted research in Europe and has been instrumental in planning research and evaluation in teacher education.

* * *

WILK, Max 1920-

PERSONAL: Born July 3, 1920, in New York, N.Y.; son of Jacob and Eva (Zalk) Wilk; married Barbara Balensweig, 1949; children: David, Richard, Mary Frances. *Education:* Yale University, B.A., 1941. *Home:* 29 Surf Rd., Westport, Conn. *Agent:* Monica McCall, International Creative Management, 40 West 57th St., New York, N.Y. 10019.

CAREER: Formerly worked in several capacities for Columbia Broadcasting System-Television, New York, N.Y.; free-lance writer, 1948—. *Military service:* U.S. Army. *Member:* Players Club and Yale Club (both New York). *Awards, honors:* Emmy, Peabody, and Writers Guild of America East awards for scripts; American Society of Composers, Authors and Publishers Deems Taylor Award, 1974, for best book on American popular music.

WRITINGS: *Don't Raise the Bridge, Lower the River,* Macmillan, 1960; *Rich Is Better,* Macmillan, 1962; *Help! Help! Help!; or, Atrocity Stories from All Over,* Macmillan, 1963; *The Beard,* Simon & Schuster, 1965; *One of Our Brains Is Draining,* Norton, 1967; *The Yellow Submarine,* New American Library, 1968; *A Dirty Mind Never Sleeps,* Norton, 1969; *My Masterpiece,* Norton, 1970; *The Wit and Wisdom of Hollywood,* Atheneum, 1971; *They're Playing Our Song,* Atheneum, 1973; *Memory Lane,* Studio International (London), 1973; *Eliminate the Middleman,* Norton, 1974; *Every Day's a Matinee,* Norton, 1975; *The Kissinger Noodles; or, Westward Mr. Ho,* Norton, 1976; *The Golden Age of Television,* Delacorte, 1977; *The Moving Picture Boys,* Norton, 1978; *Get Out and Get Under,* Norton, 1981. Also author of screenplays and numerous television scripts and adaptations, including "Melina Mecouri's Greece," American Broadcasting Companies, Inc., 1965. Contributor to magazines.

WORK IN PROGRESS: A film, "Moving Picture Boys," based on his book of the same title.

BIOGRAPHICAL/CRITICAL SOURCES: *New York Times Book Review,* February 28, 1960, March 10, 1968, March 24, 1974; *New Yorker,* March 12, 1960, November 6, 1978; *Saturday Review,* March 19, 1960; *Chicago Sunday Tribune,*

April 3, 1960; *New York Herald Tribune Books,* April 1, 1962; *San Francisco Chronicle,* May 13, 1962; *Books and Bookmen,* May, 1968, July, 1974, May, 1975; *Best Sellers,* May 15, 1969, October 1, 1970; *Variety,* July 14, 1971; *Life,* July 30, 1971; *Cue,* August 14, 1971; *Vogue,* September 1, 1971.

* * *

WILKINSON, Rosemary C(halloner) 1924-

PERSONAL: Born February 21, 1924, in New Orleans, La.; daughter of William Lindsay (in wholesale jewelry materials) and Julia (Sellen) Challoner; married Henry Bertram Wilkinson, 1949; children: Denis, Marian, Paul, Richard. *Education:* Attended College of San Mateo, 1964-66; University of Minnesota, student by correspondence, 1967. *Politics:* Democrat. *Religion:* Catholic. *Home:* 1239 Bernal Ave., Burlingame, Calif. 94010.

CAREER: Bookkeeper at hospitals in Lafayette and New Albany, Ind., 1939-44; St. James Hospital, Chicago Heights, Ill., administrative supervisor, 1944-47; St. Joseph Hospital, Phoenix, Ariz., administrative supervisor, 1947-48; West Disinfecting Co., San Francisco, Calif., bookkeeper, 1948-51; Peninsula Hospital, Burlingame, Calif., billing officer, 1961-62; full-time writer, 1964—. Advisor to Third World Congress of Poets, 1976, member of board, Fourth World Congress of Poets, and chairman of organizing committee and president, Fifth World Congress of Poets; member of board of trustees, World Academy of Arts and Culture. Coordinator of California's second chapter of Hospital Audiences, Inc., 1972. Has given poetry readings to schools and hospitals. *Member:* International Academy of Poets, United Poets Laureate International (Philippines), Poetry Society of England, National League of American Pen Women, Tagore Institute of Creative Writing (India), Cosmosynthesis League (honorary life member), California Federation of Chaparral Poets (president of Toyon chapter, 1972-74), California Writers Club, Ina Coolbrith Circle (member of board; San Francisco). *Awards, honors:* Certificate of merit from American Poets Fellowship Society, Charleston, Ill., 1973; International Woman of 1975 with laureate honors; D.H.L., Libre University, 1975.

WRITINGS: A Girl's Will (poems), Prairie Press, 1973; *An Historical Epic,* [Republic of China], 1975; *California Poet,* Burlingame Press, 1976. Also author of *Earth's Compromise, It Happened to Me, The Captain Artist, I Am Earth Woman,* 1979, and *The Poet and the Painter,* 1980.

* * *

WILL, Frederic 1928-

PERSONAL: Born December 4, 1928, in New Haven, Conn.; son of Samuel (a professor) and Constance (Bicknell) Will; married Elizabeth Lyding (a professor), July 13, 1951; children: Alex, Barbara. *Education:* Indiana University, A.B., 1949; Yale University, Ph.D., 1954. *Religion:* Roman Catholic. *Home:* 84 High Point Dr., Amherst, Mass. 01002. *Office:* South College, University of Massachusetts, Amherst, Mass. 01002.

CAREER: Dartmouth College, Hanover, N.H., instructor in classics, 1953-55; Pennsylvania State University, University Park, assistant professor of classics, 1954-59; University of Texas, Main University (now University of Texas at Austin), assistant professor of classics, 1960-64; University of Iowa, Iowa City, associate professor of English and comparative literature, 1964-66, professor of comparative literature, 1966-71; University of Massachusetts—Amherst, professor of comparative literature, 1971—. Lecturer on poetry and criticism at various colleges and universities in the United States and Canada, including Harvard University, Yale University, and Princeton University. Conducts poetry readings at various universities and institutions, including State University of New York at Buffalo, Carleton University, and San Francisco State Poetry Center.

AWARDS, HONORS: Fulbright grants, 1950-51, 1955, 1956-57, 1975-76, and 1980-81; American Council of Learned Societies grant, 1958; annual poetry prize, Texas Institute of Letters, 1963; Voertman Poetry Prize; first periodical prose award, Texas Institute of Letters; National Endowment for the Arts grant and Coordinating Council for Literary Magazines grant, both for poetry journal, *Micromegas.*

WRITINGS: Intelligible Beauty in Aesthetic Thought: From Winckelmann to Victor Cousin, M. Niemeyer, 1958; *Mosaic, and Other Poems,* Pennsylvania State University Press, 1959; *A Wedge of Words* (poems), University of Texas, Main University, 1962; (translator and author of introduction) Kostes Palamas, *The Twelve Words of the Gypsy,* University of Nebraska Press, 1964; (editor) *Hereditas: Seven Essays on the Modern Experience of the Classical,* University of Texas Press, 1964; (editor and author of introduction) *Metaphrasis: An Anthology from the University of Iowa Translation Workshop, 1964-65,* Verb, 1965; *Flumen historicum: Victor Cousin's Aesthetic and Its Sources,* University of North Carolina Press, 1965; *Literature Inside Out: Ten Speculative Essays,* Press of Western Reserve University, 1966; *Planets* (poems), Golden Quill, 1966; (translator and author of introduction) Palamas, *The King's Flute,* University of Nebraska Press, 1967; *From a Year in Greece,* University of Texas Press, 1967; *Archilochos,* Twayne, 1969.

Herondas, Twayne, 1972; *Brandy in the Snow* (poems), New Rivers Press, 1972; (translator with Knut Tarnowski) Theodor Adorno, *The Jargon of Authenticity,* Northwestern University Press, 1973; *The Knife in the Stone,* Mouton, 1973; *The Fact of Literature,* Rodopi, 1973; *Guatemala,* Bellevue, 1973; *Botulism* (poems), Micromegas, 1975; *The Generic Demands of Greek Literature,* Rodopi, 1976; *Belphagor,* Rodopi, 1977; *Epics of America* (poems), Panache, 1977; *Our Thousand Year Old Bodies: Selected Poems, 1956-1976,* University of Massachusetts Press, 1980. Contributor of numerous poems and articles to various publications. Editor, *Micromegas.*

WORK IN PROGRESS: Selected Poems, 1976-1981; Selected Critical Essays, 1957-1975.

SIDELIGHTS: Frederic Will told *CA:* "I see writing as an obsolescent rear-guard action against a new oral culture. The writer's obligation is to defend the values of the classical tradition without failing to see that they are no longer his. Hope and the future are intimately linked to the whole process of writing."

* * *

WILLIAMS, Barbara 1925-

PERSONAL: Born January 1, 1925, in Salt Lake City, Utah; daughter of Walter (a lawyer) and Emily (Jeremy) Wright; married J. D. Williams (a professor of political science), July 5, 1946; children: Kirk, Gil, Taylor, Kimberly. *Education:* Attended Banff School of Fine Arts, 1945; University of Utah, B.A., 1946, M.A., 1972; Boston University, additional study, 1949-50. *Politics:* Democrat. *Home:* 3399 East Loren Von Dr., Salt Lake City, Utah 84117.

CAREER: Deseret News, Salt Lake City, Utah, occasional

society reporter and columnist, 1944-50; Library of Congress, Washington, D.C., secretary, 1946-48, 1951; University of Utah, Salt Lake City, remedial English teacher, 1960-71; *Marriage*, St. Meinrad, Ind., children's book reviewer, 1974-76. *Awards, honors:* First place winner in Utah Fine Arts Writing Contest, 1965, for *William H. McGuffey: Boy Reading Genius*, 1971, for *The Secret Name*, 1975, for *Desert Hunter and Other Stories*, and 1978, for *Where Are You, Angela von Hauptmann, Now that I Need You?*; awarded bronze medallion from the Christophers, 1979, for *Chester Chipmunk's Thanksgiving*.

WRITINGS—Juvenile, except as indicated: *Let's Go to an Indian Cliff Dwelling*, Putnam, 1965; *I Know a Policeman*, Putnam, 1966; *I Know a Fireman*, Putnam, 1967; *I Know a Mayor*, Putnam, 1967; *I Know a Garageman*, Putnam, 1968; *William H. McGuffey: Boy Reading Genius*, Bobbs-Merrill, 1968; *I Know a Bank Teller*, Putnam, 1968; *Twelve Steps to Better Exposition* (textbook), C. E. Merrill, 1968; *Boston: Seat of American History*, McGraw, 1969; *I Know a Weatherman*, Putnam, 1970; *The Well-Structured Paragraph* (textbook), C. E. Merrill, 1970; *The Secret Name*, Harcourt, 1972; *Gary and the Very Terrible Monster*, Childrens Press, 1973; *We Can Jump*, Childrens Press, 1973; *Albert's Toothache* (Junior Literary Guild selection), Dutton, 1974; *Kevin's Grandma*, Dutton, 1975; *Desert Hunter and Other Stories*, Harvey House, 1975; *Someday, Said Mitchell* (Junior Literary Guild selection), Dutton, 1976; *Cornzapoppin'!* (Junior Literary Guild selection), Holt, 1976; *If He's My Brother*, Harvey House, 1976; *Never Hit a Porcupine*, Dutton, 1977; *Pins, Picks and Popsicle Sticks*, Holt, 1977; *Twenty-six Lively Letters* (adult book), Taplinger, 1977; *Seven True Elephant Stories*, Hastings House, 1978; *Chester Chipmunk's Thanksgiving*, Dutton, 1978; *Guess Who's Coming to My Tea Party*, Holt, 1978; *Brigham Young and Me, Clarissa*, Doubleday, 1978; *I Know a Salesperson*, Putnam, 1978; *Jeremy Isn't Hungry* (Junior Literary Guild selection), Dutton, 1978; *Whatever Happened to Beverly Bigler's Birthday?*, Harcourt, 1978; *Hello, Dandelions!*, Holt, 1979; *Breakthrough: Women in Politics*, Walker & Co., 1979; *Where Are You, Angela von Hauptmann, Now that I Need You?*, Holt, 1979; *A Valentine for Cousin Archie*, Dutton, 1980; *So What If I'm a Sore Loser?*, Harcourt, 1981.

Plays: *Eternally Peggy* (three-act), Deseret News Press, 1957; *The Ghost of Black Jack* (one-act), Samuel French, 1961; *Just the Two of Us* (one-act), Utah Printing, 1965.

WORK IN PROGRESS: A book of poetry for children.

SIDELIGHTS: Barbara Williams wrote *CA:* "As I look back upon it, I feel sure I must have turned to pencils and typewriters in self-defense. The only non-athlete in the neighborhood (I failed courses in beginning swimming seven times, among other things), no captain ever chose me for his team; and I had to find something to do while all the other kids were playing football and baseball. As a result, I spent a good part of my childhood living in the realm of my imagination and setting down my ideas on an antique typewriter which I attacked with one finger.

"Like many other writers for children, I didn't turn to this genre until I had children of my own to read to and realized how interesting and how satisfying children's books could be. Although my college textbooks (which I wrote while I was teaching at the University of Utah) earn far more money than my children's books do, no reader of one of those books has ever sent me a 'thank you' letter. Children are the most appreciative readers in the world!"

BIOGRAPHICAL/CRITICAL SOURCES: Mountain West, December, 1979; *New York Times*, February 17, 1980; *New York Times Book Review*, February 24, 1980.

*   *   *

WILLIAMS, Brad 1918-

PERSONAL: Born April 20, 1918, in New York, N.Y.; son of Arthur Herbert and Sophie W. (Baker) Williams; married, 1951; wife's name, Harriet; children: Kevin, Wendy, Suzanne. *Education:* Attended Mexico City College. *Home:* 1207 Tenth St., Manhattan Beach, Calif. *Agent:* Paul R. Reynolds, Inc., 12 East 41st St., New York, N.Y. 10017.

CAREER: Associated Press, reporter in Denver, Colo., and in New Mexico, 1946-49; United Press, reporter in Mexico City, Mexico, 1949-53; *Oregon Journal*, Portland, Ore., reporter, 1953-58; *Los Angeles Times*, Los Angeles, Calif., reporter, 1958-60; writer, 1960—. *Military service:* U.S. Army Air Corps; became sergeant.

WRITINGS: A Borderline Case, Morrow, 1960; *Due Process*, Morrow, 1960; *Make a Killing*, Morrow, 1961; *Death Lies in Waiting*, Jenkins Publishing, 1961; *A Well Dressed Skeleton*, Morrow, 1962; *Flight 967*, Morrow, 1963; *A Stranger to Herself*, Doubleday, 1964; (with Choral Pepper) *The Mysterious West*, World Publishing, 1967; *Anatomy of an Airline*, Doubleday, 1970; (with Pepper) *Lost Legends of the West*, Holt, 1970; (with Jake Ehrlich) *A Conflict of Interest*, Holt, 1971; *Tumulto*, Avon, 1974; (with Ehrlich) *A Matter of Confidence*, Holt, 1974; (with Pepper) *Lost Treasures of the West*, Holt, 1975; *Legendary Outlaws of the West*, McKay, 1976; *Legendary Women of the West*, McKay, 1978. Also author of television scripts. Contributor of articles and short stories to numerous magazines.

WORK IN PROGRESS: The Touch of Siva; The Apollo Extortion.

*   *   *

WILLIAMS, Daniel Day 1910-1973

PERSONAL: Born September 12, 1910, in Denver, Colo.; died December 3, 1973, in New York, N.Y.; son of Wayne Cullen and Lena (Day) Williams; married Eulalia Westberg, June 15, 1935. *Education:* University of Denver, A.B., 1931; University of Chicago, M.A., 1933; Chicago Theological Seminary, B.D., 1934; Columbia University, Ph.D., 1940. *Home:* 99 Claremont Ave., New York, N.Y. 10027. *Office:* Union Theological Seminary, Broadway at 120th St., New York, N.Y.

CAREER: First Congregational Church, Colorado Springs, Colo., minister, 1936-38; Colorado College, Colorado Springs, dean of chapel and instructor in religion, 1938-39; University of Chicago, Chicago, Ill., professor, federated theological faculty, 1939-54; Union Theological Seminary, New York, N.Y., professor of systematic theology, 1954-59, Roosevelt Professor of Systematic Theology, 1959-73. Rauschenbush Lecturer, Colgate-Rochester Divinity School, 1947; Mead-Swing Lecturer, Oberlin College, 1951; lecturer, general council of Congregational Churches, 1952; Nathaniel Taylor Lecturer, Yale Divinity School, 1953; Alden-Tuthill Lecturer, Chicago Theological Seminary, 1959; Earl Lecturer, Pacific School of Religion, 1959; lecturer, Theological Faculties Institute, Singapore, 1962. Member of commission on basis of social action, 1953; associate director, survey of theological education, 1954-55; delegate of United Church of Christ, Faith and Order Commission, World Council of Churches, 1971-73. *Member:* American Theological Society (president, Midwest division, 1947), Sigma Alpha Epsilon,

Duodecim. *Awards, honors:* D.D. from Colorado College, 1965, Chicago Theological Seminary, 1966, and Bloomfield College, 1973.

WRITINGS: The Andover Liberals: A Study in American Theology, Columbia University Press, 1941, reprinted, Octagon, 1970; *God's Grace and Man's Hope,* Harper, 1949, reprinted, 1965; *What Present Day Theologians Are Thinking,* Harper, 1952 (published in England as *Interpreting Theology, 1918-1952,* SCM Press, 1953), 3rd edition, 1967; (contributor) *The Theology of Reinhold Niebuhr: A Companion to the Study of St. Augustine,* Scribner, 1956; (editor with Helmut Richard Niebuhr) *The Ministry in Historical Perspectives,* Harper, 1956; (with H. R. Niebuhr and James Gustafson) *The Advancement of Theological Education,* Harper, 1957; *The Minister and the Care of Souls,* Harper, 1961, reprinted, 1977; (contributor) Ivor Leclerc, editor, *The Relevance of Whitehead,* Macmillan, 1961; (contributor) *The Shaping of American Religion,* Princeton University Press, 1961; (contributor) *Alfred North Whitehead: Essays on His Philosophy,* Macmillan, 1963; (contributor) Robert W. Bretall, editor, *The Empirical Theology of Henry Nelson Weiman,* Macmillan, 1963; (contributor) William Lewis Reese and Eugene Freeman, editors, *Process and Divinity: Philosophical Essays Presented to Charles Hartshorne,* Open Court, 1964; (with Roger Lincoln Shinn) *We Believe: An Interpretation of the United Church Statement of Faith,* United Church Press, 1966; *The Spirit and the Forms of Love,* Harper, 1968. American editor, *Library of Constructive Theology.* Contributor to professional journals.

SIDELIGHTS: Daniel Day Williams was a proponent of process theology, a method of analysis based on the philosophy of Alfred North Whitehead. He used process theology in *The Spirit and the Forms of Love,* a discussion of the history of love in Western culture and its Old and New Testament roots, regarding which William A. Sadler, Jr. wrote in the *Christian Century,* "It presents an argument that is well reasoned, highly informed and clearly stated; it is broad in scope and yet illuminating of everyday existence and its possibilities."

AVOCATIONAL INTERESTS: Music, mountain climbing.

BIOGRAPHICAL/CRITICAL SOURCES: Christian Century, June 4, 1969; *Commonweal,* August 22, 1969.†

* * *

WILLIAMS, George Huntston 1914-

PERSONAL: Born April 7, 1914, in Huntsburg, Ohio; son of David Rhys and Lucy (Pease) Williams; married Marjorie L. Derr, 1941; children: Portia, Jeremy, Jonathan, Roger. *Education:* Attended University of Munich, 1934-35; St. Lawrence University, A.B., 1936; Meadville Theological School (now Meadville/Lombard Theological Seminary), B.D., 1939; additional study at University of Strasbourg, 1939-40 and University of California, 1942-43; Union Theological Seminary, Th.D., 1946. *Home:* 58 Pinehurst Rd., Belmont, Mass. 02178. *Office:* Widener Library K, Harvard University, Cambridge, Mass. 02138.

CAREER: Church of the Christian Union, Rockford, Ill., assistant minister, 1940-41; Starr King School of Ministry, and Pacific School of Religion, Berkeley, Calif., 1941-47, began as instructor, became assistant professor of church history; Harvard University, Divinity School, Cambridge, Mass., lecturer, 1947-53, associate professor, 1953-55, professor of church history, 1955-56, Winn Professor of Ecclesiastical History, 1956-63, Hollis Professor of Divinity, 1963—, acting dean, 1953-55. Fulbright lecturer, University of Strasbourg, France, 1960-61. Delegated as observer to Second Vatican Council, 1962, 1963, 1964, and 1965. *Member:* American Society of Church History (president, 1957-58), American Academy of Arts and Sciences, Reformation Research Society (member of council), Americans United for Life (chairman, 1970-77), North American Committee for Documentation of Free Church Origins (chairman), Massachusetts Council of Churches (chairman of committee on church and state, 1963-68), Phi Beta Kappa. *Awards, honors:* Cruft traveling fellowship, 1939; D.D., St. Lawrence University, 1953; Harvard research grant, 1956; Lilly Endowment grant, 1959; Litt.D., Meadville Theological School (now Meadville/Lombard Theological Seminary), 1964; Guggenheim fellow, University of Lublin, 1972-73; Papal Knight of the Order of St. Gregory the Great, 1979; National Endowment for the Humanities fellow, 1979-80; D.H.L., Loyola University (New Orleans, La.), 1980.

WRITINGS: The Norman Anonymous of 1100 A.D., Harvard University Press, 1951; (editor) *Harvard Divinity School,* Beacon Press, 1954; (editor with Angel M. Mergal) *Spiritual and Anabaptist Writers,* Westminster, 1957; *The Theological Idea of the University,* National Council of Churches, 1958; *Anselm: Communion and Atonement,* Concordia, 1960; *Wilderness and Paradise in Christian Thought,* Harper, 1962; *The Radical Reformation,* Westminster Press, 1962, revised and enlarged edition published in Spanish as *Reformacion Radial,* Fondode Cultura Economica, 1978; (author of introduction) *Ecumenical Dialogue at Harvard: The Roman Catholic-Protestant Colloquium,* Belknap, 1964; (editor) *Church, State, and Education: A New Look,* Beacon Press, 1968; (editor with Isadore Twersky) *Studies in the History of Philosophy and Religion,* Harvard University Press, 1973; (editor) *Thomas Hooker: Writings in England and Holland, 1626-1633,* Harvard University Press, 1975; (editor with Twersky) *Religious Philosophy,* Harvard University Press, 1977; *Polish Brethren: 1601-1685,* Scholars' Press, 1978; *Continuity and Discontinuity in Church History,* E. J. Brill, 1979.

Contributor: Arnold Nash, editor, *Protestant Thought in the Twentieth Century,* Macmillan, 1951; H. Richard Niebuhr and Daniel D. Williams, editors, *The Ministry in Historical Perspective,* Harper, 1956; Joe Park, editor, *Selected Readings in the Philosophy of Education,* Macmillan, 1958; Stephen Neill and Hans R. Weber, editor, *The Layman in Christian History,* S.C.M. Press, 1963; John Tedeschi, editor, *Italian Reformation Studies,* Le Monnier, 1965; D. B. Robertson, editor, *Voluntary Associations,* John Knox, 1966; Theodore K. Rabb and Jerrold E. Seigel, editors, *Action and Conviction in Early Modern Europe,* Princeton University Press, 1969; James L. Garrett, Jr., *The Concept of the Believers' Church,* Herald Press, 1969; *The Morality of Abortion,* Harvard University Press, 1970; Harvey Cox, editor, *Military Chaplains: From a Religious Military to a Military Religion,* American Report Press, 1971; L. P. Buck and J. W. Zophy, editors, *The Social History of the Reformation,* Ohio State University Press, 1972; Thomas W. Hilgers and Dennis J. Horan, *Abortion and Social Justice,* Sheed, 1972; T. Gill, editor, *To God Be the Glory,* Abingdon, 1973; Thomas Bird and Andrew Blane, *The Ecumenical World of Orthodox Civilization,* Mouton, 1974; Alexander McKelway and E. David Willis, editors, *The Context of Contemporary Theology,* John Knox, 1974; Canon Michael Hamilton, editor, *The Charismatics: Confusion or Blessing?,* Eerdmans, 1975; David Wells and John Woodbridge, editors, *The Evangelical Resurgence,* Abingdon, 1975, revised edition, Baker Book, 1977; Zenon Kohut, editor, *Church and Religion in*

Early Modern Ukraine, Harvard University Press, 1979; Ihor Sercenko, editor, *Essays in Honor of Omeljan Pritsak,* Harvard University Press, 1980.

Also author of forewords and introductions in numerous books. Contributor of many articles to periodicals including *Polish Review, Journal of Liberal Religion, Studies of Romanticism,* and *Reflections.* Member of editorial boards, *Harvard Theological Review, Mennonite Quarterly Review,* and *Church History.*

WORK IN PROGRESS: The Mind and Spirit of Pope John Paul II, for Seabury; contributing chapters to *The Ecumenical World of Orthodox Civilization, Shapers of Traditions in Germany, Switzerland, and Poland,* and a critical edition of *History of the Polish Reformation.*

AVOCATIONAL INTERESTS: Conservation.

* * *

WILLIAMS, Jerome 1926-

PERSONAL: Born July 15, 1926, in Toronto, Ontario, Canada; son of Maurice Edward (in social services) and Bertha (Bronstein) Williams; married Lelia K. Holden (a proofreader), March 1, 1953; children: Pamela Jean, Robert Stuart. *Education:* University of Maryland, B.S., 1950; Johns Hopkins University, M.A., 1952. *Politics:* Liberal. *Religion:* Unitarian Universalist. *Home:* 2804 Pine Dr., Annapolis, Md. 21401. *Office:* Department of Oceanography, United States Naval Academy, Annapolis, Md. 21402.

CAREER: Chesapeake Bay Institute, Annapolis, Md., research associate, 1951-69; United States Naval Academy, Annapolis, Md., assistant professor, 1957-65, associate professor, 1965-74, professor of oceanography, 1974—. *Military service:* U.S. Navy, 1944-46; served in Pacific theater. *Member:* American Geophysical Union, American Society of Limnology and Oceanography, American Association for the Advancement of Science, Marine Technology Society, American Association of Physics Teachers, Estuarine Research Federation (vice-president, 1971-73; secretary, 1973-75; executive director, 1975—), Atlantic Estuarine Research Society (president, 1967). *Awards, honors:* First prize in poetry reading from Anne Arundel Poetry Association, 1971.

WRITINGS: Oceanography: An Introduction to the Marine Sciences, Little, Brown, 1962; (with John J. Higginson and John D. Rohrbough) *Sea and Air,* U.S. Naval Institute, 1968, revised edition, 1973; *Optical Properties of the Sea,* U.S. Naval Institute, 1970; *Oceanography: A First Book,* F. Watts, 1972; *Oceanographic Instrumentation,* U.S. Naval Institute, 1973; *Introduction to Marine Pollution Control,* Wiley, 1979; (with wife, Lelia K. Williams) *Science Puzzles,* F. Watts, 1979. Contributor to transactions and to *Journal of Marine Technology.*

WORK IN PROGRESS: Research in marine optics and pollution; ocean engineering text.

SIDELIGHTS: Jerome Williams wrote *CA* that he "believes that science writing does not have to be as bad as it usually is and children's science books should be written by scientists rather than journalists."

* * *

WILLIAMS, Selma R(uth) 1925-

PERSONAL: Born October 26, 1925, in Malden, Mass.; married Burton L. Williams (a lawyer), June 26, 1949; children: Pamela, Wendy. *Education:* Radcliffe College, A.B. (cum laude), 1946; Tufts University, Ed.M., 1964. *Politics:* "Independent-liberal." *Home:* 17 Dane Rd., Lexington, Mass. 02173.

CAREER: Harvard Law Record, Cambridge, Mass., executive director, 1946-50; Diamond Junior High School, Lexington, Mass., history teacher, 1964-67; Concord-Carlisle Senior High School, Concord, Mass., history teacher, 1967-68; Middlesex Community College, Bedford, Mass., lecturer in history, 1973-76; professional lecturer, 1976—. *Member:* Authors Guild, American Historical Association, Organization of American Historians, League of Women Voters (member of local executive board, 1955-60), New England Association of Women Historians.

WRITINGS: Fifty-Five Fathers: The Story of the Constitutional Convention, Dodd, 1970; *Kings, Commoners, and Colonists: Puritan Politics in Old and New England, 1603-1660,* Atheneum, 1974; *Demeter's Daughters: The Women Who Founded America,* Atheneum, 1976; *Riding the Nightmare: Women and Witchcraft,* Atheneum, 1978.

WORK IN PROGRESS: A biography of Anne Hutchinson, for Holt.

SIDELIGHTS: Selma R. Williams wrote *CA:* "In my undergraduate days I constantly bewailed missing out on the suffrage campaign. Only after teaching history to students of all ages, from junior high to university graduate level, did I finally discover what I wanted to be when I grew up—an activist uncovering deep female roots in history and spreading the word.

"Each book had led directly to the next. *Fifty-Five Fathers: The Story of the Constitutional Convention* made me seek the roots of our government in England and early Massachusetts and resulted in *Kings, Commoners, and Colonists.* This book in turn led me to wonder about the role of women in colonization and produced *Demeter's Daughters.* And a chapter here on women and witchcraft inspired [*Riding the Nightmare*]—uncovering the reasons why hundreds of thousands, perhaps millions, of women were put to death as witches in Europe and America."

* * *

WILLS, Garry 1934-

PERSONAL: Born May 22, 1934, in Atlanta, Ga.; son of John H. and Mayno (Collins) Wills; married Natalie Cavallo, 1959; children: John Christopher, Garry Laurence, Lydia Mayno. *Education:* St. Louis University, A.B., 1957; Xavier University, M.A., 1958; Yale University, M.A., 1959, Ph.D., 1961. *Office:* Humanities Center, Johns Hopkins University, Baltimore, Md. 21218.

CAREER: Richmond News Leader, Richmond, Va., associate editor, 1961; Center for Hellenic Studies, Washington, D.C., fellow, 1961-62; Johns Hopkins University, Baltimore, Md., assistant professor, 1962-67, visiting lecturer in classics, 1968-69, adjunct professor of humanities, Johns Hopkins University, 1973—; writer. Regents' Lecturer, University of California, 1971. *Awards, honors:* Organization of American Historians Merle Curti Award 1978, National Book Critics Circle Award, 1979, and John D. Rockefeller III Award, 1979, all for *Inventing America.*

WRITINGS: Chesterton: Man and Mask, Sheed, 1961; *Politics and Catholic Freedom,* Regnery, 1964; (contributor) Frank S. Meyer, *What Is Conservatism?,* Holt, 1964; (contributor) Daniel Callahan, *Generation of the Third Eye,* Sheed, 1965; (editor) *Roman Culture: Weapons and the Man,* Braziller, 1966; (with Ovid Demaris) *Jack Ruby,* New American Library, 1968; *The Second Civil War: Arming for*

Armageddon, New American Library, 1968; *Nixon Agonistes: The Crisis of the Self-Made Man,* Houghton, 1970, revised edition, New American Library, 1979; *Bare Ruined Choirs: Doubt, Prophecy, and Radical Religion,* Doubleday, 1972; (editor) *Values Americans Live By,* Arno, 1974; *Inventing America: Jefferson's Declaration of Independence,* Doubleday, 1978; *Confessions of a Conservative,* Doubleday, 1979; *At Button's* (novel), Andrews & McMeel, 1979; *Explaining America: The Federalist,* Doubleday, 1980. Author of column, "Outrider," Universal Press Syndicate, 1970—. Contributor of articles and book reviews to numerous periodicals. Contributing editor, *Esquire,* 1967-70.

SIDELIGHTS: Although his formal educational background is in classical studies, Garry Wills has written on topics as diverse as Jack Ruby, race relations in America, and the Catholic Church. Wills, however, is probably best known to his readers for his incisive political commentaries, especially as they appear in such books as *Nixon Agonistes* and *Inventing America.* A critic of both the America liberal and conservative establishments, Wills was once described by a *New York Times Book Review* commentator as "an undogmatic conservative who is ready to let his experiences influence his conclusions. . . . He is cheerfully resigned to being a singular conservative, a renegade in the eyes of others who crowd under that rubric."

But Wills is not only a "renegade" in the eyes of self-proclaimed conservatives; the words "provocative" and "controversial" appear quite frequently in reviews of his work. For example, in the case of his study of Richard Nixon's political career, *Nixon Agonistes,* most reviewers were "quite startled to receive a description of Richard M. Nixon as a liberal," reports George Reedy in the *Washington Post.* "But that is precisely the characterization set forth by Garry Wills in *Nixon Agonistes,* and he marshals an impressive array of quotations to support his thesis. . . . It is quite obvious that he did not write this book to make friends. He finds all contemporary political philosophies wanting . . . and his attitude towards academicians verges on the savage. . . . Basically, Mr. Wills regards Richard M. Nixon as a framework for studying the philosophical patterns of that part of the electorate which is politically effective. . . . In the analysis that follows, [the book] becomes fascinating, although controversial, reading. . . . [But] even though many of his conclusions are arguable, Mr. Wills has produced a very good book."

John Leonard of the *New York Times* agrees. Calling the book "astonishing," he writes: "Mr. Wills achieves the not inconsiderable feat of making Richard Nixon a sympathetic—even tragic—figure, while at the same time being appalled by him. But superb as it is, his 'psycho-biography' of Mr. Nixon is merely prelude to a provocative essay on political theory. . . . One is tempted to quote constantly from *Nixon Agonistes* because Mr. Wills writes with a scalpel, to wound in Technicolor, drawing on literary sources both apposite and various. The reporter in him is as eager for the revealing detail as the theorist in him is eager for the abstraction. . . . His book is a stunning attempt to possess [the] past, that we may all of us escape it."

Others, however, do not feel that Wills and his book are quite so stunning. The *Newsweek* critic, for example, notes: "Garry Wills is a bright young man who left his Yale Ph.D. in classics behind him only to bring the academic vices of preciosity and obfuscation to his new career as a political journalist. Now Wills has produced a galumphing, endless and endlessly roundabout tome on Richard Nixon and how he got that way. . . . In the course of his chaotic book . . . Wills roams wide and far and everywhere. It could be said that he has inadvertently covered enough territory to make his book a textbook of post-Truman politics. As that, it would be a useful, if barely readable compendium of what can be said at so early a date. . . . [This is] a book that manipulates historical abstractions instead of asking the hard and pressing practical questions of policy and direction that have made our current political life almost a day-to-day crisis."

Frank S. Meyer of the *National Review* is even more critical of Wills and his approach. "This is a strange book," he begins. "Its avowed subject is Richard Nixon; yet its real subject is America today—an America about which there is nothing good to be said. . . . The book is strange also in another way. Since it is an indictment of America couched as an indictment of Richard Nixon, the seriousness of the indictment would seem to demand serious argument; what argument there is, however, is scattered here and there in a few dozen of its 617 pages. The ideas are insinuated through a kaleidoscope of sketches of personalities, personal adventures of the author, [and] landscape mood pieces. . . . This style has in his hands . . . all the honesty, all the straightforward openness to rational discourse of the TV commercial. . . . I have not been Mr. Nixon's warmest admirer, but this book has raised him inestimably in my esteem."

Finally, a *New York* reviewer feels that in spite of its faults, *Nixon Agonistes* is worth reading. He writes: "Much of the book is given over to painstaking, if at times pedantic, refutations of such card-carrying contemporary liberals as Schlesinger, Goodwin and Galbraith, all of whom [the author] holds—in the late Robert S. Kerr's classic phrase of senatorial courtesy—in minimum high regard. In the course of supporting his thesis, Wills writes convincingly of academia as aristocracy and of radicalism's abhorrence of backsliding liberalism as he perceives it to be on the American campus. All this is not to say, however, that Nixon emerges simply as a bit player. Wills provides some of the most revealing insights into the roots and nature of the man yet written. . . . Although [the author] devotes more space to grappling with theory than with personality, his quick, deft thrusts at leading political figures of the day, inserted throughout, enliven [*Nixon Agonistes*]. . . . There are, of course, invitations to arguments in this long book, . . . but in the main, Wills paints a broad and provocative landscape of the nation's—and now Nixon's—travail."

A later Wills effort, the award-winning *Inventing America,* has been almost equally controversial. Basically a revisionist account of the life of Thomas Jefferson and his most famous written work, the Declaration of Independence, *Inventing America* seeks to prove that Jefferson was influenced primarily by philosophers of the Scottish Enlightenment rather than by John Locke and that our interpretation of the Declaration does not correspond to what the Founding Fathers originally intended. The result of Wills' "demystification" attempt, according to *Time,* "is a scintillating tour de force of historical detective work. Wills is writing intellectual history, but even the most abstruse ideas come to life in his sharp, intelligent prose. . . . His most original achievement is his exorcism of John Locke as Jefferson's alleged inspiration. . . . To Locke, society was an aggregation of fundamentally separate individuals, but to the Scots, sociability was the very essence of man. If Wills is right—and his case is formidable—the roots of our political culture are far less individualistic than they are communal."

"No one has offered so drastic a revision or so close or convincing an analysis of the [Declaration] itself as Wills has now presented," writes the *New York Review of Books* critic. "[His] interpretation offers a fresh perspective both on Jefferson and on the Congress. And like most new insights in history it raises as many questions as it answers. Since Wills gives us so much to think about in this brilliant book, it is perhaps churlish to suggest that he might have given us more. But one cannot help wishing that he had persued [certain questions] somewhat further than he did."

A *New Republic* reviewer feels that *Inventing America* is incomplete for a different reason: "Garry Wills is an investigative reporter uncovering a conspiracy to distort the *Declaration of Independence*. . . . Since [he] is prosecuting charlatans rather than arguing with fellow-scholars he uses evidence selectively to score points, and his tone is generally sly and snide. The outcome is terrible intellectual history, but oddly a convincing picture of Jefferson does emerge. [Nevertheless,] we are still without a really good book on the *Declaration*."

Arthur Schlesinger, Jr., commenting in *Saturday Review*, calls *Inventing America* a "discursive but often brilliant book [that] illuminates both the men who wrote the Declaration of Independence and the nation that thereafter revered it. . . . [Wills] restores the world of the young Jefferson through reasonable conjecture derived from close textual analysis. [The book] is a tour de force of speculative scholarship. . . . [The author] sustains [his thesis] persuasively. He carries forward his exploration of the mind of the young Jefferson through a series of ingenious suggestions and digressions. . . . In short, *Inventing America* is a rich and original, if somewhat disorderly, book."

A *Commonweal* critic concludes: "Make no mistake, this is an important book, perhaps one of the most important books published in American history in the last ten years. Its subject is the Declaration of Independence and the author has approached it with such originality and high scholarship that the results of his research and thinking are little less than breathtaking. . . . Because Wills is a scholar, classicist, and journalist, he perceived the need to examine the document in the context of the world that actually produced it, not as 'invented' by the nineteenth century, and in so doing he has produced a radically altered reading of the Declaration, one so profound as to necessitate sharp revisions in all history textbooks dealing with the subject. . . . Wills uncovers new meaning in the Declaration and he tells us things about Jefferson that are revealing and important. Phrases in the document come into clearer focus. What was vague becomes precise. What once seemed like rhetorical flourishes assume the kind of meaning that they had for Jefferson and other men of the Enlightenment who appreciated them. . . . This penetrating, original and exciting book, written at times with a Jeffersonian felicity, only begins to uncover the lost world of Thomas Jefferson and his contemporaries. Much more remains to be revealed. Perhaps in the future Wills will help provide it."

BIOGRAPHICAL/CRITICAL SOURCES: *Book World*, January 14, 1968, June 18, 1978, April 15, 1979, June 17, 1979; *National Review*, April 9, 1968, June 4, 1968, July 18, 1970, October 20, 1975, July 7, 1978; *New York Times*, May 6, 1968, October 15, 1970, October 20, 1972, March 19, 1979, April 26, 1979; *Christian Century*, August 22, 1968; *Newsweek*, October 19, 1970, July 17, 1978; *New York*, October 19, 1970; *Washington Post*, October 22, 1970; *Village Voice*, October 29, 1970, August 28, 1978; *Time*, November 2, 1970, July 31, 1978; *Best Sellers*, December 1, 1970, November, 1978; *Christian Science Monitor*, December 5, 1970; *Commonweal*, April 30, 1971, October 27, 1978; *New Leader*, November 16, 1971; *New York Times Book Review*, June 16, 1978, July 15, 1979; *Saturday Review*, August, 1978; *New York Review of Books*, August 17, 1978; *New Republic*, August 26, 1978; *Los Angeles Times*, March 22, 1979.†

—*Sketch by Deborah A. Straub*

* * *

WILSON, Beth P(ierre)

PERSONAL: Born in Tacoma, Wash.; daughter of Samuel Deal (a tailor) and Mae (Conna) Pierre; married William Douglas Wilson (a dentist); children: Diane M. Wilson Thomas. *Education:* University of Puget Sound, B.A.; graduate study at University of California, Los Angeles. *Residence:* Berkeley, Calif. 94707.

CAREER: Oakland Public Schools, Oakland, Calif., elementary teacher, 1936-44, elementary assistant, 1945-60; editorial consultant and author, 1972—. Member of Links, Inc., and Jack and Jill of America, Inc. *Member:* National Association for the Advancement of Colored People (life member), National Council of Negro Women, Parent-Teacher Association (life member), Alpha Kappa Alpha. *Awards, honors:* Senior citizens award, 1971, and Cate award from California Association of Teachers of English, 1972, both for *Martin Luther King, Jr.;* Delta Sigma Theta award for published books, 1975.

WRITINGS: *Martin Luther King, Jr.*, Putnam, 1971; *Muhammed Ali*, Putnam, 1974; *The Great Minu*, Follett, 1974; *Giants for Justice*, Harcourt, 1978; *Stevie Wonder*, Putnam, 1979. Also author of *I Like Nighttime* and *Hannibal Jeffrey and the Big Surprise*.

SIDELIGHTS: Beth Wilson has travelled throughout Europe, Canada, Hawaii, Mexico, Scandinavia, and western Africa. Her song, "The Wheel of Life," was recorded on Stax Records, 1978. *Avocational interests:* Youth groups.

* * *

WILSON, Colin 1931-

PERSONAL: Born June 26, 1931, in Leicester, England; son of Arthur (a factory worker) and Anetta (Jones) Wilson; married Dorothy Betty Troop, 1951 (divorced, 1952); married Pamela Joy Stewart (a librarian), 1960; children: (first marriage) Roderick; (second marriage) Sally, John Damon, Christopher Rowan. *Education:* Attended schools in Leicester until he was sixteen. *Politics:* "Moderate right." *Religion:* "My deepest interest is religion. My deepest need—to create my own." *Home and office:* Tetherdown, Gorran Haven, Cornwall, England. *Agent:* Georges Borchardt, 136 East 57th St., New York, N.Y. 10022.

CAREER: Employed by Cranbourne Products Ltd. (wool company), Leicester, England, 1947; laboratory assistant at Gateway Secondary Technical School, 1947-48; tax collector, 1947-49; held various jobs as laborer and office worker; hospital porter in Fulham, England; spent some time in Paris and Strasbourg in the early fifties, working in Paris on *Merlin* and *Paris Review*, 1954; lecturer in American universities. Writer-in-residence, Hollins College, 1966-67; visiting professor, University of Washington, 1967-68, Rutgers University, 1974. *Military service:* Royal Air Force, 1949-50; became aircraftman second grade. *Member:* Society of Authors, Gentleman's Club (St. Austell, Cornwall), Savage Club (London). *Awards, honors:* Ford Foundation grant, 1961.

WRITINGS—Nonfiction: *The Outsider*, Houghton, 1956; *Religion and the Rebel*, Houghton, 1957, reprinted, Greenwood Press, 1974; (contributor) Tom Maschler, editor, *Dec-*

laration, Dutton, 1958; *The Stature of Man,* Houghton, 1959 (published in England as *Age of Defeat,* Gollancz, 1959); *The Strength to Dream,* Houghton, 1962; *Origins of the Sexual Impulse,* Putnam, 1962; (with Patricia Pitman) *An Encyclopedia of Murder,* Putnam, 1962; *Rasputin and the Fall of the Romanovs,* Farrar, Straus, 1964; *The Brandy of the Damned* (essays on music), John Baker, 1964, published as *Chords and Discords,* Atheneum, 1966, published as *Colin Wilson on Music,* Pan, 1967; *Beyond the Outsider,* Houghton, 1965; *Eagle and Earwig* (essays on literature), John Baker, 1965; *Introduction to the New Existentialism,* Hutchinson, 1966, Houghton, 1967; *Sex and the Intelligent Teenager,* Arrow, 1966; (author of introduction) James Drought, *Drugoth,* new edition, Skylight Press, 1966; *Voyage to a Beginning: A Preliminary Autobiography,* Crown, 1969; (contributor) James F. T. Bugental, editor, *Challenges of Humanistic Psychology,* McGraw, 1967; *Bernard Shaw: A Reassessment,* Atheneum, 1969; *A Casebook of Murder,* Ferwin, 1969, Cowles, 1970; *Poetry and Mysticism,* City Lights, 1969, expanded edition, Hutchinson, 1970.

(With J. B. Pick and E. H. Visiak) *The Strange Genius of David Lindsay,* John Baker, 1970, published as *The Haunted Man: The Strange Genius of David Lindsay,* Borgo Press, 1979; *The Occult,* Random House, 1971; (with Piero Rimaldi) *L'Amour: The Ways of Love,* Crown, 1972; *New Pathways in Psychology: Maslow and the Post-Freudian Revolution,* Taplinger, 1972; *Order of Assassins,* Hart-Davis, 1972; (author of introduction) Alexander Garfield Kelly, *Jack the Ripper: A Bibliography and Review of the Literature,* Association of Assistant Librarians (London), 1973; *Tree by Tolkien,* Covent Garden Press, 1973, Capra, 1974; *Strange Powers,* Latimer New Dimensions, 1973, Random House, 1975; *A Book of Booze,* Gollancz, 1974; *Hesse-Reich-Borges,* Leaves of Grass Press, 1974; *The Craft of the Novel,* Gollancz, 1975; *Mysterious Powers,* Aldus Books, 1975, published as *They Had Strange Powers,* Doubleday, 1975, published with *Minds without Boundaries,* by Stuart Holroyd, as *Mysteries of the Mind,* Aldus Books, 1978; *The Unexplained,* edited by Robert Durand and Roberta Dyer, Lost Pleiade Press, 1975; *Enigmas and Mysteries,* Doubleday, 1976; *The Geller Phenomena,* Aldus Books, 1976; (editor) *Dark Dimensions: A Celebration of the Occult,* Everest House, 1978; *Mysteries: An Investigation into the Occult, the Paranormal, and the Supernatural,* Putnam, 1978; *Science Fiction as Existentialism,* Bran's Head Books, 1978; (with George Hay) *Necronomicon,* Spearman, 1978.

Fiction: *Ritual in the Dark,* Houghton, 1960; *Adrift in Soho,* Houghton, 1961; *The Violent World of Hugh Greene,* Houghton, 1963 (published in England as *The World of Violence,* Gollancz, 1963); *Man without a Shadow: The Diary of an Existentialist,* Barker, 1963; *The Sex Diary of Gerard Sorme,* Dial, 1963; *Necessary Doubt,* Simon & Schuster, 1964; *The Mind Parasites,* Barker, 1966, Arkham, 1967, 3rd edition, Oneiric, 1972; *The Glass Cage,* Random House, 1967; *The Philosopher's Stone,* John Baker, 1969, Crown, 1971; *The Killer,* New English Library, 1970, published as *Lingard,* Crown, 1970; *The God of the Labyrinth,* Hart-Davis, 1970, published as *The Hedonists,* New American Library, 1971; *Strindberg: Playscript 31,* Calder & Boyars, 1970, Random House, 1972; *The Black Room,* Weidenfeld and Nicolson, 1971, Pyramid Publications, 1975; *The Schoolgirl Murder Case,* Crown, 1974; *Return of the Lloigor,* Village Press, 1974; *The Space Vampires,* Hart-Davis, 1975, Random House, 1976.

Plays: "Viennese Interlude," 1960; "The Metal Flower Blossom," 1960; "The Death of God," 1966; "Pictures in a Bath of Acid," 1970.

Also editor of *Fiery Angel,* by Valeri Briussov, Spearman, 1976. Editor, "Occult" series, Aldus Books, 1975. Contributor to *Encounter, Time and Tide, London Magazine, Chicago Review,* and other periodicals.

WORK IN PROGRESS: A novel, *Lulu; The Quest for Wilhelm Reich.*

SIDELIGHTS: "On the one hand," Colin Wilson writes, "there is the world, an immense and complex and beautiful place, with enough interests in it to occupy a man for a million years. And on the other hand there is the curious narrowness, the limitedness, of human consciousness." It is this problem and the possible methods of resolving it that form the central concern of Wilson's writing.

Beginning with his first book, *The Outsider,* Wilson has been developing a kind of "optimistic existentialism" to enlarge man's consciousness. "Existentialism," Wilson states, "is the revolt against mere logic and reason. It is a plea for intuition and vision." In *The Outsider,* Wilson discusses those people who see life as chaos and the logical rules of society as false order. "The 'Outsider's' ultimate problem," he writes, "is to become a visionary."

In subsequent books, Wilson has explored various methods of achieving this visionary state, a state he has come to believe is a harbinger of an evolutionary advancement for mankind. He has written of psychological, occult, sexual, and other methods of evoking this evolutionary change. "What Wilson has searched for," Richard Hack writes in *Chicago Review,* "is a path to the human energy centers, the springs of evolution that drive all life, and especially humanity, up to higher levels of consciousness and achievement."

Wilson's books have been published in over fourteen languages.

AVOCATIONAL INTERESTS: Collecting opera records (owns a collection of several thousand); mathematics.

BIOGRAPHICAL/CRITICAL SOURCES: London Evening News, May 24, 1956; *New York Times Book Review,* July 1, 1956, November 15, 1959, March 6, 1960, December 13, 1964, June 14, 1970, January 28, 1973; *Nation,* August 25, 1956, April 16, 1960; *Saturday Review,* September 8, 1956, March 12, 1960, March 20, 1965, January 15, 1972; *Life,* October 1, 1956, December 31, 1971; *Times Literary Supplement,* October 25, 1957, June 14, 1963, February 27, 1964, January 28, 1965, November 6, 1969, February 5, 1971; Kenneth Allsop, *The Angry Decade,* P. Owen, 1958; Tom Maschler, editor, *Declaration,* MacGibbon & Kee, 1959, reprinted, Kennikat, 1972; *New Statesman,* September 5, 1959, March 5, 1960, May 24, 1963, January 15, 1965, December 22, 1978; *Atlantic,* December, 1959, January, 1972, July, 1974; *Christian Science Monitor,* December 24, 1959, September 4, 1969.

New Republic, February 1, 1960, November 22, 1969; *New York Herald Tribune Book Review,* March 6, 1960; *San Francisco Chronicle,* March 13, 1960; *Commonweal,* April 1, 1960; *Chicago Sunday Tribune,* April 10, 1960; *New Yorker,* August 20, 1960, June 3, 1967, November 29, 1969, September 16, 1974; Sidney Campion, *The World of Colin Wilson,* Muller, 1962; James Gindin, *Postwar British Fiction,* University of California Press, 1962; *Time,* May 31, 1963; *Harper's,* November, 1963; *New York Review of Books,* December 31, 1964; John W. Aldridge, *Time to Murder and Create: The Contemporary Novel in Crisis,* McKay, 1966; *Observer,* September 18, 1966; *Punch,* October 5, 1966, May

29, 1974; *Manchester Guardian,* February 9, 1967; *Listener,* February 16, 1967; *Christian Century,* April 5, 1967; *Hollins Critic,* October, 1967; *Magazine of Fantasy and Science Fiction,* January, 1968, August, 1972; Colin Wilson, *Voyage to a Beginning: A Preliminary Autobiography,* Crown, 1969; *Antioch Review,* summer, 1969; *Spectator,* June 28, 1969; *Newsweek,* July 21, 1969.

Books and Bookmen, January, 1970, December, 1971; *Science Fiction Review,* February, 1970; *Book World,* July 12, 1970, March 18, 1973, December 24, 1978; *American Scholar,* fall, 1971; *Economist,* November 6, 1971; *Chicago Review,* winter, 1972; *Choice,* April, 1972; *American Poetry Review,* January-February, 1973; *Critic,* October, 1974; John A. Weigel, *Colin Wilson,* Twayne, 1975; *Contemporary Literary Criticism,* Volume III, Gale, 1975; *Book List,* June 1, 1976; *Wall Street Journal,* June 17, 1976; *Illustrated London News,* October, 1978.

* * *

WILSON, Edmund 1895-1972

PERSONAL: Born May 8, 1895, in Red Bank, N.J.; died June 12, 1972; buried in Wellfleet, Mass.; son of Edmund (a lawyer) and Helen Mather (Kimball) Wilson; married Mary Blair, 1923; married Margaret Canby, 1930; married Mary McCarthy, 1938; married Elena Thornton, 1946; children: Rosalind (first marriage), Reuel (third marriage), Helen (fourth marriage). *Education:* Princeton University, A.B., 1916.

CAREER: New York Evening Sun, New York City, reporter, 1916-17; managing editor, *Vanity Fair* magazine, 1920-21; associate editor, *New Republic* magazine, 1926-31; *New Yorker* magazine, New York City, book reviewer, 1944-48. *Military service:* U.S. Army, 1917-1919; served as enlisted man at Base Hospital 36, in France, and in the Intelligence Corps. *Member:* Charter Club (Princeton), Princeton Club (New York). *Awards, honors:* Guggenheim fellowship, 1935; National Institute of Arts and Letters Gold Medal Award, 1955, for essays and criticism; Presidential Medal of Freedom, 1963; Edward MacDowell Medal, 1964; Emerson-Thoreau Medal, 1966; National Medal for Literature, National Book Committee, 1966; Golden Eagle Award, 1971.

WRITINGS: I Thought of Daisy (novel; also see below), Scribner, 1929; *The American Jitters: A Year of the Slump* (essay collection), Scribner, 1932, reprinted, Books for Libraries, 1968 (published in England as *Devil Take the Hindmost,* Scribner, 1932); *Travels in Two Democracies* (essays and story collection), Harcourt, 1936; *To the Finland Station: A Study in the Writing and Acting of History,* Harcourt, 1940, revised edition, Farrar, Straus, 1972; *Memoirs of Hecate County* (story collection), Doubleday, 1946, revised edition, W. H. Allen, 1958, Farrar, Straus, 1959, reprinted, Octagon, 1979; *Europe Without Baedeker: Sketches among the Ruins of Italy, Greece, and England,* Doubleday, 1947, revised edition published as *Europe Without Baedeker: Sketches among the Ruins of Italy, Greece, and England, Together with Notes from a European Diary: 1963-64,* Farrar, Straus, 1966; *The Scrolls from the Dead Sea,* Oxford University Press, 1955, revised edition published as *The Dead Sea Scrolls: 1947-1969,* 1969; *Red, Black, Blond, and Olive: Studies in Four Civilizations; Zuni, Haiti, Soviet Russia, Israel,* Oxford University Press, 1956; *A Piece of My Mind: Reflections at Sixty,* Farrar, Straus, 1957; *The American Earthquake: A Documentary of the Twenties and Thirties,* Doubleday, 1958.

Apologies to the Iroquois, Farrar, Straus, 1960, reprinted, Octagon, 1978; (contributor) Donald Alfred Stauffer, editor, *The Intent of the Critic,* Peter Smith, 1963; *The Cold War and the Income Tax: A Protest,* Farrar, Straus, 1963; *O Canada: An American's Notes on Canadian Culture,* Farrar, Straus, 1965; *A Prelude: Landscapes, Characters, and Conversations from the Earlier Years of My Life,* Farrar, Straus, 1967; *Galahad* [and] *I Thought of Daisy* (novels), Farrar, Straus, 1967; (with Marianne Moore) *Homage to Henry James,* Appel, 1971; *Upstate: Records and Recollections of Northern New York,* Farrar, Straus, 1971; *The Twenties: From Notebooks and Diaries of the Period,* edited by Leon Edel, Farrar, Straus, 1975; *Letters on Literature and Politics, 1912-1972,* edited by wife, Elena Wilson, Farrar, Straus, 1977; *The Nabakov-Wilson Letters: Correspondence Between Vladimir Nabakov and Edmund Wilson,* edited by Simon Karlinsky, Harper, 1979; *The Thirties,* Farrar, Straus, 1980.

Literary criticism: *Axel's Castle: A Study in the Imaginative Literature of 1870-1930,* Scribner, 1931, reprinted, 1969; *The Triple Thinkers: Ten Essays on Literature,* Harcourt, 1938, revised edition published as *The Triple Thinkers: Twelve Essays on Literary Subjects,* Oxford University Press, 1948, reprinted, Octagon, 1976; *The Boys in the Back Room: Notes on California Novelists,* Colt Press, 1941; *The Wound and the Bow: Seven Studies in Literature,* Houghton, 1941, revised edition, Oxford University Press, 1965; *Classics and Commercials: A Literary Chronicle of the Forties,* Farrar, Straus, 1950, reprinted, 1967; *The Shores of Light: A Literary Chronicle of the Twenties and Thirties,* Farrar, Straus, 1952, reprinted, 1980; *Patriotic Gore: Studies in the Literature of the American Civil War,* Oxford University Press, 1962; *The Bit Between My Teeth: A Literary Chronicle of 1950-1965,* Farrar, Straus, 1965; *A Window on Russia for the Use of Foreign Readers,* Farrar, Straus, 1972; *The Devils and Canon Barham: Ten Essays on Poets, Novelists, and Monsters,* Farrar, Straus, 1973.

Poetry: (With John Peale Bishop) *The Undertaker's Garland,* Knopf, 1922, reprinted, Haskell House, 1974; *Poets, Farewell!,* Scribner, 1929; *Note-Books of Night,* Colt Press, 1942; *Night Thoughts,* Farrar, Straus, 1961. Also author of several poetry pamphlets.

Plays: "The Crime in the Whistler Room," produced in New York City, 1924; *Discordant Encounters: Plays and Dialogues,* Boni, 1926; *This Room and This Gin and These Sandwiches: Three Plays* (contains "The Crime in the Whistler Room," "Beppo and Beth," and "A Winter in Beech Street"), New Republic, 1937; *The Little Blue Light* (produced in Cambridge, Mass., 1950), Farrar, Straus, 1950; *Five Plays: Cyprian's Prayer, The Crime in the Whistler Room, This Room and This Gin and These Sandwiches, Beppo and Beth, The Little Blue Light,* Farrar, Straus, 1954; *The Duke of Palermo and Other Plays, with an Open Letter to Mike Nichols* (includes "The Duke of Palermo," "Dr. McGrath," and "Osbert's Career; or, The Poet's Progress"), Farrar, Straus, 1969.

Editor: F. Scott Fitzgerald, *The Last Tycoon: An Unfinished Novel by F. Scott Fitzgerald, Together with The Great Gatsby and Selected Stories,* Scribner, 1941; *The Shock of Recognition: The Development of Literature in the United States Recorded by the Men Who Made It,* Doubleday, 1943, revised edition, Farrar, Straus, 1955, reprinted, Octagon, 1974; Fitzgerald, *The Crack-Up: With Other Uncollected Pieces, Note-Books, and Unpublished Letters,* New Directions, 1945; John Peale Bishop, *The Collected Essays of John Peale Bishop,* Scribner, 1948; Anton Chekhov, *Peasants and Other Stories,* Doubleday, 1956; (with Malcolm

Cowley) Fitzgerald, *Three Novels* (contains *The Great Gatsby, Tender Is the Night,* and *The Last Tycoon*), Scribner, 1970. Contributor to numerous periodicals.

SIDELIGHTS: As one of the nation's foremost literary critics, Edmund Wilson enjoyed a high position in American letters. L. E. Sissman called him "the greatest of our critics of this century, and among the three or four greatest—along with T. S. Eliot, Wallace Stevens, and F. Scott Fitzgerald—of our literary men." Wilson, according to T. S. Matthews, was "the foremost American man of letters of the twentieth century." Norman Podhoretz judged Wilson as "one of the greatest men of letters this country has ever produced."

Wilson's influence upon American literature was substantial. Warner Berthoff said that "for nearly every important development in contemporary writing Edmund Wilson was in some way a spokesman—an arbiter of taste, a supplier of perspective, at the least (to adapt his own phrase for Hemingway) a gauge of intellectual morale." Leonard Kriegel described Wilson's writing as "one of the standards of sanity in this culture." Despite misgivings about some of Wilson's strongly-held opinions, Berthoff believed that "all who have to do with literature have played parasite to his writings, his discoveries and revaluations, and are too much in his debt to allow much complaining. He has been one of his time's indispensable teachers and transmitters of important news."

One of Wilson's most important contributions was his role in giving an international perspective to American literature. Speaking of this, Sissman praised Wilson for his "destruction of the literary isolationism of this continent." "No man," Anthony Burgess wrote, "has had a profounder influence on the capacity of a couple of generations (including my own) to form its own judgements on a very large and important sector of European literature." A reviewer for *Times Literary Supplement* cited Wilson's "incontestably important task" as "explaining the world to America and explaining America to itself."

Axel's Castle, Wilson's first book of literary criticism, established his reputation as a critic and still stands as one of his most important works. Sherman Paul explained that the book, a study of the Symbolist literary movement, "established the writers of the *avant garde* in the consciousness of the general reader: not only did it place them in a significant historical development, it taught the uninitiated how to read them." Pointing out the book's lasting value, Taylor stated that "it is that rare work that can never really be dated or superceded." Kriegel agreed, writing that "the book remains one of the truly seminal works of literary criticism published in our century."

Wilson's strongly-held opinions were expressed in a manner that drew respect from even those readers who did not agree with him. When reading Wilson, Burgess claimed, one was "enlightened with conclusions that, so well are they stated and so logically arrived at, appear inevitable and hence obvious." George H. Douglas believed that "even when we find [Wilson's] ideas eccentric, perverse, and opinionated, as at times all of his readers must, we cannot but admire his ability to think through all of his problems for himself, his ceaseless endeavor to understand the world that confronts him and bring some order to it." Alfred Kazin wrote that Wilson "fascinates even when he is wrong." Joseph Epstein complained that "the stamp of Wilson's personality was on every sentence he wrote, yet nothing he wrote could by any stretch of the imagination be called 'personable'." Nevertheless, he admired Wilson as "a living embodiment of the belief in literature . . . as a guide to life, and a weapon . . . with which to bring some sort of order to an otherwise possibly quite senseless world."

Wilson's concern with literary values was reflected in his concern for political values as well. "He always retained his strong faith in our American democratic traditions," Douglas wrote, "even though he found the original dream of the founding fathers foundering in a sea of commercial ethics and impersonal, insensate government." After a brief interest in socialism, culminating in *To the Finland Station,* a study of the subject, Wilson grew disillusioned with politics. His writings after the Second World War ignored the contemporary scene. "Having lived through two World Wars in which he did not believe," Robert Emmet Long wrote, "[Wilson could] no longer believe in the power of rationality to create a humane and meaningful world." Despite his disillusionment with politics, Wilson protested the Cold War of the 1950s by not paying his income taxes for nine years on the grounds that the money was used to purchase nuclear and bacteriological weapons.

"Some years before he died," Luckett stated, "[Wilson] attempted an assessment of his own contribution to modern literature, and seemed content to stand on his achievements as an interpreter, explaining the characteristics of the literatures of other nations to readers in the United States. This was absurdly modest." Matthews believed that Wilson's "place in the hall of literary immortals is secure." Summing up Wilson's career, Douglas wrote: "He was not only an imaginative writer of the first rank but a great democratic idealist, and a spokesman for liberal learning in the best sense. And the combination of these virtues produced for us a remarkable body of works which is sure to remain one of the great contributions to American literature of the 20th century."

BIOGRAPHICAL/CRITICAL SOURCES—Books: Alfred Kazin, *On Native Grounds,* Reynal, 1942; Elmer Edgar Stoll, *From Shakespeare to Joyce: Authors and Critics, Literature and Life,* Doubleday, 1944; Kerker Quinn and Charles Shattuck, editors, *Accent Anthology,* Harcourt, 1946; Stanley Edgar Hyman, *The Armed Vision,* Knopf, 1948; F. O. Matthiessen, *Responsibilities of the Critic,* Oxford University Press, 1952; C. I. Glicksberg, editor, *American Literary Criticism, 1900-1950,* Farrar, Straus, 1952; Gilbert Highet, *People, Places and Books,* Oxford University Press, 1953; Kazin, *The Inmost Leaf,* Harcourt, 1955; Murray Kempton, *Part of Our Time: Some Ruins and Monuments of the Thirties,* Simon & Schuster, 1955; John Paul Pritchard, *Criticism in America: An Account of the Development of Critical Technique,* University of Oklahoma Press, 1956; Harvey Breit, *The Writer Observed,* World Publishing, 1956; Robert Graves, *Five Pens in Hand,* Doubleday, 1958; Louis Frailberg, *Psychoanalysis and American Literary Criticism,* [Detroit], 1960; Kenneth Rexroth, *Assays,* New Directions, 1961; Daniel Aaron, *Writers on the Left,* Harcourt, 1961; Kazin, *Contemporaries,* Little, Brown, 1962; Frank Kermode, *Puzzles and Epiphanies,* Routledge & Kegan Paul, 1962; William Goldhurst, *F. Scott Fitzgerald and His Contemporaries,* World Publishing, 1963; Irving Howe, *A World More Attractive: A View of Modern Literature and Politics,* Horizon, 1963; Norman Podhoretz, *Doings and Undoings,* Farrar, Straus, 1964; Sherman Paul, *Edmund Wilson: A Study of Literary Vocation in Our Time,* University of Illinois Press, 1965; John W. Aldridge, *Time to Murder and Create: The Contemporary Novel in Crisis,* McKay, 1966; Edmund Wilson, *A Prelude: Landscapes, Characters, and Conversations from the Earlier Years of My Life,* Farrar, Straus, 1967; Anthony Burgess, *Urgent Copy: Literary Studies,* Norton, 1968; Charles P. Frank, *Edmund Wilson,* Twayne, 1970; Warner Berthoff, *Fiction and Events: Essays in Criticism and Literary History,* Dutton, 1971; Leonard Kriegel, *Edmund Wilson,* Southern Illinois University Press, 1971; Richard David Ramsey, *Edmund Wilson: A Bibliography,* David Lewis, 1971; *Contemporary Literary Criticism,* Gale, Volume I, 1973, Volume II, 1974, Volume III, 1975, Volume VIII, 1978; John Wain, editor, *Edmund Wilson: The Man and His Work,* New York University Press, 1978; Simon Karlinsky, editor, *The Nabakov-Wilson Letters: Correspondence Between Vladimir Nabakov and Edmund Wilson,* Harper, 1979.

Periodicals: *New Republic,* December 12, 1934, June 3, 1936, October 7, 1940, March 25, 1946, June 25, 1962, November 30, 1963, May 9, 1970, January 17, 1976; *Commonweal,* July 8, 1938, December 12, 1952, May 13, 1960, November 5, 1971, July 14, 1972; *Time,* November 13, 1939, May 4, 1962, September 13, 1971; *Newsweek,* March 11, 1946, November 12, 1956, August 30, 1971; *Antioch Review,* December, 1946, summer, 1976; *Furioso,* spring, 1948; *Sewanee Review,* April, 1948; *Nation,* October 16, 1948, December 8, 1956, June 26, 1972, August 7, 1972, October 2, 1972; *New York Times Book Review,* February 9, 1958, March 20, 1960, December 10, 1961, July 2, 1972, July 29, 1973, June 5, 1975, June 8, 1980; *Spectator,* April 25, 1958, May 27, 1960, November 17, 1973; *Times Literary Supplement,* April 25, 1958, June 3, 1960, May 19, 1972; *New Statesman,* April 26, 1958, May 21, 1960, June 22, 1962; *New Yorker,* July 5, 1958, June 24, 1972; *New York Herald Tribune Book Review,* March 13, 1960, December 24, 1961, April 29, 1962; *Saturday Review,* June 4, 1960, April 28, 1962, August 28, 1971; *Atlantic,* December, 1961, May, 1962, July, 1967, September, 1972; *Christian Science Monitor,* April 26, 1962; *Commentary,* August, 1962; *Esquire,* July, 1963, May, 1972; *Books,* May, 1965; *Book Week,* May 9, 1965; *Village Voice,* August 26, 1965, May 26, 1975; *Encounter,* May, 1966; *Virginia Quarterly Review,* winter, 1968; *Bulletin of Bibliography,* May, 1968; *Harper's,* January, 1971, June, 1975; *Wall Street Journal,* September 16, 1971; *New York Review of Books,* October 7, 1971; *New York Times,* June 13, 1972, October 6, 1977; *America,* June 24, 1972; *Prairie Schooner,* summer, 1972; *World,* August 15, 1972; *New Leader,* September 4, 1972; *Progressive,* August, 1973; *Listener,* November 29, 1973; *Texas Quarterly,* winter, 1974; *Books & Bookmen,* March, 1974; *National Review,* September 12, 1975; *Progressive,* December, 1977.†

—*Sketch by Thomas Wiloch*

* * *

WILSON, F(rank) P(ercy) 1889-1963

PERSONAL: Born October 11, 1889, in Worcestershire, England; died May 29, 1963; married Joanna Perry-Keene, March 15, 1924; children: three sons, one daughter. *Education:* University of Birmingham, M.A., 1912, B.Litt., 1913, D.Litt., 1922; Oxford University, postdoctoral study, 1922. *Home:* 30 Cumnor Hill, Oxford, England.

CAREER: University of Birmingham, Birmingham, England, lecturer in English literature, 1919-21; Oxford University, Oxford, England, lecturer, 1921-25, reader in English literature, 1925-29; University of Leeds, Leeds, England, professor of English literature, 1929-36; University of London, London, England, Hildred Carlile Professor of English Literature, 1936-46; Oxford University, professor of English literature, 1947-57, senior research fellow, Merton College, 1957-60, professor emeritus, 1957-63. Visiting fellow, Huntington Library, 1933, 1952-53, 1958; visiting Carnegie Professor, Columbia University, 1943; Alexander Lecturer, University of Toronto, 1943; Clark Lecturer, Trinity College, University of Cambridge, 1951; Turnbull Lecturer, Johns Hopkins University, 1952; visiting fellow, Folger Shakespeare Library, 1957; Ewing Lecturer, University of California, 1958.

MEMBER: British Academy (fellow), Modern Language Association of America, Renaissance English Text Society, Elizabethan Club (Yale University, honorary member), Tudor and Stuart Club (Johns Hopkins University, honorary member). *Awards, honors:* LL.D., University of Birmingham; honorary fellow, Lincoln College, Oxford University.

WRITINGS: (Editor) Thomas Dekker, *The Plague Pamphlets of Thomas Dekker,* Oxford University Press, 1925, reprinted, Folcroft Library Editions, 1970; *The Plague in Shakespeare's London,* Oxford University Press, 1927, reprinted, 1963; *Elizabethan and Jacobean,* Oxford University Press, 1945, reprinted, 1960; *Shakespeare and the New Bibliography,* Bibliographical Society, 1945, reprinted, Oxford University Press, 1970; (editor) Nathaniel Woodes, *The Conflict of Conscience,* Norwood, 1952; *Marlowe and the Early Shakespeare,* Oxford University Press, 1953; *The Elizabethan Theatre,* J. B. Wolters, 1955, reprinted, Folcroft Library Editions, 1976; *Seventeenth Century Prose: Five Lectures,* University of California Press, 1960, reprinted, Greenwood Press, 1976; *The English Drama, 1485-1585,* edited by G. K. Hunter, Oxford University Press, 1969; *Shakespearian and Other Studies,* edited by Helen Gardner, Oxford University Press, 1969; *Shakespeare and the Diction of Common Life,* Folcroft Library Editions, 1970; (editor with William G. Smith) *The Oxford Dictionary of English Proverbs,* 3rd edition (Wilson not associated with previous editions), Oxford University Press, 1970; *The Proverbial Wisdom of Shakespeare,* Folcroft Library Editions, 1977.

SIDELIGHTS: F. P. Wilson, "the most learned Elizabethan scholar in the world," as Helen Gardner once called him, was more interested in the accumulation of primary material in his field of study than in the debates concerning that material's interpretation. "He practiced a high, disinterested, and minute scholarship," Frank Kermode wrote in the *New York Review of Books,* "and commanded an enormous range of information, having done the kind of reading that only a few men in any generation can or will undertake."

BIOGRAPHICAL/CRITICAL SOURCES: Elizabethan and Jacobean Studies: Presented to Frank Percy Wilson in Honour of His Seventieth Birthday, Oxford University Press, 1959; *New York Times,* May 31, 1963; *English Studies,* August, 1963; *South Atlantic Quarterly,* Volume LXVIII, number 3, summer, 1969; *New Statesman,* October 9, 1970; *New York Review of Books,* November 19, 1970.†

* * *

WILSON, Jacqueline 1945-

PERSONAL: Born December 17, 1945, in Bath, England; daughter of Harry Albert (a civil servant) and Margaret (Clibbens) Aitken; married William Millar Wilson (a police sergeant), August 28, 1965; children: Emma Fiona. *Education:* Attended Carshalton Technical College. *Politics:* None. *Religion:* None. *Home:* 1B Beaufort Rd., Kingston-on-Thames, Surrey, England. *Agent:* Rosemary Gould, Laurence Pollinger Ltd., 18 Maddox St., London W1R OEU, England.

CAREER: Journalist. Employed by D. C. Thomsons, Dundee, Scotland, 1963-65; currently free-lance magazine writer. *Member:* Society of Women Writers and Journalists, Crime Writers Association.

WRITINGS—Suspense novels; published by Macmillan (London), except as indicated: *Hide and Seek,* 1972, Doubleday, 1973; *Truth or Dare,* Doubleday, 1973; (contributor) Virginia Whitaker, editor, *Winter's Crimes,* 1973; *Snap,* 1974; *Let's Pretend,* 1976; *Making Hate,* 1977, St. Martin's, 1978.

WORK IN PROGRESS: A teenage novel and radio plays.

* * *

WILSON, Sloan 1920-

PERSONAL: Born May 8, 1920, in Norwalk, Conn.; son of Albert Frederick and Ruch (Danenhower) Wilson; married Elise Pickhardt, February 4, 1941 (divorced); married Betty Stephens, 1962; children: (first marriage) Lisa, Rebecca, David Sloan; (second marriage) Jessica Ruth. *Education:* Harvard University, B.A., 1942. *Office:* Department of English, Rollins College, Winter Park, Fla. 32789.

CAREER: *Providence Journal,* Providence, R.I., reporter, 1946-47; Time, Inc., New York City, writer, 1947-49; assistant director, National Citizens Commission for the Public Schools, 1949-52; University of Buffalo (now State University of New York at Buffalo), assistant professor of English, 1952-55; education editor, *Parents' Magazine,* 1955-57, and *New York Herald Tribune,* 1956-57; free-lance writer, 1958—. Distinguished writer-in-residence, Rollins College, 1980—. Assistant director, White House Conference on Education, 1956. *Military service:* U.S. Coast Guard, 1942-45; became lieutenant. *Member:* Harvard Club (New York), Rogers Rock Club.

WRITINGS: *Voyage to Somewhere,* Wyn, 1947; *The Man in the Gray Flannel Suit* (Literary Guild selection), Simon & Schuster, 1955; *A Summer Place* (Literary Guild selection), Simon & Schuster, 1958; *A Sense of Values,* Harper, 1960; *Georgie Winthrop,* Harper, 1963; *Janus Island,* Little, Brown, 1967; *Away from It All* (autobiography), Putnam, 1970; *What Shall We Wear to This Party?* (autobiography), Arbor House, 1976; *Small Town,* Arbor House, 1978; *Ice Brothers,* Arbor House, 1979; *Crime of the Century,* Arbor House, 1980. Contributor to the *New Yorker, Harper's, Reader's Digest, Life,* and to boating and other magazines.

SIDELIGHTS: Sloan Wilson's *The Man in the Gray Flannel Suit,* referred to by an *Atlantic* reviewer as "one of the great artifacts of popular culture in the fifties," marked the author's first and—with the possible exception of *A Summer Place*—only big success. It was so popular, in fact, that the title became a part of the American language; for many years, its image of the ordinary, upper-middle-class man who works in the city and leaves each day at five p.m. to return to his wife and children in the suburbs was regarded as a metaphor for middle-class America. A *New York Herald Tribune Book Review* critic called *The Man in the Gray Flannel Suit* a "thoughtful, searching novel," while a *Christian Science Monitor* colleague judged Wilson to be "an expert writer. His characters fit that section of extreme civilization which centers on Rockefeller Center and Fairfield County, Connecticut. His dialogue could have been piped from any of thousands of offices or living rooms in those areas. If his novel cannot be called major with capital letters, it is because its subject matter does not cover universal experiences."

"Unlike certain novels of advertising, publishing, and Big Business that have milked sensational aspects beyond all recognition, this one conveys more effect than excitement," writes a *Saturday Review* critic. "It is a consequential novel, if not a definitive one, by a mature writer who knows unwaveringly what he is about." A *San Francisco Chronicle* reviewer notes: "An inexact but rough impression of Mr. Wilson's style is that he writes like a younger, less expert J. P. Marquand. . . . In his calm way, he brings to the mind's eye a man we all know, and most of us rather like."

Others, however, did not find much to praise in *The Man in the Gray Flannel Suit.* A *Commonweal* reviewer, for example, writes: "What is the moral of the novel supposed to be anyway: the self-pitying shall inherit the earth? The sloppily happy ending with its emphasis on material rewards certainly implies no more than that, although Sloan Wilson probably imagined that there was a deal of moral fiber in this story of the faceless man who, as it turns out, is faceless, not because he is Everyman, but because he is no man at all." A *Time* critic brings up a point which has haunted Wilson in his later works as well: the charge that his novels are nothing more than "literate soap operas"—theatrical and extremely conventional. As the *Time* critic notes: "Unfortunately, too much of [*The Man in the Gray Flannel Suit*] verges on upper-middle-class soap opera baited with tune-in-tomorrow-for-the-next-upsetting-episode slickness. Author Wilson has something to say, but his title sums up his book better than his story does."

The Man in the Gray Flannel Suit was filmed by Twentieth Century-Fox in 1956, and *A Summer Place* was filmed by Warner Brothers in 1959.

AVOCATIONAL INTERESTS: Sailing.

BIOGRAPHICAL/CRITICAL SOURCES: *Chicago Sunday Tribune,* July 17, 1955, April 13, 1958; *New York Herald Tribune Book Review,* July 17, 1955, April 13, 1958; *New York Times,* July 17, 1955, April 13, 1958; *Time,* July 18, 1955, April 14, 1958; *Christian Science Monitor,* July 21, 1955, November 2, 1967; *Saturday Review,* July 23, 1955, May 3, 1958, April 5, 1969; *San Francisco Chronicle,* July 25, 1955, April 14, 1958; *New Republic,* August 8, 1955, October 28, 1978; *Commonweal,* August 26, 1955, June 20, 1958; *Catholic World,* September, 1955; *New Yorker,* April 12, 1958; *Spectator,* August 15, 1958; *Manchester Guardian,* August 19, 1958; *Books and Bookmen,* June, 1967; *Best Sellers,* October 1, 1967, April 15, 1969, November 1, 1970, February, 1979; *New York Times Book Review,* October 15, 1967; *Books,* November, 1969, March, 1970; Sloan Wilson, *Away from It All* (autobiography), Putnam, 1970; Wilson, *What Shall We Wear to This Party?* (autobiography), Arbor House, 1976; *Atlantic,* July, 1976; *Washington Post,* December 15, 1978; *New York Times Book Review,* December 9, 1979.

* * *

WILSON, William J. 1935-

PERSONAL: Born December 20, 1935, in Derry Township, Pa.; son of Pauline (Bracy) Wilson; married first wife, Mildred, August 31, 1957; married Beverly Huebner (a manuscript editor), July 31, 1971; children: Colleen, Lisa, Carter, Paula. *Education:* Wilberforce University, B.A., 1958; Bowling Green State University, M.A., 1961; Washington State University, Ph.D., 1966. *Home:* 5228 South Greenwood, Chicago, Ill. 60615. *Office:* Department of Sociology, University of Chicago, 1126 East 59th St., Chicago, Ill. 60637.

CAREER: University of Massachusetts—Amherst, assistant

professor 1965-69, associate professor of sociology, 1969-71; University of Chicago, Chicago, Ill., associate professor, 1971-75, professor of sociology, 1975—, chairman of department, 1978—. Visiting professor at Harvard University, summer, 1972. Visiting scholar-in-residence at Concordia College, 1968. Associate of Institute of the Black World, 1971. Chairman of advisory committee, Chicago Urban League, 1976—, and Lilly Endowment, 1976-78. Member of social sciences research review committee of National Institute of Mental Health, 1972-75; research consultant to Russell Sage Foundation, 1971; member of editorial board, Warner Modular Publications, 1972-75; member of board of university publications, University of Chicago Press, 1975-79. Member of advisory board of Social Science Book Club, 1980—. *Military service:* U.S. Army.

MEMBER: International Sociological Association (member of executive committee on ethnic, race, and minority relations, 1971—), American Sociological Association, Society for the Study of Social Problems, Association of Social and Behavioral Scientists. *Awards, honors:* Grant from National Institute of Child Health Development; Bobbs-Merrill Award, 1963; named distinguished teacher of the year, University of Massachusetts, 1970; Sidney M. Spivack Award, American Sociological Association, 1977.

WRITINGS: Power, Racism, and Privilege: Race Relations in Theoretical and Sociohistorical Perspectives, Macmillan, 1973; (editor with Peter I. Rose and Stanley Rothman) *Through Different Eyes: Black and White Perspectives on American Race Relations,* Oxford University Press, 1973; *The Declining Significance of Race: Blacks and Changing American Institutions,* University of Chicago Press, 1978.

Contributor: Donald A. Read, editor, *New Directions in Health Education,* Macmillan, 1971; Dennis P. Forcese and Stephen Richer, editors, *Social Research Methods,* Prentice-Hall, 1972; Rose, *Nation of Nations: The Ethnic Experience and the Racial Crisis,* Random House, 1972; Edgar G. Epps, editor, *Black Students in White Colleges,* Charles A. Jones Publishing, 1973; James E. Blackwell and Morris Janowitz, editors, *The Black Sociologists: Historical and Contemporary Perspectives,* University of Chicago Press, 1974; John Stone, editor, *Race, Ethnicity and Social Change,* 1977; Hubert M. Blalock, editor, *Sociological Theories and Research: A Critical Appraisal,* Free Press, 1980. Contributor to *University Desk Encyclopedia,* 1977. Also contributor of articles and reviews to professional journals, including *School Review, Journal of Black Studies, Journal of Social and Behavior Scientists, American Sociological Review, Contemporary Sociology and International Review of History and Political Science.* Associate editor of *International Journal of Contemporary Sociology,* 1971-75, *American Journal of Sociology,* 1972-74, *American Sociologists,* 1974-78, *Social Forces,* 1977, and *Ethnic and Racial Studies,* 1977—.

WORK IN PROGRESS: Research on ethnicity, class, and public policy in comparative perspective.

* * *

WINSTON, Daoma 1922-

PERSONAL: Born November 3, 1922, in Washington, D.C.; daughter of Joel (a businessman) and Ray (Freedman) Winston; married Murray Strasberg (a physicist), August 26, 1944. *Education:* George Washington University, A.B. (with distinction), 1946. *Residence:* Washington, D.C. *Agent:* Jay Garon-Brooke Associates, 415 Central Park W., New York, N.Y. 10025.

CAREER: Novelist. *Member:* Authors League of America, Mystery Writers of America, Phi Beta Kappa.

WRITINGS: Doubtful Mercy (poems), Decker Press, 1950.

Novels: *Tormented Lovers,* Monarch, 1962; *Love Her, She's Yours,* Monarch, 1964; *Secrets of Cromwell Crossing,* Lancer Books, 1965; *Sinister Stone,* Paperback Library, 1966; *The Wakefield Witches,* Universal Publishing and Distributing, 1966; *Mansion of Smiling Masks,* New American Library, 1967; *Shadow of an Unknown Woman,* Lancer Books, 1967; *Castle of Closing Doors* (bound with *Night of Evil,* by Genevieve St. John), Belmont-Tower, 1967; *The Carnaby Curse* (bound with *House of Hell,* by Virginia Coffmann), Belmont-Tower, 1967; *Shadow on Mercer Mountain,* Lancer Books, 1967; *Pity My Love,* Belmont-Tower, 1967; *The Traficante Treasure,* Lancer Books, 1968; *Moderns,* Pyramid Publications, 1968; *Long and Living Shadow,* Belmont-Tower, 1968; *Bracken's World No. 1,* Paperback Library, 1969.

Mrs. Berrigan's Dirty Book, Lancer Books, 1970; *Beach Generation,* Lancer Books, 1970; *Bracken's World No. 2: Wild Country,* Paperback Library, 1970; *Dennison Hill,* Paperback Library, 1970; *House of Mirror Images,* Lancer Books, 1970; *Bracken's World No. 3: Sound Stage,* Paperback Library, 1970; *Vampire Curse,* Paperback Library, 1971; *Love of Lucifer,* Lancer Books, 1971; *Flight of a Fallen Angel,* Lancer Books, 1971; *Devil's Daughter,* Lancer Books, 1971; *Devil's Princess,* Lancer Books, 1971; *Seminar in Evil,* Lancer Books, 1972; *The Victim,* Popular Library, 1972; *The Return,* Avon, 1972; *The Inheritance,* Avon, 1972; *Kingdom's Castle,* Berkley Publishing, 1972; *Moorhaven,* Avon, 1973; *The Trap,* Popular Library, 1973; *The Unforgotten,* Berkley Publishing, 1973; *Emerald Station,* Avon, 1974; *Return to Elysium,* Avon, 1975; *The Haversham Legacy,* Simon & Schuster, 1975; *A Visit after Dark,* Ace Books, 1975; *Death Watch,* Ace Books, 1975; *The Golden Valley,* Simon & Schuster, 1976; *The Dream Killers,* Ace Books, 1976; *Pity My Love,* Pocket Books, 1977; *Gallows Way,* Simon & Schuster, 1978; *The Adventuress,* Simon & Schuster, 1978; *Walk around the Square,* Ace Books, 1979; *Mills of the Gods,* Simon & Schuster, 1979; *The Mayeroni Myth,* Pocket Books, 1979; *The Lotteries* (Literary Guild alternate selection), Morrow, 1980. Contributor to *Mirror, Mirror, Fatal Mirror,* 1973. Contributor to *Writer.*

SIDELIGHTS: Daoma Winston wrote *CA:* "I didn't begin a career in writing. I always wrote, and always knew that that would be my major interest in life. I wanted to tell stories about people; their needs hopes and dreams; about their weaknesses and their strengths. When on a book, I work about six hours a day, seven days a week, with small bites of time taken from each day to attend to those chores everyone must deal with."

Winston continues: "I tell aspiring writers who ask me, first of all to read, read, read. Then to write only what they themselves most enjoy reading. And thirdly to make a habit of writing every single day, even if it's only a few words. But I am always uneasy about giving advice to hopefuls. Survival as a professional writer is difficult, demanding emotionally and physically. And publishing today makes it more and more risky for the beginner."

* * *

WINTER, Ginny Linville 1925-

PERSONAL: Born December 11, 1925, in West Lafayette, Ind.; daughter of James Edward Linville (a mechanical engineer) and Nellie (Kendall) Linville; married Munroe Adams

Winter, July 6, 1951; children: Mary Adams, Kendall Linville. *Education:* Attended Art Institute of Chicago, 1943-46, American Academy of Arts, 1946-47, and Illinois Institute of Technology, 1948-50. *Politics:* Republican. *Religion:* Episcopalian. *Home:* 333 Crescent Dr., Lake Bluff, Ill. 60044.

CAREER: J. Walter Thompson Co., Chicago, Ill., artist, 1943-47; free-lance cartoonist and artist, Chicago, Ill., 1947—. Designer of Easter Seal and posters for National Association of Crippled Children, 1960. Has done illustrations for Western Publishing Co., Inc., 1965—. *Member:* Art Institute of Chicago, Chicago Historical Society, Chicago Museum of Natural History. *Awards, honors:* American Institute of Graphic Arts Children's Book Show Award, 1962, for *The Ballet Book;* Layton School of Art Award, 1964, for *What's in My Tree?.*

WRITINGS—Self-illustrated; all published by Obolensky: *The Ballet Book,* 1962; *What's in My Tree?,* 1962; *The Riding Book,* 1963; *The Skating Book,* 1963; *The Swimming Book,* 1964.

Illustrator; all published by Atheneum: *Seeing What Plants Do,* 1972; *How Plants Travel,* 1973; *Grocery Store Botany,* 1974; *More about What Plants Do,* 1975; *How Plants Are Pollinated,* 1975; *The Metric System,* 1976; *Alfalfa, Beans and Clover,* 1976; *Grocery Store Zoology,* 1977. Contributor of poems, stories, and illustrations to *Humpty Dumpty's Magazine.*

SIDELIGHTS: Ginny Linville Winter has done murals for the Lake Forest Hospital Nursery, Lake Forest, Ill., and Condell Memorial Hospital pediatrics ward, Libertyville, Ill. *The Ballet Book* is part of the Kerlan Collection at the University of Minnesota. *Avocational interests:* Ballet and character dancing, skating, riding, doing benefit work for charities and cultural organizations.

* * *

WISEMAN, James R(ichard) 1934-

PERSONAL: Born August 29, 1934, in North Little Rock, Ark.; married Margaret Lucille Mayhue, August 20, 1954; children: James Alexander, Stephen Michael. *Education:* University of Missouri, B.A., 1957; University of Chicago, M.A., 1960, Ph.D., 1966; also studied at American School of Classical Studies, Athens, Greece, 1959-60. *Home:* 60 Browne St., Brookline, Mass. 02146. *Office:* Department of Classical Studies, Boston University, Boston, Mass. 02215.

CAREER: University of Texas at Austin, instructor, 1960-64, assistant professor, 1964-66, associate professor, 1966-70, professor of classics, 1970-73, director of excavations in ancient Corinth, Greece, 1965-72; Boston University, Boston, Mass., professor of classics, 1973—, professor of art history, 1975—, chairman of classical studies department, 1974—, director, Archaeological Studies Program, 1979—. Lecturer in the United States and Canada for Archaeological Institute of America, 1968—; visiting associate professor, University of Colorado, spring, 1970; visiting research professor, American School of Classical Studies at Athens, 1978-79. Member of University of Chicago Isthmian excavation staff in Greece, 1960-61; conducted field surveys in Greece, 1959-72, including archaeological field survey and excavation for American School of Classical Studies and Greek Archaeological Service, 1967; co-director of Yugoslav-American archaeological excavation in Stobi, Yugoslavia, for Smithsonian Institution, 1970—; member of managing committee, American School of Classical Studies (member of executive committee, 1972-76). *Military service:* U.S. Navy, 1952-55; served in Mediterranean and Caribbean theaters.

MEMBER: Archaeological Institute of America (founder and organizer of Central Texas Society; former president; member of executive committee, 1962—; member of national executive committee, 1973-78), Association for Field Archaeology (member of founding committee; member of executive committee, 1970—), Phi Beta Kappa. *Awards, honors:* Woodrow Wilson fellowship, 1957-58; American Council of Learned Societies fellowship to study ancient Corinth, 1967-68, and 1978-79; Ford Foundation grant to train students in archaeological field work, 1968-72; National Endowment for the Humanities grants for archaeological excavations in ancient Corinth, 1968, 1969, and for archaeological research at Stobi, Yugoslavia, 1976-80; Smithsonian Institution grants for excavation in Stobi, Yugoslavia, 1970-75, 1979-80; Guggenheim fellowship, 1971-72.

WRITINGS: (Editor and contributor) *Introduction to Old World Art and Archaeology,* University of Texas Co-op, 1962, 2nd edition, 1967; *Stobi: A Guide to the Excavations,* University of Texas and National Museum of Titov Veles, 1973; (editor with Djordje Mano-Zissi, and contributor) *Studies in the Antiquities of Stobi I,* University of Texas and National Museum of Titov Veles, 1973; (editor with Mano-Zissi, and contributor) *Studies in the Antiquities of Stobi II,* Boston University and National Museum of Titov Veles, 1975; *The Land of the Ancient Corinthians,* Paul Astrom, 1978. Author of "Excavations at Corinth," a series of radio broadcasts, 1967. Contributor to *Encyclopedia Americana* and *Princeton Dictionary of Classical Archaeology.* Contributor of more than a hundred articles, abstracts, and reviews to journals, including *Journal of Field Archaeology, Hesperia, American Journal of Archaeology, Archaiologikon Deltion, Archaeology, Klio,* and *Texas Quarterly.* Member of board of editors, *Vergilius.* Founding editor, *Journal of Field Archaeology,* 1974—.

WORK IN PROGRESS: Editing and contributing to a series of volumes on excavations at Stobi, Yugoslavia. Research for a historical commentary on the *Hellenica* of Xenophon; studying inscriptions from Turkey, Macedonia, and Corinth.

* * *

WISEMAN, T(imothy) P(eter) 1940-

PERSONAL: Born February 3, 1940, in Bridlington, England; son of Stephen (an educational psychologist) and Winifred A. (Rigby) Wiseman; married Anne Williams (a teacher), September 15, 1962. *Education:* Balliol College, Oxford, B.A., 1961, M.A., 1964, D. Phil., 1967. *Home:* 22 Hillcrest Park, Exeter, England. *Office:* Classics Department, University of Exeter, Exeter, England.

CAREER: University of Leicester, Leicester, England, lecturer in classics, 1963-73, reader in Roman history, 1973-76; University of Exeter, Exeter, England, professor of classics, 1977—.

WRITINGS: *Catullan Questions,* Humanities, 1969; *New Men in the Roman Senate 139 B.C.-A.D. 14,* Oxford University Press, 1971; *Cinna the Poet and Other Roman Essays,* Humanities, 1974; *Clio's Cosmetics,* Rowman & Littlefield, 1979. Contributor to *Journal of Roman Studies, Classical Quarterly, Classical Review,* and other journals in his field.

WORK IN PROGRESS: Research in Roman history, literature, and topography.

* * *

WITHERSPOON, Irene Murray 1913- (Irene Murray)

PERSONAL: Born April 4, 1913, in Silvis, Ill.; daughter of

Michael Wallace (a railroad roundhouse foreman) and Grace (Tubbs) Murray; Married Glenn J. Witherspoon (an Air Force chaplain), November 10, 1972 (died, February 19, 1978). *Education:* Attended special writing courses at Northwestern University and American University. *Religion:* Baptist. *Home:* 621 Trail View Lane, Garland, Tex. 75043.

CAREER: Comptometer operator in Rock Island, Ill., 1937-45; secretary in East Moline, Ill., Chicago, Ill., Silvis, Ill., Davenport, Iowa, Bettendorf, Iowa, and High Point, N.C., 1945-57; General Commission on Chaplains, Washington, D.C., assistant editor of *Link* and *The Chaplain,* 1957-72. *Member:* National Secretaries Association (former officer, Thomasville, N.C., chapter).

WRITINGS—All under name, Irene Murray; published by Zondervan: *The Yielded Heart,* 1959; *The Green Olive Tree,* 1962. Contributor of short stories and articles to periodicals.

SIDELIGHTS: Irene Murray Witherspoon told *CA:* "My aim in writing is to study and articulate experiences that have been helpful to me and hope that they also will be helpful to other people. I would like to bring joy and happiness and enlightenment to other people through my own writing."

* * *

WITKIN, Herman A. 1916-1979

PERSONAL: Born August 2, 1916, in New York, N.Y.; died July 8, 1979; son of Abraham and Anna (Baer) Witkin; married Evelyn Maisel, 1943; children: Joseph, Andrew. *Education:* Attended Cornell University, 1932-34; New York University, A.B., 1935, A.M., 1936, Ph.D., 1939. *Home:* 88 Balcort Dr., Princeton, N.J. 08540. *Office:* Psychological Development Research Division, Educational Testing Service, Princeton, N.J. 08541.

CAREER: New York University, New York, N.Y., assistant in psychology, 1936-39; Swarthmore College, Swarthmore, Pa., research associate, 1939-40; Brooklyn College (now Brooklyn College of the City University of New York), Brooklyn, N.Y., 1940-52, began as instructor, became associate professor; State University of New York, Downstate Medical Center, Brooklyn, professor of psychology, 1952-71; Educational Testing Service, Psychological Development Research Division, Princeton, N.J., senior research psychologist and chairman of personality and social behavior research group, 1971-79. *Military service:* U.S. Army Air Forces, 1945-46. *Member:* American Psychological Association.

WRITINGS: Personality through Perception: An Experimental and Clinical Study, Harper, 1954, reprinted, Greenwood Press, 1972; *Psychological Differentiation,* Wiley, 1962; (editor) *Experimental Studies of Dreaming,* Random House, 1967; *Cognitive Styles in Personal and Cultural Adaptation,* Clark University Press, 1978. Contributor to professional journals.

* * *

WITT, Harold (Vernon) 1923-

PERSONAL: Born February 6, 1923, in Santa Ana, Calif.; son of Oscar Solomon (an orange rancher) and Blanche (Talcott) Witt; married Beth Hewitt, September 8, 1948; children: Emily, Eric, Jessamyn. *Education:* University of California, Berkeley, B.A., 1943, B.L.S., 1953; University of Michigan, M.A., 1947. *Home:* 39 Claremont Ave., Orinda, Calif. 94563.

CAREER: Washoe County Library, Reno, Nev., reference librarian, 1953-55; San Jose State College (now Univeristy), San Jose, Calif., reference librarian, 1956-59; free-lance writer, 1959—. Has displayed collages accompanied by poems at several exhibitions, including a one-man show at Trinity Gallery, Berkeley, 1977. *Member:* Poetry Society of America, Phi Beta Kappa, Alpha Mu Gamma. *Awards, honors:* Hopwood Award for poetry, 1947; Phelan Award for narrative poetry, 1960; first prize, San Francisco Poetry Center poetic drama competition, 1963, for "Eros on the Shield"; Poetry Society of America Emily Dickinson Award, 1972.

WRITINGS: Family in the Forest, Porpoise Bookshop, 1956; *Superman Unbound,* New Orleans Poetry Journal, 1956; *The Death of Venus* (Book Club for Poetry selection), Golden Quill, 1958; *Beasts in Clothes,* Macmillan, 1961; *Winesburg by the Sea: A Preview,* Hearse Press, 1970; *Population by 1940: 40,000,* Best Cellar Press, 1971; *Now, Swim,* Ashland Poetry Press, 1974; *Surprised by Others at Fort Cronkhite,* Sparrow, 1975; *Winesburg by the Sea: Poems,* Thorp Springs Press, 1979.

Contributor to anthologies, including: *Eight American Poets,* Villiers, 1952; *A Western Sampler: Nine Contemporary Poets,* Talisman Press, 1963; William Cole, editor, *Erotic Poetry,* Random House, 1963; *The New Yorker Book of Poems,* Viking, 1969; S. Dunning and others, editors, *Some Haystacks Don't Even Have Any Needle,* Scott, Foresman, 1969; Thomas Lask, editor, *The New York Times Book of Verse,* Macmillan, 1970; Jean Burden, editor, *A Celebration of Cuts,* Eriksson, 1974; Lawrence P. Spingarn, editor, *Poets West,* Perivale, 1975; David Kherdian, editor, *Traveling America with Today's Poets,* Macmillan, 1977.

Also author of a play, "Eros on the Shield," and a novel, *Handled with a Chain.* Contributor of poetry to *Atlantic, New Yorker, Saturday Review, Nation, New Republic, Hudson Review, Poetry, Kenyon Review, Poetry Northwest,* and other magazines and journals. Co-editor, *California State Poetry Quarterly,* 1976—, and *Blue Unicorn,* 1977—; consulting editor, *Poet Lore,* 1976—.

WORK IN PROGRESS: The Snow Prince, a book of poems; *Over Fifty,* a collection of sonnets on the subject of aging; *Winesburg by the Sea: Book Two; Witt's Mythology,* poems which personalize or reinterpret the classic myths..

SIDELIGHTS: Harold Witt told *CA:* "I am not a believer in throwing away the past, and I have built my poetry on what has gone before, preferring a memorable music and meaning to disposable lines. I have used old forms for new purposes and have particularly varied the sonnet to make it my own, discovering its confinement of fourteen lines, if not slavishly rhymed, can be almost limitless.

"In *Winesburg by the Sea* I have written a book about growing up in a pre-World War II southern California town, which might be everywhere U.S.A., and its people, sometimes looked back on from the present, sometimes then and there as told by the voices of citizens. It is not only nostalgia but an attempted insight into where we have come from and why we stay the same in spite of changes. If that weren't true the literature of the past would be incomprehensible today, and no one would find Shakespeare or the Greek dramatists as modern as ever. I am continuing to write of the changes and samenesses in a second volume, in which some of the characters age and new ones appear, confronted by today's technology, discoveries and morality, and usually no happier or wiser. The tragedy and comedy remain even if the setting has become more urban than rural and, as advertisers like to boast, the products are 'new and improved.'

"In the past few years I have also become interested in another artform—collage. I have produced many collages which accompany poems, some of which have been published in magazines, some of which have been in shows, and my intention is—if a publisher can be found—to bring out books of poems and collages."

*   *   *

WOLFF, Kurt H(einrich) 1912-

PERSONAL: Born May 20, 1912, in Darmstadt, Germany; came to United States in 1939, naturalized in 1945; son of Oscar Louis and Ida Bertha (Kohn) Wolff; married Carla Elisabeth Bruck, June 11, 1936; children: Carlo Thomas. *Education:* Attended University of Frankfurt, 1930-31 and 1932-33, and University of Munich, 1931-32; University of Florence, laurea (doctorate), 1935; postdoctoral study, University of Chicago, 1943-44, and Harvard University, 1955-56. *Home:* 58 Lombard St., Newton, Mass. 02158. *Office:* Department of Sociology, Brandeis University, Waltham, Mass. 02154.

CAREER: Teacher, Schule am Mittelmeer, Recco, Italy, 1934-36, and Istituti Mare-Monti, Ruta, Italy, 1936-38; Southern Methodist University, Dallas, Tex., research assistant in sociology, 1939-43; Earlham College, Richmond, Ind., assistant professor of sociology, 1944-45; Ohio State University, Columbus, assistant professor, 1945-52, associate professor of sociology, 1952-59; Brandeis University, Waltham, Mass., professor of sociology, 1959-69, Yellen Professor of Social Relations, 1969—, chairman of department of sociology, 1959-62. Visiting professor, College of the Pacific, summer, 1948, New School for Social Research, summer, 1950, Institute of Social Research (Oslo, Norway), 1959, Sir George Williams University, 1965, University of Freiburg, summer, 1966, University of Frankfurt, 1966-67, University of Paris-Nanterre, spring, 1967, York University, 1971, and University of Leeds, June, 1980; senior Fulbright Lecturer, University of Rome, 1963-64; Simon Visiting Professor, University of Manchester, May, 1980. Member of Social Science Research Council summer seminar, Northwestern University, 1952; U.S. Department of State specialist, Frankfurt Institute of Social Research, 1952 and 1953. *Member:* International Sociological Association (chairman of research committee on the sociology of knowledge, 1966-72), International Society for the Sociology of Knowledge (president, 1972—), American Sociological Association (fellow), American Association of University Professors, American Civil Liberties Union. *Awards, honors:* Social Science Research Council fellowship, 1943-44, grant, 1966-67; Viking Fund (now Wenner-Gren Foundation for Anthropological Research) grant, 1947 and 1949; Fund for Advancement of Education faculty fellow, Harvard University, 1955-56; senior Fulbright scholar, La Trobe University (Australia), fall, 1980.

WRITINGS: (Editor and translator) Georg Simmel, *The Sociology of Georg Simmel,* Free Press of Glencoe, 1950; (translator with Reinhold Bendix) Simmel, *Conflict and the Web of Group Affiliations,* Free Press of Glencoe, 1955; (editor, contributor, and translator) *Georg Simmel, 1858-1918,* Ohio State University Press, 1959, published as *Essays on Sociology, Philosophy and Aesthetics,* Harper, 1965; (editor, contributor, and translator) *Emile Durkheim, 1858-1917,* Ohio State University Press, 1960, published as *Essays on Sociology and Philosophy,* Harper, 1964; (editor and contributor) *Transactions of the Fourth World Congress of Sociology,* Volume 4, International Sociological Association, 1961; (editor and author of introduction) Karl Mannheim, *Wissenssoziologie,* Luchterhand, 1964; (editor with Barrington Moore, Jr., and contributor) *The Critical Spirit: Essays in Honor of Herbert Marcuse,* Beacon Press, 1967; *The Sociology of Knowledge in the United States of America,* Mouton, 1967; *Versuch zu einer Wissenssoziologie,* Luchterhand, 1968; *Hingeburg und Begriff,* Luchterhand, 1968; (editor, translator, and author of introduction) Mannheim, *From Karl Mannheim,* Oxford University Press, 1971; *Trying Sociology,* Wiley, 1974; *Surrender and Catch: Experience and Inquiry Today,* D. Reidel, 1976; *Vorgang und immer-waehrende Revolution,* Heymann, 1978. Contributor to symposia and to professional journals. Member of board of directors, *Sociological Abstracts,* 1963—; member of editorial advisory board, *Praxis,* 1966-73, *International Journal of Contemporary Sociology,* 1971—, *Phenomenology and Social Science,* 1973—, and *Annals of Phenomenological Sociology,* 1976-77; member of editorial board, *Sociological Focus,* 1972—.

WORK IN PROGRESS: A book on "Loma."

AVOCATIONAL INTERESTS: Drawing and painting.

BIOGRAPHICAL/CRITICAL SOURCES: Salmagundi, winter, 1978; *Society,* January-February, 1978; *Phenomenological Sociology,* March, 1978; *La critica sociologica,* summer, 1978; *Philosophy and Social Criticism,* spring, 1979.

*   *   *

WOLFSKILL, George 1921-

PERSONAL: Born July 28, 1921, in Alton, Ill.; son of Casper George and Mabel (Haggard) Wolfskill; married Alberta Schnick, 1943; children: Regina, Martha, Jeffrey, Rachel, Sarah, Andrew. *Education:* St. Louis University, B.S., 1941; Baylor University, M.A., 1947; University of Texas, Ph.D., 1952. *Religion:* Baptist. *Home:* 2253 Spanish Trail, Arlington, Tex. *Office:* Department of History, University of Texas, Arlington, Tex. 76019.

CAREER: William Jewell College, Liberty, Mo., associate professor, 1952-55; University of Texas at Arlington, professor of history, 1955—. *Military service:* U.S. Marine Corps, 1942-45; became technical sergeant. *Member:* American Historical Association, Organization of American Historians, Texas Institute of Letters, Alpha Sigma Nu. *Awards, honors:* Piper Professor of the Year Award ($1000 prize) for Texas, 1959; "Texas Writer of the Year" award in general history, Theta Sigma Phi, 1962; Texas Institute of Letters award, 1963; "Teacher of the Year" award, Amoco Foundation, 1976.

WRITINGS: The Revolt of the Conservatives, Houghton, 1962; *All but the People: Franklin Roosevelt and His Critics, 1933-1939,* Macmillan, 1969; *Happy Days Are Here Again!,* Dryden, 1974. Contributor to *Encyclopaedia Britannica* and professional journals.

WORK IN PROGRESS: A Land Worth Saving: The New Deal and the South.

*   *   *

WOLLHEIM, Donald A(llen) 1914- (David Grinnell)

PERSONAL: Born October 1, 1914, in New York, N.Y.; son of J. L. (a doctor) and Rose (Grinnell) Wollheim; married Elsie Balter, June 25, 1943; children: Elizabeth. *Education:* New York University, B.A. *Home:* 66-17 Clyde St., Rego Park, N.Y. 11374. *Agent:* Scott Meredith Literary Agency, Inc., 845 Third Ave., New York, N.Y. 10022. *Office:* DAW Books, Inc., 1633 Broadway, New York, N.Y. 10019.

CAREER: Albing Publications, Inc., New York City, editor, 1941-42; Ace Magazines, New York City, editor, 1942-47; Avon Books, New York City, editor, 1947-52; Ace Books, New York City, vice-president and editor-in-chief, 1952-71; DAW Books, New York City, publisher, president, and editor, 1971—. *Member:* Mystery Writers of America, Western Writers of America (director), Science Fiction Writers of America, British Science Fiction Association, Overseas Press Club, British Model Soldier Society, Burroughs Bibliophiles, Miniature Figure Collectors of America, Count Dracula Society, Twenty-five Year Club. *Awards, honors:* Hugo Award, World Science Fiction Convention, 1963, for book publishing; named to First Fandom Hall of Fame, 1975; Ann Radcliffe Award, Count Dracula Society, 1975; received commendation from 33rd World Science Fiction Convention, 1975, as "The Fan Who Has Done Everything"; and numerous other awards.

WRITINGS—Novels: *The Secret of Saturn's Rings,* Winston, 1954; *The Secret of the Martian Moons,* Winston, 1955; *One Against the Moon,* World, 1956; *The Secret of the Ninth Planet,* Winston, 1959; Bouregy, 1959; *The Mystery Satellite,* Doubleday, 1963.

"Mike Mars" series; published by Doubleday, except as indicated: *Mike Mars: Astronaut,* 1961; . . . *Flies the X-15,* 1961; . . . *at Cape Canaveral,* 1961, published as . . . *at Cape Kennedy,* Paperback Library, 1966; . . . *in Orbit,* 1961; . . . *Flies the Dyna-Soar,* 1962; . . .*: South Pole Spaceman,* 1962; . . . *and the Mystery Satellite,* 1963; . . . *Around the Moon,* 1964.

Other: *Lee DeForrest* (biography), Britannica Press Books, 1962; (contributor) *Editors on Editing,* Grosset, 1962; *Two Dozen Dragon Eggs* (collected stories), Powell, 1969; *The Universe Makers* (nonfiction), Harper, 1971.

Editor of anthologies: *The Pocket Book of Science Fiction,* Pocket Books, 1943; *Portable Novels of Science,* Viking, 1945; *Avon Book of New Stories of the Great Wild West,* Avon, 1949; *The New Avon Bedside Companion,* Avon, 1949, *The Girl with the Hungry Eyes and Other Stories,* Avon, 1949; *Giant Mystery Reader,* Avon, 1950; *Flight into Space,* Fell, 1950; *Every Boy's Book of Science Fiction,* Fell, 1951; *Let's Go Naked,* Pyramid Books, 1952; *Prize Science Fiction,* McBride, 1953 (published in England as *Prize Stories of Space and Time,* Weidenfeld & Nicolson, 1953); *Tales of Outer Space,* Ace Books, 1954; *Adventures in the Far Future,* Ace Books, 1954; *The Ultimate Invader and Other Science Fiction,* Ace Books, 1954; *Adventures on Other Planets,* Ace Books, 1955; *Terror in the Modern Vein,* Hanover House, 1955 (abridged edition published in England as *More Terror in the Modern Vein,* Digit, 1961); *The End of the World,* Ace Books, 1956; *The Earth in Peril,* Ace Books, 1957; *Men on the Moon,* Ace Books, 1957; *The Macabre Reader,* Ace Books, 1959; *The Hidden Planet,* Ace Books, 1959; *More Macabre,* Ace Books, 1961; *More Adventures on Other Planets,* Ace Books, 1963; *Swordsmen in the Sky,* Ace Books, 1964; *Operation Phantasy,* Donald M. Grant, 1967; *A Quintet of Sixes,* Ace Books, 1969; *Ace Science Fiction Reader.* Ace Books, 1971 (published in England as *Trilogy of the Future,* Sidgwick & Jackson, 1972; *DAW Science Fiction Reader,* DAW Books, 1976; *The Best from the Rest of the World,* Doubleday, 1976.

Editor of series: "Avon Fantasy Reader" series, eighteen books, Avon, 1946-52; "Avon Science Fiction Reader" series, three books, Avon, 1951-52; (with Terry Carr) "World's Best Science Fiction" series, seven books, Ace Books, 1965-71; (with Arthur W. Saha) "The Annual World's Best Science Fiction" series, DAW Books, 1972—.

Under pseudonym David Grinnell; all published by Avalon, except as indicated: *Across Time,* 1957; *Edge of Time,* 1958; *The Martian Missile,* 1959; *Destiny's Orbit,* 1961; (with Lin Carter) *Destination: Saturn,* 1967; *To Venus! To Venus!,* Ace Books, 1970.

Contributor of many articles and short stories to popular magazines since 1932.

WORK IN PROGRESS: An anthology of East European science fiction.

SIDELIGHTS: In 1972, after thirty years working as editor and editor-in-chief in the publishing field, Donald A. Wollheim established a new publishing house, using his own initials for its name. DAW Books is a co-publishing venture with New American Library, which is also the distributor for the firm. As Wollheim told Robert Dahlin in an interview for *Publishers Weekly:* "At one time, I thought of branching out into Westerns and mysteries, but the science fiction market is getting stronger. More companies have gotten into the field and there is more science fiction on the stands. And, despite the competition, our sales have slowly gone up."

Throughout his long career, Wollheim has always encouraged new writers. He has edited and published the first novels of many of today's more important science fiction writers, including Ursula K. LeGuin, Marion Zimmer Bradley, Andre Norton, Philip K. Dick, C. J. Cherryh, Samuel R. Delany, and John Brunner.

Wollheim owns and maintains one of the largest collections of science fiction books in the world. His works have been translated into twelve languages.

AVOCATIONAL INTERESTS: Interplanetary flights; collecting and painting model soldiers.

BIOGRAPHICAL/CRITICAL SOURCES: Fantasy and Science Fiction, October, 1968; *Publishers Weekly,* January 20, 1969, March 10, 1977, *Library Journal,* June 15, 1971; *National Review,* November 5, 1971; Damon Knight, *The Futurians,* John Day, 1977; Frederick Pohl, *The Way the Future Was,* Ballantine, 1978.

* * *

WOLSELEY, Roland E. 1904-

PERSONAL: Born March 9, 1904, in New York, N.Y.; son of Enrique de G. and Erminie (Rath) Wolseley; married Bernice Mather Browne, November 28, 1928. *Education:* Attended Schuylkill College (now Albright College), 1923-24; Northwestern University, B.S., 1928, M.S. 1934. *Politics:* Independent. *Religion:* Methodist. *Home:* 1307 Westmoreland Ave., Syracuse, N.Y. 13210. *Office:* School of Public Communications, Syracuse University, Syracuse, N.Y. 13210.

CAREER: Herald-Telegram, Reading, Pa., reporter, 1922-23; *News-Times,* Reading, reporter, 1923-24; *Tribune,* Reading, reporter, 1924; *Daily News-Index,* Evanston, Ill., copy editor, 1927; *Pennsylvania Railroad-News,* Chicago, Ill., editorial assistant to managing editor, 1928-31; *Daily News-Index,* Evanston, 1934-37, began as reporter and copyreader, became managing editor; Northwestern University, Evanston, instructor, assistant professor, 1938-46; Syracuse University, Syracuse, N.Y., associate professor, 1946-47, professor of journalism, 1946-72, professor emeritus, 1972—, chairman of magazine department, 1947-69. Fulbright lecturer, Nagpur University, Nagpur, India, 1952-53. *Member:* Association for Education in Journalism (president, 1948-49), American Association of University Professors, Religion Newswriters Association, Society of Professional Journalists, Sigma Delta Chi. *Awards, honors:* D. Litt., Albright College, 1955; Kappa Tau Alpha citation, 1972, for *The Black Press, U.S.A.*

WRITINGS: (With Bastian and Case) *Around the Copydesk,* Macmillan, 1933; (with H. F. Harrington) *The Copyreader's Workshop,* Heath, 1934; (compiler) *The Journalist's Bookshelf,* Burgess, 1939, 7th edition, Chilton, 1961; (with L. R. Campbell) *Exploring Journalism,* Prentice-Hall, 1943, 3rd edition, 1957; (with others) *New Survey of Journalism,* Barnes & Noble, 1947, 4th edition, 1959; (with L. R. Campbell) *Newsmen at Work,* Houghton, 1949; *The Magazine World,* Prentice-Hall, 1951; *Interpreting the Church through Press and Radio,* Muhlenberg, 1951; (co-author and editor) *Journalism in Modern India,* Asia Publishing House, 1954, 2nd edition, 1964; *Face to Face with India,* Friendship, 1954; *Careers in Religious Journalism,* Association Press, 1955, 3rd edition, Herald Press, 1977; (co-author and editor) *Writing for the Religious Market,* Association Press, 1956; *Critical Writing for the Journalist,* Chilton, 1959; (with L. R. Campbell) *How to Report and Write the News,* Prentice-Hall, 1961; *Understanding Magazines,* Iowa State University Press, 1965, 2nd edition, 1969; (with P. D. Tandon) *Gandhi,* National Book Trust, 1969; *The Low Countries,* Thomas Nelson, 1969; *The Black Press, U.S.A.,* Iowa State University Press, 1971; *The Changing Magazine,* Hastings House, 1973; (with Tandon) *Three Women to Remember,* St. Paul Press, 1975. Contributor to *Encyclopedia Americana, Academic American Encyclopedia,* and others. Contributor of articles to some 250 newspapers and magazines in United States, England, Sweden, and India, including *Christian Science Monitor, Economic Times, Journalism Educator, Cleveland Plain Dealer, Washington Post, Dallas News,* and *Scanorama.*

WORK IN PROGRESS: Book on women magazine editors; *Nansen; Black Deadlines;* new editions of *The Journalist's Bookshelf; Understanding Magazines.*

SIDELIGHTS: Roland Wolseley told *CA:* "One of my strongest motivations for writing is my belief that teachers of journalism and other types of writing are more effective if they can do well what they teach. It does not follow that only those who can do what they teach can be able as teachers, for there are excellent teachers who, nevertheless, are not as competent technically as some of their students. But the teacher-cum-writer is less likely than the unproductive teacher to lose sight of the problems involved in modern writing and therefore is both more practical in teaching and better understands student writers. . . . Another strong motivation is attempting to fill needs for books on communications. Five of my books were the first in their fields, largely because when I searched for a text for some new course I found there was none. So I wrote it. Or joined with others to provide it. These materials were tested for a few years in the classroom before being shaped into books."

BIOGRAPHICAL/CRITICAL SOURCES: Quill & Scroll, December, 1951, January, 1952, April/May, 1969; *Journal of Education,* January, 1952; *The Hindi Udyama,* July, 1953; *Lutheran Magazine,* September 14, 1955.

* * *

WOOD, James (Alexander Fraser) 1918-

PERSONAL: Born September 29, 1918, in Elgin, Scotland. *Education:* Attended Robert Gordon's College, Aberdeen. *Home and office:* 2, Gordon St., Elgin 1V30 1JQ, Scotland. *Agent:* Sterling Lord Agency, Inc., 660 Madison Ave., New York, N.Y. 10021.

CAREER: Employee in whisky distillery, three years; precision engineer, optical instrument specialist, four years; deep-sea fisherman and deck-hand, three years; free-lance writer; currently conducting fresh-water fishery research for the British government. *Military service:* British Army, six and a half years; became warrant officer. *Member:* Imperial Club and Newmarket Club (both Elgin, Scotland).

WRITINGS—All published by Hutchinson, except as indicated: *The Rain Islands,* Duckworth, 1957; *The Sealer,* Vanguard, 1959; *The Lisa Bastian,* Vanguard, 1961; *Cry of the Kestrel,* 1962, reprinted, Remploy, 1980; *Tipple in the Deep* (autobiography), 1962; *Bay of Seals,* 1964, reprinted, Remploy, 1980; *Beer for Christmas* (autobiography), 1964; *Rare Summer,* 1965; *Fire Rock,* 1965, Vanguard, 1966; *Be Thou My Judge,* 1966, published as *Voyage into Nowhere,* Vanguard, 1968; *A Drop of Himself: A Distillation in Four Phases,* 1967; *The Friday Run,* 1967, Vanguard, 1971; *Sport Fishing for Beginners,* Ward, Lock, 1969; *Three Blind Mice,* Vanguard, 1969; *Highland Gathering,* 1970; *Road to Canossa,* 1971; *A Black Horse Running,* 1972, Vanguard, 1977; *Star Witness,* 1972; *North Beat,* 1973; *The Uist Project,* 1973; *The Shop in Loch Street,* Chivers, 1974; *North Kill,* 1975. Also author of radio and television scripts for the British Broadcasting Corp. and for Scottish Television. Contributor to newspapers and magazines in England and Scotland.

SIDELIGHTS: James Wood told *CA:* "I'm a rabid Scottish Nationalist. I hate the Tory Government. And, although I never wear a kilt or play the bagpipes, I sometimes swear violently in the Gaelic when I am drunk." *Avocational interests:* Wildfowling, fly-fishing, ornithology, and drinking.

* * *

WOODCOCK, George 1912-

PERSONAL: Born May 8, 1912, in Winnipeg, Manitoba, Canada; son of Samuel Arthur (a musician) and Margaret Gertrude (Lewis) Woodcock; married Ingeborg Hedwig Elisabeth Linzer (an artist), February 10, 1949. *Education:* Attended Morley College, London, England, 1935-36. *Home:* 6429 McCleery St., Vancouver, British Columbia, Canada V6N 1G5.

CAREER: Worked as farmer and railway administrator; writer, 1946—; University of Washington, Seattle, lecturer in English, 1954-55; University of British Columbia, Vancouver, lecturer, 1956-57, assistant professor, 1958-61, associate professor of English, 1961-63. Editorial adviser for Porcupine Press, 1946-48, and for Canadian Broadcasting Corp. program, "Anthology," 1955-61. *Member:* Royal Society of Canada (fellow), Royal Geographical Society (fellow), Tibetan Refugee Aid Society (chairman, 1962-74). *Awards, honors:* Guggenheim fellow, 1951-52; Canadian Government overseas fellow, 1957-58; Canada Council, travel grants to India, 1961, Asia, 1963, and Kerala, 1965, Killam fellow, 1970, senior arts fellow, 1975; Governor General's Award for Nonfiction, 1967; Molson Prize, 1973; University of British Columbia Medal for Popular Biography, 1973 and 1976. LL.D., University of Victoria, 1967, and University of Winnepeg, 1975; D.Litt., Sir George Williams University, 1970, University of Ottawa, 1974, and University of British Columbia, 1977.

WRITINGS: New Life to the Land: Anarchist Proposals for Agriculture, Freedom Press, 1942; *Railways and Society,* Freedom Press, 1943; *Anarchy or Chaos,* Freedom Press, 1944; *William Godwin: A Biographical Study,* Irving Ravin, 1946; *The Basis of Communal Living,* Freedom Press, 1947; *The Incomparable Aphra,* Boardman, 1948; *The Writer and*

Politics, Porcupine Press, 1948; *The Paradox of Oscar Wilde,* Boardman, 1949, Macmillan, 1950; (with Ivan Avakumovic) *The Anarchist Prince: A Biographical Study of Peter Kropotkin,* Boardman, 1950; *Ravens and Prophets: An Account of Journeys in British Columbia, Alberta and Southern Alaska,* Wingate, 1953; *Pierre-Joseph Proudhon: A Biography,* Macmillan, 1956; *To the City of the Dead: An Account of Travels in Mexico,* Faber, 1957; *Incas and Other Men: Travels in the Andes,* Faber, 1959.

Anarchism: A History of Libertarian Ideas and Movements, Meridian, 1962; *Faces of India: A Travel Narrative,* Faber, 1964; *Civil Disobedience,* Canadian Broadcasting Corp., 1966; *The Greeks in India,* Faber, 1966; *Asia, Gods and Cities: Aden to Tokyo,* Faber, 1966; *The Crystal Spirit: A Study of George Orwell,* Little, Brown, 1966; *Kerala: A Portrait of the Malabar Coast,* Faber, 1967; (with Ivan Avakumovic) *The Doukhobors,* Oxford University Press, 1968; *The British in the Far East,* Atheneum, 1969; *Hugh MacLennan,* McGill-Queen's University Press, 1969; *Henry Walter Bates: Naturalist of the Amazons,* Barnes & Noble, 1969.

Odysseus Ever Returning: Essays on Canadian Writers and Writing, McClelland & Stewart, 1970; *The Hudson's Bay Company,* Crowell Collier, 1970; *Canada and the Canadians,* Stackpole, 1970, revised edition, Faber, 1973; *Mordecai Richler,* McClelland & Stewart, 1970; *Into Tibet: The Early British Explorers,* Barnes & Noble, 1971; *Mohandas Gandhi,* Viking, 1971 (published in England as *Gandhi,* Fontana, 1972); *Dawn and the Darkest Hour: A Study of Aldous Huxley,* Viking, 1972; *Herbert Read: The Stream and the Source,* Faber, 1972; *Who Killed the British Empire?: An Inquest,* Quadrangle, 1974; *Gabriel Dumont,* Hurtig, 1975; *The Canadian Novel in the Twentieth Century,* McClelland & Stewart, 1975; *Canadian Poets, 1960-1973,* Golden Dog (Ottawa), 1976; *South Sea Journey,* Faber, 1976; *Peoples of the Coast,* Hurtig, 1977; *Two Plays,* Talon Press, 1977; *Thomas Merton: Monk and Poet,* Douglas & MacIntyre, 1978; *Faces from History,* Hurtig, 1978; *The Canadians,* Harvard University Press, 1979; *The World of Canadian Writing,* Douglas & MacIntyre, 1980.

Poetry: *The White Island,* Fortune Press, 1940; *The Centre Cannot Hold,* Routledge & Kegan Paul, 1943; *Imagine the South,* Untide Press, 1947; *Selected Poems,* Irwin Clarke, 1967; *Notes on Visitations,* House of Anansi, 1975. Also author of *The Kestrel,* a book of verse, 1978.

Editor: *A Hundred Years of Revolution: 1848 and After,* Porcupine Press, 1948, reprinted, Haskell House, 1974; *The Letters of Charles Lamb,* Grey Walls Press, 1950; *A Choice of Critics,* Oxford University Press, 1966; *Variations on the Human Theme,* Ryerson, 1966; *The Sixties: Canadian Writers and Writing of the Decade,* University of British Columbia Press, 1969; *Malcolm Lowry: The Man and His Work,* University of British Columbia Press, 1971; *Wyndham Lewis in Canada,* University of British Columbia Press, 1971; Herman Melville, *Typee: A Peep at Polynesian Life,* Penguin, 1972; *Poets and Critics: Essays from Canadian Literature, 1966-1974,* Oxford University Press, 1974; *Colony and Confederation: Early Canadian Poets and Their Background,* University of British Columbia Press, 1974.

Author of numerous scripts for British Broadcasting Corp. and Canadian Broadcasting Corp., including "Maskerman," 1960, "The Island of Demons," 1962, "The Benefactor," 1963, and "The Brideship," 1967. Contributor to numerous British and American periodicals, including *Horizon, New Yorker, Saturday Review, New Republic, London Magazine,* and *Encounter.* Editor, *Now,* 1940-47; contributing editor, *Dissent,* 1954—; editor, *Canadian Literature,* 1959-77; contributing editor, *Arts Magazine,* 1962-66. Advisory editor, *Tamarack Review,* 1956-60.

WORK IN PROGRESS: A three-volume autobiography.

SIDELIGHTS: George Woodcock's journeys in Canada, the United States, Mexico, Peru, Egypt, India, Ceylon, Southeast Asia, Japan, Pakistan, Lebanon, Iran, Oceana, and most of Western Europe have resulted in a number of highly-acclaimed travel books. In addition, he has become noted as a poet, essayist, historian, and biographer.

One of his most controversial books is his study of George Orwell. Malcolm Muggeridge calls *The Crystal Spirit,* "far and away the best of the numerous books, essays, and other writings about [Orwell] since his death. There are some interesting and perceptive reminiscences of Orwell whom Woodcock knew well over a number of years, a valuable analysis of Orwell's work, and an attempted statement of his philosophical and political views." And Julian Symons writes: "Mr. Woodcock, ex-anarchist and now free-wheeling radical, has produced an excellent survey of Orwell's ideas, beginning with an account of personal friendship from 1942 onwards and going on to consider the books, the social attitudes, the figure behind them. . . . This lucid exposition conveys very well the things that have made Orwell's work and personality increasingly important since his death in 1950." But many critics find the book lacking, both as a biography and as a study of the writer's works. Tom Nairn says that Woodcock "fails to look critically at the cultural tradition Orwell sprang from, and at the vital relationship between Orwell's work and the political and social realities of his time—surely a major omission in such a committed and moralising writer. . . . It is absurd to be neutral about someone like Orwell. Yet Mr. Woodcock almost manages it." A reviewer for the *Times Literary Supplement* points out several instances in which he or she feels that Woodcock is in error about the details of Orwell's motivation and his talent. The reviewer calls *The Crystal Spirit,* "a doggedly rambling book, sometimes good, sometimes extremely boring, quite often irrelevantly tetchy, at moments plain silly. . . ."

With the exception of some relatively minor criticism, most of Woodcock's historical works have been well received by book reviewers. For instance, Pat Barr writes that, in *The British in the Far East,* the author "swings his wide-screen lens between 1604 and 1961, between Bencoolen and Bangkok, Peking and Penang, Kobe and Kuala Lumpur and has produced a 'lively, fact-packed, colourful panorama,' as they say. He is nimble footed and well informed, focusing now upon the fortunes of Malayan rubber planting, now upon the administration of treaty-port Shanghai, upon the influential careers of Francis Light of Penang, James Brook of Sarawak, Robert Morrison of Canton, upon shipboard life on the early P and Os, the building of Hong Kong, Raffles's grand plans for Singapore, the hierarchies of the Overseas Clubs. . . ." A *Times Literary Supplement* reviewer calls the book "a fascinating pot-pourri of British life in the Orient, covering a period from the first arrival of the East India Company in the early seventeenth century to the traumatic years of the Second World War." Finally, D. J. Enright writes: "The indefatigable George Woodcock displays synoptic gifts of a high order in this handsome account of the British in Hong Kong, Singapore, Malaysia and the treaty ports of China and Japan, from the earliest times up to nearly the latest. Woodcock is fair-minded in a field where fair minds are still rare. . . ."

George Woodcock told *CA:* "I think the uniting feature in

my work has been an immense and zestful and lasting curiosity about the world and the beings who inhabit it; I was aware of this already as a small boy reading the great books of the nineteenth century travellers and naturalists. Related to that curiosity is a desire to understand and empathize, which has led me into the study of Asian philosophies and, if not into fiction, certainly into drama as a means of understanding human motives by personifying them. The curiosity, the striving for empathy, underly my anarchism (a desire to see a society emerging out of natural impulses rather than imposed on them), my perennial urge to wander that has produced so many travel books, and my effort to understand the present through the past that has led me into history and biography. Finally there has been the hope of synthesizing everything through art, which has led me into criticism. The journey is endless; one's curiosity is depthless; one's empathies are never complete. The next stage of the journey—which in terms of writing means the book—is always the important one. The last book immediately finds its way into a cupboard, to be read perhaps years later in curiosity again, about a lost self."

BIOGRAPHICAL/CRITICAL SOURCES: Commonweal, April 28, 1967, April 4, 1969; *Esquire,* May, 1967; *Saturday Night,* June, 1967; *Punch,* June 7, 1967; *Books and Bookmen,* July, 1967, February, 1971; *Times Literary Supplement,* July 13, 1967, July 20, 1967, June 5, 1969, December 11, 1969; *New Statesman,* July 14, 1967; *Listener,* December 28, 1967; *Saturday Review,* January 18, 1969; *Statesman,* March 14, 1969; *Spectator,* November 15, 1969; *Book World,* March 8, 1970; *Canadian Forum,* September, 1970, March, 1971; *Detroit News,* June 25, 1972.

* * *

WOOLF, Harry 1923-

PERSONAL: Born August 12, 1923, in New York, N.Y.; son of Abraham and Anna (Frankman) Woolf; married Patricia Kelsh, 1961; children: Susan D., Alan, Aaron, Sara Anna. *Education:* University of Chicago, B.S., 1948, M.A., 1949; Cornell University, Ph.D., 1955. *Office:* Institute for Advanced Study, Princeton University, Princeton, N.J. 08540.

CAREER: Boston University, Boston, Mass., instructor in physics, 1953-55; Brandeis University, Waltham, Mass., instructor in history, 1954-55; University of Washington, Seattle, assistant professor, 1955-58, associate professor, 1958-59, professor of history of science, 1959-61; Johns Hopkins University, Baltimore, Md., Willis K. Shepard Professor of History of Science, 1961-76, chairman of department, 1961-72, provost, 1972-76; Princeton University, Princeton, N.J., Institute for Advanced Study, director, 1976—. Member of joint committee on health policy, National Association of State Universities and Land Grant Colleges and Association of American Universities, 1976—; member of National Advisory Child Health and Human Development Council, National Institutes of Health, 1977—; Johns Hopkins Program for International Education in Gynecology and Obstetrics, Inc., president and chairman of board, 1973-76, trustee, 1976—. Trustee of Associated Universities, Inc., Brookhaven National Laboratories, 1972—, and Hampshire College, 1977—; member of advisory council, School of Advanced International Studies, 1973-76, and Smithsonian research awards, 1975—; member of visiting committees, department of linguistics and philosophy, Massachusetts Institute of Technology, 1977—, Research Center for Language Sciences, Indiana University, 1977—, and Vanderbilt University Graduate School, 1977—; member of board of governors, Tel-Aviv University, 1977—. *Military service:* U.S. Army, 1943-46; became sergeant. *Member:* History of Science Society (member of executive council), American Association for the Advancement of Science (fellow; vice-president, 1960), Royal Astronomical Society (fellow), Academie Internationale d'Histoire des Sciences (membre effective), Phi Beta Kappa, Sigma Xi. *Awards, honors:* National Science Foundation senior fellowship, 1961-62, and 1965-69.

WRITINGS: The Transits of Venus, Princeton University Press, 1959; *Quantification,* Bobbs-Merrill, 1961; *Science as a Cultural Force,* Johns Hopkins Press, 1964; (contributor) *J. J. Sylvester Symposium on Algebraic Geometry,* Johns Hopkins Press, 1977; *Albert Einstein Centennial Celebration,* Addison-Wesley, 1980. Contributor of articles to professional journals. Editor, *Isis,* 1958-64, and *The Sources of Science;* associate editor, *Dictionary of Scientific Biography,* 1965—; member of editorial advisory board, *The Writings of Albert Einstein,* 1977—.

WORK IN PROGRESS: A history of astrophysics.

* * *

WRIGHT, Charles Alan 1927-

PERSONAL: Born September 3, 1927, in Philadelphia, Pa.; son of Charles A. (a public relations representative) and Helen (McCormack) Wright; married Mary Joan Herriott, July 8, 1950 (divorced, 1955); married Eleanor Custis Broyles, December 17, 1955; children: (first marriage) Charles Edward; (second marriage) Henrietta, Cecily; (stepchildren) Eleanor Clarke, Margot Clarke. *Education:* Wesleyan University, A.B., 1947; Yale University, LL.B., 1949. *Politics:* Republican. *Religion:* Episcopalian. *Home:* 5304 Western Hills Dr., Austin, Tex. 78731. *Office:* School of Law, University of Texas, Austin, Tex. 78705.

CAREER: University of Minnesota, Minneapolis, assistant professor, 1950-53, associate professor of law, 1953-55; University of Texas at Austin, associate professor, 1955-58, professor of law, 1958-65, Charles T. McCormick Professor of Law, 1965—. Member of board of trustees, St. Stephen's Episcopal School, 1962-66; Capitol Broadcasting Association, member of board of trustees, 1966—, chairman, 1969—; Austin Symphony Orchestra Society, member of board of trustees, 1966—, member of executive committee, 1966-70, 1973—; St. Andrews Episcopal School, member of board of trustees, 1971-74, 1977-80, chairman, 1973-74, 1979-80. *Member:* American Bar Association, Institute of Judicial Administration, American Judicature Society, American Law Institute (member of council, 1969—), Order of the Coif, Country Club of Austin, Tarry House, Headliners Club, Century Association, Yale Club of New York.

WRITINGS: Wright's Minnesota Rules, Callaghan, 1954; *Cases on Remedies,* West Publishing, 1955; (with C. T. McCormick and J. H. Chadbourn) *Cases on Federal Courts,* Foundation Press, 4th edition (Wright was not associated with earlier editions), 1962, 6th edition, 1976; *Handbook of the Law of Federal Courts,* West Publishing, 1963, 3rd edition, 1976; (with H. M. Reasoner) *Procedure: The Handmaid of Justice,* West Publishing, 1965; *Federal Practice and Procedure: Criminal,* three volumes, West Publishing, 1969; (with A. R. Miller) *Federal Practice and Procedure: Civil,* ten volumes, West Publishing, 1969-73; *Ships, Footballs, and Other Diversions,* privately printed, 1972; (with Miller and E. H. Cooper) *Federal Practice and Procedure: Jurisdiction,* six volumes, West Publishing, 1975-80; (with K. W. Graham) *Federal Practice and Procedure: Evidence,* three volumes, West Publishing, 1977-80.

WRIGHT, Charles R(obert) 1927-

PERSONAL: Born February 26, 1927, in Pennsauken, N.J.; son of Frank Watson and Elizabeth (Price-Demme) Wright; married Anne Marie Krefft, July 1, 1950. *Education:* Columbia University, A.B., 1949, M.A., 1950, Ph.D., 1954. *Home:* 57 Woodcroft Rd., Havertown, Pa. 19083. *Office:* Annenberg School of Communications, University of Pennsylvania, Philadelphia, Pa. 19104.

CAREER: Columbia University, New York, N.Y., research assistant in Bureau of Applied Social Research, 1951-53, lecturer, 1953-54, instructor in sociology, 1954-56, researcher in Bureau of Applied Social Research, 1954-56; University of California, Los Angeles, assistant professor, 1956-60, associate professor, 1960-65, professor of sociology, 1965-69; University of Pennsylvania, Annenberg School of Communications, Philadelphia, professor of communications and sociology, 1969—, director of research and chairman of doctoral program in communications, 1970-76, associate dean, 1971-72. Visiting lecturer, University of British Columbia, summer, 1962; Organization of American States' Professor at Universidad Catolica, Santiago, Chile, 1963; special researcher, United Nations Research Institute for Social Development, summer, 1965; program director for sociology and social psychology, National Science Foundation, 1967-69. National Center for Health Services Research and Development, member of scientific and technical advisory board, 1967-71, member of publications advisory board, 1969-71; consultant to U.S. Department of Health, Education, and Welfare, 1969-71. *Military service:* U.S. Navy, 1944-46.

MEMBER: International Communications Association, American Sociological Association, American Association for Public Opinion Research (president of Pacific chapter, 1962), Society for the Study of Social Problems, Society for Applied Anthropology, American Association for the Advancement of Science (fellow), Eastern Sociological Society. *Awards, honors:* Research training grant from National Institute of General Medical Sciences, 1963-67.

WRITINGS: Evaluation of Mass Media Effectiveness, Bureau of Applied Social Research, Columbia University, 1955; (with Herbert H. Hyman) *Youth in Transition: An Evaluation of the Contribution of the Encampment for Citizenship to the Education of Youth,* Bureau of Applied Social Research, Columbia University, 1956; *Mass Communication: A Sociological Perspective,* Random House, 1959, 2nd edition, 1975; (with Wendell Bell and Richard J. Hill) *Public Leadership,* Chandler Publishing, 1961; (with Hyman and Terence Hopkins) *Applications of Methods of Evaluation: Four Studies of the Encampment for Citizenship,* University of California Press, 1962.

(With Hyman and Gene N. Levine) *Methods to Induce Change at the Local Level: A Survey of Expert Opinion,* United Nations Research Institute for Social Development, 1966; (with Hyman and Levine) *Inducing Social Change in Developing Communities: An International Survey of Expert Advice,* United Nations Research Institute for Social Development, 1967; (with Hyman and John Shelton Reed) *The Enduring Effects of Education,* University of Chicago Press, 1975; (with Hyman) *Education's Lasting Influence on Values,* University of Chicago Press, 1979.

Contributor: Eric Larrabee and Rolf Meyersohn, editors, *Mass Leisure,* Free Press, 1958; Kimball Young and Raymond Mack, editors, *Readings in Sociology,* American Book Co., 1960, 2nd edition, 1962; Robert O'Brien, Clarence Schrag, and William Martin, editors, *Readings in General Sociology,* Houghton, 1964, 4th edition, 1969; Lewis Dexter and David White, editors, *People, Society and Mass Communication,* Free Press, 1964; Phillip Hammond, editor, *Sociologists at Work,* Basic Books, 1964; Otto Lerbinger and Albert Sullivan, editors, *Information, Influence and Communication,* Basic Books, 1965.

Roland Warren, editor, *Perspectives on the American Community,* Rand McNally, 1966; Murray A. Strauss and Joel I. Nelson, editors, *Sociological Analysis,* Harper, 1966; William Glaser and David Sills, editors, *The Government of Associations,* Free Press, 1966; Peter Rose, editor, *The Study of Society,* Random House, 1967, 2nd edition, 1970; Betty Zisk, editor, *American Political Interest Groups,* Wadsworth, 1969; David T. Kollat and others, editors, *Research in Consumer Behavior,* Holt, 1970; Francis Caro, editor, *Readings in Evaluation Research,* Russell Sage, 1971; Jay G. Blume and Elihu Katz, editors, *The Uses of Mass Communications,* Sage Publications, 1974; Lewis A. Coser, editor, *The Idea of Social Structure: Papers in Honor of Robert K. Merton,* Harcourt, 1975; Alex Inkeles, James Coleman, and Ralph H. Turner, editors, *Annual Review of Sociology,* Annual Reviews, Inc., 1979.

Contributor to proceedings of various organizations; also contributor to *International Encyclopedia of Statistics, International Encyclopedia of the Social Sciences,* and *Grolier's Encyclopedia International.* Contributor of articles and reviews to social science journals, including *American Sociological Review, Journal of Abnormal and Social Psychology, International Social Science Bulletin, Journal of Broadcasting, Teachers College Record, Public Opinion Quarterly, Sociological Inquiry,* and *Sociology of Education. American Sociological Review,* member of editorial staff, 1956-57, associate editor, 1969-73; associate editor of *Pacific Sociological Review,* 1962-64, *Sociological Inquiry,* 1964-67, *Journal of Health and Social Behavior,* 1966-69, and *Sociometry,* 1973-76; member of editorial board, *Public Opinion Quarterly,* 1970—, and *Health and Society,* 1973-75.

WORK IN PROGRESS: Research on personal and mass communications behavior.

SIDELIGHTS: Charles R. Wright's books have been translated into French, Spanish, Japanese, Italian, and Portuguese.

* * *

WRIGHT, George Nelson 1921-

PERSONAL: Born December 10, 1921, in Earlington, Ky.; son of James Nelson and Jennie (Carr) Wright; married Patricia Gilmer, June 8, 1952; children: John Nelson, Elizabeth, Robert James, James Nelson. *Education:* Indiana University, B.S., 1947; Purdue University, M.S., 1954, Ph.D., 1959. *Home:* 492 Presidential Lane, Madison, Wis. 53711. *Office:* School of Education, University of Wisconsin, Madison, Wis. 53706.

CAREER: Missouri Valley Bridge and Iron Co., Evansville, Ind., personnel interviewer, 1942-45; Indiana Division of Vocational Rehabilitation, West Lafayette, rehabilitation counselor, 1947-58; National Epilepsy League, Chicago, Ill., director of national program, 1959-62; University of Wisconsin, School of Education, Madison, lecturer, 1962-64, associate professor, 1964-69, professor of rehabilitation counselor education, 1969—, director of Rehabilitation Research Institute, 1962—. Chairman of research meeting, Twelfth World Rehabilitation Congress, Sydney, Australia, 1972; participant in World Congress on Rehabilitation Medicine, Mexico City, 1974; seminar and discussion group leader; lecturer. Developer and consultant, Rehabilitation Counseling

Program, Bar Ilan University, Israel, 1969—; co-founder and research consultant, Council on Rehabilitation Education. Consultant to Social Security Administration, 1966—; national consultant on rehabilitation, Epilepsy Foundation of America, 1972—; member of advisory council, Public Information Program on Epilepsy, National Institute of Health, and National Institute of Neurological Disease and Stroke, 1972; member of advisory board, Project Skill, Wisconsin Department of Administration, 1974—.

MEMBER: American Psychological Association (fellow), American Personnel and Guidance Association (member of board of directors, 1975-77), American Rehabilitation Counseling Association (president, 1976), National Council of Rehabilitation Counselor Educators (secretary, 1970), National Rehabilitation Association, National Vocational Guidance Association, Wisconsin Epilepsy Association (cofounder; director, 1972—), Sigma Xi. *Awards, honors:* U.S. Office of Vocational Rehabilitation research fellowship, 1958; Silver Medal for Service, Government of Israel, 1969.

WRITINGS: Report on Epilepsy and Handicapping Conditions, White House Conference on Children and Youth, 1960; (with H. H. Remmers) *Handicap Problems Inventory,* Purdue Research Foundation, 1960; (editor with F. A. Gibbs and S. M. Linde) *Total Rehabilitation of Epileptics: Gateway to Employment,* U.S. Government Printing Office, 1962; *Employment Problems of Persons with Epilepsy,* American Electroencephalography Association, 1966; *The Vocational Rehabilitation of the Culturally Disadvantaged,* Research Utilization Conference, Northeastern University, 1968; (with A. B. Trotter) *Rehabilitation Research,* University of Wisconsin—Madison, 1968; (with A. J. Butler) *Rehabilitation Counselor Functions: Annotated References,* University of Wisconsin—Madison, 1968; (with K. W. Reagles and S. Katz) *Rehabilitation in Israel,* B'nai B'rith International (Washington, D.C.), 1974; (editor and contributor) *Epilepsy Rehabilitation,* Little, Brown, 1975; *Rehabilitation,* Little, Brown, 1980.

All published by Rehabilitation Research Institute, University of Wisconsin: (Editor) *Madison Lectures on Vocational Rehabilitation: The Counselor in Our Time,* 1966; (with M. J. Aldridge and A. J. Butler) *A Procedure for Estimating Rehabilitation Need,* 1967; (editor) *Madison Lectures on Vocational Rehabilitation: History and Philosophy, International Aspects, the Big Challenge,* 1967; (editor and contributor) *Wisconsin Studies in Vocational Rehabilitation,* 1968; (with Aldridge) *A Survey of Rehabilitation Need: Preliminary Report on Methodology,* 1968; (with Butler and K. W. Reagles) *The Wood County Project: An Expanded Program of Vocational Rehabilitation,* three volumes, 1969; (editor with Butler and Reagles) *Selected Research Papers from the Wood County Project,* 1970; (editor) *Long-term Success of Rehabilitated Public Welfare Recipients,* 1970; (with Reagles and others) *The Development of a Research-based Mechanism for the Evaluation and Accreditation of Rehabilitation Counselor Education Programs,* 1974. Editor, with Butler and Aldridge, of "Rehabilitation Information" series, nine volumes, 1968.

Author of numerous monographs; also author of papers presented to professional organizations. Contributor of articles to professional journals.

* * *

WRIGHT, Louis Booker 1899-

PERSONAL: Born March 1, 1899, in Greenwood, S.C.; son of Thomas Fleming and Lena (Booker) Wright; married Frances Black, 1925; children: Christopher. *Education:* Wofford College, A.B., 1920; University of North Carolina, M.A., 1924, Ph.D., 1926. *Politics:* Democrat. *Home:* 3702 Leland St., Chevy Chase, Md. 20015. *Office:* National Geographic Society, Washington, D.C. 20036.

CAREER: Newspaper correspondent and editor, 1918-23; University of North Carolina, Chapel Hill, 1926-32, began as instructor, became associate professor of English; Huntington Library, San Marino, Calif., member of permanent research group, 1932-48; Folger Shakespeare Library, Washington, D.C., director, 1948-68; National Geographic Society, Washington, D.C., consultant in history, 1971—. Johnston Research Professor, Johns Hopkins University, 1927-28; visiting scholar, Huntington Library, 1931-32; visiting professor at several universities. Chairman of advisory board, John Simon Guggenheim Memorial Foundation, 1950-71; member of board of directors, Winterthur Museum, 1955-76; vice-chairman of board of directors, Council on Library Resources, 1956—; member of board of directors, Harry S Truman Library Institute for National and International Affairs, 1956—; vice-chairman of board of directors, American Council of Learned Societies, 1958-60; National Geographic Society, trustee, 1964—, member of research committee, 1976—. *Military service:* U.S. Army, 1918.

MEMBER: Modern Language Association of America, Royal Society of Literature (fellow), American Historical Association, American Antiquarian Society, American Philosophical Society, American Academy of Arts and Sciences, Royal Society of Arts (fellow), Colonial Society of Massachusetts, Massachusetts Historical Society, Phi Beta Kappa (senate), Elizabethan Club (Yale); Grolier Club, Century Association (both New York); Cosmos Club (Washington, D.C.); Hamilton Street Club (Baltimore). *Awards, honors:* Guggenheim fellow, 1928-29, 1930; Commonwealth Club of California Gold Medal, 1947, for *The Atlantic Frontier;* Order of the British Empire, 1968; Benjamin Franklin Award, Royal Society of Arts, 1969; honorary degrees from twenty-nine universities and colleges, including Princeton University, Amherst College, University of British Columbia, Northwestern University, University of North Carolina, Yale University, St. Andrews University, Scotland, and University of Birmingham, England.

WRITINGS: Middle-Class Culture in Elizabethan England, University of North Carolina Press, 1935, reprinted, Cornell University Press, 1958; (with Mary Isabel Fry) *Puritans in the South Seas,* Huntington Library, 1936; *The First Gentlemen of Virginia,* Huntington Library, 1940, reprinted, Dominion Books, 1964; *Religion and Empire: The Alliance between Piety and Commerce in English Expansion, 1558-1625,* University of North Carolina Press, 1943, reprinted, Octagon, 1965; (with Julia MacLeod) *The First Americans in North Africa,* Princeton University Press, 1945; *The Atlantic Frontier: Colonial American Civilization, 1607-1763,* Knopf, 1947, published as *The Colonial Civilization of North America, 1607-1763,* Eyre & Spottiswoode, 1949; (contributor) Robert E. Spiller, editor, *Literary History of the United States,* Macmillan, 1948; *The Colonial Search for a Southern Eden,* University of Alabama Press, 1953, reprinted, Haskell House, 1973; *Culture on the Moving Frontier,* Indiana University Press, 1955; *The British Tradition in America,* privately printed, 1955; *The Cultural Life of the American Colonies, 1607-1763,* Harper, 1957; (with others) *The Democratic Experience: A Short American History,* Scott, Foresman, 1963; *Shakespeare for Everyman,* Washington Square Press, 1964; *The Dream of Prosperity in Colonial America,* New York University Press, 1965; *Everyday Life in Colonial America,* Putnam, 1965; (with others) *The Arts in America: The Colonial Period,* Scribner, 1966; (with others) *The American Heritage History of the Thirteen Colonies,* American Heritage Publishing, 1967; *The Folger Library: Two Decades of Growth,* University Press of Virginia, 1968; (with Virginia A. La Mar) *The Folger Guide to Shakespeare,* Washington Square Press, 1969; *Gold, Glory, and the Gospel: The Adventurous Lives and Times of the Renaissance Explorers,* Atheneum, 1970; (with others) *The Renaissance: Maker of Modern Man,* National Geographic Society, 1970; (with Elaine W. Fowler) *Everyday Life in the New Nation,* Putnam, 1972; *Barefoot in Arcadia,* University of South Carolina Press, 1974; *Tradition and the Founding Fathers,* University Press of Virginia, 1975; (with Fowler) *A Visual Guide to Shakespeare's Life and Times,* Pocket Books, 1975; *South Carolina: A Bicentennial History,* Norton, 1976; *Of Books and Men,* University of South Carolina Press, 1976.

Editor: (With others) *Royster Memorial Studies,* University of North Carolina Press, 1931; *Letters of Robert Carter, 1720-1727,* Huntington Library, 1940; (with Marion Tinling) *The Secret Diary of William Byrd of Westover, 1709-1712,* Dietz, 1941; (with H. T. Swedenberg, Jr.) *The American Tradition,* Crofts, 1941; (with Tinling) *Quebec to Carolina in 1785-1786,* Huntington Library, 1943; *An Essay upon the Government of the English Plantation on the Continent of America, 1701,* Huntington Library, 1945; *Newes from the New-World,* Huntington Library, 1946; Robert Beverley, *The History and Present State of Virginia,* University of North Carolina Press, 1947; (with Virginia L. Freund) William Strachey, *The Historie of Travell into Virginia Britania,* Hakluyt Society, 1953; (with Leon Howard and Carl Bode) *American Heritage: An Anthology and Interpretative Survey of Our Literature,* Heath, 1955; (with Tinling) *William Byrd of Virginia: The London Diary, 1717-1721, and Other Writings,* Oxford University Press, 1958; Christopher Marlowe, *Doctor Faustus,* Washington Square Press, 1959; John Webster, *Duchess of Malfi,* Washington Square Press, 1959.

Advice to a Son, Cornell University Press, 1962; Richard Eburne, *A Plain Pathway to Plantations,* Cornell University Press, 1962, reprinted, Folger Library Editions, 1978; (with La Mar) *Life and Letters in Tudor and Stuart England,* Cornell University Press, 1962; (with La Mar) *Four Famous Tudor and Stuart Plays,* Washington Square Press, 1963; (with La Mar) *Four Great Restoration Plays,* Washington Square Press, 1964; *A Voyage to Virginia in 1609,* University of Virginia Press, 1964; *The Elizabethan's America: A Collection of Reports,* Harvard University Press, 1965; *Shakespeare Celebrated,* Cornell University Press, 1966; William Byrd, *Prose Works: Narratives of a Colonial Virginia,* Harvard University Press, 1966; John W. Dodds, *Everyday Life in Twentieth-Century America,* Putnam, 1966; (with Fowler) *English Colonization of North America,* St. Martin's, 1968; (with La Mar) Ben Jonson, *Wolpone,* Washington Square Press, 1970; (with Fowler) *West and by North: North America Seen through the Eyes of Its Seafaring Discoverers,* Delacorte, 1971; (with Fowler) *The Moving Frontier: North America Seen through the Eyes of Its Pioneer Discoverers,* Delacorte, 1972.

"Folger Library General Reader's Shakespeare" series; all by William Shakespeare; edited with Virginia A. La Mar, except as indicated; published by Washington Square Press, except as indicated: (With Virginia L. Freund) *The Life of King Henry the Fifth,* Penguin, 1957; *The Tragedy of King Lear,* Pocket Books, 1957; (with Freund) *The Tragedy of Othello, the Moor of Venice,* Pocket Books, 1957; *The Merchant of Venice,* Pocket Books, 1957; (with Freund) *The Tragedy of Hamlet, Prince of Denmark,* Pocket Books, 1958; *A Midsummer Night's Dream,* Pocket Books, 1958; *The Tragedy of Julius Caesar,* Pocket Books, 1958; *The Tragedy of Macbeth,* Pocket Books, 1959; *The Tragedy of Romeo and Juliet,* 1959; *As You Like It,* 1960; *Twelfth Night; or, What You Will,* 1960; *Richard III,* 1960; *Henry IV, Part I,* 1960; *Henry IV, Part II,* 1961; *Love's Labour's Lost,* 1962; *Coriolanus,* 1962; *Richard II,* 1962; *A Comedy of Errors,* 1963; *The Taming of the Shrew,* 1963; *Much Ado about Nothing,* 1964; *The Two Gentlemen of Verona,* 1964; *The Merry Wives of Windsor,* 1964; *Measure for Measure,* 1965; *All's Well that Ends Well,* 1965; *Cymbeline,* 1965; *The First Part of Henry the Sixth,* 1966; *Troilus and Cressida,* 1966; *The Life of Timon of Athens,* 1967; *The Third Part of Henry the Sixth,* 1967; *Sonnets,* 1967; *The Famous History of the Life of King Henry the Eighth,* 1968; *Pericles, Prince of Tyre,* 1968; *Titus Andronicus,* 1968; *Shakespeare's Poems,* 1969.

Also author of numerous monographs and published lectures. Associate editor, *Journal of the History of Ideas,* 1940-55, *William and Mary Quarterly,* 1944-45, 1958—, and *Pacific Spectator,* 1947-48; editor, *Huntington Library Quarterly,* 1946-48; member of editorial board, History Book Club, 1951—, and John Harvard Library.

SIDELIGHTS: Louis Wright served for many years as director of the Folger Shakespeare Library. During this time, he built the Library's already-vast collection into one of the largest of its kind in the world. More than seventy-eight thousand books from the Sixteenth and Seventeenth Centuries, many of them rare or scarce, were added to the Library's collection under Wright's direction. W. K. Jordan states that "Dr. Wright has made the Folger into a great and famous research library, one of the truly great libraries for scholars in the Western World." In his present position with the National Geographic Society, Wright has traveled extensively in Europe, the Middle East, and South America.

AVOCATIONAL INTERESTS: Fishing, gardening, travel.

BIOGRAPHICAL/CRITICAL SOURCES: Journal of American History, June, 1965, March, 1977; *American Historical Review,* October, 1965; *New York Times Book Review,* February 27, 1966; *South Atlantic Quarterly,* autumn, 1966; *New Yorker,* November 26, 1966; *Atlantic,* December, 1966; *National Review,* December 13, 1966; *Louis B. Wright: A Bibliography and an Appreciation,* University Press of Virginia, 1968; *National Observer,* April 29, 1968; *Times Literary Supplement,* May 29, 1969; *New York Review of Books,* November 5, 1970; *Book World,* November 22, 1970, June 15, 1974; *Washington Post,* December 10, 1970; *Virginia Quarterly Review,* spring, 1971; *New England Quarterly,* March, 1976.

* * *

WRIGHT, Stephen 1922-

PERSONAL: Born November 30, 1922, in New York, N.Y.; son of Martin (a painter) and Yolanda K. Wright; married Sylvia Halpert, May, 1954 (divorced, 1960). *Education:* Long Island University, B.A., 1949; New York University, M.A., 1950. *Residence:* New York, N.Y. *Office:* P.O. Box 1341, F.D.R. Postal Station, New York, N.Y. 10022.

CAREER: Writer. Has held "a long line of jobs, too numerous to mention." *Military service:* U.S. Navy, pharmacist's mate, 1943-46. *Member:* Authors Guild, Authors League of America, Mystery Writers of America.

WRITINGS: *Crime in the Schools* (novel), Contemporary Research Library, 1959; (editor and author of introduction) *Different: An Anthology of Homosexual Short Stories,* Bantam, 1974; *Brief Encyclopedia of Homosexuality,* Steven Wright Press, 1978; "The Greatest Thrill" (play), 1980.

WORK IN PROGRESS: A mystery novel.

SIDELIGHTS: Stephen Wright told *CA* that his advice to aspiring writers is "begin writing at an early age. Get published any way you can, in whatever medium; what you earn is not important at first. Write regular hours, whether after work or weekends (and holidays). Only by writing at specific times or days can you 1) develop the habit of writing, 2) achieve a measure of skill and some knowledge of your craft, and 3) turn out a quantity of work, which is almost always necessary if you ever hope to become a professional writer. Above all, . . . you must be motivated to write, especially if you have to write (as all beginning writers do) in your leisure time, after a hard day or week at work . . . you must think that writing is (one of) the most important things in the world.

"Some say you must consider it a pleasure to write. This attitude is not necessarily a valid one. Writing can be fun but more often it is probably the hardest thing you'll ever do. Try not to think of the possible commercial value of what you are writing; write something that is especially appealing to you, but do write it as well as you can. Get the words down, get the [piece] finished. Revise after you have completed the work. One last word: try to be as original as you possibly can."

AVOCATIONAL INTERESTS: Early silent and sound films, ragtime music, old records (particularly those of Ruth Etting), collecting books (has first editions of Somerset Maugham's work).

* * *

WYND, Oswald Morris 1913-
(Gavin Black)

PERSONAL: Born July 4, 1913, in Tokyo, Japan; son of William Oswald and Anna (Morris) Wynd; married Janet Muir. *Education:* Attended University of Edinburgh, four years. *Home and office:* St. Adrian's, Crail, Fife, Scotland. *Agent:* Curtis Brown Ltd., 60 East 56th St., New York, N.Y.

CAREER: Professional writer. Town Councillor, Crail, Fife, Scotland, 1956-59. Society of Authors representative at booksellers conference, 1964. *Military service:* British Intelligence Corps, six years; became lieutenant; was Japanese prisoner of war; mentioned in dispatches. *Member:* Society of Authors (committee for Scotland), Crime Writers Association, P.E.N. *Awards, honors:* Doubleday prize, 1947, for *Black Fountains.*

WRITINGS—All published by Doubleday, except as indicated: *Black Fountains,* 1947; *Red Sun South,* 1948; *When Ape Is King,* Horne & Van Thal, 1949; *Friend of the Family,* 1950; *The Gentle Pirate,* 1951; *Stars in the Heather,* Blackwood, 1956; *Moon of the Tiger,* 1958; *Summer Can't Last,* Cassell, 1959; *The Devil Came on Sunday,* 1961; *A Walk in the Long Dark Night,* Cassell, 1962; *Death the Red Flower,* Harcourt, 1965; *Walk Softly, Men Praying,* Harcourt, 1967; *Sumatra Seven Zero,* Harcourt, 1968; *The Hawser Pirates,* Harcourt, 1970; *The Forty Days,* Collins, 1972, Harcourt, 1973; *The Ginger Tree,* Harper, 1977.

Under pseudonym, Gavin Black; all published by Harper, except as indicated: *Suddenly at Singapore,* Collins, 1960, reprinted, 1977; *Dead Man Calling,* Random House, 1962, reprinted, Fontana, 1977; *Dragon for Christmas,* 1963, reprinted, 1979; *The Eyes around Me,* 1964; *You Want to Die, Johnny?,* 1966; *A Wind of Death,* 1967; *The Cold Jungle,* 1969; *A Time for Pirates,* 1971; *The Bitter Tea,* 1972; *The Golden Cockatrice,* Collins, 1974, Harper, 1975; *A Big Wind for Summer,* 1975, published as *Gale Force,* Fontana, 1978; *A Moon for Killers,* Collins, 1976, published as *Killer Moon,* Fontana, 1978. Author of television play, "Killer Lie Waiting." Contributor of short stories to *Saturday Evening Post, Woman's Day, Toronto Star,* and other newspapers and periodicals in United States, England, and Europe.

SIDELIGHTS: As the son of missionary parents, Oswald Wynd spent his first 18 years in Japan. He started to write seriously as a Japanese prisoner of war and reckons "that over the years I have turned out about 2,000,000 words—hackwork if you like—keeping us in bread and butter. That subsidizes the more ambitious work."

Generally, Wynd's adventure and suspense books have been well received. He has been commended by a *Times Literary Supplement* reviewer for his "moderation and good sense"; Anthony Boucher notes his books' "happy absence of sex"; Newgate Callendar characterizes the hero of many of the Gavin Black stories as "a thinking man with principles." Martin Levin, who classes Wynd among "blue chip adventure writers," writes of *The Hawser Pirates:* "It has everything a good adventure novel should have: clearly visible personalities, suspense as taut as a tow line, and an exotic expertise unobtrusively spliced into the action." In spite of this, P. L. Marr terms it a "rather feeble attempt," while a reviewer for the *New York Times* notes that Wynd "writes like an intelligent and over-polite visitor from another planet."

D. B. Hughes has few complaints, however. He comments that Wynd's "irresistible social commentary, his inventive characterizations, and his knowledge of the Far East make his books pure joy to read." In a later review Hughes elaborates, "[Wynd] doesn't just develop a pressure plot entangled in suspense, he adds uninfected wit, character, charm, and sharp knowledge . . . to make rereading as keen as the first race-through."

Wynd's novels have been translated into seven languages, and his serials have been sold throughout the world. He also has written for television and radio.

AVOCATIONAL INTERESTS: Japanese color prints, ceramics, gardening.

BIOGRAPHICAL/CRITICAL SOURCES: *New York Times,* March 16, 1947, September 12, 1948; *New York Herald Tribune Weekly Book Review,* March 16, 1947; *Christian Science Monitor,* April 12, 1947; *Catholic World,* June, 1947; *Saturday Review of Literature,* May 5, 1951; *Scottish Daily Express,* May 13, 1961; *Scottish Daily Mail,* November 8, 1961; *Book Week,* September 27, 1964, August 14, 1966; *New York Times Book Review,* July 9, 1967, August 30, 1970, January 14, 1973, June 8, 1975; *Times Literary Supplement,* June 20, 1968, May 1, 1969; *Library Journal,* September 15, 1970; *Best Sellers,* October 15, 1970.†

Y

YANKOWITZ, Susan 1941-

PERSONAL: Born February 20, 1941, in Newark, N.J.; daughter of Irving N. and Ruth (Katz) Yankowitz; married Herbert Leibowitz, 1978; children: Gabriel. *Education:* Sarah Lawrence College, B.A., 1963; Yale University, M.F.A., 1968. *Home:* 205 West 89th St., New York, N.Y. *Agent:* Gloria Loomis, A. Watkins, Inc., 77 Park Ave., New York, N.Y.

CAREER: Writer. *Awards, honors:* Joseph E. Levine fellowship in screenwriting, 1968-69; Vernon Rice Drama Desk Award for Most Promising Playwright, 1969; MacDowell Colony fellowship, 1971; National Endowment for the Arts creative writing fellowship grant, 1972-73, 1979; Rockefeller Foundation grant in playwriting, 1973-74; Guggenheim fellowship, 1975.

WRITINGS—Plays: "The Cage" (one-act), first produced in New York, N.Y. at Omar Khayyam Cafe, 1965; "Nightmare" (one-act), first produced in New Haven, Conn. at Yale University Theatre, 1967; "That Old Rock-A-Bye" (one-act), first produced Off-Off-Broadway at Cooper Square Arts Theatre, 1968; "Terminal" (full-length; published in *Scripts,* October, 1971), first produced Off-Broadway at American Place Theatre, 1969; "The Ha-Ha Play" (one-act; published in *Scripts,* October, 1972), first produced Off-Off-Broadway at Cubiculo Theatre, 1970; "The Lamb" (one-act), first produced Off-Off-Broadway at Cubiculo Theatre, 1970; "Transplant" (full-length), first produced in Omaha, Neb. at Magic Theatre, 1971; "Slaughterhouse Play" (full-length; published in *Yale/Theatre,* summer, 1969), first produced Off-Broadway at Public Theatre, 1971; "Positions" (one-act), first produced in New York, N.Y., 1972; "Boxes" (full-length), first produced in Berkeley, Calif. at Magic Theatre, 1972; "Acts of Love" (full-length), first produced in Atlanta, Ga. at Academy Theatre, 1973; "Wooden Nickels" (full-length), first produced in New York, N.Y. at Theatre for the New City, 1973; "Still Life" (full-length), first produced in New York, N.Y. at Interart Theatre, 1976; "True Romances" (full-length), first produced in Los Angeles, Calif. at Mark Taper Lab, 1978; "Qui est Anna Marks" (full-length), first produced in Paris, France, 1979.

Other: *Silent Witness* (novel), Knopf, 1976; "The Prison Game" (teleplay), produced on "Visions" series, KCET-TV (Los Angeles), 1976; "Milk and Honey" (musical teleplay), produced on "Visions" series, KCET-TV, 1977. Also author of a radio play, "Rats' Alley," 1969, a film story, "Danny Awol," 1969, and a series of monologues in "The Wicked Women Revue," 1973.

Plays anthologized in *New American Plays,* edited by William M. Hoffman, Hill & Wang, 1971, and *Playwrights for Tomorrow,* edited by Arthur H. Ballet, University of Minnesota Press, 1973. Contributor to *Yale/Theatre, African Forum,* and *Performance.*

WORK IN PROGRESS: A second novel; a teleplay on the life of Charlotte Perkins Gilman; a book musical for Broadway production, with Richard Maltby and David Shire.

* * *

YAUKEY, Grace S(ydenstricker) 1899-
(Cornelia Spencer)

PERSONAL: Born May 12, 1899, in Chinkiang, China; daughter of Absalom and Caroline (Stulting) Sydenstricker; married Jesse Baer Yaukey; children: Raymond, David, Jean Yaukey Matlack. *Education:* Maryville College, A.B., 1922; Columbia University, M.A., 1930. *Religion:* Quaker. *Home:* 17204 Quaker Lane, Sandy Spring, Md. 20860.

CAREER: Writer. *Member:* Authors Guild, Authors League of America, Society of Women Geographers, Childrens Book Guild (Washington, D.C.), East and West Association (Washington branch).

WRITINGS—Under pseudonym Cornelia Spencer; juvenile books, except as indicated; published by John Day, except as indicated: *Three Sisters,* 1938; *China Trader* (adult novel), 1940; *Elizabeth, England's Modern Queen,* 1941; *Made in China,* Knopf, 1943, 2nd edition, 1952; *The Exile's Daughter: A Biography of Pearl S. Buck,* Coward, 1944; *The Land of the Chinese People,* Lippincott, 1945, 2nd edition published as *The Land and People of China,* 1972; *Made in India,* Knopf, 1946, 2nd edition, 1953; *The Missionary* (adult novel), 1947; *Let's Read about China,* Fideler, 1948, published as *China,* 1958; *Japan,* Holiday House, 1948; *Nehru of India,* 1948; *Straight Furrow: The Biography of Harry S Truman for Young People,* 1949; *Understanding the Japanese,* Aladdin Books, 1949.

Seven Thousand Islands: The Story of the Philippines, Aladdin Books, 1951; *Romulo: Voice of Freedom,* 1953; *More Hands for Man: The Story of the Industrial Revolution,* 1960; *The Song in the Streets: A Brief History of the French

Revolution, 1960; *Claim to Freedom,* 1962; *How Art and Music Speak to Us,* 1963; *The Yangtze: China's River Highway,* Garrard, 1963; *Made in Japan,* Knopf, 1963; *Ancient China,* 1964; *Pearl S. Buck: Revealing the Human Heart,* Encyclopaedia Britannica Press, 1964; *Keeping ahead of Machines: The Human Side of the Automation Revolution,* 1965; *China's Leaders in Ideas and Action,* Macrae Smith, 1966; *Sun Yat-Sen: Founder of the Chinese Republic,* 1967; *Chiang Kai-Shek: Generalissimo of Nationalist China,* 1968; *Modern China,* 1969.

Also author of *The Low Countries,* Holiday House, and *Akbar,* Row, Peterson & Co., and editor of abridged edition of *My Several Worlds,* by Pearl S. Buck.

SIDELIGHTS: The sister of Pearl S. Buck, Grace S. Yaukey was born in central China and, until 1935, lived in various Chinese provinces. Her writings first appeared in *Asia* magazine and were short stories about China and its people.

* * *

YEE, Albert H(oy) 1929-

PERSONAL: Born June 14, 1929, in Santa Barbara, Calif.; son of George H. (a merchant) and Bertha (Lee) Yee; married Irene Tang (a home management teacher), August 24, 1958; children: Lisa D., Hoyt B., Cynthia R. *Education:* Attended Lingnan University, 1947-48; Santa Rosa Junior College, A.A., 1950; University of California, Berkeley, B.A., 1952; San Francisco State College (now University), M.A., 1959; Stanford University, Ed.D., 1965; University of Oregon, postdoctoral study, 1966-67. *Home:* 3822 Lincoln Rd., Missoula, Mont. 59801. *Office:* School of Education, University of Montana, Missoula, Mont. 59812.

CAREER: Elementary school teacher in Sonoma County, Calif., 1955-59; San Francisco State College (now University), San Francisco, Calif., instructor, 1959-63, assistant professor of education, 1963-64; University of Texas at Austin, lecturer, 1964-65, assistant professor of curriculum and instruction, 1965-67; University of Wisconsin—Madison, associate professor, 1967-70, professor of curriculum and instruction, 1970-73; California State University, Long Beach, professor of educational psychology and dean of graduate studies and research, 1973-79; University of Montana, Missoula, professor of education and dean of School of Education, 1979—. Lecturer, Chinese Academy of Sciences and Chinese Psychological Society, 1980. Chairman, advisory committee to the U.S. Census Bureau for the 1980 Census, 1976—; member of numerous state and national advisory boards; consultant to state and U.S. government agencies, including National Institute of Education, U.S. Office of Education, and Education Commission of the States. *Military service:* U.S. Army, Signal Corps, 1952-55; served in Korea and Japan; became staff sergeant.

MEMBER: American Association for the Advancement of Science (fellow), American Educational Research Association, American Psychological Association (fellow), National Conference on Research in English (fellow), Society for the Psychological Study of Social Issues, Asian American Psychological Association (president, 1979—), Western Psychological Association. *Awards, honors:* U.S. Office of Education research grants, 1965-66, 1970-73; Fulbright lecturer in Japan, 1972; first Fulbright scholar to People's Republic of China, 1972.

WRITINGS: (Contributor) Wayne Otto and Karl Koenke, editors, *Remedial Teaching,* Houghton, 1969; (contributor) M. Vere DeVault, editor, *Research, Development and the Classroom Teacher Producer/Consumer,* Association for Childhood Education International, 1970; (editor) *Social Interaction in Educational Settings,* Prentice-Hall, 1971; (with Carl Personke) *Comprehensive Spelling Instruction: Theory, Research and Application,* International Publishing Co., 1971; (editor) *Perspectives on Management Systems Approaches in Education: A Symposium,* Educational Technology Publications, 1973; (contributor) Dwight Allen and Jeffrey Hecht, editors, *Controversies in Education,* Saunders, 1974. Work represented in anthologies, including *Issues and Problems in the Elementary Language Arts,* Allyn & Bacon, 1968. Contributor to proceedings. Contributor of more than seventy-five articles to education and psychology journals. Consultant to *Review of Educational Research, American Psychologist, Educational Researcher, Chinese Education, Peace and Change,* and *Journal of Educational Psychology.*

* * *

YEP, Laurence Michael 1948-

PERSONAL: Born June 14, 1948, in San Francisco, Calif.; son of Thomas Gim (a postal clerk) and Franche (Lee) Yep. *Education:* Attended Marquette University, 1966-68; University of California, Santa Cruz, B.A., 1970; State University of New York at Buffalo, Ph.D., 1975. *Home:* 921 Populus Pl., Sunnyvale, Calif. 94086. *Agent:* Pat Berens, Sterling Lord Agency, 660 Madison Ave., New York, N.Y. 10021.

CAREER: Writer. *Awards, honors:* Book-of-the-Month Club writing fellowship, 1970.

WRITINGS—Juvenile novels, except as indicated; all published by Harper: *Sweetwater,* 1973; *Dragonwings,* 1975; *Child of the Owl,* 1977; *Seademons* (adult novel), 1977; *Sea Glass,* 1979; *The Green Darkness,* 1980.

Work is represented in anthologies, including: *World's Best Science Fiction of 1969,* edited by Donald A. Wollheim and Terry Carr, Gollancz, 1969; *Quark Number Two,* edited by Samuel Delaney and Marilyn Hacker, Paperback Library, 1971; *Protostars,* edited by David Gerrold, Ballantine, 1971; *Strange Bedfellows: Sex and Science Fiction,* edited by Thomas N. Scortia, Random House, 1973; *The Demon Children,* Avon, 1973.

WORK IN PROGRESS: Of Bones Are Coral Made, an adult novel.

BIOGRAPHICAL/CRITICAL SOURCES: Francelia Butler, editor, *Children's Literature: Annual of the Modern Language Association Seminar on Children's Literature and the Children's Literature Association,* Temple University Press, 1975; *New York Times Book Review,* November 16, 1975, May 22, 1977; *Vector 78,* November-December, 1976; *Reading Teacher,* January, 1977; *Book World,* May 1, 1977; *Children's Literature Review,* Volume III, Gale, 1978.

* * *

YIN, Robert K(uo-zuir) 1941-

PERSONAL: Born March 31, 1941, in New York, N.Y. *Education:* Harvard University, B.A., 1962; Massachusetts Institute of Technology, Ph.D., 1970. *Office:* Massachusetts Institute of Technology, Building 10, Room 485, Cambridge, Mass. 02139; and 1527 New Hampshire Ave. N.W., Washington, D.C. 20036.

CAREER: Rand Corporation, Washington, D.C., research psychologist, 1970-78; Massachusetts Institute of Technology, Cambridge, assistant professor, beginning 1972, currently visiting associate professor of urban studies and planning; independent consultant, 1978—.

WRITINGS: (Editor) *The City in the Seventies,* F. E. Peacock, 1972; (editor) *Race, Creed, Color, or National Origin,* F. E. Peacock, 1973; *Street-Level Governments,* Lexington Books, 1975; *Changing Urban Bureaucracies,* Lexington Books, 1979; *Improving America's Neighborhoods,* Plenum, in press.

WORK IN PROGRESS: Urban policy research.

* * *

YLVISAKER, Paul 1921-

PERSONAL: Born November 28, 1921, in St. Paul, Minn.; son of Sigurd C. and Norma (Norem) Ylvisaker; married Barbara Ewing; children: Elizabeth, Mark, Peter, David. *Education:* Bethany Lutheran College, A.A., 1940; Mankato State College, B.S., 1942; University of Minnesota, additional study, 1942-43; Harvard University, M.P.A., 1945, Ph.D., 1948. *Home:* 18 Hilliard St., Cambridge, Mass. 02138. *Office:* Graduate School of Education, Longfellow Hall, Harvard University, Cambridge, Mass. 02138.

CAREER: Bethany Lutheran College, Mankato, Minn., instructor, 1942, 1943-44; Harvard University, Cambridge, Mass., tutor and instructor in department of government, 1945-48; Swarthmore College, Swarthmore, Pa., assistant professor, 1948-53, associate professor of political science, 1953-55; executive secretary and consultant to the mayor of Philadelphia, Philadelphia, Pa., 1954-55; Ford Foundation, Public Affairs Program, New York, N.Y., executive associate, 1955-58, associate director, 1958-59, director, 1959-67; commissioner, New Jersey Department of Community Affairs, 1967-70; Princeton University, Princeton, N.J., professor of public affairs and urban planning, 1970-72; Harvard University, Graduate School of Education, Charles William Eliot Professor of Education and dean of faculty, 1972—. Visiting professor at Princeton University, 1961-62, 1965-66, Harvard University, 1968-69, and Yale University, 1970-71. Member of health exchange mission to U.S.S.R. for U.S. Public Health Service, 1964, Blue Earth County Council on Inter-governmental Relations, 1943-46, and United Nation's team of advisers to Japan on planning of Hanshin metropolitan region, 1960, 1964. Member of board and advisory boards of numerous companies, organizations, and foundations. *Awards, honors:* D.H.L. from New York Medical College, 1967, Princeton University, 1970, and Jersey City State College, 1978; LL.D. from St. Peter's College, 1968, Bloomfield College, 1968, Upsala College, 1969, and Swarthmore College, 1978.

WRITINGS: *Battle of Blue Earth County,* Alabama University Press, 1949, revised edition, 1955; *The Natural Cement Controversy,* Alabama University Press, 1950; *Inter-governmental Relations at the Grassroots,* University of Minnesota Press, 1956; (contributor) *Area and Power,* Free Press of Glencoe, 1960; (contributor) *America 1980,* U.S. Department of Agriculture, 1965; (contributor) *The Environment, the University, and the Welfare of Man,* Pitman Medical, 1969; (contributor) *Agenda for Survival,* Yale University Press, 1971; (author of introduction) Milton Viorst, *The Citizen Poor of the 1960's: An Examination into a Social Experiment,* Kettering Foundation, 1977; (author of introduction) M. Carter McFarland, *Federal Government and Urban Problems,* Westview Press, 1978. Editor with Martin Meyerson, *Metropolis in Ferment,* 1957. Contributor of articles to *Life, American Institute of Planning Journal, National Municipal Review, Saturday Review,* and other periodicals.

YORKE, Susan 1915-

PERSONAL: Original name, Suzette Telenga; name legally changed; born March 24, 1915, in Mannheim, Germany. *Education:* Vassar College, B.A., 1936; additional study at New School for Social Research, 1937-39, University of Hamburg, 1939, University of Chicago, 1940, University of Buenos Aires, 1942, and Sorbonne, University of Paris. *Home:* 422/290 Jersey Rd., Woollahra, New South Wales 2025, Australia.

CAREER: Author. *Member:* P.E.N. International (secretary), Australia Society of Authors, Fellowship of Australian Writers, Society of Women Writers Australia (co-president).

WRITINGS—Novels: *The Widow,* Harcourt, 1950; *Naked to Mine Enemies,* Harcourt, 1952; *Freighter,* Day, 1956; *Poule de Luxe,* Macdonald & Co., 1956; *The Seduction,* Farrar, Straus, 1960; *The Time and the Place,* Macdonald & Co., 1960; *Agency House Malaya,* Farrar, Straus, 1961; *Captain China,* Macdonald & Co., 1961; *Star Sapphire,* Macdonald & Co., 1966; *The Adventuress,* Macdonald & Co., 1966.

Plays: "My Country Right or Left" (musical satire), first produced Off-Broadway, 1935; "Freighter" (based on Yorke's novel of same title), first produced in Sydney, Australia, 1977. Contributor of stories, book reviews, and articles to numerous magazines in United States, United Kingdom, Europe, South America, Canada, Australia, Malaysia, Africa, and Mexico.

SIDELIGHTS: Susan Yorke was born in a German prisoner of war camp. Her parents were Belgian and Dutch.

The Widow was made into a movie in 1954. Many of Yorke's books have been published in other languages including French, Italian, Spanish, and German.

* * *

YOUNG, John 1920-

PERSONAL: Born March 6, 1920, in Tientsin, China; naturalized U.S. citizen; son of Samuel and Helen (Han) Yang; married Elizabeth Jen, July 1, 1949 (died February, 1957); married Peggy Chang (a professor), March 1, 1960; children: (first marriage) Alice (Mrs. Glenn LauKee), Peter, Nancy. *Education:* Tokyo Imperial University, B.A., 1942; Georgetown University, B.S.F.S., 1949, M.S.F.S., 1951; Johns Hopkins University, Ph.D., 1955. *Home:* 377 North Wyoming Ave., South Orange, N.J. 07079. *Office:* Institute of Far Eastern Studies, Seton Hall University, South Orange, N.J. 07079.

CAREER: Republic of China, Ministry of Foreign Affairs, foreign service officer, 1942-46; Chinese Delegation to Far East Commission, delegate and secretary, 1946-51; Georgetown University, Washington, D.C., lecturer, 1951-56, assistant professor, 1956-60, associate professor of Japanese history and language, 1960-62; University of Maryland, College Park, professor of languages, 1962-64; University of Hawaii, Honolulu, professor in department of Asian and Pacific languages, 1964-74, chairman of department, 1964-70; Seton Hall University, South Orange, N.J., professor of Asian studies, 1974—, chairman of department, 1974-78, director of Institute of Far Eastern Studies, 1978—. Training instructor and language supervisor, Foreign Service Institute, U.S. Department of State, 1960-61; member, University Seminar, Columbia University, 1960—.

MEMBER: Chinese Language Teachers Association (member of board of directors, 1967-70; president, 1969-70), Association for Teachers of Japanese (member of executive committee, 1970-73), American Council on the Teaching of Foreign Languages (member of executive council, 1971-74), American Oriental Society, Kokugo Gakkai, Linguistic Society of Japan, Association for Asian Studies, Modern Language Association of America, Nihongo Kyoiku Gakkai, National Association for Bilingual Education, National Association for Asian American and Pacific Education, Linguistic Circle of Tokyo, Pacific Area Inter-Collegiate Council on Asian Studies (member of executive committee, 1967-70), P.E.N. (secretary treasurer of Hawaii Center, 1971-74), New Jersey State Advisory Committee on Bilingual Education (member of council, 1976-78). *Awards, honors:* Ford Foundation grants, 1958, 1959-60; East-West Center senior fellow, 1966-67; U.S. Office of Education grants.

WRITINGS: The Location of Yamatai: A Case Study of Japanese Historiography, 720-1945, Johns Hopkins Press, 1957; *Checklist of Microfilmed Reproduction of Selected Archives of the Japanese Army, Navy and Other Government Agencies, 1868-1945,* Georgetown University Press, 1959; (with Kyochahn Rhee, Young-Sook Lee, and Byounghye Chang) *Learn Korean: Pattern Approach,* four volumes, University of Maryland, 1963-64; *The Research Activities of the South Manchurian Railway Company, 1907-45,* Columbia University, 1966; (with Kimiko Nakajimo) *Learn Japanese: Pattern Approach,* four volumes, East-West Center, 1967-68; (with Nagashima Fukutaro) *Tradional Air of Japanese Chanoyu,* Tanko-Shinsha (Kyoto), 1968; (with Nobuko Hasegawa, Bernice Hirai, Kazuko Tsuruoka, and Janet Fong) *Learn Japanese: Secondary School Text,* eight volumes, Tongg Publishing, 1969-71; (with Yaeko Habein, Amy Takayesu, and Edward Smith) *Learn Japanese: Elementary School Text,* eight volumes, Tongg Publishing, 1969-71; (with M. Hashimoto, M. P. Hagiwara, and E. Sato) *Teachers Manual for Learn Japanese Series and Accompanying Materials,* University of Hawaii, 1971; (with Kimiko Nakajima) *Learn Japanese: Cultural Material for College Text,* four volumes, CALM, 1972. Contributor to professional journals. Asian books review editor, *Modern Language Journal,* 1971-77.

WORK IN PROGRESS: Further volumes in the "Learn Japanese" series; cultural materials for college text.

Z

ZASLAVSKY, Claudia 1917-

PERSONAL: Born January 12, 1917, in New York, N.Y.; daughter of Morris N. (a businessman) and Olga (Reisman) Cogan; married Sam Zaslavsky (a college mathematics teacher), July 19, 1941; children: Thomas, Alan. *Education:* Hunter College (now Hunter College of the City University of New York), B.A., 1937; University of Michigan, M.A., 1938; graduate study at Wesleyan University, 1962-64, and New York University, 1969-70; currently Ph.D. candidate at Columbia University. *Home:* 45 Fairview Ave., New York, N.Y. 10040.

CAREER: Block Drug Co., Jersey City, N.J., cost accountant, 1938-42; Remington Arms Co., Ilion, N.Y., engineer, 1942-43; New Rochelle Academy, New Rochelle, N.Y., teacher of mathematics and department chairman, 1959-65; Woodlands High School, Hartsdale, N.Y., teacher of mathematics, 1965-77; College of New Rochelle, New Rochelle, adjunct assistant professor of education, 1979—. Lecturer at various colleges. *Member:* National Council of Teachers of Mathematics, American Federation of Teachers. Women's International League for Peace and Freedom, Authors League, Society of Children's Book Writers, League of Women Voters, Phi Beta Kappa. *Awards, honors:* Delta Kappa Gamma Society honorable mention award, 1974, for *Africa Counts.*

WRITINGS: (Contributor) Stanley Brown, editor, *Realm of Science,* Volume IV, Touchstone, 1972; (contributor) Dan Matthews, editor, *A Current Bibliography on African Affairs,* African Bibliographic Center, 1972; *Africa Counts: Number and Pattern in African Culture,* Prindle, 1973; *Preparing Young Children for Math: A Book of Games,* Schocken, 1979; *Count On Your Fingers African Style,* Crowell, 1980. Contributor to *Mathematics Teacher, Journal of Cameroon Affairs, Summation, Arithmetic Teacher,* and other publications.

WORK IN PROGRESS: Contributing to *Reflections on the Mathematics Experience,* edited by Marshall Gordon.

SIDELIGHTS: Jeremy Bernstein writes in the *New Yorker* that Claudia Zaslavsky's book *Africa Counts* is a study of "how the African's number systems, their geometrical designs, and their exceedingly subtle mathematical games have developed and are being used." Citing his belief that "an awareness of the complexity and beauty of African culture should dissolve certain prejudices," Bernstein concludes that *Africa Counts* is "an extraordinary valuable book" and that "anyone who reads [it] will never again view the African peoples in quite the same light."

AVOCATIONAL INTERESTS: Playing chamber music on the violin, singing a capella music, peace movement and community activities, prison reform.

BIOGRAPHICAL/CRITICAL SOURCES: Scientific American, March, 1974; *Natural History,* April, 1974; *Science & Society,* summer, 1974; *New Yorker,* October 14, 1974.

* * *

ZAVALA, Iris M(ilagros) 1936-

PERSONAL: Born December 27, 1936, in Ponce, Puerto Rico; daughter of Romualdo and Maria M. (Zapata) Zavala. *Education:* University of Salamanca, Lic.en Letras, 1961, Dr.en Phil. y Letras, 1962. *Politics:* None. *Religion:* None. *Home:* 440 East 62nd St., New York, N.Y. 10021. *Office:* Department of Hispanic Language, State University of New York, Stony Brook, N.Y. 11790.

CAREER: University of Puerto Rico, Rio Piedras, assistant professor of Spanish literature, 1962-63; El Colegio de Mexico, Mexico City, researcher, 1964; Hunter College of the City University of New York, New York, N.Y., assistant professor of Hispanic literature, 1967-68; State University of New York at Stony Brook, associate professor, 1968-71, professor of Hispanic and comparative literature, 1971—. Director of publications for Instituto de Cultura Puertorriquena, 1962-64. *Member:* Modern Language Association of America, American Association of Teachers of Spanish and Portuguese, Society for Spanish and Portuguese Historical Studies (member of executive council, 1969—). *Awards, honors:* Premio de Literatura Puertorriquena, 1964, 1973, 1978; Guggenheim fellowship, 1967-68; grant from American Council of Learned Societies and Social Science Research Council, 1972.

WRITINGS: Unamuno y su teatro de consciencia (title means "Unamuno and His Philosophical Theatre"), Acta Salmanticensia, 1963; *Barro doliente* (poems; title means "Repenting Clay"), Publicaciones la Isla de los Ratones, 1964; *La angustia y la busqueda del hombre* (title means "Literature of Anguish in the 19th Century"), Universidad Veracruzana, 1965; (editor with Clara E. Lida) *La Revolucion de 1868: Historia, pensamiento, literatura* (title means "Revolution of 1868: History, Thought, and Literature"),

Las Americas, 1970; *Masones, comuneros y carbonarios,* Editorial Siglo Veinte Uno, 1971; *Ideologia y politica en la novela espanola del siglo XIX* (title means "Ideology and Politics in the 19th Century Spanish Novel"), Anaya, 1971; *Poemas prescindibles* (title means "Dispensable Poems"), Antiediciones Villa Mseria, 1971; (editor with Rafael Rodriguez) *Libertad y critica en el ensayo politico puertorriqueno,* Puerto, 1973; (editor) Alejandra Sawa, *Illuminaciones en la sombra,* [Madrid], 1977; *Clandestinidad y libertinaje erudito en los albores del siglo XVIII,* Ariel, 1978; (with Carlos Blanco Aguinaga and Julio Rodriguez Puertolas) *Historia social de la literatura espanola (en lengua castellana),* three volumes, Castalia, 1978-79. Contributor to American, Latin American, and European journals of Hispanic literature and thought.

WORK IN PROGRESS: Espacio y tiempo romanticos: 1789-1850, a book on Spanish Romanticism and politics, for Espasa-Calpe; *Kiliagonia,* a novella; a translation of *Libertad y critica,* for Monthly Review Press; revision of *Historia social de la literatura espanola.*

SIDELIGHTS: Iris M. Zavala told *CA:* "I continue to maintain my adolescent goals: that scholarship and creation are the same creative process and that I will try to merge them. Therefore, the reader (if any) will find that my books of poetry and my novella make wide use of history, philosophy, art, literature and foreign languages. Many friends have helped me in writing my books, most are dead and illustrious: Dante, Cervantes, Erasmus, Goethe, Marx. Their peculiar erudition will save me, I hope, from lamentable blunders. Indefatigable research in archives and libraries has given me whatever understanding I have of memories, expectations and disappointments.

"Since in the capitalist age a human being must dutifully put on layers of makeup and dress, Ms. Zavala is a professor of Hispanic and comparative literature at SUNY at Stony Brook. I earnestly hope that I have been able to slip out of each new fashion, reappraising to my students the nature of literature, bedfellow of truth."

* * *

ZAVATSKY, William Alexander 1943- (Bill Zavatsky)

PERSONAL: Born June 1, 1943, in Bridgeport, Conn.; son of Alexander (an auto mechanic) and Jane (Henderson) Zavatsky; married Phyllis Geffen, June 29, 1968. *Education:* Columbia University, B.A., M.F.A., 1974. *Politics:* "Leftist, nonaligned." *Religion:* "Pursue the spiritual but belong to no formal religious organization." *Home:* 456 Riverside Dr., Apt. 5B, New York, N.Y. 10027.

CAREER: Former professional musician (jazz pianist) and journalist; creative writing teacher for Teachers and Writers Collaborative and New York State Poets in the Schools Program, New York, N.Y., 1971-77, Bedford-Lincoln Neighborhood Museum, Brooklyn, N.Y., 1971-73, Long Island University, C. W. Post Center, Greenvale, N.Y., 1974-75, and University of Texas at Austin, 1977-79. Editor, SUN (publishing house and magazine), 1971—. *Awards, honors:* Creative Artists Public Service fellowship, New York State Council of the Arts, 1975; Creative Writing fellowship in poetry, National Endowment for the Arts, 1979.

WRITINGS—Under name Bill Zavatsky: *Theories of Rain and Other Poems,* SUN, 1975; (translator with Ron Padgett) Valery Larbaud, *The Poems of A. O. Barnabooth,* Mushinsha Books (Tokyo), 1977; (editor with Padgett) *The Whole World Catalogue 2,* McGraw, 1977. Contributor of poems and translations to literary magazines, including *Unmuzzled Ox, Marxist Perspectives,* and *Adventures in Poetry,* and reviews and essays to *New York Times Book Review, Small Press Review, Poetry Project Newsletter,* and *TriQuarterly.* Editor, *Roy Rogers,* 1971—.

WORK IN PROGRESS: Translating poetry and prose by Andre Breton, Robert Desnos, Paul Morand, and Ramon Gomez de la Serna; working on essays, including essays about contemporary poetry; writing short stories.

SIDELIGHTS: William Zavatsky told *CA:* "My enthusiasm for writing drawn predominantly from the unconscious—dream, fantasy, composition through chance occurrence—has tempered with the years. I am now working to integrate intuitive strengths with attention to perception of the world ('the outside world,' so called). Simply put, I am now shifting emphasis from my interior life to the world of relationships. I want to write about what has happened to me and to those I care about and thus have found myself turning more towards narrative modes, fiction included. I have become extremely concerned about the communication of feeling in writing; I want my reader to be touched emotionally by what I write. Most writers, especially poets, don't care about this anymore, I think."

* * *

ZEHNA, Peter W(illiam) 1925-

PERSONAL: Born September 17, 1925, in Pueblo, Colo.; son of Anthony D. and Sarah (Glasgow) Zehna; married Veronica Vigil, 1946; children: Donna, Theresa, Margaret, Patricia. *Education:* Colorado State College of Education (now University of Northern Colorado), A.B., 1950, A.M., 1951; University of Kansas, A.M., 1956; Stanford University, Ph.D., 1959. *Home:* 1196 Castro Rd., Monterey, Calif. *Office:* Department of Operations Research, U.S. Naval Postgraduate School, Monterey, Calif. 93940.

CAREER: Colorado State College of Education (now University of Northern Colorado), Greeley, acting instructor in mathematics, 1953-54; University of Kansas, Lawrence, instructor, 1954-56; Stanford University, Stanford, Calif., research assistant, 1956-59; Colorado State College (now University of Northern Colorado), assistant professor of mathematics, 1959-61; CEIR, Inc., Los Altos, Calif., statistician, 1961-62; U.S. Naval Postgraduate School, Monterey, Calif., associate professor of mathematics, 1962—. Consultant to Decision Studies Group, 1964-68. *Military service:* U.S. Navy, 1943-46; became pharmacist's mate. U.S. Army Reserve, four years; became second lieutenant. *Member:* Institute of Mathematical Statistics, Mathematical Association of America, American Statistical Association, Phi Beta Kappa, Sigma Xi.

WRITINGS: Elements of Set Theory, Allyn & Bacon, 1962, 2nd edition, 1972; (contributor) *Studies in Applied Probability and Management Science,* Stanford University Press, 1962; *Sets with Applications,* Allyn & Bacon, 1966; *Finite Probability,* Allyn & Bacon, 1969; *Probability Distributions and Statistics,* Allyn & Bacon, 1970; (with Donald R. Barr) *Probability,* Brooks/Cole, 1971; (editor) *Selected Methods and Models in Military Operations Research,* U.S. Government Printing Office, 1972; *Introductory Statistics,* Prindle, 1974.

WORK IN PROGRESS: Calculator Probability and Statistics.†

ZEKOWSKI, Arlene 1922-
(Zephyr Jans)

PERSONAL: Born May 13, 1922, in Long Island, N.Y.; daughter of Harry (an advertising executive) and Belle (Sargoy) Zekowski; married Stanley Berne (a writer and university professor), May 17, 1953. *Education:* Brooklyn College (now Brooklyn College of the City University of New York), B.A., 1944; Duke University, M.A., 1945; Sorbonne, University of Paris, licence es lettres, 1948; Louisiana State University, further additional study, 1958-62; also studied at Columbia University and Southern Methodist University. *Office:* Department of English, Eastern New Mexico University, Portales, N.M. 88130.

CAREER: University of Bridgeport, Bridgeport, Conn., lecturer in French, 1946; Associated Colleges of Upper New York, Plattsburgh and Utica, instructor in French and Spanish, 1946-48; Berlitz School, Paris, France, teacher of English and speech, 1949; Eastern New Mexico University, Portales, assistant professor, 1963-67, associate professor of English, 1968—, associate research professor, Llano Estacado Center, 1978—. Free-lance writer and reporter. Guest lecturer on French literature at Queens College (now Queens College of the City University of New York), 1955, University of the Americas, 1965, University of South Dakota, 1968, and Styrian Hauptschulen Paedagogische Akademie (Graz), 1969. Executive chairman, American-Canadian Publishing, Inc., 1973—. Producer and host with husband, Stanley Berne, of television series, "Future Writing Today," for Public Broadcasting System. Has appeared on over 150 radio and television interview programs in the United States and Canada, speaking about the arts and literature, and on television programs including "Avant-Garde Goes West" and "Noonday." *Member:* P.E.N., Committee of Small Magazine Editors and Publishers, New England Small Press Association, Western Independent Publishers, Rio Grande Writers Association, Phi Kappa Phi.

WRITINGS: (Under pseudonym Zephyr Jans) *Thursday's Season* (poems), Parnasse Press, 1950; (with husband, Stanley Berne) *A First Book of the Neo-Narrative,* Wittenborn, 1954; (with Stanley Berne) *Cardinals and Saints,* Wittenborn, 1958; *Concretions,* Wittenborn, 1962; *Abraxas,* Wittenborn, 1964; *Seasons of the Mind,* Wittenborn, 1969; *The Age of Iron and Other Interludes,* American-Canadian Publishing, 1973; *Image Breaking Images: A New Mythology of Language,* Horizon Press, 1976; *Histories and Dynasties,* Horizon Press, 1980. Work is represented in numerous anthologies, including *Breakthrough Fictioneers,* edited by Richard Kostelanetz, Something Else Press, 1973, *Voices from the Rio Grande,* Rio Grande, 1976, *Polish-American Anthology,* University of Kansas Press, 1980, *Boundary 2, Third Assembling,* and *American Writing Today.*

SIDELIGHTS: Arlene Zekowski wrote *CA:* "The problem for literature today is not just a problem of language in terms of how we are accustomed to use it, but of extending the communication of thought so that we can penetrate and go beyond already mundane known human experience, into the unknown untapped realms of higher human consciousness surrounding us in an ever expanding universe. Our Twentieth-Twenty-first Century world today is no longer the circumscribed static Eighteenth Century domain where grammar and the 'logic' of the sentence were born as a paradigm of Newtonian classical mechanics absolutes and Western cause-effect either-or rational psychology.

"In my own writing, the unit of thought has always been the liberated word, which is structured in clusters of *images,* basic to all literary form, past, present and future."

Zekowski is a descendant of the Russian poet, Vasily Andreyevich Zhukonsky.

AVOCATIONAL INTERESTS: Alpine skiing, backpacking, trail hiking, camping, sailing, bicycling, gardening, collecting rocks and shells.

BIOGRAPHICAL/CRITICAL SOURCES: *New World Writing No. 11,* Horizon Press, 1958; *Surfiction,* Swallow Press, 1975; *Intermedia,* winter, 1976; *Saturday Review,* September 29, 1979.

* * *

ZELKO, Harold Philip 1908-

PERSONAL: Born September 15, 1908, in Orange, N.J.; son of Benjamin H. and Sarah (Weiner) Zelko; married Sarah Ann Favish, 1935 (divorced, 1978); married Betty Frazier, 1980; children (first marriage): Marjorie Elaine, Karen Joy, Gary William. *Education:* Ohio State University, LL.B., 1933, M.A. (speech), 1939, J.D., 1970. *Residence:* Tucson, Ariz. *Office:* Southern Arizona Legal Aid, Tucson, Ariz. 85706.

CAREER: Lawyer in Columbus, Ohio, 1933-35; Pennsylvania State University, University Park, professor of speech, 1936-68, professor emeritus, 1968—; currently serving as VISTA volunteer with Southern Arizona Legal Aid, Tucson. Fulbright lecturer, University of Amsterdam, 1966. On leave from Pennsylvania State University, serving as assistant director of training, Corps of Engineers, U.S. Army, Washington, D.C., 1944-47, and director of training with Office of Price Stabilization, Washington, D.C., 1950-51, and Internal Revenue Service, Washington, D.C., 1952-53. Consultant, Area Redevelopment Administration, Washington, D.C., 1962—. Consultant to E. I. du Pont Company, American Telephone and Telegraph Company, and General Telephone and Electronics Corp. Director of workshops in industrial and business communication and frequent lecturer at numerous universities.

MEMBER: Speech Association of America, International Communication Association (president, 1966), American Society of Training Directors, American Association of University Professors, Society for Personnel Administration, Speech Association of Eastern States, Pennsylvania Speech Association (president-elect), B'nai B'rith (president, State College, Pa. branch, 1951), Delta Sigma Rho. *Awards, honors:* Meritorious civilian award, Department of the Army, 1947.

WRITINGS: (With R. Oliver and P. Holtzman) *Communicative Speech,* Holt, 1949, 4th edition, 1969; *How to Become a Successful Speaker,* National Foremen's Institute, 1950; *Successful Conference and Discussion Techniques,* McGraw, 1957, revised edition published as *The Business Conference,* 1969; (with H. O'Brien) *Management-Employee Communication in Action,* Howard Allen, 1957; (with F. Dance) *Business and Professional Speech Communication,* Holt, 1965, 2nd edition, 1978; (with daughter, Marjorie E. Zelko) *How to Make Speeches for All Occasions,* Doubleday, 1971. Also author of training manuals for government agencies and booklets on speech, conference management, training, and selling. Contributor of articles to numerous periodicals.

AVOCATIONAL INTERESTS: Sports, automobiles.

* * *

ZIESLER, J(ohn) A(nthony) 1930-

PERSONAL: Born December 7, 1930, in Timaru, New Zealand; son of Erling (a business executive) and Daisy (Dailey) Ziesler; married Sally Horwood (a teacher), January 30, 1960; children: Kaja Irene, Karen Jane, Sarah Nell. *Education:* University of Otago, B.A., 1953; University of London, B.D., 1956, Ph.D., 1969; University of Bristol, M.A., 1958. *Office:* Department of Theology, University of Bristol, Bristol, England.

CAREER: Didsbury College, Bristol, England, assistant tutor in Old and New Testament, 1956-58; minister of Methodist church in Hastings, New Zealand, 1958-62; Trinity College, Auckland, New Zealand, lecturer in New Testament, 1962-72; St. Matthias' College, Fishponds, Bristol, senior lecturer in theology 1972-77; University of Bristol, Bristol, lecturer in theology, 1977—. *Member:* Studiorum Novi Testamenti Societas.

WRITINGS: The Meaning of Righteousness in Paul: A Linguistic and Theological Inquiry, Cambridge University Press, 1972; *Christian Asceticism,* S.P.C.K., 1973; *The Jesus Question,* Lutterworth, 1980.

WORK IN PROGRESS: An introduction to *Paul and Pauline Christianity,* for Oxford Univeristy Press.

* * *

ZINER, Florence 1921-
(Feenie Ziner)

PERSONAL: Born March 22, 1921, in Brooklyn, N.Y.; daughter of Morris (a diamond merchant) and Sophie (Guttman) Katz; married Zeke Ziner (an artist and sculptor), September 17, 1941; children: Marc, Joe, Amie Ziner Mills, Ted, Eric. *Education:* Brooklyn College (now Brooklyn College of the City University of New York), B.A., 1941; Columbia University, M.S.S., 1944. *Home:* 85 Myrtle Ave., Dobbs Ferry, N.Y. 10522. *Agent:* Rita Scott, 25 Sutton Pl. S., New York, N.Y. 10022. *Office:* Department of English, University of Connecticut, Storrs, Conn. 06268.

CAREER: Connecticut Children's Aid Society, Hartford, caseworker, 1944-45; Veterans Administration, Mental Hygiene Clinic, Chicago, Ill., psychiatric social worker, 1946; Institute for Juvenile Research, Chicago, psychiatric social worker, 1947; Park Ridge School for Girls, Chicago, intake, 1949-52; Sir George Williams University and McGill University, Montreal, Quebec, lecturer in contemporary literature, 1967-70; New School for Social Research, New York, N.Y., instructor of literature and writing, 1971-73; State University of New York College at Purchase, lecturer, 1971-73; University of Connecticut, Storrs, visiting professor of English, 1974—. *Member:* American Association of University Professors, Authors Guild, P.E.N. American Center.

WRITINGS—Under name Feenie Ziner: (With E. S. Thompson) *The Book of Time,* Children's Press, 1956, published as *Time,* Grosset, 1959 (published in England as *The Junior Book of Time,* Muller, 1959); *Hiding,* Golden Gate, 1957; *Little Sailor's Big Pet,* Parnassus, 1958; *Wonderful Wheels,* Melmont, 1959; *Pilgrims and Plymouth Colony,* American Heritage, 1961; (with Paul Galdone) *Counting Carnival,* Coward, 1962; *Dark Pilgrim* (biography of an Indian), Chilton, 1965; *A Guide to Expo,* Tundra Books, 1967; *A Full House,* Simon & Schuster, 1967; *Bluenose, Queen of the Grand Banks,* Chilton, 1970; *The Duck of Billingsgate Market,* Four Winds Press, 1974; *Cricket Boy: A Chinese Tale Retold,* Doubleday, 1978; *Within This Wilderness,* Norton, 1978. Children's book reviewer, *Montreal Star,* 1968-70, *New York Times Book Review,* 1970-74. Contributor of articles to *Canadian, Parents', American Journal of Psychoanalysis, Redbook,* and *Good Housekeeping.*

WORK IN PROGRESS: A novel on Arthurian mythology.

SIDELIGHTS: Feenie Ziner told *CA:* "Although I have been writing for years I feel I have only become 'a writer' with my most recent book. . . . *Within This Wilderness* was my second book about my family. The first was *A Full House,* which described a thinking woman's struggle to be, simultaneously, both a parent and a person. One could say *A Full House* dealt with taking on children, and *Within This Wilderness* explored the process of letting them go."

In *Within This Wilderness,* Ziner traces her journey to visit her son who seven years earlier at the age of sixteen had left home and was now living on an island off British Columbia. Anatole Brayard comments in the *New York Times:* "Ziner is a pretty good writer and an even better mother, because it took an almost superhuman emotional balance on her part to get her son to accept a pinch of love and common sense. . . . Mrs. Ziner's willingness to turn maternal love into an adventure may have just a soupcon of self-consciousness in it, but that is only natural. Mothers have egos too, and there's nothing wrong with the author exalting a bit in her emotional and psychological agility as she learns new skills, such as relieving herself from a plank or not crowding in on her son's spiritual space. . . . Most of the time, though, the author . . . is likable, perhaps even admirable, as she tries to smuggle a little mother love into her son when he's not on guard."

The writer for the *New York Times Book Review* calls *Within This Wilderness* "one of the most realistic accounts yet to emerge from that strange 60's generation." He continues: "[This book] describes the wretchedness that can arise when parent and child, both loving, are forced to face the fact that they no longer share the same assumptions about life; it also discusses the possibilities of coming to terms with the separation that follows. . . . It is a very tricky thing to convey this tension without lapsing into excessive explaining or stream-of-consciousness emotionalism, and it is greatly to Mrs. Ziner's credit that she does neither. She has produced a beautifully understated, yet painful, journey of revelation." Writing in *Saturday Review,* Doris Grumbach finds this book "moving, understanding, compelling. . . . You will not come upon a better piece of autobiographical writing this year."

BIOGRAPHICAL/CRITICAL SOURCES: New York Times, January 18, 1978; *Christian Science Monitor,* February 2, 1978; *Saturday Review,* February 18, 1978; *Washington Post,* March 18, 1978; *New York Times Book Review,* April 2, 1978.

* * *

ZINNES, Harriet

PERSONAL: Born in Hyde Park, Mass.; daughter of Assir N. (a pharmacist) and Sara (Goldberg) Fich; married Irving I. Zinnes (a professor of physics), September 24, 1943; children: Clifford, Alice. *Education:* Hunter College (now Hunter College of the City University of New York), B.A., 1939; Brooklyn College (now Brooklyn College of the City University of New York), M.A., 1944; New York University, Ph.D., 1953. *Residence:* Great Neck, N.Y. 11021. *Office:* Department of English, Queens College of the City University of New York, Flushing, N.Y. 11367.

CAREER: Raritan Arsenal, Raritan, N.J., editor in publications division, 1942-43; *Harper's Bazaar,* New York City, associate editor, 1944-46; Hunter College (now Hunter College of the City University of New York), New York City, tutor, 1946-49; Queens College (now Queens College of the City University of New York), Flushing, N.Y., tutor, 1949-53; Rutgers University, New Brunswick, N.J., lecturer in

English, 1961-62; Queens College of the City University of New York, 1962—, began as instructor, professor of creative writing and modern literature, 1978—. Visiting professor of American literature, University of Geneva, 1968. *Member:* Academy of American Poets, P.E.N., Poetry Society of America. *Awards, honors:* MacDowell Art Colony fellowships, 1972, 1973, 1974, and 1977; Virginia Center for the Creative Arts fellowships, 1975 and 1976; nominated for Elliston Award, 1976, for *I Wanted to See Something Flying;* YADDO fellowship, 1978; American Council of Learned Socities grant, 1978; City University of New York summer grant, 1979.

WRITINGS: Waiting (poems), Goosetree Press, 1964; *An Eye for an I* (poems, with oil and watercolor reproductions), Folder Editions, 1966; (contributor of criticism) Robert Zaller, editor, *Casebook of Anais Nin,* World Publishing, 1973; *I Wanted to See Something Flying* (poems), Folder Editions, 1976; *Entropisms* (prose poems), Gallimaufry, 1978. Poetry and fiction is represented in anthologies, including: *A New Folder: Americans,* edited by Daisy Aldan, Folder Editions, 1959; *Out of the War Shadow,* editied by Denise Levertov, Grossman, 1967; *The New York Times Book of Verse,* edited by Thomas Lask, Macmillan, 1970; *New Directions 27,* edited by James Laughlin, New Directions, 1973; *New Directions 30,* edited by Laughlin, New Directions, 1975; *Solo: Women on Women Alone,* edited by Linda Hamalian and Leo Hamalian, Dell, 1977.

Contributor of poetry and criticism to periodicals, including *Nation, American Scholar, New York Times, Prairie Schooner, Chelsea, Voyages, Mademoiselle, New Leader, Choice, Centennial Review, New York Quarterly, Carleton Miscellany, Parnassus,* and *Southern Review.* Art and literary critic, *Weekly Tribune* (Geneva), 1968-70; art critic, *Pictures on Exhibit,* 1971—.

WORK IN PROGRESS: Editing a book for New Directions, tentatively titled *Ezra Pound and the Visual Arts*; a collection of poems, tentatively titled *Five Pieces of Wire*; a book of poems, *Book of Ten*; a collection of short stories, *Ancient Ritual*; a novel on the New York art scene; translating the poems of Jacques Prevert.

SIDELIGHTS: Harriet Zinnes told *CA*: "Each poem, it seems to me, begs its own music. And without music, lyrical, cacophonous, or strangely rooted in prose, there is no line. I am devoted to the Pound line. [Ezra] Pound's way with verse has given today's poet that freedom with rigor that turns poetic expression into necessary order and vision. I always need the excitement of the visual: paintings are feasts to me. So from the ear, the eye to the word in form.

"I should add that [recently] I have been writing fiction, perhaps unconsciously directed toward that medium after writing a book of prose poems that are essentially dramatic, reductive narrations exposing the absurdity and contradictions of our time. In summary, I may say that I am drawn to the poems of the French poet Jacques Prevert because he too emphasizes sound, syntactical play, and the absurd human situation. And like Prevert, it is the total human that I admire, cajole, and caress, as I write both prose and poetry."

* * *

ZIOMEK, Henryk 1922-

PERSONAL: Surname is pronounced *Zyoh*-mek; born January 8, 1922, in Druzbin, Poland; son of Walenty (a manufacturer) and Jozefa (Fijalkowski) Ziomek; married Patricia Ann De Moor (a piano teacher), August 16, 1956; children: Stanley, John Josef, Paul Henry. *Education:* Attended University of Warsaw, 1939-41; Indiana State University, B.A., 1955; Indiana University, M.A., 1956; University of Minnesota, Ph.D., 1960. *Home:* 370 Rivermont Rd., Athens, Ga. 30601. *Office:* Department of Romance Languages, University of Georgia, Athens, Ga. 30601.

CAREER: Wisconsin State University—Oshkosh (now University of Wisconsin—Oshkosh), 1956-60, began as instructor, became assistant professor of Latin, Spanish, and French; Butler University, Indianapolis, Ind., assistant professor of Spanish and French, 1960-62; Colorado State University, Fort Collins, associate professor of Spanish and French, 1962-64; Ohio University, Athens, professor of Spanish and French, 1964-66; University of Georgia, Athens, professor of Spanish and literature of the Spanish Golden Age, 1966—. Visiting professor of Spanish, University of Warsaw, 1978. Has worked as commercial artist and as an anthropologist. *Military service:* Polish Underground Army, 1942-44. U.S. Army, 1945; served in France; became second lieutenant. *Member:* Asociacion Internacional de Hispanistas, Modern Language Association of America, American Association of Teachers of Spanish and Portuguese, Polish Institute of Arts and Sciences in America, South Atlantic Modern Language Association, Sigma Delta Pi.

WRITINGS: Reflexiones del Quijote, Editorial M. Molina, 1971; (annotator) Vern G. Williamson, editor, *An Annotated, Analytical Bibliography of Tirso de Molina Studies,* University of Missouri Press, 1979.

Editor: (And author of introduction) Lope de Vega, *La nueva victoria de D. Gonzalo de Cordoua* (play), Hispanic Institute of the United States, Columbia University, 1962; *Papers of French-Spanish-Spanish American-Luso-Brazilian Relations,* University of Georgia Press, 1966; (and author of introduction) de Vega, *El poder en el discreto* (play; critical edition), Editorial M. Molina, 1971; (and author of introduction) de Vega, *La batalla del honor* (play), University of Georgia Press, 1972; *Papers on Romance Literary Relations,* University of Georgia Press, 1972; (and author of notes and introduction) de Vega, *La prueba de los amigos,* University of Georgia Press, 1973; (with Robert W. Linker) Luis Velez de Guevara, *La creacion del mundo* (play; critical edition), University of Georgia Press, 1974; de Guevara, *El amor en vizcaino y el principe vinador* (play), Editorial Ebro, 1975; de Guevara, *Mas pesa el rey que la sangre, y blason de los Guzmanes* (play), Editorial Ebro, 1976.

WORK IN PROGRESS: Impresiones de lo grotesco en la literatura del siglo de oro, for Editorial Alcala; *Spanish Golden Age Comedia,* for Twayne.

* * *

ZOLOTOW, Maurice 1913-

PERSONAL: Born November 23, 1913; son of Harry and Pauline (Edelstein) Zolotow; married Charlotte Shapiro (a writer; divorced, 1969); children: Stephen, Ellen. *Education:* Attended New York University, 1932-33; University of Wisconsin, B.A., 1936. *Home:* 8440 Fountain Ave., Hollywood, Calif. 90069. *Agent:* Scott Meredith Literary Agency, Inc., 845 Third Ave., New York, N.Y. 10022.

CAREER: Billboard magazine, New York City, reporter, 1936-37; publicity agent in New York City, 1937-39; freelance writer, 1939—. *Member:* Society of Magazine Writers (founder; first president, 1948).

WRITINGS: *Never Whistle in a Dressing Room,* Dutton, 1944; *The Great Balsamo,* Random House, 1946; *No People Like Show People,* Random House, 1951; *It Takes All Kinds,* Random House, 1952; *Oh Careless Love,* Harcourt, 1959; *Marilyn Monroe: A Biography,* Harcourt, 1960; *Stagestruck: The Romance of Alfred Lunt and Lynn Fontanne,* Harcourt, 1965; (with Allen Sherman) *A Gift of Laughter,* Atheneum, 1965; *Shooting Star: A Biography of John Wayne,* Simon & Schuster, 1974, revised edition, 1979; *Billy Wilder in Hollywood,* Putnam, 1977. Contributor of articles to *Reader's Digest, Playboy,* and other national magazines. Contributing editor, *Los Angeles Magazine.*

SIDELIGHTS: Maurice Zolotow has been called "The Boswell of Broadway," in reference to his biographies of stage and movie stars. Zolotow speaks and reads French and has traveled in France, England, Germany, and Holland. *Avocational interests:* Jazz, backgammon, poker, blackjack, and bird watching.

* * *

ZURHORST, Charles (Stewart, Jr.) 1913-
(Charles Stewart)

PERSONAL: Surname is pronounced *Zur*-hurst; born December 3, 1913, in Washington, D.C.; son of Charles S. and Edwinetta (Schroeder) Zurhorst; married Esther May McGinnis, August 19, 1936 (divorced, 1950); married Susan Mylroie, June 3, 1951; children: (first marriage) Charles S. III; (second marriage) Craig G. *Education:* Attended St. John's College, Annapolis, Md., 1932-33. *Politics:* Independent. *Religion:* Christian. *Home address:* Roque Bluffs, Machias, Me. 04654.

CAREER: Guide and general deputy forest fire warden in Maine woods, 1933-40; press agent for Fulton Lewis Jr. (radio commentator), 1940-48; producer of "American Forum of the Air" (radio program), 1941-43; public relations consultant to industry, 1948-56; free-lance writer, 1956—. *Member:* National Press Club, Overseas Press Club, National Cowboy Hall of Fame.

WRITINGS: *Conservation Is a Dirty Word,* Books for Business, 1968; *The Conservation Fraud,* Cowles, 1970; *The First Cowboys,* Abelard-Schuman, 1973; *The First Cowboy and Those Who Followed,* Cassell, 1974. Contributor to *Grolier Encyclopedia.* Contributor, sometimes under pseudonym Charles Stewart, to magazines and newspapers, including *Better Camping, Pageant, Continental,* and *New York Times.*

WORK IN PROGRESS: A book on pirates of the Maine coast.

SIDELIGHTS: Charles Zurhorst told *CA*: "While I thoroughly enjoy being a writer, I do not always enjoy writing. To me, writing is a business. It requires a schedule and adherence to that schedule, and this is often quite difficult and very demanding. Yet, I would not exchange my chosen profession for any other. Being a writer allows me the freedom to live where I please, which at the moment is Maine, and in the style I please, which at the moment is in a log cabin. The only requirement I must accept is adherence to that writing schedule, and even that can be from midnight to 4:00 a.m. if I so desire. What other profession could beat this way of life?"